MLA
Directory of Periodicals

A Guide to Journals and Series
in Languages and Literatures
Seventh Edition • 1993–95

Complete International Listings

A Companion to the *MLA International Bibliography*

Compiled by
KATHLEEN L. KENT

PUBLISHED BY
The Modern Language Association of America

The *Directory* is available in a clothbound volume, which contains listings for all journals and series on the Master List, and in a paperbound volume, which contains listings for journals and series published in the Americas. This volume contains listings for all titles on the Master List.

ISBN 0-87352-650-3

Copyright © 1993 by The Modern Language Association of America
10 Astor Place, New York, NY 10003-6981

Contents

Guide for Users	v
MLA Directory of Periodicals Staff	vii
Master List of Periodicals	viii
Journals and Series Listings	1
Index to Subjects	755
Index to Sponsoring Organizations	778
Index to Editorial Personnel	789
Index to Languages Published	809
Periodicals with Author-Anonymous Submission Policy	810

Guide for Users of the 1993–95 *MLA Directory of Periodicals*

The *MLA Directory of Periodicals*, a companion volume to the *MLA International Bibliography*, contains all information available on the journals and series on the *Bibliography*'s Master List. This information has been gathered by the MLA staff with the cooperation of field bibliographers and the editors represented in these listings. This edition of the *Directory* contains listings for journals and series on the Master List as of 19 February 1993. The *Directory* is available in a clothbound volume, which contains listings for all 3,277 journals and series on the Master List, and in a paperbound volume, which contains listings for the 1,344 journals and series published in North and South America.

Scope

Any regularly published journal available to libraries and/or universities that prints articles on language, literature, or folklore with some frequency is eligible for inclusion on the Master List. Any series that publishes books on language, literature, or folklore, regardless of the frequency of the series, is also eligible. Editors of journals or series not currently included on the Master List are invited to send a sample copy of the journal or series to the MLA Center for Bibliographical Services for consideration.

Verification

Information gathered by the MLA staff was sent to the editors for verification and update. Approximately 80% of the entries have been verified by the editors; these listings are preceded by an asterisk (*). If no verification was received from the editor, the MLA staff updated the entries whenever possible by examining recent copies of the publication. If verification was not received by the editor and we were unable to locate the publication, the original information was assumed to be correct.

Arrangement

The *Directory* is arranged alphabetically by the titles of the journals or series. A sequence number, printed within parentheses, has been assigned to each title for easy reference from the indexes. Under each title, data have been arranged in separate sections for general, editorial, advertising, subscription, and manuscript information. This edition is the first to include telephone and fax numbers and e-mail addresses.

Acronyms, ISSNs

The journal and series acronyms listed are those used in citations in the *MLA International Bibliography*. Historical variations in the title are listed only if the title of the journal or series has changed recently. International Standard Serial Numbers (ISSNs) have been indicated when they are known.

Editorial Information

For those publications that have not supplied an editorial address, the subscription address has been substituted. When there are multiple editors, the editorial address is that of the first editor listed, but if other editorial addresses have been supplied, they are listed as additional editorial addresses. Scope notes have been taken from the wording supplied either in the journal or series or by the editor. If no scope note was provided by the editor, one was provided by the MLA staff upon examination of the publication. There has been no attempt to standardize the vocabulary used in the scope notes.

Subscription Information

Subscription rates have been quoted as provided by the editor. No attempt has been made to express foreign-currency prices in United States equivalents, but if the editor has supplied both the foreign-currency price and the United States–currency price, the United States–currency price is noted in parentheses. Many editors of non–United States journals and series have chosen to indicate only a United States–currency price, and no attempt has been made to express this in foreign-currency equivalents.

Manuscript Submission Information

Information on the time it takes editors to make publication decisions or the number of times manuscripts are read is based on estimates provided by the editors. Users are urged to read carefully sections on special requirements and restrictions on contributors since these sections will often contain information vital to a manuscript's chances of acceptance. Whether a rejected manuscript is returned to the author often depends on whether or not the author has enclosed return postage. Authors submitting manuscripts are well advised to enclose a self-addressed envelope with sufficient unattached postage for return of the manuscript. When submitting to foreign journals and series, authors should enclose international reply coupons.

Indexes

Five indexes accompany the *Directory*. The Index to Editorial Personnel lists all personal names represented in the listings; the Index to Languages Published includes the languages published by the journals and series, with the exception of English, French, German, Italian, and Spanish; the Index to Sponsoring Organizations includes all sponsoring organizations represented in the listings; and Periodicals with Author-Anonymous Submission Policy includes those titles that review materials anonymously. The Index to Subjects has been compiled on the basis of the scope notes furnished by the editors. On occasion, subject-index entries have also been taken from the titles of the journals and series, particularly when no scope note has been given. We have retained insofar as possible the terminology provided by the respondent editors. Journals and series listed under the heading "Book reviews" publish only, or primarily, book reviews. Many others publish book reviews in addition to other articles in their fields: this information appears in individual entries in the main section of the *Directory*. The numbers referred to in the indexes are the entry numbers for the journals and series, not the page numbers of the text. In all indexes, except for Periodicals with Author-Anonymous Submission Policy, a range of numbers has been supplied when a particular index term refers to a number of titles in sequence, so that 124–130 refers to entries 124 through 130.

Availability

The *Directory* is available on an individual and standing-order basis. Orders should be sent to Member and Customer Services, MLA, 10 Astor Place, New York, NY 10003-6981.

MLA Directory of Periodicals Staff

EDITORIAL

KATHLEEN L. KENT
Coordinator
Master List and Directory of Periodicals

Daniel J. Uchitelle
Director
Center for Information Services

Andrew F. B. LaCroix
Assistant to the Director
Center for Information Services

CENTER FOR BIBLIOGRAPHICAL SERVICES

E. Terence Ford
Director

Janet L. Anderson
Index Editor

Brigitte A. Agna
Associate Index Editor

Amy J. Colley
Assistant Index Editor

Albert P. Mobilio
Assistant Index Editor

James B. Stack
Assistant Index Editor

John Gould
Indexer

Shirley A. Newman
Indexer

William N. Ostrow
Indexer

Bibi B. Rahamatulla
Indexer

Edward Willis
Indexer

Susan B. Lincoln
Associate Thesaurus Editor

Walter S. Achtert
Assistant Thesaurus Editor

Glenna Young
Assistant Thesaurus Editor

Christopher M. Joseph
Editorial Assistant

Laura Matis
Administrative Assistant

Gary Green
Keyboard Operator

COMPUTER CENTER

David B. Feinberg
Manager
MLA Computer Center

J. C. Cabunag
Computer Operator

Frances R. Meilak
Programmer
Textual Systems Development

Cuyler W. Bleecker
Operations Manager
MLA Computer Center

Neil J. Balavram
Programmer
Textual Systems Development

Kinglen L. Wang
Manager
Information Systems

The editorial staff is grateful to the editors represented in these listings for their cooperation. It also extends its appreciation to James R. Keller, Marta Williams-Šušmelj, Judith Altreuter, and Judy Goulding for their invaluable assistance.

MASTER LIST OF PERIODICALS

AA	American Anthropologist
AAA	Archivio per l'Alto Adige: Rivista di Studi Alpini
AAASH	Acta Antiqua Academiae Scientiarum Hungaricae
AAD	Afroasiatic Dialects
AAF	Anglo-American Forum
A&A	Anglica et Americana
A&CS	Area and Culture Studies (Tokyo, Japan)
A&E	Anglistik & Englischunterricht
AAR	African American Review [Formerly *Black American Literature Forum*]
AArmL	Annual of Armenian Linguistics (Cleveland, OH)
AAS	Asian and African Studies
AASF	Annales Academiae Scientiarum Fennicae. Dissertationes Humanarum Litterarum
AASFB	Annales Academiae Scientiarum Fennicae/Suomalaisen Tiedeakatemian Toimituksia
AAWG	Abhandlungen der Akademie der Wissenschaften in Göttingen: Philologisch-Historische Klasse; Folge 3
AB	Acta Baltica: Liber Annalis Instituti Baltici
ABäG	Amsterdamer Beiträge zur Älteren Germanistik
ABalzac	L'Année Balzacienne
ABC	American Book Collector
ABI	Accademie e Biblioteche d'Italia
ABK	Aachener Beiträge zur Komparatistik
ABLS	The Albert Bates Lord Studies in Oral Tradition
ABnG	Amsterdamer Beiträge zur Neueren Germanistik
ABORI	Annals of the Bhandarkar Oriental Research Institute
ABPR	The African Book Publishing Record
ABR	American Benedictine Review
Abr-Nahrain	
ABS	Acta Baltico-Slavica: Archaeologia, Historia, Etnographia, et Linguarum Scientia (Warsaw, Poland)
ABSt	A/B: Auto/Biography Studies
ACar	Analecta Cartusiana
ACCP	Arquivos do Centro Cultural Português (Paris, France)
ACer	Anales Cervantinos
ACF	Annali di Ca' Foscari: Rivista della Facoltà di Lingue e Letterature Straniere dell'Università di Venezia
ACiL	Amsterdam Studies in the Theory and History of Linguistic Science I: Amsterdam Classics in Linguistics 1800-1925
ACist	Analecta Cisterciensia
ACM	The Aligarh Critical Miscellany
Acme: Annali della Facoltà di Lettere e Filosofia dell'Università degli Studi di Milano	
ACP	Amitié Charles Péguy: Bulletin d'Informations et de Recherches
ACRAA	Annales du Centre de Recherches sur l'Amérique Anglophone
ACS	Australian-Canadian Studies: A Journal for the Humanities & Social Sciences
Acta (Binghamton, NY)	
ActaA	Acta Asiatica: Bulletin of the Institute of Eastern Culture
ActaG	Acta Germanica: Jahrbuch des Germanistenverbandes im Südlichen Afrika (Frankfurt, Germany) [Formerly *Acta Germanica: Jahrbuch des Südafrikanischen Germanistenverbandes*]
ActaLit	Acta Literaria
ActN	L'Action Nationale
Actualidades: Consejo Nacional de la Cultura, Centro de Estudios Latinoamericanos "Romulo Gallegos"/Caracas, Venezuela	
Adam	ADAM International Review
ADEB	ADE Bulletin
ADFLB	ADFL Bulletin
AdI	Annali d'Italianistica
AdLB	Brahmavidya, The Adyar Library Bulletin
AdM	Annales du Midi: Revue de la France Méridionale
ADML	Automatic Documentation and Mathematical Linguistics
ADPh	Német Filológiai Tanulmányok/Arbeiten zur Deutschen Philologie
ADS	Australasian Drama Studies
AdTb	Altdeutsche Textbibliothek
AdUA	Annales de l'Université d'Abidjan: Serie D: Lettres
ADz	Akadēmiskā Dzīve
AEASH	Acta Ethnographica Academiae Scientiarum Hungaricae
AEB	Analytical & Enumerative Bibliography
AEFil	Anuario de Estudios Filológicos
Aegyptus: Rivista Italiana di Egittologia et di Papirologia	
AEM	Archeion Euvoikōn Meletōn
AES	Abstracts of English Studies
Aevum: Rassegna di Scienze Storiche, Linguistiche, Filologiche	
AF	Anglistische Forschungen
AfB	Africana Bulletin
AFH	Archivum Franciscanum Historicum
AFLFP	Annali della Facoltà di Lettere e Filosofia dell'Università di Perugia
AFLFUM	Annali della Facoltà di Lettere e Filosofia dell'Università di Macerata
AFLSHS	Annales de la Faculté des Lettres et Sciences Humaines: Philosophie, Littérature, Langues, Sciences Humaines (Dakar, Senegal)
AFLSHY	Annales de la Faculté des Lettres et Sciences Humaines de Yaoundé/Annals of Faculty of Letters and Social Sciences of Yaounde
AfrA	African Arts
AfrF	Afrika Focus
Africa: Rivista Trimestrale di Studi e Documentazione dell'Istituto Italo-Africano (Rome, Italy)	
AfricaL	Africa: Journal of the International African Institute/Revue de l'Institut Africain International
AfricaR	Africa Report
AfrL	Africana Linguistica (Tervuren, Belgium)
AfrLit	American University Studies XVIII: African Literature
AfrLJ	Africana Journal: A Bibliographic Library Journal and Review Quarterly
AfrN	African Notes: Journal of the Institute of African Studies
AfrS	African Studies (Johannesburg, S. Africa)
AfrSR	The African Studies Review
Afr-T	Africa-Tervuren
AfrWS	African Writers Series
AFS	Asian Folklore Studies
AGald	Anales Galdosianos
AGB	Archiv für Geschichte des Buchwesens
Agenda	
AGI	Archivio Glottologico Italiano
Agora: A Journal in the Humanities and Social Sciences	
AGP	Archiv für Geschichte der Philosophie
AHDLMA	Archives d'Histoire Doctrinale et Littéraire du Moyen Âge
AHR	Afro-Hispanic Review
Aidai (Brooklyn, NY)	
AiH	Ånd i Hanske: Tidsskrift for Norsk Dukketeaterforening
AILAR	AILA Review
AiolikaG	Aiolika Grammata
AION-SO	Annali Istituto Universitario Orientale, Napoli: Rivista del Dipartimento di Studi Asiatici e del Dipartimento di Studi e Ricerche su Africa e Paesi Arabi
AION-SR	Annali Istituto Universitario Orientale, Napoli, Sezione Romanza
AIPHOS	Annuaire de l'Institut de Philologie et d'Histoire Orientales et Slaves
AIQ	American Indian Quarterly
AIV	Atti del R. Istituto Veneto di Scienze, Lettere ed Arti. Venezia. Classe di Scienze Morali e Lettere
AJ	The Age of Johnson: A Scholarly Annual
AJES	The Aligarh Journal of English Studies
AJFS	Australian Journal of French Studies
AJGLL	American Journal of Germanic Linguistics and Literatures
AJL	Australian Journal of Linguistics: Journal of the Australian Linguistic Society
AJP	The American Journal of Psychoanalysis
AJS	The American Journal of Semiotics

AKG	Archiv für Kulturgeschichte		Anales	Anales del Instituto Ibero-Americano (Göteborg, Sweden)

AKG	Archiv für Kulturgeschichte
AKML	Abhandlungen zur Kunst-, Musik- und Literaturwissenschaft
Akzente: Zeitschrift für Literatur	
AL	American Literature: A Journal of Literary History, Criticism, and Bibliography
ALA	L'Afrique Littéraire
Alaluz: Revista de Poesia, Narracion y Ensayo	
AL&C	African Languages and Cultures
Alcance: Revista Literaria	
ALCGP	Annali del Liceo Classico "G. Garibaldi" di Palermo
AldeAm	Alba de América: Revista Literaria
ALE	Anales de Literatura Española
ALEC	Anales de la Literatura Española Contemporánea
Alfa: Revista de Lingüística	
ALFA-C	ALFA: Actes de Langue Française et de Linguistique/Symposium on French Language and Linguistics
Alföld: Irodalmi Művelődési és Kritikai Folyóirat	
ALG	Auslandsdeutsche Literatur der Gegenwart: Beiträge zur Literatur- und Kulturgeschichte
ALH	Acta Linguistica Hafniensia: International Journal of General Linguistics
Alif: Journal of Comparative Poetics	
Alighieri	L'Alighieri: Rassegna Bibliografica Dantesca
ALIL	Anuar de Lingvistică şi Istorie Literară
ALitASH	Acta Litteraria Academiae Scientiarum Hungaricae
Alizés: Revue Angliciste de la Réunion	
AlJ	Alemannisches Jahrbuch
AllaB	Alla Bottega: Rivista Bimestrale di Cultura ed Arte
Allegorica	
ALM	Archives des Lettres Modernes: Etudes de Critique et d'Histoire Littéraire
ALMA	Archivum Latinitatis Medii Aevi (Bulletin du Cange)
AlP	Altro Polo: A Volume of Italian Studies
ALR	American Literary Realism, 1870-1910
ALS	Australian Literary Studies
ALT	African Literature Today
AmasJ	Amerasia Journal
AmDram	American Drama (Cincinnati, OH)
Américas	
Amérindia: Revue d'Ethnolinguistique Amérindienne	
AmerS	American Studies
Ameryka: A Ukrainian Catholic Daily (Philadelphia, PA)	
AmLH	American Literary History
AmLit	American University Studies XXIV: American Literature
AmLS	American Literary Scholarship: An Annual
AmNov	The American Novel
AmP	American Psychologist
AmPer	American Periodicals: A Journal of History, Criticism, and Bibliography
AmRev	The Americas Review: A Review of Hispanic Literature and Art of the USA
AMSAP	AMS Ars Poetica
AmSeph	The American Sephardi: Journal of the Sephardic Studies Program of Yeshiva University
AMSGLC	AMS Studies in German Literature and Culture
AMSML	AMS Studies in Modern Literature
AMSR	AMS Studies in the Renaissance
AMSS	AMS Studies in the Eighteenth Century
AMSSC	AMS Studies in the Seventeenth Century
AMSSE	AMS Studies in the Emblem
AMSSMA	AMS Studies in the Middle Ages
AMSSN	AMS Studies in the Nineteenth Century
Amst	Amerikastudien/American Studies
Amstel	Amstelodamum: Maandblad voor de Kennis van Amsterdam. Orgaan van Het Genootschap Amstelodamum
AmStScan	American Studies in Scandinavia
AmStudies	Amerikastudien/American Studies: A Monograph Series
AMus	Asian Music: Journal of the Society for Asian Music
AN	Acta Neophilologica (Ljubljana, Slovenia)
Anais: An International Journal	
Anales	Anales del Instituto Ibero-Americano (Göteborg, Sweden)
Analysis: Quaderni di Anglistica	
Anatolica: Annuaire International pour les Civilisations de l'Asie Antérieure	
AnBol	Analecta Bollandiana
AnBret	Annales de Bretagne et des Pays de l'Ouest
AnCNT	L'Anello Che Non Tiene: Journal of Modern Italian Literature [Formerly L'Anello Che Non Tiene: Journal of Modern Literature]
ANF	Arkiv för Nordisk Filologi/Archives for Scandinavian Philology
Angelicum: Periodicum Trimestre Pontificae Studiorum Universitatis a Sancto Thoma Aquinate in Urbe	
Angles	Angles on the English Speaking World
Anglia: Zeitschrift für Englische Philologie	
AnL	Anthropological Linguistics
ANLMSF	Atti della Accademia Nazionale dei Lincei. Rendiconti della Classe di Scienze Morali, Storiche e Filologiche
AnMal	Analecta Malacitana: Revista de la Seccion de Filología de la Facultad de Filosofia y Letras
ANQ: A Quarterly Journal of Short Articles, Notes, and Reviews	
AnSch	Annals of Scholarship: An International Quarterly in the Humanities and Social Sciences [Formerly Annals of Scholarship: Metastudies of the Humanities and Social Sciences]
ANSDSL	Australian and New Zealand Studies in German Language and Literature/Australisch-Neuseeländische Studien zur Deutschen Sprache und Literatur (Bern, Switzerland)
AnST	Analecta Sacra Tarraconensia: Revista de Ciencias Historico-Eclesiasticas Balmesiana
ÁNT	Általános Nyelvészeti Tanulmányok
AntC	L'Antiquité Classique
Anthropologica	
Anthropos: International Review of Ethnology and Linguistics (Fribourg, Switzerland)	
AnthroposS	Anthropos: Revista de Documentación Científica de la Cultura (Sant Cugat del Vallés, Spain)
AntigR	The Antigonish Review
Antípodas: Journal of Hispanic Studies of the University of Auckland and La Trobe University [Formerly Antípodas: Journal of Hispanic Studies of the University of Auckland]	
Antipodes: A North American Journal of Australian Literature	
Antonianum	
AntQ	Anthropological Quarterly
ANTS	Anglo-Norman Text Society
ANYAS	Annals of the New York Academy of Sciences
ANZSC	Australian and New Zealand Studies in Canada
AOASH	Acta Orientalia Academiae Scientiarum Hungaricae
AÖAW	Anzeiger der Philosophisch-Historischen Klasse der Österreichischen Akademie der Wissenschaften
AODNS	Acta Orientalia (Societates Orientales Danica, Fennica, Norvegica, Svecica) (Copenhagen, Denmark)
AP	Aurea Parma: Rivista Quadrimestrale di Storia, Letteratura e Arte
APK	Aufsätze zur Portugiesischen Kulturgeschichte (Subseries of Portugiesische Forschungen der Görresgesellschaft)
AppalJ	Appalachian Journal: A Regional Studies Review
AppLing	Applied Linguistics (Oxford, England)
APR	The American Poetry Review
APSL	Amsterdamer Publikationen zur Sprache und Literatur
APsy	Applied Psycholinguistics (New York, NY)
ApTS	Approaches to Translation Studies
AQ	American Quarterly
AR	The Antioch Review
ArAA	Arbeiten aus Anglistik und Amerikanistik
Arabica: Revue d'Etudes Arabes	
Arabiyya	Al-'Arabiyya: Journal of the American Association of Teachers of Arabic
ARAL	Annual Review of Applied Linguistics
ARB	Africana Research Bulletin

	Arbor: Ciencia, Pensamiento y Cultura
Arc	L'Arc (Aix-en-Provence, France)
	Arcadia: Zeitschrift für Vergleichende Literaturwissenschaft
Archiv	Archiv für das Studium der Neueren Sprachen und Literaturen
	Archīvs: Raksti par Latviskām Problēmām (Melbourne, Australia)
ARCS	The Annual Report on Cultural Science
ARG	Archiv für Reformationsgeschichte
	Ariel: A Review of Arts and Letters in Israel (Jerusalem, Israel)
ArielE	Ariel: A Review of International English Literature (Calgary, Canada)
ArielK	Ariel (Lexington, KY)
ARIPUC	Annual Report of the Institute of Phonetics, University of Copenhagen
ArkQ	The Arkansas Quarterly: A Journal of Criticism
ArmD	Armchair Detective: A Quarterly Journal Devoted to the Appreciation of Mystery, Detective, and Suspense Fiction
ArO	Archív Orientální: Quarterly Journal of African, Asian, and Latin-American Studies
ArQ	Arizona Quarterly: A Journal of American Literature, Culture, and Theory
ARS	Augustan Reprint Society
ARSCJ	Association for Recorded Sound Collections Journal
ArsL	Ars Lyrica: Journal of Lyrica, Society for Word-Music Relations
ArthY	The Arthurian Yearbook
	Arv: Scandinavian Yearbook of Folklore
ARWWR	The Annual Review of Women in World Religions
AS	American Speech: A Quarterly of Linguistic Usage
ASBFC	Archivio Storico di Belluno, Feltre e Cadore
ASch	The American Scholar
ASE	Anglo-Saxon England
ASEA	Asiatische Studien/Etudes Asiatiques: Zeitschrift der Schweizerischen Asiengesellschaft/Revue de la Société Suisse-Asie [Formerly *Asiatische Studien/Etudes Asiatiques: Zeitschrift der Schweizerischen für Asienkunde/Revue de la Société Suisse d'Etudes Asiatiques*]
ASEES	Australian Slavonic & East European Studies
ASEL	Acta Semiotica et Lingvistica: International Review of Semiotics and Linguistics (São Paulo, Brazil)
	Asemka: A Literary Journal of the University of Cape Coast
ASGM	Atti del Sodalizio Glottologico Milanese (Milan, Italy)
ASI	Archivio Storico Italiano
ASILO	Adalbert Stifter Institut des Landes Oberösterreich: Vierteljahresschrift
ASInt	American Studies International
AsMj	Asia Major
ASNSP	Annali della Scuola Normale Superiore di Pisa: Classe di Lettere e Filosofia
	Assaph: Studies in the Theatre
	Assays: Critical Approaches to Medieval and Renaissance Texts
Astrado	L'Astrado: Revisto Bilengo de Prouvènço/Revue Bilingue de Provence
Astraea	Collection Astraea
AŞUI	Analele Ştiintifice ale Universităţii "Al.I. Cuza" din Iaşi (Serie nouă), e. Lingvistică
ASWL	Authoritative Studies in World Literature
ATAS	American Translators Association Series
	Atenea: Revista de Ciencia, Arte y Literatura de la Universidad de Concepción
	Athanor (Ravenna, Italy)
	Athēna: Syngramma Periodikon tēs en Athēnais Epistēmonikēs Hetaireias
	Athenaeum: Studi Periodici di Letteratura e Storia dell'Antichità
	Athēnaïka: Periodikē Ekdosis tou Syllogou ton Athenaion
ATJ	Asian Theatre Journal
	Atlantis: A Women's Studies Journal/Revue d'Etudes sur la Femme [Formerly *Atlantis: A Women's Studies Journal/Journal d'Etudes sur la Femme*]
AtlantisR	Atlantis: Revista de la Asociacion Española de Estudios Anglo-Norteamericanos
ATQ	American Transcendental Quarterly
AtS	Approaches to Semiotics
AÜ	Afrika und Übersee: Sprachen-Kulturen
AuA	Anglistik und Amerikanistik
AUC	Anales de la Universidad de Chile
AuE	Arheoloğija un Etnogrāfija
	Augustinianum
	Augustinus: Quarterly Review of The Fathers Augustinian Recollects
AUMLA	*Journal of the Australasian Universities Language and Literature Association: A Journal of Literary Criticism and Linguistics*
AUNS	Al'manakh Ukraïns'koho Narodnoho Soiuzu (Jersey City, NJ)
	Aurora: Jahrbuch der Eichendorff Gesellschaft
AuroraB	Aurora-Buchreihe
AUS-AG&R	Acta Universitatis Szegediensis de Attila József Nominatae: Acta Romanica
AUS-AHLH	Acta Universitatis Szegediensis de Attila József Nominatae: Acta Historiae Litterarum Hungaricarum
	Ausblick: Zeitschrift für Deutsch-Skandinavische Beziehungen
AUS-E&L	Acta Universitatis Szegediensis de Attila József Nominatae: Sectio Ethnographica et Linguistica/Néprajz és Nyelvtudomány/Volkskunde und Sprachwissenschaft
AusFolk	Australian Folklore: A Journal of Folklore Studies
AusPl	Australian Playwrights
	Aut Aut: Rivista di Filosofia e di Cultura
AUUSAU	Acta Universitatis Upsaliensis, Studia Anglistica Upsaliensia
AUUSGU	Acta Universitatis Upsaliensis, Studia Germanistica Upsaliensia
AUUSRU	Acta Universitatis Upsaliensis, Studia Romanica Upsaliensia
AUUSSlU	Acta Universitatis Upsaliensis, Studia Slavica Upsaliensia
AUUSSU	Acta Universitatis Upsaliensis, Studia Semitica Upsaliensia
AUUSUU	Acta Universitatis Upsaliensis, Studia Uralica Upsaliensia
AUUUSH	Acta Universitatis Umensis, Umeå Studies in the Humanities
AV	Ateneo Veneto: Rivista di Scienze, Lettere ed Arti
AvG	Avant Garde: Revue Interdisciplinaire et Internationale des Arts et Littératures du XXe Siècle/Interdisciplinary and International Review of Literature and Arts of the 20th Century
AzSL	Abhandlungen zur Sprache und Literatur
	Aztlán: A Journal of Chicano Studies
BAA	Braunschweiger Anglistische Arbeiten
BAAG	Bulletin des Amis d'André Gide
	Babel: Revue Intérnationale de la Traduction/International Journal of Translation
BAC	Boletín de la Academia Colombiana
BADL	Bonner Arbeiten zur Deutschen Literatur
BAFAS	Bibliotheca Afroasiatica
BAGB	Bulletin de l'Association Guillaume Budé
BALCAM	Bulletin de l'ALCAM: Revue de Linguistique Camerounaise
	Balcanica: Annuaire de l'Institut des Etudes Balkaniques
BALI	Bollettino dell'Atlante Linguistico Italiano
BALit	Biblioteka Analiz Literackich
BALM	Bollettino dell'Atlante Linguistico Mediterraneo
BalSt	Balkan Studies
	Baltistica: Baltų Kalbų Tyrinėjimai (Vilnius, Lithuania)
B&L	Brain and Language
BAnglia	Buchreihe der Anglia
BANLE	Boletín de la Academia Norteamericana de la Lengua Española
BAR	Bulletin de l'Association des Amis de Rabelais et de La Devinière
BARLLF	Bulletin de l'Académie Royale de Langue et de Littérature Françaises

BArn	Bibliotheca Arnamagnæana
Baroque: Revue Internationale	
Barroco (Minas Gerais, Brazil)	
BaumB	The Baum Bugle
BAWS	Bayerische Akademie der Wissenschaften. Philosophisch-Historische Klasse, Sitzungsberichte
Bazmavep	Revue Bazmavep: Hayagitakan-Banasirakan-Grakan Handēs/Revue d'Etudes Arméniennes
BB	Bulletin of Bibliography
BBA	Berliner Byzantinistische Arbeiten
BBaud	Bulletin Baudelairien
BBCS	Bulletin of the Board of Celtic Studies/Bwletin y Bwrdd Gwybodau Celtaidd (Cardiff, Wales)
BBH	Books in Bosnia and Herzegovina: A Yugoslav Literary Journal
BBMP	Boletín de la Biblioteca de Menéndez Pelayo
BBN	Berliner Beiträge zur Namenforschung
BBr	Books at Brown
BBSIA	Bulletin Bibliographique de la Société Internationale Arthurienne
BC	The Book Collector
BCB	Boletin Cultural y Bibliografico (Bogotá, Colombia)
BCH	Bulletin de Correspondance Hellénique
BCILA	Bulletin CILA: Organe de la Commission Interuniversitaire Suisse de Linguistique Appliquée
BCILL	Bibliothèque des Cahiers de l'Institut de Linguistique de Louvain
BCom	Bulletin of the Comediantes
BCSM	Bulletin of the Cantigueiros de Santa Maria
BCSV	Bollettino del Centro di Studi Vichiani
BDBU	Bulletin of Daito Bunka University: The Humanities
BdF	Boletim de Filologia
BDLM	Bibliographien zur Deutschen Literatur des Mittelalters
BDM	Bollettino della Domus Mazziniana
BDP	Beiträge zur Deutschen Philologie
BDVA	Beiträge zur Deutschen Volks- und Altertumskunde
BE	Bŭlgarski Ezik: Organ na Instituta za Bŭlgarski Ezik pri Bŭlgarskata Akademiia na Naukite (Sofia, Bulgaria)
Béaloideas: The Journal of the Folklore of Ireland Society	
BEBS	Bochum-Essener Beiträge zur Sprachwandelforschung
Beckettiana: Cuadernos del Seminario Beckett	
Belfagor: Rassegna di Varia Umanità	
BelL	Belaruskaia Linhvistyka
Bellmansstudier	Bellmansstudier Utg. av Bellmanssällskapet
BEP&S	Bulletin d'Etudes Parnassiennes et Symbolistes
Bergomum: Bollettino della Civica Biblioteca	
Bestia: Yearbook of the Beast Fable Society	
BêteN	Bête Noire
BEV	Bulletin des Etudes Valéryennes
BEz	Balkansko Ezikoznanie/Linguistique Balkanique
BF	Books from Finland
BFFGL	Boletín de la Fundación Federico García Lorca
BFil	Boletín de Filología (Santiago, Chile)
BForum	Book Forum: An International Transdisciplinary Quarterly
BG	Bungaku
BGDSL	Beiträge zur Geschichte der Deutschen Sprache und Literatur
BGPTM	Beiträge zur Geschichte der Philosophie und Theologie des Mittelalters
BGU	Bluegrass Unlimited
BH	Bulletin Hispanique
BHe	Baltische Hefte
BHEA	Biblioteca Hispanoamericana y Española de Amsterdam
BHF	Bonner Historische Forschungen
BHR	Bibliothèque d'Humanisme et Renaissance
BHS	Bulletin of Hispanic Studies
BhV	Bharatiya Vidya
BI	Books at Iowa
BibA	Biblical Archaeologist
Biblio 17	
Bibliofilia: Rivista di Storia del Libro e di Bibliografia	
Biblioteca	Biblioteca/The Library: Monthly Journal for Bibliography [Formerly *Biblioteca/The Library: Quarterly Bulletin for Librarianship*]
Bibliotheck	The Bibliotheck: A Scottish Journal of Bibliography and Allied Topics
BIEA	Boletín del Real Instituto de Estudios Asturianos [Formerly *Boletín del Instituto de Estudios Asturianos*]
Biḳoret u-Parshanut: Ketav-'et le-Sifrut, Lashon, Historiah ve-Esteṭiḳah (Ramat Gan, Israel)	
BILC	Boletim do Istituto Luís de Camões (Macao, Asia)
Biography: An Interdisciplinary Quarterly	
BiP	Biuletyn Polonistyczny: Kwartalnik
BIPr	Bulletin d'Informations Proustiennes
Bitzaron: Quarterly Review of Hebrew Letters/Riv'on Sifrut, Hagut, Meḥkar	
BJA	British Journal of Aesthetics
BJECS	British Journal for Eighteenth-Century Studies
BJL	Belgian Journal of Linguistics
BJP	British Journal of Psychology
BJRL	Bulletin of the John Rylands University Library of Manchester
Blake: An Illustrated Quarterly	
BLE	Bulletin de Littérature Ecclésiastique
BLJ	The British Library Journal
BLM	Bonniers Litterära Magasin
Bloch-Almanach: Periodicum des Ernst-Bloch-Archivs des Kulturbüros der Stadt Ludwigshafen [Formerly *Bloch-Almanach: Eine Veröffentlichung des Ernst-Bloch-Archivs der Stadtbibliothek Ludwigshafen*]	
BLR	Bodleian Library Record
BMFEA	Bulletin of the Museum of Far Eastern Antiquities
BMM	Belaruskaia Mova: Mizhvuzaŭski Zbornik
BMP	Bulletin Marcel Proust
BN	Beiträge zur Namenforschung
BN&R	Botswana Notes and Records
BNL	Beiträge zur neueren Literaturgeschichte
BO	Black Orpheus: Journal of African and Afro-American Literature
Bokvännen	
BolSt	Bolivian Studies
BoundaryII	Boundary 2: An International Journal of Literature and Culture
BP	Banasthali Patrika
BPS	Bulletin of the Psychonomic Society
BPTJ	Biuletyn Polskiego Towarzystwa Językoznawczego/Bulletin de la Société Polonaise de Linguistique
BRAE	Boletín de la Real Academia Española
BrechtJ	The Brecht Yearbook/Das Brecht-Jahrbuch
BrenS	Brenner-Studien
BRev	Boston Review
BRG	Blätter der Rilke-Gesellschaft
Bridges: A Senegalese Journal of English Studies/Revue Sénégalaise d'Etudes Anglaises	
BRIES	Bibliothèque Russe de l'Institut d'Etudes Slaves
Brotéria: Cultura e Informação	
BR/RB	The Bilingual Review/La Revista Bilingüe
BRT	Behavior Research and Therapy: An International Multi-Disciplinary Journal
BRTS	Biblioteca della Ricerca: Testi Stranieri
BSAM	Bulletin de la Société des Amis de Montaigne
BSAPLF	Bulletin de la Société Américaine de Philosophie de Langue Française
BSDSL	Basler Studien zur Deutschen Sprache und Literatur
BSE	Brno Studies in English
BSEAA	Bulletin de la Société d'Etudes Anglo-Américaines des XVIIᵉ et XVIIIᵉ Siècles
BSJ	The Baker Street Journal: An Irregular Quarterly of Sherlockiana
BSl	Byzantinoslavica: Revue Internationale des Etudes Byzantines

BslBzl	Brasil/Brazil: Revista de Literatura Brasileira/A Journal of Brazilian Literature
BSLP	Bulletin de la Société de Linguistique de Paris
BSNotes	Browning Society Notes
BSOAS	Bulletin of the School of Oriental and African Studies
BST	Brontë Society Transactions
BSTG	Bulletin de la Société Théophile Gautier
BStu	Bunyan Studies: John Bunyan and His Times
BTLV	Bijdragen tot de Taal-, Land- en Volkenkunde
BTMG	Blätter der Thomas Mann Gesellschaft
BU	Blues Unlimited
BuR	Bucknell Review: A Scholarly Journal of Letters, Arts and Sciences
BWR	Black Warrior Review
BWVACET	The Bulletin of the West Virginia Association of College English Teachers
ByronJ	The Byron Journal
BYUS	Brigham Young University Studies
Byzantion: Revue Internationale des Etudes Byzantines	
BZ	Byzantinische Zeitschrift
BZCP	Buchreihe der Zeitschrift für Celtische Philologie
BzE	Beihefte zum Euphorion: Zeitschrift für Literaturgeschichte
BzNH	Byzantion—Nea Hellas
BZRP	Beihefte zur Zeitschrift für Romanische Philologie
CA	Cuadernos Americanos
CACM	Communications of the ACM
CahiersE	Cahiers Elisabéthains: Late Medieval and Renaissance Studies [Formerly *Cahiers Elisabéthains: Etudes sur la Pré-Renaissance et la Renaissance Anglaises*]
CahiersS	Cahiers Staëliens
CAIEF	Cahiers de l'Association Internationale des Etudes Françaises
CAld	Cuadernos de Aldeeu
Caliban (Toulouse, France)	
Calibano (Rome, Italy)	
Callaloo: A Journal of African-American and African Arts and Letters [Formerly *Callaloo: An Afro-American and African Journal of Arts and Letters*]	
CalR	Calcutta Review
CALS	Cambridge Applied Linguistics Series
CalSS	California Slavic Studies
CalWPL	Calgary Working Papers in Linguistics
CamObsc	Camera Obscura: A Journal of Feminism and Film Theory
C&L	Christianity and Literature
C&T	Culture & Tradition
CanL	Canadian Literature
CAnn	The Carlyle Annual
CanPo	Canadian Poetry: Studies, Documents, Reviews
CanRom	Canadiana Romanica
CAnth	Current Anthropology: A World Journal of the Human Sciences
ČaR	Čakavska Rič
CARA: Actes du Centre Aixois de Recherches Anglaises	
CARB	Cahiers des Amis de Robert Brasillach
CarmP	Carmina Philosophiae: Journal of the International Boethius Society
CarnEx	Les Carnets de l'Exotisme [Supersedes *Revue Pierre Loti*]
Carrell	The Carrell: Journal of the Friends of the University of Miami Library
CarSP	The Carlyle Society Papers
CarteI	Carte Italiane: A Journal of Italian Studies
CArts	Critical Arts: A Journal of Cultural Studies
CasaA	Casa de las Américas
CAsJ	Central Asiatic Journal: International Periodical for the Languages, Literature, History and Archeology of Central Asia
CASS	Canadian-American Slavic Studies
Castilla: Boletín del Departamento de Literatura Española	
CathSt	Cather Studies
CAtI	Contemporary Approaches to Ibsen
CAtL	Cambridge Approaches to Linguistics
CaudaP	Cauda Pavonis: Studies in Hermeticism
CBAA	A Current Bibliography on African Affairs
CBalk	Cahiers Balkaniques
CBunH	Chūgoku Bungaku Hō
CCC	College Composition and Communication
CCCist	Cîteaux Commentarii Cistercienses (Brecht, Belgium)
CCIEP	Courrier du Centre International d'Études Poétiques
CCM	Cahiers de Civilisation Médiévale (X^e-XIIe Siècles)
CComp	Chinese Comparatist
CCon	Cahiers Confrontation
CCR	The Claflin College Review
CCRev	Comparative Civilizations Review
CCrit	Comparative Criticism: A Yearbook
CCRLH	Cahiers CRLH-CIRAOI
CCTEP	Conference of College Teachers of English Studies
CCur	Cross Currents: A Yearbook of Central European Culture (New Haven, CT)
CCV	Cahiers Charles V
CD	Child Development
CD&S	Country Dance and Song
CdD	La Ciudad de Dios: Revista Agustiniana
CdDLSL	Cahiers du Département des Langues et des Sciences du Langage
CdDS	Cahiers du Dix-septième: An Interdisciplinary Journal
CdIL	Cahiers de l'Institut de Linguistique de Louvain
CdL	Cahiers de Lexicologie
CdP	Cuadernos de Poética
CE	College English
CEA	CEA Critic: An Official Journal of the College English Association
CEAfr	Cahiers d'Etudes Africaines
CEAL	Critical Essays on American Literature
CE&S	Commonwealth Essays and Studies
CEBL	Critical Essays on British Literature
CEc	Corps Ecrit
CEd	Communication Education
CEG	Cuadernos de Estudios Gallegos
CEGe	Cahiers d'Etudes Germaniques
CEL	Cadernos de Estudos Lingüísticos
Celestinesca: Boletín Informativo Internacional	
CelfanR	Revue Celfan/Celfan Review
Celtica	
CEM	Cahiers d'Etudes Médiévales
CEMC	Centro de Estudios Mayas-Cuadernos
Cenobio: Rivista Trimestrale di Cultura	
CentR	The Centennial Review (East Lansing, MI)
CEP	Conference on Editorial Problems. University of Toronto
CER	Cahiers d'Etudes Romanes
Cervantes: Bulletin of the Cervantes Society of America	
CeS	Cultura e Scuola
CEStudies	Canadian Ethnic Studies/Etudes Ethniques au Canada
CEWL	Critical Essays on World Literature
CFAQV	Cahiers du Français des Années Quatre-Vingts
CFC	Cuadernos de Filología Clásica
CFMA	Classiques Français du Moyen Âge
CFMB	Canadian Folk Music Bulletin
CFMJ	Canadian Folk Music Journal
CFolkC	Canadian Folklore Canadien
CFR	Children's Folklore Review
CFS	Cahiers Ferdinand de Saussure: Revue de Linguistique Générale
CGFT	Critical Guides to French Texts
CGGT	Critical Guides to German Texts
CGN	Cahiers Gérard de Nerval
CGP	Carleton Germanic Papers
CGST	Critical Guides to Spanish Texts
CH	Crítica Hispánica
CHA	Cuadernos Hispanoamericanos: Revista Mensual de Cultura Hispanica
Chasqui: Revista de Literatura Latinoamericana	

ChauR	The Chaucer Review: A Journal of Medieval Studies and Literary Criticism
CHB	Cahiers Henri Bosco
ChC	Chinese Culture: A Quarterly Review
CHelv	Colloquium Helveticum: Cahiers Suisses de Littérature Comparée/Schweizer Hefte für Allgemeine und Vergleichende Literaturwissenschaft/Quaderni Svizzeri di Letteratura Generale e Comparata
ChibaR	Chiba Review
ChildL	Children's Literature: An International Journal, Inc. Annual of the Modern Language Association Division on Children's Literature and the Children's Literature Association
ChinL	Chinese Literature
ChiR	Chicago Review
Chiricú	
ChLB	Charles Lamb Bulletin
Chloe: Beihefte zum Daphnis	
CHLSSF	Commentationes Humanarum Litterarum Societatis Scientiarum Fennicae
ChrE	Chronique d'Egypte
ChSigne	Champs du Signe: Cahiers de Stylistique
CHum	Computers and the Humanities
CIBS	Communications from the International Brecht Society
CICIM: Revue pour le Cinéma Français	
CICPB	Les Cahiers de l'I.C.P.: Bulletin de la Communication
CICPR	Les Cahiers de l'I.C.P.: Rapport de Recherche
CIEFLB	Central Institute of English and Foreign Languages Bulletin
CIF	Cuadernos de Investigación Filológica
CIFM	Contributi dell'Istituto di Filologia Moderna. Ser. Ital. 1. Univ. Cattolica del Sacro Cuore
CILT	Amsterdam Studies in the Theory and History of Linguistic Science IV: Current Issues in Linguistic Theory
CImm	Campi Immaginabili: Rivista Quadrimenstrale di Cultura [Supersedes *Ipotesi 80*]
CimR	Cimarron Review
Cineaste: America's Leading Magazine on the Art and Politics of the Cinema	
Cinefocus (Bloomington, IN)	
CinJ	Cinema Journal
CiP	Amsterdam Studies in the Theory and History of Linguistic Science II: Classics in Psycholinguistics
Círculo: Revista de Cultura	
CIRRI	Centre Interuniversitaire de Recherche sur la Renaissance Italienne
CIS	Cahiers Internationaux de Symbolisme
Cithara: Essays in the Judaeo-Christian Tradition	
CJ	The Classical Journal
CJAS	Canadian Journal of African Studies/Revue Canadienne des Etudes Africaines
CJC	Cahiers Jean Cocteau
CJG	Cahiers Jean Giraudoux
CJIS	Canadian Journal of Irish Studies
CJItS	Canadian Journal of Italian Studies
CJL	Canadian Journal of Linguistics/Revue Canadienne de Linguistique
CJNS	Canadian Journal of Netherlandic Studies/Revue Canadienne d'Etudes Néerlandaises
CJPhil	Canadian Journal of Philosophy
CJVŠ	Cizí Jazyky ve Škole
CL	Comparative Literature (Eugene, OR)
ČL	Česká Literatura: Časopis pro Literární Vědu
CLAJ	College Language Association Journal
CLAO	Cahiers de Linguistique—Asie Orientale
CLAQ	Children's Literature Association Quarterly
ClassQ	The Classical Quarterly
ClaudelS	Claudel Studies
CLC	Columbia Library Columns
CLE	Children's Literature in Education
CLEAR	Chinese Literature: Essays, Articles, Reviews (Bloomington, IN)
CLeg	Contemporary Legend: The Journal of the International Society for Contemporary Legend Research
ČLid	Český Lid: Národopisný Časopis/Ethnological Journal
CLing	Cercetări de Lingvistică
ClioI	CLIO: A Journal of Literature, History, and the Philosophy of History
CLL	Creole Language Library
CLO	Cahiers Linguistiques d'Ottawa
ClQ	Colby Quarterly
CLS	Comparative Literature Studies
CLTL	Cadernos de Lingüística e Teoria da Literatura
CLTT	Child Language Teaching and Therapy
Clues: A Journal of Detection	
CMat	Critical Matrix: Princeton Working Papers in Women's Studies
CMC	Crosscurrents/Modern Critiques (Carbondale, IL)
CMCS	Cambridge Medieval Celtic Studies
ČMF	Časopis pro Moderní Filologii
CMHLB	Cahiers du Monde Hispanique et Luso-Brésilien/Caravelle
CML	Classical and Modern Literature: A Quarterly (Terre Haute, IN)
CMLR	Canadian Modern Language Review/La Revue Canadienne des Langues Vivantes
CMRLFC	Collection Monographique Rodopi en Littérature Française Contemporaine
CMRS	Cahiers du Monde Russe et Soviétique
CN	Cultura Neolatina
CNat	Les Cahiers Naturalistes
CNIE	Commonwealth Novel in English
CNLR	Council on National Literatures/World Report
CoA	The Coat of Arms: An Heraldic Quarterly Magazine
CogLi	Cognitive Linguistics
CogN	Cognitive Neuropsychology
Cognition: International Journal of Cognitive Science	
Collections (Newark, DE)	
CollG	Colloquia Germanica, Internationale Zeitschrift für Germanische Sprach- und Literaturwissenschaft
CollL	College Literature
Colóquio	Colóquio/Letras
Comhar	
Comitatus: A Journal of Medieval and Renaissance Studies	
ComM	Communication Monographs
Commentary	
Comparatist	The Comparatist: Journal of the Southern Comparative Literature Association
CompD	Comparative Drama
Compendia: Computer Generated Aids to Literary and Linguistic Research	
CompL	American University Studies III: Comparative Literature
CompLing	Computational Linguistics
ComQ	Commonwealth Quarterly
Comunità: Rivista di Informazione Culturale	
Conch	The Conch: A Sociological Journal of African Cultures and Literatures
Confluencia: Revista Hispánica de Cultura y Literatura	
ConL	Contemporary Literature (Madison, WI)
ConLit	Convorbiri Literare
Connotations: A Journal for Critical Debate	
Conradian	The Conradian
Conradiana: A Journal of Joseph Conrad Studies	
Constructions	
ContempR	Contemporary Review (London, England)
Continuum: Problems in French Literature from the Late Renaissance to the Early Enlightenment	
Contrastes: Revue de l'Association pour le Développement des Etudes Contrastives	
Coranto: Journal of the Friends of the Libraries, University of Southern California	

CoRev	The Commonwealth Review
Corona: Marking the Edges of Many Circles	
Corónica	La Corónica: Spanish Medieval Language and Literature Journal and Newsletter
Costerus	
Co-textes	
Courier	Syracuse University Library Associates Courier
Cowrie: A Chinese Journal of Comparative Literature	
CPA	Culture Populaire Albanaise
CPALS	Carleton Papers in Applied Language Studies
CPe	Castrum Peregrini
CPsy	Cognitive Psychology
CQ	The Cambridge Quarterly
CR	The Critical Review (Canberra, Australia)
CRCL	Canadian Review of Comparative Literature/Revue Canadienne de Littérature Comparée
CREDIF	Bulletin Bibliographique du C.R.E.D.I.F. (Centre de Recherche et d'Etude pour la Diffusion du Français Service de Documentation)
CREL	Cahiers Roumains d'Etudes Littéraires: Revue Trimestrielle de Critique, d'Esthétique et d'Histoire Littéraires
CRev	The Chesterton Review: The Journal of the Chesterton Society
CRevAS	Canadian Review of American Studies
CRevB	Conch Review of Books: A Literary Supplement on Africa
CrF	Creative Forum: A Quarterly Journal of Contemporary Writing
Crisol	
Cristallo: Rassegna di Varia Umanità (Bolzano, Italy)	
Crit	Critique: Studies in Contemporary Fiction
CritI	Critical Inquiry
Criticism: A Quarterly for Literature and the Arts (Detroit, MI)	
Criticón	
Critique: Revue Générale des Publications Françaises et Etrangères (Paris, France)	
CritLett	Critica Letteraria
CritQ	Critical Quarterly
CritSt	Critical Studies [Formerly *Critical Studies: A Journal of Critical Theory, Literature and Culture*]
CritT	Critical Texts: A Review of Theory and Criticism
CritTh	Critical Theory: Interdisciplinary Approaches to Language, Discourse and Ideology
CRLN	The Comparative Romance Linguistics Newsletter
CrossC	Cross/Cultures: Readings in the Post/Colonial Literatures in English
Crosscurrents	Cross Currents (New Rochelle, NY)
CRR	Cincinnati Romance Review
CrSurv	Critical Survey
CRUX: A Journal on the Teaching of English	
CSALC	Cambridge Studies in American Literature and Culture
CSASE	Cambridge Studies in Anglo-Saxon England
CSci	Cognitive Science: A Multidisciplinary Journal of Artificial Intelligence, Linguistics, Neuroscience, Philosophy, Psychology
CSF	Cambridge Studies in French
CSG	Cambridge Studies in German
CSGLL	Canadian Studies in German Language and Literature
CSiL	Copenhagen Studies in Language
CSJP	Cahiers Saint-John Perse
CSL	Cambridge Studies in Linguistics
CSLAIL	Cambridge Studies in Latin American and Iberian Literature
CSLBull	CSL: The Bulletin of the New York C. S. Lewis Society [Formerly *Bulletin of the New York C. S. Lewis Society*]
CSLing	Current Studies in Linguistics
CSLL	Cardozo Studies in Law and Literature
CSP	Canadian Slavonic Papers: An Inter-Disciplinary Quarterly Devoted to Central and Eastern Europe [Formerly *Canadian Slavonic Papers: An Inter-Disciplinary Quarterly Devoted to the Soviet Union and Eastern Europe*]
CSR	Christian Scholar's Review
CSRL	Cambridge Studies in Russian Literature
CSW	Cahiers Simone Weil
CSWL	Contributions to the Study of World Literature
CT	Ciencia Tomista: Publicación Cuatrimestral del Centro de Estudios Teológicos de San Esteban
CTC	Cuadernos de Teatro Clásico
CTR	Canadian Theatre Review
CultCrit	Cultural Critique
CUNYF	CUNYForum: Papers in Linguistics
Cupey: Revista de la Universidad Metropolitana	
CUWPL	Columbia University Working Papers in Linguistics
CuyahogaR	Cuyahoga Review
CV	Città di Vita: Bimestrale di Religione Arte e Scienza
CVE	Cahiers Victoriens et Edouardiens: Revue du Centre d'Etudes et de Recherches Victoriennes et Edouardiennes de l'Université Paul Valéry, Montpellier
CWLM	Chung-wai Literary Monthly: Studies in Chinese and Foreign Literatures [Formerly *Chung-wai Literary Monthly: Publicación Cuatrimestral del Centro di Estudios Teológicos de San Esteban*]
CWPL	Cornell Working Papers in Linguistics
Cycnos	
Dactylus	
Dada	Dada/Surrealism
Dædalus: Journal of the American Academy of Arts and Sciences	
DAEM	Deutsches Archiv für Erforschung des Mittelalters
DaF	Deutsch als Fremdsprache: Zeitschrift zur Theorie und Praxis des Deutschunterrichts für Auslaender
DAI	Dissertation Abstracts International
DanF	Danske Folkemål
Dansk Udsyn (Askov, Denmark)	
DAO	Danske Afhandlinger om Oversættelse
Daphnis: Zeitschrift für Mittlere Deutsche Literatur	
DASDJ	Deutsche Akademie für Sprache und Dichtung, Darmstadt. Jahrbuch
Daugava: Literaturno-Khudozhestvennyĭ i Obshchestvenno-Politicheskiĭ Ezhemesiachnyĭ Zhurnal Soiuza Pisateleĭ Latvii [Formerly *Daugava: Literaturno-Khudozhestvennyĭ i Obshchestvenno-Politicheskiĭ Ezhemesiachnyĭ Zhurnal Soiuza Sovetskikh Pisateleĭ Latvii*]	
DC	Dutch Crossing: A Journal of Low Countries Studies
DDG	Deutsche Dialektgeographie/Dialektographie
DDJ	Deutsches Dante-Jahrbuch
DdW	Les Dialectes de Wallonie
Degrés: Revue de Synthèse à Orientation Sémiologique	
Delo: Mesečni Književni Časopis (Belgrade, Yugoslavia)	
DevB	Devil's Box
DFS	Dalhousie French Studies
DHA	Diálogos Hispánicos de Amsterdam
DHLR	The D. H. Lawrence Review
DHS	Dix-Huitième Siècle
Diachronica: International Journal for Historical Linguistics/Revue Internationale pour la Linguistique Historique/Internationale Zeitschrift für Historische Linguistik	
Diacritics: A Review of Contemporary Criticism	
Dialoghi: Rivista Bimestrale di Letteratura Arti Scienze	
Dialogi: Revija za Kulturo	
Dialogue: Canadian Philosophical Review/Revue Canadienne de Philosophie	
DialogW	Dialog: Miesięcznik Poświęcony Dramaturgii Współczesnej: Teatralnej, Filmowej, Radiowej, Telewizyjnej (Warsaw, Poland)
Dickensian	The Dickensian
DicS	Dickinson Studies: Emily Dickinson (1830-86), U.S. Poet
Dictionaries: Journal of the Dictionary Society of North America	
DidS	Diderot Studies
Dieciocho: Hispanic Enlightenment, Aesthetics, and Literary Theory	
Differentia: Review of Italian Thought	
DilR	Diliman Review (Quezon City, Philippines)

Dimension: Contemporary German Arts and Letters	
Diogenes	
Dionysos: The Literature and Addiction TriQuarterly [Formerly *Dionysos: The Literature and Intoxication TriQuarterly*]	
Dires: Revue du Centre d'Etudes Freudiennes	
Discourse: Journal for Theoretical Studies in Media and Culture	
Discurso: Revista de Estudios Iberoamericanos	
Dispatch	The Dispatch
Dispositio: Revista Americana de Estudios Semióticos y Culturales/American Journal of Semiotic and Cultural Studies	
DLB	Dictionary of Literary Biography
DLE	Documents sur l'Espéranto
DLN	Doris Lessing Newsletter
DMLS	Durham Modern Languages Series
DMT	Durham Medieval Texts
Dnipro: Literaturno-Khudozhniĭ ta Hromads'ko-Polityčnyĭ Zhurnal	
DNR	Dime Novel Roundup: A Magazine Devoted to the Collecting, Preservation and Literature of the Old-Time Dime and Nickel Novels, Libraries and Popular Story Papers
DocCRLLI	Documents du Centre de Recherche de Langue et Littérature Italiennes et du Centre de Recherches Italiennes [Formerly *Documents du Centre de Recherche de Langue et Littérature Italiennes*]
DocumentosA	Documentos A: Genealogia Cientifica de la Cultura
Dolphin	The Dolphin: Publications of the English Department, University of Aarhus
DownR	Downside Review: A Quarterly of Catholic Thought
DP	Developmental Psychology
DPPNGL	Data Papers in Papua New Guinea Languages
DPr	Discourse Processes: A Multidisciplinary Journal
DQ	Denver Quarterly
DQu	Dickens Quarterly
DR	Dalhousie Review
DrSt	Dreiser Studies
DruzhN	Druzhba Narodov: Ezhemesiachnyĭ Literaturno-Khudozhestvennyĭ i Obshchestvenno-Politicheskiĭ Zhurnal
DS	Danske Studier
DSA	Dickens Studies Annual: Essays on Victorian Fiction
DSALL	Dutch Studies in Armenian Language and Literature
DSARDS	Dante Studies, with the Annual Report of the Dante Society
DSec	Degré Second: Studies in French Literature
DSFNS	Deutsch-Slawische Forschungen zur Namenkunde und Siedlungsgeschichte
DSGW	Deutsche Shakespeare-Gesellschaft West: Jahrbuch
DSLL	Duquesne Studies in Language and Literature
DSp	Deutsche Sprache: Zeitschrift für Theorie, Praxis, Dokumentation
DSS	Dix-Septième Siècle
DS/SD	Discours Social/Social Discourse: Analyse du Discours et Sociocritique des Textes/Discourse Analysis and Text Sociocriticism [Formerly *Discours Social/Social Discourse: International Research Papers in Comparative Literature*]
DSt	Deutsche Studien
DStudies	Dostoevsky Studies: Journal of the International Dostoevsky Society
DT	Divus Thomas: Commentarium de Philosophia et Theologia
DTM	Deutsche Texte des Mittelalters
DU	Der Deutschunterricht: Beiträge zu Seiner Praxis und Wissenschaftlichen Grundlegung
DUJ	Durham University Journal
DVLG	Deutsche Vierteljahrsschrift für Literaturwissenschaft und Geistesgeschichte
DWB	Dietsche Warande en Belfort: Tijdschrift voor Letterkunde en Geestesleven
DzD	Dzejas Diena
EA	Etudes Anglaises: Grande-Bretagne, Etats-Unis
EAA	Estudos Anglo-Americanos (São Paulo, Brazil)
EAL	Early American Literature
E&H	Ear and Hearing: Official Journal of the American Auditory Society
E&S	Essays and Studies (London, England)
EAS	Essays in Arts and Sciences
EBaud	Etudes Baudelairiennes
EBC	Etudes Britanniques Contemporaines: Revue de la Société d'Etudes Anglaises Contemporaines
EBSK	Erlanger Beiträge zur Sprach- und Kunstwissenschaft
EBT	Les Etudes Balkaniques Tchécoslovaques
EC	Etudes Celtiques
ECAMML	The Edward C. Armstrong Monographs on Medieval Literature
ECent	The Eighteenth Century: Theory and Interpretation
ECF	Eighteenth-Century Fiction
ECl	Les Etudes Classiques
ECLife	Eighteenth-Century Life
ECM	Estudios de Cultura Maya: Publicación Periódica del Centro de Estudios Mayas
ECN	Estudios de Cultura Náhuatl
Eco: Revista de la Cultura de Occidente	
ECon	L'Epoque Conradienne
ECr	L'Esprit Créateur
ECS	Eighteenth-Century Studies (Cincinnati, OH)
ECW	Essays on Canadian Writing
EDAMMS	Early Drama, Art, and Music Monograph Series
EDAMRef	Early Drama, Art, and Music Reference Series
EDAMRvw	The Early Drama, Art, and Music Review [Incorporates *Medieval Music-Drama News*]
EdArn	Editiones Arnamagnæanæ
Edda: Nordisk Tidsskrift for Litteraturforskning/Scandinavian Journal of Literary Research	
EdF	Erträge der Forschung
EDH	Essays by Divers Hands
Editio: Internationales Jahrbuch für Editionswissenschaft/International Yearbook of Scholarly Editing/Revue Internationale des Sciences de l'Edition Critique	
EDJ	The Emily Dickinson Journal
EdL	Etudes de Lettres
EDLA	Estudios de Lingüística Aplicada
EdLing	Estudios de Lingüística
EdN	Editors' Notes
EdO	Edad de Oro
EDoc	Esperanto Documents
EDS	English Dance and Song
EEPSAPT	Epistēmonikē Epetērida Philosophikēs Scholēs Aristoteleiou Panepistēmiou Thessalonikēs
EES	Explorations in Ethnic Studies: The Journal of the National Association for Ethnic Studies
EEsc	Estudis Escènics: Quaderns de l'Institut del Teatre de la Diputació de Barcelona
EETS	Early English Text Society
EF	Etudes Françaises
EFG	Erlanger Forschungen A: Geisteswissenschaften
EFil	Estudios Filológicos
EFL	Essays in French Literature (Nedlands, Western Australia)
EFO	Etudes Finno-Ougriennes
EG	Etudes Germaniques
EGA	Etudes Germano-Africaines: Revue Annuelle de Germanistique Africaine/Jahresschrift für Afrikanische Germanistik/Annual Review of German Studies in Africa
EGN	Ellen Glasgow Newsletter
EHBS	Epetēris Hetaireias Byzantinōn Spoudōn
EI	Etudes Irlandaises: Revue Française d'Histoire, Civilisation et Littérature de l'Irelande
EIC	Essays in Criticism: A Quarterly Journal of Literary Criticism (Oxford, England)
EIDOS: The International Prosody Bulletin	

EigoS	Eigo Seinen		ERBr	Etudes Romanes de Brno

EigoS   Eigo Seinen
Éigse: A Journal of Irish Studies
EinA   English in Africa
EiP   Essays in Poetics: The Journal of the British Neo-Formalist School
EIRC   Explorations in Renaissance Culture
Éire   Éire-Ireland: A Journal of Irish Studies
EiTET   Essays in Theatre/Etudes Théâtrales [Formerly *Essays in Theatre*]
EJ   The English Journal (Urbana, IL)
EJDC   European Journal of Disorders of Communication [Formerly *British Journal of Disorders of Communication*]
EJS   European Joyce Studies
EKEEK   Epetēris tou Kentrou Epistēmonikon Ereunōn Kyprou
EKEHL   Epetēris tou Kentrou Ereunēs tēs Hellēnikēs Laographias
ELA   Etudes de Linguistique Appliquée
EL&L   American University Studies IV: English Language and Literature
ELawr   Etudes Lawrenciennes
Elementa: Schriften zur Philosophie und ihrer Problemgeschichte
ELet   Esperienze Letterarie: Rivista Trimestrale di Critica e Cultura
ELF   Etudes Littéraires Françaises
ELH
ELing   Etudes Linguistiques: Revue du Département de Linguistique de l'Université de Niamey
ELit   Etudes Littéraires
ElizS   Salzburg Studies in English Literature: Elizabethan & Renaissance Studies
ELkT   Epitheōrēsē Logou kai Technēs
ELLF   Etudes de Langue et Littérature Françaises
ELLS   English Literature and Language (Tokyo, Japan)
ELN   English Language Notes (Boulder, CO)
ELR   English Literary Renaissance
ELS   English Literary Studies Monograph Series
ELSt   Exeter Linguistic Studies
ELT   English Literature in Transition (1880-1920)
ELWIU   Essays in Literature (Macomb, IL)
Emblematica: An Interdisciplinary Journal of Emblem Studies
Emérita: Revista de Lingüística y Filología Clásica (Madrid, Spain)
EMong   Cahiers d'Etudes Mongoles et Siberiennes
EMS   English Manuscript Studies 1100-1700
EmSA   Emakeele Seltsi Aastaraamat
EN   Enemy News: Journal of the Wyndham Lewis Society
Enclitic
Encomia: Bibliographical Bulletin of the International Courtly Literature Society
Encyclia: The Journal of the Utah Academy of Sciences, Arts, and Letters
EngLing   English Linguistics: Journal of the English Linguistic Society of Japan (Tokyo, Japan)
English: The Journal of the English Association (London, England)
EngR   English Record
Ensayistas   Los Ensayistas: Georgia Series on Hispanic Thought
EnT   English Today: The International Review of the English Language
Envoi: A Review Journal of Medieval Literature
EOMC   Estudios de Asia y Africa (Mexico City, Mexico)
EONR   The Eugene O'Neill Review
Eos.: Commentarii Societatis Philologae Polonorum (Wrocław, Poland)
EP   Etudes Philosophiques
EPA   Estudos Portugueses e Africanos
EPC   El Popola Ĉinio
ĒpH   Ēpeirōtikē Hestia
Epos: Revista de Filología
EPSS   Ezra Pound Scholarship Series
Equivalences: Revue de l'Institut Supérieur de Traduction et d'Interprètes de Bruxelles
Equivalencias   Equivalencias/Equivalences: Revista Internacional de Poesía/International Journal of Poetry
ER   Etudes Rabelaisiennes
Eranos: Acta Philologica Suecana

ERBr   Etudes Romanes de Brno
Ériu
ERP   English Renaissance Prose
ERR   European Romantic Review
ERUO   Etudes Romanes de l'Université d'Odense
ES   English Studies: A Journal of English Language and Literature (Lisse, Netherlands)
ESA   English Studies in Africa: A Journal of the Humanities (Johannesburg, South Africa)
ESC   English Studies in Canada
Escritos: Revista del Centro de Ciencias del Lenguaje
Escritura: Revista de Teoría y Crítica Literarias
ESef   Estudios Sefardíes
ESELL   Tohoku Gakuin University Review: Essays and Studies in English Language and Literature [Tohoku Gakuin Daigaku Ronshu, Eigo-Eibungaku] (Sendai, Japan)
ESJ   European Studies Journal
ESMSLCC   The Edward Sapir Monograph Series in Language, Culture, and Cognition
EspA   Español Actual
EspDok   Esperanto-Dokumentoj
Esperanto (Rotterdam, Netherlands)
Esprit (Paris, France)
ESQ: A Journal of the American Renaissance
ESRS   Emporia State Research Studies
ESt   Erlanger Studien
Estreno: Cuadernos del Teatro Español Contemporáneo
ETC.: A Review of General Semantics
EtCr   Etudes Créoles
ETh   Elizabethan Theatre
EthF   Ethnologia Fennica/Finnish Studies in Ethnology
EthnoE   Ethnologia Europaea
EthnoF   Ethnologie Française: Revue Trimestrielle de la Société d'Ethnologie Française
Ethnographia: A Magyar Néprajzi Társaság Folyóirata
Ethnology: An International Journal of Cultural and Social Anthropology (Pittsburgh, PA)
Ethnomusicology: Journal of the Society for Ethnomusicology
Ethology
EthS   Ethnologia Slavica
EthSc   Ethnologia Scandinavica: A Journal for Nordic Ethnology
EtIE   Etudes Indo-Européennes
Etnolog: Glasnik Slovenskega Etnografskega Muzeja/Bulletin of the Slovene Ethnographic Museum [Formerly *Slovenski Etnograf*]
Etudes (Paris, France)
Euphorion: Zeitschrift für Literaturgeschichte
EurH   Europäische Hochschulschriften/Publications Universitaire Européennes/European University Studies
Europe: Revue Littéraire Mensuelle
Eutopias: Teorías/Historia/Discurso
EuWN   Eudora Welty Newsletter
EW   East-West Film Journal
EWhR   Edith Wharton Review [Formerly *Edith Wharton Newsletter*]
EWNS   Evelyn Waugh Newsletter and Studies [Formerly *Evelyn Waugh Newsletter*]
EWW   English World-Wide: A Journal of Varieties of English
Exemplaria: A Journal of Theory in Medieval and Renaissance Studies
Expl   Explicator
ExplorSp   Explorations: Special Series
ExTL   Explicación de Textos Literarios
Extrapolation: A Journal of Science Fiction and Fantasy
FAB   Frankfurter Afrikanistische Blätter
Fabu   Fabula (Villeneuve d'Ascq, France)
Fabula: Zeitschrift für Erzählforschung/Journal of Folktale Studies/Revue d'Etudes sur le Conte Populaire
Face: Revista de Semiótica e Comunicação
Fachsprache: International Journal of LSP (Vienna, Austria)
FAF   Festival of American Folklife
FaN   Le Français au Nigéria
FantCo   Fantasy Commentator

Fataburen: Nordiska Museets och Skansens Årsbok
FaulkSt   Faulkner Studies (Kyoto, Japan)
FauxT   Faux Titre: Etudes de Langue et Littérature Françaises
FB   Fontane Blätter (Potsdam, Germany)
FBG   Frankfurter Beiträge zur Germanistik
FBS   Franco-British Studies: Journal of the British Institute in Paris
FCB   The Flannery O'Connor Bulletin
FCN   Folklife Center News
FCS   Fifteenth-Century Studies
FCSt   French Cultural Studies
FdL   Forum der Letteren: Tijdschrift voor Taal- en Letterkunde
Feminaria (Buenos Aires, Argentina)
FFC   Folklore Fellows' Communications
FForum   Folklore Forum
FGADL   Forschungen zur Geschichte der Älteren Deutschen Literatur
FGO   Forschungen zur Geschichte Oberösterreichs
FH   Die Neue Gesellschaft/Frankfurter Hefte
FHP   Fort Hare Papers (Alice, Republic of Ciskei, South Africa)
FI   Forum Italicum
Field: Contemporary Poetry and Poetics
FilmC   Film Criticism
FilmQ   Film Quarterly
Filología (Buenos Aires, Argentina)
FirstL   First Language
FIZ   Farhang-e Irān Zamīn: Revue des Etudes Iranologiques
FJ   The Faulkner Journal
FJS   Fu Jen Studies: Literature & Linguistics (Taipei)
FK   Filológiai Közlöny
FLits   Foreign Literatures
Florilegium: Carleton University Annual Papers on Late Antiquity and the Middle Ages
FLS   French Literature Series (Columbia, SC)
FLTR   Foreign Language Teaching and Research: A Quarterly of Foreign Languages and Cultures
FM   Le Français Moderne: Revue de Linguistique Française
FMAS   Frühmittelalterliche Studien: Jahrbuch des Instituts für Frühmittelalterforschung der Universität Münster
FMJ   Folk Music Journal (London, England)
FMLS   Forum for Modern Language Studies
FMonde   Le Français dans le Monde
FN   Filologicheskie Nauki
FNS   Frank Norris Studies
FoK   Folk og Kultur: Årbog for Dansk Etnologi og Folkemindevidenskab
FoL   Folk Life: Journal of Ethnological Studies
FoLi   Folia Linguistica: Acta Societatis Linguisticae Europaeae
FoliaO   Folia Orientalia (Cracow, Poland)
FolkH   The Folklore Historian: Journal of the Folklore and History Section of the American Folklore Society
Folklore (London, England)
FolkloreC   Folklore: English Monthly Devoted to the Cause of Indian Folklore Society
FolkS   Folklore Suisse/Folclore Svizzero: Bulletin de la Société Suisse des Traditions Populaires/Bolletino della Società Svizzera per le Tradizioni Populari
ForL   Forum Linguisticum (Bern, Switzerland)
ForLing   Forum Linguisticum (Lake Bluff, IL)
ForoL   Foro Literario: Revista de Literatura y Lenguaje
ForumHL   Forum Homosexualität und Literatur (Siegen, Germany)
ForumS   Forum: A Ukrainian Review (Scranton, PA)
ForumZ   Forum (Zagreb, Croatia)
FoS   Foundations of Semiotics
Foundation: The Review of Science Fiction
Foxfire
FPhon   Folia Phoniatrica: International Journal of Phoniatrics, Speech Therapy and Communication Pathology
FPVRV   Forschungen zu Paul Valéry—Recherches Valéryennes
FR   The French Review: Journal of the American Association of Teachers of French

Francofonia: Studi e Ricerche Sulle Letterature di Lingua Francese
Francographies: Bulletin de la Société des Professeurs Français et Francophones d'Amérique [Supersedes *Bulletin de la Société des Professeurs Français d'Amérique*]
FranS   Franciscan Studies
FrF   French Forum
FrFM   French Forum Monographs
FRG&C   Focus on Robert Graves and His Contemporaries
FrH   Französisch Heute
FrL   La France Latine
Fróðskaparrit: Annales Societatis Scientiarum Faeroensis (Tórshavn, Faroe Islands)
FrontenacR   Revue Frontenac Review
Frontiers: A Journal of Women Studies
FrSt   Franziskanische Studien
FS   French Studies: A Quarterly Review
FSB   French Studies Bulletin: A Quarterly Supplement (Leeds, England)
FSSA   French Studies in Southern Africa
FSt   Feminist Studies
FSUC   Florida State University Conference on Literature and Film
FT   Finsk Tidskrift
FUF   Finnisch-Ugrische Forschungen: Zeitschrift für Finnisch-Ugrische Sprach- und Volkskunde
Función (Guadalajara, Mexico)
FurmS   Furman Studies
Fusta   La Fusta: Journal of Literature and Culture
FV   Fortuna Vitrea
FZPT   Freiburger Zeitschrift für Philosophie und Theologie
GA   Germanistische Abhandlungen
GAG   Göppinger Arbeiten zur Germanistik
GAGL   Groninger Arbeiten zur Germanistischen Linguistik
Gaia: Collana di Studi di Letteratura Comparata
GaiS   Gai Saber: Revista de l'Escòla Occitana (Toulouse, France)
GaR   The Georgia Review
Gardar: Årsbok för Samfundet Sverige-Island i Lund-Malmö
GB   Grazer Beiträge: Zeitschrift für die Klassische Altertumswissenschaft
GCBI   Godisnjak Centar za Balkanoloska Ispitivanja (Sarajevo, Bosnia and Herzegovina)
GCFI   Giornale Critico della Filosofia Italiana
GCY   German-Canadian Yearbook/Deutschkanadisches Jahrbuch
GdG   Grundlagen der Germanistik
GDRB   GDR Bulletin (St. Louis, MO)
GEGHLS   George Eliot-George Henry Lewes Studies [Formerly *The George Eliot-George Henry Lewes Newsletter*]
Genders
GenL   American University Studies XIX: General Literature
Genre (Norman, OK)
Geolinguistics: Journal of the American Society of Geolinguistics
GER   The George Eliot Review: Journal of the George Eliot Fellowship [Formerly *George Eliot Fellowship Review*]
Germanistik: Internationales Referatenorgan mit Bibliographischen Hinweisen
GerSR   German Studies Review
Gestos: Teoria y Practica del Teatro Hispánico
Gestus: The Electronic Journal of Brechtian Studies [Full text available online through EIES, NWI, COSY (Canada)]
GettR   The Gettysburg Review
GezellianaK   Gezelliana: Kroniek van de Gezellestudie
GGF   Göteborger Germanistische Forschungen
GHJ   George Herbert Journal
Gids   De Gids
GIF   Giornale Italiano di Filologia
GissingJ   The Gissing Journal [Formerly *The Gissing Newsletter*]
GJ   Gutenberg-Jahrbuch
GJLL   The Georgetown Journal of Languages and Linguistics
GK   Gengo Kenkyū: Journal of the Linguistic Society of Japan

GKa	Gimtoji Kalba
GL	General Linguistics (Binghamton, NY)
GL&L	German Life and Letters
GliA	Gli Annali Università per Stranieri
GLing	Germanistische Linguistik
GLL	American University Studies I: Germanic Languages and Literature
GLML	Garland Library of Medieval Literature

Glotta: Zeitschrift für Griechische und Lateinische Sprache

GlottaC	Glotta: Organo de Difusión Lingüística

Glottodidactica: An International Journal of Applied Linguistics (Poznań, Poland)

GLS	Grazer Linguistische Studien
GlyphT	Glyph Textual Studies
GMit	Germanistische Mitteilungen: Zeitschrift für Deutsche Sprache, Literatur und Kultur in Wissenschaft und Praxis
GMT	Garland Medieval Texts

Gnomon: Kritische Zeitschrift für die Gesamte Klassische Altertumswissenschaft

GNR	Germanic Notes and Reviews [Formerly *Germanic Notes*]
Goethe	Goethe-Jahrbuch
GoldK	Di Goldene Keyt
GothSE	Gothenburg Studies in English
GPQ	Great Plains Quarterly
GQ	The German Quarterly
GR	Germanic Review

Gradiva: International Journal of Italian Literature

GrandS	Grand Street

Grani: Zhurnal Literatury, Iskusstva, Nauki i Obshchestvenno-Politicheskoĭ Mysli

Gratia: Bamberger Schriften zur Renaissanceforschung

Grial: Revista Galega de Cultura (Vigo, Spain)

Griot: Official Journal of the Southern Conference on Afro-American Studies, Inc.

GRLH	Garland Reference Library of the Humanities
GRM	Germanisch-Romanische Monatsschrift
Grundzüge	
GSA	Germanic Studies in America
GSJ	Gaskell Society Journal
GSlav	Germano-Slavica: A Canadian Journal of Germanic and Slavic Comparative Studies
GSLI	Giornale Storico della Letteratura Italiana
GSLS	Georgia State Literary Studies Series
GSNA	Goethe Yearbook: Publications of the Goethe Society of North America
GSS	George Sand Studies
GStud	Grundtvig-Studier
GTS	Germanistische Texte und Studien (Hildesheim, Germany)
GURT	Georgetown University Round Table on Languages and Linguistics

Gymnasium: Zeitschrift für Kultur der Antike und Humanistische Bildung

HA	Handēs Amsōreay: Zeitschrift für Armenische Philologie
Haiku	Haiku Review

Halcyon: A Journal of the Humanities

HAR	Hebrew Annual Review
HBK	Hoppo Bunka Kenkyu: Bulletin of the Institute for the Study of North Eurasian Cultures, Hokkaido University
HBl	Hofmannsthal Blätter
HBR	Heidelberger Beiträge zur Romanistik
HBSÅ	Hjalmar Bergman Samfundet Årsbok (Stockholm, Sweden)
HC	The Hollins Critic
HCad	Hors Cadre: Le Cinéma à Travers Champs Disciplinaires
HCompL	Hebrew Linguistics: A Journal for Hebrew Formal, Computational, Applied Linguistics, and Modern Hebrew
HD	Human Development
HDNews	H. D. Newsletter
HEAS	Harvard East Asian Monographs
HebSt	Hebrew Studies: A Journal Devoted to Hebrew Language and Literature
HEI	History of European Ideas
HeineJ	Heine Jahrbuch
HelikonI	Helikon: Irodalomtudányi Szemle (Budapest, Hungary) [Formerly *Helikon: Világirodalmi Figyelő*]

Hellas: A Journal of Poetry and the Humanities

Hellenika	(Bochum, Germany)
HellēnikaS	Hellēnika: Philologikon, Historikon kai Laographikon Periodikon Syngramma

Hermaea: Germanistische Forschungen

Hermes: Zeitschrift für Klassische Philologie

HES	Harvard English Studies
HF	Heidelberger Forschungen
HisJ	Hispanic Journal (Indiana, PA)
Hispam	Hispamerica: Revista de Literatura

Hispania: A Journal Devoted to the Interests of the Teaching of Spanish and Portuguese

Hispano	Hispanófila (Chapel Hill, NC)
HispIss	Hispanic Issues
HJA&S	Hitotsubashi Journal of Arts and Sciences
HJAS	Harvard Journal of Asiatic Studies
HJb	Hebbel-Jahrbuch
HJR	The Henry James Review
HK	Heritage of the Great Plains
HL	Historiographia Linguistica: International Journal for the History of the Language Sciences/Revue Internationale pour l'Histoire des Sciences du Langage/Internationale Zeitschrift für die Geschichte der Sprachwissenschaften
HLB	Harvard Library Bulletin
HLing	Hispanic Linguistics
HLQ	Huntington Library Quarterly: A Journal for the History and Interpretation of English and American Civilization
HLS	Historiska och Litteraturhistoriska Studier (Helsinki, Finland)
HN	The Hemingway Review
HofP	Horns of Plenty: Malcolm Cowley and his Generation
HöJb	Hölderlin-Jahrbuch
HOL	Hefte für Ostasiatische Literatur
Homme	L'Homme: Revue Française d'Anthropologie
Horen	Die Horen: Zeitschrift für Literatur, Kunst und Kritik
Horisont	Kulturtidskriften HORISONT

Horizontes: Revista de la Universidad Católica de Puerto Rico

Hor Yezh

HP	Hispanica Posnaniensia
HPEN	The Hungarian P.E.N./Le P.E.N. Hongrois
HPLR	High Plains Literary Review
HPS	Hamburger Philologische Studien
HQ	The Hopkins Quarterly
HR	Hispanic Review
HRD	Hamburger Romanistische Dissertationen
HS	Humanities in the South: Newsletter of the Southern Humanities Council
HSCL	Harvard Studies in Comparative Literature
HSE	Hungarian Studies in English (Debrecen, Hungary)
HSELL	Hiroshima Studies in English Language and Literature
HSHL	Historische Sprachforschung/Historical Linguistics
HSJ	Housman Society Journal
HSL	University of Hartford Studies in Literature: A Journal of Interdisciplinary Criticism
HSR	Hungarian Studies Review
HSRL	Harvard Studies in Romance Languages
HSt	Hamlet Studies: An International Journal of Research on The Tragedie of Hamlet, Prince of Denmarke *(New Delhi, India)*
HStudien	Hispanistische Studien
HT	Historisk Tidskrift (Stockholm, Sweden)
HTR	Harvard Theological Review
HudR	The Hudson Review

HumanS	Human Studies: A Journal for Philosophy and the Social Sciences
HumB	Humanitas: Rivista bimestrale di Cultura (Brescia, Italy)
HumLov	Humanistica Lovaniensia: Journal of Neo-Latin Studies (Louvain, Belgium)

Humor: International Journal of Humor Research

HungQ	The Hungarian Quarterly [Formerly *The New Hungarian Quarterly*]
HUS	Harvard Ukrainian Studies
HUSL	Hebrew University Studies in Literature and the Arts
HymnM	Hymnologiske Meddelelser: Tidsskrift om Salmer
HZM	Handelingen van de Koninklijke Zuidnederlandse Maatschappij voor Taal- en Letterkunde en Geschiedenis
IAL	Issues in Applied Linguistics
IAN	Izvestiia Akademii Nauk, Seriia Literatury i Iazyka (Moscow, Russia) [Formerly *Izvestiia Akademii Nauk S.S.S.R., Seriia Literatury i Iazyka*]
IASL	Internationales Archiv für Sozialgeschichte der Deutschen Literatur
IASOP	Institute of African Studies, Occasional Publications (Ibadan, Nigeria)
IAT	Izvestiia Akademii Nauk Turkmenskoĭ SSR, Seriia Obshchestvennykh Nauk
IBD	Infant Behavior and Development: An International and Interdisciplinary Journal
Ibero	Iberoromania: Zeitschrift für die Iberoromanischen Sprachen und Literaturen in Europa und Amerika/Revista Dedicada a las Lenguas y Literaturas Iberorrománicas de Europa y América
IBK	Innsbrucker Beiträge zur Kulturwissenschaft: Germanistische Reihe

IBLA: Revue de l'Institut des Belles Lettres Arabes

IBP	Italian Books and Periodicals: Cultural and Bibliographic Review
I/C	Information/Communication

ICarbS (Carbondale, IL)

ID	L'Italia Dialettale: Rivista di Dialettologia Italiana
Idc	L'Intermédiaire des Casanovistes (Rome, Italy)
IdD	Ilha do Desterro: A Journal of Language and Literature
IdF	Impulse der Forschung

Idiomatica: Veröffentlichungen der Tübinger Arbeitsstelle 'Sprache in Südwestdeutschland'

IEY	Iowa English Bulletin
IF	Indogermanische Forschungen: Zeitschrift für Indogermanistik und Allgemeine Sprachwissenschaft
IFr	Italia Francescana
IFR	International Fiction Review
IFRev	International Folklore Review: Folklore Studies from Overseas
IG	L'Information Grammaticale
IHS	Irish Historical Studies
IIJ	Indo-Iranian Journal
IJAL	International Journal of American Linguistics
IJDL	International Journal of Dravidian Linguistics
IJL	Indian Journal of Linguistics/Praci-Bhasha-Vijnan
IJLex	International Journal of Lexicography [Incorporates *The EURALEX Newsletter*]
IJMES	International Journal of Middle East Studies
IJOAL	Indian Journal of Applied Linguistics
IJPP	Interpretation: A Journal of Political Philosophy
IJŠ	Inostrannye Iazyki v Shkole
IJSL	International Journal of the Sociology of Language
IJSLing	Internationales Journal of Sign Linguistics
IJSLP	International Journal of Slavic Linguistics and Poetics
IJT	International Journal of Translation
IK	Irodalomtörténeti Közlemények
IKw	Inmun Kwahak: The Journal of Humanities
IL	L'Information Littéraire: Revue Paraissant Cinq Fois par An
ILing	Initiation à la Linguistique
ILML	Istituto Lombardo, Accademia di Scienze e Lettere, Memorie
ILR	The Indian Literary Review: A Tri-Quarterly of Indian Literature
ILRL	Istituto Lombardo, Accademia di Scienze e Lettere, Rendiconti della Classe di Lettere

Imprévue (Montpellier, France)

IMU	Italia Medioevale e Umanistica

Incipit (Buenos Aires, Argentina)

IndH	Indian Horizons
IndL	Indian Literature
IndLing	Indian Linguistics: Journal of the Linguistic Society of India

Indonesia (Ithaca, NY)

Infini	L'Infini
InG	In Geardagum: Essays on Old and Middle English Language and Literature
Initiales	Initiales/Initials: Travaux des Etudiants de Cycle Supérieur, Département de Français, Université Dalhousie/Graduate Students' Writings, Department of French, Dalhousie University
INJAL	International Journal of Applied Linguistics

Inklings: Jahrbuch für Literatur und Ästhetik

InLi	Incontri Linguistici
InozF	Inozemna Filolohiia

Insula: Revista de Letras y Ciencias Humanas

Interface: Journal of Applied Linguistics/Tijdschrift voor Toegepaste Linguïstiek

Interplay: Proceedings of Colloquia in Comparative Literature and the Arts

Interprete	L'Interprete (Ravenna, Italy)

Inti: Revista de Literatura Hispánica

IonC	Index on Censorship
IowaR	The Iowa Review
IPAJ	Journal of the International Phonetic Association
IPEN	The Indian P.E.N.
IPOAPR	IPO Annual Progress Report
IQ	Italian Quarterly
IQdG	I Quaderni di Gaia: Rivista Semestrale di Letteratura Comparata e di Cultura Transdisciplinare
IqR	Iqbal Review: Journal of the Iqbal Academy Pakistan
IRAL	International Review of Applied Linguistics in Language Teaching

Iran: Journal of the British Institute of Persian Studies

IranS	Iranian Studies: Journal of the Society for Iranian Studies

Irian: Bulletin of Irian Jaya

Iris (Montpellier, France)

IrishSt	Irish Studies
IrisW	Iris: Graduate Journal of French Critical Studies
IRLI	Italianistica: Rivista di Letteratura Italiana
IrodalF	Irodalomtörténeti Füzetek
Irodalom	Irodalomtörténet: History of Literature (Budapest, Hungary)
IS	Italian Studies (Edinburgh, Scotland)
ISh	The Independent Shavian
Islam	Der Islam: Zeitschrift für Geschichte und Kultur des Islamischen Orients
ISlSt	Irish Slavonic Studies
ISSJ	International Social Science Journal
ItalAm	Italian Americana
Italianist	The Italianist: Journal of the Department of Italian Studies, University of Reading

Italica

ItalienischZ	Italienisch: Zeitschrift für Italienische Sprache und Literatur
ItB	It Beaken: Tydskrift fan de Fryske Akademy
ItC	Italian Culture
ItF	Italyan Filolojisi/Filologia Italiana

ITL: Review of Applied Linguistics

IUPUAS	Indiana University Uralic and Altaic Series
IUR	Irish University Review: A Journal of Irish Studies

Izraz: Časopis za Književnu i Umjetničku Kritiku (Sarajevo, Bosnia and Herzegovina)
JAAC	Journal of Aesthetics and Art Criticism
JAAL	Journal of Afroasiatic Languages
JAAR	Journal of the American Academy of Religion

Jabberwocky: The Journal of the Lewis Carroll Society
JAC	Journal of Advanced Composition
JACult	Journal of American Culture
JAF	Journal of American Folklore
JAIS	Journal of Anglo-Italian Studies (Malta)
JALL	Journal of African Languages and Linguistics (Leiden, Netherlands)
JAmS	Journal of American Studies
JAOS	Journal of the American Oriental Society
JAP	Journal of Abnormal Psychology
JapQ	Japan Quarterly
JAR	Journal of Anthropological Research
JARAAS	Journal of the American Romanian Academy of Arts and Sciences
JArabL	Journal of Arabic Literature
JAS	Journal of the Acoustical Society of America
JASA	Journal of the Appalachian Studies Association
JASAT	Journal of the American Studies Association of Texas
JASB	Journal of the Asiatic Society of Bombay
JAsiat	Journal Asiatique
JASt	Journal of Asian Studies
JATJ	Journal of the Association of Teachers of Japanese
JAusL	Journal of Australian Literature
JBalS	Journal of Baltic Studies
JBeckS	Journal of Beckett Studies
JC	Journal of Communication (New York, NY)
JCeltL	Journal of Celtic Linguistics
JCF	Journal of Canadian Fiction
JCG	Journal of Cultural Geography
JCHAS	Journal of the Cork Historical and Archaeological Society
JChinL	Journal of Chinese Linguistics (Berkeley, CA)
JChinP	Journal of Chinese Philosophy
JChL	Journal of Child Language
JChSt	Journal of Chinese Studies
JCL	The Journal of Commonwealth Literature
JCLA	Journal of Comparative Literature and Aesthetics
JCLS	Jyväskylä Cross-Language Studies
JCLTA	Journal of the Chinese Language Teachers Association
JCM	The Journal of Country Music
JCP	Journal of Canadian Poetry
JCS	Journal of Croatian Studies: Annual Review of the Croatian Academy of America, Inc.
JCSJ	John Clare Society Journal
JCSR	Journal of Canadian Studies/Revue d'Etudes Canadiennes
JCSt	Journal of Caribbean Studies
JCunS	Journal of Cuneiform Studies
JD	Journal of Documentation
JDECU	Journal of the Department of English (Calcutta Univ.)
JDHLS	D. H. Lawrence: The Journal of the D. H. Lawrence Society
JDJ	John Donne Journal: Studies in the Age of Donne
JDN	James Dickey Newsletter
JDS	Salzburg Studies in English: Jacobean Drama Studies
JDSG	Jahrbuch der Deutschen Schillergesellschaft
JDTC	Journal of Dramatic Theory and Criticism
JDurS	Journal of Durassian Studies
JEAL	Journal of East Asian Linguistics
JEFL	Journal of English and Foreign Languages
JEGP	Journal of English and Germanic Philology
JEI	Journal of the English Institute
JELL	The Journal of English Language and Literature
JELL-CB	Journal of the English Language and Literature (Chungbuk Branch, English Language and Literature Assn. of Korea)
JEn	Journal of English
JEngL	Journal of English Linguistics
JEngS	Journal of English Studies
JENS	Journal of the Eighteen Nineties Society
JEP	Journal of Evolutionary Psychology
JES	Journal of European Studies
JExPH	Journal of Experimental Psychology: Human Perception and Performance
JExPLMC	Journal of Experimental Psychology: Learning, Memory, and Cognition

Jezik: Časopis za Kulturu Hrvatskoga Književnog Jezika (Zagreb, Croatia)
JF	Južnoslovenski Filolog
JFDH	Jahrbuch des Freien Deutschen Hochstifts (Tübingen, Germany)
JFDL	Jahrbuch für Finnisch-Deutsche Literaturbeziehungen: Mitteilungen aus der Deutschen Bibliothek
JFER	Jewish Folklore and Ethnology Review
JFL	Jahrbuch für Fränkische Landesforschung
JFLS	Journal of French Language Studies
JFR	Journal of Folklore Research (Bloomington, IN)
JGa	Jaunā Gaita

JGE: The Journal of General Education
JGG	Jahrbuch der Grillparzer-Gesellschaft
JGJRI	Journal of the Ganganatha Jha Kendriya Sanskrit Vidyapeetha
JGLS	Journal of the Gypsy Lore Society
JH	Journal of Humanities
JHD	Journal of the Hellenic Diaspora
JHI	Journal of the History of Ideas
JHP	Journal of Hispanic Philology (Tallahassee, FL)
JIES	Journal of Indo-European Studies
JIG	Jahrbuch für Internationale Germanistik
JIGA	Jahrbuch für Internationale Germanistik: Reihe A: Kongressberichte
JIL	Journal of Irish Literature
JILS	Journal of Interdisciplinary Literary Studies/Cuadernos Interdisciplinarios de Estudios Literarios
JIP	Journal of Indian Philosophy
JiS	Jezik in Slovstvo (Ljubljana, Slovenia)
JISHS	Illinois Historical Journal
JIWE	The Journal of Indian Writing in English
JJCL	Jadavpur Journal of Comparative Literature
JJPG	Jahrbuch der Jean-Paul-Gesellschaft
JJQ	James Joyce Quarterly
JJS	The Journal of Japanese Studies
JKMG	Jahrbuch der Karl-May-Gesellschaft
JKSA	Journal of the Kafka Society of America
JKSUA	Journal of King Saud University, Arts
JKWJC	Journal of Kyoritsu Women's Junior College
JL	Journal of Linguistics (Cambridge, England)
JLAL	Journal of Latin American Lore
JLD	Journal of Learning Disabilities
JLDS	Journal of the Lancashire Dialect Society
JLS	Journal of Literary Semantics
JLSP	Journal of Language and Social Psychology
JLSTL	Journal of Literary Studies/Tydskrif Vir Literaturwetenskap
JMacL	Journal of Macrolinguistics
JMAS	The Journal of Modern African Studies
JMemL	Journal of Memory and Language
JMGS	Journal of Modern Greek Studies
JML	Journal of Modern Literature
JMLing	Journal of Mayan Linguistics
JMMD	Journal of Multilingual and Multicultural Development
JMMLA	The Journal of the Midwest Modern Language Association
JMRS	Journal of Medieval and Renaissance Studies
JMSUB	Journal of the Maharaja Sayajirao University of Baroda
JNB	Journal of Nonverbal Behavior
JNES	Journal of Near Eastern Studies (Chicago, IL)
JNMD	Journal of Nervous and Mental Disease
JNPH	Journal of Newspaper and Periodical History
JNT	Journal of Narrative Technique

JNWSL	Journal of Northwest Semitic Languages (Stellenbosch, South Africa)
JÖBG	Jahrbuch der Österreichischen Byzantinistik
JOCI	Journal of Communication Inquiry
JoHS	Journal of Hellenic Studies
JOIB	Journal of the Oriental Institute (Baroda, India)
Jolan: Journal of the Linguistic Association of Nigeria	
JoS	Journal of Semantics: An International Journal for the Interdisciplinary Study of the Semantics of Natural Language (Oxford, England)
JP	Journal of Philosophy
JPC	Journal of Popular Culture
JPCL	Journal of Pidgin and Creole Languages
JPFT	Journal of Popular Film and Television
JPhon	Journal of Phonetics
JPL	Journal of Philosophical Logic
JPol	Język Polski
JPrag	Journal of Pragmatics: An Interdisciplinary Monthly of Language Studies [Formerly Journal of Pragmatics: An Interdisciplinary Bi-Monthly of Language Studies]
JPRS	The Journal of Pre-Raphaelite Studies
JPS	Journal of the Polynesian Society (Auckland, New Zealand)
JPSP	Journal of Personality and Social Psychology
JPsyR	Journal of Psycholinguistic Research
JQ	Journalism Quarterly
JRAS	Journal of the Royal Asiatic Society of Great Britain and Ireland
JRASM	Journal of the Malaysian Branch of the Royal Asiatic Society
JRG	Jahrbuch der Raabe-Gesellschaft
JRMMRA	Journal of the Rocky Mountain Medieval and Renaissance Association
JRR	Jean Rhys Review
JRSAI	Journal of the Royal Society of Antiquaries of Ireland
JRStud	Journal of Ritual Studies
JRUL	Journal of the Rutgers University Libraries
JS	Journal des Savants
JSA	Joyce Studies Annual
JSBSA	Journal of the Society of Basque Studies in America
JSem	Journal for Semitics/Tydskrif vir Semitistiek
JSHR	Journal of Speech and Hearing Research
JSK	Jahrbuch der Sammlung Kippenberg (Düsseldorf, Germany)
JSL	Journal of the School of Languages
JSoAL	Journal of South Asian Literature
JSS	Journal of Semitic Studies
JSSB	Journal of the Siam Society (Bangkok, Thailand)
JSSE	Journal of the Short Story in English
JSSR	Journal for the Scientific Study of Religion (Akron, OH)
JSw	Journal of the Southwest
JTamS	Journal of Tamil Studies
Judaism: A Quarterly Journal of Jewish Life and Thought	
JUkGS	Journal of Ukrainian Studies
JV	Jahrbuch für Volksliedforschung
JWAL	The Journal of West African Languages
JWCI	Journal of the Warburg and Courtauld Institutes
JWGV	Jahrbuch des Wiener Goethe-Vereins
JWIL	Journal of West Indian Literature
JWMS	The Journal of the William Morris Society
Kadmos: Zeitschrift für Vor- und Frühgriechische Epigraphik	
KAL	Kyushu American Literature (Fukuoka, Japan)
Kalbotyra: Lietuvos Aukštųjų Mokyklų Mokslo Darbai (Vilnius, Lithuania)	
Kalki: Studies in James Branch Cabell	
Kanava	
K&K: Kultur og Klasse. Kritik og Kulturanalyse [Formerly Kultur & Klasse]	
Káñina: Revista de Artes y Letras de la Universidad de Costa Rica	
KanQ	Kansas Quarterly
KAr	Kansatieteellinen Arkisto
Karogs (Riga, Latvia)	
KASL	Kasseler Arbeiten zur Sprache und Literatur: Anglistik-Germanistik-Romanistik
KB	Kultūros Barai
KBCJ	Jaarboek Koninklijke Belgische Commissie voor Volkskunde, Vlaamse Afdeling
KBGL	Kopenhagener Beiträge zur Germanistischen Linguistik
KDSL	Konzepte der Sprach- und Literaturwissenschaft
KDVS	Kongelige Danske Videnskabernes Selskab. Historisk-Filosofiske Meddelelser (Copenhagen, Denmark)
KeK	Keiryō Kokugogaku/Mathematical Linguistics
KerC	Kerkyraïka Chronika
KGad	Kritikas Gadagrāmata (Riga, Latvia)
KGGJ	Klaus-Groth-Gesellschaft Jahresgabe
KGUAS	Kwansei Gakuin University Annual Studies
KiJ	Književnost i Jezik
Kiswahili	
KJ	The Kipling Journal
KjK	Keel ja Kirjandus (Tallinn, Estonia)
KL	Kypriakos Logos
Klage: Kölner Linguistische Arbeiten—Germanistik	
Klasgids: By die Studie van die Afrikaanse Taal en Letterkunde	
KN	Kwartalnik Neofilologiczny (Warsaw, Poland)
Knji	Književnost
KnjiK	Književna Kritika: Časopis za Estetiku Književnosti
KnjiNov	Književne Novine: List za Književnost i Kulturu (Belgrade, Yugoslavia)
KnjIst	Književna Istorija
Knygotyra: Vilniaus Universiteto Mokslo Darbai (Vilnius, Lithuania) [Formerly Knygotyra: Lietuvos TSR Aukštųjų Mokyklų Mokslo Darbai]	
Kodikas	Kodikas/Code/Ars semeiotica
KoJ	Korea Journal
Kontekst: Literary Theory Studies	
Kortárs	Kortárs: Irodalmi és Kritikai Folyóirat
Korunk (Cluj-Kolozsvar, Romania)	
KPR	Kentucky Philological Review
KPS	Korespondence Pomembnih Slovencev
KR	The Kenyon Review
KRA	Kölner Romanistische Arbeiten
KRev	The Kentucky Review
Kritik: Tidsskrift for Litteratur, Forskning, Undervisning (Copenhagen, Denmark)	
KRQ	Romance Quarterly
KSGT	Kleine Schriften der Gesellschaft für Theatergeschichte
KSJ	Keats-Shelley Journal: Keats, Shelley, Byron, Hunt, and Their Circles
KSl	Kul'tura Slova
KSMB	Keats-Shelley Review
KSV	Kirjallisuudentutkijain Seuran Vuosikirja (Helsinki, Finland)
KSVK	Kalevalaseuran Vuosikirja
Kuka: Journal of Creative and Critical Writing (Zaria, Nigeria)	
KulturaP	Kultura: Szkice, Opowiadania, Sprawozdania (Paris, France)
Kunapipi	
KVNS	Korrespondenzblatt des Vereins für Niederdeutsche Sprachforschung
KyS	Kypriakai Spoudai
LA	Linguistica Antverpiensia
LA&LD	Language Acquisition & Language Disorders
LAcq	Language Acquisition: A Journal of Developmental Linguistics
LAf	Linguistique Africaine
LAILJ	Latin American Indian Literatures Journal: A Review of American Indian Texts and Studies
LAkt	Linguistik Aktuell
LAL	Library of Arabic Linguistics
LAlb	Les Lettres Albanaises: Revue Littéraire et Artistique
LaLit	Louisiana Literature: A Review of Literature and Humanities
LALR	Latin American Literary Review

LAmer	Letterature d'America: Rivista Trimestrale
LAMR	Latin American Music Review/Revista de Música Latinoamericana
L&B	Literature and Belief
L&C	Language & Communication: An Interdisciplinary Journal
L&Comp	Language and Computers: Studies in Practical Linguistics
L&E	Linguistics and Education: An International Research Journal

Landfall: A New Zealand Quarterly

L&H	Literature and History
L&LC	Literary and Linguistic Computing: Journal of the Association for Literary and Linguistic Computing
L&LifeA	Literature and Life: American Writers
L&LifeB	Literature and Life: British Writers
L&LifeW	Literature and Life: World Writers
L&LinM	Language and Linguistics in Melanesia: Journal of the Linguistic Society of Papua New Guinea
L&M	Literature and Medicine
L&P	Literature and Psychology
L&S	Language and Speech
L&Soc	Langage et Société
L&T	Literature & Theology: An Interdisciplinary Journal of Theory and Criticism
L&U	The Lion and the Unicorn: A Critical Journal of Children's Literature

Langages (Paris, France)

Lang&C	Language and Culture (Hokkaido Univ.)
Lang&H	Le Langage et l'Homme: Recherches Pluridisciplinaires sur le Langage
Lang&Lit	Language and Literature: Journal of the Poetics and Linguistics Association
Lang&S	Language and Style: An International Journal
LangF	Language Forum: A Half-Yearly Journal of Language and Literature
LangQ	The Language Quarterly (Tampa, FL)
LangR	Language Research
LangS	Language Sciences
LangT	Language Testing

Language: Journal of the Linguistic Society of America

Langues&L	Langues et Linguistique
LanM	Les Langues Modernes
LArb	Linguistische Arbeiten
LArm	Literaturnaia Armeniia: Ezhemesiachnyĭ Literaturno-Khudozhestvennyĭ i Obshchestvenno-Politicheskiĭ Zhurnal
LAS	Living Author Series
LatAL	American University Studies XXII: Latin American Literature

Latinitas: Commentarii Linguae Latinae Excolendae
Latomus: Revue d'Etudes Latines

LATR	Latin American Theatre Review
LB	Leuvense Bijdragen: Contributions in Linguistics and Philology
LBib	Linguistica Biblica: Interdisziplinäre Zeitschrift für Theologie und Linguistik
LBl	Living Blues: A Journal of the African-American Blues Tradition [Formerly *Living Blues: A Journal of the Black American Blues Tradition*]
LBR	Luso-Brazilian Review
LC&C	Language, Culture, and Curriculum
LCC	Léachtaí Cholm Cille
LCP	Language and Cognitive Processes
LCRC	Literature and Contemporary Revolutionary Culture: Journal of the Society of Contemporary Hispanic and Lusophone Revolutionary Literatures
LCrit	The Literary Criterion (Mysore, India)
LCUT	Library Chronicle of the University of Texas
LDant	Lectura Dantis: A Forum for Dante Research and Interpretation
LdBA	Letras de Buenos Aires
LdC	Lletra de Canvi
LdD	Letras de Deusto
LdProv	Il Lettore di Provincia
LE	Linguistica Extranea
LEA	Lingüística Española Actual
LE&W	Literature East and West
LeedsSE	Leeds Studies in English

Legacy: A Journal of American Women Writers [Formerly *Legacy: A Journal of Nineteenth-Century American Women Writers*]
Lendemains: Etudes Comparées sur la France/Vergleichende Frankreichforschung

LengM	Lenguas Modernas

Lenguaje (Cali, Colombia)

LeS	Lingua e Stile: Trimestrale di Filosofia del Linguaggio, Linguistica e Analisi Letteraria (Bologna, Italy) [Formerly *Lingua e Stile: Trimestrale di Linguistica e Critica Letteraria*]
Leshonenu	Leshonenu/Lĕšonénu: A Journal for the Study of the Hebrew Language and Cognate Subjects/Ketav-'Et le-Ḥeqer ha-Lashon ha-'Ivrit ve-ha-Teḥumim ha-Semukhim Lah
LetC	Letture Classensi
LetP	Letras Peninsulares

Letterato: Periodico di Attualità e Cultura
Letture: Libro e Spettacolo/Mensile di Studi e Rassegne
Lexicographica: International Annual for Lexicography/Revue Internationale de Lexicographie/Internationales Jahrbuch für Lexikographie

LexicographicaS	Lexicographica: Series Maior

Lexique (Villeneuve d'Ascq, France)
Lexis: Revista de Lingüística y Literatura

LF	Listy Filologické: Folia Philologica
LFC	Letteratura Francese Contemporanea le Correnti d'Avanguardia: Berenice
LFem	Letras Femeninas
LfL	Literatur für Leser
LFoiro	Literatura Foiro: Kultura Revuo en Esperanto
LForum	Literaturen Forum: Sedmichnik na Nesavisimite Balgarski Pisateli (Sofia, Bulgaria) [Formerly *Literaturen Front: Organ na Suiuza na Bulgarskite Pisateli*]
LFQ	Literature/Film Quarterly
LFr	Langue Française
LG	Literaturnaia Gazeta
LGF	Lunder Germanistische Forschungen
LGGL	Literatur in der Geschichte, Geschichte in der Literatur
LGJ	Lost Generation Journal
LGriot	The Literary Griot: International Journal of Black Oral and Literary Studies
LHRev	The Langston Hughes Review
LHY	Literary Half-Yearly
LI	Lettere Italiane
Lib&C	Libraries & Culture: A Journal of Library History

Liberté (Montréal, Canada)
Librarium: Zeitschrift der Schweizerischen Bibliophilen-Gesellschaft/Revue de la Société Suisse des Bibliophiles

Library	The Library: The Transactions of the Bibliographical Society

Libri: International Library Review (Copenhagen, Denmark)

LIC	Letteratura Italiana Contemporaneo: Rivista Quadrimestrale di Studi Sul Novecento
Licorne	La Licorne

LiLi: Zeitschrift für Literaturwissenschaft und Linguistik

LiMen	Literatūra ir Menas
LimR	Limba Română
Ling	American University Studies XIII: Linguistics
LingA	Linguistic Analysis
LingAb	Linguistics Abstracts
Ling&L	Língua e Literatura: Revista dos Departamentos de Letras da Faculdade de Filosofia, Letras e Ciêncas Humanas da Universidade de São Paulo
Ling&P	Linguistics and Philosophy: An International Journal
LingB	Linguistische Berichte
LingI	Linguistic Inquiry

LingInv	Lingvisticæ Investigationes: Revue Internationale de Linguistique Française et de Linguistique Générale
Lingua: International Review of General Linguistics	
Linguist	The Linguist
Linguistica (Ljubljana, Slovenia)	
Linguistics: An Interdisciplinary Journal of the Language Sciences	
Linguistique	La Linguistique: Revue de la Société Internationale de Linguistique Fonctionnelle/Journal of the International Society of Functional Linguistics (Paris, France)
LiNQ: (Literature in North Queensland)	
LinS	Language in Society (Oxford, England)
LIS	Lingvisticæ Investigationes: Supplementa: Studies in French & General Linguistics/Etudes en Linguistique Française et Générale
LiSa	Litteratur og Samfund
LISL	Amsterdam Studies in the Theory and History of Linguistic Science V: Library and Information Sources in Linguistics
Lit	Littérature (Paris, France)
LIT	Lit: Literature Interpretation Theory
LitAS	Literatur als Sprache: Literaturtheorie—Interpretation—Sprachkritik
LitC	Literatura Chilena: Creación y Crítica
LitE	The Literary Endeavour: A Quarterly Journal Devoted to English Studies
Literator: Tydskrif vir Besondere en Vergelykende Taal- en Literatuurstudie/Journal of Literary Criticism, Comparative Linguistics and Literary Studies	
Literatura (Budapest, Hungary)	
Literatūra: Lietuvos Aukštųjų Mokyklų Mokslo Darbai (Vilnius, Lithuania)	
LitLeks	Literarni Leksikon
LitR	The Literary Review: An International Journal of Contemporary Writing (Madison, NJ)
Litt	Littératures (Toulouse, France)
Litteraria: Teoria Literatury. Metodologia. Kultura. Humanistyka	
LittéRéalité	
LittSlov	Litterae Slovenicae: A Slovene Literary Magazine (Ljubljana, Slovenia) [Formerly *Le Livre Slovène*]
Lituanus: Baltic States Quarterly of Arts & Sciences	
LJb	Lutherjahrbuch
LJGG	Literaturwissenschaftliches Jahrbuch im Auftrage der Görres-Gesellschaft
LJH	Legon Journal of the Humanities (Legon, Ghana)
LJHum	Lamar Journal of the Humanities
LKK	Lietuvių Kalbotyros Klausimai
LL	Language Learning: A Journal of Applied Linguistics
LLa	Leshonenu La'Am
Llên Cymru	
LLNL	Les Langues Néo-Latines: Bulletin Trimestriel de la Société de Langues Néo-Latines
LLSEE	Linguistic and Literary Studies in Eastern Europe
LLud	Literatura Ludowa
LMex	Literatura Mexicana
LMHS	Liverpool Monographs in Hispanic Studies
LMi	Literaturna Misŭl (Sofia, Bulgaria)
LN	Lingua Nostra
LnL	Language and Literature (San Antonio, TX)
LO	Literaturnoe Obozrenie: Organ Soiuza Pisateleĭ SSSR
LoomingE	Looming: Eesti Kirjanike Liidu Kuukiri (Tallinn, Estonia)
Lore&L	Lore and Language
LP	Lingua Posnaniensis: Czasopismo Poświecone Językoznawstwu Porównawczemu i Ogólnemu
LPFMRD	Lingvisticheskie Problemy Funktsional'nogo Modelirovaniia Rechevoĭ Deiatel'nosti
LPLP	Language Problems and Language Planning/Lingvaj Problemoj kaj Lingvo-Planado
LQ	Lettres Québécoises
LR	Les Lettres Romanes
LRB	London Review of Books
LRN	Literary Research: A Journal of Scholarly Method and Technique
LSE	Lund Studies in English
LSil	Linguistica Silesiana
LSoc	Language in Society (New York, NY)
LSp	Lebende Sprachen: Zeitschrift für Fremde Sprachen in Wissenschaft und Praxis
LSPd	Literary Studies in Poland/Etudes Littéraires en Pologne
LSS	Leyte-Samar Studies
LSt	Lovecraft Studies
LT	Levende Talen
LTBA	Linguistics of the Tibeto-Burman Area
LTeach	Language Teaching: The International Abstracting Journal for Language Teachers and Applied Linguists
LTM	Leeds Texts and Monographs
Luc	Luceafărul (Bucharest, Romania)
Lucero: A Journal of Iberian and Latin American Studies	
Lud: Organ Polskiego Towarzystwa Ludoznawczego i Komitetu Nauk Etnologicznych Polskiej Akademii Nauk/Organe de la Société Polonaise d'Ethnologie et du Comité des Sciences Ethnologiques	
LuG	Literatur und Geschichte: Eine Schriftenreihe
LuK	Literatur und Kritik (Salzburg, Austria)
LuM	Literatura un Māksla
LUral	Linguistica Uralica
Luther: Zeitschrift der Luther-Gesellschaft	
LV&C	Language Variation and Change
LWU	Literatur in Wissenschaft und Unterricht (Kiel, Germany)
LY	Lessing Yearbook/Jahrbuch
LyC	Lenguaje y Ciencias
LyL	Literatura y Lingüística (Santiago, Chile)
LyLit	Lingüística y Literatura (Medellín, Colombia)
Lyrikvännen (Stockholm, Sweden)	
LyT	Lenguaje y Texto
LZ	Literaturen Zbor: Spisanie na Sojuzot na Društvata za Makedonski Jazik i Literatura na SR Makedonija
LZAV	Latvijas Zinātņu Akadēmijas Vēstis (Riga, Latvia) [Formerly *Latvijas PSR Zinātņu Akadēmijas Vēstis*]
MA	Le Moyen Âge: Revue d'Histoire et de Philologie [Formerly *Le Moyen Age: Revue Historique*]
Maatstaf	
MachT	Machine Translation
MACLCL	Memórias da Academia das Ciências de Lisboa, Classe de Letras
MacR	Macedonian Review: History, Culture, Literature, Arts
MÆ	Medium Ævum
Magazine (Abington, PA)	
MagLitt	Magazine Littéraire
MagN	Magyar Nyelvőr
Maia: Rivista di Letterature Classiche	
Makedonika	
MAL	Modern Austrian Literature
Maladosts': Literaturno-Mastatski i Hramadska-Palitychny Chasopis	
Maledicta: The International Journal of Verbal Aggression	
Mallorn: The Journal of the Tolkien Society	
Mana	
M&C	Memory & Cognition
M&H	Medievalia et Humanistica: Studies in Medieval and Renaissance Culture
M&L	Music & Letters
M&N	Man and Nature/L'Homme et La Nature: Proceedings of the Canadian Society for Eighteenth-Century Studies/Actes de la Société Canadienne d'Etude du Dix-Huitième Siècle
M&SA	Metaphor and Symbolic Activity
ManQ	The Mankind Quarterly
Manuscripta (St. Louis, MO)	
Manuscriptum: Revistă Trimestrială Editată de Muzeul Literaturii Române	
MAPS	Memoirs of the American Philosophical Society
MARev	Mid-American Review
Marges	

Marginalien: Zeitschrift für Buchkunst und Bibliophilie
Marianum
Markers: The Journal of the Association for Gravestone Studies
MarM   Marbacher Magazin
MASO   Meijerbergs Arkiv för Svensk Ordforskning
Matatu: Journal for African Culture and Society
MAWAR   MAWA Review
Mawazo: The Makerere Journal of the Faculties of Arts and Social Sciences
MayR   The Maynooth Review/Reiviú Mhá Nuad: A Journal of the Arts
MBMRF   Münchener Beiträge zur Mediävistik u. Renaissance-Forschung
MCL   Modern Chinese Literature
McNR   McNeese Review
MCRel   Mythes, Croyances et Religions dans le Monde Anglo-Saxon
MCul   Material Culture: Journal of the Pioneer American Society
McWPL   McGill Working Papers in Linguistics/Cahiers Linguistiques de McGill
MD   Modern Drama
MDAM   Majalle(h)-ye Dāneshkade(h)-ye Adabiyyāt-e va Olume-e Ensanie-e Danashga(h)-e Ferdowsi
MDOG   Mitteilungen der Deutschen Orient-Gesellschaft zu Berlin
MEAH   Miscelanea de Estudios Arabes y Hebraicos: II. Filologia Hebrea, Biblia y Judaismo
Meanjin
Meddelelser
Mediaevalia: A Journal of Mediaeval Studies
Medien   Medien in Forschung + Unterricht: Series A
Médiévales: Langue, Textes, Histoire
MedLR   Mediterranean Language Review
MedPers   Medieval Perspectives
MedR   Medioevo Romanzo
MELUS: The Journal of the Society for the Study of the Multi-Ethnic Literature of the United States
Menckeniana: A Quarterly Review
Merkur: Deutsche Zeitschrift für europäisches Denken
MertAn   The Merton Annual: Studies in Thomas Merton, Religion, Culture, Literature and Social Concerns
Mester
MET   Middle English Texts
Meta: Journal des Traducteurs/Translators' Journal
METh   Medieval English Theatre
METhMST   Medieval English Theatre Modern-Spelling Texts
Metmenys
MFCG   Mitteilungen und Forschungsbeiträge der Cusanus-Gesellschaft
MFra   Le Moyen Français
MFS   Modern Fiction Studies
MFSJ   Missouri Folklore Society Journal
MGB   Münchener Germanistische Beiträge
MGS   Michigan Germanic Studies
MGSL   Minas Gerais, Suplemento Literário
MGv   Molodaia Gvardiia: Ezhemesiachnyĭ Literaturno-Khudozhestvennyĭ i Obshchestvenno-Politicheskiĭ Zhurnal
MH   Museum Helveticum: Schweizerische Zeitschrift für Klassische Altertumswissenschaft/Revue Suisse pour l'Etude de l'Antiquité Classique/Rivista svizzera di Filologia Classica
MHG   Mitteilungen der E.T.A. Hoffmann-Gesellschaft-Bamberg e.V.
MHL   Modern Hebrew Literature
MHRADS   Modern Humanities Research Association Texts and Dissertations Series
MichA   Michigan Academician
Midamerica: The Yearbook of the Society for the Study of Midwestern Literature
MidF   Midwestern Folklore
MidSF   Mid-America Folklore

MiltonQ   Milton Quarterly
MiltonS   Milton Studies
Mimesis: Untersuchungen zu den Romanischen Literaturen der Neuzeit/Recherches sur les Littératures Romanes depuis la Renaissance
Mind: A Quarterly Review of Philosophy
MinnR   The Minnesota Review
Minos: Revista de Filologia Egea (Salamanca, Spain)
Miorița: A Journal of Romanian Studies
MiscMed   Miscellanea Mediaevalia
MissFR   Mississippi Folklore Register
MissQ   Mississippi Quarterly: The Journal of Southern Culture
MissR   The Missouri Review
MitJ   Mittellateinisches Jahrbuch: Internationale Zeitschrift für Mediävistik/International Journal of Medieval Studies/Revue Internationale des Etudes Médiévales/Rivista Internazionale di Studi Medievali
MITOPL   MIT Occasional Papers in Linguistics
MITWPL   MIT Working Papers in Linguistics
MJ   Makedonski Jazik
MJCL&L   Meerut Journal of Comparative Literature and Language
MK   Magyar Könyvszemle: Könyvtörténeti Folyóirat/Revue pour l'Histoire du Livre et de la Presse
MKNAL   Mededelingen der Koninklijke Nederlandse Akademie van Wetenschappen, Afdeling Letterkunde, Nieuwe Reeks
MKS   Mon-Khmer Studies: A Journal of Southeast Asian Languages
Mladika (Trieste, Italy)
MLing   Modèles Linguistiques
MLit   Miesięcznik Literacki (Warsaw, Poland)
MLJ   The Modern Language Journal
MLN (Baltimore, MD)
MLNew   The Malcolm Lowry Review
MLQ   Modern Language Quarterly
MLR   The Modern Language Review
MLS   Modern Language Studies
MM   Maal og Minne
MMisc   Midwestern Miscellany
MML   Monographs in Modern Languages
MN   Monumenta Nipponica
MNCDN   Mededelingen van de Nijmeegse Centrale voor Dialect- en Naamkunde
Mnemosyne: Bibliotheca Classica Batava
MnēmosynēA   Mnēmosynē: Etēsion Periodikon tēs Hetaireias Historikōn Spoudōn epi tou Neōterou Hellēnismou (Athens, Greece)
MNy   Magyar Nyelv
MNyj   Magyar Nyelvjárások
ModA   Modern Age: A Quarterly Review
Modellanalysen: Literatur
Mogućnosti: Književnost, Umjetnost, Kulturni Problemi
MOII   Metodika Obuchenia Inostrannym Iazykam: Romanskoe i Germanskoe Iazykoznanie (Minsk, Belarus)
Monatshefte   Monatshefte für Deutschen Unterricht, Deutsche Sprache und Literatur
MontS   Montaigne Studies: An Interdisciplinary Forum
MOR   Mount Olive Review
Moreana: Bulletin Thomas More
Morphé: Ciencias del Lenguaje [Formerly *Morphé: Semiótica y Lingüística*]
Mosaic: A Journal for the Interdisciplinary Study of Literature
Mostovi
Motif: International Review of Research in Folklore & Literature
Mov   Movoznavstvo: Naukovo-Teoretychnyĭ Zhurnal Viddilennia Literatury, Movy i Mystetstvoznavstva Akademiĭ Nauk Ukraine (Kiev, Ukraine) [Formerly *Movoznavstvo: Naukovo-Teoretychnyĭ Zhurnal Viddilennia Literatury, Movy i Mystetstvoznavstva Akademiĭ Nauk Ukrains'oĭ RSR*]

Moznayim: Yarḥon Agudat ha-Soferim ha-'Ivrim be-Medinat Yiśrael/ Monthly of the Association of Hebrew Writers in Israel (Tel Aviv, Israel)
MP   Modern Philology: A Journal Devoted to Research in Medieval and Modern Literature
MPR   The Mervyn Peake Review
MQ   Midwest Quarterly: A Journal of Contemporary Thought (Pittsburg, KS)
MQR   Michigan Quarterly Review
MR   Massachusetts Review: A Quarterly of Literature, the Arts and Public Affairs
MRD   Memoirs of the Research Department of the Tōyō Bunko (Tokyo, Japan)
MRDE   Medieval & Renaissance Drama in England: An Annual Gathering of Research, Criticism and Reviews
MRMS   Medieval and Renaissance Monograph Series
MRom   Marche Romane
MRRM   Monographic Review/Revista Monográfica
MRS   Michigan Romance Studies
MRTS   Medieval & Renaissance Texts & Studies
MS   Mediaeval Studies (Toronto, Canada)
MSAS   Monographs in International Studies, Africa Series. Ohio University Center for International Studies
MSB   Mongolian Studies: Journal of the Mongolia Society
MSC   Michigan Slavic Contributions
MScan   Mediaeval Scandinavia
MSE   Massachusetts Studies in English
MSEx   Melville Society Extracts
MSFL   Metodologia delle Scienze e Filosofia del Linguaggio
MSFO   Suomalais-Ugrilaisen Seuran Toimituksia/Mémoires de la Société Finno-Ougrienne (Helsinki, Finland)
MSH   Michigan Studies in the Humanities
MSI   Moody Street Irregulars: A Jack Kerouac Magazine
MSNH   Mémoires de la Société Néophilologique de Helsinki
MSpr   Moderna Språk
MSR   Mélanges de Science Religieuse
MSS   Manuscripts
MSTSC   Monograph Series of the Toronto Semiotic Circle
MSzA   Mainzer Studien zur Amerikanistik: Eine Europäische Hochschulreihe
MSzS   Münchener Studien zur Sprachwissenschaft
MTJ   Mark Twain Journal
MTUDLM   Münchener Texte und Untersuchungen zur Deutschen Literatur des Mittelalters
MuK   Maske und Kothurn: Internationale Beiträge zur Theaterwissenschaft
Multilingua: Journal of Cross-Cultural and Interlanguage Communication
MultM   Multilingual Matters
Muse   The Muse: Literary Journal of the English Association at Nsukka
MuseumsJ   Museums Journal
MusilS   Musil Studien
Muttersprache: Zeitschrift zur Pflege und Erforschung der Deutschen Sprache
MVdA   Mitteilungen des Verbandes deutscher Anglisten
MW   The Muslim World (Hartford, CT)
MysticsQ   Mystics Quarterly
Mythlore: A Journal of J. R. R. Tolkien, C. S. Lewis, Charles Williams, and the Genres of Myth and Fantasy Studies
Nabokovian   The Nabokovian
NAc   New Accents
NADS   Newsletter of the American Dialect Society
Names: Journal of the American Name Society
N&Q   Notes and Queries
N&T   Now and Then
NArg   Nuovi Argomenti
NAS   Norwegian-American Studies
NatP   Nationalities Papers
NB   Namn och Bygd: Tidskrift för Nordisk Ortnamnsforskning/Journal for Nordic Place-Name Research
NCarF   North Carolina Folklore Journal

NCC   Nineteenth-Century Contexts
NCF   Nineteenth-Century Literature
NCFS   Nineteenth-Century French Studies
NCHR   North Carolina Historical Review
NConL   Notes on Contemporary Literature
NCP   Nineteenth-Century Prose
NCS   Nineteenth-Century Studies (Charleston, SC)
NCSS   New Cultural Studies Series
NCTR   Nineteenth Century Theatre
NDAT   Nashriyye(h)-ye Däneshkade(h)-ye Adabiyyāt va Olum-e Ensāni-ye Tabriz
NDH   Neue Deutsche Hefte
NdL   Neudrucke Deutscher Literaturwerke: Neue Folge
NDQ   North Dakota Quarterly
NdW   Niederdeutsches Wort: Beiträge zur Niederdeutschen Philologie
NegCap   Negative Capability
Neman: Literaturno-Khudozhestvennyĭ i Obshchestvenno-Politicheskiĭ Zhurnal (Minsk, Belarus)
NemlaIS   Nemla Italian Studies
Nëntori: Organ i Lidhjes së Shkrimtarëve dhe Artistëve të Shqipërisë (Tirana, Albania)
Neohelicon: Acta Comparationis Litterarum Universarum
Neophil   Neophilologus (Groningen, Netherlands)
NEQ   The New England Quarterly: A Historical Review of New England Life and Letters
NERMS   New England Review [Formerly *New England Review and Bread Loaf Quarterly*]
NETJ   New England Theatre Journal
Neurolinguistik: Zeitschrift für Aphasieforschung und -therapie
Neva (St. Petersburg, Russia)
NewC   The New Criterion
NewComp   New Comparison: A Journal of Comparative and General Literary Studies
NewL   New Letters
NewS   New Scholar: An Americanist Review
Newsboy
NFJ   Nordfriesisches Jahrbuch
NFS   Nottingham French Studies
NGC   New German Critique: An Interdisciplinary Journal of German Studies
NGR   New German Review: A Journal of Germanic Studies
NGS   New German Studies
NH   New Historicism: Studies in Cultural Poetics
NHLS   North-Holland Linguistic Series
NHR   The Nathaniel Hawthorne Review
NietzscheS   Nietzsche Studien: Internationales Jahrbuch für die Nietzsche-Forschung
NIK   Nyelv-és Irodalomtudományi Közlemények
NJ   Niederdeutsches Jahrbuch: Jahrbuch des Vereins für Niederdeutsche Sprachforschung
NJe   Naš Jezik (Belgrade, Yugoslavia)
NJF   New Jersey Folklife
NJL   Nordic Journal of Linguistics
NK   Nyelvtudományi Közlemények
Nku   Naamkunde
NLÅ   Norsk Litterær Årbok
NL&LT   Natural Language & Linguistic Theory
NLauR   New Laurel Review
NLCHAIBS   The Newberry Library Center for the History of the American Indian Bibliographical Series
NLH   New Literary History: A Journal of Theory and Interpretation
NLib   Notre Librairie: Revue du Livre: Afrique, Caraïbes, Océan Indien
NLing   Notes on Linguistics
NLitsR   New Literatures Review
NLT   Norsk Lingvistisk Tidsskrift
NLWJ   The National Library of Wales Journal/Cylchgrawn Llyfrgell Genedlaethol Cymru
NM   Neuphilologische Mitteilungen: Bulletin de la Société

	Néophilologique/Bulletin of the Modern Language Society
NMHR	New Mexico Humanities Review
NMIL	Notes on Modern Irish Literature
NMS	Nottingham Medieval Studies
NMW	Notes on Mississippi Writers
NNy	Nord Nytt: Nordisk Tidsskrift for Folkelivsforskning
Noaj: Revista Literaria	
NoEF	Northeast Folklore
Nomina: A Journal of Name Studies Relating to Great Britain and Ireland	
NOQ	Northwest Ohio Quarterly
NOR	New Orleans Review
Nordelbingen: Beiträge zur Kunst- und Kulturgeschichte	
Nordlyd: Tromsø University Working Papers on Language & Linguistics	
Norte: Revista Hispano-Americana	
NOT	Notes on Translation
NouvAS	Nouveaux Actes Sémiotiques
Novel: A Forum on Fiction (Providence, RI)	
NovM	Novyi Mir: Literaturno-Khudozhestvennyĭ i Obshchestvenno-Politicheskiĭ Zhurnal
NovŽ	Novyĭ Zhurnal/The New Review (New York, NY)
NOWELE: North-Western European Language Evolution	
Nowi Dni	
NP	Nea Poreia
NR	The Nassau Review: The Journal of Nassau Community College Devoted to Arts, Letters, and Sciences
NŘeč	Naše Řeč
NRF	Nouvelle Revue Française
NRFH	Nueva Revista de Filología Hispánica (Mexico City, Mexico)
NRL	Nouvelles de la République des Lettres
NRO	Nouvelle Revue d'Onomastique
NRP	Nueva Revista del Pacífico
NRs	Neue Rundschau
NRSS	Nouvelle Revue du XVIe Siècle
NS	Die Neueren Sprachen
NSAA	Neue Studien zur Anglistik und Amerikanistik
NSammlung	Neue Sammlung: Vierteljahres-Zeitschrift für Erziehung und Gesellschaft
NsM	Neusprachliche Mitteilungen aus Wissenschaft und Praxis
NSov	Nash Sovremennik: Literaturno-Khudozhestvennyĭ i Obshchestvenno-Politicheskiĭ Zhurnal
NSSVD	Naučni Sastanak Slavista u Vukove Dane (Belgrade, Yugoslavia)
NStv	Narodno Stvaralaštvo. Folklor
NTBB	Nordisk Tidskrift för Bok- och Biblioteksväsen
NTE	Narodna Tvorchist' ta Etnohrafiia
NTg	De Nieuwe Taalgids: Tijdschrift voor Neerlandici
NTQ	New Theatre Quarterly
NUm	Narodna Umjetnost (Zagreb, Croatia)
Numen: International Review for the History of Religions	
NUWPL	Northwestern University Working Papers in Linguistics
NVS	New Vico Studies
NwFolk	Northwest Folklore
NWi	North Wind: Journal of the George MacDonald Society
NWR	Northwest Review
NWRev	The New Welsh Review
NYRB	The New York Review of Books
NYRSF	The New York Review of Science Fiction
NYSNDL	New Yorker Studien zur Neueren Deutschen Literaturgeschichte
NysS	Nysvenska Studier: Tidskrift för Svensk Stil- och Språkforskning
NZJFS	New Zealand Journal of French Studies
NZSJ	New Zealand Slavonic Journal
O&C	Oeuvres & Critiques: Revue Internationale d'Etude de la Réception Critique d'Etude des Oeuvres Littéraires de Langue Française
ÖAS	Österreich in Amerikanischer Sicht: Das Österreichbild im Amerikanischen Schulunterricht
OB	Ord och Bild
Obsidian II: Black Literature in Review	
Oceania	
OcL	Oceanic Linguistics
October (Cambridge, MA)	
Odra (Wrocław, Poland)	
Odù: A Journal of West African Studies	
OE	Oriens Extremus: Zeitschrift für Sprache, Kunst und Kultur der Länder des Fernen Ostens
OEM	Oxford English Monographs
OENews	Old English Newsletter
OENS	Old English Newsletter, Subsidia
OG	Orientalia Gandensia (Ghent, Belgium)
Ogam: Tradition Celtique	
OGE	Ons Geestelijk Erf: Driemaandelijks Tijdschrift voor de Geschiedenis van de Vroomheid in de Nederlanden
OGK	Onsei Gakkai Kaihô [Bulletin of the Phonetic Society of Japan]
ÖGL	Österreich in Geschichte und Literatur (mit Geographie)
OGS	Oxford German Studies
OhR	The Ohio Review
Ojáncano: Revista de Literatura Española	
Okike: An African Journal of New Writing	
Okt	Oktiabr': Literaturno-Khudozhestvennyĭ i Obshchestvenno-Politicheskiĭ Zhurnal
OL	Orbis Litterarum: International Review of Literary Studies
Olifant: A Publication of the Société Rencesvals, American-Canadian Branch	
OLP	Orientalia Lovaniensia Periodica
OLR	The Oxford Literary Review
OLSP	Oceanic Linguistics Special Publications
OM	Objets et Mondes: La Revue du Musée de l'Homme
OMLLM	Oxford Modern Languages and Literature Monographs
ON	The Old Northwest: A Journal of Regional Life and Letters
Onoma: Bibliographical and Information Bulletin	
Onomastica: Pismo Poświęcone Nazewnictwu Geograficznemu i Osobowemu	
OnomasticaC	Onomastica Canadiana
OnsE	Ons Erfdeel: Algemeen-Nederlands Tweemaandelijks Cultureel Tijdschrift
OntarioR	Ontario Review
OPDT	Oklahoma Project for Discourse and Theory
OPLing	Occasional Papers on Linguistics (Carbondale, IL)
OPLLL	Occasional Papers in Language, Literature and Linguistics
OralH	Oral History: The Journal of the Oral History Society
OralHR	The Oral History Review: Journal of the Oral History Association
OrGoth	Orientalia Gothoburgensia
Orizont: Revista a Uniunii Scriitorilor din Republica Socialistă România	
Orpheus: Rivista di Umanità Classica e Cristiana	
OS	Orientalia Suecana (Uppsala, Sweden)
Osamayor: Graduate Student Review	
OSP	Oxford Slavonic Papers
Osteuropa: Zeitschrift für Gegenwartsfragen des Ostens	
ÖstO	Österreichische Osthefte: Zeitschrift für Mittel-, Ost- und Südosteuropaforschung
OT	Oral Tradition
OUÅ	Ortnamnssällskapets i Uppsala Årsskrift
OUSE	Odense University Studies in English
Overland (Melbourne, Australia)	
OZČSAV	Onomastický Zpravodaj ČSAV: Zpravodaj Místopisné Komise ČSAV [Onomastic Bulletin of the Czechoslovak Academy of Sciences: Bulletin of the Topographic Board of the Czechoslovak Academy of Sciences]
ÖZV	Österreichische Zeitschrift für Volkskunde
PA	Présence Africaine: Revue Culturelle du Monde Noir/Cultural Review of the Negro World
PAAS	Proceedings of the American Antiquarian Society: A Journal of American History and Culture Through 1876
PAC	Papers of the Algonquian Conference/Actes du Congrès des Algonquistes

PADS	Publication of the American Dialect Society
PAFS	Publications of the American Folklore Society

Paideia: Rivista Letteraria di Informazione Bibliografica (Brescia, Italy)
Paideuma: A Journal Devoted to Ezra Pound Scholarship (Orono, ME)

PaideumaM	Paideuma: Mitteilungen zur Kulturkunde (Stuttgart, Germany)

Paintbrush: A Journal of Poetry, Translations, and Letters

Palacio	El Palacio: Magazine of the Museum of New Mexico

Palaestra: Untersuchungen aus der Deutschen, Englischen, und Scandinavischen Philologie (Göttingen, Germany)

Palimpsest	
PAMAPLA	Papers from the Annual Meeting of the Atlantic Provinces Linguistic Association/Actes du Colloque Annuel de l'Association de Linguistique des Provinces Atlantiques
PAMWS	Proceedings of the Annual Meeting of the Western Society for French History
P&B	Pragmatics & Beyond: New Series
P&L	Philosophy and Literature
P&P	Perception & Psychophysics
P&R	Philosophy and Rhetoric
PANPJ	Prace Językoznawcze
PANPKS	Prace Komisji Słowianoznawstwa
PAPA	Publications of the Arkansas Philological Association
PAPS	Proceedings of the American Philosophical Society Held at Philadelphia for Promoting Useful Knowledge
PAR	Performing Arts Resources

Parabola: The Magazine of Myth and Tradition

ParadeS	Parade Sauvage

Paragone: Rivista Mensile di Arte Figurativa e Letteratura
Paragraph: A Journal of Modern Critical Theory
Parergon: Bulletin of the Australian and New Zealand Association for Medieval and Renaissance Studies
Parnasso (Helsinki, Finland)

ParnassosL	Parnassos: Philologikon Periodikon/Literary Journal of the Parnassos Literary Society (Athens, Greece)

Parnassus: Poetry in Review

PArtsJ	Performing Arts Journal

PASAA: A Journal of Language Teaching and Learning in Thailand

PaSlow	Pamiętnik Słowiański
PaT	Pamiętnik Teatralny: Kwartalnik Poświęcony Historii I Krytyce Teatru
Paunch	
PAusL	Papers in Australian Linguistics (Subseries of Pacific Linguistics. Series A: Occasional Papers)
PBA	Proceedings of the British Academy
PBH	Patma-Banasirakan Handes: Istoriko-Filologičeskiĭ Zhurnal
PBML	Prague Bulletin of Mathematical Linguistics
PBSA	Papers of the Bibliographical Society of America
PBSC	Papers of the Bibliographical Society of Canada/Cahiers de la Société Bibliographique du Canada
PCP	Pacific Coast Philology
PCS	Papers in Comparative Studies
PD	Salzburg Studies in English Literature: Poetic Drama & Poetic Theory
PdD	Probleme der Dichtung
PeakeSt	Peake Studies
PE&W	Philosophy East and West: A Quarterly of Comparative Philosophy [Formerly *Philosophy East and West: A Quarterly of Asian and Comparative Thought*]
PEGS	Publications of the English Goethe Society
Pensée	La Pensée: Revue du Rationalisme Moderne

Pequod: A Journal of Contemporary Literature and Literary Criticism
Peritia: Journal of the Medieval Academy of Ireland
Persuasions: Journal of the Jane Austen Society of North America

PF	Pennsylvania Folklife
PFr	Présence Francophone: Revue Internationale de Langue et de Littérature
PFSCL	Papers on French Seventeenth Century Literature
PG	Paroles Gelées: UCLA French Studies
PH	La Palabra y el Hombre: Revista de la Universidad Veracruzana

Philobiblon: Eine Vierteljahrsschrift für Buch- und Graphiksammler

PHist	Printing History (New York, NY)
PhoenixC	Phoenix: The Journal of the Classical Association of Canada/Revue de la Société Canadienne des Etudes Classiques
PhoenixK	Phoenix (Seoul, Korea)

Phonai: Lautbibliothek der Deutschen Sprache
Phonetica: International Journal of Speech Science

PhoneticaS	Phonetica Saraviensia: Veröffentlichungen des Instituts für Phonetik

Phonology (Cambridge, England)

PhQ	The Philosophical Quarterly
PhR	Philosophical Review
PhS	Philosophical Studies: An International Journal for Philosophy in the Analytic Tradition
PhSR	Philippine Sociological Review
PHT	Personhistorisk Tidskrift
PHum	Przegląd Humanistyczny

Phylon: A Review of Race and Culture [Formerly *Phylon: The Atlanta University Review of Race and Culture*]

PIMSST	Pontifical Institute of Mediaeval Studies, Studies and Texts
PintR	The Pinter Review: Annual Essays
PJ	Poradnik Językowy (Warsaw, Poland)
PJGG	Philosophisches Jahrbuch der Görres-Gesellschaft (Freiburg, Germany)
PJL	Philippine Journal of Linguistics
PK	Philologikē Kypros
PKJ	Prace Komisji Językoznawstwa
PKn	Primerjalna Književnost
PKy	Pneumatikē Kypros
PL	Pamiętnik Literacki: Czasopismo Kwartalne Poświęcone Historii i Krytyce Literatury Polskiej

Plamŭk: Mesechno Spisanie za Literatura, Izkustvo i Publitsistika
Pleiades (Warrensburg, MO)

PLG	Probleme de Lingvistică Generală
PLL	Papers on Language and Literature: A Journal for Scholars and Critics of Language and Literature

Ploughshares

PLPLS-LHS	Proceedings of the Leeds Philosophical and Literary Society, Literary & Historical Section

Plural: Revista Cultural de Excelsior

PM	Pembroke Magazine
PMC	Postmodern Culture: An Electronic Journal of Interdisciplinary Criticism
PmdnS	Postmodern Studies
PMHB	Pennsylvania Magazine of History and Biography
PMHS	Proceedings of the Massachusetts Historical Society

PMLA: Publications of the Modern Language Association of America

PMPA	Publications of the Missouri Philological Association
PMS	Perceptual and Motor Skills
PNotes	Pynchon Notes
PNR	PN Review
Po&sie	Po&sie
PoeS	Poe Studies: Dark Romanticism: History, Theory, Interpretation

Poesía (Valencia, Venezuela)
Poetica: Zeitschrift für Sprach- und Literaturwissenschaft (Munich, Germany)

PoeticsJ	Poetics: Journal for Empirical Research on Literature, the Media and the Arts

Poétique: Revue de Théorie et d'Analyse Littéraires

PoetryR	Poetry Review (London, England)

Poeziia (Kiev, Ukraine)
Polonica

PolP	Polish Perspectives
PolR	The Polish Review

Polymia

POMPA	Publications of the Mississippi Philological Association

Ponte	Il Ponte: Rivista Mensile de Politica e Letteratura Fondata da Piero Calamandrei
Portico	Il Portico: Biblioteca di Lettere e Arti
PostB	Postilla Bohemica/Postylla Bohemica: Vierteljahrsschrift der Konstanzer Hus-Gesellschaft e.V.
PostS	Post Script: Essays in Film and the Humanities
PoT	Poetics Today
PowN	Powys Notes
PPCL	Papers in Pidgin and Creole Linguistics (Subseries of Pacific Linguistics. Series A: Occasional Papers)
PPJ	Prilozi Proučavanju Jezika
PPMRC	Proceedings of the PMR Conference: Annual Publication of the International Patristic, Mediaeval and Renaissance Conference
PPol	Il Pensiero Politico: Rivista di Storia delle Idee Politiche e Sociali
PPR	Philosophy and Phenomenological Research
PPS	Publications of the Philological Society
PQ	Philological Quarterly (Iowa City, IA)
PQCS	Philippine Quarterly of Culture and Society
PR	Partisan Review

Pragmatics: Quarterly Publication of the International Pragmatics Association

PRAN	Proust Research Association Newsletter

Prapor: Literaturno-Khudozhniĭ ta Hromads'ko-Politychnyĭ Zhurnal (Kharkov, Ukraine)

Praxis: A Journal of Culture and Criticism

Prépub	(Pré)publications (Aarhus, Denmark)

Pre/Text: A Journal of Rhetorical Theory

Pretexts: Studies in Writing and Culture

PRev	The Powys Review
PRF	Publications Romanes et Françaises
Prilozi	Prilozi za Književnost, Jezik, Istoriju i Folklor

Prismal/Cabral: Revista de Literatura Hispánica/Caderno Afro-Brasileiro Asiático Lusitano

Problemi: Periodico Quadrimestrale di Cultura

Probus: International Journal of Latin and Romance Linguistics

Profession

ProL	Pro Lingua
Proměny	

Prooftexts: A Journal of Jewish Literary History

Prospects: An Annual Journal of American Cultural Studies

Proteus: A Journal of Ideas

ProverbiumY	Proverbium: Yearbook of International Proverb Scholarship (Burlington, VT)
PRQ	Publishing Research Quarterly [Formerly *Book Research Quarterly*]
PSAm	PSA: The Official Publication of the Pirandello Society of America
PSCL	Papers and Studies in Contrastive Linguistics
PSEAL	Papers in South East Asian Linguistics (Subseries of Pacific Linguistics. Series A: Occasional Papers)
PSEKUT	Paar Sammukest Eesti Kirjanduse Uurimise Teed
PSem	Problemata Semiotica
PSM	Philippine Studies (Manila, Philippines)
PSP	Papers in Slavic Philology
PSSEAS	Monographs in International Studies, Southeast Asia Series. Ohio University Center for International Studies
PSt	Prose Studies: History, Theory, Criticism (London, England)
PStud	Portuguese Studies
PsyB	Psychological Bulletin

Psychiatry: Interpersonal and Biological Processes

PsychologR	Psychological Review
PSzL	Polska Sztuka Ludowa: Konteksty. Antropologia Kultury. Etnografia. Sztuka
PText	Papiere zur Textlinguistik/Papers in Textlinguistics
PTFS	Publications of the Texas Folklore Society
PTRSC	Proceedings & Transactions Royal Society of Canada
PU	Problemi di Ulisse
PubCult	Public Culture: Bulletin of the Society for Transnational Cultural Studies
PubHist	Publishing History: The Social, Economic and Literary History of Book, Newspaper and Magazine Publishing
PULC	Princeton University Library Chronicle
PURBA	Panjab University Research Bulletin (Arts)
PuW	Poesie und Wissenschaft
PVR	Platte Valley Review
PWJ	Peter Weiss Jahrbuch
PZKA	Philologus: Zeitschrift für Klassische Philologie
PzL	Papiere zur Linguistik
Q&F	Quondam et Futurus: A Journal of Arthurian Interpretations
Qanṭara	Al-Qanṭara: Revista de Estudios Arabes
QDLLSM	Quaderni del Dipartimento di Lingue e Letterature Straniere Moderne, Universita di Genova
QFG	Quaderni di Filologia Germanica della Facoltà di Lettere e Filosofia dell'Università di Bologna
QFSK	Quellen und Forschungen zur Sprach- und Kulturgeschichte der Germanischen Völker
QI	Quaderni d'Italianistica: Official Journal of the Canadian Society for Italian Studies
QIA	Quaderni Ibero-Americani: Attualità Culturale della Penisola Iberica e America Latina
QJS	The Quarterly Journal of Speech
QL	La Quinzaine Littéraire
QLing	Quantitative Linguistics
QLL	Quaderni di Lingue e Letterature
QPar	Qui Parle: A Journal of Literary and Critical Studies
QQ	Queen's Quarterly
QRFV	Quarterly Review of Film and Video
QSem	Quaderni di Semantica: Rivista Internazionale di Semantica Teorica e Applicata/An International Journal of Theoretical and Applied Semantics (Bologna, Italy)
QSGLL	Queensland Studies in German Language and Literature
Qu	Quadrant (Montpellier, France)

Quadrant (Victoria, Australia)

Quest	New Quest (Pune, India)

Quimera: Revista de Literatura

QVen	Quaderni Veneti
RA	Romanistische Arbeitshefte (Tübingen, FRG)
RAAD	Revue de l'Académie Arabe de Damas
RACLA	Revue de l'ACLA/Journal of the CAAL [Formerly *Bulletin de l'ACLA/Bulletin of the CAAL*]
Rad	Rad Jugoslavenske Akademije Znanosti i Umjetnosti
RAdL	Revista Argentina de Lingüística
Raduga	
RAEI	Revista Alicantina de Estudios Ingleses

Raft: A Journal of Armenian Poetry and Criticism

RagL	Il Ragguaglio Librario: Rassegna Mensile Bibliografica Culturale
RAIP	Rapport d'Activités de l'Institut de Phonétique
RaJAH	The Rackham Journal of the Arts and Humanities
RAL	Research in African Literatures
RALS	Resources for American Literary Study
RAMR	Revue André Malraux Review
R&L	Religion and Literature (Notre Dame, IN)
R&W	Reading and Writing: An Interdisciplinary Journal
RANNAM	Recherches Anglaises et Nord-Américaines
RAQL	Revue Québécoise de Linguistique Théorique et Appliquée

Raritan: A Quarterly Review

Razgledi: Spisanie za Literatura Umetnost i Kultura

Raz SAZU	Razprave Razreda za Filološke in Literarne vede Slovenske Akademije Znanosti in Umetnosti
RB	Revue Bénédictine
RBL	Revista Brasileira de Lingüística
RBLL	Revista Brasileira de Língua e Literatura
RBML	Rare Books & Manuscripts Librarianship
RBPH	Revue Belge de Philologie et d'Histoire/Belgisch Tijdschrift voor Filologie en Geschiedenis

RBSL	Regensburger Beiträge zur Deutschen Sprach- und Literaturwissenschaft. Reihe B: Untersuchungen (Bern, Switzerland)
RC	Ruperto Carola: Heidelberger Universitätshefte
RCCM	Rivista di Cultura Classica e Medievale
RCEH	Revista Canadiense de Estudios Hispánicos
RCEI	Revista Canaria de Estudios Ingleses
RCEPRC	La Revista del Centro de Estudios Avanzados de Puerto Rico y el Caribe
RCF	The Review of Contemporary Fiction
RChL	Revista Chilena de Literatura
RCLL	Revista de Critica Literaria Latinoamericana
RcRt	Salzburg Studies in English Literature: Romantic Reassessment
RCSCSPL	Russian, Croatian and Serbian, Czech and Slovak, Polish Literature
RD	La Rivista Dalmatica
RdE	Rivista di Estetica
RdH	Revista de História
RDidE	Recherches sur Diderot et sur l'*Encyclopédie*
RdLing	Rivista di Linguistica
RdSO	Rivista degli Studi Orientali
RdT	Revista de Teatro
RDTP	Revista de Dialectología y Tradiciones Populares
RdVV	Reihe der Villa Vigoni: Deutsch-Italienische Studien
RE	Revue d'Esthétique
REA	Revue des Etudes Augustiniennes
Reader: Essays in Reader-Oriented Theory, Criticism, and Pedagogy	
REAL	RE Arts & Letters: A Liberal Arts Forum
REALB	REAL: The Yearbook of Research in English and American Literature (Tübingen, Germany)
REAnc	Revue des Etudes Anciennes
ReapprC	Reappraisals: Canadian Writers
REArmNS	Revue des Etudes Arméniennes
RechA	Recherches Augustiniennes
RechSR	Recherches de Science Religieuse
RecL	Recovering Literature: A Journal of Contextualist Criticism
RECTR	Restoration and 18th Century Theatre Research
REE	Revista de Estudios Extremeños
REEDN	Records of Early English Drama Newsletter
REF	Revista de Etnografie şi Folclor
REG	Revue des Etudes Grecques
REH	Revista de Estudios Hispánicos (St. Louis, MO)
REH-PR	Revista de Estudios Hispánicos (Río Piedras, Puerto Rico)
REI	Revue des Etudes Italiennes
Reinardus: Yearbook of the International Reynard Society/Annuaire de la Société Internationale Renardienne	
REIsl	Revue des Etudes Islamiques
RELat	Revue des Etudes Latines
RELC	RELC Journal: A Journal of Language Teaching and Research in Southeast Asia
Ren&R	Renaissance and Reformation/Renaissance et Réforme
Renascence: Essays on Value in Literature	
RenB	The Renaissance Bulletin
RenD	Renaissance Drama
Renditions: A Chinese-English Translation Magazine	
RenM	Renaissance Monographs
RenP	Renaissance Papers
RenQ	Renaissance Quarterly
RenSt	Renaissance Studies: Journal of the Society for Renaissance Studies
Representations	
RES	Review of English Studies: A Quarterly Journal of English Literature and the English Language
REspL	Revista Española de Lingüística
Restant: Tijdschrift voor Recente Semiotische Teorievorming en de Analyse van Teksten/Review for Semiotic Theories and the Analysis of Texts	
Restoration: Studies in English Literary Culture, 1660-1700	
Rev	Review (Blacksburg, VA)
RevI	Revista/Review Interamericana
Review: Latin American Literature and Arts (New York, NY)	
RevIMA	RIMA: Review of Indonesian and Malaysian Affairs
Revisor	De Revisor
RevPL	Revue de Phonétique Appliquée
RevR	Revue Romane
RF	Romanische Forschungen
RFdL	Revue Francophone de Louisiane
RFE	Revista de Filología Española
RFEA	Revue Française d'Etudes Américaines
RFLUCR	Revista de Filología y Lingüística de la Universidad de Costa Rica
RFNS	Rivista di Filosofia Neo-Scolastica
RFP	Recherches sur le Français Parlé
RFR	Robert Frost Review
RFULL	Revista de Filologia de la Universidad de La Laguna
RG	Revue Générale
RGad	Raiņa Gadagrāmata (Riga, Latvia)
RGer	Recherches Germaniques
RGL	Reihe Germanistische Linguistik
RHE	Revue d'Histoire Ecclésiastique
Rhetorica: A Journal of the History of Rhetoric	
RhetRev	Rhetoric Review
RHistM	Römische Historische Mitteilungen
RHL	Revue d'Histoire Littéraire de la France
RHM	Revista Hispánica Moderna
RHT	Revue d'Histoire du Théâtre
RhV	Rheinische Vierteljahrsblätter
RI	Revista Iberoamericana
RIB	Revista Interamericana de Bibliografía/Inter-American Review of Bibliography
RIber	Rassegna Iberistica
RID	Rivista Italiana di Dialettologia: Lingue Dialetti Società [Formerly *Rivista Italiana di Dialettologia: Scuola Società Territorio*]
RIL	Rendiconti dell'Istituto Lombardo Accademia di Scienze e Lettere
RILA	Rassegna Italiana di Linguistica Applicata
RILCE: Revista de Filología Hispánica	
Rinascimento: Rivista dell'Istituto Nazionale di Studi sul Rinascimento	
RíoPla	Río de la Plata: Culturas (Paris, France)
RIPh	Revue Internationale de Philosophie (Brussels, Belgium)
Riscontri: Rivista Trimestrale di Cultura e di Attualità	
RITL	Revista de Istorie şi Teorie Literară
RJ	Romanistisches Jahrbuch
RJN	Robinson Jeffers Newsletter
RJR	Russkiĭ Iazyk za Rubezhom
RJŠ	Russkiĭ Iazyk v Shkole: Metodicheskiĭ Zhurnal
RJV	Rheinisches Jahrbuch für Volkskunde
RKH	Rocznik Komisji Historycznoliterackiej
RKJ	Rozprawy Komisji Językowej
RL	Revista de Literatura
RLAn	RLA: Romance Languages Annual (West Lafayette, IN)
RL&LR	Romance Linguistics & Literature Review
RL&LS	Romance Languages and Linguistics Series
RLC	Revue de Littérature Comparée
RLdV	Recherches Linguistiques de Vincennes
RLet	Revista Letras (Paraná, Brazil)
RLetras	República de las Letras
RLI	Rassegna della Letteratura Italiana
RLiR	Revue de Linguistique Romane
RLit	Russkaia Literatura: Istoriko-Literaturnyĭ Zhurnal (St. Petersburg, Russia)
RLJ	Russian Language Journal
RLL	American University Studies II: Romance Languages and Literature
RLM	La Revue des Lettres Modernes: Histoire des Idées et des Littératures
RLMC	Rivista di Letterature Moderne e Comparate (Pisa, Italy)
RLR	Revue des Langues Romanes

RLS	Regional Language Studies—Newfoundland (St. John's, Newfoundland)	*RTSS*	Revue Tunisienne de Sciences Sociales
RLTA	RLA: Revista de Lingüística Teórica y Aplicada (Concepción, Chile)	*RTT*	Research in Text Theory/Untersuchungen zur Texttheorie
RM	Rowohlts Monographien	*RuchL*	Ruch Literacki
RMM	Revue de Métaphysique et de Morale	*RUSEng*	Rajasthan University Studies in English
RMon	Romance Monographs	*RusF*	Russkiĭ Fol'klor: Materialy i Issledovaniia
RMP	Rheinisches Museum für Philologie	*RuskGaz*	The Ruskin Gazette
RMR	Rocky Mountain Review of Language and Literature	*RuskN*	Ruskin Newsletter
RMS	Renaissance & Modern Studies	*RusLing*	Russian Linguistics: International Journal for the Study of the Russian Language
RMSt	Reading Medieval Studies	*RusR*	The Russian Review: An American Quarterly Devoted to Russia Past and Present
RNL	Review of National Literatures		
RO	Revista de Occidente	*RusRe*	Russkaia Rech': Nauchno-Populiarnyĭ Zhurnal
RocO	Rocznik Orientalistyczny (Warsaw, Poland)	*RVC*	Roman 20-50: Revue d'Etude du Roman du XXe Siècle
RoHum	Roczniki Humanistyczne: Annales de Lettres et Sciences Humaines/Annals of Arts (Lublin, Poland)	*RyF*	Razón y Fe: Revista Hispanoamericana de Cultura
		RYLL	Research in Yoruba Language and Literature
ROLIG	Rolig-Papir	*RZSF*	Radovi Zavoda za Slavensku Filologiju
RoLit	România Literară: Săptăminal de Literatură și Artă Editat de Uniunea Scriitorilor din Republica Socialistă România	*SAA*	Schweizer Anglistische Arbeiten
		SAC	Studies in the Age of Chaucer: The Yearbook of the New Chaucer Society
Romania: Revue Consacrée à l'Etude des Langues et des Literatures Romanes		*SacE*	Sacris Eruditi: Jaarboek voor Godsdienstwetenschappen
Romantisme: Revue du Dix-Neuvième Siècle		*SAD*	Studies in American Drama, 1945-Present
Romantist	The Romantist	*SAF*	Studies in American Fiction
RomG	Romanica Gandensia	*SAfrL*	Studies in African Literature
RomGoth	Romanica Gothoburgensia	*SAG*	Stuttgarter Arbeiten zur Germanistik
RomLi	Romance Linguistics [Croon Helm Romance Linguistics]	*Saga-Book* (London, England)	
		SagaS	Saga och Sed. Kungl. Gustav Adolfs Akademiens Årsbok
RomN	Romance Notes	*SAGE: A Scholarly Journal on Black Women*	
RomSl	Romanoslavica	*SagetriebIO*	Sagetrieb: A Journal Devoted to Poets in the Imagist/Objectivist Tradition
ROO	Room of One's Own: A Feminist Journal of Literature and Criticism		
		SAH	Svenska Akademiens Handlingar
RoR	Romanian Review	*SAHQ*	Swedish-American Historical Quarterly
RORD	Research Opportunities in Renaissance Drama	*SAIL*	Studies in American Indian Literatures: The Journal of the Association for the Study of American Indian Literatures
RoSlaw	Rocznik Slawistyczny/Revue Slavistique		
RPF	Revista Portuguesa de Filologia	*SAJAL*	South African Journal of African Languages/Suid-Afrikaanse Tydskrif vir Afrikatale (Pretoria, South Africa)
RPFilos	Revista Portuguesa de Filosofia		
RPh	Romance Philology		
RPLHA	Revue de Philologie de Littérature et d'Histoire Anciennes	*SAJL*	Studies in American Jewish Literature
RPLit	Res Publica Litterarum: Studies in the Classical Tradition	*SAL*	Studies in African Linguistics
RPML	Rodopi Perspectives on Modern Literature	*SAlb*	Studia Albanica (Tirana, Albania)
RPsych	Reading Psychology: An International Quarterly	*SALCT*	Studies in Austrian Literature, Culture, and Thought
RQ	Riverside Quarterly	*SALit*	Chu-Shikoku Studies in American Literature
RQCAK	Römische Quartalschrift für Christliche Altertumskunde und Kirchengeschichte	*Salmagundi*	
		Samlaren: Tidskrift för Svensk Litteraturvetenskaplig Forskning	
RQdL	Revue Québécoise de Linguistique	*Samtiden: Tidsskrift for Politikk, Litteratur og Samfunnsspørsmål*	
RR	Romanic Review	*Sananjalka: Suomen Kielen Seuran Vuosikirja*	
RRL	Revue Roumaine de Linguistique [Incorporates *Cahiers de Linguistique Théorique et Appliquée*]	*S&I*	Sprache und Information: Beiträge zur Philologischen und Linguistischen Datenverarbeitung, Informatik, und Informationswissenschaft
RRQ	Reading Research Quarterly		
RSA	RSA Journal: Rivista di Studi Nord-Americani (Florence, Italy)	*S&K*	Sprache & Kognition: Zeitschrift für Sprach- und Kognitionspsychologie und ihre Grenzgebiete
RSBN	Rivista di Studi Bizantini e Neoellenici	*S&S*	Syntax and Semantics
RSFPP	Rongorongo Studies: A Forum for Polynesian Philology	*SAnt*	Suomen Antropologi/Antropologi i Finland
RSH	Revue des Sciences Humaines	*SAP*	Studia Anglica Posnaniensia: An International Review of English Studies
RSI	Rivista Storica Italiana		
RSieg	Reihe Siegen: Beiträge zur Literatur-, Sprach- und Medienwissenschaft	*Sapienza: Rivista di Filosofia e di Teologia*	
		SAQ	South Atlantic Quarterly
RSiL	Russian Studies in Literature: A Journal of Translations [Formerly *Soviet Studies in Literature*]	*SAR*	Studies in the American Renaissance
		SARE	Southeast Asian Review of English (Kuala Lumpur, Malaysia)
RSItal	Rivista di Studi Italiani		
RSl	Ricerche Slavistiche	*SARev*	South Asian Review
RsLI	Recherches sur l'Imaginaire	*SArt*	Speculum Artium (Ravenna, Italy)
RSLR	Rivista di Storia e Letteratura Religiosa	*SaS*	Slovo a Slovesnost
RSQ	Rhetoric Society Quarterly	*SATF*	Société des Anciens Textes Français
RSR	Rassegna Storica del Risorgimento	*SATJ*	South African Theatre Journal
RSSI	Recherches Sémiotiques/Semiotic Inquiry	*SAV*	Schweizerisches Archiv für Volkskunde
RSt	Romance Studies (Swansea, Wales)	*Savacou: A Journal of the Caribbean Artists Movement* (Jamaica, West Indies)	
RSV	Revista Signos: Estudios de Lengua y Literatura		
RTAM	Recherches de Théologie Ancienne et Médiévale	*Savremenik: Mesečni Književni Časopis*	
RThom	Revue Thomiste: Revue Doctrinale de Théologie et de Philosophie	*SB*	Studies in Bibliography: Papers of the Bibliographical Society of the University of Virginia

SBHC	Studies in Browning and His Circle: A Journal of Criticism, History, and Bibliography
SBLL	Selected Bibliographies in Language and Literature
SBN	Saul Bellow Journal
SBoc	Studi sul Boccaccio
SBR	Swedish Book Review
SC	Stendhal Club: Revue Internationale d'Etudes Stendhaliennes. Nouvelle Série. Revue Trimestrielle
Scan	Scandinavica: An International Journal of Scandinavian Studies
ScanR	Scandinavian Review
ScEc	Science et Esprit
SCen	The Seventeenth Century
SCFS	Seventeenth-Century French Studies
SCh	Sources Chrétiennes
Schatzkammer	Schatzkammer der Deutschen Sprache, Dichtung und Geschichte
Schlesien: Arts, Science, Folklore	
SchP	Scholarly Publishing: A Journal for Authors and Publishers
ScI	Scripta Islandica: Isländska Sällskapets Årsbok
SCJ	The Sixteenth Century Journal
SCL	Studies in Canadian Literature/Etudes en Littérature Canadienne
SCLing	Siouan and Caddoan Linguistics
SCLit	Studies in Comparative Literature
ScLJ	Scottish Literary Journal [Formerly *Scottish Literary Journal: A Review of Studies in Scottish Language and Literature*]
SCN	Seventeenth-Century News
ScotL	Scottish Language
SCR	South Carolina Review
SCr	Strumenti Critici: Rivista Quadrimestrale di Cultura e Critica Letteraria
Screen (Glasgow, Scotland)	
SCRev	South Central Review: The Journal of the South Central Modern Language Association
Scriblerian	The Scriblerian and the Kit Cats: A Newsjournal Devoted to Pope, Swift, and Their Circle
Scripsi	
Scriptorium: Revue Internationale des Etudes Relatives aux Manuscrits/International Review of Manuscript Studies	
ScS	Scottish Studies (Edinburgh, Scotland)
SCSSL	Semiosis: Seminario de Semiótica, Teoría, Análsis
SCUL	Soundings: Collections of the University Library, University of California, Santa Barbara
SD	Studi Danteschi
SdBS	Simone de Beauvoir Studies
SDi	Slovenské Divadlo: Revue Dramatických Umení
SDL	Studies in Descriptive Linguistics
SDLNZJ	Studien zur Deutschen Literatur des 19. und 20. Jahrhunderts
SDR	South Dakota Review
SDv	Sprache und Datenverarbeitung: International Journal for Language Data Processing
SEA	Studies in English and American (Budapest, Hungary)
SEALLC	Studies in English and American Literature, Linguistics, and Culture
SEAS	Salzburg English & American Studies [Formerly *Salzburger Studien zur Anglistik und Amerikanistik*]
SECC	Studies in Eighteenth-Century Culture
SECL	Studies in English and Comparative Literature
SECOLASA	SECOLAS Annals: Journal of the Southeastern Council on Latin American Studies
SECOLB	The SECOL Review: Southeastern Conference on Linguistics
SEEA	Slavic and East European Arts
SEEJ	Slavic and East European Journal
SEER	The Slavonic and East European Review
Sefarad: Revista de Estudios Hebraicos, Sefardies y de Oriente Proximo	
Seges: Etudes et Textes de Philologie et Littérature. Université de Fribourg Suisse/Studien und Texte zur Philologie und Literatur. Universität Freiburg Schweiz/Studi e Testi di Filologia e Letteratura. Università di Friburgo Svizzera	
SEL: Studies in English Literature, 1500-1900	
Selecta: Journal of the Pacific Northwest Council on Foreign Languages	
SELit	Studies in English Literature (Tokyo, Japan)
SELL	Studies in English Language and Literature (Kyushu University)
SELL-SG	Studies in English Language and Literature (Seinan Gakuin University)
SemCross	Semiotic Crossroads
Seminar: A Journal of Germanic Studies	
Semiosis: Internationale Zeitschrift für Semiotik und Ästhetik	
Semiotext(e)	
Semiotica: Journal of the International Association for Semiotic Studies/Revue de l'Association Internationale de Sémiotique	
SeN	Seara Nova
Senara: Revista de Filoloxía	
SerL	Serie Linguistica (Brasilia, Brazil)
Serpe: Rivista Letteraria	
SES	Sophia English Studies
SeSL	Studi e Saggi Linguistici
SEzik	Sŭpostavitelno Ezikoznanie/Sopostavitel'noe Jazykoznanie/Contrastive Linguistics (Sofia, Bulgaria)
SF&R	Scholars' Facsimiles & Reprints
SFenE	Studia Fennica Ethnologica [Supersedes *Studia Fennica*]
SFenF	Studia Fennica Folkloristica [Supersedes *Studia Fennica*]
SFenL	Studia Fennica Linguistica [Supersedes *Studia Fennica*]
SFI	Studi di Filologia Italiana: Bollettino Annuale dell'Accademia della Crusca
SFic	Science Fiction: A Review of Speculative Literature
SFil	Studime Filologjike (Tirana, Albania)
SFIS	Stanford French and Italian Studies
SFolk	Southern Folklore
SFr	Studi Francesi
SFR	Stanford French Review
SFran	Studi Francescani: Trimestrale di Vita Culturale e Religiosa a Cura dei Frati Minori d'Italia
SFS	Science-Fiction Studies
SGAK	Studien zur Germanistik, Anglistik und Komparatistik
SGerS	Stanford German Studies
SGF	Stockholmer Germanistische Forschungen
SGG	Studia Germanica Gandensia
SGh	Studia Ghisleriana (Pavia, Italy)
SGLLC	Studies in German Literature, Linguistics, and Culture
SGoldoniani	Studi Goldoniani
SGS	Scottish Gaelic Studies
SGT	Schriften der Gesellschaft für Theatergeschichte
SGym	Siculorum Gymnasium
SH	Studia Hibernica (Dublin, Ireland)
ShakB	Shakespeare Bulletin: A Journal of Performance Criticism and Scholarship
ShakS	Shakespeare Studies (New York, NY)
Shandean	The Shandean: An Annual Devoted to Laurence Sterne and His Works
Shavian	The Shavian: The Journal of the Shaw Society
ShawR	Shaw: The Annual of Bernard Shaw Studies
Shenandoah: The Washington & Lee University Review [Formerly *Shenendoah*]	
Shiron	
ShJE	Shakespeare-Jahrbuch (Weimar, Germany)
SHL	Amsterdam Studies in the Theory and History of the Language Sciences III: Studies in the History of the Language Sciences
ShLR	Shoin Literary Review
ShN	The Shakespeare Newsletter
SHnd	The Single Hound: The Poetry and Image of Emily Dickinson
SHR	Southern Humanities Review

ShS	Shakespeare Survey: An Annual Survey of Shakespeare Studies and Production
ShSA	Shakespeare in Southern Africa: Journal of the Shakespeare Society of Southern Africa
ShStud	Shakespeare Studies (Tokyo, Japan)
SHum	Scripta Humanistica
SHUR	Sacred Heart University Review
SHW	Studies in Hogg and his World
ShY	Shakespeare Yearbook
SIAA	Studi d'Italianistica nell'Africa Australe/Italian Studies in Southern Africa
SIcon	Studies in Iconography
Sig	Sigma: Linguistique Anglaise-Linguistique Générale [Formerly *Sigma: Revue de Centre d'Etudes Linguistiques d'Aix*]
Sight&S	Sight and Sound
Siglo	Siglo XX/20th Century

Signs: Journal of Women in Culture and Society
Sìlarus: Rassegna Bimestrale di Cultura

SILTA	Studi Italiani di Linguistica Teorica ed Applicata
SILUTAPL	Summer Institute of Linguistics and the University of Texas at Arlington Publications in Linguistics
SiM	Studies in Medievalism
Sing Out	Sing Out!: The Folk Song Magazine
SINSU	Skrifter Utgivna av Institutionen för Nordiska Språk vid Uppsala Universitet

Sipario: Il Mensile Italiano dello Spettacolo

SiPC	Studies in Popular Culture
SIPL	Studies in Philippine Linguistics
SIR	Studies in Romanticism (Boston, MA)
SIs	Studi Ispanici (Pisa, Italy)
SiTZ	Sprache im Technischen Zeitalter
SJ	Silliman Journal
SJL	Southwest Journal of Linguistics
SJS	San José Studies
SjV	Sirp ja Vasar

Skandinavistik: Zeitschrift für Sprache, Literatur und Kultur der Nordischen Länder

SKDS	Studien zum Kleinen Deutschen Sprachatlas
SkGgD	Sammlung Kurzer Grammatiken Germanischer Dialekte

Skírnir: Tímarit Hins Íslenska Bókmenntafélags (Reykjavik, Iceland)

SKS	Suomalaisen Kirjallisuuden Seuran Toimituksia (Helsinki, Finland)
SL	Studia Linguistica (Lund, Sweden)
SL&Li	American University Studies XII: Slavic Languages and Literature
SLang	Studies in Language: International Journal Sponsored by the Foundation "Foundations of Language"
SLAPC	Studies in Latin American Popular Culture
SlavH	Slavica Helvetica

Slavia: Časopis pro Slovanskou Filologii

SlavO	Slavica Othiniensia
SlavR	Slavic Review: American Quarterly of Russian, Eurasian and East European Studies [Formerly *Slavic Review: American Quarterly of Soviet and East European Studies*]
SlavS	Slavistički Studii: Spisanie za Rusistika, Polonistika i Bohemistika
SLCS	Studies in Language Companion Series (Amsterdam, Netherlands)
SLD	Studia Litteraria (Debrecen, Hungary)
SLF	Skrifter Utgivna av Svenska Litteratursällskapet i Finland
SlfÅ	Svensklärarföreningens Årsskrift
SLIA	Studi di Letteratura Ispano-Americana
SLitI	Studies in the Literary Imagination
SLJ	Southern Literary Journal
SLL	Studies in Language Learning: An Interdisciplinary Review of Language Acquisition, Language Pedagogy, Stylistics and Language Planning
SLog	Studia Logica: An International Journal for Symbolic Logic
SlOr	Slavia Orientalis

Slovakia

SlovLit	Slovenská Literatúra: Revue Pre Literárnu Vedu (Bratislava, Slovak Republic)
SlovN	Slovenský Národopis

Slovo: Časopis Staroslavenskog Zavoda u Zagrebu

SlovP	Slovenské Pohl'ady na Literatúru a Umenie (Bratislava, Slovak Republic)
SlovS	Slovene Studies: Journal of the Society for Slovene Studies
SLP	Serie Lingüística Peruana (Lima, Peru)
SlR	Slavistična Revija
SLRAAA	Sprache und Literatur: Regensburger Arbeiten zur Anglistik und Amerikanistik (Bern, Switzerland)
SLRe	Second Language Research
SlReč	Slovenská Reč: Časopis Pre Výskum Slovenského Jazyka (Bratislava, Slovak Republic)
SLRev	Stanford Literature Review
SLRJ	Saint Louis University Research Journal of the Graduate School of Arts and Sciences
SLS	Sign Language Studies
SLSc	Studies in the Linguistic Sciences
SLSF	Svenska Landsmål och Svenskt Folkliv (Uppsala, Sweden)
SM	Sammlung Metzler
SMC	Studies in Medieval Culture (Kalamazoo, MI)
SMEA	Studi Micenei ed Egeo-Anatolici
SMed	Studi Medievali
SMELL	Studies in Medieval English Language and Literature
SMGL	Studies in Modern German Literature
SMS	Studier i Modern Språkvetenskap
SMus	Studia Musicologica Academiae Scientiarum Hungaricae (Budapest, Hungary)
SMV	Studi Mediolatini e Volgari
SMy	Studia Mystica
SN	Studia Neophilologica: A Journal of Germanic and Romance Languages and Literature
SNew	Sidney Newsletter & Journal [Formerly *Sidney Newsletter*]
SNNTS	Studies in the Novel (Denton, TX)
SNov	Studi Novecenteschi: Revista Semestrale di Storia della Letteratura Italiana Contemporanea (Padua, Italy)
SNS	Slovo na Storozhi
SNSS	Skrifter Utgivna av Svenska Språknämnden
SO	Symbolae Osloenses
SOÅ	Sydsvenska Ortnamnssällskapets Årsskrift/The Annual Journal of the South Swedish Place-Name Society
SoAR	South Atlantic Review
SÖAW	Sitzungsberichte der Österreichischen Akademie der Wissenschaften in Wien, Philosophisch-Historische Klasse

Sociocriticism

Socioling	Sociolinguistics (Dordrecht, Netherlands)

Sodobnost (Ljubljana, Slovenia)

SOF	Südost-Forschungen
SoK	Sprog og Kultur (Aarhus, Denmark)
SophiaT	Sophia (Tokyo, Japan)
SoQ	The Southern Quarterly: A Journal of the Arts in the South (Hattiesburg, MS)
SoR	The Southern Review (Baton Rouge, LA)
SoRA	Southern Review: Literary and Interdisciplinary Essays (Adelaide, Australia)
SoS	Syn og Segn: Norsk Tidsskrift
SoSt	Southern Studies: An Interdisciplinary Journal of the South

Soundings: An Interdisciplinary Journal
Southerly: A Review of Australian Literature (Sydney, Australia)

SovH	Sovetish Heymland/Sovetskaia Rodina: Ezhemesiachnyĭ Literaturno-Khudozhestvennyĭ Zhurnal
SovL	Soviet Literature
SP	Studies in Philology

SPAN: Journal of the South Pacific Association for Commonwealth Literature and Language Studies

SPAS	Studies in Puritan American Spirituality
SPCT	Studi e Problemi di Critica Testuale
Speculum: A Journal of Medieval Studies	
Spektator: Tijdschrift voor Neerlandistiek (Assen, Netherlands)	
SPELL	Swiss Papers in English Language and Literature
SPFFBUA	Sborník Prací Filosofické Fakulty Brněnské University: Řada Jazykovědná—A
SPFFBUD	Sborník Prací Filosofické Fakulty Brněnské University: Řada Literárněvědná—D
SPh	Studia Phonetica
SPIL: (Stellenbosch Papers in Linguistics)	
Spirit: A Magazine of Poetry	
SpL	Spiegel der Letteren: Tijdschrift voor Nederlandse Literatuurgeschiedenis en voor Literatuurwetenschap
SpM	Spicilegio Moderno: Letteratura, Lingua, Idee
Sprachdienst	Der Sprachdienst
Sprache	Die Sprache: Zeitschrift für Sprachwissenschaft (Wiesbaden, Germany)
Sprachkunst: Beiträge zur Literaturwissenschaft	
SprachstrukA	Sprachstrukturen, Reihe A: Historische Sprachstrukturen
Sprachwiss	Sprachwissenschaft
Språkvård: Tidskrift Utgiven av Svenska Språknämnden	
Spr&Spr	Sprachpflege und Sprachkultur: Zeitschrift für Gutes Deutsch
SpRi	Spunti e Ricerche: Rivista d'Italianistica
SpringE	Spring: The Journal of the E. E. Cummings Society
Spsp	Sprachspiegel: Schweizerische Zeitschrift für die deutsche Muttersprache
SPsy	Social Psychology Quarterly
SPWVSRA	Shakespeare and Renaissance Association of West Virginia—Selected Papers [Also known as *Selected Papers from the West Virginia Shakespeare and Renaissance Association*]
SQ	Shakespeare Quarterly
SR	Sewanee Review
SRC	Studies in Religion/Sciences Religieuses: Revue Canadienne/A Canadian Journal
SRIELA	Selected Reports in Ethnomusicology
SRL	Studies in Romance Languages
SRo	Studi Romani: Rivista Trimestrale dell'Istituto Nazionale di Studi Romani
SS	Scandinavian Studies
SSASH	Studia Slavica Academiae Scientiarum Hungaricae
SSAWL	Sitzungsberichte der Sächsischen Akademie der Wissenschaften zu Leipzig: Philologisch-Historische Klasse
SSBL	Stockholm Studies in Baltic Languages
SSCP	SUNY Series in Cultural Perspectives
SSe	Studi Secenteschi
SSEL	Stockholm Studies in English
SSEng	Sydney Studies in English
SSF	Studies in Short Fiction
SSFin	Studia Slavica Finlandensia
SSG	Schriften der Theodor-Storm-Gesellschaft
SSGL	Studies in Slavic and General Linguistics
SSI	Social Science Information/Information sur les Sciences Sociales
SSl	Scando-Slavica (Copenhagen, Denmark)
SSL	Studies in Scottish Literature (Columbia, SC)
SSLA	Studies in Second Language Acquisition
SSLP	Studies in Slavic Literature and Poetics
SSLS	Studies in the Sciences of Language Series
SSLSN	Skrifter Utgivna av Svenska Litteratursällskapet. Studier i Nordisk Filologi
SSMLN	Society for the Study of Midwestern Literature Newsletter
SSO	Studier fra Sprog- og Oldtidsforskning
SSPCL	Studies in Speech Pathology and Clinical Linguistics
SSR	Scottish Slavonic Review: An International Journal Promoting East-West Contacts
SSRL	Stockholm Studies in Russian Literature
SSt	Spenser Studies: A Renaissance Poetry Annual
SStud	Swift Studies: The Annual of the Ehrenpreis Center
ST	Studi Tassiani
StAH	Studies in American Humor
StAS	Studia Anthroponymica Scandinavica: Tidskrift för Nordisk Personnamnsforskning
Stasinos: The Bulletin of the Greek Philologists	
StBoT	Studien zu den Boğazköy-Texten (Wiesbaden, Germany)
StC	Studia Celtica
StCL	Studii și Cercetări Lingvistice
StCS	Studies in Contemporary Satire: A Creative and Critical Journal
Steaua	
SText	Social Text
STFM	Société des Textes Français Modernes
StG	Studi Germanici
Stgr	Studia Grammatica
StGrI	Studi di Grammatica Italiana
StH-LPS	Studies in the Humanities: Literature-Politics-Society (New York, NY)
StHR	Stanford Humanities Review
StHum	Studies in the Humanities (Indiana, PA)
StII	Studien zur Indologie und Iranistik
StIL	Studi dell'Istituto Linguistico
StIR	Stanford Italian Review
StIS	Studies in Interactional Sociolinguistics
StIsl	Studia Islamica
StLD	Studies on Lucette Desvignes and the Twentieth Century
StLF	Studi di Letteratura Francese
STLing	Studien zur Theoretischen Linguistik
StLM	Studien zur Literatur der Moderne
StM	Studia Monastica
StMed	Studia Mediewistyczne
StMS	Steinbeck Monograph Series
StQ	Steinbeck Quarterly
STr	Studi Trentini di Scienze Storiche
Strindbergiana	
STS	Scottish Text Society
STSL	Studien und Texte zur Sozialgeschichte der Literatur
StSS	Stanford Slavic Studies
StTCL	Studies in Twentieth Century Literature
StudaI	Studia Iranica
Studiekamraten [Formerly *Studiekamraten: Tidskrift för det Fria Bildningsarbetet*]	
Studies: An Irish Quarterly Review (Dublin, Ireland)	
StudIm	Studia Imagologica: Comparative Literature and European Diversity/Littérature Comparée et Diversité Européenne/Vergleichende Literaturwissenschaft und Europäische Diversität
StudIsl	Studia Islandica: Íslenzk Fræði
Studium (Rome, Italy)	
StuSta	Studia Staropolskie
Stvaranje: Časopis za Književnost i Kulturu	
StWF	Studies in Weird Fiction
Style (DeKalb, IL)	
SubStance: A Review of Theory and Literary Criticism	
SuD	Sprache und Dichtung
Sudetenland	
SUDFU	Skrifter Utgivna genom Dialekt- och Folkminnesarkivet i Uppsala
SüdoA	Südostdeutsches Archiv
SuF	Sinn und Form: Beiträge zur Literatur
SUGIA	Sprache und Geschichte in Afrika
SULI	Skrifter Utgivna av Litteraturvetenskapliga Institutionen vid Uppsala Universitet
SULLA	Studi Urbinati, Serie B3: Linguistica, Letteratura, Arte
Sumlen: Årsbok för Vis- och Folkmusikforskning	
SupA	Suplementos Anthropos: Materiales de Trabajo Intelectual
Surfaces	Surfaces [Electronic publication]
SUS	Susquehanna University Studies (Selinsgrove, PA)
SuvL	Suvremena Lingvistika
SUVSL	Skrifter Utgivna av Vetenskaps-Societeten i Lund

SV   Schweizer Volkskunde: Korrespondenzblatt der Schweizerischen Gesellschaft für Volkskunde
Svantevit: Dansk Tidsskrift for Slavistik
SVDI   Serie de Vocabularios y Diccionarios Indigenas "Mariano Silva y Aceves"
SVEC   Studies on Voltaire and the Eighteenth Century
Svoboda: Ukrainian Daily
SWR   Southwest Review
SXX   Secolul 20
Symposium: A Quarterly Journal in Modern Foreign Literatures
Synthese: An International Journal for Epistemology, Methodology and Philosophy of Science
Synthesis: Bulletin du Comité National Roumain de Littérature Comparée et de l'Institut d'Histoire et de Théorie Littéraire "G. Călinescu" de l'Académie Roumaine (Bucharest, Romania)
Syria: Revue d'Art Orientale et d'Archéologie
SZ   Stimmen der Zeit
SzDL   Studien zur Deutschen Literatur
SzEP   Studien zur Englischen Philologie
Szinház: Theatre, Theoretical and Critical Journal of Theatrical Arts
TA   Theatre Annual
TAI   T. A. Informations: Revue Internationale du Traitement Automatique du Langage
Talisman: A Journal of Contemporary Poetry and Poetics
Tamarack: Journal of the Edna St. Vincent Millay Society
T&C   Text & Context: A Journal of Interdisciplinary Studies
T&D   Testi e Discorsi: Strumenti Linguistici e Letterari
T&K   Text & Kontext
T&P   Text & Presentation: The Journal of the Comparative Drama Conference [Formerly *Comparative Drama Conference Papers*]
T&T   Tools & Tillage: A Journal on the History of the Implements of Cultivation and Other Agricultural Processes
Tangence
Tarbiz: A Quarterly for Jewish Studies
Target: International Journal of Translation Studies
TASJ   The Transactions of the Asiatic Society of Japan
TCBS   Transactions of the Cambridge Bibliographical Society
TCEL   Thought Currents in English Literature
TCHN   Twayne's Critical History of the Novel
TCHPS   Twayne's Critical History of Poetry Series
TCL   Twentieth Century Literature: A Scholarly and Critical Journal
TCrit   Texto Crítico
TdL   Taller de Letras [Formerly *Taller de Letras: Revista del Instituto de Letras de la Ponfifica Universidad Católica de Chile*]
TDRev   TDR: The Drama Review: A Journal of Performance Studies
TE   Teología Espiritual
Teanga: Bliainiris na Teangeolaíochta Feidhmi in Éirinn/The Yearbook of Applied Linguistics [Formerly *Teanga: Iris Chumann na Teangeolaíochta Feidhmí/Joural of the Irish Association for Applied Linguistics*]
Teangeolas
TEAS   Twayne's English Authors Series
TekstyD   Teksty Drugie: Teoria Literatury—Krytyka—Interpretacja
Temenos: Studies in Comparative Religion Presented by Scholars in Denmark, Finland, Norway and Sweden
TENotes   T. E. Notes: A T. E. Lawrence Newsletter
TENSO: Bulletin of the Societe Guilhem IX
Te Reo: Journal of the Linguistic Society of New Zealand
TESOLQ   TESOL Quarterly
Tessera
TeT   Taal en Tongval
TexasR   The Texas Review
TexP   Textual Practice
Text: Transactions of the Society for Textual Scholarship
Texte: Revue de Critique et de Théorie Littéraire
Textus: Annual of the Hebrew University Bible Project

TfL   Tidskrift för Litteraturvetenskap
TFS   Twayne's Filmmakers Series
TFSB   Tennessee Folklore Society Bulletin
TGSI   Transactions of the Gaelic Society of Inverness
Thalia: Studies in Literary Humor
ThD   Themes in Drama
Theater (New Haven, CT)
TheatreS   Theatre Studies
Theatron: Studien zur Geschichte und Theorie der Dramatischen Künste
Theoria: A Journal of Studies in the Arts, Humanities and Social Sciences (Natal, S. Africa)
Thēsaurismata
Thesaurus: Boletín del Instituto Caro y Cuervo
THeth   Texte der Hethiter
THIC   Theatre History in Canada/Histoire du Théâtre au Canada
ThirdR   Third Rail: A Review of International Arts & Literature
THJ   The Thomas Hardy Journal
THJCS   Tsing Hua Journal of Chinese Studies
THL   Theory and History of Literature
ThMS   Thomas-Mann-Studien
Thought: A Review of Culture and Idea
ThR   Theatre Research International
THR   Travaux d'Humanisme et Renaissance
ThS   Theatre Survey: The Journal of the American Society for Theatre Research
THSC   Transactions of the Honourable Society of Cymmrodorion
THStud   Theatre History Studies
THY   The Thomas Hardy Yearbook
TICOJ   Transactions of the International Conference of Orientalists in Japan
TiLDoc   Trends in Linguistics: Documentation
TiLSaM   Trends in Linguistics: Studies and Monographs
TiLSAR   Trends in Linguistics: State-of-the-Art Reports
Tinta
Tirade
TiS   Topics in Sociolinguistics
TJ   Theatre Journal
TkR   Tamkang Review: A Quarterly of Comparative Studies between Chinese and Foreign Literatures
TL   Travaux de Linguistique: Revue Internationale de Linguistique Française (Louvain-la-Neuve, Belgium) [Formerly *Travaux de Linguistique: Publications du Service de Linguistique Française de l'Université de l'Etat à Gand*]
TLA   Trabalhos em Linguistica Aplicada
Tlalocan: Revista de Fuentes para el Conocimiento de las Culturas Indigenas de México (Mexico City, Mexico)
TLF   Textes Littéraires Français
TLit   Teoría Literária: Texto y Teoría
TLQ   Travaux de Linguistique Quantitative
TLR   The Linguistic Review
TLS   [London] Times Literary Supplement
TM   Temps Modernes
TMJ   Thomas Mann Jahrbuch
TMS   Twayne's Masterwork Studies
TN   Theatre Notebook: A Journal of the History and Technique of the British Theatre
TNCIS   Twayne's New Critical Introductions to Shakespeare
TNTL   Tijdschrift voor Nederlandse Taal- en Letterkunde (Leiden, Netherlands)
Tōhōgaku: Eastern Studies
Topic: A Journal of the Liberal Arts (Washington, PA)
Torre   La Torre: Revista de la Universidad de Puerto Rico
TPA   T'oung Pao: Revue Internationale de Sinologie
TPAS   Texas Pan American Series
TPB   Tennessee Philological Bulletin: Proceedings of the Annual Meeting of the Tennessee Philological Association
TPQ   Text and Performance Quarterly
TPS   Transactions of the Philological Society (Oxford, England)
Tradisjon: Tidsskrift for Folkeminnevitskap
Traditio: Studies in Ancient and Medieval History, Thought, and Religion

Tradition: A Journal of Orthodox Jewish Thought	
TraLiPhi	Travaux de Linguistique et de Philologie
TraLit	Travaux de Littérature
Translation (New York, NY)	
Travessia	
TRB	The Tennyson Research Bulletin
TrCIEREC	Travaux du CIEREC (Centre Interdisciplinaire d'Etudes et de Recherches sur l'Expression Contemporaine)
TRev	Translation Review
Trimestre (Chieti, Italy)	
TriQ	TriQuarterly (Evanston, IL)
Tristania: A Journal Devoted to Tristan Studies	
Triveni: Journal of Indian Renaissance	
Trivium (Dyfed, Wales)	
TrM	Traditional Music
Tropelías: Revista de Teoría de la Literatura y Literatura Comparada	
Tropismes	
Tropos	
TrP	Translation Perspectives
TS	Tijdschrift voor Skandinavistiek
TSB	Thoreau Society Bulletin
TSDL	Tübinger Studien zur Deutschen Literatur
TSJ	Tolstoy Studies Journal
TSJSNW	Transactions of the Samuel Johnson Society of the Northwest
TSLang	Typological Studies in Language
TSLit	Trierer Studien zur Literatur
TSLL	Texas Studies in Literature and Language
TSM	Texte des Späten Mittelalters und der Frühen Neuzeit
TSMon	Tennyson Society Monographs
TSO	Teatro del Siglo de Oro: Ediciones Críticas
TSOL	Teatro del Siglo de Oro: Estudios de Literatura
TSSF	Twayne's Studies in Short Fiction
TStL	Tennessee Studies in Literature
TSWL	Tulsa Studies in Women's Literature
TTR	TTR: Traduction, Terminologie, Rédaction: Etudes Sur le Texte et Ses Transformations
TTT: Interdisciplinair Tijdschrift voor Taal- & Tekstwetenschap	
TUBWPL	Technische Universität Berlin Arbeitspapiere zur Linguistik/Working Papers in Linguistics
TuK	Text + Kritik: Zeitschrift für Literatur
Tulimuld: Eesti Kirjanduse ja Kultuuri Ajakiri	
TUSAS	Twayne's United States Authors Series
TvG	Tydskrif vir Geesteswetenskappe
TvL	Tydskrif vir Letterkunde
Tw	Twórczość
TWA	Transactions of the Wisconsin Academy of Sciences, Arts, and Letters
TWAS	Twayne's World Authors Series
TWLS	Twayne's Women and Literature Series
TWN	The Thomas Wolfe Review
TWP	Trondheim Workingpapers
TYDS	Transactions of the Yorkshire Dialect Society (Leeds Univ.)
TZ	Zapiski Russkoi Akademicheskoi Gruppy v S.Sh.A./ Transactions of the Association of Russian-American Scholars in the U.S.A.
TzF	Texte zur Forschung
TZI	Traditiones: Zbornik Inštituta za Slovensko Narodopisje
TZS	TheaterZeitSchrift: Beiträge zu Theater, Medien, Kulturpolitik
UAJ	Ural-Altaische Jahrbücher/Ural-Altaic Yearbook: Internationale Zeitschrift für Nord-Eurasien
UAM	Uniwersytet im. Adama Mickiewicza w Poznaniu: Seria Filologia Angielska
UCAL	Understanding Contemporary American Literature
UCBL	Understanding Contemporary British Literature
UCLAOPL	UCLA Occasional Papers in Linguistics
UCPFS	University of California Publications, Folklore and Mythology Studies
UCPL	University of California Publications in Linguistics
UCPMP	University of California Publications in Modern Philology
UCrow	The Upstart Crow
UDL	Untersuchungen zur Deutschen Literaturgeschichte
UdLH	Universidad de La Habana
UDR	University of Dayton Review
UeL	Uomini e Libri: Periodico Bimestrale di Critica ed Informazione Letteraria
UES	Unisa English Studies: Journal of the Department of English
UF	Ulster Folklife
Ufahamu: Journal of the African Activist Association	
UFMH	University of Florida Monographs, Humanities Series
UKPHS	University of Kansas Humanistic Studies
UkrI	Ukraïns'kyĭ Istoryk
UkrMov	Ukraïns'ke Movoznavstvo: Mizhvidomchyĭ Naukovyĭ Zbirnyk
UkrR	The Ukrainian Review: A Quarterly Journal Devoted to the Study of Ukraine
ULR	University of Leeds Review
ULULA: Graduate Studies in Romance Languages	
ULz	Ukraïns'ke Literaturoznavstvo: Mizhvidomchyĭ Respublikans'kyĭ Zbirnyk
UMELAL	Understanding Modern European and Latin American Literature
Umma: A Magazine of Original Writing	
UMSE	University of Mississippi Studies in English
Uncoverings: Research Papers of the American Quilt Study Group	
UNCSCL	University of North Carolina Studies in Comparative Literature
UNCSGLL	University of North Carolina Studies in the Germanic Languages and Literatures
UNCSRLL	North Carolina Studies in the Romance Languages and Literatures
Unilit (Secunderabad, India)	
Unitas: A Quarterly for the Arts and Sciences (Manila, Philippines)	
Univ	Universitas: Zeitschrift für Wissenschaft, Kunst und Literatur (Stuttgart, Germany)
UP	Die Unterrichtspraxis
UPAL	Utrechtse Publikaties voor Algemene Literatuurwetenschap/Utrecht Publications in General and Comparative Literature
UPSSA	University of Pennsylvania Studies on South Asia
UQ	Ukrainian Quarterly: Journal of East European and Asian Affairs
Urbe: Rivista Romana di Storia, Arte, Lettere, Costumanze (Rome, Italy)	
USLL	Utah Studies in Literature and Linguistics
USSE	The University of Saga Studies in English
USTSLL	Università degli Studi di Torino. Dipartimento di Scienze e del Linguaggio e Letterature Moderne e Comparate
UTFS	University of Toronto Romance Series
UTIS	University of Toronto Italian Studies
UTQ	University of Toronto Quarterly: A Canadian Journal of the Humanities
UW	Us Wurk: Tydskrift foar Frisistyk
Vagant	
Vagartha: Critical Quarterly of Indian Literature	
VANBel	Vestsi Akadėmii Navuk Belarusi [Formerly *Vestsi Akadėmii Navuk BSSR*]
V&I	Voix et Images: Littérature Québécoise
Varaviksne	
Variétés	
VC	Virginia Cavalcade
VChrist	Vetera Christianorum
VDASD	Veröffentlichungen der Deutschen Akademie für Sprache und Dichtung
VEAW	Varieties of English Around the World
Veltro	Il Veltro: Rivista della Civiltà Italiana
Ventanal: Revista de Creación y Crítica	
Verba: Anuario Galego de Filoloxía	
Verbatim: The Language Quarterly	
Verri	Il Verri: Rivista di Letteratura

	Versants: Revue Suisse des Littératures Romanes/Rivista Svizzera di Letterature Romanze/Schweizerische Zeitschrift für Romanische Literaturen
	Versus: Quaderni di Studi Semiotici
	Vértice: Revista de Cultura e Arte
VFR	Victorian Fiction Research Guides
VGIEMTP	Veröffentlichungen des Grabmann Instituts zur Erforschung der Mittelalterlichen Theologie und Philosophie
	VIA: Voices in Italian Americana
	Viator: Medieval and Renaissance Studies
VigC	Vigiliae Christianae: A Review of Early Christian Life and Language
	VIJ: Victorians Institute Journal
VIndJ	Vishveshvaranand Indological Journal
	Vinduet (Oslo, Norway)
Vir	Virittäjä: Journal de Kotikielen Seura
ViR	Viaţa Românească (Bucharest, Romania)
	Vitchyzna: Literaturno-Khudozhniĭ ta Hromads'ko-Politychnyĭ Misiachnyk (Kiev, Ukraine)
	Vivarium: An International Journal for the Philosophy and Intellectual Life of the Middle Ages and Renaissance
VJa	Voprosy Iazykoznaniia (Moscow, Russia)
VLang	Visible Language: The Quarterly Concerned with All That Is Involved in Our Being Literate
VLC	Victorian Literature and Culture [Formerly *Browning Institute Studies*]
VlG	De Vlaamse Gids
VLit	Voprosy Literatury
VLT	The Velvet Light Trap
VLU	Vestnik Leningradskogo Universiteta. Seriia 2, Istoriia, Iazykoznanie, Literaturovedenie
VMKAN	Verslagen en Mededelingen van de Koninklijke Academie voor Nederlandse Taal- en Letterkunde
VMU	Vestnik Moskovskogo Universiteta. Seriia 9, Filologiia
VN	Victorian Newsletter
VOEI	Veröffentlichungen der Abteilung für Slavische Sprachen und Literaturen des Osteuropa-Instituts (Slavisches Seminar) an der Freien Universität Berlin
	Volkskunde: Driemaandelijks Tijdschrift voor de Studie van het Volksleven (Antwerp, Belgium)
VP	Victorian Poetry
VPR	Victorian Periodicals Review
VQR	Virginia Quarterly Review: A National Journal of Literature and Discussion (Richmond, VA)
VR	Vox Romanica: Annales Helvetici Explorandis Linguis Romanicis Destinati
VRev	Victorian Review: The Journal of the Victorian Studies Association of Western Canada
VRL	Voprosy Russkoĭ Literatury: Respublikanskiĭ Mezhvedomstvennyĭ Nauchnyĭ Sbornik
VS	Victorian Studies: A Journal of the Humanities, Arts and Sciences
	Vsesvit: Zhurnal Inozemnoï Literatury. Literaturno-Mystets'kyĭ ta Hromads'ko-Politychnyĭ Misiachnyk. Orhan Spilky Pys'mennykiv Ukraïny, Ukraïns'koho Tovarystva Druzhby i Kul'turnykh Zv'iazkiv z Zarubizhnymy Kraïnamy, Ukraïns'koï Rady Myru
VSLÅ	Vetenskaps-Societeten i Lund Årsbok
VT	Vinyar Tengwar
	Vuelta
vwa	[vwa]
VWM	Virginia Woolf Miscellany
VyV	Verdad y Vida: Revista de las Ciencias del Espiritu (Madrid, Spain)
VyzSh	Vyzvol'nyĭ Shliakh/Liberation Path
WADL	Wiener Arbeiten zur Deutschen Literatur
	Waiguoyu [Foreign Languages]
WAL	Western American Literature
WAn	Wide Angle: A Film Quarterly of Theory, Criticism, and Practice
W&D	Works and Days: Essays in the Socio-Historical Dimensions of Literature and the Arts
W&I	Word & Image: A Journal of Verbal/Visual Enquiry
W&L	Women & Literature
W&Lang	Women and Language
W&P	Women & Performance: A Journal of Feminist Theory
WascanaR	Wascana Review
WAWN	Wild About Wilde Newsletter
WB	Weimarer Beiträge: Zeitschrift für Literaturwissenschaft, Ästhetik und Kulturwissenschaften [Formerly *Weimarer Beiträge: Zeitschrift für Literaturwissenschaft, Ästhetik und Kulturtheorie*]
WBEP	Wiener Beiträge zur Englischen Philologie
WBN	Wolfenbütteler Barock-Nachrichten
WC	The Wordsworth Circle
WCPMN	Willa Cather Pioneer Memorial Newsletter
WCSJ	Wilkie Collins Society Journal
WCWR	William Carlos Williams Review
WdF	Wege der Forschung
WE	The Winesburg Eagle: The Official Publication of the Sherwood Anderson Society
Wellsian	The Wellsian: The Journal of the H. G. Wells Society
WEng	World Englishes: Journal of English as an International and Intranational Language
	Westerly: A Quarterly Review
WF	Western Folklore
WGCR	West Georgia College Review
WGY	Women in German Yearbook: Feminist Studies in German Literature and Culture [Formerly *Women in German Yearbook: Feminist Studies and German Culture*]
WHR	Western Humanities Review
WI	Die Welt des Islams: Internationale Zeitschrift für die Geschichte des Islams in der Neuzeit
WL&A	War, Literature, and the Arts
WLG	Wiener Linguistische Gazette
WLT	World Literature Today: A Literary Quarterly of the University of Oklahoma
WLWE	World Literature Written in English
WMQ	The William and Mary Quarterly: A Magazine of Early American History and Culture
WO	Die Welt des Orients: Wissenschaftliche Beiträge zur Kunde des Morgenlandes
WolfenbüttelerB	Wolfenbütteler Beiträge: Aus den Schätzen der Herzog August Bibliothek
Word	WORD: Journal of the International Linguistic Association
WPL	Working Papers in Linguistics (Columbus, OH)
WPLU	Working Papers (Lund University Department of Linguistics)
WPo	Winterthur Portfolio: A Journal of American Material Culture
WPP	UCLA Working Papers in Phonetics
WPSILUNDS	Work Papers of the Summer Institute of Linguistics, University of North Dakota Session
WS	Women's Studies: An Interdisciplinary Journal
WSA	Wolfenbütteler Studien zur Aufklärung
WSaR	The Wicazo SA Review: A Journal of Indian Studies
WSJ	Wiener Slavistisches Jahrbuch
WSJour	The Wallace Stevens Journal: A Publication of the Wallace Stevens Society
WSl	Die Welt der Slaven: Halbjahresschrift für Slavistik (Munich, Germany)
WSlA	Wiener Slawistischer Almanach
WStu	Weber Studies: An Interdisciplinary Humanities Journal
WT	Wetenschappelijke Tijdingen op het Gebied van de Geschiedenis van de Vlaamse Beweging
WVUPP	West Virginia University Philological Papers
WWays	Word Ways: The Journal of Recreational Linguistics
WWort	Wirkendes Wort: Deutsche Sprache und Literatur in Forschung und Lehre
WWQR	Walt Whitman Quarterly Review

WWS	Western Writers Series (Boise State University)
WZKS	Wiener Zeitschrift für die Kunde Südasiens und Archiv für Indische Philosophie
WZUB	Wissenschaftliche Zeitschrift der Humboldt-Universität zu Berlin: Gesellschaftswissenschaftliche Reihe
WZUH	Wissenschaftliche Zeitschrift der Martin-Luther Universität Halle-Wittenberg. Gesellschafts- und Sprachwissenschaftliche Reihe
WZUJ	Wissenschaftliche Zeitschrift der Friedrich-Schiller-Universität Jena. Gesellschaftswissenschaftliche Reihe
WZUR	Wissenschaftliche Zeitschrift der Wilhelm-Pieck-Universität Rostock. Gesellschaftswissenschaftliche Reihe
XUS	Xavier Review
YA	Yed'a-'Am/Yeda-Am: Bamah le-Folklor Yehudi/Journal of the Israel Folklore Society
YAlm	Yerushalaymer Almanakh
YCC	Yearbook of Comparative Criticism
YCGL	Yearbook of Comparative and General Literature
YeA	Yeats Annual

Yeats: An Annual of Critical and Textual Studies

YER	Yeats Eliot Review: A Journal of Criticism and Scholarship
YES	Yearbook of English Studies
YFS	Yale French Studies

Yiddish (Flushing, NY)

YIS	Yearbook of Italian Studies (Florence, Italy)
YJC	The Yale Journal of Criticism: Interpretation in the Humanities
YJLH	Yale Journal of Law & the Humanities
YK	Yiddishe Kultur
YLS	The Yearbook of Langland Studies
YOD	Revue des Etudes Hébraïques et Juives Modernes et Contemporaines
YR	The Yale Review
YRS	Yearbook of Romanian Studies: A Publication of the Romanian Studies Association of America
YSPS	The Yearbook of the Society for Pirandello Studies [Formerly *Yearbook of the British Pirandello Society*]
YTM	Yearbook for Traditional Music

Y Traethodydd (Caernarvon, Wales)

YULG	Yale University Library Gazette
YWES	Year's Work in English Studies
YWMLS	The Year's Work in Modern Language Studies

Z: Filmtidsskrift

Z-A	Zaïre-Afrique
ŽA	Živa Antika
ZAA	Zeitschrift für Anglistik und Amerikanistik
ZAH	Zeitschrift für Althebraistik
ZAL	Zeitschrift für Arabische Linguistik

Zambezia: The Journal of the University of Zimbabwe
Zapisy (Rutherford, NJ)

ZAVA	Zeitschrift für Assyriologie und Vorderasiatische Archäologie
ZB	Zeitschrift für Balkanologie
ZbirP	Zbirnyk Prats' Naukovoï Shevchenkivs'koï Konferentsiï
ZCP	Zeitschrift für Celtische Philologie
ZD	Zielsprache Deutsch: Zeitschrift für Unterrichtsmethodik und Angewandte Sprachwissenschaft
ZDA	Zeitschrift für Deutsches Altertum und Deutsche Literatur
ZDFALP	Z Dziejów Form Artystycznych W Literaturze Polskiej
ZDL	Zeitschrift für Dialektologie und Linguistik
ZDMG	Zeitschrift der Deutschen Morgenländischen Gesellschaft
ZDP	Zeitschrift für Deutsche Philologie (Berlin, Germany)

Zeta: Rivista Internazionale di Poesia (Udine, Italy)

ZfK	Zeitschrift für Katalanistik: Revista d'Estudis Catalans
ZFSL	Zeitschrift für Französische Sprache und Literatur
ZG	Zeitschrift für Germanistik
ZGL	Zeitschrift für Germanistische Linguistik

Život: Časopis za Književnost i Kulturu

ZL	Zeszyty Literackie
ŻLit	Życie Literackie

Znak: Miesięcznik (Cracow, Poland)
Znamenje (Ljubljana, Slovenia)
Znamia: Literaturno-Khudozhestvennyĭ i Obshchestvenno-Politicheskiĭ Zhurnal (Moscow, Russia)

ZNHF	The Zora Neale Hurston Forum
ZOF	Zeitschrift für Ostforschung: Länder und Völker im Östlichen Mitteleuropa
ZR	Zadarska Revija: Časopis za Kulturu i Društvena Pitanja
ZRL	Zagadnienia Rodzajów Literackich: Woprosy Literaturnych Żanrov/Les Problèmes des Genres Littéraires
ZRP	Zeitschrift für Romanische Philologie
ZS	Zeitschrift für Slawistik
ZSP	Zeitschrift für Slavische Philologie
ZV	Zeitschrift für Volkskunde: Halbjahreschrift der Deutschen Ges. f. Volkskunde

Zvezda (St. Petersburg, Russia)

(1)
Aachener Beiträge zur Komparatistik

Hugo Dyserinck, Editor
Lehr- und Forschungsgebiet Komparatistik
Philosophische Fakultät der RWTH Aachen
Templergraben 55
5100 Aachen, Germany

First published: 1977
Sponsoring organization: European Cultural Foundation
ISSN: 0342-4081
MLA acronym: ABK

SUBSCRIPTION INFORMATION

Frequency of publication: Irregular
Available in microform: No
Subscription address: Bouvier Verlag Herbert Grundmann, Am Hof 32, Postfach 1268, 5300 Bonn, Germany
Additional subscription address: Otto Harrassowitz, Postfach 2929, 6200 Wiesbaden 1, Germany

ADVERTISING INFORMATION

Advertising accepted: No

EDITORIAL DESCRIPTION

Scope: Publishes monographs on the history and theory of comparative literature, international cultural relations, European studies, and national stereotypes.
Reviews books: No
Publishes notes: Yes
Languages accepted: German; English; French
Prints abstracts: No

SUBMISSION REQUIREMENTS

Author pays submission fee: No
Author pays page charges: No
Length of books: 60,000 words minimum
Number of copies required: 3
Special requirements: Submit original typescript; include a 400-word abstract.
Copyright ownership: Bouvier Verlag Herbert Grundmann
Rejected manuscripts: Returned
Time before publication decision: 2 mos.
Time between decision and publication: 6 mos.
Number of reviewers: 2

(2)
*A/B: Auto/Biography Studies

Rebecca Hogan, Thomas Smith, Timothy Dow Adams, Joseph Hogan, & William Andrews, Editors
English Dept.
Univ. of Wisconsin
Whitewater, WI 53190-1790

Telephone: 414 472-5060; 414 472-5048
Fax: 414 472-1518 (R. Hogan)
E-mail: HOGANR@UWWVAX.UWW.EDU; HOGANJ@UWWVAX.UWW.EDU
First published: 1985
Sponsoring organization: Autobiography Soc.
ISSN: 0898-9575
MLA acronym: ABSt

SUBSCRIPTION INFORMATION

Frequency of publication: 2 times/yr.
Circulation: 220
Available in microform: No
Subscription price: $45.00/yr. institutions; $15.00/yr. individuals
Year to which price refers: 1992
Subscription address: Brad Born, Managing Editor, Hall Center for the Humanities, Univ. of Kansas, Lawrence, KS 66045-2967
Subscription telephone: 913 864-4798
Subscription fax: 913 864-5272

ADVERTISING INFORMATION

Advertising accepted: Yes
Advertising rates: $50.00/half page; $100.00/full page

EDITORIAL DESCRIPTION

Scope: Deals with all aspects of autobiography, biography, diaries, and letters, as well as with relations between life-writing and other forms. Subject matter may be drawn from any period or genre but must show clear connections to the theory and practice of life-writing.
Reviews books: Yes
Publishes notes: Yes
Languages accepted: English
Prints abstracts: No
Author-anonymous submission: No

SUBMISSION REQUIREMENTS

Restrictions on contributors: None
Author pays submission fee: No
Author pays page charges: No
Length of articles: 3,750-8,750 words
Length of book reviews: 1,000-2,000 words
Length of notes: 500 words
Style: MLA
Number of copies required: 3
Copyright ownership: Journal
Rejected manuscripts: Returned; enclose SASE.
Time before publication decision: 6 mos.
Time between decision and publication: 6-12 mos.
Number of reviewers: 2
Articles submitted per year: 40
Articles published per year: 20
Book reviews submitted per year: 10
Book reviews published per year: 10
Notes submitted per year: 10
Notes published per year: 5

(3)
*Abhandlungen der Akademie der Wissenschaften in Göttingen: Philologisch-Historische Klasse; Folge 3

Akademie der Wissenschaften in Göttingen
Theaterstr. 7
3400 Göttingen, Germany

Telephone: (49) 551 395362
Fax: (49) 551 395365
First published: 1752
Sponsoring organization: Akademie der Wissenschaften in Göttingen
MLA acronym: AAWG

SUBSCRIPTION INFORMATION

Frequency of publication: Irregular
Available in microform: No
Subscription address: Vandenhoeck & Ruprecht, Theaterstr. 13, 3400 Göttingen, Germany
Subscription telephone: (49) 551 695916
Subscription fax: (49) 551 695917

ADVERTISING INFORMATION

Advertising accepted: No

EDITORIAL DESCRIPTION

Scope: Publishes monographs on philosophy, history, and philology.
Reviews books: No
Publishes notes: No
Languages accepted: German; English; French; Latin; Greek
Prints abstracts: No
Author-anonymous submission: No

SUBMISSION REQUIREMENTS

Restrictions on contributors: Papers must be presented by a member of the Academy at a meeting. Author need not be a member.
Author pays submission fee: No
Author pays page charges: No
Length of books: No restrictions
Style: None
Number of copies required: 1
Special requirements: Submit typescript.
Copyright ownership: Vandenhoeck & Ruprecht
Rejected manuscripts: Returned
Time before publication decision: 6 mos.
Time between decision and publication: 6-9 mos.
Number of reviewers: 1
Books submitted per year: 2-8
Books published per year: 2-8

(4)
*Abhandlungen zur Kunst-, Musik- und Literaturwissenschaft

Verlag Bouvier GmbH & Co.
Postfach 1268, Am Hof 28
5300 Bonn 1, Germany

Telephone: (49) 228 72901-24
Fax: (49) 228 72901-79
First published: 1957
ISSN: 0567-4999
MLA acronym: AKML

SUBSCRIPTION INFORMATION

Frequency of publication: Irregular
Available in microform: No
Additional subscription address: VVA, Vereinigte Verlagsauslieferung, An der Autobahn 100, 4830 Gütersloh, Germany

ADVERTISING INFORMATION

Advertising accepted: No

EDITORIAL DESCRIPTION

Scope: Publishes studies in literature, music, and art.
Reviews books: No
Publishes notes: No
Languages accepted: German; English
Prints abstracts: No

SUBMISSION REQUIREMENTS

Restrictions on contributors: None
Copyright ownership: Editor
Rejected manuscripts: Returned
Time before publication decision: 6 weeks
Books published per year: 2-3

(5)
*Abhandlungen zur Sprache und Literatur

Richard Baum, Frank-Rutger Hausmann, & Jürgen Grimm, Editors
Romanistischer Verlag
Hochkreuzallee 46
5300 Bonn 2, Germany

Telephone: (49) 228 310961
Fax: (49) 228 312842
First published: 1986
ISSN: 0178-8515
MLA acronym: AzSL

SUBSCRIPTION INFORMATION

Frequency of publication: Irregular
Available in microform: No

ADVERTISING INFORMATION

Advertising accepted: No

EDITORIAL DESCRIPTION

Scope: Publishes monographs and collections on language, linguistics, and literature, with an emphasis on Romance literature and linguistics.
Reviews books: No
Publishes notes: No
Languages accepted: German; French; Spanish; Italian
Prints abstracts: Yes
Author-anonymous submission: No

SUBMISSION REQUIREMENTS

Restrictions on contributors: None
Author pays submission fee: No
Author pays page charges: Yes, for doctoral dissertations
Cost of page charges: 7.50 DM/page
Length of books: 100-500 pp.
Number of copies required: 1
Copyright ownership: Author
Rejected manuscripts: Returned
Time before publication decision: 1-2 mos.
Time between decision and publication: 2 mos.
Number of reviewers: 2-3
Books submitted per year: 10
Books published per year: 5-6

(6) *Abr-Nahrain

G. Bunnens, Editor
Dept. of Classical & Near Eastern Studies
Univ. of Melbourne
Parkville, Victoria 3052, Australia

Telephone: (61) 3 3444173
Fax: (61) 3 3444161
E-mail: GUY—BUNNENS.-CANES@MUWAYF.UNIMELB.EDU.AU
First published: 1959-60
Sponsoring organization: Dept. of Classical & Near Eastern Studies, Univ. of Melbourne
MLA acronym: Abr-Nahrain

SUBSCRIPTION INFORMATION

Frequency of publication: Annual
Circulation: 250
Available in microform: No
Subscription price: 1,200 BF/yr.
Year to which price refers: 1992
Subscription address: Peeter's Press, P.B. 41, 3000 Louvain, Belgium
Subscription telephone: (31) 16 1235170
Subscription fax: (31) 16 1228500

ADVERTISING INFORMATION

Advertising accepted: No

EDITORIAL DESCRIPTION

Scope: Publishes articles on Middle Eastern studies.
Reviews books: Yes
Publishes notes: No
Languages accepted: English; French; German
Prints abstracts: No
Author-anonymous submission: Yes

SUBMISSION REQUIREMENTS

Restrictions on contributors: None
Author pays submission fee: No
Author pays page charges: No
Length of articles: No restrictions
Length of book reviews: No restrictions
Style: None
Number of copies required: 1
Special requirements: Make minimum use of Semitic scripts.
Copyright ownership: Dept. of Classical & Near Eastern Studies, Univ. of Melbourne
Rejected manuscripts: Not returned
Time before publication decision: 3 mos.
Time between decision and publication: 1 yr. maximum
Number of reviewers: 2
Articles submitted per year: 10
Articles published per year: 5
Book reviews submitted per year: 7-8
Book reviews published per year: 5-6

(7) Abstracts of English Studies

William Monday & Jerre Paquette, Editors
English Dept.
Mount Royal College
4825 Richard Rd. SW
Calgary, AB T3E 6K6, Canada

First published: 1958
ISSN: 0001-3560
MLA acronym: AES

SUBSCRIPTION INFORMATION

Frequency of publication: 4 times/yr.
Circulation: 1,500
Available in microform: Yes
Subscription address: Basil Blackwell, Journals Dept., 108 Cowley Rd., Oxford OX4 1JF, England
Additional subscription address: Blackwell Publishers, 238 Main St., Suite 501, Cambridge, MA 02142

ADVERTISING INFORMATION

Advertising accepted: Yes

EDITORIAL DESCRIPTION

Scope: Publishes abstracts of journals that deal with critical articles on American and English literature, world literature in English and related languages, and English language.
Reviews books: No
Publishes notes: No
Languages accepted: English
Author-anonymous submission: No

SUBMISSION REQUIREMENTS

Author pays submission fee: No
Author pays page charges: No
Style: MLA
Number of copies required: 1
Special requirements: Abstracts should be 200 words in length.
Copyright ownership: Journal
Rejected manuscripts: Not returned
Time before publication decision: 6-12 mos.
Time between decision and publication: 3 mos.
Articles submitted per year: 3,000
Articles published per year: 2,800

(8) *Accademie e Biblioteche d'Italia

Ministero per i Beni Culturali e Ambientali
Ufficio Centrale per i Beni Librari e gli Istituti Culturali
Via Michele Mercati, 4
00197 Rome, Italy

Telephone: (39) 6 3215636
Fax: (39) 6 3216437
First published: 1927
ISSN: 0393-4451
MLA acronym: ABI

SUBSCRIPTION INFORMATION

Frequency of publication: 4 times/yr.
Circulation: 2,000
Available in microform: No
Subscription price: 65,000 Lit/yr. Italy; 110,000 Lit/yr. elsewhere
Year to which price refers: 1991
Subscription address: Organizzazione Rab S.R.-L., C.P. 30101, 00100 Rome 47, Italy
Subscription telephone: (39) 6 6381177; (39) 6 632595

EDITORIAL DESCRIPTION

Scope: Publishes articles on the activities of libraries and cultural institutions; Italian literature; and book history.
Reviews books: Yes
Publishes notes: Yes
Languages accepted: Italian
Prints abstracts: Yes

SUBMISSION REQUIREMENTS

Author pays submission fee: No
Author pays page charges: No
Length of notes: 1 p.
Number of copies required: 1
Special requirements: Submit original typescript.
Copyright ownership: Author
Rejected manuscripts: Not returned
Time before publication decision: 1-2 mos.
Time between decision and publication: 1-2 mos.
Articles submitted per year: 30
Articles published per year: 24
Book reviews published per year: 30

(9) *Acme: Annali della Facoltà di Lettere e Filosofia dell'Università degli Studi di Milano

Guido Bézzola, Editor
Fac. di Lettere e Filosofia
Univ. degli Studi
Via Festa del Perdono, 7
Milan, Italy

First published: 1948
Sponsoring organization: Univ. di Milano
ISSN: 0001-494X
MLA acronym: Acme

SUBSCRIPTION INFORMATION

Frequency of publication: 3 times/yr.
Circulation: 750
Available in microform: No
Subscription address: Ist. Ed. Cisalpino-La Goliardica, Via Rezia 4, Milan, Italy

ADVERTISING INFORMATION

Advertising accepted: No

EDITORIAL DESCRIPTION

Scope: Publishes studies relative to the material taught in the Department of Literature and Philosophy of the Università degli Studi di Milano.
Reviews books: No
Publishes notes: No
Languages accepted: Italian; French; English; German; Russian; Spanish
Prints abstracts: No

SUBMISSION REQUIREMENTS

Restrictions on contributors: Contributors must be members of the Univ. degli Studi faculty, or be comissioned by a faculty member.
Author pays submission fee: No
Author pays page charges: No
Length of articles: No restrictions
Number of copies required: 1
Copyright ownership: Univ. degli Studi
Rejected manuscripts: Returned
Time before publication decision: 6 mos.

Time between decision and publication: 6 mos.
Number of reviewers: 7
Articles published per year: 22

(10)
*Acta

Center for Medieval & Early Renaissance Studies
State Univ. of New York
Binghamton, NY 13902-6000

First published: 1974
Sponsoring organization: State Univ. of New York at Binghamton, Center for Medieval & Early Renaissance Studies
ISSN: 0361-7491
MLA acronym: Acta

SUBSCRIPTION INFORMATION

Frequency of publication: Annual
Circulation: 400
Available in microform: No
Subscription address: State Univ. of New York Press, Box 6525, Ithaca, NY 14850

ADVERTISING INFORMATION

Advertising accepted: Yes, on an exchange basis

EDITORIAL DESCRIPTION

Scope: Publishes interdisciplinary studies concerning the Middle Ages, presented at SUNY regional conferences.
Reviews books: No
Publishes notes: No
Languages accepted: English
Prints abstracts: No
Author-anonymous submission: No

SUBMISSION REQUIREMENTS

Restrictions on contributors: Unsolicited manuscripts are not accepted.
Author pays submission fee: No
Author pays page charges: Yes
Style: MLA
Number of copies required: 2
Copyright ownership: Center for Medieval & Early Renaissance Studies
Rejected manuscripts: Returned
Time before publication decision: 3 mos.
Time between decision and publication: 1 yr.
Number of reviewers: 2
Articles submitted per year: 6-8

(11)
*Acta Antiqua Academiae Scientiarum Hungaricae

Zsigmond Ritoók, Editor
Mátyás utca 20
1093 Budapest, Hungary

Additional editorial address: Akadémiai Kiadó, P.O. Box 24, 1363 Budapest, Hungary
Telephone: (36) 1 1812130
Fax: (36) 1 1666466
First published: 1951
Sponsoring organization: Magyar Tudományos Akadémia
ISSN: 0044-5975
MLA acronym: AAASH

SUBSCRIPTION INFORMATION

Frequency of publication: 2 double issues/yr.
Circulation: 590
Available in microform: No
Subscription price: $80.00/yr.
Year to which price refers: 1992

ADVERTISING INFORMATION

Advertising accepted: Yes
Advertising rates: $300.00/full page

EDITORIAL DESCRIPTION

Scope: Publishes articles in the field of ancient studies, including history, literature, language, religion, law, and material culture.
Reviews books: Yes
Publishes notes: Yes
Languages accepted: English; French; German; Latin; Russian
Prints abstracts: No
Author-anonymous submission: No

SUBMISSION REQUIREMENTS

Restrictions on contributors: None
Author pays submission fee: No
Author pays page charges: No
Length of articles: 15,000 words maximum
Length of book reviews: 2,000-2,500 words
Length of notes: 1,500-2,000 words
Style: None
Number of copies required: 2
Special requirements: Submit original typescript.
Copyright ownership: Author
Rejected manuscripts: Returned
Time before publication decision: 2 mos.
Time between decision and publication: 18-24 mos.
Number of reviewers: 2
Articles submitted per year: 30-40
Articles published per year: 30-35
Book reviews submitted per year: 3-4
Book reviews published per year: 3-4
Notes submitted per year: 3-5
Notes published per year: 3-5

(12)
*Acta Asiatica: Bulletin of the Institute of Eastern Culture

Jikidō Takasaki, Editor
Tōhō Gakkai/Inst. of Eastern Culture
4-1, Nishi-Kanda 2-chōme
Chiyoda-ku
Tokyo 101, Japan

Telephone: (81) 3 32627221
Fax: (81) 3 32627227
First published: 1960
Sponsoring organization: Tōhō Gakkai
ISSN: 0567-7254
MLA acronym: ActaA

SUBSCRIPTION INFORMATION

Frequency of publication: 2 times/yr.
Available in microform: No
Subscription price: 4,000 yen/yr. plus postage
Year to which price refers: 1992

ADVERTISING INFORMATION

Advertising accepted: No

EDITORIAL DESCRIPTION

Scope: Publishes articles on Oriental studies.
Reviews books: No
Publishes notes: No
Languages accepted: English
Prints abstracts: No
Author-anonymous submission: No

SUBMISSION REQUIREMENTS

Restrictions on contributors: Unsolicited manuscripts are not accepted.
Author pays submission fee: No
Style: Chicago
Number of copies required: 1
Copyright ownership: Tōhō Gakkai
Articles published per year: 10

(13)
*Acta Baltica: Liber Annalis Instituti Baltici

Ernst Benz, Editor
Inst. Balticum
Albertus-Magnus-Kolleg
Bischof-Kaller-Str. 3
6240 Königstein/Ts., Germany

Telephone: (49) 6174 299123
First published: 1962
Sponsoring organization: Albertus-Magnus-Kolleg Haus der Begegnung e.V.
ISSN: 0567-7289
MLA acronym: AB

SUBSCRIPTION INFORMATION

Frequency of publication: Annual
Circulation: 700
Available in microform: No
Subscription price: $30.00 (40 DM)/yr.
Year to which price refers: 1992

ADVERTISING INFORMATION

Advertising accepted: No

EDITORIAL DESCRIPTION

Scope: Publishes articles on Baltic studies (including history and literature), as well as on the Church in Estonia, Latvia, and Lithuania.
Reviews books: Yes
Publishes notes: No
Languages accepted: German
Prints abstracts: No
Author-anonymous submission: No

SUBMISSION REQUIREMENTS

Restrictions on contributors: None
Author pays submission fee: Varies
Author pays page charges: No
Length of articles: 20-80 pp.
Length of book reviews: 1-2 pp.
Style: None
Number of copies required: 1
Special requirements: Accepted articles written in English, Lithuanian, Latvian, Estonian, or Russian will be translated into German for publication.
Copyright ownership: Inst. Balticum
Rejected manuscripts: Returned
Time before publication decision: 2 mos.
Time between decision and publication: 6-12 mos.
Number of reviewers: 2
Articles submitted per year: 12-15
Articles published per year: 5-9
Book reviews submitted per year: 2-4
Book reviews published per year: 1-2

(14)
*Acta Baltico-Slavica: Archaeologia, Historia, Etnographia, et Linguarum Scientia

Jan Safarewicz & Krzysztof Luczyk, Editors
Inst. Słowianoznawstwa Polskiej Akademii Nauk
Pałac Kultury i Nauki
p. 1913, Skr. Poczt. 24
00-901 Warsaw, Poland

First published: 1964
Sponsoring organization: Polska Akademia Nauk, Inst. Słowianoznawstwa
ISSN: 0065-1044
MLA acronym: ABS

SUBSCRIPTION INFORMATION

Frequency of publication: Annual
Circulation: 500
Available in microform: No

Subscription address: Slawistyczny Ośrodek Wydawniczy, Inst. Słowianioznawstwa PAN, Pałac Kultury i Nauki VI p., Skr. Poczt. 24, 00-644 Warsaw, Poland

ADVERTISING INFORMATION

Advertising accepted: No

EDITORIAL DESCRIPTION

Scope: Deals with the political, social, and cultural relations between the Baltic peoples (the ancient Prussians, the Lithuanians, and the Letts) and the Slavonic peoples (the Poles, the Whiterussians, and the Russians) in the past and in our times. Discusses the traditions and the scientific achievement of the Baltic and Slavonic peoples.
Reviews books: Yes
Publishes notes: Yes
Languages accepted: English; French; Polish; Russian; German
Prints abstracts: Yes

SUBMISSION REQUIREMENTS

Restrictions on contributors: None
Author pays submission fee: No
Author pays page charges: No
Length of articles: 15-20 pp.
Length of book reviews: 10 pp. maximum
Length of notes: 3 pp. maximum
Number of copies required: 2
Special requirements: Submit original typescript.
Copyright ownership: Assigned by author to journal
Rejected manuscripts: Returned
Time before publication decision: 2 mos.
Time between decision and publication: 12-18 mos.
Number of reviewers: 1 plus Editorial Board
Articles submitted per year: 12-18
Articles published per year: 10-15
Book reviews submitted per year: 5-6
Book reviews published per year: 5-6

(15)
*Acta Ethnographica Academiae Scientiarum Hungaricae

Béla Gunda & Gábor Barna, Editors
MTA Néprajzi Kutató Csoport
Országház u. 30
Posta fiók 29
1250 Budapest I, Hungary

First published: 1950
Sponsoring organization: Magyar Tudományos Akadémia
ISSN: 0001-5628
MLA acronym: AEASH

SUBSCRIPTION INFORMATION

Frequency of publication: 2 double issues/yr.
Available in microform: No
Subscription address: Kultura Foreign Trade Co., P.O. Box 149, 1389 Budapest 62, Hungary

ADVERTISING INFORMATION

Advertising accepted: No

EDITORIAL DESCRIPTION

Scope: Publishes articles on social and cultural anthropology, ethnography, and folklore. Emphasis is on subjects related to Hungarian ethnography and folklore as well as on works presenting Hungarian folklore in the context of East European and Eurasian cultures.
Reviews books: Yes
Publishes notes: Yes
Languages accepted: English; French; German; Russian
Prints abstracts: No

SUBMISSION REQUIREMENTS

Restrictions on contributors: None
Author pays submission fee: No
Author pays page charges: No
Length of articles: 40 double-spaced typescript pp.
Length of book reviews: 800 words
Length of notes: 2,000 words maximum
Number of copies required: 2
Special requirements: Use form of *American Anthropologist* for citations.
Copyright ownership: Author
Rejected manuscripts: Returned
Time before publication decision: 2 mos.
Time between decision and publication: 1 yr.
Number of reviewers: 2
Articles submitted per year: 20
Articles published per year: 10
Book reviews published per year: 25-30

(16)
*Acta Germanica: Jahrbuch des Germanistenverbandes im Südlichen Afrika

Walter Köppe, Editor
Dept. of German
Univ. of Stellenbosch
7600 Stellenbosch, South Africa

Telephone: (27) 2231 772034
Fax: (27) 2231 774499
E-mail: WGHK@MATIES.SUN.AC.ZA
First published: 1966
Historical variations in title: Formerly Acta Germanica: Jahrbuch des Südafrikanischen Germanistenverbandes
Sponsoring organization: Germanistenverband im Südlichen Afrika
ISSN: 0065-1273
MLA acronym: ActaG

SUBSCRIPTION INFORMATION

Frequency of publication: Annual
Circulation: 600
Available in microform: No
Subscription price: 30 R/yr.
Year to which price refers: 1992
Subscription address: Verlag Peter Lang, Eschborner Landstr. 42-50, 6000 Frankfurt a. M. 90, Germany

ADVERTISING INFORMATION

Advertising accepted: Yes

EDITORIAL DESCRIPTION

Scope: Publishes articles on German literature.
Reviews books: Yes
Publishes notes: No
Languages accepted: German; English; French
Prints abstracts: No
Author-anonymous submission: Yes

SUBMISSION REQUIREMENTS

Restrictions on contributors: None
Author pays submission fee: No
Author pays page charges: No
Length of articles: No restrictions
Length of book reviews: No restrictions
Style: Harvard
Number of copies required: 1
Copyright ownership: Author
Rejected manuscripts: Returned
Time before publication decision: 6 mos.
Time between decision and publication: 6 mos.
Number of reviewers: 1
Articles submitted per year: 18
Articles published per year: 12
Book reviews submitted per year: 3
Book reviews published per year: 3

(17)
Acta Linguistica Hafniensia: International Journal of General Linguistics

Henning Andersen, Sóren Egerod, Jørgen Rischel, Michael Fortescue, & Jens Elmegård Rasmussen, Editors
Inst. of Linguistics
Njalsgade 96
2300 Copenhagen S, Denmark

First published: 1939
Sponsoring organization: Danish Research Council for the Humanities
ISSN: 0374-0463
MLA acronym: ALH

SUBSCRIPTION INFORMATION

Frequency of publication: 2 times/yr. (Apr., Oct.)
Circulation: 500
Available in microform: No
Subscription address: C. A. Reitzels Boghandel, Nørregade 20, 1165 Copenhagen K, Denmark

ADVERTISING INFORMATION

Advertising accepted: No

EDITORIAL DESCRIPTION

Scope: Publishes articles presenting original research in all branches of theoretical linguistics. Especially interested in papers dealing with typological aspects of language structure and papers presenting documented and critical discussions of the methodology, terminology, and subject matter of linguistics.
Reviews books: Yes
Publishes notes: Yes
Languages accepted: English; French; German
Prints abstracts: Yes

SUBMISSION REQUIREMENTS

Restrictions on contributors: None
Author pays submission fee: No
Author pays page charges: No
Length of articles: 9,000 words
Length of book reviews: 2,500 words
Length of notes: 1,500 words
Style: MLA; journal
Number of copies required: 3
Special requirements: Include a 10-15 line abstract.
Copyright ownership: Linguistic Circle of Copenhagen
Rejected manuscripts: Returned
Time before publication decision: 3 mos.
Time between decision and publication: 3-9 mos.
Articles published per year: 10-14

(18)
*Acta Literaria

Luis Muñoz G., Editor
Dept. de Español
Fac. de Educación, Humanidades y Arte
Univ. de Concepción
Casilla 82-C, Correo 3
Concepción, Chile

Telephone: (56) 41 234985 ext. 2313, 2530
Fax: (56) 41 240280
First published: 1975
Sponsoring organization: Univ. de Concepción
ISSN: 0716-0909
MLA acronym: ActaLit

SUBSCRIPTION INFORMATION

Frequency of publication: Annual
Available in microform: No
Subscription price: $7.00/yr. plus postage
Year to which price refers: 1991

Subscription address: Administración *Acta Literaria,* at above address

ADVERTISING INFORMATION

Advertising accepted: No

EDITORIAL DESCRIPTION

Scope: Publishes articles on Latin American literature and literary theory.
Reviews books: Yes
Publishes notes: Yes
Languages accepted: Spanish; French; English
Prints abstracts: No
Author-anonymous submission: No

SUBMISSION REQUIREMENTS

Restrictions on contributors: None
Author pays submission fee: No
Author pays page charges: No
Length of articles: No restrictions
Length of book reviews: No restrictions
Length of notes: No restrictions
Number of copies required: 1
Special requirements: See *ActaLit,* nos. 10-11, pp. 245-247.
Copyright ownership: Journal
Time before publication decision: 1 yr.
Time between decision and publication: 6 mos.
Number of reviewers: 5
Articles submitted per year: 8
Articles published per year: 6
Book reviews submitted per year: 2-3
Book reviews published per year: 2-3
Notes submitted per year: 3-4
Notes published per year: 3-4

(19) Acta Litteraria Academiae Scientiarum Hungaricae

Katalin Kulin, Managing Editor
Eötvös Loránd Tudományegyetem
P.O. Box 107
1364 Budapest, Hungary

First published: 1957
Sponsoring organization: Hungarian Academy of Sciences
ISSN: 0567-7661
MLA acronym: ALitASH

SUBSCRIPTION INFORMATION

Frequency of publication: 4 times/yr.
Circulation: 380
Subscription address: Akadémiai Kiadó, P.O. Box 245, 1519 Budapest, Hungary

ADVERTISING INFORMATION

Advertising accepted: Yes

EDITORIAL DESCRIPTION

Scope: Publishes papers dealing with problems in Hungarian and European history of literature, especially those where stress is laid on the relation between Hungarian literature and the literatures of other European countries in the past (during the Middle Ages, Humanism, Reformation, Enlightenment, etc.) as well as on the place and role of Hungarian letters in world literature. Reviews the latest results achieved by Hungarian scholars.
Reviews books: Yes
Publishes notes: Yes
Languages accepted: English; French; German; Italian; Russian; Spanish
Prints abstracts: No

SUBMISSION REQUIREMENTS

Restrictions on contributors: None
Author pays submission fee: No
Author pays page charges: No
Length of articles: 15,000 words maximum
Length of book reviews: 3,750 words
Style: Journal
Number of copies required: 1
Special requirements: Submit original typescript.
Copyright ownership: Author
Rejected manuscripts: Not returned
Time before publication decision: 2 mos.
Time between decision and publication: 1-2 yrs.
Number of reviewers: 2
Articles submitted per year: 50
Articles published per year: 30
Book reviews submitted per year: 20
Book reviews published per year: 12
Notes submitted per year: 10
Notes published per year: 8

(20) *Acta Neophilologica

Janez Stanonik, Editor
Dept. of Germanic Languages and Literatures
Faculty of Philosophy
Aškerčeva 12
61000 Ljubljana, Slovenia

First published: 1968
Sponsoring organization: Ljubljana Univ., Faculty of Philosophy
ISSN: 0567-784X
MLA acronym: AN

SUBSCRIPTION INFORMATION

Frequency of publication: Annual
Circulation: 400
Available in microform: No
Subscription price: $10.00/yr.
Year to which price refers: 1992

ADVERTISING INFORMATION

Advertising accepted: No

EDITORIAL DESCRIPTION

Scope: Publishes articles on Western European and American literatures.
Reviews books: Yes
Languages accepted: English; French; German; Spanish; Italian; Swedish
Prints abstracts: Yes, in Slovene
Author-anonymous submission: No

SUBMISSION REQUIREMENTS

Author pays submission fee: No
Author pays page charges: No
Length of articles: 2,000-15,000 words; occasionally 30,000 words maximum
Length of book reviews: 2,000 words maximum
Style: MLA
Number of copies required: 1
Copyright ownership: Journal
Rejected manuscripts: Returned
Time before publication decision: 1 yr.
Time between decision and publication: 6 mos.
Number of reviewers: 2
Articles submitted per year: 8
Articles published per year: 4-8
Book reviews published per year: 3

(21) *Acta Orientalia Academiae Scientiarum Hungaricae

Alice Sárközi, Editor
Akademiai Kiadó
Publishing House of the Hungarian Academy of Sciences
P.O. Box 24
1363 Budapest, Hungary

Additional editorial address: Eötvös Loránd Univ., Izabella u. 46, 1064 Budapest, Hungary

First published: 1950
Sponsoring organization: Magyar Tudományos Akadémia (Hungarian Academy of Sciences)
ISSN: 0001-6446
MLA acronym: AOASH

SUBSCRIPTION INFORMATION

Frequency of publication: 4 times/yr.
Available in microform: No
Subscription price: $75.00/yr.
Year to which price refers: 1992

ADVERTISING INFORMATION

Advertising accepted: Yes

EDITORIAL DESCRIPTION

Scope: Publishes papers on Oriental studies, including Turkish, Mongolian, Manchurian, Chinese, Tibetan, Indian, Iranian, and Semitic philology, literature, and history.
Reviews books: Yes
Publishes notes: Yes
Languages accepted: English; French; German; Russian
Prints abstracts: No
Author-anonymous submission: No

SUBMISSION REQUIREMENTS

Author pays submission fee: No
Author pays page charges: No
Number of copies required: 2
Copyright ownership: Journal
Rejected manuscripts: Returned
Time before publication decision: 2 weeks
Time between decision and publication: 2 yrs.
Number of reviewers: 5
Articles published per year: 18-20
Book reviews published per year: 30

(22) *Acta Orientalia (Societates Orientales Danica, Fennica, Norvegica, Svecica)

Søren Egerod, Editor
East Asian Inst.
Univ. of Copenhagen
Njalsgade 80
2300 Copenhagen S, Denmark

Telephone: (45) 33 542211
Fax: (45) 32 961518
First published: 1922
Sponsoring organization: Danish, Norwegian, Finnish and Swedish Oriental Societies; Nordiska Publiceringsnämnden för Humanistiska Tidskrifter/Nordic Publications Board for Humanistic Studies (NOP-H)
ISSN: 0001-6438
MLA acronym: AODNS

SUBSCRIPTION INFORMATION

Frequency of publication: Annual
Circulation: 250
Available in microform: No
Subscription price: 377 Dkr (£36.00, 103 DM, $55.00)/yr.
Subscription address: Munksgaard International Publishers Ltd., Nørre Søgade 35, P.O. Box 2148, 1016 Copenhagen K, Denmark
Additional subscription address: Munksgaard International Publishers, Three Cambridge Center, Suite 208, Cambridge, MA 02142

ADVERTISING INFORMATION

Advertising accepted: No

EDITORIAL DESCRIPTION

Scope: Publishes scholarly articles concerned with the languages, history, archaeology, and religions of the Orient from the earliest times to the present.
Reviews books: Yes
Publishes notes: No
Languages accepted: English; French; German
Prints abstracts: No
Author-anonymous submission: No

SUBMISSION REQUIREMENTS

Restrictions on contributors: None
Author pays submission fee: No
Author pays page charges: No
Length of articles: No restrictions
Length of book reviews: No restrictions
Style: None
Number of copies required: 1
Special requirements: Submit original double-spaced typescript.
Copyright ownership: Assigned by author to journal.
Rejected manuscripts: Returned at author's request
Time before publication decision: 1-3 mos.
Time between decision and publication: 6-12 mos.
Number of reviewers: 2-4
Articles submitted per year: 8-15
Articles published per year: 6-10
Book reviews submitted per year: 20-40
Book reviews published per year: 20-40

(23)
Acta Semiotica et Lingvistica: International Review of Semiotics and Linguistics

Cidmar Teodoro Pais, Editor
Univ. de São Paulo
São Paulo, Brazil

First published: 1977
Sponsoring organization: Brazilian Soc. of Professors of Linguistics; Ed. de Humanismo, Ciencia & Tecnologia
ISSN: 0102-4264
MLA acronym: ASEL

SUBSCRIPTION INFORMATION

Frequency of publication: 2 times/yr.
Subscription address: Maria de Fátima Gonçalves Moreira, Editora de Humanismo, Ciência e Tecnologia HUCITEC Ltda., Alameda Jaú, 404, 01420 São Paulo, Brazil

EDITORIAL DESCRIPTION

Scope: Encourages the exchange of ideas among professors and researchers in the social sciences interested in problems of signification and language, whether verbal or non-verbal. Accepts articles which advance different theoretical positions and which express the thinking of various schools in the treatment of semiotic questions. Is primarily interested in the study of linguistic and non-linguistic signification, and of their division into universes of discourse; reaffirming the concept of linguistics and of semiotics as sciences; and maintaining the distinction between semiology and semiotics. Another concern of the journal is the pragmatic dimension of language, according to which one considers significance as a relation between sign and user.
Reviews books: Yes
Languages accepted: English; French; Spanish
Prints abstracts: Yes

SUBMISSION REQUIREMENTS

Style: Journal
Number of copies required: 2
Special requirements: Include a 250-word abstract in English and French.

Rejected manuscripts: Not returned
Articles published per year: 16

(24)
Acta Universitatis Szegediensis de Attila József Nominatae: Acta Historiae Litterarum Hungaricarum

B. Keserü & F. Grezsa, Editors
Attila József Univ.
Egyetem u. 2-6
6722 Szeged, Hungary

First published: 1961
Sponsoring organization: Attila József Univ.
ISSN: 0586-3708
MLA acronym: AUS-AHLH

SUBSCRIPTION INFORMATION

Frequency of publication: Annual
Available in microform: No
Subscription address: József Attila Tudományegyetem, Központi Könyvtar, Dugonics Tér 13, P.O. Box 393, 6701 Szeged, Hungary

ADVERTISING INFORMATION

Advertising accepted: No

EDITORIAL DESCRIPTION

Scope: Publishes articles on Hungarian literary history.
Reviews books: No
Publishes notes: No
Prints abstracts: No

SUBMISSION REQUIREMENTS

Restrictions on contributors: None
Author pays submission fee: No
Author pays page charges: No
Length of articles: 7,000 words
Style: Hungarian Academy of Sciences
Number of copies required: 1
Copyright ownership: Author
Rejected manuscripts: Returned at author's request
Time before publication decision: 1 mo.
Time between decision and publication: 1 yr.
Number of reviewers: 1
Articles submitted per year: 10
Articles published per year: 9

(25)
*Acta Universitatis Szegediensis de Attila József Nominatae: Acta Romanica

Attila József Univ.
Faculty of Arts
Egyetem u. 2
6722 Szeged, Hungary

First published: 1966
Sponsoring organization: Attila József Univ.
ISSN: 0567-8099
MLA acronym: AUS-AG&R

SUBSCRIPTION INFORMATION

Frequency of publication: Annual
Circulation: 300
Available in microform: No
Subscription address: Kultura Foreign Trade Co., Box 149, 1389 Budapest, Hungary

ADVERTISING INFORMATION

Advertising accepted: No

EDITORIAL DESCRIPTION

Scope: Publishes scholarly essays by the staff of the Department of Romance Studies, Attila József University.
Reviews books: No
Languages accepted: French; Italian; Hungarian
Prints abstracts: No

SUBMISSION REQUIREMENTS

Restrictions on contributors: Contributors are usually members of the Dept. of Romance Languages, Attila József Univ.
Author pays submission fee: No
Author pays page charges: No
Length of articles: No restrictions
Number of copies required: 2
Copyright ownership: Attila József Univ.
Rejected manuscripts: Returned
Time between decision and publication: 1 yr.
Number of reviewers: 2
Articles submitted per year: 10-15
Articles published per year: 10-13

(26)
Acta Universitatis Szegediensis de Attila József Nominatae: Sectio Ethnographica et Linguistica/Néprajz és Nyelvtudomány/Volkskunde und Sprachwissenschaft

S. Károly, T. Mikola, & A. Róna Tas, Editors
Attila József Univ.
Egyetem u. 2
6722 Szeged, Hungary

First published: 1957
Sponsoring organization: Dept. of Philosophy, Attila József Univ.
ISSN: 0586-3716
MLA acronym: AUS-E&L

SUBSCRIPTION INFORMATION

Frequency of publication: Annual
Circulation: 500
Available in microform: No
Subscription address: József Attila Tudományegyetem, Kozponti Konyvtar, Dugonics Ter 13, 6722 Szeged, Hungary

ADVERTISING INFORMATION

Advertising accepted: No

EDITORIAL DESCRIPTION

Scope: Publishes articles on Hungarian, Uralic, Altaic languages and ethnography.
Reviews books: Yes
Languages accepted: Hungarian; German; English; Russian
Prints abstracts: Yes

SUBMISSION REQUIREMENTS

Restrictions on contributors: Contributors must be members or guests of the Dept. of Philosophy, Attila József Univ.
Author pays submission fee: No
Author pays page charges: No
Length of articles: 20,000-40,000 characters
Length of book reviews: 10,000 characters maximum
Number of copies required: 1
Copyright ownership: Author
Rejected manuscripts: Returned
Time before publication decision: 2-4 mos.
Time between decision and publication: 12-20 mos.
Number of reviewers: 2
Articles submitted per year: 10-20
Articles published per year: 10-20
Book reviews submitted per year: 3-5
Book reviews published per year: 3-5

(27)
Acta Universitatis Umensis, Umeå Studies in the Humanities

Per Råberg, Editor
Humanistiska fakulteten
Umeå Univ.
901 87 Umeå, Sweden

First published: 1975
Sponsoring organization: Humanistisk-Samhällsvetenskapliga Forskningsrådet
ISSN: 0345-0155
MLA acronym: AUUUSH

SUBSCRIPTION INFORMATION

Frequency of publication: Irregular

ADVERTISING INFORMATION

Advertising accepted: No

EDITORIAL DESCRIPTION

Scope: Publishes books focusing on the humanities.
Reviews books: No
Languages accepted: English
Prints abstracts: No

(28)
*Acta Universitatis Upsaliensis, Studia Anglistica Upsaliensia

Gunnar Sorelius, Mats Rydén, & Rolf Lundén, Editors
Editorial Office
Uppsala Univ.
P.O. Box 256
751 05 Uppsala, Sweden

Telephone: (46) 18 181229 (G. Sorelius); (46) 18 181818 (Editorial Office)
Fax: (46) 18 181817
First published: 1963
Sponsoring organization: Uppsala Univ.
ISSN: 0562-2719
MLA acronym: AUUSAU

SUBSCRIPTION INFORMATION

Frequency of publication: Irregular
Circulation: 700
Available in microform: No
Subscription address: Almqvist & Wiksell International, P.O. Box 4627, 116 91 Stockholm, Sweden
Subscription telephone: (46) 8 6408800
Subscription fax: (46) 8 6411180

ADVERTISING INFORMATION

Advertising accepted: No

EDITORIAL DESCRIPTION

Scope: Publishes monographs on British, American, and Irish literatures and the English language.
Reviews books: No
Publishes notes: No
Languages accepted: English
Prints abstracts: Yes
Author-anonymous submission: No

SUBMISSION REQUIREMENTS

Restrictions on contributors: Contributors must be associated with the English Dept. at Uppsala Univ.
Author pays submission fee: No
Author pays page charges: No
Length of books: 50,000-60,000 words
Style: Chicago
Number of copies required: 1
Special requirements: Submit a 100-500 word abstract.
Copyright ownership: Author after 3 yrs.
Rejected manuscripts: Returned
Time before publication decision: 3 mos.
Time between decision and publication: 8 mos.
Number of reviewers: 1-3
Books published per year: 2-7

(29)
*Acta Universitatis Upsaliensis, Studia Germanistica Upsaliensia

John Evert Härd, Editor
Uppsala Univ.
Box 513
751 20 Uppsala, Sweden

First published: 1964
Sponsoring organization: Uppsala Univ.
ISSN: 0585-5160
MLA acronym: AUUSGU

SUBSCRIPTION INFORMATION

Frequency of publication: Irregular
Available in microform: No
Subscription address: Almqvist & Wiksell International, P.O. Box 4627, 116 91 Stockholm, Sweden

ADVERTISING INFORMATION

Advertising accepted: No

EDITORIAL DESCRIPTION

Scope: Publishes scholarly works written at the University of Uppsala in the field of German language and literature.
Reviews books: No
Languages accepted: German
Prints abstracts: Yes

SUBMISSION REQUIREMENTS

Restrictions on contributors: Contributors must be associated with the German Institute at Uppsala Univ.
Author pays submission fee: No
Author pays page charges: No
Length of books: 750,000 words
Number of copies required: 1
Copyright ownership: Series
Rejected manuscripts: Returned
Time before publication decision: 6 mos.
Time between decision and publication: 1 yr.
Number of reviewers: 1-2

(30)
*Acta Universitatis Upsaliensis, Studia Romanica Upsaliensia

Mats Forsgren & Sven Åke Hed, Editors
Uppsala Univ., Editorial Office
P.O. Box 256
751 05 Uppsala, Sweden

Telephone: (46) 18 181821
Fax: (46) 18 181817
First published: 1961
Sponsoring organization: Uppsala Univ.
ISSN: 0562-3022
MLA acronym: AUUSRU

SUBSCRIPTION INFORMATION

Frequency of publication: Irregular
Circulation: 50
Available in microform: No
Subscription address: Almqvist & Wiksell International, P.O. Box 4627, 116 91 Stockholm, Sweden
Subscription telephone: (46) 8 6408800

ADVERTISING INFORMATION

Advertising accepted: No

EDITORIAL DESCRIPTION

Scope: Publishes monographs on Romance languages and literatures.
Reviews books: No
Publishes notes: Yes
Languages accepted: French; Italian; Spanish
Prints abstracts: Yes
Author-anonymous submission: No

SUBMISSION REQUIREMENTS

Restrictions on contributors: Contributors must be associated with the Dept. of Romance Languages & Literatures at Uppsala Univ.
Author pays submission fee: No
Author pays page charges: No
Length of books: 200 pp.
Number of copies required: 1
Special requirements: Submit a 100-500 word abstract.
Copyright ownership: Author
Rejected manuscripts: Returned
Time before publication decision: 2 mos.
Time between decision and publication: 8 mos.
Number of reviewers: 1-2
Books submitted per year: 2-3
Books published per year: 2-3

(31)
*Acta Universitatis Upsaliensis, Studia Semitica Upsaliensia

Tryggve Kronholm, Editor
Uppsala Univ.
Editorial Office
P.O. Box 256
751 05 Uppsala, Sweden

Telephone: (46) 18 182500
Fax: (46) 18 181817
First published: 1968
Sponsoring organization: Uppsala Univ.
ISSN: 0585-5535
MLA acronym: AUUSSU

SUBSCRIPTION INFORMATION

Frequency of publication: Irregular
Circulation: 500-700
Available in microform: No
Subscription address: Almqvist & Wiksell International, P.O. Box 4627, 116 91 Stockholm, Sweden
Subscription telephone: (46) 8 6408800

ADVERTISING INFORMATION

Advertising accepted: No

EDITORIAL DESCRIPTION

Scope: Publishes monographs on Semitic literatures.
Reviews books: No
Languages accepted: English; German; French
Prints abstracts: Yes
Author-anonymous submission: No

SUBMISSION REQUIREMENTS

Restrictions on contributors: Contributors must be associated with the Dept. of Afro-Asian Languages at Uppsala Univ.
Author pays submission fee: No
Author pays page charges: No
Number of copies required: 1
Special requirements: Submit a 100-500 word abstract.
Copyright ownership: Author after 3 yrs.
Rejected manuscripts: Returned
Time before publication decision: 3 mos.
Time between decision and publication: 6 mos.
Number of reviewers: 1-3
Books submitted per year: 0-2
Books published per year: 0-2

(32)
*Acta Universitatis Upsaliensis, Studia Slavica Upsaliensia

Sven R. Gustavsson & Lennart Lönngren, Editors
Uppsala Univ.
Editorial Office
P.O. Box 256
751 05 Uppsala, Sweden

First published: 1960
Sponsoring organization: Uppsala Univ.
ISSN: 0562-3030
MLA acronym: AUUSSlU

SUBSCRIPTION INFORMATION

Frequency of publication: Irregular
Circulation: 600-700
Available in microform: No
Subscription address: Almqvist & Wiksell International, P.O. Box 4627, 116 91 Stockholm, Sweden

ADVERTISING INFORMATION

Advertising accepted: No

EDITORIAL DESCRIPTION

Scope: Publishes monographs on Slavic languages, literatures, and history.
Reviews books: No
Publishes notes: No
Languages accepted: English; German; Swedish; Polish; Russian
Prints abstracts: Yes

SUBMISSION REQUIREMENTS

Restrictions on contributors: Contributors must be associated with the Dept. of Slavic Languages at Uppsala Univ.
Author pays submission fee: No
Author pays page charges: No
Special requirements: Submit a 100-500 word abstract.
Copyright ownership: Author after 3 yrs.
Rejected manuscripts: Returned
Time before publication decision: 3 mos.
Time between decision and publication: 6 mos.
Number of reviewers: 1-2

(33)
*Acta Universitatis Upsaliensis, Studia Uralica Upsaliensia

Lars-Gunnar Larsson, Editor
Uppsala Univ.
Finsk-ugriska Inst.
Box 513
751 20 Uppsala, Sweden

Telephone: (46) 18 181314
Fax: (46) 18 181314
First published: 1964
Sponsoring organization: Uppsala Univ.
ISSN: 1101-7430
MLA acronym: AUUSUU

SUBSCRIPTION INFORMATION

Frequency of publication: Irregular
Circulation: 500
Available in microform: No
Subscription address: Almqvist & Wiksell International, P.O. Box 4627, 116 91 Stockholm, Sweden

ADVERTISING INFORMATION

Advertising accepted: No

EDITORIAL DESCRIPTION

Scope: Publishes monographs on Uralic linguistics. Includes studies on bilingualism and on Uralic languages, including Finnish, Estonian, and Hungarian.
Reviews books: No
Publishes notes: No
Languages accepted: English; German; Swedish; Finnish; Russian
Prints abstracts: Yes
Author-anonymous submission: No

SUBMISSION REQUIREMENTS

Author pays submission fee: No
Author pays page charges: No
Length of books: 160-200 pp.
Number of copies required: 2
Copyright ownership: Author
Time before publication decision: 2-5 mos.
Time between decision and publication: 11 weeks
Number of reviewers: 1-3
Books submitted per year: 1-2
Books published per year: 1-2

(34)
*L'Action Nationale

Rosaire Morin, Editor
82 ouest, rue Sherbrooke
Montreal, Québec H2X 1X3, Canada

First published: 1917
Sponsoring organization: Ligue d'Action Nationale
ISSN: 0001-7469
MLA acronym: ActN

SUBSCRIPTION INFORMATION

Frequency of publication: 10 times/yr. (Sept.-June)
Circulation: 3,300
Available in microform: No

ADVERTISING INFORMATION

Advertising accepted: Yes

EDITORIAL DESCRIPTION

Scope: Publishes articles on Canadian national interests with a focus on Quebec. Includes studies on French-Canadian literature and language policy in Canada.
Reviews books: Yes
Publishes notes: Yes
Languages accepted: French
Prints abstracts: No
Author-anonymous submission: No

SUBMISSION REQUIREMENTS

Restrictions on contributors: None
Author pays submission fee: No
Author pays page charges: No
Length of articles: 10 pp.
Length of book reviews: 1-10 pp.
Number of copies required: 1
Copyright ownership: Author & journal
Rejected manuscripts: Returned at author's request
Time before publication decision: 1 mo.
Time between decision and publication: 1 mo.
Number of reviewers: 2-3
Articles submitted per year: 80
Articles published per year: 60
Book reviews submitted per year: 10
Book reviews published per year: 5-6

(35)
Actualidades: Consejo Nacional de la Cultura, Centro de Estudios Latinoamericanos "Romulo Gallegos"/ Caracas, Venezuela

Eduardo Casanova, Editor
Centro des Estudios Latinoamericanos
"Romulo Gallegos"
Septima Ave. Altanura
Apt. 75667
Caracas 1062, Venezuela

First published: 1976
Sponsoring organization: Centro de Estudios Latinoamericanos "Romulo Gallegos"
MLA acronym: Actualidades

SUBSCRIPTION INFORMATION

Frequency of publication: Annual
Available in microform: No

ADVERTISING INFORMATION

Advertising accepted: No

EDITORIAL DESCRIPTION

Scope: Publishes Latin American studies.
Reviews books: Yes
Languages accepted: Spanish
Prints abstracts: No

SUBMISSION REQUIREMENTS

Restrictions on contributors: Unsolicited manuscripts are not accepted.
Copyright ownership: Journal

(36)
Adalbert Stifter Institut des Landes Oberösterreich: Vierteljahresschrift

Johann Lachinger, Editor
Adalbert-Stifter-Inst. des Landes Oberösterreich
Adalbert-Stifter-Platz 1
4020 Linz-Donau, Austria

Telephone: (43) 732 27201295
First published: 1952
Sponsoring organization: Government of the Land Oberösterreich
ISSN: 0001-799X
MLA acronym: ASILO

SUBSCRIPTION INFORMATION

Frequency of publication: 2 double issues/yr.
Circulation: 450
Available in microform: No

ADVERTISING INFORMATION

Advertising accepted: Yes

EDITORIAL DESCRIPTION

Scope: Publishes articles on the work of Adalbert Stifter as well as the literary history and language of Austria.
Reviews books: Yes
Publishes notes: Yes
Languages accepted: German; English; French
Prints abstracts: No
Author-anonymous submission: No

SUBMISSION REQUIREMENTS

Restrictions on contributors: None
Author pays submission fee: No
Author pays page charges: No
Length of articles: 20-30 pp.
Length of book reviews: 3-6 pp.
Length of notes: 2-5 pp.
Style: MLA or similar
Number of copies required: 2

Special requirements: Submit original typescript.
Copyright ownership: Editor
Rejected manuscripts: Returned
Time before publication decision: 2 mos.
Time between decision and publication: 1 yr.
Number of reviewers: 2
Articles submitted per year: 20
Articles published per year: 15
Book reviews submitted per year: 10
Book reviews published per year: 6-10
Notes submitted per year: 2-5
Notes published per year: 2-5

(37) ADAM International Review

Miron Grindea, Editor
28 Emperor's Gate
London SW7, England

First published: 1941
ISSN: 0001-8015
MLA acronym: Adam

SUBSCRIPTION INFORMATION

Frequency of publication: 4 times/yr.

ADVERTISING INFORMATION

Advertising accepted: Yes

EDITORIAL DESCRIPTION

Scope: Publishes articles on contemporary arts, drama, architecture, and music.
Reviews books: Yes
Publishes notes: Yes
Languages accepted: English; French
Prints abstracts: Yes

SUBMISSION REQUIREMENTS

Length of articles: 1,000-1,800 words
Number of copies required: 1
Copyright ownership: Journal & author

(38) *ADE Bulletin

David Laurence & Stephen Olsen, Editors
ADE
10 Astor Place
New York, NY 10003-6981

Telephone: 212 614-6318
Fax: 212 477-9863
First published: 1962
Sponsoring organization: Assn. of Depts. of English
ISSN: 0001-0898
MLA acronym: ADEB

SUBSCRIPTION INFORMATION

Frequency of publication: 3 times/yr. (Dec., Apr., Sept.)
Circulation: 2,200
Available in microform: Yes
Subscription price: $30.00/yr. institutions; $15.00/yr. individuals
Year to which price refers: 1992

ADVERTISING INFORMATION

Advertising accepted: Yes
Advertising rates: $90.00/half page; $160.00/full page

EDITORIAL DESCRIPTION

Scope: A journal of opinion on life and work in English departments. Publishes essays, surveys, and reviews dealing with scholarly, pedagogical, curricular, and professional matters in English studies.
Reviews books: Yes
Publishes notes: No
Languages accepted: English
Prints abstracts: No
Author-anonymous submission: No

SUBMISSION REQUIREMENTS

Restrictions on contributors: None
Author pays submission fee: No
Author pays page charges: No
Length of articles: 2,500-7,500 words
Length of book reviews: 1,250-3,750 words
Style: MLA
Number of copies required: 2
Copyright ownership: ADE
Rejected manuscripts: Returned; enclose SASE.
Time before publication decision: 2-3 mos.
Time between decision and publication: 1-12 mos.
Number of reviewers: 2-3
Articles submitted per year: 90
Articles published per year: 30-35
Book reviews submitted per year: 4-6
Book reviews published per year: 4-6

(39) *ADFL Bulletin

John Cross & David Goldberg, Editors
ADFL
10 Astor Place
New York, NY 10003-6981

Telephone: 212 614-6320
Fax: 212 477-9863
First published: 1969
Sponsoring organization: Assn. of Depts. of Foreign Languages
ISSN: 0148-7639
MLA acronym: ADFLB

SUBSCRIPTION INFORMATION

Frequency of publication: 3 times/yr. (Sept., Jan., Apr.)
Circulation: 1,650
Available in microform: Yes
Subscription price: $30.00/yr. institutions; $15.00/yr. individuals
Year to which price refers: 1991-92

ADVERTISING INFORMATION

Advertising accepted: Yes

EDITORIAL DESCRIPTION

Scope: Publishes articles on professional and pedagogical issues involving foreign language departments in colleges and universities.
Reviews books: No
Publishes notes: Yes
Languages accepted: English
Prints abstracts: No
Author-anonymous submission: Yes

SUBMISSION REQUIREMENTS

Restrictions on contributors: None
Author pays submission fee: No
Author pays page charges: No
Length of articles: 3,500 words
Style: MLA
Number of copies required: 3
Special requirements: Submit original double-spaced typescript and 2 copies.
Copyright ownership: Journal
Rejected manuscripts: Returned at author's request
Time before publication decision: 3 mos.

Time between decision and publication: 3-9 mos.
Number of reviewers: 3
Articles submitted per year: 80
Articles published per year: 25
Notes submitted per year: 100
Notes published per year: 35

(40) Aegyptus: Rivista Italiana di Egittologia et di Papirologia

Orsolina Montevecchi, Editor
Scuola di Papirologia
Univ. Cattolica del Sacro Cuore
Largo A. Gemelli, 1
20123 Milan, Italy

First published: 1920
Sponsoring organization: Univ. Cattolica del Sacro Cuore
ISSN: 0001-9046
MLA acronym: Aegyptus

SUBSCRIPTION INFORMATION

Frequency of publication: Annual
Available in microform: No
Subscription address: Pubblicazioni Periodiche, Vita e Pensiero, at the above address
Additional subscription address: For review and/or exchange requests write to: Biblioteca/Scambi Periodici, at the above address.

ADVERTISING INFORMATION

Advertising accepted: Yes

EDITORIAL DESCRIPTION

Scope: Publishes scientific research on Egyptology and papyrology.
Reviews books: Yes
Publishes notes: No
Languages accepted: English; French; German; Italian; Spanish; Latin
Prints abstracts: No
Author-anonymous submission: No

SUBMISSION REQUIREMENTS

Author pays submission fee: No
Author pays page charges: No
Length of articles: No restrictions
Length of book reviews: No restrictions
Number of copies required: 1
Copyright ownership: Assigned by author to journal
Rejected manuscripts: Returned
Time before publication decision: 2 mos.
Time between decision and publication: 1 yr. maximum
Number of reviewers: 3

(41) *Aevum: Rassegna di Scienze Storiche, Linguistiche, Filologiche

Mirella Ferrari, Editor
Univ. Cattolica del Sacro Cuore
Largo A. Gemelli, 1
20123 Milan, Italy

Telephone: (39) 2 8856335
Fax: (39) 2 8856260
First published: 1927
Sponsoring organization: Univ. Cattolica Milano, Facoltà di Lettere
ISSN: 0001-9593
MLA acronym: Aevum

SUBSCRIPTION INFORMATION

Frequency of publication: 3 times/yr. (Apr., Sept., Dec.)
Circulation: 1,000

Available in microform: No
Subscription price: 85,000 Lit/yr. Italy; 130,000 Lit/yr. elsewhere
Year to which price refers: 1991
Subscription telephone: (39) 2 8856310

ADVERTISING INFORMATION

Advertising accepted: No

EDITORIAL DESCRIPTION

Scope: Publishes articles on ancient, medieval, Renaissance, and modern languages, literatures, philology, and history.
Reviews books: Yes
Publishes notes: Yes
Languages accepted: English; French; Italian; German; Spanish
Prints abstracts: No
Author-anonymous submission: No

SUBMISSION REQUIREMENTS

Restrictions on contributors: None
Author pays submission fee: No
Author pays page charges: No
Length of articles: 20-40 pp.
Length of book reviews: 5-15 pp.
Style: Journal; see 1988; 62
Number of copies required: 1
Special requirements: Submit original typescript. Submissions on diskette are welcome.
Copyright ownership: Assigned by author to journal
Rejected manuscripts: Returned
Time before publication decision: 1 mo.
Time between decision and publication: 8-18 mos.
Number of reviewers: 3
Articles submitted per year: 50-60
Articles published per year: 30-35
Book reviews published per year: 70-80

(42)
*Africa: Journal of the International African Institute/Revue de l'Institut Africain International

Murray Last, Editor
Dept. of Anthropology
Univ. College London
Gower St.
London WC1E 6BT, England

Telephone: (44) 71 3877050 ext. 2446
Fax: (44) 71 3807728
First published: 1928
Sponsoring organization: International African Inst.
ISSN: 0001-9720
MLA acronym: AfricaL

SUBSCRIPTION INFORMATION

Frequency of publication: 4 times/yr. (Mar., June, Sept., Dec.) plus annual bibliography
Circulation: 1,200
Available in microform: Yes
Subscription price: £105.00/yr. institutions United Kingdom & Europe (including Bibliography); £215.00/yr. institutions N. America (including Bibliography); £112.00/yr. institutions elsewhere (including Bibliography); £51.00/yr. individuals United Kingdom & Europe (including Bibliography); £30.00/yr. individuals United Kingdom & Europe (excluding Bibliography); £106.00/yr. individuals N. America (including Bibliography); £78.00/yr. individuals N. America (excluding Bibliography); £55.00/yr. individuals elsewhere (including Bibliography); £40.00/yr. individuals elsewhere (excluding Bibliography); add £20.00 ($40.00)/yr. for airmail
Year to which price refers: 1993
Subscription address: Edinburgh Univ. Press, 22 George Square, Edinburgh EH8 9LF, Scotland

ADVERTISING INFORMATION

Advertising accepted: Yes, on an exchange basis

EDITORIAL DESCRIPTION

Scope: Publishes original papers on African societies, cultures, and languages. Includes an annual bibliography.
Reviews books: Yes
Publishes notes: Yes
Languages accepted: English; French
Prints abstracts: Yes
Author-anonymous submission: No

SUBMISSION REQUIREMENTS

Restrictions on contributors: Book reviews are commissioned.
Author pays submission fee: No
Author pays page charges: No, except for extra illustrative materials
Length of articles: 8,000 words maximum
Length of book reviews: 500-800 words
Length of notes: 4,000 words maximum
Style: Journal
Number of copies required: 2
Copyright ownership: International African Inst.
Rejected manuscripts: Not returned
Time before publication decision: 6 mos.
Time between decision and publication: 6 mos.
Number of reviewers: 3
Articles submitted per year: 40
Articles published per year: 20
Book reviews published per year: 50
Notes submitted per year: 4
Notes published per year: 4

(43)
*Africa: Rivista Trimestrale di Studi e Documentazione dell'Istituto Italo-Africano

Teobaldo Filesi, Editor
Ist. Italo-Africano
via U. Aldrovandi, 16
00197 Rome, Italy

Telephone: (39) 6 3221297
Fax: (39) 6 3225348
First published: 1946
Sponsoring organization: Ist. Italo-Africano
ISSN: 0001-9747
MLA acronym: Africa

SUBSCRIPTION INFORMATION

Frequency of publication: 4 times/yr.
Circulation: 1,300
Available in microform: No
Subscription price: 30,000 Lit/yr. Italy; 40,000 Lit/yr. elsewhere
Year to which price refers: 1992

ADVERTISING INFORMATION

Advertising accepted: No

EDITORIAL DESCRIPTION

Scope: Publishes original studies, notes, and documents on various aspects of Africa, past and present, with particular attention given to the history, political and legal institutions, and socio-economic problems of independent Africa. Solicits contributions from all areas, and particularly from Africa, that apply, on a scientific level, to African studies.
Reviews books: Yes
Publishes notes: No
Languages accepted: English; French; Italian; Spanish
Prints abstracts: Yes
Author-anonymous submission: No

SUBMISSION REQUIREMENTS

Author pays submission fee: No
Author pays page charges: No
Length of articles: 30 pp.
Length of book reviews: 2 pp.
Number of copies required: 2
Special requirements: Abstracts are published in the languages not used in text.
Time before publication decision: 3 mos. minimum
Time between decision and publication: 3 mos. minimum
Number of reviewers: 2
Articles submitted per year: 20
Articles published per year: 12
Book reviews submitted per year: 50
Book reviews published per year: 25

(44)
Africa Report

Margaret A. Novicki, Editor
African-American Inst.
833 United Nations Plaza
New York, NY 10017

First published: 1956
Sponsoring organization: African-American Inst.
ISSN: 0001-9836
MLA acronym: AfricaR

SUBSCRIPTION INFORMATION

Frequency of publication: 6 times/yr.
Circulation: 12,200
Available in microform: Yes
Subscription price: $37.00/yr. institutions US; $43.00/yr. institutions Canada; $61.00/yr. institutions elsewhere; $30.00/yr. individuals US; $36.00/yr. individuals Canada; $54.00/yr. individuals elsewhere
Year to which price refers: 1993
Subscription address: Africa Report Subscription Services, P.O. Box 3000, Dept. AR, Denville, NJ 07834

ADVERTISING INFORMATION

Advertising accepted: Yes

EDITORIAL DESCRIPTION

Scope: Publishes articles on African political, economic, social, and cultural affairs.
Reviews books: Yes
Publishes notes: No
Languages accepted: English
Prints abstracts: No
Author-anonymous submission: Yes

SUBMISSION REQUIREMENTS

Restrictions on contributors: None
Author pays submission fee: No
Author pays page charges: No
Length of articles: 2,500 words
Length of book reviews: 500 words
Style: Chicago
Number of copies required: 1
Special requirements: Black and white photographs for illustrations are requested.
Copyright ownership: Journal
Rejected manuscripts: Returned; enclose return postage.
Time before publication decision: 1 mo.
Time between decision and publication: 2 mos.
Number of reviewers: 2
Articles submitted per year: 200
Articles published per year: 60
Book reviews submitted per year: 20
Book reviews published per year: 6

(45)
Africa-Tervuren

J.-B. Cuypers, Editor
De Vriender van het Koninklijk Museum voor Midden-Afrika
Steenweg Op Leuven 13
1980 Tervuren, Belgium

First published: 1955
Sponsoring organization: Musée Royal de l'Afrique Centrale
ISSN: 0001-9879
MLA acronym: Afr-T

SUBSCRIPTION INFORMATION

Frequency of publication: 4 times/yr.
Circulation: 500
Available in microform: No
Subscription address: Verantwoordelijke Uitgever J.-B. Cuypers, Steenweg op Leuven 11, Tervuren, Belgium

ADVERTISING INFORMATION

Advertising accepted: No

EDITORIAL DESCRIPTION

Scope: Publishes articles on the culture and material arts of Sub-Saharan Africa.
Reviews books: No
Languages accepted: Dutch; English; French
Prints abstracts: Yes

SUBMISSION REQUIREMENTS

Author pays submission fee: No
Author pays page charges: No

(46)
*African American Review

Joe Weixlmann, Editor
Dept. of English
Indiana State Univ.
Terre Haute, IN 47809

Telephone: 812 237-2968
Fax: 812 237-4382
First published: 1967
Historical variations in title: Formerly *Black American Literature Forum*
Sponsoring organization: Indiana State Univ.
ISSN: 1062-4783
MLA acronym: AAR

SUBSCRIPTION INFORMATION

Frequency of publication: 4 times/yr. (Mar., June, Sept., Dec.)
Circulation: 1,350
Available in microform: Yes
Subscription price: $40.00/yr. institutions; $20.00/yr. individuals; add $7.00/yr. postage outside US
Year to which price refers: 1992

ADVERTISING INFORMATION

Advertising accepted: Yes
Advertising rates: $105.00/half page; $180.00/full page

EDITORIAL DESCRIPTION

Scope: Publishes essays on African American literature, theater, film, visual arts, and culture in general. Also publishes poetry, fiction, interviews, bibliographies, and book reviews.
Reviews books: Yes
Publishes notes: No
Languages accepted: English
Prints abstracts: No
Author-anonymous submission: No

SUBMISSION REQUIREMENTS

Author pays submission fee: No
Author pays page charges: No
Length of articles: 6,000-10,000 words
Length of book reviews: 2,000 words
Style: MLA
Number of copies required: 2
Copyright ownership: Author
Rejected manuscripts: Returned; enclose return postage
Time before publication decision: 3 mos.
Time between decision and publication: 9-15 mos.
Number of reviewers: 3
Articles submitted per year: 200
Articles published per year: 35
Book reviews submitted per year: 25
Book reviews published per year: 15

(47)
*African Arts

Donald J. Consentino & Doran H. Ross, Editors
J. S. Coleman African Studies Center
Univ. of California
405 Hilgard Ave.
Los Angeles, CA 90024-1310

Telephone: 310 825-1218
Fax: 310 206-3555
First published: 1967
Sponsoring organization: Univ. of California, Los Angeles
ISSN: 0001-9933
MLA acronym: AfrA

SUBSCRIPTION INFORMATION

Frequency of publication: 4 times/yr. (Jan., Apr., July, Oct.)
Circulation: 4,000
Available in microform: Yes
Subscription price: $60.00/yr. institutions US; $68.00/yr. institutions elsewhere; $38.00/yr. individuals US; $46.00/yr. individuals elsewhere
Year to which price refers: 1992

ADVERTISING INFORMATION

Advertising accepted: Yes

EDITORIAL DESCRIPTION

Scope: Publishes articles on African arts and culture.
Reviews books: Yes
Publishes notes: Yes
Languages accepted: English
Prints abstracts: No
Author-anonymous submission: No

SUBMISSION REQUIREMENTS

Restrictions on contributors: Reviews are commissioned.
Author pays submission fee: No
Author pays page charges: No
Length of articles: 20 pp.
Length of book reviews: 10 pp.
Length of notes: 5 pp.
Style: Chicago
Number of copies required: 1
Special requirements: Photographs printed in color or black and white.
Copyright ownership: Regents of the Univ. of California
Rejected manuscripts: Returned
Time before publication decision: 4 mos. minimum
Number of reviewers: 3 minimum
Articles submitted per year: 30
Articles published per year: 16
Book reviews published per year: 40

(48)
*The African Book Publishing Record

Hans M. Zell & Mary Jay, Editors
P.O. Box 56
Oxford OX1 2SJ, England

Telephone: (44) 865 511428
Fax: (44) 865 311534
First published: 1975
ISSN: 0306-0322
MLA acronym: ABPR

SUBSCRIPTION INFORMATION

Frequency of publication: 4 times/yr.
Circulation: 700
Available in microform: No
Subscription price: $140.00 (£85.00)/yr.
Year to which price refers: 1992
Subscription address: Hans Zell Publishers, c/o Butterworth & Co. Ltd., Borough Green, Sevenoaks, Kent TN15 8PH, England
Subscription telephone: (44) 732 884567
Subscription fax: (44) 732 884530

ADVERTISING INFORMATION

Advertising accepted: Yes
Advertising rates: £70.00 ($120.00)/half page; £110.00 ($190.00)/full page; £120.00 ($220.00)/back cover

EDITORIAL DESCRIPTION

Scope: Provides extensive bibliographic coverage of new and forthcoming African publications in English and French, and significant new titles in the African languages. Serves as a medium of communication between the African book professions, and features news, reports, interviews, and articles about African book trade activities and developments, and an annual list of new African reference sources. Includes an extensive book review section, as well as reviews of new periodicals and magazines published in Africa.
Reviews books: Yes
Publishes notes: Yes
Languages accepted: English; French
Prints abstracts: No
Author-anonymous submission: No

SUBMISSION REQUIREMENTS

Restrictions on contributors: Book reviews and most articles/features are solicited.
Author pays submission fee: No
Author pays page charges: No
Length of articles: 3,000-4,000 words
Length of book reviews: 350 words
Length of notes: 1,800-2,500 words
Style: Chicago
Number of copies required: 1
Special requirements: Submit double-spaced typescript on size A4 (8 1/4 in. x 11 3/4 in.) paper with notes at the end of article.
Copyright ownership: Author
Rejected manuscripts: Returned
Time before publication decision: 2-3 mos.
Time between decision and publication: 3-9 mos.
Number of reviewers: 1-2
Articles submitted per year: 20
Articles published per year: 4-6
Book reviews published per year: 250-350
Notes submitted per year: 6
Notes published per year: 30

(49)
*African Languages and Cultures

Philip J. Jaggar, Editor
School of Oriental & African Studies
Thornhaugh St.
Russell Square
London WC1H 0XG, England

Telephone: (44) 71 6372388
Fax: (44) 71 4363844
First published: 1988
Sponsoring organization: School of Oriental & African Studies
ISSN: 0954-416X
MLA acronym: AL&C

SUBSCRIPTION INFORMATION

Frequency of publication: 2 times/yr.
Circulation: 130
Available in microform: No
Subscription price: £10.00 ($25.00)/yr.
Year to which price refers: 1992
Subscription address: ALC Subscriptions, The Publications Officer, at the above address

ADVERTISING INFORMATION

Advertising accepted: Yes, on an exchange basis

EDITORIAL DESCRIPTION

Scope: Publishes articles on all aspects of African language studies and language-based cultural studies.
Reviews books: No
Publishes notes: No
Languages accepted: English; French
Prints abstracts: No
Author-anonymous submission: No

SUBMISSION REQUIREMENTS

Restrictions on contributors: None
Author pays submission fee: No
Author pays page charges: No
Length of articles: 25 pp.
Style: Journal
Number of copies required: 2
Copyright ownership: School of Oriental & African Studies
Rejected manuscripts: Returned; enclose return postage
Time before publication decision: 4-6 weeks
Time between decision and publication: 6 mos.
Number of reviewers: 2
Articles submitted per year: 20-25
Articles published per year: 10-12

(50)
*African Literature Today

Eldred Durosimi Jones, Eustace J. T. Palmer, & Marjorie Jones, Editors
Fourah Bay College
Univ. of Sierra Leone
Freetown, Sierra Leone

First published: 1968
ISSN: 0065-4000
MLA acronym: ALT

SUBSCRIPTION INFORMATION

Frequency of publication: Annual
Available in microform: No
Subscription address: James Currey Publisher, 54b Thornhill Square, Islington, London N1 1BE, England

ADVERTISING INFORMATION

Advertising accepted: No

EDITORIAL DESCRIPTION

Scope: Surveys the field of African literature. Each issue concentrates on a particular area of literature.
Reviews books: No
Publishes notes: No
Languages accepted: English
Prints abstracts: No

SUBMISSION REQUIREMENTS

Restrictions on contributors: None
Author pays submission fee: No
Author pays page charges: No
Length of articles: 3,000 words
Style: MLA
Number of copies required: 1
Rejected manuscripts: Returned; enclose return postage
Time before publication decision: 2-3 mos.
Time between decision and publication: 1 yr.
Articles submitted per year: 20-24
Articles published per year: 12-14

(51)
*African Notes: Journal of the Institute of African Studies

Dele Layiwola, Editor
Inst. of African Studies
Univ. of Ibadan
Ibadan, Nigeria

First published: 1963
ISSN: 0002-0087
MLA acronym: AfrN

SUBSCRIPTION INFORMATION

Frequency of publication: 1-2 times/yr.
Circulation: 200-300
Available in microform: No
Subscription price: $10.00 (£8.00, 20 N)/yr.
Year to which price refers: 1991

ADVERTISING INFORMATION

Advertising accepted: Yes
Advertising rates: $50.00/full page

EDITORIAL DESCRIPTION

Scope: Contributions concerned with aspects of Nigerian/African traditional culture are particularly welcome. Aims to serve primarily as a forum for contributions from people who are professionally involved with the study of traditional and modern culture, e.g., archaeologists, linguists, musicologists, anthropologists, dance researchers. Also welcomes notes or articles from interested amateurs which draw attention to cultural phenomena meriting future professional study.
Reviews books: Yes
Publishes notes: Yes
Languages accepted: English
Prints abstracts: No
Author-anonymous submission: Yes

SUBMISSION REQUIREMENTS

Restrictions on contributors: None
Author pays submission fee: No
Author pays page charges: No
Length of articles: 10,000 words maximum
Length of book reviews: 5,000 words
Length of notes: 500 words
Style: MLA
Number of copies required: 2
Special requirements: Submit original manuscript.
Copyright ownership: Inst. of African Studies
Rejected manuscripts: Returned; enclose SASE.
Time before publication decision: 2-4 mos.
Time between decision and publication: 4-6 mos.
Number of reviewers: 1-2
Articles submitted per year: 50
Articles published per year: 20
Book reviews submitted per year: 5-10
Book reviews published per year: 4-5
Notes submitted per year: 2
Notes published per year: 2

(52)
African Studies

W. D. Hammond-Tooke, Editor
c/o Publications Officer
Witwatersrand Univ. Press
1 Jan Smuts Ave.
2001 Johannesburg, South Africa

First published: 1921
Sponsoring organization: Univ. of Witwatersrand
ISSN: 0002-0184
MLA acronym: AfrS

SUBSCRIPTION INFORMATION

Frequency of publication: 2 times/yr. (June, Dec.)
Circulation: 800
Available in microform: No

ADVERTISING INFORMATION

Advertising accepted: Yes

EDITORIAL DESCRIPTION

Scope: Publishes research in African anthropology, government, history, and languages.
Reviews books: Yes
Publishes notes: No
Languages accepted: Afrikaans; English; French; Portuguese
Prints abstracts: No
Author-anonymous submission: Yes

SUBMISSION REQUIREMENTS

Restrictions on contributors: None
Author pays submission fee: No
Author pays page charges: No
Length of articles: 4,000 words
Length of book reviews: 250 words
Style: Journal
Number of copies required: 1
Special requirements: Submit original typescript.
Copyright ownership: Witwatersrand Univ. Press
Rejected manuscripts: Returned
Time before publication decision: 2-3 mos.
Time between decision and publication: 3-6 mos.
Number of reviewers: 2
Articles submitted per year: 15-25
Articles published per year: 12-15
Book reviews submitted per year: 20-30
Book reviews published per year: 18-25

(53)
*The African Studies Review

Mark W. DeLancey, Editor
G.I.N.T.
Univ. of South Carolina
Columbia, SC 29208

Telephone: 803 777-3108
Fax: 803 777-8255
First published: 1957
Sponsoring organization: African Studies Assn.
ISSN: 0002-0206
MLA acronym: AfrSR

SUBSCRIPTION INFORMATION

Frequency of publication: 3 times/yr. (Apr., Sept., Dec.) plus occasional special issues
Circulation: 2,200

Available in microform: No
Subscription address: African Studies Assn., Credit Union Bldg., Emory Univ., Atlanta, GA 30322
Subscription telephone: 404 329-6410

ADVERTISING INFORMATION

Advertising accepted: Yes, primarily on an exchange basis

EDITORIAL DESCRIPTION

Scope: Publishes articles and reviews on African topics of interest to an interdisciplinary readership.
Reviews books: Yes
Publishes notes: Yes
Languages accepted: English
Prints abstracts: No
Author-anonymous submission: Yes

SUBMISSION REQUIREMENTS

Restrictions on contributors: Book reviews are solicited.
Author pays submission fee: No
Author pays page charges: No
Length of articles: 6,000-8,000 words
Length of book reviews: 500-1,000 words
Length of notes: 2,500-5,000 words
Style: Chicago
Number of copies required: 3
Special requirements: Manuscripts are submitted without name of author to 3 outside readers. Include a removable cover page giving title, authorship, affiliation, and address. Submit an abstract of 250-words maximum and a statement of sole submission.
Copyright ownership: African Studies Assn.
Rejected manuscripts: Returned at author's request
Time before publication decision: 3-4 mos.
Time between decision and publication: 6-12 mos.
Number of reviewers: 3
Articles submitted per year: 150
Articles published per year: 15-20
Book reviews submitted per year: 70-75
Book reviews published per year: 65-70
Notes submitted per year: 6-10
Notes published per year: 2-3

(54)
*African Writers Series

Vicky Unwin, Editor
Heinemann International
Halley Court
Jordan Hill
Oxford OX2 8EJ, England

Telephone: (44) 865 314163
Fax: (44) 865 314169
First published: 1962
ISSN: 0065-4108
MLA acronym: AfrWS

SUBSCRIPTION INFORMATION

Frequency of publication: 2 times/yr. (Spring, Fall)
Circulation: 5,000-100,000
Available in microform: No
Subscription address: Heinemann Educational Books Inc., 361 Hanover St., Portsmouth, NH 03801-3959

ADVERTISING INFORMATION

Advertising accepted: No

EDITORIAL DESCRIPTION

Scope: Presents the works of African writers.
Reviews books: No
Publishes notes: No
Languages accepted: English
Prints abstracts: No

Author-anonymous submission: No

SUBMISSION REQUIREMENTS

Restrictions on contributors: Contributors must have been born in Africa or spent formative years there.
Author pays submission fee: No
Author pays page charges: No
Length of books: 150-250 pp.
Style: Oxford
Number of copies required: 1
Copyright ownership: Heinemann International on behalf of author
Rejected manuscripts: Returned
Time before publication decision: 4 mos.
Time between decision and publication: 6-12 mos.
Number of reviewers: 3
Books submitted per year: 150
Books published per year: 12

(55)
*Africana Bulletin

Bogodar Winid, Editor
Inst. Krajów Rozwijających się
Uniw. Warszawski
Ul. Karowa 20
00-324 Warsaw, Poland

Telephone: (48) 22 6330340
Fax: (48) 22 261965
E-mail: GRK01@PLEARN
First published: 1964
Sponsoring organization: Uniw. Warszawski
ISSN: 0002-029X
MLA acronym: AfB

SUBSCRIPTION INFORMATION

Frequency of publication: Irregular
Circulation: 1,000
Available in microform: No

ADVERTISING INFORMATION

Advertising accepted: No

EDITORIAL DESCRIPTION

Scope: Publishes articles on interdisciplinary studies.
Reviews books: Yes
Publishes notes: Yes
Languages accepted: English; French
Prints abstracts: Yes

SUBMISSION REQUIREMENTS

Restrictions on contributors: Contributors must be Polish.
Author pays submission fee: No
Author pays page charges: No
Length of articles: 20-30 pp.
Length of book reviews: 1-2 pp.
Length of notes: 1-2 pp.
Style: None
Number of copies required: 3
Special requirements: Submit original manuscript.
Copyright ownership: Author
Time before publication decision: 1 mo.
Time between decision and publication: 1 yr.
Number of reviewers: 2
Articles submitted per year: 10
Articles published per year: 5-6
Book reviews submitted per year: 20
Book reviews published per year: 10-15
Notes submitted per year: 15
Notes published per year: 10

(56)
Africana Journal: A Bibliographic Library Journal and Review Quarterly

David Gardinier, Editor
Dept. of History
Marquette Univ.
Milwaukee, WI 53233

First published: 1970
ISSN: 0095-1080
MLA acronym: AfrLJ

SUBSCRIPTION INFORMATION

Frequency of publication: 4 times/yr. (Spring, Summer, Fall, Winter)
Circulation: 1,000
Available in microform: No
Subscription address: Africana Publishing Co., Holmes & Meier Pubs., Inc., 30 Irving Place, New York, NY 10003

ADVERTISING INFORMATION

Advertising accepted: Yes

EDITORIAL DESCRIPTION

Scope: Publishes bibliographic articles, reports on research and teaching resources, book reviews, and a comprehensive current bibliography of recently published books. Intended as a source for reference and review materials for scholars, researchers, and librarians in all areas relating to African studies. Also emphasizes articles on culture, art, literature, politics, history, etc.
Reviews books: Yes
Publishes notes: No
Languages accepted: English
Prints abstracts: No
Author-anonymous submission: No

SUBMISSION REQUIREMENTS

Restrictions on contributors: Most articles are solicited.
Author pays submission fee: No
Author pays page charges: No
Length of articles: 4,000-9,000 words
Length of book reviews: 400-600 words
Style: Chicago
Number of copies required: 2
Special requirements: Submit original typescript.
Copyright ownership: Assigned by author to journal
Rejected manuscripts: Returned
Time before publication decision: 2 mos.
Time between decision and publication: 8 mos.
Number of reviewers: 1-2
Articles published per year: 15-20
Book reviews published per year: 130-160

(57)
Africana Linguistica

Cl. Gregoire, Editor
Musée Royal de l'Afrique Centrale
3080 Tervuren, Belgium

Telephone: (32) 2 7675401
Fax: (32) 2 7670242
First published: 1962
Sponsoring organization: Musée Royal de l'Afrique Centrale
ISSN: 0065-4124
MLA acronym: AfrL

SUBSCRIPTION INFORMATION

Frequency of publication: Irregular
Circulation: 600

ADVERTISING INFORMATION

Advertising accepted: No

EDITORIAL DESCRIPTION

Scope: Publishes articles on African linguistics, especially Bantu.
Reviews books: No
Publishes notes: No
Languages accepted: Dutch; English; French; German
Prints abstracts: No
Author-anonymous submission: No

SUBMISSION REQUIREMENTS

Restrictions on contributors: None
Author pays submission fee: No
Author pays page charges: No
Length of articles: 10,000 words
Style: None
Number of copies required: 1
Special requirements: Provide tonal notation for tonal languages.
Copyright ownership: Author
Rejected manuscripts: Returned
Time before publication decision: 6 mos.
Time between decision and publication: 2 yrs.
Number of reviewers: 3
Articles submitted per year: 20
Articles published per year: 8

(58)
*Africana Research Bulletin

Arthur Abraham, Editor
Inst. of African Studies
Fourah Bay College
Univ. of Sierra Leone
Freetown, Sierra Leone

First published: 1970
Sponsoring organization: Univ. of Sierra Leone
ISSN: 0259-9651
MLA acronym: ARB

SUBSCRIPTION INFORMATION

Frequency of publication: 2 times/yr.
Circulation: 250
Available in microform: No
Subscription price: $15.00 (£9.00)/yr.
Year to which price refers: 1992

ADVERTISING INFORMATION

Advertising accepted: No

EDITORIAL DESCRIPTION

Scope: Focuses attention on Sierra Leone, but articles relating to any part of Africa will be considered.
Reviews books: Yes
Publishes notes: Yes
Languages accepted: English
Prints abstracts: No

SUBMISSION REQUIREMENTS

Restrictions on contributors: None
Author pays submission fee: No
Author pays page charges: No
Length of articles: 30 pp. maximum
Length of book reviews: 1,500 words maximum
Length of notes: 2,000 words maximum
Style: MLA
Number of copies required: 2
Special requirements: Submit camera-ready maps and diagrams no more than quarto size. Submit original typescript and 1 copy.
Copyright ownership: Journal
Rejected manuscripts: Not returned
Time before publication decision: 2 mos.
Time between decision and publication: 6 mos.
Number of reviewers: 2
Articles submitted per year: 15
Articles published per year: 9
Book reviews submitted per year: 4
Book reviews published per year: 3
Notes submitted per year: 10
Notes published per year: 9

(59)
*Afrika Focus

Afrika Brug V.Z.W.
Coupure Links 653
9000 Ghent, Belgium

Telephone: (32) 91 646089
Fax: (32) 91 646245
First published: 1972
Sponsoring organization: Afrika Brug V.Z.W.
ISSN: 0772-084X
MLA acronym: AfrF

SUBSCRIPTION INFORMATION

Frequency of publication: 4 times/yr.
Circulation: 500
Available in microform: No
Subscription price: 2,000 BF/yr. institutions; 500 BF/yr. individuals
Year to which price refers: 1991

ADVERTISING INFORMATION

Advertising accepted: Yes

EDITORIAL DESCRIPTION

Scope: Publishes scholarly articles and multidisciplinary research on African languages and literatures, African history, Africa in the global perspective, and global education.
Reviews books: Yes
Publishes notes: Yes
Languages accepted: English; French; Dutch; German
Prints abstracts: Yes
Author-anonymous submission: No

SUBMISSION REQUIREMENTS

Restrictions on contributors: None
Author pays submission fee: No
Author pays page charges: No
Length of articles: 10-15 pp.
Length of book reviews: 1-2 pp.
Length of notes: 1/2-1 p.
Number of copies required: 4
Special requirements: Submit original typescript plus 3 copies and a diskette with the article in WordStar or WordPerfect; include a summary and at least three English key words.
Copyright ownership: Author
Rejected manuscripts: Not returned
Time before publication decision: 3 mos.
Time between decision and publication: 4-8 mos.
Number of reviewers: 3-4
Articles submitted per year: 40
Articles published per year: 20-30
Book reviews submitted per year: 20
Book reviews published per year: 10-20
Notes submitted per year: 20
Notes published per year: 10-20

(60)
*Afrika und Übersee: Sprachen-Kulturen

E. Dammann, L. Gerhardt, E. Kähler-Meyer, H. Meyer-Bahlburg, S. Uhlig, & J. Zwernemann, Editors
c/o Hilke Meyer-Bahlburg
Seminar für Afrikanische Sprachen und Kulturen
Univ. Hamburg
Rothenbaumchaussee 67-69
2000 Hamburg 13, Germany

First published: 1910
Sponsoring organization: Deutsche Forschungsgemeinschaft; Univ. Hamburg
ISSN: 0002-0427
MLA acronym: AÜ

SUBSCRIPTION INFORMATION

Frequency of publication: 2 times/yr. (Summer, Winter)
Circulation: 185
Available in microform: No
Subscription price: 145 DM/yr.
Year to which price refers: 1992
Subscription address: Dietrich Reimer Verlag, Unter den Eichen 57, 1 Berlin 45, Germany

ADVERTISING INFORMATION

Advertising accepted: No

EDITORIAL DESCRIPTION

Scope: Publishes articles on African languages.
Reviews books: Yes
Publishes notes: No
Languages accepted: German; English; French
Prints abstracts: No
Author-anonymous submission: No

SUBMISSION REQUIREMENTS

Restrictions on contributors: None
Author pays submission fee: No
Author pays page charges: No
Length of articles: 20-30 pp.
Length of book reviews: 1-2 pp.
Number of copies required: 1
Copyright ownership: Dietrich Reimer Verlag
Rejected manuscripts: Returned
Time before publication decision: 2-4 mos.
Time between decision and publication: 6-12 mos.
Number of reviewers: 2-3
Articles submitted per year: 20-25
Articles published per year: 12-15
Book reviews submitted per year: 30-40
Book reviews published per year: 30-40

(61)
L'Afrique Littéraire

Paulette Decraene, Editor
Société Afrique Littéraire
2, rue Cretet
75009 Paris, France

First published: 1968
ISSN: 0002-0508
MLA acronym: ALA

SUBSCRIPTION INFORMATION

Frequency of publication: 4 times/yr.
Circulation: 3,000
Available in microform: No

ADVERTISING INFORMATION

Advertising accepted: No

EDITORIAL DESCRIPTION

Scope: Publishes articles on African arts.
Reviews books: Yes
Languages accepted: French
Prints abstracts: No

SUBMISSION REQUIREMENTS

Author pays submission fee: No
Author pays page charges: No
Length of articles: 1,500-3,000 words
Length of book reviews: 300 words
Length of notes: 1,500-3,000 words
Number of copies required: 1
Copyright ownership: Author
Rejected manuscripts: Returned
Time before publication decision: 1 mo.
Time between decision and publication: 3-6 mos.
Number of reviewers: 3
Articles submitted per year: 120
Articles published per year: 50

(62)
*Afro-Hispanic Review

Marvin A. Lewis & Edward J. Mullen, Editors
Romance Languages
Univ. of Missouri
143 Arts & Science Bldg.
Columbia, MO 65211

Telephone: 314 882-2030
First published: 1982
Sponsoring organization: Univ. of Missouri, Columbia
ISSN: 0278-8969
MLA acronym: AHR

SUBSCRIPTION INFORMATION

Frequency of publication: 3 times/yr. (Jan., May, Sept.)
Circulation: 500
Available in microform: No

ADVERTISING INFORMATION

Advertising accepted: Yes

EDITORIAL DESCRIPTION

Scope: Publishes scholarly articles on the literature of Blacks in Spanish-speaking nations; includes interdisciplinary studies focusing on sociology, anthropology, and history. Translations of works by and about Afro-Hispanic literature are also published.
Reviews books: Yes
Publishes notes: No
Languages accepted: Spanish; English
Prints abstracts: No
Author-anonymous submission: Yes

SUBMISSION REQUIREMENTS

Restrictions on contributors: Authors may publish only one article per year in journal.
Author pays submission fee: No
Author pays page charges: No
Length of articles: 15-20 typescript pp.
Length of book reviews: 4-8 typescript pp.
Style: MLA (1984)
Number of copies required: 2
Copyright ownership: Journal
Rejected manuscripts: Returned
Time before publication decision: 3 mos.
Time between decision and publication: 6-12 mos.
Number of reviewers: 4
Articles submitted per year: 40
Articles published per year: 21
Book reviews submitted per year: 10
Book reviews published per year: 10

(63)
*Afroasiatic Dialects

Tom Penchoen, Editor
Undena Publications
P.O. Box 97
Malibu, CA 90265

First published: 1973
ISSN: 0732-6416
MLA acronym: AAD

SUBSCRIPTION INFORMATION

Frequency of publication: Irregular
Circulation: 200
Available in microform: No
Subscription address: Crescent Academic Services, 29528 Madera Ave., Shafter, CA 93263
Subscription telephone: 805 746-5870
Subscription fax: 805 746-2728

ADVERTISING INFORMATION

Advertising accepted: No

EDITORIAL DESCRIPTION

Scope: The series publishes descriptions of individual languages of the Afroasiatic family. It is primarily data oriented.
Reviews books: Yes
Publishes notes: No
Languages accepted: English
Prints abstracts: Yes
Author-anonymous submission: No

SUBMISSION REQUIREMENTS

Restrictions on contributors: None
Author pays submission fee: No
Author pays page charges: No
Length of books: 40-50 pp.
Length of book reviews: No restrictions
Style: Chicago
Number of copies required: 2
Special requirements: Submission of camera-ready copy is preferred.
Copyright ownership: Author or publisher
Rejected manuscripts: Returned; enclose SASE.
Time before publication decision: 1-3 mos.
Time between decision and publication: 6-8 mos.
Number of reviewers: 2

(64)
*The Age of Johnson: A Scholarly Annual

Paul J. Korshin, Editor
Dept. of English
Univ. of Pennsylvania
Philadelphia, PA 19104-6273

Telephone: 215 387-5520
Fax: 215 573-2063
First published: 1987
ISSN: 0884-5816
MLA acronym: AJ

SUBSCRIPTION INFORMATION

Frequency of publication: Annual
Available in microform: No
Subscription price: $50.00/yr.
Year to which price refers: 1992
Subscription address: AMS Press, Inc., 56 East 13th St., New York, NY 10003

ADVERTISING INFORMATION

Advertising accepted: No

EDITORIAL DESCRIPTION

Scope: Publishes articles on English literature, history, and culture relating to the period of Samuel Johnson's life (1709-84) to about 1820.
Reviews books: Yes
Publishes notes: No
Languages accepted: English
Prints abstracts: No
Author-anonymous submission: No

SUBMISSION REQUIREMENTS

Author pays submission fee: No
Author pays page charges: No
Length of articles: 8,000-10,000 words
Length of book reviews: 1,500-3,000 words
Style: Chicago
Copyright ownership: AMS Press
Rejected manuscripts: Returned
Time before publication decision: 3 mos.
Time between decision and publication: 1 yr.
Number of reviewers: 2-3
Articles submitted per year: 35
Articles published per year: 14
Book reviews submitted per year: 20-25
Book reviews published per year: 20-25

(65)
*Agenda

William Cookson & Peter Dale, Editors
5 Cranbourne Court
Albert Bridge Rd.
London SW11 4PE, England

Telephone: (44) 71 228440700
First published: 1959
Sponsoring organization: Arts Council of Great Britain
ISSN: 0002-0796
MLA acronym: Agenda

SUBSCRIPTION INFORMATION

Frequency of publication: 4 times/yr.
Circulation: 2,000
Available in microform: Yes

ADVERTISING INFORMATION

Advertising accepted: Yes

EDITORIAL DESCRIPTION

Scope: Includes poetry, criticism, translations, and articles on translations, with occasional special issues on individual authors.
Reviews books: Yes
Languages accepted: English
Prints abstracts: No
Author-anonymous submission: Yes

SUBMISSION REQUIREMENTS

Restrictions on contributors: Most reviews are commissioned.
Author pays submission fee: No
Author pays page charges: No
Length of articles: No restrictions
Length of book reviews: No restrictions
Style: None
Number of copies required: 1
Copyright ownership: Author
Rejected manuscripts: Returned; enclose return postage.
Time before publication decision: 3 mos.
Time between decision and publication: 3-6 mos.
Number of reviewers: 3
Articles submitted per year: 50
Articles published per year: 16
Book reviews published per year: 25

(66)
Agora: A Journal in the Humanities and Social Sciences

Martin A. Bertman, Editor
Dept. of Philosophy
State Univ. of New York at Potsdam
Potsdam, NY 13676

First published: 1969
Sponsoring organization: State Univ. of New York, College at Potsdam
ISSN: 0002-1016
MLA acronym: Agora

SUBSCRIPTION INFORMATION

Frequency of publication: Irregular
Circulation: 800

ADVERTISING INFORMATION

Advertising accepted: No

EDITORIAL DESCRIPTION

Scope: Welcomes contributions pertinent to the humanities and social sciences, with emphasis on critical and theoretical approaches.
Reviews books: Yes
Languages accepted: English
Prints abstracts: No

Book reviews published per year: 8-12
Notes published per year: 10

SUBMISSION REQUIREMENTS

Restrictions on contributors: None
Author pays submission fee: No
Author pays page charges: No
Length of articles: 4,500 words
Length of book reviews: 900 words
Style: MLA
Number of copies required: 1
Copyright ownership: Journal
Rejected manuscripts: Returned; enclose return postage.
Time before publication decision: 6-8 weeks
Time between decision and publication: 10 mos.
Number of reviewers: 2
Articles submitted per year: 60
Articles published per year: 12
Book reviews published per year: 5

(67)
Aidai

Leonardas Andriekus, O.F.M., Editor
361 Highland Blvd.
Brooklyn, NY 11207

First published: 1945
Sponsoring organization: Lithuanian Franciscan Friars
ISSN: 0002-208X
MLA acronym: Aidai

SUBSCRIPTION INFORMATION

Frequency of publication: 4 times/yr.
Circulation: 1,200
Available in microform: No
Subscription price: $20.00/yr.
Year to which price refers: 1991
Subscription address: Aidai, Franciscan Fathers, 361 Highland Blvd., Brooklyn, NY 11207

ADVERTISING INFORMATION

Advertising accepted: No

EDITORIAL DESCRIPTION

Scope: Publishes articles on Lithuanian literature and culture.
Reviews books: Yes
Publishes notes: Yes
Languages accepted: Lithuanian
Prints abstracts: No

SUBMISSION REQUIREMENTS

Restrictions on contributors: None
Author pays submission fee: No
Author pays page charges: No
Length of articles: No restrictions
Length of book reviews: No restrictions
Number of copies required: 1
Copyright ownership: Author
Rejected manuscripts: Returned
Time before publication decision: 1 mo.
Time between decision and publication: 1 mo.
Number of reviewers: 2
Articles submitted per year: 40
Articles published per year: 35-40
Book reviews submitted per year: 40-42
Book reviews published per year: 20-25

(68)
*AILA Review

Johan F. Matter, Editor
Vakgroep TTW
Vrije Univ.
De Boelelaan 1105
1087 HV Amsterdam, Netherlands

Telephone: (31) 20 5483075
Fax: (31) 20 6426355
E-mail: AILA@VU.LET.NL

First published: 1984
Sponsoring organization: Assn. Internationale de Linguistique Appliquée (AILA)
MLA acronym: AILAR

SUBSCRIPTION INFORMATION

Frequency of publication: Annual
Circulation: 5,500
Available in microform: No
Subscription price: 10 f/yr.
Year to which price refers: 1990
Additional subscription address: Single issues can be ordered from Free University Press, De Boelelaan 1105, 1081 HV Amsterdam, Netherlands
Subscription telephone: (31) 20 6444355
Subscription fax: (31) 20 6462719

ADVERTISING INFORMATION

Advertising accepted: Yes
Advertising rates: 300 f/half page; 500 f/full page

EDITORIAL DESCRIPTION

Scope: Publishes articles on applied linguistics.
Reviews books: No
Languages accepted: English; French; German
Author-anonymous submission: No

SUBMISSION REQUIREMENTS

Restrictions on contributors: Contribution is by invitation only.
Author pays submission fee: No
Author pays page charges: No
Length of articles: 10 pp.
Copyright ownership: Author
Time before publication decision: 2 mos. maximum
Time between decision and publication: 4 mos. maximum
Articles published per year: 6-8

(69)
*Aiolika Grammata

Kostas Valetas, Editor
Prighipissis Ekaterinis 4
Callithea
17676 Athens, Greece

Telephone: (30) 1 3600142
First published: 1971
MLA acronym: AiolikaG

SUBSCRIPTION INFORMATION

Frequency of publication: 6 times/yr.
Circulation: 5,000
Available in microform: No

ADVERTISING INFORMATION

Advertising accepted: Yes

EDITORIAL DESCRIPTION

Scope: Publishes articles on literature, history, and literary criticism, as well as theater, art, and sociology.
Reviews books: Yes
Publishes notes: Yes
Languages accepted: Greek; Italian; French
Prints abstracts: Yes

SUBMISSION REQUIREMENTS

Author pays submission fee: No
Author pays page charges: No
Length of articles: No restrictions
Length of book reviews: No restrictions
Length of notes: No restrictions
Number of copies required: 2
Copyright ownership: Editor
Time before publication decision: 5 mos.
Time between decision and publication: 4 mos.

Articles submitted per year: 2,100
Articles published per year: 140-300
Book reviews submitted per year: 60-100
Notes submitted per year: 1,000
Notes published per year: 805

(70)
*Akadēmiskā Dzīve

Magdalēne Rozentāle, Aina Dravnieks, Eižens Skurupijs, & Sulamite Ozolins, Editors
Akadēmiskā Dzīve
1 Vincent Ave. S.
Minneapolis, MN 55405

Telephone: 612 374-3009
First published: 1958
Sponsoring organization: Latvian Academic Club
ISSN: 0516-3145
MLA acronym: ADz

SUBSCRIPTION INFORMATION

Frequency of publication: Annual
Circulation: 1,000
Available in microform: No
Subscription price: $5.00/yr.
Year to which price refers: 1991

ADVERTISING INFORMATION

Advertising accepted: No

EDITORIAL DESCRIPTION

Scope: Publishes articles on Latvian culture, particularly in the fields of history, sociology, political science, philosophy, philology, and science.
Reviews books: Yes
Publishes notes: Yes
Languages accepted: Latvian
Prints abstracts: Yes
Author-anonymous submission: No

SUBMISSION REQUIREMENTS

Restrictions on contributors: None
Author pays submission fee: No
Author pays page charges: No
Length of articles: 8-10 typescript pp.
Length of book reviews: 1-2 typescript pp.
Length of notes: 1 p. maximum
Style: None
Number of copies required: 1
Special requirements: Submit double-spaced typescript.
Copyright ownership: Journal
Rejected manuscripts: Returned at author's request
Time before publication decision: 1 mo.
Time between decision and publication: 4 mos.
Number of reviewers: 3
Articles submitted per year: 25
Articles published per year: 15
Book reviews submitted per year: 10
Book reviews published per year: 8
Notes submitted per year: 2
Notes published per year: 1

(71)
*Akzente: Zeitschrift für Literatur

Michael Krüger, Editor
Carl Hanser Verlag
Kolbergerstr. 22
8 Munich 80, Germany

Telephone: (49) 89 998300
First published: 1954
ISSN: 0002-3957
MLA acronym: Akzente

SUBSCRIPTION INFORMATION

Frequency of publication: 6 times/yr.
Circulation: 4,500
Available in microform: No

ADVERTISING INFORMATION

Advertising accepted: Yes
Advertising rates: 650 DM/full page

EDITORIAL DESCRIPTION

Scope: Publishes articles on modern literature.
Reviews books: No
Publishes notes: No
Languages accepted: German
Prints abstracts: No
Author-anonymous submission: No

SUBMISSION REQUIREMENTS

Restrictions on contributors: None
Author pays submission fee: No
Author pays page charges: No
Style: None
Number of copies required: 1
Special requirements: Articles in English, French, and Italian will be published in German translation.
Copyright ownership: Carl Hanser Verlag for 1 yr.
Rejected manuscripts: Returned
Time before publication decision: 6 mos.
Time between decision and publication: 4 mos.
Number of reviewers: 1
Articles submitted per year: 1,000
Articles published per year: 200

(72)
*Al-'Arabiyya: Journal of the American Association of Teachers of Arabic

Mushira Eid, Editor
Middle East Center, Bldg. 113
Univ. of Utah
Salt Lake City, UT 84112

Telephone: 801 581-6181
Fax: 801 581-6183
E-mail: ARABIYYA@cc.utah.edu
First published: 1967
Sponsoring organization: American Assn. of Teachers of Arabic
ISSN: 0889-8731
MLA acronym: Arabiyya

SUBSCRIPTION INFORMATION

Frequency of publication: 1-2 times/yr.
Circulation: 275
Available in microform: No
Subscription price: $20.00/yr. (includes membership)
Year to which price refers: 1991
Subscription address: American Assn. of Teachers of Arabic, David M. Kennedy Center, 280 HCRB, Brigham Young Univ., Provo, UT 84602
Subscription telephone: 801 378-6528
Subscription fax: 801 378-6528

ADVERTISING INFORMATION

Advertising accepted: Yes
Advertising rates: $30.00/half page; $50.00/full page

EDITORIAL DESCRIPTION

Scope: Publishes articles and reviews that contribute to the advancement of study, criticism, research, and teaching in the fields of Arabic language, literature, linguistics, and teaching.
Reviews books: Yes
Publishes notes: Yes
Languages accepted: Arabic; English; French
Author-anonymous submission: Yes

SUBMISSION REQUIREMENTS

Restrictions on contributors: None
Author pays submission fee: No
Author pays page charges: No
Length of articles: No restrictions
Length of book reviews: 500-750 words
Length of notes: 1,000 words maximum
Style: Chicago; journal
Number of copies required: 3
Special requirements: Include a 100-150 word abstract in English. Author's name, affiliation, address, and phone number should be on a cover sheet, not on the manuscript. Footnotes should be typed double-spaced at the end of the manuscript. Submit original typescript plus 2 copies. Authors are requested to avoid sexist language. Diskettes are required for accepted submissions.
Copyright ownership: American Assn. of Teachers of Arabic
Rejected manuscripts: Original returned
Time before publication decision: 5 mos.
Time between decision and publication: 4 mos.
Number of reviewers: 2-4
Articles submitted per year: 25-30
Articles published per year: 10-12
Book reviews submitted per year: 8-10
Book reviews published per year: 3-6
Notes submitted per year: 5-10
Notes published per year: 3-6

(73)
*Alaluz: Revista de Poesia, Narracion y Ensayo

Ann Maria Fagundo, Editor
Dept. of Spanish & Portuguese
Univ. of California
Riverside, CA 92521

Additional editorial address: During summer: Ann Maria Fagundo, Valdevarnes 13, 5° D, Madrid 28039, Spain
Telephone: 714 787-3406
Fax: 714 787-2294
First published: 1969
Sponsoring organization: Univ. California at Riverside
ISSN: 0044-7094
MLA acronym: Alaluz

SUBSCRIPTION INFORMATION

Frequency of publication: 2 times/yr.
Circulation: 1,000
Available in microform: No
Subscription price: $40.00/yr.
Year to which price refers: 1992

ADVERTISING INFORMATION

Advertising accepted: No

EDITORIAL DESCRIPTION

Scope: Devoted to contemporary Hispanic literature and poetry.
Reviews books: Yes
Publishes notes: No
Languages accepted: Spanish
Prints abstracts: No
Author-anonymous submission: No

SUBMISSION REQUIREMENTS

Restrictions on contributors: Articles are solicited and must be previously unpublished.
Author pays submission fee: No
Author pays page charges: No
Length of articles: 10 pp.
Length of book reviews: 3-4 pp.
Style: MLA
Number of copies required: 2
Copyright ownership: Journal
Rejected manuscripts: Returned
Time before publication decision: 1 mo.

Number of reviewers: 1
Articles submitted per year: 10-20
Articles published per year: 2-3
Book reviews submitted per year: 20-30
Book reviews published per year: 6-10

(74)
*Alba de América: Revista Literaria

Juana Alcira Arancibia, Director
Inst. Literario & Cultural Hispánico
8452 Furman Ave.
Westminster, CA 92683

Telephone: 714 892-8285
Fax: 714 892-0883
First published: 1982
Sponsoring organization: Inst. Literario & Cultural Hispánico
ISSN: 0888-3181
MLA acronym: AldeAm

SUBSCRIPTION INFORMATION

Frequency of publication: 2 times/yr.
Circulation: 500
Available in microform: No
Subscription price: $25.00/yr. Latin America; $35.00/yr. elsewhere
Year to which price refers: 1992

ADVERTISING INFORMATION

Advertising accepted: Yes, on an exchange basis

EDITORIAL DESCRIPTION

Scope: Publishes articles on Spanish and Latin American literature. Includes creative writing.
Reviews books: Yes
Publishes notes: No
Languages accepted: Spanish
Prints abstracts: No
Author-anonymous submission: Yes

SUBMISSION REQUIREMENTS

Restrictions on contributors: None
Author pays submission fee: No
Author pays page charges: No
Length of articles: 6,000 words
Length of book reviews: 750-1,000 words
Style: MLA
Number of copies required: 3
Special requirements: Submit original typescript.
Copyright ownership: Inst. Literario & Cultural Hispánico
Rejected manuscripts: Returned at author's request
Time before publication decision: 3-5 mos.
Time between decision and publication: 12-15 mos.
Number of reviewers: 2-3
Articles submitted per year: 200
Articles published per year: 35
Book reviews submitted per year: 20-30
Book reviews published per year: 15

(75)
*The Albert Bates Lord Studies in Oral Tradition

John Miles Foley, Editor
Center for Studies in Oral Tradition
301 Read Hall
Univ. of Missouri
Columbia, MO 65211

Additional editorial address: Garland Publishing, Inc., 717 Fifth Ave., New York, NY 10022
Telephone: 314 882-9720
First published: 1987

Sponsoring organization: Center for Studies in Oral Tradition, Univ. of Missouri
MLA acronym: ABLS

SUBSCRIPTION INFORMATION

Frequency of publication: Irregular
Available in microform: No
Subscription address: Garland Publishing, Inc., 1000A Sherman Ave., Hamden, CT 06514
Subscription telephone: 800 627-6273; 203 230-4487
Subscription fax: 203 230-1186

ADVERTISING INFORMATION

Advertising accepted: No

EDITORIAL DESCRIPTION

Scope: Publishes monographs and collections of essays on comparative studies on oral traditions from around the world.
Reviews books: No
Publishes notes: No
Languages accepted: English
Prints abstracts: No
Author-anonymous submission: No

SUBMISSION REQUIREMENTS

Restrictions on contributors: None
Author pays submission fee: No
Author pays page charges: No
Length of books: 150-300 pp.
Style: Chicago
Number of copies required: 1
Copyright ownership: Author
Rejected manuscripts: Returned
Time before publication decision: 4-5 mos.
Time between decision and publication: 6-8 mos.
Number of reviewers: 2
Books submitted per year: 12-15
Books published per year: 2-3

(76)
Alcance: Revista Literaria

Franklin Gutiérrez, Editor
520 W. 163 St. Suite A-8
New York, NY 10032

First published: 1982
MLA acronym: Alcance

SUBSCRIPTION INFORMATION

Frequency of publication: 3 times/yr.
Available in microform: No

ADVERTISING INFORMATION

Advertising accepted: Yes

EDITORIAL DESCRIPTION

Scope: Publishes articles on Latin American literature, theater, poetry, history, sociology, and philosophy.
Reviews books: Yes
Publishes notes: Yes
Languages accepted: Spanish
Prints abstracts: Yes
Author-anonymous submission: No

SUBMISSION REQUIREMENTS

Restrictions on contributors: None
Author pays submission fee: No
Author pays page charges: No
Length of articles: No restrictions
Length of book reviews: No restrictions
Length of notes: No restrictions
Number of copies required: 2
Time before publication decision: 1 mo.
Time between decision and publication: 4 mos.
Number of reviewers: 2
Articles published per year: 15-20

Book reviews submitted per year: 30
Book reviews published per year: 20
Notes submitted per year: 50
Notes published per year: 30

(77)
*Alemannisches Jahrbuch

Alemannisches Inst.
Mozartstr. 30
7800 Freiburg i.Br., Germany

First published: 1953
Sponsoring organization: Alemannisches Inst.
MLA acronym: AlJ

SUBSCRIPTION INFORMATION

Frequency of publication: Annual
Available in microform: No
Subscription address: Konkordia Verlag, Eisenbahnstr. 31, 7580 Bühl/Baden, Germany

ADVERTISING INFORMATION

Advertising accepted: No

EDITORIAL DESCRIPTION

Scope: Publishes articles on the geography, history, language, and folklore of the Alemannic-Suebian regions: Alsace, Liechtenstein, Vorarlberg, Baden-Würtemberg, and Bavarian Swabia.
Reviews books: No
Publishes notes: No
Languages accepted: German
Prints abstracts: No
Author-anonymous submission: Yes

SUBMISSION REQUIREMENTS

Restrictions on contributors: None
Author pays submission fee: No
Author pays page charges: No
Length of articles: 30 pp.
Number of copies required: 1
Copyright ownership: Editor & Konkordia Verlag
Rejected manuscripts: Returned
Time before publication decision: 3 mos.
Time between decision and publication: 1-2 yrs.
Number of reviewers: 2
Articles submitted per year: 15
Articles published per year: 8

(78)
*ALFA: Actes de Langue Française et de Linguistique/Symposium on French Language and Linguistics

Rostislav Kocourek, Editor
Dept. of French
Dalhousie Univ.
Halifax, NS B3H 3J5, Canada

Telephone: 902 492-2430
Fax: 902 492-2319
First published: 1989
Sponsoring organization: Dept. of French, Dalhousie Univ.
ISSN: 0838-1321
MLA acronym: ALFA-C

SUBSCRIPTION INFORMATION

Frequency of publication: Annual
Circulation: 50
Available in microform: No
Subscription price: C$30.00/yr.
Year to which price refers: 1992

ADVERTISING INFORMATION

Advertising accepted: No

EDITORIAL DESCRIPTION

Scope: Aims to provide a Canadian, North American, and international forum for the type of linguistic and language-oriented reflection, knowledge and understanding which is one of the central areas of research in university departments of French studies.
Reviews books: No
Publishes notes: No
Languages accepted: French; English
Prints abstracts: No
Author-anonymous submission: No

SUBMISSION REQUIREMENTS

Restrictions on contributors: Many contributors are invited to present their studies at the Dalhousie International Symposium on French Language and Linguistics; other submissions are invited by the editor.
Author pays submission fee: No
Author pays page charges: No
Length of articles: 18,000 words maximum
Style: MLA or Linguistic Soc. of America preferred
Number of copies required: 1
Special requirements: Deadline for submission is usually in Dec.
Rejected manuscripts: Returned
Time before publication decision: 3 mos.
Time between decision and publication: 1 yr.
Number of reviewers: 2 minimum
Articles submitted per year: 30
Articles published per year: 18

(79)
*Alfa: Revista de Lingüística

Roberto Gomes Camacho, Editor
FUNDUNESP
Directoria de Publicações
Av. Rio Branco, 1210
Campos Elíseos
01206 São Paulo SP, Brazil

First published: 1962
Sponsoring organization: Univ. Estadual Paulista
ISSN: 0002-5216
MLA acronym: Alfa

SUBSCRIPTION INFORMATION

Frequency of publication: Annual
Available in microform: No

ADVERTISING INFORMATION

Advertising accepted: No

EDITORIAL DESCRIPTION

Scope: Publishes articles on topics in linguistics including both general and language-specific studies.
Reviews books: Yes
Publishes notes: No
Languages accepted: English; French; German; Portuguese; Spanish; Italian
Prints abstracts: Yes
Author-anonymous submission: No

SUBMISSION REQUIREMENTS

Restrictions on contributors: Preference is given to those affiliated with Univ. Estadual Paulista.
Author pays submission fee: No
Author pays page charges: No
Length of articles: 45,000 characters
Length of book reviews: 9,500 characters
Number of copies required: 3
Special requirements: Submit a 200-word abstract in Portuguese and English or French.
Copyright ownership: Univ. Estadual Paulista
Rejected manuscripts: Returned
Time before publication decision: 8 mos.
Time between decision and publication: 5 mos.

(80)
*Alföld: Irodalmi Művelődési és Kritikai Folyóirat

Márkus Béla, Editor
Piac u. 26/A I.em.
Debrecen, Hungary

Additional editorial address: P.O. Box 144, 4001 Debrecen, Hungary
Telephone: (36) 52 12626
First published: 1950
Sponsoring organization: Debrecen Town Local Government
ISSN: 0401-3174
MLA acronym: Alföld

SUBSCRIPTION INFORMATION

Frequency of publication: 12 times/yr.
Circulation: 2,000
Available in microform: No
Subscription price: 360 Ft/yr.
Year to which price refers: 1992
Subscription address: Posta Központi Hirlapirodánál, József nádor ter I, 1900 Budapest V., Hungary

ADVERTISING INFORMATION

Advertising accepted: No

EDITORIAL DESCRIPTION

Scope: Publishes articles on literature, public education, arts, and criticism with an emphasis on Hungarian literature.
Reviews books: Yes
Publishes notes: Yes
Languages accepted: Hungarian
Prints abstracts: No
Author-anonymous submission: No

SUBMISSION REQUIREMENTS

Restrictions on contributors: None
Author pays submission fee: No
Author pays page charges: No
Length of articles: No restrictions
Length of book reviews: 3-6 pp.
Length of notes: 3-5 pp.
Style: None
Number of copies required: 1
Copyright ownership: Author
Rejected manuscripts: Not returned
Time before publication decision: 1 mo.
Time between decision and publication: 1-3 mos.
Number of reviewers: 3
Articles submitted per year: 120
Articles published per year: 50
Book reviews submitted per year: 120
Book reviews published per year: 90
Notes submitted per year: 110
Notes published per year: 80

(81)
*Alif: Journal of Comparative Poetics

Ferial J. Ghazoul, Editor
American Univ. in Cairo
Dept. of English & Comparative Literature
113 Kasr el Aini St.
P.O. Box 2511
Cairo, Egypt

Telephone: (20) 2 3575107
Fax: (20) 2 3557565 attn. Alif
First published: 1981

Sponsoring organization: Dept. of English & Comparative Literature, American Univ. in Cairo
MLA acronym: Alif

SUBSCRIPTION INFORMATION

Frequency of publication: Annual
Circulation: 600
Available in microform: No
Subscription price: $30.00/yr. institutions; $15.00/yr. individuals
Year to which price refers: 1992

ADVERTISING INFORMATION

Advertising accepted: No

EDITORIAL DESCRIPTION

Scope: Publishes articles on comparative literature, poetics, cultural studies, Arabic studies, the Middle East, and philosophy. Each issue is thematic.
Reviews books: No
Publishes notes: No
Languages accepted: English; Arabic; French
Prints abstracts: Yes
Author-anonymous submission: Yes

SUBMISSION REQUIREMENTS

Restrictions on contributors: Most articles are solicited.
Author pays submission fee: No
Author pays page charges: No
Length of articles: 10,000 words maximum
Style: MLA
Number of copies required: 1
Special requirements: Submit double-space typescript, and if possible, a Macintosh diskette.
Copyright ownership: Publisher
Rejected manuscripts: Returned
Time before publication decision: 3-4 mos.
Time between decision and publication: 6 mos.
Number of reviewers: 2
Articles submitted per year: 20
Articles published per year: 10-15

(82)
The Aligarh Critical Miscellany

Asloob Ahmad Ansari, Editor
"Gulfishan" Civil Lines
Aligarh 202 001, India

First published: 1988
MLA acronym: ACM

SUBSCRIPTION INFORMATION

Frequency of publication: 2 times/yr.
Available in microform: No
Subscription price: £5.00 ($10.00)/yr.
Year to which price refers: 1993

ADVERTISING INFORMATION

Advertising accepted: Yes

EDITORIAL DESCRIPTION

Scope: Publishes articles on Shakespeare.
Reviews books: Yes
Languages accepted: English
Prints abstracts: No
Author-anonymous submission: No

SUBMISSION REQUIREMENTS

Restrictions on contributors: None
Author pays submission fee: No
Author pays page charges: No
Length of articles: 3,000 words
Length of book reviews: 600-700 words
Style: MLA; Modern Humanities Research Assn.
Number of copies required: 1
Time before publication decision: 1 yr.
Time between decision and publication: 3 mos.
Articles submitted per year: 16-20
Articles published per year: 12-16
Book reviews submitted per year: 4-6
Book reviews published per year: 3-6

(83)
*The Aligarh Journal of English Studies

A. Tariq, Editor
Dept. of English
Aligarh Muslim Univ.
202002 Aligarh, India

First published: 1976
Sponsoring organization: Aligarh Muslim Univ.
ISSN: 0258-0365
MLA acronym: AJES

SUBSCRIPTION INFORMATION

Frequency of publication: 2 times/yr. (Apr., Oct.)
Circulation: 1,000
Available in microform: No
Subscription price: $6.00 (£3.50)/yr.
Year to which price refers: 1992

ADVERTISING INFORMATION

Advertising accepted: No

EDITORIAL DESCRIPTION

Scope: Publishes critical and research articles dealing with subjects in all the main areas of English studies, with special attention to Shakespeare.
Reviews books: Yes
Publishes notes: No
Languages accepted: English
Prints abstracts: No
Author-anonymous submission: No

SUBMISSION REQUIREMENTS

Restrictions on contributors: None
Author pays submission fee: No
Author pays page charges: No
Length of articles: 3,000-10,000 words
Length of book reviews: 1,000 words
Style: Modern Humanities Research Assn.
Number of copies required: 1
Special requirements: Submit original typescript.
Copyright ownership: Author
Rejected manuscripts: Returned
Time before publication decision: 3 mos.
Time between decision and publication: 1 yr.
Number of reviewers: 2
Articles submitted per year: 20
Articles published per year: 12
Book reviews submitted per year: 12
Book reviews published per year: 6

(84)
L'Alighieri: Rassegna Bibliografica Dantesca

Aldo Vallone, Editor
Via F. Portinari, 37
00151 Rome, Italy

First published: 1960
Sponsoring organization: Casa di Dante
ISSN: 0516-6551
MLA acronym: Alighieri

SUBSCRIPTION INFORMATION

Frequency of publication: 2 times/yr.
Circulation: 2,000
Available in microform: No
Subscription address: Silvio Zennaro, Casa di Dante, Piazza Sonnino, 5, Rome, Italy

ADVERTISING INFORMATION

Advertising accepted: Yes

EDITORIAL DESCRIPTION

Scope: Publishes studies relating to Dante.
Reviews books: Yes
Publishes notes: Yes
Languages accepted: Italian; English; French; German
Prints abstracts: No

SUBMISSION REQUIREMENTS

Author pays submission fee: No
Author pays page charges: No
Length of articles: 15-20 pp.
Length of book reviews: 1-2 pp.
Length of notes: 1-2 pp.
Number of copies required: 1
Copyright ownership: Author
Time before publication decision: 6 mos.
Time between decision and publication: 1 yr.
Number of reviewers: 1
Articles submitted per year: 20
Articles published per year: 4
Book reviews submitted per year: 50
Book reviews published per year: 20
Notes submitted per year: 60
Notes published per year: 20

(85)
Alizés: Revue Angliciste de la Réunion

Alain Geoffroy, Editor
Univ. de La Réunion
Fac. des Lettres
26 av. de la Victoire
97400 Saint Denis, Ile de la Réunion

Telephone: (262) 215299
First published: 1991
Sponsoring organization: Fac. des Lettres de l'Univ. de La Réunion
ISSN: 1155-4363
MLA acronym: Alizés

SUBSCRIPTION INFORMATION

Frequency of publication: 2 times/yr.
Available in microform: No
Subscription price: 65 F/issue
Year to which price refers: 1992
Subscription address: Secrétariat de la Recherche & des Publications, at the above address

ADVERTISING INFORMATION

Advertising accepted: No

EDITORIAL DESCRIPTION

Scope: Publishes articles on the literature, history, and culture of the English-speaking world.
Reviews books: No
Publishes notes: No
Languages accepted: French; English
Prints abstracts: No
Author-anonymous submission: No

SUBMISSION REQUIREMENTS

Author pays submission fee: No
Length of articles: 27,000 characters
Style: MLA
Number of copies required: 1
Copyright ownership: Author
Rejected manuscripts: Returned
Time before publication decision: 3 mos.
Time between decision and publication: 4 mos.
Number of reviewers: 1
Articles submitted per year: 40
Articles published per year: 30

(86)
Alla Bottega: Rivista Bimestrale di Cultura ed Arte

Pino Lucano, Editor
Via Plinio, 38
20129 Milan, Italy

Telephone: (39) 2 29528413
First published: 1963
ISSN: 0002-5631
MLA acronym: AllaB

SUBSCRIPTION INFORMATION

Frequency of publication: 6 times/yr.
Available in microform: No

EDITORIAL DESCRIPTION

Scope: Publishes articles on culture and art.
Reviews books: Yes
Publishes notes: Yes
Languages accepted: Italian
Prints abstracts: No
Author-anonymous submission: No

SUBMISSION REQUIREMENTS

Author pays submission fee: No
Author pays page charges: No
Length of articles: No restrictions
Length of book reviews: No restrictions
Length of notes: No restrictions
Copyright ownership: Editor
Rejected manuscripts: Not returned
Time before publication decision: 3-4 mos.
Time between decision and publication: 3-4 mos.
Articles submitted per year: 40
Articles published per year: 40
Book reviews submitted per year: 70

(87)
*Allegorica

Craig Kallendorf, Editor
Dept. of English
Texas A&M Univ.
College Station, TX 77843

Telephone: 409 845-3452
Fax: 409 862-2292
First published: 1976
Sponsoring organization: Dept. of English & Dept. of Modern Languages, Texas A&M Univ.
ISSN: 0363-2377
MLA acronym: Allegorica

SUBSCRIPTION INFORMATION

Frequency of publication: Annual
Circulation: 200
Available in microform: No
Subscription price: $10.00/yr. US & Canada; $12.00/yr. elsewhere
Year to which price refers: 1992

ADVERTISING INFORMATION

Advertising accepted: Yes
Advertising rates: $50.00/half page; $100.00/full page

EDITORIAL DESCRIPTION

Scope: Devoted to making available to scholars literal translations of Medieval and Renaissance literary works and documents which heretofore have been available only in their original languages or in outmoded or inadequate English translations. Also publishes scholarly articles on Medieval and Renaissance topics from the Early Christian period through the Rococo. Invites the submission of translations, articles, and review articles.
Reviews books: Yes
Publishes notes: No
Languages accepted: English
Prints abstracts: No
Author-anonymous submission: Yes

SUBMISSION REQUIREMENTS

Restrictions on contributors: Book reviews are solicited.
Author pays submission fee: No
Author pays page charges: No
Length of articles: 15-40 pp.
Length of book reviews: 10-15 pp.
Style: MLA (pre-1985)
Number of copies required: 3
Special requirements: Translate extensive foreign language quotations in footnotes. Send a xerox copy of the texts translated and obtain from the publishers of the texts permission to reprint.
Copyright ownership: Journal
Rejected manuscripts: Returned; enclose return postage.
Time before publication decision: 3 mos.
Time between decision and publication: 3-12 mos.
Number of reviewers: 2-3
Articles submitted per year: 35
Articles published per year: 7
Book reviews published per year: 4

(88)
*Al'manakh Ukraïns'koho Narodnoho Soiuzu

Zenon Snylyk, Editor
Ukrainian National Assn., Inc.
P.O. Box 17a, 30 Montgomery St.
Jersey City, NJ 07303

Telephone: 201 434-0237
Fax: 201 451-5486
First published: 1910
Sponsoring organization: Ukrainian National Assn., Inc.
ISSN: 0883-7368
MLA acronym: AUNS

SUBSCRIPTION INFORMATION

Frequency of publication: Annual
Circulation: 13,000
Available in microform: No
Subscription price: $10.00/yr.
Year to which price refers: 1992

ADVERTISING INFORMATION

Advertising accepted: Yes
Advertising rates: $33.00/quarter page; $50.00/half page; $90.00/full page

EDITORIAL DESCRIPTION

Scope: Publishes articles on Ukrainian politics, as well as Ukrainian culture, arts, history, and literature in Ukraine and other parts of the world.
Reviews books: No
Languages accepted: English; Ukrainian
Prints abstracts: Yes
Author-anonymous submission: No

SUBMISSION REQUIREMENTS

Restrictions on contributors: None
Author pays submission fee: No
Author pays page charges: No
Length of articles: 1,500 words maximum
Number of copies required: 1
Copyright ownership: Svoboda Press
Rejected manuscripts: Returned at author's request
Time between decision and publication: 3 mos.
Articles submitted per year: 35
Articles published per year: 20-25

(89)
*Általános Nyelvészeti Tanulmányok

Ferenc Kiefer, Editor
Magyar Tudományos Akadémia
Nyelvtudomány Intézete
P.O. Box 19
Budapest 1, Hungary

First published: 1963
Sponsoring organization: Magyar Tudományos Akadémia Nyelvtudomány Intézete
ISSN: 0569-1338
MLA acronym: ÁNT

SUBSCRIPTION INFORMATION

Frequency of publication: Irregular
Available in microform: No
Subscription address: Akadémiai Kiadó, Alkotmány Utca 21, 1054 Budapest, Hungary

ADVERTISING INFORMATION

Advertising accepted: No

EDITORIAL DESCRIPTION

Scope: Provides a forum for papers concerning general linguistics. Modern approaches are preferred, but no approach is excluded.
Reviews books: Yes
Publishes notes: No
Languages accepted: Hungarian
Prints abstracts: No
Author-anonymous submission: Yes

SUBMISSION REQUIREMENTS

Author pays submission fee: No
Author pays page charges: No
Length of articles: 24 pp.
Length of book reviews: 8 pp.
Style: None
Number of copies required: 2
Copyright ownership: Akadémiai Kiadó
Rejected manuscripts: Not returned
Time before publication decision: 1 yr.
Time between decision and publication: 1 yr.
Number of reviewers: 2

(90)
*Altdeutsche Textbibliothek

Burghart Wachinger, Editor
Wilhelmstr., 50
7400 Tübingen, Germany

First published: 1882
ISSN: 0342-6661
MLA acronym: AdTb

SUBSCRIPTION INFORMATION

Frequency of publication: Irregular
Available in microform: No
Subscription address: Max Niemeyer Verlag, Postfach 2140, 7400 Tübingen, Germany

ADVERTISING INFORMATION

Advertising accepted: No

EDITORIAL DESCRIPTION

Scope: The series publishes editions of German texts from the beginnings of German literature until 1500.
Reviews books: No
Publishes notes: No
Languages accepted: German
Prints abstracts: No
Author-anonymous submission: No

SUBMISSION REQUIREMENTS

Author pays submission fee: No
Author pays page charges: No
Number of copies required: 1
Copyright ownership: Max Niemeyer Verlag
Rejected manuscripts: Returned
Number of reviewers: 1

(91)
*Altro Polo: A Volume of Italian Studies

Frederick May Foundation for Italian Studies
Dept. of Italian
Univ. of Sydney
Sydney, NSW 2006, Australia

Telephone: (61) 2 6922875
Fax: (61) 2 6924203
First published: 1978
Sponsoring organization: Frederick May Foundation for Italian Studies
ISSN: 0727-0046
MLA acronym: AlP

SUBSCRIPTION INFORMATION

Frequency of publication: Annual
Circulation: 250
Available in microform: No
Subscription address: Honorary Secretary, at the above address

ADVERTISING INFORMATION

Advertising accepted: No

EDITORIAL DESCRIPTION

Scope: Provides an international and interdisciplinary forum for the exchange of information on all aspects of Italian studies, including modern Italian literature, poetry, history, political thought, economics, and language, and the arts.
Reviews books: No
Publishes notes: No
Languages accepted: English; Italian
Prints abstracts: No

SUBMISSION REQUIREMENTS

Restrictions on contributors: Unsolicited manuscripts are generally not accepted.
Author pays submission fee: No
Author pays page charges: No
Length of articles: 6,000-7,000 words (20 typescript pp. including footnotes)
Style: MLA
Number of copies required: 3
Special requirements: Submit orginal typescript and 2 copies.
Copyright ownership: Frederick May Foundation for Italian Studies
Rejected manuscripts: Returned; enclose return postage.
Time before publication decision: 3-6 mos.
Time between decision and publication: 1 yr.
Number of reviewers: 1-2
Articles submitted per year: 8-10
Articles published per year: 8

(92)
*Amerasia Journal

Russell C. Leong & Glenn Omatsu, Editors
Asian American Studies Center
3230 Campbell Hall
Univ. of California
Los Angeles, CA 90024-1546

Telephone: 310 825-3415; 310 206-2892
Fax: 310 206-9844
First published: 1971
Sponsoring organization: UCLA Asian American Studies Center
ISSN: 0044-7471
MLA acronym: AmasJ

SUBSCRIPTION INFORMATION

Frequency of publication: 3 times/yr.
Circulation: 1,100
Available in microform: Yes
Subscription price: $21.00/yr. institutions; $15.00/yr. individuals; add $3.00/yr. postage outside US
Year to which price refers: 1992
Subscription telephone: 310 825-2968

ADVERTISING INFORMATION

Advertising accepted: Yes
Advertising rates: $120.00/half page; $180.00/ full page

EDITORIAL DESCRIPTION

Scope: Publishes articles on historical and contemporary issues of Asian Pacific Americans. Includes studies on social science, literature, health, and inter-ethnic issues.
Reviews books: Yes
Publishes notes: Yes
Languages accepted: English
Prints abstracts: No
Author-anonymous submission: Yes

SUBMISSION REQUIREMENTS

Author pays submission fee: No
Author pays page charges: No
Length of articles: 5,000 words
Length of book reviews: 800 words
Style: MLA; Chicago
Number of copies required: 3
Copyright ownership: Univ. of California, Los Angeles
Rejected manuscripts: Returned
Time before publication decision: 4 mos.
Time between decision and publication: 4-6 mos.
Number of reviewers: 2
Articles submitted per year: 80-100
Articles published per year: 20-30
Book reviews submitted per year: 30-40
Book reviews published per year: 25

(93)
*American Anthropologist

Janet Dixon Keller, Editor
American Anthropological Assn.
1703 New Hampshire Ave., NW
Washington, DC 20009

Telephone: 202 667-5345
First published: 1888
Sponsoring organization: American Anthropological Assn.
ISSN: 0002-7294
MLA acronym: AA

SUBSCRIPTION INFORMATION

Frequency of publication: 4 times/yr. (Mar., June, Sept., Dec.)
Circulation: 8,500
Available in microform: No

ADVERTISING INFORMATION

Advertising accepted: Yes

EDITORIAL DESCRIPTION

Scope: Publishes cross-field, theoretical, and review articles, book and audiovisual reviews, reports, and comments.
Reviews books: Yes
Publishes notes: Yes
Languages accepted: English
Prints abstracts: Yes

SUBMISSION REQUIREMENTS

Restrictions on contributors: Considers unsolicited manuscripts by nonmembers, but manuscripts must be accompanied by a nonrefundable processing fee of $25.00.
Author pays submission fee: Yes, if nonmember
Author pays page charges: No
Length of articles: 40 pp. maximum
Style: MLA; Chicago
Number of copies required: 5
Special requirements: Submit original manuscript, abstract, biography of author.
Copyright ownership: American Anthropological Assn.
Rejected manuscripts: Not returned
Articles published per year: 30; 40 reports & comments
Book reviews published per year: 40

(94)
*American Benedictine Review

Terrence Kardong, Editor
Assumption Abbey
Richardton, ND 58652

Telephone: 701 974-3315
First published: 1950
Sponsoring organization: Abbeys & Priories of the American Cassinese Federation of Benedictines
ISSN: 0002-7650
MLA acronym: ABR

SUBSCRIPTION INFORMATION

Frequency of publication: 4 times/yr. (Mar., June, Sept., Dec.)
Circulation: 1,100
Available in microform: Yes
Subscription price: $15.00/yr.
Year to which price refers: 1992
Subscription address: Box A, at the above address

ADVERTISING INFORMATION

Advertising accepted: No

EDITORIAL DESCRIPTION

Scope: Publishes articles on the theory and history of the religious life, philosophy, theology, science and the humanities. Is particularly concerned with the religious aspect of the arts and sciences.
Reviews books: No
Publishes notes: No
Languages accepted: English
Prints abstracts: No
Author-anonymous submission: Yes

SUBMISSION REQUIREMENTS

Restrictions on contributors: None
Author pays submission fee: No
Author pays page charges: No
Length of articles: 15-30 pp.
Style: MLA
Number of copies required: 1
Special requirements: Submit original typescript.
Copyright ownership: Journal & author
Rejected manuscripts: Returned; enclose return postage.
Time before publication decision: 6 mos.
Time between decision and publication: 18 mos.
Number of reviewers: 4
Articles submitted per year: 60
Articles published per year: 30

(95)
American Book Collector

Bernard McTigue, Editor
Moretus Press, Inc.
P.O. Box 1080
Ossining, NY 10562-1080

First published: 1932
ISSN: 0196-5654
MLA acronym: ABC

SUBSCRIPTION INFORMATION

Frequency of publication: 12 times/yr.
Circulation: 2,200
Available in microform: No

ADVERTISING INFORMATION

Advertising accepted: Yes

EDITORIAL DESCRIPTION

Scope: Magazine is of interest to book collectors, book dealers, librarians, bibliophiles, and anyone in the book trade. Articles deal with every aspect of American and European rare books and collected authors.
Reviews books: Yes
Publishes notes: Yes
Languages accepted: English
Prints abstracts: No
Author-anonymous submission: No

SUBMISSION REQUIREMENTS

Restrictions on contributors: None
Author pays submission fee: No
Author pays page charges: No
Length of articles: 1,000-3,500 words
Length of book reviews: 750-1,000 words
Length of notes: 200 words
Style: Chicago
Number of copies required: 2
Special requirements: Submit original typescript; send 200-word summary in advance to editor.
Copyright ownership: Moretus Press; returned to author upon request
Rejected manuscripts: Returned; enclose SASE.
Time before publication decision: 1 mo.
Time between decision and publication: 1-6 mos.
Number of reviewers: 2
Articles submitted per year: 150-180
Articles published per year: 50-80
Book reviews submitted per year: 180-250
Book reviews published per year: 180-250
Notes submitted per year: 5-10
Notes published per year: 2-10

(96)
*American Drama

Norma Jenckes & Yashdip Bains, Editors
Dept. of English
ML 69
Univ. of Cincinnati
Cincinnati, OH 45221-0069

Telephone: 513 556-3914
First published: 1991
Sponsoring organization: American Drama Inst.; Univ. of Cincinnati, Helen Weinberger Center for the Study of Drama & Playwriting; Univ. of Cincinnati, College of Arts & Sciences
ISSN: 1061-0057
MLA acronym: AmDram

SUBSCRIPTION INFORMATION

Frequency of publication: 2 times/yr.
Available in microform: No
Subscription price: $25.00/yr. institutions; $15.00/yr. individuals
Year to which price refers: 1992-93

EDITORIAL DESCRIPTION

Scope: Publishes articles on American writing for stage, radio, film, and television. Explores the legacy of dramatic literature from the earliest to the most recent playwrights, featuring discussions of American dramatic diversity and promoting critical examination of trends in the writing of drama.
Reviews books: Yes
Publishes notes: No
Languages accepted: English
Prints abstracts: No
Author-anonymous submission: Yes

SUBMISSION REQUIREMENTS

Restrictions on contributors: None
Author pays submission fee: No
Author pays page charges: No
Length of articles: 2,500-5,000 words
Style: MLA
Number of copies required: 2
Special requirements: Submit original typescript and 1 copy. Accepted articles must be submitted on diskette.
Copyright ownership: American Drama Inst.
Rejected manuscripts: Returned; enclose return postage.
Time before publication decision: 2-4 mos.
Time between decision and publication: 4 mos.
Number of reviewers: 2

(97)
*American Indian Quarterly

Morris Foster, Editor
Dept. of Anthropology
Univ. of Oklahoma
Norman, OK 73019

Additional editorial address: Robert A. Black, Book Review Editor, Univ. of California, Native American Studies, 3415 Dwinelle Hall, Berkeley, CA 94720
First published: 1974
Sponsoring organization: Univ. of Oklahoma
ISSN: 0095-182X
MLA acronym: AIQ

SUBSCRIPTION INFORMATION

Frequency of publication: 4 times/yr.
Circulation: 700
Available in microform: No
Subscription price: $45.00/yr. institutions; $25.00/yr. individuals
Year to which price refers: 1992

ADVERTISING INFORMATION

Advertising accepted: Yes
Advertising rates: $60.00/quarter page; $100.00/half page; $175.00/full page

EDITORIAL DESCRIPTION

Scope: An interdisciplinary focus on American Indian studies including the fields of history, anthropology, literature, and the arts. Provides a forum for contemporary research and scholarship and is especially interested in encouraging contributions of Native Americans.
Reviews books: Yes
Publishes notes: Yes
Languages accepted: English
Prints abstracts: No
Author-anonymous submission: No

SUBMISSION REQUIREMENTS

Restrictions on contributors: None
Author pays submission fee: No
Author pays page charges: No
Length of articles: 5,000-15,000 words
Length of book reviews: 700-800 words
Length of notes: 50-100 words
Style: Chicago
Number of copies required: 2

Rejected manuscripts: Returned; enclose return postage.
Time before publication decision: 6 weeks
Time between decision and publication: 6 mos.
Number of reviewers: 2-3
Articles submitted per year: 15
Articles published per year: 12
Book reviews submitted per year: 100
Book reviews published per year: 80
Notes submitted per year: 20
Notes published per year: 15

(98)
*American Journal of Germanic Linguistics and Literatures

Richard K. Seymour, Editor
College of Languages, Linguistics & Literature
2528 The Mall, Webster 202
Univ. of Hawaii, Manoa
Honolulu, HI 96822

Telephone: 808 956-8516
Fax: 808 956-9879
First published: 1989
Sponsoring organization: Soc. for Germanic Philology; College of Languages, Linguistics & Literature, Univ. of Hawaii
ISSN: 1040-8207
MLA acronym: AJGLL

SUBSCRIPTION INFORMATION

Frequency of publication: 2 times/yr. (Jan., July)
Circulation: 140
Available in microform: No
Subscription price: $40.00/yr. institutions; $25.00/yr. individuals; $15.00/yr. students
Year to which price refers: 1992
Subscription address: Soc. for Germanic Philology, P.O. Box 020225, Brooklyn, NY 11202-0005
Subscription telephone: 718 997-5587
Subscription fax: 718 997-5566

ADVERTISING INFORMATION

Advertising accepted: No

EDITORIAL DESCRIPTION

Scope: Publishes articles on all aspects of Germanic languages, including English and Scandinavian, from the earliest phases to the present, as well as on the linguistic facets of works of literature in those languages prior to the eighteenth century. Topics may include, but are not limited to, the historical development of those languages, their European and pre-Indo-European antecedents, word formations, lexicology, syntax, semantics, pragmatics, dialectology, language use, and folklore.
Reviews books: Yes
Publishes notes: No
Languages accepted: English; German
Prints abstracts: Yes
Author-anonymous submission: Yes

SUBMISSION REQUIREMENTS

Restrictions on contributors: Book reviews are solicited.
Author pays submission fee: No
Author pays page charges: No
Length of articles: No restrictions
Length of book reviews: No restrictions
Style: MLA, with modifications; Journal
Number of copies required: 3
Special requirements: See "Instructions for Authors" in first issue of every odd-numbered volume.
Copyright ownership: College of Languages, Linguistics & Literature, Univ. of Hawaii
Rejected manuscripts: Returned
Time before publication decision: 3 mos. maximum
Time between decision and publication: 6-12 mos.

Number of reviewers: 2-4
Articles submitted per year: 25
Articles published per year: 8-10
Book reviews submitted per year: 11-15
Book reviews published per year: 8-10

(99)
*The American Journal of Psychoanalysis

Douglas H. Ingram, Editor
329 E. 62nd St.
New York, NY 10021

Telephone: 212 838-8044
First published: 1940
Sponsoring organization: Assn. for the Advancement of Psychoanalysis
ISSN: 0002-9548
MLA acronym: AJP

SUBSCRIPTION INFORMATION

Frequency of publication: 4 times/yr. (Mar., June, Sept., Dec.)
Circulation: 800
Available in microform: Yes
Subscription price: $95.00/yr. institutions US; $110.00/yr. institutions elsewhere; $29.00/yr. individuals US; $37.00/yr. individuals elsewhere
Year to which price refers: 1992
Subscription address: Journal Subscription Dept., Human Sciences Press, 233 Spring St., New York, NY 10013
Subscription telephone: 212 620-8000
Subscription fax: 212 807-1047

ADVERTISING INFORMATION

Advertising accepted: No

EDITORIAL DESCRIPTION

Scope: Aims to communicate modern concepts of psychoanalytic theory and practice, and related investigations in allied fields. Includes articles on psychology and its relation to literature and linguistics.
Reviews books: Yes
Publishes notes: Yes
Languages accepted: English
Prints abstracts: No
Author-anonymous submission: No

SUBMISSION REQUIREMENTS

Restrictions on contributors: Many articles and all notes are solicited.
Author pays submission fee: No
Author pays page charges: No
Length of articles: 2,000-7,000 words
Length of book reviews: 500 words
Length of notes: 300 words
Style: Chicago
Number of copies required: 4
Copyright ownership: Human Sciences Press
Rejected manuscripts: Not returned
Time before publication decision: 4-6 weeks
Time between decision and publication: 6-9 mos.
Number of reviewers: 3
Articles submitted per year: 90
Articles published per year: 30
Book reviews submitted per year: 20
Book reviews published per year: 12
Notes submitted per year: 8
Notes published per year: 6

(100)
The American Journal of Semiotics

Dean MacCannell & Juliet Flower MacCannell, Editors
1452 Huston Rd.
Lafayette, CA 94549

Additional editorial address: Comparative Literature, Univ. of California at Irvine, Irvine, CA 92717
First published: 1981
Sponsoring organization: Semiotic Soc. of America
ISSN: 0277-7126
MLA acronym: AJS

SUBSCRIPTION INFORMATION

Frequency of publication: 4 times/yr.
Circulation: 790
Available in microform: No
Subscription price: $45.00 (£22.50)/yr. institutions; $30.00 (£15.00)/yr. individuals
Year to which price refers: 1991
Subscription address: Indiana Univ. Press, 601 North Morton St., Bloomington, IN 47404

ADVERTISING INFORMATION

Advertising accepted: Yes

EDITORIAL DESCRIPTION

Scope: Publishes analyses of texts, events, groups, cultural and natural objects utilizing a semiotic methodology as well as essays that examine the theory and method of semiotics and the theory and methods of academic disciplines in relationship to semiotics.
Reviews books: Yes
Publishes notes: Yes
Languages accepted: English
Prints abstracts: No
Author-anonymous submission: Yes

SUBMISSION REQUIREMENTS

Restrictions on contributors: Contributors must be members of the Semiotic Soc.
Author pays submission fee: No
Author pays page charges: No
Length of articles: No restrictions
Length of book reviews: No restrictions
Style: Semiotic Soc. of America
Special requirements: Submit double-spaced typescript on 8 1/2 x 11 in. paper divided into the following sections: Title page, Text, Notes, References, Tables, Figure captions, Figures. Each section starts on a new page.
Copyright ownership: Author
Rejected manuscripts: Returned
Time before publication decision: 3 mos.
Time between decision and publication: 1 yr.
Number of reviewers: 3
Articles submitted per year: 80
Articles published per year: 20
Book reviews published per year: 12
Notes submitted per year: 10
Notes published per year: 5

(101)
*American Literary History

Gordon Hutner, Editor
Dept. of English
Univ. of Wisconsin, Madison
600 N. Park St.
Madison, WI 53706

Telephone: 608 263-3797
First published: 1989
ISSN: 0896-7148
MLA acronym: AmLH

SUBSCRIPTION INFORMATION

Frequency of publication: 4 times/yr. (Mar., June, Sept., Dec.)
Circulation: 1,000
Available in microform: Yes
Subscription address: Journals Dept., Oxford Univ. Press, 2001 Evans Rd., Cary, NC 27513
Subscription telephone: 212 679-7300; 919 677-0977

ADVERTISING INFORMATION

Advertising accepted: Yes

EDITORIAL DESCRIPTION

Scope: Publishes articles on American literature and culture from all periods. Bringing together work in history, theory, and interpretation, it seeks not simply to reflect but to extend and challenge the terms of recent literary inquiry.
Reviews books: Yes
Publishes notes: No
Languages accepted: English
Prints abstracts: No
Author-anonymous submission: Yes

SUBMISSION REQUIREMENTS

Author pays submission fee: No
Author pays page charges: No
Length of articles: 5,000-8,000 words
Length of book reviews: 3,000 words
Style: MLA
Number of copies required: 3
Special requirements: Submit original, double-spaced typescript and 2 copies.
Copyright ownership: Oxford Univ. Press
Rejected manuscripts: Returned; enclose SASE.
Time before publication decision: 1-4 mos.
Time between decision and publication: 9-12 mos.
Number of reviewers: 2-4
Articles submitted per year: 500
Articles published per year: 40
Book reviews submitted per year: 25
Book reviews published per year: 12-15

(102)
*American Literary Realism, 1870-1910

Robert E. Fleming & Gary Scharnhorst, Editors
Dept. of English
Humanities 217
Univ. of New Mexico
Albuquerque, NM 87131

Telephone: 505 277-5027
Fax: 505 277-5573
First published: 1967
Sponsoring organization: Dept. of English, Univ. of New Mexico
ISSN: 0002-9823
MLA acronym: ALR

SUBSCRIPTION INFORMATION

Frequency of publication: 3 times/yr. (Fall, Winter, Spring)
Circulation: 600
Available in microform: No
Subscription price: $25.00/yr.
Year to which price refers: 1992
Subscription address: McFarland & Co., Inc., Box 611, Jefferson, NC 28640

ADVERTISING INFORMATION

Advertising accepted: Yes
Advertising rates: $45.00/full page

EDITORIAL DESCRIPTION

Scope: Primary focus is critical, but the editors consider bibliographic articles of special merit and notes of interest to their readers.
Reviews books: Yes
Publishes notes: Yes
Languages accepted: English
Prints abstracts: No
Author-anonymous submission: Yes

SUBMISSION REQUIREMENTS

Restrictions on contributors: None
Author pays submission fee: No
Author pays page charges: No
Length of articles: 2,500-7,500 words
Length of book reviews: 500 words
Length of notes: 500-2,500 words
Style: MLA, 2nd ed.
Number of copies required: 2
Special requirements: Notes should follow text; submit double-spaced typescript.
Copyright ownership: McFarland & Co., Inc.
Rejected manuscripts: Returned; enclose SASE.
Time before publication decision: 4 mos.
Time between decision and publication: 1 yr.
Number of reviewers: 3
Articles submitted per year: 100
Articles published per year: 18
Book reviews submitted per year: 20
Book reviews published per year: 20
Notes submitted per year: 6
Notes published per year: 3

(103)
*American Literary Scholarship: An Annual

David J. Nordloh, Editor
Dept. of English
Indiana Univ.
Bloomington, IN 47405

Telephone: 812 855-7748
Fax: 812 855-5678
First published: 1963
Sponsoring organization: MLA, American Literature Section
ISSN: 0065-9142
MLA acronym: AmLS

SUBSCRIPTION INFORMATION

Frequency of publication: Annual
Circulation: 2,400
Available in microform: No
Subscription price: $40.00/yr.
Year to which price refers: 1992
Subscription address: Duke Univ. Press, 6697 College Station, Durham, NC 27708

ADVERTISING INFORMATION

Advertising accepted: No

EDITORIAL DESCRIPTION

Scope: Reviews scholarship in American literature for the calendar year, including scholarship published in major foreign languages.
Reviews books: Yes
Publishes notes: No
Languages accepted: English
Prints abstracts: No
Author-anonymous submission: No

SUBMISSION REQUIREMENTS

Restrictions on contributors: Unsolicited manuscripts are not accepted.
Author pays submission fee: No
Author pays page charges: No
Style: MLA
Copyright ownership: Duke Univ. Press
Articles published per year: 22

(104)
*American Literature: A Journal of Literary History, Criticism, and Bibliography

Cathy Davidson & Michael Moon, Editors
304E Allen Bldg.
Duke Univ.
Durham, NC 27706

Telephone: 919 684-3948
Fax: 919 684-4871
First published: 1929
Sponsoring organization: MLA, American Literature Section
ISSN: 0002-9831
MLA acronym: AL

SUBSCRIPTION INFORMATION

Frequency of publication: 4 times/yr. (Mar., June, Oct., Dec.)
Circulation: 5,550
Available in microform: Yes, through Univ. Microfilms International
Subscription price: $44.00/yr. institutions; $24.00/yr. individuals & school libraries
Year to which price refers: 1992
Subscription address: Duke Univ. Press, P.O. Box 6697 College Station, Durham, NC 27708
Subscription telephone: 919 684-2173

ADVERTISING INFORMATION

Advertising accepted: Yes
Advertising rates: $200.00/half page; $300.00/full page

EDITORIAL DESCRIPTION

Scope: Publishes scholarly and critical writings on American literature: literary history, criticism, bibliography.
Reviews books: Yes
Publishes notes: Yes
Languages accepted: English
Prints abstracts: No
Author-anonymous submission: No

SUBMISSION REQUIREMENTS

Restrictions on contributors: Unsolicited reviews are not accepted.
Author pays submission fee: No
Author pays page charges: No
Length of articles: 7,500 words
Length of book reviews: 500 words
Length of notes: 1,500 words
Style: Chicago
Number of copies required: 1
Special requirements: Submit original, double-spaced typescript.
Copyright ownership: Duke Univ. Press
Rejected manuscripts: Returned; enclose return postage.
Time before publication decision: 3 mos.
Time between decision and publication: 1 yr.
Number of reviewers: 2
Articles submitted per year: 425
Articles published per year: 25-30
Book reviews published per year: 140
Notes published per year: 2-3

(105)
*The American Novel

Emory Elliot, Editor
Cambridge Univ. Press
40 West 20th St.
New York, NY 10011

Telephone: 212 924-3900 ext. 409
Fax: 212 691-3239
MLA acronym: AmNov

EDITORIAL DESCRIPTION

Scope: Publishes critical guides to American novels. Each volume is devoted to a single novel and includes an introduction which presents details of the novel's composition, publication history, and contemporary reception, in addition to essays which present a distinct point of view.
Reviews books: No
Publishes notes: No
Languages accepted: English
Prints abstracts: No
Author-anonymous submission: No

SUBMISSION REQUIREMENTS

Length of books: 125 pp. maximum
Number of copies required: 2
Copyright ownership: Cambridge Univ. Press
Time before publication decision: 3-6 mos.
Time between decision and publication: 1 yr.
Books published per year: 3-6

(106)
*American Periodicals: A Journal of History, Criticism, and Bibliography

James T. F. Tanner, Editor
Dept. of English
Univ. of North Texas
P.O. Box 5096, UNT
Denton, TX 76203-5096

Additional editorial address: David E. E. Sloane, Book Review Editor, Dept. of English, Univ. of New Haven, West Haven, CT 06516
Telephone: 817 565-2134; 817 565-2124
Fax: 817 565-6464
First published: 1991
Sponsoring organization: Research Soc. for American Periodicals
ISSN: 1054-7479
MLA acronym: AmPer

SUBSCRIPTION INFORMATION

Frequency of publication: Annual
Circulation: 500
Subscription price: $15.00/yr.
Year to which price refers: 1991

ADVERTISING INFORMATION

Advertising accepted: Yes
Advertising rates: $25.00/half page; $50.00/full page

EDITORIAL DESCRIPTION

Scope: Publishes articles that treat any aspect of American periodicals, both magazines and newspapers, from the beginnings of American culture to the present. Submissions that treat such topics as the editorial policy, financing, production, readership, design, illustration, and circulation of one or more periodicals are welcome, as are those which explore the position of American periodicals within the larger culture. Articles which cross the boundaries of several disciplines and explore the complex ways that periodicals have shaped, and have been shaped by, American culture are particularly welcome.
Reviews books: Yes
Publishes notes: Yes
Languages accepted: English
Prints abstracts: No

SUBMISSION REQUIREMENTS

Author pays submission fee: No
Author pays page charges: No
Length of articles: 3,000-6,000 words
Length of book reviews: 1,000 words
Style: MLA
Number of copies required: 2
Special requirements: Submit typescript and 5.25 in. diskette using WordPerfect. Include a complete list of works cited.
Rejected manuscripts: Returned; enclose return postage and SAE
Time before publication decision: 2-4 mos.
Time between decision and publication: 6-18 mos.
Number of reviewers: 2-5
Articles submitted per year: 25
Articles published per year: 8
Book reviews published per year: 10-12

(107)
*The American Poetry Review

David Bonanno, Stephen Berg, & Arthur Vogelsang, Editors
1721 Walnut St.
Philadelphia, PA 19103

Telephone: 215 496-0439
First published: 1972
ISSN: 0360-3709
MLA acronym: APR

SUBSCRIPTION INFORMATION

Frequency of publication: 6 times/yr.
Circulation: 20,000
Available in microform: Yes
Subscription price: $14.00/yr.
Year to which price refers: 1992
Subscription address: Dept. S, at the above address

ADVERTISING INFORMATION

Advertising accepted: Yes
Advertising rates: $725.00/full page

EDITORIAL DESCRIPTION

Scope: Publishes poetry, criticism, fiction, columns, translations, and interviews.
Reviews books: Yes
Publishes notes: Yes
Languages accepted: English
Prints abstracts: No
Author-anonymous submission: No

SUBMISSION REQUIREMENTS

Restrictions on contributors: None
Author pays submission fee: No
Author pays page charges: No
Length of articles: 3,000 words
Length of book reviews: 3,000 words
Length of notes: 1,000 words
Style: Chicago
Number of copies required: 1
Copyright ownership: Author
Rejected manuscripts: Returned; enclose return postage.
Time before publication decision: 2-3 mos.
Time between decision and publication: 6-24 mos.
Number of reviewers: 3
Articles submitted per year: 1,000
Articles published per year: 24

(108)
*American Psychologist

Raymond D. Fowler, Editor
American Psychological Assn.
750 First St. NE
Washington, DC 20002-4242

Telephone: 202 336-6010
First published: 1946
Sponsoring organization: American Psychological Assn.
ISSN: 0003-066X
MLA acronym: AmP

SUBSCRIPTION INFORMATION

Frequency of publication: 12 times/yr.
Circulation: 90,000
Available in microform: Yes
Subscription price: $120.00/yr. individuals
Year to which price refers: 1992
Subscription address: Subscription Dept., at the above address
Subscription telephone: 202 336-5600

ADVERTISING INFORMATION

Advertising accepted: Yes
Advertising rates: Contact Advertising Dept. at: 202 336-5565

EDITORIAL DESCRIPTION

Scope: Contains archival documents. Also publishes articles on current issues in psychology, and theoretical articles on broad aspects of psychology.
Reviews books: No
Publishes notes: Yes
Languages accepted: English
Prints abstracts: Yes
Author-anonymous submission: Yes

SUBMISSION REQUIREMENTS

Restrictions on contributors: Contributors must hold terminal degrees in their field.
Author pays submission fee: No
Author pays page charges: No
Length of articles: 6,000-7,000 words
Length of notes: 250-500 words
Style: American Psychological Assn.
Number of copies required: 5
Special requirements: Include a 100-120 word abstract.
Copyright ownership: American Psychological Assn.
Rejected manuscripts: 3 copies returned
Time before publication decision: 11 mos. maximum
Time between decision and publication: 6 mos.
Number of reviewers: 3
Articles submitted per year: 500
Articles published per year: 55
Notes submitted per year: 100
Notes published per year: 30

(109)
*American Quarterly

Gary Kulik, Editor
Room 4601
National Museum of American History
Smithsonian Inst.
Washington, DC 20560

Telephone: 202 357-1853
First published: 1949
Sponsoring organization: American Studies Assn.
ISSN: 0003-0678
MLA acronym: AQ

SUBSCRIPTION INFORMATION

Frequency of publication: 4 times/yr. (Spring, Summer, Fall, Winter)
Circulation: 5,000
Available in microform: Yes
Subscription price: $55.50/yr. institutions US; $59.50/yr. institutions Canada & Mexico; $65.80/yr. institutions elsewhere
Year to which price refers: 1993
Subscription address: Johns Hopkins Univ. Press, Journals Publishing Division, 2715 North Charles St., Baltimore, MD 21218-4319
Subscription telephone: 800 537-5487
Subscription fax: 410 516-6998

ADVERTISING INFORMATION

Advertising accepted: Yes

EDITORIAL DESCRIPTION

Scope: Editors and contributors concern themselves not only with the areas of American life which they know best but with the relation of those areas to the entire American scene and to world society. Publishes interdisciplinary articles dealing with all aspects of American life, including history, literature, religion, art, music, politics, folklore, customs, popular culture, women's studies, and minority studies.
Reviews books: Yes
Publishes notes: No
Languages accepted: English
Prints abstracts: No
Author-anonymous submission: Yes

SUBMISSION REQUIREMENTS

Restrictions on contributors: None
Author pays submission fee: No
Author pays page charges: No
Length of articles: 30 typescript pp. including footnotes
Length of book reviews: 10 typescript pp.
Style: Chicago
Number of copies required: 3
Copyright ownership: Assigned by author to American Studies Assn.
Rejected manuscripts: Returned; enclose return postage.
Time before publication decision: 4 mos.
Time between decision and publication: 1 yr.
Number of reviewers: 2 plus Editorial Board
Articles submitted per year: 250
Articles published per year: 12-16
Book reviews published per year: 28

(110)
*The American Scholar

Joseph Epstein, Editor
1811 Q St., NW
Washington, DC 20009

Telephone: 202 265-3808
First published: 1932
Sponsoring organization: Phi Beta Kappa
ISSN: 0003-0937
MLA acronym: ASch

SUBSCRIPTION INFORMATION

Frequency of publication: 4 times/yr. (Mar., June, Sept., Dec.)
Circulation: 26,000
Available in microform: Yes
Subscription price: $21.00/yr., $38.00/2 yrs.
Year to which price refers: 1992

ADVERTISING INFORMATION

Advertising accepted: Yes
Advertising rates: $675.00/full page

EDITORIAL DESCRIPTION

Scope: Publishes articles on the arts, sciences, social sciences, and literature. Articles should be written in non-technical language for an intelligent audience. Fills the gap between learned journals and good magazines for a popular audience.
Reviews books: Yes
Publishes notes: No
Languages accepted: English
Prints abstracts: No
Author-anonymous submission: No

SUBMISSION REQUIREMENTS

Restrictions on contributors: None
Author pays submission fee: No
Author pays page charges: No
Length of articles: 3,500-5,000 words
Length of book reviews: 1,500-2,000 words
Style: Chicago preferred
Number of copies required: 1

Special requirements: Submit original double-spaced typescript.
Copyright ownership: Author
Rejected manuscripts: Returned; enclose SASE.
Time before publication decision: 2-4 weeks
Time between decision and publication: 3-6 mos.
Number of reviewers: 2 plus Editorial Board & Editor
Articles submitted per year: 500
Articles published per year: 40
Book reviews submitted per year: 250
Book reviews published per year: 25-30

(111)
*The American Sephardi: Journal of the Sephardic Studies Program of Yeshiva University

Herman P. Salomon & Tomás L. Ryan, Editors
c/o Rabbi M. Mitchell Serels
Yeshiva Univ.
500 West 185 St.
New York, NY 10033

Telephone: 212 960-5235
Fax: 212 960-5228
First published: 1967
Sponsoring organization: Yeshiva Univ.
ISSN: 0003-102X
MLA acronym: AmSeph

SUBSCRIPTION INFORMATION

Frequency of publication: Irregular
Circulation: 4,000
Available in microform: No
Subscription price: $15.00/yr.
Year to which price refers: 1992

ADVERTISING INFORMATION

Advertising accepted: No

EDITORIAL DESCRIPTION

Scope: Publishes Sephardic studies.
Reviews books: Yes
Publishes notes: Yes
Languages accepted: English; French; Spanish
Prints abstracts: No

SUBMISSION REQUIREMENTS

Restrictions on contributors: None
Author pays submission fee: No
Author pays page charges: No
Length of articles: 6-10 pp.
Length of book reviews: 400 words
Style: None
Number of copies required: 3
Copyright ownership: Yeshiva Univ.
Rejected manuscripts: Returned at author's request
Time before publication decision: 3 mos.
Time between decision and publication: 7 mos.
Number of reviewers: 5
Articles submitted per year: 20
Articles published per year: 10
Book reviews published per year: 6

(112)
*American Speech: A Quarterly of Linguistic Usage

Ronald R. Butters, Editor
English Dept.
Duke Univ.
Durham, NC 27706

Telephone: 919 684-6561
Fax: 919 684-4871
First published: 1925
Sponsoring organization: American Dialect Soc.
ISSN: 0003-1283
MLA acronym: AS

SUBSCRIPTION INFORMATION

Frequency of publication: 4 times/yr. (Mar., June, Sept., Dec.)
Circulation: 1,800
Available in microform: Yes
Subscription price: $25.00/yr.
Year to which price refers: 1992
Subscription address: Allan Metcalf, Executive Secretary, American Dialect Soc., MacMurray College, Jacksonville, IL 62650
Additional subscription address: Journals Dept., Univ. of Alabama Press, Box 870380, Tuscaloosa, AL 35487-0380
Subscription telephone: 217 245-6151
Subscription fax: 217 245-5214

ADVERTISING INFORMATION

Advertising accepted: No

EDITORIAL DESCRIPTION

Scope: Concerned with the English language in the western hemisphere, although contributions dealing with English in other parts of the world, with other languages influencing English or influenced by it, and with general linguistic theory may also be submitted. Welcomes articles dealing with current usage, dialectology, and the history and structure of English. Is not committed to any particular theoretical framework, but preference is given to articles that are likely to be of interest to a wide readership.
Reviews books: Yes
Publishes notes: Yes
Languages accepted: English
Prints abstracts: No
Author-anonymous submission: Yes

SUBMISSION REQUIREMENTS

Restrictions on contributors: None
Author pays submission fee: No
Author pays page charges: No
Length of articles: 2,000-8,000 words
Length of book reviews: 750-2,500 words
Length of notes: 1,500 words maximum
Style: MLA
Number of copies required: 2
Special requirements: Articles accepted for publication must be submitted on diskette.
Copyright ownership: Univ. of Alabama Press
Rejected manuscripts: Returned; enclose return postage.
Time before publication decision: 6 mos.
Time between decision and publication: 15 mos.
Number of reviewers: 3
Articles submitted per year: 100
Articles published per year: 25
Book reviews submitted per year: 15
Book reviews published per year: 15
Notes submitted per year: 100
Notes published per year: 25

(113)
*American Studies

David Katzman & Norman Yetman, Editors
2120 Wescoe
Univ. of Kansas
Lawrence, KS 66045

Telephone: 913 864-4878
First published: 1960
Sponsoring organization: Mid-America American Studies Assn., Univ. of Kansas
ISSN: 0026-3079
MLA acronym: AmerS

SUBSCRIPTION INFORMATION

Frequency of publication: 2 times/yr. (Spring, Fall)
Circulation: 1,600
Available in microform: Yes

Subscription price: $25.00/yr. institutions; $15.00/yr. individuals; add $8.00/yr. outside US
Year to which price refers: 1993
Subscription address: Business Manager, at the above address

ADVERTISING INFORMATION

Advertising accepted: Yes
Advertising rates: $150.00/full page; $200.00/ inside cover; $250.00/back cover

EDITORIAL DESCRIPTION

Scope: The journal is an interdisciplinary magazine concerned with American culture and society approached through history, literature, political science, sociology, anthropology, art, architecture, and music. Accepts articles in these fields when the work reported is clearly of interest to Americanists in general.
Reviews books: Yes
Publishes notes: Yes
Languages accepted: English
Prints abstracts: No
Author-anonymous submission: Yes

SUBMISSION REQUIREMENTS

Restrictions on contributors: Unsolicited reviews or reviews written by graduate students are not accepted.
Author pays submission fee: No
Author pays page charges: No
Length of articles: 20-30 typescript pp.
Length of book reviews: 100-250 words
Style: Journal
Number of copies required: 4
Special requirements: Submit a signed statement that the essay is not being submitted elsewhere and 100-word abstract.
Copyright ownership: Mid-America American Studies Assn.
Rejected manuscripts: Returned at author's request
Time before publication decision: 4 mos.
Time between decision and publication: 6-12 mos.
Number of reviewers: 3
Articles submitted per year: 75
Articles published per year: 10
Book reviews published per year: 30-50

(114)
*American Studies in Scandinavia

Niels Thorsen, Paul Levine, & Niels Bjerre-Poulsen, Editors
Dept. of English
Univ. of Copenhagen
Njalsgade 84
2300 Copenhagen S, Denmark

Telephone: (45) 31 542211
First published: 1969
Sponsoring organization: Nordic Assn. for American Studies
ISSN: 0044-8060
MLA acronym: AmStScan

SUBSCRIPTION INFORMATION

Frequency of publication: 2 times/yr.
Circulation: 450
Available in microform: Yes
Subscription price: 140 Dkr/yr. Scandinavia; $28.00/yr. elsewhere
Year to which price refers: 1992

ADVERTISING INFORMATION

Advertising accepted: Yes
Advertising rates: $200.00/full page

EDITORIAL DESCRIPTION

Scope: Publishes articles on American studies, including American literature and American history, written by Scandinavians.
Reviews books: Yes
Publishes notes: Yes
Languages accepted: English
Prints abstracts: No
Author-anonymous submission: No

SUBMISSION REQUIREMENTS

Restrictions on contributors: Contributors must be scholars in Scandinavian countries or visiting scholars.
Author pays submission fee: No
Author pays page charges: No
Length of articles: 10,000-11,000 words
Length of book reviews: 1,000 words
Length of notes: 500 words
Style: MLA
Number of copies required: 1
Copyright ownership: Nordic Assn. for American Studies
Rejected manuscripts: Returned
Time before publication decision: 3 mos.
Time between decision and publication: 4-6 mos.
Number of reviewers: 2-3
Articles submitted per year: 15-25
Articles published per year: 8-9
Book reviews submitted per year: 25-30
Book reviews published per year: 20-25
Notes submitted per year: 8-10
Notes published per year: 8-10

(115)
*American Studies International

Bernard Mergen, Senior Editor
George Washington Univ.
2108 G. St.
Washington, DC 20052

Telephone: 202 994-7368
Fax: 202 994-0458
First published: 1962
Sponsoring organization: George Washington Univ.
ISSN: 0003-1321
MLA acronym: ASInt

SUBSCRIPTION INFORMATION

Frequency of publication: 2 times/yr. (Apr., Oct.) plus 2 newsletters/yr. (Jan., July)
Circulation: 2,000
Available in microform: Yes, through Univ. Microfilms International
Subscription price: $30.00/yr. institutions US; $22.00/yr. individuals US; $30.00/yr. elsewhere
Year to which price refers: 1992

ADVERTISING INFORMATION

Advertising accepted: Yes
Advertising rates: Journal: $150.00/full page; $175.00/inside back cover. Newsletter: $100.00/half back cover

EDITORIAL DESCRIPTION

Scope: Includes bibliographic essays on American studies, original articles by foreign scholars, and book reviews.
Reviews books: Yes
Publishes notes: No
Languages accepted: English
Prints abstracts: No
Author-anonymous submission: No

SUBMISSION REQUIREMENTS

Restrictions on contributors: Bibliographic essays are accepted only from US scholars; original articles by foreign scholars are accepted. Reviews are written by journal's staff.
Author pays submission fee: No
Author pays page charges: No
Length of articles: 5,000-10,000 words
Length of book reviews: 500 words
Style: Chicago
Number of copies required: 1
Special requirements: Bibliographers should cite least expensive paperback editions when possible.
Copyright ownership: George Washington Univ.
Rejected manuscripts: Returned at author's request
Time before publication decision: 3 mos.
Time between decision and publication: 6 mos.
Number of reviewers: 3
Articles submitted per year: 15-20
Articles published per year: 10-12
Book reviews published per year: 70-100

(116)
*American Transcendental Quarterly

Josie P. Campbell, Editor
Dept. of English
Univ. of Rhode Island
Kingston, RI 02881-0812

Telephone: 401 792-2576
First published: 1969
ISSN: 0149-9017
MLA acronym: ATQ

SUBSCRIPTION INFORMATION

Frequency of publication: 4 times/yr.
Circulation: 400
Available in microform: Yes
Subscription price: $25.00/yr. US; $26.00/yr. elsewhere
Year to which price refers: 1992

ADVERTISING INFORMATION

Advertising accepted: No

EDITORIAL DESCRIPTION

Scope: Publishes studies of literary works and authors, as well as nontechnical articles on all other aspects of 19th-century American culture and society.
Reviews books: No
Publishes notes: No
Languages accepted: English
Prints abstracts: No
Author-anonymous submission: Yes

SUBMISSION REQUIREMENTS

Restrictions on contributors: None
Author pays submission fee: No
Author pays page charges: No
Length of articles: 3,000-7,500 words
Style: MLA
Number of copies required: 1
Copyright ownership: Univ. of Rhode Island
Rejected manuscripts: Returned
Time before publication decision: 6 weeks maximum
Time between decision and publication: 6 mos.
Number of reviewers: 3
Articles submitted per year: 50
Articles published per year: 28-30

(117)
*American Translators Association Series

Marilyn Gaddis Rose, Editor
Center for Research in Translation
P.O. Box 6000
State Univ. of New York
Binghamton, NY 13902-6000

Telephone: 607 777-6765

Fax: 607 777-4000
First published: 1987
Sponsoring organization: American Translators Assn.; State Univ. of New York, Binghamton
ISSN: 0890-4111
MLA acronym: ATAS

SUBSCRIPTION INFORMATION

Frequency of publication: Annual
Circulation: 500
Available in microform: No
Subscription price: $25.00/yr.
Year to which price refers: 1991

ADVERTISING INFORMATION

Advertising accepted: No

EDITORIAL DESCRIPTION

Scope: Publishes monographs on issues in translation as an art and as a profession, as well as issues in translation studies.
Reviews books: No
Publishes notes: No
Languages accepted: English
Prints abstracts: No
Author-anonymous submission: No

SUBMISSION REQUIREMENTS

Restrictions on contributors: All essays are solicited by guest editor.
Author pays submission fee: No
Author pays page charges: No
Length of articles: 2,500-3,000 words
Style: MLA
Number of copies required: 1
Special requirements: Submit typescript and 1 diskette.
Copyright ownership: State Univ. of New York at Binghamton
Rejected manuscripts: Returned
Time before publication decision: 2-4 weeks
Time between decision and publication: 1 yr.
Number of reviewers: 2-3
Articles submitted per year: 25-30
Articles published per year: 15-20

(118)
*American University Studies I: Germanic Languages and Literature

Michael J. Flamini, Editor
Peter Lang Publishing, Inc.
62 West 45th St., 4th Floor
New York, NY 10036-4202

Telephone: 212 302-6740
Fax: 212 302-7574
ISSN: 0721-1392
MLA acronym: GLL

SUBSCRIPTION INFORMATION

Available in microform: No
Subscription telephone: 212 764-1471

ADVERTISING INFORMATION

Advertising accepted: No

EDITORIAL DESCRIPTION

Scope: Publishes monographs and critical texts in the humanities with an emphasis on Germanic languages and literature.
Languages accepted: English; French; German; Spanish; Italian
Author-anonymous submission: No

SUBMISSION REQUIREMENTS

Restrictions on contributors: None
Author pays submission fee: No
Author pays page charges: No
Style: MLA
Number of copies required: 1
Copyright ownership: Peter Lang Publishing, Inc.
Rejected manuscripts: Returned; enclose return postage
Time before publication decision: 3-6 mos.
Time between decision and publication: 9 mos.
Number of reviewers: 1-4
Books submitted per year: 180
Books published per year: 60

(119)
*American University Studies II: Romance Languages and Literature

Michael J. Flamini, Editor
Peter Lang Publishing, Inc.
62 West 45th St., 4th Floor
New York, NY 10036-4202

Telephone: 212 302-6740
Fax: 212 302-7574
First published: 1982
ISSN: 0740-9257
MLA acronym: RLL

SUBSCRIPTION INFORMATION

Available in microform: No
Subscription telephone: 212 764-1471

ADVERTISING INFORMATION

Advertising accepted: No

EDITORIAL DESCRIPTION

Scope: Publishes monographs and critical texts in the humanities with an emphasis on French and Spanish literature.
Author-anonymous submission: No

SUBMISSION REQUIREMENTS

Restrictions on contributors: None
Author pays submission fee: No
Author pays page charges: No
Length of books: 200 pp. minimum
Style: MLA
Number of copies required: 1
Copyright ownership: Peter Lang Publishing, Inc.
Rejected manuscripts: Returned; enclose return postage
Time before publication decision: 3-6 mos.
Time between decision and publication: 9 mos.
Number of reviewers: 1-4
Books submitted per year: 150
Books published per year: 25-30

(120)
*American University Studies III: Comparative Literature

Michael J. Flamini, Editor
Peter Lang Publishing, Inc.
62 West 45th St., 4th Floor
New York, NY 10036-4202

Telephone: 212 302-6740
Fax: 212 302-7574
ISSN: 0724-1445
MLA acronym: CompL

SUBSCRIPTION INFORMATION

Available in microform: No
Subscription telephone: 212 764-1471

ADVERTISING INFORMATION

Advertising accepted: No

EDITORIAL DESCRIPTION

Scope: Publishes monographs and critical texts in the humanities with an emphasis on comparative literature.
Languages accepted: English; French; German; Spanish; Italian
Prints abstracts: No
Author-anonymous submission: No

SUBMISSION REQUIREMENTS

Restrictions on contributors: None
Author pays submission fee: No
Author pays page charges: No
Style: MLA
Number of copies required: 1
Copyright ownership: Peter Lang Publishing, Inc.
Rejected manuscripts: Returned; enclose return postage
Time before publication decision: 3-6 mos.
Time between decision and publication: 9 mos.
Number of reviewers: 1-4
Books submitted per year: 50
Books published per year: 6

(121)
*American University Studies IV: English Language and Literature

Michael J. Flamini, Editor
Peter Lang Publishing, Inc.
62 West 45th St., 4th Floor
New York, NY 10036-4202

Telephone: 212 302-6740
Fax: 212 302-7574
First published: 1982
ISSN: 0741-0700
MLA acronym: EL&L

SUBSCRIPTION INFORMATION

Available in microform: No
Subscription telephone: 212 764-1471

ADVERTISING INFORMATION

Advertising accepted: No

EDITORIAL DESCRIPTION

Scope: Publishes monographs and critical texts in the humanities with an emphasis on English language and literature.
Languages accepted: English; French; German; Spanish; Italian
Author-anonymous submission: No

SUBMISSION REQUIREMENTS

Restrictions on contributors: None
Author pays submission fee: No
Author pays page charges: No
Style: MLA
Number of copies required: 1
Copyright ownership: Peter Lang Publishing, Inc.
Rejected manuscripts: Returned; enclose return postage
Time before publication decision: 3-6 mos.
Time between decision and publication: 9 mos.
Number of reviewers: 1-4
Books submitted per year: 200
Books published per year: 40-50

(122)
*American University Studies XII: Slavic Languages and Literature

Michael J. Flamini, Editor
Peter Lang Publishing, Inc.
62 West 45th St., 4th Floor
New York, NY 10036-4202

Telephone: 212 302-6740
Fax: 212 302-7574
First published: 1982
ISSN: 0740-0497
MLA acronym: SL&Li

SUBSCRIPTION INFORMATION

Available in microform: No
Subscription telephone: 212 764-1471

ADVERTISING INFORMATION

Advertising accepted: No

EDITORIAL DESCRIPTION

Scope: Publishes monographs and critical texts in the humanities with an emphasis on Slavic languages and literature.
Languages accepted: English; French; German; Spanish; Italian

SUBMISSION REQUIREMENTS

Restrictions on contributors: None
Author pays submission fee: No
Author pays page charges: No
Style: MLA
Number of copies required: 1
Copyright ownership: Peter Lang Publishing, Inc.
Rejected manuscripts: Returned; enclose return postage
Time before publication decision: 3-6 mos.
Time between decision and publication: 9 mos.
Number of reviewers: 1-4
Books submitted per year: 50
Books published per year: 6

(123)
*American University Studies XIII: Linguistics

Michael J. Flamini, Editor
Peter Lang Publishing, Inc.
42 West 45th St., 4th Floor
New York, NY 10036-4202

Telephone: 212 302-6740
Fax: 212 302-7574
First published: 1982
ISSN: 0740-4557
MLA acronym: Ling

SUBSCRIPTION INFORMATION

Available in microform: No
Subscription telephone: 212 764-1471

ADVERTISING INFORMATION

Advertising accepted: No

EDITORIAL DESCRIPTION

Scope: Publishes monographs and critical texts in the humanities with an emphasis on linguistics.
Languages accepted: English; French; German; Spanish; Italian
Author-anonymous submission: No

SUBMISSION REQUIREMENTS

Restrictions on contributors: None
Author pays submission fee: No
Author pays page charges: No
Length of books: 150 pp. minimum
Style: MLA
Number of copies required: 1
Copyright ownership: Peter Lang Publishing, Inc.
Rejected manuscripts: Returned; enclose return postage
Time before publication decision: 3-6 mos.
Time between decision and publication: 9 mos.
Number of reviewers: 1-4
Books submitted per year: 15
Books published per year: 2

(124)
*American University Studies XVIII: African Literature

Michael J. Flamini, Editor
Peter Lang Publishing, Inc.
62 West 45th St., 4th Floor
New York, NY 10036-4202

Telephone: 212 302-6740
Fax: 212 302-7574
ISSN: 0742-1923
MLA acronym: AfrLit

SUBSCRIPTION INFORMATION

Available in microform: No
Subscription telephone: 212 764-1471

ADVERTISING INFORMATION

Advertising accepted: No

EDITORIAL DESCRIPTION

Scope: Publishes monographs and critical texts in the humanities with an emphasis on African literature.
Languages accepted: English; French; German; Spanish; Italian
Author-anonymous submission: No

SUBMISSION REQUIREMENTS

Restrictions on contributors: None
Author pays submission fee: No
Author pays page charges: No
Style: MLA
Number of copies required: 1
Copyright ownership: Peter Lang Publishing, Inc.
Rejected manuscripts: Returned; enclose return postage
Time before publication decision: 3-6 mos.
Time between decision and publication: 9 mos.
Number of reviewers: 1-4
Books submitted per year: 20
Books published per year: 2

(125)
*American University Studies XIX: General Literature

Michael J. Flamini, Editor
Peter Lang Publishing, Inc.
62 West 45th St., 4th Floor
New York, NY 10036-4202

Telephone: 212 302-6740
Fax: 212 302-7574
First published: 1982
ISSN: 0743-6645
MLA acronym: GenL

SUBSCRIPTION INFORMATION

Frequency of publication: Irregular
Available in microform: No
Subscription telephone: 212 764-1471

ADVERTISING INFORMATION

Advertising accepted: No

EDITORIAL DESCRIPTION

Scope: Publishes monographs and critical texts in the humanities with an emphasis on literary theory and literary criticism.
Languages accepted: English; French; German; Spanish; Italian
Author-anonymous submission: No

SUBMISSION REQUIREMENTS

Restrictions on contributors: None
Author pays submission fee: No
Author pays page charges: No
Length of books: 150 pp. minimun
Style: MLA
Number of copies required: 1
Copyright ownership: Peter Lang Publishing, Inc.
Rejected manuscripts: Returned; enclose return postage
Time before publication decision: 3-6 mos.
Time between decision and publication: 9 mos.
Number of reviewers: 1-4
Books submitted per year: 15
Books published per year: 4

(126)
*American University Studies XXII: Latin American Literature

Michael J. Flamini, Editor
Peter Lang Publishing Co.
62 West 45th St., 4th Floor
New York, NY 10036-4202

Telephone: 212 302-6740
Fax: 212 302-7574
First published: 1988
ISSN: 0895-0490
MLA acronym: LatAL

SUBSCRIPTION INFORMATION

Available in microform: No
Subscription telephone: 212 764-1471

ADVERTISING INFORMATION

Advertising accepted: No

EDITORIAL DESCRIPTION

Scope: Publishes monographs and critical texts in the humanities with an emphasis on Latin American literature.
Languages accepted: English; Spanish; Portuguese
Author-anonymous submission: No

SUBMISSION REQUIREMENTS

Restrictions on contributors: None
Author pays submission fee: No
Author pays page charges: No
Length of books: 150 pp. minimum
Style: MLA
Number of copies required: 1
Copyright ownership: Peter Lang Publishing, Inc.
Rejected manuscripts: Returned; enclose return postage
Time before publication decision: 9 mos.
Time between decision and publication: 6 weeks minimum
Number of reviewers: 3

(127)
*American University Studies XXIV: American Literature

Michael J. Flamini, Editor
Peter Lang Publishing, Inc.
62 West 45th St., 4th Floor
New York, NY 10036-4202

Telephone: 212 302-6740
Fax: 212 302-7574
First published: 1988
ISSN: 0895-0512
MLA acronym: AmLit

SUBSCRIPTION INFORMATION

Available in microform: No
Subscription telephone: 212 764-1471

ADVERTISING INFORMATION

Advertising accepted: No

EDITORIAL DESCRIPTION

Scope: Publishes monographs and critical texts in the humanities with an emphasis on American literature.
Languages accepted: English; French; German; Spanish; Italian
Author-anonymous submission: No

SUBMISSION REQUIREMENTS

Restrictions on contributors: None
Author pays submission fee: No
Author pays page charges: No
Length of books: 200-300 pp.
Style: MLA
Number of copies required: 1
Copyright ownership: Peter Lang Publishing, Inc.
Rejected manuscripts: Returned; enclose return postage.
Time before publication decision: 3-6 mos.
Time between decision and publication: 9 mos.
Number of reviewers: 2
Books submitted per year: 50
Books published per year: 10

(128)
*Américas

Rebecca Read Medrano, Editor
19th & Constitution Ave., NW
Washington, DC 20006

Telephone: 202 458-6218
Fax: 201 458-6217
First published: 1948
Sponsoring organization: Organization of American States
ISSN: 0003-1577
MLA acronym: Américas

SUBSCRIPTION INFORMATION

Frequency of publication: 6 times/yr.
Circulation: 50,000
Available in microform: Yes
Subscription price: $15.00/yr.
Year to which price refers: 1992
Subscription address: Américas Subscription Service Dept., P.O. Box 2103, Knoxville, IA 50197
Subscription telephone: 800 284-6746

ADVERTISING INFORMATION

Advertising accepted: No

EDITORIAL DESCRIPTION

Scope: To promote mutual understanding among the peoples of the member nations of the Organization of American States by publishing articles on apolitical topics of general interest. Focuses on Latin American culture, art, history, and happenings.
Reviews books: Yes
Publishes notes: Yes
Languages accepted: English; Spanish
Prints abstracts: No
Author-anonymous submission: No

SUBMISSION REQUIREMENTS

Restrictions on contributors: None
Author pays submission fee: No
Author pays page charges: No
Length of articles: 2,000-4,000 words
Length of book reviews: 650 words
Style: MLA
Number of copies required: 1
Special requirements: Provide original version of translated quotations.
Copyright ownership: Author on request
Rejected manuscripts: Not returned
Time before publication decision: 2-3 mos.
Time between decision and publication: 3 mos.
Number of reviewers: 4
Articles submitted per year: 500
Articles published per year: 66
Book reviews published per year: 40
Notes published per year: 24

(129)
The Americas Review: A Review of Hispanic Literature and Art of the USA

Julián Olivares & Evangelina Vigil-Piñón, Editors
Univ. of Houston
Houston, TX 77204-2090

Telephone: 713 749-4768
Fax: 713 749-2499
First published: 1973
ISSN: 1042-6213
MLA acronym: AmRev

SUBSCRIPTION INFORMATION

Frequency of publication: 3 times/yr.
Circulation: 1,500
Available in microform: No

ADVERTISING INFORMATION

Advertising accepted: Yes

EDITORIAL DESCRIPTION

Scope: Primarily publishes creative literature and art by U.S. Hispanics. Also includes literary criticism and book reviews of Chicano, Puerto Rican, and Latino literature.
Reviews books: Yes
Publishes notes: No
Languages accepted: English; Spanish
Prints abstracts: No
Author-anonymous submission: No

SUBMISSION REQUIREMENTS

Restrictions on contributors: Subscription is required upon submission of creative work and articles. In exchange, in the case of rejections, the submitter receives editorial comments. Authors of creative work receive a payment of not less than $25.00. Book reviews are solicited by editor.
Author pays submission fee: No
Author pays page charges: No
Length of articles: 25 pp. maximum
Length of book reviews: 500-1,000 words
Style: MLA
Number of copies required: 2
Copyright ownership: Journal
Rejected manuscripts: Returned; enclose SASE.
Time before publication decision: 3 mos.
Time between decision and publication: 1 yr.
Number of reviewers: 3
Articles submitted per year: 120
Articles published per year: 20
Book reviews published per year: 15-20

(130)
*Amerikastudien/American Studies

Alfred Hornung, Reinhard R. Doerries, Renate Hof, Gerhard Hoffmann, Heinz Ickstadt, & Peter Lösche, Editors
Seminar für Englische Philologie
Amerikanistische Abteilung
Johannes Gutenberg-Univ.
Jakob Welder-Weg 18
6500 Mainz, Germany

Telephone: (49) 6131 392146
Fax: (49) 6131 395100
First published: 1956
Sponsoring organization: Deutsche Gesellschaft für Amerikastudien
ISSN: 0340-2827
MLA acronym: Amst

SUBSCRIPTION INFORMATION

Frequency of publication: 4 times/yr.
Circulation: 1,000
Available in microform: No
Subscription price: 112 DM/yr.
Year to which price refers: 1992
Subscription address: Wilhelm Fink GmbH., Ohmstr. 5, 8000 Munich 40, Germany
Additional subscription address: Schöningh Verlag, Postfach 2540, 4790 Paderborn, Germany
Subscription telephone: (49) 5251 290167
Subscription fax: (49) 5251 290135

ADVERTISING INFORMATION

Advertising accepted: Yes
Advertising rates: 200 DM/half page; 380 DM/full page

EDITORIAL DESCRIPTION

Scope: Publishes articles on American language, literature, history, politics, culture, and sociology.
Reviews books: Yes
Publishes notes: Yes
Languages accepted: English; German
Prints abstracts: Yes
Author-anonymous submission: Yes

SUBMISSION REQUIREMENTS

Restrictions on contributors: None
Author pays submission fee: No
Author pays page charges: No
Length of articles: 20 pp.
Length of book reviews: 500-1,000 words
Length of notes: 200-300 words
Style: MLA
Number of copies required: 2
Special requirements: Include a 200-word summary in English.
Copyright ownership: Wilhelm Fink Verlag; Reverts to author 1 yr. after publication
Rejected manuscripts: Returned; enclose return postage.
Time before publication decision: 6 mos.
Time between decision and publication: 6 mos.
Number of reviewers: 2-3
Articles submitted per year: 150
Articles published per year: 30
Book reviews submitted per year: 100
Book reviews published per year: 50
Notes submitted per year: 20
Notes published per year: 10

(131)
***Amerikastudien/American Studies: A Monograph Series**

Gerhard Hoffmann, Reinhard R. Dörries, & Alfred Hornung, Editors
Inst. for English Philology
Univ. Würzburg
Am Hubland
8700 Würzburg, Germany

Telephone: (49) 931 8885656
Fax: (49) 931 8884615
First published: 1957
Sponsoring organization: Deutsche Gesellschaft für Amerikastudien
MLA acronym: AmStudies

SUBSCRIPTION INFORMATION

Frequency of publication: 3-5 times/yr.
Circulation: 500
Available in microform: No
Subscription address: Wilhelm Fink Verlag, Ohmstr. 5, 8000 Munich 40, Germany

ADVERTISING INFORMATION

Advertising accepted: No

EDITORIAL DESCRIPTION

Scope: Publishes monographs on American literature, language, history, politics, culture, sociology.
Reviews books: No
Publishes notes: No
Languages accepted: German; English
Prints abstracts: Occasionally
Author-anonymous submission: No

SUBMISSION REQUIREMENTS

Restrictions on contributors: None
Author pays submission fee: No
Author pays page charges: No
Length of books: 250 pp.
Style: MLA
Number of copies required: 1
Copyright ownership: Wilhelm Fink Verlag
Rejected manuscripts: Returned; enclose return postage.
Time before publication decision: 6 mos.
Time between decision and publication: 3-6 mos.
Number of reviewers: 3
Books submitted per year: 20
Books published per year: 3-5

(132)
***Amérindia: Revue d'Ethnolinguistique Amérindienne**

André Cauty, Editor
A.E.A., B.P. 431
75233 Paris Cédex 05, France

First published: 1976
Sponsoring organization: Centre National de la Recherche Scientifique
ISSN: 0221-8852
MLA acronym: Amérindia

SUBSCRIPTION INFORMATION

Frequency of publication: Annual
Circulation: 100-150
Available in microform: No
Subscription price: 75 F/yr., 120 F/2 yrs.
Year to which price refers: 1991-92

ADVERTISING INFORMATION

Advertising accepted: Yes, on an exchange basis

EDITORIAL DESCRIPTION

Scope: Publishes articles on American Indian linguistics and ethnolinguistics.
Reviews books: Yes
Publishes notes: Yes
Languages accepted: English; French; Portuguese; Spanish
Prints abstracts: Yes

SUBMISSION REQUIREMENTS

Restrictions on contributors: None
Author pays submission fee: No
Author pays page charges: No
Length of articles: 30 typescript pp. maximum
Length of book reviews: 1-2 pp.
Length of notes: 1-4 pp.
Number of copies required: 1
Special requirements: Include an abstract of 10 lines or less.
Copyright ownership: Journal
Rejected manuscripts: Destroyed unless otherwise requested by author
Time before publication decision: 1-3 mos.
Time between decision and publication: 6-12 mos.
Number of reviewers: 2-4
Articles submitted per year: 10-15
Articles published per year: 5-9
Book reviews submitted per year: 3-6
Book reviews published per year: 3-6

(133)
Ameryka: A Ukrainian Catholic Daily

Mstyslaw B. Dolnycky, Editor
817 N. Franklin St.
Philadelphia, PA 19123

First published: 1912
Sponsoring organization: Providence Assn. for Ukrainian Catholics in America
ISSN: 0279-6201
MLA acronym: Ameryka

SUBSCRIPTION INFORMATION

Frequency of publication: 5 times/week
Circulation: 4,000
Available in microform: Yes

ADVERTISING INFORMATION

Advertising accepted: Yes

EDITORIAL DESCRIPTION

Scope: Publishes articles on international and national news and commentary, with an emphasis on Ukrainian problems.
Reviews books: Yes
Languages accepted: English; Ukrainian

SUBMISSION REQUIREMENTS

Author pays submission fee: Occasionally
Number of copies required: 1
Special requirements: Submit typescript.
Rejected manuscripts: Not returned
Time before publication decision: 1 week
Time between decision and publication: 3 days

(134)
***Amitié Charles Péguy: Bulletin d'Informations et de Recherches**

Jean Bastaire, Director
Chez Françoise Gerbod
12, rue Notre Dame des Champs
75006 Paris, France

Additional editorial address: Jean Bastaire, Chemin Clos-Buisson, Les Villaux, 38240 Meylan, France
First published: 1978
Sponsoring organization: Amitié Charles Péguy
ISSN: 0180-8567
MLA acronym: ACP

SUBSCRIPTION INFORMATION

Frequency of publication: 4 times/yr.
Circulation: 800
Available in microform: No
Subscription price: 125 F/yr. France; 135 F/yr. elsewhere
Year to which price refers: 1991

ADVERTISING INFORMATION

Advertising accepted: No

EDITORIAL DESCRIPTION

Scope: Publishes items of interest concerning the life and work of Charles Péguy (1873-1914).
Reviews books: Yes
Publishes notes: Yes
Languages accepted: French
Prints abstracts: No

SUBMISSION REQUIREMENTS

Restrictions on contributors: None
Author pays submission fee: No
Author pays page charges: No
Length of articles: 10-15 pp.
Length of book reviews: 2 pp.
Length of notes: 1 p.
Number of copies required: 2
Special requirements: Submit typescript.
Copyright ownership: Journal
Rejected manuscripts: Returned
Time before publication decision: 3 mos.
Time between decision and publication: 6 mos.
Number of reviewers: 3
Articles submitted per year: 30
Articles published per year: 20
Book reviews published per year: 10
Notes published per year: 20

(135)
***AMS Ars Poetica**

John Hopper, Editor
AMS Press, Inc.
56 E. 13th St.
New York, NY 10003

Telephone: 212 777-4700
Fax: 212 995-5413
First published: 1983
ISSN: 0734-7618
MLA acronym: AMSAP

SUBSCRIPTION INFORMATION

Available in microform: No

ADVERTISING INFORMATION

Advertising accepted: No

EDITORIAL DESCRIPTION

Scope: Publishes monographs on literature and philology.
Reviews books: No
Publishes notes: No
Languages accepted: English
Prints abstracts: No
Author-anonymous submission: No

SUBMISSION REQUIREMENTS

Author pays submission fee: No
Author pays page charges: No
Length of books: No restrictions
Style: Chicago
Number of copies required: 1
Special requirements: Submit double-spaced typescript.
Copyright ownership: AMS Press

Rejected manuscripts: Returned; enclose SASE.
Time before publication decision: 3 mos.
Time between decision and publication: 6 mos.
Number of reviewers: 2
Books submitted per year: 5-10
Books published per year: 0-1

(136) AMS Studies in German Literature and Culture

Peter M. Daly, Editor
AMS Press
56 E. 13th St.
New York, NY 10003

Telephone: 212 777-4700
Fax: 212 995-5413
First published: 1991
ISSN: 1045-6023
MLA acronym: AMSGLC

SUBSCRIPTION INFORMATION

Frequency of publication: Irregular
Available in microform: No

ADVERTISING INFORMATION

Advertising accepted: No

EDITORIAL DESCRIPTION

Scope: Publishes studies in German literature and culture.
Reviews books: No
Publishes notes: No
Languages accepted: English
Prints abstracts: No
Author-anonymous submission: No

SUBMISSION REQUIREMENTS

Author pays submission fee: No
Author pays page charges: No
Style: Chicago
Copyright ownership: AMS Press
Rejected manuscripts: Returned

(137) *AMS Studies in Modern Literature

John Hopper, Editor
AMS Press, Inc.
56 E. 13th St.
New York, NY 10003

Telephone: 212 777-4700
Fax: 212 995-5413
First published: 1974
ISSN: 0270-2983
MLA acronym: AMSML

SUBSCRIPTION INFORMATION

Frequency of publication: Irregular
Available in microform: No

ADVERTISING INFORMATION

Advertising accepted: No

EDITORIAL DESCRIPTION

Scope: Publishes critical studies, reference works, and bibliographies, about 20th-century literature.
Reviews books: No
Publishes notes: No
Languages accepted: English
Prints abstracts: No
Author-anonymous submission: No

SUBMISSION REQUIREMENTS

Author pays submission fee: No

Author pays page charges: No
Length of books: No restrictions
Style: Chicago
Number of copies required: 1
Special requirements: Submit double-spaced typescript.
Copyright ownership: AMS Press
Rejected manuscripts: Returned; enclose SASE.
Time before publication decision: 3-6 mos.
Time between decision and publication: 9-12 mos.
Number of reviewers: 2
Books submitted per year: 15
Books published per year: 1-2

(138) *AMS Studies in the Eighteenth Century

John Hopper, Editor
AMS Press, Inc.
56 E. 13th St.
New York, NY 10003

Telephone: 212 777-4700
Fax: 212 995-5413
First published: 1970
ISSN: 0196-6561
MLA acronym: AMSS

SUBSCRIPTION INFORMATION

Frequency of publication: Irregular
Available in microform: No

ADVERTISING INFORMATION

Advertising accepted: No

EDITORIAL DESCRIPTION

Scope: Publishes studies in the 18th century.
Publishes notes: No
Languages accepted: English
Prints abstracts: No
Author-anonymous submission: No

SUBMISSION REQUIREMENTS

Restrictions on contributors: None
Author pays submission fee: No
Author pays page charges: No
Length of books: No restrictions
Style: Chicago
Number of copies required: 1
Special requirements: Submit double-spaced typescript.
Copyright ownership: AMS Press
Rejected manuscripts: Returned; enclose SASE.
Time before publication decision: 3 mos.
Time between decision and publication: 6-9 mos.
Books submitted per year: 30
Books published per year: 15

(139) *AMS Studies in the Emblem

Peter M. Daly & Daniel S. Russell, Editors
Dept. of German
McGill Univ.
Montreal, Quebec H3A 1G5, Canada

Additional editorial address: Dept. of French & Italian, Univ. of Pittsburgh, Pittsburgh, PA 15260
Telephone: 412 624-5220 (D. Russell); 514 398-3647 (P. Daly)
Fax: 412 624-4575 (D. Russell); 514 398-8239 (P. Daly)
E-mail: Russell@vms.cis.pitt.edu; erl0@musica.mcgill.ca
First published: 1988
ISSN: 0892-4201
MLA acronym: AMSSE

SUBSCRIPTION INFORMATION

Frequency of publication: Irregular
Available in microform: No
Subscription address: AMS Press, Inc., 56 E. 13th St., New York, NY 10003
Subscription telephone: 212 777-4700
Subscription fax: 212 995-5413

ADVERTISING INFORMATION

Advertising accepted: No

EDITORIAL DESCRIPTION

Scope: Publishes studies of the emblem from the Middle Ages to the 20th century.
Reviews books: No
Publishes notes: No
Languages accepted: English
Prints abstracts: No
Author-anonymous submission: No

SUBMISSION REQUIREMENTS

Author pays submission fee: No
Author pays page charges: No
Length of books: No restrictions
Style: MLA
Number of copies required: 2
Copyright ownership: AMS Press
Rejected manuscripts: Returned
Time before publication decision: 3 mos.
Time between decision and publication: 12-16 mos.
Number of reviewers: 4
Books submitted per year: 5
Books published per year: 3

(140) *AMS Studies in the Middle Ages

John Hopper, Editor
AMS Press, Inc.
56 E. 13th St.
New York, NY 10003

Telephone: 212 777-4700
Fax: 212 995-5413
First published: 1978
ISSN: 0270-6261
MLA acronym: AMSSMA

SUBSCRIPTION INFORMATION

Frequency of publication: Irregular
Available in microform: No

ADVERTISING INFORMATION

Advertising accepted: No

EDITORIAL DESCRIPTION

Scope: Publishes studies in the Middle Ages.
Reviews books: No
Publishes notes: No
Languages accepted: English
Prints abstracts: No
Author-anonymous submission: No

SUBMISSION REQUIREMENTS

Restrictions on contributors: None
Author pays submission fee: No
Author pays page charges: No
Length of books: No restrictions
Style: Chicago
Number of copies required: 1
Special requirements: Submit double-spaced typescript.
Copyright ownership: AMS Press
Rejected manuscripts: Returned; enclose SASE.
Time before publication decision: 3 mos.
Time between decision and publication: 6 mos.
Books submitted per year: 20
Books published per year: 2

(141)
*AMS Studies in the Nineteenth Century

John Hopper, Editor
AMS Press, Inc.
56 E. 13th St.
New York, NY 10003

Telephone: 212 777-4700
Fax: 212 995-5413
First published: 1980
ISSN: 0196-657X
MLA acronym: AMSSN

SUBSCRIPTION INFORMATION

Frequency of publication: Irregular
Available in microform: No

ADVERTISING INFORMATION

Advertising accepted: No

EDITORIAL DESCRIPTION

Scope: Publishes studies in the 19th century.
Reviews books: No
Publishes notes: No
Languages accepted: English
Prints abstracts: No
Author-anonymous submission: No

SUBMISSION REQUIREMENTS

Author pays submission fee: No
Author pays page charges: No
Length of books: No restrictions
Style: Chicago
Special requirements: Submit double-spaced typescript.
Copyright ownership: AMS Press
Rejected manuscripts: Returned; enclose SASE.
Time before publication decision: 3 mos.
Time between decision and publication: 6-9 mos.
Number of reviewers: 2
Books submitted per year: 20
Books published per year: 3

(142)
*AMS Studies in the Renaissance

John Hopper, Editor
AMS Press, Inc.
56 E. 13th St.
New York, NY 10003

Telephone: 212 777-4700
Fax: 212 995-5413
First published: 1976
ISSN: 0195-8011
MLA acronym: AMSR

SUBSCRIPTION INFORMATION

Frequency of publication: Irregular
Available in microform: No

ADVERTISING INFORMATION

Advertising accepted: No

EDITORIAL DESCRIPTION

Scope: Publishes studies in the Renaissance.
Reviews books: No
Publishes notes: No
Languages accepted: English
Prints abstracts: No
Author-anonymous submission: No

SUBMISSION REQUIREMENTS

Author pays submission fee: No
Author pays page charges: No
Length of books: No restrictions
Style: Chicago
Number of copies required: 1
Special requirements: Submit double-spaced typescript
Copyright ownership: AMS Press
Rejected manuscripts: Returned; enclose SASE.
Time before publication decision: 3 mos.
Time between decision and publication: 6 mos.
Number of reviewers: 2
Books submitted per year: 25-30
Books published per year: 2-3

(143)
*AMS Studies in the Seventeenth Century

John Hopper, Editor
AMS Press, Inc.
56 E. 13th St.
New York, NY 10003

Telephone: 212 777-4700
Fax: 212 995-5413
First published: 1986
ISSN: 0731-2342
MLA acronym: AMSSC

SUBSCRIPTION INFORMATION

Frequency of publication: Irregular
Available in microform: No

ADVERTISING INFORMATION

Advertising accepted: No

EDITORIAL DESCRIPTION

Scope: Publishes studies in the literature, history, psychology, and theater of the 17th century.
Reviews books: No
Publishes notes: No
Languages accepted: English
Prints abstracts: No
Author-anonymous submission: No

SUBMISSION REQUIREMENTS

Author pays submission fee: No
Author pays page charges: No
Length of books: No restrictions
Style: Chicago
Number of copies required: 1
Special requirements: Submit double-spaced typescript.
Copyright ownership: AMS Press
Rejected manuscripts: Returned; enclose SASE.
Time before publication decision: 3 mos.
Time between decision and publication: 9-12 mos.
Number of reviewers: 2
Books submitted per year: 15
Books published per year: 2

(144)
*Amstelodamum: Maandblad voor de Kennis van Amsterdam. Orgaan van Het Genootschap Amstelodamum

J. H. van den Hoek Ostende, Editor
Binnen Wieringerstraat 22
1013 EB Amsterdam, Netherlands

First published: 1914
ISSN: 0165-9278
MLA acronym: Amstel

SUBSCRIPTION INFORMATION

Frequency of publication: 6 times/yr.
Circulation: 1,400
Available in microform: No
Subscription price: 65 f/yr.
Year to which price refers: 1992
Subscription address: Amstel 59, 1018 EJ Amsterdam, Netherlands

ADVERTISING INFORMATION

Advertising accepted: No

EDITORIAL DESCRIPTION

Scope: Publishes articles on the history of Amsterdam.
Reviews books: Yes
Publishes notes: Yes
Languages accepted: Dutch
Prints abstracts: No
Author-anonymous submission: No

SUBMISSION REQUIREMENTS

Restrictions on contributors: None
Author pays submission fee: No
Author pays page charges: No
Length of articles: 2,000-2,500 words
Length of book reviews: 500-600 words
Length of notes: 10-15 words
Style: None
Number of copies required: 2
Copyright ownership: Author
Rejected manuscripts: Returned
Time before publication decision: 1 mo.
Time between decision and publication: 3-6 mos.
Number of reviewers: 1-3
Articles submitted per year: 35
Articles published per year: 35
Book reviews submitted per year: 20
Book reviews published per year: 20
Notes submitted per year: 120
Notes published per year: 120

(145)
*Amsterdam Studies in the Theory and History of Linguistic Science I: Amsterdam Classics in Linguistics 1800-1925

E. F. Konrad Koerner, Editor
Dept. of Linguistics
Univ. of Ottawa
Ottawa, Ontario K1N 6N5, Canada

First published: 1974
ISSN: 0304-0712
MLA acronym: ACiL

SUBSCRIPTION INFORMATION

Frequency of publication: Irregular
Available in microform: No
Subscription address: John Benjamins North America, Inc., 821 Bethlehem Pike, Philadelphia, PA 19118
Additional subscription address: John Benjamins B.V., Amsteldijk 44, P.O. Box 75577, 1070 AN Amsterdam, Netherlands

ADVERTISING INFORMATION

Advertising accepted: No

EDITORIAL DESCRIPTION

Scope: Publishes new editions of important 19th- and 20th-century linguistics works together with present-day introductions evaluating the present-day relevance of the work in question.
Reviews books: No
Publishes notes: No
Languages accepted: English; German
Prints abstracts: No

SUBMISSION REQUIREMENTS

Author pays submission fee: No
Author pays page charges: No
Length of books: 600 pp. maximum
Style: Linguistic Soc. of America with modifications
Number of copies required: 2

Special requirements: Consult with editor prior to submission.
Copyright ownership: John Benjamins B.V.
Rejected manuscripts: Returned
Time before publication decision: 6-12 mos.
Time between decision and publication: 3-6 mos.
Number of reviewers: 2
Books submitted per year: 5-8
Books published per year: 1-2

(146)
*Amsterdam Studies in the Theory and History of Linguistic Science II: Classics in Psycholinguistics

E. F. Konrad Koerner, Editor
Dept. of Linguistics
Univ. of Ottawa
Ottawa, Ontario, K1N 6N5, Canada

First published: 1978
ISSN: 0165-716X
MLA acronym: CiP

SUBSCRIPTION INFORMATION

Frequency of publication: Irregular
Subscription address: John Benjamins North America, Inc., 821 Bethlehem Pike, Philadelphia, PA 19118
Additional subscription address: John Benjamins B.V., Amsteldijk 44, P.O. Box 75577, 1070 AN Amsterdam, Netherlands

EDITORIAL DESCRIPTION

Scope: Publishes new editions and evaluations by present-day specialists of seminal works from Europe and America which appeared at the end of the 19th and at the beginning of the 20th century when psycholinguistics emerged as an important area of interdisciplinary study.
Reviews books: No
Publishes notes: No
Languages accepted: English; German
Prints abstracts: No

SUBMISSION REQUIREMENTS

Author pays submission fee: No
Author pays page charges: No
Length of books: 600 pp. maximum
Style: Linguistic Soc. of America with modifications
Number of copies required: 2
Special requirements: Consult with editor prior to submission.
Copyright ownership: John Benjamins B.V.
Rejected manuscripts: Returned
Time before publication decision: 3-6 mos.
Time between decision and publication: 6-12 mos.
Number of reviewers: 2 minimum

(147)
*Amsterdam Studies in the Theory and History of Linguistic Science IV: Current Issues in Linguistic Theory

E. F. Konrad Koerner, Editor
Dept. of Linguistics
Univ. of Ottawa
Ottawa, Ontario K1N 6N5, Canada

First published: 1975
ISSN: 0304-0763
MLA acronym: CILT

SUBSCRIPTION INFORMATION

Frequency of publication: Irregular
Available in microform: No
Subscription address: John Benjamins B.V., P.O. Box 75577, Amsteldijk 44, 1070 AN Amsterdam, Netherlands
Additional subscription address: John Benjamins North America, Inc., 821 Bethlehem Pike, Philadelphia, PA 19118
Subscription telephone: (31) 20 6738156; 215 836-1200
Subscription fax: (31) 20 6739773; 215 836-1204

ADVERTISING INFORMATION

Advertising accepted: No

EDITORIAL DESCRIPTION

Scope: Publishes monographs on issues in current linguistic theory.
Reviews books: No
Publishes notes: No
Languages accepted: English
Prints abstracts: No
Author-anonymous submission: Yes

SUBMISSION REQUIREMENTS

Author pays submission fee: No
Author pays page charges: No
Length of books: 250-350 pp.
Style: Series; request from editor.
Copyright ownership: John Benjamins Publishing Co.
Rejected manuscripts: Returned
Time before publication decision: 6 mos.
Time between decision and publication: 1 yr.
Number of reviewers: 2

(148)
*Amsterdam Studies in the Theory and History of Linguistic Science V: Library and Information Sources in Linguistics

E. F. Konrad Koerner, Editor
Dept. of Linguistics
Univ. of Ottawa
Ottawa, Ontario K1N 6N5, Canada

First published: 1977
ISSN: 0165-7267
MLA acronym: LISL

SUBSCRIPTION INFORMATION

Frequency of publication: Irregular
Circulation: 600-1,000
Available in microform: No
Subscription address: John Benjamins North America, Inc., 821 Bethlehem Pike, Philadelphia, PA 19118
Additional subscription address: John Benjamins B.V., P.O. Box 75577, Amsteldijk 44, 1070 AN Amsterdam, Netherlands

ADVERTISING INFORMATION

Advertising accepted: No

EDITORIAL DESCRIPTION

Scope: Publishes monographs on biographical and bibliographical information on particular subjects and authors in linguistics.
Reviews books: No
Publishes notes: No
Languages accepted: English; German (occasionally); French (occasionally)
Prints abstracts: No

SUBMISSION REQUIREMENTS

Author pays submission fee: No
Author pays page charges: No
Length of books: Manuscripts must be book length.
Style: Linguistic Soc. of America
Number of copies required: 2 minimum
Copyright ownership: John Benjamins B.V.
Rejected manuscripts: Returned
Time before publication decision: 4-6 mos.
Time between decision and publication: 6-12 mos.
Number of reviewers: 2
Books submitted per year: 10
Books published per year: 2-3

(149)
*Amsterdam Studies in the Theory and History of the Language Sciences III: Studies in the History of the Language Sciences

E. F. Konrad Koerner, Editor
Dept. of Linguistics
Univ. of Ottawa
Ottawa, Ontario K1N 6N5, Canada

First published: 1973
ISSN: 0165-7763
MLA acronym: SHL

SUBSCRIPTION INFORMATION

Frequency of publication: Irregular
Available in microform: No
Subscription address: John Benjamins Publishing Co., P.O. Box 75577, Amsteldijk 44, 1070 AN Amsterdam, Netherlands
Additional subscription address: John Benjamins North America, Inc., 821 Bethlehem Pike, Philadelphia, PA 19118
Subscription telephone: (31) 20 6738156; 215 836-1200
Subscription fax: (31) 20 6739773; 215 836-1204

ADVERTISING INFORMATION

Advertising accepted: No

EDITORIAL DESCRIPTION

Scope: Publishes monographs on the history of linguistic thought and scholarship.
Reviews books: No
Publishes notes: No
Languages accepted: English
Prints abstracts: No

SUBMISSION REQUIREMENTS

Author pays submission fee: No
Author pays page charges: No
Style: Series; request from editor.
Copyright ownership: John Benjamins Publishing Co.
Books submitted per year: 10
Books published per year: 3-4

(150)
*Amsterdamer Beiträge zur Älteren Germanistik

Arend Quak & Paula Vermeyden, Editors
Univ. van Amsterdam
Afd. Oudgermanistiek
Spuistraat 210
Amsterdam, Netherlands

First published: 1972
ISSN: 0165-7305
MLA acronym: ABäG

SUBSCRIPTION INFORMATION

Frequency of publication: Irregular (1-2 times/yr.)
Circulation: 300
Available in microform: No
Subscription address: Editions Rodopi B.V., Keizersgracht 302-304, 1016 EX Amsterdam, Netherlands

Additional subscription address: In N. America: Editions Rodopi, 233 Peachtree St., N.E., Suite 404, Atlanta, GA 30303-1504
Subscription telephone: (31) 20 6227507; 404 523-1964; 800 225-3998
Subscription fax: (31) 20 6380948; 404 522-7116

ADVERTISING INFORMATION

Advertising accepted: Yes, on an exchange basis

EDITORIAL DESCRIPTION

Scope: Promotes the old Germanic languages.
Reviews books: Yes
Publishes notes: No
Languages accepted: English; German; Dutch; Norwegian; Danish; Swedish; French; Icelandic
Prints abstracts: Yes
Author-anonymous submission: Yes

SUBMISSION REQUIREMENTS

Restrictions on contributors: None
Author pays submission fee: No
Author pays page charges: No
Length of articles: No restrictions
Length of book reviews: No restrictions
Number of copies required: 1
Copyright ownership: Author
Rejected manuscripts: Returned
Time before publication decision: 1-2 mos.
Time between decision and publication: 6-12 mos.
Number of reviewers: 1-2
Articles submitted per year: 11
Articles published per year: 9
Book reviews submitted per year: 15
Book reviews published per year: 15

(151)
*Amsterdamer Beiträge zur Neueren Germanistik

Gerd Labroisse, Editor
Vrije Univ.
Duitse taal- en letterkunde
Postbus 7161/De Boelelaan 1105
Amsterdam, Netherlands

First published: 1972
ISSN: 0304-6257
MLA acronym: ABnG

SUBSCRIPTION INFORMATION

Frequency of publication: 2 times/yr.
Circulation: 700
Available in microform: No
Subscription address: Editions Rodopi B.V., Keizersgracht 302-304, 1016 EX Amsterdam, Netherlands
Additional subscription address: In N. America: Editions Rodopi, 233 Peachtree St. N.E., Suite 404, Atlanta, GA 30303-1504
Subscription telephone: (31) 20 6227507; 404 523-1964
Subscription fax: (31) 20 6380948; 404 522-7116

ADVERTISING INFORMATION

Advertising accepted: Yes

EDITORIAL DESCRIPTION

Scope: Publishes collections of articles on modern German language and literature, primarily from the 18th century to the present.
Reviews books: No
Publishes notes: No
Languages accepted: German; English
Prints abstracts: No
Author-anonymous submission: No

SUBMISSION REQUIREMENTS

Restrictions on contributors: None
Author pays submission fee: No
Author pays page charges: No
Length of articles: No restrictions
Style: MLA
Number of copies required: 1
Copyright ownership: Editions Rodopi B.V.
Rejected manuscripts: Returned; enclose return postage.
Time before publication decision: 1 mo.
Time between decision and publication: 6 mos.
Number of reviewers: 2
Articles submitted per year: 20-30
Articles published per year: 20-30
Books published per year: 2

(152)
*Amsterdamer Publikationen zur Sprache und Literatur

Arend Quak, Editor
Univ. van Amsterdam
Afdeling Oudgermanistiek
Spuistraat 210
Amsterdam, Netherlands

First published: 1972
ISSN: 0169-0221
MLA acronym: APSL

SUBSCRIPTION INFORMATION

Frequency of publication: Irregular (2-6 times/yr.)
Circulation: 500
Available in microform: No
Subscription address: Editions Rodopi, Keizersgracht 302-304, 1016 EX Amsterdam, Netherlands
Additional subscription address: In N. America: Editions Rodopi, 233 Peachtree St., N.E., Suite 404, Atlanta, GA 30303-1504
Subscription telephone: (31) 20 6227507; 404 523-1964; 800 225-3998
Subscription fax: (31) 20 6380948; 404 522-7116

ADVERTISING INFORMATION

Advertising accepted: No

EDITORIAL DESCRIPTION

Scope: Publishes studies on Germanic languages and literatures.
Reviews books: No
Publishes notes: No
Languages accepted: English; German
Prints abstracts: No
Author-anonymous submission: Yes

SUBMISSION REQUIREMENTS

Restrictions on contributors: None
Author pays submission fee: No
Author pays page charges: Varies
Length of books: 200-500 pp.
Style: MLA; Chicago
Number of copies required: 1
Copyright ownership: Editions Rodopi
Rejected manuscripts: Returned; enclose return postage.
Time before publication decision: 2-3 mos.
Time between decision and publication: 3-6 mos.
Number of reviewers: 1-2
Books submitted per year: 10
Books published per year: 5

(153)
*Anais: An International Journal

Gunther Stuhlmann, Editor
P.O. Box 276
Becket, MA 01223

First published: 1983
Sponsoring organization: Anaïs Nin Foundation
MLA acronym: Anais

SUBSCRIPTION INFORMATION

Frequency of publication: Annual (Feb.)
Circulation: 1,000
Available in microform: No
Subscription price: $7.50/yr. US; $8.50/yr. elsewhere
Year to which price refers: 1992
Subscription address: Anaïs Nin Foundation, 2335 Hidalgo Ave., Los Angeles, CA 90039
Subscription telephone: 213 665-5017

ADVERTISING INFORMATION

Advertising accepted: No

EDITORIAL DESCRIPTION

Scope: Publishes critical/biographical material on Anaïs Nin, her circle, in the US and Europe, writers in her orbit, diary writing, and feminism.
Reviews books: Yes
Publishes notes: Yes
Languages accepted: English
Prints abstracts: No

SUBMISSION REQUIREMENTS

Restrictions on contributors: Query editor prior to submission. Book reviews and most articles are solicited.
Author pays submission fee: No
Author pays page charges: No
Length of articles: No restrictions
Length of book reviews: No restrictions
Length of notes: No restrictions
Style: Journal
Number of copies required: 2
Special requirements: Submit original typescript and a carbon copy. Articles are accepted in French, Spanish, and German for translation into English.
Copyright ownership: Editor
Rejected manuscripts: Returned; enclose SASE.
Time before publication decision: 1 mo.
Articles published per year: 20
Book reviews published per year: 10-15
Notes published per year: 3-5

(154)
*Analecta Bollandiana

Soc. des Bollandistes
24, boulevard Saint-Michel
1040 Brussels, Belgium

First published: 1882
Sponsoring organization: Soc. des Bollandistes
ISSN: 0003-2468
MLA acronym: AnBol

SUBSCRIPTION INFORMATION

Frequency of publication: 2 times/yr. (June, Dec.)
Available in microform: No
Subscription price: 3,000 BF/yr.
Year to which price refers: 1992

ADVERTISING INFORMATION

Advertising accepted: No

EDITORIAL DESCRIPTION

Scope: Publishes articles on pre-sixteenth century critical ecclesiastical history and lives of the saints up to the 16th century.
Reviews books: Yes
Publishes notes: Yes
Languages accepted: English; French; German; Italian
Prints abstracts: Yes
Author-anonymous submission: No

SUBMISSION REQUIREMENTS

Restrictions on contributors: None
Author pays submission fee: No
Author pays page charges: No
Length of articles: 32 printed pp. maximum
Length of book reviews: 1-2 pp.
Length of notes: 1-2 pp.
Style: MLA
Number of copies required: 1
Copyright ownership: Soc. des Bollandistes
Rejected manuscripts: Returned at author's request
Time before publication decision: 1 yr.
Time between decision and publication: 1 yr.
Number of reviewers: 3
Articles published per year: 15
Book reviews published per year: 150
Notes published per year: 150

(155)
*Analecta Cartusiana

James Hogg, Editor
Inst. für Anglistik und Amerikanistik
Univ. Salzburg
Akademiestr. 24
5020 Salzburg, Austria

Telephone: (43) 6217 7084
First published: 1970
ISSN: 0253-1593
MLA acronym: ACar

SUBSCRIPTION INFORMATION

Frequency of publication: Irregular
Circulation: 200
Available in microform: No
Subscription price: 65 DM/yr.
Year to which price refers: 1992

ADVERTISING INFORMATION

Advertising accepted: No

EDITORIAL DESCRIPTION

Scope: Publishes monographs on Carthusian history and spirituality.
Reviews books: No
Publishes notes: Yes
Languages accepted: German; English; French; Spanish; Italian; Latin
Prints abstracts: No
Author-anonymous submission: No

SUBMISSION REQUIREMENTS

Restrictions on contributors: None
Author pays submission fee: No
Author pays page charges: No
Length of books: No restrictions
Length of notes: No restrictions
Style: None
Number of copies required: 1
Copyright ownership: Author
Rejected manuscripts: Returned; enclose return postage.
Time before publication decision: 1 mo.
Time between decision and publication: 2 mos.
Number of reviewers: 1
Books submitted per year: 15
Books published per year: 8

(156)
*Analecta Cisterciensia

P. Polycarpus Zakar, Editor
Edizioni Cisterciensi
Piazza de Tempio di Diana, 14
00153 Rome, Italy

Telephone: (39) 6 5743694; (39) 6 5755110
Fax: (39) 6 5741827
First published: 1945
Sponsoring organization: Curia Generalis Ordinis Cisterciensis
ISSN: 0003-2476
MLA acronym: ACist

SUBSCRIPTION INFORMATION

Frequency of publication: 2 times/yr.
Circulation: 300
Available in microform: No
Subscription price: 85,000 Lit/yr.
Year to which price refers: 1992

ADVERTISING INFORMATION

Advertising accepted: No

EDITORIAL DESCRIPTION

Scope: Publishes articles on the history, law, liturgy, spirituality of the Cistercian Order.
Reviews books: Yes
Publishes notes: Yes
Languages accepted: English; French; German; Italian; Spanish
Prints abstracts: No
Author-anonymous submission: No

SUBMISSION REQUIREMENTS

Restrictions on contributors: None
Author pays submission fee: No
Author pays page charges: No
Length of articles: No restrictions
Length of book reviews: No restrictions
Number of copies required: 1
Copyright ownership: Journal
Rejected manuscripts: Returned
Time before publication decision: 2-3 mos.
Time between decision and publication: 8-10 mos.
Number of reviewers: 2-3
Articles submitted per year: 10-12
Articles published per year: 6-8
Book reviews submitted per year: 25
Book reviews published per year: 15

(157)
*Analecta Malacitana: Revista de la Seccion de Filología de la Facultad de Filosofia y Letras

Olegario García de la Fuente, Editor
Fac. de Filosofia & Letras
Campus de Teatinos
29071 Malaga, Spain

Telephone: (34) 5 2131836; (34) 5 2131812
First published: 1978
Sponsoring organization: Univ. de Malaga
ISSN: 0211-934X
MLA acronym: AnMal

SUBSCRIPTION INFORMATION

Frequency of publication: 2 times/yr.
Circulation: 400
Available in microform: No
Subscription price: 3,000 Pta/yr. Spain; $34.00/yr. elsewhere
Year to which price refers: 1990

ADVERTISING INFORMATION

Advertising accepted: No

EDITORIAL DESCRIPTION

Scope: Publishes articles on Spanish, Latin, Greek, English, and French philology and literature.
Reviews books: Yes
Publishes notes: Yes
Languages accepted: Spanish; Italian; English; French; German
Prints abstracts: No
Author-anonymous submission: No

SUBMISSION REQUIREMENTS

Author pays submission fee: No
Author pays page charges: No
Length of articles: 25-30 pp.
Length of book reviews: 1-3 pp.
Length of notes: 8-12 pp.
Style: Chicago
Number of copies required: 1
Copyright ownership: Publisher
Rejected manuscripts: Returned
Time before publication decision: 2-4 weeks
Time between decision and publication: 6-8 mos.
Number of reviewers: 2
Articles submitted per year: 23-26
Articles published per year: 16-18
Book reviews submitted per year: 6-8
Book reviews published per year: 6-8
Notes submitted per year: 8-10
Notes published per year: 5-7

(158)
Analecta Sacra Tarraconensia: Revista de Ciencias Historico-Eclesiasticas Balmesiana

Francisco de P. Solà, S.J., Editor
c/o Biblioteca Balmes
Duran y Bas 9, Apdo. 1382
08002 Barcelona, Spain

First published: 1925
Sponsoring organization: Biblioteca Balmes
ISSN: 0304-4300
MLA acronym: AnST

SUBSCRIPTION INFORMATION

Circulation: 1,000
Available in microform: Yes

EDITORIAL DESCRIPTION

Scope: Publishes articles on Ecclesiatical history.
Reviews books: No
Languages accepted: English; Spanish; Catalan; French; German; Latin
Prints abstracts: Yes

SUBMISSION REQUIREMENTS

Restrictions on contributors: None
Author pays submission fee: No
Number of copies required: 1
Rejected manuscripts: Returned at author's request
Articles published per year: 12

(159)
Analele Ştiintifice ale Universităţii "Al.I. Cuza" din Iaşi (Serie nouă), e. Lingvistică

Al. Andriescu & D. Irimia, Editors
Univ. Al. I. Cuza
Calea 23 August, nr. 11
Iaşi, 6600, Romania

First published: 1900
Sponsoring organization: Al. I Cuza Univ.
ISSN: 0379-7880

MLA acronym: ASUI

SUBSCRIPTION INFORMATION

Frequency of publication: Annual
Circulation: 250
Available in microform: No

ADVERTISING INFORMATION

Advertising accepted: No

EDITORIAL DESCRIPTION

Scope: Publishes articles on linguistics and literature.
Reviews books: Yes
Publishes notes: Yes
Languages accepted: English; French; Romanian; Spanish; German; Russian; Italian
Prints abstracts: Yes
Author-anonymous submission: No

SUBMISSION REQUIREMENTS

Restrictions on contributors: None
Author pays submission fee: No
Author pays page charges: No
Length of articles: 3,000 words
Length of book reviews: 500 words
Length of notes: 200 words
Style: MLA
Number of copies required: 2
Copyright ownership: Author
Rejected manuscripts: Not returned
Time before publication decision: 4 mos.
Time between decision and publication: 6 mos.
Number of reviewers: 3
Articles submitted per year: 50
Articles published per year: 20
Book reviews submitted per year: 20
Book reviews published per year: 10
Notes submitted per year: 10
Notes published per year: 4

(160)
Anales Cervantinos

Alberto Sánchez, Editor
Inst. de Filología
Consejo Superior de Investigaciones Científicas
Medinaceli, 6
28014 Madrid, Spain

First published: 1951
Sponsoring organization: Inst. de Filología, Consejo Superior de Investigaciones Científicas (C.S.I.C.)
ISSN: 0569-9878
MLA acronym: ACer

SUBSCRIPTION INFORMATION

Frequency of publication: Annual
Circulation: 800
Available in microform: No
Subscription address: Servicio de Publicaciones, Vitrubio 8, 28006 Madrid, Spain

ADVERTISING INFORMATION

Advertising accepted: No

EDITORIAL DESCRIPTION

Scope: Publishes articles on Cervantes.
Reviews books: Yes
Publishes notes: Yes
Languages accepted: Spanish
Prints abstracts: No

SUBMISSION REQUIREMENTS

Restrictions on contributors: None
Author pays submission fee: No
Author pays page charges: No
Length of articles: No restrictions
Length of book reviews: No restrictions
Length of notes: No restrictions
Style: MLA
Number of copies required: 2
Special requirements: Submit original typescript and 1 copy.
Copyright ownership: Author
Rejected manuscripts: Returned
Time before publication decision: 3-6 mos.
Time between decision and publication: 1-2 yrs.
Number of reviewers: 2
Articles submitted per year: 20
Articles published per year: 8-12
Book reviews submitted per year: 75
Book reviews published per year: 80
Notes submitted per year: 2-8
Notes published per year: 2-6

(161)
*Anales de la Literatura Española Contemporánea

Luis T. González-del-Valle, Editor
Dept. of Spanish & Portuguese
Univ. of Colorado
McKenna Lang. Building, Campus Box 278
Boulder, CO 80309-0278

Telephone: 303 492-7308
Fax: 303 492-3699
First published: 1973
Sponsoring organization: Univ. de Santiago de Compostela; Univ. of Colorado; Soc. of Spanish & Spanish-American Studies; Twentieth Century Spanish Assn. of America
ISSN: 0272-1635
MLA acronym: ALEC

SUBSCRIPTION INFORMATION

Frequency of publication: 1-3 times/yr.
Circulation: 900
Available in microform: Yes
Subscription price: $45.00/yr.
Year to which price refers: 1992

ADVERTISING INFORMATION

Advertising accepted: No

EDITORIAL DESCRIPTION

Scope: Publishes scholarly articles dealing with the literature of 20th-century Spain.
Reviews books: Yes
Publishes notes: Yes
Languages accepted: English; Spanish
Prints abstracts: Yes
Author-anonymous submission: No

SUBMISSION REQUIREMENTS

Restrictions on contributors: None
Author pays submission fee: No
Author pays page charges: No
Length of articles: 12-25 pp.
Length of book reviews: 3-5 pp.
Length of notes: 8-12 pp.
Style: MLA
Number of copies required: 3
Special requirements: Submit original manuscript, an abstract in the language of the essay, and 2 copies of both.
Copyright ownership: Journal
Rejected manuscripts: Returned; enclose return postage.
Time before publication decision: 2-3 mos.
Time between decision and publication: 1 yr.
Number of reviewers: 6
Articles submitted per year: 160
Articles published per year: 15
Book reviews submitted per year: 45
Book reviews published per year: 30
Notes submitted per year: 10
Notes published per year: 3

(162)
Anales de la Universidad de Chile

Univ. de Chile
Casilla 9578
Santiago, Chile

First published: 1843
Sponsoring organization: Univ. de Chile
ISSN: 0365-7779
MLA acronym: AUC

SUBSCRIPTION INFORMATION

Subscription address: Editorial Universitaria S.A., San Francisco 454, Santiago, Chile

EDITORIAL DESCRIPTION

Scope: Publishes university work and festschriften for university professors.
Languages accepted: Spanish

(163)
*Anales de Literatura Española

Guillermo Carnero, Editor
Dept. de Literatura Española
Facultad de Letras/Univ. de Alicante
Carretera San Vicente
Apartado 99
03080 Alicante, Spain

Telephone: (34) 6 5903419
Fax: (34) 6 5903464
First published: 1982
Sponsoring organization: Univ. de Alicante
ISSN: 0212-5889
MLA acronym: ALE

SUBSCRIPTION INFORMATION

Frequency of publication: Annual
Available in microform: No
Subscription price: $25.00/yr.
Year to which price refers: 1992

ADVERTISING INFORMATION

Advertising accepted: Yes, on an exchange basis

EDITORIAL DESCRIPTION

Scope: Publishes articles on Spanish and comparative literature, Latin American literature, literary theory, and related topics in history and political science concerning the eighteenth, nineteenth, and twentieth centuries.
Reviews books: No
Publishes notes: Yes
Languages accepted: Spanish; English; French; Italian; Catalan
Prints abstracts: No

SUBMISSION REQUIREMENTS

Restrictions on contributors: None
Author pays submission fee: No
Author pays page charges: No
Length of articles: 10,000 words
Length of notes: 3,000 words
Style: MLA
Number of copies required: 1
Copyright ownership: Univ. de Alicante for 1 yr.; reverts to author
Rejected manuscripts: Not returned
Time before publication decision: 2 mos. minimum
Time between decision and publication: 2-10 mos.
Number of reviewers: 3
Articles submitted per year: 40-50
Articles published per year: 12-15
Notes submitted per year: 10-15
Notes published per year: 5

(164)
*Anales del Instituto Ibero-Americano

Carlos Foresti, Director
c/o Inst. Iberoamericano
Göteborgs Univ.
412 98 Göteborg, Sweden

Telephone: (46) 31 7731804; (46) 31 7731796
Fax: (46) 31 7734911
First published: 1989
Sponsoring organization: Inst. de Lenguas Románicas, Göteborgs Univ.
ISSN: 1101-4148; 1101-4156 (*Anejo*)
MLA acronym: Anales

SUBSCRIPTION INFORMATION

Frequency of publication: Annual
Available in microform: No
Subscription price: $15.00/yr. plus postage
Year to which price refers: 1992

ADVERTISING INFORMATION

Advertising accepted: No

EDITORIAL DESCRIPTION

Scope: Publishes articles on Ibero-American studies, including literature, languages, history, and economics. Focuses on Chilean studies of the 19th century. Includes the supplement, *Anejo*, which publishes thematic issues on an irregular basis.
Reviews books: No
Publishes notes: No
Languages accepted: Spanish; Portuguese; English; French
Prints abstracts: No
Author-anonymous submission: No

SUBMISSION REQUIREMENTS

Author pays submission fee: No
Author pays page charges: No
Rejected manuscripts: Returned
Articles published per year: 15

(165)
*Anales Galdosianos

Peter A. Bly, Editor
Dept. of Spanish & Italian
Queen's Univ.
Kingston, Ontario, K7L 3N6, Canada

Telephone: 613 545-2112
Fax: 613 545-6300
E-mail: BLYP@QUEENSU.CA
First published: 1966
Sponsoring organization: Cabildo Insular de Gran Canaria; International Galdós Assn.
ISSN: 0569-9924
MLA acronym: AGald

SUBSCRIPTION INFORMATION

Frequency of publication: Annual
Circulation: 500-1,000
Available in microform: No

ADVERTISING INFORMATION

Advertising accepted: Yes, on an exchange basis

EDITORIAL DESCRIPTION

Scope: Publishes articles, book reviews, notices, and documents on the works of Benito Pérez Galdós; texts and documents on the intellectual history of Galdós's Spain; articles on the theoretical problems of the realistic novel and on nineteenth-century Spanish narrative.
Reviews books: Yes
Publishes notes: Yes
Languages accepted: English; Spanish
Prints abstracts: No
Author-anonymous submission: Yes

SUBMISSION REQUIREMENTS

Restrictions on contributors: None
Author pays submission fee: No
Author pays page charges: No
Length of articles: 9,000 words maximum
Length of book reviews: 1,000-2,500 words
Length of notes: 3,000 words
Style: MLA
Number of copies required: 2
Special requirements: Submit original typescript and 1 copy.
Copyright ownership: Author
Rejected manuscripts: Returned
Time before publication decision: 2-4 mos.
Time between decision and publication: 2 yrs. maximum
Number of reviewers: 2-3
Articles submitted per year: 25-35
Articles published per year: 12-15
Book reviews submitted per year: 9-10
Book reviews published per year: 7-8
Notes submitted per year: 4-5
Notes published per year: 2-3

(166)
Analysis: Quaderni di Anglistica

Anthony L. Johnson, Editor
Ist. di Letteratura Inglese e Angloamericana
Via della Faggiola, 7
56100 Pisa, Italy

First published: 1983
Sponsoring organization: Assn. Italiana di Anglistica; the British Council
MLA acronym: Analysis

SUBSCRIPTION INFORMATION

Frequency of publication: 2 times/yr.
Circulation: 120
Available in microform: No
Subscription address: ETS, Piazza Torricelli 4, 56100 Pisa, Italy

ADVERTISING INFORMATION

Advertising accepted: Yes

EDITORIAL DESCRIPTION

Scope: Publishes studies on English language and the literature and culture of Britain and the Commonwealth.
Reviews books: No
Publishes notes: No
Languages accepted: Italian; English
Prints abstracts: No
Author-anonymous submission: No

SUBMISSION REQUIREMENTS

Restrictions on contributors: None
Author pays submission fee: No
Author pays page charges: No
Length of articles: 4,000-6,000 words
Style: Poetics Today
Number of copies required: 3
Copyright ownership: Author
Rejected manuscripts: Not returned
Time before publication decision: 3-6 mos.
Time between decision and publication: 3-6 mos.
Number of reviewers: 3
Articles published per year: 8-10

(167)
*Analytical & Enumerative Bibliography

William P. Williams, Editor
Dept. of English
Northern Illinois Univ.
DeKalb, IL 60115

First published: 1977
Sponsoring organization: Bibliographical Soc. of Northern Illinois
ISSN: 0161-0376
MLA acronym: AEB

SUBSCRIPTION INFORMATION

Frequency of publication: 4 times/yr.
Circulation: 250
Available in microform: No

ADVERTISING INFORMATION

Advertising accepted: Yes

EDITORIAL DESCRIPTION

Scope: Publishes scholarly articles, notes, and reviews in bibliography, textual criticism, and publishing history.
Reviews books: Yes
Publishes notes: Yes
Languages accepted: English
Prints abstracts: No
Author-anonymous submission: No

SUBMISSION REQUIREMENTS

Restrictions on contributors: Unsolicited book reviews are not accepted.
Author pays submission fee: No
Author pays page charges: No
Length of articles: No restrictions
Length of book reviews: No restrictions
Length of notes: No restrictions
Style: MLA; Modern Humanities Research Assn.; Chicago
Number of copies required: 1
Copyright ownership: Bibliographical Soc. of Northern Illinois
Rejected manuscripts: Returned
Time before publication decision: 4 mos.
Time between decision and publication: 1 yr.
Number of reviewers: 3
Articles submitted per year: 20
Articles published per year: 6-8
Book reviews published per year: 30
Notes submitted per year: 6
Notes published per year: 1-3

(168)
*Anatolica: Annuaire International pour les Civilisations de l'Asie Antérieure

B. Flemming, D. J. W. Meijer, C. Nijland, M. Özdogan, J. J. Roodenberg, & J. De Roos, Editors
Nederlands Inst. voor het Nabije Oosten
Witte Singel 25, P.O.B. 9515
2300 RA Leiden, Netherlands

Additional editorial address: Nederlands Historisch-Archaeologisch Inst., P.K. 132, Istanbul-Beyoglu, Turkey
Telephone: (31) 71 272036
Fax: (31) 71 272038
First published: 1967
Sponsoring organization: Inst. Historique & Archéologique Néerlandais à Istanbul
ISSN: 0066-1554
MLA acronym: Anatolica

SUBSCRIPTION INFORMATION

Frequency of publication: Annual
Circulation: 250
Available in microform: No

ADVERTISING INFORMATION

Advertising accepted: No

EDITORIAL DESCRIPTION

Scope: Publishes articles on languages and cultures of Asia Minor from prehistoric to modern times.
Reviews books: Yes
Publishes notes: Yes
Languages accepted: English; French; German
Prints abstracts: No
Author-anonymous submission: No

SUBMISSION REQUIREMENTS

Restrictions on contributors: None
Author pays submission fee: No
Author pays page charges: No
Length of articles: No restrictions
Length of notes: 1,000 words
Number of copies required: 1
Copyright ownership: Nederlands Inst. voor het Nabije Oosten
Rejected manuscripts: Returned
Time between decision and publication: 12-18 mos.
Number of reviewers: 2
Articles published per year: 6-10
Book reviews published per year: 5-10

(169)
*Ånd i Hanske: Tidsskrift for Norsk Dukketeaterforening

Anne Helgesen, Editor
Storgt. 88
8000 Bodø, Norway

Telephone: (47) 81 25077
Fax: (47) 81 24816
First published: 1982
Sponsoring organization: UNIMA
ISSN: 0800-2479
MLA acronym: AiH

SUBSCRIPTION INFORMATION

Frequency of publication: 4 times/yr.
Circulation: 400
Available in microform: No
Subscription price: 100 NKr/yr.
Year to which price refers: 1992
Subscription address: Norsk Dukketeaterforening, Hovinun 1, 0576 Oslo 5, Norway
Subscription telephone: (47) 2 677356
Subscription fax: (47) 2 689634

ADVERTISING INFORMATION

Advertising accepted: No

EDITORIAL DESCRIPTION

Scope: Publishes articles on Norwegian and Scandinavian puppet theater.
Reviews books: Yes
Publishes notes: Yes
Languages accepted: Norwegian; Swedish; Danish
Prints abstracts: No

SUBMISSION REQUIREMENTS

Author pays submission fee: No
Author pays page charges: No
Length of articles: 500-1,000 words
Length of book reviews: 250 words
Length of notes: 200 words
Number of copies required: 1
Copyright ownership: UNIMA
Rejected manuscripts: Returned
Time before publication decision: 3 mos. maximum
Time between decision and publication: 1 mo.
Articles published per year: 100
Book reviews submitted per year: 40
Book reviews published per year: 25

Notes submitted per year: 70
Notes published per year: 50

(170)
*L'Anello Che Non Tiene: Journal of Modern Italian Literature

Ernesto Livorni, Editor
Italian Dept.
P.O. Box 4067, Yale Station
Yale Univ.
New Haven, CT 06520-4067

Telephone: 203 624-4011
First published: 1988
Historical variations in title: Formerly *L'Anello Che Non Tiene: Journal of Modern Literature*
ISSN: 0899-5273
MLA acronym: AnCNT

SUBSCRIPTION INFORMATION

Frequency of publication: 2 times/yr. (Spring, Fall)
Available in microform: No
Subscription price: $25.00/yr. institutions US; $30.00/yr. institutions elsewhere; $15.00/yr. individuals US; $20.00/yr. individuals elsewhere
Year to which price refers: 1992

ADVERTISING INFORMATION

Advertising accepted: Yes

EDITORIAL DESCRIPTION

Scope: Focuses on 19th- and 20th-century Italian literature. Also publishes articles on other literatures and other centuries.
Reviews books: Yes
Publishes notes: Yes
Languages accepted: English; Italian
Prints abstracts: No
Author-anonymous submission: Yes

SUBMISSION REQUIREMENTS

Author pays submission fee: No
Author pays page charges: No
Length of articles: 2,000-3,500 words
Length of book reviews: 500-1,200 words
Style: MLA
Number of copies required: 2
Special requirements: Submit double-spaced typescript.
Copyright ownership: Journal
Rejected manuscripts: Not returned
Time before publication decision: 1-2 mos.
Time between decision and publication: 6-12 mos.
Number of reviewers: 3
Articles submitted per year: 12-15
Articles published per year: 6-8
Book reviews submitted per year: 15-20
Book reviews published per year: 12-15

(171)
*Angelicum: Periodicum Trimestre Pontificae Studiorum Universitatis a Sancto Thoma Aquinate in Urbe

Stjepan Krasić, O.P., Editor
Univ. S. Tommaso
Largo Angelicum, 1
00184 Rome, Italy

Telephone: (39) 6 6702255
Fax: (39) 6 6790407
First published: 1924
Sponsoring organization: Univ. S. Tommaso
ISSN: 0003-3081
MLA acronym: Angelicum

SUBSCRIPTION INFORMATION

Frequency of publication: 4 times/yr.
Circulation: 800
Available in microform: No
Subscription price: $30.00/yr.; $8.00/single issue
Year to which price refers: 1992

ADVERTISING INFORMATION

Advertising accepted: No

EDITORIAL DESCRIPTION

Scope: Publishes articles on theology, philosophy, Canon Law. Includes literary and language studies pertaining to religion and philosophy.
Reviews books: Yes
Publishes notes: No
Languages accepted: English; French; German; Italian; Spanish; Latin
Prints abstracts: No
Author-anonymous submission: No

SUBMISSION REQUIREMENTS

Restrictions on contributors: Contributors must be professors at Univ. S. Tommaso or treat Thomistic material.
Author pays submission fee: No
Author pays page charges: No
Length of articles: 6,000 words
Length of book reviews: 500 words
Style: MLA; Chicago
Number of copies required: 1
Special requirements: Submit typescript.
Copyright ownership: Univ. S. Tommaso
Rejected manuscripts: Returned
Time before publication decision: 1 mo.
Time between decision and publication: 3 mos. minimum
Number of reviewers: 2
Articles submitted per year: 30
Articles published per year: 20-24
Book reviews submitted per year: 100-140
Book reviews published per year: 100-140

(172)
*Angles on the English Speaking World

Peter Harder, Niels Bugge Hansen, & Jørgen Sevaldsen, Editors
Dept. of English
Copenhagen Univ.
Njalsgade 84
2300 Copenhagen S, Denmark

Telephone: (46) 45 542211
First published: 1986
Sponsoring organization: Københavns Univ., Faculty of Humanities
MLA acronym: Angles

SUBSCRIPTION INFORMATION

Frequency of publication: 1-2 times/yr.
Available in microform: No

ADVERTISING INFORMATION

Advertising accepted: No

EDITORIAL DESCRIPTION

Scope: Publishes articles on the language and culture of the English-speaking world.
Reviews books: Yes
Publishes notes: No
Languages accepted: English
Prints abstracts: No
Author-anonymous submission: No

Restrictions on contributors: Articles written by Danish scholars or on subjects with a Scandinavian angle are particularly welcome.
Author pays submission fee: No
Author pays page charges: No
Length of articles: 7,000 words
Length of book reviews: 2,000 words
Number of copies required: 1
Special requirements: Articles which are scholarly, but which avoid scholarly jargon, are preferred.
Copyright ownership: Author & English Dept., Københavns Univ.
Rejected manuscripts: Returned
Number of reviewers: 2
Articles published per year: 5-10
Book reviews published per year: 5-15

(173)
*Anglia: Zeitschrift für Englische Philologie

Helmut Gneuss, Hans Käsmann, Erwin Wolff, & Theodor Wolpers, Editors
Inst. für Englische Philologie
Univ. München
Schellingstr. 3
8000 Munich 40, Germany

Additional editorial address: Contributions on English language and medieval literature should be sent to: Helmut Gneuss, at the above address or Hans Käsmann, Anglistisches Seminar, Univ. Heidelberg, Kettengasse 12, 6900 Heidelberg, Germany. Contributions on English literature (after 1500) and American and Commonwealth literature should be sent to: Erwin Wolff, Inst. für Anglistik, Univ. Erlangen-Nürnberg, Bismarckstr. 1, 8520 Erlangen, Germany; or Theodor Wolpers, Seminar für Englische Philologie, Univ. Göttingen, Humboldtallee 13, 3400 Göttingen, Germany
Telephone: (49) 89 21803270
Fax: (49) 89 21802322
First published: 1878
ISSN: 0340-5222
MLA acronym: Anglia

SUBSCRIPTION INFORMATION

Frequency of publication: 2 double issues/yr.
Circulation: 750
Available in microform: No
Subscription price: 186 DM/yr.
Year to which price refers: 1991
Subscription address: Max Niemeyer Verlag, Postfach 2140, 7400 Tübingen, Germany
Subscription telephone: (49) 7071 81104
Subscription fax: (49) 7071 87419

ADVERTISING INFORMATION

Advertising accepted: Yes
Advertising rates: Request from Max Niemeyer Verlag.

EDITORIAL DESCRIPTION

Scope: Publishes articles on English language (historical and descriptive); medieval and modern English literature; American literature; Commonwealth literature.
Reviews books: Yes
Publishes notes: Yes
Languages accepted: English; German
Prints abstracts: No
Author-anonymous submission: No

SUBMISSION REQUIREMENTS

Restrictions on contributors: Unsolicited reviews are not accepted.
Author pays submission fee: No
Author pays page charges: No
Length of articles: 12,000 English words or 10,000 German words maximum
Length of book reviews: 1,500 English words or 1,200 German words maximum
Length of notes: 5,000 English words or 4,000 German words maximum
Style: Journal
Number of copies required: 1
Copyright ownership: Max Niemeyer Verlag
Rejected manuscripts: Returned; enclose return postage.
Time before publication decision: 3 mos.
Time between decision and publication: 12-18 mos.
Number of reviewers: 2 minimum
Articles submitted per year: 50
Articles published per year: 15-20
Book reviews published per year: 65-80

(174)
Anglica et Americana

Bruce Clunies Ross, Steen Schousboe, & Niels Thorsen, Editors
Dept. of English
Univ. of Copenhagen
Njalsgade 84
2300 Copenhagen S, Denmark

First published: 1977
Sponsoring organization: Faculty of Humanities, Univ. of Copenhagen
ISSN: 0105-9963
MLA acronym: A&A

SUBSCRIPTION INFORMATION

Frequency of publication: Irregular
Available in microform: No
Subscription address: Atheneum, Nørregade 6, 1165 Copenhagen K, Denmark

ADVERTISING INFORMATION

Advertising accepted: No

EDITORIAL DESCRIPTION

Scope: Publishes monographs on English and American language, literature, culture, and history written by members of the English department at the University of Copenhagen.
Reviews books: No
Publishes notes: No
Languages accepted: English; Danish
Prints abstracts: No
Author-anonymous submission: Yes

SUBMISSION REQUIREMENTS

Restrictions on contributors: Contributors must be staff members of the Department of English of the University of Copenhagen.
Author pays submission fee: No
Author pays page charges: No
Number of copies required: 1
Copyright ownership: Author & Dept. of English, Univ. of Copenhagen
Rejected manuscripts: Returned
Time between decision and publication: 2
Books submitted per year: 4 maximum
Books published per year: 3 maximum

(175)
*Anglistik und Amerikanistik

Wissenschaftliche Buchgesellschaft
Hindenburgstr. 40
6100 Darmstadt 11, Germany

Telephone: (49) 6151 3308-0
Fax: (49) 6151 314128
First published: 1971
MLA acronym: AuA

SUBSCRIPTION INFORMATION

Frequency of publication: Irregular
Available in microform: No

EDITORIAL DESCRIPTION

Scope: Publishes studies on British and American literature, language, and culture.
Reviews books: No
Publishes notes: No
Languages accepted: English; German
Prints abstracts: No
Author-anonymous submission: No

SUBMISSION REQUIREMENTS

Length of books: 150-250 pp.
Special requirements: Submit original typescript.
Copyright ownership: Wissenschaftlich Buchgesellschaft
Rejected manuscripts: Returned
Time between decision and publication: 7-12 mos.
Number of reviewers: 1-3
Books published per year: 1-4

(176)
*Anglistik & Englischunterricht

Hans-Jürgen Diller, Stephan Kohl, Joachim Kornelius, Erwin Otto, & Gerd Stratmann, Editors
c/o J. Kornelius & M. Buschmeier
English Dept.
Ruhr Univ. Bochum
Universitätsstr. 150
4630 Bochum 1, Germany

Telephone: (49) 234 7002601
First published: 1977
ISSN: 0344-8266
MLA acronym: A&E

SUBSCRIPTION INFORMATION

Frequency of publication: 3 times/yr.
Circulation: 1,200
Available in microform: No
Subscription price: 60 DM/yr.; 50 DM/yr. students
Year to which price refers: 1991-92
Subscription address: Carl Winter Universitätsverlag, Lutherstr. 59, 6900 Heidelberg 1, Germany
Subscription telephone: (49) 6221 41490
Subscription fax: (49) 6221 415941

ADVERTISING INFORMATION

Advertising accepted: Yes

EDITORIAL DESCRIPTION

Scope: Publishes articles on British and American language, literature, and cultural studies. Issues are thematic.
Reviews books: Yes
Publishes notes: No
Languages accepted: English; German
Prints abstracts: No
Author-anonymous submission: No

SUBMISSION REQUIREMENTS

Restrictions on contributors: Most articles are specially commissioned for each volume.
Author pays submission fee: No
Author pays page charges: No
Length of articles: 15-25 pp.
Length of book reviews: 1/3 p.
Style: Journal
Number of copies required: 2
Copyright ownership: Journal
Rejected manuscripts: Returned at author's request
Time before publication decision: 4-6 weeks
Time between decision and publication: 6 mos.
Number of reviewers: 5
Articles submitted per year: 35
Articles published per year: 25-30

Book reviews submitted per year: 40-60
Book reviews published per year: 40-60

(177)
*Anglistische Forschungen

Carl Winter, Editor
Carl Winter Universitätsverlag GmbH
Lutherstr. 59
6900 Heidelberg, Germany

First published: 1900
ISSN: 0179-1389
MLA acronym: AF

SUBSCRIPTION INFORMATION

Frequency of publication: Irregular
Circulation: 600-3,000
Available in microform: No

ADVERTISING INFORMATION

Advertising accepted: No

EDITORIAL DESCRIPTION

Scope: Publishes collections of articles on English and American language, literature, and cultural history.
Reviews books: No
Publishes notes: No
Languages accepted: German; English; French
Author-anonymous submission: No

SUBMISSION REQUIREMENTS

Restrictions on contributors: None
Length of books: No restrictions
Style: MLA preferred
Number of copies required: 1
Copyright ownership: Carl Winter Universitätsverlag GmbH
Rejected manuscripts: Returned
Time before publication decision: 8 mos.
Time between decision and publication: 1 yr.
Number of reviewers: 1-2
Books submitted per year: 10-20
Books published per year: 5-10

(178)
Anglo-American Forum

Christoph Gutknecht, Editor
Univ. Hamburg
Seminar für Englische Sprache und Kultur
Von-Melle-Park 6
2 Hamburg 13, Germany

First published: 1975
ISSN: 0170-8163
MLA acronym: AAF

SUBSCRIPTION INFORMATION

Frequency of publication: Irregular
Circulation: 200-1,000
Available in microform: No
Subscription address: Verlag Peter Lang AG, Jupiterstr. 15, P.O. Box 277, 3000 Bern 15, Switzerland

ADVERTISING INFORMATION

Advertising accepted: No

EDITORIAL DESCRIPTION

Scope: Includes bibliographies, source publications, essays, monographs, and review essays, with the aim of promoting the interdisciplinary interpretation and understanding of English (British, U.S., and Commonwealth) language, life, and literature.
Reviews books: Yes
Publishes notes: Yes
Languages accepted: English
Prints abstracts: No

SUBMISSION REQUIREMENTS

Restrictions on contributors: None
Author pays submission fee: No
Author pays page charges: Yes
Length of books: No restrictions
Length of book reviews: 20,000 words
Length of notes: 20,000 words
Style: MLA
Number of copies required: 1
Special requirements: Submit reproducible typescript, size A4 (8 1/4 in. x 11 3/4 in.); use IBM typewriter, plastic or film ribbon. Prepared paper should be ordered from: Verlag P. Lang, Eschborner Landstr. 42-50, 6000 Frankfurt a.M. 90, Germany.
Copyright ownership: Assigned by author to Verlag Peter Lang AG
Rejected manuscripts: Returned
Time before publication decision: 1 mo.
Time between decision and publication: 5 mos.
Number of reviewers: 2-3
Books submitted per year: 5-10
Books published per year: 2-3
Book reviews published per year: 2-3
Notes published per year: 2-3

(179)
*Anglo-Norman Text Society

c/o Hon. Secretary
Anglo-Norman Text Soc.
Birkbeck College
Malet St.
London WC1E 7HX, England

Telephone: (44) 71 6316233
First published: 1939
Sponsoring organization: Anglo-Norman Text Soc.
ISSN: 0066-183X
MLA acronym: ANTS

SUBSCRIPTION INFORMATION

Frequency of publication: Annual
Circulation: 400
Available in microform: No
Subscription address: c/o Hon. Treasurer A.N.-T.S., Dept. of French, The University, St. Andrews KY16 9PH, Scotland

ADVERTISING INFORMATION

Advertising accepted: No

EDITORIAL DESCRIPTION

Scope: Publishes Anglo-Norman texts.
Reviews books: Yes
Publishes notes: No
Languages accepted: English; French
Prints abstracts: No

SUBMISSION REQUIREMENTS

Restrictions on contributors: None
Author pays submission fee: No
Author pays page charges: No
Length of books: No restrictions
Style: Series
Number of copies required: 2
Special requirements: Consult with Hon. Secretary before submission.
Copyright ownership: Anglo-Norman Text Soc.
Rejected manuscripts: Returned
Time between decision and publication: 2-3 yrs.
Number of reviewers: 3
Books published per year: 1

(180)
*Anglo-Saxon England

Michael Lapidge, Malcolm Godden, & Simon Keynes, Editors
Cambridge Univ. Press
Edinburgh Bldg.
Shaftesbury Rd.
Cambridge CB2 2RU, England

First published: 1972
ISSN: 0263-6751
MLA acronym: ASE

SUBSCRIPTION INFORMATION

Frequency of publication: Annual
Circulation: 2,000
Subscription price: $96.00/yr. institutions; $60.00/yr. individuals
Year to which price refers: 1992
Additional subscription address: In US & Canada: Cambridge Univ. Press, 40 W. 20th St., New York, NY 10011-4211

ADVERTISING INFORMATION

Advertising accepted: Yes

EDITORIAL DESCRIPTION

Scope: Publishes articles on all aspects of Anglo-Saxon studies. Includes a bibliography of the previous year's publications in the field.
Reviews books: No
Languages accepted: English
Prints abstracts: No

SUBMISSION REQUIREMENTS

Restrictions on contributors: None
Length of articles: 7,000 words
Style: Journal
Number of copies required: 1
Copyright ownership: Cambridge Univ. Press
Rejected manuscripts: Returned
Time before publication decision: 3-6 mos.
Time between decision and publication: 1-2 yrs.
Number of reviewers: 2
Articles published per year: 15

(181)
*Annales Academiae Scientiarum Fennicae. Dissertationes Humanarum Litterarum

Pekka Suvanto, Editor
Ohjaajantie 34 B
00400 Helsinki, Finland

Fax: (358) 0 6221121
First published: 1973
ISSN: 0355-113X
MLA acronym: AASF

SUBSCRIPTION INFORMATION

Frequency of publication: Irregular
Circulation: 500
Subscription address: Suomalainen Tiedeakatemia-Academia Scientiarum Fennica, Mariankatu 5, 00170 Helsinki 17, Finland

EDITORIAL DESCRIPTION

Scope: Publishes doctoral dissertations in the humanities.
Reviews books: No
Languages accepted: English; French; German; Latin
Prints abstracts: No

SUBMISSION REQUIREMENTS

Number of copies required: 1
Special requirements: Submit original typescript.

Copyright ownership: Assigned by author to Suomalainen Tiedeakatemia-Academia Scientiarum Fennica
Rejected manuscripts: Returned
Time before publication decision: 1-3 mos.
Time between decision and publication: 18 mos.
Number of reviewers: 1
Books published per year: 3-4

(182)
*Annales Academiae Scientiarum Fennicae/Suomalaisen Tiedeakatemian Toimituksia

Pekka Suvanto, Editor
Ohjaajantie 34B
00400 Helsinki, Finland

Additional editorial address: Hannu Heikkila, FFSS, Mariankatu 5, 00170 Helsinki, Finland
Telephone: (358) 0 652572
Fax: (358) 0 6221121
First published: 1909
Sponsoring organization: Academia Scientiarum Fennica
ISSN: 0066-2011
MLA acronym: AASFB

SUBSCRIPTION INFORMATION

Frequency of publication: Irregular
Circulation: 500
Available in microform: No
Subscription address: Tiedekurja Bookstore, Kirkkokatu 14, 00170 Helsinki, Finland
Additional subscription address: Academic Bookstore, Keskuskatu 2, 00100 Helsinki, Finland
Subscription telephone: (358) 0 635177

ADVERTISING INFORMATION

Advertising accepted: No

EDITORIAL DESCRIPTION

Scope: Publishes monographs on the humanities.
Reviews books: No
Publishes notes: No
Languages accepted: English; German; French
Prints abstracts: No

SUBMISSION REQUIREMENTS

Author pays page charges: No
Length of books: 200-300 pp.
Copyright ownership: Publisher
Rejected manuscripts: Returned
Time before publication decision: 1 mo.
Books published per year: 10

(183)
*Annales de Bretagne et des Pays de l'Ouest

J. Queniart, Managing Editor
Univ. de Haute-Bretagne (Rennes II)
6, Avenue Gaston-Bergen
35000 Rennes, France

Telephone: (33) 99333252 ext. 1631
First published: 1886
Sponsoring organization: Assn. pour la publication des *AnBret*
ISSN: 0003-391X
MLA acronym: AnBret

SUBSCRIPTION INFORMATION

Frequency of publication: 4 times/yr.
Circulation: 700
Available in microform: No
Subscription address: Mme Margat, at the above address

ADVERTISING INFORMATION

Advertising accepted: No

EDITORIAL DESCRIPTION

Scope: Publishes articles on the history, in the widest sense of the term, of western France.
Reviews books: Yes
Publishes notes: Yes
Languages accepted: French
Prints abstracts: No
Author-anonymous submission: Yes

SUBMISSION REQUIREMENTS

Author pays submission fee: No
Length of articles: 10-25 printed pp.
Number of copies required: 1
Copyright ownership: Journal
Rejected manuscripts: Returned
Time before publication decision: 6-12 mos.
Time between decision and publication: 6-12 mos.
Articles published per year: 25-30

(184)
*Annales de la Faculté des Lettres et Sciences Humaines: Philosophie, Littérature, Langues, Sciences Humaines

Faculté des Lettres & Sciences Humaines
Univ. Cheikh Anta Diop de Dakar
Dakar, Senegal

Telephone: (221) 255073
Fax: (221) 254977
First published: 1971
Sponsoring organization: Univ. Cheikh Anta Diop de Dakar
ISSN: 0850-1254
MLA acronym: AFLSHS

SUBSCRIPTION INFORMATION

Frequency of publication: Annual
Available in microform: No
Subscription price: 2,000 CFAF (40 F)/yr.
Year to which price refers: 1992

ADVERTISING INFORMATION

Advertising accepted: Yes, on an exchange basis

EDITORIAL DESCRIPTION

Scope: Publishes articles on philosophy, literature, language, and human sciences.
Reviews books: No
Publishes notes: No
Languages accepted: French; English; Spanish; Portuguese
Prints abstracts: Yes
Author-anonymous submission: No

SUBMISSION REQUIREMENTS

Restrictions on contributors: Priority is given to staff members of the Faculté des Lettres & Sciences Humaines of the Univ. Cheikh Anta Diop de Dakar.
Author pays submission fee: No
Author pays page charges: No
Length of articles: 8,500 words
Number of copies required: 3
Special requirements: Submit a 225-word abstract, preferably in English.
Copyright ownership: Publisher
Rejected manuscripts: Not returned
Time before publication decision: 2-3 mos.
Time between decision and publication: 8 mos. maximum
Number of reviewers: 2-3
Articles submitted per year: 25
Articles published per year: 12-15

(185)
*Annales de la Faculté des Lettres et Sciences Humaines de Yaoundé/ Annals of Faculty of Letters and Social Sciences of Yaounde

Pierre Ngijol Ngijol, Jean Louis Dongmo, Pius Ondona, Paul Mbangwana, Ambroise Kom, & Hansel Eyoh, Editors
Faculté des Lettres et Sciences Humaines
Univ. Fédérale de Yaoundé
B.P. 755
Yaoundé, Cameroun

Telephone: (237) 220978
First published: 1969
Sponsoring organization: Faculté des Lettres & Sciences Humaines de Yaoundé, Univ. de Yaoundé
ISSN: 0379-1793
MLA acronym: AFLSHY

SUBSCRIPTION INFORMATION

Frequency of publication: 2 times/yr.
Circulation: 500
Available in microform: No
Subscription price: $20.00/yr.
Year to which price refers: 1991

ADVERTISING INFORMATION

Advertising accepted: No

EDITORIAL DESCRIPTION

Scope: Publishes research on modern French, English, German, and Spanish letters, as well as the social sciences, including history, sociology, philosophy, and language sciences.
Reviews books: No
Publishes notes: No
Languages accepted: French; English
Prints abstracts: Yes

SUBMISSION REQUIREMENTS

Restrictions on contributors: None
Author pays submission fee: No
Author pays page charges: No
Length of articles: 10,000 words
Style: MLA
Number of copies required: 2
Special requirements: Submit original typescript.
Copyright ownership: Assigned by author to journal
Rejected manuscripts: Not returned
Time before publication decision: 6-9 mos.
Time between decision and publication: 1-2 yrs.
Number of reviewers: 3
Articles submitted per year: 50
Articles published per year: 12-20

(186)
*Annales de l'Université d'Abidjan: Serie D: Lettres

Gilles Vilasco & Touré Bakary, Editors
Services des Publications de l'Univ. d'Abidjan
01 B.P. V.34
Abidjan 01, Ivory Coast

Telephone: (225) 445649
First published: 1965
Sponsoring organization: Univ. d'Abidjan
ISSN: 0587-4114
MLA acronym: AdUA

SUBSCRIPTION INFORMATION

Frequency of publication: Annual
Available in microform: No

ADVERTISING INFORMATION

Advertising accepted: No

EDITORIAL DESCRIPTION

Scope: Publishes studies written at the Université d'Abidjan including works in the fields of literature, history, art, archaeology, and the sciences.
Reviews books: Yes
Languages accepted: French; English; Spanish
Prints abstracts: No
Author-anonymous submission: No

SUBMISSION REQUIREMENTS

Restrictions on contributors: None
Author pays submission fee: No
Author pays page charges: No
Length of articles: 25 pp. maximum
Length of book reviews: 200-300 words
Style: None
Number of copies required: 2
Copyright ownership: Univ. d'Abidjan
Rejected manuscripts: Returned
Time before publication decision: 6 weeks
Time between decision and publication: 6 mos.
Articles submitted per year: 20-50
Articles published per year: 10-20

(187)
*Annales du Centre de Recherches sur l'Amérique Anglophone

Jean Berenger, Jean Cazemajou, Jean-Michel LaCroix, & Pierre Spriet, Editors
Centre de Recherches sur l'Amérique Anglophone
Maison des Sciences de l'Homme d'Aquitaine
Esplanade des Antilles
Domaine Universitaire
33405 Talence Cedex, France

Telephone: (33) 56846800
Fax: (33) 56846810
First published: 1975
Sponsoring organization: Centre de Recherches sur l'Amérique Anglophone
ISSN: 0399-0443
MLA acronym: ACRAA

SUBSCRIPTION INFORMATION

Frequency of publication: Annual (July)
Circulation: 100
Available in microform: No
Subscription price: 120 F/yr.
Year to which price refers: 1992
Subscription address: Presses Universitaires de Bordeaux, Univ. Michel de Montaigne-Bordeaux III, Domaine Universitaire, 33405 Talence Cedex, France
Subscription telephone: (33) 56845022
Subscription fax: (33) 56845135

ADVERTISING INFORMATION

Advertising accepted: No

EDITORIAL DESCRIPTION

Scope: Publishes collections of articles on American and Canadian literature. Includes works on ethnic literatures of the United States.
Reviews books: No
Publishes notes: No
Languages accepted: French; English
Prints abstracts: Yes
Author-anonymous submission: No

SUBMISSION REQUIREMENTS

Author pays submission fee: No
Author pays page charges: No
Length of articles: 40,000 characters
Number of copies required: 1
Copyright ownership: Presses Universitaires de Bordeaux
Time between decision and publication: 6-7 mos.
Number of reviewers: 3
Articles published per year: 16-17

(188)
*Annales du Midi: Revue de la France Méridionale

M. Taillefer & J. B. Marquette, Editors
Ed. Privat
14, rue des Arts
31068 Toulouse Cédex, France

Telephone: (33) 61230926
First published: 1889
Sponsoring organization: Univ. de Toulouse; Univ. de Bordeaux; Univ. d'Aix; Univ. de Marseille; Univ. de Montpellier; Univ. de Nice; Univ. de Pau; Univ. de Limoges; Univ. de Perpignan
ISSN: 0003-4398
MLA acronym: AdM

SUBSCRIPTION INFORMATION

Frequency of publication: 4 times/yr.
Circulation: 550
Available in microform: No
Subscription price: 265 F/yr. France; 395 F/yr. elsewhere
Year to which price refers: 1992

ADVERTISING INFORMATION

Advertising accepted: No

EDITORIAL DESCRIPTION

Scope: Pubishes articles on the history and culture of Southern France.
Reviews books: Yes
Publishes notes: Yes
Languages accepted: French
Prints abstracts: Yes
Author-anonymous submission: No

SUBMISSION REQUIREMENTS

Author pays submission fee: No
Author pays page charges: No
Length of articles: 25 pp.
Length of book reviews: 2 pp.
Length of notes: 5 pp.
Number of copies required: 1
Time before publication decision: 1 yr. maximum
Time between decision and publication: 1 yr. maximum
Number of reviewers: 2
Articles submitted per year: 20-30
Articles published per year: 10-12
Book reviews submitted per year: 60
Book reviews published per year: 40
Notes submitted per year: 10-20
Notes published per year: 6-8

(189)
Annali del Liceo Classico "G. Garibaldi" di Palermo

Giuseppe Guttilla, Editor
Liceo Classico "G. Garibaldi" di Palermo
Via Canonico Rotolo, 2
90143 Palermo, Italy

Additional editorial address: Via Cl. Monteverdi 43, 90145 Palermo, Italy
First published: 1964
Sponsoring organization: Liceo Classico G. Garibaldi di Palermo; Assessorato Regionale Beni Culturali
MLA acronym: ALCGP

SUBSCRIPTION INFORMATION

Frequency of publication: Irregular
Circulation: 600
Available in microform: No

ADVERTISING INFORMATION

Advertising accepted: No

EDITORIAL DESCRIPTION

Scope: Publishes articles on classic and modern languages and literatures, history, philosophy, archaeology, art, and sciences that are of significant cultural interest. Also publishes notices on Liceo life.
Reviews books: No
Publishes notes: Yes
Languages accepted: Italian; Latin; Greek; French; Spanish; English; German
Prints abstracts: No
Author-anonymous submission: No

SUBMISSION REQUIREMENTS

Restrictions on contributors: None
Author pays submission fee: No
Author pays page charges: No
Length of articles: 2-50 pp.
Style: Journal
Number of copies required: 1
Special requirements: Submit original typescript before 1 Sept.
Copyright ownership: Assigned by author to journal
Rejected manuscripts: Not returned
Time before publication decision: 2 mos.
Time between decision and publication: 15 mos.
Number of reviewers: Editorial Board
Articles submitted per year: 40-45
Articles published per year: 30

(190)
*Annali della Facoltà di Lettere e Filosofia dell'Università di Macerata

Univ. di Macerata
Facoltà di Lettere e Filosofia
Via Don Minzoni
62100 Macerata, Italy

First published: 1968
Sponsoring organization: Univ. degli Studi di Macerata
MLA acronym: AFLFUM

SUBSCRIPTION INFORMATION

Frequency of publication: Annual
Circulation: 400
Available in microform: No

ADVERTISING INFORMATION

Advertising accepted: No

EDITORIAL DESCRIPTION

Scope: Publishes letters, stories, and philosophy.
Reviews books: No
Publishes notes: No
Languages accepted: Italian; French; English; German; Spanish
Prints abstracts: No

SUBMISSION REQUIREMENTS

Restrictions on contributors: None
Author pays submission fee: No
Author pays page charges: No
Length of articles: No restrictions
Style: None
Number of copies required: 1
Rejected manuscripts: Returned
Time before publication decision: 1 mo.
Time between decision and publication: 1 yr.
Articles published per year: 15-25

(191)
*Annali della Facoltà di Lettere e Filosofia dell'Università di Perugia

Antonio Pieretti, Editor
Facoltà di Lettere e Filosofia
Univ. degli Studi di Perugia
Piazza Moriacchi, 11
Perugia, Italy

First published: 1962
Sponsoring organization: Univ. degli Studi di Perugia
ISSN: 0553-8289
MLA acronym: AFLFP

SUBSCRIPTION INFORMATION

Frequency of publication: Annual
Circulation: 1,000
Available in microform: No

ADVERTISING INFORMATION

Advertising accepted: No

EDITORIAL DESCRIPTION

Scope: Publishes articles on literature, philosophy, and philology.
Reviews books: No
Publishes notes: No
Languages accepted: Italian; Spanish; French; German; English
Prints abstracts: No

SUBMISSION REQUIREMENTS

Restrictions on contributors: None
Author pays page charges: No
Length of articles: No restrictions
Style: None
Number of copies required: 1
Rejected manuscripts: Returned
Time before publication decision: 2 mos.
Time between decision and publication: 15 mos.
Articles submitted per year: 50
Articles published per year: 40

(192)
*Annali della Scuola Normale Superiore di Pisa: Classe di Lettere e Filosofia

Giuseppe Nenci, Editor
Scuola Normale Superiore di Pisa
Piazza dei Cavalieri, 7
56100 Pisa, Italy

Telephone: (39) 50 597111
Fax: (39) 50 563513
First published: 1873
ISSN: 0392-095X
MLA acronym: ASNSP

SUBSCRIPTION INFORMATION

Frequency of publication: 4 times/yr.
Circulation: 1,500
Available in microform: No

ADVERTISING INFORMATION

Advertising accepted: No

EDITORIAL DESCRIPTION

Scope: Publishes papers on literature, philosophy, history, archaeology, linguistics, and history of the arts.
Reviews books: Yes
Languages accepted: English; French; German; Italian; Spanish
Prints abstracts: No

SUBMISSION REQUIREMENTS

Number of copies required: 1
Copyright ownership: Journal
Time before publication decision: 2 mos.
Time between decision and publication: 1 yr.
Number of reviewers: 3
Articles submitted per year: 70
Articles published per year: 50
Book reviews submitted per year: 200
Book reviews published per year: 180

(193)
*Annali di Ca' Foscari: Rivista della Facoltà di Lingue e Letterature Straniere dell'Università di Venezia

Giuliano Tamani, Editor
Dipto. di Studi Eurasiatici
San Polo 2035
30125 Venice, Italy

First published: 1962
Sponsoring organization: Univ. degli Studi di Venezia
ISSN: 0506-6379
MLA acronym: ACF

SUBSCRIPTION INFORMATION

Frequency of publication: 3-4 times/yr.
Circulation: 500
Available in microform: No
Subscription address: Editoriale Programma, Via S. Eufemia 5, 35121 Padua, Italy

ADVERTISING INFORMATION

Advertising accepted: No

EDITORIAL DESCRIPTION

Scope: Publishes articles on modern and Oriental languages and literatures.
Reviews books: Yes
Publishes notes: Yes
Languages accepted: All European languages
Prints abstracts: No
Author-anonymous submission: No

SUBMISSION REQUIREMENTS

Restrictions on contributors: None
Author pays submission fee: No
Author pays page charges: No
Length of articles: 24 double-spaced typescript pp.
Length of book reviews: 2,000-3,000 words
Style: MLA
Number of copies required: 2
Copyright ownership: Univ. degli Studi di Venezia
Rejected manuscripts: Returned; enclose return postage.
Time before publication decision: 6 mos.
Time between decision and publication: 10-12 mos.
Number of reviewers: 2
Articles submitted per year: 60
Articles published per year: 50
Book reviews submitted per year: 8
Book reviews published per year: 4
Notes submitted per year: 4
Notes published per year: 4

(194)
*Annali d'Italianistica

Dino S. Cervigni, Editor
CB 3170, 141 Dey Hall
Univ. of North Carolina
Chapel Hill, NC 27599-3170

First published: 1983
ISSN: 0741-7527
MLA acronym: AdI

SUBSCRIPTION INFORMATION

Frequency of publication: Annual
Circulation: 600
Available in microform: No
Subscription price: $19.00/yr. institutions US; $12.00/yr. individuals US; $21.00/yr. elsewhere
Year to which price refers: 1992

ADVERTISING INFORMATION

Advertising accepted: Yes

EDITORIAL DESCRIPTION

Scope: Publishes articles on Italian literature and culture. Monograph themes are announced two years ahead.
Reviews books: Yes
Publishes notes: Yes
Languages accepted: Italian; English
Prints abstracts: Yes

SUBMISSION REQUIREMENTS

Author pays submission fee: No
Author pays page charges: No
Length of articles: 20-30 pp.
Length of book reviews: 3-5 pp.
Length of notes: No restrictions
Style: MLA for English articles; journal style sheet for Italian articles
Number of copies required: 2
Copyright ownership: Journal
Rejected manuscripts: Returned
Time before publication decision: 3 mos.
Time between decision and publication: 3 mos.
Number of reviewers: 2-3
Articles published per year: 15-20
Book reviews published per year: 20-30
Notes published per year: 1-2

(195)
*Annali Istituto Universitario Orientale, Napoli: Rivista del Dipartimento di Studi Asiatici e del Dipartimento di Studi e Ricerche su Africa e Paesi Arabi

Luigi Cagni, Editor
Dipt. di Studi Asiatici
Ist. Universitario Orientale di Napoli
Piazza S. Domenico Maggiore, 12
Palazzo Corigliano
80134 Naples, Italy

Telephone: (39) 81 5521678
Fax: (39) 81 5517852
First published: 1929
Sponsoring organization: Dipt. di Studi Asiatici & Dipt. di Studi e Ricerche su Africa e Paesi Arabi, Ist. Universitario Orientale
MLA acronym: AION-SO

SUBSCRIPTION INFORMATION

Frequency of publication: 4 times/yr. & 4 supplements/yr.
Circulation: 120
Available in microform: No
Subscription address: Herder Editrice & Liberia, Piazza Montecitocio 120, 00186 Rome, Italy

ADVERTISING INFORMATION

Advertising accepted: No

EDITORIAL DESCRIPTION

Scope: Publishes articles on the Near, Middle, and Far East as well as on Africa, including archaeology, art history, literature, linguistics, religion, philosophy, history, and pre-history.
Reviews books: Yes
Publishes notes: Yes

Languages accepted: English; French; German; Italian
Prints abstracts: Yes
Author-anonymous submission: No

SUBMISSION REQUIREMENTS

Restrictions on contributors: None
Author pays submission fee: No
Author pays page charges: No
Length of articles: 30-35 pp. maximum
Length of books: 110 pp. maximum for supplements
Length of book reviews: No restrictions
Length of notes: No restrictions
Style: None
Number of copies required: 1
Copyright ownership: Ist. Universitario Orientale, Napoli
Rejected manuscripts: Returned
Time before publication decision: 12-15 mos.
Time between decision and publication: 12-15 mos.
Number of reviewers: 1-2
Articles submitted per year: 20-25
Articles published per year: 20-25
Books submitted per year: 10-15
Books published per year: 4 supplements
Book reviews published per year: 10-15

(196)
Annali Istituto Universitario Orientale, Napoli, Sezione Romanza

Raffaele Sirri, Editor
viale Nicola Fornelli, 16/B
80132 Naples, Italy

First published: 1959
Sponsoring organization: Ist. Universitario Orientale, Napoli
ISSN: 0547-2121
MLA acronym: AION-SR

SUBSCRIPTION INFORMATION

Frequency of publication: 2 times/yr.
Circulation: 800
Available in microform: No
Subscription address: Ist. Universitario Orientale di Napoli, Largo S. Giovanni Maggiore, 30, 80134 Naples, Italy

ADVERTISING INFORMATION

Advertising accepted: No

EDITORIAL DESCRIPTION

Scope: Publishes studies in Romance languages, from a philological and critical point of view.
Reviews books: Yes
Publishes notes: No
Languages accepted: English; French; German; Italian; Portuguese; Spanish; Romanian
Prints abstracts: Yes
Author-anonymous submission: No

SUBMISSION REQUIREMENTS

Restrictions on contributors: None
Author pays submission fee: No
Author pays page charges: No
Length of articles: No restrictions
Number of copies required: 2
Special requirements: Submit final version.
Copyright ownership: Ist. Universitario Orientale, Napoli
Rejected manuscripts: Not returned
Time before publication decision: 6 mos.
Time between decision and publication: 6 mos.
Number of reviewers: 3
Articles submitted per year: 150
Articles published per year: 30
Book reviews submitted per year: 10
Book reviews published per year: 10

(197)
Gli Annali Università per Stranieri

Giorgio Spitella, Director
Univ. Italiana per Stranieri
Palazzo Gallenga
Perugia, Italy

Telephone: (39) 75 64344
First published: 1981
Sponsoring organization: Univ. Italiana per Stranieri
MLA acronym: GliA

SUBSCRIPTION INFORMATION

Frequency of publication: 2 times/yr.
Subscription address: Case Editrice Le Monnier, Via Antonio Meucci 2, 50015 Grassina (FI), Italy
Subscription telephone: (39) 55 6491402

EDITORIAL DESCRIPTION

Scope: Publishes articles on Italian literature, history, and language.
Publishes notes: Yes
Languages accepted: Italian
Prints abstracts: Yes
Author-anonymous submission: Yes

SUBMISSION REQUIREMENTS

Articles published per year: 16

(198)
*Annals of Scholarship: An International Quarterly in the Humanities and Social Sciences

Ruth Graham, Marie-Rose Logan, Nina daVinci Nichols, & Paul-Bernard Newman, Editors
1841 Broadway
New York, NY 10023-7602

Telephone: 212 765-3988
First published: 1980
Historical variations in title: Formerly *Annals of Scholarship: Metastudies of the Humanities and Social Sciences*
ISSN: 0192-2858
MLA acronym: AnSch

SUBSCRIPTION INFORMATION

Frequency of publication: 4 times/yr. (Winter, Spring, Summer, Fall)
Circulation: 600-700
Available in microform: No
Subscription price: $60.00/yr. institutions; $32.00/yr. individuals; add $8.00/yr. postage outside US
Year to which price refers: 1991
Subscription address: Wayne State Univ. Press, Leonard N. Simons Bldg., 5959 Woodward Ave., Detroit, MI 48202
Subscription telephone: 313 577-6120

ADVERTISING INFORMATION

Advertising accepted: Yes

EDITORIAL DESCRIPTION

Scope: The journal publishes studies of the history and current development of the disciplines, methodologies, and manners in which scholars and their scholarship influence and are influenced by institutional, political, and social structures.
Reviews books: Yes
Publishes notes: Yes
Languages accepted: English
Prints abstracts: No
Author-anonymous submission: Yes

SUBMISSION REQUIREMENTS

Restrictions on contributors: Unsolicited reviews are not accepted.
Author pays submission fee: No
Author pays page charges: No
Length of articles: 12,500-15,000 words
Length of book reviews: No restrictions
Length of notes: No restrictions
Style: Chicago
Number of copies required: 2
Special requirements: Articles in French, Italian, German, and Spanish are accepted for translation into English.
Copyright ownership: Journal
Rejected manuscripts: Returned
Time before publication decision: 3-6 mos.
Time between decision and publication: 6-12 mos.
Number of reviewers: 2
Articles submitted per year: 50
Articles published per year: 20
Book reviews published per year: 10-12
Notes submitted per year: 1
Notes published per year: 1

(199)
*Annals of the Bhandarkar Oriental Research Institute

R. N. Dandekar & S. D. Laddu, Editors
Bhandarkar Oriental Research Inst.
Pune 411004, India

First published: 1919
Sponsoring organization: Bhandarkar Oriental Research Inst.
ISSN: 0378-1143
MLA acronym: ABORI

SUBSCRIPTION INFORMATION

Frequency of publication: Annual
Circulation: 800
Available in microform: No
Subscription price: 200 Re/yr.
Year to which price refers: 1990
Subscription address: Secretary, at the above address

ADVERTISING INFORMATION

Advertising accepted: No

EDITORIAL DESCRIPTION

Scope: Publishes articles on Sanskrit and Indological subjects. Serial articles are accepted.
Reviews books: Yes
Publishes notes: Yes
Languages accepted: English; Sanskrit
Prints abstracts: No
Author-anonymous submission: No

SUBMISSION REQUIREMENTS

Restrictions on contributors: None
Author pays submission fee: No
Author pays page charges: No
Length of articles: 3,000-8,000 words
Length of book reviews: 500-1,000 words
Length of notes: 1,500-2,500 words
Style: Journal
Number of copies required: 1
Special requirements: Only original contributions are accepted.
Copyright ownership: Author & Bhandarkar Oriental Research Inst.
Rejected manuscripts: Returned
Time before publication decision: 1 yr.
Time between decision and publication: 10 mos.
Number of reviewers: 2
Articles submitted per year: 30-40
Articles published per year: 20-25
Book reviews submitted per year: 70
Book reviews published per year: 50
Notes submitted per year: 20
Notes published per year: 12

(200)
*Annals of the New York Academy of Sciences

Bill Boland, Editor
2 East 63rd St.
New York, NY 10021

Telephone: 212 838-0230
Fax: 212 888-2894
First published: 1824
Sponsoring organization: New York Academy of Sciences
ISSN: 0077-8923
MLA acronym: ANYAS

SUBSCRIPTION INFORMATION

Frequency of publication: Irregular
Circulation: 5,500
Available in microform: Yes
Subscription price: $2,800.00/yr.; single volumes are also available
Year to which price refers: 1992

ADVERTISING INFORMATION

Advertising accepted: No

EDITORIAL DESCRIPTION

Scope: Each volume is the published record of a conference. Includes topics on science, literature, linguistics.
Reviews books: No
Publishes notes: No
Languages accepted: English
Prints abstracts: No
Author-anonymous submission: No

SUBMISSION REQUIREMENTS

Restrictions on contributors: Unsolicited manuscripts are not accepted. Papers must be have been presented at conference.
Author pays submission fee: No
Author pays page charges: No
Length of books: 5,000 words
Number of copies required: 3
Special requirements: Submit original manuscript and 2 copies.
Copyright ownership: New York Academy of Sciences
Rejected manuscripts: Returned
Articles submitted per year: 1,200
Articles published per year: 1,200
Books published per year: 32

(201)
*L'Année Balzacienne

Madeleine Ambrière-Fargeaud & Michel Lichtlé, Editors
Les Parcs de la Noue, Bt 5
13, rue de la Noue
93170 Bagnolet, France

First published: 1960
Sponsoring organization: Groupe d'Etudes Balzaciennes
ISSN: 0084-6473
MLA acronym: ABalzac

SUBSCRIPTION INFORMATION

Frequency of publication: Annual
Circulation: 2,500
Available in microform: No
Subscription price: 270 F/yr.
Year to which price refers: 1992
Subscription address: Nathalie Preiss, 47, rue Raynouard, 75016 Paris, France

ADVERTISING INFORMATION

Advertising accepted: No

EDITORIAL DESCRIPTION

Scope: Publishes research articles (thematic, historic, stylistic, etc.) on the personality and works of Balzac.
Reviews books: Yes
Publishes notes: Yes
Languages accepted: French
Prints abstracts: No
Author-anonymous submission: No

SUBMISSION REQUIREMENTS

Restrictions on contributors: None
Author pays submission fee: No
Author pays page charges: No
Length of articles: 25 pp. maximum
Length of book reviews: 1-3 pp.
Length of notes: 4-8 pp.
Number of copies required: 2
Special requirements: Submit papers before 15 Jan.
Copyright ownership: Assigned by author to journal
Rejected manuscripts: Not returned
Time before publication decision: 3 mos.
Time between decision and publication: 10 mos.
Number of reviewers: 3
Articles published per year: 15

(202)
Annuaire de l'Institut de Philologie et d'Histoire Orientales et Slaves

Marie Onatzky-Malin, Aristide Théodoridès, & René van Compernolle, Editors
Inst. de Philologie et d'Histoire Orientale et Slaves
Univ. Libre de Bruxelles
Brussels, Belgium

First published: 1932
Sponsoring organization: Inst. de Philologie & d'Histoire Orientales, Groupe d'Etudes Orientales & Slaves; Univ. Libre de Bruxelles, Faculté de Philosophie & Lettres, Section de Slavistique
ISSN: 0773-5812
MLA acronym: AIPHOS

SUBSCRIPTION INFORMATION

Frequency of publication: Annual
Available in microform: No
Subscription address: Editions de l'Univ. de Bruxelles, 26 Ave. Paul Héger, C.P. 163, 1050 Brussels, Belgium

ADVERTISING INFORMATION

Advertising accepted: No

EDITORIAL DESCRIPTION

Scope: Publishes articles on Oriental and Slavic history.
Reviews books: No
Languages accepted: English; French; German
Prints abstracts: No

SUBMISSION REQUIREMENTS

Author pays submission fee: No
Author pays page charges: No
Number of copies required: 1
Articles submitted per year: 6-10
Articles published per year: 6-10

(203)
*Annual of Armenian Linguistics

John A. C. Greppin, Editor
Program in Linguistics
Cleveland State Univ.
Cleveland, OH 44115

Telephone: 216 687-3967
Fax: 216 687-9366
First published: 1980
ISSN: 0271-9800
MLA acronym: AArmL

SUBSCRIPTION INFORMATION

Frequency of publication: Annual
Circulation: 200
Available in microform: No
Subscription price: $20.00/2 yrs. individuals
Year to which price refers: 1992

ADVERTISING INFORMATION

Advertising accepted: Yes
Advertising rates: $100.00/back cover

EDITORIAL DESCRIPTION

Scope: Publishes articles on Armenian linguistics.
Reviews books: Yes
Publishes notes: Yes
Languages accepted: English; French; German; Italian
Prints abstracts: No
Author-anonymous submission: Yes

SUBMISSION REQUIREMENTS

Restrictions on contributors: None
Author pays submission fee: No
Author pays page charges: No
Length of book reviews: 300 words
Length of notes: No restrictions
Style: None
Number of copies required: 1
Copyright ownership: Author
Rejected manuscripts: Returned
Time before publication decision: 1 mo.
Time between decision and publication: 1 yr.
Number of reviewers: 2-3
Articles submitted per year: 10
Articles published per year: 7
Book reviews submitted per year: 8-10
Book reviews published per year: 8-10
Notes submitted per year: 1
Notes published per year: 1

(204)
Annual Report of the Institute of Phonetics, University of Copenhagen

Jørgen Rischel, Editor
Inst. of Phonetics
Univ. of Copenhagen
96 Njalsgade
2300 Copenhagen, Denmark

First published: 1966
Sponsoring organization: Univ. of Copenhagen
ISSN: 0589-6681
MLA acronym: ARIPUC

SUBSCRIPTION INFORMATION

Frequency of publication: Annual
Available in microform: No

ADVERTISING INFORMATION

Advertising accepted: No

EDITORIAL DESCRIPTION

Scope: Publishes results of research in experimental phonetics and phonology.
Reviews books: No
Publishes notes: Yes
Languages accepted: English
Prints abstracts: Yes
Author-anonymous submission: No

SUBMISSION REQUIREMENTS

Restrictions on contributors: Contributors must be students, staff members, or guest researchers at the Inst. of Phonetics.
Author pays submission fee: No
Author pays page charges: No
Number of copies required: 1
Copyright ownership: Author

(205)
*The Annual Report on Cultural Science

Hokkaido Univ.
North 8, West 5
Kitaku, Sapporo 060, Japan

First published: 1952
Sponsoring organization: Hokkaido Univ.
ISSN: 0437-6668
MLA acronym: ARCS

SUBSCRIPTION INFORMATION

Frequency of publication: Annual
Available in microform: No

ADVERTISING INFORMATION

Advertising accepted: No

EDITORIAL DESCRIPTION

Scope: Publishes articles on literature, linguistics, and literary theory with an emphasis on Asian literatures.
Reviews books: No
Publishes notes: No
Languages accepted: Japanese
Prints abstracts: Yes

SUBMISSION REQUIREMENTS

Restrictions on contributors: Contributors must be faculty members of Hokkaido Univ.
Author pays submission fee: No
Author pays page charges: No
Length of articles: No restrictions
Number of copies required: 1
Copyright ownership: Hokkaido Univ.
Time before publication decision: 6 mos.
Time between decision and publication: 6 mos.
Number of reviewers: 2

(206)
*Annual Review of Applied Linguistics

William Grabe, Robert B. Kaplan, Charles Ferguson, G. Richard Tucker, & H. G. Widdowson, Editors
English Dept., Box 6032
Northern Arizona Univ.
Flagstaff, AZ 86011

Telephone: 602 523-4911
Fax: 602 523-2626
First published: 1980
ISSN: 0267-1905
MLA acronym: ARAL

SUBSCRIPTION INFORMATION

Frequency of publication: Annual
Circulation: 600
Available in microform: No
Subscription price: $49.00/yr. institutions; $27.00/yr. individuals
Year to which price refers: 1992
Subscription address: Journals Division, Cambridge Univ. Press, 40 W. 20th St., New York, NY 10011-4211
Additional subscription address: Cambridge Univ. Press, Edinburgh Bldg., Shaftesbury Rd., Cambridge CB2 2RU, England
Subscription telephone: 800 872-7423

ADVERTISING INFORMATION

Advertising accepted: No

EDITORIAL DESCRIPTION

Scope: Publishes articles on applied linguistics.
Reviews books: No
Publishes notes: No
Languages accepted: English
Prints abstracts: No
Author-anonymous submission: No

SUBMISSION REQUIREMENTS

Restrictions on contributors: Unsolicited manuscripts are not accepted.
Author pays submission fee: No
Author pays page charges: No
Length of articles: 5,000-6,000 words plus up to 20 annotated bibliographic citations and up to 60 other bibliographic citations
Style: Journal
Number of copies required: 1
Special requirements: Submit original typescript; outlines are required 6 mos. prior to copy deadline.
Copyright ownership: Cambridge Univ. Press
Rejected manuscripts: Not returned
Time before publication decision: 6 mos.
Number of reviewers: 5
Articles submitted per year: 12-15
Articles published per year: 12-15

(207)
*The Annual Review of Women in World Religions

Arvind Sharma & Katherine K. Young, Editors
Faculty of Religious Studies
McGill Univ.
3520 University St.
Montreal, PQ H3A 2A7, Canada

Telephone: 514 398-4121
Fax: 514 398-6665
First published: 1991
ISSN: 1056-4578
MLA acronym: ARWWR

SUBSCRIPTION INFORMATION

Frequency of publication: Annual
Subscription address: SUNY Press, c/o CUP Services, P.O. Box 6525, Ithaca, NY 14851
Subscription telephone: 800 666-2211; 607 277-2211
Subscription fax: 800 688-2877

ADVERTISING INFORMATION

Advertising accepted: No

EDITORIAL DESCRIPTION

Scope: Publishes interdisciplinary, polymethodic articles on the field of women and religion. Topics covered include the study of women in religion in the fields of literature and folklore.
Reviews books: Yes
Languages accepted: English
Prints abstracts: No

SUBMISSION REQUIREMENTS

Author pays submission fee: No
Author pays page charges: No
Length of articles: 5,000-7,530 words
Style: Chicago
Number of copies required: 1
Special requirements: Include a 500-word abstract and curriculum vitae.
Copyright ownership: State Univ. of New York Press
Rejected manuscripts: Returned
Articles published per year: 4-8

(208)
*ANQ: A Quarterly Journal of Short Articles, Notes, and Reviews

Arthur Wrobel, Editor
Dept. of English
Univ. of Kentucky
1321 Patterson Office Tower
Lexington, KY 40506-0027

Telephone: 606 257-6975
E-mail: Engaw@ukcc.uky.edu
First published: 1962
ISSN: 0003-0171
MLA acronym: ANQ

SUBSCRIPTION INFORMATION

Frequency of publication: 4 times/yr.
Circulation: 1,000
Available in microform: Yes
Subscription price: $14.00/yr.
Year to which price refers: 1992
Subscription address: Univ. Press of Kentucky, 663 South Limestone, Lexington, KY 40506-0336
Subscription telephone: 606 257-8439

ADVERTISING INFORMATION

Advertising accepted: No

EDITORIAL DESCRIPTION

Scope: Publishes articles on American and English literature, bibliography, and minority and women's studies.
Reviews books: Yes
Publishes notes: Yes
Languages accepted: English
Prints abstracts: No
Author-anonymous submission: No

SUBMISSION REQUIREMENTS

Restrictions on contributors: None
Author pays submission fee: No
Author pays page charges: No
Length of articles: 1,750 words maximum
Length of book reviews: 600-1,200 words
Length of notes: 1,750 words maximum
Style: MLA
Number of copies required: 2
Special requirements: Submit double-spaced typescript. Author's name and address should be in upper left of first text page.
Copyright ownership: Univ. Press of Kentucky
Rejected manuscripts: Returned; enclose SASE.
Time before publication decision: 2-6 weeks
Time between decision and publication: 2-10 mos.
Number of reviewers: 2
Articles submitted per year: 300
Articles published per year: 60-80
Book reviews submitted per year: 25-30
Book reviews published per year: 25-30

(209)
*Anthropologica

Mathias G. Guenther, Andrew P. Lyons, & Harriet D. Lyons, Editors
Dept. of Sociology & Anthropology
Wilfrid Laurier Univ.
Waterloo, Ontario N2L 3C5, Canada

Telephone: 519 884-1970
Fax: 519 886-9351
First published: 1955
Sponsoring organization: Wilfrid Laurier Univ.
ISSN: 0003-5459
MLA acronym: Anthropologica

SUBSCRIPTION INFORMATION

Frequency of publication: 2 times/yr.
Circulation: 340
Available in microform: Yes

Subscription price: C$40.00/yr. Canada; $40.00/yr. elsewhere
Year to which price refers: 1992-93
Subscription address: Wilfrid Laurier Univ. Press, University Ave., Wilfrid Laurier Univ., Waterloo, Ontario N2L 3C5, Canada

ADVERTISING INFORMATION

Advertising accepted: Yes

EDITORIAL DESCRIPTION

Scope: Publishes articles in the fields of cultural and social anthropology and related disciplines.
Reviews books: Yes
Publishes notes: Yes
Languages accepted: English; French
Prints abstracts: Yes
Author-anonymous submission: Yes

SUBMISSION REQUIREMENTS

Author pays submission fee: No
Author pays page charges: No
Length of articles: 8,000 words
Length of book reviews: 800 words
Style: Chicago
Number of copies required: 2
Special requirements: Submit double-spaced original typescript. Include an abstract of not more than 100 words, in French if possible.
Copyright ownership: Journal
Rejected manuscripts: Returned at author's request
Time before publication decision: 4-6 mos.
Time between decision and publication: 1 yr.
Number of reviewers: 3-5
Articles submitted per year: 20
Articles published per year: 10
Book reviews published per year: 10-15

(210)
Anthropological Linguistics

Martha B. Kendall, Editor
Indiana Univ.
Rawles Hall 108
Bloomington, IN 47405

First published: 1959
Sponsoring organization: Dept. of Anthropology, Indiana Univ.
ISSN: 0003-5483
MLA acronym: AnL

SUBSCRIPTION INFORMATION

Frequency of publication: 4 times/yr. (Spring, Summer, Fall, Winter)
Circulation: 1,150
Available in microform: Yes

ADVERTISING INFORMATION

Advertising accepted: Yes, on an exchange basis

EDITORIAL DESCRIPTION

Scope: Welcomes theoretical and methodological papers on the use of language in its social settings, particularly those focused on ethnolinguistics, ethnography of communication, psycholinguistics, or sociolinguistics.
Reviews books: Yes
Publishes notes: Yes
Languages accepted: English
Prints abstracts: Yes
Author-anonymous submission: No

SUBMISSION REQUIREMENTS

Restrictions on contributors: Papers should be previously unpublished, and not under consideration elsewhere.
Author pays submission fee: No

Author pays page charges: Yes, for corrections made at proof stage.
Length of articles: 10-30 double-spaced typescript pp.; 50 pp. maximum
Length of book reviews: 500 words
Length of notes: 1,000 words
Style: Journal; Linguistic Soc. of America
Number of copies required: 3
Special requirements: Tables, charts, and figures must be provided camera-ready. Submit a 50-75 word abstract. No appendices or concluding sections which merely summarize or repeat paper's findings should be included. Submit original typescript and 2 copies.
Copyright ownership: Journal
Rejected manuscripts: Returned; enclose return postage.
Time before publication decision: 3 mos.
Time between decision and publication: 2 mos.
Number of reviewers: 2-3
Articles submitted per year: 55
Articles published per year: 31
Book reviews submitted per year: 6
Book reviews published per year: 6
Notes submitted per year: 2
Notes published per year: 2

(211)
*Anthropological Quarterly

Phyllis Pease Chock, Editor
Dept. of Anthropology
Catholic Univ. of America
Washington, DC 20064

Telephone: 202 319-5080
Fax: 202 319-5579
E-mail: CHOCK@CUAVAX.DNET.CUA.EDU
First published: 1929
Sponsoring organization: Dept. of Anthropology, Catholic Univ. of America
ISSN: 0003-5491
MLA acronym: AntQ

SUBSCRIPTION INFORMATION

Frequency of publication: 4 times/yr. (Jan., Apr., July, Oct.)
Circulation: 900
Available in microform: No
Subscription price: $30.00/yr. institutions; $24.00/yr. individuals
Year to which price refers: 1992
Subscription address: Business Office, 303 Administration, Catholic Univ. of America Press, 620 Michigan Ave., NE, Washington, DC 20064
Subscription telephone: 202 319-5052
Subscription fax: 202 319-5802

ADVERTISING INFORMATION

Advertising accepted: Yes
Advertising rates: $100.00/half page; $150.00/full page

EDITORIAL DESCRIPTION

Scope: Publishes articles on social and cultural anthropology.
Reviews books: Yes
Publishes notes: No
Languages accepted: English
Prints abstracts: Yes
Author-anonymous submission: Yes

SUBMISSION REQUIREMENTS

Restrictions on contributors: Book reviews are commissioned.
Author pays submission fee: No
Author pays page charges: No
Length of articles: 8,000-14,000 words
Length of book reviews: 1,000-2,000 words
Style: American Anthropologist
Number of copies required: 3

Special requirements: Final versions of manuscripts accepted for publication must be submitted on disk or on-line. Request specifications from editor.
Copyright ownership: Journal
Rejected manuscripts: Returned; enclose SASE.
Time before publication decision: 6 mos.
Time between decision and publication: 6-12 mos.
Number of reviewers: 1-4
Articles submitted per year: 37-40
Articles published per year: 16-18
Book reviews published per year: 15

(212)
*Anthropos: International Review of Ethnology and Linguistics

Anton Quack, Joachim Piepke, & Othmar Gächter, Editors
Anthropos-Inst.
Arnold-Janssen-Str. 20
5205 St. Augustin 1, Germany

Fax: (49) 2241 29142
First published: 1906
Sponsoring organization: Anthropos-Inst.
ISSN: 0257-9774
MLA acronym: Anthropos

SUBSCRIPTION INFORMATION

Frequency of publication: 2 times/yr.
Circulation: 1,000
Available in microform: No
Subscription price: 175 SwF/yr.
Year to which price refers: 1992
Subscription address: Editions Saint-Paul/Paulusverlag, Boulevard de Pérolles 42, 1700 Fribourg, Switzerland

ADVERTISING INFORMATION

Advertising accepted: Yes

EDITORIAL DESCRIPTION

Scope: Publishes articles on all anthropological fields, including linguistics.
Reviews books: Yes
Publishes notes: Yes
Languages accepted: English; French; German; Spanish; Portuguese; Italian
Prints abstracts: Yes
Author-anonymous submission: Yes

SUBMISSION REQUIREMENTS

Restrictions on contributors: None
Author pays submission fee: No
Author pays page charges: No
Length of articles: 30-40 pp. maximum
Length of book reviews: 1,500 words
Length of notes: 150-200 words
Style: Chicago preferred
Number of copies required: 2
Special requirements: Submit original double-spaced typescript. Use 1 inch margins. Include a 150-word biographical sketch and a 100-word summary, preferably in English.
Copyright ownership: Assigned by author to journal
Rejected manuscripts: Returned
Time before publication decision: 5 mos.
Time between decision and publication: 1 yr.
Number of reviewers: 2-3
Articles submitted per year: 50
Articles published per year: 40-50
Book reviews submitted per year: 180
Book reviews published per year: 150
Notes submitted per year: 15
Notes published per year: 10

(213)
*Anthropos: Revista de Documentación Científica de la Cultura

Ramón Gabarrós Cardona, Editor
Aptd. 387
08190 Sant Cugat del Vallés, Spain

Telephone: (34) 3 5894884
Fax: (34) 3 6741713
First published: 1981
ISSN: 0211-5611
MLA acronym: AnthroposS

SUBSCRIPTION INFORMATION

Frequency of publication: 10 times/yr.
Circulation: 4,000
Available in microform: No
Subscription price: 9,164 Pta/yr.
Year to which price refers: 1992
Additional subscription address: In US: Literal Books, P.O. Box 713, Adelphi, MD 20783
Subscription telephone: US: 800 366-8680; elsewhere: (34) 3 5894884

ADVERTISING INFORMATION

Advertising accepted: Yes
Advertising rates: 195,000 Pta/full page

EDITORIAL DESCRIPTION

Scope: Publishes scholarly articles on Spanish and Latin American literature, culture, and thought.
Reviews books: Yes
Publishes notes: Yes
Languages accepted: Spanish
Prints abstracts: No
Author-anonymous submission: No

SUBMISSION REQUIREMENTS

Restrictions on contributors: Contributions are solicited.
Author pays submission fee: No
Author pays page charges: No
Length of articles: 5,000-6,000 words
Length of book reviews: 500-700 words
Length of notes: 40-50 words
Number of copies required: 1
Copyright ownership: Anthropos Editorial
Articles published per year: 100
Book reviews submitted per year: 1,000
Book reviews published per year: 300
Notes submitted per year: 200
Notes published per year: 150

(214)
*The Antigonish Review

George Sanderson, Editor
St. Francis Xavier Univ.
Antigonish, Nova Scotia B2G 1C0, Canada

Telephone: 902 867-3962
Fax: 902 867-5153
First published: 1970
Sponsoring organization: St. Francis Xavier Univ.; Canada Council
ISSN: 0003-5661
MLA acronym: AntigR

SUBSCRIPTION INFORMATION

Frequency of publication: 4 times/yr.
Circulation: 700
Available in microform: Yes
Subscription price: $18.00/yr.
Year to which price refers: 1992-93
Subscription address: Business Manager, at the above address

ADVERTISING INFORMATION

Advertising accepted: No

EDITORIAL DESCRIPTION

Scope: Publishes poetry, short fiction, light critical articles on modern and contemporary writers, and book reviews of both national and international authors.
Reviews books: Yes
Languages accepted: English
Prints abstracts: No
Author-anonymous submission: No

SUBMISSION REQUIREMENTS

Restrictions on contributors: None
Author pays submission fee: No
Author pays page charges: No
Length of articles: 2,000-3,000 words
Length of book reviews: 500 words
Style: MLA
Number of copies required: 1
Copyright ownership: Author
Rejected manuscripts: Returned; enclose return postage or international reply coupons.
Time before publication decision: 4 mos.
Time between decision and publication: 6 mos.
Number of reviewers: 3
Articles submitted per year: 30-40
Articles published per year: 9-13
Book reviews submitted per year: 30-40
Book reviews published per year: 20-30

(215)
*The Antioch Review

Robert S. Fogarty, Editor
P.O. Box 148
Yellow Springs, OH 45387

Telephone: 513 767-6389
First published: 1941
Sponsoring organization: Antioch College
ISSN: 0003-5769
MLA acronym: AR

SUBSCRIPTION INFORMATION

Frequency of publication: 4 times/yr.
Circulation: 3,600
Available in microform: Yes
Subscription price: $36.00/yr. institutions; $25.00/yr. individuals
Year to which price refers: 1992

ADVERTISING INFORMATION

Advertising accepted: Yes

EDITORIAL DESCRIPTION

Scope: Publishes articles on literary and social commentary.
Reviews books: Yes
Publishes notes: No
Languages accepted: English
Prints abstracts: No

SUBMISSION REQUIREMENTS

Restrictions on contributors: Accepts book reviews by Antioch College faculty only.
Author pays submission fee: No
Author pays page charges: No
Length of articles: 5,000 words maximum
Style: Chicago
Number of copies required: 1
Copyright ownership: Journal
Rejected manuscripts: Returned; enclose SASE.
Time before publication decision: 4-6 weeks
Time between decision and publication: 3-6 mos.
Number of reviewers: 2-3
Articles submitted per year: 400 nonfiction; 2,500 fiction
Articles published per year: 19 nonfiction; 13 fiction
Book reviews published per year: 50

(216)
*Antípodas: Journal of Hispanic Studies of the University of Auckland and La Trobe University

Roy C. Boland & Sally Harvey, Editors
Dept. of Romance Languages
Univ. of Auckland
Privat Bag
Auckland, New Zealand

Additional editorial address: Dept. of Spanish, La Trobe Univ., Bundoora, Victoria 3083, Australia
Telephone: (61) 3 4792428
Fax: (61) 3 4791700
First published: 1988
Historical variations in title: Formerly Antípodas: Journal of Hispanic Studies of the University of Auckland
Sponsoring organization: Univ. of Auckland; Inst. Vox, Madrid; La Trobe Univ.
ISSN: 0113-2415
MLA acronym: Antípodas

SUBSCRIPTION INFORMATION

Frequency of publication: Annual
Circulation: 350
Available in microform: No
Subscription price: $30.00/yr. institutions; $25.00/yr. individuals
Year to which price refers: 1992

ADVERTISING INFORMATION

Advertising accepted: Yes

EDITORIAL DESCRIPTION

Scope: A monographic journal on Hispanic studies, including language, literature, and culture.
Reviews books: Yes
Publishes notes: No
Languages accepted: English; Spanish
Prints abstracts: No
Author-anonymous submission: Yes

SUBMISSION REQUIREMENTS

Restrictions on contributors: Contributors must be subscribers. Book reviews are by invitation only.
Author pays submission fee: No
Author pays page charges: No
Length of articles: 3,000-5,000 words
Length of book reviews: 500-750 words
Style: MLA (1977)
Number of copies required: 2
Special requirements: Manuscripts must be accompanied by a 3.5 in. Macintosh diskette.
Copyright ownership: Journal
Rejected manuscripts: Returned; enclose international mail coupons.
Time before publication decision: 6-18 mos.
Time between decision and publication: 6-12 mos.
Number of reviewers: 2
Articles submitted per year: 40
Articles published per year: 15-20
Book reviews published per year: 5-6

(217)
*Antipodes: A North American Journal of Australian Literature

Robert Ross, Editor
Edward A. Clark Center for Australian Studies
Univ. of Texas
Austin, TX 78712

Telephone: 512 471-9607
Fax: 512 471-8869
First published: 1987
Sponsoring organization: American Assn. of Australian Literary Studies
ISSN: 0893-5580

MLA acronym: Antipodes

SUBSCRIPTION INFORMATION

Frequency of publication: 2 times/yr. (Spring, Winter)
Circulation: 400
Available in microform: No
Subscription price: $35.00/yr. institutions; $20.00/yr. individuals
Year to which price refers: 1992
Subscription address: 190 Sixth Ave., Brooklyn, NY 11217
Subscription telephone: 718 789-5826
Subscription fax: 718 482-5599

ADVERTISING INFORMATION

Advertising accepted: Yes
Advertising rates: $150.00/half page; $250.00/full page

EDITORIAL DESCRIPTION

Scope: Informs general and scholarly readers on Australian literature, especially contemporary, through articles, reviews, interviews, and creative work by major Australian writers.
Reviews books: Yes
Publishes notes: No
Languages accepted: English
Prints abstracts: No
Author-anonymous submission: Yes

SUBMISSION REQUIREMENTS

Restrictions on contributors: Preference is given to AAALS members. Book reviews are commissioned.
Author pays submission fee: No
Author pays page charges: No
Length of articles: 3,000-4,000 words
Length of book reviews: 750 words
Style: MLA
Number of copies required: 1
Copyright ownership: Author
Rejected manuscripts: Returned
Time before publication decision: 6 mos.
Time between decision and publication: 4 mos.
Number of reviewers: 2-3
Articles submitted per year: 35
Articles published per year: 12
Book reviews published per year: 40

(218)
*L'Antiquité Classique

Jules Labarbe, G. Raepsaet, T. Hackens, & H. van Looy, Editors
c/o T. Hackens
Inst. d'Archéologie
Collège Erasme
Place Blaise Pascal 31
1348 Louvain-la-Neuve, Belgium

Telephone: (32) 20 474850
Fax: (32) 20 472579
First published: 1932
ISSN: 0770-2817
MLA acronym: AntC

SUBSCRIPTION INFORMATION

Frequency of publication: 1 double issue/yr.
Circulation: 1,000
Available in microform: No
Subscription price: 2,500 BF/yr.
Year to which price refers: 1992

ADVERTISING INFORMATION

Advertising accepted: Yes

EDITORIAL DESCRIPTION

Scope: Publishes articles on Greek and Roman philology, literature, history, and archaeology, including the pre-Roman and pre-Hellenic as well as early Byzantine periods.

Reviews books: Yes
Publishes notes: Yes
Languages accepted: French; English; Dutch; German; Italian; Spanish
Prints abstracts: Yes

SUBMISSION REQUIREMENTS

Author pays submission fee: No
Author pays page charges: Yes, for manuscripts longer than 12 pp.
Length of articles: 12 double-spaced typescript pp.
Length of book reviews: 2 pp.
Length of notes: 1-6 pp.
Style: Journal
Number of copies required: 1
Special requirements: If line drawings are required, originals must be provided. Only excellent photographs are accepted.
Copyright ownership: Journal
Rejected manuscripts: Returned; enclose return postage.
Time before publication decision: 4 mos. maximum
Time between decision and publication: 2 yrs.
Number of reviewers: 1-4
Articles submitted per year: 30
Articles published per year: 20
Book reviews submitted per year: 200
Book reviews published per year: 150
Notes submitted per year: 20
Notes published per year: 15

(219)
*Antonianum

Pontificio Ateneo Antonianum, Editor
Via Merulana, 124
00185 Rome, Italy

Telephone: (39) 6 70373462
Fax: (39) 6 779749
First published: 1926
ISSN: 0003-6064
MLA acronym: Antonianum

SUBSCRIPTION INFORMATION

Frequency of publication: 4 times/yr.
Circulation: 850
Available in microform: No
Subscription price: $65.00/yr.
Year to which price refers: 1992

ADVERTISING INFORMATION

Advertising accepted: No

EDITORIAL DESCRIPTION

Scope: Publishes articles on theology, philosophy, spirituality, and church history.
Reviews books: Yes
Publishes notes: Yes
Languages accepted: English; French; German; Italian; Latin; Spanish
Prints abstracts: Yes
Author-anonymous submission: No

SUBMISSION REQUIREMENTS

Author pays page charges: No
Length of articles: 30,000 words
Length of book reviews: 2,000 words
Length of notes: 8,000 words
Number of copies required: 1
Copyright ownership: Editor
Rejected manuscripts: Not returned
Time before publication decision: 2 mos.
Time between decision and publication: 1 yr.
Number of reviewers: 2
Articles submitted per year: 20
Articles published per year: 15
Book reviews submitted per year: 50
Book reviews published per year: 40
Notes submitted per year: 15
Notes published per year: 12

(220)
*Anuar de Lingvistică și Istorie Literară

Stelian Dumistrăcel & Remus Zăstroiu, Editors
Inst. de Filologie Română "A. Philippide"
Academia Română, Filiala Iași
Str. Codrescu, nr. 2
6600 Iași 6, Romania

Additional editorial address: Editura Academiei Române, Calea Victoriei, nr. 125, 79717 Bucharest 22, Romania
Telephone: (40) 981 45617
First published: 1965
Sponsoring organization: Academia Română
ISSN: Series A: 1220-4900; Series B: 1220-4919
MLA acronym: ALIL

SUBSCRIPTION INFORMATION

Frequency of publication: Annual
Available in microform: No

ADVERTISING INFORMATION

Advertising accepted: Yes

EDITORIAL DESCRIPTION

Scope: Series A publishes articles on linguistics including the history of Romanian language, phonetics, dialectology, onomastics, literary language, and stylistics. Series B publishes articles on literature including literary history, literary theory and criticism, and folklore.
Reviews books: Yes
Publishes notes: Yes
Languages accepted: Romanian; English; French; German; Spanish; Italian
Prints abstracts: Yes
Author-anonymous submission: No

SUBMISSION REQUIREMENTS

Author pays submission fee: No
Length of articles: 20 pp.
Length of book reviews: 2 pp.
Length of notes: 1 p.
Style: MLA
Number of copies required: 2
Copyright ownership: Editorial Board
Rejected manuscripts: Not returned
Time before publication decision: 2 mos.
Number of reviewers: —
Articles submitted per year: 15
Articles published per year: 10
Book reviews published per year: 10
Notes published per year: 25

(221)
*Anuario de Estudios Filologicos

Antonio Viudas Camarasa, Editor
Fac. de Filosofía y Letras
Univ. de Extremadura
10071 Cáceres, Spain

First published: 1978
ISSN: 0210-8178
MLA acronym: AEFil

SUBSCRIPTION INFORMATION

Frequency of publication: Annual
Available in microform: No
Subscription price: 1,500 Pta/yr.
Year to which price refers: 1992
Subscription address: Servicio de Publicaciones, Univ. de Extremadura, 10071 Cáceres, Spain

ADVERTISING INFORMATION

Advertising accepted: No

EDITORIAL DESCRIPTION

Scope: Publishes articles on Spanish literature and philology.
Reviews books: No
Publishes notes: No
Languages accepted: Spanish; English; French; Italian; Portuguese
Prints abstracts: Yes

SUBMISSION REQUIREMENTS

Author pays submission fee: No
Author pays page charges: No
Length of articles: 12,500 words
Number of copies required: 1
Copyright ownership: Author & editor
Time before publication decision: 6 mos.
Time between decision and publication: 10-12 mos.
Number of reviewers: 2
Articles submitted per year: 25-35
Articles published per year: 20-30

(222)
*Anzeiger der Philosophisch-Historischen Klasse der Österreichischen Akademie der Wissenschaften

Verlag der Österreichischen Akademie der Wissenschaften
Dr.-Ignaz-Seipel-Platz 2
1010 Vienna, Austria

Telephone: (43) 222 515810
Fax: (43) 222 5139541
First published: 1864
Sponsoring organization: Österreichische Akademie der Wissenschaften
ISSN: 0378-8652
MLA acronym: AÖAW

SUBSCRIPTION INFORMATION

Frequency of publication: Annual
Available in microform: No

ADVERTISING INFORMATION

Advertising accepted: No

EDITORIAL DESCRIPTION

Scope: Publishes research in all fields from the University of Vienna and the Academy of Vienna, including philosophy, philology, music, history, and literature.
Reviews books: No
Publishes notes: No
Languages accepted: German; French; English
Prints abstracts: No
Author-anonymous submission: No

SUBMISSION REQUIREMENTS

Restrictions on contributors: Contributors must be members of the Austrian Academy or the book must be presented by a member.
Author pays submission fee: No
Author pays page charges: No
Length of articles: No restrictions
Number of copies required: 1
Special requirements: Submit original typescript.
Copyright ownership: Österreichische Akademie der Wissenschaften

(223)
*Appalachian Journal: A Regional Studies Review

J. W. Williamson, Editor
Univ. Hall
Appalachian State Univ.
Boone, NC 28608

Telephone: 704 262-4072
Fax: 704 262-2553
First published: 1972
Sponsoring organization: Appalachian State Univ., Center for Appalachian Studies
ISSN: 0090-3779
MLA acronym: AppalJ

SUBSCRIPTION INFORMATION

Frequency of publication: 4 times/yr. (Oct., Jan., Mar., July)
Circulation: 1,000
Available in microform: No
Subscription price: $18.00/yr. US; $24.00/yr. elsewhere
Year to which price refers: 1992

ADVERTISING INFORMATION

Advertising accepted: No

EDITORIAL DESCRIPTION

Scope: Publishes a broad spectrum of cross-disciplinary scholarship and opinion on the Appalachian region, including folklore and regional literature.
Reviews books: Yes
Publishes notes: Yes
Languages accepted: English
Prints abstracts: No
Author-anonymous submission: Yes

SUBMISSION REQUIREMENTS

Restrictions on contributors: Reviews are commissioned.
Author pays submission fee: No
Author pays page charges: No
Length of articles: 15-40 pp.
Length of book reviews: 800-1,000 words
Style: None
Number of copies required: 2
Copyright ownership: Assigned by author to journal.
Rejected manuscripts: Returned
Time before publication decision: 1 mo.
Time between decision and publication: 9 mos.
Number of reviewers: 1-3
Articles submitted per year: 100
Articles published per year: 50
Book reviews published per year: 25

(224)
*Applied Linguistics

Craig Chaudron & Rosamond Mitchell, Editors
Oxford Univ. Press
Walton St.
Oxford OX2 6DP, England

Additional editorial address: Craig Chaudron, Dept. of English as a Second Language, Univ. of Hawaii at Manoa, 1890 East-West Rd., Honolulu, HI 96822; Rosamond Mitchell, Centre for Language in Education, School of Education, Univ. of Southampton, Southampton SO9 5NB, England; Koes de Bot, Reviews Editor, Dept. of Applied Linguistics, Catholic Univ. of Nijmegen, Erasmusplein 1, 6525 HT Nijmegen, Netherlands
First published: 1980
Sponsoring organization: American Assn. for Applied Linguistics; British Assn. for Applied Linguistics
ISSN: 0142-6001
MLA acronym: AppLing

SUBSCRIPTION INFORMATION

Frequency of publication: 4 times/yr. (Mar., June, Sept., Dec.)
Circulation: 1,400
Available in microform: Yes
Subscription price: £58.00 ($115.00)/yr. institutions; £30.00 ($65.00)/yr. individuals
Year to which price refers: 1992
Subscription address: Journals Subscriptions Dept., Oxford Univ. Press, Pinkhill House, Southfield Rd., Eynsham, Oxford OX8 1JJ, England
Subscription telephone: (44) 865 882283
Subscription fax: (44) 865 882890

ADVERTISING INFORMATION

Advertising accepted: Yes
Advertising rates: £105.00/quarter page; £145.00/half page; £250.00/full page

EDITORIAL DESCRIPTION

Scope: To promote a principled approach to language education and other language related concerns by encouraging enquiry into the relationship between theoretical and practical studies.
Reviews books: Yes
Publishes notes: No
Languages accepted: English
Prints abstracts: Yes
Author-anonymous submission: No

SUBMISSION REQUIREMENTS

Restrictions on contributors: None
Author pays submission fee: No
Author pays page charges: No
Length of articles: No restrictions
Length of book reviews: No restrictions
Style: Oxford Univ. Press
Number of copies required: 3
Special requirements: Papers should not have been published previously or be being considered for publication.
Copyright ownership: Oxford Univ. Press
Rejected manuscripts: Returned
Time before publication decision: 3 mos.
Time between decision and publication: 18-24 mos.
Number of reviewers: 3
Articles submitted per year: 120
Articles published per year: 20
Book reviews submitted per year: 40
Book reviews published per year: 20

(225)
*Applied Psycholinguistics

Catherine Snow & John Locke, Editors
Larsen Hall, 3rd floor
Harvard Graduate School of Education
Cambridge, MA 02138

First published: 1980
ISSN: 0142-7164
MLA acronym: APsy

SUBSCRIPTION INFORMATION

Frequency of publication: 4 times/yr.
Circulation: 850
Available in microform: No
Subscription price: $88.00/yr. institutions US & Canada; £65.00/yr. institutions elsewhere; $44.00/yr. individuals US & Canada; £31.00/yr. individuals elsewhere
Year to which price refers: 1992
Subscription address: Cambridge Univ. Press, 40 W. 20th St., New York, NY 10011

ADVERTISING INFORMATION

Advertising accepted: No

EDITORIAL DESCRIPTION

Scope: Publishes articles on both normal and disordered language and communicative development in children and normal and disordered language and communicative functioning in adults.
Reviews books: Yes
Publishes notes: No
Languages accepted: English
Prints abstracts: Yes
Author-anonymous submission: No

SUBMISSION REQUIREMENTS

Restrictions on contributors: Book reviews are solicited.
Author pays submission fee: No
Author pays page charges: No
Length of articles: 50 typescript pp.
Length of book reviews: 4-8 pp.
Style: American Psychological Assn.
Number of copies required: 3
Special requirements: Include an abstract of 120 words maximum.
Copyright ownership: Cambridge Univ. Press
Rejected manuscripts: Not returned
Time before publication decision: 1-2 mos.
Time between decision and publication: 6-9 mos.
Number of reviewers: 2
Articles submitted per year: 60
Articles published per year: 20
Book reviews published per year: 20-24

(226)
*Approaches to Semiotics

Thomas A. Sebeok, Editor
Research Center for Language & Semiotic Studies
Indiana Univ.
P.O. Box 10
Bloomington, IN 47402-0010

Telephone: 812 855-1567
Fax: 812 855-1273
E-mail: SEBEOK@IUBACS
First published: 1969
ISSN: 0066-5576
MLA acronym: AtS

SUBSCRIPTION INFORMATION

Frequency of publication: Irregular
Available in microform: No
Subscription address: Mouton Publishers, 200 Saw Mill River Rd., Hawthorne, NY 10532
Subscription telephone: 914 747-0110
Subscription fax: 914 747-1326

ADVERTISING INFORMATION

Advertising accepted: No

EDITORIAL DESCRIPTION

Scope: Embraces studies in the humanities, the social and behavioral sciences, and the life sciences which deal with signification and interpretation in, or communication and interaction among and between, human beings and the speechless creatures.
Reviews books: No
Publishes notes: No
Languages accepted: English; French
Prints abstracts: No
Author-anonymous submission: No

SUBMISSION REQUIREMENTS

Restrictions on contributors: None
Author pays submission fee: No
Author pays page charges: No
Length of books: 350 pp.
Style: Mouton de Gruyter
Number of copies required: 1
Copyright ownership: Mouton Publishers
Rejected manuscripts: Returned at author's request; enclose return postage

Time before publication decision: 6 mos.
Time between decision and publication: 18 mos.
Books submitted per year: 12
Books published per year: 6

(227)
*Approaches to Translation Studies

Raymond van den Broeck & Kitty van Leuven-Zwart, Editors
Editions Rodopi B.V.
Keizersgracht 302-304
1016 EX Amsterdam, Netherlands

Telephone: (31) 20 6227507
Fax: (31) 20 6380948
ISSN: 0169-0523
MLA acronym: ApTS

SUBSCRIPTION INFORMATION

Circulation: 700
Available in microform: No
Additional subscription address: In N. America: Editions Rodopi, 233 Peachtree St. N.E., Suite 404, Atlanta, GA 30303-1504
Subscription telephone: 404 523-1964; 800 225-3998
Subscription fax: 404 522-7116

ADVERTISING INFORMATION

Advertising accepted: No

EDITORIAL DESCRIPTION

Scope: Publishes monographs on translation.
Reviews books: No
Publishes notes: No
Languages accepted: English
Prints abstracts: No
Author-anonymous submission: Yes

SUBMISSION REQUIREMENTS

Author pays submission fee: No
Author pays page charges: No
Length of books: 100 pp. minimum
Style: MLA; Chicago
Number of copies required: 2
Copyright ownership: Editions Rodopi B.V.
Time before publication decision: 6-12 mos.
Time between decision and publication: 3-9 mos.
Books published per year: 1-2

(228)
*Arabica: Revue d'Etudes Arabes

Mohammad Arkoun, Director
Univ. de la Sorbonne Nouvelle
13, rue de Santeuil
75231 Paris Cedex 5, France

Telephone: (33) 1 40180337
Fax: (33) 1 45874175
First published: 1954
Sponsoring organization: Centre National de Recherche Scientifique
ISSN: 0570-5398
MLA acronym: Arabica

SUBSCRIPTION INFORMATION

Frequency of publication: 3 times/yr.
Available in microform: No
Subscription price: 160 f ($80.00)/yr.
Year to which price refers: 1991
Subscription address: E. J. Brill, N.V., P.O. Box 9000, 2300 PA Leiden, Netherlands
Additional subscription address: In US & Canada: E. J. Brill, 24 Hudson St., Kinderhook, NY 12106

ADVERTISING INFORMATION

Advertising accepted: No

EDITORIAL DESCRIPTION

Scope: Publishes studies, documents, and notes on the language, literature, and civilization of the Arab world, as well as on the influence of the Arab culture on Western culture; a critical bulletin; a chronicle of the Arab world.
Reviews books: Yes
Publishes notes: Yes
Languages accepted: French; English; German; Arabic
Prints abstracts: No
Author-anonymous submission: No

SUBMISSION REQUIREMENTS

Author pays submission fee: No
Author pays page charges: No
Length of articles: 30 pp. maximum
Length of book reviews: No restrictions
Length of notes: 10 pp.
Number of copies required: 1
Special requirements: Use *Arabica*'s Arabic transcription.
Copyright ownership: E. J. Brill
Time before publication decision: 3 mos.
Time between decision and publication: 1 yr.
Number of reviewers: 2
Articles submitted per year: 40-50
Articles published per year: 15-20

(229)
*Arbeiten aus Anglistik und Amerikanistik

Bernhard Kettemann, Editor
Inst. für Anglistik
Univ. Graz
Heinrichstr. 36
8010 Graz, Austria

Telephone: (43) 316 3802488; (43) 316 3802487
Fax: (43) 316 31358
E-mail: KETTEMANN@edvz.uni-graz.ada.at
First published: 1976
Sponsoring organization: Bundesministerium für Wissenschaft & Forschung, Vienna
ISSN: 0171-5410
MLA acronym: ArAA

SUBSCRIPTION INFORMATION

Frequency of publication: 2 times/yr.
Circulation: 250
Available in microform: No
Subscription price: 78 DM/yr. institutions; 56 DM/yr. individuals; 42 DM/single issue
Year to which price refers: 1991
Subscription address: Gunter Narr Verlag, Postfach 2567, 7400 Tübingen, Germany
Subscription telephone: (49) 7071 78091
Subscription fax: (49) 7071 75288

ADVERTISING INFORMATION

Advertising accepted: Yes

EDITORIAL DESCRIPTION

Scope: Publishes articles on English and American studies, including language, language teaching and learning, literature, and civilization.
Reviews books: Yes
Publishes notes: Yes
Languages accepted: English; German
Prints abstracts: Yes
Author-anonymous submission: No

SUBMISSION REQUIREMENTS

Restrictions on contributors: None
Author pays submission fee: No
Author pays page charges: No
Length of articles: 15-25 pp.

Length of book reviews: 3-5 pp.
Length of notes: 1-3 pp.
Style: MLA; Modern Humanities Research Assn.; Linguistic Soc. of America
Number of copies required: 1
Special requirements: Articles must be preceded by a 15-line English abstract. Submit hard copy and diskette.
Copyright ownership: Gunter Narr Verlag
Rejected manuscripts: Returned at author's request
Time before publication decision: 3 mos.
Time between decision and publication: 3 mos.
Number of reviewers: 3
Articles submitted per year: 40-60
Articles published per year: 10-15
Book reviews submitted per year: 30-40
Book reviews published per year: 15-20
Notes submitted per year: 0-5
Notes published per year: 0-2

(230)
Arbor: Ciencia, Pensamiento y Cultura

Miguel Angel Quintanilla, Editor
Vitrubio, 8
28006 Madrid, Spain

Telephone: (34) 1 5855589
Fax: (34) 1 2612833
First published: 1941
Sponsoring organization: Consejo Superior de Investigaciones Científicas (C.S.I.C.)
ISSN: 0210-1963
MLA acronym: Arbor

SUBSCRIPTION INFORMATION

Frequency of publication: 12 times/yr.
Circulation: 2,500
Available in microform: No
Subscription price: 6,000 Pta/yr. Spain; 9,500 Pta/yr. elsewhere
Year to which price refers: 1992
Subscription address: Servicio de Publicaciones del C.S.I.C., at the above address

ADVERTISING INFORMATION

Advertising accepted: Yes

EDITORIAL DESCRIPTION

Scope: Publishes articles dealing with culture.
Reviews books: Yes
Publishes notes: Yes
Languages accepted: Spanish
Prints abstracts: Yes
Author-anonymous submission: Yes

SUBMISSION REQUIREMENTS

Restrictions on contributors: None
Author pays submission fee: Yes
Author pays page charges: Yes
Length of articles: 15-20 typescript pp.
Length of book reviews: 2-3 pp.
Length of notes: 8-12 pp.
Number of copies required: 1
Special requirements: Include 100-word abstract.
Copyright ownership: Author
Rejected manuscripts: Returned at author's request
Number of reviewers: 8
Articles submitted per year: 150
Articles published per year: 70-80
Book reviews submitted per year: 100
Book reviews published per year: 60-70
Notes submitted per year: 100
Notes published per year: 60

(231)
L'Arc

Jean-François Guesnier & Zoé Guesnier, Editors
Le Jas
04230 Le Revest Saint Martin, France

First published: 1958
ISSN: 0003-7974
MLA acronym: Arc

SUBSCRIPTION INFORMATION

Frequency of publication: 6 issues/yr.
Available in microform: No

ADVERTISING INFORMATION

Advertising accepted: Yes

EDITORIAL DESCRIPTION

Scope: Publishes articles on international literature, arts, philosophy, and science.
Reviews books: No
Languages accepted: French
Prints abstracts: No

SUBMISSION REQUIREMENTS

Time before publication decision: 6 mos.

(232)
*Arcadia: Zeitschrift für Vergleichende Literaturwissenschaft

Maria Moog-Grünewald & Jürgen Wertheimer, Editors
Neuphilologikum
Wilhelmstr. 50
7400 Tübingen, Germany

Telephone: (49) 7071 292907; (49) 7071 296135
First published: 1966
ISSN: 0003-7982
MLA acronym: Arcadia

SUBSCRIPTION INFORMATION

Frequency of publication: 3 times/yr.
Circulation: 1,500
Available in microform: No
Subscription address: Walter de Gruyter & Co., Genthiner Str. 13, 1000 Berlin 30, Germany

ADVERTISING INFORMATION

Advertising accepted: Yes

EDITORIAL DESCRIPTION

Scope: Publishes articles on comparative literature.
Reviews books: Yes
Publishes notes: Yes
Languages accepted: English; French; German; Italian; Spanish
Prints abstracts: No
Author-anonymous submission: No

SUBMISSION REQUIREMENTS

Restrictions on contributors: None
Author pays submission fee: No
Author pays page charges: No
Length of articles: 18 pp.
Length of book reviews: 2-4 pp.
Length of notes: 1/2 p.
Style: Journal
Number of copies required: 2
Copyright ownership: Walter de Gruyter for 2 yrs.
Rejected manuscripts: Returned; enclose return postage.
Time before publication decision: 2 mos.
Time between decision and publication: 1 yr.
Number of reviewers: 2
Articles submitted per year: 50

Articles published per year: 10-15
Book reviews submitted per year: 45
Book reviews published per year: 40
Notes submitted per year: 7
Notes published per year: 5

(233)
*Archeion Euvoikōn Meletōn

Soc. of Euboean Studies
Harilaou Trikoypi 60
Athens 10680, Greece

Telephone: (30) 1 3629504
First published: 1935
Sponsoring organization: Soc. of Euboean Studies
ISSN: 1010-3724
MLA acronym: AEM

SUBSCRIPTION INFORMATION

Frequency of publication: Annual
Available in microform: No
Subscription price: 4,000 Dr/yr.
Year to which price refers: 1992

ADVERTISING INFORMATION

Advertising accepted: No

EDITORIAL DESCRIPTION

Scope: Publishes articles on the history, archaeology, and popular art of Euboea.
Reviews books: Yes
Publishes notes: Yes
Languages accepted: Greek; English; French; German
Prints abstracts: Yes
Author-anonymous submission: No

SUBMISSION REQUIREMENTS

Restrictions on contributors: None
Author pays submission fee: No
Author pays page charges: No
Length of articles: 50 pp.
Length of book reviews: 5 pp.
Length of notes: 5 pp.
Style: None
Number of copies required: 1
Special requirements: Submit original typescript.
Copyright ownership: Soc. of Euboean Studies
Rejected manuscripts: Returned
Time before publication decision: 1-8 mos.
Time between decision and publication: 1-8 mos.
Number of reviewers: 5
Articles submitted per year: 10-12
Articles published per year: 8-10
Book reviews submitted per year: 3-4
Book reviews published per year: 3-4
Notes submitted per year: 3-5
Notes published per year: 3-5

(234)
*Archiv für das Studium der Neueren Sprachen und Literaturen

Dieter Mehl, Klaus Heitmann, & Horst Brunner, Editors
Englisches Seminar der Univ. Bonn
Regina-Pacis-Weg 5
5300 Bonn 1, Germany

Additional editorial address: Send English and American studies to Dieter Mehl at the above address. Send Romance studies to Klaus Heitmann, Romanisches Seminar, Seminarstr. 3, 69 Heidelberg, Germany; send Germanic studies to Horst Brunner, Germanistische Seminar, Am Hubland, 7800 Würzburg, Germany
Telephone: (49) 228 737623
First published: 1848

Sponsoring organization: Deutsche Forschungs-
  gemeinschaft, Bonn
ISSN: 0003-8970
MLA acronym: Archiv

SUBSCRIPTION INFORMATION

Frequency of publication: 2 times/yr.
Circulation: 800
Available in microform: No
Subscription price: 120 DM/yr.
Year to which price refers: 1992
Subscription address: Erich Schmidt Verlag,
  Genthinerstr. 30 G, 1000 Berlin 30, Germany
Subscription telephone: (49) 30 25008560

ADVERTISING INFORMATION

Advertising accepted: Yes

EDITORIAL DESCRIPTION

Scope: Publishes general studies of modern and medieval language and literature.
Reviews books: Yes
Publishes notes: Yes
Languages accepted: English; French; German; Italian; Spanish
Prints abstracts: No
Author-anonymous submission: No

SUBMISSION REQUIREMENTS

Restrictions on contributors: None
Author pays submission fee: No
Author pays page charges: No
Length of articles: 18 pp. maximum
Length of book reviews: 1,400 words
Length of notes: 2,000 words
Style: MLA
Number of copies required: 1
Copyright ownership: Erich Schmidt Verlag
Rejected manuscripts: Returned; enclose return postage.
Time before publication decision: 5 weeks
Time between decision and publication: 1 yr.
Number of reviewers: 1
Articles submitted per year: 80
Articles published per year: 15
Book reviews submitted per year: 100
Book reviews published per year: 80
Notes submitted per year: 25
Notes published per year: 10

(235)
*Archiv für Geschichte der Philosophie

Rainer Specht & Edwin M. Curley, Editors
Philosophisches Seminar, Schloss
Univ. der Mannheim
6800 Mannheim 1, Germany

Additional editorial address: Edwin M. Curley, Dept. of Philosophy, Univ. of Illinois, Chicago, IL 60680
First published: 1888
ISSN: 0003-9101
MLA acronym: AGP

SUBSCRIPTION INFORMATION

Frequency of publication: 3 times/yr.
Available in microform: No
Subscription price: 188 DM ($120.00)/yr.
Year to which price refers: 1992
Subscription address: Walter de Gruyter Inc., 200 Saw Mill River Road, Hawthorne, NY 10532

ADVERTISING INFORMATION

Advertising accepted: Yes

EDITORIAL DESCRIPTION

Scope: Publishes articles on the history of philosophy.

Reviews books: Yes
Publishes notes: No
Languages accepted: English; German; French; Italian
Prints abstracts: No
Author-anonymous submission: Yes, in American office; occasionally in European office

SUBMISSION REQUIREMENTS

Restrictions on contributors: Book reviews are solicited.
Author pays submission fee: No
Author pays page charges: No
Length of articles: 30 typescript pp. maximum
Length of book reviews: 1,500-2,000 words
Style: None
Number of copies required: 1
Copyright ownership: Journal
Rejected manuscripts: Returned; enclose SASE.
Time before publication decision: 3-6 mos.
Time between decision and publication: 2 yrs.
Number of reviewers: 2
Articles submitted per year: 75
Articles published per year: 12
Book reviews published per year: 20

(236)
*Archiv für Geschichte des Buchwesens

Monika Estermann, Reinhard Wittmann, & Rafaela Stein, Editors
Historische Kommission des Börsenvereins des Deutschen Buchhandels
Postfach 100442
6000 Frankfurt, Germany

Telephone: (49) 69 1306287
Fax: (49) 69 1306201
First published: 1956
Sponsoring organization: Börsenverein des Deutschen Buchhandels
ISSN: 0066-6327
MLA acronym: AGB

SUBSCRIPTION INFORMATION

Frequency of publication: 2 times/yr.
Circulation: 600
Available in microform: No
Subscription address: Buchhändler-Vereinigung GmbH, at the above address

ADVERTISING INFORMATION

Advertising accepted: No

EDITORIAL DESCRIPTION

Scope: Contains scholarly studies on all aspects of the book and the book trade, ranging from printing, publishing, binding, and illustration to the history of collecting, reading, and libraries.
Reviews books: No
Publishes notes: No
Languages accepted: German
Prints abstracts: Yes, in English and French.

SUBMISSION REQUIREMENTS

Restrictions on contributors: None
Author pays submission fee: No
Author pays page charges: No
Length of articles: No restrictions
Style: Journal
Number of copies required: 1
Copyright ownership: Assigned by author to journal
Rejected manuscripts: Returned
Time between decision and publication: 9 mos.
Number of reviewers: 3
Articles published per year: 10-15

(237)
*Archiv für Kulturgeschichte

Egon Boshof, Editor
Böhlau Verlag
Theodor-Heuss-Str. 76
5000 Cologne 90, Germany

Telephone: (49) 2203 307021
Fax: (49) 2203 307349
First published: 1903
ISSN: 0003-9233
MLA acronym: AKG

SUBSCRIPTION INFORMATION

Frequency of publication: 2 times/yr.
Circulation: 650
Available in microform: No

ADVERTISING INFORMATION

Advertising accepted: Yes

EDITORIAL DESCRIPTION

Scope: Publishes articles on every epoch and from various disciplines, especially old, Medieval and modern history, art, legal, religious and church history, folklore, German studies, sociology, political science and philosophy, insofar as it touches on the totality of historical life. Focuses on the European cultural sphere, but includes other cultural areas, especially when they are brought in by way of comparison.
Reviews books: Yes
Publishes notes: No
Languages accepted: German; English; French
Prints abstracts: No
Author-anonymous submission: No

SUBMISSION REQUIREMENTS

Restrictions on contributors: None
Author pays submission fee: No
Author pays page charges: No
Length of articles: 30 pp.
Length of book reviews: 1 p.
Number of copies required: 1
Copyright ownership: Böhlau Verlag
Rejected manuscripts: Returned
Time before publication decision: 1 mo.
Time between decision and publication: 6 mos.
Number of reviewers: 1-2
Articles submitted per year: 25
Articles published per year: 15
Book reviews submitted per year: 40-60
Book reviews published per year: 30-40

(238)
*Archiv für Reformationsgeschichte

Hans R. Guggisberg & Gottfried G. Krodel, Editors
Bruderholzallee 20
4059 Basel, Switzerland

Additional editorial address: Papers from N. America should be submitted to: Gottfried G. Krodel, Valparaiso Univ., Valparaiso, IN 46383
Telephone: (41) 61 357350; 219 462-9690; 219 464-5302
First published: 1904
Sponsoring organization: Verein für Reformationsgeschichte; American Soc. for Reformation Research
ISSN: 0003-9381
MLA acronym: ARG

SUBSCRIPTION INFORMATION

Frequency of publication: Annual
Circulation: 1,100
Available in microform: No
Subscription price: $52.00/yr.
Year to which price refers: 1991

Subscription address: Gütersloher Verlagshaus Gerd Mohn, Carl-Bertelsmann-Str. 256, P.O. Box 1343, 4830 Gütersloh 100, Germany
Additional subscription address: For subscriptions in N. America contact: Center for Reformation Research, 6477 San Bonita Ave., St. Louis, MO 63105
Subscription telephone: (49) 524 74050
Subscription fax: (49) 524 740548

ADVERTISING INFORMATION

Advertising accepted: Yes

EDITORIAL DESCRIPTION

Scope: An international journal concerned with the history of the Reformation, its significance in social cultural history, and its impact on world cultures.
Reviews books: Yes
Publishes notes: No
Languages accepted: English; German; French; Italian
Prints abstracts: Yes
Author-anonymous submission: No

SUBMISSION REQUIREMENTS

Restrictions on contributors: None
Author pays submission fee: No
Author pays page charges: No
Length of articles: No restrictions
Length of book reviews: No restrictions
Style: Chicago
Number of copies required: 2
Special requirements: Abstract must accompany final draft.
Copyright ownership: Author
Rejected manuscripts: Returned
Time before publication decision: 12-15 mos.
Time between decision and publication: 1 yr.
Articles submitted per year: 12-20
Articles published per year: 12-14
Book reviews published per year: 1-2

(239)
*Archív Orientální: Quarterly Journal of African, Asian, and Latin-American Studies

Blahoslav Hruška & B. Řichová, Editors
Lázeňská 4
118 37 Prague 1, Czech Republic

First published: 1929
Sponsoring organization: Československá Akademie Věd, Oriental Inst.
ISSN: 0044-8699
MLA acronym: ArO

SUBSCRIPTION INFORMATION

Frequency of publication: 4 times/yr.
Circulation: 800
Available in microform: Yes
Subscription price: 288 f ($174.00)/yr.
Year to which price refers: 1993
Subscription address: John Benjamins B.V., Amsteldijk 44, P.O. Box 75577, 1071 AN Amsterdam, Netherlands
Additional subscription address: John Benjamins North America, Inc., 821 Bethlehem Pike, Philadelphia, PA 19118
Subscription telephone: (31) 20 6738156; 215 836-1200
Subscription fax: (31) 20 6739773; 215 836-1204

ADVERTISING INFORMATION

Advertising accepted: No

EDITORIAL DESCRIPTION

Scope: Publishes articles on history, economy, culture, and society of African, Asian, and Latin American countries.
Reviews books: Yes
Publishes notes: Yes
Languages accepted: English; French; German; Russian; Spanish
Prints abstracts: Yes
Author-anonymous submission: No

SUBMISSION REQUIREMENTS

Restrictions on contributors: None
Author pays submission fee: No
Author pays page charges: No
Length of articles: 20 pp. maximum
Length of book reviews: 300-500 words
Length of notes: 100-200 words
Number of copies required: 1
Special requirements: Include an abstract (2 pp. maximum) in English for articles written in other languages.
Copyright ownership: Oriental Inst. of the Czechoslovak Academy of Sciences
Rejected manuscripts: Returned at author's request
Time before publication decision: 2 mos.
Time between decision and publication: 6-14 mos.
Number of reviewers: Editorial Board
Articles submitted per year: 50
Articles published per year: 28-32
Book reviews submitted per year: 190-215
Book reviews published per year: 180-200
Notes submitted per year: 30
Notes published per year: 20

(240)
*Archives des Lettres Modernes: Etudes de Critique et d'Histoire Littéraire

Michel J. Minard, Editor
Lettres Modernes-Minard
73, rue du Cardinal-Lemoine
75005 Paris, France

Telephone: (33) 1 43544609
First published: 1957
ISSN: 0003-9675
MLA acronym: ALM

SUBSCRIPTION INFORMATION

Available in microform: No
Subscription price: 570 F/yr.
Year to which price refers: 1992

ADVERTISING INFORMATION

Advertising accepted: No

EDITORIAL DESCRIPTION

Scope: Each issue is dedicated to a single subject, including: editorials (present state of a question, etc.) or original studies of literary history.
Reviews books: No
Publishes notes: No
Languages accepted: French
Prints abstracts: No

SUBMISSION REQUIREMENTS

Author pays submission fee: Yes
Author pays page charges: No
Length of books: 150 pp.
Style: Journal
Number of copies required: 1
Rejected manuscripts: Returned; enclose return postage or international reply coupons.
Time before publication decision: 4 mos.
Time between decision and publication: 4 mos.
Number of reviewers: 2
Books submitted per year: 10
Books published per year: 7

(241)
*Archives d'Histoire Doctrinale et Littéraire du Moyen Âge

Françoise Hudry, Editor
Librairie Philosophique J. Vrin
6, Place de la Sorbonne
75005 Paris, France

First published: 1926-27
Sponsoring organization: Centre National de la Recherche Scientifique
ISSN: 0373-5478
MLA acronym: AHDLMA

SUBSCRIPTION INFORMATION

Frequency of publication: Annual
Circulation: 750
Available in microform: No

ADVERTISING INFORMATION

Advertising accepted: No

EDITORIAL DESCRIPTION

Scope: A purely historical publication which publishes only studies devoted to medieval thought and to literary history of writings wherein this thought is expressed. Publishes only original memoirs, unpublished or only partially published texts.
Reviews books: No
Publishes notes: Yes
Languages accepted: English; French; German; Latin; Spanish; Italian
Prints abstracts: Yes
Author-anonymous submission: No

SUBMISSION REQUIREMENTS

Author pays submission fee: No
Author pays page charges: No
Length of articles: 50 pp.
Length of notes: 10 pp.
Number of copies required: 1
Special requirements: Submit Macintosh or IBM diskette, if possible.
Copyright ownership: Lib. Philosophique J. Vrin
Rejected manuscripts: Returned at author's request
Time before publication decision: 6-10 mos.
Time between decision and publication: 1 yr.
Number of reviewers: 2
Articles submitted per year: 4-7
Articles published per year: 5-6
Notes submitted per year: 5
Notes published per year: 3

(242)
*Archivio Glottologico Italiano

Editoriale & Finanziaria le Monnier Firenze
C.P. 202
50100 Florence, Italy

Additional editorial address: Editoriale & Finanziaria le Monnier Firenze, Via Meucci 2, 50015 Grassina FI, Italy
Telephone: (39) 55 6491402
Fax: (39) 55 643983
First published: 1873
ISSN: 0004-0207
MLA acronym: AGI

SUBSCRIPTION INFORMATION

Frequency of publication: 2 times/yr.
Circulation: 1,000
Available in microform: No
Subscription price: 64,500 Lit/yr. Italy; 90,000 Lit/yr. elsewhere
Year to which price refers: 1992

ADVERTISING INFORMATION

Advertising accepted: Yes

EDITORIAL DESCRIPTION

Scope: Publishes studies on Italian linguistics, with an emphasis on the interrelationships between methodological and historical studies in the field of linguistics, and the comparison of research findings in Indo-European, Romance, and Italian linguistics.
Reviews books: Yes
Publishes notes: Yes
Languages accepted: Italian
Prints abstracts: No
Author-anonymous submission: No

SUBMISSION REQUIREMENTS

Author pays submission fee: No
Author pays page charges: No
Length of articles: 25 pp.
Length of book reviews: 6 pp.
Length of notes: 2 pp.
Number of copies required: 1
Copyright ownership: Editor
Rejected manuscripts: Not returned
Time before publication decision: 6 mos.
Time between decision and publication: 6 mos.
Number of reviewers: 5
Articles submitted per year: 20
Articles published per year: 10
Book reviews submitted per year: 40
Book reviews published per year: 20

(243)
*Archivio per l'Alto Adige: Rivista di Studi Alpini

Carlo Alberto Mastrelli, Editor
Ist. di Studi per l'Alto Adige
Via Cesare Battisti, 4
50122 Florence, Italy

Telephone: (39) 55 211355
First published: 1906
Sponsoring organization: Dante Alighieri; Soc. Italiana di Geografia; Soc. per il Progresso delle Scienze (Rome)
ISSN: 0392-1050
MLA acronym: AAA

SUBSCRIPTION INFORMATION

Frequency of publication: Annual
Circulation: 600
Available in microform: No

ADVERTISING INFORMATION

Advertising accepted: No

EDITORIAL DESCRIPTION

Scope: Publishes articles on the study and description of the Alto Adige region and nearby territories from linguistic and historical points of view.
Reviews books: Yes
Publishes notes: Yes
Languages accepted: Italian; German; English; French; Spanish; Latin
Prints abstracts: Yes
Author-anonymous submission: No

SUBMISSION REQUIREMENTS

Restrictions on contributors: None
Author pays submission fee: No
Author pays page charges: No
Length of articles: 2,000-15,000 words
Length of book reviews: 300 words minimum
Length of notes: No restrictions
Style: None
Number of copies required: 1
Special requirements: Submit original typescript.

Copyright ownership: Assigned by author to journal
Rejected manuscripts: Returned
Time before publication decision: 2 weeks
Time between decision and publication: 1-12 mos.
Number of reviewers: 2
Articles submitted per year: 5-20
Articles published per year: 5-20
Book reviews submitted per year: 5-10
Book reviews published per year: 5-10
Notes submitted per year: 1
Notes published per year: 1

(244)
*Archivio Storico di Belluno, Feltre e Cadore

Bartolomeo Zanenga, Adriano Alpago-Novello, Luisa Alpago-Novello Ferrerio, Ester Cason Angelini, Sergio Claut, Paolo Conte, Giorgio Maggioni, Franco Sartori, Ferdinando Tamis, Flavio Vizzutti, & Giandomenico Zanderigo Rosolo, Editors
C.P. 34
32100 Belluno, Italy

Telephone: (39) 437 34177
First published: 1929
MLA acronym: ASBFC

SUBSCRIPTION INFORMATION

Frequency of publication: 4 times/yr.
Circulation: 500
Available in microform: No
Subscription price: 30,000 Lit/yr. Italy; 60,000 Lit/yr. elsewhere
Year to which price refers: 1992
Subscription telephone: (39) 437 213858

ADVERTISING INFORMATION

Advertising accepted: Yes

EDITORIAL DESCRIPTION

Scope: Publishes artistic, scientific, linguistic, historical, and literary articles on the province of Veneto.
Reviews books: Yes
Publishes notes: Yes
Languages accepted: Italian
Prints abstracts: No

SUBMISSION REQUIREMENTS

Author pays submission fee: No
Author pays page charges: No
Length of articles: 1,000-12,000 words
Length of book reviews: 500 words maximum
Length of notes: 100-200 words maximum
Style: None
Number of copies required: 1
Copyright ownership: Author
Rejected manuscripts: Not returned
Time before publication decision: 1 mo.
Time between decision and publication: 3 mos.
Number of reviewers: 1-3
Articles submitted per year: 30-40
Articles published per year: 30
Book reviews submitted per year: 50-60
Book reviews published per year: 50
Notes submitted per year: 7-8
Notes published per year: 7-8

(245)
Archivio Storico Italiano

Arnaldo D'Addario, Editor
Deputazione di Storia Patria per la Toscana
Piazza dei Giudici, 1
50122 Florence, Italy

First published: 1842

Sponsoring organization: Deputazione di Storia Patria, Toscana
ISSN: 0004-0339
MLA acronym: ASI

SUBSCRIPTION INFORMATION

Frequency of publication: 4 times/yr.
Available in microform: No
Subscription price: 64,000 Lit/yr. Italy; 80,000 Lit/yr. elsewhere
Year to which price refers: 1991
Subscription address: Casa Editrice Leo S. Olschki, Viuzzo del Pozzetto (Viale Europa), C.P. 66, 50100 Florence, Italy

ADVERTISING INFORMATION

Advertising accepted: Yes

EDITORIAL DESCRIPTION

Scope: Publishes studies of historic nature and of documentary sources.
Reviews books: Yes
Publishes notes: Yes
Languages accepted: Italian
Prints abstracts: No

SUBMISSION REQUIREMENTS

Restrictions on contributors: None
Author pays submission fee: No
Author pays page charges: No
Length of articles: 2,500-44,000 words
Length of book reviews: 2,500 words
Length of notes: 950 words
Number of copies required: 1
Special requirements: Submit original typescript. Articles not written in Italian are accepted for translation.
Copyright ownership: Journal
Rejected manuscripts: Returned
Time before publication decision: 10-12 mos.
Time between decision and publication: 2 mos.
Number of reviewers: 2-3
Articles submitted per year: 50
Articles published per year: 10-20
Book reviews submitted per year: 50-60
Book reviews published per year: 20
Notes submitted per year: 150-200
Notes published per year: 100

(246)
*Archīvs: Raksti par Latviskām Problēmām

Edgars Dunsdorfs, Editor
3 Dickens St.
Elwood, Victoria 3184, Australia

First published: 1960
Sponsoring organization: World Federation of Free Latvians; Karla Zarina Fonds
MLA acronym: Archīvs

SUBSCRIPTION INFORMATION

Frequency of publication: Annual
Circulation: 1,600
Available in microform: No
Subscription address: E. Verzemnieks, 5814 108th Ave. CT E., Puyallup, WA 98372-2701

ADVERTISING INFORMATION

Advertising accepted: No

EDITORIAL DESCRIPTION

Scope: Investigates all aspects of the life of Latvians in the free world.
Reviews books: No
Publishes notes: Yes
Languages accepted: Latvian
Prints abstracts: No
Author-anonymous submission: No

SUBMISSION REQUIREMENTS

Restrictions on contributors: None
Author pays submission fee: No
Author pays page charges: No
Length of articles: No restrictions
Length of notes: No restrictions
Style: John Wiley & Sons, Inc.
Number of copies required: 1
Copyright ownership: Journal
Rejected manuscripts: Returned at author's request
Time before publication decision: 1-2 yrs.
Time between decision and publication: 1 yr.
Number of reviewers: 2
Articles submitted per year: 15-20
Articles published per year: 10-12
Notes submitted per year: 2-5
Notes published per year: 2-5

(247)
*Archivum Franciscanum Historicum

Francisco Víctor Sánchez Gil, Editor
Collegio San Bonaventura
Via Vecchia di Marino, 28-30
00046 Grottaferrata (Rome), Italy

Telephone: (39) 6 94315318; (39) 6 9410781
First published: 1908
Sponsoring organization: Collegio San Bonaventura, Historical Commission
ISSN: 0004-0665
MLA acronym: AFH

SUBSCRIPTION INFORMATION

Frequency of publication: 4 times/yr.
Circulation: 900
Available in microform: No
Subscription price: 60,000 Lit/yr.
Year to which price refers: 1992

ADVERTISING INFORMATION

Advertising accepted: No

EDITORIAL DESCRIPTION

Scope: Publishes articles on the history of the Franciscan Order.
Reviews books: Yes
Publishes notes: Yes
Languages accepted: English; French; German; Italian; Latin; Spanish
Prints abstracts: No
Author-anonymous submission: No

SUBMISSION REQUIREMENTS

Restrictions on contributors: None
Author pays submission fee: No
Author pays page charges: No
Length of articles: No restrictions
Length of book reviews: No restrictions
Length of notes: No restrictions
Style: Journal
Number of copies required: 1
Copyright ownership: Collegio San Bonaventura
Rejected manuscripts: Returned
Time before publication decision: 1 mo.
Time between decision and publication: 6 mos.
Number of reviewers: 2
Articles submitted per year: 15-20
Articles published per year: 20
Book reviews submitted per year: 15-20
Book reviews published per year: 20
Notes submitted per year: 20
Notes published per year: 120-150

(248)
*Archivum Latinitatis Medii Aevi (Bulletin du Cange)

Jacques Monfrin, Editor
c/o Ecole des Chartes
19 rue de la Sorbonne
75005 Paris, France

First published: 1924
Sponsoring organization: International Union of Academies
MLA acronym: ALMA

SUBSCRIPTION INFORMATION

Frequency of publication: Annual
Available in microform: No
Subscription address: Librairie Droz, S.A., 11 rue Massot, 1211 Geneva, Switzerland
Subscription telephone: (41) 22 466666

ADVERTISING INFORMATION

Advertising accepted: No

EDITORIAL DESCRIPTION

Scope: Publishes articles on lexicography and medieval Latin literature.
Reviews books: Yes
Publishes notes: Yes
Languages accepted: French; English; German; Italian; Spanish
Prints abstracts: No
Author-anonymous submission: No

SUBMISSION REQUIREMENTS

Restrictions on contributors: None
Author pays submission fee: No
Author pays page charges: No
Length of articles: 16,000-64,000 words
Length of book reviews: 5,000-6,000 words
Length of notes: 8,000-15,000 words
Number of copies required: 1
Rejected manuscripts: Not returned
Time before publication decision: 1 mo.
Time between decision and publication: 1 yr.
Number of reviewers: 2
Articles submitted per year: 8
Articles published per year: 5
Book reviews submitted per year: 20
Book reviews published per year: 20
Notes submitted per year: 15

(249)
Area and Culture Studies

Koretada Sakamoto, Editor
Tokyo Univ. of Foreign Studies
4-51-21 Nishigahara
Kita-ku
Tokyo, Japan

First published: 1952
Sponsoring organization: Tokyo Univ. of Foreign Studies
ISSN: 0493-4342
MLA acronym: A&CS

SUBSCRIPTION INFORMATION

Frequency of publication: Annual
Circulation: 1,000

EDITORIAL DESCRIPTION

Scope: Publishes articles on linguistics, literature, and area and culture studies.
Reviews books: Yes
Languages accepted: Japanese; English; French; German; Spanish
Prints abstracts: Yes

SUBMISSION REQUIREMENTS

Restrictions on contributors: Contributors must be members of the teaching staff of Tokyo Univ. of Foreign Studies.
Style: None
Number of copies required: 1
Copyright ownership: Author
Rejected manuscripts: Returned
Time between decision and publication: 6 mos.

(250)
Arheoloğija un Etnogrāfija

Ē. Mugurēvičs, Editor
Inst. of History
Academy of Sciences, Latvia
Turgeneva 19
226524 Riga, Latvia

First published: 1957
Sponsoring organization: Latvian Academy of Sciences
ISSN: 0320-9415
MLA acronym: AuE

SUBSCRIPTION INFORMATION

Frequency of publication: Irregular
Circulation: 3,000
Available in microform: No

ADVERTISING INFORMATION

Advertising accepted: Yes

EDITORIAL DESCRIPTION

Scope: Publishes articles on Latvian archaeology and ethnography.
Reviews books: Yes
Publishes notes: No
Languages accepted: Latvian; Russian (summaries); German (summaries)
Prints abstracts: Yes
Author-anonymous submission: No

SUBMISSION REQUIREMENTS

Restrictions on contributors: None
Author pays submission fee: No
Author pays page charges: No
Length of articles: 5,000-20,000 words
Length of book reviews: No restrictions
Style: None
Number of copies required: 3
Special requirements: Submit original typescript and 2 copies. Include a 400-word abstract.
Copyright ownership: Author
Rejected manuscripts: Not returned
Time before publication decision: 2 mos.
Time between decision and publication: 10 mos.
Number of reviewers: 2
Articles submitted per year: 10-20
Articles published per year: 10
Book reviews submitted per year: 3
Book reviews published per year: 3

(251)
*Ariel

Patricia Bolaños, Editor
Dept. of Spanish & Italian
1115 Patterson Office Tower
Univ. of Kentucky
Lexington, KY 40506-0027

Telephone: 606 257-1565
First published: 1983
Sponsoring organization: Spanish & Italian Graduate Student Assn., Univ. of Kentucky
ISSN: 0895-8920
MLA acronym: ArielK

SUBSCRIPTION INFORMATION

Frequency of publication: Annual
Available in microform: No
Subscription price: Free
Year to which price refers: 1992

ADVERTISING INFORMATION

Advertising accepted: No

EDITORIAL DESCRIPTION

Scope: To foster scholarship among graduate students in the areas of Hispanic/Hispanic American language and literature.
Reviews books: Yes
Publishes notes: Yes
Languages accepted: English; Spanish; other languages considered on an individual basis
Prints abstracts: No
Author-anonymous submission: Yes

SUBMISSION REQUIREMENTS

Restrictions on contributors: None
Author pays submission fee: No
Author pays page charges: No
Length of articles: 3,500 words
Length of book reviews: 350-500 words
Length of notes: 40-60 words
Style: MLA
Number of copies required: 2
Copyright ownership: Author
Rejected manuscripts: Returned
Time before publication decision: 4-6 mos.
Time between decision and publication: 6 mos.
Number of reviewers: 2-5
Articles submitted per year: 25-30
Articles published per year: 7-10
Book reviews submitted per year: 5-6
Book reviews published per year: 1-4
Notes submitted per year: 5-10
Notes published per year: 5-10

(252)
*Ariel: A Review of Arts and Letters in Israel

Asher Weill, Editor
214, Jaffa St.
Jerusalem 91130, Israel

Telephone: (972) 2 381515
Fax: (972) 2 254896
First published: 1962
Sponsoring organization: Israel Ministry of Foreign Affairs
ISSN: 0004-1343
MLA acronym: Ariel

SUBSCRIPTION INFORMATION

Frequency of publication: 4 times/yr. in each language
Circulation: 25,000
Available in microform: No
Subscription price: $27.00 ($36.00 airmail)/yr.
Year to which price refers: 1992
Subscription address: Youval Tal, Ltd., P.O. Box 2160, Jerusalem 91021, Israel
Subscription telephone: (972) 2 248897

ADVERTISING INFORMATION

Advertising accepted: Yes

EDITORIAL DESCRIPTION

Scope: Publishes articles on Israeli culture including literature, poetry, criticism, painting and sculpture, archaeology, theater, film, music, dance, ethnography, Judaica, etc. The journal is published in English, French, German, Spanish, and Russian editions.
Reviews books: Yes
Publishes notes: No
Languages accepted: English; French; German; Spanish; Russian
Prints abstracts: No
Author-anonymous submission: No

SUBMISSION REQUIREMENTS

Restrictions on contributors: None
Author pays submission fee: No
Author pays page charges: No
Length of articles: 2,000-5,000 words
Length of book reviews: 1,000-2,000 words
Style: Oxford Univ. Press
Number of copies required: 1
Copyright ownership: Author & Journal
Rejected manuscripts: Returned
Time before publication decision: 2-4 weeks
Time between decision and publication: 2 yrs. maximum
Number of reviewers: 1
Articles published per year: 32
Book reviews published per year: 8

(253)
*Ariel: A Review of International English Literature

Victor Ramraj, Pamela McCallom, David Oakleaf, & Patricia Srebrnik, Editors
Dept. of English
Univ. of Calgary
2500 University Dr., NW
Calgary, Alberta T2N 1N4, Canada

Telephone: 403 220-4679
Fax: 403 284-0848
First published: 1970
Sponsoring organization: Univ. of Calgary
ISSN: 0004-1327
MLA acronym: ArielE

SUBSCRIPTION INFORMATION

Frequency of publication: 4 times/yr. (Jan., Apr., July, Oct.)
Circulation: 850
Available in microform: No
Subscription price: C$25.00/yr. institutions; C$17.00/yr. individuals
Year to which price refers: 1993
Subscription telephone: 403 220-4657

ADVERTISING INFORMATION

Advertising accepted: Yes
Advertising rates: $75.00/half page; $110.00/full page; $115.00/inside cover; $125.00/back cover

EDITORIAL DESCRIPTION

Scope: Publishes articles on international English literature. Emphasis is on commonwealth or postcolonial literature and its relationship with British and American literature.
Reviews books: Yes
Publishes notes: No
Languages accepted: English
Prints abstracts: No
Author-anonymous submission: Yes

SUBMISSION REQUIREMENTS

Restrictions on contributors: None
Author pays submission fee: No
Author pays page charges: No
Length of articles: 3,000-6,000 words
Length of book reviews: 750-1,000 words
Style: MLA
Number of copies required: 2
Special requirements: No multiple submissions. Submit original typescript and 1 copy. Typescripts should be submitted on diskette in WordPerfect upon acceptance.
Copyright ownership: Univ. of Calgary
Rejected manuscripts: Returned; enclose return postage or international reply coupons.
Time before publication decision: 2-3 mos.
Time between decision and publication: 1 yr.
Number of reviewers: 3
Articles submitted per year: 100-120
Articles published per year: 26
Book reviews submitted per year: 20
Book reviews published per year: 16

(254)
*Arizona Quarterly: A Journal of American Literature, Culture, and Theory

Edgar A. Dryden, Editor
B-541, Main Library
Univ. of Arizona
Tucson, AZ 85721

First published: 1945
Sponsoring organization: Univ. of Arizona
ISSN: 0004-1610
MLA acronym: ArQ

SUBSCRIPTION INFORMATION

Frequency of publication: 4 times/yr.
Circulation: 600
Available in microform: Yes
Subscription price: $16.00/yr., $32.00/2 yrs. institutions; $12.00/yr., $24.00/2 yrs. individuals; add $4.00/yr. postage outside N. America
Year to which price refers: 1992

ADVERTISING INFORMATION

Advertising accepted: Yes
Advertising rates: $150.00/full page

EDITORIAL DESCRIPTION

Scope: Publishes scholarly articles on all periods and genres of literature and film of the Americas in English, with a particular emphasis on contemporary theoretical approaches to both canonical and noncanonical texts.
Reviews books: Yes
Publishes notes: No
Languages accepted: English
Prints abstracts: No
Author-anonymous submission: No

SUBMISSION REQUIREMENTS

Restrictions on contributors: Book reviews are commissioned.
Author pays submission fee: No
Author pays page charges: No
Length of articles: 3,500-10,000 words
Length of book reviews: 3,500-10,000 words
Style: MLA with modifications
Number of copies required: 2
Copyright ownership: Arizona Board of Regents
Rejected manuscripts: Returned; enclose return postage.
Time before publication decision: 2-4 mos.
Time between decision and publication: 6-16 mos.
Number of reviewers: 2-3
Articles submitted per year: 250
Articles published per year: 16-24
Book reviews submitted per year: 10
Book reviews published per year: 1-4

(255)
*The Arkansas Quarterly: A Journal of Criticism

Dora Rainey, Floyd Collins, & Susan Smith Nash, Editors
P.O. Box 2691
Univ. of Arkansas
Fayetteville, AR 72601-2691

Additional editorial address: 88 Dawn Hill Rd., Siloam Springs, AR 72761
Telephone: 501 524-3326
First published: 1992
MLA acronym: ArkQ

SUBSCRIPTION INFORMATION

Frequency of publication: 4 times/yr.
Circulation: 550
Available in microform: No
Subscription price: $12.00/yr. US; $22.00/yr. elsewhere
Year to which price refers: 1993
Subscription address: 88 Dawn Hill Rd., Siloam Springs, AR 72761
Additional subscription address: Epiphany Publications Inc., 408 E. Tulsa, Siloam Springs, AR 72761

ADVERTISING INFORMATION

Advertising accepted: Yes
Advertising rates: $25.00/quarter page; $50.00/half page; $100.00/full page

EDITORIAL DESCRIPTION

Scope: Presents a forum for scholars commenting on the literature and literary theory of the 20th century, preferably the latter half of the century. Texts of other ages are addressed by comparing and contrasting older texts with those of the 20th century. The purpose of this approach is to focus on the present and to address developing ideas of current thought.
Reviews books: Yes
Publishes notes: Yes
Languages accepted: English
Prints abstracts: No
Author-anonymous submission: Yes

SUBMISSION REQUIREMENTS

Restrictions on contributors: Book reviews are by invitation.
Author pays submission fee: No
Author pays page charges: No
Length of articles: 10,000 words maximum
Length of book reviews: 500 words maximum
Style: MLA
Number of copies required: 1
Special requirements: Articles longer than 5 pp. should be submitted on diskette.
Copyright ownership: Journal; reverts to author upon publication
Rejected manuscripts: Returned at author's request; enclose return postage
Time before publication decision: 3-4 mos.
Time between decision and publication: 2-3 mos.
Number of reviewers: 3 minimum
Articles submitted per year: 250
Articles published per year: 50
Book reviews published per year: 40

(256)
*Arkiv för Nordisk Filologi/Archives for Scandinavian Philology

Bengt Pamp & Christer Platzack, Editors
Helgonabacken 14
223 62 Lund, Sweden

Telephone: (46) 46 107470
Fax: (46) 46 152381
First published: 1882
Sponsoring organization: Scandinavian Councils of the Humanities
ISSN: 0066-7668
MLA acronym: ANF

SUBSCRIPTION INFORMATION

Frequency of publication: Annual
Circulation: 470
Available in microform: No
Subscription price: 356 Skr/yr. institutions; 302 Skr/yr. individuals
Year to which price refers: 1991
Subscription address: Lund Univ. Press, Box 141, 221 00 Lund, Sweden
Subscription telephone: (46) 46 312000
Subscription fax: (46) 46 305338

ADVERTISING INFORMATION

Advertising accepted: No

EDITORIAL DESCRIPTION

Scope: Publishes articles on Scandinavian languages and Old Norse and medieval Scandinavian literature.
Reviews books: Yes
Publishes notes: No
Languages accepted: Danish; English; French; German; Norwegian; Swedish; Icelandic
Prints abstracts: No
Author-anonymous submission: No

SUBMISSION REQUIREMENTS

Restrictions on contributors: Book reviews are written by the editors.
Author pays submission fee: No
Author pays page charges: No
Length of articles: 12,000 words maximum
Length of book reviews: 3,000 words
Number of copies required: 3
Special requirements: Notes should be numbered consecutively and placed at end of article. Texts and titles should be quoted according to Swedish printing punctuation norm, meaning that full stops and commas are to be placed after the quotation marks.
Copyright ownership: Journal
Rejected manuscripts: Returned at author's request
Time before publication decision: 2-4 mos.
Time between decision and publication: 1-2 yrs.
Number of reviewers: 2-3
Articles submitted per year: 15-20
Articles published per year: 10-15
Book reviews submitted per year: 2-4
Book reviews published per year: 1-3

(257)
*Armchair Detective: A Quarterly Journal Devoted to the Appreciation of Mystery, Detective, and Suspense Fiction

Kate Stine & Barbara Norton, Editors
129 W. 56 St.
New York, NY 10019

Telephone: 212 765-0902
Fax: 212 265-5478
First published: 1967
ISSN: 0004-217X
MLA acronym: ArmD

SUBSCRIPTION INFORMATION

Frequency of publication: 4 times/yr.
Circulation: 3,500
Available in microform: No
Subscription price: $26.00/yr., $48.00/2 yrs. US; $30.00 ($42.00 airmail)/yr. elsewhere
Year to which price refers: 1992

ADVERTISING INFORMATION

Advertising accepted: Yes
Advertising rates: $400.00/quarter page; $675.00/half page; $1,100.00/full page

EDITORIAL DESCRIPTION

Scope: Publishes bibliographical, biographical, short fiction, critical, survey, and commentary material about mystery, detective, and suspense fiction, as well as relevant reviews and letters.
Reviews books: Yes
Publishes notes: No
Languages accepted: English
Prints abstracts: No

SUBMISSION REQUIREMENTS

Restrictions on contributors: None
Author pays submission fee: No
Author pays page charges: No
Length of articles: 4,000-10,000 words
Length of book reviews: 250-1,000 words
Number of copies required: 1
Copyright ownership: Journal
Rejected manuscripts: Returned; enclose SASE.
Time before publication decision: 3 mos.
Time between decision and publication: 3 mos.
Number of reviewers: 2
Articles submitted per year: 100
Articles published per year: 20
Book reviews submitted per year: 700
Book reviews published per year: 400

(258)
*Arquivos do Centro Cultural Português

Maria de Lourdes Belchior, Director
Centro Cultural Português
Fundação Calouste Gulbenkian
51, avenue d'Iéna
Paris 75116, France

Telephone: (33) 1 47208684
Fax: (33) 1 40709879
First published: 1969
Sponsoring organization: Fundação Calouste Gulbenkian
ISSN: 0590-966X
MLA acronym: ACCP

SUBSCRIPTION INFORMATION

Frequency of publication: Annual
Available in microform: No
Subscription price: 350 F/yr.
Year to which price refers: 1992
Subscription address: Jean Touzot, Libraire Editeur, 38, rue Saint-Sulpice, 75278 Paris Cedex 06, France

ADVERTISING INFORMATION

Advertising accepted: No

EDITORIAL DESCRIPTION

Scope: Publishes studies concerning Portuguese culture and Franco-Portuguese cultural exchanges of a general, historical, or artistic nature. Studies of other subjects pertinent to Portuguese culture are also occasionally accepted.
Reviews books: Yes
Publishes notes: Yes
Languages accepted: English; French; Italian; Portuguese; Spanish
Prints abstracts: No
Author-anonymous submission: No

SUBMISSION REQUIREMENTS

Restrictions on contributors: None
Author pays submission fee: No
Author pays page charges: No
Length of articles: 25-35 pp.
Style: None
Number of copies required: 1
Special requirements: Submissions are accepted from Jan. through May.
Copyright ownership: Author
Rejected manuscripts: Returned
Time before publication decision: 2 mos.
Time between decision and publication: 6-9 mos.
Number of reviewers: 1
Articles submitted per year: 25-30
Articles published per year: 20-25

(259)
Ars Lyrica: Journal of Lyrica, Society for Word-Music Relations

Louis E. Auld, Editor
90 Church St.
Guilford, CT 06437

First published: 1981
Sponsoring organization: Lyrica Soc.
ISSN: 1043-3848
MLA acronym: ArsL

SUBSCRIPTION INFORMATION

Frequency of publication: Irregular
Available in microform: No

ADVERTISING INFORMATION

Advertising accepted: Yes, on an exchange basis.

EDITORIAL DESCRIPTION

Scope: Publishes articles on all approaches to the interrelations of music and words.
Reviews books: Yes
Publishes notes: Yes
Languages accepted: English; French; German; Spanish
Prints abstracts: Yes, for non-English contributions.
Author-anonymous submission: Yes

SUBMISSION REQUIREMENTS

Author pays submission fee: No
Author pays page charges: No
Length of articles: 3,000-8,000 words
Length of book reviews: 1,500 words
Length of notes: 1,500 words
Style: MLA; Chicago
Number of copies required: 1
Special requirements: Submit typescript and diskette, if possible.
Copyright ownership: Lyrica Soc.
Rejected manuscripts: Returned; enclose SASE.
Time before publication decision: 1 yr.
Time between decision and publication: 2 yrs.
Number of reviewers: 2
Articles published per year: 6-8
Book reviews published per year: 4-8

(260)
*The Arthurian Yearbook

Keith Busby, Editor
Dept. of Modern Languages
Univ. of Oklahoma
780 Van Vleet Oval, Rm. 202
Norman, OK 73019

Telephone: 405 325-6181
Fax: 405 325-5068
E-mail: AA1726@UOKMVSA
First published: 1991
ISSN: 1053-3877
MLA acronym: ArthY

SUBSCRIPTION INFORMATION

Frequency of publication: Annual
Circulation: 500
Available in microform: No
Subscription price: $37.00/yr.
Year to which price refers: 1992
Subscription address: Garland Publishing, 1000A Sherman Ave., Hamden, CT 06514
Subscription telephone: 800 627-6273

EDITORIAL DESCRIPTION

Scope: Publishes articles on any aspect, medieval or modern, of the cultural manifestation of the Arthurian legend. Areas covered include literature, art, music, film, and the relations between them.

Reviews books: Yes
Languages accepted: English
Prints abstracts: No
Author-anonymous submission: Yes

SUBMISSION REQUIREMENTS

Author pays submission fee: No
Author pays page charges: No
Length of articles: No restrictions
Style: MLA
Number of copies required: 2
Special requirements: Submit typescript and MS-DOS diskette for final version.
Copyright ownership: Editor
Rejected manuscripts: Returned at author's request
Time before publication decision: 2 mos.
Time between decision and publication: 6-9 mos.
Number of reviewers: 2
Articles submitted per year: 20
Articles published per year: 12
Books published per year: 1

(261)
*Arv: Scandinavian Yearbook of Folklore

Ulrika Wolf-Knuts, Editor
Folkloristik
Åbo Akademi
20500 Åbo, Finland

Telephone: (358) 21 654342
Fax: (358) 21 517553
First published: 1945
Sponsoring organization: Kungliga Gustav Adolfs Akademien
ISSN: 0066-8176
MLA acronym: Arv

SUBSCRIPTION INFORMATION

Frequency of publication: Annual
Available in microform: No
Subscription price: 200 Skr/yr.; 150 Skr/yr. members; 100 Skr/yr. students
Year to which price refers: 1993

ADVERTISING INFORMATION

Advertising accepted: No

EDITORIAL DESCRIPTION

Scope: Publishes articles on folklore.
Reviews books: Yes
Publishes notes: No
Languages accepted: English
Prints abstracts: Yes
Author-anonymous submission: No

SUBMISSION REQUIREMENTS

Author pays submission fee: No
Author pays page charges: No
Style: Chicago
Number of copies required: 3
Special requirements: Submit original typescript and 2 copies, along with diskette, if possible.
Copyright ownership: Publisher
Rejected manuscripts: Returned
Time before publication decision: 2-3 weeks
Time between decision and publication: 9 mos.
Articles published per year: 10-20
Book reviews published per year: 10-20

(262)
*Asemka: A Literary Journal of the University of Cape Coast

Y. S. Boafo, Editor
French Dept.
Univ. of Cape Coast
Cape Coast, Ghana

First published: 1974
Sponsoring organization: Univ. of Cape Coast
ISSN: 0855-000X
MLA acronym: Asemka

SUBSCRIPTION INFORMATION

Frequency of publication: Annual
Circulation: 1,000
Available in microform: No

ADVERTISING INFORMATION

Advertising accepted: Yes

EDITORIAL DESCRIPTION

Scope: Publishes articles on African, Caribbean, modern European, and American literatures, languages, and civilizations.
Reviews books: Yes
Publishes notes: No
Languages accepted: English; French
Prints abstracts: Yes
Author-anonymous submission: No

SUBMISSION REQUIREMENTS

Author pays submission fee: No
Author pays page charges: No
Length of articles: 3,000-6,000 words
Length of book reviews: 1,500 words maximum
Style: MLA
Number of copies required: 2
Copyright ownership: Author
Rejected manuscripts: Not returned
Time before publication decision: 8 mos.
Time between decision and publication: 6 mos.
Number of reviewers: 2
Articles submitted per year: 20
Articles published per year: 10
Book reviews submitted per year: 8
Book reviews published per year: 4

(263)
Asia Major

Howard L. Goodman, Managing Editor
211 Jones Hall
Princeton Univ.
Princeton, NJ 08544

First published: 1988
Sponsoring organization: Program in East Asian Studies, Princeton Univ.
ISSN: 0004-4482
MLA acronym: AsMj

SUBSCRIPTION INFORMATION

Frequency of publication: 2 times/yr.
Circulation: 150
Available in microform: No
Subscription address: P.O. Box 465, Hanover, PA 17331

ADVERTISING INFORMATION

Advertising accepted: Yes

EDITORIAL DESCRIPTION

Scope: Publishes articles on all periods of Chinese history, literature, ideas, and culture. Also includes the history and culture of other East Asian and central Asian people in their relations with China.
Reviews books: Yes
Publishes notes: Yes

Languages accepted: English
Prints abstracts: No
Author-anonymous submission: No

SUBMISSION REQUIREMENTS

Author pays submission fee: No
Author pays page charges: No
Length of articles: 8,000-10,000 words
Length of book reviews: 6,000-8,000 words
Length of notes: 60-75 words maximum
Style: Chicago
Number of copies required: 3
Special requirements: Submissions for Western language portion are preferred on diskette in WordPerfect, accompanied by typescript. Manuscripts must include legible East Asian characters and must be printed with a good quality, high resolution printer.
Copyright ownership: Trustees of Princeton Univ.
Rejected manuscripts: Not returned
Time before publication decision: 5-8 mos.
Time between decision and publication: 4-6 mos.
Number of reviewers: 1-3
Articles submitted per year: 25
Articles published per year: 10
Book reviews submitted per year: 2-3
Book reviews published per year: 1
Notes submitted per year: 5
Notes published per year: 1

(264)
*Asian and African Studies

Gabriel R. Warburg & Gad G. Gilbar, Editors
Gustav Heinemann Inst. of Middle Eastern Studies
Univ. of Haifa
Mt. Carmel, Haifa 31999, Israel

Telephone: (972) 4 240655
Fax: (972) 4 342104
E-mail: FHHM401@HAIFAUVM
First published: 1965
ISSN: 0066-8281
MLA acronym: AAS

SUBSCRIPTION INFORMATION

Frequency of publication: 3 times/yr.
Circulation: 800
Available in microform: Yes, through Univ. Microfilms International
Subscription price: $60.00/yr.
Year to which price refers: 1992

ADVERTISING INFORMATION

Advertising accepted: Yes
Advertising rates: $150.00/half page; $300.00/full page

EDITORIAL DESCRIPTION

Scope: Publishes articles on the social, economic, and political history of Middle Eastern and Asian and African countries. Includes medieval, modern, and contemporary periods.
Reviews books: Yes
Publishes notes: No
Languages accepted: English
Prints abstracts: No
Author-anonymous submission: No

SUBMISSION REQUIREMENTS

Restrictions on contributors: Book reviews are by invitation only.
Author pays submission fee: No
Author pays page charges: No
Length of articles: 8,000 words
Length of book reviews: 2,000 words
Style: Available on request.
Number of copies required: 2
Special requirements: Submit double-spaced typescript with liberal margins.
Copyright ownership: Publisher

Rejected manuscripts: Returned at author's request.
Time before publication decision: 3-6 mos.
Time between decision and publication: 2 yrs.
Number of reviewers: 4
Articles submitted per year: 80-100
Articles published per year: 15-20
Book reviews published per year: 15-20

(265)
*Asian Folklore Studies

Peter Knecht, Editor
Nanzan Univ.
18, Yamazato-cho, Showa-ku
466 Nagoya, Japan

Telephone: (81) 52 8323111
Fax: (81) 52 8336157
First published: 1942
Sponsoring organization: Nanzan Anthropological Inst.
ISSN: 0385-2342
MLA acronym: AFS

SUBSCRIPTION INFORMATION

Frequency of publication: 2 times/yr.
Circulation: 350
Available in microform: Yes
Subscription price: $35.00/yr. institutions; $18.00/yr. individuals
Year to which price refers: 1992

ADVERTISING INFORMATION

Advertising accepted: Yes, on an exchange basis.

EDITORIAL DESCRIPTION

Scope: Publishes articles on folklore and folklife, including religion, oral tradition, music, and art.
Reviews books: Yes
Publishes notes: Yes
Languages accepted: English
Prints abstracts: Yes
Author-anonymous submission: No

SUBMISSION REQUIREMENTS

Restrictions on contributors: None
Author pays submission fee: No
Author pays page charges: No
Length of articles: 30 printed pp.
Length of book reviews: 2-3 double-spaced typescript pp.
Length of notes: 1 double-spaced typescript p.
Style: Chicago
Number of copies required: 1
Special requirements: Use pinyin system for transcription of Chinese, Hepburn for Japanese, and McCure-Reischauer for Korean. Provide original characters and English translations for Chinese, Japanese, and Korean words.
Copyright ownership: Publisher
Rejected manuscripts: Returned
Time before publication decision: 3 mos.
Time between decision and publication: 1 yr. maximum
Number of reviewers: 1-2
Articles submitted per year: 28-30
Articles published per year: 10-15
Book reviews submitted per year: 50-55
Book reviews published per year: 45-50
Notes submitted per year: 8-10
Notes published per year: 8-10

(266)
*Asian Music: Journal of the Society for Asian Music

Martin Hatch, Editor
Music Dept.
Lincoln Hall
Cornell Univ.
Ithaca, NY 14853-0254

Telephone: 607 255-5049
Fax: 607 255-1454
First published: 1968-69
Sponsoring organization: Soc. for Asian Music
ISSN: 0004-9202
MLA acronym: AMus

SUBSCRIPTION INFORMATION

Frequency of publication: 2 times/yr.
Circulation: 600
Available in microform: No
Subscription price: $35.00/yr. institutions; $25.00/yr. individuals; $15.00/yr. students
Year to which price refers: 1991-92
Subscription address: Dept. of Asian Studies, 388 Rockefeller Hall, Cornell Univ., Ithaca, NY 14853-2502

ADVERTISING INFORMATION

Advertising accepted: No

EDITORIAL DESCRIPTION

Scope: Publishes articles on musical styles and music cultures of Asia (Near East to Far East), including dance and theater.
Reviews books: Yes
Publishes notes: No
Languages accepted: English; French; German
Prints abstracts: No
Author-anonymous submission: Yes

SUBMISSION REQUIREMENTS

Restrictions on contributors: None
Author pays submission fee: No
Author pays page charges: No
Length of articles: No restrictions
Length of book reviews: No restrictions
Style: Journal
Number of copies required: 2
Copyright ownership: Soc. for Asian Music
Rejected manuscripts: Returned
Time before publication decision: 2-4 mos.
Time between decision and publication: 1 yr.
Number of reviewers: 2
Articles submitted per year: 15-25
Articles published per year: 12-15
Book reviews submitted per year: 10
Book reviews published per year: 8-10

(267)
*Asian Theatre Journal

Samuel L. Leiter, Editor
137-29 79th St.
Howard Beach, NY 11414

Telephone: 718 780-5666
Fax: 718 843-0946
First published: 1984
Sponsoring organization: Assn. for Asian Performance
ISSN: 0742-5457
MLA acronym: ATJ

SUBSCRIPTION INFORMATION

Frequency of publication: 2 times/yr. (Fall, Spring)
Circulation: 500
Available in microform: Yes
Subscription price: $30.00/yr. institutions US & Canada; $35.00/yr. institutions elsewhere; $15.00/yr. individuals US & Canada; $18.00/yr. individuals elsewhere

Year to which price refers: 1992
Subscription address: Journals Dept., Univ. of Hawaii Press, 2840 Kolowalu St., Honolulu, HI 96822
Subscription telephone: 808 956-8833

ADVERTISING INFORMATION

Advertising accepted: Yes
Advertising rates: $95.00/half page; $150.00/full page

EDITORIAL DESCRIPTION

Scope: Publishes scholarly articles on traditional and modern Asian theater, and relations between Asian and Western theater.
Reviews books: Yes
Publishes notes: Yes
Languages accepted: English
Prints abstracts: No

SUBMISSION REQUIREMENTS

Restrictions on contributors: Book reviews are commissioned.
Author pays submission fee: No
Author pays page charges: No
Length of articles: 10-25 pp.
Length of book reviews: 700-1,000 words
Style: Chicago
Number of copies required: 2
Special requirements: Submit double-spaced typescript.
Copyright ownership: Univ. of Hawaii Press
Rejected manuscripts: Returned
Time between decision and publication: 1 yr.
Number of reviewers: 4
Articles submitted per year: 15-20
Articles published per year: 7-10
Book reviews published per year: 10-15
Notes published per year: 1-2

(268)
*Asiatische Studien/Etudes Asiatiques: Zeitschrift der Schweizerischen Asiengesellschaft/Revue de la Société Suisse-Asie

Robert Gassmann, Jacques May, Johannes Bronkhorst, J. Christoph Bürgel, Gregor Schoeler, & Eduard Klopfenstein, Editors
Ostasiatisches Seminar
der Univ. Zürich
Zürichbergstr. 4
8032 Zürich, Switzerland

Telephone: (41) 1 2573181
Fax: (41) 1 2615687
First published: 1947
Historical variations in title: Formerly *Asiatische Studien/Etudes Asiatiques: Zeitschrift der Schweizerischen für Asienkunde/Revue de la Société Suisse d'Etudes Asiatiques*
Sponsoring organization: Schweizerische Asiengesellschaft/Soc. Suisse-Asie; Schweizerische Akademie der Geisteswissenschaften/Swiss Academy of Humanities & Social Sciences
ISSN: 0004-4717
MLA acronym: ASEA

SUBSCRIPTION INFORMATION

Frequency of publication: 4 times/yr.
Circulation: 500
Available in microform: No
Subscription address: Verlag Peter Lang AG, Jupiterstr. 15, Postfach 277, 3000 Bern 15, Switzerland

ADVERTISING INFORMATION

Advertising accepted: Yes

EDITORIAL DESCRIPTION

Scope: Publishes articles on Asia General, East Asia, and South Asia.
Reviews books: Yes
Publishes notes: Yes
Languages accepted: English; French; German
Prints abstracts: No
Author-anonymous submission: No

SUBMISSION REQUIREMENTS

Restrictions on contributors: None
Author pays submission fee: No
Author pays page charges: No
Length of articles: 50 pp. maximum
Length of book reviews: 2 pp.
Length of notes: 200 words
Style: Journal
Number of copies required: 2
Special requirements: Request style sheet from editor prior to submission.
Copyright ownership: Author & Schweizerische Asiengesellschaft
Rejected manuscripts: Returned
Time before publication decision: 2 mos.
Time between decision and publication: 12-18 mos.
Number of reviewers: 2-3
Articles submitted per year: 15-20
Articles published per year: 12-16
Book reviews submitted per year: 30-40
Book reviews published per year: 20-30
Notes submitted per year: 10-15
Notes published per year: 10-15

(269)
*Assaph: Studies in the Theatre

Eli Rozik, Editor
Dept. of Theatre Arts
Tel Aviv Univ.
69 978 Tel Aviv, Israel

Telephone: (972) 3 6408612
Fax: (972) 3 6409482
First published: 1984
Sponsoring organization: Tel Aviv Univ.
ISSN: 0334-5963
MLA acronym: Assaph

SUBSCRIPTION INFORMATION

Frequency of publication: Annual (Apr.-May)
Available in microform: No
Subscription price: $12.00/yr. institutions; $7.00/yr. individuals
Year to which price refers: 1992

ADVERTISING INFORMATION

Advertising accepted: No

EDITORIAL DESCRIPTION

Scope: Publishes articles on theater studies including theory, aesthetics, history and criticism, performance, and design. Includes a section on Israeli theater.
Reviews books: No
Publishes notes: No
Languages accepted: English
Prints abstracts: No
Author-anonymous submission: No

SUBMISSION REQUIREMENTS

Restrictions on contributors: None
Author pays submission fee: No
Author pays page charges: No
Length of articles: 5,000 words
Style: MLA
Number of copies required: 2
Copyright ownership: Tel Aviv Univ.
Rejected manuscripts: Not returned
Time before publication decision: 4-5 mos.
Time between decision and publication: 3-15 mos.
Number of reviewers: 3

Articles submitted per year: 40
Articles published per year: 9-10

(270)
*Assays: Critical Approaches to Medieval and Renaissance Texts

Peggy A. Knapp, Editor
Dept. of English
Carnegie Mellon Univ.
Pittsburgh, PA 15213

Telephone: 412 268-6453
Fax: 412 268-5288
E-mail: PK07@ANDREW.CMU.EDU
First published: 1981
ISSN: 0275-0058
MLA acronym: Assays

SUBSCRIPTION INFORMATION

Frequency of publication: Annual
Circulation: 100
Available in microform: No
Subscription price: $33.00/yr.
Year to which price refers: 1991
Subscription address: Carnegie Mellon Univ. Press, Baker Hall, Carnegie Mellon Univ., Pittsburgh, PA 15213
Subscription telephone: 412 268-6348

ADVERTISING INFORMATION

Advertising accepted: No

EDITORIAL DESCRIPTION

Scope: Functions as a forum for debate about the connections between contemporary critical theory and early texts.
Reviews books: No
Publishes notes: No
Languages accepted: English
Prints abstracts: No
Author-anonymous submission: Yes

SUBMISSION REQUIREMENTS

Restrictions on contributors: None
Author pays submission fee: No
Author pays page charges: Author's alterations above 5% of composition costs
Length of articles: No restrictions
Style: MLA
Number of copies required: 2
Copyright ownership: Carnegie Mellon Univ. Press
Rejected manuscripts: Returned; enclose SASE.
Time before publication decision: 3 mos.
Time between decision and publication: 1 yr.
Number of reviewers: 3
Articles submitted per year: 35
Articles published per year: 6-7

(271)
*Association for Recorded Sound Collections Journal

Ted P. Sheldon, Managing Editor
Miller Nichols Library
5100 Rockhill Rd.
Kansas City, MO 64110-2499

Telephone: 816 235-1531
Fax: 816 333-5584
E-mail: TSHELDON@UMKCVAX1
First published: 1967-68
Sponsoring organization: Assn. for Recorded Sound Collections
ISSN: 0004-5438
MLA acronym: ARSCJ

SUBSCRIPTION INFORMATION

Frequency of publication: 2 times/yr.
Circulation: 1,000

Available in microform: Yes
Subscription price: $30.00/yr.
Year to which price refers: 1992
Subscription address: Executive Director, ARSC, P.O. Box 10162, Silver Spring, MD 20914
Subscription telephone: 301 593-6552

ADVERTISING INFORMATION

Advertising accepted: Yes
Advertising rates: $40.00/quarter page; $65.00/half page; $100.00/full page; $200.00/cover

EDITORIAL DESCRIPTION

Scope: Focuses on bibliographic, discographic, technical, and historical aspects of recorded sound.
Reviews books: Yes
Publishes notes: Yes
Languages accepted: English
Prints abstracts: No
Author-anonymous submission: Yes

SUBMISSION REQUIREMENTS

Restrictions on contributors: None
Author pays submission fee: No
Author pays page charges: No
Length of articles: 50 pp. maximum
Length of book reviews: 10 pp. maximum
Length of notes: No restrictions
Style: Chicago
Number of copies required: 2
Special requirements: Submit original manuscript
Copyright ownership: Author
Rejected manuscripts: Returned
Time before publication decision: 4 mos.
Time between decision and publication: 2-8 mos.
Number of reviewers: 2
Articles submitted per year: 30
Articles published per year: 7-10
Book reviews submitted per year: 20
Book reviews published per year: 15
Notes submitted per year: 2
Notes published per year: 2

(272)
*L'Astrado: Revisto Bilengo de Prouvènço/Revue Bilinque de Provence

Michel Courty, Editor
L'Astrado Prouvençalo
7, les Fauvettes
13130 Berre L'Etang, France

First published: 1965
ISSN: 0004-6116
MLA acronym: Astrado

SUBSCRIPTION INFORMATION

Frequency of publication: Annual
Circulation: 1,000
Available in microform: No
Subscription price: 120 F/yr. France; 160 F/yr. elsewhere
Year to which price refers: 1991

ADVERTISING INFORMATION

Advertising accepted: No

EDITORIAL DESCRIPTION

Scope: Publishes articles on Provençal language, literature, and culture.
Reviews books: Yes
Publishes notes: No
Languages accepted: French; Occitan
Prints abstracts: Yes
Author-anonymous submission: No

SUBMISSION REQUIREMENTS

Author pays submission fee: No
Author pays page charges: No
Number of copies required: 1
Copyright ownership: Journal
Rejected manuscripts: Not returned
Time before publication decision: 6 mos.
Articles published per year: 30

(273)
Atenea: Revista de Ciencia, Arte y Literatura de la Universidad de Concepción

Tito Castillo Peralta, Director
Biblioteca Central Campus Universitario
Univ. de Concepción
Casilla 1557
Concepción, Chile

First published: 1924
Sponsoring organization: Univ. de Concepción
ISSN: 0716-1840
MLA acronym: Atenea

SUBSCRIPTION INFORMATION

Frequency of publication: 2 times/yr.
Circulation: 1,500
Available in microform: No

ADVERTISING INFORMATION

Advertising accepted: Yes

EDITORIAL DESCRIPTION

Scope: Publishes philosophical and historical essays and work about art and literature. Includes writings by foreign authors as well as Chilean collaborators.
Reviews books: No
Publishes notes: No
Languages accepted: Spanish
Prints abstracts: No
Author-anonymous submission: No

SUBMISSION REQUIREMENTS

Restrictions on contributors: None
Author pays submission fee: No
Author pays page charges: No
Length of articles: 1,500-3,000 words
Style: None
Number of copies required: 2
Special requirements: Submit original typescript.
Time before publication decision: 3 mos.
Time between decision and publication: 3 mos.
Articles submitted per year: 60
Articles published per year: 40

(274)
*Ateneo Veneto: Rivista di Scienze, Lettere ed Arti

Marino Zorzi, Editor
Campo S. Fantin, 1897
Venice, Italy

Telephone: (39) 41 5224459
Fax: (39) 41 5224459
First published: 1812
Sponsoring organization: Ateneo Veneto
ISSN: 0004-6558
MLA acronym: AV

SUBSCRIPTION INFORMATION

Frequency of publication: Annual
Circulation: 1,000
Available in microform: No

ADVERTISING INFORMATION

Advertising accepted: No

EDITORIAL DESCRIPTION

Scope: Publishes articles on Venetian culture.
Reviews books: Yes
Publishes notes: Yes
Languages accepted: Italian; English; French
Prints abstracts: No
Author-anonymous submission: No

SUBMISSION REQUIREMENTS

Restrictions on contributors: None
Author pays submission fee: No
Author pays page charges: No
Length of articles: 5-30 pp.
Length of book reviews: 2-5 pp.
Length of notes: 2-5 pp.
Number of copies required: 1
Copyright ownership: Journal
Rejected manuscripts: Returned
Time before publication decision: 2 mos.
Time between decision and publication: 6-10 mos.
Number of reviewers: 2
Articles submitted per year: 25
Articles published per year: 20
Book reviews submitted per year: 12
Book reviews published per year: 2
Notes submitted per year: 10
Notes published per year: 10

(275)
*Athanor

Augusto Ponzio & Claude Gandelman, Editors
A. Longo Editore
Via P. Costa 33
48100 Ravenna, Italy

Telephone: (39) 544 217026
Fax: (39) 544 217026
First published: 1990
Sponsoring organization: Univ. di Bari, Ist. Filosofia del Linguaggio
MLA acronym: Athanor

SUBSCRIPTION INFORMATION

Frequency of publication: Annual
Circulation: 1,500
Available in microform: No
Subscription price: 40,000 Lit/yr.
Year to which price refers: 1993

ADVERTISING INFORMATION

Advertising accepted: Yes
Advertising rates: 500,000 Lit/half page; 800,000 Lit/full page

EDITORIAL DESCRIPTION

Scope: Publishes texts and criticism on literature, arts, semiotics, and the philosophy of language.
Reviews books: Yes
Publishes notes: Yes
Languages accepted: Italian; French; English
Prints abstracts: No
Author-anonymous submission: No

SUBMISSION REQUIREMENTS

Author pays submission fee: No
Author pays page charges: No
Length of articles: 5,000-7,000 words
Length of book reviews: 2,500 words
Length of notes: 2,000-2,500 words
Style: MLA
Number of copies required: 2
Special requirements: Submit original typescript and IBM- or Macintosh-compatible diskette.
Copyright ownership: A. Longo Editrice
Rejected manuscripts: Not returned
Time before publication decision: 6 mos.

Time between decision and publication: 1 yr.
Number of reviewers: 2
Articles submitted per year: 50-100
Articles published per year: 20-25
Book reviews submitted per year: 50-100
Book reviews published per year: 10
Notes submitted per year: 50-100
Notes published per year: 10

(276)
Athēna: Syngramma Periodikon tēs en Athēnais Epistēmonikēs Hetaireias

En Athenais Epistemonike
Hetaireia
Odos Erssou 74
Athens 148, Greece

First published: 1889
MLA acronym: Athēna

SUBSCRIPTION INFORMATION

Frequency of publication: Annual

EDITORIAL DESCRIPTION

Reviews books: Yes
Languages accepted: English; French; Greek
Prints abstracts: Yes

(277)
*Athenaeum: Studi Periodici di Letteratura e Storia dell'Antichità

Emilio Gabba, Editor
Amministrazione di Athenaeum
Univ. di Pavia
27100 Pavia, Italy

Telephone: (39) 382 25697
First published: 1913
ISSN: 0004-6574
MLA acronym: Athenaeum

SUBSCRIPTION INFORMATION

Frequency of publication: 2 times/yr.
Circulation: 750
Available in microform: No
Subscription price: $78.00/yr.
Year to which price refers: 1993

ADVERTISING INFORMATION

Advertising accepted: No

EDITORIAL DESCRIPTION

Scope: Publishes articles on history, poetry, and literature of the Greek and Roman ancient worlds.
Reviews books: Yes
Publishes notes: Yes
Languages accepted: English; French; German; Italian; Spanish
Prints abstracts: No
Author-anonymous submission: No

SUBMISSION REQUIREMENTS

Author pays page charges: No
Length of articles: 25 pp.
Length of book reviews: 1,500 words
Length of notes: 3,000 words
Number of copies required: 1
Rejected manuscripts: Not returned
Time before publication decision: 1-2 mos.
Time between decision and publication: 1 yr.
Number of reviewers: 3
Articles submitted per year: 25-30
Articles published per year: 20
Book reviews submitted per year: 60
Book reviews published per year: 40
Notes submitted per year: 30
Notes published per year: 15

(278)
Athēnaïka: Periodikē Ekdosis tou Syllogou ton Athenaion

Syllogos ton Athinaion
Odos Kydathinaion 20
Athens 119, Greece

First published: 1955
ISSN: 0403-8185
MLA acronym: Athēnaïka

SUBSCRIPTION INFORMATION

Frequency of publication: 3 times/yr.

EDITORIAL DESCRIPTION

Reviews books: Yes

(279)
*Atlantis: A Women's Studies Journal/Revue d'Etudes sur la Femme

Deborah C. Poff, Editor
Mount Saint Vincent Univ.
Halifax, Nova Scotia, B3M 2J6, Canada

Telephone: 902 443-4450 ext. 319
Fax: 902 443-1352
First published: 1975
Historical variations in title: Formerly Atlantis: A Women's Studies Journal/Journal d'Etudes sur la Femme
Sponsoring organization: Social Sciences & Humanities Research Council of Canada; Mount Saint Vincent Univ.
ISSN: 0702-7818
MLA acronym: Atlantis

SUBSCRIPTION INFORMATION

Frequency of publication: 2 times/yr.
Circulation: 600
Available in microform: Yes
Subscription price: C$40.00/yr. institutions Canada; C$50.00/yr. institutions US; C$55.00/yr. institutions elsewhere; C$20.00/yr. individuals Canada; C$30.00/yr. individuals US; C$35.00/yr. individuals elsewhere
Year to which price refers: 1991-92

ADVERTISING INFORMATION

Advertising accepted: Yes
Advertising rates: C$50.00/quarter page; C$75.00/half page; C$150.00/full page

EDITORIAL DESCRIPTION

Scope: Publishes complete manuscripts of critical and creative writing on the topic of women. Book and film reviews, photography, and graphic work will also be considered for inclusion.
Reviews books: Yes
Publishes notes: Yes
Languages accepted: English; French
Prints abstracts: Yes
Author-anonymous submission: Yes

SUBMISSION REQUIREMENTS

Restrictions on contributors: Preference is given to Canadian scholarship.
Author pays submission fee: No
Author pays page charges: No
Length of articles: 10,000 words maximum
Length of book reviews: 500-1,000 words
Length of notes: 500 words
Style: MLA; American Psychological Assn.
Number of copies required: 3
Special requirements: Submit clean, double-spaced original typescript and 3 copies.
Copyright ownership: Journal

Rejected manuscripts: Returned; enclose return postage.
Time before publication decision: 6-8 mos.
Time between decision and publication: 1-6 mos.
Number of reviewers: 3
Articles submitted per year: 100
Articles published per year: 20
Book reviews submitted per year: 30
Book reviews published per year: 25
Notes submitted per year: 1-3
Notes published per year: 0-3

(280)
Atlantis: Revista de la Asociacion Española de Estudios Anglo-Norteamericanos

José S. Gómez-Soliño, Editor
Dpto. de Filología Moderna
Fac. de Filología
Univ. de La Laguna
38200 La Laguna, Tenerife
Canary Islands, Spain

Sponsoring organization: Asoc. Española de Estudios Anglo-Norteamericanos (ANDEAN)
MLA acronym: AtlantisR

EDITORIAL DESCRIPTION

Scope: Publishes articles on English linguistics and the teaching of the English language; English literature; North American literature; other English language literatures; and the history of English-speaking countries.
Reviews books: Yes
Languages accepted: Spanish; English

SUBMISSION REQUIREMENTS

Style: MLA

(281)
*Atti del R. Istituto Veneto di Scienze, Lettere ed Arti. Venezia. Classe di Scienze Morali e Lettere

Leopoldo Mazzarolli, Editor
Ist. Veneto di Scienze Lettere ed Arti
Campo S. Stefano, 2945 (Palazzo Loredan)
30124 Venice, Italy

Telephone: (39) 41 5210177
Fax: (39) 41 5210598
First published: 1840
ISSN: 0392-1336
MLA acronym: AIV

SUBSCRIPTION INFORMATION

Frequency of publication: Annual
Available in microform: No

EDITORIAL DESCRIPTION

Scope: Publishes articles on literature, science, and the arts.
Reviews books: No
Languages accepted: Italian; English; French
Prints abstracts: Yes

SUBMISSION REQUIREMENTS

Author pays submission fee: No
Author pays page charges: No
Number of copies required: 1

(282)
Atti del Sodalizio Glottologico Milanese

Vittore Pisani, Editor
c/o Roberto Giacomelli
Largo C. Treves, 5
20121 Milan, Italy

First published: 1947
Sponsoring organization: Sodalizio Glottologico Milanese
MLA acronym: ASGM

SUBSCRIPTION INFORMATION

Frequency of publication: Annual
Circulation: 1,000
Available in microform: No
Subscription address: Casa Editrice Paideia, Via Corsica 130, 25100 Brescia, Italy

ADVERTISING INFORMATION

Advertising accepted: No

EDITORIAL DESCRIPTION

Scope: Publishes articles on historical linguistics.
Reviews books: Yes
Publishes notes: Yes
Languages accepted: English; French; Spanish; Italian; German
Prints abstracts: Yes

SUBMISSION REQUIREMENTS

Author pays submission fee: No
Author pays page charges: No
Number of copies required: 1
Time before publication decision: 1 yr.
Articles submitted per year: 10
Articles published per year: 10

(283)
*Atti della Accademia Nazionale dei Lincei. Rendiconti della Classe di Scienze Morali, Storiche e Filologiche

C. F. Golisano, Editor
Accademia Nazionale dei Lincei
Via della Lungara, 10
00165 Rome, Italy

Telephone: (39) 6 6838831
Fax: (39) 6 6893616
First published: 1873
ISSN: 0391-8181
MLA acronym: ANLMSF

SUBSCRIPTION INFORMATION

Frequency of publication: 3 times/yr.
Circulation: 950
Available in microform: No
Subscription price: 50,000 Lit/yr. Italy; 60,000 Lit/yr. elsewhere
Year to which price refers: 1992

ADVERTISING INFORMATION

Advertising accepted: No

EDITORIAL DESCRIPTION

Scope: Journal focuses on philology and linguistics, archaeology, criticism of art and poetry, history and geography, philosophy, judicial science, and social and political sciences.
Reviews books: No
Publishes notes: Yes
Languages accepted: Italian; English; German; Latin; French; Spanish
Prints abstracts: Yes
Author-anonymous submission: No

SUBMISSION REQUIREMENTS

Restrictions on contributors: Contributors must be Fellows of the Accademia dei Lincei or scholars sponsored by Fellows.
Author pays submission fee: No
Author pays page charges: No
Number of copies required: 2
Special requirements: Submit original typescript and a 200-word abstract.
Copyright ownership: Accademia Nazionale dei Lincei
Rejected manuscripts: Not returned
Time before publication decision: 1 mo.
Time between decision and publication: 10 mos.
Number of reviewers: 1
Articles submitted per year: 30
Articles published per year: 30

(284)
*Aufsätze zur Portugiesischen Kulturgeschichte (Subseries of Portugiesische Forschungen der Görresgesellschaft)

Dietrich Briesemeister, Hans Flasche, & Karl-Hermann Körner, Editors
Verlag Aschendorff
Soesterstr. 13
P.O. Box 1124
4400 Münster in Westf., Germany

Additional editorial address: H. Flasche at Ordentlichen Prof. de Romanischen Philologie an der Univ. Hamburg, 2 Hamburg 13, Germany
Telephone: (49) 251 6900
Fax: (49) 251 690405
First published: 1960
Sponsoring organization: Görres-Gesellschaft zur Pflege der Wissenschaft
ISSN: 0079-421X
MLA acronym: APK

SUBSCRIPTION INFORMATION

Frequency of publication: Annual
Circulation: 250
Available in microform: No

ADVERTISING INFORMATION

Advertising accepted: No

EDITORIAL DESCRIPTION

Scope: Publishes studies on culture, language, literature, history, philosophy, and theology in Portuguese-speaking countries.
Reviews books: No
Publishes notes: No
Languages accepted: Portuguese; French; German; Italian; English; Spanish
Prints abstracts: No
Author-anonymous submission: No

SUBMISSION REQUIREMENTS

Restrictions on contributors: None
Author pays submission fee: No
Author pays page charges: No
Length of articles: 32 printed pp. maximum
Number of copies required: 1
Special requirements: Submit original typescript.
Copyright ownership: Author & journal
Rejected manuscripts: Returned
Time before publication decision: 2 mos.
Time between decision and publication: 15 mos.
Number of reviewers: 2
Articles submitted per year: 8
Articles published per year: 8

(285)
*Augustan Reprint Society

Maximilian Novak, Editor
Dept. of English
Univ. of California
405 Hilgard Ave.
Los Angeles, CA 90024-1433

Telephone: 310 825-1975
First published: 1946
Sponsoring organization: Univ. of California, Los Angeles; Augustan Reprint Soc.
ISSN: 0885-7954
MLA acronym: ARS

SUBSCRIPTION INFORMATION

Frequency of publication: Annual
Circulation: 1,000
Available in microform: No
Subscription address: AMS Press, Inc., 56 E. 13th St., New York, NY 10003
Subscription telephone: 212 777-4700
Subscription fax: 212 995-5413

ADVERTISING INFORMATION

Advertising accepted: No

EDITORIAL DESCRIPTION

Scope: Publishes facsimile reprints, with introductions of rare 17th- and 18th-century works relating to British and American literature and culture.
Reviews books: No
Publishes notes: No
Languages accepted: English
Prints abstracts: No
Author-anonymous submission: No

SUBMISSION REQUIREMENTS

Restrictions on contributors: None
Author pays submission fee: No
Author pays page charges: No
Length of books: 10 double-spaced typescript pp. for introduction & notes
Style: Chicago
Number of copies required: 1
Special requirements: Essay should be in the form of a brief, scholarly introduction to the accompanying facsimile. The work proposed should be rare, photographically reproducible, and under 50 pp. (for a single issue) or 100 pp. (for a double issue).
Copyright ownership: Augustan Reprint Soc.
Rejected manuscripts: Returned at author's request
Time before publication decision: 1 yr.
Time between decision and publication: 1 yr.
Number of reviewers: 3

(286)
*Augustinianum

V. Grossi, Editor
Inst. Patristicum Augustinianum
Via Paolo VI, 25
00193 Rome, Italy

Telephone: (39) 6 6861163
Fax: (39) 6 6866227
First published: 1961
Sponsoring organization: Augustinian Order
ISSN: 0004-8011
MLA acronym: Augustinianum

SUBSCRIPTION INFORMATION

Frequency of publication: 2 times/yr.
Circulation: 800
Available in microform: No
Subscription price: 45,000 Lit/yr. Italy; 50,000 Lit/yr. elsewhere
Year to which price refers: 1991

ADVERTISING INFORMATION

Advertising accepted: Yes

EDITORIAL DESCRIPTION

Scope: Focuses on patristic studies.
Reviews books: Yes
Publishes notes: Yes
Languages accepted: Italian; French; English; German; Spanish
Prints abstracts: Yes
Author-anonymous submission: No

SUBMISSION REQUIREMENTS

Author pays submission fee: No
Author pays page charges: No
Length of articles: 20-25 pp.
Length of book reviews: 200 words
Number of copies required: 1
Special requirements: Submit typescript and diskette.
Copyright ownership: Journal
Time before publication decision: 10 weeks
Time between decision and publication: 1 yr.
Articles submitted per year: 10
Articles published per year: 25
Book reviews submitted per year: 10
Book reviews published per year: 15

(287)
*Augustinus: Quarterly Review of The Fathers Augustinian Recollects

José Oroz Reta, Editor
Order of Augustinian Recollects
General Dávila, 5
28003 Madrid, Spain

Telephone: (34) 1 5342070
First published: 1956
ISSN: 0004-802X
MLA acronym: *Augustinus*

SUBSCRIPTION INFORMATION

Frequency of publication: 4 times/yr.
Circulation: 700
Available in microform: No
Subscription price: $45.00/yr.
Year to which price refers: 1992

ADVERTISING INFORMATION

Advertising accepted: No

EDITORIAL DESCRIPTION

Scope: Publishes articles on the works, influence, and time of St. Augustine.
Reviews books: Yes
Publishes notes: No
Languages accepted: Spanish; French; English; Italian; German
Prints abstracts: No
Author-anonymous submission: No

SUBMISSION REQUIREMENTS

Restrictions on contributors: None
Author pays submission fee: No
Author pays page charges: No
Length of articles: No restrictions
Length of book reviews: No restrictions
Style: None
Number of copies required: 1
Copyright ownership: Editors
Time before publication decision: 3 mos.
Time between decision and publication: 6 mos.
Articles submitted per year: 20
Articles published per year: 16
Book reviews submitted per year: 100
Book reviews published per year: 75

(288)
*AUMLA: Journal of the Australasian Universities Language and Literature Association: A Journal of Literary Criticism and Linguistics

Margaret Burrell, Editor
Dept. of English
Univ. of Canterbury
Christchurch 1, New Zealand

Telephone: (64) 3 667001 ext. 8544
Fax: (64) 3 642999
E-mail: Fren010@csc.canterbury.ac.nz
First published: 1953
Sponsoring organization: Australasian Universities Language & Literature Assn.
ISSN: 0001-2793
MLA acronym: *AUMLA*

SUBSCRIPTION INFORMATION

Frequency of publication: 2 times/yr. (May, Nov.)
Circulation: 1,200
Available in microform: No
Subscription address: R. White/Secretary, AUMLA, c/o Dept. of French, Univ. of Sydney, Sydney, N.S.W. 2006, Australia
Subscription telephone: (61) 2 6922381
Subscription fax: (61) 2 6924757

ADVERTISING INFORMATION

Advertising accepted: Yes
Advertising rates: NZ$100.00/half page

EDITORIAL DESCRIPTION

Scope: Publishes literary criticism, literary theory, and linguistics. All literatures are covered but emphasis is on English, French, German, Italian, Scandinavian, Slavonic, Spanish, and Asian literatures.
Reviews books: Yes
Publishes notes: Yes
Languages accepted: English; French; German; Spanish; Italian
Prints abstracts: No
Author-anonymous submission: No

SUBMISSION REQUIREMENTS

Restrictions on contributors: None
Author pays submission fee: No
Author pays page charges: No
Length of articles: 4,000-9,000 words
Length of book reviews: 800-1,200 words
Length of notes: 500 words
Style: MLA; Australian Government Publishing Service
Number of copies required: 2
Special requirements: Submit preferably on an MS DOS 2 IBM-compatible diskette formatted in Wordperfect/ASCII or compatible software, accompanied by 2 hard copies of the text.
Copyright ownership: Journal
Rejected manuscripts: Returned
Time before publication decision: 3 mos.
Time between decision and publication: 6-12 mos.
Number of reviewers: 2-3
Articles submitted per year: 50
Articles published per year: 18-20
Book reviews submitted per year: 40-50
Book reviews published per year: 15-20
Notes submitted per year: 5-10
Notes published per year: 2-3

(289)
Aurea Parma: Rivista Quadrimestrale di Storia, Letteratura e Arte

Aldo Curti, Editor
c/o G.D.P. Editrice s.r.l.
Via Emilio Casa, 5/A
43100 Parma, Italy

First published: 1912
ISSN: 0004-8062
MLA acronym: *AP*

SUBSCRIPTION INFORMATION

Frequency of publication: 3 times/yr.
Available in microform: Yes

ADVERTISING INFORMATION

Advertising accepted: Yes

EDITORIAL DESCRIPTION

Reviews books: Yes
Publishes notes: Yes
Languages accepted: Italian
Prints abstracts: No

SUBMISSION REQUIREMENTS

Author pays submission fee: No
Author pays page charges: No
Length of articles: 10-20 pp.
Number of copies required: 1
Time before publication decision: 1 mo.
Time between decision and publication: 2 mos.
Articles submitted per year: 20
Articles published per year: 15
Book reviews submitted per year: 30
Book reviews published per year: 25

(290)
*Aurora: Jahrbuch der Eichendorff Gesellschaft

Wolfgang Frühwald, Franz Heiduk, Helmut Koopmann, & Peter Horst Neumann, Editors
c/o P. H. Neumann
Erlenstegenstr. 28
8500 Numberg, Germany

Additional editorial address: H. Koopmann, Univ. Augsburg, 8900 Augsburg, Germany
First published: 1929
Sponsoring organization: Eichendorff-Gesellschaft
ISSN: 0341-1230
MLA acronym: *Aurora*

SUBSCRIPTION INFORMATION

Frequency of publication: Annual
Circulation: 1,000
Available in microform: No
Subscription address: Jan Thorbecke Verlag, Postfach 546, 7480 Sigmaringen, Germany

ADVERTISING INFORMATION

Advertising accepted: No

EDITORIAL DESCRIPTION

Scope: Publishes articles on the life and work of Joseph von Eichendorff as well as the literature and art of Romanticism and its reception in the 19th and 20th centuries.
Reviews books: Yes
Publishes notes: Yes
Languages accepted: German; English
Prints abstracts: Yes
Author-anonymous submission: No

SUBMISSION REQUIREMENTS

Restrictions on contributors: None

Author pays submission fee: No
Author pays page charges: No
Length of articles: 6,000 words
Length of book reviews: 1,800 words
Length of notes: 1,000 words
Number of copies required: 1
Special requirements: Submit original typescript, accompanied by a diskette, if possible.
Copyright ownership: Editor
Rejected manuscripts: Returned
Time before publication decision: 2-3 mos.
Time between decision and publication: 10 mos.
Number of reviewers: 3
Articles submitted per year: 15
Articles published per year: 12
Book reviews published per year: 15
Notes published per year: 5

(291)
*Aurora-Buchreihe

Franz Heiduk, Helmut Koopmann, & Peter Horst Neumann, Editors
Jan Thorbecke Verlag GmbH
Karlstr. 10
Postfach 546
7480 Sigmaringen, Germany

Telephone: (49) 7571 728100
Fax: (49) 7571 728280
First published: 1974
ISSN: 0171-6530
MLA acronym: AuroraB

SUBSCRIPTION INFORMATION

Frequency of publication: Irregular

ADVERTISING INFORMATION

Advertising accepted: No

EDITORIAL DESCRIPTION

Scope: Publishes monographs on the life and works of Joseph Karl Benedict von Eichendorff.
Reviews books: No
Publishes notes: No
Languages accepted: German
Author-anonymous submission: No

SUBMISSION REQUIREMENTS

Author pays submission fee: No
Author pays page charges: No
Copyright ownership: Jan Thorbecke Verlag

(292)
*Ausblick: Zeitschrift für Deutsch-Skandinavische Beziehungen

Karsten Jessen, Editor
Deutsche Auslandsgesellschaft
Holstenstr. 17
Lübeck, Germany

First published: 1949
MLA acronym: Ausblick

SUBSCRIPTION INFORMATION

Frequency of publication: 2 double issues/yr. (June, Dec.)
Circulation: 2,500
Available in microform: No

ADVERTISING INFORMATION

Advertising accepted: Yes

EDITORIAL DESCRIPTION

Scope: Publishes articles on cultural relations between the Scandinavian countries and Germany.
Reviews books: Yes
Publishes notes: No
Languages accepted: German
Prints abstracts: No

SUBMISSION REQUIREMENTS

Restrictions on contributors: None
Author pays page charges: No
Length of articles: No restrictions
Length of book reviews: No restrictions
Number of copies required: 1
Copyright ownership: Author
Rejected manuscripts: Returned
Time before publication decision: 1 mo.
Time between decision and publication: 3-5 mos.
Articles published per year: 8
Book reviews published per year: 100

(293)
*Auslandsdeutsche Literatur der Gegenwart: Beiträge zur Literatur- und Kulturgeschichte

Georg Olms Verlag
Hagentorwall 7
3200 Hildesheim, Germany

Additional editorial address: Georg Olms Verlag, 111 W. 57th St., New York. NY 10019
Telephone: (49) 5121 37007
Fax: (49) 5121 32007
First published: 1974
MLA acronym: ALG

SUBSCRIPTION INFORMATION

Frequency of publication: Irregular

ADVERTISING INFORMATION

Advertising accepted: No

EDITORIAL DESCRIPTION

Scope: Publishes monographs on literature by German writers living outside of Germany, as well as critical editions of works by such authors.
Reviews books: No
Publishes notes: No
Languages accepted: German
Prints abstracts: No

(294)
*Australasian Drama Studies

Richard Fotheringham & Veronica Kelly, Editors
Dept. of English
Univ. of Queensland
Queensland 4072, Australia

Telephone: (61) 7 3652135
Fax: (61) 7 3652799
First published: 1982
ISSN: 0810-4123
MLA acronym: ADS

SUBSCRIPTION INFORMATION

Frequency of publication: 2 times/yr. (Apr., Oct.)
Circulation: 400
Subscription price: A$30.00/yr. Australia; A$40.00/yr. elsewhere
Year to which price refers: 1992

ADVERTISING INFORMATION

Advertising accepted: Yes

EDITORIAL DESCRIPTION

Scope: Publishes articles on drama, theater, film and television in the region of Australasia.
Reviews books: Yes
Publishes notes: No
Languages accepted: English
Prints abstracts: No
Author-anonymous submission: No

SUBMISSION REQUIREMENTS

Author pays submission fee: No
Author pays page charges: No
Length of articles: 4,000-8,000 words
Length of book reviews: 1,000-2,000 words
Style: MLA with endnotes
Number of copies required: 1
Copyright ownership: Author
Rejected manuscripts: Returned
Time before publication decision: 6 mos.
Time between decision and publication: 6 mos.
Number of reviewers: 2
Articles submitted per year: 40
Articles published per year: 12-14
Book reviews submitted per year: 30
Book reviews published per year: 20

(295)
*Australian and New Zealand Studies in Canada

Thomas E. Tausky, Editor
Dept. of English
Univ. of Western Ontario
London, Ontario N6A 3K7, Canada

Telephone: 519 679-2111 ext. 5782
Fax: 519 661-3292
First published: 1989
Sponsoring organization: Faculty of Arts, Univ. of Western Ontario; Australian Government; New Zealand Government; Australia Council
ISSN: 0843-5049
MLA acronym: ANZSC

SUBSCRIPTION INFORMATION

Frequency of publication: 2 times/yr. (Spring, Fall)
Circulation: 200
Available in microform: No
Subscription price: C$15.00/yr. institutions N. America, Australia, & New Zealand; C$10.00/yr. individuals N. America, Australia, & New Zealand
Year to which price refers: 1992

ADVERTISING INFORMATION

Advertising accepted: Yes
Advertising rates: C$100.00/full page

EDITORIAL DESCRIPTION

Scope: Publishes articles on literature and the related arts in Australia and New Zealand.
Reviews books: Yes
Publishes notes: No
Languages accepted: English
Prints abstracts: No
Author-anonymous submission: No

SUBMISSION REQUIREMENTS

Restrictions on contributors: Book reviews are commissioned.
Author pays submission fee: No
Author pays page charges: No
Length of articles: 5,000-10,000 words
Length of book reviews: 1,000-3,000 words
Style: MLA
Number of copies required: 1
Copyright ownership: Author
Rejected manuscripts: Returned
Time before publication decision: 3 mos.
Time between decision and publication: 6 mos.
Number of reviewers: 1-2

Articles published per year: 15
Book reviews published per year: 4-6

(296)
*Australian and New Zealand Studies in German Language and Literature/ Australisch-Neuseeländische Studien zur Deutschen Sprache und Literatur

Gerhard Schulz & J. A. Asher, Editors
Dept. of Germanic Studies
Univ. of Melbourne
AUS-Parkville, Victoria 3052, Australia

Telephone: (61) 3 3705660
Fax: (41) 31 321131
First published: 1971
ISSN: 0171-6867
MLA acronym: ANSDSL

SUBSCRIPTION INFORMATION

Frequency of publication: Irregular
Available in microform: No
Subscription address: Verlag Peter Lang AG, Jupiterstr. 15, 3015 Bern, Switzerland
Subscription telephone: (41) 31 321122

ADVERTISING INFORMATION

Advertising accepted: No

EDITORIAL DESCRIPTION

Scope: Publishes studies on German language and literature.
Reviews books: No
Publishes notes: No
Languages accepted: English; German
Prints abstracts: No

SUBMISSION REQUIREMENTS

Author pays submission fee: No
Author pays page charges: No
Copyright ownership: Verlag Peter Lang AG
Rejected manuscripts: Returned
Time before publication decision: 2 mos.
Time between decision and publication: 5-7 mos.
Number of reviewers: 2
Books published per year: 1

(297)
*Australian-Canadian Studies: A Journal for the Humanities & Social Sciences

Gerry Turcotte, Editor
Dept. of English
Univ. of Wollongong
P.O. Box 1144
Wollongong 2500, Australia

Telephone: (61) 42 213737
Fax: (61) 42 213179
First published: 1983
Sponsoring organization: Assn. for Canadian Studies in Australia & New Zealand; Univ. of New England, Armidale, Australia
ISSN: 0810-1906
MLA acronym: ACS

SUBSCRIPTION INFORMATION

Frequency of publication: 2 times/yr. (May, Sept.)
Circulation: 300
Available in microform: No
Subscription price: A$30.00/yr. institutions Australia; A$33.00/yr. institutions elsewhere; A$15.00/yr. individuals Australia; A$18.00/yr. individuals elsewhere
Year to which price refers: 1992

ADVERTISING INFORMATION

Advertising accepted: Yes
Advertising rates: A$40.00/half page; A$80.00/full page

EDITORIAL DESCRIPTION

Scope: Focuses on comparative, interdisciplinary research in the humanities and social sciences, especially concerning issues of common interest in Australia, Canada, and New Zealand.
Reviews books: Yes
Publishes notes: Yes
Languages accepted: English
Prints abstracts: No
Author-anonymous submission: Yes

SUBMISSION REQUIREMENTS

Restrictions on contributors: None
Author pays submission fee: No
Author pays page charges: No
Length of articles: 5,000-10,000 words
Length of book reviews: 800-2,000 words
Length of notes: 500-800 words
Style: Chicago
Number of copies required: 3
Special requirements: Submit double-spaced typescript.
Copyright ownership: Journal
Rejected manuscripts: Returned; enclose SASE.
Time before publication decision: 4-6 mos.
Time between decision and publication: 2-4 mos.
Number of reviewers: 2
Articles submitted per year: 25-35
Articles published per year: 10-14
Book reviews published per year: 12-15
Notes published per year: 20-25

(298)
Australian Folklore: A Journal of Folklore Studies

J. S. Ryan, Editor
Dept. of English & Communication Studies
Univ. of New England
Armidale, NSW 2351, Australia

Additional editorial address: Send book reviews to: Hugh Anderson, c/o Red Rooster Press, 13 Fernhill St., Ascot Vale, Victoria 3032, Australia
First published: 1987
Sponsoring organization: Australian Folklore Assn.
ISSN: 0819-0852
MLA acronym: AusFolk

SUBSCRIPTION INFORMATION

Frequency of publication: 2 times/yr.
Circulation: 120
Available in microform: No
Subscription price: A$25.00/yr. institutions; A$20.00/yr. individuals
Year to which price refers: 1992
Subscription address: Jill Stubington, Dept. of Music, Univ. of New South Wales, Kensington, NSW 2033, Australia

ADVERTISING INFORMATION

Advertising accepted: Yes

EDITORIAL DESCRIPTION

Scope: Publishes articles on folklore. Emphasis is on Australian folklore.
Reviews books: Yes
Publishes notes: Yes
Languages accepted: English
Prints abstracts: No
Author-anonymous submission: No

SUBMISSION REQUIREMENTS

Author pays submission fee: No
Author pays page charges: No
Length of articles: 2,000-5,000 words
Length of notes: 500 words
Number of copies required: 2
Copyright ownership: Author & publisher
Time before publication decision: 1 yr. maximum
Number of reviewers: 2-5
Articles submitted per year: 20
Articles published per year: 10
Book reviews submitted per year: 8
Book reviews published per year: 8
Notes submitted per year: 10
Notes published per year: 10

(299)
*Australian Journal of French Studies

Wallace Kirsop, Editor
Dept. of Romance Languages
French Section
Monash Univ.
Clayton, Victoria 3168, Australia

Telephone: (61) 3 5652217
Fax: (61) 3 5652948
First published: 1964
Sponsoring organization: Monash Univ.
ISSN: 0004-9468
MLA acronym: AJFS

SUBSCRIPTION INFORMATION

Frequency of publication: 3 times/yr.
Circulation: 500
Available in microform: No
Subscription price: A$25.00/yr. Australia & New Zealand; A$35.00 ($35.00, £16.00)/yr. elsewhere
Year to which price refers: 1992

ADVERTISING INFORMATION

Advertising accepted: Yes, on an exchange basis

EDITORIAL DESCRIPTION

Scope: Publishes articles on French literature and civilization.
Reviews books: Yes
Publishes notes: Yes
Languages accepted: English; French
Prints abstracts: No
Author-anonymous submission: No

SUBMISSION REQUIREMENTS

Restrictions on contributors: Unsolicited reviews and notes are not accepted.
Author pays submission fee: No
Author pays page charges: No
Length of articles: No restrictions
Length of book reviews: No restrictions
Length of notes: No restrictions
Style: Journal
Number of copies required: 1
Special requirements: Submit original typescript and diskette using WordPerfect.
Copyright ownership: Journal
Rejected manuscripts: Returned
Time before publication decision: 3-6 mos.
Time between decision and publication: 2 yrs.
Number of reviewers: 2
Articles submitted per year: 50
Articles published per year: 20-25
Book reviews published per year: 3-5
Notes published per year: 5

(300)
*Australian Journal of Linguistics: Journal of the Australian Linguistic Society

Barbara Horvath & Cynthia Allen, Editors
Dept. of Linguistics
Univ. of Sydney
Sydney 2006, Australia

Additional editorial address: C. Allen, Dept. of Linguistics, Australian National Univ., Canberra 2600, Australia; Peter Petersen, Book Review Editor, Dept. of Linguistics, Univ. of Newcastle, Newcastle 2308, Australia; Graham Scott, Business Manager, Dept. of Linguistics, La Trobe Univ., Bundoora, Victoria 3083, Australia
Telephone: (61) 3 4792447
Fax: (61) 3 4791700; (61) 3 4785814
First published: 1981
Sponsoring organization: Australian Linguistic Soc.
ISSN: 0726-8602
MLA acronym: AJL

SUBSCRIPTION INFORMATION

Frequency of publication: 2 times/yr. (June, Dec.)
Circulation: 550
Available in microform: No
Subscription price: A$44.00 (£24.00, $43.00)/yr.
Year to which price refers: 1993
Subscription address: Business Manager, Linguistics Dept., La Trobe Univ., Bundoora, Victoria 3083, Australia

ADVERTISING INFORMATION

Advertising accepted: Yes
Advertising rates: A$100.00/full page; also available on an exchange basis

EDITORIAL DESCRIPTION

Scope: Publishes articles on all branches of linguistics, with an emphasis on theory and Australian English and Australian aboriginal languages.
Reviews books: Yes
Publishes notes: Yes
Languages accepted: English
Prints abstracts: No
Author-anonymous submission: No

SUBMISSION REQUIREMENTS

Restrictions on contributors: None
Author pays submission fee: No
Author pays page charges: No
Length of book reviews: 1,800-2,000 words
Length of notes: 600-800 words
Style: Journal
Number of copies required: 3
Special requirements: Final submission on diskette is preferred.
Copyright ownership: Australian Linguistic Soc.
Rejected manuscripts: Returned
Time before publication decision: 2-4 mos.
Time between decision and publication: 6-12 mos.
Number of reviewers: 2-4
Articles submitted per year: 22
Articles published per year: 9
Book reviews submitted per year: 13
Book reviews published per year: 11
Notes submitted per year: 8
Notes published per year: 6

(301)
*Australian Literary Studies

L. T. Hergenhan, Editor
Dept. of English
Univ. of Queensland
St. Lucia, Queensland 4067, Australia

Telephone: (61) 7 3652799
First published: 1963
Sponsoring organization: Univ. of Queensland; Australia Council, Literature Board
ISSN: 0004-9697
MLA acronym: ALS

SUBSCRIPTION INFORMATION

Frequency of publication: 2 times/yr. (May, Oct.)
Circulation: 1,250
Available in microform: Yes
Subscription price: A$40.00/yr. institutions; A$30.00/yr. individuals
Year to which price refers: 1992
Subscription address: Box 88, St. Lucia, Queensland 4067, Australia

ADVERTISING INFORMATION

Advertising accepted: Yes

EDITORIAL DESCRIPTION

Scope: Includes critical assessments of writers; sociocultural studies; discussions of general issues such as colonialism, nationalism, links with overseas writing; the Australian tradition and its relation to others; an annual bibliography; notes presenting the results of current and original research; and interviews.
Reviews books: Yes
Publishes notes: Yes
Languages accepted: English
Prints abstracts: No

SUBMISSION REQUIREMENTS

Restrictions on contributors: None
Author pays submission fee: No
Author pays page charges: No
Length of articles: 4,000-5,000 words
Length of book reviews: 2,000 words
Length of notes: 2,000-3,000 words
Style: MLA, but use single inverted commas for quotations
Number of copies required: 2
Copyright ownership: Author
Rejected manuscripts: Returned; enclose return postage.
Time before publication decision: 3 mos.
Time between decision and publication: 1 yr.
Number of reviewers: 2
Articles submitted per year: 40
Articles published per year: 16
Book reviews submitted per year: 12
Book reviews published per year: 12
Notes submitted per year: 20
Notes published per year: 12

(302)
*Australian Playwrights

Ortrun Zuber-Skerritt, Editor
Griffith Univ.
Centre for Advancement of Learning & Teaching
Nathan, Brisbane, Australia

First published: 1987
ISSN: 0921-2531
MLA acronym: AusPl

SUBSCRIPTION INFORMATION

Frequency of publication: Irregular
Circulation: 1,000
Available in microform: No
Subscription address: Editions Rodopi B.V., Keizersgracht 302-304, 1016 EX Amsterdam, Netherlands
Additional subscription address: In N. America: Editions Rodopi, 233 Peachtree St. N.E., Suite 404, Atlanta, GA 30303-1504
Subscription telephone: (31) 20 6227507; 404 523-1964; 800 225-3998
Subscription fax: (31) 20 6380948; 404 522-7116

ADVERTISING INFORMATION

Advertising accepted: No

EDITORIAL DESCRIPTION

Scope: Publishes monographs on Australian playwrights and their works.
Reviews books: No
Publishes notes: No
Languages accepted: English
Prints abstracts: No
Author-anonymous submission: No

SUBMISSION REQUIREMENTS

Author pays submission fee: No
Author pays page charges: No
Length of books: 70,000 words
Style: MLA
Number of copies required: 1
Copyright ownership: Editions Rodopi B.V.
Time before publication decision: 2 mos.
Time between decision and publication: 6 mos.

(303)
*Australian Slavonic & East European Studies

Paul Cubberley, Editor
Dept. of Russian
Univ. of Melbourne
Parkville, Victoria 3052, Australia

Telephone: (61) 3 3445193
Fax: (61) 3 3447821
E-mail: CUBBE@ARIEL.UCS.UNIMELB.EDU.AU
First published: 1967
Sponsoring organization: Univ. of Melbourne; Australia & New Zealand Slavists' Assn.
ISSN: 0818-8149
MLA acronym: ASEES

SUBSCRIPTION INFORMATION

Frequency of publication: 2 times/yr.
Circulation: 200
Available in microform: Yes
Subscription price: A$25.00/yr.
Year to which price refers: 1992

ADVERTISING INFORMATION

Advertising accepted: Yes

EDITORIAL DESCRIPTION

Scope: Publishes articles on Slavonic and East European language, literature, history, and political science.
Reviews books: Yes
Publishes notes: Yes
Languages accepted: English; Russian
Prints abstracts: No
Author-anonymous submission: No

SUBMISSION REQUIREMENTS

Restrictions on contributors: None
Author pays submission fee: No
Author pays page charges: No
Length of articles: 10,000 words maximum
Length of book reviews: 4,000 words maximum
Length of notes: 1,000 words maximum
Style: MLA
Number of copies required: 2

Special requirements: Quotations in any Slavonic language and in all modern European languages are permitted.
Copyright ownership: Author & Publisher
Rejected manuscripts: Returned; enclose return postage.
Time before publication decision: 3 mos.
Time between decision and publication: 6-12 mos.
Number of reviewers: 2-3
Articles submitted per year: 20
Articles published per year: 15-18
Book reviews published per year: 10-15
Notes published per year: 5-10

(304)
*Aut Aut: Rivista di Filosofia e di Cultura

Pier Aldo Rovatti, Editor
Via Catalani 61
20131 Milan, Italy

Telephone: (39) 2 26149142
First published: 1951
ISSN: 0005-0601
MLA acronym: Aut Aut

SUBSCRIPTION INFORMATION

Frequency of publication: 6 times/yr.
Available in microform: No
Subscription address: La Nuova Italia Editrice, C.P. 183, 50100 Florence, Italy

ADVERTISING INFORMATION

Advertising accepted: Yes

EDITORIAL DESCRIPTION

Scope: Publishes articles on philosophy and culture.
Reviews books: Yes
Publishes notes: Yes
Languages accepted: Italian
Prints abstracts: No
Author-anonymous submission: No

SUBMISSION REQUIREMENTS

Author pays submission fee: Yes
Author pays page charges: No
Length of articles: 10,000-11,000 words
Length of book reviews: 2,500 words
Length of notes: 5,000 words
Number of copies required: 4
Copyright ownership: Author
Rejected manuscripts: Not returned
Time before publication decision: 6 mos.
Time between decision and publication: 3 mos.
Number of reviewers: 3

(305)
*Authoritative Studies in World Literature

Saad Elkhadem, Editor
York Press
P.O. Box 1172
Fredricton N.B., E3B 5C8, Canada

Telephone: 506 458-8748
First published: 1984
MLA acronym: ASWL

SUBSCRIPTION INFORMATION

Frequency of publication: 6 vols./yr.
Circulation: 500
Available in microform: No
Subscription price: $6.95/issue
Year to which price refers: 1992

ADVERTISING INFORMATION

Advertising accepted: No

EDITORIAL DESCRIPTION

Scope: Publishes studies dealing with the life, work, and criticism of world writers.
Reviews books: No
Publishes notes: No
Languages accepted: English
Prints abstracts: No
Author-anonymous submission: No

SUBMISSION REQUIREMENTS

Restrictions on contributors: Contributors must be recognized scholars in the field.
Author pays submission fee: No
Author pays page charges: No
Length of books: 17,000 words
Style: MLA; York Press Style Manual
Number of copies required: 2
Copyright ownership: York Press
Rejected manuscripts: Returned
Time before publication decision: 3 weeks
Time between decision and publication: 9 mos.
Number of reviewers: 3
Books submitted per year: 12
Books published per year: 6

(306)
*Automatic Documentation and Mathematical Linguistics

A. I. Mikhailov, Editor
Allerton Press, Inc.
150 Fifth Ave.
New York, NY 10011

First published: 1967
ISSN: 0005-1055
MLA acronym: ADML

SUBSCRIPTION INFORMATION

Frequency of publication: 6 times/yr.
Subscription price: $745.00/yr. US & Canada; $785.00/yr. elsewhere
Year to which price refers: 1992
Subscription telephone: 212 924-3950
Subscription fax: 212 463-9684

EDITORIAL DESCRIPTION

Scope: Publishes selected major articles from Nauchno-Tekhnicheskaya Informatsiya, Seriya 2.
Reviews books: No
Languages accepted: English
Prints abstracts: No

(307)
*Avant Garde: Revue Interdisciplinaire et Internationale des Arts et Littératures du XXe Siècle/ Interdisciplinary and International Review of Literature and Arts of the 20th Century

Fernand Drijkoningen, Director
c/o Klaus Beekman, Secretary
P. C. Hooftuis
Spuistraat 134
1012 VB Amsterdam, Netherlands

Telephone: (31) 20 5254721
First published: 1987
ISSN: 0921-2515
MLA acronym: AvG

SUBSCRIPTION INFORMATION

Frequency of publication: 3 times/yr.
Available in microform: No
Subscription price: 100 f/yr. institutions; 35 f/yr. individuals
Year to which price refers: 1991
Subscription address: Editions Rodopi B.V., Keizersgracht 302-304, 1016 EX Amsterdam, Netherlands
Subscription telephone: (31) 20 6227507
Subscription fax: (31) 20 6380948

ADVERTISING INFORMATION

Advertising accepted: Yes
Advertising rates: Request from Editions Rodopi

EDITORIAL DESCRIPTION

Scope: Publishes studies to promote the international exchange of ideas among researchers working in the areas of modern and postmodern art, literature, and music.
Reviews books: No
Publishes notes: Yes
Languages accepted: English; French; German
Prints abstracts: No
Author-anonymous submission: No

SUBMISSION REQUIREMENTS

Author pays submission fee: No
Author pays page charges: No
Length of articles: 7,500 words
Length of books: 126 pp.
Number of copies required: 2
Copyright ownership: Author
Rejected manuscripts: Returned
Time before publication decision: 2 mos.
Time between decision and publication: 9 mos.
Articles published per year: 16
Books published per year: 3

(308)
Aztlán: A Journal of Chicano Studies

Raymund A. Paredes, Editor
Chicano Studies Research Center
Univ. of California, Berkeley
405 Hilgard Ave.
Los Angeles, CA 90024

First published: 1970
Sponsoring organization: UCLA Chicano Studies Research Center
ISSN: 0005-2604
MLA acronym: Aztlán

SUBSCRIPTION INFORMATION

Frequency of publication: 2 times/yr.
Circulation: 800
Available in microform: Yes

ADVERTISING INFORMATION

Advertising accepted: No

EDITORIAL DESCRIPTION

Scope: Publishes articles on the Chicano experience as it relates to Mexico and the United States. Includes works on the humanities, social sciences, education, and the arts.
Reviews books: Yes
Publishes notes: Yes
Languages accepted: English; Spanish
Prints abstracts: No
Author-anonymous submission: Yes

SUBMISSION REQUIREMENTS

Restrictions on contributors: None
Author pays submission fee: No
Author pays page charges: No
Length of articles: 7,000 words
Length of book reviews: 1,500-2,000 words
Length of notes: 2,000-3,000 words
Style: Chicago
Number of copies required: 3
Copyright ownership: Journal & author

Rejected manuscripts: Not returned
Time before publication decision: 5 mos.
Time between decision and publication: 9 mos.
Number of reviewers: 2-3
Articles submitted per year: 40
Articles published per year: 8
Book reviews submitted per year: 6
Book reviews published per year: 6
Notes published per year: 4

(309)
*Babel: Revue Intérnationale de la Traduction/International Journal of Translation

René Haeseryn, Editor
Heiveldstr. 245
9040 Sint Amandsberg, Belgium

Telephone: (32) 91 283971
First published: 1955
Sponsoring organization: UNESCO
ISSN: 0521-9744
MLA acronym: Babel

SUBSCRIPTION INFORMATION

Frequency of publication: 4 times/yr.
Circulation: 800
Available in microform: No
Subscription price: 125 f ($75.00)/yr.
Year to which price refers: 1993
Subscription address: John Benjamins Publishing Co., P.O. Box 75577, Amsteldijk 44, 1070 AN Amsterdam, Netherlands
Additional subscription address: John Benjamins North America, Inc., 821 Bethlehem Pike, Philadelphia, PA 19118
Subscription telephone: (31) 20 6738156; 215 836-1200
Subscription fax: (31) 20 6739773; 215 836-1204

ADVERTISING INFORMATION

Advertising accepted: Yes
Advertising rates: 650 f ($325.00)/full page

EDITORIAL DESCRIPTION

Scope: Publishes articles on translation and translators, applied linguistics, and terminology.
Reviews books: Yes
Publishes notes: Yes
Languages accepted: English; French; German; Russian; Spanish; Italian
Prints abstracts: Yes

SUBMISSION REQUIREMENTS

Author pays submission fee: No
Author pays page charges: No
Length of articles: 6,000 words
Length of book reviews: 300 words
Length of notes: 150 words
Style: Journal; request from editor
Number of copies required: 2
Special requirements: Submit original typescript; electronic submission is preferred.
Copyright ownership: Journal
Rejected manuscripts: Not returned
Time before publication decision: 4 mos.
Time between decision and publication: 8 mos.
Number of reviewers: 3
Articles published per year: 20
Book reviews published per year: 30
Notes published per year: 20

(310)
*The Baker Street Journal: An Irregular Quarterly of Sherlockiana

William R. Cochran, Editor
517 N. Vine St.
DuQuoin, IL 62832

First published: 1946
Sponsoring organization: Baker Street Irregulars
ISSN: 0005-4070
MLA acronym: BSJ

SUBSCRIPTION INFORMATION

Frequency of publication: 4 times/yr. (Mar., June, Sept., Dec.)
Circulation: 1,800
Available in microform: Yes
Subscription address: Fordham Univ. Press, University Box L, Bronx, NY 10458

ADVERTISING INFORMATION

Advertising accepted: Yes

EDITORIAL DESCRIPTION

Scope: Publishes articles and editorials about Sherlock Holmes and the Sherlockian Scene, and news from the Scion Societies of The Baker Street Irregulars as well as reviews of Sherlockian books.
Reviews books: Yes
Publishes notes: No
Languages accepted: English
Prints abstracts: No
Author-anonymous submission: No

SUBMISSION REQUIREMENTS

Restrictions on contributors: Unsolicited reviews are not accepted.
Author pays submission fee: No
Author pays page charges: No
Length of articles: 500-3,750 words
Style: MLA
Number of copies required: 1
Copyright ownership: Journal
Rejected manuscripts: Returned
Time before publication decision: 1-3 mos.
Time between decision and publication: 6-24 mos.
Number of reviewers: 1-2
Articles submitted per year: 100
Articles published per year: 40-50

(311)
*Balcanica: Annuaire de l'Institut des Etudes Balkaniques

Nikola Tasić, Editor
Balkanološki Inst.
Srpska Akademija Nauka i Umetnosti
Kneza Mihaila 35/IV
11000 Belgrade, Yugoslavia

Telephone: (38) 11 639830
First published: 1970
Sponsoring organization: Srpska Akademija Nauka i Umetnosti, Balkanološki Inst.
ISSN: 0350-7653
MLA acronym: Balcanica

SUBSCRIPTION INFORMATION

Frequency of publication: Annual
Available in microform: No

ADVERTISING INFORMATION

Advertising accepted: No

EDITORIAL DESCRIPTION

Scope: Publishes articles on Balkan and East European studies.
Reviews books: Yes
Publishes notes: Yes
Languages accepted: English; French; Russian; German; Serbo-Croatian
Prints abstracts: Yes

SUBMISSION REQUIREMENTS

Restrictions on contributors: None
Author pays submission fee: No
Author pays page charges: No
Length of articles: 32 pp.
Length of book reviews: 1,000 words
Length of notes: No restrictions
Style: None
Number of copies required: 1
Special requirements: Submit double-spaced typescript.
Copyright ownership: Author
Rejected manuscripts: Returned
Time before publication decision: 2 mos.
Time between decision and publication: 3-5 mos.
Number of reviewers: 2
Articles submitted per year: 20
Articles published per year: 20
Book reviews submitted per year: 10
Book reviews published per year: 10
Notes submitted per year: 5
Notes published per year: 5

(312)
*Balkan Studies

B. Kondis, Editor
Inst. for Balkan Studies
31a Meg. Alexandrou Str.
P.O. Box 10611
54110 Thessaloniki, Greece

Telephone: (30) 31 832143
Fax: (30) 31 831429
First published: 1961
Sponsoring organization: Inst. for Balkan Studies
ISSN: 0005-4313
MLA acronym: BalSt

SUBSCRIPTION INFORMATION

Frequency of publication: 2 times/yr.
Circulation: 2,000
Available in microform: No
Subscription price: $30.00/yr.
Year to which price refers: 1990
Additional subscription address: F. W. Faxon Co., 515 Hyde Park Ave., Boston, MA 02131; Ebsco Subscription Services, 17-19 Washington Ave., Tenafly, NJ 07670

ADVERTISING INFORMATION

Advertising accepted: No

EDITORIAL DESCRIPTION

Scope: Publishes articles on history and culture in the Balkans.
Reviews books: Yes
Languages accepted: English; French; German; Italian
Prints abstracts: Yes
Author-anonymous submission: No

SUBMISSION REQUIREMENTS

Restrictions on contributors: None
Author pays submission fee: No
Author pays page charges: No
Length of articles: 8-30 typescript pp.
Length of book reviews: 1-3 printed pp.
Style: MLA
Number of copies required: 1
Special requirements: Submit original typescript.
Copyright ownership: Inst. for Balkan Studies
Rejected manuscripts: Returned
Time before publication decision: 6 mos.
Time between decision and publication: 1 yr.

Number of reviewers: 2
Articles submitted per year: 20-25
Articles published per year: 15-20
Book reviews published per year: 25-38

(313)
Balkansko Ezikoznanie/Linguistique Balkanique

Ivan V. Duridanov, Editor
Académie Bulgare des Sciences
ul. Chapaev, 52, bl. 17
1113 Sofia, Bulgaria

First published: 1957
Sponsoring organization: Bŭlgarska Akademija na Naukite
ISSN: 0324-1653
MLA acronym: BEz

SUBSCRIPTION INFORMATION

Frequency of publication: 4 times/yr.
Circulation: 1,300
Available in microform: No
Subscription address: Hemus, Bd. Ruski, 6, 1000 Sofia, Bulgaria

ADVERTISING INFORMATION

Advertising accepted: Yes

EDITORIAL DESCRIPTION

Scope: Publishes studies in morphology, onomastics, history, and other areas of linguistics relating to the languages of the Balkan area, including non-Slavic, substratum languages, and Indo-European languages.
Reviews books: Yes
Publishes notes: Yes
Languages accepted: Russian; English; French; German
Prints abstracts: No

SUBMISSION REQUIREMENTS

Restrictions on contributors: None
Author pays submission fee: No
Author pays page charges: Yes
Length of articles: 20-30 pp.
Length of book reviews: 3-5 pp.
Length of notes: 2,000 words
Style: None
Number of copies required: 2
Copyright ownership: Author
Rejected manuscripts: Original is not returned.
Time before publication decision: 6 mos.
Time between decision and publication: 1 yr.
Articles published per year: 30-40
Book reviews submitted per year: 15-20
Book reviews published per year: 15-20

(314)
Baltische Hefte

Harro V. Hirschheydt, Editor
Postfach 281769
3000 Hannover-Döhren, Germany

First published: 1954
ISSN: 0005-4534
MLA acronym: BHe

SUBSCRIPTION INFORMATION

Frequency of publication: Annual
Circulation: 1,100

EDITORIAL DESCRIPTION

Reviews books: Yes

(315)
Baltistica: Baltų Kalbų Tyrinėjimai

"Mokslas"
Vilniaus Univ. Baltu Filologijos Katedra
232734 Vilnius, Lithuania

First published: 1965
Sponsoring organization: Ministerstvo Vysšego Obrazovanija Litovskoj S.S.R.
ISSN: 0132-6503
MLA acronym: Baltistica

SUBSCRIPTION INFORMATION

Frequency of publication: 2 times/yr.
Circulation: 1,200
Available in microform: No

ADVERTISING INFORMATION

Advertising accepted: No

EDITORIAL DESCRIPTION

Scope: Publishes articles concerning historical and comparative studies in Baltic linguistics.
Reviews books: Yes
Publishes notes: Yes
Languages accepted: English; French; German; Latvian; Russian; Lithuanian
Prints abstracts: Yes

SUBMISSION REQUIREMENTS

Author pays page charges: No
Number of copies required: 3
Special requirements: Summaries are published in one of the above languages. Submit original typescript plus 2 copies.
Rejected manuscripts: Not returned
Time before publication decision: 6 mos.
Time between decision and publication: 18 mos.
Number of reviewers: 2
Articles submitted per year: 26-28
Articles published per year: 21-23
Book reviews submitted per year: 5-11
Book reviews published per year: 4-10
Notes submitted per year: 5-9
Notes published per year: 4-8

(316)
Banasthali Patrika

Rameshwar Gupta, Editor
Banasthali Vidyapith
Jaipur, Rajasthan, India

First published: 1964
Sponsoring organization: Banasthali-Vidyapith
ISSN: 0970-4825
MLA acronym: BP

SUBSCRIPTION INFORMATION

Frequency of publication: 4 times/yr. (Jan. & July in English, Apr. & Oct. in Hindi)
Circulation: 1,000

EDITORIAL DESCRIPTION

Scope: Journal is devoted primarily to English, American, and Indo-English literature.
Reviews books: Yes
Languages accepted: English; Hindi
Prints abstracts: No

SUBMISSION REQUIREMENTS

Restrictions on contributors: None
Length of articles: 2,000 words
Style: MLA

Number of copies required: 2
Copyright ownership: Banasthali-Vidyapith
Rejected manuscripts: Returned
Time before publication decision: 2 mos.
Time between decision and publication: 6 mos.
Number of reviewers: 2
Articles published per year: 30

(317)
*Baroque: Revue Internationale

Félix Castan, Editor
Centre International de Synthèse du Baroque
30, rue de la Banque
82000 Montauban, France

Telephone: (33) 63630567
First published: 1965
Sponsoring organization: Centre International de Synthèse du Baroque
ISSN: 0067-4222
MLA acronym: Baroque

SUBSCRIPTION INFORMATION

Frequency of publication: Irregular
Available in microform: No

ADVERTISING INFORMATION

Advertising accepted: Yes

EDITORIAL DESCRIPTION

Scope: Interdisciplinary review of the phenomenon of the baroque (late 16th-late 18th century) in all the arts and in all European and Latin American countries.
Reviews books: No
Languages accepted: French
Prints abstracts: No

SUBMISSION REQUIREMENTS

Author pays page charges: No
Time before publication decision: 2 yrs.

(318)
Barroco

Univ. Federal de Minas Gerais
C.P. 1621
30000 Belo Horizonte
Minas Gerais, Brazil

First published: 1969
Sponsoring organization: Univ. Federal de Minas Gerais, Centro de Estudos Mineiros
ISSN: 0525-5708
MLA acronym: Barroco

SUBSCRIPTION INFORMATION

Frequency of publication: Annual
Circulation: 1,000

EDITORIAL DESCRIPTION

Reviews books: Yes
Prints abstracts: Yes

SUBMISSION REQUIREMENTS

Restrictions on contributors: None
Length of articles: 20-40 typescript pp.
Number of copies required: 1
Special requirements: Include illustrations if possible.
Copyright ownership: Author
Rejected manuscripts: Not returned
Time before publication decision: 6 mos.
Time between decision and publication: 6 mos.
Number of reviewers: 2
Articles published per year: 4-5

Frequency of publication: Annual
Circulation: 1,100

(319)
*Basler Studien zur Deutschen Sprache und Literatur

K. G. Saur Verlag
Ortlesstr. 8
8000 Munich 70, Germany

First published: 1954
ISSN: 0067-4508
MLA acronym: BSDSL

SUBSCRIPTION INFORMATION

Frequency of publication: Irregular

ADVERTISING INFORMATION

Advertising accepted: No

EDITORIAL DESCRIPTION

Scope: Publishes monographs on German language and literature.
Reviews books: No
Languages accepted: German
Prints abstracts: No

(320)
*The Baum Bugle

Michael Gessel, Editor
P.O. Box 748
Arlington, VA 22216

Telephone: 703 532-4261
First published: 1957
Sponsoring organization: International Wizard of Oz Club, Inc.
ISSN: 0005-6677
MLA acronym: BaumB

SUBSCRIPTION INFORMATION

Frequency of publication: 3 times/yr. (Spring, Fall, Winter)
Circulation: 3,000
Available in microform: No
Subscription price: $15.00/yr.
Year to which price refers: 1992
Subscription address: Fred M. Meyer, 220 N. 11th St., Escanaba, MI 49829

ADVERTISING INFORMATION

Advertising accepted: No

EDITORIAL DESCRIPTION

Scope: Promotes interest in the Land of Oz, its authors, and illustrators.
Reviews books: Yes
Publishes notes: No
Languages accepted: English
Prints abstracts: No
Author-anonymous submission: No

SUBMISSION REQUIREMENTS

Restrictions on contributors: None
Author pays submission fee: No
Author pays page charges: No
Length of articles: 2,000-7,000 words
Length of book reviews: 500-1,000 words
Style: Chicago
Number of copies required: 1
Special requirements: Submit original double-spaced typescript with wide margins, using one side of page only.
Copyright ownership: Assigned by author to the International Wizard of Oz Club, Inc.
Rejected manuscripts: Returned; enclose SAE.
Time before publication decision: 1-4 mos.
Time between decision and publication: 6-12 mos.
Number of reviewers: 3
Articles submitted per year: 25
Articles published per year: 30-35
Book reviews submitted per year: 15
Book reviews published per year: 15

(321)
*Bayerische Akademie der Wissenschaften. Philosophisch-Historische Klasse, Sitzungsberichte

Bayerische Akademie der Wissenschaften
Marstallplatz 8
8000 Munich 22, Germany

First published: 1871
Sponsoring organization: Bayerische Akademie der Wissenschaften
ISSN: 0342-5991
MLA acronym: BAWS

SUBSCRIPTION INFORMATION

Frequency of publication: Irregular
Circulation: 800
Available in microform: No
Subscription address: C. H. Beck, Wilhelmstr. 9, 8000 Munich 40, Germany

ADVERTISING INFORMATION

Advertising accepted: No

EDITORIAL DESCRIPTION

Scope: Covers all aspects of the humanities.
Reviews books: No
Publishes notes: Yes
Languages accepted: German; English; French
Prints abstracts: No
Author-anonymous submission: No

SUBMISSION REQUIREMENTS

Restrictions on contributors: Contributors must be sponsored by a member of the academy.
Author pays submission fee: No
Author pays page charges: No
Length of books: No restrictions
Length of notes: No restrictions
Style: None
Number of copies required: 1
Special requirements: Submit either manuscript or typescript.
Copyright ownership: Bayerische Akademie der Wissenschaften
Rejected manuscripts: Returned
Time before publication decision: 1 mo.
Time between decision and publication: 3 mos.

(322)
*Béaloideas: The Journal of the Folklore of Ireland Society

Pádraig Ó Héalaí & Bo Almqvist, Editors
Roinn na Nua-Ghaeilge
Coláiste na hOllscoile
Gaillinh, Ireland

Telephone: (353) 91 24411
Fax: (353) 91 25700
First published: 1927
Sponsoring organization: Folklore of Ireland Soc.
ISSN: 0332-270X
MLA acronym: Béaloideas

SUBSCRIPTION INFORMATION

Frequency of publication: Annual
Circulation: 500
Available in microform: No
Subscription price: $19.00/yr.
Year to which price refers: 1991
Subscription address: An Cumann le Béaloideas Éireann, c/o Roinn Bhéaloideasa Éireann, An Coláiste Ollscoile, Baile Átha Cliath 4, Ireland
Subscription telephone: (353) 1 693244 ext. 8216

ADVERTISING INFORMATION

Advertising accepted: No

EDITORIAL DESCRIPTION

Scope: Publishes articles on Irish and Celtic folklore.
Reviews books: Yes
Publishes notes: No
Languages accepted: English; Irish Gaelic
Prints abstracts: No
Author-anonymous submission: No

SUBMISSION REQUIREMENTS

Restrictions on contributors: None
Author pays submission fee: No
Author pays page charges: No
Length of articles: 10,000-20,000 words maximum
Length of book reviews: 1,000 words
Style: None
Number of copies required: 1
Copyright ownership: An Cumann le Béaloideas Éireann
Rejected manuscripts: Returned
Time before publication decision: 1-2 mos.
Time between decision and publication: 6-8 mos.
Number of reviewers: 4
Articles submitted per year: 10
Articles published per year: 5-6
Book reviews submitted per year: 10-15
Book reviews published per year: 10-15

(323)
*Beckettiana: Cuadernos del Seminario Beckett

Laura Cerrato, Editor
Tomás Guido 135
1834 Temperley, Argentina

Additional editorial address: Facultad de Filosofía & Letras, Puan 470, Buenos Aires, Argentina
First published: 1992
Sponsoring organization: Fac. de Filosofía & Letras, Univ. de Buenos Aires
ISSN: 0327-7550
MLA acronym: Beckettiana

SUBSCRIPTION INFORMATION

Frequency of publication: Annual
Available in microform: No
Subscription price: $5.00/yr.
Year to which price refers: 1992

ADVERTISING INFORMATION

Advertising accepted: Yes
Advertising rates: $80.00/full page

EDITORIAL DESCRIPTION

Scope: Publishes research papers of the Beckett Seminar of the University of Buenos Aires, and bibliographical material concerning Samuel Beckett.
Reviews books: Yes
Publishes notes: Yes
Languages accepted: Spanish
Prints abstracts: Yes
Author-anonymous submission: No

SUBMISSION REQUIREMENTS

Author pays submission fee: No
Author pays page charges: No
Length of articles: 5,000 words
Length of book reviews: 1,000 words
Length of notes: 3,000 words
Style: MLA
Number of copies required: 3
Special requirements: Contributions in English, French, Italian, and Portuguese are accepted for translation into Spanish.

Copyright ownership: Author
Rejected manuscripts: Returned
Time before publication decision: 2 mos.
Time between decision and publication: 4 mos.
Number of reviewers: 3

(324)
*Behavior Research and Therapy: An International Multi-Disciplinary Journal

S. Rachman, Editor
Dept. of Psychology
Univ. of British Columbia
Vancouver, BC V6T 1Y7, Canada

First published: 1963
MLA acronym: BRT

SUBSCRIPTION INFORMATION

Frequency of publication: 6 times/yr.
Available in microform: No
Subscription address: Pergamon Press, Inc., 660 White Plains Rd., Tarrytown, NY 10591-5153
Subscription telephone: 914 524-9200
Subscription fax: 914 333-2444

ADVERTISING INFORMATION

Advertising accepted: Yes

EDITORIAL DESCRIPTION

Scope: Publishes articles on behavior research and therapy.
Reviews books: Yes
Publishes notes: No
Languages accepted: English
Prints abstracts: Yes
Author-anonymous submission: Yes

SUBMISSION REQUIREMENTS

Restrictions on contributors: Book reviews are solicited.
Author pays submission fee: No
Author pays page charges: No
Length of articles: 2,000-10,000 words
Length of book reviews: 500 words
Number of copies required: 2
Copyright ownership: Author
Rejected manuscripts: Returned
Time before publication decision: 3 mos.
Time between decision and publication: 6-9 mos.
Number of reviewers: 2
Articles submitted per year: 215-250
Articles published per year: 60
Book reviews published per year: 60

(325)
Beihefte zum Euphorion: Zeitschrift für Literaturgeschichte

Rainer Gruenter, Editor
Carl Winter Universitätsverlag
Lutherstr. 59
Postfach 106140
6900 Heidelberg 1, Germany

Telephone: (49) 6221 41490
Fax: (49) 6221 414941
First published: 1964
ISSN: 0531-2167
MLA acronym: BzE

SUBSCRIPTION INFORMATION

Frequency of publication: Irregular
Circulation: 250
Available in microform: No
Subscription telephone: (49) 6221 414920

ADVERTISING INFORMATION

Advertising accepted: No

EDITORIAL DESCRIPTION

Scope: Publishes monographs on German literary history.
Reviews books: No
Publishes notes: No
Languages accepted: German; English
Prints abstracts: No

SUBMISSION REQUIREMENTS

Author pays submission fee: No
Author pays page charges: Occasionnally
Style: MLA
Number of copies required: 1
Copyright ownership: Carl Winter Universitätsverlag
Rejected manuscripts: Returned
Time before publication decision: 2 mos.
Time between decision and publication: 6-12 mos.
Books submitted per year: 12
Books published per year: 1-2

(326)
*Beihefte zur Zeitschrift für Romanische Philologie

Max Pfister, Editor
Max Niemeyer Verlag
Postfach 2140
7400 Tübingen, Germany

First published: 1905
ISSN: 0084-5396
MLA acronym: BZRP

SUBSCRIPTION INFORMATION

Frequency of publication: Irregular
Available in microform: No

ADVERTISING INFORMATION

Advertising accepted: No

EDITORIAL DESCRIPTION

Scope: Publishes monographs on romance languages and linguistics.
Reviews books: No
Publishes notes: No
Languages accepted: German; French; Spanish; Italian; English
Prints abstracts: No
Author-anonymous submission: Yes

SUBMISSION REQUIREMENTS

Author pays submission fee: No
Author pays page charges: No
Style: None
Number of copies required: 2
Copyright ownership: Max Niemeyer Verlag
Rejected manuscripts: Returned
Time before publication decision: 6 mos.
Time between decision and publication: 1 yr.
Number of reviewers: 1
Books published per year: 6

(327)
*Beiträge zur Deutschen Philologie

H. Ramge, L. E. Schmitt, & C. Wiedemann, Editors
Wilhelm Schmitz Verlag
Staufenbergerweg 22
6304 Lollar, Germany

First published: 1954
ISSN: 0522-6341
MLA acronym: BDP

SUBSCRIPTION INFORMATION

Frequency of publication: Irregular
Circulation: 100
Available in microform: No

ADVERTISING INFORMATION

Advertising accepted: Yes

EDITORIAL DESCRIPTION

Scope: Publishes monographs on linguistic and literary criticism.
Reviews books: Yes
Publishes notes: Yes
Languages accepted: German
Prints abstracts: No
Author-anonymous submission: No

SUBMISSION REQUIREMENTS

Author pays submission fee: No
Author pays page charges: No
Copyright ownership: Wilhelm Schmitz Verlag

(328)
*Beiträge zur Deutschen Volks- und Altertumskunde

Jörgen Bracker, Editor
Museum für Hamburgische Geschichte
Holstenwall 24
2000 Hamburg 36, Germany

Telephone: (49) 40 35042365
Fax: (49) 40 34973103
First published: 1954
Sponsoring organization: Museum für Hamburgische Geschichte
ISSN: 0408-8220
MLA acronym: BDVA

SUBSCRIPTION INFORMATION

Frequency of publication: Annual
Circulation: 500
Available in microform: No

ADVERTISING INFORMATION

Advertising accepted: No

EDITORIAL DESCRIPTION

Scope: Publishes articles on folklore, cultural history, and museum studies.
Reviews books: Yes
Publishes notes: No
Languages accepted: German
Prints abstracts: No
Author-anonymous submission: No

SUBMISSION REQUIREMENTS

Restrictions on contributors: None
Author pays submission fee: No
Author pays page charges: No
Style: None
Number of copies required: 1
Copyright ownership: Editor
Rejected manuscripts: Returned
Number of reviewers: 2

(329)
***Beiträge zur Geschichte der Deutschen Sprache und Literatur**

Klaus Grubmüller, Marga Reis, & Burghart Wachinger, Editors
Deutsches Seminar
Wilhelmstr. 50
7400 Tübingen, Germany

Additional editorial address: Hans Fromm, Inst. für Deutsche Philologie der Univ. Munich, Schellingstr. 3, 8000 Munich 40, Germany
First published: 1873
ISSN: 0005-8076
MLA acronym: BGDSL

SUBSCRIPTION INFORMATION

Frequency of publication: 3 times/yr.
Circulation: 800
Available in microform: No
Subscription address: Max Niemeyer Verlag, Postfach 2140, 7400 Tübingen, Germany

ADVERTISING INFORMATION

Advertising accepted: Yes

EDITORIAL DESCRIPTION

Scope: Focuses on all aspects of present-day German, as well as Medieval German, Latin, and Nordic literatures, and the history of the German language.
Reviews books: Yes
Publishes notes: No
Languages accepted: English; French; German
Prints abstracts: No
Author-anonymous submission: No

SUBMISSION REQUIREMENTS

Restrictions on contributors: None
Author pays submission fee: No
Author pays page charges: No
Length of articles: 25-30 pp. maximum
Length of book reviews: 5 pp.
Style: Journal
Number of copies required: 1
Special requirements: Submit original typescript; type footnotes in separate section.
Copyright ownership: Assigned by author to journal
Rejected manuscripts: Returned
Time before publication decision: 6 weeks
Time between decision and publication: 6-24 mos.
Number of reviewers: 3
Articles submitted per year: 60
Articles published per year: 20
Book reviews submitted per year: 40
Book reviews published per year: 40

(330)
***Beiträge zur Geschichte der Philosophie und Theologie des Mittelalters**

Ludwig Hödl & Wolfgang Kluxen, Editors
Verlag Aschendorff
Soester Str. 13
4400 Münster, Germany

Telephone: (49) 251 6900
Fax: (49) 251 690405
First published: 1891
Sponsoring organization: Görres-Gesellschaft zur Pflege der Wissenschaft
ISSN: 0067-5024
MLA acronym: BGPTM

SUBSCRIPTION INFORMATION

Frequency of publication: Irregular
Circulation: 500-550
Available in microform: No

ADVERTISING INFORMATION

Advertising accepted: No

EDITORIAL DESCRIPTION

Scope: Publishes research on medieval European philosophy and theology.
Reviews books: No
Publishes notes: No
Languages accepted: German; French; English
Prints abstracts: No
Author-anonymous submission: No

SUBMISSION REQUIREMENTS

Restrictions on contributors: None
Author pays submission fee: No
Author pays page charges: No
Length of books: 240-280 pp.
Style: None
Number of copies required: 1
Special requirements: Submit original typescript.
Copyright ownership: Verlag Aschendorff
Rejected manuscripts: Returned
Time before publication decision: 2-3 mos.
Time between decision and publication: 12-18 mos.
Number of reviewers: 2
Books submitted per year: 2
Books published per year: 2

(331)
***Beiträge zur Namenforschung**

Rudolf Schützeichel, Rolf Bergmann, Jürgen Untermann, Ulrich Obst, & H. von Gadow, Editors
Potstiege 16
4400 Münster, Germany

First published: 1965
ISSN: 0005-8114
MLA acronym: BN

SUBSCRIPTION INFORMATION

Frequency of publication: 4 times/yr.
Circulation: 440
Available in microform: No
Subscription address: Carl Winter Universitätsverlag, Lutherstr. 59, 6900 Heidelberg, Germany

ADVERTISING INFORMATION

Advertising accepted: No

EDITORIAL DESCRIPTION

Scope: Publishes articles on European languages.
Reviews books: Yes
Publishes notes: Yes
Languages accepted: English; German; Russian; French; Spanish
Prints abstracts: No

SUBMISSION REQUIREMENTS

Restrictions on contributors: None
Author pays submission fee: No
Author pays page charges: No
Length of articles: No restrictions
Length of book reviews: No restrictions
Length of notes: No restrictions
Style: Journal; request from editor
Number of copies required: 1
Special requirements: Submit original typescript.
Copyright ownership: Author
Rejected manuscripts: Returned
Time before publication decision: 6-12 mos.
Time between decision and publication: 3-6 mos.
Number of reviewers: 1-3
Articles submitted per year: 30-40
Articles published per year: 20-30
Book reviews submitted per year: 100
Book reviews published per year: 80-100
Notes submitted per year: 10
Notes published per year: 5-10

(332)
***Beiträge zur neueren Literaturgeschichte**

Carl Winter, Editor
Carl Winter Universitätsverlag GmbH
Lutherstr. 59
6900 Heidelberg, Germany

First published: 1908
ISSN: 0179-4027
MLA acronym: BNL

SUBSCRIPTION INFORMATION

Frequency of publication: Irregular
Circulation: 400-1,000
Available in microform: No

ADVERTISING INFORMATION

Advertising accepted: No

EDITORIAL DESCRIPTION

Scope: Publishes monographs on modern literary history.
Reviews books: No
Publishes notes: No
Languages accepted: German; English; French
Prints abstracts: No
Author-anonymous submission: No

SUBMISSION REQUIREMENTS

Restrictions on contributors: None
Author pays submission fee: No
Author pays page charges: Occasionally
Length of books: No restrictions
Style: MLA
Number of copies required: 1
Copyright ownership: Carl Winter Universitätsverlag GmbH
Rejected manuscripts: Returned
Time before publication decision: 2 mos.
Time between decision and publication: 2-10 mos.
Number of reviewers: 1-2
Books submitted per year: 30
Books published per year: 8-10

(333)
Belaruskaia Linhvistyka

A. I. Padluzhny, Editor
Akademiia Navuk Belaruskaï
Inst. Movaznaŭstva im. Iakuba Kolasa
Skaryna Str. 25
220072 Minsk 72, Belarus

First published: 1972
Sponsoring organization: Akademiia Nauk
MLA acronym: BelL

SUBSCRIPTION INFORMATION

Frequency of publication: 2 times/yr.
Circulation: 500
Available in microform: Yes

ADVERTISING INFORMATION

Advertising accepted: No

EDITORIAL DESCRIPTION

Scope: Publishes articles on the study and research of Belorussian language. Is of interest to those specializing in the study of Belorussian and other slavonic languages, and general and applied linguistics.
Reviews books: Yes

Publishes notes: Yes
Languages accepted: Belorussian
Prints abstracts: No
Author-anonymous submission: No

SUBMISSION REQUIREMENTS

Restrictions on contributors: None
Author pays submission fee: No
Author pays page charges: No
Length of articles: 12 typescript pp.
Length of book reviews: 5 typescript pp.
Length of notes: 2-4 pp.
Number of copies required: 2
Special requirements: See instructions on page 3 of each issue.
Copyright ownership: Author
Rejected manuscripts: Returned
Time before publication decision: 1 yr.
Time between decision and publication: 6 mos.
Number of reviewers: 3
Articles submitted per year: 30
Articles published per year: 20
Book reviews submitted per year: 2-3
Book reviews published per year: 2-3
Notes submitted per year: 8-10
Notes published per year: 8-10

(334)
*Belaruskaia Mova: Mizhvuzaŭski Zbornik

V. V. Anichenko, Editor
Gomel', Sovetskaia 108
Gomel'skiĭ Gosudarstvennyĭ Univ.
Minsk, Belarus

Telephone: (7) 172 238665
First published: 1973
Sponsoring organization: Gomel'skiĭ Gosudarstvennyĭ Univ.
ISSN: 1010-3996
MLA acronym: BMM

SUBSCRIPTION INFORMATION

Frequency of publication: Annual
Circulation: 1,000
Available in microform: Yes

ADVERTISING INFORMATION

Advertising accepted: Yes
Advertising rates: Free

EDITORIAL DESCRIPTION

Scope: Publishes articles on the Belorussian language and comparative linguistics.
Reviews books: Yes
Languages accepted: Belorussian
Author-anonymous submission: No

SUBMISSION REQUIREMENTS

Restrictions on contributors: None
Author pays submission fee: No
Author pays page charges: No
Length of articles: 12-15 typescript pp.
Length of book reviews: 7 pp. maximum
Style: MLA
Number of copies required: 2
Special requirements: Must include scientific data and discuss applications thereof; submit typescript copies.
Copyright ownership: Author
Rejected manuscripts: Not returned
Time before publication decision: 1 mo.
Time between decision and publication: 1 yr.
Number of reviewers: 2
Articles submitted per year: 30
Articles published per year: 20
Book reviews submitted per year: 2
Book reviews published per year: 2

(335)
*Belfagor: Rassegna di Varia Umanità

Carlo Ferdinando Russo, Editor
"La Belfagoriana"
C.P. 66
50100 Florence, Italy

Telephone: (39) 55 6530684
Fax: (39) 55 6530214
First published: 1946
ISSN: 0005-8351
MLA acronym: Belfagor

SUBSCRIPTION INFORMATION

Frequency of publication: 6 times/yr.
Circulation: 4,000
Available in microform: No
Subscription price: 55,000 Lit/yr. Italy; 85,000 Lit/yr. elsewhere
Year to which price refers: 1992

ADVERTISING INFORMATION

Advertising accepted: Yes

EDITORIAL DESCRIPTION

Scope: Major focus is on literary and historical criticism, with attention to contemporary situations. The journal is known for its political and cultural independence. Every issue is divided into six sections: essays and studies, portraits of contemporaries, documents, short notes and discussions, reviews, and books received.
Reviews books: Yes
Publishes notes: Yes
Languages accepted: Italian; French; English
Prints abstracts: No
Author-anonymous submission: No

SUBMISSION REQUIREMENTS

Restrictions on contributors: None
Author pays submission fee: No
Author pays page charges: No
Length of articles: 2-36 printed pp.
Length of book reviews: 2-4 pp.
Length of notes: 2-4 pp.
Style: Journal
Number of copies required: 1
Special requirements: Submit typescript.
Copyright ownership: Author
Rejected manuscripts: Returned at author's request
Time before publication decision: 1 mo.
Time between decision and publication: 6 mos.
Number of reviewers: 4
Articles submitted per year: 288
Articles published per year: 66
Book reviews submitted per year: 100
Book reviews published per year: 36-40
Notes submitted per year: 50
Notes published per year: 18

(336)
*Belgian Journal of Linguistics

Marc Dominicy, Editor
C.P. 175 ULB
Avenue Roosevelt, 50
1050 Brussels, Belgium

Telephone: (32) 2 6502454
Fax: (32) 2 6502450
E-mail: MDOMINI@BBRFU60 (Bitnet)
First published: 1986
Sponsoring organization: Linguistic Soc. of Belgium
ISSN: 0774-5141
MLA acronym: BJL

SUBSCRIPTION INFORMATION

Frequency of publication: Annual (Nov.)
Circulation: 80

Available in microform: No
Subscription price: 835 BF/yr.
Year to which price refers: 1991
Subscription address: Editions de l'Univ. de Bruxelles, Avenue Paul Héger 26, C.P. 163, 1050 Brussels, Belgium
Subscription telephone: (32) 2 6503789
Subscription fax: (32) 2 6503794

ADVERTISING INFORMATION

Advertising accepted: Yes

EDITORIAL DESCRIPTION

Scope: Publishes articles on all aspects of linguistics. Each issue is devoted to the topic of the Fall meeting of the Linguistic Society of Belgium.
Reviews books: No
Publishes notes: No
Languages accepted: English primarily; French; German; Dutch
Prints abstracts: Yes
Author-anonymous submission: No

SUBMISSION REQUIREMENTS

Restrictions on contributors: Contributions must be related to the topic of a session of the Linguistic Society of Belgium.
Author pays submission fee: No
Author pays page charges: No
Length of articles: 10,000 words
Style: Linguistic Soc. of Belgium
Number of copies required: 2
Special requirements: Submit a 200-word abstract.
Copyright ownership: Editions de l'Univ. de Bruxelles
Rejected manuscripts: Returned
Time before publication decision: 6 mos.
Time between decision and publication: 3 mos.
Number of reviewers: 3
Articles submitted per year: 12
Articles published per year: 8

(337)
*Bellmansstudier Utg. av Bellmanssällskapet

c/o Catharina von Essen
Margrethelund
184 60 Åkersberga, Sweden

First published: 1924
Sponsoring organization: Bellmanssällskapet
ISSN: 0405-3923
MLA acronym: Bellmansstudier

SUBSCRIPTION INFORMATION

Frequency of publication: Once every 4 yrs.
Available in microform: No
Subscription price: 100 Skr/volume
Year to which price refers: 1989

ADVERTISING INFORMATION

Advertising accepted: No

EDITORIAL DESCRIPTION

Scope: Publishes articles on Carl Michael Bellman and his time.
Reviews books: No
Publishes notes: No
Languages accepted: Swedish; Danish; Norwegian; German; English
Prints abstracts: No
Author-anonymous submission: No

SUBMISSION REQUIREMENTS

Author pays submission fee: No
Author pays page charges: No
Length of articles: 20-30 pp.
Number of copies required: 2

(338)
*Bergomum: Bollettino della Civica Biblioteca

Biblioteca Civica Angelo Mai
Piazza Vecchia, 15
24100 Bergamo, Italy

Telephone: (39) 35 399430; (39) 35 399431
Fax: (39) 35 240655
First published: 1907
Sponsoring organization: Comune di Bergamo
ISSN: 0005-8955
MLA acronym: Bergomum

SUBSCRIPTION INFORMATION

Frequency of publication: 4 times/yr.
Circulation: 500
Available in microform: No
Subscription price: 80,000 Lit/yr.
Year to which price refers: 1992

ADVERTISING INFORMATION

Advertising accepted: Yes

EDITORIAL DESCRIPTION

Scope: Publishes articles about the city of Bergamo.
Reviews books: Yes
Publishes notes: No
Languages accepted: Italian
Prints abstracts: No
Author-anonymous submission: No

SUBMISSION REQUIREMENTS

Restrictions on contributors: Contributors must be members of Comune de Bergamo.
Author pays submission fee: No
Author pays page charges: Yes
Length of articles: 10 pp.
Length of book reviews: 5 pp.
Style: Tondo Romano
Number of copies required: 1
Copyright ownership: Author
Rejected manuscripts: Not returned
Time before publication decision: 2 mos.
Time between decision and publication: 2 mos.
Number of reviewers: 3
Articles submitted per year: 25
Articles published per year: 20
Book reviews submitted per year: 5
Book reviews published per year: 3

(339)
Berliner Beiträge zur Namenforschung

K. Gutschmidt, G. Schlinpert, H. Schmidt, & T. Witkowski, Editors
Verlag Herman Böhlaus Nachfolger
Meyerstr. 50a
Postfach 260
5300 Weimar, Germany

First published: 1967
Sponsoring organization: Akademie der Wissenschaften Berlin, Zentralinst. für Sprachwissenschaft
ISSN: 0572-6263
MLA acronym: BBN

SUBSCRIPTION INFORMATION

Frequency of publication: Irregular
Available in microform: No
Subscription address: Verlag Herman Böhlaus Nachfolger, Karlstr. 10, Postfach 546, 7480 Sigmaringen, Germany

EDITORIAL DESCRIPTION

Scope: Publishes monographs on the linguistic history of place names in East Germany.
Reviews books: No
Publishes notes: No
Languages accepted: German
Prints abstracts: No

SUBMISSION REQUIREMENTS

Restrictions on contributors: None
Author pays submission fee: No
Length of books: No restrictions
Style: None
Special requirements: Submit original typescript.
Rejected manuscripts: Returned

(340)
*Berliner Byzantinistische Arbeiten

Friedhelm Winkelmann, Editor
Akademie-Verlag
Leipziger Str. 3-4
1086 Berlin, Germany

First published: 1956
ISSN: 0067-6055
MLA acronym: BBA

SUBSCRIPTION INFORMATION

Frequency of publication: Irregular
Available in microform: No

ADVERTISING INFORMATION

Advertising accepted: No

EDITORIAL DESCRIPTION

Scope: Publishes monographs on Byzantine political, social, economic, and cultural development.
Reviews books: No
Publishes notes: No
Languages accepted: German; English; French; Italian
Prints abstracts: No
Author-anonymous submission: No

SUBMISSION REQUIREMENTS

Restrictions on contributors: None
Author pays submission fee: No
Author pays page charges: No
Length of books: 200,000 words
Style: Series
Number of copies required: 2
Special requirements: Submit original typescript.
Copyright ownership: Akademie-Verlag Berlin
Time before publication decision: 2 mos.
Time between decision and publication: 1 yr.
Number of reviewers: 2
Books submitted per year: 1-2
Books published per year: 1-2

(341)
*Bestia: Yearbook of the Beast Fable Society

Benjamin Bennani, Editor
Northeast Missouri State Univ.
Kirksville, MO 63501

Telephone: 816 785-4185
Fax: 816 785-4181
First published: 1989
Sponsoring organization: Northeast Missouri State Univ.
ISSN: 1041-2212
MLA acronym: Bestia

SUBSCRIPTION INFORMATION

Frequency of publication: Annual (May)
Available in microform: No
Subscription price: 90 f ($55.00)/yr.
Year to which price refers: 1993
Subscription address: Institutions contact: John Benjamins Publishing Co., Amsteldijk 44, P.O. Box 75577, 1070 AN Amsterdam, Netherlands
Subscription telephone: (31) 20 6738156
Subscription fax: (31) 20 6739773

ADVERTISING INFORMATION

Advertising accepted: No

EDITORIAL DESCRIPTION

Scope: Publishes articles on the beast fable and related genres. Articles are chosen from papers delivered at the annual congress of the Beast Fable Society.
Reviews books: No
Publishes notes: No
Languages accepted: English
Prints abstracts: Yes
Author-anonymous submission: Yes

SUBMISSION REQUIREMENTS

Restrictions on contributors: Contributor must have read paper at the annual congress of the Beast Fable Soc.
Author pays submission fee: No
Author pays page charges: No
Length of articles: 4,000-6,000 words
Style: MLA
Number of copies required: 2
Copyright ownership: Beast Fable Soc.
Time before publication decision: 1 yr.
Time between decision and publication: 6 mos.
Articles submitted per year: 60
Articles published per year: 12

(342)
Bête Noire

John Osborne, Editor
American Studies
The University
Cottingham Rd.
Hull
Humberside, HU6 7RX, England

First published: 1986
Sponsoring organization: Lincolnshire & Humberside Arts Assn.
MLA acronym: BêteN

SUBSCRIPTION INFORMATION

Frequency of publication: 2 times/yr. (Spring, Winter)
Circulation: 500
Available in microform: No

ADVERTISING INFORMATION

Advertising accepted: No

EDITORIAL DESCRIPTION

Scope: Publishes contemporary literature and criticism thereof.
Reviews books: Yes
Publishes notes: No
Languages accepted: English
Prints abstracts: No

SUBMISSION REQUIREMENTS

Restrictions on contributors: None
Author pays submission fee: No
Author pays page charges: No
Length of articles: 10,000 words
Length of book reviews: 1,000 words
Style: MLA preferred
Number of copies required: 1

Copyright ownership: Author
Rejected manuscripts: Returned
Articles submitted per year: 3-4 every 4 yrs.
Articles published per year: 3-4 every 4 yrs.

(343)
*Bharatiya Vidya

J. H. Dave & S. A. Upadhyaya, Editors
Bharatiya Vidya Bhavan
Kulapnati K.M. Munshi Marg
Bombay 400 007, India

Telephone: (91) 22 3634462
First published: 1939
Sponsoring organization: Bharatiya Vidya Bhavan
ISSN: 0378-1984
MLA acronym: BhV

SUBSCRIPTION INFORMATION

Frequency of publication: 4 times/yr.
Circulation: 75
Available in microform: No
Subscription price: 60 Re/yr.
Year to which price refers: 1991-92

ADVERTISING INFORMATION

Advertising accepted: No

EDITORIAL DESCRIPTION

Scope: Publishes articles on Indian culture and Indological studies.
Reviews books: Yes
Publishes notes: Yes
Languages accepted: English; Sanskrit
Prints abstracts: No
Author-anonymous submission: No

SUBMISSION REQUIREMENTS

Restrictions on contributors: None
Author pays submission fee: No
Author pays page charges: No
Length of articles: 1-15 printed pp.
Length of book reviews: No restrictions
Length of notes: 500 words
Number of copies required: 1
Special requirements: Submit double-spaced typescript with diacritical marks.
Copyright ownership: Publisher
Rejected manuscripts: Returned
Time before publication decision: 1 mo.
Time between decision and publication: 1 yr.
Number of reviewers: 2
Articles submitted per year: 50
Articles published per year: 35
Book reviews submitted per year: 15
Book reviews published per year: 8
Notes submitted per year: 5
Notes published per year: 1

(344)
*Biblical Archaeologist

Eric M. Meyers, Editor
P.O. Box H.M.
Duke Station
Durham, NC 27706

Telephone: 919 684-3075
Fax: 919 660-3530
First published: 1938
Sponsoring organization: American Schools of Oriental Research
ISSN: 0006-0895
MLA acronym: BibA

SUBSCRIPTION INFORMATION

Frequency of publication: 4 times/yr.
Circulation: 4,500
Available in microform: Yes
Subscription price: $35.00/yr.
Year to which price refers: 1992
Subscription address: ASOR Membership/Subscription Services, P.O. Box 15399, Atlanta, GA 30333-0399
Subscription telephone: 404 636-4757
Subscription fax: 404 636-8301

ADVERTISING INFORMATION

Advertising accepted: Yes

EDITORIAL DESCRIPTION

Scope: Publishes articles on the languages, cultures, and archaeology of ancient Near East.
Reviews books: Yes
Publishes notes: No
Languages accepted: English
Prints abstracts: No
Author-anonymous submission: No

SUBMISSION REQUIREMENTS

Restrictions on contributors: None
Author pays submission fee: No
Author pays page charges: No
Length of articles: 4,000 words
Length of book reviews: 750 words
Style: Chicago
Number of copies required: 1
Special requirements: Submit original typescript and diskette.
Copyright ownership: American Schools of Oriental Research
Rejected manuscripts: Returned
Time before publication decision: 3 mos.
Time between decision and publication: 1 yr.
Number of reviewers: 2
Articles submitted per year: 30
Articles published per year: 16
Book reviews submitted per year: 25
Book reviews published per year: 25

(345)
*Biblio 17

Wolfgang Leiner, Editor
Wilhelmstr. 50
7400 Tübingen, Germany

First published: 1981
ISSN: 0343-0758
MLA acronym: Biblio 17

SUBSCRIPTION INFORMATION

Frequency of publication: Irregular
Circulation: 300-500
Available in microform: No

ADVERTISING INFORMATION

Advertising accepted: Yes

EDITORIAL DESCRIPTION

Scope: The series publishes monographs on 17th-century French literature.
Reviews books: No
Publishes notes: No
Languages accepted: English; French; German
Prints abstracts: No
Author-anonymous submission: No

SUBMISSION REQUIREMENTS

Style: MLA
Number of copies required: 2
Copyright ownership: Series & Author
Rejected manuscripts: Not returned
Time before publication decision: 1-2 mos.
Time between decision and publication: 2-4 mos.
Number of reviewers: 3
Books published per year: 5-8

(346)
*Bibliofilia: Rivista di Storia del Libro e di Bibliografia

Luigi Balsamo, Editor
Via Saragozza, 12
40123 Bologna, Italy

Telephone: (39) 51 331499
First published: 1899
ISSN: 0006-0941
MLA acronym: Bibliofilia

SUBSCRIPTION INFORMATION

Frequency of publication: 3 times/yr.
Circulation: 700
Available in microform: No
Subscription price: 101,000 Lit/yr.
Year to which price refers: 1992
Subscription address: Casa Editrice Leo S. Olschki, Viuzzo del Pozzetto (Viale Europa), C.P. 66, 50100 Florence, Italy
Subscription telephone: (39) 55 6530684
Subscription fax: (39) 55 6530214

ADVERTISING INFORMATION

Advertising accepted: Yes
Advertising rates: 580,000 Lit/full page

EDITORIAL DESCRIPTION

Scope: Publishes articles on the history of books, bibliography, and printing.
Reviews books: Yes
Publishes notes: Yes
Languages accepted: French; German; Italian
Prints abstracts: No
Author-anonymous submission: No

SUBMISSION REQUIREMENTS

Restrictions on contributors: None
Author pays submission fee: No
Author pays page charges: No
Length of articles: 6,000-8,000 words
Length of book reviews: 600-800 words
Style: Olschki
Number of copies required: 1-2
Copyright ownership: Olschki
Rejected manuscripts: Returned
Time before publication decision: 2 mos.
Number of reviewers: 1
Articles published per year: 13-15
Book reviews submitted per year: 90-100
Book reviews published per year: 60-90
Notes submitted per year: 4-6
Notes published per year: 3-4

(347)
Bibliographien zur Deutschen Literatur des Mittelalters

Ulrich Pretzel & Wolfgang Bachofer, Editors
Erich Schmidt
Genthiner Str., 30G
1000 Berlin 30, Germany

First published: 1966
ISSN: 0523-2767
MLA acronym: BDLM

SUBSCRIPTION INFORMATION

Frequency of publication: Irregular
Available in microform: No
Subscription address: Erich Schmidt Verlag, Viktoriastr., 44a, 4800 Bielefeld 1, Germany

ADVERTISING INFORMATION

Advertising accepted: No

Copyright ownership: Author
Rejected manuscripts: Returned; enclose SAE.
Time before publication decision: 2 mos.
Time between decision and publication: 6 mos.
Number of reviewers: 2
Articles published per year: 12
Book reviews published per year: 6

(348)
*Biblioteca della Ricerca: Testi Stranieri

Giovanni Dotoli, Editor
Schena Editore
Viale Stazione 177
72015 Fasano DI P. (BR), Italy

Additional editorial address: Via Di Crollalanza 2, 70121 Bari, Italy
Telephone: (39) 80 714681
Fax: (39) 80 714681
First published: 1983
Sponsoring organization: Univ. of Italy; Consiglio Nationale della Ricerche, Italy; Ministero dell'educazione Nationale, Italy
MLA acronym: BRTS

SUBSCRIPTION INFORMATION

Frequency of publication: 12 times/yr.
Available in microform: No

ADVERTISING INFORMATION

Advertising accepted: No

EDITORIAL DESCRIPTION

Scope: Publishes monograph studies of foreign literatures including extensive introductory material, annotations, and notes. Also includes essays on literature and mentality, translation, and linguistics from the Middle Ages to the 20th century.
Reviews books: Yes
Publishes notes: Yes
Languages accepted: Italian; French; Spanish; German; English; Arabic; Greek; Serbo-Croatian; Portuguese
Prints abstracts: No
Author-anonymous submission: No

SUBMISSION REQUIREMENTS

Author pays submission fee: No
Author pays page charges: Yes
Length of books: 200-300 pp.
Length of book reviews: 1 p.
Number of copies required: 1
Copyright ownership: Author
Time before publication decision: 1 mo.
Time between decision and publication: 6 mos.
Number of reviewers: 2
Books submitted per year: 15
Books published per year: 10-15
Book reviews submitted per year: 500
Book reviews published per year: 100

(349)
Biblioteca Hispanoamericana y Española de Amsterdam

Guillermo Araya, Editor
Keizersgracht 746
1017 EX Amsterdam, Netherlands

First published: 1982
MLA acronym: BHEA

SUBSCRIPTION INFORMATION

Subscription address: Humanities Press International, Inc., Atlantic Highlands, NJ 07716

EDITORIAL DESCRIPTION

Scope: The series publishes monograph studies on major figures and themes in Spanish and Latin American literature.
Languages accepted: Spanish; English

(350)
*Biblioteca/The Library: Monthly Journal for Bibliography

Ioana Lupu, Editor
Ministerul Culturii
Redacția Revistei "Biblioteca"
Piața Presei Libere 1
71341 Bucharest, Romania

First published: 1948
Historical variations in title: Formerly Biblioteca/The Library: Quarterly Bulletin for Librarianship
Sponsoring organization: Ministerul Culturii
ISSN: 1220-3386
MLA acronym: Biblioteca

SUBSCRIPTION INFORMATION

Frequency of publication: 12 times/yr.
Circulation: 6,000
Available in microform: No
Subscription price: $48.00/yr.
Year to which price refers: 1992
Additional subscription address: Outside Romania: Orion S.R.L., Splaiul Independenței 202 A, Sector 6, Bucharest, Romania

ADVERTISING INFORMATION

Advertising accepted: Yes

EDITORIAL DESCRIPTION

Scope: Publishes articles in the field of modern librarianship, bibliography, and book history. Other topics covered include reading, library science, and publishing.
Reviews books: Yes
Publishes notes: Yes
Languages accepted: Romanian
Prints abstracts: Yes

SUBMISSION REQUIREMENTS

Restrictions on contributors: None
Author pays submission fee: No
Author pays page charges: No
Length of articles: 2,500-10,000 words
Length of book reviews: 500-2,500 words
Length of notes: 250-2,500 words
Style: None
Number of copies required: 2
Copyright ownership: Author
Rejected manuscripts: Not returned
Time before publication decision: 3 weeks
Time between decision and publication: 3 mos.
Number of reviewers: 2
Articles submitted per year: 400-420
Articles published per year: 300-320
Book reviews published per year: 100-120
Notes published per year: 80-100

(351)
*Biblioteka Analiz Literackich

Wydawnictwa Szkolne i Pedagogiczne
pl. Dąbrowskiego 8
00-950 Warsaw, Poland

Telephone: (48) 22 265451
Fax: (48) 22 279204
First published: 1959
Sponsoring organization: Wydawnictwa Szkolne & Pedagogiczne
ISSN: 0519-7929
MLA acronym: BALit

SUBSCRIPTION INFORMATION

Frequency of publication: Irregular
Circulation: 10,000-150,000
Available in microform: No

ADVERTISING INFORMATION

Advertising accepted: No

EDITORIAL DESCRIPTION

Scope: Publishes analyses and interpretations of Polish and general literary masterpieces.
Publishes notes: Yes
Languages accepted: Polish
Prints abstracts: No
Author-anonymous submission: No

SUBMISSION REQUIREMENTS

Restrictions on contributors: None
Author pays submission fee: No
Author pays page charges: No
Length of articles: No restrictions
Length of books: 110-220 typescript pp.
Length of notes: No restrictions
Style: Standard Polish
Number of copies required: 2
Copyright ownership: Wydawnictwa Szkolne & Pedagogiczne
Rejected manuscripts: Returned
Time before publication decision: 6 mos.
Time between decision and publication: 2 yrs.
Number of reviewers: 3
Books submitted per year: 1-2
Books published per year: 1-2

(352)
*Bibliotheca Afroasiatica

John L. Hayes, Editor
Undena Publications
P.O. Box 97
Malibu, CA 90265

First published: 1980
ISSN: 0742-1117
MLA acronym: BAFAS

SUBSCRIPTION INFORMATION

Frequency of publication: Irregular
Circulation: 200
Available in microform: No
Subscription address: Crescent Academic Services, 29528 Madera Ave., Schafter, CA 93263
Subscription telephone: 805 746-5870
Subscription fax: 805 746-2728

ADVERTISING INFORMATION

Advertising accepted: No

EDITORIAL DESCRIPTION

Scope: Publishes linguistic and lexical studies on the Afroasiatic language group. Both primary data and comparative analyses are included.
Reviews books: No
Publishes notes: No
Languages accepted: English
Prints abstracts: Yes
Author-anonymous submission: No

SUBMISSION REQUIREMENTS

Author pays submission fee: No
Author pays page charges: No
Length of books: 150-200 pp.
Style: Chicago
Number of copies required: 1
Special requirements: Subsidies or camera-ready copy is required.
Copyright ownership: Publisher or Author
Rejected manuscripts: Returned; enclose SASE.
Time before publication decision: 2-3 mos.

Time between decision and publication: 1 yr.
Number of reviewers: 2

(353)
*Bibliotheca Arnamagnæana

Det Arnamagnæanske Inst.
Københavns Univ. Amager
Njalsgade 76
2300 Copenhagen S, Denmark

First published: 1941
Sponsoring organization: Arnamagnæan Commission of Københavns Univ.
ISSN: 0067-7841
MLA acronym: BArn

SUBSCRIPTION INFORMATION

Frequency of publication: Irregular
Available in microform: No
Subscription address: C. A. Reitzels Boghandel A/S, Nørregade 20, 1165 Copenhagen K, Denmark

ADVERTISING INFORMATION

Advertising accepted: No

EDITORIAL DESCRIPTION

Scope: Publishes editions and monographs primarily in the area of Old Norse-Icelandic philology and literature.
Reviews books: No
Languages accepted: Norwegian; Danish; Swedish; English; German; Icelandic
Prints abstracts: No

SUBMISSION REQUIREMENTS

Author pays submission fee: No
Author pays page charges: No
Number of copies required: 1
Copyright ownership: Arnamagnæan Commission

(354)
*The Biblioteck: A Scottish Journal of Bibliography and Allied Topics

W. A. Kelly, Editor
Dept. of Printed Books
National Library of Scotland
George IV Bridge
Edinburgh EA1 1EW, Scotland

Telephone: (44) 31 2264531 ext. 2307
Fax: (44) 31 2206662
First published: 1956
Sponsoring organization: Library Assn., Univ., College, and Research Section, Scottish Group
ISSN: 0006-193X
MLA acronym: Bibliotheck

SUBSCRIPTION INFORMATION

Frequency of publication: 3 times/yr. plus 1 supplement
Circulation: 350
Available in microform: No
Subscription price: £12.00 ($27.50)/yr. institutions; £14.00 ($22.00)/yr. individuals
Year to which price refers: 1992

ADVERTISING INFORMATION

Advertising accepted: Yes

EDITORIAL DESCRIPTION

Scope: Publishes bibliographical and related articles and notes (which may incorporate short descriptive bibliographies, check-lists, or catalogues) of Scottish interest or association. An annual Supplement contains a bibliography of books, reviews, essays, and articles in the field of Scottish literature published during the preceding year.
Reviews books: Yes
Publishes notes: Yes
Languages accepted: English
Prints abstracts: No

SUBMISSION REQUIREMENTS

Restrictions on contributors: None
Author pays submission fee: No
Author pays page charges: No
Length of articles: 6,000 words maximum
Length of book reviews: 300 words
Style: MLA; Modern Humanities Research Assn.
Number of copies required: 1
Copyright ownership: Author & publisher
Rejected manuscripts: Returned
Time before publication decision: 2 mos.
Time between decision and publication: 18 mos.
Number of reviewers: 1-2

(355)
*Bibliothèque des Cahiers de l'Institut de Linguistique de Louvain

Peeters
Bondgenotenlaan 153
3000 Leuven, Belgium

Telephone: (32) 16 235170
Fax: (32) 16 228500
First published: 1976
MLA acronym: BCILL

SUBSCRIPTION INFORMATION

Available in microform: No

ADVERTISING INFORMATION

Advertising accepted: No

EDITORIAL DESCRIPTION

Scope: Publishes monographs on linguistics.
Reviews books: No
Publishes notes: No
Languages accepted: French; English; Italian; Spanish; German; Dutch
Prints abstracts: Yes
Author-anonymous submission: Yes

SUBMISSION REQUIREMENTS

Author pays submission fee: No
Number of copies required: 1
Copyright ownership: Peeters
Time before publication decision: 4 mos.
Time between decision and publication: 6 mos.
Books submitted per year: 10
Books published per year: 4

(356)
*Bibliothèque d'Humanisme et Renaissance

A. Dufour, Editor
Librairie Droz S.A.
11, rue Massot
1211 Geneva 12, Switzerland

Telephone: (41) 22 466666
Fax: (41) 22 472391
First published: 1933
Sponsoring organization: Assn. d'Humanisme & Renaissance
ISSN: 0006-1999
MLA acronym: BHR

SUBSCRIPTION INFORMATION

Frequency of publication: 3 times/yr.
Circulation: 1,000
Available in microform: No
Subscription price: 90 SwF/yr.
Year to which price refers: 1992

ADVERTISING INFORMATION

Advertising accepted: No

EDITORIAL DESCRIPTION

Scope: Focuses on the 15th and 16th centuries. Contains articles that bring together the contributions of the best specialists in history, literature, politics, religion, art, and economics.
Reviews books: Yes
Publishes notes: Yes
Languages accepted: English; French; German; Italian
Prints abstracts: No
Author-anonymous submission: No

SUBMISSION REQUIREMENTS

Restrictions on contributors: Book reviews are solicited.
Author pays submission fee: No
Author pays page charges: No
Length of articles: 20 typescript pp. maximum
Length of book reviews: 2 pp.
Length of notes: 2-10 pp.
Style: None
Number of copies required: 1
Copyright ownership: Librairie DROZ S.A.
Rejected manuscripts: Returned
Time before publication decision: 8 mos.
Time between decision and publication: 6 mos.
Articles submitted per year: 60
Articles published per year: 20
Book reviews published per year: 100
Notes submitted per year: 40
Notes published per year: 20-30

(357)
*Bibliothèque Russe de l'Institut d'Etudes Slaves

Institut d'Etudes Slaves
9, rue Michelet
75006 Paris, France

Telephone: (33) 1 43265089
Fax: (33) 1 43261623
First published: 1946
ISSN: 0078-9976
MLA acronym: BRIES

SUBSCRIPTION INFORMATION

Frequency of publication: Irregular; 2-3 times/yr.
Circulation: 350
Available in microform: No

ADVERTISING INFORMATION

Advertising accepted: No

EDITORIAL DESCRIPTION

Scope: Publishes a monographic series devoted to major figures in Russian literature and linguistics.
Reviews books: Yes
Publishes notes: No
Languages accepted: French; Russian
Prints abstracts: No
Author-anonymous submission: No

SUBMISSION REQUIREMENTS

Author pays submission fee: No

Author pays page charges: No
Style: French Code Typographique; Manuel Typographique du Russiste
Number of copies required: 2
Copyright ownership: Institut d'Etudes Slaves
Time before publication decision: 18-24 mos.
Time between decision and publication: 12-18 mos.
Number of reviewers: 2
Books submitted per year: 8
Books published per year: 3

(358)
*Bijdragen tot de Taal-, Land- en Volkenkunde

Henri J. M. Claessen & Maria J. L. van Yperen, Editors
Koninklijk Inst. voor Taal-, Land- en Volkenkunde
Reuvensplaats 2
Postbus 9515
2300 RA Leiden, Netherlands

Telephone: (31) 71 272463
Fax: (31) 71 272638
First published: 1853
Sponsoring organization: Koninklijk Inst. voor Taal-, Land- en Volkenkunde (KITLV)
ISSN: 0006-2294
MLA acronym: BTLV

SUBSCRIPTION INFORMATION

Frequency of publication: 3 times/yr. (Spring, Summer, Fall)
Circulation: 2,300
Available in microform: No
Subscription price: 100 f/yr.
Year to which price refers: 1992

ADVERTISING INFORMATION

Advertising accepted: Yes
Advertising rates: 125 f/quarter page; 225 f/half page; 400 f/full page

EDITORIAL DESCRIPTION

Scope: Publishes articles on the anthropology, history, and linguistics of Southeast Asia, with special emphasis on Indonesia, and Oceania.
Reviews books: Yes
Publishes notes: Yes
Languages accepted: English; Dutch
Prints abstracts: No
Author-anonymous submission: Yes

SUBMISSION REQUIREMENTS

Restrictions on contributors: None
Author pays submission fee: No
Author pays page charges: No
Length of articles: 30 pp. maximum
Length of book reviews: 350 words
Length of notes: 2-8 pp.
Style: Journal
Number of copies required: 1
Special requirements: Submit on diskette with a printout in accordance with KITLV's "Information on the Preparation of Manuscripts for Publication".
Copyright ownership: Koninklijk Inst. voor Taal-, Land- en Volkenkunde
Rejected manuscripts: Returned
Time before publication decision: 1-2 mos.
Time between decision and publication: 1-2 yrs.
Number of reviewers: 2-3
Articles submitted per year: 48
Articles published per year: 27
Book reviews submitted per year: 65
Book reviews published per year: 50
Notes submitted per year: 5
Notes published per year: 3

(359)
*Biḳoret u-Parshanut: Ketav-'et le-Sifrut, Lashon, Historiah ve-Esteṭiḳah

H. Weiss, Editor
Dept. of Literature of the Jewish People
Bar-Ilan Univ.
52900 Ramat-Gan, Israel

First published: 1970
Sponsoring organization: Bar-Ilan Univ.
ISSN: 0084-9456
MLA acronym: Biḳoret u-Parshanut

SUBSCRIPTION INFORMATION

Frequency of publication: 2 times/yr.
Circulation: 1,500

ADVERTISING INFORMATION

Advertising accepted: No

EDITORIAL DESCRIPTION

Scope: Publishes articles on Hebrew literature.
Reviews books: Yes
Publishes notes: Yes
Languages accepted: Hebrew
Prints abstracts: Yes
Author-anonymous submission: No

SUBMISSION REQUIREMENTS

Restrictions on contributors: None
Author pays submission fee: No
Author pays page charges: No
Length of articles: 3,000-4,000 words
Length of book reviews: 1,000 words
Length of notes: 600 words
Style: None
Number of copies required: 3
Special requirements: Submit typescript.
Copyright ownership: Author & journal
Rejected manuscripts: Returned; enclose return postage.
Time before publication decision: 3-6 mos.
Time between decision and publication: 1-2 yrs.
Number of reviewers: 2
Articles published per year: 25-30
Book reviews published per year: 6-8
Notes submitted per year: 2

(360)
*The Bilingual Review/La Revista Bilingüe

Gary D. Keller & Karen S. Van Hooft, Editors
Hispanic Research Center
Arizona State Univ.
Tempe, AZ 85287-2702

Telephone: 602 965-3867
Fax: 602 965-8309
First published: 1974
Sponsoring organization: Hispanic Research Center, Arizona State Univ.
ISSN: 0094-5366
MLA acronym: BR/RB

SUBSCRIPTION INFORMATION

Frequency of publication: 3 times/yr.
Circulation: 1,000
Available in microform: Yes
Subscription price: $28.00/yr. institutions; $16.00/yr. individuals
Year to which price refers: 1992

ADVERTISING INFORMATION

Advertising accepted: Yes
Advertising rates: $90.00/half page; $150.00/full page; $175.00/inside back cover; $200.00/back cover

EDITORIAL DESCRIPTION

Scope: Focuses on the linguistics and literature of English-Spanish bilingualism and bilingual education in the US. Publishes research and scholarship in bilingualism, bilingual education, and US Hispanic literature (e.g. Chicano, Puerto Rican, Cuban American literature, etc.). Also publishes material dealing with bilingualism other than Spanish-English if of theoretical significance.
Reviews books: Yes
Publishes notes: No
Languages accepted: English; Spanish
Prints abstracts: Yes
Author-anonymous submission: No

SUBMISSION REQUIREMENTS

Restrictions on contributors: Review articles are assigned.
Author pays submission fee: No
Author pays page charges: No, unless articles contain more than 2 tables or charts. Authors are charged $20-$25 for each table or chart in excess of 2.
Length of articles: 20-40 pp.
Style: MLA, Chicago, linguistics, or social sciences formats accepted
Number of copies required: 2
Special requirements: Submit original typescript.
Copyright ownership: Assigned by author to journal
Rejected manuscripts: Returned; enclose return postage.
Time before publication decision: 2 mos.
Time between decision and publication: 1 yr.
Number of reviewers: 2
Articles submitted per year: 200
Articles published per year: 15-16
Book reviews published per year: 9-10 review articles

(361)
*Biography: An Interdisciplinary Quarterly

George Simson, Editor
Center for Biographical Research
Univ. of Hawaii
Honolulu, HI 96822

Telephone: 808 956-3774
Fax: 808 956-3774
First published: 1978
Sponsoring organization: Center for Biographical Research, Univ. of Hawaii
ISSN: 0162-4962
MLA acronym: Biography

SUBSCRIPTION INFORMATION

Frequency of publication: 4 times/yr. (Winter, Spring, Summer, Fall)
Circulation: 475
Available in microform: Yes
Subscription price: $26.00/yr. institutions; $20.00/yr. individuals
Year to which price refers: 1992
Subscription address: Journals Manager, Univ. of Hawaii Press, 2840 Kolowalu St., Honolulu, HI 96822
Subscription telephone: 808 956-8873

ADVERTISING INFORMATION

Advertising accepted: Yes
Advertising rates: $95.00/half page; $150.00/full page; $200.00/back cover

EDITORIAL DESCRIPTION

Scope: Publishes interdisciplinary articles, essays, reviews, and an annual bibliography in the field of biographical scholarship. Acts as a forum to stimulate the multidisciplinary criticism and theory of life-writing by presenting new information, sharper definitions, fresh interpretations, and well-argued evaluations. Welcomes contributions from all points of view on all topics concerning life-writing.
Reviews books: Yes
Publishes notes: Yes
Languages accepted: English
Prints abstracts: Yes
Author-anonymous submission: No

SUBMISSION REQUIREMENTS

Restrictions on contributors: None
Author pays submission fee: No
Author pays page charges: Yes, if galleys are altered more than 5%
Length of articles: 2,500-7,500 words
Length of book reviews: 500-2,000 words
Length of notes: 100-1,500 words
Style: MLA; Author's field
Number of copies required: 2
Special requirements: Submit original typescript accompanied by a 50-word abstract and a biographical note of 1 or 2 sentences on the author. Footnotes, numbered consecutively, should be placed at end. Texts in other languages will be accepted if accompanied by an English translation.
Copyright ownership: Biographical Research Center unless prior agreement
Rejected manuscripts: Returned with critique; enclose first-class return postage for US, airmail postage elsewhere.
Time before publication decision: 2-3 mos.
Time between decision and publication: 6-9 mos.
Number of reviewers: 2-5
Articles submitted per year: 50-100
Articles published per year: 20-25
Book reviews published per year: 20-25
Notes submitted per year: 1-3
Notes published per year: 1-3

(362)
Bitzaron: Quarterly Review of Hebrew Letters/Riv'on Sifrut, Hagut, Meḥkar

Hayim Leaf, Editor
P.O. Box 623
Cooper Station
New York, NY 10003

Additional editorial address: C/o Faculty of Arts & Science, Skirball Dept. of Hebrew & Judaic Studies, 51 Washington Square South, New York, NY 10012
First published: 1939
Sponsoring organization: Hebrew Literary Foundation; New York Univ., School of Education, Inst. of Hebrew Culture & Education
ISSN: 0006-3932
MLA acronym: Bitzaron

SUBSCRIPTION INFORMATION

Frequency of publication: 4 times/yr.
Circulation: 4,500
Available in microform: No

ADVERTISING INFORMATION

Advertising accepted: Yes

EDITORIAL DESCRIPTION

Scope: Publishes creative writing, scholarly and literary articles, philosophical essays, and comments on the cultural and social scene in America and Israel.
Reviews books: Yes
Publishes notes: Yes
Languages accepted: Hebrew; English

Prints abstracts: Yes

SUBMISSION REQUIREMENTS

Restrictions on contributors: None
Author pays submission fee: No
Author pays page charges: No
Length of articles: 1,000-5,000 words
Length of book reviews: 500-1,000 words
Length of notes: 150 words
Number of copies required: 1
Special requirements: Include an abstract.
Copyright ownership: Author
Rejected manuscripts: Returned at author's request
Time before publication decision: 1-4 mos.
Time between decision and publication: 3-12 mos.
Number of reviewers: 2-3
Articles submitted per year: 100-150
Articles published per year: 60
Book reviews submitted per year: 50-100
Book reviews published per year: 20-30
Notes submitted per year: 40-50
Notes published per year: 30-40

(363)
Biuletyn Polonistyczny: Kwartalnik

Krystyna Sierocka, Editor
Ossolineum Publishing House of the Polish Academy of Sciences
Rynek 9
50-106 Wrocław, Poland

Additional editorial address: Inst. Badan Literackich PAN, Biuletyn Polonistyczny Redakcja, Nowy Swiat 72, Pok. 123, 00-330 Warsaw, Poland
First published: 1958
Sponsoring organization: Inst. Badan Literackich, Polska Akademia Nauk
ISSN: 0067-902X
MLA acronym: BiP

SUBSCRIPTION INFORMATION

Frequency of publication: 4 times/yr.
Circulation: 1,600
Subscription address: Foreign Trade Enterprise "Ars Polona", Krakowskie Przedmieście 7, 00-068 Warsaw, Poland

ADVERTISING INFORMATION

Advertising accepted: No

EDITORIAL DESCRIPTION

Scope: Publishes articles on Polish literary history and literary theory.
Reviews books: No
Publishes notes: Yes
Languages accepted: Polish
Prints abstracts: Yes
Author-anonymous submission: No

SUBMISSION REQUIREMENTS

Restrictions on contributors: None
Author pays submission fee: No
Author pays page charges: No
Length of articles: 6 pp.
Length of notes: 18 lines
Number of copies required: 2
Copyright ownership: Ossolineum
Rejected manuscripts: Returned
Time before publication decision: 1 week
Time between decision and publication: 1 yr.
Articles submitted per year: 40-50
Articles published per year: 40-50
Notes submitted per year: 500
Notes published per year: 500

(364)
*Biuletyn Polskiego Towarzystwa Językoznawczego/Bulletin de la Société Polonaise de Linguistique

Ruta Nagucka, Krystyna Pisarkowa, Aleksander Szulc, & Kazimierz Polański, Editors
A. Mickiewicza 9/11
31-120 Cracow, Poland

First published: 1927
Sponsoring organization: Polish Linguistics Assn.
ISSN: 0032-3802
MLA acronym: BPTJ

SUBSCRIPTION INFORMATION

Frequency of publication: Annual
Circulation: 1,200
Available in microform: No
Subscription price: 60,000 Zł/yr.
Year to which price refers: 1992
Subscription address: Wydawnictwo Energeia, ul. Wiktorska 91B/1, 02-582 Warsaw, Poland
Subscription telephone: (48) 22 447671

ADVERTISING INFORMATION

Advertising accepted: Yes

EDITORIAL DESCRIPTION

Scope: Publishes articles on general linguistics.
Reviews books: Yes
Publishes notes: Yes
Languages accepted: English; French; German; Polish; Russian
Prints abstracts: Yes, of texts written in Polish
Author-anonymous submission: No

SUBMISSION REQUIREMENTS

Restrictions on contributors: None
Author pays submission fee: No
Author pays page charges: No
Length of articles: 20 pp. maximum
Length of book reviews: No restrictions
Length of notes: No restrictions
Style: MLA
Number of copies required: 2
Copyright ownership: Journal
Rejected manuscripts: Not returned
Time before publication decision: 1 mo.
Time between decision and publication: 18 mos.
Number of reviewers: 2
Articles submitted per year: 20-25
Articles published per year: 15-18
Book reviews submitted per year: 2-3
Book reviews published per year: 1-3

(365)
Black Orpheus: Journal of African and Afro-American Literature

T. Vincent, Editor
Univ. of Lagos
Yaba, Lagos, Nigeria

First published: 1957
ISSN: 0067-9100
MLA acronym: BO

SUBSCRIPTION INFORMATION

Frequency of publication: 2 times/yr.
Circulation: 2,000
Subscription address: Business Manager, Univ. of Lagos Bookshop, Univ. of Lagos, Lagos, Nigeria

EDITORIAL DESCRIPTION

Scope: Publishes articles on African and African American literature.
Reviews books: Yes
Languages accepted: English

SUBMISSION REQUIREMENTS

Special requirements: Considers manuscripts in African languages.

(366) *Black Warrior Review

Glenn Mott, Editor
P.O. Box 2936
Tuscaloosa, AL 35486-2936

Telephone: 205 348-4518
First published: 1974
Sponsoring organization: Univ. of Alabama
ISSN: 0193-6301
MLA acronym: BWR

SUBSCRIPTION INFORMATION

Frequency of publication: 2 times/yr.
Circulation: 2,000
Available in microform: No

ADVERTISING INFORMATION

Advertising accepted: Yes

EDITORIAL DESCRIPTION

Scope: Publishes articles on all aspects of contemporary literature.
Reviews books: Yes
Publishes notes: No
Languages accepted: English
Prints abstracts: No
Author-anonymous submission: No

SUBMISSION REQUIREMENTS

Restrictions on contributors: None
Author pays submission fee: No
Author pays page charges: No
Length of articles: 7,500 words
Length of book reviews: 500-1,000 words
Style: None
Number of copies required: 1
Special requirements: Submit typescript. Do not use footnotes.
Copyright ownership: Journal
Rejected manuscripts: Returned; enclose SASE.
Time before publication decision: 2-8 weeks
Time between decision and publication: 3 mos.
Number of reviewers: 5
Articles submitted per year: 3,000
Articles published per year: 50
Book reviews submitted per year: 20-30
Book reviews published per year: 5-10

(367) *Blake: An Illustrated Quarterly

Morris Eaves & Morton D. Paley, Editors
Dept. of English
Univ. of Rochester
Rochester, NY 14627

Additional editorial address: Morton D. Paley, Dept. of English, Univ. of California, Berkeley, CA 94720
Telephone: 716 275-3820
Fax: 716 442-5769
E-mail: PNPJ@DB1.cc.rochester.edu
First published: 1967
Sponsoring organization: Dept. of English, Univ. of Rochester
ISSN: 0160-628X
MLA acronym: Blake

SUBSCRIPTION INFORMATION

Frequency of publication: 4 times/yr.
Circulation: 700
Available in microform: No
Subscription price: $40.00/yr. institutions; $20.00/yr. individuals

Year to which price refers: 1992

ADVERTISING INFORMATION

Advertising accepted: Yes
Advertising rates: $80.00/half page; $115.00/full page insert; $120.00/full page

EDITORIAL DESCRIPTION

Scope: Publishes a variety of material, scholarly and critical, on the life and work of William Blake and certain of his contemporaries and followers; news; essays and notes; discussion; bibliographical tools; reviews; queries; reproductions.
Reviews books: Yes
Publishes notes: Yes
Languages accepted: English
Prints abstracts: No
Author-anonymous submission: No

SUBMISSION REQUIREMENTS

Restrictions on contributors: Unsolicited book reviews are not accepted.
Author pays submission fee: No
Author pays page charges: No
Length of articles: No restrictions
Length of book reviews: No restrictions
Length of notes: No restrictions
Style: MLA; Chicago
Number of copies required: 2
Special requirements: Submit diskette, preferably MS-DOS WordPerfect 5.0, with contribution.
Copyright ownership: Assigned by author to editors
Rejected manuscripts: Returned; enclose return postage.
Time before publication decision: 3 mos.
Time between decision and publication: 6-12 mos.
Number of reviewers: 1-2 plus editors
Articles submitted per year: 150
Articles published per year: 15
Book reviews published per year: 25
Notes submitted per year: 20
Notes published per year: 12

(368) *Blätter der Rilke-Gesellschaft

c/o Hansgeorg Schmidt-Bergmann
Kollegium am Schloss
7500 Karlsruhe 1, Germany

Additional editorial address: R. Luck, c/o Schweizer Landesbibliothek, 3003 Bern, Switzerland
First published: 1972
Sponsoring organization: Rilke-Gesellschaft
MLA acronym: BRG

SUBSCRIPTION INFORMATION

Frequency of publication: Annual
Circulation: 700
Available in microform: No
Subscription price: 60 DM/yr.
Year to which price refers: 1992
Subscription address: Thorbecke-Verlag, Karlstr. 10, 7480 Sigmaringen, Germany

ADVERTISING INFORMATION

Advertising accepted: Yes

EDITORIAL DESCRIPTION

Scope: Publishes research papers, sources, bibliographies, and lectures on Rilke and his times.
Reviews books: Yes
Publishes notes: Yes
Languages accepted: English; French; German
Prints abstracts: No

SUBMISSION REQUIREMENTS

Restrictions on contributors: None
Author pays submission fee: No
Author pays page charges: No
Length of articles: 30 typescript pp. maximum
Length of book reviews: 5 typescript pp. maximum
Length of notes: 30 words
Number of copies required: 1; 2 preferred
Special requirements: Submit original typescript.
Copyright ownership: Author
Rejected manuscripts: 1 copy returned
Time before publication decision: 2 mos.
Time between decision and publication: 6 mos.
Number of reviewers: 5
Articles submitted per year: 5-10
Articles published per year: 5-9
Book reviews submitted per year: 1-3
Book reviews published per year: 1-3
Notes submitted per year: 1-5
Notes published per year: 1-5

(369) *Blätter der Thomas Mann Gesellschaft

Heinrich Rumpel, Editor
Thomas Mann Gesellschaft
c/o Europa Verlag Zürich
Rämistr. 5
Postfach
8001 Zurich, Switzerland

Telephone: (41) 1 2611629
First published: 1958
Sponsoring organization: Thomas Mann Gesellschaft
ISSN: 0082-4186
MLA acronym: BTMG

SUBSCRIPTION INFORMATION

Frequency of publication: Irregular
Circulation: 1,000
Available in microform: No

ADVERTISING INFORMATION

Advertising accepted: No

EDITORIAL DESCRIPTION

Scope: Publishes articles on Thomas Mann.
Reviews books: No
Publishes notes: No
Languages accepted: German
Prints abstracts: No
Author-anonymous submission: No

SUBMISSION REQUIREMENTS

Restrictions on contributors: None
Author pays submission fee: No
Author pays page charges: No
Length of articles: 20-30 typescript pp.
Copyright ownership: Thomas Mann Gesellschaft
Rejected manuscripts: Returned
Articles published per year: 1-2

(370) *Bloch-Almanach: Periodicum des Ernst-Bloch-Archivs des Kulturbüros der Stadt Ludwigshafen

Karl-Heinz Weigand, Editor
Ernst-Bloch-Archiv
Bismarckstr., 44-48
6700 Ludwigshafen, Germany

Telephone: (49) 621 5042592
Fax: (49) 621 5042259
First published: 1981

Historical variations in title: Formerly *Bloch-Almanach: Eine Veröffentlichung des Ernst-Bloch-Archivs der Stadtbibliothek Ludwigshafen*
Sponsoring organization: Stadt Ludwigshafen
ISSN: 0721-3743
MLA acronym: Bloch-Almanach

SUBSCRIPTION INFORMATION

Frequency of publication: Annual
Circulation: 700
Available in microform: No
Subscription address: Kulturburo, Stadtverwaltung, Postfach 21 12 25, 6700 Ludwigshafen, Germany
Subscription telephone: (49) 621 5042261
Subscription fax: (49) 621 5043782

ADVERTISING INFORMATION

Advertising accepted: No

EDITORIAL DESCRIPTION

Scope: Publishes articles about the life and work of Ernst Bloch.
Reviews books: No
Languages accepted: German; English; French
Prints abstracts: No

SUBMISSION REQUIREMENTS

Author pays submission fee: Yes
Author pays page charges: No
Length of articles: 20-30 pp.
Number of copies required: 2
Copyright ownership: Journal
Rejected manuscripts: Returned
Time before publication decision: 6 mos.
Time between decision and publication: 3 mos.
Number of reviewers: 1
Articles submitted per year: 12-15
Articles published per year: 10-12

(371)
*Bluegrass Unlimited

Peter V. Kuykendall, Editor
P.O. Box 111
Broad Run, VA 22014

Telephone: 703 349-8181
First published: 1966
ISSN: 0006-5137
MLA acronym: BGU

SUBSCRIPTION INFORMATION

Frequency of publication: 12 times/yr.
Circulation: 21,575
Available in microform: No
Subscription price: $20.00/yr. US; $27.00/yr. elsewhere
Year to which price refers: 1991

ADVERTISING INFORMATION

Advertising accepted: Yes

EDITORIAL DESCRIPTION

Scope: Publishes articles on popular bluegrass music, musicians, and musical instruments.
Reviews books: Yes
Languages accepted: English
Prints abstracts: No

SUBMISSION REQUIREMENTS

Restrictions on contributors: None
Author pays submission fee: No
Author pays page charges: No
Length of articles: 500-5,000 words
Length of book reviews: 200-300 words
Style: None
Number of copies required: 1
Special requirements: Submit double-spaced typescript. Query editor before submitting book reviews.

Copyright ownership: Journal holds first rights; other rights returned to author on request
Rejected manuscripts: Returned
Time before publication decision: 1 mo.
Time between decision and publication: 12-14 weeks
Number of reviewers: 2
Articles submitted per year: 50-200
Articles published per year: 40-50
Book reviews submitted per year: 10-20
Book reviews published per year: 25

(372)
Blues Unlimited

Bez Turner, Bill Greensmith, & Mike Rowe, Editors
36 Belmont Park
Lewisham
London SE13 5DB, England

First published: 1963
Sponsoring organization: BU Publications Ltd.
ISSN: 0006-5153
MLA acronym: BU

SUBSCRIPTION INFORMATION

Frequency of publication: 4 times/yr.
Circulation: 3,500
Available in microform: No

ADVERTISING INFORMATION

Advertising accepted: Yes

EDITORIAL DESCRIPTION

Scope: Publishes articles on all aspects of blues music.
Reviews books: Yes
Publishes notes: Yes
Languages accepted: English
Prints abstracts: No

SUBMISSION REQUIREMENTS

Restrictions on contributors: None
Author pays submission fee: No
Author pays page charges: No
Length of articles: 2,000 words maximum
Length of book reviews: 500 words
Style: None
Number of copies required: 1
Copyright ownership: Author & journal
Rejected manuscripts: Not returned
Time before publication decision: 1 mo.
Time between decision and publication: 2 mos.
Number of reviewers: 2
Articles submitted per year: 45
Articles published per year: 30
Book reviews published per year: 10
Notes published per year: 10

(373)
*Bochum-Essener Beiträge zur Sprachwandelforschung

Norbert Boretzky, Werner Enninger, Thomas Stolz, & Benedict Jessing, Editors
Universitätsverlag Dr. Norbert Brockmeyer
Uni-Tech-Center-Gebäude MC
4630 Bochum 1, Germany

Telephone: (49) 234 706978; (49) 234 9706124
Fax: (49) 234 9706122
First published: 1985
MLA acronym: BEBS

SUBSCRIPTION INFORMATION

Available in microform: No

EDITORIAL DESCRIPTION

Reviews books: No
Languages accepted: German; English; Spanish

(374)
*Bodleian Library Record

D. S. Porter, Editor
c/o Publications Officer
Bodleian Library
Oxford OX1 3BG, England

Telephone: (44) 865 277213
Fax: (44) 865 277182
First published: 1938
Sponsoring organization: Bodleian Library
ISSN: 0067-9488
MLA acronym: BLR

SUBSCRIPTION INFORMATION

Frequency of publication: 2 times/yr.
Circulation: 1,500
Available in microform: No, beginning with vol. 9; previous volumes available from Univ. Microfilms International
Subscription price: £14.00/yr.
Year to which price refers: 1992

ADVERTISING INFORMATION

Advertising accepted: No

EDITORIAL DESCRIPTION

Scope: Publishes bibliographies and articles on library history, principally related to the Bodleian Library and its collections.
Reviews books: No
Publishes notes: Yes
Languages accepted: English
Prints abstracts: No
Author-anonymous submission: No

SUBMISSION REQUIREMENTS

Restrictions on contributors: None
Author pays submission fee: No
Author pays page charges: No
Length of articles: 5,000 words maximum
Length of notes: 500 words maximum
Style: Oxford Univ. Press
Number of copies required: 1
Copyright ownership: Bodleian Library & author
Rejected manuscripts: Returned
Time before publication decision: 6-12 mos.
Time between decision and publication: 1 yr.
Number of reviewers: 4
Articles submitted per year: 10-15
Articles published per year: 8-10
Notes submitted per year: 5-8
Notes published per year: 2-5

(375)
*Bokvännen

Lars-Ove Pollack, Editor
Box 10285
100 55 Stockholm, Sweden

Telephone: (46) 8 6605364
First published: 1946
Sponsoring organization: Sällskapet Bokvännerna
ISSN: 0006-5846
MLA acronym: Bokvännen

SUBSCRIPTION INFORMATION

Frequency of publication: 6 times/yr.
Circulation: 1,700
Available in microform: No

ADVERTISING INFORMATION

Advertising accepted: Yes

EDITORIAL DESCRIPTION

Scope: Focuses on book collecting, bibliography, graphic arts, history of literature, and allied subjects.
Reviews books: Yes
Publishes notes: Yes
Languages accepted: Swedish; Norwegian; Danish
Prints abstracts: No
Author-anonymous submission: No

SUBMISSION REQUIREMENTS

Restrictions on contributors: None
Author pays submission fee: No
Author pays page charges: No
Length of articles: 2,000-5,000 words
Length of book reviews: 500-1,000 words
Length of notes: 100-500 words
Number of copies required: 1
Special requirements: Submit typescript.
Copyright ownership: Journal & author
Rejected manuscripts: Returned
Time before publication decision: 2-3 weeks
Time between decision and publication: 4 mos.
Number of reviewers: 1-2
Articles submitted per year: 40
Articles published per year: 25
Book reviews submitted per year: 35
Book reviews published per year: 35
Notes submitted per year: 50
Notes published per year: 35

(376)
*Boletim de Filologia

I. Castro, Editor
Centro de Linguística da Univ. de Lisboa
Av. 5 de Outubro, 85-5°
1000 Lisbon, Portugal

Telephone: (351) 1 7967110
First published: 1932
Sponsoring organization: Univ. de Lisboa
ISSN: 0870-4600
MLA acronym: BdF

SUBSCRIPTION INFORMATION

Frequency of publication: Annual
Circulation: 750
Available in microform: No
Subscription address: Imprensa Nacional-Casa da Moeda, R. Marquês Sá da Bandeira, 162A-B, 1000 Lisbon, Portugal
Subscription telephone: (351) 1 693414

ADVERTISING INFORMATION

Advertising accepted: Yes

EDITORIAL DESCRIPTION

Scope: Publishes articles on linguistics and philology. Includes studies on Portuguese, Romance, and general linguistics.
Reviews books: Yes
Publishes notes: Yes
Languages accepted: Portuguese; French; Spanish; English; Italian; Galician
Prints abstracts: No
Author-anonymous submission: No

SUBMISSION REQUIREMENTS

Restrictions on contributors: None
Author pays submission fee: No
Author pays page charges: No
Style: Journal
Number of copies required: 2
Special requirements: Submit original typescript.
Copyright ownership: Author
Rejected manuscripts: Returned
Time before publication decision: 6 mos.
Time between decision and publication: 1 yr.
Number of reviewers: 2
Articles submitted per year: 12-15
Articles published per year: 8-10

(377)
Boletim do Istituto Luís de Camões

Manuel Teixeira, Editor
Istituto Luís de Camões
Edificio da Biblioteca Chinesa Ho Tung
Largo de Santo Agostinho
Macao, Asia

First published: 1965
Sponsoring organization: Leal Senado (City Council)
MLA acronym: BILC

SUBSCRIPTION INFORMATION

Frequency of publication: 4 times/yr. (Spring, Summer, Fall, Winter)
Available in microform: No

ADVERTISING INFORMATION

Advertising accepted: No

EDITORIAL DESCRIPTION

Scope: Publishes articles on Portuguese history and culture in Asia.
Reviews books: Yes
Languages accepted: Portuguese; English; French; Italian; Spanish
Prints abstracts: Yes

SUBMISSION REQUIREMENTS

Restrictions on contributors: None
Author pays submission fee: No
Author pays page charges: No
Length of articles: No restrictions
Length of book reviews: No restrictions
Number of copies required: 1
Rejected manuscripts: Returned
Time before publication decision: 1 week
Time between decision and publication: 3 mos.
Number of reviewers: 1

(378)
*Boletin Cultural y Bibliografico

Biblioteca Luis-Angel Arango
Barrio de La Candelaria
Calle 11, No. 4-14
Bogotá, Colombia

First published: 1958
Sponsoring organization: Banco de la Republica; Subgerencia Cultural; Biblioteca Luis Angel Arang
ISSN: 0006-6184
MLA acronym: BCB

SUBSCRIPTION INFORMATION

Frequency of publication: 4 times/yr.
Circulation: 4,000
Available in microform: No

ADVERTISING INFORMATION

Advertising accepted: No

EDITORIAL DESCRIPTION

Scope: Publishes articles on Colombian literature and culture.
Reviews books: Yes
Publishes notes: No
Languages accepted: Spanish
Prints abstracts: No
Author-anonymous submission: No

SUBMISSION REQUIREMENTS

Restrictions on contributors: None
Author pays submission fee: No
Author pays page charges: No
Length of articles: 2,000-5,000 words
Length of book reviews: 1,000-1,500 words
Style: Chicago
Number of copies required: 2
Special requirements: Submit original typescript.
Copyright ownership: Author
Rejected manuscripts: Returned
Time before publication decision: 2 mos.
Time between decision and publication: 2 mos.
Articles submitted per year: 40
Articles published per year: 20
Book reviews submitted per year: 140
Book reviews published per year: 120

(379)
*Boletín de Filología

Alfredo Matus Olivier, Editor
Univ. de Chile, Dept. de Linguistica
Casilla 10136
Correo Central
Santiago, Chile

Telephone: (56) 2 2725977 ext. 47
Fax: (56) 2 2716823
First published: 1934
Sponsoring organization: Dept. de Linguistica, Univ. de Chile
ISSN: 0067-9674
MLA acronym: BFil

SUBSCRIPTION INFORMATION

Frequency of publication: Annual
Available in microform: No
Subscription price: $25.00/yr.
Year to which price refers: 1992

ADVERTISING INFORMATION

Advertising accepted: No

EDITORIAL DESCRIPTION

Scope: Publishes scholarly articles in general linguistics, dialectology, the history of linguistics, sociolinguistics, stylistics, and text analysis.
Reviews books: Yes
Publishes notes: Yes
Languages accepted: Spanish; French; English; German
Prints abstracts: No
Author-anonymous submission: No

SUBMISSION REQUIREMENTS

Author pays submission fee: No
Length of articles: 8,000 words
Length of book reviews: 1,600 words
Length of notes: 2,000 words
Style: Linguistic Soc. of America, adapted
Number of copies required: 3
Special requirements: Submit original typescript, 2 copies, and a 100-word abstract.
Copyright ownership: Journal
Rejected manuscripts: Not returned
Time before publication decision: 2 mos.
Time between decision and publication: 7 mos.
Number of reviewers: 3
Articles submitted per year: 10-15
Articles published per year: 8
Book reviews submitted per year: 10
Book reviews published per year: 4
Notes submitted per year: 4
Notes published per year: 2

(380)
Boletín de la Academia Colombiana

Manuel-José Forero, Editor
Academia Colombiana
Carrera 3-A, Número 17-34
Bogotá, Colombia

First published: 1936
ISSN: 0001-3773
MLA acronym: BAC

SUBSCRIPTION INFORMATION

Frequency of publication: 4 times/yr.
Circulation: 1,000
Available in microform: No

ADVERTISING INFORMATION

Advertising accepted: No

EDITORIAL DESCRIPTION

Scope: Publishes a register of new words and connotations for the Dictionary of the Real Academia Española, articles of a grammatical nature, and selected prose.
Reviews books: Yes
Languages accepted: Spanish
Prints abstracts: Yes

(381)
*Boletín de la Academia Norteamericana de la Lengua Española

Eugenio Chang-Rodríguez, Editor
Dept. of Romance Languages
Queens College, CUNY
Flushing, NY 11367

Telephone: 212 751-3779
Fax: 212 751-3779
First published: 1976
Sponsoring organization: Academia Norteamericana de la Lengua Española
ISSN: 0884-0091
MLA acronym: BANLE

SUBSCRIPTION INFORMATION

Frequency of publication: Annual
Circulation: 3,000
Available in microform: No
Subscription price: $12.00/yr.
Year to which price refers: 1992
Subscription address: D. Odón Betanzos, 125 Queen St., Staten Island, NY 10314
Subscription telephone: 718 761-0556
Subscription fax: 212 941-5793

ADVERTISING INFORMATION

Advertising accepted: No

EDITORIAL DESCRIPTION

Scope: Publishes linguistic studies on Spanish spoken in the US and studies of Hispanic tradition in the US.
Reviews books: No
Publishes notes: Yes
Languages accepted: Spanish
Prints abstracts: No
Author-anonymous submission: No

SUBMISSION REQUIREMENTS

Restrictions on contributors: Contributors must be subscribers.
Author pays submission fee: No
Author pays page charges: No
Length of articles: 2,500-8,000 words
Length of notes: 1,000-1,500 words
Style: MLA
Number of copies required: 3
Special requirements: Submit original typescript and 2 copies.
Copyright ownership: Assigned by author to journal
Rejected manuscripts: Returned; enclose return postage.
Time before publication decision: 2 mos.
Time between decision and publication: 6 mos.
Number of reviewers: 2
Articles submitted per year: 30
Articles published per year: 10
Notes submitted per year: 20
Notes published per year: 10

(382)
*Boletín de la Biblioteca de Menéndez Pelayo

Manuel Revuelta Sañudo, Editor
Biblioteca de Menéndez Pelayo
Rubio 6
Santander, Spain

Telephone: (34) 42 234534
Fax: (34) 42 372445
First published: 1919
Sponsoring organization: Soc. Menéndez Pelayo
ISSN: 0006-1646
MLA acronym: BBMP

SUBSCRIPTION INFORMATION

Frequency of publication: Annual
Available in microform: No

ADVERTISING INFORMATION

Advertising accepted: No

EDITORIAL DESCRIPTION

Scope: Publishes criticism of Spanish and Spanish American literature.
Reviews books: Yes
Publishes notes: No
Languages accepted: Spanish
Prints abstracts: No

SUBMISSION REQUIREMENTS

Author pays submission fee: No
Author pays page charges: No
Length of articles: 15-30 pp.
Length of book reviews: 2-3 pp.
Style: MLA
Number of copies required: 2
Time before publication decision: 3 mos.
Articles published per year: 10-12
Book reviews published per year: 15-25

(383)
*Boletín de la Fundación Federico García Lorca

Manuel Fernandez-Montesinos, Andrew A. Anderson, Isabel García Lorca, Mario Hernández, Christopher Maurer, Piero Menarini, & Margarita Ucelay, Editors
Fundación Federico García Lorca
C.S.I.C.
c/ Jorge Manrique, 27
28006 Madrid, Spain

Additional editorial address: Anthony A. Anderson, Univ. of Michigan, Dept. of Romance Languages & Literatures, Ann Arbor, MI 48109-1275
First published: 1987
Sponsoring organization: Fundación Federico García Lorca
ISSN: 0214-3771
MLA acronym: BFFGL

SUBSCRIPTION INFORMATION

Frequency of publication: 2 times/yr.
Circulation: 1,500
Available in microform: No
Subscription price: 1,700 Pta/yr., 3,200 Pta/2 yrs. N. America
Year to which price refers: 1992
Subscription telephone: (34) 1 5615779
Subscription fax: (34) 1 5644202

ADVERTISING INFORMATION

Advertising accepted: No

EDITORIAL DESCRIPTION

Scope: Publishes articles on all aspects of the life and work of Federico García Lorca and of his major and secondary contemporaries in the Generation of 1927. Also publishes Spanish and Latin American poetry.
Reviews books: Yes
Publishes notes: Yes
Languages accepted: Spanish
Prints abstracts: No
Author-anonymous submission: No

SUBMISSION REQUIREMENTS

Restrictions on contributors: Book reviews are commissioned.
Author pays submission fee: No
Author pays page charges: No
Length of articles: 9,000 words maximum
Length of book reviews: 500-1,000 words
Length of notes: 2,000 words maximum
Number of copies required: 1
Special requirements: Submit double-spaced typescript on size A4 (8 1/4 in. x 11 3/4 in.) or US letter-sized paper.
Copyright ownership: Author
Rejected manuscripts: Returned at author's request
Time before publication decision: 2-3 mos.
Time between decision and publication: 4-12 mos.
Number of reviewers: 3
Articles submitted per year: 30
Articles published per year: 20
Book reviews published per year: 3-4
Notes submitted per year: 5
Notes published per year: 2-3

(384)
*Boletín de la Real Academia Española

Real Academia Española
Felipe IV, 4
28014 Madrid, Spain

Telephone: (34) 1 4201478
Fax: (34) 1 4200079
First published: 1914
ISSN: 0210-4822
MLA acronym: BRAE

SUBSCRIPTION INFORMATION

Frequency of publication: 3 times/yr.
Circulation: 2,000
Available in microform: No
Subscription price: 5,600 Pta/yr.
Year to which price refers: 1992
Subscription address: Editorial Gedos, Sánchez Pacheco, 81, 28002 Madrid, Spain
Subscription telephone: (34) 1 4156836
Subscription fax: (34) 1 5192033

ADVERTISING INFORMATION

Advertising accepted: No

EDITORIAL DESCRIPTION

Scope: Publishes studies on the Spanish language and literature.
Reviews books: No
Languages accepted: Spanish
Prints abstracts: No

SUBMISSION REQUIREMENTS

Number of copies required: 2
Articles submitted per year: 15-20
Articles published per year: 15

(385)
*Boletín del Real Instituto de Estudios Asturianos

Real Inst. de Estudios Asturianos
Plaza Porlien 9, 1°
33003 Oviedo, Spain

First published: 1947
Historical variations in title: Formerly *Boletín del Instituto de Estudios Asturianos*
Sponsoring organization: Real Inst. de Estudios Asturianos
ISSN: 0020-0384
MLA acronym: BIEA

SUBSCRIPTION INFORMATION

Frequency of publication: 2 times/yr.
Available in microform: No
Subscription price: 3,000 Pta/yr.
Year to which price refers: 1992

ADVERTISING INFORMATION

Advertising accepted: No

EDITORIAL DESCRIPTION

Scope: Publishes studies on Asturias in the humanities and natural sciences.
Reviews books: Yes
Publishes notes: Yes
Languages accepted: Spanish
Prints abstracts: No
Author-anonymous submission: No

SUBMISSION REQUIREMENTS

Restrictions on contributors: None
Author pays submission fee: Yes
Author pays page charges: No
Length of articles: 70 pp. maximum
Length of book reviews: 4 pp.
Style: None
Number of copies required: 1
Rejected manuscripts: Returned
Time before publication decision: 2 mos.
Time between decision and publication: 2 mos.
Number of reviewers: 2
Articles submitted per year: 100
Articles published per year: 40

(386)
*Bolivian Studies

Ricardo Pastor, Editor
Dept. of Modern Foreign Languages
Saginaw Valley State Univ.
University Center, MI 48710

Telephone: 517 790-4486
First published: 1990
Sponsoring organization: Inst. of Bolivian Studies
MLA acronym: BolSt

SUBSCRIPTION INFORMATION

Frequency of publication: Annual (Spring)
Available in microform: No
Subscription price: $10.00/yr.
Year to which price refers: 1991

ADVERTISING INFORMATION

Advertising accepted: Yes
Advertising rates: $250.00/full page

EDITORIAL DESCRIPTION

Scope: Publishes articles on Bolivian culture, folklore, history, literature, anthropology, history, and social sciences.
Reviews books: Yes
Languages accepted: English; Spanish
Prints abstracts: No
Author-anonymous submission: No

SUBMISSION REQUIREMENTS

Author pays submission fee: Yes
Cost of submission fee: $100.00
Author pays page charges: No
Length of articles: 5,000-6,000 words
Length of book reviews: 300-400 words
Style: MLA
Number of copies required: 4
Special requirements: Submission must not have been previously published, except for translations of published works.
Copyright ownership: Author
Time before publication decision: 2 mos.
Time between decision and publication: 2 mos.
Number of reviewers: 4
Articles published per year: 8-10
Book reviews published per year: 5 maximum

(387)
*Bollettino del Centro di Studi Vichiani

Giuseppe Giarrizzo & Fulvio Tessitore, Editors
Centro di Studi Vichiani
Facoltá di Lettere e Filosofia
dell'Univ. di Napoli
Via Porta di Massa 1
80133 Naples, Italy

Telephone: (39) 81 5420276
First published: 1971
Sponsoring organization: Centro di Studi Vichiani, Consiglio Nazionale delle Ricerche
ISSN: 0392-7334
MLA acronym: BCSV

SUBSCRIPTION INFORMATION

Frequency of publication: Annual
Circulation: 1,000
Available in microform: No
Subscription price: 40,000 Lit/yr.
Year to which price refers: 1990
Subscription address: Edizioni Bibliopolis, Via Arangis Ruiz 83, 80122 Naples, Italy
Subscription telephone: (39) 81 664606

ADVERTISING INFORMATION

Advertising accepted: No

EDITORIAL DESCRIPTION

Scope: Promotes the study of Giambattista Vico's thought.
Reviews books: Yes
Publishes notes: Yes
Languages accepted: Italian; English; French; Spanish
Prints abstracts: No
Author-anonymous submission: No

SUBMISSION REQUIREMENTS

Restrictions on contributors: None
Author pays submission fee: No
Author pays page charges: No
Length of articles: No restrictions
Length of book reviews: No restrictions
Length of notes: No restrictions
Style: None
Number of copies required: 1
Special requirements: Submit original typescript.
Copyright ownership: Centro di Studi Vichiani
Rejected manuscripts: Not returned
Time before publication decision: 2 mos.
Time between decision and publication: 8 mos.

Number of reviewers: 2
Articles published per year: 6-8
Book reviews published per year: 6-8
Notes published per year: 60-130

(388)
*Bollettino della Domus Mazziniana

Giacomo Adami, Editor
Domus Mazziniana
Via Mazzini, 71
56100 Pisa, Italy

First published: 1955
Sponsoring organization: Domus Mazziniana
ISSN: 0012-5385
MLA acronym: BDM

SUBSCRIPTION INFORMATION

Frequency of publication: 2 times/yr.
Circulation: 200
Available in microform: No

ADVERTISING INFORMATION

Advertising accepted: No

EDITORIAL DESCRIPTION

Scope: Publishes articles concerning the history and bibliography of studies on Giuseppe Mazzini and his movement.
Reviews books: Yes
Publishes notes: Yes
Languages accepted: Italian; English; French; German
Prints abstracts: No

SUBMISSION REQUIREMENTS

Restrictions on contributors: None
Author pays submission fee: No
Author pays page charges: No
Length of articles: No restrictions
Length of book reviews: No restrictions
Length of notes: No restrictions
Style: None
Number of copies required: 1
Copyright ownership: Domus Mazziniana
Rejected manuscripts: Not returned
Time before publication decision: 1 mo.
Time between decision and publication: 6 mos.
Number of reviewers: 2
Articles submitted per year: 20
Articles published per year: 5
Book reviews submitted per year: 120
Book reviews published per year: 90

(389)
*Bollettino dell'Atlante Linguistico Italiano

Lorenzo Massobrio, Editor
Ist. dell'Atlante Linguistico Italiano
Palazzo delle Facoltà Umanistische dell'Univ.
Via Sant'Ottavio, 20
10124 Torino, Italy

Telephone: (39) 11 874848
First published: 1933
Sponsoring organization: Soc. Filologica Friulana "G.I. Ascoli" di Udine; Univ. di Torino; Consiglio Nazionale delle Ricerche
MLA acronym: BALI

SUBSCRIPTION INFORMATION

Frequency of publication: Irregular
Circulation: 500
Available in microform: No
Subscription address: Opus Libri s.r.l., Via della Torretta 16, 50137 Florence, Italy
Subscription telephone: (39) 55 660833
Subscription fax: (39) 55 670604

ADVERTISING INFORMATION

Advertising accepted: No

EDITORIAL DESCRIPTION

Scope: Publishes information on the state of the work of the *Atlante Linguistico Italiano* as well as studies of a linguistic nature related to the *Atlas*.
Reviews books: Yes
Publishes notes: Yes
Languages accepted: Italian; French; Spanish
Prints abstracts: No
Author-anonymous submission: No

SUBMISSION REQUIREMENTS

Restrictions on contributors: None
Author pays submission fee: No
Author pays page charges: No
Length of articles: 40 pp. maximum
Number of copies required: 1
Copyright ownership: Univ. di Torino
Rejected manuscripts: Not returned
Time before publication decision: 1 mo.
Time between decision and publication: 6 mos.
Number of reviewers: 2

(390) Bollettino dell'Atlante Linguistico Mediterraneo

Gianfranco Folena & Manlio Cortelazzo, Editors
Comitato per L'Atlante Linguistico Mediterraneo
Fondazione G. Cini-Ist. di Lettere e Teatro
Isola di S. Giorgio Maggiore
30100 Venice, Italy

First published: 1959
Sponsoring organization: Fondazione G. Cini-CNRS It.
ISSN: 0067-9879
MLA acronym: BALM

SUBSCRIPTION INFORMATION

Frequency of publication: Annual
Available in microform: No
Subscription address: Casa Editrice Leo S. Olschki, Viuzzo del Pozzetto, C.P. 66, 50100 Florence, Italy

ADVERTISING INFORMATION

Advertising accepted: No

EDITORIAL DESCRIPTION

Scope: Publishes articles on Mediterranean nautical languages.
Reviews books: Yes
Publishes notes: Yes
Languages accepted: Italian; French; Spanish; English; German
Prints abstracts: No

SUBMISSION REQUIREMENTS

Author pays submission fee: No
Author pays page charges: No
Length of articles: 3,000 words
Length of book reviews: 1,000 words
Length of notes: 2,000 words
Style: MLA
Number of copies required: 1
Copyright ownership: Author
Time before publication decision: 3 mos.
Time between decision and publication: 18 mos.
Number of reviewers: 2
Articles submitted per year: 10
Articles published per year: 5
Book reviews submitted per year: 10
Book reviews published per year: 5
Notes submitted per year: 5
Notes published per year: 2

(391) *Bonner Arbeiten zur Deutschen Literatur

Benno von Wiese, Norbert Oellers, & Peter Pütz, Editors
Bouvier Verlag Herbert Grundmann
Postfach 1268
Am Hof 32
5300 Bonn 1, Germany

First published: 1957
ISSN: 0068-001X
MLA acronym: BADL

SUBSCRIPTION INFORMATION

Frequency of publication: Irregular
Available in microform: No
Subscription address: Vereinigte Verlagsauslieferung, P.O. Box 7777, 4830 Gütersloh, Germany

ADVERTISING INFORMATION

Advertising accepted: No

EDITORIAL DESCRIPTION

Scope: Publishes studies on German literature.
Reviews books: No
Publishes notes: No
Languages accepted: German
Prints abstracts: No

SUBMISSION REQUIREMENTS

Copyright ownership: Editor
Rejected manuscripts: Returned
Time before publication decision: 6 weeks

(392) *Bonner Historische Forschungen

Raymund Kottje, Editor
Historisches Seminar
Univ. Bonn
Konviktstr. 11
5300 Bonn 1, Germany

Telephone: (49) 228 735167
Fax: (49) 228 735579 (Univ. Bonn)
First published: 1952
Sponsoring organization: Univ. Bonn, Historisches Seminar
MLA acronym: BHF

SUBSCRIPTION INFORMATION

Frequency of publication: Irregular
Available in microform: No
Subscription address: Verlag Franz Schmitt, Kaiserstr. 99-101, Postfach 1831, 5200 Siegburg, Germany

ADVERTISING INFORMATION

Advertising accepted: No

EDITORIAL DESCRIPTION

Reviews books: No
Publishes notes: No
Languages accepted: German; all European languages
Prints abstracts: No

SUBMISSION REQUIREMENTS

Author pays submission fee: No
Author pays page charges: No
Copyright ownership: Verlag Franz Schmitt
Time between decision and publication: 1 yr.
Number of reviewers: 2-3

(393) *Bonniers Litterära Magasin

Maria Schottenius, Editor
Albert Bonniers Förlag AB
P.O. Box 3159
103 63 Stockholm 3,
Sweden

Telephone: (46) 8 229120
Fax: (46) 8 208451
First published: 1932
ISSN: 0005-3198
MLA acronym: BLM

SUBSCRIPTION INFORMATION

Frequency of publication: 6 times/yr.
Circulation: 8,500
Available in microform: No
Subscription address: Pressdata, P.O. Box 3263, 103 65 Stockholm 3, Sweden

ADVERTISING INFORMATION

Advertising accepted: Yes

EDITORIAL DESCRIPTION

Scope: Literary magazine
Reviews books: Yes
Publishes notes: Yes
Languages accepted: Swedish
Prints abstracts: No
Author-anonymous submission: No

SUBMISSION REQUIREMENTS

Restrictions on contributors: None
Author pays submission fee: No
Author pays page charges: No
Length of articles: 10 pp.
Length of book reviews: 3 pp.
Length of notes: No restrictions
Number of copies required: 1
Copyright ownership: Author
Rejected manuscripts: Returned
Time before publication decision: 2 mos.
Number of reviewers: 2-3
Articles submitted per year: 200-300
Articles published per year: 30-40
Book reviews submitted per year: 100
Book reviews published per year: 100
Notes submitted per year: 100-150
Notes published per year: 100-150

(394) *The Book Collector

Nicolas Barker, Editor
The Collector Ltd.
68 Neal St.
Covent Garden
London WC2H 9PA, England

Telephone: (44) 71 3795416
Fax: (44) 71 3790132
First published: 1952
ISSN: 0006-7237
MLA acronym: BC

SUBSCRIPTION INFORMATION

Frequency of publication: 4 times/yr.
Available in microform: Yes
Subscription price: $57.00/yr.
Year to which price refers: 1992

ADVERTISING INFORMATION

Advertising accepted: Yes

EDITORIAL DESCRIPTION

Scope: Focuses on book collecting and bibliography.
Reviews books: Yes
Publishes notes: Yes

Languages accepted: English
Prints abstracts: No

SUBMISSION REQUIREMENTS

Restrictions on contributors: None
Author pays submission fee: No
Length of articles: 3,000-5,000 words
Length of book reviews: 500-1,000 words
Length of notes: No restrictions
Style: None
Number of copies required: 1
Copyright ownership: Author
Rejected manuscripts: Returned
Number of reviewers: 3

(395)
Book Forum: An International Transdisciplinary Quarterly

Clarence Driskill, Editor
Crescent Publishing Co.
Box 585
Niantic, CT 06357

First published: 1974
ISSN: 0094-9426
MLA acronym: BForum

SUBSCRIPTION INFORMATION

Frequency of publication: 4 times/yr.
Circulation: 5,300
Available in microform: No

ADVERTISING INFORMATION

Advertising accepted: Yes

EDITORIAL DESCRIPTION

Scope: A transdisciplinary quarterly devoted to essays, reviews, and previews of current scholarly books. Noted scholars review the new books in the major disciplines that are of wide-ranging significance. Each issue contains book reviews, forthcoming scholarly books, essays, and review essays, arranged by subject.
Reviews books: Yes
Publishes notes: Yes
Languages accepted: English
Prints abstracts: No
Author-anonymous submission: No

SUBMISSION REQUIREMENTS

Restrictions on contributors: None
Author pays submission fee: No
Author pays page charges: No
Length of articles: 1,200-3,500 words
Length of book reviews: 500-800 words
Length of notes: 200-300 words
Style: MLA
Number of copies required: 1
Special requirements: Inquire before submission.
Copyright ownership: Author
Rejected manuscripts: Returned
Time before publication decision: 1 mo.
Time between decision and publication: 3-4 mos.
Number of reviewers: 3
Articles submitted per year: 400-600
Articles published per year: 80-120
Book reviews published per year: 150-200

(396)
Books at Brown

John H. Stanley, Editor
Friends of the Library
Brown Univ. Library
P.O. Box A
Providence, RI 02912

Telephone: 401 863-1518

First published: 1938
Sponsoring organization: Brown Univ., Friends of the Library
ISSN: 0147-0787
MLA acronym: BBr

SUBSCRIPTION INFORMATION

Frequency of publication: Annual
Circulation: 800
Available in microform: No

ADVERTISING INFORMATION

Advertising accepted: No

EDITORIAL DESCRIPTION

Scope: Prints articles and bibliographic essays resulting from research based on the collections in the Brown University Library. Also considers profiles of book collectors, articles on book collecting, fine printing, and graphic arts. Articles should appeal to a literate audience and should present a contribution to knowledge or a fresh appraisal based on scholarly research.
Reviews books: No
Publishes notes: No
Languages accepted: English
Prints abstracts: No
Author-anonymous submission: No

SUBMISSION REQUIREMENTS

Restrictions on contributors: None
Author pays submission fee: No
Author pays page charges: No
Length of articles: No restrictions
Style: MLA
Number of copies required: 2
Special requirements: Submit double-spaced typescript on 8 1/2 in. x 11 in. sheets, numbered consecutively with 1 1/2 in. margins, and footnotes in a separate section. Include a 50-word biographical sketch.
Copyright ownership: Brown Univ.
Rejected manuscripts: Returned
Time before publication decision: 2-3 mos.
Number of reviewers: 4
Articles submitted per year: 12-15
Articles published per year: 8-10

(397)
*Books at Iowa

Robert A. McCown, Margaret Richardson, & David E. Schoonover, Editors
Friends of the Univ. of Iowa Libraries
Univ. of Iowa
Iowa City, IA 52242

Telephone: 319 335-5921
Fax: 319 335-5830
E-mail: CADRMCTS@UIAMUS.Bitnet
First published: 1964
Sponsoring organization: Friends of the Univ. of Iowa Libraries
ISSN: 0006-7474
MLA acronym: BI

SUBSCRIPTION INFORMATION

Frequency of publication: 2 times/yr.
Circulation: 750
Available in microform: No
Subscription price: $25.00/yr.
Year to which price refers: 1992
Subscription address: Barbara I. Dewey, at the above address

ADVERTISING INFORMATION

Advertising accepted: No

EDITORIAL DESCRIPTION

Scope: Prints descriptions of resource materials available in the University of Iowa libraries.
Reviews books: No
Publishes notes: No
Languages accepted: English
Prints abstracts: No
Author-anonymous submission: No

SUBMISSION REQUIREMENTS

Restrictions on contributors: Articles are generally solicited.
Author pays submission fee: No
Author pays page charges: No
Length of articles: 3,000-8,000 words
Style: Chicago
Number of copies required: 1
Copyright ownership: Univ. of Iowa
Rejected manuscripts: Returned postpaid
Time before publication decision: 6 weeks
Time between decision and publication: 6-12 mos.
Number of reviewers: 3
Articles submitted per year: 8-10
Articles published per year: 6-8

(398)
*Books from Finland

Erkka Lehtola & Soila Lehtonen, Editors
P.O. Box 312
00171 Helsinki, Finland

Telephone: (358) 0 1357942
Fax: (358) 0 1357942
First published: 1967
Sponsoring organization: Helsingfors Universitetsbibliotek
ISSN: 0006-7490
MLA acronym: BF

SUBSCRIPTION INFORMATION

Frequency of publication: 4 times/yr.
Circulation: 1,300
Available in microform: No
Subscription price: $35.00/yr.
Year to which price refers: 1992

ADVERTISING INFORMATION

Advertising accepted: Yes
Advertising rates: 3,000 Fmk/full page

EDITORIAL DESCRIPTION

Scope: Publishes fiction, nonfiction, poetry, and drama written in Finnish, Swedish, or Lappish languages by Finnish writers, Lappish writers, and Swedish writers in Finland.
Reviews books: Yes
Publishes notes: Yes
Languages accepted: English; Finnish; Swedish
Prints abstracts: No
Author-anonymous submission: No

SUBMISSION REQUIREMENTS

Restrictions on contributors: Most contributions are commissioned.
Author pays submission fee: No
Author pays page charges: No
Length of articles: 900-3,000 words
Length of book reviews: 600-1,200 words
Length of notes: 600 words maximum
Number of copies required: 1
Copyright ownership: Author
Rejected manuscripts: Returned
Time before publication decision: 1 mo.
Time between decision and publication: 2 mos. minimum
Number of reviewers: 3

(399)
Books in Bosnia and Herzegovina: A Yugoslav Literary Journal

Tvrtko Kulenović, Editor
Petra Preradovića, 3
Sarajevo, Bosnia and Herzegovina

ISSN: 0352-1044
MLA acronym: BBH

SUBSCRIPTION INFORMATION

Circulation: 1,500

EDITORIAL DESCRIPTION

Scope: Publishes essays about writers from Bosnia and Herzegovina and includes excerpts from their works.

(400)
*Boston Review

Joshua Cohen, Editor
33 Harrison Ave., 2nd Floor
Boston, MA 02111

Telephone: 617 350-5353
First published: 1975
Sponsoring organization: Boston Critic, Inc.
ISSN: 0734-2306
MLA acronym: BRev

SUBSCRIPTION INFORMATION

Frequency of publication: 6 times/yr.
Circulation: 9,000
Available in microform: Yes
Subscription price: $15.00/yr., $25.00/2 yrs.
Year to which price refers: 1992

ADVERTISING INFORMATION

Advertising accepted: Yes
Advertising rates: $106.00/sixteenth page; $848.00/full page

EDITORIAL DESCRIPTION

Scope: The journal publishes critical articles on politics, literature and the arts and culture including music, dance, theater, painting, film, and photography.
Reviews books: Yes
Publishes notes: No
Languages accepted: English
Prints abstracts: No
Author-anonymous submission: No

SUBMISSION REQUIREMENTS

Author pays submission fee: No
Author pays page charges: No
Length of articles: 800-3,000 words
Length of book reviews: 800-1,000 words
Style: Chicago
Number of copies required: 1
Copyright ownership: Author
Rejected manuscripts: Returned; enclose SASE.
Time before publication decision: 8-10 weeks
Time between decision and publication: 2-6 mos.
Number of reviewers: 1-2
Articles submitted per year: 600
Articles published per year: 60
Book reviews submitted per year: 200
Book reviews published per year: 20

(401)
*Botswana Notes and Records

Doreen A. N. Nteta, Editor
Botswana Soc.
P.O. Box 71
Gaborone, Botswana

Telephone: (267) 351500
Fax: (267) 359321
First published: 1968
Sponsoring organization: Botswana Soc.
ISSN: 0525-5090
MLA acronym: BN&R

SUBSCRIPTION INFORMATION

Frequency of publication: Annual
Circulation: 1,500
Available in microform: No
Subscription price: £12.00 ($25.00)/yr.
Year to which price refers: 1992

ADVERTISING INFORMATION

Advertising accepted: No

EDITORIAL DESCRIPTION

Scope: Publishes papers and notes of archaeological, historical, linguistic, scientific, and other permanent interest concerning Botswana. Considers scholarly and nonscholarly items for publication. In particular, it is hoped that officers in the service of the Government of Botswana will make use of the journal to publish something of what they have learned during their period of service in Botswana.
Reviews books: Yes
Publishes notes: Yes
Languages accepted: English
Prints abstracts: No
Author-anonymous submission: No

SUBMISSION REQUIREMENTS

Restrictions on contributors: None
Author pays submission fee: No
Author pays page charges: No
Length of articles: 5,000-8,000 words
Length of book reviews: 1,000 words
Length of notes: 500 words
Style: Journal, see vol. 14 for details
Number of copies required: 1
Special requirements: Deadline for submission is 31 March; submit original typescript.
Copyright ownership: Author through Botswana Soc.
Rejected manuscripts: Returned at author's request
Time before publication decision: 3 mos.
Time between decision and publication: 9 mos.
Number of reviewers: 3-4
Articles submitted per year: 35
Articles published per year: 20-30
Book reviews submitted per year: 1-2
Book reviews published per year: 1-2
Notes submitted per year: 6-10
Notes published per year: 6-10

(402)
*Boundary 2: An International Journal of Literature and Culture

Paul A. Bové, Editor
Dept. of English
Univ. of Pittsburgh
Pittsburgh, PA 15260

Telephone: 412 624-6523
Fax: 412 624-6639
E-mail: Bove@pittvms
First published: 1972
Sponsoring organization: Dept. of English, Univ. of Pittsburgh
ISSN: 0190-3659
MLA acronym: BoundaryII

SUBSCRIPTION INFORMATION

Frequency of publication: 3 times/yr. (Fall, Winter, Spring)
Circulation: 1,250
Available in microform: No
Subscription price: $40.00/yr. institutions; $20.00/yr. individuals
Year to which price refers: 1991-92
Subscription address: Duke Univ. Press, 6697 College Station, Durham, NC 27708
Subscription telephone: 919 684-2173

ADVERTISING INFORMATION

Advertising accepted: Yes
Advertising rates: $85.00/half page; $150.00/full page

EDITORIAL DESCRIPTION

Scope: Publishes essays on the relation of literature to culture, on critical theory, and on cultural studies, especially feminism, minority, and third world studies. Essays should be informed by modern and postmodern criticism and theory. Also publishes review-essays on theory and literature.
Reviews books: Yes
Publishes notes: No
Languages accepted: English
Prints abstracts: No
Author-anonymous submission: No

SUBMISSION REQUIREMENTS

Restrictions on contributors: None
Author pays submission fee: No
Author pays page charges: No
Length of articles: 20-40 pp.
Length of book reviews: 15-18 pp.
Style: Chicago
Number of copies required: 2
Special requirements: Submit double-spaced endnotes. Quotations should be double-spaced.
Copyright ownership: Duke Univ. Press
Rejected manuscripts: Returned; enclose return postage.
Time before publication decision: 3-6 mos.
Time between decision and publication: 6-9 mos.
Number of reviewers: 2 minimum
Articles submitted per year: 200-250
Articles published per year: 40
Book reviews submitted per year: 20
Book reviews published per year: 6-10

(403)
*Brahmavidya, The Adyar Library Bulletin

Radha Burnier, K. Kunjunni Raja, E. R. Sreekrishna Sarma, K. V. Sarma, & S. Sankaranarayanan, Editors
Adyar Library and Research Centre
Theosophical Soc.
Adyar, Madras 600020, India

First published: 1937
Sponsoring organization: Adyar Library & Research Centre, The Theosophical Soc.
ISSN: 0001-910X
MLA acronym: AdLB

SUBSCRIPTION INFORMATION

Frequency of publication: Annual
Circulation: 400
Available in microform: No
Subscription address: Librarian, at the above address

ADVERTISING INFORMATION

Advertising accepted: No

EDITORIAL DESCRIPTION

Scope: Publishes studies on religion, philosophy, civilizations, and various aspects of Sanskrit and other Oriental literatures; includes ancient texts and English translations or studies of those texts.
Reviews books: Yes
Publishes notes: Yes
Languages accepted: English; Sanskrit; French; German
Prints abstracts: No
Author-anonymous submission: No

SUBMISSION REQUIREMENTS

Restrictions on contributors: None
Author pays submission fee: No
Author pays page charges: No
Length of articles: 20-25 printed pp. maximum
Length of book reviews: 500 words
Length of notes: No restrictions
Style: Oxford for English; Journal for Sanskrit
Number of copies required: 1
Special requirements: Submit original double-spaced typescript.
Copyright ownership: Adyar Library and Research Centre
Rejected manuscripts: Returned
Time before publication decision: 3-4 mos.
Time between decision and publication: 15 mos.
Number of reviewers: Editorial Board
Articles submitted per year: 10
Articles published per year: 6-8
Book reviews submitted per year: 60
Book reviews published per year: 50
Notes submitted per year: 2
Notes published per year: 2

(404)
Brain and Language

Harry A. Whitaker, Editor
Editorial Office
1250 Sixth Ave., 7th floor
San Diego, CA 92101

First published: 1974
ISSN: 0093-934X
MLA acronym: B&L

SUBSCRIPTION INFORMATION

Frequency of publication: 8 times/yr. in 2 vols.
Circulation: 2,000
Available in microform: No
Subscription price: $296.00/yr. US & Canada; $370.00/yr. elsewhere
Year to which price refers: 1993
Subscription address: Academic Press, 6277 Sea Harbor Dr., Orlando, FL 32887-4900

ADVERTISING INFORMATION

Advertising accepted: Yes

EDITORIAL DESCRIPTION

Scope: Publishes original research articles, case histories, critical reviews, and scholarly notes; each contribution will be concerned with human language or communication related to any aspect of the brain or brain function. Each will have theoretical import, either formulating new hypotheses, or supporting or refuting new or previously established ones. The interdisciplinary focus includes the fields of neurology, linguistics, neurophysiology, psychology, neuroanatomy, psychiatry, neurosurgery, and speech pathology. Manuscripts of several different types are solicited: regular articles, single or multiple case history studies, critical reviews of books of interest to the journal's readership, and short, scholarly notes and comments discussing issues of topical interest.
Reviews books: Yes
Publishes notes: Yes
Languages accepted: English

Prints abstracts: Yes
Author-anonymous submission: Yes, at author's request

SUBMISSION REQUIREMENTS

Restrictions on contributors: None
Author pays submission fee: No
Author pays page charges: No
Length of articles: No restrictions
Length of book reviews: No restrictions
Length of notes: 1-10 pp.
Style: Journal
Number of copies required: 4
Special requirements: Include a 100-word abstract.
Copyright ownership: Assigned by author to Academic Press
Rejected manuscripts: Returned
Time before publication decision: 3 mos.
Time between decision and publication: 9 mos.
Number of reviewers: 2
Articles submitted per year: 200
Articles published per year: 80-90
Book reviews published per year: 5
Notes published per year: 10

(405)
*Brasil/Brazil: Revista de Literatura Brasileira/A Journal of Brazilian Literature

Nelson H. Vieira, Regina Zilberman, Luiz Fernando Valente, & Maria da Glória Bordoni, Editors
Center for Portuguese & Brazilian Studies
Brown Univ.—Box 0
Providence, RI 02912

Additional editorial address: Editora Mercado Aberto Ltda., Rua da Conceição 195—1º-andar, 90037 Porto Alegre-RS, Brazil
Telephone: 401 863-3042; Brazil: (55) 512 214022
Fax: 401 863-3700; Brazil: (55) 512 218601
First published: 1988
Sponsoring organization: Brown Univ.; Pontifícia Univ. Católica, Rio Grande do Sul
ISSN: 0103-751X
MLA acronym: BslBzl

SUBSCRIPTION INFORMATION

Frequency of publication: 2 times/yr.
Available in microform: No
Subscription price: $40.00/yr. institutions; $15.00/yr. individuals
Year to which price refers: 1992

ADVERTISING INFORMATION

Advertising accepted: No

EDITORIAL DESCRIPTION

Scope: Publishes articles on Brazilian literature and in comparative literature with a focus on Brazilian literature, as well as book reviews, English language translations of Brazilian literature, and original prose and poetry by Brazilian authors.
Reviews books: Yes
Publishes notes: No
Languages accepted: English; Portuguese
Prints abstracts: Yes
Author-anonymous submission: Yes

SUBMISSION REQUIREMENTS

Author pays submission fee: No
Author pays page charges: No
Length of articles: 6,000-7,500 words
Length of book reviews: 500-750 words
Style: MLA preferred
Number of copies required: 2
Special requirements: Submit original typescript and 1 copy. Include a 50-100 word abstract.
Rejected manuscripts: Returned
Time before publication decision: 6-12 mos.

Time between decision and publication: 3-6 mos.
Number of reviewers: 2
Articles submitted per year: 20
Articles published per year: 8-10
Book reviews submitted per year: 8
Book reviews published per year: 6

(406)
*Braunschweiger Anglistische Arbeiten

Viktor Link & H.-J. Possin, Editors
Technische Univ. Braunschweig
Seminar für Anglistik & Amerikanistik
Mühlenpfordtstr. 22/23
3300 Braunschweig, Germany

Telephone: (49) 531 3913500; (49) 531 3913507
Fax: (49) 531 3915933
First published: 1970
MLA acronym: BAA

SUBSCRIPTION INFORMATION

Frequency of publication: Irregular
Circulation: 150-200
Available in microform: No

ADVERTISING INFORMATION

Advertising accepted: No

EDITORIAL DESCRIPTION

Scope: Publishes monographs on the English language and on literature written in English.
Reviews books: No
Publishes notes: No
Languages accepted: English; German
Prints abstracts: No
Author-anonymous submission: No

SUBMISSION REQUIREMENTS

Author pays submission fee: No
Author pays page charges: No
Length of books: 100-150 pp.
Style: MLA
Number of copies required: 1
Copyright ownership: Author after 2 yrs.
Rejected manuscripts: Returned
Time before publication decision: 3 mos. maximum
Time between decision and publication: 2 mos.
Number of reviewers: 2-3
Books submitted per year: 1-3

(407)
*The Brecht Yearbook/Das Brecht-Jahrbuch

Marc Silberman, Managing Editor
Dept. of German
818 Van Hise Hall
Univ. of Wisconsin
Madison, WI 53706

Telephone: 608 262-2192
E-mail: Marcs@macc.wisc.edu
First published: 1971
Sponsoring organization: International Brecht Soc.
ISSN: 0734-8665
MLA acronym: BrechtJ

SUBSCRIPTION INFORMATION

Frequency of publication: Annual
Circulation: 400
Available in microform: No
Subscription price: $30.00/yr. institutions; $20.00-$25.00/yr. individuals; $15.00/yr. students
Year to which price refers: 1992

Subscription address: Ward B. Lewis, Secretary/Treasurer, International Brecht Soc., Dept. of Germanic & Slavic Languages, Univ. of Georgia, Athens, GA 30602
Subscription telephone: 404 542-3663

ADVERTISING INFORMATION

Advertising accepted: No

EDITORIAL DESCRIPTION

Scope: Promotes discussion of issues related to theater performance, theory and history, in particular with reference to Bertolt Brecht.
Reviews books: Yes
Publishes notes: No
Languages accepted: English; French; German; Spanish
Prints abstracts: Yes
Author-anonymous submission: No

SUBMISSION REQUIREMENTS

Restrictions on contributors: Book reviews are commissioned.
Author pays submission fee: No
Author pays page charges: No
Length of articles: 6,000-7,000 words
Length of book reviews: 1,000 words
Style: MLA
Number of copies required: 3
Copyright ownership: International Brecht Soc.
Rejected manuscripts: Not returned
Time before publication decision: 4-9 mos.
Time between decision and publication: 8-12 mos.
Number of reviewers: 3 minimum
Articles submitted per year: 30-40
Articles published per year: 10
Book reviews published per year: 10

(408)
*Brenner-Studien

Walter Methlagl, Sigurd Paul Scheichl, Wolfgang Wiesmüller, & Allan Janik, Editors
Brenner-Archiv
Univ. Innsbruck
Innrain 52
6020 Innsbruck, Austria

Telephone: (43) 512 5073471
First published: 1969
MLA acronym: BrenS

SUBSCRIPTION INFORMATION

Frequency of publication: Irregular
Available in microform: No
Subscription address: Haymon-Verlag, Koch-Str. 10, 6020 Innsbruck, Austria

ADVERTISING INFORMATION

Advertising accepted: No

EDITORIAL DESCRIPTION

Scope: Publishes monographs on the periodical *Der Brenner* and its contributors (1910-1954).
Reviews books: No
Publishes notes: No
Languages accepted: German
Prints abstracts: No
Author-anonymous submission: No

SUBMISSION REQUIREMENTS

Restrictions on contributors: None
Author pays submission fee: No
Author pays page charges: No
Style: None
Number of copies required: 2
Copyright ownership: Haymon-Verlag or author
Rejected manuscripts: Returned
Time before publication decision: 6 mos.
Time between decision and publication: 1 yr.

Number of reviewers: 2-5
Books submitted per year: 1-2
Books published per year: 1-2

(409)
*Bridges: A Senegalese Journal of English Studies/Revue Sénégalaise d'Etudes Anglaises

Mamadou Kandji, Editor
Inst. Sénégalo-Britannique
rue du 18 juin
B.P. 35
Dakar, Senegal

Telephone: (221) 224023; (221) 222870
First published: 1990
Sponsoring organization: Inst. Sénégalo-Britannique
ISSN: 0850-1335
MLA acronym: Bridges

SUBSCRIPTION INFORMATION

Frequency of publication: 2 times/yr.
Available in microform: No
Subscription price: 20 F/yr. Senegal; 30 F/yr. elsewhere
Year to which price refers: 1992

ADVERTISING INFORMATION

Advertising accepted: Yes
Advertising rates: $20.00/full page

EDITORIAL DESCRIPTION

Scope: Publishes articles on English-language literature, comparative literature, literary theory, linguistics, and English language teaching. Includes studies on English, American, and African literatures, and English for specific purposes.
Reviews books: Yes
Publishes notes: Yes
Languages accepted: English; French
Prints abstracts: No
Author-anonymous submission: No

SUBMISSION REQUIREMENTS

Restrictions on contributors: None
Author pays submission fee: No
Author pays page charges: No
Length of articles: 7,200 words
Length of book reviews: 480 words
Length of notes: 1 p.
Style: MLA
Number of copies required: 3
Copyright ownership: Author
Rejected manuscripts: Not returned
Time before publication decision: 2 mos. maximum
Time between decision and publication: 3-4 mos.
Number of reviewers: 2
Articles submitted per year: 41
Articles published per year: 20
Book reviews submitted per year: 5
Book reviews published per year: 2
Notes submitted per year: 2
Notes published per year: 2

(410)
*Brigham Young University Studies

John W. Welch, Editor
522 JRCB
Brigham Young Univ.
Provo, UT 84602

Telephone: 801 378-6691
Fax: 801 378-3595
First published: 1959
Sponsoring organization: Brigham Young Univ.
ISSN: 0007-0106

MLA acronym: BYUS

SUBSCRIPTION INFORMATION

Frequency of publication: 4 times/yr. (Winter, Spring, Summer, Fall)
Circulation: 3,000
Available in microform: Yes
Subscription price: $10.00/yr.
Year to which price refers: 1992

ADVERTISING INFORMATION

Advertising accepted: No

EDITORIAL DESCRIPTION

Scope: Seeks contributions in thought, letters, history, theology, from a latter-day saint point of view. Articles should conform to the highest scholarly standards, but should be written for the informed nonspecialist. High quality fiction, poetry, drama, and personal essays are also welcome.
Reviews books: Yes
Publishes notes: Yes
Languages accepted: English
Prints abstracts: No
Author-anonymous submission: No

SUBMISSION REQUIREMENTS

Restrictions on contributors: None
Author pays submission fee: No
Author pays page charges: No
Length of articles: 5,000 words maximum
Length of book reviews: 500-700 words
Length of notes: 200-300 words
Style: Chicago
Number of copies required: 2
Special requirements: Submit original typescript.
Copyright ownership: Journal; reverts to author upon publication
Rejected manuscripts: Returned; enclose return postage.
Time before publication decision: 2-4 mos.
Time between decision and publication: 1 yr.
Number of reviewers: 3-4
Articles submitted per year: 75-125
Articles published per year: 30-40
Book reviews published per year: 20-30
Notes submitted per year: 10-20
Notes published per year: 5-10

(411)
*British Journal for Eighteenth-Century Studies

Brean Hammond, Editor
Dept. of English
Univ. College of Wales, Aberystwyth
Hugh Owen Bldg.
Penglais
Aberystwyth SY23 3DY, Wales

Telephone: (44) 970 622534
Fax: (44) 970 622530
E-mail: BBH@wk.ac.aber
First published: 1978
Sponsoring organization: British Soc. for Eighteenth-Century Studies
ISSN: 0141-876X
MLA acronym: BJECS

SUBSCRIPTION INFORMATION

Frequency of publication: 2 times/yr. (Spring, Fall)
Circulation: 500
Available in microform: Yes
Subscription address: Voltaire Foundation, Taylor Inst., Oxford OX1 3NA, England

ADVERTISING INFORMATION

Advertising accepted: Yes

EDITORIAL DESCRIPTION

Scope: Publishes articles on 18th-century studies.
Reviews books: Yes
Publishes notes: No
Languages accepted: English
Prints abstracts: No

SUBMISSION REQUIREMENTS

Author pays submission fee: No
Author pays page charges: No
Length of articles: 6,000 words
Length of book reviews: 300-700 words
Style: Modern Humanities Research Assn.
Number of copies required: 1
Copyright ownership: Author
Rejected manuscripts: Returned
Time before publication decision: 3 mos.
Time between decision and publication: 2 yrs.
Number of reviewers: 1-3
Articles published per year: 13
Book reviews published per year: 90

(412)
*British Journal of Aesthetics

T. J. Diffey, Editor
Univ. of Sussex
School of Cultural & Community Studies
Arts Building, Falmer
Brighton, BN1 9QN, England

First published: 1960
Sponsoring organization: British Soc. of Aesthetics
ISSN: 0007-0904
MLA acronym: BJA

SUBSCRIPTION INFORMATION

Frequency of publication: 4 times/yr. (Jan., Apr., July, Oct.)
Circulation: 1,500
Available in microform: Yes
Subscription price: £48.00/yr. United Kingdom & Europe; $100.00/yr. elsewhere
Year to which price refers: 1992
Subscription address: Oxford Univ. Press, Journals Subscription Dept., Pinkhill House, Southfield Rd., Eynsham, Oxford OX8 1JJ, England
Additional subscription address: Individuals desiring to subscribe by membership to the British Soc. of Aesthetics should contact Richard Woodfield, Hon. Sec., BSA, School of Art & Design, Nottingham Polytechnic, Burton St., Nottingham NG1 4BU, England
Subscription telephone: (44) 865 882283
Subscription fax: (44) 865 882890

ADVERTISING INFORMATION

Advertising accepted: Yes
Advertising rates: Request from publisher.

EDITORIAL DESCRIPTION

Scope: Promotes study, research, and discussion in aesthetics as a theoretical study of the arts and related types of experience, predominantly from a philosophical standpoint, but psychological, sociological, scientific, historical, critical, or educational viewpoints are also admitted.
Reviews books: Yes
Publishes notes: No
Languages accepted: English
Prints abstracts: No
Author-anonymous submission: Yes, if paper is prepared for it

SUBMISSION REQUIREMENTS

Restrictions on contributors: Unsolicited book reviews are not accepted.
Author pays submission fee: No

Author pays page charges: No, except for illustrations
Length of articles: 5,500 words
Length of book reviews: 900 words
Style: Journal
Number of copies required: 1
Special requirements: Double space typescript including indented quotations and references. Cost of reproducing illustrations and photographs is charged to the author.
Copyright ownership: Oxford Univ. Press
Rejected manuscripts: Returned; enclose return postage.
Time before publication decision: 3 mos. maximum
Time between decision and publication: 12-18 mos.
Number of reviewers: 1-2
Articles published per year: 30-35
Book reviews published per year: 35-40

(413)
*British Journal of Psychology

Antony J. Chapman, Editor
Dept. of Psychology
Univ. of Leeds
Leeds LS2 9JT, England

First published: 1904
Sponsoring organization: British Psychological Soc.
ISSN: 0007-1269
MLA acronym: BJP

SUBSCRIPTION INFORMATION

Frequency of publication: 4 times/yr. (Feb., May, Aug., Nov.)
Circulation: 3,900
Available in microform: Yes
Subscription address: Distribution Center, Blackhorse Rd., Letchworth, Hertfordshire SG6 1HN, England

ADVERTISING INFORMATION

Advertising accepted: Yes

EDITORIAL DESCRIPTION

Scope: Publishes articles on all aspects of psychology.
Reviews books: Yes
Publishes notes: No
Languages accepted: English
Prints abstracts: Yes
Author-anonymous submission: Yes

SUBMISSION REQUIREMENTS

Restrictions on contributors: None
Author pays submission fee: No
Author pays page charges: No
Length of articles: 5,000-7,000 words
Length of book reviews: 700 words
Style: Journal
Number of copies required: 4
Copyright ownership: British Psychological Soc.
Rejected manuscripts: Returned
Time before publication decision: 4 mos.
Time between decision and publication: 9 mos.;
Number of reviewers: 2-3
Articles submitted per year: 150
Articles published per year: 46
Book reviews published per year: 60

(414)
*The British Library Journal

C. J. Wright, Editor
The British Library
Great Russell St.
London WC1B 3DG, England

Telephone: (44) 71 3237516
Fax: (44) 71 3237754
First published: 1975
Sponsoring organization: British Library
ISSN: 0305-5167
MLA acronym: BLJ

SUBSCRIPTION INFORMATION

Frequency of publication: 2 times/yr. (Spring, Fall)
Circulation: 730
Available in microform: No
Subscription price: £35.00/yr. United Kingdom; £40.00/yr. elsewhere
Year to which price refers: 1992
Subscription address: Publication Sales Unit, The British Library, Boston Spa Wetherby, West Yorkshire LS23 7BQ, England

ADVERTISING INFORMATION

Advertising accepted: Yes
Advertising rates: £150.00/half page; £250.00/full page

EDITORIAL DESCRIPTION

Scope: Publishes articles partly or entirely based on the British Library's holdings and its history.
Reviews books: No
Publishes notes: Yes
Languages accepted: English
Prints abstracts: No
Author-anonymous submission: No

SUBMISSION REQUIREMENTS

Restrictions on contributors: None
Author pays submission fee: No
Author pays page charges: No
Length of articles: 1,000-10,000 words
Length of notes: 300-1,000 words
Style: Journal
Number of copies required: 2
Special requirements: Submit typescript.
Copyright ownership: British Library Board
Rejected manuscripts: Returned
Time before publication decision: 3-6 mos.
Time between decision and publication: 6-24 mos.
Number of reviewers: 2-3
Articles published per year: 10-12
Notes published per year: 4

(415)
*Brno Studies in English

Josef Hladký & Jan Firbas, Editors
Sbornik praci a Spisy Filozofické Fakulty
Masarykovy Univ.
A. Novaka 1
660 88 Brno, Czech Republic

Telephone: (42) 5 750050
Fax: (42) 5 753050
First published: 1959
ISSN: 0231-5351
MLA acronym: BSE

SUBSCRIPTION INFORMATION

Frequency of publication: Once every 2 yrs.
Circulation: 500
Available in microform: No
Subscription address: Knihkupectoí-Antikvanát, Miroslav Manžel, Dittrichova 13, 120 00 Prague 2, Czech Republic

Additional subscription address: Outside Czech & Slovak Republics: Knizní Velkoobchod, Opatovická 18, 10381 Prague 1 Nové Mesto, Czech Republic

ADVERTISING INFORMATION

Advertising accepted: No

EDITORIAL DESCRIPTION

Scope: Focuses on English and American language and literatures.
Reviews books: Yes
Publishes notes: No
Languages accepted: English
Prints abstracts: Yes
Author-anonymous submission: No

SUBMISSION REQUIREMENTS

Restrictions on contributors: Most contributors are members of Brno Dept. of English.
Author pays submission fee: No
Author pays page charges: No
Length of articles: No restrictions
Length of book reviews: 2,000 words
Number of copies required: 2
Special requirements: Submit original typescript plus 1 copy.
Copyright ownership: Masarykovy Univ.
Rejected manuscripts: Not returned
Time before publication decision: 3 mos.
Time between decision and publication: 1 yr.
Number of reviewers: 2
Articles submitted per year: 5
Articles published per year: 5
Book reviews submitted per year: 5
Book reviews published per year: 5

(416)
*Brontë Society Transactions

Mark R. D. Seaward, Editor
Brontë Parsonage
Haworth
Keighley
West Yorkshire BD22 8DR, England

Telephone: (44) 535 642323
Fax: (44) 535 647131
First published: 1895
Sponsoring organization: Brontë Soc.
ISSN: 0309-7765
MLA acronym: BST

SUBSCRIPTION INFORMATION

Frequency of publication: 2 times/yr.
Circulation: 3,300
Available in microform: Yes
Subscription price: £6.00/yr. United Kingdom & Europe; £10.00/yr. elsewhere
Year to which price refers: 1992

ADVERTISING INFORMATION

Advertising accepted: Yes
Advertising rates: £125.00/half page; £250.00/full page

EDITORIAL DESCRIPTION

Scope: Publishes articles on the life and works of the Brontë family and their circle.
Reviews books: Yes
Publishes notes: Yes
Languages accepted: English
Prints abstracts: No
Author-anonymous submission: No

SUBMISSION REQUIREMENTS

Author pays submission fee: No
Author pays page charges: No
Length of articles: No restrictions
Number of copies required: 2
Copyright ownership: Publisher
Rejected manuscripts: Returned

Time before publication decision: 3-4 mos.
Time between decision and publication: 3-6 mos.
Number of reviewers: 2
Articles submitted per year: 40
Articles published per year: 20
Book reviews submitted per year: 8
Book reviews published per year: 8

(417)
*Brotéria: Cultura e Informação

António da Silva, Editor
R. Maestro António Taborda, 14
1293 Lisbon Codex, Portugal

Telephone: (351) 1 3961660
First published: 1925
ISSN: 0870-7618
MLA acronym: Brotéria

SUBSCRIPTION INFORMATION

Frequency of publication: 10 times/yr.
Available in microform: No
Subscription price: 2,500 Esc/yr. Portugal; $35.00/yr. US
Year to which price refers: 1992

ADVERTISING INFORMATION

Advertising accepted: No

EDITORIAL DESCRIPTION

Scope: Publishes articles on humanities, philosophy, and theology.
Reviews books: Yes
Publishes notes: Yes
Languages accepted: Portuguese
Prints abstracts: No

SUBMISSION REQUIREMENTS

Restrictions on contributors: Submission is by invitation.
Articles published per year: 100
Book reviews published per year: 300

(418)
Browning Society Notes

Michael Meredith, Editor
English Dept.
Eton College
Windsor
Berkshire SL4 6HB, England

First published: 1970
Sponsoring organization: Browning Soc.
ISSN: 0950-6349
MLA acronym: BSNotes

SUBSCRIPTION INFORMATION

Frequency of publication: 2 times/yr.
Circulation: 200
Available in microform: No

ADVERTISING INFORMATION

Advertising accepted: Yes

EDITORIAL DESCRIPTION

Scope: Studies the lives and works of Robert Browning, Elizabeth Barrett Browning, and other Victorian writers.
Reviews books: Yes
Publishes notes: No
Languages accepted: English
Prints abstracts: No
Author-anonymous submission: No

SUBMISSION REQUIREMENTS

Author pays submission fee: No
Author pays page charges: No
Length of articles: 7,500 words
Length of book reviews: 2,000 words
Style: MLA
Number of copies required: 2
Copyright ownership: Author & Browning Soc.
Rejected manuscripts: Returned; enclose return postage or international reply coupons
Time before publication decision: 6 weeks maximum
Time between decision and publication: 6 mos.
Number of reviewers: 2

(419)
*Buchreihe der Anglia

Helmut Gneuss, Hans Käsmann, Erwin Wolff, & Theodor Wolpers, Editors
Max Niemeyer Verlag
Postfach 2140
7400 Tübingen, Germany

Telephone: (49) 7071 81104
Fax: (49) 7071 87419
First published: 1952
ISSN: 0340-5435
MLA acronym: BAnglia

SUBSCRIPTION INFORMATION

Frequency of publication: Irregular
Available in microform: No

ADVERTISING INFORMATION

Advertising accepted: No

EDITORIAL DESCRIPTION

Scope: Publishes monographs on English language; medieval and modern English literature; American literature; Commonwealth literature.
Reviews books: No
Publishes notes: No
Languages accepted: German; English
Prints abstracts: No
Author-anonymous submission: No

SUBMISSION REQUIREMENTS

Restrictions on contributors: None
Author pays submission fee: No
Length of books: No restrictions
Style: Series
Number of copies required: 2
Copyright ownership: Max Niemeyer Verlag
Rejected manuscripts: Returned
Time before publication decision: 6 mos.
Time between decision and publication: 6-12 mos.
Number of reviewers: 2 minimum
Books submitted per year: 3-4
Books published per year: 1-2

(420)
*Buchreihe der Zeitschrift für Celtische Philologie

Karl Horst Schmidt, Editor
Sprachwissenschaftliches Inst. der Univ. Bonn
An der Schlosskirche 2
5300 Bonn 1, Germany

First published: 1959
ISSN: 0931-4261
MLA acronym: BZCP

SUBSCRIPTION INFORMATION

Frequency of publication: Irregular
Available in microform: No

Subscription address: Max Niemeyer Verlag, Postfach 2140, 7400 Tübingen, Germany

ADVERTISING INFORMATION

Advertising accepted: No

EDITORIAL DESCRIPTION

Scope: Publishes monographs in the fields of Celtic philology and linguistics.
Reviews books: No
Publishes notes: No
Languages accepted: German; English; French
Prints abstracts: No
Author-anonymous submission: No

SUBMISSION REQUIREMENTS

Restrictions on contributors: None
Author pays submission fee: No
Author pays page charges: No
Style: None
Number of copies required: 1
Copyright ownership: Max Niemeyer Verlag
Rejected manuscripts: Returned
Time before publication decision: 2-6 mos.
Time between decision and publication: 3-12 mos.
Number of reviewers: 1-3

(421)
*Bucknell Review: A Scholarly Journal of Letters, Arts and Sciences

Pauline Fletcher, Editor
Bucknell Univ.
Lewisburg, PA 17837

Telephone: 717 524-1184
Fax: 717 524-3760
First published: 1941
Sponsoring organization: Bucknell Univ. Press
ISSN: 0007-2869
MLA acronym: BuR

SUBSCRIPTION INFORMATION

Frequency of publication: 2 times/yr.
Circulation: 700
Available in microform: No
Subscription price: $32.00/yr.
Year to which price refers: 1992
Subscription address: Associated Univ. Presses, 440 Forsgate Dr., Cranbury, NJ 08512
Subscription telephone: 609 655-4770
Subscription fax: 609 655-8366

ADVERTISING INFORMATION

Advertising accepted: No

EDITORIAL DESCRIPTION

Scope: A scholarly, interdisciplinary journal, each issue of which is devoted to a major theme or movement in the humanities or sciences.
Reviews books: No
Publishes notes: No
Languages accepted: English
Prints abstracts: No
Author-anonymous submission: No

SUBMISSION REQUIREMENTS

Restrictions on contributors: None
Author pays submission fee: No
Author pays page charges: No
Length of articles: 15-25 double-spaced typescript pp.
Style: Chicago
Number of copies required: 1
Copyright ownership: Journal
Rejected manuscripts: Returned; enclose SASE.
Time before publication decision: 20-60 days
Time between decision and publication: 1-2 yrs.
Number of reviewers: 2-4

Articles submitted per year: 260
Articles published per year: 18-24

(422)
Bŭlgarski Ezik: Organ na Instituta za Bŭlgarski Ezik pri Bŭlgarskata Akademiia na Naukite

K. Ivanova, Sv. Ivanchev, Iv. Kochev, D. Mircheva, V. Stankov, Kr. Cholakova
Inst. za Bŭlgarski Ezik pri BAN
ul. Chapaev 52, bl. 17
1113 Sofia, Bulgaria

First published: 1951
Sponsoring organization: Inst. za Bŭlgarski Ezik pri Bŭlgarskata, Bŭlgarska Akademija na Naukite
ISSN: 0005-4283
MLA acronym: BE

SUBSCRIPTION INFORMATION

Frequency of publication: 6 times/yr.
Circulation: 2,550
Available in microform: No

ADVERTISING INFORMATION

Advertising accepted: No

EDITORIAL DESCRIPTION

Scope: Publishes articles, discussions, notes, and views on phonological, grammatical, and lexical problems of modern Bulgarian and its historical development, as well as discussions on writers' styles. Also contains commentary on the usage of words and structures.
Reviews books: Yes
Publishes notes: Yes
Languages accepted: Bulgarian
Prints abstracts: No

SUBMISSION REQUIREMENTS

Restrictions on contributors: None
Author pays submission fee: No
Author pays page charges: No
Length of articles: 15 pp
Length of book reviews: 12 pp.
Length of notes: 10 pp.
Number of copies required: 2
Copyright ownership: Author
Rejected manuscripts: Not returned
Time before publication decision: 3 mos.
Time between decision and publication: 9 mos.
Number of reviewers: 2
Articles submitted per year: 220
Articles published per year: 140
Book reviews submitted per year: 15
Book reviews published per year: 15
Notes submitted per year: 20
Notes published per year: 20

(423)
*Bulletin Baudelairien

Claude Pichois & James S. Patty, Editors
Box 6325, Station B
Vanderbilt Univ.
Nashville, TN 37235

Telephone: 615 343-0372
First published: 1965
Sponsoring organization: Vanderbilt Univ., W. T. Bandy Center for Baudelaire Studies
ISSN: 0007-4128
MLA acronym: BBaud

SUBSCRIPTION INFORMATION

Frequency of publication: 2 times/yr.
Circulation: 300
Available in microform: No

Subscription price: $10.00/yr. N. America; $14.00/yr. elsewhere
Year to which price refers: 1992

ADVERTISING INFORMATION

Advertising accepted: No

EDITORIAL DESCRIPTION

Scope: Publishes documents and articles specifically dealing with Baudelaire.
Reviews books: No
Publishes notes: Yes
Languages accepted: French
Prints abstracts: No
Author-anonymous submission: No

SUBMISSION REQUIREMENTS

Restrictions on contributors: None
Author pays submission fee: No
Author pays page charges: No
Length of articles: 4,500 words maximum
Length of notes: 300-500 words
Style: RHLF (French)
Number of copies required: 1
Copyright ownership: Author
Rejected manuscripts: Returned
Time before publication decision: 4 mos.
Time between decision and publication: 6 mos.
Number of reviewers: 3-4
Articles submitted per year: 6-10
Articles published per year: 5-8
Notes submitted per year: 3-6
Notes published per year: 2-5

(424)
*Bulletin Bibliographique de la Société Internationale Arthurienne

Philippe Ménard & Douglas Kelly, Editors
1, rue Victor-Cousin
75005 Paris, France

First published: 1949
Sponsoring organization: International Arthurian Soc.
ISSN: 0074-1388
MLA acronym: BBSIA

SUBSCRIPTION INFORMATION

Frequency of publication: Annual
Circulation: 1,500
Available in microform: No
Subscription address: Douglas Kelly, International Secretary, Dept. of French & Italian, Univ. of Wisconsin, Madison, WI 53706

ADVERTISING INFORMATION

Advertising accepted: No

EDITORIAL DESCRIPTION

Scope: Lists all books and articles published on subjects of direct interest to the study of Brittany. Also includes articles dealing with courtly love or the style and structure of romances, but only as they relate to Arthurian studies. Includes studies on the Arthurian tradition after the 16th century. Does not publish works of a fictional nature or works generally dealing with the history of literature or civilization.
Reviews books: Yes, as part of the critical bibliography only
Publishes notes: Yes
Languages accepted: English; French; German; Italian; Spanish
Prints abstracts: No

SUBMISSION REQUIREMENTS

Restrictions on contributors: Contributors must be members of the International Arthurian Soc.
Author pays submission fee: No

Author pays submission fee: No
Author pays page charges: Yes, for articles over 20 pp.
Length of articles: 1,500-2,000 words
Length of book reviews: 200 words maximum
Style: MLA preferred
Number of copies required: 1
Special requirements: Consult with editor prior to submission.
Copyright ownership: Journal
Rejected manuscripts: Returned
Time before publication decision: 2-4 mos.
Time between decision and publication: 1 yr.
Number of reviewers: 2
Articles submitted per year: 2-3
Articles published per year: 2-3
Notes published per year: 3-4

(425)
**Bulletin Bibliographique du C.R.E.D.I.F. (Centre de Recherche et d'Etude pour la Diffusion du Français Service de Documentation)

R. Adda & C. Robine, Editors
L'Ecole Normale Supérieure de Fontenay-St.-Cloud
Grille d'Honneur
Le Parc
92211 St.-Cloud Cédex, France

First published: 1972
Sponsoring organization: Ecole Normale Supérieure de Fontenay-St.-Cloud
ISSN: 0765-1937
MLA acronym: CREDIF

SUBSCRIPTION INFORMATION

Frequency of publication: 7 times/yr.
Circulation: 250
Available in microform: No
Subscription price: 145 F/yr. France; 225 F/yr. elsewhere
Year to which price refers: 1992
Subscription address: C.R.E.D.I.F., at the above address

ADVERTISING INFORMATION

Advertising accepted: No

EDITORIAL DESCRIPTION

Scope: Publishes monographs on general and applied linguistics, psychology, and pedagogy.
Reviews books: Yes
Publishes notes: No
Languages accepted: French
Prints abstracts: Yes

SUBMISSION REQUIREMENTS

Copyright ownership: C.R.E.D.I.F., Ecole Normale Supérieure de Fontenay-St.-Cloud

(426)
**Bulletin CILA: Organe de la Commission Interuniversitaire Suisse de Linguistique Appliquée

Gérard Merkt, Editor
Inst. de Linguistique
Espace Louis-Agassiz 1
Univ. de Neuchâtel
2000 Neuchâtel, Switzerland

Telephone: (41) 38 208894
Fax: (41) 38 213760
First published: 1966
Sponsoring organization: Commission Interuniversitaire Suisse de Linguistique Appliquée (CILA)
ISSN: 0251-7256
MLA acronym: BCILA

SUBSCRIPTION INFORMATION

Frequency of publication: 2 times/yr. (April, Oct.)
Circulation: 600-700
Available in microform: No
Subscription price: 40 SwF/yr. institutions; 20 SwF/yr. individuals Switzerland; 25 SwF/yr. individuals elsewhere
Year to which price refers: 1991

ADVERTISING INFORMATION

Advertising accepted: Yes

EDITORIAL DESCRIPTION

Scope: Publishes articles on applied linguistics and the teaching of foreign languages.
Reviews books: Yes
Publishes notes: No
Languages accepted: French; German; English; Italian
Prints abstracts: No

SUBMISSION REQUIREMENTS

Restrictions on contributors: Book reviews are commissioned.
Author pays submission fee: No
Author pays page charges: No
Length of articles: No restrictions
Length of book reviews: 2-3 pp.
Number of copies required: 1
Copyright ownership: Univ. de Neuchâtel, Inst. de Linguistique
Rejected manuscripts: Returned
Time before publication decision: 6 mos.
Time between decision and publication: 6 mos.
Number of reviewers: 1
Articles submitted per year: 12-20
Articles published per year: 10-15
Book reviews submitted per year: 20
Book reviews published per year: 10

(427)
**Bulletin de Correspondance Hellénique

Olivier Picard, Editor
Ecole Française d'Athènes
6 rue Didotou
106 80 Athens, Greece

Telephone: (30) 1 3612521
Fax: (30) 1 3612101
First published: 1877
Sponsoring organization: Ecole Française d'Athenes
ISSN: 0007-4217
MLA acronym: BCH

SUBSCRIPTION INFORMATION

Frequency of publication: 2 times/yr.
Circulation: 1,000
Available in microform: No
Subscription price: 750 F/yr.
Year to which price refers: 1991
Subscription address: Diffusion de Boccard, 11, rue de Médicis, 75006 Paris, France

ADVERTISING INFORMATION

Advertising accepted: No

EDITORIAL DESCRIPTION

Scope: Focuses on the archaeology of the Greek world in ancient and Byzantine times. Includes articles on ancient Greek language.
Reviews books: No
Publishes notes: No
Languages accepted: French; English; German
Prints abstracts: Yes
Author-anonymous submission: No

SUBMISSION REQUIREMENTS

Restrictions on contributors: None
Author pays submission fee: No
Author pays page charges: No
Length of articles: No restrictions
Style: None
Number of copies required: 1
Special requirements: Submit 150-200 word abstract and a subject index with manuscript.
Copyright ownership: Editor
Rejected manuscripts: Returned
Time before publication decision: 3 mos.
Time between decision and publication: 7 mos.
Number of reviewers: 1
Articles submitted per year: 60
Articles published per year: 40

(428)
**Bulletin de la Société Américaine de Philosophie de Langue Française

Colette Michael, Editor
5 Morraine Terrace
DeKalb, IL 60115

Telephone: 815 756-4639
Fax: 815 753-6302
E-mail: TC0CVM1@NIU
First published: 1989
Sponsoring organization: Northern Illinois Univ.; Soc. Américaine de Philosophie de Langue Française
ISSN: 1040-6833
MLA acronym: BSAPLF

SUBSCRIPTION INFORMATION

Frequency of publication: 3 times/yr.
Circulation: 300
Available in microform: No
Subscription price: $20.00/yr. institutions; $15.00/yr. individuals
Year to which price refers: 1992
Subscription address: Treasurer, at the above address
Additional subscription address: Treasurer, Soc. Américaine de Philosophie, Foreign Languages & Literatures, Northern Illinois Univ., DeKalb, IL 60115-2854
Subscription telephone: 815 756-4156; 815 753-6463

ADVERTISING INFORMATION

Advertising accepted: Yes
Advertising rates: $100.00/full page

EDITORIAL DESCRIPTION

Scope: Publishes articles devoted to the study of applications of theories of French philosophers to numerous disciplines including art, literature, language, and political science. Is also interested in problems and theories of translation, and publishes bibliographies.
Reviews books: Yes
Publishes notes: Yes
Languages accepted: French preferred; English
Prints abstracts: No
Author-anonymous submission: Yes

SUBMISSION REQUIREMENTS

Restrictions on contributors: Contributors must be members of the Soc. Américaine de Philosophie de Langue Française. Majority of book reviews are solicited; contact editor before submission.
Author pays submission fee: No
Author pays page charges: No
Length of articles: 2,500-5,000 words
Length of book reviews: 500-2,000 words
Length of notes: 1,000-2,000 words
Style: MLA preferred
Number of copies required: 2
Copyright ownership: Journal & author
Rejected manuscripts: Returned; enclose SASE.
Time before publication decision: 3-4 mos.

Time between decision and publication: 3 mos.
Number of reviewers: 2-4
Articles submitted per year: 60-80
Articles published per year: 15-25
Book reviews published per year: 15-20
Notes submitted per year: 5-10
Notes published per year: 5-10

(429)
Bulletin de la Société de Linguistique de Paris

Jean Perrot, Gilbert Lazard, & Françoise Bader, Editors
Secrétariat de la Soc. de Linguistique
Ecole des Hautes-Etudes, à la Sorbonne
75005 Paris, France

First published: 1865
Sponsoring organization: Centre National de la Recherche Scientifique
ISSN: 0037-9069
MLA acronym: BSLP

SUBSCRIPTION INFORMATION

Frequency of publication: Annual
Circulation: 1,200
Available in microform: No

ADVERTISING INFORMATION

Advertising accepted: No

EDITORIAL DESCRIPTION

Scope: Publishes the minutes of Society proceedings for the past year, articles on general, descriptive, and historical linguistics, and book reviews.
Reviews books: Yes
Languages accepted: French
Prints abstracts: Yes

SUBMISSION REQUIREMENTS

Restrictions on contributors: Contributors must be members of the Soc. de Linguistique de Paris.
Author pays submission fee: No
Author pays page charges: No
Length of articles: 10,000 words
Length of book reviews: 1,000 words
Style: MLA
Number of copies required: 1
Copyright ownership: Journal
Rejected manuscripts: Returned
Time before publication decision: 6 mos.
Time between decision and publication: 6 mos.
Number of reviewers: 2
Articles submitted per year: 30
Articles published per year: 15
Book reviews published per year: 170

(430)
*Bulletin de la Société des Amis de Montaigne

Françoise Charpentier & Claude Blum, Editors
17, rue de Babylone
75007 Paris, France

First published: 1913
Sponsoring organization: Soc. Internationale des Amis de Montaigne (S.I.A.M.)
ISSN: 0037-9182
MLA acronym: BSAM

SUBSCRIPTION INFORMATION

Frequency of publication: 2 double issues/yr.
Circulation: 550
Available in microform: No
Subscription address: Soc. Internationale des Amis de Montaigne, B.P. Paris Bourse 913, 75073 Paris Cédex 02, France

ADVERTISING INFORMATION

Advertising accepted: No

EDITORIAL DESCRIPTION

Scope: Focuses on the study of Montaigne and his times.
Reviews books: Yes
Publishes notes: Yes
Languages accepted: French
Prints abstracts: No
Author-anonymous submission: No

SUBMISSION REQUIREMENTS

Author pays submission fee: No
Author pays page charges: No
Length of articles: 15-20 double-spaced typescript pp.
Length of book reviews: 2 double-spaced typescript pp.
Length of notes: 700 words
Number of copies required: 2
Copyright ownership: Author
Rejected manuscripts: Not returned
Time before publication decision: 6 mos.
Time between decision and publication: 1-2 yrs.
Number of reviewers: 5
Articles submitted per year: 30
Articles published per year: 15-20
Book reviews submitted per year: 12
Book reviews published per year: 6
Notes submitted per year: 4
Notes published per year: 4

(431)
*Bulletin de la Société d'Etudes Anglo-Américaines des XVIIe et XVIIIe Siècles

Paul Denizot, Editor
Les Hauts de Roquefavour
Route de Vauvenargues
13100 Aix-en-Provence, France

First published: 1975
Sponsoring organization: Soc. d'Etudes Anglo-Américaines des XVIIe & XVIIIe Siècles
ISSN: 0291-3798
MLA acronym: BSEAA

SUBSCRIPTION INFORMATION

Frequency of publication: 2 times/yr. (June, Nov.)
Circulation: 300-400
Available in microform: No
Subscription price: $30.00/yr.
Year to which price refers: 1992
Subscription address: Pierre Arnaud, Soc. d'Etudes Anglo-Américaines 17e-18e, 18, rue du Ranelagh, 75016 Paris, France

ADVERTISING INFORMATION

Advertising accepted: No

EDITORIAL DESCRIPTION

Scope: Publishes articles on studies in 17th- and 18th-century Anglo-American literature and civilization.
Reviews books: Yes
Languages accepted: French; English

SUBMISSION REQUIREMENTS

Restrictions on contributors: None
Author pays submission fee: No
Author pays page charges: No
Length of articles: 15 pp.
Style: MLA
Number of copies required: 3
Special requirements: Submit original typescript.
Rejected manuscripts: Returned
Time before publication decision: 3 mos.
Time between decision and publication: 2 mos.
Number of reviewers: 3
Articles published per year: 15

(432)
Bulletin de la Société Théophile Gautier

Claudine Lacoste, Editor
Univ. Paul Valéry
B.P. 5043
34032 Montpellier, France

First published: 1979
Sponsoring organization: Soc. Théophile Gautier
ISSN: 0221-7945
MLA acronym: BSTG

SUBSCRIPTION INFORMATION

Frequency of publication: Annual
Available in microform: No
Additional subscription address: For payment in US or Canadian currencies, contact Andrew Gann, Mount Allison Univ., Sackville, NB E0A 3C0, Canada

EDITORIAL DESCRIPTION

Scope: Publishes scholarly articles on the life and works of Théophile Gautier; includes surveys of research.
Reviews books: Yes
Languages accepted: English; French
Prints abstracts: No

SUBMISSION REQUIREMENTS

Restrictions on contributors: None
Author pays submission fee: No
Author pays page charges: No
Length of articles: 30 pp. maximum
Length of book reviews: 150 words
Number of copies required: 2
Special requirements: French abstract must accompany articles not written in French.
Rejected manuscripts: Returned
Time before publication decision: June-Sept.
Time between decision and publication: 6 mos.
Number of reviewers: 3
Articles submitted per year: 18-20
Articles published per year: 12-15
Book reviews submitted per year: 8-10
Book reviews published per year: 8-10

(433)
*Bulletin de l'Académie Royale de Langue et de Littérature Françaises

Académie Royale de Langue & de Littérature Françaises
Palais des Académies
Rue Ducale, 1
1000 Brussels, Belgium

First published: 1922
Sponsoring organization: Académie Royale de Langue & de Littérature Françaises
ISSN: 0378-0708
MLA acronym: BARLLF

SUBSCRIPTION INFORMATION

Frequency of publication: 2 double-issues/yr.
Circulation: 1,000

EDITORIAL DESCRIPTION

Scope: Focuses on French language and literature. Publishes texts of lectures given at the Academy.
Reviews books: No
Languages accepted: French
Prints abstracts: No

SUBMISSION REQUIREMENTS

Length of articles: 10-20 pp.

(434)
Bulletin de l'ALCAM: Revue de Linguistique Camerounaise

Inst. des Sciences Humaines
B.P. 73
Yaoundé, Cameroon

First published: 1976
Sponsoring organization: Onarest-Inst. des Sciences Humaines
ISSN: 0258-1302
MLA acronym: BALCAM

EDITORIAL DESCRIPTION

Scope: Publishes articles on African linguistics.
Reviews books: No
Languages accepted: French
Prints abstracts: No

(435)
*Bulletin de l'Association des Amis de Rabelais et de La Devinière

Jack Vivier, Editor
Amis de Rabelais
43, Rue de Sebastopol
37000 Tours, France

Telephone: (33) 47200100
First published: 1951
Sponsoring organization: Assn. des Amis de Rabelais & de la Devinière
ISSN: 0571-5350
MLA acronym: BAR

SUBSCRIPTION INFORMATION

Frequency of publication: Annual
Circulation: 750
Available in microform: No
Subscription price: 100 F/yr.
Year to which price refers: 1992

ADVERTISING INFORMATION

Advertising accepted: Yes

EDITORIAL DESCRIPTION

Scope: Publishes articles on Rabelais.
Reviews books: Yes
Languages accepted: French; English
Prints abstracts: No
Author-anonymous submission: No

SUBMISSION REQUIREMENTS

Restrictions on contributors: Contributors must be members of Assn. des Amis de Rabelais et de la Devinière.
Author pays page charges: No
Length of articles: 3-4 pp.
Number of copies required: 2
Special requirements: Submit typescript.
Copyright ownership: Assn. des Amis de Rabelais et de la Devinière
Rejected manuscripts: Returned; enclose return postage.
Time before publication decision: 2-3 mos.
Time between decision and publication: 1 yr.
Number of reviewers: 2
Articles submitted per year: 10
Articles published per year: 4

(436)
Bulletin de l'Association Guillaume Budé

M. Michel, Editor
Assn. Guillaume Budé
95, boulevard Raspail
75006 Paris, France

Telephone: (33) 1 42226915
First published: 1923
Sponsoring organization: Assn. Guillaume Budé
ISSN: 0004-5527
MLA acronym: BAGB

SUBSCRIPTION INFORMATION

Frequency of publication: 4 times/yr.
Circulation: 4,000
Available in microform: No

ADVERTISING INFORMATION

Advertising accepted: Yes

EDITORIAL DESCRIPTION

Scope: Publishes articles on Greek and Latin culture and literature.
Reviews books: Yes
Publishes notes: Yes
Languages accepted: French
Prints abstracts: No
Author-anonymous submission: No

SUBMISSION REQUIREMENTS

Restrictions on contributors: None
Author pays submission fee: No
Author pays page charges: No
Length of articles: 8-10 pp.
Length of notes: 100-300 words
Style: MLA
Number of copies required: 2
Special requirements: Submit original typescript.
Rejected manuscripts: Returned
Time before publication decision: 6 mos.
Time between decision and publication: 1 yr.
Number of reviewers: 2
Articles submitted per year: 30
Articles published per year: 20
Book reviews published per year: 30
Notes published per year: 10

(437)
*Bulletin de Littérature Ecclésiastique

Inst. Catholique de Toulouse
31, rue de la Fonderie
31068 Toulouse Cédex, France

Telephone: (33) 61368117
First published: 1899
Sponsoring organization: Inst. Catholique de Toulouse
ISSN: 0007-4322
MLA acronym: BLE

SUBSCRIPTION INFORMATION

Frequency of publication: 4 times/yr.
Available in microform: No
Subscription price: 273 F/yr.
Year to which price refers: 1992

ADVERTISING INFORMATION

Advertising accepted: No

EDITORIAL DESCRIPTION

Scope: Publishes articles on the history of religious literature.
Reviews books: Yes
Publishes notes: Yes
Languages accepted: French
Prints abstracts: Yes

Author-anonymous submission: No

SUBMISSION REQUIREMENTS

Restrictions on contributors: Unsolicited manuscripts are not accepted.
Author pays submission fee: No
Author pays page charges: No
Number of copies required: 1
Time before publication decision: 1 mo.
Time between decision and publication: 1 yr.
Number of reviewers: 3
Articles submitted per year: 15
Articles published per year: 12
Book reviews submitted per year: 130
Book reviews published per year: 100
Notes submitted per year: 10
Notes published per year: 10

(438)
*Bulletin des Amis d'André Gide

Pierre Masson, Editor
Centre d'Etudes Gidiennes
Univ. Lumière-Lyon 2
18 quai Claude Bernert
69365 Lyon Cédex 07, France

First published: 1968
Sponsoring organization: Centre d'Etudes Gidiennes; Centre National des Lettres
ISSN: 0044-8133
MLA acronym: BAAG

SUBSCRIPTION INFORMATION

Frequency of publication: 4 times/yr.
Circulation: 1,100
Available in microform: No
Subscription address: Henri Heinemann, 59 avenue Carnot, 80410 Cayeux sur Mer, France

ADVERTISING INFORMATION

Advertising accepted: No

EDITORIAL DESCRIPTION

Scope: Publishes articles on 20th-century French literature, André Gide, La NRF, and associated writers of this journal.
Reviews books: Yes
Publishes notes: Yes
Languages accepted: French
Prints abstracts: No
Author-anonymous submission: No

SUBMISSION REQUIREMENTS

Restrictions on contributors: None
Author pays submission fee: No
Author pays page charges: No
Length of articles: No restrictions
Length of book reviews: No restrictions
Length of notes: No restrictions
Style: MLA preferred
Number of copies required: 2
Copyright ownership: Author
Rejected manuscripts: Returned; enclose return postage.
Time before publication decision: 3 mos.
Time between decision and publication: 1 yr.
Number of reviewers: 2
Articles published per year: 40

(439)
*Bulletin des Etudes Valéryennes

Serge Bourjea, Editor
Service des Publications
Univ. Paul Valéry
B.P. 5043
34032 Montpellier-Cedex, France

Telephone: (33) 67142393
First published: 1974

Sponsoring organization: Centre d'Etudes Valéryennes, Univ. Paul Valéry
ISSN: 0335-508X
MLA acronym: BEV

SUBSCRIPTION INFORMATION

Frequency of publication: 3 times/yr.
Circulation: 600
Available in microform: No
Subscription price: 135 F/yr.
Year to which price refers: 1993
Subscription address: Publications de la Recherche, Univ. de Montpellier, at the above address

ADVERTISING INFORMATION

Advertising accepted: No

EDITORIAL DESCRIPTION

Scope: Publishes research on Paul Valéry including articles, book reviews, announcements, and reports of research in progress.
Reviews books: Yes
Publishes notes: Yes
Languages accepted: French; English; Spanish
Prints abstracts: Yes
Author-anonymous submission: No

SUBMISSION REQUIREMENTS

Restrictions on contributors: None
Author pays submission fee: No
Author pays page charges: No
Length of articles: 20-30 typescript pp.
Length of book reviews: 1-8 pp.
Length of notes: 150 words
Style: None
Number of copies required: 2
Special requirements: Submit a 100-200 word abstract.
Copyright ownership: Centre d'Etudes Valéryennes
Rejected manuscripts: Returned
Time before publication decision: 3 mos. maximum
Time between decision and publication: 1 yr.
Number of reviewers: 2
Articles submitted per year: 6-10
Articles published per year: 6-8
Book reviews submitted per year: 10-12
Book reviews published per year: 10-12
Notes submitted per year: 10-12
Notes published per year: 10-12

(440)
*Bulletin d'Etudes Parnassiennes et Symbolistes

Edgard Pich, Editor
A.L.D.R.U.I.
40, rue de Gerland
69007 Lyon, France

Telephone: (33) 78692504
First published: 1988
Sponsoring organization: Assn. Lyonnaise pour le Développement des Relations Universitaires Internationales
MLA acronym: BEP&S

SUBSCRIPTION INFORMATION

Frequency of publication: 2 times/yr.
Circulation: 20
Available in microform: No

EDITORIAL DESCRIPTION

Scope: Publishes articles on French 19th-century Parnassian and symbolist poets.
Reviews books: Yes
Publishes notes: Yes
Languages accepted: French
Prints abstracts: Yes
Author-anonymous submission: No

SUBMISSION REQUIREMENTS

Author pays submission fee: No
Author pays page charges: No
Length of articles: 2-20 pp.
Number of copies required: 1
Rejected manuscripts: Returned
Time before publication decision: 6-12 mos.
Time between decision and publication: 1 yr.
Number of reviewers: 2
Articles submitted per year: 10
Articles published per year: 6
Book reviews submitted per year: 30
Book reviews published per year: 30

(441)
*Bulletin d'Informations Proustiennes

Bernard Brun, Editor
Ecole Normale Supérieure
45, rue d'Ulm
75230 Paris Cedex 05, France

Telephone: (33) 1 44323176
First published: 1974
Sponsoring organization: Ecole Normale Supérieure; Centre National de la Recherche Scientifique
ISSN: 0338-0548
MLA acronym: BIPr

SUBSCRIPTION INFORMATION

Frequency of publication: Annual
Circulation: 500
Available in microform: No
Subscription price: 145 F/yr. plus postage
Year to which price refers: 1992
Subscription address: Presses de l'Ecole Normale Supérieure, 48 boulevard Jourdan, 75690 Paris Cedex 14, France

ADVERTISING INFORMATION

Advertising accepted: Yes
Advertising rates: Free

EDITORIAL DESCRIPTION

Scope: Publishes articles on Marcel Proust's works including first drafts, manuscripts, proofs, and galleys.
Reviews books: Yes
Publishes notes: Yes
Languages accepted: French; English
Prints abstracts: No
Author-anonymous submission: No

SUBMISSION REQUIREMENTS

Author pays submission fee: No
Author pays page charges: No
Length of articles: 15 pp.
Length of book reviews: 2 pp.
Length of notes: 1/2 p.
Number of copies required: 1
Copyright ownership: Author
Rejected manuscripts: Returned
Time before publication decision: 6 mos.
Time between decision and publication: 6 mos.
Number of reviewers: 4
Articles submitted per year: 12
Articles published per year: 10
Book reviews submitted per year: 10
Book reviews published per year: 10
Notes submitted per year: 20
Notes published per year: 20

(442)
*Bulletin Hispanique

D. Sartor, Secretaire de Redaction
Inst. d'Etudes Ibériques & Ibéro-américaines
Univ. de Bordeaux III
Domaine Universitaire
33405 Talence, France

First published: 1899
Sponsoring organization: Univ. de Bordeaux; Univ. de Toulouse; Univ. de Poitiers
ISSN: 0007-4640
MLA acronym: BH

SUBSCRIPTION INFORMATION

Frequency of publication: 2 times/yr.
Circulation: 1,500
Subscription address: Editions Bière, 18 à 22, rue du Peugue, 33000 Bordeaux, France

EDITORIAL DESCRIPTION

Scope: Publishes scholarly articles and notes on the language, literature, and history of countries on the Iberian Peninsula and in Latin America; abstracts or indexes works in all languages related to these areas; provides a regular chronicle of world-wide Hispanic activities.
Reviews books: Yes
Languages accepted: English; French; Italian; Spanish
Prints abstracts: Yes

(443)
*Bulletin Marcel Proust

Elyane Dezon-Jones, Editor
Dept. of Romance Languages
Washington Univ.
Saint Louis, MO 63130

Additional editorial address: Anne Borrel, Secrétaire Générale, Soc. des Amis de Marcel Proust & des Amis de Combray, 11 rue Martel, 75010 Paris, France
Telephone: (33) 1 42468964
First published: 1950
Sponsoring organization: Soc. des Amis de Marcel Proust & des Amis de Combray
ISSN: 0583-8452
MLA acronym: BMP

SUBSCRIPTION INFORMATION

Frequency of publication: Annual
Circulation: 800-900
Available in microform: No
Subscription price: 150 F/yr. institutions; 160 F/yr. individuals; 80 F/yr. students
Year to which price refers: 1992
Subscription address: 11 rue Martel, 75010 Paris, France
Additional subscription address: 4 rue du Dr Proust, 28120 Illiers-Combray, France
Subscription telephone: (33) 1 42468964

ADVERTISING INFORMATION

Advertising accepted: No

EDITORIAL DESCRIPTION

Scope: Publishes studies on Marcel Proust, a bibliography, and information on activities of the Society as well as book reviews and unpublished Proust texts.
Reviews books: Yes
Publishes notes: Yes
Languages accepted: French
Prints abstracts: No

SUBMISSION REQUIREMENTS

Restrictions on contributors: Priority is given to members of the Soc. des Amis de Marcel Proust et des Amis de Combray. Unsolicited book reviews are not accepted. Accepts only previously unpublished texts.
Author pays submission fee: No
Author pays page charges: No
Length of articles: 15-20 pp. including footnotes
Length of book reviews: 1-3 pp.
Length of notes: 1-3 pp.
Style: Nouvelle Revue Française
Number of copies required: 2
Special requirements: Authors are encouraged to send their submissions on diskette.
Copyright ownership: Author
Rejected manuscripts: Not returned
Time before publication decision: 3 mos.
Time between decision and publication: 3-24 mos.
Number of reviewers: 5
Articles submitted per year: 15-20
Articles published per year: 12
Book reviews published per year: 15-20
Notes published per year: 5-10

(444)
Bulletin of Bibliography

Bernard F. McTigue, Editor
Greenwood Publishing Group
P.O. Box 5007
88 Post Rd. West
Westport, CT 06881-9990

Telephone: 203 226-3571
First published: 1897
ISSN: 0190-745X
MLA acronym: BB

SUBSCRIPTION INFORMATION

Frequency of publication: 4 times/yr. (Mar., June, Sept., Dec.)
Circulation: 1,500
Available in microform: Yes, through Univ. Microfilms International
Subscription price: $95.00/yr. US; $115.00/yr. elsewhere
Year to which price refers: 1992

ADVERTISING INFORMATION

Advertising accepted: Yes

EDITORIAL DESCRIPTION

Scope: Publishes bibliographies on a wide range of topics in the humanities and social sciences. Welcomes submissions on topics of scholarly and general interest which contain material not accessible through published sources.
Reviews books: Yes
Publishes notes: Yes
Languages accepted: English
Prints abstracts: No
Author-anonymous submission: No

SUBMISSION REQUIREMENTS

Restrictions on contributors: None
Author pays submission fee: No
Author pays page charges: No
Length of articles: 60 pp. maximum
Length of book reviews: 1,000 words
Length of notes: 100 words
Style: MLA; Chicago; American National Standards Inst.
Number of copies required: 2
Special requirements: Include a brief introduction outlining article's scope and citing previous bibliographical research on its subject.
Copyright ownership: Greenwood Publishing
Rejected manuscripts: Returned; enclose return postage.
Time before publication decision: 2-3 weeks
Time between decision and publication: 12-18 mos.

Number of reviewers: 1
Articles submitted per year: 50
Articles published per year: 18
Book reviews submitted per year: 50
Book reviews published per year: 30

(445)
Bulletin of Daito Bunka University: The Humanities

Junichi Kohsaka, Editor
Daito Bunka Univ.
1-9-1 Takashima-Daira
Itabashi-ku
Tokyo 175, Japan

First published: 1962
Sponsoring organization: Daito Bunka Univ.
MLA acronym: BDBU

SUBSCRIPTION INFORMATION

Frequency of publication: Annual

EDITORIAL DESCRIPTION

Scope: The journal publishes articles on a wide range of subjects including Asian and European literatures and linguistics with an emphasis on Japanese studies.
Reviews books: No
Languages accepted: Japanese; English; German; French; Chinese languages
Prints abstracts: Yes

SUBMISSION REQUIREMENTS

Restrictions on contributors: Contributors must be members of faculty of Daito Bunka Univ.
Author pays submission fee: No
Author pays page charges: No
Copyright ownership: Author

(446)
*Bulletin of Hispanic Studies

Dorothy Sherman Severin & Ann Logan Mackenzie, Editors
School of Hispanic Studies
Univ. of Liverpool
P.O. Box 147
Liverpool L69 3BX, England

Telephone: (44) 51 7942774
Fax: (44) 51 7086502
First published: 1923
Sponsoring organization: Univ. of Liverpool
ISSN: 0007-490X
MLA acronym: BHS

SUBSCRIPTION INFORMATION

Frequency of publication: 4 times/yr. (Jan., Apr., July, Oct.)
Circulation: 1,000
Available in microform: Yes
Subscription price: £120.00/yr. institutions; £45.00/yr. individuals
Year to which price refers: 1992
Subscription address: Liverpool Univ. Press, Distribution Centre, Blackhorse Rd., Letchworth SG6 1HN, England
Subscription telephone: (44) 462 672555
Subscription fax: (44) 462 480947

ADVERTISING INFORMATION

Advertising accepted: Yes
Advertising rates: £40.00/quarter page; £80.00/half page; £150.00/full page

EDITORIAL DESCRIPTION

Scope: Devoted to the languages, literatures, and civilizations of Spain, Portugal, and Latin America.

Reviews books: Yes
Publishes notes: Yes
Languages accepted: Catalan; English; French; Portuguese; Spanish
Prints abstracts: No
Author-anonymous submission: No

SUBMISSION REQUIREMENTS

Restrictions on contributors: Unsolicited reviews are not accepted.
Author pays submission fee: No
Author pays page charges: No
Length of articles: 12,000 words maximum
Length of book reviews: 800 words maximum
Length of notes: 2,500 words
Style: Modern Humanities Research Assn. with modifications
Number of copies required: 2
Copyright ownership: Assigned by author to journal
Rejected manuscripts: Returned by ordinary mail unless airmail postage paid in advance
Time before publication decision: 3 mos.
Time between decision and publication: 21 mos.
Number of reviewers: 2
Articles submitted per year: 60
Articles published per year: 20
Book reviews submitted per year: 200
Book reviews published per year: 200
Notes submitted per year: 20
Notes published per year: 8

(447)
*Bulletin of the Board of Celtic Studies/Bwletin y Bwrdd Gwybodau Celtaidd

D. Ellis Evans, J. Beverly Smith, & Robin G. Livens, Editors
Jesus College
Oxford, England

Additional editorial address: J. Beverly Smith, Univ. College of Wales, Aberystwyth, Wales; Robin G. Livens, Univ. College of North Wales, Bangor, Wales
Telephone: (44) 222 231919
Fax: (44) 222 230908
First published: 1921
Sponsoring organization: Univ. of Wales, Board of Celtic Studies
ISSN: 0142-3363
MLA acronym: BBCS

SUBSCRIPTION INFORMATION

Frequency of publication: Annual (Nov.)
Available in microform: No
Subscription price: £20.00/yr.
Year to which price refers: 1992-93
Subscription address: Univ. of Wales Press, 6 Gwennyth St., Cathays, Cardiff, Wales

ADVERTISING INFORMATION

Advertising accepted: Yes

EDITORIAL DESCRIPTION

Scope: Publishes articles on Celtic language, literature, history, law, archaeology, and art, with a special emphasis on Wales, the Welsh language, Welsh literature, and Welsh history.
Reviews books: No
Publishes notes: Yes
Languages accepted: English; Welsh; French; German
Prints abstracts: No
Author-anonymous submission: No

SUBMISSION REQUIREMENTS

Restrictions on contributors: None
Author pays submission fee: No
Length of articles: No restrictions
Style: None
Number of copies required: 2

Copyright ownership: Univ. of Wales, Board of Celtic Studies
Rejected manuscripts: Returned

(448)
*Bulletin of the Cantigueiros de Santa Maria

John E. Keller & Connie L. Scarborough, Editors
Dept. of Spanish & Italian
Univ. of Kentucky
Lexington, KY 40506

Telephone: 513 556-1835; 513 241-1194
First published: 1987
Sponsoring organization: Soc. of the Cantigueiros de Santa Maria
ISSN: 0898-8463
MLA acronym: BCSM

SUBSCRIPTION INFORMATION

Frequency of publication: Annual
Circulation: 200
Available in microform: No
Subscription price: $10.00/yr. institutions; $5.00/yr. individuals
Year to which price refers: 1992
Subscription address: Connie Scarborough, Dept. of Romance Languages, ML 377, Univ. of Cincinnati, Cincinnati, OH 45221

ADVERTISING INFORMATION

Advertising accepted: Yes

EDITORIAL DESCRIPTION

Scope: Publishes articles pertaining to any aspect of Alfonso X, el Sabio's, *Cantigas de Santa Maria.*
Reviews books: Yes
Publishes notes: Yes
Languages accepted: English; Spanish
Prints abstracts: No
Author-anonymous submission: No

SUBMISSION REQUIREMENTS

Restrictions on contributors: Book reviews are solicited.
Author pays submission fee: No
Author pays page charges: No
Length of articles: 15-25 pp.
Length of book reviews: 700 words
Length of notes: 1,800-4,500 words
Style: MLA
Number of copies required: 2
Special requirements: Submit original double-spaced typescript, 1 copy, and a diskette.
Copyright ownership: Soc. of the Cantigueiros de Santa Maria
Rejected manuscripts: Returned; enclose SAE and loose postage.
Time before publication decision: 3 mos.
Time between decision and publication: 6-12 mos.
Number of reviewers: 3 minimum
Articles submitted per year: 20
Articles published per year: 5-7
Book reviews published per year: 2-4
Notes submitted per year: 3-5

(449)
*Bulletin of the Comediantes

James A. Parr, Editor
Dept. of Spanish & Portuguese
Univ. of California, Riverside
Riverside, CA 92521-0222

Telephone: 714 787-7339; 714 787-7334
Fax: 714 787-2294
First published: 1948
Sponsoring organization: Comediantes
ISSN: 0007-5108
MLA acronym: BCom

SUBSCRIPTION INFORMATION

Frequency of publication: 2 times/yr. (Winter, Summer)
Circulation: 550
Available in microform: No
Subscription price: $15.00/yr.
Year to which price refers: 1992
Subscription address: José A. Madrigal, Managing Editor, Dept. of Foreign Languages, Auburn Univ., Auburn, AL 36830
Subscription telephone: 205 844-4345
Subscription fax: 205 844-2378

ADVERTISING INFORMATION

Advertising accepted: Yes

EDITORIAL DESCRIPTION

Scope: Includes notes and articles on Spanish Renaissance and Baroque drama, annual bibliography, book reviews, forum, announcements, and news.
Reviews books: Yes
Publishes notes: Yes
Languages accepted: English; Spanish
Prints abstracts: Yes
Author-anonymous submission: No

SUBMISSION REQUIREMENTS

Restrictions on contributors: Contributors must subscribe to journal. Unsolicited book reviews are not accepted.
Author pays submission fee: No
Author pays page charges: No
Length of articles: 10-30 pp.
Length of book reviews: 500-800 words
Length of notes: 500-1,500 words
Style: MLA
Number of copies required: 2
Special requirements: Submit original typescript, one copy, and abstract.
Copyright ownership: Author
Rejected manuscripts: Returned; enclose return postage.
Time before publication decision: 3-6 mos.
Time between decision and publication: 6-12 mos.
Number of reviewers: 2
Articles submitted per year: 25-30
Articles published per year: 15-18
Book reviews published per year: 8-10
Notes submitted per year: 5-6
Notes published per year: 2-3

(450)
*Bulletin of the John Rylands University Library of Manchester

Dorothy J. Clayton, Editor
John Rylands Univ. Library of Manchester
Oxford Road,
Manchester, M13 9PP, England

Telephone: (44) 61 2753757
First published: 1903
Sponsoring organization: John Ryland Univ. Library of Manchester
ISSN: 0301-102X
MLA acronym: BJRL

SUBSCRIPTION INFORMATION

Frequency of publication: 3 times/yr.
Circulation: 700
Available in microform: Yes
Subscription price: £35.00/yr.
Year to which price refers: 1992

ADVERTISING INFORMATION

Advertising accepted: Yes

EDITORIAL DESCRIPTION

Scope: Publishes methodological interpretative, or substantive articles in any subject area from the arts and social studies and on the historical or philosophical aspects of the natural and physical sciences. Contributions which are of an interdisciplinary nature and/or which incorporate the results of research on the extensive collections of the John Rylands University Library are especially welcome.
Reviews books: No
Publishes notes: Yes
Languages accepted: English; French; German
Prints abstracts: No
Author-anonymous submission: No

SUBMISSION REQUIREMENTS

Restrictions on contributors: None
Author pays submission fee: No
Author pays page charges: No
Length of articles: 8,000 words including references
Length of notes: 3,000-4,000 words
Style: Hart's Rules
Number of copies required: 2
Special requirements: Submit original typescript and 1 copy. Articles should be typed, double-spaced throughout and with first lines of paragraphs indented, on one side of good quality A4 size (8 1/4 in. x 11 3/4 in.) paper with generous margins on all four sides. Footnotes should be numbered consecutively in superscript and appear on separate sheets at the end of the main text.
Copyright ownership: John Rylands Univ. Library of Manchester
Rejected manuscripts: Returned; enclose SASE or international reply coupons.
Time before publication decision: 6-8 weeks
Time between decision and publication: 6-12 mos.
Number of reviewers: 2-3
Articles submitted per year: 40
Articles published per year: 25
Notes submitted per year: 2-3
Notes published per year: 1-2

(451)
*Bulletin of the Museum of Far Eastern Antiquities

Jan Wirgin, Editor
Östasiatiska Museet
Skeppsholmen, Box 16381
10327 Stockholm, Sweden

Telephone: (46) 8 6664400; (46) 8 6664401
Fax: (46) 8 6112845
First published: 1929
Sponsoring organization: Humanistisk-Samhällsvetenskapliga Forskningsrådet; Chiang Ching-kuo Foundation
ISSN: 0081-5691
MLA acronym: BMFEA

SUBSCRIPTION INFORMATION

Frequency of publication: Annual
Circulation: 800
Available in microform: No
Subscription price: 250 Skr/yr.
Year to which price refers: 1991

ADVERTISING INFORMATION

Advertising accepted: No

EDITORIAL DESCRIPTION

Scope: Publishes articles on Chinese, Japanese, and Korean art, archaeology, language, and literature.
Reviews books: No
Publishes notes: No
Languages accepted: English
Prints abstracts: No
Author-anonymous submission: No

SUBMISSION REQUIREMENTS

Restrictions on contributors: None
Author pays submission fee: No
Author pays page charges: No
Number of copies required: 1
Copyright ownership: Journal
Rejected manuscripts: Returned
Time before publication decision: 3 mos.
Time between decision and publication: 6-12 mos.
Number of reviewers: 1-2
Articles published per year: 1-3

(452)
*Bulletin of the Psychonomic Society

Anne Matson Dossett, Managing Editor
Psychonomic Soc.
1710 Fortview Rd.
Austin, TX 78704

Telephone: 512 462-2442
First published: 1973
Sponsoring organization: Psychonomic Soc., Inc.
ISSN: 0090-5054
MLA acronym: BPS

SUBSCRIPTION INFORMATION

Frequency of publication: 6 times/yr.
Circulation: 1,400
Available in microform: Yes
Subscription price: $85.00/yr. institutions; $40.00/yr. individuals; add $8.00/yr. postage outside US
Year to which price refers: 1992

ADVERTISING INFORMATION

Advertising accepted: Yes
Advertising rates: $110.00/full page

EDITORIAL DESCRIPTION

Scope: Publishes brief articles authored or co-authored by members of the Psychonomic Society.
Reviews books: No
Publishes notes: Yes
Languages accepted: English
Prints abstracts: Yes
Author-anonymous submission: No

SUBMISSION REQUIREMENTS

Restrictions on contributors: Contributors must be members or be sponsored by members of the Psychonomic Soc.
Author pays submission fee: No
Author pays page charges: No
Length of articles: 4 printed pp. maximum (55 characters/line, 59 lines/column)
Length of notes: 100 words maximum
Style: American Psychological Assn.
Number of copies required: 1
Special requirements: Include a 100-150 word abstract. If possible, submit also on IBM or compatible diskette.
Copyright ownership: Assigned by author to journal
Rejected manuscripts: Returned
Time between decision and publication: 4 mos.
Articles submitted per year: 225
Articles published per year: 225
Notes submitted per year: 6
Notes published per year: 6

(453)
*Bulletin of the School of Oriental and African Studies

c/o D. N. Matias, Editorial Secretary
School of Oriental & African Studies
Univ. of London
Thornhaugh St., Russell Square
London WC1H OXG, England

Telephone: (44) 71 6372388
Fax: (44) 71 4363844
First published: 1917
Sponsoring organization: Univ. of London, School of Oriental & African Studies
ISSN: 0041-977X
MLA acronym: BSOAS

SUBSCRIPTION INFORMATION

Frequency of publication: 3 times/yr. (Feb., June, Oct.)
Circulation: 1,100
Available in microform: No
Subscription address: M. J. Daly, at the above address

ADVERTISING INFORMATION

Advertising accepted: Yes
Advertising rates: £90.00/half page; £110.00/full page

EDITORIAL DESCRIPTION

Scope: Focuses on advanced research in Oriental and African studies.
Reviews books: Yes
Publishes notes: Yes
Languages accepted: English; French; German
Prints abstracts: No
Author-anonymous submission: No

SUBMISSION REQUIREMENTS

Restrictions on contributors: No multiple submissions; notes should be brief academic contributions, not announcements or news items.
Author pays submission fee: No
Author pays page charges: No
Length of articles: 15,000-20,000 words
Length of book reviews: 1,000 words
Length of notes: 500-1,500 words
Style: Journal
Number of copies required: 1
Special requirements: Submit printer-ready typescript.
Copyright ownership: School of Oriental & African Studies
Rejected manuscripts: Returned
Time before publication decision: 4 mos.
Time between decision and publication: 12-15 mos.
Articles submitted per year: 100
Articles published per year: 30-35
Book reviews submitted per year: 300
Book reviews published per year: 250
Notes published per year: 50

(454)
*The Bulletin of the West Virginia Association of College English Teachers

Robert Gerke, Director
Dept. of English
Marshall Univ.
Huntington, WV 25755-2646

Telephone: 304 696-6600
First published: 1955
Sponsoring organization: Marshall Univ., West Virginia Assn. of College Teachers of English
ISSN: 0301-7525
MLA acronym: BWVACET

SUBSCRIPTION INFORMATION

Frequency of publication: Annual
Circulation: 500
Available in microform: No

ADVERTISING INFORMATION

Advertising accepted: No

EDITORIAL DESCRIPTION

Scope: Accepts papers and reviews on traditional areas of criticism and scholarship on all periods.
Reviews books: Yes
Languages accepted: English
Prints abstracts: No

SUBMISSION REQUIREMENTS

Restrictions on contributors: Contributors must have presented their paper at a conference of the West Virginia Assn. of College English Teachers. Book reviews are assigned.
Author pays submission fee: No
Author pays page charges: No
Length of articles: 5,000 words maximum
Length of book reviews: 400-800 words
Style: MLA
Number of copies required: 1
Special requirements: Submit original typescript.
Copyright ownership: Author
Rejected manuscripts: Returned
Time before publication decision: 1-3 mos.
Time between decision and publication: 6 mos.
Number of reviewers: 2-4
Articles submitted per year: 25
Articles published per year: 10-12
Book reviews published per year: 4-6

(455)
Bungaku

Iwanami Shoten Publishers
2-5-5 Hitotsubashi
Chiyoda-ku
Tokyo, Japan

First published: 1933
ISSN: 0389-4029
MLA acronym: BG

SUBSCRIPTION INFORMATION

Frequency of publication: 12 times/yr.
Circulation: 10,000
Available in microform: No

ADVERTISING INFORMATION

Advertising accepted: Yes

EDITORIAL DESCRIPTION

Reviews books: Yes
Languages accepted: Japanese
Prints abstracts: No

SUBMISSION REQUIREMENTS

Restrictions on contributors: None
Author pays submission fee: No
Author pays page charges: No
Length of articles: 14,000 letters
Length of book reviews: 7,000 letters
Number of copies required: 1
Copyright ownership: Author
Rejected manuscripts: Returned
Time before publication decision: 6 mos.
Time between decision and publication: 3 mos. maximum
Articles submitted per year: 180
Articles published per year: 120
Book reviews published per year: 5-6

(456)
*Bunyan Studies: John Bunyan and His Times

W. R. Owens, Editor
The Open Univ.
Parsifal College
527 Finchley Rd.
London NW3 7BG, England

First published: 1988
ISSN: 0954-0970
MLA acronym: BStu

SUBSCRIPTION INFORMATION

Frequency of publication: 2 times/yr.
Circulation: 150
Available in microform: No
Subscription price: £20.00/yr. institutions United Kingdom; £24.00/yr. institutions elsewhere; £10.00/yr. individuals United Kingdom; £12.00/yr. individuals elsewhere
Year to which price refers: 1992
Subscription address: Anne Laurence, Faculty of Arts, The Open Univ., Milton Keynes MK7 6AA, England

ADVERTISING INFORMATION

Advertising accepted: Yes

EDITORIAL DESCRIPTION

Scope: Publishes articles on John Bunyan, and the religious, historical, and literary contexts within which his works were produced.
Reviews books: Yes
Publishes notes: Yes
Languages accepted: English
Prints abstracts: No
Author-anonymous submission: No

SUBMISSION REQUIREMENTS

Restrictions on contributors: None
Author pays submission fee: No
Author pays page charges: No
Length of articles: 6,000 words maximum
Length of book reviews: 600-1,000 words
Length of notes: 1,000-2,000 words
Style: Modern Humanities Research Assn.
Number of copies required: 1
Copyright ownership: Journal & author
Rejected manuscripts: Returned
Time before publication decision: 3 mos.
Time between decision and publication: 6-12 mos.
Number of reviewers: 2
Articles submitted per year: 20
Articles published per year: 8
Book reviews published per year: 15
Notes submitted per year: 4
Notes published per year: 2

(457)
*The Byron Journal

Bernard Beatty, Elma Dangerfield, Anne Fleming, Vincent Newey, & Derek Wise, Editors
Dept. of English Language & Literature
Univ. of Liverpool
Liverpool L69 5BX, England

Additional editorial address: Vincent Newey, Reviews Editor, Dept. of English, Univ. of Leicester, Leicester LE1 7RH, England
Telephone: (44) 51 7942711
First published: 1973
Sponsoring organization: Byron Soc., UK; International Byron Soc.
ISSN: 0301-7257
MLA acronym: ByronJ

SUBSCRIPTION INFORMATION

Frequency of publication: Annual
Circulation: 2,000
Available in microform: No
Subscription address: Byron House, 6, Gertrude St., London SW10 OJN, England

ADVERTISING INFORMATION

Advertising accepted: Yes

EDITORIAL DESCRIPTION

Scope: Publishes articles on the life and work of Lord Byron and his contemporaries.
Reviews books: Yes
Publishes notes: Yes
Languages accepted: English
Prints abstracts: Yes
Author-anonymous submission: No

SUBMISSION REQUIREMENTS

Restrictions on contributors: Unsolicited book reviews are not accepted.
Author pays submission fee: No
Author pays page charges: No
Length of articles: 4,000 words
Length of book reviews: 500 words maximum
Length of notes: 500 words maximum
Style: Oxford; Hart-Davis; Modern Humanities Research Assn. preferred
Number of copies required: 2 minimum
Special requirements: Deadline for submission is October of each year.
Copyright ownership: Author
Rejected manuscripts: Returned at author's request; enclose return postage
Time before publication decision: 2-14 mos.
Time between decision and publication: 2-14 mos.
Number of reviewers: 2
Articles submitted per year: 20
Articles published per year: 6-7
Book reviews published per year: 5-10
Notes submitted per year: 6
Notes published per year: 4-5

(458)
*Byzantinische Zeitschrift

Peter Schreiner, Editor
Univ. zu Köln
Abt. Byzantinistik
Albertus-Magnus-Platz
5000 Cologne 41, Germany

Telephone: (49) 221 4702524
Fax: (49) 221 4705151
First published: 1892
ISSN: 0007-7704
MLA acronym: BZ

SUBSCRIPTION INFORMATION

Frequency of publication: 2 times/yr.
Circulation: 800
Available in microform: No
Subscription address: B. G. Teubner Verlag, Industriestr. 15, 7000 Stuttgart 80, Germany

ADVERTISING INFORMATION

Advertising accepted: Occasionally

EDITORIAL DESCRIPTION

Scope: Focuses on Byzantine studies, including history, literature, and art.
Reviews books: Yes
Publishes notes: Yes
Languages accepted: English; German; French; Italian; Greek
Prints abstracts: No
Author-anonymous submission: No

SUBMISSION REQUIREMENTS

Restrictions on contributors: None
Author pays submission fee: No
Author pays page charges: No
Length of articles: No restrictions
Length of book reviews: 3 pp.
Length of notes: No restrictions
Number of copies required: 1
Special requirements: Submit typescript.
Copyright ownership: B. G. Teubner-Verlag
Rejected manuscripts: Returned
Time before publication decision: 1 mo.
Time between decision and publication: 6-8 mos.
Number of reviewers: 1-2
Articles submitted per year: 10-15
Articles published per year: 10-12
Book reviews submitted per year: 50-70
Book reviews published per year: 40-45

(459)
*Byzantinoslavica: Revue Internationale des Etudes Byzantines

Vladimír Vavřínek, Editor
Inst. for Classical Studies
Římská 14
120 00 Prague 2, Czech Republic

Telephone: (42) 2 2361672
First published: 1929
Sponsoring organization: Československá Akademie Věd
ISSN: 0007-7712
MLA acronym: BSl

SUBSCRIPTION INFORMATION

Frequency of publication: 2 times/yr.
Circulation: 900
Available in microform: No
Subscription price: 230 f ($131.00)/yr.
Year to which price refers: 1991
Subscription address: John Benjamins B.V., Periodical Trade, Amsteldijk 44, P.O. Box 75577, 1070 AN Amsterdam, Netherlands
Additional subscription address: John Benjamins North America, Inc., 821 Bethlehem Pike, Philadelphia, PA 19118
Subscription telephone: (31) 20 6738156; 215 836-1200
Subscription fax: (31) 20 6739773; 215 836-1204

ADVERTISING INFORMATION

Advertising accepted: Yes

EDITORIAL DESCRIPTION

Scope: Covers all fields of Byzantine studies with an emphasis on the problems of Byzantino-Slav relations. Also provides a current annotated bibliography of Byzantine studies emphasizing Byzantino-Slav relations and providing full coverage of the scholarly Byzantinological production published in the Central and East European countries.
Reviews books: Yes
Publishes notes: Yes, bibliographical notes
Languages accepted: English; French; German; Italian; Russian
Prints abstracts: No

SUBMISSION REQUIREMENTS

Restrictions on contributors: None
Author pays submission fee: No
Author pays page charges: No
Length of articles: 10-25 typescript pp.
Length of book reviews: 3-6 typescript pp.
Length of notes: 40-60 words
Number of copies required: 2
Copyright ownership: Publishing House Academia, Prague
Rejected manuscripts: Returned
Time before publication decision: 2-3 mos.
Time between decision and publication: 1-2 yrs.
Number of reviewers: 1-2
Articles published per year: 8-10
Book reviews published per year: 20
Notes published per year: 2,000

(460)
*Byzantion: Revue Internationale des Etudes Byzantines

Alice Leroy-Molinghen & Justin Mossay, Editors
Fondation Byzantine
4, boulevard de l'Empereur
1000 Brussels, Belgium

First published: 1924
ISSN: 0378-2506
MLA acronym: Byzantion

SUBSCRIPTION INFORMATION

Frequency of publication: 1-2 times/yr.
Available in microform: No
Subscription address: Editions Universa, 24, Hoenderstr., 9200 Wetteren, Belgium

ADVERTISING INFORMATION

Advertising accepted: No

EDITORIAL DESCRIPTION

Scope: Publishes studies on the Byzantine empire: history, art, literature, and philology.
Reviews books: Yes
Publishes notes: Yes
Languages accepted: English; French; German; Italian; Greek
Prints abstracts: No

SUBMISSION REQUIREMENTS

Restrictions on contributors: None
Author pays submission fee: No
Author pays page charges: No
Length of articles: No restrictions
Length of book reviews: 1-4 pp.
Number of copies required: 1
Special requirements: Submit original typescript.
Copyright ownership: Assn. "Byzantion"
Rejected manuscripts: Returned
Number of reviewers: 2
Articles submitted per year: 40
Articles published per year: 30

(461)
*Byzantion—Nea Hellas

Aldjandro Zorbas, Editor
Pabellón Helènico
Facultad de Filosofía & Humanidades
Univ. de Chile
Casilla 10.136
Santiago, Chile

Telephone: (56) 2 2236639
Fax: (56) 2 2725977 ext. 73
First published: 1970
Sponsoring organization: Univ. de Chile, Centro de Estudios Bizantinos & Neohelénicos
ISSN: 0716-2138
MLA acronym: BzNH

SUBSCRIPTION INFORMATION

Frequency of publication: Annual
Circulation: 1,000
Available in microform: No

ADVERTISING INFORMATION

Advertising accepted: No

EDITORIAL DESCRIPTION

Scope: Publishes articles on medieval and modern Greek history, literature, art, economics, and linguistics.
Reviews books: Yes
Publishes notes: No
Languages accepted: Spanish; English; French
Prints abstracts: Yes
Author-anonymous submission: No

SUBMISSION REQUIREMENTS

Restrictions on contributors: None
Author pays submission fee: No
Author pays page charges: No
Length of articles: No restrictions
Length of book reviews: No restrictions
Style: None
Number of copies required: 2
Special requirements: Submit original manuscript.
Copyright ownership: Centro de Estudios Bizantinos & Neohelénicos
Rejected manuscripts: Returned
Time before publication decision: 3 mos.
Time between decision and publication: 3 mos.
Number of reviewers: 1

(462)
Cadernos de Estudos Lingüísticos

UNICAMP-Inst. de Estudos da Linguagem
Setor de Publicações
C.P. 6045
13081 Campinas-SP, Brazil

First published: 1979
Sponsoring organization: Dept. de Lingüística do Inst. de Estudos da Linguagem, Univ. Estadual de Campinas
ISSN: 0102-5767
MLA acronym: CEL

SUBSCRIPTION INFORMATION

Frequency of publication: 2 times/yr.
Circulation: 800
Available in microform: No

EDITORIAL DESCRIPTION

Scope: Publishes articles on the theory of linguistics, Portuguese language, native languages of Brazil, syntax, semantics, and pragmatics.
Reviews books: Yes
Publishes notes: No
Languages accepted: Portuguese; English; French; Spanish
Prints abstracts: No
Author-anonymous submission: No

SUBMISSION REQUIREMENTS

Time before publication decision: 6 mos.
Time between decision and publication: 6 mos.
Articles published per year: 12-16

(463)
Cadernos de Lingüística e Teoria da Literatura

Dept. de Lingüística e Teoria da Literatura
Univ. Federal de Minas Gerais
Faculdade de Letras
C.P. 905
30,000 Belo Horizonte, Minas Gerais, Brazil

First published: 1978
Sponsoring organization: Univ. Federal de Minas Gerais
ISSN: 0101-3548
MLA acronym: CLTL

SUBSCRIPTION INFORMATION

Frequency of publication: Annual
Circulation: 1,000
Available in microform: No

ADVERTISING INFORMATION

Advertising accepted: No

EDITORIAL DESCRIPTION

Scope: Publishes articles on Portuguese linguistics, literary theory, and general linguistics.
Reviews books: No
Publishes notes: No
Languages accepted: Germanic languages; Romance languages
Prints abstracts: Yes
Author-anonymous submission: No

SUBMISSION REQUIREMENTS

Restrictions on contributors: None
Author pays submission fee: No
Author pays page charges: No
Length of articles: 30 pp. maximum
Style: Chicago
Number of copies required: 2
Copyright ownership: Journal; reverts to author after 1 yr.
Rejected manuscripts: Returned
Time before publication decision: 3 mos.
Time between decision and publication: 6 mos.
Number of reviewers: 2
Articles submitted per year: 15
Articles published per year: 10

(464)
*Cahiers Balkaniques

Jack Feuillet, Henri Tonnet, L. Kovacs, B. Lory, & T. Velmans, Editors
2, rue de Lille
75007 Paris, France

Telephone: (33) 1 49264259
Fax: (33) 1 49264299
First published: 1981
Sponsoring organization: Inst. National des Langues & Civilisations Orientales (INALCO)
ISSN: 0290-7402
MLA acronym: CBalk

SUBSCRIPTION INFORMATION

Frequency of publication: 2 times/yr.
Circulation: 50
Available in microform: No
Subscription price: 70 F/yr.
Year to which price refers: 1990

ADVERTISING INFORMATION

Advertising accepted: No

EDITORIAL DESCRIPTION

Scope: Publishes articles on Balkan languages, literatures, and history. Each issue is devoted to a specific theme.
Reviews books: Yes
Publishes notes: Yes
Languages accepted: French; Italian; Greek; German; English
Prints abstracts: No

SUBMISSION REQUIREMENTS

Author pays submission fee: No
Author pays page charges: No
Length of articles: 10,000 words
Length of book reviews: 1,000 words
Number of copies required: 1
Special requirements: If possible, submit on Macintosh-compatible diskette.
Copyright ownership: Author
Rejected manuscripts: Returned
Time before publication decision: 6 mos. maximum
Time between decision and publication: 1 yr. maximum
Number of reviewers: 1-2
Articles submitted per year: 20-25
Articles published per year: 15
Book reviews submitted per year: 10
Book reviews published per year: 5-6
Notes submitted per year: 12
Notes published per year: 5-6

(465)
*Cahiers Charles V

Claire Bruyère, Editor
Inst. d'Anglais Charles V
10, rue Charles V
75004 Paris, France

Telephone: (33) 1 42742754
Fax: (33) 1 42781247
First published: 1979
Sponsoring organization: Inst. d'Anglais Charles V; Univ. de Paris VII-Denis Diderot
MLA acronym: CCV

SUBSCRIPTION INFORMATION

Frequency of publication: Annual
Circulation: 600-700
Available in microform: No
Subscription price: 60 F/yr.; 50 F/yr. students
Year to which price refers: 1991

ADVERTISING INFORMATION

Advertising accepted: Yes

EDITORIAL DESCRIPTION

Scope: The series is meant as the place of publication of some of the research under way at the Institut d'Anglais (Université de Paris VII-Denis Diderot), which is devoted to a field or a special topic related to American and English literature and linguistics, English studies, American studies, and translation from English into French.
Reviews books: No
Publishes notes: No
Languages accepted: French; English
Prints abstracts: Yes
Author-anonymous submission: No

SUBMISSION REQUIREMENTS

Restrictions on contributors: Some contributors, including the editor, must be members of the Inst. d'Anglais Charles V. No more than half the contributions can be in English. All contributions are solicited.
Author pays submission fee: No
Author pays page charges: No
Length of articles: 5,000-6,000 words
Style: Adapted MLA
Number of copies required: 2
Copyright ownership: Inst. d'Anglais Charles V & Univ. de Paris VII-Denis Diderot
Rejected manuscripts: Returned
Time before publication decision: 3 mos.
Time between decision and publication: 6 mos.
Number of reviewers: 2
Articles published per year: 12-14

(466)
*Cahiers Confrontation

René Major, Editor
23, quai Bourbon
75004 Paris, France

Fax: (33) 1 43269197
First published: 1979
Sponsoring organization: Centre National des Lettres
ISSN: 0222-5966
MLA acronym: CCon

SUBSCRIPTION INFORMATION

Frequency of publication: 2 times/yr.
Circulation: 1,500
Available in microform: No
Subscription address: Editions AUBIER, 13, quai de Conti, 75006 Paris, France
Subscription telephone: (33) 1 40513040

ADVERTISING INFORMATION

Advertising accepted: No

EDITORIAL DESCRIPTION

Scope: Publishes articles on literary theory, psychoanalysis, and philosophical approaches to literature.
Reviews books: No
Publishes notes: No
Languages accepted: French
Prints abstracts: No
Author-anonymous submission: No

SUBMISSION REQUIREMENTS

Author pays submission fee: No
Author pays page charges: No
Length of articles: 20 typed double-spaced pp.
Number of copies required: 1
Copyright ownership: Author

(467)
*Cahiers CRLH-CIRAOI

Jean-Michel Racault, Editor
Univ. de la Réunion
Fac. des Lettres & Sciences Humaines
26, av. de la Victoire
97489 St.-Denis Cédex, Ile de la Réunion

Additional editorial address: Editions l'Harmattan, 16-21 rue des Ecoles, 75005 Paris, France
Telephone: (33) 1 43564757 (Editorial Board); (33) 1 43547910 (Editions l'Harmattan)
First published: 1984
Sponsoring organization: Conseil Général de la Réunion; Centre de Recherches Littéraires & Historiques (CRLH) ; Centre Inter-Disciplinaire de Recherches Afro-Indian-Océaniques (CIRAOI)
ISSN: 0299-0628
MLA acronym: CCRLH

SUBSCRIPTION INFORMATION

Frequency of publication: Annual
Circulation: 500
Available in microform: No

ADVERTISING INFORMATION

Advertising accepted: No

EDITORIAL DESCRIPTION

Scope: Publishes interdisciplinary studies with an emphasis on French and comparative literature, Anglo-American literature and civilization, and history. Each volume focuses on a specific subject.
Reviews books: No
Publishes notes: No
Languages accepted: French; English occasionally
Prints abstracts: Yes
Author-anonymous submission: No

SUBMISSION REQUIREMENTS

Restrictions on contributors: Contributions are solicited.
Author pays submission fee: No
Author pays page charges: No
Length of articles: 15 pp.
Style: RHLF (French); MLA (English)
Number of copies required: 2
Copyright ownership: Author
Rejected manuscripts: Not returned
Time before publication decision: 1 yr.
Time between decision and publication: 6 mos.
Number of reviewers: 3
Articles published per year: 20
Books submitted per year: 1-2
Books published per year: 1

(468)
*Cahiers de Civilisation Médiévale (X^e-XIIe Siècles)

Pierre Bec & Robert Favreau, Editors
Centre d'Etudes Supérieures de Civilisation Médiévale
Univ. de Poitiers
24, rue de la Chaîne
86022 Poitiers, France

Telephone: (33) 49410386
First published: 1958
Sponsoring organization: Centre National de la Recherche Scientifique
ISSN: 0007-9731
MLA acronym: CCM

SUBSCRIPTION INFORMATION

Frequency of publication: 4 times/yr. plus annual bibliography
Circulation: 1,700
Available in microform: No
Subscription price: 390 F/yr. France; 430 F/yr. elsewhere
Year to which price refers: 1992

ADVERTISING INFORMATION

Advertising accepted: Yes

EDITORIAL DESCRIPTION

Scope: Publishes articles on all aspects of medieval civilization including history, art history, literature, and philosophy.
Reviews books: Yes
Publishes notes: Yes
Languages accepted: French
Prints abstracts: Yes
Author-anonymous submission: No

SUBMISSION REQUIREMENTS

Restrictions on contributors: None
Author pays submission fee: No
Author pays page charges: No
Length of articles: 20-25 printed pp.
Length of book reviews: 2 pp.
Length of notes: 1/2 p.
Number of copies required: 2
Special requirements: Submit French and English abstracts with manuscript.
Copyright ownership: Centre d'Etudes Supérieures de Civilisation Médiévale
Rejected manuscripts: Not returned
Time before publication decision: 2 mos.
Time between decision and publication: 6-24 mos.
Number of reviewers: 2
Articles submitted per year: 25
Articles published per year: 15
Book reviews submitted per year: 130
Book reviews published per year: 100
Notes submitted per year: 30-35
Notes published per year: 20-25

(469)
*Cahiers de l'Association Internationale des Etudes Françaises

Charles Mazouer, Editor
Assn. Internationale des Etudes Françaises
11, place Marcelin-Berthelot
75005 Paris, France

Additional editorial address: Univ. de Bordeaux III, Domaine Universitaire, 33405 Talence Cedex, France
First published: 1951
Sponsoring organization: Assn. Internationale des Etudes Françaises
ISSN: 0571-5865
MLA acronym: CAIEF

SUBSCRIPTION INFORMATION

Frequency of publication: Annual
Circulation: 800
Available in microform: No
Subscription price: 150 F/yr.
Year to which price refers: 1992

ADVERTISING INFORMATION

Advertising accepted: No

EDITORIAL DESCRIPTION

Scope: Publishes articles on French studies including literature, philosophy, and the arts.
Reviews books: No
Publishes notes: No
Languages accepted: French
Prints abstracts: No

SUBMISSION REQUIREMENTS

Restrictions on contributors: Publishes the proceedings of the annual congress.
Author pays submission fee: No
Author pays page charges: No
Length of articles: 5,500 words
Number of copies required: 1
Copyright ownership: Assn. Internationale des Etudes Françaises
Articles submitted per year: 18
Articles published per year: 18

(470)
*Cahiers de Lexicologie

Bernard Quemada, Editor
Inst. National de la Langue Française
52 Blvd. de Magenta
75010 Paris, France

First published: 1959
Sponsoring organization: Inst. National de la Langue Française (C.N.R.S.)
ISSN: 0007-9871
MLA acronym: CdL

SUBSCRIPTION INFORMATION

Frequency of publication: 2 times/yr.
Available in microform: No
Subscription address: Soc. Nouvelle, Didier-Erudition, 6, rue de la Sorbonne, 75005 Paris, France

ADVERTISING INFORMATION

Advertising accepted: Yes

EDITORIAL DESCRIPTION

Scope: Publishes leading articles on contemporary trends in lexicology, lexicography, and semantics that are of significant interest to scholars and specialists concerned with the methodology of the above matters.
Reviews books: Yes
Publishes notes: Yes
Languages accepted: French; English
Prints abstracts: Yes
Author-anonymous submission: No

SUBMISSION REQUIREMENTS

Author pays submission fee: No
Author pays page charges: No
Length of articles: 5,000-7,000 words
Length of book reviews: 500-700 words
Length of notes: 1,000-3,000 words
Style: Chicago
Number of copies required: 2
Copyright ownership: Journal & author
Time before publication decision: 2-3 mos.
Time between decision and publication: 8-12 mos.
Number of reviewers: 3
Articles submitted per year: 30-40
Articles published per year: 15-20

Book reviews submitted per year: 15-20
Notes submitted per year: 4-5
Notes published per year: 2-3

(471)
Les Cahiers de l'I.C.P.: Bulletin de la Communication

Dominique Vuillet, Secretary
Inst. de la Communication Parlée
Univ. Stendhal
B.P. 25
38040 Grenoble Cedex 9, France

Telephone: (33) 76824337
Fax: (33) 76824335
First published: 1991
Sponsoring organization: Inst. de la Communication Parlée
ISSN: 1163-7641
MLA acronym: CICPB

SUBSCRIPTION INFORMATION

Frequency of publication: Annual
Subscription price: 100 F/yr.
Year to which price refers: 1992

ADVERTISING INFORMATION

Advertising accepted: No

EDITORIAL DESCRIPTION

Scope: Publishes articles on all aspects of speech sciences.
Languages accepted: French; English
Prints abstracts: Yes

(472)
Les Cahiers de l'I.C.P.: Rapport de Recherche

Dominique Vuillet, Editor
Inst. de la Communication Parlée
Univ. Stendhal
B.P. 25
38040 Grenoble Cedex 9, France

Telephone: (33) 76824337
Fax: (33) 76824335
First published: 1991
Sponsoring organization: Inst. de la Communication Parlée
ISSN: 1163-765X
MLA acronym: CICPR

SUBSCRIPTION INFORMATION

Frequency of publication: Annual
Subscription price: 100 F/yr.
Year to which price refers: 1992

ADVERTISING INFORMATION

Advertising accepted: No

EDITORIAL DESCRIPTION

Scope: Publishes articles on language and linguistics published by members of the Institut de la Communication Parlée in major French and international journals.
Reviews books: No
Languages accepted: French; English
Prints abstracts: Yes

SUBMISSION REQUIREMENTS

Restrictions on contributors: Contributors must be members of the Institut de la Communication Parlée.

(473)
*Cahiers de Linguistique—Asie Orientale

Alain Lucas & Waltraud Paul, Editors
Ecole des Hautes Etudes en Sciences Sociales
Centre de Recherches Linguistiques sur l'Asie Orientale
54, blvd. Raspail
75270 Paris Cedex 06, France

Additional editorial address: W. Paul, Ostasien-Inst., Heinrich-Heine-Univ., Brinckmannstr. 8-10, 4000 Dusseldorf, Germany
Telephone: (33) 1 49542404 (A. Lucas); (49) 211 9330547 (W. Paul)
Fax: (33) 1 49542671 (A. Lucas); (49) 211 9330560 (W. Paul)
First published: 1977
Sponsoring organization: Centre National de la Recherche Scientifique
ISSN: 0153-3320
MLA acronym: CLAO

SUBSCRIPTION INFORMATION

Frequency of publication: 2 times/yr.
Circulation: 120
Available in microform: No
Subscription price: 180 F/yr. institutions; 150 F/yr. individuals European Community; 180 F/yr. inividuals elsewhere
Year to which price refers: 1992

ADVERTISING INFORMATION

Advertising accepted: Yes

EDITORIAL DESCRIPTION

Scope: Publishes articles on East Asian linguistics.
Reviews books: Yes
Publishes notes: Yes
Languages accepted: French; English; German; Chinese languages
Prints abstracts: Yes
Author-anonymous submission: Yes

SUBMISSION REQUIREMENTS

Author pays submission fee: No
Author pays page charges: No
Length of articles: 40 pp. maximum
Length of book reviews: 1-5 pp.
Length of notes: 1 p.
Style: Journal
Number of copies required: 2
Special requirements: Submit camera-ready copy for maps, diagrams, etc. Also submit an abstract in French and in English.
Copyright ownership: Journal
Rejected manuscripts: Returned at author's request
Time before publication decision: 6-12 mos.
Time between decision and publication: 6 mos.
Number of reviewers: 2-3
Articles submitted per year: 20
Articles published per year: 10-14
Book reviews submitted per year: 8-10
Book reviews published per year: 8
Notes submitted per year: 2
Notes published per year: 1

(474)
*Cahiers de l'Institut de Linguistique de Louvain

Guy Jucquois & Yves Duhoux, Editors
Inst. de Linguistique
Place Blaise Pascal
1348 Louvain-la-Neuve, Belgium

First published: 1972
Sponsoring organization: Univ. Catholique de Louvain, Inst. de Linguistique
ISSN: 0771-6524
MLA acronym: CdIL

SUBSCRIPTION INFORMATION

Frequency of publication: 2 times/yr.
Available in microform: No
Subscription price: 1,200 BF/yr.
Year to which price refers: 1992
Subscription address: Peeters, Grand'Rue 56, 1348 Louvain-la-Neuve, Belgium

ADVERTISING INFORMATION

Advertising accepted: Yes

EDITORIAL DESCRIPTION

Scope: Publishes articles, collections on a specific theme, and monographs. Linguistics is regarded in its broadest sense including traditional problems and contemporary research. A very special place has been given to the peripheral domains of linguistics: anthropology, psychoanalysis, psychology, sociology, etc.
Reviews books: Yes
Publishes notes: Yes
Languages accepted: English; French; German; Dutch; Spanish
Prints abstracts: Yes
Author-anonymous submission: No

SUBMISSION REQUIREMENTS

Restrictions on contributors: None
Author pays submission fee: No
Author pays page charges: No
Length of articles: 25 pp.
Length of book reviews: 1 p.
Number of copies required: 1
Special requirements: Submit original typescript.
Copyright ownership: Journal
Rejected manuscripts: Not returned
Time before publication decision: 1 mo.
Time between decision and publication: 8 mos.
Number of reviewers: 2
Articles submitted per year: 40
Articles published per year: 20
Book reviews submitted per year: 60
Book reviews published per year: 40

(475)
Cahiers des Amis de Robert Brasillach

Dominique Gallarques, Editor
Assn. des Amis de Robert Brasillach
C.P. 2755
1002 Lausanne, Switzerland

First published: 1947
Sponsoring organization: Assn. des Amis de Robert Brasillach
ISSN: 0409-8536
MLA acronym: CARB

SUBSCRIPTION INFORMATION

Frequency of publication: Annual
Available in microform: No

ADVERTISING INFORMATION

Advertising accepted: No

EDITORIAL DESCRIPTION

Scope: Publishes articles about the work of Robert Brasillach.
Reviews books: No
Publishes notes: No
Languages accepted: French
Prints abstracts: Yes

SUBMISSION REQUIREMENTS

Author pays submission fee: No
Author pays page charges: No
Length of articles: No restrictions
Number of copies required: 3
Copyright ownership: Journal
Rejected manuscripts: Returned

(476)
*Cahiers d'Etudes Africaines

Jean-Loup Amselle, Editor
Ecole des Hautes Etudes en Sciences Sociales
54, boulevard Raspail
75006 Paris, France

Telephone: (33) 1 49542469
Fax: (33) 1 45449311
First published: 1960
Sponsoring organization: Ecole des Hautes Etudes en Sciences Sociales
ISSN: 0008-0055
MLA acronym: CEAfr

SUBSCRIPTION INFORMATION

Frequency of publication: 4 times/yr.
Circulation: 1,100
Available in microform: No
Subscription price: 390 F/yr. institutions France; 446 F/yr. institutions elsewhere; 255 F/yr. individuals
Year to which price refers: 1991
Subscription address: CDR, Centrale des Revues, 11 rue Gossin, 92543 Montrouge Cedex, France

ADVERTISING INFORMATION

Advertising accepted: Yes, on an exchange basis

EDITORIAL DESCRIPTION

Scope: Publishes articles on the social sciences in Africa, including anthropology, economics, ethnology, history, geography, linguistics, and political sciences.
Reviews books: Yes
Publishes notes: Yes
Languages accepted: English; French
Prints abstracts: Yes
Author-anonymous submission: No

SUBMISSION REQUIREMENTS

Restrictions on contributors: None
Author pays submission fee: No
Author pays page charges: No
Length of articles: 25-30 double-spaced typescript pp.
Length of book reviews: 2-3 double-spaced typescript pp.
Length of notes: 10-15 double-spaced typescript pp.
Style: French: *Code typographique*; English: *Hart*, Oxford Univ. Press
Number of copies required: 2
Special requirements: Submit original typescript.
Copyright ownership: Ecole des Hautes Etudes en Sciences Sociales
Rejected manuscripts: Not returned
Time before publication decision: 3 mos.
Time between decision and publication: 18 mos.
Number of reviewers: 3
Articles submitted per year: 70
Articles published per year: 40
Book reviews submitted per year: 80-90

Book reviews published per year: 25 full-length and 70 short notes
Notes submitted per year: 10
Notes published per year: 5-10

(477)
Cahiers d'Etudes Germaniques

Marie-Hélène Varnier, Editor
Bibliothèque de l'U.E.R. d'Etudes Germaniques
Univ. de Provence
29, ave. Robert Schuman
13621 Aix-en-Provence, France

ISSN: 0751-4239
MLA acronym: CEGe

SUBSCRIPTION INFORMATION

Frequency of publication: Annual

(478)
*Cahiers d'Etudes Médiévales

Guy H. Allard, Editor
Inst. d'Etudes Médiévales
Univ. de Montréal
C.P. 6128 succ. A
Montreal, Quebec H3C 3J7, Canada

Telephone: 514 745-4290
Fax: 514 745-4299
First published: 1972
Sponsoring organization: Inst. d'Etudes Médiévales de l'Univ. de Montréal; Conseil de Recherches en Sciences Humaines du Canada
ISSN: 0381-1719
MLA acronym: CEM

SUBSCRIPTION INFORMATION

Frequency of publication: Annual
Available in microform: No
Subscription address: Editions Bellarmin, 165 rue Deslauriers, Ville St. Laurent, Quebec H4N 2S4, Canada

ADVERTISING INFORMATION

Advertising accepted: No

EDITORIAL DESCRIPTION

Scope: Publishes monographs that focus on new approaches to medieval civilization and which emphasize relatively unknown aspects of medieval culture.
Reviews books: No
Publishes notes: No
Languages accepted: French; English
Prints abstracts: No
Author-anonymous submission: No

SUBMISSION REQUIREMENTS

Restrictions on contributors: None
Author pays submission fee: Yes
Author pays page charges: Yes
Length of articles: 25-30 pp.
Length of books: 200-300 pp.
Number of copies required: 3
Copyright ownership: Editions Bellarmin
Rejected manuscripts: Not returned
Time before publication decision: 3-4 mos.
Time between decision and publication: 3-4 mos.
Number of reviewers: 3
Books submitted per year: 2-3
Books published per year: 1

(479)
*Cahiers d'Etudes Mongoles et Siberiennes

Marie-Lise Beffa, Editor
Centre d'Etudes Mongoles
Laboratoire d'Ethnologie & de Sociologie Comparative
Univ. de Paris X
200 av. de la République
92001 Nanterre, France

Telephone: (33) 1 40977755
Fax: (33) 1 40977117
First published: 1970
Sponsoring organization: Centre National de la Recherche Scientifique; Univ. de Paris X-Nanterre
ISSN: 0766-5075
MLA acronym: EMong

SUBSCRIPTION INFORMATION

Frequency of publication: Annual
Circulation: 500
Available in microform: No
Subscription price: 75 F/yr.
Year to which price refers: 1992
Subscription address: Service de Publication, at the above address

ADVERTISING INFORMATION

Advertising accepted: Yes, on an exchange basis

EDITORIAL DESCRIPTION

Scope: Presents various documents and studies with regard to Mongolia and Siberia, giving preference to those dealing with linguistic and cultural aspects. Also publishes articles on the peoples of eastern Siberia.
Reviews books: Yes
Languages accepted: French; English; Mongol languages
Prints abstracts: Yes

SUBMISSION REQUIREMENTS

Restrictions on contributors: None
Author pays submission fee: No
Author pays page charges: No
Length of articles: No restrictions
Length of book reviews: No restrictions
Number of copies required: 2
Special requirements: Submit typescript.
Copyright ownership: Laboratoire d'Ethnologie & de Sociologie Comparative
Rejected manuscripts: Returned
Time before publication decision: 6 mos.
Time between decision and publication: 1 yr.
Number of reviewers: 5

(480)
Cahiers d'Etudes Romanes

J. Battesti Pelegrin, Editor
Univ. de Provence (Aix-Marseille I)
13621 Aix-en-Provence, France

First published: 1974
ISSN: 0180-684X
MLA acronym: CER

SUBSCRIPTION INFORMATION

Subscription address: Klincksieck, 11, rue de Lille, 75007 Paris, France

EDITORIAL DESCRIPTION

Scope: Publishes articles on Romance language literatures.
Languages accepted: French; Spanish; Portuguese

(481)
Cahiers du Département des Langues et des Sciences du Langage

G. Peter Winnington, Editor
Dépt. des Langues et des Sciences du Langage
Section de Linguistique, Fac. des Lettres
BFSH 2
Univ. de Lausanne
1015 Lausanne, Switzerland

First published: 1985
Sponsoring organization: Dépt. des Langues & des Sciences du Langage, Univ. de Lausanne
ISSN: 0256-1565
MLA acronym: CdDLSL

SUBSCRIPTION INFORMATION

Frequency of publication: 2 times/yr.
Available in microform: No

ADVERTISING INFORMATION

Advertising accepted: No

EDITORIAL DESCRIPTION

Scope: Publishes working papers in linguistics, psycholinguistics, neurolinguistics, and related fields, derived from research and lectures at the Université de Lausanne.
Reviews books: No
Publishes notes: No
Languages accepted: French; English; German
Prints abstracts: No

SUBMISSION REQUIREMENTS

Restrictions on contributors: Unsolicited contributions are not accepted.
Copyright ownership: Author

(482)
*Cahiers du Dix-septième: An Interdisciplinary Journal

Francis B. Assaf, Editor
Dept. of Romance Languages
Univ. of Georgia
Athens, GA 30602

Telephone: 706 542-3164
Fax: 706 542-3287
E-mail: FASSAF@UGA.BITNET
First published: 1987
Sponsoring organization: Southeast American Soc. for French Seventeenth-Century Studies; Dept. of Romance Languages, Univ. of Georgia
ISSN: 1040-3647
MLA acronym: CdDS

SUBSCRIPTION INFORMATION

Frequency of publication: 2 times/yr.
Circulation: 90
Available in microform: No
Subscription price: $17.00/yr. institutions US; $19.00/yr. institutions elsewhere; $15.00/yr. individuals US; $17.00/yr. individuals elsewhere
Year to which price refers: 1992

ADVERTISING INFORMATION

Advertising accepted: Yes
Advertising rates: $140.00/half page; $250.00/full page

EDITORIAL DESCRIPTION

Scope: Publishes articles on French 17th-century studies, including literature, art, music, history, and philosophy.
Reviews books: Yes
Publishes notes: No
Languages accepted: English; French
Prints abstracts: No
Author-anonymous submission: Yes

SUBMISSION REQUIREMENTS

Restrictions on contributors: None
Author pays submission fee: No
Author pays page charges: No
Length of articles: 4,000-20,000 words
Length of book reviews: 250-750 words
Style: MLA
Number of copies required: 2
Special requirements: Submission of IBM-formatted Microsoft Word or unformatted ASCII diskette is also acceptable. Book reviews are solicited.
Copyright ownership: Journal
Rejected manuscripts: Returned; enclose SASE.
Time before publication decision: 6 mos.
Number of reviewers: 2
Articles submitted per year: 37-40
Articles published per year: 29-30
Book reviews published per year: 5-10

(483)
*Cahiers du Français des Années Quatre-Vingts

Marie-Anne Mochet & Charmian O'Neil, Editors
C.R.E.D.I.F.
Ecole Normale Supérieure de Fontenay-St.-Cloud
Grille d'Honneur
Parc de Saint-Cloud
92211 Saint-Cloud Cédex, France

Telephone: (33) 1 47719111
Fax: (33) 1 46023911
First published: 1985
Sponsoring organization: Ecole Normale Supérieure de Fontenay-St.-Cloud
ISSN: 0765-068X
MLA acronym: CFAQV

SUBSCRIPTION INFORMATION

Frequency of publication: Annual
Circulation: 300
Available in microform: No
Subscription address: Didier Erudition, 6 rue de la Sorbonne, 75007 Paris, France
Subscription telephone: (33) 1 43544757

ADVERTISING INFORMATION

Advertising accepted: No

EDITORIAL DESCRIPTION

Scope: Publishes articles on the work carried out by the group *Variété des pratiques Langagières dans le français des Années quatre-vingts* on variations in the French language in the 1980s.
Reviews books: No
Publishes notes: No
Languages accepted: French
Prints abstracts: Yes

SUBMISSION REQUIREMENTS

Author pays submission fee: No
Author pays page charges: No
Length of articles: 14,000-23,000 words
Number of copies required: 1
Special requirements: Submit on diskette.
Copyright ownership: Ecole Normale Supérieure de Fontenay-Saint-Cloud
Time between decision and publication: 6 mos.
Articles published per year: 5-8

(484)
*Cahiers du Monde Hispanique et Luso-Brésilien/Caravelle

Georges Baudot, Director
c/o Annie Paradis
Inst. Pluridisciplinaire d'Etudes sur l'Amérique Latine à Toulouse
56, rue du Taur
31069 Toulouse Cedex, France

Telephone: (33) 61225831
First published: 1963
Sponsoring organization: Centre National des Lettres; Univ. de Toulouse-Le Mirail; Centre National de la Recherche Scientifique
ISSN: 0008-0152
MLA acronym: CMHLB

SUBSCRIPTION INFORMATION

Frequency of publication: 2 times/yr.
Circulation: 1,000
Available in microform: No
Subscription price: 160 F/yr.
Year to which price refers: 1992
Subscription address: Presses Universitaires de l'Univ. de Toulouse-Le Mirail, 56, rue du Taur, 31000 Toulouse, France

ADVERTISING INFORMATION

Advertising accepted: Yes

EDITORIAL DESCRIPTION

Scope: Publishes on all aspects of Hispanic American and Luso-Brazilian culture. Includes original short literary works and many articles on literary criticism. Occasionally devotes an issue to one particular country, subject, or author.
Reviews books: Yes
Publishes notes: Yes
Languages accepted: French; Portuguese; Spanish
Prints abstracts: Yes

SUBMISSION REQUIREMENTS

Restrictions on contributors: None
Author pays submission fee: No
Author pays page charges: No
Length of articles: 20 pp.
Length of book reviews: 1 p.
Length of notes: 1/2 p.
Style: Times
Number of copies required: 1
Special requirements: Submit original typescript.
Copyright ownership: Assigned by author to journal
Rejected manuscripts: Not returned
Time before publication decision: 1 yr.
Time between decision and publication: 6 mos.
Number of reviewers: 2 minimum
Articles submitted per year: 25
Articles published per year: 16
Book reviews published per year: 80

(485)
*Cahiers du Monde Russe et Soviétique

Dominique Négrel, Editor
Ecole des Hautes Etudes en Sciences Sociales
Centre d'Etudes sur la Russie & l'Europe Orientale
54, boulevard Raspail
75270 Paris Cedex 06, France

Telephone: (33) 1 49542596
Fax: (33) 1 49542672
First published: 1960
Sponsoring organization: Ecole des Hautes Etudes en Sciences Sociales
ISSN: 0008-0160
MLA acronym: CMRS

SUBSCRIPTION INFORMATION

Frequency of publication: 4 times/yr.
Circulation: 800
Available in microform: No
Subscription price: 435 F/yr. institutions; 255 F/yr. students
Year to which price refers: 1992
Subscription address: CDR Gauthier-Villars—Centrale des Revues, 11, rue Gossin, 92543 Montrouge Cedex, France

ADVERTISING INFORMATION

Advertising accepted: No

EDITORIAL DESCRIPTION

Scope: Publishes articles on Russian literature and history.
Reviews books: No
Languages accepted: English; French
Prints abstracts: Yes

SUBMISSION REQUIREMENTS

Restrictions on contributors: None
Author pays submission fee: No
Author pays page charges: No
Length of articles: 20-25 pp.
Style: None
Number of copies required: 2
Special requirements: Submit original typescript. Submit camera-ready copy for documents and maps and include a 10-line abstract.
Copyright ownership: Author
Rejected manuscripts: Returned
Time before publication decision: 6 mos.
Time between decision and publication: 18 mos.
Number of reviewers: 3
Articles submitted per year: 40
Articles published per year: 24

(486)
*Cahiers Elisabéthains: Late Medieval and Renaissance Studies

Jean-Marie Maguin, Editor
Centre d'Etudes & de Recherches Elisabéthaines
Univ. Paul Valéry
B.P. 5043
34032 Montpellier-Cedex, France

Telephone: (33) 67142200
Fax: (33) 67142200
First published: 1971
Historical variations in title: Formerly Cahiers Elisabéthains: Etudes sur la Pré-Renaissance et la Renaissance Anglaises
Sponsoring organization: Univ. Paul Valéry, Centre d'Etudes et de Recherches Elisabéthaines; Centre National de la Recherche Scientifique
ISSN: 0184-7678
MLA acronym: CahiersE

SUBSCRIPTION INFORMATION

Frequency of publication: 2 times/yr. (Apr., Oct.)
Circulation: 400
Available in microform: No
Subscription price: 140 F/yr. France; 180 F/yr. elsewhere
Year to which price refers: 1992

ADVERTISING INFORMATION

Advertising accepted: Yes, on an exchange basis

EDITORIAL DESCRIPTION

Scope: Publishes articles and reviews on all aspects of the English Renaissance. The term is given its broadest connotation; subjects have ranged from Chaucer to Restoration drama and beyond. The literature and drama of the Elizabethan period is, however, the main focus of our interests. Theater reviews and a discography of English Renaissance music are occasional features.
Reviews books: Yes
Publishes notes: Yes
Languages accepted: English; French
Prints abstracts: Yes
Author-anonymous submission: No

SUBMISSION REQUIREMENTS

Restrictions on contributors: Articles and reviews contributed mainly by members and associates of the Univ. of Montpellier. Publishes two or three guest articles in each number; articles may be submitted for consideration.
Author pays submission fee: No
Author pays page charges: No
Length of articles: 8-20 pp.
Length of book reviews: 1/2-2 pp.
Length of notes: 4 pp. maximum
Style: MLA
Number of copies required: 2
Special requirements: Submit double-spaced typescript or MacWrite II word processed files on 3.5 inch disks, or Microsoft Word 4.
Copyright ownership: Author
Rejected manuscripts: Returned; enclose return postage or international reply coupons.
Time before publication decision: 3 mos.
Time between decision and publication: 18 mos.
Number of reviewers: 2-3
Articles submitted per year: 30
Articles published per year: 10-12
Book reviews submitted per year: 60
Book reviews published per year: 50
Notes submitted per year: 10
Notes published per year: 5

(487)
Cahiers Ferdinand de Saussure: Revue de Linguistique Générale

Rudolf Engler & René Amacker, Editors
Fac. des Lettres
Univ. de Genève
1211 Geneva 4, Switzerland

Additional editorial address: René Amacker, Rue des Charmilles 5, 1203 Geneva, Switzerland
First published: 1941
Sponsoring organization: Cercle Ferdinand de Saussure
ISSN: 0068-516X
MLA acronym: CFS

SUBSCRIPTION INFORMATION

Frequency of publication: Annual
Circulation: 800
Available in microform: No
Subscription address: Librairie Droz, 11, rue Massot, 1211 Geneva 12, Switzerland

ADVERTISING INFORMATION

Advertising accepted: No

EDITORIAL DESCRIPTION

Scope: Publishes articles on general linguistics with regard to Saussurean or Geneva structuralism; includes Saussurean documents.
Reviews books: Yes
Publishes notes: Yes
Languages accepted: French; English; German; Italian
Prints abstracts: No
Author-anonymous submission: No

SUBMISSION REQUIREMENTS

Restrictions on contributors: None
Author pays submission fee: No
Author pays page charges: No
Length of articles: 3,500-12,000 words
Length of book reviews: 1,500 words
Length of notes: 1,500 words
Style: None
Number of copies required: 1
Copyright ownership: Cercle Ferdinand de Saussure
Rejected manuscripts: Returned
Time before publication decision: 2-3 mos.
Time between decision and publication: 6-12 mos.
Number of reviewers: 3-7
Articles submitted per year: 12
Articles published per year: 6-10
Book reviews submitted per year: 5-6
Book reviews published per year: 3-4
Notes submitted per year: Notes are generally written upon invitation and therefore automatically published.
Notes published per year: 0-2

(488)
*Cahiers Gérard de Nerval

Jacques Huré, Editor
58, Ave. Roger Salengro
68100 Mulhouse, France

Telephone: (33) 89456989
First published: 1978
Sponsoring organization: Soc. Gérard de Nerval
ISSN: 0222-1578
MLA acronym: CGN

SUBSCRIPTION INFORMATION

Frequency of publication: Annual
Circulation: 500
Available in microform: No
Subscription price: 100 F/yr.
Year to which price refers: 1992
Subscription address: Mireille Kachanian-Toutenu, 4E rue Aristide Briand, 90300 Offemont, France

ADVERTISING INFORMATION

Advertising accepted: No

EDITORIAL DESCRIPTION

Scope: Publishes articles on Nerval's writings and studies of his work.
Reviews books: Yes
Publishes notes: Yes
Languages accepted: French
Author-anonymous submission: No

SUBMISSION REQUIREMENTS

Restrictions on contributors: Priority is given to articles by members.
Author pays submission fee: No
Author pays page charges: No
Length of articles: 1,500-2,000 words
Length of notes: 800 words
Number of copies required: 2
Special requirements: Submit typescript.
Copyright ownership: Soc. Gérard de Nerval
Rejected manuscripts: Returned
Time before publication decision: 11 mos. maximum
Time between decision and publication: 11 mos. maximum
Number of reviewers: 2
Articles submitted per year: 12
Articles published per year: 6-10
Book reviews submitted per year: 2-3
Notes submitted per year: 4
Notes published per year: 2

(489)
*Cahiers Henri Bosco

Claude Girault, Editor-in-Chief
Amitié Henri Bosco
Palais Aurore, Entrée C
33 Bd. Tzarewitch
06000 Nice, France

Additional editorial address: Diffusion Edisud, La Calade R.N. 7, 13090 Aix-en-Provence, France
Telephone: (33) 93 375555
Fax: (33) 93 375599
First published: 1972
Sponsoring organization: Amitié Henri Bosco; Comité Doyeu Jean Lépine, Nice
ISSN: 0753-4590
MLA acronym: CHB

SUBSCRIPTION INFORMATION

Frequency of publication: Annual
Circulation: 420
Available in microform: No
Subscription price: 120 F/yr.
Year to which price refers: 1992

ADVERTISING INFORMATION

Advertising accepted: No

EDITORIAL DESCRIPTION

Scope: Publishes critical studies on the works of Henri Bosco, unedited works and editions of works by Bosco, and an annual bibliography, as well as studies on friends of Bosco including Jules Roy, Jean Amrouche, Armand Guibert, and Blaise Cendrars.
Reviews books: Yes
Publishes notes: Yes
Languages accepted: French
Prints abstracts: No

SUBMISSION REQUIREMENTS

Author pays submission fee: No
Author pays page charges: No
Number of copies required: 1
Copyright ownership: Publisher
Rejected manuscripts: Not returned

(490)
*Cahiers Internationaux de Symbolisme

Claire Lejeune, Editor
Ciéphum
Univ. de Mons-Hainaut
20, place du Parc
7000 Mons, Belgium

Telephone: (32) 65 335084; (32) 65 373736
Fax: (32) 65 373054
First published: 1962
Sponsoring organization: Univ. de Mons (Ciéphum), Assn. sans But Lucratif Centre Interdisciplinaire d'Etudes Philosophiques
ISSN: 0008-0284
MLA acronym: CIS

SUBSCRIPTION INFORMATION

Frequency of publication: 3 times/yr.
Circulation: 1,200
Available in microform: No
Subscription price: 1,500 BF/yr.
Year to which price refers: 1992

ADVERTISING INFORMATION

Advertising accepted: No

EDITORIAL DESCRIPTION

Scope: Publishes studies on symbolism.
Reviews books: Yes
Publishes notes: Yes
Languages accepted: French
Prints abstracts: No

(491)
*Cahiers Jean Cocteau

Soc. des Amis de Jean Cocteau
17, rue de Lau
91490 Milly-la-Forêt, France

Additional editorial address: Secrétariat, 174 av. du Maine, 75014 Paris, France
First published: 1969
Sponsoring organization: Soc. des Amis de Jean Cocteau
ISSN: 0068-5178
MLA acronym: CJC

SUBSCRIPTION INFORMATION

Frequency of publication: Annual
Circulation: 500
Available in microform: No

ADVERTISING INFORMATION

Advertising accepted: No

EDITORIAL DESCRIPTION

Scope: Promotes the memory of Jean Cocteau.
Reviews books: No
Languages accepted: French
Prints abstracts: No

SUBMISSION REQUIREMENTS

Restrictions on contributors: Contributors must be members of the Soc. des Amis de Jean Cocteau.
Author pays submission fee: No
Author pays page charges: No
Length of articles: No restrictions
Copyright ownership: Author
Time between decision and publication: 1 yr.
Number of reviewers: 1

(492)
*Cahiers Jean Giraudoux

Editions Bernard Grasset
61, rue des Saints-Pères
75006 Paris, France

First published: 1972
Sponsoring organization: Soc. des Amis de Jean Giraudoux
ISSN: 0150-6943
MLA acronym: CJG

SUBSCRIPTION INFORMATION

Frequency of publication: Annual
Circulation: 1,000
Available in microform: No
Subscription address: Soc. des Amis de Jean Giraudoux, rue Louis-Jouvet, 87300 Bellac, France

ADVERTISING INFORMATION

Advertising accepted: No

EDITORIAL DESCRIPTION

Scope: Publishes articles on Jean Giraudoux.
Reviews books: Yes
Languages accepted: French
Prints abstracts: No

SUBMISSION REQUIREMENTS

Restrictions on contributors: Submissions must be previously unpublished.
Author pays submission fee: No

Author pays page charges: No
Length of articles: 5-30 pp.
Length of book reviews: 200 words
Number of copies required: 1
Copyright ownership: Author after 2 yrs.
Rejected manuscripts: Not returned
Time before publication decision: 6 mos.
Time between decision and publication: 1 yr.
Number of reviewers: 6
Articles published per year: 12-14

(493)
*Cahiers Linguistiques d'Ottawa

John T. Jensen, Editor
Dept. of Linguistics
Univ. of Ottawa
Ottawa, Ontario K1N 6N5, Canada

Telephone: 613 564-4207
Fax: 613 564-9067
First published: 1971
Sponsoring organization: Dept. of Linguistics, Univ. of Ottawa
ISSN: 0315-3967
MLA acronym: CLO

SUBSCRIPTION INFORMATION

Frequency of publication: Annual (Nov.)
Circulation: 150
Available in microform: No
Subscription price: C$8.00/yr.
Year to which price refers: 1992

ADVERTISING INFORMATION

Advertising accepted: No

EDITORIAL DESCRIPTION

Scope: Publishes new research in formal, experimental, and applied linguistics in a form which lies between that of an informal working papers series and a formal publication in a standard journal of the discipline. Most articles are of a theoretical nature, but submissions of a bibliographical nature, translations of inaccessible materials, etc., are also welcome. Notes and replies to articles appearing in any number of *CLO* are also encouraged, as are shorter notes dealing with any aspect of linguistics.
Reviews books: Yes
Publishes notes: Yes
Languages accepted: English; French
Prints abstracts: No

SUBMISSION REQUIREMENTS

Restrictions on contributors: None
Author pays submission fee: No
Author pays page charges: No
Length of articles: 30 pp. maximum
Length of book reviews: 10 pp.
Length of notes: 5 pp.
Style: Journal
Number of copies required: 2
Special requirements: Include a 200-word abstract in English or French.
Copyright ownership: Journal
Rejected manuscripts: Returned
Time before publication decision: 6 mos.
Time between decision and publication: 3 mos.
Number of reviewers: 2
Articles submitted per year: 7-8
Articles published per year: 5-6

(494)
*Les Cahiers Naturalistes

Alain Pagès, Editor
B.P. 12
77580 Villers/Morin, France

First published: 1955
Sponsoring organization: Soc. Littéraire des Amis d'Emile Zola
ISSN: 0008-0365
MLA acronym: CNat

SUBSCRIPTION INFORMATION

Frequency of publication: Annual
Circulation: 1,000
Available in microform: No
Subscription price: 160 F ($30.00)/yr.
Year to which price refers: 1992

ADVERTISING INFORMATION

Advertising accepted: Yes

EDITORIAL DESCRIPTION

Scope: The journal is not limited to the study of the life and works of Emile Zola. It is dedicated equally to the study of the Naturalist movement and to the history of the Dreyfus affair. Also publishes an annual bibliography of works dedicated to Zola and to Naturalism.
Reviews books: Yes
Publishes notes: Yes
Languages accepted: French
Prints abstracts: No

SUBMISSION REQUIREMENTS

Restrictions on contributors: Submissions must be previously unpublished.
Author pays submission fee: No
Author pays page charges: No
Length of articles: 10-15 typescript pp. with 1,800 characters per page
Length of book reviews: 1 p.
Length of notes: 1 p.
Style: MLA
Number of copies required: 2
Copyright ownership: Assigned by author to journal
Rejected manuscripts: Not returned
Time before publication decision: 2 mos.
Time between decision and publication: 18-24 mos.
Number of reviewers: 2
Articles submitted per year: 20-30
Articles published per year: 15-25
Book reviews submitted per year: 5-10
Book reviews published per year: 5-10
Notes submitted per year: 5-10
Notes published per year: 5-10

(495)
Cahiers Roumains d'Etudes Littéraires: Revue Trimestrielle de Critique, d'Esthétique et d'Histoire Littéraires

Romul Munteanu, Editor
Maison d'Edition UNIVERS
Piaţa Scînteii 1
Bucharest 1, Romania

First published: 1973
MLA acronym: CREL

SUBSCRIPTION INFORMATION

Frequency of publication: 4 times/yr.
Circulation: 1,600
Available in microform: No
Subscription address: Rompresfilatelia, Dep., Exportation-Importation Press, P.O. Box 12-201, Calea Griviţei 64-66, Bucharest, Romania

ADVERTISING INFORMATION

Advertising accepted: No

EDITORIAL DESCRIPTION

Scope: Publishes scholarly and critical articles on literary criticism, literary history, comparative literature (Romanian and world literature), and literary aesthetics. Publishes news items about Romanian and non-Romanian literature, and conferences of scholars.
Reviews books: Yes
Publishes notes: Yes
Languages accepted: English; French; German; Italian; Russian; Spanish
Prints abstracts: No
Author-anonymous submission: No

SUBMISSION REQUIREMENTS

Restrictions on contributors: None
Author pays submission fee: No
Author pays page charges: No
Length of articles: 6,500-10,000 words
Length of book reviews: 1,000-2,500 words
Length of notes: 500-1,000 words
Style: None
Number of copies required: 2
Copyright ownership: Author
Rejected manuscripts: Not returned
Time before publication decision: 1-2 mos.
Time between decision and publication: 6-12 mos.
Number of reviewers: 1
Articles submitted per year: 100
Articles published per year: 48-50
Book reviews submitted per year: 80-100
Book reviews published per year: 60-65
Notes submitted per year: 45-60
Notes published per year: 32-35

(496)
*Cahiers Saint-John Perse

Jean-Louis Lalanne, Editor
Gallimard Editions
5 rue Sébastien-Bottin
75007 Paris, France

Telephone: (33) 1 49544200
First published: 1978
Sponsoring organization: Fondation Saint-John Perse
ISSN: 0181-7779
MLA acronym: CSJP

SUBSCRIPTION INFORMATION

Frequency of publication: Once every 2 yrs.
Available in microform: No
Subscription address: Fondation Saint-John Perse, Espace Méjanes, 8,10 rue des Allumettes, 13098 Aix-en-Provence Cédex 2, France
Subscription telephone: (33) 42259885

ADVERTISING INFORMATION

Advertising accepted: No

EDITORIAL DESCRIPTION

Scope: Publishes critical articles, an exhaustive bibliography, rare unpublished texts of the poet, documents, correspondence, and other information on Saint-John Perse.
Reviews books: Yes
Publishes notes: Yes
Languages accepted: French

SUBMISSION REQUIREMENTS

Author pays submission fee: No
Author pays page charges: No
Length of articles: 10-30 pp.
Style: Chicago
Number of copies required: 1
Copyright ownership: Gallimard Editions; Fondation St. John Perse
Rejected manuscripts: Returned
Time before publication decision: 3 mos.
Time between decision and publication: 4 mos.
Number of reviewers: 6

Articles submitted per year: 30
Articles published per year: 6

(497)
*Cahiers Simone Weil

Michel Narcy, Editor
14, Résidence du Bois du Roi
91940 Les Ulis, France

Telephone: (33) 1 64467389
First published: 1978
Sponsoring organization: Assn. pour l'Etude de la Pensée de Simone Weil
ISSN: 0181-1126
MLA acronym: CSW

SUBSCRIPTION INFORMATION

Frequency of publication: 4 times/yr.
Circulation: 500
Available in microform: No
Subscription price: 180 F/yr. France; 190 F (240 F airmail)/yr. elsewhere; 60 F/single issue
Year to which price refers: 1992
Subscription address: Assn. pour l'Etude de la Pensée de Simone Weil, c/o Georges Charot, Les Buis B, 38 Avenue Philippe Solari, 13090 Aix-en-Provence, France
Subscription telephone: (33) 42232513

ADVERTISING INFORMATION

Advertising accepted: No

EDITORIAL DESCRIPTION

Scope: Publishes articles on the times, life, and work of Simone Weil.
Reviews books: Yes
Publishes notes: Yes
Languages accepted: French; English
Prints abstracts: Yes
Author-anonymous submission: No

SUBMISSION REQUIREMENTS

Restrictions on contributors: None
Author pays submission fee: No
Author pays page charges: No
Length of articles: 7,000 words
Length of book reviews: 2,500 words
Length of notes: 500 words
Number of copies required: 1
Special requirements: Submit typescript with 3 cm margin on all sides. Footnotes should be numbered consecutively throughout the article.
Copyright ownership: Assn. pour l'Etude de la Pensée de Simone Weil
Rejected manuscripts: Returned
Time before publication decision: 6 mos.
Time between decision and publication: 6 mos.
Number of reviewers: 2
Articles submitted per year: 30
Articles published per year: 25
Book reviews submitted per year: 20
Book reviews published per year: 20
Notes submitted per year: 50
Notes published per year: 50

(498)
*Cahiers Staëliens

Norman King, Editor
25 St. Vincent Crescent
Glasgow G3 8LQ, Scotland

Telephone: (44) 41 2214482
First published: 1964
Sponsoring organization: Soc. des Etudes Staëliennes; Centre National des Lettres
ISSN: 0575-1126
MLA acronym: CahiersS

SUBSCRIPTION INFORMATION

Frequency of publication: Annual
Circulation: 300
Available in microform: No
Subscription price: 120 F/yr.
Year to which price refers: 1991
Subscription address: Librairie Jean Touzot, 38, rue Saint-Suplice, 75278 Paris Cedex 06, France
Additional subscription address: Philippe Carton, Treasurer, 6 rue de Vouillé, 75015 Paris, France

EDITORIAL DESCRIPTION

Scope: Publishes studies on Mme de Staël, the Groupe de Coppet, and European Romanticism.
Reviews books: Yes
Publishes notes: No
Languages accepted: French
Prints abstracts: No
Author-anonymous submission: No

SUBMISSION REQUIREMENTS

Restrictions on contributors: None
Author pays submission fee: No
Author pays page charges: No
Length of articles: 2,000-10,000 words
Length of book reviews: 2 pp. maximum
Number of copies required: 1
Rejected manuscripts: Not returned
Number of reviewers: 2
Articles published per year: 6
Book reviews published per year: 6

(499)
*Cahiers Victoriens et Edouardiens: Revue du Centre d'Etudes et de Recherches Victoriennes et Edouardiennes de l'Université Paul Valéry, Montpellier

Jean-Claude Amalric, Editor
Univ. Paul Valéry
B.P. 5043
34032 Montpellier Cédex, France

Telephone: (33) 67142071
Fax: (33) 67142052
First published: 1974
Sponsoring organization: Univ. Paul Valéry, Centre d'Etudes & de Recherches Victoriennes & Edouardiennes
ISSN: 0220-5610
MLA acronym: CVE

SUBSCRIPTION INFORMATION

Frequency of publication: 2 times/yr. (Apr., Oct.)
Circulation: 350
Available in microform: Yes, through Univ. Microfilms International
Subscription price: 130 F/yr. France; 150 F/yr. elsewhere
Year to which price refers: 1992

ADVERTISING INFORMATION

Advertising accepted: Yes

EDITORIAL DESCRIPTION

Scope: Publishes articles on the literature and civilization of Victorian and Edwardian England (1830-1915).
Reviews books: Yes
Publishes notes: Yes
Languages accepted: English; French
Prints abstracts: Yes
Author-anonymous submission: No

SUBMISSION REQUIREMENTS

Restrictions on contributors: None
Author pays submission fee: No
Author pays page charges: No
Length of articles: 10-20 typescript pp.
Length of book reviews: 300-500 words
Length of notes: 500-600 words
Style: MLA
Number of copies required: 2
Special requirements: Submit a 200-word abstract.
Copyright ownership: Journal
Rejected manuscripts: Returned; enclose return postage or reply coupons.
Time before publication decision: 3-4 mos.
Time between decision and publication: 6-18 mos.
Number of reviewers: 2-3
Articles submitted per year: 20
Articles published per year: 10-15
Book reviews submitted per year: 10-20
Book reviews published per year: 10-15
Notes submitted per year: 3-6
Notes published per year: 2-5

(500)
Čakavska Rič

Radovan Vidović, Editor
Književni Krug, za "Čakavsku rič"
Bosanska 4
58000 Split, Croatia

First published: 1971
ISSN: 0350-7831
MLA acronym: ČaR

SUBSCRIPTION INFORMATION

Frequency of publication: 2 times/yr.

EDITORIAL DESCRIPTION

Scope: Focuses on linguistics of Cakavian dialect.
Reviews books: No
Languages accepted: Serbo-Croatian
Prints abstracts: No

(501)
Calcutta Review

Amalendu Bose, Editor
Asutosh Building
Calcutta Univ.
Calcutta-12, India

First published: 1842
ISSN: 0045-3846
MLA acronym: CalR

SUBSCRIPTION INFORMATION

Frequency of publication: 4 times/yr.
Subscription address: Calcutta Univ. Press, Sri Sibendra Nath Kanjilal, 48 Hazra Rd., Calcutta 19, West Bengal, India

EDITORIAL DESCRIPTION

Scope: Publishes articles on subjects of intellectual and educational interest as well as articles on current political, economic, social, and cultural topics and movements of national and international significance. Discourages excessively technical articles except when they aim at a high standard of scholarship and literary excellence.
Reviews books: Yes
Languages accepted: English
Prints abstracts: No

(502)
*Calgary Working Papers in Linguistics

Lorna Rowsell, Editor
Univ. of Calgary
Dept. of Linguistics
2500 University Dr. NW
Calgary, AB T2N 1N4, Canada

Telephone: 403 220-5469
Fax: 403 282-8606
E-mail: 13422@UCDASVM1
First published: 1975
Sponsoring organization: Graduate Student Assn., Univ. of Calgary
ISSN: 0823-0579
MLA acronym: CalWPL

SUBSCRIPTION INFORMATION

Frequency of publication: Annual (Fall-Winter)
Circulation: 50
Available in microform: No
Subscription price: C$6.00/yr. Canada; C$7.00/yr. US; C$8.00/yr. elsewhere
Year to which price refers: 1992

ADVERTISING INFORMATION

Advertising accepted: No

EDITORIAL DESCRIPTION

Scope: Publishes papers by faculty and students of the University of Calgary, and elsewhere, on theoretical linguistics and related topics.
Reviews books: No
Publishes notes: No
Languages accepted: Primarily English
Prints abstracts: No
Author-anonymous submission: No

SUBMISSION REQUIREMENTS

Author pays submission fee: No
Author pays page charges: No
Length of articles: 20-30 pp.
Style: Linguistic Soc. of America
Number of copies required: 3
Special requirements: Submission on 3.5 in. Macintosh diskette in Microsoft Word format is preferred.
Copyright ownership: Author
Rejected manuscripts: Not returned
Time before publication decision: 3 mos.
Time between decision and publication: 9 mos.
Number of reviewers: 3
Articles submitted per year: 5-6
Articles published per year: 5-6

(503)
*Caliban

Marcienne Rocard, Editor
19, rue Paul Vidal
31000 Toulouse, France

Telephone: (33) 61232317
First published: 1964
Sponsoring organization: Univ. de Toulouse-Le Mirail
ISSN: 0575-2124
MLA acronym: Caliban

SUBSCRIPTION INFORMATION

Frequency of publication: Annual
Circulation: 500
Available in microform: No
Subscription price: 80 F/yr.
Year to which price refers: 1992
Subscription address: Presses Univ. de Mirail, Univ. de Toulouse-Le Mirail, 56, rue du Taur, 31000 Toulouse 2, France
Subscription telephone: (33) 61225831
Subscription fax: (33) 61218420

ADVERTISING INFORMATION

Advertising accepted: Yes

EDITORIAL DESCRIPTION

Scope: Publishes articles on English language literature. Each issue has a separate theme.
Reviews books: No
Publishes notes: No
Languages accepted: English; French
Prints abstracts: No

SUBMISSION REQUIREMENTS

Restrictions on contributors: None
Author pays submission fee: No
Author pays page charges: No
Length of articles: 3,000-4,500 words
Style: MLA
Number of copies required: 1
Copyright ownership: Author
Rejected manuscripts: Returned
Time before publication decision: 1 yr.
Time between decision and publication: 1 yr.
Number of reviewers: 3
Articles submitted per year: 14-16
Articles published per year: 10-12

(504)
Calibano

Paola Colaiacomo, Editor
Via Tevere 44
Rome, Italy

First published: 1977
ISSN: 0391-237X
MLA acronym: Calibano

SUBSCRIPTION INFORMATION

Frequency of publication: 2 times/yr.

EDITORIAL DESCRIPTION

Scope: Publishes articles on English and American literature.
Reviews books: No
Languages accepted: Italian

(505)
*California Slavic Studies

Nicholas V. Riasanovsky, Thomas Eekman, Henrik Birnbaum, & Hugh McLean, Editors
Univ. of California Press
2120 Berkeley Way
Berkeley, CA 94720

First published: 1960
Sponsoring organization: Univ. of California
MLA acronym: CalSS

SUBSCRIPTION INFORMATION

Frequency of publication: Irregular
Available in microform: No

ADVERTISING INFORMATION

Advertising accepted: No

EDITORIAL DESCRIPTION

Scope: Publishes studies on the history, literature, and culture of Slavic countries.
Reviews books: No
Publishes notes: No
Languages accepted: English; Russian
Prints abstracts: No
Author-anonymous submission: No

SUBMISSION REQUIREMENTS

Restrictions on contributors: None
Author pays submission fee: No
Author pays page charges: No
Length of articles: No restrictions
Style: Chicago
Number of copies required: 1
Copyright ownership: Regents of the Univ. of California
Rejected manuscripts: Returned
Time between decision and publication: 1 yr. maximum
Number of reviewers: 5-6

(506)
Callaloo: A Journal of African-American and African Arts and Letters

Charles H. Rowell, Editor
Dept. of English
Univ. of Virginia
Charlottesville, VA 22903

First published: 1976
Historical variations in title: Formerly Callaloo: An Afro-American and African Journal of Arts and Letters
Sponsoring organization: Univ. of Virginia
ISSN: 0161-2492
MLA acronym: Callaloo

SUBSCRIPTION INFORMATION

Frequency of publication: 4 times/yr. (Winter, Spring, Summer, Fall)
Circulation: 1,200
Available in microform: No
Subscription price: $47.00/yr. institutions US; $22.00/yr. individuals US; add $5.30/yr. postage Canada & Mexico, $17.00/yr. elsewhere
Year to which price refers: 1993
Subscription address: Johns Hopkins Univ. Press, Journals Publishing Division, 2715 North Charles St., Baltimore, MD 21218-4319
Subscription telephone: 800 537-5487
Subscription fax: 410 516-6998

ADVERTISING INFORMATION

Advertising accepted: Yes

EDITORIAL DESCRIPTION

Scope: Devoted to the publication of creative and critical writings by and about African and Afro-American writers of the United States, the Caribbean, Canada, and South America. In addition to poetry, fiction, drama, and literary criticism, the journal also publishes interviews with writers, bibliographies, and book reviews. Also publishes articles on visual arts and interviews with visual artists.
Reviews books: Yes
Publishes notes: No
Languages accepted: English
Prints abstracts: No
Author-anonymous submission: No

SUBMISSION REQUIREMENTS

Author pays submission fee: No
Author pays page charges: No
Length of articles: No restrictions
Length of book reviews: No restrictions
Style: MLA
Number of copies required: 1
Special requirements: Submit typescript.
Copyright ownership: Journal
Rejected manuscripts: Returned; enclose return postage.
Time before publication decision: 3-6 mos.
Time between decision and publication: 3-6 mos.
Number of reviewers: 5
Articles submitted per year: 50-60
Articles published per year: 10-15
Book reviews submitted per year: 20-40
Book reviews published per year: 10-25

(507)
*Cambridge Applied Linguistics Series

Michael H. Long & Jack C. Richards, Editors
c/o Mary Vaughn, Executive Editor, ESL/EFL
Cambridge Univ. Press
40 W. 20th St.
New York, NY 10011

Additional editorial address: Jack C. Richards, Head, Dept. of English, City Polytechnic of Hong Kong, Tat Chee Ave., Kowloon Tong, Hong Kong; Michael H. Long, Dept. of ESL, Univ. of Hawaii at Manoa, 1890 East-West Rd., Honolulu, HI 96822
Telephone: 212 924-3900 ext. 406
Fax: 212 691-3239
First published: 1988
MLA acronym: CALS

SUBSCRIPTION INFORMATION

Frequency of publication: Irregular
Available in microform: No

ADVERTISING INFORMATION

Advertising accepted: No

EDITORIAL DESCRIPTION

Scope: Publishes monographs on recent research in applied linguistics in a form readily accessible to language teachers, researchers, and students of applied linguistics.
Reviews books: No
Publishes notes: No
Languages accepted: English
Prints abstracts: No
Author-anonymous submission: No

SUBMISSION REQUIREMENTS

Author pays submission fee: No
Author pays page charges: No
Length of books: 200-336 pp.
Style: Chicago
Number of copies required: 4
Special requirements: For single or multiple-author volumes, include rationale, table of contents, and 2 sample chapters. For edited collections, include rationale, table of contents listing contributors and length of paper, and abstracts, outlines, or draft chapters from each contributor.
Copyright ownership: Cambridge Univ. Press
Rejected manuscripts: Solicited manuscripts are return; unsolicited manuscripts are returned if return postage is supplied
Time before publication decision: 4 mos.
Time between decision and publication: 9-12 mos.
Number of reviewers: 3
Books submitted per year: 10
Books published per year: 4

(508)
*Cambridge Approaches to Linguistics

Jean Aitchison, Editor
Cambridge Univ. Press
Edinburgh Bldg.
Shaftesbury Rd.
Cambridge CB2 2RU, England

Additional editorial address: Cambridge Univ. Press, 40 W. 20th St., New York, NY 10011-4211
Telephone: (44) 223 325745
Fax: (44) 223 315052
E-mail: Jaa10@phx.cam.ac.uk
First published: 1991
MLA acronym: CAtL

SUBSCRIPTION INFORMATION

Frequency of publication: Irregular
Available in microform: No

EDITORIAL DESCRIPTION

Scope: Presents current findings in linguistics in a nontechnical way. Concentrates on what is recent rather than on surveying the past. Aims to provide links between branches of linguistics which are traditionally separate.
Reviews books: No
Publishes notes: No
Languages accepted: English
Prints abstracts: No
Author-anonymous submission: No

SUBMISSION REQUIREMENTS

Author pays submission fee: No
Author pays page charges: No
Length of books: 250 printed pp.
Style: MLA preferred
Number of copies required: 1
Copyright ownership: Cambridge Univ. Press
Rejected manuscripts: Returned
Time before publication decision: 3 mos.
Time between decision and publication: 8-12 mos.
Books submitted per year: 4
Books published per year: 2

(509)
*Cambridge Medieval Celtic Studies

Patrick Sims-Williams, Editor
St. John's College
Cambridge CB2 1TP, England

First published: 1981
Sponsoring organization: Dept. of Anglo-Saxon, Norse, & Celtic, Univ. of Cambridge
ISSN: 0260-5600
MLA acronym: CMCS

SUBSCRIPTION INFORMATION

Frequency of publication: 2 times/yr.
Circulation: 500
Available in microform: No
Subscription price: £14.00/yr. institutions; £10.00/yr. individuals
Year to which price refers: 1992
Subscription address: CMCS Publications, Dept. of Anglo-Saxon, Norse & Celtic, 9 West Rd., Cambridge CB3 9DP, England

ADVERTISING INFORMATION

Advertising accepted: Yes

EDITORIAL DESCRIPTION

Scope: Publishes articles on all aspects of current research on the Celtic countries from 400-1500. Includes articles on archaeology, art, folklore, history, historical geography, language, literature, palaeography, place-name studies, and the relations of the Celtic countries to the rest of the British Isles and the Continent.
Reviews books: Yes
Publishes notes: Yes
Languages accepted: English
Prints abstracts: No
Author-anonymous submission: No

SUBMISSION REQUIREMENTS

Restrictions on contributors: Unsolicited book reviews are not accepted.
Author pays submission fee: No
Author pays page charges: No
Style: Modern Humanities Research Assn.
Number of copies required: 2
Special requirements: Submit double-spaced typescript.
Copyright ownership: Journal
Rejected manuscripts: Not returned
Time before publication decision: 1 mo.
Time between decision and publication: 1 yr.
Number of reviewers: 2
Articles submitted per year: 15
Articles published per year: 12
Book reviews published per year: 18

(510)
*The Cambridge Quarterly

A. P. Newton, H. A. Mason, R. D. Gooder, F. M. Rosslyn, & D. C. Gervais, Editors
c/o The Forbes Mellon Library
Clare College
Cambridge CB2 ITL, England

Telephone: (44) 223 461009
First published: 1965
ISSN: 0008-199X
MLA acronym: CQ

SUBSCRIPTION INFORMATION

Frequency of publication: 4 times/yr.
Circulation: 900
Available in microform: Yes
Subscription price: £46.00/yr. European Economic Community; $94.00/yr. elsewhere
Year to which price refers: 1992
Subscription address: Journals Subscription Dept., Oxford Univ. Press, Pinkhill House, Southfield Rd., Eynsham, Oxford OX8 1JJ, England
Subscription telephone: (44) 865 882283
Subscription fax: (44) 865 882890

ADVERTISING INFORMATION

Advertising accepted: Yes

EDITORIAL DESCRIPTION

Scope: Publishes articles and reviews on English, American, and classical European literature primarily, but also on painting, sculpture, music, and cinema.
Reviews books: Yes
Publishes notes: Yes
Languages accepted: English
Prints abstracts: No
Author-anonymous submission: No

SUBMISSION REQUIREMENTS

Restrictions on contributors: Book reviews are commissioned.
Author pays submission fee: No
Author pays page charges: No
Length of articles: No restrictions
Length of book reviews: 2,000-3,000 words
Length of notes: 800 words
Style: Journal
Number of copies required: 3
Copyright ownership: Editors for authors
Rejected manuscripts: Returned; enclose SASE
Time before publication decision: 2-3 mos.
Time between decision and publication: 3-6 mos.
Number of reviewers: 2-5
Articles submitted per year: 50
Articles published per year: 9-12
Book reviews published per year: 12-18
Notes submitted per year: 10
Notes published per year: 5

(511)
*Cambridge Studies in American Literature and Culture

Eric Sundquist, Editor
Dept. of English
Univ. of California
Los Angeles, CA 90024

First published: 1983
MLA acronym: CSALC

SUBSCRIPTION INFORMATION

Subscription address: Cambridge Univ. Press, 40 W. 20th St., New York, NY 10011
Additional subscription address: Outside N. America: Cambridge Univ. Press, Edinburgh Bldg., Shaftesbury Rd., Cambridge CB2 2RU, England
Subscription telephone: 914 937-4712

EDITORIAL DESCRIPTION

Scope: Publishes monograph studies on American literature, painting, philosophy, cultural history, and the history of ideas.
Languages accepted: English
Prints abstracts: No
Author-anonymous submission: No

SUBMISSION REQUIREMENTS

Restrictions on contributors: None
Length of books: No restrictions
Style: MLA preferred
Number of copies required: 2
Copyright ownership: Cambridge Univ. Press
Time before publication decision: 4-6 mos.
Time between decision and publication: 1 yr.
Number of reviewers: 2

(512)
Cambridge Studies in Anglo-Saxon England

Michael Lapidge & Simon Keynes, Editors
Cambridge Univ. Press
Edinburgh Bldg.
Shaftesbury Rd.
Cambridge CB2 2RU, England

Additional editorial address: Dept. of Anglo-Saxon Studies, Univ. of Cambridge, 9 West Rd., Cambridge, England
First published: 1990
MLA acronym: CSASE

SUBSCRIPTION INFORMATION

Frequency of publication: Irregular
Available in microform: No
Additional subscription address: Cambridge Univ. Press, 40 West 20th St., New York, NY 10011

ADVERTISING INFORMATION

Advertising accepted: No

EDITORIAL DESCRIPTION

Scope: Publishes monographs on all aspects of Anglo-Saxon studies.
Languages accepted: English
Prints abstracts: No

SUBMISSION REQUIREMENTS

Length of books: 100,000 words
Style: Series
Number of copies required: 2
Copyright ownership: Cambridge Univ. Press
Time before publication decision: 3 mos.
Time between decision and publication: 14-16 mos.
Number of reviewers: 2
Books submitted per year: 10
Books published per year: 2

(513)
Cambridge Studies in French

Malcolm Bowie, Editor
Cambridge Univ. Press
Edinburgh Bldg.
Shaftesbury Rd.
Cambridge CB2 2RU, England

First published: 1981
ISSN: 0950-6322
MLA acronym: CSF

SUBSCRIPTION INFORMATION

Frequency of publication: 2-4 times/yr.
Available in microform: No
Subscription address: Cambridge Univ. Press, 40 W. 20th St., New York, NY 10011

ADVERTISING INFORMATION

Advertising accepted: No

EDITORIAL DESCRIPTION

Scope: Provides a forum for the discussion of major critical or scholarly topics within the field of French studies, including literature, poetry, and culture.
Reviews books: No
Publishes notes: No
Languages accepted: English
Prints abstracts: No
Author-anonymous submission: No

SUBMISSION REQUIREMENTS

Author pays submission fee: No
Author pays page charges: No
Length of books: 100,000 words maximum
Style: Generally MLA
Number of copies required: 2
Special requirements: Submit original typescript and 1 copy.
Copyright ownership: Cambridge Univ. Press
Rejected manuscripts: Returned
Time before publication decision: 3-6 mos.
Time between decision and publication: Depends on date of delivery of final typescript.
Number of reviewers: 1-3
Books submitted per year: 20-25
Books published per year: 2-5

(514)
*Cambridge Studies in German

H. B. Nisbet & Martin Swales, Editors
Cambridge Univ. Press
Edinburgh Bldg.
Shaftesbury Rd.
Cambridge CB2 2RU, England

First published: 1986
MLA acronym: CSG

SUBSCRIPTION INFORMATION

Frequency of publication: Irregular
Available in microform: No

ADVERTISING INFORMATION

Advertising accepted: No

EDITORIAL DESCRIPTION

Scope: Publishes studies in the field of German literary history, especially those relevant to its wider historical, philosophical, social, political, and cultural aspects.
Reviews books: No
Publishes notes: No
Languages accepted: English
Prints abstracts: No
Author-anonymous submission: No

SUBMISSION REQUIREMENTS

Author pays submission fee: No
Author pays page charges: No
Length of books: 100,000 words maximum
Style: MLA
Number of copies required: 1
Copyright ownership: Cambridge Univ. Press
Rejected manuscripts: Returned
Time before publication decision: 2-3 mos.
Number of reviewers: 1-2
Books published per year: 1-3

(515)
Cambridge Studies in Latin American and Iberian Literature

Enrique Pupo-Walker, Editor
Cambridge Univ. Press
Edinburgh Bldg.
Shaftesbury Rd.
Cambridge CB2 2RU, England

First published: 1989
MLA acronym: CSLAIL

SUBSCRIPTION INFORMATION

Frequency of publication: Irregular
Available in microform: No

ADVERTISING INFORMATION

Advertising accepted: No

EDITORIAL DESCRIPTION

Scope: Publishes monographs on Latin American, Spanish, and Portuguese literature and culture.
Reviews books: No
Publishes notes: No
Languages accepted: English
Prints abstracts: No
Author-anonymous submission: No

SUBMISSION REQUIREMENTS

Restrictions on contributors: None
Author pays submission fee: No
Author pays page charges: No
Length of books: 220-320 pp.
Style: MLA
Number of copies required: 2
Special requirements: Submit original typescript and 1 copy.
Copyright ownership: Cambridge Univ. Press
Rejected manuscripts: Returned
Time before publication decision: 3-6 mos.
Number of reviewers: 2-4
Books submitted per year: 25
Books published per year: 2-3

(516)
*Cambridge Studies in Linguistics

R. Lass, J. Lyons, S. Romaine, P. H. Matthews, R. Posner, N. V. Smith, B. Comrie, D. Lightfoot, W. Dressler, J. Bresnan, Nigel Vincent, & R. Huddleston, Editors
Cambridge Univ. Press
Edinburgh Bldg.
Shaftesbury Rd.
Cambridge CB2 2RU, England

Additional editorial address: Cambridge Univ. Press, 40 W. 20th St., New York, NY 10011
Telephone: (44) 223 325745
Fax: (44) 223 315052
E-mail: JAA10@PHX.CAM.AC.UK
First published: 1969
Sponsoring organization: Cambridge Univ. Press
ISSN: 0068-676X
MLA acronym: CSL

SUBSCRIPTION INFORMATION

Frequency of publication: Irregular
Available in microform: No

ADVERTISING INFORMATION

Advertising accepted: No

EDITORIAL DESCRIPTION

Scope: Publishes work on all aspects of theoretical linguistics.
Reviews books: No
Publishes notes: No
Languages accepted: English
Prints abstracts: No
Author-anonymous submission: No

SUBMISSION REQUIREMENTS

Restrictions on contributors: None
Author pays submission fee: No
Author pays page charges: No
Length of books: No restrictions
Style: Series
Number of copies required: 2
Copyright ownership: Cambridge Univ. Press
Rejected manuscripts: Returned
Time before publication decision: 3 mos. maximum
Time between decision and publication: 1 yr.
Number of reviewers: 2-5
Books submitted per year: 10-20
Books published per year: 5

(517)
*Cambridge Studies in Russian Literature

Malcolm Jones, Editor
Cambridge Univ. Press
Edinburgh Bldg.
Shaftesbury Rd.
Cambridge CB2 2RU, England

First published: 1981
ISSN: 0950-6292
MLA acronym: CSRL

SUBSCRIPTION INFORMATION

Frequency of publication: Irregular
Available in microform: No

ADVERTISING INFORMATION

Advertising accepted: No

EDITORIAL DESCRIPTION

Scope: Publishes monographs on Russian writers and poets.
Reviews books: No
Publishes notes: No
Languages accepted: English
Prints abstracts: No
Author-anonymous submission: No

SUBMISSION REQUIREMENTS

Author pays submission fee: No
Author pays page charges: No
Length of books: 100,000 words
Style: MLA
Number of copies required: 2
Special requirements: Submit original typescript and 1 copy.
Copyright ownership: Cambridge Univ. Press
Rejected manuscripts: Returned
Time before publication decision: 3-6 mos.
Time between decision and publication: Depends on date of delivery of final typescript.
Number of reviewers: 1-2
Books published per year: 2-3

(518)
*Camera Obscura: A Journal of Feminism and Film Theory

Constance Penley, Elsabeth Lyon, Lynn Spigel, & Sharon Willis, Editors
c/o Film Studies Program
Univ. of California
Santa Barbara, CA 93106

Telephone: 805 893-7069
Fax: 805 893-8016
First published: 1977
Sponsoring organization: Univ. of California, Santa Barbara
ISSN: 0270-5346
MLA acronym: CamObsc

SUBSCRIPTION INFORMATION

Frequency of publication: 3 times/yr. (Jan., May, Sept.)
Circulation: 1,000
Available in microform: Yes
Subscription price: $37.00/yr. institutions; $18.50/yr. individuals
Year to which price refers: 1991
Subscription address: Indiana Univ. Press, Journals, 10th & Morton Sts., Bloomington, IN 47405

ADVERTISING INFORMATION

Advertising accepted: Yes

EDITORIAL DESCRIPTION

Scope: Publishes articles and translations on women and their representation in the media.
Reviews books: Yes
Publishes notes: No
Languages accepted: English; French; German; Italian; Spanish
Prints abstracts: No
Author-anonymous submission: No

SUBMISSION REQUIREMENTS

Restrictions on contributors: None
Author pays submission fee: No
Author pays page charges: No
Length of articles: 10,000 words
Length of book reviews: 4,000-8,000 words
Style: MLA
Number of copies required: 2
Special requirements: Submit double-spaced typescript with wide margins and endnotes.
Copyright ownership: Journal
Rejected manuscripts: Returned; enclose SASE.
Time before publication decision: 2-4 mos.
Time between decision and publication: 6-8 mos.
Number of reviewers: 4-6
Articles submitted per year: 75
Articles published per year: 24
Book reviews submitted per year: 25
Book reviews published per year: 15

(519)
*Campi Immaginabili: Rivista Quadrimenstrale di Cultura

Rocco Mario Morano, Editor
Contrada Bosco De Nicola
18 strada, n. 21/49
87100 Cosenza, Italy

Telephone: (39) 984 394265
First published: 1991
Historical variations in title: Supersedes *Ipotesi 80*
MLA acronym: CImm

SUBSCRIPTION INFORMATION

Frequency of publication: 3 times/yr.
Circulation: 400
Available in microform: No
Subscription price: 40,000 Lit/yr. Italy; 60,000 Lit/yr. elsewhere
Year to which price refers: 1992

ADVERTISING INFORMATION

Advertising accepted: Yes
Advertising rates: 150,000 Lit/half page; 300,000 Lit/full page

EDITORIAL DESCRIPTION

Scope: Publishes articles on Italian literature and culture.
Reviews books: Yes
Publishes notes: Yes
Languages accepted: Italian
Prints abstracts: No
Author-anonymous submission: No

SUBMISSION REQUIREMENTS

Restrictions on contributors: None
Author pays submission fee: No
Author pays page charges: No
Length of articles: 3,000-4,500 words
Length of book reviews: 800-1,000 words
Length of notes: 1,500-2,000 words
Style: Journal
Number of copies required: 2
Special requirements: Submit original typescript and 1 copy.
Copyright ownership: Journal
Rejected manuscripts: Not returned
Time before publication decision: 3-4 mos.
Time between decision and publication: 1 yr.
Number of reviewers: 5
Articles submitted per year: 90
Articles published per year: 25
Book reviews submitted per year: 40
Book reviews published per year: 12
Notes submitted per year: 10
Notes published per year: 3

(520)
*Canadian-American Slavic Studies

Charles Schlacks, Jr., Publisher
Dept. of Languages & Literature
Univ. of Utah
Salt Lake City, UT 84112

Telephone: 801 581-5554
Fax: 801 581-7581
First published: 1967
Sponsoring organization: Univ. of Utah
ISSN: 0090-8290
MLA acronym: CASS

SUBSCRIPTION INFORMATION

Frequency of publication: 4 times/yr.
Circulation: 1,100
Available in microform: No
Subscription price: $40.00/yr. plus postage
Year to which price refers: 1992

ADVERTISING INFORMATION

Advertising accepted: Yes

EDITORIAL DESCRIPTION

Scope: Publishes original contributions addressed to the international scholarly community within the disciplines of the humanities and social sciences.
Reviews books: Yes
Publishes notes: Yes
Languages accepted: English; French; German; Russian
Prints abstracts: No
Author-anonymous submission: Yes

SUBMISSION REQUIREMENTS

Restrictions on contributors: None
Author pays submission fee: No
Author pays page charges: No

Length of articles: No restrictions
Length of book reviews: No restrictions
Length of notes: No restrictions
Style: MLA & modified Library of Congress System for transliteration
Number of copies required: 3
Copyright ownership: Journal
Rejected manuscripts: Returned; enclose return postage.
Time before publication decision: 4 mos.
Time between decision and publication: 6-12 mos.
Number of reviewers: 2-3
Articles published per year: 30
Book reviews published per year: 100
Notes published per year: 4

(521)
*Canadian Ethnic Studies/Etudes Ethniques au Canada

James Frideres & A. W. Rasporich, Editors
Univ. of Calgary
Dept. of Sociology
2500 University Dr. NW
Calgary, Alberta T2N 1N4, Canada

Telephone: 403 220-5889
Fax: 403 282-8606
E-mail: FRIDERES@UNCAMULT
First published: 1969
Sponsoring organization: Canadian Ethnic Studies Assn.
ISSN: 0008-3496
MLA acronym: CEStudies

SUBSCRIPTION INFORMATION

Frequency of publication: 3 times/yr.
Circulation: 650
Available in microform: Yes
Subscription price: C$36.00/yr. institutions; C$30.00/yr. individuals; C$12.00/yr. students
Year to which price refers: 1992
Subscription address: Canadian Ethnic Studies Assn., c/o Center for Ukrainian Studies, Univ. of Manitoba, Winnepeg, Manitoba R3T 2N2, Canada

ADVERTISING INFORMATION

Advertising accepted: Yes
Advertising rates: $125.00/half page; $250.00/full page

EDITORIAL DESCRIPTION

Scope: An interdisciplinary journal devoted to the study of ethnicity, immigration, intergroup relations, and the cultural life of ethnic groups in Canada.
Reviews books: Yes
Publishes notes: Yes
Languages accepted: English; French
Prints abstracts: Yes
Author-anonymous submission: Yes

SUBMISSION REQUIREMENTS

Restrictions on contributors: None
Author pays submission fee: Yes, if nonmember
Author pays page charges: No
Length of articles: 20-30 double-spaced pp. maximum
Length of book reviews: 750 words
Length of notes: 15 double-spaced pp. maximum
Style: MLA
Number of copies required: 3
Special requirements: Include an abstract in French and English.
Copyright ownership: Journal
Rejected manuscripts: 1 copy returned, 1 filed
Time before publication decision: 6-8 weeks
Time between decision and publication: 3 mos.
Number of reviewers: 2
Articles submitted per year: 100+
Articles published per year: 25-30
Book reviews submitted per year: 60

Book reviews published per year: 50-60
Notes submitted per year: 12-15
Notes published per year: 3-5

(522)
*Canadian Folk Music Bulletin

George Lyon & John Leeder, Editors
Soc. Canadienne pour les Traditions Musicales
Box 4232, Station C
Calgary, Alberta T2T 5N1, Canada

Additional editorial address: 224 20th Ave. NW, Calgary, Alberta T2M 1C2, Canada
Telephone: 403 230-0340
First published: 1965
Sponsoring organization: Canadian Soc. for Musical Traditions
ISSN: 0068-8746
MLA acronym: CFMB

SUBSCRIPTION INFORMATION

Frequency of publication: 4 times/yr.
Circulation: 500
Available in microform: No
Subscription price: $20.00/yr.; $16.00/yr. students & seniors
Year to which price refers: 1992

ADVERTISING INFORMATION

Advertising accepted: Yes

EDITORIAL DESCRIPTION

Scope: Publishes articles on Canadian folk music.
Reviews books: Yes
Publishes notes: Yes
Languages accepted: English; French
Prints abstracts: Yes
Author-anonymous submission: No

SUBMISSION REQUIREMENTS

Restrictions on contributors: None
Author pays submission fee: No
Author pays page charges: No
Length of articles: 3,000-6,000 words
Length of book reviews: 750-1,500 words
Length of notes: 750-1,500 words
Style: MLA
Number of copies required: 1
Special requirements: All graphics must be camera-ready.
Copyright ownership: Canadian Soc. for Musical Traditions unless requested by author.
Rejected manuscripts: Returned
Time before publication decision: 6 mos.
Time between decision and publication: 3 mos.
Number of reviewers: 1-2
Articles submitted per year: 50
Articles published per year: 40
Book reviews submitted per year: 10
Book reviews published per year: 10
Notes submitted per year: 10
Notes published per year: 8

(523)
*Canadian Folk Music Journal

Edith Fowke & Jay Rahn, Editors
5 Notley Place
Toronto, Ontario M4B 2M7, Canada

Telephone: 416 757-2984
First published: 1973
Sponsoring organization: Canadian Soc. for Musical Traditions
ISSN: 0318-2568
MLA acronym: CFMJ

SUBSCRIPTION INFORMATION

Frequency of publication: Annual

Circulation: 800
Available in microform: No
Subscription price: $20.00/yr. (includes membership)
Year to which price refers: 1992
Subscription address: Canadian Soc. for Musical Traditions, Box 4232, Station C, Calgary, Alberta T2T 5N1, Canada

ADVERTISING INFORMATION

Advertising accepted: No

EDITORIAL DESCRIPTION

Scope: Publishes articles on various aspects of folksong and music in Canada.
Reviews books: Yes
Publishes notes: Yes
Languages accepted: English; French
Prints abstracts: Yes
Author-anonymous submission: No

SUBMISSION REQUIREMENTS

Restrictions on contributors: None
Author pays submission fee: No
Author pays page charges: No
Length of articles: 4,000-5,000 words
Length of book reviews: 300-500 words
Length of notes: 300 words
Style: MLA
Number of copies required: 2
Special requirements: Summaries are printed in language other than language of the text.
Copyright ownership: Author
Rejected manuscripts: Returned
Time before publication decision: 2 mos.
Time between decision and publication: 8 mos.
Number of reviewers: 2
Articles submitted per year: 10-12
Articles published per year: 8
Book reviews submitted per year: 4
Book reviews published per year: 2-4

(524)
*Canadian Folklore Canadien

Laurier Turgeon, Editor
CELAT
Fac. des Lettres
Pavillion de Konick
Univ. Laval
Quebec, PQ G1K 7P4, Canada

Telephone: 418 656-7200
Fax: 418 656-2019
First published: 1979
Sponsoring organization: Folklore Studies Assn. of Canada/Assn. Canadienne d'Ethnologie & de Folklore
ISSN: 0225-2899
MLA acronym: CFolkC

SUBSCRIPTION INFORMATION

Frequency of publication: 2 times/yr.
Circulation: 260
Available in microform: No
Subscription price: C$40.00/yr. institutions; C$25.00/yr. individuals; C$15.00/yr. students
Year to which price refers: 1992
Subscription address: Diane Tye, Folklore Studies, Center for Canadian Studies, Mount Allison Univ., Sackville, NB E0A 3C0, Canada

ADVERTISING INFORMATION

Advertising accepted: Yes
Advertising rates: C$100.00/full page

EDITORIAL DESCRIPTION

Scope: Publishes thematic issues on Canadian folklore. Subjects covered include popular culture, material culture, oral tradition, and research methods.
Reviews books: Yes
Publishes notes: Yes

Languages accepted: French; English
Prints abstracts: Yes
Author-anonymous submission: Yes

SUBMISSION REQUIREMENTS

Restrictions on contributors: None
Author pays submission fee: No
Author pays page charges: No
Length of articles: 12,000 words
Length of book reviews: 800 words
Length of notes: No restrictions
Style: MLA
Number of copies required: 3
Special requirements: Submit 3 copies of typescript and an IBM-compatible diskette using WordPerfect, along with a short abstract.
Copyright ownership: Author
Rejected manuscripts: Returned
Time before publication decision: 2 mos.
Time between decision and publication: 3-4 mos.
Number of reviewers: 2
Articles submitted per year: 30
Articles published per year: 15
Book reviews submitted per year: 20
Book reviews published per year: 20
Notes submitted per year: 4
Notes published per year: 2

(525)
*Canadian Journal of African Studies/ Revue Canadienne des Etudes Africaines

Roger Riendeau, Rhoda Howard, & Barry Riddell, Editors
Innis College, Univ. of Toronto
2 Sussex Ave.
Toronto, ON M5S 1J5, Canada

Telephone: 416 978-3424
Fax: 416 978-7162
First published: 1967
Sponsoring organization: Canadian Assn. of African Studies
ISSN: 0008-3968
MLA acronym: CJAS

SUBSCRIPTION INFORMATION

Frequency of publication: 3 times/yr.
Circulation: 800
Available in microform: No
Subscription price: C$70.00/yr.
Year to which price refers: 1992

ADVERTISING INFORMATION

Advertising accepted: No

EDITORIAL DESCRIPTION

Scope: Publishes articles on African studies.
Reviews books: Yes
Publishes notes: Yes
Languages accepted: English; French
Prints abstracts: Yes
Author-anonymous submission: No

SUBMISSION REQUIREMENTS

Restrictions on contributors: None
Author pays submission fee: No
Author pays page charges: No
Length of articles: 3,000-6,000 words
Length of book reviews: 750 words
Length of notes: 2,000 words
Style: Chicago
Number of copies required: 4
Special requirements: Include an abstract (15 lines maximum) in English for French manuscripts, French for English manuscripts.
Copyright ownership: Canadian Assn. of African Studies
Rejected manuscripts: Not returned
Time before publication decision: 6 mos.
Time between decision and publication: 6 mos.

Number of reviewers: 3
Articles submitted per year: 125
Articles published per year: 15
Book reviews published per year: 60
Notes published per year: 9

(526)
*Canadian Journal of Irish Studies

Ron Marken, Editor
Dept. of English
Univ. of Saskatchewan
Saskatoon, Saskatchewan S7N 0W0, Canada

Additional editorial address: Denis Sampson, Book Review Editor, Dept. of English, Vanier College, 821 Ste-Croix Blvd., St. Laurent, Quebec H4L 3X9, Canada
Telephone: 306 966-5500
Fax: 306 966-8839
E-mail: MARKEN@SASK.USASK.CA
First published: 1975
Sponsoring organization: Canadian Assn. for Irish Studies
ISSN: 0703-1459
MLA acronym: CJIS

SUBSCRIPTION INFORMATION

Frequency of publication: 2 times/yr. (Jan., July)
Circulation: 575
Available in microform: No
Subscription price: $15.00/yr. US; $17.00/yr. elsewhere
Year to which price refers: 1992

ADVERTISING INFORMATION

Advertising accepted: Yes
Advertising rates: C$150.00/half page; C$200.00/full page

EDITORIAL DESCRIPTION

Scope: Publishes articles on Irish literature, history, and culture.
Reviews books: Yes
Publishes notes: Yes
Languages accepted: English; French; Irish Gaelic
Prints abstracts: Yes
Author-anonymous submission: Yes

SUBMISSION REQUIREMENTS

Restrictions on contributors: None
Author pays submission fee: No
Author pays page charges: No
Length of articles: 4,000-6,000 words
Length of book reviews: 500-750 words
Length of notes: No restrictions
Style: MLA
Number of copies required: 2
Special requirements: Submit original typescript plus 1 copy. Include English and French abstract of 200 words maximum and brief biographical note. DOS text computer diskette should accompany manuscript.
Copyright ownership: Author
Rejected manuscripts: Returned; enclose SASE.
Time before publication decision: 3 mos.
Time between decision and publication: 18 mos. maximum
Number of reviewers: 2-3
Articles submitted per year: 75
Articles published per year: 10-12
Book reviews submitted per year: 30
Book reviews published per year: 20
Notes submitted per year: 8
Notes published per year: 2

(527)
*Canadian Journal of Italian Studies

Stelio Cro, Editor
McMaster Univ.
P.O. Box 1012
Hamilton, Ontario L8S 1C0, Canada

Telephone: 416 525-9140 ext. 3761
First published: 1977
ISSN: 0705-3002
MLA acronym: CJItS

SUBSCRIPTION INFORMATION

Frequency of publication: 2 times/yr.
Circulation: 2,500
Available in microform: No
Subscription address: Symposium Press Ltd., P.O. Box 89061, Westdale Postal Outlet, Hamilton, Ontario L8S 4R5, Canada

ADVERTISING INFORMATION

Advertising accepted: Yes

EDITORIAL DESCRIPTION

Scope: An international, interdisciplinary journal, combining traditional methods of criticism with an innovative approach for a better understanding of the text in relation to the history of ideas.
Reviews books: Yes
Publishes notes: Yes
Languages accepted: English; French; Italian
Prints abstracts: No
Author-anonymous submission: Yes

SUBMISSION REQUIREMENTS

Restrictions on contributors: None
Author pays submission fee: No
Author pays page charges: No
Length of articles: 15-20 pp.
Length of book reviews: 650-750 words
Length of notes: 100-500 words
Style: MLA
Number of copies required: 2
Special requirements: Include a 200-word abstract.
Copyright ownership: Journal
Rejected manuscripts: Not returned
Time before publication decision: 3 mos.
Time between decision and publication: 6-12 mos.
Number of reviewers: 3
Articles submitted per year: 45
Articles published per year: 30
Book reviews submitted per year: 50
Book reviews published per year: 30
Notes submitted per year: 15-20
Notes published per year: 6-10

(528)
*Canadian Journal of Linguistics/ Revue Canadienne de Linguistique

William Cowan, Editor
Dept. of Linguistics
Carleton Univ.
Ottawa, Ontario K1S 5B6, Canada

Telephone: 613 788-2809
E-mail: CJLRCL@CARLETON.CA
First published: 1954
Sponsoring organization: Canadian Linguistic Assn.
ISSN: 0008-4131
MLA acronym: CJL

SUBSCRIPTION INFORMATION

Frequency of publication: 4 times/yr.
Circulation: 700
Available in microform: Yes
Subscription price: C$40.00/yr.; C$12.00/yr. students

Year to which price refers: 1992
Subscription address: Experimental Phonetics Lab, Univ. of Toronto, Toronto, Ontario M5S 1A1, Canada
Subscription telephone: 416 599-0973
Subscription fax: 416 978-9870

ADVERTISING INFORMATION

Advertising accepted: Yes
Advertising rates: C$50.00/half page; C$100.00/full page

EDITORIAL DESCRIPTION

Scope: Publishes articles on theoretical linguistics.
Reviews books: Yes
Publishes notes: No
Languages accepted: English; French
Prints abstracts: No
Author-anonymous submission: No

SUBMISSION REQUIREMENTS

Restrictions on contributors: None
Author pays submission fee: No
Author pays page charges: No
Length of articles: 8,000 words
Length of book reviews: 1,000 words
Style: Journal
Number of copies required: 3
Special requirements: Submit only xerox copies.
Copyright ownership: Canadian Linguistic Assn.
Rejected manuscripts: Not returned
Time before publication decision: 4 mos.
Time between decision and publication: 1 yr.
Number of reviewers: 2
Articles submitted per year: 30-40
Articles published per year: 8-15
Book reviews submitted per year: 40-60
Book reviews published per year: 40-60

(529)
*Canadian Journal of Netherlandic Studies/Revue Canadienne d'Etudes Néerlandaises

Basil D. Kingstone, Editor
Dept. of French
Univ. of Windsor
Windsor, Ontario N9B 3P4, Canada

Telephone: 519 253-4232 ext. 2062
Fax: 519 973-7050
First published: 1979
Sponsoring organization: Canadian Assn. for the Advancement of Netherlandic Studies
ISSN: 0225-0500
MLA acronym: CJNS

SUBSCRIPTION INFORMATION

Frequency of publication: 2 times/yr. (Spring, Fall)
Circulation: 300
Available in microform: No
Subscription price: C$15.00/yr.
Year to which price refers: 1992
Subscription address: J. Herman van Wermeskerken, 5148-11A Ave., Delta, BC V4M 3W3, Canada
Subscription telephone: 604 943-4793

ADVERTISING INFORMATION

Advertising accepted: Yes, on an exchange basis

EDITORIAL DESCRIPTION

Scope: Journal promotes the study of Netherlandic language, literature, and civilization.
Reviews books: Yes
Publishes notes: No
Languages accepted: French; English; Dutch
Prints abstracts: No
Author-anonymous submission: Yes

SUBMISSION REQUIREMENTS

Restrictions on contributors: None
Author pays submission fee: No
Author pays page charges: No
Length of articles: No restrictions
Length of book reviews: No restrictions
Number of copies required: 1
Special requirements: Submit ASCII-format diskette, if possible.
Copyright ownership: Journal
Rejected manuscripts: Not returned
Time before publication decision: 6-12 mos.
Time between decision and publication: 6-12 mos.
Number of reviewers: 6 maximum
Articles submitted per year: 15-20
Articles published per year: 10-15
Book reviews submitted per year: 3-4
Book reviews published per year: 3-4

(530)
*Canadian Journal of Philosophy

Philip Hanson, Thomas Hurka, John King-Farlow, Bernard Linsky, Mohan Matthen, Kai Nielsen, Kathleen Okruhlik, Robert Ware, & Bruce Hunter, Editors
c/o Anne Williams, Executive Secretary
Dept. of Philosophy
Univ. of Lethbridge
Lethbridge, Alberta, T1K 3M4, Canada

Telephone: 403 329-2545
Fax: 403 492-9160
E-mail: MMATTHEN@VM.UCS.UALBERTA.CA
First published: 1971
ISSN: 0045-5091
MLA acronym: CJPhil

SUBSCRIPTION INFORMATION

Frequency of publication: 4 times/yr.
Circulation: 1,180
Available in microform: Yes
Subscription price: C$40.00/yr. institutions; C$25.00/yr. individuals
Year to which price refers: 1992
Subscription address: Univ. of Calgary Press, 2500 Univ. Dr., NW, Calgary, Alberta T2N 1N4, Canada
Subscription telephone: 403 220-7578

ADVERTISING INFORMATION

Advertising accepted: Yes
Advertising rates: C$90.00/half page; C$140.00/full page

EDITORIAL DESCRIPTION

Scope: Publishes articles on any field of philosophy.
Reviews books: Yes
Publishes notes: Yes
Languages accepted: English; French
Prints abstracts: No
Author-anonymous submission: Yes

SUBMISSION REQUIREMENTS

Author pays submission fee: No
Author pays page charges: No
Length of articles: 4,000-10,000 words
Length of book reviews: 5,000-8,000 words
Length of notes: 1,200-1,400 words
Style: Chicago
Number of copies required: 3
Copyright ownership: Journal
Rejected manuscripts: Returned; enclose return postage.
Time before publication decision: 4-6 mos.
Time between decision and publication: 1 yr.
Number of reviewers: 2
Articles submitted per year: 200
Articles published per year: 25
Book reviews published per year: 10-12

(531)
*Canadian Literature

W. H. New, Editor
Univ. of British Columbia
2029 West Mall
Vancouver, British Columbia V6T 1Z2, Canada

Telephone: 604 822-2780
First published: 1959
Sponsoring organization: Univ. of British Columbia
ISSN: 0008-4360
MLA acronym: CanL

SUBSCRIPTION INFORMATION

Frequency of publication: 4 times/yr.
Circulation: 2,000
Available in microform: Yes, through Univ. Microfilms International
Subscription price: C$45.00/yr. institutions Canada; C$50.00/yr. institutions elsewhere; C$30.00/yr. individuals Canada; C$35.00/yr. individuals elsewhere
Year to which price refers: 1992
Subscription address: Circulation Manager, at above address

ADVERTISING INFORMATION

Advertising accepted: Yes
Advertising rates: C$125.00/half page; C$200.00/full page

EDITORIAL DESCRIPTION

Scope: Publishes criticism and reviews of Canadian writers and writing.
Reviews books: Yes
Publishes notes: Yes
Languages accepted: English; French
Prints abstracts: No
Author-anonymous submission: No

SUBMISSION REQUIREMENTS

Restrictions on contributors: Publishes poems by Canadian writers only.
Author pays submission fee: No
Author pays page charges: No
Length of articles: 15-20 typescript pp.
Length of book reviews: 1,000 words
Length of notes: 5-10 typescript pp.
Style: MLA
Number of copies required: 1
Special requirements: Keep footnotes to a minimum.
Copyright ownership: Author after publication
Rejected manuscripts: Returned; enclose SASE.
Time before publication decision: 1 mo.
Time between decision and publication: 1-2 yrs.
Number of reviewers: 2
Articles submitted per year: 400
Articles published per year: 40-50
Book reviews submitted per year: 120
Book reviews published per year: 100-120
Notes submitted per year: 40-50
Notes published per year: 15

(532)
*Canadian Modern Language Review/ La Revue Canadienne des Langues Vivantes

Sally Rehorick & Viviane Edwards, Editors
French Second Language Teacher Education Centre
Faculty of Education
Univ. of New Brunswick
Fredericton, NB E3B 6E3, Canada

Telephone: 506 453-5136

Fax: 506 453-3569
E-mail: SALLY@UNB.CA
First published: 1944
ISSN: 0008-4506
MLA acronym: CMLR

SUBSCRIPTION INFORMATION

Frequency of publication: 4 times/yr. (Jan., Apr., June, Oct.); occasional special issues
Circulation: 2,300
Available in microform: Yes
Subscription price: C$35.00/yr. institutions Canada; $35.00/yr. institutions US; C$25.00/yr. individuals Canada; $25.00/yr. individuals US; $45.00/yr. elsewhere
Year to which price refers: 1992-93
Subscription address: Business Office, 237 Hellems Ave., Welland, Ontario L3B 3B8, Canada
Subscription telephone: 416 734-3640
Subscription fax: 416 734-3640

ADVERTISING INFORMATION

Advertising accepted: Yes
Advertising rates: $90.00/half page; $150.00/full page; $175.00/inside cover; $200.00/back cover

EDITORIAL DESCRIPTION

Scope: Publishes literary, linguistic, and pedagogical articles and book reviews of interest to teachers of French, German, Italian, Spanish, and English as a second language and heritage languages at all levels of instruction.
Reviews books: Yes
Publishes notes: Yes
Languages accepted: English; French; Spanish; Italian; German
Prints abstracts: Yes
Author-anonymous submission: Yes

SUBMISSION REQUIREMENTS

Restrictions on contributors: Authors are encouraged to subscribe to journal.
Author pays submission fee: No
Author pays page charges: No
Length of articles: 20-25 double-spaced pp.
Length of book reviews: 600-700 words
Style: American Psychological Assn.
Number of copies required: 3
Special requirements: Include an abstract and a short biographical note about the author in English and French of about 125 words.
Copyright ownership: Editor
Rejected manuscripts: Returned; enclose return postage.
Time before publication decision: 3-6 mos.
Time between decision and publication: 9-12 mos.
Number of reviewers: 3
Articles submitted per year: 80-90
Articles published per year: 40-50
Book reviews submitted per year: 100
Book reviews published per year: 60-70
Notes published per year: 4-5

(533)
*Canadian Poetry: Studies, Documents, Reviews

D. M. R. Bentley, Editor
Dept. of English
Univ. of Western Ontario
London, Ontario N6A 3K7, Canada

Telephone: 519 673-1164
First published: 1977
Sponsoring organization: Social Sciences & Humanities Research Council of Canada; Ontario Arts Council
ISSN: 0704-5646
MLA acronym: CanPo

SUBSCRIPTION INFORMATION

Frequency of publication: 2 times/yr.
Circulation: 350
Available in microform: No
Subscription price: C$18.00/yr. institutions; C$15.00/yr. individuals
Year to which price refers: 1992
Subscription address: Circulation Manager, at the above address
Subscription telephone: 519 661-3403

ADVERTISING INFORMATION

Advertising accepted: Yes, on an exchange basis

EDITORIAL DESCRIPTION

Scope: Publishes studies, documents, and reviews relating to Canadian poetry from all periods. Contains an annual annotated bibliography of "The Year's Work in Canadian Poetry Studies."
Reviews books: Yes
Publishes notes: Yes
Languages accepted: English; French
Prints abstracts: No
Author-anonymous submission: No

SUBMISSION REQUIREMENTS

Restrictions on contributors: Book reviews are commissioned.
Author pays submission fee: No
Author pays page charges: No
Length of articles: No restrictions
Length of book reviews: No restrictions
Length of notes: No restrictions
Style: MLA
Number of copies required: 2
Copyright ownership: Author
Rejected manuscripts: Returned; enclose SAE.
Time before publication decision: 6 weeks
Time between decision and publication: 6-12 mos.
Number of reviewers: 2
Articles submitted per year: 42
Articles published per year: 14
Book reviews published per year: 8
Notes submitted per year: 6
Notes published per year: 3

(534)
*Canadian Review of American Studies

Stephen Randall & Christine Bold, Editors
Univ. of Calgary
Calgary, Alberta T2N 1N4, Canada

First published: 1970
Sponsoring organization: Canadian Assn. for American Studies
ISSN: 0007-7720
MLA acronym: CRevAS

SUBSCRIPTION INFORMATION

Frequency of publication: 3 times/yr. (Summer, Fall, Winter)
Circulation: 500
Available in microform: No
Subscription price: C$35.00/yr.
Year to which price refers: 1992

ADVERTISING INFORMATION

Advertising accepted: Yes
Advertising rates: C$75.00/half page; C$110.00/full page; C$125.00/inside cover; C$125.00/back cover

EDITORIAL DESCRIPTION

Scope: Publishes articles and review essays whose broadly-based purpose is analysis and understanding of the culture, both past and present, of the US, and of the relations between the cultures of the US and Canada.
Reviews books: Yes
Publishes notes: No
Languages accepted: English; French
Prints abstracts: No
Author-anonymous submission: Yes

SUBMISSION REQUIREMENTS

Restrictions on contributors: None
Author pays submission fee: No
Author pays page charges: No
Length of articles: 10,000 words maximum
Length of book reviews: 10,000 words maximum
Style: Chicago
Number of copies required: 2
Special requirements: Submit ribbon copy or statement that article is not being considered elsewhere, as well as a diskette using WordPerfect.
Copyright ownership: Journal, but reprint rights freely granted
Rejected manuscripts: Returned; enclose return postage.
Time before publication decision: 3 mos.
Time between decision and publication: 1 yr.
Number of reviewers: 2-3
Articles submitted per year: 50
Articles published per year: 12
Book reviews submitted per year: 50-75
Book reviews published per year: 50-75

(535)
*Canadian Review of Comparative Literature/Revue Canadienne de Littérature Comparée

M. V. Dimić, E. D. Blodgett, & S. Tötösy de Zepetnek, Editors
Research Inst. for Comparative Literature
Univ. of Alberta
Edmonton, Alberta T6G 2E6, Canada

Telephone: 403 492-4776; 403 492-4926
Fax: 403 492-5662
E-mail: STOTOSY@VM.VCS.ualberta.ca
First published: 1974
Sponsoring organization: Canadian Comparative Literature Assn./Assn. Canadienne de Littérature Comparée
ISSN: 0319-051X
MLA acronym: CRCL

SUBSCRIPTION INFORMATION

Frequency of publication: 4 times/yr. (Winter, Spring, Summer, Fall)
Circulation: 650
Available in microform: No
Subscription price: C$64.50/yr. institutions Canada; $62.00/yr. institutions elsewhere; C$37.50/yr. individuals Canada; $40.00/yr. individuals elsewhere
Year to which price refers: 1992-93
Additional subscription address: Institutions contact: Academic Printing & Publishing, P.O. Box 4834, Edmonton, Alberta T6E 5G7, Canada

ADVERTISING INFORMATION

Advertising accepted: Yes, on an exchange basis

EDITORIAL DESCRIPTION

Scope: Provides a forum for scholars engaged in the study of literature from both an international and an interdisciplinary point of view. Publishes articles on the international history of literature, theory of literature, methods of literary scholarship, and the relation of literature with other spheres of human expression. Encourages different methodological approaches and interests and is ready to pursue experiments and innovations; welcomes articles on comparative Canadian literature; encourages the study of other literatures besides the major European literatures; publishes issues devoted to single topics; supports articles of an exploratory nature that indicate new directions of research and new working hypotheses; provides a Notes and Queries Section; includes papers on the present state of research in areas of comparative literature, review articles, and shorter reviews of individual books (particularly by scholars working in Canadian universities).
Reviews books: Yes
Publishes notes: Yes
Languages accepted: English; French; German; Spanish; Italian; Russian
Prints abstracts: No
Author-anonymous submission: No

SUBMISSION REQUIREMENTS

Restrictions on contributors: None
Author pays submission fee: No
Author pays page charges: No
Length of articles: 6,000-7,500 words; longer articles may be accepted
Length of book reviews: 1,000-1,300 words; longer reviews may be accepted
Length of notes: 100 words
Style: MLA
Number of copies required: 3
Special requirements: Submit original typescript with appropriate copies, and, if possible, diskette.
Copyright ownership: Canadian Comparative Literature Assn.
Rejected manuscripts: Returned with comments, if desired
Time before publication decision: 3-4 mos.
Time between decision and publication: 6-18 mos.
Number of reviewers: 2-5
Articles submitted per year: 75
Articles published per year: 25
Book reviews submitted per year: 70-90
Book reviews published per year: 70-75
Notes submitted per year: 20
Notes published per year: 5-10

(536)
*Canadian Slavonic Papers: An Inter-Disciplinary Quarterly Devoted to Central and Eastern Europe

E. Mozejko, Editor
Dept. of Comparative Literature
Univ. of Alberta
347 Arts Bldg.
Edmonton, Alberta T6G 2E6, Canada

Telephone: 403 492-2566
E-mail: USERcspa@UALTAMTS (Bitnet); USERcspa@mts.ucs.ualberta.ca (Internet)
First published: 1956
Historical variations in title: Formerly Canadian Slavonic Papers: An Inter-Disciplinary Quarterly Devoted to the Soviet Union and Eastern Europe
Sponsoring organization: Canadian Assn. of Slavists
ISSN: 0008-5006
MLA acronym: CSP

SUBSCRIPTION INFORMATION

Frequency of publication: 4 times/yr. (Mar., June, Sept., Dec.)
Circulation: 1,000
Available in microform: No
Subscription price: C$40.00/yr. individuals Canada (includes membership); $45.00/yr. individuals elsewhere (includes membership); C$20.00/yr. students & emeritus Canada (includes membership); $25.00/yr. elsewhere (includes membership)
Year to which price refers: 1992

ADVERTISING INFORMATION

Advertising accepted: Yes
Advertising rates: C$50.00/quarter page; C$80.00/half page; C$120.00/full page

EDITORIAL DESCRIPTION

Scope: Publishes articles, notes, comments, and book reviews in the field of Central and East European studies.
Reviews books: Yes
Publishes notes: Yes
Languages accepted: English; French
Prints abstracts: No
Author-anonymous submission: Yes

SUBMISSION REQUIREMENTS

Restrictions on contributors: Unsolicited book reviews are not accepted.
Author pays submission fee: No
Author pays page charges: Yes, for graphs & maps
Length of articles: 25 pp. maximum; not considered if exceeding 35 pp.
Length of book reviews: 500 words
Length of notes: 5-10 pp.
Style: MLA; Library of Congress for transliteration
Number of copies required: 3
Copyright ownership: Journal
Rejected manuscripts: Returned; enclose return postage.
Time before publication decision: 3 mos.
Time between decision and publication: 6-12 mos.
Number of reviewers: 2-3
Articles submitted per year: 75-100
Articles published per year: 20-30
Book reviews submitted per year: 200
Book reviews published per year: 125-150
Notes submitted per year: 4
Notes published per year: 2

(537)
*Canadian Studies in German Language and Literature

Armin Arnold, Michael S. Batts, & Hans Eichner, Editors
HWV
Bifang 10
4600 Olten, Switzerland

First published: 1970
Sponsoring organization: Canadian Assn. of University Teachers of German
ISSN: 0171-6859
MLA acronym: CSGLL

SUBSCRIPTION INFORMATION

Frequency of publication: Irregular
Circulation: 150
Available in microform: No
Subscription address: Verlag Peter Lang, Jupiterstr. 15, 3015 Bern, Switzerland

ADVERTISING INFORMATION

Advertising accepted: No

EDITORIAL DESCRIPTION

Scope: Publishes monographs on German language and literature.
Reviews books: No
Publishes notes: No
Languages accepted: English; German; French
Prints abstracts: No
Author-anonymous submission: No

SUBMISSION REQUIREMENTS

Restrictions on contributors: Contributors must be Canadian authors or must write on a Canadian topic.
Author pays submission fee: No
Author pays page charges: No
Length of books: No restrictions
Style: MLA or German usage
Number of copies required: 1
Copyright ownership: Verlag Peter Lang A.G.
Rejected manuscripts: Returned
Time before publication decision: 2-6 mos.
Time between decision and publication: 6-15 mos.
Number of reviewers: 2
Books submitted per year: 6-10
Books published per year: 1-3

(538)
*Canadian Theatre Review

Alan Filewod & Natalie Rewa, Editors
Dept. of Drama
Univ. of Guelph
Guelph, Ontario N1G 2WI, Canada

Telephone: 519 824-4120 ext. 2932
Fax: 519 837-1315
First published: 1974
ISSN: 0315-0836
MLA acronym: CTR

SUBSCRIPTION INFORMATION

Frequency of publication: 4 times/yr. (Mar., June, Sept., Dec.)
Circulation: 1,500
Available in microform: Yes
Subscription price: C$37.50/yr. institutions; C$27.50/yr. individuals
Year to which price refers: 1992
Subscription address: Journals Dept., Univ. of Toronto Press, 5201 Dufferin St., Downsview, Ontario M3H 5T8, Canada
Subscription fax: 416 667-7781

ADVERTISING INFORMATION

Advertising accepted: Yes

EDITORIAL DESCRIPTION

Scope: Publishes materials relevant to Canadian theater. Publishes playscripts.
Reviews books: Yes
Publishes notes: No
Languages accepted: English; French
Prints abstracts: No
Author-anonymous submission: No

SUBMISSION REQUIREMENTS

Restrictions on contributors: Most articles are commissioned.
Author pays submission fee: No
Author pays page charges: No
Length of articles: 3,000 words
Length of book reviews: 1,000 words
Style: MLA
Number of copies required: 1
Special requirements: Submit photographs to illustrate article and a biography of author.
Copyright ownership: Author
Rejected manuscripts: Returned
Time before publication decision: 3 mos.
Time between decision and publication: 6 mos.
Articles submitted per year: 80
Articles published per year: 50-60
Book reviews submitted per year: 16
Book reviews published per year: 14

(539)
*Canadiana Romanica

Hans-Josef Niederehe & Lothar Wolf, Editors
Max Niemeyer Verlag
Postfach 2140
7400 Tübingen, Germany

Telephone: (49) 7071 81104
Fax: (49) 7071 87419
First published: 1987
Sponsoring organization: Gesellschaft für Kanada-Studien
ISSN: 0933-2421
MLA acronym: CanRom

SUBSCRIPTION INFORMATION

Frequency of publication: Irregular
Available in microform: No

ADVERTISING INFORMATION

Advertising accepted: No

EDITORIAL DESCRIPTION

Scope: Publishes collections and monographs on the French language and literature in Canada.
Reviews books: No
Publishes notes: No
Languages accepted: French; German
Prints abstracts: No
Author-anonymous submission: Yes

SUBMISSION REQUIREMENTS

Restrictions on contributors: None
Author pays submission fee: No
Author pays page charges: No
Length of books: No restrictions
Style: Series
Number of copies required: 2
Copyright ownership: Max Niemeyer Verlag
Rejected manuscripts: Returned
Time before publication decision: 2 mos.
Time between decision and publication: 6-12 mos.
Number of reviewers: 2
Books published per year: 1-3

(540)
*CARA: Actes du Centre Aixois de Recherches Anglaises

Pierre Sahel, Editor
Univ. de Provence
29, ave. Robert-Schumann
13621 Aix-en-Provence Cédex, France

Telephone: (33) 42641908
First published: 1980
Sponsoring organization: Univ. de Provence-Aix
ISSN: 0240-8864
MLA acronym: CARA

SUBSCRIPTION INFORMATION

Frequency of publication: Annual
Available in microform: No

ADVERTISING INFORMATION

Advertising accepted: No

EDITORIAL DESCRIPTION

Scope: Publishes articles on all periods of English literature and civilization.
Reviews books: No
Publishes notes: No
Languages accepted: French; English
Prints abstracts: No
Author-anonymous submission: Yes

SUBMISSION REQUIREMENTS

Author pays submission fee: No
Author pays page charges: No
Length of articles: 12 pp.
Style: MLA
Number of copies required: 2
Copyright ownership: Publications de l'Univ. de Provence
Rejected manuscripts: Returned
Time before publication decision: 9 mos.
Time between decision and publication: 6 mos.
Number of reviewers: 2
Articles submitted per year: 20
Articles published per year: 15

(541)
*Cardozo Studies in Law and Literature

Richard H. Weisberg, Editor
Jacob Burns Inst. for Advanced Legal Studies
Cardozo School of Law
55 Fifth Ave.
New York, NY 10003

Telephone: 212 790-0299
Fax: 212 790-0205
First published: 1989
Sponsoring organization: Jacob Burns Inst. for Advanced Legal Studies, Benjamin N. Cardozo School of Law of Yeshiva Univ.
ISSN: 1043-1500
MLA acronym: CSLL

SUBSCRIPTION INFORMATION

Frequency of publication: 2 times/yr. (May, Nov.)
Circulation: 600
Available in microform: No
Subscription price: $50.00/yr. institutions; $20.00/yr. individuals
Year to which price refers: 1992
Subscription telephone: 212 790-0370

ADVERTISING INFORMATION

Advertising accepted: Yes
Advertising rates: $550.00/full page

EDITORIAL DESCRIPTION

Scope: Publishes articles on the interrelation of literature and law; hermeneutics; legal themes in literature; and first amendment concerns for fiction writers and critics. Also includes original plays and stories about law.
Reviews books: Yes
Publishes notes: Yes
Languages accepted: English
Prints abstracts: No
Author-anonymous submission: Yes

SUBMISSION REQUIREMENTS

Restrictions on contributors: Most book reviews and notes are solicited.
Author pays submission fee: No
Author pays page charges: No
Length of notes: 2,500 words
Style: Journal
Number of copies required: 1
Copyright ownership: Yeshiva Univ.
Rejected manuscripts: Not returned
Time before publication decision: 3-4 mos.
Time between decision and publication: 6 mos.
Number of reviewers: 2
Articles submitted per year: 150
Articles published per year: 15
Book reviews published per year: 2-4
Notes submitted per year: 2-4

(542)
*Carleton Germanic Papers

A. Bohm, J. Dallett, J. Goheen, R. Gould, B. Mogridge, & E. Oppenheimer, Editors
Dept. of German
Carleton Univ.
Ottawa, Ontario K1S 5B6, Canada

Telephone: 613 788-2116
Fax: 613 788-3544
E-mail: GERMAN@CARLETON.CA.-BITNET
First published: 1973
Sponsoring organization: Carleton Univ.
ISSN: 0317-7254
MLA acronym: CGP

SUBSCRIPTION INFORMATION

Frequency of publication: Annual
Circulation: 190
Available in microform: No
Subscription price: C$3.00/yr.
Year to which price refers: 1992

ADVERTISING INFORMATION

Advertising accepted: Yes

EDITORIAL DESCRIPTION

Scope: Publishes scholarship and criticism in the area of *Germanistik*.
Reviews books: No
Publishes notes: Yes
Languages accepted: English; French; German
Prints abstracts: No
Author-anonymous submission: Yes

SUBMISSION REQUIREMENTS

Restrictions on contributors: None
Author pays submission fee: No
Author pays page charges: No
Length of articles: 12,000 words maximum
Length of notes: 1,500 words
Style: None
Number of copies required: 1
Copyright ownership: Author
Rejected manuscripts: Returned
Time before publication decision: 3 mos.
Time between decision and publication: 1 yr. maximum
Number of reviewers: 5
Articles submitted per year: 6-9
Articles published per year: 3-5

(543)
*Carleton Papers in Applied Language Studies

Lynne Young, Editor
Centre for Applied Language Studies
Room 215 Paterson Hall
Carleton Univ.
Ottawa, Ontario K1S 5B6, Canada

Telephone: 613 788-6612
Fax: 613 788-6641
First published: 1984
Sponsoring organization: Carleton Univ.
ISSN: 0824-7714
MLA acronym: CPALS

SUBSCRIPTION INFORMATION

Frequency of publication: Annual
Circulation: 200
Available in microform: Yes, through Univ. Microfilms International
Subscription price: C$8.00/yr. Canada; $8.00/yr. elsewhere
Year to which price refers: 1992

ADVERTISING INFORMATION

Advertising accepted: No

EDITORIAL DESCRIPTION

Scope: Publishes articles on educational linguistics, including communicative language teaching, syllabus design, second language learning, linguistic development in the first language, literacy, and writing development.
Reviews books: No
Publishes notes: No
Languages accepted: English; French
Prints abstracts: No
Author-anonymous submission: No

SUBMISSION REQUIREMENTS

Restrictions on contributors: Contributors are usually associated with Carleton University or are responding to previous articles.
Author pays submission fee: No
Author pays page charges: No
Length of articles: 6-30 pp.
Style: Chicago
Special requirements: Submit on diskette in DOS format using WordPerfect 5.1.
Copyright ownership: Author
Rejected manuscripts: Returned
Time before publication decision: 1 yr. maximum
Time between decision and publication: 1 yr. maximum
Number of reviewers: 1
Articles submitted per year: 20
Articles published per year: 8-10

(544)
*The Carlyle Annual

Michael Timko & Ian Campbell, Editors
Dept. of English
Queens College
CUNY
Flushing, NY 11367

Additional editorial address: Ian Campbell, Dept. of English, Univ. of Edinburgh, David Hume Tower, George Square, Edinburgh EH8 9JX, Scotland
Telephone: 718 520-7238
First published: 1979
Sponsoring organization: Queens College; Victorian Committee, City Univ. of New York
MLA acronym: CAnn

SUBSCRIPTION INFORMATION

Frequency of publication: Annual
Circulation: 250
Available in microform: No
Subscription price: $9.00/yr., $24.00/3 yrs.
Year to which price refers: 1992
Subscription telephone: 718 997-4476; 516 627-2654

ADVERTISING INFORMATION

Advertising accepted: Yes
Advertising rates: $100.00/full page

EDITORIAL DESCRIPTION

Scope: Publishes articles on the works of Thomas and Jane Carlyle and their circle.
Reviews books: Yes
Publishes notes: Yes
Languages accepted: English
Prints abstracts: No
Author-anonymous submission: No

SUBMISSION REQUIREMENTS

Restrictions on contributors: None
Author pays submission fee: No
Author pays page charges: No
Length of articles: 1,500 words
Length of book reviews: 500 words
Length of notes: 750 words
Style: MLA preferred
Number of copies required: 2

Copyright ownership: Journal, unless specific request is made
Rejected manuscripts: Returned
Time before publication decision: 3 mos.
Time between decision and publication: 9 mos.
Number of reviewers: 2
Articles submitted per year: 15
Articles published per year: 8
Book reviews submitted per year: 10
Book reviews published per year: 5
Notes submitted per year: 12
Notes published per year: 6-8

(545)
*The Carlyle Society Papers

Ian Campbell, Editor
Dept. of English Literature
Univ. of Edinburgh
George Square
Edinburgh EH8 9JX, Scotland

First published: 1965
Sponsoring organization: Carlyle Soc.
MLA acronym: CarSP

SUBSCRIPTION INFORMATION

Frequency of publication: Annual
Available in microform: No

ADVERTISING INFORMATION

Advertising accepted: No

EDITORIAL DESCRIPTION

Scope: Publishes papers on Thomas Carlyle which have been presented to the Carlyle Society.
Reviews books: No
Publishes notes: No
Languages accepted: English
Prints abstracts: No
Author-anonymous submission: No

SUBMISSION REQUIREMENTS

Restrictions on contributors: Papers must be presented at a lecture delivered to the Carlyle Soc.
Author pays submission fee: No
Author pays page charges: No
Special requirements: Submit word-processed typescript.
Copyright ownership: Carlyle Soc.
Number of reviewers: 3-4

(546)
*Carmina Philosophiae: Journal of the International Boethius Society

William Watts, Editor
Dept. of English
Butler Univ.
Indianapolis, IN 46208

First published: 1992
Sponsoring organization: International Boethius Soc.
MLA acronym: CarmP

SUBSCRIPTION INFORMATION

Frequency of publication: Annual
Circulation: 100
Available in microform: No
Subscription price: $16.00/yr. US; $18.00/yr. elsewhere
Year to which price refers: 1993
Subscription address: Noel H. Kaylor Jr., Dept. of English, Univ. of Northern Iowa, Cedar Falls, IA 50614-0502
Subscription telephone: 319 273-2821

ADVERTISING INFORMATION

Advertising accepted: No

EDITORIAL DESCRIPTION

Scope: Publishes articles dealing with all aspects of the works and influence of Hector Boece.
Reviews books: Yes
Publishes notes: No
Languages accepted: English; French; German
Prints abstracts: No

SUBMISSION REQUIREMENTS

Restrictions on contributors: None
Author pays submission fee: No
Author pays page charges: No
Length of articles: 10-30 pp.
Length of book reviews: No restrictions
Style: Chicago
Number of copies required: 3
Special requirements: Submit original typescript and 2 copies. Author's name should appear only on the title page.
Copyright ownership: Publisher
Rejected manuscripts: Returned
Time before publication decision: 1-2 mos.
Time between decision and publication: 2 yrs. maximum
Number of reviewers: 3
Articles submitted per year: 10-15
Articles published per year: 5-10
Book reviews submitted per year: 5-10
Book reviews published per year: 2-10

(547)
*Les Carnets de l'Exotisme

Alain Quella-Villéger, Editor
B.P. 93
86003 Poitiers Cedex, France

Telephone: (33) 49611408
First published: 1990
Historical variations in title: Supersedes *Revue Pierre Loti*
ISSN: 1148-3202
MLA acronym: CarnEx

SUBSCRIPTION INFORMATION

Frequency of publication: 2 times/yr.
Available in microform: No
Subscription price: 160 F/yr. France; 180 F/yr. elsewhere
Year to which price refers: 1992

ADVERTISING INFORMATION

Advertising accepted: No

EDITORIAL DESCRIPTION

Scope: Publishes articles on exoticism. Includes studies on literature, the arts, colonial history, history of travels, etc.
Reviews books: Yes
Publishes notes: Yes
Languages accepted: French
Prints abstracts: No
Author-anonymous submission: No

SUBMISSION REQUIREMENTS

Author pays submission fee: No
Author pays page charges: No
Number of copies required: 1
Copyright ownership: Author
Articles published per year: 30

(548)
*The Carrell: Journal of the Friends of the University of Miami Library

Laurence Donovan & Ronald P. Naylor, Editors
P.O. Box 248214
Coral Gables, FL 33124

Telephone: 305 284-4585
Fax: 305 665-7352
E-mail: RNAYLOR@UMIAMI
First published: 1960
Sponsoring organization: Friends of the Univ. of Miami Library
ISSN: 0008-6894
MLA acronym: Carrell

SUBSCRIPTION INFORMATION

Frequency of publication: Annual
Circulation: 400
Available in microform: No

ADVERTISING INFORMATION

Advertising accepted: No

EDITORIAL DESCRIPTION

Scope: Publishes poetry, literature, criticism, reviews, and art by University of Miami faculty and students, and others.
Reviews books: Yes
Publishes notes: No
Languages accepted: English
Prints abstracts: No
Author-anonymous submission: No

SUBMISSION REQUIREMENTS

Restrictions on contributors: None
Author pays submission fee: No
Author pays page charges: No
Number of copies required: 2
Copyright ownership: Journal
Rejected manuscripts: Returned
Time before publication decision: 3 mos.
Time between decision and publication: 6-12 mos.
Number of reviewers: 2

(549)
*Carte Italiane: A Journal of Italian Studies

Giovanni d'Agostino, Daniela di Gaeta, & Mauro Ferrero, Editors
Dept. of Italian, 340 Royce Hall
Univ. of California at Los Angeles
405 Hilgard Ave.
Los Angeles, CA 90024

Fax: 310 206-7727
First published: 1979
Sponsoring organization: Dept. of Italian, Univ. of California at Los Angeles
ISSN: 0747-9412
MLA acronym: CarteI

SUBSCRIPTION INFORMATION

Frequency of publication: Annual
Circulation: 300
Available in microform: No
Subscription price: $8.00/yr. institutions; $6.00/yr. individuals
Year to which price refers: 1992

ADVERTISING INFORMATION

Advertising accepted: Yes

EDITORIAL DESCRIPTION

Scope: Includes scholarly articles on all facets of Italian culture with an emphasis on literature.
Reviews books: Yes
Publishes notes: No
Languages accepted: Italian; English
Prints abstracts: No

SUBMISSION REQUIREMENTS

Restrictions on contributors: Contributors must be advanced undergraduates or graduate students.
Author pays submission fee: No
Author pays page charges: No
Length of articles: 12 pp.
Length of book reviews: 4-5 pp.
Style: MLA
Number of copies required: 2
Special requirements: Submissions must be accompanied by diskette using Microsoft Word or WordPerfect.
Copyright ownership: Regents of the Univ. of California
Rejected manuscripts: Not returned
Time before publication decision: 3 mos.
Time between decision and publication: 3 mos.
Number of reviewers: 3-6
Articles submitted per year: 15
Articles published per year: 5-7
Book reviews submitted per year: 5-8
Book reviews published per year: 5-8

(550)
*Casa de las Américas

Roberto Fernández Retamar, Editor
3ra y G. El Vedado
Havana, Cuba

Telephone: (537) 32 3587
Fax: (537) 32 7272
First published: 1960
ISSN: 0008-7157
MLA acronym: CasaA

SUBSCRIPTION INFORMATION

Frequency of publication: 4 times/yr.
Circulation: 6,000
Available in microform: No
Subscription price: $20.00/yr. N. America; $19.00/yr. S. America; $22.00/yr. Europe; $30.00/yr. elsewhere
Year to which price refers: 1992
Subscription address: Publications Exchange Inc., 8306 Mills Dr., Ste. 241, Miami, FL 33183

ADVERTISING INFORMATION

Advertising accepted: Yes

EDITORIAL DESCRIPTION

Scope: Publishes articles on Latin American literature, arts, ideas, and problems.
Reviews books: Yes
Publishes notes: Yes
Languages accepted: Spanish
Prints abstracts: No
Author-anonymous submission: No

SUBMISSION REQUIREMENTS

Restrictions on contributors: None
Author pays submission fee: No
Author pays page charges: No
Length of articles: 20 pp.
Length of book reviews: 6 pp.
Length of notes: 10 pp.
Style: None
Number of copies required: 1
Copyright ownership: Author
Time before publication decision: 3 mos.
Time between decision and publication: 3 mos.
Number of reviewers: 2
Articles submitted per year: 450
Articles published per year: 150
Book reviews submitted per year: 40
Notes submitted per year: 45
Notes published per year: 10

(551)
*Časopis pro Moderní Filologii

Jaromír Povejšil, Editor
Československá Akademie Věd
Ústav pro Jazyk Český
Letenská 4
118 51 Prague 1, Czech Republic

First published: 1911
Sponsoring organization: Československá Akademie Věd
ISSN: 0862-8459
MLA acronym: ČMF

SUBSCRIPTION INFORMATION

Frequency of publication: 2 times/yr.
Circulation: 1,000
Available in microform: No
Subscription price: $34.00/yr.
Year to which price refers: 1992
Subscription address: John Benjamins B.V., Amsteldijk 44, P.O. Box 75577, 1070 AN Amsterdam, Netherlands
Additional subscription address: John Benjamins North America, Inc., 821 Bethlehem Pike, Philadelphia, PA 19118
Subscription telephone: (31) 20 6738156; 215 836-1200
Subscription fax: (31) 20 6739773; 215 836-1204

ADVERTISING INFORMATION

Advertising accepted: No

EDITORIAL DESCRIPTION

Scope: Publishes articles on German, Romance, and Slavonic linguistics, translation studies, and interdisciplinary studies in linguistics including psycholinguistics and sociolinguistics.
Reviews books: Yes
Publishes notes: Yes
Languages accepted: Czech
Prints abstracts: Yes
Author-anonymous submission: Yes

SUBMISSION REQUIREMENTS

Restrictions on contributors: None
Author pays submission fee: No
Author pays page charges: No
Length of articles: 5,000 words
Length of book reviews: 500 words
Length of notes: 300 words
Style: None
Number of copies required: 2
Copyright ownership: Assigned by author to journal
Rejected manuscripts: Returned
Time before publication decision: 3 mos.
Time between decision and publication: 6-12 mos.
Number of reviewers: 3-4
Articles submitted per year: 12-15
Articles published per year: 8-12
Book reviews submitted per year: 10-15
Book reviews published per year: 10-12

(552)
*Castilla: Boletín del Departamento de Literatura Española

Ricardo de la Fuente, Editor
Fac. de Filosofía y Letras
Dept. de Literatura Española
Pl. de Universidad
Univ. de Valladolid,
47002 Valladolid, Spain

Telephone: (34) 83 423000 ext. 4155
Fax: (34) 83 423234
First published: 1980
Sponsoring organization: Univ. de Valladolid, Dept. de Literatura Española
ISSN: 0378-200X

MLA acronym: Castilla

SUBSCRIPTION INFORMATION

Frequency of publication: 2 times/yr.
Available in microform: No
Subscription address: Secretariado de Publicaciones, Univ. de Valladolid,, Avda. Ramón y Cajal 7, 47005 Valladolid, Spain
Subscription telephone: (34) 83 250458 ext. 2247 & 2248

ADVERTISING INFORMATION

Advertising accepted: Yes

EDITORIAL DESCRIPTION

Scope: Publishes articles on Spanish literature.
Reviews books: Yes
Publishes notes: Yes
Languages accepted: Spanish
Prints abstracts: No

SUBMISSION REQUIREMENTS

Author pays submission fee: No
Author pays page charges: No
Length of articles: 15 pp.
Length of book reviews: 3 pp. maximum
Length of notes: 8 pp.
Number of copies required: 1
Special requirements: All submissions should be on size A4 (8 1/4 in. x 11 3/4 in.) paper.
Copyright ownership: Author
Rejected manuscripts: Returned
Time before publication decision: 3 mos.
Time between decision and publication: 1 yr.
Number of reviewers: 3
Articles submitted per year: 20
Articles published per year: 10
Book reviews submitted per year: 11
Book reviews published per year: 11
Notes submitted per year: 10
Notes published per year: 6

(553)
*Castrum Peregrini

M. R. Goldschmidt, Editor
Castrum Peregrini Presse
Postbox 645
1000 AP Amsterdam, Netherlands

Telephone: (31) 20 6235287
Fax: (31) 20 6247096
First published: 1951
Sponsoring organization: Foundation Castrum Peregrini
ISSN: 0008-7556
MLA acronym: CPe

SUBSCRIPTION INFORMATION

Frequency of publication: 5 times/yr.
Circulation: 1,200
Available in microform: No
Subscription price: 70 DM (80 f)/yr.
Year to which price refers: 1992
Additional subscription address: Rheinaustr. 158, 5300 Bonn 3, Germany

ADVERTISING INFORMATION

Advertising accepted: Yes
Advertising rates: 350 DM/half page; 650 DM/full page

EDITORIAL DESCRIPTION

Scope: Publishes interpretations of works of art and literature; 20th-century bio-bibliographical essays; German-Dutch literary relations; old Persian mystics; Stefan George and his circle.
Reviews books: Yes
Publishes notes: Yes
Languages accepted: German
Prints abstracts: Yes
Author-anonymous submission: No

SUBMISSION REQUIREMENTS

Restrictions on contributors: None
Author pays submission fee: No
Author pays page charges: No
Number of copies required: 1
Copyright ownership: Castrum Peregrini Presse
Rejected manuscripts: Returned
Time between decision and publication: 6 mos.
Number of reviewers: 3
Articles submitted per year: 25
Articles published per year: 15
Book reviews submitted per year: 15
Book reviews published per year: 10
Notes submitted per year: 10
Notes published per year: 8

(554)
*Cather Studies

Susan J. Rosowski, Editor
Dept. of English
Univ. of Nebraska-Lincoln
Lincoln, NE 68588-0333

Telephone: 402 472-6645; 402 472-3191 (message)
Fax: 402 472-4636
First published: 1990
Sponsoring organization: Univ. of Nebraska-Lincoln; Willa Cather Pioneer Memorial & Educational Foundation
ISSN: 1045-9871
MLA acronym: CathSt

SUBSCRIPTION INFORMATION

Frequency of publication: Once every 2 yrs.
Available in microform: No
Subscription price: $26.50/yr.
Year to which price refers: 1990
Subscription address: Customer Service, Univ. of Nebraska Press, 901 North 17th St., Lincoln, NE 68588-0520

ADVERTISING INFORMATION

Advertising accepted: No

EDITORIAL DESCRIPTION

Scope: Publishes articles on all aspects of Willa Cather studies, including biography, various critical approaches to the art of Cather, her literary relationships and reputation, and the artistic, historical, intellectual, religious, economic, political, and social backgrounds to her work.
Reviews books: No
Publishes notes: Yes
Languages accepted: English
Prints abstracts: No
Author-anonymous submission: Yes

SUBMISSION REQUIREMENTS

Author pays submission fee: No
Author pays page charges: No
Length of articles: 3,500-12,000 words
Length of notes: 600-3,500 words
Style: MLA (1985)
Number of copies required: 2
Copyright ownership: Journal
Rejected manuscripts: Returned
Time before publication decision: 4 mos.
Time between decision and publication: 1 yr.
Number of reviewers: 2-6
Articles submitted per year: 50
Articles published per year: 9
Notes submitted per year: 15
Notes published per year: 3

(555)
*Cauda Pavonis: Studies in Hermeticism

Stanton J. Linden, Editor
Dept. of English
Washington State Univ.
Pullman, WA 99164-5020

Telephone: 509 335-3023
Fax: 509 335-2582
E-mail: HRC$14@WSUVM1
First published: 1974
Sponsoring organization: Dept. of English, Washington State Univ.
ISSN: 1059-8308
MLA acronym: CaudaP

SUBSCRIPTION INFORMATION

Frequency of publication: 2 times/yr. (Spring, Fall)
Circulation: 500
Available in microform: No
Subscription price: $10.00/yr. institutions; $7.50/yr. individuals
Year to which price refers: 1992

ADVERTISING INFORMATION

Advertising accepted: No

EDITORIAL DESCRIPTION

Scope: Publishes scholarly material on all aspects of alchemy and Hermeticism, and their influence on classical and modern literature, philosophy, art, religion, and the history of science and medicine. The approach is necessarily interdisciplinary and not limited to any particular historical period, national emphasis, or methodology.
Reviews books: Yes
Publishes notes: Yes
Languages accepted: English
Prints abstracts: No
Author-anonymous submission: No

SUBMISSION REQUIREMENTS

Restrictions on contributors: None
Author pays submission fee: No
Author pays page charges: No
Length of articles: 2,500-5,000 words
Length of book reviews: 1,200 words maximum
Length of notes: 1,500-2,000 words
Style: Chicago
Number of copies required: 1
Special requirements: Preferred form is a flat ASCII file submitted on an IBM-compatible or Macintosh diskette along with a fully-coded copy. Otherwise submit double-spaced typescript prepared with letter Gothic, Prestige Elite, or Courier typefaces to facilitate computerized photocomposition.
Copyright ownership: Author
Rejected manuscripts: Returned
Time before publication decision: 2 mos.
Time between decision and publication: 1 yr.
Number of reviewers: 2-3
Articles submitted per year: 12
Articles published per year: 6
Book reviews submitted per year: 10
Book reviews published per year: 10
Notes submitted per year: 8
Notes published per year: 3

(556)
*CEA Critic: An Official Journal of the College English Association

Bege K. Bowers & Barbara Brothers, Editors
Dept. of English
Youngstown State Univ.
Youngstown, OH 44555-3415

Telephone: 216 742-3415
First published: 1939

Sponsoring organization: College English Assn.
ISSN: 0007-8069
MLA acronym: CEA

SUBSCRIPTION INFORMATION

Frequency of publication: 3 times/yr. (Fall, Winter, Spring-Summer)
Circulation: 1,200
Available in microform: Yes
Subscription price: $30.00/yr. institutions; $25.00/yr. individuals; $7.00/yr. students
Year to which price refers: 1991-92
Subscription address: College English Assn., Marion A. Hoctor, Treasurer, Nazareth College of Rochester, Rochester, NY 14618-3790
Subscription telephone: 716 586-2525

ADVERTISING INFORMATION

Advertising accepted: Yes

EDITORIAL DESCRIPTION

Scope: Aims to provide as complete a picture as possible of the wide range of scholarship now occurring in the discipline. Manuscripts are welcomed in all areas of English studies.
Reviews books: No
Publishes notes: No
Languages accepted: English
Prints abstracts: No
Author-anonymous submission: No

SUBMISSION REQUIREMENTS

Restrictions on contributors: Nonmembers may submit, but must join prior to publication.
Author pays submission fee: No
Author pays page charges: No
Length of articles: 3,750-7,000 words
Style: MLA
Number of copies required: 2
Special requirements: If possible, submit 1 copy on IBM-compatible diskette and specify word processing program used. WordPerfect 5.1 is preferred.
Copyright ownership: College English Assn.
Rejected manuscripts: Returned; enclose return postage.
Time before publication decision: 3-4 mos.
Time between decision and publication: 1-2 yrs.
Number of reviewers: 2
Articles submitted per year: 90
Articles published per year: 25

(557)
*Celestinesca: Boletín Informativo Internacional

Joseph T. Snow, Editor
Romance & Classical Languages
Michigan State Univ.
East Lansing, MI 48824

Telephone: 517 355-8350
First published: 1977
ISSN: 0147-3085
MLA acronym: Celestinesca

SUBSCRIPTION INFORMATION

Frequency of publication: 2 times/yr. (May, Nov.)
Circulation: 500
Available in microform: No
Subscription price: $8.00/yr. US; $13.00/yr. elsewhere
Year to which price refers: 1992
Additional subscription address: D. Plácido Rodriguez, Lib. 'Corral del Almagro', Almagro 13, 28010 Madrid, Spain; Geoffrey West, Dept. of Printed Books (Hispanic), British Library, Great Russell St., London WC1B 3DG, England

ADVERTISING INFORMATION

Advertising accepted: No

EDITORIAL DESCRIPTION

Scope: Focuses on Fernando de Rojas' *Celestina*; sources, imitations, continuations, adaptations, translations; other celestinesque literature, bibliographies, illustrations, and new creative work.
Reviews books: Yes
Publishes notes: Yes
Languages accepted: English; French; Spanish; Italian
Prints abstracts: No
Author-anonymous submission: Yes

SUBMISSION REQUIREMENTS

Restrictions on contributors: None
Author pays submission fee: No
Author pays page charges: No
Length of articles: 2,000-4,000 words
Length of book reviews: 500-1,000 words
Length of notes: 500-2,000 words
Style: MLA
Number of copies required: 2
Copyright ownership: Journal for 1 yr.
Rejected manuscripts: Returned; enclose return postage.
Time before publication decision: 2-3 mos.
Time between decision and publication: 6-12 mos.
Number of reviewers: 2 minimum
Articles submitted per year: 25-30
Articles published per year: 10-15
Book reviews submitted per year: 3-10
Book reviews published per year: 3-8
Notes submitted per year: 8-10
Notes published per year: 5-7

(558)
*Celtica

10 Burlington Rd.
Dublin 4, Ireland

Telephone: (353) 1 680748 ext. 202
Fax: (353) 1 680561
First published: 1946
Sponsoring organization: School of Celtic Studies, Dublin Inst. for Advanced Studies
ISSN: 0069-1399
MLA acronym: Celtica

SUBSCRIPTION INFORMATION

Frequency of publication: Irregular
Available in microform: No
Subscription telephone: (353) 1 680748 ext. 249

ADVERTISING INFORMATION

Advertising accepted: No

EDITORIAL DESCRIPTION

Scope: Contains miscellaneous articles dealing with Celtic studies including Irish language, literature, and history.
Reviews books: No
Publishes notes: Yes
Languages accepted: English; Irish Gaelic
Prints abstracts: No

SUBMISSION REQUIREMENTS

Author pays submission fee: No
Author pays page charges: No
Length of articles: No restrictions
Length of notes: 450 words
Style: Journal
Number of copies required: 1
Special requirements: Submit legible typescript and diskette.
Copyright ownership: Publisher
Rejected manuscripts: Returned
Time before publication decision: 1-2 mos.
Time between decision and publication: 6-12 mos.
Number of reviewers: 3
Articles published per year: 10-15

(559)
*Cenobio: Rivista Trimestrale di Cultura

Pier Riccardo Frigeri, Editor
6933 Muzzano-Piodella, Switzerland

Telephone: (41) 91 581048 ext. 291
Fax: (41) 91 565156
First published: 1952
Sponsoring organization: Pro Helvetia (Zürich); Stato del Cantone Ticino (Bellinzona)
ISSN: 0008-896X
MLA acronym: Cenobio

SUBSCRIPTION INFORMATION

Frequency of publication: 4 times/yr.
Circulation: 6,500
Available in microform: No
Subscription address: C.P. 174, 6903 Lugano 3, Switzerland

ADVERTISING INFORMATION

Advertising accepted: Yes

EDITORIAL DESCRIPTION

Scope: Focus is on the defense of the Italian language on a critical level and the furthering of contact and dialogue with the active forces in Italian literary life.
Reviews books: Yes
Publishes notes: Yes
Languages accepted: French; Italian
Prints abstracts: No

SUBMISSION REQUIREMENTS

Restrictions on contributors: None
Author pays submission fee: No
Author pays page charges: No
Length of articles: No restrictions
Length of book reviews: 100-1,000 words
Length of notes: 100-300 words
Style: Chicago
Number of copies required: 1
Special requirements: Submit typescript.
Copyright ownership: Editor
Rejected manuscripts: Not returned
Time before publication decision: 2 mos.
Time between decision and publication: 2-12 mos.
Number of reviewers: 2
Articles submitted per year: 500
Articles published per year: 200
Book reviews submitted per year: 500
Book reviews published per year: 80-150
Notes submitted per year: 60
Notes published per year: 10

(560)
*The Centennial Review

R. K. Meiners, Editor
312 Linton Hall
Michigan State Univ.
East Lansing, MI 48824-1036

Telephone: 517 355-1905
Fax: 517 353-5368
E-mail: CENREV@MSU.BITNET
First published: 1957
Sponsoring organization: Michigan State Univ., College of Arts & Letters
ISSN: 0162-0177
MLA acronym: CentR

SUBSCRIPTION INFORMATION

Frequency of publication: 3 times/yr.
Circulation: 1,000
Available in microform: Yes

ADVERTISING INFORMATION

Advertising accepted: Yes

EDITORIAL DESCRIPTION

Scope: Concerned with the interrelations among the disciplines.
Reviews books: No
Publishes notes: No
Languages accepted: English
Prints abstracts: No
Author-anonymous submission: No

SUBMISSION REQUIREMENTS

Restrictions on contributors: None
Author pays submission fee: No
Author pays page charges: No
Length of articles: 20-40 pp.
Style: Chicago
Number of copies required: 2
Copyright ownership: Journal
Rejected manuscripts: Returned
Time before publication decision: 3 mos.
Time between decision and publication: 1 yr.
Number of reviewers: 1-2
Articles submitted per year: 120
Articles published per year: 20-24

(561)
*Central Asiatic Journal: International Periodical for the Languages, Literature, History and Archeology of Central Asia

Giovanni Stary, Editor
Via Card. Urbani 25
30174 Mestre-Venezia, Italy

Telephone: (39) 41 916186
Fax: (39) 41 916186
First published: 1956
ISSN: 0008-9192
MLA acronym: CAsJ

SUBSCRIPTION INFORMATION

Frequency of publication: 2 double issues/yr.
Circulation: 550
Available in microform: Yes
Subscription price: 128 DM/yr.
Year to which price refers: 1992
Subscription address: Only available through book sellers & agencies.

ADVERTISING INFORMATION

Advertising accepted: Yes
Advertising rates: 480 DM/full page

EDITORIAL DESCRIPTION

Scope: Publishes articles on Central Asia including studies on its languages, literature, history, and archaeology.
Reviews books: Yes
Publishes notes: No
Languages accepted: English; French; German; Russian
Prints abstracts: No
Author-anonymous submission: No

SUBMISSION REQUIREMENTS

Author pays submission fee: No
Author pays page charges: No
Number of copies required: 1
Special requirements: Quotations in Chinese, Japanese, and Arabic are permitted.
Copyright ownership: Verlag Otto Harrassowitz
Rejected manuscripts: Returned
Time before publication decision: 3 mos. maximum
Number of reviewers: 1
Articles submitted per year: 25-35
Articles published per year: 15-20
Book reviews submitted per year: 20-40
Book reviews published per year: 20-30

(562)
*Central Institute of English and Foreign Languages Bulletin

J. C. Mahanti, Editor
Central Inst. of English & Foreign Languages
Hyderabad 500 007, India

Telephone: (91) 842 868131
First published: 1961
Sponsoring organization: Central Inst. of English & Foreign Languages
MLA acronym: CIEFLB

SUBSCRIPTION INFORMATION

Frequency of publication: 2 times/yr.
Circulation: 500
Available in microform: No
Subscription address: Publications Unit, at the above address

ADVERTISING INFORMATION

Advertising accepted: Yes

EDITORIAL DESCRIPTION

Scope: Presents information and ideas on theories, research, methods and materials related to language studies, linguistics, phonetics and literature with special reference to the teaching of English, French, German, Russian, Arabic, and Spanish.
Reviews books: Yes
Publishes notes: Yes
Languages accepted: English
Prints abstracts: No
Author-anonymous submission: No

SUBMISSION REQUIREMENTS

Restrictions on contributors: None
Author pays submission fee: No
Author pays page charges: No
Length of articles: 3,000-5,000 words
Length of book reviews: 3,000 words
Length of notes: 1,500 words
Style: MLA
Number of copies required: 2
Special requirements: Submit double-spaced typescript with 1 1/2 in. margins on all sides.
Copyright ownership: Central Inst. of English & Foreign Languages
Rejected manuscripts: Returned; enclose return postage or international reply coupons.
Time before publication decision: 3 mos.
Time between decision and publication: 6-12 mos.
Number of reviewers: 2
Articles submitted per year: 70-80
Articles published per year: 16-20
Book reviews submitted per year: 10-15
Book reviews published per year: 2-3
Notes submitted per year: 5-10
Notes published per year: 1-2

(563)
*Centre Interuniversitaire de Recherche sur la Renaissance Italienne

Centre Interuniversitaire de la Renaissance Italienne
13, rue de Santeuil
75005 Paris, France

First published: 1972
Sponsoring organization: Centre National de la Recherche Scientifique; Univ. de Paris III (Sorbonne Nouvelle)
MLA acronym: CIRRI

SUBSCRIPTION INFORMATION

Frequency of publication: Annual (Nov./Dec.)
Circulation: 400-900
Available in microform: No

ADVERTISING INFORMATION

Advertising accepted: No

EDITORIAL DESCRIPTION

Scope: Publishes collections of articles on the literature and culture of the Italian Renaissance.
Reviews books: No
Publishes notes: No
Languages accepted: French; Italian
Prints abstracts: No
Author-anonymous submission: No

SUBMISSION REQUIREMENTS

Restrictions on contributors: None
Author pays submission fee: No
Author pays page charges: No
Length of books: 200-450 pp.
Number of copies required: 2
Copyright ownership: Author
Rejected manuscripts: Returned
Time before publication decision: 6 mos.
Time between decision and publication: 6 mos.
Number of reviewers: 8-10
Articles submitted per year: 8-10
Articles published per year: 4-6
Books submitted per year: 1
Books published per year: 1

(564)
Centro de Estudios Mayas-Cuadernos

Mercedes de la Garza, Editor
Centro de Estudios Mayas
Inst. de Investigaciones Filológicas
Circuito Mario de la Cueva
Ciudad Universitaria, UNAM
04510 Mexico, D.F., Mexico

First published: 1969
Sponsoring organization: Centro de Estudios Maya, Univ. Nacional Autónoma de México
MLA acronym: CEMC

SUBSCRIPTION INFORMATION

Frequency of publication: Irregular
Circulation: 1,000-2,000
Available in microform: No
Subscription address: Dept. de Publicaciones, Inst. de Investigaciones Filológicas, Circuito Mario de la Cueva, Ciudad Univ., UNAM, 04510 Mexico, D.F., Mexico

ADVERTISING INFORMATION

Advertising accepted: No

EDITORIAL DESCRIPTION

Scope: Focuses on all cultural aspects of the ancient and modern Mayans.
Reviews books: No
Languages accepted: Spanish; French; English
Prints abstracts: No

SUBMISSION REQUIREMENTS

Restrictions on contributors: None
Author pays submission fee: No
Author pays page charges: No
Length of books: 150 pp.
Style: None
Number of copies required: 2
Special requirements: Submit original typescript.
Copyright ownership: Author
Rejected manuscripts: Not returned
Time before publication decision: 6 mos.
Time between decision and publication: 1 yr.
Number of reviewers: 4

(565)
*Cercetări de Lingvistică

Ioan Pătruț, Editor
Inst. de Lingvistică şi Istorie Literară "Sectil Puşcariu"
Str. E.Racoviță nr. 21
3400 Cluj-Napoca, Romania

Additional editorial address: Editura Academiei Române, Calea Victoriei 125, 79717 Bucharest, Romania
Telephone: (40) 95 136205
First published: 1956
Sponsoring organization: Inst. de Lingvistică şi Istorie Literară din Cluj-Napoca
ISSN: 0373-1545
MLA acronym: CLing

SUBSCRIPTION INFORMATION

Frequency of publication: 2 times/yr.
Available in microform: No
Subscription price: $100.00/yr.
Year to which price refers: 1992
Subscription address: Rompresfilatelia, Sectorul Export-Import Presa, P.O. Box 12-201, Calea Grivitei nr. 64-66, 78104 Bucharest, Romania

ADVERTISING INFORMATION

Advertising accepted: Yes

EDITORIAL DESCRIPTION

Scope: Publishes articles on all areas of linguistics but especially on Romanian linguistics.
Reviews books: Yes
Publishes notes: No
Languages accepted: Romanian; French; English; German; Italian; Spanish
Prints abstracts: Yes
Author-anonymous submission: No

SUBMISSION REQUIREMENTS

Restrictions on contributors: None
Author pays submission fee: No
Author pays page charges: No
Length of articles: 5,000 words
Length of book reviews: 1,800 words
Style: Romanian Academy
Number of copies required: 2
Special requirements: Submit original typescript plus 1 copy.
Copyright ownership: Editura Academiei Române
Rejected manuscripts: Not returned
Time before publication decision: 3 mos.
Time between decision and publication: 3 mos.
Number of reviewers: 2
Articles submitted per year: 25
Articles published per year: 20
Book reviews submitted per year: 25
Book reviews published per year: 20

(566)
*Cervantes: Bulletin of the Cervantes Society of America

Michael McGaha, Editor
Dept. of Modern Languages & Literatures
Pomona College
Claremont, CA 91711-6333

Telephone: 714 621-8000 ext. 8616
Fax: 714 621-9609
First published: 1981
Sponsoring organization: Cervantes Soc. of America
ISSN: 0277-6995
MLA acronym: Cervantes

SUBSCRIPTION INFORMATION

Frequency of publication: 2 times/yr. (Spring, Fall)
Circulation: 245
Available in microform: No
Subscription price: $20.00/yr. institutions; $17.00/yr. individuals
Year to which price refers: 1992
Subscription address: William H. Clamurro, Dept. of Modern Languages, Denison Univ., Granville, OH 43023

ADVERTISING INFORMATION

Advertising accepted: Yes

EDITORIAL DESCRIPTION

Scope: Publishes articles on the life and works of Miguel de Cervantes Saavedra.
Reviews books: Yes
Publishes notes: Yes
Languages accepted: Spanish; English
Prints abstracts: Yes
Author-anonymous submission: Yes

SUBMISSION REQUIREMENTS

Restrictions on contributors: None
Author pays submission fee: No
Author pays page charges: No
Style: MLA
Number of copies required: 2
Copyright ownership: Journal
Rejected manuscripts: Returned
Time before publication decision: 6 weeks
Time between decision and publication: 1-2 yrs.
Number of reviewers: 2
Articles submitted per year: 15-20
Articles published per year: 9-12
Book reviews published per year: 5-10
Notes submitted per year: 5
Notes published per year: 2

(567)
*Česká Literatura: Časopis pro Literární Vědu

Miroslav Červenka, Editor
Academia, Publishing House of the Czechoslovak Academy of Sciences
Vodičkova 40
112 29 Prague, Czech Republic

First published: 1953
Sponsoring organization: Československá Akademie Věd, Ústav pro Českou a Světovou Literaturu
ISSN: 0009-0468
MLA acronym: ČL

SUBSCRIPTION INFORMATION

Frequency of publication: 6 times/yr.
Circulation: 1,850
Available in microform: No
Subscription price: 232 f ($140.00)/yr.
Year to which price refers: 1993
Subscription address: John Benjamins B.V., Amsteldijk 44, P.O. Box 75577, 1070 AN Amsterdam, Netherlands
Additional subscription address: John Benjamins North America, Inc., 821 Bethlehem Pike, Philadelphia, PA 19118
Subscription telephone: (31) 20 6738156; 215 836-1200
Subscription fax: (31) 20 6739773; 215 836-1204

ADVERTISING INFORMATION

Advertising accepted: No

EDITORIAL DESCRIPTION

Scope: Publishes articles on the history of Czech literature and the theory of literature.
Reviews books: Yes
Publishes notes: Yes
Languages accepted: Czech
Prints abstracts: Yes
Author-anonymous submission: No

SUBMISSION REQUIREMENTS

Restrictions on contributors: None
Author pays submission fee: No
Author pays page charges: No
Length of articles: 20-25 typescript pp.
Length of book reviews: 3-4 pp.
Length of notes: 2 pp.
Number of copies required: 1
Special requirements: Submit an abstract.
Copyright ownership: Academia Praha
Rejected manuscripts: Returned
Time before publication decision: 2 mos.
Time between decision and publication: 10 mos.
Number of reviewers: 3
Articles submitted per year: 40-45
Articles published per year: 25-35
Book reviews submitted per year: 40-50
Book reviews published per year: 35-45
Notes submitted per year: 10
Notes published per year: 8-10

(568)
Český Lid: Národopisný Časopis/ Ethnological Journal

Jiřina Todorovová, Editor
Římská 14
120 00 Prague 2, Czech Republic

First published: 1891
Sponsoring organization: Československá Akademie Věd, Ústav pro Etnografii & Folkloristiku
ISSN: 0009-0794
MLA acronym: ČLid

SUBSCRIPTION INFORMATION

Frequency of publication: 4 times/yr.
Circulation: 1,000
Available in microform: No
Subscription address: Kubon & Sagner, Postfach 340108, 8000 Munich 34, Germany
Additional subscription address: In Non-Western countries write to: Artia, Ve Smečkách 30, 111 27 Prague 1, Czech Republic

ADVERTISING INFORMATION

Advertising accepted: No

EDITORIAL DESCRIPTION

Scope: Publishes articles on Czech and Slovak ethnography, folklore, social anthropology, and literature.
Reviews books: Yes
Publishes notes: Yes
Languages accepted: Czech; Slovak
Prints abstracts: Yes
Author-anonymous submission: No

SUBMISSION REQUIREMENTS

Restrictions on contributors: None
Author pays submission fee: No
Author pays page charges: No
Length of articles: 10-25 typescript pp.
Length of book reviews: 2-3 typescript pp.
Length of notes: 2-3 typescript pp.
Style: None
Number of copies required: 1
Copyright ownership: Author
Time before publication decision: 6-12 mos.
Time between decision and publication: 6 mos.
Number of reviewers: 2
Articles submitted per year: 57
Articles published per year: 30
Book reviews submitted per year: 90
Book reviews published per year: 59
Notes submitted per year: 35
Notes published per year: 19

(569)
Champs du Signe: Cahiers de Stylistique

François-Charles Gaudard, Editor
Univ. de Toulouse-Le Mirail
5, allées Antonio Machado
UFR de Lettres, Langages & Musique
31058 Toulouse Cédex, France

Additional editorial address: Presses Universitaires du Mirail, 56 rue du Taur, 31069 Toulouse Cédex, France
First published: 1991
ISSN: 1157-4860
MLA acronym: ChSigne

SUBSCRIPTION INFORMATION

Frequency of publication: Annual
Circulation: 500
Available in microform: No
Subscription price: 80 F/yr. France; 100 F/yr. elsewhere
Year to which price refers: 1993
Subscription address: Presses Universitaires du Mirail, 56, rue du Taur, 31000 Toulouse, France

ADVERTISING INFORMATION

Advertising accepted: Yes

EDITORIAL DESCRIPTION

Scope: Publishes articles on textual, comparative, and historical stylistics.
Languages accepted: French; English
Author-anonymous submission: Yes

SUBMISSION REQUIREMENTS

Author pays submission fee: No
Author pays page charges: No
Length of articles: 12-15 pp.
Number of copies required: 1
Special requirements: Submit on a 3.5 inch diskette.
Copyright ownership: Presses Universitaires du Mirail
Rejected manuscripts: Not returned
Time before publication decision: 1-3 mos.
Time between decision and publication: 1 yr. maximum
Number of reviewers: 8
Articles submitted per year: 25
Articles published per year: 12-15

(570)
*Charles Lamb Bulletin

William Ruddick, Editor
9 Dale View Gardens
Crawcrook
Ryton
Tyne & Wear, NE40 4ED, England

Additional editorial address: Duncan Wu, Assistant Editor, St. Catherine's College, Oxford OX1 3UJ, England
Telephone: (44) 91 4138798
First published: 1973
Sponsoring organization: Charles Lamb Soc.
ISSN: 0308-0951
MLA acronym: ChLB

SUBSCRIPTION INFORMATION

Frequency of publication: 4 times/yr.
Circulation: 350
Available in microform: No
Subscription price: £12.00/yr. institutions United Kingdom; £21.00/yr. institutions elsewhere; £8.00/yr. individuals United Kingdom; $14.00/yr. individuals elsewhere
Year to which price refers: 1991
Subscription address: Membership Secretary, Shelley Cottage, 108 West Street, Marlow, Bucks SL7 2BP England

ADVERTISING INFORMATION

Advertising accepted: No

EDITORIAL DESCRIPTION

Scope: Publishes literary or background articles on subjects related to Charles Lamb and his circle (includes Coleridge, Wordsworth, Hazlitt, and all the older Romantics; omits Keats, Shelley, Byron).
Reviews books: Yes
Languages accepted: English
Prints abstracts: No

SUBMISSION REQUIREMENTS

Restrictions on contributors: None
Author pays submission fee: No
Author pays page charges: No
Length of articles: 3,000-6,000 words
Length of book reviews: 1,000 words maximum
Style: None
Number of copies required: 1
Copyright ownership: Charles Lamb Soc.
Rejected manuscripts: Returned
Time before publication decision: 1 mo.
Time between decision and publication: 6 mos.
Number of reviewers: 2
Articles published per year: 10-14
Book reviews published per year: 10-14
Notes published per year: 4

(571)
*Chasqui: Revista de Literatura Latinoamericana

Ted Lyon, Editor
4048 JKHB
Brigham Young Univ.
Provo, UT 84602

Telephone: 801 378-2837
First published: 1972
ISSN: 0145-8973
MLA acronym: Chasqui

SUBSCRIPTION INFORMATION

Frequency of publication: 2 times/yr. (Nov., May)
Circulation: 600
Available in microform: No
Subscription price: $9.00/yr.
Year to which price refers: 1992
Subscription address: Howard M. Fraser, Dept. of Modern Languages, College of William and Mary, Williamsburg, VA 23185

ADVERTISING INFORMATION

Advertising accepted: Yes
Advertising rates: $50.00/half page

EDITORIAL DESCRIPTION

Scope: Focuses on current Latin American literature. Includes scholarly articles, bibliographies, book reviews, extensive lists of new publications, and creative writing in Spanish and Portuguese.
Reviews books: Yes
Publishes notes: No
Languages accepted: Spanish; Portuguese; English
Prints abstracts: No
Author-anonymous submission: Yes

SUBMISSION REQUIREMENTS

Restrictions on contributors: None
Author pays submission fee: No
Author pays page charges: No
Length of articles: 10-25 pp.
Length of book reviews: 1,000-3,000 words
Style: MLA
Number of copies required: 2
Special requirements: Include a brief bio-bibliographical note. Creative works in English are not accepted.
Copyright ownership: Author
Rejected manuscripts: Returned; enclose return postage.
Time before publication decision: 2-3 mos.
Time between decision and publication: 6-12 mos.
Number of reviewers: 3-4
Articles submitted per year: 60-100
Articles published per year: 15-25
Book reviews submitted per year: 60
Book reviews published per year: 50

(572)
*The Chaucer Review: A Journal of Medieval Studies and Literary Criticism

Robert W. Frank, Jr., Editor
117 Burrowes Bldg.
Pennsylvania State Univ.
University Park, PA 16802

Telephone: 814 863-2467
Fax: 814 863-1408
First published: 1966
Sponsoring organization: MLA, Division on Chaucer
ISSN: 0009-2002
MLA acronym: ChauR

SUBSCRIPTION INFORMATION

Frequency of publication: 4 times/yr. (Summer, Fall, Winter, Spring)
Circulation: 1,300
Available in microform: Yes
Subscription price: $35.00/yr. institutions US; $40.00/yr. institutions elsewhere; $22.50/yr. individuals US; $30.00/yr. individuals elsewhere
Year to which price refers: 1992
Subscription address: Pennsylvania State Univ. Press, Suite C, Barbara Bldg., 820 N. University Dr., University Park, PA 16802

ADVERTISING INFORMATION

Advertising accepted: Yes
Advertising rates: $125.00/half page; $225.00/full page

EDITORIAL DESCRIPTION

Scope: Publishes scholarly and critical studies on Chaucer and other Middle English authors.
Reviews books: No
Publishes notes: Yes
Languages accepted: English
Prints abstracts: No

SUBMISSION REQUIREMENTS

Restrictions on contributors: None
Author pays submission fee: No
Author pays page charges: No
Length of articles: 15-30 pp.
Length of notes: 2-7 pp.
Style: Chicago
Number of copies required: 1
Special requirements: Translate extensive foreign language quotations in footnotes; identify citations of medieval works appearing in a collection according to the divisions of the original and the volume and page (or column) of the collection. Submit typescript.
Copyright ownership: Pennsylvania State Univ.
Rejected manuscripts: Returned; enclose return postage.
Time before publication decision: 2-6 mos.
Time between decision and publication: 18-24 mos.
Number of reviewers: 1-2
Articles submitted per year: 150

Articles published per year: 30
Notes submitted per year: 10
Notes published per year: 3

(573)
*The Chesterton Review: The Journal of the Chesterton Society

Ian Boyd, Sister Mary Loyola, Leo Hetzler, & Gertrude White, Editors
St. Thomas More College
1437 College Dr.
Saskatoon, Saskatchewan S7N 0W6, Canada

Telephone: 306 966-8962
Fax: 306 966-8904
First published: 1974
Sponsoring organization: G. K. Chesterton Soc.
ISSN: 0317-0500
MLA acronym: CRev

SUBSCRIPTION INFORMATION

Frequency of publication: 4 times/yr.
Circulation: 1,500
Available in microform: No
Subscription price: $30.00/yr.
Year to which price refers: 1992

ADVERTISING INFORMATION

Advertising accepted: Yes
Advertising rates: $300.00/full page

EDITORIAL DESCRIPTION

Scope: Publishes articles on all aspects of the life, work, and thought of G. K. Chesterton, of the Chesterton circle, and of twentieth-century writers in the Chesterton or in an analogous tradition.
Reviews books: Yes
Publishes notes: Yes
Languages accepted: English
Prints abstracts: No
Author-anonymous submission: No

SUBMISSION REQUIREMENTS

Restrictions on contributors: Book reviews are commissioned.
Author pays submission fee: No
Author pays page charges: No
Length of articles: 3,000-5,000 words for major articles; shorter articles also accepted
Length of book reviews: 400-2,000 words
Length of notes: 300-500 words
Style: MLA
Number of copies required: 1
Copyright ownership: Journal
Rejected manuscripts: Returned
Time before publication decision: 6 mos.
Time between decision and publication: 12-28 mos.
Number of reviewers: 2
Articles submitted per year: 20-30
Articles published per year: 18-20
Book reviews published per year: 24
Notes published per year: 100

(574)
*Chiba Review

Kiyoyuki Ono, Editor
Dept. of English
Chiba Univ.
1-33 Yayoi-cho, Chiba City 260, Japan

First published: 1978
Sponsoring organization: Chiba English Literary Soc.
ISSN: 0388-2241
MLA acronym: ChibaR

SUBSCRIPTION INFORMATION

Frequency of publication: Annual
Circulation: 370
Available in microform: No
Subscription price: 4,000 yen/yr. Japan; $15.00/yr. elsewhere
Year to which price refers: 1991

ADVERTISING INFORMATION

Advertising accepted: No

EDITORIAL DESCRIPTION

Scope: Promotes scholarship in the fields of English literature, American literature, and English language education.
Reviews books: No
Publishes notes: Yes
Languages accepted: English; Japanese
Prints abstracts: No
Author-anonymous submission: No

SUBMISSION REQUIREMENTS

Restrictions on contributors: Deadline for the submission of manuscripts is 31 May of each year.
Author pays submission fee: No
Author pays page charges: No
Length of articles: 8,000 words maximum
Length of notes: 1,500 words
Style: MLA
Number of copies required: 1
Copyright ownership: Author
Rejected manuscripts: Not returned
Time before publication decision: 2 mos.
Time between decision and publication: 2 mos.
Articles submitted per year: 5-8
Articles published per year: 4-5

(575)
*Chicago Review

David Nicholls, Editor
5801 S. Kenwood
Chicago, IL 60637

Telephone: 312 702-0887
First published: 1946
Sponsoring organization: Univ. of Chicago
ISSN: 0009-3696
MLA acronym: ChiR

SUBSCRIPTION INFORMATION

Frequency of publication: 4 times/yr.
Circulation: 2,000
Available in microform: Yes
Subscription price: $30.00/yr. institutions US; $35.00/yr. institutions elsewhere; $20.00/yr. individuals US; $25.00/yr. individuals elsewhere
Year to which price refers: 1992

ADVERTISING INFORMATION

Advertising accepted: Yes
Advertising rates: $75.00/half page; $150.00/full page

EDITORIAL DESCRIPTION

Scope: Publishes aspiring and established poets and writers, as well as literary criticism and reviews.
Reviews books: Yes
Publishes notes: No
Languages accepted: English
Prints abstracts: No
Author-anonymous submission: No

SUBMISSION REQUIREMENTS

Restrictions on contributors: None
Author pays submission fee: No
Author pays page charges: No
Length of articles: No restrictions

Length of book reviews: No restrictions
Style: None
Number of copies required: 1
Copyright ownership: Journal
Rejected manuscripts: Returned; enclose SASE.
Time before publication decision: 3 mos.
Time between decision and publication: 3 mos.
Number of reviewers: 6
Articles submitted per year: 5,000
Articles published per year: 100

(576)
*Child Development

Susan C. Somerville, Editor
Dept. of Psychology
Arizona State Univ.
Tempe, AZ 85287-1104

Telephone: 602 965-1614
Fax: 602 965-8544
First published: 1930
Sponsoring organization: Soc. for Research in Child Development, Inc.
ISSN: 0009-3920
MLA acronym: CD

SUBSCRIPTION INFORMATION

Frequency of publication: 6 times/yr. (Feb., Apr., June, Aug., Oct., Dec.)
Circulation: 8,500
Available in microform: Yes
Subscription price: $126.00/yr.
Year to which price refers: 1993
Subscription address: Univ. of Chicago Press, Journals Division, P.O. Box 37005, Chicago, IL 60637
Subscription telephone: 312 753-8038
Subscription fax: 312 753-0811

ADVERTISING INFORMATION

Advertising accepted: Yes
Advertising rates: $275.00/full page

EDITORIAL DESCRIPTION

Scope: Publishes reports of empirical research and theoretical articles or reviews that have implications for developmental research. Welcomes contributions from all disciplines concerned with developmental processes. Special consideration is given to manuscripts reporting more than one experiment.
Reviews books: No
Publishes notes: No
Languages accepted: English
Prints abstracts: Yes
Author-anonymous submission: Yes

SUBMISSION REQUIREMENTS

Author pays submission fee: No
Author pays page charges: No
Length of articles: 8-20 pp.
Style: American Psychological Assn.
Number of copies required: 4
Special requirements: Include an abstract of 100-150 words on a separate sheet of paper.
Copyright ownership: Soc. for Research in Child Development, Inc.
Rejected manuscripts: Returned at author's request; enclose return postage.
Time before publication decision: 3 mos.
Time between decision and publication: 1 yr. maximum
Number of reviewers: 2-3
Articles submitted per year: 600
Articles published per year: 135

(577)
*Child Language Teaching and Therapy

David Crystal, Editor
P.O. Box 5
Holyhead
Gwynedd LL65 1RG, United Kingdom

Fax: (44) 407 769728
First published: 1985
ISSN: 0265-6590
MLA acronym: CLTT

SUBSCRIPTION INFORMATION

Frequency of publication: 3 times/yr. (Feb., June, Oct.)
Circulation: 1,400
Available in microform: Yes
Subscription price: £41.00/yr. institutions United Kingdom; $82.00/yr. institutions US; £26.00/yr. individuals United Kingdom; $54.00/yr. individuals US
Year to which price refers: 1991
Subscription address: Edward Arnold Journals, Mill Rd., Dunton Green, Sevenoaks, Kent TN13 2YA, England
Additional subscription address: In US & Canada: Cambridge Univ. Press, 40 W. 20th St., New York, NY 10011

ADVERTISING INFORMATION

Advertising accepted: Yes

EDITORIAL DESCRIPTION

Scope: Aims to help all who are directly involved in the teaching of children handicapped by an inadequate command of spoken or written language. It will be of use to speech pathologists and therapists as well as members of other professions who have a special interest in child language problems, such as the educational psychologist or pediatrician.
Reviews books: Yes
Publishes notes: Yes
Languages accepted: English
Prints abstracts: Yes
Author-anonymous submission: No

SUBMISSION REQUIREMENTS

Restrictions on contributors: Book reviews are solicited.
Author pays submission fee: No
Author pays page charges: No
Length of articles: 3,000-5,000 words
Length of book reviews: 300-1,000 words
Length of notes: 2,000 words
Style: Harvard
Number of copies required: 3
Copyright ownership: Edward Arnold Publishers, Ltd.
Rejected manuscripts: Returned at author's request
Time before publication decision: 1-2 mos.
Time between decision and publication: 3-6 mos.
Number of reviewers: 2
Articles submitted per year: 50
Articles published per year: 26
Book reviews published per year: 50
Notes submitted per year: 6
Notes published per year: 6

(578)
*Children's Folklore Review

C. W. Sullivan III, Editor
English Dept.
East Carolina Univ.
Greenville, NC 27858-4353

Telephone: 919 757-6660
Fax: 919 757-4263
First published: 1978
Sponsoring organization: Children's Folklore Section, American Folklore Soc.
ISSN: 0739-5558
MLA acronym: CFR

SUBSCRIPTION INFORMATION

Frequency of publication: 2 times/yr. (Fall, Spring)
Circulation: 150
Available in microform: No
Subscription price: $10.00/yr.
Year to which price refers: 1991-92
Subscription address: Danielle Roemer, Dept. of Literature & Language, Northern Kentucky Univ., Highland Heights, KY 41076
Subscription telephone: 606 572-5416
Subscription fax: 606 572-5566

ADVERTISING INFORMATION

Advertising accepted: Yes
Advertising rates: $50.00/half page; $75.00/full page

EDITORIAL DESCRIPTION

Scope: Publishes articles, notes, book reviews, and other items of interest to folklorists and other scholars interested in the traditional folklore and folklife of children.
Reviews books: Yes
Publishes notes: Yes
Languages accepted: English
Prints abstracts: No
Author-anonymous submission: Yes

SUBMISSION REQUIREMENTS

Restrictions on contributors: None
Author pays submission fee: No
Author pays page charges: No
Length of articles: 2,500-5,000 words
Length of book reviews: 350-850 words
Length of notes: 100-500 words
Style: MLA
Number of copies required: 1
Copyright ownership: Children's Folklore Section, American Folklore Soc.
Rejected manuscripts: Returned
Time before publication decision: 3 mos. maximum
Time between decision and publication: 1 yr.
Number of reviewers: 2
Articles submitted per year: 10
Articles published per year: 7

(579)
*Children's Literature: An International Journal, Inc. Annual of the Modern Language Association Division on Children's Literature and the Children's Literature Association

R. H. W. Dillard & Elizabeth Keyser, Editors
Dept. of English
Hollins College
Roanoke, VA 24020

First published: 1972
Sponsoring organization: MLA, Division on Children's Literature; Children's Literature Assn.
MLA acronym: ChildL

SUBSCRIPTION INFORMATION

Frequency of publication: Annual
Circulation: 3,000
Available in microform: No
Subscription address: Yale Univ. Press, Box 92A, Yale Station, New Haven, CT 06520
Additional subscription address: Vols. 1-7 available from Children's Literature Foundation, Box 370, Windham Center, CT 06280

ADVERTISING INFORMATION

Advertising accepted: No

EDITORIAL DESCRIPTION

Scope: Publishes criticism of children's literature.
Reviews books: Yes
Publishes notes: Yes
Languages accepted: English
Prints abstracts: No
Author-anonymous submission: No

SUBMISSION REQUIREMENTS

Restrictions on contributors: None
Author pays submission fee: No
Author pays page charges: No
Length of articles: 5,000 words maximum
Length of book reviews: 1,000 words
Length of notes: No restrictions
Style: MLA
Number of copies required: 3
Special requirements: Submit original typescript.
Copyright ownership: Journal
Rejected manuscripts: Returned; enclose SASE.
Time before publication decision: 3 mos.
Time between decision and publication: 1 yr.
Number of reviewers: 8
Articles submitted per year: 75
Articles published per year: 10
Book reviews submitted per year: 20
Book reviews published per year: 10
Notes submitted per year: 5
Notes published per year: 2

(580)
*Children's Literature Association Quarterly

Gillian Adams, Editor
5906 Fairlane Dr.
Austin, TX 78731-4417

Telephone: 512 454-1799
First published: 1974
Sponsoring organization: Children's Literature Assn.
ISSN: 0885-0429
MLA acronym: CLAQ

SUBSCRIPTION INFORMATION

Frequency of publication: 4 times/yr. (Spring, Summer, Fall, Winter)
Circulation: 850
Available in microform: No
Subscription address: Children's Literature Assn., 22 Harvest Lane, Battle Creek, MI 49017
Subscription telephone: 616 965-8108

ADVERTISING INFORMATION

Advertising accepted: Yes
Advertising rates: $100.00/quarter page; $175.00/half page; $275.00/full page; $250.00/half back page

EDITORIAL DESCRIPTION

Scope: Publishes critical articles and research on children's literature and related fields (e.g., children's folklore, illustration in children's books, the teaching of children's literature, young adult literature, children's theater, media).
Reviews books: Yes
Publishes notes: No
Languages accepted: English
Prints abstracts: No
Author-anonymous submission: Yes

SUBMISSION REQUIREMENTS

Restrictions on contributors: None
Author pays submission fee: No

Author pays page charges: No
Length of articles: 3,000-6,000 words
Length of book reviews: 250-3,000 words
Style: MLA
Number of copies required: 3
Copyright ownership: Children's Literature Assn.
Rejected manuscripts: Returned
Time before publication decision: 2-6 mos.
Time between decision and publication: 3-18 mos.
Number of reviewers: 3-5
Articles submitted per year: 100
Articles published per year: 40
Book reviews submitted per year: 25
Book reviews published per year: 25

(581)
Children's Literature in Education

Anita Moss, Editor
English Dept.
Univ. of North Carolina
UNCC Station
Charlotte, NC 28223

Additional editorial address: Outside of N. America: Geoff Fox, Univ. of Exeter, School of Education, St. Luke's, Exeter EX1 2LU, Devon, England. Send books for review to: Elizabeth Segal, 5821 Wayne Rd., Pittsburgh, PA 15206
ISSN: 0045-6713
MLA acronym: CLE

SUBSCRIPTION INFORMATION

Frequency of publication: 4 times/yr.
Subscription price: $65.00/yr. institutions US; $75.00/yr. institutions elsewhere; $23.00/yr. individuals and schools (grades K-12) US; $27.00/yr. individuals and schools (grades K-12) elsewhere
Year to which price refers: 1992
Subscription address: Human Sciences Press, 233 Spring St., New York, NY 10013-1578
Subscription telephone: 800 221-9369; 212 620-8000
Subscription fax: 212 807-1047

ADVERTISING INFORMATION

Advertising accepted: No

EDITORIAL DESCRIPTION

Scope: Seeks to promote lively discussions of poetry and prose for children and young adults and to heighten professional awareness and understanding of this literature and its use. Welcomes critical evaluation of individual authors or single works, analysis or commentary on social issues reflected in books, interviews with or articles by authors and illustrators, accounts of classroom practice and experience, and examinations of the reading process and its developmental role in childhood and adolescence..
Reviews books: Yes
Languages accepted: English

SUBMISSION REQUIREMENTS

Number of copies required: 2
Special requirements: Manuscript should be original and not previously published.
Rejected manuscripts: Returned; enclose SASE.

(582)
Chinese Comparatist

Beiling Wu, Editor
Program of Comparative Literature & Theory
Northwestern Univ.
Evanston, IL 60201

First published: 1987
Sponsoring organization: American Chapter of the Chinese Comparative Literature Assn.
ISSN: 1041-3928
MLA acronym: CComp

SUBSCRIPTION INFORMATION

Frequency of publication: 2 times/yr.
Circulation: 200
Available in microform: No
Subscription address: 9614 Crawford, Skokie, IL 60076

ADVERTISING INFORMATION

Advertising accepted: Yes

EDITORIAL DESCRIPTION

Scope: Publishes articles which explore East-West literary relations, Chinese comparative literature, and Chinese and western literary criticism and theories.
Reviews books: Yes
Publishes notes: Yes
Languages accepted: English
Prints abstracts: Yes
Author-anonymous submission: No

SUBMISSION REQUIREMENTS

Author pays submission fee: No
Author pays page charges: No
Style: MLA
Number of copies required: 1
Copyright ownership: Journal
Rejected manuscripts: Returned
Time before publication decision: 2-3 mos.
Time between decision and publication: 3-6 mos.
Number of reviewers: 2

(583)
*Chinese Culture: A Quarterly Review

Sung Shee & Lo Mou-pin, Editors
P.O. Box 12
Yang Ming Shan, Taipei
Taiwan, Republic of China

Telephone: (886) 2 8610511 ext. 446, 447
First published: 1957
Sponsoring organization: China Academy, Inst. for Advanced Chinese Studies
ISSN: 0009-4544
MLA acronym: ChC

SUBSCRIPTION INFORMATION

Frequency of publication: 4 times/yr. (Mar., June, Sept., Dec.)
Circulation: 2,000
Available in microform: No
Subscription price: $40.00/yr.
Year to which price refers: 1992
Subscription address: Chinese Culture Univ. Press, Hwa Kang, Yang Ming Shan, Taipei, Taiwan, Republic of China
Subscription telephone: (886) 2 8610511 ext. 459, 460

ADVERTISING INFORMATION

Advertising accepted: Yes

EDITORIAL DESCRIPTION

Scope: Publishes articles on Chinese studies and international cultural interflow.

Reviews books: Yes
Languages accepted: English
Prints abstracts: No

SUBMISSION REQUIREMENTS

Restrictions on contributors: None
Author pays submission fee: No
Length of articles: 5,000-20,000 words
Style: MLA
Number of copies required: 1
Special requirements: Submit original typescript. Chinese quotations are permitted.
Copyright ownership: Assigned by author to journal
Rejected manuscripts: Returned
Time before publication decision: 2 mos.
Time between decision and publication: 1 yr.
Number of reviewers: 2
Articles published per year: 24-30

(584)
*Chinese Literature

He Jingzhi, Editor
Chinese Literature Press
24 Baiwanzhuang Rd.
Beijing 100037, People's Republic of China

Telephone: (86) 1 8323291
First published: 1951
Sponsoring organization: Foreign Languages Publication & Distribution Bureau
ISSN: 0009-4617
MLA acronym: ChinL

SUBSCRIPTION INFORMATION

Frequency of publication: 4 times/yr. (Spring, Summer, Autumn, Winter)
Circulation: 60,000
Available in microform: No
Subscription price: $16.50/yr.
Year to which price refers: 1992
Subscription address: International Book Trading Corp., Guoji Shudian, P.O. Box 399, Beijing, People's Republic of China

ADVERTISING INFORMATION

Advertising accepted: Yes

EDITORIAL DESCRIPTION

Scope: Publishes translations of selected ancient, modern, and contemporary Chinese works, and articles on modern and classical Chinese fiction, poetry, literary criticism, and arts.
Reviews books: Yes
Languages accepted: English; French
Prints abstracts: No
Author-anonymous submission: No

SUBMISSION REQUIREMENTS

Restrictions on contributors: Contributors are mostly Chinese writers. Writings about Chinese culture by others are accepted, but the fee must be paid in Chinese currency.
Author pays submission fee: No
Author pays page charges: No
Length of articles: 10,000 words maximum
Length of book reviews: 2,000 words
Number of copies required: 1
Copyright ownership: Chinese Literature Press
Rejected manuscripts: Returned
Time between decision and publication: 4 mos.
Number of reviewers: 2-3

(585)
*Chinese Literature: Essays, Articles, Reviews

Eugene C. Eoyang, William H. Nienhauser, Jr., & Robert E. Hegel, Editors
Ballantine Hall 402
Comparative Literature
Indiana Univ.
Bloomington, IN 47405

Additional editorial address: East Asian Languages & Cultures, Indiana Univ., Bloomington, IN 47405
E-mail: CLEAR@IUBACS (Bitnet); CLEAR@UCS.INDIANA.EDU (Internet)
First published: 1979
Sponsoring organization: Univ. of Wisconsin; Indiana Univ.; Washington Univ.
ISSN: 0161-9705
MLA acronym: CLEAR

SUBSCRIPTION INFORMATION

Frequency of publication: Annual (Dec.)
Circulation: 370
Available in microform: Yes
Subscription price: $50.00/yr. institutions US; $60.00/yr. institutions elsewhere; $25.00/yr. individuals US; $35.00/yr. individuals elsewhere
Year to which price refers: 1992-95
Additional subscription address: 221 Goodbody Hall, Indiana Univ., Bloomington, IN 47405

ADVERTISING INFORMATION

Advertising accepted: Yes
Advertising rates: $150.00/half page; $200.00/full page

EDITORIAL DESCRIPTION

Scope: Publishes articles on traditional and modern Chinese literature.
Reviews books: Yes
Publishes notes: Yes
Languages accepted: English
Prints abstracts: No
Author-anonymous submission: Yes

SUBMISSION REQUIREMENTS

Restrictions on contributors: None
Author pays submission fee: No
Author pays page charges: No
Length of articles: 7,500 words
Length of book reviews: 1,000 words minimum
Style: MLA & *Harvard Journal of Asiatic Studies*
Number of copies required: 3
Special requirements: Send double-spaced typescript with original text citations; append footnotes.
Copyright ownership: Journal
Rejected manuscripts: Returned
Time before publication decision: 6 mos.
Time between decision and publication: 12-15 mos.
Number of reviewers: 2-3
Articles submitted per year: 20
Articles published per year: 5
Book reviews submitted per year: 20-25
Book reviews published per year: 20-25
Notes submitted per year: 10
Notes published per year: 10

(586)
*Chiricú

Sean Dwyer, Editor
Chicano-Riqueño Studies
Ballantine Hall 849
Indiana Univ.
Bloomington, IN 47405

Telephone: 812 855-5257
First published: 1976
Sponsoring organization: Indiana Univ., Chicano-Riqueño Studies
ISSN: 0277-7223
MLA acronym: Chiricú

SUBSCRIPTION INFORMATION

Frequency of publication: Annual (Fall)
Circulation: 200-500
Available in microform: No
Subscription price: $7.00/yr. institutions; $5.00/yr. individuals
Year to which price refers: 1992

ADVERTISING INFORMATION

Advertising accepted: No

EDITORIAL DESCRIPTION

Scope: Publishes articles on Latin American literature and poetry. Also includes original stories, poems, and drama written by Latin Americans.
Reviews books: Yes
Publishes notes: No
Languages accepted: Spanish; Portuguese; English
Prints abstracts: No
Author-anonymous submission: No

SUBMISSION REQUIREMENTS

Author pays submission fee: No
Author pays page charges: No
Length of articles: 10-15 double-spaced typescript pp.
Length of book reviews: 3-5 double-spaced typescript pp.
Style: MLA
Number of copies required: 1
Copyright ownership: Chicano Riqueño Studies, Indiana Univ. & author
Rejected manuscripts: Returned; enclose SASE.
Time before publication decision: 6-12 mos.
Time between decision and publication: 6 mos.
Number of reviewers: 3
Articles submitted per year: 20
Articles published per year: 5
Book reviews submitted per year: 3
Book reviews published per year: 1

(587)
*Chloe: Beihefte zum Daphnis

Hans-Gert Roloff, Leonard W. Forster, Ferdinand van Ingen, Eberhard Mannack, Blake Lee Spahr, Alberto Martino, Gerhard Spellerberg, Barbara Becker-Cantarino, Wilhelm Kühlmann, Marian Szyrocki, Jean-Marie Valentin, & Martin Bircher, Editors
Freie Univ. Berlin
Fachbereich Germanistik Forschungsstelle für Mittlere Deutsche Literatur
Habelschwerdter Allee, 45
1000 Berlin 33, Germany

Telephone: (49) 30 8385007
Fax: (49) 30 8386749
First published: 1984
MLA acronym: Chloe

SUBSCRIPTION INFORMATION

Frequency of publication: Irregular
Circulation: 300-500
Available in microform: No
Subscription address: Editions Rodopi, Keizersgracht 302-304, 1016 EX Amsterdam, Netherlands

ADVERTISING INFORMATION

Advertising accepted: Yes

EDITORIAL DESCRIPTION

Scope: Publishes articles on German literature from the Reformation, Baroque period, and the Renaissance.
Reviews books: No
Publishes notes: No
Languages accepted: German; French; English
Prints abstracts: No
Author-anonymous submission: No

SUBMISSION REQUIREMENTS

Restrictions on contributors: None
Author pays submission fee: No
Author pays page charges: No
Length of books: No restrictions
Style: Series
Number of copies required: 2
Copyright ownership: Editions Rodopi
Rejected manuscripts: Returned
Time before publication decision: 6-8 weeks
Time between decision and publication: 6 mos.
Number of reviewers: 2-3
Articles submitted per year: 50
Articles published per year: 20-40
Books submitted per year: 1-3
Books published per year: 1

(588)
*Christian Scholar's Review

William Hasker, Editor
Huntington College
Huntington, IN 46750

Telephone: 219 356-6000 ext. 2037
First published: 1971
ISSN: 0017-2251
MLA acronym: CSR

SUBSCRIPTION INFORMATION

Frequency of publication: 4 times/yr.
Circulation: 4,500
Available in microform: Yes
Subscription price: $14.00/yr.
Year to which price refers: 1991-92
Subscription address: Circulation Editor, Hope College, Holland, MI 49423

ADVERTISING INFORMATION

Advertising accepted: Yes
Advertising rates: $150.00/full page

EDITORIAL DESCRIPTION

Scope: Publishes articles of high standards of original scholarship and of general interest dealing with all aspects of Christian thought and the interrelationship of Christian thought with all areas of scholarly interest. Normally articles should reflect a Christian perspective. However, articles not clearly reflecting a Christian perspective, but of general interest to the Christian community or of such a character as to promote communication between Christians and non-Christians may be included as well.
Reviews books: Yes
Publishes notes: Yes
Languages accepted: English
Prints abstracts: No
Author-anonymous submission: No

SUBMISSION REQUIREMENTS

Restrictions on contributors: None
Author pays submission fee: No
Author pays page charges: No
Length of articles: 10,000 words maximum
Length of book reviews: 1,000 words
Length of notes: 1,000 words
Style: Chicago
Number of copies required: 2
Copyright ownership: Assigned by author to journal
Rejected manuscripts: Returned; enclose SASE.
Time before publication decision: 1-4 mos.
Time between decision and publication: 6-12 mos.
Number of reviewers: 3
Articles submitted per year: 100
Articles published per year: 20

(589)
*Christianity and Literature

Robert Snyder, Editor
Dept. of English
Seattle Pacific Univ.
Seattle, WA 98119-1997

Telephone: 206 281-2404
Fax: 206 281-2500
First published: 1951
Sponsoring organization: Conference on Christianity & Literature
ISSN: 0148-3331
MLA acronym: C&L

SUBSCRIPTION INFORMATION

Frequency of publication: 4 times/yr.
Circulation: 1,300
Available in microform: No
Subscription price: $20.00/yr. institutions; $15.00/yr. individuals; $10.00/yr. students; add $5.00/yr. postage outside US
Year to which price refers: 1991-92

ADVERTISING INFORMATION

Advertising accepted: Yes
Advertising rates: $125.00/half page; $200.00/full page

EDITORIAL DESCRIPTION

Scope: Publishes articles and reviews in all areas of literature, with emphasis on the relationship between literature and Christianity.
Reviews books: Yes
Publishes notes: No
Languages accepted: English
Prints abstracts: No
Author-anonymous submission: Yes

SUBMISSION REQUIREMENTS

Restrictions on contributors: Unsolicited book reviews are not accepted.
Author pays submission fee: No
Author pays page charges: No
Length of articles: 4,000-9,000 words
Length of book reviews: 1,000-1,250 words
Style: MLA
Number of copies required: 2
Copyright ownership: Conference on Christianity & Literature
Rejected manuscripts: Returned; enclose return postage.
Time before publication decision: 3 mos.
Time between decision and publication: 6-9 mos.
Number of reviewers: 2
Articles submitted per year: 125
Articles published per year: 15-20
Book reviews submitted per year: 90
Book reviews published per year: 80

(590)
*Chronique d'Egypte

Jean Bingen & H. De Meulenaere, Editors
Fondation Egyptologique Reine Elisabeth
Parc du Cinquantenaire 10
1040 Brussels, Belgium

Telephone: (32) 2 7417364
First published: 1925
Sponsoring organization: Fondation Egyptologique Reine Elisabeth
ISSN: 0009-6067
MLA acronym: ChrE

SUBSCRIPTION INFORMATION

Frequency of publication: 2 times/yr.
Circulation: 1,000
Available in microform: No
Subscription price: 2,200 BF/yr.
Year to which price refers: 1992

ADVERTISING INFORMATION

Advertising accepted: Yes
Advertising rates: 5,000 BF/full page

EDITORIAL DESCRIPTION

Scope: Publishes research in the fields of Egyptology, Papyrology, and Ancient East history, archaeology, philosophy, and linguistics.
Reviews books: Yes
Publishes notes: Yes
Languages accepted: English; French; German; Italian; Dutch
Prints abstracts: No

SUBMISSION REQUIREMENTS

Restrictions on contributors: None
Author pays submission fee: No
Author pays page charges: No
Length of articles: 2,500-5,000 words
Length of book reviews: 1,000-3,000 words
Length of notes: 1,000-3,000 words
Number of copies required: 1
Special requirements: Submit original typescript
Copyright ownership: Author & Fondation Egyptologique Reine Elisabeth
Rejected manuscripts: Returned
Time before publication decision: 4 mos.
Time between decision and publication: 6-15 mos.
Number of reviewers: 2
Articles submitted per year: 30
Articles published per year: 20
Book reviews submitted per year: 50
Book reviews published per year: 20-40
Notes submitted per year: 10
Notes published per year: 5

(591)
*Chu-Shikoku Studies in American Literature

Osamu Hamaguchi, Katsuhiro Jinzaki, Yamato Izu, & Takashi Nishimae, Editors
Chu-Shikoku American Literature Soc.
Faculty of Letters
Hiroshima Univ.
1-1-89, Higashisenda-machi
Naka-ku, Hiroshima 730, Japan

Telephone: (81) 82 2411221 ext. 2265
First published: 1962
Sponsoring organization: Chu-Shikoku American Literature Soc.
ISSN: 0388-0176
MLA acronym: SALit

SUBSCRIPTION INFORMATION

Frequency of publication: Annual
Circulation: 300
Available in microform: No
Subscription fax: (81) 82 2468466

ADVERTISING INFORMATION

Advertising accepted: No

EDITORIAL DESCRIPTION

Scope: Publishes articles on American language and literature that are of significant interest to the entire membership of the Society.
Reviews books: Yes
Publishes notes: Yes
Languages accepted: English; Japanese
Prints abstracts: Yes
Author-anonymous submission: No

SUBMISSION REQUIREMENTS

Restrictions on contributors: Contributors must be members of Chu-Shikoku American Literature Soc.
Author pays submission fee: Yes
Cost of submission fee: 20,000 yen (if published)
Author pays page charges: No
Length of articles: 20 double-spaced typescript pp. (65 characters per line, 25 lines per page)
Length of book reviews: 1,500 words
Length of notes: 3,000 words
Style: MLA
Number of copies required: 5
Copyright ownership: Chu-Shikoku American Literature Soc.
Rejected manuscripts: Returned
Time before publication decision: 3 mos.
Time between decision and publication: 6 mos.
Number of reviewers: 4
Articles submitted per year: 10
Articles published per year: 5-6
Book reviews submitted per year: 2
Book reviews published per year: 1
Notes submitted per year: 2
Notes published per year: 1

(592)
*Chūgoku Bungaku Hō

Chinese Literature Assn.
Dept. of Chinese Language & Literature
Kyoto Univ.
Kyoto, Japan

Telephone: (81) 75 7532825
First published: 1954
Sponsoring organization: Chūgoku Bungakukai
ISSN: 0578-0934
MLA acronym: CBunH

SUBSCRIPTION INFORMATION

Frequency of publication: 2 times/yr. (Apr., Oct.)
Circulation: 900
Available in microform: No
Subscription price: 2,700 yen/yr.
Year to which price refers: 1992

ADVERTISING INFORMATION

Advertising accepted: No

EDITORIAL DESCRIPTION

Scope: Publishes articles on Chinese literature.
Reviews books: Yes
Publishes notes: No
Languages accepted: Japanese; Chinese languages
Prints abstracts: Yes
Author-anonymous submission: No

SUBMISSION REQUIREMENTS

Restrictions on contributors: None
Author pays submission fee: No
Author pays page charges: No
Length of articles: No restrictions
Length of book reviews: No restrictions
Style: None
Number of copies required: 1
Special requirements: None
Copyright ownership: Author
Rejected manuscripts: Not returned
Time before publication decision: 2 mos.
Time between decision and publication: 6 mos.
Number of reviewers: 3
Articles submitted per year: 8
Articles published per year: 6
Book reviews submitted per year: 4
Book reviews published per year: 4

(593)
*Chung-wai Literary Monthly: Studies in Chinese and Foreign Literatures

Hsien-hao Sebastian Liao, Editor
Dept. of Foreign Languages & Literature
National Taiwan Univ.
Taipei
Taiwan, Republic of China

Telephone: (886) 2 3639652
Fax: (886) 2 3639395
First published: 1972
Historical variations in title: Formerly *Chung-wai Literary Monthly: Publicación Cuatrimestral del Centro di Estudios Teológicos de San Esteban*
Sponsoring organization: National Taiwan Univ.
MLA acronym: CWLM

SUBSCRIPTION INFORMATION

Frequency of publication: 12 times/yr.
Circulation: 2,000
Available in microform: No
Subscription price: NT$850.00/yr.
Year to which price refers: 1992

ADVERTISING INFORMATION

Advertising accepted: Yes
Advertising rates: NT$2,000.00/full page

EDITORIAL DESCRIPTION

Scope: Publishes articles on Chinese, Western, and comparative literature.
Reviews books: Yes
Publishes notes: Yes
Languages accepted: Chinese languages
Prints abstracts: No
Author-anonymous submission: No

SUBMISSION REQUIREMENTS

Author pays submission fee: No
Author pays page charges: No
Length of articles: 10,000 words
Length of book reviews: 5,000 words
Length of notes: 1,000 words
Style: MLA
Number of copies required: 1
Copyright ownership: Author
Rejected manuscripts: Returned; enclose return postage.
Time before publication decision: 3 mos.
Time between decision and publication: 1 mo.
Number of reviewers: 1-2
Articles submitted per year: 210
Articles published per year: 75
Book reviews submitted per year: 30
Book reviews published per year: 10
Notes submitted per year: 20
Notes published per year: 6

(594)
*CICIM: Revue pour le Cinéma Français

Heiner Gassen, Editor
Kaulbachstr. 13
8000 Munich 22, Germany

Telephone: (49) 89 28662824
Fax: (49) 89 28662866
First published: 1982
ISSN: 0938-233X
MLA acronym: CICIM

SUBSCRIPTION INFORMATION

Frequency of publication: 3 times/yr.
Circulation: 2,000
Available in microform: No
Subscription price: 30 DM/4 issues, 55 DM/8 issues Germany; 35 DM/4 issues, 65 DM/8 issues elsewhere
Year to which price refers: 1992

ADVERTISING INFORMATION

Advertising accepted: Yes

EDITORIAL DESCRIPTION

Scope: Publishes articles on French cinema.
Reviews books: Yes
Publishes notes: No
Languages accepted: German
Prints abstracts: No
Author-anonymous submission: No

SUBMISSION REQUIREMENTS

Restrictions on contributors: None
Author pays submission fee: No
Author pays page charges: No
Number of copies required: 1
Special requirements: Contact editor before submitting manuscript. Articles in French and English are accepted for translation into German.
Copyright ownership: Journal & author for articles in German; author for articles in other languages.
Rejected manuscripts: Not returned
Time before publication decision: 2-4 weeks
Number of reviewers: 1
Articles submitted per year: 10-15
Book reviews submitted per year: 5-10

(595)
Ciencia Tomista: Publicación Cuatrimestral del Centro de Estudios Teológicos de San Esteban

Luis Lago Alba, Editor
Estudio Teologico de San Esteban
Plaza del Concilio de Trento, 4
Apartado 17
37080 Salamanca, Spain

Telephone: (34) 23 215000
Fax: (34) 23 265480
First published: 1910
Sponsoring organization: Estudio Teologico de San Esteban
ISSN: 0210-0398
MLA acronym: CT

SUBSCRIPTION INFORMATION

Frequency of publication: 3 times/yr.
Circulation: 780
Available in microform: No
Subscription price: 3,600 Pta/yr. Spain; 4,600 Pta/yr. elsewhere
Year to which price refers: 1992

ADVERTISING INFORMATION

Advertising accepted: No

EDITORIAL DESCRIPTION

Scope: Publishes articles on theology and the sciences of religion.
Reviews books: Yes
Publishes notes: Yes
Languages accepted: Spanish
Prints abstracts: No
Author-anonymous submission: No

SUBMISSION REQUIREMENTS

Author pays submission fee: No
Author pays page charges: No
Length of articles: 36,000 words
Length of book reviews: 1,800 words
Length of notes: 26,000 words
Number of copies required: 3
Copyright ownership: Journal
Rejected manuscripts: Not returned
Time before publication decision: 1 mo.
Number of reviewers: 3

Articles published per year: 18
Book reviews submitted per year: 200
Book reviews published per year: 200
Notes published per year: 10

(596)
*Cimarron Review

Gordon Weaver & Deborah Bransford, Editors
205 Morrill Hall
Oklahoma State Univ.
Stillwater, OK 74078-0135

Telephone: 405 744-9476
Fax: 405 744-6326
First published: 1967
Sponsoring organization: Oklahoma State Univ., College of Arts & Sciences
ISSN: 0009-6849
MLA acronym: CimR

SUBSCRIPTION INFORMATION

Frequency of publication: 4 times/yr. (Jan., Apr., July, Oct.)
Circulation: 600
Available in microform: Yes
Subscription price: $12.00/yr., $30.00/3 yrs. US; $15.00/yr., $40.00/3 yrs. Canada
Year to which price refers: 1992

ADVERTISING INFORMATION

Advertising accepted: No

EDITORIAL DESCRIPTION

Scope: Publishes fiction, poetry, and articles on arts and letters.
Reviews books: Yes
Publishes notes: No
Languages accepted: English
Prints abstracts: No
Author-anonymous submission: No

SUBMISSION REQUIREMENTS

Restrictions on contributors: Book reviews are assigned.
Author pays submission fee: No
Author pays page charges: No
Length of articles: 1,500-3,500 words
Length of book reviews: 500 words
Style: MLA
Number of copies required: 1
Special requirements: Submit typescript. No simultaneous submissions.
Copyright ownership: Oklahoma State Univ. Board of Regents
Rejected manuscripts: Returned; enclose SASE.
Time before publication decision: 6-8 weeks
Time between decision and publication: 1 yr.
Number of reviewers: 3
Articles submitted per year: 50
Articles published per year: 10
Book reviews published per year: 10-16

(597)
*Cincinnati Romance Review

Jean-Charles Seigneuret & Kathryn M. Lorenz, Editors
Mail location 377
Dept. of Romance Languages & Literatures
Univ. of Cincinnati
Cincinnati, OH 45221

Telephone: 513 556-1950
First published: 1982
ISSN: 0883-9816
MLA acronym: CRR

SUBSCRIPTION INFORMATION

Frequency of publication: Annual (May)
Circulation: 100

Available in microform: No
Subscription price: $10.00/yr.
Year to which price refers: 1992

ADVERTISING INFORMATION

Advertising accepted: No

EDITORIAL DESCRIPTION

Scope: Publishes articles on Romance literatures and languages selected from papers read at the annual Cincinnati Conference on Romance Languages and Literatures. Articles are selected on the basis of originality, erudition, and broad interest to scholars in the above fields.
Reviews books: No
Publishes notes: No
Languages accepted: English; French; Spanish; Italian
Prints abstracts: No
Author-anonymous submission: Yes

SUBMISSION REQUIREMENTS

Restrictions on contributors: Contributors must have read the paper at the annual Cincinnati Conference on Romance Languages and Literatures.
Author pays submission fee: No
Author pays page charges: No
Length of articles: 4,000-5,500 words
Style: MLA
Number of copies required: 3
Special requirements: Submit original typescript and 2 copies. Articles must not have been published previously.
Copyright ownership: Journal
Rejected manuscripts: Returned; enclose SASE.
Time before publication decision: 6 mos.
Time between decision and publication: 4 mos.
Number of reviewers: 2
Articles submitted per year: 75
Articles published per year: 10-14

(598)
*Cineaste: America's Leading Magazine on the Art and Politics of the Cinema

Gary Crowdus, Dan Georgakas, Roy Grundmann, Robert Sklar, Leonard Quart, & Cynthia Lucia, Editors
200 Park Ave. South, 1320
New York, NY 10003

Telephone: 212 982-1241
First published: 1967
ISSN: 0009-7004
MLA acronym: Cineaste

SUBSCRIPTION INFORMATION

Frequency of publication: 4 times/yr.
Circulation: 7,000
Available in microform: Yes
Subscription price: $30.00/yr. institutions US; $37.00/yr. institutions elsewhere; $15.00/yr. individuals US; $24.00/yr. individuals elsewhere
Year to which price refers: 1992
Subscription address: P.O. Box 2242, New York, NY 10003

ADVERTISING INFORMATION

Advertising accepted: Yes; contact Tina Margolis & Assoc., 445 Broadway, Suite 3J, Hastings-on-Hudson, NY 10706

EDITORIAL DESCRIPTION

Scope: Publishes critical articles about films as well as film reviews.
Reviews books: Yes
Publishes notes: No
Languages accepted: English

Prints abstracts: No

SUBMISSION REQUIREMENTS

Restrictions on contributors: None
Author pays submission fee: No
Author pays page charges: No
Length of articles: 3,000-4,000 words
Length of book reviews: 1,000-1,500 words
Style: Journal
Number of copies required: 1
Copyright ownership: Journal
Rejected manuscripts: Returned; enclose SASE.
Time before publication decision: 3 weeks
Time between decision and publication: 1-3 mos.
Number of reviewers: 5
Articles submitted per year: 100
Articles published per year: 10-12
Book reviews submitted per year: 75
Book reviews published per year: 40-50

(599)
*Cinefocus

Cimberli Carpenter, Yifen Tsau, Neepa Majumdar, Lahen Haddad, Katrina Boyd, & Juan Suarez, Editors
Film Studies Division BH309
Indiana Univ.
Bloomington, IN 47405

Telephone: 812 855-1072
E-mail: CINEFOCUS@IUBACS (Bitnet); CINEFOCUS@UCS.INDIANA.EDU (Internet)
First published: 1990
Sponsoring organization: College of Arts & Sciences, Indiana Univ.
ISSN: 1059-0900
MLA acronym: Cinefocus

SUBSCRIPTION INFORMATION

Frequency of publication: 2 times/yr. (Fall, Spring)
Available in microform: No
Subscription price: $10.00/yr. institutions; $8.00/yr. individuals
Year to which price refers: 1991

ADVERTISING INFORMATION

Advertising accepted: No

EDITORIAL DESCRIPTION

Scope: Publishes articles on films and other related media. A portion of each issue is devoted to a specific topic.
Reviews books: No
Publishes notes: Yes
Languages accepted: English
Prints abstracts: No
Author-anonymous submission: No

SUBMISSION REQUIREMENTS

Restrictions on contributors: None
Author pays submission fee: No
Author pays page charges: No
Length of articles: 6,000 words maximum
Style: MLA; Chicago
Number of copies required: 2
Special requirements: Submission on Macintosh-compatible diskettes is preferred.
Copyright ownership: Film Studies Division, Indiana Univ.
Rejected manuscripts: Not returned
Time between decision and publication: 1 yr. maximum
Number of reviewers: 2 minimum
Articles published per year: 8

(600)
*Cinema Journal

Dana Polan, Editor
Dept. of English
526 C.L.
Univ. of Pittsburgh
Pittsburgh, PA 15260

Telephone: 412 624-6528
Fax: 412 624-6639
First published: 1961
Sponsoring organization: Soc. for Cinema Studies
ISSN: 0009-7101
MLA acronym: CinJ

SUBSCRIPTION INFORMATION

Frequency of publication: 4 times/yr.
Circulation: 1,400
Available in microform: Yes, through Univ. Microfilms International
Subscription price: $32.00/yr. institutions US; $39.00/yr. institutions elsewhere; $25.00/yr. individuals US; $32.00/yr. individuals elsewhere
Year to which price refers: 1992
Subscription address: Univ. of Illinois Press, 54 E. Gregory Dr., Champaign, IL 61820
Subscription telephone: 217 244-0626
Subscription fax: 217 244-8082

ADVERTISING INFORMATION

Advertising accepted: Yes
Advertising rates: $95.00/half page; $160.00/full page

EDITORIAL DESCRIPTION

Scope: Publishes articles about American and international film and television, and concentrates on areas of screen studies within college programs. Includes a comprehensive section of notes regarding upcoming conferences, current research, articles on film in non-screen productions, new books, and grant opportunities.
Reviews books: No
Publishes notes: Yes
Languages accepted: English
Prints abstracts: Yes
Author-anonymous submission: Yes

SUBMISSION REQUIREMENTS

Restrictions on contributors: Contributors must be members of the Society for Cinema Studies. Author's names should not appear on manuscript.
Author pays submission fee: No
Author pays page charges: No
Length of articles: 7,500 words maximum
Style: Chicago
Number of copies required: 3
Special requirements: Authors must obtain permission to publish illustrations and frame enlargements.
Copyright ownership: Univ. of Illinois Press
Rejected manuscripts: Returned; enclose SASE.
Time before publication decision: 3-6 mos.
Time between decision and publication: 3-6 mos.
Number of reviewers: 3
Articles submitted per year: 100
Articles published per year: 12-15

(601)
*Círculo: Revista de Cultura

Elio Alba-Buffill, Editor
16 Malvern Pl.
Verona, NJ 07044

Telephone: 201 239-3125
First published: 1970
Sponsoring organization: Círculo de Cultura Panamericano

ISSN: 0009-7349
MLA acronym: Círculo

SUBSCRIPTION INFORMATION

Frequency of publication: Annual
Circulation: 775
Available in microform: No
Subscription price: $25.00/yr.
Year to which price refers: 1992

ADVERTISING INFORMATION

Advertising accepted: Yes

EDITORIAL DESCRIPTION

Scope: Publishes on Spanish-American and Spanish literature.
Reviews books: Yes
Publishes notes: Yes
Languages accepted: English; Spanish
Prints abstracts: No
Author-anonymous submission: No

SUBMISSION REQUIREMENTS

Restrictions on contributors: Publishes only original articles written by members of Círculo de Cultura Panamericano, or by special request. Reviews are by invitation only.
Author pays submission fee: No
Author pays page charges: No
Length of articles: 10 pp.
Length of book reviews: 3 pp.
Length of notes: 5 pp.
Style: MLA
Number of copies required: 2
Copyright ownership: Journal
Rejected manuscripts: Returned; enclose SASE.
Time before publication decision: 6-18 mos.
Time between decision and publication: 4-6 mos.
Number of reviewers: 2
Articles submitted per year: 70
Articles published per year: 15
Notes submitted per year: 10
Notes published per year: 2

(602)
*Cîteaux Commentarii Cistercienses

Jean-François Holthof, Editor
Abbaye de Cîteaux
21700 Saint-Nicolas-les-Cîteaux, France

Telephone: (33) 80611153
Fax: (33) 80623679
First published: 1950
Sponsoring organization: Cistercian Order
ISSN: 0009-7497
MLA acronym: CCCist

SUBSCRIPTION INFORMATION

Frequency of publication: 2 double issues/yr. (occasionally one 4-issue volume/yr.)
Circulation: 500
Available in microform: Yes, for 1950-1974.
Subscription address: Citeaux VZW, Abbaye Cistercienne, 2100 Brecht, Belgium
Additional subscription address: Abbey of the Genesee, Piffard, NY 14533

ADVERTISING INFORMATION

Advertising accepted: No

EDITORIAL DESCRIPTION

Scope: Publishes scholarly and general articles written by members of the Cistercian Order which, based on theological and spiritual doctrine and on monasticism from the 12th through the 20th centuries, deal with history, economics, law, and the arts. Also publishes bibliographies of recent research on the Cistercian Order as well as book reviews.
Reviews books: Yes

Publishes notes: Yes
Languages accepted: English; French; German; Dutch; Italian; Spanish; Portuguese
Prints abstracts: Yes
Author-anonymous submission: No

SUBMISSION REQUIREMENTS

Restrictions on contributors: Book reviews are solicited.
Author pays submission fee: No
Author pays page charges: No
Length of articles: 10,000-30,000 words
Length of book reviews: 500 words
Length of notes: 1,500-3,000 words
Number of copies required: 1; 2 preferred
Copyright ownership: Journal
Rejected manuscripts: Returned
Time before publication decision: 1-5 mos.
Time between decision and publication: 6-9 mos.
Number of reviewers: 6-7
Articles submitted per year: 20-25
Articles published per year: 10-15
Book reviews published per year: 40-60
Notes submitted per year: 10-15
Notes published per year: 5-10

(603)
Cithara: Essays in the Judaeo-Christian Tradition

John Mulryan, Editor
P.O. Box BC
St. Bonaventure Univ.
St. Bonaventure, NY 14778

First published: 1961
Sponsoring organization: St. Bonaventure Univ.
ISSN: 0009-7527
MLA acronym: Cithara

SUBSCRIPTION INFORMATION

Frequency of publication: 2 times/yr. (May, Nov.)
Circulation: 700

ADVERTISING INFORMATION

Advertising accepted: No

EDITORIAL DESCRIPTION

Scope: Publishes articles relating to the problems of the human race in the light of its heritage and future. Although investigations in the field of liberal arts will more frequently furnish materials suitable for publication, the approach to such "Essays in the Judeao-Christian tradition" should be interdepartmental and should state or imply a relationship to that religious and cultural inheritance.
Reviews books: Yes
Publishes notes: No
Languages accepted: English
Prints abstracts: No

SUBMISSION REQUIREMENTS

Author pays submission fee: No
Author pays page charges: No
Length of articles: 20-30 typescript pp.
Style: MLA
Number of copies required: 2
Special requirements: Submit original typescript.
Copyright ownership: St. Bonaventure Univ.
Rejected manuscripts: Returned
Time before publication decision: 3 mos.
Time between decision and publication: 3-6 mos.
Number of reviewers: 3
Articles published per year: 7-10

(604)
*Città di Vita: Bimestrale di Religione Arte e Scienza

Massimiliano Giuseppe Rosito, Editor
Piazza S. Croce, 16
50122 Florence, Italy

Telephone: (39) 55 242783
First published: 1946
Sponsoring organization: Provincia Toscana Frati Minori Conventuali
ISSN: 0009-7632
MLA acronym: CV

SUBSCRIPTION INFORMATION

Frequency of publication: 6 times/yr.
Circulation: 2,000
Available in microform: No
Subscription price: 50,000 Lit/yr.
Year to which price refers: 1992

ADVERTISING INFORMATION

Advertising accepted: Yes

EDITORIAL DESCRIPTION

Scope: Publishes articles on religion, art, science, and philosophy.
Reviews books: Yes
Publishes notes: Yes
Languages accepted: Italian
Prints abstracts: No
Author-anonymous submission: No

SUBMISSION REQUIREMENTS

Restrictions on contributors: None
Author pays submission fee: No
Author pays page charges: No
Length of articles: 2,400 words
Number of copies required: 1
Copyright ownership: Journal
Rejected manuscripts: Not returned
Time before publication decision: 4-6 mos.
Number of reviewers: 2-3
Articles submitted per year: 500
Articles published per year: 55
Book reviews submitted per year: 320
Book reviews published per year: 170

(605)
*La Ciudad de Dios: Revista Agustiniana

Saturnino Alvarez Turienzo, Teodoro Alonso Turienzo, & Gonzalo Díaz, Editors
Real Monasterio
28200 San Lorenzo del Escorial
Madrid, Spain

Telephone: (91) 1 8905011
Fax: (91) 1 8905421
First published: 1881
Sponsoring organization: Augustinian Fathers of the Real Monasterio de San Lorenzo de El Escorial
ISSN: 0009-7756
MLA acronym: CdD

SUBSCRIPTION INFORMATION

Frequency of publication: 3 times/yr.
Circulation: 700
Available in microform: No
Subscription price: $45.00/yr.
Year to which price refers: 1992
Subscription address: Ediciones Escurialenses, at the above address

ADVERTISING INFORMATION

Advertising accepted: No

EDITORIAL DESCRIPTION

Scope: Publishes articles on philosophy, theology, old library funds, Augustinism, and culture.
Reviews books: Yes
Publishes notes: Yes
Languages accepted: English; French; Italian; German
Prints abstracts: No
Author-anonymous submission: No

SUBMISSION REQUIREMENTS

Restrictions on contributors: None
Author pays submission fee: No
Author pays page charges: No
Length of articles: 25 pp. maximum
Length of book reviews: 20 lines
Style: None
Number of copies required: 1
Special requirements: Submit original typescript.
Copyright ownership: Assigned by author to journal
Rejected manuscripts: Returned
Time before publication decision: 1 mo.
Number of reviewers: Editorial Board
Articles submitted per year: 15-20
Articles published per year: 10-12
Book reviews published per year: 150-200
Notes submitted per year: 4-5
Notes published per year: 4-5

(606)
Cizí Jazyky ve Škole

Statni Pedagogicke Nakladatelstvi
Ostravni 30
113 01 Prague, Czech Republic

First published: 1957
Sponsoring organization: Ministerstvo Skolstvi Ceske Socialisticke Republiky; Ministerstvo Skolstva Slovenskej Socialistickej Republiky
ISSN: 0009-8205
MLA acronym: CJVŠ

SUBSCRIPTION INFORMATION

Frequency of publication: 10 times/yr.

EDITORIAL DESCRIPTION

Scope: Journal for the teaching of foreign languages, especially German, English, French, Spanish, and Latin.
Reviews books: Yes
Languages accepted: Czech; Slovak
Prints abstracts: No

(607)
The Claflin College Review

Paul R. Smith, Editor
Claflin College
Orangeburg, SC 29115

First published: 1976
Sponsoring organization: Claflin College
ISSN: 0191-216X
MLA acronym: CCR

SUBSCRIPTION INFORMATION

Frequency of publication: 2 times/yr. (Dec., May)
Circulation: 500

EDITORIAL DESCRIPTION

Scope: Articles are generally limited to materials in the arts and sciences, but poetry and art work is accepted. Art work is published in color when funds are available.
Reviews books: Yes

Languages accepted: English
Prints abstracts: No

SUBMISSION REQUIREMENTS

Restrictions on contributors: Preference is given to Claflin College faculty, but unsolicited manuscripts are published when space is available.
Length of articles: 25 double-spaced typescript pp. or longer
Style: MLA
Number of copies required: 2
Special requirements: Submit footnotes in separate section. Include a brief 100-word abstract.
Rejected manuscripts: Returned; enclose return postage.
Time before publication decision: 3 mos.
Time between decision and publication: 2 mos.
Number of reviewers: 2-3
Articles published per year: 10-12

(608)
*Classical and Modern Literature: A Quarterly

James O. Loyd & Virginia León de Vivero, Editors
P.O. Box 629
Terre Haute, IN 47808-0629

E-mail: FLLEON@ROOT.INDSTATE.EDU
First published: 1980
ISSN: 0197-2227
MLA acronym: CML

SUBSCRIPTION INFORMATION

Frequency of publication: 4 times/yr. (Oct., Jan., Apr., July)
Circulation: 500
Available in microform: No
Subscription price: $21.00/yr. institutions; $18.00/yr. individuals
Year to which price refers: 1992-93

ADVERTISING INFORMATION

Advertising accepted: Yes
Advertising rates: $40.00/half page; $75.00/full page

EDITORIAL DESCRIPTION

Scope: Focuses on the interrelationship of classical and modern literature.
Reviews books: Yes
Publishes notes: Yes
Languages accepted: English
Prints abstracts: No
Author-anonymous submission: Yes

SUBMISSION REQUIREMENTS

Restrictions on contributors: None
Author pays submission fee: No
Author pays page charges: No
Length of articles: 11,000 words
Length of book reviews: 1,500 words
Length of notes: 1,500 words
Style: Chicago
Number of copies required: 2
Copyright ownership: Journal
Rejected manuscripts: Returned; enclose SASE.
Time before publication decision: 3 mos.
Time between decision and publication: 6 mos.
Number of reviewers: 3
Articles submitted per year: 120
Articles published per year: 20
Book reviews published per year: 8

(609)
*The Classical Journal

John F. Miller, Editor
Dept. of Classics
Univ. of Virginia
146 New Cabell Hall
Charlottesville, VA 22903

Additional editorial address: For book reviews: Jenny S. Clay, at the above address
Telephone: 804 924-3008
Fax: 804 982-2002
E-mail: Jfm4j@virginia.edu
First published: 1905
Sponsoring organization: Classical Assn. of the Middle West & South, Inc.
ISSN: 0009-8353
MLA acronym: CJ

SUBSCRIPTION INFORMATION

Frequency of publication: 4 times/yr.
Circulation: 2,650
Available in microform: No
Subscription price: $30.00/yr.
Year to which price refers: 1992
Subscription address: John F. Hall, CAMWS Secretary-Treasurer, 118 KMB, Brigham Young Univ., Provo, UT 84602

ADVERTISING INFORMATION

Advertising accepted: Yes
Advertising rates: $150.00/full page

EDITORIAL DESCRIPTION

Scope: Publishes articles on Greek and Latin languages and literatures and Greek and Roman history and historiography.
Reviews books: Yes
Publishes notes: Yes
Languages accepted: English
Prints abstracts: No
Author-anonymous submission: Yes

SUBMISSION REQUIREMENTS

Restrictions on contributors: None
Author pays submission fee: No
Author pays page charges: No
Length of articles: No restrictions
Length of book reviews: No restrictions
Length of notes: No restrictions
Style: MLA; Chicago
Number of copies required: 2 without signature
Special requirements: Greek and Latin quotes are permitted.
Copyright ownership: Author
Rejected manuscripts: Returned; enclose return postage.
Time before publication decision: 3 mos.
Time between decision and publication: 3 mos.
Number of reviewers: 1-3
Articles submitted per year: 90-110
Articles published per year: 24
Book reviews published per year: 12-20
Notes published per year: 2-4

(610)
*The Classical Quarterly

P. C. Millett & A. S. Hollis, Editors
Downing College
Cambridge CB2 1DQ, England

Additional editorial address: A. S. Hollis, Keble College, Oxford OX1 3PG, England
Telephone: (44) 865 882283
Fax: (44) 865 882890
First published: 1906
Sponsoring organization: Classical Assn.
ISSN: 0009-8388
MLA acronym: ClassQ

SUBSCRIPTION INFORMATION

Frequency of publication: 2 times/yr.
Circulation: 1,600
Available in microform: Yes
Subscription price: £32.00/yr. United Kingdom & Europe; $62.00/yr. elsewhere
Year to which price refers: 1992
Subscription address: Oxford Univ. Press, Journals Subscriptions Dept., Pinkhill House, Southfield Rd., Eynsham, Oxford OX8 1JJ, England

ADVERTISING INFORMATION

Advertising accepted: Yes

EDITORIAL DESCRIPTION

Scope: Focuses on all fields of classical language, literature, history, and philosophy. Does not include articles on archaeology.
Reviews books: No
Publishes notes: Yes
Languages accepted: English
Prints abstracts: No
Author-anonymous submission: No

SUBMISSION REQUIREMENTS

Restrictions on contributors: None
Author pays submission fee: No
Author pays page charges: No
Length of articles: 20 pp. maximum
Length of notes: 600 words
Style: Style requirements given inside back cover.
Number of copies required: 1
Special requirements: Translations of submissions in languages other than English can be arranged. Articles should be typed double-spaced on size A4 (8 1/4 in. x 11 3/4 in.) paper. Footnotes should be numbered consecutively and typed on separate sheets. Greek quotations, if handwritten, should be clear and legible.
Copyright ownership: Oxford Univ. Press
Rejected manuscripts: Returned at author's request
Time before publication decision: 3 mos. maximum
Time between decision and publication: 1 yr. maximum
Number of reviewers: 2 editors; referees if necessary
Articles submitted per year: 150-200
Articles published per year: 40-50
Notes submitted per year: 50-60
Notes published per year: 12-25

(611)
*Classiques Français du Moyen Âge

H. Champion, Editor
7, quai Malaquais
75006 Paris, France

Telephone: (33) 1 46340729
Fax: (33) 1 46346406
First published: 1910
ISSN: 0755-1959
MLA acronym: CFMA

SUBSCRIPTION INFORMATION

Frequency of publication: Irregular
Available in microform: No

ADVERTISING INFORMATION

Advertising accepted: No

EDITORIAL DESCRIPTION

Scope: Publishes Medieval French texts.
Reviews books: Yes
Publishes notes: Yes
Languages accepted: French
Prints abstracts: No

SUBMISSION REQUIREMENTS

Author pays submission fee: No
Author pays page charges: No
Books submitted per year: 50
Books published per year: 20

(612)
*Claudel Studies

Moses M. Nagy, John S. Maddux, & Jean-Pierre Cap, Editors
Dept. of French
Univ. of Dallas
P.O. Box 464
Irving, TX 75062-4799

Telephone: 214 721-5229
First published: 1972
Sponsoring organization: Univ. of Dallas & Lafayette College
ISSN: 0090-1237
MLA acronym: ClaudelS

SUBSCRIPTION INFORMATION

Frequency of publication: 2 times/yr.
Circulation: 500
Available in microform: No
Subscription price: $20.00/yr. institutions; $15.00/yr. individuals US; $20.00/yr. individuals elsewhere
Year to which price refers: 1992

ADVERTISING INFORMATION

Advertising accepted: No

EDITORIAL DESCRIPTION

Scope: Accepts articles, monographs, notes, and reviews relating directly or indirectly to Paul Claudel.
Reviews books: Yes
Publishes notes: No
Languages accepted: English; French
Prints abstracts: No
Author-anonymous submission: No

SUBMISSION REQUIREMENTS

Restrictions on contributors: None
Author pays submission fee: No
Author pays page charges: No
Length of articles: 15-18 double-spaced typescript pp.
Length of book reviews: 600 words
Style: MLA
Number of copies required: 2
Copyright ownership: Editorial Board
Rejected manuscripts: Returned at author's request
Time before publication decision: 2 mos.
Time between decision and publication: 6-12 mos.
Number of reviewers: 3-4
Articles submitted per year: 25
Articles published per year: 16
Book reviews submitted per year: 10
Book reviews published per year: 10

(613)
*CLIO: A Journal of Literature, History, and the Philosophy of History

Henry Kozicki, Clark Butler, & Andrew McLean, Editors
Indiana Univ.-Purdue Univ.
Fort Wayne, IN 46805

Telephone: 219 481-6753
Fax: 219 481-6985
E-mail: CLIO@CVAX.IPFW.INDIANA.EDU
First published: 1971
Sponsoring organization: Indiana Univ.-Purdue Univ. at Fort Wayne
ISSN: 0884-2043
MLA acronym: ClioI

SUBSCRIPTION INFORMATION

Frequency of publication: 4 times/yr.
Circulation: 600
Available in microform: Yes
Subscription price: $40.00/yr. institutions; $15.00/yr. individuals; add $4.00/yr. postage outside US
Year to which price refers: 1991-92

ADVERTISING INFORMATION

Advertising accepted: Yes

EDITORIAL DESCRIPTION

Scope: Publishes critiques of literature in which history or the philosophy of history functions as an ordering principle; literary analyses of historical writing; and historiography that deals with the nature of historical and thus literary knowledge and narrative. Also interested in speculative philosophy of history and in particular with the thought of Hegel, from various perspectives, and its interdisciplinary application.
Reviews books: Yes
Publishes notes: No
Languages accepted: English
Prints abstracts: No
Author-anonymous submission: No

SUBMISSION REQUIREMENTS

Restrictions on contributors: Most reviews are assigned, but inquiries are welcome.
Author pays submission fee: No
Author pays page charges: No
Length of articles: 5,000-8,000 words
Length of book reviews: 1,000-1,500 words
Style: Chicago
Number of copies required: 2
Copyright ownership: Author
Rejected manuscripts: Returned; enclose SAE and return postage.
Time before publication decision: 3 mos.
Time between decision and publication: 1 yr.
Number of reviewers: 2-4
Articles published per year: 20
Book reviews published per year: 40

(614)
*Clues: A Journal of Detection

Pat Browne, Editor
Popular Press
Bowling Green State Univ.
Bowling Green, OH 43403

Telephone: 419 372-7867
Fax: 419 372-8095
First published: 1980
ISSN: 0742-4248
MLA acronym: Clues

SUBSCRIPTION INFORMATION

Frequency of publication: 2 times/yr.
Circulation: 1,000
Available in microform: No
Subscription price: $12.50/yr.
Year to which price refers: 1991

ADVERTISING INFORMATION

Advertising accepted: Yes
Advertising rates: $100.00/full page

EDITORIAL DESCRIPTION

Scope: Journal is dedicated to detection in the widest sense of the word and as evidenced in all the media and in all aspects of culture.
Reviews books: Yes

Publishes notes: Yes
Languages accepted: English
Prints abstracts: No
Author-anonymous submission: Yes

SUBMISSION REQUIREMENTS

Restrictions on contributors: None
Author pays submission fee: No
Author pays page charges: No
Length of articles: 12-15 pp.
Length of book reviews: 300-400 words
Length of notes: 800-1,000 words
Style: MLA
Number of copies required: 2
Copyright ownership: Journal
Rejected manuscripts: Returned; enclose SASE.
Time before publication decision: 2-3 mos.
Time between decision and publication: 3-6 mos.
Number of reviewers: 3
Articles submitted per year: 30-40
Articles published per year: 20
Book reviews submitted per year: 150-200
Book reviews published per year: 150-200
Notes submitted per year: 1-2
Notes published per year: 1-2

(615)
*Co-textes

Edmond Cros, Editor
Centre d'Etudes et Recherches Sociocritiques (U.E.R. II)
Univ. Paul-Valéry
B.P. 5043
34032 Montpellier Cedex, France

Telephone: (33) 67142172
Fax: (33) 67041823
First published: 1980
Sponsoring organization: Centre d'Etudes & Recherches Semiotiques
ISSN: 0249-6356
MLA acronym: Co-textes

SUBSCRIPTION INFORMATION

Frequency of publication: 2 times/yr.
Circulation: 300
Available in microform: No

ADVERTISING INFORMATION

Advertising accepted: No

EDITORIAL DESCRIPTION

Scope: Publishes articles on Latin American literature and literary criticism.
Reviews books: No
Publishes notes: No
Languages accepted: French; Spanish; English
Prints abstracts: No

SUBMISSION REQUIREMENTS

Restrictions on contributors: None
Author pays submission fee: No
Author pays page charges: No
Length of articles: 25 pp.
Style: MLA
Number of copies required: 2
Special requirements: Submit abstract and personal introduction.
Copyright ownership: Journal
Rejected manuscripts: Not returned
Time before publication decision: 3 mos.
Time between decision and publication: 2 mos.
Number of reviewers: 3
Articles submitted per year: 30
Articles published per year: 19

(616)
*The Coat of Arms: An Heraldic Quarterly Magazine

John P. Brooke-Little, Editor
Heyford House
Lower Heyford
Bicester
Oxon OX6 3NZ, England

Telephone: (44) 869 40337
First published: 1950
Sponsoring organization: Heraldry Soc.
ISSN: 0010-003X
MLA acronym: CoA

SUBSCRIPTION INFORMATION

Frequency of publication: 4 times/yr.
Circulation: 1,200
Available in microform: No
Subscription price: £8.00/yr.
Year to which price refers: 1992
Subscription address: Secretary, Heraldry Soc., 44/45 Museum St., London WC1A 1LY, England
Subscription telephone: (44) 71 4302172

ADVERTISING INFORMATION

Advertising accepted: Yes
Advertising rates: £20.00/eighth page; £30.00/quarter page; £60.00/half page; £95.00/full page

EDITORIAL DESCRIPTION

Scope: Publishes scholarly and popular articles on heraldry, chivalry, ceremony, precedence, genealogy, etc.
Reviews books: Yes
Publishes notes: Yes
Languages accepted: English
Prints abstracts: No
Author-anonymous submission: No

SUBMISSION REQUIREMENTS

Restrictions on contributors: None
Author pays submission fee: No
Author pays page charges: No
Length of articles: 500-2,500 words
Length of book reviews: 250 words
Length of notes: 150 words
Number of copies required: 1
Special requirements: Submit double-spaced typescript.
Copyright ownership: Author
Rejected manuscripts: Returned
Time before publication decision: 1 mo.
Time between decision and publication: 18 mos. maximum

(617)
*Cognition: International Journal of Cognitive Science

Jacques Mehler, Editor
Laboratoire de Sciences Cognitives & Psycholinguistique
54, boulevard Raspail
75006 Paris, France

Telephone: (33) 1 49542262
Fax: (33) 1 45449835
First published: 1971
ISSN: 0010-0277
MLA acronym: Cognition

SUBSCRIPTION INFORMATION

Frequency of publication: 12 times/yr.
Circulation: 2,000
Available in microform: No
Subscription address: Elsevier Science Publishers, Box 211, 1000 AE Amsterdam, Netherlands

ADVERTISING INFORMATION

Advertising accepted: Occasionally

EDITORIAL DESCRIPTION

Scope: Publishes theoretical and experimental papers on the study of the mind; notes and discussions on current trends in scientific, social or ethical matters; welcomes book reviews of recently published books or of books that should again be brought to the attention of readers.
Reviews books: Yes
Publishes notes: Yes
Languages accepted: English
Prints abstracts: Yes
Author-anonymous submission: No

SUBMISSION REQUIREMENTS

Restrictions on contributors: Articles in French and German also considered but authors are responsible for translation into English after acceptance.
Author pays submission fee: No
Author pays page charges: No
Length of articles: 1,000 words
Style: American Psychological Assn.
Number of copies required: 4
Special requirements: Include an abstract in English.
Copyright ownership: Elsevier Sequoia S. A.
Rejected manuscripts: Returned at author's request
Time before publication decision: 3 mos.
Time between decision and publication: 4 mos.
Number of reviewers: 2
Articles submitted per year: 120-150
Articles published per year: 25-30
Notes submitted per year: 5

(618)
*Cognitive Linguistics

Dirk Geeraerts, Editor
Dept. of Linguistics
Univ. of Leuven
Blijde-Inkomststraat 21
3000 Leuven, Belgium

Additional editorial address: Richard Rhodes, Review Editor, Dept. of Linguistics, Univ. of California, Berkeley, CA 94720
First published: 1990
ISSN: 0936-5907
MLA acronym: CogLi

SUBSCRIPTION INFORMATION

Frequency of publication: 4 times/yr. (Mar., June, Sept., Dec.)
Available in microform: No
Subscription price: $85.00/yr. N. America; 154 DM/yr. elsewhere
Year to which price refers: 1992
Subscription address: Walter de Gruyter, Inc., 200 Saw Mill River Rd., Hawthorne, NY 10532
Additional subscription address: Outside N. America: Walter de Gruyter & Co., Postfach 110240, 1000 Berlin 11, Germany

ADVERTISING INFORMATION

Advertising accepted: Yes
Advertising rates: 320 DM/half page; 600 DM/full page

EDITORIAL DESCRIPTION

Scope: Publishes articles on linguistic research on the interaction between language and cognition. Focuses on language as an instrument for organizing, processing and conveying information.
Reviews books: Yes
Publishes notes: Yes
Languages accepted: English

Prints abstracts: Yes
Author-anonymous submission: No

SUBMISSION REQUIREMENTS

Author pays submission fee: No
Author pays page charges: No
Length of articles: 25,000 words maximum
Length of book reviews: 3,000 words maximum
Length of notes: 2,000 words maximum
Number of copies required: 3
Special requirements: Submit double-spaced typescript on size A4 (8 1/4 in. x 11 3/4 in.) paper, accompanied by an abstract of 200 words maximum.
Copyright ownership: Walter de Gruyter & Co.
Rejected manuscripts: Not returned
Time before publication decision: 3-4 mos.
Time between decision and publication: 9 mos.
Number of reviewers: 2
Articles submitted per year: 30-40
Articles published per year: 15-20
Book reviews published per year: 10-15
Notes submitted per year: 10
Notes published per year: 5

(619)
*Cognitive Neuropsychology

Max Coltheart, Editor
Lawrence Erlbaum Assoc., Ltd.
27 Palmeira Mansions
Church Rd.
Hove
East Sussex BN3 2FA, England

Telephone: (61) 2 8058086
Fax: (61) 2 8058062
E-mail: MAX@CURRAWONG.MQCC.MQ.-OZ.AU
First published: 1984
ISSN: 0264-3294
MLA acronym: CogN

SUBSCRIPTION INFORMATION

Frequency of publication: 6 times/yr.
Circulation: 500
Available in microform: No
Subscription price: $180.00/yr. institutions; $76.00/yr. individuals
Year to which price refers: 1991
Additional subscription address: Journal Subscription Dept., Lawrence Erlbaum Assoc., Inc., 365 Broadway, Hillsdale, NJ 07642

ADVERTISING INFORMATION

Advertising accepted: Yes
Advertising rates: Request from Lawrence Erlbaum Assoc.

EDITORIAL DESCRIPTION

Scope: Publishes articles which promote the study of cognitive processes from a neuropsychological perspective. It includes work on perception, attention, object recognition, planning, language, thinking, memory, and action.
Reviews books: Yes
Languages accepted: English
Prints abstracts: Yes
Author-anonymous submission: Yes, at author's request.

SUBMISSION REQUIREMENTS

Restrictions on contributors: None
Author pays submission fee: No
Author pays page charges: No
Length of articles: No restrictions
Length of book reviews: No restrictions
Style: American Psychological Assn.
Number of copies required: 4
Copyright ownership: Lawrence Erlbaum Assoc.
Rejected manuscripts: Returned
Time before publication decision: 4-5 mos.

Time between decision and publication: 2-3 mos.
Number of reviewers: 2-3
Articles submitted per year: 50
Articles published per year: 30
Book reviews submitted per year: 4
Book reviews published per year: 4

(620)
*Cognitive Psychology

Douglas L. Medin, Editor
Dept. of Psychology
Univ. of Michigan
330 Packard Rd.
Ann Arbor, MI 48104

Fax: 313 764-3520
E-mail: Cog.psych@um.cc.umich.edu (internet)
First published: 1970
ISSN: 0010-0285
MLA acronym: CPsy

SUBSCRIPTION INFORMATION

Frequency of publication: 4 times/yr.
Subscription address: Academic Press, Inc., 1250 Sixth Ave., San Diego, CA 92101

ADVERTISING INFORMATION

Advertising accepted: Yes

EDITORIAL DESCRIPTION

Scope: Publishes original empirical, theoretical, and tutorial papers, methodological articles, and critical reviews dealing with memory, language processing, perception, problem solving, and thinking. Emphasizes work on the organization of human information processing.
Reviews books: No
Publishes notes: No
Languages accepted: English
Prints abstracts: Yes
Author-anonymous submission: Yes, at author's request

SUBMISSION REQUIREMENTS

Author pays submission fee: No
Style: American Psychological Assn.
Number of copies required: 4
Special requirements: Consult journal before submitting.
Copyright ownership: Academic Press
Rejected manuscripts: Returned
Time before publication decision: 3 mos.
Time between decision and publication: 3 mos.
Number of reviewers: 2-3
Articles submitted per year: 100
Articles published per year: 19

(621)
*Cognitive Science: A Multidisciplinary Journal of Artificial Intelligence, Linguistics, Neuroscience, Philosophy, Psychology

Martin Ringle, Keith J. Holyoak, William J. Clancey, & Jeffrey Elman, Editors
Computing & Information Systems
Reed College
Portland, OR 97202

Telephone: 503 777-7254
Fax: 503 777-7778
E-mail: Ringle@reed.edu
First published: 1977
Sponsoring organization: Cognitive Science Soc.
ISSN: 0364-0213
MLA acronym: CSci

SUBSCRIPTION INFORMATION

Frequency of publication: 4 times/yr.
Circulation: 2,500
Available in microform: No
Subscription price: $95.00/yr. institutions; $40.00/yr. individuals
Year to which price refers: 1991
Subscription address: Ablex Publishing Corp., 355 Chestnut St., Norwood, NJ 07648

ADVERTISING INFORMATION

Advertising accepted: Yes

EDITORIAL DESCRIPTION

Scope: Covers knowledge representation and cognitive processes, experimental studies, intelligent programs that exhibit some human ability, and design proposals for cognitive models.
Reviews books: No
Publishes notes: Yes
Languages accepted: English
Prints abstracts: Yes
Author-anonymous submission: Yes

SUBMISSION REQUIREMENTS

Restrictions on contributors: None
Author pays submission fee: No
Author pays page charges: No
Length of articles: 35-50 pp.
Length of notes: No restrictions
Style: American Psychological Assn.
Number of copies required: 5
Special requirements: Submit double-spaced typescript on 8 1/2 in. x 11 in. bond. Include typed endnotes and a 100-150 word abstract. See journal for more information.
Copyright ownership: Ablex Publishing Corp.
Rejected manuscripts: Returned at author's request
Time before publication decision: 3 mos.
Time between decision and publication: 6 mos.
Number of reviewers: 2-3
Articles submitted per year: 100
Articles published per year: 16-20

(622)
*Colby Quarterly

Douglas Archibald, Editor
Colby College
Waterville, ME 04901

Telephone: 207 872-3622
Fax: 207 872-3555
First published: 1943
Sponsoring organization: Colby College
ISSN: 0010-0552
MLA acronym: ClQ

SUBSCRIPTION INFORMATION

Frequency of publication: 4 times/yr. (Mar., June, Sept., Dec.)
Circulation: 750
Subscription price: $10.00/yr.
Year to which price refers: 1992
Subscription address: Patience-Anne Lenk, Special Collections, at the above address
Subscription telephone: 207 872-3284

ADVERTISING INFORMATION

Advertising accepted: No

EDITORIAL DESCRIPTION

Scope: A journal of analysis and commentary upon subjects in the humanities, with an emphasis on literature written in English. Takes an interest in regional studies including the history and literature of Maine, New England, and Canada. Also takes a special interest in authors well represented in Colby's special collections (e.g., Thomas Hardy, Henry James, W. B. Yeats, Lady Gregory, James Joyce, Brian Friel, Seamus Heaney, and other Irish writers from 1880 to the present). Concerns include Irish and American studies, the relationship of art and literature, and the relationships of psychology, history, and literature.
Reviews books: No
Publishes notes: No
Languages accepted: English
Prints abstracts: No
Author-anonymous submission: No

SUBMISSION REQUIREMENTS

Restrictions on contributors: None
Author pays submission fee: No
Author pays page charges: No
Length of articles: 2,000-7,000 words
Style: MLA
Number of copies required: 1
Copyright ownership: Author
Rejected manuscripts: Returned; enclose SAE and return postage.
Time before publication decision: 3-6 mos.
Time between decision and publication: 15 mos.
Number of reviewers: 2
Articles submitted per year: 200
Articles published per year: 20

(623)
*Collection Astraea

François G. Laroque, Editor
Centre d'Etudes & de Recherches Elisabéthaines
Univ. Paul Valéry
Route de Mende
B.P. 5043
34032 Montpellier Cedex, France

Telephone: (33) 67142200
Fax: (33) 67142200
First published: 1986
Sponsoring organization: Conseil Scientifique de l'Univ. Paul Valéry & Centre National de la Recherche Scientifique
ISSN: 0299-2388
MLA acronym: Astraea

SUBSCRIPTION INFORMATION

Frequency of publication: Irregular
Circulation: 150
Available in microform: No
Subscription price: 180 F/yr.
Year to which price refers: 1992

ADVERTISING INFORMATION

Advertising accepted: Yes, on an exchange basis

EDITORIAL DESCRIPTION

Scope: Publishes collections of papers focusing on a single theme. The general aim is to be a link between English-speaking and French-speaking scholars of the 15th through the 17th century.
Reviews books: No
Publishes notes: No
Languages accepted: English; French
Prints abstracts: No
Author-anonymous submission: No

SUBMISSION REQUIREMENTS

Author pays submission fee: No
Author pays page charges: No
Length of books: 150-250 pp.

Style: MLA
Number of copies required: 2
Special requirements: Submit camera-ready typescript or Macintosh diskette.
Copyright ownership: Series
Rejected manuscripts: Returned at author's request
Time before publication decision: 3-4 mos.
Time between decision and publication: 6-8 mos.
Number of reviewers: 2
Books submitted per year: 4
Books published per year: 1

(624)
*Collection Monographique Rodopi en Littérature Française Contemporaine

Michaël Bishop, Editor
Editions Rodopi B.V.
Keizersgracht 302-304
1016 EX Amsterdam, Netherlands

Additional editorial address: In N. America: Editions Rodopi, 233 Peachtree St. NE, Suite 404, Atlanta, GA 30303-1504
First published: 1984
ISSN: 0169-0078
MLA acronym: CMRLFC

SUBSCRIPTION INFORMATION

Frequency of publication: Irregular
Circulation: 1,000
Subscription telephone: (31) 20 6227507; 404 523-1964; 800 225-3998
Subscription fax: (31) 20 6380948; 404 522-7116

ADVERTISING INFORMATION

Advertising accepted: No

EDITORIAL DESCRIPTION

Scope: Publishes critical studies on modern French writers and their work.
Reviews books: No
Publishes notes: No
Languages accepted: French; English
Author-anonymous submission: No

SUBMISSION REQUIREMENTS

Author pays submission fee: No
Author pays page charges: No
Length of books: 80-120 pp.
Style: MLA
Number of copies required: 1
Copyright ownership: Editions Rodopi B.V.
Time before publication decision: 1 yr.
Books submitted per year: 3-4
Books published per year: 3-4

(625)
*Collections

Office of the Director
Univ. of Delaware Library
Newark, DE 19717-5267

Telephone: 302 831-2231
Fax: 302 831-1046
First published: 1984
Sponsoring organization: Univ. of Delaware Library Associates
ISSN: 8755-3473
MLA acronym: Collections

SUBSCRIPTION INFORMATION

Frequency of publication: Irregular
Circulation: 350
Available in microform: No

Subscription address: Univ. of Delaware Library Associates, Univ. of Delaware Library, Newark, DE 19717-5267

ADVERTISING INFORMATION

Advertising accepted: No

EDITORIAL DESCRIPTION

Scope: Publishes articles, principally in the fields of literature and history, about or based on the manuscript, rare book, or other collections of the University of Delaware Library.
Reviews books: No
Publishes notes: No
Languages accepted: English
Prints abstracts: No
Author-anonymous submission: No

SUBMISSION REQUIREMENTS

Restrictions on contributors: Contributors must have worked on or used manuscript, rare book, or other collections of the University of Delaware Library.
Author pays submission fee: No
Author pays page charges: No
Length of articles: 1,500-7,700 words
Style: Chicago
Number of copies required: 2
Special requirements: Articles including illustrations are encouraged.
Copyright ownership: Univ. of Delaware Library Associates
Rejected manuscripts: Returned
Time before publication decision: 6 mos.
Time between decision and publication: 12-15 mos.
Number of reviewers: 3
Articles submitted per year: 8
Articles published per year: 3

(626)
*College Composition and Communication

Richard C. Gebhardt, Editor
English Dept.
Bowling Green State Univ.
Bowling Green, OH 43403

First published: 1950
Sponsoring organization: National Council of Teachers of English, Conference on College Composition & Communication
ISSN: 0010-096X
MLA acronym: CCC

SUBSCRIPTION INFORMATION

Frequency of publication: 4 times/yr. (Feb., May, Oct., Dec.)
Circulation: 12,000
Available in microform: Yes, for issues before 1981.
Subscription price: $12.00/yr.
Year to which price refers: 1992
Subscription address: National Council of Teachers of English, 1111 Kenyon Rd., Urbana, IL 61801

ADVERTISING INFORMATION

Advertising accepted: Yes

EDITORIAL DESCRIPTION

Scope: Publishes scholarly articles, of interest to rhetoricians, linguists, and literary scholars; specialists in historical rhetoric, empirical research, and literacy; scholars studying composition and its connections to social and literary theory; and teachers and administrators seeking sound theory upon which to base composition instruction. Includes essays of speculation, application, or advocacy; and descriptions of specific instructional or administrative practice growing from recent theory or research.
Reviews books: Yes
Publishes notes: No
Languages accepted: English
Prints abstracts: No
Author-anonymous submission: Yes

SUBMISSION REQUIREMENTS

Restrictions on contributors: Unsolicited book reviews are not accepted.
Author pays submission fee: No
Author pays page charges: No
Length of articles: 4,000-7,000 words, but shorter articles are also accepted
Style: MLA
Number of copies required: 4
Special requirements: See Feb. issue for guide.
Copyright ownership: National Council of Teachers of English
Rejected manuscripts: Returned; enclose return postage.
Time before publication decision: 6-8 weeks
Time between decision and publication: 6-9 mos.
Number of reviewers: 2-4
Articles submitted per year: 300
Articles published per year: 45-50
Book reviews submitted per year: 40
Book reviews published per year: 40

(627)
College English

James C. Raymond, Editor
Drawer AL
Univ. of Alabama
Tuscaloosa, AL 35487

First published: 1939
Sponsoring organization: National Council of Teachers of English
ISSN: 0010-0994
MLA acronym: CE

SUBSCRIPTION INFORMATION

Frequency of publication: 8 times/yr. (monthly Sept.-Apr.)
Circulation: 16,000
Available in microform: No
Subscription address: National Council of Teachers of English, 1111 Kenyon Rd., Urbana, IL 61801

ADVERTISING INFORMATION

Advertising accepted: Yes

EDITORIAL DESCRIPTION

Scope: Provides a forum in which scholars working within any of the various sub-specialties of the discipline can address a broad cross-section of the profession. Appropriate subjects are literature (including nonfiction), linguistics, critical theory, reading theory, rhetoric, composition, pedagogy, and professional issues.
Reviews books: Yes
Publishes notes: No
Languages accepted: English
Prints abstracts: No
Author-anonymous submission: Yes

SUBMISSION REQUIREMENTS

Restrictions on contributors: Unsolicited book reviews are not accepted.
Author pays submission fee: No
Author pays page charges: No
Length of articles: 30 pp. maximum for articles, 5 pp. maximum for comments
Length of book reviews: 10 pp. maximum
Style: MLA
Number of copies required: 2
Copyright ownership: National Council of Teachers of English
Rejected manuscripts: Returned; enclose return postage.
Time before publication decision: 3 mos.
Time between decision and publication: 3-6 mos.
Number of reviewers: 2-3
Articles submitted per year: 500-600
Articles published per year: 60-70
Book reviews published per year: 8-12

(628)
*College Language Association Journal

Cason L. Hill, Editor
Morehouse College
Atlanta, GA 30314

Telephone: 404 681-2800 ext. 2164 or 2160
First published: 1957
Sponsoring organization: College Language Assn.
ISSN: 0007-8549
MLA acronym: CLAJ

SUBSCRIPTION INFORMATION

Frequency of publication: 4 times/yr. (Mar., June, Sept., Dec.)
Circulation: 1,400
Available in microform: No
Subscription price: $35.00/yr. US; $36.50/yr. Canada; $40.50/yr. elsewhere
Year to which price refers: 1991-92

ADVERTISING INFORMATION

Advertising accepted: Yes
Advertising rates: $225.00/half page; $300.00/full page

EDITORIAL DESCRIPTION

Scope: Publishes articles on language and literature.
Reviews books: Yes
Publishes notes: No
Languages accepted: English; French; Spanish; German
Prints abstracts: No
Author-anonymous submission: No

SUBMISSION REQUIREMENTS

Restrictions on contributors: Contributors must be members of CLA or subscribe to the journal.
Author pays submission fee: No
Author pays page charges: No
Length of articles: 10-20 pp.
Length of book reviews: 2-6 pp.
Style: MLA
Number of copies required: 2
Copyright ownership: Journal
Rejected manuscripts: Returned; enclose return postage.
Time before publication decision: 3-6 mos.
Time between decision and publication: 3-12 mos.
Number of reviewers: 2 minimum
Articles submitted per year: 50
Articles published per year: 48
Book reviews submitted per year: 10
Book reviews published per year: 10

(629)
*College Literature

Kostas Myrsiades, Editor
544 New Main
West Chester Univ.
West Chester, PA 19383

Telephone: 215 436-2901
Fax: 215 436-3150
First published: 1974
Sponsoring organization: West Chester Univ.
ISSN: 0093-3139
MLA acronym: CollL

SUBSCRIPTION INFORMATION

Frequency of publication: 3 times/yr. (Feb., June, Oct.)
Circulation: 800
Available in microform: Yes
Subscription price: $48.00/yr. institutions US; $53.00/yr. institutions elsewhere; $24.00/yr. individuals US; $29.00/yr. individuals elsewhere
Year to which price refers: 1992

ADVERTISING INFORMATION

Advertising accepted: Yes
Advertising rates: $150.00/half page; $200.00/full page

EDITORIAL DESCRIPTION

Scope: Publishes articles and notes on theory, textual interpretation and pedagogy, dedicated to providing college/university teachers with access to innovative ways of studying and teaching new bodies of literature and experiencing old literature in new ways. Encourages a variety of approaches to textual analysis and criticism (including political, feminist, and poststructuralist) on English and American literature in addition to Eastern literatures, minority and Third World literatures, oral literature, and interdisciplinary/comparative studies.
Reviews books: Yes
Publishes notes: Yes
Languages accepted: English
Prints abstracts: No
Author-anonymous submission: Yes

SUBMISSION REQUIREMENTS

Restrictions on contributors: None
Author pays submission fee: No
Author pays page charges: No
Length of articles: 5,000-7,500 words
Length of book reviews: 1,000-2,000 words
Length of notes: 1,250-3,750 words
Style: MLA
Number of copies required: 3
Special requirements: Submission on diskette in Nota Bene or any other IBM compatible ASCII format is preferred.
Copyright ownership: Assigned by author to journal
Rejected manuscripts: Returned; enclose return postage.
Time before publication decision: 3-4 mos.
Time between decision and publication: 3-12 mos.
Number of reviewers: 5
Articles submitted per year: 245
Articles published per year: 21
Book reviews submitted per year: 50
Book reviews published per year: 25-30
Notes submitted per year: 45
Notes published per year: 12-15

(630)
*Colloquia Germanica, Internationale Zeitschrift für Germanische Sprach- und Literaturwissenschaft

Bernd Kratz, Editor
Univ. of Kentucky
1055 P.O.T.
Lexington, KY 40506-0027

Telephone: 606 257-7011
Fax: 606 258-1073
E-mail: BKratz@ucc.uky.edu
First published: 1967
Sponsoring organization: Univ. of Kentucky
ISSN: 0010-1338
MLA acronym: CollG

SUBSCRIPTION INFORMATION

Frequency of publication: 4 times/yr.
Circulation: 500
Available in microform: No
Subscription price: 138 DM/yr. institutions; 96 DM/yr. individuals
Year to which price refers: 1992
Subscription address: Francke Publishers, Journals Division, P.O. Box 2560, 7400 Tübingen 5, Germany
Subscription telephone: (49) 7071 7809192
Subscription fax: (49) 7071 75288

ADVERTISING INFORMATION

Advertising accepted: Yes

EDITORIAL DESCRIPTION

Scope: Publishes articles on German language and literature with the emphasis on German literature.
Reviews books: Yes
Publishes notes: Occasionally
Languages accepted: English; German; French
Prints abstracts: No
Author-anonymous submission: No

SUBMISSION REQUIREMENTS

Restrictions on contributors: None
Author pays submission fee: No
Author pays page charges: No
Length of articles: 25 typescript pp.
Length of book reviews: 3-4 typescript pp.
Length of notes: 10 typescript pp.; notes are not regularly published.
Style: MLA with modifications
Number of copies required: 1
Copyright ownership: Francke Verlag for 1 yr. and then reverts to author
Rejected manuscripts: Returned
Time before publication decision: 2-3 mos.
Time between decision and publication: 12-15 mos.
Number of reviewers: 2
Articles submitted per year: 50
Articles published per year: 20
Book reviews submitted per year: 100
Book reviews published per year: 100

(631)
*Colloquium Helveticum: Cahiers Suisses de Littérature Comparée/ Schweizer Hefte für Allgemeine und Vergleichende Litteraturwissenschaft/ Quaderni Svizzeri di Letteratura Generale e Comparata

Yves Giraud, President
c/o Séminaire de Littérature Française
Univ. de Fribourg
1700 Fribourg, Switzerland

Additional editorial address: Michèle Stäuble, Devin 65 bis, 1012 Lausanne, Switzerland
First published: 1985
Sponsoring organization: Assn. Suisse de Littérature Générale & Comparée; Assn. Suisse des Sciences Humaines
MLA acronym: CHelv

SUBSCRIPTION INFORMATION

Frequency of publication: 2 times/yr.
Circulation: 400
Available in microform: No
Subscription price: 30 SwF/yr.
Year to which price refers: 1991
Subscription address: Verlag Peter Lang, Jupiterstr. 15, 3000 Bern 15, Switzerland

ADVERTISING INFORMATION

Advertising accepted: No

EDITORIAL DESCRIPTION

Scope: Publishes articles on general literary theory, comparative literature with practical examples, and problems of translation.
Reviews books: Yes
Languages accepted: French; German; Italian; English
Prints abstracts: Yes
Author-anonymous submission: No

SUBMISSION REQUIREMENTS

Restrictions on contributors: None
Author pays submission fee: No
Author pays page charges: No
Length of articles: 10 pp.
Length of book reviews: 500 words
Number of copies required: 1
Copyright ownership: Journal
Rejected manuscripts: Returned
Time before publication decision: 3 mos.
Time between decision and publication: 3 mos.
Number of reviewers: 6
Articles submitted per year: 10-12
Articles published per year: 6
Book reviews submitted per year: 25
Book reviews published per year: 10

(632)
*Colóquio/Letras

David Mourão-Ferreira, Editor
Fundação Calouste Gulbenkian
1093 Lisbon Codex, Portugal

Telephone: (351) 1 7935131
Fax: (351) 1 7935139
First published: 1971
Sponsoring organization: Fundação Calouste Gulbenkian
ISSN: 0010-1451
MLA acronym: Colóquio

SUBSCRIPTION INFORMATION

Frequency of publication: 6 times/yr.
Available in microform: No
Subscription address: NOBAR-Grupo Editorial, Lda., Rua da Cruz da Carreira, 4-B, 1100 Lisbon, Portugal
Subscription telephone: (351) 1 570051

ADVERTISING INFORMATION

Advertising accepted: No

EDITORIAL DESCRIPTION

Scope: Publishes literary essays on Portuguese language, theory of literature, and general literature.
Reviews books: Yes
Publishes notes: Yes
Languages accepted: Portuguese; Spanish; French
Prints abstracts: No
Author-anonymous submission: No

SUBMISSION REQUIREMENTS

Restrictions on contributors: None
Author pays submission fee: No
Author pays page charges: No
Length of articles: 3,000-4,000 words
Length of book reviews: 400-800 words
Length of notes: 600-1,000 words
Number of copies required: 1
Special requirements: Submit original typescript.
Copyright ownership: Author
Rejected manuscripts: Not returned
Time before publication decision: 2-3 weeks
Time between decision and publication: 1 yr.
Number of reviewers: 1
Articles submitted per year: 36
Articles published per year: 30
Book reviews submitted per year: 120
Book reviews published per year: 120
Notes submitted per year: 30
Notes published per year: 24

(633)
*Columbia Library Columns

Kenneth A. Lohf & Rudolph Ellenbogen, Editors
Butler Library, Sixth Floor
Columbia Univ.
New York, NY 10027

Telephone: 212 854-2231
First published: 1951
Sponsoring organization: Columbia Univ., Friends of Columbia Libraries
ISSN: 0010-1966
MLA acronym: CLC

SUBSCRIPTION INFORMATION

Frequency of publication: 3 times/yr.
Circulation: 1,000
Available in microform: No
Subscription price: $12.00/yr. US; $15.00/yr. elsewhere
Year to which price refers: 1992

ADVERTISING INFORMATION

Advertising accepted: No

EDITORIAL DESCRIPTION

Scope: Publishes articles mainly in the fields of literature and history, primarily relating to collections of books and manuscripts in the Columbia University Libraries.
Reviews books: No
Publishes notes: No
Languages accepted: English
Prints abstracts: No
Author-anonymous submission: No

SUBMISSION REQUIREMENTS

Author pays submission fee: No
Author pays page charges: No
Length of articles: 2,400 words
Number of copies required: 1
Copyright ownership: Journal
Rejected manuscripts: Returned
Time before publication decision: 2 mos.
Time between decision and publication: 6-8 mos.
Articles published per year: 9-12

(634)
*Columbia University Working Papers in Linguistics

William Diver, Editor
Box 708, Casa Italiana
Columbia Univ.
New York, NY 10027

Telephone: 212 865-7341

E-mail: WD6@CUNIXF.CC.COLUMBIA.EDU
First published: 1975
Sponsoring organization: Dept. of Linguistics, Columbia Univ.
ISSN: 0886-3229
MLA acronym: CUWPL

SUBSCRIPTION INFORMATION

Frequency of publication: Irregular
Circulation: 700
Available in microform: No

ADVERTISING INFORMATION

Advertising accepted: No

EDITORIAL DESCRIPTION

Scope: Publishes articles on linguistic research in the "Columbia School."
Reviews books: No
Publishes notes: No
Languages accepted: English
Prints abstracts: No
Author-anonymous submission: No

SUBMISSION REQUIREMENTS

Restrictions on contributors: Contributors must be members of the "Columbia School," but not necessarily at Columbia Univ.
Author pays submission fee: No
Author pays page charges: No
Length of articles: No restrictions
Style: None
Number of copies required: 2
Special requirements: Consult with editor prior to submission.
Copyright ownership: Author
Rejected manuscripts: Returned
Number of reviewers: 1

(635)
Comhar

Tomás Mac Síomóin, Editor
5 Rae Mhuirfean
Baile Átha Cliath 2, Ireland

Telephone: (353) 1 785443
First published: 1942
Sponsoring organization: Comhar Teoranta
ISSN: 0010-2369
MLA acronym: Comhar

SUBSCRIPTION INFORMATION

Frequency of publication: 12 times/yr. (monthly)
Circulation: 3,000
Available in microform: No
Subscription price: IR£18.00/yr. Ireland
Year to which price refers: 1992

ADVERTISING INFORMATION

Advertising accepted: Yes

EDITORIAL DESCRIPTION

Scope: Publishes articles on Irish literature, as well as on Irish politics and current affairs.
Reviews books: Yes
Publishes notes: No
Languages accepted: Irish Gaelic
Prints abstracts: No

SUBMISSION REQUIREMENTS

Author pays submission fee: No
Author pays page charges: No
Book reviews published per year: 36

(636)
*Comitatus: A Journal of Medieval and Renaissance Studies

Peter Moore, Managing Editor
Center for Medieval & Renaissance Studies
212 Royce Hall
UCLA
405 Hilgard Ave.
Los Angeles, CA 90024-1485

Telephone: 310 206-3173
Fax: 310 825-0655
First published: 1970
Sponsoring organization: Univ. of California, Los Angeles, Center for Medieval & Renaissance Studies
ISSN: 0069-6412
MLA acronym: Comitatus

SUBSCRIPTION INFORMATION

Frequency of publication: Annual
Circulation: 500
Available in microform: No
Subscription price: $15.00/yr. institutions; $10.00/yr. individuals
Year to which price refers: 1992

ADVERTISING INFORMATION

Advertising accepted: No

EDITORIAL DESCRIPTION

Scope: Publishes interdisciplinary articles on Medieval and Renaissance studies.
Reviews books: Yes
Publishes notes: Yes
Languages accepted: English
Prints abstracts: No
Author-anonymous submission: Yes

SUBMISSION REQUIREMENTS

Restrictions on contributors: Contributors are graduate students or new scholars (within 3 yrs. of Ph.D.)
Author pays submission fee: No
Author pays page charges: No
Length of articles: 15-30 typescript pp.
Length of book reviews: 750 words maximum
Length of notes: 250 words
Style: Chicago
Number of copies required: 2
Special requirements: Submit original typescript on nonerasable bond. Passages in other languages should be translated in text.
Copyright ownership: Univ. of California, Los Angeles, Regents
Rejected manuscripts: Returned; enclose SASE.
Time before publication decision: 1-3 mos.
Time between decision and publication: 5 mos.
Number of reviewers: 4-8
Articles submitted per year: 40-100
Articles published per year: 6-10
Book reviews submitted per year: 1-10
Book reviews published per year: 0-6
Notes submitted per year: 0-4
Notes published per year: 0-4

(637)
*Commentary

Norman Podhoretz & Neal Kozodoy, Editors
American Jewish Committee
165 E. 56th St.
New York, NY 10022

Telephone: 212 751-4000
Fax: 212 751-1174
First published: 1945
Sponsoring organization: American Jewish Committee
ISSN: 0010-2601
MLA acronym: Commentary

SUBSCRIPTION INFORMATION

Frequency of publication: 12 times/yr.
Circulation: 30,000
Available in microform: Yes
Subscription price: $39.00/yr.
Year to which price refers: 1992
Subscription telephone: 800 829-6270

ADVERTISING INFORMATION

Advertising accepted: Yes
Advertising rates: $855.00/third page; $1,145.00/half page; $1,820.00/full page; $3,975.00/full page, color

EDITORIAL DESCRIPTION

Scope: Focuses on United States and international politics, social trends, culture, and the arts. Deals with both general and Jewish issues.
Reviews books: Yes
Publishes notes: Yes
Languages accepted: English
Prints abstracts: No

SUBMISSION REQUIREMENTS

Restrictions on contributors: None
Author pays submission fee: No
Author pays page charges: No
Length of articles: 3,000-7,500 words
Length of book reviews: 1,500-2,500 words
Style: Chicago
Number of copies required: 1
Copyright ownership: American Jewish Committee
Rejected manuscripts: Returned; enclose return postage.
Time before publication decision: 1 mo.
Time between decision and publication: 3-4 mos.
Number of reviewers: 4
Articles published per year: 85
Book reviews published per year: 60

(638)
*Commentationes Humanarum Litterarum Societatis Scientiarum Fennicae

Holger Thesleff, Editor
Mariankatu 5
00170 Helsinki 17, Finland

Additional editorial address: Tiedekirja, Kirkkokatu 14, 00170 Helsinki, Finland
Telephone: (358) 0 633005
First published: 1923
Sponsoring organization: Societas Scientiarum Fennicae
ISSN: 0069-6587
MLA acronym: CHLSSF

SUBSCRIPTION INFORMATION

Frequency of publication: Irregular
Circulation: 700
Available in microform: No
Subscription address: Academic Bookstore, Keskuskatu 1, 00100 Helsinki 10, Finland

ADVERTISING INFORMATION

Advertising accepted: No

EDITORIAL DESCRIPTION

Scope: Publishes monographs on literature, history, classics, and philology.
Reviews books: No
Publishes notes: No
Languages accepted: English; German; French; Latin; Italian; Spanish
Prints abstracts: No
Author-anonymous submission: No

SUBMISSION REQUIREMENTS

Restrictions on contributors: Contributions must be recommended by one member of the Soc. Scientiarum Fennica.
Author pays submission fee: No
Author pays page charges: No
Length of books: No restrictions
Style: None
Number of copies required: 2
Special requirements: None
Copyright ownership: Soc. Scientiarum Fennica
Rejected manuscripts: Returned at author's request
Time before publication decision: 2-6 mos.
Time between decision and publication: 3-6 mos.
Number of reviewers: 1-2
Books submitted per year: 2-5
Books published per year: 1-4

(639)
*Commonwealth Essays and Studies

Jean-Pierre Durix, Editor
Faculté des Lettres
Univ. de Dijon
2, blvd. Gabriel
21000 Dijon, France

Telephone: (33) 80395619
First published: 1975
Sponsoring organization: Soc. Française d'Etudes des Pays du Commonwealth
ISSN: 0385-6989
MLA acronym: CE&S

SUBSCRIPTION INFORMATION

Frequency of publication: 2 times/yr.
Circulation: 600
Available in microform: No
Subscription price: 130 F/yr.
Year to which price refers: 1991-92

ADVERTISING INFORMATION

Advertising accepted: Yes

EDITORIAL DESCRIPTION

Scope: Publishes articles on all aspects of Commonwealth literature.
Reviews books: Yes
Publishes notes: Yes
Languages accepted: English; French
Prints abstracts: No

SUBMISSION REQUIREMENTS

Restrictions on contributors: Contributors must be members of Soc. Française d'Etudes des Pays du Commonwealth.
Author pays submission fee: No
Author pays page charges: No
Length of articles: 7,500 words
Length of book reviews: 500 words
Length of notes: 300 words
Style: MLA
Number of copies required: 2
Copyright ownership: Author
Rejected manuscripts: Returned; enclose return postage.
Time before publication decision: 6 mos.
Time between decision and publication: 6 mos.
Number of reviewers: 2
Articles published per year: 25-30

(640)
*Commonwealth Novel in English

Sudhakar Ratnakar Jamkhandi, Editor
Center for International Understanding
English Dept.
Bluefield State College
Bluefield, WV 24701

Telephone: 304 327-4036
Fax: 304 325-7747
First published: 1982
Sponsoring organization: Bluefield State College Center for International Understanding
ISSN: 0732-6734
MLA acronym: CNIE

SUBSCRIPTION INFORMATION

Frequency of publication: 2 times/yr. (Spring/Summer, Fall/Winter)
Circulation: 300
Available in microform: No
Subscription price: $16.00/yr. institutions; $14.00/yr. individuals
Year to which price refers: 1991-92

ADVERTISING INFORMATION

Advertising accepted: Yes

EDITORIAL DESCRIPTION

Scope: Publishes articles on the Commonwealth novel written in English; rhetorical, political, aesthetic, sociological, and psychological criticism; checklists, bibliographies, interviews.
Reviews books: Yes
Publishes notes: No
Languages accepted: English
Prints abstracts: No
Author-anonymous submission: No

SUBMISSION REQUIREMENTS

Restrictions on contributors: None
Author pays submission fee: No
Author pays page charges: No
Length of articles: No restrictions
Length of book reviews: No restrictions
Style: MLA
Number of copies required: 2
Copyright ownership: Bluefield State College Center for International Understanding
Rejected manuscripts: Returned; enclose SASE.
Time before publication decision: 6-12 mos.
Time between decision and publication: 6-12 mos.
Number of reviewers: 2
Articles submitted per year: 25-50
Articles published per year: 25
Book reviews submitted per year: 25
Book reviews published per year: 10-15

(641)
*Commonwealth Quarterly

S. N. Vikramraj Urs, Editor
2823, VIII Cross
V.V. Mohalla, Mysore 2
Karnataka State, India

First published: 1976
ISSN: 1013-9877
MLA acronym: ComQ

SUBSCRIPTION INFORMATION

Frequency of publication: 4 times/yr. (Dec., Mar., June, Sept.)
Circulation: 70
Available in microform: No
Subscription price: 20 Re ($10.00)/yr.
Year to which price refers: 1992
Subscription address: M. Vijaya Lakshmi, at the above address

ADVERTISING INFORMATION

Advertising accepted: Yes
Advertising rates: 500 Re/half page; 1,000 Re/full page

EDITORIAL DESCRIPTION

Scope: Publishes articles on Commonwealth literature and Indian regional literature.
Reviews books: Yes
Publishes notes: No
Languages accepted: English
Prints abstracts: No

SUBMISSION REQUIREMENTS

Restrictions on contributors: None
Author pays submission fee: No
Author pays page charges: No
Length of articles: No restrictions
Length of book reviews: No restrictions
Style: MLA
Number of copies required: 2
Special requirements: Submit double-spaced manuscript; include 2 copies of a vita.
Copyright ownership: Author
Rejected manuscripts: Returned; enclose return postage.
Time before publication decision: 1 mo.
Number of reviewers: 4
Articles submitted per year: 75
Articles published per year: 35
Book reviews published per year: 12

(642)
*The Commonwealth Review

R. K. Dhawan, Editor
J 391
New Rajinder Nagar
New Delhi 110 060, India

Additional editorial address: Send articles and books for review to: Ms. Seema, Executive Secretary, ISCS, C 129 Mansarovar Garden, New Delhi 110 015, India
Telephone: (91) 11 5737849
Fax: (91) 11 588111; (91) 11 5736111
First published: 1989
Sponsoring organization: Indian Soc. for Commonwealth Studies
MLA acronym: CoRev

SUBSCRIPTION INFORMATION

Frequency of publication: 2 times/yr. (Jan., July)
Circulation: 430
Available in microform: No
Subscription price: $25.00/yr., $60.00/3 yrs.; for airmail add $6.00/yr.
Year to which price refers: 1992

ADVERTISING INFORMATION

Advertising accepted: Yes
Advertising rates: $40.00/half page; $75.00/full page; $100.00/inside cover; $100.00/back cover

EDITORIAL DESCRIPTION

Scope: Publishes articles on new literatures in English. Prefers literary studies which search for aesthetic dimensions arising from the interaction of literature from one Commonwealth country with that of the literatures of other Commonwealth countries and with world literature.
Reviews books: Yes
Publishes notes: No
Languages accepted: English
Prints abstracts: No

SUBMISSION REQUIREMENTS

Restrictions on contributors: None
Author pays submission fee: No

Author pays page charges: No
Length of articles: 800-1,000 words
Length of book reviews: 200 words
Style: MLA
Number of copies required: 1
Copyright ownership: Indian Soc. for Commonwealth Studies
Rejected manuscripts: Returned at author's request
Time before publication decision: 1 mo.
Time between decision and publication: 6 mos.
Number of reviewers: 2
Articles submitted per year: 100
Articles published per year: 30
Book reviews submitted per year: 20
Book reviews published per year: 10

(643)
*Communication Education

Lawrence B. Rosenfeld, Editor
Dept. of Speech Communication
Univ. of North Carolina
Chapel Hill, NC 27599-3285

First published: 1952
Sponsoring organization: Speech Communication Assn.
ISSN: 0363-4523
MLA acronym: CEd

SUBSCRIPTION INFORMATION

Frequency of publication: 4 times/yr. (Jan., Apr., July, Oct.)
Circulation: 5,000
Available in microform: No
Subscription address: James L. Gaudino, Executive Director, Speech Communication Assn., 5105 Backlick Rd., Annandale, VA 22003

ADVERTISING INFORMATION

Advertising accepted: Yes

EDITORIAL DESCRIPTION

Scope: Deals with all aspects of teaching and learning speech communication in elementary, middle, junior, and senior high schools and in higher education. Publishes articles on many aspects of speech communication such as communication in instruction, interpersonal communication and small group interaction, mass communication, nonverbal communication, teacher preparation, curriculum development and classroom interaction. Welcomes feature length articles.
Reviews books: Yes
Publishes notes: No
Languages accepted: English
Prints abstracts: Yes
Author-anonymous submission: Yes

SUBMISSION REQUIREMENTS

Author pays submission fee: No
Author pays page charges: No
Length of articles: 2,000-6,000 words
Length of book reviews: 500-750 words
Style: American Psychological Assn.
Number of copies required: 4
Special requirements: Include name, address, academic rank or title, institutional affiliation, name of the article, and a 50-75 word abstract on a cover sheet of paper separate from the manuscript. Avoid including contributor's name in the manuscript proper, but leave space for it to be added later beneath the title of the first page. The Editor will submit complete manuscripts to the Editorial Board members with names of the authors deleted.
Copyright ownership: Speech Communication Assn.
Rejected manuscripts: Not returned
Time before publication decision: 2 mos.
Time between decision and publication: 10 mos.
Number of reviewers: 2
Articles submitted per year: 150-200
Articles published per year: 24-32
Book reviews published per year: 20-30

(644)
*Communication Monographs

Charles R. Bantz, Editor
Dept. of Communication
Arizona State Univ.
Tempe, AZ 85287-1205

Telephone: 602 965-4231
E-mail: ATCRB@ASUACAD
First published: 1934
Sponsoring organization: Speech Communication Assn.
ISSN: 0363-7751
MLA acronym: ComM

SUBSCRIPTION INFORMATION

Frequency of publication: 4 times/yr. (Mar., June, Sept., Dec.)
Circulation: 3,980
Available in microform: Yes
Subscription price: $75.00/yr. members
Year to which price refers: 1991
Subscription address: Speech Communication Assn., 5105 Backlick Rd., Annandale, VA 22003

ADVERTISING INFORMATION

Advertising accepted: No

EDITORIAL DESCRIPTION

Scope: Advances knowledge of communication processes through publication of theoretically relevant research reports.
Reviews books: No
Publishes notes: Yes
Languages accepted: English
Prints abstracts: Yes
Author-anonymous submission: Yes

SUBMISSION REQUIREMENTS

Restrictions on contributors: None
Author pays submission fee: No
Author pays page charges: No
Length of articles: 6,000 words
Length of notes: 2,000 words
Style: American Psychological Assn.
Number of copies required: 4
Special requirements: Submit 4 copies with author identification removed plus a title page complete with author identification.
Copyright ownership: Speech Communication Assn.
Rejected manuscripts: Not returned
Time before publication decision: 2-3 mos.
Time between decision and publication: 8-12 mos.
Number of reviewers: 3
Articles submitted per year: 250
Articles published per year: 35

(645)
*Communications from the International Brecht Society

Vera Stegmann, Editor
Dept. of Modern Foreign Languages
Maginnes Hall 9
Lehigh Univ.
Bethlehem, PA 18015

Telephone: 215 758-5026
E-mail: Vss2@ns.cc.lehigh.edu
First published: 1970
Sponsoring organization: International Brecht Soc., Inc.
ISSN: 0740-8943
MLA acronym: CIBS

SUBSCRIPTION INFORMATION

Frequency of publication: 2 times/yr.
Circulation: 250
Available in microform: No
Subscription address: Ward B. Lewis, Secretary/Treasurer, International Brecht Soc., Dept. of Germanic & Slavic Languages, Univ. of Georgia, Athens, GA 30602

ADVERTISING INFORMATION

Advertising accepted: Yes

EDITORIAL DESCRIPTION

Scope: Publishes articles about the life and work of Bertolt Brecht and his impact on modern theater and culture worldwide.
Reviews books: No
Publishes notes: Yes
Languages accepted: English; German; French; Spanish
Prints abstracts: No
Author-anonymous submission: No

SUBMISSION REQUIREMENTS

Restrictions on contributors: None
Author pays submission fee: No
Author pays page charges: No
Length of articles: 4,000 words (10-15 double-spaced typescript pp.) or consult editor
Length of notes: No restrictions
Style: MLA
Number of copies required: 1
Special requirements: Will translate manuscripts into English from major European languages.
Copyright ownership: Journal
Rejected manuscripts: Returned
Time before publication decision: 2-3 mos.
Time between decision and publication: 6-12 mos.
Number of reviewers: 1-2
Articles submitted per year: 15-20
Articles published per year: 10-12
Notes published per year: 100

(646)
Communications of the ACM

Assn. for Computing Machinery
11 West 42nd St.
New York, NY 10036

First published: 1958
Sponsoring organization: Assn. for Computing Machinery
ISSN: 0001-0782
MLA acronym: CACM

SUBSCRIPTION INFORMATION

Frequency of publication: 12 times/yr.
Circulation: 75,000
Available in microform: Yes

ADVERTISING INFORMATION

Advertising accepted: Yes

EDITORIAL DESCRIPTION

Scope: Publishes reports, articles, and features on all aspects of computing.
Reviews books: No
Publishes notes: Yes
Languages accepted: English
Prints abstracts: Yes
Author-anonymous submission: No

SUBMISSION REQUIREMENTS

Restrictions on contributors: None
Author pays submission fee: No
Author pays page charges: Yes
Length of articles: No restrictions
Length of notes: No restrictions

Style: None
Number of copies required: 3
Copyright ownership: Assn. for Computing Machinery
Rejected manuscripts: Not returned
Time before publication decision: 4 mos.
Time between decision and publication: 6 mos.
Number of reviewers: 3-4
Articles submitted per year: 400
Articles published per year: 140
Notes submitted per year: 20
Notes published per year: 10

(647)
*The Comparatist: Journal of the Southern Comparative Literature Association

Marcel Cornis-Pope, Editor
Dept. of English
Virginia Commonwealth Univ.
Richmond, VA 23284-2005

Telephone: 804 367-1667
Fax: 804 367-2171
E-mail: MCORNIS@hibbs.VCU.EDU
First published: 1977
Sponsoring organization: Southern Comparative Literature Assn.; Dept. of English, Virginia Commonwealth Univ.
ISSN: 0195-7678
MLA acronym: Comparatist

SUBSCRIPTION INFORMATION

Frequency of publication: Annual (May)
Circulation: 300
Available in microform: No
Subscription address: Carolyn R. Hodges, Dept. of German, 701 McClung Tower, Univ. of Tennessee, Knoxville, TN 37996-0470
Subscription telephone: 615 974-3421

ADVERTISING INFORMATION

Advertising accepted: No

EDITORIAL DESCRIPTION

Scope: Publishes articles on all aspects of comparative literature: literature and the other arts, literature and other areas of human expression or achievement, literary criticism, methodology, theory, genre, and period studies. Papers on inter-American, Third World, and East-West literary relations are encouraged. Analytic papers using the comparatist approach to discuss two or more literary works are especially sought.
Reviews books: Yes
Publishes notes: Yes
Languages accepted: English; French; Spanish; German
Prints abstracts: No
Author-anonymous submission: Yes

SUBMISSION REQUIREMENTS

Restrictions on contributors: Contributors must be members of the SCLA when article is published.
Author pays submission fee: No
Author pays page charges: No
Length of articles: 5,000-15,000 words
Length of book reviews: 800-2,500 words
Length of notes: 500-800 words
Style: MLA
Number of copies required: 3
Copyright ownership: Journal
Rejected manuscripts: Returned; enclose return postage.
Time before publication decision: 2-4 mos.
Time between decision and publication: 1 yr.
Number of reviewers: 3
Articles submitted per year: 25-35
Articles published per year: 6-10
Book reviews submitted per year: 8-15
Book reviews published per year: 6-8

Notes submitted per year: 4-5
Notes published per year: 3-4

(648)
*Comparative Civilizations Review

Wayne M. Bledsoe & Vytautas Kavolis, Editors
Dept. of History
Univ. of Missouri-Rolla
Rolla, MO 65401

Additional editorial address: Vytautas Kavolis, Dept. of Sociology, Dickinson College, Carlisle, PA 17013
Telephone: 314 341-4815
E-mail: C0402A@UMRVMB
First published: 1978
Sponsoring organization: International Soc. for the Comparative Study of Civilizations
ISSN: 0733-4540
MLA acronym: CCRev

SUBSCRIPTION INFORMATION

Frequency of publication: 2 times/yr.
Circulation: 600
Available in microform: No
Subscription price: $25.00/yr. institutions; $20.00/yr. individuals; $5.00/yr. students
Year to which price refers: 1992
Subscription address: Denise Guback, Program in Comparative Literature, Univ. of Illinois, Urbana, IL 61801

ADVERTISING INFORMATION

Advertising accepted: Yes

EDITORIAL DESCRIPTION

Scope: Publishes analytic studies and interpretive essays primarily concerned with the comparison of whole civilizations, the development of theories or methods especially useful in comparative civilizational studies, and significant issues in the humanities or social sciences studied from a comparative civilizational perspective.
Reviews books: Yes
Publishes notes: Yes
Languages accepted: English
Prints abstracts: No
Author-anonymous submission: Yes

SUBMISSION REQUIREMENTS

Restrictions on contributors: None
Author pays submission fee: No
Author pays page charges: No
Length of articles: 30-40 double-spaced typescript pp.
Length of book reviews: 10 pp.
Length of notes: 5-7 pp.
Style: MLA; Turabian
Number of copies required: 3
Copyright ownership: International Soc. for the Comparative Study of Civilizations
Rejected manuscripts: Returned
Time before publication decision: 3 mos.
Time between decision and publication: 1 yr.
Number of reviewers: 3
Articles submitted per year: 30
Articles published per year: 10
Book reviews submitted per year: 15
Book reviews published per year: 10-12
Notes submitted per year: 3
Notes published per year: 3

(649)
*Comparative Criticism: A Yearbook

Elinor Shaffer, Editor
Cambridge Univ. Press
Edinburgh Bldg.
Shaftesbury Rd.
Cambridge CB2 2RU, England

Additional editorial address: Reviews Editor, 9 Crammer Rd., Cambridge CB3 9BK, England
First published: 1979
Sponsoring organization: British Comparative Literature Assn.
ISSN: 0144-7564
MLA acronym: CCrit

SUBSCRIPTION INFORMATION

Frequency of publication: Annual (Summer)
Circulation: 450
Available in microform: No
Subscription price: $85.00/yr. institutions; $53.00/yr. individuals
Year to which price refers: 1992
Additional subscription address: Cambridge Univ. Press, 40 W. 20th St., New York, NY 10011

ADVERTISING INFORMATION

Advertising accepted: Yes

EDITORIAL DESCRIPTION

Scope: Publishes on questions of literary theory and criticism, comparative studies in terms of theme, genre, movement, influence and reception, and interdisciplinary questions. Includes translations of literary, scholarly, and critical works, and original writing in English; substantial reviews of major books in the field; an annual bibliography of comparative literature in Britain; and specialized bibliographies on annual themes or individual authors.
Reviews books: Yes
Publishes notes: No
Languages accepted: English
Prints abstracts: No
Author-anonymous submission: No

SUBMISSION REQUIREMENTS

Restrictions on contributors: Deadline for submission is 1 Mar. Book reviews are commissioned.
Author pays submission fee: No
Author pays page charges: Only for extensive changes at proof stage
Length of articles: 7,500 words
Length of book reviews: 2,000-3,000 words
Style: Modern Humanities Research Assn.
Number of copies required: 2
Special requirements: Submit original typescript and 1 copy. Author is responsible for securing necessary permissions.
Copyright ownership: Cambridge Univ. Press for one year. Reverts to author by arrangement.
Rejected manuscripts: Returned
Time before publication decision: 3 mos.
Time between decision and publication: 1 yr.
Number of reviewers: 3
Articles submitted per year: 40-45
Articles published per year: 15
Book reviews published per year: 5

(650)
*Comparative Drama

Clifford Davidson & John H. Stroupe, Editors
Dept. of English
Western Michigan Univ.
Kalamazoo, MI 49008-3899

Telephone: 616 387-2579; 616 387-4153
Fax: 616 387-4150
First published: 1967

ISSN: 0010-4078
MLA acronym: CompD

SUBSCRIPTION INFORMATION

Frequency of publication: 4 times/yr. (Spring, Summer, Fall, Winter)
Circulation: 800
Available in microform: Yes
Subscription price: $22.00/yr. institutions US; $25.00/yr. institutions elsewhere; $12.00/yr. individuals US; $15.00/yr. individuals elsewhere
Year to which price refers: 1991
Subscription address: Medieval Inst. Publications, Western Michigan Univ., Kalamazoo, MI 49008-3851

ADVERTISING INFORMATION

Advertising accepted: No

EDITORIAL DESCRIPTION

Scope: Publishes drama studies which are international in spirit and interdisciplinary in scope. While medieval drama is a special interest, articles may focus on drama of any period from antiquity to the present.
Reviews books: Yes
Publishes notes: No
Languages accepted: English
Prints abstracts: No
Author-anonymous submission: No

SUBMISSION REQUIREMENTS

Restrictions on contributors: Unsolicited book reviews are not accepted.
Author pays submission fee: No
Author pays page charges: No, but authors are expected to pay for printing illustrations or plates.
Length of articles: 20-30 typescript pp.
Length of book reviews: 1,500 words maximum
Style: MLA (1970)
Number of copies required: 1
Special requirements: Footnotes should be kept to a minimum. Quotations in languages other than English are permitted, but translations should be supplied. Short notes are not accepted.
Copyright ownership: Board of the Medieval Inst.
Rejected manuscripts: Returned; enclose return postage.
Time before publication decision: 1 mo.
Time between decision and publication: 6 mos.
Number of reviewers: 2-3
Articles submitted per year: 130-150
Articles published per year: 20
Book reviews published per year: 30

(651)
*****Comparative Literature**

Thomas R. Hart & Steven Rendall, Editors
223 Friendly Hall
Univ. of Oregon
Eugene, OR 97403-1233

Telephone: 503 346-4022
Fax: 503 346-4030
E-mail: PDANIELS@OREGON.UOREGON.EDU
First published: 1949
Sponsoring organization: American Comparative Literature Assn.
ISSN: 0010-4124
MLA acronym: CL

SUBSCRIPTION INFORMATION

Frequency of publication: 4 times/yr. (Feb., May, Aug., Nov.)
Circulation: 2,100
Available in microform: Yes

Subscription price: $22.50/yr. institutions US; $24.50/yr. institutions elsewhere; $12.50/yr. individuals
Year to which price refers: 1993

ADVERTISING INFORMATION

Advertising accepted: Seldomly; on an exchange basis only

EDITORIAL DESCRIPTION

Scope: Publishes articles which explore important problems of literary theory and literary history not confined to a single national literature. A broad range of theoretical and critical approaches is encouraged.
Reviews books: Yes
Publishes notes: No
Languages accepted: English; French; German; Italian; Spanish
Prints abstracts: No
Author-anonymous submission: No

SUBMISSION REQUIREMENTS

Restrictions on contributors: Unsolicited book reviews are not accepted.
Author pays submission fee: No
Author pays page charges: No
Length of articles: 5,000-12,000 words
Length of book reviews: 1,200 words
Style: MLA
Number of copies required: 1
Special requirements: Submit original typescript or a photocopy with assurance that manuscript is not being submitted elsewhere.
Copyright ownership: Author
Rejected manuscripts: Returned
Time before publication decision: 3 mos.
Time between decision and publication: 2 yrs.
Number of reviewers: 1-3
Articles submitted per year: 182
Articles published per year: 15-18
Book reviews submitted per year: 50
Book reviews published per year: 32-48

(652)
*****Comparative Literature Studies**

Robert R. Edwards, Patrick Cheney, & Gerhard Strasser, Editors
433 N. Burrowes Building
Dept. of Comparative Literature
Pennsylvania State Univ.
University Park, PA 16802

Telephone: 814 863-1336
E-mail: RRE1@PSUVM.PSU.EDU
First published: 1963
ISSN: 0010-4132
MLA acronym: CLS

SUBSCRIPTION INFORMATION

Frequency of publication: 4 times/yr. (Mar., June, Sept., Dec.)
Circulation: 1,000
Available in microform: Yes
Subscription price: $35.00/yr. institutions US; $40.00/yr. institutions elsewhere; $22.50/yr. individuals US; $30.00/yr. individuals elsewhere
Year to which price refers: 1992
Subscription address: Pennsylvania State Univ. Press, Barbara Bldg., Suite C, 820 North University Dr., University Park, PA 16802
Subscription telephone: 804 865-1327

ADVERTISING INFORMATION

Advertising accepted: Yes

EDITORIAL DESCRIPTION

Scope: Publishes comparative articles in literary history, the history of ideas, critical theory, relationships between authors, and literary relations within and beyond the Western tradition. Publishes a biennial issue on East-West relations.
Reviews books: Yes
Publishes notes: No
Languages accepted: English
Prints abstracts: No
Author-anonymous submission: No

SUBMISSION REQUIREMENTS

Restrictions on contributors: Book reviews are commissioned.
Author pays submission fee: No
Author pays page charges: No
Length of articles: 20 pp.
Length of book reviews: 750 words
Style: MLA with endnotes
Number of copies required: 2
Special requirements: Manuscripts should be prepared with endnotes.
Copyright ownership: Assigned by author to journal
Rejected manuscripts: Returned; enclose return postage.
Time before publication decision: 3-4 mos.
Time between decision and publication: 6-12 mos.
Number of reviewers: 3
Articles submitted per year: 125
Articles published per year: 20
Book reviews published per year: 25

(653)
*****The Comparative Romance Linguistics Newsletter**

Joel Rini, Editor
Dept. of Spanish
Univ. of Virginia
Charlottesville, VA 22903

Telephone: 804 924-7159
First published: 1950
Sponsoring organization: MLA, Discussion Group on Comparative Romance Linguistics
ISSN: 0010-4167
MLA acronym: CRLN

SUBSCRIPTION INFORMATION

Frequency of publication: 2 times/yr.
Circulation: 100
Available in microform: No

ADVERTISING INFORMATION

Advertising accepted: Yes

EDITORIAL DESCRIPTION

Scope: Publishes news of the field of comparative Romance linguistics and bibliography.
Reviews books: Yes
Publishes notes: No
Prints abstracts: No

(654)
*****Compendia: Computer Generated Aids to Literary and Linguistic Research**

R. A. Wisbey, Editor
King's College
Strand
London WC2R 2LS, England

First published: 1968
ISSN: 0950-6756
MLA acronym: Compendia

SUBSCRIPTION INFORMATION

Frequency of publication: Irregular
Available in microform: No
Subscription address: W. S. Maney & Son, Ltd., Hudson Road, Leeds 9, England
Subscription telephone: (44) 532 497481
Subscription fax: (44) 532 486983

ADVERTISING INFORMATION

Advertising accepted: No

EDITORIAL DESCRIPTION

Scope: Publishes concordances, word indexes, and other reference works.
Reviews books: No
Publishes notes: No
Languages accepted: European languages
Prints abstracts: No
Author-anonymous submission: No

SUBMISSION REQUIREMENTS

Restrictions on contributors: None
Author pays submission fee: No
Author pays page charges: No
Style: Modern Humanities Research Assn.
Number of copies required: 1
Special requirements: Manuscripts considered in all modern European and Classical languages. Submit specimen pages only.
Copyright ownership: Author
Rejected manuscripts: Returned
Time between decision and publication: 9-12 mos.
Number of reviewers: 1
Books published per year: 1

(655)
*Computational Linguistics

James F. Allen, Editor
Computer Science Dept.
Univ. of Rochester
Rochester, NY 14627

Telephone: 716 275-5478
Fax: 716 461-2018
E-mail: Acl@cs.rochester.edu
First published: 1973
Sponsoring organization: Assn. for Computational Linguistics
ISSN: 0362-613X
MLA acronym: CompLing

SUBSCRIPTION INFORMATION

Frequency of publication: 4 times/yr.
Circulation: 2,500
Available in microform: Yes
Subscription price: $75.00/yr. institutions; $25.00/yr. individuals
Year to which price refers: 1992
Subscription address: Donald E. Walker, Bell Communications Research, 445 South St., Morristown, NJ 07960
Additional subscription address: Institutions contact: MIT Press Journals, 55 Hayward St., Cambridge, MA 02142

ADVERTISING INFORMATION

Advertising accepted: Yes

EDITORIAL DESCRIPTION

Scope: Publishes articles on computational linguistics.
Reviews books: Yes
Publishes notes: Yes
Languages accepted: English
Prints abstracts: Yes
Author-anonymous submission: No

SUBMISSION REQUIREMENTS

Author pays submission fee: No

Author pays page charges: No
Length of articles: 45 pp. maximum
Length of book reviews: 1 p.
Length of notes: 2 pp.
Number of copies required: 5
Special requirements: Manuscripts must be double-spaced typescript, including footnotes. Submit an abstract of 150-200 words.
Copyright ownership: Assn. for Computational Linguistics
Rejected manuscripts: Not returned
Time before publication decision: 3-6 mos.
Time between decision and publication: 3-6 mos.
Number of reviewers: 3-4
Articles submitted per year: 80-90
Articles published per year: 16-20
Book reviews published per year: 20-25
Notes submitted per year: 2-4
Notes published per year: 1-2

(656)
*Computers and the Humanities

Glyn Holmes, Editor
Kluwer Academic Publishers
P.O. Box 17
3300 AA Dordrecht, Netherlands

Telephone: (31) 78 334207
Fax: (31) 78 334254
First published: 1966
Sponsoring organization: Assn. for Computers & the Humanities
ISSN: 0010-4817
MLA acronym: CHum

SUBSCRIPTION INFORMATION

Frequency of publication: 6 times/yr.
Circulation: 1,300
Available in microform: Yes, through Univ. Microfilms International
Subscription price: 354 f ($180.00)/yr.
Year to which price refers: 1992
Subscription address: Kluwer Academic Publishers, P.O. Box 322, 3300 AH Dordrecht, Netherlands
Additional subscription address: In N. America: Kluwer Academic Publishers, P.O. Box 358, Accord Station, Hingham, MA 02018-0358
Subscription telephone: (31) 78 524400
Subscription fax: (31) 78 524474

ADVERTISING INFORMATION

Advertising accepted: Yes
Advertising rates: $400.00/full page

EDITORIAL DESCRIPTION

Scope: Publishes articles on computer applications in humanities research and instruction.
Reviews books: Yes
Publishes notes: Yes
Languages accepted: English; French; German
Prints abstracts: Yes
Author-anonymous submission: No

SUBMISSION REQUIREMENTS

Restrictions on contributors: None
Author pays submission fee: No
Author pays page charges: No
Length of articles: No restrictions
Length of book reviews: No restrictions
Length of notes: No restrictions
Style: MLA recommended
Number of copies required: 4
Special requirements: Include a 250-word English abstract if article is in French or German. If possible, submit typescript accompanied by ASCII diskette, or submit by electronic mail.
Copyright ownership: Assigned by author to Kluwer Academic Publishers
Rejected manuscripts: Returned; enclose return postage.

Time before publication decision: 6 mos.
Time between decision and publication: 6 mos.
Number of reviewers: 3-4
Articles submitted per year: 70
Articles published per year: 35
Book reviews submitted per year: 50
Book reviews published per year: 50
Notes submitted per year: 5
Notes published per year: 5

(657)
Comunità: Rivista di Informazione Culturale

Renzo Zorzi, Editor
Via Manfredo Camperio 11
20123 Milan, Italy

First published: 1946
ISSN: 0010-504X
MLA acronym: Comunità

SUBSCRIPTION INFORMATION

Frequency of publication: Annual
Circulation: 7,000
Available in microform: No
Subscription address: Arnoldo Mondadori Editori, SpA, Ufficio Abbonamenti, Via Arnoldo Mondadori, 20090 Segrate, Italy

ADVERTISING INFORMATION

Advertising accepted: Yes

EDITORIAL DESCRIPTION

Scope: Publishes articles on politics, sociology, literature, arts, and architecture.
Reviews books: No
Languages accepted: Italian
Prints abstracts: No

SUBMISSION REQUIREMENTS

Restrictions on contributors: None
Author pays submission fee: No
Author pays page charges: No
Length of articles: No restrictions
Number of copies required: 1
Copyright ownership: Journal
Rejected manuscripts: Not returned
Time before publication decision: 3 mos.
Number of reviewers: 2
Articles published per year: 15

(658)
The Conch: A Sociological Journal of African Cultures and Literatures

Sunday O. Anozie, Editor
Conch Magazine Ltd.
c/o Conch Typesetting
Box 777
Buffalo, NY 14213-0777

First published: 1969
Sponsoring organization: Conch Magazine, Ltd.
ISSN: 0092-7708
MLA acronym: Conch

SUBSCRIPTION INFORMATION

Frequency of publication: 2 times/yr. (Mar., Sept.)
Circulation: 1,500
Available in microform: No
Subscription address: Subscriptions & Renewals Dept., at the above address

ADVERTISING INFORMATION

Advertising accepted: Yes

EDITORIAL DESCRIPTION

Scope: Particular, though not exclusive, interest is in the sociology of African cultures and literatures both traditional and modern. Especially interested in contributions that develop theories of the text and poetics in Africa, from a structuralist or semiotic viewpoint. Journal's primary concern is with the problems of objectivity and methodology in African studies.
Reviews books: No
Publishes notes: No
Languages accepted: English; French
Prints abstracts: No

SUBMISSION REQUIREMENTS

Restrictions on contributors: Contributors must demonstrate a special competence in subject matter. Unsolicited manuscripts are rarely accepted.
Author pays submission fee: No
Author pays page charges: No
Length of articles: 2,250 words
Style: MLA & journal
Number of copies required: 1
Special requirements: Contributors should consult with editor prior to submission. Supply English abstract for articles written in French.
Copyright ownership: Author
Rejected manuscripts: Returned
Time before publication decision: 4-6 weeks
Time between decision and publication: 3-6 mos.
Number of reviewers: 3
Articles submitted per year: 40-60
Articles published per year: 14-30

(659)
Conch Review of Books: A Literary Supplement on Africa

Sunday O. Anozie, Editor
Conch Magazine Ltd.
c/o Conch Typesetting
Box 777
Buffalo, NY 14213-0777

First published: 1973
Sponsoring organization: Conch Magazine, Inc.
ISSN: 0092-7708
MLA acronym: CRevB

SUBSCRIPTION INFORMATION

Frequency of publication: 4 times/yr. (Mar., June, Sept., Dec.)
Circulation: 2,000
Subscription address: Subscription & Renewals Dept., at the above address

EDITORIAL DESCRIPTION

Scope: Devoted to in-depth, timely, objective reviews of books and audio-visual materials about Africa. Special annual volumes on bibliographic essays, dual and multiple reviews, author, title, and reviewer's indexes.
Reviews books: Yes
Languages accepted: English; French
Prints abstracts: No

SUBMISSION REQUIREMENTS

Restrictions on contributors: None
Length of articles: 1,500-2,000 words for review articles
Length of book reviews: 1,000 words
Style: MLA; Journal
Number of copies required: 1
Special requirements: Consult with editor prior to submission; include English abstract for articles written in French.
Copyright ownership: Author
Rejected manuscripts: Returned; enclose return postage.
Time before publication decision: 3 weeks
Time between decision and publication: 2-6 mos.

Number of reviewers: 3
Articles published per year: 50

(660)
*Conference of College Teachers of English Studies

Alice Mathews, Editor
English Dept., Box 13827
Univ. of North Texas
Denton, TX 76203

First published: 1935
Sponsoring organization: Conference of College Teachers of English of Texas
ISSN: 0092-8151
MLA acronym: CCTEP

SUBSCRIPTION INFORMATION

Frequency of publication: Annual (Sept.)
Circulation: 630
Available in microform: No

ADVERTISING INFORMATION

Advertising accepted: No

EDITORIAL DESCRIPTION

Scope: Publishes articles on literature, pedagogy, rhetoric, composition, language, and linguistics, as well as creative writing, presented at the annual conference of College Teachers of English of Texas.
Reviews books: No
Publishes notes: No
Languages accepted: English
Prints abstracts: No
Author-anonymous submission: Yes

SUBMISSION REQUIREMENTS

Restrictions on contributors: Contributors must be members of CCTE and paper must have been read at CCTE convention and must not have been previously read or published.
Author pays submission fee: No
Author pays page charges: No
Length of articles: 8-10 double-spaced typescript pp.
Style: MLA
Number of copies required: 3
Special requirements: Submit a 100-word abstract.
Copyright ownership: Conference of College Teachers of English of Texas
Rejected manuscripts: Returned; enclose SASE.
Time before publication decision: 6 mos.
Time between decision and publication: 5 mos.
Number of reviewers: 7
Articles submitted per year: 60-70
Articles published per year: 10

(661)
*Conference on Editorial Problems. University of Toronto

G. E. Bentley, Jr., Editor
AMS Press, Inc.
56 East 13th St.
New York, NY 10003

First published: 1965
Sponsoring organization: Conference on Editorial Problems, Univ. of Toronto
ISSN: 0891-1908
MLA acronym: CEP

SUBSCRIPTION INFORMATION

Frequency of publication: Annual
Available in microform: No

ADVERTISING INFORMATION

Advertising accepted: No

EDITORIAL DESCRIPTION

Scope: Publishes papers delivered at the annual Conference on Editoral Problems held at the University of Toronto. Each conference focuses on a specific kind of editorial problem.
Reviews books: No
Publishes notes: No
Languages accepted: English
Prints abstracts: No
Author-anonymous submission: No

SUBMISSION REQUIREMENTS

Restrictions on contributors: Contribution is by invitation only.
Author pays submission fee: No
Author pays page charges: No
Copyright ownership: AMS Press

(662)
*Confluencia: Revista Hispánica de Cultura y Literatura

Alfonso Rodríguez & Lynn A. Sandstedt, Editors
Dept. of Hispanic Studies
Univ. of Northern Colorado
Greeley, CO 80639

Telephone: 303 351-2162; 303 351-2811
Fax: 303 351-2983
First published: 1985
Sponsoring organization: Dept. of Hispanic Studies, Univ. of Northern Colorado
ISSN: 0888-6091
MLA acronym: Confluencia

SUBSCRIPTION INFORMATION

Frequency of publication: 2 times/yr. (Fall, Spring)
Circulation: 450
Available in microform: No
Subscription price: $20.00/yr. institutions US; $25.00/yr. institutions elsewhere; $16.00/yr. individuals US; $20.00/yr. individuals elsewhere
Year to which price refers: 1991-92

ADVERTISING INFORMATION

Advertising accepted: Yes
Advertising rates: $50.00/quarter page; $100.00/half page; $200.00/full page

EDITORIAL DESCRIPTION

Scope: Publishes material dealing with Spanish and Spanish American culture and literature.
Reviews books: Yes
Publishes notes: Yes
Languages accepted: Spanish; English
Prints abstracts: No
Author-anonymous submission: No

SUBMISSION REQUIREMENTS

Restrictions on contributors: None
Author pays submission fee: No
Author pays page charges: No
Length of articles: 25 pp. maximum
Style: MLA Manual, 2nd ed.
Number of copies required: 3
Special requirements: Submit double-spaced typescript. Notes should be placed at the end of text. Submit original typescript plus 2 copies.
Copyright ownership: Univ. of Northern Colorado
Rejected manuscripts: Original returned; enclose return postage.
Time before publication decision: 6-12 mos.
Time between decision and publication: 4 mos.
Number of reviewers: 2
Articles submitted per year: 80

Articles published per year: 35-40
Book reviews submitted per year: 15
Book reviews published per year: 8-10
Notes submitted per year: 25
Notes published per year: 14

(663)
*Connotations: A Journal for Critical Debate

Inge Leimberg, Lothar Černy, Michael Steppat, & Matthias Bauer, Editors
Westfälische Wilhelms-Univ.
Dept. of English
Johannisstr. 12-20
4400 Munster, Germany

Telephone: (49) 251 834589
Fax: (49) 251 834827
First published: 1991
Sponsoring organization: Westfälische Wilhelms-Univ.
ISSN: 0939-5482
MLA acronym: Connotations

SUBSCRIPTION INFORMATION

Frequency of publication: 3 times/yr. (Mar., July, Nov.)
Available in microform: No
Subscription price: Print version: 53 DM/yr. Europe; $40.00/yr. elsewhere. Disk version: 30 DM/yr. Europe; $20.00/yr. elsewhere
Year to which price refers: 1992
Subscription address: Waxmann Verlag GmbH, Steinfurter Str. 555, 4400 Munster, Germany
Additional subscription address: Waxmann Publishing Co., P.O. Box 1318, New York, NY 10028
Subscription telephone: (49) 251 217798
Subscription fax: (49) 251 216075

ADVERTISING INFORMATION

Advertising accepted: Yes

EDITORIAL DESCRIPTION

Scope: Aims to encourage scholarly communications in the field of English literature (from the Middle English period to the present), as well as American and Commonwealth literature. It focuses on the semantic and stylistic energy of the language of literature in a historical perspective. Each issue consists of articles and a forum for discussion. The forum includes research in progress, critical hypotheses, and responses to articles published in *Connotations* and elsewhere, as well as comments on recent books, and authors' answers to reviews. The journal is available in print and on diskette.
Reviews books: No
Publishes notes: Yes
Languages accepted: English
Prints abstracts: No
Author-anonymous submission: No

SUBMISSION REQUIREMENTS

Author pays submission fee: No
Author pays page charges: No
Length of articles: 12,000 words maximum
Length of notes: 4,000 words
Style: MLA
Number of copies required: 1
Special requirements: Submit printout accompanied by DOS diskette.
Copyright ownership: Publisher
Rejected manuscripts: Returned; enclose international reply coupons.
Time before publication decision: 2-4 weeks
Time between decision and publication: 1-5 mos.
Number of reviewers: 2-3
Articles submitted per year: 60
Articles published per year: 12
Notes submitted per year: 40
Notes published per year: 20

(664)
*The Conradian

Robert Hampson & Owen Knowles, Editors
Dept. of English
Royal Holloway & Bedford New College
Egham, Surrey TW20 0EX, England

First published: 1975
Sponsoring organization: Joseph Conrad Soc.
MLA acronym: Conradian

SUBSCRIPTION INFORMATION

Frequency of publication: 2 times/yr. (May, Sept.)
Available in microform: No
Subscription price: £12.00/yr.
Year to which price refers: 1991

ADVERTISING INFORMATION

Advertising accepted: Yes

EDITORIAL DESCRIPTION

Scope: Publishes articles on Joseph Conrad, including his context and his contemporaries.
Reviews books: Yes
Publishes notes: Yes
Languages accepted: English
Prints abstracts: No

SUBMISSION REQUIREMENTS

Restrictions on contributors: Unsolicited book reviews are not accepted.
Author pays submission fee: No
Author pays page charges: No
Length of articles: 8,000-10,000 words
Length of book reviews: 2,000 words maximum
Length of notes: 2,000 words maximum
Style: MLA
Number of copies required: 1
Copyright ownership: Journal
Time before publication decision: 6 mos.
Time between decision and publication: 3 mos.
Number of reviewers: 2
Articles submitted per year: 60
Articles published per year: 14
Book reviews published per year: 15
Notes submitted per year: 40
Notes published per year: 10

(665)
*Conradiana: A Journal of Joseph Conrad Studies

David Leon Higdon, Editor
Dept. of English
P.O. Box 43091
Texas Tech Univ.
Lubbock, TX 79409-3091

Telephone: 806 742-2527
Fax: 806 742-2527
First published: 1968
ISSN: 0010-6356
MLA acronym: Conradiana

SUBSCRIPTION INFORMATION

Frequency of publication: 3 times/yr. (Jan., May, Sept.)
Circulation: 800
Available in microform: Yes
Subscription price: $16.00/yr. US; $19.00/yr. elsewhere
Year to which price refers: 1992
Subscription address: Sales Office, Texas Tech Univ. Press, Lubbock, TX 79409-1037
Subscription telephone: 806 742-0158

ADVERTISING INFORMATION

Advertising accepted: Yes

EDITORIAL DESCRIPTION

Scope: An international journal devoted to all aspects and periods of the life and works of Joseph Conrad.
Reviews books: Yes
Publishes notes: Yes
Languages accepted: English
Prints abstracts: No
Author-anonymous submission: No

SUBMISSION REQUIREMENTS

Restrictions on contributors: None
Author pays submission fee: No
Author pays page charges: No
Length of articles: 50 typescript pp. maximum
Length of book reviews: 2,000 words maximum
Length of notes: No restrictions
Style: Chicago
Number of copies required: 2
Special requirements: Manuscripts should be submitted in hard copy as well as on IBM-compatible diskettes, preferably as ASCII files.
Copyright ownership: Texas Tech Univ. Press
Rejected manuscripts: Returned; enclose return postage.
Time before publication decision: 2 mos.
Time between decision and publication: 12-18 mos.
Number of reviewers: 3
Articles submitted per year: 75
Articles published per year: 18
Book reviews submitted per year: 10-12
Book reviews published per year: 10
Notes submitted per year: 15
Notes published per year: 3

(666)
*Constructions

Michelle R. Wright, Editor
Dept. of French & Italian
Stanford Univ.
Stanford, CA 94305-2010

Telephone: 415 723-4183
E-mail: Mrw@leland.stanford.edu
First published: 1984
Sponsoring organization: Dept. of French & Italian, Stanford Univ.; Dept. of Comparative Literature, Stanford Univ.; Program of Interdisciplinary Research, Stanford Univ.; Assoc. Students of Stanford Univ.
ISSN: 0898-8609
MLA acronym: Constructions

SUBSCRIPTION INFORMATION

Frequency of publication: Annual
Available in microform: No
Subscription price: $10.00/yr.
Year to which price refers: 1992

ADVERTISING INFORMATION

Advertising accepted: Yes

EDITORIAL DESCRIPTION

Scope: Publishes critical essays in the fields of literature and culture including art, philosophy, and history. Submissions from all humanistic disciplines and interdisciplinary approaches are welcome. Interviews, conference reviews, and book reviews are also published.
Reviews books: Yes
Publishes notes: Yes
Languages accepted: French; English
Prints abstracts: No
Author-anonymous submission: Yes

SUBMISSION REQUIREMENTS

Restrictions on contributors: Contributors must be graduate students.
Author pays submission fee: No
Author pays page charges: No

Length of articles: 15-20 double-spaced typescript pp.
Length of book reviews: 5-10 pp.
Length of notes: No restrictions
Style: MLA
Number of copies required: 2
Special requirements: Final version must be submitted on diskette using Microsoft Word for Macintosh.
Copyright ownership: Journal
Rejected manuscripts: Returned; enclose return postage.
Time before publication decision: 2 mos.
Time between decision and publication: 5 mos.
Number of reviewers: 2 minimum
Articles submitted per year: 30
Articles published per year: 3-5
Book reviews submitted per year: 3
Book reviews published per year: 3

(667)
*Contemporary Approaches to Ibsen

Bjørn Hemmer & Vigdis Ystad, Editors
Norwegian Univ. Press
P.O. Box 2959 Tøyen
0608 Oslo 6, Norway

Telephone: (47) 2 677600
Fax: (47) 2 677575
First published: 1952
Sponsoring organization: Norges Almenvitenskapelige Forskningsråd (Norwegian Research Council for Science & Humanities)
ISSN: 0073-4365
MLA acronym: CAtI

SUBSCRIPTION INFORMATION

Frequency of publication: Once every 2 yrs.
Available in microform: No
Subscription address: Norwegian Univ. Press, Order Dept., P.O. Box 2977 Tøyen, 0608 Oslo 6, Norway
Additional subscription address: In the US: Oxford Univ. Press, 16-00 Pollitt Dr., Fair Lawn, NJ 07410; outside US & Scandinavia: Oxford Univ. Press Distribution Services, Saxon Way West, Corby, Northants NN18 9ES, England

ADVERTISING INFORMATION

Advertising accepted: No

EDITORIAL DESCRIPTION

Scope: Publishes articles on Henrik Ibsen and his work.
Reviews books: Yes
Publishes notes: Yes
Languages accepted: English
Prints abstracts: No
Author-anonymous submission: No

SUBMISSION REQUIREMENTS

Restrictions on contributors: None
Author pays submission fee: No
Author pays page charges: No
Length of articles: 10,000 words
Length of book reviews: 5,000 words
Length of notes: 500 words
Style: Norwegian Univ. Press
Number of copies required: 2
Copyright ownership: Norwegian Univ. Press
Rejected manuscripts: Returned
Time before publication decision: 6 mos.
Time between decision and publication: 6 mos.
Number of reviewers: 3
Articles published per year: 20

(668)
*Contemporary Legend: The Journal of the International Society for Contemporary Legend Research

Paul Smith, Editor
Dept. of Folklore
Memorial Univ. of Newfoundland
St. John's, Newfoundland A1C 5S7, Canada

Telephone: 709 737-8402
Fax: 709 737-4569
E-mail: IFSBAC@KEAN.UCS.MUN.CA
First published: 1991
Sponsoring organization: International Soc. for Contemporary Legend
ISSN: 0963-8334
MLA acronym: CLeg

SUBSCRIPTION INFORMATION

Frequency of publication: Annual
Circulation: 150
Available in microform: No
Subscription price: £20.00/yr. institutions United Kingdom & Europe; £22.00/yr. institutions elsewhere; £10.00 ($18.00/yr.) individuals
Year to which price refers: 1992
Additional subscription address: Hisarlik Press, 4 Catisfield Rd., Enfield Lock, Middlesex EN3 6BD, England
Subscription telephone: (44) 992 700898
Subscription fax: (44) 992 700898

ADVERTISING INFORMATION

Advertising accepted: Yes
Advertising rates: £20.00/full page

EDITORIAL DESCRIPTION

Scope: Publishes articles on contemporary legends. Aims to promote research and provide a forum for those working in the area of traditional narrative scholarship. Legend is interpreted in its broadest sense to include Sagen, dites, popular rumors, sayings and beliefs as well as narrative. Contemporary refers to modern urban legends as well as to legends in active circulation within a given community.
Reviews books: Yes
Publishes notes: Yes
Languages accepted: English
Prints abstracts: No
Author-anonymous submission: Yes

SUBMISSION REQUIREMENTS

Restrictions on contributors: None
Author pays submission fee: No
Author pays page charges: No
Length of articles: 5,000-8,000 words
Length of book reviews: 500-1,000 words
Length of notes: 2,000-4,000 words
Style: Chicago
Number of copies required: 1
Special requirements: Submission of typescript along with diskette using WordPerfect or ASCII format is preferred.
Copyright ownership: Hisarlik Press
Rejected manuscripts: Returned
Number of reviewers: 2
Articles published per year: 10
Notes published per year: 1

(669)
*Contemporary Literature

Thomas Schaub, Editor
Dept. of English
Helen C. White Hall
600 N. Park St.
Univ. of Wisconsin
Madison, WI 53706

Telephone: 608 263-3775
First published: 1960
Sponsoring organization: Univ. of Wisconsin
ISSN: 0010-7484
MLA acronym: ConL

SUBSCRIPTION INFORMATION

Frequency of publication: 4 times/yr. (Spring, Summer, Fall, Winter)
Circulation: 2,000
Available in microform: Yes
Subscription price: $47.00/yr. institutions; $20.00/yr. individuals; add $8.00/yr. postage outside US
Year to which price refers: 1992
Subscription address: Journal Division, Univ. of Wisconsin Press, 114 N. Murray St., Madison, WI 53715
Subscription telephone: 608 262-4952

ADVERTISING INFORMATION

Advertising accepted: Yes
Advertising rates: $125.00/half page; $215.00/full page

EDITORIAL DESCRIPTION

Scope: Publishes articles on all forms of contemporary literature written in English or translated into English. Publishes interviews with contemporary writers.
Reviews books: Yes
Publishes notes: No
Languages accepted: English
Prints abstracts: No
Author-anonymous submission: No

SUBMISSION REQUIREMENTS

Restrictions on contributors: Manuscripts simultaneously under consideration elsewhere are not reviewed. Book reviews are commissioned.
Author pays submission fee: No
Author pays page charges: No
Length of articles: 25-30 pp.
Style: MLA
Number of copies required: 1
Copyright ownership: Assigned by author to Univ. of Wisconsin Press
Rejected manuscripts: Returned; enclose return postage.
Time before publication decision: 3-4 mos.
Time between decision and publication: 1 yr.
Number of reviewers: 2-4
Articles submitted per year: 220
Articles published per year: 20
Book reviews published per year: 15-20

(670)
*Contemporary Review

Richard Mullen & Anselma Bruce, Editors
61 Carey St.
London WC2A 2JG, England

First published: 1866
ISSN: 0100-7565
MLA acronym: ContempR

SUBSCRIPTION INFORMATION

Frequency of publication: 12 times/yr.
Circulation: 1,800
Available in microform: Yes
Subscription price: £29.00/yr. United Kingdom; $130.00/yr. US & Canada
Year to which price refers: 1992-93

ADVERTISING INFORMATION

Advertising accepted: Yes

EDITORIAL DESCRIPTION

Scope: International subjects in the widest sense receive considerable attention. Also has a wide spectrum of interests including home affairs and politics, literature and the arts, history, travel, and religion. Has a monthly book section and occasional reviews of recent fiction.
Reviews books: Yes
Publishes notes: Yes
Languages accepted: English
Prints abstracts: No
Author-anonymous submission: Yes, if author requests with good reason.

SUBMISSION REQUIREMENTS

Restrictions on contributors: Book reviews and most other works are commissioned.
Author pays submission fee: No
Author pays page charges: No
Length of articles: 2,000-3,000 words
Length of book reviews: 300-500 words
Style: None
Number of copies required: 1-2
Special requirements: Consult journal before submitting articles.
Copyright ownership: Negotiated
Rejected manuscripts: Returned; enclose SAE or international postal coupons.
Time before publication decision: 2 weeks
Number of reviewers: 1
Articles published per year: 100
Book reviews published per year: 100

(671)
*Continuum: Problems in French Literature from the Late Renaissance to the Early Enlightenment

AMS Press, Inc.
56 E. 13th St.
New York, NY 10003

First published: 1989
Sponsoring organization: Univ. of Virginia, Center for Advanced Studies, College of Arts and Sciences, & Dept. of French
ISSN: 0899-4307
MLA acronym: Continuum

SUBSCRIPTION INFORMATION

Frequency of publication: Annual
Available in microform: No

ADVERTISING INFORMATION

Advertising accepted: No

EDITORIAL DESCRIPTION

Scope: Publishes collections on theoretical, historical, and interpretive issues in the study of early modern French literature.
Reviews books: Yes
Languages accepted: English; French
Prints abstracts: No
Author-anonymous submission: Yes

SUBMISSION REQUIREMENTS

Restrictions on contributors: All contributors are invited.
Author pays submission fee: No
Author pays page charges: No
Length of articles: 10,000 words maximum
Length of book reviews: 2,000 words
Style: MLA
Number of copies required: 2
Copyright ownership: AMS Press
Rejected manuscripts: Returned
Time before publication decision: 1 mo.
Time between decision and publication: 1 yr.
Number of reviewers: 2 minimum
Articles submitted per year: 20
Articles published per year: 10

Book reviews submitted per year: 10
Book reviews published per year: 10

(672)
Contrastes: Revue de l'Association pour le Développement des Etudes Contrastives

Anne-Marie Loffler-Laurian, Marc Tukia, & Georges Kassai, Editors
A.D.E.C.
99, bd. Saint-Michel
75005 Paris, France

Telephone: (33) 93130555
First published: 1981
Sponsoring organization: Assn. pour le Développement des Etudes Contrastives
ISSN: 0247-915X
MLA acronym: Contrastes

SUBSCRIPTION INFORMATION

Frequency of publication: 2 times/yr. (June, Dec.) plus one special issue
Circulation: 500
Available in microform: No
Subscription address: L'Editions, 15, rue Alberti, 06047 Nice Cedex, France

ADVERTISING INFORMATION

Advertising accepted: Yes, on an exchange basis

EDITORIAL DESCRIPTION

Scope: Publishes articles on contrastive linguistics including studies of applied linguistics, language instruction, and translation.
Reviews books: Yes
Publishes notes: Yes
Languages accepted: French; English; German; Spanish
Prints abstracts: No
Author-anonymous submission: No

SUBMISSION REQUIREMENTS

Restrictions on contributors: Contributors must be subscribers.
Author pays submission fee: No
Author pays page charges: No
Length of articles: 5,000-7,000 words
Length of book reviews: 400-1,200 words
Length of notes: 2,000-3,000 words
Number of copies required: 2
Copyright ownership: Journal
Time before publication decision: 1-3 mos.
Time between decision and publication: 6-18 mos.
Number of reviewers: 3
Articles published per year: 25
Book reviews submitted per year: 50-100

(673)
Contributi dell'Istituto di Filologia Moderna. Ser. Ital. 1. Univ. Cattolica del Sacro Cuore

Istituto di Filologia Moderna
Univ. del Sacro Cuore
Milan, Italy

First published: 1968
ISSN: 0544-1595
MLA acronym: CIFM

SUBSCRIPTION INFORMATION

Frequency of publication: Annual

(674)
*Contributions to the Study of World Literature

Marilyn Brownstein, Editor
Greenwood Press
88 Post Rd. West
Box 5007
Westport, CT 06881-9990

Telephone: 203 336-3571
Fax: 203 222-1502
First published: 1983
MLA acronym: CSWL

SUBSCRIPTION INFORMATION

Frequency of publication: Irregular
Available in microform: No

EDITORIAL DESCRIPTION

Scope: Publishes monographs of original scholarship on literature geared mainly to academic libraries and the profession.
Languages accepted: English
Author-anonymous submission: No

SUBMISSION REQUIREMENTS

Length of books: 50,000-100,000 words
Style: MLA; Chicago
Number of copies required: 1
Copyright ownership: Author
Rejected manuscripts: Returned
Time before publication decision: 2-3 mos.
Time between decision and publication: 8-9 mos.
Number of reviewers: 1-2

(675)
Convorbiri Literare

Corneliu Sturzu, Editor
Uniunea Scriitorilor din Republica Socialista Romania
Calea Victoriei 115
Bucharest, Romania

First published: 1867
Sponsoring organization: Iași Soc. "Junimea"; Uniuni Scriitorilor din România
ISSN: 0010-8243
MLA acronym: ConLit

SUBSCRIPTION INFORMATION

Frequency of publication: 12 times/yr.
Circulation: 5,000
Available in microform: No
Subscription address: ILEXIM, Str. 13 Decembrie, Nr. 3, Box 136-137, 70116 Bucharest, Romania

ADVERTISING INFORMATION

Advertising accepted: Yes

EDITORIAL DESCRIPTION

Scope: Publishes articles on contemporary Romanian literature.
Reviews books: Yes
Publishes notes: Yes
Languages accepted: Romanian; French; English; Russian
Prints abstracts: No

SUBMISSION REQUIREMENTS

Restrictions on contributors: No
Author pays submission fee: Yes

Author pays page charges: No
Length of articles: 1,000-1,200 words
Length of book reviews: 600-800 words
Length of notes: 150-300 words
Style: None
Number of copies required: 2
Copyright ownership: Author
Rejected manuscripts: Not returned
Time before publication decision: 1-2 mos.
Time between decision and publication: 1 mo.
Number of reviewers: 2
Articles submitted per year: 110
Articles published per year: 50
Book reviews submitted per year: 160
Book reviews published per year: 100
Notes submitted per year: 160
Notes published per year: 100

(676)
*Copenhagen Studies in Language

Niels Davidsen-Nielsen, Editor
Copenhagen Business School
Dept. of English
Dalgas Have 15
2000 Frederiksberg, Denmark

Telephone: (45) 31 191919
Fax: (45) 31 861188
First published: 1970
Sponsoring organization: Faculty of Languages, Copenhagen Business School
ISSN: 0905-9857
MLA acronym: CSiL

SUBSCRIPTION INFORMATION

Frequency of publication: Annual
Available in microform: No
Subscription price: 100 Dkr/yr.
Year to which price refers: 1991
Additional subscription address: Nyt Nordisk Forlag, Købmagergade 49, 1150 Copenhagen K, Denmark
Subscription telephone: (45) 33 111103
Subscription fax: (45) 33 934490

ADVERTISING INFORMATION

Advertising accepted: No

EDITORIAL DESCRIPTION

Scope: Publishes studies in both general and specialized language, social and institutional background, and language teaching methods. Focuses on language for special purposes, and theoretical and applied linguistics.
Reviews books: Yes
Publishes notes: Yes
Languages accepted: English; French; German; Italian; Spanish
Prints abstracts: Yes
Author-anonymous submission: No

SUBMISSION REQUIREMENTS

Restrictions on contributors: Contributors are mainly faculty of the Copenhagen Business School, but papers by other contributors are accepted.
Author pays submission fee: No
Author pays page charges: No
Length of articles: 10,000 words
Length of book reviews: 2,500 words
Length of notes: 1,000 words
Style: MLA; Linguistic Soc. of America
Number of copies required: 3
Copyright ownership: Handelshøjskolens Forlag
Rejected manuscripts: Returned
Time before publication decision: 2 mos.
Time between decision and publication: 6 mos.
Number of reviewers: 2
Articles published per year: 3-8
Book reviews published per year: 1-2

(677)
*Coranto: Journal of the Friends of the Libraries, University of Southern California

Gerald Lange, Managing Editor
USC Fine Arts Press
USC Research Annex 122
3716 South Hope St.
Los Angeles, CA 90007

Telephone: 213 743-3939
First published: 1963
Sponsoring organization: Univ. of Southern California, Friends of the Univ. of Southern California Libraries
ISSN: 0010-8669
MLA acronym: Coranto

SUBSCRIPTION INFORMATION

Frequency of publication: Annual

ADVERTISING INFORMATION

Advertising accepted: No

EDITORIAL DESCRIPTION

Reviews books: No
Publishes notes: No
Languages accepted: English
Prints abstracts: No
Author-anonymous submission: No

SUBMISSION REQUIREMENTS

Author pays submission fee: No
Author pays page charges: No
Style: Chicago
Copyright ownership: Univ. of Southern California

(678)
Cornell Working Papers in Linguistics

Wayne Harbert, Editor
Dept. of Modern Languages & Linguistics
Cornell Univ.
Ithaca, NY 14853-4701

First published: 1980
Sponsoring organization: Dept. of Modern Languages & Linguistics, Cornell Univ.
ISSN: 0888-3122
MLA acronym: CWPL

SUBSCRIPTION INFORMATION

Frequency of publication: Irregular
Circulation: 200
Available in microform: No

ADVERTISING INFORMATION

Advertising accepted: No

EDITORIAL DESCRIPTION

Scope: Publishes papers in linguistics written by the faculty and students of Cornell University.
Reviews books: No
Publishes notes: No
Languages accepted: English
Prints abstracts: No

SUBMISSION REQUIREMENTS

Restrictions on contributors: Contributors must be faculty members or students at Cornell Univ. or be invited contributors.
Author pays submission fee: No
Author pays page charges: No
Length of articles: 12-20 pp.
Style: Linguistic Soc. of America
Number of copies required: 1

Special requirements: Submit camera-ready copy and a 100-word abstract.
Copyright ownership: Author
Rejected manuscripts: Returned
Time between decision and publication: 3 mos.
Number of reviewers: 2
Articles submitted per year: 15
Articles published per year: 11

(679)
*Corona: Marking the Edges of Many Circles

Lynda Sexson & Michael Sexson, Editors
Dept. of History & Philosophy
Montana State Univ.
Bozeman, MT 59717

First published: 1980
Sponsoring organization: National Endowment for the Humanities; Montana Committee for the Humanities; Montana State Univ. Research & Endowment Organization
ISSN: 0270-6687
MLA acronym: Corona

SUBSCRIPTION INFORMATION

Frequency of publication: Irregular
Circulation: 1,500
Available in microform: No

ADVERTISING INFORMATION

Advertising accepted: Yes

EDITORIAL DESCRIPTION

Scope: Includes speculative essays, criticism, musical scores, artwork, photography, short stories, and poetry.
Reviews books: Yes
Publishes notes: No
Languages accepted: English
Prints abstracts: No
Author-anonymous submission: No

SUBMISSION REQUIREMENTS

Author pays submission fee: No
Author pays page charges: No
Length of articles: No restrictions
Length of book reviews: No restrictions
Style: Chicago
Number of copies required: 1
Special requirements: Previously published work is not accepted.
Copyright ownership: Copyright reverts from journal to author after 1 yr.
Rejected manuscripts: Returned; enclose return postage.
Time before publication decision: 1-6 mos.
Number of reviewers: 3-8
Articles submitted per year: 2,000
Articles published per year: 20
Book reviews published per year: 10

(680)
La Corónica: Spanish Medieval Language and Literature Journal and Newsletter

Spurgeon Baldwin, Editor
Dept. of Romance Languages & Classics
Univ. of Alabama
Tuscaloosa, AL 35487

First published: 1972
Sponsoring organization: MLA, Division on Spanish Medieval Language & Literature
ISSN: 0193-3892
MLA acronym: Corónica

SUBSCRIPTION INFORMATION

Frequency of publication: 2 times/yr.

Circulation: 375
Available in microform: No
Subscription price: $25.00/yr. institutions; $10.00/yr., $18.00/2 yrs. individuals
Year to which price refers: 1992
Subscription address: Barbara Weissgerger, Managing Editor, Dept. of Foreign Languages & Literatures, Old Dominion Univ., Norfolk, VA 23529

ADVERTISING INFORMATION

Advertising accepted: No

EDITORIAL DESCRIPTION

Scope: Publishes articles, notes, bibliographies, reports, reviews, short texts, miscellanea, personalia, and announcements in the area of Spanish Medieval language and literature, with an emphasis on the latter.
Reviews books: Yes
Publishes notes: Yes
Languages accepted: English; Spanish
Prints abstracts: Yes
Author-anonymous submission: No

SUBMISSION REQUIREMENTS

Restrictions on contributors: None
Author pays submission fee: No
Author pays page charges: No
Length of articles: 5,000 words
Length of book reviews: 1,500 words
Length of notes: 2,400 words
Style: MLA
Number of copies required: 2
Special requirements: Submission on diskette in ASCII format is suggested.
Copyright ownership: Journal
Rejected manuscripts: Returned; enclose SASE.
Time before publication decision: 2 mos.
Time between decision and publication: 6 mos.
Number of reviewers: 2
Articles submitted per year: 25
Articles published per year: 12
Book reviews submitted per year: 15
Book reviews published per year: 10
Notes submitted per year: 12
Notes published per year: 8

(681)
Corps Ecrit

Béatrice Didier, Editor
Maison Honnorat
21 bd. Jourdan
75014 Paris, France

First published: 1982
Sponsoring organization: Centre National des Letters
ISSN: 0751-5022
MLA acronym: CEc

SUBSCRIPTION INFORMATION

Frequency of publication: 4 times/yr.
Available in microform: No

ADVERTISING INFORMATION

Advertising accepted: No

EDITORIAL DESCRIPTION

Scope: Publishes articles in such diverse disciplines as literature, drama, art, film, poetry, aesthetics, and philosophy.
Reviews books: No
Publishes notes: No
Languages accepted: French
Prints abstracts: No

SUBMISSION REQUIREMENTS

Author pays submission fee: Yes
Author pays page charges: Yes
Style: Journal

Number of copies required: 2
Copyright ownership: Publisher
Time before publication decision: 1 yr.
Time between decision and publication: 6 mos.
Number of reviewers: 27
Articles submitted per year: 200
Articles published per year: 100

(682)
*Costerus

Theo D'haen, C. C. Barfoot, Erik Kooper, & Hans Bertens, Editors
Rijksuniversiteit Leiden
Dept. of English
2300 RA Leiden, Netherlands

Telephone: (31) 71 272158
First published: 1972
ISSN: 0165-9618
MLA acronym: Costerus

SUBSCRIPTION INFORMATION

Circulation: 500
Available in microform: No
Subscription address: Editions Rodopi, Keizersgracht 302-304, 1016 EX Amsterdam, Netherlands
Additional subscription address: Editions Rodopi, 233 Peachtree St. N.E., Suite 404, Atlanta, GA 30303-1504
Subscription telephone: (31) 20 6227507; 404 523-1964

ADVERTISING INFORMATION

Advertising accepted: No

EDITORIAL DESCRIPTION

Scope: Publishes essays on all periods and genres of English and American literature. Many articles are solicited or commissioned, but unsolicited material is welcome. Rarely publishes essays that are exclusively critical in focus, but editors are interested in heavily-researched, fully documented articles on authors' lives, writings, and professional careers. Original source materials, authors' manuscripts, letters and other such documents, are particularly solicited. Editors also interested in textual, bibliographical, and canonical scholarship.
Reviews books: Yes
Publishes notes: No
Languages accepted: English
Prints abstracts: No

SUBMISSION REQUIREMENTS

Author pays submission fee: No
Author pays page charges: No
Length of books: 100-125 pp.
Style: MLA
Number of copies required: 2
Special requirements: Include a 100-word abstract.
Copyright ownership: Editions Rodopi
Rejected manuscripts: Returned; enclose return postage
Time before publication decision: 1 mo.
Time between decision and publication: 3 mos.
Books published per year: 2 minimum

(683)
*Council on National Literatures/World Report

Anne Paolucci, Editor
Council on National Literatures
P.O. Box 81
Whitestone, NY 11357

Telephone: 718 767-8380; 718 767-5364
Fax: 718 767-8380

First published: 1974
Sponsoring organization: Council on National Literatures
ISSN: 0145-6873
MLA acronym: CNLR

SUBSCRIPTION INFORMATION

Frequency of publication: Annual
Circulation: 1,000
Available in microform: No
Subscription price: $35.00/yr. US; $45.00/yr. elsewhere
Year to which price refers: 1992

ADVERTISING INFORMATION

Advertising accepted: Yes
Advertising rates: $90.00/half page; $150.00/full page; $200.00/back cover

EDITORIAL DESCRIPTION

Scope: Serves as the medium for the Council's continuing world-wide dialogue among comparatists and special literatures experts on matters pertaining to the future of comparative literary studies. Publishes papers delivered at the annual CNL/MLA meetings, brief translations of articles published elsewhere, and author and subject issues
Reviews books: Yes
Publishes notes: Yes
Languages accepted: English
Prints abstracts: Yes
Author-anonymous submission: Yes

SUBMISSION REQUIREMENTS

Restrictions on contributors: None
Author pays submission fee: No
Author pays page charges: No
Length of articles: 5-10 double-spaced typescript pp.
Length of book reviews: 300-500 words
Length of notes: 300-500 words
Style: MLA
Number of copies required: 2
Special requirements: Type footnotes at end.
Copyright ownership: Council on National Literatures
Rejected manuscripts: Returned; enclose SASE.
Time before publication decision: 8 mos.
Time between decision and publication: 8 mos.
Number of reviewers: 2
Articles submitted per year: 15-20
Articles published per year: 4-6
Book reviews submitted per year: 12
Book reviews published per year: 4

(684)
*Country Dance and Song

David E. E. Sloane, Editor
Univ. of New Haven
300 Orange Ave.
West Haven, CT 06516

Telephone: 203 777-0677; 203 932-7371
Fax: 203 932-1469
First published: 1970
Sponsoring organization: Country Dance & Song Soc. of America
MLA acronym: CD&S

SUBSCRIPTION INFORMATION

Frequency of publication: Annual
Circulation: 2,500-3,000
Subscription price: $15.00/yr.
Year to which price refers: 1992
Subscription address: Country Dance & Song Soc. of America, 17 New South St., Northampton, MA 01060
Subscription telephone: 413 584-9913

EDITORIAL DESCRIPTION

Scope: Publishes articles on social dance and music in England and America, and related historical materials.
Reviews books: Yes
Publishes notes: Yes
Languages accepted: English
Prints abstracts: No
Author-anonymous submission: Yes

SUBMISSION REQUIREMENTS

Restrictions on contributors: None
Author pays submission fee: No
Author pays page charges: No
Length of articles: 2,000-5,000 words
Length of book reviews: 1,000-1,500 words
Length of notes: 500-1,500 words
Style: None
Number of copies required: 3
Special requirements: Accepted articles should be submitted on diskette in WordPerfect.
Copyright ownership: Journal
Rejected manuscripts: Returned
Time before publication decision: 3 mos. maximum
Time between decision and publication: 6-10 mos.
Number of reviewers: 3
Articles submitted per year: 1-10
Articles published per year: 3-5
Notes submitted per year: 1-2
Notes published per year: 1-2

(685)
*Courrier du Centre International d'Études Poétiques

F. Verhesen & F. De Haes, Editors
Boulevard de L'Empereur 4
1000 Brussels, Belgium

Telephone: (32) 2 5195580
Fax: (32) 2 5195533
First published: 1954
Sponsoring organization: Archives & Musée de la Littérature
ISSN: 0771-6443
MLA acronym: CCIEP

SUBSCRIPTION INFORMATION

Frequency of publication: 4 times/yr.
Available in microform: No
Subscription price: 800 BF/yr.
Year to which price refers: 1992

ADVERTISING INFORMATION

Advertising accepted: No

EDITORIAL DESCRIPTION

Scope: Publishes articles on the studies of modern poetical writing.
Reviews books: No
Publishes notes: No
Languages accepted: French
Prints abstracts: No
Author-anonymous submission: No

SUBMISSION REQUIREMENTS

Author pays submission fee: No
Author pays page charges: No
Length of articles: 15-20 pp.
Number of copies required: 2
Copyright ownership: Author
Rejected manuscripts: Returned
Time before publication decision: 5-12 mos.
Time between decision and publication: 4-6 mos.
Articles submitted per year: 20-25
Articles published per year: 15-16

(686)
Cowrie: A Chinese Journal of Comparative Literature

Jingyao Sun & Mark Bender, Editors
Comparative Literature Center
Guangxi Univ.
Nanning
Guangxi Zhuang Autonomous Region, People's Republic of China

First published: 1983
MLA acronym: Cowrie

SUBSCRIPTION INFORMATION

Frequency of publication: Annual (Spring)
Available in microform: No

ADVERTISING INFORMATION

Advertising accepted: No

EDITORIAL DESCRIPTION

Scope: The journal publishes articles on comparative literature and arts with an emphasis on Asia.
Reviews books: Yes
Publishes notes: No
Languages accepted: Chinese languages; English
Prints abstracts: No

SUBMISSION REQUIREMENTS

Restrictions on contributors: Articles from China must have appeared in other Chinese publications. Footnotes must appear at the end of the article.
Author pays submission fee: No
Author pays page charges: No
Length of articles: 3,000-3,500 words
Number of copies required: 2
Special requirements: Submit query before sending manuscript.
Rejected manuscripts: Returned if solicited
Time before publication decision: 6 mos.
Time between decision and publication: 6-8 mos.
Number of reviewers: 4-8
Articles published per year: 7

(687)
*Creative Forum: A Quarterly Journal of Contemporary Writing

Ravinder K. Bahri & Ujjal Singh Bahri, Editors
Bahri Books & Periodicals
997A, Street No. 9
P.O. Box 4453
Gobindpuri, Kalkaji
New Delhi 110019, India

Telephone: (91) 11 6448606; (91) 11 6445710
Fax: (91) 11 6460796
First published: 1988
MLA acronym: CrF

SUBSCRIPTION INFORMATION

Frequency of publication: 2 times/yr.
Circulation: 190
Available in microform: No
Subscription price: $40.00/yr.
Year to which price refers: 1992

ADVERTISING INFORMATION

Advertising accepted: Yes
Advertising rates: $100.00/full page

EDITORIAL DESCRIPTION

Scope: Focuses on contemporary literary studies, latest trends and critical methods with a balanced coverage of late 20th-century literature, and current literary practices in India and elsewhere. Includes short stories and poems, both original and in translation.
Reviews books: Yes
Languages accepted: English
Prints abstracts: No
Author-anonymous submission: No

SUBMISSION REQUIREMENTS

Restrictions on contributors: None
Author pays submission fee: Yes, if paper exceeds 20 pp.
Cost of submission fee: $30.00-$50.00
Author pays page charges: No
Length of articles: 12-16 pp.
Length of book reviews: 8-10 pp.
Style: MLA
Number of copies required: 2
Special requirements: Use size A4 (8 1/4 in. x 11 3/4 in.) paper. Include a 150-word abstract.
Copyright ownership: Bahri Publications; reverts to author after 3 yrs.
Rejected manuscripts: Returned; enclose return postage.
Time before publication decision: 10 weeks
Time between decision and publication: 3-4 mos.
Number of reviewers: 2
Articles submitted per year: 60-70
Articles published per year: 56-60
Book reviews submitted per year: 10-15
Book reviews published per year: 10-15

(688)
*Creole Language Library

Pieter Muysken & John V. Singler, Editors
Dept. of General Linguistics
Spuistraat 210
1012 VT Amsterdam, Netherlands

Additional editorial address: John Singler, Dept. of Linguistics, New York Univ., 719 Broadway, Room 502, New York, NY 10003
First published: 1986
ISSN: 0920-9026
MLA acronym: CLL

SUBSCRIPTION INFORMATION

Frequency of publication: Irregular
Available in microform: No
Subscription address: John Benjamins Publishing Co., Amsteldijk 44, P.O. Box 75577, 1070 AN Amsterdam, Netherlands
Additional subscription address: John Benjamins North America, Inc., 821 Bethlehem Pike, Philadelphia, PA 19118

ADVERTISING INFORMATION

Advertising accepted: No

EDITORIAL DESCRIPTION

Scope: Publishes monographs on descriptive and theoretical studies designed to add significantly to the data available on pidgin and creole languages.
Reviews books: No
Publishes notes: No
Languages accepted: English
Prints abstracts: No
Author-anonymous submission: Yes

SUBMISSION REQUIREMENTS

Author pays submission fee: No
Author pays page charges: No
Style: MLA
Number of copies required: 2
Copyright ownership: John Benjamins B.V.

(689)
Crisol

Charles Minguet & Bernard Sesé, Editors
Centre de Recherches Ibériques & Ibéro-Américaines
Univ. de Paris X-Nanterre
200, Av. de la République
92001 Nanterre Cedex, France

First published: 1983
Sponsoring organization: Centre de Recherches Ibériques & Ibéro-Américaines, Univ. de Paris X-Nanterre
ISSN: 0764-7611
MLA acronym: Crisol

SUBSCRIPTION INFORMATION

Frequency of publication: 2 times/yr.
Available in microform: No
Subscription address: PUBLIDIX-Univ. de Paris X, 200, Av. de la République, 92001 Nanterre Cedex, France

ADVERTISING INFORMATION

Advertising accepted: No

EDITORIAL DESCRIPTION

Scope: Publishes articles on all subjects pertaining to Iberia; this includes but is not limited to the literature and language of Spain, Portugal, Latin America, and Brazil.
Reviews books: Yes
Publishes notes: Yes
Languages accepted: French; Spanish; Portuguese
Prints abstracts: No
Author-anonymous submission: No

SUBMISSION REQUIREMENTS

Author pays submission fee: No
Author pays page charges: No
Length of articles: 10-20 pp.
Time before publication decision: 6 mos.
Number of reviewers: 2
Rejected manuscripts: Returned
Time before publication decision: 2-3 mos.
Time between decision and publication: 6 mos.
Number of reviewers: 2
Books submitted per year: 6-8
Books published per year: 2-3

(690)
*Cristallo: Rassegna di Varia Umanità

Giuseppe Negri, Editor
Centro di Cultura dell'Alto Adige
Via Napoli-1
39100 Bolzano, Italy

Telephone: (39) 471 201354
First published: 1959
Sponsoring organization: Centro di Cultura dell'Alto Adige
ISSN: 0011-1449
MLA acronym: Cristallo

SUBSCRIPTION INFORMATION

Frequency of publication: 3 times/yr. (Apr., Aug., Dec.)
Circulation: 3,000
Available in microform: No

ADVERTISING INFORMATION

Advertising accepted: No

EDITORIAL DESCRIPTION

Scope: Publishes articles on literature, poetry, history, philosophy, and art.
Reviews books: Yes
Publishes notes: Yes
Languages accepted: Italian
Prints abstracts: Yes
Author-anonymous submission: No

SUBMISSION REQUIREMENTS

Restrictions on contributors: None
Author pays submission fee: No
Author pays page charges: No
Length of articles: 20 pp.
Length of book reviews: 2 pp.
Number of copies required: 1
Copyright ownership: Journal
Rejected manuscripts: Not returned
Time before publication decision: 2 mos.
Time between decision and publication: 2 mos.
Number of reviewers: 3
Articles submitted per year: 50
Articles published per year: 35
Book reviews submitted per year: 60
Book reviews published per year: 30
Notes submitted per year: 18
Notes published per year: 12

(691)
*Crítica Hispánica

Gregorio C. Martín, Editor
Duquesne Univ.
Dept. of Modern Languages
Pittsburgh, PA 15282

Telephone: 412 434-6415
Fax: 412 434-5197
First published: 1979
Sponsoring organization: Duquesne Univ., Dept. of Modern Languages
ISSN: 0278-7261
MLA acronym: CH

SUBSCRIPTION INFORMATION

Frequency of publication: 2 times/yr. (Spring, Fall)
Circulation: 225
Available in microform: No
Subscription price: $27.00/yr. institutions US & Canada; $38.00/yr. institutions elsewhere; $12.00/yr. individuals US & Canada; $18.00/yr. individuals elsewhere
Year to which price refers: 1991

ADVERTISING INFORMATION

Advertising accepted: Yes
Advertising rates: $150.00/full page

EDITORIAL DESCRIPTION

Scope: Publishes articles and notes on Spanish and Spanish American literature and linguistics.
Reviews books: Yes
Publishes notes: Yes
Languages accepted: English; Spanish
Prints abstracts: No
Author-anonymous submission: No

SUBMISSION REQUIREMENTS

Restrictions on contributors: None
Author pays submission fee: No
Author pays page charges: No
Length of articles: 20 double-spaced typescript pp.
Length of book reviews: 4 pp.
Length of notes: 5-8 pp.
Style: MLA
Number of copies required: 3
Special requirements: Submit original typescript and 2 copies.
Copyright ownership: Author
Rejected manuscripts: Returned; enclose return postage.
Time before publication decision: 3-5 mos.
Time between decision and publication: 2 yrs.
Number of reviewers: 3
Articles submitted per year: 60
Articles published per year: 10
Book reviews submitted per year: 30
Book reviews published per year: 10
Notes submitted per year: 5
Notes published per year: 2

(692)
Critica Letteraria

Pompeo Giannantonio, Editor
Via Stazio, 15
80123 Naples, Italy

ISSN: 0390-0142
MLA acronym: CritLett

SUBSCRIPTION INFORMATION

Frequency of publication: 4 times/yr.

EDITORIAL DESCRIPTION

Scope: Publishes articles on Italian literature.
Reviews books: Yes
Languages accepted: Italian

(693)
*Critical Arts: A Journal of Cultural Studies

Keyan Gray Tomaselli, Editor
Centre for Cultural & Media Studies
Univ. of Natal
King George V Ave.
Durban 4001, South Africa

Telephone: (27) 31 8162505
Fax: (27) 31 8162214
First published: 1980
Sponsoring organization: Critical Arts Projects
ISSN: 0256-0046
MLA acronym: CArts

SUBSCRIPTION INFORMATION

Frequency of publication: 2 times/yr.
Circulation: 700
Available in microform: No
Subscription price: $56.00/yr.
Year to which price refers: 1993

ADVERTISING INFORMATION

Advertising accepted: Yes, on an exchange basis

EDITORIAL DESCRIPTION

Scope: Publishes articles on language, cinema, television, print, theater, performance, cultural studies, and applications of semiology and semiotics, ideology, popular culture, and sociology.
Reviews books: Yes
Publishes notes: Yes
Languages accepted: English
Prints abstracts: No
Author-anonymous submission: Yes

SUBMISSION REQUIREMENTS

Restrictions on contributors: None
Author pays submission fee: No
Author pays page charges: No
Length of articles: 6,000 words
Length of book reviews: 750 words
Length of notes: 500 words
Style: Journal
Number of copies required: 3
Copyright ownership: Journal & author

Rejected manuscripts: Not returned
Time before publication decision: 2 mos.
Time between decision and publication: 9 mos.
Number of reviewers: 2-5
Articles submitted per year: 25
Articles published per year: 15
Book reviews submitted per year: 5
Book reviews published per year: 5
Notes submitted per year: 6
Notes published per year: 6

(694)
*Critical Essays on American Literature

James Nagel, Editor
Dept. of English
Univ. of Georgia
Athens, GA 30602

Telephone: 404 542-2145
First published: 1979
MLA acronym: CEAL

SUBSCRIPTION INFORMATION

Frequency of publication: 12 times/yr.
Circulation: 3,500
Available in microform: No
Subscription address: G. K. Hall & Co., Macmillan Publishing Co., 866 Third Ave., New York, NY 10022

ADVERTISING INFORMATION

Advertising accepted: No

EDITORIAL DESCRIPTION

Scope: Publishes collections of critical essays about themes, individual works, and individual figures in American literature of all periods.
Reviews books: No
Publishes notes: Yes
Languages accepted: English
Prints abstracts: No
Author-anonymous submission: No

SUBMISSION REQUIREMENTS

Restrictions on contributors: Unsolicited manuscripts are not accepted.
Author pays submission fee: No
Author pays page charges: No
Style: Chicago
Copyright ownership: Editor
Rejected manuscripts: Returned
Time before publication decision: 15 mos.
Time between decision and publication: 3 mos.
Books submitted per year: 100
Books published per year: 12

(695)
*Critical Essays on British Literature

Zack Bowen, Editor
Dept. of English
Univ. of Miami
Coral Gables, FL 33124

Telephone: 305 284-2182
First published: 1985
MLA acronym: CEBL

SUBSCRIPTION INFORMATION

Frequency of publication: Irregular
Available in microform: No
Subscription address: G. K. Hall & Co., Macmillan Publishing Co., 866 Third Ave., New York, NY 10022

ADVERTISING INFORMATION

Advertising accepted: No

EDITORIAL DESCRIPTION

Scope: Publishes collections of critical essays about themes, individual works, and individual figures in British and Irish literature of all periods.
Reviews books: No
Publishes notes: No
Languages accepted: English
Prints abstracts: No
Author-anonymous submission: No

SUBMISSION REQUIREMENTS

Restrictions on contributors: Unsolicited manuscripts are not accepted.
Author pays submission fee: No
Author pays page charges: No
Length of books: 250 pp.
Style: Chicago
Number of copies required: 1
Copyright ownership: G. K. Hall
Rejected manuscripts: Returned
Time before publication decision: 3 mos.
Time between decision and publication: 18 mos.
Number of reviewers: 2
Books submitted per year: 8-10
Books published per year: 8

(696)
*Critical Essays on World Literature

Robert Lecker, Editor
Dept. of English
McGill Univ.
Montreal, Quebec H3A 2T6, Canada

First published: 1986
MLA acronym: CEWL

SUBSCRIPTION INFORMATION

Frequency of publication: Irregular
Available in microform: No
Subscription address: G. K. Hall & Co., Macmillan Publishing Co., 866 Third Ave., New York, NY 10022

ADVERTISING INFORMATION

Advertising accepted: No

EDITORIAL DESCRIPTION

Scope: Publishes collections of critical essays about themes, individual works, and individual figures in literature.
Reviews books: No
Publishes notes: No
Languages accepted: English
Prints abstracts: No
Author-anonymous submission: No

SUBMISSION REQUIREMENTS

Restrictions on contributors: Unsolicited manuscripts are not accepted.
Author pays submission fee: No
Author pays page charges: No
Length of books: 250 pp.
Style: Chicago
Copyright ownership: G. K. Hall & Co.
Time before publication decision: 3 mos.
Time between decision and publication: 18 mos.
Books published per year: 5

(697)
*Critical Guides to French Texts

Roger Little, Wolfgang van Emden, & David Williams, Editors
Grant & Cutler Ltd.
55-57 Great Marlborough St.
London W1V 2AY, England

Telephone: (44) 71 7342012
Fax: (44) 71 7342013
First published: 1980
MLA acronym: CGFT

SUBSCRIPTION INFORMATION

Frequency of publication: Irregular
Available in microform: No

ADVERTISING INFORMATION

Advertising accepted: No

EDITORIAL DESCRIPTION

Scope: Publishes criticism on works of French literature.
Reviews books: No
Publishes notes: No
Languages accepted: English
Prints abstracts: No

SUBMISSION REQUIREMENTS

Author pays submission fee: No
Author pays page charges: No
Length of books: 35,500 words
Copyright ownership: Grant & Cutler, Ltd.
Books published per year: 6

(698)
*Critical Guides to German Texts

Martin Swales, Editor
Grant & Cutler Ltd.
55-57 Great Marlborough St.
London W1V 2AY, England

Telephone: (44) 71 4943130
Fax: (44) 71 7342013
First published: 1985
MLA acronym: CGGT

SUBSCRIPTION INFORMATION

Frequency of publication: Irregular
Available in microform: No

ADVERTISING INFORMATION

Advertising accepted: No

EDITORIAL DESCRIPTION

Scope: Publishes criticism on works of German literature.
Reviews books: No
Publishes notes: No
Languages accepted: English
Prints abstracts: No

SUBMISSION REQUIREMENTS

Author pays submission fee: No
Author pays page charges: No
Length of articles: 35,500 words
Length of books: 90 pp.
Style: Modern Humanities Research Assn.
Copyright ownership: Grant & Cutler, Ltd.
Number of reviewers: 1
Books published per year: 1-2

(699)
*Critical Guides to Spanish Texts

J. E. Varey & A. D. Deyermond, Editors
Grant & Cutler Ltd.
55-57 Great Marlborough St.
London W1V 2AY, England

First published: 1971
MLA acronym: CGST

SUBSCRIPTION INFORMATION

Frequency of publication: Irregular

Available in microform: No
Subscription telephone: (44) 71 7342012
Subscription fax: (44) 71 7342013

ADVERTISING INFORMATION

Advertising accepted: No

EDITORIAL DESCRIPTION

Scope: Publishes critical monographs on works of Spanish and Spanish-American literature.
Reviews books: No
Publishes notes: No
Languages accepted: English
Prints abstracts: No
Author-anonymous submission: No

SUBMISSION REQUIREMENTS

Author pays submission fee: No
Author pays page charges: No
Length of books: 35,500 words
Style: Modern Humanities Research Assn.
Number of copies required: 2
Special requirements: Submit table of contents and draft chapter before submitting complete manuscript.
Copyright ownership: Grant & Cutler, Ltd.
Rejected manuscripts: Returned
Time before publication decision: 6 mos.
Time between decision and publication: 1 yr.
Number of reviewers: 2
Books published per year: 3

(700)
*Critical Inquiry

W. J. T. Mitchell, Arnold I. Davidson, Françoise Meltzer, Joel Snyder, Elizabeth Helsinger, Harry Harootunian, & Lauren Berlant, Editors
Wieboldt Hall 202
Univ. of Chicago
1050 E. 59th St.
Chicago, IL 60637

Telephone: 312 702-8477
Fax: 312 702-3397
First published: 1974
Sponsoring organization: Univ. of Chicago Press
ISSN: 0093-1896
MLA acronym: CritI

SUBSCRIPTION INFORMATION

Frequency of publication: 4 times/yr. (Sept., Dec., Mar., June)
Circulation: 4,500
Available in microform: Yes
Subscription price: $31.00/yr.
Year to which price refers: 1992
Subscription address: Univ. of Chicago Press, 11030 S. Langley Ave., Chicago, IL 60628
Subscription telephone: 312 753-3347

ADVERTISING INFORMATION

Advertising accepted: Yes

EDITORIAL DESCRIPTION

Scope: Publishes articles dealing with theory, method, and exploration of critical principles in the fields of literature, music, visual arts, film, philosophy, and popular culture.
Reviews books: Yes, review essays
Publishes notes: No
Languages accepted: English
Prints abstracts: No
Author-anonymous submission: No

SUBMISSION REQUIREMENTS

Restrictions on contributors: None
Author pays submission fee: No
Author pays page charges: No
Length of articles: 7,500 words
Style: Chicago
Number of copies required: 2
Special requirements: Submit original double-spaced typescript.
Copyright ownership: Univ. of Chicago
Rejected manuscripts: Returned; enclose return postage.
Time before publication decision: 3 mos.
Time between decision and publication: 1 yr. maximum
Number of reviewers: 2-3
Articles submitted per year: 500
Articles published per year: 40

(701)
*Critical Matrix: Princeton Working Papers in Women's Studies

Gwen Bergner & Linda Lierheimer, Editors
Program in Women's Studies
Princeton Univ.
113 Dickinson Hall
Princeton, NJ 08544-1017

Telephone: 609 258-5430
First published: 1985
MLA acronym: CMat

SUBSCRIPTION INFORMATION

Frequency of publication: 2 times/yr.
Available in microform: No
Subscription price: $24.00/yr. institutions; $12.00/yr. individuals; $7.50/single issue
Year to which price refers: 1992

ADVERTISING INFORMATION

Advertising accepted: No

EDITORIAL DESCRIPTION

Scope: Publishes articles on women's studies. Includes works on literature, history, philosophy, and social issues.
Reviews books: No
Publishes notes: No
Languages accepted: English
Prints abstracts: No

SUBMISSION REQUIREMENTS

Author pays submission fee: No
Author pays page charges: No
Number of copies required: 2
Copyright ownership: Author
Rejected manuscripts: Returned; enclose return postage
Articles published per year: 6

(702)
*Critical Quarterly

C. Brian Cox, Colin MacCabe, Kate Pahl, & Margaret Philips, Editors
Programme in Literary Linguistics
Univ. of Strathclyde
Glasgow G1 1XH, Scotland

Additional editorial address: Sandy Russo, Dept. of English, Univ. of Pittsburgh, Pittsburgh, PA 15260
First published: 1959
Sponsoring organization: Manchester Univ.
ISSN: 0011-1562
MLA acronym: CritQ

SUBSCRIPTION INFORMATION

Frequency of publication: 4 times/yr.
Circulation: 2,500
Available in microform: No
Subscription price: £36.00/yr. United Kingdom & Europe; $65.00/yr. N. America
Year to which price refers: 1992
Subscription address: Journals Dept., Basil Blackwell, Cowley Rd., Oxford OX4 1JF, England
Additional subscription address: In N. America: Basil Blackwell Inc., 238 Main St., Suite 501, Cambridge, MA 02142

ADVERTISING INFORMATION

Advertising accepted: Yes
Advertising rates: £130.00/half page; £200.00/full page

EDITORIAL DESCRIPTION

Scope: Particular, though not exclusive, interest is in 20th-century literature. Interested in poems and fiction, by writers known and unknown, all of which will receive sympathetic attention.
Reviews books: No
Publishes notes: No
Languages accepted: English
Prints abstracts: No
Author-anonymous submission: No

SUBMISSION REQUIREMENTS

Restrictions on contributors: Critical articles are solicited.
Author pays submission fee: No
Author pays page charges: No
Length of articles: 3,000-5,000 words
Style: MLA
Number of copies required: 1
Copyright ownership: Author
Rejected manuscripts: Not returned
Time before publication decision: 1 mo.
Time between decision and publication: 6 mos.
Number of reviewers: 2
Articles submitted per year: 600
Articles published per year: 24
Book reviews published per year: 80

(703)
The Critical Review

S. L. Goldberg, Editor
Dept. of Philosophy, Research School of Social Science
Australian National Univ.
P.O. Box 4, Canberra, ACT 2600, Australia

Fax: (61) 62 489062
First published: 1958
Sponsoring organization: Australian National Univ., Research School of Social Sciences
ISSN: 0070-1548
MLA acronym: CR

SUBSCRIPTION INFORMATION

Frequency of publication: Annual
Circulation: 500-1,000
Available in microform: No

ADVERTISING INFORMATION

Advertising accepted: No

EDITORIAL DESCRIPTION

Scope: Publishes literary and cultural criticism.
Reviews books: No
Publishes notes: No
Languages accepted: English
Prints abstracts: No
Author-anonymous submission: No

SUBMISSION REQUIREMENTS

Restrictions on contributors: None
Author pays submission fee: No
Author pays page charges: No
Length of articles: 4,000-8,000 words
Style: Journal
Number of copies required: 1
Copyright ownership: Author upon request

Rejected manuscripts: Returned; enclose return postage.
Time before publication decision: 2 mos.
Time between decision and publication: 1-9 mos.
Number of reviewers: 6-9
Articles submitted per year: 25-30
Articles published per year: 7-10

(704)
*Critical Studies

Myriam Díaz-Diocaretz, Editor
P.O. Box 10004
1001 EA Amsterdam, Netherlands

Telephone: (31) 20 6730659
First published: 1989
Historical variations in title: Formerly *Critical Studies: A Journal of Critical Theory, Literature and Culture*
ISSN: 0923-411X
MLA acronym: CritSt

SUBSCRIPTION INFORMATION

Frequency of publication: 2 times/yr.
Circulation: 600
Available in microform: No
Subscription address: Editions Rodopi B.V., Keizersgracht 302-304, 1016 EX Amsterdam, Netherlands
Additional subscription address: In N. America: Editions Rodopi, 233 Peachtree St. N.E., Suite 404, Atlanta, GA 30303-1504
Subscription telephone: (31) 20 6227507
Subscription fax: (31) 20 6380948

ADVERTISING INFORMATION

Advertising accepted: Yes

EDITORIAL DESCRIPTION

Scope: Publishes articles in the fields of literary theory, philosophy and history, explorations of discourse, culture, and communication, and the interrrelations between theory and critical practices.
Reviews books: No
Publishes notes: No
Languages accepted: English
Prints abstracts: No
Author-anonymous submission: Yes

SUBMISSION REQUIREMENTS

Restrictions on contributors: None
Author pays submission fee: No
Author pays page charges: No
Length of articles: 28-30 pp.
Style: Chicago
Number of copies required: 3
Special requirements: Avoid prejudicial language. Submission on diskette is welcome.
Copyright ownership: Editions Rodopi
Rejected manuscripts: Returned; enclose SASE.
Articles published per year: 6-13

(705)
*Critical Survey

Bryan Loughrey, Editor
c/o The Secretary
Roehampton Inst.
Digby Stuart College
Roehampton Lane
London SW15 5PU, England

Telephone: (44) 81 8768273
First published: 1989
Sponsoring organization: Critical Quarterly Soc.
ISSN: 0011-1570
MLA acronym: CrSurv

SUBSCRIPTION INFORMATION

Frequency of publication: 3 times/yr.
Circulation: 600
Available in microform: Yes
Subscription price: £25.00/yr. United Kingdom & Europe; $52.00/yr. institutions elsewhere; $30.00/yr. individuals
Year to which price refers: 1992
Subscription address: Journals Subscriptions Dept., Oxford Univ. Press, Pinkhill House, Southfield Rd., Eynsham, Oxford OX8 1JJ, England
Subscription telephone: (44) 865 882283
Subscription fax: (44) 865 882890

ADVERTISING INFORMATION

Advertising accepted: Yes

EDITORIAL DESCRIPTION

Scope: Publishes articles on literary studies, as well as cultural analysis. Each issue focuses on one author.
Reviews books: Yes
Publishes notes: Yes
Languages accepted: English
Prints abstracts: No
Author-anonymous submission: No

SUBMISSION REQUIREMENTS

Restrictions on contributors: None
Author pays submission fee: No
Author pays page charges: No
Length of articles: 3,000-3,500 words
Length of book reviews: 1,000 words
Length of notes: 1,500 words maximum
Style: Modern Humanities Research Assn.
Number of copies required: 2
Copyright ownership: Journal
Rejected manuscripts: Returned
Time before publication decision: 1 mo.
Number of reviewers: 2
Articles published per year: 20-30

(706)
Critical Texts: A Review of Theory and Criticism

Joseph Childers, Jon Anderson, Martha Buskirk, James Buzard, Susan Fraiman, Gary Hentzi, Ina Lipkowitz, Eric Lott, & Richard Moye, Editors
Dept. of English
602 Philosophy Hall
Columbia Univ.
New York, NY 10027

Additional editorial address: Joseph Childers, Dept. of English, Univ. of California, Riverside, CA 92521
First published: 1983
ISSN: 0730-2304
MLA acronym: CritT

SUBSCRIPTION INFORMATION

Frequency of publication: 3 times/yr.
Circulation: 850
Available in microform: No

ADVERTISING INFORMATION

Advertising accepted: Yes

EDITORIAL DESCRIPTION

Scope: An oppositional journal that publishes interviews, articles, translations, and reviews concerned with theory in literature, art, film, music, language, and the human sciences.
Reviews books: Yes
Publishes notes: No
Languages accepted: English
Prints abstracts: No
Author-anonymous submission: No

SUBMISSION REQUIREMENTS

Restrictions on contributors: None
Author pays submission fee: No
Author pays page charges: No
Length of articles: 15-45 pp.
Length of book reviews: 8-12 pp.
Style: MLA
Number of copies required: 2
Special requirements: Submit typescript and 5.25 or 3.5 in. IBM-compatible diskette in Microsoft Word, WordPerfect, Wordstar, or in DCA, RTF, or ASCII format.
Copyright ownership: Journal
Rejected manuscripts: Returned; enclose SASE.
Time before publication decision: 2 mos.
Time between decision and publication: 4 mos.
Number of reviewers: 9
Articles submitted per year: 50
Articles published per year: 6-9
Book reviews submitted per year: 75
Book reviews published per year: 25

(707)
*Critical Theory: Interdisciplinary Approaches to Language, Discourse and Ideology

Iris M. Zavala & Myriam Díaz-Diocaretz, Editors
Rijksuniv. te Utrecht
Fac. der Letteren
Kromme Nieuwe Gracht 29
3512 HD Utrecht, Netherlands

Additional editorial address: Myriam Diaz-Diocaretz, P.O. Box 10004, 1001 EA Amsterdam, Netherlands
First published: 1985
ISSN: 0920-3060
MLA acronym: CritTh

SUBSCRIPTION INFORMATION

Frequency of publication: Irregular
Available in microform: No
Subscription address: John Benjamins Publishing Co., Amsteldijk 44, P.O. Box 75577, 1070 AN Amsterdam, Netherlands
Additional subscription address: John Benjamins North America, Inc., 821 Bethlehem Pike, Philadelphia, PA 19118

ADVERTISING INFORMATION

Advertising accepted: No

EDITORIAL DESCRIPTION

Scope: Publishes studies on the areas of investigation which involve the scrutiny of the role of discourse in society and which experiment with new ideas and literary criticism.
Reviews books: No
Publishes notes: No
Languages accepted: English
Prints abstracts: No
Author-anonymous submission: Yes

SUBMISSION REQUIREMENTS

Author pays submission fee: No
Author pays page charges: No
Style: MLA
Copyright ownership: John Benjamins B.V.
Rejected manuscripts: Returned
Time before publication decision: 3 mos.
Time between decision and publication: 6 mos.
Number of reviewers: 2
Books submitted per year: 6-8
Books published per year: 2-3

(708)
*Criticism: A Quarterly for Literature and the Arts

Arthur F. Marotti, Editor
Dept. of English
Wayne State Univ.
Detroit, MI 48202

Telephone: 313 577-3409
Fax: 313 577-4626
First published: 1959
ISSN: 0011-1589
MLA acronym: Criticism

SUBSCRIPTION INFORMATION

Frequency of publication: 4 times/yr. (Winter, Spring, Summer, Fall)
Circulation: 1,150
Available in microform: Yes
Subscription price: $45.00/yr. institutions; $28.00/yr. individuals
Year to which price refers: 1992
Subscription address: Wayne State Univ. Press, Leonard N. Simons Bldg., 5959 Woodward Ave., Detroit, MI 48202

ADVERTISING INFORMATION

Advertising accepted: Yes
Advertising rates: $100.00/half page; $200.00/full page

EDITORIAL DESCRIPTION

Scope: A journal of literary criticism, designed to offer new approaches to literary problems, genres, texts, authors, and literary history as well as studies relating literature to the other arts. The reviews and review essays deal with the most current works of criticism and theory.
Reviews books: Yes
Publishes notes: No
Languages accepted: English
Prints abstracts: No
Author-anonymous submission: No

SUBMISSION REQUIREMENTS

Restrictions on contributors: None
Author pays submission fee: No
Author pays page charges: No
Length of articles: 15-50 pp.
Length of book reviews: 800-1,500 words
Style: Chicago
Number of copies required: 1
Special requirements: Submit original typescript.
Copyright ownership: Wayne State Univ. Press
Rejected manuscripts: Returned; enclose return postage.
Time before publication decision: 1-3 mos.
Time between decision and publication: 6-9 mos.
Number of reviewers: 2-3
Articles submitted per year: 300
Articles published per year: 24
Book reviews submitted per year: 50
Book reviews published per year: 30-40

(709)
Criticón

Robert Jammes, Odette Gorsse, Frédéric Serralta, & Marc Vitse, Editors
France-Ibérie Recherche
Inst. d'Etudes Hispaniques
Univ. de Toulouse-Le Mirail
5, allées Antonio Machado
31058 Toulouse Cedex, France

Telephone: (33) 61504349
Fax: (33) 61504209
First published: 1980
ISSN: 0247-381X
MLA acronym: Criticón

SUBSCRIPTION INFORMATION

Frequency of publication: 4 times/yr. (Mar., June, Oct., Dec.)
Circulation: 200
Available in microform: No
Subscription price: 180 F/yr.
Year to which price refers: 1992
Subscription address: Presses Universitaires du Mirail, 56 rue du Taur, 31000 Toulouse, France
Subscription telephone: (33) 61225831
Subscription fax: (33) 61218420

ADVERTISING INFORMATION

Advertising accepted: Yes

EDITORIAL DESCRIPTION

Scope: Publishes articles on the literature and language of the Spanish Golden Age (15th-17th centuries).
Reviews books: Yes
Publishes notes: Yes
Languages accepted: Spanish
Prints abstracts: Yes
Author-anonymous submission: Yes

SUBMISSION REQUIREMENTS

Restrictions on contributors: Contributors must be subscribers.
Length of articles: No restrictions
Style: Journal
Number of copies required: 2
Special requirements: Submit 10-line abstract in Spanish and English.
Copyright ownership: France-Ibérie Recherche
Rejected manuscripts: Returned; enclose return postage.
Time before publication decision: 6 mos.
Time between decision and publication: 3 mos.
Number of reviewers: 3
Articles submitted per year: 25
Articles published per year: 12-15
Book reviews submitted per year: 25
Book reviews published per year: 15

(710)
Critique: Revue Générale des Publications Françaises et Etrangères

Jean Piel, Editor
Editions de Minuit
7, rue Bernard-Palissy
75006 Paris, France

Telephone: (33) 1 45442316
First published: 1946
ISSN: 0011-1600
MLA acronym: Critique

SUBSCRIPTION INFORMATION

Frequency of publication: 12 times/yr.
Available in microform: No

ADVERTISING INFORMATION

Advertising accepted: No

EDITORIAL DESCRIPTION

Scope: Strives to achieve a living synthesis of contemporary culture by analyzing the essential and newest aspects of French and foreign intellectual production.
Reviews books: Yes
Publishes notes: Yes
Languages accepted: French
Prints abstracts: No

(711)
*Critique: Studies in Contemporary Fiction

Helen Strang, Managing Editor
Heldref Publications
1319 Eighteenth St. NW
Washington, DC 20036

Telephone: 202 296-6267 ext. 216
Fax: 202 296-5149
First published: 1956
ISSN: 0011-1619
MLA acronym: Crit

SUBSCRIPTION INFORMATION

Frequency of publication: 4 times/yr. (Spring, Summer, Fall, Winter)
Circulation: 1,500
Available in microform: Yes
Subscription price: $45.00/yr. institutions; $25.00/yr. individuals; add $10.00/yr. outside US
Year to which price refers: 1992
Subscription telephone: 202 296-6267 ext. 264

ADVERTISING INFORMATION

Advertising accepted: Yes
Advertising rates: $150.00/half page; $190.00/full page

EDITORIAL DESCRIPTION

Scope: Devoted to essays on contemporary fiction. Gives particular consideration to critical essays on the fiction of writers from any country who are alive and without great reputations.
Reviews books: Yes
Publishes notes: No
Languages accepted: English
Prints abstracts: No
Author-anonymous submission: No

SUBMISSION REQUIREMENTS

Restrictions on contributors: Book reviews are assigned.
Author pays submission fee: No
Author pays page charges: No
Length of articles: 2,500-8,000 words
Length of book reviews: 1,500 words
Style: MLA with endnotes
Number of copies required: 2
Special requirements: Submit original typescript.
Copyright ownership: Heldref Publications
Rejected manuscripts: Returned; enclose SASE.
Time before publication decision: 6-8 weeks
Time between decision and publication: 1 yr.
Number of reviewers: 2-3
Articles submitted per year: 70
Articles published per year: 20
Book reviews published per year: 6

(712)
*Cross Currents

Joseph Cunneen, William Birmingham, & Nancy M. Malone, Editors
College of New Rochelle
New Rochelle, NY 10805-2308

Telephone: 914 654-5425
Fax: 914 654-5554
First published: 1950
Sponsoring organization: Convergence, Inc.
ISSN: 0011-1953
MLA acronym: Crosscurrents

SUBSCRIPTION INFORMATION

Frequency of publication: 4 times/yr.
Circulation: 4,700
Available in microform: Yes

Subscription address: P.O. Box 147, Pearl River, NY 10965

ADVERTISING INFORMATION

Advertising accepted: Yes

EDITORIAL DESCRIPTION

Scope: Publishes articles on the relation of religion, especially Judaism and Christianity, to modern culture. Strives to aid members in resolving the conflict between religious values and intellectual ideology.
Reviews books: Yes
Publishes notes: Yes
Languages accepted: English
Prints abstracts: No
Author-anonymous submission: No

SUBMISSION REQUIREMENTS

Restrictions on contributors: Unsolicited book reviews are not accepted, but inquiries on possible reviews are welcome.
Author pays submission fee: No
Author pays page charges: No
Length of articles: 4,000-7,000 words
Length of book reviews: 1,500 words
Length of notes: 1,500 words
Style: MLA
Number of copies required: 1
Special requirements: Submit original typescript.
Copyright ownership: Assigned by author to journal
Rejected manuscripts: Returned
Time before publication decision: 6 weeks.
Time between decision and publication: 6 mos.
Number of reviewers: 3 minimum
Articles submitted per year: 350
Articles published per year: 26-30
Book reviews published per year: 120
Notes submitted per year: 30
Notes published per year: 5

(713)
*Cross Currents: A Yearbook of Central European Culture

Yale Univ. Press
92A Yale Station
New Haven, CT 06520

First published: 1982
Sponsoring organization: Slavic Dept., Univ. of Michigan
ISSN: 0748-0164
MLA acronym: CCur

SUBSCRIPTION INFORMATION

Frequency of publication: Annual
Available in microform: No
Subscription price: $20.00/yr.
Year to which price refers: 1991

ADVERTISING INFORMATION

Advertising accepted: No

EDITORIAL DESCRIPTION

Scope: Publishes articles on East European literature, film, and culture.
Reviews books: No
Publishes notes: No
Languages accepted: English
Prints abstracts: No

SUBMISSION REQUIREMENTS

Restrictions on contributors: None
Author pays submission fee: No
Author pays page charges: No
Style: Chicago
Copyright ownership: Editor
Rejected manuscripts: Not returned

(714)
*Cross/Cultures: Readings in the Post/Colonial Literatures in English

Gordon Collier, Geoffrey Davis, & Hena Maes-Jelinek, Editors
Dept. of English
Justus Liebig Univ.
Otto-Behaghel-Str. 10
6300 Giessen, Germany

Additional editorial address: Geoffrey Davis, Dept. of English, RWTH, Karmanstr. 17-19, 5100 Aachen, Germany; Hena Maes-Jelinek, Dept. of English, Univ. of Liege, 3 Place Cockerill, 4000 Liege, Belgium
First published: 1990
ISSN: 0924-1426
MLA acronym: CrossC

SUBSCRIPTION INFORMATION

Frequency of publication: Irregular
Circulation: 500
Available in microform: No
Subscription address: Fred van der Zee, Editions Rodopi B.V., Keizersgracht 302-304, 1016 EX Amsterdam, Netherlands
Additional subscription address: Editions Rodopi, 233 Peachtree St. N.E., Suite 404, Atlanta, GA 30303-1504
Subscription telephone: (31) 20 6227507; 404 523-1964; 800 225-3998
Subscription fax: (31) 20 6380948; 404 522-7116

ADVERTISING INFORMATION

Advertising accepted: No

EDITORIAL DESCRIPTION

Scope: A critical series devoted to the study of the English-speaking world (except the United States and United Kingdom). Encourages comparative approaches to multicultural societies, provides a forum for theoretical studies, and stimulates in-depth analysis of the work of individual writers as well as the investigation of thematic concerns specific to the post/colonial environment.
Reviews books: No
Publishes notes: No
Languages accepted: English
Author-anonymous submission: No

SUBMISSION REQUIREMENTS

Author pays submission fee: No
Author pays page charges: No
Length of books: 250-500 pp.
Style: MLA with modifications
Number of copies required: 3
Special requirements: Submission of 1 copy and a 3.5" diskette is acceptable.
Copyright ownership: Editions Rodopi b.v.
Rejected manuscripts: Returned
Time between decision and publication: 3 mos.
Number of reviewers: 3
Books submitted per year: 10
Books published per year: 4

(715)
Crosscurrents/Modern Critiques

Jerome Klinkowitz, Editor
c/o Southern Illinois Univ. Press
P.O. Box 3697
Carbondale, IL 62902-3697

First published: 1962
MLA acronym: CMC

SUBSCRIPTION INFORMATION

Frequency of publication: Irregular
Available in microform: No

ADVERTISING INFORMATION

Advertising accepted: No

EDITORIAL DESCRIPTION

Scope: Publishes avant-garde criticism.
Reviews books: No
Publishes notes: No
Languages accepted: English
Prints abstracts: No
Author-anonymous submission: No

SUBMISSION REQUIREMENTS

Author pays submission fee: No
Author pays page charges: No
Length of books: 45,000-50,000 words
Style: Chicago
Number of copies required: 2
Copyright ownership: Southern Illinois Univ. Press
Rejected manuscripts: Returned
Time before publication decision: 6 mos.
Time between decision and publication: 10 mos.
Number of reviewers: 2
Books submitted per year: 50
Books published per year: 4

(716)
*CRUX: A Journal on the Teaching of English

M. M. Hacksley, Editor
Private Bag 1019
Grahamstown 6140, South Africa

Telephone: (27) 461 27042
Fax: (27) 461 22582
First published: 1967
Sponsoring organization: Foundation for Education, Science & Technology
ISSN: 0250-0035
MLA acronym: CRUX

SUBSCRIPTION INFORMATION

Frequency of publication: 4 times/yr.
Circulation: 3,900
Available in microform: No
Subscription price: 11 R/yr.
Year to which price refers: 1992
Subscription address: P.O. Box 1758, Pretoria 0001, South Africa
Subscription telephone: (27) 461 3226404

ADVERTISING INFORMATION

Advertising accepted: Yes

EDITORIAL DESCRIPTION

Scope: Deals with aspects of English teaching, including ESL, EFL, applied linguistics, and media studies.
Reviews books: Yes
Publishes notes: Yes
Languages accepted: English
Prints abstracts: No
Author-anonymous submission: No

SUBMISSION REQUIREMENTS

Restrictions on contributors: None
Author pays submission fee: No
Author pays page charges: No
Length of articles: 6,000 words maximum
Length of book reviews: 250-1,000 words
Length of notes: 300-1,000 words
Style: None
Number of copies required: 1
Copyright ownership: Journal
Rejected manuscripts: Returned
Time before publication decision: 2 mos.
Time between decision and publication: 4 mos.
Number of reviewers: 2
Articles submitted per year: 50-60
Articles published per year: 40-50
Book reviews submitted per year: 10

Book reviews published per year: 7
Notes submitted per year: 4
Notes published per year: 4

(717)
*CSL: The Bulletin of the New York C. S. Lewis Society

James Como, Editor
York College
City Univ. of New York
Jamaica, NY 11451

First published: 1969
Historical variations in title: Formerly *Bulletin of the New York C. S. Lewis Society*
Sponsoring organization: New York C. S. Lewis Soc.
ISSN: 0883-9980
MLA acronym: CSLBull

SUBSCRIPTION INFORMATION

Frequency of publication: 12 times/yr.
Circulation: 550
Available in microform: No
Subscription price: $10.00/yr.
Year to which price refers: 1992
Subscription address: Clara Sarrocco, 84-23 77th Ave., Glendale, NY 11385

ADVERTISING INFORMATION

Advertising accepted: No

EDITORIAL DESCRIPTION

Scope: Focuses on the works of C. S. Lewis.
Reviews books: Yes
Publishes notes: Yes
Languages accepted: English
Prints abstracts: No

SUBMISSION REQUIREMENTS

Restrictions on contributors: None
Author pays submission fee: No
Author pays page charges: No
Length of articles: 500-5,000 words
Length of notes: 1,000 words
Number of copies required: 1
Rejected manuscripts: Returned
Time before publication decision: 1 mo.
Time between decision and publication: 3 mos.
Number of reviewers: 1-3
Articles submitted per year: 45
Articles published per year: 20
Book reviews submitted per year: 15
Book reviews published per year: 10
Notes submitted per year: 100
Notes published per year: 50

(718)
*Cuadernos Americanos

Leopoldo Zea, Editor
P.B. Torre I de Humanidades
Ciudad Universitaria
04510 Mexico City, D.F., Mexico

Telephone: (52) 5 5505745
Fax: (52) 5 5489662
First published: 1942
Sponsoring organization: Univ. Nacional Autónoma de México
ISSN: 0185-156X
MLA acronym: CA

SUBSCRIPTION INFORMATION

Frequency of publication: 6 times/yr.
Circulation: 2,500
Available in microform: No
Subscription price: $120.00/yr.
Year to which price refers: 1992

Subscription address: Apartado Postale 965, 06000 Mexico City, D.F., Mexico

ADVERTISING INFORMATION

Advertising accepted: Yes
Advertising rates: $300.00/full page

EDITORIAL DESCRIPTION

Scope: Publishes articles on Latin American cultural studies.
Reviews books: Yes
Publishes notes: Yes
Languages accepted: Spanish
Prints abstracts: No
Author-anonymous submission: No

SUBMISSION REQUIREMENTS

Author pays submission fee: No
Author pays page charges: No
Length of articles: 8,400 words
Length of book reviews: 1,260 words
Length of notes: 2,520 words
Number of copies required: 1
Special requirements: Submit original typescript. Submission on diskette is acceptable.
Copyright ownership: Journal for 1 yr.
Rejected manuscripts: Not returned
Time before publication decision: 6 mos.
Time between decision and publication: 9-12 mos.
Number of reviewers: 2
Articles published per year: 70
Book reviews published per year: 18
Notes published per year: 6

(719)
*Cuadernos de Aldeeu

Juan Fernández-Jiménez, Editor
Pennsylvania State Univ. at Erie
Behrend College
Station Rd.
Erie, PA 16563

Telephone: 814 898-6446
Fax: 814 898-6032
First published: 1983
Sponsoring organization: Asoc. de Licenciados y Doctores en los Estados Unidos (Spanish Professionals in America)
ISSN: 0740-0632
MLA acronym: CAld

SUBSCRIPTION INFORMATION

Frequency of publication: 2 times/yr. (Apr., Nov.)
Available in microform: No
Subscription price: $26.00/yr. institutions; $18.00/yr. individuals
Year to which price refers: 1992

ADVERTISING INFORMATION

Advertising accepted: Yes
Advertising rates: $100.00/full page

EDITORIAL DESCRIPTION

Scope: Publishes articles, notes, and reviews in all fields represented by the members of Asoc. de Licenciados y Doctores en los Estados Unidos. The major focus is on Spanish literature, history, and art; Spanish American literature; and cultural relations between Spain and the United States.
Reviews books: Yes
Publishes notes: Yes
Languages accepted: Spanish; English
Prints abstracts: No
Author-anonymous submission: No

SUBMISSION REQUIREMENTS

Restrictions on contributors: Preference is given to members of the association. Reviews are usually solicited.
Author pays submission fee: No
Author pays page charges: No
Length of articles: 10-20 pp.
Length of book reviews: 700-1,000 words
Length of notes: 4-8 pp.
Number of copies required: 2
Copyright ownership: Journal
Rejected manuscripts: Returned; enclose return postage.
Time before publication decision: 2-5 mos.
Time between decision and publication: 8-15 mos.
Number of reviewers: 2 minimum
Articles submitted per year: 20-25
Articles published per year: 12-15
Book reviews published per year: 12-20
Notes submitted per year: 3-4
Notes published per year: 2-3

(720)
Cuadernos de Estudios Gallegos

Consejo Superior de Investigaciones Científicas
Vitruvio 8
Apartado 14.458
28006 Madrid, Spain

First published: 1944
ISSN: 0210-847X
MLA acronym: CEG

SUBSCRIPTION INFORMATION

Frequency of publication: 3 times/yr.
Subscription address: Duque de Medinaceli, 4, Madrid-14, Spain

EDITORIAL DESCRIPTION

Reviews books: No
Languages accepted: English; Italian; Spanish
Prints abstracts: No

(721)
Cuadernos de Filología Clásica

Antonio Ruiz de Elvira, Editor
Fac. de Filología
Edificio A
Cuidad Univ.
Madrid-3, Spain

Additional editorial address: Send books for review to: Jośe S. Lasso de la Vega, at editorial address.
ISSN: 0210-0746
MLA acronym: CFC

SUBSCRIPTION INFORMATION

Subscription address: Editorial de la Univ. Complutense de Madrid, Edificio de Estomatologia Bajos, Cuidad Univ., Madrid-3, Spain

EDITORIAL DESCRIPTION

Languages accepted: Spanish

(722)
*Cuadernos de Investigación Filológica

Maria Jesús Salinero Cascante, Editor
Colegio Univ. de la Rioja
Servicio de Publicaciones
Obispo Bustamante, 3
26001 Logroño, Spain

Telephone: (34) 41 231699 ext. 18
First published: 1975

Sponsoring organization: Colegio Univ. de la Rioja
ISSN: 0211-0547
MLA acronym: CIF

SUBSCRIPTION INFORMATION

Frequency of publication: 2 times/yr.
Circulation: 500
Available in microform: Yes
Subscription price: 1,500 Pta/yr. Spain; 1,800 Pta/yr. elsewhere
Year to which price refers: 1992

ADVERTISING INFORMATION

Advertising accepted: Yes, on an exchange basis

EDITORIAL DESCRIPTION

Scope: Publishes articles on philology, language, and literature.
Reviews books: Yes
Publishes notes: Yes
Languages accepted: Spanish; French; English
Prints abstracts: Yes
Author-anonymous submission: No

SUBMISSION REQUIREMENTS

Restrictions on contributors: None
Author pays submission fee: No
Author pays page charges: No
Length of articles: 9,000 words
Length of book reviews: 900 words
Length of notes: 3,000 words
Style: MLA
Number of copies required: 2
Special requirements: Submit original typescript and 1 copy. Include two ten-line abstracts, one in Spanish and the other in English or French. Corrections are the responsibility of the author.
Copyright ownership: Colegio Univ. de la Rioja
Rejected manuscripts: Returned
Time before publication decision: 5 mos.
Time between decision and publication: 5 mos.
Number of reviewers: 4
Articles submitted per year: 15-20
Articles published per year: 10-12
Book reviews submitted per year: 3
Book reviews published per year: 2-3
Notes submitted per year: 2-4
Notes published per year: 1-2

(723)
*Cuadernos de Poética

Diógenes Céspedes, Editor
P.O. Box 1736
Santo Domingo D. N., Dominican Republic

First published: 1983
ISSN: 0257-6457
MLA acronym: CdP

SUBSCRIPTION INFORMATION

Frequency of publication: 3 times/yr. (Winter, Spring, Summer)
Circulation: 300
Available in microform: No
Subscription price: $30.00/yr. institutions US & Europe; $40.00/yr. institutions Africa, Asia, & Oceania; $25.00/yr. individuals US & Europe; $30.00/yr. individuals Africa, Asia, & Oceania
Year to which price refers: 1992

ADVERTISING INFORMATION

Advertising accepted: Yes
Advertising rates: $50.00/full page

EDITORIAL DESCRIPTION

Scope: Devoted to research in the theory of poetry and writing, literary criticism, and linguistics as a dialectic whole. Publishes fiction (poems, short stories) and book reviews.
Reviews books: Yes
Publishes notes: Yes
Languages accepted: Spanish; English; French
Prints abstracts: No
Author-anonymous submission: Yes

SUBMISSION REQUIREMENTS

Restrictions on contributors: Book reviews are solicited.
Author pays submission fee: No
Author pays page charges: No
Length of articles: 5,000 words maximum
Length of book reviews: 500-1,000 words
Length of notes: No restrictions
Style: MLA; Chicago
Number of copies required: 3
Special requirements: Manuscripts must be submitted in Spanish, English, and French. Footnotes, not endnotes, are published. Manuscripts must be typed, double-spaced and accompanied by a brief bio-bibliography.
Copyright ownership: Author
Rejected manuscripts: Returned at author's request
Time before publication decision: 1-6 mos.
Time between decision and publication: 1 yr.
Number of reviewers: 3
Articles submitted per year: 50
Articles published per year: 15
Book reviews submitted per year: 9-10
Book reviews published per year: 9-10
Notes submitted per year: 10
Notes published per year: 4-6

(724)
*Cuadernos de Teatro Clásico

Luciano García Lorenzo, Director
Compañía Nacional de Teatro Clásico
C/ Príncipe, n°. 14
28012 Madrid, Spain

Telephone: (34) 1 5327928
Fax: (34) 1 5224690
Sponsoring organization: Compañía Nacional de Teatro Clásico
ISSN: 0214-1388
MLA acronym: CTC

SUBSCRIPTION INFORMATION

Frequency of publication: 2 times/yr.
Available in microform: No

ADVERTISING INFORMATION

Advertising accepted: Yes

EDITORIAL DESCRIPTION

Scope: Publishes articles on classical Spanish theater.
Reviews books: No
Publishes notes: Yes
Languages accepted: Spanish
Prints abstracts: No

SUBMISSION REQUIREMENTS

Restrictions on contributors: None
Author pays submission fee: No
Author pays page charges: No
Number of copies required: 3
Copyright ownership: Compañía Nacional de Teatro Clásico
Articles published per year: 20

(725)
*Cuadernos Hispanoamericanos: Revista Mensual de Cultura Hispanica

Félix Grande, Editor
Avenida de los Reyes Católicos, 4
Inst. de Cooperación Iberoamericana
Ciudad Univ.
28040 Madrid, Spain

Telephone: (34) 1 5838399
Fax: (34) 1 5838264
First published: 1948
Sponsoring organization: Inst. de Cooperación Iberoamericana
ISSN: 0011-250X
MLA acronym: CHA

SUBSCRIPTION INFORMATION

Frequency of publication: 14 times/yr.
Circulation: 10,000
Available in microform: No
Subscription price: $120.00/yr.
Year to which price refers: 1992

ADVERTISING INFORMATION

Advertising accepted: No

EDITORIAL DESCRIPTION

Scope: Publishes articles on Spanish and Spanish American literature and art.
Reviews books: Yes
Publishes notes: Yes
Languages accepted: Spanish
Prints abstracts: No
Author-anonymous submission: No

SUBMISSION REQUIREMENTS

Restrictions on contributors: None
Author pays submission fee: No
Author pays page charges: No
Length of articles: No restrictions
Length of book reviews: 3-5 pp.
Length of notes: No restrictions
Style: None
Number of copies required: 1
Copyright ownership: Author
Rejected manuscripts: Returned
Time before publication decision: 2 mos.
Number of reviewers: 5
Articles submitted per year: 300-400
Articles published per year: 200
Book reviews submitted per year: 1,500
Book reviews published per year: 350
Notes submitted per year: 5,000
Notes published per year: 100

(726)
*Cultura e Scuola

Vittorio Mathieu, Director
Via Dandolo, 19a
00153 Rome, Italy

First published: 1961
Sponsoring organization: Ist. Enciclopedia Italiana
ISSN: 0011-2771
MLA acronym: CeS

SUBSCRIPTION INFORMATION

Frequency of publication: 4 times/yr.
Subscription address: Ist. della Enciclopedia Italiana, Piazza Paganica, 4, 00186 Rome, Italy

EDITORIAL DESCRIPTION

Scope: Publishes articles on culture.
Reviews books: No
Languages accepted: Italian
Prints abstracts: No

(727)
Cultura Neolatina

Aurelio Roncaglia, Editor
Mucchi Editore srl
Via Emilia Est 1527
41100 Modena, Italy

First published: 1941
Sponsoring organization: Univ. di Roma, Ist. di Filologia Romanza
ISSN: 0391-5654
MLA acronym: CN

SUBSCRIPTION INFORMATION

Frequency of publication: 6 times/yr.
Available in microform: No
Subscription price: 100,000 Lit/yr. Italy; 120,000 Lit/yr. elsewhere
Year to which price refers: 1991

EDITORIAL DESCRIPTION

Reviews books: Yes
Languages accepted: Italian
Prints abstracts: No

SUBMISSION REQUIREMENTS

Restrictions on contributors: None
Length of articles: No restrictions
Number of copies required: 2
Copyright ownership: Mucchi Editore srl
Time before publication decision: 3 mos.
Time between decision and publication: 6 mos.
Number of reviewers: 1
Articles published per year: 32

(728)
*Cultural Critique

Donna Przybylowicz & Abdul Jan Mohamed, Editors
Dept. of English
Univ. of Minnesota
Minneapolis, MN 55455

Telephone: 612 625-8082
First published: 1985
Sponsoring organization: Soc. for Cultural Critique
ISSN: 0882-4371
MLA acronym: CultCrit

SUBSCRIPTION INFORMATION

Frequency of publication: 3 times/yr.
Circulation: 1,000
Available in microform: Yes
Subscription price: $48.00/yr. institutions US; $59.00/yr. institutions elsewhere; $24.00/yr. individuals US; $35.00/yr. individuals elsewhere
Year to which price refers: 1992
Subscription address: Journal Customer Service, Oxford Univ. Press, 2001 Evans Rd., Cary, NC 27513
Subscription telephone: 800 852-7323
Subscription fax: 919 677-1714

ADVERTISING INFORMATION

Advertising accepted: Yes
Advertising rates: $150.00/half page; $200.00/full page

EDITORIAL DESCRIPTION

Scope: Publishes studies on cultural phenomena. Includes studies on popular culture, folk culture, literary theory, critical theory, feminist studies, and minority discourse.
Reviews books: Yes
Publishes notes: No
Languages accepted: English
Prints abstracts: No
Author-anonymous submission: Yes

SUBMISSION REQUIREMENTS

Restrictions on contributors: Contributions must not have been previously published.
Author pays submission fee: No
Author pays page charges: No
Length of articles: 5,000-10,000 words
Style: MLA
Number of copies required: 3
Copyright ownership: Journal
Rejected manuscripts: Returned; enclose SASE.
Time before publication decision: 4 mos.
Time between decision and publication: 6 mos.
Number of reviewers: 2-3
Articles submitted per year: 250
Articles published per year: 20-25

(729)
*Culture & Tradition

Anita Best & Marie-France St. Laurent, Editors
Box 115, Arts & Administration
Memorial Univ. of Newfoundland
St. John's, Newfoundland A1C 5S7, Canada

Additional editorial address: CELAT, Pavillon de Koninck, Univ. Laval, Ste. Foy, Quebec G1K 7P4, Canada
Telephone: 709 737-2166
Fax: 709 737-4569
E-mail: CULTURE@KEAN.UCS.MUN.CA
First published: 1976
ISSN: 0701-0184
MLA acronym: C&T

SUBSCRIPTION INFORMATION

Frequency of publication: Annual
Circulation: 200
Available in microform: No

ADVERTISING INFORMATION

Advertising accepted: No

EDITORIAL DESCRIPTION

Scope: Publishes articles on folklore or of interest to folklorists, with special emphasis on Canadian folklore.
Reviews books: Yes
Publishes notes: Yes
Languages accepted: English; French
Prints abstracts: Yes
Author-anonymous submission: No

SUBMISSION REQUIREMENTS

Restrictions on contributors: None
Author pays submission fee: No
Author pays page charges: No
Length of articles: 10-20 pp.
Length of book reviews: 200 words
Length of notes: 50 words
Style: MLA
Number of copies required: 1
Special requirements: Submit typescript and diskette using ASCII, Scribe, or WordPerfect software.
Copyright ownership: Author
Rejected manuscripts: Returned
Time before publication decision: Decision made in Sept. or Oct.
Time between decision and publication: 2 mos.
Number of reviewers: 3
Articles submitted per year: 8-12
Articles published per year: 8-10
Book reviews submitted per year: 2-4
Book reviews published per year: 1-2

(730)
Culture Populaire Albanaise

Dalan Shapllo, Editor
Inst. de Culture Populaire
rue Kont Urani, no. 3
Tirana, Albania

Sponsoring organization: Inst. de Culture Populaire, Académie des Sciences de la RPS d'Albanie
MLA acronym: CPA

SUBSCRIPTION INFORMATION

Frequency of publication: Annual

ADVERTISING INFORMATION

Advertising accepted: No

EDITORIAL DESCRIPTION

Scope: Publishes articles on Albanian popular culture and folklore. Articles are selected from the journal *Kultura Popullore*.
Reviews books: Yes
Publishes notes: Yes
Languages accepted: French

(731)
CUNYForum: Papers in Linguistics

Robert M. Vago, Editor
Ph.D. Program in Linguistics
Graduate Center, City Univ. of New York
33 W. 42 St.
New York, NY 10036

First published: 1976
Sponsoring organization: City Univ. of New York-Graduate Center, Ph.D. Program in Linguistics
ISSN: 0884-4275
MLA acronym: CUNYF

SUBSCRIPTION INFORMATION

Frequency of publication: Annual
Circulation: 150-200
Available in microform: No

ADVERTISING INFORMATION

Advertising accepted: No

EDITORIAL DESCRIPTION

Scope: Publishes linguistics studies.
Reviews books: No
Publishes notes: No
Languages accepted: English
Prints abstracts: No
Author-anonymous submission: No

SUBMISSION REQUIREMENTS

Restrictions on contributors: None
Author pays submission fee: No
Author pays page charges: No
Length of articles: No restrictions
Style: Journal
Number of copies required: 1
Special requirements: Submit camera-ready copy.
Copyright ownership: Author
Rejected manuscripts: Returned
Time before publication decision: 4-6 weeks
Time between decision and publication: 2-3 mos.
Number of reviewers: 2
Articles submitted per year: 10
Articles published per year: 7

(732)
*Cupey: Revista de la Universidad Metropolitana

Olga Nolla, Editor
Call Box 21150
Río Piedras, PR 00928

Telephone: 809 766-1717 ext. 463
Fax: 809 766-1717 ext. 507
First published: 1984
Sponsoring organization: Univ. Metropolitana
MLA acronym: Cupey

SUBSCRIPTION INFORMATION

Frequency of publication: Annual
Available in microform: No
Subscription price: $20.00/2 yrs.
Year to which price refers: 1992

ADVERTISING INFORMATION

Advertising accepted: No

EDITORIAL DESCRIPTION

Scope: Publishes poetry, short stories, and other creative writing that expresses intellectual activity in Puerto Rico, as well as critical works on plastic arts, comics, history, education, and science in Puerto Rico as they are related to society and literature.
Reviews books: Yes
Publishes notes: No
Languages accepted: Spanish
Prints abstracts: No
Author-anonymous submission: No

SUBMISSION REQUIREMENTS

Author pays submission fee: No
Author pays page charges: No
Length of articles: 3,500 words
Length of book reviews: 1,000-1,500 words
Number of copies required: 1
Special requirements: Submission of typescript accompanied by a computer cassette is preferred.
Copyright ownership: Journal for 2 yrs.
Rejected manuscripts: Returned at author's request
Time before publication decision: 6-12 mos.
Time between decision and publication: 6-12 mos.
Number of reviewers: 3
Articles submitted per year: 25
Articles published per year: 10
Book reviews submitted per year: 6-10
Book reviews published per year: 3-4

(733)
*Current Anthropology: A World Journal of the Human Sciences

Adam J. Kuper, Editor
Office of the Editor
Brunel Univ.
Uxbridge, Middlesex UB8 3PH, England

First published: 1960
Sponsoring organization: Wenner-Gren Foundation for Anthropological Research
ISSN: 0011-3204
MLA acronym: CAnth

SUBSCRIPTION INFORMATION

Frequency of publication: 5 times/yr.
Circulation: 4,985
Available in microform: Yes
Subscription price: $120.00/yr. institutions; $45.00/yr. individuals
Year to which price refers: 1992
Subscription address: Univ. of Chicago Press, Journals Division, 5720 S. Woodlawn Ave., Chicago, IL 60637
Subscription fax: 312 753-0811

ADVERTISING INFORMATION

Advertising accepted: Yes

EDITORIAL DESCRIPTION

Scope: Journal focuses on communication within a world-wide community of individual scholars concerning all aspects of the human sciences.
Reviews books: Yes
Publishes notes: Yes
Languages accepted: English
Prints abstracts: Yes
Author-anonymous submission: No

SUBMISSION REQUIREMENTS

Restrictions on contributors: Papers submitted in languages other than English will be reviewed and journal will pay translation costs if a paper is accepted.
Author pays submission fee: No
Author pays page charges: No
Length of articles: 10-50 typescript pp.
Length of book reviews: 1,500-2,000 words
Length of notes: 3,000 words
Style: Chicago
Number of copies required: 1
Copyright ownership: Wenner-Gren Foundation
Rejected manuscripts: Returned
Time before publication decision: 6 weeks
Time between decision and publication: 6-8 mos.
Number of reviewers: 7-10
Articles submitted per year: 140
Articles published per year: 45
Book reviews submitted per year: 30
Book reviews published per year: 23

(734)
*A Current Bibliography on African Affairs

Paula Boesch, Editor
Baywood Publishing Co.
26 Austin Ave.
Amityville, NY 11701

Telephone: 516 691-1470
Fax: 516 691-1770
First published: 1962
ISSN: 0011-3255
MLA acronym: CBAA

SUBSCRIPTION INFORMATION

Frequency of publication: 4 times/yr.
Circulation: 1,000
Available in microform: No

ADVERTISING INFORMATION

Advertising accepted: Yes, on an exchange basis

EDITORIAL DESCRIPTION

Scope: Publishes bibliographic articles, bibliographies, and book reviews on African affairs. Includes a bibliography of 500 entries per issue.
Reviews books: Yes
Publishes notes: No
Languages accepted: English
Prints abstracts: Yes
Author-anonymous submission: Yes

SUBMISSION REQUIREMENTS

Author pays submission fee: No
Author pays page charges: No
Length of articles: 10 pp.
Style: Chicago
Number of copies required: 2
Special requirements: Contributions must be in the form of a bibliography or a bibliographic essay.
Copyright ownership: Baywood Publishing Co., Inc.
Rejected manuscripts: Returned
Time before publication decision: 3-6 mos.
Time between decision and publication: 3-6 mos.
Number of reviewers: 1
Articles submitted per year: 20
Articles published per year: 10
Book reviews submitted per year: 20
Book reviews published per year: 16

(735)
*Current Studies in Linguistics

Samuel Jay Keyser, Editor
MIT Press
55 Hayward St.
Cambridge, MA 02142

First published: 1972
MLA acronym: CSLing

SUBSCRIPTION INFORMATION

Frequency of publication: Irregular
Available in microform: No

ADVERTISING INFORMATION

Advertising accepted: No

EDITORIAL DESCRIPTION

Scope: Publishes monograph studies in linguistics.
Reviews books: No
Publishes notes: No
Languages accepted: English
Prints abstracts: No
Author-anonymous submission: No

SUBMISSION REQUIREMENTS

Author pays submission fee: No
Author pays page charges: No
Style: Chicago
Number of copies required: 1
Copyright ownership: MIT
Rejected manuscripts: Returned
Number of reviewers: 2-4
Books published per year: 2-3

(736)
Cuyahoga Review

Richard Charnigo, Jerome M. McKeever, & Barbara A. Charnigo, Editors
Cuyahoga Community College
11000 Pleasant Valley Rd.
Parma, OH 44130

First published: 1983
ISSN: 0737-139X
MLA acronym: CuyahogaR

SUBSCRIPTION INFORMATION

Circulation: 400
Available in microform: No

ADVERTISING INFORMATION

Advertising accepted: No

EDITORIAL DESCRIPTION

Scope: Publishes articles on literature, culture, and pedagogy.
Reviews books: No
Languages accepted: English
Prints abstracts: No

SUBMISSION REQUIREMENTS

Restrictions on contributors: None

Author pays submission fee: No
Author pays page charges: No
Length of articles: 2,000-5,000 words
Style: MLA
Number of copies required: 2
Copyright ownership: Journal
Rejected manuscripts: Returned
Time before publication decision: 1-6 mos.
Time between decision and publication: 1-6 mos.
Number of reviewers: 1-3
Articles submitted per year: 35-40
Articles published per year: 20

(737)
*Cycnos

André Viola, Editor
U.F.R. Lettres, Arts & Sciences Humaines
98, Bd. Edouard Herriot
B.P. 369
06007 Nice Cedex, France

First published: 1985
Sponsoring organization: Centre de Recherche sur les Écritures de Langue Anglaise (C.R.E.L.A.), Univ. de Nice
ISSN: 0992-1893
MLA acronym: Cycnos

SUBSCRIPTION INFORMATION

Frequency of publication: 2 times/yr.
Available in microform: No

ADVERTISING INFORMATION

Advertising accepted: No

EDITORIAL DESCRIPTION

Scope: Publishes issues organized around a specific theme concerning the English language or literatures written in English. Also publishes articles on the history of ideas in Anglophone countries.
Reviews books: No
Publishes notes: Yes
Languages accepted: French; English
Prints abstracts: Yes
Author-anonymous submission: No

SUBMISSION REQUIREMENTS

Restrictions on contributors: No
Author pays submission fee: No
Author pays page charges: No
Length of articles: 5,000 words
Length of notes: 2,000 words
Style: MLA
Number of copies required: 1
Copyright ownership: Journal
Rejected manuscripts: Returned; enclose return postage.
Time before publication decision: 2 mos.
Time between decision and publication: 4 mos.
Number of reviewers: 2
Articles submitted per year: 15
Articles published per year: 10-14

(738)
*D. H. Lawrence: The Journal of the D. H. Lawrence Society

Peter Preston, Editor
7 Brornley Rd.
West Bridgford
Nottingham NG2 7AP, England

Telephone: (44) 602 810738
Sponsoring organization: D. H. Lawrence Soc.
MLA acronym: JDHLS

SUBSCRIPTION INFORMATION

Frequency of publication: Annual
Available in microform: No
Subscription price: £7.00/yr. United Kingdom; £10.00/yr. Europe; £15.00/yr. elsewhere
Year to which price refers: 1991-92
Subscription address: Monica Rothe-Rotowski, 23 Lincoln Court, Bilborough, Nottingham NG8 4FQ, England

ADVERTISING INFORMATION

Advertising accepted: Yes

EDITORIAL DESCRIPTION

Scope: Publishes articles on the life and works of D. H. Lawrence.
Reviews books: Yes
Publishes notes: No
Languages accepted: English
Prints abstracts: No
Author-anonymous submission: No

SUBMISSION REQUIREMENTS

Restrictions on contributors: Reviews are solicited.
Author pays submission fee: No
Author pays page charges: No
Length of articles: 3,000-5,000 words
Style: Journal
Number of copies required: 1
Copyright ownership: Author
Rejected manuscripts: Returned
Time before publication decision: 3 mos.
Time between decision and publication: 3-12 mos.
Number of reviewers: 2
Articles published per year: 4-6
Book reviews published per year: 6-8

(739)
*The D. H. Lawrence Review

Dennis Jackson, Editor
English Dept., 204 Memorial Hall
Univ. of Delaware
Newark, DE 19716

Telephone: 302 454-1480
First published: 1968
ISSN: 0011-4936
MLA acronym: DHLR

SUBSCRIPTION INFORMATION

Frequency of publication: 3 times/yr. (Spring, Summer, Fall)
Circulation: 800
Available in microform: Yes
Subscription price: $20.00/yr. institutions US; $14.00/yr. individuals US; $15.00/yr. elsewhere
Year to which price refers: 1992

ADVERTISING INFORMATION

Advertising accepted: Yes
Advertising rates: $60.00/half page; $120.00/full page

EDITORIAL DESCRIPTION

Scope: Publishes criticism, scholarship, reviews, and bibliography of D. H. Lawrence and his circle. Occasional special numbers are devoted to particular areas of Lawrence's work or to other figures associated with him.
Reviews books: Yes
Publishes notes: Yes
Languages accepted: English
Prints abstracts: No
Author-anonymous submission: No

SUBMISSION REQUIREMENTS

Restrictions on contributors: Multiple submissions are not accepted.
Author pays submission fee: No
Author pays page charges: No
Length of articles: 7,500 words maximum
Length of book reviews: 1,000 words
Length of notes: 1,000 words
Style: MLA
Number of copies required: 2
Copyright ownership: Journal
Rejected manuscripts: Returned; enclose SASE.
Time before publication decision: 3 mos.
Time between decision and publication: 6-12 mos.
Number of reviewers: 3
Articles submitted per year: 60-75
Articles published per year: 12-15
Book reviews submitted per year: 20
Book reviews published per year: 20
Notes submitted per year: 12
Notes published per year: 4

(740)
*Dactylus

David Julseth & Benjamín Milano, Editors
Univ. of Texas, Austin
Dept. of Spanish & Portuguese
Batts Hall 110
Austin, TX 78712

Telephone: 512 471-4936
First published: 1984
Sponsoring organization: Dept. of Spanish & Portuguese, Univ. of Texas, Austin
MLA acronym: Dactylus

SUBSCRIPTION INFORMATION

Frequency of publication: Annual
Circulation: 350
Available in microform: No
Subscription price: $5.00/yr. US; $7.00/yr. Europe & Latin America
Year to which price refers: 1991

ADVERTISING INFORMATION

Advertising accepted: Yes

EDITORIAL DESCRIPTION

Scope: Publishes original articles and creative works regarding the literature of Spanish- and Portuguese-speaking countries.
Reviews books: Yes
Publishes notes: Yes
Languages accepted: Spanish; English; Portuguese
Prints abstracts: No
Author-anonymous submission: No

SUBMISSION REQUIREMENTS

Restrictions on contributors: None
Author pays submission fee: No
Author pays page charges: No
Length of articles: 2,500-3,500 words
Length of book reviews: 500 words
Length of notes: 500 words
Style: MLA
Number of copies required: 2
Special requirements: Submit 2 typescript copies and a 3.5 in. Macintosh diskette.
Copyright ownership: Journal
Rejected manuscripts: Not returned
Time before publication decision: 2 mos.
Time between decision and publication: 4 mos.
Number of reviewers: 3
Articles submitted per year: 30
Articles published per year: 25

(741)
*Dada/Surrealism

Mary Ann Caws & Rudolf E. Kuenzli, Editors
Dept. of Comparative Literature, 425 EPB
Univ. of Iowa
Iowa City, IA 52242

Telephone: 319 335-0330
First published: 1971
Sponsoring organization: Assn. for the Study of Dada & Surrealism; Peyre Inst., City Univ. of New York Graduate Center
ISSN: 0084-9537
MLA acronym: Dada

SUBSCRIPTION INFORMATION

Frequency of publication: Annual
Circulation: 1,000
Available in microform: No

ADVERTISING INFORMATION

Advertising accepted: Yes

EDITORIAL DESCRIPTION

Scope: Publishes articles on topics in the fields of Dada and Surrealism.
Reviews books: No
Publishes notes: No
Languages accepted: English
Prints abstracts: No
Author-anonymous submission: No

SUBMISSION REQUIREMENTS

Restrictions on contributors: None
Author pays submission fee: No
Author pays page charges: No
Length of articles: 8-15 pp. maximum
Style: MLA
Number of copies required: 2
Special requirements: Quotes may be printed in languages other than English, but translations should be provided. Topics for articles are announced in advance.
Copyright ownership: Author & Assn. for the Study of Dada and Surrealism
Rejected manuscripts: Returned
Time before publication decision: 2-4 mos.
Time between decision and publication: 1 yr.
Number of reviewers: 1-3
Articles submitted per year: 20-25
Articles published per year: 10-15

(742)
*Dædalus: Journal of the American Academy of Arts and Sciences

Stephen R. Graubard, Editor
Norton's Woods
136 Irving St.
Cambridge, MA 02138

Telephone: 617 491-2600
Fax: 617 576-5088
First published: 1958
Sponsoring organization: American Academy of Arts & Sciences
ISSN: 0011-5266
MLA acronym: Dædalus

SUBSCRIPTION INFORMATION

Frequency of publication: 4 times/yr.
Circulation: 20,000
Available in microform: Yes
Subscription price: $40.00/yr. institutions; $25.00/yr. individuals; add $5.00/yr. outside US
Year to which price refers: 1992
Subscription address: Dædalus Business Office, at the above address
Subscription telephone: 800 327-0229

ADVERTISING INFORMATION

Advertising accepted: No

EDITORIAL DESCRIPTION

Scope: Focuses on interdisciplinary scholarship.
Reviews books: No
Publishes notes: No
Languages accepted: English
Prints abstracts: No
Author-anonymous submission: No

SUBMISSION REQUIREMENTS

Restrictions on contributors: Unsolicited manuscripts are not accepted.
Author pays submission fee: No
Author pays page charges: No
Length of articles: No restrictions
Special requirements: Submit typescript and diskette.
Copyright ownership: American Academy of Arts & Sciences
Rejected manuscripts: Returned; enclose return postage.
Time between decision and publication: 6 mos.
Number of reviewers: 4-20
Articles published per year: 50

(743)
*Dalhousie French Studies

Hans R. Runte, Editor
Dept. of French
Dalhousie Univ.
Halifax, Nova Scotia B3H 3J5, Canada

Telephone: 902 494-2430
First published: 1978
Sponsoring organization: Dalhousie Univ.
ISSN: 0711-8813
MLA acronym: DFS

SUBSCRIPTION INFORMATION

Frequency of publication: 2 times/yr. (Spring-Summer, Fall-Winter)
Circulation: 250
Available in microform: No
Subscription price: $16.00/yr.
Year to which price refers: 1992

ADVERTISING INFORMATION

Advertising accepted: Yes

EDITORIAL DESCRIPTION

Scope: Publishes critical essays on French and Francophone literature as well as poetry and essays.
Reviews books: No
Publishes notes: No
Languages accepted: English; French
Prints abstracts: No
Author-anonymous submission: Yes

SUBMISSION REQUIREMENTS

Restrictions on contributors: None
Author pays submission fee: No
Author pays page charges: No
Length of articles: 3,500-5,000 words
Style: MLA
Number of copies required: 2
Copyright ownership: Author
Rejected manuscripts: Returned
Time before publication decision: 2 mos.
Time between decision and publication: 9 mos.
Number of reviewers: 3
Articles submitted per year: 50-60
Articles published per year: 12-20

(744)
*Dalhousie Review

Alan Andrews & J. A. Wainwright, Editors
Sir James Dunn Bldg., Suite 314
Dalhousie Univ.
Halifax, Nova Scotia B3H 3J5, Canada

Telephone: 902 494-2541
Fax: 902 492-2319
First published: 1921
Sponsoring organization: Dalhousie Univ.; Social Sciences & Humanities Research Council of Canada
ISSN: 0011-5827
MLA acronym: DR

SUBSCRIPTION INFORMATION

Frequency of publication: 4 times/yr.
Circulation: 1,000
Available in microform: Yes
Subscription price: C$19.00/yr. Canada; C$28.00/yr. elsewhere
Year to which price refers: 1992
Subscription address: Office Manager, at the above address

ADVERTISING INFORMATION

Advertising accepted: Yes

EDITORIAL DESCRIPTION

Scope: Invites contributions in such fields as history, literature, political science, and philosophy as well as fiction and verse from both new and established writers.
Reviews books: Yes
Publishes notes: No
Languages accepted: English
Prints abstracts: No
Author-anonymous submission: Yes

SUBMISSION REQUIREMENTS

Restrictions on contributors: Preference is given to Canadian authors; book reviews are commissioned.
Author pays submission fee: No
Author pays page charges: No
Length of articles: 5,000 words maximum
Length of book reviews: 1,000 words maximum
Style: Canadian preferred; MLA accepted
Number of copies required: 2
Special requirements: Submission on IBM or IBM-compatible diskettes using Wordperfect is preferred. Other systems and programs are often acceptable, including electronic mail.
Copyright ownership: Dalhousie Univ. Press, Ltd.
Rejected manuscripts: Returned; enclose Canadian postage or international reply coupons, and SAE.
Time before publication decision: 2-12 mos.
Time between decision and publication: 2-24 mos.
Number of reviewers: 1-2
Articles submitted per year: 65
Articles published per year: 40
Book reviews published per year: 50

(745)
*Dansk Udsyn

Askov Højskole
6600 Vejen, Denmark

First published: 1921
ISSN: 0106-4622
MLA acronym: Dansk Udsyn

SUBSCRIPTION INFORMATION

Frequency of publication: 6 times/yr. (Feb., Apr., June, Aug., Oct., Dec.)
Circulation: 1,500
Available in microform: No

ADVERTISING INFORMATION

Advertising accepted: No

EDITORIAL DESCRIPTION

Scope: Publishes essays on literary, social, and cultural subjects.
Reviews books: Yes
Languages accepted: Danish
Prints abstracts: No

SUBMISSION REQUIREMENTS

Restrictions on contributors: Book reviews are commissioned.
Author pays submission fee: No
Author pays page charges: No
Length of articles: 10-20 pp.
Length of book reviews: 2 pp.
Style: None
Number of copies required: 1
Copyright ownership: Author
Rejected manuscripts: Returned
Time before publication decision: 2-4 mos.
Time between decision and publication: 3-6 mos.
Number of reviewers: 4
Articles submitted per year: 45
Articles published per year: 30
Book reviews published per year: 12

(746)
*Danske Afhandlinger om Oversættelse

Cay Dollerup & Viggo Hjørnager Pedersen, Editors
Københavns Univ.
Center for Oversættelsesvidenskab & Leksikografi
Njalsgade 96
2300 Copenhagen S, Denmark

Telephone: (45) 31 542211
Fax: (45) 32 961518
First published: 1991
Sponsoring organization: Københavns Univ., Center for Oversættelsesvidenskab & Leksikografi
ISSN: 0906-9178
MLA acronym: DAO

SUBSCRIPTION INFORMATION

Frequency of publication: Irregular
Circulation: 100
Available in microform: No

ADVERTISING INFORMATION

Advertising accepted: Yes

EDITORIAL DESCRIPTION

Scope: Publishes studies on translation and lexicography.
Reviews books: No
Publishes notes: No
Languages accepted: Danish
Prints abstracts: Yes
Author-anonymous submission: No

SUBMISSION REQUIREMENTS

Author pays submission fee: No
Author pays page charges: No
Copyright ownership: Author
Rejected manuscripts: Returned at author's request; enclose return postage
Time before publication decision: 3 mos.
Time between decision and publication: 1-2 mos.
Books published per year: 1-3

(747)
*Danske Folkemål

Inst. for Dansk Dialektforskning
Njalsgade 80
2300 Copenhagen S, Denmark

First published: 1927
Sponsoring organization: Københavns Univ.
ISSN: 0106-4630
MLA acronym: DanF

SUBSCRIPTION INFORMATION

Frequency of publication: Annual
Circulation: 200
Available in microform: No
Subscription price: 180 Dkr/yr.
Year to which price refers: 1992
Subscription address: C. A. Reitzels Forlag, Nørregade 20, 1165 Copenhagen K, Denmark

ADVERTISING INFORMATION

Advertising accepted: No

EDITORIAL DESCRIPTION

Scope: Publishes articles on Danish dialects and local variants of the standard language, from different points of view: phonetics, phonology, lexicography, sociolinguistics, rural culture, etc.
Reviews books: No
Languages accepted: Danish
Prints abstracts: No

SUBMISSION REQUIREMENTS

Restrictions on contributors: Contributors must be on the staff of the Inst. for Dansk Dialektforskning.

(748)
*Danske Studier

Iver Kjær & Flemming Lundgreen-Nielsen, Editors
Rolighedsvej 27
3460 Birkerød, Denmark

First published: 1904
Sponsoring organization: Univ.-Jubilæets Danske Samfund
ISSN: 0106-4525
MLA acronym: DS

SUBSCRIPTION INFORMATION

Frequency of publication: Annual
Circulation: 1,000
Available in microform: No
Subscription price: 200 Dkr/yr.
Year to which price refers: 1991
Subscription address: C. A. Reitzels Forlag, Nørregade 20, 1165 Copenhagen K, Denmark

ADVERTISING INFORMATION

Advertising accepted: No

EDITORIAL DESCRIPTION

Scope: Publishes articles on Danish language, literature, and folklore.
Reviews books: Yes
Publishes notes: Yes
Languages accepted: Danish; Swedish; Norwegian; English; German
Prints abstracts: No
Author-anonymous submission: No

SUBMISSION REQUIREMENTS

Restrictions on contributors: None
Author pays submission fee: No
Author pays page charges: No
Length of articles: 5-20 pp.
Length of book reviews: 2-5 pp.
Length of notes: 1/2-1 1/2 pp.
Style: MLA
Number of copies required: 1
Special requirements: Submit original typescript.
Copyright ownership: Author & Univ.-Jubilæets Danske Samfund
Rejected manuscripts: Returned
Time before publication decision: Publication decision by 1 Sept.
Time between decision and publication: 7 mos.
Number of reviewers: 3
Articles submitted per year: 15-20
Articles published per year: 5-6
Book reviews submitted per year: 15
Book reviews published per year: 13
Notes submitted per year: 6-7
Notes published per year: 3-4

(749)
*Dante Studies, with the Annual Report of the Dante Society

Christopher Kleinhenz, Editor
Dept. of French & Italian
618 Van Hise Hall
1220 Linden Dr.
Univ. of Wisconsin
Madison, WI 53706

Telephone: 608 262-5816; 608 262-3941
Fax: 608 262-4747
E-mail: CKLEIN@MACC.WISC.EDU
First published: 1882
Sponsoring organization: Dante Soc. of America
ISSN: 0070-2862
MLA acronym: DSARDS

SUBSCRIPTION INFORMATION

Frequency of publication: Annual
Circulation: 500
Available in microform: No
Subscription price: $19.95/yr.
Year to which price refers: 1991
Subscription address: State Univ. of New York Press, SUNY Plaza, Albany, NY 12246
Subscription telephone: 518 472-5000

ADVERTISING INFORMATION

Advertising accepted: Yes

EDITORIAL DESCRIPTION

Scope: Publishes articles on the life, work, and influence of Dante.
Reviews books: Occasionally
Publishes notes: Occasionally
Languages accepted: English; Italian; French
Prints abstracts: No
Author-anonymous submission: No

SUBMISSION REQUIREMENTS

Restrictions on contributors: Book reviews are commissioned.
Author pays submission fee: No
Author pays page charges: No
Length of articles: 5,000-8,000 words
Length of notes: 1,000-1,500 words
Style: Journal
Number of copies required: 2
Special requirements: Submit a 200-word abstract. Submission of final accepted manuscript should be on diskette using WordPerfect or ASCII format.
Copyright ownership: Dante Soc. of America
Rejected manuscripts: Returned
Time before publication decision: 1-6 mos.
Time between decision and publication: 6-9 mos.
Number of reviewers: 5
Articles submitted per year: 10-15
Articles published per year: 6-7
Notes submitted per year: 2-5
Notes published per year: 1-2

(750)
*Daphnis: Zeitschrift für Mittlere Deutsche Literatur

Hans-Gert Roloff, Leonard W. Forster, Ferdinand van Ingen, Eberhard Mannack, Blake Lee Spahr, Alberto Martino, Gerhard Spellberg, Barbara Becker-Cantarino, Wilhelm Kühlmann, Marian Szyrocki, Jean-Marie Valentin, & Martin Bircher, Editors
Forschungsstelle für Mittlere Deutsche Literatur
Freie Univ. Berlin
Habelschwerdter Allee 45
1000 Berlin 33, Germany

Telephone: (49) 30 8384078
Fax: (49) 30 8386749
First published: 1972
ISSN: 0300-693X
MLA acronym: Daphnis

SUBSCRIPTION INFORMATION

Frequency of publication: 4 times/yr.
Circulation: 400
Available in microform: No
Subscription address: Editions Rodopi B.V., Keizersgracht 302-304, 1016 EX Amsterdam, Netherlands
Subscription telephone: (31) 20 6227507
Subscription fax: (31) 20 380948

ADVERTISING INFORMATION

Advertising accepted: Yes

EDITORIAL DESCRIPTION

Scope: Publishes articles on German literature between 1380 and 1750, including Neo-Latin, Late Middle Ages, Humanism, Reformation, Renaissance, Baroque, Mannerism, Enlightenment, and Rococo.
Reviews books: Yes
Publishes notes: Yes
Languages accepted: English; German; French
Prints abstracts: No
Author-anonymous submission: Yes

SUBMISSION REQUIREMENTS

Restrictions on contributors: None
Author pays submission fee: No
Author pays page charges: No
Length of articles: No restrictions
Length of book reviews: No restrictions
Length of notes: 1,000 words
Style: Journal
Number of copies required: 1
Copyright ownership: Author
Rejected manuscripts: Returned
Time before publication decision: 1-2 mos.
Time between decision and publication: 6-10 mos.
Number of reviewers: 2-3
Articles submitted per year: 40-50
Articles published per year: 25-30
Book reviews submitted per year: 60
Book reviews published per year: 25-30
Notes submitted per year: 5-15
Notes published per year: 5-10

(751)
Data Papers in Papua New Guinea Languages

John M. Clifton, Editor
Summer Inst. of Linguistics
Box 418
Ukarumpa via Lae, Papua New Guinea

First published: 1973
Sponsoring organization: Summer Inst. of Linguistics
MLA acronym: DPPNGL

SUBSCRIPTION INFORMATION

Frequency of publication: 2 times/yr.
Circulation: 200
Available in microform: Yes
Subscription address: Summer Inst. of Linguistics, Academic Publications, Box 397, Ukarumpa via Lae, Papua New Guinea

ADVERTISING INFORMATION

Advertising accepted: No

EDITORIAL DESCRIPTION

Scope: Publishes articles on languages of Papua New Guinea by members of the Summer Institute of Linguistics.
Reviews books: No
Publishes notes: No
Languages accepted: English
Prints abstracts: No
Author-anonymous submission: No

SUBMISSION REQUIREMENTS

Restrictions on contributors: Contributors normally must be members of the Summer Inst. of Linguistics or be Papua New Guinea national linguists.
Author pays submission fee: No
Author pays page charges: No
Length of books: 250 pp. maximum
Style: Chicago
Number of copies required: 1
Special requirements: Submit camera-ready copy or computer diskette (3 1/2 or 5 1/4).
Copyright ownership: Summer Inst. of Linguistics
Rejected manuscripts: Returned; enclose return postage.
Time before publication decision: 3 mos.
Time between decision and publication: 6-12 mos.
Number of reviewers: 1-2
Books published per year: 1-3

(752)
*Daugava: Literaturno-Khudozhestvennyĭ i Obshchestvenno-Politicheskiĭ Ezhemesiachnyĭ Zhurnal Soiuza Pisateleĭ Latvii

R. Dobrovenskiĭ, Editor
Balasta Dambī, 3
Riga, 1081, Latvia

First published: 1977
Historical variations in title: Formerly *Daugava: Literaturno-Khudozhestvennyĭ i Obshchestvenno-Politicheskiĭ Ezhemesiachnyĭ Zhurnal Soiuza Sovetskikh Pisateleleĭ Latvii*
Sponsoring organization: Soiuz Pisateleĭ Latvii
ISSN: 0207-4001
MLA acronym: Daugava

SUBSCRIPTION INFORMATION

Frequency of publication: 6 times/yr.
Available in microform: No
Subscription address: Izdatel'stvo Daugava, Riga, Latvia

EDITORIAL DESCRIPTION

Scope: Publishes articles on literature and socio-political topics.
Reviews books: No
Languages accepted: Russian
Prints abstracts: No

SUBMISSION REQUIREMENTS

Rejected manuscripts: Not returned

(753)
Degré Second: Studies in French Literature

W. Pierre Jacoebée, James P. McNab, & Jack Undank, Editors
Dept. of Foreign Languages & Literatures
Virginia Polytechnic Inst. & State Univ.
Blacksburg, VA 24061

First published: 1977
ISSN: 0148-561X
MLA acronym: DSec

SUBSCRIPTION INFORMATION

Frequency of publication: Annual
Circulation: 220
Available in microform: No

ADVERTISING INFORMATION

Advertising accepted: Yes

EDITORIAL DESCRIPTION

Scope: Publishes essays on French literature and, occasionally, on Francophone literature.
Reviews books: Yes
Publishes notes: No
Languages accepted: English; French; German
Prints abstracts: No
Author-anonymous submission: Yes

SUBMISSION REQUIREMENTS

Restrictions on contributors: Unsolicited book reviews are not accepted.
Author pays submission fee: No
Author pays page charges: No
Length of articles: No restrictions
Length of book reviews: No restrictions
Style: MLA; Chicago; Modern Humanities Research Assn.
Number of copies required: 1
Copyright ownership: Journal
Rejected manuscripts: Returned
Time before publication decision: 3-5 mos.
Time between decision and publication: 3-15 mos.
Number of reviewers: 3
Articles submitted per year: 35-50
Articles published per year: 12 maximum
Book reviews published per year: 5-10

(754)
*Degrés: Revue de Synthèse à Orientation Sémiologique

André Helbo, Editor
Pl. Constantin Meunier, 2, bte 13
1180 Brussels, Belgium

Telephone: (32) 2 3450083
First published: 1973
ISSN: 0770-8378
MLA acronym: Degrés

SUBSCRIPTION INFORMATION

Frequency of publication: 4 times/yr.
Circulation: 5,000
Available in microform: No
Subscription price: 1,250 BF/yr. plus postage
Year to which price refers: 1992

ADVERTISING INFORMATION

Advertising accepted: Yes

EDITORIAL DESCRIPTION

Scope: Studies the interdisciplinary problem of the transfer of operative concepts of semiotics to literature, aesthetic communication, mass media, etc.
Reviews books: Yes
Publishes notes: Yes
Languages accepted: English; French; German; Spanish; Italian
Prints abstracts: Yes
Author-anonymous submission: Yes

SUBMISSION REQUIREMENTS

Restrictions on contributors: None
Author pays submission fee: No
Author pays page charges: No
Length of articles: No restrictions
Length of book reviews: 150 words
Length of notes: 50 words
Style: None
Number of copies required: 2
Copyright ownership: Journal
Rejected manuscripts: Not returned
Time before publication decision: 3 mos.
Time between decision and publication: 3 mos. minimum
Number of reviewers: 5
Articles submitted per year: 400
Articles published per year: 60
Book reviews submitted per year: 1,000
Book reviews published per year: 200
Notes submitted per year: 400
Notes published per year: 60

(755)
*Delo: Mesečni Književni Časopis

Slobodan Blagojević, Editor
Nolit, Terazije 27/II
Belgrade, Yugoslavia

First published: 1955
ISSN: 0011-7935
MLA acronym: Delo

SUBSCRIPTION INFORMATION

Frequency of publication: 12 times/yr.
Circulation: 1,000
Available in microform: Yes
Subscription price: $30.00/yr. Yugoslavia; $50.00/yr. elsewhere
Year to which price refers: 1991
Subscription address: Delo, Terazije 13/IV, Belgrade, Yugoslavia

ADVERTISING INFORMATION

Advertising accepted: No

EDITORIAL DESCRIPTION

Scope: Publishes articles on literary theory, criticism, poetry, and new ideas.
Reviews books: No
Publishes notes: No
Languages accepted: Serbo-Croatian; English; Russian; German; French; Italian; Spanish
Prints abstracts: Yes
Author-anonymous submission: No

SUBMISSION REQUIREMENTS

Restrictions on contributors: None
Author pays submission fee: No
Author pays page charges: No
Length of articles: 40 pp. maximum
Style: None
Number of copies required: 1
Special requirements: Include 100-word abstract.
Copyright ownership: Author
Rejected manuscripts: Returned; enclose return postage.
Time before publication decision: 1 mo.
Time between decision and publication: 2-3 mos.

Number of reviewers: 2
Articles submitted per year: 500
Articles published per year: 200

(756)
*Denver Quarterly

Donald Revell, Editor
Univ. of Denver
Denver, CO 80208

Telephone: 303 871-2892
First published: 1966
Sponsoring organization: Dept. of English, Univ. of Denver
ISSN: 0011-8869
MLA acronym: DQ

SUBSCRIPTION INFORMATION

Frequency of publication: 4 times/yr. (Apr., July, Sept., Dec.)
Circulation: 900
Available in microform: Yes
Subscription price: $15.00/yr.

ADVERTISING INFORMATION

Advertising accepted: Yes
Advertising rates: $150.00/full page

EDITORIAL DESCRIPTION

Scope: Publishes short fiction, novel excerpts, poetry, essays, and reviews of significant books. Perhaps one issue a year is devoted to a special theme or literary figure. Also publishes translations of important continental and South American writers.
Reviews books: Yes
Publishes notes: No
Languages accepted: English
Prints abstracts: No
Author-anonymous submission: No

SUBMISSION REQUIREMENTS

Author pays submission fee: No
Author pays page charges: No
Length of articles: No restrictions
Length of book reviews: 1,000-2,000 words
Style: MLA
Number of copies required: 1
Copyright ownership: Journal for 1 yr., then reverts to author upon request
Rejected manuscripts: Returned at author's request; enclose SASE.
Time before publication decision: 2-4 weeks
Time between decision and publication: 18 mos. maximum
Number of reviewers: 1-3
Articles submitted per year: 100
Articles published per year: 6

(757)
*Deutsch als Fremdsprache: Zeitschrift zur Theorie und Praxis des Deutschunterrichts für Auslaender

Gerhard Helbig, Editor
Herder-Inst. der Univ. Leipzig
Lumumbastr. 4
7022 Leipzig, Germany

First published: 1964
ISSN: 0011-9741
MLA acronym: DaF

SUBSCRIPTION INFORMATION

Frequency of publication: 4 times/yr.
Available in microform: No
Subscription price: 38 DM/yr.
Year to which price refers: 1992

Additional subscription address: Verlag Langenscheidt KG, Crellestr. 28-30, 1000 Berlin, Germany

ADVERTISING INFORMATION

Advertising accepted: Yes

EDITORIAL DESCRIPTION

Scope: Publishes articles on Germanic linguistics, teaching German, the methodology of foreign language instruction, languages for special purposes, the study of geography and civilization, and the psychology of language learning.
Reviews books: Yes
Publishes notes: Yes
Languages accepted: German
Prints abstracts: Yes

SUBMISSION REQUIREMENTS

Restrictions on contributors: None
Author pays submission fee: No
Author pays page charges: No
Length of articles: 15 typescript pp. (30 lines per page)
Length of book reviews: 3-4 pp.
Length of notes: 20 lines
Style: None
Number of copies required: 3
Special requirements: Submit original typescript plus 2 copies.
Copyright ownership: Verlag Langenscheidt KG & author
Rejected manuscripts: Returned
Time before publication decision: 6 mos.
Time between decision and publication: 6-12 mos.
Number of reviewers: 3-6
Articles submitted per year: 80
Articles published per year: 40
Book reviews submitted per year: 30
Book reviews published per year: 25
Notes submitted per year: 15
Notes published per year: 8

(758)
*Deutsch-Slawische Forschungen zur Namenkunde und Siedlungsgeschichte

Ernst Eichler, Wolfgang Fleischer, Rudolf Grosse, & Hans Walther, Editors
Sprachwissenschaftliche Kommission der Sächsischen Akademie der Wissenschaften zu Leipzig
Goethestr. 3-5
7010 Leipzig, Germany

Telephone: (37) 41 7192973
First published: 1956
Sponsoring organization: Sächsische Akademie der Wissenschaften; Deutsche Forschungsgemeinschaft
ISSN: 0070-3893
MLA acronym: DSFNS

SUBSCRIPTION INFORMATION

Frequency of publication: Irregular
Circulation: 500
Available in microform: No
Subscription address: Akademie Verlag GmbH, Leipziger Str. 3-4, 1086 Berlin, Germany

ADVERTISING INFORMATION

Advertising accepted: No

EDITORIAL DESCRIPTION

Scope: Publishes monographs on German-Slavic research on onomastics and the history of settlement.
Reviews books: No
Publishes notes: No
Languages accepted: German
Prints abstracts: No

SUBMISSION REQUIREMENTS

Restrictions on contributors: None
Author pays submission fee: No
Author pays page charges: No
Length of books: No restrictions
Style: None
Number of copies required: 2
Copyright ownership: Akademie Verlag
Rejected manuscripts: Returned
Time before publication decision: 1 yr.
Time between decision and publication: 1 yr.
Number of reviewers: 2
Books submitted per year: 1
Books published per year: 1

(759)
*Deutsche Akademie für Sprache und Dichtung, Darmstadt. Jahrbuch

Michael Assmann, Editor
Deutsche Akademie für Sprache und Dichtung
Alexandraweg 23 (Glückert-Haus)
6100 Darmstadt, Germany

Telephone: (49) 6151 44823
Fax: (49) 6151 46268
First published: 1953
Sponsoring organization: Deutsche Akademie für Sprache & Dichtung
ISSN: 0070-3923
MLA acronym: DASDJ

SUBSCRIPTION INFORMATION

Frequency of publication: Annual
Available in microform: No
Subscription address: Luchterhand Literaturverlag, Mühlenkamp 6c, 2000 Hamburg 60, Germany
Additional subscription address: Luchterhand Literaturverlag, c/o Arche Verlag, Hölderlinstr. 15, Zurich, Switzerland
Subscription telephone: (41) 1 2522952 (Zurich)

ADVERTISING INFORMATION

Advertising accepted: No

EDITORIAL DESCRIPTION

Scope: Publishes papers delivered at the Spring and Fall conferences of the German Academy of Language and Literature; includes essays, and news of the Academy.
Reviews books: No
Publishes notes: No
Languages accepted: German
Prints abstracts: No

SUBMISSION REQUIREMENTS

Restrictions on contributors: Contributions are by invitation only.
Length of articles: No restrictions
Number of copies required: 1
Copyright ownership: Author
Rejected manuscripts: Returned
Time before publication decision: 3 mos.
Time between decision and publication: 6 mos.
Articles published per year: 16-20

(760)
*Deutsche Dialektgeographie/ Dialektographie

Reiner Hildebrandt & Ludwig Erich Schmitt, Editors
Forschungs Inst. für Deutsche Sprache
Deutscher Sprachatlas
Kaffweg 3
3350 Marburg/Lahn, Germany

Telephone: (49) 6421 282483
Fax: (49) 6421 287050
First published: 1908
Sponsoring organization: Forschungsinst. für Deutsche Sprache; Deutscher Sprachatlas
ISSN: 0179-3233
MLA acronym: DDG

SUBSCRIPTION INFORMATION

Frequency of publication: Irregular
Circulation: 250
Available in microform: No
Subscription address: N. G. Elwert Verlag, Reitgasse 7/9, Postfach 1228, 3550 Marburg/Lahn, Germany

ADVERTISING INFORMATION

Advertising accepted: No

EDITORIAL DESCRIPTION

Scope: Publishes monographs on German areal linguistics.
Reviews books: No
Publishes notes: No
Languages accepted: German
Prints abstracts: No
Author-anonymous submission: No

SUBMISSION REQUIREMENTS

Restrictions on contributors: None
Author pays submission fee: No
Author pays page charges: Yes
Number of copies required: 1
Special requirements: Submit original typescript.
Copyright ownership: Editor
Rejected manuscripts: Returned
Time before publication decision: 6 weeks
Time between decision and publication: 8 mos.
Number of reviewers: 2
Books submitted per year: 1
Books published per year: 1

(761)
*Deutsche Shakespeare-Gesellschaft West: Jahrbuch

Werner Habicht, Editor
Rathaus
4630 Bochum, Germany

Additional editorial address: Werner Habicht, c/o Inst. für Englische Philologie, Am Hubland, 8700 Würzburg, Germany
Telephone: (49) 931 8885657
First published: 1964
Sponsoring organization: Deutsche Shakespeare-Gesellschaft West
ISSN: 0070-4326
MLA acronym: DSGW

SUBSCRIPTION INFORMATION

Frequency of publication: Annual
Circulation: 2,000
Available in microform: No
Subscription price: 86 DM/yr.
Year to which price refers: 1992
Subscription address: Verlag Ferdinand Kamp, Widumestr. 6-8, 4630 Bochum 1, Germany
Subscription telephone: (49) 234 15071

ADVERTISING INFORMATION

Advertising accepted: No

EDITORIAL DESCRIPTION

Scope: Publishes critical studies on Shakespearean drama, poetry, and theater. Also publishes studies which relate to Shakespeare.
Reviews books: Yes
Publishes notes: Yes
Languages accepted: German; English
Prints abstracts: No
Author-anonymous submission: No

SUBMISSION REQUIREMENTS

Restrictions on contributors: Book reviews are solicited.
Author pays submission fee: No
Author pays page charges: No
Length of articles: 4,000 words
Length of notes: 900 words
Style: MLA
Number of copies required: 2
Special requirements: Submit original typescript plus 1 copy.
Copyright ownership: Deutsche Shakespeare-Gesellschaft West; reverts to author after 1 yr.
Rejected manuscripts: Returned
Time before publication decision: 2-4 mos.
Time between decision and publication: 1 yr.
Number of reviewers: 4
Articles submitted per year: 40
Articles published per year: 8
Notes submitted per year: 10
Notes published per year: 2-5

(762)
Deutsche Sprache: Zeitschrift für Theorie, Praxis, Dokumentation

Siegfried Grosse, Odo Leys, Gerhard Stickel, & Johannes Schwitalla, Editors
Inst. für deutsche Sprache
Postfach 10 16 21
6800 Mannheim 1, Germany

Telephone: (49) 621 1581118
First published: 1973
Sponsoring organization: Inst. für Deutsche Sprache, Mannheim
ISSN: 0340-9341
MLA acronym: DSp

SUBSCRIPTION INFORMATION

Frequency of publication: 4 times/yr.
Circulation: 600
Available in microform: No
Subscription address: Erich Schmidt Verlag, Genthiner Str. 30g, 1000 Berlin 30, Germany

ADVERTISING INFORMATION

Advertising accepted: Yes

EDITORIAL DESCRIPTION

Scope: Serves members of academic communities, both in Germany and abroad, who are interested in the research of German language and linguistic theory. Major emphasis is given to Modern German.
Reviews books: No
Publishes notes: Yes
Languages accepted: German
Prints abstracts: Yes
Author-anonymous submission: No

SUBMISSION REQUIREMENTS

Restrictions on contributors: None
Author pays submission fee: No
Author pays page charges: No
Length of articles: 2,000-14,000 words
Length of notes: 2,000 words maximum
Style: Journal
Number of copies required: 1
Special requirements: Submit a 300-word abstract.
Copyright ownership: Assigned by author to journal
Rejected manuscripts: Returned
Time before publication decision: 6 weeks
Time between decision and publication: 6 mos.
Number of reviewers: 4
Articles submitted per year: 30-35
Articles published per year: 16-20
Notes submitted per year: 40
Notes published per year: 40

(763)
Deutsche Studien

H.-P. Schäfer, W. Hildebrandt, B. Schalhorn, & G. Zaluskowski, Editors
Ost-Akademie
Herderstr. 1-11
2120 Lüneburg, Germany

First published: 1963
Sponsoring organization: Ministry of Intergerman Relations
ISSN: 0012-0812
MLA acronym: DSt

SUBSCRIPTION INFORMATION

Frequency of publication: 4 times/yr.
Circulation: 1,200
Available in microform: No
Subscription address: Verlag Ost-Akademie e.V., at the above address

ADVERTISING INFORMATION

Advertising accepted: Yes

EDITORIAL DESCRIPTION

Scope: Publishes articles on German studies and East-West relations.
Reviews books: Yes
Publishes notes: Yes
Languages accepted: German
Prints abstracts: No
Author-anonymous submission: No

SUBMISSION REQUIREMENTS

Restrictions on contributors: None
Author pays submission fee: No
Author pays page charges: No
Length of articles: 15 pp.
Length of book reviews: 1 p.
Length of notes: 1/2 p.
Number of copies required: 1
Special requirements: Submit original typescript.
Copyright ownership: Verlag Ost-Akademie
Rejected manuscripts: Returned
Time before publication decision: 1 mo.
Time between decision and publication: 1 mo.
Number of reviewers: 2
Articles submitted per year: 100
Articles published per year: 25
Book reviews submitted per year: 15
Book reviews published per year: 10

(764)
*Deutsche Texte des Mittelalters

Rudolf Bentringer, Editor
Arbeitsstelle Deutsche Texte des Mittelalters
Prenzlauer Promenade 149-152
1100 Berlin, Germany

Telephone: (37) 2 4797145
First published: 1904
Sponsoring organization: Akademie der Wissenschaften Berlin/Brandenburg
ISSN: 0070-4334
MLA acronym: DTM

SUBSCRIPTION INFORMATION

Frequency of publication: Irregular
Available in microform: No
Subscription address: Akademie Verlag, Leipziger Str. 3-4, 1086 Berlin, Germany

ADVERTISING INFORMATION

Advertising accepted: No

EDITORIAL DESCRIPTION

Scope: Publishes editions of literature in verse and prose form, technical and commercial prose of literary, sociological, cultural-historical, and linguistic importance, descriptions of medieval German manuscripts to the end of the 16th century, and catalogues of manuscript collections in libraries.
Reviews books: No
Publishes notes: No
Languages accepted: German
Prints abstracts: No

SUBMISSION REQUIREMENTS

Restrictions on contributors: None
Author pays submission fee: No
Author pays page charges: No
Number of copies required: 2
Special requirements: Submit typescript.
Copyright ownership: Akademie Verlag
Rejected manuscripts: Returned
Time before publication decision: 1 yr.
Time between decision and publication: 6-12 mos.
Number of reviewers: 2
Books submitted per year: 1
Books published per year: 1

(765)
*Deutsche Vierteljahrsschrift für Literaturwissenschaft und Geistesgeschichte

Richard Brinkmann, Gerhart Graevenitz, & Walter Haug, Editors
Im Rotbad 30
7400 Tübingen, Germany

Additional editorial address: Gerhart V. Graevenitz, Univ. Konstanz, Philosophische Fakultät, Fachgruppe Literaturwissenschaft, Postfach 5560, 7750 Constance, Germany; Walter Haug, Im Tannengrund 9, 7400 Tübingen 4, Germany
Telephone: (49) 711 229020
Fax: (49) 711 2290290
First published: 1923
ISSN: 0012-0936
MLA acronym: DVLG

SUBSCRIPTION INFORMATION

Frequency of publication: 4 times/yr.
Circulation: 1,600
Available in microform: No
Subscription price: 172 DM/yr.; 136 DM/yr. students & assistants; 52 DM/single issue
Year to which price refers: 1992
Subscription address: J. B. Metzlersche Verlagsbuchhandlung, Kernerstr. 43, P.O. Box 10 32 41, 7000 Stuttgart 10, Germany

ADVERTISING INFORMATION

Advertising accepted: Yes

EDITORIAL DESCRIPTION

Scope: Publishes articles on medieval and modern literatures, as well as on subjects from other fields of the humanities.
Reviews books: No
Publishes notes: No
Languages accepted: German; English; French
Prints abstracts: Yes
Author-anonymous submission: No

SUBMISSION REQUIREMENTS

Restrictions on contributors: None
Author pays submission fee: No
Author pays page charges: No
Length of articles: 2,500-12,500 words
Style: MLA
Number of copies required: 1
Special requirements: Submit original typescript as well as an abstract in English and German consisting of not more than 375 characters each.
Copyright ownership: Assigned by author to journal
Rejected manuscripts: Returned; enclose return postage.
Time before publication decision: 1 mo.
Time between decision and publication: 1 yr.
Number of reviewers: 2-3
Articles published per year: 25-30

(766)
*Deutsches Archiv für Erforschung des Mittelalters

Horst Fuhrmann & Hans Martin Schaller, Editors
Monumenta Germaniae Historica
Ludwigstr. 16, Postfach 34 02 23
8000 Munich 34, Germany

Telephone: (49) 89 28638389
Fax: (49) 89 281419
First published: 1937
Sponsoring organization: Monumenta Germaniae Historica; Deutsche Forschungsgemeinschaft
ISSN: 0012-1223
MLA acronym: DAEM

SUBSCRIPTION INFORMATION

Frequency of publication: 2 times/yr.
Circulation: 900
Available in microform: No
Subscription address: Böhlau-Verlag, Theodor Heuss Str. 76, 5000 Cologne 90, Germany

ADVERTISING INFORMATION

Advertising accepted: Yes

EDITORIAL DESCRIPTION

Scope: Publishes critical analyses and descriptions of sources of the history of the Middle Ages (500-1500 AD) and reports on scholarly literature on the subject.
Reviews books: Yes
Publishes notes: Yes
Languages accepted: German
Prints abstracts: No
Author-anonymous submission: No

SUBMISSION REQUIREMENTS

Restrictions on contributors: None
Author pays submission fee: No
Author pays page charges: No
Length of articles: No restrictions
Length of book reviews: No restrictions
Length of notes: No restrictions
Style: Monumenta Germaniae Historica
Number of copies required: 1
Special requirements: Consult with editor prior to submission.
Copyright ownership: Monumenta Germaniae Historica & Böhlau-Verlag; reverts to author after 1 yr.
Rejected manuscripts: Returned
Time before publication decision: 2 mos.
Time between decision and publication: 6 mos. minimum
Number of reviewers: 2-5
Articles submitted per year: 30
Articles published per year: 15
Book reviews submitted per year: 1,200
Book reviews published per year: 1,200
Notes submitted per year: 20
Notes published per year: 10

(767)
*Deutsches Dante-Jahrbuch

Marcella Roddewig, Editor
Bohlau Verlag GmbH & CIE
Theodor Heuss Str. 76
5000 Cologne 90, Germany

Telephone: (49) 2203 307021
Fax: (49) 2203 307349
First published: 1867
Sponsoring organization: Deutsche Dante-Gesellschaft E.V.
ISSN: 0070-444X
MLA acronym: DDJ

SUBSCRIPTION INFORMATION

Frequency of publication: Annual
Available in microform: No
Subscription price: 68 DM/yr.
Year to which price refers: 1991

ADVERTISING INFORMATION

Advertising accepted: Yes

EDITORIAL DESCRIPTION

Scope: Publishes articles on Dante.
Reviews books: Yes
Publishes notes: Yes
Languages accepted: German; English; French; Italian; Spanish
Prints abstracts: No
Author-anonymous submission: No

SUBMISSION REQUIREMENTS

Restrictions on contributors: None
Author pays submission fee: No
Author pays page charges: No
Length of articles: 7,400 words
Length of book reviews: 1,480 words
Length of notes: 200 words
Style: MLA
Number of copies required: 1
Special requirements: Submit original typescript and diskette.
Copyright ownership: Bohlau Verlag
Rejected manuscripts: Returned
Time before publication decision: 3 weeks
Time between decision and publication: 6-18 mos.
Number of reviewers: 1
Articles submitted per year: 10
Articles published per year: 7
Book reviews published per year: 15
Notes submitted per year: 3
Notes published per year: 2-3

(768)
*Der Deutschunterricht: Beiträge zu Seiner Praxis und Wissenschaftlichen Grundlegung

Gerhard Augst, Wilhelm Dehn, Stephan Lohr, Eva Neuland, Helmut Scheuer, & Michael Sauer, Editors
Friedrich-Verlag
Im Brande 15a
3016 Seelze 6, Germany

Telephone: (49) 511 4000418
Fax: (49) 511 4000419
First published: 1948
ISSN: 0340-2258
MLA acronym: DU

SUBSCRIPTION INFORMATION

Frequency of publication: 6 times/yr.
Circulation: 7,000
Available in microform: No
Subscription price: 78.40 DM/yr. (includes Friedrich Yearbook)
Year to which price refers: 1992
Subscription telephone: (49) 511 4000453

ADVERTISING INFORMATION

Advertising accepted: Yes

EDITORIAL DESCRIPTION

Scope: Publishes essays on the application and theoretical foundations of German instruction.
Reviews books: No
Publishes notes: Yes
Languages accepted: German
Prints abstracts: Yes
Author-anonymous submission: No

SUBMISSION REQUIREMENTS

Restrictions on contributors: None
Author pays submission fee: No
Author pays page charges: No
Length of articles: 12 printed pp.
Length of notes: No restrictions
Number of copies required: 1
Special requirements: Submit original typescript.
Copyright ownership: Erhard Friedrich Verlag GmbH & Cokg.
Rejected manuscripts: Returned
Time before publication decision: 4 mos.
Time between decision and publication: 4-12 mos.
Number of reviewers: 4-6
Articles submitted per year: 70-90
Articles published per year: 40-50
Notes submitted per year: 15
Notes published per year: 10

(769)
Developmental Psychology

Carolyn Zahn-Waxler, Editor
4305 Dresden St.
Kensington, MD 20895

First published: 1969
Sponsoring organization: American Psychological Assn.
ISSN: 0012-1649
MLA acronym: DP

SUBSCRIPTION INFORMATION

Frequency of publication: 6 times/yr.
Circulation: 5,200
Available in microform: Yes, through Johnson Assn., Box 1017, Greenwich CT, 06830
Subscription address: Subscription Section, American Psychological Assn., 750 First St. NE, Washington, DC 20002-4242

ADVERTISING INFORMATION

Advertising accepted: Yes

EDITORIAL DESCRIPTION

Scope: Publishes articles that advance knowledge about growth and development. The journal is primarily intended for reports of empirical research in which the developmental implications are clear and convincing. Any variable or set of variables that helps to promote understanding of psychological processes and their development within the life span is appropriate.
Reviews books: No
Languages accepted: English
Prints abstracts: Yes

SUBMISSION REQUIREMENTS

Restrictions on contributors: None
Author pays submission fee: No
Author pays page charges: Only for author alterations
Length of articles: 15-20 pp.
Style: American Psychological Assn.
Number of copies required: 3
Copyright ownership: Assigned by author to American Psychological Assn.
Rejected manuscripts: 1 copy returned
Time before publication decision: 6 weeks
Time between decision and publication: 9 mos.
Number of reviewers: 2
Articles published per year: 125

(770)
Devil's Box

Stephen F. Davis, Editor
1524 Washington
Emporia, KS 66801

First published: 1967
Sponsoring organization: Tennessee Folklore Soc.
ISSN: 0092-0789
MLA acronym: DevB

SUBSCRIPTION INFORMATION

Frequency of publication: 4 times/yr.
Circulation: 800
Subscription address: 305 Stella Dr., Madison, WI 35758

EDITORIAL DESCRIPTION

Reviews books: Yes

(771)
*Diachronica: International Journal for Historical Linguistics/Revue Internationale pour la Linguistique Historique/Internationale Zeitschrift für Historische Linguistik

E. F. Konrad Koerner, Sheila M. Embleton, & Brian D. Joseph, Editors
Dept. of Linguistics
Univ. of Ottawa
Ottawa, Ontario K1N 6N5, Canada

Additional editorial address: Managing Editor: Sheila M. Embleton, Dept. of Languages, Literatures & Linguistics, York Univ., 561 S Ross Bldg., North York, Ontario M3J 1P3, Canada; Review Editor: Brian D. Joseph, Dept. of Linguistics, Ohio State Univ., Columbus, OH 43210
First published: 1984
ISSN: 0176-4225
MLA acronym: Diachronica

SUBSCRIPTION INFORMATION

Frequency of publication: 2 times/yr. (Spring, Fall)
Circulation: 300
Available in microform: No
Subscription price: 157 f ($95.00)/yr.
Year to which price refers: 1993
Subscription address: John Benjamins Publishing Co., 821 Bethlehem Pike, Philadelphia, PA 19118
Additional subscription address: John Benjamins B.V., P.O. Box 75577, Amsteldijk 44, 1070 AN Amsterdam, Netherlands
Subscription telephone: 215 836-1200; (31) 20 6738156
Subscription fax: 215 836-1204; (31) 20 6739773

ADVERTISING INFORMATION

Advertising accepted: Yes

EDITORIAL DESCRIPTION

Scope: Provides a forum for the exchange and synthesis of information concerning all aspects of historical linguistics and pertaining to all language families. It includes both theory-oriented and data-oriented contributions.
Reviews books: Yes

Publishes notes: Yes
Languages accepted: English; French; German
Prints abstracts: Yes
Author-anonymous submission: No

SUBMISSION REQUIREMENTS

Restrictions on contributors: Book reviews are generally solicited.
Author pays submission fee: No
Author pays page charges: No
Length of articles: 15-35 pp.
Length of book reviews: 3-8 pp.
Length of notes: 1-4 pp.
Style: Linguistic Soc. of America with modifications
Number of copies required: 3
Special requirements: One of the editors should be contacted prior to submission. Journal will sometimes also publish articles in Italian and Spanish.
Copyright ownership: Journal
Rejected manuscripts: Returned
Time before publication decision: 3-6 mos.
Time between decision and publication: 6-12 mos.
Number of reviewers: 3
Articles published per year: 6-10
Book reviews published per year: 10-20

(772)
*Diacritics: A Review of Contemporary Criticism

Richard Klein, Editor
Dept. of Romance Studies
Cornell Univ.
Ithaca, NY 14853

Telephone: 607 255-1374
Fax: 607 255-1454
First published: 1970
Sponsoring organization: Dept. of Romance Studies, Cornell Univ.
ISSN: 0300-7162
MLA acronym: Diacritics

SUBSCRIPTION INFORMATION

Frequency of publication: 4 times/yr. (Spring, Summer, Fall, Winter)
Circulation: 1,750
Available in microform: Yes, through Univ. Microfilms International
Subscription price: $53.00/yr. institutions US; $21.00/yr. individuals US; add $3.40/yr. postage Canada & Mexico, $8.60/yr. elsewhere
Year to which price refers: 1993
Subscription address: Johns Hopkins Univ. Press, Journals Publishing Division, 2715 North Charles St., Baltimore, MD 21218-4319
Subscription telephone: 410 516-6987; 800 537-5487
Subscription fax: 410 516-6998

ADVERTISING INFORMATION

Advertising accepted: Yes
Advertising rates: $170.00/half page; $230.00/full page

EDITORIAL DESCRIPTION

Scope: A review of contemporary criticism in literature, cinema, and the arts, as well as a preview of important work in progress. Invites critical responses from all quarters to published opinion. While the journal is concerned primarily with the problems of criticism, the editors have adopted no formal policy governing the choice of books to be reviewed or critical perspectives to be explored. Diacritical discussion entails distinguishing the methodological and ideological issues which critics encounter and setting forth a critical position in relation to them. Review articles, which are the principal component of each issue, should both provide a serious account of the work(s) under consideration and allow the reviewers to respond by developing their own ideas or positions.
Reviews books: Yes
Publishes notes: No
Languages accepted: English
Prints abstracts: No
Author-anonymous submission: No

SUBMISSION REQUIREMENTS

Restrictions on contributors: None
Author pays submission fee: No
Author pays page charges: No
Length of articles: 5,000 words
Length of book reviews: 5,000 words
Style: MLA
Number of copies required: 2
Special requirements: Correspondence with editors prior to submission of manuscripts is recommended. Submit diskette.
Copyright ownership: Johns Hopkins Univ. Press
Rejected manuscripts: Returned at author's request
Time before publication decision: 6 mos.
Time between decision and publication: 6 mos.
Number of reviewers: 4
Articles submitted per year: 80
Articles published per year: 26
Book reviews submitted per year: 60
Book reviews published per year: 20

(773)
*Les Dialectes de Wallonie

Jean Lechanteur, Editor
Rue Beckers, 11
4630 Soumagne, Belgium

Telephone: (32) 41 771321
First published: 1972
Sponsoring organization: Soc. de Langue & de Littérature Wallonnes; Ministère de la Communauté Française
ISSN: 0773-7688
MLA acronym: DdW

SUBSCRIPTION INFORMATION

Frequency of publication: Annual
Circulation: 600
Available in microform: No
Subscription address: Soc. de Langue et de Littérature Wallonnes, Univ. de l'Etat à Liège, 7 Place du XX Août, 4000 Liège, Belgium
Additional subscription address: Bibliothèque des Dialectes de Wallonie, Place des Carmes 8, 4000 Liège, Belgium

ADVERTISING INFORMATION

Advertising accepted: No

EDITORIAL DESCRIPTION

Scope: Publishes articles on Wallonian, Picardian, Lorrainian, and Belgian French dialectology and onomastics.
Reviews books: Yes
Publishes notes: Yes
Languages accepted: French
Prints abstracts: No
Author-anonymous submission: No

SUBMISSION REQUIREMENTS

Restrictions on contributors: None
Author pays submission fee: No
Author pays page charges: No
Length of articles: 30 pp. maximum
Length of book reviews: 2 pp. maximum
Length of notes: 3 pp. maximum
Style: None
Number of copies required: 1
Special requirements: Submit original typescript.
Copyright ownership: Assigned by author to journal
Rejected manuscripts: Returned
Time before publication decision: 3-6 mos.
Time between decision and publication: 1 yr.
Number of reviewers: 3
Articles submitted per year: 15
Articles published per year: 10
Book reviews submitted per year: 2-3
Book reviews published per year: 2-3
Notes submitted per year: 2-3
Notes published per year: 2-10

(774)
*Dialog: Miesięcznik Poświęcony Dramaturgii Współczesnej: Teatralnej, Filmowej, Radiowej, Telewizyjnej

Jacek Sieradzki, Editor
ul. Puławska 61
02-595 Warsaw, Poland

Telephone: (48) 22 455475; (48) 22 455583
First published: 1956
ISSN: 0012-2041
MLA acronym: DialogW

SUBSCRIPTION INFORMATION

Frequency of publication: 12 times/yr.
Circulation: 3,500
Available in microform: No
Subscription address: "Prasa-Książka-Ruch", Centrala Kolportażu Prasy i Wydawnictw, ul. Towarowa 28, 00-958 Warsaw, Poland

ADVERTISING INFORMATION

Advertising accepted: Yes
Advertising rates: $200.00/full page

EDITORIAL DESCRIPTION

Scope: Publishes modern plays, including both Polish and foreign, as well as essays, criticism, and general information on contemporary drama and theater.
Reviews books: Yes
Publishes notes: Yes
Languages accepted: Polish
Prints abstracts: No

SUBMISSION REQUIREMENTS

Restrictions on contributors: None
Author pays submission fee: No
Author pays page charges: No
Length of articles: 10-15 typescript pp.
Length of book reviews: 5-10 typescript pp.
Length of notes: 5-10 typescript pp.
Style: None
Number of copies required: 1
Copyright ownership: Assigned by author to journal
Rejected manuscripts: Returned
Time before publication decision: 2 mos.
Time between decision and publication: 4-5 mos.
Number of reviewers: 1-5
Articles submitted per year: 150-160
Articles published per year: 75-85
Book reviews submitted per year: 10

Book reviews published per year: 6
Notes submitted per year: 100-150
Notes published per year: 75-85

(775)
Dialoghi: Rivista Bimestrale di Letteratura Arti Scienze

N. F. Cimmino, Editor
Via Acciaioli, 7
Rome, Italy

First published: 1953
ISSN: 0012-205X
MLA acronym: Dialoghi

SUBSCRIPTION INFORMATION

Frequency of publication: 6 times/yr.

EDITORIAL DESCRIPTION

Reviews books: Yes

(776)
*Dialogi: Revija za Kulturo

Bernard Rajh, Editor
Gospejna 10
P.P. 223
62000 Maribor, Slovenia

First published: 1965
ISSN: 0012-2068
MLA acronym: Dialogi

SUBSCRIPTION INFORMATION

Frequency of publication: 12 times/yr.
Subscription address: Art Consulting, d.o.o., Slovenska 36, 62000 Maribor, Slovenia
Subscription telephone: (38) 62 222096

ADVERTISING INFORMATION

Advertising accepted: Yes

EDITORIAL DESCRIPTION

Scope: Publishes articles on literature and culture.
Reviews books: Yes
Publishes notes: Yes
Languages accepted: Slovenian
Prints abstracts: No

SUBMISSION REQUIREMENTS

Restrictions on contributors: None
Author pays page charges: No
Length of articles: 1 p.
Length of book reviews: 1 p.
Length of notes: 1 p.
Number of copies required: 1
Copyright ownership: Author
Time before publication decision: 1 mo.
Time between decision and publication: 1 week
Articles submitted per year: 1,000
Articles published per year: 140
Book reviews submitted per year: 6
Book reviews published per year: 4
Notes submitted per year: 30
Notes published per year: 30

(777)
*Diálogos Hispánicos de Amsterdam

Henk Haverkate, Editor
Spaans Seminarium
Spuistraat 134
1012 VB Amsterdam, Netherlands

First published: 1980
ISSN: 0167-8744
MLA acronym: DHA

SUBSCRIPTION INFORMATION

Frequency of publication: Annual
Circulation: 300-600
Available in microform: No
Subscription address: Editions Rodopi B.V., Keizersgracht 302-304, 1016 EX Amsterdam, Netherlands
Additional subscription address: In N. American: Editions Rodopi, 233 Peachtree St. N.E., Suite 404, Atlanta, GA 30303-1504
Subscription telephone: (31) 20 6227507; 404 523-1964; 800 225-3998
Subscription fax: (31) 20 6380948; 404 522-7116

ADVERTISING INFORMATION

Advertising accepted: Yes, on an exchange basis

EDITORIAL DESCRIPTION

Scope: Publishes articles on Spanish and Spanish American literature and linguistics.
Reviews books: No
Publishes notes: No
Languages accepted: Spanish; English
Prints abstracts: No
Author-anonymous submission: No

SUBMISSION REQUIREMENTS

Restrictions on contributors: Contributors must have read a paper at the Round Table Conference.
Author pays submission fee: No
Author pays page charges: No
Length of articles: 10,000-20,000 words
Style: MLA
Number of copies required: 3
Special requirements: Sumbit typescript.
Copyright ownership: Editions Rodopi
Rejected manuscripts: Returned
Time before publication decision: 3 mos.
Time between decision and publication: 1 yr. maximum
Number of reviewers: 2-4
Articles published per year: 8-10

(778)
*Dialogue: Canadian Philosophical Review/Revue Canadienne de Philosophie

Claude Panaccio & Steven Davis, Editors
Dépt. de Philosophie
Univ. du Québec à Trois-Rivières
C.P. 500
Trois-Rivières, PQ G9A 5H7, Canada

Additional editorial address: Send French articles to above address; send English articles to: Steven Davis, Dept. of Philosophy, Simon Fraser Univ., Burnaby, BC V5A 1S6, Canada
Telephone: 604 291-4979
Fax: 604 291-4455
E-mail: Dialogue@SFU.CA
First published: 1962
Sponsoring organization: Canadian Philosophical Assn.
ISSN: 0012-2173
MLA acronym: Dialogue

SUBSCRIPTION INFORMATION

Frequency of publication: 4 times/yr.
Circulation: 1,300
Available in microform: No
Subscription price: C$45.00/yr.
Year to which price refers: 1991-92
Subscription address: Wilfrid Laurier Univ. Press, Wilfrid Laurier Univ., Waterloo, Ontario N2L 3C5, Canada
Additional subscription address: For individual subscriptions & membership: Canadian Philosophical Assn., Morisset Hall, Univ. of Ottawa, Ottawa, ON K1N 6N5, Canada

ADVERTISING INFORMATION

Advertising accepted: Yes
Advertising rates: C$125.00/half page; C$200.00/full page

EDITORIAL DESCRIPTION

Scope: Publishes articles in the various fields of philosophy. Includes studies on literary theory, linguistic theory, and the philosophy of language.
Reviews books: Yes
Publishes notes: Yes
Languages accepted: English; French
Prints abstracts: No
Author-anonymous submission: Yes

SUBMISSION REQUIREMENTS

Restrictions on contributors: None
Author pays submission fee: No
Author pays page charges: Yes
Length of articles: 1,000-7,000 words
Length of book reviews: 750-1,500 words
Length of notes: 1,250 words maximum
Style: Journal
Number of copies required: 3
Special requirements: Submit original double-spaced typescript plus 2 copies; notes must be double-spaced at the end of the text.
Copyright ownership: Assigned by author to journal
Rejected manuscripts: Returned at author's request
Time before publication decision: 3 mos.
Time between decision and publication: 1 yr.
Number of reviewers: 2-3
Articles submitted per year: 100-120
Articles published per year: 25-30
Book reviews submitted per year: 55-70
Book reviews published per year: 50-65
Notes submitted per year: 10-15
Notes published per year: 7-10

(779)
*Dickens Quarterly

David Paroissien, Mary Rosner, Heather Henderson, & William G. Wall, Editors
Dept. of English
Univ. of Massachusetts
Amherst, MA 01003

Additional editorial address: Send all review copies to: Dept. of English, Mount Holyoke College, South Hadley, MA 01075-1484
Telephone: 502 588-5494
Fax: 413 545-3880
First published: 1970
Sponsoring organization: Dickens Soc.; Univ. of Louisville, Academic Publications
ISSN: 0742-5473
MLA acronym: DQu

SUBSCRIPTION INFORMATION

Frequency of publication: 4 times/yr. (Mar., June, Sept., Dec.)
Circulation: 550
Available in microform: No
Subscription price: $15.00/yr.
Year to which price refers: 1992
Subscription address: Office of the President, Graweymeyer Hall, Univ. of Louisville, Louisville, KY 40292
Subscription telephone: 502 588-5417
Subscription fax: 502 588-5682

ADVERTISING INFORMATION

Advertising accepted: Yes
Advertising rates: $50.00/half page; $75.00/full page

EDITORIAL DESCRIPTION

Scope: Publishes articles about the life, times, and literature of Charles Dickens.
Reviews books: Yes
Publishes notes: Yes
Languages accepted: English
Prints abstracts: No
Author-anonymous submission: No

SUBMISSION REQUIREMENTS

Restrictions on contributors: None
Author pays submission fee: No
Author pays page charges: No
Length of articles: 2,000-3,000 words
Length of book reviews: No restrictions
Length of notes: 500-1,000 words
Style: MLA
Number of copies required: 2
Copyright ownership: Dickens Soc.
Rejected manuscripts: Returned; enclose return postage.
Time before publication decision: 2-4 mos.
Time between decision and publication: 2-15 mos.
Number of reviewers: 2
Articles submitted per year: 50
Articles published per year: 12
Book reviews submitted per year: 15
Book reviews published per year: 10
Notes submitted per year: 15
Notes published per year: 5

(780)
*Dickens Studies Annual: Essays on Victorian Fiction

Fred Kaplan, Michael Timko, & Edward Guiliano, Editors
Graduate School & Univ. Center
City Univ. of New York
33 W. 42nd St.
New York, NY 10036

Telephone: 212 642-2228; 212 642-2206
Fax: 212 924-8352
First published: 1970
Sponsoring organization: Graduate Center, City Univ. of New York; Queen's College
ISSN: 0084-9812
MLA acronym: DSA

SUBSCRIPTION INFORMATION

Frequency of publication: Annual
Circulation: 1,000
Available in microform: No
Subscription price: $45.00/yr. institutions; $25.00/yr. individuals
Year to which price refers: 1991
Subscription address: AMS Press, 56 E. 13th St., New York, NY 10003
Subscription telephone: 212 777-4700

ADVERTISING INFORMATION

Advertising accepted: No

EDITORIAL DESCRIPTION

Scope: Publishes essay and monograph-length contributions on Charles Dickens as well as on other Victorian novelists and on the history or aesthetics of Victorian fiction.
Reviews books: Yes
Publishes notes: No
Languages accepted: English
Prints abstracts: No
Author-anonymous submission: Yes

SUBMISSION REQUIREMENTS

Restrictions on contributors: None
Author pays submission fee: No
Author pays page charges: No
Length of articles: 3,750-30,000 words (15-120 typescript pp.)
Length of book reviews: 3,750-10,000 words
Style: MLA
Number of copies required: 2
Special requirements: Original typescript is preferred. Publishes review essays.
Copyright ownership: AMS Press
Rejected manuscripts: Returned with comments; enclose return postage or international reply coupons.
Time before publication decision: 3-6 mos.
Time between decision and publication: 6-12 mos.
Number of reviewers: 2-5
Articles submitted per year: 100
Articles published per year: 14-18

(781)
*The Dickensian

Malcolm Andrews, Editor
Eliot College
Univ. of Kent
Canterbury
Kent G2 7NS, England

Telephone: (44) 227 764000 ext. 3335
Fax: (44) 227 475471
First published: 1905
Sponsoring organization: Dickens Fellowship
ISSN: 0012-2440
MLA acronym: Dickensian

SUBSCRIPTION INFORMATION

Frequency of publication: 3 times/yr. (Spring, Summer, Autumn)
Circulation: 2,250
Available in microform: Yes
Subscription price: £11.00/yr. institutions United Kingdom; £13.00/yr. institutions elsewhere; £9.00/yr. individuals United Kingdom; £10.00/yr. individuals elsewhere
Year to which price refers: 1992
Subscription address: Edward Preston, Secretary, Dickens House, 48 Doughty St., London WC1N 2LF, England
Subscription telephone: (44) 71 4052127

ADVERTISING INFORMATION

Advertising accepted: Yes
Advertising rates: £40.00/half page; £80.00/full page

EDITORIAL DESCRIPTION

Scope: Publishes articles on the work and life of Charles Dickens and on the literature, art, and culture of the Victorian period.
Reviews books: Yes
Publishes notes: Yes
Languages accepted: English
Prints abstracts: No
Author-anonymous submission: No

SUBMISSION REQUIREMENTS

Restrictions on contributors: Book reviews are commissioned.
Author pays submission fee: No
Author pays page charges: No
Length of articles: 2,000-5,000 words
Length of book reviews: 500-600 words
Length of notes: 1,000-2,000 words
Number of copies required: 1
Copyright ownership: Author
Rejected manuscripts: Returned at author's request; enclose return postage.
Time before publication decision: 3 mos.
Time between decision and publication: 6-24 mos.
Number of reviewers: 1
Articles submitted per year: 45-50
Articles published per year: 15-20
Book reviews published per year: 14-20
Notes submitted per year: 6-10
Notes published per year: 3-5

(782)
*Dickinson Studies: Emily Dickinson (1830-86), U.S. Poet

Frederick L. Morey, Editor
1330 Massachusetts Ave., NW, Apt. 503
Washington, DC 20005-4150

First published: 1968
ISSN: 0164-1492
MLA acronym: DicS

SUBSCRIPTION INFORMATION

Frequency of publication: 2 times/yr. (June, Dec.)
Circulation: 300
Available in microform: No

ADVERTISING INFORMATION

Advertising accepted: Yes

EDITORIAL DESCRIPTION

Scope: Publishes scholarly articles, notes and queries on the life and work of Emily Dickinson.
Reviews books: Yes
Publishes notes: Yes
Languages accepted: English
Prints abstracts: No
Author-anonymous submission: No

SUBMISSION REQUIREMENTS

Restrictions on contributors: Most reviews are solicited.
Author pays submission fee: No
Author pays page charges: Yes
Length of articles: 4,000 words maximum
Length of book reviews: 600 words
Length of notes: 300 words
Style: MLA preferred
Number of copies required: 1
Special requirements: Submission of an abstract is preferred. Poetry and translations may be in any language.
Copyright ownership: Editor; reprint rights to author.
Rejected manuscripts: Returned; enclose SASE.
Time before publication decision: 1-2 weeks
Time between decision and publication: 1-2 yrs.
Number of reviewers: 1-2
Articles submitted per year: 50
Articles published per year: 24
Book reviews published per year: 12
Notes published per year: 6

(783)
*Dictionaries: Journal of the Dictionary Society of North America

William S. Chisholm, Editor
Dept. of English
Cleveland State Univ.
Cleveland, OH 44115

Telephone: 216 687-3985
Fax: 216 687-9366
E-mail: R1505@CSUOhio
First published: 1979
Sponsoring organization: Dictionary Soc. of North America
ISSN: 0197-6745
MLA acronym: Dictionaries

SUBSCRIPTION INFORMATION

Frequency of publication: Annual
Circulation: 500
Available in microform: No
Subscription price: $20.00/yr. (includes membership)
Year to which price refers: 1992
Subscription address: Dictionary Soc. of North America, RT-937, Cleveland State Univ., Cleveland, OH 44115-2403

Subscription telephone: 216 687-4830

ADVERTISING INFORMATION

Advertising accepted: No

EDITORIAL DESCRIPTION

Scope: Publishes essays and reviews concerned with monolingual and bilingual lexicography.
Reviews books: Yes
Publishes notes: Yes
Languages accepted: English; French
Prints abstracts: No
Author-anonymous submission: No

SUBMISSION REQUIREMENTS

Restrictions on contributors: Contributors must be members of the Dictionary Soc. of North America in the year in which their submission is published.
Author pays submission fee: No
Author pays page charges: No
Length of articles: 20-50 typescript pp.
Length of book reviews: 3,000-5,000 words
Length of notes: 500 words
Style: Chicago
Number of copies required: 1
Special requirements: Submit typescript and diskette.
Copyright ownership: Dictionary Soc. of North America
Rejected manuscripts: Returned
Time before publication decision: 2 mos.
Time between decision and publication: 8 mos.
Number of reviewers: 2
Articles submitted per year: 20-25
Articles published per year: 8-10
Book reviews submitted per year: 12-15
Book reviews published per year: 10-12
Notes submitted per year: 1-2
Notes published per year: 1-2

(784)
*Dictionary of Literary Biography

Matthew J. Bruccoli, Richard Layman, & C. E. Frazer Clark, Editors
2006 Sumter St.
Columbia, SC 29201

First published: 1978
MLA acronym: DLB

SUBSCRIPTION INFORMATION

Frequency of publication: Irregular
Available in microform: No
Subscription address: Gale Research Co., Book Tower, Detroit, MI 48226

ADVERTISING INFORMATION

Advertising accepted: No

EDITORIAL DESCRIPTION

Scope: Publishes biographies of writers.
Reviews books: Yes
Publishes notes: No
Languages accepted: English
Prints abstracts: No

SUBMISSION REQUIREMENTS

Restrictions on contributors: Reviews are commissioned.
Author pays submission fee: No
Author pays page charges: No
Style: Chicago
Number of copies required: 2
Copyright ownership: Gale Research Co.
Rejected manuscripts: Returned

(785)
*Diderot Studies

Otis Fellows & Diana Guiragossian Carr, Editors
Dept. of French & Italian
635 Ballantine Hall
Indiana Univ.
Bloomington, IN 47405

Telephone: 812 332-9920
First published: 1949
ISSN: 0070-4806
MLA acronym: DidS

SUBSCRIPTION INFORMATION

Frequency of publication: Once every 2 yrs.
Circulation: 800-1,000
Available in microform: No
Subscription address: Librairie Droz S.A., 11, rue Massot, 1211 Geneva 12, Switzerland

ADVERTISING INFORMATION

Advertising accepted: No

EDITORIAL DESCRIPTION

Scope: Publishes articles on Diderot and the *Encyclopédie*. Welcomes contributions representing various critical approaches and diverse points of view.
Reviews books: Yes
Languages accepted: English; French
Prints abstracts: No
Author-anonymous submission: Yes

SUBMISSION REQUIREMENTS

Author pays submission fee: No
Author pays page charges: No
Length of articles: 30 pp. maximum
Length of book reviews: 600-800 words
Style: MLA
Number of copies required: 2
Copyright ownership: Journal
Rejected manuscripts: Returned; enclose return postage.
Time before publication decision: 3 mos.
Time between decision and publication: 2 yrs.
Number of reviewers: 3

(786)
*Dieciocho: Hispanic Enlightenment, Aesthetics, and Literary Theory

Eva M. Kahiluoto Rudat, Ciriaco Moron Arroyo, & Jesús Gutiérrez, Editors
53 King Charles Lane
Newton, PA 18940-2312

Telephone: 215 579-2995
First published: 1978
ISSN: 0163-0415
MLA acronym: Dieciocho

SUBSCRIPTION INFORMATION

Frequency of publication: 2 times/yr. or 1 double issue/yr.
Circulation: 140
Available in microform: No
Subscription price: $17.00/yr. institutions US; $12.00/yr. individuals US; add $1.00 ($5.00 airmail)/yr. postage elsewhere
Year to which price refers: 1992

ADVERTISING INFORMATION

Advertising accepted: No

EDITORIAL DESCRIPTION

Scope: Dedicated to studies of Hispanic Enlightenment (Spanish, Portuguese, Latin American), and theoretical and methodological studies on any area of Hispanic literary criticism and aesthetics.
Reviews books: Yes
Publishes notes: No
Languages accepted: English; Portuguese; Spanish
Prints abstracts: No
Author-anonymous submission: Yes

SUBMISSION REQUIREMENTS

Restrictions on contributors: Contributors must be subscribers unless manuscript is solicited.
Author pays submission fee: No
Author pays page charges: No
Length of articles: 20-30 double-spaced typescript pp. maximum for articles; 6-8 pp. for review articles
Style: MLA
Number of copies required: 2
Copyright ownership: Journal
Rejected manuscripts: Returned; enclose return postage.
Time before publication decision: 1-2 mos.
Time between decision and publication: 6-12 mos.
Number of reviewers: 2-3
Articles submitted per year: 30
Articles published per year: 10-15 articles; 5-6 review articles

(787)
*Dietsche Warande en Belfort: Tijdschrift voor Letterkunde en Geestesleven

Marcel Janssens, Editor
Postbus 137
3000 Leuven 3, Belgium

Telephone: (32) 16 488102
First published: 1855
Sponsoring organization: Ministerie van de Vlaamse Gemeenschap
ISSN: 0012-2645
MLA acronym: DWB

SUBSCRIPTION INFORMATION

Frequency of publication: 6 times/yr.
Circulation: 2,000
Available in microform: No
Subscription address: Peeters, Bondgenotenlaan 153, 3000 Leuven, Belgium

ADVERTISING INFORMATION

Advertising accepted: Yes

EDITORIAL DESCRIPTION

Scope: Publishes creative and critical literature.
Reviews books: Yes
Publishes notes: Yes
Languages accepted: Dutch
Prints abstracts: No

SUBMISSION REQUIREMENTS

Restrictions on contributors: None
Author pays submission fee: No
Author pays page charges: No
Length of articles: No restrictions
Length of book reviews: No restrictions
Length of notes: No restrictions
Number of copies required: 1
Copyright ownership: Author
Rejected manuscripts: Returned; enclose return postage.
Time before publication decision: 2 mo.
Time between decision and publication: 6 mos.
Number of reviewers: 3
Articles submitted per year: 500
Articles published per year: 80
Book reviews submitted per year: 200
Book reviews published per year: 50
Notes submitted per year: 100
Notes published per year: 50

(788)
*Differentia: Review of Italian Thought

Peter Carravetta, Editor
Kiely Hall 243
CUNY/Queens College
Flushing, NY 11367-0904

Telephone: 718 997-5660
Fax: 718 358-4542
E-mail: DIFFERE1@QCVAX; DIFFERE2@QCVAX
First published: 1986
Sponsoring organization: Queens College, City Univ. of New York
ISSN: 0890-4294
MLA acronym: Differentia

SUBSCRIPTION INFORMATION

Frequency of publication: 2 times/yr.
Circulation: 300
Available in microform: No
Subscription price: $30.00/yr. institutions US & Canada; $35.00/yr. institution elsewhere; $20.00/yr. individuals US & Canada; $25.00/yr. individuals elsewhere
Year to which price refers: 1992

ADVERTISING INFORMATION

Advertising accepted: Yes
Advertising rates: $250.00/full page

EDITORIAL DESCRIPTION

Scope: Publishes material on contemporary Italian philosophy, social, aesthetic, and political criticism.
Reviews books: Yes
Publishes notes: Yes
Languages accepted: English
Prints abstracts: No
Author-anonymous submission: No

SUBMISSION REQUIREMENTS

Restrictions on contributors: None
Author pays submission fee: No
Author pays page charges: No
Length of articles: 3,000-7,000 words
Length of book reviews: 750-1,250 words
Length of notes: 500-750 words
Style: MLA
Number of copies required: 2
Special requirements: Translated articles should be accompanied by originals. Submit typescript and diskette, if possible.
Copyright ownership: Journal
Rejected manuscripts: Returned; enclose SASE.
Time before publication decision: 6-9 mos.
Time between decision and publication: 3-6 mos.
Number of reviewers: 3-5
Articles submitted per year: 40
Articles published per year: 20
Book reviews submitted per year: 15
Book reviews published per year: 10-12
Notes published per year: 2-3

(789)
*Diliman Review

Consuelo Paz, Roger Posadas, Rogelio Sicat, Lilia Quindoza-Santiago, Vivencio Abastillas, & Roberto Tangco, Editors
College of Social Sciences & Philosophy
Room 10, Palma Hall Annex Ext.
Univ. of the Philippines
Diliman, Quezon City, D-505, Philippines

First published: 1952
Sponsoring organization: Univ. of the Philippines, College of Social Sciences & Philosophy, College of Science, College of Arts & Letters
ISSN: 0012-2858

MLA acronym: DilR

SUBSCRIPTION INFORMATION

Frequency of publication: 4 times/yr.
Circulation: 5,000
Available in microform: No
Subscription price: $65.00/yr., $130.00/2 yrs.
Year to which price refers: 1992
Subscription address: Portia L. Reyes, at above address

ADVERTISING INFORMATION

Advertising accepted: No

EDITORIAL DESCRIPTION

Scope: Journal analyzes contemporary Philippine history and culture, serving as a forum for the exchange of ideas.
Reviews books: Yes
Publishes notes: No
Languages accepted: English; Tagalog
Prints abstracts: No
Author-anonymous submission: No

SUBMISSION REQUIREMENTS

Restrictions on contributors: None
Author pays submission fee: No
Author pays page charges: No
Length of articles: 1,200 words
Length of book reviews: 1,200 words
Style: Chicago
Number of copies required: 2
Special requirements: Authors may not reprint without permission.
Copyright ownership: Author
Rejected manuscripts: Returned; enclose SASE.
Time before publication decision: 1-2 mos.
Time between decision and publication: 2-8 weeks
Number of reviewers: 4
Articles submitted per year: 180-200
Articles published per year: 102-120
Book reviews submitted per year: 50
Book reviews published per year: 20

(790)
*Dime Novel Roundup: A Magazine Devoted to the Collecting, Preservation and Literature of the Old-Time Dime and Nickel Novels, Libraries and Popular Story Papers

Edward T. LeBlanc, Editor
87 School St.
Fall River, MA 02720

Telephone: 508 672-2082
First published: 1931
Sponsoring organization: Happy Hours Brotherhood
ISSN: 0012-2874
MLA acronym: DNR

SUBSCRIPTION INFORMATION

Frequency of publication: 6 times/yr. (Feb., Apr., June, Aug., Oct., Dec.)
Circulation: 360
Available in microform: No
Subscription price: $10.00/yr.
Year to which price refers: 1992

ADVERTISING INFORMATION

Advertising accepted: Yes
Advertising rates: $6.00/quarter page; $20.00/full page

EDITORIAL DESCRIPTION

Scope: Publishes articles on dime and nickel novels, and on children's series books.
Reviews books: Yes
Publishes notes: Yes

Languages accepted: English
Prints abstracts: No
Author-anonymous submission: No

SUBMISSION REQUIREMENTS

Restrictions on contributors: None
Author pays submission fee: No
Author pays page charges: No
Length of articles: 2,500 words
Length of book reviews: 150 words
Length of notes: 175-200 words
Style: None
Number of copies required: 1
Special requirements: Submit double-spaced typescript.
Copyright ownership: Not copyrighted
Rejected manuscripts: Returned; enclose SASE.
Time before publication decision: 3-6 mos.
Time between decision and publication: 3-6 mos.
Number of reviewers: 1
Articles submitted per year: 12-15
Articles published per year: 12-15
Book reviews submitted per year: 15
Book reviews published per year: 10
Notes submitted per year: 10
Notes published per year: 8

(791)
Dimension: Contemporary German Arts and Letters

A. Leslie Willson, Editor
P.O. Box 26673
Austin, TX 78755-0673

First published: 1968
Sponsoring organization: Univ. of Texas at Austin; Inter Nationes
ISSN: 0012-2882
MLA acronym: Dimension

SUBSCRIPTION INFORMATION

Frequency of publication: 3 times/yr. (Spring, Summer, Fall)
Circulation: 810
Available in microform: Yes
Subscription price: $24.00/yr. institutions US; $29.00/yr. institutions elsewhere; $20.00/yr. individuals US; $25.00/yr. individuals elsewhere
Year to which price refers: 1992

ADVERTISING INFORMATION

Advertising accepted: No

EDITORIAL DESCRIPTION

Scope: Publishes contemporary German-language literature and criticism in a bilingual form.
Reviews books: No
Publishes notes: No
Languages accepted: German; English
Prints abstracts: No
Author-anonymous submission: No

SUBMISSION REQUIREMENTS

Restrictions on contributors: Contributors must have published in Europe.
Author pays submission fee: No
Author pays page charges: No
Length of articles: No restrictions
Style: MLA
Number of copies required: 1
Special requirements: Include originals for all translations.
Copyright ownership: Journal
Rejected manuscripts: Returned; enclose SASE.
Time before publication decision: 3 mos.
Time between decision and publication: 1-2 yrs.
Number of reviewers: 2
Articles submitted per year: 40
Articles published per year: 20

(792)
*Diogenes

Jean d'Ormesson & Paola Costa, Editors
UNESCO House
1, rue Miollis
75732 Paris Cedex 15, France

Telephone: (33) 1 45682734
Fax: (33) 1 40659480
First published: 1952
Sponsoring organization: International Council for Philosophy & Humanistic Studies, UNESCO
ISSN: 0012-303X
MLA acronym: Diogenes

SUBSCRIPTION INFORMATION

Frequency of publication: 4 times/yr.
Circulation: 1,500 (English edition)
Available in microform: Yes
Subscription price: $60.00/yr.
Year to which price refers: 1991
Subscription address: Order English language edition from Berg Publishers, c/o Ellen Maly, Providence, RI 02906
Subscription telephone: 401 273-0061

ADVERTISING INFORMATION

Advertising accepted: Yes

EDITORIAL DESCRIPTION

Scope: Publishes articles on the philosophy of science, history of religion, linguistics, aesthetics, anthropology and ethnology, literary history, and psychology, etc. Serves as a link between the different disciplines of the humanistic sciences. Available in English, French, Spanish, and Arabic editions.
Reviews books: No
Publishes notes: No
Languages accepted: English; French; Spanish
Prints abstracts: No
Author-anonymous submission: No

SUBMISSION REQUIREMENTS

Restrictions on contributors: None
Author pays submission fee: No
Author pays page charges: No
Length of articles: 50,000 characters (20-25 pp.)
Number of copies required: 2
Special requirements: Include a 200-word abstract.
Copyright ownership: Journal
Rejected manuscripts: Returned; enclose return postage.
Time before publication decision: 2-3 mos.
Time between decision and publication: 6 mos.
Number of reviewers: 4
Articles submitted per year: 130
Articles published per year: 28

(793)
*Dionysos: The Literature and Addiction TriQuarterly

Roger Forseth, Editor
Sundquist Hall 238
Univ. of Wisconsin-Superior
1800 Grand Ave.
Superior, WI 54880-2898

Telephone: 715 394-8465
Fax: 715 394-8454
First published: 1989
Historical variations in title: Formerly Dionysos: The Literature and Intoxication TriQuarterly
Sponsoring organization: Univ. of Wisconsin, Superior
ISSN: 1044-4149
MLA acronym: Dionysos

SUBSCRIPTION INFORMATION

Frequency of publication: 3 times/yr.
Circulation: 150
Available in microform: No
Subscription price: $12.00/yr. institutions US & Canada; $15.00/yr. institutions elsewhere; $8.00/yr. individuals US & Canada; $10.00/yr. individuals elsewhere
Year to which price refers: 1991-92

ADVERTISING INFORMATION

Advertising accepted: Yes

EDITORIAL DESCRIPTION

Scope: Publishes critical and scholarly articles concerning both the destructive and creative dimensions of intoxication in literary text and biography.
Reviews books: Yes
Publishes notes: Yes
Languages accepted: English
Prints abstracts: No
Author-anonymous submission: No

SUBMISSION REQUIREMENTS

Restrictions on contributors: Book reviews are commissioned.
Author pays submission fee: No
Author pays page charges: No
Length of articles: 4,000 words
Length of book reviews: 1,500 words
Length of notes: 1,000 words
Style: MLA (1985)
Number of copies required: 2
Copyright ownership: Univ. of Wisconsin, Superior
Rejected manuscripts: Returned
Time before publication decision: 2 mos.
Time between decision and publication: 3 mos.
Number of reviewers: 2-3
Articles submitted per year: 25
Articles published per year: 12-15
Book reviews submitted per year: 12-15
Book reviews published per year: 12-15
Notes submitted per year: 3
Notes published per year: 3

(794)
*Dires: Revue du Centre d'Etudes Freudiennes

Paule Plouvier, Editor
Centre d'Etudes Freudiennes
Univ. Paul Valéry
Route de Mende, B.P. 5043
34032 Montpellier Cédex, France

Telephone: (33) 67142326
Fax: (33) 67142052
First published: 1983
Sponsoring organization: Centre d'Etudes Freudiennes du Montpellier
ISSN: 0766-5350
MLA acronym: Dires

SUBSCRIPTION INFORMATION

Frequency of publication: Annual
Circulation: 600
Available in microform: No
Subscription price: 100 F/yr.
Year to which price refers: 1992

ADVERTISING INFORMATION

Advertising accepted: Yes

EDITORIAL DESCRIPTION

Scope: Publishes articles on psychoanalysis and literature.
Reviews books: No
Publishes notes: No
Languages accepted: French
Prints abstracts: No
Author-anonymous submission: No

SUBMISSION REQUIREMENTS

Restrictions on contributors: None
Author pays submission fee: No
Author pays page charges: No
Length of articles: 10 pp.
Style: MLA
Number of copies required: 3
Special requirements: Submit manuscript 1 yr. before next publication.
Copyright ownership: Journal
Rejected manuscripts: Returned
Time before publication decision: 6 mos.
Time between decision and publication: 6 mos.
Number of reviewers: 2
Articles published per year: 15

(795)
*Discours Social/Social Discourse: Analyse du Discours et Sociocritique des Textes/Discourse Analysis and Text Sociocriticism

Robert Franklin Barsky & Marc Argenot, Editors
Pavillon Sainte-Catherine Ouest
Univ. de Québec à Montréal
C.P. 8888, Succ. "A"
Montreal, PQ H3C 3P8, Canada

Telephone: 514 987-7719
Fax: 514 987-3523
First published: 1987
Historical variations in title: Formerly Discours Social/Social Discourse: International Research Papers in Comparative Literature
Sponsoring organization: Inter-University Center for Discourse Analysis & Text Sociocriticism (ICDATS), McGill Univ.
ISSN: 0842-1420
MLA acronym: DS/SD

SUBSCRIPTION INFORMATION

Frequency of publication: 4 times/yr.
Circulation: 200
Available in microform: No
Subscription price: C$65.00/yr. institutions; C$40.00/yr. individuals; C$30.00/yr. students; add C$5.00/yr. postage outside Canada
Year to which price refers: 1992

ADVERTISING INFORMATION

Advertising accepted: Yes
Advertising rates: C$200.00/full page; also on an exchange basis

EDITORIAL DESCRIPTION

Scope: Publishes articles on theories of social discourse which expand the knowledge of interaction within and amongst different cultures.
Reviews books: Yes
Publishes notes: Yes
Languages accepted: English; French; German; Italian; Spanish
Prints abstracts: Yes
Author-anonymous submission: Yes

SUBMISSION REQUIREMENTS

Restrictions on contributors: None
Author pays submission fee: No
Author pays page charges: No
Length of articles: 5,000 words maximum
Length of book reviews: 500 words
Length of notes: 250-500 words
Style: MLA
Number of copies required: 2
Special requirements: Submit abstracts in French, if possible. Translation assistance will be provided if necessary.
Copyright ownership: Author
Rejected manuscripts: Returned
Time before publication decision: 1-3 mos.
Time between decision and publication: 1-3 mos.

(796)
*Discourse: Journal for Theoretical Studies in Media and Culture

Roswitha Mueller & Kathleen Woodward, Editors
Center for Twentieth Century Studies
P.O. Box 413
Univ. of Wisconsin-Milwaukee
Milwaukee, WI 53201

Telephone: 414 229-4141
Fax: 414 229-5964
First published: 1978
Sponsoring organization: Center for Twentieth Century Studies, Univ. of Wisconsin-Milwaukee
ISSN: 0730-1081
MLA acronym: Discourse

SUBSCRIPTION INFORMATION

Frequency of publication: 3 times/yr. (Fall, Winter, Spring)
Circulation: 500
Available in microform: No
Subscription price: $50.00/yr. institutions; $25.00/yr. individuals; add $10.00 ($20.00 airmail)/yr. postage elsewhere
Year to which price refers: 1992
Subscription address: Indiana Univ. Press, 10th & Morton Sts., Bloomington, IN 47405
Subscription telephone: 812 855-9449
Subscription fax: 812 855-7931

ADVERTISING INFORMATION

Advertising accepted: Yes, on an exchange basis

EDITORIAL DESCRIPTION

Scope: Explores a variety of topics in continental philosophy, theories of media and literature, and the politics of sexuality, including questions of language and psychoanalysis.
Reviews books: Yes
Publishes notes: No
Languages accepted: English
Prints abstracts: No
Author-anonymous submission: No

SUBMISSION REQUIREMENTS

Restrictions on contributors: None
Author pays submission fee: No
Author pays page charges: No
Length of articles: 5,000-6,000 words
Length of book reviews: 1,500 words
Style: MLA
Number of copies required: 3
Special requirements: Submit original typescript and 2 copies.
Copyright ownership: Regents of Univ. of Wisconsin; revents to author upon publication
Rejected manuscripts: Returned; enclose SASE.
Time before publication decision: 2-3 mos.
Time between decision and publication: 3-6 mos.
Number of reviewers: 2-3
Articles published per year: 12-20
Book reviews published per year: 4-8

Number of reviewers: 3
Articles submitted per year: 200
Articles published per year: 20-25
Book reviews submitted per year: 20
Book reviews published per year: 15
Notes submitted per year: 10
Notes published per year: 8

(797)
*Discourse Processes: A Multidisciplinary Journal

Roy O. Freedle, Editor
Educational Testing Service
Research Building
Princeton, NJ 08540

Telephone: 609 734-5712
First published: 1978
ISSN: 0163-853X
MLA acronym: DPr

SUBSCRIPTION INFORMATION

Frequency of publication: 4 times/yr.
Subscription address: Ablex Publishing Corp., 355 Chestnut St., Norwood, NJ 07648

ADVERTISING INFORMATION

Advertising accepted: Yes

EDITORIAL DESCRIPTION

Scope: Publishes articles on discourse studies, empirical studies and research, including sociolinguistics, psycholinguistics, ethnomethodology and the study of language, educational psychology, philosophy of language, etc.
Reviews books: No
Languages accepted: English
Prints abstracts: Yes
Author-anonymous submission: No

SUBMISSION REQUIREMENTS

Restrictions on contributors: None
Author pays submission fee: No
Author pays page charges: No
Length of articles: 35 double-spaced typescript pp.
Style: American Psychological Assn.
Number of copies required: 4
Special requirements: Submit typescript on 8 1/2 in. x 11 in. bond with 1 in. margins on all sides. Include footnotes at end and a 100-150 word abstract. See journal for more information.
Copyright ownership: Ablex Publishing Corp. & author
Rejected manuscripts: Returned
Time before publication decision: 3 mos.
Time between decision and publication: 16 mos.
Number of reviewers: 2
Articles submitted per year: 80
Articles published per year: 25

(798)
*Discurso: Revista de Estudios Iberoamericanos

Javier Restrepo & Juan Manuel Marcos, Editors
Centro de Estudios de Economía & Sociedad
Estados Unidos 1461
Asunción, Paraguay

Telephone: (595) 21 73608
Fax: (595) 21 73640
First published: 1983
Sponsoring organization: Centro de Estudios de Economía & Sociedad (CEDES); Univ. del Norte, Asunción
ISSN: 0737-8742
MLA acronym: Discurso

SUBSCRIPTION INFORMATION

Frequency of publication: 2 times/yr.
Circulation: 1,000
Available in microform: No
Subscription price: $60.00/yr. institutions; $40.00/yr. individuals
Year to which price refers: 1993
Subscription address: Javier Restrepo, Rca. Francesa 728, Asunción, Paraguay

ADVERTISING INFORMATION

Advertising accepted: Yes
Advertising rates: $125.00/half page; $200.00/full page

EDITORIAL DESCRIPTION

Scope: Publishes articles on Latin American, Portuguese, and Spanish literatures. Also includes works on linguistics, and social sciences, including economics, history, anthropology, sociology, and international relations.
Reviews books: Yes
Publishes notes: Yes
Languages accepted: Spanish; English; Portuguese
Prints abstracts: No
Author-anonymous submission: Yes

SUBMISSION REQUIREMENTS

Restrictions on contributors: Contributors should subscribe to the journal.
Author pays submission fee: No
Author pays page charges: No
Length of articles: 4,500 words
Length of book reviews: 2,500 words
Length of notes: 2,500 words
Style: MLA
Number of copies required: 3
Special requirements: Submit typescript.
Copyright ownership: CEDES
Rejected manuscripts: Not returned
Time before publication decision: 2 mos.
Time between decision and publication: 6-24 mos.
Number of reviewers: 2-3
Articles submitted per year: 45
Articles published per year: 22
Book reviews submitted per year: 10
Book reviews published per year: 5
Notes submitted per year: 6
Notes published per year: 2

(799)
*The Dispatch

Jack Salzman, Editor
Center for American Culture Studies
603 Lewisohn Hall
Columbia Univ.
New York, NY 10027

First published: 1984
Sponsoring organization: Columbia Univ., Center for American Culture Studies
MLA acronym: Dispatch

SUBSCRIPTION INFORMATION

Frequency of publication: 2 times/yr. (Spring, Fall)
Available in microform: No
Subscription price: $10.00/yr.
Year to which price refers: 1992

ADVERTISING INFORMATION

Advertising accepted: No

EDITORIAL DESCRIPTION

Scope: Reports on various activities of the Center for American Culture Studies. Includes a wide range of commentary on interdisciplinary approaches to American culture studies.
Reviews books: No
Publishes notes: No
Languages accepted: English
Prints abstracts: No

SUBMISSION REQUIREMENTS

Author pays submission fee: No
Author pays page charges: No
Length of articles: 10-20 pp.
Style: MLA; Chicago
Number of copies required: 1

Time before publication decision: 6 mos.
Time between decision and publication: 1 yr.
Number of reviewers: 1
Articles published per year: 2

(800)
*Dispositio: Revista Americana de Estudios Semióticos y Culturales/ American Journal of Semiotic and Cultural Studies

Walter D. Mignolo, Editor
Dept. of Romance Languages
Univ. of Michigan
Ann Arbor, MI 48109-1275

Telephone: 313 764-5363; 313 747-2383
First published: 1976
Sponsoring organization: Dept. of Romance Languages, Program in American Culture, Univ. of Michigan
ISSN: 0734-0591
MLA acronym: Dispositio

SUBSCRIPTION INFORMATION

Frequency of publication: 2-3 times/yr.
Circulation: 900
Available in microform: No

ADVERTISING INFORMATION

Advertising accepted: Yes

EDITORIAL DESCRIPTION

Scope: Aims to contribute to the advancement the understanding of the plurilingual and multicultural realities of the Americas. Publishes articles related to language-centered disciplines as well as to Mesoamerican and Andean writing systems, popular culture and mass media.
Reviews books: Yes
Publishes notes: Yes
Languages accepted: English; Spanish
Prints abstracts: No
Author-anonymous submission: No

SUBMISSION REQUIREMENTS

Restrictions on contributors: None
Author pays submission fee: No
Author pays page charges: No
Length of articles: 50 pp. maximum
Length of book reviews: 1,500 words
Length of notes: 500 words
Style: MLA; Semiotica
Number of copies required: 2
Special requirements: Submit an abstract.
Copyright ownership: Dept. of Romance Languages, Univ. of Michigan
Rejected manuscripts: Returned
Time before publication decision: 6 mos.
Time between decision and publication: 1 yr.
Number of reviewers: 2-3
Articles submitted per year: 40-60
Articles published per year: 30
Book reviews submitted per year: 10-15
Book reviews published per year: 10
Notes submitted per year: 10
Notes published per year: 3

(801)
*Dissertation Abstracts International

David J. Billick, Editor
Univ. Microfilms International
300 N. Zeeb Rd.
Ann Arbor, MI 48106

Telephone: 313 761-4700
Fax: 313 973-6436
First published: 1938
Sponsoring organization: Univ. Microfilms International

ISSN: Pt. A, 0419-4209; Pt. B, 0419-4217; Pt. C, 1042-7279
MLA acronym: DAI

SUBSCRIPTION INFORMATION

Frequency of publication: 12 times/yr.
Circulation: 2,000 (Combined)
Available in microform: Yes
Subscription price: Pt. A & Pt. B: $715.00/yr. US & Canada; $915.00/yr. elsewhere. Pt. A or Pt. B: $475.00/yr. US & Canada; $675.00/yr. elsewhere. Pt. C: $750.00/yr. US & Canada; $850.00/yr. elsewhere
Year to which price refers: 1992

ADVERTISING INFORMATION

Advertising accepted: No

EDITORIAL DESCRIPTION

Scope: Section A: Humanities and Social Sciences; Section B: Sciences & Engineering; Section C: Primarily European Abstracts
Reviews books: No
Publishes notes: No
Languages accepted: English; French
Prints abstracts: Yes

SUBMISSION REQUIREMENTS

Restrictions on contributors: Abstracts must be submitted from an accredited school.
Author pays submission fee: Yes
Author pays page charges: No
Length of articles: 350 words doctoral; 150 words masters
Style: None
Number of copies required: 2
Special requirements: Submit double-spaced typescript.
Copyright ownership: Author
Time before publication decision: 4 mos.
Time between decision and publication: 3 mos.
Articles submitted per year: 38,000 abstracts
Articles published per year: 38,000 abstracts

(802)
Divus Thomas: Commentarium de Philosophia et Theologia

Edizioni Studio Domenicano
Via Osservanza 72
40136 Bologna, Italy

Telephone: (39) 51 582034
Fax: (39) 51 331583
First published: 1880
ISSN: 0012-4257
MLA acronym: DT

SUBSCRIPTION INFORMATION

Frequency of publication: 4 times/yr.
Circulation: 600
Available in microform: No
Subscription price: 40,000 Lit/yr. Italy; 65,000 Lit (80,000 Lit airmail)/yr. elsewhere
Year to which price refers: 1992

ADVERTISING INFORMATION

Advertising accepted: No

EDITORIAL DESCRIPTION

Scope: Publishes studies on new theoretical problems in philosophy and theology. Preference is given to articles that deal with the thought of St. Thomas Aquinas or are based on his doctrine.
Reviews books: Yes
Publishes notes: Yes
Languages accepted: English; French; German; Italian; Latin; Spanish
Prints abstracts: Yes
Author-anonymous submission: Yes

SUBMISSION REQUIREMENTS

Restrictions on contributors: None
Author pays submission fee: No
Author pays page charges: No
Length of articles: 12,000 words
Length of book reviews: 800 words
Length of notes: 4,000 words
Style: MLA
Number of copies required: 1
Special requirements: Submit original typescript.
Copyright ownership: Author
Rejected manuscripts: Returned
Time before publication decision: 1 mo.
Time between decision and publication: 8 mos.
Number of reviewers: 1 plus Editorial Board
Articles submitted per year: 15
Articles published per year: 12
Book reviews submitted per year: 120
Book reviews published per year: 100
Notes submitted per year: 12
Notes published per year: 10

(803)
*Dix-Huitième Siècle

Roland Desné, Director
23, quai de Grenelle
75015 Paris, France

Telephone: (33) 1 45790932
First published: 1969
Sponsoring organization: Soc. Française d'Etude du 18ᵉ Siècle; Centre National de la Recherche Scientifique
ISSN: 0070-6760
MLA acronym: DHS

SUBSCRIPTION INFORMATION

Frequency of publication: Annual
Circulation: 3,000
Available in microform: No
Subscription price: 200 F/yr.
Year to which price refers: 1992
Subscription address: Robert Granderoute, Aspin 2, 12 ave. du Stade Nautique, 64000 Pau, France

ADVERTISING INFORMATION

Advertising accepted: Yes
Advertising rates: 600 F/half page; 900 F/full page

EDITORIAL DESCRIPTION

Scope: Publishes interdisciplinary studies on the Enlightenment and 18th century.
Reviews books: Yes
Publishes notes: Yes
Languages accepted: French
Prints abstracts: Yes
Author-anonymous submission: Yes

SUBMISSION REQUIREMENTS

Restrictions on contributors: None
Author pays submission fee: No
Author pays page charges: No
Length of articles: 5,000 words
Length of book reviews: 250 words
Length of notes: 1,000 words
Style: MLA
Number of copies required: 2
Special requirements: Include a 100-word abstract in English.
Copyright ownership: Journal
Rejected manuscripts: Not returned
Time before publication decision: 4-6 mos.
Time between decision and publication: 2-24 mos.
Number of reviewers: 1-2
Articles submitted per year: 50
Articles published per year: 25-30
Book reviews submitted per year: 300
Book reviews published per year: 260

Notes submitted per year: 2-3
Notes published per year: 1-2

(804)
*Dix-Septième Siècle

G. Molinié, Editor
Soc. d'Etude du XVIIe Siècle
c/o Collège de France
11, place Marcelin-Berthelot
75231 Paris Cedex 05, France

First published: 1948
Sponsoring organization: Soc. d'Etude du XVIIe Siècle
ISSN: 0012-4273
MLA acronym: DSS

SUBSCRIPTION INFORMATION

Frequency of publication: 4 times/yr.
Circulation: 1,500
Available in microform: No
Subscription price: 360 F/yr.
Year to which price refers: 1992

ADVERTISING INFORMATION

Advertising accepted: No

EDITORIAL DESCRIPTION

Scope: Publishes articles on all topics concerning the 17th century.
Reviews books: Yes
Publishes notes: No
Languages accepted: French
Prints abstracts: No
Author-anonymous submission: No

SUBMISSION REQUIREMENTS

Restrictions on contributors: None
Author pays submission fee: No
Author pays page charges: No
Length of articles: 12 pp.
Length of book reviews: 1 p.
Number of copies required: 2
Copyright ownership: Assigned by author to Soc. d'Etude du XVIIe Siècle
Rejected manuscripts: Not returned
Time before publication decision: 6 mos.
Time between decision and publication: 1 yr.
Number of reviewers: 3
Articles submitted per year: 50
Articles published per year: 20-30
Book reviews submitted per year: 120
Book reviews published per year: 120

(805)
Dnipro: Literaturno-Khudozhniĭ ta Hromads'ko-Politychnyĭ Zhurnal

Mykola Lukiv, Editor
Izdatel'stvo Molod
38-42 Parkhomenko St.
Kiev, Ukraine

First published: 1927
Sponsoring organization: CK LKSMU
ISSN: 0012-4354
MLA acronym: Dnipro

SUBSCRIPTION INFORMATION

Frequency of publication: 12 times/yr.
Circulation: 76,000

EDITORIAL DESCRIPTION

Scope: Focuses on the education of young people in the spirit of patriotism and internationalism, ideals of peace, friendship among peoples, and communism. Publishes literary, critical, and journalistic works, preferably by or about young people.
Reviews books: Yes
Languages accepted: Russian; Ukrainian
Prints abstracts: No

SUBMISSION REQUIREMENTS

Restrictions on contributors: None
Length of articles: 25 pp.
Style: None
Number of copies required: 1
Special requirements: Submit original typescript.
Copyright ownership: Assigned by author to journal
Rejected manuscripts: Returned
Time before publication decision: 2-3 mos.
Time between decision and publication: 1 yr.
Number of reviewers: 2 plus Editorial Board
Articles published per year: 100

(806)
*Documentos A: Genealogia Cientifica de la Cultura

Ángel Nogueira Dobarro, Editor
Anthropos. Editorial del Hombre
Aptdo. 387
08190 Sant Cugat del Vallés, Spain

Telephone: (34) 3 5894884
Fax: (34) 3 6741733
First published: 1991
ISSN: 1130-4936
MLA acronym: DocumentosA

SUBSCRIPTION INFORMATION

Frequency of publication: 2 times/yr.
Circulation: 2,000
Available in microform: No
Subscription price: 4,415 Pta/yr.
Year to which price refers: 1992
Additional subscription address: In US: Literal Books, P.O. Box 713, Adelphi, MD 20783
Subscription telephone: US: 800 366-8680; elsewhere: (34) 3 5894884

ADVERTISING INFORMATION

Advertising accepted: Yes
Advertising rates: 180,000 Pta/inside back cover; 195,000/inside front cover

EDITORIAL DESCRIPTION

Scope: A multidisciplinary journal that publishes articles on Spanish and Latin American literature, culture, and thought. Each subject covered is analyzed genealogically in its history, its evolution, its diffusion, etc.
Reviews books: No
Publishes notes: No
Languages accepted: Spanish
Prints abstracts: No

SUBMISSION REQUIREMENTS

Restrictions on contributors: Contributions are solicited.
Copyright ownership: Anthropos Editorial
Articles published per year: 40

(807)
*Documents du Centre de Recherche de Langue et Littérature Italiennes et du Centre de Recherches Italiennes

Gérard Genot, Paul Larivaille, & Marie-Hélène Caspar, Editors
C.R.I.X.
Univ. de Paris X
92001 Nanterre Cédex, France

First published: 1973
Historical variations in title: Formerly Documents du Centre de Recherche de Langue et Littérature Italiennes
Sponsoring organization: Centre de Recherches Italiennes de Paris X (C.R.I.X.)
ISSN: 0152-707X
MLA acronym: DocCRLLI

SUBSCRIPTION INFORMATION

Frequency of publication: 4 times/yr.
Circulation: 300
Available in microform: No
Subscription address: Centre de Diffusion, Univ. de Paris X, 92001 Nanterre Cedex, France

ADVERTISING INFORMATION

Advertising accepted: No

EDITORIAL DESCRIPTION

Scope: Publishes monographs on Italian and general linguistics and literature.
Reviews books: No
Publishes notes: No
Languages accepted: French; Italian; English
Prints abstracts: No

SUBMISSION REQUIREMENTS

Restrictions on contributors: Contributors must be invited or be members of C.R.I.X.
Author pays submission fee: No
Author pays page charges: No
Style: None
Number of copies required: 1
Special requirements: Submit camera-ready manuscript.
Copyright ownership: C.R.I.X.
Rejected manuscripts: Not returned.
Time before publication decision: 1 mo.
Time between decision and publication: 6-12 mos.
Number of reviewers: 2 minimum
Books submitted per year: 6-8
Books published per year: 4

(808)
*Documents sur l'Espéranto

Thomas Bormann, Editor
Assn. Universelle d'Espéranto
Nieuwe Binnenweg 176
3015 BJ Rotterdam, Netherlands

Telephone: (31) 10 4361044
Fax: (31) 10 4361751
Sponsoring organization: Universala Esperanto-Asocio
ISSN: 0165-2621
MLA acronym: DLE

SUBSCRIPTION INFORMATION

Frequency of publication: Irregular
Available in microform: No
Subscription price: $22.50/10 issues
Year to which price refers: 1992

ADVERTISING INFORMATION

Advertising accepted: Yes

EDITORIAL DESCRIPTION

Scope: Publishes articles on the work, organization, culture, and history of the movement for the adoption of the international language Esperanto as a second language for international use. Many documents also appear in the associated publications *Esperanto Documents* and *Esperanto-Dokumentoj.*
Reviews books: No
Publishes notes: No
Languages accepted: French
Prints abstracts: No
Author-anonymous submission: No

SUBMISSION REQUIREMENTS

Author pays submission fee: No
Author pays page charges: No
Length of books: 3,000-12,000 words
Number of copies required: 1
Copyright ownership: Not copyrighted
Rejected manuscripts: Returned
Books published per year: 1-4

(809)
*The Dolphin: Publications of the English Department, University of Aarhus

Tim Caudery, Editor
English Dept.
Univ. of Aarhus
Building 326
8000 Aarhus C, Denmark

Telephone: (45) 86 136711
Fax: (45) 86 136711
First published: 1979
Sponsoring organization: Dept. of English, Univ. of Aarhus
ISSN: 0106-4487
MLA acronym: Dolphin

SUBSCRIPTION INFORMATION

Frequency of publication: 2 times/yr.
Circulation: 125
Available in microform: No
Subscription price: $38.00/yr.
Year to which price refers: 1992
Subscription address: Aarhus Univ. Press, Aarhus Univ., 8000 Aarhus C, Denmark
Subscription telephone: (45) 86 197033
Subscription fax: (45) 86 198433

ADVERTISING INFORMATION

Advertising accepted: Yes

EDITORIAL DESCRIPTION

Scope: Publishes articles on English, American, and Commonwealth studies. Issues are thematic.
Reviews books: No
Publishes notes: No
Languages accepted: English
Prints abstracts: Yes
Author-anonymous submission: No

SUBMISSION REQUIREMENTS

Restrictions on contributors: None
Author pays submission fee: No
Author pays page charges: No
Length of articles: 6,000 words
Style: MLA
Number of copies required: 1
Copyright ownership: Publisher
Rejected manuscripts: Returned
Time before publication decision: 6 mos.
Time between decision and publication: 18 mos.
Number of reviewers: 2
Articles submitted per year: 25
Articles published per year: 20

(810)
Doris Lessing Newsletter

Ruth Saxton, Editor
Mills College
Dept. of English
5000 MacArthur Blvd.
Oakland, CA 94613

Additional editorial address: Mona Knapp, Associate Editor, 2490 E. Murray-Holladay Rd., Salt Lake City, UT 84117
First published: 1977
Sponsoring organization: Doris Lessing Soc.
ISSN: 0882-486X
MLA acronym: DLN

SUBSCRIPTION INFORMATION

Frequency of publication: 2 times/yr. (Fall, Spring)
Circulation: 150-200
Available in microform: No
Subscription address: Katherine Fishburn, Dept. of English, Michigan State Univ., East Lansing, MI 48824-1036

ADVERTISING INFORMATION

Advertising accepted: Yes

EDITORIAL DESCRIPTION

Scope: Publishes articles, reviews, and bibliography on Doris Lessing.
Reviews books: Yes
Publishes notes: Yes
Languages accepted: English
Prints abstracts: No
Author-anonymous submission: No

SUBMISSION REQUIREMENTS

Restrictions on contributors: Contributors must be members of the Doris Lessing Soc.
Author pays submission fee: No
Author pays page charges: No
Length of articles: 1,000-5,000 words
Length of book reviews: 500-1,500 words
Length of notes: 25-1,000 words
Style: MLA
Number of copies required: 2 preferred
Special requirements: Camera-ready artwork is required.
Copyright ownership: Brooklyn College Press
Rejected manuscripts: Returned
Time before publication decision: 3 mos.
Time between decision and publication: 2-12 mos.
Number of reviewers: 2-3
Articles submitted per year: 10-25
Articles published per year: 6-15
Book reviews submitted per year: 3-6
Book reviews published per year: 6-10
Notes submitted per year: 40
Notes published per year: 25

(811)
*Dostoevsky Studies: Journal of the International Dostoevsky Society

Charles Schlacks, Jr., Editor
c/o Dept. of Languages & Literature
Univ. of Utah
Salt Lake City, UT 84112

Additional editorial address: Rudolf Neuhäuser, European Editor, Inst. für Slawistik, Univ. of Bildungswissenschaften, 9022 Klagenfurt, Austria
Telephone: 801 581-5554
Fax: 801 581-7581
First published: 1980
Sponsoring organization: International Dostoevsky Soc.
ISSN: 0047-0686
MLA acronym: DStudies

SUBSCRIPTION INFORMATION

Frequency of publication: 2 times/yr.
Circulation: 300
Available in microform: No
Subscription price: $30.00/yr. plus postage
Year to which price refers: 1992

ADVERTISING INFORMATION

Advertising accepted: Yes
Advertising rates: $100.00/full page

EDITORIAL DESCRIPTION

Scope: Publishes extensive bibliographies, book reviews, research papers, and information of interest in the area of Dostoevsky research.
Reviews books: Yes
Publishes notes: Yes
Languages accepted: English; French; German; Russian
Prints abstracts: No
Author-anonymous submission: Yes

SUBMISSION REQUIREMENTS

Restrictions on contributors: Unsolicited book reviews are not accepted.
Author pays submission fee: No
Author pays page charges: No
Length of articles: 25 pp. maximum
Length of book reviews: 1-2 pp.
Length of notes: 10 pp. maximum
Style: MLA with modifications for submissions in English; generally accepted transliteration systems in other languages
Number of copies required: 3
Copyright ownership: Journal
Rejected manuscripts: Returned
Time before publication decision: 6-12 mos.
Time between decision and publication: 3-12 mos.
Number of reviewers: 2-3
Articles submitted per year: 15-20
Articles published per year: 10-15
Book reviews submitted per year: 10-15
Book reviews published per year: 5-10
Notes submitted per year: 3-5
Notes published per year: 1-5

(812)
Downside Review: A Quarterly of Catholic Thought

Dom Daniel Rees, Editor
Downside Abbey
Stratton-on-the-Fosse
Bath BA3 4RH, England

First published: 1880
ISSN: 0012-5806
MLA acronym: DownR

SUBSCRIPTION INFORMATION

Frequency of publication: 4 times/yr.
Subscription address: Newman Bookshop, Downside Abbey, Stratton-on-the-Fosse, Bath BA3 4RH, England

EDITORIAL DESCRIPTION

Reviews books: Yes
Languages accepted: English
Prints abstracts: No

(813)
*Dreiser Studies

Frederic E. Rusch & David Vancil, Editors
Dept. of English
Indiana State Univ.
Terre Haute, IN 47809

Telephone: 812 237-3163
Fax: 812 237-2567
E-mail: LIBVANC@INDST.BITNET
First published: 1970
Sponsoring organization: Dept. of English, Indiana State Univ., Terre Haute
ISSN: 0896-6362
MLA acronym: DrSt

SUBSCRIPTION INFORMATION

Frequency of publication: 2 times/yr. (Spring, Fall)
Circulation: 300

Available in microform: No
Subscription price: $10.00/yr. institutions N. America; $7.00/yr. individuals N. America; $15.00/yr. elsewhere
Year to which price refers: 1992

ADVERTISING INFORMATION

Advertising accepted: No

EDITORIAL DESCRIPTION

Scope: Publishes articles on Theodore Dreiser and his circle.
Reviews books: Yes
Publishes notes: Yes
Languages accepted: English
Prints abstracts: No
Author-anonymous submission: No

SUBMISSION REQUIREMENTS

Restrictions on contributors: Featured book reviews are solicited.
Author pays submission fee: No
Author pays page charges: No
Length of articles: 12,500 words maximum
Length of book reviews: 2,000 words for featured review; 200-500 words for short reviews
Length of notes: 500-2,000 words
Style: MLA
Number of copies required: 1
Special requirements: Submit on diskette in WordStar 5.0+, WordPerfect 5.0+, Nota Bene, or ASCII.
Copyright ownership: Journal
Rejected manuscripts: Returned; enclose SASE.
Time before publication decision: 3-12 weeks
Time between decision and publication: 3-6 mos.
Number of reviewers: 2 minimum
Articles submitted per year: 20-30
Articles published per year: 7-8
Book reviews submitted per year: 2 featured; 7-15 short reviews
Book reviews published per year: 2 featured; 7-15 short reviews
Notes submitted per year: 2-3
Notes published per year: 2-3

(814)
Druzhba Narodov: Ezhemesiachnyĭ Literaturno-Khudozhestvennyĭ i Obshchestvenno-Politicheskiĭ Zhurnal

Aleksandr Rudenko-Desniak, Editor
ul. Vorovskogo, 52
121827 GSP Moscow G-69, Russia

First published: 1938
ISSN: 0012-6756
MLA acronym: DruzhN

SUBSCRIPTION INFORMATION

Frequency of publication: 12 times/yr.

EDITORIAL DESCRIPTION

Scope: Publishes articles on Soviet literatures and culture.

(815)
*Duquesne Studies in Language and Literature

Albert C. Labriola, Editor
Dept. of English
Duquesne Univ.
Pittsburgh, PA 15282

Telephone: 412 434-6420
Fax: 412 434-5197
First published: 1978
Sponsoring organization: English Dept., Duquesne Univ.
ISSN: 0070-7694
MLA acronym: DSLL

SUBSCRIPTION INFORMATION

Frequency of publication: Annual
Available in microform: No
Subscription address: Duquesne Univ. Press, 600 Forbes Ave., Pittsburgh, PA 15282

ADVERTISING INFORMATION

Advertising accepted: No

EDITORIAL DESCRIPTION

Scope: Publishes monographs on Spenser, Milton, and their classical and medieval antecedents.
Reviews books: No
Publishes notes: No
Languages accepted: English
Prints abstracts: No
Author-anonymous submission: No

SUBMISSION REQUIREMENTS

Restrictions on contributors: None
Author pays submission fee: No
Author pays page charges: No
Length of books: 200-250 pp.
Style: MLA
Number of copies required: 2
Special requirements: Query editor before submission.
Copyright ownership: Duquesne Univ. Press
Rejected manuscripts: Returned
Time before publication decision: 4-6 mos.
Time between decision and publication: 1-2 yrs.
Number of reviewers: 2-3
Books published per year: 1

(816)
*Durham Medieval Texts

Paul Bibire, Joyce Hill, John McKinnell, & Meg Twycross, Editors
Office for English Language & Medieval Literature
School of English
Elvet Riverside
New Elvet, Durham DH1 3JT, England

Telephone: (44) 91 3742644
First published: 1978
ISSN: 0955-0666
MLA acronym: DMT

SUBSCRIPTION INFORMATION

Frequency of publication: Irregular
Circulation: 500
Available in microform: No

ADVERTISING INFORMATION

Advertising accepted: No

EDITORIAL DESCRIPTION

Scope: Publishes scholarly editions of Medieval literary works for the use of scholars and students.
Reviews books: No
Publishes notes: No
Languages accepted: English
Prints abstracts: No
Author-anonymous submission: No

SUBMISSION REQUIREMENTS

Restrictions on contributors: None
Author pays submission fee: No
Author pays page charges: No
Length of books: 250 pp. maximum
Style: Modern Humanities Research Assn. preferred
Number of copies required: 4
Special requirements: Submission of camera-ready copy is preferred.
Copyright ownership: Editor
Rejected manuscripts: Returned
Time before publication decision: 6 mos.
Number of reviewers: 4

(817)
*Durham Modern Languages Series

D. Hillery, Editor
Univ. of Durham
Elvet Riverside
New Elvet, Durham DH1 3JT, England

Telephone: (44) 91 3742718; (44) 91 3742954
First published: 1980
Sponsoring organization: Univ. of Durham
MLA acronym: DMLS

SUBSCRIPTION INFORMATION

Frequency of publication: 2 times/yr.
Available in microform: No

ADVERTISING INFORMATION

Advertising accepted: No

EDITORIAL DESCRIPTION

Scope: Publishes scholarly monographs and texts in the major modern languages.
Reviews books: No
Publishes notes: No
Languages accepted: French; German; Spanish; Russian
Prints abstracts: No

SUBMISSION REQUIREMENTS

Restrictions on contributors: None
Author pays submission fee: No
Author pays page charges: No
Length of books: 96-120 pp.
Style: Modern Humanities Research Assn.
Number of copies required: 1
Special requirements: Submission of camera-ready copy is preferred.
Copyright ownership: Author
Rejected manuscripts: Returned
Time before publication decision: 1-2 mos.
Time between decision and publication: 2 yrs.
Number of reviewers: 2
Books published per year: 2

(818)
*Durham University Journal

Peter E. Lewis, Editor
School of English
Univ. of Durham
Elvet Riverside
New Elvet, Durham DH1 3JT, England

Telephone: (44) 91 3742744
Fax: (44) 91 3743716
First published: 1876
Sponsoring organization: Univ. of Durham, Senate
ISSN: 0012-7280
MLA acronym: DUJ

SUBSCRIPTION INFORMATION

Frequency of publication: 2 times/yr. (Jan., July)
Circulation: 500
Available in microform: Yes, 1876-1967 issues
Subscription price: £19.00/yr. United Kingdom; £22.00/yr. elsewhere
Year to which price refers: 1992
Subscription address: Secretary, at above address

ADVERTISING INFORMATION

Advertising accepted: Yes

EDITORIAL DESCRIPTION

Scope: Publishes articles on the arts, the humanities, and Christian theology.
Reviews books: Yes
Publishes notes: Yes
Languages accepted: English; French
Prints abstracts: No
Author-anonymous submission: Yes

SUBMISSION REQUIREMENTS

Restrictions on contributors: Scientific articles are not accepted unless of general or local interest.
Author pays submission fee: No
Author pays page charges: No
Length of articles: 7,000 words
Length of book reviews: 800 words
Length of notes: 1,200 words
Style: Hart's Rules for Compositors and Readers at the Oxford University Press
Number of copies required: 1
Copyright ownership: Univ. of Durham, Senate
Rejected manuscripts: Returned
Time before publication decision: 3-6 mos.
Time between decision and publication: 2 yrs.
Number of reviewers: 1-2
Articles submitted per year: 60-70
Articles published per year: 20-24
Book reviews submitted per year: 66
Book reviews published per year: 66
Notes submitted per year: 2
Notes published per year: 2

(819)
*Dutch Crossing: A Journal of Low Countries Studies

J. Fenoulhet, C. Ford, T. Hermans, & M. Wintle, Editors
Dept. of Dutch
Univ. College London
Gower Street
London WC1E 6BT, England

Telephone: (44) 71 3877050 ext. 3113
First published: 1977
Sponsoring organization: Nederlandse Taalunie (Dutch Language Union)
ISSN: 0309-6564
MLA acronym: DC

SUBSCRIPTION INFORMATION

Frequency of publication: 3 times/yr.
Circulation: 150
Available in microform: No
Subscription price: £11.25/yr.
Year to which price refers: 1991

ADVERTISING INFORMATION

Advertising accepted: Yes

EDITORIAL DESCRIPTION

Scope: Publishes articles on Dutch language, literature, history, art history, politics, and economics.
Reviews books: Yes
Publishes notes: Yes
Languages accepted: English
Prints abstracts: No
Author-anonymous submission: No

SUBMISSION REQUIREMENTS

Author pays submission fee: No
Author pays page charges: No
Length of articles: 7,000 words
Length of book reviews: 1,000 words
Length of notes: 400 words
Style: MLA
Number of copies required: 1

Copyright ownership: Author
Rejected manuscripts: Returned
Time before publication decision: 8 mos.
Time between decision and publication: 6 mos.
Number of reviewers: 2
Articles submitted per year: 25
Articles published per year: 18
Book reviews submitted per year: 17
Book reviews published per year: 15
Notes submitted per year: 3
Notes published per year: 5

(820)
Dutch Studies in Armenian Language and Literature

J. J. S. Weitenberg & Th. van Lint, Editors
Editions Rodopi B.V.
Keizersgracht 302-304
1016 EX Amsterdam, Netherlands

First published: 1992
ISSN: 0927-7501
MLA acronym: DSALL

SUBSCRIPTION INFORMATION

Additional subscription address: Editions Rodopi, 233 Peachtree St. N.E., Suite 404, Atlanta, GA 30303-1504
Subscription telephone: 404 523-1964; 800 225-3998
Subscription fax: 404 522-7116

ADVERTISING INFORMATION

Advertising accepted: No

EDITORIAL DESCRIPTION

Scope: Publishes monographs on Armenian language and literature.

SUBMISSION REQUIREMENTS

Copyright ownership: Editions Rodopi B.V.

(821)
Dzejas Diena

Izdevnieciba "Liesma"
Padomju bulvari 24
Riga, Latvia

MLA acronym: DzD

SUBSCRIPTION INFORMATION

Frequency of publication: Annual

(822)
*Ear and Hearing: Official Journal of the American Auditory Society

Susan Jerger, Editor
Division of Audiology, NA 200
Baylor College of Medicine
One Baylor Plaza
Houston, TX 77030-3498

Telephone: 713 798-5916
Fax: 713 798-6002
E-mail: SJERGER@BCM.TMC.Edu
First published: 1977
Sponsoring organization: American Auditory Soc.
ISSN: 0196-0202
MLA acronym: E&H

SUBSCRIPTION INFORMATION

Frequency of publication: 6 times/yr.
Available in microform: Yes

Subscription address: Williams & Wilkins, 428 E. Preston St., Baltimore, MD 21203-9990
Additional subscription address: Williams & Wilkins, Broadway House, 2-6 Fulham Broadway, London SW6 1AA, England

ADVERTISING INFORMATION

Advertising accepted: Yes

EDITORIAL DESCRIPTION

Scope: Focuses on assessment, diagnosis, and management of audiology disorders; includes articles on psycholinguistics, neurolinguistics, speech, learning disabilities, language, and medical aspects of the science.
Reviews books: Yes
Publishes notes: Yes
Languages accepted: English
Prints abstracts: Yes
Author-anonymous submission: No

SUBMISSION REQUIREMENTS

Restrictions on contributors: None
Author pays submission fee: No
Author pays page charges: No
Length of articles: 15 pp.
Length of notes: 3 pp.
Style: American Psychological Assn.
Number of copies required: 4
Copyright ownership: Williams & Wilkins
Rejected manuscripts: Returned
Time before publication decision: 10 weeks
Time between decision and publication: 6 mos.
Number of reviewers: 1-2
Articles submitted per year: 150
Articles published per year: 60-70
Book reviews published per year: 20-30
Notes published per year: 6

(823)
*Early American Literature

Philip F. Gura, Editor
Univ. of North Carolina
Campus Box 3520
Chapel Hill, NC 27599-3520

Telephone: 919 962-5481
First published: 1966
Sponsoring organization: MLA, Division on American Literature to 1800; Univ. of North Carolina at Chapel Hill, Dept. of English
ISSN: 0012-8163
MLA acronym: EAL

SUBSCRIPTION INFORMATION

Frequency of publication: 3 times/yr.
Circulation: 780
Available in microform: No
Subscription price: $22.00/yr. institutions US; $16.50/yr. individuals US; $26.00/yr. elsewhere
Year to which price refers: 1992
Subscription address: Univ. of North Carolina Press, Box 2288, Chapel Hill, NC 27515-2288
Subscription telephone: 919 966-3561

ADVERTISING INFORMATION

Advertising accepted: Yes

EDITORIAL DESCRIPTION

Scope: Publishes articles on American literature through the early national period (about 1820).
Reviews books: Yes
Publishes notes: Yes
Languages accepted: English
Prints abstracts: No
Author-anonymous submission: No

SUBMISSION REQUIREMENTS

Restrictions on contributors: Book reviews are commissioned.
Author pays submission fee: No
Author pays page charges: No
Length of articles: 2,000-7,000 words
Length of book reviews: 500-2,000 words
Length of notes: 500-1,500 words
Style: MLA
Number of copies required: 1
Copyright ownership: Univ. of North Carolina at Chapel Hill, Dept. of English
Rejected manuscripts: Returned; enclose return postage.
Time before publication decision: 4 mos.
Time between decision and publication: 1 yr.
Number of reviewers: 2
Articles submitted per year: 60
Articles published per year: 15
Book reviews submitted per year: 20
Book reviews published per year: 20
Notes submitted per year: 8
Notes published per year: 2

(824)
*Early Drama, Art, and Music Monograph Series

Clifford Davidson, Editor
Medieval Inst.
Western Michigan Univ.
Kalamazoo, MI 49008

Telephone: 616 387-4153
Fax: 616 387-4150
First published: 1977
Sponsoring organization: Medieval Inst.
MLA acronym: EDAMMS

SUBSCRIPTION INFORMATION

Frequency of publication: 1-2 times/yr.
Circulation: 800
Available in microform: No
Subscription address: Medieval Inst. Publications, Western Michigan Univ., Kalamazoo, MI 49008
Subscription telephone: 616 387-4155

ADVERTISING INFORMATION

Advertising accepted: No

EDITORIAL DESCRIPTION

Scope: Publishes monographs focusing on interdisciplinary research about Medieval and Renaissance drama and the other arts.
Reviews books: No
Publishes notes: No
Languages accepted: English
Prints abstracts: No
Author-anonymous submission: No

SUBMISSION REQUIREMENTS

Author pays submission fee: No
Author pays page charges: No
Length of books: 125-400 pp.
Style: MLA (1970) with modifications; request style sheet from editor
Number of copies required: 1
Special requirements: Computer diskettes using WordPerfect should be supplied whenever possible.
Copyright ownership: Board of the Medieval Inst.
Rejected manuscripts: Returned; enclose return postage.
Time before publication decision: 6 mos. maximum
Time between decision and publication: 2 yrs. maximum
Number of reviewers: 1-3
Books submitted per year: 6-8
Books published per year: 1-2

(825)
*Early Drama, Art, and Music Reference Series

Clifford Davidson, Editor
Medieval Inst.
Western Michigan Univ.
Kalamazoo, MI 49008

Telephone: 616 387-4153
Fax: 616 387-4150
First published: 1978
Sponsoring organization: Medieval Inst.
MLA acronym: EDAMRef

SUBSCRIPTION INFORMATION

Frequency of publication: Irregular
Available in microform: No
Subscription address: Medieval Inst. Publications, Western Michigan Univ., Kalamazoo, MI 49008
Subscription telephone: 616 387-4155

ADVERTISING INFORMATION

Advertising accepted: No

EDITORIAL DESCRIPTION

Scope: Reference volumes in medieval and early Renaissance drama and related fields. Publishes surveys and indexes on drama, regional iconography for areas in which theater was active, and music in drama.
Reviews books: No
Publishes notes: No
Languages accepted: English
Prints abstracts: No
Author-anonymous submission: No

SUBMISSION REQUIREMENTS

Author pays submission fee: No
Author pays page charges: No
Length of books: 150-400 pp.
Style: MLA with modifications; request style sheet from editor
Number of copies required: 1
Copyright ownership: Board of the Medieval Inst.
Rejected manuscripts: Returned
Time before publication decision: 22 mos.
Time between decision and publication: 18 mos.
Number of reviewers: 2-5
Books submitted per year: 1-2
Books published per year: 0-1

(826)
*The Early Drama, Art, and Music Review

Clifford Davidson, Editor
Medieval Inst.
Western Michigan Univ.
Kalamazoo, MI 49008

Telephone: 616 387-4153
Fax: 616 387-4150
First published: 1978
Historical variations in title: Incorporates *Medieval Music-Drama News*
Sponsoring organization: Medieval Inst.
ISSN: 0148-9401
MLA acronym: EDAMRvw

SUBSCRIPTION INFORMATION

Frequency of publication: 2 times/yr. (Fall, Spring)
Circulation: 200
Available in microform: No
Subscription price: $8.00/yr. institutions; $6.00/yr. individuals
Year to which price refers: 1991-92
Subscription address: Medieval Inst. Publications, Western Michigan Univ., Kalamazoo, MI 49008

ADVERTISING INFORMATION

Advertising accepted: No

EDITORIAL DESCRIPTION

Scope: Publishes short articles, notes, reviews, and notices of interest to persons working in interdisciplinary studies focusing on the early theater or drama and the related fields of music and art.
Reviews books: Yes
Publishes notes: Yes
Languages accepted: English
Prints abstracts: No
Author-anonymous submission: No

SUBMISSION REQUIREMENTS

Restrictions on contributors: Book reviews are commissioned.
Author pays submission fee: No
Author pays page charges: No
Length of articles: 900-2,500 words
Length of book reviews: 200-500 words
Length of notes: 350-900 words
Style: MLA with modifications; request from editor
Number of copies required: 1
Copyright ownership: Board of Medieval Inst.
Rejected manuscripts: Returned
Time before publication decision: 6 mos.
Time between decision and publication: 5 mos.
Number of reviewers: 2
Articles submitted per year: 15
Articles published per year: 5-7
Book reviews published per year: 6-8
Notes published per year: 3-5

(827)
Early English Text Society

Oxford Univ. Press, Inc.
200 Madison Ave.
New York, NY 10016

First published: 1864
ISSN: 0070-7872
MLA acronym: EETS

SUBSCRIPTION INFORMATION

Frequency of publication: Irregular
Available in microform: No

ADVERTISING INFORMATION

Advertising accepted: No

EDITORIAL DESCRIPTION

Scope: Brings the mass of unprinted Early English literature within the reach of students.
Reviews books: No
Languages accepted: English
Prints abstracts: No

(828)
*East-West Film Journal

Wimal Dissanayake & Paul Clark, Editors
Inst. of Culture & Communication
East-West Center
1777 East-West Rd.
Honolulu, HI 96848

Telephone: 808 944-7302
Fax: 808 944-7670
E-mail: MACMILLM@EWC (Bitnet)
First published: 1986
Sponsoring organization: Inst. of Culture & Communication
ISSN: 0891-6780
MLA acronym: EW

SUBSCRIPTION INFORMATION

Frequency of publication: 2 times/yr. (June, Dec.)
Circulation: 200
Available in microform: No
Subscription price: $25.00/yr. institutions US & Canada; $30.00/yr. institutions elsewhere; $15.00/yr. individuals US & Canada; $17.00/yr. individuals elsewhere
Year to which price refers: 1992
Subscription address: Journals Dept., Univ. of Hawaii Press, 2840 Kolowalu St., Honolulu, HI 96822
Subscription telephone: 808 956-8833

ADVERTISING INFORMATION

Advertising accepted: Yes
Advertising rates: $95.00/half page; $150.00/full page

EDITORIAL DESCRIPTION

Scope: Publishes articles that emphasize the cross-cultural aspects of the film of the East and the West.
Reviews books: Yes
Publishes notes: No
Languages accepted: English
Prints abstracts: No
Author-anonymous submission: No

SUBMISSION REQUIREMENTS

Restrictions on contributors: None
Author pays submission fee: No
Author pays page charges: No
Length of articles: 8,000 words
Length of book reviews: 1,500 words
Style: Chicago
Number of copies required: 2
Copyright ownership: East-West Center
Rejected manuscripts: Returned
Time before publication decision: 6-18 mos.
Time between decision and publication: 6-12 mos.
Number of reviewers: 1
Articles submitted per year: 30-50
Articles published per year: 16-20
Book reviews submitted per year: 5-10
Book reviews published per year: 5-10

(829)
Eco: Revista de la Cultura de Occidente

J. G. Cobo Borda, Editor
Librería Buchholz
Av. Jiminez de Quesada 8-40
Bogota, Colombia

First published: 1961
ISSN: 0012-9410
MLA acronym: Eco

SUBSCRIPTION INFORMATION

Frequency of publication: 12 times/yr.
Available in microform: No

ADVERTISING INFORMATION

Advertising accepted: Yes

EDITORIAL DESCRIPTION

Scope: Publishes articles on the literature and culture of the Western world, with an emphasis on Latin American literature.
Reviews books: Yes
Languages accepted: Spanish

(830)
*Edad de Oro

Pablo Jauralde Pou, Editor
Dept. of Spanish Philology
Univ. Autónoma
Cuidad Univ. de Canto Blanco
28049 Madrid, Spain

Additional editorial address: Fernán González 75, 28009 Madrid, Spain
Telephone: (34) 1 3974016
Fax: (34) 1 3973930
First published: 1981
Sponsoring organization: Univ. Autónoma, Madrid
MLA acronym: EdO

SUBSCRIPTION INFORMATION

Frequency of publication: Annual
Available in microform: No
Subscription address: Publicaciones, Univ. Autónoma, Cuidad Univ. de Canto Blanco, 28049 Madrid, Spain

ADVERTISING INFORMATION

Advertising accepted: Yes
Advertising rates: 25,000 Pta/full page

EDITORIAL DESCRIPTION

Scope: Publishes articles on 16th- and 17th-century Spanish literature.
Reviews books: Yes
Publishes notes: Yes
Languages accepted: Spanish
Prints abstracts: No
Author-anonymous submission: Yes

SUBMISSION REQUIREMENTS

Restrictions on contributors: Contributors must have participated in the international seminars of *Edad de Oro*.
Author pays submission fee: No
Author pays page charges: No
Length of articles: 15 pp.
Length of book reviews: 7 pp.
Length of notes: 10 pp.
Style: MLA
Number of copies required: 2
Copyright ownership: Journal
Time before publication decision: 8 mos.
Time between decision and publication: 6 mos.
Number of reviewers: 3
Articles submitted per year: 12-20
Articles published per year: 12-20
Book reviews submitted per year: 5-10
Book reviews published per year: 5-10
Notes submitted per year: 3-5
Notes published per year: 3-5

(831)
*Edda: Nordisk Tidsskrift for Litteraturforskning/Scandinavian Journal of Literary Research

Jorunn Hareide, Editor
Dept. of Scandinavian
Univ. of Trondheim
College of Arts & Sciences
7055 Dragvoll, Norway

Telephone: (47) 7 596410; (47) 7 596416
Fax: (47) 7 596411
First published: 1914
Sponsoring organization: Norges Almenvitenskapelige Forskningsråd (Norwegian Research Council for Science & Humanities)
ISSN: 0013-0818
MLA acronym: Edda

SUBSCRIPTION INFORMATION

Frequency of publication: 4 times/yr.
Circulation: 800
Available in microform: No
Subscription price: 470 NKr ($81.00)/yr. institutions
Year to which price refers: 1992
Subscription address: Scandinanian Univ. Press, Abonnementsavdelingen, Box 2959-Tøyen, 0608 Oslo, Norway
Additional subscription address: Scandinavian Univ. Press, 200 Meacham Ave., Elmont, NY 11003
Subscription telephone: (47) 2 677600
Subscription fax: (47) 2 677575

ADVERTISING INFORMATION

Advertising accepted: Yes

EDITORIAL DESCRIPTION

Scope: Publishes literary research by Scandinavian scholars and research on Scandinavian literature by scholars from other countries.
Reviews books: Yes
Publishes notes: Yes
Languages accepted: Norwegian; Danish; Swedish; English; German
Prints abstracts: No
Author-anonymous submission: No

SUBMISSION REQUIREMENTS

Restrictions on contributors: None
Author pays submission fee: No
Author pays page charges: No
Length of articles: 6,000-12,000 words
Length of book reviews: 1,000-3,000 words
Length of notes: 100 words
Style: MLA
Number of copies required: 1
Copyright ownership: Universitetsforlaget
Rejected manuscripts: Returned
Time before publication decision: 1-2 mos.
Time between decision and publication: 6-12 mos.
Number of reviewers: 2
Articles submitted per year: 50-60
Articles published per year: 25-30
Book reviews submitted per year: 25-30
Book reviews published per year: 25-30
Notes submitted per year: 4-5
Notes published per year: 4-5

(832)
Edith Wharton Review

Annette Zilversmit, Editor
Edith Wharton Soc.
Dept. of English
Long Island Univ.
Brooklyn, NY 11201

First published: 1984
Historical variations in title: Formerly *Edith Wharton Newsletter*
Sponsoring organization: Edith Wharton Soc.
MLA acronym: EWhR

SUBSCRIPTION INFORMATION

Frequency of publication: 2 times/yr. (Spring, Fall)
Circulation: 300
Available in microform: No
Subscription price: $10.00/yr. (includes membership)
Year to which price refers: 1992

ADVERTISING INFORMATION

Advertising accepted: Yes

EDITORIAL DESCRIPTION

Scope: Publishes articles on Edith Wharton's work, life, and background.
Reviews books: Yes
Publishes notes: Yes
Languages accepted: English
Prints abstracts: No

Author-anonymous submission: No

SUBMISSION REQUIREMENTS

Restrictions on contributors: Book reviews are solicited.
Author pays submission fee: No
Author pays page charges: No
Length of articles: 500-1,500 words
Length of book reviews: 500-1,000 words
Length of notes: 250-500 words
Style: MLA
Number of copies required: 3
Special requirements: Submit original typescript and 2 copies.
Copyright ownership: Journal
Rejected manuscripts: Returned; enclose SASE.
Time before publication decision: 1-3 mos.
Time between decision and publication: 6-12 mos.
Number of reviewers: 2
Articles submitted per year: 20-30
Articles published per year: 4-8
Book reviews submitted per year: 4-8
Book reviews published per year: 2-8
Notes submitted per year: 5-10
Notes published per year: 2-5

(833)
*Editio: Internationales Jahrbuch für Editionswissenschaft/International Yearbook of Scholarly Editing/Revue Internationale des Sciences de l'Edition Critique

Winfried Woesler, Editor
Editionswissenschaftliche Forschungsstelle
Univ. Osnabrück
Postfach 4469
4500 Osnabrück, Germany

First published: 1987
ISSN: 0931-3079
MLA acronym: Editio

SUBSCRIPTION INFORMATION

Frequency of publication: Annual
Available in microform: No
Subscription address: Max Niemeyer Verlag, Postfach 2140, 7400 Tübingen, Germany

ADVERTISING INFORMATION

Advertising accepted: Yes

EDITORIAL DESCRIPTION

Scope: Publishes articles on scholarly editing.
Reviews books: Yes
Publishes notes: Yes
Languages accepted: German; English; French
Prints abstracts: Yes
Author-anonymous submission: No

SUBMISSION REQUIREMENTS

Author pays submission fee: No
Author pays page charges: No
Length of articles: 15-20 pp.
Length of book reviews: 2-3 pp.
Length of notes: 5 pp. maximum
Style: Journal
Number of copies required: 2
Copyright ownership: Max Niemeyer Verlag
Number of reviewers: 1-2

(834)
*Editiones Arnamagnæanæ

Det Arnamagnæanske Inst.
Københavns Univ. Amager
2300 Copenhagen S, Denmark

First published: 1958
Sponsoring organization: Arnamagnæan Commission of Københavns Univ.
ISSN: 0070-9069
MLA acronym: EdArn

SUBSCRIPTION INFORMATION

Frequency of publication: Irregular
Available in microform: No
Subscription address: C. A. Reitzels Boghandel A/S, Nørregade 20, 1165 Copenhagen, Denmark

ADVERTISING INFORMATION

Advertising accepted: No

EDITORIAL DESCRIPTION

Scope: Publishes critical editions primarily of Old Norse-Icelandic medieval literature.
Reviews books: No
Languages accepted: Norwegian; Danish; Swedish; English; German; Icelandic
Prints abstracts: No

SUBMISSION REQUIREMENTS

Author pays submission fee: No
Author pays page charges: No
Number of copies required: 1
Copyright ownership: Arnamagnæan Commission

(835)
*Editors' Notes

Edna L. Steeves & Peter Schmidt, Editors
English Dept.
Univ. of Rhode Island
Kingston, RI 02881

First published: 1981
Sponsoring organization: Council of Editors of Learned Journals
ISSN: 0888-3173
MLA acronym: EdN

SUBSCRIPTION INFORMATION

Frequency of publication: 2 times/yr. (Spring, Fall)
Circulation: 425
Available in microform: No
Subscription price: $30.00/yr.
Year to which price refers: 1991
Subscription address: John N. Serio, CELJ Secty.-Treas., English Dept., Clarkson Univ., Potsdam, NY 13699

ADVERTISING INFORMATION

Advertising accepted: Yes
Advertising rates: $50.00/half page; $100.00/full page

EDITORIAL DESCRIPTION

Scope: The journal is the bulletin of the Council of Editors of Learned Journals. It focuses on the interests and concerns of scholarly publishers.
Reviews books: Yes
Publishes notes: Yes
Languages accepted: English
Prints abstracts: No
Author-anonymous submission: No

SUBMISSION REQUIREMENTS

Restrictions on contributors: None
Author pays submission fee: No
Author pays page charges: No
Length of articles: 1,000-2,500 words
Length of book reviews: 250 words
Length of notes: 100 words
Style: MLA
Number of copies required: 2
Copyright ownership: Council of Editors of Learned Journals
Rejected manuscripts: Returned
Time before publication decision: 3 mos.
Time between decision and publication: 3 mos.
Number of reviewers: 2
Articles submitted per year: 25-35
Articles published per year: 15-20
Book reviews submitted per year: 4-6
Book reviews published per year: 2-3

(836)
*The Edward C. Armstrong Monographs on Medieval Literature

Karl D. Uitti, Editor
Dept. of Romance Languages
Princeton Univ.
Princeton, NJ 08544

Telephone: 606 885-1446
First published: 1979
Sponsoring organization: French Forum Publishers, Inc.
MLA acronym: ECAMML

SUBSCRIPTION INFORMATION

Frequency of publication: Irregular
Available in microform: No
Subscription address: French Forum Publishers, Inc., P.O. Box 130, Nicholasville, KY 40430

ADVERTISING INFORMATION

Advertising accepted: No

EDITORIAL DESCRIPTION

Scope: Publishes monographs on Medieval French literature.
Reviews books: No
Publishes notes: No
Languages accepted: English; French
Prints abstracts: No
Author-anonymous submission: No

SUBMISSION REQUIREMENTS

Restrictions on contributors: None
Author pays submission fee: No
Cost of submission fee: No
Length of books: 60,000 words
Style: MLA
Number of copies required: 2
Copyright ownership: Assigned by author to series
Rejected manuscripts: Returned
Time before publication decision: 3-4 mos.
Time between decision and publication: 9-12 mos.
Number of reviewers: 2
Books published per year: 1-2

(837)
The Edward Sapir Monograph Series in Language, Culture, and Cognition

Adam Makkai & Valerie Becker Makkai, Editors
c/o Jupiter Press
P.O. Box 101
Lake Bluff, IL 60044

First published: 1977
Sponsoring organization: Linguistic Assn. of Canada & the United States
ISSN: 0163-3848
MLA acronym: ESMSLCC

SUBSCRIPTION INFORMATION

Frequency of publication: Irregular
Circulation: 1,000
Available in microform: No

ADVERTISING INFORMATION

Advertising accepted: No

EDITORIAL DESCRIPTION

Scope: Publishes monographs on all areas of linguistics, both theoretical and descriptive, and its humanistic applications to related disciplines and the general human condition.
Reviews books: No
Publishes notes: No
Languages accepted: English; French; German; Spanish
Prints abstracts: No
Author-anonymous submission: Yes

SUBMISSION REQUIREMENTS

Restrictions on contributors: None
Author pays submission fee: No
Author pays page charges: Yes
Length of books: No restrictions
Style: Linguistic Soc. of America with modifications; request specifications.
Number of copies required: 1
Copyright ownership: Jupiter Press
Rejected manuscripts: Returned; enclose return postage.
Time before publication decision: 2-3 mos.
Time between decision and publication: 4-6 mos.
Number of reviewers: 3
Books submitted per year: 6
Books published per year: 2-4

(838)
EIDOS: The International Prosody Bulletin

Eleanor Berry, Editor
R.R. 1, Box 58A
Cedar Grove, WI 53013

First published: 1984
ISSN: 8755-3198
MLA acronym: EIDOS

SUBSCRIPTION INFORMATION

Frequency of publication: 4 times/yr.
Circulation: 100
Available in microform: No

ADVERTISING INFORMATION

Advertising accepted: No

EDITORIAL DESCRIPTION

Scope: Serves as an exchange of up-to-date information on publications, conferences, problems, and advances in prosodic studies.
Reviews books: Yes
Publishes notes: Yes
Languages accepted: English
Prints abstracts: No
Author-anonymous submission: No

SUBMISSION REQUIREMENTS

Restrictions on contributors: None
Author pays submission fee: No
Author pays page charges: No
Length of articles: 2,500 words maximum
Length of book reviews: 1,000 words maximum
Length of notes: 1,000 words maximum
Style: MLA; Chicago
Number of copies required: 1
Copyright ownership: Author
Rejected manuscripts: Returned
Time before publication decision: 2 mos. maximum
Time between decision and publication: 6 mos. maximum
Number of reviewers: 1-2

(839)
*The Eighteenth Century: Theory and Interpretation

Bruce Clarke, Robert M. Markley, & Joel Reed, Editors
P.O. Box 43091
Texas Tech Univ.
Lubbock, TX 79409-3091

Telephone: 806 742-2501
E-mail: TECTI@TTACS.bitnet
First published: 1959
Sponsoring organization: Texas Tech Univ.
ISSN: 0193-5380
MLA acronym: ECent

SUBSCRIPTION INFORMATION

Frequency of publication: 3 times/yr. (Fall, Winter, Spring)
Circulation: 750
Available in microform: No
Subscription price: $28.00/yr. institutions; $16.00/yr. individuals
Year to which price refers: 1992
Subscription address: Sales Office, Texas Tech Univ. Press, P.O. Box 4139, Lubbock, TX 79409-1037
Subscription telephone: 806 742-0158

ADVERTISING INFORMATION

Advertising accepted: Yes
Advertising rates: $125.00/full page

EDITORIAL DESCRIPTION

Scope: Welcomes essays on all aspects of British, American, and Continental culture from 1660-1800, including literature, history, art, science, music, history of ideas, and popular culture. Concerned with the application of 20th-century theory and methodology to the 18th century. The editors also invite commentaries on essays published in the journal or on other matters of concern to its readers.
Reviews books: Yes
Publishes notes: No
Languages accepted: English
Prints abstracts: No
Author-anonymous submission: No

SUBMISSION REQUIREMENTS

Restrictions on contributors: None
Author pays submission fee: No
Author pays page charges: No
Length of articles: 4,000-8,000 words
Length of book reviews: 2,500-5,000 words
Style: Chicago
Number of copies required: 2
Copyright ownership: Texas Tech Univ. Press
Rejected manuscripts: Returned; enclose return postage.
Time before publication decision: 3 mos.
Time between decision and publication: 1-2 yrs.
Number of reviewers: 2-3
Articles submitted per year: 50-75
Articles published per year: 10-15
Book reviews submitted per year: 8-10
Book reviews published per year: 3-5

(840)
*Eighteenth-Century Fiction

David Blewett, Editor
McMaster Univ.
Chester New Hall-321
Hamilton, Ontario L8S 4L9, Canada

Telephone: 416 525-9140 ext. 7123
Fax: 416 521-0689
E-mail: ECF@MCMASTER.CA
First published: 1988
Sponsoring organization: McMaster Univ.
ISSN: 0840-6286
MLA acronym: ECF

SUBSCRIPTION INFORMATION

Frequency of publication: 4 times/yr. (Jan., Apr., July, Oct.)
Circulation: 575
Available in microform: No
Subscription price: $50.00/yr. institutions; $30.00/yr. individuals; $23.00/yr. students
Year to which price refers: 1991-92
Subscription address: Univ. of Toronto Press, 5201 Dufferin St., Downsview, Ontario M3H 5T8, Canada
Subscription telephone: 416 667-7782
Subscription fax: 416 667-7832

ADVERTISING INFORMATION

Advertising accepted: Yes
Advertising rates: $249.00/full page

EDITORIAL DESCRIPTION

Scope: Publishes articles on the historical and critical investigation of imaginative prose from 1660-1832.
Reviews books: Yes
Publishes notes: No
Languages accepted: English; French
Prints abstracts: No
Author-anonymous submission: Yes

SUBMISSION REQUIREMENTS

Restrictions on contributors: None
Author pays submission fee: No
Author pays page charges: No
Length of articles: 6,000 words
Length of book reviews: 1,000 words
Style: Chigaco
Number of copies required: 1
Copyright ownership: McMaster Univ.
Rejected manuscripts: Returned
Time before publication decision: 3 mos.
Time between decision and publication: 1 yr.
Number of reviewers: 3-4
Articles submitted per year: 80-100
Articles published per year: 16-18
Book reviews submitted per year: 32-44
Book reviews published per year: 32-40

(841)
*Eighteenth-Century Life

Robert P. Maccubbin, Editor
Dept. of English
College of William & Mary
Williamsburg, VA 23185

Telephone: 804 221-3904
Fax: 804 221-1021
First published: 1974
ISSN: 0098-2601
MLA acronym: ECLife

SUBSCRIPTION INFORMATION

Frequency of publication: 3 times/yr.
Circulation: 750
Available in microform: No
Subscription price: $37.00/yr. institutions US; $19.00/yr. individuals US; add $5.60/yr. postage Canada & Mexico, $7.40/yr. elsewhere
Year to which price refers: 1993
Subscription address: Johns Hopkins Univ. Press, Journals Publishing Division, 2715 North Charles St., Baltimore, MD 21218-4319
Subscription telephone: 410 516-6944; 800 537-5487
Subscription fax: 410 516-6998

ADVERTISING INFORMATION

Advertising accepted: Yes
Advertising rates: $110.00/half page; $170.00/full page; $195.00/inside back cover; $210.00/back cover

EDITORIAL DESCRIPTION

Scope: Publishes articles, notes, and documents in all areas of 18th-century European, Near Eastern, and Asian life, especially literature, history, philosophy, social studies, nontechnical science, art, religion, and music.
Reviews books: Yes, review essays
Publishes notes: Yes
Languages accepted: English; French
Prints abstracts: No
Author-anonymous submission: Yes

SUBMISSION REQUIREMENTS

Restrictions on contributors: Review essays are commissioned.
Author pays submission fee: No
Author pays page charges: No
Length of articles: 2,000-10,000 words
Length of book reviews: 2,000-5,000 words
Length of notes: 750-1,750 words
Style: Chicago
Number of copies required: 3
Special requirements: Submit original typescript. Entire manuscript, including endnotes, must be typescript. Author's name should not appear on manuscript.
Copyright ownership: Assigned by author to journal
Rejected manuscripts: Original returned; enclose return postage.
Time before publication decision: 3-4 mos.
Time between decision and publication: 4-9 mos.
Number of reviewers: 2-4
Articles submitted per year: 160
Articles published per year: 26
Book reviews published per year: 3 review essays
Notes submitted per year: 10
Notes published per year: 2

(842)
*Eighteenth-Century Studies

Arthur McGuinness, Editor
Dept. of English
Univ. of California
Davis, CA 95616

Telephone: 916 752-2249
First published: 1967
Sponsoring organization: American Soc. for Eighteenth-Century Studies
ISSN: 0013-2586
MLA acronym: ECS

SUBSCRIPTION INFORMATION

Frequency of publication: 4 times/yr. (Fall, Winter, Spring, Summer)
Circulation: 2,950
Available in microform: Yes
Subscription price: $52.00/yr.
Year to which price refers: 1992
Subscription address: Edward P. Harris, Executive Secretary, American Soc. for Eighteenth-Century Studies, Univ. of Cincinnati, Cincinnati, OH 45221-0368
Subscription telephone: 513 556-3820

ADVERTISING INFORMATION

Advertising accepted: Yes

EDITORIAL DESCRIPTION

Scope: Welcomes contributions on all aspects of the 18th century, especially those that are interdisciplinary or that are of general interest to scholars working in other disciplines.
Reviews books: Yes
Publishes notes: No
Languages accepted: English
Prints abstracts: No
Author-anonymous submission: Yes

SUBMISSION REQUIREMENTS

Restrictions on contributors: None
Author pays submission fee: No
Author pays page charges: No
Length of articles: 6,500 words maximum
Length of book reviews: 1,500 words
Style: Chicago
Number of copies required: 2
Special requirements: Place author's name on title page only. Book reviews are commissioned.
Copyright ownership: American Soc. for Eighteenth-Century Studies
Rejected manuscripts: Returned; enclose return postage.
Time before publication decision: 6 mos.
Time between decision and publication: 1 yr.
Number of reviewers: 7-8
Articles submitted per year: 110
Articles published per year: 12-14
Book reviews published per year: 80

(843)
Eigo Seinen

Mineo Moriya, Editor
Kenkyusha Publishing Co.
11-3, Fujimi 2-chome
Chiyoda-ku, Tokyo 102 Japan

First published: 1898
ISSN: 0287-2706
MLA acronym: EigoS

SUBSCRIPTION INFORMATION

Frequency of publication: 12 times/yr.
Available in microform: No

ADVERTISING INFORMATION

Advertising accepted: Yes

EDITORIAL DESCRIPTION

Scope: Publishes articles on English language and literature.
Reviews books: Yes
Publishes notes: No
Languages accepted: Japanese; English
Prints abstracts: No
Author-anonymous submission: No

SUBMISSION REQUIREMENTS

Author pays submission fee: No
Author pays page charges: No
Length of articles: 1,600 words
Style: MLA
Number of copies required: Submit original typescript.
Copyright ownership: Author & Kenkyusha Publishing Co.
Rejected manuscripts: Not returned
Time before publication decision: Several mos.
Articles published per year: 200
Book reviews published per year: 100

(844)
*Éigse: A Journal of Irish Studies

Pádraig A. Breatnach, Editor
National Univ. of Ireland
49 Merrion Square
Dublin 2, Ireland

Telephone: (353) 1 767246; (353) 1 763429
Fax: (353) 1 619665
First published: 1939
Sponsoring organization: National Univ. of Ireland
ISSN: 0013-2608
MLA acronym: Éigse

SUBSCRIPTION INFORMATION

Frequency of publication: Annual
Circulation: 300
Available in microform: No
Subscription price: IR£12.00/yr.
Year to which price refers: 1991

ADVERTISING INFORMATION

Advertising accepted: No

EDITORIAL DESCRIPTION

Scope: Publishes articles on Irish language and literary studies.
Reviews books: Yes
Publishes notes: Yes
Languages accepted: English; Irish Gaelic; Scottish Gaelic
Prints abstracts: No
Author-anonymous submission: No

SUBMISSION REQUIREMENTS

Restrictions on contributors: None
Author pays submission fee: No
Author pays page charges: No
Length of articles: 1,000-8,000 words
Length of book reviews: 400-800 words
Length of notes: 400-800 words
Style: Journal
Number of copies required: 1
Special requirements: Submit original typescript.
Copyright ownership: Author & Journal
Rejected manuscripts: Returned
Time before publication decision: 1 mo.
Time between decision and publication: 1-2 yrs.
Number of reviewers: 1
Articles submitted per year: 25
Articles published per year: 20
Book reviews submitted per year: 11
Book reviews published per year: 7
Notes submitted per year: 6-8
Notes published per year: 4-5

(845)
*Éire-Ireland: A Journal of Irish Studies

Thomas Dillon Redshaw, Editor
Mail 5026
Univ. of St. Thomas
St. Paul, MN 55105

Additional editorial address: Robert Ward, Book Review Editor, Dept. of English, Univ. of Western Kentucky, Bowling Green, KY 42101
Telephone: 612 647-4112
First published: 1966
Sponsoring organization: Irish American Cultural Inst.
ISSN: 0013-2683
MLA acronym: Éire

SUBSCRIPTION INFORMATION

Frequency of publication: 4 times/yr.
Circulation: 4,230
Available in microform: Yes, through Univ. Microfilms International
Subscription price: $24.00/yr. institutions; $35.00/yr. individuals (includes membership)

ADVERTISING INFORMATION

Advertising accepted: Yes

EDITORIAL DESCRIPTION

Scope: Publishes articles related to any aspect of Irish culture in Ireland or abroad.
Reviews books: Yes
Publishes notes: Yes
Languages accepted: English; Irish Gaelic
Prints abstracts: No
Author-anonymous submission: No

SUBMISSION REQUIREMENTS

Restrictions on contributors: None
Author pays submission fee: No
Author pays page charges: No
Length of articles: 3,000-5,000 words
Length of book reviews: 500-1,000 words
Length of notes: 100-300 words
Style: Chicago
Number of copies required: 2
Special requirements: Author's name and address should appear on cover sheet only. Include English abstract with articles written in Irish.
Copyright ownership: Irish American Cultural Inst.
Rejected manuscripts: Returned; enclose return postage.
Time before publication decision: 3-5 mos.
Time between decision and publication: 6-12 mos.
Number of reviewers: 3-4
Articles submitted per year: 120
Articles published per year: 40
Book reviews submitted per year: 100
Book reviews published per year: 20-30
Notes submitted per year: 10-25
Notes published per year: 10-15

(846)
*El Popola Ĉinio

Wu Xunnan, Editor
Cina Esperanto-Ligo
P.O. Kesto 77
Beijing, People's Republic of China

Telephone: (86) 1 8322718
Fax: (86) 1 8315599-2318
First published: 1950
ISSN: 0032-4361
MLA acronym: EPC

SUBSCRIPTION INFORMATION

Frequency of publication: 12 times/yr.
Circulation: 7,000
Available in microform: No
Subscription address: Internacia Libro-Komerca Kompanio de Ĉinio, Guoji Shudian, Esperanto Sekcio, P.O. Kesto 313, Beijing, People's Republic of China
Subscription telephone: (86) 1 8411144-432

ADVERTISING INFORMATION

Advertising accepted: Yes
Advertising rates: $1,700.00/back cover

EDITORIAL DESCRIPTION

Scope: Publishes Esperanto-language articles on Chinese culture, economy, and social life in general.
Reviews books: Yes
Publishes notes: No
Languages accepted: Esperanto
Prints abstracts: Yes
Author-anonymous submission: Yes

SUBMISSION REQUIREMENTS

Restrictions on contributors: None
Author pays submission fee: Yes
Length of articles: 2,000 words
Length of book reviews: 1,500 words
Number of copies required: 1
Special requirements: Submit original typescript.
Copyright ownership: Journal
Rejected manuscripts: Not returned
Time before publication decision: 1-2 weeks
Time between decision and publication: 2-3 mos.
Number of reviewers: 3
Articles submitted per year: 280
Articles published per year: 265
Book reviews submitted per year: 6
Book reviews published per year: 5

(847)
*Elementa: Schriften zur Philosophie und ihrer Problemgeschichte

Rudolph Berlinger & Wiebke Schrader, Editors
Frankenstr. 35
8702 Eisingen, Germany

First published: 1975
ISSN: 0013-5933
MLA acronym: Elementa

SUBSCRIPTION INFORMATION

Frequency of publication: Irregular
Circulation: 400-800
Available in microform: No
Subscription address: Editions Rodopi B.V., Keizersgracht 302-304, 1016 EX Amsterdam, Netherlands
Additional subscription address: In N. America: Editions Rodopi, 233 Peachtree St. N.E., Suite 404, Atlanta, GA 30303-1504
Subscription telephone: (31) 20 6227507; 404 523-1964; 800 225-3998
Subscription fax: (31) 20 6380948; 404 522-7116

ADVERTISING INFORMATION

Advertising accepted: No

EDITORIAL DESCRIPTION

Scope: Publishes monographs on philosophy.
Reviews books: No
Publishes notes: No
Languages accepted: German; English
Prints abstracts: No
Author-anonymous submission: Yes

SUBMISSION REQUIREMENTS

Author pays submission fee: No
Author pays page charges: No
Length of books: 300,000-600,000 words
Style: MLA
Number of copies required: 1
Copyright ownership: Editions Rodopi B.V.
Time before publication decision: 3 mos.
Time between decision and publication: 3-9 mos.
Books submitted per year: 10
Books published per year: 2-4

(848)
*ELH

Ronald Paulson, Editor
Dept. of English
Johns Hopkins Univ.
Baltimore, MD 21218

Telephone: 410 516-8948
First published: 1934
Sponsoring organization: Johns Hopkins Univ. Press
ISSN: 0013-8304
MLA acronym: ELH

SUBSCRIPTION INFORMATION

Frequency of publication: 4 times/yr. (Spring, Summer, Fall, Winter)
Circulation: 1,940
Available in microform: Yes
Subscription price: $65.00/yr. institutions US; $20.00/yr. individuals US; add $4.60/yr. postage Canada & Mexico, $11.40/yr. elsewhere
Year to which price refers: 1993
Subscription address: Johns Hopkins Univ. Press, Journals Publishing Division, 2715 North Charles St., Baltimore, MD 21218-4319
Subscription telephone: 410 516-6988; 800 537-5487
Subscription fax: 410 516-6998

ADVERTISING INFORMATION

Advertising accepted: Yes

EDITORIAL DESCRIPTION

Scope: Publishes critical, historical, and theoretical studies of English and American literature.
Reviews books: Yes
Publishes notes: No
Languages accepted: English
Prints abstracts: No
Author-anonymous submission: No

SUBMISSION REQUIREMENTS

Restrictions on contributors: Review articles are commissioned.
Author pays submission fee: No
Author pays page charges: No
Length of articles: 4,000-10,000 words
Style: Chicago
Number of copies required: 1
Special requirements: Submit double-spaced manuscripts (including notes).
Copyright ownership: Johns Hopkins Univ. Press
Rejected manuscripts: Returned; enclose return postage.
Time before publication decision: 1-2 mos.
Time between decision and publication: 1 yr.
Number of reviewers: 2
Articles submitted per year: 350
Articles published per year: 35-40

(849)
*Elizabethan Theatre

A. L. Magnusson & C. E. McGee, Editors
P. D. Meany Publishers
Box 118
Streetsville, Ontario L5M 2B7, Canada

Telephone: 416 567-5803
Fax: 416 567-1687
First published: 1969
ISSN: 0317-4964
MLA acronym: ETh

SUBSCRIPTION INFORMATION

Frequency of publication: Once every 2 yrs.
Available in microform: No

ADVERTISING INFORMATION

Advertising accepted: No

EDITORIAL DESCRIPTION

Scope: Represents the University of Waterloo Proceedings of International Conference on Elizabethan Theatre.
Reviews books: No
Publishes notes: No
Prints abstracts: No
Author-anonymous submission: No

SUBMISSION REQUIREMENTS

Restrictions on contributors: Contributions are pre-selected by Editor as papers for the University of Waterloo International Conference on Elizabethan Theatre.
Author pays submission fee: No
Author pays page charges: No
Copyright ownership: P. D. Meany Publishers

(850)
*Ellen Glasgow Newsletter

Catherine Rainwater, Editor
School of Humanities
St. Edward's Univ.
Austin, TX 78704

Telephone: 512 837-6579
First published: 1974
Sponsoring organization: Ellen Glasgow Soc.
ISSN: 0160-7545
MLA acronym: EGN

SUBSCRIPTION INFORMATION

Frequency of publication: 2 times/yr. (Mar., Oct.)
Circulation: 250
Available in microform: No
Subscription price: $5.00/yr.
Year to which price refers: 1993
Subscription address: 9901 Oak Run Dr., Austin, TX 78758

ADVERTISING INFORMATION

Advertising accepted: No

EDITORIAL DESCRIPTION

Scope: Publishes short, factual articles about Ellen Glasgow and her contemporaries on the Richmond literary scene, as well as news of scholarship and publications.
Reviews books: Yes
Publishes notes: Yes
Languages accepted: English
Prints abstracts: No
Author-anonymous submission: No

SUBMISSION REQUIREMENTS

Restrictions on contributors: None
Author pays submission fee: No
Author pays page charges: No
Length of articles: 200-4,000 words
Length of book reviews: 1,000 words
Length of notes: 200-500 words
Style: MLA
Number of copies required: 1
Copyright ownership: Author
Rejected manuscripts: Returned
Time before publication decision: 1 mo.
Time between decision and publication: 2-6 mos.
Number of reviewers: 2
Articles published per year: 4-8
Book reviews published per year: 2-3
Notes published per year: 20-25

(851)
*Emakeele Seltsi Aastaraamat

Mart Meri, Editor
Mother Tongue Society
Estonian Academy of Sciences
Roosikrantsi 6
EE0106 Tallinn, Estonia

Telephone: (7) 142 449331
Fax: (7) 142 441800
First published: 1954
Sponsoring organization: Mother Tongue Soc., Estonian Academy of Sciences
ISSN: 0206-3735
MLA acronym: EmSA

SUBSCRIPTION INFORMATION

Frequency of publication: Annual
Circulation: 800
Available in microform: No
Subscription address: Scientific Library, Academy of Sciences, Rävala pst. 10, EE0104 Tallinn, Estonia
Subscription telephone: (7) 142 440649

ADVERTISING INFORMATION

Advertising accepted: No

EDITORIAL DESCRIPTION

Scope: Publishes articles on Estonian language, Finno-Ugric linguistics, and folklore.
Reviews books: No
Publishes notes: No
Languages accepted: Estonian
Author-anonymous submission: No

SUBMISSION REQUIREMENTS

Restrictions on contributors: None
Author pays submission fee: No
Author pays page charges: No
Length of articles: 5-25 typescript pp.
Number of copies required: 2
Copyright ownership: Journal
Rejected manuscripts: Not returned
Time before publication decision: 2 mos.
Time between decision and publication: 1 yr.
Number of reviewers: 5
Articles submitted per year: 30
Articles published per year: 20-25

(852)
Emblematica: An Interdisciplinary Journal of Emblem Studies

Peter M. Daly & Daniel S. Russell, Editors
McGill Univ.
Dept. of German
1001 Sherbrooke St. W.
Montreal, PQ H3A 1G5, Canada

Additional editorial address: Daniel S. Russell, Dept. of French & Italian, Univ. of Pittsburgh, Pittsburgh, PA 15260
First published: 1986
ISSN: 0885-968X
MLA acronym: Emblematica

SUBSCRIPTION INFORMATION

Frequency of publication: 2 times/yr. (Spring, Fall)
Circulation: 500
Available in microform: No
Subscription address: AMS Press, 56 E. 13th St., New York, NY 10003

ADVERTISING INFORMATION

Advertising accepted: Yes

EDITORIAL DESCRIPTION

Scope: Publishes original articles, essays, and specialized bibliographies in all areas of emblem studies.
Reviews books: Yes
Publishes notes: Yes
Languages accepted: English; French
Prints abstracts: No
Author-anonymous submission: Yes

SUBMISSION REQUIREMENTS

Restrictions on contributors: None
Author pays submission fee: No
Author pays page charges: No
Length of articles: No restrictions
Length of book reviews: No restrictions
Length of notes: No restrictions
Style: MLA
Number of copies required: 2
Special requirements: Authors will be expected to provide high-quality glossy prints of any illustrations.
Copyright ownership: AMS Press
Rejected manuscripts: Returned; enclose return postage.
Time before publication decision: 3-6 mos.
Time between decision and publication: 6-12 mos.
Number of reviewers: 2-4

(853)
*Emérita: Revista de Lingüística y Filología Clasica

Francisco R. Adrados, Editor
Duque de Medinaceli, 6
28014 Madrid, Spain

First published: 1933
Sponsoring organization: Inst. de Filología, Consejo Superior de Investigaciones Científicas (C.S.I.C.)
ISSN: 0013-6662
MLA acronym: Emérita

SUBSCRIPTION INFORMATION

Frequency of publication: 2 times/yr.
Circulation: 1,000
Available in microform: No
Subscription address: Librería Científica Medinaceli, at the above address

ADVERTISING INFORMATION

Advertising accepted: No

EDITORIAL DESCRIPTION

Scope: Publishes articles on classical philology, classical antiquity, Greek, Latin, and the languages of ancient Spain.
Reviews books: Yes
Publishes notes: No
Languages accepted: Spanish; German; French; Italian; English
Prints abstracts: Yes

SUBMISSION REQUIREMENTS

Restrictions on contributors: None
Length of articles: 10-30 pp.
Length of book reviews: 2 pp.
Number of copies required: 1
Copyright ownership: Consejo Superior de Investigaciones Científicas
Time before publication decision: 3 mos.
Time between decision and publication: 1 yr.
Articles published per year: 20
Book reviews published per year: 40

(854)
The Emily Dickinson Journal

Suzanne Juhasz, Editor
Dept. of English
Campus Box 226
Univ. of Colorado
Boulder, CO 80309

First published: 1992
Sponsoring organization: Emily Dickinson International Soc.
ISSN: 1059-6879
MLA acronym: EDJ

SUBSCRIPTION INFORMATION

Frequency of publication: 2 times/yr.
Subscription address: Univ. Press of Colorado, P.O. Box 849, Niwot, CO 80544

EDITORIAL DESCRIPTION

Scope: Publishes articles and review essays on Emily Dickinson and her works, to showcase the poet at the center of current critical practices and perspectives.
Reviews books: Yes, review essays
Languages accepted: English

SUBMISSION REQUIREMENTS

Style: MLA
Number of copies required: 2

(855)
*Emporia State Research Studies

Faye N. Vowell, Carl W. Prophet, Melvin Storm, Tom Isern, & Jeffrey H. Bair, Editors
Office of Graduate Studies & Research
Emporia State Univ.
1200 Commercial St.
Emporia, KS 66801-5087

Telephone: 316 341-5508
First published: 1952
Sponsoring organization: Emporia State Univ., Office of Graduate Studies & Research
ISSN: 0424-9399
MLA acronym: ESRS

SUBSCRIPTION INFORMATION

Circulation: 2,000-4,000
Available in microform: No
Subscription address: Director of Library Services, W. A. White Library, 1200 Commercial St., Emporia, KS 66801-5087
Subscription telephone: 316 341-5208

ADVERTISING INFORMATION

Advertising accepted: No

EDITORIAL DESCRIPTION

Scope: Publishes papers on literature and culture written by faculty members or students whose studies are conducted in residence under the supervision of a faculty member.
Reviews books: No
Publishes notes: No
Languages accepted: English
Prints abstracts: Yes
Author-anonymous submission: Yes

SUBMISSION REQUIREMENTS

Author pays submission fee: No
Author pays page charges: No
Number of copies required: 1
Copyright ownership: Author
Rejected manuscripts: Returned
Number of reviewers: 5

(856)
*Enclitic

John O'Kane, Editor
P.O. Box 36098
Los Angeles, CA 90036-0098

First published: 1977
ISSN: 0193-5798
MLA acronym: Enclitic

SUBSCRIPTION INFORMATION

Frequency of publication: 4 times/yr.
Circulation: 6,500
Available in microform: No
Subscription price: $36.00/yr. institutions; $16.00/yr. individuals
Year to which price refers: 1992-93

ADVERTISING INFORMATION

Advertising accepted: Yes

EDITORIAL DESCRIPTION

Scope: Publishes articles on contemporary literature, critical theories, film, and politics.
Reviews books: Yes
Publishes notes: Yes
Languages accepted: English
Prints abstracts: No
Author-anonymous submission: No

SUBMISSION REQUIREMENTS

Restrictions on contributors: None
Author pays submission fee: No
Author pays page charges: No
Length of articles: 5-25 typescript pp.
Length of book reviews: 5-15 typescript pp.
Style: None
Number of copies required: 2
Copyright ownership: Journal
Rejected manuscripts: Returned; enclose return postage.
Time before publication decision: 2-3 mos.
Time between decision and publication: 2-4 mos.
Number of reviewers: 5-8
Articles submitted per year: 400-500
Articles published per year: 50-60
Book reviews submitted per year: 30-40
Book reviews published per year: 10-15

(857)
*Encomia: Bibliographical Bulletin of the International Courtly Literature Society

Maria Dobozy, Editor
Dept. of Languages
Univ. of Utah
Salt Lake City, UT 84112

Telephone: 801 581-7561
First published: 1975
Sponsoring organization: International Courtly Literature Soc.
ISSN: 0363-4841
MLA acronym: Encomia

SUBSCRIPTION INFORMATION

Frequency of publication: Annual
Circulation: 850
Available in microform: No
Subscription price: $10.00/yr.
Year to which price refers: 1992
Subscription address: Dhira Mahoney, Dept. of English, Arizona State Univ., Tempe, AZ 85287-0302

ADVERTISING INFORMATION

Advertising accepted: Yes

EDITORIAL DESCRIPTION

Scope: Publishes bibliographies on courtly literature and the adjacent disciplines of the Western European Middle Ages.
Reviews books: Yes
Publishes notes: No
Languages accepted: English; French; German
Prints abstracts: No

SUBMISSION REQUIREMENTS

Restrictions on contributors: Unsolicited manuscripts are not accepted.
Author pays submission fee: No
Style: MLA
Copyright ownership: International Courtly Literature Soc.
Time before publication decision: 2 weeks
Book reviews published per year: 6-10

(858)
*Encyclia: The Journal of the Utah Academy of Sciences, Arts, and Letters

Thomas F. Rogers, Editor
4089A Jesse Knight Humanities Bldg.
Brigham Young Univ.
Provo, UT 84602

First published: 1918
Sponsoring organization: Utah Academy of Sciences, Arts, & Letters
ISSN: 0083-4823
MLA acronym: Encyclia

SUBSCRIPTION INFORMATION

Frequency of publication: Annual
Circulation: 1,000
Available in microform: No
Subscription address: 990 SWKT, Brigham Young Univ., Provo, UT 84602
Subscription telephone: 801 378-3615

ADVERTISING INFORMATION

Advertising accepted: No

EDITORIAL DESCRIPTION

Scope: Publishes articles in arts, biological sciences, business, education, engineering, health, physical education, recreation, letters, library science, physical sciences, and social sciences.
Reviews books: No
Publishes notes: No
Languages accepted: English
Prints abstracts: Yes, for papers read at Academy conferences
Author-anonymous submission: Yes

SUBMISSION REQUIREMENTS

Restrictions on contributors: Contributors must be members of the Utah Academy of Sciences, Arts, & Letters.
Author pays submission fee: No
Author pays page charges: No
Length of articles: 2,500 words
Style: Chicago
Number of copies required: 3
Special requirements: Accepted articles must be submitted on diskette.
Copyright ownership: Author
Rejected manuscripts: Returned; enclose SASE.
Time before publication decision: 6 mos.
Time between decision and publication: 1 yr.
Number of reviewers: 2-3
Articles submitted per year: 30-40
Articles published per year: 15-20

(859)
*Enemy News: Journal of the Wyndham Lewis Society

Paul O'Keeffe, Editor
Dept. of English Language & Literature
Univ. of Liverpool
P.O. Box 147
Liverpool L69 3BX, England

First published: 1974
Sponsoring organization: Wyndham Lewis Soc.
ISSN: 0142-6214
MLA acronym: EN

SUBSCRIPTION INFORMATION

Frequency of publication: 2 times/yr. (June, Dec.)
Circulation: 150
Available in microform: No
Subscription price: £7.30/yr. institutions United Kingdom & Ireland; $21.00/yr. institutions elsewhere; £5.60/yr. individuals United Kingdom & Ireland; $16.00/yr. individuals elsewhere
Year to which price refers: 1991
Subscription address: Frank Fitzpatrick, 148 Bellahouston Dr., Glasgow G52 1HL, Scotland

ADVERTISING INFORMATION

Advertising accepted: No

EDITORIAL DESCRIPTION

Scope: Publishes articles on the art, literature, and thought of Wyndham Lewis. Includes inaccessible Lewis writings and reproduces inaccessible Lewis paintings.
Reviews books: Yes
Publishes notes: Yes
Languages accepted: English
Prints abstracts: No
Author-anonymous submission: No

SUBMISSION REQUIREMENTS

Restrictions on contributors: None
Author pays submission fee: No
Author pays page charges: No
Length of articles: 3,000-5,000 words
Length of book reviews: 750 words
Length of notes: 1,500-2,000 words
Style: MLA
Number of copies required: 1
Copyright ownership: Author
Rejected manuscripts: Returned
Time before publication decision: 1-3 mos.
Time between decision and publication: 2-12 mos.
Number of reviewers: 4
Articles submitted per year: 10-12
Articles published per year: 6
Book reviews submitted per year: 6
Book reviews published per year: 4
Notes submitted per year: 2-3
Notes published per year: 2

(860)
*English: The Journal of the English Association

Peter Barry & Michael Baron, Editors
Dept. of English
La Sainte Union College
The Avenue
Southampton SO9 5HB, England

Additional editorial address: Send reviews to Michael Baron, English Dept., Birkbeck College, Malet St., London WC1E 7HX, England
Telephone: (44) 703 228761 ext. 2222
Fax: (44) 703 230944
First published: 1936
Sponsoring organization: English Assn., London
ISSN: 0013-8215
MLA acronym: English

SUBSCRIPTION INFORMATION

Frequency of publication: 3 times/yr. (Spring, Summer, Autumn)
Circulation: 1,700
Available in microform: No
Subscription price: $2L36.50 ($83.00)/yr.
Year to which price refers: 1991
Subscription address: Noreen Pleavin, 64 Endcliffe Hall Ave., Fulwood, Sheffield SI0 3EL, England
Subscription telephone: (44) 742 665377

ADVERTISING INFORMATION

Advertising accepted: Yes
Advertising rates: $50.00/half page; $80.00/full page

EDITORIAL DESCRIPTION

Scope: Critical articles on major literatures in English or of major critical interest complement the large review section.
Reviews books: Yes
Publishes notes: No
Languages accepted: English
Prints abstracts: No
Author-anonymous submission: No

SUBMISSION REQUIREMENTS

Restrictions on contributors: Reviews are commissioned.
Author pays submission fee: No
Author pays page charges: No
Length of articles: No restrictions
Length of book reviews: 2,000 words
Style: None
Number of copies required: 1
Copyright ownership: English Assn.
Rejected manuscripts: Returned; enclose return postage.
Time before publication decision: 3-4 mos.
Time between decision and publication: 1 yr.
Number of reviewers: 1-2
Articles submitted per year: 80-100
Articles published per year: 7-8
Book reviews submitted per year: 30
Book reviews published per year: 24

(861)
English Dance and Song

David Arthur, Editor
South Hill Court
4 Chilston Rd.
Tunbridge Wells
Kent TN4 9LR, England

Telephone: (44) 892 510251
Fax: (44) 892 520716
First published: 1936
Sponsoring organization: Soc. of English Folk Dance & Song
ISSN: 0013-8231
MLA acronym: EDS

SUBSCRIPTION INFORMATION

Frequency of publication: 4 times/yr.
Circulation: 11,000
Available in microform: No
Subscription price: £18.00/yr.; £9.00/yr. students
Year to which price refers: 1993
Subscription address: English Folk Dance & Song Soc., Sharp House, 2 Regents Park Rd., London NW1 7AY, England
Subscription telephone: (44) 71 4852206

ADVERTISING INFORMATION

Advertising accepted: Yes

EDITORIAL DESCRIPTION

Scope: Publishes articles on English folk music and folklore.
Reviews books: Yes
Languages accepted: English
Prints abstracts: No

SUBMISSION REQUIREMENTS

Author pays submission fee: No
Author pays page charges: No
Length of articles: 2,000-2,500 words
Copyright ownership: Author
Articles published per year: 20
Book reviews published per year: 20

(862)
*English in Africa

Gareth Cornwell, Editor
Inst. for the Study of English in Africa
Rhodes Univ.
Grahamstown 6140, South Africa

Telephone: (27) 461 26093
Fax: (27) 461 25642
First published: 1974
Sponsoring organization: Inst. for the Study of English in Africa, Rhodes Univ.
ISSN: 0376-8902
MLA acronym: EinA

SUBSCRIPTION INFORMATION

Frequency of publication: 2 times/yr. (May, Oct.)
Circulation: 550
Available in microform: No
Subscription price: 27.50 R/yr. institutions Africa; 16.50 R/yr. individuals Africa; $20.00 (£15.00)/yr. elsewhere
Year to which price refers: 1992

ADVERTISING INFORMATION

Advertising accepted: Yes
Advertising rates: Request from editor.

EDITORIAL DESCRIPTION

Scope: Publishes articles on African literature and the English language in Africa; collections of early South African writing and criticism not easily available to scholars; and book reviews in areas germane to these fields.
Reviews books: Yes
Publishes notes: Yes
Languages accepted: English
Prints abstracts: No
Author-anonymous submission: Yes

SUBMISSION REQUIREMENTS

Restrictions on contributors: None
Author pays submission fee: No
Author pays page charges: No
Length of articles: 2,500-8,000 words
Length of book reviews: 500-1,500 words
Length of notes: 500-1,500 words
Style: MLA
Number of copies required: 1
Copyright ownership: Author; republication requires notification and acknowledgment to journal.
Rejected manuscripts: Returned
Time before publication decision: 3 mos.
Time between decision and publication: 1 yr.
Number of reviewers: 2-3
Articles submitted per year: 40
Articles published per year: 10-15
Book reviews submitted per year: 5-10
Book reviews published per year: 3-7
Notes submitted per year: 1-4
Notes published per year: 1-4

(863)
The English Journal

Alleen Nilsen & Ken Donelson, Editors
College of Education
Arizona State Univ.
Tempe, AZ 85281

First published: 1912
Sponsoring organization: National Council of Teachers of English
ISSN: 0013-8274
MLA acronym: EJ

SUBSCRIPTION INFORMATION

Frequency of publication: 8 times/yr. (Sept.-Apr.)
Circulation: 55,000
Available in microform: Yes
Subscription address: National Council of Teachers of English, 1111 Kenyon Rd., Urbana, IL 61801

ADVERTISING INFORMATION

Advertising accepted: Yes

EDITORIAL DESCRIPTION

Scope: Publishes articles on English and education.
Reviews books: Yes
Languages accepted: English

Prints abstracts: No

SUBMISSION REQUIREMENTS

Restrictions on contributors: Book reviews are commissioned.
Author pays submission fee: No
Author pays page charges: No
Length of articles: 10-15 typescript pp.
Style: Chicago
Number of copies required: 1
Special requirements: Manuscripts may not be under consideration elsewhere.
Copyright ownership: National Council of Teachers of English
Rejected manuscripts: Returned; enclose SASE.
Time before publication decision: 3-6 weeks
Time between decision and publication: 1 yr.
Number of reviewers: 2
Articles submitted per year: 1,500
Articles published per year: 150
Book reviews published per year: 120

(864)
*English Language Notes

J. Wallace Donald, Editor
Dept. of English, Box 226
Hellems Bldg.
Univ. of Colorado at Boulder
Boulder, CO 80309

Telephone: 303 492-7176
First published: 1963
Sponsoring organization: Univ. of Colorado
ISSN: 0013-8282
MLA acronym: ELN

SUBSCRIPTION INFORMATION

Frequency of publication: 4 times/yr. (Sept., Dec., Mar., June)
Circulation: 1,100
Available in microform: No
Subscription price: $40.00/yr. institutions US & Canada; $47.00/yr. institutions elsewhere; $27.00/yr. individuals
Year to which price refers: 1992

ADVERTISING INFORMATION

Advertising accepted: Yes
Advertising rates: $250.00/full page

EDITORIAL DESCRIPTION

Scope: Publishes articles and scholarly notes pertaining to English and American language and literature. Ordinarily explication unsupported by biographical, historical, or bibliographical evidence is not accepted.
Reviews books: Yes
Publishes notes: Yes
Languages accepted: English
Prints abstracts: No
Author-anonymous submission: Yes

SUBMISSION REQUIREMENTS

Restrictions on contributors: None
Author pays submission fee: No
Author pays page charges: No
Length of articles: 1,000-6,000 words
Length of book reviews: 500-750 words
Length of notes: 800 words
Style: MLA for endnotes
Number of copies required: 2
Copyright ownership: Board of Regents, Univ. of Colorado
Rejected manuscripts: Returned
Time before publication decision: 3-6 mos.
Time between decision and publication: 9-12 mos.
Number of reviewers: 2-3
Articles submitted per year: 250
Articles published per year: 50
Book reviews published per year: 30

(865)
*English Linguistics: Journal of the English Linguistic Society of Japan

Secretariat
English Linguistic Soc. of Japan
c/o Kirihara Shoten
44-5 Koenji-minami 2-chome
Suginami-ku, Tokyo, 166, Japan

Telephone: (81) 3 33148181
Fax: (81) 3 33144469
First published: 1984
Sponsoring organization: English Linguistic Soc. of Japan
MLA acronym: EngLing

SUBSCRIPTION INFORMATION

Frequency of publication: Annual
Circulation: 1,300
Available in microform: No
Subscription price: 8,000 yen/yr. institutions; 6,000 yen/yr. individuals Japan; 7,000 yen/yr. individuals elsewhere
Year to which price refers: 1991
Subscription address: Kaitakusha Publishing Co., 5 Kanda-Jinbocho 2-chome, Chiyoda-ku, Tokyo, 101, Japan
Additional subscription address: Individuals contact: English Linguistic Soc. of Japan, Business Center for Academic Socs. of Japan, 5-16-9 Honkomagome, Bunkyou-ku, Tokyo, 113, Japan
Subscription telephone: Institutions: (81) 3 32657641; Individuals: (81) 3 58145810
Subscription fax: Institutions: (81) 3 32652989; Individuals: (81) 3 58145825

ADVERTISING INFORMATION

Advertising accepted: Yes

EDITORIAL DESCRIPTION

Scope: Publishes articles on synchronic and diachronic English linguistics. Includes studies on linguistic theory, and comparisons of English with other languages, especially Japanese.
Reviews books: Yes
Publishes notes: Yes
Languages accepted: English
Prints abstracts: Yes
Author-anonymous submission: Yes

SUBMISSION REQUIREMENTS

Restrictions on contributors: Contributors must be members of the English Linguistic Society of Japan.
Author pays submission fee: No
Author pays page charges: No
Length of articles: 8,700 words maximum
Length of book reviews: 8,700 words maximum
Length of notes: 2,000 words maximum
Style: Journal
Number of copies required: 3
Special requirements: Submit a 100-word abstract for articles.
Copyright ownership: English Linguistic Soc. of Japan
Rejected manuscripts: Not returned
Time before publication decision: 2-12 mos.
Time between decision and publication: 4 mos.
Number of reviewers: 2
Articles submitted per year: 20-30
Articles published per year: 8-12
Book reviews submitted per year: 3-7
Book reviews published per year: 3-7
Notes submitted per year: 4-8
Notes published per year: 1-4

(866)
*English Literary Renaissance

Arthur F. Kinney, Editor
Dept. of English
Univ. of Massachusetts
Amherst, MA 01003

Telephone: 413 545-5465
Fax: 413 545-3880
First published: 1971
Sponsoring organization: Univ. of Massachusetts, Graduate School & Dept. of English
ISSN: 0013-8312
MLA acronym: ELR

SUBSCRIPTION INFORMATION

Frequency of publication: 3 times/yr.; index and abstracts issued separately
Circulation: 1,050
Available in microform: No
Subscription price: $25.00/yr. institutions; $20.00/yr. individuals
Year to which price refers: 1992
Subscription address: Business Manager, at the above address

ADVERTISING INFORMATION

Advertising accepted: Yes
Advertising rates: $75.00/half page; $125.00/full page; $150.00/back cover

EDITORIAL DESCRIPTION

Scope: Publishes texts, studies, and bibliographies on the intellectual context and literary achievement of Tudor and Stuart England.
Reviews books: No
Publishes notes: No
Languages accepted: All modern languages
Prints abstracts: Yes
Author-anonymous submission: No

SUBMISSION REQUIREMENTS

Restrictions on contributors: None
Author pays submission fee: No
Author pays page charges: No
Length of articles: 10-50 pp.
Style: Chicago
Number of copies required: 1; 2-3 preferred
Special requirements: Submit original double-spaced typescript or a note stating that submission is not being considered simultaneously by another publication. Texts should be prepared in old spelling with notes typed separately.
Copyright ownership: Journal
Rejected manuscripts: Returned; enclose return postage.
Time before publication decision: 8-10 weeks
Time between decision and publication: 1-2 yrs.
Number of reviewers: 3 minimum
Articles submitted per year: 250
Articles published per year: 15-20

(867)
*English Literary Studies Monograph Series

Samuel L. Macey, Editor
Dept. of English
Univ. of Victoria
P.O. Box 3045
Victoria, BC V8W 3P4, Canada

Telephone: 604 721-7237
Fax: 604 721-7212
First published: 1975
Sponsoring organization: Univ. of Victoria
ISSN: 0829-7681
MLA acronym: ELS

SUBSCRIPTION INFORMATION

Frequency of publication: Annual (Aug.)

Circulation: 500
Available in microform: No

ADVERTISING INFORMATION

Advertising accepted: No

EDITORIAL DESCRIPTION

Scope: Publishes monographs representing new scholarship related to English literature.
Reviews books: No
Publishes notes: No
Languages accepted: English
Prints abstracts: No
Author-anonymous submission: No

SUBMISSION REQUIREMENTS

Restrictions on contributors: None
Author pays submission fee: No
Author pays page charges: No
Length of books: 45,000-60,000 words
Style: MLA; Chicago
Number of copies required: 1
Copyright ownership: Author
Rejected manuscripts: Returned
Time before publication decision: 2-3 mos.
Time between decision and publication: 3 mos.
Number of reviewers: 3
Books published per year: 3-5

(868)
English Literature and Language

Hiroshi Yamamoto, Editor
English Literature Dept.
Sophia Univ.
7 Kioi-cho
Chiyoda-ku
Tokyo 102, Japan

First published: 1963
Sponsoring organization: Sophia Univ., Faculty of Literature
ISSN: 0289-1050
MLA acronym: ELLS

SUBSCRIPTION INFORMATION

Frequency of publication: Annual
Circulation: 700
Available in microform: No

ADVERTISING INFORMATION

Advertising accepted: No

EDITORIAL DESCRIPTION

Scope: Publishes articles on English literature and language.
Reviews books: No
Publishes notes: No
Languages accepted: English; Japanese
Prints abstracts: No
Author-anonymous submission: No

SUBMISSION REQUIREMENTS

Restrictions on contributors: Contributors must be on the faculty of the English Literature Dept. of Sophia Univ.
Author pays submission fee: No
Author pays page charges: No
Length of articles: 2,500-12,500 English words or 12,000 Japanese characters
Style: MLA
Number of copies required: 1
Copyright ownership: Assigned by author to journal
Rejected manuscripts: Returned
Time before publication decision: 1 mo.
Time between decision and publication: 4 mos.
Number of reviewers: 3
Articles submitted per year: 6
Articles published per year: 6

(869)
*English Literature in Transition (1880-1920)

Robert Langenfeld, Editor
Dept. of English
Univ. of North Carolina
Greensboro, NC 27412-5001

Telephone: 919 334-5446
Fax: 919 334-3281
E-mail: Langen@Steffi.UNCG.EDU
First published: 1957
ISSN: 0013-8339
MLA acronym: ELT

SUBSCRIPTION INFORMATION

Frequency of publication: 4 times/yr. (irregular)
Circulation: 800
Available in microform: Yes
Subscription price: $16.00/yr. US; $20.00/yr. elsewhere
Year to which price refers: 1992

ADVERTISING INFORMATION

Advertising accepted: Yes
Advertising rates: $75.00/full page

EDITORIAL DESCRIPTION

Scope: Publishes scholarly articles, book reviews, and secondary and primary bibliographies concerning English literature and culture from 1880-1920.
Reviews books: Yes
Publishes notes: Yes
Languages accepted: English
Prints abstracts: No
Author-anonymous submission: No

SUBMISSION REQUIREMENTS

Restrictions on contributors: None
Author pays submission fee: No
Author pays page charges: No
Length of articles: 3,000-6,000 words
Length of book reviews: 1,000-1,200 words
Length of notes: No restrictions
Style: Chicago
Number of copies required: 2
Special requirements: Submit original typescript plus 1 copy.
Copyright ownership: Journal
Rejected manuscripts: Returned; enclose return postage.
Time before publication decision: 3 mos.
Time between decision and publication: 6-12 mos.
Number of reviewers: 2-3
Articles submitted per year: 80-100
Articles published per year: 12-15
Book reviews submitted per year: 100-110
Book reviews published per year: 100-110
Notes submitted per year: 2-4
Notes published per year: 1

(870)
*English Manuscript Studies 1100-1700

Jeremy Griffiths & Peter Beal, Editors
St. John's College
Oxford OX1 3JP, England

Telephone: (44) 71 4085298 (P. Beal)
Fax: (44) 71 4936863 (P. Beal)
First published: 1989
Sponsoring organization: British Library
MLA acronym: EMS

SUBSCRIPTION INFORMATION

Frequency of publication: Annual
Circulation: 600
Available in microform: No

Subscription price: £40.00/yr.
Year to which price refers: 1992
Subscription address: British Library, Marketing & Publishing, 41 Russell Square, London WC1B 3DG, England
Subscription telephone: (44) 71 3237726
Subscription fax: (44) 71 3237736

ADVERTISING INFORMATION

Advertising accepted: No

EDITORIAL DESCRIPTION

Scope: Publishes articles that reflect the growth of scholarly interest in manuscript sources for literature and intellectual history from medieval to early modern times. Provides a forum for the study of medieval and Renaissance manuscripts produced in the British Isles between the Conquest and the end of the seventeenth century.
Reviews books: No
Publishes notes: No
Languages accepted: English
Prints abstracts: No
Author-anonymous submission: No

SUBMISSION REQUIREMENTS

Author pays submission fee: No
Author pays page charges: No
Length of articles: 10-60 pp.
Style: Journal; request from editor
Number of copies required: 1
Copyright ownership: British Library
Rejected manuscripts: Returned
Time before publication decision: 1 mo.
Time between decision and publication: 1 yr.
Articles published per year: 11

(871)
English Record

Thomas J. Reigstad, Editor
English Dept.
SUNY College at Buffalo
1300 Elmwood Ave.,
Buffalo, NY 14222

First published: 1950
Sponsoring organization: New York State English Council
ISSN: 0013-8363
MLA acronym: EngR

SUBSCRIPTION INFORMATION

Frequency of publication: 4 times/yr. (Fall, Winter, Spring, Summer)
Circulation: 1,500
Available in microform: No

ADVERTISING INFORMATION

Advertising accepted: Yes

EDITORIAL DESCRIPTION

Scope: General articles of interest to English teachers on all levels of instruction are invited.
Reviews books: Yes
Publishes notes: No
Languages accepted: English
Prints abstracts: No

SUBMISSION REQUIREMENTS

Author pays submission fee: No
Author pays page charges: No
Length of articles: 1,500-2,000 words
Length of book reviews: 350 words
Style: None
Number of copies required: 2
Rejected manuscripts: Returned; enclose return postage.
Time before publication decision: 6-8 weeks
Articles submitted per year: 150

Articles published per year: 28
Book reviews published per year: 2-4

(872)
English Renaissance Prose

Committee for English Renaissance Literature
Purdue Univ.
Dept. of English
West Lafayette, IN 47907

First published: 1987
MLA acronym: ERP

SUBSCRIPTION INFORMATION

Frequency of publication: Annual
Available in microform: No

ADVERTISING INFORMATION

Advertising accepted: No

EDITORIAL DESCRIPTION

Scope: Publishes articles and bibliographies on English Renaissance prose.
Reviews books: No
Publishes notes: No
Languages accepted: English
Prints abstracts: No
Author-anonymous submission: No

SUBMISSION REQUIREMENTS

Restrictions on contributors: None
Author pays submission fee: No
Author pays page charges: No
Length of articles: 7,000 words
Style: MLA
Number of copies required: 2
Copyright ownership: English Dept., Purdue Univ.
Rejected manuscripts: Returned
Time before publication decision: 1 mo.
Time between decision and publication: 1 yr.
Number of reviewers: 2

(873)
*English Studies: A Journal of English Language and Literature

T. A. Birrell & J. M. Blom, Editors
Erasmusplein 1
6500 HD Nijmegen, Netherlands

Telephone: (31) 80 512841
Fax: (31) 80 615939
First published: 1919
ISSN: 0013-838X
MLA acronym: ES

SUBSCRIPTION INFORMATION

Frequency of publication: 6 times/yr. (Feb., Apr., June, Aug., Oct., Dec.)
Circulation: 1,800
Available in microform: Yes
Subscription price: $190.00/yr. institutions; $143.25/yr. individuals
Year to which price refers: 1992
Subscription address: Swets & Zeitlinger, Publishing Dept., 347B Heereweg, 2161 CA Lisse, Netherlands
Subscription telephone: (31) 2521 35111
Subscription fax: (31) 2521 15888

ADVERTISING INFORMATION

Advertising accepted: Yes
Advertising rates: Request from Swets & Zeitlinger

EDITORIAL DESCRIPTION

Scope: Publishes articles ranging from Old English to Modern English (including American and Commonwealth) language and literature.
Reviews books: Yes
Publishes notes: Yes
Languages accepted: English
Prints abstracts: No
Author-anonymous submission: No

SUBMISSION REQUIREMENTS

Restrictions on contributors: None
Author pays submission fee: No
Author pays page charges: No
Length of articles: 3,000-8,000 words
Length of book reviews: 400-800 words
Length of notes: 200-300 words
Style: Journal; see 1990 Apr.; 71(2), pp. 183-184
Number of copies required: 1
Copyright ownership: Assigned by author to Swets & Zeitlinger
Rejected manuscripts: Returned; enclose international reply coupons.
Time before publication decision: 2 mos.
Time between decision and publication: 18 mos.
Number of reviewers: 2
Articles published per year: 50
Book reviews published per year: 70
Notes published per year: 10

(874)
*English Studies in Africa: A Journal of the Humanities

G. I. Hughes, Editor
Dept. of English
Univ. of Witwatersrand
P.O. WITS
2050, South Africa

First published: 1958
ISSN: 0013-8398
MLA acronym: ESA

SUBSCRIPTION INFORMATION

Frequency of publication: 2 times/yr. (Mar., Sept.)
Circulation: 250
Available in microform: No
Subscription price: $20.00/yr. institutions; $10.00/yr. individuals
Year to which price refers: 1992

ADVERTISING INFORMATION

Advertising accepted: Yes

EDITORIAL DESCRIPTION

Scope: Publishes articles on English, Commonwealth, and American literature, as well as general topics in the humanities.
Reviews books: No
Publishes notes: Yes
Languages accepted: English
Prints abstracts: No
Author-anonymous submission: Yes

SUBMISSION REQUIREMENTS

Restrictions on contributors: None
Author pays submission fee: No
Author pays page charges: No
Length of articles: 5,000-10,000 words
Length of notes: 1,000 words
Style: MLA
Number of copies required: 1
Special requirements: Submit double-spaced typescript on one side of paper only with endnotes.
Copyright ownership: Assigned by author to Witwatersrand Univ. Press
Rejected manuscripts: Returned
Time before publication decision: 2 mos.
Time between decision and publication: 6 mos.
Number of reviewers: 2
Articles submitted per year: 30
Articles published per year: 8-10

(875)
*English Studies in Canada

Douglas J. Wurtele & F. Guildenhuys, Editors
Dept. of English
Carleton Univ.
Ottawa, Ontario K1S 5B6, Canada

Telephone: 613 788-2600 ext. 2317
Fax: 613 788-3544
First published: 1975
Sponsoring organization: Assn. of Canadian Univ. Teachers of English
ISSN: 0317-0802
MLA acronym: ESC

SUBSCRIPTION INFORMATION

Frequency of publication: 4 times/yr. (Mar., June, Sept., Dec.)
Circulation: 1,300
Available in microform: No
Subscription price: C$45.00/yr.
Year to which price refers: 1992

ADVERTISING INFORMATION

Advertising accepted: No

EDITORIAL DESCRIPTION

Scope: Publishes scholarship and criticism concerned with all literature written in the English language.
Reviews books: Yes
Publishes notes: No
Languages accepted: English
Prints abstracts: No
Author-anonymous submission: Yes

SUBMISSION REQUIREMENTS

Restrictions on contributors: Contributors must be members of the Canadian academic or literary community. Book reviews are assigned.
Author pays submission fee: No
Author pays page charges: No
Length of articles: 6,000 words maximum
Length of book reviews: 1,000 words maximum
Style: MLA
Number of copies required: 2
Special requirements: Submit original typescript plus 1 copy.
Copyright ownership: Assn. of Canadian Univ. Teachers of English or author
Rejected manuscripts: Returned
Time before publication decision: 3 mos.
Time between decision and publication: 1 yr.
Number of reviewers: 2
Articles submitted per year: 100
Articles published per year: 25-30
Book reviews published per year: 30-35

(876)
*English Today: The International Review of the English Language

Tom McArthur & David Crystal, Editors
22-23 Ventress Farm Court
Cherry Hinton Rd.
Cambridge CB1 4HD, England

Telephone: (44) 223 245934
Fax: (44) 223 315052
First published: 1985
ISSN: 0266-0784
MLA acronym: EnT

SUBSCRIPTION INFORMATION

Frequency of publication: 4 times/yr. (Jan., Apr., July, Oct.)

Circulation: 2,000
Available in microform: No
Subscription price: $68.00 (£41.00)/yr. institutions; $31.00 (£19.00)/yr. individuals; $22.00 (£16.00)/yr. students
Year to which price refers: 1992
Subscription address: Cambridge Univ. Press, 40 W. 20th St., New York, NY 10011
Additional subscription address: Cambridge Univ. Press, Edinburgh Bldg., Shaftesbury Rd., Cambridge CB2 2RU, England

ADVERTISING INFORMATION

Advertising accepted: Yes

EDITORIAL DESCRIPTION

Scope: Focuses on the uses and users of the English language.
Reviews books: Yes
Publishes notes: Yes
Languages accepted: English
Prints abstracts: No
Author-anonymous submission: No

SUBMISSION REQUIREMENTS

Restrictions on contributors: Most book reviews are commissioned.
Author pays submission fee: No
Author pays page charges: No
Length of articles: 2,000-4,000 words
Length of book reviews: 500-1,500 words
Length of notes: 500 words
Number of copies required: 2
Copyright ownership: Cambridge Univ. Press
Rejected manuscripts: Returned at author's request; enclose return postage.
Time before publication decision: 1 mo.
Time between decision and publication: 3-9 mos.
Number of reviewers: 2
Articles submitted per year: 60
Articles published per year: 30
Book reviews published per year: 12-36
Notes published per year: 30

(877)
*English World-Wide: A Journal of Varieties of English

Manfred Görlach, Editor
Univ. zu Köln
Englisches Seminar
Albertus-Magnus-Platz
5000 Cologne 41, Germany

First published: 1980
ISSN: 0172-8865
MLA acronym: EWW

SUBSCRIPTION INFORMATION

Frequency of publication: 2 times/yr.
Circulation: 500
Available in microform: Yes
Subscription price: 222 f ($121.00)/yr. institutions; 70 f ($40.00)/yr. individuals
Year to which price refers: 1992
Subscription address: John Benjamins B.V., P.O. Box 75577, Amsteldijk 44, 1070 AN Amsterdam, Netherlands
Additional subscription address: John Benjamins North America, Inc., 821 Bethlehem Pike, Philadelphia, PA 19118
Subscription telephone: (31) 20 6738156; 215 836-1200
Subscription fax: (31) 20 6739773; 215 836-1204

ADVERTISING INFORMATION

Advertising accepted: No

EDITORIAL DESCRIPTION

Scope: Publishes current research in the fields of English dialects and sociolects, and the users and uses of English around the globe. The journal also provides information on English-based Pidgins and Creoles.
Reviews books: Yes
Publishes notes: Yes
Languages accepted: English
Prints abstracts: No
Author-anonymous submission: No

SUBMISSION REQUIREMENTS

Author pays submission fee: No
Author pays page charges: No
Length of book reviews: 1,000 words
Length of notes: 1,000 words
Style: MLA
Number of copies required: 2
Special requirements: Submissions must not have been published previously or be under consideration elsewhere.
Copyright ownership: John Benjamins B.V.
Rejected manuscripts: Not returned
Time before publication decision: 3 mos.
Time between decision and publication: 6-12 mos.
Number of reviewers: 2
Articles submitted per year: 12-15
Articles published per year: 8-10
Book reviews submitted per year: 20
Book reviews published per year: 20
Notes submitted per year: 2
Notes published per year: 2

(878)
*Los Ensayistas: Georgia Series on Hispanic Thought

José Luis Gómez-Martínez & Carmen Chaves McClendon, Editors
Dept. of Romance Languages
Moore College
Univ. of Georgia
Athens, GA 30602

Telephone: 706 542-3123
Fax: 706 542-3287
First published: 1976
Sponsoring organization: Georgia Series on Hispanic Thought, Univ. of Georgia
ISSN: 0148-8627
MLA acronym: Ensayistas

SUBSCRIPTION INFORMATION

Frequency of publication: Annual
Circulation: 400
Available in microform: No
Subscription price: $15.00/yr. US; $17.50/yr. elsewhere
Year to which price refers: 1991

ADVERTISING INFORMATION

Advertising accepted: No

EDITORIAL DESCRIPTION

Scope: Focuses on the essay and Hispanic thought.
Reviews books: Yes
Publishes notes: Yes
Languages accepted: English; Portuguese; Spanish
Prints abstracts: No
Author-anonymous submission: No

SUBMISSION REQUIREMENTS

Restrictions on contributors: None
Author pays submission fee: No
Author pays page charges: No
Length of articles: 22 pp.
Length of book reviews: 250 words
Length of notes: 250-1,000 words
Style: MLA

Number of copies required: 1
Copyright ownership: Journal
Rejected manuscripts: Returned
Time before publication decision: 50 days
Time between decision and publication: 1 yr.
Number of reviewers: 2
Articles published per year: 12
Book reviews published per year: 5
Notes published per year: 4

(879)
*Envoi: A Review Journal of Medieval Literature

Paul Spillenger, Editor
Dept. of English
Univ. of Central Arkansas
Conway, AR 72032

Telephone: 501 450-5131
E-mail: Pauls@vm1.uca.edu
First published: 1988
Sponsoring organization: Dept. of English, Univ. of Central Arkansas; Dept. of English & Comparative Literature, Columbia Univ.
ISSN: 0897-4888
MLA acronym: Envoi

SUBSCRIPTION INFORMATION

Frequency of publication: 2 times/yr. (Spring, Autumn)
Circulation: 500
Available in microform: No
Subscription price: $55.00/yr. institutions; $27.50/yr. individuals; $16.00/yr. students
Year to which price refers: 1991
Subscription address: AMS Press, Inc., 56 E. 13th St., New York, NY 10003
Subscription telephone: 212 777-4700

ADVERTISING INFORMATION

Advertising accepted: Yes
Advertising rates: $90.00/half page; $140.00/full page

EDITORIAL DESCRIPTION

Scope: Aims to review new books on medieval literature within a year of publication and provides a forum for the discussion of ideas related to this field.
Reviews books: Yes
Publishes notes: Yes
Languages accepted: English; French; Italian
Prints abstracts: No
Author-anonymous submission: No

SUBMISSION REQUIREMENTS

Restrictions on contributors: Manuscripts are solicited.
Author pays submission fee: No
Author pays page charges: No
Length of articles: 4,000-6,000 words
Length of book reviews: 2,000 words
Length of notes: 750 words
Style: Chicago with additional guidelines
Number of copies required: 1
Special requirements: Submit a diskette in addition to the manuscript, if possible.
Copyright ownership: AMS Press
Rejected manuscripts: Returned
Time before publication decision: 1 mo.
Time between decision and publication: 4-6 mos.
Number of reviewers: 1
Articles published per year: 6
Book reviews published per year: 60
Notes submitted per year: 55-60
Notes published per year: 55

(880)
*Eos.: Commentarii Societatis Philologae Polonorum

Silvester Dworacki & Andreas Wójcik, Editors
Inst. Filologii Klasycznej
Ul. Marchlewskiego 124-126
61-874 Poznan, Poland

Telephone: (48) 61 521191 ext. 146
Fax: (48) 61 526425; (48) 61 535535
E-mail: CYCERO@PLPUAM11
First published: 1894
Sponsoring organization: Polska Akademia Nauk
ISSN: 0012-7825
MLA acronym: Eos.

SUBSCRIPTION INFORMATION

Frequency of publication: 2 times/yr.
Circulation: 550
Available in microform: No
Subscription address: Ars Polona, Krakowskie Przedmieście 7, 00-068 Warsaw, Poland
Subscription telephone: (48) 22 261201

ADVERTISING INFORMATION

Advertising accepted: No

EDITORIAL DESCRIPTION

Scope: Publishes articles on Greek and Roman antiquity and later reception.
Reviews books: Yes
Publishes notes: Yes
Languages accepted: English; French; German; Latin; Polish; Italian
Prints abstracts: Yes
Author-anonymous submission: No

SUBMISSION REQUIREMENTS

Restrictions on contributors: None
Author pays submission fee: No
Author pays page charges: No
Length of articles: 20 typescript pp. maximum
Length of book reviews: 10 pp. maximum
Length of notes: 2 pp.
Style: MLA
Number of copies required: 2
Special requirements: Submit double-spaced typescript including footnotes.
Copyright ownership: Zakład Narodowy im Ossolińskich, Wydawnictwo, Wrocław
Rejected manuscripts: Returned
Time before publication decision: 3 mos.
Time between decision and publication: 1 yr.
Number of reviewers: 1-3
Articles submitted per year: 45
Articles published per year: 30
Book reviews submitted per year: 25
Book reviews published per year: 20
Notes submitted per year: 5
Notes published per year: 5

(881)
Ēpeirōtikē Hestia

Demosthenes Kokkinos, Editor
M. Geografou 53
Yannina 45333, Greece

First published: 1952
ISSN: 0425-1431
MLA acronym: ĒpH

SUBSCRIPTION INFORMATION

Frequency of publication: 12 times/yr. (often double issues)
Available in microform: No

ADVERTISING INFORMATION

Advertising accepted: Yes

EDITORIAL DESCRIPTION

Scope: Publishes articles on literature, folklore, history, and arts.
Reviews books: Yes
Publishes notes: Yes
Languages accepted: Greek; French; English; Italian
Prints abstracts: Yes

SUBMISSION REQUIREMENTS

Restrictions on contributors: None
Author pays submission fee: No
Author pays page charges: No
Length of articles: No restrictions
Length of book reviews: No restrictions
Length of notes: No restrictions
Number of copies required: 2
Special requirements: All manuscripts will be translated into Greek.
Copyright ownership: Author
Time before publication decision: 2 weeks
Time between decision and publication: 1 week
Articles submitted per year: 400
Articles published per year: 150
Book reviews submitted per year: 200
Book reviews published per year: 100
Notes submitted per year: 200
Notes published per year: 100

(882)
Epetēris Hetaireias Byzantinōn Spoudōn

N. B. Tomadakis, Editor
Aristidou 8
Athens 122, Greece

First published: 1924
Sponsoring organization: Hetaireia Byzantinōn Spoudōn
ISSN: 0253-391X
MLA acronym: EHBS

SUBSCRIPTION INFORMATION

Frequency of publication: Annual
Circulation: 750
Subscription address: Assn. d'Etudes Byzantines, Rue Aristidou 8/8, Athens 122, Greece

EDITORIAL DESCRIPTION

Scope: Publishes articles on Byzantine literature, history, and art.
Reviews books: Yes
Languages accepted: Greek; English; French; German; Italian
Prints abstracts: Yes

SUBMISSION REQUIREMENTS

Restrictions on contributors: None
Length of articles: 32 pp.
Number of copies required: 1
Special requirements: Submit original typescript.
Rejected manuscripts: Returned
Time before publication decision: 2-3 mos.
Time between decision and publication: 6 mos.
Number of reviewers: 2
Articles published per year: 10-15

(883)
*Epetēris tou Kentrou Epistēmonikon Ereunōn Kyprou

G. S. Georghallides, Editor
Cyprus Research Centre
P.O. Box 1952
Nicosia, Cyprus

Telephone: (357) 30 3263; (357) 30 3202; (357) 30 3365
First published: 1967-68
Sponsoring organization: Cyprus Research Centre
MLA acronym: EKEEK

SUBSCRIPTION INFORMATION

Frequency of publication: Annual
Circulation: 500
Available in microform: No
Subscription price: C£18.00/yr.
Year to which price refers: 1992

ADVERTISING INFORMATION

Advertising accepted: No

EDITORIAL DESCRIPTION

Scope: Publishes studies of the history, ethnology, folklore, and linguistics of Cyprus.
Reviews books: Yes
Publishes notes: Yes
Languages accepted: Greek; English; French; German; Italian; Russian; Turkish
Prints abstracts: Yes

SUBMISSION REQUIREMENTS

Restrictions on contributors: None
Author pays submission fee: No
Author pays page charges: No
Length of articles: No restrictions
Length of book reviews: No restrictions
Style: Journal
Number of copies required: 1
Copyright ownership: Cyprus Research Centre
Rejected manuscripts: Not returned
Time before publication decision: 1-4 mos.
Time between decision and publication: 12-18 mos.
Number of reviewers: 1-3
Articles submitted per year: 15-20
Articles published per year: 8-10
Book reviews submitted per year: 1-3
Book reviews published per year: 1-3
Notes published per year: 1-3

(884)
*Epetēris tou Kentrou Ereunēs tēs Hellēnikēs Laographias

Anna Papamichael-Koutroubas, Editor
Leophoros Sygrou 129, B. Dipla 1
Athens, 117.45 Greece

Telephone: (30) 1 9344811
First published: 1939
Sponsoring organization: Akadēmia Athēnōn
MLA acronym: EKEHL

SUBSCRIPTION INFORMATION

Frequency of publication: Annual
Circulation: 500
Available in microform: No

ADVERTISING INFORMATION

Advertising accepted: No

EDITORIAL DESCRIPTION

Scope: Publishes articles on Greek folklore, ethnography, and ethnology.
Reviews books: No
Publishes notes: Yes
Languages accepted: English; French; German; Greek
Prints abstracts: Yes
Author-anonymous submission: No

SUBMISSION REQUIREMENTS

Restrictions on contributors: None
Author pays submission fee: No
Author pays page charges: No
Length of articles: No restrictions
Style: None

Number of copies required: 1
Copyright ownership: Folklore Research Center
Rejected manuscripts: Not returned
Time before publication decision: 2-3 mos.
Number of reviewers: 1

(885)
Epistēmonikē Epetērida Philosophikēs Scholēs Aristoteleiou Panepistēmiou Thessalonikēs

A.-Ph. Christidis, Editor
Philosophike Schole
Aristoteleio Panepistemio
54006 Thessalonike, Greece

First published: 1927
Sponsoring organization: Univ. of Thessaloniki, Faculty of Philosophy
ISSN: 0495-4742
MLA acronym: EEPSAPT

SUBSCRIPTION INFORMATION

Frequency of publication: Annual
Circulation: 1,000
Available in microform: No

ADVERTISING INFORMATION

Advertising accepted: No

EDITORIAL DESCRIPTION

Scope: Publishes articles on various subjects in the humanities.
Reviews books: No
Publishes notes: No
Languages accepted: Greek; Latin; English; French; German; Italian
Prints abstracts: Yes

SUBMISSION REQUIREMENTS

Restrictions on contributors: Contributors must be members or guests of the Faculty of Philosophy, Univ. of Thessaloniki.
Author pays submission fee: No
Author pays page charges: No
Length of articles: 32 printed pp. maximum
Style: Journal
Number of copies required: 1
Special requirements: Submit original typescript.
Copyright ownership: Assigned by author to journal
Rejected manuscripts: Returned
Time before publication decision: 1 mo.
Time between decision and publication: 1 yr.
Number of reviewers: 2
Articles submitted per year: 20-25
Articles published per year: 15-20

(886)
Epitheōrēsē Logou kai Technēs

Editorial Board
Korytsas 4B
Nicosia, Cyprus

First published: 1974
MLA acronym: ELkT

SUBSCRIPTION INFORMATION

Frequency of publication: 12 times/yr.
Circulation: 1,000

ADVERTISING INFORMATION

Advertising accepted: Yes

EDITORIAL DESCRIPTION

Scope: Publishes articles on culture and literature.
Reviews books: Yes
Languages accepted: Greek
Prints abstracts: Yes

SUBMISSION REQUIREMENTS

Restrictions on contributors: None
Author pays submission fee: Yes
Author pays page charges: No
Length of articles: No restrictions
Number of copies required: 1
Copyright ownership: Journal
Rejected manuscripts: Not returned

(887)
*L'Epoque Conradienne

Jacques Darras & Jean-Pierre Moreau, Editors
Fac. des Lettres
39E, rue Camille-Guérin
87036 Limoges Cedex, France

Telephone: (33) 55012619
Fax: (33) 55013806
First published: 1975
Sponsoring organization: Soc. Conradienne Française; Fac. des Lettres & Sciences Humaines de Limoges
ISSN: 0294-6904
MLA acronym: ECon

SUBSCRIPTION INFORMATION

Frequency of publication: Annual
Circulation: 60
Available in microform: No
Subscription price: 70 F/yr.
Year to which price refers: 1991

ADVERTISING INFORMATION

Advertising accepted: Yes
Advertising rates: 1,000 F/full page

EDITORIAL DESCRIPTION

Scope: Publishes articles on the works and literary influence of Joseph Conrad, as well as on late Victorian and Edwardian literature.
Reviews books: Yes
Publishes notes: No
Languages accepted: English; French
Prints abstracts: No
Author-anonymous submission: No

SUBMISSION REQUIREMENTS

Author pays submission fee: No
Author pays page charges: No
Length of articles: 7,000 words
Length of book reviews: 1,000 words
Number of copies required: 1
Copyright ownership: Soc. Conradienne Française
Rejected manuscripts: Returned
Time before publication decision: 3 mos.
Time between decision and publication: 4-12 mos.
Number of reviewers: 1
Articles submitted per year: 12
Articles published per year: 10
Book reviews submitted per year: 4-5
Book reviews published per year: 4-5

(888)
Epos: Revista de Filología

Miguel Angel Pérez Priego, Editor
Facultad de Filología
U.N.E.D.
Ciudad Univ.
28040 Madrid, Spain

First published: 1984
Sponsoring organization: Fac. de Filología, Univ. Nacional de Educacion a Distancia (U.N.E.D.)
ISSN: 0213-201X
MLA acronym: Epos

SUBSCRIPTION INFORMATION

Frequency of publication: Annual
Circulation: 500
Available in microform: No
Subscription address: Marcial Pons (Librero), Dpt. de Revistas, c/Tamayo y Baus 7, 28004 Madrid, Spain

ADVERTISING INFORMATION

Advertising accepted: No

EDITORIAL DESCRIPTION

Scope: Publishes articles on Spanish literature and linguistics.
Reviews books: Yes
Publishes notes: Yes
Languages accepted: Spanish
Prints abstracts: No
Author-anonymous submission: Yes

SUBMISSION REQUIREMENTS

Author pays submission fee: No
Author pays page charges: No
Length of articles: 20 pp.
Length of book reviews: 3 pp.
Length of notes: 5 pp.
Style: MLA
Number of copies required: 1
Time before publication decision: 6 mos.
Time between decision and publication: 6 mos.
Number of reviewers: 1
Articles published per year: 20
Book reviews published per year: 10
Notes submitted per year: 10

(889)
Equivalences: Revue de l'Institut Supérieur de Traduction et d'Interprètes de Bruxelles

Jean-Marie van der Meerschen, Editor
rue Hazard, 34
1180 Brussels, Belgium

First published: 1970
Sponsoring organization: Assn. pour la Promotion de l'Etude des Langues Modernes; Inst. Superieur de l'Etat de Traducteurs & d'Interprètes
ISSN: 0751-9532
MLA acronym: Equivalences

SUBSCRIPTION INFORMATION

Frequency of publication: 3 times/yr.
Circulation: 500
Available in microform: No
Subscription address: Inst. Superieur de l'Etat de Traducteurs, Assn. pour la Promotion de l'Etude des Langues Modernes, at above address

ADVERTISING INFORMATION

Advertising accepted: Yes

EDITORIAL DESCRIPTION

Scope: Publishes articles on translation.
Reviews books: Yes
Languages accepted: French; Dutch; English; German; Italian; Spanish
Prints abstracts: No

SUBMISSION REQUIREMENTS

Restrictions on contributors: None
Author pays submission fee: No

Author pays page charges: No
Length of articles: 7,000 words
Length of book reviews: 1,000 words
Number of copies required: 2
Special requirements: Submit typescript.
Copyright ownership: Assigned by author to journal
Rejected manuscripts: Returned
Time before publication decision: 2 mos.
Time between decision and publication: 6-12 mos.
Number of reviewers: 2
Articles published per year: 10-15
Book reviews published per year: 10-15

(890)
Equivalencias/Equivalences: Revista Internacional de Poesía/International Journal of Poetry

Justo Jorge Padrón, Editor
Jorge Juan 102, 2B
28009 Madrid, Spain

Telephone: (34) 1 5754091
First published: 1982
Sponsoring organization: Fernando Rielo Foundation
ISSN: 0211-8181
MLA acronym: Equivalencias

SUBSCRIPTION INFORMATION

Frequency of publication: 3 times/yr.
Available in microform: No
Subscription address: Editorial Fundación Fernando Rielo, Apartado de Correos no. 54, 41450 Constantina (Seville), Spain
Subscription telephone: (34) 5 4880055

ADVERTISING INFORMATION

Advertising accepted: No

EDITORIAL DESCRIPTION

Scope: Publishes contemporary poetry and essays.
Reviews books: Yes
Languages accepted: All languages
Prints abstracts: No

SUBMISSION REQUIREMENTS

Articles published per year: 4

(891)
*Eranos: Acta Philologica Suecana

Sten Eklund, Birger Bergh, J. F. Kindstrand, & L. Rydén, Editors
Dept. of Classical Philology
P.O. Box 513
751 20 Uppsala, Sweden

Fax: (46) 18 181421
First published: 1896
Sponsoring organization: Humanistisk-Samhällsvetenskapliga Forskningsrådet; Gunvor & Josef Arnérs Stiftelse
ISSN: 0013-9947
MLA acronym: Eranos

SUBSCRIPTION INFORMATION

Frequency of publication: 2 times/yr.
Circulation: 800
Available in microform: No
Subscription price: 400 NKr ($67.00)/yr.
Year to which price refers: 1992
Subscription address: Scandinavian Univ. Press, P.O. Box 2959 Tøyen, 0608 Oslo, Norway
Additional subscription address: Scandinavian Univ. Press, 200 Meacham Ave., Elmont, NY 11003
Subscription telephone: (46) 8 6135935

Subscription fax: (46) 8 209982

ADVERTISING INFORMATION

Advertising accepted: No

EDITORIAL DESCRIPTION

Scope: Publishes articles on Greek and Latin philology, including Medieval Latin and Byzantine Greek, and on Antiquity in general.
Reviews books: No
Publishes notes: Yes
Languages accepted: English; German; French
Prints abstracts: No
Author-anonymous submission: No

SUBMISSION REQUIREMENTS

Restrictions on contributors: None
Author pays submission fee: No
Author pays page charges: No
Length of articles: 25 typescript pp. maximum
Style: None
Number of copies required: 2
Copyright ownership: Journal
Rejected manuscripts: Returned
Time before publication decision: 1 yr. maximum
Time between decision and publication: 1 yr.
Number of reviewers: 1-2
Articles submitted per year: 20-30
Articles published per year: 10-15
Notes published per year: 4-8

(892)
*Ériu

Proinsias Mac Cana, Rolf Baumgarten & Liam Breatnach, Editors
Royal Irish Academy
19, Dawson St.
Dublin 2, Ireland

Telephone: (353) 1 764222
Fax: (353) 1 762346
First published: 1904
Sponsoring organization: Royal Irish Academy
ISSN: 0332-0758
MLA acronym: Ériu

SUBSCRIPTION INFORMATION

Frequency of publication: Annual (Dec.)
Circulation: 500
Available in microform: No
Subscription price: IR£20.00/yr. institutions; IR£15.00/yr. individuals
Year to which price refers: 1991

ADVERTISING INFORMATION

Advertising accepted: No

EDITORIAL DESCRIPTION

Scope: Devoted to the study of the Irish language and of the literature written in that language, together with ancillary studies (e.g., paleography, Hiberno-Latin, Irish history before the Norman invasion).
Reviews books: No
Publishes notes: Yes
Languages accepted: English; Irish Gaelic
Prints abstracts: No
Author-anonymous submission: No

SUBMISSION REQUIREMENTS

Restrictions on contributors: None
Author pays submission fee: No
Author pays page charges: No
Length of articles: 10,000 words maximum
Length of notes: 600-1,000 words
Style: None
Number of copies required: 2
Special requirements: Submit typescript.
Copyright ownership: Assigned by author to journal

Rejected manuscripts: Returned
Time before publication decision: 2 mos.
Time between decision and publication: 15 mos. maximum
Number of reviewers: 3-5
Articles submitted per year: 15-20
Articles published per year: 8-12
Notes submitted per year: 10-15
Notes published per year: 4-8

(893)
*Erlanger Beiträge zur Sprach- und Kunstwissenschaft

Bernhard Rupprecht, Editor
Inst. für Kunstgeschichte
Schlossgarten 1, Orangerie
8520 Erlangen, Germany

Telephone: (49) 9131 852395
First published: 1958
ISSN: 0425-2268
MLA acronym: EBSK

SUBSCRIPTION INFORMATION

Frequency of publication: Irregular
Available in microform: No
Subscription address: Verlag Hans Carl, Breite Gasse 58-60, Postfach 9110, 8500 Nuremberg 1, Germany

ADVERTISING INFORMATION

Advertising accepted: No

EDITORIAL DESCRIPTION

Scope: Publishes monographs in language, literature, and art history.
Publishes notes: No
Languages accepted: German
Prints abstracts: No
Author-anonymous submission: No

SUBMISSION REQUIREMENTS

Restrictions on contributors: Contributors must be affiliated with Univ. Erlangen-Nürnberg.
Author pays submission fee: No
Author pays page charges: Yes
Length of books: No restrictions
Style: None
Number of copies required: 1
Copyright ownership: Verlag Hans Carl
Rejected manuscripts: Returned
Time before publication decision: 1 yr.
Time between decision and publication: 1 yr.
Number of reviewers: 2
Books submitted per year: 2
Books published per year: 1-2

(894)
*Erlanger Forschungen A: Geisteswissenschaften

Universitätsbibliothek Erlangen-Nürnberg
Universitätsstr. 4
Postfach 3509
8520 Erlangen, Germany

Telephone: (49) 9131 852150
Fax: (49) 9131 852131
First published: 1954
Sponsoring organization: Universitätsbund Erlangen-Nürnberg e.V.
ISSN: 0423-3433
MLA acronym: EFG

SUBSCRIPTION INFORMATION

Frequency of publication: 3-4 times/yr.
Available in microform: No

ADVERTISING INFORMATION

Advertising accepted: No

EDITORIAL DESCRIPTION

Scope: Publishes monograph studies about literature, poetry, and drama.
Reviews books: No
Publishes notes: No
Languages accepted: German; French; English
Prints abstracts: No

SUBMISSION REQUIREMENTS

Author pays submission fee: No
Author pays page charges: No
Length of books: No restrictions
Number of copies required: 1
Copyright ownership: Editor
Rejected manuscripts: Returned
Time before publication decision: 4-6 mos.
Time between decision and publication: 4-6 mos.
Number of reviewers: 12

(895)
*Erlanger Studien

Detlef B. Leistner-Opfermann & Dietmar Peschel-Rentsch, Editors
Univ. Erlangen-Nürnberg
Inst. für Deutsche Sprach- und Literaturwissenschaft
Bismarckstr. 1
8520 Erlangen, Germany

Telephone: (49) 9131 209612
First published: 1973
ISSN: 0179-1710
MLA acronym: ESt

SUBSCRIPTION INFORMATION

Frequency of publication: Irregular
Available in microform: No
Subscription address: Verlag Palm & Enke Erlangen, Universitätsstr. 2140, Postfach 140, 8520 Erlangen 10, Germany

ADVERTISING INFORMATION

Advertising accepted: No

EDITORIAL DESCRIPTION

Scope: Publishes monographs focusing on the humanities.
Reviews books: No
Publishes notes: No
Languages accepted: German; English
Prints abstracts: No
Author-anonymous submission: No

SUBMISSION REQUIREMENTS

Author pays submission fee: No
Author pays page charges: No
Length of books: No restrictions
Number of copies required: 1
Special requirements: Consult with editors.
Copyright ownership: Author
Rejected manuscripts: Returned
Time before publication decision: 4-6 weeks
Time between decision and publication: 4-6 weeks
Number of reviewers: 2
Books submitted per year: 5-8
Books published per year: 5-8

(896)
Erträge der Forschung

Wissenschaftliche Buchgesellschaft
Hindenburgstr., 40
6100 Darmstadt, Germany

First published: 1966
ISSN: 0174-0695
MLA acronym: EdF

SUBSCRIPTION INFORMATION

Frequency of publication: Irregular

EDITORIAL DESCRIPTION

Languages accepted: German

SUBMISSION REQUIREMENTS

Author pays submission fee: No
Author pays page charges: No
Length of books: 160-200 pp.
Number of copies required: 2
Copyright ownership: Wissenschaftliche Buchgesellschaft & Author
Rejected manuscripts: Returned
Number of reviewers: 2

(897)
*Escritos: Revista del Centro de Ciencias del Lenguaje

Francisco Serrano Osorio, Director
Maximino Ávila Camacho 219, 2 piso
Aptdo. Postal 229
C.P. 72000 Puebla
Puebla, Mexico

Telephone: (52) 22 325346
Fax: (52) 22 326067
First published: 1986
Sponsoring organization: Centro de Ciencias del Lenguaje, Univ. Autónoma de Puebla
ISSN: 0188-6126
MLA acronym: Escritos

SUBSCRIPTION INFORMATION

Frequency of publication: 2 times/yr.
Circulation: 500
Available in microform: No
Subscription price: Mex$40,000.00/yr. Mexico; $25.00/yr. elsewhere
Year to which price refers: 1993

ADVERTISING INFORMATION

Advertising accepted: Yes, on an exchange basis

EDITORIAL DESCRIPTION

Scope: Publishes articles on Mexican and Hispanic American linguistics, semiotics, and literary studies.
Reviews books: Yes
Publishes notes: Yes
Languages accepted: Spanish
Prints abstracts: Yes

SUBMISSION REQUIREMENTS

Author pays submission fee: No
Author pays page charges: No
Length of articles: 3,750-7,500 words
Length of book reviews: 1,500 words
Length of notes: 2,000-3,500 words
Style: MLA; Chicago; American Psychological Assn.
Number of copies required: 2
Special requirements: Submission must not be previously published.
Copyright ownership: Journal
Rejected manuscripts: Not returned
Time before publication decision: 3 mos.

Time between decision and publication: 3-9 mos.
Number of reviewers: 5
Articles submitted per year: 36
Articles published per year: 18
Book reviews submitted per year: 20
Book reviews published per year: 9

(898)
*Escritura: Revista de Teoría y Crítica Literarias

Rafael Di Prisco, Editor
Apartado de Correos 65603
Caracas 1066-A, Venezuela

First published: 1976
Sponsoring organization: Univ. Central de Venezuela
ISSN: 1011-7989
MLA acronym: Escritura

SUBSCRIPTION INFORMATION

Frequency of publication: 2 times/yr.
Circulation: 1,000
Available in microform: No
Subscription price: $35.00/yr. institutions; $15.00/yr. individuals
Year to which price refers: 1991

ADVERTISING INFORMATION

Advertising accepted: Yes

EDITORIAL DESCRIPTION

Scope: Publishes articles on literature, with an emphasis on Hispanic American literature.
Reviews books: No
Publishes notes: No
Languages accepted: Spanish
Prints abstracts: No
Author-anonymous submission: No

SUBMISSION REQUIREMENTS

Restrictions on contributors: None
Author pays submission fee: No
Author pays page charges: No
Length of articles: 7,000 words
Number of copies required: 1
Special requirements: Submit original typescript and 2 copies.
Copyright ownership: Author
Rejected manuscripts: Not returned
Time before publication decision: 2-3 mos.
Time between decision and publication: 3 mos.
Number of reviewers: 3
Articles published per year: 5-20

(899)
Español Actual

Manuel Alvar, Editor
Agencia Española de Cooperación Internacional
Avda. Reyes Católicos, 4
28040 Madrid, Spain

First published: 1963
Sponsoring organization: Inst. de Cooperación Iberoamericana
ISSN: 0425-2772
MLA acronym: EspA

SUBSCRIPTION INFORMATION

Frequency of publication: 2 times/yr.
Available in microform: No
Subscription address: Editorial Arco Libros S.-A., Juan Bautista de Toledo 28, 28002 Madrid, Spain

ADVERTISING INFORMATION

Advertising accepted: No

EDITORIAL DESCRIPTION

Scope: Publishes articles on Spanish language and literature.
Reviews books: No
Languages accepted: Spanish
Prints abstracts: Yes

SUBMISSION REQUIREMENTS

Author pays submission fee: No
Author pays page charges: No
Length of articles: No restrictions
Style: None
Rejected manuscripts: Returned
Time before publication decision: 3 weeks
Time between decision and publication: 2 mos.
Number of reviewers: 3
Articles submitted per year: 12
Articles published per year: 9

(900) *Esperanto

István Ertl, Editor
Universala Esperanto-Asocio
Nieuwe Binnenweg 176
3015 BJ Rotterdam, Netherlands

Telephone: (31) 10 4361044
Fax: (31) 10 4361751
First published: 1905
Sponsoring organization: Universala Esperanto-Asocio
ISSN: 0014-0635
MLA acronym: Esperanto

SUBSCRIPTION INFORMATION

Frequency of publication: 11 times/yr.
Circulation: 6,200
Available in microform: No
Subscription price: $27.00/yr.
Year to which price refers: 1992

ADVERTISING INFORMATION

Advertising accepted: Yes

EDITORIAL DESCRIPTION

Scope: Publishes articles on the Esperanto movement, language, literature, and the world language problem.
Reviews books: Yes
Publishes notes: Yes
Languages accepted: Esperanto
Prints abstracts: No
Author-anonymous submission: No

SUBMISSION REQUIREMENTS

Restrictions on contributors: None
Author pays submission fee: No
Author pays page charges: No
Length of articles: 800 words
Length of book reviews: 250-350 words
Length of notes: 100 words
Number of copies required: 1
Special requirements: Submit double-spaced typescript.
Copyright ownership: Author
Rejected manuscripts: Returned; enclose return postage.
Time before publication decision: 1-4 mos.
Time between decision and publication: 1 mo.
Number of reviewers: 1 minimum
Articles submitted per year: 70
Articles published per year: 30
Book reviews submitted per year: 65
Book reviews published per year: 60
Notes submitted per year: 50
Notes published per year: 200

(901) *Esperanto Documents

Thomas Bormann, Editor
Universala Esperanto-Asocio
Nieuwe Binnenweg 176
3015 BJ Rotterdam, Netherlands

Telephone: (31) 10 4361044
Fax: (31) 10 4361751
First published: 1975
Sponsoring organization: Universala Esperanto-Asocio
ISSN: 0165-2575
MLA acronym: EDoc

SUBSCRIPTION INFORMATION

Frequency of publication: Irregular
Circulation: 140
Available in microform: No
Subscription price: $22.50/10 issues
Year to which price refers: 1992

ADVERTISING INFORMATION

Advertising accepted: No

EDITORIAL DESCRIPTION

Scope: Publishes articles in English on the work, organization, culture, and history of the movement for the adoption of the international language Esperanto as a second language for international use. Many documents also appear in the associated publications *Documents sur l'Esperanto* and *Esperanto-Dokumentoj*.
Reviews books: No
Publishes notes: No
Languages accepted: English
Prints abstracts: No
Author-anonymous submission: No

SUBMISSION REQUIREMENTS

Author pays submission fee: No
Author pays page charges: No
Number of copies required: 1
Copyright ownership: Not copyrighted
Rejected manuscripts: Returned
Number of reviewers: 1
Books submitted per year: 6
Books published per year: 2

(902) *Esperanto-Dokumentoj

Thomas Bormann, Editor
Universala Esperanto-Asocio
Nieuwe Binnenweg 176
3015 BJ Rotterdam, Netherlands

Additional editorial address: H3, 13, 6800 Mannheim 1, Germany
Telephone: (31) 10 4361044; (49) 621 153885
Fax: (31) 10 4361751
First published: 1975
Sponsoring organization: Universala Esperanto-Asocio
ISSN: 0165-2524
MLA acronym: EspDok

SUBSCRIPTION INFORMATION

Frequency of publication: Irregular
Circulation: 140
Available in microform: No
Subscription price: $22.50/10 issues
Year to which price refers: 1992

ADVERTISING INFORMATION

Advertising accepted: No

EDITORIAL DESCRIPTION

Scope: Publishes articles in Esperanto on the work, organization, culture, and history of the movement for the adoption of the international language Esperanto as a second language for international use. Many documents also appear in the associated publications *Documents sur l'Esperanto* and *Esperanto Documents*.
Reviews books: No
Publishes notes: No
Languages accepted: Esperanto
Prints abstracts: No
Author-anonymous submission: No

SUBMISSION REQUIREMENTS

Author pays submission fee: No
Author pays page charges: No
Number of copies required: 1
Copyright ownership: Not copyrighted
Rejected manuscripts: Returned
Number of reviewers: 1
Articles submitted per year: 6
Articles published per year: 3
Books submitted per year: 6
Books published per year: 2

(903) *Esperienze Letterarie: Rivista Trimestrale di Critica e Cultura

Marco Santoro, Editor
Via R. R. Pereira, 21
00136 Rome, Italy

Telephone: (39) 6 3498698
First published: 1976
ISSN: 0392-3495
MLA acronym: ELet

SUBSCRIPTION INFORMATION

Frequency of publication: 4 times/yr.
Available in microform: No
Subscription price: 70,000 Lit/yr. Italy; 100,000 Lit/yr. elsewhere
Year to which price refers: 1992
Subscription address: Federico e Ardia, Via Ventaglieri 85, 80138 Naples, Italy

ADVERTISING INFORMATION

Advertising accepted: Yes

EDITORIAL DESCRIPTION

Scope: Publishes critical and methodological articles on Italian, other European, and English literatures, with an emphasis on the relationship between literature and society.
Reviews books: Yes
Publishes notes: Yes
Languages accepted: Italian; English; French; German; Spanish
Prints abstracts: Yes

SUBMISSION REQUIREMENTS

Author pays submission fee: No
Author pays page charges: No
Length of articles: 30 pp. maximum
Length of book reviews: 4 pp. typescript
Length of notes: 2 pp. typescript
Style: RICA
Number of copies required: 2
Special requirements: Submit a 200-word abstract in Italian and English, French, German, or Spanish.
Copyright ownership: Author
Rejected manuscripts: Not returned
Time before publication decision: 1-2 mos.
Time between decision and publication: 6-12 mos.
Number of reviewers: 6
Articles submitted per year: 60-80
Articles published per year: 30
Book reviews submitted per year: 60-80

Book reviews published per year: 20-30
Notes submitted per year: 100
Notes published per year: 60

(904)
Esprit

Olivier Mongin, Director
212 Rue Saint-Martin
75003 Paris, France

First published: 1932
ISSN: 0014-0759
MLA acronym: Esprit

SUBSCRIPTION INFORMATION

Frequency of publication: 11 times/yr.
Circulation: 14,000
Available in microform: Yes

ADVERTISING INFORMATION

Advertising accepted: Yes

EDITORIAL DESCRIPTION

Scope: Publishes critical perspectives on society and politics with regard to artistic and intellectual life, particularly the humanities. Concerned with political philosophy, anthropology, sociology, literary criticism, theology, economics, the philosophy of science, and the interdisciplinary approaches of these different fields.
Reviews books: Yes
Publishes notes: Yes
Languages accepted: French
Prints abstracts: No

SUBMISSION REQUIREMENTS

Restrictions on contributors: None
Author pays submission fee: No
Author pays page charges: No
Length of articles: 10,000 words
Length of book reviews: 2,000 words
Length of notes: 2,000 words
Style: None
Number of copies required: 1
Copyright ownership: Journal
Rejected manuscripts: Returned
Time before publication decision: 2 mos.
Time between decision and publication: 2-3 mos.
Number of reviewers: 2-3
Articles submitted per year: 400
Articles published per year: 100
Book reviews submitted per year: 150
Book reviews published per year: 120
Notes submitted per year: 300
Notes published per year: 150

(905)
*L'Esprit Créateur

John D. Erickson, Editor
Box 25333
Baton Rouge, LA 70894

Telephone: 504 388-6713
Fax: 504 388-6628
First published: 1961
Sponsoring organization: Dept. of French & Italian, Louisiana State Univ.
ISSN: 0014-0767
MLA acronym: ECr

SUBSCRIPTION INFORMATION

Frequency of publication: 4 times/yr. (Spring, Summer, Fall, Winter)
Circulation: 1,200
Available in microform: Yes; vols. 1-6 (1961-1966) only
Subscription price: $30.00/yr. institutions; $17.00/yr. individuals N. America; $21.00/yr. individuals elsewhere
Year to which price refers: 1991

ADVERTISING INFORMATION

Advertising accepted: Yes
Advertising rates: $60.00/quarter page; $85.00/half page; $140.00/full page

EDITORIAL DESCRIPTION

Scope: Publishes studies in French literature and criticism and their interrelations with other literatures and fields of human inquiry. Each issue presents essays on the literary production of a single author or of works falling within a literary/critical movement or mode. All periods of French literature are reflected. Critical studies, of all methological persuasions, that observe the primacy of the literary text, are welcome.
Reviews books: Yes
Publishes notes: No
Languages accepted: English; French
Prints abstracts: No
Author-anonymous submission: Yes

SUBMISSION REQUIREMENTS

Restrictions on contributors: None
Author pays submission fee: No
Author pays page charges: No
Length of articles: 4,800 words maximum
Length of book reviews: 500 words
Style: MLA
Number of copies required: 2
Special requirements: Submit double-spaced typescript.
Copyright ownership: Journal
Rejected manuscripts: Returned; enclose SASE.
Time before publication decision: 3-6 mos.
Time between decision and publication: 6-9 mos.
Number of reviewers: 3
Articles submitted per year: 60-80
Articles published per year: 35-40
Book reviews published per year: 15-25

(906)
ESQ: A Journal of the American Renaissance

Robert C. McLean, Editor
Dept. of English
Washington State Univ.
Pullman, WA 99164-5020

First published: 1955
Sponsoring organization: Dept. of English, Washington State Univ.
ISSN: 0093-8297
MLA acronym: ESQ

SUBSCRIPTION INFORMATION

Frequency of publication: 4 times/yr.
Circulation: 800
Available in microform: No
Subscription address: Washington State Univ. Press, Pullman, WA 99164-5020

ADVERTISING INFORMATION

Advertising accepted: Yes

EDITORIAL DESCRIPTION

Scope: Devoted to the study of 19th-century American literature. Focuses on all aspects of the Romantic Transcendental tradition emanating from New England, of which Emerson is a principal figure. The journal's coverage, however, encompasses influences upon and responses to mid-century Romanticism generally, from Charles Brockden Brown to Henry James, from Philip Freneau to E. A. Robinson. Critical essays, source and influence studies, biographical and bibliographical studies of all figures in the century are invited as well as more general discussions of literary theory, literary history, and the history of ideas. Includes commissioned review-essays that examine a body of recent critical, historical, or bibliographical work relating to particular authors or to such general issues as the Gothic or the critical approaches to American romanticism.
Reviews books: Yes
Publishes notes: No
Languages accepted: English
Prints abstracts: No

SUBMISSION REQUIREMENTS

Restrictions on contributors: Reviews are solicited.
Author pays submission fee: No
Author pays page charges: No
Length of book reviews: No restrictions
Style: MLA
Number of copies required: 2
Special requirements: Manuscripts must be typed on an IBM Selectric or printed on a letter-quality printer in letter gothic, courier, or prestige elite typeface with unjustified right margins preferred.
Rejected manuscripts: Returned
Time before publication decision: 2-4 mos.
Time between decision and publication: 3 mos.
Number of reviewers: 2-5
Articles submitted per year: 250
Articles published per year: 25
Book reviews published per year: 4

(907)
Essays and Studies

English Assn.
The Vicarage, Priory Gardens, Bedford Park
London W4 1TT, England

First published: 1910
Sponsoring organization: English Assn., London
ISSN: 0071-1357
MLA acronym: E&S

SUBSCRIPTION INFORMATION

Frequency of publication: Annual
Circulation: 2,500
Available in microform: No

ADVERTISING INFORMATION

Advertising accepted: No

EDITORIAL DESCRIPTION

Scope: Publishes articles on literature and language.
Reviews books: No
Publishes notes: No
Languages accepted: English
Prints abstracts: No

SUBMISSION REQUIREMENTS

Restrictions on contributors: Unsolicited articles are not accepted.
Author pays submission fee: No
Author pays page charges: No
Length of articles: 5,000 words

(908) Essays by Divers Hands

Royal Soc. of Literature of the United Kingdom
1 Hyde Park Gardens
London W2 2LT, England

First published: 1921
Sponsoring organization: Royal Soc. of Literature
ISSN: 0080-4584
MLA acronym: EDH

SUBSCRIPTION INFORMATION

Frequency of publication: Once every 2 yrs.
Available in microform: No

ADVERTISING INFORMATION

Advertising accepted: No

EDITORIAL DESCRIPTION

Scope: Publishes papers read before the Royal Society of Literature.
Reviews books: No
Languages accepted: English
Prints abstracts: No

SUBMISSION REQUIREMENTS

Restrictions on contributors: Manuscripts are not accepted from outside contributors.
Author pays submission fee: No
Author pays page charges: No
Copyright ownership: Author

(909) *Essays in Arts and Sciences

David E. E. Sloane, Editor
Univ. of New Haven
300 Orange Ave.
West Haven, CT 06516

Telephone: 203 932-7371
Fax: 203 932-1469
First published: 1970
Sponsoring organization: Univ. of New Haven
ISSN: 0361-5634
MLA acronym: EAS

SUBSCRIPTION INFORMATION

Frequency of publication: Annual plus special issues
Circulation: 500
Available in microform: No
Subscription price: $5.00/yr. institutions; $10.00/yr. individuals
Year to which price refers: 1992

ADVERTISING INFORMATION

Advertising accepted: Yes
Advertising rates: $100.00/full page

EDITORIAL DESCRIPTION

Scope: A scholarly journal devoted to a broad range of interests, including literature, the arts, the social sciences, the natural sciences, and mathematics.
Reviews books: Yes
Publishes notes: Yes
Languages accepted: English
Prints abstracts: No
Author-anonymous submission: Yes

SUBMISSION REQUIREMENTS

Restrictions on contributors: None
Author pays submission fee: No
Author pays page charges: No
Length of articles: 3,000-5,000 words
Length of book reviews: 1,000-1,500 words
Length of notes: 1,500 words
Style: None
Number of copies required: 2
Special requirements: Accepted articles should be submitted on diskette in WordPerfect.
Copyright ownership: Journal
Rejected manuscripts: Returned; enclose return postage.
Time before publication decision: 3 mos. maximum
Time between decision and publication: 18 mos. maximum
Number of reviewers: 4-5
Articles submitted per year: 30-50
Articles published per year: 5-10
Book reviews published per year: 0-5
Notes published per year: 0-4

(910) *Essays in Criticism: A Quarterly Journal of Literary Criticism

Stephen Wall & Christopher Ricks, Editors
6A Rawlinson Rd.
Oxford OX2 6UE, England

First published: 1951
ISSN: 0014-0856
MLA acronym: EIC

SUBSCRIPTION INFORMATION

Frequency of publication: 4 times/yr. (Jan., Apr., July, Oct.)
Circulation: 2,250
Available in microform: Yes
Subscription price: $68.00/yr.; $18.00/single issue
Year to which price refers: 1992
Subscription address: Business Manager, at the above address

ADVERTISING INFORMATION

Advertising accepted: Yes

EDITORIAL DESCRIPTION

Scope: An Oxford journal with an English bias, but suitable articles from abroad are welcome.
Reviews books: Yes
Publishes notes: No
Languages accepted: English
Prints abstracts: No

SUBMISSION REQUIREMENTS

Restrictions on contributors: Unsolicited book reviews are not accepted.
Author pays submission fee: No
Author pays page charges: No
Length of articles: 6,000-7,500 words
Length of book reviews: 2,000-3,000 words
Number of copies required: 1
Copyright ownership: Journal & author
Rejected manuscripts: Returned; enclose return postage.
Time before publication decision: 2-6 weeks
Time between decision and publication: 1 yr.
Number of reviewers: 1-2
Articles submitted per year: 80-120
Articles published per year: 14-16
Book reviews published per year: 16

(911) *Essays in French Literature

Denis Boak, Editor
Dept. of French Studies
Univ. of Western Australia
Nedlands, Western Australia 6009, Australia

Telephone: (61) 9 3802173
Fax: (61) 9 3801080
First published: 1964
Sponsoring organization: Dept. of French Studies, Univ. of Western Australia
ISSN: 0071-139X
MLA acronym: EFL

SUBSCRIPTION INFORMATION

Frequency of publication: Annual
Circulation: 400
Available in microform: No
Subscription address: Univ. Bookshop, at the above address

ADVERTISING INFORMATION

Advertising accepted: No

EDITORIAL DESCRIPTION

Scope: Publishes articles on all aspects of French literature from the Middle Ages to the present day. Methods of approach and points of view expressed vary widely and range from literary history and the history of ideas to explication. Major emphasis is given, however, to the detailed reading and critical evaluation of individual works.
Reviews books: No
Publishes notes: No
Languages accepted: English; French
Prints abstracts: No
Author-anonymous submission: No

SUBMISSION REQUIREMENTS

Restrictions on contributors: None
Author pays submission fee: No
Author pays page charges: No
Length of articles: 20,000 words maximum
Style: MLA; Modern Humanities Research Assn.
Number of copies required: 1
Special requirements: Submit xerox copy.
Copyright ownership: Journal
Rejected manuscripts: Not returned
Time before publication decision: 3-6 mos.
Time between decision and publication: 1 yr.
Number of reviewers: 3
Articles submitted per year: 20
Articles published per year: 8

(912) *Essays in Literature

Thomas P. Joswick, Daniel L. Colvin, & Morris Vos, Editors
114 Simpkins Hall
Dept. of English
Western Illinois Univ.
Macomb, IL 61455

Telephone: 309 298-2212
First published: 1974
Sponsoring organization: Western Illinois Univ., College of Arts & Sciences
ISSN: 0094-5404
MLA acronym: ELWIU

SUBSCRIPTION INFORMATION

Frequency of publication: 2 times/yr. (Spring, Fall)
Circulation: 800
Available in microform: No
Subscription price: $8.00/yr. institutions US; $5.00/yr. individuals US; $9.00/yr. elsewhere
Year to which price refers: 1991

ADVERTISING INFORMATION

Advertising accepted: No

EDITORIAL DESCRIPTION

Scope: Focuses on literature and literary theory in the British and American traditions and the modern European languages. The editors welcome studies concerning any literary period, figure, genre, or work, as well as studies of literary theories or critical practices.
Reviews books: No
Publishes notes: Yes
Languages accepted: English
Prints abstracts: No
Author-anonymous submission: No

SUBMISSION REQUIREMENTS

Restrictions on contributors: None
Author pays submission fee: No
Author pays page charges: No
Length of articles: 5,000-9,000 words
Length of notes: 2,250-5,000 words
Style: MLA
Number of copies required: 1; 2 preferred
Special requirements: Submit original typescript.
Copyright ownership: Assigned by author to journal
Rejected manuscripts: Returned; enclose SASE or return postage.
Time before publication decision: 10 weeks
Time between decision and publication: 1 yr.
Number of reviewers: 2 minimum
Articles submitted per year: 200
Articles published per year: 24
Notes submitted per year: 10
Notes published per year: 1

(913)
*Essays in Poetics: The Journal of the British Neo-Formalist School

Joseph M. Andrew & Robert Reid, Editors
Dept. of Russian Studies
Univ. of Keele
Keele, Staffs., ST5 5BG, England

Telephone: (44) 782 621111 ext. 3291
Fax: (44) 782 713036
First published: 1976
ISSN: 0308-888X
MLA acronym: EiP

SUBSCRIPTION INFORMATION

Frequency of publication: 2 times/yr. (Apr., Sept.)
Circulation: 300
Available in microform: No
Subscription price: £24.00/yr.
Year to which price refers: 1991
Subscription address: Oxon Publishers, Market House, Deddington, Oxford OX5 4SW, England

ADVERTISING INFORMATION

Advertising accepted: Yes

EDITORIAL DESCRIPTION

Scope: Publishes articles on formalist, structuralist, and poststructuralist theories of literature and poetics.
Reviews books: Yes
Publishes notes: Yes
Languages accepted: English
Prints abstracts: No
Author-anonymous submission: No

SUBMISSION REQUIREMENTS

Restrictions on contributors: None
Author pays submission fee: No
Author pays page charges: No
Length of articles: 10,000 words

Length of book reviews: 5,000 words maximum
Length of notes: 2,000 words maximun
Style: Journal
Number of copies required: 1
Copyright ownership: Author
Rejected manuscripts: Returned
Time before publication decision: 1-2 mos.
Time between decision and publication: 6-12 mos.
Number of reviewers: 2
Articles submitted per year: 15
Articles published per year: 10
Book reviews submitted per year: 2
Book reviews published per year: 2

(914)
*Essays in Theatre/Etudes Théâtrales

Harry Lane & Ann Wilson, Editors
Dept. of Drama
Univ. of Guelph
Guelph, Ontario N1G 2W1, Canada

Telephone: 519 824-4120 ext. 3147
Fax: 519 837-1315
E-mail: DRMLANE@VM.UOGUELPH.CA
First published: 1982
Historical variations in title: Formerly *Essays in Theatre*
Sponsoring organization: Dept. of Drama, Univ. of Guelph
ISSN: 0821-4425
MLA acronym: EiTET

SUBSCRIPTION INFORMATION

Frequency of publication: 2 times/yr.
Available in microform: No
Subscription price: C$20.00/yr. institutions Canada; $20.00/yr. institutions elsewhere; C$15.00/yr. individuals Canada; $15.00/yr. individuals elsewhere
Year to which price refers: 1992-93

ADVERTISING INFORMATION

Advertising accepted: No

EDITORIAL DESCRIPTION

Scope: Publishes articles on dramatic theory, aesthetics, literature, theater history, and production.
Reviews books: Yes
Publishes notes: No
Languages accepted: English; French
Prints abstracts: No
Author-anonymous submission: Yes

SUBMISSION REQUIREMENTS

Restrictions on contributors: Book reviews are commissioned.
Author pays submission fee: No
Author pays page charges: No
Length of articles: 5,000 words
Length of book reviews: 1,000 words
Style: MLA
Number of copies required: 2
Copyright ownership: Author
Rejected manuscripts: Returned
Time before publication decision: 2 mos.
Time between decision and publication: 6 mos.
Number of reviewers: 2 minimum
Articles submitted per year: 50
Articles published per year: 10
Book reviews published per year: 8-10

(915)
*Essays on Canadian Writing

Jack David & Robert Lecker, Editors
Dept. of English
McGill Univ.
853 Sherbrooke St. West
Montreal, Quebec H3A 2T6, Canada

Telephone: 514 398-8326
Fax: 514 398-8220
E-mail: CYRL@MUSICA.MCGILL.CA
First published: 1974
ISSN: 0313-0300
MLA acronym: ECW

SUBSCRIPTION INFORMATION

Frequency of publication: 3 times/yr.
Circulation: 1,200
Available in microform: Yes
Subscription price: $20.00/yr.
Year to which price refers: 1991
Subscription address: ECW Press, 1980 Queen St. E., 2nd Floor, Toronto, Ontario M4L 1J2, Canada
Subscription telephone: 416 694-3348
Subscription fax: 416 698-9906

ADVERTISING INFORMATION

Advertising accepted: Yes

EDITORIAL DESCRIPTION

Scope: Publishes articles, reviews, interviews, bibliographies, and criticism on Canadian literature.
Reviews books: Yes
Publishes notes: Yes
Languages accepted: English; French
Prints abstracts: No
Author-anonymous submission: Yes

SUBMISSION REQUIREMENTS

Restrictions on contributors: None
Author pays submission fee: No
Author pays page charges: No
Length of articles: 1,500-50,000 words
Length of book reviews: 3,000 words
Length of notes: 2,000 words
Style: MLA
Number of copies required: 1
Special requirements: For all material quoted in text, submit photocopies from original source.
Copyright ownership: Journal
Rejected manuscripts: Returned with comments; enclose return postage.
Time before publication decision: 1 mo.
Time between decision and publication: 12-18 mos.
Number of reviewers: 3
Articles submitted per year: 200
Articles published per year: 20
Book reviews submitted per year: 40
Book reviews published per year: 35
Notes submitted per year: 5
Notes published per year: 1

(916)
*Estreno: Cuadernos del Teatro Español Contemporáneo

Martha T. Halsey, Editor
Pennsylvania State Univ.
350 N. Burrowes Bldg.
University Park, PA 16802

Telephone: 814 865-4252
Fax: 814 863-7944
First published: 1975
ISSN: 0097-8663
MLA acronym: Estreno

SUBSCRIPTION INFORMATION

Frequency of publication: 2 times/yr.

Circulation: 550
Available in microform: No
Subscription price: $23.00/yr. institutions; $14.00/yr. individuals
Year to which price refers: 1992

ADVERTISING INFORMATION

Advertising accepted: Yes

EDITORIAL DESCRIPTION

Scope: Publishes unpublished theatrical works directed toward the Spanish audience by the professional or semi-professional author, by those at home or abroad, as well as by those well-known or unknown. Selection is based on the value, interest, and theatrical novelty of the work, without political or ideological considerations. Journal also publishes interviews, articles, and documents of 20th century Spanish theater, as well as information about first performances, criticism, censorship, works in progress and, in general, any facts of interest to professionals and students of the contemporary Spanish theater.
Reviews books: Yes
Publishes notes: Yes
Languages accepted: English; Spanish
Prints abstracts: No
Author-anonymous submission: Yes

SUBMISSION REQUIREMENTS

Restrictions on contributors: Most book reviews are solicited.
Author pays submission fee: No
Author pays page charges: No
Length of articles: 2,000-4,000 words
Length of book reviews: 200 words
Length of notes: 50-400 words
Style: MLA
Number of copies required: 2
Special requirements: Play manuscripts must be accompanied by permission of the author to publish a work; an introduction (in English or Spanish) about the author and the work presented; conditions concerning performing the work with the name and address of the agent; whenever possible, a photograph of the author or pictures of the stage cast.
Copyright ownership: Author
Rejected manuscripts: Returned
Time before publication decision: 1-2 mos.
Time between decision and publication: 10-20 mos.
Number of reviewers: 2 minimum
Articles submitted per year: 50-60
Articles published per year: 5-8
Book reviews submitted per year: 20
Book reviews published per year: 15
Notes submitted per year: 15-20
Notes published per year: 5-10

(917)
*Estudios de Asia y Africa

Guillermo Quartucci, Editor
El Colegio de México
Camino al Ajusco 20
Mexico City, D.F., 01000, Mexico

Telephone: (52) 5 6455955 ext. 388, 297
Fax: (52) 5 6450464
First published: 1966
Sponsoring organization: El Colegio de México
ISSN: 0185-0164
MLA acronym: EOMC

SUBSCRIPTION INFORMATION

Frequency of publication: 3 times/yr. (May, Sept., Jan.)
Circulation: 350
Available in microform: No
Subscription price: $50.00/yr. institutions; $32.00/yr. individuals
Year to which price refers: 1992

Subscription address: El Colegio de México, Dpto. de Publicaciones, Camino al Ajusco 20, Pedregal de Sta. Teresa, 10740 Mexico City, D.F., Mexico

ADVERTISING INFORMATION

Advertising accepted: Yes

EDITORIAL DESCRIPTION

Scope: Journal focuses on Asia and Africa for Latin American scholars.
Reviews books: Yes
Publishes notes: Yes
Languages accepted: Spanish; English; French
Prints abstracts: Yes
Author-anonymous submission: No

SUBMISSION REQUIREMENTS

Restrictions on contributors: Some articles are commissioned.
Author pays submission fee: No
Author pays page charges: No
Length of articles: 5,000 words
Length of book reviews: 2,000 words
Length of notes: 300 words
Style: Chicago
Number of copies required: 1
Special requirements: Submit original typescript and a 200-word abstract.
Copyright ownership: El Colegio de México
Rejected manuscripts: Returned at author's request
Time before publication decision: 2 mos.
Time between decision and publication: 4-6 mos.
Number of reviewers: 3
Articles submitted per year: 40
Articles published per year: 15-20
Book reviews submitted per year: 40-50
Book reviews published per year: 40-50
Notes submitted per year: 12-15
Notes published per year: 12-15

(918)
*Estudios de Cultura Maya: Publicación Periódica del Centro de Estudios Mayas

Gerardo Bustos Trejo, Editor
Centro de Estudios Mayas
Inst. de Investigaciones Filológicas
Circuito Mario de la Cueva
Ciudad Univ., UNAM
04510 Mexico City, D.F., Mexico

Telephone: (52) 5 6227490
Fax: (52) 5 6657874
First published: 1961
Sponsoring organization: Centro de Estudios Mayas, Univ. Nacional Autónoma de México
ISSN: 0185-2574
MLA acronym: ECM

SUBSCRIPTION INFORMATION

Frequency of publication: Irregular
Circulation: 2,000
Available in microform: No
Subscription address: Dept. de Publicaciones, Inst. de Investigaciones Filologicas, Circuito Mario de la Cueva, Ciudad Univ., UNAM, 04510 Mexico City, D.F., Mexico

ADVERTISING INFORMATION

Advertising accepted: No

EDITORIAL DESCRIPTION

Scope: Publishes articles about Mayan languages and cultures and all cultural aspects of the ancient and modern Mayans.
Reviews books: Yes
Publishes notes: Yes
Languages accepted: English; Spanish; French
Prints abstracts: No
Author-anonymous submission: No

SUBMISSION REQUIREMENTS

Restrictions on contributors: None
Author pays submission fee: No
Author pays page charges: No
Length of articles: 50-60 pp.
Length of book reviews: 5 pp. maximum
Length of notes: 1 p.
Style: None
Number of copies required: 2
Special requirements: Submit original typescript.
Copyright ownership: Univ. Nacional Autónoma de México
Rejected manuscripts: Returned
Time before publication decision: 6 mos.
Time between decision and publication: 1 yr.
Number of reviewers: 4
Articles submitted per year: 17
Articles published per year: 15

(919)
*Estudios de Cultura Náhuatl

Miguel León-Portilla & Guadalupe Borgonio, Editors
Inst. de Investigaciones Históricas
Circuito Cultural
Ciudad de las Humanidades
Ciudad Univ. (UNAM)
04510 Mexico City, D.F., Mexico

Telephone: (52) 5 6650070
Fax: (52) 5 6650070
First published: 1959
Sponsoring organization: Univ. National Autónoma de México, Inst. de Investigaciones Historicas
ISSN: 0071-1675
MLA acronym: ECN

SUBSCRIPTION INFORMATION

Frequency of publication: Annual
Circulation: 2,000
Available in microform: No
Subscription address: Distribuidora de Libros Universitarios, Insurgentes 299 Sur, Mexico City 11, D.F., Mexico

ADVERTISING INFORMATION

Advertising accepted: Yes, on an exchange basis

EDITORIAL DESCRIPTION

Scope: Publishes articles on the culture, idiom, history, and bibliography of the Aztecs and other Nahua groups.
Reviews books: Yes
Publishes notes: Yes
Languages accepted: English; French; Spanish
Prints abstracts: No
Author-anonymous submission: No

SUBMISSION REQUIREMENTS

Restrictions on contributors: None
Author pays submission fee: No
Author pays page charges: No
Length of articles: 5,000-7,000 words
Length of book reviews: 250-500 words
Length of notes: 150-300 words
Style: American Anthropologist; Hispanic American Historical Review
Number of copies required: 2
Copyright ownership: Author
Rejected manuscripts: Not returned
Time before publication decision: 2 mos.
Time between decision and publication: 6 mos.
Number of reviewers: 3
Articles submitted per year: 25
Articles published per year: 15
Book reviews submitted per year: 6
Book reviews published per year: 8-10

Notes submitted per year: 10
Notes published per year: 8

(920)
Estudios de Lingüística

Ana Isabel Navarro Carrosco & José Luis Cifuentes Honrubia, Coordinators, Editors
Dept. de Filología Española, Lingüística General & Teoría de la Literatura
Fac. de Filosofía & Letras
Univ. de Alicante
03071 Alicante, Spain

First published: 1983
Sponsoring organization: Univ. de Alicante
ISSN: 0212-7636
MLA acronym: EdLing

SUBSCRIPTION INFORMATION

Frequency of publication: Annual (Nov.)
Available in microform: No
Subscription address: Secretariado de Publicaciones, Univ. de Alicante, 03071 Alicante, Spain

ADVERTISING INFORMATION

Advertising accepted: Yes

EDITORIAL DESCRIPTION

Scope: Publishes articles on general linguistics, contrastive linguistics, textual linguistics, pragmatics, sociolinguistics and literary theory with an emphasis on the Spanish language.
Reviews books: Yes
Publishes notes: Yes
Languages accepted: Spanish; English; French; German; Italian; Catalan; Portuguese
Prints abstracts: Yes
Author-anonymous submission: Yes

SUBMISSION REQUIREMENTS

Restrictions on contributors: None
Author pays submission fee: No
Author pays page charges: No
Length of articles: 10,000 words
Length of book reviews: 1,400 words
Length of notes: 2,500 words
Style: MLA
Number of copies required: 2
Special requirements: Submit English-language abstract.
Copyright ownership: Author
Rejected manuscripts: Returned
Time before publication decision: 8 mos.
Time between decision and publication: 4 mos.
Number of reviewers: 3
Articles submitted per year: 30-40
Articles published per year: 12-14
Book reviews submitted per year: 6-8
Book reviews published per year: 1-2
Notes submitted per year: 4-5
Notes published per year: 1-2

(921)
*Estudios de Lingüística Aplicada

Anna De Fina, Ilse Heckel, Natalia Ignatieva, Dietrich Rall, Phyllis Ryan, & Jacqueline Okuma, Editors
Centro de Enseñanza de Lenguas Extranjeras
Univ. Nacional Autónoma de México
Ciudad Univ.
04510 Mexico City, D.F., Mexico

Telephone: (52) 5 5480944; (52) 5 6220676; (52) 5 6220678
Fax: (52) 5 5487832
First published: 1981
Sponsoring organization: Univ. Nacional Autónoma de México, Centro de Enseñanza de Lenguas Extranjeras

ISSN: 0185-2647
MLA acronym: EDLA

SUBSCRIPTION INFORMATION

Frequency of publication: 2 times/yr.
Circulation: 400
Available in microform: No
Subscription price: $25.00/yr.
Year to which price refers: 1992

ADVERTISING INFORMATION

Advertising accepted: No

EDITORIAL DESCRIPTION

Scope: Publishes articles dealing with theoretical and practical aspects of second language learning, with an emphasis on sociolinguistics, psycholinguistics, contrastive linguistics, and the theory of language.
Reviews books: Yes
Publishes notes: No
Languages accepted: English; Spanish
Prints abstracts: Yes
Author-anonymous submission: Yes

SUBMISSION REQUIREMENTS

Restrictions on contributors: None
Author pays submission fee: No
Author pays page charges: No
Length of articles: 2,500-5,000 words
Length of book reviews: 250 words
Style: None
Number of copies required: 2
Special requirements: Submit double-spaced typescript and diskette using Word Star; include name and affiliation on the title page; include 120-150 word abstract.
Copyright ownership: Univ. Nacional Autonoma de Mexico
Rejected manuscripts: Not returned
Time before publication decision: 45 days
Time between decision and publication: 6-12 mos.
Number of reviewers: 2
Articles submitted per year: 20
Articles published per year: 12
Book reviews submitted per year: 10
Book reviews published per year: 6

(922)
*Estudios Filológicos

Claudio Wagner, Editor
Fac. de Filosofia & Humanidades
Casilla 142
Univ. Austral de Chile
Valdivia, Chile

Fax: (56) 63 212589
First published: 1965
Sponsoring organization: Univ. Austral de Chile
ISSN: 0071-1713
MLA acronym: EFil

SUBSCRIPTION INFORMATION

Frequency of publication: Annual
Available in microform: No
Subscription price: $15.00/yr. Latin America; $20.00/yr. elsewhere
Year to which price refers: 1991

ADVERTISING INFORMATION

Advertising accepted: Yes, on an exchange basis

EDITORIAL DESCRIPTION

Scope: Publishes studies on linguistics and literature, especially themes related to the Spanish language and Spanish and Hispano-American literatures.
Reviews books: Yes

Publishes notes: Yes
Languages accepted: Spanish
Prints abstracts: Yes
Author-anonymous submission: No

SUBMISSION REQUIREMENTS

Restrictions on contributors: None
Author pays submission fee: No
Author pays page charges: No
Length of articles: 3,000-17,000 words
Length of book reviews: 500-3,000 words
Length of notes: 3,000-8,000 words
Style: None
Number of copies required: 2
Special requirements: Submit original typescript and an abstract.
Copyright ownership: Univ. Austral de Chile
Rejected manuscripts: Not returned
Time before publication decision: 3 mos.
Time between decision and publication: 6 mos.
Number of reviewers: 2 plus Editorial Board
Articles submitted per year: 10-15
Articles published per year: 10
Book reviews submitted per year: 5
Book reviews published per year: 3-5
Notes submitted per year: 4
Notes published per year: 2-3

(923)
Estudios Sefardíes

Iacob M. Hassán & Elena Romero, Editors
Dept. Arias Montano, Inst. di Fililogía, C.S.I.C.
Duque de Medinaceli, 6
Madrid 28014, Spain

First published: 1978
Sponsoring organization: Consejo Superior de Investigaciones Científicas (C.S.I.C.)
ISSN: 0210-9077
MLA acronym: ESef

SUBSCRIPTION INFORMATION

Frequency of publication: Annual
Available in microform: No
Subscription address: Dept. de Publicaciones de C.S.I.C., Servicio de Distribución, Vitrubio, 16, Madrid 28016, Spain

ADVERTISING INFORMATION

Advertising accepted: No

EDITORIAL DESCRIPTION

Scope: Publishes studies and articles on Judeo-Spanish literature and language and on Sephardic culture.
Reviews books: Yes
Publishes notes: Yes
Languages accepted: Spanish; French; English
Prints abstracts: No

SUBMISSION REQUIREMENTS

Author pays submission fee: No
Author pays page charges: Occasionally
Length of articles: 15-25 pp.
Length of book reviews: 1-3 pp.
Length of notes: 2-7 pp.
Style: MLA; Chicago; Journal
Number of copies required: 1
Special requirements: Consult editor prior to submission.
Copyright ownership: Consejo Superior de Investigaciones
Rejected manuscripts: Returned
Time before publication decision: 2 mos.
Time between decision and publication: 6-18 mos.
Number of reviewers: 1-2
Articles submitted per year: 12
Articles published per year: 7

(924)
Estudis Escènics: Quaderns de l'Institut del Teatre de la Diputació de Barcelona

Jordi Coca & Joan-Enric Lahosa, Editors
Carrer Nou de la Rambla 3
Palau Güell, 3
08001-Barcelona, Spain

First published: 1957
Sponsoring organization: Diputació de Barcelona
ISSN: 0212-3819
MLA acronym: EEsc

SUBSCRIPTION INFORMATION

Frequency of publication: 2 times/yr.
Available in microform: No

ADVERTISING INFORMATION

Advertising accepted: No

EDITORIAL DESCRIPTION

Scope: Publishes articles on the performing arts.
Reviews books: No
Publishes notes: Yes
Languages accepted: Catalan
Author-anonymous submission: No

SUBMISSION REQUIREMENTS

Author pays submission fee: Yes
Author pays page charges: No
Length of articles: No restrictions
Length of notes: No restrictions
Number of copies required: 1
Special requirements: Submit original typescript.
Copyright ownership: Inst. de Teatre
Time before publication decision: 6 mos.
Time between decision and publication: 1 yr.
Number of reviewers: 11

(925)
Estudos Anglo-Americanos

Paolo Vizioli, Alfredo Leme Coelho de Carvalho, Carlos Daghlian, M. Antonieta A. Celani, Francisco Gomes de Matos, & Hilario I. Bohn, Editors
ABRAPUI
C.P. 164
15001 São José do Rio Preto
São Paulo, Brazil

First published: 1977
Sponsoring organization: Assoc. Brasileira de Professores Universitários de Inglés (ABRAPUI)
ISSN: 0102-4906
MLA acronym: EAA

SUBSCRIPTION INFORMATION

Frequency of publication: Annual
Circulation: 500
Available in microform: No

ADVERTISING INFORMATION

Advertising accepted: No

EDITORIAL DESCRIPTION

Scope: Publishes papers, mainly by Brazilian scholars, on English language and literature in English.
Reviews books: Yes
Languages accepted: English; Portuguese
Prints abstracts: Yes

SUBMISSION REQUIREMENTS

Restrictions on contributors: None
Author pays submission fee: No
Author pays page charges: No
Length of articles: 20 typescript pp.
Length of book reviews: 2,000 words
Style: MLA preferred
Number of copies required: 1
Special requirements: Include an abstract.
Copyright ownership: Author
Rejected manuscripts: Returned
Time before publication decision: 3 mos.
Time between decision and publication: 3 mos.
Number of reviewers: 3
Articles submitted per year: 10
Articles published per year: 8
Book reviews submitted per year: 1
Book reviews published per year: 1

(926)
*Estudos Portugueses e Africanos

João Wanderley Geraldi, Editor
UNICAMP-Inst. de Estudos da Linguagem
Setor de Publicações
C.P. 6045
13081 Campinas-SP, Brazil

Telephone: (55) 192 398252
Fax: (55) 192 391501
E-mail: NECEPO@CCVAX.UNICAP.ANSP.-BR
First published: 1983
Sponsoring organization: Núcleo de Estudos de Cultura de Expressão Portuguesa do Inst. de Estudos da Linguagem, Univ. Estadual de Campinas
ISSN: 0103-1821
MLA acronym: EPA

SUBSCRIPTION INFORMATION

Frequency of publication: 2 times/yr.
Circulation: 400
Available in microform: No

ADVERTISING INFORMATION

Advertising accepted: No

EDITORIAL DESCRIPTION

Scope: Publishes articles on African and Portuguese culture and literature.
Reviews books: Yes
Publishes notes: Yes
Languages accepted: Portuguese; English; French; Spanish
Prints abstracts: No
Author-anonymous submission: No

SUBMISSION REQUIREMENTS

Author pays page charges: No
Copyright ownership: Journal
Number of reviewers: 5

(927)
*ETC.: A Review of General Semantics

Jeremy Klein, Editor
International Soc. for General Semantics
P.O. Box 728
Concord, CA 94522

Telephone: 510 798-0311
First published: 1943
Sponsoring organization: International Soc. for General Semantics
ISSN: 0014-164X
MLA acronym: ETC.

SUBSCRIPTION INFORMATION

Frequency of publication: 4 times/yr. (Mar., June, Sept., Dec.)
Circulation: 2,400
Available in microform: Yes
Subscription price: $30.00/yr.
Year to which price refers: 1992

ADVERTISING INFORMATION

Advertising accepted: Yes

EDITORIAL DESCRIPTION

Scope: Focuses on the role of symbols in human behavior. Explores the relationships between language, thought, and behavior, and questions of improving human communication.
Reviews books: Yes
Publishes notes: Yes
Languages accepted: English
Prints abstracts: No
Author-anonymous submission: No

SUBMISSION REQUIREMENTS

Author pays submission fee: No
Author pays page charges: No
Length of articles: 750-3,000 words
Length of book reviews: 500-2,000 words
Length of notes: 1,000 words maximum
Style: Chicago
Number of copies required: 2
Copyright ownership: International Soc. for General Semantics or author
Rejected manuscripts: Returned; enclose return postage.
Time before publication decision: 3-9 mos.
Time between decision and publication: 3-6 mos.
Number of reviewers: 2-3
Articles submitted per year: 200
Articles published per year: 50
Book reviews published per year: 12-14
Notes published per year: 12

(928)
*Ethnographia: A Magyar Néprajzi Társaság Folyóirata

László Lukács, Editor
Magyar Néprajzi Társaság
Kossuth Lajos tér 12
1055 Budapest, Hungary

Telephone: (36) 1 1326340; (36) 1 1759011
Fax: (36) 1 1759764
First published: 1890
Sponsoring organization: Magyar Tudományos Akadémia
ISSN: 0014-1798
MLA acronym: Ethnographia

SUBSCRIPTION INFORMATION

Frequency of publication: 2 times/yr.
Circulation: 900
Available in microform: No
Subscription price: 212 Ft/yr.
Year to which price refers: 1991
Subscription address: Kultura Foreign Trade Co., Box 149, 1389 Budapest, Hungary

ADVERTISING INFORMATION

Advertising accepted: No

EDITORIAL DESCRIPTION

Scope: Publishes articles on ethnography, folklore, and social and cultural anthropology.
Reviews books: Yes
Publishes notes: Yes
Languages accepted: Hungarian
Prints abstracts: Yes

SUBMISSION REQUIREMENTS

Author pays submission fee: No
Author pays page charges: No
Length of articles: 40 pp.
Length of book reviews: 800 words
Length of notes: 2,000 words
Number of copies required: 2
Copyright ownership: Author
Rejected manuscripts: Returned
Time before publication decision: 6 mos.
Time between decision and publication: 1 yr.
Number of reviewers: 1
Articles submitted per year: 20
Articles published per year: 14
Book reviews submitted per year: 50
Book reviews published per year: 40
Notes submitted per year: 60
Notes published per year: 40

(929)
*Ethnologia Europaea

Bjarne Stoklund, Editor
Dept. of European Ethnology
Univ. of Copenhagen
Brede Alle 69
2800 Lyngby, Denmark

Telephone: (45) 42 854477
First published: 1967
Sponsoring organization: Nordiska Publicerings-snämnden för Humanistiska Tidskrifter (Nordic Publications Committee for Humanist Periodicals)
ISSN: 0109-8713
MLA acronym: EthnoE

SUBSCRIPTION INFORMATION

Frequency of publication: 2 times/yr.
Circulation: 500
Available in microform: No
Subscription price: 200 Dkr/yr. institutions; 180 Dkr/yr. individuals
Year to which price refers: 1991
Subscription address: AIO-Tryk, Cikorievej 8, 5220 Odense 50, Denmark
Subscription telephone: (45) 66 121030

ADVERTISING INFORMATION

Advertising accepted: Yes

EDITORIAL DESCRIPTION

Scope: Presents the results of research on the ethnic culture (folk culture) of different regions of Europe, and serves as a forum for discussion appropriate to the establishment of a synthesis of the different branches and tendencies of European ethnology.
Reviews books: No
Publishes notes: No
Languages accepted: English; German; French
Prints abstracts: Yes

SUBMISSION REQUIREMENTS

Restrictions on contributors: None
Author pays submission fee: No
Author pays page charges: No
Length of articles: 10-20 printed pp.
Number of copies required: 1
Special requirements: An abstract of 100-125 words in the language of the paper should be included.
Copyright ownership: Author & journal
Time before publication decision: 3 mos.
Time between decision and publication: 6 mos. minimum
Articles submitted per year: 20
Articles published per year: 12

(930)
*Ethnologia Fennica/Finnish Studies in Ethnology

Kaija Heikkinen, Anna-Maria Åström, Leena Sammallahti, Matti Räsänen, Hannu Sinisalo, & Jukka Pennanen, Editors
Ethnos r.y.
P.O. Box 913
00101 Helsinki, Finland

Telephone: (358) 0 4050241
Fax: (358) 0 4050300
First published: 1971
Sponsoring organization: Academia Scientiarum Fennica
ISSN: 0355-1776
MLA acronym: EthF

SUBSCRIPTION INFORMATION

Frequency of publication: Annual
Circulation: 40
Available in microform: No
Subscription price: 40 Fmk/yr. plus postage
Year to which price refers: 1992
Subscription address: Tiedekirja, Kirkkokatu 14, 00170 Helsinki, Finland
Subscription telephone: (358) 0 635177
Subscription fax: (358) 0 6221121

ADVERTISING INFORMATION

Advertising accepted: Yes
Advertising rates: 250 Fmk/quarter page; 500 Fmk/half page; 1,000 Fmk/full page

EDITORIAL DESCRIPTION

Scope: Publishes articles on material, social, and general ethnology.
Reviews books: Yes
Publishes notes: Yes
Languages accepted: English; German
Prints abstracts: Yes
Author-anonymous submission: No

SUBMISSION REQUIREMENTS

Restrictions on contributors: None
Author pays submission fee: No
Author pays page charges: No
Length of articles: 1,000-10,000 words
Length of book reviews: 200-600 words
Length of notes: 200-600 words
Number of copies required: 1
Copyright ownership: Author
Rejected manuscripts: Returned
Time before publication decision: 1 mo.
Time between decision and publication: 1 yr.
Number of reviewers: 3-7
Articles submitted per year: 4
Articles published per year: 3-7
Book reviews submitted per year: 3-6
Book reviews published per year: 3-6
Notes submitted per year: 0-4
Notes published per year: 0-4

(931)
*Ethnologia Scandinavica: A Journal for Nordic Ethnology

Nils-Arvid Bringéus, Editor
Folklivsarkivet
Finngatan 8
Univ. of Lund
223 62 Lund, Sweden

Telephone: (46) 46 291314
First published: 1971
Sponsoring organization: Kungliga Gustav Adolfs Akademien; Nordic Humanities Research Councils
ISSN: 0348-9698
MLA acronym: EthSc

SUBSCRIPTION INFORMATION

Frequency of publication: Annual
Circulation: 1,000
Available in microform: No
Subscription price: 220 NKr ($36.00)/yr.
Year to which price refers: 1992
Subscription address: Scandinavian Univ. Press, P.O. Box 2959 Tøyen, 0608 Oslo, Norway
Additional subscription address: Scandinavian Univ. Press, 200 Meacham Ave., Elmont, NY 11003
Subscription telephone: (47) 2 677600
Subscription fax: (47) 2 677575

ADVERTISING INFORMATION

Advertising accepted: No

EDITORIAL DESCRIPTION

Scope: Publishes articles on Scandinavian ethnology, and includes studies in all branches of material and social culture.
Reviews books: Yes
Publishes notes: Yes
Languages accepted: English; German; Swedish
Prints abstracts: No

SUBMISSION REQUIREMENTS

Author pays submission fee: No
Author pays page charges: No
Length of articles: 8,190-16,380 words
Length of book reviews: 736-2,208 words
Length of notes: 736-1,104 words
Number of copies required: 1
Special requirements: Submit original typescript.
Copyright ownership: Author
Rejected manuscripts: Returned
Time between decision and publication: 6 mos.
Number of reviewers: 2
Articles submitted per year: 7-9
Articles published per year: 7-9
Book reviews published per year: 30
Notes published per year: 3

(932)
*Ethnologia Slavica

Ján Podolák, Editor
Dept. of Ethnology
Comenius Univ.
Gondova 2
81801 Bratislava, Slovak Republic

Telephone: (42) 7 56471
Fax: (42) 7 51549
First published: 1970
Sponsoring organization: Comenius Univ.
ISSN: 0083-4106
MLA acronym: EthS

SUBSCRIPTION INFORMATION

Frequency of publication: Annual
Circulation: 1,000
Available in microform: No
Subscription address: Central Library, Faculty of Philosophy, Comenius Univ., Šafárikovo 6, 81806 Bratislava, Slovak Republic

ADVERTISING INFORMATION

Advertising accepted: No

EDITORIAL DESCRIPTION

Scope: Publishes articles on Slavic ethnology.
Reviews books: Yes
Publishes notes: Yes
Languages accepted: English; German; French
Prints abstracts: Yes
Author-anonymous submission: No

SUBMISSION REQUIREMENTS

Restrictions on contributors: Contributors must be specialists in Slavic ethnology.
Author pays submission fee: Yes
Author pays page charges: No
Length of articles: 20-25 typescript pp.
Length of book reviews: 3-5 pp.
Length of notes: 3-5 pp.
Style: MLA
Number of copies required: 2
Copyright ownership: Comenius Univ.
Rejected manuscripts: Returned
Time before publication decision: 6 mos.
Time between decision and publication: 1 yr.
Number of reviewers: 2 plus Editorial Board
Articles submitted per year: 20
Articles published per year: 10-15
Book reviews published per year: 5-10
Notes submitted per year: 5-10
Notes published per year: 5-10

(933)
*Ethnologie Française: Revue Trimestrielle de la Société d'Ethnologie Française

Gérard Collomb, Editor
Musée National des Arts & Traditions Populaires
6, route du Mahatma Gandhi
75116 Paris, France

Telephone: (33) 1 44176084
Fax: (33) 1 44176060
First published: 1971
Sponsoring organization: Centre d'Ethnologie Française; Centre National de la Recherche Scientifique; Réunion des Musées Nationaux
ISSN: 0046-2616
MLA acronym: EthnoF

SUBSCRIPTION INFORMATION

Frequency of publication: 4 times/yr.
Circulation: 1,800
Available in microform: No
Subscription address: Armand Colin Editeur, 103, boulevard St. Michel, 75240 Paris Cedex 05, France
Additional subscription address: Armand Colin, B.P. 22, 41353 Vineuil Cedex, France

ADVERTISING INFORMATION

Advertising accepted: Yes, on an exchange basis

EDITORIAL DESCRIPTION

Scope: Concerned with all French-speaking cultures and societies of the past and present. Journal is characterized by an interdisciplinary approach to ethnology and publishes detailed studies on controversial subjects, monographs on an object, workshop, or event, and technical documents.
Reviews books: Yes
Publishes notes: Yes
Languages accepted: French
Prints abstracts: Yes

SUBMISSION REQUIREMENTS

Restrictions on contributors: None
Author pays submission fee: No
Author pays page charges: No
Length of articles: 15-30 double-spaced typescript pp.
Length of book reviews: 6-12 double-spaced typescript pp.
Style: Le Tapuscrit, Paris: Ecole Pratique des Hautes Etudes
Number of copies required: 3
Special requirements: Submit original typescript.
Copyright ownership: Author & editor
Rejected manuscripts: Returned
Time before publication decision: 3-6 mos.
Time between decision and publication: 1 yr.
Number of reviewers: 3 plus Editorial Board
Articles submitted per year: 75
Articles published per year: 66
Book reviews submitted per year: 15
Book reviews published per year: 15

(934)
*Ethnology: An International Journal of Cultural and Social Anthropology

E. Dolores Donohue, Managing Editor
Dept. of Anthropology
Univ. of Pittsburgh
Pittsburgh, PA 15260

First published: 1962
Sponsoring organization: Univ. of Pittsburgh
ISSN: 0014-1828
MLA acronym: Ethnology

SUBSCRIPTION INFORMATION

Frequency of publication: 4 times/yr. (Jan., Apr., July, Oct.)
Circulation: 3,000
Available in microform: Yes
Subscription price: $32.00/yr.
Year to which price refers: 1992

ADVERTISING INFORMATION

Advertising accepted: No

EDITORIAL DESCRIPTION

Scope: Welcomes scientific articles on any aspect of cultural anthropology. Theoretical or methodological discussions are published only if they specifically relate to some body of substantive data.
Reviews books: No
Publishes notes: No
Languages accepted: English
Prints abstracts: No
Author-anonymous submission: Yes

SUBMISSION REQUIREMENTS

Restrictions on contributors: None
Author pays submission fee: Yes
Cost of submission fee: $15.00
Author pays page charges: Yes
Length of articles: 2-30 printed pp.
Number of copies required: 2
Copyright ownership: Journal
Rejected manuscripts: Returned; enclose return postage.
Time before publication decision: 3 mos.
Time between decision and publication: 3 mos.
Number of reviewers: 3
Articles submitted per year: 100-125
Articles published per year: 25-30

(935)
*Ethnomusicology: Journal of the Society for Ethnomusicology

Jaff Todd Titon, Editor
Dept. of Music, Box 1924
Brown Univ.
Providence, RI 02912

Telephone: 401 863-3645
E-mail: Jtiton@brownvm.brown.edu
First published: 1957
Sponsoring organization: Soc. for Ethnomusicology
ISSN: 0014-1836
MLA acronym: Ethnomusicology

SUBSCRIPTION INFORMATION

Frequency of publication: 3 times/yr.
Circulation: 2,500
Available in microform: Yes
Subscription price: $50.00/yr. US (includes membership)
Year to which price refers: 1992
Subscription address: Journals Division, Univ. of Illinois Press, 54 E. Gregory Dr., Champaign, IL 61820

ADVERTISING INFORMATION

Advertising accepted: Yes

EDITORIAL DESCRIPTION

Scope: Publishes original articles in the field of ethnomusicology, broadly defined. Contributions are not limited to members of the Society. Favors the publication of papers revealing new areas and studies, both in content and geographical coverage, and of a speculative and theoretical nature rather than a mainly descriptive one.
Reviews books: Yes
Publishes notes: No
Languages accepted: English
Prints abstracts: No
Author-anonymous submission: Yes

SUBMISSION REQUIREMENTS

Restrictions on contributors: None
Author pays submission fee: No
Author pays page charges: No
Length of articles: 25-45 typescript pp.
Length of book reviews: 600 words
Style: Chicago
Number of copies required: 3
Special requirements: Foreign members may submit manuscripts in idiomatic English, along with a copy of the manuscript in their original language or, preferably, in French, German, or Spanish. Include a 50-100 word abstract and brief biographical data on the author with all manuscripts.
Copyright ownership: Univ. of Illinois Press
Rejected manuscripts: Returned
Time before publication decision: 2-5 mos.
Time between decision and publication: 3-12 mos.
Number of reviewers: 2
Articles submitted per year: 50
Articles published per year: 10-12
Book reviews submitted per year: 40-50
Book reviews published per year: 40-50

(936)
*Ethology

Jane Brockmann, Walter Pflumm, Wolfgang Wickler, & C. Lessells, Editors
Dept. of Zoology
Bartram Hall
Univ. of Florida
Gainesville, FL 32611

Additional editorial address: Wolfgang Wickler, Max-Planck-Inst. für Verhaltensphysiologie, 8130 Seewiesen Post Starnberg, Germany
Telephone: 904 392-1297
Fax: 904 392-3704
First published: 1937
ISSN: 0179-1613
MLA acronym: Ethology

SUBSCRIPTION INFORMATION

Frequency of publication: 12 times/yr.
Circulation: 600
Available in microform: No
Subscription price: 1,044 DM/yr.
Year to which price refers: 1993
Subscription address: Paul Parey Scientific Publishers, 35 West 38th St., Suite 3W, New York, NY 10018
Additional subscription address: Paul Parey Scientific Publishers, Seelbüschring 9-17, P.O. Box 490866, 1000 Berlin 42, Germany
Subscription telephone: (49) 30 707840
Subscription fax: (49) 30 70784199

ADVERTISING INFORMATION

Advertising accepted: No

EDITORIAL DESCRIPTION

Scope: Publishes articles in the field of behavioral research.
Reviews books: Yes
Publishes notes: Yes
Languages accepted: English; German
Prints abstracts: Yes
Author-anonymous submission: No

SUBMISSION REQUIREMENTS

Restrictions on contributors: None
Author pays submission fee: No
Author pays page charges: No
Length of articles: 12 pp.
Length of book reviews: No restrictions
Length of notes: 5-6 pp.
Style: Scientific
Number of copies required: 3
Special requirements: Consult *Instructions to authors*
Copyright ownership: Publisher
Rejected manuscripts: Returned
Time before publication decision: 2 mos.
Time between decision and publication: 5 mos.
Number of reviewers: 2-3
Articles submitted per year: 160
Articles published per year: 80
Book reviews published per year: 100
Notes submitted per year: 6
Notes published per year: 4

(937)
*Etnolog: Glasnik Slovenskega Etnografskega Muzeja/Bulletin of the Slovene Ethnographic Museum

Inja Smerdel, Editor
Slovenski Etnografski Muzej
Prešernova 20
61000 Ljubljana, Slovenia

Telephone: (38) 61 218886; (38) 61 218862
Fax: (38) 61 218844
First published: 1926
Historical variations in title: Formerly *Slovenski Etnograf*
Sponsoring organization: Ministrstva za Kulturo Republike Slovenije
ISSN: 0354-0316
MLA acronym: Etnolog

SUBSCRIPTION INFORMATION

Frequency of publication: Annual
Available in microform: No
Subscription price: $8.00/yr.
Year to which price refers: 1991-92

ADVERTISING INFORMATION

Advertising accepted: No

EDITORIAL DESCRIPTION

Scope: Publishes articles on ethnology.
Reviews books: Yes
Publishes notes: Yes
Languages accepted: Slovenian; English; German; French
Prints abstracts: Yes

SUBMISSION REQUIREMENTS

Author pays submission fee: No
Author pays page charges: No
Length of articles: 15-40 pp.
Length of book reviews: 1-5 pp.
Length of notes: 1/2-2 pp.
Number of copies required: 1
Copyright ownership: Author
Number of reviewers: 7

(938)
*Etudes

Jean-Yves Calvez, Editor
14, rue d'Assas
75006 Paris, France

Telephone: (33) 1 44394829
First published: 1856
ISSN: 0014-1941
MLA acronym: Etudes

SUBSCRIPTION INFORMATION

Frequency of publication: 11 times/yr.
Circulation: 14,000
Available in microform: No
Subscription price: 395 F/yr. France; 490 F/yr. elsewhere
Year to which price refers: 1991

ADVERTISING INFORMATION

Advertising accepted: Yes

EDITORIAL DESCRIPTION

Scope: Publishes articles on culture, society, and religion.
Reviews books: Yes
Publishes notes: Yes
Languages accepted: French
Prints abstracts: No
Author-anonymous submission: No

SUBMISSION REQUIREMENTS

Restrictions on contributors: None
Author pays submission fee: No
Author pays page charges: No
Length of articles: 5,000 words
Length of book reviews: 250 words
Length of notes: 10,000 words
Number of copies required: 2
Copyright ownership: Journal
Rejected manuscripts: Not returned
Time before publication decision: 2 weeks
Time between decision and publication: 4 mos.
Number of reviewers: 6-12
Articles submitted per year: 200
Articles published per year: 90
Book reviews submitted per year: 1,500
Book reviews published per year: 600
Notes submitted per year: 50
Notes published per year: 40

(939)
*Etudes Anglaises: Grande-Bretagne, Etats-Unis

Serge Soupel, Editor
2 à 4, quai George Sand
78360 Montesson, France

Telephone: (33) 1 39138857
First published: 1937
Sponsoring organization: Centre National de la Recherche Scientifique & Centre National des Lettres
ISSN: 0014-195X
MLA acronym: EA

SUBSCRIPTION INFORMATION

Frequency of publication: 4 times/yr. (Mar., June, Sept., Dec.)
Circulation: 1,000
Available in microform: Yes
Subscription price: 290 F/yr. France; 410 F/yr. elsewhere; 282 F/yr. students France; 390 F/yr. students elsewhere
Year to which price refers: 1991
Subscription address: Didier-Erudition, 6, rue de la Sorbonne, 75005 Paris, France
Subscription telephone: (33) 1 43544757
Subscription fax: (33) 1 40517385

ADVERTISING INFORMATION

Advertising accepted: Yes
Advertising rates: 2,000 F/full page

EDITORIAL DESCRIPTION

Scope: Publishes articles on English and American studies, including literature, language, and culture.
Reviews books: Yes
Publishes notes: Yes
Languages accepted: English; French
Prints abstracts: Yes
Author-anonymous submission: Yes

SUBMISSION REQUIREMENTS

Restrictions on contributors: None
Author pays submission fee: No
Author pays page charges: No
Length of articles: 10-12 printed pp.
Length of book reviews: No restrictions
Length of notes: 2,500-3,000 words minimum
Style: MLA
Number of copies required: 2
Special requirements: Submit 2 copies of 100-word abstract in English.
Copyright ownership: Didier Erudition
Rejected manuscripts: Not returned
Time before publication decision: 1 yr.
Time between decision and publication: 6 mos.
Number of reviewers: 2 plus Editor
Articles submitted per year: 50
Articles published per year: 25
Book reviews submitted per year: 100-120
Book reviews published per year: 100-120
Notes submitted per year: 10
Notes published per year: 2-3

(940)
Les Etudes Balkaniques Tchécoslovaques

Jan Petr, Čestmír Amort, & Zdeněk Urban, Editors
c/o Filosofická Fakulta
Univ. Karlova v Praze
116 38 Prague 1, Czech Republic

First published: 1966
Sponsoring organization: Univ. Karlova v Praze, Filosofická Fakulta
ISSN: 0425-4783
MLA acronym: EBT

SUBSCRIPTION INFORMATION

Frequency of publication: Irregular
Circulation: 500
Available in microform: No

ADVERTISING INFORMATION

Advertising accepted: No

EDITORIAL DESCRIPTION

Scope: Publishes studies in Balkan languages, literatures, and folklore.
Reviews books: No
Publishes notes: No
Languages accepted: French; English; German
Prints abstracts: No

SUBMISSION REQUIREMENTS

Restrictions on contributors: None
Length of articles: 5-40 typescript pp.
Number of copies required: 2
Copyright ownership: Charles Univ.
Rejected manuscripts: Returned
Time before publication decision: 6 mos.
Number of reviewers: 5

(941)
*Etudes Baudelairiennes

Claude Pichois, Editor
Editions de la Baconnière SA
19 ave. du Collège
C.P. 185
2017 Boudry, Switzerland

Telephone: (41) 38 421004
First published: 1970
MLA acronym: EBaud

SUBSCRIPTION INFORMATION

Frequency of publication: Irregular
Available in microform: No

ADVERTISING INFORMATION

Advertising accepted: No

EDITORIAL DESCRIPTION

Scope: Publishes studies on the works of Baudelaire.
Reviews books: No
Publishes notes: No
Languages accepted: French
Author-anonymous submission: No

SUBMISSION REQUIREMENTS

Author pays submission fee: No
Author pays page charges: No
Length of books: 180-250 pp.
Number of copies required: 1
Copyright ownership: Editions de la Baconnière
Rejected manuscripts: Returned
Number of reviewers: 2-3
Books published per year: 0-1

(942)
*Etudes Britanniques Contemporaines: Revue de la Société d'Etudes Anglaises Contemporaines

Alain Blayac, Editor
Publications de la Recherche
Univ. Paul Valéry-Montpellier III
B.P. 5043
34032 Montpellier Cedex, France

Telephone: (33) 67142201
Fax: (33) 67142052
First published: 1992
Sponsoring organization: Soc. d'Etudes Anglaises Contemporaines (S.E.A.C.)
ISSN: 1168-4917
MLA acronym: EBC

SUBSCRIPTION INFORMATION

Frequency of publication: 2 times/yr.
Circulation: 250
Available in microform: No
Subscription price: 120 F/yr.
Year to which price refers: 1993

ADVERTISING INFORMATION

Advertising accepted: No

EDITORIAL DESCRIPTION

Scope: Publishes articles on contemporary studies on Britain. Includes studies on British literature, culture, and politics.
Reviews books: Yes
Publishes notes: Yes
Languages accepted: French; English
Prints abstracts: No
Author-anonymous submission: No

SUBMISSION REQUIREMENTS

Author pays submission fee: No

Author pays page charges: No
Length of articles: 13,000-15,000 words
Length of book reviews: 2,500 words
Style: MLA
Number of copies required: 1
Special requirements: Submit typescript and diskette.
Copyright ownership: Univ. Paul Valéry, Montpellier
Time before publication decision: 6 mos.
Time between decision and publication: 3 mos.
Number of reviewers: 2
Articles published per year: 15-20

(943)
Etudes Celtiques

Edward Bachellery, Editor
Editions du CNRS
1 Place Aristide Briand
92195 Meudon Cedex, France

First published: 1936
Sponsoring organization: Centre National de la Recherche Scientifique
ISSN: 0373-1928
MLA acronym: EC

SUBSCRIPTION INFORMATION

Frequency of publication: Annual
Available in microform: No
Subscription address: Presses du CNRS, 20-22 rue Saint-Amand, 75015 Paris, France

ADVERTISING INFORMATION

Advertising accepted: No

EDITORIAL DESCRIPTION

Scope: Publishes articles from various scholarly disciplines which deal with the Celtic world, past and present: ancient and modern linguistics and philology, archaeology, epigraphy, numismatics, the history of literature, of art, of law, and of religion. Includes news items and a bibliographical section.
Reviews books: Yes
Publishes notes: Yes
Languages accepted: French; English; German; Spanish; Italian
Prints abstracts: No
Author-anonymous submission: No

SUBMISSION REQUIREMENTS

Restrictions on contributors: None
Author pays submission fee: No
Author pays page charges: No
Length of articles: 25 pp. maximum
Length of book reviews: 2 pp. maximum
Length of notes: 4 pp.
Number of copies required: 1
Copyright ownership: Centre National de la Recherche Scientifique
Rejected manuscripts: Returned
Time before publication decision: 2 mos.
Time between decision and publication: 8 mos.
Number of reviewers: 1
Articles submitted per year: 19
Articles published per year: 15
Book reviews submitted per year: 20
Book reviews published per year: 11
Notes submitted per year: 8
Notes published per year: 6

(944)
*Les Etudes Classiques

W. Derouau, A. Wankenne, S.J., L. Isebaert, & P. Marchetti, Editors
Fac. Notre-Dame de la Paix
Faculté de Philosophie et Lettres
61, rue de Bruxelles
5000 Namur, Belgium

Telephone: (33) 81 724189
Fax: (33) 81 724203
First published: 1932
Sponsoring organization: A.S.B.L. Société des Etudes Classiques
ISSN: 0014-200X
MLA acronym: ECl

SUBSCRIPTION INFORMATION

Frequency of publication: 4 times/yr. (Jan., Apr., July, Oct.)
Circulation: 1,000
Available in microform: No
Subscription price: 1,200 BF/yr.
Year to which price refers: 1992

ADVERTISING INFORMATION

Advertising accepted: Yes

EDITORIAL DESCRIPTION

Scope: Publishes articles on classical studies, writings of the ancients, and the connections between classical culture and modern European literature.
Reviews books: Yes
Publishes notes: Yes
Languages accepted: French
Prints abstracts: No
Author-anonymous submission: No

SUBMISSION REQUIREMENTS

Restrictions on contributors: None
Author pays submission fee: No
Author pays page charges: No
Length of articles: 10-12 pp.
Length of book reviews: 1/2 p.
Length of notes: 150-300 words
Style: None
Number of copies required: 1
Special requirements: Include 200-word abstract.
Copyright ownership: Journal
Rejected manuscripts: Returned
Time before publication decision: 6 mos.
Time between decision and publication: 6 mos.
Number of reviewers: 4
Articles submitted per year: 70
Articles published per year: 24
Book reviews submitted per year: 300
Book reviews published per year: 250
Notes submitted per year: 20
Notes published per year: 10

(945)
*Etudes Créoles

Marie-Christine Hazael-Massieux, Editor
Univ. de Provence
29 av. R. Schumann
13621 Aix-en-Provence, France

Telephone: (33) 42643990
Fax: (33) 42590019
First published: 1978
Sponsoring organization: L'Association des Universités Partiellement ou Entièrement de Langue Française; L'Agence de Coopération Culturelle & Technique
ISSN: 0708-2398
MLA acronym: EtCr

SUBSCRIPTION INFORMATION

Frequency of publication: 2 times/yr.

Circulation: 800
Available in microform: No
Subscription price: 150 F ($30.00)/yr.
Year to which price refers: 1992
Subscription address: Soc. Nouvelle, Didier Erudition, 6, rue de la Sorbonne, 75005 Paris, France
Additional subscription address: APRODEC, Inst. d'Etudes Creoles, 29 av. Schuman, 13621 Aix-en-Provence, France
Subscription telephone: (33) 1 43544757

ADVERTISING INFORMATION

Advertising accepted: Yes

EDITORIAL DESCRIPTION

Scope: Publishes articles on Creole, Caribbean, and Indian Ocean language, literature, culture, folklore, and civilization.
Reviews books: Yes
Publishes notes: No
Languages accepted: French; French Creole; English
Prints abstracts: No
Author-anonymous submission: Yes

SUBMISSION REQUIREMENTS

Restrictions on contributors: None
Author pays submission fee: No
Author pays page charges: No
Length of articles: 15-30 pp.
Number of copies required: 2
Special requirements: Submit short abstract.
Copyright ownership: AUPELF
Time before publication decision: 5-12 mos.
Time between decision and publication: 5-12 mos.
Number of reviewers: 2-3
Articles submitted per year: 30
Articles published per year: 15
Book reviews submitted per year: 25
Book reviews published per year: 15

(946)
Etudes de Langue et Littérature Françaises

Katsumi Kawamura, Editor
Soc. Japonaise de Langue & Littérature Françaises
Maison Franco-Japonaise
2-3 Kanda-Surugadai
Chiyoda-ku
Tokyo, Japan

Sponsoring organization: Soc. Japonaise de Langue & Littérature Françaises
ISSN: 0425-4929
MLA acronym: ELLF

EDITORIAL DESCRIPTION

Reviews books: No
Languages accepted: French
Prints abstracts: No

(947)
Etudes de Lettres

Eric Hicks, Editor
Fac. des Lettres
BFSH 2
1015 Lausanne-Dorigny, Switzerland

First published: 1926
Sponsoring organization: Univ. de Lausanne, Fac. des Lettres; Soc. des Etudes de Lettres
ISSN: 0014-2026
MLA acronym: EdL

SUBSCRIPTION INFORMATION

Frequency of publication: 4 times/yr.
Available in microform: No

Subscription price: 50 SwF/yr. Switzerland; 60 SwF/yr. elsewhere
Year to which price refers: 1992

ADVERTISING INFORMATION

Advertising accepted: No

EDITORIAL DESCRIPTION

Scope: Publishes articles and studies written by members of the Faculty of Arts.
Reviews books: Yes
Publishes notes: No
Languages accepted: French; English; German; Italian
Prints abstracts: Yes

SUBMISSION REQUIREMENTS

Restrictions on contributors: First priority is given to Lausanne students and professors; second to French-speaking Swiss; and lastly to authors from other countries.
Author pays submission fee: No
Author pays page charges: No
Length of articles: No restrictions
Length of book reviews: No restrictions
Style: None
Number of copies required: 1
Copyright ownership: Journal & author
Rejected manuscripts: Returned
Time before publication decision: 3 mos.
Time between decision and publication: 1 yr.
Number of reviewers: 2

(948)
Etudes de Linguistique Appliquée

Robert Galisson, D. Coste, & F. Marchand, Editors
Didier Erudition
6, rue de la Sorbonne
75005 Paris, France

First published: 1962
ISSN: 0071-190X
MLA acronym: ELA

SUBSCRIPTION INFORMATION

Frequency of publication: 4 times/yr.
Circulation: 1,500
Available in microform: Yes

ADVERTISING INFORMATION

Advertising accepted: Yes

EDITORIAL DESCRIPTION

Scope: Publishes articles on applied linguistics and language teaching and learning. Issues are thematically organized.
Reviews books: No
Publishes notes: No
Languages accepted: French
Prints abstracts: Yes
Author-anonymous submission: No

SUBMISSION REQUIREMENTS

Author pays submission fee: No
Author pays page charges: No
Length of articles: 4,500 words
Style: MLA
Number of copies required: 2
Copyright ownership: Assigned by author to publisher
Rejected manuscripts: Not returned
Time before publication decision: 2 mos.
Time between decision and publication: 1 yr.
Number of reviewers: 2-3
Articles submitted per year: 100
Articles published per year: 25

(949)
*Etudes Finno-Ougriennes

Jean Perrot, Editor
Centre d'Etudes Finno-Ougriennes
13, Rue de Santeuil
75005 Paris, France

Fax: (33) 1 45874175
First published: 1972
Sponsoring organization: Assn. pour le Développement des Etudes Finno-Ougriennes (A.D.E.F.O.)
MLA acronym: EFO

SUBSCRIPTION INFORMATION

Frequency of publication: Annual
Available in microform: No
Subscription price: 200 F/yr. (includes A.D.E.F.O. membership)
Year to which price refers: 1991

ADVERTISING INFORMATION

Advertising accepted: No

EDITORIAL DESCRIPTION

Scope: Publishes articles on Finno-Ugric linguistics, Finno-Ugric languages, and peoples speaking Finno-Ugric languages.
Reviews books: Yes
Publishes notes: Yes
Languages accepted: French; English; Russian; German
Prints abstracts: No
Author-anonymous submission: No

SUBMISSION REQUIREMENTS

Author pays submission fee: No
Author pays page charges: No
Number of copies required: 2
Copyright ownership: A.D.E.F.O.
Rejected manuscripts: Returned
Time before publication decision: 3 mos.
Time between decision and publication: 20 mos. maximum
Number of reviewers: 2
Articles published per year: 10
Book reviews published per year: 10
Notes published per year: 6

(950)
*Etudes Françaises

Ginette Michaud, Editor
Dept. d'Etudes Françaises
Univ. de Montréal
C.P. 6128, Succ. A.
Montreal, Quebec H3C 3J7, Canada

Telephone: 514 343-7366
Fax: 514 343-2256
First published: 1965
Sponsoring organization: Presses de l'Univ. de Montréal
ISSN: 0014-2085
MLA acronym: EF

SUBSCRIPTION INFORMATION

Frequency of publication: 3 times/yr. (Spring, Fall, Winter)
Circulation: 1,200
Available in microform: Yes
Subscription address: Presses de l'Univ. de Montréal, at the above address

ADVERTISING INFORMATION

Advertising accepted: No

EDITORIAL DESCRIPTION

Scope: Publishes articles on French and Québécois literature, as well as on literary theory.

Reviews books: No
Publishes notes: Yes
Languages accepted: French
Prints abstracts: No
Author-anonymous submission: No

SUBMISSION REQUIREMENTS

Restrictions on contributors: None
Author pays submission fee: No
Author pays page charges: No
Length of articles: 4,000 words
Length of notes: 1,500-2,000 words
Style: None
Number of copies required: 1
Copyright ownership: Presses de l'Univ. de Montréal
Rejected manuscripts: Returned
Time before publication decision: 1 mo.
Time between decision and publication: 6-12 mos.
Number of reviewers: 10
Articles submitted per year: 50-75
Articles published per year: 20-25
Notes submitted per year: 10-15
Notes published per year: 6

(951)
*Etudes Germaniques

Jean-Marie Valentin, Editor
Centre Universitaire du Grand Palais
Cours-la-Reine
75008 Paris, France

Telephone: (33) 1 42259640
First published: 1946-47
Sponsoring organization: Soc. des Etudes Germaniques
ISSN: 0014-2115
MLA acronym: EG

SUBSCRIPTION INFORMATION

Frequency of publication: 4 times/yr.
Circulation: 1,600
Available in microform: Yes
Subscription price: 291 F/yr. France; 411 F/yr. elsewhere; 283 F/yr. students France; 391 F/yr. students elsewhere
Year to which price refers: 1991
Subscription address: Didier Erudition, 6, rue de la Sorbonne, 75005 Paris, France

ADVERTISING INFORMATION

Advertising accepted: Yes
Advertising rates: 400 F/full page

EDITORIAL DESCRIPTION

Scope: Publishes articles on Germany, Austria, Switzerland, and Scandinavian and Netherlandic countries.
Reviews books: Yes
Publishes notes: Yes
Languages accepted: French; German; English
Prints abstracts: No

SUBMISSION REQUIREMENTS

Author pays submission fee: No
Author pays page charges: No
Length of articles: 20 pp.
Length of book reviews: 20 lines
Length of notes: 3-4 pp.
Style: MLA
Number of copies required: 1
Copyright ownership: Soc. des Etudes Germaniques
Time before publication decision: 6-10 mos.
Time between decision and publication: 3-4 mos.
Number of reviewers: 5
Articles submitted per year: 30
Articles published per year: 15
Book reviews published per year: 200
Notes submitted per year: 20
Notes published per year: 12-14

(952)
*Etudes Germano-Africaines: Revue Annuelle de Germanistique Africaine/Jahresschrift für Afrikanische Germanistik/Annual Review of German Studies in Africa

Amadou Booker Sadji, Editor
B.P. 8421
Dakar, Senegal

Telephone: (221) 243415
First published: 1983
ISSN: 0850-640X
MLA acronym: EGA

SUBSCRIPTION INFORMATION

Frequency of publication: Annual
Circulation: 500
Available in microform: No
Subscription price: $25.00/yr. institutions; $15.00/yr. individuals
Year to which price refers: 1992
Subscription address: For US subscriptions: Carter G. Woodson Inst., Univ. of Virginia, 1512 Jefferson Park Ave., Charlottesville, VA 22903
Additional subscription address: In Europe: G. Tiedemann, Kreisauerstr. 4, 1000 Berlin 42, Germany
Subscription telephone: 804 924-3109; (49) 30 8222436

ADVERTISING INFORMATION

Advertising accepted: Yes
Advertising rates: $250.00/full page

EDITORIAL DESCRIPTION

Scope: Publishes articles on the interdisciplinary relationships between German and African cultures and languages.
Reviews books: Yes
Publishes notes: Yes
Languages accepted: French; English; German
Prints abstracts: Yes
Author-anonymous submission: No

SUBMISSION REQUIREMENTS

Restrictions on contributors: None
Author pays submission fee: No
Author pays page charges: No
Length of articles: 4,000 words
Length of book reviews: 700 words
Length of notes: 350 words
Style: None
Number of copies required: 1
Copyright ownership: Journal
Rejected manuscripts: Not returned
Time before publication decision: 9-12 mos.
Time between decision and publication: 6-9 mos.
Number of reviewers: 2
Articles submitted per year: 20
Articles published per year: 10-17
Book reviews submitted per year: 10
Book reviews published per year: 5-10
Notes submitted per year: 15
Notes published per year: 10

(953)
*Etudes Indo-Européennes

Jean-Paul Allard, Editor
Inst. d'Etudes Indo-Européennes
Univ. de Lyon III
74, rue Pasteur
69007 Lyon, France

Telephone: (33) 72722174
First published: 1982
ISSN: 0750-3547
MLA acronym: EtIE

SUBSCRIPTION INFORMATION

Frequency of publication: Annual
Circulation: 20
Available in microform: No
Subscription price: 180 F/yr.
Year to which price refers: 1992

ADVERTISING INFORMATION

Advertising accepted: Yes

EDITORIAL DESCRIPTION

Scope: Publishes articles on Indo-European studies, including language, literature, culture, anthropology, and prehistory.
Reviews books: Yes
Languages accepted: French
Prints abstracts: Yes

SUBMISSION REQUIREMENTS

Restrictions on contributors: None
Author pays page charges: No
Number of copies required: 1
Copyright ownership: Journal
Rejected manuscripts: Not returned
Time before publication decision: 1 mo.
Time between decision and publication: 1 mo.
Number of reviewers: 2

(954)
Etudes Irlandaises: Revue Française d'Histoire, Civilisation et Littérature de l'Irelande

Univ. de Lille III
B.P. 20
59262 Sainghinen en Melantois, France

First published: 1972
Sponsoring organization: Univ. de Lille; Univ. de Rennes; Univ. de Caen; Centre National de la Recherche Scientifique
ISSN: 0183-973X
MLA acronym: EI

SUBSCRIPTION INFORMATION

Frequency of publication: 2 times/yr.
Circulation: 300
Available in microform: No

ADVERTISING INFORMATION

Advertising accepted: Yes

EDITORIAL DESCRIPTION

Scope: Publishes articles on the history, civilization, and literature of Ireland.
Reviews books: Yes
Publishes notes: No
Languages accepted: English; French
Prints abstracts: Yes
Author-anonymous submission: No

SUBMISSION REQUIREMENTS

Restrictions on contributors: None
Author pays submission fee: No
Author pays page charges: No
Length of articles: 5,000 words
Length of book reviews: 600 words
Style: MLA
Number of copies required: 1
Special requirements: Submit typescript on size A4 (8 1/4 in. x 11 3/4 in.) paper.
Copyright ownership: Univ. de Lille, Univ. de Rennes, & Univ. de Caen
Rejected manuscripts: Returned
Time before publication decision: 2-4 mos.
Time between decision and publication: 6 mos.
Number of reviewers: 2
Articles submitted per year: 40
Articles published per year: 20

Book reviews submitted per year: 40
Book reviews published per year: 20

(955)
*Etudes Lawrenciennes

Ginette Katz-Roy, Editor
Univ. de Paris X-Nanterre
200 Avenue de la République
92001 Nanterre Cedex, France

Additional editorial address: 135 rue du Mont Cenis, 75018 Paris, France
Telephone: (33) 1 42588133
Fax: (33) 1 47216744
First published: 1986
Sponsoring organization: Univ. de Paris X-Nanterre
ISSN: 0994-5490
MLA acronym: ELawr

SUBSCRIPTION INFORMATION

Frequency of publication: Annual
Circulation: 250
Available in microform: No
Subscription price: 75 F/yr.
Year to which price refers: 1991
Subscription address: Editions de l'Espace Européan, 89 rue Sartoris, 92250 La Garenne-Colombes, France
Subscription telephone: (33) 1 47829732

ADVERTISING INFORMATION

Advertising accepted: No

EDITORIAL DESCRIPTION

Scope: Publishes articles on the works of D. H. Lawrence.
Reviews books: Yes
Publishes notes: No
Languages accepted: English; French
Prints abstracts: Yes
Author-anonymous submission: No

SUBMISSION REQUIREMENTS

Author pays submission fee: No
Author pays page charges: No
Length of articles: 8,500 words
Length of book reviews: 720 words
Style: MLA
Number of copies required: 2
Special requirements: Submit typescript and diskette.
Copyright ownership: Publisher
Rejected manuscripts: Not returned
Time before publication decision: 6 mos.
Time between decision and publication: 6 mos.
Number of reviewers: 2
Articles submitted per year: 8-16
Articles published per year: 6-8
Book reviews submitted per year: 5
Book reviews published per year: 3

(956)
Etudes Linguistiques: Revue du Département de Linguistique de l'Université de Niamey

Dept. de Linguistique
Univ. de Niamey
B.P. 418
Niamey, Niger

First published: 1979
ISSN: 0255-0393
MLA acronym: ELing

SUBSCRIPTION INFORMATION

Frequency of publication: 2 times/yr. (June, Dec.)
Circulation: 185

EDITORIAL DESCRIPTION

Scope: Publishes articles on African languages and linguistics.
Reviews books: Yes
Languages accepted: English; French
Prints abstracts: Yes

SUBMISSION REQUIREMENTS

Restrictions on contributors: None
Length of articles: 40 typescript pp. maximum
Style: Journal
Number of copies required: 2
Special requirements: Include a 200-word abstract.
Rejected manuscripts: Not returned
Time before publication decision: 3 mos.
Time between decision and publication: 3 mos.
Number of reviewers: 2
Articles published per year: 10

(957)
*Etudes Littéraires

Monique Moser-Verrey, Editor
c/o Assistante à la Rédaction
Fac. des Lettres
Univ. Laval, Ste-Foy
Quebec G1K 7P4, Canada

Telephone: 418 656-7844
Fax: 418 656-2019
First published: 1968
Sponsoring organization: Conseil de Recherches en Sciences Humaines du Canada; Fonds F.C.A.R. pour l'Aide et le Soutien à la Recherche
ISSN: 0014-214X
MLA acronym: ELit

SUBSCRIPTION INFORMATION

Frequency of publication: 3 times/yr.
Circulation: 750
Available in microform: No
Subscription price: C$36.00/yr. institutions; C$22.00/yr. individuals Canada; C$26.00/yr. individuals elsewhere; C$16.00/yr. students Canada
Year to which price refers: 1992
Subscription address: Raymond Dufour, Pavillon Jean-Durand, Univ. Laval, Ste.-Foy, Quebec G1K 7P4, Canada
Subscription telephone: 418 656-3809
Subscription fax: 418 656-2600

ADVERTISING INFORMATION

Advertising accepted: No

EDITORIAL DESCRIPTION

Scope: Publishes articles on literary theory, French and other literatures, cinema, and theater.
Reviews books: Yes
Publishes notes: No
Languages accepted: French
Prints abstracts: Yes
Author-anonymous submission: Yes

SUBMISSION REQUIREMENTS

Restrictions on contributors: Half of the contributions are solicited.
Author pays submission fee: No
Author pays page charges: No
Length of articles: 6,000 words
Length of book reviews: 500 words
Style: Journal
Number of copies required: 4
Special requirements: Submit floppy disk (Microsoft Word 4.01), abstract in French and English, and short bibliography.
Copyright ownership: Journal
Rejected manuscripts: Not returned
Time before publication decision: 2 mos.
Time between decision and publication: 6-9 mos.
Number of reviewers: 3
Articles submitted per year: 35-45
Articles published per year: 25-30
Book reviews submitted per year: 20
Book reviews published per year: 10

(958)
*Etudes Littéraires Françaises

Wolfgang Leiner, Jacqueline Leiner, & Ernst Behler, Editors
Gunter Narr Verlag
P.O. Box 2567
7400 Tübingen, Germany

Telephone: (49) 7071 78091
Fax: (49) 7071 75288
First published: 1978
ISSN: 0338-1900
MLA acronym: ELF

SUBSCRIPTION INFORMATION

Frequency of publication: Irregular
Available in microform: No
Subscription price: 68 DM/yr.
Year to which price refers: 1992
Additional subscription address: In France and French-speaking countries: Editions Sedes, 88, Boulevard Saint-Germain, 75005 Paris, France

ADVERTISING INFORMATION

Advertising accepted: No

EDITORIAL DESCRIPTION

Scope: Publishes monographs on French and francophone literature.
Reviews books: No
Publishes notes: Yes
Languages accepted: French; English; German
Prints abstracts: No
Author-anonymous submission: No

SUBMISSION REQUIREMENTS

Author pays submission fee: No
Author pays page charges: No
Length of books: 200-300 pp.
Style: MLA
Number of copies required: 1
Copyright ownership: Gunter Narr Verlag
Rejected manuscripts: Returned
Time before publication decision: 3-4 weeks
Time between decision and publication: 6 mos.
Number of reviewers: 1
Books published per year: 2-3

(959)
Etudes Philosophiques

Pierre Aubenque, Editor
2-8, rue Francis-de-Croisset
75018 Paris, France

Telephone: (33) 1 46061749
First published: 1926
Sponsoring organization: Soc. d'Etudes Philosophiques
ISSN: 0014-2166
MLA acronym: EP

SUBSCRIPTION INFORMATION

Frequency of publication: 4 times/yr.
Circulation: 2,300
Available in microform: Yes
Subscription price: 315 F/yr. France; 380 F/yr. elsewhere
Year to which price refers: 1992
Subscription address: Presses Universitaires de France, 108, bd. Saint-Germain, 75279 Paris Cedex 06, France

ADVERTISING INFORMATION

Advertising accepted: Yes, on an exchange basis with other journals only

EDITORIAL DESCRIPTION

Scope: Publishes articles on philosophy.
Reviews books: Yes
Publishes notes: Yes
Languages accepted: French
Prints abstracts: Yes

SUBMISSION REQUIREMENTS

Restrictions on contributors: None
Author pays submission fee: No
Author pays page charges: No
Length of articles: 20 pp.
Length of book reviews: 600 words
Length of notes: 2,000 words
Number of copies required: 2
Special requirements: Include a summary in English.
Copyright ownership: Journal
Rejected manuscripts: Returned
Time before publication decision: 1 yr.
Time between decision and publication: 3 mos.
Number of reviewers: 2
Articles submitted per year: 100
Articles published per year: 20-25
Book reviews published per year: 70
Notes published per year: 4

(960)
*Etudes Rabelaisiennes

Librairie Droz S.A.
11, rue Massot
1211 Geneva 12, Switzerland

Telephone: (41) 22 3466666
Fax: (41) 22 3472391
First published: 1956
ISSN: 0531-1969
MLA acronym: ER

SUBSCRIPTION INFORMATION

Frequency of publication: Annual
Available in microform: No

ADVERTISING INFORMATION

Advertising accepted: No

EDITORIAL DESCRIPTION

Scope: Publishes articles on Rabelais.
Reviews books: No
Publishes notes: No
Languages accepted: French; English; Italian
Prints abstracts: No

SUBMISSION REQUIREMENTS

Restrictions on contributors: None
Author pays submission fee: No
Author pays page charges: No
Length of articles: No restrictions
Style: None
Number of copies required: 1
Copyright ownership: Librairie Droz S.A.
Rejected manuscripts: Returned
Time before publication decision: 1 yr.
Time between decision and publication: 1 yr.

(961)
*Etudes Romanes de Brno

Ivan Seidl, Editor
Sborník prací a Spisy Filozofické Fakulty
Masarykovy Univ.
A. Nováka 1
660 88 Brno, Czech Republic

First published: 1965
Sponsoring organization: Masarykovy Univ.
ISSN: 0231-7532
MLA acronym: ERBr

SUBSCRIPTION INFORMATION

Frequency of publication: Annual
Circulation: 500
Available in microform: No
Subscription address: Kníhkupectví-Antikvariát, Dr. Miroslav Mazněl, Dittrichova 13, 12000 Prague 2, Czech Republic

ADVERTISING INFORMATION

Advertising accepted: No

EDITORIAL DESCRIPTION

Scope: Publishes articles on Romance languages and literatures, general linguistics, and literary theory.
Reviews books: Yes
Publishes notes: No
Languages accepted: French; Spanish; Italian
Prints abstracts: No
Author-anonymous submission: No

SUBMISSION REQUIREMENTS

Restrictions on contributors: None
Author pays submission fee: No
Author pays page charges: No
Length of articles: 20 pp. maximum
Length of books: 300 pp. maximum
Length of book reviews: 600 words
Number of copies required: 2
Copyright ownership: Assigned by author to journal
Rejected manuscripts: Returned
Time before publication decision: 6 mos.
Time between decision and publication: 1 yr.
Number of reviewers: 1 plus Editorial Board
Articles submitted per year: 10
Articles published per year: 10
Book reviews submitted per year: 10
Book reviews published per year: 6

(962)
*Etudes Romanes de l'Université d'Odense

Morten Nøjgaard, Editor
Odense Univ.
Centers of Romance Language
Campusvej 55
5230 Odense M, Denmark

Telephone: (45) 66 158600
Fax: (45) 66 158696
First published: 1971
Sponsoring organization: Odense Univ.
ISSN: 0107-7392
MLA acronym: ERUO

SUBSCRIPTION INFORMATION

Frequency of publication: Irregular
Available in microform: No
Subscription address: Odense Univ. Press, at the above address

ADVERTISING INFORMATION

Advertising accepted: No

EDITORIAL DESCRIPTION

Scope: Publishes articles on Romance languages and literatures, linguistics, and literary theory.
Reviews books: No
Publishes notes: No
Languages accepted: French; Italian; Spanish; Portuguese
Prints abstracts: Yes
Author-anonymous submission: No

SUBMISSION REQUIREMENTS

Number of copies required: 3
Copyright ownership: Odense Univ. Press
Rejected manuscripts: Returned
Time before publication decision: 1-2 mos.
Time between decision and publication: 3 mos.
Number of reviewers: 3

(963)
*Eudora Welty Newsletter

W. U. McDonald, Jr., Editor
Dept. of English
Univ. of Toledo
Toledo, OH 43606

Telephone: 419 537-2318
First published: 1977
ISSN: 0146-7220
MLA acronym: EuWN

SUBSCRIPTION INFORMATION

Frequency of publication: 2 times/yr. (Winter, Summer)
Circulation: 150
Available in microform: No
Subscription price: $2.00/yr. US & Canada; $3.00/yr. elsewhere
Year to which price refers: 1992

ADVERTISING INFORMATION

Advertising accepted: No

EDITORIAL DESCRIPTION

Scope: Publishes bibliographical scholarship on Eudora Welty, including short bibliographic notes, checklists of writings by and about Welty, queries from Welty scholars and collectors, want lists, information about collections and acquisitions of Welty materials, and news about Welty.
Reviews books: No
Publishes notes: Yes
Languages accepted: English
Prints abstracts: No
Author-anonymous submission: No

SUBMISSION REQUIREMENTS

Restrictions on contributors: Unsolicited book reviews are not accepted.
Author pays submission fee: No
Author pays page charges: No
Length of notes: 1,600 words maximum
Style: MLA
Number of copies required: 1
Special requirements: Submit original typescript.
Copyright ownership: Not copyrighted; copyright application on individual notes will be applied for if author requests.
Rejected manuscripts: Returned; enclose SASE.
Time before publication decision: 2-3 weeks
Time between decision and publication: 6 mos. maximum
Number of reviewers: 1-2
Notes published per year: 8-10

(964)
*The Eugene O'Neill Review

Frederick Wilkins, Editor
Dept. of English
Suffolk Univ.
Boston, MA 02114

Additional editorial address: Steven F. Bloom, Book Review Editor, Dept. of English, Emmanuel College, Boston, MA 02115; Yvonne Shafer, Play Review Editor, Dept. of Theater, Univ. of Colorado, Boulder, CO 80309
Telephone: 617 573-8272
First published: 1977
Sponsoring organization: Suffolk Univ.; Eugene O'Neill Soc.
ISSN: 1040-9843
MLA acronym: EONR

SUBSCRIPTION INFORMATION

Frequency of publication: 2 times/yr. (Spring, Fall)
Circulation: 450
Available in microform: No
Subscription price: $15.00/yr. institutions; $10.00/yr. individuals US & Canada; $15.00/yr. individuals elsewhere
Year to which price refers: 1992

ADVERTISING INFORMATION

Advertising accepted: Yes
Advertising rates: $50.00/half page; $100.00/full page

EDITORIAL DESCRIPTION

Scope: Publishes articles on O'Neill's life and works, illustrated reviews of productions, reviews of books about the playwright and the plays, abstracts of articles on O'Neill published elsewhere, and news, notes, and queries.
Reviews books: Yes
Publishes notes: Yes
Languages accepted: English
Prints abstracts: No
Author-anonymous submission: No

SUBMISSION REQUIREMENTS

Restrictions on contributors: None
Author pays submission fee: No
Author pays page charges: No
Length of articles: 1,000-2,500 words
Length of book reviews: 750-1,500 words; longer articles are accepted
Length of notes: 100-500 words
Style: MLA preferred
Number of copies required: 2
Copyright ownership: Journal
Rejected manuscripts: Returned with comments
Time before publication decision: 3-6 mos.
Time between decision and publication: 6-12 mos.
Number of reviewers: 2-6
Articles submitted per year: 30
Articles published per year: 15-20
Book reviews submitted per year: 15
Book reviews published per year: 10-15
Notes submitted per year: 120
Notes published per year: 80-100

(965)
*Euphorion: Zeitschrift für Literaturgeschichte

Wolfgang Adam, Editor
Univ. Osnabrück
Fachbereich Sprach- & Literaturwissenschaft
Postfach 4469
4500 Osnabrück, Germany

Additional editorial address: Bergische Univ./Gesamthochschule Wuppertal, Gauss Str. 20, 5600 Wuppertal 1, Germany
First published: 1894
ISSN: 0014-2328
MLA acronym: Euphorion

SUBSCRIPTION INFORMATION

Frequency of publication: 4 times/yr. (Mar., June, Sept., Dec.)
Circulation: 1,100
Available in microform: No
Subscription address: Carl Winter Universitätsverlag, Lutherstr. 59, Postfach 106140, 6900 Heidelberg 1, Germany

ADVERTISING INFORMATION

Advertising accepted: Yes

EDITORIAL DESCRIPTION

Scope: Publishes articles on European literary history through the present.
Reviews books: No
Publishes notes: Yes
Languages accepted: German; English; French
Prints abstracts: No

SUBMISSION REQUIREMENTS

Author pays submission fee: No
Author pays page charges: No
Style: Journal
Number of copies required: 1
Special requirements: Submit original typescript.

(966)
*Europäische Hochschulschriften/Publications Universitaire Européennes/European University Studies

Verlag Peter Lang AG
Jupiterstr. 15
Postfach 277
3015 Bern, Switzerland

Telephone: (41) 31 9411122
Fax: (41) 31 9411131
First published: 1967
ISSN: 0531-240X
MLA acronym: EurH

SUBSCRIPTION INFORMATION

Frequency of publication: Irregular
Available in microform: No
Additional subscription address: Verlag Peter Lang GmbH, Eschborner Landstr. 42-50, 6000 Frankfurt am Main 90, Germany
Subscription telephone: (49) 69 7807050; (41) 31 941122
Subscription fax: (49) 69 785893

ADVERTISING INFORMATION

Advertising accepted: No

EDITORIAL DESCRIPTION

Scope: Publishes monographs on scholarly information and development.
Publishes notes: Yes
Languages accepted: English; German; French; Spanish; Italian
Prints abstracts: No

SUBMISSION REQUIREMENTS

Restrictions on contributors: None
Author pays submission fee: No
Author pays page charges: No
Length of books: 150-600 pp.
Number of copies required: 1
Copyright ownership: Verlag Peter Lang AG
Rejected manuscripts: Returned
Time before publication decision: 1 mo.
Time between decision and publication: 3 mos.
Number of reviewers: 1-2
Articles submitted per year: 1,500
Articles published per year: 1,000

(967)
*Europe: Revue Littéraire Mensuelle

Charles Dobzynski & Jean Baptiste Para, Editors
146, rue du Fg. Poissonnière
75010 Paris, France

Telephone: (33) 1 42819103
Fax: (33) 1 48741999
First published: 1923
ISSN: 0014-2751
MLA acronym: Europe

SUBSCRIPTION INFORMATION

Frequency of publication: 8 times/yr.
Circulation: 10,000
Available in microform: No
Subscription price: 550 F/yr.
Year to which price refers: 1992

ADVERTISING INFORMATION

Advertising accepted: Yes
Advertising rates: 3,000 F/full page

EDITORIAL DESCRIPTION

Scope: Literary review
Reviews books: Yes
Publishes notes: Yes
Languages accepted: French
Prints abstracts: No

SUBMISSION REQUIREMENTS

Restrictions on contributors: None
Author pays submission fee: No
Author pays page charges: No
Length of articles: 10 double-spaced typescript pp. of 25 lines each
Length of book reviews: 1 typescript p.
Length of notes: 1 typescript p.
Number of copies required: 1
Copyright ownership: Author
Rejected manuscripts: Returned; enclose return postage.
Time before publication decision: 2-3 mos.
Time between decision and publication: 2 mos.
Number of reviewers: 3
Articles submitted per year: 400-500
Articles published per year: 250
Notes submitted per year: 300
Notes published per year: 100

(968)
*European Journal of Disorders of Communication

Evelyn Abberton, Editor
Dept. of Phonetics & Linguistics
Univ. College London
Gower St.
London WC1E 6BT, England

Telephone: (44) 71 3877050
Fax: (44) 71 3834108
E-mail: Uclyera@uk.ac.ucl
First published: 1965
Historical variations in title: Formerly *British Journal of Disorders of Communication*
Sponsoring organization: College of Speech & Language Therapists, London
ISSN: 0963-7273
MLA acronym: EJDC

SUBSCRIPTION INFORMATION

Frequency of publication: 4 times/yr.
Circulation: 6,000
Available in microform: Yes
Subscription price: $125.00 (£70.00)/yr. institutions; $80.00 (£45.00)/yr. individuals

Year to which price refers: 1992
Subscription address: Whurr Publishers Ltd., 19B Compton Terrace, London N1 2UN, England
Additional subscription address: In N. America: Whurr Publishers, P.O. Box 1897, Lawrence, KS 66044-8897
Subscription telephone: (44) 71 3595979; 913 843-1221
Subscription fax: (44) 71 2265290; 913 843-1274

ADVERTISING INFORMATION

Advertising accepted: Yes
Advertising rates: £225.00/half page; £375.00/full page

EDITORIAL DESCRIPTION

Scope: Publishes articles on normal communication and communication disorders, including hearing, speech, writing, and nonverbal communication, as well as relevant contributions in subjects such as audiology, phonetics, linguistics, education, psycholinguistics, sociolinguistics, child psychology, information technology, neuropsychology, neurology, ENT surgery and medicine.
Reviews books: Yes
Publishes notes: Yes
Languages accepted: English
Prints abstracts: Yes
Author-anonymous submission: No

SUBMISSION REQUIREMENTS

Author pays submission fee: No
Author pays page charges: No
Length of articles: 7,000 words
Length of book reviews: 500 words
Length of notes: 1,500 words
Style: British Psychological Soc.
Number of copies required: 4
Special requirements: Include a 200-word abstract and key words.
Copyright ownership: College of Speech & Language Therapists
Rejected manuscripts: Not returned
Time before publication decision: 6-12 mos.
Time between decision and publication: 3 mos.
Number of reviewers: 2
Articles published per year: 20-25
Book reviews published per year: 12-16
Notes published per year: 5

(969)
European Joyce Studies

Fritz Senn & Christine van Boheemen, Editors
Zurich James Joyce Foundation
Augustinergasse 9
8001 Zurich, Switzerland

Additional editorial address: Prinsengracht 666, 1017 KW Amsterdam, Netherlands
First published: 1989
MLA acronym: EJS

SUBSCRIPTION INFORMATION

Frequency of publication: Irregular
Circulation: 350
Available in microform: No
Subscription address: Editions Rodopi, Keizersgracht 302-304, 1016 EX Amsterdam, Netherlands
Additional subscription address: Editions Rodopi, 233 Peachtree St. NE, Suite 404, Atlanta, GA 30303-1504

ADVERTISING INFORMATION

Advertising accepted: No

EDITORIAL DESCRIPTION

Scope: Publishes British and European studies on James Joyce and his works and influence.
Reviews books: No
Publishes notes: No
Languages accepted: English
Prints abstracts: No
Author-anonymous submission: No

SUBMISSION REQUIREMENTS

Author pays submission fee: No
Author pays page charges: No
Length of books: 250 pp. maximum
Style: MLA
Number of copies required: 2
Copyright ownership: Rodopi
Rejected manuscripts: Returned
Articles submitted per year: 35
Articles published per year: 18
Books submitted per year: 3-4
Books published per year: 1

(970)
European Romantic Review

Frederick Burwick, Editor
Dept. of English
Univ. of California, Los Angeles
Los Angeles, CA 90024

Additional editorial address: Grant F. Scott, Review Editor, English Dept., Muhlenberg College, Allentown, PA 18104
Telephone: 213 825-1275
First published: 1990
ISSN: 1050-9585
MLA acronym: ERR

SUBSCRIPTION INFORMATION

Frequency of publication: 2 times/yr. (Summer, Winter)
Circulation: 400
Available in microform: No
Subscription price: $22.00/yr. institutions; $14.00/yr. individuals
Year to which price refers: 1992
Subscription address: Logos Press, P.O. Box 591402, San Francisco, CA 94159
Subscription telephone: 415 681-5853

ADVERTISING INFORMATION

Advertising accepted: No
Advertising rates: $50.00/half page; $100.00/full page

EDITORIAL DESCRIPTION

Scope: Publishes articles on European literature of the Romantic period. Dedicated to the interdisciplinary study of history, philosophy, art, and literature of the early nineteenth century.
Reviews books: Yes
Publishes notes: No
Languages accepted: English
Prints abstracts: No
Author-anonymous submission: Yes

SUBMISSION REQUIREMENTS

Restrictions on contributors: None
Author pays submission fee: No
Author pays page charges: No
Length of articles: 4,000-10,000 words
Length of book reviews: 2,500 words
Style: MLA
Number of copies required: 2
Copyright ownership: Logos Press
Rejected manuscripts: Returned; enclose SASE
Time before publication decision: 4 mos.
Time between decision and publication: 1 yr.
Number of reviewers: 2
Articles submitted per year: 60
Articles published per year: 10
Book reviews submitted per year: 10
Book reviews published per year: 10-15

(971)
*European Studies Journal

Reinhold Bubser, Editor
Dept. of Modern Languages
Univ. of Northern Iowa
Cedar Falls, IA 50614-0504

Telephone: 319 273-3887; 319 273-2749
Fax: 319 273-2921
First published: 1984
Sponsoring organization: Univ. of Northern Iowa
ISSN: 0820-6244
MLA acronym: ESJ

SUBSCRIPTION INFORMATION

Frequency of publication: 2 times/yr. (Spring, Fall)
Circulation: 500
Available in microform: No
Subscription price: $30.00/yr. institutions; $20.00/yr. individuals
Year to which price refers: 1992-93

ADVERTISING INFORMATION

Advertising accepted: No

EDITORIAL DESCRIPTION

Scope: Publishes articles about European literature, thought, culture, economics, and politics.
Reviews books: Yes
Publishes notes: Yes
Languages accepted: English
Prints abstracts: No
Author-anonymous submission: Yes

SUBMISSION REQUIREMENTS

Restrictions on contributors: None
Author pays submission fee: No
Author pays page charges: No
Length of articles: 10-20 double-spaced typescript pp.
Length of book reviews: 500-1,500 words
Length of notes: 200-1,000 words
Style: MLA
Number of copies required: 3
Special requirements: Enclose SASE and a postcard for acknowledgement of manuscript receipt. Author's name should not appear on manuscript, but should be on a separate sheet.
Copyright ownership: Author
Rejected manuscripts: Returned
Time before publication decision: 6-12 mos.
Time between decision and publication: 3-6 mos.
Number of reviewers: 3
Articles submitted per year: 60
Articles published per year: 9-15
Book reviews submitted per year: 30-50
Book reviews published per year: 25
Notes submitted per year: 10-15
Notes published per year: 5

(972)
Eutopias: Teorías/Historia/Discurso

Jenaro Talens, René Jara, & Nicholas Spadaccini, Editors
Inst. de Cine & RTV
Alvaro de Bazán, 16
Valencia 46010, Spain

First published: 1985
Sponsoring organization: Dept. of Spanish & Portuguese, Univ. of Minnesota; Inst. de Cine & RTV/Fundación Inst. Shakespeare, Valencia, Spain
ISSN: 0213-246X
MLA acronym: Eutopias

SUBSCRIPTION INFORMATION

Frequency of publication: 2 times/yr.

Subscription address: Dept. of Spanish & Portuguese, Univ. of Minnesota, 34 Folwell Hall, 9 Pleasant St., SE, Minneapolis, MN 55455

EDITORIAL DESCRIPTION

Scope: Publishes articles on issues related to critical theory, cultural criticism, and literary history, with the purpose of reviewing and redefining the canonical agreements marking these areas of research. The focus is the multidisciplinary inscription of general theory of discourse following the revolutionary emergency of mass media.
Reviews books: No
Publishes notes: Yes
Languages accepted: English; French; Italian; Portuguese; Spanish
Prints abstracts: No

SUBMISSION REQUIREMENTS

Author pays submission fee: No
Author pays page charges: No
Length of articles: 20-30 pp.
Style: MLA
Number of copies required: 2
Special requirements: Contributions must comply with the focus and purpose of the publication. Include a Macintosh or other compatible diskette.
Copyright ownership: Dept. of Spanish & Portuguese, Univ. of Minnesota; Inst. de Cine & RTV/Fundacíon Inst. Shakespeare
Rejected manuscripts: Returned
Time before publication decision: 6 mos.
Time between decision and publication: 4 mos.
Number of reviewers: 3
Articles submitted per year: 35-40
Articles published per year: 25

(973)
*Evelyn Waugh Newsletter and Studies

Paul A. Doyle, Winnifred M. Bogaards, Alfred W. Borrello, Robert Murray Davis, Heinz Kosok, & Charles E. Linck, Jr., Editors
English Dept.
Nassau Community College
State Univ. of New York
Garden City, NY 11530

Telephone: 516 222-7187
First published: 1967
Historical variations in title: Formerly *Evelyn Waugh Newsletter*
Sponsoring organization: Evelyn Waugh Soc.
ISSN: 0014-3693
MLA acronym: EWNS

SUBSCRIPTION INFORMATION

Frequency of publication: 3 times/yr. (Apr., Sept., Dec.)
Circulation: 200
Available in microform: No
Subscription price: $8.00/yr.
Year to which price refers: 1992

ADVERTISING INFORMATION

Advertising accepted: Yes
Advertising rates: $15.00/half page; $30.00/full page

EDITORIAL DESCRIPTION

Scope: Includes notes, brief essays, and news items designed to stimulate research and continue interest in the life and writings of Evelyn Waugh.
Reviews books: Yes
Publishes notes: Yes
Languages accepted: English
Prints abstracts: No
Author-anonymous submission: Yes

SUBMISSION REQUIREMENTS

Restrictions on contributors: None
Author pays submission fee: No
Author pays page charges: No
Length of articles: 200-600 words
Length of book reviews: 200-250 words
Length of notes: 50-200 words
Style: MLA
Number of copies required: 1
Copyright ownership: Author
Rejected manuscripts: Returned; enclose SASE.
Time before publication decision: 3-8 mos.
Time between decision and publication: 1-3 yrs.
Number of reviewers: 2-3
Articles submitted per year: 20
Articles published per year: 12
Book reviews submitted per year: 3-7
Book reviews published per year: 5-6
Notes submitted per year: 10
Notes published per year: 8

(974)
*Exemplaria: A Journal of Theory in Medieval and Renaissance Studies

R. A. Shoaf, Patrick Geary, Barrie Ruth Straus, Julian N. Wasserman, & Judith P. Shoaf, Editors
Dept. of English
Univ. of Florida
Gainesville, FL 32611-2036

Additional editorial address: Dept. of English, Loyola Univ., New Orleans, LA 70118
Telephone: 904 392-0795; 904 392-5299
E-mail: EXEMPLA@NERVM.Bitnet
First published: 1989
Sponsoring organization: Univ. of Florida; Loyola Univ.; Center for Medieval & Early Renaissance Studies and Medieval & Renaissance Texts & Studies, State Univ. of New York at Binghamton
ISSN: 1041-2573
MLA acronym: Exemplaria

SUBSCRIPTION INFORMATION

Frequency of publication: 2 times/yr. (Spring, Autumn)
Circulation: 400
Available in microform: No
Subscription price: $35.00/yr. institutions; $20.00/yr. individuals; add $7.00/yr. postage outside US
Year to which price refers: 1992
Subscription address: MRTS, LNG99, State Univ. of New York, Binghamton, NY 13901
Subscription telephone: 607 777-6758

ADVERTISING INFORMATION

Advertising accepted: Yes
Advertising rates: $80.00/half page; $120.00/full page

EDITORIAL DESCRIPTION

Scope: Publishes articles on medieval and Renaissance studies, including literature, history, anthropology, and music. Aims to provide a forum where different methods, different terminologies, and different approaches can communicate without sacrificing any of their distinctiveness.
Reviews books: No
Publishes notes: No
Languages accepted: English
Prints abstracts: No
Author-anonymous submission: No

SUBMISSION REQUIREMENTS

Restrictions on contributors: None
Author pays submission fee: No
Author pays page charges: No
Length of articles: 7,000-13,000 words
Style: Chicago
Number of copies required: 2

Special requirements: Submit original typescript and 1 copy along with IBM-compatible diskette in WordPerfect.
Copyright ownership: Medieval & Renaissance Texts & Studies and State Univ. of New York, Binghamton
Rejected manuscripts: Returned
Time before publication decision: 4-6 mos.
Time between decision and publication: 10-15 mos.
Number of reviewers: 2
Articles submitted per year: 60-80
Articles published per year: 15-18

(975)
*Exeter Linguistic Studies

R. R. K. Hartmann, Editor
Dept. of Applied Linguistics
Queen's Building
Univ. of Exeter, Queen's Drive
Exeter EX4 4QH, England

Telephone: (44) 392 264303
Fax: (44) 392 264377
First published: 1976
Sponsoring organization: Univ. of Exeter
ISSN: 0309-4375
MLA acronym: ELSt

SUBSCRIPTION INFORMATION

Frequency of publication: Annual
Circulation: 500
Available in microform: No
Subscription address: University of Exeter Press, Hailey Wing, Reed Hall, Exeter EX4 4QR, England
Subscription telephone: (44) 392 263066
Subscription fax: (44) 392 264420

ADVERTISING INFORMATION

Advertising accepted: No

EDITORIAL DESCRIPTION

Scope: Publishes monograph studies and collections of papers on linguistics and related subjects.
Reviews books: No
Publishes notes: No
Languages accepted: English
Prints abstracts: No
Author-anonymous submission: No

SUBMISSION REQUIREMENTS

Restrictions on contributors: None
Author pays submission fee: No
Author pays page charges: No
Length of articles: 20 pp.
Length of books: 100-200 pp.
Style: Series
Number of copies required: 1
Special requirements: Preparation on word processor is preferred.
Copyright ownership: Univ. of Exeter Press
Rejected manuscripts: Returned
Time before publication decision: 3 mos.
Time between decision and publication: 8 mos.
Number of reviewers: 2
Books submitted per year: 2
Books published per year: 1

(976)
*Explicación de Textos Literarios

Jorge A. Santana, Harry J. Dennis, & Fausto Avendaño, Editors
Dept. of Foreign Languages
California State Univ.
6000 J. St.
Sacramento, CA 95819-6087

Telephone: 916 278-5862

First published: 1972
Sponsoring organization: Dept. of Foreign Languages, California State Univ., Sacramento
ISSN: 0361-9621
MLA acronym: ExTL

SUBSCRIPTION INFORMATION

Frequency of publication: 2 times/yr.
Circulation: 1,500
Available in microform: No

ADVERTISING INFORMATION

Advertising accepted: Yes
Advertising rates: $75.00/quarter page; $100.00/half page; $150.00/full page

EDITORIAL DESCRIPTION

Scope: Publishes studies by scholars dealing with literary works in Castilian.
Reviews books: Yes
Publishes notes: Yes
Languages accepted: Spanish
Prints abstracts: No
Author-anonymous submission: No

SUBMISSION REQUIREMENTS

Restrictions on contributors: None
Author pays submission fee: No
Author pays page charges: No
Length of articles: 15 pp. maximum
Length of book reviews: 500 words
Style: MLA
Number of copies required: 2
Special requirements: Submission of manuscript accompanied by a Macintosh diskette is preferred.
Copyright ownership: Journal
Rejected manuscripts: Returned
Time before publication decision: 1 yr.
Time between decision and publication: 8 mos.
Number of reviewers: 4
Articles submitted per year: 50
Articles published per year: 20
Book reviews submitted per year: 14
Book reviews published per year: 10

(977)
*Explicator

Nancy Lenihan Geltman, Managing Editor
Heldref Publications
1319 18th St. NW
Washington, DC 20038-1802

Telephone: 202 296-6267
Fax: 202 296-5149
First published: 1942
Sponsoring organization: Helen Dwight Reid Educational Foundation
ISSN: 0014-4940
MLA acronym: Expl

SUBSCRIPTION INFORMATION

Frequency of publication: 4 times/yr.
Circulation: 2,300
Available in microform: Yes
Subscription price: $41.00/yr. institutions; $25.00/yr. individuals
Year to which price refers: 1992

ADVERTISING INFORMATION

Advertising accepted: Yes

EDITORIAL DESCRIPTION

Scope: Welcomes short contributions relevant to *explication de texte* in prose or poetry. Material concerned with genesis, parallelism, or biography cannot be accepted unless it has a direct bearing upon the interpretation of the texts.
Reviews books: No
Publishes notes: Yes

Languages accepted: English
Prints abstracts: No

SUBMISSION REQUIREMENTS

Restrictions on contributors: None
Author pays submission fee: No
Author pays page charges: No
Length of articles: 1,200 words maximum
Style: MLA
Number of copies required: 2
Copyright ownership: Heldref Publications
Rejected manuscripts: Returned
Time before publication decision: 2-5 mos.
Time between decision and publication: 6-12 mos.
Number of reviewers: 2-3
Articles submitted per year: 300
Articles published per year: 100

(978)
*Explorations: Special Series

Maurice W. duQuesnay, Albert W. Fields, & James A. Marino, Editors
P.O. Box 44612
USL Station
Lafayette, LA 70504

Telephone: 318 231-6857
E-mail: Awf6623@USL.EDU
First published: 1987
Sponsoring organization: Levy Humanities Series (Flora Levy Endowment)
ISSN: 1043-2493
MLA acronym: ExplorSp

SUBSCRIPTION INFORMATION

Frequency of publication: Annual
Circulation: 60
Available in microform: No
Subscription price: $5.00/yr.
Year to which price refers: 1992

ADVERTISING INFORMATION

Advertising accepted: No

EDITORIAL DESCRIPTION

Scope: Publishes interdisciplinary articles in the humanities, with an emphasis on British and American literature. Each issue focuses on a topic which is reflected in the issue's subtitle.
Reviews books: Yes
Publishes notes: No
Languages accepted: English
Prints abstracts: No
Author-anonymous submission: No

SUBMISSION REQUIREMENTS

Restrictions on contributors: Many articles and all book reviews are solicited.
Author pays submission fee: No
Author pays page charges: No
Length of articles: 8,000-12,000 words
Length of book reviews: 2,000 words
Style: MLA
Number of copies required: 2
Copyright ownership: Journal
Rejected manuscripts: Returned
Time before publication decision: 8-14 weeks
Time between decision and publication: 1 yr.
Number of reviewers: 2-3
Articles submitted per year: 25-35
Articles published per year: 5-7
Book reviews published per year: 2-3

(979)
Explorations in Ethnic Studies: The Journal of the National Association for Ethnic Studies

Gretchen M. Bataille, Barbara L. Hiura, & Phillips G. Davies, Editors
NAES Publications
Dept. of English
Arizona State Univ.
Tempe, AZ 85287-0302

First published: 1978
Sponsoring organization: National Assn. for Ethnic Studies
ISSN: 0730-904X
MLA acronym: EES

SUBSCRIPTION INFORMATION

Frequency of publication: 2 times/yr. (Jan., July)
Circulation: 270
Available in microform: Yes, through Univ. Microfilms International

ADVERTISING INFORMATION

Advertising accepted: Yes

EDITORIAL DESCRIPTION

Scope: The journal is devoted to the study of ethnicity, ethnic groups, intergroup relations, and the cultural life of ethnic minorities.
Reviews books: No
Publishes notes: No
Languages accepted: English
Prints abstracts: No
Author-anonymous submission: Yes

SUBMISSION REQUIREMENTS

Restrictions on contributors: Unsolicited reviews are not accepted. Contributors must be members of the National Assn. for Ethnic Studies at time of publication.
Author pays submission fee: No
Author pays page charges: No
Length of articles: 5,000 words
Style: Journal
Number of copies required: 4
Special requirements: Submit double-spaced typescript. Author's name should appear on separate title page.
Copyright ownership: National Assn. for Ethnic Studies
Rejected manuscripts: Returned; enclose SASE.
Time before publication decision: 6 mos.
Time between decision and publication: 1 yr.
Number of reviewers: 2-3
Articles submitted per year: 15
Articles published per year: 6-8

(980)
*Explorations in Renaissance Culture

Albert W. Fields, Editor
P.O. Box 44612
Univ. of Southwestern Louisiana
Lafayette, LA 70504-4612

Telephone: 318 231-6857
E-mail: Awf6623@USL.edu
First published: 1974
Sponsoring organization: South-Central Renaissance Conference; Levy Humanities Series
ISSN: 0098-2474
MLA acronym: EIRC

SUBSCRIPTION INFORMATION

Frequency of publication: Annual
Circulation: 300
Available in microform: No
Subscription price: $5.00/yr.
Year to which price refers: 1991

ADVERTISING INFORMATION

Advertising accepted: No

EDITORIAL DESCRIPTION

Scope: Publishes articles on all areas of Renaissance studies including art history, literature, music, philosophy, and history.
Reviews books: No
Publishes notes: No
Languages accepted: English
Prints abstracts: No
Author-anonymous submission: No

SUBMISSION REQUIREMENTS

Restrictions on contributors: Contributors must be members of the South-Central Renaissance Conference.
Author pays submission fee: No
Author pays page charges: No
Length of articles: 12-20 double-spaced typescript pp.
Style: MLA with modifications
Number of copies required: 2
Special requirements: Contributors must obtain permissions for use of all copyrighted materials.
Copyright ownership: Journal
Rejected manuscripts: Returned; enclose SASE.
Time before publication decision: 3 mos.
Time between decision and publication: 9 mos.
Number of reviewers: 3-4
Articles submitted per year: 50-75
Articles published per year: 7-9

(981)
*Extrapolation: A Journal of Science Fiction and Fantasy

Donald M. Hassler, Editor
Dept. of English
Kent State Univ.
Kent, OH 44242

Telephone: 216 672-2676
Fax: 216 672-3152
First published: 1959
ISSN: 0014-5483
MLA acronym: Extrapolation

SUBSCRIPTION INFORMATION

Frequency of publication: 4 times/yr. (Mar., June, Sept., Dec.)
Circulation: 1,000
Available in microform: Yes
Subscription price: $15.00/yr.
Year to which price refers: 1992
Subscription address: Sandy Clark, Kent State Univ. Press, Kent, OH 44242
Subscription telephone: 216 672-7913

ADVERTISING INFORMATION

Advertising accepted: Yes

EDITORIAL DESCRIPTION

Scope: Serving the members of the MLA and the Science Fiction Research Association, the journal undertakes the historical, critical, and bibliographical study of science fiction and fantasy.
Reviews books: Yes
Publishes notes: Yes
Languages accepted: English
Prints abstracts: No
Author-anonymous submission: No

SUBMISSION REQUIREMENTS

Restrictions on contributors: None
Author pays submission fee: No
Author pays page charges: No
Length of articles: 6,000-8,000 words
Length of book reviews: 1,500 words
Length of notes: 1,000 words

Style: MLA
Number of copies required: 2
Copyright ownership: Kent State Univ. Press
Rejected manuscripts: Returned
Time before publication decision: 6-8 weeks
Time between decision and publication: 6-9 mos.
Number of reviewers: 2-4
Articles submitted per year: 80-100
Articles published per year: 30-40
Book reviews submitted per year: 40
Book reviews published per year: 40
Notes submitted per year: 2-10
Notes published per year: 2-6

(982)
*Ezra Pound Scholarship Series

Carroll F. Terrell, Editor
National Poetry Foundation
302 Neville Hall
Univ. of Maine at Orono
Orono, ME 04469

First published: 1975
Sponsoring organization: National Poetry Foundation
MLA acronym: EPSS

SUBSCRIPTION INFORMATION

Frequency of publication: Irregular

ADVERTISING INFORMATION

Advertising accepted: No

EDITORIAL DESCRIPTION

Scope: Publishes monograph studies about Ezra Pound's works, sources, and influences.
Reviews books: No
Languages accepted: English
Prints abstracts: No
Author-anonymous submission: No

SUBMISSION REQUIREMENTS

Author pays submission fee: No
Author pays page charges: No
Style: MLA
Number of copies required: 2
Special requirements: Submission on IBM-compatible diskette using Microsoft Word is preferred.
Copyright ownership: National Poetry Foundation
Rejected manuscripts: Returned; enclose SASE.
Number of reviewers: 2

(983)
Fabula

Jean-Claude Dupas, R. Durand, & H. Quere, Editors
Presses Univ. de Lille
rue du Barreau, BP 199
59654 Villeneuve d'Ascq Cédex, France

First published: 1983
Sponsoring organization: Univ. de Lille III; Centre National de la Recherche Scientifique
ISSN: 0755-0960
MLA acronym: Fabu

SUBSCRIPTION INFORMATION

Frequency of publication: 2 times/yr. (Spring, Autumn)
Circulation: 250
Available in microform: No

ADVERTISING INFORMATION

Advertising accepted: Yes, on an exchange basis

EDITORIAL DESCRIPTION

Scope: Publishes articles on literary theory with an emphasis on English-language literature.
Reviews books: No
Publishes notes: Yes
Languages accepted: French; English
Prints abstracts: Yes

SUBMISSION REQUIREMENTS

Restrictions on contributors: None
Author pays submission fee: No
Author pays page charges: No
Length of articles: 6,000-8,000 words
Length of notes: 2,000-4,000 words
Style: MLA
Number of copies required: 2
Special requirements: Submit French and English abstracts.
Copyright ownership: Presses Univ. de Lille
Rejected manuscripts: Returned
Time before publication decision: 6-10 mos.
Time between decision and publication: 3 mos.
Number of reviewers: 2
Articles submitted per year: 20
Articles published per year: 12-14
Notes submitted per year: 16
Notes published per year: 8-12

(984)
*Fabula: Zeitschrift für Erzählforschung/Journal of Folktale Studies/Revue d'Etudes sur le Conte Populaire

Rolf Wilhelm Brednich & Hans-Jörg Uther, Editors
Seminar für Volkskunde
Friedländer Weg 2
3400 Göttingen, Germany

First published: 1958
ISSN: 0014-6242
MLA acronym: Fabula

SUBSCRIPTION INFORMATION

Frequency of publication: 2 times/yr.
Circulation: 600
Available in microform: No
Subscription price: 148 DM/yr.
Year to which price refers: 1991
Subscription address: Walter de Gruyter & Co., Genthiner Str. 13, 1000 Berlin 30, Germany

ADVERTISING INFORMATION

Advertising accepted: No

EDITORIAL DESCRIPTION

Scope: Publishes studies in folklore, popular narrative, and popular literature.
Reviews books: Yes
Publishes notes: Yes
Languages accepted: German; French; English
Prints abstracts: No
Author-anonymous submission: No

SUBMISSION REQUIREMENTS

Restrictions on contributors: None
Author pays submission fee: No
Author pays page charges: No
Length of articles: 20-40 typescript pp.
Length of book reviews: 2 typescript pp.
Length of notes: 1/2 typescript page
Style: Enzyklopädie des Märchens; no abbreviations are used.
Number of copies required: 1
Special requirements: Submit original typescript.
Copyright ownership: Walter de Gruyter & Co.
Rejected manuscripts: Returned
Time before publication decision: 3 mos.
Time between decision and publication: 1-2 yrs.
Number of reviewers: 2-3

Articles submitted per year: 30-40
Articles published per year: 10-15
Book reviews submitted per year: 160
Book reviews published per year: 60-70
Notes submitted per year: 20-40
Notes published per year: 20-40

(985)
*Face: Revista de Semiótica e Comunicação

Lucia Santaella, Editor
Programa de Pós-Graduação em Comunicação e Semiótica
PUCSP
Rua Monte Alegre 984
Prédio Novo-4 andar
CEP 05014 São Paulo SP, Brazil

Telephone: (55) 11 2631793
Fax: (55) 11 8722413
First published: 1988
Sponsoring organization: Pontificia Univ. Católica de São Paulo (PUCSP); Conselho Nacional de Pesquisa (CNPq)
ISSN: 0103-1562
MLA acronym: Face

SUBSCRIPTION INFORMATION

Frequency of publication: 2 times/yr. (June, Dec.)
Circulation: 150
Available in microform: No
Subscription price: $20.00/yr.
Year to which price refers: 1991

ADVERTISING INFORMATION

Advertising accepted: Yes

EDITORIAL DESCRIPTION

Scope: Publishes analyses of texts utilizing a semiotic methodology as well as articles that examine the theory of semiotics. Includes essays on how semiotics is applied to literature, communication, and music.
Reviews books: Yes
Languages accepted: English; French; Spanish; Portuguese
Prints abstracts: Yes
Author-anonymous submission: No

SUBMISSION REQUIREMENTS

Restrictions on contributors: None
Author pays submission fee: No
Author pays page charges: No
Length of articles: 20 pp.
Length of book reviews: 3-5 pp.
Number of copies required: 1
Special requirements: Include a short biography and abstract.
Rejected manuscripts: Not returned
Time before publication decision: 3 mos.
Time between decision and publication: 1 yr.
Number of reviewers: 3
Articles submitted per year: 40
Articles published per year: 20
Book reviews submitted per year: 15
Book reviews published per year: 8

(986)
*Fachsprache: International Journal of LSP

Lothar Hoffman, Dieter Möhn, & Peter Bierbaumer, Editors
c/o Joseph Wieser
Jakob Trinksgeldgasse 29-31
2380 Perchtoldsdorf, Austria

Telephone: (43) 222 348124
Fax: (43) 222 3102805
First published: 1979
Sponsoring organization: Austrian Ministry of Science
ISSN: 0256-2510
MLA acronym: Fachsprache

SUBSCRIPTION INFORMATION

Frequency of publication: 2 times/yr.
Circulation: 400
Available in microform: No
Subscription price: 620 S/yr.
Year to which price refers: 1991
Subscription address: Wilhelm Braumüller, Universitäts-Verlagbuchhandlung GmbH, Servitengasse 5, 1092 Vienna, Austria

ADVERTISING INFORMATION

Advertising accepted: Yes

EDITORIAL DESCRIPTION

Scope: Publishes articles on special and technical terminology from a linguistic standpoint, on LSP text linguistics, and didactics.
Reviews books: Yes
Publishes notes: Yes
Languages accepted: German; French; English
Prints abstracts: Yes
Author-anonymous submission: No

SUBMISSION REQUIREMENTS

Restrictions on contributors: None
Author pays submission fee: No
Author pays page charges: No
Length of articles: 25 pp.
Length of book reviews: 2-4 pp.
Length of notes: 1 p.
Style: Journal
Number of copies required: 2
Special requirements: Submit typescript and an 8-12 line abstract.
Copyright ownership: Publisher
Rejected manuscripts: Returned
Time before publication decision: 1 mo.
Time between decision and publication: 4 mos.
Number of reviewers: 4
Articles submitted per year: 8-10
Articles published per year: 8
Book reviews submitted per year: 8
Book reviews published per year: 8
Notes submitted per year: 6
Notes published per year: 10

(987)
*Fantasy Commentator

A. Langley Searles, Editor
48 Highland Circle
Bronxville, NY 10708

Telephone: 914 961-6799
First published: 1943
ISSN: 1051-5001
MLA acronym: FantCo

SUBSCRIPTION INFORMATION

Frequency of publication: 2 times/yr. (Spring, Fall)
Circulation: 500
Available in microform: No
Subscription price: $5.00/single issue; $25.00/6 issues
Year to which price refers: 1991

ADVERTISING INFORMATION

Advertising accepted: No

EDITORIAL DESCRIPTION

Scope: Publishes articles, book reviews, and verse in the field of science fiction and fantasy fiction.
Reviews books: Yes
Publishes notes: Yes
Languages accepted: English
Prints abstracts: No
Author-anonymous submission: No

SUBMISSION REQUIREMENTS

Restrictions on contributors: None
Author pays submission fee: No
Author pays page charges: No
Length of articles: 6,000-8,000 words
Length of book reviews: 1,500-3,000 words
Length of notes: 500-1,500 words
Number of copies required: 1
Special requirements: Notes are printed in the form of correspondence.
Copyright ownership: Editor for first N. American serial rights
Rejected manuscripts: Returned
Time before publication decision: 6-18 weeks
Time between decision and publication: 6-18 mos.
Number of reviewers: 1-2
Articles submitted per year: 15-20
Articles published per year: 10-12
Book reviews submitted per year: 30-35
Book reviews published per year: 25-30
Notes submitted per year: 10-12
Notes published per year: 8-10

(988)
*Farhang-e Irān Zamin: Revue des Etudes Iranologiques

Iraj Afshar, Editor
P.O. Box 19575-583
Tehran, Iran

First published: 1952
ISSN: 0014-7788
MLA acronym: FIZ

SUBSCRIPTION INFORMATION

Frequency of publication: Annual
Circulation: 1,500
Available in microform: Yes

ADVERTISING INFORMATION

Advertising accepted: Yes

EDITORIAL DESCRIPTION

Scope: Publishes articles on Iranian studies and Persian classical texts.
Reviews books: Yes
Publishes notes: Yes
Languages accepted: Persian; English (occasionally); French (occasionally); German (occasionally)
Prints abstracts: Yes

SUBMISSION REQUIREMENTS

Length of articles: No restrictions
Length of book reviews: 3 pp.
Number of copies required: 1
Time before publication decision: 2 yrs.
Articles submitted per year: 10
Articles published per year: 10-15

(989)
*Fataburen: Nordiska Museets och Skansens Årsbok

Nordiska Museet
Box 27820
115 93 Stockholm, Sweden

Telephone: (46) 8 6664600
Fax: (46) 8 6653853
First published: 1906
ISSN: 0348-971X
MLA acronym: Fataburen

SUBSCRIPTION INFORMATION

Frequency of publication: Annual
Circulation: 7,000
Available in microform: No

ADVERTISING INFORMATION

Advertising accepted: No

EDITORIAL DESCRIPTION

Scope: Publishes articles on Swedish cultural history.
Reviews books: No
Publishes notes: No
Languages accepted: Swedish
Prints abstracts: Yes

SUBMISSION REQUIREMENTS

Restrictions on contributors: None
Author pays submission fee: No
Author pays page charges: No
Copyright ownership: Nordiska Museet & author
Articles published per year: 10

(990)
*The Faulkner Journal

Dawn Trouard, John T. Matthews, & James B. Carothers, Editors
Dept. of English
Univ. of Akron
Akron, OH 44325-1906

Additional editorial address: John T. Matthews, Dept. of English, Boston Univ., Boston, MA 02215
Telephone: 216 972-5194
Fax: 216 972-6990
First published: 1985
Sponsoring organization: Univ. of Akron
ISSN: 0884-2949
MLA acronym: FJ

SUBSCRIPTION INFORMATION

Frequency of publication: 2 times/yr. (Sept., Mar.)
Circulation: 500
Available in microform: Yes
Subscription price: $15.00/yr. institutions US; $9.00/yr. individuals US; $15.00/yr. elsewhere
Year to which price refers: 1992

ADVERTISING INFORMATION

Advertising accepted: Yes

EDITORIAL DESCRIPTION

Scope: Publishes scholarly criticism on William Faulkner.
Reviews books: No
Publishes notes: Yes
Languages accepted: English
Prints abstracts: No
Author-anonymous submission: Yes

SUBMISSION REQUIREMENTS

Restrictions on contributors: None
Author pays submission fee: No
Author pays page charges: No
Length of articles: 2,000-10,000 words
Length of notes: 400-1,000 words
Style: MLA
Number of copies required: 2
Copyright ownership: Univ. of Akron
Rejected manuscripts: Returned; enclose SASE.
Time before publication decision: 2-6 mos.
Time between decision and publication: 6-12 mos.
Number of reviewers: 2-3
Articles submitted per year: 30-40
Articles published per year: 12-16

Notes submitted per year: 3-5
Notes published per year: 1-2

(991)
*Faulkner Studies

Michel Gresset, Kenzaburo Ohashi, Kiyoyuki Ono, & Noel Polk, Editors
c/o Kiyoyuki Ono
Dept. of English
Faculty of Letters
Chiba Univ.
Chiba 260, Japan

Telephone: (81) 472 511111 ext. 2338
Fax: (81) 472 530255
First published: 1991
ISSN: 0917-4265
MLA acronym: FaulkSt

SUBSCRIPTION INFORMATION

Frequency of publication: 2 times/yr.
Circulation: 1,000
Available in microform: No
Subscription price: $15.00/yr.
Year to which price refers: 1992
Subscription address: Yamaguchi Publishing House, 72 Tsukuda-Cho, Iehijoji, Sakyo-ku, Kyoto 606, Japan

ADVERTISING INFORMATION

Advertising accepted: Yes
Advertising rates: 30,000 yen ($200.00)/full page

EDITORIAL DESCRIPTION

Scope: Publishes articles on William Faulkner and his work.
Reviews books: Yes
Publishes notes: Yes
Languages accepted: English
Prints abstracts: No
Author-anonymous submission: No

SUBMISSION REQUIREMENTS

Restrictions on contributors: None
Author pays submission fee: No
Author pays page charges: No
Length of articles: 4,500 words maximum
Length of book reviews: 1,500 words maximum
Length of notes: 1,000 words maximum
Style: MLA
Number of copies required: 5
Copyright ownership: Author
Rejected manuscripts: Not returned
Time before publication decision: 3 mos.
Time between decision and publication: 6 mos. maximum
Number of reviewers: 4
Articles submitted per year: 15
Articles published per year: 8
Book reviews submitted per year: 2-3
Book reviews published per year: 2-4
Notes submitted per year: 2-4
Notes published per year: 2 maximum

(992)
*Faux Titre: Etudes de Langue et Littérature Françaises

Keith Busby, Paul Pelckmans, Co Vet, M. J. Freeman, & Sjef Houppermans, Editors
Dept. of Modern Languages
Univ. of Oklahoma
780 Van Vleet Oval, Rm. 202
Norman, OK 73019

Telephone: 405 325-6181
First published: 1980
ISSN: 0167-9392
MLA acronym: FauxT

SUBSCRIPTION INFORMATION

Frequency of publication: Irregular
Circulation: 600
Available in microform: No
Subscription address: Editions Rodopi B.V., Keizersgracht 302-304, 1016 EX Amsterdam, Netherlands
Additional subscription address: In US & Canada: Editions Rodopi, 233 Peachtree St., N.E., Suite 404, Atlanta, GA 30303-1504. In France: NORDEAL, 30 rue de Verlinghem, B.P. 139, 59832 Lambersart Cedex, France
Subscription telephone: (31) 20 6227507; 404 523-1964; 800 225-3998
Subscription fax: (31) 20 6227507; 404 522-7116

ADVERTISING INFORMATION

Advertising accepted: No

EDITORIAL DESCRIPTION

Scope: Publishes monographs on French language and literature.
Reviews books: No
Publishes notes: No
Languages accepted: English; French
Prints abstracts: No
Author-anonymous submission: No

SUBMISSION REQUIREMENTS

Restrictions on contributors: None
Author pays submission fee: No
Author pays page charges: No
Length of books: 100 pp. minimum
Style: MLA
Number of copies required: 1
Copyright ownership: Editions Rodopi B.V.
Rejected manuscripts: Returned
Time before publication decision: 3 mos.
Time between decision and publication: 1 yr.
Number of reviewers: 2
Books submitted per year: 7
Books published per year: 4

(993)
*Feminaria

Lea Fletcher, Editor
C.C. 402
1000 Buenos Aires, Argentina

Telephone: (54) 1 5683029
Fax: (54) 1 3815878
First published: 1988
MLA acronym: Feminaria

SUBSCRIPTION INFORMATION

Frequency of publication: 2 times/yr.
Circulation: 1,000
Available in microform: No
Subscription price: $20.00/yr. US & Europe; $15.00/yr. Latin America; $10.00/yr. Argentina
Year to which price refers: 1992
Additional subscription address: In the US: Andrés Avellaneda, Dept. of Romance Languages & Literatures, Univ. of Florida, Gainesville, FL 32611

ADVERTISING INFORMATION

Advertising accepted: Yes

EDITORIAL DESCRIPTION

Scope: Publishes literary criticism and articles on feminist theory.
Reviews books: No
Publishes notes: Yes
Languages accepted: Spanish
Prints abstracts: No
Author-anonymous submission: Yes

(994)
*Feminist Studies

Claire G. Moses, Editor
c/o Women's Studies Program
Univ. of Maryland
College Park, MD 20742

Telephone: 301 405-7413
First published: 1972
Sponsoring organization: Univ. of Maryland
ISSN: 0046-3663
MLA acronym: FSt

SUBSCRIPTION INFORMATION

Frequency of publication: 3 times/yr.
Circulation: 8,000
Available in microform: Yes
Subscription price: $55.00/yr. institutions; $25.00/yr. individuals; add $5.00 ($20.00 airmail)/yr. postage outside US
Year to which price refers: 1992
Subscription telephone: 301 405-7415

ADVERTISING INFORMATION

Advertising accepted: Yes
Advertising rates: $250.00/full page

EDITORIAL DESCRIPTION

Scope: Publishes articles on all areas of feminist analysis, debate, theory, and discussion.
Reviews books: Yes
Publishes notes: Yes
Languages accepted: English
Prints abstracts: No
Author-anonymous submission: Yes

SUBMISSION REQUIREMENTS

Restrictions on contributors: Book reviews are commissioned.
Author pays submission fee: No
Author pays page charges: No
Length of articles: 20-30 double-spaced pp.
Length of book reviews: 12-15 double-spaced pp.
Style: Chicago
Number of copies required: 3
Special requirements: Author's name should be on a separate sheet. Submit a 1 page abstract.
Copyright ownership: Journal or author
Rejected manuscripts: Not returned
Time before publication decision: 4 mos.
Time between decision and publication: 3-6 mos.
Number of reviewers: 3-5
Articles submitted per year: 300
Articles published per year: 20
Book reviews published per year: 3-8
Notes published per year: 60

SUBMISSION REQUIREMENTS

Restrictions on contributors: Contributions of original fiction and poetry can be by women only.
Author pays submission fee: No
Author pays page charges: No
Number of copies required: 2
Copyright ownership: Author & journal
Rejected manuscripts: Returned; enclose return postage
Time before publication decision: 1 mo.
Time between decision and publication: 1 yr.
Number of reviewers: 2
Articles published per year: 8-10

(995)
*Festival of American Folklife

Peter Seitel, Editor
Center for Folklife Programs & Cultural Studies
955 L'Enfant Plaza
Rm. 2600
Smithsonian Inst.
Washington, DC 20560

Telephone: 202 287-3424
Fax: 202 287-3699
First published: 1967
Sponsoring organization: Smithsonian Inst.; National Park Service
ISSN: 1056-6805
MLA acronym: FAF

SUBSCRIPTION INFORMATION

Frequency of publication: Annual
Available in microform: No
Subscription price: $3.00/yr.
Year to which price refers: 1992

ADVERTISING INFORMATION

Advertising accepted: No

EDITORIAL DESCRIPTION

Scope: Provides contextual information for cultural traditions presented at the Festival of American Folklife.
Reviews books: No
Publishes notes: No
Languages accepted: English; Spanish
Prints abstracts: No

SUBMISSION REQUIREMENTS

Restrictions on contributors: Contributions are solicited.
Author pays submission fee: No
Author pays page charges: No
Copyright ownership: Publisher
Articles published per year: 15-40

(996)
*Field: Contemporary Poetry and Poetics

Stuart Friebert & David Young, Editors
Rice Hall
Oberlin College
Oberlin, OH 44074

Telephone: 216 775-8408
Fax: 216 775-8124
First published: 1969
Sponsoring organization: Oberlin College
ISSN: 0015-0657
MLA acronym: Field

SUBSCRIPTION INFORMATION

Frequency of publication: 2 times/yr. (Spring, Fall)
Circulation: 2,200
Available in microform: No
Subscription price: $12.00/yr., $20.00/2 yrs.
Year to which price refers: 1992

ADVERTISING INFORMATION

Advertising accepted: No

EDITORIAL DESCRIPTION

Scope: Publishes poetry, poetry in translation, and essays by poets on contemporary poetics.
Reviews books: Yes
Publishes notes: Yes
Languages accepted: English
Prints abstracts: No
Author-anonymous submission: Yes

SUBMISSION REQUIREMENTS

Restrictions on contributors: Unsolicited book reviews are not accepted.
Author pays submission fee: No
Author pays page charges: No
Length of articles: 1-25 pp.
Length of notes: 1-10 pp.
Style: MLA
Number of copies required: 1
Special requirements: Rights to translations are the translator's responsibility.
Copyright ownership: Journal; reverts to author
Rejected manuscripts: Returned; enclose SASE.
Time before publication decision: 2-3 weeks
Time between decision and publication: 3-6 mos.
Number of reviewers: 4
Articles submitted per year: 30
Articles published per year: 4-8
Book reviews published per year: 4
Notes submitted per year: 20
Notes published per year: 1-2

(997)
*Fifteenth-Century Studies

Edelgard E. DuBruck & William C. McDonald, Editors
Marygrove College
Detroit, MI 48221

Additional editorial address: William C. McDonald, Germanic Languages, Univ. of Virginia, Charlottesville, VA 22903
Telephone: 313 338-4948
First published: 1978
Sponsoring organization: Medieval Inst., Kalamazoo, MI
ISSN: 0164-0933
MLA acronym: FCS

SUBSCRIPTION INFORMATION

Frequency of publication: Annual
Circulation: 150
Available in microform: No
Subscription address: Medieval Inst. Publications, Western Michigan Univ., Kalamazoo, MI 49008-3851
Subscription telephone: 616 387-4155
Subscription fax: 616 387-4150

ADVERTISING INFORMATION

Advertising accepted: No

EDITORIAL DESCRIPTION

Scope: Publishes on 15th-century languages, literatures, history, and culture.
Reviews books: Yes
Publishes notes: No
Languages accepted: English; French; German; Spanish
Prints abstracts: No
Author-anonymous submission: No

SUBMISSION REQUIREMENTS

Restrictions on contributors: None
Author pays submission fee: No
Author pays page charges: Yes, if manuscript is not submitted on diskette.
Length of articles: No restrictions
Length of book reviews: No restrictions
Style: Chicago
Number of copies required: 2
Special requirements: Request guidelines. Submit original typescript and 1 copy.
Copyright ownership: Editors
Rejected manuscripts: Returned; enclose return postage.
Time before publication decision: 3 mos.
Time between decision and publication: 6 mos.
Number of reviewers: 2-3
Articles submitted per year: 30
Articles published per year: 20

Book reviews submitted per year: 10-20
Book reviews published per year: 15-20

(998)
*Film Criticism

I. Lloyd Michaels, Editor
Allegheny College
Meadville, PA 16335

Telephone: 814 332-4333
First published: 1976
Sponsoring organization: Allegheny College
ISSN: 0163-5069
MLA acronym: FilmC

SUBSCRIPTION INFORMATION

Frequency of publication: 3 times/yr. (Fall, Winter, Spring)
Circulation: 500
Available in microform: No
Subscription price: $15.00/yr.
Year to which price refers: 1992-93

ADVERTISING INFORMATION

Advertising accepted: No

EDITORIAL DESCRIPTION

Scope: Publishes articles, reviews, and interviews related to film scholarship.
Reviews books: Yes
Publishes notes: No
Languages accepted: English
Author-anonymous submission: Yes

SUBMISSION REQUIREMENTS

Author pays submission fee: No
Author pays page charges: No
Length of articles: 2,500-4,500 words
Length of book reviews: 750-1,000 words
Style: MLA
Number of copies required: 2
Copyright ownership: Journal
Rejected manuscripts: Returned; enclose SASE.
Time before publication decision: 2-3 mos.
Time between decision and publication: 3-4 mos.
Number of reviewers: 3
Articles submitted per year: 100
Articles published per year: 20
Book reviews submitted per year: 10
Book reviews published per year: 5

(999)
*Film Quarterly

Ann Martin, Editor
Univ. of California Press
2120 Berkeley Way
Berkeley, CA 94720

Telephone: 510 601-9070
Fax: 510 601-9036
First published: 1945
Sponsoring organization: Univ. of California Press
ISSN: 0015-1386
MLA acronym: FilmQ

SUBSCRIPTION INFORMATION

Frequency of publication: 4 times/yr.
Circulation: 6,500
Available in microform: Yes
Subscription price: $40.00/yr. institutions; $19.00/yr. individuals; add $6.00/yr. postage outside US
Year to which price refers: 1992
Subscription telephone: 510 642-9129
Subscription fax: 510 643-7127

ADVERTISING INFORMATION

Advertising accepted: Yes
Advertising rates: $65.00/eighth page; $110.00/quarter page; $215.00/half page; $375.00/full page; $390.00/cover

EDITORIAL DESCRIPTION

Scope: Journal of film criticism, theory, and history.
Reviews books: Yes
Languages accepted: English
Prints abstracts: No
Author-anonymous submission: No

SUBMISSION REQUIREMENTS

Restrictions on contributors: None
Author pays submission fee: No
Author pays page charges: No
Length of articles: 6,250 words maximum
Length of book reviews: 1,250 words maximum
Style: Chicago
Number of copies required: 1
Special requirements: Submit double-spaced typescript. Contributions produced on a dot-matrix printer are not considered.
Copyright ownership: Regents of the Univ. of California
Rejected manuscripts: Returned; enclose SASE.
Time before publication decision: 3 mos. maximum
Time between decision and publication: 3-9 mos.
Number of reviewers: 6
Articles submitted per year: 100
Articles published per year: 15
Book reviews submitted per year: 80
Book reviews published per year: 70

(1000)
*Filología

Ana Maria Barrenechea, Editor
Inst. de Filología y Literaturas Hispánicas "Dr. Amado Alonso"
Fac. de Filosofia y Letras
Univ. de Buenos Aires
25 de Mayo 217
1002 Buenos Aires, Argentina

First published: 1949
Sponsoring organization: Inst. de Filología y Literaturas Hispánicas "Dr. Amado Alonso", Fac. de Filosofía & Letras, Univ. de Buenos Aires; Fundación Amado Alonso
ISSN: 0071-495X
MLA acronym: Filología

SUBSCRIPTION INFORMATION

Frequency of publication: 2 times/yr.
Circulation: 1,000
Available in microform: No
Subscription address: Oficina de Venta de Publicaciones, Fac. de Filosofia y Letras, Puán 470, 1406 Buenos Aires, Argentina
Additional subscription address: Ana María Barrenechea, c/o Columbia Univ. Post Office, P.O. Box 250202, New York, NY 10025

ADVERTISING INFORMATION

Advertising accepted: No

EDITORIAL DESCRIPTION

Scope: Publishes papers dealing with Hispanic language and literature, both peninsular and American. Also publishes works of general Romanic interest and literary and linguistic theory.
Reviews books: Yes
Publishes notes: Yes
Languages accepted: Spanish
Prints abstracts: No
Author-anonymous submission: Yes

SUBMISSION REQUIREMENTS

Author pays submission fee: No
Author pays page charges: No
Length of articles: 15-20 pp.
Style: None
Number of copies required: 2
Special requirements: Submit original typescript.
Copyright ownership: Journal
Rejected manuscripts: Not returned
Time before publication decision: 2 mos.
Time between decision and publication: 2 yrs.
Number of reviewers: 2

(1001)
*Filológiai Közlöny

Imre Szabics, Editor
Amerikai út 96
1145 Budapest, Hungary

Additional editorial address: P.O. Box 107, 1364 Budapest, Hungary
First published: 1955
Sponsoring organization: Magyar Tudományos Akadémia
ISSN: 0015-1785
MLA acronym: FK

SUBSCRIPTION INFORMATION

Frequency of publication: 4 times/yr.
Circulation: 600
Available in microform: No
Subscription address: HELIR, Lehel u. 10/a, 1900 Budapest, Hungary
Additional subscription address: Foreign subscribers write to: Kultura, P.O. Box 149, 1389 Budapest, Hungary

ADVERTISING INFORMATION

Advertising accepted: No

EDITORIAL DESCRIPTION

Scope: Publishes articles on literatures in modern languages.
Reviews books: Yes
Publishes notes: No
Languages accepted: Hungarian
Prints abstracts: No
Author-anonymous submission: No

SUBMISSION REQUIREMENTS

Restrictions on contributors: None
Author pays submission fee: No
Author pays page charges: No
Length of articles: 15-25 typescript pp.
Length of book reviews: 4-8 typescript pp.
Length of notes: 2-4 typescript pp.
Style: None
Number of copies required: 2
Special requirements: Submit original typescript plus 1 copy on size A4 (8 1/4 in. x 11 3/4 in.) paper.
Copyright ownership: Journal
Rejected manuscripts: Returned
Time before publication decision: 6 mos.
Time between decision and publication: 12-18 mos.
Number of reviewers: 2
Articles submitted per year: 40-50
Articles published per year: 30-35
Book reviews submitted per year: 25-30
Book reviews published per year: 40
Notes submitted per year: 5-6
Notes published per year: 3-5

(1002)
Filologicheskie Nauki

Izdatel'stvo Vysshaia Shkola
Prosp. Marksa, 18
103009 Moscow, K-9, Russia

First published: 1958
Sponsoring organization: Nauchnye Doklady Vysshej Shkoly
ISSN: 0130-9730
MLA acronym: FN

SUBSCRIPTION INFORMATION

Frequency of publication: 6 times/yr.

EDITORIAL DESCRIPTION

Reviews books: Yes
Languages accepted: Russian
Prints abstracts: No

(1003)
*Finnisch-Ugrische Forschungen: Zeitschrift für Finnisch-Ugrische Sprach- und Volkskunde

Alho Alhoniemi, Erkki Itkonen, Lauri Honko, & Ingrid Schellbach-Kopra, Editors
Castrenianum
Fabianinkatu 33
00170 Helsinki, Finland

Additional editorial address: Fennicum, Henrikinkatu 3, 20500 Turku, Finland
Fax: (358) 0 1913329; (358) 21 6336360
First published: 1901
Sponsoring organization: Suomalais-ugrilainen Seura
ISSN: 0355-1253
MLA acronym: FUF

SUBSCRIPTION INFORMATION

Frequency of publication: Irregular
Circulation: 100
Available in microform: No
Subscription address: Suomalais-ugrilainen Seura, Kirjavarainhoitaja, PL 320, 00171 Helsinki, Finland

ADVERTISING INFORMATION

Advertising accepted: No

EDITORIAL DESCRIPTION

Scope: Publishes articles on Finno-Ugric linguistics, ethnology, and folklore research.
Reviews books: Yes
Publishes notes: Yes
Languages accepted: English; German; French
Prints abstracts: Yes
Author-anonymous submission: Yes

SUBMISSION REQUIREMENTS

Restrictions on contributors: None
Author pays submission fee: No
Author pays page charges: No
Length of articles: 10-40 pp.
Length of book reviews: 3-10 pp.
Length of notes: 3-10 pp.
Style: Journal
Number of copies required: 1
Special requirements: Submit original typescript.
Copyright ownership: Author
Rejected manuscripts: Returned
Time before publication decision: 2-3 mos.
Time between decision and publication: 16 mos.
Number of reviewers: 2-3
Articles submitted per year: 10-12
Articles published per year: 6-8
Book reviews submitted per year: 15-18
Book reviews published per year: 10-15

Notes submitted per year: 1-3
Notes published per year: 1

(1004)
Finsk Tidskrift

Carina Nynäs, Editorial Secretary
P.B. 28
20501 Åbo, Finland

Telephone: (358) 21 322468
Fax: (358) 21 654585
First published: 1876
Sponsoring organization: Föreningen Granskaren
ISSN: 0015-248X
MLA acronym: FT

SUBSCRIPTION INFORMATION

Frequency of publication: 10 times/yr.
Circulation: 1,200
Available in microform: No
Subscription address: Åbo Akademi Univ., Dept. of Public Administration, Biskopsgatan 15, 20500 Åbo, Finland

ADVERTISING INFORMATION

Advertising accepted: Yes

EDITORIAL DESCRIPTION

Scope: Publishes articles on culture, economics, and politics.
Reviews books: Yes
Publishes notes: Yes
Languages accepted: Swedish; Norwegian; Danish; Finnish
Prints abstracts: No
Author-anonymous submission: No

SUBMISSION REQUIREMENTS

Restrictions on contributors: None
Author pays submission fee: No
Author pays page charges: No
Length of articles: 5-10 pp.
Length of book reviews: 5 pp.
Length of notes: 4 pp.
Style: None
Number of copies required: 1
Copyright ownership: Author
Rejected manuscripts: Not returned
Time before publication decision: 1 mo.
Time between decision and publication: 2-6 mos.
Number of reviewers: 2-3
Articles submitted per year: 80
Articles published per year: 40
Book reviews published per year: 30
Notes submitted per year: 20
Notes published per year: 10

(1005)
*First Language

Kevin Durkin, Editor
Dept. of Psychology
Univ. of Western Australia
Nedlands
Western Australia 6009, Australia

Additional editorial address: Send books for review to: Martyn Barrett, Dept. of Psychology, Royal Holloway & Bedford New College, Egham Hall, Egham, Surrey TW20 0EX, England
Telephone: (61) 9 3802479
Fax: (61) 9 3801006
E-mail: Kevin@psy.uwa.oz.au
First published: 1980
ISSN: 0142-7237
MLA acronym: FirstL

SUBSCRIPTION INFORMATION

Frequency of publication: 3 times/yr. (Feb., June, Oct.)
Circulation: 380
Available in microform: No
Subscription price: A$75.00/yr. institutions; A$45.00/yr. individuals
Year to which price refers: 1991
Subscription address: Alpha Academic, Halfpenny Furze, Mill Lane, Chalfont St. Giles, Buck HP8 4NR, England

ADVERTISING INFORMATION

Advertising accepted: Yes

EDITORIAL DESCRIPTION

Scope: Publishes research, theoretical articles and reviews concerned with all aspects of first language acquisition.
Reviews books: Yes
Publishes notes: Yes
Languages accepted: English
Prints abstracts: Yes
Author-anonymous submission: Yes

SUBMISSION REQUIREMENTS

Restrictions on contributors: Book reviews are solicited.
Author pays submission fee: No
Author pays page charges: No
Length of articles: No restrictions
Length of book reviews: 500-800 words
Length of notes: 1,000 words
Style: Journal
Number of copies required: 3
Special requirements: Submit double-spaced typescript on size A4 (8 1/4 in. x 11 3/4 in.) paper. If word-processed, submit IBM-compatible diskette, preferably in ASCII format, in addition to typescript. Consult journal cover for complete details.
Copyright ownership: Alpha Academic
Rejected manuscripts: Not returned
Time before publication decision: 2-3 mos.
Time between decision and publication: 9-12 mos.
Number of reviewers: 2
Articles submitted per year: 80
Articles published per year: 16-20
Book reviews published per year: 10
Notes submitted per year: 6
Notes published per year: 2

(1006)
*The Flannery O'Connor Bulletin

Sarah Gordon, Editor
English Dept.
Box 44
Georgia College
Milledgeville, GA 31061

Telephone: 912 453-5568
Fax: 912 453-4581
First published: 1972
Sponsoring organization: Georgia College
ISSN: 0091-4924
MLA acronym: FCB

SUBSCRIPTION INFORMATION

Frequency of publication: Annual
Circulation: 600
Available in microform: Yes
Subscription price: $6.00/yr. institutions; $5.00/yr. individuals; add $5.00/yr. postage outside US & Canada
Year to which price refers: 1991

ADVERTISING INFORMATION

Advertising accepted: Yes
Advertising rates: $150.00/half page; $300.00/full page

EDITORIAL DESCRIPTION

Scope: Publishes critical articles on the fiction of Flannery O'Connor.
Reviews books: Yes
Publishes notes: Yes
Languages accepted: English
Prints abstracts: No
Author-anonymous submission: Yes

SUBMISSION REQUIREMENTS

Author pays submission fee: No
Author pays page charges: No
Length of articles: 20 pp. maximum
Length of book reviews: 1,000 words
Length of notes: 1,000 words
Style: MLA
Number of copies required: 2
Copyright ownership: Journal
Rejected manuscripts: Returned; enclose SASE.
Time before publication decision: 6 mos.
Time between decision and publication: 6 mos.
Number of reviewers: 4
Articles submitted per year: 25
Articles published per year: 10
Book reviews published per year: 3
Notes submitted per year: 2
Notes published per year: 1

(1007)
*Florida State University Conference on Literature and Film

Florida State Univ. Press
c/o Univ. Presses of Florida
15 NW 15th St.
Gainesville, FL 32603

Telephone: 904 392-1351
Fax: 904 392-7302
Sponsoring organization: Florida State Univ. Comparative Literature & Film Circle; Florida State Univ. College of Arts & Sciences
MLA acronym: FSUC

SUBSCRIPTION INFORMATION

Frequency of publication: Annual
Available in microform: No

ADVERTISING INFORMATION

Advertising accepted: No

EDITORIAL DESCRIPTION

Scope: Publishes papers selected from the annual Florida State University Conference on Literature and Film.
Reviews books: No
Publishes notes: No
Languages accepted: English
Prints abstracts: No
Author-anonymous submission: No

SUBMISSION REQUIREMENTS

Restrictions on contributors: Contributors must have presented the paper at the annual Florida State Univ. Conference on Literature & Film.
Author pays submission fee: No
Cost of page charges: No
Style: Chicago
Number of copies required: 2
Copyright ownership: Board of Regents of the State of Florida
Rejected manuscripts: Returned; enclose SASE.
Time between decision and publication: 1 yr.
Number of reviewers: 2 minimum

(1008)
*Florilegium: Carleton University Annual Papers on Late Antiquity and the Middle Ages

Douglas J. Wurtele & Roger C. Blockley, Editors
Dept. of English
Carleton Univ.
Ottawa, Ontario K1S 5B6, Canada

Telephone: 613 788-2600 ext. 2317
Fax: 613 788-3544
First published: 1979
Sponsoring organization: Carleton Univ.
ISSN: 0709-5201
MLA acronym: Florilegium

SUBSCRIPTION INFORMATION

Frequency of publication: Annual
Circulation: 200
Available in microform: No

ADVERTISING INFORMATION

Advertising accepted: No

EDITORIAL DESCRIPTION

Scope: Material dealing with all subjects within the period relating to history, literature, and other relevant areas of study is welcome.
Reviews books: No
Publishes notes: No
Languages accepted: English; French
Prints abstracts: No
Author-anonymous submission: Yes

SUBMISSION REQUIREMENTS

Restrictions on contributors: None
Author pays submission fee: No
Author pays page charges: Generally no; if article contains half-tone illustrations, charge is negotiated.
Length of articles: 2,500-10,000 words
Style: MLA
Number of copies required: 2
Copyright ownership: Journal
Rejected manuscripts: Returned with comments; enclose return postage.
Time before publication decision: 3 mos.
Time between decision and publication: 1 yr.
Number of reviewers: 2-3
Articles submitted per year: 40
Articles published per year: 13

(1009)
*Focus on Robert Graves and His Contemporaries

Patrick Quinn, Editor
Univ. of Maryland
European Division
APO NY 09102

Additional editorial address: 6 Pound Close, Kirtlington, Oxforshire DX5 3JR, England
Telephone: (44) 869 50817
First published: 1972
Sponsoring organization: Univ. of Maryland, European Division
MLA acronym: FRG&C

SUBSCRIPTION INFORMATION

Frequency of publication: 2 times/yr.
Circulation: 500
Available in microform: No
Subscription price: $5.00/yr.
Year to which price refers: 1992

ADVERTISING INFORMATION

Advertising accepted: No

EDITORIAL DESCRIPTION

Scope: Publishes articles on Robert Graves and other World War I literary figures.
Reviews books: Yes
Publishes notes: Yes
Languages accepted: English
Prints abstracts: No
Author-anonymous submission: No

SUBMISSION REQUIREMENTS

Restrictions on contributors: None
Author pays submission fee: No
Author pays page charges: No
Length of articles: No restrictions
Length of book reviews: No restrictions
Length of notes: No restrictions
Style: MLA preferred
Number of copies required: 2
Copyright ownership: Editor
Rejected manuscripts: Returned
Time before publication decision: 6 weeks
Time between decision and publication: 3 mos.
Number of reviewers: 3
Articles submitted per year: 8-10
Articles published per year: 6
Book reviews submitted per year: 3-4
Book reviews published per year: 2
Notes published per year: 2-4

(1010)
*Folia Linguistica: Acta Societatis Linguisticae Europaeae

Wolfgang U. Dressler, Editor
Inst. für Sprachwissenschaft der Universität
Berggasse 11
1090 Vienna, Austria

Telephone: (43) 222 3103886
First published: 1967
Sponsoring organization: Soc. Linguistica Europaea
ISSN: 0165-4004
MLA acronym: FoLi

SUBSCRIPTION INFORMATION

Frequency of publication: 2 times/yr.
Circulation: 1,600
Available in microform: No
Subscription price: 35 DM/yr. (includes membership)
Year to which price refers: 1992
Subscription address: Dieter Kastovsky, Inst. für Anglistik, Univ. Wien, Universitätsstr. 7/III, 1010 Vienna, Austria
Additional subscription address: Mouton de Gruyter, Genthinerstr. 13, 1000 Berlin, Germany
Subscription telephone: (43) 222 401032513

ADVERTISING INFORMATION

Advertising accepted: No

EDITORIAL DESCRIPTION

Scope: Publishes articles on general and comparative linguistics that are of significant interest to the entire membership of the association.
Reviews books: Yes
Publishes notes: Yes
Languages accepted: English; German; French
Prints abstracts: Yes
Author-anonymous submission: No

SUBMISSION REQUIREMENTS

Restrictions on contributors: Contributors must be members of the Soc. Linguistica Europaea.
Author pays submission fee: No
Author pays page charges: No
Length of articles: 50,000 words maximum
Length of book reviews: 1,500 words
Length of notes: 1,500 words
Style: Journal

Number of copies required: 2
Special requirements: Submit double-spaced typescript with wide margins.
Copyright ownership: Soc. Linguistica Europaea
Rejected manuscripts: Returned
Time before publication decision: 3 mos.
Time between decision and publication: 18 mos.
Number of reviewers: 3
Articles submitted per year: 30
Articles published per year: 21
Book reviews submitted per year: 1-2
Book reviews published per year: 1-2

(1011)
Folia Orientalia

Stanisław Stachowski & Zdzisław Kapera, Editors
Komisja Orientalistyczna
Polska Akademia Nauk
ul. Sławkowska 17
31-016 Cracow, Poland

First published: 1958
Sponsoring organization: Polska Akademia Nauk, Cracow Branch, Komisja Orientalistyczna
ISSN: 0015-5675
MLA acronym: FoliaO

SUBSCRIPTION INFORMATION

Frequency of publication: Annual
Circulation: 1,000
Available in microform: No
Subscription address: Ars Polona, ul. Krakowskie Przedmieście 7, 000-068 Warsaw, Poland

ADVERTISING INFORMATION

Advertising accepted: No

EDITORIAL DESCRIPTION

Scope: Publishes articles on Oriental research.
Reviews books: Yes
Publishes notes: Yes
Languages accepted: English; French; German
Prints abstracts: No
Author-anonymous submission: No

SUBMISSION REQUIREMENTS

Restrictions on contributors: None
Author pays submission fee: No
Author pays page charges: No
Length of articles: 4,000 words
Length of book reviews: 800 words
Length of notes: 200 words
Style: Journal
Number of copies required: 2
Special requirements: Submit original typescript; include footnotes at end of article. Allow maximum of 31 lines per page of text.
Copyright ownership: Ossolineum Publishing House
Rejected manuscripts: Returned at author's request
Time before publication decision: 3 mos.
Time between decision and publication: 18-24 mos.
Number of reviewers: 2
Articles submitted per year: 30
Articles published per year: 20-25
Book reviews submitted per year: 15
Book reviews published per year: 10-15
Notes submitted per year: 5-10
Notes published per year: 5-10

(1012)
*Folia Phoniatrica: International Journal of Phoniatrics, Speech Therapy and Communication Pathology

E. Loebell, K. G. Butler, S. Fex, N. Kotby, R. Luchsinger, H. Oyer, & J. Perelló, Editors
S. Karger AG
Editorial Dept.
4009 Basel, Switzerland

Additional editorial address: Communications for *IALP News* should be sent to: A. Muller, Avenue de la Gare 6, 1003 Lausanne, Switzerland
Telephone: (41) 61 3061111
Fax: (41) 61 3061234
First published: 1947
Sponsoring organization: International Assn. of Logopedics & Phoniatrics (IALP)
ISSN: 0015-5705
MLA acronym: FPhon

SUBSCRIPTION INFORMATION

Frequency of publication: 6 times/yr.
Circulation: 1,600
Available in microform: Yes
Subscription price: 280 SwF (359 DM, £122.00, $187.00)/yr. institutions; 196 SwF (252 DM, £86.00, $131.00)/yr. individuals
Year to which price refers: 1992
Subscription address: S. Karger AG, P.O. Box, 4009 Basel, Switzerland
Additional subscription address: S. Karger Publishers, Inc., 26 West Avon Rd., P.O. Box 529, Farmington, CT 06085
Subscription telephone: 203 675-7834
Subscription fax: 203 675-7302

ADVERTISING INFORMATION

Advertising accepted: Yes

EDITORIAL DESCRIPTION

Scope: Publishes articles concerning experimental and quantitive methods for the study of physiology and pathology of speech and the vocal organs.
Reviews books: Yes
Publishes notes: No
Languages accepted: English; French; German
Prints abstracts: No
Author-anonymous submission: No

SUBMISSION REQUIREMENTS

Restrictions on contributors: None
Author pays submission fee: No
Author pays page charges: Yes, for more than 5 printed pp.
Length of articles: No restrictions
Length of book reviews: No restrictions
Style: Journal; see "Instructions to Authors"
Number of copies required: 2
Special requirements: Submit original double-spaced typescript plus 1 copy. Include a 10-line (maximum) summary in each of the two languages not used in the paper. Consult publisher for further details.
Copyright ownership: S. Karger AG
Rejected manuscripts: Returned
Time before publication decision: 6 mos.
Time between decision and publication: 1 yr.
Number of reviewers: 2
Articles submitted per year: 50
Articles published per year: 30
Book reviews published per year: 5; 20 in *IALP News* section
Notes published per year: 25 in *IALP News* section

(1013)
*Folk Life: Journal of Ethnological Studies

Roy Brigden, Editor
Museum of English Rural Life
Univ. of Reading
Whiteknights Park, Reading, England

First published: 1963
Sponsoring organization: Soc. for Folk Life Studies
ISSN: 0430-8778
MLA acronym: FoL

SUBSCRIPTION INFORMATION

Frequency of publication: Annual
Circulation: 550
Available in microform: No
Subscription price: £12.50/yr.
Year to which price refers: 1992
Subscription address: C. Stevens, Hon. Treasurer, Welsh Folk Museum, St. Fagans, Cardiff, Wales
Subscription telephone: (44) 222 569441
Subscription fax: (44) 222 578413

ADVERTISING INFORMATION

Advertising accepted: Yes
Advertising rates: £50.00/half page

EDITORIAL DESCRIPTION

Scope: Publishes articles on studies of traditional and changing ways of life in Great Britain and Ireland. Includes articles which explore a variety of approaches to the practice and methodology of ethnological studies through architecture, geography, history, linguistics, onomastics, material culture, folklore, etc.
Reviews books: Yes
Publishes notes: Yes
Languages accepted: English
Prints abstracts: No
Author-anonymous submission: Yes

SUBMISSION REQUIREMENTS

Restrictions on contributors: None
Author pays submission fee: No
Author pays page charges: No
Length of articles: 3,000-7,000 words
Length of notes: 1,000 words
Style: Modern Humanities Research Assn.
Number of copies required: 1
Copyright ownership: Author
Rejected manuscripts: Returned
Time before publication decision: 2 weeks
Time between decision and publication: 6-18 mos.
Number of reviewers: 2
Articles submitted per year: 10-18
Articles published per year: 8-10
Book reviews submitted per year: 15-17
Book reviews published per year: 15-17
Notes submitted per year: 5-10
Notes published per year: 2-3

(1014)
*Folk Music Journal

Ian Russell, Editor
Bridge House
Unstone
Sheffield SI8 5AF, England

Telephone: (44) 246 417315
First published: 1965
Sponsoring organization: English Folk Dance & Song Soc.
ISSN: 0531-9684
MLA acronym: FMJ

SUBSCRIPTION INFORMATION

Frequency of publication: Annual

Circulation: 5,000
Available in microform: No
Subscription price: £12.00/yr. institutions United Kingdom; $24.00/yr. institutions US; £7.50/yr individuals United Kingdom; $15.00/yr. individuals US
Year to which price refers: 1992
Subscription address: Cecil Sharp House, 2 Regent's Park Rd., London NW1 7AY, England
Subscription telephone: (44) 71 4852206

ADVERTISING INFORMATION

Advertising accepted: Yes

EDITORIAL DESCRIPTION

Scope: Focuses on the study of folk/traditional music, song, dance, and drama.
Reviews books: Yes
Publishes notes: Yes
Languages accepted: English
Prints abstracts: No
Author-anonymous submission: No

SUBMISSION REQUIREMENTS

Restrictions on contributors: None
Author pays submission fee: No
Author pays page charges: No
Length of articles: 4,000-15,000 words
Length of book reviews: 600-1,200 words
Length of notes: 300-4,000 words
Style: Modern Humanities Research Assn.
Number of copies required: 1
Special requirements: Submit original manuscript.
Copyright ownership: Journal
Rejected manuscripts: Returned; enclose SASE.
Time before publication decision: Decisions made 1 Nov.
Time between decision and publication: 9-12 mos.
Number of reviewers: 10
Articles submitted per year: 6
Articles published per year: 3-4
Book reviews submitted per year: 25
Book reviews published per year: 20
Notes submitted per year: 1-5
Notes published per year: 1-5

(1015)
*Folk og Kultur: Årbog for Dansk Etnologi og Folkemindevidenskab

George Nellemann, Bengt Holbek, Iørn Piö, & Poul Moustgaard, Editors
c/o Nationalmuseets 3. Afdeling
Brede
2800 Lyngby, Denmark

First published: 1972
Sponsoring organization: Arthur Christensens Folkemindefond
ISSN: 0105-1024
MLA acronym: FoK

SUBSCRIPTION INFORMATION

Frequency of publication: Annual
Circulation: 1,600
Available in microform: No
Subscription address: Foreningen Danmarks Folkeminder, c/o Dansk Folkemindesamling, Birketinget 6, 2300 Copenhagen S, Denmark

ADVERTISING INFORMATION

Advertising accepted: No

EDITORIAL DESCRIPTION

Scope: Publishes articles on ethnology and folk life, particularly in Denmark.
Reviews books: Yes
Publishes notes: No
Languages accepted: Danish
Prints abstracts: Yes

SUBMISSION REQUIREMENTS

Author pays submission fee: No
Author pays page charges: No
Length of articles: 4,000-16,000 words
Length of book reviews: 600-700 words
Style: None
Number of copies required: 3
Special requirements: Submit typescript.
Copyright ownership: Author
Rejected manuscripts: Returned
Time before publication decision: 2-3 mos.
Time between decision and publication: 8-9 mos.
Number of reviewers: 4
Articles submitted per year: 7
Articles published per year: 6-8
Book reviews published per year: 20

(1016)
*Folklife Center News

James Hardin, Editor
American Folklife Center
Library of Congress
Washington, DC 20540

Telephone: 202 707-1741
First published: 1978
Sponsoring organization: American Folklife Center, Library of Congress
ISSN: 0149-6840
MLA acronym: FCN

SUBSCRIPTION INFORMATION

Frequency of publication: 4 times/yr.
Circulation: 10,000
Available in microform: No
Subscription price: Free
Year to which price refers: 1992
Subscription telephone: 202 707-6590

ADVERTISING INFORMATION

Advertising accepted: No

EDITORIAL DESCRIPTION

Scope: Publishes articles on the programs and activities of the American Folklife Center, as well as other articles on traditional expressive culture.
Reviews books: No
Publishes notes: No
Languages accepted: English
Prints abstracts: No
Author-anonymous submission: No

SUBMISSION REQUIREMENTS

Author pays submission fee: No
Author pays page charges: No
Length of articles: 1,000-4,000 words
Style: Chicago
Number of copies required: 1
Special requirements: Submit typescript and diskette using WordPerfect.
Copyright ownership: Author
Rejected manuscripts: Returned
Time before publication decision: 1 mo.
Time between decision and publication: 1-6 mos.
Number of reviewers: 2

(1017)
*Folklore

Jacqueline Simpson, Editor
9 Christchurch Rd.
Worthing
West Sussex BN11 1JH, England

Telephone: (44) 903 200163
First published: 1878
Sponsoring organization: Folklore Soc.
ISSN: 0015-587X
MLA acronym: Folklore

SUBSCRIPTION INFORMATION

Frequency of publication: 2 times/yr. (Spring, Fall)
Circulation: 1,200
Available in microform: No
Subscription price: $45.00 (£18.00)/yr.
Year to which price refers: 1991
Subscription address: Hon. Secretary, Folklore Soc., Univ. College, Gower St., London WC1E 6BT, England
Subscription telephone: (44) 71 3875894

ADVERTISING INFORMATION

Advertising accepted: Yes
Advertising rates: £25.00/half page; £50.00/full page

EDITORIAL DESCRIPTION

Scope: Publishes articles on folklore from any area or period, with particular emphasis on British, European, and related cultural traditions.
Reviews books: Yes
Publishes notes: Yes
Languages accepted: English
Prints abstracts: No
Author-anonymous submission: No

SUBMISSION REQUIREMENTS

Restrictions on contributors: None
Author pays submission fee: No
Author pays page charges: No
Length of articles: 2,000-15,000 words
Length of book reviews: 200-1,000 words
Length of notes: 500-1,000 words
Style: Journal
Number of copies required: 2
Copyright ownership: Journal
Rejected manuscripts: Returned; enclose return postage.
Time before publication decision: 6 weeks
Time between decision and publication: 18 mos.
Number of reviewers: 3-4
Articles submitted per year: 35
Articles published per year: 20
Book reviews submitted per year: 25
Book reviews published per year: 25
Notes submitted per year: 4
Notes published per year: 4

(1018)
Folklore: English Monthly Devoted to the Cause of Indian Folklore Society

Kanad Dasgupta, Editor
172/22 Acharya Jagadish Bose Rd.
Calcutta 14, India

First published: 1956
Sponsoring organization: Indian Publications Devoted to the Cause of Indian Folklore Soc.
ISSN: 0015-5896
MLA acronym: FolkloreC

SUBSCRIPTION INFORMATION

Frequency of publication: 12 times/yr.
Circulation: 5,000
Available in microform: Yes
Subscription address: Indian Publications, 3 British Indian St., Calcutta 700069, India

ADVERTISING INFORMATION

Advertising accepted: Yes

EDITORIAL DESCRIPTION

Scope: Publishes articles on folklore, sociology, anthropology, social work, agriculture, social and physical education, behavioral and field sciences, as well as traditional literature, song, music, dance, folk arts, crafts, and tribal studies. Emphasis is on Indian studies.
Reviews books: Yes
Publishes notes: Yes
Languages accepted: English; Hindi-Urdu
Prints abstracts: No
Author-anonymous submission: No

SUBMISSION REQUIREMENTS

Restrictions on contributors: None
Author pays submission fee: No
Author pays page charges: No
Length of articles: 2,500-10,000 words
Length of book reviews: 500-1,500 words
Length of notes: 200-750 words
Style: MLA
Number of copies required: 1; 2 preferred
Special requirements: Submit original typescript; cite quotations in original language with English translation. Notes should be based on important events in folklore, obituary notice of folklore scholars, or significant achievement in folklore studies.
Copyright ownership: Assigned by author to journal for 3 yrs.
Rejected manuscripts: Returned; enclose return postage.
Time before publication decision: 3 mos.
Time between decision and publication: 15 mos.
Number of reviewers: 2
Articles submitted per year: 150
Articles published per year: 45-50
Book reviews submitted per year: 100
Book reviews published per year: 20-30
Notes submitted per year: 71-80
Notes published per year: 50-55

(1019)
*Folklore Fellows' Communications

Lauri Honko, Editor
FFC Editorial Office
Hämeenkatu 2 A 12
20500 Turku, Finland

Additional editorial address: Satakielenkatu 8, 20610 Turku, Finland
Telephone: (358) 21 6335241
Fax: (358) 21 6336360
First published: 1910
Sponsoring organization: Academia Scientiarum Fennica
ISSN: 0014-5815
MLA acronym: FFC

SUBSCRIPTION INFORMATION

Frequency of publication: 2-4 times/yr.
Circulation: 120
Available in microform: No
Subscription address: Federation of Finnish Scientific Socs., Bookstore Tiedekirja, Kirkkokatu 14, 00170 Helsinki, Finland
Additional subscription address: Akateeminen Kirjakauppa, Postbox 128, 00101 Helsinki 10, Finland
Subscription telephone: (358) 0 635177

ADVERTISING INFORMATION

Advertising accepted: No

EDITORIAL DESCRIPTION

Scope: Publishes monographs on oral literature, folklore, folk customs, myth, folk belief, and ritual.
Reviews books: No
Publishes notes: No
Languages accepted: English; French; German
Prints abstracts: No
Author-anonymous submission: No

SUBMISSION REQUIREMENTS

Restrictions on contributors: None
Author pays submission fee: No
Author pays page charges: Yes, for doctoral dissertations over 200 pp.
Length of books: No restrictions
Style: Series
Number of copies required: 1
Copyright ownership: Academia Scientiarum Fennica & author upon request
Rejected manuscripts: Returned
Time before publication decision: 1-4 mos.
Time between decision and publication: 3-6 mos.
Number of reviewers: 2-3
Books submitted per year: 6-8
Books published per year: 2-4

(1020)
*Folklore Forum

Charles Greg Kelley & Jill Terry Rudy, Editors
504 N. Fess St.
Bloomington, IN 47405

Telephone: 812 855-0426
First published: 1968
ISSN: 0015-5926
MLA acronym: FForum

SUBSCRIPTION INFORMATION

Frequency of publication: 2 times/yr.
Circulation: 250
Available in microform: No
Subscription price: $10.00/yr. institutions; $8.00/yr. individuals; $6.00/yr. students; add $2.00/yr. postage outside US
Year to which price refers: 1992

ADVERTISING INFORMATION

Advertising accepted: Yes

EDITORIAL DESCRIPTION

Scope: Publishes analytical articles, translations, and reviews on topics in folklore and folklife. Journal is international in scope.
Reviews books: Yes
Publishes notes: Yes
Languages accepted: English
Prints abstracts: No
Author-anonymous submission: Yes

SUBMISSION REQUIREMENTS

Restrictions on contributors: None
Author pays submission fee: No
Author pays page charges: No
Length of articles: No restrictions
Length of book reviews: 200 words minimum
Style: Chicago
Number of copies required: 2
Special requirements: Include a short biography of author. Submit manuscript and diskette in ASCII or WordPerfect format.
Copyright ownership: Author & Journal
Rejected manuscripts: Returned; enclose SASE.
Time before publication decision: 8-16 weeks
Time between decision and publication: 6 mos.
Number of reviewers: 3-4
Articles submitted per year: 25
Articles published per year: 10
Book reviews submitted per year: 30-50
Book reviews published per year: 20-24 including record & film reviews
Notes submitted per year: 10
Notes published per year: 6

(1021)
*The Folklore Historian: Journal of the Folklore and History Section of the American Folklore Society

Ronald L. Baker, Editor
Dept. of English
Indiana State Univ.
Terre Haute, IN 47809

Telephone: 812 237-3160
Fax: 812 237-4382
First published: 1984
Sponsoring organization: Folklore & History Section, American Folklore Soc.
ISSN: 1041-8644
MLA acronym: FolkH

SUBSCRIPTION INFORMATION

Frequency of publication: Annual (Summer)
Circulation: 350
Available in microform: No
Subscription price: $7.00/yr.
Year to which price refers: 1992

ADVERTISING INFORMATION

Advertising accepted: No

EDITORIAL DESCRIPTION

Scope: Publishes articles on the history of folklore studies, historical folk narratives, folk biography, museology, and other topics treating the relations of folklore and history or utilizing historical methodology in folklore research.
Reviews books: Yes
Publishes notes: Yes
Languages accepted: English
Prints abstracts: No
Author-anonymous submission: Yes

SUBMISSION REQUIREMENTS

Restrictions on contributors: None
Author pays submission fee: No
Author pays page charges: No
Length of articles: 3,000-9,000 words
Length of book reviews: 1,000 words
Length of notes: 1,000-2,000 words
Style: Chicago
Number of copies required: 1
Special requirements: Accepted articles should be submitted on an IBM-compatible diskette.
Copyright ownership: Author
Rejected manuscripts: Returned
Time before publication decision: 6-12 mos.
Time between decision and publication: 3 mos.
Number of reviewers: 3
Articles submitted per year: 25
Articles published per year: 6-8
Book reviews published per year: 0-2
Notes published per year: 0-2

(1022)
*Folklore Suisse/Folclore Svizzero: Bulletin de la Société Suisse des Traditions Populaires/Bolletino della Società Svizzera per le Tradizioni Populari

Schweizerische Gesellschaft für Volkskunde
Augustinergasse 19
4051 Basel, Switzerland

Additional editorial address: Bernard Schüle, Scientific Editor, Musée Nationale Suisse, C.P. 6789, 8023 Zurich, Switzerland
Telephone: (41) 61 2619900
First published: 1911
Sponsoring organization: Schweizerische Gesellschaft für Volkskunde/Soc. Suisse des Traditions Populaires
ISSN: 0015-5989
MLA acronym: FolkS

SUBSCRIPTION INFORMATION

Frequency of publication: 6 times/yr.
Circulation: 850
Available in microform: No
Subscription price: 44 SwF/yr.
Year to which price refers: 1992

ADVERTISING INFORMATION

Advertising accepted: No

EDITORIAL DESCRIPTION

Scope: Publishes studies on Swiss folklore, including articles on popular poetry, popular beliefs, folklife, manners and customs, arts and crafts, costume, and foodways.
Reviews books: Yes
Publishes notes: Yes
Languages accepted: French; Italian
Prints abstracts: Yes
Author-anonymous submission: Yes

SUBMISSION REQUIREMENTS

Restrictions on contributors: None
Author pays submission fee: No
Author pays page charges: No
Number of copies required: 1
Copyright ownership: Schweizerische Gesellschaft für Volkskunde
Rejected manuscripts: Returned
Time before publication decision: 3 weeks
Time between decision and publication: 3 mos.
Number of reviewers: 2
Articles published per year: 5-15
Book reviews published per year: 0-15
Notes published per year: 5-10

(1023)
*Fontane Blätter

Theodor Fontane Archiv
Postfach 59
Dortustr. 30/34
1561 Potsdam, Germany

First published: 1965
ISSN: 0015-6175
MLA acronym: FB

SUBSCRIPTION INFORMATION

Frequency of publication: 2 times/yr.
Circulation: 1,100
Available in microform: No
Subscription price: 8.50 DM/yr. plus postage
Year to which price refers: 1992

ADVERTISING INFORMATION

Advertising accepted: Yes

EDITORIAL DESCRIPTION

Scope: Publishes articles on Theodor Fontane.
Reviews books: Yes
Publishes notes: Yes
Languages accepted: German
Prints abstracts: No
Author-anonymous submission: No

SUBMISSION REQUIREMENTS

Author pays page charges: No
Length of articles: 25 pp.
Length of book reviews: 3 pp. maximum
Length of notes: 5 pp.
Style: Journal
Number of copies required: 2
Copyright ownership: Journal
Rejected manuscripts: Not returned
Time before publication decision: 6 mos.
Time between decision and publication: 6 mos.
Number of reviewers: 4-8
Articles submitted per year: 24
Articles published per year: 20
Book reviews submitted per year: 10

Book reviews published per year: 10
Notes submitted per year: 8
Notes published per year: 6

(1024)
*Foreign Language Teaching and Research: A Quarterly of Foreign Languages and Cultures

Xu Guozhang, Yao Xiaoping, & Chen Guohua, Editors
Editor's Dept.
Box 169
P.O. Box 8110
Beijing, People's Republic of China

Additional editorial address: Editor's Dept., 2 North Xisanhuan Ave., Beijing 100081, People's Republic of China
Telephone: (86) 1 8422277 ext. 467
Fax: (86) 1 8423144
First published: 1957
Sponsoring organization: Beijing Foreign Studies Univ.
MLA acronym: FLTR

SUBSCRIPTION INFORMATION

Frequency of publication: 4 times/yr. (Mar., June, Sept., Dec.)
Circulation: 13,000
Available in microform: No
Subscription address: China International Book Trading Corp., P.O. Box 2820, Beijing, People's Republic of China

ADVERTISING INFORMATION

Advertising accepted: Yes

EDITORIAL DESCRIPTION

Scope: Publishes articles on foreign second language teaching (methodology & theory) and non-Chinese linguistics. Includes works on linguistic theory, comparative linguistics, psycholinguistics, sociolinguistics, applied linguistics, pragmatics, grammar, phonology, semantics, lexicology, stylistics, translation, and cultural studies.
Reviews books: Yes
Publishes notes: Yes
Languages accepted: Chinese languages; English
Prints abstracts: Yes
Author-anonymous submission: No

SUBMISSION REQUIREMENTS

Restrictions on contributors: None
Author pays submission fee: No
Author pays page charges: No
Length of articles: 4,000-10,000 words
Length of book reviews: 1,000-5,000 words
Length of notes: 500-1,000 words
Style: MLA with modifications
Number of copies required: 1
Special requirements: Submit a 200-word abstract (in Chinese and, if possible, in English).
Copyright ownership: Journal; reverts to author after 1 yr.
Rejected manuscripts: Returned; enclose return postage.
Time before publication decision: 3 mos.
Time between decision and publication: 6 mos.
Number of reviewers: 2-3
Articles submitted per year: 300-400
Articles published per year: 30-40
Book reviews submitted per year: 60-80
Book reviews published per year: 15-20
Notes submitted per year: 100-150
Notes published per year: 20-30

(1025)
*Foreign Literatures

Wang Zuoliang & Li De-en, Editors
Letter Box 91
Beijing Foreign Studies Univ.
19 North Xisanhuan Ave.
Beijing 100081, People's Republic of China

Telephone: (86) 1 8422277-730
Fax: (86) 1 8423144
First published: 1980
Sponsoring organization: Inst. of Research in Foreign Literatures; Publishing House of Foreign Language Teaching & Research; Beijing Foreign Studies Univ.
MLA acronym: FLits

SUBSCRIPTION INFORMATION

Frequency of publication: Bimonthly
Circulation: 15,000
Available in microform: No

ADVERTISING INFORMATION

Advertising accepted: No

EDITORIAL DESCRIPTION

Scope: Publishes Chinese translations of contemporary fiction, poetry, drama, and literary criticism as well as original Chinese language articles about foreign literatures.
Reviews books: Yes
Publishes notes: No
Languages accepted: Chinese languages; other languages are considered
Prints abstracts: No
Author-anonymous submission: Yes

SUBMISSION REQUIREMENTS

Restrictions on contributors: Articles in languages other than Chinese are occasionally accepted and Chinese translations are arranged.
Author pays submission fee: No
Author pays page charges: No
Length of articles: 3,000-5,000 characters
Length of book reviews: 3,000 characters
Number of copies required: 2
Rejected manuscripts: Returned
Time before publication decision: 2 mos.
Time between decision and publication: 1 mo.
Number of reviewers: 2
Articles submitted per year: 1,000
Articles published per year: 200
Book reviews submitted per year: 100
Book reviews published per year: 40

(1026)
Foro Literario: Revista de Literatura y Lenguaje

Julio Ricci & Rima de Vallbona, Editors
El Viejo Pancho, 2585
Montevideo, Uruguay

Additional editorial address: Rima de Vallbona, Univ. of St. Thomas, Houston, TX 77006
First published: 1977
Sponsoring organization: Univ. of St. Thomas, Houston, TX
MLA acronym: ForoL

SUBSCRIPTION INFORMATION

Frequency of publication: 6 times/yr.
Available in microform: No

ADVERTISING INFORMATION

Advertising accepted: Yes

EDITORIAL DESCRIPTION

Scope: Publishes original work and critical writings on Latin American literature and languages.
Reviews books: Yes
Publishes notes: Yes
Languages accepted: Spanish
Prints abstracts: No

SUBMISSION REQUIREMENTS

Author pays submission fee: No
Author pays page charges: No
Length of articles: 5,000-5,500 words
Length of book reviews: 500-700 words
Length of notes: 100 words
Style: MLA
Number of copies required: 1
Special requirements: Will consider, in special cases, submissions in English, French, Italian, and Portuguese. Include check for $2.00 to defray mailing charges.
Copyright ownership: Author
Rejected manuscripts: Not returned
Time before publication decision: 6 mos.
Time between decision and publication: 6-12 mos.
Articles published per year: 8-10
Book reviews submitted per year: 30
Book reviews published per year: 20-25

(1027)
*Forschungen zu Paul Valéry—Recherches Valéryennes

Karl Alfred Blüher & Jürgen Schmidt-Radefeldt, Editors
Romanisches Seminar
Univ. Kiel
Leibnizstr. 10
2300 Kiel, Germany

Telephone: (49) 431 8802266
Fax: (49) 431 8801512
First published: 1988
ISSN: 0934-5337
MLA acronym: FPVRV

SUBSCRIPTION INFORMATION

Frequency of publication: 1-2 times/yr.
Circulation: 100
Available in microform: No

ADVERTISING INFORMATION

Advertising accepted: Yes

EDITORIAL DESCRIPTION

Scope: Publishes research on Paul Valéry and his work. Includes interdisciplinary articles, book reviews, announcements, reports on research in progress, and bibliographical surveys.
Reviews books: Yes
Publishes notes: Yes
Languages accepted: German; French; English
Prints abstracts: No
Author-anonymous submission: Yes

SUBMISSION REQUIREMENTS

Author pays submission fee: No
Author pays page charges: No
Length of articles: 8,000 words maximum
Length of book reviews: 3,600 words
Style: Journal; see 1988; 1
Number of copies required: 2
Copyright ownership: Editors
Rejected manuscripts: Returned
Time before publication decision: 2 mos.
Time between decision and publication: 5 mos.
Number of reviewers: 3
Articles submitted per year: 5
Articles published per year: 5
Book reviews submitted per year: 3-4
Book reviews published per year: 3-4

Notes submitted per year: 8
Notes published per year: 8

(1028)
*Forschungen zur Geschichte der Älteren Deutschen Literatur

Joachim Bumke, Thomas Cramer, Klaus Grubmüller, Gert Kaiser, & Horst Wenzel, Editors
c/o Thomas Cramer
Inst. für Deutsche Philologie
der Technischen Univ. Berlin
Str. des 17. Juni 135
1000 Berlin 12, Germany

First published: 1980
ISSN: 0177-9370
MLA acronym: FGADL

SUBSCRIPTION INFORMATION

Frequency of publication: Irregular
Circulation: 600
Available in microform: No
Subscription address: Wilhelm Fink Verlag, Ohmstr. 5, 8000 Munich 40, Germany

ADVERTISING INFORMATION

Advertising accepted: No

EDITORIAL DESCRIPTION

Scope: Publishes monographs on Medieval German literature.
Reviews books: No
Publishes notes: No
Languages accepted: German; English; French
Prints abstracts: No

SUBMISSION REQUIREMENTS

Restrictions on contributors: None
Author pays submission fee: No
Author pays page charges: No
Length of books: No restrictions
Style: None
Number of copies required: 1
Copyright ownership: Wilhelm Fink Verlag
Rejected manuscripts: Returned
Time before publication decision: 1-2 mos.
Time between decision and publication: 6-12 mos.
Number of reviewers: 2

(1029)
*Forschungen zur Geschichte Oberösterreichs

Siegfried Haider & Georg Heilingsetzer, Editors
Oberösterreichisches Landesarchiv
Anzengruberstr. 19
4020 Linz, Austria

Telephone: (43) 732 655523
Fax: (43) 732 655523-4619
First published: 1952
Sponsoring organization: Land Oberösterreich
ISSN: 0429-1565
MLA acronym: FGO

SUBSCRIPTION INFORMATION

Frequency of publication: Irregular
Circulation: 500
Available in microform: No

ADVERTISING INFORMATION

Advertising accepted: Yes

EDITORIAL DESCRIPTION

Scope: Publishes monographs on the history of Upper Austria.
Reviews books: No

Publishes notes: No
Languages accepted: German
Prints abstracts: No
Author-anonymous submission: No

SUBMISSION REQUIREMENTS

Restrictions on contributors: None
Author pays submission fee: No
Author pays page charges: No
Number of copies required: 1
Special requirements: Submit typescript.
Copyright ownership: Assigned by author to Oberösterreichisches Landesarchiv
Rejected manuscripts: Returned
Time before publication decision: 1 mo.
Time between decision and publication: 1 yr.
Number of reviewers: 2

(1030)
*Fort Hare Papers

M. J. Prins, Editor
Fort Hare Univ. Press
Private Bag 1314
Alice, Republic of Ciskei, South Africa

Telephone: (27) 404 32011 ext. 2084
Fax: (27) 404 31643
First published: 1945
Sponsoring organization: Fort Hare Univ.
ISSN: 0015-8054
MLA acronym: FHP

SUBSCRIPTION INFORMATION

Frequency of publication: Once every 18 mos.
Circulation: 180
Available in microform: No
Subscription price: 5 R/yr.
Year to which price refers: 1992
Subscription address: Fort Hare Univ. Press, Private Bag 322, Alice, Republic of Ciskei, South Africa

ADVERTISING INFORMATION

Advertising accepted: No

EDITORIAL DESCRIPTION

Scope: Publishes original research, thought, or collocation of material which constitutes a significant contribution to art or science. Articles which have a bearing on the African scene and African development are particularly welcome.
Reviews books: No
Publishes notes: No
Languages accepted: English; Afrikaans
Prints abstracts: Yes
Author-anonymous submission: No

SUBMISSION REQUIREMENTS

Restrictions on contributors: Contributors must be staff members of Fort Hare Univ.
Author pays submission fee: No
Author pays page charges: No
Length of articles: 10,000 words
Style: Journal; request guidelines.
Number of copies required: 3
Special requirements: Submit original double-spaced typescript plus 2 copies and a diskette using WordPerfect; include a 250-word abstract.
Copyright ownership: Author with restrictions
Rejected manuscripts: Returned
Time before publication decision: 3 mos.
Time between decision and publication: 1 yr.
Number of reviewers: 5
Articles submitted per year: 8
Articles published per year: 3-4

(1031)
Fortuna Vitrea

Walter Haug & Burghart Wachinger, Editors
Max Niemeyer Verlag
Postfach 2140
7400 Tübingen, Germany

ISSN: 0938-9660
MLA acronym: FV

EDITORIAL DESCRIPTION

Scope: Publishes studies on European literature.
Reviews books: No
Publishes notes: No
Languages accepted: German

(1032)
*Forum

Slavko Mihalić, Editor
Hrvatska Akademija Znanosti i Umjetnosti
Razred za Književnost
Zrinjski trg 11
41000 Zagreb, Croatia

First published: 1961
Sponsoring organization: Jugoslavenska Akademija Znanosti i Umjetnosti
ISSN: 0015-8445
MLA acronym: ForumZ

SUBSCRIPTION INFORMATION

Frequency of publication: 8 times/yr.
Circulation: 3,000
Available in microform: No
Subscription price: $60.00/yr.
Year to which price refers: 1992
Subscription address: Ulica Andrije Hebranga 1, 41000 Zagreb, Croatia

ADVERTISING INFORMATION

Advertising accepted: Yes
Advertising rates: $300.00/full page

EDITORIAL DESCRIPTION

Scope: Publishes articles on literature.
Reviews books: Yes
Publishes notes: Yes
Languages accepted: Serbo-Croatian
Prints abstracts: No
Author-anonymous submission: Yes

SUBMISSION REQUIREMENTS

Author pays submission fee: No
Length of articles: 30,000-60,000 words
Length of book reviews: 15,000-30,000 words
Length of notes: 50 words
Number of copies required: 1
Copyright ownership: Author
Rejected manuscripts: Not returned
Time before publication decision: 2 weeks
Time between decision and publication: 2-24 mos.
Number of reviewers: 1
Articles submitted per year: 400
Articles published per year: 100
Book reviews submitted per year: 100
Book reviews published per year: 40
Notes submitted per year: 300
Notes published per year: 300

(1033)
Forum: A Ukrainian Review

Andrew Gregorovich, Editor
314 Oriole Pkwy.
Toronto, Ontario M5P 2H5, Canada

Telephone: 416 480-2440
First published: 1967
Sponsoring organization: Ukrainian Fraternal Assn.
ISSN: 0015-8399
MLA acronym: ForumS

SUBSCRIPTION INFORMATION

Frequency of publication: 4 times/yr. (Mar., June, Sept., Dec.)
Circulation: 3,500
Available in microform: No
Subscription price: $10.00/yr. US & Canada
Year to which price refers: 1992
Subscription address: Box 350, 440 Wyoming Ave., Scranton, PA 18503-0350

ADVERTISING INFORMATION

Advertising accepted: No

EDITORIAL DESCRIPTION

Scope: Publishes articles on the arts, culture, history, and achievements of Ukraine and Ukrainians in the US, Canada, and Ukraine.
Reviews books: Yes
Publishes notes: Yes
Languages accepted: English
Prints abstracts: No

SUBMISSION REQUIREMENTS

Restrictions on contributors: None
Author pays submission fee: No
Author pays page charges: No
Length of articles: 2,000 words
Length of book reviews: 500 words
Length of notes: 100 words
Number of copies required: 2
Special requirements: Query the editor before writing a feature-length article. Submit original typescript.
Copyright ownership: Publisher
Rejected manuscripts: Returned; enclose return postage.
Time before publication decision: 7 weeks
Time between decision and publication: 6-9 mos.
Number of reviewers: 2
Articles published per year: 40
Book reviews submitted per year: 35
Book reviews published per year: 30
Notes submitted per year: 30
Notes published per year: 30

(1034)
*Forum der Letteren: Tijdschrift voor Taal- en Letterkunde

Saskia van As, Matthias Hüning, Jan van Luxemburg, Arie Verhagen, Wardy Poelstra, & Ann Rigbey, Editors
Postbus 232
2300 AE Leiden, Netherlands

Additional editorial address: Margreet den Buurman, Secretariat, Levendaal 132a, 2311 JP Leiden, Netherlands
Telephone: (31) 71 127062
First published: 1960
Sponsoring organization: Nederlandse Organisatie voor Zuiver-Wetenschappelijk Onderzoek
ISSN: 0015-8496
MLA acronym: FdL

SUBSCRIPTION INFORMATION

Frequency of publication: 4 times/yr. (Mar., June, Sept., Dec.)
Circulation: 500
Available in microform: No
Subscription address: Uitgeverij Smits bv, Postbus 276, 2501 CG Den Haag, Netherlands

ADVERTISING INFORMATION

Advertising accepted: Yes

EDITORIAL DESCRIPTION

Scope: Publishes articles on the humanities, literature, and linguistics.
Reviews books: Yes
Publishes notes: Yes
Languages accepted: Dutch
Prints abstracts: Yes
Author-anonymous submission: Yes

SUBMISSION REQUIREMENTS

Restrictions on contributors: None
Author pays submission fee: No
Author pays page charges: No
Length of articles: 10-15 printed pp.
Length of book reviews: 1,000 words
Length of notes: 100 words
Style: MLA
Number of copies required: 3
Special requirements: Include a summary.
Copyright ownership: Publisher & Editor
Rejected manuscripts: Returned
Time before publication decision: 3 mos.
Time between decision and publication: 7-8 mos.
Number of reviewers: 4-6
Articles submitted per year: 60
Articles published per year: 18
Book reviews submitted per year: 24
Book reviews published per year: 24
Notes submitted per year: 30
Notes published per year: 8

(1035)
*Forum for Modern Language Studies

J. R. Ashcroft, D. D. R. Owen, & I. R. W. Higgins, Editors
Buchanan Building
Univ. of St. Andrews
St. Andrews,
Fife KY16 9PH, Scotland

Telephone: (44) 334 76161 ext. 394/344/217
Fax: (44) 334 74674
E-mail: Jra@uk.ac.st-andrews
First published: 1965
Sponsoring organization: Univ. of St. Andrews
ISSN: 0015-8518
MLA acronym: FMLS

SUBSCRIPTION INFORMATION

Frequency of publication: 4 times/yr.
Circulation: 500
Available in microform: Yes
Subscription price: $98.00/yr. institutions; $44.00/yr. individuals
Year to which price refers: 1992
Subscription address: Oxford Univ. Press, Pinkhill House, Southfield Rd., Eynsham, Oxford, OX8 1JJ, England
Subscription telephone: (44) 865 882283
Subscription fax: (44) 865 882890

ADVERTISING INFORMATION

Advertising accepted: Yes
Advertising rates: Request from Oxford Univ. Press

EDITORIAL DESCRIPTION

Scope: Publishes articles on European and American languages and literatures from the Middle Ages to the present. Includes short notices and occasional review articles.
Reviews books: Yes
Publishes notes: Yes
Languages accepted: English
Prints abstracts: No
Author-anonymous submission: No

SUBMISSION REQUIREMENTS

Restrictions on contributors: Notes are commissioned.
Author pays submission fee: No

Author pays page charges: No
Length of articles: 6,000 words for articles; 3,000 words for review articles
Length of book reviews: 3,000 words
Length of notes: 150 words
Style: MLA
Number of copies required: 2
Special requirements: Submit original typescript and 1 copy.
Copyright ownership: Author & journal
Rejected manuscripts: Returned; enclose return postage.
Time before publication decision: 2 mos.
Time between decision and publication: 1-2 yrs.
Number of reviewers: 2
Articles submitted per year: 60
Articles published per year: 28
Notes published per year: 140

(1036)
*Forum Homosexualität und Literatur

Wolfgang Popp, Editor
Fachbereich 3
Universität-Gesamthochschule
Adolf-Reichweinstr.
5900 Siegen, Germany

Additional editorial address: Gerhard Härle, Gladenbacher Weg 69, 3550 Marburg, Germany
Telephone: (49) 271 7404597
Fax: (49) 271 7402330
First published: 1987
Sponsoring organization: Gesellschaft zur Förderung Literaturwissenschaftlicher Homostudien
ISSN: 0931-4091
MLA acronym: ForumHL

SUBSCRIPTION INFORMATION

Frequency of publication: 2-3 times/yr.
Available in microform: No

ADVERTISING INFORMATION

Advertising accepted: Yes

EDITORIAL DESCRIPTION

Scope: Publishes articles on homosexuality as it pertains to literature.
Reviews books: Yes
Publishes notes: Yes
Languages accepted: German
Prints abstracts: No
Author-anonymous submission: No

SUBMISSION REQUIREMENTS

Restrictions on contributors: None
Author pays submission fee: No
Author pays page charges: No
Length of articles: 7,000 words
Length of book reviews: 1,000 words
Length of notes: 200 words
Number of copies required: 1
Copyright ownership: Journal
Rejected manuscripts: Returned
Time before publication decision: 3 mos.
Time between decision and publication: 9 mos.
Number of reviewers: 5
Articles submitted per year: 20-25
Articles published per year: 12
Book reviews submitted per year: 15-18
Book reviews published per year: 9-12
Notes submitted per year: 10
Notes published per year: 5-8

(1037)
*Forum Italicum

M. Ricciardelli, Editor
Center for Italian Studies
State Univ. of New York at Stony Brook
Stony Brook, NY 11794-3359

Telephone: 516 632-7444
Fax: 516 632-6900
First published: 1967
Sponsoring organization: Forum Italicum, Inc.
ISSN: 0014-5858
MLA acronym: FI

SUBSCRIPTION INFORMATION

Frequency of publication: 2 times/yr. (Spring, Fall)
Circulation: 850
Available in microform: No
Subscription price: $30.00/yr. institutions US; $32.00/yr. institutions elsewhere; $20.00/yr. individuals US; $25.00/yr. individuals elsewhere; $15.00/yr. students US; $18.00/yr. students elsewhere
Year to which price refers: 1991

ADVERTISING INFORMATION

Advertising accepted: Yes
Advertising rates: $80.00/half page; $125.00/full page; $150.00/inside cover

EDITORIAL DESCRIPTION

Scope: Intended as a meeting-place where scholars, critics, and teachers can present their views on the language, literature, and culture of Italy and of other countries in relation to Italy. Besides critical and informative articles, *FI* contains the sections Poetry, Translation, and Fiction which give creative writers an opportunity to offer original works, such as poems, short stories, or artistic translations of works of merit. Young and hitherto unpublished scholars are encouraged to contribute their critical or creative work.
Reviews books: Yes
Publishes notes: Yes
Languages accepted: French; Portuguese; Spanish; Italian; English
Prints abstracts: No
Author-anonymous submission: No

SUBMISSION REQUIREMENTS

Restrictions on contributors: Book reviews are commissioned.
Author pays submission fee: No
Author pays page charges: No
Length of articles: 20-25 pp.
Length of book reviews: 2 pp.
Length of notes: 3-4 pp.
Style: MLA
Number of copies required: 2
Copyright ownership: Journal
Rejected manuscripts: Returned: enclose return postage.
Time before publication decision: 3 mos.
Time between decision and publication: 1-2 yrs.
Number of reviewers: 3
Articles submitted per year: 50
Articles published per year: 25
Book reviews submitted per year: 35-40
Book reviews published per year: 30
Notes submitted per year: 55
Notes published per year: 35

(1038)
Forum Linguisticum

Adam Makkai & Valerie Becker Makkai, Editors
c/o Jupiter Press
P.O. Box 101
Lake Bluff, IL 60044

First published: 1976

Sponsoring organization: Linguistic Assn. of Canada & the United States
ISSN: 0163-0768
MLA acronym: ForLing

SUBSCRIPTION INFORMATION

Frequency of publication: 3 times/yr. (Apr., Aug., Dec.)
Circulation: 1,000
Available in microform: No

ADVERTISING INFORMATION

Advertising accepted: Yes

EDITORIAL DESCRIPTION

Scope: Publishes articles on all areas of linguistics, both theoretical and descriptive, and its humanistic applications to related disciplines and to the general human condition.
Reviews books: Yes
Publishes notes: Yes
Languages accepted: English; French; German; Spanish
Prints abstracts: Yes
Author-anonymous submission: Yes

SUBMISSION REQUIREMENTS

Restrictions on contributors: None
Author pays submission fee: No
Author pays page charges: No
Length of articles: 10-20 pp.
Length of book reviews: 2-3 pp.
Length of notes: 1 p.
Style: Linguistic Soc. of America with some modifications; request specifications.
Number of copies required: 3
Special requirements: A 250-word or less abstract should preceed manuscript.
Copyright ownership: Journal
Rejected manuscripts: Returned; enclose return postage.
Time before publication decision: 3 mos.
Time between decision and publication: 6 mos.
Number of reviewers: 3
Articles submitted per year: 35-40
Articles published per year: 15
Book reviews submitted per year: 10
Book reviews published per year: 6-8
Notes submitted per year: 5
Notes published per year: 3

(1039)
Forum Linguisticum

Christoph Gutknecht, Editor
Baumkamp 26
2 Hamburg 60, Germany

First published: 1974
ISSN: 0163-0768
MLA acronym: ForL

SUBSCRIPTION INFORMATION

Frequency of publication: Irregular
Circulation: 200-1,000
Available in microform: No
Subscription address: Verlag Peter Lang AG, Jupiterstr. 15, 3015 Bern, Switzerland

ADVERTISING INFORMATION

Advertising accepted: No

EDITORIAL DESCRIPTION

Scope: Publishes articles or monographs on all aspects of linguistics, both general and applied, and on the teaching of foreign languages.
Reviews books: Yes
Publishes notes: Yes
Prints abstracts: No

SUBMISSION REQUIREMENTS

Restrictions on contributors: None
Author pays submission fee: No
Author pays page charges: Yes
Length of books: No restrictions
Length of book reviews: 20,000 words
Length of notes: 20,000 words
Style: MLA
Number of copies required: 1
Special requirements: Submit reproducible typescript, size A4 paper (8 1/4 in. x 11 3/4 in.). Order prepared paper from: Verlag P. Lang, Eschborner Landstr. 42-50, 6000 Frankfurt a.-M. 90, Germany. Use IBM typewriter, plastic or film ribbon.
Copyright ownership: Assigned by author to Verlag Peter Lang AG
Rejected manuscripts: Returned
Time before publication decision: 1 mo.
Time between decision and publication: 5 mos.
Number of reviewers: 2-3
Books submitted per year: 5-10
Books published per year: 2-3
Book reviews published per year: 5-10
Notes published per year: 4-6

(1040)
*Foundation: The Review of Science Fiction

Edward James & Colin Greenland, Editors
Science Fiction Foundation
Polytechnic of East London
Longbridge Rd.
Dagenham,
Essex RM8 2AS, England

Additional editorial address: Edward James, Univ. of York, King's Manor, York YO1 2EP, England
Telephone: (44) 904 433915
First published: 1972
Sponsoring organization: Science Fiction Foundation
ISSN: 0306-4964
MLA acronym: Foundation

SUBSCRIPTION INFORMATION

Frequency of publication: 3 times/yr. (Spring, Summer, Autumn)
Circulation: 1,200
Available in microform: No

ADVERTISING INFORMATION

Advertising accepted: Yes
Advertising rates: $100.00/full page

EDITORIAL DESCRIPTION

Scope: Publishes critical, historical, and sociological articles on science fiction and autobiographical articles by science fiction writers as well as reviews and criticism of science fiction.
Reviews books: Yes
Publishes notes: Yes
Languages accepted: English
Prints abstracts: No
Author-anonymous submission: No

SUBMISSION REQUIREMENTS

Author pays submission fee: No
Author pays page charges: No
Length of articles: 2,000-8,000 words
Length of book reviews: 750-1,250 words
Style: None
Number of copies required: 1
Special requirements: Submit double-spaced typescript.
Copyright ownership: Author
Rejected manuscripts: Returned at author's request; enclose return postage.
Time before publication decision: 1-2 mos.
Time between decision and publication: 6-9 mos.
Number of reviewers: 3

Articles published per year: 12-15
Book reviews published per year: 40-50

(1041)
*Foundations of Semiotics

Achim Eschbach, Editor
Inst. of Semiotic & Communication Research
Dept. 4
Univ. of Essen
4300 Essen, Germany

First published: 1983
ISSN: 0168-2555
MLA acronym: FoS

SUBSCRIPTION INFORMATION

Frequency of publication: Irregular
Available in microform: No
Subscription address: John Benjamins B.V., P.O. Box 75577, Amsteldijk 44, 1070 AN Amsterdam, Netherlands
Additional subscription address: John Benjamins North America, Inc., 821 Bethlehem Pike, Philadelphia, PA 19118

ADVERTISING INFORMATION

Advertising accepted: No

EDITORIAL DESCRIPTION

Scope: The series is a forum for fundamental research in the field of semiotics. Designed to accomodate book length contributions to the theory of signs. Includes reprints, as well as translations, collections, relevant conference proceedings and analyses and syntheses of current research in semiotics.
Reviews books: No
Publishes notes: No
Languages accepted: English
Prints abstracts: No
Author-anonymous submission: Yes

SUBMISSION REQUIREMENTS

Author pays submission fee: No
Author pays page charges: No
Length of books: 250-350 pp.
Style: Series; request specifications from editor
Copyright ownership: John Benjamins Publishing Co.
Rejected manuscripts: Returned
Time before publication decision: 3 mos.
Time between decision and publication: 1 yr.
Number of reviewers: 2
Books submitted per year: 4-6
Books published per year: 2-3

(1042)
*Foxfire

Eliot Wigginton, Editor
Foxfire Fund, Inc.
Rabun Gap, GA 30568

Telephone: 404 746-5828
Fax: 404 746-5829
First published: 1967
Sponsoring organization: Foxfire Fund, Inc.
ISSN: 0015-9220
MLA acronym: Foxfire

SUBSCRIPTION INFORMATION

Frequency of publication: 4 times/yr.
Circulation: 4,000
Available in microform: Yes
Subscription price: $9.00/yr., $16.00/2 yrs.
Year to which price refers: 1992

ADVERTISING INFORMATION

Advertising accepted: No

EDITORIAL DESCRIPTION

Scope: Publishes articles on folklore and oral history of Appalachian Georgia and North Carolina, as collected by high school students.
Reviews books: No
Publishes notes: No
Languages accepted: English
Prints abstracts: No

SUBMISSION REQUIREMENTS

Restrictions on contributors: Manuscripts are not accepted.
Copyright ownership: Foxfire Fund, Inc.

(1043)
*Le Français au Nigéria

A. U. Iwara, Editor
Dept. of Modern Languages
Univ. of Ibadan
Ibadan, Nigeria

First published: 1966
Sponsoring organization: Nigerian Assn. of French Teachers
ISSN: 0015-9387
MLA acronym: FaN

SUBSCRIPTION INFORMATION

Frequency of publication: 3 times/yr.
Circulation: 500
Available in microform: No
Subscription price: 20 N/yr.
Year to which price refers: 1992

ADVERTISING INFORMATION

Advertising accepted: Yes
Advertising rates: 3,000 N/inside front cover; 2,500 N/back cover

EDITORIAL DESCRIPTION

Scope: Publishes articles on French literature and other French studies.
Reviews books: Yes
Publishes notes: No
Languages accepted: English; French
Prints abstracts: No
Author-anonymous submission: Yes

SUBMISSION REQUIREMENTS

Restrictions on contributors: Contributors must be members of the Nigerian Assn. of French Teachers.
Author pays submission fee: Yes
Cost of submission fee: 50 N
Author pays page charges: No
Length of articles: 15-20 pp.
Length of book reviews: 1-2 pp.
Style: MLA
Number of copies required: 2
Rejected manuscripts: Returned
Time before publication decision: 6 mos.
Time between decision and publication: 6 mos.
Number of reviewers: 1
Articles submitted per year: 30
Articles published per year: 12
Book reviews submitted per year: 5
Book reviews published per year: 3-4

(1044)
*Le Français dans le Monde

Jacques Pécheur, Editor
58, rue Jean Bleuzen
92178 Vanves Cédex, France

Telephone: (33) 1 46621010
Fax: (33) 1 40951133
First published: 1961
ISSN: 0015-9395

MLA acronym: FMonde

SUBSCRIPTION INFORMATION

Frequency of publication: 8 times/yr.
Circulation: 15,000
Available in microform: Yes
Subscription price: 475 F/yr.
Year to which price refers: 1992
Subscription address: 99, rue d'Amsterdam, 75008 Paris, France
Subscription telephone: (33) 1 42806855
Subscription fax: (33) 1 45262480

ADVERTISING INFORMATION

Advertising accepted: Yes

EDITORIAL DESCRIPTION

Scope: Pedagogical magazine for teachers of French as a foreign language: theoretical and practical materials, experiments, and reviews are published.
Reviews books: Yes
Publishes notes: No
Languages accepted: French
Prints abstracts: No
Author-anonymous submission: No

SUBMISSION REQUIREMENTS

Restrictions on contributors: None
Author pays submission fee: No
Author pays page charges: No
Length of articles: 3,500-18,000 words
Length of book reviews: 1,500 words
Style: Journal
Number of copies required: 1
Special requirements: Contributions not in French are accepted for translation into French.
Copyright ownership: Journal
Rejected manuscripts: Not returned
Time before publication decision: 3-6 mos. minimum
Time between decision and publication: 2 mos. minimum
Number of reviewers: 1-3
Articles submitted per year: 200
Articles published per year: 45
Book reviews submitted per year: 1,200
Book reviews published per year: 400

(1045)
*Le Français Moderne: Revue de Linguistique Française

J. Chaurand, Editor
Conseil International de la Langue Française
142 bis, rue de Grenelle
75007 Paris, France

Additional editorial address: O. Soutet, 119 rue de la Convention, 75015 Paris, France; J. M. Klinkenberg, Univ. de Liège, 3 place Cockerill, 4000 Liège, Belgium
Telephone: (33) 1 47050405; (33) 1 47050793; (33) 1 45512292
Fax: (33) 1 45554116
First published: 1933
ISSN: 0015-9409
MLA acronym: FM

SUBSCRIPTION INFORMATION

Frequency of publication: 2 times/yr.
Circulation: 2,000
Available in microform: No
Subscription price: 160 F (210 F airmail)/yr.
Year to which price refers: 1991
Subscription address: C.I.L.F., 21 bis, rue du Cardinal Lemoine, 75005 Paris, France

ADVERTISING INFORMATION

Advertising accepted: Yes

EDITORIAL DESCRIPTION

Scope: Publishes a wide range of articles on modern French descriptive grammar and stylistics, as well as general linguistics. Some, though not all, issues have articles dealing with a common topic.
Reviews books: Yes
Publishes notes: Yes
Languages accepted: French
Prints abstracts: No
Author-anonymous submission: No

SUBMISSION REQUIREMENTS

Author pays submission fee: No
Author pays page charges: No
Length of articles: 30 typescript pp. maximum
Number of copies required: 2
Special requirements: Submit on IBM-compatible or Macintosh diskette.
Copyright ownership: Author
Rejected manuscripts: Not returned
Time before publication decision: 3 mos.
Time between decision and publication: 15 mos.
Number of reviewers: 2-3
Articles submitted per year: 40-50
Articles published per year: 15-20
Book reviews submitted per year: 40-50
Book reviews published per year: 40-50
Notes submitted per year: 6-8
Notes published per year: 2-3

(1046)
*La France Latine

George Bonifassi, Vincent Armendarés, & Suzanne Thiolier-Méjean, Editors
16, rue de la Sorbonne
75005 Paris, France

Telephone: (33) 1 40462744
First published: 1960
Sponsoring organization: Inst. de Langue & Littérature d'Oc; Union des Amis de la France Latine
ISSN: 0222-0326
MLA acronym: FrL

SUBSCRIPTION INFORMATION

Frequency of publication: 2 times/yr.
Circulation: 300
Available in microform: No
Subscription price: 100 F/yr.
Year to which price refers: 1992
Subscription telephone: (33) 1 48050623

ADVERTISING INFORMATION

Advertising accepted: Yes

EDITORIAL DESCRIPTION

Scope: Journal focuses on Provençal literature.
Reviews books: Yes
Publishes notes: Yes
Languages accepted: French; Catalan; Spanish; Italian; Occitan
Prints abstracts: No
Author-anonymous submission: No

SUBMISSION REQUIREMENTS

Restrictions on contributors: None
Author pays submission fee: No
Author pays page charges: No
Length of articles: 4,500 words
Length of book reviews: 200 words
Length of notes: 600 words
Number of copies required: 1
Copyright ownership: Author
Rejected manuscripts: Returned at author's request; enclose return postage.
Time before publication decision: 2 mos.
Time between decision and publication: 4-12 mos.
Number of reviewers: 4
Book reviews published per year: 30

(1047)
*Franciscan Studies

Conrad L. Harkins, O.F.M., Editor
Franciscan Inst.
St. Bonaventure Univ.
St. Bonaventure, NY 14778

Telephone: 716 375-2159
Fax: 716 375-2389
First published: 1941
Sponsoring organization: Franciscan Inst.
ISSN: 0080-5459
MLA acronym: FranS

SUBSCRIPTION INFORMATION

Frequency of publication: Annual
Circulation: 775
Available in microform: Yes
Subscription telephone: 716 375-2105

ADVERTISING INFORMATION

Advertising accepted: No

EDITORIAL DESCRIPTION

Scope: Publishes articles, texts, and translations concerned with Franciscan contributions to theological, philosophical, and scientific thought, literature, and the historical evolution of the Franciscan movement, particularly in the medieval period.
Reviews books: Yes
Publishes notes: Yes
Languages accepted: English
Prints abstracts: No
Author-anonymous submission: No

SUBMISSION REQUIREMENTS

Restrictions on contributors: None
Author pays submission fee: Yes
Cost of submission fee: $20.00
Author pays page charges: No
Length of articles: 6,000 words
Style: MLA
Number of copies required: 2
Special requirements: Request guidelines from editor.
Copyright ownership: Franciscan Inst.
Rejected manuscripts: Returned
Time before publication decision: 4 mos.
Time between decision and publication: 1 yr.
Number of reviewers: 2
Articles submitted per year: 25
Articles published per year: 12

(1048)
*Franco-British Studies: Journal of the British Institute in Paris

Christophe Campos, David Horner, Adrian Kempton, Adrian Matthews, Douglas Oliver, Jean-Claude Sergeant, Dunstan Ward, & Elaine Williamson, Editors
Inst. Britannique de Paris
11, rue de Constantine
75007 Paris, France

Telephone: (33) 1 45447199
Fax: (33) 1 45503155
First published: 1986
Sponsoring organization: British Inst. in Paris
ISSN: 0952-8571
MLA acronym: FBS

SUBSCRIPTION INFORMATION

Frequency of publication: 2 times/yr. (Spring, Fall)
Circulation: 300
Available in microform: No
Subscription price: £25.00/yr.
Year to which price refers: 1992

Subscription address: British Inst. in Paris, Senate House, Univ. of London, Malet St., London WC1E 7HU, England

ADVERTISING INFORMATION

Advertising accepted: No

EDITORIAL DESCRIPTION

Scope: Publishes articles on French and English historical, literary, and linguistic studies, focusing on work on cross-cultural relations, comparisons and translation.
Reviews books: Occasionally
Publishes notes: Yes
Languages accepted: English; French
Prints abstracts: Yes
Author-anonymous submission: No

SUBMISSION REQUIREMENTS

Restrictions on contributors: Book reviews are commissioned.
Author pays submission fee: No
Author pays page charges: No
Length of articles: 2,000-6,000 words
Length of book reviews: 1,000-2,000 words
Length of notes: 500 words minimum
Style: MLA
Number of copies required: 1
Special requirements: Submission on diskette accompanied by printout is preferred.
Copyright ownership: Journal & Author
Rejected manuscripts: Returned
Time before publication decision: 2-6 mos.
Time between decision and publication: 6-12 mos.
Number of reviewers: 2
Articles submitted per year: 25
Articles published per year: 8-10
Book reviews published per year: 1-3
Notes submitted per year: 4
Notes published per year: 1-2

(1049)
*Francofonia: Studi e Ricerche Sulle Letterature di Lingua Francese

Liano Petroni, Editor
Dipt. di Lingue & Lett. Straniere Moderne
via Cartoleria 5
40124 Bologna, Italy

Telephone: (39) 51 217111; (39) 51 217126
Fax: (39) 51 264722
First published: 1981
Sponsoring organization: Univ. di Bologna
MLA acronym: Francofonia

SUBSCRIPTION INFORMATION

Frequency of publication: 2 times/yr.
Available in microform: No
Subscription price: 46,000 Lit/yr. Italy; 59,000 Lit/yr. elsewhere
Year to which price refers: 1992
Subscription address: Olschki Editore, C.P. 66, 50100 Florence, Italy
Subscription telephone: (39) 55 6530684
Subscription fax: (39) 55 6530214

ADVERTISING INFORMATION

Advertising accepted: Yes

EDITORIAL DESCRIPTION

Scope: Publishes studies and essays on literatures of French-speaking countries.
Reviews books: Yes
Publishes notes: Yes
Languages accepted: French; English; German; Italian; Spanish
Prints abstracts: Yes
Author-anonymous submission: No

SUBMISSION REQUIREMENTS

Restrictions on contributors: None
Author pays submission fee: No
Author pays page charges: No
Length of articles: 5,000-8,000 words
Length of book reviews: 750 words
Length of notes: 200 words
Style: Olschki
Number of copies required: 1
Copyright ownership: Author & journal
Rejected manuscripts: Not returned
Time before publication decision: 6 mos.
Time between decision and publication: 8 mos.
Number of reviewers: 7
Articles submitted per year: 35
Articles published per year: 20
Book reviews submitted per year: 25
Book reviews published per year: 20
Notes submitted per year: 25
Notes published per year: 20

(1050)
*Francographies: Bulletin de la Société des Professeurs Français et Francophones d'Amérique

Jean Macary, Editor
SPFFA
22 E. 60th St.
New York, NY 10022

Telephone: 212 410-7405
First published: 1992
Historical variations in title: Supersedes *Bulletin de la Société des Professeurs Français d'Amérique*
Sponsoring organization: Soc. des Professeurs Français & Francophones d'Amérique (SPFFA)
MLA acronym: Francographies

SUBSCRIPTION INFORMATION

Frequency of publication: Annual
Available in microform: No

ADVERTISING INFORMATION

Advertising accepted: No

EDITORIAL DESCRIPTION

Scope: Publishes articles on Francophone literature, culture, and civilization.
Reviews books: Yes
Publishes notes: No
Languages accepted: French
Prints abstracts: No
Author-anonymous submission: No

SUBMISSION REQUIREMENTS

Author pays submission fee: No
Author pays page charges: No
Length of articles: 20 pp.
Length of book reviews: 2 pp.
Number of copies required: 2
Special requirements: If possible, submit on diskette using WordPerfect 5.1.
Rejected manuscripts: Not returned
Time before publication decision: 6-12 mos.
Time between decision and publication: 2-6 mos.
Number of reviewers: 5
Articles submitted per year: 30
Articles published per year: 12

(1051)
*Frank Norris Studies

Jesse S. Crisler & Robert C. Leitz III, Editors
Language, Literature, & Communications
Brigham Young Univ.-Hawaii Campus
Laie, HI 96762

Additional editorial address: Robert C. Leitz III, Dept. of English, Louisiana State Univ. at Shreveport, Shreveport, LA 71115
First published: 1986
Sponsoring organization: Frank Norris Soc.
MLA acronym: FNS

SUBSCRIPTION INFORMATION

Frequency of publication: 2 times/yr. (Oct., Apr.)
Circulation: 52
Available in microform: No
Subscription price: $10.00/yr.
Year to which price refers: 1992
Subscription address: Dept. of English, Florida State Univ., Tallahassee, FL 32306

ADVERTISING INFORMATION

Advertising accepted: No

EDITORIAL DESCRIPTION

Scope: Disseminates information concerning the life and works of Frank Norris.
Reviews books: Yes
Publishes notes: Yes
Languages accepted: English; French
Prints abstracts: No

SUBMISSION REQUIREMENTS

Author pays submission fee: No
Author pays page charges: No
Length of articles: 1,500 words
Length of book reviews: 500 words
Length of notes: 500 words maximum
Style: Chicago
Number of copies required: 1
Rejected manuscripts: Returned
Time before publication decision: 1 mo.
Time between decision and publication: 6-12 mos.
Number of reviewers: 2
Articles submitted per year: 10-20
Articles published per year: 5-6
Book reviews submitted per year: 2-4
Book reviews published per year: 2-4
Notes submitted per year: 10-20
Notes published per year: 5-10

(1052)
*Frankfurter Afrikanistische Blätter

Jörg Adelberger, Eleonore Adwiraah, Ulrich Kleinewillinghöfer, Rudolf Leger, & Kerstin Winkelmann, Editors
Praunheimer Landstr. 70
6000 Frankfurt 90, Germany

Telephone: (49) 69 7988264
First published: 1989
ISSN: 0937-3039
MLA acronym: FAB

SUBSCRIPTION INFORMATION

Frequency of publication: 1-2 times/yr.
Circulation: 50
Available in microform: No
Subscription price: 45 DM/2 issues institutions; 30 DM/2 issues individuals
Year to which price refers: 1991
Subscription address: Stadt- & Universitätsbibliothek, Bockenheimer Landstr. 134-138, 6000 Frankfurt 1, Germany

ADVERTISING INFORMATION

Advertising accepted: No

EDITORIAL DESCRIPTION

Scope: Publishes articles on the linguistics, ethnology, and history of Africa.
Reviews books: Yes
Publishes notes: Yes
Languages accepted: English; French; German
Prints abstracts: No
Author-anonymous submission: No

SUBMISSION REQUIREMENTS

Restrictions on contributors: None
Author pays submission fee: No
Author pays page charges: No
Length of articles: 15 pp.
Length of book reviews: 2-3 pp.
Length of notes: 5 pp. maximum
Number of copies required: 1
Special requirements: Submit camera-ready typescript, or diskette.
Copyright ownership: Author
Rejected manuscripts: Returned; enclose return postage.
Time before publication decision: 3 mos.
Time between decision and publication: 6-12 mos.
Number of reviewers: 2-3
Articles submitted per year: 20-30
Articles published per year: 10
Book reviews submitted per year: 5
Book reviews published per year: 2
Notes submitted per year: 4
Notes published per year: 4

(1053)
Frankfurter Beiträge zur Germanistik

Klaus von See & Norbert Altenhofer, Editors
Carl Winter Universitätsverlag
Lutherstr. 59
Postfach 106140
6900 Heidelberg, Germany

First published: 1967
ISSN: 0071-9226
MLA acronym: FBG

SUBSCRIPTION INFORMATION

Frequency of publication: Irregular
Circulation: 600-1,000
Available in microform: No

ADVERTISING INFORMATION

Advertising accepted: No

EDITORIAL DESCRIPTION

Scope: Publishes monographs on Germanic language and literature.
Reviews books: No
Publishes notes: No
Languages accepted: German
Prints abstracts: No
Author-anonymous submission: No

SUBMISSION REQUIREMENTS

Restrictions on contributors: None
Author pays submission fee: No
Author pays page charges: Occasionally
Length of books: No restrictions
Style: MLA
Number of copies required: 1
Copyright ownership: Carl Winter Universitätsverlag
Rejected manuscripts: Returned
Time before publication decision: 2 mos.
Time between decision and publication: 1 yr.
Number of reviewers: 2
Books published per year: 1-2

(1054)
*Franziskanische Studien

Ildefons Vanderheyden, Editor
Hörsterplatz 4
4400 Münster, Germany

Telephone: (49) 251 57677
First published: 1914
Sponsoring organization: Franciscan Order
ISSN: 0016-0067
MLA acronym: FrSt

SUBSCRIPTION INFORMATION

Frequency of publication: 4 times/yr.
Circulation: 300
Available in microform: No
Subscription address: Dietrich-Coelde Verlag, Steinergraben 53, 4760 Werl/Westfalen, Germany

ADVERTISING INFORMATION

Advertising accepted: No

EDITORIAL DESCRIPTION

Scope: Publishes articles on the history of the Franciscan influence.
Reviews books: Yes
Publishes notes: Yes
Languages accepted: English; German; French; Spanish; Italian
Prints abstracts: No
Author-anonymous submission: No

SUBMISSION REQUIREMENTS

Restrictions on contributors: None
Author pays submission fee: No
Author pays page charges: No
Length of articles: No restrictions
Style: None
Number of copies required: 1
Copyright ownership: Author & Dietrich-Coelde Verlag
Rejected manuscripts: Not returned
Time before publication decision: 1-2 weeks
Time between decision and publication: 1 yr.
Number of reviewers: 2

(1055)
*Französisch Heute

Jürgen Olbert & Ulf Wielandt, Editors
Verlag Moritz Diesterweg
Wächtersbacher Str. 89
6000 Frankfurt 63, Germany

Telephone: (49) 69 42081234
Fax: (49) 69 42081299
First published: 1972
Sponsoring organization: Vereinigung der Französischlehrer e.V.
ISSN: 0342-2895
MLA acronym: FrH

SUBSCRIPTION INFORMATION

Frequency of publication: 4 times/yr.
Circulation: 2,800
Available in microform: No
Subscription price: 30 DM/yr. members; 36 DM/yr. nonmembers; 20 DM/yr. students
Year to which price refers: 1992
Subscription telephone: (49) 69 42081131

ADVERTISING INFORMATION

Advertising accepted: Yes

EDITORIAL DESCRIPTION

Scope: Publishes articles on methods of teaching French, applied linguistics, French literature and civilization, and French literature outside France.
Reviews books: Yes
Publishes notes: Yes
Languages accepted: French; German
Prints abstracts: No
Author-anonymous submission: No

SUBMISSION REQUIREMENTS

Author pays submission fee: No
Author pays page charges: No
Length of articles: 10-14 printed pp.
Length of book reviews: 2 printed pp.
Length of notes: 1/2 printed p.
Style: MLA
Number of copies required: 2
Copyright ownership: Vereinigung der Französischlehrer e.V.
Rejected manuscripts: Returned
Time before publication decision: 2 mos.
Time between decision and publication: 3-9 mos.
Number of reviewers: 3
Articles submitted per year: 30-45
Articles published per year: 24-34
Book reviews submitted per year: 30
Book reviews published per year: 20-25
Notes submitted per year: 30-40
Notes published per year: 25

(1056)
*Freiburger Zeitschrift für Philosophie und Theologie

J.-B. Brantschen, R. Imbach, G. Vergauwen, & M. Gut, Editors
Univ. of Freiburg
1700 Freiburg, Switzerland

First published: 1886
Sponsoring organization: Soc. Suisse de Philosophie
ISSN: 0016-0725
MLA acronym: FZPT

SUBSCRIPTION INFORMATION

Frequency of publication: 2 times/yr. (June double issue, Nov. or Dec.)
Circulation: 650
Available in microform: No
Subscription address: Editions St. Paul, Perolles 42, 1700 Freiburg, Switzerland

ADVERTISING INFORMATION

Advertising accepted: No

EDITORIAL DESCRIPTION

Reviews books: Yes
Publishes notes: No
Languages accepted: French; German; English; Italian; Spanish
Prints abstracts: No

SUBMISSION REQUIREMENTS

Restrictions on contributors: None
Author pays submission fee: No
Author pays page charges: No
Length of articles: 20 pp.
Length of book reviews: 3-4 pp.
Number of copies required: 1
Time before publication decision: 3-6 mos.
Time between decision and publication: 6-12 mos.
Number of reviewers: 3
Articles submitted per year: 35
Articles published per year: 15-20
Book reviews submitted per year: 10-15
Book reviews published per year: 10-15

(1057)
*French Cultural Studies

Brian Rigby, Editor
Dept. of French Studies
Univ. of Warwick
Coventry CV4 7AL, England

First published: 1990
ISSN: 0957-1558
MLA acronym: FCSt

SUBSCRIPTION INFORMATION

Frequency of publication: 3 times/yr. (Feb., June, Oct.)
Available in microform: No
Subscription price: £35.00/yr. institutions United Kingdom; $76.00/yr. institutions North & South America & Japan; £38.00/yr. institutions elsewhere; £20.00/yr. individuals United Kingdom; $42.00/yr. individuals North & South America & Japan; £22.00/yr. individuals elsewhere
Year to which price refers: 1992
Subscription address: Alpha Academic, Halfpenny Furze, Mill Lane, Chalfont St. Giles, Bucks HP8 4NR, England
Subscription telephone: (44) 2407 2509

ADVERTISING INFORMATION

Advertising accepted: Yes

EDITORIAL DESCRIPTION

Scope: Provides a forum for studies of modern French cultural life (cinema, television, press, theater, visual arts, popular culture) as well as changing patterns of language and literature that now encompass modern French culture.
Reviews books: Yes
Publishes notes: Yes
Languages accepted: English; French
Prints abstracts: No
Author-anonymous submission: Yes

SUBMISSION REQUIREMENTS

Author pays submission fee: No
Author pays page charges: No
Length of articles: 6,000-8,000 words
Length of book reviews: 1,500 words
Style: MLA
Number of copies required: 3
Copyright ownership: Alpha Academic
Rejected manuscripts: Returned
Time before publication decision: 3 mos.
Time between decision and publication: 3-12 mos.
Articles published per year: 15-18

(1058)
*French Forum

Raymond C. La Charité & Virginia A. La Charité, Editors
French Forum Publishers
P.O. Box 130
Nicholasville, KY 40430

Telephone: 606 885-1446
First published: 1976
Sponsoring organization: French Forum Publishers, Inc.
ISSN: 0098-9355
MLA acronym: FrF

SUBSCRIPTION INFORMATION

Frequency of publication: 3 times/yr. (Winter, Spring, Fall)
Circulation: 550
Available in microform: No
Subscription price: $35.00/yr. institutions; $15.00/yr. individuals
Year to which price refers: 1992

ADVERTISING INFORMATION

Advertising accepted: Yes
Advertising rates: $55.00/half page; $90.00/full page

EDITORIAL DESCRIPTION

Scope: Publishes criticism on French literature of all periods.
Reviews books: Yes
Publishes notes: No
Languages accepted: English; French
Prints abstracts: No
Author-anonymous submission: Yes

SUBMISSION REQUIREMENTS

Restrictions on contributors: Unsolicited book reviews are not accepted.
Author pays submission fee: No
Author pays page charges: No
Length of articles: 6,000 words maximum
Length of book reviews: 700 words
Style: MLA
Number of copies required: 2
Copyright ownership: Assigned by author to journal
Rejected manuscripts: Returned; enclose SASE.
Time before publication decision: 3 mos.
Time between decision and publication: 9-12 mos.
Number of reviewers: 2
Articles submitted per year: 150
Articles published per year: 25
Book reviews published per year: 50

(1059)
*French Forum Monographs

Raymond C. La Charité & Virginia A. La Charité, Editors
French Forum Publishers
P.O. Box 130
Nicholasville, KY 40430

Telephone: 606 885-1446
First published: 1976
Sponsoring organization: French Forum Publishers, Inc.
MLA acronym: FrFM

SUBSCRIPTION INFORMATION

Frequency of publication: Irregular
Available in microform: No

ADVERTISING INFORMATION

Advertising accepted: No

EDITORIAL DESCRIPTION

Scope: Publishes monographs on French literature and literary criticism.
Reviews books: No
Publishes notes: No
Languages accepted: French; English
Prints abstracts: No
Author-anonymous submission: No

SUBMISSION REQUIREMENTS

Restrictions on contributors: None
Author pays submission fee: No
Author pays page charges: No
Length of books: 60,000 words
Style: MLA
Number of copies required: 2
Copyright ownership: Assigned by author to series
Rejected manuscripts: Returned
Time before publication decision: 3 mos.
Time between decision and publication: 9 mos.
Number of reviewers: 2
Books submitted per year: 14-18
Books published per year: 5-6

(1060)
*French Literature Series

Freeman G. Henry, Editor
Dept. of French & Classics
Univ. of South Carolina
Columbia, SC 29208

Telephone: 803 777-2845
First published: 1974
Sponsoring organization: Dept. of French & Classics, Univ. of South Carolina
ISSN: 0271-6607
MLA acronym: FLS

SUBSCRIPTION INFORMATION

Frequency of publication: Annual
Circulation: 300
Available in microform: No
Subscription price: $25.00/yr. institutions; $15.00/yr. individuals
Year to which price refers: 1992

ADVERTISING INFORMATION

Advertising accepted: Yes

EDITORIAL DESCRIPTION

Scope: FLS is the official publication of the annual French Literature Conference which was established in 1973 at the University of South Carolina. The Conference (usually in March) focuses on a pre-announced topic, and papers, notes, and bibliographical contributions are invited for consideration. Articles accepted for the Conference are published within one year. Other articles for the volume may be solicited on an individual basis.
Reviews books: No
Publishes notes: Yes
Languages accepted: English; French
Prints abstracts: No
Author-anonymous submission: Yes

SUBMISSION REQUIREMENTS

Restrictions on contributors: Submissions must have been submitted previously at the French Literature Conference or be scholarly short notes on the given subject, unless solicited individually.
Author pays submission fee: No
Author pays page charges: No
Length of articles: 4,000 words maximum including footnotes
Length of notes: 5 pp. maximum
Style: MLA; Chicago; standard French format
Number of copies required: 2
Copyright ownership: Univ. of South Carolina
Rejected manuscripts: Returned; enclose return postage and self-addressed envelope.
Time before publication decision: 1-2 mos.
Time between decision and publication: 1 yr.
Number of reviewers: 3-4
Articles published per year: 12-15
Notes submitted per year: 4-5
Notes published per year: 2-5

(1061)
*The French Review: Journal of the American Association of Teachers of French

Ronald W. Tobin, Editor
Dept. of French & Italian
Univ. of California
Santa Barbara, CA 93106

Telephone: 805 893-2419
Fax: 805 893-8373
E-mail: Acp1@UCSBVM.bitnet
First published: 1927
Sponsoring organization: American Assn. of Teachers of French
ISSN: 0016-111X
MLA acronym: FR

SUBSCRIPTION INFORMATION

Frequency of publication: 6 times/yr. (Oct., Dec., Feb., Mar., Apr., May)
Circulation: 12,000
Available in microform: No
Subscription price: $35.00/yr.
Year to which price refers: 1991-92
Subscription address: Fred Jenkins, Executive Director, American Assn. of Teachers of French, 57 E. Armory Ave., Champaign, IL 61820
Subscription telephone: 217 333-2842

ADVERTISING INFORMATION

Advertising accepted: Yes

EDITORIAL DESCRIPTION

Scope: Publishes articles on all aspects of French language, literature, film, and civilization.
Reviews books: Yes
Publishes notes: Yes
Languages accepted: English; French
Prints abstracts: Yes
Author-anonymous submission: Yes

SUBMISSION REQUIREMENTS

Restrictions on contributors: Contributors must be members of the American Assn. of Teachers of French. Book reviews are solicited.
Author pays submission fee: No
Author pays page charges: No
Length of articles: 5,000 words maximum
Length of book reviews: 650 words maximum
Length of notes: 1,000 words maximum
Style: MLA
Number of copies required: 3
Special requirements: Enclose $3.00 in stamps with each submission.
Copyright ownership: Journal
Rejected manuscripts: Not returned
Time before publication decision: 2-4 mos.
Time between decision and publication: 12-18 mos.
Number of reviewers: 2-3
Articles submitted per year: 200
Articles published per year: 55
Book reviews published per year: 300
Notes submitted per year: 15
Notes published per year: 10

(1062)
French Studies: A Quarterly Review

Taylor Inst.
St. Giles
Oxford OX1 3NA, England

First published: 1947
Sponsoring organization: Soc. for French Studies
ISSN: 0016-1128
MLA acronym: FS

SUBSCRIPTION INFORMATION

Frequency of publication: 4 times/yr. (Jan., Apr., July, Oct.)
Circulation: 1,800
Available in microform: No
Subscription address: Nonmembers of the Soc. for French Studies write to: J. M. Lewis, Dept. of French, Queen's Univ., Belfast BT7 INN, Northern Ireland

ADVERTISING INFORMATION

Advertising accepted: Yes

EDITORIAL DESCRIPTION

Scope: Publishes scholarly articles and reviews on French language, literature, history, and civilization.
Reviews books: Yes
Publishes notes: No
Languages accepted: English; French
Prints abstracts: No
Author-anonymous submission: No

SUBMISSION REQUIREMENTS

Restrictions on contributors: All book reviews are commissioned.
Author pays submission fee: No
Author pays page charges: No
Length of articles: 6,000 words
Length of book reviews: 100-800 words
Style: Modern Humanities Research Assn.
Number of copies required: 2
Special requirements: Submit original typescript.
Copyright ownership: Soc. for French Studies
Rejected manuscripts: Returned
Time before publication decision: 3 mos.
Time between decision and publication: 12-18 mos.
Number of reviewers: 3
Articles submitted per year: 50-60
Articles published per year: 16-20
Book reviews published per year: 300-350

(1063)
*French Studies Bulletin: A Quarterly Supplement

Alan Hindley, Editor
Dept. of French
Univ. of Hull
Hull HU6 7RX, England

Telephone: (44) 482 465833
Fax: (44) 482 465991
First published: 1981
Sponsoring organization: Soc. for French Studies
ISSN: 0262-2750
MLA acronym: FSB

SUBSCRIPTION INFORMATION

Frequency of publication: 4 times/yr.
Circulation: 1,900
Available in microform: No
Subscription address: Roger H. Middleton, Dept. of French, The University, Nottingham, England
Additional subscription address: Nonmembers of the Soc. for French Studies write to: C. B. Radford, Dept. of French, Queen's Univ., Belfast BT7 1NN, Northern Ireland
Subscription telephone: (44) 602 484848
Subscription fax: (44) 602 420825

ADVERTISING INFORMATION

Advertising accepted: No

EDITORIAL DESCRIPTION

Scope: Publishes articles on French literature, language, history, philosophy, and art cinema.
Reviews books: No
Publishes notes: Yes
Languages accepted: English; French
Prints abstracts: No
Author-anonymous submission: No

SUBMISSION REQUIREMENTS

Restrictions on contributors: None
Author pays submission fee: No
Author pays page charges: No
Length of articles: 1,000 words
Style: Modern Humanites Research Assn.
Number of copies required: 2
Copyright ownership: Soc. for French Studies
Rejected manuscripts: Returned
Time before publication decision: 2 mos.
Time between decision and publication: 9-12 mos.
Number of reviewers: 2
Articles submitted per year: 50
Articles published per year: 25
Notes submitted per year: 16
Notes published per year: 14

(1064)
*French Studies in Southern Africa

Leopold Peeters, Editor
Univ. of Pretoria
Pretoria 0002, South Africa

Telephone: (27) 21 6502895
Fax: (27) 21 6503726
First published: 1971
Sponsoring organization: Assn. for French Studies in Southern Africa
ISSN: 0259-0247
MLA acronym: FSSA

SUBSCRIPTION INFORMATION

Frequency of publication: Annual
Circulation: 300
Available in microform: No
Subscription price: 30 R/yr. institutions South Africa; $15.00/yr. elsewhere
Year to which price refers: 1992
Subscription address: Secretary, Assn. for French Studies in Southern Africa, Univ. of Cape Town, Private Bag, Rondebosch 7700, South Africa

ADVERTISING INFORMATION

Advertising accepted: Yes

EDITORIAL DESCRIPTION

Scope: Publishes research publications in French literature and linguistics with special reference to Southern African context.
Reviews books: Yes
Publishes notes: Yes
Languages accepted: French; English
Prints abstracts: No
Author-anonymous submission: No

SUBMISSION REQUIREMENTS

Restrictions on contributors: Reviews are limited to books published by the Association.
Author pays submission fee: No
Author pays page charges: Yes
Cost of page charges: 50 R/page
Length of articles: 10-18 pp.
Length of book reviews: 800-1,000 words
Length of notes: 1,200 words
Style: Harvard
Number of copies required: 2
Special requirements: Submit original double-spaced typescript on size A4 (8 1/4 in. x 11 3/4 in.) paper and 1 copy.
Copyright ownership: Assn. for French Studies in Southern Africa
Rejected manuscripts: Returned
Time before publication decision: 3-5 mos.
Time between decision and publication: 6 mos.
Number of reviewers: 2-3
Articles submitted per year: 25
Articles published per year: 5-7
Book reviews submitted per year: 1-2
Book reviews published per year: 1-2
Notes submitted per year: 2
Notes published per year: 1-2

(1065)
*Fróðskaparrit: Annales Societatis Scientiarum Faeroensis

Jóan Hendrik W. Poulsen, Joan Pauli Joensen, Arne Nörrevang, & Elin Súsanna Jacobsen, Editors
Föroya Fróðskaparfelag
P.O. Box 209
FR 100 Tórshavn, Faroe Islands

First published: 1952

Sponsoring organization: Mentunargrunnur Føroya Løgtings
ISSN: 0085-0896
MLA acronym: Fróðskaparrit

SUBSCRIPTION INFORMATION

Frequency of publication: Annual
Circulation: 1,000
Available in microform: No

ADVERTISING INFORMATION

Advertising accepted: No

EDITORIAL DESCRIPTION

Scope: Publishes recent observations and results of research from all branches of knowledge. Treatises do not have to deal with Faroese subjects but should preferably be written in Faroese with a summary in another language.
Publishes notes: No
Languages accepted: Faroese; English
Prints abstracts: Yes
Author-anonymous submission: Yes

SUBMISSION REQUIREMENTS

Author pays submission fee: No
Author pays page charges: No
Number of copies required: 1
Copyright ownership: Author after publication
Rejected manuscripts: Returned
Time before publication decision: 2 mos.
Time between decision and publication: 3 mos.
Number of reviewers: 2
Articles submitted per year: 8-10
Articles published per year: 6-8

(1066)
*Frontiers: A Journal of Women Studies

Louise Lamphere, Jane Slaughter, & Elizabeth Cahn, Editors
Mesa Vista Hall 2142
Univ. of New Mexico
Albuquerque, NM 87131-1586

Telephone: 505 277-1198
Fax: 505 277-0267
First published: 1975
Sponsoring organization: Frontiers Editorial Collective
ISSN: 0160-9009
MLA acronym: Frontiers

SUBSCRIPTION INFORMATION

Frequency of publication: 3 times/yr.
Circulation: 1,000
Available in microform: Yes
Subscription price: $33.00/yr. institutions; $20.00/yr. individuals; $8.00/single issue
Year to which price refers: 1992
Subscription address: Univ. Press of Colorado, P.O. Box 849, Niwot, CO 80544
Subscription telephone: 303 530-5337
Subscription fax: 303 530-5306

ADVERTISING INFORMATION

Advertising accepted: Yes
Advertising rates: $80.00/quarter page; $150.00/half page; $250.00/full page

EDITORIAL DESCRIPTION

Scope: Publishes articles on all aspects of women studies and feminist scholarship, including academic articles, personal essays, exceptional creative work, review essays, and criticism. Interdisciplinary and collaborative work is encouraged.
Reviews books: Yes
Publishes notes: Yes
Languages accepted: English

Prints abstracts: No
Author-anonymous submission: Yes

SUBMISSION REQUIREMENTS

Restrictions on contributors: None
Author pays submission fee: No
Author pays page charges: No
Length of articles: 30 double-spaced typescript pp. maximum for text
Length of book reviews: 10-20 double-spaced typescript pp.
Style: Chicago
Number of copies required: 3
Special requirements: Manuscripts must not have been published elsewhere or be under consideration by another journal, in entirety or in part. Author's name should appear on title page only. Notes should follow text. Creative work (especially poetry) may be submitted in any language if accompanied by translation.
Copyright ownership: Journal unless first North American serial rights are requested by author prior to publication
Rejected manuscripts: Returned; enclose SASE.
Time before publication decision: 3-6 mos.
Time between decision and publication: 2-12 mos.
Number of reviewers: 3-9
Articles submitted per year: 400
Articles published per year: 50
Book reviews submitted per year: 25
Book reviews published per year: 5

(1067)
*Frühmittelalterliche Studien: Jahrbuch des Instituts für Frühmittelalterforschung der Universität Münster

Hagen Keller & Joachim Wollasch, Editors
Inst. für Frühmittelalterforschung
Univ. Münster
Salzstr. 41,
4400 Münster, Germany

Telephone: (49) 44251 832070
Fax: (49) 44251 832090
First published: 1967
ISSN: 0071-9706
MLA acronym: FMAS

SUBSCRIPTION INFORMATION

Frequency of publication: Annual
Circulation: 700
Available in microform: No
Subscription price: 298 DM/yr.
Year to which price refers: 1991
Subscription address: Walter de Gruyter & Co., Genthiner Str. 13, 1000 Berlin 30, Germany
Subscription telephone: (49) 4430 260050
Subscription fax: (49) 4430 26005251

ADVERTISING INFORMATION

Advertising accepted: No

EDITORIAL DESCRIPTION

Scope: Publishes articles on medieval history, literature, archaeology, philosophy, and art history.
Reviews books: No
Publishes notes: No
Languages accepted: German; English; French
Prints abstracts: No
Author-anonymous submission: No

SUBMISSION REQUIREMENTS

Restrictions on contributors: None
Author pays submission fee: No
Author pays page charges: No
Style: Journal
Number of copies required: 1

Special requirements: Submit camera-ready figures, diagrams, illustrations, and reproductions.
Copyright ownership: Walter de Gruyter & Co.
Rejected manuscripts: Returned
Time before publication decision: 6 mos.
Time between decision and publication: 1 yr.
Number of reviewers: 2
Articles submitted per year: 25-35
Articles published per year: 15-20

(1068)
*Fu Jen Studies: Literature & Linguistics

Heliéna Krenn, Editor
c/o English Dept.
Fu Jen Univ., Hsinchuang 24205
Taipei
Taiwan, Republic of China

Telephone: (886) 2 9031111 ext. 2563
Fax: (886) 2 9014733
First published: 1968
Sponsoring organization: Fu Jen Univ., College of Foreign Languages
ISSN: 1015-0021
MLA acronym: FJS

SUBSCRIPTION INFORMATION

Frequency of publication: Annual
Circulation: 300
Available in microform: No
Subscription price: $5.00/yr.
Year to which price refers: 1991

ADVERTISING INFORMATION

Advertising accepted: No

EDITORIAL DESCRIPTION

Scope: Publishes articles on literature and linguistics, with an emphasis on exchange between China and the West.
Reviews books: No
Publishes notes: No
Languages accepted: English; German; French; Spanish
Prints abstracts: No
Author-anonymous submission: No

SUBMISSION REQUIREMENTS

Restrictions on contributors: None
Author pays submission fee: No
Author pays page charges: No
Length of articles: 4,000-7,000 words
Style: MLA for literature; Linguistic Soc. of America for linguistics
Number of copies required: 2
Copyright ownership: Author
Rejected manuscripts: Returned
Time before publication decision: 1-2 mos.
Time between decision and publication: 6-8 mos.
Number of reviewers: 2-3
Articles submitted per year: 15-20
Articles published per year: 6-10

(1069)
*Función

José Luis Iturrioz Leza, Director
Apdo. Postal 1-1379
44101 Guadalajara, Jal., Mexico

Telephone: (52) 36 159742
First published: 1986
Sponsoring organization: Univ. de Guadalajara
ISSN: 0186-7687
MLA acronym: Función

SUBSCRIPTION INFORMATION

Frequency of publication: 2 times/yr.
Available in microform: No
Subscription price: $20.00/yr.
Year to which price refers: 1992

ADVERTISING INFORMATION

Advertising accepted: Yes

EDITORIAL DESCRIPTION

Scope: Publishes articles and monograph issues on the languages of the Americas, linguistic theory and philosophy of language. Includes studies on typology and universals, and functional linguistics.
Reviews books: Yes
Publishes notes: Yes
Languages accepted: English; Spanish
Prints abstracts: Yes
Author-anonymous submission: No

SUBMISSION REQUIREMENTS

Restrictions on contributors: None
Author pays submission fee: No
Author pays page charges: No
Length of articles: 12,000 words
Length of book reviews: 1,500 words
Number of copies required: 1
Copyright ownership: Author
Rejected manuscripts: Returned
Time before publication decision: 1 mo.
Time between decision and publication: 3 mos.
Number of reviewers: 3
Articles submitted per year: 15
Articles published per year: 10

(1070)
Furman Studies

Gilbert Allen, Editor
Furman Univ.
Greenville, SC 29613

First published: 1912
Sponsoring organization: Furman Univ.
ISSN: 0190-4701
MLA acronym: FurmS

SUBSCRIPTION INFORMATION

Frequency of publication: Annual (Dec.)
Circulation: 500
Available in microform: No

ADVERTISING INFORMATION

Advertising accepted: No

EDITORIAL DESCRIPTION

Scope: Focuses on studies in the liberal arts.
Reviews books: No
Publishes notes: No
Languages accepted: English
Prints abstracts: No
Author-anonymous submission: No

SUBMISSION REQUIREMENTS

Restrictions on contributors: Contributors must be members of the Furman community or invited to submit article.
Author pays submission fee: No
Author pays page charges: No
Length of articles: 1,500-5,000 words
Number of copies required: 1
Copyright ownership: Furman Univ.
Time before publication decision: 1 mo.
Time between decision and publication: 3-12 mos.
Number of reviewers: 1
Articles published per year: 1-10

(1071)
*La Fusta: Journal of Literature and Culture

David Del Principe, Editor
Rutgers Univ.
Dept. of Italian
18 Seminary Pl.
New Brunswick, NJ 08903

Telephone: 908 932-7031
First published: 1975
Sponsoring organization: Dept. of Italian, Rutgers Univ.
ISSN: 0742-8561
MLA acronym: Fusta

SUBSCRIPTION INFORMATION

Frequency of publication: Annual
Circulation: 200
Available in microform: No
Subscription price: $20.00/yr. institutions; $10.00/yr. individuals
Year to which price refers: 1992

ADVERTISING INFORMATION

Advertising accepted: Yes
Advertising rates: $75.00/half page; $100.00/full page

EDITORIAL DESCRIPTION

Scope: Publishes literary criticism, cultural material, creative writing, reviews, and translations.
Reviews books: Yes
Publishes notes: Yes
Languages accepted: Italian; English
Prints abstracts: No
Author-anonymous submission: No

SUBMISSION REQUIREMENTS

Restrictions on contributors: None
Author pays submission fee: No
Author pays page charges: No
Length of articles: 10-15 pp.
Length of book reviews: 1,500 words
Style: MLA
Number of copies required: 2
Special requirements: Submit on diskette if possible.
Copyright ownership: Journal
Rejected manuscripts: Returned; enclose return postage
Time before publication decision: 3 mos.
Time between decision and publication: 1 yr.
Number of reviewers: 2
Articles submitted per year: 30
Articles published per year: 10
Book reviews submitted per year: 5-10
Book reviews published per year: 5
Notes submitted per year: 5
Notes published per year: 2

(1072)
*Gai Saber: Revista de l'Escòla Occitana

Philippe Carbonne, Editor
Lieu dit "Les Dames"
Auréville
31320 Castanet-Talosan, France

First published: 1919
Sponsoring organization: Escòla Occitana
ISSN: 0047-4916
MLA acronym: GaiS

SUBSCRIPTION INFORMATION

Frequency of publication: 4 times/yr.
Circulation: 550
Available in microform: No
Subscription price: 80 F/yr. France; 90 F/yr. elsewhere
Year to which price refers: 1991

ADVERTISING INFORMATION

Advertising accepted: No

EDITORIAL DESCRIPTION

Scope: Publishes articles on Occitan language and literature.
Reviews books: Yes
Languages accepted: French; Occitan; Catalan
Prints abstracts: No

SUBMISSION REQUIREMENTS

Restrictions on contributors: None
Author pays submission fee: No
Author pays page charges: No
Length of articles: No restrictions
Length of book reviews: No restrictions
Style: None
Number of copies required: 1
Copyright ownership: Journal
Rejected manuscripts: Not returned
Articles published per year: 30-40
Book reviews published per year: 20-30

(1073)
Gaia: Collana di Studi di Letteratura Comparata

Armando Gnisci, Editor
Cattedra du Letterature Comparate
Fac. di Lettere, Dpto. di Italianistica
Univ. "La Sapienza"
Piazzale A. Moro 5
00185 Rome, Italy

Additional editorial address: Carucci Editore, Viale Trastevere 60, 00153 Rome, Italy
Telephone: (39) 6 5806274
Fax: (39) 6 491609
First published: 1989
MLA acronym: Gaia

SUBSCRIPTION INFORMATION

Frequency of publication: Irregular
Subscription address: Carucci Editore, Viale Trastevere 60, 00153 Rome, Italy

EDITORIAL DESCRIPTION

Scope: Publishes monographes on Italian comparative literature studies.
Reviews books: No
Publishes notes: No
Languages accepted: Italian

SUBMISSION REQUIREMENTS

Copyright ownership: Carruci Editore

(1074)
*Gardar: Årsbok för Samfundet Sverige-Island i Lund-Malmö

Gunilla Byrman & Alan Crozier, Editors
Skattebergra PL 36
240 17 Södra Sandby, Sweden

Telephone: (46) 46 51145
Fax: (46) 46 51145
First published: 1970
Sponsoring organization: Samfundet Sverige-Island; Humanistisk-Samhällsvetenskapliga Forskningsrådet
ISSN: 0280-6487
MLA acronym: Gardar

SUBSCRIPTION INFORMATION

Frequency of publication: Annual
Circulation: 550
Available in microform: No

Subscription price: 75 Skr/yr.
Year to which price refers: 1992
Subscription address: Sten Rundgren, Blåtungavägen 14, 223 75 Lund, Sweden

ADVERTISING INFORMATION

Advertising accepted: Yes
Advertising rates: 1,500 Skr/full page

EDITORIAL DESCRIPTION

Scope: Publishes articles on Iceland, with an emphasis on language and literature.
Reviews books: Yes
Publishes notes: Yes
Languages accepted: Danish; English; Norwegian; Swedish
Prints abstracts: Yes
Author-anonymous submission: No

SUBMISSION REQUIREMENTS

Restrictions on contributors: None
Author pays submission fee: No
Author pays page charges: No
Length of articles: 20 pp.
Length of book reviews: 300-500 words
Length of notes: No restrictions
Number of copies required: 1
Special requirements: Submit typescript and an abstract.
Copyright ownership: Journal & author
Rejected manuscripts: Returned
Time before publication decision: 2-3 weeks
Time between decision and publication: 5 mos.
Number of reviewers: 1
Articles submitted per year: 5-7
Articles published per year: 4
Book reviews submitted per year: 5-10
Book reviews published per year: 5-10

(1075)
Garland Library of Medieval Literature

James J. Wilhelm & Lowry Nelson, Jr., Editors
Garland Publishing, Inc.
717 Fifth Ave.
New York, NY 10022

Telephone: 212 751-7447
Fax: 212 308-9399
First published: 1980
MLA acronym: GLML

SUBSCRIPTION INFORMATION

Frequency of publication: Irregular
Available in microform: No
Subscription address: Garland Publishing, Inc., 1000A Sherman Ave., Hamden, CT 06514
Subscription telephone: 800 627-7273; 203 281-4487

ADVERTISING INFORMATION

Advertising accepted: No

EDITORIAL DESCRIPTION

Scope: Publishes modern translations of medieval texts. Most volumes contain introductions featuring a biography of the author or a discussion of the problem of authorship, an objective discussion of the literary style of the original, a consideration of sources and influences, and a statement of editorial policy for each edition and translation.
Reviews books: No
Publishes notes: No
Languages accepted: English; Western European languages
Prints abstracts: No
Author-anonymous submission: Yes

SUBMISSION REQUIREMENTS

Restrictions on contributors: None
Author pays submission fee: No
Author pays page charges: No
Length of books: 300 pp.
Style: Series
Number of copies required: 2
Special requirements: Submit camera-ready typescript.
Copyright ownership: Author
Rejected manuscripts: Returned
Time before publication decision: 1 mo.
Time between decision and publication: 9 mos.
Books published per year: 12

(1076)
*Garland Medieval Texts

A. S. G. Edwards, Editor
Garland Publishing Co.
717 Fifth Ave.
New York, NY 10022

Telephone: 212 751-7447
Fax: 212 308-9399
First published: 1981
MLA acronym: GMT

SUBSCRIPTION INFORMATION

Available in microform: No
Subscription address: Garland Publishing Co., 1000A Sherman Ave., Hamden, CT 06514
Subscription telephone: 800 627-6273; 203 281-4487

ADVERTISING INFORMATION

Advertising accepted: Yes

EDITORIAL DESCRIPTION

Scope: Publishes critical editions of texts from the Middle Ages.
Reviews books: No
Publishes notes: No
Languages accepted: English
Prints abstracts: No
Author-anonymous submission: No

SUBMISSION REQUIREMENTS

Author pays page charges: No
Copyright ownership: Author
Rejected manuscripts: Returned
Books published per year: 4

(1077)
Garland Reference Library of the Humanities

Gary Kuris, Phyllis Korper, & Paula Ladenburg, Editors
Garland Publishing, Inc.
717 Fifth Ave.
New York, NY 10022

Telephone: 212 751-7447
Fax: 212 308-9399
First published: 1975
MLA acronym: GRLH

SUBSCRIPTION INFORMATION

Frequency of publication: 150 titles/yr.
Available in microform: No
Subscription address: Garland Publishing Co., 1000A Sherman Ave., Hamden, CT 06514
Subscription telephone: 800 627-7273; 203 281-4487

ADVERTISING INFORMATION

Advertising accepted: No

EDITORIAL DESCRIPTION

Scope: Aims to facilitate research in all areas of the humanities and social sciences by making available to scholars, encyclopedias, bibliographies, concordances, journal indexes, library catalogues, and textual editions.
Reviews books: No
Publishes notes: No
Languages accepted: English
Prints abstracts: No

SUBMISSION REQUIREMENTS

Restrictions on contributors: None
Author pays submission fee: No
Author pays page charges: No
Length of books: 100 pp. minimum
Style: Chicago
Number of copies required: 2
Copyright ownership: Author
Rejected manuscripts: Returned
Time before publication decision: 1 mo.
Time between decision and publication: 6 mos.
Number of reviewers: 1-2
Books submitted per year: 300
Books published per year: 150

(1078)
*Gaskell Society Journal

Alan Shelston, Editor
Dept. of English
Univ. of Manchester
Manchester M13 9PL, England

Telephone: (44) 61 2753158
Fax: (44) 61 2753031
First published: 1987
Sponsoring organization: Gaskell Soc.
ISSN: 0951-7200
MLA acronym: GSJ

SUBSCRIPTION INFORMATION

Frequency of publication: Annual (Mar.)
Circulation: 300
Available in microform: No
Subscription price: £5.00/yr. United Kingdom; £10.00/yr. elsewhere
Year to which price refers: 1992
Subscription address: c/o Joan Leach, Far Yew Tree House, Over Tabley, Knutsford, Cheshire WA16 0HN, England

ADVERTISING INFORMATION

Advertising accepted: Yes
Advertising rates: £25.00/half page; £50.00/full page

EDITORIAL DESCRIPTION

Scope: Publishes critical and scholarly articles on the life and works of Elisabeth Gaskell.
Reviews books: Yes
Publishes notes: Yes
Languages accepted: English
Prints abstracts: No
Author-anonymous submission: No

SUBMISSION REQUIREMENTS

Restrictions on contributors: None
Author pays submission fee: No
Author pays page charges: No
Length of articles: 2,500-7,500 words
Length of book reviews: 1,000-1,500 words
Style: MLA
Number of copies required: 1
Copyright ownership: Gaskell Soc.
Rejected manuscripts: Returned
Time before publication decision: 2 mos.
Time between decision and publication: 1 yr.
Number of reviewers: 2
Articles submitted per year: 10-15
Articles published per year: 6-8
Book reviews published per year: 2-3

(1079)
GDR Bulletin

Thomas C. Fox, Editor
Dept. of Germanic Languages & Literatures
Washington Univ.
Box 1104
One Brookings Dr.
St. Louis, MO 63130-4899

Telephone: 314 935-5106
First published: 1975
Sponsoring organization: Dept. of Germanic Languages & Literatures, Washington Univ.
MLA acronym: GDRB

SUBSCRIPTION INFORMATION

Frequency of publication: 2 times/yr.
Circulation: 400
Available in microform: No
Subscription price: $10.00/yr. institutions; $3.00/yr. individuals; add $2.00/yr. postage outside US
Year to which price refers: 1992

ADVERTISING INFORMATION

Advertising accepted: Yes

EDITORIAL DESCRIPTION

Scope: An interdisciplinary journal of East German studies, *GDRB* focuses primarily on the literature of the former German Democratic Republic. In addition to articles, the journal features interviews with East German writers.
Reviews books: Yes
Publishes notes: Yes
Languages accepted: English; German
Prints abstracts: No

SUBMISSION REQUIREMENTS

Special requirements: Submission should be made on diskette.

(1080)
*Genders

Ann Kibbey, Editor
Univ. of Colorado
Campus Box 226
Boulder, CO 80309

Telephone: 303 492-2853
First published: 1988
Sponsoring organization: Univ. of Colorado, Boulder
ISSN: 0894-9832
MLA acronym: Genders

SUBSCRIPTION INFORMATION

Frequency of publication: 3 times/yr. (Apr., Aug., Dec.)
Circulation: 1,000
Available in microform: Yes
Subscription price: $40.00/yr. institutions; $24.00/yr. individuals; add $16.50/yr. postage outside US
Year to which price refers: 1992
Subscription address: Univ. of Texas Press, P.O. Box 7819, Austin, TX 78713
Subscription telephone: 512 471-4531

ADVERTISING INFORMATION

Advertising accepted: Yes

EDITORIAL DESCRIPTION

Scope: Focuses on the theory and representation of gender in literature, art, history, music, photography, television, and film.
Reviews books: Yes
Publishes notes: No
Languages accepted: English
Prints abstracts: No
Author-anonymous submission: Yes

SUBMISSION REQUIREMENTS

Restrictions on contributors: None
Author pays submission fee: No
Author pays page charges: No
Length of articles: 6,000-9,000 words
Length of book reviews: 6,000-9,000 words
Style: Chicago
Number of copies required: 1
Special requirements: Submit typescript.
Copyright ownership: Univ. of Texas Press
Rejected manuscripts: Returned at author's request
Time before publication decision: 4 mos.
Time between decision and publication: 6-8 mos.
Number of reviewers: 1-4
Articles submitted per year: 150
Articles published per year: 21-25
Book reviews submitted per year: 10
Book reviews published per year: 2

(1081)
*General Linguistics

Ernst A. Ebbinghaus, Saul Levin, & Philip H. Baldi, Editors
S 332 Burrowes
Pennsylvania State Univ.
University Park, PA 16802

First published: 1955
ISSN: 0016-6553
MLA acronym: GL

SUBSCRIPTION INFORMATION

Frequency of publication: 4 times/yr. (Spring, Summer, Fall, Winter)
Circulation: 950
Available in microform: No
Subscription address: MRTS-LN G 99, State Univ. of New York, Binghamton, NY 13902-6000

ADVERTISING INFORMATION

Advertising accepted: Yes

EDITORIAL DESCRIPTION

Scope: Invites articles in all fields of linguistics, especially historical, comparative, and descriptive.
Reviews books: Yes
Publishes notes: Yes
Languages accepted: English; French; German; Russian
Prints abstracts: No
Author-anonymous submission: Yes

SUBMISSION REQUIREMENTS

Restrictions on contributors: None
Author pays submission fee: No
Author pays page charges: No
Length of articles: No restrictions
Length of book reviews: No restrictions
Length of notes: No restrictions
Style: Chicago
Number of copies required: 2
Special requirements: Submit typescript.
Copyright ownership: Assigned by author to journal
Rejected manuscripts: Returned
Time before publication decision: 4 mos.
Time between decision and publication: 18 mos.
Number of reviewers: 4
Articles submitted per year: 50-60
Articles published per year: 12-15
Book reviews submitted per year: 20
Book reviews published per year: 20
Notes submitted per year: 30
Notes published per year: 5-10

(1082)
*Gengo Kenkyū: Journal of the Linguistic Society of Japan

Masayoshi Shibatani, Editor
Linguistic Soc. of Japan
c/o The Sanseido Co.
2-22-14 Misaki-cho
Chiyoda-ku, Tokyo 101, Japan

Telephone: (81) 3 32309526
First published: 1939
Sponsoring organization: Linguistic Soc. of Japan
ISSN: 0024-3914
MLA acronym: GK

SUBSCRIPTION INFORMATION

Frequency of publication: 2 times/yr.
Circulation: 1,800
Available in microform: No
Subscription price: 7,000 yen/yr. individuals Japan; 8,500 yen/yr. individuals elsewhere
Year to which price refers: 1992
Subscription address: Business Centre for Academic Socs. of Japan, 5-16-9 Honkomagome, Bunkyō-ku, Tokyo, 113, Japan
Subscription telephone: (81) 3 58145801
Subscription fax: (81) 3 58145820

ADVERTISING INFORMATION

Advertising accepted: No

EDITORIAL DESCRIPTION

Scope: Publishes articles on all aspects of linguistics.
Reviews books: Yes
Publishes notes: No
Languages accepted: Japanese; English; French; German
Prints abstracts: Yes
Author-anonymous submission: Yes

SUBMISSION REQUIREMENTS

Restrictions on contributors: Contributors must be members of the Linguistic Soc. of Japan.
Author pays submission fee: No
Author pays page charges: No
Length of articles: 600 lines or 16,000 Japanese characters
Length of book reviews: 12,000 characters
Style: Linguistic Soc. of Japan
Number of copies required: 3
Special requirements: Submit original manuscript. Submit a 20-line abstract in English if article is in Japanese; submit a 400-character abstract in Japanese if article is in language other than Japanese.
Copyright ownership: Linguistic Soc. of Japan
Rejected manuscripts: Not returned
Time before publication decision: 3 mos.
Time between decision and publication: 3 mos.
Number of reviewers: 2
Articles submitted per year: 25
Articles published per year: 10
Book reviews submitted per year: 7
Book reviews published per year: 6

(1083)
*Genre

Ronald Schleifer, Editor
Dept. of English
Univ. of Oklahoma
Norman, OK 73019

First published: 1968
Sponsoring organization: Univ. of Oklahoma
ISSN: 0016-6928
MLA acronym: Genre

SUBSCRIPTION INFORMATION

Frequency of publication: 4 times/yr. (Spring, Summer, Fall, Winter)
Circulation: 750
Available in microform: No
Subscription price: $27.00/yr. institutions; $14.00/yr. individuals; $30.00/yr. outside US
Year to which price refers: 1992

ADVERTISING INFORMATION

Advertising accepted: Yes
Advertising rates: $75.00/full page

EDITORIAL DESCRIPTION

Scope: Devoted to generic criticism. Publishes articles dealing with questions of genre in relation to interpretation of major literary texts, historical development of specific genres, and theoretical discussion of the concept of genre itself.
Reviews books: Yes
Publishes notes: No
Languages accepted: English
Prints abstracts: No
Author-anonymous submission: No

SUBMISSION REQUIREMENTS

Restrictions on contributors: None
Author pays submission fee: No
Author pays page charges: No
Length of articles: 25 pp.
Length of book reviews: 1,000 words
Style: MLA
Number of copies required: 2
Copyright ownership: Univ. of Oklahoma
Rejected manuscripts: Returned; enclose return postage.
Time before publication decision: 2-3 mos.
Time between decision and publication: 8-12 mos.
Number of reviewers: 3
Articles submitted per year: 250
Articles published per year: 25-30
Book reviews submitted per year: 15-20
Book reviews published per year: 15-20

(1084)
*Geolinguistics: Journal of the American Society of Geolinguistics

Jesse Levitt, Editor
485 Brooklawn Ave.
Fairfield, CT 06432-1805

Telephone: 203 333-8920
First published: 1974
Sponsoring organization: American Soc. of Geolinguistics
ISSN: 0190-4671
MLA acronym: Geolinguistics

SUBSCRIPTION INFORMATION

Frequency of publication: Annual (Dec.)
Circulation: 100
Available in microform: No
Subscription price: $25.00/yr.; $15.00/yr. students & retired members
Year to which price refers: 1992
Subscription address: L. Barbara Richardson, Treasurer, American Soc. of Geolinguistics, P.O. Box 6337, FDR Station, New York, NY 10150

ADVERTISING INFORMATION

Advertising accepted: Yes

EDITORIAL DESCRIPTION

Scope: Publishes articles on distribution, use, relative practical importance, identification, and interrelationships of present-day languages; includes selected materials in other areas of linguistics, especially languages in contact, sociolinguistics, language education, linguistic geography, and language politics.
Reviews books: Yes
Publishes notes: Yes
Languages accepted: English; French; Spanish
Prints abstracts: No
Author-anonymous submission: No

SUBMISSION REQUIREMENTS

Restrictions on contributors: Preference is given to members and invited speakers, but other contributions are welcome.
Author pays submission fee: No
Author pays page charges: No
Length of articles: 5-25 pp.
Length of book reviews: 1,000-2,000 words
Length of notes: 1,000-3,000 words
Style: MLA
Number of copies required: 3
Special requirements: For camera-ready contributions, submit single-spaced typescript with blank lines between paragraphs, and wide margins (1.5 inches, left and right margins). If not camera-ready, submit double-spaced typescript. Abstract is preferred for unsolicited items (1.5 inches, left and right margins). Clear photocopies are acceptable; do not submit carbon copies (1.5 inches, left and right margins). English is the preferred language of publication. Last manuscript to be considered must be received by 1 August.
Copyright ownership: Author
Rejected manuscripts: Returned
Time before publication decision: 2 mos.
Time between decision and publication: Manuscripts are evaluated Jan.-Aug.
Number of reviewers: 2-3
Articles submitted per year: 12-20
Articles published per year: 10-15
Book reviews submitted per year: 3-10
Book reviews published per year: 4-7
Notes submitted per year: 1-3
Notes published per year: 1-2

(1085)
*George Eliot-George Henry Lewes Studies

William Baker, Editor
English Dept.
Northern Illinois Univ.
DeKalb, IL 60115-2868

Telephone: 815 753-1857
Fax: 815 753-2003
First published: 1982
Historical variations in title: Formerly *The George Eliot-George Henry Lewes Newsletter*
Sponsoring organization: Northern Illinois Univ. Graduate School, Dept. of English, & University Libraries
ISSN: 0953-0754
MLA acronym: GEGHLS

SUBSCRIPTION INFORMATION

Frequency of publication: 1-2 times/yr.
Circulation: 350
Available in microform: No
Subscription price: $6.00 (£3.00)/yr.
Year to which price refers: 1991

ADVERTISING INFORMATION

Advertising accepted: Yes

EDITORIAL DESCRIPTION

Scope: Includes articles and notes relating to George Eliot, George Henry Lewes, and the relationship between them and their circle.
Reviews books: Yes
Publishes notes: Yes
Languages accepted: English
Prints abstracts: No
Author-anonymous submission: No

SUBMISSION REQUIREMENTS

Restrictions on contributors: None
Author pays submission fee: No
Author pays page charges: No
Length of articles: No restrictions
Length of book reviews: No restrictions
Length of notes: No restrictions
Style: MLA
Number of copies required: 2
Special requirements: Submit double-spaced typescript. Materials for the April issue should arrive in March, for the September issue in August.
Copyright ownership: Journal & Author
Rejected manuscripts: Returned
Time before publication decision: 1 mo.
Number of reviewers: 2
Articles submitted per year: 10-15
Articles published per year: 5-6
Book reviews submitted per year: 5
Book reviews published per year: 5
Notes submitted per year: 5
Notes published per year: 5

(1086)
*The George Eliot Review: Journal of the George Eliot Fellowship

Graham Handley & Beryl Gray, Editors
Glasgow Stud Farmhouse
Crews Hill
Enfield, Middlesex EN2 9DY, England

Telephone: (44) 81 3631460
First published: 1970
Historical variations in title: Formerly *George Eliot Fellowship Review*
Sponsoring organization: Univ. of Warwick, Dept. of English
MLA acronym: GER

SUBSCRIPTION INFORMATION

Frequency of publication: Annual (July)
Circulation: 400
Available in microform: No
Subscription address: Kathleen Adams, 71 Stepping Stones Rd., Coventry CV5 8JT, Warwickshire, England
Subscription telephone: (44) 203 592231

ADVERTISING INFORMATION

Advertising accepted: Yes
Advertising rates: £25.00/half page; £50.00/full page

EDITORIAL DESCRIPTION

Scope: Includes short biographical and critical articles on George Eliot, reviews, reports on addresses to the Fellowship and notes of interest to members.
Reviews books: Yes
Publishes notes: Yes
Languages accepted: English
Prints abstracts: No
Author-anonymous submission: No

SUBMISSION REQUIREMENTS

Restrictions on contributors: None
Author pays submission fee: No
Author pays page charges: No
Length of articles: 1,500 words
Length of book reviews: 800 words
Style: MLA
Number of copies required: 1
Rejected manuscripts: Returned
Time between decision and publication: 2 mos.
Number of reviewers: 2
Articles submitted per year: 7-10

Articles published per year: 5-7
Book reviews published per year: 6-7

(1087)
*George Herbert Journal

Sidney Gottlieb, Editor
English Dept.
Sacred Heart Univ.
5151 Park Ave.
Fairfield, CT 06432-1023

Telephone: 908 846-8487
First published: 1977
ISSN: 0161-7435
MLA acronym: GHJ

SUBSCRIPTION INFORMATION

Frequency of publication: 2 times/yr. (Fall, Spring)
Circulation: 400
Available in microform: No
Subscription price: $15.00/yr. institutions; $7.00/yr. individuals US; $10.00/yr. individuals elsewhere
Year to which price refers: 1992

ADVERTISING INFORMATION

Advertising accepted: Yes
Advertising rates: $40.00/half page; $70.00/full page

EDITORIAL DESCRIPTION

Scope: Focuses primarily on the life and works of George Herbert (1593-1633); reviews often touch on topics more generally relevant to 17th-century (particularly metaphysical) poetry. Occasional special numbers cover related authors and/or themes.
Reviews books: Yes
Publishes notes: Yes
Languages accepted: English
Prints abstracts: No
Author-anonymous submission: No

SUBMISSION REQUIREMENTS

Restrictions on contributors: Book reviews are assigned.
Author pays submission fee: No
Author pays page charges: No
Length of articles: 5,000 words maximum
Length of book reviews: No restrictions
Length of notes: No restrictions
Style: Chicago
Number of copies required: 2
Special requirements: Final versions of accepted articles should be submitted on IBM-compatible diskette.
Copyright ownership: Journal
Rejected manuscripts: Returned; enclose return postage.
Time before publication decision: 4 mos.
Time between decision and publication: 6 mos. maximum
Number of reviewers: 2 minimum
Articles submitted per year: 25
Articles published per year: 8
Book reviews published per year: 8-10
Notes submitted per year: 12-15
Notes published per year: 6-8

(1088)
*George Sand Studies

Natalie Datlof & David A. Powell, Editors
Hofstra Cultural Center
Hofstra Univ.
Hempstead, NY 11550

Telephone: 516 463-5669; 516 463-5417
Fax: 516 564-4297
First published: 1977
Sponsoring organization: Friends of George Sand
ISSN: 0161-6544
MLA acronym: GSS

SUBSCRIPTION INFORMATION

Frequency of publication: Annual (Spring)
Circulation: 250
Available in microform: No
Subscription price: $15.00/yr. institutions; $12.00/yr. individuals; $7.00/yr. students

ADVERTISING INFORMATION

Advertising accepted: Yes
Advertising rates: $25.00/half page; $50.00/full page

EDITORIAL DESCRIPTION

Scope: Publishes articles on the life, works, and influence of George Sand, as well as articles on her contemporaries.
Reviews books: Yes
Publishes notes: Yes
Languages accepted: English; French
Prints abstracts: No
Author-anonymous submission: Yes

SUBMISSION REQUIREMENTS

Author pays submission fee: No
Author pays page charges: No
Length of articles: No restrictions
Length of book reviews: No restrictions
Length of notes: No restrictions
Style: MLA
Number of copies required: 2
Copyright ownership: Journal
Rejected manuscripts: Returned; enclose return postage.
Time before publication decision: 1 yr.
Time between decision and publication: 6 mos.
Number of reviewers: 3
Articles submitted per year: 20
Articles published per year: 6-8
Book reviews submitted per year: 6-12
Book reviews published per year: 8

(1089)
*The Georgetown Journal of Languages and Linguistics

James E. Alatis, Editor
Georgetown Univ.
Washington, DC 20057-0988

Telephone: 202 687-6045
Fax: 202 687-5712
E-mail: GJLL@GUVAX (Bitnet); GJLL@GUVAX.GEORGETOWN.EDU (Internet)
First published: 1990
Sponsoring organization: Georgetown Univ., School of Languages & Linguistics
ISSN: 1048-4205
MLA acronym: GJLL

SUBSCRIPTION INFORMATION

Frequency of publication: 4 times/yr.
Circulation: 300
Available in microform: No
Subscription price: $15.00/yr. US; $30.00/yr. elsewhere
Year to which price refers: 1992
Subscription address: Order Dept., Georgetown Univ. Press, Georgetown Univ., Washington, DC 20057-1079
Subscription telephone: 202 687-5889

ADVERTISING INFORMATION

Advertising accepted: No

EDITORIAL DESCRIPTION

Scope: Publishes articles on all areas of languages and linguistics. Also includes studies on literary history, theory, and criticism.
Reviews books: Yes
Publishes notes: Yes
Languages accepted: Primarily English; French; German; Italian; Spanish; Portuguese; Russian; Japanese; Chinese languages; Arabic
Prints abstracts: No

SUBMISSION REQUIREMENTS

Author pays submission fee: No
Author pays page charges: No
Length of articles: No restrictions
Length of book reviews: No restrictions
Length of notes: No restrictions
Style: Linguistic Soc. of America
Number of copies required: 1
Special requirements: Submission of typescript and diskette is preferred.
Copyright ownership: Georgetown Univ.
Rejected manuscripts: Returned with comments
Number of reviewers: 2-3
Articles published per year: 20-25
Book reviews published per year: 8-12
Notes published per year: 30-35

(1090)
*Georgetown University Round Table on Languages and Linguistics

James E. Alatis, Editor
Georgetown Univ. Press
Intercultural Center, Room 111
Georgetown Univ.
Washington, DC 20057-1067

Telephone: 202 687-6063
Fax: 202 687-6340
E-mail: GURT@GUVAX (bitnet); GURT@GUVAX.GEORGETOWN.EDU
First published: 1971
Sponsoring organization: Georgetown Univ., School of Languages & Linguistics
ISSN: 0186-7207
MLA acronym: GURT

SUBSCRIPTION INFORMATION

Frequency of publication: Annual
Circulation: 300
Available in microform: Yes, for out-of-print issues only
Subscription price: $35.00/yr.
Year to which price refers: 1991
Subscription address: Order Dept., at the above address

ADVERTISING INFORMATION

Advertising accepted: No

EDITORIAL DESCRIPTION

Scope: Publishes proceedings of the annual Georgetown University Round Table on Languages and Linguistics.
Reviews books: No
Publishes notes: No
Languages accepted: English
Prints abstracts: No
Author-anonymous submission: No

SUBMISSION REQUIREMENTS

Restrictions on contributors: Contributors are the invited speakers at annual meeting.
Author pays submission fee: No
Author pays page charges: No
Style: Linguistic Soc. of America
Number of copies required: 1
Copyright ownership: Georgetown Univ.
Rejected manuscripts: Returned at author's request

(1091)
*The Georgia Review

Stanley W. Lindberg, Editor
Univ. of Georgia
Athens, GA 30602-9009

Telephone: 706 542-3481
First published: 1947
Sponsoring organization: Univ. of Georgia
ISSN: 0016-8386
MLA acronym: GaR

SUBSCRIPTION INFORMATION

Frequency of publication: 4 times/yr. (Mar., June, Sept., Dec.)
Circulation: 5,700
Available in microform: Yes
Subscription price: $18.00/yr., $30.00/2 yrs.
Year to which price refers: 1992-93
Subscription fax: 706 542-0047

ADVERTISING INFORMATION

Advertising accepted: Yes
Advertising rates: $225.00/half page; $350.00/full page

EDITORIAL DESCRIPTION

Scope: Publishes essays in literary criticism, philosophy, history, art history, film criticism, linguistics, music, psychology; book reviews in these fields; poetry; fiction.
Reviews books: Yes
Publishes notes: No
Languages accepted: English
Prints abstracts: No
Author-anonymous submission: No

SUBMISSION REQUIREMENTS

Restrictions on contributors: Unsolicited manuscripts are not considered during June, July, and August. Book reviews are assigned, but queries are welcomed.
Author pays submission fee: No
Author pays page charges: No
Length of articles: 2,500-10,000 words
Style: MLA
Number of copies required: 1
Copyright ownership: Univ. of Georgia; reverts to author upon publication.
Rejected manuscripts: Returned at author's request; enclose SASE.
Time before publication decision: 2-3 mos.
Time between decision and publication: 6-12 mos.
Number of reviewers: 2-4
Articles submitted per year: 350
Articles published per year: 20
Book reviews submitted per year: 100
Book reviews published per year: 30

(1092)
*Georgia State Literary Studies Series

Victor A. Kramer, Editor
Dept. of English
Georgia State Univ.
University Plaza
Atlanta, GA 30303

First published: 1987
Sponsoring organization: Georgia State Univ.
ISSN: 0884-8696
MLA acronym: GSLS

SUBSCRIPTION INFORMATION

Frequency of publication: 1-2 times/yr.
Available in microform: No
Subscription address: AMS Press, Inc., 56 E. 13th St., New York, NY 10003

ADVERTISING INFORMATION

Advertising accepted: No

EDITORIAL DESCRIPTION

Scope: Publishes book collections on topics which were first subjects of issues of *Studies in the Literary Imagination*. Selected issues of *SLitI* are used as the basis for expansion into these books. Some articles from the journal are selected and revised; many additional essays are commissioned; a new introduction as well as a new bibliography are added so that the book stands as a comprehensive study in its particular topic.
Reviews books: No
Publishes notes: No
Languages accepted: English
Prints abstracts: No
Author-anonymous submission: No

SUBMISSION REQUIREMENTS

Restrictions on contributors: Contributions are solicited.
Author pays submission fee: No
Author pays page charges: No
Length of articles: 5,000-7,000 words
Length of books: 300 pp.
Style: MLA
Number of copies required: 1
Special requirements: Submit on diskette using WordPerfect.
Copyright ownership: AMS Press, Inc.
Rejected manuscripts: Returned
Time before publication decision: 1-2 mos.
Time between decision and publication: 11-12 mos.
Number of reviewers: 2
Books published per year: 1-2

(1093)
*German-Canadian Yearbook/ Deutschkanadisches Jahrbuch

Hartmut Froeschle & Lothar Zimmermann, Editors
Historical Soc. of Mecklenburg Upper Canada
P.O. Box 1251, Station K
Toronto, Ontario M4P 3E5, Canada

Additional editorial address: Georg K. Weissenborn, Univ. of Toronto, St. Michael's College, 81 St. Mary St., Toronto, Ontario M5S 1J4, Canada
Telephone: 416 926-1300 ext. 3294 (Weissenborn)
First published: 1973
Sponsoring organization: Historical Soc. of Mecklenburg Upper Canada Inc.
ISSN: 0316-8603
MLA acronym: GCY

SUBSCRIPTION INFORMATION

Frequency of publication: Once every 18 mos.
Circulation: 1,200
Available in microform: No
Subscription price: C$29.00/yr.
Year to which price refers: 1991
Subscription telephone: 416 635-6529

ADVERTISING INFORMATION

Advertising accepted: No

EDITORIAL DESCRIPTION

Scope: Publishes articles on German-Canadiana.
Reviews books: Yes
Publishes notes: Yes
Languages accepted: English; German; French
Prints abstracts: Yes
Author-anonymous submission: No

SUBMISSION REQUIREMENTS

Restrictions on contributors: None
Author pays submission fee: No
Author pays page charges: No
Length of articles: 5-30 typescript pp.
Length of book reviews: 1-5 typescript pp.
Style: MLA
Number of copies required: 2
Special requirements: Include English abstracts for German and French articles.
Copyright ownership: Journal
Rejected manuscripts: Returned
Time before publication decision: 2 mos.
Time between decision and publication: 1 yr.
Number of reviewers: 2
Articles submitted per year: 30-40
Articles published per year: 20-30
Book reviews submitted per year: 20
Book reviews published per year: 15-20
Notes submitted per year: 5
Notes published per year: 3

(1094)
*German Life and Letters

Leonard W. Forster, G. P. G. Butler, G. Gillespie, J. M. Ritchie, J. Sandford, H. Watanabe, & J. J. White, Editors
c/o Inst. of Germanic Studies
29 Russell Square
London WC1 B 5DP, England

First published: 1936
ISSN: 0016-8777
MLA acronym: GL&L

SUBSCRIPTION INFORMATION

Frequency of publication: 4 times/yr. (Oct., Jan., Apr., July)
Circulation: 750
Available in microform: No
Subscription price: $165.00/yr. institutions; $79.00/yr. individuals
Year to which price refers: 1992
Subscription address: Basil Blackwell, 108 Cowley Rd., Oxford OX4 1JF, England

ADVERTISING INFORMATION

Advertising accepted: Yes
Advertising rates: Request from Basil Blackwell

EDITORIAL DESCRIPTION

Scope: Publishes scholarly articles on aspects of German literature, culture, and society.
Reviews books: No
Publishes notes: Yes
Languages accepted: English; German
Prints abstracts: No
Author-anonymous submission: Yes

SUBMISSION REQUIREMENTS

Restrictions on contributors: None
Author pays submission fee: No
Author pays page charges: No
Length of articles: No restrictions
Length of notes: 3,000 words
Style: Journal
Number of copies required: 1
Special requirements: Use British spelling.
Copyright ownership: Journal
Rejected manuscripts: Returned
Time before publication decision: 2 mos.
Time between decision and publication: 12-18 mos.
Number of reviewers: 5
Articles published per year: 35
Notes published per year: 2

(1095)
*The German Quarterly

Reinhold Grimm, Editor
Dept. of Languages & Literatures
Univ. of California
Riverside, CA 92521

Telephone: 714 787-5017
First published: 1928
Sponsoring organization: American Assn. of Teachers of German
ISSN: 0016-8831
MLA acronym: GQ

SUBSCRIPTION INFORMATION

Frequency of publication: 4 times/yr. (Winter, Spring, Summer, Fall)
Circulation: 5,500
Available in microform: No
Subscription price: $35.00/yr. US; $45.00/yr. elsewhere
Year to which price refers: 1992
Subscription address: American Assn. of Teachers of German, Administrative Office, 112 Haddontowne Court, No. 104, Cherry Hill, NJ 08034

ADVERTISING INFORMATION

Advertising accepted: Yes
Advertising rates: $200.00/half page; $275.00/full page; $350.00/inside back cover; $395.00/back cover

EDITORIAL DESCRIPTION

Scope: Publishes scholarly articles on German literature and language.
Reviews books: Yes
Publishes notes: No
Languages accepted: English; German
Prints abstracts: Yes
Author-anonymous submission: Yes

SUBMISSION REQUIREMENTS

Restrictions on contributors: Unsolicited book reviews are not accepted.
Author pays submission fee: No
Author pays page charges: No
Length of articles: 30 double-spaced pp.
Length of book reviews: 500-600 words
Style: MLA
Number of copies required: 3
Special requirements: Type name and address on separate sheet or in cover letter for anonymous review. Articles accepted for submission must be submitted on diskette.
Copyright ownership: Journal
Rejected manuscripts: Returned; enclose SASE.
Time before publication decision: 1-4 mos.
Time between decision and publication: 4-8 mos.
Number of reviewers: 1-3
Articles submitted per year: 110
Articles published per year: 33
Book reviews published per year: 225

(1096)
*German Studies Review

Gerald R. Kleinfeld, Editor
Arizona State Univ.
Tempe, AZ 85287-4205

Telephone: 602 965-4839
Fax: 602 965-8989
First published: 1978
Sponsoring organization: German Studies Assn.
ISSN: 0149-7952
MLA acronym: GerSR

SUBSCRIPTION INFORMATION

Frequency of publication: 3 times/yr.
Circulation: 1,400
Available in microform: No

ADVERTISING INFORMATION

Advertising accepted: Yes

EDITORIAL DESCRIPTION

Scope: Publishes articles and book reviews on literature, history, and political science of the German-speaking area. Interdisciplinary articles are also welcome.
Reviews books: Yes
Publishes notes: No
Languages accepted: English; German
Prints abstracts: No
Author-anonymous submission: Yes

SUBMISSION REQUIREMENTS

Restrictions on contributors: None
Author pays submission fee: No
Author pays page charges: No
Length of articles: 25 typescript pp.
Length of book reviews: 450 words
Style: MLA; Chicago
Number of copies required: 2
Copyright ownership: Journal
Rejected manuscripts: Returned; enclose return postage.
Time before publication decision: 3 mos.
Time between decision and publication: 6 mos.
Number of reviewers: 3
Articles submitted per year: 125
Articles published per year: 20
Book reviews published per year: 160

(1097)
*Germanic Notes and Reviews

Richard F. Krummel, Editor
Dept. of Modern Languages
Bemidji State Univ.
Bemidji, MN 56601

Telephone: 218 751-6265
First published: 1970
Historical variations in title: Formerly *Germanic Notes*
ISSN: 0016-8882
MLA acronym: GNR

SUBSCRIPTION INFORMATION

Frequency of publication: 2 times/yr.
Circulation: 500
Available in microform: Yes
Subscription price: $10.00/yr. US; $11.00/yr. elsewhere
Year to which price refers: 1992
Subscription address: Evelyn Krummel, Business Manager, Route 7, Box 179 B2, Bemidji, MN 56601

ADVERTISING INFORMATION

Advertising accepted: Yes

EDITORIAL DESCRIPTION

Scope: Includes notes, queries, critical reviews of scholarly works and annotated lists of works basic to research libraries supporting advanced programs in Germanic areas, on literature, language, folklore, genealogy, numismatics, prehistory, and onomastics, when pertinent to broader fields.
Reviews books: Yes
Publishes notes: Yes
Languages accepted: English; German
Prints abstracts: No
Author-anonymous submission: No

SUBMISSION REQUIREMENTS

Restrictions on contributors: Book reviews are solicited.
Author pays submission fee: No
Author pays page charges: No
Length of articles: 300-3,000 words
Length of book reviews: 300-1,000 words
Length of notes: 300-1,000 words
Style: MLA
Number of copies required: 2
Special requirements: Put full address on upper left of first page. Submit typescript; submission on MS-DOS diskette in addition to typescript is appreciated.
Copyright ownership: Journal
Rejected manuscripts: Returned; enclose return postage.
Time before publication decision: 1 mo.
Time between decision and publication: 1 yr.
Number of reviewers: 3
Articles submitted per year: 30
Articles published per year: 12
Book reviews submitted per year: 26
Book reviews published per year: 24
Notes submitted per year: 30
Notes published per year: 20

(1098)
*Germanic Review

Inge D. Halpert, Editor
320 Hamilton Hall
Columbia Univ.
New York, NY 10027

Telephone: 212 854-3202
First published: 1926
Sponsoring organization: Dept. of Germanic Languages, Columbia Univ.
ISSN: 0016-8890
MLA acronym: GR

SUBSCRIPTION INFORMATION

Frequency of publication: 4 times/yr. (Feb., May, Aug., Nov.)
Circulation: 1,400
Available in microform: Yes
Subscription price: $55.00/yr. institutions; $28.00/yr. individuals
Year to which price refers: 1992
Subscription address: Heldref Publications, 1319 18th St., NW, Washington, DC 20036-1802
Subscription telephone: 800 365-9753
Subscription fax: 202 296-5149

ADVERTISING INFORMATION

Advertising accepted: Yes
Advertising rates: $75.00/quarter page; $150.00/half page; $190.00/full page

EDITORIAL DESCRIPTION

Scope: Devoted to studies dealing with German literature from the medieval period to the present, and literary criticism.
Reviews books: Yes
Publishes notes: No
Languages accepted: English; German
Prints abstracts: No
Author-anonymous submission: Yes

SUBMISSION REQUIREMENTS

Restrictions on contributors: None
Author pays submission fee: No
Author pays page charges: No
Length of articles: 20-25 typescript pp.
Length of book reviews: 500-750 words
Style: MLA
Number of copies required: 2
Copyright ownership: Helen Dwight Reed Foundation
Rejected manuscripts: Returned; enclose return postage.
Time before publication decision: 3 mos.
Time between decision and publication: 1 yr.
Number of reviewers: 2
Articles submitted per year: 80
Articles published per year: 16-20
Book reviews submitted per year: 30
Book reviews published per year: 15-20

(1099)
*Germanic Studies in America

Katharina Mommsen, Editor
Dept. of German Studies, Bldg. 240
Stanford Univ.
Stanford, CA 94305

First published: 1969
ISSN: 0721-3727
MLA acronym: GSA

SUBSCRIPTION INFORMATION

Frequency of publication: Irregular
Available in microform: No
Subscription address: Verlag Peter Lang AG, Jupiterstr. 15, 3015 Bern, Switzerland

ADVERTISING INFORMATION

Advertising accepted: No

EDITORIAL DESCRIPTION

Scope: Publishes books on German and comparative literature and germanic philology written by American scholars.
Reviews books: No
Publishes notes: No
Languages accepted: English; German
Prints abstracts: No

SUBMISSION REQUIREMENTS

Author pays submission fee: No
Author pays page charges: Varies
Length of books: 100-500 pp.
Number of copies required: 1
Special requirements: Camera-ready computer typescript is preferred.
Copyright ownership: Verlag Peter Lang AG
Rejected manuscripts: Returned
Time before publication decision: 1 mo.
Time between decision and publication: 4-12 mos.
Number of reviewers: 1-3
Books submitted per year: 12-15
Books published per year: 4

(1100)
*Germanisch-Romanische Monatsschrift

Conrad Wiedemann, H. O. Burger, Johannes Janota, Sebastian Neumeister, Franz Karl Stanzel, & Renate Stauf, Editors
Inst. für Deutsche Philologie, Allgemeine & Vergleichende Literaturwissenschaft
Technische Univ. Berlin
Strasse des 17. Juni 135
1000 Berlin 12, Germany

Telephone: (49) 30 31422231
First published: 1909
ISSN: 0016-8904
MLA acronym: GRM

SUBSCRIPTION INFORMATION

Frequency of publication: 4 times/yr.
Circulation: 1,100
Available in microform: No
Subscription price: 135 DM/yr.
Year to which price refers: 1992
Subscription address: Carl Winter Universitätsverlag, Lutherstr. 59, Postfach 106140, 6900 Heidelberg 1, Germany
Subscription telephone: (49) 6221 49111

ADVERTISING INFORMATION

Advertising accepted: Yes

EDITORIAL DESCRIPTION

Scope: Publishes articles on literary history and literary theory in Germanic, Romance, and English studies with special emphasis on comparative aspects.
Reviews books: Yes
Publishes notes: Yes
Languages accepted: German; occasionally English; occasionally French
Prints abstracts: No
Author-anonymous submission: No

SUBMISSION REQUIREMENTS

Restrictions on contributors: None
Author pays submission fee: No
Author pays page charges: No
Length of articles: 16 pp.
Length of book reviews: 2-4 pp.
Length of notes: 1-4 pp.
Number of copies required: 1
Copyright ownership: Carl Winter Universitätsverlag
Rejected manuscripts: Returned
Time before publication decision: 2 mos.
Time between decision and publication: 6-18 mos.
Number of reviewers: 2
Articles submitted per year: 90
Articles published per year: 25
Book reviews submitted per year: 40
Book reviews published per year: 35
Notes submitted per year: 10
Notes published per year: 5

(1101)
*Germanistik: Internationales Referatenorgan mit Bibliographischen Hinweisen

Matthias Reifegerste, Editor
c/o Max Niemeyer Verlag
Postfach 2140
7400 Tübingen 1, Germany

Telephone: (49) 7071 87640
Fax: (49) 7071 87419
First published: 1960
Sponsoring organization: Trägerverein Germanistik e.V.
ISSN: 0016-8912
MLA acronym: Germanistik

SUBSCRIPTION INFORMATION

Frequency of publication: 4 times/yr.
Circulation: 1,900
Available in microform: No
Subscription price: 126 DM/yr. plus postage
Year to which price refers: 1991

ADVERTISING INFORMATION

Advertising accepted: Yes
Advertising rates: 1,200 DM/full page

EDITORIAL DESCRIPTION

Scope: Publishes reviews of books and bibliographical registration of articles on: German language (including historical stages, dialectology, onomastics) and literature, general linguistics, general and comparative literature, German folklore, and Old Norse language and literature.
Reviews books: Yes
Publishes notes: Yes
Languages accepted: German
Prints abstracts: No
Author-anonymous submission: No

SUBMISSION REQUIREMENTS

Restrictions on contributors: Unsolicited manuscripts are not accepted.
Author pays submission fee: No
Author pays page charges: No
Style: None
Number of copies required: 1
Special requirements: Submit original typescript.
Copyright ownership: Max Niemeyer Verlag
Rejected manuscripts: Returned
Time before publication decision: 3 weeks maximum
Time between decision and publication: 3 mos. maximum
Number of reviewers: 2
Book reviews published per year: 8,000 bibliographical entries

(1102)
*Germanistische Abhandlungen

J. B. Metzlersche Verlagsbuchhandlung
Kernerstr. 43
Postfach 529
7000 Stuttgart, Germany

Telephone: (49) 711 2290243
Fax: (49) 711 2290290
First published: 1962
Sponsoring organization: Deutsche Forschungsgemeinschaft
ISSN: 0435-5903
MLA acronym: GA

SUBSCRIPTION INFORMATION

Frequency of publication: Irregular
Circulation: 1,200
Available in microform: No

ADVERTISING INFORMATION

Advertising accepted: No

EDITORIAL DESCRIPTION

Scope: Publishes monographs on German literature.
Reviews books: No
Publishes notes: No
Languages accepted: German
Prints abstracts: No
Author-anonymous submission: No

SUBMISSION REQUIREMENTS

Restrictions on contributors: None
Author pays submission fee: No
Author pays page charges: No
Length of books: No restrictions
Style: None
Number of copies required: 1
Copyright ownership: J. B. Metzlersche Verlag
Rejected manuscripts: Returned
Time before publication decision: 2 mos.
Time between decision and publication: 6 mos.
Number of reviewers: 2
Books submitted per year: 10-20
Books published per year: 1-2

(1103)
*Germanistische Linguistik

Ulrich Knoop, Friedrich Debus, Wolfgang Putschke, Ludwig Erich Schmitt, & Herbert Ernst Wiegand, Editors
Forschungsinst. für Deutsche Sprache
Kaffweg 3
3550 Marburg/Lahn, Germany

Telephone: (49) 5121 37007
Fax: (49) 5121 32007
First published: 1969
ISSN: 0721-460X
MLA acronym: GLing

SUBSCRIPTION INFORMATION

Frequency of publication: Irregular
Available in microform: No

Subscription address: Georg Olms Verlag AG, Hagentorwall 7, 3200 Hildesheim, Germany
Additional subscription address: Georg Olms Verlag, 111 W. 57th St., New York, NY 10019

ADVERTISING INFORMATION

Advertising accepted: Yes

EDITORIAL DESCRIPTION

Scope: Publishes monographs on German language and linguistics.
Reviews books: No
Publishes notes: No
Languages accepted: German
Prints abstracts: No

SUBMISSION REQUIREMENTS

Books published per year: 4-6

(1104)
*Germanistische Mitteilungen: Zeitschrift für Deutsche Sprache, Literatur und Kultur in Wissenschaft und Praxis

Rudolf Kern & Peter Nelde, Editors
Belgischer Germanisten- und Deutschlehrerverband
Vrijheidslaan 17, Av. de la Liberté
1080 Brussels, Belgium

Telephone: (32) 2 4124231
Fax: (32) 2 4124200
First published: 1975
Sponsoring organization: Belgischer Germanisten- & Deutschlehrerverband
ISSN: 0771-3703
MLA acronym: GMit

SUBSCRIPTION INFORMATION

Frequency of publication: 2 times/yr.
Circulation: 1,000
Available in microform: No
Subscription price: 44 DM/yr.
Year to which price refers: 1992
Subscription address: F. Dümmler Verlag, Postfach 1480, 5300 Bonn, Germany

ADVERTISING INFORMATION

Advertising accepted: Yes
Advertising rates: 600 DM/full page

EDITORIAL DESCRIPTION

Scope: Publishes articles on German literature and linguistics.
Reviews books: Yes
Publishes notes: Yes
Languages accepted: German
Prints abstracts: No
Author-anonymous submission: No

SUBMISSION REQUIREMENTS

Restrictions on contributors: None
Author pays submission fee: No
Author pays page charges: No
Length of articles: 4,000-8,000 words
Length of book reviews: 1,000-2,000 words
Length of notes: 1-2 pp.
Style: Journal
Number of copies required: 1
Copyright ownership: Editor
Rejected manuscripts: Not returned
Time before publication decision: 1 mo.
Time between decision and publication: 6 mos.
Number of reviewers: 2
Articles submitted per year: 50
Articles published per year: 20
Book reviews submitted per year: 30
Book reviews published per year: 10-15

(1105)
*Germanistische Texte und Studien

Georg Olms Verlag AG
Hagentorwall 7
3200 Hildesheim, Germany

Additional editorial address: Georg Olms Verlag, 111 West 57th St., New York, NY 10019
Telephone: (49) 5121 37007
Fax: (49) 5121 32007
First published: 1975
ISSN: 0721-460X
MLA acronym: GTS

SUBSCRIPTION INFORMATION

Frequency of publication: Irregular
Available in microform: No

ADVERTISING INFORMATION

Advertising accepted: No

EDITORIAL DESCRIPTION

Scope: Publishes monographs on German literature.
Reviews books: No
Publishes notes: No
Languages accepted: German; English
Prints abstracts: Yes
Author-anonymous submission: No

SUBMISSION REQUIREMENTS

Author pays submission fee: No
Author pays page charges: Yes
Number of copies required: 1
Special requirements: Submit original typescript.
Copyright ownership: Author
Rejected manuscripts: Returned
Time before publication decision: 3 weeks
Time between decision and publication: 3 mos.
Number of reviewers: 2-3
Books submitted per year: 8-10
Books published per year: 3-4

(1106)
*Germano-Slavica: A Canadian Journal of Germanic and Slavic Comparative Studies

J. Whiton, Editor
Dept. of Germanic & Slavic Languages & Literatures
Univ. of Waterloo
Waterloo, Ontario N2L 3G1, Canada

Telephone: 519 885-1211 ext. 3683
First published: 1973
Sponsoring organization: Univ. of Waterloo
ISSN: 0317-4956
MLA acronym: GSlav

SUBSCRIPTION INFORMATION

Frequency of publication: Annual
Circulation: 400
Available in microform: No
Subscription price: $12.00/yr.
Year to which price refers: 1992

ADVERTISING INFORMATION

Advertising accepted: Yes
Advertising rates: $30.00/half page; $50.00/full page; $60.00/inside back cover; $75.00/back cover

EDITORIAL DESCRIPTION

Scope: Publishes articles on Germanic and Slavic comparative studies.
Reviews books: Yes
Publishes notes: Yes
Languages accepted: English; French; German

Prints abstracts: Yes
Author-anonymous submission: No

SUBMISSION REQUIREMENTS

Restrictions on contributors: None
Author pays submission fee: No
Author pays page charges: No
Length of articles: 8,000 words maximum
Style: MLA
Number of copies required: 1
Copyright ownership: Author
Rejected manuscripts: Returned
Time before publication decision: 3-12 weeks
Time between decision and publication: 1-6 mos.
Number of reviewers: 2
Articles published per year: 6-8
Book reviews published per year: 6-8
Notes published per year: 2

(1107)
*Gestos: Teoria y Practica del Teatro Hispánico

Juan Villegas, Editor
Dept. of Spanish & Portuguese
Univ. of California
Irvine, CA 92717

Telephone: 714 856-7171
Fax: 714 725-2803
First published: 1986
Sponsoring organization: Univ. of California, Irvine
ISSN: 1040-483X
MLA acronym: Gestos

SUBSCRIPTION INFORMATION

Frequency of publication: 2 times/yr. (Apr., Nov.)
Available in microform: No
Subscription price: $30.00/yr. institutions; $18.00/yr. individuals
Year to which price refers: 1992
Subscription telephone: 714 856-6901

ADVERTISING INFORMATION

Advertising accepted: Yes
Advertising rates: $50.00/full page

EDITORIAL DESCRIPTION

Scope: Publishes articles on Spanish, Latin American and Mexican American theater. Each issue includes reports of theater performances and features one unpublished play by a prominent dramatist.
Reviews books: Yes
Publishes notes: Yes
Languages accepted: Spanish; English
Prints abstracts: No
Author-anonymous submission: No

SUBMISSION REQUIREMENTS

Restrictions on contributors: None
Author pays submission fee: No
Author pays page charges: No
Length of articles: 25 pp. maximum
Length of book reviews: 3 pp.
Style: MLA
Number of copies required: 2
Special requirements: Submit original typescript and 1 copy.
Copyright ownership: Author
Rejected manuscripts: Original is returned.
Time before publication decision: 2-3 mos.
Time between decision and publication: 6-12 mos.
Number of reviewers: 2
Articles published per year: 14-18
Book reviews published per year: 18-22
Notes published per year: 4-6

(1108)
Gestus: The Electronic Journal of Brechtian Studies

Dwight Steward, Editor
Brecht Soc. of America
59 S. New St.
Dover, DE 19901

First published: 1985
Historical variations in title: Full text available online through EIES, NWI, COSY (Canada)
Sponsoring organization: Brecht Soc. of America
ISSN: 0749-7644
MLA acronym: Gestus

SUBSCRIPTION INFORMATION

Frequency of publication: 4 times/yr. (May, Aug., Nov., Feb.)
Circulation: 250
Available in microform: Yes
Additional subscription address: Gestus is published electronically and may be accessed over EIES and NWI, with E-Mail queries from most other networks via DASnet.

ADVERTISING INFORMATION

Advertising accepted: No

EDITORIAL DESCRIPTION

Scope: Publishes articles on all aspects of Bertolt Brecht, with special emphasis on his influence on modern theatre. Articles also welcomed on technology and its influence on theatre, translation, and scholarship.
Reviews books: Yes
Publishes notes: Yes
Languages accepted: English; German; French; Italian; Spanish
Prints abstracts: No

SUBMISSION REQUIREMENTS

Restrictions on contributors: Author must agree to electronic publication.
Author pays submission fee: No
Author pays page charges: No
Length of articles: 500-5,000 words
Length of book reviews: 400-3,000 words
Length of notes: 500 words
Style: Paper: MLA or Chicago; electronic: plain ASCII
Number of copies required: 2
Special requirements: Paper manuscripts should be typed in a font suitable for machine scanning. If article is not in English, submit 2 copies plus English translation. Electronic manuscripts accepted on diskette or via telephone modem. Submit a plain ASCII file with margins set for 50 characters per line plus a paper copy for verification.
Copyright ownership: Brecht Soc. of America
Rejected manuscripts: Returned
Time before publication decision: 1-2 mos.
Time between decision and publication: 3-6 mos.
Number of reviewers: 2
Articles submitted per year: 50
Articles published per year: 30
Book reviews submitted per year: 20
Book reviews published per year: 12
Notes submitted per year: 20
Notes published per year: 12

(1109)
*The Gettysburg Review

Peter Stitt, Editor
Gettysburg College
Gettysburg, PA 17325-1491

Telephone: 717 337-6770
Fax: 717 337-6775
First published: 1988
Sponsoring organization: Gettysburg College
ISSN: 0898-4557
MLA acronym: GettR

SUBSCRIPTION INFORMATION

Frequency of publication: 4 times/yr. (Jan., Apr., July, Oct.)
Circulation: 2,500
Available in microform: No
Subscription price: $15.00/yr., $27.00/2 yrs.
Year to which price refers: 1992
Subscription telephone: 717 337-6774

ADVERTISING INFORMATION

Advertising accepted: Yes
Advertising rates: $150.00/full page; $225.00/inside cover

EDITORIAL DESCRIPTION

Scope: Publishes interdisciplinary articles but focuses on American and contemporary literature. Also publishes poetry and fiction.
Reviews books: Yes
Publishes notes: No
Languages accepted: English
Prints abstracts: No
Author-anonymous submission: No

SUBMISSION REQUIREMENTS

Restrictions on contributors: None
Author pays submission fee: No
Author pays page charges: No
Length of articles: 3,000-7,000 words
Length of book reviews: 3,000-7,000 words
Style: Chicago
Number of copies required: 1
Special requirements: Submissions should be gracefully written, and not for specialists.
Copyright ownership: Author
Rejected manuscripts: Returned; enclose SASE.
Time before publication decision: 1-3 mos.
Time between decision and publication: 3-12 mos.
Number of reviewers: 2-3
Articles submitted per year: 90-100
Articles published per year: 15
Book reviews submitted per year: 20
Book reviews published per year: 15

(1110)
*Gezelliana: Kroniek van de Gezellestudie

P. Couttenier, N. Bakker, L. Simons, & A. De Vos, Editors
Centrum voor Gezellestudie
UFSIA
Prinsstraat 13
2000 Antwerp, Belgium

Telephone: (32) 3 2204291
First published: 1989
Sponsoring organization: Centrum voor Gezellestudie, Univ. Faculteiten Sint-Ignatius (UFSIA, Univ. Antwerp)
ISSN: 0776-4111
MLA acronym: GezellianaK

SUBSCRIPTION INFORMATION

Frequency of publication: 2 times/yr.
Circulation: 300
Available in microform: No
Subscription price: 600 BF/yr.
Year to which price refers: 1991
Subscription telephone: (32) 3 2204289

ADVERTISING INFORMATION

Advertising accepted: No

EDITORIAL DESCRIPTION

Scope: Focuses on the study of the life and works of the Flemish poet Guido Gezelle (1830-1899), in the context of 19th century literature and culture.
Reviews books: Yes
Publishes notes: Yes
Languages accepted: Dutch; English; German; French
Prints abstracts: No
Author-anonymous submission: Yes

SUBMISSION REQUIREMENTS

Restrictions on contributors: None
Author pays submission fee: No
Author pays page charges: No
Length of articles: 8,000-10,000 words
Length of book reviews: 2,000 words
Style: None
Special requirements: Submit original typescript.
Copyright ownership: Author
Rejected manuscripts: Returned
Time before publication decision: 2 mos.
Time between decision and publication: 6 mos.
Number of reviewers: 4
Articles submitted per year: 15
Articles published per year: 10
Book reviews submitted per year: 10
Book reviews published per year: 8

(1111)
*De Gids

G. van Benthem van den Bergh, Editor
Meulenhoff Nederland B.V.
Postbus 100
1000 AC Amsterdam, Netherlands

Telephone: (31) 20 6267555
Fax: (31) 20 6205516
First published: 1837
ISSN: 0016-9730
MLA acronym: Gids

SUBSCRIPTION INFORMATION

Frequency of publication: 12 times/yr.
Circulation: 3,000
Available in microform: No
Subscription price: 105 f/yr.
Year to which price refers: 1992
Subscription address: Meulenhoff B.V., Antwoordnummer 2619, Postbus 197, Amsterdam, Netherlands

ADVERTISING INFORMATION

Advertising accepted: Yes

EDITORIAL DESCRIPTION

Scope: Publishes articles on science and literature.
Reviews books: No
Publishes notes: No
Languages accepted: Dutch; English
Prints abstracts: No
Author-anonymous submission: No

SUBMISSION REQUIREMENTS

Author pays submission fee: No
Author pays page charges: No
Length of articles: 4,000 words
Number of copies required: 2
Copyright ownership: Author
Time before publication decision: 2 mos.
Time between decision and publication: 1-6 mos.
Articles published per year: 60

(1112)
*Gimtoji Kalba

Aldonas Pupkis, Editor
Sierakausko 15
2600 Vilnius, Lithuania

Telephone: (7) 122 628149
First published: 1990
Sponsoring organization: Lietuvos Respublikos Kultūros ir Švietimo Ministerija
ISSN: 0868-5134
MLA acronym: GKa

SUBSCRIPTION INFORMATION

Frequency of publication: 12 times/yr.
Circulation: 4,150
Available in microform: No
Subscription price: 36 Rbl/yr. Lithuania; $25.00/yr. elsewhere
Year to which price refers: 1992

ADVERTISING INFORMATION

Advertising accepted: Yes

EDITORIAL DESCRIPTION

Scope: Publishes articles on Lithuanian language. Includes studies on Lithuanian culture and linguistic education, and reports on the activities of the Society of Lithuanian Language. Covers problems of standard Lithuanian.
Reviews books: Yes
Publishes notes: Yes
Languages accepted: Lithuanian
Prints abstracts: No
Author-anonymous submission: No

SUBMISSION REQUIREMENTS

Restrictions on contributors: Book reviews are solicited.
Author pays submission fee: Yes
Author pays page charges: Yes
Length of articles: 1,700-2,000 words
Length of book reviews: 800-1,000 words
Length of notes: 500-700 words
Number of copies required: 2
Special requirements: Submit original typescript and 1 copy.
Copyright ownership: Author
Rejected manuscripts: Not returned
Time before publication decision: 1-2 mos.
Time between decision and publication: 3-4 mos.
Number of reviewers: 3
Articles submitted per year: 85-90
Articles published per year: 75-80
Book reviews submitted per year: 12-15
Book reviews published per year: 10-12
Notes submitted per year: 25-30
Notes published per year: 25-30

(1113)
Giornale Critico della Filosofia Italiana

Eugenio Garin, Director
Case Editrice Le Lettere
Costa San Giorgio 28
50125 Florence, Italy

ISSN: 0017-0089
MLA acronym: GCFI

SUBSCRIPTION INFORMATION

Frequency of publication: 4 times/yr.
Subscription price: 90,000 Lit/yr. Italy; 120,000 Lit/yr. elsewhere
Year to which price refers: 1991
Subscription address: Licosa SpA, Via Duca di Calabria, 1/1, 50125 Florence, Italy

EDITORIAL DESCRIPTION

Reviews books: Yes
Languages accepted: English; French; Italian
Prints abstracts: No

(1114)
*Giornale Italiano di Filologia

Nino Scivoletto, Editor
Via Ettore Romagnoli, 9
00137 Rome-Montesacro, Italy

Telephone: (39) 6 86802336
First published: 1948
ISSN: 0017-0461
MLA acronym: GIF

SUBSCRIPTION INFORMATION

Frequency of publication: 2 times/yr. (May, Nov.)
Circulation: 1,300
Available in microform: No
Subscription price: 52,000 Lit/yr. Italy; 64,000 Lit/yr. elsewhere; 35,000 Lit/single issue
Year to which price refers: 1991
Subscription address: Herder International Book Center, Piazza Montecitorio, 120, 00186 Rome, Italy
Subscription telephone: (39) 6 6795304

ADVERTISING INFORMATION

Advertising accepted: No

EDITORIAL DESCRIPTION

Scope: Publishes studies in Greco-Latin, medieval, and humanist philology.
Reviews books: Yes
Publishes notes: No
Languages accepted: Italian; French; English; German; Latin
Prints abstracts: No
Author-anonymous submission: No

SUBMISSION REQUIREMENTS

Restrictions on contributors: None
Author pays submission fee: No
Author pays page charges: No
Length of articles: 30 pp.
Length of book reviews: 2-3 pp.
Style: Chicago
Number of copies required: 1
Special requirements: Submit original typescript.
Copyright ownership: Assigned by author to journal
Rejected manuscripts: Not returned
Time before publication decision: 2 mos.
Time between decision and publication: 6 mos.
Number of reviewers: 2
Articles published per year: 15-20

(1115)
*Giornale Storico della Letteratura Italiana

E. Bigi, M. Marti, E. Bonora, & M. Pozzi, Editors
c/o Casa Editrice Loescher
Via Vittorio Amedeo, 18
10121 Torino, Italy

Telephone: (39) 11 549333
Fax: (39) 11 547614
First published: 1883
ISSN: 0017-0496
MLA acronym: GSLI

SUBSCRIPTION INFORMATION

Frequency of publication: 4 times/yr.
Circulation: 1,200
Available in microform: No
Subscription price: 94,000 Lit/yr. Italy; 122,000 Lit/yr. elsewhere
Year to which price refers: 1991

ADVERTISING INFORMATION

Advertising accepted: No

EDITORIAL DESCRIPTION

Scope: Publishes articles on the history of Italian literature.
Reviews books: Yes
Publishes notes: Yes
Languages accepted: Italian
Prints abstracts: No

SUBMISSION REQUIREMENTS

Author pays submission fee: No
Author pays page charges: No
Number of copies required: 1
Copyright ownership: Assigned by author to journal
Rejected manuscripts: Not returned
Time before publication decision: 2-4 weeks
Time between decision and publication: 1 mo.
Number of reviewers: 5
Articles submitted per year: 25-30
Articles published per year: 20
Book reviews submitted per year: 120
Book reviews published per year: 120
Notes submitted per year: 10
Notes published per year: 4

(1116)
*The Gissing Journal

Pierre Coustillas, Editor
10, rue Gay-Lussac
59110 La Madeleine, France

Telephone: (33) 20512927
Historical variations in title: Formerly The Gissing Newsletter
Sponsoring organization: Gissing Trust, Wakefield
ISSN: 0017-0615
MLA acronym: GissingJ

SUBSCRIPTION INFORMATION

Frequency of publication: 4 times/yr.
Circulation: 250
Available in microform: No
Subscription price: £12.00/yr. institutions; £8.00/yr. individuals
Year to which price refers: 1992
Subscription address: Ros Stinton, 7 Town Lane, Idle, Bradford BD10 8PR, England
Subscription telephone: (44) 274 613737

ADVERTISING INFORMATION

Advertising accepted: No

EDITORIAL DESCRIPTION

Scope: Publishes articles, notes, bibliographies, queries, and reviews on George Gissing and his circle.
Reviews books: Yes
Publishes notes: Yes
Languages accepted: English
Prints abstracts: No
Author-anonymous submission: No

SUBMISSION REQUIREMENTS

Restrictions on contributors: None
Author pays submission fee: No
Author pays page charges: No
Length of articles: 8,000 words maximum
Length of book reviews: 1,200 words
Length of notes: 500-1,000 words
Style: MLA
Number of copies required: 1
Copyright ownership: Author
Rejected manuscripts: Returned

Time before publication decision: 3 mos. maximum
Time between decision and publication: 6 mos.
Number of reviewers: 1-2
Articles submitted per year: 12
Articles published per year: 10
Book reviews submitted per year: 6
Book reviews published per year: 6
Notes submitted per year: 8
Notes published per year: 8

(1117)
Glotta: Organo de Difusión Lingüística

Clemencia Pineda de Valderrama, Director
P.O. Box 43789, Calle 17 No. 10-16, Piso 8o
Bogotá D.E., Colombia

First published: 1986
Sponsoring organization: Inst. Meyer
ISSN: 0120-6516
MLA acronym: GlottaC

SUBSCRIPTION INFORMATION

Frequency of publication: 3 times/yr.
Circulation: 3,500
Available in microform: No

ADVERTISING INFORMATION

Advertising accepted: Yes

EDITORIAL DESCRIPTION

Scope: Publishes articles on linguistics. Main focus is scientific and educational.
Reviews books: Yes
Publishes notes: No
Languages accepted: Spanish
Prints abstracts: Yes
Author-anonymous submission: No

SUBMISSION REQUIREMENTS

Author pays submission fee: No
Author pays page charges: No
Style: Colombian Standards ICFES/ICONTEC
Number of copies required: 1
Copyright ownership: Author
Rejected manuscripts: Returned at author's request
Time before publication decision: 6 mos.
Time between decision and publication: 3 mos.
Number of reviewers: 3
Articles submitted per year: 20
Articles published per year: 12-15
Book reviews submitted per year: 20
Book reviews published per year: 12

(1118)
Glotta: Zeitschrift für Griechische und Lateinische Sprache

Hartmut Erbse, Klaŭs Nickaŭ, & Klaus Strunk, Editors
Vandenhoeck & Ruprecht
Theaterstr. 13, Postfach 3753
3400 Göttingen, Germany

First published: 1908
Sponsoring organization: Deutsche Forschungsgemeinschaft
ISSN: 0017-1298
MLA acronym: Glotta

SUBSCRIPTION INFORMATION

Frequency of publication: 2 double issues/yr.
Circulation: 500
Available in microform: No

ADVERTISING INFORMATION

Advertising accepted: Yes

EDITORIAL DESCRIPTION

Scope: Publishes articles on Greek and Latin languages.
Reviews books: No
Publishes notes: No
Languages accepted: English; German; French; Italian; Latin
Prints abstracts: No

SUBMISSION REQUIREMENTS

Author pays submission fee: No
Author pays page charges: No
Length of articles: No restrictions
Number of copies required: 1
Special requirements: Manuscripts must be typescript, including Greek words.
Copyright ownership: Reverts from journal to author after 1 yr.
Rejected manuscripts: Returned
Time before publication decision: 1-2 mos.
Articles published per year: 20

(1119)
*Glottodidactica: An International Journal of Applied Linguistics

Waldemar Pfeiffer, Editor
Adam Mickiewicz Univ.
H. Wieniawskiego 1
61-712 Poznań, Poland

Telephone: (48) 61 311219
Fax: (48) 61 535535
First published: 1966
Sponsoring organization: Dept. of Glottodidactics, Adam Mickiewicz Univ.
ISSN: 0072-4769
MLA acronym: Glottodidactica

SUBSCRIPTION INFORMATION

Frequency of publication: Annual
Circulation: 800
Available in microform: No
Subscription address: Adam Mickiewicz Univ. Press, H. Wieniawskiego 1, 61-712 Poznań, Poland

ADVERTISING INFORMATION

Advertising accepted: Yes, on an exchange basis

EDITORIAL DESCRIPTION

Scope: Publishes articles on the theory and practice of foreign language teaching in Poland and abroad. Aimed at scientists and teachers of foreign languages.
Reviews books: Yes
Publishes notes: Yes
Languages accepted: English; French; German; Russian
Prints abstracts: Yes
Author-anonymous submission: No

SUBMISSION REQUIREMENTS

Restrictions on contributors: None
Author pays submission fee: No
Author pays page charges: No
Length of articles: 20 pp.
Length of book reviews: 750-1,500 words
Length of notes: 500 words
Style: MLA
Number of copies required: 3
Special requirements: Submit original typescript; include a 200-word abstract.
Copyright ownership: Journal
Rejected manuscripts: Returned
Time before publication decision: 3 mos.
Time between decision and publication: 1 yr.
Number of reviewers: 2-3
Articles submitted per year: 20
Articles published per year: 10
Book reviews submitted per year: 20-30
Book reviews published per year: 8-10

Notes submitted per year: 20
Notes published per year: 10

(1120)
*Glyph Textual Studies

Wlad Godzich, Samuel Weber, & Henry Sussman, Editors
Univ. of Minnesota Press
2037 University Ave., SE
Minneapolis, MN 55414-3092

First published: 1977
Sponsoring organization: Univ. of Minnesota Press
MLA acronym: GlyphT

SUBSCRIPTION INFORMATION

Frequency of publication: Annual
Available in microform: No
Subscription telephone: 800 388-3863

ADVERTISING INFORMATION

Advertising accepted: No

EDITORIAL DESCRIPTION

Reviews books: No
Languages accepted: English
Prints abstracts: No

SUBMISSION REQUIREMENTS

Restrictions on contributors: None
Author pays submission fee: No
Author pays page charges: No
Length of books: 20-40 pp.
Style: Chicago
Number of copies required: 2
Copyright ownership: Journal
Rejected manuscripts: Returned; enclose return postage.
Time before publication decision: 3 mos. maximum
Time between decision and publication: 9-12 mos.
Number of reviewers: 2-3
Books submitted per year: 60-75
Books published per year: 15-20

(1121)
*Gnomon: Kritische Zeitschrift für die Gesamte Klassische Altertumswissenschaft

Erich Burck, Carl Joachim Classen, Walter Schmitthenner, Ernst Vogt, & Paul Zanker, Editors
Inst. für Klassische Philologie
Univ. München
Geschwister-Scholl-Platz 1
8000 Munich 22, Germany

First published: 1925
ISSN: 0017-1417
MLA acronym: Gnomon

SUBSCRIPTION INFORMATION

Frequency of publication: 8 times/yr.
Available in microform: No
Subscription address: C. H. Beck'sche Verlagsbuchhandlung, (Oscar Beck), Wilhelmstr. 9, 8000 Munich 40, Germany

ADVERTISING INFORMATION

Advertising accepted: Yes

EDITORIAL DESCRIPTION

Scope: Publishes reviews of recent books on all fields of classical studies (Greek and Latin languages, literatures, culture, ancient history; classical archaeology; reception of antiquity in the Middle Ages and afterwards). Publishes a bibliographical survey four times a year.
Reviews books: Yes
Publishes notes: Yes
Languages accepted: English; German; Italian; French; Latin
Prints abstracts: No

SUBMISSION REQUIREMENTS

Restrictions on contributors: Contributions are solicited.
Author pays submission fee: No
Author pays page charges: No
Length of articles: 6-8 pp.
Number of copies required: 1
Special requirements: Submit print-ready typescript.
Copyright ownership: Author
Rejected manuscripts: Returned
Time before publication decision: Immediate
Time between decision and publication: 1-2 yrs.
Number of reviewers: 1
Articles published per year: 230
Book reviews published per year: 226
Notes published per year: 50

(1122)
Godisnjak Centar za Balkanoloska Ispitivanja

Alojz Benac, Editor
Centar za Balkanoloska Ispitivanja
6 Novemra 7
71000 Sarajevo, Bosnia and Herzegovina

First published: 1965
Sponsoring organization: Akademija Nauka i Umjetnosti Bosne i Hercegovine Sarajevo
ISSN: 0350-0020
MLA acronym: GCBI

SUBSCRIPTION INFORMATION

Frequency of publication: Annual
Circulation: 800
Available in microform: No

ADVERTISING INFORMATION

Advertising accepted: No

EDITORIAL DESCRIPTION

Scope: Publishes multidisciplinary Balkanistic studies, especially on Illyrian material and spiritual culture.
Reviews books: Yes
Publishes notes: No
Languages accepted: Serbo-Croatian; French; German; English; Italian
Prints abstracts: Yes
Author-anonymous submission: No

SUBMISSION REQUIREMENTS

Restrictions on contributors: None
Author pays submission fee: Yes
Author pays page charges: No
Length of articles: 60 typescript pp.
Length of book reviews: 1,500 words
Number of copies required: 2
Copyright ownership: Akademija Nauka i Umjetnosti Bosne i Hercegovine Sarajevo
Rejected manuscripts: Returned
Time before publication decision: 2 mos.
Time between decision and publication: 6 mos.
Number of reviewers: 2
Articles submitted per year: 10-15
Articles published per year: 10-12
Book reviews submitted per year: 1-2
Book reviews published per year: 1-2

(1123)
***Goethe-Jahrbuch**

Werner Keller, Editor
Goethe-Gesellschaft in Weimar e.V.
Hans-Wahl-Str. 4
Postfach 251
5300 Weimar/Thüringen, Germany

First published: 1880
Sponsoring organization: Goethe-Gesellschaft in Weimar e.V.
ISSN: 0323-4207
MLA acronym: Goethe

SUBSCRIPTION INFORMATION

Frequency of publication: Annual
Circulation: 4,900
Available in microform: No

ADVERTISING INFORMATION

Advertising accepted: No

EDITORIAL DESCRIPTION

Scope: Publishes articles on Goethe and his times.
Reviews books: No
Publishes notes: Yes
Languages accepted: German
Prints abstracts: No
Author-anonymous submission: No

SUBMISSION REQUIREMENTS

Author pays submission fee: No
Author pays page charges: No
Length of articles: 25 pp.
Length of notes: No restrictions
Style: None
Number of copies required: 3
Copyright ownership: Journal
Rejected manuscripts: Returned
Number of reviewers: 3
Articles submitted per year: 25-30
Articles published per year: 16-18

(1124)
***Goethe Yearbook: Publications of the Goethe Society of North America**

Thomas P. Saine, Editor
Dept. of German
Univ. of California
Irvine, CA 92717

First published: 1982
Sponsoring organization: Goethe Soc. of North America
ISSN: 0734-3329
MLA acronym: GSNA

SUBSCRIPTION INFORMATION

Frequency of publication: Annual
Circulation: 1,000
Available in microform: No
Subscription address: Camden House, Inc., Drawer 2025, Columbia, SC 29202

ADVERTISING INFORMATION

Advertising accepted: Yes

EDITORIAL DESCRIPTION

Scope: Publishes studies on Goethe and the Goethe period in Germany.
Reviews books: Yes
Publishes notes: Yes
Languages accepted: German; English
Prints abstracts: No
Author-anonymous submission: Sometimes

SUBMISSION REQUIREMENTS

Restrictions on contributors: None
Author pays submission fee: No
Author pays page charges: No
Style: Chicago
Number of copies required: 1
Copyright ownership: Goethe Soc. of North America
Rejected manuscripts: Returned
Time before publication decision: 2 mos.
Time between decision and publication: 1 yr. maximum
Number of reviewers: 1-3
Articles submitted per year: 15-20
Articles published per year: 10-12

(1125)
Di Goldene Keyt

Avrom Sutzkever, Editor
General Federation of Labor in Israel
Rechov Weizmann 30
Tel Aviv 62091, Israel

First published: 1948
Sponsoring organization: General Federation of Labor in Israel
ISSN: 0017-1638
MLA acronym: GoldK

SUBSCRIPTION INFORMATION

Frequency of publication: 4 times/yr.
Available in microform: No

ADVERTISING INFORMATION

Advertising accepted: No

EDITORIAL DESCRIPTION

Scope: Publishes articles on Yiddish literature and culture.
Reviews books: Yes
Languages accepted: Yiddish
Prints abstracts: No

(1126)
***Göppinger Arbeiten zur Germanistik**

Ulrich Müller, Franz Hundsnurscher, & Cornelius Sommer, Editors
Verlag Kümmerle GmbH
Staibengasse 1
7073 Lorch 2, Germany

Telephone: (49) 7172 4844
Fax: (49) 7172 4844
First published: 1968
ISSN: 0179-1834
MLA acronym: GAG

SUBSCRIPTION INFORMATION

Frequency of publication: Irregular
Circulation: 300-3,000
Available in microform: No

ADVERTISING INFORMATION

Advertising accepted: Yes

EDITORIAL DESCRIPTION

Scope: Deals exclusively with scholarship on old Germanic languages, literatures, and linguistics.
Reviews books: Yes
Languages accepted: English; French; German; Italian
Prints abstracts: No

SUBMISSION REQUIREMENTS

Restrictions on contributors: None

Author pays submission fee: No
Author pays page charges: No
Length of books: 80 pp. minimum
Style: None
Number of copies required: 1
Special requirements: Submit camera-ready copy.
Copyright ownership: Kümmerle Verlag
Rejected manuscripts: Returned
Time between decision and publication: 3-6 mos.
Number of reviewers: 1

(1127)
*Göteborger Germanistische Forschungen

Sven-Gunnar Andersson, Editor
Acta Universitatis Gothoburgensis
Box 5096
402 22 Göteborg, Sweden

First published: 1955
ISSN: 0072-4793
MLA acronym: GGF

SUBSCRIPTION INFORMATION

Frequency of publication: Irregular
Available in microform: No

ADVERTISING INFORMATION

Advertising accepted: No

EDITORIAL DESCRIPTION

Scope: Publishes monographs on German language and literature.
Reviews books: No
Publishes notes: No
Languages accepted: German
Prints abstracts: Sometimes
Author-anonymous submission: No

SUBMISSION REQUIREMENTS

Copyright ownership: Editor & author

(1128)
*Gothenburg Studies in English

Lennart A. Björk & Aimo Seppänen, Editors
Acta Universitatis Gothoburgensis
Box 5096
402 22 Göteborg, Sweden

First published: 1952
Sponsoring organization: Göteborgs Univ., Publications Committee
ISSN: 0072-503X
MLA acronym: GothSE

SUBSCRIPTION INFORMATION

Frequency of publication: Irregular
Circulation: 800
Available in microform: No

ADVERTISING INFORMATION

Advertising accepted: No

EDITORIAL DESCRIPTION

Scope: Includes theses and other studies by members of the English Department of Göteborgs University.
Reviews books: Yes
Publishes notes: No
Languages accepted: English
Prints abstracts: No

SUBMISSION REQUIREMENTS

Restrictions on contributors: Contributors are usually members or former members of the English Dept. at Göteborgs Univ.
Author pays submission fee: No
Author pays page charges: No
Length of books: 100,000 words
Style: MLA recommended
Number of copies required: 1
Copyright ownership: Author
Rejected manuscripts: Returned
Time before publication decision: 2 mos.
Number of reviewers: 1-2

(1129)
*Gradiva: International Journal of Italian Literature

Luigi Fontanella, Editor
Dept. of French & Italian
State Univ. of New York at Stony Brook
Stony Brook, NY 11794-3359

Telephone: 516 632-7440; 516 632-7448
Fax: 516 632-6252
First published: 1976
ISSN: 0363-8057
MLA acronym: Gradiva

SUBSCRIPTION INFORMATION

Frequency of publication: Annual
Circulation: 300
Available in microform: No
Subscription price: $25.00/yr.
Year to which price refers: 1991
Subscription address: P.O. Box 831, Stony Brook, NY 11790

ADVERTISING INFORMATION

Advertising accepted: Yes
Advertising rates: $50.00/half page; $100.00/full page

EDITORIAL DESCRIPTION

Scope: International scholarly journal devoted to modern Italian literary criticism and theory. Each issue presents essays on literary theory and criticism, reviews, and translations. Original articles of significance appear in English or Italian.
Reviews books: Yes
Publishes notes: Yes
Languages accepted: English; Italian
Prints abstracts: No
Author-anonymous submission: No

SUBMISSION REQUIREMENTS

Restrictions on contributors: None
Author pays submission fee: No
Author pays page charges: No
Length of articles: 20 pp. maximum
Length of book reviews: 6 pp. maximum
Length of notes: 8 pp. maximum
Style: MLA
Number of copies required: 2
Special requirements: Submit typescript.
Copyright ownership: Journal
Rejected manuscripts: Returned; enclose SASE.
Time before publication decision: 3 mos.
Time between decision and publication: 1 yr.
Number of reviewers: 2-3
Articles submitted per year: 15
Articles published per year: 5
Book reviews submitted per year: 6-8
Book reviews published per year: 6
Notes submitted per year: 15
Notes published per year: 5

(1130)
*Grand Street

Jean Stein, Editor
135 Central Park West
New York, NY 10023

Telephone: 212 807-6548
Fax: 212 807-6544
First published: 1981
ISSN: 0734-5496
MLA acronym: GrandS

SUBSCRIPTION INFORMATION

Frequency of publication: 4 times/yr.
Circulation: 3,000
Available in microform: No
Subscription price: $24.00/yr. US; $34.00/yr. elsewhere
Year to which price refers: 1992
Subscription address: Subscription Services, Dept. GRS, Box 3000, Denville, NJ 07834

ADVERTISING INFORMATION

Advertising accepted: Yes
Advertising rates: $450.00/full page

EDITORIAL DESCRIPTION

Scope: Publishes articles on literature and politics. Also publishes poetry, fiction, nonfiction, art, and photography.
Reviews books: No
Publishes notes: No
Languages accepted: English
Prints abstracts: No
Author-anonymous submission: No

SUBMISSION REQUIREMENTS

Author pays submission fee: No
Author pays page charges: No
Length of articles: 2,500-8,000 words
Number of copies required: 1
Copyright ownership: Author
Rejected manuscripts: Returned; enclose SASE.
Time before publication decision: 4 mos. maximum
Time between decision and publication: 6-12 mos.
Number of reviewers: 4
Articles published per year: 80

(1131)
*Grani: Zhurnal Literatury, Iskusstva, Nauki i Obshchestvenno-Politicheskoĭ Mysli

E. Breitbart-Samsonowa, Editor
c/o Possev-Verlag
Flurscheidweg 15
6230 Frankfurt 80, Germany

Telephone: (49) 69 344671
First published: 1946
ISSN: 0017-3185
MLA acronym: Grani

SUBSCRIPTION INFORMATION

Frequency of publication: 4 times/yr.
Circulation: 1,000
Available in microform: No

ADVERTISING INFORMATION

Advertising accepted: No

EDITORIAL DESCRIPTION

Scope: Publishes articles on literature.
Reviews books: Yes
Publishes notes: Yes
Languages accepted: Russian
Prints abstracts: Yes
Author-anonymous submission: No

SUBMISSION REQUIREMENTS

Restrictions on contributors: None
Author pays submission fee: No
Author pays page charges: No
Length of articles: No restrictions
Length of book reviews: 500 words
Length of notes: 100 words
Style: None
Number of copies required: 1
Copyright ownership: Possev-Verlag
Rejected manuscripts: Not returned
Time before publication decision: 1 yr. maximum
Time between decision and publication: 1 yr.
Number of reviewers: 5
Articles submitted per year: 250
Articles published per year: 100
Book reviews submitted per year: 200
Book reviews published per year: 20
Notes submitted per year: 80
Notes published per year: 20

(1132)
*Gratia: Bamberger Schriften zur Renaissanceforschung

Dieter Wuttke, Stephan Füssel, & Joachim Knape, Editors
Otto-Friedrich-Univ.
Postfach 1549
8600 Bamberg, Germany

Telephone: (49) 951 863286
Fax: (49) 951 863301
First published: 1977
MLA acronym: Gratia

SUBSCRIPTION INFORMATION

Frequency of publication: 2-3 times/yr.
Circulation: 500-600
Available in microform: No
Subscription address: Verlag Otto Harrassowitz, Taunusstr. 14, 6200 Wiesbaden, Germany

ADVERTISING INFORMATION

Advertising accepted: No

EDITORIAL DESCRIPTION

Scope: Publishes monographs on the Renaissance, Reformation, and the era of humanism, with a focus on German, English, French, Italian, and Latin literatures.
Reviews books: No
Publishes notes: No
Languages accepted: English; French; German; Italian; Latin
Prints abstracts: No
Author-anonymous submission: No

SUBMISSION REQUIREMENTS

Restrictions on contributors: None
Author pays submission fee: No
Author pays page charges: No
Length of books: No restrictions
Number of copies required: 1
Copyright ownership: Verlag Otto Harrassowitz
Rejected manuscripts: Returned; enclose return postage.
Time before publication decision: 1 mo.
Time between decision and publication: 6 mos.
Number of reviewers: 1-3
Books published per year: 2-3

(1133)
Grazer Beiträge: Zeitschrift für die Klassische Altertumswissenschaft

Gerhard Petersmann, Franz Stoessel, Ferdinand Schwarz, Walker Pötscher, & Joachim Dalfen, Editors
Inst. für Klassische Philologie
Univ. Salzburg
Residenplatz 1,
5020 Salzburg, Austria

First published: 1973
Sponsoring organization: Bundesministerium für Wissenschaft & Forschung, Vienna
ISSN: 0376-5253
MLA acronym: GB

SUBSCRIPTION INFORMATION

Frequency of publication: Annual
Circulation: 1,000
Available in microform: No
Subscription address: Verlag Ferdinand Berger & Söhne OHG, Wiener Str. 21-23, 3580 Horn, Austria

ADVERTISING INFORMATION

Advertising accepted: Yes

EDITORIAL DESCRIPTION

Scope: Publishes articles that promote knowledge of Greek-Roman antiquity (philology, history, philosophy, archaeology).
Reviews books: Yes
Publishes notes: No
Languages accepted: English; French; German; Italian; Latin; Spanish
Prints abstracts: Yes

SUBMISSION REQUIREMENTS

Restrictions on contributors: None
Author pays submission fee: No
Author pays page charges: No
Length of articles: 40 pp. maximum
Length of book reviews: 1,000 words
Number of copies required: 1
Copyright ownership: Editors
Time before publication decision: 2-3 mos.
Time between decision and publication: 1-2 yrs.
Number of reviewers: 4
Articles submitted per year: 30
Articles published per year: 15-20
Book reviews submitted per year: 30
Book reviews published per year: 15-20

(1134)
*Grazer Linguistische Studien

Norman Denison, Hanspeter Gadler, Hans Grassegger, & Karl Sornig, Editors
Inst. für Sprachwissenschaft
Karl-Franzens-Univ. Graz
Mozartgasse, 8/II
8010 Graz, Austria

First published: 1975
Sponsoring organization: Austrian Ministry of Science
MLA acronym: GLS

SUBSCRIPTION INFORMATION

Frequency of publication: 2 times/yr.
Circulation: 120
Available in microform: No

ADVERTISING INFORMATION

Advertising accepted: Yes, on an exchange basis

EDITORIAL DESCRIPTION

Scope: Publishes articles on general and applied linguistics.
Reviews books: Yes
Publishes notes: No
Languages accepted: German; French; English; Spanish; Italian; Serbo-Croatian
Prints abstracts: No
Author-anonymous submission: No

SUBMISSION REQUIREMENTS

Restrictions on contributors: None
Author pays submission fee: No
Author pays page charges: No
Length of articles: 12-15 pp.
Length of book reviews: 5-7 pp.
Style: Journal
Number of copies required: 1
Copyright ownership: Author
Rejected manuscripts: Returned
Time before publication decision: 6 mos.
Time between decision and publication: 6 mos.
Number of reviewers: 1-2
Articles submitted per year: 30
Articles published per year: 24
Book reviews submitted per year: 8
Book reviews published per year: 6

(1135)
*Great Plains Quarterly

Frances W. Kaye, Editor
1214 Oldfather
Univ. of Nebraska-Lincoln
Lincoln, NE 68588-0313

Telephone: 402 472-6058
Fax: 402 472-1123
First published: 1981
Sponsoring organization: Center for Great Plains Studies
ISSN: 0275-7664
MLA acronym: GPQ

SUBSCRIPTION INFORMATION

Frequency of publication: 4 times/yr. (Jan., Apr., July, Oct.)
Circulation: 700
Available in microform: Yes
Subscription price: $20.00/yr. institutions US; $23.00/yr. institutions Canada; $26.00/yr. institutions elsewhere; $15.00/yr. individuals US; $18.00/yr. individuals Canada; $21.00/yr. individuals elsewhere
Year to which price refers: 1992

ADVERTISING INFORMATION

Advertising accepted: Yes
Advertising rates: $50.00/half page; $100.00/full page

EDITORIAL DESCRIPTION

Scope: Publishes articles on the literature, history, folklore, politics, fine arts, and anthropology of the Great Plains.
Reviews books: Yes
Publishes notes: Yes
Languages accepted: English
Prints abstracts: No
Author-anonymous submission: Yes

SUBMISSION REQUIREMENTS

Restrictions on contributors: None
Author pays submission fee: No
Author pays page charges: No
Length of articles: 9,000 words maximum
Length of book reviews: 400 words; some 100-word reviews are published.
Style: Chicago
Number of copies required: 3
Special requirements: Submit 1 ribbon copy and 2 photocopies or 3 high quality photocopies.

Copyright ownership: Center for Great Plains Studies
Rejected manuscripts: 1 copy retained; others returned. Enclose SASE.
Time before publication decision: 2-9 mos.
Time between decision and publication: 2-18 mos.
Number of reviewers: 7
Articles submitted per year: 50-60
Articles published per year: 15-16
Book reviews submitted per year: 49
Book reviews published per year: 44

(1136)
*Grial: Revista Galega de Cultura

Carlos Casares, Editor
Editorial Galaxia
Reconquista, 1
36201 Vigo, Spain

Telephone: (34) 86 432100
Fax: (34) 86 223205
First published: 1963
ISSN: 0017-4181
MLA acronym: Grial

SUBSCRIPTION INFORMATION

Frequency of publication: 4 times/yr.
Available in microform: No
Subscription price: 3,350 Pta/yr. Spain; 4,000 Pta/yr. elsewhere
Year to which price refers: 1992

ADVERTISING INFORMATION

Advertising accepted: No

EDITORIAL DESCRIPTION

Scope: Publishes articles on Galician language and culture.
Reviews books: Yes
Publishes notes: Yes
Languages accepted: Galician
Prints abstracts: No
Author-anonymous submission: No

SUBMISSION REQUIREMENTS

Restrictions on contributors: None
Author pays submission fee: No
Author pays page charges: No
Length of articles: No restrictions
Length of book reviews: No restrictions
Number of copies required: 1
Copyright ownership: Galaxia, S.A.
Time before publication decision: 2 mos.
Time between decision and publication: 1-2 mos.
Number of reviewers: 3
Articles published per year: 50
Book reviews published per year: 20
Notes published per year: 30

(1137)
*Griot: Official Journal of the Southern Conference on Afro-American Studies, Inc.

Andrew Baskin, Editor
c/o Black Cultural Center
CPO 134, Berea College
Berea, KY 40404

Telephone: 606 986-9341 ext. 6515 or 6516
First published: 1981
Sponsoring organization: Southern Conference on Afro-American Studies, Inc.; Black Cultural Center, Berea College
ISSN: 0737-0873
MLA acronym: Griot

SUBSCRIPTION INFORMATION

Frequency of publication: 2 times/yr.
Circulation: 200
Available in microform: No
Subscription price: $25.00/yr.
Year to which price refers: 1992
Subscription address: Howard J. Jones, Southern Conference on Afro-American Studies, Inc., P.O. Box 33163, Houston, TX 77233
Subscription telephone: 713 641-9711

ADVERTISING INFORMATION

Advertising accepted: Yes
Advertising rates: $150.00/half page; $250.00/full page

EDITORIAL DESCRIPTION

Scope: Publishes articles on African American, African, and Caribbean literatures and folklore.
Reviews books: Yes
Publishes notes: No
Languages accepted: English
Prints abstracts: No
Author-anonymous submission: No

SUBMISSION REQUIREMENTS

Restrictions on contributors: No restrictions on scholarly materials, but creative writing and oral tradition materials must be by Blacks.
Author pays submission fee: No
Author pays page charges: No
Length of articles: 15-20 pp.
Length of book reviews: 1-3 pp.
Style: MLA
Number of copies required: 2
Special requirements: Submit biographical data and English summary if article is not in English.
Copyright ownership: Journal
Rejected manuscripts: Returned; enclose SASE.
Time before publication decision: 3-6 mos.
Time between decision and publication: 3 mos.
Number of reviewers: 4
Articles published per year: 15-20

(1138)
*Groninger Arbeiten zur Germanistischen Linguistik

Werner Abraham, Editor
Germanistisch Inst.
Rijksuniv. Groningen, Letteren
Oude Kijk in 't Jatstraat 26
Postbus 716
9700 AS Groningen, Netherlands

Telephone: (31) 50 635820
Fax: (31) 50 635821
E-mail: ABRAHAM@LET.RUG.NL
First published: 1974
Sponsoring organization: Rijksuniv. te Groningen
MLA acronym: GAGL

SUBSCRIPTION INFORMATION

Frequency of publication: Irregular
Circulation: 80
Available in microform: No

ADVERTISING INFORMATION

Advertising accepted: Yes

EDITORIAL DESCRIPTION

Scope: Publishes materials on German and Germanic linguistics.
Reviews books: No
Publishes notes: No
Languages accepted: English; German
Prints abstracts: No
Author-anonymous submission: No

SUBMISSION REQUIREMENTS

Restrictions on contributors: Only solicited articles are accepted.
Author pays submission fee: No
Author pays page charges: No
Style: Language; Studies in Language
Number of copies required: 1
Copyright ownership: Author
Rejected manuscripts: Returned
Time before publication decision: 1 mo.
Time between decision and publication: 6 mos. maximum

(1139)
Grundlagen der Germanistik

Hugo Moser, Werner Besch, & Hartmut Steinecke, Editors
Erich Schmidt Verlag
Genthiner Str., 30G
1000 Berlin 30, Germany

First published: 1966
ISSN: 0533-3350
MLA acronym: GdG

SUBSCRIPTION INFORMATION

Frequency of publication: Irregular
Available in microform: No
Subscription address: Erich Schmidt Verlag, Viktoria Str., 44A, 4800 Bielefeld 1, Germany

ADVERTISING INFORMATION

Advertising accepted: No

EDITORIAL DESCRIPTION

Scope: Publishes scholarly monographs on all subjects relating to German philology.
Reviews books: No
Publishes notes: No
Languages accepted: German
Prints abstracts: No

SUBMISSION REQUIREMENTS

Restrictions on contributors: None
Author pays page charges: No
Copyright ownership: Erich Schmidt Verlag
Rejected manuscripts: Returned
Time between decision and publication: 1 yr.

(1140)
*Grundtvig-Studier

Gustav Albeck, William Michelsen, Jens Holger Schjørring, & Helmut Toftdahl, Editors
Jens Baggesensvej 104
8200 Aarhus, Denmark

Additional editorial address: William Michelsen, H. C. Brydesens Allé 3, 3060 Espergærde, Denmark; Jens H. Schjørring, Enemærket 26, 8240 Risskov, Denmark; Hellmut Toftdahl, Hvidbjergvej, Ølsted, 8280 Trige, Denmark
First published: 1948
Sponsoring organization: Grundtvig-Center
ISSN: 0107-4164
MLA acronym: GStud

SUBSCRIPTION INFORMATION

Frequency of publication: Annual
Circulation: 500
Available in microform: No
Subscription price: 150 Dkr/yr.
Year to which price refers: 1991
Subscription address: Grundtvig-Selskabet, Vartov, Farvergade 27, 1463 Copenhagen, Denmark

Additional subscription address: Centre for Grundtvig-Studies, Faculty of Theology, Univ. Aarhus, Main Bldg., Ndr. Ringgade, 8000 Aarhus C, Denmark
Subscription telephone: (45) 86 136711
Subscription fax: (45) 86 130490

ADVERTISING INFORMATION

Advertising accepted: No

EDITORIAL DESCRIPTION

Scope: Publishes studies on Danish writer Nikolai Frederik Severin Grundtvig (1783-1872). Promotes knowledge of his life and contribution to Danish and international culture.
Reviews books: Yes
Publishes notes: Yes
Languages accepted: Danish; English; German; French; Swedish; Norwegian
Prints abstracts: Yes
Author-anonymous submission: No

SUBMISSION REQUIREMENTS

Restrictions on contributors: None
Author pays submission fee: No
Author pays page charges: No
Length of articles: 9,000 words
Length of book reviews: 2,000 words
Style: None
Number of copies required: 1
Special requirements: Submit original typescript. Include a 200-400 word abstract in Danish or English.
Copyright ownership: Author
Rejected manuscripts: Returned
Time before publication decision: 6 mos.
Time between decision and publication: 1-2 yrs.
Number of reviewers: 2
Articles submitted per year: 6-12
Articles published per year: 5-8
Book reviews submitted per year: 2-4
Book reviews published per year: 2-4

(1141)
Grundzüge

Wissenschaftliche Buchgesellschaft
Hindenburgstr., 40
Postfach 11 11 29
6100 Darmstadt 11, Germany

First published: 1964
ISSN: 0533-344X
MLA acronym: Grundzüge

SUBSCRIPTION INFORMATION

Frequency of publication: Irregular
Available in microform: No

ADVERTISING INFORMATION

Advertising accepted: No

EDITORIAL DESCRIPTION

Scope: Publishes monograph studies on German language and literature and other scientific disciplines.
Reviews books: No
Publishes notes: No
Languages accepted: German
Prints abstracts: No

SUBMISSION REQUIREMENTS

Author pays submission fee: No
Author pays page charges: No
Length of books: 160-240 pp.
Number of copies required: 2
Copyright ownership: Wissenschaftliche Buchgesellschaft & author
Rejected manuscripts: Returned
Time between decision and publication: 2-3 yrs.
Number of reviewers: 2

(1142)
Gutenberg-Jahrbuch

H.-J. Koppitz, Editor
Inst. für Buchwesen
Johannes Gutenburg Univ.
Saarstr. 21
6500 Mainz 1, Germany

First published: 1926
Sponsoring organization: Gutenberg-Gesellschaft e.V.
ISSN: 0072-9094
MLA acronym: GJ

SUBSCRIPTION INFORMATION

Frequency of publication: Annual
Circulation: 2,100
Available in microform: No

ADVERTISING INFORMATION

Advertising accepted: Yes

EDITORIAL DESCRIPTION

Scope: Publishes articles on the history and present state of book printing and Gutenberg research. Includes a bibliography.
Reviews books: No
Publishes notes: Yes
Languages accepted: German; French; English; Spanish; Italian
Prints abstracts: No
Author-anonymous submission: No

SUBMISSION REQUIREMENTS

Restrictions on contributors: None
Author pays submission fee: No
Author pays page charges: No
Length of articles: 15 pp. maximum
Length of notes: 50 words
Style: None
Number of copies required: 1
Copyright ownership: Gutenberg-Gesellschaft
Rejected manuscripts: Returned
Time before publication decision: 1 yr.
Time between decision and publication: 9 mos.
Number of reviewers: 2
Articles submitted per year: 30-40
Articles published per year: 20-30

(1143)
Gymnasium: Zeitschrift für Kultur der Antike und Humanistische Bildung

Franz Bömer & Hermann Steinthal, Editors
Mozartweg 32
2000 Norderstedt 3, Germany

First published: 1890
Sponsoring organization: Deutscher Altphilologenverband
ISSN: 0342-5231
MLA acronym: Gymnasium

SUBSCRIPTION INFORMATION

Frequency of publication: 6 times/yr.
Circulation: 2,800
Available in microform: No
Subscription address: Carl Winter Universitätsverlag, Lutherstr. 59, 6900 Heidelberg 1, Germany

ADVERTISING INFORMATION

Advertising accepted: Yes

EDITORIAL DESCRIPTION

Scope: Focuses on the classics, ancient history, archaeology, and classical instruction.
Reviews books: Yes
Publishes notes: Yes
Languages accepted: German; English; French
Prints abstracts: No

SUBMISSION REQUIREMENTS

Restrictions on contributors: None
Author pays submission fee: No
Author pays page charges: No
Length of articles: 25 pp. maximum
Length of book reviews: 600 words
Length of notes: No restrictions
Number of copies required: 1
Special requirements: Submit original typescript.
Copyright ownership: Carl Winter Universitätsverlag
Rejected manuscripts: Returned
Time before publication decision: 2 mos.
Time between decision and publication: 9-18 mos.
Number of reviewers: 2
Articles published per year: 25-30
Book reviews submitted per year: 80
Book reviews published per year: 80-120
Notes submitted per year: 20
Notes published per year: 10

(1144)
*H. D. Newsletter

Eileen Gregory, Editor
Dallas Inst. of Humanities
2719 Routh St.
Dallas, TX 75201

Telephone: 214 721-5342
First published: 1987
Sponsoring organization: Dallas Inst. of Humanities & Culture
ISSN: 1040-4015
MLA acronym: HDNews

SUBSCRIPTION INFORMATION

Frequency of publication: 2 times/yr. (Spring, Winter)
Circulation: 150
Available in microform: No
Subscription price: $10.00/yr. US; $15.00/yr. elsewhere
Year to which price refers: 1993

ADVERTISING INFORMATION

Advertising accepted: No

EDITORIAL DESCRIPTION

Scope: Publishes articles on the works of H. D. (Hilda Doolittle). Welcomes specific information that might aid research, including chronologies, bibliographies, and essays reflecting work with primary biographical or textual materials, as well as notes, queries, and notices of work-in-progress.
Reviews books: No
Publishes notes: Yes
Languages accepted: English
Prints abstracts: No
Author-anonymous submission: No

SUBMISSION REQUIREMENTS

Author pays submission fee: No
Author pays page charges: No
Length of articles: 5-20 pp.
Length of notes: 4-6 pp.
Style: MLA
Number of copies required: 1
Special requirements: Submission of articles or notes on IBM-compatible diskettes is encouraged.
Copyright ownership: Journal & author
Rejected manuscripts: Returned at author's request
Time before publication decision: 3-6 mos.
Time between decision and publication: 1-5 mos.
Number of reviewers: 1
Articles submitted per year: 10

Articles published per year: 8
Notes submitted per year: 6
Notes published per year: 4

(1145)
Haiku Review

Randy Brooks & Shirley Brooks, Editors
4634 Hale Dr.
Decatur, IL 62526-1117

E-mail: Rbrooks@millikin.edu
First published: 1980
Sponsoring organization: HIGH/COO Press
MLA acronym: Haiku

SUBSCRIPTION INFORMATION

Frequency of publication: Irregular
Circulation: 350
Available in microform: No

ADVERTISING INFORMATION

Advertising accepted: No

EDITORIAL DESCRIPTION

Scope: Journal is a reference guide to books, journals, articles, and scholarship on *haiku* in English. Bibliographies are updated every two or three years, and critical essays on new developments in *haiku* in English are published.
Reviews books: Yes
Publishes notes: Yes
Languages accepted: English; French; Japanese; Spanish; German; Portuguese
Prints abstracts: No
Author-anonymous submission: No

SUBMISSION REQUIREMENTS

Restrictions on contributors: Contributors must be informed on *haiku* in English and the Japanese tradition.
Author pays submission fee: No
Author pays page charges: No
Length of articles: 1,500-2,000 words
Length of book reviews: 500-1,000 words
Length of notes: 500 words
Style: MLA
Number of copies required: 1
Copyright ownership: Author
Rejected manuscripts: Returned; enclose SASE.
Time before publication decision: 6-12 mos.
Time between decision and publication: 6-12 mos.
Number of reviewers: 2
Articles submitted per year: 15-20
Articles published per year: 3
Notes submitted per year: 10
Notes published per year: 2-3

(1146)
*Halcyon: A Journal of the Humanities

Thomas C. Wright, Editor
Dept. of History
Univ. of Nevada, Las Vegas
Las Vegas, NV 89154

Telephone: 702 739-3349
Fax: 702 597-4097
First published: 1979
Sponsoring organization: Nevada Humanities Committee; Univ. of Nevada Press
ISSN: 0198-6449
MLA acronym: Halcyon

SUBSCRIPTION INFORMATION

Frequency of publication: Annual (Apr.)
Circulation: 2,000
Available in microform: No
Subscription price: Free
Year to which price refers: 1993
Subscription address: Nevada Humanities Committee, P.O. Box 8029, Reno, NV 89507
Subscription telephone: 702 784-6587
Subscription fax: 702 784-1300

ADVERTISING INFORMATION

Advertising accepted: No

EDITORIAL DESCRIPTION

Scope: Publishes articles on a broad spectrum in the humanities. Topics covered include literature and the arts, oral tradition, European traditions, cultural criticism, education, politics, economics, and Nevada history.
Reviews books: No
Publishes notes: No
Languages accepted: English
Prints abstracts: No
Author-anonymous submission: No

SUBMISSION REQUIREMENTS

Author pays submission fee: No
Author pays page charges: No
Length of articles: 3,750-5,500 words
Style: Chicago
Number of copies required: 2
Copyright ownership: Author
Rejected manuscripts: Returned
Time before publication decision: 10 weeks
Time between decision and publication: 18 mos. maximum
Number of reviewers: 3
Articles submitted per year: 25
Articles published per year: 15

(1147)
*Hamburger Philologische Studien

Helmut Buske Verlag Hamburg
Postfach 760244
Richardstr. 47
2000 Hamburg 76, Germany

Telephone: (49) 40 296842
Fax: (49) 40 2993614
First published: 1967
ISSN: 0072-9582
MLA acronym: HPS

SUBSCRIPTION INFORMATION

Frequency of publication: Irregular
Circulation: 400
Available in microform: No

ADVERTISING INFORMATION

Advertising accepted: No

EDITORIAL DESCRIPTION

Scope: Publishes monographs in linguistics and literature.
Reviews books: No
Publishes notes: No
Languages accepted: English; German; French
Prints abstracts: No

SUBMISSION REQUIREMENTS

Restrictions on contributors: None
Author pays submission fee: No
Author pays page charges: No
Length of books: No restrictions
Style: MLA preferred
Number of copies required: 1
Copyright ownership: Helmut Buske Verlag
Time before publication decision: 1 mo.
Time between decision and publication: 6 mos.
Number of reviewers: 1

(1148)
*Hamburger Romanistische Dissertationen

Margot Kruse, Editor
Romanisches Seminar
Univ. Hamburg
Von-Melle-Park 6
2000 Hamburg 13, Germany

Telephone: (49) 40 41232731
First published: 1966
MLA acronym: HRD

SUBSCRIPTION INFORMATION

Frequency of publication: Irregular
Available in microform: No

ADVERTISING INFORMATION

Advertising accepted: No

EDITORIAL DESCRIPTION

Scope: Publishes selected Romance dissertations from the University of Hamburg.
Reviews books: No
Publishes notes: No
Languages accepted: German; French; Italian; Spanish
Prints abstracts: No

SUBMISSION REQUIREMENTS

Restrictions on contributors: Contributors must have written a Romance dissertation for the University of Hamburg.
Author pays submission fee: No
Author pays page charges: Yes
Length of books: 150-350 pp.
Copyright ownership: Author
Rejected manuscripts: Returned
Number of reviewers: 1

(1149)
Hamlet Studies: An International Journal of Research on The Tragedie of Hamlet, Prince of Denmarke

R. W. Desai, Editor
"Rangoon Villa"
1/10 West Patel Nagar
New Delhi 110008, India

Telephone: (91) 11 5747399
First published: 1979
ISSN: 0256-2480
MLA acronym: HSt

SUBSCRIPTION INFORMATION

Frequency of publication: 2 times/yr. (Summer, Winter)
Circulation: 500
Available in microform: Yes
Subscription price: $18.00/yr.
Year to which price refers: 1992

ADVERTISING INFORMATION

Advertising accepted: Yes
Advertising rates: $25.00/full page

EDITORIAL DESCRIPTION

Scope: Publishes articles, notes, book reviews, and reports on significant stage productions of *Hamlet*. Includes a digest of articles on *Hamlet* in other journals and comments by readers.
Reviews books: Yes
Publishes notes: Yes
Languages accepted: English
Prints abstracts: Yes
Author-anonymous submission: Yes

(1150)
Handelingen van de Koninklijke Zuidnederlandse Maatschappij voor Taal- en Letterkunde en Geschiedenis

Rudolf De Smet, Editor
Azalealaan, 57
9470 Denderleeuw, Belgium

First published: 1946
Sponsoring organization: Ministère de l'Education Nationale
ISSN: 0774-3254
MLA acronym: HZM

SUBSCRIPTION INFORMATION

Frequency of publication: Annual
Available in microform: No

ADVERTISING INFORMATION

Advertising accepted: No

EDITORIAL DESCRIPTION

Scope: Publishes articles on linguistics, literature, history, and classical philology.
Reviews books: No
Publishes notes: No
Languages accepted: Dutch; French (occasionally); German (occasionally); English (occasionally)
Prints abstracts: No
Author-anonymous submission: No

SUBMISSION REQUIREMENTS

Restrictions on contributors: None
Author pays submission fee: No
Author pays page charges: No
Length of articles: 16-20 pp.
Style: None
Number of copies required: 1
Copyright ownership: Editor
Time before publication decision: 2 mos.
Time between decision and publication: 1 yr.
Articles submitted per year: 14-16
Articles published per year: 14-16

(1151)
*Handēs Amsōreay: Zeitschrift für Armenische Philologie

P. Augustin Szekula, C.M.V.
Mechitharisten-Congregation in Wien
Mechitharistengasse 4
1070 Vienna, Austria

Telephone: (43) 222 93641711
Fax: (43) 222 935446
First published: 1887
Sponsoring organization: Mechitarist Congregation
ISSN: 0017-7377
MLA acronym: HA

SUBSCRIPTION INFORMATION

Frequency of publication: 12 times/yr.
Available in microform: No
Subscription price: 1,100 S/yr.
Year to which price refers: 1992

ADVERTISING INFORMATION

Advertising accepted: No

EDITORIAL DESCRIPTION

Scope: Publishes articles on Armenian philology.
Reviews books: Yes
Publishes notes: No
Languages accepted: Armenian; German; English; Italian; Spanish; Russian; French
Prints abstracts: Occasionnally
Author-anonymous submission: No

SUBMISSION REQUIREMENTS

Restrictions on contributors: None
Author pays submission fee: No
Author pays page charges: No
Length of articles: No restrictions
Length of book reviews: No restrictions
Number of copies required: 1
Rejected manuscripts: Returned at author's request
Time between decision and publication: 1 mo.
Number of reviewers: 2

(1152)
*Harvard East Asian Monographs

Katherine Keenum, Editor
Room 203
1737 Cambridge St.
Cambridge, MA 02138

Telephone: 617 496-2804
Fax: 617 495-9976
First published: 1956
Sponsoring organization: Council on East Asian Studies, Harvard Univ.
ISSN: 0073-0491
MLA acronym: HEAS

SUBSCRIPTION INFORMATION

Frequency of publication: Irregular
Available in microform: No
Subscription address: Harvard Univ. Press, 79 Garden St., Cambridge, MA 02138

ADVERTISING INFORMATION

Advertising accepted: No

EDITORIAL DESCRIPTION

Scope: Publishes works about East Asian history, culture, and social sciences.
Reviews books: Yes
Languages accepted: English
Prints abstracts: No
Author-anonymous submission: No

SUBMISSION REQUIREMENTS

Restrictions on contributors: None
Author pays submission fee: No
Author pays page charges: No
Style: Chicago; Series
Number of copies required: 2
Special requirements: Include a brief abstract and author's C.V.
Copyright ownership: President & Fellows of Harvard College
Rejected manuscripts: Returned
Time before publication decision: 2-18 mos.
Time between decision and publication: 1-5 yrs.
Number of reviewers: 2-4 plus committee
Books submitted per year: 15-25
Books published per year: 6-10

(1153)
*Harvard English Studies

Dept. of English
Warren House
Harvard Univ.
Cambridge, MA 02138

First published: 1970
Sponsoring organization: Dept. of English & American Literature & Language, Harvard Univ.
ISSN: 0073-0513
MLA acronym: HES

SUBSCRIPTION INFORMATION

Frequency of publication: Annual
Available in microform: No
Subscription address: Harvard Univ. Press, 79 Garden St., Cambridge, MA 02138

ADVERTISING INFORMATION

Advertising accepted: No

EDITORIAL DESCRIPTION

Scope: Publishes studies of English and American literature.
Reviews books: No
Publishes notes: No
Languages accepted: English
Prints abstracts: No

SUBMISSION REQUIREMENTS

Restrictions on contributors: All contributions are solicited.
Author pays submission fee: No
Author pays page charges: No
Copyright ownership: Dept. of English, Harvard Univ.

(1154)
*Harvard Journal of Asiatic Studies

Howard S. Hibbett & Joanna Handlin Smith, Editors
2 Divinity Ave.
Cambridge, MA 02138

Telephone: 617 495-2758
Fax: 617 495-7798
First published: 1936
Sponsoring organization: Harvard-Yenching Inst.
ISSN: 0073-0548
MLA acronym: HJAS

SUBSCRIPTION INFORMATION

Frequency of publication: 2 times/yr. (June, Dec.)
Circulation: 1,100
Available in microform: No
Subscription price: $45.00/yr. institutions; $30.00/yr. individuals
Year to which price refers: 1992

ADVERTISING INFORMATION

Advertising accepted: No

EDITORIAL DESCRIPTION

Scope: Concerned primarily with the literatures, cultures, and histories of the countries of Eastern and Central Asia, dealing with modern scholarship and publication on these subjects but not with contemporary political and social matters.
Reviews books: Yes
Publishes notes: No
Languages accepted: English
Prints abstracts: No
Author-anonymous submission: No

SUBMISSION REQUIREMENTS

Restrictions on contributors: None
Author pays submission fee: No
Author pays page charges: No
Length of articles: No restrictions
Length of book reviews: No restrictions
Style: Journal
Number of copies required: 2
Copyright ownership: Harvard-Yenching Inst. & Author
Rejected manuscripts: Returned
Time before publication decision: 2-3 weeks
Time between decision and publication: 1 yr. maximum
Number of reviewers: 3 minimum
Articles submitted per year: 40
Articles published per year: 12-13
Book reviews submitted per year: 15
Book reviews published per year: 12

(1155)
*Harvard Library Bulletin

Kenneth E. Carpenter & Daniel J. Griffin, Editors
Harvard Library Publications Office
25 Mt. Auburn St., Rm. 206
Cambridge, MA 02138

Telephone: 617 495-7746; 617 495-7793
Fax: 617 496-8344
First published: 1947
Sponsoring organization: Harvard Univ. Library
ISSN: 0017-8136
MLA acronym: HLB

SUBSCRIPTION INFORMATION

Frequency of publication: 4 times/yr.
Circulation: 1,500
Available in microform: Yes
Subscription price: $35.00/yr.; $15.00/single issue
Year to which price refers: 1991

ADVERTISING INFORMATION

Advertising accepted: No

EDITORIAL DESCRIPTION

Scope: Publishes articles in all humanistic areas, with priority for those growing out of research based on Harvard Library collections.
Reviews books: No
Publishes notes: Yes
Languages accepted: English
Prints abstracts: No
Author-anonymous submission: Yes

SUBMISSION REQUIREMENTS

Restrictions on contributors: None
Author pays submission fee: No
Author pays page charges: No
Length of articles: 1,000-15,000 words
Length of notes: 500-1,000 words
Style: Chicago
Number of copies required: 1
Copyright ownership: President & Fellows of Harvard College
Rejected manuscripts: Returned
Time before publication decision: 3 mos.
Time between decision and publication: 1 yr.
Number of reviewers: 2
Articles published per year: 22-30

(1156)
*Harvard Studies in Comparative Literature

Chairman, Dept. of Comparative Literature
401 Boylston Hall
Harvard Univ.
Cambridge, MA 02138

First published: 1910
Sponsoring organization: Dept. of Comparative Literature, Harvard Univ.
ISSN: 0073-0696
MLA acronym: HSCL

SUBSCRIPTION INFORMATION

Frequency of publication: Irregular
Available in microform: No
Subscription address: Harvard Univ. Press, 79 Garden St., Cambridge, MA 02138

ADVERTISING INFORMATION

Advertising accepted: No

EDITORIAL DESCRIPTION

Scope: Publishes scholarly monographs in comparative literature.
Reviews books: No
Publishes notes: No
Languages accepted: English
Prints abstracts: No
Author-anonymous submission: No

SUBMISSION REQUIREMENTS

Restrictions on contributors: None
Author pays submission fee: No
Author pays page charges: No
Style: MLA
Number of copies required: 1
Copyright ownership: President & Fellows of Harvard College
Rejected manuscripts: Returned
Number of reviewers: 2
Books submitted per year: 2-3
Books published per year: 1-2

(1157)
Harvard Studies in Romance Languages

Dept. of Romance Languages & Literatures
Harvard Univ.
Cambridge, MA 02138

First published: 1915
Sponsoring organization: Dept. of Romance Languages, Harvard Univ.
ISSN: 0073-0718
MLA acronym: HSRL

SUBSCRIPTION INFORMATION

Frequency of publication: Irregular
Circulation: 600-800
Available in microform: No
Subscription address: French Forum Publishers, P.O. Box 130, Nicholasville, KY 40430

ADVERTISING INFORMATION

Advertising accepted: No

EDITORIAL DESCRIPTION

Scope: Publishes critical studies on works in the Romance languages as well as editions of texts.
Reviews books: No
Languages accepted: English; French; Italian; Portuguese; Romanian; Spanish
Prints abstracts: No

SUBMISSION REQUIREMENTS

Restrictions on contributors: Contributors must be present or past members of the Dept. of Romance Languages at Harvard. Acceptance will be based on a recommendation by any active senior professor of Romance Languages made according to a rotation system established by the professor's date of retirement.
Author pays submission fee: No
Author pays page charges: No
Length of books: 350 pp.
Style: MLA
Number of copies required: 1
Special requirements: Author is responsible for all costs incurred in the preparation of the manuscript.
Copyright ownership: President & Fellows of Harvard Univ.
Rejected manuscripts: Returned
Time between decision and publication: 1 yr.

(1158)
*Harvard Theological Review

Helmut Koester, Editor
Harvard Divinity School
45 Francis Ave.
Cambridge, MA 02138

Telephone: 617 495-5786
Fax: 617 495-9489
First published: 1908
Sponsoring organization: Harvard Univ., Divinity School
ISSN: 0017-8160
MLA acronym: HTR

SUBSCRIPTION INFORMATION

Frequency of publication: 4 times/yr.
Circulation: 1,800

Available in microform: No

ADVERTISING INFORMATION

Advertising accepted: Yes

EDITORIAL DESCRIPTION

Scope: Embraces theology, ethics, the history and philosophy of religion, and cognate subjects. Aims to publish investigations, discussions, and reviews which contribute to the enlargement of knowledge or the advancement of thought.
Reviews books: No
Publishes notes: Yes
Languages accepted: English
Prints abstracts: No
Author-anonymous submission: No

SUBMISSION REQUIREMENTS

Restrictions on contributors: None
Author pays submission fee: No
Author pays page charges: No
Length of articles: 10,000 words maximum
Length of notes: 500-1,000 words
Style: Chicago
Number of copies required: 2
Copyright ownership: Assigned by author to journal
Rejected manuscripts: Returned
Time before publication decision: 1-2 mos.
Time between decision and publication: 8-10 mos.
Number of reviewers: 2 plus Editor & Editorial Board if readers recommend publication
Articles submitted per year: 250
Articles published per year: 25
Notes published per year: 4

(1159)
*Harvard Ukrainian Studies

Omeljan Pritsak, Ihor Ševčenko, George G. Grabowicz, Michael S. Flier, & Roman Szporluk, Editors
Ukrainian Research Inst.
Harvard Univ.
1581-83 Massachusetts Ave.
Cambridge, MA 02138

Telephone: 617 495-4243
Fax: 617 495-8097
E-mail: Kdt@wjh12.harvard.edu
First published: 1977
Sponsoring organization: Harvard Univ., Ukrainian Research Inst.
ISSN: 0363-5570
MLA acronym: HUS

SUBSCRIPTION INFORMATION

Frequency of publication: 2 times/yr.
Circulation: 350-400
Available in microform: No
Subscription price: $28.00/yr. US & Canada; $32.00/yr. elsewhere
Year to which price refers: 1992

ADVERTISING INFORMATION

Advertising accepted: Yes, on an exchange basis

EDITORIAL DESCRIPTION

Scope: Publishes original, scholarly articles, review articles, documents, notes, and book reviews on topics of Ukrainian history, literature, linguistics, and related disciplines. Attention is given to European, East European, and Eurasian contexts.
Reviews books: Yes
Publishes notes: Yes
Languages accepted: English; French; German
Prints abstracts: No
Author-anonymous submission: No

SUBMISSION REQUIREMENTS

Restrictions on contributors: None
Author pays submission fee: No
Author pays page charges: No
Length of articles: 25-30 typescript pp.
Length of book reviews: 750-1,000 words
Length of notes: 200 words
Style: Chicago
Number of copies required: 3
Special requirements: Submit original typescript and 2 copies.
Copyright ownership: President & Fellows of Harvard College
Rejected manuscripts: Returned at author's request
Time before publication decision: 4 mos.
Time between decision and publication: 1 yr.
Number of reviewers: 3-5
Articles submitted per year: 25-35
Articles published per year: 15-20
Book reviews submitted per year: 40
Book reviews published per year: 30-35
Notes submitted per year: 1-5
Notes published per year: 1-2

(1160)
*Hebbel-Jahrbuch

Günter Häntzschel & Volker Schulz, Editors
Hebbel-Gesellschaft
Österstr. 6
2244 Wesselburen, Germany

Telephone: (49) 4833 72079
Fax: (49) 4833 8126
First published: 1939
Sponsoring organization: Hebbel-Gesellschaft; Land Schleswig-Holstein
ISSN: 0073-1560
MLA acronym: HJb

SUBSCRIPTION INFORMATION

Frequency of publication: Annual
Circulation: 1,000
Available in microform: No
Subscription address: Westholsteinische Verlagsanstalt Boyens & Co., Wulf-Isebrand-Platz 1, 2240 Heide, Germany

ADVERTISING INFORMATION

Advertising accepted: No

EDITORIAL DESCRIPTION

Scope: Publishes articles concerning Friedrich Hebbel and his time.
Reviews books: Yes
Publishes notes: Yes
Languages accepted: German; English
Prints abstracts: No
Author-anonymous submission: No

SUBMISSION REQUIREMENTS

Restrictions on contributors: None
Author pays submission fee: No
Author pays page charges: No
Length of articles: No restrictions
Length of book reviews: No restrictions
Length of notes: No restrictions
Style: None
Number of copies required: 1
Special requirements: See 1983 and 1984 volumes for requirements.
Copyright ownership: Author
Rejected manuscripts: Returned
Time before publication decision: 3 mos.
Time between decision and publication: 6 mos.
Number of reviewers: 2
Articles submitted per year: 8-10
Articles published per year: 6-8
Book reviews submitted per year: 4
Book reviews published per year: 4
Notes submitted per year: 2
Notes published per year: 2

(1161)
*Hebrew Annual Review

Theodore Lewis, Editor
Dept. of Judaic & Near Eastern Languages & Literatures
Ohio State Univ.
1841 Millikin Road
Columbus, OH 43210

First published: 1978
Sponsoring organization: Melton Center for Jewish Studies, Ohio State Univ.
ISSN: 0193-7162
MLA acronym: HAR

SUBSCRIPTION INFORMATION

Frequency of publication: Annual
Circulation: 400
Available in microform: Yes
Subscription price: $35.00/yr.
Year to which price refers: 1991

ADVERTISING INFORMATION

Advertising accepted: No

EDITORIAL DESCRIPTION

Scope: Promotes scholarship in Biblical and Hebraic studies.
Reviews books: No
Publishes notes: No
Languages accepted: English
Prints abstracts: No
Author-anonymous submission: Yes

SUBMISSION REQUIREMENTS

Restrictions on contributors: None
Author pays submission fee: No
Author pays page charges: No
Length of articles: 7,000 words
Style: Chicago
Number of copies required: 3
Copyright ownership: Dept. of Judaic & Near Eastern Languages & Literatures, Ohio State Univ.
Rejected manuscripts: Returned
Time before publication decision: 9-12 mos.
Time between decision and publication: 6-9 mos.
Number of reviewers: 2
Articles submitted per year: 40
Articles published per year: 17-23

(1162)
*Hebrew Linguistics: A Journal for Hebrew Descriptive, Computational and Applied Linguistics

Maya Fruchtman, Editor
Dept. of Hebrew & Semitic Languages
Bar-Ilan Univ.
52900 Ramat-Gan, Israel

First published: 1969
Sponsoring organization: Bar-Ilan Univ.
ISSN: 0334-3472
MLA acronym: HCompL

SUBSCRIPTION INFORMATION

Frequency of publication: 2 times/yr.
Circulation: 500
Available in microform: No
Subscription address: Bar-Ilan Univ. Press, Bar-Ilan Univ., 52900 Ramat-Gan, Israel

ADVERTISING INFORMATION

Advertising accepted: No

EDITORIAL DESCRIPTION

Scope: Publishes articles on modern linguistic theories. Subjects treated are: computational linguistics, stylistics, phonology and morphophonemics, lexicology and lexical representation, phonetics, syntax and semantics. In addition to the articles there are two regular sections: "The News" section which chronicles lectures, conferences, research projects, and other events in the field of computational, formal, or applied linguistics, and "In the Literature" section which lists recent books and articles.
Reviews books: Yes
Publishes notes: Yes
Languages accepted: English; Hebrew
Prints abstracts: Yes
Author-anonymous submission: No

SUBMISSION REQUIREMENTS

Restrictions on contributors: None
Author pays submission fee: No
Author pays page charges: No
Length of articles: 15-25 pp.
Length of book reviews: 5-10 pp.
Length of notes: 350 words
Style: Chicago
Number of copies required: 2
Special requirements: Submit double-spaced typescript; footnotes and references should follow article. Include a 200-word English abstract with every Hebrew article, and a Hebrew abstract with every English article. Omit author's name from all but the first page.
Copyright ownership: Bar-Ilan Univ.
Rejected manuscripts: Returned at author's request
Time before publication decision: 2-3 weeks
Time between decision and publication: 6-24 mos.
Number of reviewers: 2-3
Articles submitted per year: 15-20
Articles published per year: 14-20
Book reviews published per year: 2
Notes submitted per year: 1-2

(1163)
*Hebrew Studies: A Journal Devoted to Hebrew Language and Literature

Michael V. Fox & Gilead Morahg, Editors
National Assn. of Professors of Hebrew in American Insts. of Higher Learning
c/o Dept. of Hebrew & Semitic Studies
1346 Van Hise Hall
Univ. of Wisconsin
Madison, WI 53706

Additional editorial address: Frederick E. Greenspahn, Book Review Editor, Center for Judaic Studies, Univ. of Denver, Denver, CO 80208-0292
Telephone: 608 262-3204
Fax: 608 262-4747
E-mail: MICHAELFOX@WISCMACC (Bitnet)
First published: 1954
Sponsoring organization: National Assn. of Professors of Hebrew in American Insts. of Higher Learning; Dept. of Hebrew & Semitic Studies, Univ. of Wisconsin, Madison; Golden Gate Baptist Theological Seminary
ISSN: 0146-0494
MLA acronym: HebSt

SUBSCRIPTION INFORMATION

Frequency of publication: Annual (Fall)
Circulation: 600
Available in microform: Yes, through Univ. Microfilms International
Subscription price: $35.00/yr.
Year to which price refers: 1992

ADVERTISING INFORMATION

Advertising accepted: Yes

Advertising rates: $125.00/half page; $200.00/full page

EDITORIAL DESCRIPTION

Scope: Publishes articles on Hebrew language and literature from all periods with a literary, linguistic, or philological focus.
Reviews books: Yes
Languages accepted: English; Hebrew
Author-anonymous submission: Yes

SUBMISSION REQUIREMENTS

Restrictions on contributors: Book reviews are assigned.
Author pays submission fee: No
Author pays page charges: No
Length of articles: No restrictions
Length of book reviews: 1,000-1,500 words
Style: Chicago with modifications
Number of copies required: 1
Special requirements: Submit an abstract in English of 300-400 words. Use Hebrew (and Greek) characters in quotations. Submission on diskette is encouraged.
Copyright ownership: Journal
Rejected manuscripts: Returned
Time before publication decision: 4-6 weeks
Time between decision and publication: 1 yr. maximum
Number of reviewers: 3
Articles submitted per year: 25
Articles published per year: 2-8
Book reviews published per year: 35-45

(1164)
Hebrew University Studies in Literature and the Arts

Ruth Nevo, Lawrence Besserman, Shlomit Rimmon-Kenan, Emily Budick, & Elizabeth Freund, Editors
Inst. of Languages, Literature, & Arts
Hebrew Univ.
91905 Jerusalem, Israel

First published: 1973
Sponsoring organization: Hebrew Univ. of Jerusalem, Inst. of Languages & Literatures
ISSN: 0792-0393
MLA acronym: HUSL

SUBSCRIPTION INFORMATION

Frequency of publication: 2 times/yr.
Circulation: 1,000
Available in microform: No
Subscription address: Magnes Press, Hebrew Univ., P.O. Box 7695, 91076 Jerusalem, Israel

ADVERTISING INFORMATION

Advertising accepted: No

EDITORIAL DESCRIPTION

Scope: Focuses on particular issues or problems in literary and artistic representation and literary theory.
Reviews books: No
Publishes notes: No
Languages accepted: English
Prints abstracts: No
Author-anonymous submission: No

SUBMISSION REQUIREMENTS

Restrictions on contributors: None
Author pays submission fee: No
Author pays page charges: No
Length of articles: 2,500-12,500 words
Style: MLA
Number of copies required: 2
Copyright ownership: Journal
Rejected manuscripts: Returned
Time before publication decision: 4 mos.
Time between decision and publication: 1-2 yrs.
Number of reviewers: 2-3

Articles submitted per year: 20-22
Articles published per year: 13-15

(1165)
*Hefte für Ostasiatische Literatur

Wolf Baus, Volker Klöpsch, Otto Putz, & Wolfgang Schamoni, Editors
Auf dem Backenberg 13
4630 Bochum, Germany

Additional editorial address: For articles on Japanese literature contact: Wolfgang Schamoni, Erzäckerweg 9, 6900 Heidelberg, Germany
Telephone: (49) 234 702473
First published: 1983
ISSN: 0933-8721
MLA acronym: HOL

SUBSCRIPTION INFORMATION

Frequency of publication: 2 times/yr.
Circulation: 500
Available in microform: No
Subscription price: 28 DM/yr.
Year to which price refers: 1992
Subscription address: Iudicium Verlag, Postfach 70 10 67, 8000 Munich, Germany
Subscription telephone: (49) 89 718747
Subscription fax: (49) 89 7142039

ADVERTISING INFORMATION

Advertising accepted: Yes

EDITORIAL DESCRIPTION

Scope: Publishes articles on the art of translation of Far Eastern languages. Includes translations of works of Chinese, Japanese, and Korean literature, as well as a bibliography of all translations from these languages and all articles in German on these literatures.
Reviews books: Yes
Publishes notes: Yes
Languages accepted: German
Prints abstracts: No
Author-anonymous submission: No

SUBMISSION REQUIREMENTS

Author pays submission fee: No
Author pays page charges: No
Length of articles: No restrictions
Number of copies required: 1
Copyright ownership: Translator for translations; editor otherwise
Rejected manuscripts: Returned
Time before publication decision: 3-6 mos.
Time between decision and publication: 3-9 mos.
Number of reviewers: 2
Articles submitted per year: 30-40
Articles published per year: 10-15
Book reviews published per year: 10-20
Notes submitted per year: 100-200
Notes published per year: 80-100

(1166)
*Heidelberger Beiträge zur Romanistik

Bodo Müller, Editor
Romanisches Seminar der Universität
6900 Heidelberg, Germany

Telephone: (49) 6221 542742
Fax: (49) 6221 543153
First published: 1974
ISSN: 0170-8821
MLA acronym: HBR

SUBSCRIPTION INFORMATION

Frequency of publication: 1-2 times/yr.

Available in microform: No
Subscription address: Peter Lang Verlag GmbH, Eschborner Landstr. 42-50, 6000 Frankfurt a.M. 90, Germany

ADVERTISING INFORMATION

Advertising accepted: No

EDITORIAL DESCRIPTION

Scope: Publishes articles on Romance languages; includes linguistics and literature.
Reviews books: No
Publishes notes: No
Languages accepted: German; French; Spanish; Italian; English
Prints abstracts: No

SUBMISSION REQUIREMENTS

Restrictions on contributors: Articles must be research studies such as doctoral dissertations.
Author pays submission fee: No
Author pays page charges: Yes
Number of copies required: 1
Copyright ownership: Peter Lang Verlag GmbH
Rejected manuscripts: Returned
Time before publication decision: 1 mo.
Time between decision and publication: 6 weeks
Number of reviewers: 1
Books submitted per year: 2-4
Books published per year: 1-2

(1167)
*Heidelberger Forschungen

Albrecht Dihle, Peter Michelsen, Reiner Wiehl, Eike Wolgast, & Hans-Joachim Zimmermann, Editors
Carl Winter Universitätsverlag GmbH
Lutherstr. 59
Postfach 106140
6900 Heidelberg, Germany

Telephone: (49) 6221 41490
First published: 1952
Sponsoring organization: Gesellschaft der Freunde der Univ. Heidelberg
ISSN: 0440-6044
MLA acronym: HF

SUBSCRIPTION INFORMATION

Frequency of publication: Irregular
Circulation: 400-800
Available in microform: No

ADVERTISING INFORMATION

Advertising accepted: No

EDITORIAL DESCRIPTION

Scope: Publishes articles on German studies, English studies, philosophy, history, and the classics.
Reviews books: No
Publishes notes: No
Languages accepted: German
Prints abstracts: No
Author-anonymous submission: No

SUBMISSION REQUIREMENTS

Restrictions on contributors: None
Author pays submission fee: No
Author pays page charges: Occasionally
Cost of page charges: 10-35 DM/page
Length of books: No restrictions
Style: MLA
Number of copies required: 2
Copyright ownership: Carl Winter Universitätsverlag
Rejected manuscripts: Returned
Time before publication decision: 2 mos.
Time between decision and publication: 8 mos.
Number of reviewers: 5

Books submitted per year: 3-5
Books published per year: 1-2

(1168)
*Heine Jahrbuch

Joseph A. Kruse, Editor
Bilker Str. 12-14
Postfach 1120
4000 Düsseldorf 1, Germany

Telephone: (49) 211 8992901
Fax: (49) 211 8993645
First published: 1962
Sponsoring organization: Heinrich-Heine-Inst. der Landeshauptstadt, Düsseldorf; Heinrich-Heine-Gesellschaft e.V.
ISSN: 0073-1962
MLA acronym: HeineJ

SUBSCRIPTION INFORMATION

Frequency of publication: Annual
Circulation: 1,500
Available in microform: No
Subscription address: Hoffmann & Campe Verlag, Harvestehuder Weg 45, Postfach 132092, 2000 Hamburg 13, Germany

ADVERTISING INFORMATION

Advertising accepted: No

EDITORIAL DESCRIPTION

Scope: Publishes articles on Heinrich Heine, young Germany, and *Vormärz*.
Reviews books: Yes
Publishes notes: Yes
Languages accepted: English; German; French
Prints abstracts: No, except for articles in French and English

SUBMISSION REQUIREMENTS

Restrictions on contributors: None
Author pays submission fee: No
Author pays page charges: No
Length of articles: 20-30 pp.
Length of book reviews: 2-3 pp.
Length of notes: 1-8 pp.
Style: MLA; Duden
Number of copies required: 1
Copyright ownership: Editor
Rejected manuscripts: Returned
Time before publication decision: 3 mos.
Time between decision and publication: 1-2 yrs.
Number of reviewers: 2
Articles published per year: 10-15
Book reviews published per year: 10-15
Notes published per year: 2-5

(1169)
*Helikon: Irodalomtudányi Szemle

Béla Köpeczi, Editor
Ménesi út 11-13
1118 Budapest XI., Hungary

Telephone: (36) 1 664819
Fax: (36) 1 853876
First published: 1955
Historical variations in title: Formerly *Helikon: Világirodalmi Figyelő*
Sponsoring organization: Magyar Tudományos Akadémia, Irodalomtudományi Intézetének Folyóirata
MLA acronym: HelikonI

SUBSCRIPTION INFORMATION

Frequency of publication: 4 times/yr.
Circulation: 1,500
Available in microform: No
Subscription price: 416 Ft/yr.
Year to which price refers: 1992

Subscription address: HELIR, Lehet út 10/a, 1900 Budapest XIII., Hungary

ADVERTISING INFORMATION

Advertising accepted: No

EDITORIAL DESCRIPTION

Scope: Publishes information and documentation in the field of literary science, theory, and history.
Reviews books: Yes
Publishes notes: Yes
Languages accepted: Hungarian
Prints abstracts: Yes
Author-anonymous submission: No

SUBMISSION REQUIREMENTS

Restrictions on contributors: None
Author pays submission fee: No
Author pays page charges: No
Length of articles: No restrictions
Length of book reviews: No restrictions
Length of notes: No restrictions
Number of copies required: 2
Copyright ownership: Académie Hongroise des Sciences, Inst. d'Études Littéraires
Rejected manuscripts: Returned
Time before publication decision: 6 mos.
Time between decision and publication: 18 mos.
Number of reviewers: 10
Articles submitted per year: 90
Articles published per year: 60
Book reviews submitted per year: 60
Book reviews published per year: 80
Notes submitted per year: 10
Notes published per year: 6

(1170)
*Hellas: A Journal of Poetry and the Humanities

Gerald Harnett, Editor
304 South Tyson Ave.
Glenside, PA 19038

Telephone: 215 884-1086
First published: 1990
ISSN: 1044-5331
MLA acronym: Hellas

SUBSCRIPTION INFORMATION

Frequency of publication: 2 times/yr. (Spring, Fall)
Circulation: 250
Available in microform: No
Subscription price: $42.00/yr.
Year to which price refers: 1992

ADVERTISING INFORMATION

Advertising accepted: Yes, on an exchange basis

EDITORIAL DESCRIPTION

Scope: Publishes poetry and studies in Classicism, Renaissance literature and modern poetry.
Reviews books: No
Publishes notes: No
Languages accepted: English
Prints abstracts: No
Author-anonymous submission: No

SUBMISSION REQUIREMENTS

Restrictions on contributors: None
Author pays submission fee: No
Author pays page charges: No
Length of articles: 10,000 words maximum
Style: Chicago
Number of copies required: 2
Copyright ownership: Author
Rejected manuscripts: Returned; enclose SASE.

Time before publication decision: 2-5 mos.
Time between decision and publication: 3-12 mos.
Number of reviewers: 2-3
Articles submitted per year: 60
Articles published per year: 1

(1171)
Hellēnika

Isidora Rosenthal-Kamarinea, Editor
Am Dornbusch 28
4630 Bochum, Germany

First published: 1964
Sponsoring organization: Vereinigung der Deutsch-Griechischen Gesellschaften
ISSN: 0018-0084
MLA acronym: Hellēnika

SUBSCRIPTION INFORMATION

Frequency of publication: Annual
Circulation: 3,000
Available in microform: No
Subscription address: Ausgaben Neugriechische Studien, Am Dornbusch 28, 4630 Bochum, Germany

ADVERTISING INFORMATION

Advertising accepted: Yes

EDITORIAL DESCRIPTION

Scope: Publishes articles on Greek language, literature, and culture, especially Modern Greek.
Reviews books: Yes
Languages accepted: German
Prints abstracts: No

SUBMISSION REQUIREMENTS

Restrictions on contributors: None
Author pays submission fee: No
Author pays page charges: No
Length of articles: No restrictions
Style: Journal
Number of copies required: 1
Special requirements: Submit original typescript.
Copyright ownership: Assigned by author to journal
Rejected manuscripts: Returned
Time before publication decision: 1 mo.
Time between decision and publication: 6 mos.
Number of reviewers: 2

(1172)
*Hellēnika: Philologikon, Historikon kai Laographikon Periodikon Syngramma

Soc. for Macedonian Studies
4 Ethnikis Amynis
54621 Salonika, Greece

Telephone: (30) 31 271195; (30) 31 268710
Fax: (30) 31 271195
First published: 1928
Sponsoring organization: Soc. for Macedonian Studies
ISSN: 0013-6336
MLA acronym: HellēnikaS

SUBSCRIPTION INFORMATION

Frequency of publication: 2 times/yr.
Circulation: 1,000
Available in microform: No
Subscription price: $30.00/yr.
Year to which price refers: 1992

ADVERTISING INFORMATION

Advertising accepted: No

EDITORIAL DESCRIPTION

Scope: Publishes articles on Greek literature, history, folklore, linguistics, archaeology, and general research in the humanities.
Reviews books: Yes
Publishes notes: Yes
Languages accepted: English; French; German; Greek; Italian
Prints abstracts: Yes
Author-anonymous submission: No

SUBMISSION REQUIREMENTS

Restrictions on contributors: None
Author pays submission fee: No
Author pays page charges: No
Length of articles: 5-30 pp.
Length of book reviews: 1-10 pp.
Length of notes: 1-5 pp.
Number of copies required: 1
Special requirements: Submit original typescript and summary.
Copyright ownership: Soc. for Macedonian Studies
Rejected manuscripts: Not returned
Time before publication decision: 3 mos.
Time between decision and publication: 6 mos.
Number of reviewers: 4
Articles submitted per year: 25
Articles published per year: 15-20
Book reviews submitted per year: 30
Book reviews published per year: 15-30
Notes published per year: 8-10

(1173)
*The Hemingway Review

Susan F. Beegel, Editor
180 Polpis Rd.
Nantucket, MA 02554

Telephone: 508 325-7157
Fax: 508 325-7157
First published: 1970
Sponsoring organization: Hemingway Soc.; Univ. of West Florida
ISSN: 0276-3362
MLA acronym: HN

SUBSCRIPTION INFORMATION

Frequency of publication: 2 times/yr. (Oct., Apr.)
Circulation: 850
Available in microform: Yes
Subscription price: $18.00/yr. (includes membership)
Year to which price refers: 1992
Subscription address: President, Hemingway Soc., Dept. of English, Univ. of North Dakota, Grand Forks, ND 58202-8237
Subscription telephone: 701 777-3321
Subscription fax: 701 777-3650

ADVERTISING INFORMATION

Advertising accepted: No

EDITORIAL DESCRIPTION

Scope: Publishes articles of interest to readers of Ernest Hemingway.
Reviews books: Yes
Publishes notes: Yes
Languages accepted: English
Prints abstracts: No
Author-anonymous submission: Yes

SUBMISSION REQUIREMENTS

Restrictions on contributors: None
Author pays submission fee: No
Author pays page charges: No
Length of articles: 7,000 words maximum
Length of book reviews: 1,000 words maximum
Length of notes: 1,500 words maximum
Style: MLA
Number of copies required: 2
Copyright ownership: Hemingway Foundation
Rejected manuscripts: Returned; enclose SASE
Time before publication decision: 2-6 mos.
Time between decision and publication: 1-2 yrs.
Number of reviewers: 3
Articles submitted per year: 150-200
Articles published per year: 12-15
Book reviews submitted per year: 10-12
Book reviews published per year: 10-15
Notes submitted per year: 15-20
Notes published per year: 6-8

(1174)
*The Henry James Review

Daniel Mark Fogel, Editor
Dept. of English
Louisiana State Univ.
Baton Rouge, LA 70803-5001

Telephone: 504 388-2865
Fax: 504 388-6447
First published: 1979
Sponsoring organization: Henry James Soc.; Louisiana State Univ.
ISSN: 0273-0340
MLA acronym: HJR

SUBSCRIPTION INFORMATION

Frequency of publication: 3 times/yr.
Circulation: 840
Available in microform: No
Subscription price: $37.00/yr. institutions US; $22.00/yr. individuals US; add $2.60/yr. postage Canada & Mexico, $6.20/yr. elsewhere
Year to which price refers: 1993
Subscription address: Johns Hopkins Univ. Press, Journals Publishing Division, 2715 North Charles St., Baltimore, MD 21218-4319
Subscription telephone: 800 537-5487
Subscription fax: 410 516-6998

ADVERTISING INFORMATION

Advertising accepted: Yes
Advertising rates: $100.00/half page; $170.00/full page; $195.00/inside front cover; $210.00/inside back cover; $220.00/back cover

EDITORIAL DESCRIPTION

Scope: Journal covers all aspects of the life and work of Henry James and includes an annual, analytic review of James studies.
Reviews books: Yes
Publishes notes: Yes
Languages accepted: English
Prints abstracts: No
Author-anonymous submission: Yes

SUBMISSION REQUIREMENTS

Restrictions on contributors: None
Author pays submission fee: No
Author pays page charges: No
Length of articles: 2,000 words minimum
Length of book reviews: 2,000 words
Length of notes: No restrictions
Style: MLA
Number of copies required: 2
Special requirements: Submit original manuscript. Name and address should appear only on a cover sheet.
Copyright ownership: Johns Hopkins Univ. Press
Rejected manuscripts: Returned; enclose return postage.
Time before publication decision: 3-5 mos.
Time between decision and publication: 4-9 mos.
Number of reviewers: 6-9
Articles submitted per year: 100
Articles published per year: 15-20
Book reviews submitted per year: 10-14
Book reviews published per year: 8-12
Notes submitted per year: 15-20
Notes published per year: 5-9

(1175)
*Heritage of the Great Plains

Joseph V. Hickey, Editor
Great Plains Center
Emporia State Univ.
Emporia, KS 66801

First published: 1957
Sponsoring organization: Emporia State Univ.
ISSN: 0739-4772
MLA acronym: HK

SUBSCRIPTION INFORMATION

Frequency of publication: 4 times/yr.
Circulation: 300
Available in microform: No
Subscription price: $7.00/yr.
Year to which price refers: 1992

ADVERTISING INFORMATION

Advertising accepted: No

EDITORIAL DESCRIPTION

Scope: Welcomes manuscripts on the literature, language, history, folklore, art, music, or life in general in Kansas or the Great Plains. Some poetry and short fiction may be accepted.
Reviews books: No
Languages accepted: English
Prints abstracts: No
Author-anonymous submission: Yes

SUBMISSION REQUIREMENTS

Author pays submission fee: No
Author pays page charges: No
Length of articles: 2,500 words
Style: Chicago
Number of copies required: 1
Special requirements: Include author's vita.
Copyright ownership: Journal
Rejected manuscripts: Returned; enclose return postage.
Time before publication decision: 2 mos.
Time between decision and publication: 9 mos.
Number of reviewers: 2-3
Articles submitted per year: 40
Articles published per year: 16

(1176)
*Hermaea: Germanistische Forschungen

Hans Fromm & Hans-Joachim Mähl, Editors
Roseggerstr. 35a
8012 Ottobrunn bei Munich, Germany

Additional editorial address: Hans-Joachim Mähl, Faulstr. 27, 2301 Surendorf uber Kiel, Germany
Telephone: (49) 89 605882
First published: 1952
ISSN: 0440-7164
MLA acronym: Hermaea

SUBSCRIPTION INFORMATION

Frequency of publication: Irregular
Available in microform: No
Subscription address: Max Niemeyer Verlag, Postfach 2140, 7400 Tübingen, Germany

ADVERTISING INFORMATION

Advertising accepted: No

EDITORIAL DESCRIPTION

Scope: Publishes monographs on German literature and language.
Reviews books: No
Publishes notes: No
Languages accepted: German

Prints abstracts: No

SUBMISSION REQUIREMENTS

Restrictions on contributors: None
Author pays submission fee: No
Author pays page charges: No
Length of books: No restrictions
Style: Series
Number of copies required: 1
Copyright ownership: Max Niemeyer Verlag
Rejected manuscripts: Returned
Time before publication decision: 6 mos.
Time between decision and publication: 1 yr.
Number of reviewers: 2-3
Books submitted per year: 5
Books published per year: 2

(1177)
*Hermes: Zeitschrift für Klassische Philologie

Jochen Bleicken, Harmut Erbse, & Willy Schetter, Editors
Althistorisches Seminar
Platz der Göttinger Sieben 5
3400 Göttingen, Germany

Additional editorial address: Philologisches Seminar der Univ. Bonn, Am Hof 1e/II, 53 Bonn, Germany
Telephone: (49) 5504 381
First published: 1866
ISSN: 0018-0777
MLA acronym: Hermes

SUBSCRIPTION INFORMATION

Frequency of publication: 4 times/yr.
Circulation: 850
Available in microform: No
Subscription address: Franz Steiner Verlag, Birkenwaldstr. 44, Postfach 101526, 7000 Stuttgart 10, Germany

ADVERTISING INFORMATION

Advertising accepted: Yes

EDITORIAL DESCRIPTION

Scope: Publishes research on Classical Antiquity including literature, language, and history.
Reviews books: No
Publishes notes: Yes
Languages accepted: German; English; French; Italian; Latin
Prints abstracts: No
Author-anonymous submission: No

SUBMISSION REQUIREMENTS

Restrictions on contributors: Journal accepts manuscripts from researchers only.
Author pays submission fee: No
Author pays page charges: No
Length of articles: 60,000 words maximum
Length of notes: 15,000 words maximum
Style: Request from editor
Number of copies required: 1
Copyright ownership: Publisher; reverts to author after 1 yr.
Rejected manuscripts: Returned
Time before publication decision: 3-6 mos.
Time between decision and publication: 1-2 yrs.
Number of reviewers: 3
Articles published per year: 35
Notes published per year: 15

(1178)
*High Plains Literary Review

Robert O. Greer, Jr., Editor
180 Adams St.
Suite 250
Denver, CO 80206

Telephone: 303 320-6828
First published: 1986
ISSN: 0888-4153
MLA acronym: HPLR

SUBSCRIPTION INFORMATION

Frequency of publication: 3 times/yr.
Circulation: 800
Available in microform: No
Subscription price: $20.00/yr.
Year to which price refers: 1992

ADVERTISING INFORMATION

Advertising accepted: Yes
Advertising rates: $50.00/half page; $100.00/full page

EDITORIAL DESCRIPTION

Scope: Publishes poetry, essays, fiction, reviews, and interviews.
Reviews books: Yes
Publishes notes: No
Languages accepted: English
Prints abstracts: No
Author-anonymous submission: No

SUBMISSION REQUIREMENTS

Author pays submission fee: No
Author pays page charges: No
Length of articles: 3,000-8,000 words
Length of book reviews: 1,500-3,000 words
Style: MLA; Chicago
Number of copies required: 1
Copyright ownership: Author
Rejected manuscripts: Returned; enclose SASE.
Time before publication decision: 8-10 weeks
Time between decision and publication: 7-9 mos.
Number of reviewers: 3
Articles published per year: 3-5
Book reviews submitted per year: 20-30
Book reviews published per year: 9-12

(1179)
Hiroshima Studies in English Language and Literature

Hiroshi Matsumoto, Editor
Dept. of English
Hiroshima Univ.
Hiroshima 730, Japan

First published: 1944
Sponsoring organization: Hiroshima Univ., English Literary Assn.
MLA acronym: HSELL

SUBSCRIPTION INFORMATION

Frequency of publication: Annual
Available in microform: No
Subscription address: Secretary, at the above address

ADVERTISING INFORMATION

Advertising accepted: No

EDITORIAL DESCRIPTION

Reviews books: Yes
Publishes notes: No
Languages accepted: English; Japanese
Prints abstracts: Yes

SUBMISSION REQUIREMENTS

Restrictions on contributors: Contributors must be members of English Literary Assn.
Author pays submission fee: No
Author pays page charges: No
Length of articles: 6,000 words maximum
Style: MLA
Number of copies required: 1
Rejected manuscripts: Returned
Number of reviewers: 8

(1180)
*Hispamerica: Revista de Literatura

Saúl Sosnowski, Editor
5 Pueblo Ct.
Gaithersburg, MD 20878

Telephone: 301 948-3494
Fax: 301 314-9752 (c/o Latin American Studies Center-UMCP)
First published: 1972
ISSN: 0363-0471
MLA acronym: Hispam

SUBSCRIPTION INFORMATION

Frequency of publication: 3 times/yr. (Apr., Aug., Dec.)
Circulation: 1,000
Available in microform: No
Subscription price: $30.00/yr. institutions; $21.00/yr. individuals
Year to which price refers: 1992

ADVERTISING INFORMATION

Advertising accepted: Yes
Advertising rates: $75.00/half page; $100.00/full page

EDITORIAL DESCRIPTION

Scope: Publishes essays, interviews, poetry, prose fiction, and reviews dealing exclusively with Spanish American literature.
Reviews books: Yes
Publishes notes: Yes
Languages accepted: Spanish
Prints abstracts: No
Author-anonymous submission: No

SUBMISSION REQUIREMENTS

Restrictions on contributors: None
Author pays submission fee: No
Author pays page charges: No
Length of articles: 15-20 pp.
Length of book reviews: 500 words
Length of notes: 2,000 words maximum
Style: Journal
Number of copies required: 2
Copyright ownership: Journal & author
Rejected manuscripts: Returned; enclose return postage.
Time before publication decision: 1-3 mos.
Time between decision and publication: 6-9 mos.
Number of reviewers: 2-3
Articles submitted per year: 45-50
Articles published per year: 8-10
Book reviews submitted per year: 50-60
Book reviews published per year: 20-25
Notes submitted per year: 30-35
Notes published per year: 5-10

(1181)
*Hispania: A Journal Devoted to the Interests of the Teaching of Spanish and Portuguese

Theodore A. Sackett, Editor
Dept. of Spanish & Portuguese
Univ. of Southern California
Los Angeles, CA 90089-0358

Telephone: 601 325-2041
Fax: 601 325-3299
First published: 1917
Sponsoring organization: American Assn. of Teachers of Spanish & Portuguese, Inc.
ISSN: 0018-2133
MLA acronym: Hispania

SUBSCRIPTION INFORMATION

Frequency of publication: 4 times/yr. (Mar., May, Sept., Dec.)
Circulation: 13,000
Available in microform: No
Subscription address: James R. Chatham, Mississippi State Univ., P.O. Box 6349, Mississippi State, MS 39762-6349

ADVERTISING INFORMATION

Advertising accepted: Yes

EDITORIAL DESCRIPTION

Scope: Publishes articles, notes, and book reviews on Spanish, Spanish American, Portuguese, and Brazilian literature, language, linguistics, and pedagogy as well as news on cultural, literary, and political events. Includes bibliographies. Journal includes a section on computers for research and teaching, and occasional information on international Hispanism.
Reviews books: Yes
Publishes notes: Yes
Languages accepted: English; Portuguese; Spanish
Prints abstracts: No
Author-anonymous submission: Yes

SUBMISSION REQUIREMENTS

Restrictions on contributors: Only members of the American Assn. of Teachers of Spanish & Portuguese may submit manuscripts. Unsolicited book reviews are not accepted.
Author pays submission fee: No
Author pays page charges: No
Length of articles: 12-30 pp.
Length of book reviews: 500-1,000 words
Length of notes: 7 pp. maximum
Style: MLA
Number of copies required: 2
Special requirements: Submit original typescript.
Copyright ownership: Journal
Rejected manuscripts: Returned; enclose loose postage or international reply coupons and SAE.
Time before publication decision: 4 mos.
Time between decision and publication: 2 yrs.
Number of reviewers: 2-3
Articles submitted per year: 800
Articles published per year: 40
Book reviews published per year: 140
Notes submitted per year: 25
Notes published per year: 15

(1182)
*Hispanic Issues

Nicholas Spadaccini, Gwendolyn Barnes-Karol, Antonio Ramos-Gascón, & Jenaro Talens, Editors
Prisma Inst.
3 Folwell Hall
9 Pleasant St. SE
Minneapolis, MN 55455

Telephone: 612 626-0532
First published: 1987
Sponsoring organization: Univ. of Minnesota
ISSN: 0893-2395
MLA acronym: HispIss

SUBSCRIPTION INFORMATION

Frequency of publication: 1-3 times/yr.
Circulation: 500
Available in microform: No
Subscription address: Univ. of Minnesota Press, 2037 University Ave. SE, Minneapolis, MN 55414
Subscription telephone: 800 388-3863
Subscription fax: 612 626-7313

ADVERTISING INFORMATION

Advertising accepted: No

EDITORIAL DESCRIPTION

Scope: Publishes collections on theoretical and methodological issues in Spanish and Spanish American literary history and criticism.
Reviews books: No
Publishes notes: No
Languages accepted: English
Prints abstracts: No
Author-anonymous submission: No

SUBMISSION REQUIREMENTS

Author pays submission fee: No
Author pays page charges: No
Style: MLA
Number of copies required: 1
Copyright ownership: Univ. of Minnesota Press
Rejected manuscripts: Not returned
Books published per year: 1-3

(1183)
*Hispanic Journal

David A. Foltz, Editor
Dept. of Spanish & Classical Languages
462 Sutton Hall
Indiana Univ. of Pennsylvania
Indiana, PA 15705

Telephone: 412 357-2326
First published: 1979
Sponsoring organization: Indiana Univ. of Pennsylvania, Graduate School & Dept. of Spanish and Classical Languages
ISSN: 0271-0986
MLA acronym: HisJ

SUBSCRIPTION INFORMATION

Frequency of publication: 2 times/yr.
Circulation: 450
Available in microform: No
Subscription price: $30.00/yr. institutions; $15.00/yr. individuals
Year to which price refers: 1992
Subscription address: José Carranza, Managing Editor, at the above address

ADVERTISING INFORMATION

Advertising accepted: No

EDITORIAL DESCRIPTION

Scope: Publishes articles on literary criticism, linguistics, and Spanish and Latin American thought and culture.
Reviews books: Yes
Publishes notes: Yes
Languages accepted: English; Spanish
Prints abstracts: No
Author-anonymous submission: No

SUBMISSION REQUIREMENTS

Restrictions on contributors: None
Author pays submission fee: No
Author pays page charges: No
Length of articles: 2,500-5,000 words
Length of book reviews: 500-2,000 words
Length of notes: 500-1,200 words
Style: MLA
Number of copies required: 2
Special requirements: Submit contributions from letter-quality or laser printers.
Copyright ownership: Journal
Rejected manuscripts: Original typescript returned
Time before publication decision: 1-8 mos.
Time between decision and publication: 1-2 yrs.
Number of reviewers: 2-3
Articles submitted per year: 80-100
Articles published per year: 24-28
Book reviews submitted per year: 15-30
Book reviews published per year: 15-30
Notes submitted per year: 2-5
Notes published per year: 2-5

(1184)
*Hispanic Linguistics

Carol A. Klee, Editor
Dept. of Spanish & Portuguese
34 Folwell Hall
9 Pleasant St. SE
Univ. of Minnesota
Minneapolis, MN 55455

Telephone: 612 625-9521
Fax: 612 626-0532
E-mail: Klee@vx.acs.umn.edu
First published: 1984
Sponsoring organization: College of Liberal Arts, Univ. of Minnesota; Dept. of Spanish & Portuguese, Univ. of Minnesota
ISSN: 0742-5287
MLA acronym: HLing

SUBSCRIPTION INFORMATION

Frequency of publication: 2 times/yr. (Spring, Fall)
Circulation: 300
Available in microform: No
Subscription price: $30.00/yr. institutions; $18.00/yr. individuals; $12.00/yr. students
Year to which price refers: 1992
Subscription address: Prisma Inst., at the above address
Subscription telephone: 612 625-9028

ADVERTISING INFORMATION

Advertising accepted: No

EDITORIAL DESCRIPTION

Scope: Publishes articles on synchronic studies of the languages and dialects originating on the Iberian peninsula, wherever they now exist. Historical studies utilizing a synchronic methodology, and diachronic studies of merit are also encouraged. Also publishes articles on interlinguistic studies which focus on a Hispanic language.
Reviews books: Yes
Publishes notes: Yes
Languages accepted: English; Spanish; Portuguese; Galician; Catalan
Prints abstracts: Yes
Author-anonymous submission: Yes

SUBMISSION REQUIREMENTS

Restrictions on contributors: None
Author pays submission fee: No
Author pays page charges: No
Length of articles: No restrictions
Length of book reviews: No restrictions
Length of notes: No restrictions
Style: Linguistic Soc. of America
Number of copies required: 3
Special requirements: Submit original typescript and 2 copies along with either IBM or Macintosh compatible diskette. diskette.
Copyright ownership: Prisma Inst., Dept. of Spanish & Portuguese, Univ. of Minnesota
Rejected manuscripts: Returned; enclose SASE.
Time before publication decision: 3 mos.
Time between decision and publication: 6-12 mos.
Number of reviewers: 2-3
Articles published per year: 14-18
Book reviews published per year: 4-6

(1185)
*Hispanic Review

Russell P. Sebold, Editor
512 Williams Hall
Univ. of Pennsylvania
Philadelphia, PA 19104-6305

Telephone: 215 898-7420
Fax: 215 898-0933
First published: 1933
Sponsoring organization: Univ. of Pennsylvania; Hispanic Soc. of America
ISSN: 0018-2176
MLA acronym: HR

SUBSCRIPTION INFORMATION

Frequency of publication: 4 times/yr. (Winter, Spring, Summer, Fall)
Circulation: 1,800
Available in microform: Yes
Subscription price: $32.50/yr. institutions; $22.50/yr. individuals; add $3.00/yr. outside US
Year to which price refers: 1992
Subscription address: Evelyn Phillips, at the above address

ADVERTISING INFORMATION

Advertising accepted: Yes

EDITORIAL DESCRIPTION

Scope: Devoted to research in the Hispanic languages and literatures.
Reviews books: Yes
Publishes notes: No
Languages accepted: English; French; German; Italian; Portuguese; Spanish
Prints abstracts: No
Author-anonymous submission: No

SUBMISSION REQUIREMENTS

Restrictions on contributors: Book reviews are solicited.
Author pays submission fee: No
Author pays page charges: No
Length of articles: 7,500 words maximum
Length of book reviews: 500-1,000 words
Style: MLA
Number of copies required: 1
Special requirements: Only original typescripts are considered. Do not include xerox or carbon copies.
Copyright ownership: Trustees of the Univ. of Pennsylvania
Rejected manuscripts: Returned; enclose return postage or international reply coupons.
Time before publication decision: 2-4 weeks
Time between decision and publication: 2 yrs.
Number of reviewers: 3
Articles submitted per year: 130
Articles published per year: 25-30
Book reviews submitted per year: 100
Book reviews published per year: 75

(1186)
Hispanica Posnaniensia

Rostislav Pazukhin, Editor
Adam Mickiewicz Univ.
Dept. of Hispanic Studies
ul. Slowackiego 20
60-822 Poznan, Poland

First published: 1990
Sponsoring organization: Adam Mickiewicz Univ.
ISSN: 0867-020X
MLA acronym: HP

SUBSCRIPTION INFORMATION

Frequency of publication: Annual
Available in microform: No
Subscription price: $15.00/yr.
Year to which price refers: 1991
Subscription address: Adam Mickiewicz Univ. Press, ul. Nowowiejskiego 55, 61-734 Poznan, Poland

ADVERTISING INFORMATION

Advertising accepted: Yes

EDITORIAL DESCRIPTION

Scope: Publishes articles on the study of the language and culture of the Ibero-Romanic world, including native Latin American cultures.
Reviews books: Yes
Publishes notes: Yes
Languages accepted: Spanish; Portuguese; Catalan; English occasionally; French occasionally
Prints abstracts: No
Author-anonymous submission: Yes

SUBMISSION REQUIREMENTS

Author pays submission fee: No
Author pays page charges: No
Length of articles: 20 pp.
Length of book reviews: 2-10 pp.
Length of notes: 1-10 pp.
Number of copies required: 1
Copyright ownership: Adam Mickiewicz Univ. Press
Rejected manuscripts: Returned
Time before publication decision: 1-6 mos.
Time between decision and publication: 8-10 mos.
Number of reviewers: 1 minimum

(1187)
*Hispanistische Studien

Rafael Gutiérrez Girardot, Editor
Verlag Peter Lang GmbH
Eschborner Landstr. 42-50
6000 Frankfurt am Main 90, Germany

First published: 1974
ISSN: 0170-8570
MLA acronym: HStudien

SUBSCRIPTION INFORMATION

Frequency of publication: Irregular
Available in microform: No

ADVERTISING INFORMATION

Advertising accepted: No

EDITORIAL DESCRIPTION

Scope: Publishes monographs on Spanish and Spanish American literature.
Reviews books: No
Publishes notes: No
Languages accepted: German; Spanish; Portuguese; English; Catalan
Prints abstracts: No

SUBMISSION REQUIREMENTS

Restrictions on contributors: None
Author pays submission fee: No
Length of books: No restrictions
Number of copies required: 2
Copyright ownership: Editor
Time before publication decision: 2 mos.
Time between decision and publication: 6 mos.
Books published per year: 1-2

(1188)
*Hispanófila

Fred M. Clark, Editor
Dept. of Romance Languages
Dey Hall CB no. 3170
Univ. of North Carolina
Chapel Hill, NC 27599-3170

Telephone: 919 962-2062
Fax: 919 962-1025
First published: 1957
Sponsoring organization: Dept. of Romance Languages, Univ. of North Carolina, Chapel Hill
ISSN: 0018-2206
MLA acronym: Hispano

SUBSCRIPTION INFORMATION

Frequency of publication: 3 times/yr.
Circulation: 600
Available in microform: Yes
Subscription price: $21.00/yr. institutions; $18.00/yr. individuals; $8.00/yr. students
Year to which price refers: 1992

ADVERTISING INFORMATION

Advertising accepted: No

EDITORIAL DESCRIPTION

Scope: Publishes articles dedicated to Spanish and Spanish American literature (including Brazilian-Portuguese) with attention given to newer critical methodology as well as the traditional approach to Hispanic literature.
Reviews books: Yes
Publishes notes: No
Languages accepted: English; Spanish; Portuguese
Prints abstracts: No
Author-anonymous submission: No

SUBMISSION REQUIREMENTS

Restrictions on contributors: None
Author pays submission fee: No
Author pays page charges: No
Length of articles: No restrictions
Length of book reviews: No restrictions
Style: MLA
Number of copies required: 2
Copyright ownership: Journal
Rejected manuscripts: Returned
Time before publication decision: 3 mos.
Time between decision and publication: 1 yr.
Number of reviewers: 2
Articles submitted per year: 60
Articles published per year: 30
Book reviews submitted per year: 24
Book reviews published per year: 12

(1189)
*Historiographia Linguistica: International Journal for the History of the Language Sciences/Revue Internationale pour l'Histoire des Sciences du Langage/Internationale Zeitschrift für die Geschichte der Sprachwissenschaften

E. F. Konrad Koerner & Hans-Josef Niederehe, Editors
Dept. of Linguistics
Univ. of Ottawa
Ottawa, Ontario K1N 6N5, Canada

Additional editorial address: H.-J. Niederehe, Associate Editor, FB II: Romanistik, Univ. Trier, 5500 Trier, Germany
First published: 1974
ISSN: 0302-5160
MLA acronym: HL

SUBSCRIPTION INFORMATION

Frequency of publication: 3 times/yr. (Apr., Aug., Dec.)
Circulation: 700
Available in microform: No
Subscription price: 312 f ($189.00)/yr.
Year to which price refers: 1993
Subscription address: John Benjamins B.V., Amsteldijk 44, P.O. Box 75577, 1070 AN Amsterdam, Netherlands
Additional subscription address: John Benjamins North America, Inc., 821 Bethelem Pike, Philadelphia, PA 19118
Subscription telephone: (31) 20 6738156; 215 836-1200
Subscription fax: (31) 20 6739773; 215 836-1204

ADVERTISING INFORMATION

Advertising accepted: Yes
Advertising rates: 400 f ($200.00)/full page

EDITORIAL DESCRIPTION

Scope: Serves the scholarly interests of linguists, psycholinguists, historians of ideas and of science, and philosophers of language of divergent persuasions in the history of linguistic thought. Each issue contains at least three major articles, one review article, and/or a bibliography devoted to a particular topic in the field, a number of reviews of recent publications, and short book notices.
Reviews books: Yes
Publishes notes: Yes
Languages accepted: English; French; German; Italian; Spanish
Prints abstracts: Yes

SUBMISSION REQUIREMENTS

Restrictions on contributors: No multiple submissions; book reviews are solicited.
Author pays submission fee: No
Author pays page charges: No
Length of articles: 25-35 typescript pp. maximum
Length of book reviews: 3,000 words
Length of notes: 1,200-1,500 words
Style: Linguistic Soc. of America with modifications
Number of copies required: 3
Copyright ownership: John Benjamins B.V.
Rejected manuscripts: Returned with comments
Time before publication decision: 2-3 mos.
Time between decision and publication: 6-12 mos.
Number of reviewers: 2 minimum
Articles submitted per year: 30-40
Articles published per year: 12-15
Book reviews published per year: 10-15
Notes submitted per year: 10-15
Notes published per year: 8-10

(1190)
*Historische Sprachforschung/ Historical Linguistics

Alfred Bammesberger & Günter Neumann, Editors
Richard-Strauss Str. 48
8078 Eichstätt, Germany

Additional editorial address: Günter Neumann, Thüringer Str. 20, 8700 Würzburg, Germany
Telephone: (49) 84213176
Fax: (49) 842120599
First published: 1852
Sponsoring organization: Deutsche Forschungsgemeinschaft
ISSN: 0044-3646
MLA acronym: HSHL

SUBSCRIPTION INFORMATION

Frequency of publication: 2 times/yr.
Circulation: 550
Available in microform: No
Subscription address: Vandenhoeck & Ruprecht, P.F. 3753, 3400 Gottingen, Germany

ADVERTISING INFORMATION

Advertising accepted: Yes

EDITORIAL DESCRIPTION

Scope: Publishes work on comparative philology and historical linguistics.
Reviews books: Yes
Publishes notes: Yes
Languages accepted: English; German; French
Prints abstracts: No
Author-anonymous submission: No

SUBMISSION REQUIREMENTS

Restrictions on contributors: None
Author pays submission fee: No
Author pays page charges: No
Length of articles: No restrictions
Length of book reviews: No restrictions
Length of notes: No restrictions
Style: None
Number of copies required: 1
Copyright ownership: Journal
Rejected manuscripts: Returned; enclose return postage.
Time before publication decision: 2 mos.
Time between decision and publication: 9-15 mos.
Number of reviewers: 2
Articles submitted per year: 50-60
Articles published per year: 30-40
Book reviews submitted per year: 15-20
Book reviews published per year: 10-15
Notes submitted per year: 1-5
Notes published per year: 1-5

(1191)
*Historisk Tidskrift

Lars Magnusson, Editor
Svenska Historiska Föreningen
P.O. Box 5405
114 84 Stockholm, Sweden

Telephone: (46) 8 7832502
Fax: (46) 8 7832515
First published: 1881
ISSN: 0345-469X
MLA acronym: HT

SUBSCRIPTION INFORMATION

Frequency of publication: 4 times/yr.
Circulation: 1,500
Available in microform: No
Subscription price: 200 Skr/yr.
Year to which price refers: 1992

ADVERTISING INFORMATION

Advertising accepted: No

EDITORIAL DESCRIPTION

Scope: Publishes articles on general and Scandinavian history.
Reviews books: Yes
Publishes notes: Yes
Languages accepted: English; German; French; Norwegian; Swedish; Danish
Prints abstracts: Yes
Author-anonymous submission: No

SUBMISSION REQUIREMENTS

Restrictions on contributors: None
Author pays submission fee: No
Author pays page charges: No
Length of articles: 10,000 words maximum
Length of book reviews: 3,000 words maximum
Length of notes: 1,000 words
Number of copies required: 3
Copyright ownership: Author
Rejected manuscripts: Returned
Time before publication decision: 6 mos.
Time between decision and publication: 3-6 mos.
Number of reviewers: 2-10
Articles submitted per year: 35
Articles published per year: 12
Book reviews submitted per year: 100
Book reviews published per year: 70
Notes submitted per year: 15
Notes published per year: 5-10

(1192)
*Historiska och Litteraturhistoriska Studier

Helena Solstrand-Pipping, Editor
Svenska Litteratursällskapet i Finland
Mariegatan 8
00170 Hfors, Finland

Telephone: (358) 0 263301
Fax: (358) 0 632820
First published: 1925
Sponsoring organization: Svenska Litteratursällskapet i Finland
ISSN: 0073-2702
MLA acronym: HLS

SUBSCRIPTION INFORMATION

Frequency of publication: Annual
Circulation: 2,000
Available in microform: No
Subscription price: 50 Fmk/yr.
Year to which price refers: 1992

ADVERTISING INFORMATION

Advertising accepted: No

EDITORIAL DESCRIPTION

Scope: Publishes articles on the history of Finland; history, ethnology, and culture of the Swedish-speaking population in Finland; Swedish literature in Finland.
Reviews books: No
Publishes notes: Yes
Languages accepted: Swedish; Danish; Norwegian
Prints abstracts: No
Author-anonymous submission: No

SUBMISSION REQUIREMENTS

Restrictions on contributors: None
Author pays submission fee: No
Author pays page charges: No
Length of articles: 20-70 pp.
Number of copies required: 1
Special requirements: Submit original typescript.
Copyright ownership: Author

Rejected manuscripts: Returned
Time before publication decision: 4 mos.
Time between decision and publication: 1-12 mos.
Number of reviewers: 1
Articles submitted per year: 7-12
Articles published per year: 7-12

(1193)
*History of European Ideas

Ezra Talmor & Sascha Talmor, Editors
Kibbutz Nachshonim
D.N. Mercaz 73190, Israel

Additional editorial address: Dept. of Philosophy, Haifa Univ., Mount Carmel, Haifa 31999, Israel
Telephone: (972) 3 9386445
Fax: (972) 3 9386500; (972) 3 9386591
First published: 1979
Sponsoring organization: European Cultural Foundation
ISSN: 0191-6599
MLA acronym: HEI

SUBSCRIPTION INFORMATION

Frequency of publication: 6 times/yr.
Circulation: 900
Available in microform: Yes
Subscription price: $495.00/yr. institutions
Year to which price refers: 1992
Subscription address: Pergamon Press, Inc., 660 White Plains Rd., Tarrytown, NY 10591-5153
Additional subscription address: Outside N. America: Pergamon Journals, Headington Hill Hall, Oxford OX3 0BW, England
Subscription telephone: 914 524-9200; (44) 865 794141
Subscription fax: 914 333-2444; (44) 865 743911

ADVERTISING INFORMATION

Advertising accepted: Yes

EDITORIAL DESCRIPTION

Scope: Publishes articles on multidisciplinary European studies, including literature, philosophy, history, linguistics, history of religion, art, science, sociology, education, and women's studies.
Reviews books: Yes
Publishes notes: Yes
Languages accepted: English; French
Prints abstracts: No
Author-anonymous submission: Yes

SUBMISSION REQUIREMENTS

Restrictions on contributors: Articles for special issues and book reviews are commissioned.
Author pays submission fee: No
Author pays page charges: No
Length of articles: 6,000 words maximum
Length of book reviews: 800 words maximum
Length of notes: 500-800 words
Style: MLA
Number of copies required: 2
Special requirements: Submit original double-spaced typescript and 1 copy.
Copyright ownership: Pergamon Journals Ltd.
Rejected manuscripts: Returned; enclose SAE and return postage.
Time before publication decision: 6 mos.
Time between decision and publication: 1 yr.
Number of reviewers: 2
Articles submitted per year: 60
Articles published per year: 30
Book reviews published per year: 120
Notes submitted per year: 2-3
Notes published per year: 2-3

(1194)
*Hitotsubashi Journal of Arts and Sciences

Hiroshi Arai, Editor
Hitotsubashi Academy
Hitotsubashi Univ.
Kunitachi, Tokyo 186, Japan

E-mail: Fukabori@hitcc.hit-u.ac.jp
First published: 1960
Sponsoring organization: Hitotsubashi Daigaku Koenkai
ISSN: 0073-2788
MLA acronym: HJA&S

SUBSCRIPTION INFORMATION

Frequency of publication: Annual
Circulation: 900
Available in microform: No
Subscription address: Japan Publications Trading Co., Ltd., P.O. Box 5030, Tokyo International, Tokyo 100, Japan
Subscription telephone: (81) 3 32923751

ADVERTISING INFORMATION

Advertising accepted: No

EDITORIAL DESCRIPTION

Scope: Publishes articles related to arts and sciences, as well as language, literature, mathematics, sports, physical training, and education.
Reviews books: No
Publishes notes: Yes
Languages accepted: English; French; German; Russian; Chinese languages
Prints abstracts: No

SUBMISSION REQUIREMENTS

Restrictions on contributors: Contributors must be members of the staff of Hitotsubashi Academy.
Author pays submission fee: No
Author pays page charges: No
Length of articles: 30-33 pp. (65 characters/line, 23 lines/page)
Style: Chicago
Number of copies required: 3
Special requirements: Submit double-spaced manuscript.
Copyright ownership: Journal & author
Rejected manuscripts: Not returned
Articles submitted per year: 3-5
Articles published per year: 3-5

(1195)
Hjalmar Bergman Samfundet Årsbok

c/o Albert Bonniers Förlag AB
P.O. Box 3159
103 63 Stockholm, Sweden

First published: 1959
ISSN: 0441-0084
MLA acronym: HBSÅ

SUBSCRIPTION INFORMATION

Frequency of publication: Annual
Available in microform: No
Subscription address: c/o G. Pehrson, Sjög. 4 E, 710 60 Grythyttan, Sweden

ADVERTISING INFORMATION

Advertising accepted: No

EDITORIAL DESCRIPTION

Scope: Publishes articles on Hjalmar Bergman.
Reviews books: No
Languages accepted: Swedish
Prints abstracts: No

SUBMISSION REQUIREMENTS

Author pays page charges: No
Articles published per year: 2-3

(1196)
*Hofmannsthal Blätter

Leonhard M. Fiedler, Editor
Inst. für Deutsche Sprache & Literatur II
Johann Wolfgang Goethe-Universität
Gräfstr. 76
6000 Frankfurt am Main, Germany

First published: 1968
Sponsoring organization: Hugo von Hofmannsthal-Gesellschaft
ISSN: 0441-6813
MLA acronym: HBl

SUBSCRIPTION INFORMATION

Frequency of publication: 2 times/yr.
Circulation: 1,000
Available in microform: No

ADVERTISING INFORMATION

Advertising accepted: No

EDITORIAL DESCRIPTION

Scope: Promotes research in the life, work, and reception of Hugo von Hofmannsthal, especially by publishing unknown materials and compiling the Hofmannsthal bibliography.
Reviews books: No
Publishes notes: Yes
Languages accepted: German
Prints abstracts: No
Author-anonymous submission: No

SUBMISSION REQUIREMENTS

Restrictions on contributors: None
Author pays submission fee: No
Author pays page charges: No
Length of articles: No restrictions
Number of copies required: 2
Copyright ownership: Hugo von Hofmannsthal-Gesellschaft
Rejected manuscripts: Returned
Time before publication decision: 4 mos.
Time between decision and publication: 6-8 mos.
Number of reviewers: 2-4
Articles published per year: 10-14

(1197)
*Hölderlin-Jahrbuch

Bernhard Böschenstein & Ulrich Gaier, Editors
Verlag J. B. Metzler
Postfach 103241
7000 Stuttgart, Germany

First published: 1947
Sponsoring organization: Hölderlin-Gesellschaft
ISSN: 0340-6849
MLA acronym: HöJb

SUBSCRIPTION INFORMATION

Frequency of publication: Once every 2 yrs.
Circulation: 2,300
Available in microform: No
Subscription address: Hölderlin-Gesellschaft, Hölderlinhaus, Bursagasse 6, 7400 Tübingen, Germany

ADVERTISING INFORMATION

Advertising accepted: No

EDITORIAL DESCRIPTION

Scope: Reviews research on Friedrich Hölderlin.
Reviews books: Yes
Publishes notes: Yes
Languages accepted: German
Prints abstracts: No
Author-anonymous submission: No

SUBMISSION REQUIREMENTS

Restrictions on contributors: None
Author pays submission fee: No
Author pays page charges: No
Length of articles: No restrictions
Length of book reviews: No restrictions
Length of notes: No restrictions
Style: Journal
Number of copies required: 1
Copyright ownership: Hölderlin-Gesellschaft
Rejected manuscripts: Returned
Time before publication decision: 1 mo.
Time between decision and publication: 1 yr.
Number of reviewers: 2
Articles submitted per year: 20-30
Articles published per year: 20-25
Book reviews submitted per year: 6
Book reviews published per year: 3
Notes submitted per year: 4
Notes published per year: 4

(1198)
*The Hollins Critic

John Rees Moore, Editor
P.O. Box 9538
Hollins College, VA 24020

Telephone: 703 362-6317
Fax: 703 362-6642
First published: 1964
Sponsoring organization: Hollins College
ISSN: 0018-3644
MLA acronym: HC

SUBSCRIPTION INFORMATION

Frequency of publication: 5 times/yr. (Feb., Apr., June, Oct., Dec.)
Circulation: 550
Available in microform: Yes
Subscription price: $6.00/yr. US; $7.50/yr. elsewhere
Year to which price refers: 1992

ADVERTISING INFORMATION

Advertising accepted: No

EDITORIAL DESCRIPTION

Scope: Offers single essay reviews of new books, in terms of author's entire work as well as brief sketch and checklist of author's work. Poems and brief book reviews are also published.
Reviews books: Yes
Publishes notes: No
Languages accepted: English
Prints abstracts: No
Author-anonymous submission: No

SUBMISSION REQUIREMENTS

Restrictions on contributors: Unsolicited manuscripts are not accepted.
Author pays submission fee: No
Length of articles: 5,000 words
Length of book reviews: 300 words
Style: None
Number of copies required: 1
Copyright ownership: Journal
Rejected manuscripts: Returned; enclose SASE.
Articles published per year: 5
Book reviews published per year: 14

(1199)
*L'Homme: Revue Française d'Anthropologie

Jean Pouillon, Editor
Laboratoire d'Anthropologie Sociale
Collège de France
52, rue du Cardinal Lemoine
75005 Paris, France

Telephone: (33) 1 44271730
Fax: (33) 1 44271766
First published: 1961
Sponsoring organization: Editions de l'Ecole des Hautes Etudes en Sciences Sociales
ISSN: 0439-4216
MLA acronym: Homme

SUBSCRIPTION INFORMATION

Frequency of publication: 4 times/yr.
Circulation: 750
Available in microform: No
Subscription price: 390 F/yr. institutions France; 446 F/yr. institutions elsewhere; 300 F/yr. individuals
Year to which price refers: 1992
Subscription address: Centrale des Revues, 11 rue Gossin, 92543 Montrouge Cedex, France
Additional subscription address: For single issues: Navarin Editeur, Dept. Diffusion, 31 rue de Navarin, 75009 Paris, France
Subscription telephone: (33) 1 46565266
Subscription fax: (33) 1 46574069 (CDR); (33) 1 48749949 (Navarin Editeur)

ADVERTISING INFORMATION

Advertising accepted: Yes
Advertising rates: Free

EDITORIAL DESCRIPTION

Scope: Focuses on anthropology.
Reviews books: Yes
Publishes notes: Yes
Languages accepted: French; English
Prints abstracts: Yes
Author-anonymous submission: No

SUBMISSION REQUIREMENTS

Restrictions on contributors: None
Author pays submission fee: No
Author pays page charges: No
Length of articles: 12,000 words maximum
Length of book reviews: 8,000 words maximum
Length of notes: 2,000 words
Style: None
Number of copies required: 2
Special requirements: Submit original typescript plus 1 copy. Camera-ready advertising copy should be sent to Rédaction de L'Homme, Laboratoire d'Anthropologie Sociale, 52 rue du Cardinal Lemoine, 75005 Paris, France
Copyright ownership: Editions de l'Ecole des Hautes Etudes en Sciences Sociales & author
Rejected manuscripts: Returned
Time before publication decision: 1-3 mos.
Time between decision and publication: 1 yr.
Number of reviewers: 2
Articles submitted per year: 50
Articles published per year: 16-20
Book reviews submitted per year: 90
Book reviews published per year: 80
Notes submitted per year: 10-15

(1200)
*The Hopkins Quarterly

Richard F. Giles, Editor
Language Studies Dept., Mohawk College
P.O. Box 2034
Hamilton, Ontario L8N 3T2, Canada

Telephone: 416 575-1212 ext. 3008
First published: 1974

Sponsoring organization: International Hopkins Assn.
ISSN: 0094-9086
MLA acronym: HQ

SUBSCRIPTION INFORMATION

Frequency of publication: 4 times/yr. (Spring, Summer, Fall, Winter)
Circulation: 390
Available in microform: No
Subscription price: C$8.00/yr. Canada; $8.00/yr. elsewhere
Year to which price refers: 1991
Subscription address: Joaquin Kuhn, Treasurer, Dept. of English, St. Michael's College, 81. St. Mary St., Toronto, Ontario M5S IJ4, Canada

ADVERTISING INFORMATION

Advertising accepted: Yes
Advertising rates: $25.00/half page; $50.00/full page

EDITORIAL DESCRIPTION

Scope: Devoted to all aspects of the work, life, and thought of Gerard Manley Hopkins and his circle: Robert Bridges, Richard W. Dixon, and Coventry Patmore. Articles, notes, and queries are welcome.
Reviews books: Yes
Publishes notes: Yes
Languages accepted: English; French
Prints abstracts: No
Author-anonymous submission: No

SUBMISSION REQUIREMENTS

Restrictions on contributors: None
Author pays submission fee: No
Author pays page charges: No
Length of articles: No restrictions
Length of book reviews: No restrictions
Length of notes: No restrictions
Style: None
Number of copies required: 3
Special requirements: Other languages are considered for publication. Inquire in advance of submission. Submission of typescript accompanied by a diskette in ASCII format is preferred.
Copyright ownership: Journal
Rejected manuscripts: Returned; enclose return postage.
Time before publication decision: 6 mos.
Time between decision and publication: 1 yr.
Number of reviewers: 3
Articles submitted per year: 35
Articles published per year: 8-10
Book reviews published per year: 4-6
Notes published per year: 8-10

(1201)
Hoppo Bunka Kenkyu: Bulletin of the Institute for the Study of North Eurasian Cultures, Hokkaido University

Inst. for the Study of North Eurasian Cultures
Fac. of Letters
Hokkaido Univ.
Sapporo, Japan

Sponsoring organization: Hokkaido Univ.
ISSN: 0385-6046
MLA acronym: HBK

EDITORIAL DESCRIPTION

Scope: Publishes articles on Asian linguistics and culture.
Reviews books: No
Languages accepted: Japanese; English
Prints abstracts: Yes, in English for articles in Japanese

(1202)
Hor Yezh

Per Denez, Editor
Le Ris, Ploare
29100 Douarnenez, France

First published: 1954
MLA acronym: Hor Yezh

SUBSCRIPTION INFORMATION

Frequency of publication: 4 times/yr.
Circulation: 400
Available in microform: No
Subscription address: 1, plasenn Charles Péguy, 29260 Lesneven, France

ADVERTISING INFORMATION

Advertising accepted: Yes

EDITORIAL DESCRIPTION

Scope: Publishes articles on Breton and other Celtic languages and literatures.
Reviews books: Yes
Publishes notes: Yes
Languages accepted: Breton
Prints abstracts: No

SUBMISSION REQUIREMENTS

Restrictions on contributors: None
Author pays submission fee: No
Author pays page charges: No
Length of articles: No restrictions
Style: None
Number of copies required: 2
Copyright ownership: Journal
Rejected manuscripts: Returned at author's request
Time before publication decision: 2 mos.
Time between decision and publication: 6-12 mos.
Number of reviewers: 2

(1203)
***Die Horen: Zeitschrift für Literatur, Kunst und Kritik**

Kurt Morawietz, Editor
Leinstr. 17
3000 Hannover 1, Germany

Sponsoring organization: Kulturamt der Landeshauptstadt Hannover; Niedersächsisches Ministerium für Wissenschaft & Kunst, Hannover; Hannoverscher Künstlerverein
ISSN: 0018-4942
MLA acronym: Horen

SUBSCRIPTION INFORMATION

Frequency of publication: 4 times/yr.
Circulation: 5,000
Available in microform: No
Subscription address: Wirtschaftsverlag NW, Postfach 101110, 2850 Bremerhaven, Germany
Subscription fax: (49) 471 42765

ADVERTISING INFORMATION

Advertising accepted: Yes

EDITORIAL DESCRIPTION

Scope: Publishes articles on literature, art, and criticism.
Reviews books: Yes
Publishes notes: No
Languages accepted: German
Prints abstracts: No
Author-anonymous submission: No

SUBMISSION REQUIREMENTS

Restrictions on contributors: Issues are organized on a thematic basis. Consult editor prior to submission.
Author pays page charges: No
Length of book reviews: 1/2-6 pp.
Number of copies required: 1
Time before publication decision: 6-9 mos.
Time between decision and publication: 6-9 mos.
Articles published per year: 200-300
Book reviews submitted per year: 400
Book reviews published per year: 180-250

(1204)
Horizontes: Revista de la Universidad Católica de Puerto Rico

María de los Milagros Pérez, Editor
Univ. Católica de Puerto Rico
Ponce, PR 00732

First published: 1957
Sponsoring organization: Univ. Católica de Puerto Rico
ISSN: 0018-5027
MLA acronym: Horizontes

SUBSCRIPTION INFORMATION

Frequency of publication: 2 times/yr. (Oct., Apr.)
Circulation: 1,100
Available in microform: No

ADVERTISING INFORMATION

Advertising accepted: No

EDITORIAL DESCRIPTION

Scope: Publishes scholarly articles from various departments of the university.
Reviews books: Yes
Publishes notes: No
Languages accepted: English; Spanish
Prints abstracts: No
Author-anonymous submission: No

SUBMISSION REQUIREMENTS

Restrictions on contributors: Contributors must be members of the faculty of the Univ. Católica de Puerto Rico.
Author pays submission fee: No
Author pays page charges: No
Length of articles: 5,000 words
Length of book reviews: 1,000 words
Style: MLA
Number of copies required: 1
Copyright ownership: Author
Rejected manuscripts: Returned; enclose return postage and SAE.
Time before publication decision: 8 mos.
Time between decision and publication: 6 mos.
Number of reviewers: 4
Articles submitted per year: 20
Articles published per year: 16
Book reviews submitted per year: 6 minimum
Book reviews published per year: 6 minimum

(1205)
Horns of Plenty: Malcolm Cowley and his Generation

William Butts & Yolanda Butts, Editors
P.O. Box 65
Crete, IL 60417

Telephone: 312 728-4671
First published: 1988
ISSN: 0896-9965
MLA acronym: HofP

SUBSCRIPTION INFORMATION

Frequency of publication: 4 times/yr. (Mar., June, Sept., Dec.)
Circulation: 100
Available in microform: No

ADVERTISING INFORMATION

Advertising accepted: No

EDITORIAL DESCRIPTION

Scope: Publishes articles on the latest in creative and critical thought on Malcolm Cowley and the generation of writers born around the turn of the century.
Reviews books: Yes
Publishes notes: Yes
Languages accepted: English
Prints abstracts: No
Author-anonymous submission: No

SUBMISSION REQUIREMENTS

Restrictions on contributors: Book reviews are solicited.
Author pays submission fee: No
Author pays page charges: No
Length of articles: 3,000 words
Length of book reviews: 1,000 words
Length of notes: 100 words
Style: MLA
Number of copies required: 1
Copyright ownership: Journal
Rejected manuscripts: Returned; enclose SASE.
Time before publication decision: 6 weeks
Time between decision and publication: 2 mos.
Number of reviewers: 3
Articles submitted per year: 40
Articles published per year: 20
Book reviews published per year: 16
Notes submitted per year: 40
Notes published per year: 40

(1206)
*Hors Cadre: Le Cinéma à Travers Champs Disciplinaires

Michèle Lagny, Marie-Claire Ropars, & Pierre Sorlin, Editors
Presses Universitaires de Paris
Univ. de Paris VIII
2, rue de la Liberté
93526 Saint-Denis Cedex 02, France

Additional editorial address: Marie-Claire Ropars, 12 rue Emile Faguet, 75014 Paris, France
Telephone: (33) 1 45405866
Fax: (33) 1 48210446
First published: 1983
ISSN: 0755-0863
MLA acronym: HCad

SUBSCRIPTION INFORMATION

Frequency of publication: Annual (Mar.)
Available in microform: No
Subscription price: 70 F/yr.
Year to which price refers: 1991
Additional subscription address: Michèle Lagny, 149 boulevard Magenta, 75010 Paris, France

ADVERTISING INFORMATION

Advertising accepted: No

EDITORIAL DESCRIPTION

Scope: Seeks to shift the emphasis of the field of film thought by outlining changes which can lead to film analysis in areas other than film. Focuses on making film a critical mirror instead of an object of study in itself.
Reviews books: No
Publishes notes: No
Languages accepted: French

Prints abstracts: No
Author-anonymous submission: No

SUBMISSION REQUIREMENTS

Restrictions on contributors: Articles are solicited.
Author pays submission fee: No
Author pays page charges: No
Length of articles: 30,000 characters
Number of copies required: 1
Copyright ownership: Editor
Number of reviewers: 3
Articles published per year: 15

(1207)
*Housman Society Journal

Alan W. Holden, Editor
58, Willow Dr.
Bromsgrove
Worcestershire B61 8PU, England

Telephone: (44) 527 31437
First published: 1974
Sponsoring organization: Housman Soc.
ISSN: 0305-926X
MLA acronym: HSJ

SUBSCRIPTION INFORMATION

Frequency of publication: Annual
Circulation: 400
Available in microform: No
Subscription address: R. Shaw, 78, Kidderminster Rd., Bromsgrove, Worcestershire, England

ADVERTISING INFORMATION

Advertising accepted: Yes

EDITORIAL DESCRIPTION

Scope: Researches the poetry, prose, and classical scholarship of A. E. Housman and the works of his brother Laurence and sister Clemence.
Reviews books: Yes
Publishes notes: Yes
Languages accepted: English
Prints abstracts: No

SUBMISSION REQUIREMENTS

Restrictions on contributors: None
Author pays submission fee: No
Author pays page charges: No
Length of articles: 3,000 words
Length of book reviews: 1,000 words
Length of notes: 200 words
Style: None
Number of copies required: 1
Special requirements: Copyright on all quotations must be cleared.
Copyright ownership: Assigned by author to journal
Rejected manuscripts: Returned; enclose return postage.
Time before publication decision: 1 mo.
Number of reviewers: 1
Articles submitted per year: 12
Articles published per year: 10
Book reviews submitted per year: 1-2
Book reviews published per year: 1-2
Notes submitted per year: 2-3
Notes published per year: 2-3

(1208)
*The Hudson Review

Paula Deitz & Frederick Morgan, Editors
684 Park Ave.
New York, NY 10021

First published: 1948

Sponsoring organization: Hudson Review, Inc.
ISSN: 0018-702X
MLA acronym: HudR

SUBSCRIPTION INFORMATION

Frequency of publication: 4 times/yr.
Circulation: 3,100
Available in microform: Yes

ADVERTISING INFORMATION

Advertising accepted: Yes

EDITORIAL DESCRIPTION

Scope: Publishes literary and cultural criticism.
Reviews books: Yes
Languages accepted: English
Prints abstracts: No

SUBMISSION REQUIREMENTS

Restrictions on contributors: None
Author pays submission fee: No
Author pays page charges: No
Length of articles: 10,000 words
Length of book reviews: 2,000 words
Style: Chicago
Number of copies required: 1
Special requirements: Submit previously unpublished typescript. Unsolicited nonfiction is read from 1 Jan.-31 Mar. and 1 Oct.-31 Dec.; unsolicited poetry is read 1 Apr.-30 Sept.; unsolicited fiction is read 1 June-30 Nov. Unsolicited manuscripts received at other times are returned unread.
Copyright ownership: Author, except work-made-for-hire
Rejected manuscripts: Returned; enclose return postage.
Time before publication decision: 6-8 weeks
Time between decision and publication: 1 yr.
Articles published per year: 8
Book reviews published per year: 25

(1209)
*Human Development

D. Kuhn, Editor
Box 119
Teachers College
Columbia Univ.
New York, NY 10027

First published: 1958
ISSN: 0018-716X
MLA acronym: HD

SUBSCRIPTION INFORMATION

Frequency of publication: 6 times/yr.
Circulation: 1,475
Available in microform: Yes
Subscription address: S. Karger Pubs., Inc., 26 W. Avon Rd., P.O. Box 529, Farmington, CT 06085
Additional subscription address: S. Karger, P.O. Box, 4009 Basel, Switzerland

ADVERTISING INFORMATION

Advertising accepted: Yes

EDITORIAL DESCRIPTION

Scope: Publishes articles to promote the integration of knowledge on human development across the disciplines of psychology, sociology, history, philosophy, etc. Preference is given to theoretical contributions and critical reviews of the literature on development across the life span. In addition, manuscripts on the following topics are viewed favorably, when related to developmental issues: theoretical orientations; history of developmental psychology; historical perspectives on development; methodological issues in the study of development; philosophy of science; cross-cultural comparisons; anthropological studies; and other topics that would be of interdisciplinary interest.
Reviews books: Yes
Publishes notes: Yes
Languages accepted: English
Prints abstracts: Yes
Author-anonymous submission: Yes, at author's request.

SUBMISSION REQUIREMENTS

Author pays submission fee: No
Author pays page charges: No
Length of articles: 6,000 words
Length of book reviews: 1,000 words
Length of notes: 1,000 words
Style: American Psychological Assn.
Number of copies required: 4
Special requirements: Manuscripts should be submitted in quadruplicate (with three sets of illustrations of which one is an original), typewritten double-spaced, with a wide margin. Include an abstract (10 lines maximum). Further details available from the editors. See statement of editorial policy in 1988; 31(1), 1-2.
Copyright ownership: S. Karger Pubs., Inc.
Rejected manuscripts: Returned at author's request
Time before publication decision: 3 mos.
Time between decision and publication: 1 yr.
Number of reviewers: 3
Articles submitted per year: 150
Articles published per year: 30
Book reviews submitted per year: 10
Book reviews published per year: 10
Notes submitted per year: 15
Notes published per year: 3

(1210)
*Human Studies: A Journal for Philosophy and the Social Sciences

George Psathas, Editor
Dept. of Sociology
Boston Univ.
100 Cummington St.
Boston, MA 02215

Telephone: 617 353-2591
Fax: 617 353-2053
First published: 1978
Sponsoring organization: Soc. for Phenomenology & the Human Sciences
ISSN: 0163-8548
MLA acronym: HumanS

SUBSCRIPTION INFORMATION

Frequency of publication: 4 times/yr.
Circulation: 400
Available in microform: No
Subscription price: $127.50/yr. institutions; $62.50/yr. individuals
Year to which price refers: 1991
Subscription address: Kluwer Academic Publishers, P.O. Box 322, 3300 AH Dordrecht, Netherlands

ADVERTISING INFORMATION

Advertising accepted: Yes

EDITORIAL DESCRIPTION

Scope: Dedicated to advancing the dialogue between philosophy and the human sciences; addresses such issues as the logic of inquiry, methodology, epistemology and foundational issues in the human sciences as exemplified by original empirical, theoretical and philosophical investigations. Phenomenological perspectives are a primary, though not exclusive, focus. Publishes articles on sociology, psychology, anthropology, history, geography, linguistics, semiotics, ethnomethodology, political science, and philosophy.
Reviews books: Yes
Publishes notes: Yes
Languages accepted: English
Prints abstracts: No
Author-anonymous submission: Yes

SUBMISSION REQUIREMENTS

Restrictions on contributors: None
Author pays submission fee: No
Author pays page charges: No
Length of articles: 15-20 pp.
Length of book reviews: 8 pp.
Length of notes: 4-8 pp.
Style: Chicago
Number of copies required: 3
Special requirements: Submit double-spaced typescript on 8 1/2 in. x 11 in. bond; include footnotes at end. See journal for more information.
Copyright ownership: Kluwer Academic Publishers
Rejected manuscripts: Not returned
Time before publication decision: 4 mos.
Time between decision and publication: 10-12 mos.
Number of reviewers: 2
Articles submitted per year: 70
Articles published per year: 25
Book reviews submitted per year: 12
Book reviews published per year: 8
Notes submitted per year: 10
Notes published per year: 5

(1211)
*Humanistica Lovaniensia: Journal of Neo-Latin Studies

Jozef IJsewijn, Gilbert Tournoy, Constant Matheeusen, & Dirk Sacré, Editors
Seminarium Philologiae Humanisticae
Katholieke Univ. Leuven
Erasmushuis
Blijde Inkomststraat 21
3000 Leuven, Belgium

Telephone: (32) 16 285019; (32) 16 285022
Fax: (32) 16 285025
First published: 1928
Sponsoring organization: Katholieke Univ. Leuven, Seminarium Philologiae Humanisticae
ISSN: 0774-2908
MLA acronym: HumLov

SUBSCRIPTION INFORMATION

Frequency of publication: Annual
Circulation: 500
Available in microform: No
Subscription price: 2,300 BF/yr.
Year to which price refers: 1992
Subscription address: Leuven Univ. Press, Krakenstraat 3, 3000 Leuven, Belgium
Additional subscription address: Uitgeverij Peeters, Bondgenotenlaan 153, 3000 Leuven, Belgium
Subscription telephone: (32) 16 284175

ADVERTISING INFORMATION

Advertising accepted: Yes
Advertising rates: Request from Leuven Univ. Press

EDITORIAL DESCRIPTION

Scope: Focuses on humanistic and Neo-Latin studies. Publishes critical editions, often with translation of Neo-Latin texts (14th-20th centuries), as well as historical, literary, and bibliographical studies on Latin authors of the Renaissance, Baroque, and modern periods. Includes an annual Neo-Latin bibliography.
Reviews books: Yes
Publishes notes: Yes
Languages accepted: English; German; French; Italian; Spanish; Latin
Prints abstracts: No
Author-anonymous submission: No

SUBMISSION REQUIREMENTS

Restrictions on contributors: None
Author pays submission fee: No
Author pays page charges: No
Length of articles: No restrictions
Length of book reviews: 1,000 words
Length of notes: 500 words maximum
Style: Modern Humanities Research Assn.
Number of copies required: 2
Special requirements: Sources should be quoted in the original language.
Copyright ownership: Leuven Univ. Press
Rejected manuscripts: Returned
Time before publication decision: 3 mos.
Time between decision and publication: 1 yr.
Number of reviewers: 2-3
Articles submitted per year: 20-30
Articles published per year: 10-16
Book reviews submitted per year: 30-40
Book reviews published per year: 30-40
Notes submitted per year: 10
Notes published per year: 1-5

(1212)
*Humanitas: Rivista bimestrale di Cultura

Stefano Minelli, Editor
Via G. Rosa, 71
25100 Brescia, Italy

Telephone: (39) 30 46451-57522
Fax: (39) 30 2400605
First published: 1946
ISSN: 0018-7461
MLA acronym: HumB

SUBSCRIPTION INFORMATION

Frequency of publication: 6 times/yr.
Circulation: 2,500
Available in microform: No
Subscription price: 42,000 Lit/yr.
Year to which price refers: 1992
Subscription address: Via G. Rosa 71, 25121 Brescia, Italy

ADVERTISING INFORMATION

Advertising accepted: No

EDITORIAL DESCRIPTION

Scope: Publishes articles on topics related to Catholic culture including theology, philosophy, and history.
Reviews books: Yes
Publishes notes: Yes
Languages accepted: Italian
Prints abstracts: No
Author-anonymous submission: No

SUBMISSION REQUIREMENTS

Restrictions on contributors: None
Author pays submission fee: No
Author pays page charges: No
Length of articles: 6,000 words
Length of book reviews: 300 words
Length of notes: 2,500 words
Style: None
Number of copies required: 2

Copyright ownership: Journal
Rejected manuscripts: Returned
Time before publication decision: 2 mos.
Time between decision and publication: 4 mos.
Number of reviewers: 3
Articles submitted per year: 30
Articles published per year: 24
Book reviews submitted per year: 130
Book reviews published per year: 100
Notes submitted per year: 40
Notes published per year: 30

(1213)
*****Humanities in the South: Newsletter of the Southern Humanities Council**

Carol Wilson, Editor
Division of Humanities
Lander College
Greenwood, SC 29646

Telephone: 803 229-8255
Fax: 803 229-8890
First published: 1951
Sponsoring organization: Southern Humanities Council
ISSN: 0018-7577
MLA acronym: HS

SUBSCRIPTION INFORMATION

Frequency of publication: 2 times/yr.
Circulation: 12,000
Available in microform: No
Subscription price: $15.00/yr.
Year to which price refers: 1992
Additional subscription address: John Phillips, Executive Director, Southern Humanities Council, Univ. of Tennessee at Chattanooga, Chattanooga, TN 37403
Subscription telephone: 615 755-4153

ADVERTISING INFORMATION

Advertising accepted: No

EDITORIAL DESCRIPTION

Scope: Focuses on ideas, directions, and methods in the humanities with emphasis on higher education.
Reviews books: Yes
Publishes notes: Yes
Languages accepted: English
Prints abstracts: No
Author-anonymous submission: No

SUBMISSION REQUIREMENTS

Restrictions on contributors: None
Author pays submission fee: No
Author pays page charges: No
Length of articles: 750-1,000 words
Length of book reviews: 500 words
Length of notes: 250 words
Style: MLA
Number of copies required: 2
Special requirements: Submit original typescript and 1 copy.
Copyright ownership: Author
Rejected manuscripts: Returned
Time before publication decision: 1-2 mos.
Time between decision and publication: 3-6 mos.
Number of reviewers: 2
Articles submitted per year: 20
Articles published per year: 8

(1214)
*****Humor: International Journal of Humor Research**

Victor Raskin, Editor
Dept. of English
324 Heavilon Hall
Purdue Univ.
West Lafayette, IN 47907-1356

Telephone: 317 494-3782
Fax: 317 494-3780
E-mail: Raskin@j.cc.purdue.edu
First published: 1988
Sponsoring organization: International Soc. for Humor Studies
ISSN: 0933-1719
MLA acronym: Humor

SUBSCRIPTION INFORMATION

Frequency of publication: 4 times/yr.
Circulation: 400
Available in microform: No
Subscription price: $37.00/yr.
Year to which price refers: 1992
Subscription address: Don L. F. Nilson, Secretary-Treasurer, International Soc. for Humor Studies, Dept. of English, Arizona State Univ., Tempe, AZ 85287
Additional subscription address: Institutions in US: Walter de Gruyter, Inc., 200 Saw Mill River Rd., Hawthorne, NY 10532; institutions elsewhere: Walter de Gruyter & Co., Postfach 11 02 40, 1000 Berlin 11, Germany

ADVERTISING INFORMATION

Advertising accepted: Yes, on an exchange basis

EDITORIAL DESCRIPTION

Scope: Publishes interdisciplinary articles on research on humor as an important and universal human faculty. Having emerged as an interdisciplinary field, humor research draws upon a wide range of academic disciplines including anthropology, computer science, folklore, history, linguistics, literature, mathematics, medicine, philosophy, psychology, and sociology.
Reviews books: Yes
Publishes notes: Yes
Languages accepted: English
Prints abstracts: Yes
Author-anonymous submission: No

SUBMISSION REQUIREMENTS

Restrictions on contributors: Book reviews are solicited.
Author pays submission fee: No
Author pays page charges: No
Length of articles: No restrictions
Length of book reviews: No restrictions
Length of notes: No restrictions
Style: Chicago
Number of copies required: 4
Special requirements: Submit double-spaced typescript using size A4 (8 1/4 in. x 11 3/4 in.) paper. Include a 200-word maximum abstract. Figures and plates must be reproducible originals.
Copyright ownership: Mouton de Gruyter
Rejected manuscripts: Returned; enclose SASE.
Time before publication decision: 3-6 mos.
Time between decision and publication: 6-18 mos.
Number of reviewers: 4
Articles submitted per year: 90
Articles published per year: 18
Book reviews published per year: 30
Notes submitted per year: 5
Notes published per year: 3

(1215)
*****The Hungarian P.E.N./Le P.E.N. Hongrois**

Imre Szász, Editor
Hungarian P.E.N. Club
Vorosmarty Ter 1
1051 Budapest, Hungary

First published: 1961
Sponsoring organization: Hungarian P.E.N. Club
ISSN: 0439-9080
MLA acronym: HPEN

SUBSCRIPTION INFORMATION

Frequency of publication: Annual
Circulation: 1,000

ADVERTISING INFORMATION

Advertising accepted: No

EDITORIAL DESCRIPTION

Scope: Publishes articles on Hungarian literature.
Reviews books: Yes
Languages accepted: English; French
Prints abstracts: No
Author-anonymous submission: No

SUBMISSION REQUIREMENTS

Restrictions on contributors: None
Author pays submission fee: No
Author pays page charges: No
Length of articles: 10,000-15,000 words
Length of book reviews: 1,000 words
Number of copies required: 2
Copyright ownership: Author
Rejected manuscripts: Not returned
Time before publication decision: 1 mo.
Time between decision and publication: 1 yr.
Number of reviewers: 3
Articles submitted per year: 20-22
Articles published per year: 15-20
Book reviews submitted per year: 15-20
Book reviews published per year: 10-12

(1216)
*****The Hungarian Quarterly**

Miklós Vajda, Editor
P.O. Box 3
1426 Budapest, Hungary

Telephone: (36) 1 1756722 ext. 1114, 1117
Fax: (36) 1 1188297
First published: 1960
Historical variations in title: Formerly *The New Hungarian Quarterly*
Sponsoring organization: Hungarian Ministry of Foreign Affairs
ISSN: 0028-5390
MLA acronym: HungQ

SUBSCRIPTION INFORMATION

Frequency of publication: 4 times/yr.
Circulation: 3,500
Available in microform: No
Subscription price: $45.00/yr. institutions; $34.00/yr. individuals; add $10.00/yr. airmail postage
Year to which price refers: 1992

ADVERTISING INFORMATION

Advertising accepted: Yes
Advertising rates: $107.00/quarter page; $166.00/half page; $285.00/full page, black & white; $450.00/full page, color; $536.00/inside cover, color

EDITORIAL DESCRIPTION

Scope: Publishes Hungarian literature in English, and essays and documents on Hungarian fine arts, cinema, theater, philosophy, music, politics, sociology, and history.
Reviews books: Yes
Publishes notes: No
Languages accepted: English; Hungarian; German; French
Prints abstracts: No
Author-anonymous submission: No

SUBMISSION REQUIREMENTS

Restrictions on contributors: None
Author pays submission fee: No
Author pays page charges: No
Length of articles: 2,000-3,000 words
Length of book reviews: 1,500 words
Number of copies required: 2
Copyright ownership: Author or translator
Rejected manuscripts: Returned at author's request
Time before publication decision: 1 mo.
Time between decision and publication: 6 mos.
Number of reviewers: 2
Articles submitted per year: 400
Articles published per year: 200
Book reviews submitted per year: 40-50
Book reviews published per year: 40

(1217)
*Hungarian Studies in English

Zoltán Abádi-Nagy, Editor
Inst. of English & American Studies
Kossuth Lajos Tudomanyegyetem
4010 Debrecen, Pf. 73, Hungary

Telephone: (36) 52 16666
Fax: (36) 52 12336
E-mail: H3560NAG@HLLA.HU
First published: 1963
Sponsoring organization: English Dept., Kossuth Lajos Tudomanyegyetem
ISSN: 0209-6552
MLA acronym: HSE

SUBSCRIPTION INFORMATION

Frequency of publication: Annual
Circulation: 500
Available in microform: No

ADVERTISING INFORMATION

Advertising accepted: No

EDITORIAL DESCRIPTION

Scope: Publishes articles of scholarly value treating English, American, Canadian, and Australian literature and culture.
Reviews books: Yes
Publishes notes: No
Languages accepted: English
Prints abstracts: No
Author-anonymous submission: No

SUBMISSION REQUIREMENTS

Restrictions on contributors: None
Author pays submission fee: No
Author pays page charges: No
Length of articles: 6,000-7,000 words
Length of book reviews: 300-500 words
Style: MLA
Number of copies required: 2
Special requirements: Submit original typescript plus a photocopy.
Copyright ownership: Assigned by author to publisher
Rejected manuscripts: Not returned
Time before publication decision: 4 mos.
Time between decision and publication: 18 mos.
Number of reviewers: 2 plus Editorial Board
Articles submitted per year: 10

Articles published per year: 5-6
Book reviews published per year: 1-2

(1218)
*Hungarian Studies Review

George Bisztray & Nandor F. Dreisziger, Editors
21 Sussex Ave.
Univ. of Toronto
Toronto, Ontario M5S 1A1, Canada

Additional editorial address: N. Dreisziger, Dept. of History, Royal Military College of Canada, Kingston, Ontario, Canada
Telephone: 416 978-4157; 613 541-6224
Fax: 416 578-5593; 613 542-5055
First published: 1974
Sponsoring organization: Hungarian Readers' Service Inc.; Univ. of Toronto, Chair of Hungarian Studies
ISSN: 0713-8083
MLA acronym: HSR

SUBSCRIPTION INFORMATION

Frequency of publication: 2 times/yr. (Spring, Fall)
Circulation: 400
Available in microform: Yes
Subscription price: $12.00/yr.
Year to which price refers: 1991
Additional subscription address: Eva Tomory, 14623 Hwy. 48, RR2, Stouffville, Ontario, L4A 7X3, Canada

ADVERTISING INFORMATION

Advertising accepted: No

EDITORIAL DESCRIPTION

Scope: Publishes interdisciplinary articles and critical book reviews relating to Hungary and Hungarians.
Reviews books: Yes
Publishes notes: No
Languages accepted: English; Hungarian; French
Prints abstracts: No
Author-anonymous submission: No

SUBMISSION REQUIREMENTS

Restrictions on contributors: None
Author pays submission fee: No
Author pays page charges: No
Length of articles: 5,000-10,000 words
Length of book reviews: 600-1,000 words
Style: Chicago
Number of copies required: 2
Special requirements: Electronic submission is preferred.
Copyright ownership: Publisher
Rejected manuscripts: Returned at author's request
Time before publication decision: 3 mos.
Time between decision and publication: 1 yr.
Number of reviewers: 3-5
Articles submitted per year: 10-15
Articles published per year: 8
Book reviews submitted per year: 15
Book reviews published per year: 10-15

(1219)
*Huntington Library Quarterly: A Journal for the History and Interpretation of English and American Civilization

Guilland Sutherland, Editor
Henry E. Huntington Library & Art Collections
1151 Oxford Rd.
San Marino, CA 91108

Telephone: 818 405-2172
Fax: 818 405-0225

First published: 1931
Sponsoring organization: Huntington Library, Art Collections, and Botanical Gardens
ISSN: 0018-7895
MLA acronym: HLQ

SUBSCRIPTION INFORMATION

Frequency of publication: 4 times/yr.
Circulation: 1,100
Available in microform: Yes
Subscription price: $40.00/yr.
Year to which price refers: 1992

ADVERTISING INFORMATION

Advertising accepted: No

EDITORIAL DESCRIPTION

Scope: Publishes scholarly articles with special attention to the research fields of the Huntington Library collections, concentrating particularly on the literature, history, and art of the sixteenth to eighteenth centuries in Britain and America. Interdisciplinary articles are frequently illustrated from rare items in the library. Also publishes long book reviews and describes recent acquisitions to the collections.
Reviews books: Yes
Publishes notes: Yes
Languages accepted: English
Prints abstracts: No
Author-anonymous submission: Yes

SUBMISSION REQUIREMENTS

Restrictions on contributors: None
Author pays submission fee: No
Author pays page charges: No
Length of articles: 10-35 typescript pp.
Length of book reviews: 1,000-2,500 words
Length of notes: 5-10 typescript pp.
Style: Chicago
Number of copies required: 1
Special requirements: Short notes must be based only on research in Huntington Library materials.
Copyright ownership: Assigned by author to journal
Rejected manuscripts: Returned; enclose return postage.
Time before publication decision: 3 mos.
Time between decision and publication: 1 yr.
Number of reviewers: 2-4
Articles submitted per year: 80
Articles published per year: 16
Book reviews submitted per year: 10
Book reviews published per year: 10
Notes submitted per year: 20
Notes published per year: 6-8

(1220)
*Hymnologiske Meddelelser: Tidsskrift om Salmer

Peter Balslev-Clausen, Jens Lyster, & Vagner Lund, Editors
Ahlmanns Allé 14
2900 Hellerup, Denmark

First published: 1972
Sponsoring organization: Salmehistorisk Selskab; Nordisk Inst. for Hymnologi
ISSN: 0106-4940
MLA acronym: HymnM

SUBSCRIPTION INFORMATION

Frequency of publication: 4 times/yr.
Circulation: 500
Available in microform: No
Subscription price: 150 Dkr/yr.
Year to which price refers: 1992
Subscription address: Inst. for Kirkehistorie, Københavns Univ., Købmagergade 44-46, 1150 Copenhagen K, Denmark

ADVERTISING INFORMATION

Advertising accepted: No

EDITORIAL DESCRIPTION

Scope: Publishes new hymns (texts and melodies), historical and analytical hymnological articles (scholarly), and reviews.
Reviews books: Yes
Publishes notes: Yes
Languages accepted: Danish; Norwegian; Swedish
Prints abstracts: Yes, in German or English
Author-anonymous submission: No

SUBMISSION REQUIREMENTS

Restrictions on contributors: None
Author pays submission fee: No
Author pays page charges: No
Length of articles: 3,500-10,000 words
Length of book reviews: 300-1,800 words
Length of notes: 250-1,000 words
Style: None
Number of copies required: 2
Special requirements: Submit original typescript.
Copyright ownership: Author
Rejected manuscripts: Returned
Time before publication decision: 3 mos.
Time between decision and publication: 2-3 mos.
Number of reviewers: 2
Articles submitted per year: 10-15
Articles published per year: 8-12
Book reviews submitted per year: 15-20
Book reviews published per year: 10-15
Notes submitted per year: 15
Notes published per year: 15

(1221)
*****Iberoromania: Zeitschrift für die Iberoromanischen Sprachen und Literaturen in Europa und Amerika/ Revista Dedicada a las Lenguas y Literaturas Iberorrománicas de Europa y América**

Heinrich Bihler, Dietrich Briesemeister, Hans-Martin Gauger, Horst Geckeler, Hans-Jörg Neuschäfer, Klaus Pörtl, & Gustav Siebenmann, Editors
Max Niemeyer Verlag
Postfach 2140
7400 Tübingen, Germany

Telephone: (49) 7071 81104
Fax: (49) 7071 87419
First published: 1969
Sponsoring organization: Deutsche Forschungsgemeinschaft
ISSN: 0019-0993
MLA acronym: Ibero

SUBSCRIPTION INFORMATION

Frequency of publication: 2 times/yr.
Available in microform: No
Subscription price: 86 DM/yr.
Year to which price refers: 1991

ADVERTISING INFORMATION

Advertising accepted: Yes
Advertising rates: 600 DM/full page

EDITORIAL DESCRIPTION

Scope: Publishes articles on the study of Ibero-Romance languages and literatures in Europe and America.
Reviews books: Yes
Publishes notes: Yes
Languages accepted: German; Portuguese; French; Italian; Spanish; English; Catalan
Prints abstracts: Yes
Author-anonymous submission: No

SUBMISSION REQUIREMENTS

Restrictions on contributors: None
Author pays submission fee: No
Author pays page charges: No
Length of articles: 20 pp.
Length of book reviews: 2-3 pp.
Length of notes: 5 pp.
Style: MLA; "Normas para la redacción de artículos"
Number of copies required: 1
Special requirements: Submit printer-ready original typescript.
Copyright ownership: Max Niemeyer Verlag
Rejected manuscripts: Returned; enclose international reply coupons.
Time before publication decision: 3 mos.
Time between decision and publication: 7-24 mos.
Number of reviewers: 2-3
Articles published per year: 16-18
Book reviews published per year: 15-20

(1222)
*****IBLA: Revue de l'Institut des Belles Lettres Arabes**

Jean Fontaine, Editor
Inst. des Belles Lettres Arabes
12, rue Jamaâ Al Haoua
1008 Tunis, Tunisia

Telephone: (216) 1 560133
First published: 1937
Sponsoring organization: Inst. des Belles Lettres Arabes
ISSN: 0018-862X
MLA acronym: IBLA

SUBSCRIPTION INFORMATION

Frequency of publication: 2 times/yr.
Circulation: 1,000
Available in microform: Yes, for 1937-1988
Subscription price: $26.00/yr.
Year to which price refers: 1992

ADVERTISING INFORMATION

Advertising accepted: Yes

EDITORIAL DESCRIPTION

Scope: Publishes articles on socio-human problems in Arab-Moslem civilization.
Reviews books: Yes
Languages accepted: French; English; Arabic
Prints abstracts: No

SUBMISSION REQUIREMENTS

Author pays submission fee: No
Author pays page charges: No
Length of articles: 15-30 pp.
Length of book reviews: 750 words
Number of copies required: 1
Copyright ownership: Journal
Rejected manuscripts: Returned
Time before publication decision: 2-6 mos.
Time between decision and publication: 6-12 mos.
Number of reviewers: 3
Articles published per year: 15
Book reviews submitted per year: 100-120
Book reviews published per year: 25

(1223)
ICarbS

David V. Koch & Alan M. Cohn, Editors
Morris Library
Southern Illinois Univ.
Carbondale, IL 62901

First published: 1973
Sponsoring organization: Southern Illinois Univ., Carbondale, Friends of Morris Library
ISSN: 0360-8409
MLA acronym: ICarbS

SUBSCRIPTION INFORMATION

Frequency of publication: Irregular
Circulation: 750
Available in microform: No
Subscription address: Barbara Rhea, Circulation Manager, at the above address

ADVERTISING INFORMATION

Advertising accepted: No

EDITORIAL DESCRIPTION

Scope: Publishes original scholarly articles and bibliographical research emanating primarily from the special collections of Morris Library, Southern Illinois University, Carbondale.
Reviews books: No
Publishes notes: Yes
Languages accepted: English
Prints abstracts: No

SUBMISSION REQUIREMENTS

Restrictions on contributors: Most articles are solicited; consult with editor before submission.
Author pays submission fee: No
Author pays page charges: No
Length of articles: 2,500-5,000 words
Style: MLA
Number of copies required: 1
Special requirements: Submit original typescript.
Copyright ownership: Assigned on request
Rejected manuscripts: Returned; enclose return postage.
Time before publication decision: 6-8 weeks
Time between decision and publication: 2-6 mos.
Number of reviewers: 3-6
Articles published per year: 16

(1224)
*****Idiomatica: Veröffentlichungen der Tübinger Arbeitsstelle 'Sprache in Südwestdeutschland'**

Arno Ruoff, Editor
Tübinger Arbeitsstelle 'Sprache in Südwestdeutschland'
Römerstr. 27
7401 Wolfenhausen, Germany

Telephone: (49) 7457 1095
First published: 1973
ISSN: 0344-6719
MLA acronym: Idiomatica

SUBSCRIPTION INFORMATION

Frequency of publication: Irregular
Subscription address: Max Niemeyer Verlag, Postfach 2140, 7400 Tübingen, Germany

ADVERTISING INFORMATION

Advertising accepted: No

EDITORIAL DESCRIPTION

Scope: Publishes monographs on research on spoken language, with an emphasis on southwestern Germany.
Reviews books: No
Publishes notes: No
Languages accepted: German
Prints abstracts: No

SUBMISSION REQUIREMENTS

Author pays submission fee: No

Author pays page charges: No
Copyright ownership: Max Niemeyer Verlag

(1225)
*Ilha do Desterro: A Journal of Language and Literature

Susana Bornéo Funck, Editor
Univ. Federal de Santa Catarina
Dpto. de Lingua e Literatura Estrangeiras
Centro de Comunicação e Expressão
88049 Florianópolis-SC, Brazil

Telephone: (55) 482 319455
Fax: (55) 482 344069
First published: 1979
Sponsoring organization: Univ. Federal de Santa Catarina
MLA acronym: IdD

SUBSCRIPTION INFORMATION

Frequency of publication: 2 times/yr.
Circulation: 500-800
Available in microform: No
Subscription price: 5,500 Cz/yr.
Year to which price refers: 1991-92

ADVERTISING INFORMATION

Advertising accepted: Yes

EDITORIAL DESCRIPTION

Scope: Publishes critical articles on Anglo-American literature, linguistics, discourse analysis, and foreign language teaching.
Reviews books: Yes
Publishes notes: Yes
Languages accepted: English; Portuguese
Prints abstracts: No
Author-anonymous submission: No

SUBMISSION REQUIREMENTS

Restrictions on contributors: None
Author pays submission fee: No
Author pays page charges: No
Length of articles: 4,000-8,000 words
Length of book reviews: 1,000 words
Length of notes: 1,000-2,000 words
Style: MLA preferred
Number of copies required: 1
Copyright ownership: Author
Rejected manuscripts: Returned
Time before publication decision: 6 mos.
Time between decision and publication: 3 mos.
Number of reviewers: 2
Articles submitted per year: 40
Articles published per year: 20
Book reviews submitted per year: 5
Book reviews published per year: 5
Notes submitted per year: 5
Notes published per year: 5

(1226)
*Illinois Historical Journal

E. Duane Elbert, Editor
Illinois Historic Preservation Agency
Old State Capitol
Springfield, IL 62701

Telephone: 217 782-4836
First published: 1908
Sponsoring organization: Illinois State Historical Soc.; Illinois Historic Preservation Agency
ISSN: 0019-2287
MLA acronym: JISHS

SUBSCRIPTION INFORMATION

Frequency of publication: 4 times/yr. (Spring, Summer, Fall, Winter)
Circulation: 2,900
Available in microform: Yes
Subscription price: $20.00/yr. institutions; $25.00/yr. individuals (includes membership)
Year to which price refers: 1992
Subscription telephone: 217 782-2635

ADVERTISING INFORMATION

Advertising accepted: No

EDITORIAL DESCRIPTION

Scope: Publishes articles that make an original contribution to Illinois history or culture, interpreted to include native or resident Illinoisans, Illinois as frontier, Civil War, etc.
Reviews books: Yes
Publishes notes: No
Languages accepted: English
Prints abstracts: No
Author-anonymous submission: Yes

SUBMISSION REQUIREMENTS

Restrictions on contributors: Reviews are commissioned.
Author pays submission fee: No
Author pays page charges: No
Length of articles: 20-25 typescript pp.
Length of book reviews: 250-500 words
Style: MLA
Number of copies required: 3
Special requirements: Submit original typescript and 2 copies.
Copyright ownership: Assigned by author to journal
Rejected manuscripts: Returned; enclose SASE.
Time before publication decision: 3 mos.
Time between decision and publication: 2 yrs.
Number of reviewers: 2 plus editorial staff
Articles submitted per year: 60
Articles published per year: 16
Book reviews submitted per year: 60
Book reviews published per year: 60

(1227)
*Imprévue

Edmond Cros, Editor
Centre d'Etudes & Recherches Sociocritiques (U.E.R.2)
Univ. Paul Valéry
B.P. 5043
34032 Montpellier Cedex, France

Telephone: (33) 67142172
Fax: (33) 67041823
First published: 1977
Sponsoring organization: Centre d'Etudes & Recherches Sociocritiques
ISSN: 0242-5149
MLA acronym: Imprévue

SUBSCRIPTION INFORMATION

Frequency of publication: 2 times/yr. (June, Dec.)
Circulation: 30-50
Available in microform: No

ADVERTISING INFORMATION

Advertising accepted: Yes, on an exchange basis only

EDITORIAL DESCRIPTION

Scope: Publishes articles on literary criticism. Focuses on sociology of literature; may include semiological studies. Focuses mainly on Spanish literature.
Reviews books: Yes
Publishes notes: Yes
Languages accepted: French; Spanish
Prints abstracts: No
Author-anonymous submission: No

SUBMISSION REQUIREMENTS

Restrictions on contributors: None
Author pays submission fee: No
Author pays page charges: No
Length of articles: 20 pp. maximum
Length of book reviews: 3 pp.
Length of notes: 3 pp.
Style: MLA preferred
Number of copies required: 2
Special requirements: Include personal introduction and abstract.
Copyright ownership: Journal
Rejected manuscripts: Not returned
Time before publication decision: 2-3 mos.
Time between decision and publication: 2-3 mos.
Number of reviewers: 3
Articles submitted per year: 30-35
Articles published per year: 20-25
Book reviews submitted per year: 30
Book reviews published per year: 10
Notes submitted per year: 4
Notes published per year: 3

(1228)
Impulse der Forschung

Wissenschaftliche Buchgesellschaft
Hindenburgstr. 40
Postfach 11-11-29
6100 Darmstadt, Germany

First published: 1970
ISSN: 0174-0687
MLA acronym: IdF

SUBSCRIPTION INFORMATION

Frequency of publication: Irregular
Available in microform: No

ADVERTISING INFORMATION

Advertising accepted: No

EDITORIAL DESCRIPTION

Scope: Publishes monograph studies about German literature and language and literature in general, and other scientific disciplines.
Reviews books: No
Publishes notes: No
Languages accepted: German
Prints abstracts: No

SUBMISSION REQUIREMENTS

Author pays submission fee: No
Author pays page charges: No
Length of books: 160-240 pp.
Number of copies required: 2
Copyright ownership: Wissenschaftliche Buchgesellschaft & author
Rejected manuscripts: Returned
Time between decision and publication: 2-3 yrs.
Number of reviewers: 2

(1229)
*In Geardagum: Essays on Old and Middle English Language and Literature

Loren C. Gruber & Dean Loganbill, Editors
Soc. for New Language Study
Box 42
Ravenwood, IA 64479

Telephone: 816 937-2928
First published: 1974
Sponsoring organization: Soc. for New Language Study
MLA acronym: InG

SUBSCRIPTION INFORMATION

Frequency of publication: Annual
Circulation: 100
Available in microform: No

Subscription price: $10.00/yr.
Year to which price refers: 1992
Subscription address: Soc. for New Language Study, P.O. Box 10596, Denver, CO 80210
Subscription telephone: 303 777-6115

ADVERTISING INFORMATION

Advertising accepted: Yes
Advertising rates: $100.00/full page

EDITORIAL DESCRIPTION

Scope: Publishes articles on Old and Middle English literature, language, and poetry.
Reviews books: Yes
Publishes notes: Yes
Languages accepted: English
Prints abstracts: No
Author-anonymous submission: No

SUBMISSION REQUIREMENTS

Restrictions on contributors: None
Author pays submission fee: No
Author pays page charges: No
Length of articles: 5,000 words
Length of book reviews: 2,000-4,000 words
Length of notes: 1,500-2,000 words
Style: None
Number of copies required: 2
Copyright ownership: Soc. for New Language Study
Rejected manuscripts: Returned; enclose SASE.
Time before publication decision: 1 mo.
Time between decision and publication: 6-12 mos.
Number of reviewers: 2
Articles submitted per year: 10-12
Articles published per year: 5-7
Book reviews submitted per year: 2-3
Book reviews published per year: 1-2
Notes submitted per year: 4-5
Notes published per year: 1-2

(1230)
*Incipit

Germán Orduna, Editor
Seminario de Edición y Crítica Textual
Riobamba 950 (5⁰ T)
1116 Buenos Aires, Argentina

First published: 1981
Sponsoring organization: Consejo Nacional de Investigaciones Científicas y Técnicas de la República Argentina
ISSN: 0326-0941
MLA acronym: Incipit

SUBSCRIPTION INFORMATION

Frequency of publication: Annual
Circulation: 400
Available in microform: No
Subscription price: $18.00/yr. institutions; $12.00/yr. individuals
Year to which price refers: 1992

ADVERTISING INFORMATION

Advertising accepted: Yes
Advertising rates: $60.00/half page; $100.00/ full page

EDITORIAL DESCRIPTION

Scope: Publishes articles dealing with textual criticism of Spanish literary texts.
Reviews books: Yes
Publishes notes: Yes
Languages accepted: Spanish
Prints abstracts: No
Author-anonymous submission: No

SUBMISSION REQUIREMENTS

Restrictions on contributors: Contributors must be members of Consejo Asesor.
Author pays submission fee: No
Author pays page charges: No
Length of articles: 19,000 words
Length of book reviews: 1,000 words maximum
Length of notes: 5,000 words
Style: Journal
Number of copies required: 1
Special requirements: Submit original typescript; include notes at end.
Copyright ownership: German Orduna
Rejected manuscripts: Returned
Time before publication decision: 1 mo.
Time between decision and publication: 1 yr.
Number of reviewers: 1
Articles submitted per year: 5
Articles published per year: 5
Book reviews submitted per year: 7
Book reviews published per year: 7
Notes submitted per year: 3
Notes published per year: 3

(1231)
*Incontri Linguistici

G. Cifoletti, F. Crevatin, M. Doria, G. Francesca, & V. Orioles, Editors
Giardini Editori e Stampatori in Pisa, S.r.l.
Via Delle Sorgenti, 23
56010 Agnano Pisano, Italy

Additional editorial address: Ist. di Glottologia, Via dell'Università, Univ. di Trieste, 34100 Trieste, Italy
Telephone: (39) 50 855390
Fax: (39) 50 856106
First published: 1974
Sponsoring organization: Univ. degli Studi di Udine e Trieste
ISSN: 0390-2412
MLA acronym: InLi

SUBSCRIPTION INFORMATION

Frequency of publication: Annual
Circulation: 400
Available in microform: No
Subscription price: 170,000 Lit/yr.
Year to which price refers: 1992

ADVERTISING INFORMATION

Advertising accepted: Yes

EDITORIAL DESCRIPTION

Scope: Publishes articles on all aspects of current research in the field of linguistic sciences.
Reviews books: Yes
Languages accepted: English; French; German; Italian; Spanish
Prints abstracts: No

SUBMISSION REQUIREMENTS

Restrictions on contributors: None
Author pays submission fee: No
Author pays page charges: No
Length of articles: 15 typescript pp. maximum
Length of book reviews: 1 typescript p. maximum
Style: Journal
Number of copies required: 1
Copyright ownership: Journal
Rejected manuscripts: Returned
Time before publication decision: 2 mos.
Time between decision and publication: 1 yr.
Number of reviewers: 4

(1232)
*The Independent Shavian

Richard Nickson & Douglas Laurie, Editors
Bernard Shaw Soc.
Box 1159 Madison Square Station
New York, NY 10159-1159

First published: 1957
Sponsoring organization: Bernard Shaw Soc.
ISSN: 0019-3763
MLA acronym: ISh

SUBSCRIPTION INFORMATION

Frequency of publication: 3 times/yr. (Fall, Winter, Spring)
Circulation: 400
Available in microform: Yes
Subscription price: $18.00/yr. US; $20.00/yr. elsewhere
Year to which price refers: 1992
Subscription telephone: 212 989-7833

ADVERTISING INFORMATION

Advertising accepted: Yes

EDITORIAL DESCRIPTION

Scope: Publishes articles on Bernard Shaw and items related to his life and works.
Reviews books: Yes
Publishes notes: Yes
Languages accepted: English
Prints abstracts: No
Author-anonymous submission: No

SUBMISSION REQUIREMENTS

Restrictions on contributors: None
Author pays submission fee: No
Author pays page charges: No
Length of articles: 500-5,000 words
Length of book reviews: 1,000 words
Length of notes: 100 words
Style: MLA
Number of copies required: 1
Copyright ownership: Author
Rejected manuscripts: Returned at author's request; enclose return postage.
Time before publication decision: 1 mo.
Time between decision and publication: 3 mos.
Number of reviewers: 4
Articles submitted per year: 25
Articles published per year: 18
Book reviews submitted per year: 12
Book reviews published per year: 9
Notes published per year: 25

(1233)
*Index on Censorship

Andrew Graham-Yooll, Editor
39c Highbury Place
London N5 1QP, England

Telephone: (44) 71 3590161
Fax: (44) 71 3548665
First published: 1972
Sponsoring organization: Writers & Scholars International Ltd.
ISSN: 0306-4220
MLA acronym: IonC

SUBSCRIPTION INFORMATION

Frequency of publication: 10 times/yr.
Circulation: 5,000
Available in microform: Yes
Subscription price: $39.00/yr.
Year to which price refers: 1992

ADVERTISING INFORMATION

Advertising accepted: Yes
Advertising rates: $450.00/half page; $800.00/ full page

EDITORIAL DESCRIPTION

Scope: The journal specializes in contemporary writers and journalists worldwide who are censored or otherwise silenced on account of their opinions or ideas. It publishes examples of their banned work (novel extracts, plays, poems, essays, statements); provides primary sources on unofficial and samizdat publications, and a platform for writers to describe their experience or opinions of censorship. It includes profiles of banned writers and a country-by-country chronicle listing acts of censorship.
Reviews books: Yes
Publishes notes: Yes
Languages accepted: English; Czech; Spanish; Russian
Prints abstracts: No
Author-anonymous submission: No

SUBMISSION REQUIREMENTS

Restrictions on contributors: None
Author pays submission fee: No
Author pays page charges: No
Length of articles: 1,000-3,000 words
Length of book reviews: 750 words
Length of notes: 400 words
Style: None
Number of copies required: 1
Copyright ownership: Author
Rejected manuscripts: Returned at author's request
Time before publication decision: 3 mos.
Time between decision and publication: 3 mos.
Number of reviewers: 2
Articles submitted per year: 200
Articles published per year: 100
Book reviews submitted per year: 40
Book reviews published per year: 20
Notes submitted per year: 200
Notes published per year: 100

(1234)
*Indian Horizons

A. Srinivasan, Editor
Indian Council for Cultural Relations
Azad Bhavan
Indraprastha Estate
New Delhi 110002, India

Telephone: (91) 11 3318647; (91) 11 3319309
Fax: (91) 11 3712639
First published: 1952
Sponsoring organization: Indian Council for Cultural Relations
ISSN: 0019-7203
MLA acronym: IndH

SUBSCRIPTION INFORMATION

Frequency of publication: 4 times/yr.
Circulation: 1,700
Available in microform: Yes
Subscription price: $10.00/yr., $25.00/3 yrs.; $2.50/single issue
Year to which price refers: 1992

ADVERTISING INFORMATION

Advertising accepted: No

EDITORIAL DESCRIPTION

Scope: Publishes articles on Indian culture, fiction, performing and fine arts, and on intercultural themes involving India.
Reviews books: Yes
Publishes notes: Yes
Languages accepted: English; Spanish; French; Arabic
Prints abstracts: No
Author-anonymous submission: No

SUBMISSION REQUIREMENTS

Restrictions on contributors: Most articles are commissioned; some uncommissioned articles are accepted.
Author pays submission fee: No
Author pays page charges: No
Length of articles: 5,000 words
Length of book reviews: 700 words
Length of notes: 300 words
Style: IH, ICCR, New Delhi
Number of copies required: 2
Special requirements: Submit original double-spaced typescript and 1 copy.
Copyright ownership: Indian Council for Cultural Relations
Rejected manuscripts: Returned
Time before publication decision: 1 mo.
Time between decision and publication: 6-12 mos.
Number of reviewers: 1
Articles submitted per year: 40-45
Articles published per year: 25
Book reviews submitted per year: 40-45
Book reviews published per year: 20
Notes submitted per year: 50-60
Notes published per year: 15-20

(1235)
*Indian Journal of Applied Linguistics

Ujjal Singh Bahri, Editor
Bahri Books & Periodicals
997A, Street No. 9
P.O. Box 4453
Gobindpuri, Kalkaji
New Delhi 110019, India

Telephone: (91) 11 6445710; (91) 11 6448606
Fax: (91) 11 6460796
First published: 1975
ISSN: 0379-0037
MLA acronym: IJOAL

SUBSCRIPTION INFORMATION

Frequency of publication: 2 times/yr. (Jan., July)
Circulation: 870
Available in microform: No
Subscription price: $40.00/yr. institutions; $30.00/yr. individuals
Year to which price refers: 1993

ADVERTISING INFORMATION

Advertising accepted: Yes
Advertising rates: $100.00/full page

EDITORIAL DESCRIPTION

Scope: Publishes articles on theoretical and methodological ideas and research from the several disciplines engaged in applied linguistics.
Reviews books: Yes
Publishes notes: Yes
Languages accepted: English
Prints abstracts: Yes
Author-anonymous submission: Yes

SUBMISSION REQUIREMENTS

Restrictions on contributors: None
Author pays submission fee: Yes, if paper is lengthy.
Cost of submission fee: $50.00
Author pays page charges: No
Length of articles: 20-25 pp.
Length of book reviews: 12 pp.
Length of notes: 10 pp.
Style: MLA
Number of copies required: 2
Special requirements: Submit double-spaced typescript on A4 sized (8 1/4 in. x 11 3/4 in.) paper. Maps, drawings, and tables should be drawn on film strip to facilitate camera use.
Copyright ownership: Bahri Publications
Rejected manuscripts: Returned; enclose return postage.
Time before publication decision: 2-8 mos.
Time between decision and publication: 10 weeks
Number of reviewers: 2
Articles submitted per year: 20-30
Articles published per year: 18-20
Book reviews submitted per year: 5-6
Book reviews published per year: 2-3
Notes submitted per year: 2-3
Notes published per year: 2-3

(1236)
Indian Journal of Linguistics/Praci-Bhasha-Vijnan

Bhakti P. Mallik, U. N. Singh, Swapan Banerjee, & Krishna Bhattacharya, Editors
Bangiya Vijnan Parishad
P-23 Raja Rajkrishna St.
Calcutta 700006, India

First published: 1974
Sponsoring organization: West Bengal Inst. of Linguistics
MLA acronym: IJL

SUBSCRIPTION INFORMATION

Frequency of publication: 2 times/yr.
Circulation: 325
Available in microform: No
Subscription address: 7 Iswar Mill Bye Lane, Calcutta 700006, India

ADVERTISING INFORMATION

Advertising accepted: Yes

EDITORIAL DESCRIPTION

Scope: Invites theoretical and experimental papers on linguistics and interdisciplinary studies throughout the world. Gives particular emphasis to papers on linguistic problems related to India and surrounding countries.
Reviews books: Yes
Publishes notes: Yes
Languages accepted: English
Prints abstracts: No

SUBMISSION REQUIREMENTS

Restrictions on contributors: None
Author pays submission fee: No
Author pays page charges: No
Length of articles: 5,000 words
Length of book reviews: No restrictions
Length of notes: 1,000 words
Style: Linguistic Soc. of India, Poona
Number of copies required: 2
Special requirements: Submit original double-spaced typescript.
Copyright ownership: Journal
Rejected manuscripts: Not returned
Time before publication decision: 3 mos.
Time between decision and publication: 6-12 mos.
Number of reviewers: 2
Articles submitted per year: 24
Articles published per year: 14
Book reviews submitted per year: 6
Book reviews published per year: 6
Notes submitted per year: 1-2
Notes published per year: 1-2

(1237)
*Indian Linguistics: Journal of the Linguistic Society of India

Suresh Kumar, K. V. Subbarao, Anvita Abbi, & Y. Wadhwani, Editors
Linguistic Soc. of India
Deccan College
Pune 411006, India

First published: 1931
Sponsoring organization: Linguistic Soc. of India
ISSN: 0378-0759
MLA acronym: IndLing

SUBSCRIPTION INFORMATION

Frequency of publication: Annual
Circulation: 1,500
Available in microform: No
Subscription price: $20.00/yr.
Year to which price refers: 1991
Subscription address: Secretary, at the above address

ADVERTISING INFORMATION

Advertising accepted: No

EDITORIAL DESCRIPTION

Scope: Publishes articles and reviews of interest to the scientific study of language, especially the languages of India.
Reviews books: Yes
Publishes notes: Yes
Languages accepted: English
Prints abstracts: Yes
Author-anonymous submission: No

SUBMISSION REQUIREMENTS

Restrictions on contributors: Contributors must be members of the Linguistic Soc. of India.
Author pays submission fee: No
Author pays page charges: No
Length of articles: 50 typescript pp. maximum
Length of book reviews: 5 pp. maximum
Length of notes: 100-150 words
Style: Linguistic Soc. of India
Number of copies required: 3
Special requirements: Submit original typescript.
Copyright ownership: Linguistic Soc. of India
Rejected manuscripts: 1 copy returned at author's request
Time before publication decision: 3 mos.
Time between decision and publication: 3 mos.
Number of reviewers: 1-2
Articles submitted per year: 60-70
Articles published per year: 30-35
Book reviews submitted per year: 15-20
Book reviews published per year: 15-20
Notes submitted per year: 5-10
Notes published per year: 5-10

(1238)
The Indian Literary Review: A Tri-Quarterly of Indian Literature

Devindra Kohli & Suresh Kohli, Editors
T-58 D C M School Marg
New Rohtak Rd.
New Delhi 110005, India

First published: 1978
MLA acronym: ILR

SUBSCRIPTION INFORMATION

Frequency of publication: 3 times/yr. (Jan., Apr., Oct.)
Circulation: 300
Available in microform: No

ADVERTISING INFORMATION

Advertising accepted: Yes

EDITORIAL DESCRIPTION

Scope: Seeks to present the distinctly Indian identity of English writing in India as well as to make available in English translation some of the outstanding work being done in other Indian languages.
Reviews books: Yes
Publishes notes: No
Languages accepted: English
Prints abstracts: No
Author-anonymous submission: No

SUBMISSION REQUIREMENTS

Restrictions on contributors: Book reviews are commissioned.
Author pays submission fee: No
Author pays page charges: No
Length of articles: 3,000-5,000 words
Length of book reviews: 1,000-1,500 words
Style: The Sewanee Review
Number of copies required: 1
Special requirements: Submit typescript.
Copyright ownership: Author
Rejected manuscripts: Returned; enclose SASE or international reply coupons.
Time before publication decision: 2 mos.
Time between decision and publication: 6 mos.
Number of reviewers: 3
Articles submitted per year: 300
Articles published per year: 60
Book reviews published per year: 30

(1239)
*Indian Literature

K. Satchidanandan, Editor
Sahitya Akademi
Rabindra Bhavan
35 Ferozeshah Rd.
New Delhi 110001, India

First published: 1957
Sponsoring organization: Sahitya Akademi
ISSN: 0019-5804
MLA acronym: IndL

SUBSCRIPTION INFORMATION

Frequency of publication: 6 times/yr.
Circulation: 2,000
Available in microform: No
Subscription price: 80 Re ($35.00)/yr.
Year to which price refers: 1992
Subscription address: Sahitya Akademi, Sales Dept., "Swati", Mandir Marg, New Delhi 110001, India

ADVERTISING INFORMATION

Advertising accepted: No

EDITORIAL DESCRIPTION

Scope: Publishes articles on Indian literatures, as well as poems, stories, plays, etc. in translation from twenty-two Indian languages.
Reviews books: Yes
Publishes notes: Yes
Languages accepted: English
Prints abstracts: No
Author-anonymous submission: No

SUBMISSION REQUIREMENTS

Restrictions on contributors: None
Author pays submission fee: No
Author pays page charges: No
Length of articles: 2,500 words
Length of book reviews: 800 words
Length of notes: 2,000 words
Style: MLA
Number of copies required: 1
Special requirements: Submit original typescript.
Copyright ownership: Author
Rejected manuscripts: Returned
Time before publication decision: 1 mo.
Time between decision and publication: 1 yr.
Number of reviewers: 1
Articles submitted per year: 500
Articles published per year: 100
Book reviews submitted per year: 120
Book reviews published per year: 50
Notes submitted per year: 100
Notes published per year: 25-50

(1240)
*The Indian P.E.N.

Nissim Ezekiel, Editor
Theosophy Hall
40 New Marine Lines
Bombay 400 020, India

Telephone: (91) 22 292175
First published: 1934
Sponsoring organization: PEN All-India Centre
ISSN: 0019-6053
MLA acronym: IPEN

SUBSCRIPTION INFORMATION

Frequency of publication: 4 times/yr. (Mar., June, Sept., Dec.)
Circulation: 500
Available in microform: No
Subscription price: 30 Re ($7.50, £4.00)/yr.
Year to which price refers: 1992
Subscription telephone: (91) 22 299024

ADVERTISING INFORMATION

Advertising accepted: Yes
Advertising rates: 600 Re ($50.00)/full page; 750 Re ($60.00)/inside back cover; 900 Re ($70.00)/inside front cover; 1,000 Re ($90.00)/back cover

EDITORIAL DESCRIPTION

Scope: Promotes Indian literature.
Reviews books: Yes
Publishes notes: Yes
Languages accepted: English
Prints abstracts: No
Author-anonymous submission: No

SUBMISSION REQUIREMENTS

Restrictions on contributors: None
Author pays submission fee: No
Author pays page charges: No
Length of articles: 1,200-1,500 words
Length of book reviews: 1,000 words
Length of notes: 200 words
Style: MLA
Number of copies required: 1
Copyright ownership: Author
Rejected manuscripts: Returned; enclose return postage or international reply coupons.
Time before publication decision: 2 weeks
Time between decision and publication: 6 mos.
Number of reviewers: 2
Articles submitted per year: 50
Articles published per year: 12
Book reviews submitted per year: 20
Book reviews published per year: 10
Notes submitted per year: 20
Notes published per year: 10

(1241)
*Indiana University Uralic and Altaic Series

Denis Sinor, Editor
Goodbody Hall
Indiana Univ.
Bloomington, IN 47405

Telephone: 812 855-1605
Fax: 812 855-7500
First published: 1960
Sponsoring organization: Research Inst. for Inner Asian Studies, Indiana Univ.
ISSN: 0893-2913
MLA acronym: IUPUAS

SUBSCRIPTION INFORMATION

Frequency of publication: 1-2 times/yr.
Available in microform: No

ADVERTISING INFORMATION

Advertising accepted: No

EDITORIAL DESCRIPTION

Scope: Publishes works on languages, linguistics, history, and civilization of the Uralic and Inner Asian (Turkic, Mongol, Tunguz, Tibetan) peoples.
Reviews books: No
Publishes notes: No
Languages accepted: English
Prints abstracts: No

SUBMISSION REQUIREMENTS

Author pays submission fee: No
Author pays page charges: No
Length of books: 20,000-25,000 words
Number of copies required: 1
Special requirements: Submit camera-ready copy according to specifications of series.
Copyright ownership: Research Inst. for Inner Asian Studies
Rejected manuscripts: Returned
Time before publication decision: 1-2 mos.
Time between decision and publication: 3-12 mos.
Number of reviewers: 2
Books submitted per year: 4-5
Books published per year: 1-3

(1242)
*Indo-Iranian Journal

J. W. de Jong, Michael Witzel, & H. W. Bodewitz, Editors
c/o H. W. Bodewitz
Inst. voor Oosterse Talen
Drift 15
3512 BR Utrecht, Netherlands

Additional editorial address: M. Witzel, Dept. of Sanskrit & Indian Studies, Phillips Brook House, Harvard Univ., Cambridge, MA 02138
First published: 1957
ISSN: 0019-7246
MLA acronym: IIJ

SUBSCRIPTION INFORMATION

Frequency of publication: 4 times/yr. (Jan., Apr., July, Oct.)
Circulation: 550
Available in microform: Yes
Subscription price: 302 f ($154.00)/yr.
Year to which price refers: 1992
Subscription address: Kluwer Academic Publisher Group, P.O. Box 322, 3300 AH Dordrecht, Netherlands
Additional subscription address: Kluwer Academic Publishers, P.O. Box 358, Accord Station, Hingham, MA 02018-0358

ADVERTISING INFORMATION

Advertising accepted: Yes

EDITORIAL DESCRIPTION

Scope: Publishes articles on Old and Middle Iranian, Indology in the widest sense of the word (with the exception of archaeology and history proper), Tibetology and Buddhist studies, and Munda and Dravidian studies.
Reviews books: Yes
Publishes notes: Yes
Languages accepted: English; German; French
Prints abstracts: No
Author-anonymous submission: No

SUBMISSION REQUIREMENTS

Restrictions on contributors: None
Author pays submission fee: No
Author pays page charges: Yes
Length of articles: 25 pp. maximum
Length of book reviews: 4 pp. maximum
Length of notes: 2 pp. maximum
Style: Journal
Number of copies required: 1
Special requirements: Submit original typescript.
Copyright ownership: Assigned by author to journal
Rejected manuscripts: Returned
Time before publication decision: 1 mo.
Time between decision and publication: 1-2 yrs.
Number of reviewers: 1-2
Articles submitted per year: 15
Articles published per year: 10
Book reviews submitted per year: 40
Book reviews published per year: 40
Notes submitted per year: 6
Notes published per year: 5

(1243)
*Indogermanische Forschungen: Zeitschrift für Indogermanistik und Allgemeine Sprachwissenschaft

Wolfgang P. Schmid, Editor
Schladeberg 20
3403 Friedland 5 (OT. Niedernjesa), Germany

Telephone: (49) 5509 1336
First published: 1891
ISSN: 0019-7262
MLA acronym: IF

SUBSCRIPTION INFORMATION

Frequency of publication: Annual
Circulation: 400
Available in microform: No
Subscription price: 196 DM/yr.
Year to which price refers: 1991
Subscription address: Walter de Gruyter & Co., Genthiner Str. 13, 1000 Berlin 30, Germany
Subscription telephone: (49) 30 260050

ADVERTISING INFORMATION

Advertising accepted: No

EDITORIAL DESCRIPTION

Scope: Focuses on historical linguistics, primarily of Indo-European languages.
Reviews books: Yes
Publishes notes: No
Languages accepted: English; French; German; Italian
Prints abstracts: No
Author-anonymous submission: No

SUBMISSION REQUIREMENTS

Restrictions on contributors: Contributors must be post-graduates.
Author pays submission fee: No
Author pays page charges: No
Length of articles: 10-15 pp.
Length of book reviews: 2-3 pp.
Style: Journal
Number of copies required: 1
Special requirements: Submit original typescript on size A4 (8 1/4 in. x 11 3/4 in.) paper.
Copyright ownership: Assigned by author to journal
Rejected manuscripts: Returned
Time before publication decision: 1 mo.
Time between decision and publication: 2 yrs.
Number of reviewers: 1
Articles submitted per year: 30-35
Articles published per year: 20-25
Book reviews submitted per year: 40-50
Book reviews published per year: 35-40

(1244)
*Indonesia

Audrey Kahin, Editor
Cornell Modern Indonesia Project
640 Stewart Ave.
Ithaca, NY 14850

Telephone: 607 255-4359
First published: 1966
Sponsoring organization: Cornell Univ., Southeast Asia Program
MLA acronym: Indonesia

SUBSCRIPTION INFORMATION

Frequency of publication: 2 times/yr.
Circulation: 700
Available in microform: Yes, through Univ. Microfilms International
Subscription price: $18.00/yr. US; $23.00/yr. elsewhere
Year to which price refers: 1992
Subscription address: Southeast Asia Program Publications, Cornell Univ., East Hill Plaza, Ithaca, NY 14850
Subscription telephone: 607 255-8038

ADVERTISING INFORMATION

Advertising accepted: No

EDITORIAL DESCRIPTION

Scope: Publishes articles on all fields relating to Indonesia, including history, anthropology, and linguistics. Also publishes translations of short stories and documents.
Reviews books: Yes
Publishes notes: No
Languages accepted: English
Prints abstracts: No
Author-anonymous submission: No

SUBMISSION REQUIREMENTS

Restrictions on contributors: Reviews are usually solicited.
Author pays submission fee: No
Author pays page charges: No
Length of articles: 4,000-7,000 words
Length of book reviews: 1,500-2,500 words
Style: Chicago
Number of copies required: 1
Special requirements: Include a short statement of author's institutional affiliation and status.
Copyright ownership: Southeast Asia Program
Rejected manuscripts: Returned
Time before publication decision: 1-4 mos.
Time between decision and publication: 3-6 mos.
Number of reviewers: 2-3
Articles submitted per year: 30-40
Articles published per year: 14
Book reviews published per year: 4-6

(1245)
*Infant Behavior and Development: An International and Interdisciplinary Journal

Carolyn K. Rovee-Collier, Editor
Dept. of Psychology
Busch Campus
Rutgers Univ.
New Brunswick, NJ 08903

Telephone: 908 932-3364
Fax: 908 932-2263
E-mail: GCOLLIER@ZODIAC.RUTGERS.-EDU
First published: 1978
Sponsoring organization: International Soc. for Infant Studies
ISSN: 0163-6383
MLA acronym: IBD

SUBSCRIPTION INFORMATION

Frequency of publication: 4 times/yr.
Circulation: 1,500
Available in microform: No
Subscription price: $105.00/yr. institutions; $45.00/yr. individuals
Year to which price refers: 1992
Subscription address: Ablex Publishing Corp., 355 Chestnut St., Norwood, NJ 07648
Subscription telephone: 201 767-8450
Subscription fax: 201 767-6717

ADVERTISING INFORMATION

Advertising accepted: No

EDITORIAL DESCRIPTION

Scope: Covers experimental psychology, developmental biology, pediatrics, psychiatry, nutrition, anthropometry, sociology, anthropology, vision, audition, speech, and hearing and all other fields relating to infant and child development.
Reviews books: No
Publishes notes: Yes
Languages accepted: English
Prints abstracts: Yes
Author-anonymous submission: No

SUBMISSION REQUIREMENTS

Restrictions on contributors: None
Author pays submission fee: No
Author pays page charges: No
Length of articles: 20-25 pp. maximum
Length of notes: 4 pp.
Style: American Psychological Assn.
Number of copies required: 4
Special requirements: Submit double-spaced typescript on 8 1/2 in. x 11 in. bond with 1 in. margins on all sides. Include footnotes at end and a 100-150 word abstract. No originals of artwork should be submitted. No DMP accepted. See journal for more information.
Copyright ownership: Ablex Publishing Corp.
Rejected manuscripts: Returned; enclose return postage.
Time before publication decision: 2-4 mos.
Time between decision and publication: 6-12 mos.
Number of reviewers: 3
Articles submitted per year: 120-130
Articles published per year: 40-55
Notes submitted per year: 4
Notes published per year: 2

(1246)
L'Infini

Philippe Sollers, Editor
Editions Gallimard
5, rue Sébastien-Bottin
75007 Paris, France

Telephone: (33) 1 49544200
ISSN: 0040-2419
MLA acronym: Infini

SUBSCRIPTION INFORMATION

Frequency of publication: 4 times/yr.
Available in microform: No
Subscription price: 287 F/yr. France; 336 F/yr. elsewhere
Year to which price refers: 1992

ADVERTISING INFORMATION

Advertising accepted: No

EDITORIAL DESCRIPTION

Scope: Publishes articles on literature, philosophy, science, and politics.
Reviews books: Yes
Publishes notes: Yes
Languages accepted: French
Prints abstracts: No

SUBMISSION REQUIREMENTS

Author pays page charges: No
Special requirements: Quotations in English are permitted.

(1247)
*L'Information Grammaticale

Guy Serbat & Irène Tamba, Editors
Sorbonne
1, rue Victor-Cousin
75005 Paris, France

First published: 1979
Sponsoring organization: Soc. pour l'Information Grammaticale
ISSN: 0222-9838
MLA acronym: IG

SUBSCRIPTION INFORMATION

Frequency of publication: 4 times/yr. (Jan., Mar., June, Oct.)
Available in microform: No
Subscription price: 200 F/yr.
Year to which price refers: 1992

ADVERTISING INFORMATION

Advertising accepted: Yes

EDITORIAL DESCRIPTION

Scope: Publishes articles on linguistics with an emphasis on the French language.
Reviews books: Yes
Publishes notes: Yes
Languages accepted: French; English; German; Spanish; Italian
Prints abstracts: Yes
Author-anonymous submission: No

SUBMISSION REQUIREMENTS

Restrictions on contributors: Contributors must be members of Soc. pour l'Information Grammaticale.
Author pays submission fee: No
Author pays page charges: No
Length of articles: 5,400 words
Length of book reviews: 1,500 words
Length of notes: 500 words
Number of copies required: 1
Rejected manuscripts: Not returned
Time before publication decision: 2-6 mos.
Time between decision and publication: 1-3 mos.
Number of reviewers: 2
Articles submitted per year: 45-50
Articles published per year: 40
Book reviews submitted per year: 20-30
Book reviews published per year: 20-25
Notes submitted per year: 12
Notes published per year: 8

(1248)
*L'Information Littéraire: Revue Paraissant Cinq Fois par An

M. Néraudau & M. Desgranges, Editors
Société d'Edition les Belles Lettres
95, Bd. Raspail
75006 Paris, France

Telephone: (33) 1 45487055
Fax: (33) 1 45449288
First published: 1949
Sponsoring organization: Soc. d'Edition les Belles Lettres
ISSN: 0020-0123
MLA acronym: IL

SUBSCRIPTION INFORMATION

Frequency of publication: 5 times/yr. (Feb., Apr., June, Oct., Dec.)
Circulation: 6,000
Available in microform: No
Subscription price: 260 F/yr.
Year to which price refers: 1992

ADVERTISING INFORMATION

Advertising accepted: Yes

EDITORIAL DESCRIPTION

Scope: Publishes articles on French literature.
Reviews books: Yes
Publishes notes: Yes
Languages accepted: French
Prints abstracts: No
Author-anonymous submission: No

SUBMISSION REQUIREMENTS

Author pays submission fee: No
Author pays page charges: No
Length of articles: 6 pp.
Length of book reviews: 20 lines
Length of notes: 2 pp.
Number of copies required: 2
Copyright ownership: Author
Rejected manuscripts: Returned
Time before publication decision: 6 mos.
Time between decision and publication: 1 mo.
Number of reviewers: 2
Articles submitted per year: 30
Articles published per year: 25
Book reviews submitted per year: 60
Book reviews published per year: 60
Notes submitted per year: 12
Notes published per year: 12

(1249)
*Information/Communication

Parth Bhatt, Editor
Canadian Scholars' Press, Inc.
211 Grenadier St.
Toronto, ON M6R 1R9, Canada

Additional editorial address: Dept. of French, 7 King's College Circle, Univ. of Toronto, Toronto, Ontario M5S 1A1, Canada
Telephone: 416 978-8131
Fax: 416 978-8131
First published: 1980
Sponsoring organization: Experimental Phonetics Lab, Univ. of Toronto
ISSN: 0842-0130
MLA acronym: I/C

SUBSCRIPTION INFORMATION

Frequency of publication: Irregular
Circulation: 200
Available in microform: No

Subscription price: C$10.00/yr.
Year to which price refers: 1991
Additional subscription address: Didier Erudition, 6 rue de la Sorbonne, 75005 Paris, France

ADVERTISING INFORMATION

Advertising accepted: No

EDITORIAL DESCRIPTION

Scope: Publishes articles on linguistics and subjects related to communication.
Reviews books: Yes
Publishes notes: Yes
Languages accepted: French; English
Prints abstracts: Yes
Author-anonymous submission: Yes

SUBMISSION REQUIREMENTS

Restrictions on contributors: None
Author pays submission fee: No
Author pays page charges: No
Length of articles: 10 pp.
Length of book reviews: 500 words
Style: Chicago
Number of copies required: 2
Copyright ownership: Canadian Scholars' Press
Rejected manuscripts: Not returned
Time before publication decision: 2 weeks
Number of reviewers: 4
Articles submitted per year: 50
Articles published per year: 20
Book reviews submitted per year: 10-20
Book reviews published per year: 10-20

(1250)
*Initiales/Initials: Travaux des Etudiants de Cycle Supérieur, Département de Français, Université Dalhousie/Graduate Students' Writings, Department of French, Dalhousie University

Rostislav Kocourek & Hans R. Runte, Editors
Dept. of French
Dalhousie Univ.
Halifax, NS B3H 3H3, Canada

Telephone: 902 492-2430
Fax: 902 494-2319
First published: 1981
Sponsoring organization: Dept. of French, Dalhousie Univ.
ISSN: 0710-4278
MLA acronym: Initiales

SUBSCRIPTION INFORMATION

Frequency of publication: Annual
Circulation: 30
Available in microform: No
Subscription price: C$9.00/yr.
Year to which price refers: 1992

ADVERTISING INFORMATION

Advertising accepted: No

EDITORIAL DESCRIPTION

Scope: Publishes articles by graduate students at Dalhousie University, and other universities, in the areas of French literature and linguistics in the broad sense, including stylistics, poetics, text linguistics, semiotics, terminology, translation, Acadian dialectology, and French language studies.
Reviews books: No
Publishes notes: No
Languages accepted: French; English
Prints abstracts: No
Author-anonymous submission: No

SUBMISSION REQUIREMENTS

Author pays submission fee: No
Author pays page charges: No
Length of articles: 12,000 words maximum
Style: MLA; Linguistic Soc. of America
Number of copies required: 2
Rejected manuscripts: Not returned
Time before publication decision: 2 mos.
Time between decision and publication: 10 mos.
Number of reviewers: 2-3
Articles submitted per year: 12
Articles published per year: 6

(1251)
Initiation à la Linguistique

Pierre Guiraud & Alain Rey, Editors
Klincksieck
11, rue de Lille
75007 Paris, France

First published: 1970
ISSN: 0073-8018
MLA acronym: ILing

SUBSCRIPTION INFORMATION

Frequency of publication: Irregular

(1252)
*Inklings: Jahrbuch für Literatur und Ästhetik

Gisbert Kranz, Editor
Erster Rote-Haag-Weg 31
5100 Aachen, Germany

Telephone: (49) 241 61876
First published: 1983
Sponsoring organization: Inklings-Gesellschaft
ISSN: 0176-3733
MLA acronym: Inklings

SUBSCRIPTION INFORMATION

Frequency of publication: Annual
Circulation: 400
Available in microform: No
Subscription price: 150 DM/yr. institutions; 50 DM/yr. individuals; 25 DM/yr. students
Year to which price refers: 1992

ADVERTISING INFORMATION

Advertising accepted: Yes

EDITORIAL DESCRIPTION

Scope: Publishes articles on the Oxford Inklings and their forerunners and followers.
Reviews books: Yes
Publishes notes: Yes
Languages accepted: German; English
Prints abstracts: Yes
Author-anonymous submission: No

SUBMISSION REQUIREMENTS

Restrictions on contributors: None
Author pays submission fee: No
Author pays page charges: No
Length of articles: 5,000 words
Length of book reviews: 500-1,000 words
Length of notes: 1,000 words
Style: MLA
Number of copies required: 2
Special requirements: Submissions should be made exclusively.
Copyright ownership: Author
Rejected manuscripts: Returned; enclose SASE.
Time before publication decision: 6 mos. maximum
Time between decision and publication: 6-24 mos.
Number of reviewers: 7

Articles submitted per year: 25
Articles published per year: 12-20
Book reviews submitted per year: 40
Book reviews published per year: 30
Notes submitted per year: 8
Notes published per year: 4

(1253)
Inmun Kwahak: The Journal of Humanities

Chong-young Lee, Editor
Inst. of Humanistic Studies
Liberal Arts College
Yonsei Univ.
Shinchon, Seoul, 120, Korea

First published: 1957
Sponsoring organization: Yonsei Univ., Liberal Arts College
ISSN: 0537-7137
MLA acronym: IKw

SUBSCRIPTION INFORMATION

Frequency of publication: 2 times/yr.
Circulation: 1,600
Subscription address: Yonsei Univ. Press, 134 Sinchon-Dong, Seodaemoon-Ku, Seoul, Korea

EDITORIAL DESCRIPTION

Scope: Publishes articles on humanities.
Reviews books: Yes
Languages accepted: Korean; Chinese languages; English; French; German
Prints abstracts: Yes

SUBMISSION REQUIREMENTS

Restrictions on contributors: Unsolicited manuscripts are not accepted.
Length of articles: 20 double-spaced typescript pp.
Style: MLA for literature; Linguistic Soc. of America for linguistics
Number of copies required: 1
Special requirements: Submit abstract (in other language).
Copyright ownership: Author
Rejected manuscripts: Returned
Time before publication decision: 2 mo.
Time between decision and publication: 3 mos.
Number of reviewers: 3
Articles published per year: 12-15

(1254)
*Innsbrucker Beiträge zur Kulturwissenschaft: Germanistische Reihe

Johann Holzner, Hans Moser, Oskar Putzer, Sigurd Paul Scheichl, & Max Siller, Editors
Inst. für Germanistik
Univ. Innsbruck
Innrain 52
6020 Innsbruck, Austria

Telephone: (43) 512 5073452
Fax: (43) 512 5072777
MLA acronym: IBK

SUBSCRIPTION INFORMATION

Frequency of publication: Irregular
Available in microform: No

ADVERTISING INFORMATION

Advertising accepted: Yes

EDITORIAL DESCRIPTION

Languages accepted: German
Prints abstracts: Yes

Author-anonymous submission: No

SUBMISSION REQUIREMENTS

Author pays submission fee: No
Author pays page charges: No
Books published per year: 4

(1255)
*Inostrannye Iazyki v Shkole

N. P. Kamenetskaya & V. I. Yuniyev, Editors
Kedrov St. 8
Moscow 117804, Russia

First published: 1934
ISSN: 0130-6073
MLA acronym: IJŠ

SUBSCRIPTION INFORMATION

Frequency of publication: 6 times/yr.
Circulation: 130,000
Available in microform: No
Subscription price: $23.00/yr.
Year to which price refers: 1993
Additional subscription address: Victor Kamkin Inc., 4956 Boiling Brook Pkwy., Rockville, MD 20852

ADVERTISING INFORMATION

Advertising accepted: Yes
Advertising rates: $100.00/full page; $200.00/cover

EDITORIAL DESCRIPTION

Scope: Publishes articles on the teaching of language, including methods, psychology, linguistics, and culture of the countries.
Reviews books: Yes
Publishes notes: Yes
Languages accepted: Russian; English; French; German
Prints abstracts: Yes
Author-anonymous submission: No

SUBMISSION REQUIREMENTS

Restrictions on contributors: None
Author pays submission fee: No
Author pays page charges: No
Length of articles: 1,600-2,000 words
Length of book reviews: 800-1,000 words
Length of notes: 600-800 words
Number of copies required: 2
Special requirements: Submit original typescript and 1 copy.
Copyright ownership: Journal; reverts to author after 2 yrs.
Rejected manuscripts: Returned; enclose return postage
Time before publication decision: 2 mos.
Time between decision and publication: 4 mos.
Number of reviewers: 2-4
Articles submitted per year: 200-250
Articles published per year: 150-160
Book reviews submitted per year: 5-10
Book reviews published per year: 3-5
Notes submitted per year: 50-70
Notes published per year: 20-30

(1256)
*Inozemna Filolohiia

K. Ja. Kusko, & B. V. Maksimchuk, Editors
L'vov Univ.
L'vov, Ukraine

Additional editorial address: A. O. Biletski, Boulevard Shevchenko 14, Kiev-17, Ukraine
First published: 1948
Sponsoring organization: L'vov Univ.; Ministry of Higher Education
ISSN: 0320-2372

MLA acronym: InozF

SUBSCRIPTION INFORMATION

Frequency of publication: 4 times/yr.
Circulation: 600-1,000
Available in microform: No
Subscription price: $8.00/yr.
Year to which price refers: 1991

ADVERTISING INFORMATION

Advertising accepted: No

EDITORIAL DESCRIPTION

Scope: Publishes scientific articles on modern European (Roman and German) languages and literature, classical philology, the history of European languages, and translations in Ukrainian of classical works.
Reviews books: No
Publishes notes: No
Languages accepted: Ukrainian; English
Prints abstracts: Yes
Author-anonymous submission: No

SUBMISSION REQUIREMENTS

Restrictions on contributors: None
Author pays submission fee: No
Author pays page charges: No
Length of articles: 8-10 typescript pp.
Style: None
Number of copies required: 2
Special requirements: Submit original typescript and 1 copy.
Copyright ownership: Assigned by author to journal
Rejected manuscripts: Not returned
Time before publication decision: 3-6 mos.
Time between decision and publication: 6-12 mos.
Number of reviewers: 2-3
Articles submitted per year: 100-140
Articles published per year: 80-100

(1257)
*Institute of African Studies, Occasional Publications

Dele Layiwola, Editor
Inst. of African Studies
Univ. of Ibadan
Ibadan, Nigeria

First published: 1964
Sponsoring organization: Univ. of Ibadan, Inst. of African Studies
ISSN: 0002-0087
MLA acronym: IASOP

SUBSCRIPTION INFORMATION

Frequency of publication: 1-2 times/yr.
Circulation: 1,900
Available in microform: No
Subscription price: $10.00 (£8.00)/yr.
Year to which price refers: 1992
Subscription address: Inst. of African Studies, Univ. of Ibadan Press, Ibadan, Nigeria

ADVERTISING INFORMATION

Advertising accepted: Yes
Advertising rates: $25.00/half page; $50.00/full page

EDITORIAL DESCRIPTION

Scope: Publishes monographs on African linguistics, anthropology, history, oral tradition, literature, art, music, and traditional medicine.
Reviews books: Yes
Publishes notes: Yes
Languages accepted: English
Prints abstracts: No
Author-anonymous submission: Yes

SUBMISSION REQUIREMENTS

Restrictions on contributors: None
Author pays submission fee: No
Author pays page charges: No
Length of articles: 5,000 words
Length of books: 75-100 pp.
Length of book reviews: 500 words
Style: MLA
Number of copies required: 3
Special requirements: Submit original typescript.
Copyright ownership: Inst. of African Studies
Rejected manuscripts: Returned; enclose return postage.
Time before publication decision: 4 mos.
Time between decision and publication: 6 mos.
Number of reviewers: 2
Articles published per year: 12
Books submitted per year: 2-5
Books published per year: 1-2
Book reviews submitted per year: 4
Book reviews published per year: 2-4

(1258)
Insula: Revista de Letras y Ciencias Humanas

Víctor García de la Concha, Editor
Insula, Librería, Ediciones y Publicaciones, S.A.
Carretera de Irún, Km. 12,200
28049 Madrid, Spain

First published: 1946
ISSN: 0020-4536
MLA acronym: Insula

SUBSCRIPTION INFORMATION

Frequency of publication: 12 times/yr.
Circulation: 5,000
Available in microform: Yes
Subscription address: Mercedes del Amo, at the above address

ADVERTISING INFORMATION

Advertising accepted: Yes

EDITORIAL DESCRIPTION

Reviews books: Yes
Publishes notes: Yes
Languages accepted: Spanish
Prints abstracts: No

SUBMISSION REQUIREMENTS

Restrictions on contributors: None
Length of articles: 1,700-2,500 words
Length of book reviews: 1,000 words
Length of notes: 500 words
Style: MLA
Number of copies required: 1
Special requirements: Submit original typescript.
Copyright ownership: Assigned by author to journal
Rejected manuscripts: Returned
Time before publication decision: 2 mos.
Time between decision and publication: 15 mos.
Number of reviewers: 5 plus Editorial Board
Articles submitted per year: 90
Articles published per year: 40
Book reviews published per year: 60
Notes published per year: 200

(1259)
*Interface: Journal of Applied Linguistics/Tijdschrift voor Toegepaste Linguïstiek

Fred van Besien, Editor
Vlaamse Economische Hogeschool
Koningsstr. 336
1210 Brussels, Belgium

Telephone: (32) 2 2211211
First published: 1986
Sponsoring organization: Dept. of Translation, Vlaamse Economische Hogeschool
MLA acronym: Interface

SUBSCRIPTION INFORMATION

Frequency of publication: 2 times/yr. (Fall, Spring)
Circulation: 150
Available in microform: No
Subscription price: 300 BF/yr. Belgium; 350 BF/yr. elsewhere
Year to which price refers: 1991-92

ADVERTISING INFORMATION

Advertising accepted: Yes
Advertising rates: 10,000 BF/full page

EDITORIAL DESCRIPTION

Scope: Publishes articles on all aspects of applied linguistics. Contributions deal with native and foreign language teaching, contrastive linguistics, error analysis, translation theory, terminology, discourse analysis, stylistics, and psycholinguistics.
Reviews books: Yes
Publishes notes: No
Languages accepted: English; German; French; Dutch
Prints abstracts: Yes
Author-anonymous submission: No

SUBMISSION REQUIREMENTS

Restrictions on contributors: None
Author pays submission fee: No
Author pays page charges: No
Length of articles: 15 pp.
Length of book reviews: 1 p.
Style: None
Number of copies required: 1
Special requirements: Include a 120-word maximum abstract in English typed on a separate sheet.
Copyright ownership: Author
Rejected manuscripts: Returned
Time before publication decision: 6 mos.
Time between decision and publication: 6 mos.
Number of reviewers: 2
Articles submitted per year: 10
Articles published per year: 8
Book reviews published per year: 8

(1260)
*L'Intermédiaire des Casanovistes

Helmut Watzlawick & Furio Luccichenti, Editors
22, Chemin de l'esplanade
1214 Vernier
Geneva, Switzerland

Additional editorial address: Furio Luccichenti, 1 via Ciro Menotti, 00195, Rome, Italy
First published: 1984
ISSN: 0259-4366
MLA acronym: Idc

SUBSCRIPTION INFORMATION

Frequency of publication: Annual
Circulation: 250

ADVERTISING INFORMATION

Advertising accepted: Yes

EDITORIAL DESCRIPTION

Scope: Focuses on Giacomo Casanova de Seingalt and 18th-century studies.
Reviews books: Yes
Publishes notes: Yes
Languages accepted: English; French; Italian
Prints abstracts: No
Author-anonymous submission: No

SUBMISSION REQUIREMENTS

Restrictions on contributors: None
Author pays submission fee: No
Author pays page charges: No
Length of articles: 1,000-2,500 words
Length of book reviews: 300 words
Length of notes: 300 words
Style: MLA
Number of copies required: 3
Special requirements: Submit typescript.
Copyright ownership: Journal
Rejected manuscripts: Returned; enclose SASE.
Time before publication decision: 9 mos.
Time between decision and publication: 3 mos.
Number of reviewers: 3
Articles submitted per year: 8
Articles published per year: 5
Book reviews submitted per year: 10
Notes submitted per year: 10
Notes published per year: 8

(1261)
*International Fiction Review

Saad Elkhadem, Editor
Dept. of German & Russian
Univ. of New Brunswick
Fredericton, New Brunswick E3B 5A3, Canada

Telephone: 506 453-4636
First published: 1974
Sponsoring organization: International Fiction Assn.
ISSN: 0315-4149
MLA acronym: IFR

SUBSCRIPTION INFORMATION

Frequency of publication: 2 times/yr.
Circulation: 500
Available in microform: Yes
Subscription price: C$15.00/yr. institutions; C$12.00/yr. individuals
Year to which price refers: 1992

ADVERTISING INFORMATION

Advertising accepted: No

EDITORIAL DESCRIPTION

Scope: Devoted to international fiction. Publishes essays on contemporary fiction of many countries as well as reviews of recently published novels and scholarly works on fiction.
Reviews books: Yes
Publishes notes: Yes
Languages accepted: English
Prints abstracts: No
Author-anonymous submission: Yes

SUBMISSION REQUIREMENTS

Restrictions on contributors: None
Author pays submission fee: No
Author pays page charges: No
Length of articles: 1,500-4,500 words
Length of book reviews: 500-750 words
Length of notes: 1,500 words
Style: MLA; York Press Style Manual
Number of copies required: 2
Copyright ownership: Assigned by author to journal
Rejected manuscripts: Returned
Time before publication decision: 6-8 weeks
Time between decision and publication: 3-6 mos.
Number of reviewers: 2 plus Editor
Articles submitted per year: 60
Articles published per year: 30
Book reviews submitted per year: 50
Book reviews published per year: 30
Notes submitted per year: 20
Notes published per year: 10

(1262)
*International Folklore Review: Folklore Studies from Overseas

Venetia Newall, Editor
14 Sloane Terrace Mansions
Sloane Terrace
London SW1X 9DG, England

First published: 1981
Sponsoring organization: New Abbey Pubs.
ISSN: 0264-2573
MLA acronym: IFRev

SUBSCRIPTION INFORMATION

Frequency of publication: Annual
Circulation: 1,000
Available in microform: No
Subscription price: £15.00 ($33.00)/yr.
Year to which price refers: 1991
Subscription address: Fourth Estate, 289 Westbourne Grove, London W2 2QA, England

ADVERTISING INFORMATION

Advertising accepted: Yes

EDITORIAL DESCRIPTION

Scope: Aims to make the work of folklorists throughout the world available to folklorists in England, to show how folklore is studied and interpreted in other countries, and to promote international cooperation and understanding.
Reviews books: Yes
Publishes notes: Yes
Languages accepted: English
Prints abstracts: No
Author-anonymous submission: No

SUBMISSION REQUIREMENTS

Restrictions on contributors: Only articles by contributors outside the British Isles are accepted.
Author pays submission fee: No
Author pays page charges: No
Length of articles: No restrictions
Length of book reviews: No restrictions
Length of notes: No restrictions
Style: MLA
Number of copies required: 3
Copyright ownership: New Abbey Pubs. & author
Rejected manuscripts: Returned
Time before publication decision: 1 mo.
Time between decision and publication: 1 yr.
Number of reviewers: 3
Articles submitted per year: 30-40
Articles published per year: 16
Book reviews submitted per year: 9-12
Book reviews published per year: 9-12

(1263)
*International Journal of American Linguistics

David S. Rood & Nora C. England, Editors
Linguistics Dept.
Campus Box 295
Univ. of Colorado
Boulder, CO 80309

Additional editorial address: Send notes to Nora C. England, Univ. of Iowa, Dept. of Anthropology, Iowa City, IA 52242
Telephone: 303 492-7082; 319 335-0533 (reviews)
First published: 1917
ISSN: 0020-7071
MLA acronym: IJAL

SUBSCRIPTION INFORMATION

Frequency of publication: 4 times/yr. (Jan., Apr., July, Oct.)
Circulation: 1,200
Available in microform: No
Subscription price: $75.00/yr. institutions US; $36.00/yr. individuals US; $26.00/yr. students US
Year to which price refers: 1992
Subscription address: Orlie Higgins, Journals Division, Univ. of Chicago Press, P.O. Box 37005, Chicago, IL 60637
Subscription telephone: 312 702-7600

ADVERTISING INFORMATION

Advertising accepted: Yes
Advertising rates: Request from Univ. of Chicago Press

EDITORIAL DESCRIPTION

Scope: Devoted to scholarly studies of all the languages native to North, Central, and South America, including Eskimo-Aleut and certain creoles and pidgins of the hemisphere. Concentrates on the investigation of linguistic data and on the presentation of grammars, historical reconstruction, grammatical fragments, and other discussions relevant to American Indian languages.
Reviews books: Yes
Publishes notes: Yes
Languages accepted: English
Prints abstracts: No
Author-anonymous submission: No

SUBMISSION REQUIREMENTS

Restrictions on contributors: None
Author pays submission fee: No
Author pays page charges: No
Length of articles: 10,000 words
Length of book reviews: 1,750 words
Length of notes: 1,750 words
Style: Linguistic Soc. of America
Number of copies required: 3
Special requirements: All languages are accepted for review but translation into English may be required for publication.
Copyright ownership: Assigned by author to journal
Rejected manuscripts: Returned
Time before publication decision: 4 mos.
Time between decision and publication: 9-12 mos.
Number of reviewers: 2-3
Articles submitted per year: 35-40
Articles published per year: 25
Book reviews submitted per year: 30-40
Book reviews published per year: 20
Notes submitted per year: 40-50
Notes published per year: 20

(1264)
*International Journal of Applied Linguistics

Ernst Håkon Jahr & Geirr Wiggen, Editors
Inst. for Språk & Litteratur
Univ. i Tromsø
9037 Tromsø, Norway

Additional editorial address: G. Wiggen, Senter for Laererutdanning & Skoletjeneste, Univ. i Oslo, P.O. Box 1099 Blindern, 0316 Oslo, Norway
Telephone: (47) 83 44273 (E. H. Jahr); (47) 2 855031 (G. Wiggen)
Fax: (47) 83 44239
E-mail: Ernsthj@mack.uit.no
First published: 1991
Sponsoring organization: Nordiska Publiceringsnämnden för Humanistiska Tidskrifter (Nordic Publications Committee for Humanist Periodicals)
ISSN: 0802-6106
MLA acronym: INJAL

SUBSCRIPTION INFORMATION

Frequency of publication: 2 times/yr.
Circulation: 100
Available in microform: No
Subscription price: 530 NKr ($82.00)/yr. institutions; 295 NKr ($49.00)/yr. individuals
Year to which price refers: 1992
Subscription address: Novus Forlag, Postboks 748 Sentrum, 0106 Oslo, Norway
Subscription telephone: (47) 2 717450
Subscription fax: (47) 2 718107

ADVERTISING INFORMATION

Advertising accepted: Yes
Advertising rates: 1,500 NKr/full page

EDITORIAL DESCRIPTION

Scope: Publishes articles on all areas of applied linguistics represented by the various commissions of the Association Internationale de Linguistique Appliquée (AILA). Also encourages the development of new fields of applied language study.
Reviews books: Yes
Publishes notes: Yes
Languages accepted: English
Prints abstracts: Yes
Author-anonymous submission: No

SUBMISSION REQUIREMENTS

Author pays submission fee: No
Author pays page charges: No
Style: MLA
Number of copies required: 3
Special requirements: Submit a 15-line abstract.
Copyright ownership: Novus Forlag
Rejected manuscripts: Returned
Time before publication decision: 1-3 mos.
Time between decision and publication: 1-5 mos.
Number of reviewers: 4

(1265)
International Journal of Dravidian Linguistics

V. I. Subramoniam, Editor
Dravidian Linguistics Assn.
Kerala Paanini Buildings, Kunnum Puram
Trivandrum-695001
Kerala, India

Sponsoring organization: Dravidian Linguistics Assn.
ISSN: 0378-2484
MLA acronym: IJDL

SUBSCRIPTION INFORMATION

Frequency of publication: 2 times/yr. (Jan., June)
Available in microform: No

ADVERTISING INFORMATION

Advertising accepted: Yes

EDITORIAL DESCRIPTION

Scope: Publishes articles on Dravidian linguistics.
Reviews books: Yes
Publishes notes: Yes
Languages accepted: English
Prints abstracts: No
Author-anonymous submission: No

SUBMISSION REQUIREMENTS

Restrictions on contributors: Preference is given to life members of the Dravidian Linguistics Assn.
Author pays submission fee: No
Author pays page charges: No
Style: Language
Number of copies required: 3
Special requirements: Submit double-spaced typescript.
Copyright ownership: Dravidian Linguistics Assn.
Time before publication decision: 6 mos.
Time between decision and publication: 1 yr.
Number of reviewers: 2
Articles submitted per year: 100
Articles published per year: 30
Book reviews submitted per year: 20-30
Book reviews published per year: 10-15
Notes submitted per year: 50-75
Notes published per year: 25-30

(1266)
*International Journal of Lexicography

Robert Ilson, Editor
58, Antrim Mansions
Antrim Rd.
London NW3, England

First published: 1988
Historical variations in title: Incorporates *The EURALEX Newsletter*
Sponsoring organization: European Assn. for Lexicography; Dictionary Soc. of North America
ISSN: 0950-3846
MLA acronym: IJLex

SUBSCRIPTION INFORMATION

Frequency of publication: 4 times/yr. (Spring, Summer, Fall, Winter)
Circulation: 770
Available in microform: Yes
Subscription price: £46.00/yr. United Kingdom & Europe; $90.00/yr. elsewhere
Year to which price refers: 1992
Subscription address: Journals Subscription Dept., Oxford Univ. Press, Pinkhill House, Southfield Rd., Eynsham, Oxford OX8 1JJ, England
Subscription telephone: (44) 865 882283
Subscription fax: (44) 865 882890

ADVERTISING INFORMATION

Advertising accepted: Yes
Advertising rates: £130.00/half page; £200.00/full page

EDITORIAL DESCRIPTION

Scope: Publishes articles that investigate dictionaries and all other types of reference work.
Reviews books: Yes
Publishes notes: Yes

Prints abstracts: Yes
Author-anonymous submission: Yes

SUBMISSION REQUIREMENTS

Restrictions on contributors: None
Author pays submission fee: No
Author pays page charges: No
Length of articles: No restrictions
Length of book reviews: No restrictions
Length of notes: No restrictions
Style: Journal
Number of copies required: 3-4
Special requirements: Submit double-spaced typescript and 150-word maximum abstract.
Copyright ownership: Oxford Univ. Press
Rejected manuscripts: Returned at author's request
Time between decision and publication: 14 weeks
Number of reviewers: 2

(1267)
*International Journal of Middle East Studies

Leila Fawaz, Editor
Cabot International Center
Fletcher School of Law & Diplomacy
Tufts Univ.
Medford, MA 02155

First published: 1970
Sponsoring organization: Middle East Studies Assn. of North America, Inc.
ISSN: 0020-7438
MLA acronym: IJMES

SUBSCRIPTION INFORMATION

Frequency of publication: 4 times/yr.
Circulation: 3,000
Available in microform: Yes
Subscription price: $117.00/yr.
Year to which price refers: 1993
Subscription address: Cambridge Univ. Press, 40 W. 20th St., New York, NY 10011-4211
Additional subscription address: Cambridge Univ. Press, Edinburgh Bldg., Shaftesbury Rd., Cambridge CB2 2RU, England
Subscription telephone: 800 431-1580 ext. 175

ADVERTISING INFORMATION

Advertising accepted: Yes

EDITORIAL DESCRIPTION

Scope: Publishes articles and reviews concerning the area encompassing Iran, Turkey, Afghanistan, Israel, Pakistan, and the countries of the Arab World from the 7th century to modern times. Spain, Southeastern Europe, and the Soviet Union are also included for the periods in which their territories were part of Middle Eastern empires or were under the influence of Middle Eastern civilization. Particular attention is given to works dealing with history, political science, economics, anthropology, sociology, philology and literature, folklore, comparative religion and theology, law and philosophy.
Reviews books: Yes
Publishes notes: Yes
Languages accepted: English
Prints abstracts: No
Author-anonymous submission: Yes

SUBMISSION REQUIREMENTS

Restrictions on contributors: None
Author pays submission fee: No
Author pays page charges: No
Length of articles: 40 double-spaced pp.
Length of book reviews: 1,200 words
Length of notes: 5 double-spaced pp.
Style: Chicago
Number of copies required: 1
Copyright ownership: Cambridge Univ. Press

Rejected manuscripts: Returned at author's request
Time before publication decision: 3-5 mos.
Time between decision and publication: 1 yr.
Number of reviewers: 3-4
Articles submitted per year: 180
Articles published per year: 25-30
Book reviews submitted per year: 100-120
Book reviews published per year: 100-120
Notes submitted per year: 10
Notes published per year: 10

(1268)
*International Journal of Sign Linguistics

William Edmondson, Editor
Multilingual Matters Ltd.
Frankfurt Lodge, Clevedon Hall
Victoria Rd.
Clevedon
Avon BS21 7SJ, England

Additional editorial address: Computer Science Dept., Univ. of Birmingham, Edgbaston, Birmingham B15 2TT, England
First published: 1990
Sponsoring organization: International Sign Linguistics Assn.
ISSN: 0959-6402
MLA acronym: IJSLing

SUBSCRIPTION INFORMATION

Frequency of publication: 2 times/yr.
Circulation: 250
Available in microform: No
Subscription price: £56.00 ($116.00)/yr. institutions; £19.00 ($40.00)/yr. individuals; £11.00 ($23.00)/yr. students
Year to which price refers: 1992

ADVERTISING INFORMATION

Advertising accepted: Yes
Advertising rates: £35.00/half page; £60.00/full page

EDITORIAL DESCRIPTION

Scope: Promotes the linguistic study of sign language. Welcomes articles on all aspects of linguistics, provided they bear directly on the study of sign language.
Reviews books: Yes
Publishes notes: Yes
Languages accepted: English
Prints abstracts: Yes
Author-anonymous submission: No

SUBMISSION REQUIREMENTS

Author pays submission fee: No
Author pays page charges: No
Length of articles: 7,000 words
Length of book reviews: 500-2,500 words
Length of notes: 100-200 words
Number of copies required: 4
Copyright ownership: Author
Rejected manuscripts: Returned at author's request
Time before publication decision: 3 mos.
Time between decision and publication: 6-8 mos.
Number of reviewers: 3
Articles submitted per year: 10
Articles published per year: 6
Book reviews submitted per year: 6
Book reviews published per year: 4

(1269)
*International Journal of Slavic Linguistics and Poetics

Dean S. Worth, Edward Stankiewicz, Walter N. Vickery, & C. H. van Schooneveld, Editors
Dept. of Slavic Languages
Univ. of California
Los Angeles, CA 90024

Telephone: 310 825-2676
First published: 1959
ISSN: 0538-8228
MLA acronym: IJSLP

SUBSCRIPTION INFORMATION

Frequency of publication: 2 times/yr.
Circulation: 400
Available in microform: No
Subscription price: $40.00/yr. institutions; $20.00.yr. individuals
Year to which price refers: 1991
Subscription address: Slavica Publishers, Inc., P.O. Box 14388, Columbus, OH 43214
Additional subscription address: Humanities Press, 171 Fifth Ave., Atlantic Highlands, NJ 07716

ADVERTISING INFORMATION

Advertising accepted: No

EDITORIAL DESCRIPTION

Scope: Publishes current research on Slavic and Baltic linguistics and poetics.
Reviews books: Yes
Publishes notes: Yes
Languages accepted: English; French; German; all Slavic languages
Prints abstracts: No
Author-anonymous submission: No

SUBMISSION REQUIREMENTS

Restrictions on contributors: Reviews are solicited.
Author pays submission fee: No
Author pays page charges: No
Length of articles: 20-30 typescript pp.
Length of book reviews: No restrictions
Length of notes: No restrictions
Style: None
Number of copies required: 2
Copyright ownership: Author
Rejected manuscripts: Returned; enclose SASE.
Time before publication decision: 1-3 mos.
Time between decision and publication: 3-12 mos.
Number of reviewers: 1-3
Articles submitted per year: 20-30
Articles published per year: 10-15

(1270)
*International Journal of the Sociology of Language

Joshua A. Fishman, Editor
Ferkauf Graduate School
Yeshiva Univ.
1300 Morris Park Ave.
Bronx, NY 10461

Additional editorial address: Unsolicited single articles: Florian Coulmas, 1-5-2 Hamadayama, Suginami-KU, Tokyo 168, Japan
Telephone: 212 881-5413
Fax: 212 881-5413
First published: 1974
ISSN: 0165-2516
MLA acronym: IJSL

SUBSCRIPTION INFORMATION

Frequency of publication: 6 times/yr.
Circulation: 750
Available in microform: No

Subscription price: $190.00/yr. institutions; $62.00/yr. individuals
Year to which price refers: 1992
Subscription address: Walter de Gruyter & Co., P.O. Box 110240, 1000 Berlin 11, Germany
Additional subscription address: In US & Canada: Walter de Gruyter Inc., 200 Saw Mill River Rd., Hawthorne, NY 10532
Subscription telephone: (49) 30 26005257
Subscription fax: (49) 30 26005251

ADVERTISING INFORMATION

Advertising accepted: Yes

EDITORIAL DESCRIPTION

Scope: Publishes articles on the development of the sociology of language in its broadest sense, as a truly international and interdisciplinary field in which various approaches, theoretical and empirical, supplement and complement each other, contributing thereby to the growth of language related knowledge, applications, values and sensitivities. Most issues are devoted to specific topics and articles appearing in these issues are commissioned or result from a call-for-papers.
Reviews books: Yes
Publishes notes: Yes
Languages accepted: English; French; Spanish; German; Italian
Prints abstracts: Yes, for non-English articles
Author-anonymous submission: No

SUBMISSION REQUIREMENTS

Restrictions on contributors: Most articles are commissioned or come as a result of a relatively long lead time call-for-papers on a particular subject. One issue comprised of unrelated articles is published annually.
Author pays submission fee: No
Author pays page charges: No
Length of articles: 20 double-spaced typescript pp.
Length of book reviews: 6 double-spaced typescript pp.
Length of notes: 500 words
Style: Journal; Chicago
Number of copies required: 2
Special requirements: Submit English abstract of articles not written in English.
Copyright ownership: Mouton de Gruyter
Rejected manuscripts: Returned; enclose return postage.
Time before publication decision: 6 mos.
Time between decision and publication: 1 yr.
Number of reviewers: 4
Articles submitted per year: 100-120
Articles published per year: 30-40
Book reviews submitted per year: 8-12
Book reviews published per year: 6-8
Notes submitted per year: 10-12
Notes published per year: 2-4

(1271)
*International Journal of Translation

Ramakant Agnihotri & Ujjal Singh Bahri, Editors
Dept. of Linguistics
Univ. of Delhi
Delhi 110007, India

First published: 1989
ISSN: 0970-9819
MLA acronym: IJT

SUBSCRIPTION INFORMATION

Frequency of publication: 2 times/yr. (Jan., June)
Circulation: 490
Available in microform: No
Subscription price: $40.00/yr. institutions; $30.00/yr. individuals
Year to which price refers: 1992
Subscription address: Bahri Books & Periodicals, 997A, Street No. 9, P.O. Box 4453, Gobindpuri, Kalkaji, New Delhi 110019, India
Subscription telephone: (91) 11 6448606; (91) 11 6445710

ADVERTISING INFORMATION

Advertising accepted: Yes
Advertising rates: $100.00/full page

EDITORIAL DESCRIPTION

Scope: Publishes research exploring the processes involved in literary and technical translation both from a theoretical and methodological point of view.
Reviews books: Yes
Publishes notes: Yes
Languages accepted: English
Prints abstracts: Yes
Author-anonymous submission: No

SUBMISSION REQUIREMENTS

Restrictions on contributors: None
Author pays submission fee: Yes, if paper exceeds 20 pp.
Cost of submission fee: $50.00/page
Author pays page charges: No
Length of articles: 20 pp. maximum
Length of book reviews: 15 pp.
Length of notes: 5-8 pp.
Style: MLA
Number of copies required: 2
Special requirements: Use size A4 (8 1/4 in. x 11 3/4 in.) paper. Submit a 150-word abstract.
Copyright ownership: Bahri Publications
Rejected manuscripts: Returned; enclose return postage.
Time before publication decision: 6 weeks
Time between decision and publication: 6-8 mos.
Number of reviewers: 2
Articles submitted per year: 15-25
Articles published per year: 12-18
Book reviews submitted per year: 3-6
Book reviews published per year: 2-4
Notes submitted per year: 2-4
Notes published per year: 2-4

(1272)
*International Review of Applied Linguistics in Language Teaching

Gerhard Nickel, Bertil Malmberg, & Dietrich Nehls, Editors
Inst. für Linguistik: Anglistik
Univ. Stuttgart
Keplerstr. 17
7000 Stuttgart 1, Germany

Additional editorial address: Bertil Malmberg, Inst. of Linguistics, Univ. of Lund, Helgonabacken 12, 223 62 Lund, Sweden
First published: 1963
ISSN: 0019-042X
MLA acronym: IRAL

SUBSCRIPTION INFORMATION

Frequency of publication: 4 times/yr. (Feb., May, Aug., Nov.)
Circulation: 2,200
Available in microform: Yes
Subscription price: $95.00/yr. institutions; $50.00/yr. individuals
Year to which price refers: 1991
Subscription address: Julius Groos Verlag, P.O. Box 102423, 6900 Heidelberg 1, Germany

ADVERTISING INFORMATION

Advertising accepted: Yes

EDITORIAL DESCRIPTION

Scope: Publishes articles on problems of general and applied linguistics in all their various forms.
Reviews books: Yes
Publishes notes: Yes
Languages accepted: English; French; German
Prints abstracts: Yes
Author-anonymous submission: No

SUBMISSION REQUIREMENTS

Restrictions on contributors: None
Author pays submission fee: No
Author pays page charges: No
Length of articles: 25 double-spaced typescript pp. maximum
Length of book reviews: 3 double-spaced typescript pp.
Length of notes: 10-15 double-spaced typescript pp.
Style: MLA
Number of copies required: 2
Special requirements: Provide an abbreviated short title (maximum 40 characters) plus a short summary of about a half typewritten page.
Copyright ownership: Julius Groos Verlag
Rejected manuscripts: Not returned
Time before publication decision: 10 weeks
Time between decision and publication: 2 yrs.
Number of reviewers: 2-4
Articles submitted per year: 40
Articles published per year: 10
Book reviews submitted per year: 30
Book reviews published per year: 20-25
Notes submitted per year: 40
Notes published per year: 10

(1273)
*International Social Science Journal

Ali Kazancigil, Editor
UNESCO
7, place de Fontenoy
75700 Paris, France

Telephone: (33) 1 45683798; (33) 1 45683828
Fax: (33) 1 45678206
E-mail: SHMAK@FRUNES21
First published: 1949
Sponsoring organization: UNESCO
ISSN: 0020-8701 (English ed.); 0304-3037 (French ed.)
MLA acronym: ISSJ

SUBSCRIPTION INFORMATION

Frequency of publication: 4 times/yr. (Feb., May, Aug., Nov.)
Circulation: 12,000
Available in microform: No
Subscription price: £42.50/yr. institutions United Kingdom & Europe; $88.00/yr. institutions N. America; £24.00 ($40.50) institutions & individuals Third World; £28.50/yr. institutions elsewhere; £24.00/yr. individuals United Kingdom & Europe; $48.00/yr. individuals N. America; £28.50/yr. individuals elsewhere
Year to which price refers: 1992
Subscription address: Basil Blackwell Ltd., 108 Cowley Rd., Oxford, OX4 1JF, England
Additional subscription address: Blackwell Publishers, 238 Main St., Suite 501, Cambridge, MA 02142
Subscription telephone: (44) 865 791100
Subscription fax: (44) 865 791347

ADVERTISING INFORMATION

Advertising accepted: Yes, on an exchange basis

EDITORIAL DESCRIPTION

Scope: Publishes thematic issues covering all social science disciplines and substantive areas of focus. Publishes English, French, Spanish, Chinese, and Arabic editions.
Reviews books: No
Publishes notes: No
Languages accepted: English; French; Spanish
Prints abstracts: No
Author-anonymous submission: No

SUBMISSION REQUIREMENTS

Restrictions on contributors: Articles are generally commissioned.
Author pays submission fee: No
Author pays page charges: No
Length of articles: 5,000 words
Style: None
Number of copies required: 3
Special requirements: Articles should reflect an international viewpoint or deal with matters of wide concern.
Copyright ownership: UNESCO
Rejected manuscripts: Returned
Time before publication decision: 1-2 mos.
Time between decision and publication: 1 yr.
Number of reviewers: Editorial staff
Articles submitted per year: 80
Articles published per year: 50

(1274)
*Internationales Archiv für Sozialgeschichte der Deutschen Literatur

Wolfgang Frühwald, Georg Jäger, Dieter Langewiesche, & Alberto Martino, Editors
Inst. für Deutsche Philologie
Schellingstr. 3
8000 Munich 40, Germany

First published: 1976
Sponsoring organization: Inst. für Deutsche Philologie, Munich
ISSN: 0340-4528
MLA acronym: IASL

SUBSCRIPTION INFORMATION

Frequency of publication: 2 times/yr.
Circulation: 800
Available in microform: No
Subscription address: Max Niemeyer Verlag, Postfach 2140, 7400 Tübingen, Germany

ADVERTISING INFORMATION

Advertising accepted: Yes

EDITORIAL DESCRIPTION

Scope: Concerns itself with the social history of German literature.
Reviews books: Yes
Publishes notes: No
Languages accepted: English; German
Prints abstracts: Yes
Author-anonymous submission: No

SUBMISSION REQUIREMENTS

Restrictions on contributors: Book reviews are commissioned.
Author pays submission fee: No
Author pays page charges: No
Length of articles: 25-40 pp.
Length of book reviews: 10 pp.
Style: MLA
Number of copies required: 1
Special requirements: Submit original typescript.
Copyright ownership: Assigned by author to journal
Rejected manuscripts: Returned
Time before publication decision: 2 mos.

Time between decision and publication: 8-12 mos.
Number of reviewers: 5
Articles submitted per year: 18-20
Articles published per year: 5-8
Book reviews published per year: 30

(1275)
*Interplay: Proceedings of Colloquia in Comparative Literature and the Arts

Moshe Lazar, Ronald Gottesman, & Robert S. Ellwood, Editors
Undena Publications
P.O. Box 97
Malibu, CA 90265

First published: 1982
Sponsoring organization: Comparative Literature Program, Univ. of Southern California
ISSN: 0742-1176
MLA acronym: Interplay

SUBSCRIPTION INFORMATION

Frequency of publication: Irregular
Available in microform: No
Subscription address: Crescent Academic Services, 29528 Madera Ave., Shafter, CA 93263
Subscription telephone: 805 746-5870
Subscription fax: 805 746-2728

ADVERTISING INFORMATION

Advertising accepted: No

EDITORIAL DESCRIPTION

Scope: Publishes proceedings of colloquia in comparative literature and the arts.
Reviews books: No
Publishes notes: No
Languages accepted: English

SUBMISSION REQUIREMENTS

Restrictions on contributors: No submissions are accepted. Publishes only proceeding of colloquia in comparative literature and the arts.
Copyright ownership: Undena Publications

(1276)
*Interpretation: A Journal of Political Philosophy

Hilail Gildin, Editor
Queens College, King Hall 101
65-30 Kissena Blvd.
Flushing, NY 11367-0904

Additional editorial address: 13 Patton Ave., Princeton, NJ 08540
Telephone: 718 520-7099
First published: 1970
ISSN: 0020-9635
MLA acronym: IJPP

SUBSCRIPTION INFORMATION

Frequency of publication: 3 times/yr.
Circulation: 900
Available in microform: No
Subscription price: $40.00/yr. institutions; $25.00/yr. individuals; $16.00/yr. students
Year to which price refers: 1992-93

ADVERTISING INFORMATION

Advertising accepted: Yes, on an exchange basis

EDITORIAL DESCRIPTION

Scope: Promotes the philosophic study of politics, literature, jurisprudence, and theology.
Reviews books: Yes
Publishes notes: No
Languages accepted: English
Prints abstracts: No
Author-anonymous submission: Yes

SUBMISSION REQUIREMENTS

Restrictions on contributors: None
Author pays submission fee: No
Author pays page charges: Yes, for alterations
Length of articles: 12,000 words
Length of book reviews: 4,000 words
Style: Chicago
Number of copies required: 3
Copyright ownership: Journal
Rejected manuscripts: Returned
Time before publication decision: 9 weeks
Time between decision and publication: 8 mos.
Number of reviewers: 3
Articles submitted per year: 150
Articles published per year: 15
Book reviews submitted per year: 25
Book reviews published per year: 10

(1277)
*L'Interprete

Aldo Scaglione, Editor
New York Univ.
24 W. 12th St.
New York, NY 10011

First published: 1975
MLA acronym: Interprete

SUBSCRIPTION INFORMATION

Frequency of publication: 2 times/yr.
Circulation: 400
Available in microform: No
Subscription address: Angelo Longo Editore, Via Rocca ai Fossi 6, C.P. 431, 48100 Ravenna, Italy

ADVERTISING INFORMATION

Advertising accepted: No

EDITORIAL DESCRIPTION

Scope: Publishes methodologically up-to-date scholarship in literary criticism without prejudice toward more traditional methods. Both newer and older methods are welcome insofar as they offer intrinsically convincing results.
Reviews books: No
Publishes notes: No
Languages accepted: Italian; English; French
Prints abstracts: Yes
Author-anonymous submission: No

SUBMISSION REQUIREMENTS

Restrictions on contributors: None
Author pays submission fee: No
Author pays page charges: Yes
Length of books: No restrictions
Style: MLA
Number of copies required: 1
Copyright ownership: Longo Editore
Rejected manuscripts: Returned
Time before publication decision: 2 mos.
Time between decision and publication: 2 yrs.
Number of reviewers: 2
Books submitted per year: 7
Books published per year: 3

(1278)
*Inti: Revista de Literatura Hispánica

Roger B. Carmosino, Gwen Kirkpatrick, Antonio
    Carreño, Pedro Lastra, & Julio Ortega, Editors
Dept. of Modern Languages
Providence College
Providence, RI 02918

Telephone: 401 865-2111
Fax: 401 865-2057
First published: 1974
Sponsoring organization: Providence College
ISSN: 0732-6750
MLA acronym: Inti

SUBSCRIPTION INFORMATION

Frequency of publication: 2 times/yr. (Nov., Apr.)
Circulation: 1,000
Available in microform: No
Subscription price: $40.00/yr. institutions US; $25.00/yr. individuals US; $40.00/yr. elsewhere; $20.00/single issue
Year to which price refers: 1992

ADVERTISING INFORMATION

Advertising accepted: Yes
Advertising rates: $90.00/half page; $125.00/full page

EDITORIAL DESCRIPTION

Scope: Publishes scholarly articles on Spanish Peninsular and Spanish American literatures. Also includes poetry, short stories, book and film reviews, interviews, bibliographies, and notes.
Reviews books: Yes
Publishes notes: Yes
Languages accepted: Spanish; English
Prints abstracts: No
Author-anonymous submission: No

SUBMISSION REQUIREMENTS

Restrictions on contributors: Priority is given to members/subscribers.
Author pays submission fee: No
Author pays page charges: No
Length of articles: 20-25 typescript pp. maximum including bibliography and notes
Length of book reviews: 600 words maximum
Length of notes: 600 words maximum
Style: MLA
Number of copies required: 3
Special requirements: Include very brief biographical note; do not send resume or C.V.
Copyright ownership: Journal
Rejected manuscripts: Returned; enclose return postage.
Time before publication decision: 2-3 mos.
Time between decision and publication: 2-3 mos.
Number of reviewers: 3
Articles submitted per year: 80
Articles published per year: 20-25
Book reviews submitted per year: 25-30
Book reviews published per year: 15
Notes submitted per year: 30
Notes published per year: 10

(1279)
*Iowa English Bulletin

Joanne Brown & Bruce Horner, Editors
Dept. of English
Drake Univ.
Des Moines, IA 50311

Telephone: 515 271-3828; 515 271-3857
Fax: 515 271-3977
First published: 1956
Sponsoring organization: Iowa Council of Teachers of English
ISSN: 0444-4663

MLA acronym: IEY

SUBSCRIPTION INFORMATION

Frequency of publication: Annual
Circulation: 875
Available in microform: Yes
Subscription price: $5.00/yr.
Year to which price refers: 1991

ADVERTISING INFORMATION

Advertising accepted: No

EDITORIAL DESCRIPTION

Scope: Publishes articles of general scholarly and pedagogical interest for English teachers at all levels.
Reviews books: No
Publishes notes: No
Languages accepted: English
Prints abstracts: No
Author-anonymous submission: No

SUBMISSION REQUIREMENTS

Restrictions on contributors: None
Author pays submission fee: No
Author pays page charges: No
Length of articles: 6,000 words maximum
Style: MLA
Number of copies required: 2
Special requirements: Include a 100-150 word abstract.
Copyright ownership: Iowa Council of Teachers of English
Rejected manuscripts: Returned; enclose SASE.
Time before publication decision: 4 mos.
Time between decision and publication: 6-12 mos.
Number of reviewers: 2
Articles submitted per year: 20-30
Articles published per year: 7-10

(1280)
*The Iowa Review

David Hamilton, Editor
308 EPB
Univ. of Iowa
Iowa City, IA 52242

Telephone: 319 335-0249; 319 335-0462
First published: 1970
Sponsoring organization: Univ. of Iowa, School of Letters & Graduate College
ISSN: 0021-065X
MLA acronym: IowaR

SUBSCRIPTION INFORMATION

Frequency of publication: 3 times/yr. (Winter, Spring-Summer, Fall)
Circulation: 1,000
Available in microform: No
Subscription price: $20.00/yr. institutions; $15.00/yr. individuals
Year to which price refers: 1992
Subscription telephone: 800 235-2665

ADVERTISING INFORMATION

Advertising accepted: Yes
Advertising rates: $80.00/half page; $150.00/full page

EDITORIAL DESCRIPTION

Scope: Publishes short fiction, poetry, prose, criticism, book reviews, and essays.
Reviews books: Yes
Publishes notes: No
Languages accepted: English
Prints abstracts: No
Author-anonymous submission: No

SUBMISSION REQUIREMENTS

Restrictions on contributors: None
Author pays submission fee: No
Author pays page charges: No
Length of articles: No restrictions
Length of book reviews: 1,000-2,000 words
Style: Chicago
Number of copies required: 1
Copyright ownership: Univ. of Iowa; reverts to author upon publication
Rejected manuscripts: Returned; enclose return postage.
Time before publication decision: 1-3 mos.
Time between decision and publication: 6-12 mos.
Number of reviewers: 1-7
Articles submitted per year: 200
Articles published per year: 12-15
Book reviews submitted per year: 50-100
Book reviews published per year: 20

(1281)
*IPO Annual Progress Report

Inst. for Perception Research/IPO
P.O. Box 513
5600 MB Eindhoven, Netherlands

Telephone: (31) 40 773873
Fax: (31) 40 773876
E-mail: Secr@heiipo5.bitnet
First published: 1966
Sponsoring organization: Inst. for Perception Research/IPO
ISSN: 0921-2566
MLA acronym: IPOAPR

SUBSCRIPTION INFORMATION

Frequency of publication: Annual
Available in microform: No

ADVERTISING INFORMATION

Advertising accepted: No

EDITORIAL DESCRIPTION

Scope: Publishes studies on perception research. Topics covered include hearing and speech, vision and reading, cognition and communication, information ergonomics, and communication aids.
Reviews books: No
Publishes notes: No
Languages accepted: English
Prints abstracts: Yes
Author-anonymous submission: No

SUBMISSION REQUIREMENTS

Restrictions on contributors: Contributions should be staff members or associates of IPO.
Author pays submission fee: No
Author pays page charges: No
Length of articles: 5,500 words maximum
Style: Times
Number of copies required: 4
Copyright ownership: IPO
Time before publication decision: 2 weeks
Time between decision and publication: 7-8 mos.
Number of reviewers: 2-3
Articles submitted per year: 12
Articles published per year: 11

(1282)
*Iqbal Review: Journal of the Iqbal Academy Pakistan

Muhammad Munawwar, Editor
Iqbal Academy Pakistan
116-Mcleod Rd.
Lahore, Pakistan

First published: 1960
Sponsoring organization: Iqbal Academy
ISSN: 0891-9356
MLA acronym: IqR

SUBSCRIPTION INFORMATION

Frequency of publication: 4 times/yr.
Circulation: 1,000
Available in microform: No

ADVERTISING INFORMATION

Advertising accepted: No

EDITORIAL DESCRIPTION

Scope: Devoted to research studies on the life, poetry, and thought of Iqbal and on those branches of learning in which he was interested: Islamics, philosophy, history, sociology, comparative religion, literature, art, and archaeology.
Reviews books: Yes
Publishes notes: No
Languages accepted: English; Hindi-Urdu
Prints abstracts: Yes
Author-anonymous submission: No

SUBMISSION REQUIREMENTS

Restrictions on contributors: None
Author pays submission fee: No
Author pays page charges: No
Length of articles: 5-20 pp.
Length of book reviews: 2-4 pp.
Number of copies required: 2
Special requirements: Submit typescript.
Copyright ownership: Iqbal Academy
Rejected manuscripts: Returned; enclose return postage.
Number of reviewers: 4
Articles submitted per year: 40-50
Articles published per year: 20-25
Book reviews submitted per year: 20-25
Book reviews published per year: 8-10

(1283)
Iran: Journal of the British Institute of Persian Studies

Vesta Curtis & Edmund Bosworth, Editors
British Academy
20/21 Cornwall Terrace
London NW1 4QP, England

First published: 1963
Sponsoring organization: British Inst. of Persian Studies
ISSN: 0578-6867
MLA acronym: Iran

SUBSCRIPTION INFORMATION

Frequency of publication: Annual (Mar.-Apr.)
Circulation: 800
Available in microform: No
Subscription address: M. E. Gueritz, M.B.E., 13 Cambrian Rd., Richmond, Surrey TW10 6JQ, England

ADVERTISING INFORMATION

Advertising accepted: No

EDITORIAL DESCRIPTION

Scope: Publishes on aspects of Iranian culture, especially archaeology, art, history, literature. Does not publish on economics or current affairs.
Reviews books: No
Languages accepted: English; French; German
Prints abstracts: No

SUBMISSION REQUIREMENTS

Restrictions on contributors: None
Author pays submission fee: No
Author pays page charges: No
Length of articles: 2,500-10,000 words
Style: Suggested styles for transliterations: (1) Old Persian, use table in Kent, *Old Persian Grammar, Texts, Lexicon,* p. 12; (2) Manichaean Middle Persian, Parthan, use Andreas-Henning, *Milletiranische Manichaica,* vol. 3, p. 66; (3) Pahlavi, use Nyberg, *A Manual of Pahlavi,* New Edition, p. 129; (4) Islamic, Modern Persian use *Cambridge History of Islam.*
Number of copies required: 2
Special requirements: Submit typescript.
Copyright ownership: Author
Rejected manuscripts: Returned
Number of reviewers: 2

(1284)
Iranian Studies: Journal of the Society for Iranian Studies

Abbas Amanat, Editor
Dept. of History
Yale Univ.
P.O. Box 1504A, Yale Station
New Haven, CT 06520

First published: 1968
Sponsoring organization: Soc. for Iranian Studies
ISSN: 0021-0862
MLA acronym: IranS

SUBSCRIPTION INFORMATION

Frequency of publication: 4 times/yr. (Winter, Spring, Summer, Fall)
Circulation: 1,000
Available in microform: Yes
Subscription price: $40.00/yr. institutions; $35.00/yr. individuals (includes membership)
Year to which price refers: 1992
Subscription address: Executive Secretary, Soc. for Iranian Studies, Columbia Univ., Middle East Inst., 420 W. 118th St., New York, NY 10027

ADVERTISING INFORMATION

Advertising accepted: Yes

EDITORIAL DESCRIPTION

Scope: Publishes the results of original research, conducted in any discipline, on Iranian society and culture. Also publishes translations of Iranian literature, particularly of the contemporary period.
Reviews books: Yes
Publishes notes: Yes
Languages accepted: English; French; German
Prints abstracts: No

SUBMISSION REQUIREMENTS

Restrictions on contributors: None
Author pays submission fee: No
Author pays page charges: No
Length of articles: 20-40 double-spaced pp.
Length of book reviews: 3-5 pp.
Length of notes: 2-4 pp.
Style: Chicago; transliteration system is based on the Persian Romanization System, available from Editor.
Number of copies required: 3
Special requirements: Submit double-spaced typescript and diskette.
Copyright ownership: Journal
Rejected manuscripts: Not returned
Time before publication decision: 3 mos.
Time between decision and publication: 1 yr.
Number of reviewers: 4
Articles submitted per year: 50-60
Articles published per year: 15-20
Book reviews submitted per year: 32
Book reviews published per year: 30
Notes submitted per year: 5
Notes published per year: 5

(1285)
*Irian: Bulletin of Irian Jaya

Daan Dimara & Peter J. Silzer, Editors
P.O. Box 1800
Jayapura 99018
Irian Jaya, Indonesia

First published: 1972
Sponsoring organization: Univ. of Cenderawasih
ISSN: 0304-2189
MLA acronym: Irian

SUBSCRIPTION INFORMATION

Frequency of publication: Annual
Circulation: 200
Available in microform: Yes
Subscription price: 20,000 Rp/yr. Indonesia; $20.00 ($26.00 airmail)/yr. elsewhere
Year to which price refers: 1992
Subscription address: Manager, at the above address

ADVERTISING INFORMATION

Advertising accepted: No

EDITORIAL DESCRIPTION

Scope: Publishes articles on Irian Jaya linguistics and anthropology, education, etc.
Reviews books: No
Publishes notes: No
Languages accepted: English; Bahasa Malay dialect
Prints abstracts: Yes
Author-anonymous submission: No

SUBMISSION REQUIREMENTS

Restrictions on contributors: None
Author pays submission fee: No
Author pays page charges: No
Length of articles: 10-60 pp. maximum
Style: MLA preferred
Number of copies required: 2
Special requirements: Submit double-spaced typescript and 1 diskette in ASCII format accompanied by (1) a 200-400 word abstract; and (2) a brief biographical note on the author.
Copyright ownership: Journal
Rejected manuscripts: Returned; enclose return postage.
Time before publication decision: 2 mos.
Time between decision and publication: 8 mos. maximum
Number of reviewers: 3
Articles submitted per year: 10
Articles published per year: 5-8

(1286)
*Iris

Centre de Recherche sur les Littératures Ibériques
 & Ibéro-Américaines
Univ. Paul-Valéry (U.E.R. II)
B.P. 5043
34032 Montpellier Cedex, France

First published: 1980
Sponsoring organization: Univ. Paul Valéry
ISSN: 0291-2066
MLA acronym: Iris

SUBSCRIPTION INFORMATION

Frequency of publication: Annual
Circulation: 250-300
Available in microform: No
Subscription price: 100 F/yr.
Year to which price refers: 1992

ADVERTISING INFORMATION

Advertising accepted: Yes

EDITORIAL DESCRIPTION

Scope: Publishes articles on modern Spanish, Portuguese, and Spanish American languages and literatures.
Reviews books: Yes
Publishes notes: No
Languages accepted: French; Portuguese; Spanish; English
Prints abstracts: No
Author-anonymous submission: No

SUBMISSION REQUIREMENTS

Restrictions on contributors: None
Author pays submission fee: No
Author pays page charges: No
Length of articles: 20-30 pp.
Length of book reviews: 5 pp.
Style: Journal
Number of copies required: 1
Copyright ownership: Centre de Recherche sur les Littératures Ibériques & Ibéro-Américaines
Rejected manuscripts: Not returned
Time before publication decision: 1 yr.
Time between decision and publication: 6 mos.
Number of reviewers: 4
Articles submitted per year: 15-20
Articles published per year: 10-15
Book reviews submitted per year: 4-6
Book reviews published per year: 2-4

(1287)
Iris: Graduate Journal of French Critical Studies

Jean-Louis Ratsimihah, Editor
Dept. of French & Italian
Univ. of Wisconsin
1220 Linden Drive
Madison, WI 53706

First published: 1985
Sponsoring organization: Dept. of French & Italian, Univ. of Wisconsin, Madison
ISSN: 0884-3570
MLA acronym: IrisW

SUBSCRIPTION INFORMATION

Frequency of publication: 2 times/yr. (Winter, Summer)
Available in microform: No

ADVERTISING INFORMATION

Advertising accepted: Yes

EDITORIAL DESCRIPTION

Scope: Graduate journal open to all approaches and time periods in the study of French literature.
Reviews books: Yes
Publishes notes: No
Languages accepted: French; English
Prints abstracts: No
Author-anonymous submission: No

SUBMISSION REQUIREMENTS

Restrictions on contributors: None
Author pays submission fee: No
Author pays page charges: No
Length of articles: 2,000-2,500 words
Length of book reviews: 500 words
Style: MLA
Number of copies required: 2
Special requirements: If author uses word processor, include copy of diskette as well. Diskette will be returned.
Copyright ownership: Dept. of French & Italian; Univ. of Wisconsin, Madison
Rejected manuscripts: Returned; enclose SASE.
Time before publication decision: 2-5 mos.
Time between decision and publication: 2 mos.
Number of reviewers: 4

(1288)
*Irish Historical Studies

J. I. McGuire & Keith Jeffery, Editors
Dept. of History
Univ. College
Dublin, Ireland

Telephone: (353) 1 7068322
Fax: (353) 1 2837022
First published: 1938
Sponsoring organization: Irish Historical Soc.; Ulster Soc. for Irish Historical Studies
ISSN: 0021-1214
MLA acronym: IHS

SUBSCRIPTION INFORMATION

Frequency of publication: 2 times/yr.
Circulation: 1,000
Subscription address: W. E. Vaughan, Dept. of Modern History, Trinity College, Dublin 2, Ireland

ADVERTISING INFORMATION

Advertising accepted: Yes
Advertising rates: IR£100.00/full page

EDITORIAL DESCRIPTION

Scope: Publishes research and writing in Irish history.
Reviews books: Yes
Languages accepted: English
Prints abstracts: No

SUBMISSION REQUIREMENTS

Restrictions on contributors: None
Author pays submission fee: No
Length of articles: 8,000 words
Length of book reviews: 750-900 words
Style: Journal
Number of copies required: 2
Copyright ownership: Author
Rejected manuscripts: Returned
Time before publication decision: 2 mos.
Time between decision and publication: 18 mos.
Number of reviewers: 2-3
Articles published per year: 8
Book reviews published per year: 35

(1289)
*Irish Slavonic Studies

Ronald Hill, Patrick O'Meara, & Sarah Smyth, Editors
Dept. of Russian
Trinity College
Dublin 2, Ireland

Telephone: (353) 1 772941
Fax: (353) 1 770546
First published: 1980
Sponsoring organization: Irish Slavists' Assn.
ISSN: 0260-2067
MLA acronym: ISlSt

SUBSCRIPTION INFORMATION

Frequency of publication: Annual (Fall)
Circulation: 250
Available in microform: No
Subscription price: $15.00/yr. institutions; $10.00/yr. individuals
Year to which price refers: 1992

ADVERTISING INFORMATION

Advertising accepted: Yes
Advertising rates: IR£30.00 ($50.00)/full page

EDITORIAL DESCRIPTION

Scope: Publishes articles on Russian, Soviet, and East European literature, language, history, society, and politics. It also includes topics of Irish-Slavic interest.
Reviews books: Yes
Publishes notes: Yes
Languages accepted: English
Prints abstracts: No
Author-anonymous submission: No

SUBMISSION REQUIREMENTS

Restrictions on contributors: None
Author pays submission fee: No
Author pays page charges: No
Length of articles: 5,000 words
Length of book reviews: 650 words
Length of notes: 1,000 words
Style: SEER; Modern Humanities Research Assn.
Number of copies required: 1-2
Copyright ownership: Journal & author
Rejected manuscripts: Returned; enclose return postage.
Time before publication decision: 3 mos.
Time between decision and publication: 6-12 mos.
Number of reviewers: 2-3
Articles published per year: 7-8
Book reviews published per year: 50

(1290)
*Irish Studies

Richard Fallis, Editor
Syracuse Univ. Press
1600 Jamesville Ave.
Syracuse, NY 13244-5160

Telephone: 315 443-5543 (C. Maude-Gembler, Executive Editor, Syracuse Univ. Press)
Fax: 315 443-5545
First published: 1981
MLA acronym: IrishSt

SUBSCRIPTION INFORMATION

Available in microform: No

ADVERTISING INFORMATION

Advertising accepted: No

EDITORIAL DESCRIPTION

Scope: Publishes monographs on scholarship and criticism of Anglo-Irish literature and Irish history and culture.
Reviews books: No
Publishes notes: No
Languages accepted: English
Prints abstracts: No
Author-anonymous submission: No

SUBMISSION REQUIREMENTS

Restrictions on contributors: None
Author pays submission fee: No
Author pays page charges: No
Length of books: 200-300 pp.
Style: MLA; Chicago
Number of copies required: 2
Special requirements: Submit original typescript and a photocopy; typescript should not be produced with dot-matrix.
Copyright ownership: Returned
Time before publication decision: 3-6 mos.
Time between decision and publication: 6-12 mos.
Number of reviewers: 2-3
Books submitted per year: 30
Books published per year: 6

(1291)
*Irish University Review: A Journal of Irish Studies

Christopher Murray, Editor
Room K203
Arts Bldg.
Univ. College
Dublin 4, Ireland

Telephone: (353) 1 7067625
Fax: (353) 1 2830328
First published: 1970
Sponsoring organization: Univ. College, Dublin
ISSN: 0021-1427
MLA acronym: IUR

SUBSCRIPTION INFORMATION

Frequency of publication: 2 times/yr.
Circulation: 1,000
Available in microform: Yes
Subscription price: IR£20.00 ($40.00)/yr. institutions; IR£15.00 ($30.00)/yr. individuals
Year to which price refers: 1992

ADVERTISING INFORMATION

Advertising accepted: Yes
Advertising rates: IR£80.00/full page

EDITORIAL DESCRIPTION

Scope: Publishes articles on modern Irish literature.
Reviews books: Yes
Publishes notes: No
Languages accepted: English; Irish Gaelic
Prints abstracts: No
Author-anonymous submission: No

SUBMISSION REQUIREMENTS

Restrictions on contributors: None
Author pays submission fee: No
Author pays page charges: No
Length of articles: 2,500-6,500 words
Length of book reviews: 800 words
Style: Journal
Number of copies required: 1
Copyright ownership: Journal
Rejected manuscripts: Returned
Time before publication decision: 3 mos.
Time between decision and publication: 1 yr.
Number of reviewers: 2-3
Articles submitted per year: 50
Articles published per year: 15-18
Book reviews submitted per year: 25-35
Book reviews published per year: 30

(1292)
*Irodalomtörténet: History of Literature

Péter Nagy, Editor
Pesti Barnabás u.I. III. 51/c.
1052 Budapest, Hungary

Telephone: (36) 1 1377819
First published: 1912
Sponsoring organization: Magyar Irodalomtörténeti Társaság
ISSN: 0324-4970
MLA acronym: Irodalom

SUBSCRIPTION INFORMATION

Frequency of publication: 4 times/yr.
Circulation: 1,000
Available in microform: No
Subscription address: Akadémiai Kiadó, Publishing House of the Hungarian Academy of Sciences, P.O. Box 24, 1363 Budapest, Hungary

ADVERTISING INFORMATION

Advertising accepted: No

EDITORIAL DESCRIPTION

Scope: Publishes articles on Hungarian literary history.
Reviews books: Yes
Publishes notes: Yes
Languages accepted: Hungarian
Prints abstracts: No

SUBMISSION REQUIREMENTS

Restrictions on contributors: None
Author pays submission fee: No
Author pays page charges: No
Length of articles: 20-30 typescript pp.
Length of book reviews: 2-5 typescript pp.
Length of notes: 1-3 pp.
Style: None
Number of copies required: 1
Special requirements: Submit original typescript.
Copyright ownership: Author
Rejected manuscripts: Returned
Time before publication decision: 3-6 weeks
Time between decision and publication: 1 yr.
Number of reviewers: 2-3
Articles submitted per year: 2-300
Articles published per year: 100
Book reviews submitted per year: 350
Book reviews published per year: 150
Notes submitted per year: 10-30
Notes published per year: 15

(1293)
*Irodalomtörténeti Füzetek

István Fenyő, Editor
Ménesi út 11-13
1118 Budapest, Hungary

Telephone: (36) 1 1155614
First published: 1950
Sponsoring organization: Magyar Tudományos Akadémia
ISSN: 0075-0840
MLA acronym: IrodalF

SUBSCRIPTION INFORMATION

Frequency of publication: Irregular
Circulation: 1,000
Available in microform: No
Subscription address: Argumentum Kiadó, VIII. Mária Utca 36, Budapest Hungary
Subscription telephone: (36) 1 1344372

ADVERTISING INFORMATION

Advertising accepted: No

EDITORIAL DESCRIPTION

Scope: Publishes monographs on Hungarian literature.
Reviews books: No
Publishes notes: No
Languages accepted: Hungarian
Prints abstracts: No
Author-anonymous submission: No

SUBMISSION REQUIREMENTS

Restrictions on contributors: None
Author pays submission fee: No
Author pays page charges: No
Length of articles: No restrictions
Length of books: 120-220 pp.
Number of copies required: 2
Copyright ownership: Author & Argumentum Kiadó
Rejected manuscripts: Returned
Time before publication decision: 6 mos.
Time between decision and publication: 2 yrs.
Number of reviewers: 2
Books submitted per year: 4
Books published per year: 4

(1294)
*Irodalomtörténeti Közlemények

Tibor Komlovszki, Editor
Inst. d'Etudes Littéraires de l'Académie Hongroise des Sciences
Ménesi út 11-13
1118 Budapest XI., Hungary

Telephone: (36) 1 1665938
Fax: (36) 1 1853876
First published: 1891
Sponsoring organization: Magyar Tudományos Akadémia, Irodalomtudományi Intézet
ISSN: 0021-1486
MLA acronym: IK

SUBSCRIPTION INFORMATION

Frequency of publication: 6 times/yr.
Circulation: 700
Available in microform: No
Subscription price: 342 Ft/yr.; 57 Ft/single issue
Year to which price refers: 1991
Subscription address: Posta Központi Hírlapiroda, József nádor tér 1, 1900 Budapest V., Hungary

ADVERTISING INFORMATION

Advertising accepted: No

EDITORIAL DESCRIPTION

Scope: Publishes articles on Hungarian literature, criticism, and unknown texts and sources.
Reviews books: Yes
Publishes notes: No
Languages accepted: Hungarian
Prints abstracts: Yes
Author-anonymous submission: No

SUBMISSION REQUIREMENTS

Restrictions on contributors: None
Author pays submission fee: No
Author pays page charges: No
Length of articles: 5-40 typescript pp.
Length of book reviews: 2-10 pp.
Style: None
Number of copies required: 1
Copyright ownership: Author
Rejected manuscripts: Returned
Time before publication decision: 3 mos.
Time between decision and publication: 6-8 mos.
Number of reviewers: 2
Articles submitted per year: 150
Articles published per year: 60-80

Book reviews submitted per year: 50-60
Book reviews published per year: 50-60

(1295)
*Der Islam: Zeitschrift für Geschichte und Kultur des Islamischen Orients

Albrecht Noth, Editor
Univ. Hamburg
Rothenbaumchaussee 36
2000 Hamburg 13, Germany

Telephone: (49) 40 41233180
Fax: (49) 40 41235674
First published: 1910
Sponsoring organization: Deutsche Forschungsgemeinschaft
ISSN: 0021-1818
MLA acronym: Islam

SUBSCRIPTION INFORMATION

Frequency of publication: 2 times/yr.
Circulation: 500
Available in microform: No
Subscription address: Walter de Gruyter & Co., Genthiner Str. 13, 1000 Berlin 30, Germany
Subscription telephone: (49) 30 260050
Subscription fax: (49) 30 26005251

ADVERTISING INFORMATION

Advertising accepted: No

EDITORIAL DESCRIPTION

Scope: Publishes articles on Islamic culture, history, and languages.
Reviews books: Yes
Publishes notes: No
Languages accepted: English; German; French; Italian
Prints abstracts: No
Author-anonymous submission: No

SUBMISSION REQUIREMENTS

Restrictions on contributors: Book reviews are commissioned.
Author pays submission fee: No
Author pays page charges: No
Length of articles: 40 printed pp. maximum; some exceptions are made
Length of book reviews: 1-3 pp.
Style: Scientific
Number of copies required: 1
Special requirements: Manuscripts should be submitted in their definitive form.
Copyright ownership: Author & Walter de Gruyter & Co.
Rejected manuscripts: Returned
Time before publication decision: 6 mos.
Time between decision and publication: 2 yrs.
Number of reviewers: 1
Articles submitted per year: 30-85
Articles published per year: 10
Book reviews submitted per year: 150
Book reviews published per year: 80

(1296)
*Issues in Applied Linguistics

Joseph R. Plummer, Editor
Univ. of California, Los Angeles
Dept. of TESL/Applied Linguistics
3300 Rolfe Hall
405 Hilgard Ave.
Los Angeles, CA 90024

Fax: 310 206-4118
E-mail: lhw1037@uclamvs.bitnet
First published: 1990
Sponsoring organization: UCLA Dept. of Applied Linguistics & Graduate Students' Assn.
ISSN: 1050-4273
MLA acronym: IAL

SUBSCRIPTION INFORMATION

Frequency of publication: 2 times/yr. (June, Dec.)
Available in microform: No
Subscription price: $35.00/yr. institutions; $25.00/yr. individuals
Year to which price refers: 1992

ADVERTISING INFORMATION

Advertising accepted: Yes

EDITORIAL DESCRIPTION

Scope: Publishes articles on language acquisition, language analysis, language education, language testing, language use, and research methodology.
Reviews books: Yes
Publishes notes: Yes
Languages accepted: English
Prints abstracts: Yes
Author-anonymous submission: Yes

SUBMISSION REQUIREMENTS

Restrictions on contributors: Submission by graduate students is preferred.
Author pays submission fee: No
Author pays page charges: No
Style: American Psychological Assn.
Number of copies required: 4
Special requirements: Accepted contributions must be submitted on Macintosh-compatible diskette using Microsoft Word.
Copyright ownership: Univ. of California Regents
Rejected manuscripts: Not returned
Time before publication decision: 1-2 mos.
Number of reviewers: 3
Articles submitted per year: 25
Articles published per year: 10
Book reviews submitted per year: 8
Book reviews published per year: 8

(1297)
Istituto Lombardo, Accademia di Scienze e Lettere, Memorie

Alfonso Giordano, Editor
Ist. Lombardo
Accademia di Scienze e Lettere
Via Borgonuovo, 25
20121 Milan, Italy

First published: 1840
Sponsoring organization: Ist. Lombardo
MLA acronym: ILML

SUBSCRIPTION INFORMATION

Frequency of publication: Irregular
Circulation: 300
Available in microform: No

ADVERTISING INFORMATION

Advertising accepted: No

EDITORIAL DESCRIPTION

Reviews books: No
Prints abstracts: No

SUBMISSION REQUIREMENTS

Restrictions on contributors: Submissions must be presented by a member of the Ist. Lombardo.
Author pays submission fee: Yes
Style: None
Number of copies required: 1

(1298)
Istituto Lombardo, Accademia di Scienze e Lettere, Rendiconti della Classe di Lettere

Alfonso Giordano, Editor
Ist. Lombardo
Accademia di Scienze e Lettere
Via Borgonuovo, 25
20121 Milan, Italy

First published: 1864
Sponsoring organization: Ist. Lombardo
ISSN: 0021-2504
MLA acronym: ILRL

SUBSCRIPTION INFORMATION

Frequency of publication: Annual
Available in microform: No

ADVERTISING INFORMATION

Advertising accepted: No

EDITORIAL DESCRIPTION

Scope: Publishes articles on literature and science.
Reviews books: No
Languages accepted: Italian; French; English; Spanish
Prints abstracts: Yes

SUBMISSION REQUIREMENTS

Restrictions on contributors: Submissions must be presented by a member of the Ist. Lombardo.
Author pays submission fee: No
Author pays page charges: Yes, if article exceeds 12 pp.
Length of articles: 12 pp. maximum
Style: None
Number of copies required: 1
Copyright ownership: Ist. Lombardo
Time between decision and publication: 1 yr.
Number of reviewers: 2
Articles submitted per year: 36
Articles published per year: 36

(1299)
*It Beaken: Tydskrift fan de Fryske Akademy

G. H. Jelsma, Editor
Fryske Akademy
Coulonhûs
Doelestrjitte 8
8911 DX Ljouwert/Leeuwarden, Netherlands

Telephone: (31) 58 131414
Fax: (31) 58 131409
First published: 1938
Sponsoring organization: Fryske Akademy
ISSN: 0005-738X
MLA acronym: ItB

SUBSCRIPTION INFORMATION

Frequency of publication: 4 times/yr.
Circulation: 3,100
Available in microform: No
Subscription price: 42.50 f/yr.
Year to which price refers: 1992

ADVERTISING INFORMATION

Advertising accepted: No

EDITORIAL DESCRIPTION

Scope: Publishes articles on Frisian language, history, and social sciences in relation to Friesland.
Reviews books: Yes
Publishes notes: No

Languages accepted: Dutch; English; Frisian; German
Prints abstracts: No
Author-anonymous submission: No

SUBMISSION REQUIREMENTS

Restrictions on contributors: None
Author pays submission fee: No
Author pays page charges: No
Length of articles: 5-20 pp.
Length of book reviews: 1-2 pp.
Number of copies required: 1
Special requirements: Submit original typescript.
Copyright ownership: Assigned by author to journal
Rejected manuscripts: Returned
Time before publication decision: 1-3 mos.
Time between decision and publication: 2-4 mos.
Number of reviewers: 2-3
Articles submitted per year: 30-40
Articles published per year: 15-25
Book reviews submitted per year: 15
Book reviews published per year: 15

(1300)
*L'Italia Dialettale: Rivista di Dialettologia Italiana

Tristano Bolelli, Editor
Lungarno Mediceo 40
56127 Pisa, Italy

Telephone: (39) 50 542485
First published: 1925
ISSN: 0085-2295
MLA acronym: ID

SUBSCRIPTION INFORMATION

Frequency of publication: Annual
Circulation: 600
Available in microform: No
Subscription price: 70,000 Lit/yr. Italy; 140,000 Lit/yr. elsewhere
Year to which price refers: 1992
Subscription address: Giardini Editori, Via S. Bibbiana 28, 56100 Pisa, Italy
Subscription telephone: (39) 50 855390

ADVERTISING INFORMATION

Advertising accepted: No

EDITORIAL DESCRIPTION

Scope: Publishes articles on descriptive and historical Italian dialectology.
Reviews books: Yes
Publishes notes: Yes
Languages accepted: Italian
Prints abstracts: No
Author-anonymous submission: No

SUBMISSION REQUIREMENTS

Restrictions on contributors: None
Author pays submission fee: No
Author pays page charges: No
Length of notes: No restrictions
Copyright ownership: Journal
Rejected manuscripts: Not returned
Time before publication decision: 6 mos.
Time between decision and publication: 6 mos.
Articles submitted per year: 18-20
Articles published per year: 8-10
Book reviews submitted per year: 6
Book reviews published per year: 0-6
Notes submitted per year: 2-6

(1301)
Italia Francescana

Via V. Veneto, 27
00187 Rome, Italy

First published: 1927
Sponsoring organization: Capuchin Italian Inst.
MLA acronym: IFr

SUBSCRIPTION INFORMATION

Frequency of publication: 6 times/yr.
Circulation: 1,000
Available in microform: No

ADVERTISING INFORMATION

Advertising accepted: No

EDITORIAL DESCRIPTION

Scope: Publishes articles on culture.
Reviews books: Yes
Languages accepted: Italian
Prints abstracts: Yes

SUBMISSION REQUIREMENTS

Restrictions on contributors: None
Author pays submission fee: No
Author pays page charges: No
Length of articles: 20 pp.
Length of book reviews: No restrictions
Style: None
Number of copies required: 1
Special requirements: Submit typescript.
Copyright ownership: Journal
Rejected manuscripts: Returned
Time before publication decision: 2 mos.
Time between decision and publication: 2 mos.
Number of reviewers: 3
Articles published per year: 40

(1302)
Italia Medioevale e Umanistica

Giovanni Berti, Editor
Editrice Antenore
Via G. Rusca, 15
35100 Padua, Italy

First published: 1958
ISSN: 0391-7495
MLA acronym: IMU

SUBSCRIPTION INFORMATION

Frequency of publication: Annual
Available in microform: No

ADVERTISING INFORMATION

Advertising accepted: No

EDITORIAL DESCRIPTION

Scope: Publishes articles on cultural history of the Italian Middle Ages and Renaissance with an emphasis on literature.
Reviews books: No
Publishes notes: Yes
Languages accepted: English; French; Italian; German; Spanish
Prints abstracts: No
Author-anonymous submission: No

SUBMISSION REQUIREMENTS

Restrictions on contributors: None
Author pays submission fee: No
Author pays page charges: No
Number of copies required: 1
Copyright ownership: Journal
Rejected manuscripts: Returned
Time before publication decision: 4-5 mos.
Time between decision and publication: 12-15 mos.

Number of reviewers: 5
Articles published per year: 12-15
Notes published per year: 8-10

(1303)
*Italian Americana

Carol Bonomo Albright, Editor
Univ. of Rhode Island
College of Continuing Education
199 Promenade St.
Providence, RI 02908-5090

Additional editorial address: John Paul Russo, Review Editor, English Dept., Univ. of Miami, Coral Gables, FL 33124
Telephone: 401 277-6180
First published: 1974
Sponsoring organization: American Italian Historical Assn.; Univ. of Rhode Island, Providence
ISSN: 0096-8846
MLA acronym: ItalAm

SUBSCRIPTION INFORMATION

Frequency of publication: 2 times/yr. (Spring-Summer, Fall-Winter) plus supplement
Circulation: 1,000
Subscription price: $22.50/yr. institutions; $25.00/yr. individual nonmembers; $15.00/yr. individual members; $15.00/yr. student nonmembers; $5.00/yr. student members; $35.00/yr. outside US
Year to which price refers: 1993

ADVERTISING INFORMATION

Advertising accepted: Yes
Advertising rates: $150.00/full page

EDITORIAL DESCRIPTION

Scope: The journal is a cultural and historical review devoted to the Italian experience in the New World, including studies and commentary in the humanities and social sciences, fiction, poetry, bibliographies, and reviews of significant books, films, plays, and art.
Reviews books: Yes
Publishes notes: Yes
Languages accepted: English
Prints abstracts: No
Author-anonymous submission: Yes

SUBMISSION REQUIREMENTS

Restrictions on contributors: None
Author pays submission fee: No
Author pays page charges: No
Length of articles: 15-20 pp.
Length of book reviews: 600-1,000 words
Length of notes: 500-600 words
Style: MLA
Number of copies required: 3
Special requirements: Submit original typescript and 2 copies.
Rejected manuscripts: Returned; enclose return postage.
Time before publication decision: 2-4 mos.
Time between decision and publication: 2-12 mos.
Number of reviewers: 3
Articles submitted per year: 50
Articles published per year: 6-8
Book reviews submitted per year: 40-50
Book reviews published per year: 30-35

(1304)
*Italian Books and Periodicals: Cultural and Bibliographic Review

Elio Silvestro, Editor
Ministero per i Beni Culturali ed Ambientali
Via del Collegio Romano 27
00186 Rome, Italy

Fax: (39) 6 6723380
First published: 1958
ISSN: 0021-2881
MLA acronym: IBP

SUBSCRIPTION INFORMATION

Frequency of publication: Annual
Available in microform: No
Subscription price: 87,000 Lit/yr.
Year to which price refers: 1991
Subscription address: Ist. Poligrafico e Zecca della Stato, Piazza Verdi, 10, 00198 Rome, Italy

ADVERTISING INFORMATION

Advertising accepted: No

EDITORIAL DESCRIPTION

Scope: Publishes information on Italian books and periodicals.
Reviews books: Yes
Publishes notes: Yes
Languages accepted: Italian; English; French; German; Spanish
Prints abstracts: No
Author-anonymous submission: No

SUBMISSION REQUIREMENTS

Author pays submission fee: No
Author pays page charges: No
Length of articles: 3,000 words
Length of book reviews: 700 words
Length of notes: 80 words
Number of copies required: 3
Articles published per year: 6-7
Book reviews published per year: 270
Notes published per year: 30

(1305)
*Italian Culture

Mario Aste, Editor
Dept. of Languages
Univ. of Massachusetts at Lowell
One University Ave.
Lowell, MA 01854

Telephone: 508 934-4123
Fax: 508 934-1035
First published: 1978
Sponsoring organization: American Assn. for Italian Studies (AAIS)
ISSN: 0161-4622
MLA acronym: ItC

SUBSCRIPTION INFORMATION

Frequency of publication: Annual
Circulation: 700
Available in microform: No
Subscription price: $20.00/yr. institutions & individuals; $15.00/yr. students, retirees, & unemployed
Year to which price refers: 1992
Subscription address: Carla Lucente, Modern Languages Dept., Duquesne Univ., Pittsburgh, PA 15282
Subscription telephone: 412 434-6404; 412 434-6415
Subscription fax: 412 434-5197

ADVERTISING INFORMATION

Advertising accepted: Yes
Advertising rates: $50.00/full page

EDITORIAL DESCRIPTION

Scope: Publishes articles on Italian culture, including language, literature, fine arts, music, film, and politics. Includes studies in comparative literature.
Reviews books: Yes
Publishes notes: Yes
Languages accepted: English; French; Italian
Prints abstracts: No
Author-anonymous submission: No

SUBMISSION REQUIREMENTS

Restrictions on contributors: Unsolicited manuscripts will be considered, but if accepted, author must join the American Assn. for Italian Studies. Articles and book reviews cannot have been published elsewhere.
Author pays submission fee: No
Author pays page charges: No
Length of articles: 18 pp. with footnotes
Length of book reviews: 1,000 words
Length of notes: 600 words
Style: MLA
Number of copies required: 2
Special requirements: Submit double-spaced typescript. If word processed, submit diskette with typescript.
Copyright ownership: Journal
Rejected manuscripts: Returned; enclose return postage.
Time before publication decision: 3 mos.
Time between decision and publication: 12-15 mos.
Number of reviewers: 2-3
Articles submitted per year: 25-45
Articles published per year: 18-25
Book reviews submitted per year: 30
Book reviews published per year: 6-15
Notes submitted per year: 5
Notes published per year: 1

(1306)
Italian Quarterly

Guido Guarino, Editor
Dept. of Italian
Rutgers Univ.
New Brunswick, NJ 08903

First published: 1957
Sponsoring organization: Rutgers Univ.
ISSN: 0021-2954
MLA acronym: IQ

SUBSCRIPTION INFORMATION

Frequency of publication: 4 times/yr.
Circulation: 500
Available in microform: No

ADVERTISING INFORMATION

Advertising accepted: Yes

EDITORIAL DESCRIPTION

Scope: Publishes major Italian literary criticism, cultural material, and creative writing.
Reviews books: Yes
Publishes notes: No
Languages accepted: English; Italian
Prints abstracts: No
Author-anonymous submission: No

SUBMISSION REQUIREMENTS

Restrictions on contributors: Book reviews are solicited.
Author pays submission fee: No
Author pays page charges: No
Length of articles: 20 pp.
Length of book reviews: 1,500 words
Style: MLA
Number of copies required: 2
Copyright ownership: Journal
Rejected manuscripts: Returned; enclose return postage.
Time before publication decision: 3 mos.
Time between decision and publication: 1 yr.
Number of reviewers: 2
Articles submitted per year: 100
Articles published per year: 25
Book reviews published per year: 25

(1307)
*Italian Studies

L. Pertile, G. Lepschy, M. Caesar, J. Lorch, & B. Richardson, Editors
Dept. of Italian
Univ. of Edinburgh
David Hume Tower, George Square
Edinburgh EH8 9JX, Scotland

Additional editorial address: For book reviews contact: M. McLaughlin, Christ Church, Oxford OX1 1DP, England
Telephone: (44) 31 6503646
Fax: (44) 31 6620772
E-mail: L.pertile@uk.ac.edinburgh
First published: 1937
Sponsoring organization: Soc. for Italian Studies
ISSN: 0075-1634
MLA acronym: IS

SUBSCRIPTION INFORMATION

Frequency of publication: Annual
Circulation: 750
Available in microform: No
Subscription price: £16.00/yr. institutions United Kingdom & Ireland; $40.00/yr. institutions elsewhere; £15.00/yr. individuals United Kingdom & Ireland; $35.00/yr. individuals elsewhere
Year to which price refers: 1991
Subscription address: Treasurer, Soc. for Italian Studies, Dept. of Italian, Hetherington Bldg., The University, Glasgow G12 8QL, Scotland
Subscription telephone: (44) 41 3398855 ext. 7327

ADVERTISING INFORMATION

Advertising accepted: Yes
Advertising rates: Request from Hon. Treasurer

EDITORIAL DESCRIPTION

Scope: Publishes the results of research in Italian studies.
Reviews books: Yes
Publishes notes: Yes
Languages accepted: English; Italian
Prints abstracts: No
Author-anonymous submission: Yes

SUBMISSION REQUIREMENTS

Restrictions on contributors: Preference is given to scholars working in Great Britain or with strong U.K. connections. Book reviews are commissioned.
Author pays submission fee: No
Author pays page charges: No
Length of articles: No restrictions
Style: Modern Humanities Research Assn.
Number of copies required: 2
Copyright ownership: Soc. for Italian Studies
Rejected manuscripts: Returned
Time before publication decision: 6 weeks
Time between decision and publication: 6 mos.
Number of reviewers: 6
Articles submitted per year: 15
Articles published per year: 6-9
Book reviews published per year: 20-25
Notes submitted per year: 1-2

(1308)
*The Italianist: Journal of the Department of Italian Studies, University of Reading

Zygmunt G. Barański & Shirley W. Vinall, Editors
Dept. of Italian Studies
Univ. of Reading
Whiteknights, Reading RG6 2AA, Berks, England

Telephone: (44) 734 318401
Fax: (44) 734 314404
First published: 1981
Sponsoring organization: Dept. of Italian Studies, Univ. of Reading
ISSN: 0261-4340
MLA acronym: Italianist

SUBSCRIPTION INFORMATION

Frequency of publication: Annual (Fall)
Circulation: 350
Available in microform: No
Subscription price: £9.00/yr.
Year to which price refers: 1991

ADVERTISING INFORMATION

Advertising accepted: Yes

EDITORIAL DESCRIPTION

Scope: Publishes articles on methodology and on all aspects of Italian art, culture, literature, and life.
Reviews books: No
Publishes notes: Yes
Languages accepted: Italian; English
Prints abstracts: No
Author-anonymous submission: No

SUBMISSION REQUIREMENTS

Restrictions on contributors: Review articles are commissioned.
Author pays submission fee: No
Author pays page charges: No
Length of articles: No restrictions
Length of notes: No restrictions
Style: Modern Humanities Research Assn.
Number of copies required: 2
Copyright ownership: Author
Rejected manuscripts: Returned
Time before publication decision: 4-6 weeks
Time between decision and publication: 6-18 mos.
Number of reviewers: 3-5
Articles submitted per year: 12-15
Articles published per year: 6-7
Notes submitted per year: 6-7
Notes published per year: 3-4

(1309)
*Italianistica: Rivista di Letteratura Italiana

Davide De Camilli, Michele Dell'Aquila, & Bruno Porcelli, Editors
Giardini Editori e Stampatori
Via delle Sorgenti, 23
56010 Agnano Pisano, Italy

Telephone: (39) 50 855390
Fax: (39) 50 856106
First published: 1972
ISSN: 0391-3368
MLA acronym: IRLI

SUBSCRIPTION INFORMATION

Frequency of publication: 3 times/yr.
Circulation: 2,000
Available in microform: No
Subscription price: 170,000 Lit/yr. Italy; 270,000 Lit/yr. elsewhere
Year to which price refers: 1991

ADVERTISING INFORMATION

Advertising accepted: Yes

EDITORIAL DESCRIPTION

Scope: Publishes articles on Italian literature.
Reviews books: Yes
Publishes notes: Yes
Languages accepted: Italian; English; French
Prints abstracts: Yes

SUBMISSION REQUIREMENTS

Author pays submission fee: No
Author pays page charges: No
Length of articles: 30 pp.
Length of book reviews: 2 pp.
Length of notes: 10 pp.
Number of copies required: 1
Special requirements: Submit original typescript.
Copyright ownership: Journal
Rejected manuscripts: Not returned
Time before publication decision: 3 mos.
Time between decision and publication: 1 yr.
Number of reviewers: 3
Articles published per year: 9
Book reviews published per year: 30
Notes published per year: 12

(1310)
*Italica

Robert J. Rodini, Editor
618 Van Hise Hall
Univ. of Wisconsin
Madison, WI 53706

Telephone: 608 262-4076
Fax: 608 262-4747
E-mail: RJRODIN@macc.wisc.edu
First published: 1924
Sponsoring organization: American Assn. of Teachers of Italian
ISSN: 0021-3020
MLA acronym: Italica

SUBSCRIPTION INFORMATION

Frequency of publication: 4 times/yr. (Spring, Summer, Fall, Winter)
Circulation: 1,700
Available in microform: No
Subscription price: $40.00/yr. institutions; $30.00/yr. individuals
Year to which price refers: 1992
Subscription address: Louis Kibler, Dept. of Modern Romance Languages & Literatures, Wayne State Univ., Detroit, MI 48202
Subscription telephone: 313 577-3219

ADVERTISING INFORMATION

Advertising accepted: Yes

EDITORIAL DESCRIPTION

Scope: Focuses on Italian literature, language, and pedagogy.
Reviews books: Yes
Publishes notes: Yes
Languages accepted: English; Italian; French; Spanish; German
Prints abstracts: No
Author-anonymous submission: Yes

SUBMISSION REQUIREMENTS

Restrictions on contributors: Book reviews are commissioned.
Author pays submission fee: No
Author pays page charges: No
Length of articles: 20-25 double-spaced typescript pp.
Style: MLA
Number of copies required: 2
Special requirements: Submit original typescript.
Copyright ownership: Journal
Rejected manuscripts: Returned; enclose return postage.
Time before publication decision: 4 mos.
Time between decision and publication: 2 yrs. maximum
Number of reviewers: 3
Articles submitted per year: 50
Articles published per year: 18
Book reviews published per year: 40
Notes published per year: 4

(1311)
*Italienisch: Zeitschrift für Italienische Sprache und Literatur

Arno Euler, Gerhard Goebel-Schilling, Salvatore A. Sanna, & Hermann H. Wetzel, Editors
Arndtstr. 12
6000 Frankfurt 1, Germany

Telephone: (49) 69 746752
First published: 1979
Sponsoring organization: Deutsch-Italienische Vereinigung
ISSN: 0171-4996
MLA acronym: ItalienischZ

SUBSCRIPTION INFORMATION

Frequency of publication: 2 times/yr.
Available in microform: No
Subscription price: 25 DM/yr. institutions & individuals; 18 DM/yr. students
Year to which price refers: 1992
Subscription address: Diesterweg Verlag, Wächtersbacher Str. 89, Postfach 63 01 80, 6000 Frankfurt 63, Germany
Subscription telephone: (49) 69 420810

ADVERTISING INFORMATION

Advertising accepted: Yes
Advertising rates: 130 DM/quarter page; 250 DM/half page; 480 DM/full page

EDITORIAL DESCRIPTION

Scope: Publishes papers on Italian in study and teaching. These include articles on Italian literature, Italian language, Italian linguistics, and Italian culture.
Reviews books: Yes
Publishes notes: Yes
Languages accepted: Italian; German
Prints abstracts: Yes
Author-anonymous submission: No

SUBMISSION REQUIREMENTS

Restrictions on contributors: None
Author pays submission fee: No
Author pays page charges: No
Length of articles: 4,100 words
Length of book reviews: 810 words
Length of notes: 600 words
Number of copies required: 2
Special requirements: Submit a 200-word abstract.
Copyright ownership: Editor for 1 yr.
Rejected manuscripts: Not returned
Time before publication decision: 1-3 mos.
Time between decision and publication: 4-6 mos.
Number of reviewers: 5
Articles submitted per year: 20-24
Articles published per year: 14-17
Book reviews submitted per year: 25-30
Book reviews published per year: 16-20
Notes submitted per year: 20
Notes published per year: 18

(1312)
Italyan Filolojisi/Filologia Italiana

Italyan Filolojisi Kürsüsü
D.T.C. Fakültesi
Ankara, Turkey

First published: 1969
Sponsoring organization: Italian Cultural Centre
MLA acronym: ItF

SUBSCRIPTION INFORMATION

Frequency of publication: Annual
Circulation: 700
Available in microform: Yes

ADVERTISING INFORMATION

Advertising accepted: Yes

EDITORIAL DESCRIPTION

Scope: Publishes research on Italian language and literature, translations, and unedited literary works.
Reviews books: Yes
Publishes notes: No
Languages accepted: Italian; Turkish
Prints abstracts: No

SUBMISSION REQUIREMENTS

Author pays submission fee: Yes
Author pays page charges: Yes
Length of articles: 10 typescript pp.
Length of book reviews: No restrictions
Style: None
Number of copies required: 1
Copyright ownership: Author
Rejected manuscripts: Not returned
Time before publication decision: 2 mos.
Time between decision and publication: 4 mos.
Number of reviewers: 3
Articles submitted per year: 10
Articles published per year: 10
Book reviews submitted per year: 10
Book reviews published per year: 10

(1313)
***ITL: Review of Applied Linguistics**

N. Delbecque, Editor
Blijde-Inkomststr. 21
3000 Louvain, Belgium

Telephone: (32) 16 285030
Fax: (32) 16 285025
First published: 1968
Sponsoring organization: Katholieke Univ. te Leuven, Afdeling Toegepaste Linguïstiek; Belgian Government
ISSN: 0019-0810
MLA acronym: ITL

SUBSCRIPTION INFORMATION

Frequency of publication: 2 times/yr.
Circulation: 800
Available in microform: No
Subscription price: 900 BF/yr.
Year to which price refers: 1992

ADVERTISING INFORMATION

Advertising accepted: No

EDITORIAL DESCRIPTION

Scope: Publishes articles on applied linguistics.
Reviews books: Yes
Publishes notes: Yes
Languages accepted: Dutch; English; French; German; Spanish
Prints abstracts: Yes
Author-anonymous submission: Yes

SUBMISSION REQUIREMENTS

Restrictions on contributors: None
Author pays submission fee: No
Author pays page charges: No
Length of articles: No restrictions
Length of book reviews: No restrictions
Length of notes: No restrictions
Style: MLA
Number of copies required: 1
Special requirements: Abstract is recommended, but not required.
Copyright ownership: Author
Rejected manuscripts: Returned
Time before publication decision: 2 mos.
Time between decision and publication: 1 yr. for articles; 18 mos. for reviews
Number of reviewers: 3
Articles submitted per year: 45-50
Articles published per year: 20-25
Book reviews submitted per year: 10-12
Book reviews published per year: 10
Notes submitted per year: 4
Notes published per year: 2-3

(1314)
Izraz: Časopis za Književnu i Umjetničku Kritiku

Dževad Karahasan, Editor
P. Preradovića 3
Poštanski fah 129,
Sarajevo, Bosnia and Herzegovina

First published: 1957
Sponsoring organization: Republican Union of Culture
ISSN: 0021-3381
MLA acronym: Izraz

SUBSCRIPTION INFORMATION

Frequency of publication: 12 times/yr.
Circulation: 1,000
Available in microform: No
Subscription address: SOUR "Svjetlost," at the above address

ADVERTISING INFORMATION

Advertising accepted: No

EDITORIAL DESCRIPTION

Scope: Publishes articles on literary and art criticism.
Reviews books: Yes
Languages accepted: Serbo-Croatian
Prints abstracts: No

SUBMISSION REQUIREMENTS

Restrictions on contributors: None
Author pays submission fee: No
Author pays page charges: No
Length of articles: 3-60 pp.
Length of book reviews: 2-5 pp.
Style: None
Number of copies required: 1
Copyright ownership: Author
Rejected manuscripts: Not returned
Time before publication decision: 1 mo.
Time between decision and publication: 1-3 mos.
Number of reviewers: 2-3
Articles submitted per year: 400-600
Articles published per year: 150-200
Book reviews submitted per year: 50-80
Book reviews published per year: 60-70

(1315)
Izvestiia Akademii Nauk, Seriia Literatury i Iazyka

V. N. Iartseva, Editor
ul. Kachalova 6/2
121069 Moscow, Russia

Telephone: (7) 95 2901709
First published: 1940
Historical variations in title: Formerly *Izvestiia Akademii Nauk S.S.S.R., Seriia Literatury i Iazyka*
Sponsoring organization: Otdelenie Literatury i Iazyka AN
ISSN: 0321-1711
MLA acronym: IAN

SUBSCRIPTION INFORMATION

Frequency of publication: 6 times/yr.
Subscription address: Mezhdunarodnaia Kniga, Moscow G-200, Russia

EDITORIAL DESCRIPTION

Scope: Publishes articles on language and literature, with an emphasis on Russian language and literature.
Reviews books: Yes
Languages accepted: Russian
Prints abstracts: No

SUBMISSION REQUIREMENTS

Author pays submission fee: No
Author pays page charges: No
Length of articles: 40,000 characters
Length of book reviews: 10,000 characters
Number of copies required: 2
Special requirements: Submit original typescript plus 1 copy.
Rejected manuscripts: Not returned
Time before publication decision: 1-3 mos.
Time between decision and publication: 2 mos.
Number of reviewers: 2-3
Articles submitted per year: 100-120
Articles published per year: 80
Book reviews submitted per year: 30
Book reviews published per year: 12

(1316)
Izvestiia Akademii Nauk Turkmenskoĭ SSR, Seriia Obshchestvennykh Nauk

A. A. Rosliakov, Editor
Turkmen Academy of Sciences
ul. Gogolia, 15
744000 Ashkhabad, Turkmenistan

First published: 1960
ISSN: 0205-9932
MLA acronym: IAT

SUBSCRIPTION INFORMATION

Frequency of publication: 6 times/yr.

EDITORIAL DESCRIPTION

Scope: Publishes articles on Turkmen politics, literature, and culture.

(1317)
***Jaarboek Koninklijke Belgische Commissie voor Volkskunde, Vlaamse Afdeling**

Koninklijke Belgische Commissie voor Volkskunde
Markiesstr. 1
1000 Brussels, Belgium

First published: 1939

MLA acronym: KBCJ

SUBSCRIPTION INFORMATION

Frequency of publication: Annual
Available in microform: No

ADVERTISING INFORMATION

Advertising accepted: No

EDITORIAL DESCRIPTION

Scope: Publishes the annual report of commission proceedings and an annual bibliography of Flemish folklore.
Reviews books: No
Publishes notes: Yes
Languages accepted: Dutch
Prints abstracts: No

SUBMISSION REQUIREMENTS

Author pays submission fee: No
Author pays page charges: No
Copyright ownership: Author

(1318)
*Jabberwocky: The Journal of the Lewis Carroll Society

Selwyn H. Goodacre,
69 Ashby Rd.
Woodville
Burton-on-Trent
Staffs DE11 7BZ, England

Telephone: (44) 283 221652
First published: 1969
Sponsoring organization: Lewis Carroll Soc.
ISSN: 0305-8182
MLA acronym: Jabberwocky

SUBSCRIPTION INFORMATION

Frequency of publication: 2-4 times/yr.
Circulation: 300
Available in microform: No
Subscription price: £10.00/yr. institutions; £8.00/yr. individuals
Year to which price refers: 1990
Subscription address: Lewis Carroll Soc., 36 Bradgers Hill Road, Luton, Beds. England LU2 3EL

ADVERTISING INFORMATION

Advertising accepted: Yes, inserts only

EDITORIAL DESCRIPTION

Scope: Includes original articles, reviews, and letters to the Editor concerning the life and works of Charles L. Dodgson.
Reviews books: Yes
Publishes notes: Yes
Languages accepted: English
Prints abstracts: No
Author-anonymous submission: No

SUBMISSION REQUIREMENTS

Restrictions on contributors: None
Author pays submission fee: No
Author pays page charges: No
Length of articles: 1,000-4,000 words
Length of book reviews: 500-1,500 words
Length of notes: 100-200 words
Style: Journal
Number of copies required: 1
Special requirements: Submit original, double-spaced typescript on A4 (8 1/4 in. x 11 3/4 in.) paper.
Copyright ownership: Assigned by author to the Lewis Carroll Soc.
Rejected manuscripts: Returned
Time before publication decision: 1 mo.
Time between decision and publication: 6-18 mos.
Number of reviewers: 1
Articles submitted per year: 20-25
Articles published per year: 16-20
Book reviews submitted per year: 5-10
Book reviews published per year: 5-10
Notes submitted per year: 5-10
Notes published per year: 5-10

(1319)
*Jadavpur Journal of Comparative Literature

Amiya Dev, Editor
Dept. of Comparative Literature
Jadavpur Univ.
Calcutta 700 032, India

First published: 1961
Sponsoring organization: Jadavpur Univ.
ISSN: 0048-1143
MLA acronym: JJCL

SUBSCRIPTION INFORMATION

Frequency of publication: Annual
Circulation: 500
Available in microform: No
Subscription price: $15.00/yr.
Year to which price refers: 1993
Subscription address: Accounts Officer, Jadavpur Univ., Calcutta 700 032, India

ADVERTISING INFORMATION

Advertising accepted: No

EDITORIAL DESCRIPTION

Scope: Publishes articles on all aspects of comparative literature.
Reviews books: Yes
Publishes notes: Yes
Languages accepted: Bengali; English
Prints abstracts: No

SUBMISSION REQUIREMENTS

Restrictions on contributors: None
Author pays submission fee: No
Author pays page charges: No
Length of articles: 2,500-10,000 words
Length of book reviews: 500-2,000 words
Style: MLA with slight variations
Number of copies required: 1
Special requirements: Submit original typescript.
Copyright ownership: Assigned by author to journal
Rejected manuscripts: Returned; enclose return postage.
Time before publication decision: 3 mos.
Time between decision and publication: 1 yr.
Number of reviewers: 3
Articles published per year: 8-10
Book reviews published per year: 1-3
Notes published per year: 1-10

(1320)
*Jahrbuch der Deutschen Schillergesellschaft

Wilfried Barner, Walter Müller-Seidel, & Ulrich Ott, Editors
Jahrbuch-Redaktion
Albrecht Bergold
Schiller Nationalmuseum/Deutsches Literaturarchiv
Postfach 1162
7142 Marbach a. N., Germany

Telephone: (49) 7144 84800
Fax: (49) 7144 15976
First published: 1957
Sponsoring organization: Deutsche Schillergesellschaft e.V.
ISSN: 0070-4318
MLA acronym: JDSG

SUBSCRIPTION INFORMATION

Frequency of publication: Annual
Circulation: No
Available in microform: No
Subscription price: 48 DM/yr.
Year to which price refers: 1992
Subscription address: Alfred Kröner Verlag, Postfach 10 28 62, Reinsburgstr. 56, 7000 Stuttgart 10, Germany
Subscription telephone: (49) 711 620221
Subscription fax: (49) 711 6159946

ADVERTISING INFORMATION

Advertising accepted: No

EDITORIAL DESCRIPTION

Scope: Focuses on the study of German language and literature since 1750.
Reviews books: No
Publishes notes: No
Languages accepted: German
Prints abstracts: No
Author-anonymous submission: No

SUBMISSION REQUIREMENTS

Author pays submission fee: No
Author pays page charges: No
Length of articles: 40 pp. maximum
Style: Merkblatt der Redaktion
Number of copies required: 2
Special requirements: Submit original typescript; type using one and one-half space.
Copyright ownership: Journal for 5 yrs.
Rejected manuscripts: Returned
Time before publication decision: 3-6 mos.
Time between decision and publication: 6 mos.
Number of reviewers: 3
Articles submitted per year: 40-60
Articles published per year: 20-25

(1321)
*Jahrbuch der Grillparzer-Gesellschaft

Robert Pichl & Hubert Reitterer, Editors
Gumpendorferstr. 15/1
1060 Vienna, Austria

Additional editorial address: Inst. für Germanistik an der Univ. Wien, Dr. Karl Lueger-Ring 1/Stg. 7, 1010 Vienna, Austria
Telephone: (43) 1 22240103 ext. 2034 & 2036
Fax: (43) 1 2224088725
First published: 1891
MLA acronym: JGG

SUBSCRIPTION INFORMATION

Frequency of publication: Once every 2 yrs.
Available in microform: No
Subscription price: 465 S/volume
Year to which price refers: 1992
Subscription address: Hora-Verlag, Hackhofergasse 8-10, 1195 Vienna, Austria
Subscription telephone: (43) 1 222374495
Subscription fax: (43) 1 222376393

ADVERTISING INFORMATION

Advertising accepted: Yes
Advertising rates: 10,000 S/full page

EDITORIAL DESCRIPTION

Scope: Publishes articles on the works of Grillparzer, his contemporaries, and important Austrian authors of the 20th century, e.g. Ingeborg Bachmann.
Reviews books: Yes
Publishes notes: Yes
Languages accepted: German

Prints abstracts: No
Author-anonymous submission: No

SUBMISSION REQUIREMENTS

Author pays submission fee: No
Author pays page charges: No
Length of articles: 50,000 words
Length of book reviews: 5,000 words
Length of notes: 5,000 words
Style: MLA preferred
Number of copies required: 3
Special requirements: Submit original typescript and 2 copies.
Copyright ownership: Journal
Rejected manuscripts: Not returned
Time before publication decision: 6 mos. maximum
Time between decision and publication: 6 mos. maximum
Number of reviewers: 3
Articles submitted per year: 15
Articles published per year: 10
Book reviews submitted per year: 5
Book reviews published per year: 5
Notes submitted per year: 2
Notes published per year: 2

(1322)
*Jahrbuch der Jean-Paul-Gesellschaft

Kurt Wölfel, Editor
Germanistisches Seminar der Univ. Bonn
Am Hof 1d
5300 Bonn 1, Germany

First published: 1966
Sponsoring organization: Jean-Paul Gesellschaft
ISSN: 0075-3580
MLA acronym: JJPG

SUBSCRIPTION INFORMATION

Frequency of publication: Annual
Circulation: 750
Available in microform: No

ADVERTISING INFORMATION

Advertising accepted: No

EDITORIAL DESCRIPTION

Scope: Publishes articles on Johann Paul Friedrich Richter and topics from the 18th and 19th centuries connected with his work.
Reviews books: Yes
Publishes notes: Yes
Languages accepted: German
Prints abstracts: No
Author-anonymous submission: No

SUBMISSION REQUIREMENTS

Restrictions on contributors: Book reviews are solicited.
Author pays submission fee: No
Author pays page charges: No
Length of articles: 50 pp. maximum
Length of book reviews: No restrictions
Length of notes: No restrictions
Style: None
Number of copies required: 1
Copyright ownership: Author
Rejected manuscripts: Returned
Time before publication decision: 2 mos.
Time between decision and publication: 6-18 mos.
Number of reviewers: 1
Articles submitted per year: 5-10
Articles published per year: 6-8
Book reviews published per year: 3

(1323)
*Jahrbuch der Karl-May-Gesellschaft

Claus Roxin, Heinz Stolte, & Hans Wollschläger, Editors
Karl-May-Gesellschaft
Maximiliankorso 45
1000 Berlin 28, Germany

Telephone: (49) 30 4061033
First published: 1970
Sponsoring organization: Karl-May-Gesellschaft
ISSN: 0300-1989
MLA acronym: JKMG

SUBSCRIPTION INFORMATION

Frequency of publication: Annual
Circulation: 1,500
Available in microform: No
Subscription price: 48 DM/yr.
Year to which price refers: 1991
Subscription address: Hansa-Verlag, Postfach 1480, 2250 Husum, Germany
Subscription telephone: (49) 4841 6081
Subscription fax: (49) 4841 61397

ADVERTISING INFORMATION

Advertising accepted: Yes
Advertising rates: Request from Hansa-Verlag

EDITORIAL DESCRIPTION

Scope: Publishes research on the life and works of Karl May from a literary, psychological, sociological, and interdisciplinary viewpoint.
Reviews books: Yes
Publishes notes: Yes
Languages accepted: German
Prints abstracts: No
Author-anonymous submission: No

SUBMISSION REQUIREMENTS

Restrictions on contributors: None
Author pays submission fee: No
Author pays page charges: No
Length of articles: 10-100 pp.
Length of book reviews: 2-3 pp.
Length of notes: 5-7 pp.
Style: MLA
Number of copies required: 1
Special requirements: Submit typescript. Texts submitted in languages other than German will be translated.
Copyright ownership: Assigned by author to Karl-May-Gesellschaft
Rejected manuscripts: Returned
Time before publication decision: 1 mo.
Time between decision and publication: 6-12 mos.
Number of reviewers: 3
Articles submitted per year: 25-30
Articles published per year: 10-15
Book reviews submitted per year: 6
Book reviews published per year: 3
Notes submitted per year: 7-10
Notes published per year: 3-5

(1324)
*Jahrbuch der Österreichischen Byzantinistik

Herbert Hunger & Wolfram Hörandner, Editors
Inst. für Byzantinistik & Neogräzistik
Univ. Wien
Postgasse 7-9
1010 Vienna, Austria

Telephone: (43) 222 51581404
Fax: (43) 222 5139541
First published: 1951
Sponsoring organization: Österreichische Akademie der Wissenschaften, Kommission für Byzantinistik; Univ. Wien, Inst. für Byzantinistik & Neogräzistik
ISSN: 0378-8660
MLA acronym: JÖBG

SUBSCRIPTION INFORMATION

Frequency of publication: Annual
Available in microform: No
Subscription address: Österreichische Akademie der Wissenschaften, Ignaz Seipel-Platz II, 1010 Vienna, Austria
Subscription telephone: (43) 222 51581

ADVERTISING INFORMATION

Advertising accepted: No

EDITORIAL DESCRIPTION

Scope: Publishes articles concerning history, literature, art, and culture of Byzantium.
Reviews books: Yes
Publishes notes: Yes
Languages accepted: English; German; Italian; French; Latin; Greek
Prints abstracts: No

SUBMISSION REQUIREMENTS

Restrictions on contributors: None
Author pays submission fee: No
Author pays page charges: No
Length of articles: 3-30 typescript pp. (30 lines per page)
Length of book reviews: 30-150 lines
Length of notes: 30 lines maximum
Style: Journal
Number of copies required: 1
Special requirements: Submit original typescript.
Copyright ownership: Editor
Rejected manuscripts: Returned
Time before publication decision: 2 mos.
Time between decision and publication: 1-2 yrs.
Number of reviewers: 2
Articles submitted per year: 25
Articles published per year: 15-20
Book reviews submitted per year: 40
Book reviews published per year: 40
Notes submitted per year: 20
Notes published per year: 20

(1325)
Jahrbuch der Raabe-Gesellschaft

Hans-Jürgen Schrader & Josef Daum, Editors
173, route d'Aïre
1219 Aïre/Geneva Switzerland

First published: 1960
Sponsoring organization: Raabe-Gesellschaft
ISSN: 0075-2371
MLA acronym: JRG

SUBSCRIPTION INFORMATION

Frequency of publication: Annual
Circulation: 1,100
Available in microform: No
Subscription address: Max Niemeyer Verlag, Postfach 2140, 7400 Tübingen, Germany
Additional subscription address: Members of Raabe-Society: Raabe-Gesellschaft, Geschäftsstelle, Leonhardstr. 29a, 3300 Braunschweig, Germany

ADVERTISING INFORMATION

Advertising accepted: Yes

EDITORIAL DESCRIPTION

Scope: Publishes works by Wilhelm Raabe and about 19th century literature studies in German realism.
Reviews books: Yes
Publishes notes: No
Languages accepted: German
Prints abstracts: No

SUBMISSION REQUIREMENTS

Restrictions on contributors: Book reviews are solicited.
Author pays submission fee: No
Author pays page charges: No
Length of articles: 5-25 pp.
Length of book reviews: 1-4 p.
Style: Journal
Number of copies required: 1
Copyright ownership: Max Niemeyer Verlag
Rejected manuscripts: Returned
Time before publication decision: 8 mos.
Time between decision and publication: 8 mos.
Number of reviewers: 1-2
Articles submitted per year: 30
Articles published per year: 10
Book reviews submitted per year: 5
Book reviews published per year: 4

(1326)
*Jahrbuch der Sammlung Kippenberg

Jörn Göres, Editor
Goethe-Museum Düsseldorf
Anton-und-Katharina-Kippenberg-Stiftung
Jacobi-Str. 2
4000 Düsseldorf 1, Germany

Telephone: (49) 211 8996262
First published: 1963
Sponsoring organization: Anton-und-Katharina-Kippenberg-Stiftung
MLA acronym: JSK

SUBSCRIPTION INFORMATION

Frequency of publication: Irregular
Available in microform: No
Subscription address: Insel Verlag, Lindenstr. Suhrkamp-Haus, Postfach 3325, 6000 Frankfurt, Germany

ADVERTISING INFORMATION

Advertising accepted: No

EDITORIAL DESCRIPTION

Scope: Publishes articles on Goethe's life and work, as documented by the Goethe-Museum Düsseldorf collection.
Reviews books: No
Publishes notes: No
Languages accepted: German
Prints abstracts: No

SUBMISSION REQUIREMENTS

Restrictions on contributors: None
Author pays submission fee: No
Author pays page charges: No
Length of articles: No restrictions
Style: Journal
Number of copies required: 1
Copyright ownership: Goethe-Museum Düsseldorf
Rejected manuscripts: Returned
Time between decision and publication: 1 yr.
Number of reviewers: 3

(1327)
*Jahrbuch des Freien Deutschen Hochstifts

Christoph Perels, Ernst Dietrich Eckhardt, & Gerda Gmoser, Editors
Freies Deutsches Hochstift
Frankfurter Goethe-Museum
Grosser Hirschgraben 23-25
6000 Frankfurt am Main 1, Germany

Telephone: (49) 69 282824
First published: 1861
ISSN: 0071-9463
MLA acronym: JFDH

SUBSCRIPTION INFORMATION

Frequency of publication: Annual (Dec.)
Circulation: 1,000
Available in microform: No
Subscription price: 50 DM/yr. members; 86 DM/yr. nonmembers
Year to which price refers: 1991
Subscription address: Max Niemeyer Verlag, Postfach 2140, 7400 Tübingen, Germany
Subscription telephone: (49) 7071 81104
Subscription fax: (49) 7071 87419

ADVERTISING INFORMATION

Advertising accepted: No

EDITORIAL DESCRIPTION

Scope: Publishes articles on German literature and art, especially during Goethe's period.
Reviews books: No
Publishes notes: No
Languages accepted: German
Prints abstracts: No
Author-anonymous submission: No

SUBMISSION REQUIREMENTS

Restrictions on contributors: None
Author pays submission fee: No
Length of articles: No restrictions
Number of copies required: 1
Special requirements: Articles should contain the results of recent research.
Copyright ownership: Journal & author
Rejected manuscripts: Returned
Time before publication decision: 3-6 mos.
Time between decision and publication: 9-18 mos.
Number of reviewers: 3
Articles submitted per year: 30-40
Articles published per year: 10-15

(1328)
*Jahrbuch des Wiener Goethe-Vereins

Herbert Zeman, Editor
Wiener Goethe-Verein
Stallburgasse, 2
1010 Vienna, Austria

First published: 1886
Sponsoring organization: Austrian Ministry of Education
ISSN: 0250-443X
MLA acronym: JWGV

SUBSCRIPTION INFORMATION

Frequency of publication: Annual
Circulation: 750
Available in microform: No
Subscription price: 200 S/yr.
Year to which price refers: 1992
Subscription address: Verlag Fassbänder, Lichtgasse 10, 1150 Vienna, Austria
Subscription telephone: (43) 222 839524
Subscription fax: (43) 222 859855

ADVERTISING INFORMATION

Advertising accepted: Yes

EDITORIAL DESCRIPTION

Scope: Publishes research in Goethe's works, his literary period, and Austrian literature.
Reviews books: Yes
Publishes notes: No
Languages accepted: German; English
Prints abstracts: No
Author-anonymous submission: No

SUBMISSION REQUIREMENTS

Restrictions on contributors: None
Author pays submission fee: No
Author pays page charges: No
Length of articles: 20-35 typescript pp.
Length of book reviews: 2 typescript pp.
Number of copies required: 1
Copyright ownership: Wiener Goethe-Verein
Rejected manuscripts: Not returned
Time before publication decision: 2-3 mos.
Time between decision and publication: 1-3 yrs.
Number of reviewers: 3
Articles submitted per year: 8-12
Articles published per year: 8-12
Book reviews submitted per year: 8-10
Book reviews published per year: 8-10

(1329)
*Jahrbuch für Finnisch-Deutsche Literaturbeziehungen: Mitteilungen aus der Deutschen Bibliothek

Hans Fromm, Maria-Liisa Nevala, Kurt Nyholm, & Ingrid Schellbach-Kopra, Editors
Deutsche Bibliothek
PL 13
00130 Helsinki, Finland

Telephone: (358) 0 669363
Fax: (358) 0 654010
First published: 1967
Sponsoring organization: Deutsche Bibliothek, Helsinki; Finnish Ministry of Education
ISSN: 0781-3619
MLA acronym: JFDL

SUBSCRIPTION INFORMATION

Frequency of publication: Annual (Nov.-Dec.)
Circulation: 750
Available in microform: No
Subscription price: 100 Fmk/yr. plus postage
Year to which price refers: 1992

ADVERTISING INFORMATION

Advertising accepted: Yes
Advertising rates: 460 Fmk/half page; 800 Fmk/full page

EDITORIAL DESCRIPTION

Scope: Publishes articles on Finnish-German relations in literature and culture, historical/cultural background of these relations, translations of Finnish literature (including works written in Swedish and Sámi), and presentations of authors (with an emphasis on contemporary literature).
Reviews books: Yes
Publishes notes: No
Languages accepted: German
Prints abstracts: No
Author-anonymous submission: No

SUBMISSION REQUIREMENTS

Restrictions on contributors: Many contributions are solicited; unsolicited manuscripts are accepted.
Author pays submission fee: No
Author pays page charges: No
Length of articles: 12 pp. maximum
Length of book reviews: 4 pp. maximum
Number of copies required: 2
Special requirements: Articles in English, French, Finnish, and Swedish are accepted for translation into German.
Copyright ownership: Publisher
Rejected manuscripts: Returned
Time before publication decision: 6 weeks
Number of reviewers: 4
Articles submitted per year: 15-25
Articles published per year: 10-20
Book reviews submitted per year: 10-30
Book reviews published per year: 10-30

(1330)
*Jahrbuch für Fränkische Landesforschung

Alfred Wendehorst, Editor
Kochstr. 4
Zentralinst. für fränkische Landeskunde & allgemeine Regionalforschung
Univ. Erlangen-Nürnberg
8520 Erlangen, Germany

Telephone: (49) 9161 2028
First published: 1935
Sponsoring organization: Friedrich-Alexander-Univ. Erlangen-Nürnberg, Zentralinst. für fränkische Landeskunde & allgemeine Regionalforschung
ISSN: 0446-3943
MLA acronym: JFL

SUBSCRIPTION INFORMATION

Frequency of publication: Annual
Circulation: 700
Available in microform: No
Subscription price: 45 DM/yr.
Year to which price refers: 1992
Subscription address: Kommissionsverlag, Degener & Co., Inh. Manfred Dreiss, 8530 Neustadt (Aisch), Germany

ADVERTISING INFORMATION

Advertising accepted: Yes

EDITORIAL DESCRIPTION

Scope: Publishes articles on Franconian regional history.
Reviews books: No
Publishes notes: Yes
Languages accepted: German; English; French
Prints abstracts: No
Author-anonymous submission: No

SUBMISSION REQUIREMENTS

Restrictions on contributors: None
Author pays submission fee: No
Author pays page charges: No
Length of articles: 50 pp. maximum
Length of notes: No restrictions
Style: Deutsches Archiv
Number of copies required: 1
Copyright ownership: Zentralinst. für fränkische Landeskunde & allgemeine Regionalforschung
Rejected manuscripts: Returned
Time before publication decision: 3 mos.
Time between decision and publication: 1 yr.
Number of reviewers: 2
Articles submitted per year: 10-15
Articles published per year: 12-15
Notes submitted per year: 4-6
Notes published per year: 4-6

(1331)
*Jahrbuch für Internationale Germanistik

Hans-Gert Roloff, Editor
Freie Univ. Berlin
Forschungsstelle für Mittlere Deutsche Literatur
Habelschwerdter Allee 45
1000 Berlin 33, Germany

Telephone: (49) 30 8385007
First published: 1969
Sponsoring organization: Internationale Vereinigung für Germanische Sprach- & Literaturwissenschaft
ISSN: 0449-5233
MLA acronym: JIG

SUBSCRIPTION INFORMATION

Frequency of publication: 2 times/yr.
Circulation: 1,000
Available in microform: No
Subscription address: Peter Lang Verlag AG, Jupiterstr. 15, 3015 Bern, Switzerland

ADVERTISING INFORMATION

Advertising accepted: Yes

EDITORIAL DESCRIPTION

Scope: Serves the scholarly pursuit of German, Dutch, and Scandinavian language and literature. Its task is to discuss central problems in German philology, give information about current or future research projects, and establish contacts with the various sides of the world-wide discipline through regular reports and announcements.
Reviews books: Yes
Publishes notes: Yes
Languages accepted: German; English; French; Dutch
Prints abstracts: No
Author-anonymous submission: No

SUBMISSION REQUIREMENTS

Restrictions on contributors: None
Author pays submission fee: No
Author pays page charges: No
Length of articles: No restrictions
Length of notes: No restrictions
Style: Journal
Number of copies required: 1
Copyright ownership: Assigned by author to journal
Rejected manuscripts: Returned
Time before publication decision: 1-2 mos.
Time between decision and publication: 6-8 mos.
Number of reviewers: 2
Articles submitted per year: 60
Articles published per year: 20-25
Notes submitted per year: 100-200
Notes published per year: 1,000-1,200

(1332)
Jahrbuch für Internationale Germanistik: Reihe A: Kongressberichte

Peter Lang Verlag AG
Jupiterstr. 15
3015 Bern, Switzerland

Sponsoring organization: Internationale Vereinigung für Germanische Sprach- & Literaturwissenschaft
MLA acronym: JIGA

EDITORIAL DESCRIPTION

Scope: Publishes collections of articles on German, Dutch, and Scandinavian language and literature.
Languages accepted: German; English

(1333)
*Jahrbuch für Volksliedforschung

Otto Holzapfel, Hartmut Braun, & Jürgen Dittmar, Editors
Deutsches Volksliedarchiv
Silberbachstr. 13
7800 Freiburg, Germany

Telephone: (49) 761 74465
First published: 1928
Sponsoring organization: Deutsches Volksliedarchiv
ISSN: 0075-2789
MLA acronym: JV

SUBSCRIPTION INFORMATION

Frequency of publication: Annual
Circulation: 350
Available in microform: No
Subscription price: 88 DM/yr.
Year to which price refers: 1990
Subscription address: Erich Schmidt Verlag, Genthiner Str. 30G, 1000 Berlin 30, Germany
Subscription telephone: (49) 30 2500850
Subscription fax: (49) 30 25008521

ADVERTISING INFORMATION

Advertising accepted: Yes, generally on an exchange basis

EDITORIAL DESCRIPTION

Scope: Publishes articles on international folk song research, including folk music, folk dance, and instruments.
Reviews books: Yes
Publishes notes: Yes
Languages accepted: German; English; French
Prints abstracts: Yes
Author-anonymous submission: No

SUBMISSION REQUIREMENTS

Restrictions on contributors: None
Author pays submission fee: No
Author pays page charges: No
Length of articles: 16 printed pp.
Length of book reviews: 1 p.
Length of notes: No restrictions
Style: MLA; journal
Number of copies required: 1
Special requirements: Submit original typescript.
Copyright ownership: Journal
Rejected manuscripts: Returned
Time before publication decision: 4 weeks
Time between decision and publication: 18 mos.
Number of reviewers: 1
Articles submitted per year: 15
Articles published per year: 8-10
Book reviews submitted per year: 100
Book reviews published per year: 100
Notes submitted per year: 15
Notes published per year: 10

(1334)
*James Dickey Newsletter

Joyce M. Pair, Editor
2101 Womack Rd.
Dunwoody, GA 30338

Telephone: 404 551-3162
Fax: 404 551-3201
First published: 1984
Sponsoring organization: DeKalb College
ISSN: 0749-0291
MLA acronym: JDN

SUBSCRIPTION INFORMATION

Frequency of publication: 2 times/yr. (Fall, Spring)
Circulation: 250
Available in microform: No
Subscription price: $10.00/yr. institutions; $5.00/yr. individuals
Year to which price refers: 1992

ADVERTISING INFORMATION

Advertising accepted: Yes
Advertising rates: $100.00/insert

EDITORIAL DESCRIPTION

Scope: Provides a forum for information on the work, bibliography, and biography of James L. Dickey.
Reviews books: Yes
Publishes notes: Yes
Languages accepted: English
Prints abstracts: No
Author-anonymous submission: No

SUBMISSION REQUIREMENTS

Restrictions on contributors: Book reviews are usually solicited.
Author pays submission fee: No
Author pays page charges: No
Length of articles: 2,500-5,000 words
Length of book reviews: 1,000-3,000 words
Length of notes: No restrictions
Style: MLA
Number of copies required: 1
Special requirements: Submit double-spaced typescript on WordPerfect ASCII file diskette, if possible.
Copyright ownership: Journal
Rejected manuscripts: Returned
Time before publication decision: 2-4 weeks
Time between decision and publication: 3-12 mos.
Number of reviewers: 1-3
Articles submitted per year: 10-30
Articles published per year: 8-10
Book reviews submitted per year: 2-8
Book reviews published per year: 2-5
Notes submitted per year: 1-3
Notes published per year: 1-3

(1335)
*James Joyce Quarterly

Robert Spoo, Editor
Univ. of Tulsa
600 S. College Ave.
Tulsa, OK 74104-3189

Telephone: 918 631-2501
Fax: 918 631-2033
First published: 1963
Sponsoring organization: Univ. of Tulsa
ISSN: 0021-4183
MLA acronym: JJQ

SUBSCRIPTION INFORMATION

Frequency of publication: 4 times/yr.
Circulation: 1,300
Available in microform: Yes
Subscription price: $15.00/yr. institutions US; $17.00/yr. institutions elsewhere; $14.00/yr. individuals US; $16.00/yr. individuals elsewhere
Year to which price refers: 1992

ADVERTISING INFORMATION

Advertising accepted: Yes
Advertising rates: $75.00/half page; $125.00/full page

EDITORIAL DESCRIPTION

Scope: All aspects of James Joyce and his milieu are considered. Comparative studies, research-oriented scholarship, bibliographical and biographical articles, and collectors' notes are desired.
Reviews books: Yes
Publishes notes: Yes
Languages accepted: English
Prints abstracts: No
Author-anonymous submission: No

SUBMISSION REQUIREMENTS

Restrictions on contributors: Much material is solicited, especially book reviews and articles in special issues.
Author pays submission fee: No
Author pays page charges: No
Length of articles: 20 pp. maximum
Length of book reviews: 1,200-1,500 words
Length of notes: 9 pp. maximum
Style: MLA (1977)
Number of copies required: 3
Special requirements: Cite references to Joyce's works and to Ellmann biography parenthetically within the body of the paper.
Copyright ownership: Journal in trust for author

Rejected manuscripts: Returned; enclose return postage.
Time before publication decision: 6-12 weeks
Time between decision and publication: 12-18 mos.
Number of reviewers: 2
Articles submitted per year: 150
Articles published per year: 50
Book reviews submitted per year: 14
Book reviews published per year: 14
Notes submitted per year: 160
Notes published per year: 25

(1336)
*Japan Quarterly

Ōishi Yūji, Editor
Asahi Shimbun
5-3-2 Tsukiji
Chuo-ku, Tokyo 104-11, Japan

Telephone: (81) 3 35450131 ext. 5440 or 5441
Fax: (81) 3 35441428
First published: 1954
ISSN: 0021-4590
MLA acronym: JapQ

SUBSCRIPTION INFORMATION

Frequency of publication: 4 times/yr. (Jan., Apr., July, Oct.)
Circulation: 5,000
Available in microform: Yes, through Univ. Microfilms International
Subscription price: $30.00 ($38.00 airmail)/yr. US
Year to which price refers: 1992
Additional subscription address: For subscriptions outside Japan write: Japan Publications Trading Co., Ltd., P.O. Box 5030, Tokyo International, Tokyo 100-31, Japan

ADVERTISING INFORMATION

Advertising accepted: Yes

EDITORIAL DESCRIPTION

Scope: Provides the reader with current information on Japanese politics, economics, society, technology, and culture.
Reviews books: Yes
Publishes notes: No
Languages accepted: English; Japanese
Prints abstracts: No
Author-anonymous submission: No

SUBMISSION REQUIREMENTS

Restrictions on contributors: Most articles are solicited.
Author pays submission fee: No
Author pays page charges: No
Length of articles: 2,000-7,500 words
Length of book reviews: 1,500 words
Style: Chicago
Number of copies required: 1
Special requirements: English submissions should be double-spaced typescript; Japanese submissions are translated into English.
Copyright ownership: Author
Rejected manuscripts: Returned
Time before publication decision: 1-3 mos.
Time between decision and publication: 2 mos.
Number of reviewers: 3-4
Articles submitted per year: 100
Articles published per year: 60-80
Book reviews submitted per year: 15-20
Book reviews published per year: 12-18

(1337)
*Jaunā Gaita

L. Zandbergs, Editor
23 Markland Drive
Etobicoke, Ontario M9C 1M8, Canada

Telephone: 416 621-0898
First published: 1955
ISSN: 0448-9179
MLA acronym: JGa

SUBSCRIPTION INFORMATION

Frequency of publication: 5 times/yr.
Circulation: 1,000
Available in microform: No
Subscription price: $29.00/yr.
Year to which price refers: 1991
Subscription address: Contact I. Bulmanis at the above address

ADVERTISING INFORMATION

Advertising accepted: No

EDITORIAL DESCRIPTION

Scope: Covers fiction, drama, literary criticism, essays, and poetry, as well as the history and languages of the East Baltic area, especially Latvia. Includes historical documents, review essays, bibliographical essays, book reviews, marginalia, and brief notes.
Reviews books: Yes
Publishes notes: Yes
Languages accepted: Latvian; English
Prints abstracts: Yes
Author-anonymous submission: No

SUBMISSION REQUIREMENTS

Restrictions on contributors: None
Author pays submission fee: No
Author pays page charges: No
Length of articles: No restrictions
Length of book reviews: 400-1,200 words
Length of notes: 150 words
Style: MLA
Number of copies required: 1
Copyright ownership: Author
Rejected manuscripts: Returned
Time before publication decision: 1-3 mos.
Time between decision and publication: 3-12 mos.
Number of reviewers: 4
Articles submitted per year: 200-400
Articles published per year: 100-125
Book reviews submitted per year: 35-45
Book reviews published per year: 30-40
Notes submitted per year: 50
Notes published per year: 30

(1338)
*Jean Rhys Review

Nora Gaines, Editor
P.O. Box 811
Planetarium Station
New York, NY 10024-0539

Telephone: 212 884-5854
First published: 1986
ISSN: 0889-759X
MLA acronym: JRR

SUBSCRIPTION INFORMATION

Frequency of publication: 2 times/yr. (Spring, Fall)
Circulation: 35
Available in microform: No
Subscription price: $20.00/yr. institutions; $14.00/yr. individuals; add $3.00/yr. postage outside US
Year to which price refers: 1992

ADVERTISING INFORMATION

Advertising accepted: No

EDITORIAL DESCRIPTION

Scope: Provides a forum for research in progress and bibliography, critical articles and reviews related to the work of Jean Rhys, as well as articles that examine Rhys's work in relation to her contemporaries, and to the context of the literary climate in which she wrote.
Reviews books: Yes
Publishes notes: Yes
Languages accepted: French; English
Prints abstracts: No
Author-anonymous submission: No

SUBMISSION REQUIREMENTS

Restrictions on contributors: None
Author pays submission fee: No
Author pays page charges: No
Length of articles: 1,300-6,500 words
Length of book reviews: 1,300-1,950 words
Length of notes: 600 words
Style: MLA
Number of copies required: 1
Copyright ownership: Journal
Rejected manuscripts: Returned
Time before publication decision: 1-3 mos.
Time between decision and publication: 2-6 mos.
Number of reviewers: 1-4
Articles submitted per year: 15
Articles published per year: 8
Book reviews submitted per year: 5
Book reviews published per year: 1-4
Notes submitted per year: 3
Notes published per year: 1

(1339)
*Jewish Folklore and Ethnology Review

Guy H. Haskell, Editor
Judaic & Near Eastern Studies
Oberlin College
Oberlin, OH 44074

Telephone: 216 775-8639
Fax: 216 775-8124
E-mail: FHASKELL@OBERLIN.BITNET
First published: 1977
Sponsoring organization: Jewish Folklore & Ethnology Section, American Folklore Soc.
ISSN: 0890-9113
MLA acronym: JFER

SUBSCRIPTION INFORMATION

Frequency of publication: 2 times/yr.
Circulation: 500
Available in microform: No
Subscription price: $20.00/yr. institutions US; $23.00/yr. institutions elsewhere; $15.00/yr. individuals US; $12.00/yr. individuals elsewhere; $12.00/yr. members US; $15.00/yr. members elsewhere; $10.00/yr. students US; $13.00/yr. students elsewhere
Year to which price refers: 1992

ADVERTISING INFORMATION

Advertising accepted: Yes

EDITORIAL DESCRIPTION

Scope: Publishes articles on Jewish folklore, folklife, anthropology, and ethnography.
Reviews books: Yes
Publishes notes: Yes
Languages accepted: English
Prints abstracts: No
Author-anonymous submission: No

SUBMISSION REQUIREMENTS

Restrictions on contributors: None

Author pays submission fee: No
Author pays page charges: No
Number of copies required: 1
Copyright ownership: Jewish Folklore & Ethnology Section, American Folklore Soc.
Rejected manuscripts: Returned
Number of reviewers: 2

(1340)
*Jezik: Časopis za Kulturu Hrvatskoga Književnog Jezika

Stjepan Babić, Radoslav Katičić, Ivo Škarić, & Antun Šojat, Editors
Salajeva 3
P.P. 171
41001 Zagreb, Croatia

Additional editorial address: Matica Hrvatska, Matičina 2, 41000 Zagreb, Croatia
Telephone: (38) 41 413060
Fax: (38) 41 425475
First published: 1952
Sponsoring organization: Hrvatsko Filološko Društvo
ISSN: 0021-6925
MLA acronym: Jezik

SUBSCRIPTION INFORMATION

Frequency of publication: 5 times/yr.
Circulation: 3,000
Available in microform: No
Subscription price: $17.00/yr.; $7.00/single issue
Year to which price refers: 1991-92
Subscription address: Školska Knjiga, Masarykova 28, 41000 Zagreb, Croatia
Subscription telephone: (38) 41 458511

ADVERTISING INFORMATION

Advertising accepted: Yes
Advertising rates: $40.00/full page

EDITORIAL DESCRIPTION

Scope: Focuses on standard Croatian language.
Reviews books: Yes
Publishes notes: Yes
Languages accepted: Croatian
Prints abstracts: Yes
Author-anonymous submission: Yes

SUBMISSION REQUIREMENTS

Restrictions on contributors: None
Author pays submission fee: No
Author pays page charges: No
Length of articles: 7,200 words maximum
Length of book reviews: 2,000 words
Length of notes: 30 words
Number of copies required: 2
Copyright ownership: Author
Rejected manuscripts: Not returned
Time before publication decision: 1-3 mos.
Time between decision and publication: 2 mos.
Number of reviewers: 4
Articles submitted per year: 30
Articles published per year: 28
Book reviews submitted per year: 10
Book reviews published per year: 10
Notes submitted per year: 7
Notes published per year: 7

(1341)
Jezik in Slovstvo

Alenka Šivic-Dular, Editor
Slavistično Društvo Slovenije, Ljubljana
Aškerčeva 12
61000 Ljubljana, Slovenia

First published: 1955
Sponsoring organization: Republiski Sekretariat nov Kulturo R Slovenije

ISSN: 0021-6933
MLA acronym: JiS

SUBSCRIPTION INFORMATION

Frequency of publication: 8 times/yr. (Oct.-May)
Circulation: 2,400
Available in microform: Yes

ADVERTISING INFORMATION

Advertising accepted: No

EDITORIAL DESCRIPTION

Scope: Publishes articles on Slovenian literature and language. Also includes studies on other Slavic literatures.
Reviews books: Yes
Publishes notes: Yes
Languages accepted: Slovenian; English
Prints abstracts: Yes

SUBMISSION REQUIREMENTS

Author pays submission fee: No
Author pays page charges: No
Number of copies required: 1
Articles submitted per year: 35-40
Articles published per year: 35-40
Book reviews submitted per year: 13-15
Book reviews published per year: 13-15
Notes submitted per year: 5-8
Notes published per year: 5-8

(1342)
Język Polski

Jan Safarewicz, Editor
Towarzystwo Miłośników Języka Polskiego
ul. Straszewskiego 27, II p.
31-113 Cracow, Poland

First published: 1913
Sponsoring organization: Towarzystwo Miłośników Języka Polskiego
ISSN: 0021-6941
MLA acronym: JPol

SUBSCRIPTION INFORMATION

Frequency of publication: 5 times/yr.
Circulation: 11,600
Subscription address: Ars Polona-Ruch, Krakowskie Przedmieście 7, Warsaw, Poland

EDITORIAL DESCRIPTION

Scope: Publishes articles on Polish language and methodology of linguistic studies.
Reviews books: Yes
Languages accepted: Polish
Prints abstracts: No

SUBMISSION REQUIREMENTS

Restrictions on contributors: None
Length of articles: 5,000-6,000 words
Number of copies required: 1
Special requirements: Submit typescript.
Copyright ownership: Author
Rejected manuscripts: Returned
Time before publication decision: 3 mos.
Time between decision and publication: 1 yr.
Number of reviewers: 1 plus Editorial Board
Articles published per year: 70

(1343)
*JGE: The Journal of General Education

James L. Ratcliff, Editor
Journals Dept.
Pennsylvania State Univ. Press
820 North University Dr.
Suite C, Barbara Bldg.
University Park, PA 16802

Telephone: 814 865-1327
Fax: 814 863-1408
First published: 1946
Sponsoring organization: Pennsylvania State Univ. Press
ISSN: 0021-3667
MLA acronym: JGE

SUBSCRIPTION INFORMATION

Frequency of publication: 4 times/yr. (Spring, Summer, Fall, Winter)
Circulation: 1,400
Available in microform: Yes
Subscription price: $30.00/yr. institutions US; $35.00/yr. institutions elsewhere; $20.00/yr. individuals US; $27.00/yr. individuals elsewhere
Year to which price refers: 1991-92
Subscription telephone: 800 326-9180

ADVERTISING INFORMATION

Advertising accepted: Yes
Advertising rates: $175.00/half page; $275.00/full page

EDITORIAL DESCRIPTION

Scope: Intended for generalists, educators who are concerned with educational problems and solutions beyond the scope of their own specialties, the journal serves as a forum for the discussion of such matters as educational policy, institutional growth and change, the relationship between academic institutions and other aspects of society, and important developments within the traditional and the newer disciplines. Articles on pedagogy should address major issues, rather than presenting isolated case-studies.
Reviews books: Yes
Publishes notes: No
Languages accepted: English
Prints abstracts: No
Author-anonymous submission: No

SUBMISSION REQUIREMENTS

Restrictions on contributors: No multiple submissions are accepted. Most book reviews are solicited; contact editor prior to submission of book reviews.
Author pays submission fee: No
Author pays page charges: No
Length of articles: 10-25 typescript pp.
Length of book reviews: 5-8 pp.
Style: MLA preferred; Chicago accepted
Number of copies required: 1
Copyright ownership: Pennsylvania State Univ. Press
Rejected manuscripts: Returned; enclose SASE.
Time before publication decision: 3-4 mos.
Time between decision and publication: 4-6 mos.
Number of reviewers: 3
Articles submitted per year: 200-250
Articles published per year: 30
Book reviews published per year: 8

(1344)
*John Clare Society Journal

John Goodridge, Editor
Dept. of English Literature
School of English
The University
Newcastle-upon-Tyne NE1 7RU, England

Telephone: (44) 91 2226000
Fax: (44) 91 2611182
First published: 1982
Sponsoring organization: John Clare Soc.
MLA acronym: JCSJ

SUBSCRIPTION INFORMATION

Frequency of publication: Annual (July)
Circulation: 350
Available in microform: No
Subscription price: £7.50/yr. United Kingdom; £10.00 ($20.00)/yr. US & Canada
Year to which price refers: 1992
Subscription address: John Clare Soc., The Stables, 1a West St., Helpston, Peterborough PE6 7DU, England
Subscription telephone: (44) 733 252678

ADVERTISING INFORMATION

Advertising accepted: Yes
Advertising rates: £60.00/full page

EDITORIAL DESCRIPTION

Scope: Journal publishes articles about the life and work of the poet John Clare (1793-1864).
Reviews books: Yes
Publishes notes: Yes
Languages accepted: English
Prints abstracts: No
Author-anonymous submission: No

SUBMISSION REQUIREMENTS

Restrictions on contributors: Submissions must not be previously published. Articles must be typescript.
Author pays submission fee: No
Author pays page charges: No
Length of articles: 4,000 words maximum
Length of book reviews: 500 words maximum
Length of notes: 500 words
Number of copies required: 2
Copyright ownership: John Clare Soc. & Author
Rejected manuscripts: Returned; enclose return postage.
Time before publication decision: 3 mos.
Time between decision and publication: 1 yr.
Number of reviewers: 2
Articles submitted per year: 10
Articles published per year: 6
Book reviews submitted per year: 3
Book reviews published per year: 3

(1345)
John Donne Journal: Studies in the Age of Donne

M. Thomas Hester & R. V. Young, Editors
Box 8105
Raleigh, NC 27695-8105

First published: 1982
Sponsoring organization: John Donne Soc.
ISSN: 0738-9655
MLA acronym: JDJ

SUBSCRIPTION INFORMATION

Frequency of publication: 2 times/yr.
Circulation: 500
Available in microform: No

ADVERTISING INFORMATION

Advertising accepted: Yes

EDITORIAL DESCRIPTION

Scope: Publishes studies of 17th-century poetry and prose in England, with an emphasis on John Donne. Includes short notes, announcements, and descriptions of manuscripts, texts, and documents.
Reviews books: Yes
Publishes notes: Yes
Languages accepted: English
Prints abstracts: No
Author-anonymous submission: No

SUBMISSION REQUIREMENTS

Restrictions on contributors: Reviews are commissioned.
Author pays submission fee: No
Author pays page charges: No
Length of articles: 50 pp. maximum
Length of book reviews: 20-50 pp.
Length of notes: 2,000 words maximum
Style: MLA
Number of copies required: 2
Copyright ownership: Journal
Rejected manuscripts: Returned
Time before publication decision: 2-3 mos.
Time between decision and publication: 6-8 mos.
Number of reviewers: 3
Articles submitted per year: 80
Articles published per year: 14
Book reviews published per year: 5-8
Notes submitted per year: 10
Notes published per year: 2

(1346)
Jolan: Journal of the Linguistic Association of Nigeria

P. Akụjụọobi Nwachukwu & Victor Manfredi, Editors
Dept. of Linguistics & Nigerian Langs.
Univ. of Nigeria
Nsuka, Nigeria

Additional editorial address: Outside Africa: Victor Manfredi, African Studies Center, Boston Univ., 270 Bay State Rd., Boston, MA 02215
First published: 1982
Sponsoring organization: Linguistic Assn. of Nigeria; Boston Univ. African Studies Center
ISSN: 0189-5680
MLA acronym: Jolan

SUBSCRIPTION INFORMATION

Frequency of publication: Annual
Circulation: 250
Available in microform: No
Subscription address: Hounkpatin C. Capo, Business Manager, Dept. of Linguistics & Nigerian Languages, Univ. of Ilorin, P.M.B. 1515 Ilorin, Kwara State, Nigeria
Additional subscription address: Outside Africa: Publications Officer at Boston Univ. address

ADVERTISING INFORMATION

Advertising accepted: Yes

EDITORIAL DESCRIPTION

Scope: Publishes articles on Nigerian linguistics.
Reviews books: No
Publishes notes: No
Languages accepted: English
Prints abstracts: No

SUBMISSION REQUIREMENTS

Author pays submission fee: No
Author pays page charges: No
Length of articles: 5,000 words
Style: Linguistic Soc. of Nigeria
Rejected manuscripts: Returned
Time before publication decision: 1 yr.

(1347)
*Journal Asiatique

Daniel Gimaret, Editor
Soc. Asiatique
3, rue Mazarine
75006 Paris, France

First published: 1822
Sponsoring organization: Soc. Asiatique; Centre National de la Recherche Scientifique
ISSN: 0021-762X
MLA acronym: JAsiat

SUBSCRIPTION INFORMATION

Frequency of publication: 2 times/yr.
Circulation: 1,500
Available in microform: No
Subscription address: Librairie Orientaliste Paul Geuthner, 12 rue Vavin, 75006 Paris, France

ADVERTISING INFORMATION

Advertising accepted: No

EDITORIAL DESCRIPTION

Scope: Publishes articles on all aspects of Orientalism.
Reviews books: No
Publishes notes: No
Languages accepted: French
Prints abstracts: Yes
Author-anonymous submission: No

SUBMISSION REQUIREMENTS

Restrictions on contributors: Contributors must be members of the Soc. Asiatique.
Author pays submission fee: No
Author pays page charges: No
Length of articles: No restrictions
Style: None
Number of copies required: 1
Special requirements: Submit an abstract in English.
Copyright ownership: Assigned by author to journal
Rejected manuscripts: Not returned
Time before publication decision: 1 mo.
Time between decision and publication: 1 yr.
Number of reviewers: 2
Articles published per year: 15

(1348)
*Journal des Savants

Pierre Toubert, Directeur
Inst. de France
23, quai de Conti
75006 Paris, France

First published: 1665
Sponsoring organization: Inst. de France, Académie des Inscriptions & Belles-Lettres
ISSN: 0021-8103
MLA acronym: JS

SUBSCRIPTION INFORMATION

Frequency of publication: 2 times/yr.
Circulation: 800
Available in microform: No
Subscription price: 480 F/yr.
Year to which price refers: 1991
Subscription address: Editions de Boccard, 11 rue de Médicis, 75006 Paris, France

ADVERTISING INFORMATION

Advertising accepted: No

Time between decision and publication: 6 mos.
Number of reviewers: 3
Articles published per year: 20

EDITORIAL DESCRIPTION

Scope: Publishes articles on archeology, history, literature, and philology.
Reviews books: No
Publishes notes: No
Languages accepted: French
Prints abstracts: No
Author-anonymous submission: No

SUBMISSION REQUIREMENTS

Author pays submission fee: No
Author pays page charges: No
Length of articles: 5,000-10,000 words
Number of copies required: 1
Copyright ownership: Inst. de France, Académie des Inscriptions & Belles-Lettres
Rejected manuscripts: Returned
Time before publication decision: 3 mos.
Time between decision and publication: 1 yr.
Number of reviewers: 3
Articles submitted per year: 50-80
Articles published per year: 12-15

(1349)
Journal for Semitics/Tydskrif vir Semitistiek

H. J. Dreyer, Editor
Dept. of Semitics
Univ. of South Africa
P.O. Box 392
1000 Pretoria, South Africa

First published: 1989
Sponsoring organization: Southern African Soc. for Semitics
ISSN: 1013-8471
MLA acronym: JSem

SUBSCRIPTION INFORMATION

Frequency of publication: 2 times/yr.

EDITORIAL DESCRIPTION

Scope: Publishes articles on the classical Semitic languages, the general and cultural history of the Ancient Near East, archaeology and iconography of the Near East, Arabic and Modern Hebrew, Judaica and Islamic studies.
Reviews books: Yes
Publishes notes: Yes
Languages accepted: English; Afrikaans; German; French; Dutch
Prints abstracts: Yes
Author-anonymous submission: Yes

SUBMISSION REQUIREMENTS

Restrictions on contributors: None
Style: Harvard method of reference
Number of copies required: 1
Special requirements: Submit original typescript or diskette (ASCII or DCA) plus print-out. Submit a 150-word maximum abstract in English.
Copyright ownership: Southern African Soc. for Semitics
Rejected manuscripts: Returned
Number of reviewers: 2

(1350)
*Journal for the Scientific Study of Religion

Armand L. Mauss, Editor
Washington State Univ.
P.O. Box 2061 C.S.
Pullman, WA 99165

Telephone: 509 335-4595
First published: 1961
Sponsoring organization: Soc. for the Scientific Study of Religion

---

ISSN: 0021-8294
MLA acronym: JSSR

SUBSCRIPTION INFORMATION

Frequency of publication: 4 times/yr. (Mar., June, Sept., Dec.)
Circulation: 3,000
Available in microform: Yes, through Univ. Microfilms International
Subscription address: Executive Office, Soc. for the Scientific Study of Religion, Dept. of Sociology & Anthropology, Purdue Univ., Pierce Hall 193, West Lafayette, IN 47907-1365
Subscription telephone: 317 494-6286

ADVERTISING INFORMATION

Advertising accepted: Yes

EDITORIAL DESCRIPTION

Scope: Publishes social scientific articles on religion and religious behavior.
Reviews books: Yes
Publishes notes: No
Languages accepted: English
Prints abstracts: Yes
Author-anonymous submission: Yes

SUBMISSION REQUIREMENTS

Restrictions on contributors: Reviews are solicited.
Author pays submission fee: Yes, for nonsubscribers
Cost of submission fee: $10.00
Author pays page charges: No
Length of articles: 30 typescript pp. maximum
Length of book reviews: 750-1,000 words
Style: Journal
Number of copies required: 3
Copyright ownership: Soc. for the Scientific Study of Religion
Rejected manuscripts: Not returned
Time before publication decision: 2 mos.
Time between decision and publication: 6-9 mos.
Number of reviewers: 3
Articles submitted per year: 180
Articles published per year: 25
Book reviews submitted per year: 50
Book reviews published per year: 50

(1351)
*Journal of Abnormal Psychology

Susan Mineka, Editor
Dept. of Psychology
Northwestern Univ.
Evanston, IL 60208

Telephone: 708 491-5676
Fax: 708 491-7859
E-mail: Mandy—spriegel@psych.nwu.edu
First published: 1906
Sponsoring organization: American Psychological Assn.
ISSN: 0021-843X
MLA acronym: JAP

SUBSCRIPTION INFORMATION

Frequency of publication: 4 times/yr.
Circulation: 5,800
Available in microform: Yes
Subscription price: $126.00/yr. institutions US; $150.00/yr. institutions elsewhere; $63.00/yr. individuals US; $75.00/yr. individuals elsewhere
Year to which price refers: 1992
Subscription address: Subscription Section, American Psychological Assn., 750 First St., NE, Washington, DC 20002

ADVERTISING INFORMATION

Advertising accepted: Yes

EDITORIAL DESCRIPTION

Scope: Publishes articles on basic research and theory in the broad field of abnormal behavior, its determinants, and its correlates.
Reviews books: No
Publishes notes: No
Languages accepted: English
Prints abstracts: Yes
Author-anonymous submission: Yes, at author's request.

SUBMISSION REQUIREMENTS

Restrictions on contributors: None
Author pays submission fee: No
Author pays page charges: No
Length of articles: 5-15 printed pp.
Style: American Psychological Assn.
Number of copies required: 5
Special requirements: Include a 100-150 word abstract. Submit original typescript plus 4 copies.
Copyright ownership: Journal
Rejected manuscripts: Not returned
Time before publication decision: 3 mos.
Time between decision and publication: 6 mos.
Number of reviewers: 2-4
Articles submitted per year: 300
Articles published per year: 70

(1352)
*Journal of Advanced Composition

Gary A. Olson, Editor
Dept. of English
Univ. of South Florida
Tampa, FL 33620-5550

Additional editorial address: Fred Reynolds, Book Review Editor, Dept. of English, Old Dominion Univ., Norfolk, VA 23529-0078
Telephone: 813 974-2193
First published: 1979
Sponsoring organization: Assn. of Teachers of Advanced Composition
ISSN: 0731-6755
MLA acronym: JAC

SUBSCRIPTION INFORMATION

Frequency of publication: 2 times/yr.
Circulation: 1,000
Available in microform: No
Subscription price: $20.00/yr. institutions; $15.00/yr. individuals; add $5.00/yr. postage outside US
Year to which price refers: 1992
Subscription address: Evelyn Ashton-Jones, Dept. of English, Univ. of Idaho, Moscow, ID 83843
Subscription telephone: 208 885-6823

ADVERTISING INFORMATION

Advertising accepted: Yes

EDITORIAL DESCRIPTION

Scope: Publishes articles on theory and research in rhetoric and composition as well as advanced composition.
Reviews books: Yes
Publishes notes: No
Languages accepted: English
Prints abstracts: No
Author-anonymous submission: Yes

SUBMISSION REQUIREMENTS

Restrictions on contributors: None
Author pays submission fee: No
Author pays page charges: No
Length of articles: 3,000-7,500 words
Length of book reviews: 350-2,000 words
Style: MLA
Number of copies required: 3
Copyright ownership: Journal
Rejected manuscripts: Returned; enclose return postage.
Time before publication decision: 10 weeks
Time between decision and publication: 6-8 mos.
Number of reviewers: 3
Articles submitted per year: 100
Articles published per year: 15-20
Book reviews submitted per year: 25
Book reviews published per year: 20

(1353)
*Journal of Aesthetics and Art Criticism

Donald W. Crawford, Editor
Dept. of Philosophy
Univ. of Wisconsin-Madison
600 North Park St.
Madison, WI 53706

First published: 1941
Sponsoring organization: American Soc. for Aesthetics
ISSN: 0021-8529
MLA acronym: JAAC

SUBSCRIPTION INFORMATION

Frequency of publication: 4 times/yr. (Winter, Spring, Summer, Fall)
Circulation: 3,000
Available in microform: Yes
Subscription price: $48.00/yr. institutions; $30.00/yr. individuals (includes membership)
Year to which price refers: 1993
Subscription address: American Soc. for Aesthetics, 4-108 Humanities Centre, Univ. of Alberta, Edmonton, Alberta T6G 2E5, Canada
Additional subscription address: Institutions contact: Journals Division, Univ. of Wisconsin Press, 114 N. Murray St., Madison, WI 53715

ADVERTISING INFORMATION

Advertising accepted: Yes
Advertising rates: $120.00/half page; $225.00/full page; $250.00/inside back cover

EDITORIAL DESCRIPTION

Scope: Publishes studies of the arts and related types of experience from a philosophic or other theoretical standpoint.
Reviews books: Yes
Publishes notes: Yes
Languages accepted: English
Prints abstracts: No
Author-anonymous submission: Yes

SUBMISSION REQUIREMENTS

Restrictions on contributors: Reviews are solicited.
Author pays submission fee: No
Author pays page charges: No
Length of articles: 4,000-8,000 words
Length of book reviews: 1,200 words
Length of notes: 1,000-4,000 words
Style: Chicago
Number of copies required: 2
Copyright ownership: Journal
Rejected manuscripts: One copy returned; enclose SASE.
Time before publication decision: 3 mos.
Time between decision and publication: 1 yr.
Number of reviewers: 3
Articles submitted per year: 350
Articles published per year: 35
Book reviews published per year: 70
Notes submitted per year: 30
Notes published per year: 6

(1354)
*Journal of African Languages and Linguistics

Gerrit J. Dimmendaal, Editor
Dept. of African Linguistics
Univ. of Leiden
Postbus 9515
2300 RA Leiden, Netherlands

First published: 1979
Sponsoring organization: Dept. of African Linguistics, Rijksuniv. te Leiden
ISSN: 0167-6164
MLA acronym: JALL

SUBSCRIPTION INFORMATION

Frequency of publication: 2 times/yr. (Apr., Oct.)
Circulation: 300
Available in microform: No
Subscription price: $74.00 (118 DM)/yr. institutions; $40.00 (62.40 DM)/yr. individuals
Year to which price refers: 1991
Subscription address: Mouton de Gruyter, Genthiner Str. 13, 1000 Berlin 30, Germany
Additional subscription address: For US, Canada, & Mexico: Walter de Gruyter, Inc., 200 Saw Mill River Rd., Hawthorne, NY 10532
Subscription telephone: (49) 30 26005235; 914 747-0110
Subscription fax: (49) 30 26005251; 914 747-1326

ADVERTISING INFORMATION

Advertising accepted: Yes
Advertising rates: Request from Mouton de Gruyter

EDITORIAL DESCRIPTION

Scope: Publishes articles on any aspect of African languages and linguistics.
Reviews books: Yes
Publishes notes: No
Languages accepted: English; French; German
Prints abstracts: Yes

SUBMISSION REQUIREMENTS

Restrictions on contributors: None
Author pays submission fee: No
Author pays page charges: No
Length of articles: No restrictions
Length of book reviews: No restrictions
Style: Chicago
Number of copies required: 2
Copyright ownership: Mouton de Gruyter
Rejected manuscripts: Not returned
Time before publication decision: 3 mos.
Time between decision and publication: 9 mos.
Number of reviewers: 2
Articles submitted per year: 28
Articles published per year: 8
Book reviews submitted per year: 20
Book reviews published per year: 18

(1355)
*Journal of Afroasiatic Languages

Robert Hetzron & Alan S. Kaye, Editors
1346 San Rafael Ave.
Santa Barbara, CA 93109

Additional editorial address: Submit reviews and books to be reviewed to Alan S. Kaye, Dept. of Linguistics, California State Univ., Fullerton, CA 92634
Telephone: 805 962-5073
First published: 1988
Sponsoring organization: Inst. of Semitic Studies
ISSN: 0894-9824
MLA acronym: JAAL

SUBSCRIPTION INFORMATION

Frequency of publication: 3 times/yr.
Circulation: 100
Available in microform: No
Subscription price: $56.00/yr. institutions; $38.00/yr. individuals
Year to which price refers: 1992
Subscription address: Subscription Dept., E. J. Brill, P.O. Box 9000, 2300 PA Leiden, Netherlands
Subscription telephone: (31) 71 31624
Subscription fax: (31) 71 317532

ADVERTISING INFORMATION

Advertising accepted: Yes

EDITORIAL DESCRIPTION

Scope: Publishes articles on historical, comparative, and theoretical linguistics that deal with Afroasiatic (Hamito-Semitic) languages.
Reviews books: Yes
Publishes notes: Yes
Languages accepted: English; French
Prints abstracts: Yes
Author-anonymous submission: No

SUBMISSION REQUIREMENTS

Author pays submission fee: No
Author pays page charges: No
Length of articles: No restrictions
Length of book reviews: No restrictions
Length of notes: No restrictions
Style: Chicago
Number of copies required: 3
Special requirements: Submit double-spaced letter-quality typescript on 8 1/2 x 11 in. paper and a 100-150 word abstract.
Copyright ownership: Inst. of Semitic Studies
Rejected manuscripts: Returned at author's request
Number of reviewers: 1-2
Articles submitted per year: 12
Articles published per year: 10

(1356)
*Journal of American Culture

Ray B. Browne, Russel B. Nye, & Tom H. Towers, Editors
Bowling Green State Univ.
Bowling Green, OH 43403

Telephone: 419 372-2981
Fax: 419 372-8095
Sponsoring organization: American Culture Assn.
MLA acronym: JACult

SUBSCRIPTION INFORMATION

Frequency of publication: 4 times/yr. (Spring, Summer, Fall, Winter)
Circulation: 1,300
Available in microform: Yes
Subscription price: $30.00/yr.
Year to which price refers: 1992

ADVERTISING INFORMATION

Advertising accepted: Yes
Advertising rates: $150.00/full page

EDITORIAL DESCRIPTION

Scope: Publishes articles on all aspects of culture of the Americas.
Reviews books: Yes
Publishes notes: No
Languages accepted: English
Prints abstracts: No
Author-anonymous submission: Yes

SUBMISSION REQUIREMENTS

Restrictions on contributors: Contributors must be subscribers.
Author pays submission fee: No
Author pays page charges: No
Length of book reviews: 300-400 words
Style: MLA with modifications
Number of copies required: 2
Copyright ownership: Journal
Rejected manuscripts: Returned; enclose SASE.
Time before publication decision: 3-6 mos.
Time between decision and publication: 3-6 mos.
Number of reviewers: 2
Articles submitted per year: 75-100
Articles published per year: 35-40
Book reviews submitted per year: 25-40
Book reviews published per year: 25-40

(1357)
*Journal of American Folklore

Burt Feintuch, Editor
Center for the Humanities
Univ. of New Hampshire
Durham, NH 03827

Telephone: 603 862-4356
First published: 1888
Sponsoring organization: American Folklore Soc., Inc.
ISSN: 0021-8715
MLA acronym: JAF

SUBSCRIPTION INFORMATION

Frequency of publication: 4 times/yr. (Jan., Apr., July, Oct.)
Circulation: 2,800
Available in microform: Yes
Subscription price: $50.00/yr.; $20.00/yr. students
Year to which price refers: 1992
Subscription address: American Folklore Soc., 1703 New Hampshire Ave., NW, Washington, DC 20009

ADVERTISING INFORMATION

Advertising accepted: Yes

EDITORIAL DESCRIPTION

Scope: Publishes scholarly studies in folklore and folklife.
Reviews books: Yes
Publishes notes: Yes
Languages accepted: English
Prints abstracts: Yes
Author-anonymous submission: No

SUBMISSION REQUIREMENTS

Restrictions on contributors: None
Author pays submission fee: Yes, for nonmembers
Cost of submission fee: $15.00
Author pays page charges: No
Length of articles: 20-50 typescript pp.
Length of book reviews: 1,000 words
Length of notes: 1-15 typescript pp.
Style: Chicago
Number of copies required: 3
Special requirements: Submit original typescript plus 2 copies.
Copyright ownership: American Folklore Soc.
Rejected manuscripts: One copy returned; enclose return postage.
Time before publication decision: 3 mos.
Time between decision and publication: 6 mos.
Number of reviewers: 2
Articles submitted per year: 100
Articles published per year: 12
Book reviews submitted per year: 60
Book reviews published per year: 50-60
Notes submitted per year: 10
Notes published per year: 5

(1358)
*Journal of American Studies

Michael Heale, Editor
History Dept.
Lancaster Univ.
Lancaster LA1 4YG, England

Telephone: (44) 524 65201
Fax: (44) 524 846102
First published: 1967
Sponsoring organization: British Assn. for American Studies
ISSN: 0021-8758
MLA acronym: JAmS

SUBSCRIPTION INFORMATION

Frequency of publication: 3 times/yr.
Circulation: 1,500
Available in microform: Yes
Subscription price: £49.00/yr. United Kingdom; $89.00/yr. elsewhere
Year to which price refers: 1991
Subscription address: Cambridge Univ. Press, Edinburgh Bldg., Shaftesbury Rd., Cambridge CB2 2RU, England
Additional subscription address: In N. America: Cambridge Univ. Press, 40 W. 20th St., New York, NY 10011

ADVERTISING INFORMATION

Advertising accepted: Yes

EDITORIAL DESCRIPTION

Scope: Publishes work on American history, literature, politics, geography, and related subjects. Articles which cross the conventional lines of those disciplines are welcome, as are comparative studies of American and other cultures. Also disseminates information about work in progress and provides a platform for the exchange of scholarly information and opinion.
Reviews books: Yes
Publishes notes: Yes
Languages accepted: English
Prints abstracts: No
Author-anonymous submission: No

SUBMISSION REQUIREMENTS

Restrictions on contributors: None
Author pays submission fee: No
Author pays page charges: No
Length of articles: 5,000 words
Length of book reviews: 400 words
Length of notes: 1,000-2,000 words
Style: Chicago
Number of copies required: 1
Copyright ownership: Cambridge Univ. Press
Rejected manuscripts: Returned; US submissions returned only if international reply coupons are sent.
Time before publication decision: 2 mos.
Time between decision and publication: 9 mos.
Number of reviewers: 2
Articles submitted per year: 120
Articles published per year: 12
Book reviews submitted per year: 150
Book reviews published per year: 140
Notes submitted per year: 20
Notes published per year: 10

(1359)
*Journal of Anglo-Italian Studies

Peter Vassallo & Edward Chaney, Editors
Inst. of Anglo-Italian Studies
Univ. of Malta, Malta

Additional editorial address: Edward Chaney, 40 Southfield Rd., Oxford OX4 1NZ, England
Telephone: (356) 336451
Fax: (356) 336450
First published: 1991

Sponsoring organization: Inst. of Anglo-Italian Studies, Univ. of Malta
MLA acronym: JAIS

SUBSCRIPTION INFORMATION

Frequency of publication: Annual
Available in microform: No
Subscription price: $30.00 (£15.00)/yr. institutions; $20.00 (£10.00)/yr. individuals
Year to which price refers: 1991

ADVERTISING INFORMATION

Advertising accepted: No

EDITORIAL DESCRIPTION

Scope: Publishes articles on literary and cultural relations in the interdisciplinary field of Anglo-Italian studies from 1300 to the present.
Reviews books: No
Publishes notes: Yes
Languages accepted: English; Italian
Prints abstracts: No
Author-anonymous submission: No

SUBMISSION REQUIREMENTS

Author pays submission fee: No
Author pays page charges: No
Length of articles: 10,000 words maximum
Style: Modern Humanities Research Assn.
Number of copies required: 2
Copyright ownership: Director, Inst. of Anglo-Italian Studies, Editors, & Author
Time before publication decision: 6-8 weeks
Number of reviewers: 2
Articles submitted per year: 15-20
Articles published per year: 10-12
Notes submitted per year: 4-6
Notes published per year: 3-4

(1360)
*Journal of Anthropological Research

Philip K. Bock, Editor
Dept. of Anthropology
Univ. of New Mexico
Albuquerque, NM 87131

Telephone: 505 277-3027
Fax: 505 277-0874
First published: 1945
Sponsoring organization: Univ. of New Mexico
ISSN: 0091-7710
MLA acronym: JAR

SUBSCRIPTION INFORMATION

Frequency of publication: 4 times/yr.
Circulation: 1,400
Available in microform: Yes
Subscription price: $40.00/yr. institutions; $20.00/yr. individuals
Year to which price refers: 1991
Subscription address: Margaret A. Colclough, Subscriptions Manager, at the above address
Subscription telephone: 505 277-4544

ADVERTISING INFORMATION

Advertising accepted: No

EDITORIAL DESCRIPTION

Scope: Includes articles on all branches of anthropology relating to peoples and cultures, past and present, in any region. Is offered as a vehicle of expression for anthropologists in all parts of the world. Occasionally publishes articles on language and literature.
Reviews books: Yes
Publishes notes: Yes
Languages accepted: English
Prints abstracts: Yes
Author-anonymous submission: Yes

SUBMISSION REQUIREMENTS

Restrictions on contributors: None
Author pays submission fee: No
Author pays page charges: No
Length of articles: 12,500 words maximum
Length of book reviews: 600 words
Length of notes: 150 words
Style: Chicago
Number of copies required: 2
Special requirements: Submit original manuscript.
Copyright ownership: Univ. of New Mexico
Rejected manuscripts: Returned; enclose SASE.
Time before publication decision: 3-4 mos.
Time between decision and publication: 3-9 mos.
Number of reviewers: 2-3
Articles submitted per year: 120
Articles published per year: 24
Book reviews submitted per year: 25
Book reviews published per year: 20
Notes submitted per year: 5
Notes published per year: 5

(1361)
Journal of Arabic Literature

M. M. Badawi, P. Cacmica, M. C. Lyons, & J. N. Mattock, Editors
E. J. Brill
P.O. Box 9000
2300 PA Leiden, Netherlands

Additional editorial address: J. N. Mattock, Dept. of Arabic, The University, Glasgow, G12 8QQ, Scotland.
First published: 1970
ISSN: 0085-2376
MLA acronym: JArabL

SUBSCRIPTION INFORMATION

Frequency of publication: 2 times/yr. (Mar., Sept.)
Circulation: 370
Available in microform: No
Subscription price: 92 f ($46.00)/yr.
Year to which price refers: 1991
Additional subscription address: In US & Canada: E. J. Brill, 24 Hudson St., Kinderhook, NY 12106

ADVERTISING INFORMATION

Advertising accepted: No

EDITORIAL DESCRIPTION

Scope: Publishes articles on all topics related to Classical and modern Arabic literature. Publishes essays in literary appreciation, assessments of trends and movements of individual authors and of single works, and bibliographics, as well as complete short stories.
Reviews books: Yes
Languages accepted: English
Prints abstracts: No

SUBMISSION REQUIREMENTS

Author pays submission fee: No
Author pays page charges: No
Style: System adopted by *Encyclopedia of Islam* preferred
Copyright ownership: E. J. Brill

(1362)
*Journal of Asian Studies

David D. Buck, Editor
Dept. of History
Univ. of Wisconsin-Milwaukee
390 Holton Hall
2442 E. Hartford Ave.
Milwaukee, WI 53201

Telephone: 313 665-2490
Fax: 313 665-3801
First published: 1941
Sponsoring organization: Univ. of Michigan; Univ. of Wisconsin
ISSN: 0021-9118
MLA acronym: JASt

SUBSCRIPTION INFORMATION

Frequency of publication: 4 times/yr. (Nov., Feb., May, Aug.)
Circulation: 9,000
Available in microform: Yes
Subscription price: $95.00/yr. institutions (includes journal, *Bibliography of Asian Studies*, & *Doctoral Dissertations on Asia*)
Year to which price refers: 1992
Subscription address: Assn. for Asian Studies Inc., One Lane Hall, Univ. of Michigan, Ann Arbor, MI 48109

ADVERTISING INFORMATION

Advertising accepted: Yes
Advertising rates: $340.00/half page; $550.00/full page

EDITORIAL DESCRIPTION

Scope: Focuses on South and Southeast Asia, China and Inner Asia, Japan and Korea. Publishes research articles, review articles, interpretive essays, research-assisting articles, and other materials stimulating and useful to a diverse readership in many geographic and disciplinary fields relating to the study of Asia.
Reviews books: Yes
Publishes notes: Yes, but rarely
Languages accepted: English
Prints abstracts: Yes
Author-anonymous submission: Yes

SUBMISSION REQUIREMENTS

Author pays submission fee: No
Author pays page charges: No
Length of articles: 35 pp. maximum
Length of book reviews: 700 words
Style: Chicago
Number of copies required: 4
Copyright ownership: Assigned by author to journal
Rejected manuscripts: Not returned
Time before publication decision: 3 mos.
Time between decision and publication: 6 mos.
Number of reviewers: 2-3
Articles submitted per year: 130
Articles published per year: 20
Book reviews submitted per year: 400
Book reviews published per year: 400

(1363)
*Journal of Australian Literature

Subhas Chandra Saha, Editor
Dept. of English
Tripura Univ.
Agartala 799 004, India

First published: 1990
ISSN: 0971-1228
MLA acronym: JAusL

SUBSCRIPTION INFORMATION

Frequency of publication: 2 times/yr.
Circulation: 500

Available in microform: No
Subscription price: $34.00/yr. institutions; $28.00/yr. individuals
Year to which price refers: 1992

ADVERTISING INFORMATION

Advertising accepted: Yes
Advertising rates: $100.00/half page; $200.00/full page

EDITORIAL DESCRIPTION

Scope: Publishes creative writing from Australia, as well as critical articles on Australian literature from any part of the world.
Reviews books: Yes
Publishes notes: Yes
Languages accepted: English
Prints abstracts: No
Author-anonymous submission: No

SUBMISSION REQUIREMENTS

Restrictions on contributors: None
Author pays submission fee: No
Author pays page charges: No
Length of articles: No restrictions
Length of book reviews: No restrictions
Length of notes: No restrictions
Style: MLA
Number of copies required: 2
Copyright ownership: Author
Rejected manuscripts: Not returned
Time before publication decision: 2 mos.
Time between decision and publication: 6 mos.
Number of reviewers: 1
Articles submitted per year: 400
Articles published per year: 100
Book reviews submitted per year: 20
Book reviews published per year: 10
Notes submitted per year: 30
Notes published per year: 16

(1364)
Journal of Baltic Studies

William Urban & Roger Noël, Editors
Dept. of History
Monmouth College
Monmount, IL 61462

Telephone: 309 457-2388
Fax: 309 457-2141
First published: 1972
Sponsoring organization: Assn. for the Advancement of Baltic Studies, Inc.
ISSN: 0162-9778
MLA acronym: JBalS

SUBSCRIPTION INFORMATION

Frequency of publication: 4 times/yr.
Circulation: 1,300
Available in microform: Yes
Subscription price: $55.00/yr. institutions; $45.00/yr. individuals; $25.00/yr. emeritus; $20.00/yr. students
Year to which price refers: 1992
Subscription address: Executive Office, Assn. for the Advancement of Baltic Studies, Inc., 111 Knob Hill Rd., Hackettstown, NJ 07840

ADVERTISING INFORMATION

Advertising accepted: Yes

EDITORIAL DESCRIPTION

Scope: Journal includes articles on Estonia, Latvia, Lithuania, and Finland and their interaction with other countries. Publishes work in a wide variety of disciplines, including literature, linguistics, history, social sciences, and musicology. Articles, review articles, book reviews, reports on conferences, and notes on the profession are included.
Reviews books: Yes
Publishes notes: Yes
Languages accepted: English; German; French
Prints abstracts: No
Author-anonymous submission: No

SUBMISSION REQUIREMENTS

Restrictions on contributors: None
Author pays submission fee: No
Author pays page charges: No
Length of articles: No restrictions
Length of book reviews: 600 words
Length of notes: No restrictions
Style: MLA with journal modifications
Number of copies required: 2
Special requirements: IBM or Macintosh diskettes are requested in addition to paper manuscripts. Request style sheet from editor.
Copyright ownership: Assn. for the Advancement of Baltic Studies, Inc.
Rejected manuscripts: Returned
Time before publication decision: 3 mos.
Time between decision and publication: 1 yr.
Number of reviewers: 2
Articles submitted per year: 50
Articles published per year: 25
Book reviews submitted per year: 45
Notes submitted per year: 12
Notes published per year: 12

(1365)
*Journal of Beckett Studies

S. E. Gontarski, Editor
Dept. of English
Florida State Univ.
Tallahassee, FL 32306

Telephone: 904 644-6038
Fax: 904 644-8817
E-mail: SGONTAR@RAI.CC.FSU.EDU
First published: 1976
Sponsoring organization: Florida State Univ., Dept. of English
ISSN: 0309-5207
MLA acronym: JBeckS

SUBSCRIPTION INFORMATION

Frequency of publication: 2 times/yr.
Circulation: 1,500
Available in microform: No
Subscription price: $25.00/yr. institutions; $15.00/yr. individuals
Year to which price refers: 1992

ADVERTISING INFORMATION

Advertising accepted: Yes

EDITORIAL DESCRIPTION

Scope: Publishes scholarship and criticism on Samuel Beckett and his circle, as well as theatrical reviews and photographs of productions.
Reviews books: Yes
Publishes notes: Yes
Languages accepted: English; French
Prints abstracts: No
Author-anonymous submission: Yes

SUBMISSION REQUIREMENTS

Restrictions on contributors: Reviews are generally commissioned.
Author pays submission fee: No
Author pays page charges: No
Length of articles: 5,000-8,000 words
Length of book reviews: 500-1,000 words
Length of notes: 500-2,500 words
Style: MLA; American or British spelling accepted
Number of copies required: 2
Special requirements: Submission on DOS or Macintosh diskette is preferred.
Copyright ownership: Author
Rejected manuscripts: Returned; enclose SASE.
Time before publication decision: 4 mos.
Time between decision and publication: 1 yr.
Number of reviewers: 2
Articles submitted per year: 75
Articles published per year: 16
Book reviews published per year: 10-12
Notes submitted per year: 15-20
Notes published per year: 6-10

(1366)
Journal of Canadian Fiction

John Robert Sorfleet, Editor
2050 Mackay St.
Montreal, Quebec H3G 2J1 Canada

First published: 1972
ISSN: 0047-2255
MLA acronym: JCF

SUBSCRIPTION INFORMATION

Frequency of publication: 4 times/yr.
Circulation: 1,500
Available in microform: No

ADVERTISING INFORMATION

Advertising accepted: Yes

EDITORIAL DESCRIPTION

Scope: Publishes Canadian fiction, interviews, articles, and in-depth reviews, plus an annual annotated bibliography of Canadian criticism.
Reviews books: Yes
Languages accepted: English; French
Prints abstracts: No

SUBMISSION REQUIREMENTS

Author pays submission fee: No
Author pays page charges: No
Length of articles: 2,500-10,000 words
Length of book reviews: 1,200-2,000 words
Style: MLA
Number of copies required: 2
Special requirements: Submit original typescript; include cover letter.
Copyright ownership: Journal & author
Rejected manuscripts: Original returned; enclose return postage.
Time before publication decision: 12-15 weeks
Time between decision and publication: 3-9 mos.
Number of reviewers: 3-5
Articles submitted per year: 75
Articles published per year: 20-25
Book reviews published per year: 40-50

(1367)
*Journal of Canadian Poetry

David Staines, Editor
Dept. of English
Univ. of Ottawa
Ottawa, Ontario K1N 6N5, Canada

Telephone: 613 564-3411
Fax: 613 564-9175
First published: 1978
ISSN: 0705-1328
MLA acronym: JCP

SUBSCRIPTION INFORMATION

Frequency of publication: Annual (Spring)
Circulation: 350
Available in microform: No
Subscription price: $12.95/yr., $25.00/2 yrs.
Year to which price refers: 1991
Subscription address: 9 Ashburn Dr., Nepean, Ontario K2E 6N4, Canada
Subscription fax: 613 224-6837

ADVERTISING INFORMATION

Advertising accepted: Yes

Advertising rates: $150.00/half page; $225.00/full page

EDITORIAL DESCRIPTION

Scope: Provides an annual review of the preceding year's publications in Canadian poetry and poetry criticism.
Reviews books: Yes
Publishes notes: Yes
Languages accepted: English; French
Prints abstracts: No
Author-anonymous submission: Yes

SUBMISSION REQUIREMENTS

Restrictions on contributors: Book reviews are solicited.
Author pays submission fee: No
Author pays page charges: No
Length of articles: No restrictions
Length of book reviews: No restrictions
Style: Chicago
Number of copies required: 1
Copyright ownership: Author & Borealis Press Ltd.
Rejected manuscripts: Returned
Time before publication decision: 3 mos.
Time between decision and publication: 1 yr.
Number of reviewers: 2-3
Articles submitted per year: 10-15
Articles published per year: 2
Book reviews submitted per year: 50
Book reviews published per year: 40-45
Notes submitted per year: 1-2
Notes published per year: 1

(1368)
*Journal of Canadian Studies/Revue d'Etudes Canadiennes

Michael A. Peterman, Editor
Trent Univ.
P.O. Box 4800
Peterborough
Ontario, K9J 7B8, Canada

Telephone: 705 748-1279
Fax: 705 748-1551
First published: 1966
Sponsoring organization: Trent Univ.
ISSN: 0021-9495
MLA acronym: JCSR

SUBSCRIPTION INFORMATION

Frequency of publication: 4 times/yr. (Spring, Summer, Fall, Winter)
Circulation: 1,300
Available in microform: Yes, through Micromedia Ltd., Toronto
Subscription price: C$45.00/yr. institutions; C$25.00/yr. students; C$15.00/yr. students
Year to which price refers: 1991

ADVERTISING INFORMATION

Advertising accepted: Yes
Advertising rates: C$66.00/quarter page; C$125.00/half page; C$200.00/full page; C$250.00/inside back cover

EDITORIAL DESCRIPTION

Scope: Publishes articles dealing with any aspect of Canada or Canadian life.
Reviews books: Yes
Languages accepted: English; French
Prints abstracts: Yes
Author-anonymous submission: Yes

SUBMISSION REQUIREMENTS

Author pays submission fee: No
Length of articles: 2,000-10,000 words
Style: MLA
Number of copies required: 2
Copyright ownership: Journal & author

Rejected manuscripts: Returned; enclose return postage.
Time before publication decision: 6 mos.
Number of reviewers: 2
Articles submitted per year: 75
Articles published per year: 30

(1369)
*Journal of Caribbean Studies

O. R. Dathorne, Editor
Assn. of Caribbean Studies
P.O. Box 22202
Lexington, KY 40522-2202

Telephone: 606 257-6966
Fax: 606 258-1072
First published: 1980
ISSN: 0190-2008
MLA acronym: JCSt

SUBSCRIPTION INFORMATION

Frequency of publication: 3 times/yr. (Winter, Spring, Fall)
Circulation: 1,500
Available in microform: No
Subscription price: $200.00/yr. institutions; $50.00/yr. individuals
Year to which price refers: 1992

ADVERTISING INFORMATION

Advertising accepted: No

EDITORIAL DESCRIPTION

Scope: Publishes articles on Caribbean studies relating to anthropology, arts, economics, folk culture, geography, history, languages, including Creoles and Pidgins, linguistics, literature, music, politics, psychology, religion, and sociology.
Reviews books: Yes
Publishes notes: No
Languages accepted: English; Spanish; French
Prints abstracts: Yes
Author-anonymous submission: Yes

SUBMISSION REQUIREMENTS

Author pays submission fee: No
Author pays page charges: No
Length of articles: 4,500-6,000 words
Length of book reviews: 200-500 words
Number of copies required: 3
Special requirements: Submit original manuscript.
Copyright ownership: Assn. of Caribbean Studies
Rejected manuscripts: Returned; enclose SASE.
Time before publication decision: 6-9 mos.
Time between decision and publication: 3-6 mos.
Number of reviewers: 3
Articles submitted per year: 200
Articles published per year: 16-20
Book reviews submitted per year: 40
Book reviews published per year: 12

(1370)
Journal of Celtic Linguistics

David Cram, Dónall P. Ó Baoill, Erich Poppe, & James Fife, Editors
Jesus College
Oxford OX1 3DW, England

Additional editorial address: D. Ó Baoill, Linguistics Inst. of Ireland, 31 Fitzwilliam Pl., Dublin 2, Ireland; E. Poppe, Dept. Anglo-Saxon, Norse & Celtic, Univ. of Cambridge, 9 West Rd., Cambridge CB3 9DP, England; J. Fife, 6655 La Jolla Blvd. # 11, La Jolla, CA 92037
First published: 1992

ISSN: 0962-1377
MLA acronym: JCeltL

SUBSCRIPTION INFORMATION

Frequency of publication: Annual
Subscription price: £10.00 ($20.00)/yr.
Year to which price refers: 1992
Subscription address: Univ. of Wales Press, 6 Gwennyth St., Cathays, Cardiff CF2 4YD, Wales
Additional subscription address: In N. America: Books International Inc., P.O. Box 605, Herndon, VA 22070
Subscription telephone: (44) 222 231919
Subscription fax: (44) 222 230908

EDITORIAL DESCRIPTION

Scope: Publishes articles on Celtic linguistics.
Reviews books: Yes
Languages accepted: English; French; German; Celtic languages
Prints abstracts: Yes
Author-anonymous submission: Yes, at author's request

SUBMISSION REQUIREMENTS

Number of copies required: 4
Special requirements: Submit an abstract of 250 words maximum. Manuscript should be submitted to the nearest regional editor. Final submission of accepted articles should be on IBM-compatible diskette. Articles in Celtic languages must be accompanied by an English abstract.

(1371)
*Journal of Child Language

Katharine Perera, Editor
Dept. of Linguistics
Univ. of Manchester
Manchester M13 9PL, England

Telephone: (44) 61 2753187
Fax: (44) 61 2753187
First published: 1974
ISSN: 0305-0009
MLA acronym: JChL

SUBSCRIPTION INFORMATION

Frequency of publication: 3 times/yr.
Circulation: 2,000
Available in microform: No
Subscription price: $124.00/yr. institutions; $55.00/yr. individuals
Year to which price refers: 1992
Subscription address: Cambridge Univ. Press, Edinburgh Bldg., Shaftesbury Rd., Cambridge CB2 2RU, England
Additional subscription address: In N. America: Cambridge Univ. Press, 40 W. 20th St., New York, NY 10011
Subscription telephone: (44) 223 312393

ADVERTISING INFORMATION

Advertising accepted: Yes

EDITORIAL DESCRIPTION

Scope: Focuses on the study of child language. Publishes material on all aspects of the scientific study of language behavior in children and the principles which underlie it. Emphasis is on the normal development of both monolingual and multilingual children, but reference may be made to pathological development where this relates to general questions of language development. In addition to articles and book reviews, the journal contains a Notes and Discussion section with short pieces of data illustrating points of general theoretical interest.
Reviews books: Yes
Publishes notes: Yes

Languages accepted: English
Prints abstracts: Yes
Author-anonymous submission: Yes

SUBMISSION REQUIREMENTS

Restrictions on contributors: None
Author pays submission fee: No
Author pays page charges: No
Length of articles: 8,000-10,000 words
Length of book reviews: 500-2,000 words
Length of notes: 2,000-3,000 words
Style: Journal
Number of copies required: 4
Special requirements: Consult back cover of journal
Copyright ownership: Cambridge Univ. Press
Rejected manuscripts: Returned at author's request
Time before publication decision: 4 mos.
Time between decision and publication: 1 yr.
Number of reviewers: 2
Articles submitted per year: 150
Articles published per year: 35
Book reviews submitted per year: 12
Book reviews published per year: 12
Notes submitted per year: 15
Notes published per year: 6

(1372)
*Journal of Chinese Linguistics

William S-Y. Wang, Editor
Project on Linguistic Analysis
Univ. of California
2222 Piedmont Ave.
Berkeley, CA 94720

Telephone: 510 642-5937
Fax: 510 283-4464
E-mail: WSYW@VIOLET.BERKELEY.EDU
First published: 1973
Sponsoring organization: Univ. of California
ISSN: 0091-3723
MLA acronym: JChinL

SUBSCRIPTION INFORMATION

Frequency of publication: 2 times/yr. (Jan., June)
Circulation: 400
Available in microform: No

ADVERTISING INFORMATION

Advertising accepted: Yes

EDITORIAL DESCRIPTION

Scope: Publishes articles on all aspects of the languages and dialects of China: historical and descriptive, theoretical and applied, spoken and written, social, psychological, and literary.
Reviews books: Yes
Publishes notes: Yes
Languages accepted: English; Chinese languages
Prints abstracts: Yes

SUBMISSION REQUIREMENTS

Author pays submission fee: No
Author pays page charges: No
Length of articles: 50 pp. maximum
Length of book reviews: 500 words
Length of notes: 200 words
Style: Journal
Number of copies required: 2
Special requirements: Include an abstract in Chinese for articles in English or an abstract in English for articles in Chinese.
Copyright ownership: Journal
Rejected manuscripts: Not returned
Time before publication decision: 1 yr.
Time between decision and publication: 6 mos.
Number of reviewers: 2
Articles submitted per year: 15
Articles published per year: 10

(1373)
*Journal of Chinese Philosophy

Chung-ying Cheng, Editor
Dialogue Publishing Co.
Box 11071
Honolulu, HI 96828

First published: 1973
Sponsoring organization: International Soc. for Chinese Philosophy; Univ. of Hawaii
ISSN: 0301-8121
MLA acronym: JChinP

SUBSCRIPTION INFORMATION

Frequency of publication: 4 times/yr.
Circulation: 500
Available in microform: No

ADVERTISING INFORMATION

Advertising accepted: Yes

EDITORIAL DESCRIPTION

Scope: Invites contributions in four major historical periods and five major fields of discipline in Chinese philosophy. The four major historical periods are Classical Chinese Philosophy in Pre-Ch'in and Han Eras, Neo-Taoism and Chinese Buddhism, Chinese Neo-Confucianism, and Modern and Contemporary Chinese Philosophy since the 19th century. The five major fields of discipline are Chinese Logic and Scientific Thinking, Chinese Moral Philosophy and Philosophy of Religion, Chinese Art Theories and Aesthetics, Chinese Metaphysical Theories, and Chinese Social and Political Philosophies. Special attention will be given to articles dealing with narrow topics with broad significances. Short and critical reviews are welcome.
Reviews books: Yes
Publishes notes: Yes
Languages accepted: English
Prints abstracts: No

SUBMISSION REQUIREMENTS

Restrictions on contributors: None
Author pays submission fee: No
Length of articles: 2,500-12,500 words
Length of book reviews: 20 pp.
Length of notes: 3-4 pp.
Style: MLA; Wade-Giles
Number of copies required: 2
Special requirements: Submit original typescript.
Copyright ownership: Assigned by author to journal
Rejected manuscripts: Returned
Time before publication decision: 3 mos.
Time between decision and publication: 15-20 mos.
Number of reviewers: 2
Articles published per year: 20
Book reviews published per year: 8-10

(1374)
Journal of Chinese Studies

Fred Gillette Sturm, Editor
American Assn. for Chinese Studies
300 Bricker Hall
Ohio State Univ.
Columbus, OH 43210

First published: 1984
Sponsoring organization: American Assn. for Chinese Studies
ISSN: 0742-5929
MLA acronym: JChSt

SUBSCRIPTION INFORMATION

Frequency of publication: 2 times/yr. (Apr., Oct.)
Circulation: 200
Available in microform: No

ADVERTISING INFORMATION

Advertising accepted: Yes

EDITORIAL DESCRIPTION

Scope: Provides a multidisciplinary forum for a discussion of all aspects of Chinese studies.
Reviews books: Yes
Publishes notes: Yes
Languages accepted: English
Prints abstracts: No
Author-anonymous submission: No

SUBMISSION REQUIREMENTS

Restrictions on contributors: None
Author pays submission fee: No
Author pays page charges: No
Length of articles: No restrictions
Length of book reviews: No restrictions
Length of notes: No restrictions
Style: Chicago
Number of copies required: 2
Copyright ownership: American Assn. for Chinese Studies
Rejected manuscripts: Returned
Time before publication decision: 2 mos.
Time between decision and publication: 4 mos.
Number of reviewers: 2
Articles submitted per year: 35
Articles published per year: 15
Book reviews published per year: 15

(1375)
*The Journal of Commonwealth Literature

John Thieme, Shirley Chew, & Ronald Warwick, Editors
Dept. of English
Univ. of Hull
Hull HU6 7RX, England

Additional editorial address: S. Chew, School of English, Univ. of Leeds, Leeds LS2 9JT, England; R. Warwick, Adult Education Officer, Commonwealth Inst., Kensington High St., London W8 6NQ, England
Telephone: (44) 482 465666
Fax: (44) 482 465641
First published: 1965
ISSN: 0021-9894
MLA acronym: JCL

SUBSCRIPTION INFORMATION

Frequency of publication: 3 times/yr. (Apr., Aug., Dec.)
Circulation: 1,200
Available in microform: No
Subscription price: £50.00 ($95.00)/yr. institutions; £30.00 ($57.00)/yr. individuals
Year to which price refers: 1992
Subscription address: Bowker-Saur Ltd., 60 Grosvenor St., London W1, England
Additional subscription address: Bailey Management Services, 127 Sandgate Rd., Folkestone, Kent CT20 2BL, England

ADVERTISING INFORMATION

Advertising accepted: Yes

EDITORIAL DESCRIPTION

Scope: Publishes bibliographies (December issue) and scholarly and/or critical articles on literature in English. Does not include studies on literature from the United States or the British Isles.
Reviews books: No
Languages accepted: English
Prints abstracts: No
Author-anonymous submission: No

SUBMISSION REQUIREMENTS

Restrictions on contributors: None
Author pays submission fee: No
Author pays page charges: No
Length of articles: 3,000-5,000 words
Style: Oxford
Number of copies required: 2
Rejected manuscripts: Returned; enclose return postage or international reply coupons.
Time before publication decision: 3 mos.
Time between decision and publication: 6 mos.
Number of reviewers: 2-3
Articles submitted per year: 80
Articles published per year: 20

(1376)
*Journal of Communication

Mark Levy, Editor
College of Journalism
Univ. of Maryland
College Park, MD 20742

Telephone: 301 405-2384
Fax: 301 314-9166
First published: 1951
Sponsoring organization: International Communication Assn.
ISSN: 0021-9916
MLA acronym: JC

SUBSCRIPTION INFORMATION

Frequency of publication: 4 times/yr.
Circulation: 6,000
Available in microform: Yes
Subscription price: $65.00/yr. institutions US; $79.00/yr. institutions elsewhere; $30.00/yr. individuals US; $44.00/yr. individuals elsewhere; $18.00/single issue institutions; $9.00/single issue individuals
Year to which price refers: 1991
Subscription address: Journals Dept., Oxford Univ. Press, 2001 Evans Rd., Cary, NC 27513
Subscription telephone: 800 852-7323

ADVERTISING INFORMATION

Advertising accepted: Yes
Advertising rates: $100.00/quarter page; $200.00/half page; $300.00/full page; $350.00/back cover

EDITORIAL DESCRIPTION

Scope: Concerned with the study of communication theory, practice, and policy. Addresses those in every field who are interested in research and policy developments and in the public impact of communication studies. Welcomes contributions (research articles and book reviews) devoted to significant problems and issues in communications and to events and work of wide professional interest.
Reviews books: Yes
Publishes notes: No
Languages accepted: English
Prints abstracts: No
Author-anonymous submission: Yes

SUBMISSION REQUIREMENTS

Restrictions on contributors: None
Author pays submission fee: No
Author pays page charges: No
Length of articles: 5,000-8,000 words
Length of book reviews: 600-1,200 words
Style: American Psychological Assn.
Number of copies required: 4
Special requirements: Include an abstract.
Copyright ownership: Journal
Rejected manuscripts: 1 copy returned; enclose SASE.
Time before publication decision: 6 mos. maximum
Time between decision and publication: 3-6 mos.
Number of reviewers: 2-3
Articles submitted per year: 325-375
Articles published per year: 30-35
Book reviews submitted per year: 80-100
Book reviews published per year: 70-85

(1377)
*Journal of Communication Inquiry

205 Communication Center
Univ. of Iowa
Iowa City, IA 52242

First published: 1974
Sponsoring organization: Iowa Center for Communication Study, School of Journalism & Mass Communication, Univ. of Iowa
ISSN: 0196-8599
MLA acronym: JOCI

SUBSCRIPTION INFORMATION

Frequency of publication: 2 times/yr. (Summer, Winter) plus special issues
Available in microform: No

ADVERTISING INFORMATION

Advertising accepted: Yes

EDITORIAL DESCRIPTION

Scope: Emphasizes interdisciplinary inquiry into communication and mass communication phenomena within cultural and historical perspectives. Such perspectives imply that an understanding of these phenomena cannot arise solely out of a narrowly focused analysis. Rather, the approaches emphasize philosophical, evaluative, empirical, legal, historical, and/or critical inquiry into relationships between mass communication and society across time and culture. The journal is a forum for such investigations.
Reviews books: Yes
Publishes notes: No
Languages accepted: English
Prints abstracts: No
Author-anonymous submission: Yes

SUBMISSION REQUIREMENTS

Restrictions on contributors: None
Author pays submission fee: No
Author pays page charges: No
Length of articles: 7,000 words
Length of book reviews: 5-10 double spaced pp.
Style: Turabian
Number of copies required: 3
Special requirements: Include cover sheet with author's name, address, phone, title. Author's name should be removed from rest of manuscript.
Copyright ownership: Univ. of Iowa, School of Journalism & Mass Communication
Rejected manuscripts: Not returned
Time before publication decision: 1-4 mos.
Time between decision and publication: 4-6 mos.
Number of reviewers: 4
Articles submitted per year: 50-60
Articles published per year: 12-18
Book reviews submitted per year: 5-10
Book reviews published per year: 2-4

(1378)
*Journal of Comparative Literature and Aesthetics

A. C. Sukla, Editor
P.O. Jyoti Vihar: 768019
B8 Jyoti Vihar
Sambalpur, Orissa, India

First published: 1978
Sponsoring organization: Vishvanatha Kaviraja Inst.
ISSN: 0252-8169
MLA acronym: JCLA

SUBSCRIPTION INFORMATION

Frequency of publication: 2 times/yr. (Summer, Winter)
Circulation: 1,000
Available in microform: No
Subscription price: £6.00 ($12.00)/yr.
Year to which price refers: 1992

ADVERTISING INFORMATION

Advertising accepted: Yes

EDITORIAL DESCRIPTION

Scope: Publishes articles on comparative studies in literature, general aesthetics, literary theory, philosophy, religion, culture, film theory, and fine arts.
Reviews books: Yes
Publishes notes: Yes
Languages accepted: English
Prints abstracts: No
Author-anonymous submission: No

SUBMISSION REQUIREMENTS

Restrictions on contributors: None
Author pays submission fee: No
Author pays page charges: No
Length of articles: 2,500-12,500 words
Length of book reviews: 500-1,000 words
Length of notes: 200-500 words
Style: MLA
Number of copies required: 1
Copyright ownership: Vishvanatha Kaviraja Inst.
Rejected manuscripts: Returned
Time before publication decision: 6 mos.
Time between decision and publication: 1 yr.
Number of reviewers: 3
Articles submitted per year: 30-40
Articles published per year: 15
Book reviews submitted per year: 25-35
Book reviews published per year: 10-15
Notes submitted per year: 15-20
Notes published per year: 5-10

(1379)
*The Journal of Country Music

Paul Kingsbury, Editor
Country Music Foundation
4 Music Square E.
Nashville, TN 37203-1639

Telephone: 615 256-1639
Fax: 615 255-2245
First published: 1970
Sponsoring organization: Country Music Foundation
ISSN: 0092-0517
MLA acronym: JCM

SUBSCRIPTION INFORMATION

Frequency of publication: 3 times/yr.
Circulation: 1,800
Available in microform: No
Subscription price: $25.00/yr. institutions; $15.00/yr. individuals US; $20.00/yr. individuals elsewhere
Year to which price refers: 1992
Subscription telephone: 800 255-2357

ADVERTISING INFORMATION

Advertising accepted: Yes
Advertising rates: $150.00/half page; $300.00/full page

EDITORIAL DESCRIPTION

Scope: Publishes articles on North American traditional and popular country music.
Reviews books: Yes

Publishes notes: No
Languages accepted: English
Prints abstracts: No
Author-anonymous submission: No

SUBMISSION REQUIREMENTS

Author pays submission fee: No
Author pays page charges: No
Length of articles: 5,000 words
Length of book reviews: 1,000 words
Style: Chicago
Number of copies required: 1
Copyright ownership: Author
Rejected manuscripts: Returned; enclose SASE.
Time before publication decision: 4 weeks
Time between decision and publication: 2-9 mos.
Number of reviewers: 3
Articles submitted per year: 20-25
Articles published per year: 12-15
Book reviews submitted per year: 20-25
Book reviews published per year: 15-20

(1380)
*Journal of Croatian Studies: Annual Review of the Croatian Academy of America, Inc.

Jerome Jareb & Karlo Mirth, Editors
Croatian Academy of America, Inc.
P.O. Box 1767 Grand Central Station
New York, NY 10163-1767

First published: 1960
Sponsoring organization: Croatian Academy of America, Inc.
ISSN: 0075-4218
MLA acronym: JCS

SUBSCRIPTION INFORMATION

Frequency of publication: Annual
Circulation: 1,000
Available in microform: No
Subscription price: $30.00/yr. institutions; $20.00/yr. individuals
Year to which price refers: 1992

ADVERTISING INFORMATION

Advertising accepted: No

EDITORIAL DESCRIPTION

Scope: Publishes critical articles pertinent to Croatian history and culture in the fields of literature, fine arts and music, sociology, history, economics, government and law, natural sciences, philology, philosophy and religion; creative translations of standard Croatian short stories and poems; reviews of recent books having a basic connection with Croatian matters; unpublished documents of Croatian historical and cultural significance (letters, diaries, and records, including Croatian Americana); registers of documentation (published or unpublished) on particular questions of Croatian historical and cultural significance.
Reviews books: Yes
Publishes notes: Yes
Languages accepted: English
Prints abstracts: No
Author-anonymous submission: No

SUBMISSION REQUIREMENTS

Restrictions on contributors: None
Author pays submission fee: No
Author pays page charges: No
Length of articles: 10,000 words
Length of book reviews: 500-2,000 words
Length of notes: 150 words
Style: Chicago; *American Historical Review*
Number of copies required: 2
Special requirements: Submit original manuscript.
Copyright ownership: Author

Rejected manuscripts: Returned; enclose return postage & SAE.
Time before publication decision: 4 mos.
Time between decision and publication: 18 mos.
Number of reviewers: 2-5
Articles published per year: 8-12
Book reviews published per year: 10
Notes published per year: 10

(1381)
*Journal of Cultural Geography

Alvar W. Carlson, Editor
Journals Dept.
Popular Press
Bowling Green State Univ.
Bowling Green, OH 43403

Telephone: 419 372-2925
Fax: 419 372-2300
First published: 1980
ISSN: 0887-3631
MLA acronym: JCG

SUBSCRIPTION INFORMATION

Frequency of publication: 2 times/yr. (Spring/Summer, Fall/Winter)
Circulation: 500
Available in microform: No
Subscription price: $15.00/yr. institutions; $12.50/yr. individuals
Year to which price refers: 1991
Subscription telephone: 419 372-2786

ADVERTISING INFORMATION

Advertising accepted: Yes

EDITORIAL DESCRIPTION

Scope: Publishes articles on material culture and cultural geography.
Reviews books: Yes
Publishes notes: Yes
Languages accepted: English
Prints abstracts: Yes
Author-anonymous submission: Yes

SUBMISSION REQUIREMENTS

Restrictions on contributors: None
Author pays submission fee: No
Author pays page charges: No
Length of articles: 3,000-4,000 words
Length of book reviews: 300 words
Length of notes: 400-500 words
Style: MLA
Number of copies required: 2
Copyright ownership: Journal
Rejected manuscripts: Returned; enclose return postage
Time before publication decision: 2 mos.
Time between decision and publication: 6-12 mos.
Number of reviewers: 2-3
Articles submitted per year: 50
Articles published per year: 20
Book reviews submitted per year: 15-20
Book reviews published per year: 15-20
Notes submitted per year: 2-3
Notes published per year: 2

(1382)
Journal of Cuneiform Studies

Piotr Michalowski, Editor
Dept. of Near Eastern Studies
3074 Frieze Bldg.
Ann Arbor, MI 48109

First published: 1947
Sponsoring organization: American Schools of Oriental Research
ISSN: 0022-0256
MLA acronym: JCunS

SUBSCRIPTION INFORMATION

Frequency of publication: 2 times/yr.
Circulation: 600
Available in microform: No
Subscription address: Journals Division, Scholars Press, P.O. Box 15399, Atlanta, GA 30333-0399
Subscription telephone: 404 636-4757
Subscription fax: 404 442-9742

ADVERTISING INFORMATION

Advertising accepted: No

EDITORIAL DESCRIPTION

Scope: Publishes works on Assyriology.
Reviews books: Yes
Languages accepted: English; French; German
Prints abstracts: No
Author-anonymous submission: No

SUBMISSION REQUIREMENTS

Restrictions on contributors: None
Author pays submission fee: No
Author pays page charges: No
Length of articles: No restrictions
Length of book reviews: No restrictions
Style: None
Number of copies required: 1
Copyright ownership: Journal
Rejected manuscripts: Returned
Time before publication decision: 1 mo.
Time between decision and publication: 6 mos.
Number of reviewers: 2-3

(1383)
*Journal of Documentation

Richard T. Kimber, Editor
Science Library
Queen's Univ. of Belfast
Chlorine Gardens
Belfast BT9 5EQ, Northern Ireland

Telephone: (353) 232 245133 ext. 4306
Fax: (353) 232 382636
First published: 1945
ISSN: 0022-0418
MLA acronym: JD

SUBSCRIPTION INFORMATION

Frequency of publication: 4 times/yr. (Mar., June, Sept., Dec.)
Circulation: 3,500
Available in microform: No
Subscription price: £55.00/yr. Aslib members, United Kingdom; £80.00/yr. Aslib members elsewhere; £60.00/yr. nonmembers, United Kingdom; £90.00/yr. nonmembers elsewhere
Year to which price refers: 1992
Subscription address: ASLIB, Information House, 20-24 Old St., London EC1V 9AP, England
Subscription telephone: (44) 71 2534488
Subscription fax: (44) 71 4300514

ADVERTISING INFORMATION

Advertising accepted: Yes

EDITORIAL DESCRIPTION

Scope: Publishes articles based on research or practice relating to the recording, organization, management, retrieval, dissemination, and use of information in systems of all kinds.
Reviews books: Yes
Publishes notes: Yes
Languages accepted: English
Prints abstracts: Yes
Author-anonymous submission: No

SUBMISSION REQUIREMENTS

Restrictions on contributors: None

Author pays submission fee: No
Author pays page charges: No
Length of articles: 5,000 words
Length of book reviews: 750 words
Length of notes: 1,500 words
Number of copies required: 2
Copyright ownership: Aslib & author
Rejected manuscripts: Returned
Time before publication decision: 3 mos.
Time between decision and publication: 6 mos.
Number of reviewers: 3
Articles published per year: 20
Book reviews published per year: 50
Notes published per year: 5

(1384)
*Journal of Dramatic Theory and Criticism

John Gronbeck-Tedesco, Editor
Dept. of Theatre & Film
Murphy Hall
Univ. of Kansas
Lawrence, KS 66045

Telephone: 913 864-3511
Fax: 913 864-5387
First published: 1986
Sponsoring organization: Univ. of Kansas; Hall Center for the Humanities
MLA acronym: JDTC

SUBSCRIPTION INFORMATION

Frequency of publication: 2 times/yr. (Fall, Spring)
Available in microform: No
Subscription price: $18.00/yr. institutions; $10.00/yr. individuals; $8.00/yr. students
Year to which price refers: 1992
Subscription address: Hall Center for the Humanities, 211 Watkins Home, Univ. of Kansas, Lawrence, KS 66045-2967
Subscription telephone: 913 864-4798

ADVERTISING INFORMATION

Advertising accepted: Yes, on an exchange basis

EDITORIAL DESCRIPTION

Scope: Publishes articles that address theoretical issues associated with performance and performance texts.
Reviews books: Yes
Publishes notes: Yes
Languages accepted: English; French
Prints abstracts: No
Author-anonymous submission: Yes

SUBMISSION REQUIREMENTS

Restrictions on contributors: None
Author pays submission fee: No
Author pays page charges: No
Length of articles: 25 pp.
Length of book reviews: 1,500 words
Style: MLA
Number of copies required: 3
Special requirements: Submit original typescript and 2 copies. Manuscripts are requested on diskette, labeled with program and title, in WordPerfect if possible.
Copyright ownership: Publisher
Rejected manuscripts: Returned; enclose SASE.
Time before publication decision: 6 weeks
Time between decision and publication: 6 mos.
Number of reviewers: 2-3
Articles submitted per year: 90
Articles published per year: 20

(1385)
*Journal of Durassian Studies

Janine Ricouart, Editor
Dept. of Foreign Languages & Literatures
George Mason Univ.
4400 University Dr.
Fairfax, VA 22030

First published: 1989
Sponsoring organization: Duras Soc.
MLA acronym: JDurS

SUBSCRIPTION INFORMATION

Frequency of publication: Annual
Available in microform: No
Subscription price: $20.00/yr. institutions US & Canada; $15.00/yr. individuals US & Canada; add $3.00 ($7.00 airmail)/yr. postage elsewhere
Year to which price refers: 1992

ADVERTISING INFORMATION

Advertising accepted: Yes

EDITORIAL DESCRIPTION

Scope: Publishes articles on any aspect of film, theater, and literature dealing with the works of Marguerite Duras.
Reviews books: Yes
Publishes notes: No
Languages accepted: French; English
Prints abstracts: No
Author-anonymous submission: Yes

SUBMISSION REQUIREMENTS

Author pays submission fee: Yes
Author pays page charges: No
Length of articles: 6,250 words
Length of book reviews: 1,250 words
Style: MLA
Number of copies required: 2
Copyright ownership: Author & journal
Rejected manuscripts: Not returned
Time before publication decision: 6-12 mos.
Time between decision and publication: 1 yr.
Number of reviewers: 2
Articles submitted per year: 10
Articles published per year: 5

(1386)
*Journal of East Asian Linguistics

C.-T. James Huang & S.-Y. Kuroda, Editors
Dept. of Linguistics
Univ. of California
Irvine, CA 92717

Additional editorial address: S.-Y. Kuroda, Linguistics Dept., Univ. of California, San Diego, CA 92093
Telephone: 714 725-2904
E-mail: Jeal@orion.oac.uci.edu; jeal@bend.ucsd.edu
First published: 1992
ISSN: 0925-8558
MLA acronym: JEAL

SUBSCRIPTION INFORMATION

Frequency of publication: 3 times/yr.
Available in microform: Yes
Subscription price: 254 f ($129.50)/yr. institutions; 127 f ($64.50)/yr. individuals
Year to which price refers: 1992
Subscription address: Kluwer Academic Publishers Group, P.O. Box 322, 3300 AH Dordrecht, Netherlands
Additional subscription address: Kluwer Academic Publishers, P.O. Box 358, Accord Station, Hingham, MA 02018-0358
Subscription telephone: 617 871-6600

ADVERTISING INFORMATION

Advertising accepted: Yes

EDITORIAL DESCRIPTION

Scope: Publishes articles on Chinese, Japanese, and Korean linguistics, and theoretical work related to other languages of the same area. Includes studies on syntax, semantics, pragmatics, and morphology of East Asian languages; comparative works among East Asian languages; grammar; and interdisciplinary studies on topics such as psycholinguistics, neurolinguistics, and computational linguistics.
Reviews books: No
Publishes notes: Yes
Languages accepted: English
Prints abstracts: Yes
Author-anonymous submission: Yes

SUBMISSION REQUIREMENTS

Author pays submission fee: No
Author pays page charges: No
Length of articles: 50 pp. maximum
Style: Journal
Number of copies required: 4
Copyright ownership: Kluwer Academic Publishers
Rejected manuscripts: Returned; enclose return postage
Time before publication decision: 4 mos.
Time between decision and publication: 6-8 mos.
Number of reviewers: 2 minimum

(1387)
Journal of English

Patricia Beam, Editor
Dept. of English
Box 1247
Sana'a Univ.
Sana'a, Yemen Arab Republic

First published: 1975
Sponsoring organization: Sana'a Univ.
ISSN: 1016-247X
MLA acronym: JEn

SUBSCRIPTION INFORMATION

Frequency of publication: Annual
Circulation: 300
Available in microform: No

ADVERTISING INFORMATION

Advertising accepted: No

EDITORIAL DESCRIPTION

Scope: Publishes articles on English literature, language, and linguistics.
Reviews books: Yes
Publishes notes: Yes
Languages accepted: English
Prints abstracts: No
Author-anonymous submission: No

SUBMISSION REQUIREMENTS

Restrictions on contributors: None
Author pays submission fee: No
Author pays page charges: No
Length of articles: 15-20 pp.
Length of book reviews: 1,000-1,500 words
Length of notes: 800-1,000 words
Number of copies required: 2
Special requirements: Include a brief biography of the author.
Copyright ownership: Journal
Rejected manuscripts: Returned
Time before publication decision: 4-6 weeks
Time between decision and publication: 2-3 mos.
Number of reviewers: 3
Articles submitted per year: 12-15

Articles published per year: 6-8
Book reviews submitted per year: 6-10
Book reviews published per year: 2-3
Notes submitted per year: 4-6
Notes published per year: 2-3

(1388)
*Journal of English and Foreign Languages

Rachel Lalitha Eapen, Editor
Central Inst. of English & Foreign Languages
Hyderabad 500 007, India

First published: 1988
Sponsoring organization: Central Inst. of English & Foreign Languages
ISSN: 0970-8332
MLA acronym: JEFL

SUBSCRIPTION INFORMATION

Frequency of publication: 2 times/yr.
Circulation: 2,000
Available in microform: No
Subscription price: 25 Re/yr. India; $12.00 (£6.00)/yr. elsewhere
Year to which price refers: 1992

ADVERTISING INFORMATION

Advertising accepted: No

EDITORIAL DESCRIPTION

Scope: Provides a forum for the sharing of experience and perceptions relevant to the theory and practice of language teaching.
Reviews books: Yes
Publishes notes: Yes
Languages accepted: English; French; German; Russian; Spanish; Arabic
Prints abstracts: No
Author-anonymous submission: No

SUBMISSION REQUIREMENTS

Author pays submission fee: No
Author pays page charges: No
Length of articles: 5,000 words maximum
Length of book reviews: 1,500 words maximum
Length of notes: 2,500 words
Style: Journal; see *JEFL*, 1989; 4
Number of copies required: 2
Special requirements: All contributions should be original and not be published elsewhere. All non-English contributions must be accompanied by English translation.
Copyright ownership: Central Inst. of English & Foreign Languages or author
Rejected manuscripts: Returned; enclose SASE.
Time before publication decision: 2-4 mos.
Time between decision and publication: 2-12 mos.
Number of reviewers: 2
Articles submitted per year: 40
Articles published per year: 15
Book reviews submitted per year: 2
Book reviews published per year: 2

(1389)
*Journal of English and Germanic Philology

Dale Kramer & Marianne Kalinke, Editors
109 English Bldg.
Univ. of Illinois
608 S. Wright St.
Urbana, IL 61801

Telephone: 217 333-2391; 217 333-7085
Fax: 217 244-8082
E-mail: Kramerdv@uxl.cso.uiuc.edu
First published: 1897
Sponsoring organization: Univ. of Illinois
ISSN: 0363-6941
MLA acronym: JEGP

SUBSCRIPTION INFORMATION

Frequency of publication: 4 times/yr. (Jan., Apr., July, Oct.)
Circulation: 1,800
Available in microform: Yes
Subscription price: $48.00/yr. institutions US; $55.00/yr. institutions elsewhere; $24.00/yr. individuals US; $31.00/yr. individuals elsewhere
Year to which price refers: 1992
Subscription address: Univ. of Illinois Press, Box 5081 Station A, Champaign, IL 61820
Subscription telephone: 217 244-0626

ADVERTISING INFORMATION

Advertising accepted: Yes
Advertising rates: $95.00/half page; $160.00/full page

EDITORIAL DESCRIPTION

Scope: Publishes essays and reviews on English, American, German, and Scandinavian languages and literatures.
Reviews books: Yes
Publishes notes: No
Languages accepted: English; German; Norwegian; Danish; Swedish
Prints abstracts: No
Author-anonymous submission: No

SUBMISSION REQUIREMENTS

Restrictions on contributors: Articles cannot be submitted elsewhere. Book reviews are commissioned.
Author pays submission fee: No
Author pays page charges: No
Length of articles: 6,000-9,000 words
Length of book reviews: 1,500-2,400 words
Style: Chicago
Number of copies required: 1-2
Special requirements: Submit original typescript or printout.
Copyright ownership: Board of Trustees, Univ. of Illinois
Rejected manuscripts: Returned; enclose return postage.
Time before publication decision: 2-3 mos.
Time between decision and publication: 12-15 mos.
Number of reviewers: 1-3
Articles submitted per year: 180
Articles published per year: 25-30
Book reviews published per year: 120

(1390)
*The Journal of English Language and Literature

Sangsup Lee, Wook-Dong Kim, Young Choi, & Yunsook Hong, Editors
English Language & Literature Assn. of Korea
89-27 Shinmoon-Ro 2-Ka, Pearson Bldg 602
Chongro-Ku
Seoul 110-062, Korea

First published: 1965
Sponsoring organization: English Language & Literature Assn. of Korea
ISSN: 1016-2283
MLA acronym: JELL

SUBSCRIPTION INFORMATION

Frequency of publication: 4 times/yr.
Circulation: 1,200
Available in microform: No
Subscription price: $45.00/yr. institutions; $35.00/yr. individuals
Year to which price refers: 1992
Subscription telephone: (82) 2 7381198
Subscription fax: (82) 2 7381198

ADVERTISING INFORMATION

Advertising accepted: Yes

EDITORIAL DESCRIPTION

Scope: Publishes articles on English and American literature and language, with the purpose of enhancing the scholarship of these fields in Korea.
Reviews books: Yes
Publishes notes: Yes
Languages accepted: English; Korean
Prints abstracts: Yes
Author-anonymous submission: No

SUBMISSION REQUIREMENTS

Author pays submission fee: No
Author pays page charges: No
Length of articles: 5,000 words
Length of book reviews: 2,000 words
Length of notes: 1,000 words
Style: MLA
Number of copies required: 1
Copyright ownership: Journal
Rejected manuscripts: Returned
Time between decision and publication: 2 mos.
Number of reviewers: 3
Articles submitted per year: 100
Articles published per year: 40-50
Book reviews submitted per year: 20
Book reviews published per year: 8
Notes submitted per year: 20
Notes published per year: 8

(1391)
*Journal of English Linguistics

William A. Kretzschmar, Jr., Editor
Univ. of Georgia
Athens, GA 30602

First published: 1967
ISSN: 0075-4242
MLA acronym: JEngL

SUBSCRIPTION INFORMATION

Frequency of publication: 2 times/yr. (Apr., Oct.)
Circulation: 600
Available in microform: No

ADVERTISING INFORMATION

Advertising accepted: Yes

EDITORIAL DESCRIPTION

Scope: Publishes articles on modern and historical periods of the English language.
Reviews books: Yes
Publishes notes: Yes
Languages accepted: English
Prints abstracts: No
Author-anonymous submission: No

SUBMISSION REQUIREMENTS

Restrictions on contributors: Reviews are solicited.
Author pays submission fee: No
Author pays page charges: No
Length of articles: 10-25 pp.
Length of book reviews: No restrictions
Length of notes: 1,000 words
Style: MLA; Linguistic Soc. of America
Number of copies required: 2
Special requirements: Notes and references should appear at the end of the article. Submit original typescript and 1 photocopy.
Copyright ownership: Journal
Rejected manuscripts: Returned; enclose SASE.
Time before publication decision: 3 mos.
Time between decision and publication: 1 yr. maximum
Number of reviewers: 2
Articles submitted per year: 20

(1392)
Journal of English Studies

A. J. Franklin & K. B. Sitaramayya, Editors
Dept. of English
Scott Christian College
Nagercoil 629 003, India

First published: 1978
Sponsoring organization: Post-Graduate Dept. of English, Scott Christian College
MLA acronym: JEngS

SUBSCRIPTION INFORMATION

Frequency of publication: Annual
Circulation: 500
Available in microform: No

ADVERTISING INFORMATION

Advertising accepted: No

EDITORIAL DESCRIPTION

Scope: Publishes articles on all aspects of English language and literature as well as Indo-Anglian literature.
Reviews books: No
Languages accepted: English
Prints abstracts: No

SUBMISSION REQUIREMENTS

Restrictions on contributors: Contributors must be students, staff, or friends of Scott Christian College.
Author pays submission fee: No
Author pays page charges: No
Length of articles: 8-10 typescript pp.
Style: MLA
Number of copies required: 2
Copyright ownership: Journal
Rejected manuscripts: Returned; enclose return postage.
Time before publication decision: 3 mos.
Time between decision and publication: 10 mos.
Number of reviewers: 2
Articles submitted per year: 15
Articles published per year: 8-10
Book reviews published per year: 6-10
Notes submitted per year: 5
Notes published per year: 2

(1393)
*Journal of European Studies

J. E. Flower & A. G. Cross, Editors
Dept. of French & Italian
Univ. of Exeter
Queen's Bldg.
Queen's Drive
Exeter EX4 4QH, England

Additional editorial address: Contributions from continental Europe should be sent to: K. M. Kuna, Inst. für Anglistik & Americanistik, Univ. für Bildungswissenschaften, 9020 Klagenfurt, Austria.
Telephone: (44) 392 264222
Fax: (44) 392 263108
First published: 1971
ISSN: 0047-2441
MLA acronym: JES

SUBSCRIPTION INFORMATION

Frequency of publication: 4 times/yr.
Circulation: 550
Available in microform: Yes
Subscription price: £51.00/yr. institutions United Kingdom; $100.00/yr. institutions Americas & Japan; £54.00/yr. institutions elsewhere; £26.00/yr. individuals United Kingdom; $52.00/yr. individuals Americas & Japan; £28.00/yr. individuals elsewhere
Year to which price refers: 1991
Subscription address: Science History Publications Ltd., Alpha Academic, Halfpenny Furze, Mill Lane, Chalfont St. Giles, Bucks HP8 4NR, England
Subscription telephone: (44) 2407 2509

ADVERTISING INFORMATION

Advertising accepted: Yes

EDITORIAL DESCRIPTION

Scope: Publishes articles on the literature and cultural history of Europe, from the Renaissance to the present day.
Reviews books: Yes
Publishes notes: Yes
Languages accepted: English
Prints abstracts: No
Author-anonymous submission: Yes

SUBMISSION REQUIREMENTS

Restrictions on contributors: None
Author pays submission fee: No
Author pays page charges: No
Length of articles: 6,000-7,000 words, but longer articles considered
Length of book reviews: 400-500 words
Length of notes: 200 words
Style: Journal
Number of copies required: 2
Special requirements: Submit double-spaced typescript of text and notes.
Copyright ownership: Journal
Rejected manuscripts: Returned; enclose return postage.
Time before publication decision: 2 mos.
Time between decision and publication: 1 yr.
Number of reviewers: 2-3
Articles submitted per year: 70
Articles published per year: 16
Book reviews submitted per year: 60
Book reviews published per year: 60
Notes submitted per year: 10
Notes published per year: 10

(1394)
*Journal of Evolutionary Psychology

Paul Neumarkt, Editor
5117 Forbes Ave.
Pittsburgh, PA 15213

First published: 1979
Sponsoring organization: Inst. for Evolutionary Psychology
ISSN: 0737-4828
MLA acronym: JEP

SUBSCRIPTION INFORMATION

Frequency of publication: 2 times/yr.
Circulation: 300
Available in microform: No

ADVERTISING INFORMATION

Advertising accepted: No

EDITORIAL DESCRIPTION

Scope: Publishes articles dealing with the psychological interpretation of literature, art, and film. Also publishes poetry.
Reviews books: Yes
Languages accepted: English
Prints abstracts: No

SUBMISSION REQUIREMENTS

Author pays submission fee: No
Author pays page charges: No
Length of articles: 15-20 double-spaced pp.
Length of book reviews: 500 words
Style: MLA; Chicago
Number of copies required: 2
Special requirements: The selection of an psychological point of view is followed by an invitation to become a member. Membership is $20.00 per year.
Copyright ownership: Journal
Rejected manuscripts: Returned
Time before publication decision: 3 weeks
Time between decision and publication: 5-6 mos.
Number of reviewers: 3
Articles submitted per year: 55
Articles published per year: 35
Book reviews submitted per year: 7
Book reviews published per year: 4

(1395)
*Journal of Experimental Psychology: Human Perception and Performance

James E. Cutting, Editor
American Psychological Assn.
750 First St., NE
Washington, DC 20002

First published: 1975
Sponsoring organization: American Psychological Assn.
ISSN: 0096-1523
MLA acronym: JExPH

SUBSCRIPTION INFORMATION

Frequency of publication: 4 times/yr.
Circulation: 2,000
Subscription price: $200.00/yr. institutions US; $224.00/yr. institutions elsewhere; $100.00/yr. individuals US; $112.00/yr. individuals elsewhere
Year to which price refers: 1992

ADVERTISING INFORMATION

Advertising accepted: Yes

EDITORIAL DESCRIPTION

Scope: Publishes articles on perception, verbal and motor performance, and cognitive processes.
Reviews books: No
Publishes notes: Yes
Languages accepted: English
Prints abstracts: Yes
Author-anonymous submission: Yes, at author's request.

SUBMISSION REQUIREMENTS

Restrictions on contributors: None
Author pays submission fee: No
Author pays page charges: No
Length of articles: No restrictions
Length of notes: No restrictions
Style: American Psychological Assn.
Number of copies required: 5
Special requirements: Submit a 960-character abstract. Contributions must not be under consideration elsewhere or have been previously published.
Copyright ownership: American Psychological Assn.
Rejected manuscripts: Not returned
Time before publication decision: 2-3 mos.
Time between decision and publication: 10 mos.
Number of reviewers: 3-4
Articles submitted per year: 200
Articles published per year: 80
Notes submitted per year: 30
Notes published per year: 8

(1396)
*Journal of Experimental Psychology: Learning, Memory, and Cognition

Keith Rayner, Lawrence W. Bassalou, Arthur M. Glenberg, & Rose T. Zacks, Editors
Dept. of Psychology
Univ. of Massachusetts
Amherst, MA 01003

Telephone: 413 545-2175; 413 545-5951
Fax: 413 545-0996
E-mail: Rayner@psych.umass.edu
Sponsoring organization: American Psychological Assn.
ISSN: 0278-7393
MLA acronym: JExPLMC

SUBSCRIPTION INFORMATION

Frequency of publication: 6 times/yr.
Available in microform: Yes
Subscription address: American Psychological Assn., 750 First St., NE, Washington, DC 20002

ADVERTISING INFORMATION

Advertising accepted: Yes

EDITORIAL DESCRIPTION

Scope: Publishes original studies on fundamental encoding, transfer, memory, reading, language, and cognitive processes in human behavior.
Reviews books: No
Publishes notes: Yes
Languages accepted: English
Prints abstracts: Yes
Author-anonymous submission: Yes, at author's request.

SUBMISSION REQUIREMENTS

Restrictions on contributors: None
Author pays submission fee: No
Style: American Psychological Assn.
Number of copies required: 5
Special requirements: Submit an 100-150 word abstract. Contributions must not be under consideration elsewhere or have been previously published.
Copyright ownership: American Psychological Assn.
Time before publication decision: 2 mos.
Time between decision and publication: 6 mos.
Number of reviewers: 3
Articles submitted per year: 285
Articles published per year: 100

(1397)
*Journal of Folklore Research

Sandra K. Dolby, Editor
Folklore Inst.
Indiana Univ.
504 N. Fess
Bloomington, IN 47408

Telephone: 812 855-0043
First published: 1964
Sponsoring organization: Indiana Univ. Folklore Inst.
ISSN: 0737-7037
MLA acronym: JFR

SUBSCRIPTION INFORMATION

Frequency of publication: 3 times/yr.
Circulation: 700
Available in microform: Yes
Subscription price: $25.00/yr. institutions; $18.00/yr. individuals; $15.00/yr. students
Year to which price refers: 1992

ADVERTISING INFORMATION

Advertising accepted: Yes
Advertising rates: $70.00/half page; $120.00/full page

EDITORIAL DESCRIPTION

Scope: Devoted to theoretical writings of high quality by the world community of folklore scholars; emphasizes articles which investigate a particular problem or assess current scholarship.
Reviews books: Yes
Publishes notes: Yes
Languages accepted: English
Prints abstracts: No
Author-anonymous submission: Yes

SUBMISSION REQUIREMENTS

Author pays submission fee: No
Author pays page charges: No
Length of articles: 20-30 pp.
Length of book reviews: 2-3 pp.
Length of notes: 2-3 pp.
Style: Chicago
Number of copies required: 2
Special requirements: Submit double-spaced typescript.
Copyright ownership: Journal
Rejected manuscripts: Returned; enclose SASE.
Time before publication decision: 3 mos.
Time between decision and publication: 3-9 mos.
Number of reviewers: 3
Articles submitted per year: 20-30
Articles published per year: 15
Book reviews submitted per year: 5-10
Book reviews published per year: 5-10
Notes submitted per year: 15
Notes published per year: 15

(1398)
*Journal of French Language Studies

Jacques Durand, R. Anthony Lodge, & Carol Sanders, Editors
Dept. of Modern Languages
Univ. of Salford
Salford M5 4WT, England

Additional editorial address: Gertrud Aub-Buscher, Reviews Editor, Language Teaching Centre, Univ. of Hull, Hull HU6 7RX, England
Telephone: (44) 61 7455193
Fax: (44) 61 7455335
First published: 1991
Sponsoring organization: Assn. for French Language Studies (AFLS)
ISSN: 0959-2695
MLA acronym: JFLS

SUBSCRIPTION INFORMATION

Frequency of publication: 2 times/yr. (Mar., Sept.)
Available in microform: No
Subscription price: $69.00/yr. institutions; $45.00/yr. individuals; $35.00/single issue
Year to which price refers: 1992
Subscription address: Cambridge Univ. Press, Journals Dept., 40 West 20th St., New York, NY 10011-4211
Additional subscription address: Outside US & Canada: Cambridge Univ. Press, Edinburgh Bldg., Shaftesbury Rd., Cambridge CB2 2RU, England

ADVERTISING INFORMATION

Advertising accepted: Yes
Advertising rates: $145.00/half page; $225.00/full page

EDITORIAL DESCRIPTION

Scope: Publishes theoretical and descriptive articles on all aspects of French language and linguistics including historical and comparative studies; sociolinguistic and variation studies; discourse, textual and pragmatic studies; and studies of French language acquisition.
Reviews books: Yes
Publishes notes: No
Languages accepted: English; French
Prints abstracts: Yes
Author-anonymous submission: Yes

SUBMISSION REQUIREMENTS

Restrictions on contributors: None
Author pays submission fee: No
Author pays page charges: No
Length of articles: 6,000-8,000 words
Number of copies required: 3
Special requirements: Submit double-spaced typescript on size A4 (8 1/4 in. x 11 3/4 in.) paper, accompanied by an abstract of 100 words on a separate page. Sexist language should be avoided.
Copyright ownership: Cambridge Univ. Press
Rejected manuscripts: Returned
Time before publication decision: 2-3 mos.
Time between decision and publication: 6-12 mos.
Number of reviewers: 3
Articles submitted per year: 40-50
Articles published per year: 12
Book reviews published per year: 20

(1399)
*Journal of Hellenic Studies

Alan H. Sommerstein, Editor
Dept. of Classical & Archaeological Studies
Univ. of Nottingham
University Park
Nottingham NG7 2RD, England

Telephone: (44) 602 484848 ext. 4507
Fax: (44) 602 420825
First published: 1880
Sponsoring organization: Soc. for the Promotion of Hellenic Studies
ISSN: 0075-4269
MLA acronym: JoHS

SUBSCRIPTION INFORMATION

Frequency of publication: Annual
Circulation: 3,000
Available in microform: No
Subscription price: £38.00 ($85.00)/yr. institutions; £25.00 ($55.00)/yr. individuals
Year to which price refers: 1992
Subscription address: Soc. for the Promotion of Hellenic Studies, 31-34 Gordon Square, London WC1H 0PP, England
Subscription telephone: (44) 71 3877495

ADVERTISING INFORMATION

Advertising accepted: Yes
Advertising rates: £100.00/half page; £200.00/full page

EDITORIAL DESCRIPTION

Scope: Publishes articles (some with illustrations) and book reviews, in the area of Ancient Greek studies (archaeology, history, language, literature, philosophy, and religion) from the Bronze Age to the Byzantine period.
Reviews books: Yes
Publishes notes: Yes
Languages accepted: English; French; German
Prints abstracts: No
Author-anonymous submission: No

SUBMISSION REQUIREMENTS

Restrictions on contributors: Book reviews are by commission only.

(1400)
*Journal of Hispanic Philology

Daniel Eisenberg, Editor
Dept. of Modern Languages & Linguistics
Florida State Univ.
Tallahassee, FL 32306

Telephone: 904 385-6130
Fax: 904 385-5392
First published: 1976
ISSN: 0147-5460
MLA acronym: JHP

SUBSCRIPTION INFORMATION

Frequency of publication: 3 times/yr.
Circulation: 500
Available in microform: Yes, vols. 4 & 5
Subscription price: $60.00/yr. US; $79.00/yr. elsewhere
Year to which price refers: 1992

ADVERTISING INFORMATION

Advertising accepted: Yes
Advertising rates: $60.00/full page

EDITORIAL DESCRIPTION

Scope: Publishes articles on literature written in Iberian peninsula or colonies through approximately 1700, regardless of language and on historical linguistics of languages of Iberian peninsula.
Reviews books: Yes
Publishes notes: Yes
Languages accepted: English; Portuguese; Spanish; French; Catalan
Prints abstracts: Yes
Author-anonymous submission: Yes, at author's request.

SUBMISSION REQUIREMENTS

Restrictions on contributors: Most reviews are commissioned.
Author pays submission fee: No
Author pays page charges: No
Length of articles: 10-30 pp.
Length of book reviews: 1,000 words
Length of notes: 500-1,000 words
Style: MLA
Number of copies required: 2
Special requirements: Submit an English abstract for Spanish articles, a Spanish abstract for English articles. Request style and electronic manuscript guide from editor.
Copyright ownership: Journal
Rejected manuscripts: Returned; enclose return postage.
Time before publication decision: 3 mos.
Time between decision and publication: 6 mos.
Number of reviewers: 1-2
Articles submitted per year: 30
Articles published per year: 12
Book reviews published per year: 25
Notes published per year: 1-2

Author pays submission fee: No
Author pays page charges: No
Length of articles: 5,000-12,000 words
Length of book reviews: 150-2,000 words
Length of notes: 300-5,000 words
Style: Journal; see 1984; 104, pp.287-8
Number of copies required: 1
Special requirements: Submit legible photocopy and diskette, if possible.
Copyright ownership: Assigned by author to Soc. for the Promotion of Hellenic Studies
Rejected manuscripts: Returned
Time before publication decision: 2 mos.
Time between decision and publication: 1-2 yrs.
Number of reviewers: 3
Articles submitted per year: 30-40
Articles published per year: 9-13
Book reviews published per year: 80-105
Notes submitted per year: 25-30
Notes published per year: 9-17

(1401)
*Journal of Humanities

Didier N. Kaphagawani & Brighton J. Uledi-Kamanga, Editors
Faculty of Humanities
Univ. of Malawi
Chancellor College
P.O. Box 280
Zomba, Malawi

Telephone: (265) 522222 ext. 179
Fax: (265) 522046; (265) 523225
First published: 1987
Sponsoring organization: Research & Publication Committee of the Univ. of Malawi
ISSN: 1016-0728
MLA acronym: JH

SUBSCRIPTION INFORMATION

Frequency of publication: Annual (Oct.)
Available in microform: No
Subscription price: 15 K/yr. institutions Malawi; $15.00/yr. institutions elsewhere; 5 K/yr. individuals Malawi; $5.00/yr. individuals Africa; $8.00/yr. individuals elsewhere
Year to which price refers: 1991

ADVERTISING INFORMATION

Advertising accepted: Yes

EDITORIAL DESCRIPTION

Scope: Publishes articles on the classics, fine and performing arts, literature and orature, linguistics, theology, and philosophy.
Reviews books: Yes
Publishes notes: No
Languages accepted: English; French
Prints abstracts: Yes, for French articles
Author-anonymous submission: No

SUBMISSION REQUIREMENTS

Restrictions on contributors: None
Author pays submission fee: No
Author pays page charges: No
Length of articles: 10,000 words
Length of book reviews: 1,500 words
Style: Journal
Number of copies required: 2
Special requirements: Submit double-spaced typescript on size A4 (8 1/4 in. x 11 3/4 in.) paper.
Copyright ownership: Faculty of Humanities, Univ. of Malawi
Rejected manuscripts: Returned; enclose return postage.
Time before publication decision: 6 mos.
Time between decision and publication: 2 mos.
Number of reviewers: 2
Articles submitted per year: 10
Articles published per year: 5
Book reviews submitted per year: 5
Book reviews published per year: 3

(1402)
Journal of Indian Philosophy

Phillis Granoff, Editor
Dept. of Religious Studies
McMaster Univ.
Hamilton, Ontario L8S 4K1, Canada

First published: 1970
ISSN: 0022-1791
MLA acronym: JIP

SUBSCRIPTION INFORMATION

Frequency of publication: 4 times/yr. (Mar., June, Sept., Dec.)
Circulation: 350
Available in microform: No
Subscription price: $210.00/yr. US & Canada; 336 f/yr. elsewhere

Year to which price refers: 1993
Subscription address: Kluwer Academic Publisher, P.O. Box 332, 3300 AH Dordrecht, Netherlands
Additional subscription address: Kluwer Academic Publishers, P.O. Box 358, Accord Station, Hingham, MA 02018-0358

ADVERTISING INFORMATION

Advertising accepted: Yes

EDITORIAL DESCRIPTION

Scope: This journal understands philosophy to include such subjects as the philosophy of language, ethics, religion, and aesthetics, as well as logic and epistemology. Welcomes contributions in neglected but important fields like Jainism, Tantrism, and Kashmir Saivism. Articles may be either analytical or historical, but they should be based on a close acquaintance with the original sources.
Reviews books: Yes
Publishes notes: No
Languages accepted: English
Prints abstracts: No
Author-anonymous submission: No

SUBMISSION REQUIREMENTS

Restrictions on contributors: None
Author pays submission fee: No
Author pays page charges: No
Length of articles: No restrictions
Length of book reviews: No restrictions
Style: MLA
Number of copies required: 1
Special requirements: Articles must be based on original Sanskrit texts.
Copyright ownership: Kluwer Academic Publishers
Rejected manuscripts: Not returned
Time before publication decision: 10 mos.
Time between decision and publication: 18 weeks
Number of reviewers: 2
Articles submitted per year: 30
Articles published per year: 18
Book reviews submitted per year: 12-16
Book reviews published per year: 4

(1403)
*The Journal of Indian Writing in English

G. S. Balarama Gupta, Editor
Dept. of English
Gulgarga Univ.
Gulbarga-585 106, India

Additional editorial address: "Niriel", 4-29, Jayanagar, Gulbarga-585 105 (Karnataka), India
Telephone: (91) 8472 24282
First published: 1973
ISSN: 0302-1319
MLA acronym: JIWE

SUBSCRIPTION INFORMATION

Frequency of publication: 2 times/yr. (Jan., July)
Circulation: 1,000
Available in microform: No
Subscription price: $24.00 ($40.00 airmail)/yr.
Year to which price refers: 1993

ADVERTISING INFORMATION

Advertising accepted: Yes
Advertising rates: 500 Re/quarter page; 1,000 Re/half page; 2,000 Re/full page

EDITORIAL DESCRIPTION

Scope: Publishes creative writing by Indians in English and critical articles on Indian writing in English by all.

Reviews books: Yes
Publishes notes: Yes
Languages accepted: English
Prints abstracts: No
Author-anonymous submission: No

SUBMISSION REQUIREMENTS

Restrictions on contributors: None
Author pays submission fee: No
Length of articles: 5,000 words
Length of book reviews: 350 words
Length of notes: 100 words
Style: MLA
Number of copies required: 2
Special requirements: Include a vita.
Copyright ownership: Journal
Rejected manuscripts: Returned; enclose return postage or international reply coupons.
Time before publication decision: 1-2 mos.
Number of reviewers: 1
Articles published per year: 8-10
Book reviews submitted per year: 20
Book reviews published per year: 15

(1404)
*Journal of Indo-European Studies

Edgar C. Polomé, Managing Editor
2701 Rock Terrace Dr.
Austin, TX 78704-3843

Additional editorial address: 1133 13th St., Suite Comm 2, Washington, DC 20005
Telephone: 512 326-4146
First published: 1973
Sponsoring organization: Inst. for the Study of Man, Inc.
ISSN: 0092-2323
MLA acronym: JIES

SUBSCRIPTION INFORMATION

Frequency of publication: 2 double issues/yr.
Circulation: 965
Available in microform: No
Subscription price: $80.00/yr. institutions; $40.00/yr. individuals; $25.00/yr. students
Year to which price refers: 1992
Subscription address: Inst. for the Study of Man, 6861 Elm St., Suite 4H, McLean, VA 22101
Subscription telephone: 703 442-8010
Subscription fax: 703 847-9524

ADVERTISING INFORMATION

Advertising accepted: Yes
Advertising rates: $250.00/full page

EDITORIAL DESCRIPTION

Scope: An interdisciplinary academic quarterly of interest to classicists, archaeologists, anthropologists, cultural historians, philologists, and mythologists, the journal is designed to serve as a medium for the exchange and synthesis of information derived from archaeology, historical anthropology, mythology, and linguistics. Brief comments, criticisms, and addenda to published articles, as well as reports on research work in progress, may be submitted for inclusion in the "Debate and Discussion" section. Reviews on works on Indo-European languages, cultures, and religion are published regularly.
Reviews books: Yes
Publishes notes: Yes
Languages accepted: English
Prints abstracts: Yes
Author-anonymous submission: Yes

SUBMISSION REQUIREMENTS

Restrictions on contributors: Book reviews are solicited.
Author pays submission fee: No
Author pays page charges: No
Length of articles: 5,000-10,000 words

Length of book reviews: 500-1,000 words
Length of notes: 1,000-2,000 words
Style: Linguistic Soc. of America
Number of copies required: 2
Special requirements: Submit typescript.
Copyright ownership: Journal
Rejected manuscripts: Not returned
Time before publication decision: 3-9 mos.
Time between decision and publication: 9-12 mos.
Number of reviewers: 2-5
Articles submitted per year: 45-50
Articles published per year: 16-24
Book reviews published per year: 20-30
Notes submitted per year: 10
Notes published per year: 6

(1405)
Journal of Interdisciplinary Literary Studies/Cuadernos Interdisciplinarios de Estudios Literarios

Catherine Nickel & Manuel L. Abellán, Editors
Dept. of Modern Languages & Literatures
1110 Oldfather Hall
Univ. of Nebraska-Lincoln
Lincoln, NE 68588-0315

Additional editorial address: In Europe contact: Manuel L. Abellán, Univ. van Amsterdam, Vakgroep Spaans-Portuges, Spuistraat 134, 1012 VB Amsterdam, Netherlands
First published: 1989
Sponsoring organization: Office of the Dean of Arts and Sciences, Univ. of Nebraska-Lincoln; Univ. van Amsterdam
ISSN: 1044-8985
MLA acronym: JILS

SUBSCRIPTION INFORMATION

Frequency of publication: 2 times/yr. (Spring, Fall)

ADVERTISING INFORMATION

Advertising accepted: Yes

EDITORIAL DESCRIPTION

Scope: Publishes articles on Hispanic literature, culture, and society from an interdisciplinary perspective.
Reviews books: Yes
Publishes notes: Yes
Languages accepted: Spanish; English; Catalan; all languages from the Iberian Peninsula

SUBMISSION REQUIREMENTS

Number of copies required: 2

(1406)
Journal of Irish Literature

Robert Hogan & Kathleen Danaher, Editors
Proscenium Press
P.O. Box 361
Newark, DE 19711

First published: 1972
ISSN: 0047-2514
MLA acronym: JIL

SUBSCRIPTION INFORMATION

Frequency of publication: 3 times/yr. (Jan., May, Sept.)
Circulation: 700
Available in microform: Yes

ADVERTISING INFORMATION

Advertising accepted: Yes

EDITORIAL DESCRIPTION

Scope: Publishes poetry, drama, fiction, criticism, book reviews, and bibliographies of Irish interest.
Reviews books: Yes
Publishes notes: Yes
Languages accepted: English; Irish Gaelic
Prints abstracts: No
Author-anonymous submission: No

SUBMISSION REQUIREMENTS

Restrictions on contributors: Book reviews are solicited.
Author pays submission fee: No
Author pays page charges: No
Length of articles: No restrictions
Length of book reviews: No restrictions
Length of notes: No restrictions
Style: MLA
Number of copies required: 1
Copyright ownership: Author
Rejected manuscripts: Returned
Time before publication decision: 2-12 mos.
Time between decision and publication: 1 yr.
Number of reviewers: 2
Articles published per year: 10
Book reviews published per year: 20
Notes published per year: 2-3

(1407)
*The Journal of Japanese Studies

Susan B. Hanley, Editor
Thomson Hall, DR-05
Univ. of Washington
Seattle, WA 98195

Telephone: 206 543-9302
Fax: 206 685-0668
First published: 1974
Sponsoring organization: Soc. for Japanese Studies
ISSN: 0095-6848
MLA acronym: JJS

SUBSCRIPTION INFORMATION

Frequency of publication: 2 times/yr. (Winter, Summer)
Circulation: 1,800
Available in microform: No
Subscription price: $25.00/yr. US; $29.00/yr. elsewhere
Year to which price refers: 1992
Subscription address: Subscriptions, at the above address

ADVERTISING INFORMATION

Advertising accepted: Yes
Advertising rates: $100.00/full page

EDITORIAL DESCRIPTION

Scope: Includes a wide variety of interdisciplinary studies on Japan.
Reviews books: Yes
Publishes notes: No
Languages accepted: English
Prints abstracts: No
Author-anonymous submission: Yes

SUBMISSION REQUIREMENTS

Restrictions on contributors: Book reviews are solicited.
Author pays submission fee: Yes, if not a subscriber
Cost of submission fee: $15.00
Author pays page charges: No; only cost of diagrams and maps.
Length of articles: 35 typescript pp.
Length of book reviews: 5-7 pp.
Style: Chicago
Number of copies required: 3

Special requirements: Submit original double-spaced typescript with double-spaced footnotes at end and 2 copies. Guidelines are specified on inside back cover of journals.
Copyright ownership: Journal
Time before publication decision: 3 mos.
Time between decision and publication: 6-12 mos.
Number of reviewers: 2-3 plus editors
Articles submitted per year: 45
Articles published per year: 8-10
Book reviews published per year: 25-45

(1408)
Journal of King Saud University, Arts

Ezzat A. Khattab, Editor
College of Arts
King Saud Univ.
P.O. Box 2456
Riyadh 11451, Saudi Arabia

Telephone: (966) 1 4675408
Fax: (966) 1 4678528
First published: 1970
Sponsoring organization: King Saud Univ.
MLA acronym: JKSUA

SUBSCRIPTION INFORMATION

Frequency of publication: 2 times/yr.
Circulation: 3,000
Available in microform: No
Subscription address: University Libraries, King Saud Univ., P.O. Box 22480, Riyadh 11495, Saudi Arabia

ADVERTISING INFORMATION

Advertising accepted: No

EDITORIAL DESCRIPTION

Scope: Publishes articles on modern languages, literatures, history, geography, archaeology, sociology, mass communication, and library science.
Reviews books: Yes
Publishes notes: Yes
Languages accepted: Arabic; English
Prints abstracts: Yes
Author-anonymous submission: Yes

SUBMISSION REQUIREMENTS

Restrictions on contributors: Affiliation with College of Arts, King Saud Univ. is preferred.
Author pays submission fee: No
Author pays page charges: No
Length of articles: 3,000-13,000 words
Length of book reviews: 1,000-2,000 words
Style: MLA
Number of copies required: 3
Special requirements: Submit original typescript and 2 copies.
Copyright ownership: Assigned by author to King Saud Univ. Libraries
Rejected manuscripts: Not returned
Time before publication decision: 3-6 mos.
Time between decision and publication: 1-2 yrs.
Number of reviewers: 2
Articles submitted per year: 80
Articles published per year: 30
Book reviews submitted per year: 3
Book reviews published per year: 2

(1409)
Journal of Kyoritsu Women's Junior College

Kyoritsu Women's Junior College
3-27 Kanda Jimbocho
Chiyoda-ku
Tokyo 101, Japan

First published: 1956
Sponsoring organization: Kyoristen Joshi Gakuen
ISSN: 0388-3647
MLA acronym: JKWJC

SUBSCRIPTION INFORMATION

Frequency of publication: Annual
Circulation: 800
Available in microform: No

ADVERTISING INFORMATION

Advertising accepted: No

EDITORIAL DESCRIPTION

Scope: Publishes the results of academic research and study of faculty members of Kyoritsu Women's Junior College.
Reviews books: No
Publishes notes: No
Languages accepted: Japanese; English; French; German
Prints abstracts: Yes
Author-anonymous submission: No

SUBMISSION REQUIREMENTS

Restrictions on contributors: Contributors must be members of the faculty of Kyoritsu Women's Junior College.
Author pays submission fee: No
Author pays page charges: No
Length of articles: 20,000 characters
Style: MLA
Number of copies required: 1
Time between decision and publication: 4 mos.
Articles submitted per year: 12
Articles published per year: 12

(1410)
*Journal of Language and Social Psychology

Kathy Kellermann & James J. Bradac, Editors
Dept. of Communication
Univ. of California
Santa Barbara, CA 93106-4020

Additional editorial address: Book reviews: John Edwards, Dept. of Psychology, St. Francis Xavier Univ., Antigonish, Nova Scotia B2G 1C0, Canada
Telephone: 805 893-8754; 805 893-4360
E-mail: 4169Kell@ucsbuxa.ucsb.edu
First published: 1982
ISSN: 0261-927X
MLA acronym: JLSP

SUBSCRIPTION INFORMATION

Frequency of publication: 4 times/yr.
Circulation: 400
Available in microform: No
Subscription price: $170.00/yr. institutions US; $176.00/yr. institutions elsewhere; $62.00/yr. individuals US; $68.00/yr. individuals elsewhere
Year to which price refers: 1993
Subscription address: Sage Publications, 2455 Teller Rd., Newbury Park, CA 91320
Subscription telephone: 805 499-0721 ext. 100
Subscription fax: 805 499-0871

ADVERTISING INFORMATION

Advertising accepted: Yes

EDITORIAL DESCRIPTION

Scope: Publishes work bridging social psychological and other approaches to the study of language.
Reviews books: Yes
Publishes notes: Yes
Languages accepted: English
Prints abstracts: Yes
Author-anonymous submission: Yes

SUBMISSION REQUIREMENTS

Author pays submission fee: No
Author pays page charges: No
Length of articles: 7,000 words maximum
Length of book reviews: 500-1,500 words
Length of notes: 100-200 words
Style: Chicago
Number of copies required: 4
Special requirements: Submit double-spaced typescript with ample left and right hand margins. Include 200-word (maximum) abstract. Submit camera-ready copy for all diagrams.
Copyright ownership: Author
Rejected manuscripts: Returned at author's request
Time before publication decision: 4 mos.
Time between decision and publication: 8 mos.
Number of reviewers: 2
Articles submitted per year: 40
Articles published per year: 16
Book reviews submitted per year: 20
Book reviews published per year: 10
Notes submitted per year: 5
Notes published per year: 5

(1411)
*Journal of Latin American Lore

Johannes Wilbert, Lawrence E. Sullivan, & Colleen Trujillo, Editors
Latin American Center
10343 Bunche Hall
Univ. of California
Los Angeles, CA 90024-1447

Telephone: 310 825-7547
Fax: 310 206-6859
E-mail: Trujill@others.sscnet.ucla.edu
First published: 1975
Sponsoring organization: Latin American Center, Univ. of California, Los Angeles
ISSN: 0360-1927
MLA acronym: JLAL

SUBSCRIPTION INFORMATION

Frequency of publication: 2 times/yr. (Summer, Winter)
Circulation: 350
Available in microform: No
Subscription price: $40.00/yr. institutions; $30.00/yr. individuals
Year to which price refers: 1992
Subscription telephone: 310 825-6634

ADVERTISING INFORMATION

Advertising accepted: Yes, on an exchange basis

EDITORIAL DESCRIPTION

Scope: Publishes articles on the lore of and about the people of Latin America. Studies focus on aspects of Latin American culture from a connotative rather than a denotative viewpoint. Emphasis is on understanding the symbolic value of cultural manifestations.
Reviews books: No
Publishes notes: No
Languages accepted: English; Spanish; Portuguese
Prints abstracts: No
Author-anonymous submission: Yes

SUBMISSION REQUIREMENTS

Restrictions on contributors: None
Author pays submission fee: No
Author pays page charges: No
Length of articles: No restrictions
Style: Chicago
Number of copies required: 3
Copyright ownership: Regents of the Univ. of California
Rejected manuscripts: Returned

Time before publication decision: 2 mos.
Time between decision and publication: 6-12 mos.
Number of reviewers: 1-2
Articles submitted per year: 30
Articles published per year: 10-15

(1412)
*Journal of Learning Disabilities

J. Lee Wiederholt, Editor
8700 Shoal Creek Blvd.
Austin, TX 78758-6897

Telephone: 512 451-3246
Fax: 512 451-8542
First published: 1968
ISSN: 0022-2194
MLA acronym: JLD

SUBSCRIPTION INFORMATION

Frequency of publication: 10 times/yr.
Circulation: 10,500
Available in microform: Yes
Subscription price: $90.00/yr. institutions US & Canada; $105.00/yr. institutions elsewhere; $45.00/yr. individuals
Year to which price refers: 1992

ADVERTISING INFORMATION

Advertising accepted: Yes
Advertising rates: $400.00/half page; $800.00/full page

EDITORIAL DESCRIPTION

Scope: Publishes articles on practice, research, and theory related to learning disabilities.
Reviews books: No
Publishes notes: No
Languages accepted: English
Prints abstracts: Yes
Author-anonymous submission: No

SUBMISSION REQUIREMENTS

Author pays submission fee: No
Author pays page charges: No
Length of articles: 30 pp. maximum
Style: American Psychological Assn.
Number of copies required: 4
Special requirements: Submit original double-spaced typescript and 3 copies.
Copyright ownership: Pro-Ed, Inc.
Rejected manuscripts: Returned
Time before publication decision: 6-8 weeks
Time between decision and publication: 9-12 mos.
Number of reviewers: 2-3
Articles submitted per year: 200
Articles published per year: 90

(1413)
*Journal of Linguistics

Nigel Vincent, Editor
Dept. of Linguistics
Univ. of Manchester
Manchester M13 9PL, England

Telephone: (44) 61 2753194
Fax: (44) 61 2753031
E-mail: N.b.vincent@uk.ac.manchester
First published: 1965
Sponsoring organization: Linguistics Assn. of Great Britain
ISSN: 0022-2267
MLA acronym: JL

SUBSCRIPTION INFORMATION

Frequency of publication: 2 times/yr. (Mar., Sept.)
Circulation: 2,300
Available in microform: Yes
Subscription price: $79.00 (£40.00)/yr.
Year to which price refers: 1992
Subscription address: Cambridge Univ. Press, Edinburgh Bldg., Shaftesbury Rd., Cambridge CB2 2RU, England
Additional subscription address: In N. America: Cambridge Univ. Press, 40 W. 20th St., New York, NY 10011

ADVERTISING INFORMATION

Advertising accepted: Yes

EDITORIAL DESCRIPTION

Scope: Is concerned with all branches of linguistics including phonetics. Preference is given to articles of general theoretical interest, but there is an attempt to cover as wide a field as possible, and to include articles on a variety of languages. Includes a section devoted to comments arising from recent articles.
Reviews books: Yes
Publishes notes: Yes
Languages accepted: English
Prints abstracts: No

SUBMISSION REQUIREMENTS

Restrictions on contributors: Book reviews are solicited.
Author pays submission fee: No
Author pays page charges: No
Length of articles: No restrictions
Length of book reviews: 1,000-2,000 words
Length of notes: 3,000-4,000 words
Style: Linguistic Soc. of America
Number of copies required: 3
Special requirements: Prior to submission consult notes for contributors printed in each issue.
Copyright ownership: Assigned by author to Cambridge Univ. Press
Rejected manuscripts: Returned; enclose return postage.
Time before publication decision: 2-3 mos.
Time between decision and publication: 9 mos.
Number of reviewers: 2
Articles submitted per year: 75
Articles published per year: 15
Book reviews published per year: 30
Notes submitted per year: 10
Notes published per year: 5

(1414)
*Journal of Literary Semantics

Trevor Eaton, Editor
Honeywood Cottage
35 Seaton Ave.
Hythe, Kent CT21 5HH, England

Fax: (44) 227 475476
First published: 1972
Sponsoring organization: Univ. of Kent, Canterbury, Academic Headquarters, School of European & Modern Language Studies
ISSN: 0341-7638
MLA acronym: JLS

SUBSCRIPTION INFORMATION

Frequency of publication: 3 times/yr. (Apr., Aug., Oct.)
Circulation: 800
Subscription price: 84 DM/yr. institutions; 68 DM/yr. individuals
Year to which price refers: 1992
Subscription address: Julius Groos Verlag, Hertzstr. 6, Postfach 10 24 23, 6900 Heidelberg 1, Germany

ADVERTISING INFORMATION

Advertising accepted: Yes

EDITORIAL DESCRIPTION

Scope: Aims to concentrate the endeavors of theoretical linguists upon those texts traditionally classed as literary, in the belief that such texts are a central, not a peripheral, concern of linguistics. Hopes also to be of interest to those who work in the field of applied linguistics. Publishes articles on all aspects of literary semantics; articles of a philosophical nature attempting to relate the study of literature to other disciplines, such as psychology, neurophysiology, mathematics, history; articles dealing with the educational problems inherent in the study of literature.
Reviews books: Yes
Publishes notes: Yes
Languages accepted: English
Prints abstracts: No
Author-anonymous submission: No

SUBMISSION REQUIREMENTS

Restrictions on contributors: None
Author pays submission fee: No
Author pays page charges: No
Length of articles: No restrictions
Length of book reviews: No restrictions
Length of notes: No restrictions
Style: International Review of Applied Linguistics in Language Teaching
Number of copies required: 1
Copyright ownership: Julius Groos Verlag
Rejected manuscripts: Returned
Time before publication decision: 1 mo.
Time between decision and publication: 1 yr.
Number of reviewers: 1
Articles published per year: 10-12
Book reviews published per year: 20

(1415)
*Journal of Literary Studies/Tydskrif Vir Literaturwetenskap

Ina Gräbe & R. Ryan, Editors
Dept. of Theory of Literature
UNISA
P.O. Box 392
0001 Pretoria, South Africa

Telephone: (27) 12 4296700
Fax: (27) 12 4293221
First published: 1985
Sponsoring organization: South African Assn. of General Literary Studies (SAVAL)
ISSN: 0025-4718
MLA acronym: JLSTL

SUBSCRIPTION INFORMATION

Frequency of publication: 4 times/yr.
Circulation: 400
Available in microform: No
Subscription price: $28.00/yr. institutions; $20.00/yr. individuals
Year to which price refers: 1992

ADVERTISING INFORMATION

Advertising accepted: Yes
Advertising rates: $90.00/half page; $180.00/full page

EDITORIAL DESCRIPTION

Scope: The journal is intended to provide a forum for the discussion of literary theory, methodology, research, and related matters.
Reviews books: Yes
Publishes notes: Yes
Languages accepted: English; Afrikaans
Prints abstracts: Yes
Author-anonymous submission: Yes

SUBMISSION REQUIREMENTS

Restrictions on contributors: None
Author pays submission fee: No
Author pays page charges: Yes

Cost of page charges: 70 R ($30.00)/page
Length of articles: 20-30 pp.
Length of book reviews: 1,000 words
Length of notes: 1,000 words
Style: MLA
Number of copies required: 3
Special requirements: Submit original double-spaced typescript plus 2 copies on size A4 (8 1/4 in. x 11 3/4 in.) paper.
Copyright ownership: South African Assn. of General Literary Studies
Rejected manuscripts: Returned
Time before publication decision: 2 mos.
Time between decision and publication: 3 mos.
Number of reviewers: 3-4
Articles submitted per year: 50
Articles published per year: 24
Book reviews submitted per year: 15
Book reviews published per year: 10
Notes submitted per year: 8
Notes published per year: 2

(1416)
*Journal of Macrolinguistics

Yip Po-Ching, Editor
14, St. Michael's Terrace
Leeds LS6 3BQ, England

Telephone: (44) 532 751768; (44) 532 783697; (44) 532 333463
Fax: (44) 532 336741 (c/o Dept. of East Asian Studies, Univ. of Leeds)
First published: 1992
ISSN: 0967-1927
MLA acronym: JMacL

SUBSCRIPTION INFORMATION

Frequency of publication: 4 times/yr.
Available in microform: No
Subscription price: £18.00/yr. institutions United Kingdom; £20.00/yr. institutions elsewhere; £15.00/yr. individuals United Kingdom; £17.00/yr. individuals elsewhere; £12.00/yr. students & retirees United Kingdom; £14.00/yr. students & retirees elsewhere
Year to which price refers: 1992-93

ADVERTISING INFORMATION

Advertising accepted: Yes

EDITORIAL DESCRIPTION

Scope: Publishes articles on the Chinese language in the context of Chinese culture and society.
Reviews books: Yes
Languages accepted: English; Chinese languages
Prints abstracts: Occasionally
Author-anonymous submission: No

SUBMISSION REQUIREMENTS

Restrictions on contributors: None
Author pays submission fee: No
Author pays page charges: No
Length of articles: 5,000-10,000 words
Length of book reviews: 500-1,000 words
Length of notes: 500-2,000 words
Number of copies required: 1
Special requirements: Articles are published in both English and Chinese. Submission of typescript and diskette is preferred.
Copyright ownership: Journal
Time before publication decision: 1 mo. minimum
Time between decision and publication: 1-2 mos.
Articles submitted per year: 150
Articles published per year: 40-50

(1417)
*Journal of Mayan Linguistics

Jill Brody, Editor
Dept. of Geography & Anthropology
Louisiana State Univ.
Baton Rouge, LA 70803

Telephone: 504 388-6245
Fax: 504 388-2912
First published: 1978
Sponsoring organization: Louisiana State Univ.
ISSN: 0195-475X
MLA acronym: JMLing

SUBSCRIPTION INFORMATION

Frequency of publication: Irregular
Circulation: 125
Available in microform: No

ADVERTISING INFORMATION

Advertising accepted: No

EDITORIAL DESCRIPTION

Scope: Publishes articles on Mayan languages, linguistics, and hieroglyphs.
Reviews books: Yes
Publishes notes: Yes
Languages accepted: English; Spanish
Prints abstracts: No

SUBMISSION REQUIREMENTS

Restrictions on contributors: None
Author pays submission fee: No
Author pays page charges: No
Length of articles: No restrictions
Length of book reviews: No restrictions
Length of notes: No restrictions
Style: Linguistic Soc. of America; journal style guide for typing is available from editor.
Number of copies required: 3
Rejected manuscripts: Not returned
Time before publication decision: 2 mos.
Time between decision and publication: 6 mos.
Number of reviewers: 2

(1418)
*Journal of Medieval and Renaissance Studies

Annabel Patterson & Marcel Tetel, Editors
4666 Duke Station
Duke Univ.
Durham, NC 27706

First published: 1971
Sponsoring organization: Duke Univ. Press
ISSN: 0047-2573
MLA acronym: JMRS

SUBSCRIPTION INFORMATION

Frequency of publication: 3 times/yr. (Winter, Spring, Fall)
Circulation: 1,000
Available in microform: No
Subscription price: $64.00/yr. institutions; $32.00/yr. individuals; add $6.00/yr. postage outside US
Year to which price refers: 1992
Subscription address: Office of Publication, Duke Univ. Press, 6697 College Station, Durham, NC 27708

ADVERTISING INFORMATION

Advertising accepted: Yes

EDITORIAL DESCRIPTION

Scope: Publishes scholarly articles on any aspect of late medieval and Renaissance culture and society, including art, literature, music, philosophy, theology, and history (intellectual, political, and social). Especially interested in studies that bring one or more of these arenas or disciplines together, and that illuminate general or specific issues in cross-disciplinary or comparative analysis; also in work that bears on the problems of change and transition—institutional, stylistic, generic, or from one period to another.
Reviews books: No
Publishes notes: No
Languages accepted: English; French; German; Italian; Spanish
Prints abstracts: No
Author-anonymous submission: No

SUBMISSION REQUIREMENTS

Restrictions on contributors: None
Author pays submission fee: No
Author pays page charges: No
Length of articles: 20-35 pp. plus notes
Style: Chicago
Number of copies required: 1
Copyright ownership: Duke Univ. Press
Rejected manuscripts: Returned
Time before publication decision: 2-3 mos.
Time between decision and publication: 12-18 mos.
Number of reviewers: 2
Articles published per year: 20

(1419)
Journal of Memory and Language

Edward J. Shoben & Gary S. Dell, Editors
Dept. of Psychology
Univ. of Illinois
603 E. Daniel St.
Champaign, IL 61820

First published: 1962
ISSN: 0749-596X
MLA acronym: JMemL

SUBSCRIPTION INFORMATION

Frequency of publication: 6 times/yr.
Circulation: 1,300
Available in microform: No
Subscription price: $182.00/yr. US & Canada; $222.00/yr. elsewhere
Year to which price refers: 1993
Subscription address: Academic Press, Inc., 6277 Sea Harbor Dr., Orlando, FL 32887-4900

ADVERTISING INFORMATION

Advertising accepted: Yes

EDITORIAL DESCRIPTION

Scope: Publishes original, experimental, theoretical, and review papers concerned with problems of language comprehension and production, human learning and memory, and other related language processes. Editorial evaluation of research papers is based on the following points: significance of the problem and precision of its statement; linkage of the problem with previous relevant work; credibility of the relation between the stated problem and the experimental design; adequacy of the experiment per se; appropriateness and sufficiency of data analysis; clarity of the relation between the results and the stated problem; and the importance of the problem-design-results package as a whole.
Reviews books: No
Publishes notes: No
Languages accepted: English
Prints abstracts: Yes

Author-anonymous submission: Yes, at author's request.

SUBMISSION REQUIREMENTS

Restrictions on contributors: None
Author pays submission fee: No
Author pays page charges: No
Length of articles: 8,000 words
Style: American Psychological Assn.
Number of copies required: 4
Special requirements: Include a 120-word abstract.
Copyright ownership: Academic Press
Rejected manuscripts: Not returned
Time before publication decision: 7 weeks
Time between decision and publication: 6 mos.
Number of reviewers: 2-3
Articles submitted per year: 120
Articles published per year: 42

(1420)
*The Journal of Modern African Studies

David Kimble, Editor
Huish, Chagford
Devon TQ13 8AR, England

Telephone: (44) 647 433569
First published: 1963
ISSN: 0022-278X
MLA acronym: JMAS

SUBSCRIPTION INFORMATION

Frequency of publication: 4 times/yr.
Circulation: 2,000
Available in microform: Yes
Subscription price: $127.00 /yr. institutions N. America; £66.00/yr. institutions elsewhere; $56.00/yr. individuals N. America; £31.00/yr. elsewhere
Year to which price refers: 1992
Subscription address: Cambridge Univ. Press, The Edinburgh Bldg., Shaftesbury Rd., Cambridge CB2 2RU, England
Additional subscription address: In the US & Canada: Cambridge Univ. Press, 40 W. 20th St., New York, NY 10011
Subscription telephone: (44) 223 312393
Subscription fax: (44) 223 315052

ADVERTISING INFORMATION

Advertising accepted: Yes

EDITORIAL DESCRIPTION

Scope: Surveys politics, economics, and related topics in contemporary Africa.
Reviews books: Yes
Publishes notes: No
Languages accepted: English
Prints abstracts: No
Author-anonymous submission: No

SUBMISSION REQUIREMENTS

Author pays submission fee: No
Author pays page charges: No
Length of articles: 4,000-6,000 words, occasional exceptions of up to 10,000 words
Length of book reviews: 700-800 words
Style: Journal
Number of copies required: 1 (not the original typescript)
Special requirements: Submit double-spaced typescript; minimize repetitive polysyllabic words.
Copyright ownership: Cambridge Univ. Press for author
Rejected manuscripts: Not returned
Time before publication decision: 1 mo.
Time between decision and publication: 5-6 mos.
Number of reviewers: 1
Articles submitted per year: 180
Articles published per year: 32

Book reviews submitted per year: 50
Book reviews published per year: 38

(1421)
*Journal of Modern Greek Studies

Peter Bien, Editor
Dept. of English
Dartmouth College
6032 Sanborn House
Hanover, NH 03755-3533

Additional editorial address: Mary Layoun, Book Review Editor, Dept. of Comparative Literature, Univ. of Wisconsin, 938 Van Hise, Madison, WI 53706
Telephone: 603 646-2316
Fax: 603 646-2754
E-mail: Peter.bien@dartmouth.edu
First published: 1983
Sponsoring organization: Modern Greek Studies Assn.
ISSN: 0738-1727
MLA acronym: JMGS

SUBSCRIPTION INFORMATION

Frequency of publication: 2 times/yr. (May, Oct.)
Circulation: 500
Available in microform: No
Subscription price: $41.00/yr. institutions US; $19.00/yr. individuals US; add $2.10/yr. postage Canada & Mexico, $4.30/yr. elsewhere
Year to which price refers: 1993
Subscription address: Johns Hopkins Univ. Press, Journals Publishing Division, 2715 North Charles St., Baltimore, MD 21218-4319
Subscription telephone: 800 537-5487; 410 516-6987
Subscription fax: 410 516-6998

ADVERTISING INFORMATION

Advertising accepted: Yes

EDITORIAL DESCRIPTION

Scope: Devoted to all aspects of Modern Greek scholarship. Welcomes articles presenting original research on, or critical analysis of, the society and culture of, the Greek-speaking peoples from the late Byzantine period to the present.
Reviews books: Yes
Publishes notes: No
Languages accepted: English
Prints abstracts: Yes
Author-anonymous submission: Yes

SUBMISSION REQUIREMENTS

Restrictions on contributors: Unsolicited book reviews are not accepted.
Author pays submission fee: No
Author pays page charges: No
Length of articles: 6,000-8,000 words
Length of book reviews: 500-1,000 words
Style: Chicago
Number of copies required: 4
Special requirements: Include a 100-word abstract.
Copyright ownership: Johns Hopkins Univ. Press
Rejected manuscripts: Returned
Time before publication decision: 3 mos.
Time between decision and publication: 1 yr.
Number of reviewers: 2
Articles submitted per year: 50
Articles published per year: 12
Book reviews published per year: 12-14

(1422)
Journal of Modern Literature

Morton P. Levitt, Editor
921 Anderson Hall
Temple Univ.
Philadelphia, PA 19122

First published: 1970
Sponsoring organization: Temple Univ.
ISSN: 0022-281X
MLA acronym: JML

SUBSCRIPTION INFORMATION

Frequency of publication: 3 times/yr.
Circulation: 2,000
Available in microform: Yes
Subscription address: Circulation Dept., at the above address

ADVERTISING INFORMATION

Advertising accepted: Yes

EDITORIAL DESCRIPTION

Scope: Devoted to scholarly studies of the literature of the 20th century, with emphasis on the Modernist period.
Reviews books: Yes
Publishes notes: Yes
Languages accepted: English
Prints abstracts: No
Author-anonymous submission: Yes

SUBMISSION REQUIREMENTS

Restrictions on contributors: None
Author pays submission fee: No
Author pays page charges: No
Length of articles: 15-30 pp.
Length of book reviews: 250 words maximum
Length of notes: 5-10 pp.
Style: MLA with modifications
Number of copies required: 1
Copyright ownership: Temple Univ.
Rejected manuscripts: Returned; enclose return postage.
Time before publication decision: 2-3 mos.
Time between decision and publication: 2 yrs.
Number of reviewers: 1-2
Articles submitted per year: 200
Articles published per year: 35
Book reviews submitted per year: 400
Book reviews published per year: 400
Notes submitted per year: 30
Notes published per year: 8

(1423)
*Journal of Multilingual and Multicultural Development

John Edwards, Editor
Multilingual Matters, Ltd.
Bank House, 8a Hill Rd.
Clevedon, Avon BS21 7HH, England

Telephone: (44) 275 876519
Fax: (44) 275 343096
First published: 1980
ISSN: 0143-4632
MLA acronym: JMMD

SUBSCRIPTION INFORMATION

Frequency of publication: 6 times/yr. (Feb., Apr., June, Aug., Oct., Dec.)
Circulation: 850
Available in microform: No
Subscription price: £73.00 ($150.00)/yr. institutions; £25.00 ($52.00)/yr. individuals; £14.00 ($30.00)/yr. students
Year to which price refers: 1992

ADVERTISING INFORMATION

Advertising accepted: Yes

Advertising rates: £30.00/half page; £60.00/full page

EDITORIAL DESCRIPTION

Scope: Journal publishes all materials relating to the benefits and problems of living in multilingual and multicultural surroundings.
Reviews books: Yes
Publishes notes: Yes
Languages accepted: English
Prints abstracts: Yes
Author-anonymous submission: No

SUBMISSION REQUIREMENTS

Restrictions on contributors: None
Author pays submission fee: No
Author pays page charges: No
Length of articles: 5,000-8,000 words
Length of book reviews: 500-2,000 words
Length of notes: 500-1,000 words
Style: Chicago
Number of copies required: 4
Special requirements: Submit camera-ready copy for all diagrams.
Copyright ownership: Author
Rejected manuscripts: Returned at author's request
Time before publication decision: 5 mos.
Time between decision and publication: 8 mos.
Number of reviewers: 1
Articles submitted per year: 80
Articles published per year: 36
Book reviews submitted per year: 35
Book reviews published per year: 20
Notes submitted per year: 10
Notes published per year: 8

(1424)
*Journal of Narrative Technique

Paul Bruss & Ian Wojcik-Andrews, Editors
Eastern Michigan Univ.
Ypsilanti, MI 48197

First published: 1971
Sponsoring organization: Eastern Michigan Univ.
ISSN: 0022-2925
MLA acronym: JNT

SUBSCRIPTION INFORMATION

Frequency of publication: 3 times/yr.
Circulation: 1,100
Available in microform: Yes
Subscription price: $20.00/yr. institutions US; $30.00/yr. institutions elsewhere
Year to which price refers: 1993

ADVERTISING INFORMATION

Advertising accepted: No

EDITORIAL DESCRIPTION

Scope: Invites manuscript submissions dealing with narrative literature, both prose and verse. Subject matter may be drawn from all periods and all literary genres, provided that in each instance the focus of the critic is on the author's management of narrative elements. Papers concerning characterization, style, biographical background, historical influences, and mythical, symbolic, or psychological patterns should demonstrate a clear relationship to the narrative movement of the work.
Reviews books: Yes
Publishes notes: Yes
Languages accepted: English
Prints abstracts: No
Author-anonymous submission: No

SUBMISSION REQUIREMENTS

Author pays submission fee: No
Author pays page charges: No
Length of articles: 15-25 typescript pp.
Length of book reviews: 200-300 words
Length of notes: 3,000 words
Style: MLA
Number of copies required: 2
Copyright ownership: Journal
Rejected manuscripts: Returned; enclose SASE.
Time before publication decision: 2-4 mos.
Time between decision and publication: 6 mos.
Number of reviewers: 3
Articles submitted per year: 200
Articles published per year: 22
Book reviews published per year: 30-40
Notes published per year: 6

(1425)
*Journal of Near Eastern Studies

Robert D. Biggs, Editor
Oriental Inst.
Univ. of Chicago
1155 E. 58 St.
Chicago, IL 60637

Telephone: 312 702-9592
Fax: 312 702-9853
E-mail: R-biggs@uchicago.edu
First published: 1884
Sponsoring organization: Dept. of Near Eastern Languages & Civilizations, Univ. of Chicago
ISSN: 0022-2968
MLA acronym: JNES

SUBSCRIPTION INFORMATION

Frequency of publication: 4 times/yr. (Jan., Apr., July, Oct.)
Circulation: 3,500
Available in microform: Yes
Subscription price: $32.00/yr. individuals
Year to which price refers: 1992
Subscription address: Univ. of Chicago Press, Journals Division, P.O. Box 37005, Chicago, IL 60637
Subscription telephone: 312 753-3347
Subscription fax: 312 753-0811

ADVERTISING INFORMATION

Advertising accepted: Yes

EDITORIAL DESCRIPTION

Scope: Journal focuses on ancient and medieval Near East, ancient Egypt, Babylonia, Palestine, Old Testament, and Islam.
Reviews books: Yes
Publishes notes: No
Languages accepted: English; French; German
Prints abstracts: No
Author-anonymous submission: No

SUBMISSION REQUIREMENTS

Restrictions on contributors: None
Author pays submission fee: No
Author pays page charges: No
Length of articles: No restrictions
Length of book reviews: 400-600 words
Style: Chicago
Number of copies required: 2
Special requirements: Photographs must be glossy prints no larger than 5 in. x 7 in.
Copyright ownership: Assigned by author to journal
Rejected manuscripts: Returned
Time before publication decision: 1 mo.
Time between decision and publication: 18 mos.
Number of reviewers: 2
Articles submitted per year: 80-100
Articles published per year: 18-25
Book reviews submitted per year: 100
Book reviews published per year: 35-40

(1426)
*Journal of Nervous and Mental Disease

Eugene B. Brody, Editor
Sheppard & Enoch Pratt Hospital
P.O. Box 6815
Towson, MD 21285-6815

Telephone: 410 938-3000 ext. 3182
Fax: 410 938-4532
First published: 1874
ISSN: 0022-3018
MLA acronym: JNMD

SUBSCRIPTION INFORMATION

Frequency of publication: 12 times/yr.
Circulation: 2,470
Available in microform: Yes
Subscription price: $150.00/yr. institutions US; $178.00/yr. institutions elsewhere; $90.00/yr. individuals US; $115.00/yr. individuals elsewhere
Year to which price refers: 1992
Subscription address: Subscription Dept., Williams & Wilkins Co., 428 E. Preston St., Baltimore, MD 21202
Subscription telephone: 800 638-6428

ADVERTISING INFORMATION

Advertising accepted: Yes

EDITORIAL DESCRIPTION

Scope: Designed for clinicians and researchers in psychiatry, psychology, the social sciences, the neurosciences, and human behavior. Includes studies on neurolinguistics, psycholinguistics, and speech disorders.
Reviews books: Yes
Publishes notes: Yes
Languages accepted: English
Prints abstracts: Yes
Author-anonymous submission: Yes

SUBMISSION REQUIREMENTS

Restrictions on contributors: None
Author pays submission fee: No
Author pays page charges: No
Length of articles: 8 printed pp., articles; 1 printed p., single case studies & brief communications
Length of book reviews: 2 double-spaced pp. maximum
Style: Journal
Number of copies required: 3
Copyright ownership: Williams & Wilkins Co.
Rejected manuscripts: Returned; enclose SASE.
Time before publication decision: 3 mos.
Time between decision and publication: 4-5 mos.
Number of reviewers: 2-4
Articles submitted per year: 350
Articles published per year: 100
Book reviews submitted per year: 100
Book reviews published per year: 50

(1427)
*Journal of Newspaper and Periodical History

Michael Harris, Editor
Birkbeck College
26 Russell Sq.
London WC1B 5DQ, England

Telephone: (44) 81 4505554
Fax: (44) 81 6316688
First published: 1984
ISSN: 0265-5942
MLA acronym: JNPH

SUBSCRIPTION INFORMATION

Frequency of publication: 2 times/yr.

Subscription address: Greenwood Press, Box 5007, 88 Post Rd. W., Westport, CT 06881

ADVERTISING INFORMATION

Advertising accepted: Yes

EDITORIAL DESCRIPTION

Scope: The journal is intended to provide a clearinghouse for information of all kinds generated through the growing and very diverse interest in the history of the press.
Reviews books: Yes
Publishes notes: Yes
Languages accepted: English
Prints abstracts: No
Author-anonymous submission: No

SUBMISSION REQUIREMENTS

Restrictions on contributors: None
Author pays submission fee: No
Author pays page charges: No
Length of articles: 5,000 words
Length of book reviews: 500 words
Style: MLA
Number of copies required: 1
Copyright ownership: Author
Rejected manuscripts: Returned
Time before publication decision: 3 mos.
Time between decision and publication: 6 mos.
Number of reviewers: 1
Articles submitted per year: 12
Articles published per year: 9
Book reviews submitted per year: 18
Book reviews published per year: 16
Notes submitted per year: 12
Notes published per year: 12

(1428)
*Journal of Nonverbal Behavior

Judith A. Hall, Editor
Dept. of Psychology
Northeastern Univ.
125 Nightingale Hall
Boston, MA 02115

Telephone: 617 437-3790; 617 437-3076
Fax: 617 437-8414
E-mail: HALL1@NUHUB
First published: 1976
ISSN: 0191-5886
MLA acronym: JNB

SUBSCRIPTION INFORMATION

Frequency of publication: 4 times/yr.
Circulation: 500
Subscription price: $145.00/yr. institutions US; $170.00/yr. institutions elsewhere; $44.00/yr. individuals US; $50.00/yr. individuals elsewhere
Year to which price refers: 1991
Subscription address: Human Sciences Press, 233 Spring St., New York, NY 10013-1578
Subscription telephone: 212 620-8000
Subscription fax: 212 807-1047; 212 463-0742

ADVERTISING INFORMATION

Advertising accepted: Yes

EDITORIAL DESCRIPTION

Scope: Publishes original theoretical, empirical, and methodological research in the areas of nonverbal behavior, including proxemics, kinesics, paralanguage, facial expression, and other areas which add significantly to our understanding of nonverbal processes, communication, and behavior.
Reviews books: No
Publishes notes: Yes
Languages accepted: English
Prints abstracts: Yes
Author-anonymous submission: Yes, at author's request

SUBMISSION REQUIREMENTS

Restrictions on contributors: None
Author pays submission fee: No
Author pays page charges: No
Length of articles: No restrictions
Length of notes: No restrictions
Style: American Psychological Assn.
Number of copies required: 4
Special requirements: A cover letter should accompany the manuscript indicating whether the author(s) wish(es) blind or open reviewing of the paper. Artwork must be camera-ready. Submit an abstract.
Copyright ownership: Human Sciences Press, Inc.
Rejected manuscripts: Returned
Time before publication decision: 2-3 mos.
Time between decision and publication: 3-6 mos.
Number of reviewers: 3
Articles submitted per year: 60-70
Articles published per year: 20-25

(1429)
*Journal of Northwest Semitic Languages

Walter T. Claassen, Editor
Dept. of Semitic Languages & Cultures
Univ. of Stellenbosch
Stellenbosch 7600, South Africa

Telephone: (27) 2231 773205
Fax: (27) 2231 774499
First published: 1971
Sponsoring organization: Assn. of Northwest Semitic Languages
ISSN: 0085-2414
MLA acronym: JNWSL

SUBSCRIPTION INFORMATION

Frequency of publication: Annual
Circulation: 500
Available in microform: No
Subscription price: $27.00/yr.
Year to which price refers: 1992

ADVERTISING INFORMATION

Advertising accepted: No

EDITORIAL DESCRIPTION

Scope: Focuses on the languages and cultures of the Ancient Near East.
Reviews books: Yes
Publishes notes: Yes
Languages accepted: English; German; French
Prints abstracts: No
Author-anonymous submission: Yes

SUBMISSION REQUIREMENTS

Restrictions on contributors: None
Author pays submission fee: No
Author pays page charges: No
Length of articles: 13,000 words
Length of book reviews: 500 words
Length of notes: No restrictions
Number of copies required: 1
Special requirements: Submit original typescript and diskette.
Copyright ownership: Author
Rejected manuscripts: Returned
Time before publication decision: 2 mos.
Time between decision and publication: 1 yr.
Number of reviewers: 2
Articles submitted per year: 15
Articles published per year: 12
Book reviews submitted per year: 8
Book reviews published per year: 8

(1430)
*Journal of Personality and Social Psychology

Abraham Tesser, Norman Miller, & Russell G. Geen, Editors
Inst. for Behavioral Research
Univ. of Georgia
111 Barrow Hall
D. W. Brooks Dr.
Athens, GA 30602

Additional editorial address: N. Miller, Dept. of Psychology, Seeley G. Mudd Bldg., Univ. of Southern California, University Park, Los Angeles, CA 90089; R. Geen, JPSP-PPID, Dept. of Psychology, Univ. of Missouri, Columbia, MO 65211
Telephone: 706 542-6100
First published: 1965
Sponsoring organization: American Psychological Assn.
ISSN: 0022-3514
MLA acronym: JPSP

SUBSCRIPTION INFORMATION

Frequency of publication: 12 times/yr. (4 vols./yr.)
Circulation: 6,500
Available in microform: Yes
Subscription address: Subscription Section, American Psychological Assn., 750 First St., NE, Washington, DC 20002

ADVERTISING INFORMATION

Advertising accepted: No

EDITORIAL DESCRIPTION

Scope: Publishes original reports of research, methodology, theory, criticism, and literature review in the fields of personality and social psychology of normal processes and populations. Submitted manuscripts should delineate an important question and provide a clear answer to it.
Reviews books: No
Publishes notes: No
Languages accepted: English
Prints abstracts: Yes
Author-anonymous submission: Yes, at author's request

SUBMISSION REQUIREMENTS

Restrictions on contributors: None
Author pays submission fee: No
Author pays page charges: Only for extensive revisions after page proof edits
Length of articles: 7,000 words
Style: American Psychological Assn.
Number of copies required: 4
Copyright ownership: American Psychological Assn.
Rejected manuscripts: Not returned
Time before publication decision: 2 mos.
Time between decision and publication: 5-8 mos.
Number of reviewers: 3-4
Articles submitted per year: 350
Articles published per year: 51

(1431)
*Journal of Philosophical Logic

J. Michael Dunn, Anil Gupta, & Terence Parsons, Editors
Dept. of Philosophy
Indiana Univ.
Bloomington, IN 47405

Additional editorial address: Terence Parsons, Dept. of Philosophy, Univ. of California, Irvine, CA 92717
Telephone: 812 855-9403
Fax: 812 855-3777

E-mail: Dunn@IUVAX.CS.INDIANA.EDU
First published: 1972
Sponsoring organization: Assn. for Symbolic Logic
ISSN: 0022-3611
MLA acronym: JPL

SUBSCRIPTION INFORMATION

Frequency of publication: 4 times/yr. (Feb., May, Aug., Nov.)
Available in microform: Yes
Subscription price: $135.00/yr. institutions; $44.00/yr. individuals
Year to which price refers: 1992
Subscription address: Kluwer Academic Publishers, P.O. Box 322, 3300 AH Dordrecht, Netherlands

ADVERTISING INFORMATION

Advertising accepted: Yes

EDITORIAL DESCRIPTION

Scope: Publishes articles on philosophical studies utilizing methods or dealing with topics in logical theory. Specifically included are: (1) contributions to branches of logical theory directly related to philosophical concerns; (2) contributions to philosophical discussions that utilize the machinery of formal logic, as in recent treatments of abstract entities, nonexistent possibles, essentialism, existence, propositional attitudes, meaning, and truth; (3) discussions of philosophical issues relating to logic and the logical structure of language, as for example, conventionalism in logic; (4) philosophical work relating to special sciences, for example, linguistics, history of logic with emphasis on foundational problems and making use of logical theory. Some instances of recent work of this kind are treatments of universal grammar, pragmatics, conceptions of possibility, theories and mathematical truth in the history of philosophy, formalization of scientific theories, logical structures in quantum mechanics.
Reviews books: No
Publishes notes: No
Languages accepted: English
Prints abstracts: Yes
Author-anonymous submission: Yes

SUBMISSION REQUIREMENTS

Restrictions on contributors: None
Author pays submission fee: No
Author pays page charges: No
Length of articles: No restrictions
Style: None
Number of copies required: 2
Special requirements: Author's name should be on sheet separate from manuscript. Photocopies of manuscript are preferred.
Copyright ownership: Kluwer Academic Publishers
Rejected manuscripts: Not returned
Time before publication decision: 2 mos.
Time between decision and publication: 18 mos.
Number of reviewers: 1
Articles submitted per year: 150
Articles published per year: 38

(1432)
*Journal of Philosophy

Michael Kelly, Managing Editor
709 Philosophy Hall
Columbia Univ.
New York, NY 10027

Telephone: 212 666-4419
Fax: 212 732-3721
First published: 1904
ISSN: 0022-362X
MLA acronym: JP

SUBSCRIPTION INFORMATION

Frequency of publication: 12 times/yr.
Circulation: 4,200
Available in microform: No
Subscription price: $50.00/yr. institutions; $30.00/yr. individuals
Year to which price refers: 1992
Subscription telephone: 212 866-1742

ADVERTISING INFORMATION

Advertising accepted: Yes

EDITORIAL DESCRIPTION

Scope: Publishes philosophical articles of current interest, argumentative rather than primarily expository, preferably on the borderline between philosophy and other disciplines.
Reviews books: Yes
Publishes notes: Yes
Languages accepted: English
Prints abstracts: No
Author-anonymous submission: No

SUBMISSION REQUIREMENTS

Restrictions on contributors: All reviews are solicited.
Author pays submission fee: No
Author pays page charges: No, unless author's excessive alterations are made
Length of articles: 7,500 words maximum
Length of book reviews: 1,500 words
Length of notes: 60 words
Style: Journal
Number of copies required: 1
Special requirements: Accepted manuscripts must be double-spaced.
Copyright ownership: Journal
Rejected manuscripts: Returned; enclose return postage.
Time before publication decision: 5-6 mos.
Time between decision and publication: 6-8 mos.
Number of reviewers: 4
Articles submitted per year: 350
Articles published per year: 35
Book reviews published per year: 25

(1433)
*Journal of Phonetics

Mary E. Beckman, Editor
Dept. of Linguistics
Ohio State Univ.
222 Oxley Hall
1712 Neil Ave.
Columbus, OH 43210-1298

Telephone: 614 292-3492
Fax: 614 292-4273
E-mail: JPHON@magnus.irec.OHIO-STATE.EDU
First published: 1973
ISSN: 0095-4470
MLA acronym: JPhon

SUBSCRIPTION INFORMATION

Frequency of publication: 4 times/yr.
Circulation: 800
Available in microform: Yes
Subscription price: £115.00 ($210.00)/yr. institutions; £58.00 ($99.00)/yr. individuals
Year to which price refers: 1992
Subscription address: Academic Press, Ltd., Footscray, Kent DA14 SHP, England
Additional subscription address: Academic Press Inc., (London) Ltd., 24-28 Oval Rd. London, NW1 7DX, England
Subscription telephone: (44) 81 3003322

ADVERTISING INFORMATION

Advertising accepted: Yes

EDITORIAL DESCRIPTION

Scope: Publishes original papers reporting experimental work primarily concerned with elucidating problems in phonetics. Theoretical papers are acceptable provided they relate to experimental findings. Short papers in the form of "Letters to the Editor" are also acceptable and may be used to report work in progress provided that there exist already some reliable findings to report.
Reviews books: Yes
Publishes notes: Yes
Languages accepted: English
Prints abstracts: Yes
Author-anonymous submission: Yes

SUBMISSION REQUIREMENTS

Restrictions on contributors: None
Author pays submission fee: No
Author pays page charges: No
Length of articles: 10 printed pp.
Length of book reviews: No restrictions
Length of notes: 1,500 words
Style: Journal
Number of copies required: 4
Special requirements: Include a 50-200 word abstract.
Copyright ownership: Academic Press
Rejected manuscripts: Returned
Time before publication decision: 6 mos.
Time between decision and publication: 3-6 mos.
Number of reviewers: 2-3
Articles submitted per year: 120
Articles published per year: 40
Book reviews submitted per year: 10
Book reviews published per year: 8
Notes submitted per year: 20
Notes published per year: 6

(1434)
*Journal of Pidgin and Creole Languages

Glenn Gilbert, Editor
Dept. of Linguistics
Southern Illinois Univ.
Carbondale, IL 62901

Additional editorial address: Send book reviews to: Salikoko Mufwene, Dept. of Linguistics, Univ. of Chicago, 1010 East 59th St., Chicago, IL 60637
First published: 1986
Sponsoring organization: The College of Liberal Arts, the Graduate School, and the Dept. of Linguistics at Southern Illinois Univ. at Carbondale.
ISSN: 0920-9034
MLA acronym: JPCL

SUBSCRIPTION INFORMATION

Frequency of publication: 2 times/yr. (Spring, Fall)
Circulation: 300
Available in microform: No
Subscription price: 197 f ($119.00)/yr.
Year to which price refers: 1993
Subscription address: John Benjamins B.V., Amsteldijk 44, P.O. Box 75577, 1070 AN Amsterdam, Netherlands
Additional subscription address: John Benjamins North America, Inc., 821 Bethlehem Pike, Philadelphia, PA 19118
Subscription telephone: (31) 20 6738156; 215 836-1200
Subscription fax: (31) 20 6739773; 215 836-1204

ADVERTISING INFORMATION

Advertising accepted: Yes
Advertising rates: 400 f ($200.00)/full page

EDITORIAL DESCRIPTION

Scope: Presents the results of current research in theory and description of pidgin and creole languages in the wider sense, and applications of this knowledge to language planning, education, and social reform in creole-speaking societies.
Reviews books: Yes
Publishes notes: Yes
Languages accepted: English
Prints abstracts: Yes
Author-anonymous submission: Yes

SUBMISSION REQUIREMENTS

Restrictions on contributors: None
Author pays submission fee: No
Author pays page charges: No
Length of articles: No restrictions
Length of book reviews: No restrictions
Length of notes: 1,500 words
Style: Linguistic Soc. of America
Number of copies required: 4
Special requirements: Submit double-spaced typescript on white A4 size (8 1/4 in. x 11 3/4 in.) paper with a wide margin. Footnotes, references, bibliographies, tables, and other illustrations should be double-spaced and presented on separate sheets.
Copyright ownership: John Benjamins Co.
Rejected manuscripts: Not returned
Time before publication decision: 4 mos.
Time between decision and publication: 6-12 mos.
Number of reviewers: 3
Articles submitted per year: 20-25
Articles published per year: 8-10
Book reviews submitted per year: 10
Book reviews published per year: 10
Notes submitted per year: 8
Notes published per year: 8

(1435)
*Journal of Popular Culture

Ray B. Browne, Editor
Center for the Study of Popular Culture
Bowling Green Univ.
Bowling Green, OH 43403

First published: 1967
Sponsoring organization: Popular Culture Assn.
ISSN: 0022-3840
MLA acronym: JPC

SUBSCRIPTION INFORMATION

Frequency of publication: 4 times/yr.
Circulation: 3,500
Available in microform: Yes
Subscription price: $30.00/yr.
Year to which price refers: 1992

ADVERTISING INFORMATION

Advertising accepted: Yes
Advertising rates: $150.00/full page

EDITORIAL DESCRIPTION

Scope: Publishes articles on "popular culture" in the broadest sense of the term. Manuscripts are invited which develop or touch on the various fields in this wide area. No limits on period or country covered.
Reviews books: Yes
Publishes notes: Yes
Languages accepted: English
Prints abstracts: No
Author-anonymous submission: No

SUBMISSION REQUIREMENTS

Restrictions on contributors: Contributors must be subscribers.
Author pays submission fee: No
Author pays page charges: No
Length of articles: 3,000 words
Length of book reviews: 150-200 words
Length of notes: 200 words
Style: MLA
Number of copies required: 2
Special requirements: Submit original manuscript.
Copyright ownership: Journal
Rejected manuscripts: Returned; enclose return postage.
Time before publication decision: 6 mos.
Time between decision and publication: 2 yrs.
Number of reviewers: 1-3
Articles submitted per year: 500
Articles published per year: 80
Book reviews submitted per year: 100
Book reviews published per year: 25
Notes submitted per year: 20
Notes published per year: 2-4

(1436)
*Journal of Popular Film and Television

Michael T. Marsden & John G. Nachbar, Editors
Popular Culture Center
Bowling Green State Univ.
Bowling Green, OH 43403

Additional editorial address: Send submissions to: Heldref Publications, 1319 Eighteenth St. NW, Washington, DC 20036-1802
Telephone: 419 372-2981
Fax: 419 372-2577
First published: 1972
Sponsoring organization: Bowling Green State Univ., Popular Culture Center
ISSN: 0195-6051
MLA acronym: JPFT

SUBSCRIPTION INFORMATION

Frequency of publication: 4 times/yr.
Circulation: 850
Available in microform: Yes
Subscription price: $48.00/yr. institutions; $24.00/yr. individuals
Year to which price refers: 1992
Subscription address: Heldref Publications, 1319 Eighteenth St. NW, Washington, DC 20036-1802
Subscription telephone: 202 296-6267
Subscription fax: 202 296-5149

ADVERTISING INFORMATION

Advertising accepted: Yes

EDITORIAL DESCRIPTION

Scope: Publishes articles about popular film and television including commercial cinema and television, film and television theory and criticism. Editorial emphasis is on film and television as social and cultural forces in society.
Reviews books: Yes
Publishes notes: Yes
Languages accepted: English
Prints abstracts: No
Author-anonymous submission: No

SUBMISSION REQUIREMENTS

Restrictions on contributors: No multiple submissions are accepted; reviews are commissioned.
Author pays submission fee: No
Author pays page charges: No
Length of articles: 10-20 pp.
Length of book reviews: 300-600 words
Length of notes: No restrictions
Style: MLA (1982)
Number of copies required: 2
Copyright ownership: Heldref Publications
Rejected manuscripts: Returned; enclose SASE.
Time before publication decision: 1-2 mos.
Time between decision and publication: 3-4 mos.
Number of reviewers: 2-4
Articles submitted per year: 75-100
Articles published per year: 15-20
Book reviews published per year: 10-20
Notes submitted per year: 3-4
Notes published per year: 1-2

(1437)
*Journal of Pragmatics: An Interdisciplinary Monthly of Language Studies

Jacob L. Mey, Richard W. Janney, Claudia Caffi, & Hartmut Haberland, Editors
Odense Univ.
Dept. of Language & Communication
Campusvej 55
5230 Odense M, Denmark

Additional editorial address: Roskilde Univ. Center, P.O. Box 260, 4000 Roskilde, Denmark
Telephone: (45) 66 158600 ext. 3404
Fax: (45) 65 932483
E-mail: Hartmut@ruc.dk; mey@ils.nwu.edu
First published: 1977
Historical variations in title: Formerly *Journal of Pragmatics: An Interdisciplinary Bi-Monthly of Language Studies*
ISSN: 0378-2166
MLA acronym: JPrag

SUBSCRIPTION INFORMATION

Frequency of publication: 12 times/yr. in 2 volumes
Available in microform: No
Subscription price: 598 f/yr. institutions
Year to which price refers: 1992
Subscription address: Elsevier Science Publishers, Journal Dept., P.O. Box 211, 1000 AE Amsterdam, Netherlands
Additional subscription address: Elsevier Science Pub. Co., Inc., 52 Vanderbilt Ave., New York, NY 10017
Subscription telephone: (31) 20 5803642
Subscription fax: (31) 20 5803598

ADVERTISING INFORMATION

Advertising accepted: Yes

EDITORIAL DESCRIPTION

Scope: The journal addresses questions essential to understanding language as an instrument of natural and societal interaction. It includes articles on sociolinguistics, psycholinguistics, psychiatric and psychoanalytic discourse, applied linguistics, human-computer interaction, metapragmatics, etc.
Reviews books: Yes
Publishes notes: Yes
Languages accepted: English; French; German
Prints abstracts: Yes
Author-anonymous submission: No

SUBMISSION REQUIREMENTS

Restrictions on contributors: None
Author pays submission fee: No
Author pays page charges: No
Length of articles: 12,000-18,000 words
Length of book reviews: 3,000-4,000 words
Length of notes: 1,500-2,000 words
Style: Journal
Number of copies required: 4
Special requirements: Submit a 500-word abstract and a 200-word biographical note. Manuscripts must be double-spaced typescript. Style sheet is published in every issue.
Copyright ownership: Elsevier Science Publishers
Rejected manuscripts: One copy retained; others returned at author's request
Time before publication decision: 3 mos.
Time between decision and publication: 3 mos.
Number of reviewers: 3
Articles submitted per year: 200-250
Articles published per year: 40-50
Book reviews submitted per year: 40-50

(1438)
*The Journal of Pre-Raphaelite Studies

Julie Codell, Editor
Arizona State Univ.
Tempe, AZ 85287-1505

Telephone: 602 965-3468
Fax: 602 965-8338
E-mail: ICJFC@ASUACAD
First published: 1987
Sponsoring organization: PRB Foundation of Pre-Raphaelite & Aesthetic Studies
ISSN: 1060-149X
MLA acronym: JPRS

SUBSCRIPTION INFORMATION

Frequency of publication: 2 times/yr. (Spring, Fall)
Circulation: 320
Available in microform: No
Subscription price: $40.00/yr. institutions; $25.00/yr. individuals; add $5.00/yr. postage outside US
Year to which price refers: 1991
Subscription address: Judy Kennedy, English Dept., Kutztown Univ. of Pennsylvania, Kutztown, PA 19530
Subscription telephone: 215 683-4343

ADVERTISING INFORMATION

Advertising accepted: No

EDITORIAL DESCRIPTION

Scope: Publishes articles and pictorial material bearing on the Pre-Raphaelite movement, its antecedents and sequelae, as well as articles on aestheticism. Includes studies on art and literature.
Reviews books: Yes
Publishes notes: Yes
Languages accepted: English; French
Prints abstracts: No
Author-anonymous submission: Yes

SUBMISSION REQUIREMENTS

Restrictions on contributors: None
Author pays submission fee: No
Author pays page charges: No
Length of articles: 4,000-5,000 words
Length of book reviews: 800-1,000 words
Length of notes: 300-600 words
Style: MLA
Number of copies required: 2
Special requirements: Illustrations must be glossy black-and-white photographs.
Copyright ownership: Author
Rejected manuscripts: Returned; enclose return postage.
Time before publication decision: 3-6 mos.
Time between decision and publication: 6-24 mos.
Number of reviewers: 2
Articles submitted per year: 25-30
Articles published per year: 8-12
Book reviews submitted per year: 10-14
Book reviews published per year: 10-14
Notes submitted per year: 6-10
Notes published per year: 6-10

(1439)
*Journal of Psycholinguistic Research

R. W. Rieber, Editor
John Jay College of Criminal Justice
City Univ. of New York
Room 5113
444 W. 56th St.
New York, NY 10019

First published: 1971
Sponsoring organization: City Univ. of New York, John Jay College
ISSN: 0090-6905
MLA acronym: JPsyR

SUBSCRIPTION INFORMATION

Frequency of publication: 6 times/yr.
Available in microform: Yes
Subscription address: Plenum Publishing Corp., 233 Spring, New York, NY 10013

ADVERTISING INFORMATION

Advertising accepted: Yes, on an exchange basis

EDITORIAL DESCRIPTION

Scope: Welcomes original theoretical and experimental papers, critical surveys, and book reviews covering a broad range of approaches to the study of the communicative process, including: the social and anthropological bases of communication; development of speech and language; semantics (problems in linguistic meaning); biological foundations; psychopathological aspects; educational psycholinguistics.
Reviews books: Yes
Publishes notes: Yes
Languages accepted: English
Prints abstracts: Yes

SUBMISSION REQUIREMENTS

Author pays submission fee: No
Author pays page charges: No
Style: American Psychological Assn.
Number of copies required: 4
Special requirements: Include an abstract of 150-words maximum.
Copyright ownership: Plenum Publishing Corp.
Time before publication decision: 6 mos.
Number of reviewers: 2-3
Notes published per year: 6

(1440)
*Journal of Ritual Studies

Ronald L. Grimes, Fred W. Clothey, & Donald S. Sutton, Editors
Dept. of Religion & Culture
Wilfrid Laurier Univ.
Waterloo, Ontario N2L 3C5, Canada

Telephone: 519 884-1970
Fax: 519 884-8854
E-mail: Rgrimes2@mach1.wlu.ca
First published: 1987
Sponsoring organization: Dept. of Religion & Culture, Wilfrid Laurier Univ.; Dept. of Religious Studies, Univ. of Pittsburgh
ISSN: 0890-1112
MLA acronym: JRStud

SUBSCRIPTION INFORMATION

Frequency of publication: 2 times/yr. (Winter, Summer)
Circulation: 300
Available in microform: No
Subscription price: $45.00/yr. institutions US & Canada; $50.00/yr. institutions elsewhere; $25.00/yr. individuals US & Canada; $30.00/yr. individuals elsewhere
Year to which price refers: 1992
Subscription address: Journal of Ritual Studies, Dept. of Religious Studies, 2604 CL; Univ. of Pittsburgh, Pittsburgh, PA 15260
Subscription telephone: 412 624-2278

ADVERTISING INFORMATION

Advertising accepted: Yes

EDITORIAL DESCRIPTION

Scope: Solicits articles, reviews, correspondence, discussion, announcements and notes from scholars treating ritual in any of its various forms. Its interdisciplinary audience includes scholars from anthropology, religious studies, sociology, psychology, performance studies, history, literature, art, and music.
Reviews books: Yes
Publishes notes: No
Languages accepted: English
Prints abstracts: Yes
Author-anonymous submission: Yes

SUBMISSION REQUIREMENTS

Author pays submission fee: No
Author pays page charges: No
Length of articles: 8,000 words maximum
Length of book reviews: 500-800 words
Style: Chicago
Number of copies required: 3
Special requirements: Articles must be aimed at interdisciplinary audience. JRS Guidelines for Authors available on request (Pittsburgh address). Submit an abstract and a 6-line maximum author biography.
Copyright ownership: Journal
Rejected manuscripts: Returned at author's request
Time before publication decision: 8-10 weeks
Time between decision and publication: 18 mos.
Number of reviewers: 3
Articles submitted per year: 35-50
Articles published per year: 12
Book reviews submitted per year: 25
Book reviews published per year: 20

(1441)
*Journal of Semantics: An International Journal for the Interdisciplinary Study of the Semantics of Natural Language

Peter Bosch, Editor
IBM Germany Scientific Center
IWBS 7000-75
P.O. Box 800880
7000 Stuttgart, Germany

First published: 1982
ISSN: 0167-5133
MLA acronym: JoS

SUBSCRIPTION INFORMATION

Frequency of publication: 4 times/yr.
Available in microform: No
Subscription address: Oxford Journals, Oxford Univ. Press, Pinkhill House, Southfield Rd., Eynsham, Oxford OX8 1JJ, England
Subscription telephone: (44) 865 882283
Subscription fax: (44) 865 882890

ADVERTISING INFORMATION

Advertising accepted: Yes

EDITORIAL DESCRIPTION

Scope: Publishes articles and discussion on natural language semantics. It is explicitly interdisciplinary, in that it aims at an integration of philosophical, psychological, and linguistic semantics as well as semantic work done in artificial intelligence and anthropology.
Reviews books: Yes
Publishes notes: Yes

Book reviews published per year: 30-40
Notes submitted per year: 10-20
Notes published per year: 5-15

Languages accepted: English
Prints abstracts: Yes
Author-anonymous submission: No

SUBMISSION REQUIREMENTS

Restrictions on contributors: None
Author pays submission fee: No
Author pays page charges: No
Length of articles: 5,000-20,000 words
Length of book reviews: 5,000 words maximum
Length of notes: 5,000 words maximum
Number of copies required: 3
Special requirements: Submit one sided, double-spaced typescript on size A4 (8 1/4 in. x 11 3/4 in.) paper with a wide margin. Must be accompanied by a 200-word summary. Footnotes and bibliographical references must appear at the end of the typescript. Figures and diagrams must be supplied camera-ready.
Copyright ownership: N.I.S. Foundation
Rejected manuscripts: Not returned
Time before publication decision: 6-8 weeks
Time between decision and publication: 2-4 mos.
Number of reviewers: 2-3
Articles submitted per year: 100
Articles published per year: 15-20
Book reviews submitted per year: 10-15
Book reviews published per year: 10-15
Notes submitted per year: 2-5
Notes published per year: 2-5

(1442)
*Journal of Semitic Studies

Philip S. Alexander, George J. Brooke, John F. Healey, Mervyn E. J. Richardson, Philip C. Sadgrove, & G. Rex Smith, Editors
Dept. of Middle Eastern Studies
Univ. of Manchester
Manchester M13 9PL, England

Telephone: (44) 61 2753073
Fax: (44) 61 2753031
E-mail: MES@UK.AC.MANCHESTER
First published: 1956
Sponsoring organization: Univ. of Manchester
ISSN: 0024-4480
MLA acronym: JSS

SUBSCRIPTION INFORMATION

Frequency of publication: 2 times/yr. (Spring, Fall)
Circulation: 750
Available in microform: Yes
Subscription price: £46.00 ($86.00)/yr.; £28.00 ($51.00)/single issue
Year to which price refers: 1992
Subscription address: Journals Subscriptions Dept., Oxford Univ. Press, Pinkhill House, Southfield Rd., Eynsham, Oxford OX8 1JJ, England
Subscription telephone: (44) 865 882283
Subscription fax: (44) 865 882890

ADVERTISING INFORMATION

Advertising accepted: Yes
Advertising rates: Call (44) 737 373544 or fax (44) 737 362813

EDITORIAL DESCRIPTION

Scope: Focuses on Semitic studies, languages, the Middle East, Jewish studies, and Islamic studies.
Reviews books: Yes
Publishes notes: Yes
Languages accepted: English; French; German
Prints abstracts: No
Author-anonymous submission: Yes

SUBMISSION REQUIREMENTS

Restrictions on contributors: None
Author pays submission fee: No
Author pays page charges: No
Length of articles: No restrictions
Length of book reviews: 600 words
Length of notes: No restrictions
Style: Cambridge
Number of copies required: 2
Special requirements: Submit 2 copies of typescript plus a diskette, if possible.
Copyright ownership: Author & Oxford Univ. Press
Rejected manuscripts: Returned
Time before publication decision: 1 mo.
Time between decision and publication: 1-2 yrs.
Number of reviewers: 3
Articles submitted per year: 50
Articles published per year: 10
Book reviews submitted per year: 50
Book reviews published per year: 50
Notes submitted per year: 10
Notes published per year: 5

(1443)
*Journal of South Asian Literature

Carlo Coppola & Surjit S. Dulai, Editors
Asian Studies Center
Center for International Programs
Michigan State Univ.
East Lansing, MI 48824-1035

Telephone: 517 353-1680
Fax: 517 336-2659
First published: 1963
Sponsoring organization: Asian Studies Center, Michigan State Univ.
ISSN: 0025-0503
MLA acronym: JSoAL

SUBSCRIPTION INFORMATION

Frequency of publication: 2 times/yr. (Summer, Winter)
Circulation: 500
Available in microform: Yes

ADVERTISING INFORMATION

Advertising accepted: Yes

EDITORIAL DESCRIPTION

Scope: Publishes English translations of South Asian literatures and critical articles dealing with all aspects of South Asian literature.
Reviews books: Yes
Publishes notes: Yes
Languages accepted: English
Prints abstracts: No
Author-anonymous submission: No

SUBMISSION REQUIREMENTS

Restrictions on contributors: None
Author pays submission fee: No
Author pays page charges: No
Length of articles: 1,500-3,000 words
Length of book reviews: 800-2,000 words
Length of notes: 300-800 words
Style: MLA; Chicago
Number of copies required: 2
Special requirements: Request from editor
Copyright ownership: Journal
Rejected manuscripts: Not returned
Time before publication decision: 6-12 mos.
Time between decision and publication: 1-2 yrs.
Number of reviewers: 2
Articles submitted per year: 75
Articles published per year: 10-12
Book reviews submitted per year: 50
Book reviews published per year: 20

(1444)
*Journal of Speech and Hearing Research

John H. Saxman, Holly K. Craig, & Arlene E. Carney, Editors
Box 146
Teachers College
Columbia Univ.
New York, NY 10027

Telephone: 212 678-3892
First published: 1958
Sponsoring organization: American Speech-Language-Hearing Assn.
ISSN: 0022-4685
MLA acronym: JSHR

SUBSCRIPTION INFORMATION

Frequency of publication: 6 times/yr. (Feb., Apr., June, Aug., Oct., Dec.)
Circulation: 34,000
Available in microform: Yes
Subscription price: $114.00/yr. institutions US; $126.00/yr. institutions elsewhere; $60.00/yr. individuals US; $72.00/yr. individuals elsewhere
Year to which price refers: 1992
Subscription address: American Speech-Language-Hearing Assn., 10801 Rockville Pike, Rockville, MD 20852
Subscription telephone: 301 897-5700 ext. 294
Subscription fax: 301 571-0457 Attn.: Subscription sales

ADVERTISING INFORMATION

Advertising accepted: Yes

EDITORIAL DESCRIPTION

Scope: Publishes articles concerning processes and disorders of speech, language, and hearing.
Reviews books: No
Publishes notes: Yes
Languages accepted: English
Prints abstracts: Yes
Author-anonymous submission: Yes, at author's request

SUBMISSION REQUIREMENTS

Author pays submission fee: No
Author pays page charges: Yes, but not mandatory
Cost of page charges: $65.00/page
Style: American Psychological Assn.
Number of copies required: 5
Special requirements: Include an abstract of 200 words maximum.
Copyright ownership: American Speech-Language-Hearing Assn.
Rejected manuscripts: Not returned
Time before publication decision: 7 mos.
Time between decision and publication: 6-9 mos.
Number of reviewers: 4-5
Articles submitted per year: 300
Articles published per year: 150
Notes submitted per year: 10
Notes published per year: 4

(1445)
*Journal of Tamil Studies

International Inst. of Tamil Studies
C.I.T. Campus, T.T.T.I. P.O.
Taramani, Madras-600 113,
Tamil Nadu, India

Telephone: 2350992
First published: 1972
Sponsoring organization: International Inst. of Tamil Studies
ISSN: 0022-4855
MLA acronym: JTamS

SUBSCRIPTION INFORMATION

Frequency of publication: 2 times/yr.
Circulation: 1,000
Available in microform: No

ADVERTISING INFORMATION

Advertising accepted: No

EDITORIAL DESCRIPTION

Scope: Covers the following fields in Tamilology: comparative literature, applied criticism, language, linguistics, history, culture, folklore, translations, textual criticism.
Reviews books: Yes
Publishes notes: No
Languages accepted: English; Tamil
Prints abstracts: No

SUBMISSION REQUIREMENTS

Restrictions on contributors: None
Author pays submission fee: No
Author pays page charges: No
Length of articles: 2,000-3,500 words
Length of book reviews: 750-1,500 words
Style: MLA
Number of copies required: 3
Special requirements: Submit typescript.
Copyright ownership: International Inst. of Tamil Studies
Rejected manuscripts: Not returned
Time before publication decision: 2 mos.
Time between decision and publication: 3 mos.
Number of reviewers: 4
Articles submitted per year: 25
Articles published per year: 10
Book reviews submitted per year: 12
Book reviews published per year: 4

(1446)
*Journal of the Acoustical Society of America

Daniel W. Martin, Editor
7349 Clough Pike
Cincinnati, OH 45244

Telephone: 513 231-5278
First published: 1929
Sponsoring organization: Acoustical Soc. of America
ISSN: 0001-4966
MLA acronym: JAS

SUBSCRIPTION INFORMATION

Frequency of publication: 12 times/yr. (plus 3 supplements)
Circulation: 8,600
Available in microform: Yes
Subscription address: American Inst. of Physics, 500 Sunnyside Blvd., Woodbury, NY 11797-2999
Subscription telephone: 516 576-2360

ADVERTISING INFORMATION

Advertising accepted: No, except for meeting programs.

EDITORIAL DESCRIPTION

Scope: Publishes results of acoustical research. Includes studies on speech.
Reviews books: Yes
Languages accepted: English
Prints abstracts: Yes
Author-anonymous submission: Yes

SUBMISSION REQUIREMENTS

Restrictions on contributors: None
Author pays submission fee: No
Author pays page charges: Page charges paid by author's institution.
Cost of page charges: $65.00/page
Length of articles: 7-8 pp.
Length of book reviews: 600 words
Style: American Inst. of Physics
Number of copies required: 3
Special requirements: Consult "Information for Contributors" in January & July issues prior to submission.
Copyright ownership: Assigned by author to the Acoustical Soc. of America
Rejected manuscripts: One copy returned
Time before publication decision: 6 mos.
Time between decision and publication: 2 mos.
Number of reviewers: 2-3
Articles submitted per year: 800
Articles published per year: 550
Book reviews submitted per year: 30
Book reviews published per year: 30

(1447)
Journal of the American Academy of Religion

William Scott Green, Editor
Dept. of Religion & Classics
Univ. of Rochester
Rochester, NY 14627

First published: 1933
Sponsoring organization: American Academy of Religion
ISSN: 0002-7189
MLA acronym: JAAR

SUBSCRIPTION INFORMATION

Frequency of publication: 4 times/yr. (Mar., June, Sept., Dec.)
Circulation: 6,000
Available in microform: Yes
Subscription address: Scholars Press, P.O. Box 15399, Atlanta, GA 30333

ADVERTISING INFORMATION

Advertising accepted: Yes

EDITORIAL DESCRIPTION

Scope: Covers all areas of the academic study of religion(s), including, but not limited to, the following: art, literature and religion; Asian religion; Biblical literature; ethics, history of Christianity; history of Judaism; religion and the social sciences; philosophy of religion; theory of religion.
Reviews books: Yes
Publishes notes: Yes
Languages accepted: English
Prints abstracts: No

SUBMISSION REQUIREMENTS

Restrictions on contributors: Book reviews are solicited.
Author pays submission fee: No
Author pays page charges: No
Length of articles: 7,500 words
Length of book reviews: 1,250 words
Length of notes: 250 words
Style: Journal
Number of copies required: 4
Copyright ownership: American Academy of Religion
Rejected manuscripts: Original returned; enclose return postage.
Time before publication decision: 2-3 mos.
Time between decision and publication: 9-12 mos.
Number of reviewers: 2-4
Articles submitted per year: 175
Articles published per year: 25
Book reviews published per year: 350
Notes submitted per year: 9-10
Notes published per year: 160

(1448)
*Journal of the American Oriental Society

Edwin Gerow, Editor
Reed College
Portland, OR 97202

First published: 1851
Sponsoring organization: American Oriental Soc.
ISSN: 0003-0279
MLA acronym: JAOS

SUBSCRIPTION INFORMATION

Frequency of publication: 4 times/yr. (Mar., June, Sept., Dec.)
Circulation: 2,150
Available in microform: Yes
Subscription address: American Oriental Soc., Harlan Hatcher Graduate Library, Univ. of Michigan, Ann Arbor, MI 48109

ADVERTISING INFORMATION

Advertising accepted: Yes

EDITORIAL DESCRIPTION

Scope: Promotes research in Oriental languages, literatures, history, and art.
Reviews books: Yes
Publishes notes: No
Languages accepted: English; French; German; Italian
Prints abstracts: Yes
Author-anonymous submission: Yes

SUBMISSION REQUIREMENTS

Restrictions on contributors: Book reviews are solicited.
Author pays submission fee: No
Author pays page charges: No
Length of articles: 2,000-6,000 words
Length of book reviews: 600-800 words
Style: Chicago
Number of copies required: 3
Special requirements: Request style sheet and submission guidelines from editor.
Copyright ownership: American Oriental Soc.
Rejected manuscripts: Returned
Time before publication decision: 1-6 mos.
Time between decision and publication: 18-24 mos.
Number of reviewers: 2
Articles submitted per year: 60
Articles published per year: 30
Book reviews published per year: 180-200

(1449)
*Journal of the American Romanian Academy of Arts and Sciences

Ion Manea, Editor
3328 Monte Vista Ave.
Davis, CA 95616

Telephone: 916 758-7720
Fax: 916 752-8630
First published: 1976
Sponsoring organization: American Romanian Academy of Arts & Sciences
ISSN: 0896-1018
MLA acronym: JARAAS

SUBSCRIPTION INFORMATION

Frequency of publication: Annual
Circulation: 500
Available in microform: No
Subscription price: $20.00/yr.
Year to which price refers: 1992
Subscription address: Secretary of ARA, 4310 Finley Ave., Los Angeles, CA 90027

ADVERTISING INFORMATION

Advertising accepted: No

EDITORIAL DESCRIPTION

Scope: Publishes research in the humanities and social sciences conducted by scholars of Romanian culture. It fosters Romanian culture and acquaints the Western World with Romanian spiritual values.
Reviews books: Yes
Publishes notes: Yes
Languages accepted: English; French; Romanian
Prints abstracts: No
Author-anonymous submission: No

SUBMISSION REQUIREMENTS

Restrictions on contributors: The majority of articles in *ARA Journal* represent contributions of members and nonmembers of the Academy made at the Congresses of this forum of Romanian culture in exile.
Author pays submission fee: No
Author pays page charges: No
Length of articles: 4,000 words
Length of book reviews: 960 words
Length of notes: 500-1,000 words
Style: MLA
Number of copies required: 2
Special requirements: Submit double-spaced typescript. Title, name, and affiliation of author should precede text. References should be consecutively numbered throughout manuscript and typewritten, double-spaced on separate sheet(s) at the end of the article.
Copyright ownership: American Romanian Academy of Arts & Sciences
Rejected manuscripts: Returned
Time before publication decision: 9-12 mos.
Time between decision and publication: 5 mos.
Number of reviewers: 2
Articles submitted per year: 30-40
Articles published per year: 25
Book reviews submitted per year: 10
Book reviews published per year: 5 maximum
Notes submitted per year: 10-15
Notes published per year: 10

(1450)
*Journal of the American Studies Association of Texas

J. R. LeMaster & Lois E. Myers, Editors
American Studies
P.O. Box 97240
Baylor Univ.
Waco, TX 76798-7240

Additional editorial address: Lois E. Myers, Managing Editor, Inst. for Oral History, Baylor Univ., P.O. Box 97271, Waco, TX 76798-7271
Telephone: 817 755-2710
First published: 1970
Sponsoring organization: American Studies Assn. of Texas
ISSN: 0587-5064
MLA acronym: JASAT

SUBSCRIPTION INFORMATION

Frequency of publication: Annual (Nov.)
Circulation: 300
Available in microform: No
Subscription price: $25.00/yr. institutions (includes membership); $15.00/yr. individuals (includes membership); $7.50/yr. students (includes membership)
Year to which price refers: 1992
Subscription address: Margaret E. Galloway, Associate Director of Libraries, Univ. of North Texas, Box 5188, North Texas Station, Denton, TX 76203
Subscription telephone: 817 565-3024

ADVERTISING INFORMATION

Advertising accepted: Yes
Advertising rates: $50.00/half page; $75.00/full page; $100.00/inside cover; $130.00/back cover

EDITORIAL DESCRIPTION

Scope: Focuses interdisciplinary attention on thematic, methodological, and pedagogical issues in American studies.
Reviews books: Yes
Publishes notes: No
Languages accepted: English
Prints abstracts: No
Author-anonymous submission: Yes

SUBMISSION REQUIREMENTS

Restrictions on contributors: Contributors must be members of the American Studies Association or the American Studies Association of Texas. Book reviews are solicited.
Author pays submission fee: No
Author pays page charges: No
Length of articles: 2,500-3,500 words
Length of book reviews: 400 words
Style: Chicago
Number of copies required: 3
Special requirements: Submit double-spaced typescript and 3.5 in. Macintosh diskette using Microsoft Word.
Copyright ownership: Baylor Univ.
Rejected manuscripts: Returned; enclose SASE.
Time before publication decision: 2-3 mos.
Time between decision and publication: 5-6 mos.
Number of reviewers: 3-4
Articles submitted per year: 25-30
Articles published per year: 10
Book reviews submitted per year: 30
Book reviews published per year: 20

(1451)
*Journal of the Appalachian Studies Association

Pat Arnow, Managing Editor
Box 70556
East Tennessee State Univ.
Johnson City, TN 37614-0556

Telephone: 615 929-5348
Fax: 615 929-5770
First published: 1983
Sponsoring organization: Appalachian Studies Assn.
ISSN: 1048-6143
MLA acronym: JASA

SUBSCRIPTION INFORMATION

Frequency of publication: Annual
Circulation: 400
Available in microform: No
Subscription price: $13.95/yr.
Year to which price refers: 1992

ADVERTISING INFORMATION

Advertising accepted: No

EDITORIAL DESCRIPTION

Scope: Publishes articles on Appalachian studies including folklore, language and literature of the region, selected from papers presented at the annual Appalachian Studies Conference.
Reviews books: No
Publishes notes: No
Languages accepted: English
Prints abstracts: No
Author-anonymous submission: No

SUBMISSION REQUIREMENTS

Restrictions on contributors: Contributors must have presented the paper at the annual Appalachian Studies Conference.
Author pays submission fee: No
Author pays page charges: No
Length of articles: 2,500 words
Style: Chicago
Number of copies required: 1
Special requirements: Submit on diskette with hard copy, or submit typescript in courier or elite type.
Copyright ownership: Center for Appalachian Studies & Services
Rejected manuscripts: Returned; enclose SASE.
Time before publication decision: 3 mos.
Time between decision and publication: 8 mos.
Number of reviewers: 1
Articles submitted per year: 75
Articles published per year: 15

(1452)
*Journal of the Asiatic Society of Bombay

K. P. Jog, Kamala Ganesh, & Shanta Tumku, Editors
Asiatic Soc. of Bombay
Town Hall
Bombay 1, India

Telephone: (91) 22 2860956
First published: 1841
Sponsoring organization: Asiatic Soc. of Bombay
ISSN: 0571-3162
MLA acronym: JASB

SUBSCRIPTION INFORMATION

Frequency of publication: Annual
Circulation: 1,000
Available in microform: No
Subscription address: European agent: Arthur Probsthain, 41 Great Russell St., London WC1, England

ADVERTISING INFORMATION

Advertising accepted: No

EDITORIAL DESCRIPTION

Scope: Focuses on Indology and other allied subjects.
Reviews books: Yes
Publishes notes: No
Languages accepted: English; Sanskrit
Prints abstracts: No
Author-anonymous submission: No

SUBMISSION REQUIREMENTS

Restrictions on contributors: None
Author pays submission fee: No
Author pays page charges: No
Length of articles: No restrictions
Length of book reviews: No restrictions
Style: None
Number of copies required: 2
Special requirements: Submit original typescript.
Copyright ownership: Asiatic Soc. of Bombay
Rejected manuscripts: Returned
Number of reviewers: 1
Articles submitted per year: 20
Articles published per year: 20
Book reviews submitted per year: 10
Book reviews published per year: 5

(1453)
*Journal of the Association of Teachers of Japanese

David O. Mills, Carol Hochstedler, Patricia Wetzel, & Marian Ury, Editors
Dept. of East Asian Languages & Literatures
Univ. of Pittsburgh
Pittsburgh, PA 15260

Telephone: 412 624-5568
Fax: 412 624-4419
E-mail: DOM@VMS.CIS.PITT.EDU
First published: 1963
Sponsoring organization: Assn. of Teachers of Japanese
ISSN: 0004-5810
MLA acronym: JATJ

SUBSCRIPTION INFORMATION

Frequency of publication: 2 times/yr.
Circulation: 1,300
Available in microform: No
Subscription price: $25.00/yr.
Year to which price refers: 1992
Subscription address: Japanese Program, Hillcrest 9, Middlebury College, Middlebury, VT 05753

ADVERTISING INFORMATION

Advertising accepted: Yes
Advertising rates: $100.00/half page; $200.00/full page; $300.00/back cover

EDITORIAL DESCRIPTION

Scope: Serves as a medium for publishing research findings, essays, reviews, and other items of interest to teachers and students of Japanese language, literature, and linguistics.
Reviews books: Yes
Publishes notes: No
Languages accepted: English
Prints abstracts: No

SUBMISSION REQUIREMENTS

Restrictions on contributors: Contributors must be members of the Assn. of Teachers of Japanese. Unsolicited book reviews are not accepted.
Author pays submission fee: No
Author pays page charges: No
Length of articles: No restrictions
Length of book reviews: No restrictions
Style: Journal; Chicago
Number of copies required: 3
Copyright ownership: Journal; reverts to author after publication.
Rejected manuscripts: Returned; enclose return postage
Time before publication decision: 6-12 mos.
Time between decision and publication: 3 mos.
Number of reviewers: 3
Articles submitted per year: 15-20
Articles published per year: 5-10
Book reviews submitted per year: 15-20
Book reviews published per year: 20

(1454)
*Journal of the Chinese Language Teachers Association

James H-Y. Tai, Editor
Dept. of East Asian Languages & Literatures
Ohio State Univ.
204 Cunz Hall
1841 Millikin Rd.
Columbus, OH 43210-1229

First published: 1966
Sponsoring organization: Ohio State Univ.; Chinese Language Teachers' Assn.
ISSN: 0009-4595
MLA acronym: JCLTA

SUBSCRIPTION INFORMATION

Frequency of publication: 3 times/yr.
Circulation: 900
Available in microform: Yes
Subscription address: Chinese Language Teachers Assn., c/o Kalamazoo College, 1200 Academy St., Kalamazoo, MI 49006-3295

ADVERTISING INFORMATION

Advertising accepted: No

EDITORIAL DESCRIPTION

Scope: Seeks contributions concerned with analysis of Chinese language and literature and their pedagogical implications.
Reviews books: Yes
Languages accepted: Chinese languages; English
Prints abstracts: No

SUBMISSION REQUIREMENTS

Restrictions on contributors: None
Author pays submission fee: No
Author pays page charges: No
Length of articles: 15 pp.
Length of book reviews: 5 pp.
Style: Journal
Number of copies required: 3
Special requirements: Chinese must be according to *Pinyin* system.
Copyright ownership: Ohio State Univ. & Chinese Language Teachers' Assn.
Rejected manuscripts: Returned
Time before publication decision: 4 mos.
Time between decision and publication: 1 yr.
Number of reviewers: 1-2
Articles submitted per year: 40
Articles published per year: 15
Book reviews submitted per year: 10
Book reviews published per year: 6-8

(1455)
*Journal of the Cork Historical and Archaeological Society

Diarmuid Ó Murchadha, Editor
Dromainn
Crosshaven
Co. Cork, Ireland

Telephone: (353) 21 831322
First published: 1892
Sponsoring organization: Cork Historical & Archaeological Soc.
ISSN: 0010-8731
MLA acronym: JCHAS

SUBSCRIPTION INFORMATION

Frequency of publication: Annual
Circulation: 600
Available in microform: No
Subscription price: IR£10.00/yr. EEC; IR£15.00 ($22.00)/yr. elsewhere
Year to which price refers: 1992
Subscription address: Anne Coleman,, 19 Briars Court, Shanakiel, Cork, Ireland
Subscription telephone: (353) 1 542824

ADVERTISING INFORMATION

Advertising accepted: No

EDITORIAL DESCRIPTION

Scope: Publishes research bearing on the history and archaeology of Cork, Munster (southern Irish province), and Ireland.
Reviews books: Yes
Publishes notes: Yes
Languages accepted: English; Irish Gaelic
Prints abstracts: No
Author-anonymous submission: No

SUBMISSION REQUIREMENTS

Restrictions on contributors: None
Author pays submission fee: No
Author pays page charges: No
Length of articles: 5,000-10,000 words
Length of book reviews: 500-1,000 words
Length of notes: 250-500 words
Style: None
Number of copies required: 1
Special requirements: Submit double-spaced typescript.
Copyright ownership: Author & Cork Historical and Archaeological Soc.
Rejected manuscripts: Returned
Time before publication decision: 3 mos.
Time between decision and publication: 1 yr.
Number of reviewers: 2
Articles submitted per year: 15
Articles published per year: 10
Book reviews submitted per year: 12
Book reviews published per year: 12
Notes submitted per year: 2
Notes published per year: 2

(1456)
Journal of the Department of English

Arun Kumar Dasgupta, Editor
Dept. of English, Journal Section
Asutosh Building
Calcutta Univ.
Calcutta-700073, India

MLA acronym: JDECU

(1457)
*Journal of the Eighteen Nineties Society

G. Krishnamurti, Editor
17 Merton Hall Rd.
Wimbledon
London SW19 3PP, England

First published: 1965
Sponsoring organization: Eighteen Nineties Soc.
ISSN: 0144-008X
MLA acronym: JENS

SUBSCRIPTION INFORMATION

Frequency of publication: Annual
Circulation: 750
Available in microform: No
Subscription price: £10.00 ($25.00)/yr.
Year to which price refers: 1992-93
Subscription address: 97-D Brixton Rd., London SW9 6EE, England

ADVERTISING INFORMATION

Advertising accepted: Yes
Advertising rates: £75.00/half page; £150.00/full page

EDITORIAL DESCRIPTION

Scope: Publishes articles on the 1890's, embracing the entire artistic and literary scene of this decade of Impressionism, Realism, Naturalism, Symbolism and of high achievement in all the arts, including theater and book production. Includes critical, biographical and bibliographical articles.
Reviews books: Yes
Publishes notes: Yes
Languages accepted: English
Prints abstracts: No
Author-anonymous submission: No

SUBMISSION REQUIREMENTS

Restrictions on contributors: None
Author pays submission fee: No
Author pays page charges: No

Length of articles: 3,000 words
Length of book reviews: 750-1,000 words
Length of notes: 200 words
Style: MLA; Chicago
Number of copies required: 2
Special requirements: Manuscripts must be double-spaced and typed on one side of the page.
Copyright ownership: Journal & author
Rejected manuscripts: Returned at author's request
Time before publication decision: 2 yrs.
Time between decision and publication: 1 yr.
Number of reviewers: 2
Articles submitted per year: 12
Articles published per year: 6
Book reviews submitted per year: 15
Book reviews published per year: 4
Notes submitted per year: 15
Notes published per year: 8

(1458)
*Journal of the English Institute

Minoru Suda, Editor
Tohoku Gakuin Univ.
English Inst.
Eigo-Eibungaku Kenkyujo
1-3-1 Tsuchitoi
Aoba-ku, Sendai 980, Japan

Telephone: (81) 22 2646401
Fax: (81) 22 2643030
First published: 1969
Sponsoring organization: Tohoku Gakuin Univ., English Inst.
ISSN: 0385-8855
MLA acronym: JEI

SUBSCRIPTION INFORMATION

Frequency of publication: Annual
Circulation: 500
Available in microform: No

ADVERTISING INFORMATION

Advertising accepted: No

EDITORIAL DESCRIPTION

Scope: Discusses British and American literature, English language, and English education.
Reviews books: No
Publishes notes: No
Languages accepted: Japanese; English
Prints abstracts: Yes
Author-anonymous submission: No

SUBMISSION REQUIREMENTS

Restrictions on contributors: Contributors must be members of the English Inst. of Tohoku Gakuin Univ.
Author pays submission fee: No
Author pays page charges: No
Length of articles: 40 pp. in Japanese; 20 pp. in English
Style: MLA
Number of copies required: 1
Copyright ownership: Author
Rejected manuscripts: Returned
Time before publication decision: 1 mo.
Time between decision and publication: 2-3 mos.
Number of reviewers: 8-10
Articles submitted per year: 4-5
Articles published per year: 4-5

(1459)
*Journal of the English Language and Literature

Seong-Jong Kim, Doo-Bon Pae, Jo-Yong Jeon, Hong-Shil Jeon, Joo-Hyun Park, & Kyu-Tae Chai, Editors
Chungbuk Branch
English Language & Literature Assn. of Korea
Dept. of English Language & Literature
Chongju Univ.
Chongju, Choongbuk 360-764, Korea

Telephone: (82) 431 518301
Fax: (82) 431 518110
First published: 1968
Sponsoring organization: Chungbuk Branch, English Language & Literature Assn. of Korea (ELLAK)
MLA acronym: JELL-CB

SUBSCRIPTION INFORMATION

Frequency of publication: Annual
Available in microform: No

ADVERTISING INFORMATION

Advertising accepted: No

EDITORIAL DESCRIPTION

Scope: Publishes articles on English literature and linguistics. Topics covered include English linguistics including syntax, phonology, and semantics; English literature including poetry, novel, and drama; and teaching English as a foreign language.
Reviews books: Yes
Publishes notes: Yes
Languages accepted: Korean; English
Prints abstracts: Yes
Author-anonymous submission: No

SUBMISSION REQUIREMENTS

Restrictions on contributors: Contributors are primarily members of the English Language & Literature Assn. of Korea but foreign contributors are welcome.
Author pays submission fee: No
Author pays page charges: No
Length of articles: 30 pp.
Length of book reviews: 15 pp.
Length of notes: 5 pp.
Style: MLA
Number of copies required: 1
Copyright ownership: Author
Rejected manuscripts: Returned
Time before publication decision: 2 mos.
Time between decision and publication: 5 mos.
Number of reviewers: 3
Articles submitted per year: 15-20
Articles published per year: 12-15

(1460)
*Journal of the Ganganatha Jha Kendriya Sanskrit Vidyapeetha

Gaya C. Tripathi & Maya Malaviya, Editors
Ganganatha Jha Kendriya Sanskrit Vidyapeetha
Azad Park
Allahabad-211002 U.P., India

Additional editorial address: Gaya C. Tripathi, 178 Allenganj, Allahabad 211002 U.P., India
Telephone: (91) 532 600957
First published: 1943
Sponsoring organization: Rashtriya Sanskrit Samsthan
ISSN: 0016-4461
MLA acronym: JGJRI

SUBSCRIPTION INFORMATION

Frequency of publication: 4 times/yr. (Mar., June, Sept., Dec.)
Circulation: 1,000
Available in microform: No
Subscription price: 60 Re/yr. India; $15.00/yr. elsewhere
Year to which price refers: 1992
Subscription address: Principal, at the above address

ADVERTISING INFORMATION

Advertising accepted: No

EDITORIAL DESCRIPTION

Scope: Publishes articles on Indology, including Indian history, and Sanskrit and Indian religion and philosophy.
Reviews books: Yes
Publishes notes: Yes
Languages accepted: English; French; German; Hindi; Sanskrit
Prints abstracts: Yes
Author-anonymous submission: No

SUBMISSION REQUIREMENTS

Restrictions on contributors: None
Author pays submission fee: No
Author pays page charges: No
Length of articles: 5-30 pp.
Length of book reviews: 1-4 pp.
Length of notes: 1-5 pp.
Style: None
Number of copies required: 2
Special requirements: Use international mode of transcription of Sanskrit. Submit original typescript and 1 copy.
Copyright ownership: Author
Rejected manuscripts: Returned at author's request
Time before publication decision: 2 mos.
Time between decision and publication: 6-12 mos.
Number of reviewers: 2
Articles submitted per year: 100-150
Articles published per year: 50-60
Book reviews submitted per year: 30-40
Book reviews published per year: 15-25
Notes submitted per year: 15-30
Notes published per year: 12-20

(1461)
*Journal of the Gypsy Lore Society

Sheila Salo, Editor
5607 Greenleaf Rd.
Cheverly, MD 20785

Telephone: 301 341-1261
First published: 1888
Sponsoring organization: Gypsy Lore Soc.
ISSN: 0017-6087
MLA acronym: JGLS

SUBSCRIPTION INFORMATION

Frequency of publication: 2 times/yr. (Feb., Aug.)
Circulation: 300
Available in microform: Yes, for 1888-1973
Subscription price: $35.00/yr. institutions; $30.00/yr. individuals; add $5.00/yr. postage outside US
Year to which price refers: 1992

ADVERTISING INFORMATION

Advertising accepted: Yes
Advertising rates: $25.00/half page; $50.00/full page

EDITORIAL DESCRIPTION

Scope: Publishes articles on the cultures of groups traditionally known as Gypsies, as well as traveler and peripatetic groups. Articles in anthropology, art, folklore and folklife, history, linguistics, literature, music, political science, and sociology are included.
Reviews books: Yes

Publishes notes: Yes
Languages accepted: English
Prints abstracts: Yes
Author-anonymous submission: Yes

SUBMISSION REQUIREMENTS

Restrictions on contributors: Book reviews are commissioned.
Author pays submission fee: No
Author pays page charges: No
Length of articles: 9,000-10,000 words
Length of book reviews: 1,000-2,000 words
Length of notes: 500 words
Style: Modified *American Anthropologist*
Number of copies required: 3
Copyright ownership: Gypsy Lore Soc.
Rejected manuscripts: Returned
Time before publication decision: 6 mos.
Time between decision and publication: 6 mos.
Number of reviewers: 2
Articles submitted per year: 10-15
Articles published per year: 6-8
Book reviews published per year: 6-8

(1462)
*Journal of the Hellenic Diaspora

Kostas Myrsiades & Alexander Kitroeff, Editors
Main 544
West Chester Univ.
West Chester, PA 19383

Telephone: 215 436-2901
Fax: 215 436-3150
E-mail: KMYRSIAD@WCU (Bitnet)
First published: 1974
ISSN: 0364-2976
MLA acronym: JHD

SUBSCRIPTION INFORMATION

Frequency of publication: 2 times/yr. (Mar., Sept.)
Circulation: 700
Available in microform: No
Subscription price: $30.00/yr. institutions US; $35.00/yr. institutions elsewhere; $20.00/yr. individuals US; $25.00/yr. individuals elsewhere
Year to which price refers: 1991

ADVERTISING INFORMATION

Advertising accepted: Yes
Advertising rates: Request from Pella Publishing Co., 337 W. 36th St., New York, NY 10018

EDITORIAL DESCRIPTION

Scope: Welcomes widely ranging approaches that embrace a variety of methodologies and perspectives. Publishes critical, theoretical, and historical studies, review articles, and translations keyed to the Greek experience of the nineteenth and twentieth centuries.
Reviews books: Yes
Publishes notes: Yes
Languages accepted: English; Greek
Prints abstracts: No
Author-anonymous submission: Yes

SUBMISSION REQUIREMENTS

Restrictions on contributors: None
Author pays submission fee: No
Author pays page charges: No
Length of articles: 5,000-7,500 words
Length of book reviews: 1,000-2,000 words
Length of notes: 1,250-3,750 words
Style: Chicago
Number of copies required: 3
Special requirements: Submit double-spaced typescript; send original text with translation.
Copyright ownership: Journal
Rejected manuscripts: Returned; enclose SASE.
Time before publication decision: 6-12 mos.
Time between decision and publication: 6 mos.

Number of reviewers: 4
Articles submitted per year: 100
Articles published per year: 12-15
Book reviews submitted per year: 50
Book reviews published per year: 15-20
Notes submitted per year: 30
Notes published per year: 5-10

(1463)
*Journal of the History of Ideas

Donald R. Kelley, Editor
Rutgers Univ.
88 College Ave.
New Brunswick, NJ 08903

Telephone: 908 932-1227
Fax: 908 932-8708
E-mail: Kelley@zodiac.rutgers.edu
First published: 1940
Sponsoring organization: Rutgers Univ.; American Council of Learned Societies
ISSN: 0022-5037
MLA acronym: JHI

SUBSCRIPTION INFORMATION

Frequency of publication: 4 times/yr. (Jan., Apr., July, Oct.)
Circulation: 3,100
Available in microform: Yes
Subscription price: $40.00/yr. institutions US; $20.00/yr. individuals US; add $4.80/yr. postage Canada & Mexico, $11.00/yr. elsewhere
Year to which price refers: 1993
Subscription address: Johns Hopkins Univ. Press, Journals Publishing Division, 2715 North Charles St., Baltimore, MD 21218-4319
Subscription telephone: 800 537-5487
Subscription fax: 410 516-6998

ADVERTISING INFORMATION

Advertising accepted: Yes

EDITORIAL DESCRIPTION

Scope: Fosters studies which emphasize the interrelations of several fields of historical study: the histories of philosophy, literature, the arts, the natural and social sciences, religion, and political and social movements.
Reviews books: Yes
Publishes notes: Yes
Languages accepted: English
Prints abstracts: No
Author-anonymous submission: Yes

SUBMISSION REQUIREMENTS

Restrictions on contributors: None
Author pays submission fee: No
Author pays page charges: No
Length of articles: 9,000 words maximum, including footnotes
Length of book reviews: 3,600-4,500 words
Length of notes: 5,000-6,000 words maximum
Style: Chicago
Number of copies required: 3
Special requirements: Submit double-spaced typescript with double-spaced endnotes. Quotations may be in the original language.
Copyright ownership: Journal & author
Rejected manuscripts: Returned; enclose return postage.
Time before publication decision: 4 mos.
Time between decision and publication: 1 yr.
Number of reviewers: 2
Articles submitted per year: 250
Articles published per year: 35-40
Book reviews submitted per year: 5-10
Book reviews published per year: 4
Notes submitted per year: 50-60
Notes published per year: 5-10

(1464)
*Journal of the International Phonetic Association

Ian Maddieson, Editor
Phonetics Lab.
Dept. of Linguistics
Univ. of California, Los Angeles
Los Angeles, CA 90024-1543

Telephone: 310 206-9877
E-mail: IDU0IAN@UCLAMVS.BITNET
First published: 1971
Sponsoring organization: International Phonetic Assn.
ISSN: 0025-1003
MLA acronym: IPAJ

SUBSCRIPTION INFORMATION

Frequency of publication: 2 times/yr.
Circulation: 1,000
Available in microform: Yes
Subscription price: £13.00 ($25.00)/yr.
Year to which price refers: 1992
Subscription address: Peter Roach, Secretary/Treasurer, International Phonetic Assn., Dept. of Psychology, Univ. of Leeds, Leeds LS2 9JT, England

ADVERTISING INFORMATION

Advertising accepted: Yes

EDITORIAL DESCRIPTION

Scope: Publishes articles, specimens, correspondence, and reviews on all aspects of phonetics and phonology.
Reviews books: Yes
Publishes notes: Yes
Languages accepted: English; French; German
Prints abstracts: No
Author-anonymous submission: No

SUBMISSION REQUIREMENTS

Restrictions on contributors: None
Author pays submission fee: No
Author pays page charges: No
Length of articles: 1,000-10,000 words
Length of book reviews: 500-2,000 words
Length of notes: 500 words
Style: Use International Phonetic Assn.'s alphabet for phonetic transcriptions.
Number of copies required: 1
Special requirements: See "Notes for Contributors" on journal cover.
Copyright ownership: Author
Rejected manuscripts: Returned
Time before publication decision: 3 mos.
Time between decision and publication: 1 yr.
Number of reviewers: 2-3
Articles submitted per year: 25
Articles published per year: 8

(1465)
*Journal of the Kafka Society of America

Maria Luise Caputo-Mayr & Julius M. Herz, Editors
German Dept., AB 335
Temple Univ. (022-35)
Philadelphia, PA 19122

Telephone: 215 787-8282
Fax: 215 787-3731
First published: 1977
Sponsoring organization: Kafka Soc. of America
ISSN: 0894-6388
MLA acronym: JKSA

SUBSCRIPTION INFORMATION

Frequency of publication: 2 times/yr.
Circulation: 300-500

Available in microform: No

ADVERTISING INFORMATION

Advertising accepted: Yes

EDITORIAL DESCRIPTION

Scope: Publishes information on current international research on Franz Kafka, events in the field, and bibliography.
Reviews books: Occasionally
Publishes notes: Yes
Languages accepted: English; German
Prints abstracts: No
Author-anonymous submission: No

SUBMISSION REQUIREMENTS

Restrictions on contributors: Contributors usually are members of the Kafka Soc. and have read paper at annual meeting.
Author pays submission fee: No
Author pays page charges: No
Length of articles: 10-15 pp.; research reports may be longer
Length of book reviews: 250 words
Length of notes: 300 words maximum
Style: MLA
Number of copies required: 3
Special requirements: Submit original manuscript.
Copyright ownership: Temple Univ.
Rejected manuscripts: Returned; enclose return postage & SAE.
Time before publication decision: 3 mos.
Time between decision and publication: 6-12 mos.
Number of reviewers: 2-3
Articles submitted per year: 20
Articles published per year: 10-12
Book reviews published per year: 10
Notes published per year: 5-10

(1466)
*Journal of the Lancashire Dialect Society

John Levitt, Editor
2 Hartington St.
Leek, Staffs, ST13 5PD, England

Additional editorial address: Peter Wright SK7 3B, 30 Broadoak Rd., Bramhall, Stockport SK7 3B, England
Telephone: (44) 538 383211
First published: 1951
ISSN: 0075-7799
MLA acronym: JLDS

SUBSCRIPTION INFORMATION

Frequency of publication: Annual
Circulation: 300
Available in microform: No
Subscription price: £3.50/yr.
Year to which price refers: 1992
Subscription address: Bob Dobson, Treasurer, 3 Staining Rise, Staining, Blackpool FY3 0BU, England
Subscription telephone: (44) 253 886103

ADVERTISING INFORMATION

Advertising accepted: No

EDITORIAL DESCRIPTION

Scope: Publishes articles on the Lancashire dialect and on the other dialects of Northern England.
Reviews books: Yes
Publishes notes: Yes
Languages accepted: English
Prints abstracts: Yes
Author-anonymous submission: No

SUBMISSION REQUIREMENTS

Restrictions on contributors: None
Author pays submission fee: No
Author pays page charges: No
Length of articles: No restrictions
Length of book reviews: 500 words
Length of notes: No restrictions
Style: None
Number of copies required: 1
Copyright ownership: Author
Rejected manuscripts: Returned
Time before publication decision: 6 mos.
Time between decision and publication: 1 yr.
Number of reviewers: 1
Articles submitted per year: 2
Articles published per year: 2
Book reviews submitted per year: 3
Book reviews published per year: 3
Notes submitted per year: 2
Notes published per year: 2

(1467)
Journal of the Maharaja Sayajirao University of Baroda

K. T. M. Hegde, S. R. Hashim, P. V. Parikh, Editors
Near Smt. Hansa Mehta Library
Journal Office
Maharaja Sayajirao Univ. of Baroda
Baroda 390002, India

First published: 1952
Sponsoring organization: Maharaja Sayajirao Univ. of Baroda
ISSN: 0025-0422
MLA acronym: JMSUB

SUBSCRIPTION INFORMATION

Frequency of publication: 1 volume/yr. in 3 parts: humanities, social sciences, science
Circulation: 500
Available in microform: Yes

ADVERTISING INFORMATION

Advertising accepted: Yes

EDITORIAL DESCRIPTION

Scope: Publishes original research papers contributed by the teachers and research scholars of the Maharaja Sayajirao University of Baroda.
Reviews books: Yes
Languages accepted: English; Gujarati; Hindi-Urdu
Prints abstracts: No

SUBMISSION REQUIREMENTS

Restrictions on contributors: None
Author pays submission fee: No
Author pays page charges: No
Length of articles: No restrictions
Number of copies required: 2
Copyright ownership: Maharaja Sayajirao Univ. of Baroda
Rejected manuscripts: Returned at author's request
Time before publication decision: 2-3 mos.
Time between decision and publication: 6-8 mos.
Number of reviewers: 2
Articles submitted per year: 50
Articles published per year: 10-12
Book reviews submitted per year: 50
Book reviews published per year: 10-12

(1468)
*Journal of the Malaysian Branch of the Royal Asiatic Society

Tan Sri Dato' & Mubin Sheppard, Editors
130M. Jalan Thamby Abdullah
Off Jalan Tun Sambanthan
Brickfields
50470 Kuala Lumpur, Malaysia

Telephone: (60) 3 2748345
Fax: (60) 3 2743458
First published: 1878
Sponsoring organization: Royal Asiatic Soc., Malaysian Branch
ISSN: 0126-7353
MLA acronym: JRASM

SUBSCRIPTION INFORMATION

Frequency of publication: 2 times/yr. (June, Dec.)
Circulation: 1,500
Available in microform: No
Subscription price: $30.00/yr. institutions; $20.00/yr. individuals
Year to which price refers: 1992

ADVERTISING INFORMATION

Advertising accepted: Yes, on an exchange basis

EDITORIAL DESCRIPTION

Scope: Focuses on increasing knowledge of Malaysia and neighboring territories including Singapore and Brunei.
Reviews books: Yes
Publishes notes: Yes
Languages accepted: English
Prints abstracts: No
Author-anonymous submission: No

SUBMISSION REQUIREMENTS

Restrictions on contributors: None
Author pays submission fee: No
Author pays page charges: No
Length of articles: 3,000-5,000 words
Length of book reviews: 400-600 words
Style: None
Number of copies required: 1
Special requirements: Submit double-spaced typescript.
Copyright ownership: Author
Rejected manuscripts: Returned
Time before publication decision: 3-6 mos.
Time between decision and publication: 6-12 mos.
Number of reviewers: 3
Articles submitted per year: 20
Articles published per year: 15
Book reviews submitted per year: 15
Book reviews published per year: 12

(1469)
*The Journal of the Midwest Modern Language Association

Rudolf E. Kuenzli, Editor
Midwest Modern Language Assn.
302 English-Philosophy Bldg.
Univ. of Iowa
Iowa City, IA 52242

Telephone: 319 335-0331
First published: 1968
Sponsoring organization: Midwest Modern Language Assn.
ISSN: 0742-5562
MLA acronym: JMMLA

SUBSCRIPTION INFORMATION

Frequency of publication: 2 times/yr. (May, Sept.)
Circulation: 2,200

Available in microform: No

ADVERTISING INFORMATION

Advertising accepted: Yes

EDITORIAL DESCRIPTION

Scope: Publishes essays on the study and teaching of language and literature, particularly in relation to political, historical, and cultural issues. Also includes studies in critical methodology, literary history, and the theory of language.
Reviews books: Yes
Publishes notes: No
Languages accepted: English
Prints abstracts: No
Author-anonymous submission: Yes

SUBMISSION REQUIREMENTS

Restrictions on contributors: None
Author pays submission fee: No
Author pays page charges: No
Length of articles: 8,000 words maximum
Length of book reviews: 1,000 words
Style: MLA; Chicago
Number of copies required: 2
Special requirements: Submit original typescript and 1 copy. Author's identity should appear on 1 copy.
Copyright ownership: Midwest Modern Language Assn.
Rejected manuscripts: Returned; enclose SASE.
Time before publication decision: 3 mos.
Time between decision and publication: 9 mos.
Number of reviewers: 1-2
Articles submitted per year: 60
Articles published per year: 9
Book reviews submitted per year: 20
Book reviews published per year: 12

(1470)
Journal of the Oriental Institute

R. T. Vyas, Editor
Oriental Inst., M. S. Univ. of Baroda
Opp. Sayaji Gunj Tower
Tilak Road
Baroda-390 002, Gujarat, India

First published: 1951
Sponsoring organization: Maharaja Sayajirao Univ. of Baroda
ISSN: 0030-5324
MLA acronym: JOIB

SUBSCRIPTION INFORMATION

Frequency of publication: 4 times/yr.
Circulation: 550
Available in microform: No

ADVERTISING INFORMATION

Advertising accepted: Yes, on an exchange basis

EDITORIAL DESCRIPTION

Scope: Publishes articles on Indological and Oriental studies.
Reviews books: Yes
Publishes notes: No
Languages accepted: English
Prints abstracts: No
Author-anonymous submission: No

SUBMISSION REQUIREMENTS

Restrictions on contributors: None
Author pays submission fee: No
Author pays page charges: No
Length of articles: No restrictions
Length of book reviews: No restrictions
Style: None
Number of copies required: 1

Special requirements: Submit original typescript.
Copyright ownership: Publisher
Rejected manuscripts: Returned
Time before publication decision: 1 mo. minimum
Time between decision and publication: 15-24 mos.
Number of reviewers: 1
Articles submitted per year: 40
Articles published per year: 30-40
Book reviews submitted per year: 20
Book reviews published per year: 16-20

(1471)
*Journal of the Polynesian Society

Richard M. Moyle, Editor
Anthropology Dept.
Univ. of Auckland
Private Bag
Auckland, New Zealand

Telephone: (64) 9 3737999
Fax: (64) 7 3737441
First published: 1892
Sponsoring organization: Polynesian Soc., Inc.
ISSN: 0032-4000
MLA acronym: JPS

SUBSCRIPTION INFORMATION

Frequency of publication: 4 times/yr.
Circulation: 1,200
Available in microform: Yes
Subscription price: NZ$55.00/yr.
Year to which price refers: 1992
Subscription address: J. Huntsman, Honorary Secretary, at the above address
Subscription fax: (64) 9 3023245

ADVERTISING INFORMATION

Advertising accepted: Yes
Advertising rates: NZ$90.00/half page; NZ$150.00/full page

EDITORIAL DESCRIPTION

Scope: Publishes articles on history, ethnology, physical anthropology, sociology, archaeology, and linguistics of the New Zealand Maori people and other Pacific peoples. Welcomes contributions from professional and amateur scholars. Editor is happy to discuss projected contributions in advance.
Reviews books: Yes
Publishes notes: No
Languages accepted: English
Prints abstracts: No
Author-anonymous submission: No

SUBMISSION REQUIREMENTS

Restrictions on contributors: Book reviews are solicited.
Author pays submission fee: No
Author pays page charges: No
Length of articles: 100 typescript pp. maximum
Length of book reviews: 1,000-1,500 words; 5,000 words for review articles; some shorter reviews accepted
Style: Harvard
Number of copies required: 2
Special requirements: Submit original typescript, 1 photocopy, and camera-ready illustrations.
Copyright ownership: Assigned by author to Polynesian Soc.
Rejected manuscripts: Returned at author's request
Time between decision and publication: 1-2 yrs.
Number of reviewers: 1-2
Articles submitted per year: 50
Articles published per year: 25
Book reviews submitted per year: 50
Book reviews published per year: 40

(1472)
*Journal of the Rocky Mountain Medieval and Renaissance Association

John S. Tanner, Editor
Dept. of English
Brigham Young Univ.
Provo, UT 84602

First published: 1980
Sponsoring organization: Rocky Mountain Medieval & Renaissance Assn.
ISSN: 0195-8453
MLA acronym: JRMMRA

SUBSCRIPTION INFORMATION

Frequency of publication: Annual
Circulation: 250
Available in microform: Yes
Subscription price: $20.00/yr. institutions; $15.00/yr. individuals
Year to which price refers: 1992
Subscription address: Steven A. Epstein, Secretary-Treasurer, Dept. of History, Univ. of Colorado, Boulder, CO 80309

ADVERTISING INFORMATION

Advertising accepted: Yes, on an exchange basis

EDITORIAL DESCRIPTION

Scope: Publishes articles on Medieval and Renaissance studies, including literature, art, and history.
Reviews books: Yes
Publishes notes: No
Languages accepted: English
Prints abstracts: No
Author-anonymous submission: Yes

SUBMISSION REQUIREMENTS

Restrictions on contributors: Send unpublished manuscripts. Book reviews are solicited.
Author pays submission fee: No
Author pays page charges: No
Length of articles: 25 pp.
Length of book reviews: 500 words
Style: Chicago
Number of copies required: 3
Special requirements: Submit original typescript and 2 copies.
Copyright ownership: Journal
Rejected manuscripts: Returned
Time before publication decision: 3 mos.
Time between decision and publication: 6 mos.
Number of reviewers: 3
Articles submitted per year: 40
Articles published per year: 8
Book reviews published per year: 20

(1473)
*Journal of the Royal Asiatic Society of Great Britain and Ireland

D. O. Morgan, Editor
Royal Asiatic Soc.
60 Queen's Gardens
London W2 3AF, England

Telephone: (44) 71 7244742
First published: 1834
Sponsoring organization: Royal Asiatic Soc.
ISSN: 0035-869X
MLA acronym: JRAS

SUBSCRIPTION INFORMATION

Frequency of publication: 3 times/yr. (Apr., July, Nov.)
Circulation: 2,000
Available in microform: Yes
Subscription price: £42.00/yr. institutions; £28.00/yr. individuals; £15.00/single issue

Year to which price refers: 1991
Subscription address: Cambridge Univ. Press, Edinburgh Bldg., Shaftesbury Rd., Cambridge CB2 2RU, England
Subscription telephone: (44) 223 312393

ADVERTISING INFORMATION

Advertising accepted: Yes
Advertising rates: £90.00/half page; £150.00/full page

EDITORIAL DESCRIPTION

Scope: Contains original articles on the archaeology, art, history, language, literature, beliefs, and customs of Asia.
Reviews books: Yes
Publishes notes: Yes
Languages accepted: English; French; German; Italian; Spanish
Prints abstracts: No

SUBMISSION REQUIREMENTS

Restrictions on contributors: None
Author pays submission fee: No
Author pays page charges: No
Length of articles: 6,000 words maximum
Length of book reviews: 300-2,500 words
Length of notes: 200 words
Style: Journal
Number of copies required: 1
Special requirements: Submit original typescript.
Copyright ownership: Assigned by author to journal
Rejected manuscripts: Returned
Time before publication decision: 3 mos. maximum
Time between decision and publication: 1 yr. maximum
Number of reviewers: 2
Articles published per year: 15-16
Book reviews submitted per year: 140-160
Book reviews published per year: 140-160
Notes submitted per year: 1-3
Notes published per year: 1-3

(1474)
Journal of the Royal Society of Antiquaries of Ireland

Michael Herity, Editor
Royal Soc. of Antiquaries of Ireland
63 Merrion Square
Dublin 2, Ireland

Telephone: (353) 1 761749
First published: 1849
Sponsoring organization: Royal Soc. of Antiquaries of Ireland
ISSN: 0035-9106
MLA acronym: JRSAI

SUBSCRIPTION INFORMATION

Frequency of publication: Annual
Circulation: 1,100
Available in microform: No

ADVERTISING INFORMATION

Advertising accepted: No

EDITORIAL DESCRIPTION

Scope: Publishes articles on antiquarian aspects of Ireland.
Reviews books: Yes
Publishes notes: Yes
Languages accepted: English; Irish Gaelic
Prints abstracts: Yes
Author-anonymous submission: No

SUBMISSION REQUIREMENTS

Restrictions on contributors: None
Author pays submission fee: No
Author pays page charges: No
Length of articles: 5,000-20,000 words
Length of book reviews: 300-1,200 words
Length of notes: 300-1,000 words
Style: Harvard Reference System
Number of copies required: 2
Special requirements: Submit original typescript plus 1 copy and a 3-4 line summary.
Copyright ownership: Royal Soc. of Antiquaries of Ireland
Rejected manuscripts: Returned
Time before publication decision: 2-3 mos.
Number of reviewers: 1
Articles published per year: 8-10
Book reviews published per year: 2-8
Notes published per year: 2-5

(1475)
*Journal of the Rutgers University Libraries

Pamela Spence Richards, Editor
Rutgers Univ. Library
New Brunswick, NJ 08903

Telephone: 908 932-7505
First published: 1937
Sponsoring organization: Rutgers Univ., Friends of the Library
ISSN: 0036-0473
MLA acronym: JRUL

SUBSCRIPTION INFORMATION

Frequency of publication: 2 times/yr. (June, Dec.)
Circulation: 500
Available in microform: No
Subscription price: $25.00/yr.
Year to which price refers: 1992
Subscription address: Subscription Dept., Alexander Library, Rutgers Univ., New Brunswick, NJ 08903

ADVERTISING INFORMATION

Advertising accepted: No

EDITORIAL DESCRIPTION

Scope: Publishes articles on topics which are based on materials in the Rutgers University Library or articles on topics concerning Rutgers, New Jersey, or the history of books and printing.
Reviews books: No
Publishes notes: Yes
Languages accepted: English
Prints abstracts: No
Author-anonymous submission: No

SUBMISSION REQUIREMENTS

Restrictions on contributors: None
Author pays submission fee: No
Author pays page charges: No
Length of articles: No restrictions
Length of notes: 300 words
Style: MLA; Chicago
Number of copies required: 1
Copyright ownership: Rutgers Univ. Library
Rejected manuscripts: Returned
Time before publication decision: 1 mo.
Time between decision and publication: 6 mos.
Number of reviewers: 1-2
Articles submitted per year: 20
Articles published per year: 10
Notes submitted per year: 2
Notes published per year: 2

(1476)
Journal of the School of Languages

H. S. Gill, Editor
Centre of Linguistics & English
Jawaharlal Nehru Univ.
New Delhi 110067, India

First published: 1973
Sponsoring organization: Jawaharlal Nehru Univ.
ISSN: 0377-0648
MLA acronym: JSL

SUBSCRIPTION INFORMATION

Frequency of publication: 2 times/yr.
Circulation: 1,000
Available in microform: No
Subscription address: Wiley Eastern Ltd., 4835/24 Ansari Rd., Daryaganj, New Delhi 110002, India

ADVERTISING INFORMATION

Advertising accepted: Yes

EDITORIAL DESCRIPTION

Scope: Publishes articles on all aspects of language and literature in society.
Reviews books: Yes
Publishes notes: Yes
Languages accepted: English
Prints abstracts: No

SUBMISSION REQUIREMENTS

Restrictions on contributors: None
Author pays submission fee: No
Author pays page charges: No
Length of articles: 3,000-6,000 words
Length of book reviews: 800-1,200 words
Length of notes: 1,500-3,000 words
Style: None
Number of copies required: 2
Special requirements: Include a 200-word abstract.
Copyright ownership: Editorial Board
Rejected manuscripts: Returned; enclose return postage.
Time before publication decision: 1-2 mos.
Time between decision and publication: 1 yr.
Number of reviewers: 2
Articles published per year: 20
Book reviews published per year: 10

(1477)
*Journal of the Short Story in English

Ben Forkner, Jeanne Devoize, Corinne Dale, & J. H. E. Paine, Editors
c/o J. H. E. Paine
Dept. of Literature & Language
Belmont Univ.
Nashville, TN 37212-3757

Additional editorial address: B. Forkner & J. Devoize, 11 boulevard Lavoisier, 49045 Angers Cedex 01, France
Telephone: 615 385-6412
Fax: 615 386-4535
First published: 1983
Sponsoring organization: Univ. d'Angers; Belmont Univ.
ISSN: 0294-0442
MLA acronym: JSSE

SUBSCRIPTION INFORMATION

Frequency of publication: 2 times/yr.
Circulation: 250
Available in microform: No
Subscription price: 156 F/yr. France; $32.00/yr. elsewhere
Year to which price refers: 1993

Additional subscription address: In France: Presses de l'Univ. d'Angers, 5 rue Le-Nôtre, boulevard Lavoisier, 49045 Angers Cedex 01, France

ADVERTISING INFORMATION

Advertising accepted: Yes
Advertising rates: 2,000 F/full page

EDITORIAL DESCRIPTION

Scope: Publishes articles and conference papers on various aspects of the short story with emphasis on American and British authors.
Reviews books: Yes
Publishes notes: Yes
Languages accepted: English
Prints abstracts: Yes

SUBMISSION REQUIREMENTS

Author pays submission fee: No
Author pays page charges: No
Length of articles: 20 pp. maximum
Style: MLA
Number of copies required: 2
Copyright ownership: Univ. d'Angers
Rejected manuscripts: Returned
Time before publication decision: 3 mos.
Time between decision and publication: 3-6 mos.
Number of reviewers: 3 minimum
Articles submitted per year: 50
Articles published per year: 16-20
Book reviews submitted per year: 4-8
Book reviews published per year: 2
Notes submitted per year: 4-8
Notes published per year: 2-4

(1478)
*Journal of the Siam Society

James V. Di Crocco, Editor
Siam Soc.
Under Royal Patronage
131 Soi Asoke
Sukhumvit Soi 21
Bangkok 10110, Thailand

Telephone: (66) 2 2583491
Fax: (66) 2 2583491
First published: 1904
Sponsoring organization: Siam Soc.
ISSN: 0807-7099
MLA acronym: JSSB

SUBSCRIPTION INFORMATION

Frequency of publication: 2 times/yr.
Circulation: 1,800
Available in microform: Yes
Subscription price: 500 B ($25.00)/yr.
Year to which price refers: 1992
Subscription address: Euayporn Kerdchouay, Administrative Secretary, at the above address

ADVERTISING INFORMATION

Advertising accepted: Yes

EDITORIAL DESCRIPTION

Scope: Publishes articles on all aspects of Thai culture in consonance with the objectives and principles of the Siam Society Under Royal Patronage, including history, arts, archaeology, anthropology, folklore, sociology, Buddhology, religion, philosophy, literature, and linguistics, as well as their relationships with other nations and cultures.
Reviews books: Yes
Publishes notes: Yes
Languages accepted: English; Thai; French; German
Prints abstracts: Yes, for non-English articles
Author-anonymous submission: No

SUBMISSION REQUIREMENTS

Restrictions on contributors: None
Author pays submission fee: No
Author pays page charges: No
Length of articles: No restrictions
Length of book reviews: No restrictions
Length of notes: No restrictions
Style: Chicago preferred
Number of copies required: 1
Special requirements: Include institutional affiliation, fields of interest, titles of major publications, and a short biographical note.
Copyright ownership: Assigned by author to Siam Soc.
Rejected manuscripts: Not returned
Time before publication decision: 1 mo.
Time between decision and publication: 2-12 mos.
Number of reviewers: 1-3
Articles submitted per year: 40-45
Articles published per year: 35-40
Book reviews submitted per year: 30-40
Book reviews published per year: 20-30
Notes submitted per year: 5-10
Notes published per year: 3-5

(1479)
Journal of the Society of Basque Studies in America

Leonard Bloom, Editor
47 Stemway Rd.
Trumbull, CT 06601

Telephone: 203 261-6748
First published: 1980
Sponsoring organization: Soc. of Basque Studies in America
ISSN: 1042-3834
MLA acronym: JSBSA

SUBSCRIPTION INFORMATION

Frequency of publication: Annual
Circulation: 400
Available in microform: No

ADVERTISING INFORMATION

Advertising accepted: No

EDITORIAL DESCRIPTION

Scope: To disseminate information covering Basque scholarship, including literature, linguistics, ethnology, folklore, and history.
Reviews books: Yes
Publishes notes: Yes
Languages accepted: English; Spanish; French; Basque
Prints abstracts: No
Author-anonymous submission: No

SUBMISSION REQUIREMENTS

Restrictions on contributors: None
Author pays submission fee: No
Author pays page charges: No
Length of articles: 3,000-7,000 words
Length of book reviews: 3 pp.
Length of notes: 1-2 pp.
Style: MLA
Number of copies required: 1
Special requirements: Submission on IBM- or Macintosh-compatible diskette is preferred.
Rejected manuscripts: Returned
Time before publication decision: 3-4 mos.
Time between decision and publication: 3-4 mos.
Number of reviewers: 2
Articles submitted per year: 10-15
Articles published per year: 7-9
Book reviews submitted per year: 4-6
Book reviews published per year: 3
Notes submitted per year: 4-6
Notes published per year: 2

(1480)
*Journal of the Southwest

Joseph Carleton Wilder, Editor
1052 North Highland Ave.
Univ. of Arizona
Tucson, AZ 85721

Telephone: 602 621-2484
First published: 1959
Sponsoring organization: Southwest Center/ Univ. of Arizona Press
ISSN: 0894-8410
MLA acronym: JSw

SUBSCRIPTION INFORMATION

Frequency of publication: 4 times/yr. (Mar., June, Sept., Dec.)
Circulation: 1,100
Available in microform: Yes
Subscription price: $24.00/yr. institutions; $18.00/yr. individuals; add $3.00/yr. postage outside US
Year to which price refers: 1992

ADVERTISING INFORMATION

Advertising accepted: Yes
Advertising rates: $100.00/full page

EDITORIAL DESCRIPTION

Scope: Publishes articles on any aspect of the greater southwestern United States and northern Mexico. Although multidisciplinary, emphasis is on history, culture, folklore, literary studies, historiography, borderlands studies, regional natural history, and public policy.
Reviews books: Yes
Publishes notes: Yes
Languages accepted: English; Spanish; all languages accepted for translation into English
Prints abstracts: No
Author-anonymous submission: Yes

SUBMISSION REQUIREMENTS

Restrictions on contributors: Book reviews are solicited.
Author pays submission fee: No
Author pays page charges: No
Length of articles: No restrictions
Length of book reviews: No restrictions
Length of notes: No restrictions
Style: Chicago
Number of copies required: 2
Copyright ownership: Univ. of Arizona Board of Regents
Rejected manuscripts: Returned
Time before publication decision: 2-6 mos.
Time between decision and publication: 6-18 mos.
Number of reviewers: 3
Articles submitted per year: 70
Articles published per year: 24
Book reviews published per year: 23

(1481)
*Journal of the Warburg and Courtauld Institutes

David Chambers, Lorne Campbell, & Elizabeth McGrath, Editors
Warburg Inst.
Univ. of London
Woburn Square
London WC1H 0AB, England

Telephone: (44) 71 5809663
Fax: (44) 71 4362852
First published: 1937
Sponsoring organization: Warburg Inst.; Courtauld Inst.
ISSN: 0075-4390
MLA acronym: JWCI

SUBSCRIPTION INFORMATION

Frequency of publication: Annual
Circulation: 1,200
Available in microform: No
Subscription price: $35.00/yr.
Year to which price refers: 1991
Subscription address: Elizabeth Witchell, at the above address

ADVERTISING INFORMATION

Advertising accepted: No

EDITORIAL DESCRIPTION

Scope: Journal deals with the history of classical tradition. Provides a forum for historians of art, religion, science, literature, social and political life, as well as for philosophers and anthropologists.
Reviews books: No
Publishes notes: Yes
Languages accepted: English
Prints abstracts: No
Author-anonymous submission: No

SUBMISSION REQUIREMENTS

Restrictions on contributors: None
Author pays submission fee: No
Author pays page charges: No
Length of articles: 5,000-6,000 words; exceptions made
Length of notes: 1,000 words
Style: Warburg (substantially Modern Humanities Research Assn. style)
Number of copies required: 1
Special requirements: Consult "Notes for *Journal* Contributors" in journal prior to submission.
Copyright ownership: Warburg Inst.
Rejected manuscripts: Returned; enclose return postage or international reply coupons.
Time before publication decision: 2-6 mos.
Number of reviewers: 2-6
Articles submitted per year: 100
Articles published per year: 8
Notes submitted per year: 50
Notes published per year: 15

(1482)
*The Journal of the William Morris Society

Peter Faulkner, Editor
William Morris Soc.
Kelmscott House, 26 Upper Mall
Hammersmith
London W6 9TA, England

First published: 1961
Sponsoring organization: William Morris Soc.
MLA acronym: JWMS

SUBSCRIPTION INFORMATION

Frequency of publication: 2 times/yr. (Spring, Autumn)
Circulation: 1,600
Available in microform: No

ADVERTISING INFORMATION

Advertising accepted: Yes
Advertising rates: £120.00/full page

EDITORIAL DESCRIPTION

Scope: Publishes articles aimed at encouraging the study of the work and life of William Morris and his associates.
Reviews books: Yes
Publishes notes: Yes
Languages accepted: English
Prints abstracts: No
Author-anonymous submission: No

SUBMISSION REQUIREMENTS

Author pays submission fee: No
Author pays page charges: No
Length of articles: 2,000-5,000 words
Length of book reviews: 700-1,000 words
Length of notes: 500 words
Style: MLA preferred
Number of copies required: 1
Special requirements: Footnotes should be placed at the end.
Rejected manuscripts: Returned
Time before publication decision: 3-15 mos.
Time between decision and publication: 3-6 mos.
Number of reviewers: 2
Articles submitted per year: 12
Articles published per year: 8
Book reviews submitted per year: 10
Book reviews published per year: 10
Notes submitted per year: 1-2
Notes published per year: 1-2

(1483)
*Journal of Ukrainian Studies

Zenon Kohut, Editor
Canadian Inst. of Ukrainian Studies
352 Athabasca Hall
Univ. of Alberta
Edmonton, Alberta T6G 2E8, Canada

Telephone: 403 492-2972
Fax: 403 492-4967
First published: 1976
Sponsoring organization: Univ. of Alberta, Canadian Inst. of Ukrainian Studies
ISSN: 0228-1635
MLA acronym: JUkGS

SUBSCRIPTION INFORMATION

Frequency of publication: 2 times/yr. (Summer, Winter)
Circulation: 600
Available in microform: Yes
Subscription price: C$20.00/yr. institutions; C$15.00/yr. individuals
Year to which price refers: 1991

ADVERTISING INFORMATION

Advertising accepted: No

EDITORIAL DESCRIPTION

Scope: Publishes articles which deal with Ukrainian-related subjects in the humanities and social sciences. The main criterion for acceptance of submission is scholarly contribution to the field of Ukrainian studies. Also publishes translations, documents, information, book reviews, guides to research, occasional journalistic articles of a problem-oriented, controversial nature, and reprints of articles from difficult to obtain past publications.
Reviews books: Yes
Publishes notes: Yes
Languages accepted: English; Ukrainian
Prints abstracts: No
Author-anonymous submission: Yes

SUBMISSION REQUIREMENTS

Restrictions on contributors: None
Author pays submission fee: No
Author pays page charges: No
Length of articles: 15-25 pp.
Length of book reviews: 1,000-1,500 words
Length of notes: 1,000-1,500 words
Style: Chicago
Number of copies required: 3
Special requirements: Include short academic biography.
Copyright ownership: Canadian Inst. of Ukrainian Studies
Rejected manuscripts: Returned; enclose return postage.

Time before publication decision: 3 mos.
Time between decision and publication: 6 mos.
Number of reviewers: 3
Articles submitted per year: 20-25
Articles published per year: 10-12
Book reviews submitted per year: 15-20
Book reviews published per year: 15-20
Notes submitted per year: 1-2
Notes published per year: 1-2

(1484)
*The Journal of West African Languages

John Bendor-Samuel, Editor
7500 W. Camp Wisdom Rd.
Dallas, TX 75236

First published: 1964
Sponsoring organization: West African Linguistic Soc.
ISSN: 0022-5401
MLA acronym: JWAL

SUBSCRIPTION INFORMATION

Frequency of publication: 2 times/yr.
Circulation: 410
Subscription price: $30.00/yr. institutions; $18.00/yr. individuals; $12.00/yr. members
Year to which price refers: 1992-93
Additional subscription address: Cambridge Univ. Press, Edinburgh Bldg., Shaftesbury Rd., Cambridge CB2 2RU, England; Univ. Bookshop (Nigeria) Ltd., Univ. of Ibadan, Ibadan, Nigeria

EDITORIAL DESCRIPTION

Scope: Publishes articles on the languages of West Africa.
Reviews books: Yes
Languages accepted: English; French
Prints abstracts: Yes

SUBMISSION REQUIREMENTS

Author pays submission fee: No
Style: Chicago
Number of copies required: 2
Special requirements: Submit diskette in ASCII or Microsoft Word format.

(1485)
*Journal of West Indian Literature

Mark McWatt & Victor L. Chang, Editors
Dept. of English
Univ. of the West Indies
Cave Hill
P.O. Box 64
Bridgetown, Barbados

Additional editorial address: Dept. of English, Univ. of the West Indies, Mona, Kingston 7, Jamaica
Telephone: 809 425-1310 ext. 378
Fax: 809 425-1327
First published: 1986
Sponsoring organization: Dept. of English, Univ. of the West Indies
ISSN: 0258-8501
MLA acronym: JWIL

SUBSCRIPTION INFORMATION

Frequency of publication: 2 times/yr.
Circulation: 380
Available in microform: No
Subscription price: $20.00/yr.
Year to which price refers: 1992
Subscription telephone: 809 425-1310 ext. 352

ADVERTISING INFORMATION

Advertising accepted: Yes

Advertising rates: $50.00/half page; $100.00/full page

EDITORIAL DESCRIPTION

Scope: Publishes the results of scholarly research in the literature of the English-speaking Caribbean as well as research into Caribbean literatures that is of a comparative nature (with English, French, Spanish, Dutch).
Reviews books: Yes
Publishes notes: Yes
Languages accepted: English
Prints abstracts: No
Author-anonymous submission: Yes

SUBMISSION REQUIREMENTS

Restrictions on contributors: None
Author pays submission fee: No
Author pays page charges: No
Length of articles: 3,500-5,000 words
Length of book reviews: 300-500 words
Length of notes: 500-1,500 words
Style: MLA
Number of copies required: 1
Copyright ownership: Author
Rejected manuscripts: Returned
Time before publication decision: 3-6 mos.
Time between decision and publication: 1 yr. maximum
Number of reviewers: 2
Articles published per year: 25-30
Book reviews submitted per year: 10-20
Book reviews published per year: 10-15

(1486)
*Journalism Quarterly

Jean Folkerts, Editor
Journalism Dept.
George Washington Univ.
Washington, DC 20052

Telephone: 202 994-6226
Fax: 202 994-5806
First published: 1924
Sponsoring organization: Assn. for Education in Journalism & Mass Communication
ISSN: 0196-3031
MLA acronym: JQ

SUBSCRIPTION INFORMATION

Frequency of publication: 4 times/yr.
Circulation: 4,650
Available in microform: Yes, through Univ. Microfilms International
Subscription price: $40.00/yr. institutions US; $50.00/yr. institutions elsewhere; $30.00/yr. individuals US; $40.00/yr. individuals elsewhere
Year to which price refers: 1992
Subscription address: AEJMC, College of Journalism, Univ. of South Carolina, Columbia, SC 29208-0251
Subscription telephone: 803 777-2005
Subscription fax: 803 777-4728

ADVERTISING INFORMATION

Advertising accepted: Yes

EDITORIAL DESCRIPTION

Scope: Publishes research in journalism and mass communication.
Reviews books: Yes
Publishes notes: Yes
Languages accepted: English
Prints abstracts: Yes
Author-anonymous submission: Yes

SUBMISSION REQUIREMENTS

Restrictions on contributors: None
Author pays submission fee: No
Author pays page charges: No
Length of articles: 4,000 words

Length of book reviews: 600 words maximum
Length of notes: 6-7 double-spaced typescript pp.
Style: AEJ Publications Manual
Number of copies required: 4
Special requirements: Submit double-spaced typescript. Manuscripts accepted for publication must be submitted on diskette.
Copyright ownership: Journal
Rejected manuscripts: Original returned
Time before publication decision: 2-3 mos.
Time between decision and publication: 9-12 mos.
Number of reviewers: 2-4
Articles submitted per year: 350
Articles published per year: 100
Book reviews published per year: 90
Notes submitted per year: 50
Notes published per year: 30

(1487)
*Joyce Studies Annual

Thomas F. Staley, Editor
P.O. Box 7219 University Station
Univ. of Texas at Austin
Austin, TX 78713

Telephone: 512 471-9113
Fax: 512 471-9646
First published: 1990
Sponsoring organization: Harry Ransom Humanities Research Center, Univ. of Texas at Austin
ISSN: 1049-0809
MLA acronym: JSA

SUBSCRIPTION INFORMATION

Frequency of publication: Annual (June)
Circulation: 700
Available in microform: No
Subscription price: $35.00/yr. institutions; $25.00/yr. individuals
Year to which price refers: 1992
Subscription address: Journals Dept., Univ. of Texas Press, P.O. Box 7819, Austin, TX 78713
Subscription telephone: 512 471-4531
Subscription fax: 512 320-0668

ADVERTISING INFORMATION

Advertising accepted: Yes
Advertising rates: $75.00/half page; $125.00/full page

EDITORIAL DESCRIPTION

Scope: Publishes articles on James Joyce and his work, including its milieu, historical context, and textual matters, as well as comparative and influence studies. Includes a secondary checklist of works on and related to Joyce as well as previously unpublished documents.
Reviews books: No
Publishes notes: Yes
Languages accepted: English
Prints abstracts: No
Author-anonymous submission: No

SUBMISSION REQUIREMENTS

Author pays submission fee: No
Author pays page charges: No
Length of articles: 4,500-7,000 words
Style: Chicago
Number of copies required: 2
Copyright ownership: Univ. of Texas Press
Rejected manuscripts: Returned; enclose SASE.
Time before publication decision: 3 mos. maximum
Time between decision and publication: 1 yr. maximum
Number of reviewers: 2-3
Articles submitted per year: 100
Articles published per year: 10-15
Notes submitted per year: 10
Notes published per year: 3

(1488)
*Judaism: A Quarterly Journal of Jewish Life and Thought

Ruth B. Waxman, Editor
American Jewish Congress
15 E. 84th St.
New York, NY 10028

Telephone: 212 879-4500
Fax: 212 249-3672
First published: 1952
Sponsoring organization: American Jewish Congress
ISSN: 0022-5762
MLA acronym: Judaism

SUBSCRIPTION INFORMATION

Frequency of publication: 4 times/yr. (Jan., Apr., July, Oct.)
Circulation: 6,000
Available in microform: Yes
Subscription price: $35.00/yr. institutions; $20.00/yr. individuals
Year to which price refers: 1992

ADVERTISING INFORMATION

Advertising accepted: Yes
Advertising rates: $150.00/half page; $250.00/full page

EDITORIAL DESCRIPTION

Scope: Nonpartisan journal dedicated to the discussion and exposition of the religious, moral, and philosophical concepts of Judaism and their relevance to the problems of modern society.
Reviews books: Yes
Publishes notes: No
Languages accepted: English
Prints abstracts: No
Author-anonymous submission: No

SUBMISSION REQUIREMENTS

Restrictions on contributors: None
Author pays submission fee: No
Author pays page charges: No
Length of articles: 5,000-7,000 words
Length of book reviews: 1,500-2,500 words
Style: MLA; Chicago
Number of copies required: 1
Special requirements: Submit original typescript.
Copyright ownership: Journal
Rejected manuscripts: Returned; enclose return postage.
Time before publication decision: 1 mo.
Time between decision and publication: 1 yr.
Number of reviewers: 2
Articles submitted per year: 200
Articles published per year: 40-50
Book reviews submitted per year: 20
Book reviews published per year: 10-15

(1489)
*Južnoslovenski Filolog

Milka Ivić, Editor
Inst. za Srpskohrvatski Jezik
Knez-Mihailova, 35/1
11000 Belgrade, Yugoslavia

Telephone: (38) 11 187144
First published: 1913
Sponsoring organization: Inst. za Srpskohrvatski Jezik
ISSN: 0350-185X
MLA acronym: JF

SUBSCRIPTION INFORMATION

Frequency of publication: Annual
Circulation: 1,000
Available in microform: No

ADVERTISING INFORMATION

Advertising accepted: No

EDITORIAL DESCRIPTION

Scope: Publishes articles and reviews concerning the Serbo-Croatian language, other Slavic languages, and general linguistics. Also publishes an annual bibliography of works in linguistics published in Yugoslavia.
Reviews books: Yes
Publishes notes: Yes
Languages accepted: English; French; Serbo-Croatian; German; Slovenian; Macedonian; Polish; Czech; Bulgarian; Russian
Prints abstracts: Yes
Author-anonymous submission: No

SUBMISSION REQUIREMENTS

Restrictions on contributors: None
Author pays submission fee: No
Author pays page charges: No
Length of articles: 50 pp. maximum
Length of book reviews: 10 pp.
Length of notes: 500 words
Style: None
Number of copies required: 1
Special requirements: Submit original typescript.
Copyright ownership: Author
Rejected manuscripts: Returned
Time before publication decision: 6 mos.
Time between decision and publication: 6 mos.
Number of reviewers: 3
Articles submitted per year: 18
Articles published per year: 16
Book reviews submitted per year: 3-4
Book reviews published per year: 3-4
Notes submitted per year: 2
Notes published per year: 1-2

(1490)
*Jyväskylä Cross-Language Studies

Kari Sajavaara & Jaakko Lehtonen, Editors
Dept. of English
Univ. of Jyväskylä
P.O. Box 35
40351 Jyväskylä, Finland

Telephone: (358) 41 601220
Fax: (358) 41 601221
E-mail: SAJAVAAR@JYLK.JYU.FI
First published: 1975
Sponsoring organization: Dept. of English, Univ. of Jyväskylä
ISSN: 0358-6464
MLA acronym: JCLS

SUBSCRIPTION INFORMATION

Frequency of publication: Irregular
Circulation: 100
Available in microform: No

ADVERTISING INFORMATION

Advertising accepted: No

EDITORIAL DESCRIPTION

Scope: Publishes articles on cross-language and cross-cultural studies, second language acquisition, and foreign language teaching.
Reviews books: No
Publishes notes: No
Languages accepted: English
Prints abstracts: Yes
Author-anonymous submission: No

SUBMISSION REQUIREMENTS

Author pays submission fee: No
Author pays page charges: No
Number of copies required: 1

Copyright ownership: Dept. of English, Univ. of Jyväskylä
Number of reviewers: 1-2

(1491)
*Kadmos: Zeitschrift für Vor- und Frühgriechische Epigraphik

Wolfgang Blümel, Editor
Leyboldstr. 68
5000 Cologne 51, Germany

First published: 1962
Sponsoring organization: Deutsche Forschungsgemeinschaft
ISSN: 0022-7498
MLA acronym: Kadmos

SUBSCRIPTION INFORMATION

Frequency of publication: 2 times/yr.
Available in microform: No
Subscription address: Walter de Gruyter & Co., Genthiner Str. 13, 1000 Berlin 30, Germany

ADVERTISING INFORMATION

Advertising accepted: No

EDITORIAL DESCRIPTION

Scope: Publishes articles on the early epigraphy of the Aegean and Cyprus.
Reviews books: No
Publishes notes: Yes
Languages accepted: English; French; German; Italian; Spanish
Prints abstracts: No
Author-anonymous submission: No

SUBMISSION REQUIREMENTS

Restrictions on contributors: None
Author pays submission fee: No
Author pays page charges: No
Length of articles: 12,000 words maximum; short communications are welcomed.
Length of notes: 400 words
Style: None
Number of copies required: 1
Copyright ownership: Walter de Gruyter & Co.
Rejected manuscripts: Returned
Time before publication decision: 2 mos.
Time between decision and publication: 1 yr.
Number of reviewers: 2-3
Articles submitted per year: 20
Articles published per year: 12
Notes published per year: 10

(1492)
*Kalbotyra: Lietuvos Aukštųjų Mokyklų Mokslo Darbai

Albertas Steponavičius, Aleksas Girdenis, Lilija Sudavičiene, & Vytautas Balaišis, Editors
Vilnius Univ.
Vilnius, Lithuania

Fax: (7) 122 613473; (7) 122 223563
First published: 1958
Sponsoring organization: Vilnius Univ.
ISSN: 0202-330X
MLA acronym: Kalbotyra

SUBSCRIPTION INFORMATION

Frequency of publication: 3 times/yr.
Circulation: 1,500
Available in microform: No

ADVERTISING INFORMATION

Advertising accepted: No

EDITORIAL DESCRIPTION

Scope: Publishes articles on linguistics with special relevance for Lithuanian, Russian, Germanic, and Romance languages.
Reviews books: Yes
Publishes notes: Yes
Languages accepted: Lithuanian; Russian; English; German; French
Prints abstracts: Yes
Author-anonymous submission: No

SUBMISSION REQUIREMENTS

Restrictions on contributors: Contributors must be on the staff of the Lithuanian higher schools.
Author pays submission fee: No
Author pays page charges: No
Length of articles: 15 typescript pp.
Length of book reviews: 15 typescript pp.
Length of notes: 1 typescript p.
Number of copies required: 3
Special requirements: Submit original typescript; include a 200-word abstract in language other than language of text.
Copyright ownership: Author
Rejected manuscripts: Returned at author's request
Time before publication decision: 3 mos.
Time between decision and publication: 1 yr.
Number of reviewers: 2
Articles submitted per year: 60
Articles published per year: 35-40
Book reviews submitted per year: 6
Book reviews published per year: 6
Notes submitted per year: 10
Notes published per year: 10

(1493)
*Kalevalaseuran Vuosikirja

Pekka Laaksonen & Sirkka-Liisa Mettomäki, Editors
Kalevalaseura
Hallituskatu 1
00170 Helsinki, Finland

Telephone: (358) 0 131231
Fax: (358) 0 13123220
First published: 1921
Sponsoring organization: Kalevalaseura; Suomalaisen Kirjallisuuden Seura
ISSN: 0355-0311
MLA acronym: KSVK

SUBSCRIPTION INFORMATION

Frequency of publication: Annual
Circulation: 2,500
Available in microform: No
Subscription price: 180 Fmk/yr.
Year to which price refers: 1991
Subscription address: Suomalaisen Kirjallisuuden Seura, Hallituskatu 1, 00170 Helsinki, Finland

ADVERTISING INFORMATION

Advertising accepted: No

EDITORIAL DESCRIPTION

Scope: Focuses on the study of Finno-Ugric folklore and ethnology, and Finnish culture in general.
Reviews books: No
Publishes notes: No
Languages accepted: Finnish
Prints abstracts: No
Author-anonymous submission: No

SUBMISSION REQUIREMENTS

Restrictions on contributors: None
Author pays submission fee: No
Author pays page charges: No
Length of articles: 1,000-3,000 words
Style: None

Number of copies required: 1
Copyright ownership: Suomalaisen Kirjallisuuden Seura & Kalevalaseura
Rejected manuscripts: Returned at author's request
Time before publication decision: 6 mos.
Time between decision and publication: 3 mos.
Number of reviewers: 1-3
Articles submitted per year: 20-30
Articles published per year: 20-30

(1494)
*Kalki: Studies in James Branch Cabell

Paul Spencer, Editor
James Branch Cabell Soc.
HC 63 Box 70A
E. Alstead, NH 03602-7705

Telephone: 603 835-6436
First published: 1965
Sponsoring organization: James Branch Cabell Soc.
ISSN: 0022-7994
MLA acronym: Kalki

SUBSCRIPTION INFORMATION

Frequency of publication: Irregular
Circulation: 200
Available in microform: No
Subscription price: $20.00/4 issues institutions; $10.00/4 issues individuals
Year to which price refers: 1992
Subscription address: Dorys C. Grover, Hall of Languages 208, East Texas State Univ., Commerce, TX 75428

ADVERTISING INFORMATION

Advertising accepted: No

EDITORIAL DESCRIPTION

Scope: Publishes analytical, biographical, and bibliographical material on Cabell.
Reviews books: Yes
Publishes notes: Yes
Languages accepted: English
Prints abstracts: No

SUBMISSION REQUIREMENTS

Restrictions on contributors: None
Author pays submission fee: No
Author pays page charges: No
Length of articles: No restrictions
Length of book reviews: No restrictions
Length of notes: No restrictions
Style: None
Number of copies required: 1
Special requirements: Submit double-spaced typescript.
Copyright ownership: Cabell Soc., but negotiable
Rejected manuscripts: Returned
Time before publication decision: 2 weeks
Number of reviewers: 1

(1495)
*Kanava

Seikko Eskola, Editor
Yhtyneet Kuvalehdet Oy
Maistraatinportti 1
00240 Helsinki, Finland

Telephone: (358) 0 1566537
Fax: (358) 0 1566500
First published: 1933
Sponsoring organization: Suomalaisuuden Liitto
ISSN: 0355-0303
MLA acronym: Kanava

SUBSCRIPTION INFORMATION

Frequency of publication: 9 times/yr.
Circulation: 6,100
Available in microform: No
Subscription price: 336 Fmk/yr.
Year to which price refers: 1992

ADVERTISING INFORMATION

Advertising accepted: Yes

EDITORIAL DESCRIPTION

Scope: Focuses on society, culture, politics, and literature.
Reviews books: Yes
Publishes notes: Yes
Languages accepted: Finnish
Prints abstracts: No

SUBMISSION REQUIREMENTS

Restrictions on contributors: None
Length of articles: 8-15 pp.
Length of book reviews: 3-6 pp.
Length of notes: 1-3 pp.
Style: None
Number of copies required: 1
Copyright ownership: Author
Rejected manuscripts: Returned
Time before publication decision: 1-2 mos.
Time between decision and publication: 1-6 mos.
Number of reviewers: 2
Articles published per year: 90
Book reviews published per year: 40
Notes published per year: 20

(1496)
Káñina: Revista de Artes y Letras de la Universidad de Costa Rica

María Amoretti H., Editor
Dept. de Publicaciones de la Univ. de Costa Rica
Apdo. 88
Univ. de Costa Rica
Ciudad Universitaria "Rodrigo Facio"
San José, Costa Rica

First published: 1977
Sponsoring organization: Univ. de Costa Rica
ISSN: 0378-0473
MLA acronym: Káñina

SUBSCRIPTION INFORMATION

Frequency of publication: 2 double issues/yr. (Spring, Fall)
Circulation: 500
Available in microform: No

ADVERTISING INFORMATION

Advertising accepted: No

EDITORIAL DESCRIPTION

Scope: Publishes academic articles on any literature, period, and method, although articles on Costa Rican, Central American, and Latin American literatures are preferred.
Reviews books: Yes
Publishes notes: Yes
Languages accepted: Spanish; English; French
Prints abstracts: Yes

SUBMISSION REQUIREMENTS

Restrictions on contributors: None
Author pays submission fee: No
Author pays page charges: No
Length of articles: 30 double-spaced typescript pp.
Length of book reviews: 2 double-spaced typescript pp.
Length of notes: 2 double-spaced typescript pp.
Style: MLA

Number of copies required: 3
Special requirements: Submit original typescript. Include an abstract in Spanish. Articles in languages other than Spanish will be translated into Spanish.
Copyright ownership: Journal & author
Rejected manuscripts: Returned; enclose return postage.
Time before publication decision: 6 mos.
Time between decision and publication: 6 mos.
Number of reviewers: 3
Articles published per year: 10-15
Book reviews published per year: 10-20
Notes published per year: 10-20

(1497)
*Kansas Quarterly

Ben Nyberg, John Rees, & G. W. Clift, Editors
Dept. of English
Kansas State Univ.
Manhattan, KS 66506

First published: 1968
Sponsoring organization: Kansas Quarterly Assn.; Kansas State Univ., English Dept.
ISSN: 0022-8745
MLA acronym: KanQ

SUBSCRIPTION INFORMATION

Frequency of publication: 4 times/yr. (Feb., May, Aug., Nov.)
Circulation: 850
Available in microform: No
Subscription price: $20.00/yr.
Year to which price refers: 1992
Subscription address: Business Manager, at the address above

ADVERTISING INFORMATION

Advertising accepted: Yes
Advertising rates: $75.00/half page; $100.00/full page; $150.00/back cover

EDITORIAL DESCRIPTION

Scope: Publishes primarily poetry and fiction. Special issues consider topics in literature, art, and film criticism and Great Plains history.
Reviews books: No
Publishes notes: Yes
Languages accepted: English
Prints abstracts: No
Author-anonymous submission: No

SUBMISSION REQUIREMENTS

Restrictions on contributors: None
Author pays submission fee: No
Author pays page charges: No
Length of articles: 2,500-10,000 words
Length of notes: 500-1,500 words
Style: MLA with modifications
Number of copies required: 1
Special requirements: Submit original typescript or photocopy.
Copyright ownership: Journal, but can be transferred to author on request for republication
Rejected manuscripts: Returned; enclose return postage.
Time before publication decision: 1-6 mos.
Time between decision and publication: 18 mos. minimum
Number of reviewers: 2-3
Articles submitted per year: 20-80
Articles published per year: 8-20
Notes submitted per year: 20-30
Notes published per year: 1-5

(1498)
*Kansatieteellinen Arkisto

Leena Sammallahti, Editor
Suomen Muinaismuistoyhdistys
P1 913
00101 Helsinki 10, Finland

First published: 1934
Sponsoring organization: Suomen Muinaismuistoyhdistys
ISSN: 0355-1830
MLA acronym: KAr

SUBSCRIPTION INFORMATION

Frequency of publication: Irregular
Circulation: 1,000
Available in microform: No

ADVERTISING INFORMATION

Advertising accepted: No

EDITORIAL DESCRIPTION

Scope: Publishes monographs on ethnology.
Reviews books: No
Publishes notes: No
Languages accepted: Finnish; English; German; Swedish
Prints abstracts: Yes
Author-anonymous submission: No

SUBMISSION REQUIREMENTS

Author pays submission fee: No
Author pays page charges: No
Length of books: 150-350 pp.
Number of copies required: 1
Copyright ownership: Suomen Muinaismuistoyhdistys
Rejected manuscripts: Returned
Time before publication decision: 2-12 weeks
Time between decision and publication: 4-12 mos.
Number of reviewers: 1-2
Books submitted per year: 1-3
Books published per year: 1-2

(1499)
Karogs

Māra Zālite, Editor
Balasta dambī, 3, P.K. 13
Rīga-81, 226081, Latvia

ISSN: 0132-6295
MLA acronym: Karogs

SUBSCRIPTION INFORMATION

Frequency of publication: 12 times/yr.

EDITORIAL DESCRIPTION

Scope: Publishes articles on literature, arts, and sociopolitics.
Reviews books: Yes
Languages accepted: Latvian
Prints abstracts: No

(1500)
*Kasseler Arbeiten zur Sprache und Literatur: Anglistik-Germanistik-Romanistik

Wolfram Buddecke, Manfred Raupach, & Martin Schulze, Editors
Gesamthochschule Kassel, FB8
3500 Kassel, Germany

Telephone: (49) 561 8043322
Fax: (49) 561 8042812
First published: 1977
Sponsoring organization: Gesamthochschule Kassel
ISSN: 0170-8805
MLA acronym: KASL

SUBSCRIPTION INFORMATION

Frequency of publication: Irregular
Available in microform: No
Subscription address: Verlag Peter H. Lang AG, Jupiterstr. 15, 3015 Bern, Switzerland

ADVERTISING INFORMATION

Advertising accepted: No

EDITORIAL DESCRIPTION

Scope: Publishes current research in German, English, and French philology.
Reviews books: No
Publishes notes: No
Languages accepted: German; English; French
Prints abstracts: No

SUBMISSION REQUIREMENTS

Author pays submission fee: No
Author pays page charges: Yes
Length of books: 100-500 pp.
Style: MLA
Number of copies required: 2
Special requirements: Submit original typescript; include a 200-word abstract.
Copyright ownership: Verlag Peter Lang
Rejected manuscripts: Returned
Time before publication decision: 3-6 mos.
Time between decision and publication: 1-2 yrs.
Number of reviewers: 3
Books submitted per year: 4-6
Books published per year: 2-4

(1501)
Keats-Shelley Journal: Keats, Shelley, Byron, Hunt, and Their Circles

Stuart Curran, Editor
Dept. of English
Bennett Hall 119
Univ. of Pennsylvania
Philadelphia, PA 19104-6273

Additional editorial address: Send books for review to: Betty T. Bennett, Book Review Editor, Dean of the College of Arts & Sciences, The American Univ., Washington, D.C. 20016
First published: 1952
Sponsoring organization: Keats-Shelley Assn. of America, Inc.
ISSN: 0453-4387
MLA acronym: KSJ

SUBSCRIPTION INFORMATION

Frequency of publication: Annual
Circulation: 1,100
Available in microform: No
Subscription address: Robert A. Hartley, Secretary, Coopers & Lybrand, 1301 Ave. of the Americas, New York, NY 10019-6013
Additional subscription address: Keats-Shelley Assn. of America, Shelley & His Circle, Room 226, New York Public Library, 5th Ave. & 42nd St., New York, NY 10018-2788

ADVERTISING INFORMATION

Advertising accepted: No

EDITORIAL DESCRIPTION

Scope: Focuses on the study of Keats, Shelley, Byron, Hunt, and their circle.
Reviews books: Yes
Publishes notes: Yes
Languages accepted: English
Prints abstracts: No
Author-anonymous submission: Yes, at author's request

SUBMISSION REQUIREMENTS

Restrictions on contributors: Book reviews are solicited.
Author pays submission fee: No
Author pays page charges: No
Length of articles: 5,000-6,000 words
Length of notes: 2,000-2,500 words
Style: Chicago
Number of copies required: 1
Copyright ownership: Keats-Shelley Assn. of America, Inc.
Rejected manuscripts: Returned
Time before publication decision: 2 mos.
Time between decision and publication: 2 yrs.
Number of reviewers: 2
Articles submitted per year: 30
Articles published per year: 8
Book reviews published per year: 10
Notes submitted per year: 12
Notes published per year: 5

(1502)
Keats-Shelley Review

Timothy Webb, Editor
Keats-Shelley Memorial Assn.
Dept. of English
Univ. of Bristol
3/5 Woodland Rd.
Bristol BS8 1TB, England

First published: 1910
Sponsoring organization: Keats-Shelley Memorial Assn.
ISSN: 0453-4395
MLA acronym: KSMB

SUBSCRIPTION INFORMATION

Frequency of publication: Annual
Circulation: 1,200

ADVERTISING INFORMATION

Advertising accepted: Yes

EDITORIAL DESCRIPTION

Scope: Publishes articles on Keats, Shelley, and their circle.
Reviews books: Yes
Languages accepted: English
Prints abstracts: No

SUBMISSION REQUIREMENTS

Length of articles: 7,000 words maximum
Special requirements: Keep footnotes to a minimum.
Rejected manuscripts: Returned; enclose SASE.

(1503)
*Keel ja Kirjandus

Aksel Tamm, Editor
Roosikrantsi 6
EE0106 Tallinn, Estonia

Telephone: (7) 142 449228
First published: 1958
Sponsoring organization: Eesti Teaduste Akadeemia (Estonian Academy of Sciences); Eesti Kirjanike Liidu (Estonian Writers' Union)
ISSN: 0131-1441
MLA acronym: KjK

SUBSCRIPTION INFORMATION

Frequency of publication: 12 times/yr.
Circulation: 2,000
Available in microform: No

Subscription price: $38.00/yr.
Year to which price refers: 1992
Subscription address: Akateeminen Kirjakauppa, 00101 Helsinki, Finland

ADVERTISING INFORMATION

Advertising accepted: Yes

EDITORIAL DESCRIPTION

Scope: Publishes articles on Estonian language and literature, Finno-Ugric languages, general linguistics and literary theory, and folklore.
Reviews books: Yes
Publishes notes: Yes
Languages accepted: Estonian
Prints abstracts: No
Author-anonymous submission: No

SUBMISSION REQUIREMENTS

Restrictions on contributors: None
Author pays submission fee: Yes
Author pays page charges: No
Length of articles: No restrictions
Length of book reviews: No restrictions
Length of notes: No restrictions
Number of copies required: 2
Copyright ownership: Editorial Board & publisher
Rejected manuscripts: Returned at author's request
Time before publication decision: 1-2 mos.
Time between decision and publication: 3-12 mos.
Number of reviewers: 2-4
Articles submitted per year: 200-250
Articles published per year: 180-200
Book reviews submitted per year: 60-75
Book reviews published per year: 50-60
Notes submitted per year: 60-80
Notes published per year: 60-80

(1504)
*Keiryō Kokugogaku/Mathematical Linguistics

Hisao Ishii, Editor
Keiryō Kokugo Gakkai
No. 3 Bldg., Rm. 118
Tokyo Woman's Christian Univ.
Zenpukuzi 2-tyōme, Suginami-ku
Tokyo 167, Japan

Telephone: (81) 3 33951211 ext. 339
First published: 1957
Sponsoring organization: Keiryō Kokugo Gakkai
ISSN: 0453-4611
MLA acronym: KeK

SUBSCRIPTION INFORMATION

Frequency of publication: 4 times/yr. (June, Sept., Dec., Mar.)
Circulation: 500
Available in microform: No
Subscription price: 3,600 yen/yr.
Year to which price refers: 1992

ADVERTISING INFORMATION

Advertising accepted: No

EDITORIAL DESCRIPTION

Scope: Publishes articles on statistical, algebraic, or computer-oriented research on Japanese or natural language.
Reviews books: Yes
Publishes notes: Yes
Languages accepted: Japanese; English; French; German
Prints abstracts: Yes
Author-anonymous submission: No

SUBMISSION REQUIREMENTS

Restrictions on contributors: Contributors must be members of the Keiryō Kokugo Gakkai.
Author pays submission fee: No
Author pays page charges: No
Length of articles: 5,000 words
Length of book reviews: 2,500 words
Length of notes: 1,500 words
Style: None
Number of copies required: 2
Special requirements: Submit abstract and 5-10 keywords in Japanese if possible.
Copyright ownership: Author
Rejected manuscripts: Not returned
Time before publication decision: 2-5 mos.
Time between decision and publication: 1-3 mos.
Number of reviewers: 2-3
Articles submitted per year: 30
Articles published per year: 16
Book reviews submitted per year: 2-3
Book reviews published per year: 2-3
Notes submitted per year: 6
Notes published per year: 4

(1505)
*Kentucky Philological Review

Katherine C. Kurk, Editor
Dept. of Literature & Language
Northern Kentucky Univ.
Highland Heights, KY 41099

Telephone: 606 572-5416
First published: 1974
Sponsoring organization: Kentucky Philological Assn.
MLA acronym: KPR

SUBSCRIPTION INFORMATION

Frequency of publication: Annual
Circulation: 250
Available in microform: No
Subscription price: $5.00/yr.
Year to which price refers: 1992

ADVERTISING INFORMATION

Advertising accepted: No

EDITORIAL DESCRIPTION

Scope: Publishes selected papers and abstracts of papers read during the annual Kentucky Philological Association meeting.
Reviews books: No
Publishes notes: No
Languages accepted: English; French; Spanish; German
Prints abstracts: No
Author-anonymous submission: No

SUBMISSION REQUIREMENTS

Restrictions on contributors: Contributors must have read paper at annual meeting.
Author pays submission fee: No
Author pays page charges: No
Length of articles: 10 pp.
Style: MLA
Number of copies required: 1
Copyright ownership: Dept. of Literature & Language, Northern Kentucky Univ.
Rejected manuscripts: Not returned
Time before publication decision: 6 mos.
Time between decision and publication: 6 mos.
Number of reviewers: 6
Articles submitted per year: 60
Articles published per year: 6

(1506)
*The Kentucky Review

Bonnie Jean Cox, Editor
Univ. of Kentucky Libraries
Lexington, KY 40506-0039

Telephone: 606 257-4351
Fax: 606 257-8379
E-mail: KLI111@ukcc.uky.edu
First published: 1979
Sponsoring organization: Univ. of Kentucky Library Associates
ISSN: 0191-1031
MLA acronym: KRev

SUBSCRIPTION INFORMATION

Frequency of publication: 3 times/yr.
Circulation: 700
Available in microform: No
Subscription price: $10.00/yr.
Year to which price refers: 1992
Subscription address: Karen T. Ellenberg, at the above address
Subscription telephone: 606 257-5895

ADVERTISING INFORMATION

Advertising accepted: No

EDITORIAL DESCRIPTION

Scope: Publishes articles and interviews on any aspect of the humanities, especially American, English, and world literature, history, philosophy, art, architecture, music, folklore, typography, and cinema.
Reviews books: No
Publishes notes: Yes
Languages accepted: English
Prints abstracts: No
Author-anonymous submission: No

SUBMISSION REQUIREMENTS

Restrictions on contributors: Most published notes relate to the Univ. of Kentucky library collections.
Author pays submission fee: No
Author pays page charges: No
Length of articles: 10-25 typescript pp.
Style: Chicago
Number of copies required: 1
Copyright ownership: Author
Rejected manuscripts: Returned
Time before publication decision: 3 mos.
Time between decision and publication: 1-2 yrs.
Number of reviewers: 2-4
Articles submitted per year: 20
Articles published per year: 9
Notes published per year: 3

(1507)
The Kenyon Review

Marilyn Hacker, David Lynn, David Baker, & Martha Finan, Editors
Kenyon College
Gambier, OH 43022

First published: 1979
Sponsoring organization: Kenyon College
ISSN: 0163-075X
MLA acronym: KR

SUBSCRIPTION INFORMATION

Frequency of publication: 4 times/yr. (Jan., Apr., July, Oct.)
Circulation: 4,000
Available in microform: Yes
Subscription price: $24.00/yr. institutions US; $32.00/yr. institutions elsewhere; $22.00/yr. individuals US; $30.00/yr. individuals elsewhere
Year to which price refers: 1992

Subscription address: P.O. Box 8062, Syracuse, NY 13217

ADVERTISING INFORMATION

Advertising accepted: Yes

EDITORIAL DESCRIPTION

Scope: Publishes poetry, fiction, criticism, autobiography, general essays, and book reviews.
Reviews books: Yes
Publishes notes: No
Languages accepted: English
Prints abstracts: No
Author-anonymous submission: No

SUBMISSION REQUIREMENTS

Restrictions on contributors: Most book reviews are solicited.
Author pays submission fee: No
Author pays page charges: No
Length of articles: 5,000-10,000 words
Length of book reviews: 2,000-3,000 words
Style: MLA
Number of copies required: 1
Copyright ownership: Author
Rejected manuscripts: Returned; enclose SASE.
Time before publication decision: 3 mos. minimum
Time between decision and publication: 3-18 mos.
Number of reviewers: 2
Articles submitted per year: 2,000
Articles published per year: 80
Book reviews published per year: 20-25

(1508)
Kerkyraīka Chronika

K. Daphnes, Editor
Sotiros St. 10
Corfu 49100, Greece

First published: 1951
Sponsoring organization: Soc. of Corfiote Studies
MLA acronym: KerC

SUBSCRIPTION INFORMATION

Frequency of publication: Annual
Circulation: 980
Available in microform: No

ADVERTISING INFORMATION

Advertising accepted: No

EDITORIAL DESCRIPTION

Scope: Publishes articles on the history, literature, and culture of the Ionian Islands.
Reviews books: No
Publishes notes: No
Languages accepted: Greek; French; Italian
Prints abstracts: Yes
Author-anonymous submission: No

SUBMISSION REQUIREMENTS

Author pays submission fee: No
Author pays page charges: No
Length of articles: No restrictions
Number of copies required: 2
Copyright ownership: Editor
Rejected manuscripts: Not returned
Time before publication decision: 6 mos.
Time between decision and publication: 1 yr.
Number of reviewers: 1
Articles submitted per year: 2-15
Articles published per year: 2-15

(1509)
*The Kipling Journal

G. H. Webb, Editor
Weavers
Danes Hill
Woking
Surrey GU22 7HQ, England

First published: 1927
Sponsoring organization: Kipling Soc.
ISSN: 0023-1738
MLA acronym: KJ

SUBSCRIPTION INFORMATION

Frequency of publication: 4 times/yr. (Mar., June, Sept., Dec.)
Circulation: 900
Available in microform: No
Subscription price: £20.00/yr. (includes membership)
Year to which price refers: 1992
Subscription address: Norman Entract, Esq., Secretary, Kipling Soc., 2nd Floor, Schomberg House, 80/82 Pall Mall, London SW1Y 5HF, England
Subscription telephone: (44) 428 652709

ADVERTISING INFORMATION

Advertising accepted: Yes

EDITORIAL DESCRIPTION

Scope: Publishes studies on aspects of the life, times, prose, and verse of Rudyard Kipling including Kipling Society lecture texts and members' correspondence.
Reviews books: Yes
Publishes notes: Yes
Languages accepted: English
Prints abstracts: No
Author-anonymous submission: No

SUBMISSION REQUIREMENTS

Restrictions on contributors: None
Author pays submission fee: No
Author pays page charges: No
Length of articles: 2,500 words maximum
Length of book reviews: 500 words maximum
Length of notes: 500 words maximum
Style: Journal
Number of copies required: 1
Copyright ownership: Author & Kipling Soc.
Rejected manuscripts: Retained unless otherwise specified and unless return postage is enclosed.
Number of reviewers: 2
Articles submitted per year: 25
Articles published per year: 10
Book reviews submitted per year: 10
Book reviews published per year: 8
Notes submitted per year: 20
Notes published per year: 10

(1510)
*Kirjallisuudentutkijain Seuran Vuosikirja

Auli Viikari, Editor
Suomalaisen Kirjallisuuden Seura
PL 259
00171 Helsinki 17, Finland

Telephone: (358) 0 131231
Fax: (358) 0 13123220
First published: 1929
Sponsoring organization: Suomalaisen Kirjallisuuden Seura
ISSN: 0355-0176
MLA acronym: KSV

SUBSCRIPTION INFORMATION

Frequency of publication: Annual
Circulation: 1,000-1,500

Available in microform: No

ADVERTISING INFORMATION

Advertising accepted: No

EDITORIAL DESCRIPTION

Scope: Publishes articles on Finnish and world literature and bibliographies on Finnish literature research.
Reviews books: Yes
Publishes notes: No
Languages accepted: Finnish
Prints abstracts: Yes

SUBMISSION REQUIREMENTS

Restrictions on contributors: None
Author pays submission fee: No
Author pays page charges: No
Length of articles: 10-20 typescript pp.
Length of book reviews: No restrictions
Number of copies required: 1
Special requirements: Submit original typescript.
Copyright ownership: Author
Rejected manuscripts: Returned
Time between decision and publication: 1-2 mos.
Number of reviewers: 2
Articles published per year: 10-15
Book reviews published per year: 4-5

(1511)
*Kiswahili

E. Wesana-Chomi & H. J. M. Maransoko, Editors
Inst. of Kiswahili Research
Univ. of Dar es Salaam
P.O. Box 35110
Dar es Salaam, Tanzania

Telephone: (255) 51 49162; (255) 51 49143
Fax: (255) 51 48274
First published: 1930
Sponsoring organization: Univ. of Dar es Salaam, Inst. of Kiswahili Research
ISSN: 0856-048X
MLA acronym: Kiswahili

SUBSCRIPTION INFORMATION

Frequency of publication: Annual
Circulation: 1,000
Available in microform: No
Subscription price: $10.00 ($15.00 airmail)/yr.
Year to which price refers: 1992
Subscription address: Director, at the above address

ADVERTISING INFORMATION

Advertising accepted: No

EDITORIAL DESCRIPTION

Scope: Publishes articles on Kiswahili language, linguistics, and literature.
Reviews books: Yes
Publishes notes: Yes
Languages accepted: English; French; German; Swahili; Arabic
Prints abstracts: Yes
Author-anonymous submission: No

SUBMISSION REQUIREMENTS

Restrictions on contributors: None
Author pays submission fee: No
Author pays page charges: No
Length of articles: 10,000 words maximum
Length of book reviews: 5,000 words maximum
Length of notes: 2,000 words maximum
Style: MLA
Number of copies required: 3
Special requirements: Submit original double-spaced typescript and 2 copies on size A4 (8 1/4 in. x 11 3/4 in.) paper.

Copyright ownership: Inst. of Kiswahili Research
Rejected manuscripts: Returned at author's request; enclose return postage.
Time before publication decision: 6 mos.
Time between decision and publication: 6 mos.
Number of reviewers: 3
Articles submitted per year: 50
Articles published per year: 15
Book reviews submitted per year: 15
Book reviews published per year: 6
Notes submitted per year: 5
Notes published per year: 3

(1512)
*K&K: Kultur og Klasse. Kritik og Kulturanalyse

Jørgen Holmgaard, Lise Busk-Jensen, & Jens F. Jensen, Editors
Forlaget Medusa
P.O. Box 1
2840 Holte, Denmark

First published: 1967
Historical variations in title: Formerly *Kultur & Klasse*
Sponsoring organization: Statens Humanistiske Forskningsråd
ISSN: 0905-6998
MLA acronym: K&K

SUBSCRIPTION INFORMATION

Frequency of publication: 2 times/yr.
Circulation: 1,000
Available in microform: No
Subscription price: 250 Dkr/yr. Denmark; $55.00/yr. US
Year to which price refers: 1992

ADVERTISING INFORMATION

Advertising accepted: Yes

EDITORIAL DESCRIPTION

Scope: Publishes theoretical articles and articles analyzing cultural phenomena, especially literature, within an historical and social context.
Reviews books: Yes
Publishes notes: No
Languages accepted: Danish; Norwegian; Swedish
Prints abstracts: No
Author-anonymous submission: No

SUBMISSION REQUIREMENTS

Restrictions on contributors: None
Author pays submission fee: No
Author pays page charges: No
Length of articles: 10-40 pp.
Length of book reviews: 2-5 pp.
Number of copies required: 1
Copyright ownership: Author
Rejected manuscripts: Returned
Time before publication decision: 3 mos.
Time between decision and publication: 6 mos.
Number of reviewers: 3
Articles submitted per year: 40
Articles published per year: 16
Book reviews submitted per year: 20
Book reviews published per year: 10

(1513)
*Klage: Kölner Linguistische Arbeiten—Germanistik

Heinz Vater, Editor
Inst. für Deutsche Sprache & Literatur
Univ. zu Köln
Albertus-Magnus-Platz
5000 Cologne 41, Germany

Telephone: (49) 2233 63550 (Gabel Verlag)

First published: 1978
ISSN: 0939-9275
MLA acronym: Klage

SUBSCRIPTION INFORMATION

Frequency of publication: Irregular
Circulation: 600-800
Available in microform: No
Subscription address: Gabel Verlag, Jülichstr. 7, 5030 Hürth-Efferen, Germany

ADVERTISING INFORMATION

Advertising accepted: No

EDITORIAL DESCRIPTION

Scope: Publishes monographs on German language and linguistics.
Reviews books: No
Publishes notes: No
Languages accepted: German
Prints abstracts: Yes
Author-anonymous submission: No

SUBMISSION REQUIREMENTS

Restrictions on contributors: None
Author pays submission fee: No
Author pays page charges: No
Length of books: 80-150 pp.
Copyright ownership: Author or Gabel Verlag
Time before publication decision: 3 mos.
Time between decision and publication: 6 mos.
Number of reviewers: 2
Books submitted per year: 4-6
Books published per year: 3-5

(1514)
*Klasgids: By die Studie van die Afrikaanse Taal en Letterkunde

Nico J. Snyman, Editor
Klasgids
Posbus 1758
Pretoria 0001, South Africa

Telephone: (27) 12 3226404
Fax: (27) 12 3207803
First published: 1965
Sponsoring organization: Foundation for Education, Science & Technology
ISSN: 1010-3465
MLA acronym: Klasgids

SUBSCRIPTION INFORMATION

Frequency of publication: 4 times/yr.
Circulation: 3,600
Available in microform: No
Subscription price: 12 R/yr.
Year to which price refers: 1992
Subscription address: SOWPT, P.O. Box 392, Pretoria 0001, South Africa

ADVERTISING INFORMATION

Advertising accepted: No

EDITORIAL DESCRIPTION

Scope: Focuses on Afrikaans language and literature, and educational aspects thereof.
Reviews books: Yes
Publishes notes: Yes
Languages accepted: Afrikaans; Dutch; English
Prints abstracts: No
Author-anonymous submission: No

SUBMISSION REQUIREMENTS

Restrictions on contributors: None
Author pays submission fee: No
Author pays page charges: No
Length of articles: 2,500-3,000 words
Length of book reviews: 400-800 words
Length of notes: 30 words

Style: MLA
Number of copies required: 1
Special requirements: Submit original typescript typed with one and a half spaces between lines.
Copyright ownership: Author
Rejected manuscripts: Returned
Time before publication decision: 1 mo.
Time between decision and publication: 3 mos.
Number of reviewers: 3
Articles submitted per year: 80
Articles published per year: 50
Book reviews submitted per year: 40
Book reviews published per year: 30
Notes submitted per year: 8
Notes published per year: 4

(1515)
*Klaus-Groth-Gesellschaft Jahresgabe

Ulf Bichel, Reimer Bull, & Erich Scheller, Editors
Klaus-Groth-Gesellschaft e.V.
Klaus-Groth Museum
Lütteinheid 48
2240 Heide in Holstein, Germany

Additional editorial address: U. Bichel, Kopenhagener Allee 12, 2300 Kiel, Germany
Telephone: (49) 431 523319
First published: 1955
Sponsoring organization: Klaus-Groth-Gesellschaft e.V.
ISSN: 0453-9842
MLA acronym: KGGJ

SUBSCRIPTION INFORMATION

Frequency of publication: Annual
Circulation: 1,000
Available in microform: No
Subscription price: 30 DM/yr.
Year to which price refers: 1991
Subscription address: Westholsteinische Verlagsanstalt Boyens & Co., Wulf-Isebrand-Platz 1/3, Postfach 1880, 2240 Heide in Holstein, Germany
Subscription telephone: (49) 481 6910
Subscription fax: (49) 481 691260

ADVERTISING INFORMATION

Advertising accepted: No

EDITORIAL DESCRIPTION

Scope: Publishes articles on the poet Klaus Groth, on Low German language and literature since 1800, and on languages and literatures of other European minorities (e.g., Basque, Breton, Provençal, Scots, Welsh). Low German verse and prose is also published.
Reviews books: No
Publishes notes: Yes
Languages accepted: German
Prints abstracts: No
Author-anonymous submission: No

SUBMISSION REQUIREMENTS

Restrictions on contributors: None
Author pays submission fee: No
Author pays page charges: No
Length of articles: No restrictions
Length of notes: No restrictions
Style: None
Number of copies required: 1
Special requirements: In most cases articles are discussed with editors prior to submission.
Copyright ownership: Klaus-Groth-Gesellschaft & author
Rejected manuscripts: Returned
Time before publication decision: 1 yr. maximum
Time between decision and publication: 1 yr. maximum
Number of reviewers: 3-5
Articles submitted per year: 20
Articles published per year: 15-20

Notes submitted per year: 3-5
Notes published per year: 3-5

(1516)
*Kleine Schriften der Gesellschaft für Theatergeschichte

Gesellschaft für Theatergeschichte
Mecklenburgische Str. 56
1000 Berlin 33, Germany

Telephone: (49) 30 82400123
Fax: (49) 30 82400111
First published: 1902
ISSN: 0176-8905
MLA acronym: KSGT

SUBSCRIPTION INFORMATION

Frequency of publication: Irregular
Circulation: 350
Available in microform: No
Subscription price: 50 DM/yr.
Year to which price refers: 1992

ADVERTISING INFORMATION

Advertising accepted: No

EDITORIAL DESCRIPTION

Scope: Publishes articles on the history of the theater.
Reviews books: No
Publishes notes: No
Languages accepted: German
Prints abstracts: No
Author-anonymous submission: No

SUBMISSION REQUIREMENTS

Restrictions on contributors: None
Author pays submission fee: No
Author pays page charges: No
Length of articles: No restrictions
Style: MLA suggested
Number of copies required: 1
Special requirements: Footnotes should come at the end of the text.
Copyright ownership: Journal
Rejected manuscripts: Returned
Time before publication decision: 4-5 mos.
Number of reviewers: 2-3

(1517)
Književna Istorija

Jovan Deretić, Editor
Kraljevića Marka 9
Belgrade, Yugoslavia

First published: 1968
Sponsoring organization: Samoupravna Interesna Zajednica Srbije
ISSN: 0350-6428
MLA acronym: KnjIst

SUBSCRIPTION INFORMATION

Frequency of publication: 4 times/yr.
Circulation: 1,500
Available in microform: No

ADVERTISING INFORMATION

Advertising accepted: No

EDITORIAL DESCRIPTION

Scope: Publishes articles on the literary history of Serbian and Yugoslavian literature.
Reviews books: Yes
Publishes notes: No
Languages accepted: Serbo-Croatian
Prints abstracts: Yes

SUBMISSION REQUIREMENTS

Restrictions on contributors: Manuscripts must not have been published previously.
Author pays submission fee: Yes
Author pays page charges: No
Number of copies required: 1
Copyright ownership: Assigned by author to journal
Rejected manuscripts: Not returned
Time before publication decision: 3 mos.
Time between decision and publication: 2 mos.
Number of reviewers: 1 plus Editorial Board
Articles submitted per year: 20-25
Articles published per year: 20
Book reviews submitted per year: 15
Book reviews published per year: 10-12

(1518)
Književna Kritika: Časopis za Estetiku Književnosti

Novica Tadić, Editor
Izdavačko preduzéce "Rad"
Moše Pijade 12
Belgrade, Yugoslavia

First published: 1970
Sponsoring organization: Zajednica za Kulturu SR Srbije
ISSN: 0350-4123
MLA acronym: KnjiK

SUBSCRIPTION INFORMATION

Frequency of publication: 6 times/yr.
Circulation: 1,200
Available in microform: No

ADVERTISING INFORMATION

Advertising accepted: No

EDITORIAL DESCRIPTION

Scope: Publishes articles on literary criticism, both theoretical and applied, covering literature in general and all world literatures, concentrating on West European.
Reviews books: Yes
Publishes notes: Yes
Languages accepted: Serbo-Croatian
Prints abstracts: Yes

SUBMISSION REQUIREMENTS

Restrictions on contributors: None
Author pays submission fee: Yes
Author pays page charges: No
Length of articles: 20 pp.
Length of book reviews: 800-1,000 words
Length of notes: 400 words
Style: MLA
Number of copies required: 2
Special requirements: Submit original typescript.
Copyright ownership: Assigned by author to journal
Rejected manuscripts: Not returned
Time before publication decision: 1 mo.
Time between decision and publication: 2-3 mos.
Number of reviewers: 2
Articles submitted per year: 150
Articles published per year: 90
Book reviews submitted per year: 30-40
Book reviews published per year: 25
Notes submitted per year: 50-60
Notes published per year: 40

(1519)
Književne Novine: List za Knjizevnost i Kulturu

Dragan M. Jeremić, Editor
Novinsko Izdavacko Preduzeće "Književne Novine"
Francuska 7
Belgrade, Yugoslavia

First published: 1965
ISSN: 0023-2416
MLA acronym: KnjiNov

SUBSCRIPTION INFORMATION

Frequency of publication: 24 times/yr.

EDITORIAL DESCRIPTION

Languages accepted: Serbo-Croatian

(1520)
Književnost

Vuk Krnjevic, Editor
Prosveta
Cika Ljubina, 1
Belgrade, Yugoslavia

Telephone: (38) 11 630120
Fax: (38) 11 182581
First published: 1945
Sponsoring organization: IRO Prosveta, OOUR Izdavačka delatnost
ISSN: 0023-2408
MLA acronym: Knji

SUBSCRIPTION INFORMATION

Frequency of publication: 12 times/yr.
Circulation: 1,500
Available in microform: No
Subscription address: Ip "Prosveta", Dobrčina 30, 11000 Belgrade, Yugoslavia

ADVERTISING INFORMATION

Advertising accepted: Yes

EDITORIAL DESCRIPTION

Scope: Publishes articles on literature.
Reviews books: Yes
Languages accepted: Serbo-Croatian
Prints abstracts: No
Author-anonymous submission: No

SUBMISSION REQUIREMENTS

Author pays submission fee: Yes
Author pays page charges: No
Length of articles: No restrictions
Number of copies required: 1
Copyright ownership: Author
Rejected manuscripts: Not returned
Time before publication decision: 1 mo.
Time between decision and publication: 8 weeks
Articles submitted per year: 300
Articles published per year: 300
Book reviews submitted per year: 80
Book reviews published per year: 80

(1521)
*Književnost i Jezik

Zlata Bojović, Editor
Knez Mixailova ul. br. 35
Belgrade, Yugoslavia

First published: 1954
Sponsoring organization: Društvo za Srpskohrvatski Jezik i Književnost nr Srbije
ISSN: 0456-0689
MLA acronym: KiJ

SUBSCRIPTION INFORMATION

Frequency of publication: 4 times/yr.
Available in microform: No
Subscription price: $20.00/yr.
Year to which price refers: 1992

ADVERTISING INFORMATION

Advertising accepted: No

EDITORIAL DESCRIPTION

Scope: Publishes articles on Serbo-Croatian language and literatures.
Reviews books: Yes
Publishes notes: No
Languages accepted: Serbo-Croatian

SUBMISSION REQUIREMENTS

Number of copies required: 1
Copyright ownership: Editor

(1522)
*Knygotyra: Vilniaus Universiteto Mokslo Darbai

Domas Kaunas, Editor
Universiteto 3
2734 Vilnius, Lithuania

Telephone: (7) 122 768961
Fax: (7) 122 613473
First published: 1961
Historical variations in title: Formerly *Knygotyra: Lietuvos TSR Aukštųjų Mokyklų Mokslo Darbai*
Sponsoring organization: Vilnius Univ.
ISSN: 0204-2061
MLA acronym: Knygotyra

SUBSCRIPTION INFORMATION

Frequency of publication: Annual
Circulation: 700
Available in microform: No

ADVERTISING INFORMATION

Advertising accepted: No

EDITORIAL DESCRIPTION

Scope: Focuses on book science, including history of books and libraries, theory of bibliography, and library science.
Reviews books: Yes
Publishes notes: No
Languages accepted: English; Russian; Lithuanian; German; Polish
Prints abstracts: Yes

SUBMISSION REQUIREMENTS

Restrictions on contributors: None
Author pays submission fee: No
Author pays page charges: No
Length of articles: 3,000 words
Length of book reviews: 1,000 words
Number of copies required: 2
Special requirements: Submit original typescript plus 1 copy and an abstract.
Rejected manuscripts: One copy returned
Time before publication decision: 2 mos.
Time between decision and publication: 1 yr.
Number of reviewers: 2-3
Articles submitted per year: 12-14
Articles published per year: 8-10
Book reviews submitted per year: 3
Book reviews published per year: 2

(1523)
*Kodikas/Code/Ars semeiotica

Achim Eschbach, Ernest W. B. Hess-Lüttich, & Jürgen Trabant, Editors
Gunter Narr Verlag
Postfach 2567
7400 Tübingen, Germany

First published: 1979
ISSN: 0171-0834
MLA acronym: Kodikas

SUBSCRIPTION INFORMATION

Frequency of publication: 2 double issues/yr.
Circulation: 500
Available in microform: No

ADVERTISING INFORMATION

Advertising accepted: Yes

EDITORIAL DESCRIPTION

Scope: Promotes research and discussion concerning semiotics.
Reviews books: Yes
Publishes notes: Yes
Languages accepted: English; French; German
Prints abstracts: No
Author-anonymous submission: No

SUBMISSION REQUIREMENTS

Restrictions on contributors: Manuscripts are solicited.
Author pays submission fee: No
Author pays page charges: No
Style: Journal
Number of copies required: 2
Rejected manuscripts: Unsolicited manuscripts are returned.
Time before publication decision: 6 mos.
Time between decision and publication: 3 mos.
Number of reviewers: 2-3
Articles submitted per year: 30
Articles published per year: 20-30
Book reviews submitted per year: 20
Book reviews published per year: 15-20

(1524)
Kölner Romanistische Arbeiten

Romanischen Seminar
Univ. Köln
Albertus-Magnus Platz
5000 Cologne, Germany

First published: 1931
Sponsoring organization: Univ. Köln
ISSN: 0075-6520
MLA acronym: KRA

SUBSCRIPTION INFORMATION

Frequency of publication: Irregular
Circulation: 500
Available in microform: No
Subscription address: Librairie Droz S.A., 11 rue Massot, 1211 Geneva 12, Switzerland

ADVERTISING INFORMATION

Advertising accepted: No

EDITORIAL DESCRIPTION

Scope: Publishes monographs focusing on Romance studies.
Reviews books: No
Publishes notes: Yes
Languages accepted: German
Prints abstracts: No
Author-anonymous submission: No

SUBMISSION REQUIREMENTS

Restrictions on contributors: None
Author pays submission fee: Yes
Author pays page charges: Yes
Number of copies required: 1
Copyright ownership: Librairie Droz S.A.
Time before publication decision: 1 mo.
Time between decision and publication: 1 mo.
Number of reviewers: 4

(1525)
*Kongelige Danske Videnskabernes Selskab. Historisk-Filosofiske Meddelelser

Poul Lindegård Hjorth, Editor
35, H.C. Andersens Blvd.
1553 Copenhagen V, Denmark

Telephone: (45) 33 113240
Fax: (45) 33 910736
First published: 1918
Sponsoring organization: Kongelige Danske Videnskabernes Selskab (Royal Danish Academy of Sciences & Letters)
ISSN: 0106-0481
MLA acronym: KDVS

SUBSCRIPTION INFORMATION

Frequency of publication: Irregular
Available in microform: No
Subscription address: Munksgaards Export & Subscription Service, 35 Nörre Sögade, 1370 Copenhagen, Denmark

ADVERTISING INFORMATION

Advertising accepted: No

EDITORIAL DESCRIPTION

Scope: Publishes monographs in the humanities, including philology, archaeology, art history, literature, and history.
Reviews books: No
Publishes notes: No
Languages accepted: English; Danish; French; German
Prints abstracts: Yes

SUBMISSION REQUIREMENTS

Restrictions on contributors: Nonmembers of the Academy are subject to review and must have some relationship to Danish scholarship.
Author pays submission fee: No
Author pays page charges: No
Number of copies required: 2
Copyright ownership: Royal Danish Academy of Sciences & Letters
Rejected manuscripts: Returned
Time before publication decision: 1-4 mos.
Time between decision and publication: 2-6 mos.
Number of reviewers: 2

(1526)
Kontekst: Literary Theory Studies

Izdatel'stvo Nauka
Profsoyuznaya ul. 90
117864 Moscow B-485, Russia

First published: 1972
Sponsoring organization: Akademiia Nauk S.S.S.R., Inst. Mirovoĭ Literatury im. A. M. Gor'kogo
MLA acronym: Kontekst

SUBSCRIPTION INFORMATION

Frequency of publication: Annual
Circulation: 10,000
Available in microform: No

ADVERTISING INFORMATION

Advertising accepted: No

EDITORIAL DESCRIPTION

Scope: Publishes articles on literary theory.
Reviews books: No
Publishes notes: No
Languages accepted: Russian
Prints abstracts: No
Author-anonymous submission: No

SUBMISSION REQUIREMENTS

Restrictions on contributors: None
Author pays submission fee: No
Author pays page charges: No
Length of articles: 60,000 words
Number of copies required: 2
Special requirements: Pages should be thirty lines long with sixty characters per line.
Copyright ownership: "Nauka" Izdatel'stvo
Rejected manuscripts: Returned
Time before publication decision: 1 yr.
Time between decision and publication: 9 mos.
Articles submitted per year: 20
Articles published per year: 8-10

(1527)
Konzepte der Sprach- und Literaturwissenschaft

Klaus Baumgärtner, Editor
Max Niemeyer Verlag
Postfach 2140
7400 Tübingen, Germany

First published: 1970
ISSN: 0344-6735
MLA acronym: KDSL

SUBSCRIPTION INFORMATION

Frequency of publication: Irregular
Available in microform: No

ADVERTISING INFORMATION

Advertising accepted: No

EDITORIAL DESCRIPTION

Scope: Publishes monographs on general linguistics, language, and literary theory.
Reviews books: No
Publishes notes: No
Languages accepted: German
Prints abstracts: No
Author-anonymous submission: Yes

SUBMISSION REQUIREMENTS

Restrictions on contributors: None
Author pays submission fee: No
Author pays page charges: No
Length of books: No restrictions
Style: MLA
Number of copies required: 2
Copyright ownership: Max Niemeyer Verlag
Rejected manuscripts: Returned
Time before publication decision: 6 mos.
Time between decision and publication: 6 mos.
Number of reviewers: 2-3
Books submitted per year: 2-3
Books published per year: 1-2

(1528)
*Kopenhagener Beiträge zur Germanistischen Linguistik

Mogens Dyhr, Karl Hyldgaard-Jensen, & Jørgen Olsen, Editors
Københavns Univ.
Inst. for Germansk Filologi
Njalsgade 80
2300 Copenhagen S, Denmark

First published: 1972
Sponsoring organization: Københavns Univ.
ISSN: 0105-0257
MLA acronym: KBGL

SUBSCRIPTION INFORMATION

Frequency of publication: Annual
Circulation: 250
Available in microform: No
Subscription address: Reitzel A/S Ltd., Nørregade 20, 1165 Copenhagen K, Denmark

ADVERTISING INFORMATION

Advertising accepted: No

EDITORIAL DESCRIPTION

Scope: Publishes essays, discussions, and reviews on all areas of Germanic linguistics, with a concentration on the contrastive aspect of the German and Danish languages.
Reviews books: Yes
Languages accepted: German
Prints abstracts: No

SUBMISSION REQUIREMENTS

Restrictions on contributors: None
Author pays submission fee: No
Author pays page charges: No
Length of articles: 10-30 pp.
Length of book reviews: 5 pp.
Number of copies required: 1
Special requirements: Submit camera-ready typescript.
Copyright ownership: Author
Rejected manuscripts: Returned
Time before publication decision: 1 mo.
Time between decision and publication: 6 mos.
Number of reviewers: 3
Articles published per year: 10

(1529)
*Korea Journal

Lee Seung-Hwan, Editor
Korean Nation Commission for UNESCO
C.P.O. Box 64
Seoul 100-022, Korea

Telephone: (82) 2 7762804
Fax: (82) 2 7743956
First published: 1961
Sponsoring organization: Korean National Commission for UNESCO
ISSN: 0023-3900
MLA acronym: KoJ

SUBSCRIPTION INFORMATION

Frequency of publication: 4 times/yr.
Circulation: 4,000
Available in microform: No
Subscription price: $22.00/yr. Korea; $35.00/yr. Asia; $40.00/yr. US, Europe, Canada, Australia, & Middle East; $45.00/yr. elsewhere
Year to which price refers: 1991
Subscription address: Section of Property Management, at the above address

ADVERTISING INFORMATION

Advertising accepted: Yes

EDITORIAL DESCRIPTION

Scope: Publishes articles on Korean studies including literature, history, education, and culture. Also publishes translations of Korean literature including short stories, poetry, and drama.
Reviews books: Yes
Publishes notes: Yes
Languages accepted: English
Prints abstracts: No
Author-anonymous submission: No

SUBMISSION REQUIREMENTS

Restrictions on contributors: None
Author pays submission fee: No
Author pays page charges: No
Length of articles: 5,000-20,000 words
Length of book reviews: 1,000-1,500 words
Length of notes: 300-500 words
Style: MLA; UNESCO
Number of copies required: 2
Special requirements: Submit original typescript and Macintosh or IBM compatible diskette, if possible. Submit Korean language original along with translation, if available.
Copyright ownership: Author
Rejected manuscripts: Not returned
Time before publication decision: 3 mos.
Time between decision and publication: 3 mos.
Number of reviewers: 5
Articles submitted per year: 120
Articles published per year: 80
Book reviews submitted per year: 30
Book reviews published per year: 25
Notes submitted per year: 100
Notes published per year: 80

(1530)
*Korespondence Pomembnih Slovencev

France Bernik & Janko Kos, Editors
Slovenska Akademija Znanosti in Umetnosti
Novi trg 3
61000 Ljubljana, Slovenia

Telephone: (38) 61 156068
Fax: (38) 61 155232
First published: 1939
Sponsoring organization: Slovenska Akademija Znanosti in Umetnosti
ISSN: 0452-5957
MLA acronym: KPS

SUBSCRIPTION INFORMATION

Frequency of publication: Irregular
Circulation: 1,000
Available in microform: No
Subscription address: Cankarjeva Založba, Kongresni trg 7, 61000 Ljubljana, Slovenia

ADVERTISING INFORMATION

Advertising accepted: No

EDITORIAL DESCRIPTION

Scope: Publishes monographs of correspondence from literary figures on literature, literary history, and history.
Reviews books: No
Publishes notes: No
Languages accepted: Slovenian
Prints abstracts: Yes

SUBMISSION REQUIREMENTS

Restrictions on contributors: None
Author pays submission fee: No
Author pays page charges: No
Number of copies required: 1

(1531)
*Korrespondenzblatt des Vereins für Niederdeutsche Sprachforschung

Vibeke Winge, Editor
Københavns Univ.
Inst. for Germansk Filologi
Njalsgade 80
Trappe 16 2. etage
2300 Copenhagen 8, Denmark

Telephone: (45) 31 542211
Fax: (45) 31 546365
First published: 1876
Sponsoring organization: Verein für Niederdeutsche Sprachforschung
ISSN: 0342-0752
MLA acronym: KVNS

SUBSCRIPTION INFORMATION

Frequency of publication: 4 times/yr.
Circulation: 800
Available in microform: No
Subscription address: Karl Wachholtz Verlag, Gänsemarkt 1/3, Postfach 2769, 2350 Neumünster, Germany

ADVERTISING INFORMATION

Advertising accepted: No

EDITORIAL DESCRIPTION

Scope: Publishes short articles on Low German language and literature as well as allusions and news of interest to the members of the Verein.
Reviews books: No
Publishes notes: Yes
Languages accepted: German; Dutch; English
Prints abstracts: No
Author-anonymous submission: No

SUBMISSION REQUIREMENTS

Restrictions on contributors: None
Author pays submission fee: No
Author pays page charges: No
Length of articles: 10 typescript pp. maximum
Length of notes: 1 typescript p.
Style: Journal
Number of copies required: 1
Copyright ownership: Assigned by author to journal
Rejected manuscripts: Returned
Time before publication decision: 1 mo.
Time between decision and publication: 3-5 mos.
Number of reviewers: 2
Articles submitted per year: 20
Articles published per year: 15
Notes submitted per year: 15
Notes published per year: 10

(1532)
*Kortárs: Irodalmi és Kritikai Folyóirat

Imre Kis Pintér, Editor
Bajza u. 18
1062 Budapest, Hungary

Telephone: (36) 1 1421520; (36) 1 1421168
Fax: (36) 1 1213419
First published: 1957
Sponsoring organization: Magyar Írószövetség
ISSN: 0023-415X
MLA acronym: Kortárs

SUBSCRIPTION INFORMATION

Frequency of publication: 12 times/yr.
Circulation: 4,800
Available in microform: No
Subscription address: Központi Hirlap Iroda, József nádor tér. 1, 1900 Budapest V., Hungary

Additional subscription address: Outside Hungary: Kultúra Külkereskedelmi Vállalat, Pf. 149, 1939 Budapest, Hungary

ADVERTISING INFORMATION

Advertising accepted: Yes

EDITORIAL DESCRIPTION

Scope: Publishes articles on Hungarian literature.
Reviews books: Yes
Publishes notes: Yes
Languages accepted: Hungarian
Prints abstracts: No
Author-anonymous submission: No

SUBMISSION REQUIREMENTS

Author pays submission fee: No
Author pays page charges: No
Length of articles: 1,500-10,000 words
Length of book reviews: 400-800 words
Length of notes: 100-300 words
Number of copies required: 1
Copyright ownership: Author
Rejected manuscripts: Returned
Time before publication decision: 2-3 weeks
Time between decision and publication: 2-5 mos.
Number of reviewers: 6-7
Articles submitted per year: 300
Articles published per year: 120
Book reviews submitted per year: 120
Book reviews published per year: 70-75
Notes submitted per year: 50-60
Notes published per year: 40

(1533)
*Korunk

Kantor Lajos, Editor
Str. Moților Nr. 3, C.P. 273
3400 Cluj-Napoca, Romania

Telephone: (40) 5 117836
First published: 1926
Sponsoring organization: CCES, Bucharest
MLA acronym: Korunk

SUBSCRIPTION INFORMATION

Frequency of publication: 12 times/yr.
Circulation: 4,000
Available in microform: No
Subscription price: $50.00/yr.
Year to which price refers: 1992
Subscription address: Orion SRL, Splaiul Independentei nr. 202/A, Sect. 6, Bucharest, Romania
Additional subscription address: Kárpáti Futár Bt, Krudy Gyula u. nr. 3, 1088 Budapest, Hungary
Subscription telephone: (40) 0 173407 (Romania); (36) 1 1340089 (Hungary)
Subscription fax: (40) 0 424169

ADVERTISING INFORMATION

Advertising accepted: No

EDITORIAL DESCRIPTION

Scope: Publishes articles on various aspects of modern human sciences, social and political theory, minority issues, history, literature, and art.
Reviews books: Yes
Publishes notes: Yes
Languages accepted: Hungarian
Prints abstracts: No

SUBMISSION REQUIREMENTS

Restrictions on contributors: None
Author pays submission fee: Yes
Author pays page charges: No
Length of articles: 7,200 words

Length of book reviews: 2,880 words
Length of notes: 1,080 words
Number of copies required: 1
Copyright ownership: Author
Rejected manuscripts: Not returned
Time before publication decision: 1 mo.
Time between decision and publication: 2 mos.
Number of reviewers: 5
Articles submitted per year: 800
Articles published per year: 300
Book reviews submitted per year: 80
Book reviews published per year: 40
Notes submitted per year: 45
Notes published per year: 30

(1534)
Kritik: Tidsskrift for Litteratur, Forskning, Undervisning

Poul Behrendt, Johs. H. Christensen, & Klaus P. Mortensen, Editors
Sortedam Dossering 29
2200 Copenhagen N, Denmark

First published: 1967
ISSN: 0454-5354
MLA acronym: Kritik

SUBSCRIPTION INFORMATION

Frequency of publication: 4 times/yr. (Jan., Apr., Sept., Nov.)
Circulation: 2,500
Available in microform: No
Subscription address: Gyldendal, Klareboderne 3, 1001 Copenhagen, Denmark

ADVERTISING INFORMATION

Advertising accepted: No

EDITORIAL DESCRIPTION

Scope: Publishes articles on Scandinavian literature and culture.
Reviews books: Yes
Publishes notes: No
Languages accepted: Danish
Prints abstracts: No

SUBMISSION REQUIREMENTS

Restrictions on contributors: None
Author pays submission fee: No
Author pays page charges: No
Length of articles: 10-30 pp.
Number of copies required: 1
Special requirements: Submit original typescript.
Copyright ownership: Gyldendal
Rejected manuscripts: Returned
Time before publication decision: 1 mo.
Time between decision and publication: 4 mos.
Number of reviewers: 3
Articles published per year: 33

(1535)
Kritikas Gadagrāmata

LIESMA
Padomju Bulvāri 24
226047 Riga, Latvia

First published: 1973
MLA acronym: KGad

SUBSCRIPTION INFORMATION

Frequency of publication: Annual

EDITORIAL DESCRIPTION

Scope: Publishes articles on Latvian literature.
Reviews books: No
Languages accepted: Latvian
Prints abstracts: No

(1536)
*Kuka: Journal of Creative and Critical Writing

Ode Ogede, Editor
Dept. of English
Ahmadu Bello Univ.
Zaria, Nigeria

First published: 1977
Sponsoring organization: Ahmadu Bello Univ., English Literary Assn.
ISSN: 0331-4545
MLA acronym: Kuka

SUBSCRIPTION INFORMATION

Frequency of publication: Annual
Available in microform: No

ADVERTISING INFORMATION

Advertising accepted: Yes

EDITORIAL DESCRIPTION

Scope: Publishes creative writing and articles on African language and literature.
Reviews books: Yes
Publishes notes: Yes
Languages accepted: English
Prints abstracts: No
Author-anonymous submission: No

SUBMISSION REQUIREMENTS

Restrictions on contributors: None
Author pays submission fee: No
Author pays page charges: No
Length of articles: 15 pp. maximum
Length of book reviews: 6 pp. maximum
Length of notes: 10 pp. maximum
Style: MLA
Number of copies required: 2
Copyright ownership: Author
Rejected manuscripts: Not returned
Time before publication decision: 2 mos.
Time between decision and publication: 2 mos.
Number of reviewers: 2-5
Book reviews published per year: 2
Notes published per year: 2

(1537)
Kultura: Szkice, Opowiadania, Sprawozdania

Jerzy Giedroyc, Editor
Inst. Littéraire
91, avenue de Poissy
Mesnil-le-Roi
78600 Maisons-Laffitte, France

Telephone: (33) 1 39621904
Fax: (33) 1 39625752
First published: 1947
Sponsoring organization: Inst. Littéraire
ISSN: 0023-5148
MLA acronym: KulturaP

SUBSCRIPTION INFORMATION

Frequency of publication: 10 times/yr.
Circulation: 9,500

ADVERTISING INFORMATION

Advertising accepted: Yes

EDITORIAL DESCRIPTION

Scope: Publishes articles on literature and culture. Emphasis is on Polish studies.
Reviews books: Yes
Publishes notes: Yes
Languages accepted: Polish
Prints abstracts: No

SUBMISSION REQUIREMENTS

Length of articles: No restrictions
Number of copies required: 1
Copyright ownership: Assigned by author to journal
Rejected manuscripts: Returned

(1538)
*Kul'tura Slova

S. Ermolenko, Editor
Akademiia Nauk Ukraïny
Inst. Ukraïns'koï Movy
Ul. Hrushevs'koho, 4
252001 MSP Kiev 1, Ukraine

First published: 1967
Sponsoring organization: Inst. Ukraïns'koï Movy, Akademiia Nauk Ukraïny
ISSN: 0201-419X
MLA acronym: KSl

SUBSCRIPTION INFORMATION

Frequency of publication: 2 times/yr.
Circulation: 1,200
Available in microform: No

ADVERTISING INFORMATION

Advertising accepted: No

EDITORIAL DESCRIPTION

Scope: Publishes articles on the problems of Ukrainian language, culture, and stylistics.
Reviews books: Yes
Publishes notes: Yes
Languages accepted: Ukrainian
Prints abstracts: No
Author-anonymous submission: No

SUBMISSION REQUIREMENTS

Restrictions on contributors: None
Author pays submission fee: No
Author pays page charges: No
Length of articles: 3,000-10,000 words
Length of notes: 2,000-2,500 words
Number of copies required: 2
Copyright ownership: Naukova dumka
Rejected manuscripts: Not returned
Time before publication decision: 3 mos.
Time between decision and publication: 18 mos.
Number of reviewers: 2
Articles submitted per year: 60-80
Articles published per year: 40-60
Notes submitted per year: 10
Notes published per year: 5

(1539)
*Kulturōs Barai

Bronys Savukynas, Editor
MTP, Universiteto 6
2600 Vilnius, Lithuania

Telephone: (7) 122 610538
First published: 1965
ISSN: 0134-3106
MLA acronym: KB

SUBSCRIPTION INFORMATION

Frequency of publication: 12 times/yr.
Available in microform: No
Subscription price: 25 Rbl/yr.
Year to which price refers: 1991

ADVERTISING INFORMATION

Advertising accepted: Yes
Advertising rates: 2,000 Rbl/full page

EDITORIAL DESCRIPTION

Scope: Publishes articles on Lithuanian and general culture, including languages, theater, art, and music.
Reviews books: Yes
Publishes notes: Yes
Languages accepted: Russian; English; Lithuanian
Prints abstracts: Yes
Author-anonymous submission: No

SUBMISSION REQUIREMENTS

Restrictions on contributors: None
Author pays submission fee: No
Author pays page charges: No
Length of articles: 1,500 words
Length of book reviews: 550 words
Length of notes: 200 words
Number of copies required: 2
Copyright ownership: Author
Rejected manuscripts: Not returned
Time before publication decision: 1 mo.
Time between decision and publication: 2 weeks
Number of reviewers: 3
Articles submitted per year: 500
Articles published per year: 260
Book reviews submitted per year: 15
Book reviews published per year: 10
Notes submitted per year: 25
Notes published per year: 10

(1540)
*Kulturtidskriften HORISONT

Maria Sandin, Editor
Handelsespl. 23A
65100 Vasa, Finland

Telephone: (358) 961 128426
First published: 1954
Sponsoring organization: Svenska Österbottens Litteraturförening
ISSN: 0439-5530
MLA acronym: Horisont

SUBSCRIPTION INFORMATION

Frequency of publication: 6 times/yr.
Circulation: 2,600
Available in microform: No
Subscription price: 150 Fmk (225 Skr)/yr.
Year to which price refers: 1992
Subscription telephone: (358) 961 177904

ADVERTISING INFORMATION

Advertising accepted: Yes

EDITORIAL DESCRIPTION

Scope: Publishes articles on literature and culture, with an emphasis on Finno-Swedish works.
Reviews books: Yes
Publishes notes: Yes
Languages accepted: Swedish; Norwegian; Danish
Prints abstracts: No

SUBMISSION REQUIREMENTS

Author pays submission fee: No
Author pays page charges: No
Length of articles: 10-20 pp.
Length of book reviews: 700 words
Length of notes: 100 words
Copyright ownership: Author
Rejected manuscripts: Returned
Time before publication decision: 2-12 mos.
Time between decision and publication: 2-18 mos.
Number of reviewers: 1-2
Articles published per year: 60
Book reviews published per year: 120
Notes published per year: 12

(1541)
Kunapipi

Anna Rutherford, Editor
Dept. of English
Univ. of Aarhus
8000 Aarhus C, Denmark

Telephone: (45) 86 136711
Fax: (45) 86 191699
First published: 1979
ISSN: 0106-5734
MLA acronym: Kunapipi

SUBSCRIPTION INFORMATION

Frequency of publication: 3 times/yr.
Circulation: 1,000
Available in microform: No
Subscription price: 200 Dkr/yr. institutions Scandinavia; $50.00 (£20.00, A$50.00)/yr. institutions elsewhere; 120 Dkr/yr. individuals Scandinavia; $30.00 (£12.00, A$30.00)/yr. individuals elsewhere
Year to which price refers: 1991

ADVERTISING INFORMATION

Advertising accepted: Yes

EDITORIAL DESCRIPTION

Scope: Publishes creative and critical material on post-colonial literature, art, and culture. Articles and reviews of related historical and sociological topics, e.g., film, will also be included as will photographs and graphics.
Reviews books: Yes
Publishes notes: Yes
Languages accepted: English
Prints abstracts: No
Author-anonymous submission: No

SUBMISSION REQUIREMENTS

Restrictions on contributors: None
Author pays submission fee: No
Author pays page charges: No
Length of articles: 3,000 words
Length of book reviews: 250 words
Style: Modern Humanities Research Assn.
Number of copies required: 1
Copyright ownership: Journal & author
Rejected manuscripts: Returned; enclose return postage.
Time before publication decision: 3 mos.
Time between decision and publication: 6-8 mos.
Articles submitted per year: 250
Articles published per year: 15
Book reviews submitted per year: 200
Book reviews published per year: 50

(1542)
*Kwansei Gakuin University Annual Studies

Kwansei Gakuin Univ.
1-1-155, Uegahara
Nishinomiya, Japan

Telephone: (81) 789 536111
Fax: (81) 789 510915
First published: 1953
Sponsoring organization: Kwansei Gakuin Univ.
ISSN: 0454-7306
MLA acronym: KGUAS

SUBSCRIPTION INFORMATION

Frequency of publication: Annual
Circulation: 800
Available in microform: No

ADVERTISING INFORMATION

Advertising accepted: No

EDITORIAL DESCRIPTION

Scope: Publishes articles by the faculty of Kwansei Gakuin University.
Reviews books: No
Publishes notes: No
Languages accepted: English; German; French
Prints abstracts: No
Author-anonymous submission: No

SUBMISSION REQUIREMENTS

Restrictions on contributors: Contributors must be affiliated with Kwansei Gakuin Univ.
Author pays submission fee: No
Author pays page charges: No
Length of articles: 2,500-10,000 words
Style: MLA
Number of copies required: 1
Special requirements: Submit original typescript or diskette.
Copyright ownership: Author
Rejected manuscripts: Returned
Time before publication decision: 2 weeks
Time between decision and publication: 6 mos.
Number of reviewers: 1
Articles submitted per year: 15
Articles published per year: 15

(1543)
Kwartalnik Neofilologiczny

Panstwowe Wydawnictwo Naukowe
Ul. Miodowa 10
Warsaw, Poland

First published: 1954
Sponsoring organization: Panstwowe Wydawnictwo Naukowe
ISSN: 0023-5911
MLA acronym: KN

SUBSCRIPTION INFORMATION

Frequency of publication: 4 times/yr.
Circulation: 600
Available in microform: No
Subscription address: Foreign Trade Enterprise, Ars Polona-Ruch, 7 Krakowskie Przedmieście, P.O. Box 1001, 00-068 Warsaw, Poland

ADVERTISING INFORMATION

Advertising accepted: No

EDITORIAL DESCRIPTION

Scope: Publishes scientific articles on linguistics and literature.
Reviews books: Yes
Publishes notes: Yes
Languages accepted: English; German; Polish; French; Italian; Spanish
Prints abstracts: Yes
Author-anonymous submission: No

SUBMISSION REQUIREMENTS

Restrictions on contributors: None
Author pays submission fee: No
Author pays page charges: No
Length of articles: 30 typescript pp. maximum
Length of book reviews: 15 typescript pp.
Length of notes: 5 typescript pp.
Number of copies required: 2
Special requirements: Type double-spaced with 30 lines per page.
Copyright ownership: Panstwowe Wydawnictwo Naukowe
Rejected manuscripts: Returned
Time before publication decision: 6 mos.
Time between decision and publication: 9 mos.
Number of reviewers: 2
Articles published per year: 35
Book reviews published per year: 30
Notes published per year: 10

(1544)
*Kypriakai Spoudai

Theodore Papadopoullos, Editor
Soc. of Cypriot Studies
P.O. Box 2031
Nicosia, Cyprus

First published: 1937
Sponsoring organization: Soc. of Cypriot Studies
ISSN: 0081-1580
MLA acronym: KyS

SUBSCRIPTION INFORMATION

Frequency of publication: Annual
Circulation: 500
Available in microform: No

ADVERTISING INFORMATION

Advertising accepted: No

EDITORIAL DESCRIPTION

Scope: Publishes articles on the history, archaeology, linguistics, and folklore of Cyprus exclusively. All works and materials included are local in scope, covering the island of Cyprus.
Reviews books: No
Languages accepted: English; French; Greek; German; Italian
Prints abstracts: No

SUBMISSION REQUIREMENTS

Restrictions on contributors: None
Author pays submission fee: No
Author pays page charges: No
Length of articles: 4-30 pp.
Style: Cambridge
Number of copies required: 1
Special requirements: Submit typescript.
Copyright ownership: Soc. of Cypriot Studies
Rejected manuscripts: Not returned
Time between decision and publication: 6-12 mos.
Number of reviewers: 1-3
Articles submitted per year: 8-18
Articles published per year: 8-15

(1545)
Kypriakos Logos

Petros S. Stylianou, Editor
Kimonos 10
Engomi, Nicosia, Cyprus

First published: 1969
ISSN: 0254-3184
MLA acronym: KL

SUBSCRIPTION INFORMATION

Frequency of publication: 6 times/yr.
Circulation: 15,000
Available in microform: Yes

ADVERTISING INFORMATION

Advertising accepted: Yes

EDITORIAL DESCRIPTION

Scope: Publishes articles on philology, history, ethnography and literature.
Reviews books: Yes
Publishes notes: Yes
Languages accepted: Greek; English; French; German
Prints abstracts: Yes

SUBMISSION REQUIREMENTS

Restrictions on contributors: None
Author pays submission fee: No
Author pays page charges: No

Length of articles: No restrictions
Length of book reviews: No restrictions
Style: None
Number of copies required: 1
Special requirements: Submit original typescript.
Copyright ownership: Author
Rejected manuscripts: Not returned
Time before publication decision: 2 mos.
Time between decision and publication: 8 mos.
Number of reviewers: 2
Articles submitted per year: 100
Articles published per year: 50
Book reviews submitted per year: 200
Book reviews published per year: 60-100
Notes submitted per year: 30
Notes published per year: 20

(1546)
*Kyushu American Literature

Hirotoshi Baba, Shogo Mitsutomi, Shinichiro Noriguchi, Kazuto Ono, Scott Pugh, Brian Quinn, & David Wood, Editors
Kyushu American Literature Soc.
Inst. of Language & Cultures
Kyushu Univ.
4-2-1 Ropponmatsu, Chuo-ku
Fukuoka 810, Japan

First published: 1958
Sponsoring organization: Kyushu American Literature Soc.
ISSN: 0454-8132
MLA acronym: KAL

SUBSCRIPTION INFORMATION

Frequency of publication: Annual
Circulation: 350
Available in microform: No

ADVERTISING INFORMATION

Advertising accepted: Yes

EDITORIAL DESCRIPTION

Scope: Publishes articles on American literature and American studies.
Reviews books: Yes
Publishes notes: Yes
Languages accepted: English
Prints abstracts: No

SUBMISSION REQUIREMENTS

Restrictions on contributors: Contributors must be members of the Kyushu American Literature Soc. unless invited.
Author pays submission fee: No
Author pays page charges: No
Length of articles: 10 double-spaced typescript pp. maximum
Length of notes: No restrictions
Style: MLA
Number of copies required: 1
Special requirements: Submit original typescript.
Copyright ownership: Assigned by author to journal
Rejected manuscripts: Returned
Time before publication decision: 3 mos.
Time between decision and publication: 8 mos.
Number of reviewers: 5
Articles submitted per year: 8
Articles published per year: 8

(1547)
*Lamar Journal of the Humanities

Ronald H. Fritze & Lloyd M. Daigrepont, Editors
College of Arts & Sciences
Lamar Univ.
P.O. Box 10023
Beaumont, TX 77710

Telephone: 409 880-2289; 409 880-8581
First published: 1973
Sponsoring organization: Lamar Univ., College of Arts & Sciences
ISSN: 0275-410X
MLA acronym: LJHum

SUBSCRIPTION INFORMATION

Frequency of publication: 2 times/yr.
Circulation: 500
Available in microform: No
Subscription price: $6.00/yr.
Year to which price refers: 1992
Subscription telephone: 409 880-8574

ADVERTISING INFORMATION

Advertising accepted: No

EDITORIAL DESCRIPTION

Scope: Publishes articles of interdisciplinary or general interest in the fields of literature, history, contemporary culture, and the fine arts. Detailed studies of highly specialized topics, literary explications which do not elucidate broader historical or ideological issues, and statistical essays in the social sciences are not encouraged but will be considered.
Reviews books: Yes
Publishes notes: No
Languages accepted: English
Prints abstracts: No

SUBMISSION REQUIREMENTS

Restrictions on contributors: None
Author pays submission fee: No
Author pays page charges: No
Length of articles: 6,000 words maximum
Length of book reviews: 1,000 words
Style: MLA; Chicago
Number of copies required: 2
Copyright ownership: Author
Rejected manuscripts: Returned; enclose return postage.
Time before publication decision: 2 mos.
Time between decision and publication: 1 yr.
Number of reviewers: 4
Articles submitted per year: 50
Articles published per year: 10
Book reviews submitted per year: 12
Book reviews published per year: 4-6

(1548)
*Landfall: A New Zealand Quarterly

Judith Baker, Mark Williams, Michelle Leggott, Anne Kennedy, & Ruth Watson, Editors
Caxton Press
P.O. Box 25-088
Christchurch, New Zealand

Telephone: (64) 3 668516
Fax: (64) 3 657840
First published: 1947
ISSN: 0023-7930
MLA acronym: Landfall

SUBSCRIPTION INFORMATION

Frequency of publication: 4 times/yr. (Mar., June, Sept., Dec.)
Circulation: 1,250
Available in microform: No
Subscription price: NZ$43.50/yr. New Zealand; NZ$46.00/yr. elsewhere
Year to which price refers: 1992

ADVERTISING INFORMATION

Advertising accepted: Yes
Advertising rates: NZ$40.00/half page; NZ$80.00/full page

EDITORIAL DESCRIPTION

Scope: Publishes new poetry and prose by New Zealand writers as well as articles on New Zealand literature.
Reviews books: Yes
Publishes notes: Yes
Languages accepted: English
Prints abstracts: No
Author-anonymous submission: No

SUBMISSION REQUIREMENTS

Restrictions on contributors: Contributors must have some connection with New Zealand.
Author pays submission fee: No
Author pays page charges: No
Length of articles: 4-12 printed pp.
Length of book reviews: 1,000-2,000 words
Length of notes: 150-500 words
Style: None
Number of copies required: 1
Special requirements: Submit double-spaced typescript on one side of page only.
Copyright ownership: Author
Rejected manuscripts: Returned; enclose return postage.
Time before publication decision: 1-3 mos.
Time between decision and publication: 1-6 mos.
Number of reviewers: 2
Articles submitted per year: 760
Articles published per year: 100-120
Book reviews submitted per year: 50
Book reviews published per year: 40

(1549)
*Le Langage et l'Homme: Recherches Pluridisciplinaires sur le Langage

Bernard Devlamminck, Editor
Inst. Libre Marie Haps
Rue d'Arlon 11
1040 Brussels, Belgium

Telephone: (32) 2 5119292
Fax: (32) 2 5119837
First published: 1966
Sponsoring organization: Inst. Libre Marie Haps
ISSN: 0458-7251
MLA acronym: Lang&H

SUBSCRIPTION INFORMATION

Frequency of publication: 3 times/yr. (Dec., Mar., June)
Circulation: 600
Available in microform: No
Subscription price: 1,500 BF/yr.
Year to which price refers: 1992

ADVERTISING INFORMATION

Advertising accepted: No

EDITORIAL DESCRIPTION

Scope: Publishes articles on linguistics, psycholinguistics, translation, literature, and paramedical aspects of language.
Reviews books: Yes
Publishes notes: Yes
Languages accepted: French; English; Dutch; German; Spanish
Prints abstracts: Yes
Author-anonymous submission: No

SUBMISSION REQUIREMENTS

Author pays submission fee: No
Author pays page charges: No
Length of articles: No restrictions

Length of book reviews: 300 words
Length of notes: 100 words
Number of copies required: 2
Copyright ownership: Author & Editor
Rejected manuscripts: Not returned
Time before publication decision: 1 mo.
Time between decision and publication: 3-6 mos.
Number of reviewers: 2
Articles submitted per year: 40
Articles published per year: 35
Book reviews submitted per year: 100
Book reviews published per year: 75
Notes submitted per year: 50
Notes published per year: 40

(1550)
*Langage et Société

Pierre Achard, Director
Maison des Sciences de l'Homme
54, boulevard Raspail
75270 Paris Cedex 06, France

Telephone: (33) 1 49542013
Fax: (33) 1 45488353
First published: 1976
Sponsoring organization: Maison des Sciences de l'Homme
ISSN: 0181-4095
MLA acronym: L&Soc

SUBSCRIPTION INFORMATION

Frequency of publication: 4 times/yr. (Mar., June, Sept., Dec.)
Circulation: 300
Available in microform: No
Subscription price: 220 F/yr. institutions France; 290 F/yr. institutions elsewhere; 180 F/yr. individuals France; 250 F/yr. individuals elsewhere
Year to which price refers: 1992

ADVERTISING INFORMATION

Advertising accepted: No

EDITORIAL DESCRIPTION

Scope: Publishes original papers and translations of articles on the relationship between the linguistic and social (historical, psychological, etc.) aspects of language.
Reviews books: Yes
Publishes notes: Yes
Languages accepted: French
Prints abstracts: Yes
Author-anonymous submission: Yes

SUBMISSION REQUIREMENTS

Author pays submission fee: No
Author pays page charges: No
Length of articles: 10,000 words
Length of book reviews: 1,600 words
Length of notes: 5,000 words
Number of copies required: 1
Copyright ownership: Journal
Rejected manuscripts: Not returned
Time before publication decision: 3 mos.
Time between decision and publication: 3 mos.
Number of reviewers: 2-3
Articles submitted per year: 25
Articles published per year: 12
Book reviews submitted per year: 15
Book reviews published per year: 15
Notes submitted per year: 5
Notes published per year: 3

(1551)
*Langages

Librairie Larousse
17, rue du Montparnasse
75298 Paris Cédex 06, France

Telephone: (33) 1 44394160
First published: 1966
ISSN: 0458-726X
MLA acronym: Langages

SUBSCRIPTION INFORMATION

Frequency of publication: 4 times/yr.
Circulation: 4,000
Available in microform: No
Subscription address: Centrale des Revues, 11, rue Gossin, 92543 Montrouge Cédex, France

ADVERTISING INFORMATION

Advertising accepted: Yes

EDITORIAL DESCRIPTION

Scope: Publishes articles on language and linguistics.
Reviews books: No
Publishes notes: No
Languages accepted: French
Prints abstracts: No

SUBMISSION REQUIREMENTS

Restrictions on contributors: None
Author pays submission fee: No
Author pays page charges: No
Length of articles: 430,000 characters
Style: None
Number of copies required: 1
Copyright ownership: Author
Time before publication decision: 1-2 yrs.
Time between decision and publication: 6 mos.
Number of reviewers: 1

(1552)
*The Langston Hughes Review

Thadious M. Davis, Editor
Box 1904
Brown Univ.
Providence, RI 02912

Telephone: 401 863-1815
Fax: 401 863-3700
First published: 1982
Sponsoring organization: Langston Hughes Soc.; Brown Univ., Afro-American Studies Program
ISSN: 0737-0555
MLA acronym: LHRev

SUBSCRIPTION INFORMATION

Frequency of publication: 2 times/yr. (Spring, Fall)
Circulation: 300
Available in microform: No
Subscription price: $10.00/yr. US; $12.00/yr. elsewhere
Year to which price refers: 1992

ADVERTISING INFORMATION

Advertising accepted: Yes

EDITORIAL DESCRIPTION

Scope: Broadly concerned with the life and writings of Langston Hughes. Publishes articles on authors, genres, literary history and theory relevant to critical study in the Hughesian tradition.
Reviews books: Yes
Publishes notes: Yes
Languages accepted: English
Prints abstracts: No

Author-anonymous submission: No

SUBMISSION REQUIREMENTS

Restrictions on contributors: Book reviews are commissioned.
Author pays submission fee: No
Author pays page charges: No
Length of articles: 3,000-5,000 words
Length of book reviews: 500-1,000 words
Length of notes: 250-750 words
Style: MLA
Number of copies required: 1
Copyright ownership: Langston Hughes Soc.
Rejected manuscripts: Returned; enclose SASE.
Time before publication decision: 3-6 mos.
Time between decision and publication: 6-12 mos.
Number of reviewers: 2
Articles submitted per year: 10-15
Articles published per year: 8-12
Book reviews published per year: 1
Notes published per year: 6-10

(1553)
*Language: Journal of the Linguistic Society of America

Sarah G. Thomason, Editor
Dept. of Linguistics
Univ. of Pittsburgh
Pittsburgh, PA 15260

Telephone: 412 624-1354
Fax: 412 624-6130
E-mail: Sgt@a.nl.cs.cmu.edu
First published: 1925
Sponsoring organization: Linguistic Soc. of America
ISSN: 0023-8260
MLA acronym: Language

SUBSCRIPTION INFORMATION

Frequency of publication: 4 times/yr.
Circulation: 7,000
Available in microform: Yes
Subscription price: $45.00/yr. individuals; $15.00/yr. students (includes membership)
Year to which price refers: 1992
Subscription address: Subscriptions Services, Linguistic Soc. of America, 428 E. Preston St., Baltimore, MD 21202

ADVERTISING INFORMATION

Advertising accepted: Yes

EDITORIAL DESCRIPTION

Scope: Publishes technical articles dealing with problems of linguistic science and reviews of recently published works.
Reviews books: Yes
Publishes notes: Yes
Languages accepted: English
Prints abstracts: Yes
Author-anonymous submission: Yes

SUBMISSION REQUIREMENTS

Restrictions on contributors: None
Author pays submission fee: No
Author pays page charges: No
Length of articles: No restrictions
Length of book reviews: 500-2,000 words
Length of notes: 2,500 words
Style: Linguistic Soc. of America
Number of copies required: 3
Copyright ownership: Assigned by author to Linguistic Soc. of America
Rejected manuscripts: One copy returned; enclose return postage.
Time before publication decision: 2-4 mos.
Time between decision and publication: 6-13 mos.
Number of reviewers: 2
Articles submitted per year: 150
Articles published per year: 18 articles

Book reviews submitted per year: 55
Book reviews published per year: 50
Notes submitted per year: 10
Notes published per year: 5

(1554)
*Language & Communication: An Interdisciplinary Journal

Roy Harris & Talbot J. Taylor, Editors
Pergamon Press, Ltd.
Headington Hill Hall
Oxford OX3 0BW, England

Additional editorial address: Pergamon Press Inc., 660 White Plains Rd., Tarrytown, NY 10591-5153
Telephone: (44) 865 794141; 914 592-7700
Fax: (44) 865 60285; 914 592-3625
First published: 1981
ISSN: 0271-5309
MLA acronym: L&C

SUBSCRIPTION INFORMATION

Frequency of publication: 4 times/yr.
Available in microform: Yes
Subscription price: £115.00/yr. institutions
Year to which price refers: 1992
Subscription telephone: (44) 865 794141; 914 524-9200
Subscription fax: (44) 865 743911; 914 333-2444

ADVERTISING INFORMATION

Advertising accepted: Yes

EDITORIAL DESCRIPTION

Scope: Publishes interdisciplinary studies of verbal and nonverbal language and communication.
Reviews books: No
Publishes notes: No
Languages accepted: English
Prints abstracts: No
Author-anonymous submission: No

SUBMISSION REQUIREMENTS

Restrictions on contributors: None
Author pays submission fee: No
Author pays page charges: No
Length of articles: No restrictions
Style: None
Number of copies required: 3
Special requirements: Submit an abstract and biographical information on the author.
Copyright ownership: Pergamon Press
Rejected manuscripts: Returned
Time before publication decision: 2-8 weeks
Time between decision and publication: 3-6 mos.
Articles published per year: 24

(1555)
*Language Acquisition: A Journal of Developmental Linguistics

Kenneth Wexler, Robert Berwick, & Thomas Roeper, Editors
Dept. of Brain & Cognitive Sciences
Massachusetts Inst. of Technology
Building E10-020
Cambridge, MA 02139

Telephone: 617 253-5797
Fax: 617 253-9767
E-mail: Wexler@psyche.mit.edu
First published: 1991
ISSN: 1048-9223
MLA acronym: LAcq

SUBSCRIPTION INFORMATION

Frequency of publication: 4 times/yr.
Available in microform: No
Subscription price: $75.00/yr. institutions US & Canada; $100.00/yr. institutions elsewhere; $25.00/yr. individuals US & Canada; $50.00/yr. individuals elsewhere
Year to which price refers: 1992
Subscription address: Journal Subscription Dept., Lawrence Erlbaum Assoc., Inc., 365 Broadway, Hillsdale, NJ 07642
Additional subscription address: Lawrence Erlbaum Assoc., 27 Palmiera Mansions, Church Rd., Hove, East Sussex BN3 2FA, England
Subscription telephone: 201 666-4110

ADVERTISING INFORMATION

Advertising accepted: Yes

EDITORIAL DESCRIPTION

Scope: Publishes articles on how language is acquired. Focuses primarily on experimental, linguistic, and computational approaches, and discusses the development of syntax, semantics, pragmatics, and phonology. Merges the data of psycholinguistics with discoveries in linguistic theory.
Reviews books: Yes
Publishes notes: Yes
Languages accepted: English
Prints abstracts: Yes
Author-anonymous submission: No

SUBMISSION REQUIREMENTS

Restrictions on contributors: None
Author pays submission fee: No
Author pays page charges: No
Style: Journal; American Psychological Assn.
Number of copies required: 4
Special requirements: Submit double-spaced typescript, along with an abstract of a maximum of 1,000 characters. Authors are responsible for obtaining permission to reprint copyrighted materials.
Copyright ownership: Lawrence Erlbaum Assoc., Inc.
Number of reviewers: 2-4
Articles published per year: 12-16

(1556)
*Language Acquisition & Language Disorders

Harald Clahsen & William Rutherford, Editors
Jakob-Krebs-Str. 126
4156 Willich, Germany

Additional editorial address: William Rutherford, Dept. of Linguistics, Univ. of Southern California, Los Angeles, CA 90089-1693
First published: 1989
ISSN: 0925-0123
MLA acronym: LA&LD

SUBSCRIPTION INFORMATION

Frequency of publication: Irregular
Available in microform: No
Subscription address: John Benjamins Publishing Co., Amsteldijk 44, P.O. Box 75577, 1070 AN Amsterdam, Netherlands
Additional subscription address: John Benjamins North America, 821 Bethlehem Pike, Philadelphia, PA 19118

ADVERTISING INFORMATION

Advertising accepted: No

EDITORIAL DESCRIPTION

Scope: A forum for research in developmental psycholinguistics from North America and from Europe. Aims to contribute to theories in language acquisition in children and adults. Focuses on language development, language attrition, language disorders, and language learning.
Reviews books: No
Publishes notes: No
Languages accepted: English
Prints abstracts: No
Author-anonymous submission: No

SUBMISSION REQUIREMENTS

Author pays submission fee: No
Author pays page charges: No
Length of books: 250-350 pp.
Copyright ownership: John Benjamins B.V.
Time before publication decision: 3-4 mos.
Time between decision and publication: 10-12 mos.
Number of reviewers: 2
Books submitted per year: 4-6
Books published per year: 2-3

(1557)
*Language and Cognitive Processes

Lorraine K. Tyler, Coordinating Editor
Dept. of Psychology
Birkbeck College
Univ. of London
Malet St.
London WC1, England

Additional editorial address: Lawrence Erlbaum Assoc. Ltd., 27 Palmeira Mansions, Church Rd., Hove, East Sussex BN3 2FA, England
Telephone: (44) 71 6316372
Fax: (44) 71 6316587
First published: 1986
ISSN: 0169-0965
MLA acronym: LCP

SUBSCRIPTION INFORMATION

Frequency of publication: 4 times/yr.
Available in microform: No
Subscription price: £75.00/yr. institutions United Kingdom; $120.00/yr. institutions US; £25.00/yr. individuals United Kingdom; $47.50/yr. individuals US
Year to which price refers: 1991
Subscription address: Linda Baker, Lawrence Erlbaum Assoc. Ltd., Distribution Centre, Blackhorse Rd., Letchworth, Herts SG6 1HN, England

ADVERTISING INFORMATION

Advertising accepted: Yes
Advertising rates: £150.00/full page

EDITORIAL DESCRIPTION

Scope: Provides an international forum for the publication of theoretical and experimental research into the mental processes and representations involved in language use.
Reviews books: Yes, review articles
Publishes notes: Yes
Languages accepted: English
Prints abstracts: Yes
Author-anonymous submission: Yes, at author's request

SUBMISSION REQUIREMENTS

Restrictions on contributors: None
Author pays submission fee: No
Author pays page charges: No
Length of articles: No restrictions
Length of book reviews: No restrictions
Length of notes: No restrictions
Style: American Psychological Assn.
Number of copies required: 4

Special requirements: Submit original typescript and 3 copies. Manuscript must not have been published previously or be under consideration elsewhere. Include an abstract of 150 words maximum.
Copyright ownership: Lawrence Erlbaum Assoc. & VSP Publications
Time before publication decision: 6-9 mos.
Time between decision and publication: 5 mos.
Number of reviewers: 2-3

(1558)
*Language and Computers: Studies in Practical Linguistics

Jan Aarts & Willem Meijs, Editors
Editions Rodopi
Keizersgracht 302-304
1016 EX Amsterdam, Netherlands

Additional editorial address: Editions Rodopi, 233 Peachtree St. NE, Suite 404, Atlanta, GA 30303-1504
ISSN: 0921-5034
MLA acronym: L&Comp

SUBSCRIPTION INFORMATION

Frequency of publication: Irregular
Circulation: 600-800
Available in microform: No
Subscription telephone: (31) 20 6227507; 404 523-1964; 800 225-3998
Subscription fax: (31) 20 6380948; 404 522-7116

ADVERTISING INFORMATION

Advertising accepted: Yes, on an exchange basis

EDITORIAL DESCRIPTION

Scope: Publishes monographs and collections of articles on studies in computer-oriented research in linguistics.
Reviews books: No
Publishes notes: No
Languages accepted: English
Prints abstracts: No

SUBMISSION REQUIREMENTS

Author pays submission fee: No
Length of books: 200-300 pp.
Style: MLA; Chicago
Number of copies required: 2
Copyright ownership: Editions Rodopi B.V.
Time before publication decision: 2 mos.
Time between decision and publication: 3-9 mos.
Books submitted per year: 2-4
Books published per year: 1-3

(1559)
*Language and Culture

Inst. of Language & Culture Studies
Hokkaido Univ.
West 8, North 17
Kita-ku, Sapporo
Hokkaido 060, Japan

First published: 1981
Sponsoring organization: Hokkaido Univ., Inst. of Language & Culture Studies
ISSN: 0286-3855
MLA acronym: Lang&C

SUBSCRIPTION INFORMATION

Frequency of publication: 2 times/yr.
Available in microform: No

ADVERTISING INFORMATION

Advertising accepted: No

EDITORIAL DESCRIPTION

Scope: Publishes scholarly articles dealing with language, culture, and literature.
Reviews books: No
Publishes notes: No
Languages accepted: English; French; German; Japanese; Spanish; Italian; all Slavic languages; Chinese languages
Prints abstracts: Yes
Author-anonymous submission: No

SUBMISSION REQUIREMENTS

Restrictions on contributors: Contributors must be faculty members of Hokkaido Univ.
Author pays submission fee: No
Author pays page charges: No
Number of copies required: 2
Copyright ownership: Author
Number of reviewers: 5
Articles submitted per year: 20
Articles published per year: 20

(1560)
*Language and Linguistics in Melanesia: Journal of the Linguistic Society of Papua New Guinea

John M. Clifton, Editor
Linguistic Soc. of Papua New Guinea
P.O. Box 418
Ukarumpa via Lae, Papua New Guinea

Additional editorial address: John Roberts, at the above address
Telephone: (675) 773544
Fax: (675) 773507
First published: 1968
Sponsoring organization: Linguistic Soc. of Papua New Guinea; Soc. on Pidgins & Creoles in Melanesia
ISSN: 0023-1959
MLA acronym: L&LinM

SUBSCRIPTION INFORMATION

Frequency of publication: 2 times/yr.
Circulation: 200
Available in microform: No
Subscription price: $35.00/yr. (A$42.00)/yr. institutions; $20.00 (A$25.00)/yr. individuals
Year to which price refers: 1992

ADVERTISING INFORMATION

Advertising accepted: Yes

EDITORIAL DESCRIPTION

Scope: Publishes articles about the languages of Melanesia and the linguistic situation there.
Reviews books: Yes
Publishes notes: Yes
Languages accepted: English; Tok Pisin English Pidgin; French; German
Prints abstracts: No
Author-anonymous submission: Yes

SUBMISSION REQUIREMENTS

Restrictions on contributors: None
Author pays submission fee: No
Author pays page charges: No
Length of articles: 5,000 words
Length of book reviews: 2,000 words maximum
Length of notes: 1,000 words
Style: Chicago
Number of copies required: 2
Special requirements: Submission of diskette in addition to hard copy is preferred.
Copyright ownership: Author
Rejected manuscripts: Returned
Time before publication decision: 3 mos.
Time between decision and publication: 6-12 mos.
Number of reviewers: 2
Articles submitted per year: 8-11
Articles published per year: 6-9
Book reviews submitted per year: 8-12
Book reviews published per year: 8-12
Notes submitted per year: 0-2
Notes published per year: 0-2

(1561)
*Language and Literature

Bates L. Hoffer, Editor
Box 47, Trinity Univ.
715 Stadium Dr.
San Antonio, TX 78212

Telephone: 512 736-7369
Fax: 512 349-8714
First published: 1975
Sponsoring organization: Trinity Univ.
ISSN: 1057-6037
MLA acronym: LnL

SUBSCRIPTION INFORMATION

Frequency of publication: Annual
Circulation: 150
Available in microform: No
Subscription price: $30.00/yr. institutions; $20.00/yr. individuals
Year to which price refers: 1992
Subscription address: Pitman Press, P.O. Box 791786, San Antonio, TX 78279-1786

ADVERTISING INFORMATION

Advertising accepted: Yes
Advertising rates: $25.00/half page; $50.00/full page

EDITORIAL DESCRIPTION

Scope: Articles analyze style and structure as necessary components of the process of literary criticism: analysis of style and structure, interpretation, evaluation, and critical commentary.
Reviews books: Yes
Publishes notes: No
Languages accepted: English; Spanish
Prints abstracts: No
Author-anonymous submission: No

SUBMISSION REQUIREMENTS

Restrictions on contributors: Contributors must be subscribers.
Author pays submission fee: No
Author pays page charges: No
Length of articles: No restrictions
Length of book reviews: No restrictions
Number of copies required: 2
Copyright ownership: Pitman Press
Rejected manuscripts: Returned
Time before publication decision: 1-3 mos.
Time between decision and publication: 15 mos. maximum
Number of reviewers: 2
Articles submitted per year: 16
Articles published per year: 5-7
Book reviews submitted per year: 1-2
Book reviews published per year: 0-1

(1562)
*Language and Literature: Journal of the Poetics and Linguistics Association

Mick Short, Katie Wales, & Tony Bex, Editors
Dept. of Linguistics & Modern English Language
Univ. of Lancaster
Bailrigg, Lancaster LA1 4YT, England

Telephone: (44) 524 65201 ext. 3035

Fax: (44) 524 843085
E-mail: Eia017@lancaster.ac.uk
First published: 1992
Sponsoring organization: Poetics & Linguistics Assn. (PALA)
ISSN: 0963-9470
MLA acronym: Lang&Lit

SUBSCRIPTION INFORMATION

Frequency of publication: 3 times/yr. (Feb., June, Sept.)
Subscription price: £46.00/yr. institutions United Kingdom; £47.00/yr. institutions Europe; $87.00/yr. institutions US & Canada; £51.00/yr. institutions elsewhere; £28.00/yr. individuals United Kingdom; £29.00/yr. individuals Europe; $53.00/yr. individuals US & Canada; £31.00/yr. individuals elsewhere
Year to which price refers: 1993
Subscription address: Subscription Dept., Longman Group UK Ltd., Fourth Ave., Harlow, Essex CM20 2JE, England
Subscription telephone: (44) 279 623924
Subscription fax: (44) 279 623841

ADVERTISING INFORMATION

Advertising accepted: Yes
Advertising rates: £120.00/half page; £175.00/full page; £175.00/insert

EDITORIAL DESCRIPTION

Scope: An international journal which brings together recent work of scholars in the field of stylistic analysis, the linguistic analysis of literary texts and related areas, including their pedagogical applications. Explores the connections between stylistics, critical theory, linguistics, and literary criticism.
Reviews books: Yes
Publishes notes: Yes
Languages accepted: English
Prints abstracts: Yes
Author-anonymous submission: Yes

SUBMISSION REQUIREMENTS

Author pays submission fee: No
Author pays page charges: No
Length of articles: 6,000 words
Length of book reviews: 750 words
Length of notes: 2,500 words maximum
Style: Journal
Number of copies required: 4
Special requirements: Contributors are responsible for copyright permissions. Submission must not be under consideration elsewhere.
Copyright ownership: Longman Group UK Ltd.
Rejected manuscripts: One copy returned
Time before publication decision: 1-2 mos.
Time between decision and publication: 5 mos.
Number of reviewers: 4-5
Articles published per year: 9-12
Book reviews published per year: 10

(1563)
*Language and Speech

Bruno H. Repp, Editor
Haskins Laboratories
270 Crown St.
New Haven, CT 06511-6695

Telephone: 203 865-6163
Fax: 203 865-8963
E-mail: LS@YALEHASK.BITNET
First published: 1958
ISSN: 0023-8309
MLA acronym: L&S

SUBSCRIPTION INFORMATION

Frequency of publication: 4 times/yr. (Mar., June, Sept., Dec.)
Circulation: 1,100
Available in microform: No
Subscription price: $180.00/yr. institutions; $90.00/yr. individuals
Year to which price refers: 1991
Subscription address: Kingston Press Services Ltd., 43 Derwent Rd., Whitton, Twickenham, Middlesex TW2 7HQ, England
Subscription fax: (44) 18 3983670

EDITORIAL DESCRIPTION

Scope: Publishes articles on the production and perception of speech, psycholinguistics, linguistic basis of reading, and sociolinguistics. Experimental approaches are preferred.
Reviews books: Yes
Languages accepted: English
Prints abstracts: Yes
Author-anonymous submission: No

SUBMISSION REQUIREMENTS

Restrictions on contributors: Book reviews are commissioned.
Author pays submission fee: No
Author pays page charges: No
Length of articles: No restrictions
Length of book reviews: 5-10 double-spaced typescript pp.
Style: Journal
Number of copies required: 3
Special requirements: Include an abstract and up to 4 keywords.
Copyright ownership: Journal
Rejected manuscripts: Not returned
Time between decision and publication: 4 mos.
Number of reviewers: 3
Articles submitted per year: 30
Articles published per year: 16
Book reviews submitted per year: 2
Book reviews published per year: 2

(1564)
*Language and Style: An International Journal

Edmund L. Epstein, Editor
Dept. of English
Queens College
Flushing, NY 11367

First published: 1968
Sponsoring organization: Queens College Press
ISSN: 0023-8317
MLA acronym: Lang&S

SUBSCRIPTION INFORMATION

Frequency of publication: 4 times/yr.
Circulation: 700
Available in microform: No
Subscription price: $22.00/yr. institutions; $16.00/yr. individuals
Year to which price refers: 1989
Subscription address: Editorial Services, Kiely 1310, Queens College of the City Univ. of New York, Flushing, NY 11367
Subscription telephone: 718 997-4476

ADVERTISING INFORMATION

Advertising accepted: No

EDITORIAL DESCRIPTION

Scope: Publishes articles on style in all of its manifestations, in all of the arts, and in all of its social and cultural contexts. There are no restrictions on theoretical approaches: any consistent and well-defined system, from mathematical linguistics to traditional rhetorical analysis, may be employed. It should be possible to employ the analytical methods in each article in a general definition.
Reviews books: Yes
Publishes notes: Yes
Languages accepted: English; French; German
Prints abstracts: No
Author-anonymous submission: No

SUBMISSION REQUIREMENTS

Restrictions on contributors: None
Author pays submission fee: No
Author pays page charges: No
Length of articles: 4,000-25,000 words
Length of book reviews: 600-2,000 words
Style: MLA
Number of copies required: 2
Special requirements: Include a 1-page abstract.
Copyright ownership: Author
Rejected manuscripts: Returned; enclose return postage.
Time before publication decision: 3-5 mos.
Time between decision and publication: 2-4 yrs.
Number of reviewers: 2
Articles submitted per year: 80-100
Articles published per year: 30-40
Book reviews published per year: 5-10

(1565)
*Language, Culture, and Curriculum

Eoghan MacAogáin & Pádraig Ó Riagáin, Editors
Linguistics Inst. of Ireland
31 Fitzwilliam Place
Dublin 2, Ireland

Telephone: (353) 1 765489
Fax: (353) 1 610004
First published: 1988
Sponsoring organization: Linguistics Inst. of Ireland
ISSN: 0790-8318
MLA acronym: LC&C

SUBSCRIPTION INFORMATION

Frequency of publication: 3 times/yr.
Circulation: 200
Available in microform: No
Subscription price: £38.00/yr.
Year to which price refers: 1992
Subscription address: Multilingual Matters Ltd., Frankfurt Lodge, Clevedon Hall, Victoria Rd., Clevedon, Avon BS21 7SJ, England
Subscription telephone: (44) 275 876519
Subscription fax: (44) 275 343096

ADVERTISING INFORMATION

Advertising accepted: Yes

EDITORIAL DESCRIPTION

Scope: Publishes articles on theoretical and empirical studies on bilingualism and multiculturalism, with a focus on language and culture, and on school-based programs designed to maintain and develop the relationship between them.
Reviews books: Yes
Publishes notes: Yes
Languages accepted: English
Prints abstracts: Yes

SUBMISSION REQUIREMENTS

Restrictions on contributors: No
Author pays submission fee: No
Author pays page charges: No
Length of articles: 7,000 words maximum
Length of book reviews: 500-1,000 words
Length of notes: 200 words maximum
Style: Chicago
Number of copies required: 4
Special requirements: Original article must not be submitted elsewhere.
Copyright ownership: Linguistics Inst. of Ireland
Rejected manuscripts: Returned at author's request
Time before publication decision: 4 mos.
Time between decision and publication: 8 mos.
Number of reviewers: 3
Articles submitted per year: 40
Articles published per year: 16
Book reviews submitted per year: 10
Book reviews published per year: 6

Notes submitted per year: 4
Notes published per year: 4

(1566)
*Language Forum: A Half-Yearly Journal of Language and Literature

Ujjal Singh Bahri, Editor
Bahri Books & Periodicals
997A, Street No. 9
Gobindpuri, Kalkaji
New Delhi 110019, India

Telephone: (91) 11 6448606
Fax: (91) 11 6460796 attn: Bahri
First published: 1975
ISSN: 0253-5071
MLA acronym: LangF

SUBSCRIPTION INFORMATION

Frequency of publication: 2 times/yr. (Jan., July)
Circulation: 260
Available in microform: No
Subscription price: $40.00/yr. institutions; $30.00/yr. individuals
Year to which price refers: 1992

ADVERTISING INFORMATION

Advertising accepted: Yes
Advertising rates: $100.00/full page

EDITORIAL DESCRIPTION

Scope: Publishes papers on curriculum planning, linguistic analyses of Indian languages and dialects, comparative literature, and linguistics in general.
Reviews books: Yes
Publishes notes: Yes
Languages accepted: English
Prints abstracts: No
Author-anonymous submission: No

SUBMISSION REQUIREMENTS

Restrictions on contributors: None
Author pays submission fee: Yes, if paper exceeds 20 pp.
Cost of submission fee: $30.00-$50.00
Author pays page charges: No
Length of articles: 20 pp.
Length of book reviews: 10-15 pp.
Style: MLA
Number of copies required: 2
Special requirements: Use size A4 (8 1/4 in. x 11 3/4 in.) paper. Include a 250-word maximum abstract.
Copyright ownership: Bahri Publications; reverts to author after 3 yrs.
Rejected manuscripts: Returned; enclose return postage.
Time before publication decision: 6-12 weeks
Time between decision and publication: 6-8 mos.
Number of reviewers: 2
Articles submitted per year: 28-30
Articles published per year: 18-20
Book reviews submitted per year: 6-8
Book reviews published per year: 3-5
Notes submitted per year: 2-4

(1567)
Language in Society

Peter Trudgill, Ralph Fasold, & William Labov, Editors
Basil Blackwell Ltd.
108 Cowley Rd.
Oxford OX4 1JF, England

Additional editorial address: Basil Blackwell Inc., 238 Main St., Suite 501, Cambridge, MA 02142
MLA acronym: LinS

ADVERTISING INFORMATION

Advertising accepted: No

EDITORIAL DESCRIPTION

Scope: Publishes monographs on language's role in and relation to the social aspects of life.
Reviews books: No
Publishes notes: No
Languages accepted: English

SUBMISSION REQUIREMENTS

Copyright ownership: Author

(1568)
Language in Society

William Bright, Suzanne Romaine, Joel Sherzer, & Deborah Tannen, Editors
1625 Mariposa Ave.
Boulder, CO 80302

Telephone: 303 938-9718
First published: 1972
ISSN: 0047-4045
MLA acronym: LSoc

SUBSCRIPTION INFORMATION

Frequency of publication: 4 times/yr. (Mar., June, Sept., Dec.)
Circulation: 1,458
Subscription price: $93.00/yr. institutions US & Canada; £67.00/yr. institutions elsewhere; $46.00/yr. individuals US & Canada; £27.00/yr. individuals elsewhere; $25.00/single issue US & Canada; £18.00/single issue elsewhere
Year to which price refers: 1992
Subscription address: Cambridge Univ. Press, 40 W. 20th St., New York, NY 10011
Additional subscription address: Cambridge Univ. Press, Edinburgh Bldg., Shaftesbury Rd., Cambridge CB2 2RU, England

ADVERTISING INFORMATION

Advertising accepted: Yes

EDITORIAL DESCRIPTION

Scope: Concerned with all branches of the theoretical and empirical study of speech and language as aspects of social life.
Reviews books: Yes
Publishes notes: Yes
Languages accepted: English
Prints abstracts: Yes
Author-anonymous submission: No

SUBMISSION REQUIREMENTS

Restrictions on contributors: None
Author pays submission fee: No
Author pays page charges: No
Length of articles: 7,000-10,000 words
Length of book reviews: 2,000-2,500 words
Length of notes: 500-750 words
Style: References according to *Linguistic Bibliography* (Permanent International Committee on Linguistics). General style is *LSoc* style sheet and *Chicago Manual of Style*.
Number of copies required: 2
Special requirements: Submit double-spaced typescript; consult style sheet.
Copyright ownership: Cambridge Univ. Press
Rejected manuscripts: 1 copy returned at author's request
Time before publication decision: 6 mos.
Time between decision and publication: 1 yr.
Number of reviewers: 2
Articles submitted per year: 100
Articles published per year: 20
Book reviews submitted per year: 64
Book reviews published per year: 50
Notes published per year: 50

(1569)
*Language Learning: A Journal of Applied Linguistics

A. Z. Guiora & J. A. Upshur, Editors
TESL Centre
Concordia Univ.
1455 de Maisonneuve Blvd. W
Montréal, Québec H3G 1M8, Canada

Additional editorial address: Dept. of Psychology, Univ. of Haifa, 31999 Haifa, Israel
First published: 1948
Sponsoring organization: Research Club in Language Learning
ISSN: 0023-8333
MLA acronym: LL

SUBSCRIPTION INFORMATION

Frequency of publication: 4 times/yr. (Mar., June, Sept., Dec.)
Circulation: 2,500
Available in microform: Yes
Subscription price: $60.00/yr. institutions; $36.00/yr. individuals
Year to which price refers: 1992
Subscription address: Language Learning, 178 Henry S. Frieze Bldg., 105 South State St., Ann Arbor, MI 48109-1285

ADVERTISING INFORMATION

Advertising accepted: No

EDITORIAL DESCRIPTION

Scope: Publishes articles that make contributions to either theoretical or practical aspects of language acquisition, language behavior, and second language pedagogy.
Reviews books: Yes
Publishes notes: No
Languages accepted: English
Prints abstracts: Yes

SUBMISSION REQUIREMENTS

Restrictions on contributors: None
Author pays submission fee: No
Author pays page charges: No
Length of articles: 25-35 pp.
Length of book reviews: 5-15 pp.
Style: American Psychological Assn.
Number of copies required: 4
Special requirements: Include an abstract (200 words maximum).
Copyright ownership: Journal
Rejected manuscripts: Returned at author's request; enclose return postage.
Time before publication decision: 2-4 mos.
Time between decision and publication: 6-8 mos.
Number of reviewers: 3
Articles submitted per year: 120
Articles published per year: 20
Book reviews submitted per year: 25
Book reviews published per year: 12

(1570)
*Language Problems and Language Planning/Lingvaj Problemoj kaj Lingvo-Planado

Humphrey Tonkin, Probal Dasgupta, & Klaus Schubert, Editors
Office of the President
Univ. of Hartford
West Hartford, CT 06117

Telephone: 203 768-4417
Fax: 203 768-5417
First published: 1977
Sponsoring organization: Center for Research & Documentation on World Language Problems
ISSN: 0272-2690
MLA acronym: LPLP

SUBSCRIPTION INFORMATION

Frequency of publication: 3 times/yr.
Circulation: 700
Available in microform: Yes
Subscription price: 132 f ($80.00)/yr.
Year to which price refers: 1993
Subscription address: John Benjamins North America, Inc., 821 Bethelehem Pike, Philadelphia, PA 19118
Additional subscription address: John Benjamins B.V., Amsteldijk 44, P.O. Box 75577, 1070 AN Amsterdam, Netherlands
Subscription telephone: 215 836-1200; (31) 20 6738156
Subscription fax: 215 836-1204; (31) 20 6739773

ADVERTISING INFORMATION

Advertising accepted: No

EDITORIAL DESCRIPTION

Scope: Journal publishes original articles and book reviews on widely shared, internationally significant problems related to human language. Each article is summarized in Esperanto and in a third language.
Reviews books: Yes
Publishes notes: Yes
Languages accepted: Esperanto; English; French; Spanish; Portuguese; German; Italian; other languages (upon consultation with editor)
Prints abstracts: Yes
Author-anonymous submission: Yes

SUBMISSION REQUIREMENTS

Restrictions on contributors: None
Author pays submission fee: No
Author pays page charges: No
Length of articles: 20 double-spaced typescript pp. maximum
Length of book reviews: 1,000-1,500 words
Length of notes: 500 words
Style: Chicago
Number of copies required: 2
Special requirements: Include a separate note of about 50 words on the career and work of each author.
Copyright ownership: John Benjamins Publishing Co.
Rejected manuscripts: Returned; enclose return postage.
Time before publication decision: 4 mos.
Time between decision and publication: 6 mos.
Number of reviewers: 2
Articles submitted per year: 60
Articles published per year: 15
Book reviews submitted per year: 30
Book reviews published per year: 25
Notes submitted per year: 10
Notes published per year: 7

(1571)
*The Language Quarterly

Roger W. Cole, Editor
CPR 107
Univ. of South Florida
Tampa, FL 33620

Telephone: 813 974-2548
First published: 1962
Sponsoring organization: Univ. of South Florida, Tampa, College of Arts & Letters, Division of Language
ISSN: 0458-7359
MLA acronym: LangQ

SUBSCRIPTION INFORMATION

Frequency of publication: 2 double issues/yr. (Dec., June)
Circulation: 500
Available in microform: Yes
Subscription price: $24.00/yr. institutions; $12.00/yr. individuals
Year to which price refers: 1991

ADVERTISING INFORMATION

Advertising accepted: Yes

EDITORIAL DESCRIPTION

Scope: Publishes articles on linguistics, literature, and language education.
Reviews books: Yes
Publishes notes: Yes
Languages accepted: English
Prints abstracts: No
Author-anonymous submission: No

SUBMISSION REQUIREMENTS

Restrictions on contributors: None
Author pays submission fee: No
Author pays page charges: No; author may advance publication time by making a donation toward the $12.00/printed page cost for extra pages.
Length of articles: 7,500 words maximum
Length of book reviews: No restrictions
Length of notes: No restrictions
Style: Linguistic Soc. of America; Chicago
Number of copies required: 2
Special requirements: Submission on 5 1/4 in. IBM-compatible diskette using WordPerfect or ASCII is preferred. If not possible, submit double-spaced typescript on 8 1/2 in. x 11 in. bond paper.
Copyright ownership: Author
Rejected manuscripts: Returned; enclose SASE.
Time before publication decision: 3-6 mos.
Time between decision and publication: 6-18 mos.
Number of reviewers: 2-3
Articles submitted per year: 40-50
Articles published per year: 20-30
Book reviews submitted per year: 1-10
Book reviews published per year: 1-6
Notes submitted per year: 1-8
Notes published per year: 1-4

(1572)
*Language Research

Chungmin Lee & San-Oak Lee, Editors
Language Research Inst.
Seoul National Univ.
Kwanak-ku
Seoul 151, Korea

Telephone: (82) 2 8805485
Fax: (82) 8 8805485
First published: 1965
Sponsoring organization: Seoul National Univ.
ISSN: 0254-4474
MLA acronym: LangR

SUBSCRIPTION INFORMATION

Frequency of publication: 4 times/yr. (Mar., June, Sept., Dec.)
Circulation: 500
Available in microform: No

ADVERTISING INFORMATION

Advertising accepted: Yes

EDITORIAL DESCRIPTION

Scope: Publishes studies on natural language, linguistic theory, formal grammar, cognitive grammar, computational linguistics, and sociolinguistics.
Reviews books: Yes
Publishes notes: Yes
Languages accepted: Korean; French; German; English
Prints abstracts: Yes
Author-anonymous submission: No

SUBMISSION REQUIREMENTS

Restrictions on contributors: None
Author pays submission fee: No
Author pays page charges: No
Length of articles: 10,000 words
Length of book reviews: 5,000 words
Length of notes: 2,000 words
Style: Journal
Number of copies required: 3
Special requirements: Submit original typescript, 2 copies, and half-page, double-spaced abstract.
Copyright ownership: Language Research Inst.
Rejected manuscripts: Not returned
Time before publication decision: 1 mo.
Time between decision and publication: 1-2 mos.
Number of reviewers: 2
Articles submitted per year: 40
Articles published per year: 25
Book reviews submitted per year: 1
Book reviews published per year: 1

(1573)
Language Sciences

Fred C. C. Peng, Editor
Dept. of Linguistics
International Christian Univ.
10-2, 3 Chome, Osawa
Mitaka, Tokyo 181, Japan

First published: 1979
Sponsoring organization: East-West Sign Language Assn.
ISSN: 0388-0001
MLA acronym: LangS

SUBSCRIPTION INFORMATION

Frequency of publication: 4 times/yr.
Circulation: 500
Available in microform: Yes
Subscription price: $190.00 (£120.00)/yr. institutions
Year to which price refers: 1992
Subscription address: Pergamon Press, Headington Hill Hall, Oxford OX3 0BW, England
Additional subscription address: Pergamon Press Inc., 660 White Plains Rd., Tarrytown, NY 10591-5153
Subscription telephone: (44) 865 794141; 914 524-9200
Subscription fax: (44) 865 743911; 914 333-2444

ADVERTISING INFORMATION

Advertising accepted: Yes

EDITORIAL DESCRIPTION

Scope: Publishes international articles on language sciences as interdisciplinary forum.
Reviews books: Yes
Publishes notes: Yes
Languages accepted: English
Prints abstracts: Yes
Author-anonymous submission: Yes

SUBMISSION REQUIREMENTS

Restrictions on contributors: None
Author pays submission fee: No
Author pays page charges: No
Length of articles: 50 pp. maximum
Length of book reviews: 8 pp. maximum
Length of notes: 3 pp.
Style: American Anthropologist
Number of copies required: 4
Special requirements: Include abstract.
Copyright ownership: Journal
Rejected manuscripts: Returned
Time before publication decision: 2-3 mos.
Time between decision and publication: 6 mos.
Number of reviewers: 3
Articles submitted per year: 20-30
Articles published per year: 10

Book reviews submitted per year: 5
Book reviews published per year: 2-5
Notes submitted per year: 2
Notes published per year: 2

(1574)
*Language Teaching: The International Abstracting Journal for Language Teachers and Applied Linguists

Valerie Kinsella, Editor
63 Long Ashton Rd.
Long Ashton, Bristol BS18 9HW, England

First published: 1965
Sponsoring organization: Centre for Information on Language Teaching & Research (CILT), Regent's College; English Language Services Dept., British Council
ISSN: 0261-4448
MLA acronym: LTeach

SUBSCRIPTION INFORMATION

Frequency of publication: 4 times/yr. (Jan., Apr., July, Oct.)
Circulation: 2,200
Available in microform: No
Subscription price: $83.00/yr. institutions US & Canada; £43.00/yr. institutions United Kingdom; £45.00/yr. institutions elsewhere; $42.00/yr. individuals US & Canada; £20.00/yr. individuals elsewhere
Year to which price refers: 1991
Subscription address: Cambridge Univ. Press, Journals Dept., 40 W. 20th St., New York, NY 10011-4211
Additional subscription address: Cambridge Univ. Press, Edinburgh Bldg., Shaftesbury Rd., Cambridge CB2 2RU, England

ADVERTISING INFORMATION

Advertising accepted: Yes
Advertising rates: $250.00/half page; $343.00/full page

EDITORIAL DESCRIPTION

Scope: Publishes abstracts of current works on language research, language testing, language studies, and applied linguistics, as well as one article per issue.
Reviews books: Yes
Publishes notes: No
Languages accepted: English
Author-anonymous submission: No

SUBMISSION REQUIREMENTS

Restrictions on contributors: Most of the abstracts are specially written by a team of abstracters. All book review annotations are written by Editor.
Author pays submission fee: No
Author pays page charges: No
Length of book reviews: 50-200 words
Copyright ownership: Cambridge Univ. Press
Articles published per year: 4

(1575)
Language Testing

Alan Davies & J. Upshur, Editors
Dept. of Applied Linguistics
Univ. of Edinburgh
14 Buccleuch Place
Edinburgh EH9 9LN, Scotland

First published: 1984
ISSN: 0265-5322
MLA acronym: LangT

SUBSCRIPTION INFORMATION

Frequency of publication: 3 times/yr. (Mar., July, Dec.)
Circulation: 570
Available in microform: No
Subscription price: $115.00/yr. institutions; $68.00/yr. individuals; $48.00/yr. single issue
Year to which price refers: 1993
Subscription address: Edward Arnold Journals, Mill Rd., Dunton Green, Sevenoaks, Kent, England
Additional subscription address: In US & Canada: Cambridge Univ. Press, 40 W. 20th St., New York, NY 10011-4211

ADVERTISING INFORMATION

Advertising accepted: Yes

EDITORIAL DESCRIPTION

Scope: Provides a forum for the exchange of ideas and information between people working in the fields of first and second language testing and assessment. These will include researchers and practitioners in English as a foreign language/English as a second language testing, mother tongue testing and assessment in child language acquistion and language pathology.
Reviews books: Yes
Publishes notes: Yes
Languages accepted: English
Prints abstracts: Yes
Author-anonymous submission: Yes

SUBMISSION REQUIREMENTS

Restrictions on contributors: Unsolicited book reviews are not accepted.
Author pays submission fee: No
Author pays page charges: No
Length of articles: 4,000-8,000 words
Length of book reviews: 1,000 words
Style: Harvard
Number of copies required: 3
Copyright ownership: Edward Arnold
Rejected manuscripts: Returned at author's request
Time before publication decision: 6 mos.
Time between decision and publication: 1 yr.
Number of reviewers: 2
Articles submitted per year: 25
Articles published per year: 14
Book reviews published per year: 6
Notes submitted per year: 3
Notes published per year: 3

(1576)
*Language Variation and Change

David Sankoff, Anthony Kroch, & William Labov, Editors
Centre de Recherches Mathematiques
Univ. de Montréal
C.P. 6128, Succursale "A"
Montreal H3C 3J7, Canada

Telephone: 514 343-7574
Fax: 514 343-2254
E-mail: Sankoff@ere.umontreal.ca
First published: 1989
ISSN: 0954-3945
MLA acronym: LV&C

SUBSCRIPTION INFORMATION

Circulation: 500
Subscription price: $52.00/yr. institutions; $27.00/yr. individuals
Year to which price refers: 1992
Subscription address: Cambridge Univ. Press, 40 W. 20th St., New York, NY 10011
Subscription telephone: 212 924-3900

ADVERTISING INFORMATION

Advertising accepted: Yes

EDITORIAL DESCRIPTION

Scope: Dedicated to the description and understanding of variability and change at the levels of the speaker/hearer and the speech community. Concentrates on the details of structure and process that have traditionally constituted the discipline of linguistics, as reflected in actual speech production and processing (or writing) and as systematically analyzed using quantitative methods.
Reviews books: No
Publishes notes: No
Languages accepted: English; French
Prints abstracts: Yes
Author-anonymous submission: No

SUBMISSION REQUIREMENTS

Author pays submission fee: No
Author pays page charges: No
Number of copies required: 3
Special requirements: Previously published articles and articles under consideration elsewhere are not acceptable.
Time before publication decision: 3 mos.
Time between decision and publication: 3 mos.
Number of reviewers: 2
Articles submitted per year: 30
Articles published per year: 15

(1577)
*Langue Française

Danielle Leeman, Editor
Larousse
17, rue du Montparnasse
75280 Paris Cédex 06, France

First published: 1969
ISSN: 0023-8368
MLA acronym: LFr

SUBSCRIPTION INFORMATION

Frequency of publication: 4 times/yr.
Circulation: 3,500
Available in microform: No
Subscription address: CDR-Centrale des Revues, 11 rue Gossin, 92543 Montrouge Cedex, France

ADVERTISING INFORMATION

Advertising accepted: Yes

EDITORIAL DESCRIPTION

Scope: Each issue is devoted to a specific topic in French (occasionally, general) linguistics, with editorial direction by a specialist or specialists in that area. There is generally a bibliography for the topic as well.
Reviews books: No
Publishes notes: No
Languages accepted: French
Prints abstracts: No

SUBMISSION REQUIREMENTS

Restrictions on contributors: None
Author pays submission fee: No
Author pays page charges: No
Number of copies required: 1
Articles published per year: 30

(1578)
*Langues et Linguistique

Dépt. de Langues & Linguistique
Pavillon de Koninck, bureau 2289
Univ. Laval
Ste-Foy, Quebec G1K 7P4, Canada

Telephone: 418 656-3263
Fax: 418 656-2019

First published: 1975
Sponsoring organization: Univ. Laval, Dépt. de Langues & Linguistique
ISSN: 0226-7144
MLA acronym: Langues&L

SUBSCRIPTION INFORMATION

Frequency of publication: Annual (May)
Circulation: 350
Available in microform: No
Subscription price: C$10.00/yr.; C$7.00/yr. students
Year to which price refers: 1991

ADVERTISING INFORMATION

Advertising accepted: Yes

EDITORIAL DESCRIPTION

Scope: Publishes articles and reviews on linguistic theories and their applications to various disciplines of linguistics, to specific languages, and to other fields.
Reviews books: Yes
Publishes notes: Yes
Languages accepted: French; English; German; Spanish
Prints abstracts: Yes
Author-anonymous submission: No

SUBMISSION REQUIREMENTS

Restrictions on contributors: None
Author pays submission fee: No
Author pays page charges: No
Length of articles: 25 pp. maximum
Length of book reviews: 5 pp. maximum
Length of notes: 10 pp. maximum
Style: Journal
Number of copies required: 1
Special requirements: Submit abstract in French and English.
Copyright ownership: Journal
Rejected manuscripts: Returned
Time before publication decision: 3-6 mos.
Time between decision and publication: 5 mos.
Number of reviewers: 4
Articles submitted per year: 20
Articles published per year: 10 minimum
Book reviews submitted per year: 10
Book reviews published per year: 5
Notes submitted per year: 4
Notes published per year: 2

(1579)
*Les Langues Modernes

Christian Punen, Editor
19, rue de la Glacière
75013 Paris, France

First published: 1903
Sponsoring organization: Assn. des Professeurs de Langues Vivantes de l'Enseignement Public
ISSN: 0023-8376
MLA acronym: LanM

SUBSCRIPTION INFORMATION

Frequency of publication: 4 times/yr.
Circulation: 6,000
Available in microform: No
Subscription price: 290 F/yr.
Year to which price refers: 1992
Subscription address: A.P.L.V., 19, rue de la Glacière, 75013 Paris, France

ADVERTISING INFORMATION

Advertising accepted: Yes

EDITORIAL DESCRIPTION

Scope: Publishes articles on the teaching of foreign languages in France.
Reviews books: Yes
Publishes notes: Yes
Languages accepted: French
Prints abstracts: Yes
Author-anonymous submission: No

SUBMISSION REQUIREMENTS

Restrictions on contributors: None
Author pays submission fee: No
Author pays page charges: No
Length of articles: 3,000 words
Length of book reviews: 500 words
Length of notes: 1,000 words
Style: Journal
Number of copies required: 1
Special requirements: Submit original typescript.
Copyright ownership: Journal
Rejected manuscripts: Not returned
Time before publication decision: 3 mos.
Time between decision and publication: 6 mos.
Number of reviewers: 2
Articles submitted per year: 90
Articles published per year: 50
Book reviews submitted per year: 40
Book reviews published per year: 30
Notes submitted per year: 10
Notes published per year: 5

(1580)
Les Langues Néo-Latines: Bulletin Trimestriel de la Société de Langues Néo-Latines

Colette Pommier, Editor
27, rue de la Chapelle
75018 Paris, France

Sponsoring organization: Soc. des Langues Néo-Latines
ISSN: 0184-7570
MLA acronym: LLNL

SUBSCRIPTION INFORMATION

Frequency of publication: 4 times/yr.
Available in microform: No
Subscription address: Marie Claire Boulas, 4 Allée des Charmes, 92500 Rueil-Malmaison, France

ADVERTISING INFORMATION

Advertising accepted: Yes

EDITORIAL DESCRIPTION

Scope: Publishes articles on Italian, Spanish, Romanian, and Portuguese literature, as well as other Romance literatures.
Reviews books: Yes
Publishes notes: No
Languages accepted: French; Spanish

SUBMISSION REQUIREMENTS

Author pays page charges: No
Length of articles: 10-20 pp.
Length of book reviews: 50 words
Number of copies required: 1
Special requirements: Submit double-spaced typescript.
Rejected manuscripts: Not returned
Time before publication decision: 1 yr.
Time between decision and publication: 3 mos.
Number of reviewers: 4
Articles submitted per year: 20-25
Articles published per year: 15
Book reviews submitted per year: 40
Book reviews published per year: 30

(1581)
*Latin American Indian Literatures Journal: A Review of American Indian Texts and Studies

Mary H. Preuss, Editor
Dept. of Spanish
Penn State Univ.
McKeesport Campus
University Drive
McKeesport, PA 15132

Telephone: 412 675-9466
First published: 1977
ISSN: 0888-5613
MLA acronym: LAILJ

SUBSCRIPTION INFORMATION

Frequency of publication: 2 times/yr. (June, Dec.)
Available in microform: No
Subscription price: $35.00/yr. institutions; $25.00/yr. individuals
Year to which price refers: 1992

ADVERTISING INFORMATION

Advertising accepted: Yes
Advertising rates: $75.00/half page; $100.00/full page

EDITORIAL DESCRIPTION

Scope: Publishes: (1) myths, songs, and other forms of oral literature of Latin American Indians, sometimes accompanied by texts in the original language; (2) short studies on Latin American Indian literatures and cultures; (3) bibliographies.
Reviews books: Yes
Publishes notes: Yes
Languages accepted: English
Prints abstracts: No
Author-anonymous submission: No

SUBMISSION REQUIREMENTS

Restrictions on contributors: None
Author pays submission fee: No
Author pays page charges: No
Length of articles: 3,700-4,300 words
Length of book reviews: 750 words
Style: Chicago
Number of copies required: 5
Special requirements: Submission on 3.5 in. IBM- or AT&T-compatible diskette using WordPerfect is preferred.
Copyright ownership: Journal
Rejected manuscripts: Returned; enclose return postage.
Time before publication decision: 3-6 mos.
Time between decision and publication: 6-12 mos.
Number of reviewers: 3
Articles submitted per year: 15
Articles published per year: 6-8
Book reviews submitted per year: 14
Book reviews published per year: 10
Notes submitted per year: 2-5
Notes published per year: 0-2

(1582)
*Latin American Literary Review

Yvette Espinosa Miller, Editor
2300 Palmer St.
Pittsburgh, PA 15218

Telephone: 412 351-1477
Fax: 412 351-6831
First published: 1972
Sponsoring organization: Univ. of Pittsburgh
ISSN: 0047-4134
MLA acronym: LALR

SUBSCRIPTION INFORMATION

Frequency of publication: 2 times/yr. (June, Dec.)
Circulation: 1,000
Available in microform: Yes
Subscription price: $35.00/yr. institutions US; $20.00/yr. individuals US; $36.00/yr. elsewhere
Year to which price refers: 1992

ADVERTISING INFORMATION

Advertising accepted: Yes
Advertising rates: $95.00/quarter page; $140.00/half page; $215.00/full page

EDITORIAL DESCRIPTION

Scope: Publishes articles on literatures of Latin America. Contains feature articles, reviews of recent literary works, translations of poetry, plays, and prose fiction, as well as articles on the arts.
Reviews books: Yes
Languages accepted: English
Prints abstracts: No
Author-anonymous submission: No

SUBMISSION REQUIREMENTS

Restrictions on contributors: None
Author pays submission fee: No
Author pays page charges: No
Length of articles: 2,500-5,000 words
Length of book reviews: 500-1,000 words
Style: MLA
Number of copies required: 2
Special requirements: Translate all quotes and titles into English. Translations of poems, short stories, plays, etc., must be accompanied by written permission from the author or party holding the copyright. Translations must also include a commentary (300 words maximum) on the author and a copy of the original work.
Copyright ownership: Journal
Rejected manuscripts: Returned; enclose SASE.
Time before publication decision: 4 mos.
Time between decision and publication: 6 mos.
Number of reviewers: 4
Articles submitted per year: 20
Articles published per year: 10
Book reviews published per year: 10

(1583)
Latin American Music Review/Revista de Música Latinoamericana

Gerard Béhague, Editor
Dept. of Music
Univ. of Texas at Austin
MRH 3.832
Austin, TX 78712

First published: 1980
Sponsoring organization: Univ. of Texas Press; Inst. of Latin-American Studies
ISSN: 0163-0350
MLA acronym: LAMR

SUBSCRIPTION INFORMATION

Frequency of publication: 2 times/yr. (Fall-Winter, Spring-Summer)
Circulation: 450
Available in microform: No
Subscription address: Univ. of Texas Press, P.O. Box 7819, Austin, TX 78713

ADVERTISING INFORMATION

Advertising accepted: Yes

EDITORIAL DESCRIPTION

Scope: Publishes studies on all aspects of written and oral music traditions (past and present) of Latin America and the Caribbean.
Reviews books: Yes
Publishes notes: Yes
Languages accepted: English; Spanish; Portuguese; French
Prints abstracts: No
Author-anonymous submission: No

SUBMISSION REQUIREMENTS

Restrictions on contributors: None
Author pays submission fee: No
Author pays page charges: No
Length of articles: 5,000-7,500 words
Length of book reviews: 1,500-2,000 words
Length of notes: 800-1,000 words
Style: MLA; Chicago
Number of copies required: 2
Special requirements: Music notations must be camera-ready.
Copyright ownership: Publisher
Rejected manuscripts: Returned at author's request
Time before publication decision: 4 mos.
Time between decision and publication: 6 mos.
Number of reviewers: 2 minimum
Articles submitted per year: 15-20
Articles published per year: 8-10
Book reviews submitted per year: 8-10
Book reviews published per year: 8-10
Notes submitted per year: 10-12
Notes published per year: 8-10

(1584)
*Latin American Theatre Review

George W. Woodyard, Editor
Center of Latin American Studies
Univ. of Kansas
Lawrence, KS 66045

Telephone: 913 864-4141
Fax: 913 864-4555
First published: 1967
Sponsoring organization: Center of Latin American Studies, Univ. of Kansas
ISSN: 0023-8813
MLA acronym: LATR

SUBSCRIPTION INFORMATION

Frequency of publication: 2 times/yr. (Fall, Spring)
Circulation: 1,000
Available in microform: No
Subscription price: $30.00/yr. institutions; $15.00/yr. individuals
Year to which price refers: 1992

ADVERTISING INFORMATION

Advertising accepted: No

EDITORIAL DESCRIPTION

Scope: Devoted to the theater and drama of Spanish and Portuguese America. Accepts articles on theater and drama in Latin America, book reviews, and summaries of plays.
Reviews books: Yes
Publishes notes: Yes
Languages accepted: English; Portuguese; Spanish
Prints abstracts: Yes
Author-anonymous submission: Yes

SUBMISSION REQUIREMENTS

Restrictions on contributors: None
Author pays submission fee: No
Author pays page charges: No
Length of articles: 3,500 words
Length of book reviews: 500 words
Length of notes: 1,000-1,500 words
Style: MLA
Number of copies required: 2
Copyright ownership: Center of Latin American Studies
Rejected manuscripts: Returned; enclose return postage.
Time before publication decision: 2-3 mos.
Time between decision and publication: 6-12 mos.
Number of reviewers: 3
Articles submitted per year: 60-80
Articles published per year: 20
Book reviews submitted per year: 10-20
Book reviews published per year: 10-12
Notes submitted per year: 10-25
Notes published per year: 10-15

(1585)
*Latinitas: Commentarii Linguae Latinae Excolendae

Carolus Egger, Editor
00120 Vatican City
Rome, Italy

Telephone: (39) 6 6984648
Fax: (39) 6 6984716
First published: 1953
Sponsoring organization: Latinitas Foundation
ISSN: 0023-883X
MLA acronym: Latinitas

SUBSCRIPTION INFORMATION

Frequency of publication: 4 times/yr.
Circulation: 1,500
Available in microform: No
Subscription price: $40.00 (£20.00)/yr.
Year to which price refers: 1992
Subscription address: Fondazione "Latinitas", at the above address

ADVERTISING INFORMATION

Advertising accepted: Yes

EDITORIAL DESCRIPTION

Scope: Publishes articles on Latin language and literature and Latin as a modern language.
Reviews books: Yes
Publishes notes: Yes
Languages accepted: Latin
Prints abstracts: Yes
Author-anonymous submission: No

SUBMISSION REQUIREMENTS

Restrictions on contributors: None
Author pays submission fee: No
Author pays page charges: No
Length of articles: No restrictions
Length of book reviews: No restrictions
Length of notes: No restrictions
Style: None
Number of copies required: 2
Special requirements: Submit original typescript.
Copyright ownership: Editor
Rejected manuscripts: Not returned
Time before publication decision: 3 mos.
Time between decision and publication: 3 mos.
Number of reviewers: 4-5
Articles submitted per year: 130-150
Articles published per year: 40-50
Book reviews submitted per year: 20-30
Book reviews published per year: 10-15

(1586)
*Latomus: Revue d'Etudes Latines

C. Deroux, Editor
Soc. d'Etudes Latines de Bruxelles
18. Avenue Van Cutsem
7500 Tournai, Belgium

Additional editorial address: Send manuscripts to: C. Deroux, B.P. 54, 1170 Brussels, Belgium
First published: 1937
Sponsoring organization: Ministère de l'Education Nationale, Fondation Universitaire

ISSN: 0023-8856
MLA acronym: Latomus

SUBSCRIPTION INFORMATION

Frequency of publication: 4 times/yr. (Feb., May, Aug., Nov.)
Circulation: 1,000
Available in microform: No
Subscription price: 2,500 BF/yr. Belgium; 2,750 BF/yr. elsewhere
Year to which price refers: 1992

ADVERTISING INFORMATION

Advertising accepted: No

EDITORIAL DESCRIPTION

Scope: Publishes articles on Latin literature, Roman history, and archaeology.
Reviews books: Yes
Publishes notes: Yes
Languages accepted: English; French; Italian; German; Latin; Spanish
Prints abstracts: No
Author-anonymous submission: No

SUBMISSION REQUIREMENTS

Author pays submission fee: No
Author pays page charges: No
Length of articles: 4,000 words
Length of book reviews: 250-800 words
Length of notes: 800 words
Number of copies required: 1
Copyright ownership: Soc. d'Etudes Latines de Bruxelles
Rejected manuscripts: Returned
Articles submitted per year: 75
Articles published per year: 65
Book reviews submitted per year: 320
Book reviews published per year: 310
Notes published per year: 10

(1587) *Latvijas Zinātņu Akadēmijas Vēstis

V. Samsons & L. Kalinka, Editors
Presidium of the Latvian Academy of Sciences
Turgenev St., 19
226524 Riga, Latvia

Telephone: (7) 132 223732; (7) 132 229830
Fax: (7) 132 228784
First published: 1947
Historical variations in title: Formerly *Latvijas PSR Zinātņu Akadēmijas Vēstis*
Sponsoring organization: Latvian Council of Science
ISSN: 0868-6556
MLA acronym: LZAV

SUBSCRIPTION INFORMATION

Frequency of publication: 12 times/yr.
Circulation: 850-1,000
Available in microform: No

ADVERTISING INFORMATION

Advertising accepted: No

EDITORIAL DESCRIPTION

Scope: Publishes articles on Baltic and Latvian linguistics and human science, including literature, folklore, art history, and theory.
Reviews books: Yes
Publishes notes: Yes
Languages accepted: Latvian; English; German; Russian
Prints abstracts: Yes
Author-anonymous submission: Yes

SUBMISSION REQUIREMENTS

Restrictions on contributors: Preference is given to writers from countries surrounding the Baltic Sea, and to subjects pertaining to the Baltic region or Latvia.
Author pays submission fee: No
Author pays page charges: No
Length of articles: 2,000-4,000 words
Length of book reviews: 450-1,000 words
Length of notes: 450-1,000 words
Style: None
Number of copies required: 2
Copyright ownership: Journal & Author
Rejected manuscripts: Returned
Time before publication decision: 1-3 mos.
Time between decision and publication: 1-8 mos.
Number of reviewers: 2-4
Articles submitted per year: 150
Articles published per year: 110
Book reviews submitted per year: 20
Book reviews published per year: 15
Notes submitted per year: 15
Notes published per year: 5

(1588) *Léachtaí Cholm Cille

Pádraig Ó Fiannachta, Editor
St. Patrick's College
Maynooth, Ireland

Telephone: (353) 1 285222
First published: 1970
Sponsoring organization: Faculty of Celtic Studies, St. Patrick's College
MLA acronym: LCC

SUBSCRIPTION INFORMATION

Frequency of publication: Annual
Circulation: 120
Available in microform: No
Subscription price: IR£6.00/yr.
Year to which price refers: 1993

ADVERTISING INFORMATION

Advertising accepted: No

EDITORIAL DESCRIPTION

Scope: Publishes articles on the history and criticism of Irish Gaelic literature.
Reviews books: No
Publishes notes: Yes
Languages accepted: Irish Gaelic
Prints abstracts: No
Author-anonymous submission: No

SUBMISSION REQUIREMENTS

Restrictions on contributors: Articles must be text of lectures.
Author pays submission fee: No
Author pays page charges: No
Length of articles: 10,000-12,000 words
Length of notes: 1,000 words
Style: DIL
Number of copies required: 1
Copyright ownership: Author
Rejected manuscripts: Returned
Time before publication decision: 9 mos.
Time between decision and publication: 1 mo.
Articles submitted per year: 1
Articles published per year: 7
Notes submitted per year: 2
Notes published per year: 2

(1589) *Lebende Sprachen: Zeitschrift für Fremde Sprachen in Wissenschaft und Praxis

Günther Haensch & Friedrich Krollmann, Editors
Langenscheidt-Verlag
Crellestr. 29-30
1000 Berlin 62, Germany

Telephone: (49) 30 7800020
Fax: (49) 30 78000215
First published: 1956
ISSN: 0023-9909
MLA acronym: LSp

SUBSCRIPTION INFORMATION

Frequency of publication: 4 times/yr.
Circulation: 4,000
Available in microform: No
Subscription price: 82 DM/yr.
Year to which price refers: 1992

ADVERTISING INFORMATION

Advertising accepted: Yes

EDITORIAL DESCRIPTION

Scope: Publishes articles on translation, interpretation in theory and practice, glossaries, and terminology.
Reviews books: Yes
Publishes notes: Yes
Languages accepted: English; French; German; Italian; Spanish
Prints abstracts: No
Author-anonymous submission: No

SUBMISSION REQUIREMENTS

Restrictions on contributors: None
Author pays page charges: No
Length of articles: 6 printed pp. maximum
Number of copies required: 2
Copyright ownership: Langenscheidt KG
Rejected manuscripts: Returned
Time before publication decision: 1-8 weeks
Time between decision and publication: 3-6 mos.
Number of reviewers: 3
Articles published per year: 80
Book reviews published per year: 20

(1590) *Lectura Dantis: A Forum for Dante Research and Interpretation

Tibor Wlassics, Editor
452 Cabell Hall
Univ. of Virginia
Charlottesville, VA 22903

First published: 1987
Sponsoring organization: Univ. of Virginia
ISSN: 0897-5280
MLA acronym: LDant

SUBSCRIPTION INFORMATION

Frequency of publication: 2 times/yr. (Spring, Fall)
Circulation: 450
Available in microform: No
Subscription price: $10.00/yr.
Year to which price refers: 1992-93

ADVERTISING INFORMATION

Advertising accepted: No

EDITORIAL DESCRIPTION

Scope: Publishes articles on Dante research and interpretation.
Reviews books: Yes

Publishes notes: Yes
Languages accepted: English; occasionally Italian
Prints abstracts: No
Author-anonymous submission: Yes

SUBMISSION REQUIREMENTS

Restrictions on contributors: None
Author pays submission fee: No
Author pays page charges: No
Length of articles: 5,000 words
Length of book reviews: 600 words
Length of notes: 2,000 words
Number of copies required: 1
Special requirements: Submit typescript. Upon acceptance, submit diskette.
Copyright ownership: Author
Rejected manuscripts: Not returned
Time before publication decision: 6 mos.
Time between decision and publication: 1 yr.
Number of reviewers: 2
Articles submitted per year: 40-50
Articles published per year: 20-25
Book reviews submitted per year: 12
Book reviews published per year: 12

(1591)
*Leeds Studies in English

Andrew Wawn, Editor
School of English
Univ. of Leeds
Leeds LS2 9JT, England

Telephone: (44) 532 4738
Fax: (44) 532 334774
First published: 1967
Sponsoring organization: Univ. of Leeds, School of English
ISSN: 0075-8556
MLA acronym: LeedsSE

SUBSCRIPTION INFORMATION

Frequency of publication: Annual
Circulation: 350
Available in microform: No
Subscription address: Secretary, at the above address

ADVERTISING INFORMATION

Advertising accepted: No

EDITORIAL DESCRIPTION

Scope: Focuses on topics related to Old and Middle English literature, the historical study of the English language, and Old Icelandic language and literature.
Reviews books: Yes
Publishes notes: No
Languages accepted: English
Prints abstracts: No
Author-anonymous submission: No

SUBMISSION REQUIREMENTS

Restrictions on contributors: Book reviews are by invitation.
Author pays submission fee: No
Author pays page charges: No
Length of articles: 6,000-12,000 words
Length of book reviews: 700-1,000 words
Style: Modern Humanities Research Assn.
Number of copies required: 1
Special requirements: None
Copyright ownership: Assigned by author to School of English, Univ. of Leeds
Rejected manuscripts: Returned; enclose return postage.
Time before publication decision: 2-3 mos.
Time between decision and publication: 12-18 mos.
Number of reviewers: 3
Articles submitted per year: 15-20
Articles published per year: 8-12
Book reviews published per year: 3-4

(1592)
*Leeds Texts and Monographs

Peter Meredith & Joyce Hill, Editors
Leeds Studies in English
School of English
Univ. of Leeds
Leeds LS2 9JT, England

Telephone: (44) 532 334738
Fax: (44) 532 334774
First published: 1967
Sponsoring organization: Univ. of Leeds, School of English
ISSN: 0075-8574
MLA acronym: LTM

SUBSCRIPTION INFORMATION

Frequency of publication: Irregular
Circulation: 300
Available in microform: No

ADVERTISING INFORMATION

Advertising accepted: No

EDITORIAL DESCRIPTION

Scope: Publishes monographs and collections of essays on topics related to the study of the English language; Old and Middle English literature; and Old Icelandic language and literature. Includes facsimiles of Medieval drama.
Reviews books: No
Publishes notes: No
Languages accepted: English
Prints abstracts: No
Author-anonymous submission: No

SUBMISSION REQUIREMENTS

Restrictions on contributors: None
Author pays submission fee: No
Author pays page charges: No
Length of books: 50,000 words
Style: Modern Humanities Research Assn. (3rd edition)
Number of copies required: 1
Copyright ownership: Assigned by author to School of English, Univ. of Leeds
Rejected manuscripts: Returned
Time before publication decision: 3 mos.
Time between decision and publication: 18 mos.
Number of reviewers: 3-4
Books submitted per year: 2
Books published per year: 1

(1593)
*Legacy: A Journal of American Women Writers

Martha Ackmann, Karen Dandurand, & Joanne Dobson, Editors
c/o Karen Dandurand
Dept. of English
Indiana Univ. of Pennsylvania
Indiana, PA 15705

Telephone: 412 357-2261 (Karen Dandurand)
First published: 1984
Historical variations in title: Formerly *Legacy: A Journal of Nineteenth-Century American Women Writers*
ISSN: 0748-4321
MLA acronym: Legacy

SUBSCRIPTION INFORMATION

Frequency of publication: 2 times/yr. (Spring, Fall)
Circulation: 450
Available in microform: No
Subscription price: $30.00/yr. institutions US; $35.00/yr. institutions elsewhere; $20.00/yr. individuals US; $23.00/yr. individuals elsewhere; $12.00/yr. students US; $14.50/yr. students elsewhere
Year to which price refers: 1993
Subscription address: Journals Dept., Penn State Press, Suite C, Barbara Bldg., 820 N. University Dr., University Park, PA 16802-1003
Subscription telephone: 800 326-9180
Subscription fax: 814 865-1408

ADVERTISING INFORMATION

Advertising accepted: Yes
Advertising rates: $100.00/half page; $200.00/full page

EDITORIAL DESCRIPTION

Scope: Publishes studies on American women writers from the 17th to early 20th centuries.
Reviews books: Yes
Publishes notes: Yes
Languages accepted: English
Prints abstracts: No
Author-anonymous submission: Yes

SUBMISSION REQUIREMENTS

Restrictions on contributors: Book reviews are commissioned.
Author pays submission fee: No
Author pays page charges: No
Length of articles: 10,000 words maximum
Length of book reviews: 750 words
Length of notes: 50 words
Style: MLA
Number of copies required: 2
Copyright ownership: Penn State Univ.
Rejected manuscripts: Returned; enclose SASE.
Time before publication decision: 4-6 mos.
Time between decision and publication: 6-12 mos.
Number of reviewers: 5
Articles submitted per year: 70
Articles published per year: 6-7
Book reviews published per year: 6-8
Notes submitted per year: 12
Notes published per year: 12

(1594)
*Legon Journal of the Humanities

J. N. DoDoo, Editor
Office of the Dean of the Faculty of Arts
P.O. Box 69
Legon, Accra, Ghana

First published: 1974
Sponsoring organization: Univ. of Ghana
MLA acronym: LJH

SUBSCRIPTION INFORMATION

Frequency of publication: Irregular
Circulation: 1,000
Available in microform: No
Subscription price: $10.00/yr.
Year to which price refers: 1992

ADVERTISING INFORMATION

Advertising accepted: Yes

EDITORIAL DESCRIPTION

Scope: Publishes the results of research in the humanities with emphasis on Africa.
Reviews books: Yes
Publishes notes: Yes
Languages accepted: English
Prints abstracts: No
Author-anonymous submission: No

SUBMISSION REQUIREMENTS

Author pays submission fee: No
Author pays page charges: No
Length of articles: 4,500-7,000 words
Length of book reviews: 1,000 words
Length of notes: 1,000 words
Style: MLA

Number of copies required: 2
Copyright ownership: Author
Rejected manuscripts: Returned; enclose return postage.
Time before publication decision: 6 mos.
Time between decision and publication: 6-12 mos.
Number of reviewers: 2
Articles submitted per year: 30
Articles published per year: 8-10
Book reviews submitted per year: 10
Book reviews published per year: 2-3
Notes submitted per year: 10
Notes published per year: 2-3

(1595)
*Lendemains: Etudes Comparées sur la France/Vergleichende Frankreichforschung

Michael Nerlich, Hans-Manfred Bock, Jacques Leenhardt, & Alain Montandon, Editors
Technische Univ. Berlin
Inst. für Französische Literaturwissenschaft
FB 1, Sekr. TEL 3
Ernst-Reuter-Platz 7
1000 Berlin 10, Germany

Telephone: (49) 30 31422958
First published: 1975
ISSN: 0170-3803
MLA acronym: Lendemains

SUBSCRIPTION INFORMATION

Frequency of publication: 4 times/yr. (Mar., Jun, Oct., Dec.)
Available in microform: No
Subscription price: 48.60 DM/yr. plus postage; 43.80/yr. plus postage students
Year to which price refers: 1992
Subscription address: Dr. Wolfram Hitzeroth-Verlag, Franz-Tuczek-Weg 1, 3550 Marburg, Germany

ADVERTISING INFORMATION

Advertising accepted: Yes

EDITORIAL DESCRIPTION

Scope: Publishes interdisciplinary research on French history, economics, politics, philosophy, arts, and literature.
Reviews books: Yes
Publishes notes: Yes
Languages accepted: German; French
Prints abstracts: Yes, in French for German contributions; in German for French contributions
Author-anonymous submission: No

SUBMISSION REQUIREMENTS

Restrictions on contributors: Book reviews are solicited.
Author pays submission fee: No
Author pays page charges: No
Length of articles: 10 pp.
Length of book reviews: 2 pp.
Style: Journal
Number of copies required: 2
Copyright ownership: Journal for 2 yrs.
Rejected manuscripts: Returned
Time before publication decision: 1 mo.
Time between decision and publication: 1 yr. maximum
Number of reviewers: 2-4
Articles submitted per year: 150
Articles published per year: 90
Book reviews published per year: 100

(1596)
Lenguaje

Luis Angel Baena Z., Editor
Dept. de Idiomas
Univ. del Valle
Apdo. Aéreo 25360
Cali, Colombia

First published: 1972
Sponsoring organization: Univ. del Valle
ISSN: 0120-3479
MLA acronym: Lenguaje

SUBSCRIPTION INFORMATION

Frequency of publication: Annual
Available in microform: No

ADVERTISING INFORMATION

Advertising accepted: No

EDITORIAL DESCRIPTION

Scope: Publishes articles on theoretical and applied linguistics.
Reviews books: Yes
Languages accepted: Spanish
Prints abstracts: No

SUBMISSION REQUIREMENTS

Author pays submission fee: No
Author pays page charges: No
Style: Linguistic Soc. of America
Number of copies required: 2
Copyright ownership: Author
Rejected manuscripts: Returned
Time before publication decision: 2 mos.
Time between decision and publication: 2 mos.
Number of reviewers: 3

(1597)
*Lenguaje y Ciencias

Ernesto Zierer, Editor
Univ. Nacional de Trujillo
Dpto. de Idiomas & Lingüística
Trujillo, Peru

First published: 1961
Sponsoring organization: Univ. Nacional de Trujillo
ISSN: 0024-0796
MLA acronym: LyC

SUBSCRIPTION INFORMATION

Frequency of publication: 2 times/yr.
Available in microform: No
Subscription price: $20.00/yr.
Year to which price refers: 1993

ADVERTISING INFORMATION

Advertising accepted: Yes
Advertising rates: $30.00/half page; $50.00/full page

EDITORIAL DESCRIPTION

Scope: Publishes articles on general and applied linguistics.
Reviews books: Yes
Publishes notes: Yes
Languages accepted: Spanish; English; French; German; Portuguese; Russian
Prints abstracts: Yes
Author-anonymous submission: No

SUBMISSION REQUIREMENTS

Restrictions on contributors: None
Author pays submission fee: No
Author pays page charges: No
Length of articles: 6-10 pp.
Length of book reviews: 1-2 pp.

Length of notes: 1 p.
Number of copies required: 2
Special requirements: Submissions should be preceded by an English abstract.
Copyright ownership: Journal
Rejected manuscripts: Returned
Time before publication decision: 1-2 mos.
Time between decision and publication: 3-6 mos.
Number of reviewers: 3
Articles submitted per year: 18
Articles published per year: 16
Book reviews submitted per year: 4
Book reviews published per year: 4-8
Notes submitted per year: 5
Notes published per year: 1

(1598)
*Lenguaje y Texto

Alfredo Rodríguez López-Vázquez, Director
Dept. de Didácticas Especiales
Paseo de Ronda 47
15011 La Coruña, Spain

Additional editorial address: S.E.D.L.L., Santísima Trinidad 37, 28010 Madrid, Spain
Telephone: (34) 81 252342 ; (34) 81 252194
Fax: (34) 81 255102
First published: 1991
Sponsoring organization: Soc. Española de Didáctica de Lengua & Literatura
MLA acronym: LyT

SUBSCRIPTION INFORMATION

Frequency of publication: 2 times/yr. plus monographic supplement
Circulation: 1,000
Available in microform: No
Subscription price: 1,600 Pta/yr. Spain; 1,800 Pta/yr. Europe; $20.00/yr. US
Year to which price refers: 1992

ADVERTISING INFORMATION

Advertising accepted: Yes
Advertising rates: 20,000 Pta/full page

EDITORIAL DESCRIPTION

Scope: Publishes articles on current trends in methods and theory in languages and literature from an educational viewpoint.
Reviews books: Yes
Publishes notes: Yes
Languages accepted: Spanish; French; English; Italian; Portuguese
Prints abstracts: No
Author-anonymous submission: Yes

SUBMISSION REQUIREMENTS

Author pays submission fee: No
Author pays page charges: No
Length of articles: 25,000 words maximum
Length of book reviews: 3,000 words maximum
Length of notes: 4,000 words maximum
Style: MLA
Number of copies required: 2
Copyright ownership: Journal
Rejected manuscripts: Returned
Time before publication decision: 6 mos.
Time between decision and publication: 6 mos.
Number of reviewers: 2
Articles submitted per year: 25
Articles published per year: 16-18
Book reviews submitted per year: 20
Book reviews published per year: 12
Notes submitted per year: 7
Notes published per year: 3

(1599)
*Lenguas Modernas

Aura Bocaz, Editor
Casilla 10136
Correo Central
Santiago, Chile

Telephone: (56) 2 2725977
Fax: (56) 2 2725977
First published: 1974
Sponsoring organization: Dept. de Linguistica, Univ. of Chile
ISSN: 0716-0542
MLA acronym: LengM

SUBSCRIPTION INFORMATION

Frequency of publication: Annual
Available in microform: No
Subscription price: $18.00/yr.
Year to which price refers: 1991

ADVERTISING INFORMATION

Advertising accepted: No

EDITORIAL DESCRIPTION

Scope: Publishes articles and reviews on different topics in the field of second and foreign language learning and teaching envisaged as interdisciplinary activities. Apart from the traditional interest in applied linguistics, particular emphasis is currently given to text linguistics and discourse analysis and their implications for TFL and TESOL. First language acquisition issues are included regularly.
Reviews books: Yes
Publishes notes: No
Languages accepted: English; Spanish
Prints abstracts: No
Author-anonymous submission: No

SUBMISSION REQUIREMENTS

Restrictions on contributors: Contributors must be faculty members of an established university.
Author pays submission fee: No
Author pays page charges: No
Length of articles: 5,000-6,000 words
Length of book reviews: 1,000 words
Style: Linguistic Soc. of America with adaptations
Number of copies required: 3
Special requirements: Submit original typescript, 2 copies, and a 100-word abstract.
Copyright ownership: Journal
Rejected manuscripts: Not returned
Time before publication decision: 2 mos.
Time between decision and publication: 1 yr.
Number of reviewers: 3
Articles submitted per year: 30-40
Articles published per year: 10-12
Book reviews submitted per year: 10-15
Book reviews published per year: 3-5

(1600)
*Leshonenu La'Am

Shoshana Bahat, Yoseph Offer, & David Talshir, Editors
Academy of the Hebrew Language
P.O. Box 3449
91034 Jerusalem, Israel

Telephone: (972) 2 632242
Fax: (972) 2 617065
First published: 1947
Sponsoring organization: Academy of the Hebrew Language, Scientific Secretariat
ISSN: 0024-1091
MLA acronym: LLa

SUBSCRIPTION INFORMATION

Frequency of publication: 5 times/yr.
Circulation: 700
Available in microform: No
Subscription price: $25.00/yr.
Year to which price refers: 1992

ADVERTISING INFORMATION

Advertising accepted: No

EDITORIAL DESCRIPTION

Scope: Publishes articles on Hebrew linguistics.
Reviews books: Yes
Publishes notes: No
Languages accepted: Hebrew
Prints abstracts: No
Author-anonymous submission: No

SUBMISSION REQUIREMENTS

Author pays submission fee: No
Author pays page charges: No
Length of articles: 3-8 pp.
Length of book reviews: 400-800 words
Style: Academy of Hebrew Language
Number of copies required: 1
Copyright ownership: Journal
Rejected manuscripts: Returned
Time before publication decision: 3 mos.
Time between decision and publication: 4 mos.
Number of reviewers: 2
Articles submitted per year: 40-60
Articles published per year: 30-40
Book reviews submitted per year: 16
Book reviews published per year: 6
Notes submitted per year: 16
Notes published per year: 10

(1601)
*Leshonenu/Lĕšonénu: A Journal for the Study of the Hebrew Language and Cognate Subjects/Ketav-'Et le-Ḥeqer ha-Lashon ha-'Ivrit ve-ha-Teḥumim ha-Semukhim Lah

Joshua Blau, Editor
P.O. Box 3449
91034 Jerusalem, Israel

Telephone: (972) 2 632242
Fax: (972) 2 617065
First published: 1929
Sponsoring organization: Academy of the Hebrew Language
ISSN: 0334-3626
MLA acronym: Leshonenu

SUBSCRIPTION INFORMATION

Frequency of publication: 4 times/yr.
Circulation: 450
Available in microform: No
Subscription price: $35.00/yr.
Year to which price refers: 1991

ADVERTISING INFORMATION

Advertising accepted: No

EDITORIAL DESCRIPTION

Scope: Publishes articles on the historical and descriptive study of Hebrew and cognate languages.
Reviews books: Yes
Publishes notes: Yes
Languages accepted: Hebrew
Prints abstracts: Yes
Author-anonymous submission: No

SUBMISSION REQUIREMENTS

Restrictions on contributors: None
Author pays submission fee: No
Author pays page charges: No
Length of articles: No restrictions
Length of book reviews: No restrictions
Length of notes: No restrictions
Style: Academy of the Hebrew Language
Number of copies required: 2
Special requirements: Manuscripts must be accompanied by an English summary.
Copyright ownership: Author & Academy of the Hebrew Language
Rejected manuscripts: Not returned
Time before publication decision: 2 mos.
Time between decision and publication: 1 yr.
Number of reviewers: 1-2
Articles submitted per year: 40-60
Articles published per year: 30-50
Book reviews submitted per year: 10-20
Book reviews published per year: 6-10
Notes submitted per year: 12-14
Notes published per year: 10-12

(1602)
*Lessing Yearbook/Jahrbuch

Richard E. Schade, Managing Editor
Lessing Soc.
Dept. of German (368)
Univ. of Cincinnati
Cincinnati, OH 45221-0372

Telephone: 513 556-2744
Fax: 513 556-1991
First published: 1969
Sponsoring organization: Lessing Soc.
ISSN: 0075-8833
MLA acronym: LY

SUBSCRIPTION INFORMATION

Frequency of publication: Annual
Circulation: 1,000
Available in microform: No

ADVERTISING INFORMATION

Advertising accepted: No

EDITORIAL DESCRIPTION

Scope: Publishes articles on Gotthold Ephraim Lessing and his contemporaries. Articles may deal with Lessing's literary, philosophical, or theological writings as well as those of other Enlightenment writers. Interdisciplinary and comparative studies are welcomed.
Reviews books: Yes
Publishes notes: Yes
Languages accepted: English; German
Prints abstracts: No
Author-anonymous submission: Yes

SUBMISSION REQUIREMENTS

Restrictions on contributors: Contributors must be members of the Lessing Society. Reviews are solicited.
Author pays submission fee: No
Author pays page charges: No
Length of articles: 20-30 typescript pp.
Length of book reviews: 1,000 words
Length of notes: 1,500 words
Style: MLA; Bangen
Number of copies required: 2
Special requirements: Manuscripts must be double-spaced.
Copyright ownership: Wayne State Univ. Press
Rejected manuscripts: Returned with critique; enclose return postage.
Time before publication decision: 10 weeks
Time between decision and publication: 18 mos.
Number of reviewers: 3
Articles submitted per year: 50
Articles published per year: 12
Book reviews published per year: 45
Notes published per year: 1

(1603)
*Letras de Buenos Aires

Victoria Pueyrredon, Director
Tagle 2572-6 P-Dto "D"
1425 Buenos Aires, Argentina

Telephone: (54) 1 8021299
First published: 1980
ISSN: 0326-2928
MLA acronym: LdBA

SUBSCRIPTION INFORMATION

Frequency of publication: 3 times/yr.
Circulation: 2,000
Available in microform: No
Subscription price: $27.00/yr.
Year to which price refers: 1993

ADVERTISING INFORMATION

Advertising accepted: Yes

EDITORIAL DESCRIPTION

Scope: Publishes articles on literature, as well as poetry and short stories. Emphasis is on Argentinian literature.
Reviews books: Yes
Publishes notes: No
Languages accepted: Spanish
Prints abstracts: No
Author-anonymous submission: No

SUBMISSION REQUIREMENTS

Author pays submission fee: No
Author pays page charges: No
Length of articles: 5 pp.
Number of copies required: 2
Copyright ownership: Author
Rejected manuscripts: Not returned
Time before publication decision: 3 mos.
Time between decision and publication: 3 mos.
Number of reviewers: 4
Book reviews submitted per year: 100
Book reviews published per year: 24

(1604)
*Letras de Deusto

María Luisa Amigo Fernandez de Arroyabe, Editor
Secretaría de la Fac. de Filosofía & Ciencias de la Educacion
Univ. de Deusto
Bilbao, Spain

Fax: (34) 91 4458916
First published: 1971
Sponsoring organization: Univ. de Deusto
ISSN: 0210-3516
MLA acronym: LdD

SUBSCRIPTION INFORMATION

Frequency of publication: 5 times/yr.
Subscription price: 4,500 Pta ($50.00)/yr.
Year to which price refers: 1992
Additional subscription address: Dept. de Publicaciones, Apartado 1, Univ. de Deusto, 48080 Bilbao, Spain

EDITORIAL DESCRIPTION

Scope: Publishes articles on Spanish language and literature.
Reviews books: Yes
Languages accepted: Spanish
Prints abstracts: No

(1605)
*Letras Femeninas

Adelaida López de Martínez, Editor
Dept. of Modern Languages
Univ. of Nebraska, Lincoln
1111 Oldfather Hall
Lincoln, NE 68588-0315

Telephone: 402 472-3710
First published: 1975
Sponsoring organization: Asoc. de Literatura Femenina Hispanica; Dept. of Modern Languages, Univ. of Nebraska, Lincoln
ISSN: 0277-1356
MLA acronym: LFem

SUBSCRIPTION INFORMATION

Frequency of publication: 2 times/yr.
Circulation: 400
Available in microform: No
Subscription price: $25.00/yr. institutions; $20.00/yr. individuals
Year to which price refers: 1992

ADVERTISING INFORMATION

Advertising accepted: Yes

EDITORIAL DESCRIPTION

Scope: Provides information on scholarship in Hispanic women's literature.
Reviews books: Yes
Publishes notes: Yes
Languages accepted: English; Portuguese; Spanish
Prints abstracts: No

SUBMISSION REQUIREMENTS

Restrictions on contributors: Contributors must be members of the Asoc. de Literatura Femenina Hispánica.
Author pays submission fee: No
Author pays page charges: No
Length of articles: 3,000-4,000 words
Length of book reviews: 750-1,000 words
Length of notes: 750-1,000 words
Style: MLA
Number of copies required: 2
Special requirements: Submit typescript or letter-quality word-processed copy and an IBM-compatible diskette using WordPerfect.
Copyright ownership: Journal & author
Rejected manuscripts: Returned
Time before publication decision: 3-4 mos.
Time between decision and publication: 12-18 mos.
Number of reviewers: 2
Articles submitted per year: 40-45
Articles published per year: 12-14
Book reviews submitted per year: 10-12
Book reviews published per year: 6
Notes published per year: 15-20

(1606)
*Letras Peninsulares

Mary S. Vásquez, Editor
Dept. of Romance & Classical Languages
Michigan State Univ.
East Lansing, MI 48824-1027

Telephone: 517 355-8350
Fax: 517 336-1858
First published: 1988
Sponsoring organization: Soc. de Letras Peninsulares
ISSN: 0897-7542
MLA acronym: LetP

SUBSCRIPTION INFORMATION

Frequency of publication: 3 times/yr. (Spring, Fall, Winter)
Circulation: 300
Available in microform: No
Subscription price: $36.00/yr. institutions US; $45.00/yr. institutions elsewhere; $24.00/yr. individuals
Year to which price refers: 1992

ADVERTISING INFORMATION

Advertising accepted: Yes

EDITORIAL DESCRIPTION

Scope: Publishes literary criticism from all serious critical foci on Peninsular Spanish literature from the 18th century through the present.
Reviews books: Yes
Publishes notes: Yes
Languages accepted: Spanish; English
Prints abstracts: No
Author-anonymous submission: Yes

SUBMISSION REQUIREMENTS

Restrictions on contributors: None
Author pays submission fee: No
Author pays page charges: No
Length of articles: 2,400-5,000 words
Length of book reviews: 600-800 words
Style: MLA
Number of copies required: 3
Special requirements: Author's name should appear only on a separate sheet. Author's identity should not be obvious from end notes.
Copyright ownership: Journal
Rejected manuscripts: Returned; enclose return postage.
Time before publication decision: 2-4 mos.
Time between decision and publication: 3-18 mos.
Number of reviewers: 2-4
Articles submitted per year: 250-300
Articles published per year: 18-24
Book reviews published per year: 16-24
Notes published per year: 4-6

(1607)
*Letterato: Periodico di Attualità e Cultura

Luigi Pellegrini, Editor
Pellegrini Editore
Via Roma, 80/b
C.P. 158
87100 Cosenza, Italy

Telephone: (39) 984 21472
Fax: (39) 984 25245
First published: 1952
ISSN: 0024-130X
MLA acronym: Letterato

SUBSCRIPTION INFORMATION

Frequency of publication: 12 times/yr.
Available in microform: No

ADVERTISING INFORMATION

Advertising accepted: Yes

EDITORIAL DESCRIPTION

Reviews books: Yes
Publishes notes: Yes
Languages accepted: Italian
Prints abstracts: No

SUBMISSION REQUIREMENTS

Author pays submission fee: Yes
Author pays page charges: Yes
Number of copies required: 2
Copyright ownership: Pellegrini Editore
Rejected manuscripts: Not returned
Time before publication decision: 1 mo.
Articles submitted per year: 280
Book reviews submitted per year: 6

(1608)
Letteratura Francese Contemporanea le Correnti d'Avanguardia: Berenice

Gabriele-Aldo Bertozzi & Luciano Lucarini, Editors
Via Trionfale 8406
00135 Rome, Italy

Additional editorial address: G. A. Bertozzi, via Ostiense 51, 00154 Rome, Italy
First published: 1980
MLA acronym: LFC

SUBSCRIPTION INFORMATION

Frequency of publication: 4 times/yr.
Available in microform: No

ADVERTISING INFORMATION

Advertising accepted: No

EDITORIAL DESCRIPTION

Scope: Publishes articles on contemporary French literature.
Reviews books: Yes
Publishes notes: Yes
Languages accepted: Italian; French
Prints abstracts: No
Author-anonymous submission: No

SUBMISSION REQUIREMENTS

Restrictions on contributors: Manuscripts are solicited.
Author pays submission fee: No
Author pays page charges: No
Length of articles: 5,000–6,000 words
Length of book reviews: 1,500 words
Length of notes: 300–400 words
Style: None
Number of copies required: 1
Copyright ownership: Journal
Time before publication decision: 2–3 mos.
Time between decision and publication: 4 mos.
Number of reviewers: 20
Articles submitted per year: 30
Articles published per year: 25
Book reviews submitted per year: 20
Book reviews published per year: 30
Notes submitted per year: 5–10
Notes published per year: 5–10

(1609)
Letteratura Italiana Contemporaneo: Rivista Quadrimestrale di Studi Sul Novecento

Gabriella D'Anna, Editor
Via Trionfale 8406
00135 Rome, Italy

First published: 1980
MLA acronym: LIC

SUBSCRIPTION INFORMATION

Frequency of publication: 4 times/yr.
Available in microform: No

ADVERTISING INFORMATION

Advertising accepted: No

EDITORIAL DESCRIPTION

Scope: Publishes articles on contemporary Italian literature.
Reviews books: Yes
Publishes notes: Yes
Languages accepted: Italian
Prints abstracts: No
Author-anonymous submission: No

SUBMISSION REQUIREMENTS

Restrictions on contributors: Manuscripts are solicited.
Author pays submission fee: No
Author pays page charges: No
Length of articles: 5,000–6,000 words
Length of book reviews: 1,500 words
Length of notes: 300–400 words
Style: None
Number of copies required: 1
Copyright ownership: Journal
Time before publication decision: 2–3 mos.
Time between decision and publication: 4 mos.
Number of reviewers: 20
Articles submitted per year: 30
Articles published per year: 25
Book reviews submitted per year: 20
Book reviews published per year: 30
Notes submitted per year: 5–10
Notes published per year: 5–10

(1610)
Letterature d'America: Rivista Trimestrale

Dario Puccini, Cristina Giorcelli, & Luciana Stegagno Picchio, Editors
Dipt. di Studi Americani
Piazza della Repubblica, 10
00185 Rome, Italy

First published: 1980
Sponsoring organization: Univ. di Roma, La Sapienza
MLA acronym: LAmer

SUBSCRIPTION INFORMATION

Frequency of publication: 4 times/yr.
Circulation: 1,000
Available in microform: No
Subscription address: Mario Bulzoni, via dei Liburni, 14, 00185 Rome, Italy

ADVERTISING INFORMATION

Advertising accepted: Yes

EDITORIAL DESCRIPTION

Scope: Features articles on North and South American literatures.
Reviews books: No
Publishes notes: No
Languages accepted: Italian; French; English; Spanish; Portuguese
Prints abstracts: No

SUBMISSION REQUIREMENTS

Restrictions on contributors: Contributions are invited.
Author pays submission fee: No
Author pays page charges: No
Length of articles: 4,500 words
Style: MLA
Number of copies required: 1
Special requirements: Submit original typescript and camera-ready copy.
Copyright ownership: Publisher
Rejected manuscripts: Not returned
Time before publication decision: 1 mo.
Time between decision and publication: 4 mos.
Number of reviewers: 1
Articles published per year: 25

(1611)
*Lettere Italiane

Vittore Branca, Editor
Ist. di Letteratura Italiana
Univ. di Padova
Padua, Italy

Telephone: (39) 55 6530684
Fax: (39) 55 6530214
First published: 1949
ISSN: 0024-1334
MLA acronym: LI

SUBSCRIPTION INFORMATION

Frequency of publication: 4 times/yr.
Circulation: 22,000
Available in microform: Yes
Subscription price: 64,000 Lit/yr. Italy; 80,000 Lit/yr. elsewhere
Year to which price refers: 1991
Subscription address: Casa Editrice Leo S. Olschki, C.P. 66, 50100 Florence, Italy

ADVERTISING INFORMATION

Advertising accepted: No

EDITORIAL DESCRIPTION

Scope: Publishes articles on Italian literature.
Reviews books: Yes
Publishes notes: Yes
Languages accepted: Italian; French; English; German
Prints abstracts: No
Author-anonymous submission: No

SUBMISSION REQUIREMENTS

Restrictions on contributors: None
Author pays submission fee: No
Author pays page charges: No
Length of articles: 30 pp.
Length of book reviews: 6 pp.
Length of notes: 10 pp.
Style: MLA
Number of copies required: 2
Special requirements: Submit original typescript.
Copyright ownership: Editor
Rejected manuscripts: Returned
Time before publication decision: 4 mos.
Time between decision and publication: 1–3 mos.
Number of reviewers: 2–3
Articles submitted per year: 100
Articles published per year: 12–15
Book reviews submitted per year: 60
Book reviews published per year: 40
Notes submitted per year: 40
Notes published per year: 20

(1612)
*Il Lettore di Provincia

Tino Dalla Valle, Editor
A. Longo Editore
P.O. Box 431
48100 Ravenna, Italy

Telephone: (39) 544 217026
Fax: (39) 544 217026
First published: 1970
ISSN: 0024-1350
MLA acronym: LdProv

SUBSCRIPTION INFORMATION

Frequency of publication: 3 times/yr.
Circulation: 2,000
Available in microform: No
Subscription price: 30,000 Lit/yr. Italy; 50,000 Lit/yr. elsewhere
Year to which price refers: 1992
Subscription address: A. Longo Editore, Via Paolo Costa 33, 48100 Ravenna, Italy

ADVERTISING INFORMATION

Advertising accepted: No

EDITORIAL DESCRIPTION

Scope: Publishes texts, research, and criticism on Italian, English, American, and French literature and poetry.

Reviews books: Yes
Publishes notes: Yes
Languages accepted: Italian
Prints abstracts: No
Author-anonymous submission: No

SUBMISSION REQUIREMENTS

Restrictions on contributors: None
Author pays submission fee: No
Author pays page charges: No
Length of articles: 5,000-7,500 words
Length of book reviews: 2,500 words
Length of notes: 2,000-2,500 words
Style: MLA
Number of copies required: 2
Special requirements: Submit original typescript.
Copyright ownership: Journal
Rejected manuscripts: Not returned
Time before publication decision: 4 mos.
Time between decision and publication: 9 mos.
Number of reviewers: 2
Articles submitted per year: 150-180
Articles published per year: 45-50
Book reviews submitted per year: 100-150
Book reviews published per year: 50-70
Notes submitted per year: 120-130
Notes published per year: 20

(1613)
Les Lettres Albanaises: Revue Littéraire et Artistique

Ismail Kadare, Editor
rue Konferencae Pezës
Tirana, Albania

First published: 1978
Sponsoring organization: Union des Ecrivains & des Artistes d'Albanie
MLA acronym: LAlb

SUBSCRIPTION INFORMATION

Subscription address: Ndermarja & Librit, Tirana, Albania

ADVERTISING INFORMATION

Advertising accepted: No

EDITORIAL DESCRIPTION

Scope: Publishes articles on Albanian studies. Includes works on literature, folklore, music, culture, and art. Also publishes creative writing.
Publishes notes: Yes
Languages accepted: French

(1614)
***Lettres Québécoises**

André Vanasse, Editor
815, rue Ontario, bureau 201
Montreal, Quebec H2L 1P1, Canada

Telephone: 514 525-9518
Fax: 514 523-9401
First published: 1976
Sponsoring organization: Conseil des Arts du Canada; Ministère des Affaires Culturelles du Québec; Commission d'Initiative & de Développement Culturels de la Ville de Montréal; Conseil des Arts de la Communauté Urbaine de Montréal
ISSN: 0382-084X
MLA acronym: LQ

SUBSCRIPTION INFORMATION

Frequency of publication: 4 times/yr.
Circulation: 2,100
Available in microform: No
Subscription price: C$23.00/yr. institutions; C$18.00/yr. individuals
Year to which price refers: 1992

ADVERTISING INFORMATION

Advertising accepted: Yes
Advertising rates: C$200.00/quarter page; C$300.00/half page; C$500.00/full page

EDITORIAL DESCRIPTION

Scope: Publishes book reviews and critical articles about Québécois writers.
Reviews books: Yes
Publishes notes: Yes
Languages accepted: French
Prints abstracts: No
Author-anonymous submission: No

SUBMISSION REQUIREMENTS

Restrictions on contributors: None
Author pays submission fee: No
Author pays page charges: No
Length of articles: 5-10 pp.
Length of book reviews: 1-3 pp.
Number of copies required: 1
Special requirements: Submit typescript and diskette.
Copyright ownership: Author
Rejected manuscripts: Returned
Time before publication decision: 1-3 mos.
Time between decision and publication: 1-2 mos.
Number of reviewers: 2-3
Articles submitted per year: 100
Articles published per year: 100
Book reviews submitted per year: 80
Book reviews published per year: 60
Notes submitted per year: 270
Notes published per year: 200

(1615)
***Les Lettres Romanes**

Georges Jacques, Editor
place Blaise Pascal, 1
1348 Louvain-la-Neuve, Belgium

Telephone: (32) 10 474921
Fax: (32) 10 472579
First published: 1947
Sponsoring organization: Fondation Universitaire de Belgique; Univ. Catholique de Louvain; Communauté Française de Belgique
ISSN: 0024-1415
MLA acronym: LR

SUBSCRIPTION INFORMATION

Frequency of publication: 4 times/yr. (Feb., May, Aug., Nov.)
Circulation: 600
Available in microform: No
Subscription price: 800 BF/yr.
Year to which price refers: 1992

ADVERTISING INFORMATION

Advertising accepted: No

EDITORIAL DESCRIPTION

Scope: Publishes original articles, critical reviews, and book reviews as well as bibliographical notes, addressed to the specialist, on Romance literature.
Reviews books: Yes
Publishes notes: Yes
Languages accepted: French
Prints abstracts: Yes
Author-anonymous submission: No

SUBMISSION REQUIREMENTS

Restrictions on contributors: None
Author pays submission fee: No
Author pays page charges: No
Length of articles: 2,000-6,000 words
Length of book reviews: 400 words
Length of notes: 100 words
Number of copies required: 1
Copyright ownership: Journal & author
Rejected manuscripts: Returned
Time before publication decision: 5 mos.
Time between decision and publication: 12-18 mos.
Number of reviewers: 7
Articles submitted per year: 20-25
Articles published per year: 15-20
Book reviews submitted per year: 40-50
Book reviews published per year: 40-50
Notes submitted per year: 25-30
Notes published per year: 25-30

(1616)
***Letture: Libro e Spettacolo/Mensile di Studi e Rassegne**

Gesuiti di San Fedele, Editors
Piazza San Fedele 4
20121 Milan, Italy

Telephone: (39) 2 804441
Fax: (39) 2 72023481
First published: 1946
Sponsoring organization: Compagnia di Gesù
ISSN: 0024-144X
MLA acronym: Letture

SUBSCRIPTION INFORMATION

Frequency of publication: 10 times/yr.
Circulation: 5,100
Available in microform: No
Subscription price: 40,000 Lit/yr. Italy; 60,000 Lit/yr. elsewhere
Year to which price refers: 1992

ADVERTISING INFORMATION

Advertising accepted: Yes
Advertising rates: 500,000 Lit/full page

EDITORIAL DESCRIPTION

Scope: Publishes reviews of books, films, plays, and music presented in Italy.
Reviews books: Yes
Publishes notes: Yes
Languages accepted: Italian
Prints abstracts: No
Author-anonymous submission: No

SUBMISSION REQUIREMENTS

Restrictions on contributors: None
Author pays submission fee: No
Author pays page charges: No
Length of articles: 1,500-10,000 words
Length of book reviews: 700 words
Length of notes: 300 words
Number of copies required: 1
Copyright ownership: Journal
Rejected manuscripts: Returned at author's request
Time between decision and publication: 1 mo.
Number of reviewers: 2
Articles submitted per year: 130
Articles published per year: 105
Book reviews submitted per year: 500
Book reviews published per year: 400
Notes submitted per year: 150
Notes published per year: 85

(1617)
***Letture Classensi**

Opera di Dante
Via Baccarini, 3
48100 Ravenna, Italy

Telephone: (39) 544 216130
Fax: (39) 544 31038

First published: 1966
Sponsoring organization: Opera di Dante-Comune di Ravenna
ISSN: 0459-1623
MLA acronym: LetC

SUBSCRIPTION INFORMATION

Frequency of publication: Annual
Circulation: 1,000
Available in microform: No
Subscription address: Angelo Longo Editore, Via Paolo Costa 33, 48100 Ravenna, Italy
Subscription telephone: (39) 544 217026
Subscription fax: (39) 544 217026

ADVERTISING INFORMATION

Advertising accepted: No

EDITORIAL DESCRIPTION

Scope: Publishes articles on Dante.
Reviews books: No
Publishes notes: No
Languages accepted: Italian
Prints abstracts: No

SUBMISSION REQUIREMENTS

Author pays submission fee: No
Author pays page charges: No
Length of articles: 7,500-10,000 words
Style: MLA
Number of copies required: 2
Special requirements: Submit original typescript with text and footnotes at end of text.
Copyright ownership: A. Longo Editore
Rejected manuscripts: Not returned
Time before publication decision: 1 yr.
Number of reviewers: 2
Articles published per year: 7

(1618)
*Leuvense Bijdragen: Contributions in Linguistics and Philology

G. Geerts, Editor
Blijde-Inkomststr. 21
3000 Louvain, Belgium

Telephone: (32) 16 285030
Fax: (32) 16 285025
First published: 1896
Sponsoring organization: Katholieke Univ. te Leuven
ISSN: 0024-1482
MLA acronym: LB

SUBSCRIPTION INFORMATION

Frequency of publication: 4 times/yr.
Circulation: 600
Available in microform: No
Subscription price: 1,500 BF/yr.
Year to which price refers: 1992

ADVERTISING INFORMATION

Advertising accepted: Yes

EDITORIAL DESCRIPTION

Scope: Publishes articles on Germanic philology and linguistics.
Reviews books: Yes
Publishes notes: Yes
Languages accepted: Dutch; English; French; German
Prints abstracts: No
Author-anonymous submission: No

SUBMISSION REQUIREMENTS

Restrictions on contributors: None
Author pays submission fee: No
Author pays page charges: No
Length of articles: No restrictions

Length of book reviews: No restrictions
Length of notes: 500 words
Style: None
Number of copies required: 1
Special requirements: Submit typescript and diskette.
Copyright ownership: Author
Time before publication decision: 1 mo.
Time between decision and publication: 6 mos. for articles; 1 yr. for reviews
Number of reviewers: 3
Articles submitted per year: 30
Articles published per year: 20
Book reviews submitted per year: 120
Book reviews published per year: 80
Notes submitted per year: 20
Notes published per year: 20

(1619)
Levende Talen

P. J. Slagter, Editor
van Goyenlaan 36
Bilthoven, Netherlands

First published: 1914
Sponsoring organization: Vereniging van Leraren in Levende Talen
ISSN: 0024-1539
MLA acronym: LT

SUBSCRIPTION INFORMATION

Frequency of publication: 6 times/yr.
Subscription address: Wolters-Noordhof B.V., Periodicals Section, P.O. Box 58, 9700 MB Groningen, Netherlands

EDITORIAL DESCRIPTION

Scope: Netherlands
Reviews books: Yes
Languages accepted: Dutch; English; French; German; Italian; Russian; Spanish
Prints abstracts: No

(1620)
Lexicographica: International Annual for Lexicography/Revue Internationale de Lexicographie/ Internationales Jahrbuch für Lexikographie

Antonín Kučera, Alain Rey, Herbert Ernst Wiegand, & Ladislav Zgusta, Editors
Max Niemeyer Verlag
Postfach 2140
7400 Tübingen, Germany

Additional editorial address: Antonín Zučera, Geschwister-Scholl-Str. 22, 6204 Taunusstein 4, Germany. Alain Rey, Dictionnaires Le Robert, 53, rue Pergolèse, 75116 Paris, France. Ladislav Zgusta, Center for Advanced Studies, Univ. of Illinois, 914 W. Illinois St., Urbana, IL 61801
First published: 1985
Sponsoring organization: Dictionary Soc. of North America; European Assn. for Lexicography
ISSN: 0175-6206
MLA acronym: Lexicographica

SUBSCRIPTION INFORMATION

Frequency of publication: Annual
Available in microform: No

ADVERTISING INFORMATION

Advertising accepted: Yes

EDITORIAL DESCRIPTION

Scope: Journal is intended as an international forum on all aspects of the theory and practice of lexicography.
Reviews books: Yes
Publishes notes: No
Languages accepted: German; English; French
Prints abstracts: Yes

SUBMISSION REQUIREMENTS

Restrictions on contributors: Submit English abstract.
Author pays page charges: No
Style: Journal
Number of copies required: 1
Copyright ownership: Max Niemeyer Verlag

(1621)
*Lexicographica: Series Maior

Sture Allén, Pierre Corbin, Reinhard R. K. Hartmann, Franz Josef Hausmann, Hans-Peder Kromann, Oskar Reichmann, & Ladislav Zgusta, Editors
Max Niemeyer Verlag
Postfach 2140
7400 Tübingen, Germany

Telephone: (49) 7071 81104
Fax: (49) 7071 87419
First published: 1984
Sponsoring organization: Dictionary Soc. of North America; European Assn. for Lexicography
ISSN: 0175-9264
MLA acronym: LexicographicaS

SUBSCRIPTION INFORMATION

Frequency of publication: Irregular
Available in microform: No

ADVERTISING INFORMATION

Advertising accepted: No

EDITORIAL DESCRIPTION

Scope: Publishes readings, proceedings and monographs on lexicography and lexicology.
Reviews books: No
Publishes notes: No
Languages accepted: German; English; French
Prints abstracts: Yes
Author-anonymous submission: Yes

SUBMISSION REQUIREMENTS

Restrictions on contributors: None
Author pays submission fee: No
Author pays page charges: No
Length of books: 100-300 pp.
Style: MLA
Number of copies required: 2
Copyright ownership: Max Niemeyer Verlag
Rejected manuscripts: Returned
Time before publication decision: 6 mos.
Time between decision and publication: 6 mos.
Number of reviewers: 2
Books submitted per year: 6-10
Books published per year: 4-8

(1622)
*Lexique

Pierre Corbin, Editor
Univ. de Lille III
B.P. 149
59653 Villeneuve d'Ascq Cedex, France

Telephone: (33) 20336132
Fax: (33) 20919171
First published: 1982
ISSN: 0756-7138

MLA acronym: Lexique

SUBSCRIPTION INFORMATION

Frequency of publication: Annual
Available in microform: No
Subscription price: 135 F/yr.
Year to which price refers: 1991
Subscription address: Presses Universitaires de Lille, Rue du Barreau, B.P. 199, 59654 Villeneuve d'Ascq Cedex, France

ADVERTISING INFORMATION

Advertising accepted: No

EDITORIAL DESCRIPTION

Scope: Devotes each issue to a theme concerning lexicons, including their relationship to lexicography, morphology, phonology, syntax, semantics, pragmatics, and theory.
Reviews books: Yes
Publishes notes: Yes
Languages accepted: French
Prints abstracts: Yes
Author-anonymous submission: No

SUBMISSION REQUIREMENTS

Author pays submission fee: No
Author pays page charges: No
Length of book reviews: 100-300 words
Length of notes: 10 lines
Number of copies required: 2
Special requirements: Submit MS-DOS diskette and camera-ready typescript. Include an abstract in French and in English.
Copyright ownership: Editors
Rejected manuscripts: Not returned
Time before publication decision: 6 mos.
Time between decision and publication: 1 yr.
Number of reviewers: 2
Articles published per year: 15-20
Book reviews published per year: 15-20

(1623)
*Lexis: Revista de Lingüística y Literatura

José Luis Rivarola, Editor
Dept. de Humanidades
Pontificia Univ. Católica del Perú
Apartado 12514
Lima 21, Peru

Telephone: (51) 14 622540 ext. 149
Fax: (51) 14 611785
First published: 1977
Sponsoring organization: Dept. de Humanidades, Pontificia Univ. Católica del Perú
ISSN: 0254-9239
MLA acronym: Lexis

SUBSCRIPTION INFORMATION

Frequency of publication: 2 times/yr.
Circulation: 100
Available in microform: No
Subscription price: $19.20/yr.
Year to which price refers: 1991
Subscription address: Fondo Editorial, at the above address

ADVERTISING INFORMATION

Advertising accepted: Yes, on an exchange basis

EDITORIAL DESCRIPTION

Scope: Publishes articles on general, Hispanic, and Andean linguistics and literature, including the theory of literature.
Reviews books: Yes
Publishes notes: Yes
Languages accepted: Spanish
Prints abstracts: No
Author-anonymous submission: No

SUBMISSION REQUIREMENTS

Restrictions on contributors: None
Author pays submission fee: No
Author pays page charges: No
Length of articles: 20-30 pp.
Length of book reviews: 2-5 pp.
Length of notes: 5-10 pp.
Style: MLA; Journal
Number of copies required: 1
Copyright ownership: Journal
Rejected manuscripts: Not returned
Time before publication decision: 2 mos.
Time between decision and publication: 8 mos.
Number of reviewers: 4
Articles published per year: 10-15
Book reviews published per year: 4
Notes published per year: 2-4

(1624)
*Leyte-Samar Studies

Gregorio C. Luangco, Editor
Divine Word Univ. of Tacloban
Tacloban City, 7101, Philippines

First published: 1967
Sponsoring organization: Divine Word Univ.
ISSN: 0024-1679
MLA acronym: LSS

SUBSCRIPTION INFORMATION

Frequency of publication: 2 times/yr.
Circulation: 1,000
Available in microform: No
Subscription price: $7.00/yr.
Year to which price refers: 1992
Subscription address: DWU Publications, Diven Word Univ. of Tacloban, Tacloban City, 6500, Philippines

ADVERTISING INFORMATION

Advertising accepted: No

EDITORIAL DESCRIPTION

Scope: Deals exclusively with aspects of Samar-Leyte culture: language, literature, biography, natural science, and especially history.
Reviews books: Occasionally
Publishes notes: Yes
Languages accepted: English; Spanish; Waray; Filipino
Prints abstracts: No
Author-anonymous submission: No

SUBMISSION REQUIREMENTS

Restrictions on contributors: None
Author pays submission fee: No
Author pays page charges: No
Length of articles: 1,000-5,000 words
Length of book reviews: 500-1,000 words
Length of notes: 500-1,000 words
Style: MLA
Number of copies required: 1
Special requirements: Submit original double-spaced typescript.
Copyright ownership: Divine Word Univ.
Rejected manuscripts: Returned
Time before publication decision: 2 mos. maximum
Time between decision and publication: 2 mos.
Number of reviewers: 5
Articles submitted per year: 10
Articles published per year: 6-8
Notes submitted per year: 4-5
Notes published per year: 2-3

(1625)
*Liberté

François Hébert, Editor
C.P. 399 Succursale Outremont
Montreal, Quebec H2V 4N3, Canada

Telephone: 514 278-4586
Fax: 514 274-0201
First published: 1959
Sponsoring organization: Canadian Council; Ministère des Affaires Culturelles du Québec; Conseil des Arts de la Communauté Urbaine de Montréal
ISSN: 0024-2020
MLA acronym: Liberté

SUBSCRIPTION INFORMATION

Frequency of publication: 6 times/yr.
Circulation: 2,000
Available in microform: Yes
Subscription price: C$40.00/yr. institutions Canada; C$45.00/yr. institutions elsewhere; C$30.00/yr. individuals Canada; C$35.00/yr. individuals elsewhere; C$25.00/yr. students Canada
Year to which price refers: 1992
Subscription address: Periodica, C.P. 444 Succursale Outremont, Montreal, Quebec H2V 4R6, Canada
Subscription telephone: 514 274-5468; 800 361-1431

ADVERTISING INFORMATION

Advertising accepted: No

EDITORIAL DESCRIPTION

Scope: Publishes articles on Québécois and world literature. Also includes creative works.
Reviews books: Yes
Publishes notes: Yes
Languages accepted: French
Prints abstracts: No
Author-anonymous submission: No

SUBMISSION REQUIREMENTS

Restrictions on contributors: None
Author pays submission fee: No
Author pays page charges: No
Length of articles: 5 pp.
Length of book reviews: 2 pp.
Length of notes: 100 words
Number of copies required: 1
Copyright ownership: Author
Rejected manuscripts: Not returned
Time before publication decision: 2 mos.
Time between decision and publication: 6-12 mos.
Number of reviewers: 4
Articles submitted per year: 200
Articles published per year: 60-75
Book reviews submitted per year: 100
Book reviews published per year: 40
Notes submitted per year: 100
Notes published per year: 30

(1626)
*Libraries & Culture: A Journal of Library History

Donald G. Davis, Jr., Editor
Graduate School of Library & Information Science
Univ. of Texas at Austin
Austin, TX 78712-1276

Telephone: 512 471-3806
Fax: 512 471-3971
First published: 1966
Sponsoring organization: Graduate School of Library & Information Science, Univ. of Texas at Austin
ISSN: 0894-8631
MLA acronym: Lib&C

SUBSCRIPTION INFORMATION

Frequency of publication: 4 times/yr. (Winter, Spring, Summer, Fall)
Circulation: 900
Available in microform: Yes
Subscription price: $36.00/yr. institutions; $24.00/yr. individuals
Year to which price refers: 1992
Subscription address: Univ. of Texas Press, Box 7819, Austin, TX 78713

ADVERTISING INFORMATION

Advertising accepted: Yes

EDITORIAL DESCRIPTION

Scope: Explores the significance of collections of recorded knowledge—their creation, organization, preservation and utilization—in the context of cultural and social history, unlimited as to time or place.
Reviews books: Yes
Publishes notes: Yes
Languages accepted: English
Prints abstracts: Yes
Author-anonymous submission: Yes

SUBMISSION REQUIREMENTS

Author pays submission fee: No
Author pays page charges: No
Length of articles: 15-25 pp.
Length of book reviews: 500-700 words
Style: Chicago
Number of copies required: 3
Special requirements: Submit double-spaced typescript with a 50-100 word abstract.
Copyright ownership: Univ. of Texas Press
Rejected manuscripts: Returned; enclose SASE.
Time before publication decision: 1-2 mos.
Time between decision and publication: 4-6 mos.
Number of reviewers: 2-4
Articles submitted per year: 30-50
Articles published per year: 20-25
Book reviews submitted per year: 60
Book reviews published per year: 50
Notes submitted per year: 4-6
Notes published per year: 3-4

(1627)
*Librarium: Zeitschrift der Schweizerischen Bibliophilen-Gesellschaft/Revue de la Société Suisse des Bibliophiles

Werner G. Zimmermann, Editor
Schweizerische Bibliophilen-Gesellschaft
Im Schilf 15
8044 Zurich, Switzerland

First published: 1958
Sponsoring organization: Schweizerische Bibliophilen-Gesellschaft
ISSN: 0024-2152
MLA acronym: Librarium

SUBSCRIPTION INFORMATION

Frequency of publication: 3 times/yr.
Circulation: 700
Available in microform: No

ADVERTISING INFORMATION

Advertising accepted: Yes

EDITORIAL DESCRIPTION

Scope: Publishes articles on all aspects of international bibliophilism, including libraries, binding, illustration, publishers, and the book trade.
Reviews books: Yes
Publishes notes: Yes

Languages accepted: French; German; Italian; English
Prints abstracts: No

SUBMISSION REQUIREMENTS

Restrictions on contributors: None
Author pays submission fee: No
Author pays page charges: No
Length of articles: 1,000-4,500 words
Style: Journal
Number of copies required: 1
Copyright ownership: Author
Rejected manuscripts: Returned
Time before publication decision: 1 mo.
Time between decision and publication: 5-8 mos.
Number of reviewers: 1
Articles published per year: 24

(1628)
*The Library: The Transactions of the Bibliographical Society

Martin Davies, Editor
British Library
Humanities & Social Sciences
Great Russell St.
London WC1B 3DG, England

Additional editorial address: Christine Ferdinand, Review Editor, Magdalen College, Oxford, England
Telephone: (44) 71 3237579
Fax: (44) 71 3237736
E-mail: BM.E3B@RLG
First published: 1889
Sponsoring organization: Bibliographical Soc., London
ISSN: 0024-2160
MLA acronym: Library

SUBSCRIPTION INFORMATION

Frequency of publication: 4 times/yr. (Mar., June, Sept., Dec.)
Circulation: 1,900
Available in microform: Yes
Subscription price: £32.00 ($80.00)/yr. nonmembers; £28.00 ($55.00)/yr. members
Year to which price refers: 1992
Subscription address: Nonmembers: Oxford Univ. Press, Journals Subscriptions Dept., Walton St., Oxford, OX2 6DP, England
Subscription telephone: (44) 865 882283
Subscription fax: (44) 865 882890

ADVERTISING INFORMATION

Advertising accepted: Yes

EDITORIAL DESCRIPTION

Scope: Focuses on historical, analytical, enumerative, descriptive, and textual bibliography; the history of printing, publishing, bookselling, collecting, binding; history of libraries; palaeography, provenance.
Reviews books: Yes
Publishes notes: Yes
Languages accepted: English
Prints abstracts: No
Author-anonymous submission: No

SUBMISSION REQUIREMENTS

Restrictions on contributors: None
Author pays submission fee: No
Author pays page charges: No
Length of articles: 20,000 words maximum
Length of book reviews: 5,000 words maximum
Length of notes: 500-3,000 words
Style: MLA; Modern Humanities Research Assn.
Number of copies required: 2

Special requirements: Glossy prints required for illustrations should be sent with dimensions of original and permission to reproduce. Long quotations may be made in French, German, Italian, Spanish, Latin, Greek, and Welsh, but translations should be provided. Submit original typescript plus 1 copy.
Copyright ownership: Author & Bibliographical Soc.
Rejected manuscripts: Returned
Time before publication decision: 2 mos. (provisional)
Time between decision and publication: 12-18 mos.
Number of reviewers: 1-2
Articles submitted per year: 20-30
Articles published per year: 12-15
Book reviews submitted per year: 30-40
Book reviews published per year: 30-40
Notes submitted per year: 20-30
Notes published per year: 15-20

(1629)
*Library Chronicle of the University of Texas

Dave Oliphant, Editor
Harry Ransom Humanities Research Center
P.O. Box 7219
Austin, TX 78713

Telephone: 512 471-8944
Fax: 512 471-9646
First published: 1944
Sponsoring organization: Univ. of Texas, General Libraries & Harry Ransom Humanities Research Center
ISSN: 0024-2241
MLA acronym: LCUT

SUBSCRIPTION INFORMATION

Frequency of publication: 4 times/yr.
Circulation: 300
Available in microform: Yes, through Univ. Microfilms International
Subscription price: $30.00/yr.
Year to which price refers: 1992

ADVERTISING INFORMATION

Advertising accepted: No

EDITORIAL DESCRIPTION

Scope: Presents information on available research materials in the humanities (especially modern American, French, and British literatures) in the special collections at the University of Texas at Austin, publishes articles based on these materials, and records matters of interest concerning new acquisitions, exhibitions, and other events related to the University's special collections.
Reviews books: No
Publishes notes: No
Languages accepted: English
Prints abstracts: No
Author-anonymous submission: No

SUBMISSION REQUIREMENTS

Author pays submission fee: No
Author pays page charges: No
Length of articles: No restrictions
Style: Chicago
Number of copies required: 1
Special requirements: Articles must be based on Center's special collection holdings.
Copyright ownership: Author
Rejected manuscripts: Returned
Time before publication decision: 6 weeks
Time between decision and publication: 6 mos.
Number of reviewers: 2
Articles submitted per year: 30
Articles published per year: 25

(1630)
Library of Arabic Linguistics

Muhammad Hasan Bakalla, Editor
King Saud Univ.
Riyadh, Saudi Arabia

MLA acronym: LAL

SUBSCRIPTION INFORMATION

Subscription address: Kegan Paul International Ltd., P.O. Box 256, 1118 Bedford Court Mansion, Bedford Ave., London WC1B 3SW, England

ADVERTISING INFORMATION

Advertising accepted: No

EDITORIAL DESCRIPTION

Scope: Publishes monograph studies of international scholarship in Arabic linguistics.
Languages accepted: Arabic; English
Prints abstracts: No

(1631)
*Libri: International Library Review

Irene Wormell, Russell Bowden, & Hans-Peter Geh, Editors
Danmarks Biblioteksskole
6, Birketinget
2300 Copenhagen S, Denmark

Telephone: (45) 31 586066
Fax: (45) 32 840200
First published: 1950
ISSN: 0024-2667
MLA acronym: Libri

SUBSCRIPTION INFORMATION

Frequency of publication: 4 times/yr. (Mar., June, Sept., Dec.)
Circulation: 1,100
Available in microform: No
Subscription price: $130.00/yr.
Year to which price refers: 1991
Subscription address: Munksgaard, International Booksellers & Publishers Ltd., 35, Nörre Sögade, 1370 Copenhagen K, Denmark

ADVERTISING INFORMATION

Advertising accepted: Yes

EDITORIAL DESCRIPTION

Scope: Publishes original papers on all aspects of librarianship, including the history of books and publishing.
Reviews books: No
Publishes notes: No
Languages accepted: English; French; German; Spanish
Prints abstracts: No
Author-anonymous submission: No

SUBMISSION REQUIREMENTS

Author pays submission fee: No
Author pays page charges: No
Length of articles: No restrictions
Style: Chicago; Oxford
Number of copies required: 3
Special requirements: Submit original typescript and consult directions to authors as printed in journal.
Copyright ownership: Author & Munksgaard International Publishers, Ltd.
Rejected manuscripts: Returned
Time before publication decision: 3-10 weeks
Time between decision and publication: 13-26 weeks
Articles submitted per year: 75
Articles published per year: 25

(1632)
La Licorne

Gérard Dessons, Editor
Fac. des Lettres & des Langues
95, avenue du Recteur Pineau
86022 Poitiers, France

Telephone: (33) 49453210
Fax: (33) 49453290
First published: 1976
Sponsoring organization: Univ. de Poitiers, Fac. des Lettres & des Langues
ISSN: 0398-9992
MLA acronym: Licorne

SUBSCRIPTION INFORMATION

Frequency of publication: 3 times/yr.
Available in microform: Yes, through the Bibliothèque Nationale, Paris
Subscription price: 290 F/yr.
Year to which price refers: 1992

ADVERTISING INFORMATION

Advertising accepted: No

EDITORIAL DESCRIPTION

Scope: Publishes articles on French literature, the history of the French language, and linguistics.
Reviews books: Yes
Publishes notes: Yes
Languages accepted: French
Prints abstracts: Yes
Author-anonymous submission: No

SUBMISSION REQUIREMENTS

Restrictions on contributors: None
Author pays submission fee: No
Author pays page charges: No
Length of articles: 20,000 words
Length of book reviews: 2,000 words
Length of notes: 2,000 words
Style: MLA; Chicago
Number of copies required: 2
Copyright ownership: Author
Rejected manuscripts: Returned
Time before publication decision: 6 weeks
Time between decision and publication: 5 mos.
Number of reviewers: 3
Articles submitted per year: 40
Articles published per year: 28-30
Book reviews submitted per year: 20
Book reviews published per year: 20
Notes submitted per year: 25
Notes published per year: 17

(1633)
*Lietuvių Kalbotyros Klausimai

A. Vanagas, S. Karaliūnas, & V. Ambrazas, Editors
Lietuvos Mokslų Akademija
Lietuvių Kalbos Inst.
Antakalnio 6
2055 Vilnius, Lithuania

Telephone: (7) 122 226126
First published: 1957
Sponsoring organization: Lietuvių Kalbos Inst.
ISSN: 0459-3324
MLA acronym: LKK

SUBSCRIPTION INFORMATION

Frequency of publication: Irregular
Available in microform: No

ADVERTISING INFORMATION

Advertising accepted: No

EDITORIAL DESCRIPTION

Scope: Publishes articles on the theory and history of Lithuanian and Baltic linguistics.
Reviews books: Yes
Publishes notes: No
Languages accepted: Russian; Lithuanian; Latvian; German; English
Prints abstracts: No
Author-anonymous submission: No

SUBMISSION REQUIREMENTS

Restrictions on contributors: None
Author pays submission fee: No
Author pays page charges: No
Length of articles: 2,000-7,000 words
Length of book reviews: 1,000-2,000 words
Number of copies required: 2
Special requirements: Submit original typescript and 1 copy and a 200-word abstract.
Rejected manuscripts: Not returned
Time before publication decision: 1-2 mos.
Time between decision and publication: 1-2 yrs.
Number of reviewers: 2-3
Articles submitted per year: 20
Articles published per year: 15
Book reviews published per year: 2

(1634)
*LiLi: Zeitschrift für Literaturwissenschaft und Linguistik

Helmut Kreuzer, Wolfgang Klein, Wolfgang Haubrichs, & Brigitte Schlieben-Lange, Editors
Univ. Siegen
Fachbereich 3
Postfach 10 12 40
5900 Siegen 21, Germany

Telephone: (49) 271 7404575 (editor); (49) 551 54031 (publisher)
Fax: (49) 271 7402330 (editor); (49) 551 46298 (publisher)
First published: 1971
Sponsoring organization: Univ. Siegen
ISSN: 0049-8653
MLA acronym: LiLi

SUBSCRIPTION INFORMATION

Frequency of publication: 4 times/yr.
Circulation: 1,200
Available in microform: No
Subscription price: 78 DM/yr.
Year to which price refers: 1991
Subscription address: Vandenhoeck & Ruprecht-Verlag, Theaterstr. 13, Postfach 3753, 3400 Göttingen, Germany

ADVERTISING INFORMATION

Advertising accepted: Yes

EDITORIAL DESCRIPTION

Scope: Publishes thematic issues with articles which reflect the modern trends in the theory of literature, literary and media criticism, linguistics, literary interpretation, and their interrelations. Also includes a laboratory column with topical notes and controversies in each issue.
Reviews books: Yes, review articles
Publishes notes: Yes
Languages accepted: German; English
Prints abstracts: Yes
Author-anonymous submission: No

SUBMISSION REQUIREMENTS

Restrictions on contributors: Articles on the main topic are by invitation. There are no restrictions for articles in the laboratory column.
Author pays submission fee: No
Author pays page charges: No
Length of articles: 20 printed pp.
Length of book reviews: 20 pp. review articles
Style: Journal

Number of copies required: 1
Special requirements: Include a 250-word abstract. Abstract should be in English for German articles; German for English articles.
Copyright ownership: Vandenhoeck & Ruprecht Verlag for 1 yr.; author thereafter
Rejected manuscripts: Returned
Time before publication decision: 2 mos.
Time between decision and publication: 1 yr.
Number of reviewers: 1-4
Articles submitted per year: 80-130
Articles published per year: 30

(1635)
Limba Română

Al. Graur, Editor
Str. Spiru Haret 12
79638 Bucharest, Romania

Additional editorial address: Editura Academiei Române, Calea Victoriei 125, 79717 Bucharest, Romania
First published: 1952
Sponsoring organization: Academia Română
ISSN: 0024-3523
MLA acronym: LimR

SUBSCRIPTION INFORMATION

Frequency of publication: 6 times/yr.
Circulation: 2,000
Available in microform: No
Subscription address: Rompresfilatelia, Sectorul Export-Import Presă, P.O. Box 12-201, Calea Griviței ur. 64-66, 79517 Bucharest, Romania

ADVERTISING INFORMATION

Advertising accepted: Yes

EDITORIAL DESCRIPTION

Scope: Focuses on the study of the Romanian language. Addresses itself to a wide audience of readers interested in linguistic problems. Publishes studies about Romanian grammar, vocabulary, literary language and stylistics, Romanian linguistic history, dialectology, language culture, orthography, etymology, history of the Romanian language, onomastics, language teaching, and philology. Also publishes articles about general linguistics.
Reviews books: Yes
Publishes notes: Yes
Languages accepted: Romanian
Prints abstracts: No

SUBMISSION REQUIREMENTS

Restrictions on contributors: None
Author pays submission fee: No
Author pays page charges: Yes
Length of articles: 15 typescript pp.
Length of book reviews: 8 typescript pp.
Length of notes: 3 typescript pp.
Style: Journal
Number of copies required: 2
Special requirements: Submit original double-spaced typescript.
Copyright ownership: Author
Rejected manuscripts: Not returned
Time before publication decision: 4 mos.
Time between decision and publication: 4 mos.
Number of reviewers: 2-3
Articles submitted per year: 200
Articles published per year: 60
Book reviews submitted per year: 15
Book reviews published per year: 12
Notes submitted per year: 40
Notes published per year: 30

(1636)
*Lingua: International Review of General Linguistics

J. M. Anderson, E. C. Garcia, N. V. Smith, & T. Hoekstra, Editors
P.O. Box 103
1000 AC Amsterdam, Netherlands

Telephone: (31) 20 5862472
Fax: (31) 20 5862616
E-mail: R.KROON@elsevier.nl
First published: 1947
ISSN: 0024-3841
MLA acronym: Lingua

SUBSCRIPTION INFORMATION

Frequency of publication: 12 times (in 3 vols.)/yr.
Available in microform: Yes
Subscription price: 984 f/yr.
Year to which price refers: 1993
Subscription address: North-Holland Publishing Co., P.O. Box 211, 1000 AE Amsterdam, Netherlands
Subscription telephone: (31) 20 5803642
Subscription fax: (31) 20 5803598

ADVERTISING INFORMATION

Advertising accepted: Yes
Advertising rates: 820 f ($450.00)/half page; 1,180 f ($630.00)/full page

EDITORIAL DESCRIPTION

Scope: Devoted to problems of general linguistics. Its aim is to present work of current interest on a variety of subjects. Contributions must contain such general theoretical implications as to be of interest to any linguist.
Reviews books: Yes
Publishes notes: Yes
Languages accepted: English; French; German
Prints abstracts: Yes
Author-anonymous submission: No

SUBMISSION REQUIREMENTS

Restrictions on contributors: None
Author pays submission fee: No
Author pays page charges: No
Length of articles: 40 typescript pp.
Length of book reviews: 10 pp.
Style: Journal
Number of copies required: 1
Special requirements: Include a summary (200 words maximum). The first page should be the title page only, stating title, author's name, full address, and an abbreviated title not exceeding 40 characters including spaces. Print this short title at the top of each page.
Copyright ownership: Journal
Rejected manuscripts: Not returned
Time before publication decision: 3 mos.
Time between decision and publication: 4 mos.
Number of reviewers: 3-4
Articles submitted per year: 120
Articles published per year: 50
Book reviews submitted per year: 80
Book reviews published per year: 60

(1637)
Língua e Literatura: Revista dos Departamentos de Letras da Faculdade de Filosofia, Letras e Ciêncas Humanas da Universidade de São Paulo

Aida Costa, Carlos Drumond, & Paolo Vizioli, Editors
Faculdade de Filosofia, Letras e Ciêncas Humanas de Univ. de São Paulo
C.P. 8105
05508 São Paulo, Brazil

ISSN: 0047-4711
MLA acronym: Ling&L

(1638)
*Lingua e Stile: Trimestrale di Filosofia del Linguaggio, Linguistica e Analisi Letteraria

Bruno Basile, Luigi Rosiello, Sergio Scalise
Soc. Editrice il Mulino
Strada Maggiore, 37
40125 Bologna, Italy

Telephone: (39) 51 256011
First published: 1966
Historical variations in title: Formerly Lingua e Stile: Trimestrale di Linguistica e Critica Letteraria
Sponsoring organization: Consiglio Nazionale delle Ricerche
ISSN: 0024-385X
MLA acronym: LeS

SUBSCRIPTION INFORMATION

Frequency of publication: 4 times/yr.
Circulation: 1,275
Available in microform: No

ADVERTISING INFORMATION

Advertising accepted: No

EDITORIAL DESCRIPTION

Scope: Focuses on philosophical, linguistic, and stylistic studies.
Reviews books: Yes
Publishes notes: Yes
Languages accepted: French; Italian; English; Spanish
Prints abstracts: Yes
Author-anonymous submission: No

SUBMISSION REQUIREMENTS

Restrictions on contributors: None
Author pays submission fee: No
Author pays page charges: No
Length of articles: 20 pp.
Length of book reviews: 4 pp.
Length of notes: 2,000 words
Style: IPA
Number of copies required: 2
Special requirements: Use IPA system of transcription; include a 10-line summary.
Copyright ownership: Soc. Editrice il Mulino
Rejected manuscripts: Not returned
Time before publication decision: 4 mos.
Time between decision and publication: 1 yr.
Number of reviewers: 2
Articles submitted per year: 40
Articles published per year: 30
Book reviews submitted per year: 50
Book reviews published per year: 50
Notes submitted per year: 10
Notes published per year: 7

(1639)
*Lingua Nostra

Ghino Ghinassi, Editor
Piazza D'Azeglio 20
50121 Florence, Italy

Telephone: (39) 55 2345626
First published: 1939
ISSN: 0024-3868
MLA acronym: LN

SUBSCRIPTION INFORMATION

Frequency of publication: 4 times/yr.
Circulation: 1,500
Available in microform: No
Subscription address: Via B. Fortini 120/10, 50125 Florence, Italy
Subscription telephone: (39) 55 646415
Subscription fax: (39) 55 641257

ADVERTISING INFORMATION

Advertising accepted: No

EDITORIAL DESCRIPTION

Scope: To promote interest in the Italian language and the study of problems with it. Discusses various concerns. Historical-philological: history of the language; grammatical history, etymology; lexicology and historical semantics; rhetoric and stylistics; metrics; history of the question of language and linguistic thought; history of grammar and lexicography; onomastics; texts and documents. Descriptive: grammar and lexicology of modern-day Italian; neologisms, foreign and contemporary dialectical phrases; special languages and technical terminology; social levels of language; regional variations; Italian abroad; linguistic testimonies of men of letters and scientists. Didactic: discussions of linguistic norms and on the teaching of language; use of mass communication; teaching experiences; teaching the language to adults; teaching Italian abroad; problems of contrastive linguistics and translation. Bibliographic: discussion and notice of important books and articles.
Reviews books: Yes
Publishes notes: Yes
Languages accepted: Italian
Prints abstracts: No
Author-anonymous submission: No

SUBMISSION REQUIREMENTS

Restrictions on contributors: None
Author pays submission fee: No
Author pays page charges: No
Length of articles: 5,000 words maximum
Length of book reviews: 1,000 words maximum
Length of notes: 1,000 words maximum
Style: MLA
Number of copies required: 2
Special requirements: Submit original typescript.
Copyright ownership: Journal
Rejected manuscripts: Returned
Time before publication decision: 2 mos.
Time between decision and publication: 3-12 mos.
Number of reviewers: 2
Articles submitted per year: 30
Articles published per year: 15
Book reviews submitted per year: 40
Book reviews published per year: 30
Notes submitted per year: 30
Notes published per year: 20

(1640)
*Lingua Posnaniensis: Czasopismo Poświecone Językoznawstwu Porównawczemu i Ogólnemu

Jerzy Bańczerowski, Editor
Wydawnictwo Poznańskiego
Towarzystwa Przyjaciół Nauk
ul. Seweryna Mielżyńskiego 27/29
61-725 Poznan, Poland

First published: 1949
Sponsoring organization: Polska Akademia Nauk
ISSN: 0079-4740
MLA acronym: LP

SUBSCRIPTION INFORMATION

Frequency of publication: Annual
Available in microform: Yes

ADVERTISING INFORMATION

Advertising accepted: Yes

EDITORIAL DESCRIPTION

Scope: Publishes articles on comparative and general linguistics. Includes in-depth studies, analyses, and book reviews.
Reviews books: Yes
Publishes notes: Yes
Languages accepted: English; French; German; Russian
Prints abstracts: No

SUBMISSION REQUIREMENTS

Restrictions on contributors: None
Author pays submission fee: No
Author pays page charges: No
Style: Journal; see back inside cover
Number of copies required: 3
Special requirements: Submit original typescript and 2 copies.
Rejected manuscripts: Returned
Time before publication decision: 1-24 weeks
Time between decision and publication: 12-18 mos.
Articles submitted per year: 14
Articles published per year: 12
Book reviews submitted per year: 15
Book reviews published per year: 10

(1641)
*The Linguist

J. L. Kettle-Williams, Editor
Inst. of Linguists
24a Highbury Grove
London N5 2EA, England

Telephone: (44) 71 3597445
Fax: (44) 71 3540202
First published: 1962
Sponsoring organization: Inst. of Linguists
ISSN: 0019-3534
MLA acronym: Linguist

SUBSCRIPTION INFORMATION

Frequency of publication: 6 times/yr. (Jan., Mar., May, July, Sept., Nov.)
Circulation: 6,500
Available in microform: No
Subscription price: £20.00/yr. United Kingdom; £27.00/yr. Europe; £30.00/yr. elsewhere
Year to which price refers: 1992

ADVERTISING INFORMATION

Advertising accepted: Yes
Advertising rates: £180.00/quarter page; £330.00/half page; £600.00/full page

EDITORIAL DESCRIPTION

Scope: Publishes articles, reviews, and news of interest to the professional linguist. Articles deal with language in general, linguistics, and translation.
Reviews books: Yes
Publishes notes: Yes
Languages accepted: Publishes in all languages using Roman alphabet; other languages published if camera-ready copy is made available.
Prints abstracts: No

SUBMISSION REQUIREMENTS

Restrictions on contributors: None
Author pays submission fee: No
Author pays page charges: No
Length of articles: 2,000-3,000 words
Length of book reviews: 400 words
Length of notes: 500-1,000 words
Style: Journal
Number of copies required: 2
Special requirements: Submit double-spaced typescript on size A4 (8 1/4 in. x 11 3/4 in.) paper.
Copyright ownership: Inst. of Linguists & author
Rejected manuscripts: Returned
Time before publication decision: 1 mo.
Time between decision and publication: 2 mos.
Number of reviewers: 1-2
Articles submitted per year: 100
Articles published per year: 25
Book reviews submitted per year: 75
Book reviews published per year: 25
Notes submitted per year: 25
Notes published per year: 10

(1642)
*Linguistic Analysis

Michael K. Brame, Editor
P.O. Box 95679
Seattle, WA 98145-2679

Additional editorial address: David R. Willingham, Managing Editor, 22525 Dockton Rd. SW, Vashon Island, WA 98070
Telephone: 206 463-3451
First published: 1975
ISSN: 0098-9053
MLA acronym: LingA

SUBSCRIPTION INFORMATION

Frequency of publication: 4 times/yr.
Circulation: 2,000
Available in microform: No
Subscription price: $105.00/yr. institutions; $52.50/yr. individuals; $35.00/yr. students; add $12.00/yr. postage outside US
Year to which price refers: 1991
Subscription address: Linguistic Analysis, P.O. Box 95679, Seattle, WA 98145-2679

ADVERTISING INFORMATION

Advertising accepted: Yes

EDITORIAL DESCRIPTION

Scope: Research journal devoted to the publication of articles on syntax, semantics, and phonology.
Reviews books: Yes
Publishes notes: Yes
Languages accepted: English; French; German; Russian
Prints abstracts: No
Author-anonymous submission: No

SUBMISSION REQUIREMENTS

Restrictions on contributors: None
Author pays submission fee: No
Author pays page charges: No
Length of articles: 5-50 pp.
Length of book reviews: 5-25 pp.

Length of notes: 3-12 pp.
Style: Linguistic Soc. of America
Number of copies required: 3
Copyright ownership: Journal
Rejected manuscripts: 1 copy returned; enclose SASE.
Time before publication decision: 2-6 mos.
Time between decision and publication: 5-12 mos.
Number of reviewers: 1-2
Articles submitted per year: 200
Articles published per year: 40
Book reviews submitted per year: 10
Book reviews published per year: 2
Notes submitted per year: 10
Notes published per year: 4

(1643) *Linguistic and Literary Studies in Eastern Europe

Petr Sgall, Editor
Ortenovo n.24
17000 Prague 7,
Czechoslovakia

First published: 1980
ISSN: 0165-7267
MLA acronym: LLSEE

SUBSCRIPTION INFORMATION

Frequency of publication: Irregular
Available in microform: No
Subscription address: John Benjamins B.V., P.O. Box 75577, Amsteldijk 44, 1070 AN Amsterdam, Netherlands
Additional subscription address: John Benjamins North America, Inc., 821 Bethlehem Pike, Philadelphia, PA 19118

ADVERTISING INFORMATION

Advertising accepted: No

EDITORIAL DESCRIPTION

Scope: Publishes monographs and collective volumes on recent developments in linguistics in Eastern Europe.
Reviews books: No
Publishes notes: No
Languages accepted: English
Prints abstracts: No
Author-anonymous submission: Yes

SUBMISSION REQUIREMENTS

Author pays submission fee: No
Author pays page charges: No
Length of books: 250-350 pp.
Style: Request from editor
Number of copies required: 2
Copyright ownership: John Benjamins Publishing Co.
Rejected manuscripts: Returned
Time before publication decision: 4-5 mos.
Time between decision and publication: 1 yr.
Number of reviewers: 2
Books submitted per year: 6-8
Books published per year: 3-4

(1644) *Linguistic Inquiry

Samuel Jay Keyser, Editor
Dept. of Linguistics & Philosophy
20D-213
Massachusetts Inst. of Technology
Cambridge, MA 02139

Telephone: 617 253-3221
First published: 1970
ISSN: 0024-3892
MLA acronym: LingI

SUBSCRIPTION INFORMATION

Frequency of publication: 4 times/yr.
Circulation: 3,000
Available in microform: Yes
Subscription price: $90.00/yr. institutions; $48.00/yr. individuals; $30.00/yr. students
Year to which price refers: 1992
Subscription address: MIT Press Journals, 55 Hayward St., Cambridge, MA 02142
Subscription telephone: 617 253-2889
Subscription fax: 617 258-6779

ADVERTISING INFORMATION

Advertising accepted: Yes
Advertising rates: $200.00/half page; $300.00/full page

EDITORIAL DESCRIPTION

Scope: Presents articles on current trends in theoretical linguistics.
Reviews books: No
Publishes notes: Yes
Languages accepted: English; French
Prints abstracts: No
Author-anonymous submission: No

SUBMISSION REQUIREMENTS

Restrictions on contributors: None
Author pays submission fee: No
Author pays page charges: No
Length of articles: 50 pp. maximum
Length of notes: 5-8 pp.
Style: Journal
Number of copies required: 3
Special requirements: Submit original typescript.
Copyright ownership: Massachusetts Inst. of Technology
Rejected manuscripts: 2 returned; 1 retained for files
Time before publication decision: 4 mos.
Time between decision and publication: 6 mos.
Number of reviewers: 2-5
Articles submitted per year: 85
Articles published per year: 19
Notes submitted per year: 62
Notes published per year: 20

(1645) *The Linguistic Review

Harry van der Hulst, Managing Editor
Vakgroep Algemene Taalwetenschap
Rijksuniv. te Leiden
Postbus 9515
2300 RA Leiden, Netherlands

Additional editorial address: Jonathan Kaye, Dept. of Phonetics & Linguistics, School of Oriental & African Studies, Thornhaugh St., London WC1H 0XG, England; Robert May, School of Social Sciences, Univ. of California, Irvine, CA 92717; Yukio Otsu, Inst. of Cultural & Linguistic Studies, Keio Univ., 2-15-45 Mita, Minato-ku, Tokyo 143, Japan; Laurie Tuller, Dépt. de Linguistique, Faculté des Lettres, 3 rue de Tanneurs, 37000 Tours, France
Telephone: (31) 71 272105
Fax: (31) 71 272615
E-mail: HULST@HLERML5.bitnet
First published: 1981
ISSN: 0167-6318
MLA acronym: TLR

SUBSCRIPTION INFORMATION

Frequency of publication: 4 times/yr.
Available in microform: No
Subscription price: 188 DM/yr. institutions; 96 DM/yr. individuals
Year to which price refers: 1991
Subscription address: Walter de Gruyter & Co., Postfach 110240, 1000 Berlin 11, Germany
Additional subscription address: In N. America: Walter de Gruyter, Inc., 200 Saw Mill River Rd., Hawthorne, NY 10532

ADVERTISING INFORMATION

Advertising accepted: Yes
Advertising rates: 320 DM/half page; 600 DM/full page

EDITORIAL DESCRIPTION

Scope: Publishes articles on syntax, semantics, phonology, and morphology, within the framework of generative grammar and related disciplines, as well as critical discussions of theoretical linguistics as a branch of cognitive psychology.
Reviews books: Yes
Publishes notes: Yes
Languages accepted: English
Prints abstracts: No
Author-anonymous submission: Yes

SUBMISSION REQUIREMENTS

Restrictions on contributors: None
Author pays submission fee: No
Author pays page charges: No
Length of articles: No restrictions
Length of book reviews: No restrictions
Length of notes: No restrictions
Style: Journal
Number of copies required: 4
Special requirements: Submit double-spaced typescript and 4 copies on size A4 (8 1/4 in. x 11 3/4 in.) paper, with wide margins on all sides. All pages, including title page, footnotes, etc., should be numbered serially. The author's name should not appear on the title page or in a running head. Manuscripts should be accompanied by a separate title page with the author's name and full address (including e-mail). Authors are strongly encouraged to submit the final version on diskette (along with 2 printed copies). The editor welcomes initiatives for thematic issues with guest editors.
Copyright ownership: Walter de Gruyter
Rejected manuscripts: Not returned
Time before publication decision: 3 mos.
Time between decision and publication: 3-6 mos.
Number of reviewers: 2-3
Articles published per year: 15-20
Notes submitted per year: 1-2
Notes published per year: 1-2

(1646) *Linguistica

Mitja Skubic, Editor
Univ. v Ljubljani
Oddelek za Romanistiko Filozofska Fakulteta
Askerceva 12
61001 Ljubljana, Slovenia

First published: 1955
Sponsoring organization: Univ. v Ljubljani, Filozofska Fakulteta
ISSN: 0024-3922
MLA acronym: Linguistica

SUBSCRIPTION INFORMATION

Frequency of publication: Annual
Circulation: 600
Available in microform: No
Subscription telephone: (38) 61 150001
Subscription fax: (38) 61 159337

ADVERTISING INFORMATION

Advertising accepted: Yes

EDITORIAL DESCRIPTION

Scope: Publishes articles on all aspects of linguistics.
Reviews books: Yes

Publishes notes: Yes
Languages accepted: Slovenian; Serbo-Croatian; Latin; French; Italian; Spanish; Catalan; Portuguese; Romanian; German; English; Russian
Prints abstracts: Yes
Author-anonymous submission: No

SUBMISSION REQUIREMENTS

Restrictions on contributors: None
Author pays submission fee: No
Author pays page charges: No
Length of articles: 16 pp. maximum
Length of book reviews: 6 pp. maximum
Length of notes: 6 pp. maximum
Number of copies required: 1
Copyright ownership: Author
Rejected manuscripts: Not returned
Time before publication decision: 1 mo.
Time between decision and publication: 1 yr.
Number of reviewers: 1
Articles submitted per year: 15-20
Articles published per year: 10
Book reviews submitted per year: 3
Book reviews published per year: 1-5
Notes submitted per year: 3
Notes published per year: 1-5

(1647)
*Linguistica Antverpiensia

M. Windross, Editor
Hoger Inst. voor Vertalers en Tolken
Schildersstr. 41
2000 Antwerp, Belgium

Telephone: (32) 3 2389833
Fax: (32) 3 2481907
First published: 1967
Sponsoring organization: Rijksuniv. Centrum Antwerpen, Hoger Inst. voor Vertalers en Tolken
ISSN: 0771-100X
MLA acronym: LA

SUBSCRIPTION INFORMATION

Frequency of publication: Annual
Available in microform: No
Subscription price: 600 BF/yr.
Year to which price refers: 1992

ADVERTISING INFORMATION

Advertising accepted: No

EDITORIAL DESCRIPTION

Scope: Publishes articles on theoretical and applied linguistics.
Reviews books: Yes
Publishes notes: Yes
Languages accepted: Dutch; English; French; German; Italian; Portuguese; Russian; Spanish
Prints abstracts: No

SUBMISSION REQUIREMENTS

Restrictions on contributors: None
Author pays submission fee: No
Author pays page charges: No
Length of articles: No restrictions
Length of book reviews: No restrictions
Length of notes: No restrictions
Number of copies required: 2
Copyright ownership: Author
Rejected manuscripts: Returned
Time before publication decision: 2 mos.
Time between decision and publication: 6-12 mos.
Number of reviewers: 3-5
Articles submitted per year: 20
Articles published per year: 13
Book reviews submitted per year: 6
Book reviews published per year: 6

(1648)
Linguistica Biblica: Interdisziplinäre Zeitschrift für Theologie und Linguistik

Erhardt Güttgemanns, Editor
Verlag Linguistica Biblica
Postfach 130154
5300 Bonn-Röttgen 1, Germany

First published: 1970
ISSN: 0342-0884
MLA acronym: LBib

SUBSCRIPTION INFORMATION

Frequency of publication: 2 times/yr.
Circulation: 600

EDITORIAL DESCRIPTION

Scope: Contains articles about the following: the present state of a research program named "Generative poetics"; the actual debate about the program of a "linguistic" theology, i.e., a theology based on an empirically controlled theory of language and texts and understood as a science in relation to speech in the form of "texts"; syntactics, semantics, and pragmatics in the field of biblical and theological language; the critical analysis of speech in church and religious activities; the influence of communication theory, information theory, theory of games, theory of graphs, theory of texts, theory of literature or poetics, theory of oral literature or folklore, semiotics, aesthetics, emblematics, rhetorics, structuralism and of other sciences of semiotic behavior or the study of biblical literature.
Reviews books: Yes
Languages accepted: English; French; German
Prints abstracts: Yes

SUBMISSION REQUIREMENTS

Restrictions on contributors: None
Length of articles: 20-40 pp.
Number of copies required: 2
Special requirements: Use decimal structuration in composition.
Copyright ownership: Journal for 2 yrs.
Time before publication decision: 1 mo.
Time between decision and publication: 3 mos.
Number of reviewers: 2
Articles published per year: 10

(1649)
Lingüística Española Actual

Manuel Alvar, Editor
Agencia Española de Cooperación Internacional
Avda. Reyes Católicos, 4
28040 Madrid, Spain

First published: 1979
Sponsoring organization: Inst. de Cooperación Iberoamericana
MLA acronym: LEA

SUBSCRIPTION INFORMATION

Frequency of publication: 2 times/yr.
Available in microform: No
Subscription address: Editorial Arco Libros, S.A., Juan Bautista de Toledo 28, 28002 Madrid, Spain

ADVERTISING INFORMATION

Advertising accepted: No

EDITORIAL DESCRIPTION

Scope: Publishes articles on Spanish language.
Reviews books: No
Languages accepted: Spanish; English; German; romance languages
Prints abstracts: No

SUBMISSION REQUIREMENTS

Author pays page charges: No
Length of articles: No
Number of copies required: 1
Time before publication decision: 1 yr.
Time between decision and publication: 6 mos.
Number of reviewers: 2
Articles published per year: 10-15

(1650)
*Linguistica Extranea

Thomas L. Markey & Patricia J. Eldridge, Editors
Karoma Publishers, Inc.
3400 Daleview Dr.
Ann Arbor, MI 48103

Telephone: 313 668-6725
First published: 1978
MLA acronym: LE

SUBSCRIPTION INFORMATION

Frequency of publication: Irregular
Available in microform: No

ADVERTISING INFORMATION

Advertising accepted: No

EDITORIAL DESCRIPTION

Languages accepted: English
Prints abstracts: No
Author-anonymous submission: No

SUBMISSION REQUIREMENTS

Restrictions on contributors: None
Author pays submission fee: No
Author pays page charges: No
Length of books: No restrictions
Style: Chicago; series
Number of copies required: 1
Copyright ownership: Karoma Publishers
Rejected manuscripts: Returned
Time before publication decision: 2 mos.
Time between decision and publication: 6-12 mos.
Number of reviewers: 3
Books published per year: 2-3

(1651)
*Linguistica Silesiana

Kazimierz Polański, Editor
Inst. of English & General Linguistics
Univ. of Silesia
10 Żytnia St.
41-205 Sosnowiec, Poland

Additional editorial address: Ossolineum Publishing House of the Polish Academy of Sciences, Rynek 9, 50-106 Wrocław, Poland
Telephone: (48) 32 667615
Fax: (48) 32 667615
First published: 1975
Sponsoring organization: Polska Akademia Nauk, Oddział w Katowicach
ISSN: 0208-4228
MLA acronym: LSil

SUBSCRIPTION INFORMATION

Frequency of publication: Annual
Circulation: 300-500
Available in microform: No
Subscription price: 30,000 Zł/yr.
Year to which price refers: 1991

ADVERTISING INFORMATION

Advertising accepted: No

EDITORIAL DESCRIPTION

Scope: Publishes articles on theoretical, historical, and contrastive linguistic studies.
Reviews books: Yes
Publishes notes: No
Languages accepted: English; French; German; Russian; Italian
Prints abstracts: No
Author-anonymous submission: No

SUBMISSION REQUIREMENTS

Restrictions on contributors: Contributors who are members of Linguistic Committee of the Polish Academy of Sciences are preferred, but others are also accepted.
Author pays submission fee: No
Author pays page charges: No
Length of articles: 25 pp. maximum
Length of book reviews: 10 pp. maximum
Style: Linguistic Soc. of America
Number of copies required: 2
Special requirements: Submit double-spaced typescript with wide margins. Request further details from publisher.
Copyright ownership: Ossolineum
Rejected manuscripts: Returned
Time before publication decision: 3-4 mos.
Time between decision and publication: 1 yr.
Number of reviewers: 2
Articles submitted per year: 10-15
Articles published per year: 8-10
Book reviews submitted per year: 5
Book reviews published per year: 2-3

(1652)
*Linguistica Uralica

Paul Kokla & Väino Klaus, Editors
Roosikrantsi 6
EE0106 Tallinn, Estonia

Telephone: (7) 142 440745
First published: 1965
Sponsoring organization: Eesti Teaduste Akadeemia
ISSN: 0868-4731
MLA acronym: LUral

SUBSCRIPTION INFORMATION

Frequency of publication: 4 times/yr.
Circulation: 1,000
Available in microform: No
Subscription price: $28.00/yr.
Year to which price refers: 1992
Subscription address: Eesti Ajakirjandus Levi, Tuukri Polk 6, EE0102 Tallinn, Estonia
Additional subscription address: Akateeminen Kirjakauppa, 128, 00101 Helsinki, Finland; Bibliotekstjänst AB 200, 22100 Lund, Sweden; Kirjastus "Perioodika", P.O. Box 107, Parnu mnt. 8, EE0090 Tallinn, Estonia
Subscription telephone: (7) 142 448820; (7) 142 425860

ADVERTISING INFORMATION

Advertising accepted: No

EDITORIAL DESCRIPTION

Scope: Invites contributions in Finno-Ugric and Samoyedic linguistics.
Reviews books: Yes
Publishes notes: No
Languages accepted: English; German; Russian; French
Prints abstracts: Yes
Author-anonymous submission: No

SUBMISSION REQUIREMENTS

Restrictions on contributors: Contributors must be professional linguists.
Author pays submission fee: No
Author pays page charges: No
Length of articles: 15 pp.
Length of book reviews: 5 pp.
Number of copies required: 2
Special requirements: Include 1/2-1 page summary.
Copyright ownership: Kirjastus "Perioodika"
Rejected manuscripts: Returned
Time before publication decision: 6-7 mos.
Time between decision and publication: 6 mos.
Number of reviewers: 1-2
Articles published per year: 25-35
Book reviews published per year: 25

(1653)
Lingüística y Literatura

Oscar Castro García, Editor
Dept. de Lingüística & Literatura
Univ. de Antioquia
Aptdo. 1226
Medellín, Colombia

Telephone: (57) 4 2630011 ext. 549
Fax: (57) 4 2638282
Sponsoring organization: Dept. de Lingüística & Literatura, Univ. de Antioquia
ISSN: 0120-5587
MLA acronym: LyLit

SUBSCRIPTION INFORMATION

Frequency of publication: 2 times/yr.
Circulation: 300
Available in microform: No
Subscription price: Col$3,000.00/yr. Colombia; $30.00/yr. elsewhere
Year to which price refers: 1992

ADVERTISING INFORMATION

Advertising accepted: Yes
Advertising rates: Col$100,000.00/full page

EDITORIAL DESCRIPTION

Scope: Publishes articles on linguistics and literature, as well as creative writing.
Reviews books: Yes
Publishes notes: Yes
Languages accepted: Spanish
Prints abstracts: No
Author-anonymous submission: No

SUBMISSION REQUIREMENTS

Author pays submission fee: No
Author pays page charges: No
Length of articles: 25 pp.
Length of book reviews: 5 pp.
Length of notes: 2-3 pp.
Style: Inst. Colombiano de Normas Técnicas
Number of copies required: 3
Copyright ownership: Author
Rejected manuscripts: Not returned
Time before publication decision: 3 mos.
Time between decision and publication: 3 mos.
Number of reviewers: 2
Articles submitted per year: 40
Articles published per year: 30
Book reviews submitted per year: 6
Book reviews published per year: 4
Notes submitted per year: 6
Notes published per year: 6

(1654)
*Linguistics: An Interdisciplinary Journal of the Language Sciences

Wolfgang Klein, Editor
Max-Planck-Inst. für Psycholinguistik
Wundtlaan 1
6525 XD Nijmegen, Netherlands

Telephone: (31) 80 521457
Fax: (31) 80 521213
E-mail: Linguistics@mpi.nl
First published: 1963

ISSN: 0024-3949
MLA acronym: Linguistics

SUBSCRIPTION INFORMATION

Frequency of publication: 6 times/yr.
Circulation: 1,000
Available in microform: Yes, through Univ. Microfilms International
Subscription price: $330.00/yr. institutions N. America; 510 DM/yr. institutions elsewhere; $143.00/yr. individuals N. America; 262 DM/yr. elsewhere
Year to which price refers: 1991
Subscription address: Walter de Gruyter, Inc., 200 Saw Mill Rd., Hawthorne, NY 10532
Additional subscription address: Outside US: Mouton de Gruyter, Postfach 110240, 1000 Berlin 11, Germany

ADVERTISING INFORMATION

Advertising accepted: Yes
Advertising rates: 300 DM/half page; 600 DM/full page

EDITORIAL DESCRIPTION

Scope: Provides an interdisciplinary forum for important new research in the language sciences. Publishes articles and short notices in the traditional disciplines of linguistics: pragmatics, semantics, syntax, morphology, phonology. Accepts articles from neighboring disciplines: experimental phonetics, psycholinguistics and neurolinguistics, and first and second language acquisition. Also publishes occasional special issues and welcomes proposals for these.
Reviews books: Yes
Publishes notes: Yes
Languages accepted: English
Prints abstracts: Yes
Author-anonymous submission: No

SUBMISSION REQUIREMENTS

Restrictions on contributors: None
Author pays submission fee: No
Author pays page charges: No
Length of articles: No restrictions
Length of book reviews: 500-1,000 words
Length of notes: 1,500 words
Style: Journal
Number of copies required: 4
Special requirements: Submit double-spaced typescript on size A4 (8 1/4 in. x 11 3/4 in.) or similar paper. Include an abstract of up to 200 words. Endnotes, tables, and figures with titles should be on separate sheets.
Copyright ownership: Mouton de Gruyter; author after 2 yrs.
Rejected manuscripts: Not returned
Time before publication decision: 8-9 weeks
Time between decision and publication: 5 mos.
Number of reviewers: 3
Articles submitted per year: 115
Articles published per year: 48
Book reviews submitted per year: 60
Book reviews published per year: 40
Notes submitted per year: 6
Notes published per year: 6

(1655)
*Linguistics Abstracts

David Crystal, Editor
P.O. Box 5
Holyhead
Gwynedd LL65 1RG, United Kingdom

Telephone: (44) 607 762764
Fax: (44) 607 769728
First published: 1985
ISSN: 0267-5498
MLA acronym: LingAb

SUBSCRIPTION INFORMATION

Frequency of publication: 4 times/yr.
Circulation: 460
Available in microform: No
Subscription price: £73.50 ($156.00)/yr. institutions; £23.00 ($55.50)/yr. individuals
Year to which price refers: 1991
Subscription address: Basil Blackwell, 108 Cowley Rd., Oxford OX4 1JF, England

ADVERTISING INFORMATION

Advertising accepted: Yes

EDITORIAL DESCRIPTION

Scope: Publishes abstracts on all branches of linguistics. Occasionally publishes survey articles.
Reviews books: No
Publishes notes: No
Languages accepted: English
Author-anonymous submission: No

SUBMISSION REQUIREMENTS

Restrictions on contributors: Abstracters are invited by editor. New abstracters are welcome and should contact editor.
Author pays submission fee: No
Author pays page charges: No
Style: Journal
Special requirements: Abstracting forms are supplied by journal.
Copyright ownership: Basil Blackwell
Articles published per year: 1,000 abstracts

(1656)
*Linguistics and Education: An International Research Journal

David Bloome, Editor
Furcolo Hall
Univ. of Massachusetts
Amherst, MA 01003

Telephone: 413 545-4247
Fax: 413 545-4491
First published: 1988
ISSN: 0898-5898
MLA acronym: L&E

SUBSCRIPTION INFORMATION

Frequency of publication: 4 times/yr.
Circulation: 600
Available in microform: No
Subscription address: Ablex Publishing Corp., 355 Chestnut St., Norwood, NJ 07648-9975

ADVERTISING INFORMATION

Advertising accepted: Yes

EDITORIAL DESCRIPTION

Scope: Publishes articles which dessimate research on all topics related to linguistics and education, broadly defined. Such topics include, but are not limited to, classroom interaction, language diversity in educational settings, language policy and curriculum, written language learning, and language disorders in educational settings.
Reviews books: Yes
Publishes notes: No
Languages accepted: English
Prints abstracts: Yes
Author-anonymous submission: Yes

SUBMISSION REQUIREMENTS

Restrictions on contributors: None
Author pays submission fee: No
Author pays page charges: No
Length of articles: 8,000-12,000 words
Length of book reviews: 1,500-6,000 words

Style: American Psychological Assn.
Number of copies required: 4
Copyright ownership: Ablex Publishing Corp.
Rejected manuscripts: Returned; enclose SASE.
Time between decision and publication: 6-9 mos.
Number of reviewers: 3
Articles submitted per year: 80-100
Articles published per year: 16-20
Book reviews submitted per year: 4-6
Book reviews published per year: 4

(1657)
Linguistics and Philosophy: An International Journal

Greg Carlson & Francis J. Pelletier, Editors
Linguistics Program
386 Dewey Hall
Univ. of Rochester
Rochester, NY 14627

Additional editorial address: Send books for review to: Francis J. Pelletier, Dept. of Philosophy, Univ. of Alberta, Edmonton, AB T6G 2E1, Canada
First published: 1977
ISSN: 0165-0157
MLA acronym: Ling&P

SUBSCRIPTION INFORMATION

Frequency of publication: 6 times/yr.
Circulation: 900
Available in microform: No
Subscription price: $258.50/yr. institutions US; 412 f/yr. institutions elsewhere; $75.00/yr. individuals US; 170 f/yr. individuals elsewhere
Year to which price refers: 1993
Subscription address: Kluwer Academic Publishers, P.O. Box 322, 3300 AH Dordrecht, Netherlands
Additional subscription address: Kluwer Academic Publishers Group, P.O. Box 358, Accord Station, Hingham, MA 02018-0358

ADVERTISING INFORMATION

Advertising accepted: Yes

EDITORIAL DESCRIPTION

Scope: Focuses on traditional areas in the philosophy of language such as meaning and truth, reference, description, entailment, speech acts; traditional areas of linguistics such as syntax, semantics and pragmatics (when the studies are of sufficient explicitness and generality to be also of philosophical interest); systems of logic with strong connections to natural language: modal logic, tense logic, epistemic logic, intentional logic; philosophical questions raised by linguistics as a science: linguistic methodology, the status of linguistic theories, the nature of linguistic universals; philosophically interesting problems at the intersection of linguistics and other disciplines: language acquisition, language and perception, language as a social convention. Contributions may be in the form of articles, review articles, notes, discussions, or remarks and replies. Reviews of books and monographs are relatively few in number and restricted to those publications of the widest possible interest.
Reviews books: Yes
Publishes notes: Yes
Languages accepted: English
Prints abstracts: No

SUBMISSION REQUIREMENTS

Restrictions on contributors: Book reviews are commissioned.
Author pays submission fee: No
Author pays page charges: No
Length of articles: 2,500-10,000 words
Length of notes: 1,000 words
Style: None

Number of copies required: 3
Special requirements: Submit double-spaced typescript with footnotes numbered consecutively.
Copyright ownership: Kluwer Academic Publishers
Rejected manuscripts: Not returned
Time before publication decision: 3-4 mos.
Time between decision and publication: 6 mos.
Number of reviewers: 2-3
Articles submitted per year: 100
Articles published per year: 20
Book reviews published per year: 5
Notes published per year: 5

(1658)
*Linguistics of the Tibeto-Burman Area

James A. Matisoff, Editor
STEDT, c/o Inst. for International Studies
Univ. of California, Berkeley
Berkeley CA 94720

E-mail: Jaisser@garnet.berkeley.edu
First published: 1974
Sponsoring organization: Univ. of California, Berkeley, Center for South & Southeast Asian Languages & Literature and Dept. of Linguistics; California State Univ., Fresno, Dept. of Linguistics
ISSN: 0731-3500
MLA acronym: LTBA

SUBSCRIPTION INFORMATION

Frequency of publication: 2 times/yr.
Circulation: 150
Available in microform: No
Subscription price: $50.00/yr.
Year to which price refers: 1992

ADVERTISING INFORMATION

Advertising accepted: Yes

EDITORIAL DESCRIPTION

Scope: Publishes occasional papers, monographs, and other materials relevant to the languages of mainland Southeast Asia and has as its focus not just Tibeto-Burman, but all the languages of mainland Southeast Asia.
Reviews books: Yes
Publishes notes: Yes
Languages accepted: English; French; German
Prints abstracts: No
Author-anonymous submission: No

SUBMISSION REQUIREMENTS

Restrictions on contributors: None
Author pays submission fee: No
Author pays page charges: No
Length of articles: No restrictions
Length of book reviews: No restrictions
Style: None
Number of copies required: 1
Special requirements: Submit typescript.
Copyright ownership: Journal
Rejected manuscripts: Returned
Time before publication decision: 6-12 mos.
Time between decision and publication: 1-2 mos.
Number of reviewers: 3

(1659)
*Linguistik Aktuell

Werner Abraham, Editor
Inst. für Deutsche Sprache & Literatur
Rijksuniv. Groningen
Oude Kijk in 't Jatstraat 26
9712 EK Groningen, Netherlands

Telephone: (31) 50 635850; (31) 50 635920

Fax: (31) 50 635821
E-mail: ABRAHAM@LET.RUG.NL
First published: 1980
ISSN: 0166-0829
MLA acronym: LAkt

SUBSCRIPTION INFORMATION

Frequency of publication: Irregular
Circulation: 300
Available in microform: No
Subscription address: John Benjamins North America, Inc., 821 Bethlehem Pike, Philadelphia, PA 19118
Additional subscription address: John Benjamins B.V., Amsteldijk 44, P.O. Box 75577, 1070 AN Amsterdam, Netherlands

ADVERTISING INFORMATION

Advertising accepted: Yes

EDITORIAL DESCRIPTION

Scope: Publishes work in linguistics and communications science with interdisciplinary interest.
Reviews books: No
Publishes notes: No
Languages accepted: English
Prints abstracts: No
Author-anonymous submission: No

SUBMISSION REQUIREMENTS

Restrictions on contributors: None
Author pays submission fee: No
Author pays page charges: No
Length of books: No restrictions
Style: MLA; Language
Number of copies required: 2
Copyright ownership: John Benjamins B.V.
Rejected manuscripts: Returned
Time before publication decision: 2-3 mos.
Time between decision and publication: 1 yr.
Number of reviewers: 2-3
Books submitted per year: 8
Books published per year: 2

(1660)
*La Linguistique: Revue de la Société Internationale de Linguistique Fonctionnelle/Journal of the International Society of Functional Linguistics

Anne Lefebvre & Jean-Pierre Goudaillier, Editors
U.F.R. de Linguistique
Univ. René-Descartes
12, rue Cujas
75230 Paris Cedex 05, France

Additional editorial address: Send books for review to: Jean-Pierre Goudaillier, at the above address.
Telephone: (33) 1 43319967
Fax: (33) 1 40462963
First published: 1965
Sponsoring organization: International Soc. of Functional Linguistics
ISSN: 0024-3957
MLA acronym: Linguistique

SUBSCRIPTION INFORMATION

Frequency of publication: 2 times/yr.
Circulation: 1,500
Available in microform: No
Subscription price: 320 F/yr.
Year to which price refers: 1992
Subscription address: Presses Universitaires de France, Dépt. des Revues, 14 ave. du Bois-de-l'Epine, B.P. 90, 91003 Evry Cedex, France

ADVERTISING INFORMATION

Advertising accepted: Yes, on an exchange basis with linguistics journals

EDITORIAL DESCRIPTION

Scope: Publishes articles on: (1) functional theory vs. other theories of language; (2) application of functional theory to phonology, syntax, morphology, semantics, synchronic linguistics, diachronic linguistics, as well as other fields of study.
Reviews books: Yes
Publishes notes: Yes
Languages accepted: English; French
Prints abstracts: No
Author-anonymous submission: No

SUBMISSION REQUIREMENTS

Restrictions on contributors: Contributors must be members of the International Soc. of Functional Linguistics.
Author pays submission fee: No
Author pays page charges: No
Length of articles: 12 pp. maximum
Length of book reviews: 250-1,000 words
Length of notes: 5,000 words
Style: Journal
Number of copies required: 2
Copyright ownership: Presses Universitaires de France
Rejected manuscripts: Not returned
Time before publication decision: 3-6 mos.
Time between decision and publication: 1 yr.
Number of reviewers: 2
Articles submitted per year: 40
Articles published per year: 15-20
Book reviews submitted per year: 50-100
Book reviews published per year: 10
Notes submitted per year: 4
Notes published per year: 1-2

(1661)
*Linguistique Africaine

Georges Herault, Editor
Univ. de Paris VII
UFR Linguistique, T.C. 9e étage
2 Place Jussieu
75251 Paris cédex 05, France

First published: 1988
Sponsoring organization: Univ. de Paris VII; Centre National de la Recherche Scientifique
ISSN: 0994-7744
MLA acronym: LAf

SUBSCRIPTION INFORMATION

Frequency of publication: 2 times/yr.
Circulation: 250
Available in microform: No
Subscription price: 150 F/yr.
Year to which price refers: 1992

ADVERTISING INFORMATION

Advertising accepted: Yes

EDITORIAL DESCRIPTION

Scope: Publishes articles on theoretical and descriptive linguistics concerning the languages of Africa.
Reviews books: Yes
Publishes notes: Yes
Languages accepted: French; English
Prints abstracts: No
Author-anonymous submission: Yes

SUBMISSION REQUIREMENTS

Author pays submission fee: No
Author pays page charges: No
Number of copies required: 1
Time before publication decision: 3 mos.
Time between decision and publication: 3-6 mos.
Number of reviewers: 2
Articles submitted per year: 25
Articles published per year: 10

Book reviews submitted per year: 2-5
Book reviews published per year: 2-5

(1662)
*Linguistische Arbeiten

Herbert E. Brekle, Hans Jürgen Heringer, Christian Rohrer, Heinz Vater, & Otmar Werner, Editors
Max Niemeyer Verlag
Postfach 2140
7400 Tübingen, Germany

Telephone: (49) 7071 81104
Fax: (49) 7071 87419
First published: 1973
ISSN: 0344-6727
MLA acronym: LArb

SUBSCRIPTION INFORMATION

Frequency of publication: Irregular
Available in microform: No

ADVERTISING INFORMATION

Advertising accepted: No

EDITORIAL DESCRIPTION

Scope: Publishes linguistic research in various areas, especially Germanic, English, and French.
Reviews books: No
Publishes notes: No
Languages accepted: English; French; German
Prints abstracts: No
Author-anonymous submission: Yes

SUBMISSION REQUIREMENTS

Restrictions on contributors: None
Author pays submission fee: No
Author pays page charges: No
Length of books: 150-250 pp.
Style: Linguistic Soc. of America recommended
Number of copies required: 1
Special requirements: Submit camera-ready typescript.
Copyright ownership: Max Niemeyer Verlag
Rejected manuscripts: Returned
Time before publication decision: 4-6 mos.
Time between decision and publication: 6 mos.
Number of reviewers: 2
Books submitted per year: 12-15
Books published per year: 12

(1663)
*Linguistische Berichte

Günther Grewendorf & Arnim V. Stechow, Editors
Univ. Frankfurt
Inst. für deutsche Sprache & Literatur II
Gräfstr. 76
6000 Frankfurt, Germany

Telephone: (49) 69 7983872
Fax: (49) 69 7983873
E-mail: Lingua.uni-frankfurt.dbp.de
First published: 1968
Sponsoring organization: Sprachwissenschaftliches Inst. & Seminaren
ISSN: 0024-3930
MLA acronym: LingB

SUBSCRIPTION INFORMATION

Frequency of publication: 6 times/yr.
Available in microform: No
Subscription price: 128 DM/yr. institutions; 72 DM/yr. individuals
Year to which price refers: 1992
Subscription address: Westdeutscher Verlag, Herrn Schäbler, Postfach 5829, 6200 Wiesbaden 1, Germany

Subscription telephone: (49) 611 160233
Subscription fax: (49) 611 160229

ADVERTISING INFORMATION

Advertising accepted: Yes

EDITORIAL DESCRIPTION

Scope: Publishes articles on linguistics.
Reviews books: Yes
Publishes notes: Yes
Languages accepted: English; German; French
Prints abstracts: Yes
Author-anonymous submission: Yes

SUBMISSION REQUIREMENTS

Author pays submission fee: No
Author pays page charges: No
Number of copies required: 3
Special requirements: Submit an abstract in English.
Copyright ownership: Westdeutscher Verlag
Rejected manuscripts: Returned
Time before publication decision: 6 mos.
Time between decision and publication: 3 mos.
Number of reviewers: 2
Articles submitted per year: 100
Articles published per year: 30-35
Book reviews submitted per year: 30
Book reviews published per year: 12

(1664)
*Lingvisticæ Investigationes: Revue Internationale de Linguistique Française et de Linguistique Générale

Christian Leclere, Jean-Claude Chevalier, & Maurice Gross, Editors
L.A.D.L. Université Paris 7
2, place Jussieu
75221 Paris Cedex 05, France

First published: 1977
Sponsoring organization: Dépt. de Linguistique, Univ. de Paris VII (Vincennes); Centre National de la Recherche Scientifique, Laboratoire d'Automatique Documentaire & Linguistique
ISSN: 0378-4169
MLA acronym: LingInv

SUBSCRIPTION INFORMATION

Frequency of publication: 2 times/yr.
Circulation: 600
Available in microform: No
Subscription price: 312 f ($189.00)/yr. institutions
Year to which price refers: 1993
Subscription address: John Benjamins B.V., Amsteldijk 44, P.O. Box 75577, 1070 AN Amsterdam, Netherlands
Additional subscription address: John Benjamins North America, Inc., 821 Bethlehem Pike, Philadelphia, PA 19118
Subscription telephone: (31) 20 6762325; 215 836-1200
Subscription fax: (31) 20 6739773; 215 836-1204

ADVERTISING INFORMATION

Advertising accepted: No

EDITORIAL DESCRIPTION

Scope: Publishes studies bearing on all languages, especially French studies. Contents are not limited to theoretical generative studies; a large amount of space is given to fundamental, descriptive studies. It is hoped that the journal will become a focus of confrontation for new theoretical positions, for example, those which avoid the artificial distinction between synchronic and diachronic linguistics. Publishes original studies in phonology, syntax, and semantics, as well as reports and reviews.
Reviews books: Yes
Publishes notes: Yes
Languages accepted: English; French
Prints abstracts: Yes
Author-anonymous submission: Yes

SUBMISSION REQUIREMENTS

Restrictions on contributors: None
Author pays submission fee: No
Author pays page charges: No
Length of articles: 8,000 words
Length of book reviews: 1,500 words
Length of notes: 1,000 words
Style: Linguistic Soc. of America
Number of copies required: 1
Special requirements: Submit original typescript.
Copyright ownership: Assigned by author to journal
Rejected manuscripts: Not returned
Time before publication decision: 3 mos.
Time between decision and publication: 1 yr.
Number of reviewers: 2
Articles submitted per year: 40
Articles published per year: 12
Book reviews published per year: 8
Notes published per year: 10

(1665)
*Lingvisticæ Investigationes: Supplementa: Studies in French & General Linguistics/Etudes en Linguistique Française et Générale

Jean-Claude Chevalier, Maurice Gross, & Christian Leclère, Editors
L.A.D.L Université Paris 7
2, place Jussieu
75221 Paris Cedex 05, France

First published: 1979
Sponsoring organization: Dept. de Linguistique, Univ. de Paris VII (Vincennes); Centre National de la Recherche Scientifique, Laboratoire d'Automatique Documentaire & Linguistique
ISSN: 0165-7569
MLA acronym: LIS

SUBSCRIPTION INFORMATION

Frequency of publication: Irregular
Available in microform: No
Subscription address: John Benjamins B.V., P.O. Box 75577, Amsteldijk 44, 1070 AN Amsterdam, Netherlands
Additional subscription address: John Benjamins North America, Inc., 821 Bethlehem Pike, Philadelphia, PA 19118
Subscription telephone: (31) 20 6738156; 215 836-1200
Subscription fax: (31) 20 6739773; 215 836-1204

ADVERTISING INFORMATION

Advertising accepted: No

EDITORIAL DESCRIPTION

Scope: Publishes international monographs on French and general linguistics.
Reviews books: No
Publishes notes: No
Languages accepted: English; French
Prints abstracts: No
Author-anonymous submission: Yes

SUBMISSION REQUIREMENTS

Length of books: No restrictions
Number of copies required: 1
Special requirements: Submit camera-ready manuscript.
Copyright ownership: John Benjamins B.V.
Time before publication decision: 3 mos.
Time between decision and publication: 1 yr.
Number of reviewers: 2

(1666)
Lingvisticheskie Problemy Funktsional'nogo Modelirovaniia Rechevoĭ Deiatel'nosti

L. A. Karpova, Editor
Universitetskaia nab. 7/9
Izdatel'stvo LGU im. A. A. Zhdanova
B-164 St. Petersburg 199164, Russia

Sponsoring organization: Leningradskiĭ Univ.
ISSN: 0130-9277
MLA acronym: LPFMRD

SUBSCRIPTION INFORMATION

Frequency of publication: Irregular

EDITORIAL DESCRIPTION

Scope: Publishes articles on semantic and syntactic analysis, mathematical linguistics, and applied linguistics.
Reviews books: No
Languages accepted: Russian
Prints abstracts: No

(1667)
*LiNQ: (Literature in North Queensland)

Elizabeth Perkins & Cheryl Taylor, Editors
LiNQ Editorial Committee
Post Office
James Cook Univ.,
Queensland 4811, Australia

Telephone: (61) 77 814276
Fax: (61) 77 814077
First published: 1971
Sponsoring organization: English Language & Literature Assn.
ISSN: 0817-458X
MLA acronym: LiNQ

SUBSCRIPTION INFORMATION

Frequency of publication: 2 times/yr. (Apr., Nov.)
Circulation: 350
Available in microform: No
Subscription price: A$25.00/yr. institutions; A$20.00/yr. individuals
Year to which price refers: 1991

ADVERTISING INFORMATION

Advertising accepted: No

EDITORIAL DESCRIPTION

Scope: Publishes creative writing and articles and reviews on literary and cultural subjects.
Reviews books: Yes
Publishes notes: Yes
Languages accepted: English; German; French
Prints abstracts: No
Author-anonymous submission: No

SUBMISSION REQUIREMENTS

Restrictions on contributors: None
Author pays submission fee: No
Author pays page charges: No
Length of articles: 3,000-4,000 words
Length of book reviews: 1,000 words
Length of notes: 200 words
Style: MLA
Number of copies required: 1
Special requirements: Include the title, page number, and author's name and address on each sheet.
Copyright ownership: Author
Rejected manuscripts: Returned; enclose return postage.
Time before publication decision: 3 mos.
Time between decision and publication: 3 mos.
Number of reviewers: 4
Articles submitted per year: 25
Articles published per year: 10
Book reviews submitted per year: 20
Book reviews published per year: 12
Notes submitted per year: 5
Notes published per year: 2

(1668)
*The Lion and the Unicorn: A Critical Journal of Children's Literature

Louisa Smith & Jack Zipes, Editors
Dept. of English, Box 53
Mankato State Univ.
Mankato, MN 56002-8400

Additional editorial address: J. Zipes, Dept. of German, Folwell Hall AH11, Univ. of Minnesota, Minneapolis, MN 55455
Telephone: 507 389-2117
First published: 1977
Sponsoring organization: Mankato State Univ.
ISSN: 0147-2593
MLA acronym: L&U

SUBSCRIPTION INFORMATION

Frequency of publication: 2 times/yr.
Circulation: 1,000
Available in microform: No
Subscription price: $34.00/yr. institutions US; $19.00/yr. individuals US; add $2.40/yr. postage Canada & Mexico, $4.40/yr. elsewhere
Year to which price refers: 1993
Subscription address: Journals Publishing Division, Johns Hopkins Univ. Press, 2715 North Charles St., Baltimore, MD 21218-4319
Subscription telephone: 410 516-6945; 800 537-5487
Subscription fax: 410 516-6998

ADVERTISING INFORMATION

Advertising accepted: Yes
Advertising rates: $115.00/half page; $190.00/full page; $215.00/inside cover; $240.00/back cover

EDITORIAL DESCRIPTION

Scope: Publishes critical essays on children's literature; interviews with writers, editors, and reviewers in the field; occasional reviews of new literature and critical works. Issues are thematic.
Reviews books: Yes
Publishes notes: No
Languages accepted: English
Prints abstracts: No

SUBMISSION REQUIREMENTS

Author pays submission fee: No
Author pays page charges: No
Length of articles: 10-40 double-spaced typescript pp.
Length of book reviews: 2,000 words
Style: MLA
Special requirements: Submit original typescript and 1 copy.
Copyright ownership: Journal
Rejected manuscripts: Returned with comments
Time before publication decision: 4-6 mos.
Time between decision and publication: 6-9 mos.
Number of reviewers: 2
Articles submitted per year: 100
Articles published per year: 20
Book reviews published per year: 4-5

(1669)
*Listy Filologické: Folia Philologica

Helena Kurzová & Alena Hadravová-Dohnalová, Editors
Ústav pro klasická studia ČSAV
Rímská 14
12000 Prague 2, Czech Republic

Telephone: (42) 2 3279905; (42) 2 2361198
First published: 1874
Sponsoring organization: Československá Akademie Věd, Inst. for Greek, Roman & Latin Studies
ISSN: 0024-4457
MLA acronym: LF

SUBSCRIPTION INFORMATION

Frequency of publication: 2 times/yr. (Spring, Fall)
Circulation: 800
Available in microform: No
Subscription price: 205 f ($124.00)/yr.
Year to which price refers: 1993
Subscription address: John Benjamins B.V., Amsteldijk 44, P.O. Box 75577, 1070 AN Amsterdam, Netherlands
Additional subscription address: John Benjamins North America, Inc., 821 Bethlehem Pike, Philadelphia, PA 19118
Subscription telephone: (31) 20 6738156; 215 836-1200
Subscription fax: (31) 20 6739773; 215 836-1204

ADVERTISING INFORMATION

Advertising accepted: No

EDITORIAL DESCRIPTION

Scope: Publishes work on Classical and Medieval Latin studies with emphasis on language and literature, medieval Czech studies, and humanistic studies.
Reviews books: Yes
Publishes notes: Yes
Languages accepted: English; French; German; Russian; Spanish; Latin; Italian; Czech
Prints abstracts: Yes
Author-anonymous submission: No

SUBMISSION REQUIREMENTS

Restrictions on contributors: None
Author pays submission fee: No
Author pays page charges: No
Length of articles: 10-25 pp. (30 lines/page)
Length of book reviews: 3-4 pp. (30 lines/page)
Length of notes: 1 p. (30 lines/page)
Style: None
Number of copies required: 2
Special requirements: Submit original typescript plus 1 copy.
Copyright ownership: Academia Publishing House for 10 yrs., then reverts to author
Rejected manuscripts: Returned
Time before publication decision: 3 mos.
Time between decision and publication: 6-12 mos.
Number of reviewers: 2
Articles submitted per year: 35-40
Articles published per year: 20
Book reviews submitted per year: 60
Book reviews published per year: 45
Notes submitted per year: 25-30
Notes published per year: 15

(1670)
*Lit: Literature Interpretation Theory

Lee A. Jacobus & Regina Barreca, Editors
Dept. of English
Univ. of Connecticut
Storrs, CT 06269

Telephone: 203 486-2570
Fax: 203 486-2570
E-mail: JACOBUS@UCONNVM
First published: 1989
Sponsoring organization: Univ. of Connecticut
ISSN: 0987-1243
MLA acronym: LIT

SUBSCRIPTION INFORMATION

Frequency of publication: 4 times/yr.
Available in microform: No
Subscription price: $74.00/yr. institutions; $38.00/yr. individuals
Year to which price refers: 1991
Subscription address: Gordon & Breach Science Publishers, Marketing Dept., P.O. Box 786 Cooper Station, New York, NY 10276
Additional subscription address: Gordon & Breach Science Publishers, Marketing Dept., P.O. Box 197, London WC2E 9PX, England
Subscription telephone: 212 206-8900
Subscription fax: 212 645-2459

ADVERTISING INFORMATION

Advertising accepted: No

EDITORIAL DESCRIPTION

Scope: Publishes theoretical and critical essays that center on literature and culture. Focuses on integration of theoretical discussions with close reading of texts.
Reviews books: No
Publishes notes: No
Languages accepted: English
Prints abstracts: No
Author-anonymous submission: No

SUBMISSION REQUIREMENTS

Author pays submission fee: No
Author pays page charges: No
Length of articles: No restrictions
Style: MLA
Number of copies required: 3
Special requirements: Contributors must secure permission for illustrations.
Copyright ownership: Journal
Rejected manuscripts: Returned
Time before publication decision: 3-6 mos.
Time between decision and publication: 3-6 mos.
Number of reviewers: 1-3
Articles submitted per year: 100
Articles published per year: 24

(1671)
*Literarni Leksikon

Janko Kos, Darko Dolinar, Majda Stanovnik, & Drago Šega, Editors
c/o Darko Dolinar
Znanstvenoraziskovalni Center SAZU
Novi trg 5
61000 Ljubljana, Slovenia

Telephone: (38) 61 156068
Fax: (38) 61 155253
First published: 1978
Sponsoring organization: Inšt. za Slovensko Literaturo in Literarne Vede, Znanstvenoraziskovalni Center Slovenska Akademije Znanosti in Umetnosti
MLA acronym: LitLeks

SUBSCRIPTION INFORMATION

Frequency of publication: Irregular

Circulation: 1,000
Available in microform: No
Subscription address: Državna Založba Slovenije, Mestni trg 26, 61000 Ljubljana, Slovenia

ADVERTISING INFORMATION

Advertising accepted: No

EDITORIAL DESCRIPTION

Scope: Publishes monographs on literary terms and literary phenomena in view of literary theory and comparative literature, with special attention to Slovenian literature and criticism.
Publishes notes: No
Languages accepted: Slovenian
Prints abstracts: Yes
Author-anonymous submission: No

SUBMISSION REQUIREMENTS

Author pays submission fee: No
Author pays page charges: No
Length of books: 50,000 words maximum
Number of copies required: 2
Special requirements: Authors are required to keep to the general contents and patterns of the basic chapters in each volume.
Copyright ownership: Znanstvenoraziskovalni Center SAZU & author
Time before publication decision: 3 mos.
Time between decision and publication: 1-2 yrs.
Number of reviewers: 3-4
Books submitted per year: 2-6
Books published per year: 2-5

(1672)
*Literary and Linguistic Computing: Journal of the Association for Literary and Linguistic Computing

Gordon Dixon, Editor
Inst. of Advanced Studies
Manchester Polytechnic
All Saints Bldg.
Oxford Rd.
Manchester, MI5 6BH, England

Additional editorial address: Thomas B. Horton, Book Reviews Editor, Dept. of Computer Science, Florida Atlantic Univ., Boca Raton, FL 33431
Telephone: (44) 61 2471947
Fax: (44) 61 2367383
E-mail: G.DIXON@UK.AC.MANCHESTER
First published: 1986
Sponsoring organization: Assn. for Literary & Linguistic Computing
ISSN: 0268-1145
MLA acronym: L&LC

SUBSCRIPTION INFORMATION

Frequency of publication: 4 times/yr. (Spring, Summer, Autumn, Winter)
Circulation: 900
Available in microform: No
Subscription price: £44.00/yr. institutions United Kingdom & Europe; $83.00/yr. institutions elsewhere; £22.00/yr. individuals United Kingdom & Europe; $42.00/yr. individuals elsewhere
Year to which price refers: 1992
Subscription address: Journals Subscription Dept., Oxford Univ. Press, Pinkhill House, Southfield Rd., Eynsham, Oxford OX8 1JJ, England
Subscription telephone: (44) 865 882283
Subscription fax: (44) 865 882890

ADVERTISING INFORMATION

Advertising accepted: Yes
Advertising rates: £110.00/half page; £200.00/full page

EDITORIAL DESCRIPTION

Scope: Focuses on computer applications in language and literature, hardware, software, computer-assisted language learning, and word-processing for humanities applications.
Reviews books: Yes
Publishes notes: Yes
Languages accepted: English; French; German
Prints abstracts: No
Author-anonymous submission: No

SUBMISSION REQUIREMENTS

Author pays submission fee: No
Author pays page charges: No
Length of articles: 5,000-9,000 words
Length of book reviews: 1,000 words
Length of notes: 500 words
Number of copies required: 2
Special requirements: Submit an abstract of 220 words or less.
Copyright ownership: Oxford Univ. Press
Rejected manuscripts: Returned
Time before publication decision: 5 mos.
Time between decision and publication: 6 weeks
Number of reviewers: 2

(1673)
*The Literary Criterion

C. D. Narasimhaiah & C. N. Srinath, Editors
Dhvanyaloka
Mysore-6, India

Telephone: (91) 821 21275
First published: 1952
Sponsoring organization: Literary Criterion Centre, Mysore
ISSN: 0024-452X
MLA acronym: LCrit

SUBSCRIPTION INFORMATION

Frequency of publication: 4 times/yr.
Circulation: 700
Available in microform: No
Subscription price: 100 Re/yr. institutions India; $25.00 (£15.00)/yr. institutions elsewhere; 60 Re/yr. individuals India
Year to which price refers: 1992
Subscription address: C. N. Srinath, Dept. of English, Bangalore Univ., Bangalore 56, India

ADVERTISING INFORMATION

Advertising accepted: Yes
Advertising rates: 2,000 Re ($100.00, £50.00)/insert, 4 issues

EDITORIAL DESCRIPTION

Scope: Focuses on the close study of significant works, authors, and movements in English, American, and Commonwealth literatures.
Reviews books: Yes
Publishes notes: Yes
Languages accepted: English
Prints abstracts: No
Author-anonymous submission: No

SUBMISSION REQUIREMENTS

Restrictions on contributors: None
Author pays submission fee: No
Author pays page charges: No
Length of articles: 3,000-4,000 words
Length of book reviews: 500 words
Length of notes: 250 words
Style: MLA
Number of copies required: 2
Special requirements: Submit original typescript.
Copyright ownership: Assigned by author to journal
Rejected manuscripts: Not returned
Time before publication decision: 2 mos.
Time between decision and publication: 2-6 mos.

Number of reviewers: 2
Articles submitted per year: 100
Articles published per year: 30
Book reviews submitted per year: 30
Book reviews published per year: 30-40
Notes submitted per year: 2-5
Notes published per year: 10

(1674)
The Literary Endeavour: A Quarterly Journal Devoted to English Studies

L. Adinarayana, Editor
Flat 3, Block 6, HIG 1st Phase
Opp. Water Tank, Baghlingampalli
Hyderabad 500 044, India

First published: 1979
ISSN: 0255-2779
MLA acronym: LitE

SUBSCRIPTION INFORMATION

Frequency of publication: 4 times/yr. (Jan., Apr., July, Oct.)
Circulation: 600
Available in microform: No

ADVERTISING INFORMATION

Advertising accepted: Yes

EDITORIAL DESCRIPTION

Scope: Aims to promote an awareness of modern creative trends and critical approaches to literature in English.
Reviews books: Yes
Publishes notes: Yes
Languages accepted: English
Prints abstracts: No
Author-anonymous submission: No

SUBMISSION REQUIREMENTS

Restrictions on contributors: None
Author pays submission fee: No
Author pays page charges: No
Length of articles: 3,000 words
Length of book reviews: 1,000 words
Length of notes: 300 words
Style: MLA
Number of copies required: 2
Special requirements: Manuscripts should include a declaration that they are original, previously unpublished works. Translators must obtain permission to translate from original authors.
Copyright ownership: Reverts from journal to author after 1 yr.
Rejected manuscripts: Returned; enclose SASE.
Time before publication decision: 3 mos.
Time between decision and publication: 3 mos.
Number of reviewers: 4
Articles submitted per year: 100
Articles published per year: 25
Book reviews submitted per year: 60
Book reviews published per year: 10
Notes submitted per year: 20
Notes published per year: 14

(1675)
The Literary Griot: International Journal of Black Oral and Literary Studies

Ousseynou B. Traoré, Editor
Dept. of African, African-American & Caribbean Studies
William Paterson College of New Jersey
Wayne, NJ 07470

Telephone: 201 595-2579
Fax: 201 595-2418
Sponsoring organization: Global Black Expressive Culture Studies Assn.

ISSN: 0737-0873
MLA acronym: *LGriot*

SUBSCRIPTION INFORMATION

Frequency of publication: 2 times/yr. (Spring, Fall)
Subscription price: $20.00/yr. institutions; $15.00/yr. individuals
Year to which price refers: 1992

EDITORIAL DESCRIPTION

Scope: Publishes articles on the literatures, oral arts, and other expressive arts of the Pan-African world (Africa, Afro-America, the Caribbean, etc.) Interested primarily in Afrocentric essays on the history, theory, and criticism of the Black expressive arts.
Reviews books: Yes
Languages accepted: English; French

SUBMISSION REQUIREMENTS

Style: MLA
Special requirements: Submission on diskette, preferably in WordPerfect, is required except for submissions from Third World countries.
Time before publication decision: 2 mos.

(1676) *Literary Half-Yearly

Anniah Gowda, Editor
"Anjali" 96, 7th Main
Jayalakshmipuran
Mysore 570 012, India

First published: 1960
Sponsoring organization: Univ. of Mysore; Inst. of Commonwealth & American Studies & English Language
ISSN: 0024-4554
MLA acronym: *LHY*

SUBSCRIPTION INFORMATION

Frequency of publication: 2 times/yr.
Circulation: 750
Available in microform: No
Subscription price: 60 Re (£10.00, $20.00)/yr.
Year to which price refers: 1991

ADVERTISING INFORMATION

Advertising accepted: Yes
Advertising rates: $250.00/full page; $500.00/cover

EDITORIAL DESCRIPTION

Scope: Devoted to comparative literature. Publishes creative and critical articles, and articles on Commonwealth literature.
Reviews books: Yes
Publishes notes: No
Languages accepted: English
Prints abstracts: No
Author-anonymous submission: Yes

SUBMISSION REQUIREMENTS

Author pays submission fee: No
Author pays page charges: No
Length of articles: 3,000 words
Length of book reviews: 300-500 words
Style: MLA
Number of copies required: 2
Copyright ownership: Editor
Rejected manuscripts: Returned; enclose return postage.
Time before publication decision: 3 mos.
Time between decision and publication: 3 mos.
Number of reviewers: 10-12
Articles submitted per year: 50
Articles published per year: 20
Book reviews published per year: 20

(1677) Literary Research: A Journal of Scholarly Method and Technique

Michael J. Marcuse, Editor
Dept. of English
Univ. of Maryland
College Park, MD 20742

First published: 1976
Sponsoring organization: Literary Research Assn.
ISSN: 0891-6365
MLA acronym: *LRN*

SUBSCRIPTION INFORMATION

Frequency of publication: 4 times/yr. (Jan., Apr., July, Oct.)
Circulation: 300
Available in microform: No

ADVERTISING INFORMATION

Advertising accepted: Yes

EDITORIAL DESCRIPTION

Scope: Publishes articles on all aspects of research (practical, pedagogical, theoretical, etc.) in modern literature, including literary scholarship and methods, bibliography, and textual studies.
Reviews books: Yes
Publishes notes: Yes
Languages accepted: English
Prints abstracts: No
Author-anonymous submission: Yes

SUBMISSION REQUIREMENTS

Restrictions on contributors: None
Author pays submission fee: No
Author pays page charges: No
Length of articles: 2,500-5,000 words
Length of book reviews: 250-1,000 words
Length of notes: 1,000-2,000 words
Style: MLA
Number of copies required: 2
Copyright ownership: Journal
Rejected manuscripts: Returned; enclose return postage.
Time before publication decision: 6 weeks
Time between decision and publication: 6-12 mos.
Number of reviewers: 3
Articles submitted per year: 40
Articles published per year: 12
Book reviews submitted per year: 40-50
Book reviews published per year: 20-30
Notes submitted per year: 80-100
Notes published per year: 75-80

(1678) *The Literary Review: An International Journal of Contemporary Writing

Walter Cummins, Martin Green, Harry Keyishian, & William Zander, Editors
Fairleigh Dickinson Univ.
285 Madison Ave.
Madison, NJ 07940

Telephone: 201 598-8564
First published: 1957
Sponsoring organization: Fairleigh Dickinson Univ.
ISSN: 0024-4589
MLA acronym: *LitR*

SUBSCRIPTION INFORMATION

Frequency of publication: 4 times/yr.
Circulation: 2,500
Available in microform: Yes
Subscription price: $18.00/yr. US; $22.00/yr. elsewhere
Year to which price refers: 1992

ADVERTISING INFORMATION

Advertising accepted: No

EDITORIAL DESCRIPTION

Scope: Publishes poetry and fiction of quality from all over the world, is an outlet for new and established writers, and reflects the best of contemporary writing in fiction and poetry by being receptive to the traditionalist as well as the experimentalist. Publishes essays dealing with major issues and trends in contemporary American and world literature, interpretive essays on the work of important and neglected figures, and essays on literary theory. Encourages the broad view of literature in its various contexts as well as the distinctly personal view of the literary response. Devotes issues to writing from a specific nation or region.
Reviews books: Yes
Publishes notes: No
Languages accepted: English
Prints abstracts: No
Author-anonymous submission: No

SUBMISSION REQUIREMENTS

Restrictions on contributors: None
Author pays submission fee: No
Author pays page charges: No
Length of articles: 2,500-5,000 words
Length of book reviews: 500 words
Style: MLA
Number of copies required: 1
Special requirements: Use minimum number of footnotes.
Copyright ownership: Assigned by author to journal; author retains all reprint rights.
Rejected manuscripts: Returned; enclose return postage.
Time before publication decision: 2-3 mos.
Time between decision and publication: 1-2 yrs.
Number of reviewers: 3-5
Articles submitted per year: 50
Articles published per year: 6-8
Book reviews submitted per year: 25
Book reviews published per year: 8-10

(1679) *Literary Studies in Poland/Etudes Littéraires en Pologne

Hanna Dziechcińska, Editor
Inst. Badán Literackich PAN
Nowy Świat 72
00-330 Warsaw, Poland

Telephone: (48) 22 269945
Fax: (48) 22 269945
First published: 1978
Sponsoring organization: Polska Akademia Nauk
ISSN: 0137-4192
MLA acronym: *LSPd*

SUBSCRIPTION INFORMATION

Frequency of publication: 2 times/yr.
Available in microform: No
Subscription address: Harry Münchberg, Wissenschaftliche Versandbuchhandlung, Postfach, 3394 Langelsheim 2, Germany

ADVERTISING INFORMATION

Advertising accepted: Request from H. Münchberg

EDITORIAL DESCRIPTION

Scope: Publishes articles on Polish literature, literary history, and theory by Polish authors.
Reviews books: Yes
Publishes notes: No
Languages accepted: English; French
Prints abstracts: No

Author-anonymous submission: No

SUBMISSION REQUIREMENTS

Author pays submission fee: No
Author pays page charges: No
Length of articles: 20-30 pp.
Length of book reviews: 7-8 pp.
Style: Journal
Number of copies required: 2
Copyright ownership: Author
Rejected manuscripts: Returned
Time before publication decision: 6 mos.
Time between decision and publication: 6 mos.
Number of reviewers: 2
Articles submitted per year: 20
Articles published per year: 15
Book reviews submitted per year: 8
Book reviews published per year: 8

(1680)
*Literator: Tydskrif vir Besondere en Vergelykende Taal- en Literatuurstudie/Journal of Literary Criticism, Comparative Linguistics and Literary Studies

D. H. Steenberg & A. L. Combrink, Editors
Bureau for Scholarly Journals
Private Bag X6001
Potchefstroom 2520, South Africa

Telephone: (27) 148 991769
Fax: (27) 148 991562
First published: 1980
Sponsoring organization: Dept. of Education & Culture; Potchefstroomse Univ. vir Christelike Hoër Onderwys; Foundation for the Creative Arts
ISSN: 0258-2279
MLA acronym: Literator

SUBSCRIPTION INFORMATION

Frequency of publication: 3 times/yr.
Circulation: 350
Available in microform: No
Subscription price: 30 R ($20.00)/yr.
Year to which price refers: 1993

ADVERTISING INFORMATION

Advertising accepted: Yes
Advertising rates: 250 R/full page

EDITORIAL DESCRIPTION

Scope: Publishes articles on languages and literature using a comparative approach. Includes studies on South African literature in English, English language in South Africa, and African languages.
Reviews books: Yes
Publishes notes: Yes
Languages accepted: English; Afrikaans; French; German; Dutch
Prints abstracts: Yes
Author-anonymous submission: Yes

SUBMISSION REQUIREMENTS

Author pays submission fee: No
Author pays page charges: Yes
Cost of page charges: 40 R/page
Length of articles: 7,000 words
Length of book reviews: 1,000-2,000 words
Length of notes: 1,000-1,500 words
Style: Harvard
Number of copies required: 4
Special requirements: Submit original double-spaced typescript and 3 copies on size A4 (8 1/4 in. x 11 3/4 in.) paper. Articles accepted for publication should be submitted on diskette using Nota Bene, DCA, or ASCII format. Include an abstract of 150-200 words.
Copyright ownership: Author
Rejected manuscripts: Returned with referees' report

Time before publication decision: 4 mos.
Time between decision and publication: 4 mos.
Number of reviewers: 3
Articles submitted per year: 50
Articles published per year: 30
Book reviews submitted per year: 5
Book reviews published per year: 4
Notes submitted per year: 3
Notes published per year: 2

(1681)
*Literatur als Sprache: Literaturtheorie—Interpretation—Sprachkritik

Helmut Arntzen, Editor
Westfälische Wilhelms-Univ. Münster
Germanistisches Inst.
Abteilung für neuere deutsche Literatur & Vergleichende Literaturwissenschaft
Domplatz 20-22
4400 Münster, Germany

Telephone: (49) 251 834437
First published: 1982
MLA acronym: LitAS

SUBSCRIPTION INFORMATION

Frequency of publication: Irregular
Available in microform: No
Subscription address: Aschendorffsche Verlagsbuchhandlung, Postfach 1124, Soester Str. 13, 44 Münster, Germany

ADVERTISING INFORMATION

Advertising accepted: No

EDITORIAL DESCRIPTION

Scope: Publishes monographs on the concept of literature as speech, with emphasis on textual criticism, linguistic and literary theory.
Reviews books: No
Publishes notes: No
Languages accepted: German
Prints abstracts: No
Author-anonymous submission: No

SUBMISSION REQUIREMENTS

Author pays submission fee: No
Author pays page charges: No
Copyright ownership: Author
Time between decision and publication: 6-8 mos.
Books submitted per year: 3
Books published per year: 2

(1682)
*Literatur für Leser

Bernhard Spies, Gerhard Kaiser, Dieter Mayer, & Maximilian Nutz, Editors
Deutsches Inst.
Univ. Mainz
Postfach 3980
6500 Mainz 1, Germany

Telephone: (49) 6131 394753
Fax: (49) 6131 393366
First published: 1978
ISSN: 0343-1657
MLA acronym: LfL

SUBSCRIPTION INFORMATION

Frequency of publication: 4 times/yr. (Mar., June, Sept., Dec.)
Circulation: 400
Available in microform: No
Subscription price: 56.80 DM/yr.; 49.80 DM/yr. students
Year to which price refers: 1992

Subscription address: Verlag Peter Lang, Eschborner Landstr. 42-50, Postfach 940225, 6000 Frankfurt, Germany
Subscription telephone: (49) 69 7893041
Subscription fax: (49) 69 785893

ADVERTISING INFORMATION

Advertising accepted: Yes
Advertising rates: 380 DM/half page; 760 DM/full page

EDITORIAL DESCRIPTION

Scope: Publishes articles on German literature from the seventeenth century to the present. Focuses on interpretation of literary texts with regard to their historical contexts.
Reviews books: No
Publishes notes: No
Languages accepted: German
Prints abstracts: No
Author-anonymous submission: No

SUBMISSION REQUIREMENTS

Author pays submission fee: No
Author pays page charges: No
Length of articles: 2,300 words
Style: MLA
Number of copies required: 1
Copyright ownership: Verlag Peter Lang
Rejected manuscripts: Not returned
Time before publication decision: 1-2 mos.
Time between decision and publication: 1-12 mos.
Number of reviewers: 4
Articles submitted per year: 35-50
Articles published per year: 22-24

(1683)
*Literatur in der Geschichte, Geschichte in der Literatur

Klaus Amann, Editor
c/o Böhlau Verlag GmbH & Co.
Sachsenplatz 4-6
1201 Vienna, Austria

Telephone: (43) 222 3302427
Fax: (43) 222 3302432
Sponsoring organization: Fonds zur Förderung der Wissenschaftlichen Forschung
MLA acronym: LGGL

SUBSCRIPTION INFORMATION

Frequency of publication: Irregular
Available in microform: No

ADVERTISING INFORMATION

Advertising accepted: No

EDITORIAL DESCRIPTION

Scope: Publishes monographs on the relationship between German and Austrian literature and history.
Publishes notes: Yes
Languages accepted: German
Prints abstracts: Yes

SUBMISSION REQUIREMENTS

Length of books: 300 pp.
Copyright ownership: Böhlau Verlag
Books published per year: 1-2

(1684)
*Literatur in Wissenschaft und Unterricht

Walter Torsten Rix, Rudolf Böhm, Dietrich Jäger, Horst Kruse, & Peter Nicolaisen, Editors
Englisches Seminar der Univ. Kiel
Neue Univ.
Olshausenstr. 40
2300 Kiel, Germany

Telephone: (49) 431 8802671
Fax: (49) 431 8802072
First published: 1968
Sponsoring organization: Schleswig-Holstein Ministry of Education
ISSN: 0024-4643
MLA acronym: LWU

SUBSCRIPTION INFORMATION

Frequency of publication: 4 times/yr.
Circulation: 1,700
Available in microform: No
Subscription price: 34 DM/yr. Germany; 38 DM/yr. elsewhere
Year to which price refers: 1992
Subscription address: Verlag Königshausen & Neumann, P.B. 6007, 8700 Würzburg 1, Germany
Subscription telephone: (49) 931 76401
Subscription fax: (49) 931 83620

ADVERTISING INFORMATION

Advertising accepted: Yes

EDITORIAL DESCRIPTION

Scope: Focuses on close readings and *explication de texte*.
Reviews books: Yes
Publishes notes: Yes, review notes
Languages accepted: English; German
Prints abstracts: No
Author-anonymous submission: No

SUBMISSION REQUIREMENTS

Restrictions on contributors: Book reviews are commissioned.
Author pays submission fee: No
Author pays page charges: No
Length of articles: 3,800 words
Length of book reviews: 750 words
Length of notes: 150 words
Style: MLA
Number of copies required: 3
Copyright ownership: Editors & Verlag Königshausen & Neumann
Rejected manuscripts: Returned
Time before publication decision: 9 mos.
Time between decision and publication: 10 mos.
Number of reviewers: 5
Articles submitted per year: 150-170
Articles published per year: 18-20
Book reviews submitted per year: 25
Book reviews published per year: 25
Notes submitted per year: 60
Notes published per year: 60

(1685)
Literatur und Geschichte: Eine Schriftenreihe

Verlag Lambert Schneider
Siemensstr. 57
Postfach 100123
7106 Gerlingen, Germany

First published: 1970
MLA acronym: LuG

SUBSCRIPTION INFORMATION

Frequency of publication: Irregular
Available in microform: No

ADVERTISING INFORMATION

Advertising accepted: No

EDITORIAL DESCRIPTION

Scope: Publishes monographs on German literature.
Reviews books: No
Languages accepted: German
Prints abstracts: No

SUBMISSION REQUIREMENTS

Restrictions on contributors: None
Length of books: No restrictions
Style: None
Number of copies required: 1
Rejected manuscripts: Returned

(1686)
*Literatur und Kritik

Karl-Markus Gauss, Editor
Ernest Thunstr. 11
5021 Salzburg, Austria

Telephone: (43) 662 88197472
Fax: (43) 662 872387
First published: 1966
Sponsoring organization: Bundesministerium für Unterricht & Kunst; Stadt Salzburg; Land Salzburg
ISSN: 0024-466X
MLA acronym: LuK

SUBSCRIPTION INFORMATION

Frequency of publication: 5 times/yr.
Circulation: 3,000
Available in microform: No
Subscription address: Otto Müller Verlag, Postfach 167, 5021 Salzburg, Austria
Subscription telephone: (43) 662 8815740
Subscription fax: (43) 662 872387

ADVERTISING INFORMATION

Advertising accepted: Yes

EDITORIAL DESCRIPTION

Scope: Publishes articles on Austrian, German, and Central European literature.
Reviews books: Yes
Publishes notes: No
Languages accepted: German
Prints abstracts: No

SUBMISSION REQUIREMENTS

Restrictions on contributors: None
Author pays submission fee: No
Author pays page charges: No
Length of articles: 10 pp. maximum
Length of book reviews: 700 words
Style: Journal
Number of copies required: 1
Copyright ownership: Author after publication
Rejected manuscripts: Returned; enclose return postage or international reply coupons
Time before publication decision: 3 mos.
Time between decision and publication: 6-12 mos.
Number of reviewers: 1-2
Articles submitted per year: 500
Articles published per year: 120
Book reviews submitted per year: 300-400
Book reviews published per year: 60

(1687)
*Literatura

Béla Pomogáts, Editor
Inst. d'Etudes Littéraires
Académie Hongroise des Sciences
Ménesi út 11-13
1118 Budapest, Hungary

Telephone: (36) 1 1667271
First published: 1974
Sponsoring organization: Magyar Tudományos Akadémia
ISSN: 0133-2368
MLA acronym: Literatura

SUBSCRIPTION INFORMATION

Frequency of publication: 4 times/yr.
Circulation: 500
Available in microform: No
Subscription address: Kultura, PF. 149, 1389 Budapest, Hungary

ADVERTISING INFORMATION

Advertising accepted: Yes

EDITORIAL DESCRIPTION

Scope: Publishes articles on modern Hungarian literature and theory of literature.
Reviews books: Yes
Publishes notes: Yes
Languages accepted: Hungarian
Prints abstracts: No

SUBMISSION REQUIREMENTS

Restrictions on contributors: None
Author pays submission fee: Yes
Author pays page charges: No
Length of articles: 4,000-6,000 words
Length of book reviews: 1,250-2,500 words
Style: None
Number of copies required: 2
Copyright ownership: Author
Rejected manuscripts: Returned
Time before publication decision: 3 mos.
Time between decision and publication: 4 mos.
Number of reviewers: 3
Articles submitted per year: 40
Articles published per year: 30
Book reviews published per year: 5

(1688)
Literatūra: Lietuvos Aukštųjų Mokyklų Mokslo Darbai

V. Areška & J. Girdzijauskas, Editors
Vilnius Univ.
Lietuvių Literatūros Katedra
Universiteto g. 3
Vilnius, Lithuania

First published: 1958
Sponsoring organization: Ministry of Higher & Special Secondary Education of Lithuania
ISSN: 0202-3296
MLA acronym: Literatūra

SUBSCRIPTION INFORMATION

Frequency of publication: Annual
Circulation: 1,000
Available in microform: No
Subscription address: Knyga Paštu, Garelio g. 9, Vilnius, Lithuania

ADVERTISING INFORMATION

Advertising accepted: No

EDITORIAL DESCRIPTION

Scope: Publishes articles on Lithuanian, Russian, Western European, classical Greek and Latin literatures, and folklore.

Reviews books: Yes
Publishes notes: Yes
Languages accepted: German; Lithuanian; Russian; English; French
Prints abstracts: Yes

SUBMISSION REQUIREMENTS

Restrictions on contributors: None
Author pays submission fee: No
Author pays page charges: No
Length of articles: 4,000 words
Length of book reviews: 2,000 words maximum
Length of notes: 200 words maximum
Style: Journal
Number of copies required: 2
Special requirements: Submit original typescript.
Copyright ownership: Vilnius State Univ.
Rejected manuscripts: 1 copy returned
Time before publication decision: 6 mos.
Time between decision and publication: 1 yr.
Number of reviewers: Editorial Board
Articles submitted per year: 20-25
Articles published per year: 15-20
Book reviews submitted per year: 3
Book reviews published per year: 1-2
Notes submitted per year: 5
Notes published per year: 1-2

(1689)
*Literatura Chilena: Creación y Crítica

David Valjalo, Editor
Ediciones de la Frontera
Box 3013
Hollywood, CA 90078

Additional editorial address: P.O. Box 3013, Hollywood, CA 90078
First published: 1977
ISSN: 0730-0220
MLA acronym: LitC

SUBSCRIPTION INFORMATION

Frequency of publication: 4 times/yr.
Circulation: 1,000
Available in microform: No

ADVERTISING INFORMATION

Advertising accepted: No

EDITORIAL DESCRIPTION

Scope: Publishes articles on Chilean and Latin American literature.
Reviews books: Yes
Publishes notes: Yes
Languages accepted: Spanish
Prints abstracts: No
Author-anonymous submission: No

SUBMISSION REQUIREMENTS

Restrictions on contributors: None
Author pays submission fee: No
Author pays page charges: No
Length of articles: 5,000 words
Length of book reviews: 600 words
Length of notes: 50 words
Style: MLA
Number of copies required: 2
Copyright ownership: Reverts to author after 60 days
Rejected manuscripts: Returned; enclose SASE.
Time before publication decision: 3 mos.
Time between decision and publication: 1 mo.
Number of reviewers: 2
Articles submitted per year: 20-30
Articles published per year: 16-20
Book reviews submitted per year: 30-40
Book reviews published per year: 24

(1690)
*Literatura Foiro: Kultura Revuo en Esperanto

Perla Ari Martinelli, Editor
P.O. Box 232
6830 Chiasso 1, Switzerland

First published: 1970
Sponsoring organization: Kooperativo de Literatura Foiro
MLA acronym: LFoiro

SUBSCRIPTION INFORMATION

Frequency of publication: 6 times/yr.
Circulation: 1,100
Available in microform: No
Subscription price: 42 SwF/yr.
Year to which price refers: 1992
Subscription address: Kooperativo de Literatura Foiro, C.P. 303, 1008 Prilly, Switzerland
Additional subscription address: In US: ELNA, P.O. Box 1129, El Cerrito, CA 94530

ADVERTISING INFORMATION

Advertising accepted: Rarely

EDITORIAL DESCRIPTION

Scope: Publishes articles on literary criticism, critical essays, and sociological and linguistic studies, as well as poetry and prose.
Reviews books: Yes
Publishes notes: Yes
Languages accepted: Esperanto
Prints abstracts: Yes
Author-anonymous submission: No

SUBMISSION REQUIREMENTS

Author pays submission fee: No
Author pays page charges: No
Length of articles: 12,000 words
Length of book reviews: 800-1,200 words
Style: Request from editor.
Number of copies required: 2
Copyright ownership: Journal
Rejected manuscripts: Not returned
Time before publication decision: 2-4 weeks
Time between decision and publication: 1 yr. maximum
Number of reviewers: 2-3
Articles submitted per year: 150-250
Articles published per year: 120-150
Book reviews submitted per year: 50
Book reviews published per year: 20-25
Notes submitted per year: 50-60
Notes published per year: 20-30

(1691)
*Literatūra ir Menas

Vytautas Rubavičius, Editor
Universiteto 4
2600 Vilnius, Lithuania

Telephone: (7) 122 612586
First published: 1946
Sponsoring organization: Writers Union of Lithuania
ISSN: 0459-5394
MLA acronym: LiMen

SUBSCRIPTION INFORMATION

Frequency of publication: 52 times/yr.
Circulation: 6,700
Available in microform: No

ADVERTISING INFORMATION

Advertising accepted: No

EDITORIAL DESCRIPTION

Scope: Publishes articles on Lithuanian culture and Lithuanian and world literature.
Reviews books: Yes
Publishes notes: Yes
Languages accepted: Lithuanian
Prints abstracts: No
Author-anonymous submission: No

SUBMISSION REQUIREMENTS

Restrictions on contributors: None
Author pays submission fee: Yes
Author pays page charges: Yes
Length of articles: 1,000-2,000 words
Length of book reviews: 500-1,000 words
Length of notes: 100-300 words
Style: Times Literary Supplement
Number of copies required: 1
Special requirements: Submit original typescript.
Copyright ownership: Author
Rejected manuscripts: Not returned
Time before publication decision: 1-2 weeks
Time between decision and publication: 1 week
Number of reviewers: 2
Articles submitted per year: 1,800-2,200
Articles published per year: 1,100
Book reviews submitted per year: 300
Book reviews published per year: 150
Notes submitted per year: 200
Notes published per year: 150

(1692)
Literatura Ludowa

Czesław Hernas, Editor
ul. Szewska 36
50-136 Wrocław, Poland

First published: 1957
Sponsoring organization: Polskie Towarzystwo Ludoznawcze
ISSN: 0024-4708
MLA acronym: LLud

SUBSCRIPTION INFORMATION

Frequency of publication: 6 times/yr.
Circulation: 1,000
Available in microform: No
Subscription address: Prasa-Książka-Ruch, Centrala Kolportażu Prasy i Wydawnictw, ul. Towarowa 28, 00-958 Warsaw, Poland

ADVERTISING INFORMATION

Advertising accepted: No

EDITORIAL DESCRIPTION

Scope: Publishes: (1) articles on Polish folklore (monographic and comparative); (2) discussions on contemporary understanding of folklore, folkloristic literary genres, differentiation of registers and topics; (3) articles on new theories and methods of folklore research; (4) unknown texts, both old and new; and (5) research on folklore and literature, mass culture, and professional subcultures.
Reviews books: Yes
Publishes notes: Yes
Languages accepted: Polish
Prints abstracts: Yes

SUBMISSION REQUIREMENTS

Restrictions on contributors: None
Author pays submission fee: No
Author pays page charges: No
Length of articles: 20 pp. (30 lines/page)
Length of book reviews: 5 pp. (30 lines/page)
Length of notes: 2 pp. (30 lines/page)
Number of copies required: 2
Special requirements: Submit original typescript.
Copyright ownership: Author
Rejected manuscripts: Returned

Time before publication decision: 6 mos.
Time between decision and publication: 15 mos.
Number of reviewers: 2-4
Articles submitted per year: 50-60
Articles published per year: 50
Book reviews submitted per year: 30-40
Book reviews published per year: 30-40
Notes submitted per year: 10-20
Notes published per year: 10-20

(1693)
*Literatura Mexicana

Margit Frenk & Adriana Sandoval, Editors
Inst. de Investigaciones Filológicas
UNAM
Circuito Mario de la Cueva
Ciudad Univ.
04510 Mexico City, D.F., Mexico

Telephone: (52) 5 6227493
Fax: (52) 5 6657874
First published: 1990
Sponsoring organization: Univ. Nacional Autónoma de México
ISSN: 0188-2546
MLA acronym: LMex

SUBSCRIPTION INFORMATION

Frequency of publication: 2 times/yr.
Available in microform: No
Subscription price: Mex$70,000/yr. Mexico; $24.00/yr. Caribbean & Latin America; $40.00/yr. US, Canada, & Europe
Year to which price refers: 1992

ADVERTISING INFORMATION

Advertising accepted: Yes, on an exchange basis

EDITORIAL DESCRIPTION

Scope: Publishes articles on Mexican literature. Includes studies on indigenous Chicano literature and on literature written by non-Mexicans in Mexico and by Mexican writers abroad.
Reviews books: Yes
Publishes notes: Yes
Languages accepted: Spanish
Prints abstracts: No
Author-anonymous submission: Yes

SUBMISSION REQUIREMENTS

Author pays submission fee: No
Author pays page charges: No
Length of articles: 30 pp.
Length of book reviews: 10 pp.
Length of notes: 15 pp.
Style: MLA
Number of copies required: 3
Special requirements: Submit original typescript and 2 copies.
Copyright ownership: Author
Rejected manuscripts: Not returned
Time before publication decision: 1 yr. maximum
Time between decision and publication: 1 yr. maximum
Number of reviewers: 2-3
Articles published per year: 4-5
Book reviews submitted per year: 8
Notes published per year: 6-7

(1694)
*Literatura un Māksla

Pēteris Bankovskis, Editor
pasta indekss 226081
Balasta dambi, 3
Riga PDP, Latvia

Telephone: (7) 132 469089

First published: 1945
MLA acronym: LuM

SUBSCRIPTION INFORMATION

Frequency of publication: 52 times/yr.
Circulation: 14,000
Available in microform: No
Subscription price: 70 Rbl ($51.00)/yr.
Year to which price refers: 1992

ADVERTISING INFORMATION

Advertising accepted: Yes

EDITORIAL DESCRIPTION

Scope: Promotes contemporary philosophy, aesthetics, literature, and arts.
Reviews books: Yes
Publishes notes: Yes
Languages accepted: Latvian
Prints abstracts: No
Author-anonymous submission: No

SUBMISSION REQUIREMENTS

Restrictions on contributors: None
Author pays submission fee: No
Author pays page charges: No
Length of articles: 800-1,000 words
Length of book reviews: 200-300 words
Length of notes: 100-200 words
Number of copies required: 1
Special requirements: Articles in English, German, and French are accepted for translation into Latvian.
Rejected manuscripts: Not returned
Time before publication decision: 2 weeks
Time between decision and publication: 1 mo.
Number of reviewers: 2
Articles submitted per year: 300-400
Articles published per year: 200-300
Book reviews submitted per year: 80-100
Book reviews published per year: 50-80
Notes submitted per year: 500-800
Notes published per year: 500-600

(1695)
*Literatura y Lingüística

Leopoldo Sáez Godoy, Editor
Carrera de Castellano
IPES "Blas Cañas"
Av. Italia 681 (Providencia)
Santiago, Chile

Telephone: (56) 2 2226537
Fax: (56) 2 391838
Sponsoring organization: Univ. Blas Cañas
ISSN: 0716-5811
MLA acronym: LyL

SUBSCRIPTION INFORMATION

Available in microform: No
Subscription price: $10.00/yr. Latin America; $12.00/yr. elsewhere
Year to which price refers: 1992

ADVERTISING INFORMATION

Advertising accepted: Yes

EDITORIAL DESCRIPTION

Scope: Publishes articles on the literature and linguistics of Spain, South America, and Central America, with an emphasis on Chile.
Reviews books: Yes
Publishes notes: Yes
Languages accepted: Spanish; English

SUBMISSION REQUIREMENTS

Author pays submission fee: No
Author pays page charges: No
Length of articles: 4,500 words
Length of book reviews: 400 words

Length of notes: 500 words
Number of copies required: 3
Special requirements: Submit on diskette using WordPerfect; include a 200-word abstract.
Copyright ownership: Author
Rejected manuscripts: Not returned
Time between decision and publication: 3 mos.
Articles published per year: 10
Book reviews published per year: 10

(1696)
*Literature and Belief

Jay Fox & Steven Walker, Editors
3076E Jesse Knight Humanities Bldg.
Brigham Young Univ.
Provo, UT 84602

Telephone: 801 378-2304
Fax: 801 378-4649
First published: 1981
Sponsoring organization: Brigham Young Univ., Center for the Study of Christian Values in Literature
ISSN: 0732-1929
MLA acronym: L&B

SUBSCRIPTION INFORMATION

Frequency of publication: Annual
Circulation: 1,000
Available in microform: Yes
Subscription price: $5.00/yr. US; $7.00/yr. elsewhere
Year to which price refers: 1992

ADVERTISING INFORMATION

Advertising accepted: No

EDITORIAL DESCRIPTION

Scope: Publishes scholarly interpretative articles that focus on the moral/religious aspects of literature or provide a critical theory of literary analysis based on moral/religious considerations.
Reviews books: Yes
Publishes notes: No
Languages accepted: English
Prints abstracts: No
Author-anonymous submission: Yes

SUBMISSION REQUIREMENTS

Restrictions on contributors: None
Author pays submission fee: No
Author pays page charges: No
Length of articles: 2,500-5,000 words
Length of book reviews: 1,500-1,750 words
Style: MLA
Number of copies required: 2
Copyright ownership: Journal
Rejected manuscripts: Returned; enclose SASE.
Time before publication decision: 3-4 mos.
Time between decision and publication: 4-6 mos.
Number of reviewers: 2-3
Articles submitted per year: 50
Articles published per year: 10-12
Book reviews submitted per year: 4-5
Book reviews published per year: 1-2

(1697)
Literature and Contemporary Revolutionary Culture: Journal of the Society of Contemporary Hispanic and Lusophone Revolutionary Literatures

Hernán Vidal, Editor
The Prisma Institute
Dept. of Spanish & Portuguese
4 Folwell Hall
Univ. of Minnesota
Minneapolis, MN 55455

Sponsoring organization: Soc. for the Study of Contemporary Hispanic & Lusophone Revolutionary Literatures
ISSN: 0885-3274
MLA acronym: LCRC

SUBSCRIPTION INFORMATION

Frequency of publication: Annual
Available in microform: No

ADVERTISING INFORMATION

Advertising accepted: No

EDITORIAL DESCRIPTION

Scope: Publishes studies of cultural production and policies of cultural production in periods of institutional rupture and state reorientation.
Reviews books: Yes
Publishes notes: No
Languages accepted: Spanish; English; Portuguese
Prints abstracts: No
Author-anonymous submission: Yes

SUBMISSION REQUIREMENTS

Restrictions on contributors: Contributors must be members of the society and open to dialogue with revolutionary processes.
Author pays submission fee: No
Author pays page charges: No
Length of articles: 40-60 pp.
Length of book reviews: 20 pp.
Style: MLA
Number of copies required: 2
Special requirements: Submit one typescript and diskette, if possible.
Copyright ownership: Soc. for the Study of Contemporary Hispanic & Lusophone Revolutionary Literatures
Rejected manuscripts: Returned
Time before publication decision: 1 yr.
Time between decision and publication: 2 mos.
Number of reviewers: 6
Articles published per year: 20

(1698)
*Literature and History

Philip Martin, Roger Richardson, John N. King, & Alan Armstrong, Editors
King Alfred's College
Winchester SO22 4NR, England

Telephone: (44) 962 841515
Fax: (44) 962 842280
First published: 1975
Sponsoring organization: King Alfred's College; Ohio State Univ.; Southern Oregon State College
ISSN: 0306-1973
MLA acronym: L&H

SUBSCRIPTION INFORMATION

Frequency of publication: 2 times/yr.
Circulation: 800
Available in microform: No
Subscription price: $45.00/yr. institutions; $30.00/yr. individuals
Year to which price refers: 1992

Subscription address: Sue Higgins, Manchester Univ. Press, Manchester M13 9PL, England
Subscription telephone: (44) 61 2735539
Subscription fax: (44) 61 2743346

ADVERTISING INFORMATION

Advertising accepted: Yes
Advertising rates: Request from Manchester Univ. Press

EDITORIAL DESCRIPTION

Scope: Investigates the relations between writing, history, and ideology.
Reviews books: Yes
Publishes notes: No
Languages accepted: English
Prints abstracts: No
Author-anonymous submission: No

SUBMISSION REQUIREMENTS

Restrictions on contributors: Book reviews are solicited.
Author pays submission fee: No
Author pays page charges: No
Length of articles: 5,000-8,000 words
Length of book reviews: 500-1,000 words
Style: Journal
Number of copies required: 2
Special requirements: Submit camera-ready material for advertisements.
Copyright ownership: Journal
Rejected manuscripts: Returned; enclose SASE
Time before publication decision: 6 mos.
Time between decision and publication: 1 yr.
Articles submitted per year: 100-120
Articles published per year: 10
Book reviews published per year: 50-60

(1699)
*Literature and Life: American Writers

Evander Lomke, Editor
Continuum/Ungar
370 Lexington Ave.
New York, NY 10017

First published: 1970
MLA acronym: L&LifeA

SUBSCRIPTION INFORMATION

Available in microform: No

ADVERTISING INFORMATION

Advertising accepted: No

EDITORIAL DESCRIPTION

Scope: Publishes bio-critical monographs on major American writers.
Reviews books: No
Publishes notes: No
Languages accepted: English
Prints abstracts: No
Author-anonymous submission: No

SUBMISSION REQUIREMENTS

Length of books: 200 pp.
Copyright ownership: Author
Books published per year: 4

(1700)
*Literature and Life: British Writers

Evander Lomke, Editor
Continuum/Ungar
370 Lexington Ave.
New York, NY 10017

First published: 1970

MLA acronym: L&LifeB

SUBSCRIPTION INFORMATION

Available in microform: No

ADVERTISING INFORMATION

Advertising accepted: No

EDITORIAL DESCRIPTION

Scope: Publishes bio-critical monographs on major British writers.
Reviews books: No
Publishes notes: No
Languages accepted: English
Prints abstracts: No
Author-anonymous submission: No

SUBMISSION REQUIREMENTS

Length of books: 200 pp.
Copyright ownership: Author
Books published per year: 4

(1701)
*Literature and Life: World Writers

Evander Lomke, Editor
Continuum/Ungar
370 Lexington Ave.
New York, NY 10017

First published: 1970
MLA acronym: L&LifeW

SUBSCRIPTION INFORMATION

Available in microform: No

ADVERTISING INFORMATION

Advertising accepted: No

EDITORIAL DESCRIPTION

Scope: Publishes bio-critical monographs on major writers from around the world.
Reviews books: No
Publishes notes: No
Languages accepted: English
Prints abstracts: No
Author-anonymous submission: No

SUBMISSION REQUIREMENTS

Length of books: 200 pp.
Copyright ownership: Author
Books published per year: 2

(1702)
*Literature and Medicine

Anne Hudson Jones, Editor
Inst. for the Medical Humanities
Univ. of Texas Medical Branch
Galveston, TX 77550

Telephone: 409 772-2376
Fax: 409 772-5640
First published: 1982
Sponsoring organization: Inst. for the Medical Humanities
ISSN: 0278-9671
MLA acronym: L&M

SUBSCRIPTION INFORMATION

Frequency of publication: 2 times/yr.
Circulation: 800
Available in microform: No
Subscription price: $34.00/yr. institutions US; $19.00/yr. individuals US; add $3.00/yr. postage Canada & Mexico, $5.00/yr. elsewhere
Year to which price refers: 1993

Subscription address: Johns Hopkins Univ. Press, Journals Publishing Division, 2715 North Charles St., Baltimore, MD 21218-4319
Subscription telephone: 800 537-5487
Subscription fax: 410 516-6998

ADVERTISING INFORMATION

Advertising accepted: Yes
Advertising rates: $115.00/half page; $190.00/full page

EDITORIAL DESCRIPTION

Scope: Publishes thematic and general issues that explore the various relationships between literature and medicine, such as images of healers, physician-writers, psychiatry and literature, use and abuse of literary concepts in medicine, literature and biomedical ethics, the art of the case history, the doctor in drama, narrative and medical knowledge, etc.
Reviews books: Yes
Publishes notes: No
Languages accepted: English
Prints abstracts: No
Author-anonymous submission: Yes

SUBMISSION REQUIREMENTS

Restrictions on contributors: Book reviews are solicited.
Author pays submission fee: No
Author pays page charges: No
Length of articles: 15-40 double-spaced pp. including notes
Length of book reviews: 1,500 words
Style: Chicago
Number of copies required: 3
Special requirements: Submit original typescript and 2 copies. Use nonsexist language.
Copyright ownership: Johns Hopkins Univ. Press
Rejected manuscripts: Returned; enclose SASE
Time before publication decision: 2-4 mos.
Time between decision and publication: 6-24 mos.
Number of reviewers: 3
Articles submitted per year: 35-50
Articles published per year: 15-20
Book reviews published per year: 5-10

(1703)
*Literature and Psychology

Morton Kaplan & Richard Feldstein, Editors
Dept. of English
Rhode Island College
Providence, RI 02908

Additional editorial address: Send contributions that apply depth psychology (psycholanalysis) to literature to M. Kaplan; send contributions that apply post-structuralist forms to psychoanalysis to theory, literature, or film and those that feature interdisciplinary approaches to R. Feldstein.
Telephone: 401 456-8670
First published: 1950
Sponsoring organization: National Assn. for Psychoanalytic Criticism; Rhode Island College
ISSN: 0024-4759
MLA acronym: L&P

SUBSCRIPTION INFORMATION

Frequency of publication: 4 times/yr.
Available in microform: Yes
Subscription price: $24.00/yr. institutions US; $15.00/yr. individuals US; $26.00/yr. elsewhere
Year to which price refers: 1992

ADVERTISING INFORMATION

Advertising accepted: Yes
Advertising rates: $100.00/full page

EDITORIAL DESCRIPTION

Scope: Publishes articles, reviews, notes, and comments pertaining to literary criticism as informed by depth psychology. The journal welcomes more theoretical articles for inclusion in special issues. We particularly encourage the submission of essays on such subjects as psychoanalysis and other modes of critical theory.
Reviews books: Yes
Languages accepted: English
Prints abstracts: No
Author-anonymous submission: No

SUBMISSION REQUIREMENTS

Restrictions on contributors: None
Author pays submission fee: No
Author pays page charges: No
Length of articles: No restrictions
Length of book reviews: No restrictions
Style: MLA
Number of copies required: 2
Copyright ownership: Journal
Rejected manuscripts: Returned; enclose SASE
Time before publication decision: 4 mos.
Time between decision and publication: 1 yr.
Number of reviewers: 3
Articles submitted per year: 100
Articles published per year: 20
Book reviews submitted per year: 5
Book reviews published per year: 5

(1704)
*Literature & Theology: An Interdisciplinary Journal of Theory and Criticism

David Jasper, Editor
Dept. of English
Univ. of Glasgow
Glasgow GL2 8QQ, Scotland

Telephone: (44) 41 3304405
Fax: (44) 41 3304601
First published: 1987
ISSN: 0269-1205
MLA acronym: L&T

SUBSCRIPTION INFORMATION

Frequency of publication: 4 times/yr.
Circulation: 400
Subscription price: $93.00/yr. institutions; $41.00/yr. individuals
Year to which price refers: 1992
Subscription address: Journals Subscriptions, Oxford Univ. Press, Pinkhill House, Southfield Rd., Eynsham, Oxford OX8 1JJ, England
Additional subscription address: In N. America: Journals Marketing Dept., Oxford Univ. Press, 2001 Evans Rd., Cary, NC 27513
Subscription telephone: (44) 865 882283
Subscription fax: (44) 865 882890

ADVERTISING INFORMATION

Advertising accepted: Yes

EDITORIAL DESCRIPTION

Scope: L&T is neither a journal of theology nor a journal of literature, but exists within the creative tension between the two disciplines. Includes articles on narrative, the intellectual and cultural context of literature, hermeneutics, myth, language and semiotics, and the art of translation.
Reviews books: Yes
Publishes notes: No
Languages accepted: English
Prints abstracts: No
Author-anonymous submission: No

SUBMISSION REQUIREMENTS

Author pays submission fee: No

Author pays page charges: No
Length of articles: 5,000 words
Length of book reviews: 500 words
Style: Oxford Univ. Press
Number of copies required: 3
Special requirements: Submit original double-spaced typescript and 2 copies on size A4 (8 1/4 in. x 11 3/4 in.) paper with ample margins.
Copyright ownership: Oxford Univ. Press
Rejected manuscripts: Returned
Time before publication decision: 2 mos.
Time between decision and publication: 9-12 mos.
Number of reviewers: 2
Articles submitted per year: 50
Articles published per year: 18
Book reviews published per year: 30

(1705)
*Literature East and West

Michael C. Hillmann, Editor
Dept. of Oriental & African Language & Literature
Univ. of Texas
Austin, TX 78712

Telephone: 512 471-1365
Fax: 512 471-8848
First published: 1953
Sponsoring organization: Dept. of Oriental & African Languages & Literatures, Univ. of Texas, Austin
ISSN: 0024-4767
MLA acronym: LE&W

SUBSCRIPTION INFORMATION

Frequency of publication: Annual
Circulation: 500
Available in microform: No
Subscription price: $9.00/yr.
Year to which price refers: 1992

ADVERTISING INFORMATION

Advertising accepted: No

EDITORIAL DESCRIPTION

Scope: Focuses on world literature, with an emphasis on nonwestern literatures.
Reviews books: Yes
Publishes notes: No
Languages accepted: English
Prints abstracts: No
Author-anonymous submission: No

SUBMISSION REQUIREMENTS

Restrictions on contributors: None
Author pays submission fee: No
Author pays page charges: No
Length of articles: 8,000 words
Length of book reviews: 500-1,000 words
Style: MLA; Chicago
Number of copies required: 2
Copyright ownership: Journal
Rejected manuscripts: Returned
Time before publication decision: 6 weeks
Time between decision and publication: 1 yr.
Number of reviewers: 1
Articles submitted per year: 20
Articles published per year: 8-10
Book reviews submitted per year: 10
Book reviews published per year: 2-4

(1706)
*Literature/Film Quarterly

James M. Welsh, Editor
Salisbury State Univ.
Salisbury, MD 21801

Telephone: 410 543-6446

Fax: 410 543-6068
First published: 1973
Sponsoring organization: Salisbury State Univ.
ISSN: 0090-4260
MLA acronym: LFQ

SUBSCRIPTION INFORMATION

Frequency of publication: 4 times/yr. (Jan., Apr., July, Oct.)
Circulation: 600
Available in microform: Yes
Subscription price: $28.00/yr. institutions; $14.00/yr. individuals US & Canada; $28.00/yr. individuals elsewhere
Year to which price refers: 1992

ADVERTISING INFORMATION

Advertising accepted: Yes
Advertising rates: $20.00/quarter page; $40.00/half page; $70.00/full page; $90.00/inside back cover

EDITORIAL DESCRIPTION

Scope: Publishes articles on individual movies, on different cinematic adaptations of a single literary work, on a director's style of adaptation, on theories of film adaptation, on the cinematic qualities of authors or works, on the reciprocal influences between film and literature, on authors' attitudes toward film and film adaptations, on the role of the screen writer, and on the teaching of film; interviews with directors, screen writers, literary figures; reviews of current film adaptations of literary works; reviews of books concerning film and the relationship between film and literature; responses to any of the articles and reviews.
Reviews books: Yes
Publishes notes: Yes
Languages accepted: English
Prints abstracts: No
Author-anonymous submission: No

SUBMISSION REQUIREMENTS

Restrictions on contributors: None
Author pays submission fee: No
Author pays page charges: No
Length of articles: 3,000 words
Length of book reviews: 1,000-1,500 words
Length of notes: 750 words
Style: MLA
Number of copies required: 2
Special requirements: Supply (if possible) stills or frame enlargements of the films discussed.
Copyright ownership: Salisbury State Univ.
Rejected manuscripts: Returned; enclose return postage.
Time before publication decision: 6 mos.
Time between decision and publication: 12-18 mos.
Number of reviewers: 3
Articles submitted per year: 200
Articles published per year: 40
Book reviews submitted per year: 10
Book reviews published per year: 4
Notes submitted per year: 10
Notes published per year: 2-3

(1707)
*Literaturen Forum: Sedmichnik na Nesavisimite Balgarski Pisateli

Marin Georgiev, Editor
Angel Kunchev 5
Sofia, Bulgaria

Telephone: (359) 2 881069
First published: 1990
Historical variations in title: Formerly *Literaturen Front: Organ na Suiuza na Bulgarskite Pisateli*
ISSN: 0861-2153
MLA acronym: LForum

SUBSCRIPTION INFORMATION

Frequency of publication: 52 times/yr.
Circulation: 20,000
Available in microform: No
Subscription address: FTO "Hemus", Dept. of Books & Periodicals, ul. Levski 7, Sofia, Bulgaria

ADVERTISING INFORMATION

Advertising accepted: No

EDITORIAL DESCRIPTION

Scope: Publishes original literary works and essays in the areas of sociopolitics and literary criticism.
Reviews books: Yes
Publishes notes: Yes
Languages accepted: Bulgarian
Prints abstracts: No

SUBMISSION REQUIREMENTS

Author pays submission fee: No
Author pays page charges: No
Length of articles: 1,440 words
Length of book reviews: 1,080 words
Length of notes: 360 words
Number of copies required: 2
Copyright ownership: Author
Rejected manuscripts: Not returned
Time before publication decision: 2 weeks
Time between decision and publication: 1 mo.
Number of reviewers: 4
Articles submitted per year: 320
Articles published per year: 160
Book reviews submitted per year: 520
Book reviews published per year: 260
Notes submitted per year: 700
Notes published per year: 350

(1708)
Literaturen Zbor: Spisanie na Sojuzot na Društvata za Makedonski Jazik i Literatura na SR Makedonija

Miodrag Drugovats, Editor
Filološki Fakultet
Skopje, Macedonia (Yugoslavia)

First published: 1954
Sponsoring organization: Sojuz na Društvata za Makedonski Jazik i Literatura na SR Makedonski
ISSN: 0024-4791
MLA acronym: LZ

SUBSCRIPTION INFORMATION

Frequency of publication: 6 times/yr. (Feb., Mar., Apr., Oct., Nov., Dec.)
Subscription address: Sojuz na Društvata za Makedonski Jazik i Literatura na SR Makedonija, Grigor Prlicev, 5, 91000 Skopje, Macedonia (Yugoslavia)

EDITORIAL DESCRIPTION

Reviews books: Yes
Languages accepted: Macedonian
Prints abstracts: No

SUBMISSION REQUIREMENTS

Rejected manuscripts: Not returned

(1709)
Literaturna Misŭl

Panteleĭ Zarev, Editor
Publishing House of the Bulgarian Academy of Sciences
Acad. G. Bonchev St., Bldg. 6
1113 Sofia, Bulgaria

First published: 1957
Sponsoring organization: Bŭlgarska Akademija na Naukite, Inst. za Bŭlgarska Literatura
ISSN: 0324-0495
MLA acronym: LMi

SUBSCRIPTION INFORMATION

Frequency of publication: 10 times/yr.
Circulation: 4,600-9,000
Available in microform: No
Subscription address: Hemus, Rouski Blvd., 6, 1000 Sofia, Bulgaria

ADVERTISING INFORMATION

Advertising accepted: No

EDITORIAL DESCRIPTION

Scope: Publishes articles on Bulgarian literature and world literature.
Reviews books: Yes
Publishes notes: Yes
Languages accepted: Bulgarian; French; Russian; English
Prints abstracts: No

SUBMISSION REQUIREMENTS

Restrictions on contributors: None
Author pays submission fee: No
Author pays page charges: No
Length of articles: 40 pp. maximum
Length of book reviews: 10 pp.
Length of notes: 40 pp.
Number of copies required: 2
Copyright ownership: Inst. za Literatura
Time between decision and publication: 2 mos.
Articles submitted per year: 200
Articles published per year: 70
Book reviews submitted per year: 30-40
Book reviews published per year: 30
Notes submitted per year: 60
Notes published per year: 50

(1710)
Literaturnaia Armeniia: Ezhemesiachnyĭ Literaturno-Khudozhestvennyĭ i Obshchestvenno-Politicheskiĭ Zhurnal

Al'bert Nalbandian, Editor
pr. Marshala Bagramiana, 3
375019 Erevan, Armenia

First published: 1958
Sponsoring organization: Soiuz Pisateleĭ Armenii
ISSN: 0130-8114
MLA acronym: LArm

SUBSCRIPTION INFORMATION

Frequency of publication: 12 times/yr.

EDITORIAL DESCRIPTION

Scope: Publishes critical articles on Armenian literature; also publishes original poetry and prose by Armenian writers.
Languages accepted: Russian

(1711)
Literaturnaia Gazeta

A. Udal'tsov, Editor
Tsvetnoĭ Bul'var, 30
103654 GSP-3
Moscow K-51, Russia

First published: 1929
Sponsoring organization: Soiuz Pisateleĭ S.S.S.R.
ISSN: 0024-4848
MLA acronym: LG

SUBSCRIPTION INFORMATION

Frequency of publication: 52 times/yr.
Circulation: 3,000,000
Available in microform: No

ADVERTISING INFORMATION

Advertising accepted: No

EDITORIAL DESCRIPTION

Scope: Publishes articles on the literatures of the U.S.S.R. and includes original poetry and works of fiction. Also includes Soviet and foreign articles on internal problems and international politics.
Reviews books: Yes
Languages accepted: Russian
Prints abstracts: No

SUBMISSION REQUIREMENTS

Author pays submission fee: No
Author pays page charges: No
Length of articles: 3-12 typescript pp.
Time before publication decision: 1-9 weeks

(1712)
Literaturnoe Obozrenie: Organ Soiuza Pisateleĭ SSSR

Leonard Lavlinskiĭ, Editor
ul. Dobroliubova 9/11
127254 Moscow I-254, Russia

First published: 1973
Sponsoring organization: Soiuz Pisateleĭ S.S.S.R.
ISSN: 0321-2904
MLA acronym: LO

SUBSCRIPTION INFORMATION

Frequency of publication: 12 times/yr.
Circulation: 30,000
Available in microform: No

ADVERTISING INFORMATION

Advertising accepted: No

EDITORIAL DESCRIPTION

Scope: Publishes criticism and a bibliography of Russian, Soviet, and world literature.
Reviews books: Yes
Publishes notes: Yes
Languages accepted: Russian
Prints abstracts: No
Author-anonymous submission: No

SUBMISSION REQUIREMENTS

Author pays submission fee: Yes
Author pays page charges: No
Number of copies required: 2
Copyright ownership: Journal
Rejected manuscripts: Not returned
Time before publication decision: 2 mos.
Time between decision and publication: 1 mo.
Articles submitted per year: 160
Articles published per year: 120
Book reviews submitted per year: 200
Book reviews published per year: 110-120
Notes submitted per year: 80-100
Notes published per year: 60-70

(1713)
*Literaturwissenschaftliches Jahrbuch im Auftrage der Görres-Gesellschaft

Theodor Berchem, Volker Kapp, Franz Link, Eckhard Heftrich, Alois Wolf, & Kurt Müller, Editors
Englisches Seminar II
Univ. Freiburg i. Br.
Kollegiengebäude IV
7800 Freiburg i. Br., Germany

Additional editorial address: Franz Link, Eiderodtstr. 1, 7800 Freiburg/Breisgau, Germany
Telephone: (49) 761 67571
First published: 1960
Sponsoring organization: Görres-Gesellschaft zur Pflege der Wissenschaft, Cologne
ISSN: 0075-997X
MLA acronym: LJGG

SUBSCRIPTION INFORMATION

Frequency of publication: Annual
Available in microform: No
Subscription price: 156 DM/yr.
Year to which price refers: 1990
Subscription address: Duncker & Humblot, Postfach 410329, Dietrich-Schäfer-Weg 9, 1000 Berlin 41-Steglitz, Germany

ADVERTISING INFORMATION

Advertising accepted: No

EDITORIAL DESCRIPTION

Scope: Publishes articles on ancient and modern literatures and languages.
Reviews books: Yes
Publishes notes: Yes
Languages accepted: German; English; French; Spanish
Prints abstracts: No
Author-anonymous submission: No

SUBMISSION REQUIREMENTS

Restrictions on contributors: None
Author pays submission fee: No
Author pays page charges: No
Length of articles: No restrictions
Length of book reviews: No restrictions
Length of notes: No restrictions
Style: MLA
Number of copies required: 1
Special requirements: Submit typescript.
Copyright ownership: Editor
Rejected manuscripts: Returned
Time before publication decision: 1-2 mos.
Time between decision and publication: 1 yr.
Number of reviewers: 5
Articles published per year: 20
Book reviews submitted per year: 15
Book reviews published per year: 15
Notes published per year: 5

(1714)
*Litterae Slovenicae: A Slovene Literary Magazine

Jani Virk, Editor
Tomšičeva 12
Ljubljana, Slovenia

Telephone: (38) 61 214144
Fax: (38) 61 214144
First published: 1962
Historical variations in title: Formerly *Le Livre Slovène*
Sponsoring organization: Assn. des Ecrivains Slovènes; Centre Slovène du PEN; Assn. des Traducteurs Littéraires de Slovènie
ISSN: 0459-6242
MLA acronym: LittSlov

SUBSCRIPTION INFORMATION

Frequency of publication: 2 double issues/yr.
Circulation: 1,500
Available in microform: No
Subscription price: Free
Year to which price refers: 1992

ADVERTISING INFORMATION

Advertising accepted: No

EDITORIAL DESCRIPTION

Scope: Publishes translations of Slovenian literature and essays and articles on Slovenian literary and cultural events.
Reviews books: Yes
Publishes notes: Yes
Languages accepted: French; English; German; Spanish
Prints abstracts: No

SUBMISSION REQUIREMENTS

Author pays page charges: No
Copyright ownership: Assn. des Ecrivians Slovènes

(1715)
*Litteraria: Teoria Literatury. Metodologia. Kultura. Humanistyka

Jan Trzynadlowski, Editor
Ossolineum Publishing House of the Polish Academy of Sciences
Rynek 9
50-106 Wrocław, Poland

Additional editorial address: Wrocław Scientific Soc., Parkowa 13, 51-616 Wrocław, Poland
Fax: (48) 71 448103
First published: 1969
Sponsoring organization: Wrocławskie Towarzystwo Naukowe, Polska Akademia Nauk
ISSN: 0084-3008
MLA acronym: Litteraria

SUBSCRIPTION INFORMATION

Frequency of publication: Annual
Circulation: 400-500
Available in microform: No
Subscription price: $9.00/yr.
Year to which price refers: 1992
Subscription address: Foreign Trade Enterprise "Ars Polona", Krakowskie Przedmieście 7, 00-068 Warsaw, Poland

EDITORIAL DESCRIPTION

Scope: Publishes articles on general Polish literary theory.
Reviews books: No
Publishes notes: Yes
Languages accepted: Polish
Prints abstracts: No
Author-anonymous submission: No

SUBMISSION REQUIREMENTS

Author pays submission fee: No
Author pays page charges: No
Length of articles: 20-25 pp.
Number of copies required: 2
Copyright ownership: Ossolineum
Rejected manuscripts: Returned
Time before publication decision: 6 mos.
Time between decision and publication: 1 yr.
Articles submitted per year: 12-15
Articles published per year: 5-10

(1716)
***Litteratur og Samfund**

Susanne Bjertrup, Henrik Blicher, Frederik Stjernfelt, Andreas Rischel, & Charlotte Jørgensen, Editors
Njalsgade 80
2300 Copenhagen S, Denmark

Telephone: (45) 31 547548
First published: 1974
Sponsoring organization: Humanistiske Forskningsråd
ISSN: 0106-620X
MLA acronym: LiSa

SUBSCRIPTION INFORMATION

Frequency of publication: 2 times/yr.
Available in microform: No
Subscription price: 280 Dkr/yr.
Year to which price refers: 1991

ADVERTISING INFORMATION

Advertising accepted: No

EDITORIAL DESCRIPTION

Scope: Publishes articles on literary criticism, as well as criticism of culture and philosophy.
Reviews books: No
Publishes notes: No
Languages accepted: Danish
Prints abstracts: No
Author-anonymous submission: No

SUBMISSION REQUIREMENTS

Restrictions on contributors: None
Author pays submission fee: No
Author pays page charges: No
Length of articles: 4,000-12,000 words
Style: None
Number of copies required: 1
Copyright ownership: Journal
Rejected manuscripts: Returned
Time before publication decision: 3 mos. maximum
Time between decision and publication: 2 mos.
Number of reviewers: 2-4
Articles submitted per year: 50
Articles published per year: 10-20

(1717)
***Littérature**

Jacques Neefs, Editor
3, rue de Turenne
75004 Paris, France

Telephone: (33) 1 42723223
First published: 1971
Sponsoring organization: Dept. de Littérature Française, Univ. de Paris VII (Vincennes)
ISSN: 0047-4800
MLA acronym: Lit

SUBSCRIPTION INFORMATION

Frequency of publication: 4 times/yr. (Feb., May, Oct., Dec.)
Available in microform: No
Subscription price: 230 F/yr. France; 270 F/yr. elsewhere; 75 F/single issue
Year to which price refers: 1992
Subscription address: CDR-Centrale des Revues, 11 rue Gossin, 92543 Montrouge Cedex, France
Subscription telephone: (33) 1 46565266
Subscription fax: (33) 1 46574069

ADVERTISING INFORMATION

Advertising accepted: Yes, on an exchange basis

EDITORIAL DESCRIPTION

Scope: Publishes articles on literary theory and French literature. The first part centers on one subject and the second part is composed of notes, critical discussions, translations, and interviews.
Reviews books: No
Publishes notes: Yes
Languages accepted: French
Prints abstracts: Yes
Author-anonymous submission: No

SUBMISSION REQUIREMENTS

Restrictions on contributors: None
Author pays submission fee: No
Author pays page charges: No
Length of articles: 40,000 characters maximum
Length of notes: 15,000 characters
Number of copies required: 1
Rejected manuscripts: Not returned
Time before publication decision: 3-6 mos.
Number of reviewers: 3
Articles submitted per year: 100-120
Articles published per year: 36

(1718)
***Littératures**

Claude Sicard, Editor
Presses Universitaires du Mirail
56, rue du Taur
31000 Toulouse, France

First published: 1952
Sponsoring organization: Univ. de Toulouse; Presses Universitaires du Mirail
ISSN: 0563-9751
MLA acronym: Litt

SUBSCRIPTION INFORMATION

Frequency of publication: 2 times/yr.
Circulation: 800
Available in microform: No
Subscription price: 150 F/yr.; 120 F/yr. students
Year to which price refers: 1992

ADVERTISING INFORMATION

Advertising accepted: No

EDITORIAL DESCRIPTION

Scope: Publishes articles on French, German, and Italian literatures, Slavic languages, music, and film.
Reviews books: Yes
Publishes notes: Yes
Languages accepted: French
Prints abstracts: No
Author-anonymous submission: No

SUBMISSION REQUIREMENTS

Restrictions on contributors: None
Author pays submission fee: No
Author pays page charges: No
Length of articles: 10 pp.
Length of book reviews: 2 pp.
Length of notes: 1/2 p.
Style: MLA
Number of copies required: 1
Special requirements: Submit original typescript.
Copyright ownership: Journal
Rejected manuscripts: Not returned
Time before publication decision: 3 mos.
Time between decision and publication: 12-18 mos.
Number of reviewers: 3
Articles submitted per year: 35
Articles published per year: 25
Book reviews submitted per year: 80
Book reviews published per year: 50
Notes submitted per year: 10
Notes published per year: 4-8

(1719)
***LittéRéalité**

Sergio Villani, Editor
Bureau no. 516, Collège Universitaire Atkinson
Univ. York
4700, rue Keele
Toronto, Ontario M3J 1P3, Canada

Telephone: 416 736-5283
Fax: 416 736-5103
First published: 1989
ISSN: 0843-4182
MLA acronym: LittéRéalité

SUBSCRIPTION INFORMATION

Frequency of publication: 2 times/yr. (Spring, Autumn)
Circulation: 300
Available in microform: No
Subscription price: C$37.00/yr. institutions; C$27.00/yr. individuals
Year to which price refers: 1993

ADVERTISING INFORMATION

Advertising accepted: No

EDITORIAL DESCRIPTION

Scope: Publishes critical articles and creative writing in all areas relating to French literary culture.
Reviews books: Yes
Publishes notes: Yes
Languages accepted: French; English
Prints abstracts: No
Author-anonymous submission: Yes

SUBMISSION REQUIREMENTS

Author pays page charges: No
Length of articles: 6,000 words maximum
Length of book reviews: 700 words
Style: MLA
Number of copies required: 2
Special requirements: Submit 2 copies of typescript along with a diskette using WordPerfect.
Copyright ownership: Author
Rejected manuscripts: Returned; enclose return postage
Time before publication decision: 6 mos.
Time between decision and publication: 6-12 mos.
Number of reviewers: 2

(1720)
***Lituanus: Baltic States Quarterly of Arts & Sciences**

Antanas Klimas, Editor
6621 S. Troy
Chicago, IL 60629-2913

Telephone: 312 434-0706
First published: 1954
Sponsoring organization: Lituanus Foundation, Inc.
ISSN: 0024-5089
MLA acronym: Lituanus

SUBSCRIPTION INFORMATION

Frequency of publication: 4 times/yr. (Spring, Summer, Fall, Winter)
Circulation: 4,000
Available in microform: Yes
Subscription price: $15.00/yr. institutions; $10.00/yr. individuals
Year to which price refers: 1992

ADVERTISING INFORMATION

Advertising accepted: No

EDITORIAL DESCRIPTION

Scope: A journal of arts and sciences, dedicated to the presentation and examination of all questions pertaining to the countries and peoples of the Baltic States, particularly Lithuania. Invites contributions concerning the Baltic countries and general problems of Eastern Europe and the former Soviet Union.
Reviews books: Yes
Publishes notes: Yes
Languages accepted: English
Prints abstracts: No

SUBMISSION REQUIREMENTS

Author pays submission fee: No
Author pays page charges: No
Length of articles: 15-20 pp.
Length of book reviews: 2-5 double-spaced pp.
Length of notes: 1-2 pp.
Style: MLA
Number of copies required: 1
Copyright ownership: Journal & publisher
Rejected manuscripts: Returned
Time before publication decision: 2 mos.
Time between decision and publication: 6-10 mos.
Number of reviewers: 2
Articles submitted per year: 30
Articles published per year: 16-20
Book reviews submitted per year: 12-14
Book reviews published per year: 8-10
Notes submitted per year: 20-22
Notes published per year: 8-12

(1721)
*Liverpool Monographs in Hispanic Studies

Peter A. Bly, James Higgins, & Roger Wright, Editors
School of Hispanic Studies
Univ. of Liverpool
P.O. Box 147
Liverpool L69 3BX, England

First published: 1982
ISSN: 0261-1538
MLA acronym: LMHS

SUBSCRIPTION INFORMATION

Frequency of publication: 1-2 volumes/yr.
Available in microform: No
Subscription address: Francis Cairns (Publications), c/o The University, Leeds LS2 9JT, England
Subscription telephone: (44) 532 333538

ADVERTISING INFORMATION

Advertising accepted: No

EDITORIAL DESCRIPTION

Scope: Publishes academic monographs in Hispanic studies with an emphasis on literary studies.
Reviews books: No
Publishes notes: No
Languages accepted: English
Prints abstracts: No

SUBMISSION REQUIREMENTS

Author pays submission fee: No
Author pays page charges: No
Length of books: 60,000-100,000 words
Style: MLA
Number of copies required: 2
Special requirements: Submit 400-word abstract.
Copyright ownership: Author
Rejected manuscripts: Returned; enclose return postage.
Time before publication decision: 3-4 mos.
Time between decision and publication: 18 mos.
Books published per year: 1-2

(1722)
*Living Author Series

James M. Haule, Editor
Dept. of English
Univ. of Texas-Pan American
Edinburg, TX 78539-2999

Telephone: 512 381-3421
Fax: 512 381-2177
E-mail: JMHEC3E@PANAM1.PANAM.EDU
First published: 1978
Sponsoring organization: Dept. of English, Univ. of Texas-Pan American
MLA acronym: LAS

SUBSCRIPTION INFORMATION

Frequency of publication: Annual
Circulation: 500
Available in microform: No

ADVERTISING INFORMATION

Advertising accepted: No

EDITORIAL DESCRIPTION

Scope: Publishes critical essays on contemporary authors, especially those who have visited the University of Texas-Pan American campus. Interviews and bibliographies are included.
Reviews books: No
Publishes notes: No
Languages accepted: English
Prints abstracts: No
Author-anonymous submission: No

SUBMISSION REQUIREMENTS

Restrictions on contributors: None
Author pays submission fee: No
Author pays page charges: No
Length of articles: 3,000-5,000 words
Style: MLA
Number of copies required: 3
Copyright ownership: Series; assignable to author upon request for republication in another form
Rejected manuscripts: Returned; enclose SASE.
Time before publication decision: 3-4 mos.
Time between decision and publication: 9 mos.
Number of reviewers: 3
Articles submitted per year: 55
Articles published per year: 12

(1723)
*Living Blues: A Journal of the African-American Blues Tradition

Peter Lee & David Nelson, Editors
Center for the Study of Southern Culture
Univ. of Mississippi
University, MS 38677

First published: 1970
Historical variations in title: Formerly *Living Blues: A Journal of the Black American Blues Tradition*
ISSN: 0024-5232
MLA acronym: LBl

SUBSCRIPTION INFORMATION

Frequency of publication: 6 times/yr.
Circulation: 16,000
Available in microform: Yes
Subscription price: $18.00/yr.
Year to which price refers: 1992
Subscription telephone: 601 232-5742
Subscription fax: 601 232-5740

ADVERTISING INFORMATION

Advertising accepted: Yes

EDITORIAL DESCRIPTION

Scope: Publishes articles on aspects of African American blues tradition.
Reviews books: Yes
Publishes notes: No
Languages accepted: English
Prints abstracts: No

SUBMISSION REQUIREMENTS

Restrictions on contributors: Book reviews are solicited.
Author pays submission fee: No
Author pays page charges: No
Length of articles: 1,500-10,000 words
Length of book reviews: 300-1,000 words
Style: Chicago
Number of copies required: 2
Copyright ownership: Negotiable
Rejected manuscripts: Held at Univ. of Mississippi Blues Archive
Time before publication decision: 3 mos.
Number of reviewers: 1-2
Articles submitted per year: 100
Articles published per year: 30

(1724)
*Llên Cymru

C. W. Lewis, Editor
Cartrefle
7 Glyncoli Rd.
Treorchy
Mid Glamorgan CF42 6SA, Wales

Telephone: (44) 443 773141
First published: 1950
Sponsoring organization: Board of Celtic Studies
ISSN: 0076-0188
MLA acronym: Llên Cymru

SUBSCRIPTION INFORMATION

Frequency of publication: Annual
Circulation: 400
Available in microform: Yes
Subscription price: £5.00/yr.
Year to which price refers: 1991
Subscription address: Univ. of Wales Press, 6 Gwennyth St., Cathays, Cardiff CF2 4YD, Wales
Subscription telephone: (44) 222 231919
Subscription fax: (44) 222 230908

ADVERTISING INFORMATION

Advertising accepted: Yes
Advertising rates: Request from Univ. of Wales Press

EDITORIAL DESCRIPTION

Scope: Publishes scholarly studies of Welsh literature and literary history.
Reviews books: Yes
Publishes notes: Yes
Languages accepted: Welsh
Prints abstracts: No
Author-anonymous submission: No

SUBMISSION REQUIREMENTS

Restrictions on contributors: None
Author pays submission fee: No
Length of articles: No restrictions
Length of book reviews: 800-4,000 words
Length of notes: 500-2,000 words
Style: MLA
Number of copies required: 2
Copyright ownership: Univ. of Wales
Rejected manuscripts: Returned
Time before publication decision: 1 mo.
Time between decision and publication: 1 yr.
Number of reviewers: 1-3
Articles submitted per year: 2-6
Articles published per year: 5-6
Book reviews submitted per year: 4-6

Book reviews published per year: 4-6
Notes submitted per year: 4-6
Notes published per year: 4-6

(1725)
Lletra de Canvi

Miguel Riera, Editor
c/o Montesinos Editor SA
Maignón 26 3°
08024 Barcelona, Spain

First published: 1987
MLA acronym: LdC

SUBSCRIPTION INFORMATION

Frequency of publication: 11 times/yr.
Circulation: 10,000
Available in microform: No

ADVERTISING INFORMATION

Advertising accepted: Yes

EDITORIAL DESCRIPTION

Scope: Publishes articles on world literature and culture.
Reviews books: Yes
Languages accepted: Catalan
Prints abstracts: No
Author-anonymous submission: Yes

SUBMISSION REQUIREMENTS

Restrictions on contributors: None
Author pays submission fee: No
Author pays page charges: No
Length of articles: 10 pp.
Length of book reviews: 5,000 characters
Number of copies required: 1
Copyright ownership: Journal
Rejected manuscripts: Not returned
Time before publication decision: 2 mos.
Time between decision and publication: 2 mos.
Number of reviewers: 1
Articles submitted per year: 1,000
Articles published per year: 200
Book reviews submitted per year: 250
Book reviews published per year: 100

(1726)
London Review of Books

Karl Miller & Mary-Kay Wilmers, Editors
Tavistock House South
Tavistock Square
London WC1H 9JZ, England

First published: 1979
Sponsoring organization: Arts Council of Great Britain
ISSN: 0260-9592
MLA acronym: LRB

SUBSCRIPTION INFORMATION

Frequency of publication: 24 times/yr.
Circulation: 16,000
Available in microform: Yes

ADVERTISING INFORMATION

Advertising accepted: Yes

EDITORIAL DESCRIPTION

Scope: Publishes critical articles and reviews of books on literature and politics, as well as poems and stories.
Reviews books: Yes
Publishes notes: No
Languages accepted: English
Prints abstracts: No
Author-anonymous submission: No

SUBMISSION REQUIREMENTS

Author pays submission fee: No
Author pays page charges: No
Length of articles: 2,500 words
Length of book reviews: 2,500 words
Number of copies required: 1
Special requirements: Submit double-spaced typescript.
Copyright ownership: Author
Rejected manuscripts: Returned
Time before publication decision: 1 mo. maximum
Time between decision and publication: 4 mos. maximum
Number of reviewers: 2
Articles submitted per year: 500-600 articles & essay-reviews
Articles published per year: 300 articles & essay-reviews

(1727)
*[London] Times Literary Supplement

Ferdinand Mount, Editor
Priory House
St. John's Lane
London EC1M 4BX, England

Telephone: (44) 71 2533000
Fax: (44) 71 2513424
First published: 1902
Sponsoring organization: Times Newspapers, Ltd.
ISSN: 0040-7895
MLA acronym: TLS

SUBSCRIPTION INFORMATION

Frequency of publication: 52 times/yr.
Circulation: 31,500
Available in microform: Yes
Subscription price: $110.00/yr.
Year to which price refers: 1992

ADVERTISING INFORMATION

Advertising accepted: Yes

EDITORIAL DESCRIPTION

Scope: Publishes reviews of new books, theater and the arts, polemical articles, news columns, letters, poetry, and listings of new books.
Reviews books: Yes
Publishes notes: Yes
Languages accepted: English
Prints abstracts: No
Author-anonymous submission: No

SUBMISSION REQUIREMENTS

Restrictions on contributors: None
Author pays submission fee: No
Author pays page charges: No
Length of notes: 150 words
Style: Oxford
Number of copies required: 1
Copyright ownership: Times Newspapers, Ltd., except by agreement
Rejected manuscripts: Returned; enclose return postage.
Time before publication decision: 3 mos. maximum
Time between decision and publication: 1 yr. maximum
Number of reviewers: 3
Articles submitted per year: 150
Articles published per year: 20
Book reviews published per year: 2,500

(1728)
*Looming: Eesti Kirjanike Liidu Kuukiri

Andres Langemets, Editor
Harju t. 1
P.O. Box 62
EE0 001 Tallinn, Estonia

Telephone: (7) 142 443262
First published: 1923
Sponsoring organization: Eesti Kirjanike Liidu (Estonian Writers' Union)
ISSN: 0134-4536
MLA acronym: LoomingE

SUBSCRIPTION INFORMATION

Frequency of publication: 12 times/yr.
Circulation: 9,000
Available in microform: No
Subscription price: $71.00/yr.
Year to which price refers: 1992
Additional subscription address: Akadeeminen Kirjakauppa, P.O. Box 128, 00101 Helsinki, Finland; Bibliotekstjänst, AB Box 200, 22100 Lund, Sweden

ADVERTISING INFORMATION

Advertising accepted: Yes

EDITORIAL DESCRIPTION

Scope: Publishes articles on Estonian and world literature, arts, and humanities.
Reviews books: Yes
Publishes notes: Yes
Languages accepted: Estonian
Prints abstracts: No
Author-anonymous submission: No

SUBMISSION REQUIREMENTS

Author pays submission fee: No
Author pays page charges: No
Number of copies required: 1
Rejected manuscripts: Returned; enclose return postage.
Time before publication decision: 1 mo.
Time between decision and publication: 3-6 mos.
Number of reviewers: 1-3

(1729)
*Lore and Language

J. D. A. Widdowson, Editor
Centre for English Cultural Tradition & Language
Univ. of Sheffield
Sheffield S10 3BP, England

Telephone: (44) 742 670043
Fax: (44) 742 670044
First published: 1969
Sponsoring organization: Univ. of Sheffield, Centre for English Cultural Tradition & Language
ISSN: 0307-7144
MLA acronym: Lore&L

SUBSCRIPTION INFORMATION

Frequency of publication: 2 times/yr.
Circulation: 1,000
Available in microform: No
Subscription price: £50.00/yr. institutions; £16.50/yr. individuals
Year to which price refers: 1990
Subscription address: Sheffield Academic Press, 343 Fulwood Rd., Sheffield S10 3BA, England

ADVERTISING INFORMATION

Advertising accepted: Yes

EDITORIAL DESCRIPTION

Scope: Publishes articles on all aspects of folklore, especially British folklore, as well as dialect and linguistic studies.
Reviews books: Yes
Publishes notes: Yes
Languages accepted: English
Prints abstracts: No
Author-anonymous submission: No

SUBMISSION REQUIREMENTS

Author pays submission fee: No
Author pays page charges: No
Length of articles: 5,000 words
Number of copies required: 1
Copyright ownership: Author and/or publisher
Rejected manuscripts: Not returned
Time before publication decision: 2 mos.
Time between decision and publication: 1 yr.
Number of reviewers: 2
Articles published per year: 15
Book reviews published per year: 300
Notes published per year: 6

(1730)
Lost Generation Journal

Deloris Gray Wood, Editor
Rural Route 5
Box 134
Salem, MO 65560

Additional editorial address: Rural Route 1, Box 1453, St. James, MO 65559
First published: 1973
ISSN: 0091-2948
MLA acronym: LGJ

SUBSCRIPTION INFORMATION

Frequency of publication: 2 times/yr.
Available in microform: No

ADVERTISING INFORMATION

Advertising accepted: Yes

EDITORIAL DESCRIPTION

Scope: Publishes articles on expatriate Americans who lived, worked, and played in Paris in the 1920s and 1930s, preserving their literature and history. Includes interviews, photographs, and reviews.
Reviews books: Yes
Publishes notes: Yes
Languages accepted: English; some French
Prints abstracts: No
Author-anonymous submission: Yes

SUBMISSION REQUIREMENTS

Restrictions on contributors: Does not publish lectures or meeting papers.
Author pays submission fee: No
Author pays page charges: No
Length of articles: 1,500 words
Length of book reviews: 100-300 words
Length of notes: 100-200 words
Style: MLA
Number of copies required: 1
Special requirements: Must have documentation. Accepted articles should be submitted on MS-DOS or Macintosh diskette.
Rejected manuscripts: Returned; enclose SASE.
Time between decision and publication: 3 yrs. maximum
Number of reviewers: 3
Articles submitted per year: 200
Articles published per year: 20
Book reviews published per year: 3
Notes submitted per year: 5
Notes published per year: 2

(1731)
*Louisiana Literature: A Review of Literature and Humanities

Tim Gautreaux, William Parrill, & Norman German, Editors
Box 792
Southeastern Louisiana Univ.
Hammond, LA 70402

Telephone: 504 549-5022; 504 549-2100
First published: 1984
Sponsoring organization: Louisiana Endowment for the Humanities
ISSN: 0890-0477
MLA acronym: LaLit

SUBSCRIPTION INFORMATION

Frequency of publication: 2 times/yr. (Spring, Fall)
Circulation: 300
Available in microform: No
Subscription price: $12.50/yr. institutions; $10.00/yr. individuals
Year to which price refers: 1992

ADVERTISING INFORMATION

Advertising accepted: Yes
Advertising rates: $50.00/half page; $80.00/full page

EDITORIAL DESCRIPTION

Scope: Publishes articles on the literature of Louisiana, as well as fiction, poetry, interviews, and reviews.
Reviews books: Yes
Publishes notes: No
Languages accepted: English
Prints abstracts: No
Author-anonymous submission: No

SUBMISSION REQUIREMENTS

Restrictions on contributors: None
Author pays submission fee: No
Author pays page charges: No
Length of articles: No restrictions
Length of book reviews: 500-750 words
Style: None
Number of copies required: 1
Copyright ownership: Southeastern Louisiana Univ.
Rejected manuscripts: Returned; enclose SASE.
Time before publication decision: 1 mo.
Time between decision and publication: 3 mos.
Number of reviewers: 3
Articles submitted per year: 15
Articles published per year: 4
Book reviews submitted per year: 12
Book reviews published per year: 10

(1732)
*Lovecraft Studies

S. T. Joshi & Steven J. Mariconda, Editors
607 First St. #3L
Hoboken, NJ 07030

First published: 1979
ISSN: 0899-8361
MLA acronym: LSt

SUBSCRIPTION INFORMATION

Frequency of publication: 2 times/yr. (Spring, Fall)
Circulation: 500
Available in microform: No
Subscription price: $4.50/issue
Year to which price refers: 1991
Subscription address: Neocronomicon Press, 101 Lockwood St., West Warwick, RI 02893

ADVERTISING INFORMATION

Advertising accepted: No

EDITORIAL DESCRIPTION

Scope: Publishes articles on the life and work of Howard Phillips Lovecraft.
Reviews books: Yes
Publishes notes: Yes
Languages accepted: English
Prints abstracts: No
Author-anonymous submission: No

SUBMISSION REQUIREMENTS

Restrictions on contributors: Reviews are assigned.
Author pays submission fee: No
Author pays page charges: No
Length of articles: 1,000-10,000 words
Length of book reviews: 500-2,000 words
Length of notes: 250 words maximum
Style: Chicago
Number of copies required: 1
Copyright ownership: Neocronomicon Press for 1 yr.
Rejected manuscripts: Returned; enclose SASE.
Time before publication decision: 1 mo.
Time between decision and publication: 3-15 mos.
Number of reviewers: 2
Articles submitted per year: 20
Articles published per year: 8-10
Book reviews published per year: 4-8
Notes submitted per year: 5-10
Notes published per year: 2-4

(1733)
Luceafărul

Nicolae Dan Runtelata, Editor
Uniunea Scriitorilor din Rupublica Socialista România
Calea Victoriei 115
Bucharest, Romania

First published: 1958
Sponsoring organization: Uniunea Scriitorilor din România
ISSN: 0458-435X
MLA acronym: Luc

SUBSCRIPTION INFORMATION

Frequency of publication: 52 times/yr.
Subscription address: ILEXIM, Str. 13 Decembrie Nr. 3, Box 136-137, 70116 Bucharest, Romania

EDITORIAL DESCRIPTION

Scope: Publishes articles dealing with contemporary national and political issues. Also publishes literary criticism, literary history, and poetry.
Reviews books: Yes
Languages accepted: Romanian
Prints abstracts: No

(1734)
*Lucero: A Journal of Iberian and Latin American Studies

Kenya C. Dworkin, Yolanda Martínez-San Miguel, & Martívon Galindo, Editors
Dept. of Spanish & Portuguese
Univ. of California, Berkeley
Berkeley, CA 94720

Telephone: 510 642-2103
First published: 1990
Sponsoring organization: Dept. of Spanish & Portuguese, Univ. of California, Berkeley
MLA acronym: Lucero

SUBSCRIPTION INFORMATION

Frequency of publication: Annual
Circulation: 500
Available in microform: No
Subscription price: $12.00/yr. institutions; $8.00/yr. individuals; $6.00/yr. students
Year to which price refers: 1991

ADVERTISING INFORMATION

Advertising accepted: Yes
Advertising rates: $30.00/half page; $55.00/full page

EDITORIAL DESCRIPTION

Scope: Publishes articles, book reviews, interviews, and other scholarly writing on any aspect of Hispanic letters including Luso-Brazilian literature, Hispanic linguistics, history, Romance philology, Afro-Hispanic literature, Lusophone literature, Catalan literature, Portuguese linguistics, Catalan linguistics, and Peninsular and Latin American history.
Reviews books: Yes
Publishes notes: Yes
Languages accepted: English; Spanish; Portuguese; Catalan
Prints abstracts: No
Author-anonymous submission: Yes

SUBMISSION REQUIREMENTS

Restrictions on contributors: None
Author pays submission fee: No
Author pays page charges: No
Length of articles: 2,500-3,500 words
Length of book reviews: 500-750 words
Length of notes: 300-500 words
Style: MLA
Number of copies required: 1
Special requirements: Submit typescript and diskette.
Copyright ownership: Regents of the Univ. of California
Rejected manuscripts: Not returned
Time before publication decision: 6-8 weeks
Time between decision and publication: 8-12 weeks
Number of reviewers: 3
Articles submitted per year: 40
Articles published per year: 15
Book reviews submitted per year: 2
Book reviews published per year: 2
Notes submitted per year: 2
Notes published per year: 2

(1735)
*Lud: Organ Polskiego Towarzystwa Ludoznawczego i Komitetu Nauk Etnologicznych Polskiej Akademii Nauk/Organe de la Société Polonaise d'Ethnologie et du Comité des Sciences Ethnologiques

Zbigniew Jasiewicz, Editor
ul. św. Marcin 78
61-809 Poznań, Poland

First published: 1895
Sponsoring organization: Polskie Towarzystwo Ludoznawcze; Komitet Nauk Etnologicznych Polskiej Akademii Nauk
ISSN: 0076-1435
MLA acronym: Lud

SUBSCRIPTION INFORMATION

Frequency of publication: Annual
Circulation: 800
Available in microform: No
Subscription address: Polskie Towarzystwo Ludoznawcze, ul. Szewska 36, 50-139 Wrocław, Poland

ADVERTISING INFORMATION

Advertising accepted: No

EDITORIAL DESCRIPTION

Scope: Focuses on ethnography, ethnology, cultural and social anthropology, and folklore.
Reviews books: Yes
Publishes notes: Yes
Languages accepted: Polish
Prints abstracts: Yes

SUBMISSION REQUIREMENTS

Restrictions on contributors: None
Author pays submission fee: No
Author pays page charges: No
Length of articles: 2,000-6,000 words
Length of book reviews: 1,000 words
Length of notes: 1,000 words
Number of copies required: 2
Copyright ownership: Polskie Towarzystwo Ludoznawcze; Komitet Nauk Etnologicznych PAN
Rejected manuscripts: Returned
Time before publication decision: 1 yr.
Time between decision and publication: 6 mos.
Number of reviewers: 2
Articles submitted per year: 15
Articles published per year: 15-20
Book reviews submitted per year: 25
Book reviews published per year: 20
Notes submitted per year: 25
Notes published per year: 15

(1736)
*Lund Studies in English

Sven Bäckman & Jan Svartvik, Editors
English Dept.
Lund Univ.
Helgonabacken 14
223 62 Lund, Sweden

First published: 1933
Sponsoring organization: Lund Univ.
ISSN: 0076-1451
MLA acronym: LSE

SUBSCRIPTION INFORMATION

Frequency of publication: Irregular
Circulation: 150
Available in microform: No
Subscription address: Lund Univ. Press, Box 141, 221 00 Lund, Sweden
Additional subscription address: Chartwell-Bratt, Old Orchard Rd., Bromley, Kent BR1 2NE, England; Krieger Publishing Co., P.O. Box 9542, Melbourne, FL 32902-9542

ADVERTISING INFORMATION

Advertising accepted: No

EDITORIAL DESCRIPTION

Scope: Publishes monographs on English language and literature in the English language.
Reviews books: No
Publishes notes: No
Languages accepted: English
Prints abstracts: Yes
Author-anonymous submission: No

SUBMISSION REQUIREMENTS

Restrictions on contributors: Authors must be affiliated with Lund Univ.
Author pays submission fee: No
Author pays page charges: No
Style: Linguistic Soc. of America
Number of copies required: 1
Copyright ownership: Author
Books published per year: 2

(1737)
*Lunder Germanistische Forschungen

Inger Rosengren, Editor
Tyska Institutionen
Lund Univ.
Helgonabacken 14
223 62 Lund, Sweden

Telephone: (46) 46 109495
Fax: (46) 46 104211
E-mail: TYSKAIR@GEMINI.LDC.LU.SE
First published: 1934
ISSN: 0348-2146
MLA acronym: LGF

SUBSCRIPTION INFORMATION

Frequency of publication: Irregular
Circulation: 200
Available in microform: No
Subscription address: Almqvist & Wiksell International, P.O. Box 4627, 116 91 Stockholm, Sweden
Subscription telephone: (46) 8 7343030

ADVERTISING INFORMATION

Advertising accepted: No

EDITORIAL DESCRIPTION

Scope: Publishes monographs on Germanic studies.
Reviews books: No
Publishes notes: No
Languages accepted: German
Prints abstracts: No

SUBMISSION REQUIREMENTS

Author pays submission fee: No
Author pays page charges: No
Copyright ownership: Author

(1738)
*Luso-Brazilian Review

Mary L. Daniel & Robert M. Levine, Editors
1470 Van Hise Hall
Univ. of Wisconsin
Madison, WI 53706

Telephone: 608 262-2811
Fax: 608 262-5161
First published: 1964
Sponsoring organization: Univ. of Wisconsin, Dept. of Spanish & Portuguese, Dept. of History, Ibero-American Center; Cyril W. Nave Foundation
ISSN: 0024-7413
MLA acronym: LBR

SUBSCRIPTION INFORMATION

Frequency of publication: 2 times/yr. (Summer, Winter); publishes occasional special issues
Circulation: 600
Available in microform: Yes
Subscription price: $70.00/yr. institutions; $27.00/yr. individuals; $13.00/yr. students
Year to which price refers: 1992
Subscription address: Journal Division, Univ. of Wisconsin Press, 114 N. Murray St., Madison, WI 53715
Subscription telephone: 608 262-4952
Subscription fax: 608 262-7560

ADVERTISING INFORMATION

Advertising accepted: Yes
Advertising rates: $110.00/half page; $200.00/full page

EDITORIAL DESCRIPTION

Scope: Provides broad coverage of scholarship in literature, language, and social science on topics related to the Portuguese-speaking world.
Reviews books: Yes
Publishes notes: Yes
Languages accepted: English; Spanish; Portuguese
Prints abstracts: No
Author-anonymous submission: No

SUBMISSION REQUIREMENTS

Restrictions on contributors: None
Author pays submission fee: No
Author pays page charges: No
Length of articles: 12-30 double-spaced typescript pp.
Length of book reviews: 750 words maximum
Length of notes: 500 words maximum
Style: Chicago
Number of copies required: 2
Copyright ownership: Board of Regents, Univ. of Wisconsin System
Rejected manuscripts: Returned; enclose SASE.
Time before publication decision: 1-12 mos.
Time between decision and publication: 1-18 mos.
Number of reviewers: 1-4
Articles submitted per year: 80
Articles published per year: 20-25
Book reviews submitted per year: 15-20
Book reviews published per year: 15-20
Notes submitted per year: 4-5
Notes published per year: 3-4

(1739)
*Luther: Zeitschrift der Luther-Gesellschaft

Hartmut Hövelmann, Editor
Vandenhoeck & Ruprecht
Postfach 3753
3400 Göttingen, Germany

Additional editorial address: Holsteiner Str. 17, 8500 Nuremberg 90, Germany
Telephone: (49) 911 315895
Fax: (49) 911 311939
First published: 1918
Sponsoring organization: Luther-Gesellschaft
ISSN: 0340-6210
MLA acronym: Luther

SUBSCRIPTION INFORMATION

Frequency of publication: 3 times/yr.
Circulation: 1,550
Available in microform: No
Subscription price: 25 DM/yr. nonmembers; 18 DM/yr. members
Year to which price refers: 1992
Additional subscription address: Members contact: Luther-Gesellschaft e.V., Bindfeldweg 49, 2000 Hamburg 61, Germany

ADVERTISING INFORMATION

Advertising accepted: Yes

EDITORIAL DESCRIPTION

Scope: Publishes articles on Luther, his contemporaries, and the Enlightenment.
Reviews books: Yes
Publishes notes: No
Languages accepted: German
Prints abstracts: No
Author-anonymous submission: No

SUBMISSION REQUIREMENTS

Author pays submission fee: No
Author pays page charges: No
Length of articles: 45,000 characters
Length of book reviews: 2,700 characters
Copyright ownership: Author
Rejected manuscripts: Returned
Time before publication decision: 2-12 weeks
Time between decision and publication: 1-10 mos.
Number of reviewers: 2
Articles submitted per year: 15
Articles published per year: 12
Book reviews submitted per year: 20
Book reviews published per year: 15-20

(1740)
*Lutherjahrbuch

Helmar Junghans, Editor
Univ. Leipzig
Theologische Fak.
Emil-Fuchs-Str. 1
7010 Leipzig, Germany

First published: 1919
Sponsoring organization: Luther-Gesellschaft
ISSN: 0342-0914
MLA acronym: LJb

SUBSCRIPTION INFORMATION

Frequency of publication: Annual
Circulation: 1,500
Available in microform: No
Subscription price: 32 DM/yr.
Year to which price refers: 1992
Subscription address: Luther-Gesellschaft, Bindfeldweg 49, 2000 Hamburg 61, Germany
Subscription telephone: (49) 4 582007

ADVERTISING INFORMATION

Advertising accepted: No

EDITORIAL DESCRIPTION

Scope: Publishes articles on Luther research.
Reviews books: Yes
Publishes notes: No
Languages accepted: German; English
Prints abstracts: No
Author-anonymous submission: No

SUBMISSION REQUIREMENTS

Restrictions on contributors: Reviews are commissioned.
Author pays submission fee: No
Author pays page charges: No
Length of articles: No restrictions
Length of book reviews: 1,000 words
Style: None
Number of copies required: 1
Special requirements: Submit original typescript, accompanied by a diskette, if possible.
Copyright ownership: Journal
Rejected manuscripts: Returned
Time before publication decision: 1 mo.
Number of reviewers: 1
Articles submitted per year: 10
Articles published per year: 10
Book reviews published per year: 15

(1741)
Lyrikvännen

Torbjörn Schmidt, Editor
Box 30184
104 25 Stockholm, Sweden

First published: 1954
ISSN: 0460-0762
MLA acronym: Lyrikvännen

SUBSCRIPTION INFORMATION

Frequency of publication: 6 times/yr.
Available in microform: No

ADVERTISING INFORMATION

Advertising accepted: Yes

EDITORIAL DESCRIPTION

Scope: Publishes articles on poetry.
Reviews books: No
Prints abstracts: No

SUBMISSION REQUIREMENTS

Number of copies required: 1
Rejected manuscripts: Returned; enclose return postage.

(1742)
*Maal og Minne

Bjarne Fidjestøl & Einar Lundeby, Editors
Nordisk Inst.
Sydneplassen 9
5007 Bergen, Norway

Additional editorial address: Einar Lundeby, Nordisk Inst., Postboks 1013, Blindern, Oslo 3, Norway
Telephone: (47) 5 212416
Fax: (47) 5 231897
E-mail: Fidjestol@hf.uib.no
First published: 1909
Sponsoring organization: Bymålslaget
ISSN: 0024-855X
MLA acronym: MM

SUBSCRIPTION INFORMATION

Frequency of publication: 2 double issues/yr.
Circulation: 500
Available in microform: No
Subscription price: 150 NKr/yr.
Year to which price refers: 1991
Subscription address: Det Norske Samlaget, Box 4672 Sofienberg, 0506 Oslo 5, Norway
Subscription telephone: (47) 2 687502

ADVERTISING INFORMATION

Advertising accepted: No

EDITORIAL DESCRIPTION

Scope: Welcomes contributions dealing with Norwegian language and linguistic relics of every kind, literature of the Middle Ages, Norwegian place names, and national folklore. Also treats Old Icelandic literature.
Reviews books: Yes
Publishes notes: No
Languages accepted: English; Norwegian; Danish; Swedish
Prints abstracts: No
Author-anonymous submission: No

SUBMISSION REQUIREMENTS

Restrictions on contributors: None
Author pays submission fee: No
Author pays page charges: No
Length of articles: 20 pp.
Length of book reviews: 10 pp.
Number of copies required: 1
Copyright ownership: Author
Rejected manuscripts: Returned
Time before publication decision: 5 weeks
Time between decision and publication: 1 yr.
Number of reviewers: 2
Articles submitted per year: 20
Articles published per year: 15
Book reviews published per year: 6

(1743)
*Maatstaf

Martin Ros, Peter de Boer, Bart Tromp, & Th. A. Sontrop, Editors
Singel 262
1016 AC Amsterdam, Netherlands

Telephone: (31) 20 5511262
Fax: (31) 20 6203509
First published: 1952
ISSN: 0464-2198
MLA acronym: Maatstaf

SUBSCRIPTION INFORMATION

Frequency of publication: 10 times/yr. (8 monthly & 2 bimonthly issues)
Circulation: 2,000
Available in microform: No
Subscription address: BV Weekbladpers, Afdeling Abonnementen, Postbus 1050, 1000 BB Amsterdam, Netherlands
Subscription telephone: (31) 20 5518417
Subscription fax: (31) 20 6229141

ADVERTISING INFORMATION

Advertising accepted: Yes

EDITORIAL DESCRIPTION

Scope: Publishes articles on literature and art.
Reviews books: Yes
Prints abstracts: No
Author-anonymous submission: No

SUBMISSION REQUIREMENTS

Restrictions on contributors: None
Author pays submission fee: Yes
Author pays page charges: No
Number of copies required: 2
Special requirements: Submit typescript.
Copyright ownership: Author
Rejected manuscripts: Returned
Time before publication decision: 2 mos.
Time between decision and publication: 1 mo.

(1744)
*Macedonian Review: History, Culture, Literature, Arts

Boris Višinski & Ljubitsa Arsovska, Editors
Ruzveltova 6
P.O. Box 85
91001 Skopje, Macedonia (Yugoslavia)

Telephone: (38) 91 239134; (38) 91 226105
First published: 1971
ISSN: 0350-3089
MLA acronym: MacR

SUBSCRIPTION INFORMATION

Frequency of publication: 3 times/yr.
Circulation: 5,000
Available in microform: Yes
Subscription price: $20.00/yr.
Year to which price refers: 1992

ADVERTISING INFORMATION

Advertising accepted: Yes
Advertising rates: $300.00/full page, 3 issues

EDITORIAL DESCRIPTION

Scope: Publishes articles on literature, arts, culture, history, and translations of Macedonian poetry and prose.
Reviews books: Yes
Publishes notes: Yes
Languages accepted: English
Prints abstracts: No
Author-anonymous submission: No

SUBMISSION REQUIREMENTS

Restrictions on contributors: None
Author pays submission fee: No
Author pays page charges: No
Length of articles: No restrictions
Length of book reviews: 600 words
Length of notes: 150 words
Style: None
Number of copies required: 2
Special requirements: Articles are translated from Macedonian into English.
Copyright ownership: Assigned by author to journal
Rejected manuscripts: Not returned
Time before publication decision: 1 mo.
Time between decision and publication: 2-3 mos.
Number of reviewers: 2
Articles submitted per year: 60-70
Articles published per year: 50-55
Book reviews submitted per year: 10-20
Book reviews published per year: 10
Notes submitted per year: 50
Notes published per year: 30-45

(1745)
Machine Translation

Sergei Nirenburg, Harold Somers, & Masaru Tomita, Editors
Center for Machine Translation
Carnegie Mellon Univ.
Pittsburgh, PA 15213

Additional editorial address: Masaru Tomita, Software Review Editor, at the above address; Harold Somers, Book Review Editor, Centre for Computational Linguistics, UMIST, P.O. Box 88, Manchester M6O 1QD, England
First published: 1986
ISSN: 0922-6567
MLA acronym: MachT

SUBSCRIPTION INFORMATION

Frequency of publication: 4 times/yr.
Available in microform: Yes, through Univ. Microfilms International
Subscription address: Kluwer Academic Publishers, P.O. Box 322, 3300 AH Dordrecht, Netherlands
Additional subscription address: Kluwer Academic Publishers, Order Dept., P.O. Box 358 Accord Station, Hingham, MA 02018-9990

ADVERTISING INFORMATION

Advertising accepted: Yes

EDITORIAL DESCRIPTION

Scope: Publishes technical articles dealing, in a theoretical, descriptive, or computational aspect, with every topic that contributes to the advancement of machine translation and machine-aided translation. Includes articles on artifical intelligence, and general linguistic studies related to translation.
Reviews books: Yes
Publishes notes: Yes
Languages accepted: English
Prints abstracts: Yes
Author-anonymous submission: No

SUBMISSION REQUIREMENTS

Author pays submission fee: No
Author pays page charges: No
Length of articles: 3,000 words
Length of book reviews: 1,000 words
Length of notes: 500 words
Style: Linguistic Soc. of America
Number of copies required: 5
Special requirements: Only papers not previously published will be accepted and authors must agree not to publish articles elsewhere once article has been accepted for publication. Request Information for Authors from editor.
Copyright ownership: Kluwer Academic Publishers
Rejected manuscripts: Returned; enclose SASE.
Time before publication decision: 1-6 mos.
Time between decision and publication: 1-6 mos.
Articles published per year: 15-20
Book reviews published per year: 8-12

(1746)
Magazine

Mel Seesholtz & Daniel Barshay, Editors
Pennsylvania State Univ.
1600 Woodland Ave.
Abington, PA 19001

Additional editorial address: Daniel Barshay, 416 N. 31st St., Philadelphia, PA 19104
First published: 1972
Sponsoring organization: Pennsylvania College English Assn.
ISSN: 0741-9805
MLA acronym: Magazine

SUBSCRIPTION INFORMATION

Frequency of publication: Annual
Circulation: 150
Available in microform: No

ADVERTISING INFORMATION

Advertising accepted: Yes

EDITORIAL DESCRIPTION

Scope: Publishes articles on English literature, general literary topics, pedagogical issues, and Pennsylvania authors.
Reviews books: Yes
Publishes notes: Yes
Languages accepted: English
Prints abstracts: No
Author-anonymous submission: Yes

SUBMISSION REQUIREMENTS

Restrictions on contributors: Contributors must be or become members of the Pennsylvania College English Assn.
Author pays submission fee: No
Author pays page charges: No
Length of articles: No restrictions
Length of book reviews: 1,000-1,500 words
Length of notes: 1,500 words
Style: Chicago
Number of copies required: 2
Special requirements: Include SASE.
Copyright ownership: Author
Rejected manuscripts: Returned
Time before publication decision: 4-5 weeks
Time between decision and publication: 1-6 mos.
Number of reviewers: 2
Articles submitted per year: 40-60
Articles published per year: 20-30
Book reviews submitted per year: 10
Book reviews published per year: 5
Notes submitted per year: 10
Notes published per year: 5

(1747)
*Magazine Littéraire

Jean Claude Fasquelle, Editor
40 rue des St. Pères
75007 Paris, France

Telephone: (33) 1 45441451
Fax: (33) 1 45489636
First published: 1966
ISSN: 0024-9807
MLA acronym: MagLitt

SUBSCRIPTION INFORMATION

Frequency of publication: 11 times/yr.
Circulation: 65,000
Available in microform: No
Subscription price: 285 F/yr. France; 400 F/yr. elsewhere
Year to which price refers: 1992

ADVERTISING INFORMATION

Advertising accepted: Yes

EDITORIAL DESCRIPTION

Scope: Publishes articles on literature, as well as book reviews and interviews.
Reviews books: Yes
Publishes notes: Yes
Languages accepted: French
Prints abstracts: No
Author-anonymous submission: No

SUBMISSION REQUIREMENTS

Author pays submission fee: No
Author pays page charges: No
Number of copies required: 1
Copyright ownership: Author & Publisher
Rejected manuscripts: Not returned

(1748)
*Magyar Könyvszemle: Könyvtörténeti Folyóirat/Revue pour l'Histoire du Livre et de la Presse

György Kókay, Editor
Ménesi út 11-13
1118 Budapest, Hungary

Telephone: (36) 1 1664819
First published: 1876
Sponsoring organization: Magyar Tudományos Akadémia
ISSN: 0025-0171
MLA acronym: MK

SUBSCRIPTION INFORMATION

Frequency of publication: 4 times/yr.
Circulation: 530
Available in microform: No
Subscription price: $20.00/yr.
Year to which price refers: 1992
Subscription address: Argumentum Kiadó, Kérő u. 4, 1112 Budapest, Hungary
Subscription telephone: (36) 1 1826118
Subscription fax: (36) 1 1344372

ADVERTISING INFORMATION

Advertising accepted: No

EDITORIAL DESCRIPTION

Scope: Focuses on the history of books, the press, and journalism.
Reviews books: Yes
Publishes notes: Yes
Languages accepted: English; German; Hungarian
Prints abstracts: Yes
Author-anonymous submission: Yes

SUBMISSION REQUIREMENTS

Restrictions on contributors: None
Author pays submission fee: Yes
Cost of submission fee: 6,000 Ft/5,000 words
Author pays page charges: No
Length of articles: 2,000-5,000 words
Length of book reviews: 1,500-3,000 words
Length of notes: 1,000-6,000 words
Number of copies required: 1
Copyright ownership: Author
Rejected manuscripts: Returned
Time before publication decision: 1-2 mos.

Time between decision and publication: 3-6 mos.
Number of reviewers: 2 plus Editorial Board
Articles submitted per year: 50-60
Articles published per year: 35-40
Book reviews submitted per year: 20-30
Book reviews published per year: 20-25
Notes submitted per year: 20
Notes published per year: 15

(1749)
Magyar Nyelv

Loránd Benkő, Editor
Akadémiai Kiadó, Publishing House of the Hungarian Academy of Sciences
P.O. Box 24
1363 Budapest, Hungary

Additional editorial address: P.O. Box 107, 1364 Budapest, Hungary
First published: 1905
Sponsoring organization: Magyar Tudományos Akadémia
ISSN: 0025-0228
MLA acronym: MNy

SUBSCRIPTION INFORMATION

Frequency of publication: 4 times/yr. (Mar., June, Sept., Dec.)
Circulation: 1,500
Available in microform: No
Subscription address: Kultura Foreign Trading Co., P.O. Box 149, 1389 Budapest, Hungary

ADVERTISING INFORMATION

Advertising accepted: No

EDITORIAL DESCRIPTION

Scope: Publishes on all topics concerning Hungarian language, historical linguistics, dialectology, phonetics, and etymology.
Reviews books: Yes
Publishes notes: Yes
Languages accepted: Hungarian
Prints abstracts: No
Author-anonymous submission: No

SUBMISSION REQUIREMENTS

Restrictions on contributors: None
Author pays submission fee: No
Author pays page charges: No
Length of articles: 10-12 pp.
Length of book reviews: 1-2 pp.
Length of notes: 2-6 pp.
Style: None
Number of copies required: 1
Special requirements: Submit original typescript.
Copyright ownership: Author
Rejected manuscripts: Returned
Time before publication decision: 2-3 mos.
Time between decision and publication: 12-18 mos.
Number of reviewers: 1-2
Articles submitted per year: 50
Articles published per year: 80-90
Book reviews submitted per year: 20
Book reviews published per year: 16
Notes submitted per year: 70
Notes published per year: 40

(1750)
*Magyar Nyelvjárások

Á. Sebestyén, Editor
Lajos Kossuth Univ.
Pf. 54
4010 Debrecen, Hungary

Telephone: (36) 52 16666
First published: 1951

Sponsoring organization: Univ. of Debrecen
ISSN: 0541-9298
MLA acronym: MNyj

SUBSCRIPTION INFORMATION

Frequency of publication: Annual
Circulation: 700
Available in microform: No
Subscription address: Kultura Foreign Trading Co., P.O. Box 149, 1389 Budapest, Hungary

ADVERTISING INFORMATION

Advertising accepted: No

EDITORIAL DESCRIPTION

Scope: Publishes articles on dialectology, onomastics, and sociolinguistics.
Reviews books: Yes
Publishes notes: Yes
Languages accepted: Hungarian; English; French; German
Prints abstracts: No

SUBMISSION REQUIREMENTS

Restrictions on contributors: None
Author pays submission fee: No
Author pays page charges: No
Length of articles: 2,000-10,000 words
Length of book reviews: 500-1,000 words
Length of notes: 100-500 words
Style: None
Number of copies required: 1
Copyright ownership: Author
Rejected manuscripts: Returned
Time before publication decision: 6 mos.
Time between decision and publication: 1-2 yrs.
Number of reviewers: 2
Articles submitted per year: 10-15
Articles published per year: 6-10
Book reviews submitted per year: 10-15
Book reviews published per year: 5-10

(1751)
Magyar Nyelvőr

Akadémiai Kaidó
P.O. Box 24
1363 Budapest, Hungary

First published: 1872
Sponsoring organization: Magyar Tudományos Akadémia
ISSN: 0025-0026
MLA acronym: MagN

SUBSCRIPTION INFORMATION

Frequency of publication: 4 times/yr.
Circulation: 5,000

EDITORIAL DESCRIPTION

Scope: Publishes articles on linguistic culture, contemporary Hungarian language, Hungarian dialects, teaching of the Hungarian language, and the language of Hungarian literature.
Reviews books: Yes
Languages accepted: Hungarian
Prints abstracts: No

(1752)
*Maia: Rivista di Letterature Classiche

Antonio La Penna & Ferruccio Bertini, Editors
Via Balbi 4, p. III
16126 Genoa, Italy

Telephone: (39) 51 239060
Fax: (39) 51 239286
First published: 1948
ISSN: 0025-0538

MLA acronym: Maia

SUBSCRIPTION INFORMATION

Frequency of publication: 3 times/yr.
Circulation: 2,000
Available in microform: No
Subscription price: $50.00/yr.
Year to which price refers: 1992
Subscription address: Casa Editrice Cappelli S.p.A., Via Farini 14, 40124 Bologna, Italy

ADVERTISING INFORMATION

Advertising accepted: Yes

EDITORIAL DESCRIPTION

Scope: Publishes critical articles on Greek and Latin literature.
Reviews books: Yes
Publishes notes: Yes
Languages accepted: Any language
Prints abstracts: No
Author-anonymous submission: No

SUBMISSION REQUIREMENTS

Restrictions on contributors: None
Author pays submission fee: No
Author pays page charges: No
Length of articles: No restrictions
Length of book reviews: No restrictions
Length of notes: No restrictions
Style: None
Number of copies required: 1
Special requirements: Submit camera-ready copy.
Copyright ownership: Assigned by author to journal
Rejected manuscripts: Not returned
Time before publication decision: 6 mos.
Time between decision and publication: 1 yr.
Number of reviewers: 2
Articles submitted per year: 40
Articles published per year: 20-30
Book reviews submitted per year: 100-130
Book reviews published per year: 100-130

(1753)
*Mainzer Studien zur Amerikanistik: Eine Europäische Hochschulreihe

Winfried Herget & Renate von Bardeleben, Editors
American Studies Division
Dept. of English
Johannes Gutenberg Univ.
65 Mainz, Germany

Additional editorial address: R. von Bandeleben, Inst. für Anglistik & Amerikanistik, Fachbereich Angewandte Sprach- & Kulturwissenschaft, Johannes Gutenberg-Univ. Mainz, 6728 Germersheim, Germany
Telephone: (49) 7274 50842
Fax: (49) 7274 50877/79
First published: 1972
ISSN: 0170-9135
MLA acronym: MSzA

SUBSCRIPTION INFORMATION

Frequency of publication: Irregular
Circulation: 250
Available in microform: No
Subscription address: Verlag Peter Lang, Jupiterstr. 15, 3015 Bern, Switzerland

ADVERTISING INFORMATION

Advertising accepted: No

EDITORIAL DESCRIPTION

Scope: Publishes studies in American literature, American English, American-German linguistic and literary relations, American culture, and American-European cultural, literary, and linguistic interrelations.
Reviews books: No
Publishes notes: No
Languages accepted: English; German
Prints abstracts: Yes
Author-anonymous submission: No

SUBMISSION REQUIREMENTS

Restrictions on contributors: Manuscript must have been accepted as a doctoral dissertation or "Habilitations-Schrift."
Author pays submission fee: No
Author pays page charges: No
Length of books: No restrictions
Style: MLA
Number of copies required: 1
Special requirements: Submit typescript; include 1-2 page abstract.
Copyright ownership: Verlag Peter Lang GmbH
Rejected manuscripts: Returned
Time before publication decision: 1-2 mos.
Time between decision and publication: 6-9 mos.
Number of reviewers: 2
Books submitted per year: 3
Books published per year: 1-2

(1754)
Majalle(h)-ye Dāneshkade(h)-ye Adabiyyāt-e va Olume-e Ensanie-e Danashga(h)-e Ferdowsi

J. Hadidi, Editor
Fac. of Letters & Humanities
Univ. of Ferdowsi
Mashad, Iran

First published: 1965
Sponsoring organization: Univ. of Ferdowsi, Faculty of Letters & Humanities
MLA acronym: MDAM

SUBSCRIPTION INFORMATION

Frequency of publication: 4 times/yr.
Circulation: 1,200

EDITORIAL DESCRIPTION

Scope: Publishes articles on Persian literature and humanities.
Reviews books: No
Languages accepted: Persian
Prints abstracts: No

SUBMISSION REQUIREMENTS

Restrictions on contributors: Contributors must be members of the Univ. of Ferdowsi Faculty of Letters and Humanities.
Copyright ownership: Univ. of Ferdowsi, Faculty of Letters & Humanities
Time before publication decision: 3 mos.
Time between decision and publication: 3 mos.

(1755)
*Makedonika

Soc. for Macedonian Studies
Ethnikis Amynis 4
54621 Thessaloniki, Greece

Telephone: (30) 31 268710
Fax: (30) 31 271195
First published: 1940
Sponsoring organization: Soc. for Macedonian Studies
ISSN: 0076-289X

MLA acronym: Makedonika

SUBSCRIPTION INFORMATION

Frequency of publication: Annual
Circulation: 1,000
Available in microform: No
Subscription price: $30.00/yr.
Year to which price refers: 1992

ADVERTISING INFORMATION

Advertising accepted: No

EDITORIAL DESCRIPTION

Scope: Publishes articles and research work in the fields of history, archaeology, linguistics and folklore concerning the northern region of Greece.
Reviews books: Yes
Publishes notes: No
Languages accepted: English; French; German; Greek
Prints abstracts: Yes
Author-anonymous submission: No

SUBMISSION REQUIREMENTS

Restrictions on contributors: None
Author pays submission fee: No
Author pays page charges: No
Length of articles: 5-50 pp.
Length of book reviews: 1-10 pp.
Number of copies required: 1
Special requirements: Submit original typescript and summary.
Copyright ownership: Soc. for Macedonian Studies
Rejected manuscripts: Not returned
Time before publication decision: 6 mos.
Time between decision and publication: 6 mos.
Number of reviewers: 4
Articles submitted per year: 20
Articles published per year: 15
Book reviews submitted per year: 10-15
Book reviews published per year: 5-10

(1756)
Makedonski Jazik

Božidar Vidoeski, Editor
Inst. za Makedonski Jazik "Krste Misirkov"
Pošt. fah. 434
91000 Skopje, Macedonia (Yugoslavia)

First published: 1950
ISSN: 0025-1089
MLA acronym: MJ

SUBSCRIPTION INFORMATION

Frequency of publication: Annual
Circulation: 1,000
Available in microform: No

ADVERTISING INFORMATION

Advertising accepted: No

EDITORIAL DESCRIPTION

Reviews books: Yes
Publishes notes: Yes
Languages accepted: All Slavic languages; French; German
Prints abstracts: Yes

SUBMISSION REQUIREMENTS

Restrictions on contributors: None
Author pays submission fee: Yes
Author pays page charges: No
Length of articles: 30 pp.
Length of book reviews: 5 pp.
Number of copies required: 2
Copyright ownership: Author
Rejected manuscripts: Not returned

(1757)
Maladosts': Literaturno-Mastatski i Hramadska-Palitychny Chasopis

Henrykh Dalidovich, Editor
Prospekt F. Skaryny 79
220041 Minsk, Belarus

First published: 1953
ISSN: 0025-1208
MLA acronym: Maladosts'

SUBSCRIPTION INFORMATION

Frequency of publication: 12 times/yr.

EDITORIAL DESCRIPTION

Languages accepted: Belorussian

(1758)
*The Malcolm Lowry Review

Paul Tiessen, Editor
Dept. of English
Wilfrid Laurier Univ.
Waterloo, Ontario N2L 3C5, Canada

First published: 1977
Sponsoring organization: Dept. of English, Wilfrid Laurier Univ.
ISSN: 0828-5020
MLA acronym: MLNew

SUBSCRIPTION INFORMATION

Frequency of publication: 2 times/yr.
Circulation: 125
Available in microform: No
Subscription price: C$80.00/10 issues institutions; C$40.00/10 issues individuals
Year to which price refers: 1992

ADVERTISING INFORMATION

Advertising accepted: Yes

EDITORIAL DESCRIPTION

Scope: Publishes an annual bibliography, reviews, scholarly articles, interviews, and notes of interest to Lowry scholars.
Reviews books: Yes
Publishes notes: Yes
Languages accepted: English
Prints abstracts: No
Author-anonymous submission: No

SUBMISSION REQUIREMENTS

Restrictions on contributors: None
Author pays submission fee: No
Author pays page charges: No
Length of articles: No restrictions
Length of book reviews: No restrictions
Length of notes: No restrictions
Style: None
Number of copies required: 1
Copyright ownership: Author & journal
Rejected manuscripts: Returned
Time before publication decision: 6 mos.
Time between decision and publication: 6 mos.
Number of reviewers: 1-4
Articles submitted per year: 10
Articles published per year: 5
Book reviews submitted per year: 3
Book reviews published per year: 3
Notes submitted per year: 15
Notes published per year: 15

Number of reviewers: 3
Articles published per year: 10-15

(1759)
*Maledicta: The International Journal of Verbal Aggression

Reinhold A. Aman, Editor
Maledicta Press
P.O. Box 14123
Santa Rosa, CA 95402-6123

Telephone: 707 523-4761
First published: 1977
Sponsoring organization: International Maledicta Soc.
ISSN: 0363-3659
MLA acronym: Maledicta

SUBSCRIPTION INFORMATION

Frequency of publication: Annual (Dec.)
Circulation: 4,000
Available in microform: No
Subscription price: $26.00/yr. institutions US; $27.00/yr. institutions elsewhere; $22.00/yr. individuals US; $23.00/yr. individuals elsewhere
Year to which price refers: 1992

ADVERTISING INFORMATION

Advertising accepted: No

EDITORIAL DESCRIPTION

Scope: Specializes in uncensored glossaries and studies of all offensive and negatively valued words and expressions, in all languages and from all cultures, past and present: their meaning, etymology, history, usage, social and psychological impact.
Reviews books: Yes
Publishes notes: Yes
Languages accepted: English
Prints abstracts: No
Author-anonymous submission: No

SUBMISSION REQUIREMENTS

Restrictions on contributors: Unsolicited manuscripts and book reviews are not accepted.
Author pays submission fee: No
Author pays page charges: No
Length of articles: 4-25 pp.
Length of book reviews: No restrictions
Length of notes: 1-4 pp.
Style: MLA; Linguistic Soc. of America; Chicago
Number of copies required: 1
Special requirements: Submit original manuscript.
Copyright ownership: Publisher; reverts to author after publication.
Rejected manuscripts: Returned; enclose return postage.
Time before publication decision: 1 week
Time between decision and publication: 2-3 yrs.
Number of reviewers: 1
Articles submitted per year: 150-200
Articles published per year: 40
Book reviews published per year: 40-50
Notes submitted per year: 50
Notes published per year: 10

(1760)
*Mallorn: The Journal of the Tolkien Society

John Ellison & Patricia Reynolds, Editors
16 Gibsons Green
Heelanos
Milton Keynes MK13 7NH, England

Telephone: (44) 908 321354
First published: 1970
Sponsoring organization: Tolkien Soc.
ISSN: 0308-6674
MLA acronym: Mallorn

SUBSCRIPTION INFORMATION

Frequency of publication: 1-2 times/yr.
Circulation: 1,000
Available in microform: No
Subscription price: £15.00/yr. individuals United Kingdom; £17.00/yr. individuals Europe; £20.00/yr. individuals N. America; £21.00/yr. individuals Australia
Year to which price refers: 1992-93
Subscription address: Chris Oakey, Flat 5, 357 High St., Cheltenham, Glostershire GL50 3HT, England

ADVERTISING INFORMATION

Advertising accepted: No

EDITORIAL DESCRIPTION

Scope: Publishes articles, poetry, artwork, and fiction on subjects related to, or inspired by, the life and works of J. R. R. Tolkien.
Reviews books: Yes
Publishes notes: No
Languages accepted: English
Prints abstracts: No
Author-anonymous submission: No

SUBMISSION REQUIREMENTS

Restrictions on contributors: None
Author pays submission fee: No
Author pays page charges: No
Length of articles: 5,000 words maximum
Length of book reviews: 2,500 words
Number of copies required: 2
Copyright ownership: Tolkien Soc.
Rejected manuscripts: Returned at author's request; enclose return postage.
Time before publication decision: 2 mos.
Time between decision and publication: 6-18 mos.
Number of reviewers: 2
Articles submitted per year: 15
Articles published per year: 6-10
Book reviews submitted per year: 6
Book reviews published per year: 2-4

(1761)
*Man and Nature/L'Homme et La Nature: Proceedings of the Canadian Society for Eighteenth-Century Studies/Actes de la Société Canadienne d'Etude du Dix-Huitième Siècle

R. J. Merrett, Managing Editor
Dept. of English
Univ. of Alberta
Edmonton, Alberta T6G 2E5, Canada

Telephone: 403 435-5878
Fax: 403 435-5852
First published: 1982
Sponsoring organization: Canadian Soc. for Eighteenth-Century Studies/Soc. Canadienne d'Etude du Dix-Huitième Siècle
ISSN: 0824-3298
MLA acronym: M&N

SUBSCRIPTION INFORMATION

Frequency of publication: Annual
Circulation: 350
Available in microform: No
Subscription price: C$25.95/yr.
Year to which price refers: 1990
Subscription address: Academic Printing & Publishing, P.O. Box 4834, Edmonton, Alberta T6E 5G7, Canada

ADVERTISING INFORMATION

Advertising accepted: Yes, on an exchange basis

EDITORIAL DESCRIPTION

Scope: Contains selected papers presented at the annual meeting of the Canadian Society for Eighteenth-Century Studies. Topics include interdisciplinary, bilingual presentations of current research in that period.
Reviews books: No
Publishes notes: No
Languages accepted: English; French
Prints abstracts: No
Author-anonymous submission: Yes

SUBMISSION REQUIREMENTS

Restrictions on contributors: Papers are selected from the annual meeting of the Canadian Soc. for Eighteenth-Century Studies. Contributors must be members of the society.
Author pays submission fee: No
Author pays page charges: No
Length of articles: 3,000-4,000 words
Style: MLA
Number of copies required: 2
Copyright ownership: Canadian Soc. for Eighteenth-Century Studies
Rejected manuscripts: Returned
Time before publication decision: 6 mos.
Time between decision and publication: 1 yr.
Number of reviewers: 2-3
Articles submitted per year: 35-40
Articles published per year: 14-16

(1762)
*Mana

Hellar Grabbi, Editor
3602 Albee Lane
Alexandria, VA 22309

First published: 1957
ISSN: 0464-8145
MLA acronym: Mana

SUBSCRIPTION INFORMATION

Frequency of publication: Irregular (2 times/yr.)
Circulation: 1,000
Available in microform: No
Subscription price: $25.00/issue
Year to which price refers: 1992

ADVERTISING INFORMATION

Advertising accepted: Yes

EDITORIAL DESCRIPTION

Scope: Focuses on Estonian culture. Includes articles on Estonian literature, art, folklore, history, and science.
Reviews books: Yes
Languages accepted: Estonian; English occasionally; German occasionally
Prints abstracts: No

SUBMISSION REQUIREMENTS

Author pays submission fee: No
Author pays page charges: No
Number of copies required: 2
Copyright ownership: Author
Time before publication decision: 2 mos.
Time between decision and publication: 6 mos.
Number of reviewers: 3

(1763)
*The Mankind Quarterly

Edgar C. Polomé, Brunetto Chiarelli, Richard Lynn, & Hans Jürgens, Editors
Inst. for the Study of Man
6861 Elm St., Suite 4H
McLean, VA 22101

Telephone: 703 442-8010
Fax: 703 847-9524
First published: 1960
Sponsoring organization: Inst. for the Study of Man
ISSN: 0025-2344
MLA acronym: ManQ

SUBSCRIPTION INFORMATION

Frequency of publication: 4 times/yr.
Circulation: 1,075
Available in microform: No
Subscription price: $70.00/yr. institutions; $35.00/yr. individuals; $25.00/yr. students
Year to which price refers: 1992

ADVERTISING INFORMATION

Advertising accepted: Yes
Advertising rates: $150.00/full page; $200.00/cover

EDITORIAL DESCRIPTION

Scope: Publishes articles on anthropology, including linguistics and mythology, with substantial Indo-European oriented articles.
Reviews books: Yes
Publishes notes: Yes
Languages accepted: English
Prints abstracts: Yes
Author-anonymous submission: Yes

SUBMISSION REQUIREMENTS

Author pays submission fee: No
Author pays page charges: No
Length of articles: 2,000-12,000 words
Length of book reviews: 1,000 words
Length of notes: 1,000-2,000 words
Style: MLA
Number of copies required: 2
Special requirements: Submit typescript. Submission on IBM-compatible diskette is preferred for accepted articles.
Copyright ownership: Journal
Rejected manuscripts: Not returned
Time before publication decision: 3-6 mos.
Time between decision and publication: 6-12 mos.
Number of reviewers: 2-5
Articles submitted per year: 40-50
Articles published per year: 20-24
Book reviews published per year: 30-50

(1764)
*Manuscripta

Charles J. Ermatinger, Editor
Pius XII Memorial Library
St. Louis Univ.
3650 Lindell Blvd.
St. Louis, MO 63108

Telephone: 314 658-3090
Fax: 314 658-3108
First published: 1957
Sponsoring organization: St. Louis Univ.
ISSN: 0025-2603
MLA acronym: Manuscripta

SUBSCRIPTION INFORMATION

Frequency of publication: 3 times/yr. (Mar., July, Nov.)
Circulation: 700

ADVERTISING INFORMATION

Advertising accepted: Yes, on an exchange basis

EDITORIAL DESCRIPTION

Scope: Publishes articles based on manuscript research, and short text editions ranging from classical antiquity to the Renaissance. Preferred subject areas are literature (Latin and Western European vernacular), science, philosophy, logic, theology, law, manuscript illumination, and history (political, religious, economic).
Reviews books: Yes
Publishes notes: Yes
Languages accepted: English; French; German; Latin
Prints abstracts: No
Author-anonymous submission: No

SUBMISSION REQUIREMENTS

Restrictions on contributors: None
Author pays submission fee: No
Author pays page charges: No
Length of articles: 25 double-spaced pp. (pica) or 21 pp. (elite) maximum
Length of book reviews: 800 words
Length of notes: 1,500 words
Style: MLA; Chicago
Number of copies required: 1
Special requirements: Submit typescript.
Rejected manuscripts: Returned; enclose return postage.
Time before publication decision: 1 mo.
Time between decision and publication: 18 mos.
Number of reviewers: 2
Articles submitted per year: 25
Articles published per year: 16
Book reviews submitted per year: 10
Book reviews published per year: 8
Notes submitted per year: 12
Notes published per year: 6

(1765)
*Manuscripts

David R. Chesnutt, Editor
Dept. of History
Univ. of South Carolina
Columbia, SC 29208

Telephone: 803 777-6525
Fax: 803 777-4494
First published: 1948
Sponsoring organization: Manuscript Soc.
ISSN: 0025-262X
MLA acronym: MSS

SUBSCRIPTION INFORMATION

Frequency of publication: 4 times/yr. (Jan., Apr., July, Oct.)
Circulation: 1,500
Available in microform: No
Subscription address: David R. Smith, 350 N. Niagara St., Burbank, CA 91505

ADVERTISING INFORMATION

Advertising accepted: Yes

EDITORIAL DESCRIPTION

Scope: Publishes articles on all types of manuscripts of interest to members of the Society.
Reviews books: Yes
Publishes notes: No
Languages accepted: English
Prints abstracts: No
Author-anonymous submission: No

SUBMISSION REQUIREMENTS

Restrictions on contributors: None
Author pays submission fee: No
Author pays page charges: No

(1766)
Manuscriptum: Revistă Trimestrială Editată de Muzeul Literaturii Române

Mihaila Ruxandra, Editor
Bd. Dacia nr. 12
Sectorul 1, 71116
Bucharest, Romania

First published: 1970
Sponsoring organization: Muzeul Literaturii Române
ISSN: 1010-5492
MLA acronym: Manuscriptum

SUBSCRIPTION INFORMATION

Frequency of publication: 4 times/yr. (Jan., Apr., July, Sept.)
Circulation: 3,000
Available in microform: No
Subscription price: $80.00/yr.
Year to which price refers: 1993
Subscription address: Rompresfilatelia, Presă P.O. 12-201, Bucharest, Romania

ADVERTISING INFORMATION

Advertising accepted: Yes

EDITORIAL DESCRIPTION

Scope: Focuses on editions of primary literary documents, particularly unpublished documents in the Museum of Literary History and other public or private archives from Romania and abroad.
Reviews books: Yes
Publishes notes: Yes
Languages accepted: Romanian; English; French; German; Russian; Latin
Prints abstracts: Yes
Author-anonymous submission: No

SUBMISSION REQUIREMENTS

Restrictions on contributors: None
Author pays submission fee: No
Author pays page charges: No
Length of articles: No restrictions
Length of book reviews: No restrictions
Length of notes: No restrictions
Number of copies required: 1
Special requirements: Submit original typescript.
Copyright ownership: Author
Rejected manuscripts: Not returned
Time before publication decision: 1 week
Time between decision and publication: 3 mos.
Number of reviewers: 2
Articles submitted per year: 400
Articles published per year: 120
Book reviews submitted per year: 20
Book reviews published per year: 8
Notes submitted per year: 200
Notes published per year: 100

Length of articles: 1,000-3,500 words
Style: Chicago preferred
Number of copies required: 2
Copyright ownership: Assigned by author to journal
Rejected manuscripts: Returned; enclose SASE.
Time before publication decision: 1-2 mos.
Time between decision and publication: 6-24 mos.
Number of reviewers: 1
Articles submitted per year: 40
Articles published per year: 24
Book reviews published per year: 1-10

(1767)
*Marbacher Magazin

Ulrich Ott, Editor
Deutsche Schillergesellschaft
7142 Marbach am Neckar, Germany

Telephone: (49) 7144 15784
Fax: (49) 7144 15976
First published: 1976
Sponsoring organization: Schiller-Nationalmuseum
MLA acronym: MarM

SUBSCRIPTION INFORMATION

Frequency of publication: Irregular (at least 3 times/yr.)
Circulation: 3,000-11,000
Available in microform: No
Subscription telephone: (49) 7144 6061

ADVERTISING INFORMATION

Advertising accepted: No

EDITORIAL DESCRIPTION

Scope: Material published comes primarily from the exhibits organized by the Schiller-Nationalmuseum.
Reviews books: No
Publishes notes: No
Languages accepted: German
Prints abstracts: No

SUBMISSION REQUIREMENTS

Restrictions on contributors: None
Author pays submission fee: No
Author pays page charges: No
Length of articles: No restrictions
Style: None
Copyright ownership: Deutsche Schillergesellschaft
Number of reviewers: 2
Articles submitted per year: 3-4
Articles published per year: 3-4

(1768)
*Marche Romane

Janine Delcourt-Angélique & Jacques Decaluwé, Editors
3, place Cockerill
4000 Liège, Belgium

Telephone: (32) 41 665648
Fax: (32) 41 665700
First published: 1951
Sponsoring organization: Académie Royale de Langue & de Littérature Françaises; Ministère de l'Education; Fonds National de la Recherche Scientifique
MLA acronym: MRom

SUBSCRIPTION INFORMATION

Frequency of publication: 1-2 times/yr.
Available in microform: No
Subscription address: c/o Christian Delcourt, 17a, quai Saint-Léonard, 4000 Liège, Belgium

ADVERTISING INFORMATION

Advertising accepted: No

EDITORIAL DESCRIPTION

Scope: Publishes Romance studies.
Reviews books: Yes
Publishes notes: Yes
Languages accepted: French; Spanish; Italian; English; German
Prints abstracts: No
Author-anonymous submission: No

SUBMISSION REQUIREMENTS

Author pays submission fee: No
Author pays page charges: No
Length of articles: 15 pp.
Length of book reviews: 2 pp.
Number of copies required: 3
Special requirements: Submit IBM or Macintosh diskette.
Copyright ownership: Journal
Time before publication decision: 3 weeks
Time between decision and publication: 1 yr.
Number of reviewers: 3
Articles submitted per year: 30
Articles published per year: 15
Book reviews published per year: 10

(1769)
Marges

Bernard Leblon & Daniel Meyran, Editors
Centre de Recherches Ibériques & Latino-Américaines
Univ. de Perpignan
Chemin de la Passió Vella
66025 Perpignan Cedex, France

First published: 1987
Sponsoring organization: Univ. de Perpignan
MLA acronym: Marges

SUBSCRIPTION INFORMATION

Frequency of publication: 2 times/yr.
Circulation: 350
Available in microform: No

ADVERTISING INFORMATION

Advertising accepted: No

EDITORIAL DESCRIPTION

Scope: Publishes monographs on problems of marginal phenomena in Spain and Latin America.
Reviews books: No
Publishes notes: No
Languages accepted: Spanish; French
Prints abstracts: No
Author-anonymous submission: No

SUBMISSION REQUIREMENTS

Restrictions on contributors: None
Author pays submission fee: No
Author pays page charges: No
Style: Series
Number of copies required: 1
Rejected manuscripts: Returned
Time before publication decision: 2-3 mos.
Time between decision and publication: 6-12 mos.
Number of reviewers: 5
Books submitted per year: 5-6
Books published per year: 2

(1770)
*Marginalien: Zeitschrift für Buchkunst und Bibliophilie

Lothar Lang, Editor
Aufbau-Verlag Berlin & Weimar
Franzoesische Str., 32
1080 Berlin, Germany

Additional editorial address: Märkische Allee 390, 1143 Berlin, Germany
First published: 1956
Sponsoring organization: Pirckheimer Gesellschaft e.V.
ISSN: 0025-2948
MLA acronym: Marginalien

SUBSCRIPTION INFORMATION

Frequency of publication: 4 times/yr.
Available in microform: No
Subscription address: VVA Bertelsmann Distribution—Zeitschriftenservice, Postfach 7777, An der Autobahn, 4830 Gütersloh, Germany

ADVERTISING INFORMATION

Advertising accepted: No

EDITORIAL DESCRIPTION

Reviews books: Yes
Languages accepted: German
Prints abstracts: No

SUBMISSION REQUIREMENTS

Restrictions on contributors: None
Author pays submission fee: No
Author pays page charges: No
Length of articles: 5-20 pp.
Number of copies required: 3
Special requirements: Submit original typescript.
Copyright ownership: Journal
Rejected manuscripts: Returned

(1771) *Marianum

Ignacio M. Calabuig Adàn, Editor
Pontificia Facolta Teologica Marianum
Viale Trenta Aprile, 6
00153 Rome, Italy

Fax: (39) 6 5880292
First published: 1939
Sponsoring organization: Pontificia Facultà Teologica Marianum
MLA acronym: Marianum

SUBSCRIPTION INFORMATION

Frequency of publication: 2 times/yr.
Circulation: 800
Available in microform: No
Subscription price: 55,000 Lit/yr.
Year to which price refers: 1991

ADVERTISING INFORMATION

Advertising accepted: No

EDITORIAL DESCRIPTION

Scope: Publishes articles on mariology and theology.
Reviews books: Yes
Publishes notes: Yes
Languages accepted: Italian; French; English; German; Spanish; Latin; Portuguese
Author-anonymous submission: No

SUBMISSION REQUIREMENTS

Restrictions on contributors: None
Author pays submission fee: No
Author pays page charges: No
Length of articles: 7,500 words
Style: Chicago preferred for English-language articles
Number of copies required: 2
Copyright ownership: Journal
Rejected manuscripts: Returned
Time before publication decision: 1 mo.
Time between decision and publication: 6-10 mos.
Number of reviewers: 3
Articles submitted per year: 20
Articles published per year: 10
Book reviews submitted per year: 50
Book reviews published per year: 40
Notes submitted per year: 20
Notes published per year: 15

(1772) *Mark Twain Journal

Thomas A. Tenney, Editor
English Dept.
College of Charleston
Charleston, SC 29424

Telephone: 803 723-0487
First published: 1936
ISSN: 0025-3499
MLA acronym: MTJ

SUBSCRIPTION INFORMATION

Frequency of publication: 2 times/yr. (Spring, Fall)
Circulation: 800
Available in microform: Yes, through Univ. Microfilms International
Subscription price: $15.00/yr. US; $16.00/yr. elsewhere
Year to which price refers: 1990

ADVERTISING INFORMATION

Advertising accepted: No

EDITORIAL DESCRIPTION

Scope: Publishes articles on Mark Twain's life and works with emphasis on original materials rather than subjective interpretations.
Reviews books: No
Publishes notes: Yes
Languages accepted: English
Prints abstracts: No
Author-anonymous submission: No

SUBMISSION REQUIREMENTS

Restrictions on contributors: None
Author pays submission fee: No
Author pays page charges: No
Length of articles: No restrictions
Style: MLA; Chicago
Number of copies required: 1
Copyright ownership: Journal, unless author reserves copyright
Rejected manuscripts: Returned; US contributors must enclose SAE.
Time before publication decision: 1 mo. maximum
Time between decision and publication: 1 yr. maximum

(1773) *Markers: The Journal of the Association for Gravestone Studies

Richard E. Meyer, Editor
Dept. of English
Western Oregon State College
345 Monmouth Ave.
Monmouth, OR 97361

Telephone: 503 838-8362
First published: 1980
Sponsoring organization: Assn. for Gravestone Studies
ISSN: 0277-8726
MLA acronym: Markers

SUBSCRIPTION INFORMATION

Frequency of publication: Annual
Circulation: 200-500
Available in microform: No
Subscription price: $20.00/yr. members; $25.00/yr. nonmembers
Year to which price refers: 1992
Subscription address: Assn. for Gravestone Studies, 30 Elm St., Worchester, MA 01609
Subscription telephone: 508 831-7753

ADVERTISING INFORMATION

Advertising accepted: No

EDITORIAL DESCRIPTION

Scope: Publishes articles on graveyards and cemeteries, grave markers, and carvers in North America and the British Isles. Includes many photographs.
Reviews books: Yes
Publishes notes: No
Languages accepted: English
Prints abstracts: No
Author-anonymous submission: No

SUBMISSION REQUIREMENTS

Restrictions on contributors: Book reviews are commissioned.
Author pays submission fee: No
Author pays page charges: No
Length of articles: 20-25 pp.
Length of book reviews: 500 words
Style: Chicago
Number of copies required: 3
Special requirements: Submit original typescript and 2 copies. Original illustrations (glossy photographs, line drawings, etc.) should accompany manuscript.
Copyright ownership: Assn. for Gravestone Studies
Rejected manuscripts: Returned
Time before publication decision: 2 mos.
Time between decision and publication: 6-18 mos.
Number of reviewers: 3
Articles submitted per year: 12-15
Articles published per year: 7-10
Book reviews published per year: 3-4

(1774) *Maske und Kothurn: Internationale Beiträge zur Theaterwissenschaft

Wolfgang Greisenegger, Editor
Inst. für Theaterwissenschaft
Univ. Vienna
Hofburg, Batthyanystiege
1010 Vienna, Austria

Telephone: (43) 222 5335086
Fax: (43) 222 5339076
First published: 1955
Sponsoring organization: Univ. Wien, Inst. für Theaterwissenschaft; Bundesministerium für Wissenschaft & Forschung, Vienna
ISSN: 0025-4606
MLA acronym: MuK

SUBSCRIPTION INFORMATION

Frequency of publication: 4 times/yr.
Circulation: 800
Available in microform: No
Subscription price: 1,280 S/yr. institutions; 990 S/yr. individuals; 392 S/yr. students
Year to which price refers: 1992
Subscription address: Böhlau Verlag, Sachsenplatz 4-6, Postfach 87, 1201 Vienna, Austria
Subscription telephone: (43) 222 3302427
Subscription fax: (43) 222 3302432

ADVERTISING INFORMATION

Advertising accepted: Yes

EDITORIAL DESCRIPTION

Scope: Publishes articles on history, theory, and research of the performing arts.
Reviews books: Yes
Publishes notes: No
Languages accepted: German; English; French
Prints abstracts: No
Author-anonymous submission: Yes

SUBMISSION REQUIREMENTS

Restrictions on contributors: None
Author pays submission fee: No
Author pays page charges: No
Length of articles: 50 pp. maximum

Length of book reviews: 10 pp. maximum
Style: MLA
Number of copies required: 2
Special requirements: Contributions in French must be accompanied by English abstracts.
Copyright ownership: Hermann Böhlaus Nachf. GmbH
Rejected manuscripts: Not returned
Time before publication decision: 2 mos.
Time between decision and publication: 2 mos.
Number of reviewers: 2
Articles submitted per year: 40
Articles published per year: 25
Book reviews submitted per year: 30
Book reviews published per year: 10

(1775)
*Massachusetts Review: A Quarterly of Literature, the Arts and Public Affairs

Jules Chametzky, Mary Heath, & Paul Jenkins, Editors
Memorial Hall
Univ. of Massachusetts
Amherst, MA 01003

First published: 1959
Sponsoring organization: Smith College; Mount Holyoke College; Amherst College; Hampshire College; Univ. of Massachusetts
ISSN: 0025-4878
MLA acronym: MR

SUBSCRIPTION INFORMATION

Frequency of publication: 4 times/yr. (Spring, Summer, Fall, Winter)
Circulation: 1,800
Available in microform: Yes
Subscription price: $20.00/yr. institutions US; $15.00/yr. individuals US; $25.00/yr. elsewhere
Year to which price refers: 1993

ADVERTISING INFORMATION

Advertising accepted: Yes

EDITORIAL DESCRIPTION

Scope: Publishes articles on the arts, literature, and public affairs as well as fiction and poetry.
Reviews books: Yes
Publishes notes: No
Languages accepted: English
Prints abstracts: No

SUBMISSION REQUIREMENTS

Restrictions on contributors: Fiction manuscripts are not considered from June to Oct.
Author pays submission fee: No
Author pays page charges: No
Length of articles: 25 pp. maximum
Number of copies required: 1
Copyright ownership: Reverts to author on publication
Rejected manuscripts: Returned; enclose SASE.
Time before publication decision: 6-8 weeks
Time between decision and publication: 6-12 mos.
Number of reviewers: 2-3
Articles submitted per year: 250
Articles published per year: 25-30

(1776)
*Massachusetts Studies in English

Marcy Tanter, Lori Paige, & Jacqueline LeBlanc, Editors
Bartlett Hall
Univ. of Massachusetts
Amherst, MA 01003

Telephone: 413 545-5502

First published: 1967
Sponsoring organization: English Dept., Univ. of Massachusetts at Amherst
ISSN: 0047-6161
MLA acronym: MSE

SUBSCRIPTION INFORMATION

Frequency of publication: 2 times/yr.
Circulation: 275
Available in microform: Yes
Subscription price: $14.00/yr. institutions; $10.00/yr. individuals; $18.00/yr. outside US
Year to which price refers: 1992

ADVERTISING INFORMATION

Advertising accepted: Yes

EDITORIAL DESCRIPTION

Scope: Publishes essays and studies on literature written in English. Encourages work from graduate students. Invites innovative approaches and essays on previously neglected authors and fields of inquiry.
Reviews books: No
Publishes notes: Yes
Languages accepted: English
Prints abstracts: No
Author-anonymous submission: Yes

SUBMISSION REQUIREMENTS

Restrictions on contributors: None
Author pays submission fee: No
Author pays page charges: No
Length of articles: 7,500 words
Length of notes: 750-1,000 words
Style: MLA
Number of copies required: 3
Special requirements: Submit original typescript plus 2 copies and a 5.25 in. diskette using WordPerfect.
Copyright ownership: Assigned by author to journal
Rejected manuscripts: Original typescript returned; enclose SASE
Time before publication decision: 3 mos.
Time between decision and publication: 6-12 mos.
Number of reviewers: 3-5
Articles submitted per year: 80-100
Articles published per year: 10-12
Notes submitted per year: 15-20
Notes published per year: 2-3

(1777)
*Matatu: Journal for African Culture and Society

Holger G. Ehling, Editor
In der Au 33
6000 Frankfurt am Main 90, Germany

Telephone: (49) 69 786310
Fax: (49) 69 786310
First published: 1987
ISSN: 0932-9714
MLA acronym: Matatu

SUBSCRIPTION INFORMATION

Frequency of publication: 2 times/yr.
Circulation: 600
Available in microform: No
Subscription address: Editions Rodopi, Keizersgracht 302-304, 1016 EX Amsterdam, Netherlands
Additional subscription address: In N. America: Editions Rodopi, 233 Peachtree St. N.E., Atlanta, GA 30303-1504
Subscription telephone: (31) 20 6227507; 404 523-1964
Subscription fax: (31) 20 6380948; 404 522-7116

ADVERTISING INFORMATION

Advertising accepted: Yes, on an exchange basis

EDITORIAL DESCRIPTION

Scope: Publishes articles on African and Caribbean literatures and arts.
Reviews books: Yes
Publishes notes: Yes
Languages accepted: English; French
Prints abstracts: Yes
Author-anonymous submission: No

SUBMISSION REQUIREMENTS

Restrictions on contributors: Reviews are solicited.
Author pays submission fee: No
Author pays page charges: No
Length of articles: 10,000-15,000 words
Length of book reviews: 3,000-5,000 words
Length of notes: 1,000 words
Style: MLA
Number of copies required: 2
Special requirements: Submit a 10-15 line abstract.
Copyright ownership: Editions Rodopi
Rejected manuscripts: Filed or returned; enclose SAE.
Time before publication decision: 6-12 mos.
Time between decision and publication: 3-9 mos.
Number of reviewers: 3
Articles submitted per year: 80-100
Articles published per year: 10
Notes submitted per year: 150
Notes published per year: 1-2

(1778)
Material Culture: Journal of the Pioneer American Society

William D. Walters, Jr., Editor
Illinois State Univ.
Dept. of Geography-Geology
Normal, IL 61701

First published: 1969
Sponsoring organization: Pioneer America Soc.
ISSN: 0032-0005
MLA acronym: MCul

SUBSCRIPTION INFORMATION

Frequency of publication: 3 times/yr. (Spring, Summer, Fall)
Circulation: 600
Available in microform: Yes
Subscription price: $20.00/yr. individuals (includes membership); $10.00/yr. students (includes membership)
Year to which price refers: 1992
Subscription address: Frank Ainsley, Secretary-Treasurer, Pioneer America Soc., Dept. of Earth Science, Univ. of North Carolina, Wilmington, NC

ADVERTISING INFORMATION

Advertising accepted: Yes

EDITORIAL DESCRIPTION

Scope: Publishes articles on material culture, cultural history, folklife artifacts, art, and architecture.
Reviews books: Yes
Publishes notes: No
Languages accepted: English
Prints abstracts: No
Author-anonymous submission: Yes

SUBMISSION REQUIREMENTS

Author pays submission fee: No
Author pays page charges: No
Length of articles: 20 pp.

(1779)
*MAWA Review

Burney J. Hollis, Editor
Morgan State Univ.
Baltimore, MD 21239

Telephone: 410 319-3090
Fax: 410 319-3743
First published: 1982
Sponsoring organization: Middle-Atlantic Writers Assn.
ISSN: 0742-9738
MLA acronym: MAWAR

SUBSCRIPTION INFORMATION

Frequency of publication: 2 times/yr. (June, Dec.)
Circulation: 300
Available in microform: No
Subscription price: $10.00/yr. US; $12.50/yr. Canada; $15.00/yr. elsewhere
Year to which price refers: 1992

ADVERTISING INFORMATION

Advertising accepted: Yes
Advertising rates: $75.00/eighth page; $125.00/quarter page; $250.00/half page; $500.00/full page

EDITORIAL DESCRIPTION

Scope: Publishes articles on African, Pan-African, African American, women's, and minority literatures.
Reviews books: Yes
Publishes notes: Yes
Languages accepted: English
Prints abstracts: No
Author-anonymous submission: No

SUBMISSION REQUIREMENTS

Restrictions on contributors: None
Author pays submission fee: No
Author pays page charges: No
Length of articles: 20 pp. maximum
Length of book reviews: 10 pp.
Length of notes: 2 pp.
Style: MLA
Number of copies required: 2
Special requirements: Include a brief biographical sketch with manuscript.
Copyright ownership: Journal
Rejected manuscripts: Returned; enclose SASE.
Time before publication decision: 2 mos.
Number of reviewers: 4
Articles submitted per year: 50
Articles published per year: 20
Book reviews submitted per year: 10
Book reviews published per year: 5
Notes submitted per year: 10
Notes published per year: 4

Length of book reviews: 4 pp.
Number of copies required: 3
Copyright ownership: Pioneer America Soc.
Rejected manuscripts: Returned
Time before publication decision: 3 mos.
Time between decision and publication: 6 mos.
Number of reviewers: 3
Articles submitted per year: 50
Articles published per year: 8
Book reviews submitted per year: 30
Book reviews published per year: 20

(1780)
Mawazo: The Makerere Journal of the Faculties of Arts and Social Sciences

Dan M. Mudoola & Fred Opali, Editors
Makere Univ.
P.O. Box 7062
Kampala, Uganda

First published: 1967
Sponsoring organization: Makerere Univ.
ISSN: 0047-6293
MLA acronym: Mawazo

SUBSCRIPTION INFORMATION

Frequency of publication: 2 times/yr. (June, Dec.)
Circulation: 2,500
Available in microform: No

ADVERTISING INFORMATION

Advertising accepted: Yes

EDITORIAL DESCRIPTION

Scope: Publishes ideas and research findings about Africa and related areas of the world. Subjects range from literature and music to politics and economics. Readers include scholars, students, administrators, and anyone who has an interest in Africa.
Reviews books: Yes
Publishes notes: No
Languages accepted: English
Prints abstracts: No
Author-anonymous submission: Yes

SUBMISSION REQUIREMENTS

Restrictions on contributors: None
Author pays submission fee: No
Author pays page charges: No
Length of articles: 5,000 words maximum
Style: MLA; Chicago
Number of copies required: 2
Special requirements: Include an introduction and a summary or conclusion.
Copyright ownership: Editorial Board
Rejected manuscripts: Not returned
Time before publication decision: 3-12 mos.
Time between decision and publication: 6 mos.
Number of reviewers: 2
Articles published per year: 12-16

(1781)
The Maynooth Review/Reiviú Mhá Nuad: A Journal of the Arts

Martin Pulbrook, Editor
St. Patrick's College
Maynooth
Co. Kildare, Ireland

First published: 1975
ISSN: 0332-4869
MLA acronym: MayR

SUBSCRIPTION INFORMATION

Frequency of publication: 2 times/yr.
Available in microform: No

ADVERTISING INFORMATION

Advertising accepted: No

EDITORIAL DESCRIPTION

Scope: The journal is devoted to the study of literature and the arts. At least one article in each issue is in Irish Gaelic.
Reviews books: No
Languages accepted: English; Irish Gaelic
Prints abstracts: No

SUBMISSION REQUIREMENTS

Restrictions on contributors: None
Author pays submission fee: No
Author pays page charges: No
Style: A. P. Herbert
Number of copies required: 1
Copyright ownership: Journal
Rejected manuscripts: Returned
Time before publication decision: 3-8 mos.
Time between decision and publication: 2 mos.
Articles published per year: 10-12

(1782)
*McGill Working Papers in Linguistics/Cahiers Linguistiques de McGill

Ben Shaer & John Matthews, Editors
Dept. of Linguistics
McGill Univ.
1001 Sherbrooke St. W.
Montreal, Quebec H3A 1G5, Canada

Telephone: 514 398-4222
Fax: 514 398-7088
First published: 1983
Sponsoring organization: Dept. of Linguistics, McGill Univ.
ISSN: 0824-5282
MLA acronym: McWPL

SUBSCRIPTION INFORMATION

Frequency of publication: 2 times/yr. (Winter, Spring)
Circulation: 75
Available in microform: No
Subscription price: $22.00/yr.
Year to which price refers: 1992

ADVERTISING INFORMATION

Advertising accepted: No

EDITORIAL DESCRIPTION

Scope: Publishes articles on current work in linguistics.
Reviews books: No
Publishes notes: No
Languages accepted: English; French
Prints abstracts: Yes
Author-anonymous submission: No

SUBMISSION REQUIREMENTS

Author pays submission fee: No
Author pays page charges: No
Length of articles: 15,000 words
Number of copies required: 2
Copyright ownership: Author
Rejected manuscripts: Returned
Time before publication decision: 6 mos.
Time between decision and publication: 3 mos.
Number of reviewers: 2
Articles submitted per year: 20
Articles published per year: 15

(1783)
*McNeese Review

Benjamin C. Harlow, Editor
McNeese State Univ.
Box 92940
Lake Charles, LA 70609-2940

Telephone: 318 475-5593
Fax: 318 475-5189
First published: 1948
Sponsoring organization: McNeese State Univ.
ISSN: 0885-467X
MLA acronym: McNR

SUBSCRIPTION INFORMATION

Frequency of publication: Annual
Circulation: 300
Available in microform: No
Subscription price: $5.00/yr.
Year to which price refers: 1992

ADVERTISING INFORMATION

Advertising accepted: No

EDITORIAL DESCRIPTION

Scope: Invites all contributions of a scholarly nature in the area of the humanities. Gives consideration to work pertaining to other academic disciplines. Does not publish creative writing.
Reviews books: No
Publishes notes: No
Languages accepted: English
Prints abstracts: No
Author-anonymous submission: No

SUBMISSION REQUIREMENTS

Restrictions on contributors: None
Author pays submission fee: No
Author pays page charges: No
Length of articles: 10-20 typescript pp.
Style: MLA
Number of copies required: 2
Special requirements: Include footnotes at end of manuscript. Avoid Latin reference tags.
Copyright ownership: Journal
Rejected manuscripts: Returned
Time before publication decision: 4 mos.
Time between decision and publication: 4 mos.
Number of reviewers: 3
Articles submitted per year: 20
Articles published per year: 8

(1784)
*Meanjin

Jenny Lee, Editor
Univ. of Melbourne
Parkville, Victoria 3052, Australia

First published: 1940
Sponsoring organization: Univ. of Melbourne
ISSN: 0025-6293
MLA acronym: Meanjin

SUBSCRIPTION INFORMATION

Frequency of publication: 4 times/yr.
Circulation: 4,000
Available in microform: Yes
Subscription price: A$28.00/yr. Australia; A$32.00/yr. elsewhere
Year to which price refers: 1992

ADVERTISING INFORMATION

Advertising accepted: Yes

EDITORIAL DESCRIPTION

Scope: Publishes reviews and articles on Australian literature, history, and culture plus some articles on non-Australian literature and culture. Includes fiction and poetry.
Reviews books: Yes
Publishes notes: No
Languages accepted: English
Prints abstracts: No
Author-anonymous submission: No

SUBMISSION REQUIREMENTS

Restrictions on contributors: Preference is given to Australian contributors; others are generally commissioned; book reviews are always commissioned.
Author pays submission fee: No
Author pays page charges: No
Length of articles: 4,000-5,000 words maximum

Length of book reviews: 1,500 words
Style: Journal
Number of copies required: 1
Copyright ownership: Author
Rejected manuscripts: Returned; enclose return postage or international reply coupons.
Time before publication decision: 2 mos.
Time between decision and publication: 3 mos.
Number of reviewers: 2
Articles submitted per year: 1,000
Articles published per year: 60
Book reviews submitted per year: 100
Book reviews published per year: 20

(1785)
*Meddelelser

Kjetil Ra Hauge, Ole Michael Selberg, Audun Mörch, & Ellen Haavaldsen, Editors
Univ. i Oslo
Slavisk-Baltisk Inst.
Postboks 1030 Blindern
0315 Oslo, Norway

Telephone: (47) 2 856797
Fax: (47) 2 854310
E-mail: Kjetilrh@hedda.uio.no
First published: 1972
Sponsoring organization: Univ. of Oslo, Inst. of Slavic & Baltic Studies
MLA acronym: Meddelelser

SUBSCRIPTION INFORMATION

Frequency of publication: Irregular
Circulation: 300
Available in microform: No

ADVERTISING INFORMATION

Advertising accepted: No

EDITORIAL DESCRIPTION

Scope: Publishes studies and bibliographies on Slavic and Baltic literatures, linguistics, and history.
Reviews books: No
Publishes notes: No
Languages accepted: Norwegian; Russian; English; German; French
Prints abstracts: No
Author-anonymous submission: No

SUBMISSION REQUIREMENTS

Restrictions on contributors: None
Author pays submission fee: No
Author pays page charges: No
Length of books: 20-100 pp. including notes
Style: None
Number of copies required: 1
Special requirements: Submit typescript.
Copyright ownership: Author
Rejected manuscripts: Returned
Time before publication decision: 2 mos.
Time between decision and publication: 2 mos.
Number of reviewers: 4
Books published per year: 1-6

(1786)
Mededelingen der Koninklijke Nederlandse Akademie van Wetenschappen, Afdeling Letterkunde, Nieuwe Reeks

F. C. Bos, Editor
Editorial Dept.
Koninklijke Nederlandse Akademie van Wetenschappen
P.O. Box 19121
1000 GC Amsterdam, Netherlands

First published: 1937

Sponsoring organization: Koninklijke Nederlandse Akademie van Wetenschappen, Amsterdam
MLA acronym: MKNAL

SUBSCRIPTION INFORMATION

Frequency of publication: Annual
Circulation: 750-1,500
Available in microform: No
Subscription address: KOK International Books, Oude Hoogstraat 14-18, 1012 CE Amsterdam, Netherlands

ADVERTISING INFORMATION

Advertising accepted: No

EDITORIAL DESCRIPTION

Scope: Publishes texts of lectures given at the monthly meetings of the Arts Division of Koninklijke Nederlandse Akademie van Wetenschappen. Topics include linguistics, philology, humanities, law, and arts.
Reviews books: Yes
Publishes notes: Yes
Languages accepted: Dutch; English; German; French
Prints abstracts: No

SUBMISSION REQUIREMENTS

Restrictions on contributors: Contributors must be members of the sponsoring organization, or manuscript must be submitted through a member.
Author pays submission fee: No
Author pays page charges: No
Length of articles: 32 pp. maximum
Style: None
Number of copies required: 1
Copyright ownership: Koninklijke Nederlandse Akademie van Wetenschappen
Time before publication decision: 1 mo.
Time between decision and publication: 3 mos.
Number of reviewers: 2
Articles submitted per year: 8
Articles published per year: 5-12

(1787)
Mededelingen van de Nijmeegse Centrale voor Dialect- en Naamkunde

A. Weijnen & A. Hagen, Editors
Katholieke Univ. Nijmegen
Erasmuslaan 40
Nijmegen, Netherlands

First published: 1961
Sponsoring organization: Katholieke Univ. Nijmegen
ISSN: 0546-1537
MLA acronym: MNCDN

SUBSCRIPTION INFORMATION

Frequency of publication: Annual
Circulation: 700

EDITORIAL DESCRIPTION

Scope: Includes scientific articles on dialectology, sociolinguistics, and onomastics. Also publishes a chronicle of the Institute.
Reviews books: Yes
Languages accepted: Dutch
Prints abstracts: Yes

SUBMISSION REQUIREMENTS

Restrictions on contributors: Contributors must be staff members of Katholieke Univ. Nijmegen, or be invited to contribute.
Length of articles: 4,000-10,000 words
Style: None
Number of copies required: 1
Copyright ownership: Author

Rejected manuscripts: Returned
Time before publication decision: 1 mo.
Time between decision and publication: 6 mos. maximum
Number of reviewers: 2
Articles published per year: 6-8

(1788)
Mediaeval Scandinavia

Hans Bekker-Nielsen, Managing Editor
Odense Univ.
Campusvej 55
5230 Odense M, Denmark

First published: 1968
Sponsoring organization: Danish Research Council for the Humanities
ISSN: 0076-5864
MLA acronym: *MScan*

SUBSCRIPTION INFORMATION

Frequency of publication: Annual
Circulation: 1,000
Available in microform: No
Subscription address: Odense Univ. Press, Campusveg 55, 5230 Odense M, Denmark

ADVERTISING INFORMATION

Advertising accepted: No

EDITORIAL DESCRIPTION

Scope: Devoted to the study of Mediaeval civilization in Scandinavia and Iceland.
Reviews books: Yes
Publishes notes: No
Languages accepted: English; German; French
Prints abstracts: No
Author-anonymous submission: No

SUBMISSION REQUIREMENTS

Restrictions on contributors: Book reviews are solicited.
Author pays submission fee: No
Author pays page charges: No
Length of articles: 20 pp. maximum
Length of book reviews: 2,000 words
Style: MLA
Number of copies required: 1
Copyright ownership: Odense Univ. Press
Rejected manuscripts: Returned
Time before publication decision: 1-12 mos.
Time between decision and publication: 6-24 mos.
Number of reviewers: 1-5
Articles submitted per year: 30
Articles published per year: 10
Book reviews published per year: 20

(1789)
Mediaeval Studies

Edward D. English, Editor
Pontifical Inst. of Mediaeval Studies
59 Queen's Park Crescent E.
Toronto, Ontario M5S 2C4, Canada

First published: 1939
Sponsoring organization: Pontifical Inst. of Mediaeval Studies
ISSN: 0076-5872
MLA acronym: *MS*

SUBSCRIPTION INFORMATION

Frequency of publication: Annual
Circulation: 1,400
Available in microform: No
Subscription address: Ron B. Thomson, at the above address

ADVERTISING INFORMATION

Advertising accepted: No

EDITORIAL DESCRIPTION

Scope: Publishes research on the Middle Ages, including that which deals with hitherto unedited manuscripts and/or archival material.
Reviews books: No
Publishes notes: Yes
Languages accepted: English; French; German; Italian; Catalan; Spanish; Latin; Greek
Prints abstracts: No
Author-anonymous submission: Yes

SUBMISSION REQUIREMENTS

Restrictions on contributors: None
Author pays submission fee: No
Author pays page charges: No
Length of articles: 100 pp. maximum
Length of notes: No restrictions
Style: Chicago; journal
Number of copies required: 2
Special requirements: Submit typescript and microfilm or xerox reproduction of medieval manuscripts being edited.
Copyright ownership: Assigned by author to journal
Rejected manuscripts: Returned
Time before publication decision: 4-5 mos.
Time between decision and publication: 18 mos.
Number of reviewers: 2
Articles submitted per year: 90
Articles published per year: 13
Notes published per year: 3

(1790)
*Mediaevalia: A Journal of Mediaeval Studies

Paul E. Szarmach, Editor
Center for Medieval & Early Renaissance Studies
State Univ. of New York
P.O. Box 6000
Binghamton, NY 13902-6000

Telephone: 607 777-2730
Fax: 607 777-4000
E-mail: PSZARMAC@BINGVAXA.BITNET
First published: 1975
Sponsoring organization: State Univ. of New York, Binghamton, Center for Medieval & Early Renaissance Studies
ISSN: 0361-946X
MLA acronym: *Mediaevalia*

SUBSCRIPTION INFORMATION

Frequency of publication: Annual
Circulation: 400
Available in microform: No
Subscription price: $25.00/yr.
Year to which price refers: 1992
Subscription address: State Univ. of New York Press, c/o CUP Services, P.O. Box 6526, Ithaca, NY 14850

ADVERTISING INFORMATION

Advertising accepted: Yes, on an exchange basis

EDITORIAL DESCRIPTION

Scope: Publishes interdisciplinary articles on the Middle Ages, as well as articles on history, literature, art history, and philosophy that, though not strictly interdisciplinary in themselves, may lead to interdisciplinary applications.
Reviews books: Yes
Publishes notes: No
Languages accepted: English
Prints abstracts: No
Author-anonymous submission: Yes

SUBMISSION REQUIREMENTS

Restrictions on contributors: Book reviews are by invitation only.
Author pays submission fee: No
Author pays page charges: Yes
Length of articles: 25 pp. maximum
Style: MLA (2nd ed.)
Number of copies required: 2
Copyright ownership: Center for Medieval & Early Renaissance Studies
Rejected manuscripts: Returned; enclose return postage.
Time before publication decision: 3 mos.
Time between decision and publication: 1 yr.
Number of reviewers: 2
Articles submitted per year: 40
Articles published per year: 10-12

(1791)
*Medien in Forschung + Unterricht: Series A

Dieter Baacke, Wolfgang Gast, & Erich Strasser, Editors
Max Niemeyer Verlag
Postfach 2140
7400 Tübingen, Germany

Telephone: (49) 7071 81104
Fax: (49) 7071 87419
First published: 1980
ISSN: 0174-4399
MLA acronym: Medien

SUBSCRIPTION INFORMATION

Frequency of publication: Irregular
Available in microform: No

ADVERTISING INFORMATION

Advertising accepted: No

EDITORIAL DESCRIPTION

Scope: Publishes monograph studies about literature and media.
Reviews books: No
Publishes notes: No
Languages accepted: German
Prints abstracts: No
Author-anonymous submission: Yes

SUBMISSION REQUIREMENTS

Restrictions on contributors: None
Author pays submission fee: No
Author pays page charges: No
Length of books: 150-250 pp.
Style: Series
Number of copies required: 1
Copyright ownership: Max Niemeyer Verlag
Rejected manuscripts: Returned
Time before publication decision: 3-6 mos.
Time between decision and publication: 6 mos.
Number of reviewers: 1-2
Books submitted per year: 2-3
Books published per year: 1-2

(1792)
Medieval & Renaissance Drama in England: An Annual Gathering of Research, Criticism and Reviews

J. Leeds Barroll, Editor
c/o James S. Shapiro
English Dept.
Columbia Univ.
New York, NY 10027

First published: 1984
ISSN: 0731-3403
MLA acronym: *MRDE*

SUBSCRIPTION INFORMATION

Frequency of publication: Annual
Available in microform: No
Subscription address: AMS Press, 56 E. 13th St., New York, NY 10003

ADVERTISING INFORMATION

Advertising accepted: No

EDITORIAL DESCRIPTION

Scope: Publishes articles on drama in England through 1640, exclusive of Shakespeare.
Reviews books: Yes
Publishes notes: No
Languages accepted: English
Prints abstracts: No
Author-anonymous submission: No

SUBMISSION REQUIREMENTS

Restrictions on contributors: Book reviews are commissioned.
Author pays submission fee: No
Author pays page charges: No
Length of articles: No restrictions
Length of book reviews: No restrictions
Style: MLA
Number of copies required: 2
Copyright ownership: AMS Press
Rejected manuscripts: Returned
Time before publication decision: 1 yr.
Time between decision and publication: 3 mos.
Number of reviewers: 2-3
Articles submitted per year: 70
Articles published per year: 14
Book reviews published per year: 15-20

(1793)
Medieval and Renaissance Monograph Series

Guy R. Mermier, Editor
Dept. of Romance Languages & Literatures
4206 MLB
Univ. of Michigan
Ann Arbor, MI 48109

First published: 1981
Sponsoring organization: Medieval & Renaissance Collegium
ISSN: 0892-9718
MLA acronym: MRMS

SUBSCRIPTION INFORMATION

Frequency of publication: Irregular
Available in microform: No
Subscription address: Marc Publishing Co., 2211 Vinewood Blvd., Ann Arbor, MI 48104

ADVERTISING INFORMATION

Advertising accepted: Yes

EDITORIAL DESCRIPTION

Scope: The series publishes monographs in various fields of research devoted to the Middle Ages and the Renaissance.
Reviews books: Yes
Publishes notes: Yes
Languages accepted: French; German; Spanish; English; Italian
Prints abstracts: No
Author-anonymous submission: Yes

SUBMISSION REQUIREMENTS

Author pays submission fee: No
Author pays page charges: Yes
Length of books: No restrictions
Length of book reviews: No restrictions
Length of notes: No restrictions
Style: MLA
Number of copies required: 2

Special requirements: Authors should request format information from editor.
Copyright ownership: Author
Rejected manuscripts: Returned
Time before publication decision: 3 mos.
Time between decision and publication: 3-6 mos.
Number of reviewers: 3
Books submitted per year: 3
Books published per year: 1

(1794)
*Medieval & Renaissance Texts & Studies

Mario A. Di Cesare, Editor
LN G99
State Univ. of New York
P.O. Box 6000
Binghamton, NY 13902-6000

Telephone: 607 777-6758
First published: 1981
Sponsoring organization: Center for Medieval & Early Renaissance Studies, State Univ. of New York, Binghamton
MLA acronym: MRTS

SUBSCRIPTION INFORMATION

Frequency of publication: Irregular
Available in microform: No

ADVERTISING INFORMATION

Advertising accepted: No

EDITORIAL DESCRIPTION

Scope: The series emphasizes texts, translations, scholarly tools, and reference works (e.g., bibliographies, manuscript catalogues) in all areas of the Middle Ages and the Renaissance.
Reviews books: No
Publishes notes: No
Languages accepted: English; French; German; Italian; Spanish; Greek; Latin
Prints abstracts: No
Author-anonymous submission: No

SUBMISSION REQUIREMENTS

Author pays submission fee: No
Author pays page charges: No
Length of books: 150 typescript pp. minimum
Style: Chicago
Number of copies required: 2
Special requirements: Books on tape or diskette are welcome.
Copyright ownership: Center for Medieval & Early Renaissance Studies, State Univ. of New York, Binghamton
Rejected manuscripts: Returned; enclose return postage.
Time before publication decision: 6 mos.
Time between decision and publication: 1 yr.
Number of reviewers: 2-4
Books submitted per year: 60-70
Books published per year: 8-10

(1795)
Medieval English Theatre

Meg Twycross, Peter Meredith, & Sarah Carpenter, Editors
English Dept.
Univ. of Lancaster
Lancaster LA1 4YT, England

First published: 1979
ISSN: 0143-3784
MLA acronym: METh

SUBSCRIPTION INFORMATION

Frequency of publication: 2 times/yr.

Circulation: 320
Available in microform: No

ADVERTISING INFORMATION

Advertising accepted: No

EDITORIAL DESCRIPTION

Scope: Publishes articles on the study of medieval theater in all its aspects from circa 980 to circa 1580. Its main focus is English and Scottish theater, but comparative articles on European theater are included, and modern survivals and parallels documented. Also publishes critical reviews of productions, and acts as a newsletter.
Reviews books: No
Publishes notes: No
Languages accepted: English; French
Prints abstracts: No
Author-anonymous submission: No

SUBMISSION REQUIREMENTS

Restrictions on contributors: Play reviews are commissioned.
Author pays submission fee: No
Author pays page charges: No
Style: Request from editor.
Number of copies required: 1
Special requirements: All photographic material must be paid for by author and evidence of world copyright clearance must be supplied.
Copyright ownership: Journal
Rejected manuscripts: Not returned
Time before publication decision: 6 weeks
Time between decision and publication: 6-12 mos.
Number of reviewers: 2-3
Articles submitted per year: 15
Articles published per year: 9

(1796)
Medieval English Theatre Modern-Spelling Texts

Meg Twycross & Peter Meredith, Editors
Centre for Medieval Studies
Univ. of Lancaster
Lancaster LA1 4YT, England

First published: 1983
ISSN: 0264-2786
MLA acronym: METhMST

SUBSCRIPTION INFORMATION

Frequency of publication: Irregular
Available in microform: No

EDITORIAL DESCRIPTION

Scope: Aims to provide individual texts of medieval and Tutor plays in modern spelling, with brief introductions and marginal glosses.
Languages accepted: English
Author-anonymous submission: No

SUBMISSION REQUIREMENTS

Length of books: 22-160 pp.
Style: Request from editor.
Number of copies required: 1
Copyright ownership: Author & series
Rejected manuscripts: Not returned

(1797)
*Medieval Perspectives

Edith Whitehurst Williams & Ordelle G. Hill, Editors
Box 22-A
Coates Bldg.
Eastern Kentucky Univ.
Richmond, KY 40475-3101

Telephone: 606 623-8494
First published: 1986
Sponsoring organization: Southeastern Medieval Assn.
MLA acronym: MedPers

SUBSCRIPTION INFORMATION

Frequency of publication: Annual
Circulation: 250
Available in microform: No
Subscription price: $7.00/yr. members; $10.00/yr. nonmembers
Year to which price refers: 1991

ADVERTISING INFORMATION

Advertising accepted: No

EDITORIAL DESCRIPTION

Scope: Publishes articles on medieval studies including literature and art, selected from papers presented at the annual conference of the Southeastern Medieval Association.
Reviews books: No
Publishes notes: No
Languages accepted: English
Prints abstracts: No
Author-anonymous submission: Yes

SUBMISSION REQUIREMENTS

Restrictions on contributors: Contributors must have presented the paper at the annual conference of the Southeastern Medieval Assn.
Author pays submission fee: No
Author pays page charges: No
Length of articles: 2,500-3,000 words
Style: MLA
Number of copies required: 2
Copyright ownership: Southeastern Medieval Assn.
Rejected manuscripts: Returned
Time before publication decision: 3 mos.
Time between decision and publication: 6 mos.
Number of reviewers: 4
Articles submitted per year: 35
Articles published per year: 15-20

(1798)
Médiévales: Langue, Textes, Histoire

Odile Redon, Director
Presses Universitaires de Vincennes
Univ. de Paris VIII
2, rue de la Liberté
93526 Saint-Denis Cedex 02, France

Telephone: (33) 1 49406750
Fax: (33) 1 48210446
First published: 1982
Sponsoring organization: Centre National des Lettres
ISSN: 0751-2708
MLA acronym: Médiévales

SUBSCRIPTION INFORMATION

Frequency of publication: 2 times/yr. (Spring, Autumn)
Available in microform: No
Subscription price: 116 F/yr., 222 F/2 yrs.
Year to which price refers: 1992

ADVERTISING INFORMATION

Advertising accepted: Yes, on an exchange basis

EDITORIAL DESCRIPTION

Scope: Publishes articles on medieval history and literature. Each issue is thematic and focuses on one aspect of the Middle Ages.
Reviews books: Yes
Publishes notes: No
Languages accepted: French
Prints abstracts: No
Author-anonymous submission: No

SUBMISSION REQUIREMENTS

Author pays submission fee: No
Author pays page charges: No
Length of articles: 10 pp.
Number of copies required: 1
Special requirements: Submit on diskette, accompanied by typescript, if possible.
Copyright ownership: Editor
Time before publication decision: 1 yr.
Number of reviewers: 6 minimum
Articles published per year: 20-30

(1799)
*Medievalia et Humanistica: Studies in Medieval and Renaissance Culture

Paul Maurice Clogan, Editor
P.O. Box 13348
North Texas Station
Denton, TX 76203

Telephone: 817 565-2050
Fax: 817 565-4919
First published: 1943
Sponsoring organization: MLA, Division on Comparative Studies in Medieval Literature
ISSN: 0076-6127
MLA acronym: M&H

SUBSCRIPTION INFORMATION

Frequency of publication: Annual
Circulation: 2,000
Available in microform: Yes
Subscription price: $38.50/yr.
Year to which price refers: 1991
Subscription address: Rowman & Littlefield Publishers, Inc., 8705 Bollman Place, Savage, MD 20763

ADVERTISING INFORMATION

Advertising accepted: No

EDITORIAL DESCRIPTION

Scope: Publishes articles in all areas of medieval and Renaissance culture. Articles should: (1) make a marked contribution to knowledge or understanding; or (2) employ an interdisciplinary approach of importance to the understanding of the subject; or (3) treat a broad theme or topic; or (4) discuss new directions in humanistic scholarship; or (5) review major areas of current concern within particular fields.
Reviews books: Yes
Publishes notes: No
Languages accepted: English
Prints abstracts: No
Author-anonymous submission: Yes

SUBMISSION REQUIREMENTS

Restrictions on contributors: None
Author pays submission fee: No
Author pays page charges: No
Length of articles: 2,500-9,000 words
Style: Chicago
Number of copies required: 4
Special requirements: Submit original typescript and 3 copies, and a 200-word abstract.
Copyright ownership: Assigned by author to series
Rejected manuscripts: Returned; enclose SASE.
Time before publication decision: 3 mos.
Time between decision and publication: 9-12 mos.
Number of reviewers: 3
Articles published per year: 15
Book reviews published per year: 30

(1800)
Medioevo Romanzo

Alberto Várvaro, D'Arco Silvio Avalle, Francesco Branciforti, Gianfranco Folena, Francesco Sabatini, & Cesare Segre, Editors
Via Porta di Massa, 1
80133 Naples, Italy

First published: 1974
ISSN: 0390-0711
MLA acronym: MedR

SUBSCRIPTION INFORMATION

Frequency of publication: 3 times/yr. (Mar., July, Nov.)
Available in microform: No
Subscription address: Società Editrice Il Mulino, Strada Maggiore 37, 40125 Bologna, Italy

ADVERTISING INFORMATION

Advertising accepted: Yes

EDITORIAL DESCRIPTION

Scope: Publishes articles on medieval Romance languages and literatures.
Reviews books: Yes
Publishes notes: Yes
Languages accepted: English; French; German; Italian; Portuguese; Romanian; Spanish; Catalan
Prints abstracts: No
Author-anonymous submission: No

SUBMISSION REQUIREMENTS

Restrictions on contributors: None
Author pays submission fee: No
Author pays page charges: No
Style: Journal
Number of copies required: 1
Copyright ownership: Author; upon request from editorial board
Rejected manuscripts: Not returned
Time before publication decision: 6-12 mos.
Time between decision and publication: 2-12 mos.
Number of reviewers: 2
Articles submitted per year: 25-50
Articles published per year: 1
Book reviews published per year: 45

(1801)
*Mediterranean Language Review

Alexander Borg & Paul Wexler, Editors
Dept. of Linguistics
Tel-Aviv Univ.
Ramat Aviv
Tel-Aviv 69978, Israel

First published: 1983
Sponsoring organization: Faculty of Humanities, Tel-Aviv Univ.
ISSN: 0724-7567
MLA acronym: MedLR

SUBSCRIPTION INFORMATION

Frequency of publication: Irregular
Circulation: 350
Available in microform: No

Subscription address: Verlag Otto Harrassowitz, Taunusstr. 14, Postfach 2929, 6200 Weisbaden 1, Germany

ADVERTISING INFORMATION

Advertising accepted: Yes, on an exchange basis

EDITORIAL DESCRIPTION

Scope: Publishes articles about past and present languages spoken around the Mediterranean including linguistic interaction; documentation of lesser known Mediterranean languages; maritime linguistics; hieratic languages; and aspects of ethnic, political, and sociocultural history.
Reviews books: Yes
Publishes notes: Yes
Languages accepted: English; French; German; Spanish; Italian
Prints abstracts: Yes
Author-anonymous submission: No

SUBMISSION REQUIREMENTS

Restrictions on contributors: None
Author pays submission fee: No
Author pays page charges: No
Length of articles: 15,000 words maximum
Length of book reviews: 1,500 words maximum
Length of notes: 1,000 words maximum
Style: Language
Number of copies required: 2
Copyright ownership: Journal
Rejected manuscripts: Not returned
Time before publication decision: 3 weeks
Time between decision and publication: 1 yr.
Number of reviewers: 2
Articles published per year: 8
Book reviews submitted per year: 8
Book reviews published per year: 10-15

(1802)
*Medium Ævum

Helen Cooper, Elspeth Kennedy, & Nigel Palmer, Editors
University College
Oxford OX1 4BH, England

Telephone: (44) 865 276633
Fax: (44) 865 276675
First published: 1932
Sponsoring organization: Soc. for the Study of Mediaeval Languages & Literature
ISSN: 0025-8385
MLA acronym: MÆ

SUBSCRIPTION INFORMATION

Frequency of publication: 2 times/yr.
Circulation: 1,100
Available in microform: Yes
Subscription price: $45.00/yr.
Year to which price refers: 1991
Subscription address: D. G. Pattison, Magdalen College, Oxford OX1 4AU, England

ADVERTISING INFORMATION

Advertising accepted: Yes

EDITORIAL DESCRIPTION

Scope: Publishes articles on Medieval languages and literature.
Reviews books: Yes
Publishes notes: Yes
Languages accepted: English; French; German; Latin; Italian; Spanish
Prints abstracts: No
Author-anonymous submission: No

SUBMISSION REQUIREMENTS

Restrictions on contributors: None
Author pays submission fee: No

Author pays page charges: No
Length of articles: 12 printed pp.
Length of book reviews: 400 words
Length of notes: 4-5 pp.
Style: Modern Humanities Research Assn.
Number of copies required: 2
Copyright ownership: Author & Soc. for the Study of Mediaeval Languages & Literature
Rejected manuscripts: Returned; enclose international reply coupons or SASE.
Time before publication decision: 3 mos.
Time between decision and publication: 18 mos.
Number of reviewers: 3
Articles published per year: 10-15
Book reviews published per year: 80
Notes published per year: 10-15

(1803)
*Meerut Journal of Comparative Literature and Language

T. R. Sharma, Editor
Dept. of English
Meerut Univ.
Meerut 250 005, India

First published: 1988
Sponsoring organization: Dept. of English, Meerut Univ.
MLA acronym: MJCL&L

SUBSCRIPTION INFORMATION

Frequency of publication: 2 times/yr. (Mar., Oct.)
Circulation: 300
Available in microform: No
Subscription price: $10.00/yr.
Year to which price refers: 1992
Subscription address: Shalabh Prakashan, 7/1055/3, Shastri Nagar, Meerut 250 005, India

ADVERTISING INFORMATION

Advertising accepted: No

EDITORIAL DESCRIPTION

Scope: Publishes articles on English literature and language in comparison with other literatures and languages.
Reviews books: Yes
Publishes notes: No
Languages accepted: English
Prints abstracts: No
Author-anonymous submission: No

SUBMISSION REQUIREMENTS

Restrictions on contributors: None
Author pays submission fee: No
Author pays page charges: No
Length of articles: 4,000-5,000 words
Length of book reviews: 1,000 words
Style: MLA
Number of copies required: 2
Copyright ownership: Editor
Rejected manuscripts: Returned; enclose SASE.
Time before publication decision: 1 mo.
Time between decision and publication: 2 mos.
Number of reviewers: 6
Articles submitted per year: 20
Articles published per year: 10
Book reviews submitted per year: 12
Book reviews published per year: 6

(1804)
Meijerbergs Arkiv för Svensk Ordforskning

Bo Ralph, Editor
Meijerbergs Inst. för Svensk Etymologisk Forskning
Inst. för Nordiska Språk
412 98 Göteborg, Sweden

First published: 1937
Sponsoring organization: Meijerbergs Inst. för Svensk Etymologisk Forskning
ISSN: 0348-7741
MLA acronym: MASO

SUBSCRIPTION INFORMATION

Frequency of publication: Once every 2 yrs.
Available in microform: No

ADVERTISING INFORMATION

Advertising accepted: No

EDITORIAL DESCRIPTION

Scope: Publishes articles on Swedish etymological research as well as articles on Germanic word research.
Reviews books: No
Languages accepted: English; Swedish; German; French; Danish; Norwegian
Prints abstracts: No

SUBMISSION REQUIREMENTS

Author pays submission fee: No
Author pays page charges: No
Length of articles: 4,000-30,000 words
Number of copies required: 1
Copyright ownership: Author
Rejected manuscripts: Returned
Time before publication decision: 1 mo.
Time between decision and publication: 1 yr.
Number of reviewers: 1
Articles submitted per year: 2
Articles published per year: 2

(1805)
Mélanges de Science Religieuse

Jacques Liébaert, Editor
60, boulevard Vauban
59016 Lille Cedex, France

First published: 1944
Sponsoring organization: Facultés Catholiques de Lille
ISSN: 0025-8911
MLA acronym: MSR

SUBSCRIPTION INFORMATION

Frequency of publication: 4 times/yr. (Mar., June, Sept., Dec.)
Circulation: 500
Available in microform: No

ADVERTISING INFORMATION

Advertising accepted: No

EDITORIAL DESCRIPTION

Scope: Deals with all questions having to do with the domain of religious knowledge: theology and related sciences, but also philosophy, history of religions, history of institutions and of law, anthropology, and religious literature.
Reviews books: Yes
Publishes notes: Yes
Languages accepted: French; English
Prints abstracts: Yes

SUBMISSION REQUIREMENTS

Restrictions on contributors: None

Author pays submission fee: No
Author pays page charges: No
Length of articles: 25-30 typescript pp.
Length of book reviews: 500-700 words
Length of notes: 2,000-3,000 words
Number of copies required: 1
Special requirements: Submit original typescript.
Copyright ownership: Journal
Rejected manuscripts: Returned
Time before publication decision: 3 mos.
Time between decision and publication: 6-12 mos.
Number of reviewers: 3
Articles submitted per year: 15-20
Articles published per year: 12
Book reviews submitted per year: 30
Book reviews published per year: 25
Notes submitted per year: 5
Notes published per year: 3

(1806)
*MELUS: The Journal of the Society for the Study of the Multi-Ethnic Literature of the United States

Joseph T. Skerrett, Jr., Editor
272 Bartlett Hall
Univ. of Massachusetts
Amherst, MA 01003

Telephone: 413 545-3166
Fax: 413 545-3880
First published: 1974
Sponsoring organization: Soc. for the Study of the Multi-Ethnic Literature of the United States
ISSN: 0163-755X
MLA acronym: MELUS

SUBSCRIPTION INFORMATION

Frequency of publication: 4 times/yr.
Circulation: 900
Available in microform: No
Subscription price: $40.00/yr. institutions US; $48.00/yr. institutions elsewhere; $35.00/yr. individuals US; $40.00/yr. individuals elsewhere
Year to which price refers: 1992

ADVERTISING INFORMATION

Advertising accepted: Yes
Advertising rates: $100.00/half page; $175.00/full page

EDITORIAL DESCRIPTION

Scope: Welcomes all news of meetings and other activities in the general area of ethnicity. Articles and book reviews may deal specifically with ethnic literature (*belles-lettres*, autobiographies, biographies of writers, critical studies) or with ethnicity in music, television and film.
Reviews books: Yes
Publishes notes: Yes
Languages accepted: English
Prints abstracts: No
Author-anonymous submission: Yes

SUBMISSION REQUIREMENTS

Restrictions on contributors: Contributors must be members of the Soc. for the Study of Multi-Ethnic Literature of the United States. Most book reviews are commissioned.
Author pays submission fee: No
Author pays page charges: No
Length of articles: 15-25 double-spaced typescript pp.
Length of book reviews: 1,000-1,200 words
Length of notes: 8-12 double-spaced typescript pp.
Style: MLA
Number of copies required: 3
Special requirements: Include name on title page only.

Copyright ownership: Journal
Rejected manuscripts: Returned; enclose return postage.
Time before publication decision: 3 mos.
Time between decision and publication: 12-18 mos.
Number of reviewers: 3
Articles submitted per year: 125
Articles published per year: 40
Book reviews submitted per year: 20
Book reviews published per year: 16
Notes submitted per year: 10
Notes published per year: 5-6

(1807)
*Melville Society Extracts

John Bryant, Editor
Dept. of English
Hofstra Univ.
Hempstead, NY 11550

Telephone: 516 463-5454
First published: 1969
Sponsoring organization: Melville Soc. of America
ISSN: 0193-8991
MLA acronym: MSEx

SUBSCRIPTION INFORMATION

Frequency of publication: 4 times/yr.
Circulation: 750
Available in microform: No
Subscription price: $10.00/yr. institutions; $7.00/yr. individuals US; $8.00/yr. individuals elsewhere
Year to which price refers: 1992
Subscription address: John Wenke, Dept. of English, Salisbury State Univ., Salisbury, MD 21801
Subscription telephone: 301 543-6447

ADVERTISING INFORMATION

Advertising accepted: Yes
Advertising rates: $50.00/insert

EDITORIAL DESCRIPTION

Scope: Publishes articles, notes, and miscellany concerning the life, times, writings, and influence of Herman Melville (1819-1891).
Reviews books: Yes
Publishes notes: Yes
Languages accepted: English
Prints abstracts: No
Author-anonymous submission: Yes

SUBMISSION REQUIREMENTS

Restrictions on contributors: None
Author pays submission fee: No
Author pays page charges: No
Length of articles: 6,000 words
Length of book reviews: 1,000 words
Length of notes: 500-1,000 words
Style: MLA
Number of copies required: 2
Copyright ownership: Author
Rejected manuscripts: Returned
Time before publication decision: 1 yr.
Time between decision and publication: 3 mos.
Number of reviewers: 3
Articles submitted per year: 60
Articles published per year: 10
Book reviews submitted per year: 8
Book reviews published per year: 5
Notes submitted per year: 20
Notes published per year: 8

(1808)
Mémoires de la Société Néophilologique de Helsinki

Soc. Néophilologique
Helsinki Univ.
Hallituskatu 11
00100 Helsinki, Finland

First published: 1893
Sponsoring organization: Soc. Néophilologique de Helsinki
ISSN: 0355-0192
MLA acronym: MSNH

SUBSCRIPTION INFORMATION

Frequency of publication: Irregular
Available in microform: No

ADVERTISING INFORMATION

Advertising accepted: No

EDITORIAL DESCRIPTION

Scope: Publishes monographs promoting philological studies and disseminating information on modern languages including both Germanic and Romance languages.
Reviews books: No
Publishes notes: No
Languages accepted: English; German; French; Italian; Spanish
Prints abstracts: No
Author-anonymous submission: No

SUBMISSION REQUIREMENTS

Restrictions on contributors: Publishes primarily Finnish studies.
Author pays submission fee: No
Author pays page charges: No
Length of books: No restrictions
Style: MLA
Number of copies required: 1
Copyright ownership: Soc. Néophilologique de Helsinki
Rejected manuscripts: Returned
Number of reviewers: 1-3
Books published per year: 1

(1809)
*Memoirs of the American Philosophical Society

Herman H. Goldstine & Carole N. LeFaivre, Editors
104 S. Fifth St.
Philadelphia, PA 19106

Telephone: 215 440-3427
Fax: 215 440-3450
First published: 1935
ISSN: 0065-9738
MLA acronym: MAPS

SUBSCRIPTION INFORMATION

Frequency of publication: 6 times/yr.
Circulation: 300
Available in microform: Yes
Subscription address: Box 40098, Philadelphia, PA 19106

ADVERTISING INFORMATION

Advertising accepted: No

EDITORIAL DESCRIPTION

Scope: Focuses on history, science, and letters.
Reviews books: No
Languages accepted: English
Prints abstracts: No

SUBMISSION REQUIREMENTS

Author pays submission fee: No
Length of books: No restrictions
Style: Chicago
Number of copies required: 2
Copyright ownership: Publisher
Rejected manuscripts: Returned
Time before publication decision: 1 yr.
Time between decision and publication: 3 yrs.
Number of reviewers: 1-2
Books submitted per year: 20
Books published per year: 7

(1810)
Memoirs of the Research Department of the Tōyō Bunko

Kazuo Enoki, Editor
Toyo Bunko (Oriental Library)
2-28-21 Honkomagome
Bunkyo-Ku
Tokyo, Japan

First published: 1926
Sponsoring organization: Japan Ministry of Education
ISSN: 0082-562X
MLA acronym: MRD

SUBSCRIPTION INFORMATION

Frequency of publication: Annual
Circulation: 500
Available in microform: No

ADVERTISING INFORMATION

Advertising accepted: No

EDITORIAL DESCRIPTION

Scope: Publishes articles on Asian history and culture.
Reviews books: Yes
Languages accepted: English
Prints abstracts: No

SUBMISSION REQUIREMENTS

Restrictions on contributors: None
Author pays submission fee: No
Author pays page charges: No
Length of articles: No restrictions
Style: None
Number of copies required: 1
Copyright ownership: Author
Rejected manuscripts: Returned
Time before publication decision: 6 mos.
Time between decision and publication: 6 mos.
Number of reviewers: 3
Articles published per year: 10

(1811)
*Memórias da Academia das Ciências de Lisboa, Classe de Letras

Rua da Academia das Ciências 19
1200 Lisbon, Portugal

Telephone: (351) 1 3463866
First published: 1797
Sponsoring organization: Academia das Ciências de Lisboa
MLA acronym: MACLCL

SUBSCRIPTION INFORMATION

Frequency of publication: Annual
Available in microform: No

ADVERTISING INFORMATION

Advertising accepted: No

EDITORIAL DESCRIPTION

Scope: Publishes articles on literature, linguistics, history, geography, sociology, and politics.
Reviews books: No
Publishes notes: No
Languages accepted: Portuguese; French; English
Prints abstracts: No
Author-anonymous submission: No

SUBMISSION REQUIREMENTS

Restrictions on contributors: Contributors must be associated with Academia das Ciências de Lisboa.
Author pays submission fee: No
Author pays page charges: No
Number of copies required: 1
Copyright ownership: Academia das Ciências de Lisboa
Articles published per year: 10

(1812)
*Memory & Cognition

Margaret Jean Intons-Peterson, Editor
Dept. of Psychology
Indiana Univ.
Bloomington, IN 47405

Telephone: 812 855-2521
Fax: 812 855-4691
E-mail: Intons@psythird.psych.indiana.edu
First published: 1973
Sponsoring organization: Psychonomic Soc.
ISSN: 0090-502X
MLA acronym: M&C

SUBSCRIPTION INFORMATION

Frequency of publication: 6 times/yr.
Circulation: 2,350
Available in microform: Yes
Subscription price: $100.00/yr. institutions; $44.00/yr. individuals; $22.00/yr. students; add $9.00/yr. postage outside US
Year to which price refers: 1992
Subscription address: Publications Office, Psychonomic Soc., 1710 Fortview Rd., Austin, TX 78704
Subscription telephone: 512 462-2442

ADVERTISING INFORMATION

Advertising accepted: Yes

EDITORIAL DESCRIPTION

Scope: Publishes articles concerned with the broad range of topics in human experimental psychology which the title of this journal encompasses. Also contains papers devoted to the development of theory and papers representing scholarly reviews of the existing literature.
Reviews books: No
Publishes notes: Yes
Languages accepted: English
Prints abstracts: Yes
Author-anonymous submission: Yes

SUBMISSION REQUIREMENTS

Restrictions on contributors: None
Author pays submission fee: No
Author pays page charges: No
Length of articles: No restrictions
Length of notes: No restrictions
Style: American Psychological Assn.
Number of copies required: 5
Special requirements: Include a 100-150 word abstract on a separate page. Also include author's address for correspondence on title page.
Copyright ownership: Psychonomic Soc., Inc.
Rejected manuscripts: Returned at author's request

Time before publication decision: 1-3 mos.
Time between decision and publication: 5-8 mos.
Number of reviewers: 2-3
Articles submitted per year: 250
Articles published per year: 60
Notes submitted per year: 2
Notes published per year: 2

(1813)
*Menckeniana: A Quarterly Review

Charles A. Fecher, Editor
Public Relations Office
Enoch Pratt Free Library
400 Cathedral St.
Baltimore, MD 21201-4484

Telephone: 410 396-5494
Fax: 410 396-5856
First published: 1962
Sponsoring organization: Enoch Pratt Free Library
ISSN: 0025-9233
MLA acronym: Menckeniana

SUBSCRIPTION INFORMATION

Frequency of publication: 4 times/yr.
Circulation: 600
Available in microform: Yes
Subscription price: $12.00/yr.
Year to which price refers: 1992
Subscription address: Publications Office, at above address
Subscription telephone: 410 396-5305

ADVERTISING INFORMATION

Advertising accepted: No

EDITORIAL DESCRIPTION

Scope: Publishes articles on H. L. Mencken.
Reviews books: Yes
Publishes notes: Yes
Languages accepted: English
Prints abstracts: No
Author-anonymous submission: No

SUBMISSION REQUIREMENTS

Author pays submission fee: No
Author pays page charges: No
Style: Chicago
Number of copies required: 1
Copyright ownership: Pratt Library
Rejected manuscripts: Returned
Time before publication decision: 1-6 mos.
Time between decision and publication: 1-3 mos.
Number of reviewers: 2
Articles submitted per year: 30
Articles published per year: 16

(1814)
*Merkur: Deutsche Zeitschrift für europäisches Denken

Karl Heinz Bohrer & Kurt Scheel, Editors
Angertorstr. 1A
8000 Munich 5, Germany

Telephone: (49) 89 2609644
Fax: (49) 89 2608307
First published: 1947
Sponsoring organization: Ernst H. Klett Stiftung Merkur
ISSN: 0026-0096
MLA acronym: Merkur

SUBSCRIPTION INFORMATION

Frequency of publication: Monthly (10 plus double issue)
Circulation: 6,000

Available in microform: No
Subscription price: 170 DM/yr.
Year to which price refers: 1992
Subscription address: Ernst Klett Verlag, Postfach 10 60 16, 7000 Stuttgart 10, Germany
Subscription telephone: (49) 711 6672551
Subscription fax: (49) 711 6672974

ADVERTISING INFORMATION

Advertising accepted: Yes
Advertising rates: 1,200 DM/full page

EDITORIAL DESCRIPTION

Scope: Publishes articles on politics, science, and literature.
Reviews books: Yes
Publishes notes: Yes
Languages accepted: German
Prints abstracts: No
Author-anonymous submission: No

SUBMISSION REQUIREMENTS

Restrictions on contributors: None
Author pays submission fee: No
Author pays page charges: No
Length of articles: 1-20 printed pp.
Length of book reviews: 1-10 printed pp.
Length of notes: 1-5 printed pp.
Style: None
Number of copies required: 1
Copyright ownership: J. G. Cotta'sche Buchhandlung Nachfolger GmbH; reverts to author after 1 yr.
Rejected manuscripts: Returned
Time before publication decision: 3 weeks
Time between decision and publication: 3-4 mos.
Number of reviewers: 2
Articles submitted per year: 300
Articles published per year: 50
Book reviews submitted per year: 200
Book reviews published per year: 50
Notes submitted per year: 200
Notes published per year: 50

(1815)
*The Merton Annual: Studies in Thomas Merton, Religion, Culture, Literature and Social Concerns

Robert E. Daggy, Patrick Hart, Dewey Weiss Kramer, & Victor A. Kramer, Editors
Merton Center
Newburg Rd.
Bellarmine College
Louisville, KY 40205-0671

Telephone: 502 452-8187
First published: 1988
Sponsoring organization: Thomas Merton Studies Center
ISSN: 0894-4857
MLA acronym: MertAn

SUBSCRIPTION INFORMATION

Frequency of publication: Annual
Available in microform: No
Subscription price: $42.50/yr.
Year to which price refers: 1992
Subscription address: AMS Press, Inc., 56 E. 13th St., New York, NY 10003
Subscription telephone: 212 777-4700

ADVERTISING INFORMATION

Advertising accepted: No

EDITORIAL DESCRIPTION

Scope: Publishes articles on Thomas Merton and on all aspects of his life and work, as well as articles related to his concerns.
Reviews books: Yes
Publishes notes: No

Languages accepted: English
Prints abstracts: No
Author-anonymous submission: No

SUBMISSION REQUIREMENTS

Author pays submission fee: No
Author pays page charges: No
Length of articles: 5,000 words
Length of book reviews: 750 words
Style: Chicago
Number of copies required: 3
Special requirements: Submit original typescript and 2 copies.
Copyright ownership: AMS Press
Rejected manuscripts: Returned; enclose SASE.
Time before publication decision: 6-8 weeks
Time between decision and publication: 9 mos.
Number of reviewers: 5
Articles published per year: 12-15
Book reviews published per year: 6-12

(1816)
*The Mervyn Peake Review

Mervyn Peake Soc.
2 Mount Park Rd.
Ealing W5 2RP, England

Telephone: (44) 81 5669307
Fax: (44) 81 9910559
First published: 1975
Sponsoring organization: Mervyn Peake Soc.
ISSN: 0309-1309
MLA acronym: MPR

SUBSCRIPTION INFORMATION

Frequency of publication: 2 times/yr. (Spring, Fall)
Circulation: 200-300
Available in microform: Yes

ADVERTISING INFORMATION

Advertising accepted: Yes

EDITORIAL DESCRIPTION

Scope: Publishes articles on Mervyn Peake's life and work as a novelist, poet, book illustrator, painter, and playwright. Reviews relevant books and includes abstracts of dissertations on Peake.
Reviews books: Yes
Publishes notes: Yes
Languages accepted: English
Prints abstracts: No

SUBMISSION REQUIREMENTS

Restrictions on contributors: Reviews are commissioned.
Author pays submission fee: No
Author pays page charges: No
Length of articles: 2,000-4,000 words; 5,000 words maximum
Length of book reviews: 500-1,000 words
Length of notes: 2,000 words maximum
Style: MLA; Chicago
Number of copies required: 2
Copyright ownership: Author
Rejected manuscripts: Returned; enclose return postage (international reply coupons preferred).
Time before publication decision: 4-6 weeks
Time between decision and publication: 1 yr.
Number of reviewers: 1-2
Articles submitted per year: 1-20
Articles published per year: 10-15
Book reviews published per year: 6-8
Notes submitted per year: 1-4
Notes published per year: 1-2

(1817)
*Mester

Jacqueline Cruz, Editor
Dept. of Spanish & Portuguese
Univ. of California
Los Angeles, CA 90024

Telephone: 310 825-6014; 310 825-1036
First published: 1970
Sponsoring organization: Univ. of California, Los Angeles, Graduate Students Assn. & Dept. of Spanish & Portuguese
ISSN: 0160-2764
MLA acronym: Mester

SUBSCRIPTION INFORMATION

Frequency of publication: 2 times/yr. (Spring, Fall)
Circulation: 500
Available in microform: No
Subscription price: $20.00/yr. institutions; $12.00/yr. individuals; $8.00/yr. students; add $4.00/yr. postage outside US, Canada, & Mexico
Year to which price refers: 1992

ADVERTISING INFORMATION

Advertising accepted: Yes
Advertising rates: $150.00/full page

EDITORIAL DESCRIPTION

Scope: Publishes articles on Spanish, Spanish American, Luso-Brazilian, and Chicano literatures as well as on comparative literature and Spanish and Portuguese linguistics.
Reviews books: Yes
Publishes notes: Yes
Languages accepted: English; Portuguese; Spanish
Prints abstracts: No
Author-anonymous submission: Yes

SUBMISSION REQUIREMENTS

Restrictions on contributors: None
Author pays submission fee: No
Author pays page charges: No
Length of articles: 4,000-4,500 words
Length of book reviews: 850 words
Length of notes: 500 words
Style: MLA
Number of copies required: 4
Special requirements: Submit original typescript plus 3 copies. Do not put author's name on manuscript; indicate complete name and address in a separate letter.
Copyright ownership: Univ. of California
Rejected manuscripts: Returned; enclose SASE.
Time before publication decision: 2-6 mos.
Time between decision and publication: 2-3 mos.
Number of reviewers: 5
Articles submitted per year: 50
Articles published per year: 20-25
Book reviews submitted per year: 10
Book reviews published per year: 5

(1818)
*Meta: Journal des Traducteurs/ Translators' Journal

André Clas, Editor
Dept. de Linguistique
Univ. de Montréal
C.P. 6128
Succursale "A"
Montreal, Quebec H3C 3J7, Canada

Telephone: 514 343-7047
Fax: 514 343-2284
E-mail: Clasand@ere.umontreal.ca
First published: 1955
ISSN: 0026-0452
MLA acronym: Meta

Metaphor

SUBSCRIPTION INFORMATION

Frequency of publication: 4 times/yr. (Mar., June, Sept., Dec.)
Circulation: 3,500
Available in microform: Yes
Subscription price: C$47.00/yr. institutions; C$23.00/yr. individuals Canada; C$27.00/yr. individuals elsewhere; C$18.00/yr. students
Year to which price refers: 1991
Subscription address: Periodica, C.P. 444, Outremont, Quebec H2V 4R6, Canada
Additional subscription address: In France, Belgium, & Switzerland: Presses Universitaires de France, Dépt. des revues, 14 Bois de l'Épine, B.P. 90, 91003 Evry Cedex, France
Subscription telephone: 514 274-5468

ADVERTISING INFORMATION

Advertising accepted: Yes, if related to scope of journal
Advertising rates: C$350.00/full page

EDITORIAL DESCRIPTION

Scope: Publishes articles and information on translation, terminology, interpretation, and lexicography.
Reviews books: Yes
Publishes notes: Yes
Languages accepted: English; French
Prints abstracts: No
Author-anonymous submission: Yes

SUBMISSION REQUIREMENTS

Restrictions on contributors: None
Author pays submission fee: No
Author pays page charges: No
Length of articles: 30 typescript pp. maximum
Length of book reviews: 500-750 words
Length of notes: 200 words
Style: MLA
Number of copies required: 2
Special requirements: Submit original typescript.
Copyright ownership: Editor & author
Rejected manuscripts: Returned
Time before publication decision: 6-12 mos.
Time between decision and publication: 10 mos.
Number of reviewers: 3
Articles submitted per year: 100
Articles published per year: 60
Book reviews submitted per year: 50
Book reviews published per year: 35
Notes submitted per year: 30
Notes published per year: 25

(1819)
*Metaphor and Symbolic Activity

Howard R. Pollio, Editor
Dept. of Psychology
Univ. of Tennessee
Knoxville, TN 37996-0900

First published: 1986
ISSN: 0885-7253
MLA acronym: M&SA

SUBSCRIPTION INFORMATION

Frequency of publication: 4 times/yr.
Circulation: 500
Available in microform: Yes
Subscription price: $100.00/yr. institutions US & Canada; $120.00/yr. institutions elsewhere; $30.00/yr. individuals US & Canada; $50.00/yr. individuals elsewhere
Year to which price refers: 1991
Subscription address: Journal Subscription Dept., Lawrence Erlbaum Assoc., 365 Broadway, Hillsdale, NJ 07642
Additional subscription address: Lawrence Erlbaum Assoc., 27 Palmeira Mansions, Church Rd., Hove, East Sussex BN3 2FA, England

ADVERTISING INFORMATION

Advertising accepted: Yes

EDITORIAL DESCRIPTION

Scope: Publishes articles on figurative language and its relationship to other topics, e.g., cognition, creativity, poetry, social analysis, and history.
Reviews books: Yes
Publishes notes: No
Languages accepted: English
Prints abstracts: Yes
Author-anonymous submission: Yes, at author's request

SUBMISSION REQUIREMENTS

Restrictions on contributors: None
Author pays submission fee: No
Author pays page charges: No
Length of articles: 2,500-5,000 words
Length of book reviews: 1,000-1,250 words
Style: American Psychological Assn.
Number of copies required: 3
Copyright ownership: Lawrence Erlbaum Assoc.
Rejected manuscripts: Returned
Time before publication decision: 3-18 mos.
Time between decision and publication: 3-6 mos.
Number of reviewers: 3
Articles submitted per year: 25-30
Articles published per year: 12-14
Book reviews submitted per year: 4-6
Book reviews published per year: 4-6

(1820)
*Metmenys

Vytautas Kavolis, Editor
Dickinson College
Carlisle, PA 17013

First published: 1959
Sponsoring organization: AM&M Publications
ISSN: 0543-615X
MLA acronym: Metmenys

SUBSCRIPTION INFORMATION

Frequency of publication: 2 times/yr.
Circulation: 800
Available in microform: No
Subscription price: $15.00/yr.
Year to which price refers: 1992
Subscription address: Aleksas Vaškelis, 3113 W. Vina del Mar Blvd., St. Petersburg Beach, FL 33706

ADVERTISING INFORMATION

Advertising accepted: No

EDITORIAL DESCRIPTION

Scope: Publishes articles on contemporary literature, history, philosophy, and the arts. Emphasis is on Lithuanian literature.
Reviews books: Yes
Publishes notes: Yes
Languages accepted: Lithuanian
Prints abstracts: No
Author-anonymous submission: Yes

SUBMISSION REQUIREMENTS

Restrictions on contributors: None
Author pays submission fee: No
Author pays page charges: No
Length of articles: No restrictions
Length of book reviews: No restrictions
Style: None
Number of copies required: 1
Copyright ownership: Author
Rejected manuscripts: Returned
Time before publication decision: 1 mo.
Time between decision and publication: 1 yr.
Number of reviewers: 2
Articles submitted per year: 40
Articles published per year: 20
Book reviews submitted per year: 8
Book reviews published per year: 8
Notes submitted per year: 10
Notes published per year: 6

(1821)
Metodika Obuchenia Inostrannym Iazykam: Romanskoe i Germanskoe Iazykoznanie

E. A. Maslyko, Editor
Minskiĭ Gosudarstvennyĭ Pedagogicheskiĭ Inst. Inostrannykh Iazykov
Redaktsionno-Izdatelskiĭ Otdel
Zakharova 21
220034 Minsk, Belarus

First published: 1971
Sponsoring organization: Minskiĭ Gosudarstvennyĭ Pedagogicheskiĭ Institut Inostrannykh Iazykov
ISSN: 0207-6233
MLA acronym: MOII

SUBSCRIPTION INFORMATION

Frequency of publication: Annual
Available in microform: No
Subscription address: Kniga-pochtoy, Magazin N 31, Ploschad Svobody 19, 220068 Minsk, Belarus

ADVERTISING INFORMATION

Advertising accepted: No

EDITORIAL DESCRIPTION

Scope: Publishes articles on semantics, grammar, phonology, lexicology, style, history, and dialects in English, German, French, and Spanish, general linguistics, typology, and methods of teaching foreign languages.
Reviews books: No
Publishes notes: No
Languages accepted: Belorussian; Russian
Prints abstracts: No
Author-anonymous submission: No

SUBMISSION REQUIREMENTS

Restrictions on contributors: Contributors are usually faculty members of institutions of higher education in Belarus.
Author pays submission fee: No, but if the article is accepted for publication, the author is expected to purchase 10 copies of the issue.
Author pays page charges: No
Length of articles: 1,800-2,400 words
Style: None
Number of copies required: 2
Special requirements: Submit original typescript.
Copyright ownership: Vysheishia Shkola Publishing House
Rejected manuscripts: Returned
Time before publication decision: Manuscripts submitted before 1 Dec. are evaluated the following Feb.
Time between decision and publication: 14 mos.
Number of reviewers: 2
Articles submitted per year: 60-70
Articles published per year: 25-30

(1822)
*Metodologia delle Scienze e Filosofia del Linguaggio

Francesco Barone & Vittorio Somenzi, Editors
Editore Armando s.r.l.
Viale Trastevere 236
00153 Rome, Italy

Telephone: (39) 6 5894525
Fax: (39) 6 5818564
First published: 1979
MLA acronym: MSFL

SUBSCRIPTION INFORMATION

Frequency of publication: Irregular
Available in microform: No

ADVERTISING INFORMATION

Advertising accepted: No

EDITORIAL DESCRIPTION

Scope: Publishes monographs dealing with the philosophy, methodology, and historiography of language, linguistics, and the natural and social sciences.
Reviews books: No
Publishes notes: No
Languages accepted: Italian
Prints abstracts: No

SUBMISSION REQUIREMENTS

Restrictions on contributors: All manuscripts are solicited.
Author pays submission fee: No
Author pays page charges: No
Copyright ownership: Author or Editore Armando s.r.l.
Books published per year: 5-6

(1823)
*Michigan Academician

Kathleen Duke, Editor
Argus II
400 S. Fourth St.
Ann Arbor, MI 48103-4816

Telephone: 313 936-2938
First published: 1969
Sponsoring organization: Michigan Academy of Science, Arts, & Letters
ISSN: 0026-2005
MLA acronym: MichA

SUBSCRIPTION INFORMATION

Frequency of publication: 4 times/yr. (Nov., Feb., May, Aug.)
Circulation: 1,200
Available in microform: No
Subscription price: $40.00/yr.
Year to which price refers: 1992

ADVERTISING INFORMATION

Advertising accepted: No

EDITORIAL DESCRIPTION

Scope: Articles are published in all academic disciplines at the college level.
Reviews books: Yes
Publishes notes: No
Languages accepted: English
Prints abstracts: No
Author-anonymous submission: Yes

SUBMISSION REQUIREMENTS

Restrictions on contributors: Papers read by Academy members at the Annual Meeting are eligible to be considered for publication (membership is open to all); unsolicited manuscripts are not accepted.
Author pays submission fee: No
Author pays page charges: Occasionally
Cost of page charges: $25.00/page
Length of articles: 4,000 words
Length of book reviews: 800 words
Style: Chicago
Number of copies required: 3
Copyright ownership: Michigan Academy of Science, Arts, & Letters
Rejected manuscripts: Not returned
Time before publication decision: 6-8 mos.
Time between decision and publication: 3-9 mos.
Number of reviewers: 2-3
Articles submitted per year: 70
Articles published per year: 35
Book reviews submitted per year: 18
Book reviews published per year: 15

(1824)
*Michigan Germanic Studies

Roy C. Cowen, Editor
Dept. of German
Univ. of Michigan
Ann Arbor, MI 48109-1275

Telephone: 313 764-8018
E-mail: R@UM.CC.UMICH.EDU
First published: 1975
Sponsoring organization: German Dept., Univ. of Michigan
ISSN: 0098-8030
MLA acronym: MGS

SUBSCRIPTION INFORMATION

Frequency of publication: 2 times/yr. (Apr., Nov.)
Circulation: 250
Available in microform: No
Subscription price: $25.00/yr. institutions; $15.00/yr. individuals; $10.00/yr. students; add $1.00/yr. postage outside US
Year to which price refers: 1992

ADVERTISING INFORMATION

Advertising accepted: Yes
Advertising rates: $20.00/quarter page; $35.00/half page; $50.00/full page

EDITORIAL DESCRIPTION

Scope: Articles may include topics in Germanic (English, German, Dutch, Scandinavian, and the older Germanic dialects) and German language and literatures. Considers articles on the relationship of literature to the other arts.
Reviews books: Yes
Publishes notes: Yes
Languages accepted: English; French; German
Prints abstracts: No
Author-anonymous submission: No

SUBMISSION REQUIREMENTS

Restrictions on contributors: Considers only contributions based on material examined in the original language(s); unsolicited reviews are not published.
Author pays submission fee: No
Author pays page charges: No
Length of articles: 5,000-8,000 words
Length of book reviews: 300-1,000 words
Length of notes: 500-1,000 words
Style: MLA; Linguistic Soc. of America
Number of copies required: 2
Copyright ownership: Assigned by author to journal
Rejected manuscripts: Returned; enclose return postage.
Time before publication decision: 1-3 mos.
Time between decision and publication: 6-12 mos.
Number of reviewers: 2
Articles submitted per year: 25
Articles published per year: 10
Book reviews published per year: 15-20

(1825)
*Michigan Quarterly Review

Laurence Goldstein, Editor
3032 Rackham Bldg.
Univ. of Michigan
Ann Arbor, MI 48109

Telephone: 313 764-9265
First published: 1962
Sponsoring organization: Univ. of Michigan
ISSN: 0026-2420
MLA acronym: MQR

SUBSCRIPTION INFORMATION

Frequency of publication: 4 times/yr. (Jan., Apr., July, Oct.)
Circulation: 1,600
Available in microform: Yes
Subscription price: $18.00/yr.
Year to which price refers: 1992

ADVERTISING INFORMATION

Advertising accepted: Yes
Advertising rates: $50.00/half page; $100.00/full page

EDITORIAL DESCRIPTION

Scope: Publishes articles and reviews on all aspects of the humanities and the social sciences.
Reviews books: Yes
Publishes notes: No
Languages accepted: English
Prints abstracts: No
Author-anonymous submission: No

SUBMISSION REQUIREMENTS

Restrictions on contributors: Book reviews are generally commissioned.
Author pays submission fee: No
Author pays page charges: No
Length of articles: 3,000-6,000 words
Length of book reviews: 1,500-2,500 words
Style: Chicago
Number of copies required: 1
Special requirements: Enclose SASE.
Copyright ownership: Author
Rejected manuscripts: Returned; enclose return postage or international postal orders.
Time before publication decision: 6 weeks
Time between decision and publication: 1 yr.
Number of reviewers: 2
Articles submitted per year: 120
Articles published per year: 20
Book reviews published per year: 20

(1826)
*Michigan Romance Studies

Floyd Gray, Editor
Dept. of Romance Languages
Univ. of Michigan
Ann Arbor, MI 48109-1275

Telephone: 313 764-5363
Fax: 313 764-8163
E-mail: Hhlv@um.cc.umich.edu
First published: 1980
Sponsoring organization: Dept. of Romance Languages, Univ. of Michigan
ISSN: 0270-3629
MLA acronym: MRS

(1827)
*Michigan Slavic Contributions

Benjamin A. Stolz & Jindrich Toman, Editors
3040 MLB, Slavic Dept.
Univ. of Michigan
Ann Arbor, MI 48109-1275

Telephone: 313 763-4496
Fax: 313 764-3521
First published: 1968
Sponsoring organization: Univ. of Michigan
MLA acronym: MSC

SUBSCRIPTION INFORMATION

Frequency of publication: Annual
Available in microform: No
Subscription price: $10.00/yr.
Year to which price refers: 1992

ADVERTISING INFORMATION

Advertising accepted: Yes, on an exchange basis

EDITORIAL DESCRIPTION

Scope: Publishes monographs on Romance language and literatures.
Reviews books: No
Publishes notes: No
Languages accepted: English; French; Spanish; Italian
Prints abstracts: No

SUBMISSION REQUIREMENTS

Restrictions on contributors: Manuscripts are commissioned.
Author pays submission fee: No
Author pays page charges: No
Style: MLA
Number of copies required: 1
Copyright ownership: Series
Time between decision and publication: 1 yr.

(1827)
*Michigan Slavic Contributions

Benjamin A. Stolz & Jindrich Toman, Editors
3040 MLB, Slavic Dept.
Univ. of Michigan
Ann Arbor, MI 48109-1275

Telephone: 313 763-4496
Fax: 313 764-3521
First published: 1968
Sponsoring organization: Univ. of Michigan
MLA acronym: MSC

SUBSCRIPTION INFORMATION

Frequency of publication: Irregular
Available in microform: No

ADVERTISING INFORMATION

Advertising accepted: No

EDITORIAL DESCRIPTION

Scope: Publishes articles on literary theory with special reference to Slavic literatures.
Reviews books: No
Publishes notes: No
Languages accepted: English; Russian; Czech; Polish; Serbo-Croatian
Prints abstracts: No
Author-anonymous submission: No

SUBMISSION REQUIREMENTS

Restrictions on contributors: None
Author pays submission fee: No
Author pays page charges: No
Length of books: No restrictions
Style: MLA; Chicago
Number of copies required: 1
Copyright ownership: Univ. of Michigan
Rejected manuscripts: Not returned

(1828)
Michigan Studies in the Humanities

Ladislav Matejka & Irwin R. Titunik, Editors
3040 MLB, Slavic Dept.
Univ. of Michigan
Ann Arbor, MI 48109-1275

First published: 1980
Sponsoring organization: Slavic Dept., Univ. of Michigan
MLA acronym: MSH

SUBSCRIPTION INFORMATION

Frequency of publication: Irregular
Available in microform: No

ADVERTISING INFORMATION

Advertising accepted: No

EDITORIAL DESCRIPTION

Scope: Publishes studies in the humanities, literary theory, and linguistics.
Reviews books: Yes
Publishes notes: No
Languages accepted: English; Russian; Czech; Polish; Serbo-Croatian
Prints abstracts: No

SUBMISSION REQUIREMENTS

Restrictions on contributors: None
Author pays submission fee: No
Author pays page charges: No
Length of books: No restrictions
Style: MLA; Chicago
Number of copies required: 1
Copyright ownership: Univ. of Michigan
Rejected manuscripts: Not returned

(1829)
*Mid-America Folklore

George Lankford, Editor
Mid-America Folklore Soc.
Arkansas College
Batesville, AR 72501

Telephone: 501 698-4346
First published: 1973
Sponsoring organization: Mid-America Folklore Soc.
ISSN: 0099-2356
MLA acronym: MidSF

SUBSCRIPTION INFORMATION

Frequency of publication: 2 times/yr.
Circulation: 300
Available in microform: No
Subscription address: W. K. McNeil, Ozark Folk Center, Mountain View, AR 72560

ADVERTISING INFORMATION

Advertising accepted: No

EDITORIAL DESCRIPTION

Scope: Publishes data-based studies of folk culture of Central United States, including Missouri, Illinois, Kansas, Oklahoma, and Arkansas.
Reviews books: Yes
Publishes notes: Yes
Languages accepted: English
Prints abstracts: No
Author-anonymous submission: No

SUBMISSION REQUIREMENTS

Restrictions on contributors: None
Author pays submission fee: No
Author pays page charges: No
Length of book reviews: 750 words
Length of notes: 750 words
Style: MLA
Number of copies required: 1
Copyright ownership: Mid-America Folklore Soc.
Rejected manuscripts: Returned; enclose return postage.
Time before publication decision: 3 mos.
Time between decision and publication: 3 mos.
Number of reviewers: 3
Articles submitted per year: 20
Articles published per year: 8
Book reviews submitted per year: 18
Book reviews published per year: 12-18
Notes submitted per year: 6-10
Notes published per year: 3-5

(1830)
*Mid-American Review

George Looney, Robert Early, & Wayne Barham, Editors
106 Hanna Hall
Dept. of English
Bowling Green State Univ.
Bowling Green, OH 43403

Telephone: 419 372-2725
First published: 1972
Sponsoring organization: Dept. of English, Bowling Green State Univ.
ISSN: 0747-8895
MLA acronym: MARev

SUBSCRIPTION INFORMATION

Frequency of publication: 2 times/yr.
Circulation: 500
Available in microform: No
Subscription price: $8.00/yr.; $15.00/2 yrs.
Year to which price refers: 1992

ADVERTISING INFORMATION

Advertising accepted: Yes

EDITORIAL DESCRIPTION

Scope: Publishes contemporary fiction, poetry, essays, critical articles, and poetry translations.
Reviews books: Yes
Publishes notes: Yes
Languages accepted: English
Prints abstracts: No
Author-anonymous submission: No

SUBMISSION REQUIREMENTS

Restrictions on contributors: None
Author pays submission fee: No
Author pays page charges: No
Length of articles: 2,500 words
Length of book reviews: 500-1,500 words
Length of notes: 300 words
Style: MLA
Number of copies required: 1
Copyright ownership: Author
Rejected manuscripts: Returned; enclose SASE.
Time before publication decision: 1-4 mos.
Time between decision and publication: 1 yr. maximum
Number of reviewers: 2-12
Articles submitted per year: 80
Articles published per year: 10-12
Book reviews submitted per year: 20-30
Book reviews published per year: 10-15
Notes submitted per year: 10-15
Notes published per year: 3-5

(1831)
*Midamerica: The Yearbook of the Society for the Study of Midwestern Literature

David D. Anderson, Editor
Soc. for the Study of Midwestern Literature
Ernst Bessey Hall
Michigan State Univ.
East Lansing, MI 48824

First published: 1974
Sponsoring organization: Soc. for the Study of Midwestern Literature
ISSN: 0190-2911
MLA acronym: Midamerica

SUBSCRIPTION INFORMATION

Frequency of publication: Annual
Circulation: 500
Available in microform: No

ADVERTISING INFORMATION

Advertising accepted: No

EDITORIAL DESCRIPTION

Scope: Publishes articles on midwestern literature.
Reviews books: Yes
Languages accepted: English
Prints abstracts: No

SUBMISSION REQUIREMENTS

Restrictions on contributors: Contributors must be members of the Soc. for Midwestern Literature.
Author pays submission fee: No
Author pays page charges: No
Length of articles: 2,000-2,500 words
Length of book reviews: 1,000 words
Style: MLA
Number of copies required: 1
Copyright ownership: Reverts to author upon request.
Time before publication decision: 3 mos.
Time between decision and publication: 9-12 mos.
Articles submitted per year: 50
Articles published per year: 12
Book reviews submitted per year: 10
Book reviews published per year: 12

(1832)
Middle English Texts

Manfred Görlach & O. S. Pickering, Editors
Englisches Seminar der Univ.
Albertus-Magnus-Platz,
5000 Cologne 41, Germany

Additional editorial address: O. S. Pickering, Brotherton Library, Univ. of Leeds, Leeds LS2 9JT, England
First published: 1975
MLA acronym: MET

SUBSCRIPTION INFORMATION

Frequency of publication: Irregular
Circulation: 400
Available in microform: No
Subscription address: Carl Winter Universitätsverlag, Lutherstr. 59, Postfach 106140, 6900 Heidelberg, Germany

ADVERTISING INFORMATION

Advertising accepted: No

EDITORIAL DESCRIPTION

Scope: Publishes scholarly editions of Middle English texts of all genres, 1100-1530, hitherto unprinted or in need of a new, reliable edition.
Reviews books: No
Publishes notes: No
Languages accepted: English
Prints abstracts: No
Author-anonymous submission: No

SUBMISSION REQUIREMENTS

Restrictions on contributors: None
Author pays submission fee: No
Length of books: 150 pp.
Style: MLA
Number of copies required: 1
Special requirements: Submit camera-ready typescript.
Copyright ownership: Carl Winter Universitätsverlag
Rejected manuscripts: Returned at author's request
Time before publication decision: 4-6 mos.
Time between decision and publication: 4 mos.
Number of reviewers: 2-3
Books submitted per year: 3-4
Books published per year: 1-2

(1833)
*Midwest Quarterly: A Journal of Contemporary Thought

James B. M. Schick, Editor
Pittsburg State Univ.
Pittsburg, KS 66762

Telephone: 316 235-4369
Fax: 316 232-7515
First published: 1959
Sponsoring organization: Pittsburg State Univ., Kansas
ISSN: 0026-3451
MLA acronym: MQ

SUBSCRIPTION INFORMATION

Frequency of publication: 4 times/yr. (Oct., Jan., Apr., July)
Circulation: 800
Available in microform: Yes
Subscription price: $10.00/yr. US; $13.00/yr. elsewhere
Year to which price refers: 1992

ADVERTISING INFORMATION

Advertising accepted: No

EDITORIAL DESCRIPTION

Scope: Publishes scholarly articles dealing with a broad range of subjects of current interest. In no way competing with the more specialized journals, the journal seeks discussions of an analytical and speculative nature rather than heavily documented research studies.
Reviews books: Yes
Publishes notes: No
Languages accepted: English
Prints abstracts: No
Author-anonymous submission: Yes

SUBMISSION REQUIREMENTS

Restrictions on contributors: Book reviews are generally commissioned.
Author pays submission fee: No
Author pays page charges: No
Length of articles: 5,000 words maximum
Length of book reviews: 500 words
Style: MLA
Number of copies required: 2
Special requirements: No footnotes
Copyright ownership: Journal
Rejected manuscripts: Returned; enclose SASE.
Time before publication decision: 6 mos.
Time between decision and publication: 9-12 mos.
Number of reviewers: 9
Articles submitted per year: 125
Articles published per year: 24
Book reviews submitted per year: 3
Book reviews published per year: 12

(1834)
*Midwestern Folklore

Ronald L. Baker, Editor
Dept. of English
Indiana State Univ.
Terre Haute, IN 47809

Telephone: 812 237-3160
Fax: 812 237-4382
First published: 1975
Sponsoring organization: Indiana State Univ.; Hoosier Folklore Soc.
ISSN: 0894-4059
MLA acronym: MidF

SUBSCRIPTION INFORMATION

Frequency of publication: 2 times/yr.
Circulation: 300
Available in microform: No
Subscription price: $7.00/yr.
Year to which price refers: 1992

ADVERTISING INFORMATION

Advertising accepted: No

EDITORIAL DESCRIPTION

Scope: Publishes articles on folklore, primarily from the Midwest, but also from other areas.
Reviews books: No
Publishes notes: No
Languages accepted: English
Prints abstracts: No
Author-anonymous submission: Yes

SUBMISSION REQUIREMENTS

Restrictions on contributors: None
Author pays submission fee: No
Author pays page charges: No
Length of articles: 15-20 typescript pp.
Style: Chicago
Number of copies required: 1
Special requirements: Accepted articles should be submitted on IBM-compatible diskette.
Copyright ownership: Author
Rejected manuscripts: Returned
Time before publication decision: 6 weeks
Time between decision and publication: 1 yr.
Number of reviewers: 3
Articles submitted per year: 24
Articles published per year: 8-10

(1835)
*Midwestern Miscellany

David D. Anderson, Editor
Soc. for the Study of Midwestern Literature
Ernst Bessey Hall
Michigan State Univ.
East Lansing, MI 48824

First published: 1974
Sponsoring organization: Soc. for the Study of Midwestern Literature
ISSN: 0885-4742
MLA acronym: MMisc

SUBSCRIPTION INFORMATION

Frequency of publication: Annual
Circulation: 500

ADVERTISING INFORMATION

Advertising accepted: No

EDITORIAL DESCRIPTION

Scope: Publishes articles on the entire range of Midwestern literature and culture.
Reviews books: Yes
Languages accepted: English
Prints abstracts: No

SUBMISSION REQUIREMENTS

Restrictions on contributors: Contributors must be members of Soc. for the Study of Midwestern Literature.
Author pays submission fee: No
Author pays page charges: No
Length of articles: 1,500-2,000 words
Length of book reviews: 500-1,000 words
Style: MLA
Number of copies required: 1
Copyright ownership: Journal; reverts to author upon request.
Rejected manuscripts: Returned
Time before publication decision: 3 mos.
Time between decision and publication: 1 yr.
Number of reviewers: 2
Articles submitted per year: 50
Articles published per year: 10
Book reviews submitted per year: 10
Book reviews published per year: 3

(1836) Miesięcznik Literacki

Włodzimierz Sokorski, Editor
Wydawnictwo Wspolczesne RSW "Prasa-Książka-Ruch"
Ul. Wiejska 12
00-420 Warsaw, Poland

First published: 1966
ISSN: 0026-3567
MLA acronym: MLit

SUBSCRIPTION INFORMATION

Frequency of publication: 12 times/yr.
Subscription address: Prasa-Książka-Ruch, Centrala Kolportażu Prasy i Wydawnictw, ul. Towarowa 28, 00-958 Warsaw, Poland

EDITORIAL DESCRIPTION

Reviews books: Yes
Languages accepted: Polish
Prints abstracts: No

(1837) *Milton Quarterly

Roy C. Flannagan, Editor
378 Ellis Hall
Dept. of English
Ohio Univ.
Athens, OH 45701-2979

Telephone: 614 593-2829
Fax: 614 593-4229
E-mail: FLANNAGA@ouaccvmb.bitnet
First published: 1967
Sponsoring organization: English Dept., Ohio Univ.; Milton Soc. of America
ISSN: 0026-4326
MLA acronym: MiltonQ

SUBSCRIPTION INFORMATION

Frequency of publication: 4 times/yr. (Mar., May, Oct., Dec.)
Circulation: 1,100
Available in microform: Yes
Subscription price: $24.00/yr. institutions; $15.00/yr. individuals; add $8.00/yr. postage outside US
Year to which price refers: 1992

ADVERTISING INFORMATION

Advertising accepted: Yes
Advertising rates: $50.00/quarter page; $100.00/half page; $150.00/full page

EDITORIAL DESCRIPTION

Scope: Solicits letters containing news interesting to Miltonists; will make an effort to print any legitimate query. Will also accept feature articles (critical, explicatory, exegetical) for which a letter of inquiry is advisable.
Reviews books: Yes
Publishes notes: Yes
Languages accepted: English; French; Italian
Prints abstracts: No
Author-anonymous submission: Yes

SUBMISSION REQUIREMENTS

Restrictions on contributors: None
Author pays submission fee: No
Author pays page charges: Yes
Length of articles: 500-7,500 words
Length of book reviews: 500-1,500 words
Length of notes: 300-1,000 words
Style: MLA
Number of copies required: 2
Special requirements: Include a 200-word abstract.
Copyright ownership: Editor
Rejected manuscripts: Returned with comments
Time before publication decision: 3-6 mos.
Time between decision and publication: 6-24 mos.
Number of reviewers: 2-3
Articles submitted per year: 75-100
Articles published per year: 15-18
Book reviews submitted per year: 15
Book reviews published per year: 12
Notes submitted per year: 20
Notes published per year: 10

(1838) *Milton Studies

Albert C. Labriola, Editor
Dept. of English
Duquesne Univ.
Pittsburgh, PA 15282

Telephone: 412 434-6420
Fax: 412 434-5197
First published: 1969
ISSN: 0076-8820
MLA acronym: MiltonS

SUBSCRIPTION INFORMATION

Frequency of publication: Annual
Circulation: 1,500
Available in microform: No
Subscription address: Univ. of Pittsburgh Press, 127 Bellefield St., Pittsburgh, PA 15260
Subscription telephone: 412 624-4110

ADVERTISING INFORMATION

Advertising accepted: No

EDITORIAL DESCRIPTION

Scope: Forum for Milton scholarship and criticism. Articles on subjects broadly related to Milton are also welcomed.
Reviews books: No
Publishes notes: No
Languages accepted: English
Prints abstracts: No

SUBMISSION REQUIREMENTS

Restrictions on contributors: None
Author pays submission fee: No
Author pays page charges: No
Length of articles: 3,000 words minimum
Style: MLA
Number of copies required: 1

Special requirements: Submit original typescript.
Copyright ownership: Univ. of Pittsburgh Press
Rejected manuscripts: Returned
Time before publication decision: 3 mos.
Time between decision and publication: 15 mos.
Number of reviewers: 2-3
Articles submitted per year: 100
Articles published per year: 10-12

(1839) *Mimesis: Untersuchungen zu den Romanischen Literaturen der Neuzeit/Recherches sur les Littératures Romanes depuis la Renaissance

Reinhold R. Grimm, Joseph Jurt, & Friedrich Wolfzettel, Editors
Romanisches Seminar
Univ. Hannover
Welfengarten 1
3000 Hannover, Germany

Additional editorial address: J. Jurt, Romanisches Seminar, Albert-Ludwigs-Univ., Werthmannplatz 3, 7800 Freiburg i.Br., Germany; F. Wolfzettel, Inst. für Romanische Sprachen & Literaturen, Goethe Univ., Gräfstr. 76, 6000 Frankfurt, Germany
First published: 1985
ISSN: 0178-7489
MLA acronym: Mimesis

SUBSCRIPTION INFORMATION

Frequency of publication: Irregular
Available in microform: No
Subscription address: Max Niemeyer Verlag, Postfach 2140, 7400 Tübingen, Germany

ADVERTISING INFORMATION

Advertising accepted: No

EDITORIAL DESCRIPTION

Scope: Publishes monographs on Romance language literature since 1500.
Reviews books: No
Publishes notes: No
Languages accepted: German; French
Author-anonymous submission: No

SUBMISSION REQUIREMENTS

Author pays submission fee: No
Author pays page charges: No
Number of copies required: 1
Copyright ownership: Max Niemeyer Verlag
Rejected manuscripts: Returned
Time before publication decision: 3 mos.
Time between decision and publication: 6 mos.
Number of reviewers: 3
Books submitted per year: 10-15
Books published per year: 3-5

(1840) *Minas Gerais, Suplemento Literário

Paschoal Motta, Editor
Imprensa Oficial do Estado de Minas Gerais
Av. Augusto de Lima, 270
30,000-Belo Horizonte, Mina Gerais, Brazil

Telephone: (55) 31 2732088 ext. 197
Fax: (55) 31 2732700
First published: 1966
Sponsoring organization: Governo do Estado de Minas Gerais
MLA acronym: MGSL

SUBSCRIPTION INFORMATION

Frequency of publication: 52 times/yr.

Circulation: Yes
Available in microform: No

ADVERTISING INFORMATION

Advertising accepted: No

EDITORIAL DESCRIPTION

Scope: Focuses on literature and art.
Reviews books: Yes
Publishes notes: Yes
Languages accepted: Portuguese
Prints abstracts: No

SUBMISSION REQUIREMENTS

Restrictions on contributors: None
Author pays submission fee: Yes
Author pays page charges: No
Length of articles: 5-6 double-spaced typescript pp.
Length of book reviews: No restrictions
Length of notes: No restrictions
Style: None
Number of copies required: 1
Rejected manuscripts: Not returned
Time before publication decision: 1 mo.
Time between decision and publication: 1 week
Number of reviewers: 3
Articles submitted per year: 500
Articles published per year: 500
Notes submitted per year: 500
Notes published per year: 1,500

(1841)
*Mind: A Quarterly Review of Philosophy

Mark Sainsbury, Editor
Dept. of Philosophy
King's College London
London WC2R 2LS, England

Additional editorial address: Send books for review to Mark Sainsbury; send all other book review correspondence to David-Hillel Rubin, Reviews Editor, Dept. of Philosophy, London School of Economics, Haughton St., London WC2A 2AE, England
Telephone: (44) 71 8732757
Fax: (44) 71 8361799
First published: 1876
Sponsoring organization: Mind Assn.
ISSN: 0026-4423
MLA acronym: Mind

SUBSCRIPTION INFORMATION

Frequency of publication: 4 times/yr.
Circulation: 3,500
Available in microform: Yes
Subscription price: £28.00/yr. institutions United Kingdom & Europe; $53.00/yr. institutions elsewhere; £17.00/yr. individuals United Kingdom & Europe; $34.00/yr. individuals elsewhere
Year to which price refers: 1992
Subscription address: Oxford Univ. Press, Journals Subscription Dept., Pinkhill House, Southfield Rd., Eynsham, Oxford OX8 1JJ, England
Subscription telephone: (44) 865 882283
Subscription fax: (44) 865 882890

ADVERTISING INFORMATION

Advertising accepted: Yes

EDITORIAL DESCRIPTION

Scope: Publishes articles with the aim of ensuring that the best philosophy is lucidly presented and open to the widest audience. Also has a major section devoted to commentary on recent literature.
Reviews books: Yes
Publishes notes: Yes
Languages accepted: English

Prints abstracts: No
Author-anonymous submission: Yes, at author's request

SUBMISSION REQUIREMENTS

Restrictions on contributors: None
Author pays submission fee: No
Author pays page charges: No
Length of articles: 6,000-9,000 words
Length of book reviews: 3,000 words maximum
Length of notes: 5,000 words maximum
Style: British punctuation
Number of copies required: 1
Special requirements: Submissions accepted for publication should be submitted on IBM- or Macintosh-compatible diskettes.
Copyright ownership: Mind Assn. or author
Rejected manuscripts: Not returned
Time before publication decision: 1-2 mos.
Time between decision and publication: 6-12 mos.
Number of reviewers: 1-3
Articles submitted per year: 250
Articles published per year: 20
Book reviews submitted per year: 80
Book reviews published per year: 80
Notes submitted per year: 100
Notes published per year: 20

(1842)
*The Minnesota Review

Jeffrey Williams, Editor
Dept. of English
East Carolina Univ.
Greenville, NC 27858

Telephone: 919 757-6388
Fax: 919 757-4263
First published: 1960
Sponsoring organization: Dept. of English, East Carolina Univ.
ISSN: 0026-5667
MLA acronym: MinnR

SUBSCRIPTION INFORMATION

Frequency of publication: 2 times/yr. (Spring, Fall)
Circulation: 700
Available in microform: Yes

ADVERTISING INFORMATION

Advertising accepted: Yes

EDITORIAL DESCRIPTION

Scope: Publishes committed writing, particularly on politics and critical theory, original fiction, poetry, literary and cultural criticism, marxist and feminist criticism, and book reviews.
Reviews books: Yes
Languages accepted: English
Prints abstracts: No
Author-anonymous submission: No

SUBMISSION REQUIREMENTS

Author pays submission fee: No
Author pays page charges: No
Length of articles: 4,000-6,000 words
Length of book reviews: 1,500-2,000 words; review essays: 2,400-4,500 words
Style: MLA preferred
Number of copies required: 1
Copyright ownership: Reverts to author on publication
Rejected manuscripts: Returned; enclose SASE.
Time before publication decision: 3-12 weeks
Time between decision and publication: 3-12 mos.
Number of reviewers: 3
Articles submitted per year: 50-100
Articles published per year: 6-10; 6-10 stories, 40-50 poems

Book reviews submitted per year: 50
Book reviews published per year: 25

(1843)
*Minos: Revista de Filologia Egea

José L. Melena, Editor
Fac. de Filología
Univ. del País Vasco
P.O. Box 2111
01080 Vitoria, Spain

First published: 1951
Sponsoring organization: Secretariado de Publicaciones, Univ. de Salamanca; Servicio Editorial, Univ. del País Vasio-Euskal Herriko Unibersitatea
ISSN: 0544-3733
MLA acronym: Minos

SUBSCRIPTION INFORMATION

Frequency of publication: Annual
Circulation: 500
Available in microform: No

ADVERTISING INFORMATION

Advertising accepted: No

EDITORIAL DESCRIPTION

Scope: Publishes articles on Aegean philology and Mycenaean Greek texts.
Reviews books: Yes
Publishes notes: Yes
Languages accepted: English; French; German; Italian; Spanish
Prints abstracts: No
Author-anonymous submission: No

SUBMISSION REQUIREMENTS

Restrictions on contributors: Contributions should be endorsed by member of editorial committee.
Author pays submission fee: No
Author pays page charges: No
Length of articles: No restrictions
Length of book reviews: 3 pp. on A4 paper
Style: None
Number of copies required: 1
Special requirements: Submit original typescript.
Copyright ownership: Journal
Rejected manuscripts: Returned
Time before publication decision: 1 mo.
Time between decision and publication: 6-12 mos.
Number of reviewers: 1-3
Articles submitted per year: 14
Articles published per year: 12
Book reviews submitted per year: 20
Book reviews published per year: 8
Notes submitted per year: 3
Notes published per year: 1

(1844)
*Miorița: A Journal of Romanian Studies

Charles M. Carlton & Norman Simms, Editors
Dept. of Foreign Languages, Literatures, & Linguistics
Univ. of Rochester
Rochester, NY 14627

Telephone: 716 275-4251; 716 275-4258
First published: 1973
Sponsoring organization: Dept. of Foreign Languages, Literatures, & Linguistics, Univ. of Rochester
ISSN: 0110-0068
MLA acronym: Miorița

SUBSCRIPTION INFORMATION

Frequency of publication: Irregular
Circulation: 200
Available in microform: No
Subscription price: $10.00/yr.
Year to which price refers: 1990

ADVERTISING INFORMATION

Advertising accepted: No

EDITORIAL DESCRIPTION

Scope: Publishes on all aspects of history, culture, languages, literature, and folklore of Romania and Romanian lands, and of coinhabiting nationalities and Romanians abroad.
Reviews books: Yes
Publishes notes: No
Languages accepted: English; French; Romanian
Prints abstracts: No
Author-anonymous submission: No

SUBMISSION REQUIREMENTS

Restrictions on contributors: None
Author pays submission fee: No
Author pays page charges: No
Length of articles: 10 pp.
Length of book reviews: 400-1,000 words
Style: None
Number of copies required: 1
Special requirements: Submission of camera-ready typescript is preferred.
Copyright ownership: Journal
Rejected manuscripts: Returned at author's request
Time before publication decision: 6 mos.
Time between decision and publication: 1 yr.
Number of reviewers: 2
Articles submitted per year: 10-15
Articles published per year: 7-10
Book reviews submitted per year: 5-10
Book reviews published per year: 5-7

(1845)
*Miscelanea de Estudios Arabes y Hebraicos: II. Filologia Hebrea, Biblia y Judaismo

M. J. Cano Pérez, Editor
Dpto. de Estudios Semíticos, Area de Hebreo & Arameo
Fac. de Filosofía
Univ. de Granada
18011 Granada, Spain

Telephone: (34) 58 243579
Fax: (34) 58 243583
First published: 1953
Sponsoring organization: Univ. de Granada
ISSN: 0544-408X
MLA acronym: MEAH

SUBSCRIPTION INFORMATION

Frequency of publication: Annual
Available in microform: No

ADVERTISING INFORMATION

Advertising accepted: No

EDITORIAL DESCRIPTION

Scope: Publishes articles on Hebrew philology, the Bible, and Judaism.
Reviews books: Yes
Publishes notes: Yes
Languages accepted: Spanish; English; French; German; Hebrew
Prints abstracts: Yes
Author-anonymous submission: Yes

SUBMISSION REQUIREMENTS

Author pays submission fee: No
Author pays page charges: No
Copyright ownership: Univ. de Granada
Rejected manuscripts: Returned
Time before publication decision: 3 mos.
Time between decision and publication: 3 mos.
Number of reviewers: 2
Articles published per year: 10-12

(1846)
*Miscellanea Mediaevalia

Albert Zimmermann, Editor
Thomas-Inst. der Univ. zu Köln
Universitätstr. 22
5000 Cologne 41, Germany

First published: 1962
Sponsoring organization: Univ. Köln, Thomas-Inst.
MLA acronym: MiscMed

SUBSCRIPTION INFORMATION

Frequency of publication: Irregular (approx. once every 2 yrs.)
Circulation: 1,000
Available in microform: No
Subscription address: Walter de Gruyter & Co., Genthiner Str. 13, Postfach 110240, 1000 Berlin 30, Germany

ADVERTISING INFORMATION

Advertising accepted: No

EDITORIAL DESCRIPTION

Scope: Publishes proceedings of the International Conventions of Medieval Scholars in Cologne.
Reviews books: No
Languages accepted: German; English; French; Italian
Prints abstracts: No

SUBMISSION REQUIREMENTS

Restrictions on contributors: Contributors must have participated in the International Conventions of Medieval Scholars in Cologne (Kölner Mediävistentagungen).
Length of articles: No restrictions
Number of copies required: 1
Copyright ownership: Walter de Gruyter & Co.
Time before publication decision: 1-2 mos.
Time between decision and publication: 9 mos.

(1847)
*Mississippi Folklore Register

Thomas S. Rankin, Editor
Box D-2
Delta State Univ.
Cleveland, MS 38733

First published: 1967
Sponsoring organization: Mississippi Folklore Soc. & Delta State Univ.
ISSN: 0026-6248
MLA acronym: MissFR

SUBSCRIPTION INFORMATION

Frequency of publication: Annual
Circulation: 350
Available in microform: No
Subscription address: William Hays, Secretary-Treasurer, Literature & Language Dept., Delta State Univ., Cleveland, MS 38733

ADVERTISING INFORMATION

Advertising accepted: Yes

EDITORIAL DESCRIPTION

Scope: Journal serves the goals of the Mississippi Folklore Society by encouraging the collection, publication, and interpretation of folk ways. Emphasis is on, although not limited to, Mississippi and Southern folklore and folklife.
Reviews books: Yes
Publishes notes: Yes
Languages accepted: English
Prints abstracts: No
Author-anonymous submission: Yes

SUBMISSION REQUIREMENTS

Restrictions on contributors: None
Author pays submission fee: No
Author pays page charges: No
Length of articles: 5-20 pp. maximum
Length of book reviews: 1,500 words maximum
Length of notes: 1,000-2,000 words
Style: MLA
Number of copies required: 2
Special requirements: Submit original typescript and 1 photocopy.
Copyright ownership: Mississippi Folklore Soc.
Rejected manuscripts: Returned; enclose return postage.
Time before publication decision: 6-8 mos.
Time between decision and publication: 6-12 mos.
Number of reviewers: 2
Articles published per year: 8-10
Book reviews published per year: 2-5
Notes published per year: 1-5

(1848)
*Mississippi Quarterly: The Journal of Southern Culture

Robert L. Phillips, Jr., Editor
P.O. Box 5272
Mississippi State, MS 39762

Telephone: 601 325-3069
Fax: 601 325-3299
First published: 1948
Sponsoring organization: College of Arts & Sciences, Mississippi State Univ.
ISSN: 0026-637X
MLA acronym: MissQ

SUBSCRIPTION INFORMATION

Frequency of publication: 4 times/yr. (Mar., June, Oct., Dec.)
Circulation: 700
Available in microform: Yes
Subscription price: $12.00/yr. US; $16.00/yr. elsewhere
Year to which price refers: 1992
Subscription address: Juanita Guyton, P.O. Box 5272, Mississippi State, MS 39762

ADVERTISING INFORMATION

Advertising accepted: Yes

EDITORIAL DESCRIPTION

Scope: Publishes articles, notes, queries, and book reviews on materials in the humanities and the social sciences dealing with the South, past and present.
Reviews books: Yes
Publishes notes: Yes
Languages accepted: English
Prints abstracts: No
Author-anonymous submission: No

SUBMISSION REQUIREMENTS

Restrictions on contributors: Book reviews are solicited.
Author pays submission fee: No
Author pays page charges: No
Length of articles: 4,000 words
Length of book reviews: 1,100 words
Length of notes: 500 words

Style: MLA
Number of copies required: 1
Copyright ownership: Journal
Rejected manuscripts: Returned; enclose return postage.
Time before publication decision: 3 mos.
Time between decision and publication: 6-18 mos.
Number of reviewers: 3
Articles submitted per year: 150
Articles published per year: 20
Book reviews published per year: 30
Notes submitted per year: 10-15
Notes published per year: 4-8

(1849)
Missouri Folklore Society Journal

Donald M. Lance, Editor
P.O. Box 1757
Columbia, MO 65205

First published: 1979
Sponsoring organization: Missouri Folklore Soc.
ISSN: 0731-2946
MLA acronym: MFSJ

SUBSCRIPTION INFORMATION

Frequency of publication: Annual
Circulation: 475
Available in microform: No

ADVERTISING INFORMATION

Advertising accepted: No

EDITORIAL DESCRIPTION

Scope: Publishes articles on folklore, folk music, and Missouri folklife.
Reviews books: Yes
Publishes notes: Yes
Languages accepted: English
Prints abstracts: No
Author-anonymous submission: No

SUBMISSION REQUIREMENTS

Restrictions on contributors: None
Author pays submission fee: No
Author pays page charges: No
Length of articles: 15-30 pp.
Length of book reviews: 2-4 pp.
Length of notes: 1-4 pp.
Style: Chicago
Number of copies required: 2
Copyright ownership: Missouri Folklore Soc.
Rejected manuscripts: Not returned
Time before publication decision: 3-10 mos.
Time between decision and publication: 3-8 mos.
Number of reviewers: 3
Articles submitted per year: 6
Articles published per year: 4
Book reviews submitted per year: 3-6
Book reviews published per year: 2-5
Notes submitted per year: 2
Notes published per year: 2

(1850)
*The Missouri Review

Speer Morgan & Greg Michalson, Editors
1507 Hillcrest Hall
Univ. of Missouri—Columbia
Columbia, MO 65211

Telephone: 314 882-4474
First published: 1978
Sponsoring organization: Curators of Univ. of Missouri
ISSN: 0191-1961
MLA acronym: MissR

SUBSCRIPTION INFORMATION

Frequency of publication: 3 times/yr.
Circulation: 4,000
Available in microform: No
Subscription price: $15.00/yr.
Year to which price refers: 1992

ADVERTISING INFORMATION

Advertising accepted: Yes
Advertising rates: $75.00/full page

EDITORIAL DESCRIPTION

Scope: Publishes articles, fiction, poetry, and interviews featuring unpublished authors as well as well-established authors. Also includes special features such as "History as Literature" and "Found Texts."
Reviews books: Yes
Publishes notes: No
Languages accepted: English
Prints abstracts: No
Author-anonymous submission: No

SUBMISSION REQUIREMENTS

Restrictions on contributors: No in-house contributors
Author pays submission fee: No
Author pays page charges: No
Length of articles: 5,000 words
Length of book reviews: 5,000 words
Style: Chicago
Number of copies required: 1
Copyright ownership: Journal; reverts to author upon request.
Rejected manuscripts: Returned; enclose SASE.
Time before publication decision: 10 weeks
Number of reviewers: 4-6
Articles submitted per year: 200
Articles published per year: 10
Book reviews submitted per year: 20
Book reviews published per year: 2

(1851)
*MIT Occasional Papers in Linguistics

Dept. of Linguistics & Philosophy, Room 20D-219
Massachusetts Inst. of Technology
Cambridge, MA 02139

Telephone: 617 253-7370
E-mail: MITWPL@athena.mit.edu
First published: 1992
Sponsoring organization: Massachusetts Inst. of Technology
MLA acronym: MITOPL

SUBSCRIPTION INFORMATION

Frequency of publication: Approx. 2 times/yr.
Available in microform: No
Subscription price: $5.00/issue
Year to which price refers: 1992

ADVERTISING INFORMATION

Advertising accepted: No

EDITORIAL DESCRIPTION

Scope: Publishes studies on theoretical linguistics. Topics covered include syntax, grammar, phonology, and morphology.
Reviews books: No
Publishes notes: No
Languages accepted: English; French
Prints abstracts: No
Author-anonymous submission: No

SUBMISSION REQUIREMENTS

Restrictions on contributors: Contributors must be MIT staff members or students.
Author pays submission fee: No
Author pays page charges: No
Length of books: 50-100 pp.
Style: Linguistic Soc. of America suggested
Number of copies required: 1
Copyright ownership: Author
Rejected manuscripts: Returned
Time before publication decision: 1 mo.
Time between decision and publication: 1 mo.
Books published per year: 1-2

(1852)
*MIT Working Papers in Linguistics

Dept. of Linguistics & Philosophy, Room 20D-219
Massachusetts Inst. of Technology
Cambridge, MA 02139

Telephone: 617 253-7370
E-mail: MITWPL@athena.mit.edu
First published: 1979
Sponsoring organization: Massachusetts Inst. of Technology
MLA acronym: MITWPL

SUBSCRIPTION INFORMATION

Frequency of publication: 1-2 times/yr.
Available in microform: No
Subscription price: $12.00/issue plus postage
Year to which price refers: 1992

ADVERTISING INFORMATION

Advertising accepted: No

EDITORIAL DESCRIPTION

Scope: Publishes articles on theoretical linguistics. Topics covered include phonology, syntax, grammar, and morphology.
Reviews books: No
Publishes notes: No
Languages accepted: English; French
Prints abstracts: No
Author-anonymous submission: No

SUBMISSION REQUIREMENTS

Restrictions on contributors: None
Author pays submission fee: No
Author pays page charges: No
Length of articles: No restrictions
Style: American Anthropological Soc.; Linguistic Soc. of America
Number of copies required: 1
Copyright ownership: Author
Rejected manuscripts: Returned
Time before publication decision: 1 mo.
Time between decision and publication: 1 mo.
Number of reviewers: 1
Articles published per year: 12-24

(1853)
*Mitteilungen der Deutschen Orient-Gesellschaft zu Berlin

Vorstand der Deutschen Orient-Gesellschaft
Altorientalisches Seminar
Bitterstr. 8-12
1000 Berlin 33, Germany

First published: 1898
Sponsoring organization: Deutsche Orient-Gesellschaft
ISSN: 0342-118X
MLA acronym: MDOG

SUBSCRIPTION INFORMATION

Frequency of publication: Annual
Circulation: 900
Available in microform: No
Subscription price: 80 DM/yr.
Year to which price refers: 1991

ADVERTISING INFORMATION

Advertising accepted: No

EDITORIAL DESCRIPTION

Scope: Publishes articles on the culture of the ancient Near and Middle East until the Islamic period.
Reviews books: No
Publishes notes: Yes
Languages accepted: German; English; French
Prints abstracts: Yes
Author-anonymous submission: No

SUBMISSION REQUIREMENTS

Restrictions on contributors: None
Author pays submission fee: No
Author pays page charges: No
Length of articles: No restrictions
Length of notes: No restrictions
Style: None
Number of copies required: 1
Copyright ownership: Author
Rejected manuscripts: Returned

(1854)
Mitteilungen der E.T.A. Hoffmann-Gesellschaft-Bamberg e.V.

E. T. A. Hoffmann-Gesellschaft
Wetzelstr. 19
8600 Bamberg, Germany

First published: 1938
ISSN: 0073-2885
MLA acronym: MHG

SUBSCRIPTION INFORMATION

Frequency of publication: Annual (irregular)
Circulation: 850
Available in microform: No

ADVERTISING INFORMATION

Advertising accepted: No

EDITORIAL DESCRIPTION

Scope: Publishes material on E. T. A. Hoffmann.
Reviews books: Yes
Publishes notes: No
Languages accepted: German

SUBMISSION REQUIREMENTS

Author pays submission fee: Yes
Author pays page charges: No

(1855)
*Mitteilungen des Verbandes deutscher Anglisten

Rüdiger Ahrens, Editor
Inst. für Englische Philologie
Univ. Würzburg
Am Hubland
8700 Würzburg, Germany

Telephone: (49) 931 8885409
Fax: (49) 931 8884615
First published: 1990
Sponsoring organization: Bayerisches Staatsministerium für Wissenschaft & Kunst, Munich; German Assn. of Univ. Professors of English
ISSN: 0938-5819
MLA acronym: MVdA

SUBSCRIPTION INFORMATION

Frequency of publication: 2 times/yr. (Mar., Sept.)
Circulation: 1,000
Available in microform: No
Subscription price: 45 DM/yr.
Year to which price refers: 1992
Subscription address: Carl Winter Universitätsverlag, Lutherstr. 59, 6900 Heidelberg, Germany
Subscription telephone: (49) 6221 414921
Subscription fax: (49) 6221 414941

ADVERTISING INFORMATION

Advertising accepted: Yes
Advertising rates: 500 DM/full page

EDITORIAL DESCRIPTION

Scope: As the official journal of the German Association of University Professors of English, it publishes articles in all fields of English and American studies with a focus on theoretical and historical dimensions of the fields and institutions.
Reviews books: Yes
Publishes notes: Yes
Languages accepted: German; English
Prints abstracts: Yes
Author-anonymous submission: No

SUBMISSION REQUIREMENTS

Restrictions on contributors: Contributors must be university teachers of English language and literature.
Author pays submission fee: No
Author pays page charges: No
Length of articles: 5,000 words
Length of book reviews: 1,000 words
Length of notes: 600 words
Style: MLA; Chicago
Number of copies required: 1
Special requirements: Submit contribution on diskette in Microsoft Word or ASCII format.
Copyright ownership: Carl Winter Universitätsverlag
Rejected manuscripts: Returned
Time before publication decision: 4 mos.
Time between decision and publication: 6 mos.
Number of reviewers: 2

(1856)
*Mitteilungen und Forschungsbeiträge der Cusanus-Gesellschaft

Rudolf Haubst, Editor
Inst. für Cusanus-Forschung an der Univ. & der Theologischen Fakultät
Domfreihof 3
5500 Trier, Germany

First published: 1961
Sponsoring organization: Cusanus Assn. Union for Cusanus Research
ISSN: 0590-451X
MLA acronym: MFCG

SUBSCRIPTION INFORMATION

Frequency of publication: Irregular
Circulation: 700
Available in microform: No
Subscription address: Paulinus-Verlag Trier, Fleischstr. 62-65, 5500 Trier, Germany

ADVERTISING INFORMATION

Advertising accepted: No

EDITORIAL DESCRIPTION

Scope: Publishes on all areas of Cusanus research and interpretation as well as the history of its influence.
Reviews books: Yes
Publishes notes: Yes
Languages accepted: German; French; English
Prints abstracts: No
Author-anonymous submission: No

SUBMISSION REQUIREMENTS

Restrictions on contributors: None
Author pays submission fee: No
Author pays page charges: No
Length of articles: No restrictions
Length of book reviews: No restrictions
Length of notes: No restrictions
Style: None
Number of copies required: 1
Special requirements: Submit typescript.
Copyright ownership: Cusanus Assn.
Rejected manuscripts: Returned at author's request
Time before publication decision: 1 yr.
Time between decision and publication: 1 yr.
Number of reviewers: 1
Articles submitted per year: 10-20
Articles published per year: 10-20

(1857)
*Mittellateinisches Jahrbuch: Internationale Zeitschrift für Mediävistik/International Journal of Medieval Studies/Revue Internationale des Etudes Médiévales/Rivista Internazionale di Studi Medievali

Fritz Wagner, Editor
Seminar für Mittellateinische Philologie
Freie Univ. Berlin
Schwendener Str. 1
1000 Berlin 33, Germany

Additional editorial address: Jürgen Stohlmann, Inst. für Altertumskunde, Mittellateinische Abteilung, Univ. zu Köln, Albertus-Magnus-Platz, 5000 Cologne 41, Germany
Telephone: (49) 30 8382659
First published: 1964
Sponsoring organization: Deutsche Forschungsgemeinschaft
ISSN: 0076-9762
MLA acronym: MitJ

SUBSCRIPTION INFORMATION

Frequency of publication: Annual
Circulation: 450
Available in microform: No
Subscription price: 156 DM/yr.
Year to which price refers: 1991
Subscription address: Anton Hiersemann Verlag, Postfach 14 01 55, 7000 Stuttgart 1, Germany
Subscription telephone: (49) 711 638264
Subscription fax: (49) 711 6369010

ADVERTISING INFORMATION

Advertising accepted: Yes
Advertising rates: Request from Anton Hiersemann Verlag

EDITORIAL DESCRIPTION

Scope: Publishes studies in Medieval Latin language and literature; editions of medieval Latin texts; studies in manuscripts, script, scriptoria, and libraries of the Middle Ages.
Reviews books: Yes
Publishes notes: Yes
Languages accepted: English; German; French; Latin; Italian
Prints abstracts: No
Author-anonymous submission: No

SUBMISSION REQUIREMENTS

Restrictions on contributors: None
Author pays submission fee: No
Author pays page charges: No
Length of articles: No restrictions
Length of book reviews: 1-10 pp.
Length of notes: No restrictions
Style: Journal; guidelines are available from the publisher and editor.

Number of copies required: 1
Special requirements: Submit camera-ready copy in journal's format.
Copyright ownership: Anton Hiersemann Verlag
Rejected manuscripts: Returned
Time before publication decision: 3 mos.
Time between decision and publication: 1-2 yrs.
Number of reviewers: 1-2
Articles submitted per year: 15-20
Articles published per year: 15-20
Book reviews submitted per year: 50
Book reviews published per year: 40-50
Notes submitted per year: 3-5
Notes published per year: 3-5

(1858)
*Mladika

Marij Maver, Editor
Ul. Donizetti 3
34133 Trst Trieste, Italy

Telephone: (39) 40 370846
Fax: (39) 40 370846
First published: 1957
ISSN: 0462-9698
MLA acronym: Mladika

SUBSCRIPTION INFORMATION

Frequency of publication: 12 times/yr.
Circulation: 1,200
Available in microform: No

ADVERTISING INFORMATION

Advertising accepted: Yes

EDITORIAL DESCRIPTION

Scope: Publishes articles on Slovenian language and literature.
Languages accepted: Slovenian
Prints abstracts: No

SUBMISSION REQUIREMENTS

Number of copies required: 1
Copyright ownership: Author
Rejected manuscripts: Not returned
Time between decision and publication: 2 weeks
Number of reviewers: 10

(1859)
*MLN

Eduardo Saccone, Harry Sieber, Werner Hamacher, Wilda Anderson, & Richard Macksey, Editors
The Humanities Center
Johns Hopkins Univ.
Baltimore, MD 21218

Telephone: 410 516-7227 [French]; 410 516-7508 [German]; 410 516-7226 [Italian & Spanish]; 410 516-7619 [comparative literature]
First published: 1886
Sponsoring organization: Johns Hopkins Univ.
ISSN: 0026-7910
MLA acronym: MLN

SUBSCRIPTION INFORMATION

Frequency of publication: 5 times/yr. (Jan. [Italian], Mar. [Hispanic], Apr. [German], Sept. [French], Dec. [Comparative Literature])
Circulation: 2,500
Available in microform: Yes
Subscription price: $74.00/yr. institutions; $29.00/yr. individuals; $27.00/3 yrs. single language, individuals only
Year to which price refers: 1993

Subscription address: Johns Hopkins Univ. Press, Journals Publishing Division, 2715 North Charles St., Baltimore, MD 21218-4319
Subscription telephone: 410 516-6987; 800 537-5487
Subscription fax: 410 516-6998

ADVERTISING INFORMATION

Advertising accepted: Yes
Advertising rates: $175.00/half page; $250.00/full page; $300.00/inside cover; $315.00/back cover

EDITORIAL DESCRIPTION

Scope: Publishes literary studies and book reviews in the areas of Italian, Spanish, French, German, and comparative literature. Each issue features one language and centers on the discussion of the literary works and related critical works of that language. Comparative literature issue also publishes articles in general critical theory, film studies, and feminist studies.
Reviews books: Yes
Publishes notes: Yes
Languages accepted: English; French; German; Italian; Spanish
Prints abstracts: No
Author-anonymous submission: No

SUBMISSION REQUIREMENTS

Restrictions on contributors: Book reviews are commissioned.
Author pays submission fee: No
Author pays page charges: No
Length of articles: 7,500 words
Length of book reviews: 1,500 words maximum
Length of notes: 2,500 words
Style: MLA
Number of copies required: 2
Special requirements: Submit double-spaced typescript (including notes).
Copyright ownership: Johns Hopkins Univ. Press
Rejected manuscripts: Returned; enclose return postage.
Time before publication decision: 3-12 mos.
Time between decision and publication: 6 mos.
Number of reviewers: 2
Articles submitted per year: 400
Articles published per year: 50
Book reviews submitted per year: 120-140
Book reviews published per year: 120
Notes submitted per year: 100
Notes published per year: 20

(1860)
Mnemosyne: Bibliotheca Classica Batava

C. J. Ruijgh, Editor
c/o L. F. Janssen
Lindenlaan, 8
3707 ER Zeist, Netherlands

First published: 1852
ISSN: 0026-7074
MLA acronym: Mnemosyne

SUBSCRIPTION INFORMATION

Frequency of publication: 2 times/yr.
Circulation: 1,000
Available in microform: No
Subscription address: E. J. Brill, Plantijnstraat 2, Postbus 9000, 2300 PA Leiden, Netherlands

ADVERTISING INFORMATION

Advertising accepted: No

EDITORIAL DESCRIPTION

Scope: Publishes articles on classical philology, ancient philosophy, history, Mycenology, Greek epigraphy, and Greek and Roman religions.
Reviews books: Yes
Publishes notes: Yes
Languages accepted: English; French; German; Latin; Italian
Prints abstracts: Yes
Author-anonymous submission: No

SUBMISSION REQUIREMENTS

Restrictions on contributors: None
Author pays submission fee: No
Author pays page charges: No
Length of articles: 10-20 pp.
Length of book reviews: 1,000-1,500 words
Length of notes: 2,000 words
Style: None
Number of copies required: 1
Special requirements: Submit typescript.
Copyright ownership: Assigned by author to journal
Rejected manuscripts: Returned
Time before publication decision: 4 mos.
Time between decision and publication: 18-24 mos.
Number of reviewers: 2-3
Articles submitted per year: 60
Articles published per year: 35
Book reviews submitted per year: 200
Book reviews published per year: 60
Notes submitted per year: 40
Notes published per year: 15

(1861)
Mnēmosynē: Etēsion Periodikon tēs Hetaireias Historikōn Spoudōn epi tou Neōterou Hellēnismou

Tassos Gritsopoulos, Editor
16, Dervenion St.
10680 Athens, Greece

First published: 1967
Sponsoring organization: Hetaireia Historikōn Spoudōn epi tou Neōterou Hellēnismou
MLA acronym: MnēmosynēA

SUBSCRIPTION INFORMATION

Frequency of publication: Annual
Circulation: 1,000
Available in microform: No

ADVERTISING INFORMATION

Advertising accepted: No

EDITORIAL DESCRIPTION

Scope: Focuses on the historical study of modern Hellenism.
Reviews books: Yes
Publishes notes: Yes
Languages accepted: Greek; English; French; German; Italian; Spanish
Prints abstracts: Yes
Author-anonymous submission: No

SUBMISSION REQUIREMENTS

Restrictions on contributors: None
Author pays submission fee: No
Author pays page charges: No
Length of articles: 6,000-12,000 words
Length of book reviews: 500-3,000 words
Length of notes: 500 words maximum
Style: MLA; Chicago
Number of copies required: 1
Copyright ownership: Hetaireia Historikōn Spoudōn epi tou Neōterou Hellēnismou
Rejected manuscripts: Returned
Time before publication decision: 2-3 mos.
Time between decision and publication: 6 mos.

Number of reviewers: 3
Articles submitted per year: 20
Articles published per year: 10
Book reviews submitted per year: 40
Book reviews published per year: 30
Notes submitted per year: 20-30
Notes published per year: 10 maximum

(1862)
Modèles Linguistiques

André Joly, Editor
Presses Universitaires de Lille
rue du Barreau, B.P. 149
59653 Villeneuve d'Ascq Cedex, France

First published: 1979
ISSN: 0249-6267
MLA acronym: MLing

SUBSCRIPTION INFORMATION

Frequency of publication: 2 times/yr.
Circulation: 500

EDITORIAL DESCRIPTION

Reviews books: Yes
Languages accepted: French
Prints abstracts: Yes

SUBMISSION REQUIREMENTS

Restrictions on contributors: None
Length of articles: No restrictions
Number of copies required: 2
Special requirements: Include an abstract.
Copyright ownership: Author
Rejected manuscripts: Returned
Time before publication decision: 6-18 mos.
Time between decision and publication: 6-18 mos.
Number of reviewers: 2
Articles published per year: 10-18

(1863)
*Modellanalysen: Literatur

Werner Zimmermann & Klaus Lindemann, Editors
Wieksiepen, 3
4300 Essen, Germany

Additional editorial address: K. Lindemann, Friedrich-Küch-str., 22, 4300 Essen 1, Germany
Telephone: (49) 201 281134 (W. Zimmermann); (49) 201 251117 (K. Lindemann)
First published: 1980
MLA acronym: Modellanalysen

SUBSCRIPTION INFORMATION

Frequency of publication: 2-3 volumes/yr.
Circulation: 3,000
Available in microform: No
Subscription price: 25 DM/volume
Year to which price refers: 1992
Subscription address: Verlag Ferdinand Schöningh, Jühenplatz, 1-3, 4790 Paderborn, Germany
Subscription telephone: (49) 5251 29010

ADVERTISING INFORMATION

Advertising accepted: No

EDITORIAL DESCRIPTION

Scope: Publishes monograph length studies on various aspects of German literature focusing on a variety of methodological approaches. Also publishes studies on special themes in German literature.
Reviews books: No
Publishes notes: Yes
Languages accepted: German
Prints abstracts: No
Author-anonymous submission: No

SUBMISSION REQUIREMENTS

Author pays submission fee: No
Author pays page charges: No
Length of books: 120 pp.
Number of copies required: 1
Copyright ownership: Verlag Ferdinand Schöningh
Rejected manuscripts: Returned
Time before publication decision: 3 mos.
Time between decision and publication: 1 yr.
Number of reviewers: 3
Books submitted per year: 5
Books published per year: 2-3

(1864)
*Modern Age: A Quarterly Review

George A. Panichas, Editor
Intercollegiate Studies Inst., Inc.
14 S. Bryn Mawr Ave.
Bryn Mawr, PA 19010

Additional editorial address: P.O. Box AB, College Park, MD 20740
Telephone: 215 525-7501
Fax: 215 525-3315
First published: 1957
Sponsoring organization: Intercollegiate Studies Inst., Inc.
ISSN: 0026-7457
MLA acronym: ModA

SUBSCRIPTION INFORMATION

Frequency of publication: 4 times/yr.
Circulation: 3,000
Available in microform: Yes
Subscription price: $15.00/yr., $25.00/2 yrs.
Year to which price refers: 1992

ADVERTISING INFORMATION

Advertising accepted: Yes

EDITORIAL DESCRIPTION

Scope: Focuses on serious discussion of foreign affairs, economics, religion, history, education, literature, and political and social philosophies in relation to conservative theory and principles. The journal seeks to pursue a conservative policy for the sake of a liberal understanding.
Reviews books: Yes
Publishes notes: Yes
Languages accepted: English
Prints abstracts: No

SUBMISSION REQUIREMENTS

Restrictions on contributors: Unsolicited book reviews are not accepted.
Author pays submission fee: No
Author pays page charges: No
Length of articles: 5,000 words
Length of book reviews: 1,500 words
Length of notes: 1,500 words
Style: Chicago
Number of copies required: 1
Special requirements: Submit original double-spaced typescript. Footnotes should be kept to a minimum.
Copyright ownership: Journal
Rejected manuscripts: Returned; enclose SASE.
Time before publication decision: 4 mos.
Time between decision and publication: 12-18 mos.
Number of reviewers: 3
Articles published per year: 40
Book reviews published per year: 40
Notes published per year: 8

(1865)
*Modern Austrian Literature

Donald G. Daviau, Editor
Dept. of Literatures & Languages
Univ. of California
Riverside, CA 92521

Telephone: 714 787-5603
Fax: 714 787-3800
First published: 1961
Sponsoring organization: International Arthur Schnitzler Research Assn.
ISSN: 0026-7503
MLA acronym: MAL

SUBSCRIPTION INFORMATION

Frequency of publication: 3-4 times/yr.
Circulation: 750
Available in microform: Yes
Subscription price: $30.00/yr. institutions US; $35.00/yr. institutions elsewhere; $20.00/yr. individuals US; $25.00/yr. individuals elsewhere
Year to which price refers: 1992
Subscription address: Jorun B. Johns, Dept. of Foreign Languages, California State Univ., San Bernardino, CA 92407
Subscription telephone: 714 880-5851

ADVERTISING INFORMATION

Advertising accepted: Yes
Advertising rates: $80.00/full page

EDITORIAL DESCRIPTION

Scope: Publishes articles on Austrian literature and culture of the 19th and 20th centuries.
Reviews books: Yes
Publishes notes: Yes
Languages accepted: English; German
Prints abstracts: Yes
Author-anonymous submission: Yes

SUBMISSION REQUIREMENTS

Restrictions on contributors: Contributors must be a members of the International Arthur Schnitzler Research Assn.
Author pays submission fee: No
Author pays page charges: No
Length of articles: 20 double-spaced typescript pp.
Length of book reviews: 500-1,200 words
Length of notes: 50-1,000 words
Style: MLA
Number of copies required: 2
Copyright ownership: Journal
Rejected manuscripts: Returned; enclose return postage.
Time before publication decision: 3-6 mos.
Time between decision and publication: 1 yr.
Number of reviewers: 2
Articles submitted per year: 60-70
Articles published per year: 25-30
Book reviews submitted per year: 100
Book reviews published per year: 100
Notes submitted per year: 5-10
Notes published per year: 2-3

(1866)
Modern Chinese Literature

Howard Goldblatt, Editor
Chinese Program
San Francisco State Univ.
1600 Holloway Ave.
San Francisco, CA 94132

First published: 1984
Sponsoring organization: San Francisco State Univ.; Univ. of California; Stanford Univ.
ISSN: 8755-8963
MLA acronym: MCL

SUBSCRIPTION INFORMATION

Frequency of publication: 2 times/yr. (Fall, Spring)
Circulation: 400
Available in microform: No

ADVERTISING INFORMATION

Advertising accepted: Yes

EDITORIAL DESCRIPTION

Scope: Publishes articles on modern and contemporary Chinese literature.
Reviews books: Yes
Publishes notes: Yes
Languages accepted: English
Prints abstracts: No

SUBMISSION REQUIREMENTS

Restrictions on contributors: Unsolicited book reviews are not accepted.
Author pays submission fee: No
Author pays page charges: No
Length of articles: No restrictions
Length of book reviews: 500-1,200 words
Length of notes: No restrictions
Style: MLA
Number of copies required: 2
Special requirements: Submit double-spaced typescript. Both Pinyin and Wade-Giles romanization are accepted.
Copyright ownership: Journal
Rejected manuscripts: Returned
Time before publication decision: 1-3 mos.
Time between decision and publication: 6-12 mos.
Number of reviewers: 1-2
Articles submitted per year: 10-20
Articles published per year: 8-10
Book reviews published per year: 5-10

(1867)
*Modern Drama

John H. Astington, Hersh Zeifman, Patricia Howard, & Christopher Innes, Editors
Graduate Centre for Study of Drama
Univ. of Toronto
214 College Street
Toronto, Ontario M5T 2Z9, Canada

Telephone: 416 978-7984
Fax: 416 971-1378
First published: 1958
Sponsoring organization: Univ. of Toronto, Graduate Centre for Study of Drama
ISSN: 0026-7694
MLA acronym: MD

SUBSCRIPTION INFORMATION

Frequency of publication: 4 times/yr. (Mar., June, Sept., Dec.)
Circulation: 2,500
Available in microform: Yes
Subscription price: C$40.00/yr. institutions; C$22.50/yr. individuals; C$15.00/yr. students; add C$5.00/yr. outside Canada
Year to which price refers: 1991
Subscription address: Journals Dept., Univ. of Toronto Press, 5201 Dufferin St., Downsview, Ontario M3H 5T8, Canada
Subscription telephone: 416 667-7781
Subscription fax: 416 667-7832

ADVERTISING INFORMATION

Advertising accepted: Yes
Advertising rates: C$200.00/half page; C$295.00/full page

EDITORIAL DESCRIPTION

Scope: Publishes critical studies in dramatic literature of the modern period, from 1850 to the present.

Reviews books: Yes
Publishes notes: Yes
Languages accepted: English; French
Prints abstracts: No
Author-anonymous submission: No

SUBMISSION REQUIREMENTS

Restrictions on contributors: None
Author pays submission fee: No
Author pays page charges: No
Length of articles: 4,000 words maximum
Length of book reviews: 500-750 words
Length of notes: 1,000 words
Style: MLA with modifications
Number of copies required: 2
Special requirements: Footnotes must be according to journal's style.
Copyright ownership: Governing Council, Univ. of Toronto
Rejected manuscripts: Not returned
Time before publication decision: 2-3 mos.
Time between decision and publication: 12-18 mos.
Number of reviewers: 2-3
Articles submitted per year: 700
Articles published per year: 35-40
Book reviews submitted per year: 60
Book reviews published per year: 45-50

(1868)
*Modern Fiction Studies

Patrick J. O'Donnell, Editor
Dept. of English
Purdue Univ., Heavilon Hall
West Lafayette, IN 47907

Telephone: 317 494-3758
Fax: 317 494-3780
E-mail: POD@PURCCVM
First published: 1955
Sponsoring organization: Dept. of English, Purdue Univ.
ISSN: 0026-7724
MLA acronym: MFS

SUBSCRIPTION INFORMATION

Frequency of publication: 4 times/yr. (Spring, Summer, Fall, Winter)
Circulation: 3,500
Available in microform: Yes
Subscription price: $21.00/yr. institutions N. America; $18.00/yr. individuals N. America; $23.00/yr. elsewhere
Year to which price refers: 1992

ADVERTISING INFORMATION

Advertising accepted: No

EDITORIAL DESCRIPTION

Scope: Invites the submission of articles offering theoretical, historical, interdisciplinary, and cultural approaches to modern narrative. The Spring and Autumn issues are special numbers dealing with special topics or individual writers; the Summer and Winter issues are general numbers concerned with various writers and subjects.
Reviews books: Yes
Publishes notes: No
Languages accepted: English
Prints abstracts: No
Author-anonymous submission: Yes

SUBMISSION REQUIREMENTS

Restrictions on contributors: Book reviews are commissioned.
Author pays submission fee: No
Author pays page charges: No
Length of articles: 6,000-10,000 words
Length of book reviews: 500 words
Style: MLA
Number of copies required: 3

Special requirements: Submit original typescript and 2 copies.
Copyright ownership: Assigned by author to Purdue Research Foundation but reprinting is available to author.
Rejected manuscripts: Returned; enclose return postage.
Time before publication decision: 2-4 mos.
Time between decision and publication: 6-18 mos.
Number of reviewers: 2-3
Articles submitted per year: 500
Articles published per year: 25
Book reviews published per year: 180-200

(1869)
*Modern Hebrew Literature

Gershon Shalsed, Editor
Inst. for the Translation of Hebrew Literature
P.O. Box 10051
Ramat-Gan 52001, Israel

Telephone: (972) 3 5796830
Fax: (972) 3 5796832
First published: 1975
ISSN: 0334-4266
MLA acronym: MHL

SUBSCRIPTION INFORMATION

Frequency of publication: 2 times/yr.
Circulation: 1,000
Available in microform: Yes
Subscription price: $9.00/yr.
Year to which price refers: 1992

ADVERTISING INFORMATION

Advertising accepted: No

EDITORIAL DESCRIPTION

Scope: Publishes critical articles on Hebrew literature as well as new translations and general articles on Hebrew literature published in English.
Reviews books: Yes
Publishes notes: Yes
Languages accepted: Hebrew; English
Prints abstracts: No
Author-anonymous submission: No

SUBMISSION REQUIREMENTS

Author pays submission fee: No
Author pays page charges: No
Length of articles: 1,200-2,000 words
Length of book reviews: 1,200 words
Style: MLA
Number of copies required: 1
Copyright ownership: Inst. for the Translation of Hebrew Literature
Rejected manuscripts: Returned
Time before publication decision: 2-3 mos.
Time between decision and publication: 1 mo.
Number of reviewers: 1
Articles submitted per year: 20
Articles published per year: 12
Book reviews submitted per year: 50
Book reviews published per year: 40

(1870)
*Modern Humanities Research Association Texts and Dissertations Series

Modern Humanities Research Assn.
King's College
Strand, London WC2R 2LS, England

First published: 1970
Sponsoring organization: Modern Humanities Research Assn.
MLA acronym: MHRADS

SUBSCRIPTION INFORMATION

Frequency of publication: Irregular
Circulation: 500
Available in microform: No

ADVERTISING INFORMATION

Advertising accepted: No

EDITORIAL DESCRIPTION

Scope: Publishes texts and dissertations.
Reviews books: No
Publishes notes: No
Languages accepted: English
Prints abstracts: No

SUBMISSION REQUIREMENTS

Restrictions on contributors: Submission by invitation only after preliminary inquiry
Author pays submission fee: No
Author pays page charges: No
Length of books: 80,000-100,000 words
Style: Modern Humanities Research Assn.
Number of copies required: 1
Special requirements: Dissertation must have been published within the last five years.
Copyright ownership: Modern Humanities Research Assn.
Rejected manuscripts: Returned if contribution was solicited.
Time before publication decision: 6 mos.
Time between decision and publication: 1 yr.

(1871)
*The Modern Language Journal

David P. Benseler, Editor
Dept. of Modern Languages & Literatures
Case Western Reserve Univ.
Cleveland, OH 44106-7118

Telephone: 216 368-3683
Fax: 216 368-2216
E-mail: DPB5@PO.CWRU.EDU
First published: 1916
Sponsoring organization: National Federation of Modern Language Teachers Assns.
ISSN: 0026-7902
MLA acronym: MLJ

SUBSCRIPTION INFORMATION

Frequency of publication: 4 times/yr. (Mar., June, Sept., Dec.)
Circulation: 7,000
Available in microform: Yes
Subscription price: $40.00/yr. institutions; $20.00/yr. individuals
Year to which price refers: 1992
Subscription address: Journal Division, Univ. of Wisconsin Press, 114 N. Murray St., Madison, WI 53715
Subscription telephone: 608 262-4952
Subscription fax: 608 262-7560

ADVERTISING INFORMATION

Advertising accepted: Yes
Advertising rates: $75.00/quarter page; $140.00/half page; $240.00/full page; $290.00/inside cover; $315.00/back cover

EDITORIAL DESCRIPTION

Scope: Devoted primarily to methods, pedagogical research, and topics of professional interest to all language teachers. Publishes articles and reviews in the areas of Italian, Spanish, French, German, and all other foreign languages, applied and general linguistics, foreign language methodology, and research.
Reviews books: Yes
Publishes notes: Yes
Languages accepted: English
Prints abstracts: No
Author-anonymous submission: Yes

SUBMISSION REQUIREMENTS

Restrictions on contributors: None
Author pays submission fee: No
Author pays page charges: No
Length of articles: 20-30 double-spaced typescript pp. (excluding notes, tables, figures, & bibliography) maximum
Length of book reviews: 500 words
Length of notes: 2,000 words maximum
Style: MLA
Number of copies required: 3
Special requirements: Manuscripts should be prepared for anonymous evaluation; author identification must be removed.
Copyright ownership: Journal
Rejected manuscripts: 1 copy returned; enclose $5.00 in loose postage & SAE.
Time before publication decision: 10-14 weeks
Time between decision and publication: 6-12 mos.
Number of reviewers: 2-3
Articles submitted per year: 200-250
Articles published per year: 35-45
Book reviews submitted per year: 200-250
Book reviews published per year: 200-250
Notes submitted per year: 4
Notes published per year: 4

(1872)
*Modern Language Quarterly

John C. Coldewey, Editor
Dept. of English, GN-30
Univ. of Washington
Seattle, WA 98195

Telephone: 206 543-6827
Fax: 206 685-2673
E-mail: Mlq@u.washington.edu
First published: 1940
Sponsoring organization: Univ. of Washington
ISSN: 0026-7929
MLA acronym: MLQ

SUBSCRIPTION INFORMATION

Frequency of publication: 4 times/yr. (Mar., June, Sept., Dec.)
Circulation: 1,700
Available in microform: Yes, through Univ. Microfilms International
Subscription price: $30.00/yr. institutions US; $38.00/yr. institutions elsewhere; $20.00/yr. individuals US; $28.00/yr. individuals elsewhere; $7.50/single issue US; $15.50/single issue elsewhere
Year to which price refers: 1991
Subscription address: Journals Dept., Duke Univ. Press, 6697 College Station, Durham, NC 27708
Subscription telephone: 919 684-6837
Subscription fax: 919 684-8644

ADVERTISING INFORMATION

Advertising accepted: Yes
Advertising rates: $150.00/half page; $250.00/full page

EDITORIAL DESCRIPTION

Scope: Publishes scholarly and critical articles and reviews dealing with British, American, Romance, Germanic, and comparative literatures, medieval to modern.
Reviews books: Yes
Publishes notes: No
Languages accepted: English
Prints abstracts: No
Author-anonymous submission: No

SUBMISSION REQUIREMENTS

Restrictions on contributors: None
Author pays submission fee: No
Author pays page charges: No
Length of articles: 3,000-8,000 words
Length of book reviews: 750-1,200 words
Style: Chicago with modifications
Number of copies required: 1
Special requirements: Contributors must provide assurance of single submission.
Copyright ownership: Univ. of Washington
Rejected manuscripts: Returned; enclose return postage.
Time before publication decision: 2-3 mos.
Time between decision and publication: 1 yr.
Number of reviewers: 1-2
Articles submitted per year: 200-250
Articles published per year: 20
Book reviews submitted per year: 32
Book reviews published per year: 30-40

(1873)
*The Modern Language Review

R. M. Walker, A. J. Gurr, M. C. Cook, J. R. Woodhouse, D. F. Henn, A. F. Bance, & R. Russell, Editors
Birkbeck College
Univ. of London
Malet St.
London WC1E 7HX, England

Telephone: (44) 71 6316145
Fax: (44) 71 6316107
First published: 1918
Sponsoring organization: Modern Humanities Research Assn.
ISSN: 0026-7937
MLA acronym: MLR

SUBSCRIPTION INFORMATION

Frequency of publication: 4 times/yr. (Jan., Apr., July, Oct.)
Circulation: 2,500
Available in microform: No
Subscription price: $110.00/yr. institutions; $35.00/yr. individuals
Year to which price refers: 1992
Subscription address: R. A. Wisbey, Dept. of German, King's College, Strand, London WC2R 2LS, England

ADVERTISING INFORMATION

Advertising accepted: No

EDITORIAL DESCRIPTION

Scope: Publishes articles on English (including US) and European languages and literatures, embodying the results of research or criticism, as well as previously unpublished texts and documents.
Reviews books: Yes
Publishes notes: No
Languages accepted: English
Prints abstracts: No
Author-anonymous submission: No

SUBMISSION REQUIREMENTS

Restrictions on contributors: None
Author pays submission fee: No
Author pays page charges: No
Length of articles: 6,000-8,000 words; shorter pieces accepted
Length of book reviews: 500-1,000 words
Style: Modern Humanities Research Assn.
Number of copies required: 2
Special requirements: Submit original typescript, preferably double-spaced on size A4 (8 1/4 in. x 11 3/4 in.) paper, and 1 copy.
Copyright ownership: Modern Humanities Research Assn.
Rejected manuscripts: Returned
Time before publication decision: 2 mos.
Time between decision and publication: 2 yrs. maximum
Number of reviewers: 2
Articles submitted per year: 100-150
Articles published per year: 40-45
Book reviews submitted per year: 450-500
Book reviews published per year: 450-500

(1874)
*Modern Language Studies

David H. Hirsch, Nelson H. Vieira, & Edna L. Steeves, Editors
Dept. of English
Box 1852
Brown Univ.
Providence, RI 02912

Telephone: 401 863-3756
First published: 1970
Sponsoring organization: Northeast Modern Language Assn.; Brown Univ.
ISSN: 0047-7729
MLA acronym: MLS

SUBSCRIPTION INFORMATION

Frequency of publication: 4 times/yr. (Winter, Spring, Summer, Fall)
Circulation: 2,500
Available in microform: No
Subscription price: $30.00/yr. nonmembers; $25.00/yr. members
Year to which price refers: 1992
Subscription address: Anne E. Berkman, Executive Director, Northeast Modern Language Assn., Dept. of English, East Stroudsburg Univ., East Stroudsburg, PA 18301-2999

ADVERTISING INFORMATION

Advertising accepted: Yes
Advertising rates: $50.00/half page; $100.00/full page

EDITORIAL DESCRIPTION

Scope: Publishes articles of interest to teachers and scholars in the areas of English, American, and comparative literatures and modern foreign languages.
Reviews books: Yes
Publishes notes: No
Languages accepted: English; German; Italian; French; Russian; Spanish
Prints abstracts: No
Author-anonymous submission: Yes

SUBMISSION REQUIREMENTS

Restrictions on contributors: Contributors must be members of Northeast Modern Language Assn. Unsolicited book reviews are not accepted.
Author pays submission fee: No
Author pays page charges: No
Length of articles: 2,500-5,000 words
Length of book reviews: 1,000 words
Style: MLA
Number of copies required: 2
Special requirements: Submit original typescript; include a 100-word English abstract for articles in foreign languages.
Copyright ownership: Northeast Modern Language Assn.
Rejected manuscripts: Returned; enclose SASE.
Time before publication decision: 3 mos.
Time between decision and publication: 1 yr.
Number of reviewers: 2
Articles submitted per year: 150
Articles published per year: 30-40
Book reviews published per year: 20

(1875)
*Modern Philology: A Journal Devoted to Research in Medieval and Modern Literature

Janel Mueller, Editor
Univ. of Chicago
1050 E. 59th St.
Chicago, IL 60637

Telephone: 312 702-8497
Fax: 312 702-9861
First published: 1903
Sponsoring organization: Univ. of Chicago, Division of Humanities; Univ. of Chicago Press
ISSN: 0026-8232
MLA acronym: MP

SUBSCRIPTION INFORMATION

Frequency of publication: 4 times/yr. (Aug., Nov., Feb., May)
Circulation: 1,600
Available in microform: Yes
Subscription price: $45.00/yr. institutions; $25.00/yr. individuals; $15.00/yr. students & MLA members; add $3.00/yr. postage outside US
Year to which price refers: 1992
Subscription address: Univ. of Chicago Press, 5801 Ellis Ave., Chicago, IL 60637
Subscription telephone: 312 753-3347
Subscription fax: 312 753-0811

ADVERTISING INFORMATION

Advertising accepted: Yes
Advertising rates: $150.00/half page; $220.00/full page

EDITORIAL DESCRIPTION

Scope: Primary emphasis is on English and American literature, but also publishes work on Continental, Eastern European, and Latin American subjects.
Reviews books: Yes
Publishes notes: Yes
Languages accepted: English; French; German; Spanish; Italian
Prints abstracts: No
Author-anonymous submission: Yes

SUBMISSION REQUIREMENTS

Restrictions on contributors: Unsolicited reviews are not accepted.
Author pays submission fee: No
Author pays page charges: No
Length of articles: 50 pp. maximum
Length of book reviews: 1,000-1,500 words
Length of notes: 1,000-3,000 words
Style: Chicago
Number of copies required: 1
Copyright ownership: Univ. of Chicago Press
Rejected manuscripts: Returned; enclose SASE.
Time before publication decision: 2-4 mos.
Time between decision and publication: 2 yrs.
Number of reviewers: 2
Articles submitted per year: 150
Articles published per year: 12-16
Book reviews published per year: 75-125
Notes submitted per year: 50
Notes published per year: 4-8

(1876)
*Moderna Språk

Claus Ohrt, Ulf Dantanus, Mats Mobärg, Olof Eriksson, Lars Lindvall, Helmut Müssener, Lars Fant, & Johan Falk, Editors
English Section - Language
C/o Mats Mobärg
Engelska Inst.
Renströmsgatan 6
412 98 Göteborg, Sweden

Additional editorial address: French Section: Olof Eriksson, Linnégatan 43, 413 08 Göteborg, Sweden; German Section: Helmut Müssener, Tuvängsvägen 36, 752 45 Uppsala, Sweden; Spanish Section: Lars Fant, Kamma Kargatan 64, 111 24 Stockholm, Sweden; English Section-Literature: Ulf Dantanus, 133 Ditchling Rd., Brighton BN1 4SE, England
Telephone: (46) 390 40604
Fax: (46) 390 40776
First published: 1907
Sponsoring organization: Modern Language Teachers' Assn. of Sweden
ISSN: 0026-8577
MLA acronym: MSpr

SUBSCRIPTION INFORMATION

Frequency of publication: 2 times/yr. (Apr.-May, Oct.-Nov.)
Circulation: 1,700
Available in microform: No
Subscription price: 180 Skr/yr.
Year to which price refers: 1992
Subscription address: Claus Ohrt, Ängen, 560 34 Visingsö, Sweden

ADVERTISING INFORMATION

Advertising accepted: Yes
Advertising rates: 1,400 Skr/half page; 2,000 Skr/full page; 2,500 Skr/back cover

EDITORIAL DESCRIPTION

Scope: Publishes articles on literature, modern languages, and the teaching of language and literature.
Reviews books: Yes
Publishes notes: Yes
Languages accepted: English; French; German; Swedish; Danish; Norwegian; Catalan; Italian; Spanish
Prints abstracts: No
Author-anonymous submission: No

SUBMISSION REQUIREMENTS

Restrictions on contributors: None
Author pays submission fee: No
Author pays page charges: No
Length of articles: 10,000 words maximum
Length of book reviews: 3,000 words maximum
Length of notes: 2,000 words
Style: MLA
Number of copies required: 1
Special requirements: Submit original typescript.
Copyright ownership: Journal
Rejected manuscripts: Returned
Time before publication decision: 1-6 mos.
Time between decision and publication: 1 yr.
Number of reviewers: 3
Articles submitted per year: 120
Articles published per year: 24
Book reviews submitted per year: 200
Book reviews published per year: 100

(1877)
Mogućnosti: Književnost, Umjetnost, Kulturni Problemi

Mirko Prelas, Josip Belamarić, Igor Fisković, Zvonko Kovač, Bratislav Lučin, Petar Opačić, & Hrvoje Čulić, Editors
Književni Krug Split
Bosanska 4/1
58000 Split, Croatia

Telephone: (38) 58 361081
Fax: (38) 58 42226
First published: 1954
Sponsoring organization: Književni Krug Split
ISSN: 0544-7267
MLA acronym: Mogućnosti

SUBSCRIPTION INFORMATION

Frequency of publication: Irregular (6-12 times/yr.)
Circulation: 900-1,000
Available in microform: No

ADVERTISING INFORMATION

Advertising accepted: No

EDITORIAL DESCRIPTION

Scope: Covers literature, the arts, and cultural problems, concentrating on Yugoslavia, and Croatian (Dalmatian) literature.
Reviews books: Yes
Publishes notes: No
Languages accepted: Serbo-Croatian

Prints abstracts: No
Author-anonymous submission: No

SUBMISSION REQUIREMENTS

Author pays submission fee: No
Author pays page charges: No
Number of copies required: 1
Copyright ownership: Author
Rejected manuscripts: Not returned
Time before publication decision: 1 mo.
Time between decision and publication: 2-6 mos.
Number of reviewers: 4
Articles submitted per year: 130
Articles published per year: 100
Book reviews submitted per year: 15-20
Book reviews published per year: 15

(1878)
Molodaia Gvardiia: Ezhemesiachnyĭ Literaturno-Khudozhestvennyĭ i Obshchestvenno-Politicheskiĭ Zhurnal

Anatoliĭ Ivanov, Editor
Novodmitrovskaia ul., 5a
125015 Moscow, Russia

First published: 1922
ISSN: 0131-2251
MLA acronym: MGv

SUBSCRIPTION INFORMATION

Frequency of publication: 12 times/yr.

EDITORIAL DESCRIPTION

Scope: Publishes articles on Russian literature; also publishes original poetry and prose.
Reviews books: Yes
Languages accepted: Russian

(1879)
*Mon-Khmer Studies: A Journal of Southeast Asian Languages

Christian Rauer, David Thomas, & Suwilai Premsrirat, Editors
Inst. of Language & Culture for Rural Development
Mahidol Univ. at Salaya
Nakorn Pathom 73170, Thailand

Telephone: (66) 2 4419327
Fax: (66) 2 4419517
First published: 1964
Sponsoring organization: Mahidol Univ.; Summer Inst. of Linguistics
ISSN: 0147-5207
MLA acronym: MKS

SUBSCRIPTION INFORMATION

Frequency of publication: Annual
Circulation: 185
Available in microform: Yes, for volumes 1-5
Additional subscription address: SIL Publications Dept., 7500 W. Camp Wisdom Rd., Dallas, TX 75236; White Lotus Books, GPO Box 1141, Bangkok 10501, Thailand

ADVERTISING INFORMATION

Advertising accepted: No

EDITORIAL DESCRIPTION

Scope: Publishes linguistic, philological, paleographical, and folklore studies on languages of the Mon-Khmer family and occasional articles on other Southeast Asian languages.
Reviews books: Yes
Publishes notes: Yes
Languages accepted: English; French

Prints abstracts: No
Author-anonymous submission: No

SUBMISSION REQUIREMENTS

Restrictions on contributors: None
Author pays submission fee: No
Author pays page charges: No
Length of articles: 8-60 pp.
Length of book reviews: 2-10 pp.
Length of notes: 1-10 pp.
Style: None
Number of copies required: 1
Special requirements: Submission of typescript and diskette is preferred.
Copyright ownership: Author
Rejected manuscripts: Returned
Time before publication decision: 1-2 mos.
Time between decision and publication: 1 yr.
Number of reviewers: 3
Articles submitted per year: 10-15
Articles published per year: 10-15
Book reviews submitted per year: 3-5
Book reviews published per year: 3-5
Notes submitted per year: 5-15
Notes published per year: 5-15

(1880)
*Monatshefte für Deutschen Unterricht, Deutsche Sprache und Literatur

Valters Nollendorfs, Salvatore Calomino, Jürgen Eichhoft, James Steakley
Dept. of German
Van Hise Hall
Univ. of Wisconsin
Madison, WI 53706

Telephone: 608 262-3008; 608 263-5091
Fax: 608 262-7949
E-mail: MONA@macc.wisc.edw
First published: 1899
Sponsoring organization: Dept. of German, Univ. of Wisconsin
ISSN: 0026-9271
MLA acronym: Monatshefte

SUBSCRIPTION INFORMATION

Frequency of publication: 4 times/yr. (Mar., June, Sept., Dec.)
Circulation: 1,300
Available in microform: Yes
Subscription price: $59.00/yr. institutions; $25.00/yr. individuals; $7.00/single issue
Year to which price refers: 1992-93
Subscription address: Journals Dept., Univ. of Wisconsin Press, 114 N. Murray St., Madison, WI 53715
Subscription telephone: 608 262-4952
Subscription fax: 608 262-7560

ADVERTISING INFORMATION

Advertising accepted: Yes
Advertising rates: $125.00/half page; $215.00/full page; $265.00/cover

EDITORIAL DESCRIPTION

Scope: Publishes articles and book reviews dealing with German literature and language, and with concerns of the German-teaching profession in the US and Canada.
Reviews books: Yes
Publishes notes: Yes
Languages accepted: English; German
Prints abstracts: Yes
Author-anonymous submission: No

SUBMISSION REQUIREMENTS

Restrictions on contributors: Only original material not published elsewhere is accepted. Dissertations are considered published material. Unsolicited book reviews are not accepted. Only scholarly books are reviewed.

Author pays submission fee: No
Author pays page charges: No
Length of articles: 15-20 pp.
Length of book reviews: 300-1,000 words
Length of notes: 150 words maximum
Style: MLA with endnote format
Number of copies required: 2
Special requirements: Articles accepted for publication and commissioned book reviews should be submitted on diskette.
Copyright ownership: Univ. of Wisconsin System, Board of Regents
Rejected manuscripts: Returned; enclose return postage.
Time before publication decision: 3 mos. minimum
Time between decision and publication: 18 mos.
Number of reviewers: 3
Articles submitted per year: 40-50
Articles published per year: 20
Book reviews published per year: 120
Notes submitted per year: 30
Notes published per year: 20

(1881)
*Mongolian Studies: Journal of the Mongolia Society

John R. Krueger, Editor
Mongolia Soc.
321-322 Goodbody Hall
Indiana Univ.
Bloomington, IN 47405-2401

First published: 1974
Sponsoring organization: Mongolia Soc.
ISSN: 0190-3667
MLA acronym: MSB

SUBSCRIPTION INFORMATION

Frequency of publication: Annual
Circulation: 400
Available in microform: No
Subscription price: $25.00/yr.
Year to which price refers: 1991

ADVERTISING INFORMATION

Advertising accepted: Yes

EDITORIAL DESCRIPTION

Scope: Welcomes scholarly contributions on Mongol-related topics in any nonscientific field or chronological era, including the 20th century.
Reviews books: Yes
Publishes notes: Yes
Languages accepted: English; French; German; Mongol languages
Prints abstracts: No
Author-anonymous submission: No

SUBMISSION REQUIREMENTS

Restrictions on contributors: None
Author pays submission fee: No
Author pays page charges: No
Length of articles: 2,500-10,000 words
Length of book reviews: 500-1,000 words
Style: Chicago; see journal for transcription & transliteration instructions.
Number of copies required: 1
Copyright ownership: Mongolia Soc.
Rejected manuscripts: Returned
Time before publication decision: 1 mo.
Time between decision and publication: 1 yr.
Number of reviewers: 3
Articles published per year: 5
Book reviews published per year: 2-5

(1882)
*Monograph Series of the Toronto Semiotic Circle

Marcel Danesi & J. Janet Gordon, Editors
NF 217
Victoria College
Univ. of Toronto
73 Queen's Park Cres.
Toronto, Ontario M5S 1K7, Canada

Telephone: 416 585-4412
Fax: 416 585-4584
First published: 1987
Sponsoring organization: Toronto Semiotic Circle
ISSN: 0838-5858
MLA acronym: MSTSC

SUBSCRIPTION INFORMATION

Frequency of publication: 2 times/yr.
Circulation: 200
Available in microform: No
Subscription price: C$40.00/yr.
Year to which price refers: 1992

ADVERTISING INFORMATION

Advertising accepted: No

EDITORIAL DESCRIPTION

Scope: Publishes monographs on semiotics, communication theory, and applications of semiotics.
Reviews books: No
Publishes notes: No
Languages accepted: English
Prints abstracts: No
Author-anonymous submission: Yes

SUBMISSION REQUIREMENTS

Author pays submission fee: No
Author pays page charges: No
Length of books: 100-150 pp.
Number of copies required: 2
Copyright ownership: Toronto Semiotic Circle
Rejected manuscripts: Returned
Time before publication decision: 1 mo.
Time between decision and publication: 6-12 mos.
Number of reviewers: 2-3
Books submitted per year: 3-4
Books published per year: 2

(1883)
*Monographic Review/Revista Monográfica

Janet Pérez & Genaro J. Pérez, Editors
Box 8401
Univ. of Texas of the Permian Basin
Odessa, TX 79762-0001

Telephone: 915 367-2249
Fax: 915 367-2115
E-mail: Bitnet: G—Perez@UTPB.PB.-UTEXAS.EDU
First published: 1985
ISSN: 0885-7512
MLA acronym: MRRM

SUBSCRIPTION INFORMATION

Frequency of publication: Annual with occasional special issues
Available in microform: No
Subscription price: $25.00/yr. US; $45.00/yr. elsewhere
Year to which price refers: 1992

ADVERTISING INFORMATION

Advertising accepted: Yes

EDITORIAL DESCRIPTION

Scope: Publishes critical monographs and articles on a single topic or writer in areas of critical neglect including Spanish children's literature, Spanish science fiction, the literature of fantasy, literature of exile and expatriation, women writers, Hispanic writers in the US, and others.
Reviews books: Occasionally
Publishes notes: Yes
Languages accepted: Spanish; English; Portuguese; French
Author-anonymous submission: No

SUBMISSION REQUIREMENTS

Restrictions on contributors: Some contributions are by invitation.
Author pays submission fee: No
Author pays page charges: No
Length of articles: No restrictions
Length of notes: No restrictions
Style: MLA
Number of copies required: 3
Copyright ownership: Editors
Rejected manuscripts: Returned
Time before publication decision: 2 mos.
Time between decision and publication: 8-10 mos.
Number of reviewers: 2
Articles submitted per year: 25
Articles published per year: 20
Notes submitted per year: 10
Notes published per year: 2-4

(1884)
Monographs in International Studies, Africa Series. Ohio University Center for International Studies

Cosmo Pieterse, Editor
Burson House
56 East Union St.
Ohio Univ.
Athens, OH 45701

First published: 1968
Sponsoring organization: Center for International Studies, Ohio Univ.
ISSN: 0078-9100
MLA acronym: MSAS

SUBSCRIPTION INFORMATION

Frequency of publication: Irregular
Circulation: 500
Available in microform: No
Subscription address: Ohio Univ. Press, Scott Quadrangle, Athens, OH 45701

ADVERTISING INFORMATION

Advertising accepted: No

EDITORIAL DESCRIPTION

Scope: Monograph series dealing with any phase of African life, literature, development, etc. Disciplines represented include history, political science, economics, geography, sociology, philosophy, anthropology, linguistics, education, literature, and bibliographies general and specific.
Reviews books: No
Publishes notes: No
Languages accepted: English
Prints abstracts: No

SUBMISSION REQUIREMENTS

Restrictions on contributors: None
Author pays submission fee: No
Author pays page charges: No
Length of books: 750-800 double-spaced pp.
Style: Chicago
Number of copies required: 2
Special requirements: Submit camera-ready copy.
Copyright ownership: Center for International Studies
Rejected manuscripts: Returned at author's request
Time before publication decision: 4 mos.
Time between decision and publication: 2-6 mos.
Number of reviewers: 1-2
Books published per year: 4

(1885)
Monographs in International Studies, Southeast Asia Series. Ohio University Center for International Studies

James L. Cobban, Editor
Burson House
56 East Union St.
Ohio Univ.
Athens, OH 45701

First published: 1968
Sponsoring organization: Center for International Studies, Ohio Univ.
ISSN: 0078-9119
MLA acronym: PSSEAS

SUBSCRIPTION INFORMATION

Frequency of publication: Irregular
Circulation: 600-1,000
Available in microform: No
Subscription address: Ohio Univ. Press, Scott Quad, Athens, OH 45701

ADVERTISING INFORMATION

Advertising accepted: No

EDITORIAL DESCRIPTION

Scope: Monograph series dealing with Southeast Asian life, literature, etc. Disciplines represented include history, politics, economics, geography, sociology, anthropology, linguistics, education, literature, and bibliographies.
Reviews books: No
Publishes notes: No
Languages accepted: English
Prints abstracts: No

SUBMISSION REQUIREMENTS

Restrictions on contributors: None
Author pays submission fee: No
Author pays page charges: No
Length of books: 250-800 double-spaced pp.
Style: Chicago
Number of copies required: 2
Special requirements: Submit camera-ready copy.
Copyright ownership: Center for International Studies
Rejected manuscripts: Returned at author's request
Time before publication decision: 3-4 mos.
Time between decision and publication: 2-6 mos.
Number of reviewers: 1-2
Books published per year: 6

(1886)
*Monographs in Modern Languages

Brian J. Levy, Editor
Dept. of French
Univ. of Hull
Hull HU6 7RX, England

Telephone: (44) 482 465367
Fax: (44) 482 465991
E-mail: BJL18@UK.AC.HULL
First published: 1966
Sponsoring organization: Univ. of Hull

ISSN: 0078-3099
MLA acronym: MML

SUBSCRIPTION INFORMATION

Frequency of publication: Irregular (usually annual)
Circulation: 500
Subscription address: Secretary, Publ. Committee, Univ. of Hull, Hull HU6 7RU, England
Subscription telephone: (44) 482 465322

ADVERTISING INFORMATION

Advertising accepted: No

EDITORIAL DESCRIPTION

Scope: Publishes literary, cultural, and linguistic studies relating to all principal European languages except English.
Reviews books: No
Publishes notes: No
Languages accepted: English
Prints abstracts: No
Author-anonymous submission: No

SUBMISSION REQUIREMENTS

Restrictions on contributors: None
Author pays submission fee: No
Author pays page charges: No
Length of books: 120 pp. maximum
Style: Oxford Univ. Press
Number of copies required: 1
Special requirements: Submit double-spaced typescript on size A4 (8 1/4 in. x 11 3/4 in.) paper.
Copyright ownership: Author
Rejected manuscripts: Returned
Time before publication decision: 3 mos.
Time between decision and publication: 1 yr.
Books published per year: 1-2

(1887)
*Montaigne Studies: An Interdisciplinary Forum

Daniel R. Martin, Director
Univ. of Massachusetts
335 Herter Hall
Amherst, MA 01003

Telephone: 413 545-0900
E-mail: MARTIN@FRITAL.UMASS.EDU
First published: 1989
ISSN: 1049-2917
MLA acronym: MontS

SUBSCRIPTION INFORMATION

Frequency of publication: 2 times/yr. (Spring, Fall)
Circulation: 145
Available in microform: No
Subscription price: $22.50/yr. institutions; $18.75/yr. individuals
Year to which price refers: 1992
Subscription address: Hestia Press, P.O. Box 2381, 559 West St., Amherst, MA 01004

ADVERTISING INFORMATION

Advertising accepted: No

EDITORIAL DESCRIPTION

Scope: Publishes interdisciplinary studies on Montaigne.
Reviews books: No
Publishes notes: No
Languages accepted: English; French; Spanish; Italian; German
Prints abstracts: No
Author-anonymous submission: No

SUBMISSION REQUIREMENTS

Restrictions on contributors: None
Author pays submission fee: No
Author pays page charges: No
Length of articles: 5,000 words
Style: MLA
Number of copies required: 2
Special requirements: Accepted articles must be submitted on IBM-compatible diskettes using Nota Bene or WordPerfect.
Copyright ownership: Hestia Press
Rejected manuscripts: Not returned
Time before publication decision: 2 mos.
Time between decision and publication: 6-12 mos.
Articles published per year: 20

(1888)
*Monumenta Nipponica

Michael Cooper, Editor
Sophia Univ.
7-1 Kioi-chō
Chiyoda-ku
Tokyo 102, Japan

Telephone: (81) 3 32383544
Fax: (81) 3 32385056
First published: 1938
Sponsoring organization: Sophia Univ.
ISSN: 0027-0741
MLA acronym: MN

SUBSCRIPTION INFORMATION

Frequency of publication: 4 times/yr.
Circulation: 1,150
Available in microform: Yes
Subscription price: $30.00/yr.
Year to which price refers: 1992

ADVERTISING INFORMATION

Advertising accepted: Yes
Advertising rates: $80.00/full page

EDITORIAL DESCRIPTION

Scope: Publishes original articles and translations dealing with Japanese literature, history, religions, and art.
Reviews books: Yes
Publishes notes: No
Languages accepted: English
Prints abstracts: No
Author-anonymous submission: Yes

SUBMISSION REQUIREMENTS

Restrictions on contributors: None
Author pays submission fee: No
Author pays page charges: No
Length of articles: 10,000-12,000 words
Length of book reviews: 1,400 words
Style: Journal
Number of copies required: 2
Special requirements: Supply *kanji* for Chinese and Japanese words.
Copyright ownership: Assigned by author to journal
Rejected manuscripts: Returned
Time before publication decision: 3 mos.
Time between decision and publication: 6-9 mos.
Number of reviewers: 2-3
Articles submitted per year: 60-70
Articles published per year: 16-18
Book reviews submitted per year: 60
Book reviews published per year: 60

(1889)
*Moody Street Irregulars: A Jack Kerouac Magazine

Joy Walsh, Editor
P.O. Box 157
Clarence Center, NY 14032

Telephone: 716 741-3393
First published: 1978
Sponsoring organization: Moody Street Irregulars, Inc.
ISSN: 0196-2605
MLA acronym: MSI

SUBSCRIPTION INFORMATION

Frequency of publication: 2-3 times/yr.
Available in microform: No
Subscription price: $30.00/yr. institutions; $20.00/yr. individuals
Year to which price refers: 1991

ADVERTISING INFORMATION

Advertising accepted: Yes

EDITORIAL DESCRIPTION

Scope: Publishes articles on Jack Kerouac, the Beats, the literature of the 1950s and its relevance today. Also publishes poetry and plays.
Reviews books: Yes
Publishes notes: Yes
Languages accepted: English; French
Prints abstracts: No
Author-anonymous submission: Yes

SUBMISSION REQUIREMENTS

Restrictions on contributors: None
Author pays submission fee: No
Author pays page charges: No
Length of articles: 5 typescript pp. suggested
Length of book reviews: 500 words
Style: Chicago
Number of copies required: 2
Special requirements: Submit original typescript.
Copyright ownership: Journal
Rejected manuscripts: Returned; enclose return postage.
Time before publication decision: 3 mos.
Time between decision and publication: 3-12 mos.
Number of reviewers: 2-3
Articles submitted per year: 20-30
Articles published per year: 15-25
Book reviews submitted per year: 25-30
Book reviews published per year: 15

(1890)
*Moreana: Bulletin Thomas More

Germain Marc'hadour, Editor
29, rue Volney
B.P. 808
49008 Angers Cedex 01, France

Telephone: (33) 41871932; (33) 41816697
First published: 1963
Sponsoring organization: Amici Thomae Mori
ISSN: 0047-8105
MLA acronym: Moreana

SUBSCRIPTION INFORMATION

Frequency of publication: 3 times/yr.
Circulation: 900
Available in microform: No
Subscription price: $60.00/yr. institutions; $46.00/yr. individuals
Year to which price refers: 1992

ADVERTISING INFORMATION

Advertising accepted: Yes, on an exchange basis

EDITORIAL DESCRIPTION

Scope: Provides a forum for research and discussion about St. Thomas More and his universe, including Erasmus and Luther; reviews books; gives news of conferences, plays, events, and people from the standpoint of More as a historical character, a major writer, and as a saint.
Reviews books: Yes
Publishes notes: Yes
Languages accepted: English; French; German; Italian; Spanish; Portuguese
Prints abstracts: Yes
Author-anonymous submission: No

SUBMISSION REQUIREMENTS

Restrictions on contributors: None
Author pays submission fee: No
Author pays page charges: No
Length of articles: 6-10 pp.
Length of book reviews: 2-3 pp.
Length of notes: 2 pp.
Style: None
Number of copies required: 3
Special requirements: Provide summaries in French and English for articles in other languages; French summary required for articles in English.
Copyright ownership: Author
Rejected manuscripts: Returned
Time before publication decision: 10 mos.
Time between decision and publication: 6 mos.
Number of reviewers: 3
Articles submitted per year: 60
Articles published per year: 30
Book reviews submitted per year: 50
Book reviews published per year: 50
Notes submitted per year: 40
Notes published per year: 30

(1891)
*Morphé: Ciencias del Lenguaje

Maria Isabel Filinich Oregui, Editor
Univ. Autónoma de Puebla
Maestría en Ciencias del Lenguaje
Maximino Avila Camacho 219
C.P. 72000 Puebla, Pue., Mexico

Historical variations in title: Formerly *Morphé: Semiótica y Lingüística*
MLA acronym: Morphé

EDITORIAL DESCRIPTION

Scope: Publishes articles on semiotics, linguistics, and philosophy of language. Includes articles on textual analysis, linguistic theory, and literary theory.
Publishes notes: No
Languages accepted: Spanish

(1892)
*Mosaic: A Journal for the Interdisciplinary Study of Literature

Evelyn J. Hinz, Editor
208 Tier Bldg.
Univ. of Manitoba
Winnipeg, Manitoba R3T 2N2, Canada

Telephone: 204 474-9763
Fax: 204 261-9086
E-mail: Hinz@ccm.UManitoba.CA
First published: 1967
Sponsoring organization: Social Sciences & Humanities Research Council of Canada; University of Manitoba
ISSN: 0027-1276
MLA acronym: Mosaic

SUBSCRIPTION INFORMATION

Frequency of publication: 4 times/yr.
Circulation: 1,700
Available in microform: Yes
Subscription price: C$32.00/yr., C$80.00/3 yrs. institutions US & Canada; C$37.00/yr., C$97.00/3 yrs. institutions elsewhere; C$20.00/yr., C$52.00/3 yrs. individuals US & Canada; C$25.00/yr., C$64.00/3 yrs. individuals elsewhere
Year to which price refers: 1992

ADVERTISING INFORMATION

Advertising accepted: Yes

EDITORIAL DESCRIPTION

Scope: Publishes articles concerned with the interdisciplinary study of literature and critical theory. One of the four yearly issues is a special issue on specific themes.
Reviews books: No
Publishes notes: No
Languages accepted: English; French
Prints abstracts: Yes
Author-anonymous submission: No

SUBMISSION REQUIREMENTS

Restrictions on contributors: Unsolicited review articles are not accepted.
Author pays submission fee: No
Author pays page charges: No
Length of articles: 20-25 typescript pp.
Style: MLA
Number of copies required: 3
Special requirements: Articles written in languages other than English and French must be translated. Footnotes are discouraged. Submit a 200-word abstract.
Copyright ownership: Journal
Rejected manuscripts: Returned; enclose return postage.
Time before publication decision: 6 mos.
Time between decision and publication: 6-12 mos.
Number of reviewers: 3
Articles submitted per year: 350
Articles published per year: 40

(1893)
*Mostovi

Drinka Gojković, Editor
Francuska 7
11000 Belgrade, Yugoslavia

Additional editorial address: Drinka Gojković, 27 Marta 20, 11000 Belgrade, Yugoslavia
Telephone: (38) 11 626081
Fax: (38) 11 333584
First published: 1970
Sponsoring organization: Udruženje Književnih Prevodilaca Srbije
ISSN: 0350-6525
MLA acronym: Mostovi

SUBSCRIPTION INFORMATION

Frequency of publication: 4 times/yr.
Circulation: 1,000
Available in microform: No
Subscription price: 400 Din/yr. Yugoslavia; $60.00/yr. elsewhere
Year to which price refers: 1992

ADVERTISING INFORMATION

Advertising accepted: Yes

EDITORIAL DESCRIPTION

Scope: Publishes translations, articles on translation, reviews of translated books, and bibliographies of translations from and into Serbo-Croatian.
Reviews books: Yes
Publishes notes: No
Languages accepted: Serbo-Croatian; English; French; German
Prints abstracts: No
Author-anonymous submission: No

SUBMISSION REQUIREMENTS

Restrictions on contributors: Reviews are commissioned.
Author pays submission fee: No
Author pays page charges: No
Length of articles: 5,000-20,000 words
Length of book reviews: 2,000-3,500 words
Number of copies required: 1
Copyright ownership: Author
Rejected manuscripts: Not returned
Time before publication decision: 1 mo.
Time between decision and publication: 1-6 mos.
Number of reviewers: 1
Articles submitted per year: 150
Articles published per year: 60-100
Book reviews submitted per year: 20-25
Book reviews published per year: 20-25

(1894)
Motif: International Review of Research in Folklore & Literature

Daniel R. Barnes, Editor
Dept. of English
Ohio State Univ.
164 W. 17 Ave.
Columbus, OH 43210

First published: 1981
Sponsoring organization: Dept. of English, Ohio State Univ.
ISSN: 0278-2286
MLA acronym: Motif

SUBSCRIPTION INFORMATION

Frequency of publication: 3 times/yr. (Feb., June, Oct.)
Circulation: 260
Available in microform: No

ADVERTISING INFORMATION

Advertising accepted: No

EDITORIAL DESCRIPTION

Scope: Publishes notes, queries, and reviews, occasionally longer essays, bibliographies, and checklists. Is directed to the international community of folklorists and literary scholars interested in the relation of folklore and literature.
Reviews books: Yes
Publishes notes: Yes
Languages accepted: English
Prints abstracts: No
Author-anonymous submission: No

SUBMISSION REQUIREMENTS

Restrictions on contributors: None
Author pays submission fee: No
Author pays page charges: No
Length of articles: 3-5 typescript pp.; occasionally 12-15 typescript pp.
Length of book reviews: 500-2,000 words
Length of notes: 250-2,500 words
Style: MLA
Number of copies required: 1
Special requirements: Reference notes are to be incorporated parenthetically in the text.
Copyright ownership: Ohio State Univ.
Rejected manuscripts: Returned
Time before publication decision: 3 mos.
Time between decision and publication: 6 mos.
Number of reviewers: 2-3
Articles submitted per year: 15-25
Articles published per year: 10
Book reviews submitted per year: 8-10
Book reviews published per year: 6-8
Notes submitted per year: 10
Notes published per year: 8

(1895)
*Mount Olive Review

Pepper Worthington & Sarah V. Clere, Editors
Mount Olive College Press
514 Henderson St.
Mount Olive College
Mont Olive, NC 28365

Telephone: 919 658-2502
First published: 1987
Sponsoring organization: Mount Olive College
ISSN: 0893-8288
MLA acronym: MOR

SUBSCRIPTION INFORMATION

Frequency of publication: Annual (Spring)
Available in microform: No
Subscription price: $8.50/yr.
Year to which price refers: 1992

ADVERTISING INFORMATION

Advertising accepted: Yes

EDITORIAL DESCRIPTION

Scope: Publishes articles on literature as it relates to various topics in the humanities. Each issue is thematic and includes articles, poems, fiction, and book reviews that relate to the theme.
Reviews books: Yes
Publishes notes: No
Languages accepted: English
Prints abstracts: No
Author-anonymous submission: Yes

SUBMISSION REQUIREMENTS

Author pays submission fee: No
Author pays page charges: No
Length of articles: 5,000 words
Length of book reviews: 500-1,000 words
Style: MLA
Number of copies required: 2
Special requirements: Articles from literature other than English may be evaluated but only in English translation.
Copyright ownership: Mount Olive College
Rejected manuscripts: Returned; enclose SASE.
Time before publication decision: 3-6 mos.
Time between decision and publication: 6 mos.
Number of reviewers: 6
Articles submitted per year: 120
Articles published per year: 20
Book reviews submitted per year: 15
Book reviews published per year: 5

(1896)
*Movoznavstvo: Naukovo-Teoretychnyĭ Zhurnal Viddilennia Literatury, Movy i Mystetstvoznavstva Akademiĭ Nauk Ukraine

O. S. Melnichuk, Editor
Akademiia Nauk Ukraïny
Ul. Hrushevs'koho, 4
252001 MSP Kiev 1, Ukraine

Telephone: (7) 44 2284383
First published: 1967
Historical variations in title: Formerly Movoznavstvo: Naukovo-Teoretychnyĭ Zhurnal Viddilennia Literatury, Movy i Mystetstvoznavstva Akademiĭ Nauk Ukraïns'oĭ RSR
Sponsoring organization: Akademiia Nauk Ukraïny, Inst. Movoznavstva
ISSN: 0027-2833
MLA acronym: Mov

SUBSCRIPTION INFORMATION

Frequency of publication: 6 times/yr.
Available in microform: No
Subscription price: 60 Rbl ($36.00)/yr.
Year to which price refers: 1993
Subscription address: "Svoboda Bookstore", 30 Montgomery St., Jersey City, NJ 07302
Subscription telephone: 201 434-0237
Subscription fax: 201 451-5486

ADVERTISING INFORMATION

Advertising accepted: Yes

EDITORIAL DESCRIPTION

Scope: Publishes studies on linguistics. Emphasis is on Ukrainian and other Slavic languages.
Reviews books: Yes
Publishes notes: No
Languages accepted: Ukrainian; Russian; English
Prints abstracts: No
Author-anonymous submission: No

SUBMISSION REQUIREMENTS

Restrictions on contributors: None
Author pays submission fee: No
Author pays page charges: No
Length of articles: 15 pp.
Length of book reviews: 6 pp.
Style: Scientific
Number of copies required: 2
Copyright ownership: Author
Rejected manuscripts: Returned
Time before publication decision: 3 mos.
Time between decision and publication: 9 mos.
Number of reviewers: 1
Articles submitted per year: 150
Articles published per year: 77
Book reviews submitted per year: 25
Book reviews published per year: 20

(1897)
*Le Moyen Âge: Revue d'Histoire et de Philologie

G. Duby, P. Toubert, A. Joris, & J. Dufournet, Editors
De Boeck-Wesmael S.A.
203 Ave. Louise-Bte. 1
1050 Brussels, Belgium

Additional editorial address: Univ. de Liege, Seminaire d'histoire, 3 Place Cockerill, Bat. A2, 4000 Liege, Belgium
Telephone: (32) 2 6273606
Fax: (32) 2 6273650
First published: 1888
Historical variations in title: Formerly Le Moyen Age: Revue Historique
Sponsoring organization: Centre National de la Recherche Scientifique
ISSN: 0027-2841
MLA acronym: MA

SUBSCRIPTION INFORMATION

Frequency of publication: 4 times/yr.
Available in microform: No
Subscription price: 2,600 BF/yr.
Year to which price refers: 1992
Subscription telephone: (32) 2 6273511
Subscription fax: (32) 2 6273519

ADVERTISING INFORMATION

Advertising accepted: Yes

EDITORIAL DESCRIPTION

Reviews books: Yes
Publishes notes: Yes
Languages accepted: French
Prints abstracts: No
Author-anonymous submission: No

SUBMISSION REQUIREMENTS

Author pays submission fee: No
Author pays page charges: No
Length of articles: No restrictions
Length of book reviews: 500 words
Length of notes: No restrictions
Style: Orator
Number of copies required: 2
Time before publication decision: 1 yr.
Time between decision and publication: 6-8 mos.
Number of reviewers: 2
Articles published per year: 30
Book reviews submitted per year: 100
Book reviews published per year: 80
Notes published per year: 10

(1898)
*Le Moyen Français

Giuseppe di Stefano & Rose M. Bidler, Editors
Editions CERES
P.O. Box 1386
Place Bonaventure
Montreal, Quebec H5A 1H3, Canada

Telephone: 514 937-7138
First published: 1977
ISSN: 0226-0174
MLA acronym: MFra

SUBSCRIPTION INFORMATION

Frequency of publication: 2 times/yr.
Circulation: 800-1,200
Available in microform: No
Subscription price: $63.20/yr.
Year to which price refers: 1993

ADVERTISING INFORMATION

Advertising accepted: Yes

EDITORIAL DESCRIPTION

Scope: Publishes studies, texts and unedited documents, and bibliographies on French language and literature of the 14th and 15th centuries.
Reviews books: Yes
Publishes notes: Yes
Languages accepted: English; French; Italian; German; Spanish
Prints abstracts: No

SUBMISSION REQUIREMENTS

Restrictions on contributors: None
Author pays submission fee: No
Author pays page charges: No
Length of articles: 35 typescript pp. maximum
Length of book reviews: 100-1,000 words
Style: MLA
Number of copies required: 2
Special requirements: Submit typescript and WordPerfect diskette.
Copyright ownership: Journal
Rejected manuscripts: Returned
Time before publication decision: 3 mos.
Time between decision and publication: 1 yr.
Number of reviewers: 3
Articles published per year: 10-15
Book reviews published per year: 13-16

(1899)
*Moznayim: Yarḥon Agudat ha-Soferim ha-'Ivrim be-Medinat Yiśrael/Monthly of the Association of Hebrew Writers in Israel

Ortsion Bartana & Moshe Ben-Shaul, Editors
P.O. Box 7098
Tel Aviv 61070, Israel

Telephone: (972) 3 6953256
Fax: (972) 3 6919681
First published: 1929

Sponsoring organization: Hebrew Writers Assn. of Israel
ISSN: 0027-2892
MLA acronym: Moznayim

SUBSCRIPTION INFORMATION

Frequency of publication: 10 times/yr. (includes 2 double issues)
Circulation: 3,500
Available in microform: No
Subscription price: $75.00/yr.
Year to which price refers: 1992

ADVERTISING INFORMATION

Advertising accepted: Yes

EDITORIAL DESCRIPTION

Scope: Publishes critical articles on contemporary literature and modern Hebrew literature, as well as poems, stories, essays, and book reviews. There are special issues on world literature.
Reviews books: Yes
Publishes notes: Yes
Languages accepted: Hebrew
Prints abstracts: No

SUBMISSION REQUIREMENTS

Restrictions on contributors: None
Author pays submission fee: No
Author pays page charges: No
Length of articles: 3,000 words
Length of book reviews: 1,000 words
Length of notes: 350 words
Style: None
Number of copies required: 1
Special requirements: Submit double-spaced typescript.
Copyright ownership: Author
Rejected manuscripts: Returned; enclose return postage.
Time before publication decision: 3-4 weeks
Time between decision and publication: 3-6 mos.
Number of reviewers: 1
Articles published per year: 80-100
Book reviews published per year: 50
Notes published per year: 50

(1900)
*Multilingua: Journal of Cross-Cultural and Interlanguage Communication

Richard J. Watts, Editor
Englisches Seminar
Univ. Bern
Gesellschaftsstr. 6
3012 Bern, Switzerland

Telephone: (41) 31 658245
Fax: (41) 31 248485
First published: 1981
ISSN: 0167-8507
MLA acronym: Multilingua

SUBSCRIPTION INFORMATION

Frequency of publication: 4 times/yr.
Circulation: 350
Available in microform: No
Subscription price: 194 DM ($120.00)/yr. plus postage institutions; 82.80 DM ($46.90)/yr. individuals
Year to which price refers: 1992
Subscription address: Walter de Gruyter, Inc., 200 Saw Mill River Rd., Hawthorne, NY 10532
Additional subscription address: Outside US: Walter de Gruyter, Postfach 110240, 1000 Berlin 11, Germany

ADVERTISING INFORMATION

Advertising accepted: Yes
Advertising rates: 300 DM/half page; 600 DM/full page

EDITORIAL DESCRIPTION

Scope: Multilingua is an international, interdisciplinary journal aimed at the enhancement of cross-cultural understanding through the study of interlingual communication. To this end it publishes articles and short notes in fields as diverse as cross-cultural differences in linguistics politeness phenomena, variety in what is traditionally regarded as one culture, conversational styles, nonstandard, oral varieties of language, strategies for the organization of verbal interaction, intercultural linguistic, variety, communication breakdown, translation, information technology and modern methods for managing and using multilingual tools.
Reviews books: Yes
Publishes notes: Yes
Languages accepted: English primary; French; German; Spanish; Italian
Prints abstracts: Yes

SUBMISSION REQUIREMENTS

Restrictions on contributors: None
Author pays submission fee: No
Author pays page charges: No
Length of articles: 6,000-9,000 words
Length of book reviews: 500-800 words
Length of notes: 500 words
Style: Journal; style sheet available from editor
Number of copies required: 4
Special requirements: Submit a 150-word abstract.
Copyright ownership: Journal for 1 yr.
Rejected manuscripts: Returned
Time before publication decision: 6 mos.
Time between decision and publication: 6 mos.
Number of reviewers: 3
Articles submitted per year: 40
Articles published per year: 15-19
Book reviews submitted per year: 50
Book reviews published per year: 15
Notes submitted per year: 10
Notes published per year: 5

(1901)
*Multilingual Matters

Derrick Sharp, Editor
Multilingual Matters, Inc.
Frankfurt Lodge, Clevedon Hall
Victoria Rd.
Clevedon
Avon BS21 7SJ, England

Telephone: (44) 275 876519
Fax: (44) 275 343096
First published: 1982
MLA acronym: MultM

SUBSCRIPTION INFORMATION

Frequency of publication: Irregular
Available in microform: No
Additional subscription address: Taylor & Francis, 1900 Frost Rd., Ste. 101, Bristol, PA 19007

ADVERTISING INFORMATION

Advertising accepted: No

EDITORIAL DESCRIPTION

Scope: Publishes monographs and collections of articles on multilingualism, multiculturalism, and second language learning.
Reviews books: No
Publishes notes: No
Languages accepted: English
Prints abstracts: No
Author-anonymous submission: No

SUBMISSION REQUIREMENTS

Author pays submission fee: No
Author pays page charges: No
Length of books: 180-250 pp.
Number of copies required: 3
Special requirements: Submit double-spaced typescript on size A4 (8 1/4 in. x 11 3/4 in.) paper.
Copyright ownership: Author
Rejected manuscripts: Returned at author's request
Time before publication decision: 4 mos.
Time between decision and publication: 9 mos.
Number of reviewers: 1
Books submitted per year: 30
Books published per year: 15

(1902)
*Münchener Beiträge zur Mediävistik u. Renaissance-Forschung

Gabriel Silagi, Editor
Arbeo-Gesellschaft
8049 Bachenhausen, Germany

First published: 1967
Sponsoring organization: Arbeo-Gesellschaft
ISSN: 0930-1127
MLA acronym: MBMRF

SUBSCRIPTION INFORMATION

Frequency of publication: Irregular
Circulation: 600
Available in microform: No

ADVERTISING INFORMATION

Advertising accepted: No

EDITORIAL DESCRIPTION

Scope: Publishes monographs on medieval, Latin, and German manuscripts and texts, as well as medieval education and history.
Reviews books: No
Publishes notes: No
Languages accepted: English; French; German
Prints abstracts: No

SUBMISSION REQUIREMENTS

Restrictions on contributors: None
Author pays submission fee: No
Author pays page charges: No
Length of books: No restrictions
Style: None
Number of copies required: 1
Copyright ownership: Author
Rejected manuscripts: Returned
Time before publication decision: 2 mos.
Time between decision and publication: 10 mos.
Number of reviewers: 2

(1903)
Münchener Germanistische Beiträge

Wolfgang Harms, Renate von Heydebrand, & Theo Vennemann, Editors
Wilhelm Fink Verlag
Ohmstr. 5
8000 Munich 40, Germany

First published: 1968
ISSN: 0077-1872
MLA acronym: MGB

SUBSCRIPTION INFORMATION

Frequency of publication: Irregular
Available in microform: No
Subscription address: Ferdinand Schöningh Verlag, Jühenplatz am Rathaus, P.O. Box 2540, 4790 Paderborn, Germany

ADVERTISING INFORMATION

Advertising accepted: No

EDITORIAL DESCRIPTION

Scope: The series publishes monograph studies and criticism on literature.
Reviews books: No
Publishes notes: No
Languages accepted: German
Prints abstracts: No
Author-anonymous submission: No

SUBMISSION REQUIREMENTS

Author pays submission fee: No
Author pays page charges: No
Length of books: No restrictions
Special requirements: Send inquiry before sending manuscripts.
Copyright ownership: Wilhem Fink Verlag
Rejected manuscripts: Returned
Time before publication decision: 6 mos.
Time between decision and publication: 1 yr.
Number of reviewers: 3

(1904)
*Münchener Studien zur Sprachwissenschaft

Heinrich Hettrich & Klaus Strunk, Editors
Inst. für Vgl. Sprachwissenschaft
Residenzplatz 2
8700 Würzburg, Germany

First published: 1950
Sponsoring organization: Münchener Sprachwissenschaftliche Studienkreis
ISSN: 0580-1346
MLA acronym: MSzS

SUBSCRIPTION INFORMATION

Frequency of publication: Annual
Circulation: 500
Available in microform: No
Subscription address: Verlag J. H. Röll, Postfach 9, 8716 Dettelbach, Germany
Subscription telephone: (49) 9324 1429
Subscription fax: (49) 9324 4257

ADVERTISING INFORMATION

Advertising accepted: No

EDITORIAL DESCRIPTION

Scope: Publishes articles on philology.
Reviews books: No
Publishes notes: No
Languages accepted: English; French; German
Prints abstracts: No
Author-anonymous submission: No

SUBMISSION REQUIREMENTS

Restrictions on contributors: None
Author pays submission fee: No
Author pays page charges: No
Length of articles: No restrictions
Style: None
Number of copies required: 1
Copyright ownership: Editors
Rejected manuscripts: Returned
Time before publication decision: 3 mos.
Time between decision and publication: 3 mos.
Number of reviewers: 2
Articles submitted per year: 12
Articles published per year: 10

(1905)
*Münchener Texte und Untersuchungen zur Deutschen Literatur des Mittelalters

Kommission für Deutsche Literatur des Mittelalters
Bayerische Akademie der Wissenschaften
Marstallplatz 8
8000 Munich 22, Germany

Telephone: (49) 89 23031183
Fax: (49) 89 23031240
First published: 1960
Sponsoring organization: Bayerische Akademie der Wissenschaften
ISSN: 0580-1362
MLA acronym: MTUDLM

SUBSCRIPTION INFORMATION

Frequency of publication: Irregular
Circulation: 600
Available in microform: No
Subscription address: Max Niemeyer Verlag, Postfach 2140, 7400 Tübingen, Germany
Subscription telephone: (49) 7071 87170
Subscription fax: (49) 7071 87419

ADVERTISING INFORMATION

Advertising accepted: No

EDITORIAL DESCRIPTION

Scope: Focuses on the publication and examination of sources, text editions, text groups, types, authors, and works of the German Middle Ages, especially the Late Middle Ages.
Reviews books: No
Publishes notes: No
Languages accepted: German; English
Prints abstracts: No
Author-anonymous submission: No

SUBMISSION REQUIREMENTS

Restrictions on contributors: Consult with editor prior to submission.
Author pays submission fee: No
Author pays page charges: No
Style: Series
Number of copies required: 3-4
Copyright ownership: Max Niemeyer Verlag
Rejected manuscripts: Returned
Time before publication decision: 6 mos.
Time between decision and publication: 14-24 mos.
Number of reviewers: 9
Books published per year: 3

(1906)
*The Muse: Literary Journal of the English Association at Nsukka

Olu Lawal, Editor
English Assn.
Dept. of English
Univ. of Nigeria
Nsukka, Nigeria

Telephone: (234) 42 771911 ext. 28
First published: 1963
Sponsoring organization: English Assn., Univ. of Nigeria, Nsukka
ISSN: 0331-3468
MLA acronym: Muse

SUBSCRIPTION INFORMATION

Frequency of publication: Annual
Circulation: 1,500
Available in microform: No
Subscription price: 30 N/yr. plus postage
Year to which price refers: 1991

ADVERTISING INFORMATION

Advertising accepted: Yes

EDITORIAL DESCRIPTION

Scope: Publishes creative and critical writing by students and members of the staff of the Department of Nigeria. Articles from other members of the university community are sometimes published.
Reviews books: Yes
Publishes notes: No
Languages accepted: English
Prints abstracts: Yes
Author-anonymous submission: No

SUBMISSION REQUIREMENTS

Restrictions on contributors: None
Author pays submission fee: No
Author pays page charges: No
Length of articles: 1,500-4,000 words
Length of book reviews: 500-1,000 words
Style: MLA
Number of copies required: 1
Special requirements: Submit original typescripts.
Copyright ownership: Assigned by author to journal
Rejected manuscripts: Returned; enclose return postage.
Time before publication decision: 2 mos.
Time between decision and publication: 4 mos.
Number of reviewers: 1 plus Editorial Board
Articles submitted per year: 70
Articles published per year: 40
Book reviews submitted per year: 1
Book reviews published per year: 1

(1907)
*Museum Helveticum: Schweizerische Zeitschrift für Klassische Altertumswissenschaft/Revue Suisse pour l'Etude de l'Antiquité Classique/ Rivista svizzera di Filologia Classica

Thomas Gelzer & Adalberto Giovannini, Editors
c/o Thomas Gelzer
Seminar für klassische Philologie
Gesellschaftsstr. 6
3012 Bern, Switzerland

Additional editorial address: Adalberto Giovannini, 75 Ch. des Voirets, 1212 Gd-Lancy, Switzerland
Telephone: (41) 31 658012
Fax: (41) 31 248485
First published: 1944
Sponsoring organization: Schweizerische Geisteswissenschaftliche Gesellschaft; Schweizerische Vereinigung für Altertumswissenschaft
ISSN: 0027-4054
MLA acronym: MH

SUBSCRIPTION INFORMATION

Frequency of publication: 4 times/yr.
Circulation: 600
Available in microform: No
Subscription price: 73 SwF/yr. plus postage
Year to which price refers: 1991
Subscription address: Verlag Schwabe & Co. AG, Steinentorstr. 13, 4010 Basel, Switzerland

ADVERTISING INFORMATION

Advertising accepted: Yes

EDITORIAL DESCRIPTION

Scope: Promotes research on, and imparts new results of studies in, classical antiquity, including Greek and Latin, literature, linguistics, ancient history, and archaeology.
Reviews books: Yes
Publishes notes: Yes

Languages accepted: English; French; German; Italian; Latin
Prints abstracts: No
Author-anonymous submission: No

SUBMISSION REQUIREMENTS

Author pays submission fee: No
Author pays page charges: No
Length of articles: 5,000-12,000 words
Length of book reviews: 300 words
Length of notes: 12,000 words
Number of copies required: 1
Rejected manuscripts: Returned
Time before publication decision: 3 mos.
Time between decision and publication: 6-12 mos.
Number of reviewers: 3
Articles submitted per year: 50-60
Articles published per year: 20-25
Book reviews submitted per year: 60-80
Book reviews published per year: 60-80
Notes submitted per year: 1-2
Notes published per year: 1-2

(1908)
Museums Journal

Maurice Davies, Editor
Museums Assn.
34 Bloomsbury Way
London WC1A 2SF, England

First published: 1901
Sponsoring organization: Museums Assn.
ISSN: 0027-416X
MLA acronym: MuseumsJ

SUBSCRIPTION INFORMATION

Frequency of publication: 12 times/yr. (monthly)
Circulation: 4,200
Available in microform: No
Subscription address: Assn. Enterprises, 852 Melton Rd., Thurmaston, Leicester LE4 8BN, England

ADVERTISING INFORMATION

Advertising accepted: Yes

EDITORIAL DESCRIPTION

Scope: Publishes articles on folklife and culture within the subject area of museum studies.
Reviews books: Yes
Publishes notes: Yes
Languages accepted: English
Prints abstracts: No

SUBMISSION REQUIREMENTS

Author pays submission fee: No
Author pays page charges: No
Length of articles: 2,000-3,000 words
Length of book reviews: 500 words
Length of notes: 500 words
Number of copies required: 1
Time before publication decision: 2 mos.

(1909)
*Music & Letters

Nigel Fortune & Timothy Carter, Editors
Dept. of Music
Royal Holloway & Bedford New College
Egham, Surrey TW20 0EX, England

Telephone: (44) 784 443532
Fax: (44) 784 437520
First published: 1920
ISSN: 0027-4224
MLA acronym: M&L

SUBSCRIPTION INFORMATION

Frequency of publication: 4 times/yr. (Feb., May, Aug., Nov.)
Circulation: 1,600
Available in microform: Yes
Subscription price: £36.00/yr. institutions United Kingdom & Europe; $72.00/yr. institutions elsewhere; £28.00/yr. individuals United Kingdom & Europe; $62.00yr. individuals elsewhere
Year to which price refers: 1991
Subscription address: Oxford Univ. Press, Journals Subscriptions, Walton St., Oxford OX2 6DP, England
Subscription telephone: (44) 865 56767

ADVERTISING INFORMATION

Advertising accepted: Yes

EDITORIAL DESCRIPTION

Scope: Publishes articles on the historical, critical, and analytic aspects of music.
Reviews books: Yes
Publishes notes: No
Languages accepted: English
Prints abstracts: No
Author-anonymous submission: No

SUBMISSION REQUIREMENTS

Restrictions on contributors: Unsolicited reviews are not accepted.
Author pays submission fee: No
Author pays page charges: No
Length of articles: 2,500-10,000 words
Style: Journal
Number of copies required: 2
Special requirements: Submit music examples separate from text. Submit double-spaced typescript with notes separate from text.
Copyright ownership: Oxford Univ. Press; author has unrestricted reproduction rights.
Rejected manuscripts: Returned unless photocopy from outside UK, in which case returned only at author's request
Time before publication decision: 2-4 mos.
Time between decision and publication: 9-21 mos.
Number of reviewers: 2-3
Articles submitted per year: 110 maximum
Articles published per year: 16 maximum
Book reviews published per year: 220

(1910)
*Musil Studien

Karl Dinklage & Josef Strutz, Editors
Wilhelm Fink Verlag
Ohmstr. 5
8000 Munich 40, Germany

Additional editorial address: Robert-Musil-Archiv, Bahnhofstr. 50, 9020 Klagenfurt, Austria
Telephone: (43) 463 54664
First published: 1971
Sponsoring organization: Robert-Musil-Archiv
ISSN: 0178-1278
MLA acronym: MusilS

SUBSCRIPTION INFORMATION

Frequency of publication: Irregular
Available in microform: No

ADVERTISING INFORMATION

Advertising accepted: No

EDITORIAL DESCRIPTION

Scope: Publishes monographs concerning literary criticism.
Reviews books: No
Publishes notes: No
Languages accepted: German

Prints abstracts: No
Author-anonymous submission: No

SUBMISSION REQUIREMENTS

Restrictions on contributors: Send inquiry before submitting manuscript.
Author pays submission fee: No
Author pays page charges: No
Length of books: No restrictions
Copyright ownership: Wilhelm Fink Verlag
Rejected manuscripts: Returned
Time before publication decision: 6 mos.
Time between decision and publication: 6-12 mos.
Number of reviewers: 4
Books submitted per year: 5
Books published per year: 1

(1911)
The Muslim World

Willem A. Bijlefeld, Wadi' Z. Haddad, & David A. Kerr, Editors
77 Sherman St.
Hartford, CT 06105

First published: 1911
Sponsoring organization: Hartford Seminary
ISSN: 0027-4909
MLA acronym: MW

SUBSCRIPTION INFORMATION

Frequency of publication: 4 times/yr. (Jan., Apr., July, Oct.)
Circulation: 1,400
Available in microform: Yes, through Univ. Microfilms International

ADVERTISING INFORMATION

Advertising accepted: Yes

EDITORIAL DESCRIPTION

Scope: Journal is devoted to the study of Islam and of Christian-Muslim relationships in the past and present.
Reviews books: Yes
Publishes notes: Yes
Languages accepted: English
Prints abstracts: No
Author-anonymous submission: No

SUBMISSION REQUIREMENTS

Restrictions on contributors: None
Author pays submission fee: No
Author pays page charges: No
Length of articles: 6,500 words maximum
Length of book reviews: 350 words
Length of notes: No restrictions
Style: Chicago
Number of copies required: 2
Special requirements: Submit original, double-spaced typescript.
Copyright ownership: Hartford Seminary
Rejected manuscripts: Returned at author's request; enclose return postage.
Time before publication decision: 2-3 mos.
Time between decision and publication: 18-24 mos.
Number of reviewers: 3 minimum
Articles submitted per year: 40-50
Articles published per year: 14
Book reviews published per year: 55

(1912)
*Muttersprache: Zeitschrift zur Pflege und Erforschung der Deutschen Sprache

Günther Pflug, Alfred Warner, Walter Otto, Rudolf Hoberg, & Matthias Schmitt, Editors
Gesellschaft für deutsche Sprache
c/o Gerhard Müller, Redaktion
Taunusstr. 11
Postfach 2669
6200 Wiesbaden 1, Germany

Telephone: (49) 611 520031
Fax: (49) 611 51313
First published: 1886
Sponsoring organization: Gesellschaft für Deutsche Sprache
ISSN: 0027-514X
MLA acronym: Muttersprache

SUBSCRIPTION INFORMATION

Frequency of publication: 4 times/yr.
Circulation: 1,000
Available in microform: No
Subscription price: 125.60 DM/yr.
Year to which price refers: 1992

ADVERTISING INFORMATION

Advertising accepted: Yes

EDITORIAL DESCRIPTION

Scope: Publishes articles on philology, theoretical bases of language cultivation, semantics, etymology, and technical language.
Reviews books: Yes
Publishes notes: Yes
Languages accepted: German
Prints abstracts: No

SUBMISSION REQUIREMENTS

Restrictions on contributors: None
Author pays submission fee: No
Author pays page charges: No
Length of articles: 25 typescript pp.
Length of book reviews: 5 typescript pp.
Style: None
Number of copies required: 1
Special requirements: Submit original typescript on size A4 (8 1/4 in. x 11 3/4 in.) paper.
Copyright ownership: Gesellschaft für Deutsche Sprache; reverts to author after 1 yr.
Rejected manuscripts: Returned
Time before publication decision: 2 mos.
Time between decision and publication: 6 mos.
Number of reviewers: 2
Articles published per year: 24-30
Book reviews published per year: 30
Notes published per year: 5

(1913)
*Mystics Quarterly

Elizabeth Psakis Armstrong, Editor
English Dept.
Univ. of Cincinnati
Cincinnati, OH 45221-0069

Telephone: 513 556-3937
Fax: 513 556-0142
First published: 1975
Sponsoring organization: Univ. of Cincinnati
ISSN: 0742-5503
MLA acronym: MysticsQ

SUBSCRIPTION INFORMATION

Frequency of publication: 4 times/yr.
Circulation: 450
Available in microform: No
Subscription price: $15.00/yr. institutions; $20.00/yr. individuals; add $3.00/yr. postage outside US
Year to which price refers: 1992

ADVERTISING INFORMATION

Advertising accepted: Yes
Advertising rates: $75.00/full page

EDITORIAL DESCRIPTION

Scope: Focuses on Continental and English mystics, especially, but not exclusively, medieval.
Reviews books: Yes
Publishes notes: Yes
Languages accepted: English
Prints abstracts: No
Author-anonymous submission: Yes

SUBMISSION REQUIREMENTS

Restrictions on contributors: None
Author pays submission fee: No
Author pays page charges: No
Length of articles: 3,000-5,000 words
Length of book reviews: 600-1,000 words
Length of notes: 250-300 words
Style: Chicago
Number of copies required: 2 (1 outside US)
Special requirements: Final version of accepted manuscripts must be submitted on diskette.
Copyright ownership: Univ. of Cincinnati; reverts to author upon publication
Rejected manuscripts: Returned; enclose return postage.
Time before publication decision: 3 mos. minimum
Time between decision and publication: 6-12 mos.
Number of reviewers: 2-3
Articles submitted per year: 30
Articles published per year: 8-10
Book reviews submitted per year: 20-25
Book reviews published per year: 30-40

(1914)
*Mythes, Croyances et Religions dans le Monde Anglo-Saxon

Maurice Abiteboul, Editor
10, rue du Grand Pré
84310 Morières, France

Telephone: (33) 90852850
First published: 1983
Sponsoring organization: Univ. d'Avignon
MLA acronym: MCRel

SUBSCRIPTION INFORMATION

Frequency of publication: Annual (Dec.)
Available in microform: No
Subscription price: 100 F/yr.
Year to which price refers: 1992
Subscription address: Dept. d'Anglais, Faculté des Lettres, Univ. d'Avignon, 5 rue Violette, 84000 Avignon, France

ADVERTISING INFORMATION

Advertising accepted: No

EDITORIAL DESCRIPTION

Scope: Publishes articles on myths, beliefs, and religion in relation to literature and civilization.
Reviews books: Yes
Languages accepted: French; English
Prints abstracts: No
Author-anonymous submission: No

SUBMISSION REQUIREMENTS

Restrictions on contributors: None
Author pays submission fee: No
Author pays page charges: No
Length of articles: 4,000-5,000 words
Length of book reviews: 500 words
Style: MLA
Number of copies required: 2
Copyright ownership: Journal
Rejected manuscripts: Not returned
Time before publication decision: 6-12 mos.
Time between decision and publication: 6 mos.
Number of reviewers: 2-3
Articles submitted per year: 15-20
Articles published per year: 10-15

(1915)
*Mythlore: A Journal of J. R. R. Tolkien, C. S. Lewis, Charles Williams, and the Genres of Myth and Fantasy Studies

Glen H. GoodKnight, Editor
742 S. Garfield Ave.
Monterey Park, CA 91754

Additional editorial address: Send articles to Frank Medlar, Submissions Editor, 74 Manet Rd., no. 2, Chestnut Hill, MA 02167
Telephone: 818 571-7727
First published: 1969
Sponsoring organization: Mythopoeic Soc.
ISSN: 0146-9339
MLA acronym: Mythlore

SUBSCRIPTION INFORMATION

Frequency of publication: 4 times/yr.
Circulation: 700
Available in microform: No
Subscription price: $20.00/yr. US; $28.50/yr. Canada; $35.00/yr. Europe & Latin America; $40.00/yr. Australia & Asia
Year to which price refers: 1991
Subscription address: Mythopoeic Soc., P.O. Box 6707, Altadena, CA 91003

ADVERTISING INFORMATION

Advertising accepted: No

EDITORIAL DESCRIPTION

Scope: Seeks to serve the further study and appreciation of all works by Tolkien, Lewis, and Williams; the realm of myth; the genre of fantasy; and the various literary, philosophical, and spiritual traditions which underlie their works, and which they have drawn from and enriched.
Reviews books: Yes
Publishes notes: No
Languages accepted: English
Prints abstracts: No
Author-anonymous submission: Yes

SUBMISSION REQUIREMENTS

Restrictions on contributors: None
Author pays submission fee: No
Author pays page charges: No
Length of articles: 3,000-6,000 words
Length of book reviews: 1,000 words
Style: MLA preferred
Number of copies required: 2
Special requirements: Submit typescript and diskette, if available.
Copyright ownership: Mythopoeic Soc.
Rejected manuscripts: Returned; enclose SASE.
Time before publication decision: 2 mos.
Time between decision and publication: 2 mos.
Number of reviewers: 3-4
Articles submitted per year: 22
Articles published per year: 19
Book reviews published per year: 20

(1916)
*Naamkunde

K. Roelandts & W. van Langendonck, Editors
Inst. voor Naamkunde
Katholieke Univ. Leuven
Blijde-Inkomstr. 21/II
3000 Leuven, Belgium

Additional editorial address: P. J. Meertens-Inst., Keizersgracht 569-571, 1017 DR Amsterdam, Netherlands
Telephone: (32) 6 284818
Fax: (32) 16 285025
First published: 1969
Sponsoring organization: Inst. voor Naamkunde, Leuven; P. J. Meertens-Inst., Amsterdam; Ministerie van de Vlaamse Gemeenschap; Univ. Stichting van België; Fakulteit Letteren & Wijsbegeerte van de Katholieke Univ. Leuven
ISSN: 0167-5357
MLA acronym: Nku

SUBSCRIPTION INFORMATION

Frequency of publication: Annual
Circulation: 825
Available in microform: No
Subscription price: 650 BF/yr.
Year to which price refers: 1991
Subscription address: Uitgeverÿ Peeters, P.O. 41, 3000 Leuven, Belgium

ADVERTISING INFORMATION

Advertising accepted: No

EDITORIAL DESCRIPTION

Scope: Publishes studies of place and personal names in the Netherlandic (Dutch and Flemish) domain.
Reviews books: Yes
Publishes notes: Yes
Languages accepted: Dutch; English; French; German
Prints abstracts: No
Author-anonymous submission: Yes

SUBMISSION REQUIREMENTS

Author pays submission fee: No
Author pays page charges: No
Length of articles: 20-50 pp.
Length of book reviews: 2 pp.
Length of notes: 1 p.
Number of copies required: 1
Copyright ownership: Author
Rejected manuscripts: Returned
Time before publication decision: 5 weeks
Time between decision and publication: 4 mos.
Number of reviewers: 3
Articles submitted per year: 25
Articles published per year: 15-20
Book reviews submitted per year: 10
Book reviews published per year: 6
Notes submitted per year: 9
Notes published per year: 6

(1917)
*The Nabokovian

Stephen Jan Parker, Editor
Slavic Languages & Literatures
Univ. of Kansas
Lawrence, KS 66045

Telephone: 913 864-3313
First published: 1978
Sponsoring organization: Vladimir Nabokov Soc.
ISSN: 0894-7120
MLA acronym: Nabokovian

SUBSCRIPTION INFORMATION

Frequency of publication: 2 times/yr. (Spring, Fall)
Circulation: 270
Available in microform: No
Subscription price: $11.00/yr. institutions; $9.00/yr. individuals
Year to which price refers: 1992

ADVERTISING INFORMATION

Advertising accepted: No

EDITORIAL DESCRIPTION

Scope: Serves to report and stimulate Nabokov scholarship and to create a link between Nabokov scholars in the United States and elsewhere.
Reviews books: Yes
Publishes notes: Yes
Languages accepted: English
Prints abstracts: No

SUBMISSION REQUIREMENTS

Restrictions on contributors: None
Author pays submission fee: No
Author pays page charges: No
Style: Library of Congress for Russian transliteration
Copyright ownership: Author
Rejected manuscripts: Returned

(1918)
*Names: Journal of the American Name Society

Thomas J. Gasque, Editor
Dept. of English
Univ. of South Dakota
Vermillion, SD 57069

Telephone: 605 677-5229
Fax: 605 677-5073
E-mail: UGTJ08@SDNET.BITNET
First published: 1953
Sponsoring organization: American Name Soc.
ISSN: 0027-7738
MLA acronym: Names

SUBSCRIPTION INFORMATION

Frequency of publication: 4 times/yr. (Mar., June, Sept., Dec.)
Circulation: 900
Available in microform: Yes
Subscription price: $25.00/yr. US; $30.00/yr. Canada; $40.00/yr. elsewhere; $15.00/yr. students & emeritus US; $20.00/yr. students & emeritus elsewhere
Year to which price refers: 1992
Subscription address: Wayne Finke, Dept. of Modern Languages & Comparative Literature, Baruch College, 17 Lexington Ave., New York, NY 10010
Subscription telephone: 212 387-1570
Subscription fax: 212 387-1591

ADVERTISING INFORMATION

Advertising accepted: No

EDITORIAL DESCRIPTION

Scope: Publishes general, regional, and topical articles, as well as the results of specialized research in place names, personal names, and literary names.
Reviews books: Yes
Languages accepted: English
Prints abstracts: Yes
Author-anonymous submission: Yes

SUBMISSION REQUIREMENTS

Restrictions on contributors: None
Author pays submission fee: No
Author pays page charges: No
Length of articles: 4,000-5,000 words
Length of book reviews: 500-1,000 words
Style: MLA (parenthetical documentation)
Number of copies required: 3
Special requirements: Include references at end of manuscript. Contributors are asked to be prepared to submit accepted articles on IBM-compatible diskettes. Submit a 100-word abstract.
Copyright ownership: Journal
Rejected manuscripts: Returned; enclose return postage.
Time before publication decision: 3 mos.
Time between decision and publication: 10 mos.
Number of reviewers: 3
Articles submitted per year: 60
Articles published per year: 20
Book reviews submitted per year: 60
Book reviews published per year: 55

(1919)
*Namn och Bygd: Tidskrift för Nordisk Ortnamnsforskning/Journal for Nordic Place-Name Research

Thorsten Andersson, Editor
Sankt Johannesgatan 11
75312 Uppsala, Sweden

Telephone: (46) 18 181289
First published: 1913
Sponsoring organization: Kungliga Gustav Adolfs Akademien; Humanistisk-Samhällsvetenskapliga Forskningsrådet
ISSN: 0077-2704
MLA acronym: NB

SUBSCRIPTION INFORMATION

Frequency of publication: Annual (Autumn)
Circulation: 300
Available in microform: No
Subscription price: 190 Skr/yr. Sweden; 160 Skr/yr. other Scandinavian countries; 175 Skr/yr. elsewhere
Year to which price refers: 1992
Subscription address: Swedish Science Press, Box 118, 75104 Uppsala, Sweden
Subscription telephone: (46) 18 365566
Subscription fax: (46) 18 365277

ADVERTISING INFORMATION

Advertising accepted: No

EDITORIAL DESCRIPTION

Scope: Publishes articles on Scandinavian place names. Presents studies in etymology, phonology, morphology, semantics and chronology of place names.
Reviews books: Yes
Publishes notes: No
Languages accepted: English; German; Swedish; Norwegian; Danish; Icelandic; Faroese
Prints abstracts: Yes
Author-anonymous submission: No

SUBMISSION REQUIREMENTS

Restrictions on contributors: None
Author pays submission fee: No
Author pays page charges: No
Length of articles: 1,000-15,000 words
Length of book reviews: 500-1,000 words
Style: None
Number of copies required: 1
Special requirements: Submit original typescript. Submit a short abstract for articles not in English or German.
Copyright ownership: Author
Rejected manuscripts: Returned
Time before publication decision: 1-2 mos.
Time between decision and publication: 6-18 mos.
Number of reviewers: 2-3
Articles submitted per year: 20-25

Articles published per year: 15-20
Book reviews submitted per year: 10-15
Book reviews published per year: 10-15

(1920)
Narodna Tvorchist' ta Etnohrafiia

O. H. Kostink, Editor
Akademiia Nauk Ukraïny
Ul. Hrushevs'koho, 4
252001 MSP Kiev 1, Ukraine

First published: 1925
Sponsoring organization: Inst. Mystetstvo-Znavstva, Folkloru ta Etnografii, Akademiia Nauk Ukraïny
ISSN: 0130-6936
MLA acronym: NTE

SUBSCRIPTION INFORMATION

Frequency of publication: 6 times/yr.
Circulation: 5,000
Available in microform: No
Subscription address: Izdatel'stvo Naukova Dumka, Ul. Repina 3, Kiev, Ukraine

ADVERTISING INFORMATION

Advertising accepted: No

EDITORIAL DESCRIPTION

Reviews books: Yes
Publishes notes: Yes
Languages accepted: Ukrainian
Prints abstracts: No
Author-anonymous submission: No

SUBMISSION REQUIREMENTS

Author pays submission fee: Yes
Author pays page charges: No
Style: Scientific
Number of copies required: 2
Rejected manuscripts: Not returned
Time before publication decision: 6 mos.
Time between decision and publication: 2-3 mos.
Number of reviewers: 2
Articles submitted per year: 200
Articles published per year: 150
Book reviews submitted per year: 40
Book reviews published per year: 30
Notes submitted per year: 60
Notes published per year: 50

(1921)
*Narodna Umjetnost

Zorica Rajković, Editor
Inst. za Etnologiju i Folkloristiku
Ulica Kralja Zvonimira 17/IV
41000 Zagreb, Croatia

Telephone: (38) 41 440880; (38) 41 410617
Fax: (38) 41 440880
First published: 1962
Sponsoring organization: Inst. za Etnologiju i Folkloristiku
ISSN: 0547-2504
MLA acronym: NUm

SUBSCRIPTION INFORMATION

Frequency of publication: Annual
Circulation: 1,500
Available in microform: No

ADVERTISING INFORMATION

Advertising accepted: No

EDITORIAL DESCRIPTION

Scope: Publishes studies and research material on oral and folk literature, music and dance folklore, folk theater, and customs.
Reviews books: Yes
Publishes notes: Yes
Languages accepted: Serbo-Croatian
Prints abstracts: Yes

SUBMISSION REQUIREMENTS

Restrictions on contributors: None
Author pays submission fee: No
Author pays page charges: No
Length of articles: 5,600-11,200 words
Length of book reviews: 900 words
Length of notes: 50-100 words
Style: YUS Times
Number of copies required: 1
Copyright ownership: Inst. za Etnologiju i Folkloristiku
Rejected manuscripts: Returned
Time before publication decision: 6 mos.
Time between decision and publication: 1 yr.
Number of reviewers: 2
Articles submitted per year: 10-12
Articles published per year: 8-10
Book reviews submitted per year: 40-50
Book reviews published per year: 40-50
Notes submitted per year: 40
Notes published per year: 40

(1922)
Narodno Stvaralaštvo. Folklor

Dušan Nedeljković, Editor
Savez Udruzenja Folklorista Jugoslavije
ul. Kneza Mihaila, 35
Belgrade, Yugoslavia

First published: 1962
Sponsoring organization: Union des Assns. des Folklorists de Yougoslavie
ISSN: 0027-8017
MLA acronym: NStv

SUBSCRIPTION INFORMATION

Frequency of publication: 4 times/yr.
Circulation: 1,000

EDITORIAL DESCRIPTION

Scope: Publishes articles on folklore.
Reviews books: Yes
Languages accepted: Serbo-Croatian
Prints abstracts: Yes

SUBMISSION REQUIREMENTS

Restrictions on contributors: None
Style: MLA
Number of copies required: 3
Copyright ownership: Author
Time before publication decision: 3 mos.
Articles published per year: 28

(1923)
*Naš Jezik

Mitar Pešikan, Editor
Inst. za Srpskokhrvatski Jezik
Knez-Mikhailova 35/1
11 000 Belgrade, Yugoslavia

First published: 1933
Sponsoring organization: Scientific Assn., Republic of Serbia
ISSN: 0027-8084
MLA acronym: NJe

SUBSCRIPTION INFORMATION

Frequency of publication: 2-5 times/yr.
Circulation: 800

Available in microform: No

ADVERTISING INFORMATION

Advertising accepted: No

EDITORIAL DESCRIPTION

Scope: Publishes articles on contemporary Serbo-Croatian language.
Reviews books: No
Publishes notes: No
Languages accepted: Serbo-Croatian
Prints abstracts: No
Author-anonymous submission: No

SUBMISSION REQUIREMENTS

Restrictions on contributors: None
Author pays submission fee: No
Author pays page charges: No
Length of articles: 16 typescript pp.
Number of copies required: 1
Copyright ownership: Author
Rejected manuscripts: Not returned
Time before publication decision: 4 mos.
Time between decision and publication: 10 weeks
Number of reviewers: 2
Articles submitted per year: 50-60
Articles published per year: 25-35

(1924)
*Naše Řeč

Jiří Kraus & Ivana Svobodová, Editors
Letenská 4
118 51 Prague 1, Czech Republic

Telephone: (42) 2 5393519
First published: 1916
Sponsoring organization: Československá Akademie Věd
ISSN: 0027-8203
MLA acronym: NŘeč

SUBSCRIPTION INFORMATION

Frequency of publication: 5 times/yr. (Feb., Apr. June, Sept., Nov.)
Circulation: 2,500
Available in microform: No
Subscription price: 35 Kčs/yr. Czechoslovakia
Year to which price refers: 1991
Additional subscription address: In western countries: Kubon & Sagner, Postfach 340108, 8000 Munich 34, Germany

ADVERTISING INFORMATION

Advertising accepted: No

EDITORIAL DESCRIPTION

Scope: Publishes articles on problems of Czech language and of language culture in general. Contains articles on the structure of Czech language, on its stylistic variants, and on the norm and codification of the standard literary language.
Reviews books: Yes
Publishes notes: Yes
Languages accepted: Czech
Prints abstracts: No
Author-anonymous submission: No

SUBMISSION REQUIREMENTS

Restrictions on contributors: None
Author pays submission fee: No
Author pays page charges: No
Length of articles: 10-15 pp.
Length of book reviews: 3-8 pp.
Length of notes: 1-4 pp.
Style: None
Number of copies required: 3
Copyright ownership: Academia, Publishing House of the Czechoslovak Academy of Sciences

Rejected manuscripts: Returned
Time before publication decision: 1-3 weeks
Time between decision and publication: 2-8 mos.
Number of reviewers: 2
Articles submitted per year: 25
Articles published per year: 19
Book reviews submitted per year: 38
Book reviews published per year: 18-20
Notes submitted per year: 36
Notes published per year: 22

(1925)
Nash Sovremennik: Literaturno-Khudozhestvennyĭ i Obshchestvenno-Politicheskiĭ Zhurnal

S. Iu. Kuniaev, Editor
Tsvetnoĭ bul'var, 30
103750 GSP Moscow, Russia

First published: 1953
Sponsoring organization: Soiuz Pisateleĭ R.S.F.S.R.
ISSN: 0027-8238
MLA acronym: NSov

SUBSCRIPTION INFORMATION

Frequency of publication: 12 times/yr.
Circulation: 205,800

EDITORIAL DESCRIPTION

Scope: Publishes prose, poetry, essays, criticism, and reviews. Emphasis is on Russian literature.
Reviews books: Yes
Languages accepted: Russian
Prints abstracts: No

SUBMISSION REQUIREMENTS

Number of copies required: 2
Special requirements: Submit double-spaced typescript.
Copyright ownership: Author
Rejected manuscripts: Returned
Time before publication decision: 3 mos.
Time between decision and publication: 4-6 mos.
Number of reviewers: 20
Articles published per year: 300

(1926)
Nashriyye(h)-ye Dāneshkade(h)-ye Adabiyyāt va Olum-e Ensāni-ye Tabriz

Nematollah Taghavi, Editor
Faculty of Arts
Univ. of Tabriz
Tabriz, Iran

First published: 1948
Sponsoring organization: Univ. of Tabriz
MLA acronym: NDAT

SUBSCRIPTION INFORMATION

Frequency of publication: 4 times/yr.
Circulation: 1,600
Available in microform: No

ADVERTISING INFORMATION

Advertising accepted: No

EDITORIAL DESCRIPTION

Scope: Publishes articles on the humanities and Persian, Azarbaijani, and Kurdish literatures and languages.
Reviews books: No
Languages accepted: Persian
Prints abstracts: No

SUBMISSION REQUIREMENTS

Restrictions on contributors: None
Author pays submission fee: No
Author pays page charges: No
Length of articles: 30 pp. maximum
Number of copies required: 1
Copyright ownership: Author
Rejected manuscripts: Not returned
Time before publication decision: 3 mos.
Time between decision and publication: 3 mo.
Number of reviewers: 6
Articles submitted per year: 30-45
Articles published per year: 24-30

(1927)
***The Nassau Review: The Journal of Nassau Community College Devoted to Arts, Letters, and Sciences**

Paul A. Doyle, Editor
English Dept.
Nassau Community College
State Univ. of New York
Garden City, NY 11530

Telephone: 516 222-7186
First published: 1964
Sponsoring organization: State Univ. of New York, Nassau Community College
ISSN: 0077-2879
MLA acronym: NR

SUBSCRIPTION INFORMATION

Frequency of publication: Annual
Circulation: 1,200
Available in microform: No
Subscription price: Free
Year to which price refers: 1992

ADVERTISING INFORMATION

Advertising accepted: No

EDITORIAL DESCRIPTION

Scope: Publishes articles in literary criticism and research, in research in history, sociology, economics, philosophy, and art, as well as poems, short stories, one-act plays, and excerpts from novels in progress.
Reviews books: No
Publishes notes: No
Languages accepted: English
Prints abstracts: No
Author-anonymous submission: Yes

SUBMISSION REQUIREMENTS

Restrictions on contributors: None
Author pays submission fee: No
Author pays page charges: No
Length of articles: 500-2,000 words
Style: MLA
Number of copies required: 3
Copyright ownership: Nassau Community College in the name of the journal
Rejected manuscripts: Returned; enclose return postage.
Time before publication decision: 6-12 mos.
Time between decision and publication: 6-10 mos.
Number of reviewers: 3-5
Articles submitted per year: 25-30
Articles published per year: 5-8

(1928)
***The Nathaniel Hawthorne Review**

John L. Idol, Jr., Editor
English Dept.
Clemson Univ.
Clemson, SC 29634

Telephone: 803 654-4545; 803 656-5395
Fax: 803 656-0258
First published: 1975
Sponsoring organization: Nathaniel Hawthorne Soc.; Clemson Univ.; Bowdoin College
ISSN: 0890-4197
MLA acronym: NHR

SUBSCRIPTION INFORMATION

Frequency of publication: 2 times/yr.
Circulation: 400
Available in microform: No
Subscription price: $10.00/yr.
Year to which price refers: 1992
Subscription address: Arthur Monke, Hawthorne-Longfellow Library, Bowdoin College, Brunswick, ME 04011

ADVERTISING INFORMATION

Advertising accepted: Yes
Advertising rates: $50.00/half page; $75.00/three-quarter page; $100.00/full page

EDITORIAL DESCRIPTION

Scope: Publishes Hawthorne Society news items, notices of research in progress, notes and queries, annual bibliography, brief book reviews, short and medium-length articles, and lists of conference papers.
Reviews books: Yes
Publishes notes: Yes
Languages accepted: English
Prints abstracts: No
Author-anonymous submission: Yes

SUBMISSION REQUIREMENTS

Restrictions on contributors: Book reviews are solicited.
Author pays submission fee: No
Author pays page charges: No
Length of articles: 2,000-2,500 words
Length of book reviews: 400-500 words
Length of notes: 400-800 words
Style: MLA
Number of copies required: 2
Special requirements: Submit original typescript.
Copyright ownership: Author
Rejected manuscripts: Returned
Time before publication decision: 4-6 weeks
Time between decision and publication: 12-18 mos.
Number of reviewers: 2-3
Articles submitted per year: 30
Articles published per year: 8
Book reviews submitted per year: 8
Book reviews published per year: 8
Notes submitted per year: 10
Notes published per year: 4

(1929)
***The National Library of Wales Journal/Cylchgrawn Llyfrgell Genedlaethol Cymru**

Brynley F. Roberts, Editor
National Library of Wales
Aberystwyth
Dyfed SY23 3BU, Wales

Telephone: (44) 970 623816
Fax: (44) 970 615709
First published: 1939
Sponsoring organization: National Library of Wales
ISSN: 0011-4421
MLA acronym: NLWJ

SUBSCRIPTION INFORMATION

Frequency of publication: 2 times/yr.
Circulation: 350
Available in microform: No
Subscription price: £10.00/yr.
Year to which price refers: 1991

ADVERTISING INFORMATION

Advertising accepted: No

EDITORIAL DESCRIPTION

Scope: Publishes articles on the collections of the National Library of Wales and on topics relating to Wales.
Reviews books: No
Publishes notes: Yes
Languages accepted: English; Welsh
Prints abstracts: No
Author-anonymous submission: No

SUBMISSION REQUIREMENTS

Restrictions on contributors: None
Author pays submission fee: No
Author pays page charges: No
Length of articles: 2,000-14,000 words
Length of notes: 100-1,000 words
Style: Hart's Rules
Number of copies required: 1
Copyright ownership: Author
Rejected manuscripts: Returned
Time before publication decision: 1-4 weeks
Time between decision and publication: 1-2 yrs.
Number of reviewers: 1-2
Articles submitted per year: 18
Articles published per year: 8-12
Notes submitted per year: 12
Notes published per year: 6

(1930)
*Nationalities Papers

Henry R. Huttenbach, Editor
City College of New York
138th St. & Convent Ave.
New York, NY 10031

Telephone: 212 650-7384
Fax: 212 650-6970
First published: 1972
Sponsoring organization: Assn. for the Study of the Nationalities (U.S.S.R. & East Europe) Inc.
ISSN: 0090-5992
MLA acronym: NatP

SUBSCRIPTION INFORMATION

Frequency of publication: 2 times/yr. (Spring, Fall)
Circulation: 1,100
Available in microform: Yes
Subscription price: $24.00/yr. institutions; $18.00/yr. individuals; $9.00/yr. students
Year to which price refers: 1992
Subscription address: Andris Skreija, Dept. of Sociology, Univ. of Nebraska, Omaha, NB 68101

ADVERTISING INFORMATION

Advertising accepted: Yes
Advertising rates: $100.00/full page

EDITORIAL DESCRIPTION

Scope: Publishes articles on social studies and humanities as related to the nationalities of Eurasia and East European ethnic minorities.
Reviews books: Yes
Publishes notes: Yes
Languages accepted: English; German; French; Russian
Prints abstracts: Yes
Author-anonymous submission: Yes

SUBMISSION REQUIREMENTS

Restrictions on contributors: Unsolicited book reviews are not accepted.
Author pays submission fee: No
Author pays page charges: No
Length of articles: 25 pp. maximum
Length of book reviews: 500 words

Length of notes: 50 words maximum
Style: Turabian; Library of Congress system of transliteration without diacritical marks
Number of copies required: 2
Special requirements: Submit double-spaced typescript; footnotes should be typed double-spaced at end of paper.
Copyright ownership: Assn. for the Study of the Nationalities (U.S.S.R. & East European) Inc.
Rejected manuscripts: Returned; enclose return postage.
Time before publication decision: 3 mos.
Time between decision and publication: 1 yr.
Number of reviewers: 2
Articles submitted per year: 70
Articles published per year: 10-12
Book reviews submitted per year: 45-60
Book reviews published per year: 45-60
Notes published per year: 2

(1931)
*Natural Language & Linguistic Theory

Joan Maling, Editor
Linguistics Program
Dept. of Psychology
Brandeis Univ.
Waltham, MA 02254

Additional editorial address: Kluwer Academic Publishers, P.O. Box 17, 3300 AA Dordrecht, Netherlands
Telephone: 617 736-3261
Fax: 617 736-3291
E-mail: Maling@brandeis.bitnet
First published: 1983
ISSN: 0167-806X
MLA acronym: NL&LT

SUBSCRIPTION INFORMATION

Frequency of publication: 4 times/yr.
Circulation: 1,400
Available in microform: No
Subscription price: $54.00/yr. individuals
Year to which price refers: 1992
Subscription address: Kluwer Academic Publishers, P.O. Box 322, 3300 AH Dordrecht, Netherlands
Additional subscription address: Kluwer Academic Publishers, P.O. Box 358, Accord Station, Hingham, MA 02018-0358
Subscription telephone: 617 871-6666; (31) 78 334317
Subscription fax: (31) 78 334254

ADVERTISING INFORMATION

Advertising accepted: Yes

EDITORIAL DESCRIPTION

Scope: Publishes articles on theoretical research concerning natural language data including syntax, semantics, phonology, and morphology. Also publishes survey articles of recent developments and replies to papers. Includes some review articles.
Reviews books: Yes
Publishes notes: Yes
Languages accepted: English
Prints abstracts: Yes
Author-anonymous submission: Yes

SUBMISSION REQUIREMENTS

Restrictions on contributors: None
Author pays submission fee: No
Author pays page charges: No
Length of articles: 50 pp.
Length of notes: 5 pp.
Style: Request specifications from Kluwer or editor
Number of copies required: 4
Special requirements: Submit author's name and address on separate page, not on manuscript. Also submit an 150-word abstract.

Copyright ownership: Kluwer Academic Publishers
Rejected manuscripts: Not returned
Time before publication decision: 3-6 mos.
Time between decision and publication: 6-9 mos.
Number of reviewers: 2-4
Articles submitted per year: 100
Articles published per year: 20
Book reviews submitted per year: 2
Book reviews published per year: 2
Notes submitted per year: 4
Notes published per year: 2

(1932)
*Naučni Sastanak Slavista u Vukove Dane

Božo Ćorić, Editor
Filololoski Fakultet
Belgrade, Yugoslavia

Telephone: (38) 11 187662
Fax: (38) 11 630039
First published: 1971
Sponsoring organization: International Slavic Center of the Republic of Serbia
MLA acronym: NSSVD

SUBSCRIPTION INFORMATION

Frequency of publication: Annual
Circulation: 500
Subscription address: Medjunarodni Slavisticki Center SR Srbije, Studentski Trg 3, Belgrade, Yugoslavia

ADVERTISING INFORMATION

Advertising accepted: No

EDITORIAL DESCRIPTION

Scope: Publishes all the papers presented at the International Slavic Symposium held in September of each year, in which both domestic and foreign scholars participate.
Reviews books: No
Publishes notes: Yes
Languages accepted: Serbo-Croatian
Prints abstracts: Yes

(1933)
*Nea Poreia

Tilemachos Alaveras, Editor
Venizelou 14
Salonika, Greece

First published: 1955
ISSN: 0470-5238
MLA acronym: NP

SUBSCRIPTION INFORMATION

Frequency of publication: 3-4 times/yr.
Circulation: 1,100
Available in microform: No

ADVERTISING INFORMATION

Advertising accepted: No

EDITORIAL DESCRIPTION

Scope: Publishes articles on literature.
Reviews books: Yes
Languages accepted: Greek
Prints abstracts: No

SUBMISSION REQUIREMENTS

Restrictions on contributors: None
Author pays submission fee: No
Author pays page charges: No
Length of articles: No restrictions

Style: None
Number of copies required: 1
Copyright ownership: Author
Rejected manuscripts: Not returned
Time between decision and publication: 2-4 mos.
Number of reviewers: 1-2

(1934)
*Negative Capability

Sue Walker, Ron Walker, & Richard Beyer, Editors
62 East Ridgelawn Dr. East
Mobile, AL 36608

Additional editorial address: English Dept., Univ. of South Alabama, Mobile, AL 36688
Telephone: 205 343-6163
Fax: 205 343-6163
First published: 1981
ISSN: 0227-5166
MLA acronym: NegCap

SUBSCRIPTION INFORMATION

Frequency of publication: 3 times/yr.
Circulation: 1,000
Available in microform: No
Subscription price: $17.00/yr. institutions; $15.00/yr. individuals
Year to which price refers: 1993

ADVERTISING INFORMATION

Advertising accepted: Yes
Advertising rates: $50.00/half page; $75.00/full page

EDITORIAL DESCRIPTION

Scope: Promotes the publication of works of contemporary poets, fiction writers, and scholars.
Reviews books: Yes
Publishes notes: Yes
Languages accepted: English; Spanish; French; German; Danish; Portuguese
Prints abstracts: No
Author-anonymous submission: No

SUBMISSION REQUIREMENTS

Author pays submission fee: No
Author pays page charges: No
Length of articles: No restrictions
Length of book reviews: No restrictions
Length of notes: No restrictions
Style: MLA; Chicago
Number of copies required: 1
Copyright ownership: Journal
Rejected manuscripts: Returned; enclose SASE.
Time before publication decision: 6 weeks
Time between decision and publication: 6 mos.
Number of reviewers: 4
Articles submitted per year: 50-100
Articles published per year: 10
Book reviews submitted per year: 40
Book reviews published per year: 12

(1935)
Neman: Literaturno-Khudozhestvennyĭ i Obshchestvenno-Politicheskiĭ Zhurnal

A. P. Kudravets, Editor
Prospekt F. Skaryny 39
220005 Minsk, Belarus

First published: 1951
ISSN: 0028-2588
MLA acronym: Neman

SUBSCRIPTION INFORMATION

Frequency of publication: 12 times/yr.

EDITORIAL DESCRIPTION

Languages accepted: Russian

(1936)
*Német Filológiai Tanulmányok/ Arbeiten zur Deutschen Philologie

Lajos Némedi, Editor
German Dept.
Kossuth Univ. of Debrecen
4010 Debrecen 10, Hungary

First published: 1965
Sponsoring organization: Kossuth Lajos Tudományegyetem
ISSN: 0418-4580
MLA acronym: ADPh

SUBSCRIPTION INFORMATION

Frequency of publication: Annual
Circulation: 500
Available in microform: No
Subscription address: Kultura Foreign Trade Co., P.O. Box 149, 1389 Budapest 62, Hungary

ADVERTISING INFORMATION

Advertising accepted: No

EDITORIAL DESCRIPTION

Scope: Publishes articles on theoretical linguistics, comparative linguistics, German historical linguistics, German literary history, and German-Hungarian literary relations.
Reviews books: Yes
Publishes notes: No
Languages accepted: German
Prints abstracts: No
Author-anonymous submission: No

SUBMISSION REQUIREMENTS

Restrictions on contributors: None
Author pays submission fee: No
Author pays page charges: No
Length of articles: 15-20 typescript pp. maximum
Length of book reviews: 3-4 typescript pp.
Style: None
Number of copies required: 2
Copyright ownership: Author
Rejected manuscripts: Not returned
Time before publication decision: 1 yr.
Time between decision and publication: 1 yr.
Number of reviewers: 2
Articles submitted per year: 10
Articles published per year: 10
Book reviews submitted per year: 4-5
Book reviews published per year: 3-4

(1937)
*Nemla Italian Studies

Umberto C. Mariani, Editor
Dept. of Italian
Rutgers Univ.
18 Seminary Pl.
New Brunswick, NJ 08903

Telephone: 908 932-7536; 908 369-5141
First published: 1977
Sponsoring organization: Dept. of Italian, Rutgers Univ.; Northeast Modern Language Assn. (NEMLA), Italian Section
MLA acronym: NemlaIS

SUBSCRIPTION INFORMATION

Frequency of publication: Annual
Circulation: 500
Available in microform: No
Subscription price: $5.00/yr.
Year to which price refers: 1992
Subscription address: 376 Zion Rd., Neshanic, NJ 08853-3012

ADVERTISING INFORMATION

Advertising accepted: Yes
Advertising rates: $60.00/full page

EDITORIAL DESCRIPTION

Scope: Publishes selected papers presented at the annual convention of the Northeast Modern Language Association. Includes papers on Italian and Italian American literature and culture.
Reviews books: No
Publishes notes: No
Languages accepted: English; Italian; French; Spanish
Prints abstracts: No
Author-anonymous submission: No

SUBMISSION REQUIREMENTS

Restrictions on contributors: Contributors must have presented the paper at the Northeast Modern Language Assn. Conference.
Author pays submission fee: No
Author pays page charges: No
Length of articles: No restrictions
Style: MLA
Number of copies required: 1
Special requirements: Authors accepted for publication must buy 24 copies at half price.
Copyright ownership: Author
Rejected manuscripts: Returned
Time before publication decision: 2 mos.
Time between decision and publication: 2 mos.
Number of reviewers: 2
Articles submitted per year: 15-20
Articles published per year: 10-12

(1938)
Nëntori: Organ i Lidhjes së Shkrimtarëve dhe Artistëve të Shqipërisë

Dalan Shapllo, Editor
Drejtoria Qendrore e Librit
Rruga Konferenca e Pezës
Tirana, Albania

First published: 1954
ISSN: 0548-1600
MLA acronym: Nëntori

SUBSCRIPTION INFORMATION

Frequency of publication: 12 times/yr.
Subscription address: Lidhja e Shkrimtanëve dhe Artistëve të Shqipërisë, at the above address

EDITORIAL DESCRIPTION

Scope: Publishes articles on Albanian literature.
Reviews books: Yes
Languages accepted: Albanian
Prints abstracts: No

(1939)
*Neohelicon: Acta Comparationis Litterarum Universarum

Miklós Szabolcsi & György Mihály Vajda, Editors
Ménesi út 11-13
1118 Budapest, Hungary

First published: 1973
Sponsoring organization: International Comparative Literature Assn.
ISSN: 0324-4652
MLA acronym: Neohelicon

SUBSCRIPTION INFORMATION

Frequency of publication: 2 times/yr.
Available in microform: No
Subscription price: 287 f ($174.00)/yr.
Year to which price refers: 1993
Subscription address: John Benjamins North America, Inc., 821 Bethlehem Pike, Philadelphia, PA 19118
Additional subscription address: John Benjamins B.V., Amsteldjk 44, P.O. Box 75577, 1070 AN Amsterdam, Netherlands
Subscription telephone: 215 836-1200; (31) 20 6738156
Subscription fax: 215 836-1204; (31) 20 6739773

ADVERTISING INFORMATION

Advertising accepted: No

EDITORIAL DESCRIPTION

Scope: Publishes studies in comparative and world literature. Welcomes studies which further a synthetic presentation of literary epochs, periods, trends, and movements from a comparative point of view.
Reviews books: Yes
Publishes notes: No
Languages accepted: English; French; German; Russian
Prints abstracts: No
Author-anonymous submission: Yes

SUBMISSION REQUIREMENTS

Restrictions on contributors: None
Author pays submission fee: No
Author pays page charges: No
Length of articles: No restrictions
Length of book reviews: No restrictions
Style: MLA
Number of copies required: 2
Copyright ownership: Akademai Kiadó
Rejected manuscripts: Returned
Time before publication decision: 2 mos.
Time between decision and publication: 10 mos.
Number of reviewers: 2
Articles submitted per year: 60
Articles published per year: 50
Book reviews submitted per year: 4-6
Book reviews published per year: 4-6

(1940)
*Neophilologus

P. J. E. Hyams & W. F. Koopman, Editors
Engels Seminarium
Spuistraat 210
1012 VT Amsterdam, Netherlands

Telephone: (31) 20 5254018
Fax: (31) 20 5253052
E-mail: WILLEMK@alf.LET.UVA.NL
First published: 1916
ISSN: 0028-2677
MLA acronym: Neophil

SUBSCRIPTION INFORMATION

Frequency of publication: 4 times/yr. (Jan., Apr., July, Oct.)
Circulation: 800
Available in microform: No
Subscription price: 265 f/yr.; 120 f/yr. students
Year to which price refers: 1992
Subscription address: Wolters-Noordhoff, P.O. Box 58, 9700 MB Groningen, Netherlands
Subscription telephone: (31) 50 226922
Subscription fax: (31) 50 264866

ADVERTISING INFORMATION

Advertising accepted: Yes

EDITORIAL DESCRIPTION

Scope: Publishes articles on modern and medieval language and literature including general linguistics, literary theory, and comparative literature.
Reviews books: No
Publishes notes: Yes
Languages accepted: English; French; German; Italian; Portuguese; Spanish
Prints abstracts: No
Author-anonymous submission: No

SUBMISSION REQUIREMENTS

Restrictions on contributors: None
Author pays submission fee: No
Author pays page charges: Yes
Cost of page charges: 50 f/page
Length of articles: 8,000 words (16 printed pp.) including footnotes maximum
Length of notes: 2,000 words
Style: MLA
Number of copies required: 1
Special requirements: Submit original typescript.
Copyright ownership: Editor
Rejected manuscripts: Returned; enclose international reply coupons.
Time before publication decision: 3-6 mos.
Time between decision and publication: 12-30 mos.
Number of reviewers: 1-2
Articles submitted per year: 250
Articles published per year: 60
Notes submitted per year: 50
Notes published per year: 10

(1941)
*Neudrucke Deutscher Literaturwerke: Neue Folge

Hans-Henrik Krummacher, Editor
Max Niemeyer Verlag
Postfach 2140
7400 Tübingen, Germany

Telephone: (49) 7071 81104
Fax: (49) 7071 87419
First published: 1876
ISSN: 0077-7668
MLA acronym: NdL

SUBSCRIPTION INFORMATION

Frequency of publication: Irregular
Available in microform: No

ADVERTISING INFORMATION

Advertising accepted: No

EDITORIAL DESCRIPTION

Scope: Publishes critical editions of German literature especially of the 16th-18th centuries.
Reviews books: No
Publishes notes: No
Languages accepted: German
Prints abstracts: No
Author-anonymous submission: No

SUBMISSION REQUIREMENTS

Restrictions on contributors: None
Author pays submission fee: No
Author pays page charges: No
Length of books: No restrictions
Style: Journal
Number of copies required: 1
Copyright ownership: Max Niemeyer Verlag
Rejected manuscripts: Returned
Time before publication decision: 6 mos.
Time between decision and publication: 1 yr.
Number of reviewers: 1
Books submitted per year: 2-3
Books published per year: 2-3

(1942)
Neue Deutsche Hefte

Joachim Günther, Editor
Kindelbergweg 7
1000 Berlin 46, Germany

First published: 1954
ISSN: 0028-3142
MLA acronym: NDH

SUBSCRIPTION INFORMATION

Frequency of publication: 4 times/yr.
Available in microform: No

ADVERTISING INFORMATION

Advertising accepted: Yes

EDITORIAL DESCRIPTION

Scope: Publishes articles on literature, criticism, culture, and art.
Reviews books: Yes
Languages accepted: German
Prints abstracts: No

SUBMISSION REQUIREMENTS

Number of copies required: 1
Copyright ownership: Author
Time before publication decision: 3 mos.

(1943)
*Die Neue Gesellschaft/Frankfurter Hefte

Holger Börner, Walter Dirkst, Johannes Rau, Hans-Jochen Vogel, Günter Grass, & Carola Stern, Editors
Godesberger Allee 139
5300 Bonn 2, Germany

Telephone: (49) 228 883541
Fax: (49) 228 883539
First published: 1946
ISSN: 0177-6738
MLA acronym: FH

SUBSCRIPTION INFORMATION

Frequency of publication: 12 times/yr.
Circulation: 11,000
Available in microform: No
Subscription price: 90 DM/yr.
Year to which price refers: 1992
Subscription address: J. H. W. Dietz Verlag, In der Raste 2, 5300 Bonn 1, Germany
Subscription telephone: (49) 228 238083
Subscription fax: (49) 228 234104

ADVERTISING INFORMATION

Advertising accepted: Yes

EDITORIAL DESCRIPTION

Scope: Publishes articles on politics and culture. Includes studies on German literature.
Reviews books: Yes
Publishes notes: Yes
Languages accepted: German
Prints abstracts: No

SUBMISSION REQUIREMENTS

Restrictions on contributors: None
Author pays submission fee: No
Author pays page charges: No
Length of articles: 35,000 characters maximum
Number of copies required: Submit original typescript.
Copyright ownership: Publisher for 1 yr.
Rejected manuscripts: Returned
Time before publication decision: 1 mo.
Number of reviewers: 3
Articles submitted per year: 360

Articles published per year: 240
Book reviews submitted per year: 100
Book reviews published per year: 60

(1944)
*Neue Rundschau

Uwe Wittstock & Günther Busch, Editors
S. Fischer Verlag
Hedderichstr. 114
Postfach 700355
6000 Frankfurt 70, Germany

Telephone: (49) 69 6062296
Fax: (49) 69 6062319
First published: 1890
ISSN: 0028-3347
MLA acronym: NRs

SUBSCRIPTION INFORMATION

Frequency of publication: 4 times/yr.
Circulation: 7,000
Available in microform: No
Subscription price: 56 DM/yr.
Year to which price refers: 1992

ADVERTISING INFORMATION

Advertising accepted: Yes

EDITORIAL DESCRIPTION

Scope: Publishes articles on literature. Focuses on German literature.
Reviews books: No
Publishes notes: No
Languages accepted: German
Prints abstracts: No

SUBMISSION REQUIREMENTS

Author pays submission fee: Yes

(1945)
*Neue Sammlung: Vierteljahres-Zeitschrift für Erziehung und Gesellschaft

Gerold Becker, Hellmut Becker, Peter Fauser, Anne Frommann, Jürgen Gidion, Hermann Giesecke, Hartmut v. Hentig, Lothar Krappmann, & Jürgen Zimmer, Editors
Cunostr. 69A
1000 Berlin, Germany

Telephone: (49) 30 8243359
First published: 1961
ISSN: 0028-3355
MLA acronym: NSammlung

SUBSCRIPTION INFORMATION

Frequency of publication: 4 times/yr.
Circulation: 2,000
Available in microform: No
Subscription price: 145 DM/yr.
Year to which price refers: 1992
Subscription address: Friedrich-Verlag, Postfach 10 01 50, 3016 Seelze, Germany
Subscription telephone: (49) 511 400040
Subscription fax: (49) 511 400041

ADVERTISING INFORMATION

Advertising accepted: Yes
Advertising rates: Request from Friedrich-Verlag

EDITORIAL DESCRIPTION

Scope: Publishes articles on the problems of education, society and their interdependency, as well as on educational history and philosophy of education.
Reviews books: Yes

Publishes notes: Yes
Languages accepted: German; English
Prints abstracts: Yes
Author-anonymous submission: No

SUBMISSION REQUIREMENTS

Restrictions on contributors: None
Author pays submission fee: No
Author pays page charges: No
Length of articles: 20 typescript pp.
Length of book reviews: 3-10 typescript pp.
Length of notes: 1/2 typescript p.
Number of copies required: 2
Copyright ownership: Author
Rejected manuscripts: Returned
Time before publication decision: 2 mos.
Time between decision and publication: 3-15 mos.
Number of reviewers: 2
Articles submitted per year: 150
Articles published per year: 30
Book reviews submitted per year: 20
Book reviews published per year: 10
Notes submitted per year: 10-20
Notes published per year: 3-8

(1946)
*Neue Studien zur Anglistik und Amerikanistik

Willi Erzgräber & Paul Goetsch, Editors
Englisches Seminar der Universität
Werthmannplatz
7800 Freiburg i.Br., Germany

First published: 1974
ISSN: 0170-8848
MLA acronym: NSAA

SUBSCRIPTION INFORMATION

Frequency of publication: Irregular
Circulation: 200-300
Available in microform: No
Subscription address: Verlag Peter Lang, Eschborner Landstr. 42-50, 6000 Frankfurt a.M. 90, Germany

ADVERTISING INFORMATION

Advertising accepted: No

EDITORIAL DESCRIPTION

Scope: Publishes studies on English and American literature of all periods.
Reviews books: Yes, occasionally
Publishes notes: No
Languages accepted: English; German
Prints abstracts: Yes
Author-anonymous submission: No

SUBMISSION REQUIREMENTS

Restrictions on contributors: Contributors are generally authors of dissertations or *habilitationsschriften* accepted by German universities.
Author pays submission fee: No
Author pays page charges: Yes
Style: MLA
Number of copies required: 1
Copyright ownership: Verlag Peter Lang
Rejected manuscripts: Returned
Time before publication decision: 6-8 weeks
Time between decision and publication: 2 mos.
Number of reviewers: 2
Books submitted per year: 3-4
Books published per year: 3-4

(1947)
*Die Neueren Sprachen

K. Schröder, E. Rattunde, F.-R. Weller, & D. Wolff, Editors
Wächtersbacher Str. 89
6000 Frankfurt 63, Germany

Telephone: (49) 69 42081234
Fax: (49) 69 42081299
First published: 1952
ISSN: 0342-3816
MLA acronym: NS

SUBSCRIPTION INFORMATION

Frequency of publication: 6 times/yr. (Feb., Apr., June, Aug., Oct., Dec.)
Circulation: 2,700
Available in microform: No
Subscription price: 54 DM/yr.; 40 DM/yr. students
Year to which price refers: 1992
Subscription telephone: (49) 69 42081131

ADVERTISING INFORMATION

Advertising accepted: Yes

EDITORIAL DESCRIPTION

Scope: Publishes articles on applied linguistics and methods of foreign language teaching.
Reviews books: Yes
Publishes notes: Yes
Languages accepted: English; French; German; Italian; Spanish
Prints abstracts: Yes
Author-anonymous submission: No

SUBMISSION REQUIREMENTS

Author pays submission fee: No
Author pays page charges: No
Length of articles: 10 printed pp.
Length of book reviews: 1 printed p.
Length of notes: 1/2 printed p.
Style: MLA
Number of copies required: 2
Special requirements: Submit a 150-word abstract.
Copyright ownership: Verlag Moritz Diesterweg
Rejected manuscripts: Returned
Time before publication decision: 8 weeks
Time between decision and publication: 6-8 mos.
Number of reviewers: 5
Articles submitted per year: 40
Articles published per year: 30
Book reviews submitted per year: 30-40
Book reviews published per year: 30
Notes submitted per year: 15-20
Notes published per year: 10

(1948)
Neuphilologische Mitteilungen: Bulletin de la Société Néophilologique/Bulletin of the Modern Language Society

Marjatta Wis, Olli Välikangas, & Matti Rissanen, Editors
c/o Pia Mänttäri, Editorial Secretary
Porthania
Univ. of Helsinki
00100 Helsinki 10, Finland

First published: 1899
Sponsoring organization: Modern Language Soc. of Helsinki
ISSN: 0028-3754
MLA acronym: NM

SUBSCRIPTION INFORMATION

Frequency of publication: 4 times/yr. (Mar., June, Sept., Dec.)

Circulation: 1,200
Available in microform: No
Subscription price: 110 Fmk/yr. nonmembers Finland; $46.00/yr. nonmembers elsewhere
Year to which price refers: 1992
Subscription address: Anna Sivula, at the above address
Additional subscription address: Nonmembers: Akateeminen Kirjakauppa, PL 128, 00101 Helsinki, Finland

ADVERTISING INFORMATION

Advertising accepted: No

EDITORIAL DESCRIPTION

Scope: Publishes articles on English, German, and Romance languages and literatures that are of significant interest to the entire membership of the Society.
Reviews books: Yes
Publishes notes: No
Languages accepted: English; French; German; Italian; Spanish
Prints abstracts: Yes
Author-anonymous submission: No

SUBMISSION REQUIREMENTS

Restrictions on contributors: None
Author pays submission fee: No
Author pays page charges: No
Length of articles: 10-15 typescript pp.
Length of book reviews: 3 typescript pp.
Style: MLA
Number of copies required: 1
Special requirements: Include a 150-word summary.
Copyright ownership: Journal
Rejected manuscripts: Returned
Time before publication decision: 1-3 mos.
Time between decision and publication: 6-24 mos.
Number of reviewers: 1-2
Articles submitted per year: 80
Articles published per year: 50
Book reviews submitted per year: 15
Book reviews published per year: 15

(1949)
*Neurolinguistik: Zeitschrift für Aphasieforschung und -therapie

Gerhard Blanken & Claus-W. Wallesch, Editors
Dept. of Neurology
Freiburg Univ.
Hansastr. 9
7800 Freiburg, Germany

First published: 1987
ISSN: 0933-2715
MLA acronym: Neurolinguistik

SUBSCRIPTION INFORMATION

Frequency of publication: 2 times/yr. (May, Nov.)
Circulation: 300
Available in microform: No
Subscription price: 50 DM/yr.
Year to which price refers: 1992
Subscription address: Hochschul Verlag GmbH, Postfach 5426, 7800 Freiburg, Germany

ADVERTISING INFORMATION

Advertising accepted: No

EDITORIAL DESCRIPTION

Scope: Publishes articles on analysis and therapy of aphasia, speech apraxia, dysarthria, language acquisition disorders and language disturbances related to other pathologies.
Reviews books: Yes
Publishes notes: Yes
Languages accepted: German
Prints abstracts: Yes
Author-anonymous submission: No

SUBMISSION REQUIREMENTS

Restrictions on contributors: None
Author pays submission fee: No
Author pays page charges: No
Length of articles: 8,000 words
Length of book reviews: 400-1,000 words
Length of notes: 1,000 words
Style: Journal
Number of copies required: 4
Copyright ownership: Hochschul Verlag GmbH
Rejected manuscripts: Returned
Time before publication decision: 3 mos.
Time between decision and publication: 6 mos. maximum
Number of reviewers: 2
Articles submitted per year: 15
Articles published per year: 8-10
Book reviews submitted per year: 5-8
Book reviews published per year: 5-8

(1950)
*Neusprachliche Mitteilungen aus Wissenschaft und Praxis

Michael Bludau, Editor
Prof.-Manegold-Str. 4
3470 Höxter, Germany

Telephone: (49) 5271 33569
First published: 1947
Sponsoring organization: Fachverband Moderne Fremdsprachen (FMF)
ISSN: 0028-3983
MLA acronym: NsM

SUBSCRIPTION INFORMATION

Frequency of publication: 4 times/yr. (Feb., May, Aug., Nov.)
Circulation: 5,500
Available in microform: No
Subscription price: 45 DM/yr. plus postage
Year to which price refers: 1992
Subscription address: Cornelsen Verlagsgesellschaft, Kammerratsheide 66, 4800 Bielefeld 1, Germany

ADVERTISING INFORMATION

Advertising accepted: Yes

EDITORIAL DESCRIPTION

Scope: Publishes material dealing with area studies, applied linguistics, goal analysis, psycholinguistics, the teaching of literature, teaching materials, audio-visual media, tests, and methods of teaching foreign languages.
Reviews books: Yes
Publishes notes: Yes
Languages accepted: English; French; German
Prints abstracts: No
Author-anonymous submission: No

SUBMISSION REQUIREMENTS

Restrictions on contributors: None
Author pays submission fee: No
Author pays page charges: No
Length of articles: 6-8 printed pp.
Length of book reviews: 500 words
Length of notes: 150 words
Style: MLA
Number of copies required: 2
Special requirements: Submit original typescript and 1 copy.
Copyright ownership: Cornelsen Verlagsgesellschaft
Rejected manuscripts: Returned
Time before publication decision: 6-12 mos.
Time between decision and publication: 12-15 mos.
Number of reviewers: 3
Articles submitted per year: 40
Articles published per year: 24
Book reviews submitted per year: 55
Book reviews published per year: 50
Notes submitted per year: 60
Notes published per year: 45

(1951)
Neva

Boris N. Nikol'skiĭ, Editor
Nevskiĭ pr., 3
191065 St. Petersburg D-65, Russia

First published: 1955
Sponsoring organization: Soiuz Pisateleĭ R.S.F.S.R.; Soiuz Pisateleĭ R.S.F.S.R., Leningradskoe Otdelenie
ISSN: 0130-741X
MLA acronym: Neva

SUBSCRIPTION INFORMATION

Frequency of publication: 12 times/yr.
Circulation: 675,000
Available in microform: No
Subscription address: Mezhdunarodnaia Kniga, Smolenskaia-Sennaia 32/34, 121200 Moscow G-200, Russia

ADVERTISING INFORMATION

Advertising accepted: No

EDITORIAL DESCRIPTION

Scope: Publishes fiction, articles, essays, and poetry. Emphasis is on Russian literature and the study of other literatures in Russia.
Reviews books: Yes
Publishes notes: Yes
Languages accepted: Russian
Prints abstracts: No

SUBMISSION REQUIREMENTS

Restrictions on contributors: None
Author pays submission fee: Yes
Author pays page charges: No
Length of articles: 1-2 pp.
Length of book reviews: 300-400 words
Length of notes: 200-300 words
Number of copies required: 2
Special requirements: Submit original typescript.
Copyright ownership: Assigned by author to journal
Rejected manuscripts: Returned
Time before publication decision: 1-2 mos.
Time between decision and publication: 3-4 mos.
Number of reviewers: 3-4 plus Editorial Board if recommended
Articles submitted per year: 600
Articles published per year: 110-120
Book reviews submitted per year: 150-155
Book reviews published per year: 50
Notes submitted per year: 80-100
Notes published per year: 60-65

(1952)
*New Accents

Terence Hawkes, Editor
Dept. of English
Univ. of Wales, College of Cardiff
P.O. Box 94
Cardiff CF1 3XE, Wales

Telephone: (44) 222 874245
Fax: (44) 222 874242
First published: 1977
MLA acronym: NAc

SUBSCRIPTION INFORMATION

Frequency of publication: Irregular
Available in microform: No

Subscription address: Routledge, 29 W. 35th St., New York, NY 10001

ADVERTISING INFORMATION

Advertising accepted: No

EDITORIAL DESCRIPTION

Scope: The series offers clear expositions of new developments in literary criticism in terms of theory and practice.
Reviews books: No
Publishes notes: No
Languages accepted: English
Prints abstracts: No
Author-anonymous submission: No

SUBMISSION REQUIREMENTS

Restrictions on contributors: None
Author pays submission fee: No
Author pays page charges: No
Length of books: 50,000 words maximum
Style: MLA
Number of copies required: 2
Copyright ownership: Author
Time before publication decision: 12-18 mos.
Time between decision and publication: 9 mos.
Number of reviewers: 1

(1953)
*New Comparison: A Journal of Comparative and General Literary Studies

Leon Burnett, Editor
Dept. of Literature
Univ. of Essex
Wivenhoe Park
Colchester CO4 35Q, England

Additional editorial address: Send book reviews to: H. M. Klein, Dept. Anglistik, Univ. Salzburg, Akademiestr. 24, 5020 Salzburg, Austria
Telephone: (44) 206 872611
First published: 1986
Sponsoring organization: British Comparative Literature Assn.
ISSN: 0950-5814
MLA acronym: NewComp

SUBSCRIPTION INFORMATION

Frequency of publication: 2 times/yr. (Summer, Autumn)
Circulation: 300
Available in microform: No
Subscription price: £24.00/yr. institutions; £12.00/yr. individuals
Year to which price refers: 1991

ADVERTISING INFORMATION

Advertising accepted: Yes

EDITORIAL DESCRIPTION

Scope: Provides a focus and a forum for scholars in Britain and abroad, who take an interest in the study of literature across national and linguistic boundaries and in relation to other disciplines.
Reviews books: Yes
Publishes notes: Yes
Languages accepted: English
Prints abstracts: No
Author-anonymous submission: No

SUBMISSION REQUIREMENTS

Restrictions on contributors: Book reviews are commissioned.
Author pays submission fee: No
Author pays page charges: No
Length of articles: 10,000 words maximum
Length of book reviews: 600 words
Length of notes: 600 words
Style: Modern Humanities Research Assn.
Number of copies required: 2
Copyright ownership: Author
Rejected manuscripts: Returned
Time before publication decision: 6-8 weeks
Time between decision and publication: 1 yr.
Number of reviewers: 2-3
Articles submitted per year: 35
Articles published per year: 24
Book reviews submitted per year: 25
Book reviews published per year: 30
Notes submitted per year: 10
Notes published per year: 6

(1954)
*The New Criterion

Hilton Kramer, Editor
Foundation for Cultural Review, Inc.
850 Seventh Ave.
New York, NY 10019

Telephone: 212 247-6980
Fax: 212 247-3217
First published: 1982
Sponsoring organization: Foundation for Cultural Review, Inc.
ISSN: 0734-0222
MLA acronym: NewC

SUBSCRIPTION INFORMATION

Frequency of publication: 10 times/yr.
Circulation: 6,000
Available in microform: Yes
Subscription price: $36.00/yr.
Year to which price refers: 1992

ADVERTISING INFORMATION

Advertising accepted: Yes
Advertising rates: $500.00/half page; $800.00/full page

EDITORIAL DESCRIPTION

Scope: Publishes articles on literature, literary criticism, drama, art, and poetry.
Reviews books: Yes
Publishes notes: No
Languages accepted: English
Prints abstracts: No
Author-anonymous submission: No

SUBMISSION REQUIREMENTS

Author pays submission fee: No
Author pays page charges: No
Length of articles: 6,000 words
Length of book reviews: 2,000 words
Number of copies required: 1
Special requirements: Submit typescript.
Copyright ownership: Author
Rejected manuscripts: Returned; enclose SASE.
Time before publication decision: 3-4 mos.
Time between decision and publication: 2-3 mos.
Articles published per year: 40
Book reviews published per year: 40

(1955)
*New Cultural Studies Series

Joan DeJean, Carroll Smith-Rosenberg, & Peter Stallybrass, Editors
Univ. of Pennsylvania Press
418 Service Dr.
1300 Blockley Hall
Philadelphia, PA 19104-6097

Telephone: 215 898-6261
Fax: 215 898-0404
First published: 1989
MLA acronym: NCSS

SUBSCRIPTION INFORMATION

Subscription address: Univ. of Pennsylvania Press, 2200 Girard Ave., Baltimore, MD 21211
Subscription telephone: 800 445-9880
Subscription fax: 410 516-6998

EDITORIAL DESCRIPTION

Scope: Explores issues in cultural studies, a field that breaks down traditional boundaries between disciplines, between high and low culture, and between public and private culture in order to study the nature of cultural constructions.
Reviews books: No
Publishes notes: No
Languages accepted: English

SUBMISSION REQUIREMENTS

Style: Chicago
Number of copies required: 2
Copyright ownership: Univ. of Pennsylvania Press
Time before publication decision: 2-3 mos.
Time between decision and publication: 9 mos.
Number of reviewers: 2
Books submitted per year: 2-3
Books published per year: 2-3

(1956)
*The New England Quarterly: A Historical Review of New England Life and Letters

William M. Fowler, Jr. & Linda Smith Rhoads, Editors
Meserve Hall 239
Northeastern Univ.
360 Huntington Ave.
Boston, MA 02115

Telephone: 617 437-2734
Fax: 617 437-2661
First published: 1928
Sponsoring organization: Colonial Soc. of Massachusetts; Northeastern Univ.
ISSN: 0028-4866
MLA acronym: NEQ

SUBSCRIPTION INFORMATION

Frequency of publication: 4 times/yr. (Mar., June, Sept., Dec.)
Circulation: 2,400
Available in microform: Yes
Subscription price: $25.00/yr. institutions; $20.00/yr., $32.50/2 yrs. individuals
Year to which price refers: 1992

ADVERTISING INFORMATION

Advertising accepted: Yes
Advertising rates: $100.00/half page; $150.00/full page

EDITORIAL DESCRIPTION

Scope: Publishes articles on all aspects of New England history, literature, and culture.
Reviews books: Yes
Publishes notes: Yes
Languages accepted: English
Prints abstracts: No
Author-anonymous submission: No

SUBMISSION REQUIREMENTS

Restrictions on contributors: None
Author pays submission fee: No
Author pays page charges: No
Length of articles: 7,500-9,000 words
Length of book reviews: 900-1,500 words
Length of notes: 3,000 words
Style: Chicago
Number of copies required: 2

Special requirements: Submit original typescript.
Copyright ownership: Journal
Rejected manuscripts: Returned; enclose return postage.
Time before publication decision: 10-12 weeks
Time between decision and publication: 6-12 mos.
Number of reviewers: 2-3
Articles submitted per year: 200
Articles published per year: 25
Book reviews submitted per year: 40
Book reviews published per year: 40
Notes submitted per year: 8
Notes published per year: 8

(1957)
*New England Review

T. R. Hummer & Devon Jersild, Editors
Middlebury College
Middlebury, VT 05753

Telephone: 802 388-3711 ext. 5075
First published: 1978
Historical variations in title: Formerly *New England Review and Bread Loaf Quarterly*
Sponsoring organization: Middlebury College
ISSN: 1053-1297
MLA acronym: NERMS

SUBSCRIPTION INFORMATION

Frequency of publication: 4 times/yr. (Fall, Winter, Spring, Summer)
Circulation: 2,000
Available in microform: Yes
Subscription price: $18.00/yr.
Year to which price refers: 1992
Subscription address: Univ. Press of New England, 23 S. Main, Hanover, NH 03755
Subscription telephone: 603 646-3340
Subscription fax: 603 643-1540

ADVERTISING INFORMATION

Advertising accepted: Yes

EDITORIAL DESCRIPTION

Scope: Publishes contemporary poetry, fiction, reviews, translations, and literary and personal essays.
Reviews books: Yes
Publishes notes: No
Languages accepted: English
Prints abstracts: No
Author-anonymous submission: No

SUBMISSION REQUIREMENTS

Restrictions on contributors: None
Author pays submission fee: No
Author pays page charges: No
Style: MLA; Chicago
Number of copies required: 1
Copyright ownership: Journal; reverts to author upon publication
Rejected manuscripts: Returned; enclose SASE.
Time before publication decision: 10-12 weeks
Time between decision and publication: 6-12 mos.
Number of reviewers: 2-3

(1958)
*New England Theatre Journal

Charles E. Combs, Editor
Berklee College of Music
1140 Boylston St.
Boston, MA 02215

Telephone: 617 266-1400 ext. 421
First published: 1990
Sponsoring organization: New England Theatre Conference (NETC)

ISSN: 1050-9720
MLA acronym: NETJ

SUBSCRIPTION INFORMATION

Frequency of publication: Annual (May)
Circulation: 800
Available in microform: No
Subscription price: $10.00/yr.
Year to which price refers: 1992
Subscription address: New England Theatre Conference, c/o Dept. of Theatre, Northeastern Univ., 360 Huntington Ave., Boston, MA 02115
Subscription telephone: 617 424-9275

ADVERTISING INFORMATION

Advertising accepted: Yes
Advertising rates: $125.00/half page; $200.00/full page

EDITORIAL DESCRIPTION

Scope: Publishes articles on theater including traditional scholarship, performance theory, and pedagogy, as well as on theater performance, design, and technology.
Reviews books: Yes
Publishes notes: No
Languages accepted: English
Prints abstracts: Yes
Author-anonymous submission: Yes

SUBMISSION REQUIREMENTS

Restrictions on contributors: None
Author pays submission fee: No
Author pays page charges: No
Length of articles: 3,500-7,000 words
Length of book reviews: 1,000 words
Style: MLA
Number of copies required: 3
Special requirements: Include a cover sheet with the article's title; author's name, affiliation, title, address, and telephone numbers; a 50- to 75-word abstract; and a brief biographical paragraph. Notes, references, charts, and figures should appear at the end of the article on separate sheets. No multiple submissions.
Copyright ownership: Author
Rejected manuscripts: Returned; enclose SASE.
Time before publication decision: 6-8 mos.
Time between decision and publication: 2 mos.
Number of reviewers: 2
Articles submitted per year: 30-40
Articles published per year: 6-9
Book reviews submitted per year: 6-8
Book reviews published per year: 6-8

(1959)
*New German Critique: An Interdisciplinary Journal of German Studies

David Bathrick, Miriam Hansen, Peter U. Hohendahl, Andreas Huyssen, Biddy Martin, Anson G. Rabinbach, & Jack Zipes, Editors
Dept. of German Studies
183 Goldwin Smith Hall
Cornell Univ.
Ithaca, NY 14853

Telephone: 607 255-5265
Fax: 607 255-1454
First published: 1973
Sponsoring organization: Cornell Univ.
ISSN: 0094-033X
MLA acronym: NGC

SUBSCRIPTION INFORMATION

Frequency of publication: 3 times/yr.
Circulation: 2,500
Available in microform: Yes
Subscription address: Telos Press Ltd., 431 E. 12th St., New York, NY 10009

ADVERTISING INFORMATION

Advertising accepted: Yes

EDITORIAL DESCRIPTION

Scope: Publishes interdisciplinary articles on German studies with focus on literature and culture.
Reviews books: Yes
Publishes notes: Yes
Languages accepted: English
Prints abstracts: No
Author-anonymous submission: No

SUBMISSION REQUIREMENTS

Author pays submission fee: No
Author pays page charges: No
Length of articles: 6,000 words
Length of book reviews: 2,000 words
Style: MLA
Number of copies required: 3
Special requirements: Submit on IBM-compatible diskette.
Copyright ownership: Journal
Rejected manuscripts: Returned
Time before publication decision: 3-4 mos.
Time between decision and publication: 3-4 mos.
Number of reviewers: 4
Articles submitted per year: 100
Articles published per year: 30
Book reviews submitted per year: 15
Book reviews published per year: 6
Notes submitted per year: 5
Notes published per year: 3

(1960)
*New German Review: A Journal of Germanic Studies

John-Thomas Siehoff, Editor
Dept. of Germanic Languages
302 Royce Hall
Univ. of California, Los Angeles
Los Angeles, CA 90024

Telephone: 310 825-3955
Fax: 310 825-9754
First published: 1985
Sponsoring organization: Graduate Students Assn. of UCLA
ISSN: 0889-0145
MLA acronym: NGR

SUBSCRIPTION INFORMATION

Frequency of publication: Annual
Circulation: 150
Available in microform: No
Subscription price: $11.00/yr. institutions; $8.00/yr. individuals
Year to which price refers: 1992

ADVERTISING INFORMATION

Advertising accepted: Yes, on an exchange basis

EDITORIAL DESCRIPTION

Scope: Publishes graduate student research in all fields of Germanic languages and literatures.
Reviews books: Yes
Publishes notes: No
Languages accepted: English; German
Prints abstracts: No
Author-anonymous submission: Yes

SUBMISSION REQUIREMENTS

Restrictions on contributors: 2/3 of published contributions are from graduate students.
Author pays submission fee: No
Author pays page charges: No
Length of articles: 5,000 words
Length of book reviews: 900 words

(1961)
*New German Studies

Alan D. Best & Alan R. Deighton, Editors
Dept. of German
Univ. of Hull
Kingston-upon-Hull HU6 7RX, England

Telephone: (44) 482 465356
Fax: (44) 482 465991
First published: 1973
Sponsoring organization: Dept. of German, Univ. of Hull
ISSN: 0307-2770
MLA acronym: NGS

SUBSCRIPTION INFORMATION

Frequency of publication: 3 times/yr. (Spring, Summer, Fall)
Circulation: 230
Available in microform: No
Subscription price: £7.00/yr. institutions; £5.00/yr. individuals
Year to which price refers: 1992

ADVERTISING INFORMATION

Advertising accepted: Yes

EDITORIAL DESCRIPTION

Scope: Publishes articles on any aspect of German studies of a general interest.
Reviews books: Yes
Publishes notes: Yes
Languages accepted: English; German
Prints abstracts: No
Author-anonymous submission: No

SUBMISSION REQUIREMENTS

Restrictions on contributors: None
Author pays submission fee: No
Author pays page charges: No
Length of articles: 4,000 words maximum
Length of book reviews: 300-500 words
Length of notes: 500-700 words
Style: MLA
Number of copies required: 1
Copyright ownership: Journal
Rejected manuscripts: Returned
Time before publication decision: 2 mos. maximum
Time between decision and publication: 6-12 mos.
Number of reviewers: 2
Articles submitted per year: 20
Articles published per year: 9
Book reviews submitted per year: 30-35
Book reviews published per year: 25-30

Style: MLA
Number of copies required: 3
Special requirements: Manuscripts should contain no author identifying marks to ensure anonymity.
Copyright ownership: Regents of University of California
Rejected manuscripts: Returned; enclose return postage.
Time before publication decision: 8 mos.
Time between decision and publication: 6 mos.
Number of reviewers: 3
Articles submitted per year: 14
Articles published per year: 5
Book reviews submitted per year: 5
Book reviews published per year: 2-3

(1962)
*New Historicism: Studies in Cultural Poetics

Stephen Greenblatt, General Editor
c/o Doris Kretschmer
Univ. of California Press
2120 Berkeley Way
Berkeley, CA 94720

Telephone: 510 642-4229
Fax: 510 643-7127
First published: 1987
MLA acronym: NH

SUBSCRIPTION INFORMATION

Frequency of publication: Irregular
Available in microform: No

ADVERTISING INFORMATION

Advertising accepted: No

EDITORIAL DESCRIPTION

Scope: Focuses on highlighting trends in literary studies and the interest in the historical embeddedness of literary production, with a concurrent awareness in history of the symbolic constructions of reality. The series is interdisciplinary and embraces studies in politics, social practices, religious beliefs, and cultural conflicts.
Reviews books: No
Publishes notes: No
Languages accepted: English
Prints abstracts: No
Author-anonymous submission: No

SUBMISSION REQUIREMENTS

Restrictions on contributors: None
Author pays submission fee: No
Author pays page charges: No
Length of books: No restrictions
Style: MLA; Chicago
Number of copies required: 1
Copyright ownership: Regents of the Univ. of California
Rejected manuscripts: Returned
Time before publication decision: 4-7 mos.
Time between decision and publication: 18 mos.
Number of reviewers: 2 minimum
Books submitted per year: 10
Books published per year: 2-3

(1963)
*New Jersey Folklife

William Westerman, Editor
New Jersey Folklore Soc.
P.O. Box 747
New Brunswick, NJ 08901

First published: 1976
Sponsoring organization: New Jersey Folklore Soc.
ISSN: 0887-8048
MLA acronym: NJF

SUBSCRIPTION INFORMATION

Frequency of publication: Annual
Circulation: 250
Available in microform: Yes
Subscription price: $15.00/yr. institutions; $12.50/yr. individuals; $8.50/yr. students
Year to which price refers: 1992
Subscription address: New Jersey Folklore Soc., P.O. Box 43203, Upper Montclair, NJ 07043

ADVERTISING INFORMATION

Advertising accepted: Yes

EDITORIAL DESCRIPTION

Scope: Publishes materials on the folklore and folklife of New Jersey.
Reviews books: No
Publishes notes: No
Languages accepted: English
Prints abstracts: No
Author-anonymous submission: No

SUBMISSION REQUIREMENTS

Restrictions on contributors: None
Author pays submission fee: No
Author pays page charges: No
Length of articles: 10-35 pp.
Style: Chicago
Number of copies required: 2
Special requirements: Submit double-spaced typescript with footnotes on separate pages at the end.
Copyright ownership: New Jersey Folklore Soc.
Articles published per year: 6-8

(1964)
*New Laurel Review

Lee Meitzen Grue, Editor
828 Lesseps St.
New Orleans, LA 70117

Telephone: 504 947-6001
First published: 1971
Sponsoring organization: New Orleans Poetry Forum
ISSN: 0145-8388
MLA acronym: NLauR

SUBSCRIPTION INFORMATION

Frequency of publication: Annual
Circulation: 400-500
Available in microform: No
Subscription price: $11.00/yr. institutions; $9.00/yr. individuals
Year to which price refers: 1992

ADVERTISING INFORMATION

Advertising accepted: No

EDITORIAL DESCRIPTION

Scope: Publishes essays on literatures which have a fresh approach and a clear lively style, so that an educated reader may be informed and perhaps engaged. The magazine also publishes the best short fiction and poetry from among the contributions submitted.
Reviews books: Yes
Publishes notes: No
Languages accepted: English
Prints abstracts: No
Author-anonymous submission: No

SUBMISSION REQUIREMENTS

Author pays submission fee: No
Author pays page charges: No
Length of articles: 10-15 pp.
Length of book reviews: 300 words
Style: MLA
Number of copies required: 1
Special requirements: Duplicated manuscripts must have a note verifying their original and unpublished status.
Copyright ownership: Assigned by author to journal
Rejected manuscripts: Returned; enclose return postage.
Time before publication decision: 1-2 mos.
Time between decision and publication: 6 mos.
Number of reviewers: 1
Articles submitted per year: 6-8
Articles published per year: 2
Book reviews submitted per year: 20
Book reviews published per year: 3-4

(1965)
New Letters

James McKinley, Editor
Univ. of Missouri-Kansas City
5100 Rockhill Rd.
Kansas City, MO 64110

Telephone: 816 235-1168
Fax: 816 235-5191
First published: 1971
Sponsoring organization: Univ. of Missouri, Kansas City
ISSN: 0146-4930
MLA acronym: NewL

SUBSCRIPTION INFORMATION

Frequency of publication: 4 times/yr.
Circulation: 1,500-2,000
Available in microform: No

ADVERTISING INFORMATION

Advertising accepted: Yes

EDITORIAL DESCRIPTION

Scope: Provides a medium for creative writing. Also includes critical articles on literature as well as interviews with writers.
Reviews books: Yes
Publishes notes: Yes
Languages accepted: English
Prints abstracts: No

SUBMISSION REQUIREMENTS

Restrictions on contributors: None
Author pays submission fee: No
Author pays page charges: No
Number of copies required: 1
Special requirements: Submit original typescript or good photocopy.
Copyright ownership: Journal
Rejected manuscripts: Returned; enclose return postage.
Time before publication decision: 1-2 mos.
Time between decision and publication: 6-12 mos.
Articles submitted per year: 60
Articles published per year: 2-4
Book reviews submitted per year: 100
Book reviews published per year: 40

(1966)
*New Literary History: A Journal of Theory and Interpretation

Ralph Cohen, Editor
236 Wilson Hall
Univ. of Virginia
Charlottesville, VA 22903

Telephone: 804 924-3887
First published: 1969
Sponsoring organization: Univ. of Virginia
ISSN: 0028-6087
MLA acronym: NLH

SUBSCRIPTION INFORMATION

Frequency of publication: 4 times/yr. (Feb., May, Aug., Nov.)
Circulation: 2,500
Available in microform: Yes
Subscription price: $71.00/yr. institutions US; $23.00/yr. individuals US; add $6.60/yr. postage Canada & Mexico, $14.90/yr. postage outside N. America
Year to which price refers: 1993
Subscription address: Johns Hopkins Univ. Press, Journals Publishing Division, 2715 North Charles St., Baltimore, MD 21218-4319
Subscription telephone: 410 516-6987; 800 537-5487
Subscription fax: 410 516-6998

ADVERTISING INFORMATION

Advertising accepted: Yes
Advertising rates: Request from Johns Hopkins Univ. Press

EDITORIAL DESCRIPTION

Scope: Welcomes two types of contributions: theoretical articles on literature that deal with such subjects as the nature of literary theory, the aims of literature, the idea of literary history, the reading process, hermeneutics, the relation of linguistics to literature, literary change, literary value, the definitions of periods and their uses in interpretation, the evolution of styles, conventions, and genres, and articles from other disciplines that help interpret or define the problems of literary history or literary study. The fourth issue of each volume is composed primarily of papers presented at the Commonwealth Center for Literary and Cultural Change at the University of Virginia.
Reviews books: No
Publishes notes: No
Languages accepted: English
Prints abstracts: No
Author-anonymous submission: No

SUBMISSION REQUIREMENTS

Restrictions on contributors: None
Author pays submission fee: No
Author pays page charges: No
Length of articles: 5,000 words maximum
Style: Chicago
Number of copies required: 1
Copyright ownership: Assigned by author to journal
Rejected manuscripts: Returned; enclose return postage.
Time before publication decision: 3 mos.
Time between decision and publication: 18-24 mos.
Number of reviewers: 2
Articles submitted per year: 210
Articles published per year: 40

(1967)
*New Literatures Review

Paul Sharrad & Bill Ashcroft, Editors
New Literatures Research Centre
Dept. of English
Univ. of Wollongong
P.O. Box 1144
Wollongong, NSW 2500, Australia

Telephone: (61) 42 213705
Fax: (61) 42 213477
First published: 1975
ISSN: 0134-7495
MLA acronym: NLitsR

SUBSCRIPTION INFORMATION

Frequency of publication: 2 times/yr.
Circulation: 300
Available in microform: No
Subscription price: A$10.00/yr.
Year to which price refers: 1992

ADVERTISING INFORMATION

Advertising accepted: Yes
Advertising rates: A$60.00/half page; A$100.00/full page

EDITORIAL DESCRIPTION

Scope: Publishes articles on the new literatures in English, theory of literature as a cultural codifier, and Australian literature.
Reviews books: Yes
Publishes notes: Yes
Languages accepted: English
Prints abstracts: No
Author-anonymous submission: No

SUBMISSION REQUIREMENTS

Restrictions on contributors: Book reviews are commissioned.
Author pays submission fee: No
Author pays page charges: No
Length of articles: 3,000-4,000 words
Length of book reviews: 500-1,000 words
Length of notes: 200 words
Style: MLA
Number of copies required: 2
Special requirements: Keep footnotes to a minimum; include frequent references to same work in text of article. Submit Macintosh-compatible diskette if possible.
Copyright ownership: Journal
Rejected manuscripts: Not returned
Time before publication decision: 1 mo.
Time between decision and publication: 6-12 mos.
Number of reviewers: 3
Articles submitted per year: 40
Articles published per year: 10-15
Book reviews published per year: 5
Notes submitted per year: 2
Notes published per year: 2

(1968)
*New Mexico Humanities Review

John Rothfork & Jerry Bradley, Editors
Humanities Dept.
New Mexico Tech
Socorro, NM 87801

Telephone: 505 835-5445
First published: 1978
Sponsoring organization: New Mexico Inst. of Mining & Technology
ISSN: 0738-9671
MLA acronym: NMHR

SUBSCRIPTION INFORMATION

Frequency of publication: 2 times/yr.
Circulation: 250
Available in microform: No
Subscription price: $11.00/yr.
Year to which price refers: 1992

ADVERTISING INFORMATION

Advertising accepted: Yes
Advertising rates: $30.00/full page

EDITORIAL DESCRIPTION

Scope: Publishes critical essays, reviews of small press books, poetry, and fiction dealing with southwest regionalism.
Reviews books: Yes
Publishes notes: No
Languages accepted: English
Prints abstracts: No
Author-anonymous submission: No

SUBMISSION REQUIREMENTS

Restrictions on contributors: None
Author pays submission fee: No
Author pays page charges: No
Length of articles: 5,000 words
Length of book reviews: 600 words
Style: MLA
Number of copies required: 1
Copyright ownership: Author
Rejected manuscripts: Returned; enclose return postage.
Time before publication decision: 2 mos.
Time between decision and publication: 9 mos.
Number of reviewers: 2
Articles submitted per year: 1,500
Articles published per year: 80
Book reviews submitted per year: 50
Book reviews published per year: 20

(1969)
*New Orleans Review

John Mosier, Editor
Box 195
Loyola Univ.
New Orleans, LA 70118

Telephone: 504 865-2294
First published: 1968
Sponsoring organization: Loyola Univ.
ISSN: 0028-6400
MLA acronym: NOR

SUBSCRIPTION INFORMATION

Frequency of publication: 4 times/yr.
Circulation: 600
Available in microform: Yes
Subscription price: $35.00/yr. institutions; $30.00/yr. individuals; $45.00/yr. outside US
Year to which price refers: 1992

ADVERTISING INFORMATION

Advertising accepted: No

EDITORIAL DESCRIPTION

Scope: Publishes contemporary fiction and poetry, translations, articles on literary and film criticism, art work, and interviews.
Reviews books: No
Publishes notes: No
Languages accepted: English
Prints abstracts: No
Author-anonymous submission: No

SUBMISSION REQUIREMENTS

Restrictions on contributors: None
Author pays submission fee: No
Author pays page charges: No
Length of articles: No restrictions
Style: MLA with modifications
Number of copies required: 2
Special requirements: Contributions should not be under consideration elsewhere.
Copyright ownership: Journal has subsidiary reprint rights. Author may reprint with acknowledgement.
Rejected manuscripts: Returned; enclose SASE.
Time before publication decision: 4 mos.
Time between decision and publication: 18 mos.
Number of reviewers: 3
Articles submitted per year: 460
Articles published per year: 50

(1970)
*New Quest

M. P. Rege, M. V. Namjoshi, & M. L. Raina, Editors
"Aboli" 850/8A Shivojinagar
Pune 411004, India

First published: 1977
Sponsoring organization: Indian Assn. for Cultural Freedom
ISSN: 0258-0381
MLA acronym: Quest

SUBSCRIPTION INFORMATION

Frequency of publication: 6 times/yr.
Circulation: 1,500
Available in microform: No
Subscription price: 40 Re/yr. institutions India; 30 Re/yr. individuals India; $10.00/yr. plus $7.00 ($14.00 airmail)/yr. postage elsewhere
Year to which price refers: 1992

ADVERTISING INFORMATION

Advertising accepted: Yes
Advertising rates: 250 Re/half page; 400 Re/full page

EDITORIAL DESCRIPTION

Scope: Publishes articles and criticism in the field of social and cultural developments in India and, secondarily, Asia and the rest of the world.
Reviews books: Yes
Publishes notes: Yes
Languages accepted: English
Prints abstracts: No

SUBMISSION REQUIREMENTS

Restrictions on contributors: None
Author pays submission fee: No
Author pays page charges: No
Length of articles: 10,000 words
Length of book reviews: 1,500-2,000 words
Length of notes: 1,500-2,000 words
Number of copies required: 2
Special requirements: Submit double-spaced typescript.
Copyright ownership: Author
Rejected manuscripts: Returned; enclose return postage.
Time before publication decision: 1 mo.
Time between decision and publication: 6 mos.
Number of reviewers: 1-2
Articles submitted per year: 50-60
Articles published per year: 30-40
Book reviews submitted per year: 60-70
Book reviews published per year: 40-50
Notes submitted per year: 20-30
Notes published per year: 10-15

(1971)
*New Scholar: An Americanist Review

Vernon Kjonegaard & Inés Talamantez, Editors
South Hall 4607
Univ. of California
Santa Barbara, CA 93106

Telephone: 805 893-8473
Fax: 805 893-2059
First published: 1969
ISSN: 0028-6613
MLA acronym: NewS

SUBSCRIPTION INFORMATION

Frequency of publication: 2 times/yr.
Circulation: 1,000
Available in microform: Yes
Subscription price: $36.00/yr. institutions; $18.00/yr. individuals; add $4.00/yr. postage outside N. America
Year to which price refers: 1992

ADVERTISING INFORMATION

Advertising accepted: Yes
Advertising rates: $110.00/half page; $190.00/full page

EDITORIAL DESCRIPTION

Scope: Provides a multidisciplinary forum for scholars seeking a fuller understanding of the unique human condition and experience in the Americas. Encourages comparative studies in an Americanist context, including indigenous societies, race relations, political and economic development, literary expression, and the comparative colonial experience.
Reviews books: Yes
Publishes notes: Yes
Languages accepted: English
Prints abstracts: No
Author-anonymous submission: Yes

SUBMISSION REQUIREMENTS

Restrictions on contributors: Reviews are commissioned.
Author pays submission fee: No
Author pays page charges: No
Length of articles: 20-40 pp.
Length of book reviews: 1,200-5,000 words
Length of notes: 3,000 words
Style: Chicago; American Anthropological Assn.
Number of copies required: 3
Special requirements: Include an abstract, a separate title page, and notes on separate pages at conclusion of manuscript. Accepted articles submitted in a language other than English are published in English translation.
Copyright ownership: Journal
Rejected manuscripts: Returned; enclose SASE.
Time before publication decision: 3 mos.
Time between decision and publication: 6 mos.
Number of reviewers: 5
Articles submitted per year: 70-90
Articles published per year: 20 articles, 30 review essays
Book reviews published per year: 100
Notes published per year: 30

(1972)
*New Theatre Quarterly

Simon Trussler & Clive Barker, Editors
Great Robhurst
Woodchurch
Ashford, Kent TN26 3TB, England

First published: 1985
ISSN: 0266-464X
MLA acronym: NTQ

SUBSCRIPTION INFORMATION

Frequency of publication: 4 times/yr. (Feb., May, Aug., Nov.)
Circulation: 1,500
Subscription price: £37.00 ($66.00)/yr. institutions; £21.00 ($32.00)/yr. individuals
Year to which price refers: 1992
Subscription address: Cambridge Univ. Press, 40 W. 20th St., New York, NY 10011
Additional subscription address: Outside N. America: Cambridge Univ. Press, Edinburgh Bldg., Shaftesbury Rd., Cambridge CB2 2RU, England

ADVERTISING INFORMATION

Advertising accepted: Yes

EDITORIAL DESCRIPTION

Scope: Publishes articles on theater and drama, with an emphasis on performance aspects.
Reviews books: Yes
Publishes notes: Yes
Languages accepted: English
Prints abstracts: No
Author-anonymous submission: No

SUBMISSION REQUIREMENTS

Restrictions on contributors: None
Author pays submission fee: No
Author pays page charges: No
Length of articles: 4,000-10,000 words
Length of book reviews: 300 words
Length of notes: 300-2,000 words
Style: Journal
Number of copies required: 2
Copyright ownership: Cambridge Univ. Press
Rejected manuscripts: Returned; enclose SASE.
Number of reviewers: 3

(1973)
*New Vico Studies

Giorgio Tagliacozzo & Donald Phillip Verene, Editors
Inst. for Vico Studies
69 Fifth Ave.
New York, NY 10003

Additional editorial address: Inst. for Vico Studies, Emory Univ., Atlanta, GA 30322

Telephone: 404 727-4320
Fax: 404 727-4959
First published: 1983
Sponsoring organization: Inst. for Vico Studies
ISSN: 0733-9542
MLA acronym: NVS

SUBSCRIPTION INFORMATION

Frequency of publication: Annual
Available in microform: No
Subscription price: $39.95/yr.
Year to which price refers: 1990
Subscription address: Humanities Press International, Inc., 171 First Ave., Atlantic Highlands, NJ 07716
Subscription fax: 908 872-0717

ADVERTISING INFORMATION

Advertising accepted: Yes

EDITORIAL DESCRIPTION

Scope: Publishes articles, reviews, abstracts, and notes that reflect the current state of the study of the thought of Giambattista Vico.
Reviews books: Yes
Publishes notes: Yes
Languages accepted: English
Prints abstracts: No
Author-anonymous submission: No

SUBMISSION REQUIREMENTS

Restrictions on contributors: None
Author pays submission fee: No
Author pays page charges: No
Style: Chicago
Copyright ownership: Humanities Press
Rejected manuscripts: Not returned
Time before publication decision: 3 mos.
Time between decision and publication: 1 yr.

(1974)
*The New Welsh Review

Robin Reeves, Editor
Dept. of English
St. David's Univ. College
Lampeter, Dyfed, SA48 7ED, Wales

Telephone: (44) 222 665529
First published: 1988
Sponsoring organization: English Language Section of Yr Academi Gymreig; Univ. of Wales Assn. for the Study of Welsh Writing in English; Welsh Arts Council
ISSN: 0954-2116
MLA acronym: NWRev

SUBSCRIPTION INFORMATION

Frequency of publication: 4 times/yr. (Jan., Apr., July, Oct.)
Circulation: 1,400
Available in microform: No
Subscription price: £15.00/yr. United Kingdom; £21.00/yr. elsewhere
Year to which price refers: 1992

ADVERTISING INFORMATION

Advertising accepted: Yes

EDITORIAL DESCRIPTION

Scope: Publishes contemporary poetry and prose in English, together with scholarly articles on English literature, with a special interest in Welsh writing in English.
Reviews books: Yes
Publishes notes: Yes
Languages accepted: English
Prints abstracts: No
Author-anonymous submission: No

SUBMISSION REQUIREMENTS

Restrictions on contributors: None
Author pays submission fee: No
Author pays page charges: No
Length of articles: 2,000-3,000 words
Length of book reviews: 500-1,000 words
Length of notes: 300 words
Style: Oxford *Hart's Rules*
Number of copies required: 1
Copyright ownership: Editor & author
Rejected manuscripts: Returned; enclose SASE.
Time before publication decision: 4 mos.
Time between decision and publication: 2-6 mos.
Number of reviewers: 2-3
Articles submitted per year: 60
Articles published per year: 24-30
Book reviews submitted per year: 45
Book reviews published per year: 40
Notes submitted per year: 20
Notes published per year: 12

(1975)
*The New York Review of Books

Robert B. Silvers & Barbara Epstein, Editors
250 W. 57 St.
New York, NY 10107

Telephone: 212 757-8070
Fax: 212 333-5374
First published: 1963
ISSN: 0028-7504
MLA acronym: NYRB

SUBSCRIPTION INFORMATION

Frequency of publication: 24 times/yr. (biweekly except monthly in Jan., July, Aug., Sept.)
Circulation: 120,000
Available in microform: Yes
Subscription price: $39.00/yr.
Year to which price refers: 1992
Subscription address: Subscription Service Dept., P.O. Box 420384, Palm Coast, FL 32142-0384
Subscription telephone: 800 829-5088

ADVERTISING INFORMATION

Advertising accepted: Yes

EDITORIAL DESCRIPTION

Scope: Publishes critical articles and reviews of books on politics, culture, and the arts.
Reviews books: Yes
Languages accepted: English
Prints abstracts: No

SUBMISSION REQUIREMENTS

Restrictions on contributors: Journal accepts no responsibility for unsolicited manuscripts.
Author pays submission fee: No
Author pays page charges: No
Length of articles: 3,000 words
Length of book reviews: 3,000 words
Number of copies required: 1
Rejected manuscripts: Returned; enclose return postage & envelope
Number of reviewers: 2
Book reviews published per year: 400

(1976)
The New York Review of Science Fiction

Kathryn Cramer, L. W. Currey, Samuel R. Delany, David G. Hartwell, Robert K. J. Killheffer, & Gordon Van Gelder, Editors
P.O. Box 78
Pleasantville, NY 10570

ISSN: 1052-9438

MLA acronym: NYRSF

SUBSCRIPTION INFORMATION

Subscription price: $29.00/yr. institutions US; $25.00/yr. individuals US; $29.00/yr. Canada; $37.00/yr. elsewhere
Year to which price refers: 1992

EDITORIAL DESCRIPTION

Scope: Publishes articles and reviews on science fiction.
Reviews books: Yes
Languages accepted: English

(1977)
New Yorker Studien zur Neueren Deutschen Literaturgeschichte

Joseph P. Strelka, Editor
State Univ. of New York, Albany
Albany, NY 12222

ISSN: 0721-4030
MLA acronym: NYSNDL

SUBSCRIPTION INFORMATION

Available in microform: No

ADVERTISING INFORMATION

Advertising accepted: Yes

EDITORIAL DESCRIPTION

Scope: Publishes monographs on literary analysis of modern German literature and language.
Reviews books: No
Publishes notes: No
Languages accepted: English; French; Spanish; Italian; German
Prints abstracts: No
Author-anonymous submission: No

SUBMISSION REQUIREMENTS

Author pays submission fee: No
Author pays page charges: No

(1978)
*New Zealand Journal of French Studies

John Dunmore, Editor
Dept. of Modern Languages
Massey Univ.
Palmerston North, New Zealand

Telephone: (64) 6 3569099
Fax: (64) 6 3505633
First published: 1980
Sponsoring organization: Dept. of Modern Languages, Massey Univ.
ISSN: 0110-7380
MLA acronym: NZJFS

SUBSCRIPTION INFORMATION

Frequency of publication: 2 times/yr.
Circulation: 250
Available in microform: No
Subscription price: NZ$16.00/yr. New Zealand; NZ$20.00/yr. elsewhere
Year to which price refers: 1992

ADVERTISING INFORMATION

Advertising accepted: Yes

EDITORIAL DESCRIPTION

Scope: Publishes articles on all aspects of French language, literature, and culture.

Reviews books: Yes
Publishes notes: Yes
Languages accepted: English; French
Prints abstracts: No
Author-anonymous submission: No

SUBMISSION REQUIREMENTS

Restrictions on contributors: None, although priority is accorded to New Zealand academics.
Author pays submission fee: No
Author pays page charges: No
Length of articles: 2,000-5,000 words
Length of book reviews: 500-1,000 words
Length of notes: 1,000 words
Style: Modern Humanities Research Assn.
Number of copies required: 1
Copyright ownership: Journal
Rejected manuscripts: Returned
Time before publication decision: 3 mos.
Time between decision and publication: 1 yr.
Number of reviewers: 2
Articles submitted per year: 15-20
Articles published per year: 8-10
Book reviews published per year: 10-15
Notes submitted per year: 1-2
Notes published per year: 1-2

(1979)
*New Zealand Slavonic Journal

P. H. Waddington, Editor
Dept. of Russian
Victoria Univ.
Box 600
Wellington, New Zealand

Telephone: (64) 4 4715322
Fax: (64) 4 4712070
First published: 1967
Sponsoring organization: Victoria Univ. of Wellington
ISSN: 0028-8683
MLA acronym: NZSJ

SUBSCRIPTION INFORMATION

Frequency of publication: Annual
Circulation: 150
Available in microform: No
Subscription price: NZ$20.00/yr. plus postage
Year to which price refers: 1992

ADVERTISING INFORMATION

Advertising accepted: No

EDITORIAL DESCRIPTION

Scope: Publishes items on the language, literature, music, art, and history of Russia, Poland, Yugoslavia, etc.
Reviews books: Yes
Publishes notes: Yes
Languages accepted: English
Prints abstracts: No
Author-anonymous submission: No

SUBMISSION REQUIREMENTS

Restrictions on contributors: Most book reviews and notes are commissioned.
Author pays submission fee: No
Author pays page charges: No
Length of articles: No restrictions
Length of book reviews: 750-1,500 words
Length of notes: 50-150 words
Style: MLA; Modern Humanities Research Assn.; *The Slavonic and East European Review* for transliteration
Number of copies required: 1
Special requirements: Quotations in Russian are permitted if on separate lines, or if incorporated in camera-ready copy prepared to the journal's specifications.
Copyright ownership: Author & Journal
Rejected manuscripts: Returned at author's request

Time before publication decision: 1 mo.
Time between decision and publication: 6-18 mos.
Number of reviewers: 1-2
Articles submitted per year: 20-30
Articles published per year: 10
Book reviews submitted per year: 5
Book reviews published per year: 20-25
Notes submitted per year: 1-2
Notes published per year: 15-20

(1980)
The Newberry Library Center for the History of the American Indian Bibliographical Series

William R. Swagerty, Editor
Newberry Library Center for the History of the American Indian
60 W. Walton
Chicago, IL 60610

First published: 1976
Sponsoring organization: Newberry Library
MLA acronym: NLCHAIBS

SUBSCRIPTION INFORMATION

Frequency of publication: Irregular
Circulation: 8,000
Available in microform: No
Subscription address: Kathleen Ketterman, Indiana Univ. Press, 10th and Morton Sts., Bloomington, IN 47401

ADVERTISING INFORMATION

Advertising accepted: No

EDITORIAL DESCRIPTION

Reviews books: Yes
Languages accepted: English
Prints abstracts: No

SUBMISSION REQUIREMENTS

Restrictions on contributors: Unsolicited manuscripts are not accepted.
Author pays submission fee: No
Author pays page charges: No
Style: Chicago
Number of copies required: 2
Special requirements: Consult with editor prior to submission.
Copyright ownership: Indiana Univ. Press
Rejected manuscripts: 1 returned
Time before publication decision: 18 mos.
Time between decision and publication: 1 yr.
Number of reviewers: 3-4
Books submitted per year: 4-5
Books published per year: 4

(1981)
*Newsboy

William R. Gowen, Editor
4907 Allison Dr.
Lansing, MI 48910-5682

Telephone: 517 882-3203
First published: 1962
Sponsoring organization: Horatio Alger Soc.
ISSN: 0028-9396
MLA acronym: Newsboy

SUBSCRIPTION INFORMATION

Frequency of publication: 6 times/yr.
Circulation: 300
Available in microform: No
Subscription price: $20.00/yr.
Year to which price refers: 1992
Subscription address: Carl T. Hartmann, at the above address

ADVERTISING INFORMATION

Advertising accepted: Yes
Advertising rates: $17.00/half page; $32.00/full page

EDITORIAL DESCRIPTION

Scope: Devoted to the study of Horatio Alger, Jr., his life, works, and influence on the culture of America.
Reviews books: Yes
Publishes notes: Yes
Languages accepted: English
Prints abstracts: No
Author-anonymous submission: No

SUBMISSION REQUIREMENTS

Restrictions on contributors: None
Author pays submission fee: No
Author pays page charges: No
Length of articles: 600-1,000 words
Length of book reviews: 500-600 words
Length of notes: 200 words
Style: MLA preferred
Number of copies required: 1
Copyright ownership: Author
Rejected manuscripts: Returned; enclose SASE.
Time before publication decision: 3 weeks
Time between decision and publication: 4 mos.
Number of reviewers: 1
Articles submitted per year: 6
Articles published per year: 6
Book reviews submitted per year: 1
Book reviews published per year: 1
Notes submitted per year: 1
Notes published per year: 1

(1982)
*Newsletter of the American Dialect Society

Allan Metcalf, Editor
English Dept.
MacMurray College
Jacksonville, IL 62650-2590

Telephone: 217 479-7049; 217 479-7000
Fax: 217 245-5214
First published: 1969
Sponsoring organization: American Dialect Soc.
ISSN: 0002-8193
MLA acronym: NADS

SUBSCRIPTION INFORMATION

Frequency of publication: 3 times/yr.
Circulation: 875
Available in microform: No
Subscription price: $25.00/yr. (includes membership)
Year to which price refers: 1992

ADVERTISING INFORMATION

Advertising accepted: Yes

EDITORIAL DESCRIPTION

Scope: Publishes reports of studies of dialects in North America as well as news of the American Dialect Society.
Reviews books: No
Publishes notes: Yes
Languages accepted: English
Prints abstracts: No
Author-anonymous submission: No

SUBMISSION REQUIREMENTS

Restrictions on contributors: None
Author pays submission fee: No
Author pays page charges: No
Length of articles: 1,000-2,000 words
Length of notes: 100-500 words
Style: None
Number of copies required: 1

Rejected manuscripts: Returned at author's request
Time before publication decision: 4 mos. maximum
Time between decision and publication: 1-16 weeks
Number of reviewers: 1
Articles submitted per year: 10
Articles published per year: 8
Notes submitted per year: 50
Notes published per year: 25

(1983)
*Niederdeutsches Jahrbuch: Jahrbuch des Vereins für Niederdeutsche Sprachforschung

Hermann Niebaum, Editor
Grosse Schulstr. 39
4500 Osnabrück-Hellern, Germany

Additional editorial address: Nedersaksisch Inst., Oude Kijk in 't Jatstr. 26, 9712 EK Groningen, Netherlands
Telephone: (49) 541 441817 (Germany); (31) 50 635963 (Netherlands)
Fax: (31) 50 635603 (Netherlands)
First published: 1875
Sponsoring organization: Verein für Niederdeutsche Sprachforschung
ISSN: 0083-5617
MLA acronym: NJ

SUBSCRIPTION INFORMATION

Frequency of publication: Annual
Circulation: 800
Available in microform: No
Subscription address: Karl Wachholtz Verlag, Rungestr. 4, Postfach 2769, 2350 Neumünster, Germany

ADVERTISING INFORMATION

Advertising accepted: No

EDITORIAL DESCRIPTION

Scope: Publishes articles on Low German language and literature.
Reviews books: Yes
Publishes notes: Yes
Languages accepted: German; English; Dutch
Prints abstracts: No
Author-anonymous submission: No

SUBMISSION REQUIREMENTS

Restrictions on contributors: None
Author pays submission fee: No
Author pays page charges: No
Style: Style Sheet in 1991; 114:255-256
Number of copies required: 1
Copyright ownership: Author & editors
Rejected manuscripts: Returned
Time before publication decision: 1 mo.
Time between decision and publication: 1 yr.
Articles submitted per year: 10-12
Articles published per year: 8-10
Book reviews submitted per year: 10-12
Book reviews published per year: 6-12
Notes published per year: 2

(1984)
*Niederdeutsches Wort: Beiträge zur Niederdeutschen Philologie

Jan Goossens, Editor
Magdalenenstr. 5
4400 Münster, Germany

Telephone: (49) 251 834413
Fax: (49) 251 838392
First published: 1960
Sponsoring organization: Landschaftsverband Westfalen-Lippe

ISSN: 0018-0545
MLA acronym: NdW

SUBSCRIPTION INFORMATION

Frequency of publication: Annual
Circulation: 500
Available in microform: No
Subscription price: 38 DM/yr.
Year to which price refers: 1991
Subscription address: Verlag Aschendorff, Soester Str. 13, 4400 Münster, Germany
Subscription telephone: (49) 251 690405
Subscription fax: (49) 251 892555

ADVERTISING INFORMATION

Advertising accepted: No

EDITORIAL DESCRIPTION

Scope: Publishes historical and synchronic studies of Low German language and literature.
Reviews books: No
Publishes notes: No
Languages accepted: German; Dutch; English
Prints abstracts: No

SUBMISSION REQUIREMENTS

Restrictions on contributors: None
Author pays submission fee: No
Author pays page charges: No
Length of articles: No restrictions
Style: Journal
Number of copies required: 1
Copyright ownership: Assigned by author to journal
Rejected manuscripts: Returned
Time before publication decision: 1 mo.
Time between decision and publication: 6-12 mos.
Number of reviewers: 2
Articles submitted per year: 10-12
Articles published per year: 8-10

(1985)
*Nietzsche Studien: Internationales Jahrbuch für die Nietzsche-Forschung

Ernst Behler, Eckhard Heftrich, Wolfgang Müller-Lauter, & Heinz Wenzel, Editors
c/o Wilhelm Haumann & Gerburg Lindner
Germanistisches Inst. der Univ. Münster
Domplatz 20-22
4400 Münster, Germany

Additional editorial address: Ernst Behler, Comparative Literature GN-32, Univ. of Washington, Seattle, WA 98195
Telephone: (49) 251 834627
First published: 1972
ISSN: 0342-1422
MLA acronym: NietzscheS

SUBSCRIPTION INFORMATION

Frequency of publication: Annual
Circulation: 1,000
Available in microform: No
Subscription price: 198 DM/yr.
Year to which price refers: 1992
Subscription address: Walter de Gruyter & Co., Genthiner Str. 13, 1000 Berlin 30, Germany
Subscription telephone: (49) 30 26005168
Subscription fax: (49) 30 26005251

ADVERTISING INFORMATION

Advertising accepted: No

EDITORIAL DESCRIPTION

Scope: Publishes articles on the epistemological, ontological, and metaphysical arguments contained in Nietzsche's philosophy, his moral, aesthetic, and critical attitudes, his relationship to other authors, and his impact on modern intellectual history.
Reviews books: Yes
Languages accepted: English; German; French
Prints abstracts: No
Author-anonymous submission: No

SUBMISSION REQUIREMENTS

Restrictions on contributors: None
Author pays submission fee: No
Author pays page charges: No
Length of articles: 30 typescript pp.
Length of book reviews: 2 typescript pp.
Style: Journal
Number of copies required: 1
Copyright ownership: Assigned by author to journal
Rejected manuscripts: Not returned
Number of reviewers: 4
Articles submitted per year: 40
Articles published per year: 15
Book reviews submitted per year: 10
Book reviews published per year: 2-3

(1986)
De Nieuwe Taalgids: Tijdschrift voor Neerlandici

W. J. van den Akker, W. P. Gerritsen, M. C. van den Toorn, M. A. Schenkeveld-Van Der Dussen, H. J. Verkuyl, & W. Zonneveld, Editors
c/o M. E. Meÿer Drees
Trans 10
3512 JK Utrecht, Netherlands

Additional editorial address: Wolters-Noordhoff B.V., Afdeling Periodieken, Postbus 58, 9700 MB Groningen, Netherlands
Telephone: (31) 30 394245
Fax: (31) 30 333380
First published: 1907
ISSN: 0028-9922
MLA acronym: NTg

SUBSCRIPTION INFORMATION

Frequency of publication: 6 times/yr. (Jan., Mar., May, July, Sept., Nov.)
Circulation: 2,000
Available in microform: No

ADVERTISING INFORMATION

Advertising accepted: Yes

EDITORIAL DESCRIPTION

Scope: Publishes articles on Netherlandic language and literature.
Reviews books: Yes
Publishes notes: Yes
Languages accepted: Dutch; German; English; French
Prints abstracts: No
Author-anonymous submission: No

SUBMISSION REQUIREMENTS

Restrictions on contributors: None
Author pays submission fee: No
Length of articles: 5 pp. including endnotes
Length of book reviews: 3 pp. including references
Length of notes: 2 pp.
Style: Journal
Number of copies required: 2
Copyright ownership: Author
Rejected manuscripts: Returned; enclose return postage.
Time before publication decision: 2 mos.
Time between decision and publication: 4-12 mos.

Number of reviewers: 2-4
Articles submitted per year: 60
Articles published per year: 30-40
Book reviews submitted per year: 10-20
Book reviews published per year: 10-20
Notes submitted per year: 2-3
Notes published per year: 2-3

(1987)
*Nineteenth-Century Contexts

Greg Kucich, Keith Hanley, & Chuck Dyke, Editors
Dept. of English
Univ. of Notre Dame
Notre Dame, IN 46556

Additional editorial address: Dept. of English, Lancaster Univ., Lancaster, PA 19122; Review Editor: Dept. of Philosophy, Temple Univ., Philadelphia, PA 19122
Telephone: 219 239-7226
Fax: 219 239-8209
E-mail: Gregory.P.Kucich.1@ND.edu
First published: 1975
Sponsoring organization: Interdisciplinary Nineteenth-Century Studies; Notre Dame Univ.; Lancaster Univ.
ISSN: 0890-5495
MLA acronym: NCC

SUBSCRIPTION INFORMATION

Frequency of publication: 2 times/yr.
Circulation: 500
Available in microform: No
Subscription price: $30.00/yr. institutions US; $33.00/yr. institutions elsewhere; $25.00/yr. individuals US: $28.00/yr. individuals elsewhere
Year to which price refers: 1993
Subscription address: Roswitha Burwick, Treasurer, INCS, Dept. of German, Scripps College, Claremont, CA 91711
Additional subscription address: Dept. of English, Lancaster Univ., Lancaster LA1 4YT, England
Subscription telephone: 714 621-8000 ext. 2502
Subscription fax: 714 621-8323; (44) 524 63806

ADVERTISING INFORMATION

Advertising accepted: Yes
Advertising rates: Request from editor.

EDITORIAL DESCRIPTION

Scope: Journal is international and interdisciplinary in its approach to its subject, 19th-century studies.
Reviews books: Yes
Publishes notes: Yes
Languages accepted: English
Prints abstracts: No
Author-anonymous submission: No

SUBMISSION REQUIREMENTS

Author pays submission fee: No
Author pays page charges: No
Length of articles: 5,000-10,000 words
Length of book reviews: 500-2,000 words
Length of notes: 500-2,000 words
Style: MLA
Number of copies required: 2
Special requirements: Submit ribbon copy. Forum contributions are solicited and may run to 5,000 words.
Copyright ownership: Journal; assignment at author's request
Rejected manuscripts: Returned; enclose SASE.
Time before publication decision: 3 mos.
Time between decision and publication: 6-12 mos.
Number of reviewers: 2-3
Articles submitted per year: 50
Articles published per year: 6
Book reviews submitted per year: 4-8
Book reviews published per year: 4-8

Notes submitted per year: 1-2
Notes published per year: 1

(1988)
*Nineteenth-Century French Studies

Thomas H. Goetz, Editor
Dept. of Foreign Languages & Literatures
State Univ. College
Fredonia, NY 14063

Telephone: 716 673-3380
First published: 1972
Sponsoring organization: State Univ. of New York, College at Fredonia
ISSN: 0146-7891
MLA acronym: NCFS

SUBSCRIPTION INFORMATION

Frequency of publication: 2 double issues/yr. (Fall-Winter, Spring-Summer)
Circulation: 800
Available in microform: Yes
Subscription price: $32.00/yr., $57.00/2 yrs. institutions; $28.00/yr., $50.00/2 yrs. individuals
Year to which price refers: 1991-92

ADVERTISING INFORMATION

Advertising accepted: Yes
Advertising rates: $30.00/half page; $50.00/full page

EDITORIAL DESCRIPTION

Scope: Publishes studies of 19th-century French literature from a philosophical, psychological, sociological, anthropological, cultural, historical, or other critical standpoints.
Reviews books: Yes
Publishes notes: Yes
Languages accepted: English; French
Prints abstracts: Yes
Author-anonymous submission: Yes

SUBMISSION REQUIREMENTS

Restrictions on contributors: Contributors should be subscribers.
Author pays submission fee: No
Author pays page charges: Page costs overrun are charged for extremely long articles.
Length of articles: 15 pp.
Length of book reviews: 3 pp.
Length of notes: 250-500 words
Style: MLA
Number of copies required: 2
Special requirements: Submit original typescript with abstract.
Copyright ownership: Editor; author may request copyright.
Rejected manuscripts: Returned; enclose return postage.
Time before publication decision: 2-3 mos.
Time between decision and publication: 2-3 yrs.
Number of reviewers: 2-4
Articles submitted per year: 65-75
Articles published per year: 25-28
Book reviews submitted per year: 70-90
Book reviews published per year: 70-80
Notes submitted per year: 2-5
Notes published per year: 2-5

(1989)
*Nineteenth-Century Literature

G. B. Tennyson & Thomas Wortham, Editors
Dept. of English
Univ. of California
Los Angeles, CA 90024

Telephone: 310 825-4920
First published: 1945

Sponsoring organization: Univ. of California Press
ISSN: 0891-9356
MLA acronym: NCF

SUBSCRIPTION INFORMATION

Frequency of publication: 4 times/yr. (June, Sept., Dec., Mar.)
Circulation: 2,500
Available in microform: Yes
Subscription price: $36.00/yr. institutions; $21.00/yr. individuals; $15.00/yr. students
Year to which price refers: 1992-93
Subscription address: Periodicals Dept., Univ. of California Press, 2120 Berkeley Way, Berkeley, CA 94720
Subscription telephone: 510 642-6221

ADVERTISING INFORMATION

Advertising accepted: Yes
Advertising rates: $120.00/half page; $200.00/full page

EDITORIAL DESCRIPTION

Scope: Publishes scholarly and critical articles on British, American, and other English language literature of the period 1800-1900. Includes reviews of scholarly and critical books in this field.
Reviews books: Yes
Publishes notes: Yes
Languages accepted: English
Prints abstracts: No
Author-anonymous submission: No

SUBMISSION REQUIREMENTS

Restrictions on contributors: All book reviews are solicited.
Author pays submission fee: No
Author pays page charges: No
Length of articles: 6,000-7,500 words
Length of book reviews: 900-1,500 words
Length of notes: 1,000-2,500 words
Style: MLA
Number of copies required: 1
Special requirements: Submit original typescript.
Copyright ownership: Assigned by author to journal
Rejected manuscripts: Returned; enclose SASE or international reply coupons. Foreign contributors may send copy rather then original. For surface mail return of manuscript, 3-5 international reply coupons are needed. Decision will be sent airmail.
Time before publication decision: 3 mos.
Time between decision and publication: 9-12 mos.
Number of reviewers: 2-4
Articles submitted per year: 300
Articles published per year: 16-20
Book reviews published per year: 40-50
Notes submitted per year: 25
Notes published per year: 4-6

(1990)
*Nineteenth-Century Prose

Barry Tharaud, Editor
Dept. of Literature & Languages
Mesa State College
Grand Junction, CO 81502

Telephone: 303 248-1385
First published: 1973
Sponsoring organization: Mesa State College
ISSN: 0160-4848
MLA acronym: NCP

SUBSCRIPTION INFORMATION

Frequency of publication: 2 times/yr.
Circulation: 400
Available in microform: No

Subscription address: Univ. Press of Colorado, P.O. Box 849, Niwot, CO 80544
Subscription telephone: 303 530-5337

ADVERTISING INFORMATION

Advertising accepted: Yes

EDITORIAL DESCRIPTION

Scope: Publishes articles, notes, bibliographical items, and essay reviews on Victorian nonfiction prose. Focuses on British, American, and Continental authors.
Reviews books: Yes
Publishes notes: Yes
Languages accepted: English
Prints abstracts: No
Author-anonymous submission: Yes

SUBMISSION REQUIREMENTS

Restrictions on contributors: Book reviews are solicited.
Author pays submission fee: No
Author pays page charges: No
Length of articles: 2,000-4,000 words
Length of book reviews: 1,000-3,000 words
Length of notes: 500-1,500 words
Style: MLA
Number of copies required: 2
Copyright ownership: Author
Rejected manuscripts: Returned; enclose SASE.
Time before publication decision: 6 mos.
Time between decision and publication: 18 mos.
Number of reviewers: 3-4
Articles submitted per year: 25-40
Articles published per year: 8-10
Book reviews published per year: 30-40
Notes submitted per year: 8-12
Notes published per year: 1-4

(1991)
*Nineteenth-Century Studies

Suzanne O. Edwards & Jack Rhodes, Editors
English Department
The Citadel
Charleston, SC 29409

Telephone: 803 792-5140
First published: 1987
Sponsoring organization: Southeastern Nineteenth-Century Studies Assn.; the Citadel
ISSN: 0893-7931
MLA acronym: NCS

SUBSCRIPTION INFORMATION

Frequency of publication: Annual
Circulation: 200
Available in microform: No
Subscription price: $25.00/yr. institutions; $15.00/yr. individuals
Year to which price refers: 1993

ADVERTISING INFORMATION

Advertising accepted: Yes

EDITORIAL DESCRIPTION

Scope: An interdisciplinary journal issued annually by the Southeastern Nineteenth-Century Studies Association. Includes studies on 19th-century American, British, and European literature.
Reviews books: Yes
Publishes notes: No
Languages accepted: English
Prints abstracts: No
Author-anonymous submission: Yes

SUBMISSION REQUIREMENTS

Restrictions on contributors: Book reviews are solicited.
Author pays submission fee: No
Author pays page charges: No

Length of articles: 3,500-7,000 words
Length of book reviews: 2,000-3,000 words
Style: MLA preferred
Number of copies required: 2
Copyright ownership: Southeastern Nineteenth-Century Studies Assn.
Rejected manuscripts: Retained in editor's files for 1 yr. unless requested by contributor
Time before publication decision: 3 mos.
Time between decision and publication: 1 yr.
Number of reviewers: 2
Articles submitted per year: 50
Articles published per year: 6
Book reviews published per year: 6

(1992)
Nineteenth Century Theatre

Joseph Donohue, Editor
Dept. of English
Univ. of Massachusetts
Amherst, MA 01003

Telephone: 413 545-0498
E-mail: Joseph.Donohue@ENGLISH.UMass.EDU
First published: 1973
Sponsoring organization: Univ. of Massachusetts; Five Colleges, Inc.
ISSN: 0893-3766
MLA acronym: NCTR

SUBSCRIPTION INFORMATION

Frequency of publication: 2 times/yr. (Summer, Winter)
Circulation: 500
Available in microform: Yes, volumes 1-4 & 6
Subscription price: $20.00/yr. institutions US & Canada; $22.00/yr. institutions elsewhere; $12.00/yr. individuals US & Canada; $14.00/yr. individuals elsewhere
Year to which price refers: 1991

ADVERTISING INFORMATION

Advertising accepted: Yes

EDITORIAL DESCRIPTION

Scope: Publishes articles, documents, bibliographies, and other research-related materials on all aspects of English-speaking and European theater for the years 1792-1914. Illustrated articles are welcome.
Reviews books: Yes
Publishes notes: Yes
Languages accepted: English
Prints abstracts: No
Author-anonymous submission: No

SUBMISSION REQUIREMENTS

Restrictions on contributors: Reviews are solicited.
Author pays submission fee: No
Author pays page charges: No
Length of articles: 5,000 words; exceptions made
Length of book reviews: 1,000 words
Length of notes: 500 words
Style: MLA
Number of copies required: 3
Special requirements: Submit original typescript and 2 copies.
Copyright ownership: Journal
Rejected manuscripts: Returned; enclose return postage or international reply coupons.
Time before publication decision: 2 mos.
Time between decision and publication: 1 yr.
Number of reviewers: 2
Articles submitted per year: 20-25
Articles published per year: 6-8
Book reviews published per year: 12-14

(1993)
*Noaj: Revista Literaria

Leonardo Senkman & Florinda F. Goldberg, Editors
P.O. Box 4658
Jerusalem 91042, Israel

Telephone: (972) 2 439468; (972) 2 768759
Fax: (972) 2 665556 (c/o F. Goldberg)
First published: 1987
Sponsoring organization: Asoc. Internacional de Escritores Judíos en Lengua Hispaña y Portuguesa
ISSN: 0792-0318
MLA acronym: Noaj

SUBSCRIPTION INFORMATION

Frequency of publication: 2 times/yr. (Autumn, Spring)
Circulation: 200
Available in microform: No
Subscription price: $20.00/yr. US & Europe; $15.00/yr. Latin America & Israel
Year to which price refers: 1992

ADVERTISING INFORMATION

Advertising accepted: Yes, on an exchange basis

EDITORIAL DESCRIPTION

Scope: Publishes articles on literature by Jewish authors and on Jewish themes originally written in Spanish or Portuguese or translated into these languages.
Reviews books: Yes
Publishes notes: Yes
Languages accepted: Spanish; Portuguese
Prints abstracts: No
Author-anonymous submission: No

SUBMISSION REQUIREMENTS

Restrictions on contributors: None
Author pays submission fee: No
Author pays page charges: No
Length of articles: 3,600 words
Length of book reviews: 600-1,000 words
Length of notes: 200-600 words
Style: None
Number of copies required: 1
Copyright ownership: Asoc. Internacional de Escritores Judíos en Lengua Hispaña y Portuguesa
Rejected manuscripts: Returned at author's request; enclose return postage.
Time before publication decision: 1 mo.
Time between decision and publication: 6 mos.
Number of reviewers: 3
Articles submitted per year: 30
Articles published per year: 15-20
Book reviews submitted per year: 10-12
Book reviews published per year: 8

(1994)
*Nomina: A Journal of Name Studies Relating to Great Britain and Ireland

John Freeman, O. J. Padel, Alexander R. Rumble, & Veronica Smart, Editors
13 Church St.
Chesterton
Cambridge CB4 IDT, England

Additional editorial address: A. R. Rumble, Dept. of English Language & Literature, Univ. of Manchester, Manchester M13 9PL, England; for reviews: V. Smart, St. John's House, 69 South Street, St. Andrews, KY16 9AL, England
Telephone: (44) 223 357585
First published: 1977
Sponsoring organization: Council for Name Studies in Great Britain & Ireland
ISSN: 0141-6340

MLA acronym: Nomina

SUBSCRIPTION INFORMATION

Frequency of publication: Annual (May-June)
Circulation: 200
Available in microform: No
Subscription price: £9.00/yr. United Kingdom; £10.00/yr. elsewhere
Year to which price refers: 1992
Subscription address: G. R. Anderson, at editorial address

ADVERTISING INFORMATION

Advertising accepted: Yes

EDITORIAL DESCRIPTION

Scope: Concerned with personal- and place-name studies relating to England, the Channel Islands, Ireland, the Isle of Man, Scotland, and Wales, the journal publishes news of research in progress, publications in preparation, annual bibliography, papers from the Council for Name Studies annual conference, and additional articles, notes, and reviews.
Reviews books: Yes
Publishes notes: Yes
Languages accepted: English
Prints abstracts: No
Author-anonymous submission: No

SUBMISSION REQUIREMENTS

Restrictions on contributors: Preference is given to CNS conference papers, but other contributions are considered. Most book reviews are commissioned.
Author pays submission fee: No
Author pays page charges: No
Length of articles: 5,000 words maximum
Length of book reviews: 1,500 words
Length of notes: 350 words
Style: Journal; see style sheet in vol. 10
Number of copies required: 2
Special requirements: Submit double-spaced typescript.
Copyright ownership: Journal
Rejected manuscripts: Returned
Time before publication decision: 3-12 wks.
Time between decision and publication: 6-10 mos.
Number of reviewers: 2-4
Articles submitted per year: 10
Articles published per year: 7-9
Book reviews submitted per year: 6-8
Book reviews published per year: 6-8
Notes submitted per year: 4
Notes published per year: 3

(1995)
*Nord Nytt: Nordisk Tidsskrift for Folkelivsforskning

Jørgen Burchardt, Editor
Nyborgvej 13
Sødinge
5750 Ringe, Denmark

Telephone: (45) 62 623617
Fax: (45) 62 623655
First published: 1963
Sponsoring organization: Nordiska Publiceringsnämnden för Humanistiska Tidskrifter (Nordic Publications Committee for Humanist Periodicals)
ISSN: 0008-1345
MLA acronym: NNy

SUBSCRIPTION INFORMATION

Frequency of publication: 4-6 times/yr.
Circulation: 1,200
Available in microform: No
Subscription price: 360 Dkr/yr.
Year to which price refers: 1992
Subscription address: Museumstjenesten, Lysgård, 8800 Viborg, Denmark

Subscription telephone: (45) 86 667666

ADVERTISING INFORMATION

Advertising accepted: Yes

EDITORIAL DESCRIPTION

Scope: Publishes articles on ethnology, folklore, folk religion, history, social sciences and psychology in Scandinavia.
Reviews books: Yes
Publishes notes: Yes
Languages accepted: Danish; Swedish; Norwegian; English
Prints abstracts: Yes, in English

SUBMISSION REQUIREMENTS

Author pays page charges: No
Length of articles: 10,000 words
Length of book reviews: 2,000 words
Length of notes: 500 words
Number of copies required: 1
Special requirements: Submit typescript and diskette.
Copyright ownership: Author & journal
Rejected manuscripts: Returned
Time before publication decision: 1 mo.
Time between decision and publication: 7 mos.
Number of reviewers: 2-6
Articles submitted per year: 120
Articles published per year: 60
Book reviews published per year: 400

(1996)
*Nordelbingen: Beiträge zur Kunst- und Kulturgeschichte

Dieter Lohmeier, Renate Paczkowski, & Ulrich Schulte-Wuelwer, Editors
Städtisches Museum Flensburg
Lutherplatz 1
2390 Flensburg, Germany

First published: 1923
Sponsoring organization: Gesellschaft für Schleswig-Holsteinische Geschichte
ISSN: 0078-1037
MLA acronym: Nordelbingen

SUBSCRIPTION INFORMATION

Frequency of publication: Annual
Circulation: 700
Available in microform: No
Subscription address: Westholsteinische Verlagsanstalt Boyens & Co., Wulf-Isebrand-Platz 1, Postfach 1880, 2240 Heide, Germany
Subscription fax: (49) 481 64890

ADVERTISING INFORMATION

Advertising accepted: No

EDITORIAL DESCRIPTION

Scope: Publishes articles on art, cultural and literary history, and folklore with respect to Schleswig-Holstein, Northern Germany, Denmark, and other northern countries.
Reviews books: Yes
Publishes notes: No
Languages accepted: German
Prints abstracts: No

SUBMISSION REQUIREMENTS

Restrictions on contributors: None
Author pays submission fee: No
Author pays page charges: No
Length of articles: 20-30 pp.
Length of book reviews: 2 pp.
Number of copies required: 1
Copyright ownership: Westholsteinische Verlagsanstalt Boyens & Co.
Rejected manuscripts: Returned
Time before publication decision: 6 mos.

Time between decision and publication: 6 mos.
Number of reviewers: 3
Articles submitted per year: 20
Articles published per year: 10-15
Book reviews submitted per year: 10
Book reviews published per year: 10

(1997)
*Nordfriesisches Jahrbuch

Nils Århammar, Rolf Kuschert, Albert A. Panten, & Brar V. Riewerts, Editors
Nordfriisk Inst.
Süderstr. 30
2257 Bräist/Bredstedt, Germany

Telephone: (49) 4671 2081
Fax: (49) 4671 1333
First published: 1965
Sponsoring organization: Verein Nordfriesisches Inst.; Nordfriesischer Verein
ISSN: 0078-1045
MLA acronym: NFJ

SUBSCRIPTION INFORMATION

Frequency of publication: Annual
Circulation: 900
Available in microform: No
Subscription price: 35 DM/yr.
Year to which price refers: 1992

ADVERTISING INFORMATION

Advertising accepted: No

EDITORIAL DESCRIPTION

Scope: Publishes articles on Frisian language, history, and nature.
Reviews books: Yes
Publishes notes: Yes
Languages accepted: German; Frisian
Prints abstracts: No
Author-anonymous submission: No

SUBMISSION REQUIREMENTS

Restrictions on contributors: None
Author pays submission fee: No
Author pays page charges: No
Length of articles: No restrictions
Length of book reviews: No restrictions
Length of notes: No restrictions
Style: Journal
Number of copies required: 1
Copyright ownership: Author
Rejected manuscripts: Returned
Time before publication decision: 1 mo.
Number of reviewers: 2
Articles submitted per year: 12
Articles published per year: 10-12
Book reviews published per year: 12
Notes submitted per year: 10-12
Notes published per year: 2-4

(1998)
*Nordic Journal of Linguistics

Thorstein Fretheim, Editor
Dept. of Linguistics
Univ. of Trondheim
7055 Dragvoll, Norway

Telephone: (47) 7 596524
Fax: (47) 7 596119
E-mail: Thorstein.Fretheim@avh.unit.no
First published: 1928
Sponsoring organization: Nordic Humanities Research Councils
ISSN: 0332-5865
MLA acronym: NJL

SUBSCRIPTION INFORMATION

Frequency of publication: 2 times/yr.

Circulation: 450
Available in microform: Yes
Subscription price: 325 NKr ($60.00)/yr.
Year to which price refers: 1992
Subscription address: Universitetsforlaget AS, Postboks 2959, Tøyen, 0608 Oslo 6, Norway
Additional subscription address: Scandinavian Univ. Press, 200 Meacham Ave., Elmont, NY 11003
Subscription telephone: (47) 2 677600
Subscription fax: (47) 2 677575

ADVERTISING INFORMATION

Advertising accepted: Yes
Advertising rates: $215.00/half page; $335.00/full page

EDITORIAL DESCRIPTION

Scope: The journal is concerned with all branches of linguistics. Preference is given to contributions of general, theoretical, or methodological interest, and to studies on Scandinavian languages (including Finnish and Lappish). Publishes articles primarily from the members of the Nordic Association of Linguistics, but contributions from nonmembers are considered.
Reviews books: Yes
Publishes notes: Yes
Languages accepted: English; German occasionally; French occasionally
Prints abstracts: Yes
Author-anonymous submission: No

SUBMISSION REQUIREMENTS

Author pays submission fee: No
Author pays page charges: No
Length of articles: 40,000-55,000 words
Length of book reviews: 10,000-20,000 words
Length of notes: 10,000 words
Style: Journal
Number of copies required: 3
Special requirements: Include an abstract in English for all article submissions.
Copyright ownership: Nordic Assn. of Linguistics
Rejected manuscripts: Returned
Time before publication decision: 2 mos.
Time between decision and publication: 4-6 mos.
Number of reviewers: 2
Articles submitted per year: 15-20
Articles published per year: 8-10
Book reviews submitted per year: 5-7
Book reviews published per year: 4-6
Notes submitted per year: 2-3
Notes published per year: 2-3

(1999)
*Nordisk Tidskrift för Bok- och Biblioteksväsen

Per S. Ridderstad, Editor
Drömstigen 5
181 65 Lidingö, Sweden

Additional editorial address: Avd. för Bok- och Bibliotekshistoria, Allhelgona Kyrkogata 14 hus V, 223 62 Lund, Sweden
Telephone: (46) 46 104271
First published: 1914
Sponsoring organization: Nordiska Publiceringsnämnden för Humanistiska Tidskrifter (Nordic Publications Committee for Humanist Periodicals)
ISSN: 0029-148X
MLA acronym: NTBB

SUBSCRIPTION INFORMATION

Frequency of publication: 4 times/yr.
Circulation: 300
Available in microform: No
Subscription price: 315 Skr/yr. institutions; 180 Skr/yr. individuals
Year to which price refers: 1993
Subscription address: Scandinavian Univ. Press, P.O. Box 2959 Tøyen, 0608 Oslo, Norway
Additional subscription address: Scandinavian Univ. Press, 200 Meacham Ave., Elmont, NY 11003

ADVERTISING INFORMATION

Advertising accepted: Yes

EDITORIAL DESCRIPTION

Scope: Publishes articles on Scandinavian bibliography and library science related to the history of learning and cultural history.
Reviews books: Yes
Publishes notes: No
Languages accepted: Danish; English; Norwegian; Swedish
Prints abstracts: Yes
Author-anonymous submission: No

SUBMISSION REQUIREMENTS

Restrictions on contributors: None
Author pays submission fee: No
Author pays page charges: No
Length of articles: 4,000-10,000 words
Length of book reviews: 500-1,500 words
Number of copies required: 1
Special requirements: Consult with editor prior to submission; articles written in a Northern language should have a summary, preferably in English.
Copyright ownership: Journal
Rejected manuscripts: Returned
Time before publication decision: 3 weeks
Time between decision and publication: 6-9 mos.
Number of reviewers: 1-2
Articles published per year: 10
Book reviews published per year: 20

(2000)
*Nordlyd: Tromsø University Working Papers on Language & Linguistics

Ernst Håkon Jahr, Editor
Inst for Språk & Litteratur
Univ. i Tromsø
9037 Tromsø, Norway

Telephone: (47) 83 44273
Fax: (47) 83 44239
E-mail: Ernsthj@mack.uit.no
First published: 1979
Sponsoring organization: Inst. for Språk & Litteratur, Univ. i Tromsø
ISSN: 0332-7531
MLA acronym: Nordlyd

SUBSCRIPTION INFORMATION

Frequency of publication: Irregular
Circulation: 500
Available in microform: No
Subscription price: Free
Year to which price refers: 1992
Subscription telephone: (47) 83 44244

ADVERTISING INFORMATION

Advertising accepted: No

EDITORIAL DESCRIPTION

Scope: Publishes working papers on linguistics and languages.
Reviews books: Seldomly
Publishes notes: Yes
Languages accepted: English; German; Norwegian
Prints abstracts: Yes, in English for non-English articles
Author-anonymous submission: No

SUBMISSION REQUIREMENTS

Restrictions on contributors: Contributors must be connected with the Univ. i Tromsø (e.g., staff, guest lecturer, etc.)
Author pays submission fee: No
Author pays page charges: No
Number of copies required: 1
Copyright ownership: Author
Rejected manuscripts: Returned
Time before publication decision: 1-2 mos.
Time between decision and publication: 6 mos. maximum
Number of reviewers: 1-2

(2001)
*Norsk Lingvistisk Tidsskrift

Ernst Håkon Jahr, Editor
Inst. for Språk & Litteratur
Univ. i Tromsø
9037 Tromsø, Norway

Telephone: (47) 83 44273
Fax: (47) 83 44239
E-mail: Ernsthj@mack.uit.no
First published: 1983
Sponsoring organization: Norges Almenvitenskapelige Forskningsråd (Norwegian Research Council for Science & Humanities)
ISSN: 0800-3076
MLA acronym: NLT

SUBSCRIPTION INFORMATION

Frequency of publication: 2 times/yr.
Circulation: 230
Available in microform: No
Subscription price: 240 NKr ($47.00)/yr. institutions; 130 NKr ($28.00)/yr. individuals
Year to which price refers: 1992
Subscription address: Novus Forlag, Postboks 748 Sentrum, 0106 Oslo, Norway
Subscription telephone: (47) 2 717450
Subscription fax: (47) 2 718107

ADVERTISING INFORMATION

Advertising accepted: Yes
Advertising rates: 1,000 NKr/full page

EDITORIAL DESCRIPTION

Scope: A forum for Norwegian linguistics, the journal publishes articles and book review on all aspects of linguistics.
Reviews books: Yes
Publishes notes: Yes
Languages accepted: Norwegian; English; German
Author-anonymous submission: No

SUBMISSION REQUIREMENTS

Author pays submission fee: No
Author pays page charges: No
Number of copies required: 3
Copyright ownership: Author & Novus Forlag
Rejected manuscripts: Returned
Time before publication decision: 1-2 mos.
Time between decision and publication: 1-5 mos.
Number of reviewers: 1-3
Articles submitted per year: 15-20
Articles published per year: 8-10
Book reviews submitted per year: 8-10
Book reviews published per year: 8-10
Notes submitted per year: 0-5
Notes published per year: 0-5

(2002)
*Norsk Litterær Årbok

Hans H. Skei & Einar Vannebo, Editors
Inst. for Nordistikk & Litteraturvitenskap
Boks 1013 Blindern
0315 Oslo, Norway

Telephone: (47) 2 854145
Fax: (47) 2 857100
E-mail: HANSHS@HEDDA.uio.NO
First published: 1966
ISSN: 0078-1266
MLA acronym: NLÅ

SUBSCRIPTION INFORMATION

Frequency of publication: Annual
Circulation: 2,000
Available in microform: No
Subscription address: Det Norske, Samlaget, Trondheimsv. 15, Oslo 5, Norway

ADVERTISING INFORMATION

Advertising accepted: No

EDITORIAL DESCRIPTION

Scope: Publishes articles on Scandinavian literature, with an emphasis on Norwegian literature. Each volume contains a bibliography of Norwegian literary scholarship published in the preceding year.
Reviews books: No
Publishes notes: No
Languages accepted: Norwegian; Danish; Swedish
Prints abstracts: No
Author-anonymous submission: No

SUBMISSION REQUIREMENTS

Restrictions on contributors: None
Author pays submission fee: No
Author pays page charges: No
Length of articles: 10-20 pp.
Number of copies required: 1
Copyright ownership: Det Norske Samlaget
Rejected manuscripts: Returned
Time before publication decision: 1 mo.
Time between decision and publication: 6 mos.
Articles published per year: 15

(2003)
*Norte: Revista Hispano-Americana

Fredo Arias de la Canal, Editor
Frente de Afirmácion Hispanista, A.C.
Lago Ginebra 47C
Mexico City 17, D.F., Mexico

Additional editorial address: Ciprés no. 384, Col. Atlampa, 06450 Mexico City, D.F., Mexico
Telephone: (52) 5 5479371
Fax: (52) 5 5411546
First published: 1929
Sponsoring organization: Frente de Afirmácion Hispanista A.C.
MLA acronym: Norte

SUBSCRIPTION INFORMATION

Frequency of publication: 6 times/yr.
Circulation: 1,000
Available in microform: No

ADVERTISING INFORMATION

Advertising accepted: No

EDITORIAL DESCRIPTION

Scope: Publishes articles on literature and the arts. Publishes poetry and psychoanalytic criticism of poetry.
Reviews books: No
Publishes notes: No
Languages accepted: Spanish; English; French; German; Portuguese
Prints abstracts: No
Author-anonymous submission: No

SUBMISSION REQUIREMENTS

Restrictions on contributors: Contributors must be members of Frente de Afirmácion Hispanista.
Author pays submission fee: No
Author pays page charges: No
Length of articles: No restrictions
Style: None
Copyright ownership: Editor
Time before publication decision: 6-12 mos.
Time between decision and publication: 6-12 mos.
Number of reviewers: 6
Articles submitted per year: 6
Articles published per year: 6

(2004)
North Carolina Folklore Journal

Thomas McGowan, Editor
Dept. of English
Appalachian State Univ.
Boone, NC 28608

First published: 1948
Sponsoring organization: North Carolina Folklore Soc.; Appalachian State Univ.
ISSN: 0029-246X
MLA acronym: NCarF

SUBSCRIPTION INFORMATION

Frequency of publication: 2 times/yr. (May, Nov.)
Circulation: 450
Available in microform: No
Subscription price: $10.00/yr. institutions; (includes membership); $5.00/yr. individuals (includes membership)
Year to which price refers: 1992
Subscription address: North Carolina Folklore Soc., Dept. of English, Appalachian State Univ., Boone, NC 28608

ADVERTISING INFORMATION

Advertising accepted: No

EDITORIAL DESCRIPTION

Scope: Publishes studies of North Carolina folklore and folklife and theoretical articles pertinent to such studies.
Reviews books: Yes
Publishes notes: Yes
Languages accepted: English
Prints abstracts: No
Author-anonymous submission: No

SUBMISSION REQUIREMENTS

Restrictions on contributors: Book reviews are solicited.
Author pays submission fee: No
Author pays page charges: No
Length of articles: 1,000-10,000 words
Length of book reviews: 500-1,000 words
Length of notes: 250-500 words
Style: MLA
Number of copies required: 1
Copyright ownership: Assigned by author to North Carolina Folklore Soc.
Rejected manuscripts: Returned
Time before publication decision: 3 weeks
Time between decision and publication: 6 mos.
Number of reviewers: 1
Articles submitted per year: 20
Articles published per year: 10
Book reviews published per year: 3
Notes submitted per year: 5
Notes published per year: 5

(2005)
*North Carolina Historical Review

Jeffrey J. Crow & Kathleen B. Wyche, Editors
Division of Archives & History
Archives & History, State Library Bldg.
109 E. Jones St.
Raleigh, NC 27611

Telephone: 919 733-1439
First published: 1924
Sponsoring organization: State of North Carolina
ISSN: 0029-2494
MLA acronym: NCHR

SUBSCRIPTION INFORMATION

Frequency of publication: 4 times/yr.
Circulation: 1,500
Available in microform: Yes
Subscription price: $25.00/yr.
Year to which price refers: 1992

ADVERTISING INFORMATION

Advertising accepted: No

EDITORIAL DESCRIPTION

Scope: Publishes scholarly articles on North Carolina history and Southern history.
Reviews books: Yes
Publishes notes: Yes
Languages accepted: English
Prints abstracts: No
Author-anonymous submission: Yes

SUBMISSION REQUIREMENTS

Restrictions on contributors: None
Author pays submission fee: No
Author pays page charges: No
Length of articles: 15-25 pp. plus footnotes
Length of book reviews: 350-450 words
Length of notes: 150-200 words
Style: Chicago
Number of copies required: 2
Special requirements: No genealogy; footnotes in journal's style
Copyright ownership: Assigned by author to Division of Archives & History
Rejected manuscripts: Returned
Time before publication decision: 8-10 weeks
Time between decision and publication: 12-18 mos.
Number of reviewers: 5
Articles submitted per year: 35
Articles published per year: 12
Book reviews published per year: 100
Notes submitted per year: 50
Notes published per year: 50

(2006)
*North Carolina Studies in the Romance Languages and Literatures

María A. Salgado, Editor
Dept. of Romance Languages
Campus Box 3170
Univ. of North Carolina
Chapel Hill, NC 27599

Telephone: 919 962-2062
First published: 1940
Sponsoring organization: Dept. of Romance Languages, Univ. of North Carolina, Chapel Hill
ISSN: 0885-6001
MLA acronym: UNCSRLL

SUBSCRIPTION INFORMATION

Frequency of publication: Irregular
Circulation: 500
Available in microform: No

Subscription address: Univ. of North Carolina Press, P.O. Box 2288, CB # 6215, Chapel Hill, NC 27514-2288
Subscription telephone: 919 966-3561

ADVERTISING INFORMATION

Advertising accepted: No

EDITORIAL DESCRIPTION

Scope: Publishes essays, texts, textual studies, and literary criticism.
Reviews books: No
Publishes notes: No
Languages accepted: English; French; Italian; Spanish
Prints abstracts: No
Author-anonymous submission: No

SUBMISSION REQUIREMENTS

Restrictions on contributors: None
Author pays submission fee: No
Author pays page charges: Yes
Cost of page charges: $18.00
Length of books: 150-250 pp.
Style: MLA
Number of copies required: 2
Special requirements: Send letter of inquiry and long abstract before submission.
Copyright ownership: Series
Rejected manuscripts: Returned
Time before publication decision: 8-12 mos.
Time between decision and publication: 6-8 mos.
Number of reviewers: 3
Books submitted per year: 40
Books published per year: 2-3

(2007)
*North Dakota Quarterly

Robert W. Lewis, Editor
Box 8237
Univ. of North Dakota
Grand Forks, ND 58202

Telephone: 701 777-3322
Fax: 701 777-3650
First published: 1910
Sponsoring organization: Univ. of North Dakota
ISSN: 0029-277X
MLA acronym: NDQ

SUBSCRIPTION INFORMATION

Frequency of publication: 4 times/yr. (Winter, Spring, Summer, Fall)
Circulation: 550
Available in microform: No
Subscription price: $20.00/yr. institutions US; $28.00/yr. institutions elsewhere; $15.00/yr. individuals US; $23.00/yr. individuals elsewhere
Year to which price refers: 1992

ADVERTISING INFORMATION

Advertising accepted: Yes
Advertising rates: $100.00/half page; $150.00/full page

EDITORIAL DESCRIPTION

Scope: Publishes articles with an emphasis on humanities and interdisciplinary studies. Also publishes short fiction, poetry, and reviews.
Reviews books: Yes
Publishes notes: No
Languages accepted: English
Prints abstracts: No
Author-anonymous submission: No

SUBMISSION REQUIREMENTS

Restrictions on contributors: None
Author pays submission fee: No

Author pays page charges: No
Length of articles: 5,000 words plus notes
Length of book reviews: 700 words
Style: MLA
Number of copies required: 1
Copyright ownership: Univ. of North Dakota
Rejected manuscripts: Returned; enclose SASE.
Time before publication decision: 3 mos.
Time between decision and publication: 1 yr.
Number of reviewers: 2-3
Articles submitted per year: 150
Articles published per year: 50
Book reviews submitted per year: 40
Book reviews published per year: 30

(2008)
North-Holland Linguistic Series

North-Holland Publishing Co.
Sara Burgerhartstr. 25
P.O. Box 2400
1000 CK Amsterdam, Netherlands

First published: 1970
ISSN: 0078-1592
MLA acronym: NHLS

SUBSCRIPTION INFORMATION

Frequency of publication: 2 times/yr.
Circulation: 500-2,500
Available in microform: No
Subscription address: Elsevier Science Publishers, Book Order Dept., P.O. Box 211, 1000 AE Amsterdam, Netherlands

ADVERTISING INFORMATION

Advertising accepted: No

EDITORIAL DESCRIPTION

Scope: Publishes high level research material in all fields of linguistics.
Reviews books: No
Publishes notes: No
Languages accepted: English
Prints abstracts: No

SUBMISSION REQUIREMENTS

Restrictions on contributors: None
Length of books: 350-650 pp.
Style: None
Number of copies required: 2
Special requirements: Submit camera-ready copy.
Copyright ownership: North-Holland/Elsevier Publishing Co.
Rejected manuscripts: Returned
Time before publication decision: 3 mos.
Time between decision and publication: 3 mos.
Number of reviewers: 2
Books published per year: 2-3

(2009)
North Wind: Journal of the George MacDonald Society

William Raeper, Editor
21, St. Mary's Rd.
Oxford OX4 IPY, England

First published: 1982
Sponsoring organization: George MacDonald Soc.
ISSN: 0265-7295
MLA acronym: NWi

SUBSCRIPTION INFORMATION

Frequency of publication: Annual (Autumn)
Circulation: 100
Available in microform: No
Subscription address: R. Johnson, 97 Hykeham Rd., Lincoln LN6 8AD, England

ADVERTISING INFORMATION

Advertising accepted: Yes

EDITORIAL DESCRIPTION

Scope: Encourages the awareness and study of the works of George MacDonald (1824-1905).
Reviews books: Yes
Publishes notes: Yes
Languages accepted: English
Prints abstracts: No
Author-anonymous submission: No

SUBMISSION REQUIREMENTS

Restrictions on contributors: None
Author pays submission fee: No
Author pays page charges: No
Length of articles: 4,000 words
Length of book reviews: 500 words
Length of notes: 500 words
Style: None
Number of copies required: 1
Copyright ownership: Author
Rejected manuscripts: Returned
Time before publication decision: 6 mos.
Time between decision and publication: 5 mos.
Number of reviewers: 1-2
Articles submitted per year: 4
Articles published per year: 3-4
Book reviews submitted per year: 4
Book reviews published per year: 2
Notes submitted per year: 1
Notes published per year: 1

(2010)
*Northeast Folklore

Edward D. Ives, Editor
Northeast Folklore Soc.
S. Stevens Hall
Univ. of Maine
Orono, ME 04469

Telephone: 207 581-1891
First published: 1958
Sponsoring organization: Dept. of Anthropology, Univ. of Maine, Orono; Northeast Archives of Folklore & Oral History; Maine Folklife Center
ISSN: 0078-1681
MLA acronym: NoEF

SUBSCRIPTION INFORMATION

Frequency of publication: Annual
Circulation: 550
Available in microform: No
Subscription price: $15.00/yr.
Year to which price refers: 1992

ADVERTISING INFORMATION

Advertising accepted: No

EDITORIAL DESCRIPTION

Scope: Annual volumes may be monographs, collections of regional material, comparative studies, or several shorter collections of studies. Topics cover the songs, legends, tales, traditions, and life styles of New England and the Atlantic Provinces of Canada.
Reviews books: No
Publishes notes: No
Languages accepted: English
Prints abstracts: No
Author-anonymous submission: No

SUBMISSION REQUIREMENTS

Restrictions on contributors: None
Author pays submission fee: No
Author pays page charges: No
Length of articles: 200 double-spaced typescript pp.
Style: Chicago
Number of copies required: 1

(2011)
Northwest Folklore

Louie W. Attebery, Editor
Regional Studies Center
College of Idaho
2112 Cleveland Blvd.
Caldwell, ID 83605

First published: 1965
Sponsoring organization: Regional Studies Center, College of Idaho; L. J. Skaggs & Mary C. Skaggs Foundation
ISSN: 0029-3369
MLA acronym: NwFolk

SUBSCRIPTION INFORMATION

Frequency of publication: 2 times/yr. (Sept., Jan.)
Circulation: 100
Available in microform: No
Subscription price: $16.00/yr. institutions; $8.00/yr. individuals
Year to which price refers: 1991

ADVERTISING INFORMATION

Advertising accepted: No

EDITORIAL DESCRIPTION

Scope: Publishes articles on all aspects of folklife—the oral-aural lore and the material culture—from and about the Great Northwest, i.e., Alaska, British Columbia, Alberta, Washington, Oregon, Idaho, and areas contiguous to them.
Reviews books: Yes
Publishes notes: No
Languages accepted: English
Prints abstracts: No
Author-anonymous submission: No

SUBMISSION REQUIREMENTS

Restrictions on contributors: None
Author pays submission fee: No
Author pays page charges: No
Length of articles: No restrictions
Length of book reviews: No restrictions
Style: MLA
Number of copies required: 3-5
Copyright ownership: Regional Studies Center
Rejected manuscripts: Returned
Time before publication decision: 1-3 mos.
Time between decision and publication: 2-12 mos.
Number of reviewers: 2-3
Articles submitted per year: 10-12
Articles published per year: 6
Book reviews submitted per year: 6
Book reviews published per year: 6

(2012)
*Northwest Ohio Quarterly

David Curtis Skaggs, Editor
Dept. of History
Bowling Green State Univ.
Bowling Green, OH 43403-0220

First published: 1929
Sponsoring organization: Maumee Valley Historical Soc.
ISSN: 0029-3407
MLA acronym: NOQ

SUBSCRIPTION INFORMATION

Frequency of publication: 4 times/yr.
Circulation: 700
Available in microform: No
Subscription price: $25.00/yr.
Year to which price refers: 1992
Subscription address: Secretary, Maumee Valley Historical Soc., 1031 River Rd., Maumee, OH 43537

ADVERTISING INFORMATION

Advertising accepted: No

EDITORIAL DESCRIPTION

Scope: Publishes articles on regional history, literature, culture, society, and science.
Reviews books: Yes
Publishes notes: Yes
Languages accepted: English
Prints abstracts: No

SUBMISSION REQUIREMENTS

Restrictions on contributors: None
Author pays submission fee: No
Author pays page charges: No
Length of articles: 3,000-8,000 words
Length of book reviews: 750-2,000 words
Length of notes: 500-2,000 words
Style: Chicago
Number of copies required: 3
Special requirements: Submit double-spaced typescript (including notes).
Copyright ownership: Journal
Rejected manuscripts: Returned
Time before publication decision: 3 mos.
Time between decision and publication: 3-12 weeks
Number of reviewers: 2
Articles submitted per year: 8-15
Articles published per year: 5-10
Book reviews submitted per year: 8-12
Book reviews published per year: 8-12
Notes submitted per year: 3-4
Notes published per year: 3-4

(2013)
*Northwest Review

John Witte, Editor
369 PLC
Univ. of Oregon
Eugene, Oregon 97403

First published: 1957
Sponsoring organization: Univ. of Oregon
ISSN: 0029-3423
MLA acronym: NWR

SUBSCRIPTION INFORMATION

Frequency of publication: 3 times/yr.
Circulation: 1,000
Available in microform: Yes
Subscription price: $14.00/yr.
Year to which price refers: 1992

ADVERTISING INFORMATION

Advertising accepted: Yes
Advertising rates: $160.00/full page

EDITORIAL DESCRIPTION

Scope: Publishes reviews, criticism, and comment on contemporary literature. Also publishes works in translation and criticism of current foreign literature.
Reviews books: Yes
Publishes notes: Yes
Languages accepted: English; all languages accepted for translation
Prints abstracts: No
Author-anonymous submission: No

SUBMISSION REQUIREMENTS

Restrictions on contributors: None
Author pays submission fee: No
Author pays page charges: No
Length of articles: 8-25 pp.
Length of book reviews: 4-6 pp.
Style: Chicago
Number of copies required: 1
Special requirements: All material must be unpublished and not currently under consideration elsewhere.
Copyright ownership: Author on request
Rejected manuscripts: Returned; enclose SASE.
Time before publication decision: 8-10 weeks
Time between decision and publication: 4 mos.
Number of reviewers: 2-3
Articles submitted per year: 75
Articles published per year: 10
Book reviews submitted per year: 80
Book reviews published per year: 18-20
Notes submitted per year: 10
Notes published per year: 3-5

(2014)
*Northwestern University Working Papers in Linguistics

Dept. of Linguistics
Northwestern Univ.
2016 Sheridan Rd.
Evanston, IL 60208

Telephone: 708 491-7020
First published: 1988
Sponsoring organization: Dept. of Linguistics, Northwestern Univ.
MLA acronym: NUWPL

SUBSCRIPTION INFORMATION

Frequency of publication: Annual (Spring)
Available in microform: No
Subscription price: $10.00/yr. plus postage
Year to which price refers: 1992

ADVERTISING INFORMATION

Advertising accepted: No

EDITORIAL DESCRIPTION

Scope: Publishes articles on current research in all areas of linguistics.
Reviews books: Yes
Publishes notes: No
Languages accepted: English
Prints abstracts: No
Author-anonymous submission: No

SUBMISSION REQUIREMENTS

Author pays submission fee: No
Author pays page charges: No
Length of articles: 3,000 words
Length of book reviews: 250 words
Style: Journal
Number of copies required: 2
Copyright ownership: Author
Rejected manuscripts: Not returned
Time before publication decision: 1-2 mos.
Time between decision and publication: 4 mos.
Number of reviewers: 2
Articles submitted per year: 8-15
Articles published per year: 8-10

(2015)
Norwegian-American Studies

Odd S. Lovoll, Editor
Norwegian-American Historical Assn.
St. Olaf College
Northfield, MN 55057-1097

First published: 1926

Copyright ownership: Maine Folklife Center
Rejected manuscripts: Returned
Time before publication decision: 2-3 mos.
Time between decision and publication: 1-2 yrs.
Number of reviewers: 2-3
Articles submitted per year: 6
Articles published per year: 1

Sponsoring organization: Norwegian-American Historical Assn.
ISSN: 0078-1983
MLA acronym: NAS

SUBSCRIPTION INFORMATION

Frequency of publication: Irregular
Circulation: 1,500
Available in microform: No

ADVERTISING INFORMATION

Advertising accepted: No

EDITORIAL DESCRIPTION

Scope: Publishes short studies and translations related to Norwegian-American life.
Reviews books: No
Publishes notes: Yes
Languages accepted: English
Prints abstracts: No
Author-anonymous submission: No

SUBMISSION REQUIREMENTS

Restrictions on contributors: None
Author pays submission fee: No
Author pays page charges: No
Length of articles: 20-30 pp.
Style: Journal
Number of copies required: 1
Special requirements: Norwegian articles are published occasionally in English translation.
Copyright ownership: Norwegian-American Historical Assn.
Rejected manuscripts: Returned
Time before publication decision: 1 mo.
Time between decision and publication: 1 yr.
Number of reviewers: 2
Articles submitted per year: 12
Articles published per year: 12

(2016)
*Notes and Queries

E. G. Stanley, L. G. Black, & D. Hewitt, Editors
Pembroke College
Oxford OX1 1DW, England

Telephone: (44) 865 276463
First published: 1849
ISSN: 0029-3970
MLA acronym: N&Q

SUBSCRIPTION INFORMATION

Frequency of publication: 4 times/yr.
Available in microform: No
Subscription price: $96.00 (£47.00)/yr.
Year to which price refers: 1992
Subscription address: Journals Subscription Dept., Oxford Univ. Press, Pinkhill House, Southfield Rd., Eynsham, Oxford OX8 1JJ, England
Subscription telephone: (44) 865 882283
Subscription fax: (44) 865 882890

ADVERTISING INFORMATION

Advertising accepted: Yes

EDITORIAL DESCRIPTION

Scope: Publishes factual contributions to the knowledge and understanding of English language and literature, lexicography, history, and scholarly antiquarianism. Each issue focuses on the works of a particular period.
Reviews books: Yes
Languages accepted: English
Prints abstracts: No
Author-anonymous submission: No

SUBMISSION REQUIREMENTS

Restrictions on contributors: None
Author pays submission fee: No
Author pays page charges: No
Length of articles: No restrictions
Length of book reviews: 600 words
Style: Hart's Rules
Number of copies required: 1
Special requirements: Submit typescript with continuously numbered footnotes at end.
Copyright ownership: Oxford Univ. Press
Rejected manuscripts: Returned; enclose British postage or international reply coupons.
Time before publication decision: 2-24 weeks
Time between decision and publication: 9-18 mos.
Articles published per year: 200-250
Book reviews published per year: 200

(2017)
*Notes on Contemporary Literature

William S. Doxey, Editor
English Dept.
West Georgia College
Carrollton, GA 30118

Telephone: 404 836-6512
First published: 1971
ISSN: 0029-4047
MLA acronym: NConL

SUBSCRIPTION INFORMATION

Frequency of publication: 5 times/yr. (Jan., Mar., May, Sept., Nov.)
Circulation: 300
Available in microform: No
Subscription price: $20.00/yr. institutions; $10.00/yr. individuals US; $20.00/yr. individuals elsewhere
Year to which price refers: 1992

ADVERTISING INFORMATION

Advertising accepted: Yes
Advertising rates: $100.00/full page

EDITORIAL DESCRIPTION

Scope: Publishes articles on contemporary literature from 1940 to the present.
Reviews books: Yes
Publishes notes: Yes
Languages accepted: English
Prints abstracts: No
Author-anonymous submission: No

SUBMISSION REQUIREMENTS

Restrictions on contributors: No multiple submissions.
Author pays submission fee: No
Author pays page charges: No
Length of articles: 1,000 words maximum
Length of book reviews: 500 words
Length of notes: 1,000 words
Number of copies required: 1
Special requirements: Incorporate notes into the text.
Copyright ownership: Editors; reassigned to author
Rejected manuscripts: Returned; enclose return postage.
Time before publication decision: 1 mo.
Time between decision and publication: 4-6 mos.
Number of reviewers: 2
Articles submitted per year: 80
Articles published per year: 35
Book reviews submitted per year: 5-10
Book reviews published per year: 5-10

(2018)
*Notes on Linguistics

Eugene Loos & Howard Law, Editors
International Linguistics Center
7500 West Camp Wisdom Rd.
Dallas, TX 75236

Telephone: 214 709-2400 ext. 2257
First published: 1977
Sponsoring organization: Summer Inst. of Linguistics, Linguistics Dept.
ISSN: 0736-0673
MLA acronym: NLing

SUBSCRIPTION INFORMATION

Frequency of publication: 4 times/yr. (Feb., May, Aug., Nov.)
Circulation: 975
Available in microform: Yes
Subscription price: $20.00/yr.
Year to which price refers: 1992
Subscription address: Bookcenter, at the above address

ADVERTISING INFORMATION

Advertising accepted: No

EDITORIAL DESCRIPTION

Scope: Publishes articles of general interest to linguistic field workers.
Reviews books: Yes
Publishes notes: Yes
Languages accepted: English
Prints abstracts: No
Author-anonymous submission: No

SUBMISSION REQUIREMENTS

Restrictions on contributors: None
Author pays submission fee: No
Author pays page charges: No
Length of articles: 2-20 pp.
Length of book reviews: 500 words
Length of notes: 300 words
Style: Linguistic Soc. of America
Number of copies required: 1
Special requirements: Submit typescript and MS DOS diskette.
Copyright ownership: Summer Inst. of Linguistics
Rejected manuscripts: Returned
Time before publication decision: 4-6 weeks
Time between decision and publication: 2-6 mos.
Number of reviewers: 2
Articles submitted per year: 15-20
Articles published per year: 18
Book reviews submitted per year: 12
Book reviews published per year: 12
Notes submitted per year: 15
Notes published per year: 15

(2019)
*Notes on Mississippi Writers

Hilton Anderson, Editor
P.O. Box 5037
Southern Station
Hattiesburg, MS 39406-5037

Telephone: 601 266-5344
First published: 1968
Sponsoring organization: Univ. of Southern Mississippi, Dept. of English
ISSN: 0029-4071
MLA acronym: NMW

SUBSCRIPTION INFORMATION

Frequency of publication: 2 times/yr.
Circulation: 250
Available in microform: No
Subscription price: $4.00/yr.
Year to which price refers: 1992

ADVERTISING INFORMATION

Advertising accepted: Yes
Advertising rates: $50.00/full page

EDITORIAL DESCRIPTION

Scope: Publishes articles on Mississippi writers.
Reviews books: Yes
Publishes notes: Yes
Languages accepted: English
Prints abstracts: No
Author-anonymous submission: No

SUBMISSION REQUIREMENTS

Restrictions on contributors: None
Author pays submission fee: No
Author pays page charges: No
Length of articles: 5,000 words maximum
Length of book reviews: 400 words
Length of notes: 300-6,000 words
Style: MLA
Number of copies required: 1
Copyright ownership: Editor
Rejected manuscripts: Returned; enclose return postage.
Time before publication decision: 1 mo.
Time between decision and publication: 1 yr.
Number of reviewers: 2-3
Articles submitted per year: 50
Articles published per year: 10-15
Book reviews submitted per year: 1-10
Book reviews published per year: 1-5
Notes submitted per year: 25-30
Notes published per year: 10-12

(2020)
*Notes on Modern Irish Literature

Edward A. Kopper, Jr., Editor
108 Farmington Dr.
Butler, PA 16001

First published: 1989
ISSN: 1045-6619
MLA acronym: NMIL

SUBSCRIPTION INFORMATION

Frequency of publication: Annual
Subscription price: $5.00/yr. US; $6.00/yr. Canada; $9.00/yr. elsewhere
Year to which price refers: 1992

ADVERTISING INFORMATION

Advertising accepted: Yes

EDITORIAL DESCRIPTION

Scope: Publishes notes on Anglo-Irish writers from about 1900 to the present. Articles on all Irish writers, standard major authors and less frequently analyzed figures, are welcome.
Reviews books: No
Publishes notes: Yes
Languages accepted: English
Prints abstracts: No
Author-anonymous submission: Yes

SUBMISSION REQUIREMENTS

Author pays submission fee: No
Author pays page charges: No
Length of articles: 3,000 words maximum
Length of notes: 3,000 words maximum
Style: MLA
Number of copies required: 1
Special requirements: Multiple submissions and articles accepted for publications elsewhere are not acceptable.
Copyright ownership: Editor
Rejected manuscripts: Returned
Time before publication decision: 2 mos.
Time between decision and publication: 6 mos.
Number of reviewers: 3

(2021)
*Notes on Translation

Katharine Barnwell, Editor
International Linguistic Center
7500 West Camp Wisdom Rd.
Dallas, TX 75236

First published: 1962
Sponsoring organization: Summer Inst. of Linguistics
ISSN: 0734-0788
MLA acronym: NOT

SUBSCRIPTION INFORMATION

Frequency of publication: 4 times/yr.
Circulation: 1,200
Available in microform: Yes
Subscription price: $17.95/yr. US; $19.95/yr. elsewhere
Year to which price refers: 1991
Subscription address: Summer Inst. of Linguistics, International Academic Bookstore, at the above address

ADVERTISING INFORMATION

Advertising accepted: No

EDITORIAL DESCRIPTION

Scope: Serves the Summer Institute of Linguistics program of translation by sharing information of a practical or theoretical nature with translators.
Reviews books: Yes
Publishes notes: Yes
Languages accepted: English
Prints abstracts: No
Author-anonymous submission: No

SUBMISSION REQUIREMENTS

Author pays submission fee: No
Author pays page charges: No
Length of articles: 8-25 pp.
Length of book reviews: 1-2 pp.
Length of notes: 1 p.
Style: Chicago
Number of copies required: 1
Copyright ownership: Summer Inst. of Linguistics
Rejected manuscripts: Not returned
Time before publication decision: 6 mos.
Number of reviewers: 3
Articles submitted per year: 30
Articles published per year: 16
Book reviews submitted per year: 6-10
Book reviews published per year: 4-8
Notes submitted per year: 6-12
Notes published per year: 4-8

(2022)
*Notre Librairie: Revue du Livre: Afrique, Caraïbes, Océan Indien

François Vuarchex, Director
CLEF
57, boulevard des Invalides
75007 Paris, France

Telephone: (33) 1 47831438
First published: 1968
Sponsoring organization: Ministère de la Coopération & du Développement; Ministère des Affaires Etrangères
ISSN: 0755-3854
MLA acronym: NLib

SUBSCRIPTION INFORMATION

Frequency of publication: 4 times/yr.
Circulation: 18,000
Available in microform: No
Subscription price: 200 F/yr. France; 280 F (320 F airmail)/yr. elsewhere
Year to which price refers: 1992

ADVERTISING INFORMATION

Advertising accepted: Yes, on an exchange basis

EDITORIAL DESCRIPTION

Scope: Publishes studies on Francophone literature from Africa, the Caribbean, and the Indian Ocean, including bibliographical overviews. Some issues are thematic and cover the literature of an area or a country.
Reviews books: Yes
Publishes notes: Yes
Languages accepted: French
Prints abstracts: No
Author-anonymous submission: No

SUBMISSION REQUIREMENTS

Restrictions on contributors: Contributions are usually solicited.
Author pays submission fee: No
Author pays page charges: No
Length of articles: 2,000-4,000 words
Length of book reviews: 1,000 words
Style: Journal
Number of copies required: 1
Copyright ownership: Editor
Rejected manuscripts: Not returned
Time before publication decision: 10 mos.
Time between decision and publication: 2 mos.
Number of reviewers: 2-3
Articles submitted per year: 85
Articles published per year: 80
Book reviews submitted per year: 50
Book reviews published per year: 50
Notes published per year: 10

(2023)
*Nottingham French Studies

S. J. Bamforth, R. E. Batchelor, R. A. Chapman, R. A. Francis, N. Hewitt, R. S. King, D. M. Knight, R. H. Middleton, & M. H. Offord, Editors
Dept. of French
Univ. of Nottingham
University Park
Nottingham NG7 2RD, England

Telephone: (44) 602 484848
Fax: (44) 602 420825
First published: 1962
Sponsoring organization: Nottingham Univ.
ISSN: 0029-4586
MLA acronym: NFS

SUBSCRIPTION INFORMATION

Frequency of publication: 2 times/yr. (May, Oct.)
Circulation: 500
Available in microform: No
Subscription price: £12.00 ($24.00)/yr. institutions; £8.00 ($16.00)/yr. individuals
Year to which price refers: 1991

ADVERTISING INFORMATION

Advertising accepted: No

EDITORIAL DESCRIPTION

Scope: Publishes articles on any aspect of French and Francophone literature, language, history, and thought.
Reviews books: No
Publishes notes: No
Languages accepted: English; French
Prints abstracts: No
Author-anonymous submission: Yes

SUBMISSION REQUIREMENTS

Restrictions on contributors: None
Author pays submission fee: No
Author pays page charges: No
Length of articles: 5,000 words maximum

Style: MLA; Modern Humanities Research Assn.
Number of copies required: 1
Special requirements: Submit original typescript accompanied by statement that manuscript is not under consideration for publication elsewhere. Omit contributor's name and affiliation from body of the manuscript.
Copyright ownership: Author
Rejected manuscripts: Returned
Time before publication decision: 3-6 mos.
Time between decision and publication: 6-12 mos.
Number of reviewers: 2
Articles submitted per year: 45-50
Articles published per year: 12

(2024)
*Nottingham Medieval Studies

Michael Jones, Editor
Dept. of History
Univ. of Nottingham
Nottingham NG7 2RD, England

Telephone: (44) 602 484848 ext. 2525
Fax: (44) 602 420825
First published: 1957
Sponsoring organization: Nottingham Univ.
ISSN: 0078-2122
MLA acronym: NMS

SUBSCRIPTION INFORMATION

Frequency of publication: Annual (Sept.)
Circulation: 500
Available in microform: No
Subscription price: £10.00 ($20.00)/yr.
Year to which price refers: 1991-92

ADVERTISING INFORMATION

Advertising accepted: No

EDITORIAL DESCRIPTION

Scope: Publishes articles concerning all aspects of medieval history.
Reviews books: Yes
Publishes notes: Yes
Languages accepted: English; French
Prints abstracts: No
Author-anonymous submission: No

SUBMISSION REQUIREMENTS

Restrictions on contributors: Book reviews are commissioned.
Author pays submission fee: No
Author pays page charges: No
Length of articles: 6,000-10,000 words
Length of book reviews: 1,000-5,000 words
Length of notes: 2,000 words
Style: Journal
Number of copies required: 2
Special requirements: Submit original typescript.
Copyright ownership: Author & Univ. of Nottingham
Rejected manuscripts: Returned
Time before publication decision: 2 mos.
Time between decision and publication: 1-2 yrs.
Number of reviewers: 2-3
Articles submitted per year: 10-20
Articles published per year: 5-8
Book reviews published per year: 3-4
Notes submitted per year: 1-2
Notes published per year: 1-2

(2025)
*Nouveaux Actes Sémiotiques

J. Fontanille, Editor
Fac. des Lettres & des Sciences Humaines
Campus Universitaire de Vanteaux
39E, rue Camille-Guérin
87036 Limoges Cedex, France

Telephone: (33) 55012619
Fax: (33) 55013806
First published: 1989
Sponsoring organization: Univ. de Limoges
MLA acronym: NouvAS

SUBSCRIPTION INFORMATION

Frequency of publication: Irregular
Subscription price: 120 F/yr.
Year to which price refers: 1992
Subscription address: John Benjamins B.V., Amsteldijk 44, P.O. Box 75577, 1070 AN Amsterdam, Netherlands
Additional subscription address: John Benjamins North America, Inc., 821 Bethlehem Pike, Philadelphia, PA 19118
Subscription telephone: (31) 20 6738156; 215 836-1200
Subscription fax: (31) 20 6739773; 215 836-1204

ADVERTISING INFORMATION

Advertising accepted: No

EDITORIAL DESCRIPTION

Scope: Publishes short monographs on semiotic studies.
Reviews books: No
Languages accepted: French
Prints abstracts: No

SUBMISSION REQUIREMENTS

Author pays submission fee: No
Author pays page charges: No
Length of books: 250 pp.
Books published per year: 1-2

(2026)
*Nouvelle Revue d'Onomastique

Pierre-Henri Billy, Editor
c/o Soc. Française d'Onomastique
87, rue Vieille-du-Temple
75003 Paris, France

First published: 1983
Sponsoring organization: Soc. Française d'Onomastique
ISSN: 0755-7752
MLA acronym: NRO

SUBSCRIPTION INFORMATION

Frequency of publication: Annual
Circulation: 250
Available in microform: No
Subscription price: 290 F/yr.
Year to which price refers: 1991
Subscription address: Secrétariat, at the above address

ADVERTISING INFORMATION

Advertising accepted: Yes

EDITORIAL DESCRIPTION

Scope: Publishes articles on French, Romance, and general onomastics.
Reviews books: Yes
Publishes notes: Yes
Languages accepted: French; Latin; Spanish; Portuguese; Italian
Prints abstracts: Yes, for articles not in French
Author-anonymous submission: No

SUBMISSION REQUIREMENTS

Restrictions on contributors: None
Author pays submission fee: No
Author pays page charges: No
Length of articles: No restrictions
Length of book reviews: No restrictions
Length of notes: No restrictions
Style: None
Number of copies required: 2
Special requirements: Submit double-spaced typescript.
Copyright ownership: Soc. Française d'Onomastique
Rejected manuscripts: Not returned
Time before publication decision: 3 mos. maximum
Time between decision and publication: 2 mos.
Number of reviewers: 2
Articles submitted per year: 17
Articles published per year: 14
Book reviews submitted per year: 25
Book reviews published per year: 25
Notes submitted per year: 20
Notes published per year: 20

(2027)
Nouvelle Revue du XVIe Siècle

S.F.D.S.
1, rue Victor Cousin
75230 Paris Cedex 05, France

First published: 1983
Sponsoring organization: Soc. Française des Seiziémistes
ISSN: 0294-1414
MLA acronym: NRSS

EDITORIAL DESCRIPTION

Scope: Publishes articles on 16th-century literature.
Languages accepted: French

(2028)
*Nouvelle Revue Française

Jacques Réda, Editor
Editions Gallimard
5, rue Sébastien-Bottin
75341 Paris Cedex 07, France

Telephone: (33) 1 49544200
First published: 1909
ISSN: 0029-4802
MLA acronym: NRF

SUBSCRIPTION INFORMATION

Frequency of publication: 12 times/yr.
Available in microform: No
Subscription price: 474 F/yr. France; 484 F/yr. elsewhere
Year to which price refers: 1992
Subscription address: 49 rue de la Vanne, 92120 Montrouge, France
Subscription telephone: (33) 1 46568900

ADVERTISING INFORMATION

Advertising accepted: No

EDITORIAL DESCRIPTION

Scope: Publishes articles on world literature with a focus on French literature.
Reviews books: Yes
Publishes notes: Yes
Languages accepted: French
Prints abstracts: No
Author-anonymous submission: No

SUBMISSION REQUIREMENTS

Author pays submission fee: No

Author pays page charges: No
Number of copies required: 1
Copyright ownership: Author
Time before publication decision: 2-3 weeks
Time between decision and publication: 2-3 mos.
Articles published per year: 180
Book reviews published per year: 110
Notes published per year: 120

(2029)
*Nouvelles de la République des Lettres

Paul Dibon & Tullio Gregory, Editors
Ist. Italiano per gli Studi Filosofici
Viale Calascione, 7
80132 Naples, Italy

Telephone: (39) 81 7612884
Fax: (39) 81 668339
First published: 1981
Sponsoring organization: Ist. Italiano per gli Studi Filosofici
ISSN: 0392-2332
MLA acronym: NRL

SUBSCRIPTION INFORMATION

Frequency of publication: 2 times/yr. (May, Nov.)
Circulation: 180
Available in microform: No
Subscription address: Prismi Editrice, via F. Caracciolo, 13, 80122 Naples, Italy

ADVERTISING INFORMATION

Advertising accepted: Yes

EDITORIAL DESCRIPTION

Scope: Publishes articles on the history of thought, science, arts, and letters, from the Renaissance to the Enlightenment, with special interest in source materials and text editions.
Reviews books: Yes
Publishes notes: Yes
Languages accepted: English; French; German; Italian; Spanish
Prints abstracts: No

SUBMISSION REQUIREMENTS

Restrictions on contributors: None
Author pays submission fee: No
Author pays page charges: No
Length of articles: No restrictions
Length of book reviews: 2,000 words
Length of notes: No restrictions
Style: None
Number of copies required: 1
Copyright ownership: Journal
Rejected manuscripts: Returned
Time before publication decision: 6 mos.
Time between decision and publication: 1 yr.
Number of reviewers: 2
Articles submitted per year: 20
Articles published per year: 12-16
Book reviews submitted per year: 30-40
Book reviews published per year: 10-12
Notes submitted per year: 10-20
Notes published per year: 10-20

(2030)
*Novel: A Forum on Fiction

Mark Spilka, Richard Pearce, & Ellen Rooney, Editors
Box 1984
Brown Univ.
Providence, RI 02912

Telephone: 401 863-3756
First published: 1967
Sponsoring organization: Brown Univ.
ISSN: 0029-5132
MLA acronym: Novel

SUBSCRIPTION INFORMATION

Frequency of publication: 3 times/yr. (Fall, Winter, Spring)
Circulation: 1,750
Available in microform: Yes

ADVERTISING INFORMATION

Advertising accepted: Yes

EDITORIAL DESCRIPTION

Scope: Publishes articles and reviews on the history and theory of fiction unrestricted by time, place, or origin. Interested in reviews of narrative theory, genre, and critical studies of fiction.
Reviews books: Yes
Publishes notes: No
Languages accepted: English
Prints abstracts: No
Author-anonymous submission: No

SUBMISSION REQUIREMENTS

Restrictions on contributors: None
Author pays submission fee: No
Author pays page charges: No
Length of articles: 20-25 pp.
Length of book reviews: 1,000-1,500 words
Style: MLA
Number of copies required: 2
Special requirements: Submit original typescript. Quotes in European languages are permitted. Book reviews are solicited.
Copyright ownership: Assigned by author to journal
Rejected manuscripts: Returned; enclose SASE.
Time before publication decision: 4 mos.
Time between decision and publication: 10-12 mos.
Number of reviewers: 2 plus Editors & Board members if recommended
Articles submitted per year: 340
Articles published per year: 12
Book reviews published per year: 20-25

(2031)
Novyi Mir: Literaturno-Khudozhestvennyĭ i Obshchestvenno-Politicheskiĭ Zhurnal

S. P. Zalygin, Editor
Izvestiia
Pushkinskaia pl. 5
1-3798 Moscow K-6, Russia

First published: 1925
ISSN: 0029-5329
MLA acronym: NovM

SUBSCRIPTION INFORMATION

Frequency of publication: 12 times/yr.
Additional subscription address: Outside the former U.S.S.R. contact: A. Neimanis Buchvertrieb & Verlag, Hans-Sachs-Str. 10, 8000 Munich, Germany

ADVERTISING INFORMATION

Advertising accepted: No

EDITORIAL DESCRIPTION

Scope: Publishes articles on Russian literature.
Reviews books: Yes
Publishes notes: No
Languages accepted: Russian
Prints abstracts: Yes

(2032)
*Novyĭ Zhurnal/The New Review

Yuri Kashkarov, Editor
New Review, Inc.
611 Broadway, Suite 842
New York, NY 10012-2608

Telephone: 212 353-1478
Fax: 212 353-1478
First published: 1942
Sponsoring organization: Julia Whitney Foundation
ISSN: 0029-5337
MLA acronym: NovŽ

SUBSCRIPTION INFORMATION

Frequency of publication: 4 times/yr.
Circulation: 1,200
Available in microform: Yes
Subscription price: $67.00/yr. institutions; $47.00/yr. individuals
Year to which price refers: 1992

ADVERTISING INFORMATION

Advertising accepted: No

EDITORIAL DESCRIPTION

Scope: Publishes articles on Russian literature.
Reviews books: Yes
Publishes notes: Yes
Languages accepted: Russian
Prints abstracts: No
Author-anonymous submission: Yes, at author's request

SUBMISSION REQUIREMENTS

Restrictions on contributors: None
Author pays submission fee: No
Author pays page charges: No
Length of articles: No restrictions
Length of book reviews: 1,200 words
Length of notes: 1,200 words
Style: Standard Russian
Number of copies required: 1
Copyright ownership: Journal
Rejected manuscripts: Not returned
Time before publication decision: 2-3 mos.
Time between decision and publication: 4-5 mos.
Number of reviewers: 2
Articles submitted per year: 25-30
Articles published per year: 25
Book reviews submitted per year: 18-20
Book reviews published per year: 15
Notes submitted per year: 15
Notes published per year: 10

(2033)
*Now and Then

Pat Arnow, Editor
Box 70556
East Tennessee State Univ.
Johnson City, TN 37614-0556

Telephone: 615 929-5348
Fax: 615 929-5770
First published: 1984
Sponsoring organization: Center for Appalachian Studies & Services, East Tennessee State Univ.
ISSN: 0896-2693
MLA acronym: N&T

SUBSCRIPTION INFORMATION

Frequency of publication: 3 times/yr.
Circulation: 800
Available in microform: No
Subscription price: $12.00/yr. institutions; $10.00/yr. individuals
Year to which price refers: 1992

ADVERTISING INFORMATION

Advertising accepted: No

EDITORIAL DESCRIPTION

Scope: Publishes articles on Appalachian issues, as well as poetry, fiction, personal essays, graphics, and photographs concerned with Appalachian life.
Reviews books: Yes
Publishes notes: No
Languages accepted: English
Prints abstracts: No
Author-anonymous submission: No

SUBMISSION REQUIREMENTS

Restrictions on contributors: Most reviews are solicited.
Author pays submission fee: No
Author pays page charges: No
Length of articles: 750-2,500 words
Length of book reviews: 750 words
Style: Associated Press
Number of copies required: 1
Copyright ownership: Center for Appalachian Studies & Services
Rejected manuscripts: Returned; enclose SASE.
Time before publication decision: 1-5 mos.
Time between decision and publication: 3-6 mos.
Number of reviewers: 1-3
Articles submitted per year: 75
Articles published per year: 15
Book reviews submitted per year: 18-20
Book reviews published per year: 18-20

(2034)
*NOWELE: North-Western European Language Evolution

Hans F. Nielsen, Managing Editor
Inst. for Sprog & Kommunication
Odense Univ.
Campusvej 55
5230 Odense M, Denmark

Additional editorial address: Michael Barnes, Dept. of Scandinavian Studies, University College London, Gower St., London WC1E 6BT, England
Telephone: (45) 66 158600 ext. 2153
Fax: (45) 65 932483
E-mail: Hfn@dou.dk
First published: 1983
ISSN: 0108-8416
MLA acronym: NOWELE

SUBSCRIPTION INFORMATION

Frequency of publication: 2 times/yr. (Mar., Sept.)
Circulation: 200
Available in microform: No
Subscription price: 180 Dkr/yr.
Year to which price refers: 1991
Subscription address: Odense Univ. Press, at the above address
Subscription telephone: (45) 66 157999

ADVERTISING INFORMATION

Advertising accepted: Yes, on an exchange basis

EDITORIAL DESCRIPTION

Scope: Publishes articles on all aspects of the (pre-)histories of Icelandic, Faroese, Norwegian, Swedish, Danish, Frisian, Dutch, German, English, Gothic and the early Runic language. Also includes studies of purely theoretical questions concerning historical language development.
Reviews books: No
Publishes notes: Yes
Languages accepted: English; German
Prints abstracts: No

Author-anonymous submission: Yes

SUBMISSION REQUIREMENTS

Author pays submission fee: No
Author pays page charges: No
Length of articles: No restrictions
Length of notes: No restrictions
Style: Journal
Number of copies required: 2
Special requirements: Submit double-space typescript on size A4 (8 1/4 in. x 11 3/4 in.) paper. See journal for complete details.
Copyright ownership: Journal & Odense Univ. Press
Rejected manuscripts: Returned
Time before publication decision: 2 mos.
Time between decision and publication: 1 yr.
Number of reviewers: 1
Articles submitted per year: 12-15
Articles published per year: 8-10

(2035)
*Nowi Dni

M. Dalney, Editor
P.O. Box 400
Station D
Toronto, Ontario M6P 3J9, Canada

Telephone: 416 767-8440
Fax: 416 535-6667
First published: 1950
ISSN: 0048-1017
MLA acronym: Nowi Dni

SUBSCRIPTION INFORMATION

Frequency of publication: 11 times/yr. (monthly, one double issue for July-Aug.)
Circulation: 1,500
Available in microform: No
Subscription price: C$27.00/yr. Canada; $25.00/yr. elsewhere
Year to which price refers: 1992

ADVERTISING INFORMATION

Advertising accepted: Yes
Advertising rates: C$50.00/quarter page; C$200.00/full page

EDITORIAL DESCRIPTION

Scope: Publishes articles on Ukrainian literature, language, and folklore.
Reviews books: Yes
Publishes notes: Yes
Languages accepted: Ukrainian
Prints abstracts: No
Author-anonymous submission: No

SUBMISSION REQUIREMENTS

Author pays submission fee: No
Author pays page charges: No
Length of articles: 2,000 words
Length of book reviews: 1,000 words
Length of notes: 150 words
Style: MLA
Number of copies required: 1
Special requirements: Submit original typescript. Articles in English, Polish, and Russian are accepted for translation into Ukrainian.
Copyright ownership: Author
Rejected manuscripts: Returned; enclose return postage.
Time before publication decision: 3 mos. maximum
Time between decision and publication: 1 mo.
Number of reviewers: 2
Articles submitted per year: 200
Articles published per year: 45
Book reviews submitted per year: 90
Book reviews published per year: 30
Notes submitted per year: 200
Notes published per year: 60

(2036)
*Nueva Revista de Filología Hispánica

Beatriz Garza Cuarón, Editor
Apartado 20-671
Camino al Ajusco 20
01000 Mexico City D.F., Mexico

Telephone: (52) 5 6455955 ext. 110
Fax: (52) 5 6450464
E-mail: COLEGIOM@UNAMVM1
First published: 1947
Sponsoring organization: El Colegio de México
ISSN: 0185-0121
MLA acronym: NRFH

SUBSCRIPTION INFORMATION

Frequency of publication: 2 times/yr.
Circulation: 2,000
Available in microform: No
Subscription price: $71.00/yr. US & Canada; $50.00/yr. South America; $80.00/yr. elsewhere
Year to which price refers: 1992
Subscription address: El Colegio de México, Dept. de Publicaciones, Camino al Ajusco 20, 01000 Mexico City D.F., Mexico
Subscription telephone: (52) 5 6455955 ext. 364, 365

ADVERTISING INFORMATION

Advertising accepted: Yes, on an exchange basis

EDITORIAL DESCRIPTION

Scope: Publishes articles and notes on Spanish and Latin American literature, Hispanic linguistics, general literary and linguistic theory and methodology; reviews of books and articles; a classified bibliography, philology, linguistics, and Spanish language literature.
Reviews books: Yes
Publishes notes: Yes
Languages accepted: Spanish
Prints abstracts: No
Author-anonymous submission: No

SUBMISSION REQUIREMENTS

Author pays submission fee: No
Author pays page charges: No
Length of articles: 75,000 words
Length of book reviews: 16,150 words
Length of notes: 34,300 words
Style: Journal
Number of copies required: 2
Copyright ownership: El Colegio de México
Rejected manuscripts: Not returned
Time before publication decision: 3-12 mos.
Time between decision and publication: 1 yr.
Number of reviewers: 2-3
Articles submitted per year: 70
Articles published per year: 30-50
Book reviews submitted per year: 100-150
Book reviews published per year: 30
Notes submitted per year: 20
Notes published per year: 10

(2037)
*Nueva Revista del Pacífico

Gilda Tassara Chávez & Eddie Morales Piña, Editors
Fac. of Humanities
Univ. of Playa Ancha de Ciencias de la Educación
Casilla 34-V,
Valparaíso, Chile

First published: 1976
Sponsoring organization: Univ. of Playa Ancha
ISSN: 0716-6346
MLA acronym: NRP

SUBSCRIPTION INFORMATION

Frequency of publication: Annual
Circulation: 100
Available in microform: No
Subscription price: $15.00/yr.
Year to which price refers: 1992
Subscription address: Biblioteca Central, Casilla 34-V, Valparaíso, Chile

ADVERTISING INFORMATION

Advertising accepted: No

EDITORIAL DESCRIPTION

Scope: Publishes articles on Hispanic and general literature and linguistics.
Reviews books: Yes
Publishes notes: Yes
Languages accepted: Spanish; English; French
Prints abstracts: Yes
Author-anonymous submission: No

SUBMISSION REQUIREMENTS

Restrictions on contributors: Contributors must be teachers of literature or linguistics.
Author pays submission fee: Yes
Author pays page charges: No
Length of articles: 5-10 double-spaced typescript pp.
Length of book reviews: 1-3 pp.
Length of notes: 1-2 pp.
Style: MLA
Number of copies required: 2
Special requirements: Submit original typescript.
Copyright ownership: Journal
Rejected manuscripts: Not returned
Time before publication decision: 1 mo.
Time between decision and publication: 3 mos.
Number of reviewers: 5
Articles submitted per year: 10-15
Articles published per year: 10-15
Book reviews submitted per year: 5-8
Book reviews published per year: 2-5
Notes submitted per year: 2-5
Notes published per year: 2-5

(2038)
*Numen: International Review for the History of Religions

Hans G. Kippenberg & E. Thomas Lawson, Editors
Univ. of Bremen
Fachbereich 9
P.O.B. 330440
2800 Bremen, Germany

Additional editorial address: In N. America: E. Thomas Lawson, Dept. of Religion, Western Michigan Univ., Kalamazoo, MI 49008
First published: 1954
Sponsoring organization: International Assn. for the History of Religions
ISSN: 0029-5973
MLA acronym: Numen

SUBSCRIPTION INFORMATION

Frequency of publication: 3 times/yr.
Available in microform: No
Subscription address: E. J. Brill, P.O.B. 9000, 2300 PA Leiden, Netherlands

ADVERTISING INFORMATION

Advertising accepted: Occasionally

EDITORIAL DESCRIPTION

Scope: Publishes articles on the history of religions.
Reviews books: Yes
Publishes notes: No
Languages accepted: English; French; German; Italian

Prints abstracts: No
Author-anonymous submission: No

SUBMISSION REQUIREMENTS

Restrictions on contributors: None
Author pays submission fee: No
Author pays page charges: No
Length of articles: No restrictions
Style: Journal
Number of copies required: 2
Special requirements: Submit double-spaced typescript with 2-inch left margin, and double-spaced footnotes on separate pages.
Copyright ownership: Journal
Rejected manuscripts: Returned; enclose SASE.
Number of reviewers: 2 plus Editorial Board
Articles published per year: 10-20

(2039)
Nuovi Argomenti

Leonardo Sciascia & Enzo Siciliano, Editors
Arnoldo Mondadori Redazione
via Sicilia, 136
00187 Rome, Italy

First published: 1953
ISSN: 0029-6295
MLA acronym: NArg

SUBSCRIPTION INFORMATION

Frequency of publication: 4 times/yr.
Circulation: 2,500
Available in microform: No
Subscription address: Periodici Mondadori, Servizio Abbonamenti, C.P. 1812, 20102 Milan, Italy

ADVERTISING INFORMATION

Advertising accepted: Yes

EDITORIAL DESCRIPTION

Scope: Publishes articles on literature and politics.
Reviews books: Yes
Publishes notes: Yes
Languages accepted: Italian
Prints abstracts: No

SUBMISSION REQUIREMENTS

Author pays submission fee: No
Author pays page charges: No
Length of articles: 3,000-6,000 words
Length of book reviews: 1,500 words
Length of notes: 1,500 words
Number of copies required: 1
Copyright ownership: Author
Rejected manuscripts: Not returned
Time before publication decision: 1-3 mos.
Time between decision and publication: 2 mos.
Number of reviewers: 2
Articles submitted per year: 500
Articles published per year: 50
Book reviews submitted per year: 30
Book reviews published per year: 16
Notes submitted per year: 100
Notes published per year: 16

(2040)
*Nyelv-és Irodalomtudományi Közlemények

Zoltán Szabó, Editor
Editura Academiei Republicii Socialiste Romania
Calea Victoriei 125
71021 Bucharest, Romania

Additional editorial address: Inst. de Linguistică, Academia Română, Str. Racovița 25, 3400 Cluj, Romania
First published: 1958

Sponsoring organization: Academia Română
ISSN: 0567-6223
MLA acronym: NIK

SUBSCRIPTION INFORMATION

Frequency of publication: 2 times/yr.
Available in microform: No
Subscription address: ILEXIM, Departamentul Export-Import Presă, P.O. Box 136-137, str. 13 Decembrie nr. 3, Bucharest, Romania

ADVERTISING INFORMATION

Advertising accepted: No

EDITORIAL DESCRIPTION

Scope: Publishes articles on the science of language and literature, and on Hungarian linguistics, ethnography, and literature.
Reviews books: Yes
Publishes notes: Yes
Languages accepted: Hungarian
Prints abstracts: Yes, in Romanian

SUBMISSION REQUIREMENTS

Restrictions on contributors: None
Length of articles: 12 pp.
Length of book reviews: 4 pp.
Style: Romanian Academy
Number of copies required: 1
Special requirements: Submit original typescript.
Copyright ownership: Editura Academiei
Rejected manuscripts: Returned
Time before publication decision: 3-4 weeks
Time between decision and publication: 2-3 mos.
Number of reviewers: 10
Articles submitted per year: 20-25
Articles published per year: 16-18
Book reviews submitted per year: 20-25
Book reviews published per year: 10-12

(2041)
Nyelvtudományi Közlemények

Péter Hajdú & Károly Rédei, Editors
A Magyar Tudományos Akadémia Nyelvtudományi Intézete
Szentháromság U. 2
1014 Budapest I, Hungary

First published: 1862
Sponsoring organization: Magyar Tudományos Akadémia
ISSN: 0029-6791
MLA acronym: NK

SUBSCRIPTION INFORMATION

Frequency of publication: 2 times/yr.
Circulation: 1,000
Available in microform: No
Subscription address: Központi Hírlap Iroda, József Nádor tér 1, 1900 Budapest V, Hungary
Additional subscription address: Akadémiai Kiadó, Alkotmány U.21, 1363 Budapest V, Hungary

ADVERTISING INFORMATION

Advertising accepted: No

EDITORIAL DESCRIPTION

Scope: Publishes articles on Uralic studies, general linguistics, phonetics, sociolinguistics, psycholinguistics, and applied linguistics.
Reviews books: Yes
Publishes notes: Yes
Languages accepted: Hungarian; German; English; Russian; Finnish; French
Prints abstracts: Yes

SUBMISSION REQUIREMENTS

Restrictions on contributors: None
Author pays submission fee: No
Author pays page charges: No
Length of articles: 1,000-15,000 words
Length of book reviews: 2,000-3,000 words
Length of notes: 500-1,000 words
Style: None
Number of copies required: 1
Special requirements: Submit original typescript, 28 lines to a page, 60 characters to a line.
Copyright ownership: Assigned by author to journal
Rejected manuscripts: Returned
Time before publication decision: 1-2 mos.
Time between decision and publication: 5-8 mos.
Number of reviewers: 3
Articles submitted per year: 35-50
Articles published per year: 15-20
Book reviews submitted per year: 40-60
Book reviews published per year: 25-40
Notes submitted per year: 10-15
Notes published per year: 4-5

(2042)
Nysvenska Studier: Tidskrift för Svensk Stil- och Språkforskning

Lennart Elmevik & Mats Thelander, Editors
Inst. för Nordiska Språk
P.O. Box 513
751 20 Uppsala, Sweden

First published: 1921
Sponsoring organization: Adolf Noreen-sällskapet för Nysvensk Språk & Stilforskning
ISSN: 0345-8768
MLA acronym: NysS

SUBSCRIPTION INFORMATION

Frequency of publication: Annual
Available in microform: No
Subscription address: Almqvist & Wiksell International, P.O. Box 4627, 116 91 Stockholm, Sweden

ADVERTISING INFORMATION

Advertising accepted: No

EDITORIAL DESCRIPTION

Scope: Publishes articles on Swedish language.
Reviews books: No
Languages accepted: Swedish; Danish; Norwegian; English
Prints abstracts: No
Author-anonymous submission: No

SUBMISSION REQUIREMENTS

Restrictions on contributors: None
Author pays submission fee: No
Author pays page charges: No
Length of articles: No restrictions
Style: None
Number of copies required: 1
Copyright ownership: Author
Rejected manuscripts: Returned

(2043)
Objets et Mondes: La Revue du Musée de l'Homme

Jean Guiart, Editor
Musée de l'Homme
Palais de Chaillot
Place du Trocadero et du 11-Novembre
75116 Paris, France

First published: 1961
Sponsoring organization: Musée de l'Homme

ISSN: 0029-7615
MLA acronym: OM

SUBSCRIPTION INFORMATION

Frequency of publication: 4 times/yr.
Circulation: 2,350
Available in microform: No

ADVERTISING INFORMATION

Advertising accepted: Yes

EDITORIAL DESCRIPTION

Scope: Publishes articles on ethnology, anthropology, and prehistory.
Reviews books: Yes
Languages accepted: French; English
Prints abstracts: Yes

SUBMISSION REQUIREMENTS

Author pays submission fee: No
Length of articles: 15 typescript pp.
Length of book reviews: No restrictions
Style: None
Number of copies required: 1
Copyright ownership: Journal
Rejected manuscripts: Returned
Number of reviewers: 10
Articles published per year: 20

(2044)
*Obsidian II: Black Literature in Review

Gerald Barrax & Joyce Pettis, Editors
Dept. of English
Box 8105
North Carolina State Univ.
Raleigh, NC 27695-8105

Telephone: 919 515-3870
First published: 1975
Sponsoring organization: North Carolina State Univ., English Dept.
ISSN: 0888-4412
MLA acronym: Obsidian II

SUBSCRIPTION INFORMATION

Frequency of publication: 3 times/yr. (Spring, Summer, Winter)
Circulation: 400
Available in microform: Yes
Subscription price: $12.00/yr. US; $13.00/yr. Canada; $15.00/yr. elsewhere
Year to which price refers: 1991-92

ADVERTISING INFORMATION

Advertising accepted: Yes
Advertising rates: $100.00/half page; $200.00/full page

EDITORIAL DESCRIPTION

Scope: Devoted to the study and cultivation of works in English by and about black writers worldwide, with scholarly critical articles on all aspects of the literature. Includes book reviews, bibliographies and bibliographical essays, short fiction, poetry, interviews, and very short plays.
Reviews books: Yes
Publishes notes: No
Languages accepted: English
Prints abstracts: No
Author-anonymous submission: No

SUBMISSION REQUIREMENTS

Restrictions on contributors: Primary material (poetry, fiction, etc.) by black writers only; no restrictions on secondary material.
Author pays submission fee: No
Author pays page charges: No

Length of articles: 2,500-3,500 words
Length of book reviews: 1,200-1,400 words
Style: MLA
Number of copies required: 2
Special requirements: Submit original typescript. Author must make a post-acceptance review of manuscript since journal provides no proofs.
Copyright ownership: Journal; reverts to author after publication.
Rejected manuscripts: Returned; enclose return postage.
Time before publication decision: 4-6 weeks
Time between decision and publication: 8-16 mos.
Number of reviewers: 2
Articles submitted per year: 125
Articles published per year: 12-16
Book reviews submitted per year: 25-30
Book reviews published per year: 6-9

(2045)
*Occasional Papers in Language, Literature and Linguistics

Orrin Frink, Editor
1509 47th St.
Des Moines, IA 50311

Telephone: 515 279-2838
Fax: 515 279-2838
First published: 1966
ISSN: 0889-6356
MLA acronym: OPLLL

SUBSCRIPTION INFORMATION

Frequency of publication: Irregular
Circulation: 200
Available in microform: No

ADVERTISING INFORMATION

Advertising accepted: No

EDITORIAL DESCRIPTION

Scope: Publishes professional articles on any topic relating to language, literature, and linguistics.
Reviews books: No
Publishes notes: Yes
Languages accepted: English
Prints abstracts: No
Author-anonymous submission: No

SUBMISSION REQUIREMENTS

Restrictions on contributors: None
Author pays submission fee: No
Author pays page charges: No
Length of articles: 800-1,200 words
Style: MLA
Number of copies required: 1
Special requirements: Submit double-spaced typescript.
Copyright ownership: Author
Rejected manuscripts: Returned
Time before publication decision: 3 mos.
Time between decision and publication: 3 mos.
Number of reviewers: 3
Articles submitted per year: 4
Articles published per year: 2

(2046)
*Occasional Papers on Linguistics

James E. Redden, Editor
Dept. of Linguistics
Southern Illinois Univ.
Carbondale, IL 62901

Telephone: 618 536-3385
Fax: 618 453-6527
E-mail: GA3606@SIUCVMB (Bitnet)
First published: 1976

Sponsoring organization: Southern Illinois Univ., Carbondale, Dept. of Linguistics
ISSN: 0885-5773
MLA acronym: OPLing

SUBSCRIPTION INFORMATION

Frequency of publication: Irregular
Circulation: 500
Available in microform: No
Subscription price: $14.00/yr.
Year to which price refers: 1991

ADVERTISING INFORMATION

Advertising accepted: No

EDITORIAL DESCRIPTION

Scope: Publishes monographs on any aspect of linguistics and language teaching.
Reviews books: No
Publishes notes: No
Languages accepted: English; Spanish; French; German
Prints abstracts: No
Author-anonymous submission: No

SUBMISSION REQUIREMENTS

Restrictions on contributors: Monographs are published by invitation only.
Author pays submission fee: No
Author pays page charges: No
Length of books: 30 pp. maximum
Style: MLA; Linguistic Soc. of America
Number of copies required: 1
Special requirements: Manuscripts must be camera-ready. Photos are not accepted.
Rejected manuscripts: Returned
Time before publication decision: 6 mos.
Time between decision and publication: 6 mos.
Number of reviewers: 2
Articles submitted per year: 15
Articles published per year: 15
Books published per year: 1-2

(2047)
*Oceania

J. R. Beckett & F. C. Merlan, Editors
Oceania Publications
116 Darlington Rd.-H.42
Univ. of Sydney
Sydney, NSW 2006, Australia

Telephone: (61) 2 6922666
Fax: (61) 2 6924293
First published: 1930
Sponsoring organization: Univ. of Sydney
ISSN: 0029-8077
MLA acronym: Oceania

SUBSCRIPTION INFORMATION

Frequency of publication: 4 times/yr.
Circulation: 1,050
Available in microform: Yes
Subscription price: $50.00/yr. institutions; $45.00/yr. individuals
Year to which price refers: 1992

ADVERTISING INFORMATION

Advertising accepted: Yes
Advertising rates: $95.00/half page; $190.00/full page

EDITORIAL DESCRIPTION

Scope: Publishes original contributions in the field of social and cultural anthropology. Its primary regional orientation is to the indigenous peoples of Australia, Melanesia, Polynesia, Micronesia, and Insular Southeast Asia.
Reviews books: Yes
Publishes notes: Yes
Languages accepted: English
Prints abstracts: Yes

Author-anonymous submission: Yes

SUBMISSION REQUIREMENTS

Restrictions on contributors: None
Author pays submission fee: No
Author pays page charges: No
Length of articles: 10,000 words
Length of book reviews: 1,000 words
Length of notes: 200 words
Number of copies required: 2
Special requirements: Submit original double-spaced typescript and 1 carbon copy or a 5 1/4 in. IBM-compatible diskette using Microsoft Word or Wordstar.
Copyright ownership: Editor
Time before publication decision: 1 mo.
Time between decision and publication: 6 mos.
Number of reviewers: 2-3
Articles submitted per year: 30
Articles published per year: 16-20
Book reviews submitted per year: 50
Book reviews published per year: 36-38
Notes submitted per year: 20
Notes published per year: 15

(2048)
*Oceanic Linguistics

Byron W. Bender, Editor
Dept. of Linguistics
Univ. of Hawaii
1890 East-West Rd.
Honolulu, HI 96822

Telephone: 808 956-8374
Fax: 808 956-9166
E-mail: Oceanic@uhunix.uhcc.hawaii.edu
First published: 1962
Sponsoring organization: Univ. of Hawaii
ISSN: 0029-8115
MLA acronym: OcL

SUBSCRIPTION INFORMATION

Frequency of publication: 2 times/yr.
Circulation: 200
Available in microform: Yes
Subscription price: $24.00/yr. institutions US & Canada; $28.00/yr. institutions elsewhere; $18.00/yr. individuals US & Canada; $19.00/yr. individuals elsewhere
Year to which price refers: 1993
Subscription address: Univ. of Hawaii Press, Journals Dept., 2840 Kolowalu St., Honolulu, HI 96822-1888
Subscription telephone: 808 956-8834

ADVERTISING INFORMATION

Advertising accepted: Yes

EDITORIAL DESCRIPTION

Scope: The journal was created at the request of the Panel on Research Needs in Pacific Languages of the Tenth Pacific Science Congress. Its object is to provide competent information and better communication across national boundaries on current research bearing on the languages of the Oceanic area. The "oceanic area" is defined for the purposes of the journal as the combined Austronesian, Papuan, and Australian language areas.
Reviews books: Yes
Publishes notes: Yes
Languages accepted: English
Prints abstracts: Yes
Author-anonymous submission: Yes

SUBMISSION REQUIREMENTS

Restrictions on contributors: None
Author pays submission fee: No
Author pays page charges: No
Length of articles: No restrictions
Length of book reviews: No restrictions
Length of notes: No restrictions
Style: Linguistic Soc. of America

Number of copies required: 3
Special requirements: Submit original typescript and 2 copies including an abstract of 100-300 words. Electronic manuscripts are encouraged.
Copyright ownership: Journal
Rejected manuscripts: Not returned
Time before publication decision: 4 mos.
Time between decision and publication: 6 mos.
Number of reviewers: 1-2
Articles submitted per year: 30
Articles published per year: 8-10
Book reviews published per year: 5-10
Notes published per year: 0-2

(2049)
*Oceanic Linguistics Special Publications

Byron W. Bender, George W. Grace, Howard P. McKaughan, Albert J. Schütz, & Donald M. Topping, Editors
Dept. of Linguistics
Univ. of Hawaii
1890 East-West Rd.
Honolulu, HI 96822

Telephone: 808 956-8374
Fax: 808 956-9166
E-mail: Oceanic@uhunix.uhcc.hawaii.edu
First published: 1966
Sponsoring organization: Univ. of Hawaii
ISSN: 0078-3188
MLA acronym: OLSP

SUBSCRIPTION INFORMATION

Frequency of publication: Irregular
Circulation: 500-1,000
Available in microform: No
Subscription address: Univ. of Hawaii Press, Book Orders, 2840 Kolowalu St., Honolulu, HI 96822
Subscription telephone: 808 956-8697

ADVERTISING INFORMATION

Advertising accepted: No

EDITORIAL DESCRIPTION

Scope: Consists of independently subsidized studies on current research bearing on the languages of the Oceanic area.
Reviews books: No
Publishes notes: No
Languages accepted: English
Prints abstracts: No
Author-anonymous submission: No

SUBMISSION REQUIREMENTS

Restrictions on contributors: None
Author pays submission fee: No
Author pays page charges: No
Length of books: No restrictions
Style: Linguistic Soc. of America
Number of copies required: 2
Copyright ownership: Univ. of Hawaii Press
Rejected manuscripts: Returned
Time before publication decision: 4 mos.
Time between decision and publication: 10-12 mos.
Number of reviewers: 2 minimum
Books published per year: 1-2

(2050)
*October

Joan Copjec, Rosalind Krauss, Annette Michelson, Yve-Alain Bois, Benjamin H. D. Buchloh, Hal Foster, Denis Hollier, & John Rajchman, Editors
19 Union Square West, 12th Floor
New York, NY 10003

Telephone: 212 255-5537

Fax: 212 633-0144
ISSN: 0162-2870
MLA acronym: October

SUBSCRIPTION INFORMATION

Frequency of publication: 4 times/yr. (Summer, Fall, Winter, Spring)
Circulation: 3,600
Available in microform: Yes
Subscription price: $75.00/yr. institutions; $30.00/yr. individuals; $20.00/yr. students & retirees
Subscription address: MIT Press Journals, 55 Hayward St., Cambridge, MA 02142
Subscription telephone: 617 253-2889
Subscription fax: 617 258-6779

ADVERTISING INFORMATION

Advertising accepted: Yes
Advertising rates: $200.00/half page; $300.00/full page

EDITORIAL DESCRIPTION

Scope: Publishes articles on art, theory, criticism, and politics.
Reviews books: Occasionally
Publishes notes: No
Languages accepted: English
Author-anonymous submission: No

SUBMISSION REQUIREMENTS

Author pays submission fee: No
Author pays page charges: No
Length of articles: 4,000-5,000 words
Style: Chicago
Number of copies required: 2
Copyright ownership: Massachusetts Inst. of Technology
Rejected manuscripts: Returned; enclose SASE.
Time before publication decision: 3-6 mos.
Time between decision and publication: 3-6 mos.
Number of reviewers: 3
Articles submitted per year: 90-100
Articles published per year: 20-24

(2051)
*Odense University Studies in English

Stefan B. Andersen, Editor
English Inst.
Odense Univ.
Campusvej 55
5230 Odense M, Denmark

Telephone: (45) 66 157999
Fax: (45) 66 158162
First published: 1969
Sponsoring organization: Odense Univ.
ISSN: 0078-3293
MLA acronym: OUSE

SUBSCRIPTION INFORMATION

Frequency of publication: Irregular
Available in microform: No
Subscription address: Odense Univ. Press, Campusvej 55, 5230 Odense M, Denmark

ADVERTISING INFORMATION

Advertising accepted: No

EDITORIAL DESCRIPTION

Scope: Publishes monographs on English language and literature.
Reviews books: No
Publishes notes: Yes
Languages accepted: English; Danish
Prints abstracts: No
Author-anonymous submission: No

SUBMISSION REQUIREMENTS

Restrictions on contributors: Contributors are primarily Odense Univ. staff.
Author pays submission fee: No
Author pays page charges: No
Length of books: No restrictions
Style: None
Number of copies required: 1
Copyright ownership: Author
Rejected manuscripts: Returned
Time before publication decision: 5 mos.
Time between decision and publication: 5 mos.
Books published per year: 1

(2052)
*Odra

Mieczysław Orski, Editor
Podwale 64
Wrocław 50-010, Poland

First published: 1961
Sponsoring organization: Polish Ministry of Culture
ISSN: 0472-5182
MLA acronym: Odra

SUBSCRIPTION INFORMATION

Frequency of publication: 11 times/yr.
Circulation: 5,500
Available in microform: No
Subscription price: $33.00/yr.
Year to which price refers: 1992

ADVERTISING INFORMATION

Advertising accepted: Yes

EDITORIAL DESCRIPTION

Reviews books: Yes
Publishes notes: Yes
Languages accepted: Polish
Prints abstracts: No

SUBMISSION REQUIREMENTS

Restrictions on contributors: None
Author pays submission fee: No
Author pays page charges: No
Length of articles: 4-30 pp. (30 lines/page)
Length of book reviews: 3-4 pp. (30 lines/page)
Length of notes: 1-3 pp.
Style: None
Number of copies required: 1
Copyright ownership: Publisher
Rejected manuscripts: Not returned
Time between decision and publication: 6 weeks minimum
Book reviews published per year: 70

(2053)
*Odù: A Journal of West African Studies

Biodun Adediran, Editor
Dept. of History
Obáfẹmi Awólọwọ Univ.
Ile-Ifẹ, Nigeria

Telephone: (234) 36 230290 ext. 2474
First published: 1964
Sponsoring organization: Obáfẹmi Awólọwọ Univ.
ISSN: 0029-8522
MLA acronym: Odù

SUBSCRIPTION INFORMATION

Frequency of publication: 2 times/yr. (Jan., July)
Circulation: 1,000-2,000
Available in microform: No
Subscription price: 35 N ($13.00, £8.00)/yr.
Year to which price refers: 1991
Subscription address: Periodicals Dept., Obáfẹmi Awólọwọ Univ., Ile-Ifẹ, Nigeria
Subscription telephone: (234) 36 230290 ext. 2955

ADVERTISING INFORMATION

Advertising accepted: No

EDITORIAL DESCRIPTION

Scope: Covers the entire spectrum of West African studies with an emphasis on intensive local research. Publishes papers which, though of particular regional reference, may serve as source material for more comprehensive studies. Thus the journal is both a contribution to international African studies, and an organ of local research.
Reviews books: Yes
Publishes notes: Yes
Languages accepted: English; French
Prints abstracts: No
Author-anonymous submission: Yes

SUBMISSION REQUIREMENTS

Restrictions on contributors: None
Author pays submission fee: No
Author pays page charges: No
Length of articles: 3,000 words minimum
Length of book reviews: 1,000 words
Length of notes: 3,000 words maximum
Style: Journal
Number of copies required: 2
Special requirements: Submit original typescript.
Copyright ownership: Assigned by author to journal
Rejected manuscripts: Returned; enclose return postage or international reply coupons.
Time before publication decision: 3 mos.
Time between decision and publication: 15-18 mos.
Number of reviewers: 3 plus Editorial Board
Articles submitted per year: 80-100
Articles published per year: 12-14
Book reviews submitted per year: 70-110
Book reviews published per year: 8-16
Notes submitted per year: 20-40
Notes published per year: 2-6

(2054)
*Oeuvres & Critiques: Revue Internationale d'Etude de la Réception Critique d'Etude des Oeuvres Littéraires de Langue Française

Wolfgang Leiner, Editor
Romanisches Seminar
Univ. Tübingen
7400 Tübingen, Germany

Additional editorial address: 67 avenue Parmentier, 75011 Paris, France
First published: 1976
Sponsoring organization: Centre National des Lettres, Paris
ISSN: 0338-1900
MLA acronym: O&C

SUBSCRIPTION INFORMATION

Frequency of publication: 2 times/yr.
Circulation: 700
Available in microform: No
Subscription address: Gunter Narr Verlag, P.O. Box 2567, 7400 Tübingen, Germany

ADVERTISING INFORMATION

Advertising accepted: Yes

EDITORIAL DESCRIPTION

Scope: Publishes articles and bibliographies concerning critical and interpretative studies of Francophone authors from the Middle Ages to the present. Also includes articles on specific authors.
Reviews books: Yes
Publishes notes: No
Languages accepted: English; French; German
Prints abstracts: No
Author-anonymous submission: No

SUBMISSION REQUIREMENTS

Restrictions on contributors: None
Author pays submission fee: No
Author pays page charges: No
Length of articles: 20 pp. maximum
Length of book reviews: 3-4 pp.
Style: MLA
Number of copies required: 2
Copyright ownership: Journal
Rejected manuscripts: Returned; enclose return postage.
Time before publication decision: 2 mos.
Time between decision and publication: 1 yr.
Number of reviewers: 2-4
Articles submitted per year: 40
Articles published per year: 25
Book reviews submitted per year: 10-15
Book reviews published per year: 10

(2055)
Ogam: Tradition Celtique

Christian J. Guyonvarc'h, Editor
Soc. des Amis de la Tradition Celtique
Postbox 574
35007 Rennes Cedex, France

First published: 1962
Sponsoring organization: Amis de la Tradition Celtique
ISSN: 0030-0691
MLA acronym: Ogam

SUBSCRIPTION INFORMATION

Frequency of publication: 4 times/yr.
Circulation: 1,800

EDITORIAL DESCRIPTION

Reviews books: Yes
Languages accepted: English; French; German
Prints abstracts: Yes

SUBMISSION REQUIREMENTS

Author pays submission fee: No
Author pays page charges: No
Length of articles: 10-20 pp. typescript
Length of book reviews: 1-2 pp.
Number of copies required: 1
Copyright ownership: Author & journal
Time before publication decision: 2-3 weeks
Articles published per year: 20-25
Book reviews published per year: 3

(2056)
*The Ohio Review

Wayne Dodd, Editor
Ellis Hall 209C
Ohio Univ.
Athens, OH 45701-2979

First published: 1959
Sponsoring organization: Ohio Univ.
ISSN: 0360-1013
MLA acronym: OhR

SUBSCRIPTION INFORMATION

Frequency of publication: 3 times/yr.
Circulation: 2,000
Available in microform: No
Subscription price: $12.00/yr., $30.00/3 yrs.
Year to which price refers: 1991-92

ADVERTISING INFORMATION

Advertising accepted: Yes
Advertising rates: $100.00/half page; $175.00/full page

EDITORIAL DESCRIPTION

Scope: A general literary review publishing fiction, poetry, and criticism. Its major focus is contemporary poetics and fiction.
Reviews books: Yes
Publishes notes: No
Languages accepted: English
Prints abstracts: No
Author-anonymous submission: No

SUBMISSION REQUIREMENTS

Restrictions on contributors: None
Author pays submission fee: No
Author pays page charges: No
Length of articles: No restrictions
Length of book reviews: No restrictions
Style: MLA
Number of copies required: 1
Copyright ownership: Journal; reverts to author after publication
Rejected manuscripts: Returned; enclose SASE.
Time before publication decision: 1 mo.
Time between decision and publication: 6-9 mos.
Number of reviewers: 2-3
Articles submitted per year: 16,000
Articles published per year: 4-6
Book reviews published per year: 15-20

(2057)
*Ojáncano: Revista de Literatura Española

Stacey L. Dolgin & Pablo Gil Casado, Editors
Dept. of Romance Languages
Univ. of Georgia
Athens, GA 30602

Additional editorial address: Pablo Gil Casado, C.B. 3170, Dept. of Romance Languages, Univ. of North Carolina, Chapel Hill, NC 27599
Telephone: 706 542-5779; 919 962-0113
Fax: 706 542-3287
First published: 1988
Sponsoring organization: Concejalía de Cultura, Excelentísimo Ayuntamiento de Santander, Cantabria
ISSN: 0899-983X
MLA acronym: Ojáncano

SUBSCRIPTION INFORMATION

Frequency of publication: 2 times/yr.
Circulation: 250
Available in microform: No
Subscription price: $40.00/yr. institutions; $18.00/yr. individuals
Year to which price refers: 1991-92

ADVERTISING INFORMATION

Advertising accepted: Yes

EDITORIAL DESCRIPTION

Scope: Publishes studies on 18th-, 19th-, and 20th-century Spanish literature. Occasionally will also publish work on other periods and on Latin American literature.
Reviews books: Yes
Publishes notes: Yes
Languages accepted: Spanish; English
Prints abstracts: No
Author-anonymous submission: No

SUBMISSION REQUIREMENTS

Author pays submission fee: No
Author pays page charges: No
Length of articles: 16-25 pp.
Length of book reviews: 4-5 pp.
Length of notes: 8-10 pp.
Style: Latest MLA, but Spanish must follow normal Spanish rules for capitalization and punctuation.
Number of copies required: 2
Special requirements: Manuscript must be unpublished. Submit quality print double-spaced typescript with clear accents and punctuation. Photographs, drawing, etc. are accepted only in black and white. Author must sign statement assuming responsibility for any liability due to copyright infringement or malicious statements.
Copyright ownership: Editor
Rejected manuscripts: Returned; enclose return postage.
Time before publication decision: 2-6 weeks
Time between decision and publication: 6-12 mos.
Number of reviewers: 2-3
Articles submitted per year: 25-35
Articles published per year: 15-18
Book reviews submitted per year: 6-10
Book reviews published per year: 6-8
Notes submitted per year: 4-6
Notes published per year: 2-3

(2058)
Okike: An African Journal of New Writing

Ossie Enekwe, Editor
P.O. Box 53
Nsukka
Enugu State, Nigeria

First published: 1971
Sponsoring organization: Okike Arts Centre
ISSN: 0331-0566
MLA acronym: Okike

SUBSCRIPTION INFORMATION

Frequency of publication: 2 times/yr.
Circulation: 1,000
Available in microform: No

ADVERTISING INFORMATION

Advertising accepted: Yes

EDITORIAL DESCRIPTION

Scope: Publishes African literature and criticism including new poetry and short fiction.
Reviews books: Yes
Publishes notes: Yes
Languages accepted: English
Prints abstracts: No
Author-anonymous submission: Yes

SUBMISSION REQUIREMENTS

Restrictions on contributors: None
Author pays submission fee: No
Author pays page charges: No
Length of articles: 3,000 words
Length of book reviews: 1,500 words
Style: MLA
Number of copies required: 2
Copyright ownership: Author
Rejected manuscripts: Destroyed unless return postage enclosed.
Time before publication decision: 1 mo.
Time between decision and publication: 6 mos.
Number of reviewers: 3
Articles submitted per year: 500
Articles published per year: 60
Book reviews submitted per year: 25
Book reviews published per year: 10

(2059)
*Oklahoma Project for Discourse and Theory

Robert Con Davis & Ronald Schleifer, Editors
760 Van Vleet Oval
Norman, OK 73019

Additional editorial address: Univ. of Oklahoma Press, 1005 Asp Ave., Norman, OK 73019
Telephone: 405 325-2908; 405 325-5111
First published: 1987
Sponsoring organization: Univ. of Oklahoma
MLA acronym: OPDT

SUBSCRIPTION INFORMATION

Frequency of publication: Irregular
Circulation: 750-1,000

ADVERTISING INFORMATION

Advertising accepted: No

EDITORIAL DESCRIPTION

Scope: Aims at integrating literary and cultural criticism within the study of a wide range of disciplines. Offers a forum for the investigation of post-Freudian, post-Sausserean, and post-Marxist questions concerning cultural theory and the discourses that constitute it.
Reviews books: No
Publishes notes: No
Languages accepted: English
Prints abstracts: No
Author-anonymous submission: No

SUBMISSION REQUIREMENTS

Author pays submission fee: No
Author pays page charges: No
Length of books: 250-300 words
Number of copies required: 1
Special requirements: Manuscripts written in languages other than English will be translated.
Copyright ownership: Univ. of Oklahoma Press
Rejected manuscripts: Returned at author's request
Time before publication decision: 4-5 mos.
Time between decision and publication: 6-12 mos.
Number of reviewers: 2
Books submitted per year: 15
Books published per year: 3-4

(2060)
Oktiabr': Literaturno-Khudozhestvennyĭ i Obshchestvenno-Politicheskiĭ Zhurnal

A. A. Anan'ev, Editor
ul. Pravda, 11
125124 GSP Moscow A-124, Russia

First published: 1924
Sponsoring organization: Soiuz Pisateleĭ R.S.F.S.R.
ISSN: 0030-1957
MLA acronym: Okt

SUBSCRIPTION INFORMATION

Frequency of publication: 12 times/yr.
Circulation: 195,000

EDITORIAL DESCRIPTION

Reviews books: Yes
Languages accepted: Russian
Prints abstracts: No

(2061)
*Old English Newsletter

Paul E. Szarmach, Carl T. Berkhout, & Joseph B. Trahean, Jr., Editors
Center for Medieval & Early Renaissance Studies
P.O. Box 6000
State Univ. of New York
Binghamton, NY 13902-6000

Telephone: 607 777-2730
Fax: 607 777-4000
E-mail: PSZARMAC@BINGVAXA.BITNET
First published: 1967
Sponsoring organization: State Univ. of New York, Binghamton, Center for Medieval & Early Renaissance Studies; MLA, Division on Old English Language & Literature
ISSN: 0030-1973
MLA acronym: OENews

SUBSCRIPTION INFORMATION

Frequency of publication: 4 times/yr. (Fall, Winter, Spring, Summer)
Circulation: 950
Available in microform: No
Subscription price: $10.00/yr. institutions; $5.00/yr. individuals
Year to which price refers: 1992

ADVERTISING INFORMATION

Advertising accepted: No

EDITORIAL DESCRIPTION

Scope: Publishes news about research and teaching in Old English; includes an annual bibliography and review.
Reviews books: Yes
Publishes notes: Yes
Languages accepted: English
Prints abstracts: No
Author-anonymous submission: Yes

SUBMISSION REQUIREMENTS

Restrictions on contributors: Reviews are published by invitation.
Author pays submission fee: No
Author pays page charges: No
Length of articles: 10 pp. maximum
Style: MLA (2nd ed.)
Number of copies required: 2
Copyright ownership: Center for Medieval & Early Renaissance Studies
Rejected manuscripts: Returned
Time before publication decision: 3 mos.
Time between decision and publication: 6 mos.
Number of reviewers: 2
Articles submitted per year: 10
Articles published per year: 6
Notes submitted per year: 4
Notes published per year: 2

(2062)
*Old English Newsletter, Subsidia

Paul E. Szarmach, Editor
CEMERS
State Univ. of New York
P.O. Box 6000
Binghamton, NY 13902-6000

Telephone: 607 777-2730
Fax: 607 777-4000
E-mail: BITNET: PSZARMAC@BINGVAXC (ANSAXNET)
First published: 1978
Sponsoring organization: Center for Medieval & Early Renaissance Studies (CEMERS), State Univ. of New York at Binghamton
ISSN: 0739-8549
MLA acronym: OENS

SUBSCRIPTION INFORMATION

Frequency of publication: Annual
Circulation: 70
Available in microform: No
Subscription price: $3.00/yr.
Year to which price refers: 1992

ADVERTISING INFORMATION

Advertising accepted: No

EDITORIAL DESCRIPTION

Scope: Publishes *ancillae* on teaching and research in the field of Anglo-Saxon studies.
Reviews books: No
Publishes notes: No
Languages accepted: English
Prints abstracts: No
Author-anonymous submission: Yes

SUBMISSION REQUIREMENTS

Author pays submission fee: No
Author pays page charges: No
Length of articles: 12,000 words maximum
Style: MLA (2nd ed.)
Number of copies required: 2
Special requirements: Submit camera-ready copy.
Copyright ownership: CEMERS
Rejected manuscripts: Returned
Number of reviewers: 2-3
Books published per year: 1

(2063)
*The Old Northwest: A Journal of Regional Life and Letters

Robert R. Kettler, Jerome H. Rosenberg, Andrew R. L. Cayton, & Guy Szuberla, Editors
302 Bachelor Hall
Miami Univ.
Oxford, OH 45056

Telephone: 513 529-5253
First published: 1975
Sponsoring organization: Miami Univ.
ISSN: 0360-5531
MLA acronym: ON

SUBSCRIPTION INFORMATION

Frequency of publication: 4 times/yr. (Spring, Summer, Fall, Winter)
Circulation: 700
Available in microform: Yes
Subscription price: $15.00/yr. institutions; $10.00/yr. individuals US; $11.00/yr. individuals Canada; $12.00/yr. individuals elsewhere
Year to which price refers: 1991

ADVERTISING INFORMATION

Advertising accepted: No

EDITORIAL DESCRIPTION

Scope: Devoted to study of the culture, early to recent, of the area in the Old Northwest Territory of the United States and the states which developed from it, including Ohio, Indiana, Illinois, Michigan, and Wisconsin.
Reviews books: Yes
Publishes notes: Yes
Languages accepted: English
Prints abstracts: No
Author-anonymous submission: Yes

SUBMISSION REQUIREMENTS

Restrictions on contributors: None
Author pays submission fee: No
Author pays page charges: No
Length of articles: 5,000-10,000 words
Length of book reviews: 600-1,000 words
Style: MLA

Number of copies required: 1
Copyright ownership: Assigned by author to journal
Rejected manuscripts: Returned
Time before publication decision: 2 mos.
Time between decision and publication: 3-6 mos.
Number of reviewers: 3
Articles submitted per year: 60-75
Articles published per year: 20
Book reviews submitted per year: 70
Book reviews published per year: 60
Notes submitted per year: 10
Notes published per year: 10

(2064)
*Olifant: A Publication of the Société Rencesvals, American-Canadian Branch

Robert Francis Cook, Editor
Dept. of French
Univ. of Virginia
Charlottesville, VA 22903

Additional editorial address: Send books for review to: Catherine Jones, Dept. of Romance Languages, Univ. of Georgia, Athens, GA 30602
Telephone: 804 924-4627
E-mail: Rfc@virginia.edu
First published: 1973
Sponsoring organization: Soc. Rencesvals, American-Canadian Branch
ISSN: 0381-9132
MLA acronym: Olifant

SUBSCRIPTION INFORMATION

Frequency of publication: 2 times/yr. (Fall, Spring)
Circulation: 400
Available in microform: No
Subscription price: $18.00/yr. institutions US & Canada; $24.00/yr. institutions elsewhere; $12.00/yr. individuals US; $13.50/yr. individuals elsewhere
Year to which price refers: 1993

ADVERTISING INFORMATION

Advertising accepted: No

EDITORIAL DESCRIPTION

Scope: Devoted to the promotion and the study of Medieval epic literature in the various Romance languages.
Reviews books: Yes
Publishes notes: Yes
Languages accepted: English; French; Spanish; German
Prints abstracts: No
Author-anonymous submission: No

SUBMISSION REQUIREMENTS

Restrictions on contributors: Reviews are solicited.
Author pays submission fee: No
Author pays page charges: No
Length of articles: No restrictions
Length of book reviews: No restrictions
Length of notes: No restrictions
Style: MLA
Number of copies required: 3
Special requirements: Submit original typescript plus 2 copies. Submission on IBM- or Macintosh-compatible diskette is preferred.
Copyright ownership: Editor
Rejected manuscripts: Returned
Time before publication decision: 4 mos.
Time between decision and publication: 4 mos.
Number of reviewers: 3
Articles submitted per year: 30
Articles published per year: 10-12
Book reviews published per year: 12

(2065)
*Onoma: Bibliographical and Information Bulletin

W. van Langendonck, Editor
International Centre of Onomastics
Blijde-Inkomststraat 21
3000 Leuven, Belgium

Telephone: (32) 16 284819
Fax: (32) 16 285025
First published: 1950
Sponsoring organization: International Committee of Onomastic Sciences
ISSN: 0078-463X
MLA acronym: Onoma

SUBSCRIPTION INFORMATION

Frequency of publication: 1-2 times/yr.
Circulation: 800
Available in microform: No
Subscription price: 1,500 BF/yr.
Year to which price refers: 1992
Subscription address: Editions Peeters, P.O. Box 41, 3000 Leuven, Belgium
Subscription telephone: (32) 16 488102
Subscription fax: (32) 16 481486

ADVERTISING INFORMATION

Advertising accepted: No

EDITORIAL DESCRIPTION

Scope: Promotes international collaboration in the field of onomastics. Publishes annual bibliography and short reports.
Reviews books: No
Publishes notes: Yes
Languages accepted: English; French; German
Prints abstracts: No
Author-anonymous submission: Yes

SUBMISSION REQUIREMENTS

Restrictions on contributors: None
Author pays submission fee: No
Author pays page charges: No
Length of articles: 10-20 printed pp.
Length of notes: 2-3 pp.
Style: None
Number of copies required: 2
Special requirements: Submit original typescript.
Copyright ownership: Assigned by author to journal
Rejected manuscripts: Not returned
Time before publication decision: 2 mos.
Time between decision and publication: 1 yr.
Number of reviewers: 2
Articles submitted per year: 5
Articles published per year: 2
Notes submitted per year: 5
Notes published per year: 5

(2066)
*Onomastica: Pismo Poświęcone Nazewnictwu Geograficznemu i Osobowemu

Kazimierz Rymut, Editor
Inst. Języka Polskiego PAN
ul. Straszewskiego, 27
31-113 Cracow, Poland

First published: 1955
Sponsoring organization: Polska Akademia Nauk, Komitet Językoznawstwa
ISSN: 0078-4648
MLA acronym: Onomastica

SUBSCRIPTION INFORMATION

Frequency of publication: Annual
Circulation: 440
Available in microform: No
Subscription address: Ars Polona, Krakowskie Przedmieście 7, 00-068 Warsaw, Poland
Additional subscription address: Earlscourt Pub., Ltd., 130 Shepherd Bush Center, London W12, England

ADVERTISING INFORMATION

Advertising accepted: No

EDITORIAL DESCRIPTION

Scope: Publishes treatises and reviews on geographical and personal names.
Reviews books: Yes
Languages accepted: Polish; German; Bulgarian; English; Russian; Serbo-Croatian; French; Czech; Slovak; Ukrainian
Prints abstracts: Yes
Author-anonymous submission: No

SUBMISSION REQUIREMENTS

Restrictions on contributors: None
Author pays submission fee: No
Author pays page charges: No
Length of articles: 20 pp. maximum
Length of book reviews: 5 pp.
Style: MLA
Number of copies required: 2
Special requirements: Submit original typescript, 1 copy, and a 200-word abstract in the language of the paper.
Copyright ownership: Zakład Narodowy im. Ossolińskich
Rejected manuscripts: Returned at author's request
Time before publication decision: 1 yr.
Time between decision and publication: 1 yr.
Number of reviewers: 1-2
Articles submitted per year: 30
Articles published per year: 25
Book reviews submitted per year: 15
Book reviews published per year: 10

(2067)
*Onomastica Canadiana

Frank Hamlin, Editor
Dept. of French
Univ. of British Columbia
Vancouver BC V6T 1Z1, Canada

Telephone: 604 822-2879
Fax: 604 822-6675
E-mail: Frank—Hamlin@mtsg.ubc.ca
First published: 1951
Sponsoring organization: Canadian Soc. for the Study of Names
ISSN: 0078-4656
MLA acronym: OnomasticaC

SUBSCRIPTION INFORMATION

Frequency of publication: 2 times/yr.
Circulation: 250
Available in microform: No
Subscription price: C$20.00 ($18.00)/yr. institutions; C$25.00 ($25.00)/yr. individuals US & Canada; C$30.00/yr. individuals elsewhere; C$20.00/yr. ($20.00)/yr. retirees US & Canada; C$25.00/yr. retirees elsewhere; C$15.00 ($15.00)/yr. students US & Canada; C$20.00/yr. students elsewhere
Year to which price refers: 1992
Subscription address: W. P. Ahrens, Secretary-Treasurer, Canadian Soc. for the Study of Names, Dept. of Languages, Literatures, & Linguistics, South 561 Ross Bldg., York Univ., 4700 Keele St., North York, ON M3J 1P3, Canada
Subscription telephone: 416 736-5016 ext. 6291
Subscription fax: 416 736-5735

ADVERTISING INFORMATION

Advertising accepted: No

EDITORIAL DESCRIPTION

Scope: Promotes the study of place names and personal names in Canada and abroad as well as the exchange of ideas among onomatologists, toponymists, and scholars in the related fields of literary onomastics and linguistic aspects of names.
Reviews books: Yes
Publishes notes: Yes
Languages accepted: English; French
Prints abstracts: Yes
Author-anonymous submission: Yes

SUBMISSION REQUIREMENTS

Restrictions on contributors: None
Author pays submission fee: No
Author pays page charges: No
Length of articles: 5,000 words
Length of book reviews: 400-1,200 words
Length of notes: 200 words
Style: The Canadian Style for English; Guide du rédacteur de l'administration fédérale for French
Number of copies required: 2
Special requirements: Maps and photographs must be camera-ready. Submit a 100-word abstract.
Copyright ownership: Author
Rejected manuscripts: Returned
Time before publication decision: 2 mos.
Time between decision and publication: 6 mos.
Number of reviewers: 2-3
Articles submitted per year: 12
Articles published per year: 5-8
Book reviews submitted per year: 8-12
Book reviews published per year: 8-12
Notes submitted per year: 1-2
Notes published per year: 1-2

(2068)
*Onomastický Zpravodaj ČSAV: Zpravodaj Místopisné Komise ČSAV

Miloslava Knappová, Editor
Ústav pro Jazyk Česky ČSAV
Onomastické Oddělení
Valentinská 1
110 46 Prague 1, Czech Republic

Telephone: (42) 2 2320137; (42) 2 2320072
First published: 1960
Historical variations in title: Onomastic Bulletin of the Czechoslovak Academy of Sciences; Bulletin of the Topographic Board of the Czechoslovak Academy of Sciences
Sponsoring organization: Československá Akademie Věd (ČSAV), Ústav pro Jazyk
MLA acronym: OZČSAV

SUBSCRIPTION INFORMATION

Frequency of publication: Annual
Circulation: 350
Available in microform: No
Subscription price: 50 Kčs/yr. Czech Republic & Slovak Republic; $12.00/yr. elsewhere
Year to which price refers: 1991

ADVERTISING INFORMATION

Advertising accepted: No

EDITORIAL DESCRIPTION

Scope: Publishes articles on onomastics. Includes studies on place names, personal names, and literary onomastics.
Reviews books: Yes
Publishes notes: Yes
Languages accepted: Czech; Russian; English; German
Prints abstracts: No
Author-anonymous submission: No

SUBMISSION REQUIREMENTS

Author pays submission fee: No

Author pays page charges: No
Length of articles: 4,200 words maximum
Length of book reviews: 2,100 words maximum
Length of notes: 2,100 words maximum
Number of copies required: 2
Special requirements: Submit original typescript and 1 copy.
Copyright ownership: Publisher
Rejected manuscripts: Returned
Time before publication decision: 3 mos. maximum
Time between decision and publication: 6-24 mos.
Number of reviewers: 4
Articles submitted per year: 25
Articles published per year: 20
Book reviews submitted per year: 3-15
Book reviews published per year: 3-15
Notes submitted per year: 100
Notes published per year: 50-100

(2069)
*Ons Erfdeel: Algemeen-Nederlands Tweemaandelijks Cultureel Tijdschrift

Jozef Deleu, Editor
Murissonstr. 260
8931 Rekkem, Belgium

Additional editorial address: Rijvoortshoef 265, 4941 VJ Raamsdonksveer, Netherlands
Telephone: (32) 56 411201
Fax: (32) 56 414707
First published: 1957
Sponsoring organization: Stichting Ons Erfdeel
ISSN: 0030-2651
MLA acronym: OnsE

SUBSCRIPTION INFORMATION

Frequency of publication: 5 times/yr.
Circulation: 10,000
Available in microform: No
Subscription price: 1,600 BF/yr. Belgium; 92 f/yr. Netherlands; 1,800 BF/yr. elsewhere
Year to which price refers: 1992
Subscription address: Postrekening 000-0907100-53, van Stichting Ons Erfdeel vzw, Murissonstr. 260, 8931 Rekkem, Belgium

ADVERTISING INFORMATION

Advertising accepted: Yes
Advertising rates: 10,000 BF/half page; 14,000 BF/full page

EDITORIAL DESCRIPTION

Scope: Publishes articles on Netherlandic literature and culture.
Reviews books: Yes
Publishes notes: Yes
Languages accepted: Dutch
Prints abstracts: No
Author-anonymous submission: No

SUBMISSION REQUIREMENTS

Restrictions on contributors: None
Author pays submission fee: No
Author pays page charges: No
Length of articles: 2,000-2,500 words
Length of book reviews: 600 words
Length of notes: 600 words
Number of copies required: 1
Copyright ownership: Journal
Rejected manuscripts: Returned
Time before publication decision: 1 mo.
Time between decision and publication: 6 mos.
Number of reviewers: Editor plus Editorial Board
Articles submitted per year: 250
Articles published per year: 150
Book reviews submitted per year: 70
Book reviews published per year: 50
Notes submitted per year: 20
Notes published per year: 15

(2070)
*Ons Geestelijk Erf: Driemaandelijks Tijdschrift voor de Geschiedenis van de Vroomheid in de Nederlanden

F. Hendrickx, Editor
Ruusbroecgenootschap
c/o UFSIA
Prinsstr. 13
2000 Antwerp, Belgium

Telephone: (32) 3 2204367
Fax: (32) 3 2204420
First published: 1927
Sponsoring organization: Universitaire Faculteiten Sint-Ignatius te Antwerpen, Ruusbroecgenootschap Centrum voor Spiritualiteit
ISSN: 0774-2827
MLA acronym: OGE

SUBSCRIPTION INFORMATION

Frequency of publication: 4 times/yr.
Circulation: 400
Available in microform: No
Subscription price: 1,550 BF/yr.
Year to which price refers: 1991
Subscription address: Th. Mertens, USFIA, D-114, Prinsstr. 13, 2000 Antwerp, Belgium
Subscription telephone: (32) 3 2204250

ADVERTISING INFORMATION

Advertising accepted: No

EDITORIAL DESCRIPTION

Scope: Publishes articles on historical and philological study of the spirituality of the Low Countries.
Reviews books: Yes
Publishes notes: No
Languages accepted: Dutch; English; French; Latin; German
Prints abstracts: Yes
Author-anonymous submission: No

SUBMISSION REQUIREMENTS

Restrictions on contributors: None
Author pays submission fee: No
Author pays page charges: No
Length of articles: No restrictions
Length of book reviews: No restrictions
Number of copies required: 2
Special requirements: Submit typescript or IBM-compatible diskette using Microsoft-Word or WordPerfect, accompanied by a printout.
Copyright ownership: Author
Rejected manuscripts: Returned
Time before publication decision: 3 mos.
Number of reviewers: 6
Articles published per year: 14
Book reviews submitted per year: 20
Book reviews published per year: 20

(2071)
Onsei Gakkai Kaihô [Bulletin of the Phonetic Society of Japan]

Masao Ōnishi, Editor
Phonetic Soc. of Japan
11-5-601
Yoyogi 2-chome
Shibuya-ku
Tokyo, 151, Japan

First published: 1926
Sponsoring organization: Phonetic Soc. of Japan
ISSN: 0911-0402
MLA acronym: OGK

SUBSCRIPTION INFORMATION

Frequency of publication: 3 times/yr.
Circulation: 1,500

Available in microform: No

ADVERTISING INFORMATION

Advertising accepted: No

EDITORIAL DESCRIPTION

Scope: Publishes articles on the study of phonetics and its applications.
Reviews books: Yes
Languages accepted: French; English; German; Russian
Prints abstracts: Yes

SUBMISSION REQUIREMENTS

Restrictions on contributors: Contributors must be members of the Phonetic Soc. of Japan.
Author pays submission fee: No
Author pays page charges: No
Length of articles: 2,000 words
Number of copies required: 1
Copyright ownership: Author & publisher
Rejected manuscripts: Not returned
Time before publication decision: 3 mos.
Time between decision and publication: 3 mos.
Number of reviewers: 5
Articles published per year: 15

(2072)
*Ontario Review

Raymond J. Smith & Joyce Carol Oates, Editors
9 Honey Brook Dr.
Princeton, NJ 08540

Telephone: 609 737-7497
First published: 1974
ISSN: 0316-4055
MLA acronym: OntarioR

SUBSCRIPTION INFORMATION

Frequency of publication: 2 times/yr. (Apr., Oct.)
Circulation: 1,000
Available in microform: Yes
Subscription price: $10.00/yr.
Year to which price refers: 1992

ADVERTISING INFORMATION

Advertising accepted: Yes
Advertising rates: $125.00/full page

EDITORIAL DESCRIPTION

Scope: Publishes poetry, fiction, essays, interviews, and graphics, but very few conventional articles.
Reviews books: No
Publishes notes: No
Languages accepted: English
Prints abstracts: No
Author-anonymous submission: No

SUBMISSION REQUIREMENTS

Restrictions on contributors: None
Author pays submission fee: No
Author pays page charges: No
Length of articles: 2,500-5,000 words
Style: None
Number of copies required: 1
Copyright ownership: Assigned by author to journal; reassigned to author after publication
Rejected manuscripts: Returned; enclose SASE.
Time before publication decision: 1 mo.
Time between decision and publication: 8 mos.
Number of reviewers: 2
Articles submitted per year: 50
Articles published per year: 2-3

(2073)
*Oral History: The Journal of the Oral History Society

Paul Thompson, Joanna Bornat, Robert Perks, Al Thomson, & Teresa Watkins, Editors
Dept. of Sociology
Univ. of Essex
Wivenhoe Park
Colchester, Essex CO4 3SQ, England

Additional editorial address: C/o National Sound Archive, 29 Exhibition Rd., London SW7 2AS, England
Telephone: (44) 71 5896603
Fax: (44) 71 8238970
First published: 1969
Sponsoring organization: Oral History Soc.
ISSN: 0143-0955
MLA acronym: OralH

SUBSCRIPTION INFORMATION

Frequency of publication: 2 times/yr.
Circulation: 800-1,000
Available in microform: No
Subscription price: £24.00/yr. institutions; £15.00/yr. (includes membership)
Year to which price refers: 1992
Subscription address: BKT Subscription Services, Lansdowne Mews, 196 High St., Tonbridge, Kent TN9 1EF, England
Subscription telephone: (44) 732 770823
Subscription fax: (44) 732 361708

ADVERTISING INFORMATION

Advertising accepted: Yes
Advertising rates: £25.00/quarter page; £50.00/half page; £95.00/full page

EDITORIAL DESCRIPTION

Scope: Publishes articles, reviews, and reports on all aspects of collecting and documenting oral history, as well as articles based on oral-historical research. Also includes information on community history, school projects, recording equipment, and recall techniques.
Reviews books: Yes
Publishes notes: Yes
Languages accepted: English
Prints abstracts: No
Author-anonymous submission: No

SUBMISSION REQUIREMENTS

Restrictions on contributors: None
Author pays submission fee: No
Author pays page charges: No
Length of articles: 8,000 words maximum
Length of book reviews: 500-1,000 words
Length of notes: 250-3,000 words
Style: Journal
Number of copies required: 2
Special requirements: Submit double-spaced typescript. Author style sheet available.
Copyright ownership: Journal & author
Rejected manuscripts: Returned
Time before publication decision: 2-3 mos.
Time between decision and publication: 1 yr. maximum
Number of reviewers: 3
Articles submitted per year: 50-100
Articles published per year: 30-40
Book reviews submitted per year: 60
Book reviews published per year: 40
Notes published per year: 10-20

(2074)
*The Oral History Review: Journal of the Oral History Association

Michael Frisch, Editor
531 Park Hall
State Univ. of New York at Buffalo
Buffalo, NY 14260

Additional editorial address: Teresa Barnett, Book Review Editor, Oral History Program, 136 Powell Library, Univ. of California at Los Angeles, Los Angeles, CA 90024
Telephone: 716 636-2181
Fax: 716 636-5954
First published: 1973
Sponsoring organization: Oral History Assn.
ISSN: 0094-0798
MLA acronym: OralHR

SUBSCRIPTION INFORMATION

Frequency of publication: 2 times/yr. (Spring, Fall)
Circulation: 1,300
Available in microform: No
Subscription price: $75.00/yr. institutions; $50.00/yr. individuals; $25.00/yr. students
Year to which price refers: 1992
Subscription address: Oral History Assn., 1093 Broxton Ave., no. 720, Los Angeles, CA 90024
Subscription telephone: 310 825-0597
Subscription fax: 310 206-1864

ADVERTISING INFORMATION

Advertising accepted: Yes
Advertising rates: $50.00/quarter page; $90.00/half page; $125.00/full page; $150.00/inside cover or back cover

EDITORIAL DESCRIPTION

Scope: Publishes articles on oral history as a mode of research. Also includes public history essays and reviews reflecting on examples, issues of theory, and projects and practice.
Reviews books: Yes
Publishes notes: No
Languages accepted: English
Prints abstracts: No
Author-anonymous submission: Yes

SUBMISSION REQUIREMENTS

Author pays submission fee: No
Author pays page charges: No
Length of articles: 7,500 words
Length of book reviews: 750 words
Style: Chicago
Number of copies required: 3
Copyright ownership: Oral History Assn.
Time before publication decision: 2 mos.
Time between decision and publication: 6-12 mos.
Number of reviewers: 2-3
Articles submitted per year: 30-40
Articles published per year: 8
Book reviews submitted per year: 70-80
Book reviews published per year: 50-60

(2075)
*Oral Tradition

John Miles Foley, Editor
Center for Studies in Oral Tradition
301 Read Hall
Univ. of Missouri
Columbia, MO 65211

Telephone: 314 882-9720
First published: 1986
Sponsoring organization: Center for Studies in Oral Tradition, Univ. of Missouri
ISSN: 0883-5365
MLA acronym: OT

SUBSCRIPTION INFORMATION

Frequency of publication: 2 times/yr.
Circulation: 500
Available in microform: No
Subscription price: $35.00/yr. institutions; $18.00/yr. individuals
Year to which price refers: 1992
Subscription address: Slavica Publishers, P.O. Box 14388, Columbia, MO 43214

ADVERTISING INFORMATION

Advertising accepted: No

EDITORIAL DESCRIPTION

Scope: Provides a comparative and interdisciplinary focus for studies in oral literature and related fields by publishing research and scholarship on the creation, transmission, and interpretation of all forms of oral traditional expression.
Reviews books: Yes
Publishes notes: Yes
Languages accepted: English
Prints abstracts: No
Author-anonymous submission: Yes

SUBMISSION REQUIREMENTS

Author pays submission fee: No
Author pays page charges: No
Length of articles: 5,000-12,000 words
Length of book reviews: 1,000-3,000 words
Length of notes: 1,000-3,000 words
Style: Journal
Number of copies required: 2
Special requirements: Final version of accepted articles must be submitted on diskette.
Copyright ownership: Author
Rejected manuscripts: Returned
Time before publication decision: 2-3 mos.
Time between decision and publication: 9 mos.
Number of reviewers: 2 minimum
Articles submitted per year: 100
Articles published per year: 15
Book reviews published per year: 10-20

(2076)
*Orbis Litterarum: International Review of Literary Studies

Morten Nøjgaard, Niels Jørgen Skydsgaard, & Bengt Algot Sørensen, Editors
Univ. of Odense
Campusvej 55
5230 Odense M, Denmark

Telephone: (45) 66 158600
Fax: (45) 65 935149
First published: 1950
ISSN: 0105-7510
MLA acronym: OL

SUBSCRIPTION INFORMATION

Frequency of publication: 6 times/yr.
Circulation: 500
Available in microform: No
Subscription price: 948 Dkr/yr.
Year to which price refers: 1991
Subscription address: Munksgaard International Booksellers & Publishers, 35 Nørre Søgade, 1370 Copenhagen K, Denmark

ADVERTISING INFORMATION

Advertising accepted: No

EDITORIAL DESCRIPTION

Scope: Publishes articles on European and American literature. Concentrates on literary theory and the principles of literary history and criticism, and publishes articles of a theoretical nature and analyses of specific works, genres, periods, etc.
Reviews books: Yes

Publishes notes: Yes
Languages accepted: English; French; German
Prints abstracts: Yes
Author-anonymous submission: No

SUBMISSION REQUIREMENTS

Restrictions on contributors: None
Author pays submission fee: No
Author pays page charges: No
Length of articles: 20 printed pp.
Length of book reviews: 2,000 words
Length of notes: 4,000 words
Style: MLA
Number of copies required: 1
Copyright ownership: Publisher
Rejected manuscripts: Returned
Time before publication decision: 6 mos.
Time between decision and publication: 1 yr.
Number of reviewers: 2-3
Articles submitted per year: 50
Articles published per year: 20
Book reviews submitted per year: 60
Book reviews published per year: 15
Notes submitted per year: 5
Notes published per year: 3

(2077)
*Ord och Bild

Johan Öberg, Editor
Box 5102
421 05 V Frölunda, Sweden

Telephone: (46) 31 293957
Fax: (46) 31 293957
First published: 1892
ISSN: 0030-4492
MLA acronym: OB

SUBSCRIPTION INFORMATION

Frequency of publication: 4 times/yr.
Circulation: 3,000
Available in microform: No
Subscription price: 225 Skr/yr.
Year to which price refers: 1992-93

ADVERTISING INFORMATION

Advertising accepted: Yes
Advertising rates: 4,000 Skr/full page

EDITORIAL DESCRIPTION

Scope: Publishes articles on Scandinavian culture, literature, philosophy, and social studies.
Reviews books: Yes
Publishes notes: Yes
Languages accepted: Swedish
Prints abstracts: No
Author-anonymous submission: No

SUBMISSION REQUIREMENTS

Restrictions on contributors: None
Author pays submission fee: No
Author pays page charges: No
Length of articles: 10-14 pp.
Length of book reviews: 6-8 pp.
Length of notes: 1 p.
Number of copies required: 1
Copyright ownership: Author
Rejected manuscripts: Returned
Time before publication decision: 1-2 mos.
Time between decision and publication: 2-4 mos.
Number of reviewers: 3
Articles published per year: 60
Book reviews submitted per year: 15
Book reviews published per year: 10
Notes submitted per year: 15
Notes published per year: 10

(2078)
*Oriens Extremus: Zeitschrift für Sprache, Kunst und Kultur der Länder des Fernen Ostens

Klaus Antoni, Roland Schneider, Hans Stumpfeldt, & Klaus Wenk, Editors
Seminar für Sprache u. Kultur Japans
Univ. Hamburg
v. Melle Park 6/VII
2000 Hamburg 13, Germany

Telephone: (49) 40 41232670
Fax: (49) 40 41234884
First published: 1954
Sponsoring organization: Deutsche Forschungsgemeinschaft
ISSN: 0030-5197
MLA acronym: OE

SUBSCRIPTION INFORMATION

Frequency of publication: 2 times/yr.
Circulation: 350
Available in microform: No
Subscription address: Verlag Otto Harrassowitz, Taunusstr. 6, Postfach 2929, 6200 Wiesbaden, Germany

ADVERTISING INFORMATION

Advertising accepted: No

EDITORIAL DESCRIPTION

Scope: Publishes articles on East Asian languages and culture.
Reviews books: Yes
Publishes notes: No
Languages accepted: English; French; German
Prints abstracts: No

SUBMISSION REQUIREMENTS

Restrictions on contributors: None
Author pays submission fee: No
Author pays page charges: No
Number of copies required: 2
Copyright ownership: Author
Rejected manuscripts: Returned
Time before publication decision: 2 mos.
Time between decision and publication: 4 mos.
Number of reviewers: 3

(2079)
*Orientalia Gandensia

L. De Meyer, Editor
Vakgroepen Oosterse Talen en Culturen
Sint-Pietersplein 6
9000 Ghent, Belgium

First published: 1964
Sponsoring organization: Rijksuniv. te Gent
ISSN: 0474-6627
MLA acronym: OG

SUBSCRIPTION INFORMATION

Frequency of publication: Annual
Available in microform: No
Subscription address: Uitgeverij Peeters, P.B. 41, 3000 Leuven, Belgium

ADVERTISING INFORMATION

Advertising accepted: No

EDITORIAL DESCRIPTION

Scope: Publishes articles on Oriental studies.
Reviews books: No
Publishes notes: Yes
Languages accepted: Dutch; English; French; German
Prints abstracts: No

(2080)
*Orientalia Gothoburgensia

Jan Retsö, Editor
Acta Universitatis Gothoburgensis
P.O. Box 5096
402 22 Göteborg, Sweden

First published: 1969
ISSN: 0078-656X
MLA acronym: OrGoth

SUBSCRIPTION INFORMATION

Frequency of publication: Irregular
Available in microform: No

ADVERTISING INFORMATION

Advertising accepted: No

EDITORIAL DESCRIPTION

Scope: Publishes monographs on Oriental and Arabic languages and literatures.
Reviews books: No
Publishes notes: No
Prints abstracts: Occasionally
Author-anonymous submission: No

SUBMISSION REQUIREMENTS

Copyright ownership: Editor & author

(2081)
*Orientalia Lovaniensia Periodica

G. Pollet, Editor
Katholieke Univ. te Leuven
Dept. Orientalistiek
Blijde Inkomststr. 21
3000 Leuven, Belgium

Telephone: (32) 16 285080
Fax: (32) 16 285025
First published: 1970
Sponsoring organization: Dept. Orientalistiek, Katholieke Univ. te Leuven
ISSN: 0085-4522
MLA acronym: OLP

SUBSCRIPTION INFORMATION

Frequency of publication: Annual
Available in microform: No

ADVERTISING INFORMATION

Advertising accepted: No

EDITORIAL DESCRIPTION

Scope: Publishes Oriental studies.
Reviews books: Yes
Languages accepted: English; French; German
Prints abstracts: No

SUBMISSION REQUIREMENTS

Author pays submission fee: No
Author pays page charges: No
Length of articles: 12,000 words maximum
Length of book reviews: 180 words
Number of copies required: 1
Copyright ownership: Author & journal
Rejected manuscripts: Returned
Time before publication decision: 6 mos.
Time between decision and publication: 8 mos.
Number of reviewers: 1-2
Articles submitted per year: 18
Articles published per year: 15
Book reviews published per year: 6

(2082)
Orientalia Suecana

Dept. of Asian & African Languages
Uppsala Univ.
Box 513
751 20 Uppsala, Sweden

First published: 1952
Sponsoring organization: Humanistisk-samhällsvetenskapliga Forskningsrådet, Stockholm
ISSN: 0078-6578
MLA acronym: OS

SUBSCRIPTION INFORMATION

Frequency of publication: Annual
Circulation: 800
Available in microform: No
Subscription address: Almqvist & Wiksell International, P.O. Box 4627, 116 91 Stockholm, Sweden

ADVERTISING INFORMATION

Advertising accepted: No

EDITORIAL DESCRIPTION

Scope: Publishes linguistic and cultural scientific papers in the oriental field.
Reviews books: Yes
Publishes notes: No
Languages accepted: English; French; German
Prints abstracts: No

SUBMISSION REQUIREMENTS

Author pays submission fee: No
Author pays page charges: No
Length of articles: 20-30 pp.
Length of book reviews: 1-3 pp.
Number of copies required: 1
Copyright ownership: Author
Rejected manuscripts: Returned at author's request
Time before publication decision: 1-2 mos.
Time between decision and publication: 1-2 yrs.
Articles published per year: 8-14
Book reviews published per year: 10-15

(2083)
Orizont: Revista a Uniunii Scriitorilor din Republica Socialista România

Ion Arieşanu, Editor
Strada Rodnei 1
Timişoara, Romania

First published: 1950
Sponsoring organization: Comitetul de Cultură şi Educaţie Socialisţă Timiş
ISSN: 0030-560X
MLA acronym: Orizont

SUBSCRIPTION INFORMATION

Frequency of publication: 52 times/yr.
Available in microform: No
Subscription address: ILEXIM, Import-Export Dept., P.O. Box 136-137, Str. 13 Decembrie 3, Bucharest, Romania

ADVERTISING INFORMATION

Advertising accepted: Yes

EDITORIAL DESCRIPTION

Scope: Publishes political, social, literary, artistic articles written mainly by writers from the Timiş region.
Reviews books: Yes
Publishes notes: Yes
Languages accepted: Romanian
Prints abstracts: Yes

SUBMISSION REQUIREMENTS

Restrictions on contributors: None
Author pays submission fee: No
Author pays page charges: No
Length of articles: No restrictions
Length of book reviews: 720 words
Length of notes: 350 words
Style: None
Number of copies required: 1
Copyright ownership: Author
Rejected manuscripts: Not returned
Time before publication decision: 2-4 weeks
Time between decision and publication: 2 weeks
Number of reviewers: 3-4
Articles submitted per year: 950
Articles published per year: 675
Book reviews submitted per year: 200
Book reviews published per year: 150
Notes submitted per year: 300
Notes published per year: 250

(2084)
*Orpheus: Rivista di Umanità Classica e Cristiana

Carmelo Curti, Director
Centro di Studi Sull'Antico Cristianesimo
Fac. di Lettere
Univ. di Catania
95124 Catania, Sicily, Italy

Telephone: (39) 95 7102659
First published: 1954
ISSN: 0030-5790
MLA acronym: Orpheus

SUBSCRIPTION INFORMATION

Frequency of publication: 2 times/yr.
Available in microform: No
Subscription price: 40,000 Lit/yr. Italy; 70,000 Lit/yr. elsewhere
Year to which price refers: 1993

ADVERTISING INFORMATION

Advertising accepted: No

EDITORIAL DESCRIPTION

Scope: Publishes articles concerning the continuity between the classical world and Christian culture in the broad context of late antiquity. Includes studies of philology, history, religion and Greek and Latin texts, as well as Byzantine and Medieval texts and studies.
Reviews books: Yes
Publishes notes: Yes
Languages accepted: English; Italian; French; German; Spanish
Prints abstracts: No
Author-anonymous submission: No

SUBMISSION REQUIREMENTS

Restrictions on contributors: None
Author pays submission fee: No
Author pays page charges: No
Style: Journal
Number of copies required: 2
Copyright ownership: Journal
Rejected manuscripts: Returned
Time before publication decision: 1 yr.
Time between decision and publication: 6 mos.

Orientalia Gothoburgensia entry (2080) continued:

Restrictions on contributors: Contributors must be affiliated with the Rijksuniv. te Gent.
Author pays submission fee: No
Author pays page charges: No
Number of copies required: 1
Copyright ownership: Journal
Rejected manuscripts: Returned
Time before publication decision: 2 mos.
Time between decision and publication: 8 mos.
Number of reviewers: 3

Number of reviewers: 2
Articles submitted per year: 20
Articles published per year: 10
Book reviews published per year: 20
Notes submitted per year: 10
Notes published per year: 5

(2085)
*Ortnamnssällskapets i Uppsala Årsskrift

Karl Inge Sandred, Managing Editor
Sankt Johannesgatan 11
753 12 Uppsala, Sweden

First published: 1936
Sponsoring organization: Ortnamnssällskapet i Uppsala
ISSN: 0473-4351
MLA acronym: OUÅ

SUBSCRIPTION INFORMATION

Frequency of publication: Annual
Circulation: 1,000
Available in microform: No
Subscription price: 50 SKr/yr.
Year to which price refers: 1991

ADVERTISING INFORMATION

Advertising accepted: No

EDITORIAL DESCRIPTION

Scope: Promotes the study of place-names and personal names in Germanic languages. Emphasizes interdisciplinary approaches.
Reviews books: Occasionally
Publishes notes: No
Languages accepted: Swedish; English; German; Danish; Norwegian
Prints abstracts: Yes
Author-anonymous submission: No

SUBMISSION REQUIREMENTS

Restrictions on contributors: None
Author pays submission fee: No
Author pays page charges: No
Length of articles: 2,500-7,500 words
Length of book reviews: 2,000-4,000 words
Style: MLA for articles in English
Number of copies required: 1
Special requirements: Submit original typescript.
Copyright ownership: Assigned by author to journal
Rejected manuscripts: Returned
Time before publication decision: 2 mos.
Time between decision and publication: 1-2 yrs.
Number of reviewers: 2
Articles submitted per year: 5-7
Articles published per year: 4-6

(2086)
Osamayor: Graduate Student Review

Dept. of Hispanic Languages & Literatures
1309 CL, Univ. of Pittsburgh
Pittsburgh, PA 15260

First published: 1989
Sponsoring organization: Dept. of Hispanic Languages & Literatures, Univ. of Pittsburgh
MLA acronym: Osamayor

SUBSCRIPTION INFORMATION

Frequency of publication: 2 times/yr. (Fall, Winter)
Available in microform: Yes

ADVERTISING INFORMATION

Advertising accepted: Yes

EDITORIAL DESCRIPTION

Scope: Publishes articles on Spanish and Latin American literature and linguistics. Includes a section on creative writing. Includes translations of works in Amerindian and Peninsular languages.
Reviews books: Yes
Publishes notes: Yes
Languages accepted: English; Portuguese; Spanish
Prints abstracts: No
Author-anonymous submission: No

SUBMISSION REQUIREMENTS

Author pays submission fee: No
Author pays page charges: No
Style: MLA
Number of copies required: 1
Time before publication decision: 3-4 mos.
Time between decision and publication: 2-8 mos.
Number of reviewers: 2
Articles submitted per year: 36
Articles published per year: 12-15
Book reviews submitted per year: 5-7

(2087)
*Österreich in Amerikanischer Sicht: Das Österreichbild im Amerikanischen Schulunterricht

Maria Luise Caputo-Mayr & Herbert Lederer, Editors
Dept. of Germanic & Slavic Languages AB335
Temple Univ. (022-35)
College of Arts & Sciences
Philadelphia, PA 19122

Telephone: 215 787-8282
Fax: 215 787-3731
First published: 1980
Sponsoring organization: Austrian Inst. of Culture
ISSN: 0082-3006
MLA acronym: ÖAS

SUBSCRIPTION INFORMATION

Frequency of publication: Irregular
Available in microform: No
Subscription address: ACSAL, Austrian Inst., 11 E. 52nd St., New York, NY 10022

ADVERTISING INFORMATION

Advertising accepted: No

EDITORIAL DESCRIPTION

Scope: Publishes scholarly and pedagogical articles of interest to teachers of German.
Reviews books: No
Publishes notes: Yes
Languages accepted: German; English
Prints abstracts: No
Author-anonymous submission: No

SUBMISSION REQUIREMENTS

Restrictions on contributors: Contributors must have presented paper at annual AATG convention on Austrian topics.
Author pays submission fee: No
Author pays page charges: No
Length of articles: 6,000-7,000 words
Style: MLA
Number of copies required: 2
Copyright ownership: Austrian Inst. of Culture
Rejected manuscripts: Returned
Time between decision and publication: 6-12 mos.
Number of reviewers: 3
Articles submitted per year: 15
Articles published per year: 6-8

(2088)
*Österreich in Geschichte und Literatur (mit Geographie)

Ernst Bruckmüller & Hermann Möcker, Editors
Inst. für Österreichkunde
Hanuschgasse 3
1010 Vienna 1, Austria

Telephone: (43) 1 5127932
First published: 1957
Sponsoring organization: Inst. für Österreichkunde
ISSN: 0029-8743
MLA acronym: ÖGL

SUBSCRIPTION INFORMATION

Frequency of publication: 6 times/yr.
Circulation: 1,500
Available in microform: No
Subscription price: 460 S/yr.
Year to which price refers: 1992
Subscription address: Verlag Wilhelm Braumüller, Servitengasse 5, 1092 Vienna, Austria
Subscription telephone: (43) 1 311159; (43) 1 348124

ADVERTISING INFORMATION

Advertising accepted: Yes

EDITORIAL DESCRIPTION

Scope: Focuses on Austria in history and literature; includes section on geography.
Reviews books: Yes
Publishes notes: Yes
Languages accepted: German
Prints abstracts: No
Author-anonymous submission: No

SUBMISSION REQUIREMENTS

Restrictions on contributors: None
Author pays submission fee: No
Author pays page charges: No
Length of articles: 10-25 printed pp.
Length of book reviews: 1-3 typescript pp.
Length of notes: 1-10 typescript pp.
Style: Journal
Number of copies required: 2
Special requirements: Submit original typescript.
Copyright ownership: Inst. für Österreichkunde
Rejected manuscripts: Returned
Time before publication decision: 1-2 mos.
Time between decision and publication: 1 yr.
Number of reviewers: 2
Articles submitted per year: 23-28
Articles published per year: 20-25
Book reviews submitted per year: 50-100
Book reviews published per year: 40-60
Notes submitted per year: 8-15
Notes published per year: 6-12

(2089)
*Österreichische Osthefte: Zeitschrift für Mittel-, Ost- und Südosteuropaforschung

Walter Lukan, Editor
Österreichisches Ost- und Südosteuropa-Inst.
Josefsplatz 6
1010 Vienna 1, Austria

Telephone: (43) 222 5124328
Fax: (43) 222 5121895-53
First published: 1959
Sponsoring organization: Österreichisches Ost- & Südosteuropa-Inst.
ISSN: 0029-9375
MLA acronym: ÖstO

SUBSCRIPTION INFORMATION

Frequency of publication: 4 times/yr. (Mar., June, Sept., Dec.)

Circulation: 800
Available in microform: No
Subscription price: 660 S/yr.
Year to which price refers: 1992
Subscription address: Typographische Anstalt, Muthgasse 56, 1190 Vienna, Austria
Subscription telephone: (43) 222 373546
Subscription fax: (43) 222 373546-150

ADVERTISING INFORMATION

Advertising accepted: No

EDITORIAL DESCRIPTION

Scope: Publishes articles on history, politics, ideology, linguistics, literatures, education, social science, economy, and geography.
Reviews books: Yes
Publishes notes: Yes
Languages accepted: German; English
Prints abstracts: No
Author-anonymous submission: No

SUBMISSION REQUIREMENTS

Author pays submission fee: No
Author pays page charges: No
Length of articles: 15 pp.
Length of book reviews: 2-3 pp.
Length of notes: 300 words
Number of copies required: 1
Special requirements: Submit original typescript.
Copyright ownership: Publisher & author
Rejected manuscripts: Returned
Articles submitted per year: 35
Articles published per year: 25
Book reviews submitted per year: 130
Book reviews published per year: 120
Notes submitted per year: 50
Notes published per year: 50

(2090)
*Österreichische Zeitschrift für Volkskunde

Klaus Beitl & Franz Grieshofer, Editors
c/o Verein für Volkskunde
Laudongasse 15-19
1080 Vienna, Austria

Telephone: (43) 222 438905
Fax: (43) 222 4085352
First published: 1895
Sponsoring organization: Verein für Volkskunde
ISSN: 0029-9669
MLA acronym: ÖZV

SUBSCRIPTION INFORMATION

Frequency of publication: 4 times/yr.
Circulation: 1,300
Available in microform: No
Subscription price: 360 S/yr. members
Year to which price refers: 1992

ADVERTISING INFORMATION

Advertising accepted: Yes
Advertising rates: 2,500 S/full page

EDITORIAL DESCRIPTION

Scope: Publishes articles on collective folklife and folklore, especially that of Austria.
Reviews books: Yes
Publishes notes: Yes
Languages accepted: German
Prints abstracts: No
Author-anonymous submission: No

SUBMISSION REQUIREMENTS

Restrictions on contributors: None
Author pays submission fee: No
Author pays page charges: No

Length of articles: 25-30 typescript pp.
Length of book reviews: 1/2-2 typescript pp.
Length of notes: No restrictions
Style: None
Number of copies required: 1
Copyright ownership: Author & editor
Rejected manuscripts: Returned
Time before publication decision: 3-6 mos.
Time between decision and publication: 6-12 mos.
Number of reviewers: 2
Articles submitted per year: 15-25
Articles published per year: 12-16
Book reviews submitted per year: 100
Book reviews published per year: 70-80
Notes submitted per year: 20-30
Notes published per year: 20-30

(2091)
Osteuropa: Zeitschrift für Gegenwartsfragen des Ostens

Alexander Steininger, Editor
Grosskölnstr. 32/34
5100 Aachen, Germany

Telephone: (49) 241 32707
Fax: (49) 241 405879
First published: 1951
Sponsoring organization: Deutsche Gesellschaft für Osteuropakunde e.V.
ISSN: 0030-6428
MLA acronym: Osteuropa

SUBSCRIPTION INFORMATION

Frequency of publication: 12 times/yr.
Circulation: 2,800
Available in microform: Yes
Subscription price: 114 DM/yr.
Year to which price refers: 1992
Subscription address: Deutsche Verlags-Anstalt, Neckarstr. 121 Postfach 106012, 7000 Stuttgart 10, Germany

ADVERTISING INFORMATION

Advertising accepted: Yes

EDITORIAL DESCRIPTION

Scope: Publishes articles on current questions about the East. Covers the Soviet Union, East European countries, other communist states, and world communism everywhere. Deals with overlapping world political themes, political change, ideology, economics, society, culture, and educational systems, analyses, current developments, and comments on current events.
Reviews books: Yes
Publishes notes: No
Languages accepted: German
Prints abstracts: No
Author-anonymous submission: No

SUBMISSION REQUIREMENTS

Restrictions on contributors: None
Author pays submission fee: No
Author pays page charges: No
Length of articles: 2,000-14,000 words
Length of book reviews: 300-400 words
Style: None
Number of copies required: 1
Special requirements: Submit original typescript.
Copyright ownership: Deutsche Gesellschaft für Osteuropakunde e.V.
Rejected manuscripts: Returned
Time before publication decision: 1 mo.
Time between decision and publication: 3 mos.
Number of reviewers: 2
Articles submitted per year: 80
Articles published per year: 60
Book reviews submitted per year: 300
Book reviews published per year: 250

(2092)
*Overland

Barrett Reid, Editor
P.O. Box 14146
Melbourne 3000, Australia

Telephone: (61) 3 8504347
Fax: (61) 3 8520527
First published: 1954
Sponsoring organization: Overland Soc.
ISSN: 0030-7416
MLA acronym: Overland

SUBSCRIPTION INFORMATION

Frequency of publication: 4 times/yr. (Apr., July, Sept., Dec.)
Circulation: 2,400
Available in microform: Yes
Subscription price: A$26.00/yr.; A$18.00/yr. students; A$40.00/yr. outside Australia
Year to which price refers: 1992

ADVERTISING INFORMATION

Advertising accepted: Yes
Advertising rates: A$180.00/half page; A$250.00/full page; A$300.00/inside back cover; A$320.00/inside front cover

EDITORIAL DESCRIPTION

Scope: Publishes articles on literature, history, and culture from an Australian point of view, as well as short stories and poetry.
Reviews books: Yes
Publishes notes: Yes
Languages accepted: English
Prints abstracts: No
Author-anonymous submission: No

SUBMISSION REQUIREMENTS

Restrictions on contributors: Unsolicited book reviews are not accepted.
Author pays submission fee: No
Author pays page charges: No
Length of articles: 4,000 words maximum
Length of book reviews: 1,200 words maximum
Style: Journal
Number of copies required: 1
Copyright ownership: Author
Rejected manuscripts: Returned; enclose return postage.
Time before publication decision: 2-3 mos.
Time between decision and publication: 2-12
Number of reviewers: 2
Articles submitted per year: 250
Articles published per year: 25
Book reviews published per year: 160

(2093)
*Oxford English Monographs

Stephen Gill, Roger Lonsdale, Douglas Gray, Emily Jones, & Christopher Butler, Editors
Oxford Univ. Press
Walton Street
Oxford OX2 6DP, England

Telephone: (44) 865 56767
Fax: (44) 865 56646
MLA acronym: OEM

SUBSCRIPTION INFORMATION

Frequency of publication: Irregular
Available in microform: No
Additional subscription address: Oxford Univ. Press, 200 Madison Ave., New York, NY 10016
Subscription telephone: 212 679-7300
Subscription fax: 212 725-2972

ADVERTISING INFORMATION

Advertising accepted: No

EDITORIAL DESCRIPTION

Scope: Publishes books derived from theses submitted to the faculty of Oxford University.
Reviews books: No
Publishes notes: No
Languages accepted: English
Prints abstracts: No
Author-anonymous submission: Yes

SUBMISSION REQUIREMENTS

Author pays submission fee: No
Author pays page charges: No
Length of books: 80,000 words
Style: Hart's Rules
Number of copies required: 2
Copyright ownership: Author
Rejected manuscripts: Returned
Books published per year: 3-5

(2094) *Oxford German Studies

T. J. Reed & N. F. Palmer, Editors
Queen's College
Oxford OX1 4AW, England

Telephone: (44) 865 279120
Fax: (44) 865 790819
First published: 1966
ISSN: 0078-7191
MLA acronym: OGS

SUBSCRIPTION INFORMATION

Frequency of publication: Annual
Circulation: 1,250
Available in microform: No
Subscription address: Willem A. Meeuws Publisher, Wightwick, Boars Hill, Oxford OX1 5DR, England

ADVERTISING INFORMATION

Advertising accepted: Yes

EDITORIAL DESCRIPTION

Scope: Publishes contributions on German literature and related subjects, social, intellectual, and art history, by both established and younger scholars. Work based on important unpublished sources is particularly welcome.
Reviews books: No
Publishes notes: Yes
Languages accepted: English; German; French
Prints abstracts: No
Author-anonymous submission: No

SUBMISSION REQUIREMENTS

Restrictions on contributors: None
Author pays submission fee: No
Author pays page charges: No
Length of articles: 50 pp. maximum
Style: Journal
Number of copies required: 2
Copyright ownership: Journal
Rejected manuscripts: Returned
Time before publication decision: 1-2 mos.
Time between decision and publication: 8-12 mos.
Number of reviewers: 2
Articles submitted per year: 15-20
Articles published per year: 10 maximum

(2095) The Oxford Literary Review

Robert Young & Geoffrey Bennington, Editors
Wadham College
Oxford OX1 3PN, England

Telephone: (44) 865 277959
Fax: (44) 865 277937
E-mail: OLR@UK.AC.OXFORD.VAX
First published: 1973
ISSN: 0305-1498
MLA acronym: OLR

SUBSCRIPTION INFORMATION

Frequency of publication: Annual
Circulation: 900
Available in microform: No
Subscription price: £17.50/yr. institutions United Kingdom; £20.00 ($35.00)/yr. institutions elsewhere; £6.95/yr. individuals United Kingdom; £9.50 ($16.75)/yr. individuals elsewhere
Year to which price refers: 1992
Subscription address: Subscriptions Manager, at the above address

ADVERTISING INFORMATION

Advertising accepted: Yes

EDITORIAL DESCRIPTION

Scope: Publishes articles on literary theory.
Reviews books: Yes
Publishes notes: No
Languages accepted: English; French
Prints abstracts: No
Author-anonymous submission: No

SUBMISSION REQUIREMENTS

Restrictions on contributors: None
Author pays submission fee: No
Author pays page charges: No
Length of articles: 6,000 words
Length of book reviews: 2,000 words
Style: MLA
Number of copies required: 2
Copyright ownership: Journal
Rejected manuscripts: Not returned
Time before publication decision: 3 mos.
Time between decision and publication: 1 yr.
Number of reviewers: 4
Articles submitted per year: 100
Articles published per year: 8-10
Book reviews submitted per year: 50
Book reviews published per year: 8-10

(2096) Oxford Modern Languages and Literature Monographs

A. W. Raitt, M. Jacobs, A. J. Krailsheimer, C. Grayson, G. C. Stone, C. N. J. Mann, & R. W. Truman, Editors
Oxford Univ. Press
200 Madison Ave.
New York, NY 10016

First published: 1979
MLA acronym: OMLLM

SUBSCRIPTION INFORMATION

Frequency of publication: Irregular
Available in microform: No

ADVERTISING INFORMATION

Advertising accepted: No

EDITORIAL DESCRIPTION

Scope: Publishes monographs based on theses submitted for higher degrees at Oxford University.
Reviews books: No
Publishes notes: No
Languages accepted: English
Prints abstracts: No
Author-anonymous submission: No

SUBMISSION REQUIREMENTS

Author pays submission fee: No
Author pays page charges: No
Length of books: 80,000 words
Copyright ownership: Author
Rejected manuscripts: Returned
Time before publication decision: 6 mos.
Time between decision and publication: 18 mos.
Number of reviewers: 1-2
Books submitted per year: 3-4
Books published per year: 2

(2097) *Oxford Slavonic Papers

G. C. Stone, C. M. MacRobert, & G. S. Smith, Editors
Hertford College
Oxford, England

First published: 1950
ISSN: 0078-7656
MLA acronym: OSP

SUBSCRIPTION INFORMATION

Frequency of publication: Annual
Circulation: 1,000
Available in microform: No
Subscription price: £30.00/yr.
Year to which price refers: 1991
Subscription address: Oxford Univ. Press, Saxon Way West, Corby, Northants NN18 9ES, England
Subscription telephone: (44) 536 741519
Subscription fax: (44) 536 746337

ADVERTISING INFORMATION

Advertising accepted: No

EDITORIAL DESCRIPTION

Scope: Publishes original contributions and documents relating to the languages, literatures, culture, and history of Russia and the other Slavonic countries. Reviews of individual books are not normally included, but bibliographical and review articles are considered.
Reviews books: No
Publishes notes: No
Languages accepted: English
Prints abstracts: No
Author-anonymous submission: No

SUBMISSION REQUIREMENTS

Restrictions on contributors: None
Author pays submission fee: No
Author pays page charges: No
Length of articles: 6,000-10,000 words
Style: Style sheet provided on request.
Number of copies required: 1
Special requirements: British System of Cyrillic transliteration (British Standard 2979; 1958); for philological work, use the International System (ISOR/9).
Copyright ownership: Oxford Univ. Press
Rejected manuscripts: Returned at author's request
Time before publication decision: 3-6 weeks
Time between decision and publication: 12-18 mos.
Number of reviewers: 3
Articles submitted per year: 15
Articles published per year: 6-8

(2098) *Paar Sammukest Eesti Kirjanduse Uurimise Teed

M. Hiiemäe, E. Ertis, E. Kalmre, E. Lüv, & H. Tering, Editors
Eesti NSV TA Fr.R. Kreutzwaldi nim. Kirjandusmuuseum
Vanemuise t. 42/44
EE2400 Tartu, Estonia

Telephone: (7) 1434 30045

First published: 1958
Sponsoring organization: Eesti Teaduste Akadeemia (Estonian Academy of Sciences)
ISSN: 0203-3194
MLA acronym: PSEKUT

SUBSCRIPTION INFORMATION

Frequency of publication: Irregular
Available in microform: No

ADVERTISING INFORMATION

Advertising accepted: No

EDITORIAL DESCRIPTION

Scope: Publishes articles on Estonian literature, folklore, and bibliography.
Reviews books: No
Languages accepted: Estonian
Prints abstracts: Yes
Author-anonymous submission: No

SUBMISSION REQUIREMENTS

Restrictions on contributors: None
Author pays submission fee: No
Author pays page charges: No
Length of articles: 7,000 words
Number of copies required: 1
Special requirements: Include an abstract.
Copyright ownership: Eesti TA Fr.R. Kreutzwaldi nim. Kirjandusmuuseum
Rejected manuscripts: Returned
Time before publication decision: 1 mo.
Time between decision and publication: 2 yrs.
Number of reviewers: 5

(2099)
*Pacific Coast Philology

Cyndia Susan Clegg, Editor
Philological Assn. of the Pacific Coast
Humanities Division
Pepperdine Univ.
Malibu, CA 90263

Telephone: 310 456-4435
First published: 1966
Sponsoring organization: Philological Assn. of the Pacific Coast
ISSN: 0078-7469
MLA acronym: PCP

SUBSCRIPTION INFORMATION

Frequency of publication: Annual
Circulation: 1,300
Available in microform: No
Subscription price: $6.00/yr.
Year to which price refers: 1992

ADVERTISING INFORMATION

Advertising accepted: Yes
Advertising rates: $10.00/column line

EDITORIAL DESCRIPTION

Scope: Publishes papers read at the annual meeting of the Philological Association of the Pacific Coast in philology, linguistics, or literature (comparative, general, or English or foreign languages).
Reviews books: No
Publishes notes: No
Languages accepted: English
Prints abstracts: No
Author-anonymous submission: No

SUBMISSION REQUIREMENTS

Restrictions on contributors: Contributors must be members of the Philological Assn. of the Pacific Coast.
Author pays submission fee: No
Author pays page charges: No

Length of articles: 10-20 double-spaced typescript pp.
Style: MLA
Number of copies required: 3
Copyright ownership: Author
Rejected manuscripts: Returned; enclose return postage.
Time before publication decision: 3 mos.
Time between decision and publication: 6 mos.
Number of reviewers: 3
Articles submitted per year: 100-150
Articles published per year: 10-15

(2100)
*Paideia: Rivista Letteraria di Informazione Bibliografica

Giuseppe Scarpat & Carlo Cordié, Editors
Via Corsica, 130
25125 Brescia, Italy

Telephone: (39) 30 222094
Fax: (39) 30 223269
First published: 1946
ISSN: 0030-9435
MLA acronym: Paideia

SUBSCRIPTION INFORMATION

Frequency of publication: 2 times/yr.
Circulation: 800
Available in microform: No

ADVERTISING INFORMATION

Advertising accepted: No

EDITORIAL DESCRIPTION

Scope: Publishes articles on the subject of bibliography and Semitic, Classical, and Modern philology.
Reviews books: Yes
Publishes notes: Yes
Languages accepted: English; French; German; Italian
Prints abstracts: No

SUBMISSION REQUIREMENTS

Author pays submission fee: No
Author pays page charges: No
Number of copies required: 1
Copyright ownership: Editor
Time before publication decision: 1 mo.
Time between decision and publication: 3 mos.
Articles submitted per year: 40
Articles published per year: 30
Book reviews submitted per year: 130
Book reviews published per year: 100

(2101)
*Paideuma: A Journal Devoted to Ezra Pound Scholarship

Hugh Kenner & Eva Hesse, Editors
c/o Carroll F. Terrell, Managing Editor
302 Neville Hall
Univ. of Maine
Orono, ME 04469

First published: 1972
Sponsoring organization: National Poetry Foundation, Inc; Univ. of Maine, Orono
ISSN: 0090-5674
MLA acronym: Paideuma

SUBSCRIPTION INFORMATION

Frequency of publication: 3 times/yr. (Spring, Fall, Winter)
Circulation: 1,200
Available in microform: No
Subscription address: National Poetry Foundation, at the above address

ADVERTISING INFORMATION

Advertising accepted: Yes

EDITORIAL DESCRIPTION

Scope: Publishes critical, biographical, and bibliographic materials on the writings and the life of Ezra Pound.
Reviews books: Yes
Publishes notes: Yes
Languages accepted: English
Prints abstracts: No
Author-anonymous submission: No

SUBMISSION REQUIREMENTS

Restrictions on contributors: None
Author pays submission fee: No
Author pays page charges: No
Length of articles: 5,000 words maximum
Length of book reviews: 1,000 words
Length of notes: 300 words minimum
Style: MLA
Number of copies required: 2
Special requirements: Submission on IBM-compatible diskette using Microsoft Word is preferred.
Copyright ownership: National Poetry Foundation, Inc.
Rejected manuscripts: Returned; enclose SASE.
Time before publication decision: 1 mo.
Time between decision and publication: 1 yr.
Number of reviewers: 1-3
Articles published per year: 50
Book reviews published per year: 10
Notes published per year: 15-20

(2102)
*Paideuma: Mitteilungen zur Kulturkunde

Eike Haberland & Beatrix Heintze, Editors
Frobenius-Inst.
Liebigstr. 41
6000 Frankfurt a.M. 1, Germany

Telephone: (49) 69 721012
Fax: (49) 69 173725
First published: 1938
Sponsoring organization: Frobenius-Gesellschaft
ISSN: 0078-7809
MLA acronym: PaideumaM

SUBSCRIPTION INFORMATION

Frequency of publication: Annual
Available in microform: No
Subscription price: 60 DM/yr.
Year to which price refers: 1991
Subscription address: Franz Steiner Verlag Wiesbaden GmbH, Postfach 10 15 26, 7000 Stuttgart 10, Germany
Subscription telephone: (49) 711 25820
Subscription fax: (49) 711 2582290

ADVERTISING INFORMATION

Advertising accepted: Yes, on an exchange basis

EDITORIAL DESCRIPTION

Scope: Publishes research on the history and culture of Africa, as well as articles of more general theoretical interest on other topics or parts of the world.
Reviews books: No
Publishes notes: Yes
Languages accepted: German; English; French
Prints abstracts: No
Author-anonymous submission: No

SUBMISSION REQUIREMENTS

Restrictions on contributors: None
Author pays submission fee: No
Author pays page charges: No
Style: Request from editor

Number of copies required: 2
Special requirements: Request from editor
Copyright ownership: Frobenius-Inst.
Rejected manuscripts: Returned
Time before publication decision: 3 mos.
Time between decision and publication: 12-18 mos.
Articles submitted per year: 20
Articles published per year: 10-15
Notes submitted per year: 0-1
Notes published per year: 0-1

(2103)
*Paintbrush: A Journal of Poetry, Translations, and Letters

Benjamin Bennani, Editor
Northeast Missouri State Univ.
Kirksville, MO 63501

Telephone: 816 785-4185
Fax: 816 785-4181
First published: 1974
Sponsoring organization: Northeast Missouri State Univ.
ISSN: 0094-1964
MLA acronym: Paintbrush

SUBSCRIPTION INFORMATION

Frequency of publication: 2 times/yr. (Spring, Fall)
Circulation: 500
Available in microform: No
Subscription price: $12.00/yr. institutions; $9.00/yr. individuals
Year to which price refers: 1992

ADVERTISING INFORMATION

Advertising accepted: Yes
Advertising rates: $150.00/full page

EDITORIAL DESCRIPTION

Scope: Publishes intertextual and comparative criticism as well as poetry, fiction, translations, and interviews.
Reviews books: Yes
Publishes notes: Yes
Languages accepted: English
Prints abstracts: No
Author-anonymous submission: No

SUBMISSION REQUIREMENTS

Restrictions on contributors: None
Author pays submission fee: No
Author pays page charges: No
Length of articles: 8-10 double-spaced typescript pp.
Length of book reviews: 500-800 words
Length of notes: 50-100 words
Style: MLA
Number of copies required: 1
Special requirements: Send original typescript with cover letter.
Copyright ownership: Author
Rejected manuscripts: Returned; enclose return postage or international reply coupons.
Time before publication decision: 2-4 weeks
Time between decision and publication: 2-5 mos.
Number of reviewers: 1-3
Articles submitted per year: 10-20
Articles published per year: 4-5
Book reviews submitted per year: 12
Book reviews published per year: 4-5
Notes published per year: 10-15

(2104)
*La Palabra y el Hombre: Revista de la Universidad Veracruzana

Raúl Hernández Viveros, Editor
Editorial de la Univ. Veracruzana
Apartádo Postal 97
Xalapa
Veracruz, Mexico

First published: 1957
Sponsoring organization: Univ. Veracruzana
ISSN: 0185-5727
MLA acronym: PH

SUBSCRIPTION INFORMATION

Frequency of publication: 4 times/yr.
Circulation: 2,000
Available in microform: No
Subscription price: $75.00/yr.
Year to which price refers: 1992

ADVERTISING INFORMATION

Advertising accepted: No

EDITORIAL DESCRIPTION

Scope: Publishes articles on the humanities.
Reviews books: Yes
Publishes notes: Yes
Languages accepted: Spanish
Prints abstracts: No
Author-anonymous submission: No

SUBMISSION REQUIREMENTS

Restrictions on contributors: None
Author pays submission fee: No
Author pays page charges: No
Length of articles: 10-25 pp.
Length of book reviews: 3-6 pp.
Length of notes: 3-6 pp.
Style: None
Number of copies required: 1
Copyright ownership: Author; cite source if published elsewhere
Rejected manuscripts: Returned at the discretion of the Editorial Board
Time before publication decision: 3 mos.
Time between decision and publication: 6 mos.
Number of reviewers: 3
Articles submitted per year: 160
Articles published per year: 1-2
Book reviews submitted per year: 32-38
Book reviews published per year: 32
Notes submitted per year: 8-10
Notes published per year: 8

(2105)
El Palacio: Magazine of the Museum of New Mexico

Karen Meadows, Editor
P.O. Box 2087
Santa Fe, NM 87504

First published: 1913
Sponsoring organization: Museum of New Mexico Foundation
ISSN: 0031-0158
MLA acronym: Palacio

SUBSCRIPTION INFORMATION

Frequency of publication: 2 times/yr. (Spring, Winter)
Circulation: 3,500
Available in microform: No
Subscription address: James Romero, Circulations Manager, Museum of New Mexico, at the above address

ADVERTISING INFORMATION

Advertising accepted: No, although the occasional sponsorship of a special issue is accepted.

EDITORIAL DESCRIPTION

Scope: Deals with anthropology, archaeology, history, fine art, folk art, and other topics related to the US Southwest and adjacent areas. Also includes essays about exhibits in the museum and related topics.
Reviews books: Yes
Publishes notes: No
Languages accepted: English; Spanish; Native American languages
Prints abstracts: Yes
Author-anonymous submission: No

SUBMISSION REQUIREMENTS

Restrictions on contributors: None
Author pays submission fee: No
Author pays page charges: No
Length of articles: 5-15 typescript pp.
Length of book reviews: 400 words
Style: Chicago
Number of copies required: 1
Special requirements: Include a biographical sketch and a bibliography or reading list on the subject. Journal encourages black and white graphics.
Copyright ownership: Publisher
Rejected manuscripts: Returned; enclose return postage.
Time before publication decision: 2 mos.
Time between decision and publication: 1 yr.
Number of reviewers: 1-2
Articles submitted per year: 60
Articles published per year: 20
Book reviews published per year: 25-30

(2106)
*Palaestra: Untersuchungen aus der Deutschen, Englischen, und Scandinavischen Philologie

Dieter Cherubim, Armin P. Frank, Walther Killy, Fritz Paul, Hans Schabram, Albrecht Schöne, Karl Stackmann, Horst Turk, Christian J. Wagenknecht, & Theodor Wolpers, Editors
Vandenhoeck & Ruprecht
Postfach 3753
Theaterstr. 13
3400 Göttingen, Germany

Telephone: (49) 551 54031
Fax: (49) 551 46298
First published: 1969
MLA acronym: Palaestra

SUBSCRIPTION INFORMATION

Frequency of publication: Irregular
Available in microform: No

ADVERTISING INFORMATION

Advertising accepted: No

EDITORIAL DESCRIPTION

Scope: Publishes monographs on German, English, and Scandinavian literature and philology.
Reviews books: No
Publishes notes: No
Languages accepted: German; English
Prints abstracts: Yes

SUBMISSION REQUIREMENTS

Author pays submission fee: No
Author pays page charges: No
Length of books: 174-635 pp.
Style: Series
Number of copies required: 1

(2107)
*Palimpsest

Ginalie Swaim, Editor
State Historical Soc. of Iowa
402 Iowa Ave.
Iowa City, IA 52240

Telephone: 319 335-3916
Fax: 319 335-3924
First published: 1920
Sponsoring organization: State Historical Soc. of Iowa
ISSN: 0031-0360
MLA acronym: Palimpsest

SUBSCRIPTION INFORMATION

Frequency of publication: 4 times/yr.
Circulation: 4,000
Available in microform: No
Subscription price: $15.00/yr.; $4.50/single issue
Year to which price refers: 1992

ADVERTISING INFORMATION

Advertising accepted: No

EDITORIAL DESCRIPTION

Scope: Encourages articles on the history of Iowa and the Midwest which may be of interest to the general reading public.
Reviews books: No
Publishes notes: No
Languages accepted: English
Prints abstracts: No
Author-anonymous submission: Yes

SUBMISSION REQUIREMENTS

Restrictions on contributors: None
Author pays submission fee: No
Author pays page charges: No
Length of articles: 15-25 pp.
Style: Chicago
Number of copies required: 2
Copyright ownership: Journal
Rejected manuscripts: Returned
Time before publication decision: 3 mos.
Time between decision and publication: 1-6 mos.
Number of reviewers: 3
Articles submitted per year: 100
Articles published per year: 20

(2108)
*Pamiętnik Literacki: Czasopismo Kwartalne Poświęcone Historii i Krytyce Literatury Polskiej

Bogdan Zakrzewski, Editor
Ossolineum Publishing House of the Polish Academy of Sciences
Rynek 9
50-106 Wrocław, Poland

Telephone: (48) 71 38625
Fax: (48) 71 448103
First published: 1902
Sponsoring organization: Polska Akademia Nauk, Inst. Badań Literackich
ISSN: 0031-0514
MLA acronym: PL

SUBSCRIPTION INFORMATION

Frequency of publication: 4 times/yr.
Circulation: 1,500-1,600
Available in microform: No
Subscription price: $84.00/yr.; $21.00/single issue
Year to which price refers: 1992

ADVERTISING INFORMATION

Advertising accepted: No

EDITORIAL DESCRIPTION

Scope: Publishes articles on Polish literary theory and literary history.
Reviews books: Yes
Publishes notes: No
Languages accepted: Polish
Prints abstracts: No
Author-anonymous submission: No

SUBMISSION REQUIREMENTS

Author pays submission fee: No
Author pays page charges: No
Length of articles: 40,000-80,000 characters
Length of book reviews: 15,000-30,000 characters
Number of copies required: 2
Copyright ownership: Ossolineum
Rejected manuscripts: Returned
Time before publication decision: 2 mos. maximum
Time between decision and publication: 6 mos.
Number of reviewers: 1-2
Articles submitted per year: 120
Articles published per year: 70
Book reviews submitted per year: 60
Book reviews published per year: 50

(2109)
Pamiętnik Słowiański

Halina Janaszek-Ivaničkova, Editor
Ossolineum Publishing House of the Polish Academy of Sciences
Rynek 9
50-106 Wrocław, Poland

Additional editorial address: KS PAN, Pamietnik Słowiański Redakcja, Patac Kultury i Nauki, POK 1719, SKR. Poczt. 24, 00-901 Warsaw, Poland
First published: 1950
Sponsoring organization: Polska Akademia Nauk, Komitet Słowianoznawstwa
ISSN: 0078-866X
MLA acronym: PaSlow

SUBSCRIPTION INFORMATION

Frequency of publication: Annual
Circulation: 500-600
Available in microform: Yes
Subscription address: Foreign Trade Enterprise "Ars Polona", Krakowskie Przedmieście 7, 00-068 Warsaw, Poland

ADVERTISING INFORMATION

Advertising accepted: No

EDITORIAL DESCRIPTION

Scope: Publishes monographs on Slavonic literature and culture.
Reviews books: Yes
Publishes notes: Yes
Languages accepted: Polish
Prints abstracts: Yes
Author-anonymous submission: No

SUBMISSION REQUIREMENTS

Author pays submission fee: Yes
Author pays page charges: No
Length of articles: 5,280 words
Length of book reviews: 940 words
Length of notes: 240 words
Style: Revue de Littérature Comparée
Number of copies required: 2
Copyright ownership: Ossolineum Publishing House
Rejected manuscripts: Returned
Time before publication decision: 9-12 mos.
Time between decision and publication: 6-12 mos.
Articles submitted per year: 30
Articles published per year: 15
Book reviews submitted per year: 15
Book reviews published per year: 10
Notes submitted per year: 5
Notes published per year: 4

(2110)
*Pamiętnik Teatralny: Kwartalnik Poświęcony Historii I Krytyce Teatru

Bohdan Korzeniewski & Zbigniew Raszewski, Editors
Inst. of Art of the Polish Academy of Sciences
Długa 26/28
P.O. Box 994
00-950 Warsaw, Poland

Telephone: (48) 22 313271 ext. 252
Fax: (48) 22 313149
First published: 1952
ISSN: 0031-0522
MLA acronym: PaT

SUBSCRIPTION INFORMATION

Frequency of publication: 4 times/yr.
Circulation: 1,500
Available in microform: No
Subscription price: 100,000 Zł/yr. Poland
Year to which price refers: 1992
Subscription address: Foreign Trade Enterprise "Ars Polona", Krakowskie Przedmieście 7, 00-068 Warsaw, Poland
Subscription telephone: (48) 22 261201

EDITORIAL DESCRIPTION

Scope: Publishes articles on the history and theory of Polish theater and drama.
Reviews books: Yes
Publishes notes: Yes
Languages accepted: Polish
Prints abstracts: Yes

SUBMISSION REQUIREMENTS

Author pays submission fee: No
Author pays page charges: No
Length of articles: 20-25 pp.
Length of book reviews: 5-10 pp.
Length of notes: 5-7 pp.
Style: Journal
Number of copies required: 2
Copyright ownership: Inst. of Art, Polska Akademia Nauk
Rejected manuscripts: Not returned
Time before publication decision: 1-2 yrs.
Time between decision and publication: 3 mos.
Number of reviewers: 3
Articles published per year: 40
Book reviews published per year: 5-8
Notes published per year: 5-8

(2111)
*Panjab University Research Bulletin (Arts)

Nirmal Mukerji, Editor
Panjab Univ. Arts Block No. I (Top Floor)
Sector 14
Chandigarh, India

First published: 1970
Sponsoring organization: Panjab Univ., Chandigarh
ISSN: 0970-5260
MLA acronym: PURBA

Copyright ownership: Vandenhoeck & Ruprecht
Rejected manuscripts: Returned
Time between decision and publication: 6-9 mos.
Books published per year: 1-3

SUBSCRIPTION INFORMATION

Frequency of publication: 2 times/yr.
Circulation: 500
Available in microform: No
Subscription price: 60 Re/yr.
Year to which price refers: 1992
Subscription address: Secretary, Panjab Univ. Publication Bureau, Chandigarh, India

ADVERTISING INFORMATION

Advertising accepted: No

EDITORIAL DESCRIPTION

Scope: Publishes articles on language, literature, comparative religion, fine arts, performing arts, history, archaeology, and philosophy.
Reviews books: Yes
Publishes notes: Yes
Languages accepted: English; Hindi-Urdu; Panjabi; Sanskrit; French; German
Prints abstracts: No
Author-anonymous submission: No

SUBMISSION REQUIREMENTS

Restrictions on contributors: None
Author pays submission fee: No
Author pays page charges: No
Length of articles: 5,000-7,000 words
Length of book reviews: 2,000 words
Length of notes: 1,000-1,500 words
Style: MLA
Number of copies required: 2
Special requirements: Submit original typescript.
Copyright ownership: Journal
Rejected manuscripts: Returned
Time before publication decision: 6 mos.
Time between decision and publication: 1 yr.
Number of reviewers: 2
Articles submitted per year: 150
Articles published per year: 36
Book reviews submitted per year: 40
Book reviews published per year: 20
Notes submitted per year: 40-50
Notes published per year: 10-15

(2112)
*Papers and Studies in Contrastive Linguistics

Jacek Fisiak, Editor
Inst. of English
Adam Mickiewicz Univ.
Marchlewskiego 124/126
61-874 Poznań, Poland

Telephone: (48) 61 528820
Fax: (48) 61 523103
First published: 1972
Sponsoring organization: Adam Mickiewicz Univ.
ISSN: 0137-2459
MLA acronym: PSCL

SUBSCRIPTION INFORMATION

Frequency of publication: Irregular
Circulation: 1,500
Available in microform: No

ADVERTISING INFORMATION

Advertising accepted: Yes

EDITORIAL DESCRIPTION

Scope: Publishes original articles and papers in contrastive linguistics as well as a bibliography of English-Polish contrastive studies in Poland.
Reviews books: Yes
Publishes notes: Yes
Languages accepted: English
Prints abstracts: No
Author-anonymous submission: No

SUBMISSION REQUIREMENTS

Restrictions on contributors: None
Author pays submission fee: No
Author pays page charges: No
Length of articles: No restrictions
Length of book reviews: No restrictions
Length of notes: No restrictions
Style: Linguistic Soc. of America
Number of copies required: 3
Special requirements: Submit original double-spaced typescript on size A4 (8 1/4 in. X 11 3/4 in.) paper.
Copyright ownership: Assigned by author to journal
Rejected manuscripts: Returned
Time before publication decision: 2 mos.
Time between decision and publication: 6-18 mos.
Number of reviewers: 3
Articles submitted per year: 40-50
Articles published per year: 20
Book reviews submitted per year: 3-5
Book reviews published per year: 1-2
Notes submitted per year: 1-3
Notes published per year: 1-3

(2113)
*Papers from the Annual Meeting of the Atlantic Provinces Linguistic Association/Actes du Colloque Annuel de l'Association de Linguistique des Provinces Atlantiques

c/o Dept. of Linguistics
Memorial Univ. of Newfoundland
St. John's, Newfoundland A1B 3X9, Canada

First published: 1977
Sponsoring organization: Atlantic Provinces Linguistic Assn.
MLA acronym: PAMAPLA

SUBSCRIPTION INFORMATION

Frequency of publication: Annual

ADVERTISING INFORMATION

Advertising accepted: No

EDITORIAL DESCRIPTION

Scope: Publishes articles on descriptive and theoretical linguistics selected from papers given at the annual meeting of the Atlantic Provinces Linguistic Association.
Reviews books: No
Languages accepted: English; French
Prints abstracts: Yes
Author-anonymous submission: No

SUBMISSION REQUIREMENTS

Restrictions on contributors: Contributors must have presented the paper at the annual meeting of the Atlantic Provinces Linguistic Assn.
Author pays submission fee: No
Author pays page charges: No
Style: Linguistic Soc. of America
Number of copies required: 1
Special requirements: Submit typescript and diskette.
Copyright ownership: Author

(2114)
*Papers in Australian Linguistics (Subseries of Pacific Linguistics. Series A: Occasional Papers)

c/o Secretary
Pacific Linguistics, Research School of Pacific Studies
Australian National Univ.
G.P.O. Box 4
Canberra, ACT 2601, Australia

Telephone: (61) 6 2492300
Fax: (61) 62 571893
E-mail: Mxk412@coombs.anu.edu.au
First published: 1967
Sponsoring organization: Dept. of Linguistics, Research School of Pacific Studies, Australian National Univ.
ISSN: 0078-9062
MLA acronym: PAusL

SUBSCRIPTION INFORMATION

Frequency of publication: Irregular
Available in microform: No
Subscription telephone: (61) 6 2492742

ADVERTISING INFORMATION

Advertising accepted: No

EDITORIAL DESCRIPTION

Scope: Publishes monographs on Australian linguistics.
Reviews books: Yes
Publishes notes: No
Languages accepted: English
Prints abstracts: No
Author-anonymous submission: No

SUBMISSION REQUIREMENTS

Author pays submission fee: No
Author pays page charges: No
Length of books: No restrictions
Length of book reviews: No restrictions
Style: Series
Number of copies required: 1
Special requirements: Request "Author's Guide"
Copyright ownership: Author
Rejected manuscripts: Returned
Time before publication decision: 1-8 weeks
Time between decision and publication: 1 yr.
Number of reviewers: 3

(2115)
*Papers in Comparative Studies

Richard Bjornson & Marilyn R. Waldman, Editors
Division of Comparative Studies
308 Dulles Hall/230 W. 17th St.
Ohio State Univ.
Columbus, OH 43210-1311

Telephone: 614 292-1265
Fax: 614 292-2282 (c/o Dept. of History)
First published: 1981
Sponsoring organization: Division of Comparative Studies, Ohio State Univ.
ISSN: 0736-9123
MLA acronym: PCS

SUBSCRIPTION INFORMATION

Frequency of publication: Irregular
Circulation: 200
Available in microform: No
Subscription price: $15.00/yr.
Year to which price refers: 1992
Subscription telephone: 614 292-2559 (Brenda Hosey)

ADVERTISING INFORMATION

Advertising accepted: Yes

EDITORIAL DESCRIPTION

Scope: Publishes papers in comparative humanities. Topics covered are of broad general concern and deal with a variety of disciplinary perspectives.
Reviews books: No
Publishes notes: No
Languages accepted: English
Prints abstracts: No
Author-anonymous submission: No

SUBMISSION REQUIREMENTS

Restrictions on contributors: All articles are commissioned, but editor welcomes inquiries.
Author pays submission fee: No
Author pays page charges: No
Length of articles: 5,000 words
Style: MLA
Number of copies required: 1
Copyright ownership: Division of Comparative Studies
Rejected manuscripts: Returned
Time before publication decision: 3-6 mos.
Time between decision and publication: 6-12 mos.
Number of reviewers: 2
Articles published per year: 10

(2116)
Papers in Pidgin and Creole Linguistics (Subseries of Pacific Linguistics. Series A: Occasional Papers)

Dept. of Linguistics
Research School of Pacific Studies
Australian National Univ.
G.P.O. Box 4, Canberra ACT 2601, Australia

Telephone: (61) 6 2492300; (61) 6 2492742
Fax: (61) 62 571893
E-mail: Mxk412@coombs.anu.edu.au
First published: 1978
Sponsoring organization: Dept. of Linguistics, Research School of Pacific Studies, Australian National Univ.
ISSN: 0811-0026
MLA acronym: PPCL

SUBSCRIPTION INFORMATION

Frequency of publication: Irregular
Available in microform: No

ADVERTISING INFORMATION

Advertising accepted: No

EDITORIAL DESCRIPTION

Scope: Publishes monographs on Pidgin and Creole languages.
Publishes notes: No
Languages accepted: English
Prints abstracts: No
Author-anonymous submission: No

SUBMISSION REQUIREMENTS

Author pays submission fee: No
Author pays page charges: No
Style: Series
Number of copies required: 1
Copyright ownership: Author
Rejected manuscripts: Returned
Time before publication decision: 1-8 weeks
Number of reviewers: 3

(2117)
Papers in Slavic Philology

Ladislav Matejka & Benjamin A. Stolz, Editors
3040 MLB, Slavic Dept.
Univ. of Michigan
Ann Arbor, MI 48109-1275

First published: 1977
Sponsoring organization: Univ. of Michigan, Slavic Dept.
ISSN: 0161-8822
MLA acronym: PSP

SUBSCRIPTION INFORMATION

Frequency of publication: Irregular
Available in microform: No

ADVERTISING INFORMATION

Advertising accepted: No

EDITORIAL DESCRIPTION

Scope: Publishes monograph series on Slavic philology.
Reviews books: No
Publishes notes: No
Languages accepted: English; Russian; Czech; Polish; Serbo-Croatian
Prints abstracts: No
Author-anonymous submission: No

SUBMISSION REQUIREMENTS

Restrictions on contributors: None
Author pays submission fee: No
Author pays page charges: No
Length of books: No restrictions
Style: MLA; Chicago
Number of copies required: 1
Copyright ownership: Univ. of Michigan
Rejected manuscripts: Not returned

(2118)
Papers in South East Asian Linguistics (Subseries of Pacific Linguistics. Series A: Occasional Papers)

Dept. of Linguistics
Research School of Pacific Studies
Australian National Univ.
G.P.O. Box 4, Canberra ACT 2601, Australia

Telephone: (61) 6 2492300; (61) 6 2492742
Fax: (61) 62 571893
E-mail: Mxk412@coombs.anu.edu.au
First published: 1967
Sponsoring organization: Dept. of Linguistics, Research School of Pacific Studies, Australian National Univ.
ISSN: 0078-9178
MLA acronym: PSEAL

SUBSCRIPTION INFORMATION

Frequency of publication: Irregular
Available in microform: No

ADVERTISING INFORMATION

Advertising accepted: No

EDITORIAL DESCRIPTION

Scope: Publishes monographs on Southeast Asian linguistics.
Publishes notes: No
Languages accepted: English
Prints abstracts: No
Author-anonymous submission: No

SUBMISSION REQUIREMENTS

Author pays submission fee: No
Author pays page charges: No
Length of articles: No restrictions
Length of books: No restrictions
Style: Series
Number of copies required: 1
Copyright ownership: Author
Rejected manuscripts: Returned
Time before publication decision: 2 mos. maximum
Time between decision and publication: 1 yr.
Number of reviewers: 3

(2119)
Papers of the Algonquian Conference/Actes du Congrès des Algonquistes

William Cowan, Editor
Dept. of Linguistics
Carleton Univ.
Ottawa, Ontario K1S 5B6 Canada

Telephone: 613 788-2809
E-mail: WILLIAM_COWAN@-CARLETON.CA
First published: 1976
ISSN: 0831-5671
MLA acronym: PAC

SUBSCRIPTION INFORMATION

Frequency of publication: Annual
Circulation: 300
Available in microform: No
Subscription price: $25.00/yr.
Year to which price refers: 1992

ADVERTISING INFORMATION

Advertising accepted: No

EDITORIAL DESCRIPTION

Scope: Publishes papers given at the annual Algonquian Conference in anthropology linguistics, history, ethnohistory, and archaeology.
Reviews books: No
Publishes notes: No
Languages accepted: French; English
Prints abstracts: No
Author-anonymous submission: No

SUBMISSION REQUIREMENTS

Restrictions on contributors: All and only papers given at the annual Algonquian Conference are accepted.
Author pays submission fee: No
Author pays page charges: No
Length of articles: No restrictions
Style: Handbook of North American Indians (Smithsonian)
Number of copies required: 1
Special requirements: All submissions must be on computer diskette or sent by electronic mail.
Copyright ownership: Carleton Univ.
Time between decision and publication: 1 yr.
Articles submitted per year: 20-30
Articles published per year: 20-30

(2120)
Papers of the Bibliographical Society of America

William S. Peterson, Editor
Dept. of English
Univ. of Maryland
College Park, MD 20742

Telephone: 301 405-3756; 202 546-2466
E-mail: WSP@WAM.UMD.EDU
First published: 1907
Sponsoring organization: Bibliographical Soc. of America
ISSN: 0006-128X

MLA acronym: PBSA

SUBSCRIPTION INFORMATION

Frequency of publication: 4 times/yr. (Mar., June, Sept., Dec.)
Circulation: 1,200
Available in microform: No
Subscription price: $30.00/yr. (includes membership)
Year to which price refers: 1992
Subscription address: P.O. Box 397, Grand Central Station, New York, NY 10163
Subscription telephone: 212 995-9151

ADVERTISING INFORMATION

Advertising accepted: Yes
Advertising rates: $45.00/quarter page; $80.00/half page; $125.00/full page

EDITORIAL DESCRIPTION

Scope: Publishes scholarly and critical papers on descriptive or analytical bibliography, the history of printing, publishing, other book trades, textual editing, and manuscript studies.
Reviews books: Yes
Publishes notes: Yes
Languages accepted: English
Prints abstracts: No
Author-anonymous submission: No

SUBMISSION REQUIREMENTS

Restrictions on contributors: Book reviews are commissioned.
Author pays submission fee: No
Author pays page charges: No
Length of articles: No restrictions
Length of notes: No restrictions
Style: Chicago preferred
Number of copies required: 1
Copyright ownership: Bibliographical Soc. of America. Author retains all rights to reprint.
Rejected manuscripts: Returned; enclose return postage.
Time before publication decision: 2-6 mos.
Time between decision and publication: 4-8 mos.
Number of reviewers: 1-2
Articles submitted per year: 35-40
Articles published per year: 10-12
Book reviews published per year: 50
Notes submitted per year: 35-50
Notes published per year: 10-15

(2121)
*Papers of the Bibliographical Society of Canada/Cahiers de la Société Bibliographique du Canada

Bruce Whiteman, Editor
Dept. of Rare Books & Special Collections
McLennan Library
McGill Univ.
3459 McTavish St.
Montreal, Quebec H3A 1Y1, Canada

Telephone: 514 398-4706
Fax: 514 398-7184
E-mail: CXD2@MUSICA.MCGILL.CA
First published: 1962
Sponsoring organization: Bibliographical Soc. of Canada/La Soc. Bibliographique du Canada
ISSN: 0067-6896
MLA acronym: PBSC

SUBSCRIPTION INFORMATION

Frequency of publication: 2 times/yr.
Circulation: 400
Available in microform: No
Subscription price: C$40.00/yr. institutions; C$30.00/yr. individuals
Year to which price refers: 1992
Subscription address: P.O. Box 575, Station P, Toronto, Ontario M5S 2T1, Canada

ADVERTISING INFORMATION

Advertising accepted: No

EDITORIAL DESCRIPTION

Scope: Promotes the study of any aspect of bibliography, including printing and publishing history, and the publication of works of bibliography.
Reviews books: Yes
Publishes notes: No
Languages accepted: English; French
Prints abstracts: No
Author-anonymous submission: No

SUBMISSION REQUIREMENTS

Restrictions on contributors: Unsolicited book reviews are not accepted.
Author pays submission fee: No
Author pays page charges: No
Length of articles: 5,000-10,000 words
Length of book reviews: 500-1,500 words
Style: Chicago
Number of copies required: 1
Copyright ownership: Bibliographical Soc. of Canada
Rejected manuscripts: Returned
Time before publication decision: 2-3 mos.
Time between decision and publication: 6-10 mos.
Number of reviewers: 3
Articles submitted per year: 10-12
Articles published per year: 5-6
Book reviews published per year: 15-20

(2122)
*Papers on French Seventeenth Century Literature

Wolfgang Leiner, Editor
Romanisches Seminar
Univ. Tübingen
Wilhelmstr. 50
7400 Tübingen, Germany

First published: 1973
ISSN: 0343-0758
MLA acronym: PFSCL

SUBSCRIPTION INFORMATION

Frequency of publication: 2 times/yr.
Circulation: 550
Available in microform: No

ADVERTISING INFORMATION

Advertising accepted: Yes

EDITORIAL DESCRIPTION

Scope: Publishes articles on French literature of the 17th century; includes papers delivered at the MLA convention and proceedings of the North American Society for French Seventeenth Century Literature conferences.
Reviews books: Yes
Publishes notes: No
Languages accepted: English; French; German
Prints abstracts: No
Author-anonymous submission: No

SUBMISSION REQUIREMENTS

Restrictions on contributors: None
Author pays submission fee: No
Author pays page charges: Yes, if manuscript exceeds 20 pp.
Length of articles: 20 pp. maximum
Length of book reviews: 3 pp.
Style: MLA
Number of copies required: 2
Special requirements: Submit camera-ready copy.
Copyright ownership: Journal
Rejected manuscripts: Returned; enclose return postage.
Time before publication decision: 2 mos.
Time between decision and publication: 6 mos.
Number of reviewers: 3
Articles submitted per year: 60
Articles published per year: 45
Book reviews published per year: 60

(2123)
*Papers on Language and Literature: A Journal for Scholars and Critics of Language and Literature

Brian Abel Ragen & Jack G. Voller, Editors
Southern Illinois Univ.
Edwardsville, IL 62026-1434

Telephone: 618 692-2119
Fax: 618 692-3509
First published: 1965
Sponsoring organization: Southern Illinois Univ. at Edwardsville
ISSN: 0031-1294
MLA acronym: PLL

SUBSCRIPTION INFORMATION

Frequency of publication: 4 times/yr. (Winter, Spring, Summer, Fall)
Circulation: 800
Available in microform: Yes
Subscription price: $48.00/yr. institutions; $24.00/yr. individuals; add $3.00/yr. outside US
Year to which price refers: 1993

ADVERTISING INFORMATION

Advertising accepted: Yes

EDITORIAL DESCRIPTION

Scope: Publishes papers devoted to literary history, analysis, stylistics, and evaluation. Welcomes papers discussing any period, genre, or national literature. Also publishes original materials relating to *belles lettres*, letters, journals, notebooks, and similar documents.
Reviews books: Yes
Publishes notes: Yes
Languages accepted: English
Prints abstracts: No
Author-anonymous submission: No

SUBMISSION REQUIREMENTS

Restrictions on contributors: Reviews are commissioned.
Author pays submission fee: No
Author pays page charges: No
Length of articles: 6,000 words
Length of book reviews: 750-1,000 words
Length of notes: 250 words
Style: MLA
Number of copies required: 2
Special requirements: Manuscripts accepted for publication must be resubmitted on diskette.
Copyright ownership: Board of Trustees, Southern Illinois Univ. at Edwardsville
Rejected manuscripts: 1 copy returned; enclose SASE.
Time before publication decision: 2-3 mos.
Time between decision and publication: 6-12 mos.
Number of reviewers: 2 minimum
Articles submitted per year: 200
Articles published per year: 36
Book reviews published per year: 4-6
Notes submitted per year: 25
Notes published per year: 4-6

(2124)
*Papiere zur Linguistik

Willi Mayerthaler & Johannes Bechert, Editors
Univ. Klagenfurt
Inst. für Sprachwissenschaft
Univ. 65-67
9010 Klagenfurt, Austria

Telephone: (43) 463 2700350
Fax: (43) 463 2700100
First published: 1979
ISSN: 0343-4133
MLA acronym: PzL

SUBSCRIPTION INFORMATION

Frequency of publication: 2 times/yr.
Available in microform: No
Subscription price: 68 DM/yr. institutions; 48 DM/yr. individuals
Year to which price refers: 1991
Subscription address: Gunter Narr Verlag, Postfach 2567, Dischingerweg 5, 7400 Tübingen 5, Germany
Subscription fax: (49) 7071 75288

ADVERTISING INFORMATION

Advertising accepted: Yes

EDITORIAL DESCRIPTION

Scope: Publishes articles on theoretical linguistics and its connections with the analytical philosophy of formal and normal language. Emphasis is on contemporary semantics and pragmatics; however, the journal is open to new developments.
Reviews books: Occasionally
Publishes notes: Occasionally
Languages accepted: English; German; occasionally French; occasionally Spanish
Prints abstracts: Yes
Author-anonymous submission: Yes

SUBMISSION REQUIREMENTS

Restrictions on contributors: None
Author pays submission fee: No
Author pays page charges: No
Style: MLA
Number of copies required: 2
Special requirements: Submit original typescript and 1 copy. Include a 15-line abstract in English.
Copyright ownership: Gunter Narr Verlag
Rejected manuscripts: Returned
Time before publication decision: 1 mo.
Time between decision and publication: 4 mos.
Number of reviewers: 2
Articles submitted per year: 15
Articles published per year: 10
Book reviews submitted per year: 2
Book reviews published per year: 1
Notes submitted per year: 3
Notes published per year: 1

(2125)
*Papiere zur Textlinguistik/Papers in Textlinguistics

Jens Ihwe, János S. Petöfi, & Hannes Rieser, Editors
Helmut Buske Verlag GmbH
Richardstr. 47
2000 Hamburg 76, Germany

Telephone: (49) 40 296842
Fax: (49) 40 2993614
First published: 1974
ISSN: 0341-3195
MLA acronym: PText

SUBSCRIPTION INFORMATION

Frequency of publication: Irregular
Circulation: 400
Available in microform: No

ADVERTISING INFORMATION

Advertising accepted: No

EDITORIAL DESCRIPTION

Scope: Publishes articles on text linguistics.
Reviews books: No
Languages accepted: German; English; French
Prints abstracts: No

SUBMISSION REQUIREMENTS

Author pays submission fee: No
Author pays page charges: No

(2126)
*Parabola: The Magazine of Myth and Tradition

Ellen Dooling Draper & Virginia Baron, Editors
656 Broadway
New York, NY 10012-2317

Telephone: 212 505-6200
Fax: 212 979-7325
First published: 1976
Sponsoring organization: Soc. for the Study of Myth & Tradition
ISSN: 0362-1596
MLA acronym: Parabola

SUBSCRIPTION INFORMATION

Frequency of publication: 4 times/yr.
Circulation: 40,000
Available in microform: Yes
Subscription price: $20.00/yr.
Year to which price refers: 1992

ADVERTISING INFORMATION

Advertising accepted: Yes
Advertising rates: $775.00/full page

EDITORIAL DESCRIPTION

Scope: Publishes articles on folklore, mythology, religion, anthropology, psychology, and comparative traditions.
Reviews books: Yes
Publishes notes: No
Languages accepted: English
Prints abstracts: No
Author-anonymous submission: No

SUBMISSION REQUIREMENTS

Restrictions on contributors: None
Author pays submission fee: No
Author pays page charges: No
Length of articles: 4,000 words maximum
Length of book reviews: 750 words maximum
Style: Chicago
Number of copies required: 1
Special requirements: Writer's guidelines are available.
Copyright ownership: Author
Rejected manuscripts: Returned; enclose SASE.
Time before publication decision: 6-8 weeks
Time between decision and publication: 3 mos.
Number of reviewers: 8
Articles submitted per year: 300
Articles published per year: 30
Book reviews submitted per year: 45
Book reviews published per year: 40

(2127)
Parade Sauvage

Steve Murphy, Editor
Musée-Bibliothèque Rimbaud
B.P. 490
08109 Charleville-Mézières, France

ISSN: 0764-471X
MLA acronym: ParadeS

EDITORIAL DESCRIPTION

Languages accepted: French

(2128)
Paragone: Rivista Mensile di Arte Figurativa e Letteratura

G. C. Sansoni, Editor
Casa Editrice G. C. Sansoni
Via Benedetto Varchi, 47
50132 Florence, Italy

First published: 1950
ISSN: 0031-1650
MLA acronym: Paragone

SUBSCRIPTION INFORMATION

Frequency of publication: 12 times/yr. (6 issues [odd numbered] dedicated to figurative art; 6 issues [even numbered] dedicated to literature)
Available in microform: No
Subscription address: Licosa SpA., Via Duca Di Calabria 1/1, 50125 Florence, Italy

EDITORIAL DESCRIPTION

Reviews books: Yes
Publishes notes: Yes
Languages accepted: Italian; English; French
Prints abstracts: No

(2129)
Paragraph: A Journal of Modern Critical Theory

Christopher Johnson, Editor
Dept. of Modern Languages
Keele Univ.
Keele, Staffordshire ST5 5BG, England

Additional editorial address: Production Dept., Oxford Univ. Press, Southfield Rd., Eynsham, Oxford OX8 1JJ, England. Send books for review to: Leslie Hill, Dept. of French Studies, Univ. of Warwick, Coventry CV4 7AL, England.
First published: 1983
Sponsoring organization: Modern Critical Theory Group
ISSN: 0264-8334
MLA acronym: Paragraph

SUBSCRIPTION INFORMATION

Frequency of publication: 3 times/yr. (Mar., July, Nov.)
Circulation: 300
Available in microform: No
Subscription price: £34.00/yr. institutions United Kingdom & Europe; $66.00/yr. institutions elsewhere; £16.00/yr. individuals United Kingdom & Europe; $30.00/yr. elsewhere
Year to which price refers: 1992
Subscription address: Subscriptions Dept., Oxford Univ. Press, Pinkhill House, Southfield Rd., Eynsham, Oxford OX8 1JJ, England
Subscription telephone: (44) 865 882283
Subscription fax: (44) 865 882890

ADVERTISING INFORMATION

Advertising accepted: Yes

EDITORIAL DESCRIPTION

Scope: Publishes articles on modern critical theory and its application to literature and other arts.
Reviews books: Yes
Publishes notes: No
Languages accepted: English
Prints abstracts: No
Author-anonymous submission: Yes

SUBMISSION REQUIREMENTS

Restrictions on contributors: Notes and review articles are commissioned. Reviews are not published.
Author pays submission fee: No
Author pays page charges: No
Length of articles: 7,000 words maximum; 2,000 words maximum for review articles
Style: Journal
Number of copies required: 2
Special requirements: All quotations in languages other than English must be accompanied by an English translation.
Copyright ownership: Oxford Univ. Press
Rejected manuscripts: Returned; enclose SASE.
Time before publication decision: 6 mos.
Time between decision and publication: 1 yr.
Number of reviewers: 8
Articles submitted per year: 30
Articles published per year: 15

(2130)
*Parergon: Bulletin of the Australian and New Zealand Association for Medieval and Renaissance Studies

D. Speed, Editor
Dept. of English
Univ. of Sydney
Sydney, NSW, 2006, Australia

Telephone: (61) 2 6922349
Fax: (61) 2 6922434
First published: 1971
Sponsoring organization: Australian & New Zealand Assn. for Medieval & Renaissance Studies
ISSN: 0313-6221
MLA acronym: Parergon

SUBSCRIPTION INFORMATION

Frequency of publication: 2 times/yr. (June, Dec.)
Circulation: 300
Available in microform: No
Subscription price: A$40.00/yr.
Year to which price refers: 1992
Subscription address: J. Quinn, Honorary Treasurer, ANZAMRS, English Dept., Univ. of Sydney, Sydney, NSW, 2006, Australia

ADVERTISING INFORMATION

Advertising accepted: No

EDITORIAL DESCRIPTION

Scope: Publishes articles on medieval and Renaissance studies.
Reviews books: Yes
Publishes notes: Yes
Languages accepted: English
Prints abstracts: No
Author-anonymous submission: Yes

SUBMISSION REQUIREMENTS

Restrictions on contributors: Book reviews are solicited.
Author pays submission fee: No
Author pays page charges: No
Length of articles: 5,000 words maximum
Length of book reviews: 500 words
Length of notes: 1,200 words
Style: Journal

Number of copies required: 1
Copyright ownership: Author
Rejected manuscripts: Returned
Time before publication decision: 3 mos.
Time between decision and publication: 9 mos.
Number of reviewers: 2
Articles submitted per year: 25
Articles published per year: 15
Book reviews submitted per year: 60
Book reviews published per year: 60
Notes submitted per year: 0-1
Notes published per year: 0-1

(2131)
*Parnasso

Jarkko Laine, Editor
Valtaojantie 2 b 1
20810 Turku, Finland

Telephone: (358) 21 354110
Fax: (358) 21 354330
First published: 1951
ISSN: 0031-2320
MLA acronym: Parnasso

SUBSCRIPTION INFORMATION

Frequency of publication: 8 times/yr.
Circulation: 6,700
Available in microform: No
Subscription price: 234 Fmk/yr. Europe; 236 Fmk/yr. elsewhere
Year to which price refers: 1991
Subscription address: Yhtyneet Kuvalehdet Oy, Maistraatinportti 1, 00240 Helsinki, Finland
Subscription telephone: (358) 0 156665
Subscription fax: (358) 0 156651

ADVERTISING INFORMATION

Advertising accepted: Yes

EDITORIAL DESCRIPTION

Scope: Publishes articles on literature, as well as short stories and poetry.
Reviews books: Yes
Languages accepted: Finnish
Prints abstracts: No
Author-anonymous submission: No

SUBMISSION REQUIREMENTS

Author pays submission fee: Yes
Cost of submission fee: Varies
Author pays page charges: Yes
Cost of page charges: Varies
Number of copies required: 1
Copyright ownership: Author
Rejected manuscripts: Returned
Time before publication decision: 3 mos.
Time between decision and publication: 1-3 mos.
Number of reviewers: 1
Articles submitted per year: 500
Articles published per year: 100
Book reviews submitted per year: 120
Book reviews published per year: 80

(2132)
*Parnassos: Philologikon Periodikon/ Literary Journal of the Parnassos Literary Society

Nikolaos Livadaras, President
Parnassos Literary Soc.
8, St. George Kazytsis Square
105.61 Athens, Greece

Telephone: (30) 1 3224679; (30) 1 3225310; (30) 1 3221917
Fax: (30) 1 3249398
First published: 1877
Sponsoring organization: Parnassos Literary Soc.

ISSN: 0048-301X
MLA acronym: ParnassosL

SUBSCRIPTION INFORMATION

Frequency of publication: Annual
Circulation: 3,500
Available in microform: No
Subscription price: $80.00/yr.
Year to which price refers: 1992

ADVERTISING INFORMATION

Advertising accepted: No

EDITORIAL DESCRIPTION

Scope: Publishes articles on philosophy and the arts, including linguistics, literature, theology, archaeology, and history.
Reviews books: Yes
Publishes notes: Yes
Languages accepted: Greek; English; French; Italian; German; Spanish
Prints abstracts: No
Author-anonymous submission: No

SUBMISSION REQUIREMENTS

Author pays submission fee: No
Author pays page charges: No
Length of articles: 2,500-12,000 words
Style: None
Number of copies required: 2
Special requirements: Submit original typescript.
Rejected manuscripts: Not returned
Time before publication decision: 3 mos.
Time between decision and publication: 6 mos.
Number of reviewers: 2
Articles submitted per year: 60
Articles published per year: 30
Book reviews submitted per year: 50
Book reviews published per year: 10

(2133)
*Parnassus: Poetry in Review

Herbert Leibowitz, Editor
41 Union Square West, Room 804
New York, NY 10003

First published: 1972
Sponsoring organization: Poetry in Review Foundation
ISSN: 0048-3028
MLA acronym: Parnassus

SUBSCRIPTION INFORMATION

Frequency of publication: 2 times/yr.
Circulation: 1,500-2,000
Available in microform: Yes, through Univ. Microfilms International
Subscription price: $36.00/yr., $68.00/2 yrs. institutions; $18.00/yr., $34.00/2 yrs. individuals; add $4.00/yr. postage outside US
Year to which price refers: 1992

ADVERTISING INFORMATION

Advertising accepted: Yes

EDITORIAL DESCRIPTION

Scope: Publishes comprehensive reviews of new books of poetry.
Reviews books: Yes
Publishes notes: No
Languages accepted: English
Prints abstracts: No
Author-anonymous submission: No

SUBMISSION REQUIREMENTS

Restrictions on contributors: Most articles are solicited.
Author pays submission fee: No
Author pays page charges: No

Length of articles: No restrictions
Length of book reviews: No restrictions
Style: MLA; Chicago
Number of copies required: 1
Copyright ownership: Assigned by journal to author if requested
Rejected manuscripts: Returned; enclose return postage.
Time before publication decision: 4-8 weeks
Time between decision and publication: 8-18 mos.
Number of reviewers: 3-4
Articles submitted per year: 250
Articles published per year: 40-50
Book reviews published per year: 40-50

(2134)
*Paroles Gelées: UCLA French Studies

Paul W. Merrill, Editor
Dept. of French
222 Royce Hall
Univ. of California at Los Angeles
405 Hilgard Ave.
Los Angeles, CA 90024-1550

Telephone: 213 825-1145
First published: 1983
Sponsoring organization: Univ. of California, Los Angeles, Graduate Students Assn.
MLA acronym: PG

SUBSCRIPTION INFORMATION

Frequency of publication: Annual (Fall)
Circulation: 350
Available in microform: No
Subscription price: $10.00/yr. institutions; $8.00/yr. individuals
Year to which price refers: 1991

ADVERTISING INFORMATION

Advertising accepted: No

EDITORIAL DESCRIPTION

Scope: Publishes articles on French studies.
Reviews books: Yes
Publishes notes: No
Languages accepted: English; French
Prints abstracts: No
Author-anonymous submission: Yes

SUBMISSION REQUIREMENTS

Restrictions on contributors: Contributors must be graduate students.
Author pays submission fee: No
Author pays page charges: No
Length of articles: 25 pp.
Length of book reviews: 750 words
Style: MLA; Chicago
Number of copies required: 2
Special requirements: Annual submission deadline is 1 Mar.
Copyright ownership: Author
Rejected manuscripts: Returned at author's request
Time before publication decision: 2-6 mos.
Time between decision and publication: 5 mos.
Number of reviewers: 3-6
Articles submitted per year: 20-30
Articles published per year: 3-6
Book reviews submitted per year: 2-9
Book reviews published per year: 1-3

(2135)
*Partisan Review

William Phillips, Editor
236 Bay State Rd.
Boston, MA 02215

Telephone: 617 353-4260
Fax: 617 353-7444
First published: 1934
Sponsoring organization: Boston Univ.
ISSN: 0031-2525
MLA acronym: PR

SUBSCRIPTION INFORMATION

Frequency of publication: 4 times/yr. (Winter, Spring, Summer, Fall)
Circulation: 8,500
Available in microform: Yes
Subscription address: Scholarly Publications, Room 230, Boston Univ., 985 Commonwealth Ave., Boston, MA 02215

ADVERTISING INFORMATION

Advertising accepted: Yes

EDITORIAL DESCRIPTION

Scope: Publishes literary intellectual and political articles, poetry, fiction, and book reviews.
Reviews books: Yes
Publishes notes: Yes
Languages accepted: English
Prints abstracts: No
Author-anonymous submission: No

SUBMISSION REQUIREMENTS

Restrictions on contributors: None
Author pays submission fee: No
Author pays page charges: No
Length of articles: No restrictions
Length of book reviews: 1,200-1,500 words
Style: Chicago
Number of copies required: 1
Copyright ownership: Author
Rejected manuscripts: Returned; enclose SASE
Time before publication decision: 1-2 mos.
Time between decision and publication: 4-8 mos.
Number of reviewers: 3 minimum
Articles submitted per year: 300
Articles published per year: 40
Book reviews submitted per year: 100
Book reviews published per year: 25-30

(2136)
*PASAA: A Journal of Language Teaching and Learning in Thailand

Pavinee Navarat, Editor
Chulalongkorn Univ. Language Inst.
4th Floor, Prem Purachatra Bldg.
Phyathai Rd.
Bangkok 10500, Thailand

Telephone: (66) 2 2521491; (66) 2 2521498
Fax: (66) 2 2525978
First published: 1970
Sponsoring organization: Chulalongkorn Univ.
ISSN: 0125-2488
MLA acronym: PASAA

SUBSCRIPTION INFORMATION

Frequency of publication: 2 times/yr. (June, Dec.)
Circulation: 500
Available in microform: No
Subscription price: 60 B/yr. Thailand; $15.00/yr. elsewhere
Year to which price refers: 1992

ADVERTISING INFORMATION

Advertising accepted: Yes

EDITORIAL DESCRIPTION

Scope: Publishes articles on language teaching in Thailand.
Reviews books: Yes
Publishes notes: No
Languages accepted: English
Prints abstracts: Yes
Author-anonymous submission: No

SUBMISSION REQUIREMENTS

Restrictions on contributors: None
Author pays submission fee: No
Author pays page charges: No
Length of articles: 3,000-10,000 words
Length of book reviews: 456-500 words
Length of notes: 400-450 words
Style: MLA; American Psychological Assn.
Number of copies required: 1
Special requirements: Submit contributions by 1 Apr. for June issue, and by 1 Sept. for Dec. issue. Include a short abstract in English and author's curriculum vitae.
Copyright ownership: Chulalongkorn Univ. Language Inst.
Rejected manuscripts: Not returned
Time before publication decision: 2 mos.
Time between decision and publication: 1 yr.
Number of reviewers: 4
Articles submitted per year: 50-60
Articles published per year: 40
Book reviews submitted per year: 5-10
Book reviews published per year: 5

(2137)
*Patma-Banasirakan Handes: Istoriko-Filologičeskiĭ Zhurnal

M. G. Nercissian, Editor
Marshal Baghramian Ave., 24-G
375019 Yerevan, Armenia

First published: 1958
Sponsoring organization: Akademiia Nauk
MLA acronym: PBH

SUBSCRIPTION INFORMATION

Frequency of publication: 3 times/yr.
Circulation: 1,000
Available in microform: No
Subscription address: Vsesoiuznoe, Ob'edinenie "Mezhdunarodnaia Kniga", G-200, 121200 Moscow, Russia

ADVERTISING INFORMATION

Advertising accepted: No

EDITORIAL DESCRIPTION

Scope: Publishes articles on Armenology, Caucasian studies, and Byzantine studies.
Reviews books: Yes
Publishes notes: Yes
Languages accepted: Armenian; Russian
Prints abstracts: No
Author-anonymous submission: No

SUBMISSION REQUIREMENTS

Restrictions on contributors: None
Author pays submission fee: No
Author pays page charges: No
Length of articles: 2,500-6,000 words
Length of book reviews: 2,000-3,000 words
Length of notes: 150-200 words
Style: None
Number of copies required: 2
Special requirements: Original typescript and summary submitted in any European language will be translated into Armenian or Russian if accepted for publication.
Copyright ownership: Editorial Board
Rejected manuscripts: Returned
Time before publication decision: 3 mos.
Time between decision and publication: 6 mos.
Number of reviewers: 3
Articles submitted per year: 120
Articles published per year: 100
Book reviews submitted per year: 18
Book reviews published per year: 12-15
Notes submitted per year: 80-100
Notes published per year: 50-60

(2138)
Paunch

Arthur Efron, Editor
State Univ. of New York at Buffalo
Dept. of English
Buffalo, NY 14260

First published: 1963
ISSN: 0031-3262
MLA acronym: Paunch

SUBSCRIPTION INFORMATION

Frequency of publication: 1 double issue/yr.
Circulation: 200
Available in microform: No

ADVERTISING INFORMATION

Advertising accepted: No

EDITORIAL DESCRIPTION

Scope: Publishes articles on the body in literature; problems in aesthetics, particularly in relation to Dewey's *Art as Experience* and Pepper's *The Basis of Criticism in the Arts*; literature in relation to the authority, and criminality, of the modern state.
Reviews books: Yes
Publishes notes: Yes
Languages accepted: English
Prints abstracts: No
Author-anonymous submission: No

SUBMISSION REQUIREMENTS

Restrictions on contributors: None
Author pays submission fee: No
Author pays page charges: No
Length of articles: 5,000-7,000 words
Length of book reviews: No restrictions
Length of notes: No restrictions
Style: None
Number of copies required: 1
Copyright ownership: Editor for first serial rights only
Rejected manuscripts: Returned; enclose return postage.
Time before publication decision: 3 mos.
Time between decision and publication: 12-18 mos.
Number of reviewers: 3
Articles submitted per year: 45
Articles published per year: 5
Book reviews submitted per year: 2-4
Book reviews published per year: 2-4

(2139)
*Peake Studies

G. Peter Winnington, Editor
Les 3 Chasseurs
1413 Orzens
Vaud, Switzerland

Telephone: (41) 21 8877976
First published: 1988
ISSN: 1013-1191
MLA acronym: PeakeSt

SUBSCRIPTION INFORMATION

Frequency of publication: Irregular (usually 2 times/yr.)
Available in microform: No

ADVERTISING INFORMATION

Advertising accepted: Yes
Advertising rates: $120.00/back cover

EDITORIAL DESCRIPTION

Scope: Publishes articles of criticism and debate of Mervyn Peake's work, information about his life, and assessments of his impact on other writers and artists.
Reviews books: Yes
Publishes notes: Yes
Languages accepted: English
Prints abstracts: No
Author-anonymous submission: No

SUBMISSION REQUIREMENTS

Restrictions on contributors: None
Author pays submission fee: No
Author pays page charges: No
Length of articles: 6,000 words maximum
Length of book reviews: No restrictions
Length of notes: No restrictions
Style: MLA preferred
Number of copies required: 1
Special requirements: Submit typescript and if possible, Macintosh or IBM MS-DOS 5.25 inch diskette.
Copyright ownership: Author
Rejected manuscripts: Returned
Time before publication decision: 1 mo.
Time between decision and publication: 6-12 mos.
Number of reviewers: 1-2

(2140)
*Pembroke Magazine

Shelby Stephenson, Editor
Pembroke Magazine
Box 60, PSU
Pembroke, NC 28372

Telephone: 919 521-4214 ext. 4433
First published: 1969
Sponsoring organization: North Carolina Arts Council; National Endowment for Arts; Coordinating Council of Literary Magazines (CCLM); Pembroke State Univ.
ISSN: 0097-496X
MLA acronym: PM

SUBSCRIPTION INFORMATION

Frequency of publication: Annual
Available in microform: Yes, through Univ. Microfilms International
Subscription price: $5.00/yr. US; $5.50/yr. elsewhere
Year to which price refers: 1991

ADVERTISING INFORMATION

Advertising accepted: Yes

EDITORIAL DESCRIPTION

Scope: Publishes poetry, stories, and critical essays. Usually, but not always, focuses on one writer in each issue.
Reviews books: Yes
Publishes notes: Yes
Languages accepted: English
Prints abstracts: No
Author-anonymous submission: Yes

SUBMISSION REQUIREMENTS

Restrictions on contributors: None
Author pays submission fee: No
Author pays page charges: No
Length of articles: 2,500 words
Length of book reviews: 500 words
Style: MLA
Special requirements: Submit double-spaced typescript.
Copyright ownership: Reverts to author
Rejected manuscripts: Returned; enclose SASE.
Time before publication decision: 6-12 mos.
Time between decision and publication: 6-12 mos.

(2141)
*Pennsylvania Folklife

Nancy K. Gaugler, Editor
Pennsylvania Folklife Soc.
Box 92
Collegeville, PA 19426

Telephone: 215 489-4111 ext. 2388
First published: 1949
Sponsoring organization: Pennsylvania Folklife Soc.; Ursinus College
ISSN: 0031-4498
MLA acronym: PF

SUBSCRIPTION INFORMATION

Frequency of publication: 3 times/yr. (Fall, Winter, Spring)
Circulation: 1,600
Available in microform: No
Subscription price: $10.00/yr.
Year to which price refers: 1992-93

ADVERTISING INFORMATION

Advertising accepted: No

EDITORIAL DESCRIPTION

Scope: Publishes articles on history and folklife of Pennsylvania with special emphasis on Pennsylvania German history, culture, folklore, and crafts. Emphasizes comparisons to other ethnic groups.
Reviews books: No
Languages accepted: English; German; Pennsylvania German dialect
Prints abstracts: No

SUBMISSION REQUIREMENTS

Author pays submission fee: No
Author pays page charges: No
Length of articles: 600-60,000 words
Style: Chicago
Number of copies required: 2
Special requirements: Articles including line drawings or photo illustrations are encouraged.
Copyright ownership: Pennsylvania Folklife Soc.
Rejected manuscripts: Returned; enclose return postage.
Time before publication decision: 6-12 weeks
Time between decision and publication: 1-2 yrs.
Number of reviewers: 1-2
Articles submitted per year: 40
Articles published per year: 15-24

(2142)
*Pennsylvania Magazine of History and Biography

Ian M. G. Quimby, Carla Mulford, & Melissa J. Greenwald, Editors
Historical Soc. of Pennsylvania
1300 Locust St.
Philadelphia, PA 19107

Telephone: 215 732-6201
Fax: 215 732-2680
First published: 1877
Sponsoring organization: Historical Soc. of Pennsylvania
ISSN: 0031-4587
MLA acronym: PMHB

SUBSCRIPTION INFORMATION

Frequency of publication: 4 times/yr. (Jan., Apr., July, Oct.)
Circulation: 3,200
Available in microform: Yes
Subscription price: $35.00/yr. institutions; $30.00/yr. individuals
Year to which price refers: 1992

ADVERTISING INFORMATION

Advertising accepted: Yes
Advertising rates: $200.00/full page

EDITORIAL DESCRIPTION

Scope: Publishes articles on the history, literature, and culture of the mid-Atlantic states from their settlement to the present.
Reviews books: Yes
Publishes notes: Occasionally
Languages accepted: English
Prints abstracts: No
Author-anonymous submission: Yes

SUBMISSION REQUIREMENTS

Restrictions on contributors: None
Author pays submission fee: No
Author pays page charges: No
Length of articles: 3,000-7,500 words
Length of book reviews: 600 words
Style: Chicago
Number of copies required: 2
Special requirements: Submission on diskette is required upon acceptance.
Copyright ownership: Assigned by author to journal
Rejected manuscripts: Returned
Time before publication decision: 6-10 weeks
Time between decision and publication: 3-6 mos.
Number of reviewers: 2-3
Articles published per year: 20
Book reviews submitted per year: 80
Book reviews published per year: 65

(2143)
La Pensée: Revue du Rationalisme Moderne

Antoine Casanova, Editor
JRM
64, boulevard Auguste-Blanqui
75013 Paris, France

Telephone: (33) 1 43364534
First published: 1939
ISSN: 0031-4773
MLA acronym: Pensée

SUBSCRIPTION INFORMATION

Frequency of publication: 6 times/yr.

EDITORIAL DESCRIPTION

Scope: Publishes articles on philosophy, history, and the social and natural sciences.
Reviews books: Yes
Publishes notes: Yes
Languages accepted: French
Prints abstracts: Yes

SUBMISSION REQUIREMENTS

Author pays page charges: No
Length of articles: 20-25 pp.
Length of book reviews: 2-3 pp.
Length of notes: 10-12 pp.
Number of copies required: 1
Copyright ownership: Journal
Rejected manuscripts: Not returned
Time before publication decision: 3 mos.
Time between decision and publication: 6 mos.
Number of reviewers: 3-4
Articles submitted per year: 140
Articles published per year: 45
Book reviews published per year: 100
Notes published per year: 40

(2144)
*Il Pensiero Politico: Rivista di Storia delle Idee Politiche e Sociali

S. Mastellone & V. I. Comparato, Editors
Dept. di Scienze Storiche
Via Pascoli
06100 Perugia, Italy

Telephone: (39) 75 5855443
Fax: (39) 75 5855449
First published: 1968
ISSN: 0031-4846
MLA acronym: PPol

SUBSCRIPTION INFORMATION

Frequency of publication: 3 times/yr.
Circulation: 1,000
Available in microform: No
Subscription price: 64,000 Lit/yr. Italy; 80,000 Lit/yr. elsewhere
Year to which price refers: 1991
Subscription address: Casa Editrice Leo S. Olschki, C.P. 66, 50100 Florence, Italy
Subscription telephone: (39) 55 6530684
Subscription fax: (39) 55 6530214

ADVERTISING INFORMATION

Advertising accepted: No

EDITORIAL DESCRIPTION

Scope: Focuses on the review of international history for political and social ideas from antiquity to the contemporary age.
Reviews books: Yes
Publishes notes: Yes
Languages accepted: French; Italian; English; German
Prints abstracts: No
Author-anonymous submission: No

SUBMISSION REQUIREMENTS

Restrictions on contributors: None
Author pays submission fee: No
Author pays page charges: No
Length of articles: 5,000-12,000 words
Length of book reviews: 300-600 words
Length of notes: 2,000-3,000 words
Style: Request instructions from Olschki
Number of copies required: 2
Copyright ownership: Journal
Rejected manuscripts: Not returned
Time before publication decision: 4 mos.
Time between decision and publication: 6-12 mos.
Number of reviewers: 2
Articles submitted per year: 15
Articles published per year: 9
Book reviews submitted per year: 120-170
Book reviews published per year: 100-150
Notes submitted per year: 20
Notes published per year: 10-15

(2145)
*Pequod: A Journal of Contemporary Literature and Literary Criticism

Mark Rudman, Editor
Dept. of English, Rm. 200
19 University Place
New York, NY 10003

First published: 1974
Sponsoring organization: New York Univ.; National Endowment for the Arts; New York State Council on the Arts
ISSN: 0149-0516
MLA acronym: Pequod

SUBSCRIPTION INFORMATION

Frequency of publication: 2 times/yr.
Circulation: 750
Available in microform: Yes

Subscription price: $18.00/yr. institutions; $12.00/yr. individuals
Year to which price refers: 1992

ADVERTISING INFORMATION

Advertising accepted: Yes

EDITORIAL DESCRIPTION

Scope: Publishes new works of poetry and fiction by young authors as well as work in translation by international writers whose work has not been widely published in the United States.
Reviews books: No
Publishes notes: No
Languages accepted: English
Prints abstracts: No
Author-anonymous submission: No

SUBMISSION REQUIREMENTS

Restrictions on contributors: None
Author pays submission fee: No
Author pays page charges: No
Length of articles: 1-20 pp.
Style: MLA
Number of copies required: 1
Special requirements: Manuscripts must be typescript and have page numbers. Author's name must be on every page, and address on first page.
Copyright ownership: Reverts to author
Rejected manuscripts: Returned; enclose SASE
Time before publication decision: 6-18 mos.
Time between decision and publication: 3-6 mos.
Number of reviewers: 2
Articles submitted per year: 75
Articles published per year: 10

(2146)
*Perception & Psychophysics

Charles W. Eriksen, Editor
Dept. of Psychology
Univ. of Illinois, Urbana-Champaign
603 E. Daniel
Champaign, IL 61820

Telephone: 217 333-3659
Fax: 217 244-5876
E-mail: Ceriksen@psych.uiuc.edu
First published: 1966
Sponsoring organization: Psychonomic Soc., Inc.
ISSN: 0031-5117
MLA acronym: P&P

SUBSCRIPTION INFORMATION

Frequency of publication: 12 times/yr.
Circulation: 2,000
Available in microform: No
Subscription price: $134.00/yr. institutions; $60.00/yr. individuals
Year to which price refers: 1992
Subscription address: Psychonomic Soc., Publications Office, 1710 Fortview Rd., Austin, TX 78704

ADVERTISING INFORMATION

Advertising accepted: Yes

EDITORIAL DESCRIPTION

Scope: Publishes articles that deal with sensory processes, perception, and psychophysics. While the majority of published articles are reports of experimental investigations in these content areas, it accepts articles that are primarily theoretical or that present interrogative and evaluative reviews. Welcomes studies employing either human or animal subjects.
Reviews books: No
Publishes notes: Yes
Languages accepted: English

Prints abstracts: Yes
Author-anonymous submission: No

SUBMISSION REQUIREMENTS

Restrictions on contributors: None
Author pays submission fee: No
Author pays page charges: No
Length of articles: No restrictions
Length of notes: No restrictions
Style: Journal
Number of copies required: 5
Special requirements: Include a 100-150 word abstract.
Copyright ownership: Psychonomic Soc.
Rejected manuscripts: Returned; enclose SASE.
Time before publication decision: 3 mos.
Time between decision and publication: 3 mos.
Number of reviewers: 2-3
Articles submitted per year: 350
Articles published per year: 150
Notes submitted per year: 40
Notes published per year: 25-30

(2147)
*Perceptual and Motor Skills

R. B. Ammons & C. H. Ammons, Editors
P.O. Box 9229
Missoula, MT 59807

Telephone: 406 228-1702
First published: 1949
ISSN: 0031-5125
MLA acronym: PMS

SUBSCRIPTION INFORMATION

Frequency of publication: 6 times/yr. (Feb., Apr., June, Aug., Oct., Dec.) plus 1-2 special issues
Circulation: 1,760
Available in microform: Yes, on 16mm positive film
Subscription price: $223.00/yr. US; $228.00/yr. elsewhere
Year to which price refers: 1992

ADVERTISING INFORMATION

Advertising accepted: No

EDITORIAL DESCRIPTION

Scope: Publishes experimental or theoretical articles dealing with perception or motor skills, especially as affected by experience; articles on general methodology; new material listing and reviews.
Reviews books: Yes
Publishes notes: Yes
Languages accepted: English
Prints abstracts: Yes
Author-anonymous submission: Yes, at author's request

SUBMISSION REQUIREMENTS

Restrictions on contributors: No outside book reviews are accepted.
Author pays submission fee: No
Author pays page charges: No, but preprint & special printing (cuts, tables, symbols) costs are paid by the author.
Length of articles: No restrictions
Length of notes: 400-800 words
Style: American Psychological Assn.
Number of copies required: 4
Copyright ownership: Journal
Rejected manuscripts: Returned
Time before publication decision: 3-6 weeks
Time between decision and publication: 6-9 weeks
Number of reviewers: 3-15
Articles submitted per year: 1,300-1,600
Articles published per year: 800-1,000
Book reviews published per year: 70-100
Notes published per year: 75

(2148)
*Performing Arts Journal

Bonnie Marranca & Gautam Dasgupta, Editors
131 Varick St., no. 902
New York, NY 10013

Telephone: 212 243-3885
First published: 1976
ISSN: 0735-8393
MLA acronym: PArtsJ

SUBSCRIPTION INFORMATION

Frequency of publication: 3 times/yr.
Circulation: 1,600-2,000
Available in microform: No
Subscription price: $37.00/yr. institutions US; $18.00/yr. individuals US; add $5.40/yr. postage Canada & Mexico, $5.70/yr. elsewhere
Year to which price refers: 1993
Subscription address: Johns Hopkins Univ. Press, Journals Publishing Division, 2715 North Charles St., Baltimore, MD 21218-4319
Subscription telephone: 800 537-5487
Subscription fax: 410 516-6998

ADVERTISING INFORMATION

Advertising accepted: Yes

EDITORIAL DESCRIPTION

Scope: Publishes articles dealing with all aspects of the performing and performance arts, dramatic and literary culture, and research in theater anthropology.
Reviews books: Yes
Publishes notes: No
Languages accepted: English
Prints abstracts: No
Author-anonymous submission: No

SUBMISSION REQUIREMENTS

Author pays submission fee: No
Author pays page charges: No
Length of articles: 2,500-5,000 words
Length of book reviews: 500-1,000 words
Style: Chicago
Number of copies required: 2
Copyright ownership: Journal
Rejected manuscripts: Returned; enclose SASE.
Time before publication decision: 4 mos. maximum
Number of reviewers: 2
Articles submitted per year: 100-150
Articles published per year: 18-24
Book reviews submitted per year: 25-75
Book reviews published per year: 12-20

(2149)
*Performing Arts Resources

Barbara Naomi Cohen-Stratyner, Editor
Theatre Library Assn.
111 Amsterdam Ave.
New York, NY 10023

Telephone: 212 870-1645
Fax: 212 787-3852
First published: 1974
Sponsoring organization: Theatre Library Assn.
ISSN: 0360-3814
MLA acronym: PAR

SUBSCRIPTION INFORMATION

Frequency of publication: Annual
Circulation: 500
Available in microform: No
Subscription price: $25.00/yr. institutions; $20.00/yr. individuals
Year to which price refers: 1992

ADVERTISING INFORMATION

Advertising accepted: No

EDITORIAL DESCRIPTION

Scope: Provides documentation for theater, film, television, and popular entertainments. Includes articles on storage and use of non-print resources, studies of curatorship, indexes, bibliographies, subject matter guides to various archives and collections and museums, descriptions of regional holdings in a particular field or subject matter, and surveys of research materials, government holdings, training and programs in the performing arts. The major portion of alternating annual volumes is devoted to describing resources for research. Even numbered volumes treat such issues as historiography, methodology, and historical essays on the states of research in the performing arts.
Reviews books: No
Publishes notes: Yes
Languages accepted: English
Prints abstracts: No
Author-anonymous submission: No

SUBMISSION REQUIREMENTS

Restrictions on contributors: None
Author pays submission fee: No
Author pays page charges: No
Length of articles: 3,000-8,000 words
Length of notes: 500-1,000 words
Style: MLA
Number of copies required: 2
Special requirements: Submit typescript; diskettes may be requested upon acceptance.
Copyright ownership: Theatre Library Assn.
Rejected manuscripts: Returned
Time before publication decision: 1 mo.
Time between decision and publication: 1 yr.
Number of reviewers: 2-3
Articles submitted per year: 25-50
Articles published per year: 10-15

(2150)
Peritia: Journal of the Medieval Academy of Ireland

Donnchadh Ó Corráin, Editor
Dept. of Irish History
University College
Cork, Ireland

First published: 1982
Sponsoring organization: Medieval Academy of Ireland
ISSN: 0332-1592
MLA acronym: Peritia

SUBSCRIPTION INFORMATION

Frequency of publication: Annual
Circulation: 600
Available in microform: No

ADVERTISING INFORMATION

Advertising accepted: Yes

EDITORIAL DESCRIPTION

Scope: Publishes articles on medieval studies, including history, language, literature, law, and archaeology.
Reviews books: Yes
Publishes notes: Yes
Languages accepted: English; French; German
Prints abstracts: Yes
Author-anonymous submission: No

SUBMISSION REQUIREMENTS

Restrictions on contributors: None
Author pays submission fee: No
Author pays page charges: No
Length of articles: 10,000 words maximum
Length of book reviews: 1,000 words
Length of notes: 400-500 words
Style: Journal
Number of copies required: 2

Special requirements: Submit 100-150 word abstract and up to 10 keywords with manuscript.
Copyright ownership: Author & journal
Rejected manuscripts: Returned
Time before publication decision: 6 mos.
Time between decision and publication: 2 yrs.
Number of reviewers: 3
Articles published per year: 20
Book reviews published per year: 10

(2151)
*Personhistorisk Tidskrift

Björn Asker, Editor
Stenhagsvägen 79 C
752 60 Uppsala, Sweden

Telephone: (46) 18 469703
First published: 1898
Sponsoring organization: Personhistoriska Samfundet
ISSN: 0031-5699
MLA acronym: PHT

SUBSCRIPTION INFORMATION

Frequency of publication: 4 times/yr. (usually double issues)
Circulation: 700
Available in microform: No
Subscription price: 100 Skr/yr. plus postage
Year to which price refers: 1992

ADVERTISING INFORMATION

Advertising accepted: No

EDITORIAL DESCRIPTION

Scope: Publishes articles on biography.
Reviews books: Yes
Publishes notes: No
Languages accepted: Swedish; English; German
Prints abstracts: Yes
Author-anonymous submission: No

SUBMISSION REQUIREMENTS

Author pays submission fee: No
Author pays page charges: No
Length of articles: 20,000 words
Length of book reviews: 2,000 words
Number of copies required: 2
Special requirements: Submit original typescript and 1 copy.
Copyright ownership: Author
Rejected manuscripts: Returned
Time before publication decision: 3 mos.
Time between decision and publication: 3 mos.
Number of reviewers: 1-3
Articles submitted per year: 20-25
Articles published per year: 6
Book reviews submitted per year: 40
Book reviews published per year: 35

(2152)
*Persuasions: Journal of the Jane Austen Society of North America

Gene Koppel, Editor
Dept. of English
Univ. of Arizona
Tucson, AZ 85721

First published: 1979
Sponsoring organization: Jane Austen Soc. of North America
ISSN: 0821-0314
MLA acronym: Persuasions

SUBSCRIPTION INFORMATION

Frequency of publication: Annual
Circulation: 2,000
Available in microform: No

Subscription price: $6.00/yr. institutions; $15.00/yr. individuals (includes membership & JASNA News)
Year to which price refers: 1992
Subscription address: Eileen Doudna, 221 Nevin St., Lancaster, PA 17603

ADVERTISING INFORMATION

Advertising accepted: No

EDITORIAL DESCRIPTION

Scope: Publishes articles on Jane Austen and her works.
Reviews books: No
Publishes notes: Yes
Languages accepted: English
Prints abstracts: No
Author-anonymous submission: No

SUBMISSION REQUIREMENTS

Restrictions on contributors: None
Author pays submission fee: No
Author pays page charges: No
Length of articles: 1,750 words maximum
Length of notes: 750 words
Style: MLA; Chicago
Number of copies required: 2
Special requirements: Manuscripts must be double-spaced typescript.
Copyright ownership: Author
Rejected manuscripts: Returned; enclose SAE.
Time before publication decision: 2 mos.
Time between decision and publication: 8 mos.
Number of reviewers: 1-2
Articles submitted per year: 20-30
Articles published per year: 13-14
Notes submitted per year: 10
Notes published per year: 5

(2153)
Peter Weiss Jahrbuch

Martin Rector, Rainer Koch, Rainer Rother, & Jochen Vogt, Editors
Univ. Hannover
Welfengarten 1
3000 Hannover 1, Germany

First published: 1992
MLA acronym: PWJ

SUBSCRIPTION INFORMATION

Frequency of publication: Annual
Available in microform: No

ADVERTISING INFORMATION

Advertising accepted: No

EDITORIAL DESCRIPTION

Scope: Publishes articles on the works of Peter Weiss, as well as book reviews and a bibliography.
Reviews books: Yes
Publishes notes: No
Languages accepted: German
Prints abstracts: No

SUBMISSION REQUIREMENTS

Author pays submission fee: No
Author pays page charges: No
Length of articles: 8,000-10,000 words
Length of book reviews: 600 words
Style: MLA
Number of copies required: 2
Copyright ownership: Westdeutscher Verlag
Time before publication decision: 1-2 mos.
Number of reviewers: 3
Book reviews published per year: 3-4

(2154)
*Philippine Journal of Linguistics

Andrew B. Gonzalez, Editor
The Secretariate
Linguistic Soc. of the Philippines
De La Salle Univ.
2401 Taft Ave.
Manila, Philippines

Telephone: (63) 2 584641
Fax: (63) 2 584641
First published: 1970
Sponsoring organization: Linguistic Soc. of the Philippines; Philippine Social Science Council; Philippine National Science Development Board; Summer Inst. of Linguistics
ISSN: 0048-3796
MLA acronym: PJL

SUBSCRIPTION INFORMATION

Frequency of publication: 2 times/yr.
Circulation: 350
Available in microform: No
Subscription price: $20.00/yr.
Year to which price refers: 1991

ADVERTISING INFORMATION

Advertising accepted: No

EDITORIAL DESCRIPTION

Scope: Publishes articles on Austronesian and Philippine linguistics.
Reviews books: Yes
Publishes notes: Yes
Languages accepted: English; Tagalog
Prints abstracts: No
Author-anonymous submission: No

SUBMISSION REQUIREMENTS

Restrictions on contributors: None
Author pays submission fee: No
Author pays page charges: No
Length of articles: 5,000 words
Length of book reviews: 750 words
Length of notes: 500 words
Style: Linguistic Soc. of America
Number of copies required: 1
Special requirements: Submit double-spaced typescript.
Copyright ownership: Author
Rejected manuscripts: Returned
Time before publication decision: 2 mos.
Time between decision and publication: 6 mos.
Number of reviewers: 1
Articles submitted per year: 15
Articles published per year: 12
Book reviews submitted per year: 8
Book reviews published per year: 6-8
Notes submitted per year: 2
Notes published per year: 2

(2155)
*Philippine Quarterly of Culture and Society

Joseph Baumgartner, Editor
San Carlos Publications
Univ. of San Carlos
6000 Cebu City, Philippines

Telephone: (63) 7 0874
First published: 1973
Sponsoring organization: Univ. of San Carlos
ISSN: 0115-0243
MLA acronym: PQCS

SUBSCRIPTION INFORMATION

Frequency of publication: 4 times/yr. (Mar., June, Sept., Dec.)
Circulation: 360
Available in microform: No
Subscription price: $25.00/yr.

Year to which price refers: 1991

ADVERTISING INFORMATION

Advertising accepted: Yes, on an exchange basis

EDITORIAL DESCRIPTION

Scope: Concentrates on Philippine culture and society. Welcomes contributions in the fields of prehistory, archaeology, anthropology, linguistics, folklore, literature, and history. As far as Philippine society is concerned, contributions may cover existing conditions and problems, their historical antecedents, their present implications, as well as their interconnections with the general national and international situation. Gives emphasis to problems concerning the Visayas and Mindanao.
Reviews books: Yes
Publishes notes: Yes
Languages accepted: English
Prints abstracts: No
Author-anonymous submission: No

SUBMISSION REQUIREMENTS

Restrictions on contributors: None
Author pays submission fee: No
Author pays page charges: No
Length of articles: No restrictions
Length of book reviews: No restrictions
Length of notes: 500 words
Style: Chicago
Number of copies required: 2
Special requirements: Line drawings, rather than photographs, are preferred. Submit original typescript plus 1 copy.
Copyright ownership: Univ. of San Carlos
Rejected manuscripts: Returned
Time before publication decision: 2 mos.
Time between decision and publication: 3 mos.
Number of reviewers: 2
Articles submitted per year: 25
Articles published per year: 17
Notes submitted per year: 10
Notes published per year: 5

(2156)
*Philippine Sociological Review

Ricardo G. Abad, Editor
Dept. of Sociology & Anthropology
Ateneo de Manila Univ.
P.O. Box 154
Manila 2801, Philippines

Additional editorial address: Philippine Social Science Council, Mariano Marcos Ave., Diliman, Quezon City, Philippines
Telephone: (63) 2 982541; (63) 2 998721, local 151
Fax: (63) 2 9216159
First published: 1953
Sponsoring organization: Philippine Sociological Soc., Inc.
ISSN: 0031-7810
MLA acronym: PhSR

SUBSCRIPTION INFORMATION

Frequency of publication: 2 times/yr. (Jan.-June, July-Dec.)
Circulation: 1,000
Available in microform: No
Subscription price: $20.00/yr.
Year to which price refers: 1991
Subscription address: PSSC Central Subscription Service, P.O. Box 655, Greenhills, Metro Manila, Philippines
Subscription telephone: (63) 2 9229621

ADVERTISING INFORMATION

Advertising accepted: No

EDITORIAL DESCRIPTION

Scope: Focuses on research and instruction in the social sciences in the Philippines. Articles should (1) be a genuine contribution to Philippine social science, that is, present either new findings or a new interpretation of old findings; (2) be written in understandable language; (3) be written in a responsible manner. For purposes of placement within an issue, manuscripts approved for publication are classified as an article, a brief communication, a research note, a news item, or a book report.
Reviews books: Yes
Publishes notes: Yes
Languages accepted: English; Filipino
Prints abstracts: Yes
Author-anonymous submission: No

SUBMISSION REQUIREMENTS

Restrictions on contributors: None
Author pays submission fee: No
Author pays page charges: No
Length of articles: 4,000-5,000 words
Length of book reviews: 500-1,500 words
Length of notes: 2,000 words
Style: American Anthropologist; Chicago
Number of copies required: 3
Special requirements: Submit original double-spaced typescript on 8 1/2 in. x 11 in. paper and submit a one-paragraph abstract.
Copyright ownership: Assigned by author to journal
Rejected manuscripts: Not returned
Time before publication decision: 4-6 weeks
Time between decision and publication: 4-6 mos.
Number of reviewers: 5
Articles submitted per year: 50-60
Articles published per year: 20-25
Book reviews submitted per year: 10
Book reviews published per year: 5-10
Notes submitted per year: 5-10
Notes published per year: 3-5

(2157)
*Philippine Studies

Joseph A. Galdon, S.J.
P.O. Box 154
Manila 1099, Philippines

First published: 1953
Sponsoring organization: Ateneo de Manila Univ.
ISSN: 0031-7837
MLA acronym: PSM

SUBSCRIPTION INFORMATION

Frequency of publication: 4 times/yr.
Circulation: 650
Available in microform: No

ADVERTISING INFORMATION

Advertising accepted: Yes, on an exchange basis

EDITORIAL DESCRIPTION

Scope: Publishes articles on literature, art, drama, history, philosophy, and the social sciences, which are of interest and related to the Philippines.
Reviews books: Yes
Publishes notes: Yes
Languages accepted: English; Philippine languages
Prints abstracts: No
Author-anonymous submission: No

SUBMISSION REQUIREMENTS

Restrictions on contributors: None
Author pays submission fee: No
Author pays page charges: No
Length of articles: 6,000-12,000 words

Length of book reviews: 700-1,200 words
Length of notes: 3,000-5,000 words
Style: Turabian
Number of copies required: 2
Special requirements: Submission of articles on diskette is preferred.
Copyright ownership: Journal
Rejected manuscripts: Returned
Time before publication decision: 1-2 mos.
Time between decision and publication: 6-9 mos.
Number of reviewers: 2-3
Articles submitted per year: 35-45
Articles published per year: 16-24
Book reviews submitted per year: 30-40
Book reviews published per year: 30-40
Notes submitted per year: 15
Notes published per year: 6-8

(2158)
*Philobiblon: Eine Vierteljahrsschrift für Buch- und Graphiksammler

Reimar W. Fuchs, Editor
Rosenbergstr. 113
Postfach 140155
7000 Stuttgart 1, Germany

Telephone: (49) 711 638265
Fax: (49) 711 6369010
First published: 1957
Sponsoring organization: Maximilian-Gesellschaft
ISSN: 0031-7969
MLA acronym: Philobiblon

SUBSCRIPTION INFORMATION

Frequency of publication: 4 times/yr. (Mar., June, Sept., Dec.)
Circulation: 1,900
Available in microform: No
Subscription price: 96 DM/yr.
Year to which price refers: 1992

ADVERTISING INFORMATION

Advertising accepted: Yes
Advertising rates: 200 DM/quarter page; 380 DM/half page; 600 DM/full page

EDITORIAL DESCRIPTION

Scope: Publishes information and hints for bibliophiles, book collectors, print collectors, and librarians.
Reviews books: No
Publishes notes: No
Languages accepted: German
Prints abstracts: No
Author-anonymous submission: No

SUBMISSION REQUIREMENTS

Restrictions on contributors: None
Author pays submission fee: No
Author pays page charges: No
Length of articles: 10-20 pp.
Number of copies required: 1
Copyright ownership: Dr. Ernst Hauswedell & Co. Verlag
Rejected manuscripts: Returned
Time before publication decision: 1 mo.
Time between decision and publication: 6 mos.
Number of reviewers: 2
Articles submitted per year: 15-20
Articles published per year: 12-16

(2159)
Philological Quarterly

William Kupersmith, Editor
311 English/Philosophy Bldg.
Univ. of Iowa
Iowa City, IA 52242-1408

First published: 1922
Sponsoring organization: Univ. of Iowa
ISSN: 0031-7977
MLA acronym: PQ

SUBSCRIPTION INFORMATION

Frequency of publication: 4 times/yr. (Winter, Spring, Summer, Fall)
Circulation: 2,000
Available in microform: Yes
Subscription price: $25.00/yr. institutions US; $28.00/yr. institutions elsewhere; $15.00/yr. individuals US; $18.00/yr. individuals elsewhere
Year to which price refers: 1992
Subscription address: Publications Order Dept., Univ. of Iowa, 100 Oakdale Campus M105 OH, Iowa City, IA 52242-5000

ADVERTISING INFORMATION

Advertising accepted: Yes

EDITORIAL DESCRIPTION

Scope: Publishes scholarship in classical and modern languages and literatures.
Reviews books: Yes
Publishes notes: Yes
Languages accepted: English
Prints abstracts: No

SUBMISSION REQUIREMENTS

Restrictions on contributors: None
Author pays submission fee: No
Author pays page charges: No
Length of articles: 8,000 words maximum
Length of book reviews: 1,500 words
Length of notes: 2,500 words
Style: Chicago
Number of copies required: 1
Special requirements: Computer-accessible articles have priority for publication.
Copyright ownership: Univ. of Iowa
Rejected manuscripts: Returned; enclose return postage.
Time before publication decision: 2 mos.
Time between decision and publication: 1-2 yrs.
Number of reviewers: 1-3
Articles submitted per year: 250
Articles published per year: 25
Book reviews submitted per year: 10
Book reviews published per year: 6
Notes published per year: 10

(2160)
Philologikē Kypros

Kypros Chrysanthis, Editor
Androkleous 2
Nicosia 135, Cyprus

First published: 1960
ISSN: 0554-0666
MLA acronym: PK

SUBSCRIPTION INFORMATION

Frequency of publication: Annual
Circulation: 700-800
Available in microform: No
Subscription address: Hellenikos Pneumatikos Omilos Kyprou, Nicosia 135, Cyprus

ADVERTISING INFORMATION

Advertising accepted: No

EDITORIAL DESCRIPTION

Reviews books: Yes
Languages accepted: Greek; English
Prints abstracts: Yes

SUBMISSION REQUIREMENTS

Author pays submission fee: No
Author pays page charges: No
Length of articles: 2,500-10,000 words
Number of copies required: 1
Copyright ownership: Author
Rejected manuscripts: Returned
Time before publication decision: 2 mos.
Time between decision and publication: 6 mos.
Number of reviewers: 3

(2161)
Philologus: Zeitschrift für Klassische Philologie

Ernst Günther Schmidt, Editor
Zentralinst. für Alte Geschichte & Archäologie
Leipziger Str. 3-4 PSF 1310
1086 Berlin, Germany

First published: 1846
Sponsoring organization: Akademie der Wissenschaften Berlin, Zentralinst. für Alte Geschichte und Archäologie
ISSN: 0031-7985
MLA acronym: PZKA

SUBSCRIPTION INFORMATION

Frequency of publication: 2 double issues/yr.
Circulation: 700
Available in microform: No
Subscription address: Akademie-Verlag, at the above address

ADVERTISING INFORMATION

Advertising accepted: Yes

EDITORIAL DESCRIPTION

Scope: Publishes scientific articles on all aspects of classical philology.
Reviews books: Yes
Publishes notes: Yes
Languages accepted: English; German; Italian; French; Latin; Russian
Prints abstracts: No

SUBMISSION REQUIREMENTS

Restrictions on contributors: None
Length of articles: 1-30 pp.
Style: None
Number of copies required: 1
Special requirements: Submit original typescript.
Copyright ownership: Akademie-Verlag
Rejected manuscripts: Returned
Time before publication decision: 2 mos.
Time between decision and publication: 18 mos.
Number of reviewers: 3
Articles published per year: 30

(2162)
*The Philosophical Quarterly

N. L. Cooper & J. E. R. Squires, Editors
Univ. of St. Andrews
St. Andrews KY16 9AL, Scotland

Additional editorial address: John Heil, Dept. of Philosophy, Davidson College, Davidson, NC 28036
Telephone: (44) 334 76161 ext. 392 or 565
Fax: (44) 334 78036
First published: 1950
Sponsoring organization: Univ. of St. Andrews; Scots Philosophical Club
ISSN: 0031-8094
MLA acronym: PhQ

SUBSCRIPTION INFORMATION

Frequency of publication: 4 times/yr.
Circulation: 1,400
Available in microform: Yes
Subscription price: $105.00/yr. institutions N. America; £46.00/yr. institutions United Kingdom & Europe; £62.00/yr. institutions elsewhere; $36.50/yr. individuals N. America; £17.00/yr. individuals United Kingdom & Europe; £21.50/yr. individuals elsewhere
Year to which price refers: 1992
Subscription address: Journals Dept., Basil Blackwell Ltd., 108 Cowley Rd., Oxford OX4 1JF, England
Additional subscription address: Blackwell Publishers, 238 Main St., Suite 501, Cambridge, MA 02142
Subscription telephone: (44) 865 791155
Subscription fax: (44) 865 791927

ADVERTISING INFORMATION

Advertising accepted: Yes

EDITORIAL DESCRIPTION

Scope: Publishes general philosophical discussions and research.
Reviews books: Yes
Publishes notes: Yes
Languages accepted: English
Prints abstracts: No
Author-anonymous submission: Yes, at author's request

SUBMISSION REQUIREMENTS

Restrictions on contributors: Book reviews are solicited.
Author pays submission fee: No
Author pays page charges: No
Length of articles: 8,000 words
Length of notes: 3,000 words
Style: None
Number of copies required: 1; 2 if submitted to US address
Copyright ownership: Journal & author
Rejected manuscripts: Returned at author's request; enclose international reply coupons or return postage.
Time before publication decision: 2 mos.
Time between decision and publication: 1 yr.
Number of reviewers: 2 minimum
Articles submitted per year: 200
Articles published per year: 20
Book reviews published per year: 100
Notes submitted per year: 60
Notes published per year: 15

(2163)
*Philosophical Review

John Rowehl, Managing Editor
327 Goldwin Smith Hall
Cornell Univ.
Ithaca, NY 14853

Telephone: 607 255-6817
Fax: 607 255-1454
E-mail: Tpr@cornelle (Bitnet); tpr@cornelle.-cit.cornell.edu (Internet)
First published: 1892
Sponsoring organization: Cornell Univ., Sage School of Philosophy
ISSN: 0081-8108
MLA acronym: PhR

SUBSCRIPTION INFORMATION

Frequency of publication: 4 times/yr. (Jan., Apr., July, Oct.)
Circulation: 3,200
Available in microform: Yes

Subscription price: $46.00/yr. institutions; $27.00/yr. individuals; $16.00/yr. students, retirees & unemployed; add $5.00/yr. postage outside US
Year to which price refers: 1992
Subscription telephone: 607 255-6830

ADVERTISING INFORMATION

Advertising accepted: Yes

EDITORIAL DESCRIPTION

Scope: Publishes articles on philosophy, including history of philosophy.
Reviews books: Yes
Publishes notes: No
Languages accepted: English
Prints abstracts: No
Author-anonymous submission: Yes

SUBMISSION REQUIREMENTS

Restrictions on contributors: Reviews are solicited.
Author pays submission fee: No
Author pays page charges: No
Length of articles: 7,500 words
Length of book reviews: 1,000 words
Style: Chicago
Number of copies required: 1
Special requirements: Submit double-spaced typescript.
Copyright ownership: Cornell Univ.
Rejected manuscripts: Returned; enclose return postage.
Time before publication decision: 3 mos.
Time between decision and publication: 1 yr.
Number of reviewers: 2-3
Articles submitted per year: 425
Articles published per year: 12-15
Book reviews published per year: 100

(2164)
*Philosophical Studies: An International Journal for Philosophy in the Analytic Tradition

Stewart Cohen, Editor
Dept. of Philosophy
Arizona State Univ.
Tucson, AZ 85287

Telephone: 602 965-9365
E-mail: Philstud@asuvm.inre.asu.edu
First published: 1950
Sponsoring organization: Arizona State Univ.
ISSN: 0031-8116
MLA acronym: PhS

SUBSCRIPTION INFORMATION

Frequency of publication: 12 times/yr.
Circulation: 1,000
Available in microform: No
Subscription address: Kluwer Academic Publishers, P.O. Box 332, 3300 AH Dordrecht, Netherlands

ADVERTISING INFORMATION

Advertising accepted: Yes

EDITORIAL DESCRIPTION

Scope: Welcomes papers in all areas of philosophy, logic, and the philosophy of language. Contributions should represent a disciplined application of methods of analysis and precise argumentation.
Reviews books: Yes
Publishes notes: Yes
Languages accepted: English
Prints abstracts: No
Author-anonymous submission: No

SUBMISSION REQUIREMENTS

Restrictions on contributors: None
Author pays submission fee: No
Author pays page charges: No
Length of articles: 10,000 words maximum
Style: MLA
Number of copies required: 3
Special requirements: Include footnotes at end.
Copyright ownership: Kluwer Academic Publishers
Rejected manuscripts: Not returned
Time before publication decision: 2 mos.
Time between decision and publication: 1 yr.
Number of reviewers: 1
Articles submitted per year: 350
Articles published per year: 40

(2165)
*Philosophisches Jahrbuch der Görres-Gesellschaft

Hermann Krings, Arno Baruzzi, Hans-Michael Baumgartner, Alois Halder, Klaus Jacobi, & Heinrich Rombach, Editors
Univ. Augsburg
Universitätsstr. 10
8900 Augsburg, Germany

First published: 1881
Sponsoring organization: Görres Gesellschaft
ISSN: 0031-8183
MLA acronym: PJGG

SUBSCRIPTION INFORMATION

Frequency of publication: 2 times/yr.
Circulation: 800
Available in microform: No
Subscription price: 94 DM/yr.
Year to which price refers: 1992
Subscription address: Verlag Karl Alber GmbH., Hermann-Herder-Str. 4, 7800 Freiburg (Breisgau), Germany

ADVERTISING INFORMATION

Advertising accepted: No

EDITORIAL DESCRIPTION

Scope: Publishes studies on philosophy.
Reviews books: Yes
Publishes notes: No
Languages accepted: German
Prints abstracts: No

SUBMISSION REQUIREMENTS

Author pays submission fee: No
Author pays page charges: No
Number of copies required: 1
Copyright ownership: Verlag Karl Alber Gmbh; reverts to author after 1 yr.
Time before publication decision: 1 yr.
Time between decision and publication: 6 mos.
Articles published per year: 28

(2166)
*Philosophy and Literature

Patrick Henry & Denis Dutton, Editors
Whitman College
Walla Walla, WA 99362

Additional editorial address: Denis Dutton, Univ. of Canterbury, Christchurch, New Zealand
First published: 1976
Sponsoring organization: Whitman College
ISSN: 0190-0013
MLA acronym: P&L

SUBSCRIPTION INFORMATION

Frequency of publication: 2 times/yr.
Circulation: 1,600
Available in microform: No
Subscription price: $38.00/yr. institutions; $19.00/yr. individuals; add $2.70/yr. postage Canada & Mexico; add $5.40/yr. postage elsewhere
Year to which price refers: 1993
Subscription address: Johns Hopkins Univ. Press, Journals Publishing Division, 2715 North Charles St., Baltimore, MD 21218-4319
Subscription telephone: 410 516-6988; 800 537-5487
Subscription fax: 410 516-6998

ADVERTISING INFORMATION

Advertising accepted: Yes

EDITORIAL DESCRIPTION

Scope: Welcomes contributions on philosophical interpretations of literature, literary investigation of classic works of philosophy, articles on the aesthetics of literature and philosophy of language relevant to literature, the theory of criticism, and the relations between philosophy and the dramatic media of theater and film.
Reviews books: Yes
Publishes notes: Yes
Languages accepted: English
Prints abstracts: No
Author-anonymous submission: Yes

SUBMISSION REQUIREMENTS

Restrictions on contributors: None
Author pays submission fee: No
Author pays page charges: No
Length of articles: 7,500 words maximum
Length of book reviews: 650 words
Length of notes: 2,000 words
Style: Chicago
Number of copies required: 2
Copyright ownership: Johns Hopkins Univ. Press
Rejected manuscripts: Returned; enclose return postage.
Time before publication decision: 4 mos. maximum
Time between decision and publication: 6-12 mos.
Articles submitted per year: 200
Articles published per year: 15-25
Book reviews published per year: 45
Notes submitted per year: 25
Notes published per year: 10

(2167)
*Philosophy and Phenomenological Research

Ernest Sosa, Editor
Box 1947
Brown Univ.
Providence, RI 02912

Telephone: 401 863-3215
Fax: 401 863-2719
E-mail: PPR@BROWNVM.brown.edu
First published: 1940
Sponsoring organization: International Phenomenological Soc.
ISSN: 0031-8205
MLA acronym: PPR

SUBSCRIPTION INFORMATION

Frequency of publication: 4 times/yr.
Available in microform: Yes
Subscription price: $42.00/yr. institutions US; $48.00/yr. institutions elsewhere; $17.00/yr. individuals US; $21.00/yr. individuals elsewhere
Year to which price refers: 1992

ADVERTISING INFORMATION

Advertising accepted: Yes

Advertising rates: $50.00/half page; $95.00/full page

EDITORIAL DESCRIPTION

Scope: Contains articles on philosophy. Journal is international in content and not restricted to the doctrines of any philosophical school.
Reviews books: Yes
Publishes notes: No
Languages accepted: English
Prints abstracts: No
Author-anonymous submission: Yes, at author's request.

SUBMISSION REQUIREMENTS

Restrictions on contributors: Book reviews are by invitation only.
Author pays submission fee: No
Author pays page charges: No
Style: Chicago
Number of copies required: 3
Special requirements: Include abstract of 150 words or less.
Copyright ownership: Publisher
Rejected manuscripts: Returned; enclose return postage.
Time before publication decision: 1-4 mos.
Time between decision and publication: 18 mos.
Number of reviewers: 1-2
Articles submitted per year: 200
Articles published per year: 25
Book reviews published per year: 45

(2168)
*Philosophy and Rhetoric

Henry W. Johnstone, Jr., Gerard A. Hauser, & Marie J. Secor, Editors
Dept. of Philosophy
Pennsylvania State Univ.
240 Sparks Bldg.
University Park, PA 16802

Additional editorial address: Send book reviews to Molly Wertheimer, Dept. of Speech Communication, Pennsylvania State Univ., Hazelton Campus, Highacres, Hazelton, PA 18201
Telephone: 814 865-1512
Fax: 814 863-7986
First published: 1968
Sponsoring organization: Pennsylvania State Univ. College of Liberal Arts
ISSN: 0031-8213
MLA acronym: P&R

SUBSCRIPTION INFORMATION

Frequency of publication: 4 times/yr. (Winter, Spring, Summer, Fall)
Circulation: 900
Available in microform: Yes
Subscription price: $35.00/yr. institutions US; $40.00/yr. institutions elsewhere; $22.50/yr. individuals US; $30.00/yr. individuals elsewhere
Year to which price refers: 1992
Subscription address: Pennsylvania State Univ. Press, 820 N. University Dr., Suite C, University Park, PA 16802
Subscription telephone: 814 865-1327
Subscription fax: 814 863-1403

ADVERTISING INFORMATION

Advertising accepted: Yes
Advertising rates: $125.00/half page; $225.00/full page

EDITORIAL DESCRIPTION

Scope: Publishes papers on theoretical issues involving the relationship between philosophy and rhetoric (including the relationship between formal or informal logic and rhetoric), articles on philosophical aspects of argumentation (including argumentation in philosophy itself), studies of philosophical views on the nature of rhetoric of historical figures and during historical periods, analyses of the relationship of rhetoric to other areas of human culture and thought, and psychological and sociological studies of rhetoric with a strong philosophical emphasis.
Reviews books: Yes
Publishes notes: Yes
Languages accepted: English
Prints abstracts: No
Author-anonymous submission: No

SUBMISSION REQUIREMENTS

Restrictions on contributors: None
Author pays submission fee: No
Author pays page charges: No
Length of articles: 7,500 words
Length of book reviews: 800 words
Length of notes: 3,000 words
Style: Chicago
Number of copies required: 4
Special requirements: Submit a 250-word abstract with manuscript.
Copyright ownership: Pennsylvania State Univ. Press
Rejected manuscripts: Not returned
Time before publication decision: 3 mos.
Time between decision and publication: 1 yr.
Number of reviewers: 3
Articles submitted per year: 150
Articles published per year: 12
Book reviews submitted per year: 20
Book reviews published per year: 18
Notes submitted per year: 5
Notes published per year: 4

(2169)
*Philosophy East and West: A Quarterly of Comparative Philosophy

Roger T. Ames, Editor
2530 Dole St.
Univ. of Hawaii
Honolulu, HI 96822

Telephone: 808 956-7288
Fax: 808 956-8859
E-mail: Rtames@uhunix.uhcc.hawaii.edu
First published: 1951
Historical variations in title: Formerly *Philosophy East and West: A Quarterly of Asian and Comparative Thought*
Sponsoring organization: Univ. of Hawaii
ISSN: 0031-8221
MLA acronym: PE&W

SUBSCRIPTION INFORMATION

Frequency of publication: 4 times/yr. (Jan., Apr., July, Oct.)
Circulation: 1,600
Available in microform: Yes
Subscription price: $20.00/yr.
Year to which price refers: 1992
Subscription address: Univ. Press of Hawaii, 2840 Kolowalu St., Honolulu, HI 96822
Subscription telephone: 808 956-8833
Subscription fax: 808 988-6052

ADVERTISING INFORMATION

Advertising accepted: Yes

EDITORIAL DESCRIPTION

Scope: Welcomes specialized articles in Asian philosophy and articles which seek to illuminate in a comparative manner the distinctive characteristics of the various philosophical traditions in the East and West. Especially welcomes articles which exhibit the relevance of philosophy for the art, literature, science, and social practice of Asian civilizations and those original contributions to philosophy which work from an intercultural basis.
Reviews books: Yes
Publishes notes: Yes
Languages accepted: English
Prints abstracts: No
Author-anonymous submission: Yes

SUBMISSION REQUIREMENTS

Restrictions on contributors: None
Author pays submission fee: No
Author pays page charges: No
Length of articles: 25 double-spaced typescript pp.
Length of book reviews: 500-1,000 words
Length of notes: No restrictions
Style: Chicago; transliteration by accepted practice
Number of copies required: 3
Copyright ownership: Univ. Press of Hawaii
Rejected manuscripts: Not returned
Time before publication decision: 2 mos.
Time between decision and publication: 12-18 mos.
Number of reviewers: 2-3
Articles submitted per year: 150
Articles published per year: 28
Book reviews submitted per year: 40
Book reviews published per year: 30-35
Notes submitted per year: 7
Notes published per year: 6

(2170)
Phoenix

Chong-wha Chung, Editor
English Literature Soc. of Korea Univ.
Dept. of English
Korea Univ.
Seoul, Korea

First published: 1955
Sponsoring organization: Korea Univ., Dept. of English
MLA acronym: PhoenixK

SUBSCRIPTION INFORMATION

Frequency of publication: Annual
Circulation: 1,000
Available in microform: No

ADVERTISING INFORMATION

Advertising accepted: No

EDITORIAL DESCRIPTION

Scope: Publishes articles on English and American literature that are of significant interest to members.
Reviews books: Yes
Publishes notes: Yes
Languages accepted: Korean; English
Prints abstracts: No

SUBMISSION REQUIREMENTS

Restrictions on contributors: Contributors must be members of the English Literature Soc.
Author pays submission fee: No
Author pays page charges: No
Length of articles: 2,500-5,000 words
Length of book reviews: 1,000-1,500 words
Length of notes: 800-1,000 words
Style: MLA
Number of copies required: 1

Special requirements: Submit original typescript.
Copyright ownership: Author
Rejected manuscripts: Returned
Time before publication decision: 3 mos.
Time between decision and publication: 1 yr. maximum
Number of reviewers: 2-3
Articles submitted per year: 20
Articles published per year: 10
Book reviews published per year: 3-5
Notes published per year: 1-2

(2171)
*Phoenix: The Journal of the Classical Association of Canada/Revue de la Société Canadienne des Etudes Classiques

C. I. R. Rubincam, Editor
Trinity College
Toronto, Ontario M5S 1H8, Canada

Telephone: 416 978-3037
Fax: 416 978-4949
E-mail: PHOENIX@EPAS.UTORONTO.CA
First published: 1946
Sponsoring organization: Classical Assn. of Canada/Soc. Canadienne des Etudes Classiques
ISSN: 0031-8299
MLA acronym: PhoenixC

SUBSCRIPTION INFORMATION

Frequency of publication: 4 times/yr.
Circulation: 1,100
Available in microform: No
Subscription price: C$45.00/yr. institutions; C$40.00/yr. individuals
Year to which price refers: 1993

ADVERTISING INFORMATION

Advertising accepted: Yes
Advertising rates: C$200.00/half page; C$295.00/full page

EDITORIAL DESCRIPTION

Scope: Publishes articles on classical antiquity.
Reviews books: Yes
Publishes notes: Yes
Languages accepted: English; French
Prints abstracts: No
Author-anonymous submission: Yes

SUBMISSION REQUIREMENTS

Restrictions on contributors: None
Author pays submission fee: No
Author pays page charges: No
Length of articles: No restrictions
Length of book reviews: No restrictions
Length of notes: 2,000 words maximum
Style: Journal
Number of copies required: 2
Copyright ownership: Classical Assn. of Canada
Rejected manuscripts: Returned; enclose SASE.
Time before publication decision: 3-4 mos.
Time between decision and publication: 6-9 mos.
Number of reviewers: 2-3
Articles submitted per year: 50
Articles published per year: 20-25
Book reviews published per year: 45
Notes submitted per year: 5
Notes published per year: 2

(2172)
*Phonai: Lautbibliothek der Deutschen Sprache

Walter Haas & Peter Wagener, Editors
Inst. für Deutsche Sprache
c/o Peter Wagener
Deutsches Spracharchiv
Friedrich-Karl-Str. 12, Postfach 10 16 21
6800 Mannheim 1, Germany

Telephone: (49) 621 4401224
Fax: (49) 621 4401200
First published: 1965
ISSN: 0554-0992
MLA acronym: Phonai

SUBSCRIPTION INFORMATION

Frequency of publication: Irregular
Available in microform: No

EDITORIAL DESCRIPTION

Scope: Publishes monographs on German linguistics and dialectology.
Reviews books: Yes
Publishes notes: Yes
Languages accepted: German
Prints abstracts: No
Author-anonymous submission: No

SUBMISSION REQUIREMENTS

Author pays submission fee: No
Author pays page charges: No
Length of books: 200-400 pp.
Length of book reviews: 1-2 pp.
Special requirements: Typescripts may be accompanied by tapes.
Copyright ownership: Max Niemeyer Verlag
Time before publication decision: 1-2 yrs.
Time between decision and publication: 6 mos.
Number of reviewers: 2
Books published per year: 1-2
Book reviews published per year: 2-3

(2173)
*Phonetica: International Journal of Speech Science

Klaus Kohler & Randy Diehl, Editors
Inst. für Phonetik & digitale Sprachverarbeitung
Univ. Kiel
Olshausenstr. 40
2300 Kiel, Germany

Additional editorial address: In North America: Randy Diehl, Dept. of Pyschology, Univ. of Texas, 330 Mezes Hall, Austin, TX 78712
Telephone: (49) 61 3061111
Fax: (49) 61 3061234
First published: 1957
ISSN: 0031-8388
MLA acronym: Phonetica

SUBSCRIPTION INFORMATION

Frequency of publication: 4 times/yr.
Circulation: 1,150
Available in microform: Occasionally
Subscription price: 321 SwF (412 DM, £140.00, $214.00)/yr. institutions; 96.30 SwF (123.60 DM, £42.00, $64.20)/yr. individuals
Year to which price refers: 1992
Subscription address: S. Karger AG, P.O. Box, 4009 Basel, Switzerland
Additional subscription address: S. Karger Publishers Inc., 26 W. Avon Rd., P.O. Box 529, Farmington, CT 06085
Subscription telephone: 203 675-7834
Subscription fax: 203 675-7302

ADVERTISING INFORMATION

Advertising accepted: Yes

EDITORIAL DESCRIPTION

Scope: Publishes articles about experimental phonetics, phonology, speech perception and production, acoustic analysis, and speech synthesis.
Reviews books: Yes
Publishes notes: No
Languages accepted: English; French; German
Prints abstracts: Yes
Author-anonymous submission: No

SUBMISSION REQUIREMENTS

Restrictions on contributors: None
Author pays submission fee: No
Author pays page charges: No
Length of articles: No restrictions
Length of book reviews: 1-2 pp.
Style: Journal
Number of copies required: 3
Special requirements: Consult journal for instructions to authors. Submit original typescript plus 2 copies.
Copyright ownership: S. Karger AG
Rejected manuscripts: Not returned
Time before publication decision: 2-3 mos.
Time between decision and publication: 4-6 mos.
Number of reviewers: 2-3
Articles submitted per year: 50
Articles published per year: 20
Book reviews submitted per year: 14
Book reviews published per year: 10

(2174)
*Phonetica Saraviensia: Veröffentlichungen des Instituts für Phonetik

William Barry, Editor
Fachrichtung 8.7
Allgemeine Linguistik
Univ. des Saarlandes
6600 Saarbrücken, Germany

First published: 1981
ISSN: 0721-6440
MLA acronym: PhoneticaS

SUBSCRIPTION INFORMATION

Frequency of publication: Irregular
Available in microform: No

ADVERTISING INFORMATION

Advertising accepted: No

EDITORIAL DESCRIPTION

Scope: The series publishes works on linguistics, in particular phonetics and phonology.
Reviews books: No
Publishes notes: No
Languages accepted: German; French; English
Prints abstracts: No
Author-anonymous submission: No

SUBMISSION REQUIREMENTS

Restrictions on contributors: Contributors must be associated with the Institute.
Author pays submission fee: No
Author pays page charges: No
Length of books: 30-100 pp.
Style: None
Number of copies required: 1
Special requirements: Submit original typescript on size A4 (8 1/4 in. x 11 3/4 in.) paper.
Copyright ownership: Author
Rejected manuscripts: Returned
Time before publication decision: 1 mo.
Time between decision and publication: 2-6 mos.
Number of reviewers: 2
Books submitted per year: 1-2
Books published per year: 0-2

(2175)
*Phonology

Colin J. Ewen, Editor
Vakgroep Engels
Rijkuniversiteit Leiden
Postbus 9515
2300 RA Leiden, Netherlands

Additional editorial address: Contributors from US submit typescript to Ellen M. Kaisse, Dept. of Linguistics, GN-40, Univ. of Washington, Seattle, WA 98195
Telephone: (31) 71 272148; 206 543-2046
Fax: (31) 71 272615
E-mail: EWEN@RULCRI.LEIDENUNIV.-NL; KAISSE@U.WASHINGTON.EDU
First published: 1984
ISSN: 0952-6757
MLA acronym: Phonology

SUBSCRIPTION INFORMATION

Frequency of publication: 2 times/yr.
Available in microform: Yes
Subscription price: $79.00 (£44.00)/yr. institutions; $46.00 (£25.00)/yr. individuals
Year to which price refers: 1991
Subscription address: Cambridge Univ. Press, 40 W. 20th St., New York, NY 10011-4211
Additional subscription address: Outside N. America: Cambridge Univ. Press, Edinburgh Bldg., Shaftesbury Rd., Cambridge CB2 2RU, England

ADVERTISING INFORMATION

Advertising accepted: Yes

EDITORIAL DESCRIPTION

Scope: Publishes articles on phonology and related disciplines.
Reviews books: Yes
Publishes notes: Yes
Languages accepted: English
Prints abstracts: No
Author-anonymous submission: Yes

SUBMISSION REQUIREMENTS

Restrictions on contributors: None
Author pays submission fee: No
Author pays page charges: No
Length of articles: 10,000-20,000 words
Length of book reviews: 1,000-2,000 words
Length of notes: 1,000-4,000 words
Style: Journal
Number of copies required: 3
Special requirements: Contributors may also submit diskettes accompanied by 1 paper copy.
Copyright ownership: Cambridge Univ. Press
Rejected manuscripts: Not returned
Time before publication decision: 2-6 mos.
Time between decision and publication: 2-6 mos.
Number of reviewers: 2-3

(2176)
Phylon: A Review of Race and Culture

Lucy C. Grigsby, Managing Editor
Clark Atlanta Univ.
James P. Brawley Dr. at Fair St., SW
Atlanta, GA 30314

First published: 1940
Historical variations in title: Formerly *Phylon: The Atlanta University Review of Race and Culture*
Sponsoring organization: Atlanta Univ.
ISSN: 0031-8906
MLA acronym: Phylon

SUBSCRIPTION INFORMATION

Frequency of publication: 4 times/yr. (Mar., June, Sept., Dec.)
Circulation: 2,000
Available in microform: Yes

ADVERTISING INFORMATION

Advertising accepted: Yes

EDITORIAL DESCRIPTION

Scope: Focuses on the achievements, problems, and concerns of minorities, with emphasis on blacks.
Reviews books: Yes
Languages accepted: English
Prints abstracts: No
Author-anonymous submission: Yes

SUBMISSION REQUIREMENTS

Restrictions on contributors: None
Author pays submission fee: No
Author pays page charges: No
Length of articles: 20 double-spaced typescript pp. maximum
Length of book reviews: 300-900 words
Style: Chicago
Number of copies required: 4
Special requirements: Submit original typescript.
Copyright ownership: Atlanta Univ.
Rejected manuscripts: Returned; enclose SASE.
Time before publication decision: 4-6 weeks
Number of reviewers: 3
Articles submitted per year: 100-120
Articles published per year: 36-40
Book reviews published per year: 10

(2177)
*The Pinter Review: Annual Essays

Francis X. Gillen & Steven H. Gale, Editors
Box 11F
Univ. of Tampa
401 West Kennedy
Tampa, FL 33606

Telephone: 813 253-3333, ext. 3321
Fax: 813 251-0016
First published: 1987
Sponsoring organization: Harold Pinter Soc., Univ. of Tampa
ISSN: 0895-9706
MLA acronym: PintR

SUBSCRIPTION INFORMATION

Frequency of publication: Annual
Circulation: 150-200
Available in microform: No
Subscription price: $30.00/yr. institutions, hard cover; $25.00/yr. institutions, soft cover; $20.00/yr. individuals, hard cover; $15.00/yr. individuals, soft cover
Year to which price refers: 1991
Subscription address: c/o Steven H. Gale, Kentucky State Univ., Frankfort, KY 40601
Additional subscription address: Institutions: same as editorial address

ADVERTISING INFORMATION

Advertising accepted: Yes

EDITORIAL DESCRIPTION

Scope: Publishes articles on all aspects of Harold Pinter's writing as well as his acting and directing activities. Also publishes articles and interviews related to Pinter and his works. Includes production notes and reviews of productions and books, as well as an annual bibliography.
Reviews books: Yes
Publishes notes: Yes
Languages accepted: English
Prints abstracts: No
Author-anonymous submission: No

SUBMISSION REQUIREMENTS

Restrictions on contributors: None
Author pays submission fee: No
Author pays page charges: No
Length of articles: No restrictions
Length of book reviews: No restrictions
Length of notes: No restrictions
Style: MLA
Number of copies required: 2
Copyright ownership: Journal
Rejected manuscripts: Returned with comments
Time before publication decision: 6-9 mos.
Time between decision and publication: 3 mos.
Number of reviewers: 2-3
Articles submitted per year: 40
Articles published per year: 8-10
Book reviews submitted per year: 4-8
Book reviews published per year: 4-8
Notes submitted per year: 4-10
Notes published per year: 2-3

(2178)
*Plamŭk: Mesechno Spisanie za Literatura, Izkustvo i Publitsistika

Gueozgui Konstantinov, Editor
Angel Kŭnchev 5
Sofia 1000, Bulgaria

Telephone: (359) 2 880031
Fax: (359) 2 835411
First published: 1957
ISSN: 0032-0528
MLA acronym: Plamŭk

SUBSCRIPTION INFORMATION

Frequency of publication: 6 times/yr.
Available in microform: Yes
Subscription price: 60 lev ($48.00)/yr.
Year to which price refers: 1992

ADVERTISING INFORMATION

Advertising accepted: Yes

EDITORIAL DESCRIPTION

Scope: Publishes original literary works and literary criticism, and poetry by writers from around the world.
Reviews books: Yes
Publishes notes: Yes
Languages accepted: Bulgarian
Prints abstracts: No
Author-anonymous submission: Yes

SUBMISSION REQUIREMENTS

Restrictions on contributors: None
Author pays submission fee: No
Author pays page charges: No
Length of articles: 20 pp. maximum
Length of book reviews: 5-8 pp.
Length of notes: 2 pp.
Number of copies required: 1
Special requirements: Submit original typescript.
Copyright ownership: Author
Rejected manuscripts: Not returned
Time before publication decision: 1 mo.
Time between decision and publication: 2 mos.
Number of reviewers: 2
Articles published per year: 30
Book reviews published per year: 15

(2179)
*Platte Valley Review

Vernon L. Plambeck, Editor
Univ. of Nebraska at Kearney
Kearney, NE 68849-0522

Telephone: 308 234-8298
First published: 1973
Sponsoring organization: Univ. of Nebraska, Kearney
ISSN: 0092-4318
MLA acronym: PVR

SUBSCRIPTION INFORMATION

Frequency of publication: 2 times/yr. (Winter, Spring)
Available in microform: No

ADVERTISING INFORMATION

Advertising accepted: No

EDITORIAL DESCRIPTION

Scope: Publishes scholarly and creative writing for the generally educated reader.
Reviews books: No
Publishes notes: No
Languages accepted: English
Prints abstracts: No
Author-anonymous submission: No

SUBMISSION REQUIREMENTS

Restrictions on contributors: Contributors are primarily Univ. of Nebraska at Kearney faculty members or graduates. Usually includes at least one outside invited author. Additional submissions are considered.
Author pays submission fee: No
Author pays page charges: No
Length of articles: 4,000 words
Number of copies required: 2
Rejected manuscripts: Returned
Time before publication decision: 2-3 mos.
Time between decision and publication: 3 mos.
Number of reviewers: 1-3
Articles submitted per year: 12-15
Articles published per year: 9

(2180)
*Pleiades

Rose Marie Kinder, Michael Mann, Judi Osborn, & Brenda Hudgens, Editors
Dept. of English
Central Missouri State Univ.
Warrensburg, MO 64093

Telephone: 816 543-4425
Fax: 816 543-8006
First published: 1939
Sponsoring organization: Dept. of English, Central Missouri State Univ.
ISSN: 1063-3391
MLA acronym: Pleiades

SUBSCRIPTION INFORMATION

Frequency of publication: 2 times/yr. (Spring, Fall)
Circulation: 100
Available in microform: No
Subscription price: $7.00/yr.
Year to which price refers: 1992-93

ADVERTISING INFORMATION

Advertising accepted: No

EDITORIAL DESCRIPTION

Scope: Publishes articles on literature, as well as original poetry, short fiction, drama, and translations.
Reviews books: No
Publishes notes: Yes
Languages accepted: English
Prints abstracts: No
Author-anonymous submission: No

SUBMISSION REQUIREMENTS

Restrictions on contributors: None
Author pays submission fee: No
Author pays page charges: No
Length of articles: 3,000-5,000 words
Length of notes: 500-1,000 words
Style: MLA
Number of copies required: 1
Copyright ownership: Journal; reverts to author after publication
Rejected manuscripts: Returned; enclose SASE
Time before publication decision: 6-12 weeks
Time between decision and publication: 3-6 mos.
Number of reviewers: 3
Articles submitted per year: 30
Articles published per year: 6-8
Notes published per year: 6

(2181)
*Ploughshares

DeWitt Henry, Editor
Emerson College
100 Beacon St.
Boston, MA 02116

Telephone: 617 578-8753
First published: 1971
Sponsoring organization: Ploughshares, Inc.; Emerson College
ISSN: 0048-4474
MLA acronym: Ploughshares

SUBSCRIPTION INFORMATION

Frequency of publication: 3 times/yr.
Circulation: 3,500
Available in microform: Yes
Subscription price: $18.00/yr. institutions US; $22.00/yr. institutions elsewhere; $15.00/yr. individuals US; $19.00/yr. individuals elsewhere
Year to which price refers: 1991

ADVERTISING INFORMATION

Advertising accepted: Yes
Advertising rates: $125.00/full page, nonprofit organizations; $250.00/full page otherwise

EDITORIAL DESCRIPTION

Scope: Journal is national and international, with focus on: (1) highest quality new poetry, fiction, and nonfiction; (2) literary judgment as problem; with editorial selections organized into continuing debate about what constitutes good writing.
Reviews books: Yes
Publishes notes: No
Languages accepted: English
Prints abstracts: No
Author-anonymous submission: No

SUBMISSION REQUIREMENTS

Restrictions on contributors: Book reviews are solicited.
Author pays submission fee: No
Author pays page charges: No
Length of articles: 6,000 words maximum
Length of book reviews: 750 words maximum
Style: None
Number of copies required: 1
Special requirements: Send a SASE for writer's guidelines prior to submission.
Rejected manuscripts: Returned; enclose return postage.
Time before publication decision: 3 mos.
Time between decision and publication: 3 mos.
Number of reviewers: 3
Articles submitted per year: 5,000-7,000
Articles published per year: 160-200
Book reviews published per year: 24-30

(2182)
*Plural: Revista Cultural de Excelsior

Jaime Labastida, Editor
Reforma 18, 1 Piso
Mexico City 1, D.F. 06600, Mexico

Telephone: (52) 5 5669360; (52) 5 5666107
Fax: (52) 5 5465215; (52) 5 5660223
First published: 1971
ISSN: 0185-4925
MLA acronym: Plural

SUBSCRIPTION INFORMATION

Frequency of publication: 12 times/yr.
Circulation: 1,200
Available in microform: No
Subscription price: $30.00/yr.
Year to which price refers: 1992
Subscription address: Excélsior, Dept. de Suscripciones, Reforma 10, Mexico City 1, D.F. 06600, Mexico
Subscription telephone: (52) 5 7054444 ext. 2176, 2177, 2178, 2179

ADVERTISING INFORMATION

Advertising accepted: Yes
Advertising rates: Mex$3,500,000.00/full page

EDITORIAL DESCRIPTION

Scope: Publishes creative works (poetry, stories) and criticism of the arts, including literature, philosophy and history.
Reviews books: Yes
Publishes notes: Yes
Languages accepted: Spanish; Portuguese
Prints abstracts: No
Author-anonymous submission: No

SUBMISSION REQUIREMENTS

Author pays submission fee: No
Author pays page charges: No
Length of articles: 10-15 pp.
Length of book reviews: 3 pp.
Length of notes: 3 pp.
Style: None
Number of copies required: 1
Special requirements: Include a biographical note on the author.
Copyright ownership: Author
Rejected manuscripts: Not returned
Time before publication decision: 1 mo.
Time between decision and publication: 2 mos.
Number of reviewers: 4
Articles submitted per year: 2,000
Articles published per year: 240
Book reviews submitted per year: 100
Book reviews published per year: 70
Notes submitted per year: 360
Notes published per year: 180

(2183)
*PMLA: Publications of the Modern Language Association of America

Domna C. Stanton, Editor
Modern Language Assn. of America
10 Astor Place
New York, NY 10003-6981

First published: 1884-85
Sponsoring organization: Modern Language Assn. of America
ISSN: 0030-8129
MLA acronym: PMLA

SUBSCRIPTION INFORMATION

Frequency of publication: 6 times/yr. (Jan., Mar., May, Sept., Oct., Nov.)
Circulation: 35,500
Available in microform: Yes

ADVERTISING INFORMATION

Advertising accepted: Yes
Advertising rates: $660.00/half page; $1,025.00/full page

EDITORIAL DESCRIPTION

Scope: Welcomes essays of interest to those concerned with the study of language and literature. As the publication of a large and heterogeneous association, the journal is receptive to a variety of topics, whether general or specific, and to all scholarly methods and theoretical perspectives. The ideal *PMLA* essay exemplifies the best of its kind, whatever the kind; addresses a significant problem; draws out clearly the implications of its findings; and engages the attention of its audience through a concise, readable presentation. Translations should accompany foreign language quotations. The MLA urges its contributors to be sensitive to the social implications of language and to seek wording free of discriminatory overtones.
Reviews books: No
Publishes notes: Yes
Languages accepted: English
Prints abstracts: Yes
Author-anonymous submission: Yes

SUBMISSION REQUIREMENTS

Restrictions on contributors: Contributors must be members of the MLA.
Author pays submission fee: No
Author pays page charges: No
Length of articles: 2,500-9,000 words (including notes but not works cited or translations)
Style: MLA
Number of copies required: 2
Special requirements: Type author's name on title page only. Manuscripts in languages other than English are accepted for review but must be accompanied by a detailed summary in English and must be translated into English if they are recommended to the Editorial Board.
Copyright ownership: Assigned by author to journal
Rejected manuscripts: Returned; enclose return postage
Time before publication decision: 8-10 weeks
Time between decision and publication: 18 mos.
Number of reviewers: 2-9
Articles submitted per year: 400-500
Articles published per year: 32-40

(2184)
*PN Review

Michael Schmidt, Editor
208 Corn Exchange Bldgs.
Manchester M4 3BQ, England

Telephone: (44) 61 8348730
Fax: (44) 61 8320084
First published: 1973
Sponsoring organization: Arts Council of Great Britain
ISSN: 0144-7076
MLA acronym: PNR

SUBSCRIPTION INFORMATION

Frequency of publication: 6 times/yr.
Circulation: 1,700
Available in microform: No
Subscription price: £28.00 ($58.00)/yr. institutions; £21.50 ($45.00)/yr. individuals
Year to which price refers: 1992

ADVERTISING INFORMATION

Advertising accepted: Yes
Advertising rates: £200.00/full page

EDITORIAL DESCRIPTION

Scope: Publishes articles on contemporary English language poetry; poetry and fiction in translation; and literary criticism.
Reviews books: Yes
Publishes notes: Yes
Languages accepted: English
Prints abstracts: No
Author-anonymous submission: No

SUBMISSION REQUIREMENTS

Restrictions on contributors: None
Author pays submission fee: No
Author pays page charges: No
Length of articles: 6,000 words maximum
Length of book reviews: 250-1,200 words
Length of notes: 50-150 words
Style: MLA
Number of copies required: 1
Special requirements: Submit original typescript.
Copyright ownership: Author
Rejected manuscripts: Returned; enclose return postage.
Time before publication decision: 1 mo.
Time between decision and publication: 1-10 mos.
Number of reviewers: 1
Articles submitted per year: 1,000
Articles published per year: 60
Book reviews published per year: 240
Notes published per year: 120

(2185)
Pneumatikē Kypros

Kypros Chrysanthis, Editor
Androkleus 2
Nicosia 135, Cyprus

First published: 1960
ISSN: 0554-3363
MLA acronym: PKy

SUBSCRIPTION INFORMATION

Frequency of publication: 11 times/yr.
Circulation: 1,600
Available in microform: No

ADVERTISING INFORMATION

Advertising accepted: Yes

EDITORIAL DESCRIPTION

Scope: Publishes articles on Greek literature, translations from various national literatures, book reviews (especially Greek), and notes.
Reviews books: Yes
Languages accepted: English; French; Greek
Prints abstracts: Yes

SUBMISSION REQUIREMENTS

Restrictions on contributors: None
Author pays submission fee: No
Author pays page charges: No
Length of articles: 2,500-5,000 words
Length of book reviews: No restrictions
Number of copies required: 1
Copyright ownership: Author
Rejected manuscripts: Returned
Time before publication decision: 4 mos.
Time between decision and publication: 6 mos.
Articles submitted per year: 1
Articles published per year: 30-40
Book reviews published per year: 30-40

(2186)
*Po&sie

Michel Deguy, Editor
Editions Belin
8, rue Férou
75278 Paris Cedex 06, France

Telephone: (33) 1 46342142
Fax: (33) 1 43251829
First published: 1977
Sponsoring organization: Centre National des Lettres
ISSN: 0152-0032
MLA acronym: Po&sie

SUBSCRIPTION INFORMATION

Frequency of publication: 4 times/yr.
Circulation: 600
Available in microform: No
Subscription price: 215 F/yr. France; 235 F/yr. elsewhere
Year to which price refers: 1992
Subscription telephone: (33) 1 46340720

ADVERTISING INFORMATION

Advertising accepted: No

EDITORIAL DESCRIPTION

Scope: Publishes articles on poetry and philosophy.
Reviews books: Yes
Publishes notes: Yes
Languages accepted: English; French; German; Italian; Portuguese; Spanish
Prints abstracts: No
Author-anonymous submission: No

SUBMISSION REQUIREMENTS

Author pays submission fee: No
Author pays page charges: No
Number of copies required: 1
Copyright ownership: Author
Rejected manuscripts: Returned
Time before publication decision: 1 mo.
Time between decision and publication: 3 mos.
Number of reviewers: 11
Articles published per year: 30-40
Book reviews published per year: 4

(2187)
*Poe Studies: Dark Romanticism: History, Theory, Interpretation

Alexander Hammond, Editor
Dept. of English
Washington State Univ.
Pullman, WA 99164-5020

Telephone: 509 335-4795
First published: 1968
Sponsoring organization: Washington State Univ., Dept. of English
ISSN: 0090-5224
MLA acronym: PoeS

SUBSCRIPTION INFORMATION

Frequency of publication: 2 times/yr. with occasional supplements
Circulation: 450
Available in microform: No
Subscription price: $15.00/yr. institutions; $10.00/yr. individuals
Year to which price refers: 1993
Subscription address: Washington State Univ. Press, Pullman, WA 99164-5910
Subscription telephone: 509 335-5817

ADVERTISING INFORMATION

Advertising accepted: Yes

EDITORIAL DESCRIPTION

Scope: Solicits manuscripts, both notes and substantial essays, on any aspect of Poe, the man and writer, from any critical, historical, or scholarly approach. Includes an annual "Poe International Bibliography," which surveys contemporary Poe criticism; reviews; and review-essays evaluating all significant Poe scholarship.
Reviews books: Yes
Publishes notes: Yes
Languages accepted: English
Prints abstracts: No

SUBMISSION REQUIREMENTS

Restrictions on contributors: Reviews are solicited.
Author pays submission fee: No
Author pays page charges: No
Length of articles: No restrictions
Length of book reviews: No restrictions
Length of notes: 1,000 words maximum
Style: Chicago
Number of copies required: 2
Special requirements: Manuscripts may also be typed on IBM Selectric or be printed on a letter-quality printer in letter gothic, courier, or prestige elite typeface with unjustified right margins. Preferred format for final versions of contributions is on diskette in ASCII format.
Rejected manuscripts: Returned
Time before publication decision: 4-12 mos.
Time between decision and publication: 6 mos.
Number of reviewers: 3-4
Articles submitted per year: 40
Articles published per year: 5
Book reviews published per year: 4
Notes submitted per year: 15
Notes published per year: 3

(2188)
*Poesía

Reynaldo Pérez Só, Editor
Dept. de Literatura (D.C.) de la Univ. de Carabobo
Apartado 3139.El Trigal
Valencia 2002
Ed. Carabobo, Venezuela

First published: 1971
Sponsoring organization: Univ. de Carabobo
MLA acronym: Poesía

SUBSCRIPTION INFORMATION

Frequency of publication: 4 times/yr.
Available in microform: No

ADVERTISING INFORMATION

Advertising accepted: No

EDITORIAL DESCRIPTION

Scope: Publishes articles on Spanish-language poetry and poetical theory.
Reviews books: Yes
Publishes notes: Yes
Languages accepted: Spanish; Latin
Prints abstracts: Yes
Author-anonymous submission: No

SUBMISSION REQUIREMENTS

Author pays submission fee: No
Author pays page charges: No
Length of articles: 3 pp.
Length of notes: 2 pp.
Number of copies required: 1
Time before publication decision: 6 mos.
Time between decision and publication: 6 mos.
Number of reviewers: 3
Book reviews submitted per year: 5
Book reviews published per year: 5

(2189)
Poesie und Wissenschaft

Lothar Stiehm, Editor
Lothar Stiehm Verlag
Siemensstr. 57
7016 Gerlingen, Germany

First published: 1967
ISSN: 0554-3762
MLA acronym: PuW

SUBSCRIPTION INFORMATION

Frequency of publication: Irregular
Available in microform: No

ADVERTISING INFORMATION

Advertising accepted: No

EDITORIAL DESCRIPTION

Scope: Publishes monographs on German literature.
Reviews books: No
Languages accepted: German
Prints abstracts: No

SUBMISSION REQUIREMENTS

Restrictions on contributors: None
Author pays page charges: No
Length of books: No restrictions
Style: None
Number of copies required: 1
Copyright ownership: Lothar Stiehm Verlag
Rejected manuscripts: Returned

(2190)
*Poetica: Zeitschrift für Sprach- und Literaturwissenschaft

Karlheinz Stierle, Ulrich Broich, Hellmut Flashar, Renate Lachmann, & Volker Schupp, Editors
Fachgruppe Literaturwissenschaft der Univ. Konstanz
Postfach 5560
7750 Constance, Germany

First published: 1967
Sponsoring organization: Deutsche Forschungsgemeinschaft
ISSN: 0303-4178
MLA acronym: Poetica

SUBSCRIPTION INFORMATION

Frequency of publication: 4 times/yr.
Circulation: 650
Available in microform: No
Subscription price: 138 DM/yr.
Year to which price refers: 1991
Subscription address: Wilhelm Fink Verlag, Ohmstr. 5, 8000 Munich 40, Germany

ADVERTISING INFORMATION

Advertising accepted: Yes

EDITORIAL DESCRIPTION

Scope: An interdisciplinary journal publishing studies in literature.
Reviews books: Yes
Publishes notes: No
Languages accepted: German
Prints abstracts: No
Author-anonymous submission: No

SUBMISSION REQUIREMENTS

Restrictions on contributors: None
Author pays submission fee: No
Author pays page charges: No
Length of articles: 5,500-9,500 words
Length of book reviews: 2,200-5,500 words
Style: Journal
Number of copies required: 2
Copyright ownership: Journal for 1 yr. and then reverts to author.
Rejected manuscripts: Returned
Time before publication decision: 3-6 mos.
Time between decision and publication: 6-8 mos.
Number of reviewers: 2
Articles submitted per year: 30-35
Articles published per year: 15-16
Book reviews submitted per year: 6-8
Book reviews published per year: 6-8

(2191)
*Poetics: Journal for Empirical Research on Literature, the Media and the Arts

Cees J. van Rees, Editor
Tilburg Univ.
Dept. of Language & Literature
P.O. Box 90153
5000 LE Tilburg, Netherlands

Telephone: (31) 13 662773
Fax: (31) 13 663110
E-mail: REES@KUB.NL
First published: 1971
ISSN: 0304-422X
MLA acronym: PoeticsJ

SUBSCRIPTION INFORMATION

Frequency of publication: 6 times/yr.
Circulation: 1,000
Available in microform: Yes
Subscription price: 355 f/yr. plus postage
Year to which price refers: 1992
Subscription address: Marlene Hamers, North Holland Publishing Co., P.O. Box 1991, 1000 BZ Amsterdam, Netherlands
Subscription telephone: (31) 20 5862467

ADVERTISING INFORMATION

Advertising accepted: Yes

EDITORIAL DESCRIPTION

Scope: Publishes articles in the fields of theoretical and empirical research on literature, the media, and the arts. Publishes not only advanced research reports, but also overview articles. Occasional special issues, guest-edited by specialists, present the "state of the art" or discuss new developments in a particular field. Some topics on which *Poetics* focuses are: psychological research on the processing of literary texts and other media; sociological research on participation in the arts, media use, the conditions under which makers of cultural products operate, the functioning of institutions which make, distribute, and/or judge cultural products, the media, and the arts; economic research on the funding, costs and benefits of organizations in the fields of art and culture; contributions from disciplines and fields such as sociology, cognitive psychology, linguistics, discourse studies, historiography, economics, and media research; techniques current in empirical research.
Reviews books: No
Publishes notes: No
Languages accepted: English
Prints abstracts: Yes
Author-anonymous submission: Yes

SUBMISSION REQUIREMENTS

Restrictions on contributors: None
Author pays submission fee: No
Author pays page charges: No
Length of articles: 5-50 typescript pp.
Style: Journal
Number of copies required: 3
Special requirements: Include a summary (200 words maximum) and a short bio-bibliographical note on author.

Copyright ownership: North Holland Publishing Co.-Elsevier Science Publishers B.V.
Rejected manuscripts: Not returned
Time before publication decision: 6-12 mos.
Time between decision and publication: 8 mos.
Number of reviewers: 3-4
Articles submitted per year: 80-100
Articles published per year: 25-30

(2192)
*Poetics Today

Itamar Even-Zohar, Brian McHale, & Ruth Ronen, Editors
Tel Aviv Univ.
Tel Aviv 69978, Israel

Additional editorial address: Porter Inst. for Poetics & Semiotics, P.O. Box 39085, Tel Aviv 61390, Israel
Telephone: (972) 3 6409420
Fax: (972) 3 6408980
E-mail: Porter@Taunivm
First published: 1979
Sponsoring organization: Porter Inst. for Poetics & Semiotics, Tel Aviv Univ.
ISSN: 0333-5372
MLA acronym: PoT

SUBSCRIPTION INFORMATION

Frequency of publication: 4 times/yr.
Circulation: 900
Available in microform: No
Subscription price: $64.00/yr. institutions; $32.00/yr. individuals; $16.00/single issue
Year to which price refers: 1993
Subscription address: Duke Univ. Press, 6697 College Station, Durham, NC 27708
Subscription telephone: 919 684-2173
Subscription fax: 919 684-8644

ADVERTISING INFORMATION

Advertising accepted: Yes
Advertising rates: Request from Duke Univ. Press

EDITORIAL DESCRIPTION

Scope: Publishes articles on contemporary literary theory, descriptive poetics of specific texts, writers or genres, language in context and communication in culture.
Reviews books: Yes
Publishes notes: No
Languages accepted: English
Prints abstracts: Yes

SUBMISSION REQUIREMENTS

Restrictions on contributors: None
Author pays submission fee: No
Author pays page charges: No
Length of articles: No restrictions
Length of book reviews: No restrictions
Style: Conforms to style of linguistics & social science journals (see PoT 9(4) for particulars)
Number of copies required: 2
Special requirements: Include references & footnotes on separate sheets, a 200-word abstract, and a biographical sketch.
Copyright ownership: Porter Inst. for Poetics & Semiotics, Tel Aviv Univ.
Rejected manuscripts: Returned at author's request
Time before publication decision: 3-6 mos.
Time between decision and publication: 1 yr.; reviews published immediately
Number of reviewers: 3
Articles submitted per year: 50-60
Articles published per year: 30-40
Book reviews submitted per year: 60-80
Book reviews published per year: 60-80

(2193)
*Poétique: Revue de Théorie et d'Analyse Littéraires

Michel Charles, Editor
Ecole Normale Supérieure
45, rue d'Ulm
75230 Paris Cedex 05, France

Telephone: (33) 1 40465050
First published: 1970
ISSN: 0032-2024
MLA acronym: Poétique

SUBSCRIPTION INFORMATION

Frequency of publication: 4 times/yr.
Circulation: 3,500
Subscription price: 330 F/yr. France; 360 F/yr. elsewhere
Year to which price refers: 1992
Subscription address: Editions du Seuil, 27 rue Jacob, 75006 Paris, France

EDITORIAL DESCRIPTION

Scope: Focuses on literary theory and its categories (genres, periods, methods of investigation, levels of analysis) in relation to concrete works of literature.
Reviews books: No
Languages accepted: French
Prints abstracts: No

SUBMISSION REQUIREMENTS

Restrictions on contributors: None
Length of articles: 50,000 characters
Style: Journal
Number of copies required: 1
Copyright ownership: Author
Rejected manuscripts: Returned at author's request
Time before publication decision: 2 mos.
Time between decision and publication: 1 yr.
Number of reviewers: 2
Articles published per year: 32

(2194)
*Poetry Review

Peter Forbes, Editor
Poetry Soc.
22 Betterton St.
London WC2H 9BU, England

Telephone: (44) 71 2404810
Fax: (44) 71 2404818
First published: 1909
Sponsoring organization: Poetry Soc.
ISSN: 0032-2156
MLA acronym: PoetryR

SUBSCRIPTION INFORMATION

Frequency of publication: 4 times/yr.
Circulation: 5,000
Available in microform: No
Subscription price: £23.00/yr. institutions United Kingdom; $45.00/yr. institutions US; £18.00/yr. individuals United Kingdom; $38.00/yr. individuals US
Year to which price refers: 1993

ADVERTISING INFORMATION

Advertising accepted: Yes

EDITORIAL DESCRIPTION

Scope: Publishes contemporary poetry and reviews.
Reviews books: Yes
Publishes notes: Yes
Languages accepted: English
Prints abstracts: No
Author-anonymous submission: No

SUBMISSION REQUIREMENTS

Restrictions on contributors: Send letter of inquiry to editor since most reviews and articles are commissioned.
Author pays submission fee: No
Author pays page charges: No
Length of articles: 1,500 words
Length of book reviews: 1,000 words
Number of copies required: 1
Copyright ownership: Author
Rejected manuscripts: Returned; enclose return postage.
Time before publication decision: 3 mos.
Time between decision and publication: 4-5 mos.
Number of reviewers: 1
Book reviews published per year: 20-30

(2195)
Poeziia

M. Nachnibida, Editor
"Radians'kyĭ Pys'mennyk"
Blvd. Lesy Ukraynky 20
Kiev, Ukraine

First published: 1967
ISSN: 0554-4084
MLA acronym: Poeziia

SUBSCRIPTION INFORMATION

Frequency of publication: 4 times/yr.

EDITORIAL DESCRIPTION

Scope: Publishes poetry and criticism of Ukrainian poets and poetry.
Reviews books: No
Languages accepted: Ukrainian
Prints abstracts: No

(2196)
Polish Perspectives

Artur Starewicz, Editor
Polski Inst. Spraw Miedzynarodowych
Warecka 1A
00-950 Warsaw, Poland

First published: 1958
Sponsoring organization: Polish Inst. of International Affairs
ISSN: 0032-2962
MLA acronym: PolP

SUBSCRIPTION INFORMATION

Frequency of publication: 4 times/yr.
Circulation: 4,500
Available in microform: Yes
Subscription address: European Publishers Representatives, Inc., 11-03 46th Ave., Long Island City, NY 11101
Additional subscription address: Ars Polona, Krakowskie Przedmieście 7, 00-068 Warsaw, Poland; addresses for other countries appear on back cover of journal

ADVERTISING INFORMATION

Advertising accepted: Yes

EDITORIAL DESCRIPTION

Scope: Publishes articles by Polish and foreign authors on the history, politics, art, culture, science, and economy of Poland. Essays, articles, and notes should refer to the past or present of Poland.
Reviews books: Yes
Publishes notes: Yes
Languages accepted: English; French; German
Prints abstracts: No
Author-anonymous submission: No

SUBMISSION REQUIREMENTS

Restrictions on contributors: None
Author pays submission fee: No
Author pays page charges: No
Length of articles: 4,000 words maximum
Length of book reviews: 500 words
Length of notes: 200 words
Style: None
Number of copies required: 1
Copyright ownership: Author
Rejected manuscripts: Not returned
Time before publication decision: 1 mo.
Time between decision and publication: 6 mos.
Number of reviewers: 3
Articles submitted per year: 100
Articles published per year: 30
Book reviews submitted per year: 200
Book reviews published per year: 12
Notes submitted per year: 1,000
Notes published per year: 150

(2197)
*The Polish Review

Joseph W. Wieczerzak, Acting Editor-in-Chief
Polish Inst. of Arts & Sciences, Inc.
208 E. 30th St.
New York, NY 10016

Telephone: 212 686-4164
First published: 1956
Sponsoring organization: Polish Inst. of Arts & Sciences of America, Inc.
ISSN: 0032-2970
MLA acronym: PolR

SUBSCRIPTION INFORMATION

Frequency of publication: 4 times/yr. (Mar., June, Sept., Dec.)
Circulation: 1,700
Available in microform: Yes
Subscription price: $30.00/yr. institutions; $25.00/yr. individuals US; $30.00/yr. individuals elsewhere
Year to which price refers: 1992

ADVERTISING INFORMATION

Advertising accepted: Yes
Advertising rates: $125.00/half page; $250.00/full page

EDITORIAL DESCRIPTION

Scope: A scholarly journal devoted to Polish affairs (social sciences and humanities).
Reviews books: Yes
Publishes notes: Yes
Languages accepted: English
Prints abstracts: No
Author-anonymous submission: Yes

SUBMISSION REQUIREMENTS

Restrictions on contributors: None
Author pays submission fee: No
Author pays page charges: No
Length of articles: 25 pp.
Length of book reviews: 4 pp.
Length of notes: 1 p.
Style: MLA; Chicago
Number of copies required: 3
Copyright ownership: Polish Inst.
Rejected manuscripts: Returned; enclose SASE.
Time before publication decision: 6 mos.
Time between decision and publication: 18 mos.
Number of reviewers: 2-3
Articles submitted per year: 50
Articles published per year: 25
Book reviews submitted per year: 55
Book reviews published per year: 35
Notes submitted per year: 28
Notes published per year: 15

(2198)
*Polonica

Henryk Wrobel & Ireneusz Bobrowski, Editors
Inst. Języka Polskiego
Polska Akademia Nauk
ul. Straszewskiego 27
31-113 Cracow, Poland

Telephone: (48) 12 222699
Fax: (48) 12 225929
First published: 1976
Sponsoring organization: Inst. Języka Polskiego, Polska Akademia Nauk
ISSN: 0137-9712
MLA acronym: Polonica

SUBSCRIPTION INFORMATION

Frequency of publication: Annual
Circulation: 400-500
Available in microform: No
Subscription price: $25.00/yr.
Year to which price refers: 1992

ADVERTISING INFORMATION

Advertising accepted: Yes

EDITORIAL DESCRIPTION

Scope: Publishes articles on Polish and general linguistics.
Reviews books: Yes
Publishes notes: Yes
Languages accepted: Polish; all Slavic languages; English; French; German
Prints abstracts: Yes
Author-anonymous submission: No

SUBMISSION REQUIREMENTS

Restrictions on contributors: None
Author pays submission fee: No
Author pays page charges: No
Length of articles: 4,000-8,000 words
Length of book reviews: 600 words
Length of notes: 1,000-1,200 words
Number of copies required: 2
Special requirements: Submit a 50-150 word abstract.
Copyright ownership: Ossolineum
Rejected manuscripts: Returned
Time before publication decision: 3 mos.
Time between decision and publication: 1 yr.
Number of reviewers: 2
Articles submitted per year: 20-25
Articles published per year: 15-20
Book reviews submitted per year: 3
Book reviews published per year: 3
Notes submitted per year: 2
Notes published per year: 2

(2199)
*Polska Sztuka Ludowa: Konteksty. Antropologia Kultury. Etnografia. Sztuka

Aleksander Jackowski & Zbigniew Benedyktowicz, Editors
Inst. Sztuki Polskiej Akademii Nauk
ul. Długa 28
00-950 Warsaw, Poland

Telephone: (48) 22 313271 ext. 227
Fax: (48) 22 313149
First published: 1947
Sponsoring organization: Polska Akademia Nauk, Inst. Sztuki
ISSN: 0032-3721
MLA acronym: PSzL

SUBSCRIPTION INFORMATION

Frequency of publication: 4 times/yr.
Circulation: 3,000
Available in microform: No
Subscription price: 16,000 Zł/yr. outside Poland
Year to which price refers: 1992
Subscription address: Foreign Trade Enterprise "Ars Polona", Krakowskie Przedmieście 7, 00-068 Warsaw, Poland
Additional subscription address: Inst Sztuki PAN, "Polska Sztuka Ludowa", ul. Długa 28, 00-950 Warsaw, Poland

ADVERTISING INFORMATION

Advertising accepted: No

EDITORIAL DESCRIPTION

Scope: Publishes articles on anthropology of culture, popular art, and folk art.
Reviews books: Yes
Publishes notes: Yes
Languages accepted: Polish
Prints abstracts: Yes
Author-anonymous submission: No

SUBMISSION REQUIREMENTS

Restrictions on contributors: None
Author pays submission fee: No
Author pays page charges: No
Length of articles: 36,000-40,000 characters
Length of book reviews: 7,000-14,000 characters
Length of notes: 7,200-9,000 characters
Number of copies required: 2
Special requirements: Submit original typescript and 1 copy, along with a 1,000-character abstract.
Copyright ownership: Author
Rejected manuscripts: Not returned
Time before publication decision: 2 weeks
Time between decision and publication: 1-2 yrs.
Number of reviewers: 1-3
Articles submitted per year: 40
Articles published per year: 25-30
Book reviews published per year: 10
Notes published per year: 8

(2200)
Polymia

Siarheĭ Zakonnikaŭ, Editor
Izdatel'stvo Polymia
ul. Zakharova 19
220005 Minsk, Belarus

First published: 1922
Sponsoring organization: Soiuz Pisateleĭ Belorussii
ISSN: 0130-8086
MLA acronym: Polymia

SUBSCRIPTION INFORMATION

Frequency of publication: 12 times/yr.
Circulation: 11,000
Subscription address: Izdatel'stvo "Polymia", at the above address

EDITORIAL DESCRIPTION

Scope: Publishes articles on literary and sociopolitical topics.
Reviews books: Yes
Languages accepted: Belorussian
Prints abstracts: No

SUBMISSION REQUIREMENTS

Restrictions on contributors: None
Length of articles: No restrictions
Number of copies required: 2
Special requirements: Submit original typescript.
Copyright ownership: Author
Rejected manuscripts: Returned
Time before publication decision: 1 mo.
Time between decision and publication: 3 mos.
Number of reviewers: 2 plus editorial staff
Articles published per year: 600-800

(2201)
Il Ponte: Rivista Mensile de Politica e Letteratura Fondata da Piero Calamandrei

Enzo Enriques Agnoletti, Editor
C.P. 183
50100 Florence, Italy

ISSN: 0032-423X
MLA acronym: Ponte

SUBSCRIPTION INFORMATION

Frequency of publication: 6 times/yr.
Subscription address: Nuova Italia Editrice, 8, via Antonio Giacomini, 50132 Florence, Italy

EDITORIAL DESCRIPTION

Scope: Publishes articles on politics and literature.
Reviews books: No
Languages accepted: Italian
Prints abstracts: No

SUBMISSION REQUIREMENTS

Rejected manuscripts: Not returned

(2202)
*Pontifical Institute of Mediaeval Studies, Studies and Texts

Dept. of Publications
Pontifical Inst. of Mediaeval Studies
59 Queen's Park Crescent East
Toronto, Ontario M5S 2C4, Canada

Telephone: 416 926-7143
Fax: 416 926-7258
E-mail: Pontifex@epds.utoronto.ca
First published: 1955
Sponsoring organization: Pontifical Inst. of Mediaeval Studies
ISSN: 0082-5328
MLA acronym: PIMSST

SUBSCRIPTION INFORMATION

Frequency of publication: Irregular
Circulation: 650
Available in microform: No

ADVERTISING INFORMATION

Advertising accepted: No

EDITORIAL DESCRIPTION

Scope: Publishes studies and critical editions of texts dealing with the Middle Ages.
Reviews books: No
Publishes notes: No
Languages accepted: English; French; Latin; Italian; German; all languages
Prints abstracts: No
Author-anonymous submission: Yes

SUBMISSION REQUIREMENTS

Restrictions on contributors: None
Author pays submission fee: No
Author pays page charges: No
Length of books: No restrictions
Style: Chicago
Number of copies required: 1
Copyright ownership: Pontifical Inst. of Mediaeval Studies
Rejected manuscripts: Returned
Time before publication decision: 4 mos.
Time between decision and publication: 1 yr.
Number of reviewers: 2
Books submitted per year: 20
Books published per year: 8

(2203)
Poradnik Językowy

Witold Doroszewski, Editor
Pałac Słaszica
ul. Nowy Świat 72
00-330 Warsaw, Poland

First published: 1901
ISSN: 0551-5343
MLA acronym: PJ

SUBSCRIPTION INFORMATION

Frequency of publication: 10 times/yr.
Subscription address: Ars Polona-Ruch, Krakowskie Przedmieście 7, P.O. Box 1001, 00-068 Warsaw, Poland

EDITORIAL DESCRIPTION

Reviews books: Yes
Languages accepted: Polish
Prints abstracts: No

(2204)
*Il Portico: Biblioteca di Lettere e Arti

Antonio Piromalli, Editor
A. Longo Editore
Via P. Costa, 33
P.O. Box 431
48100 Ravenna, Italy

Telephone: (39) 544 217026
Fax: (39) 544 217026
First published: 1967
MLA acronym: Portico

SUBSCRIPTION INFORMATION

Frequency of publication: Irregular
Circulation: 1,500-2,000
Available in microform: No

ADVERTISING INFORMATION

Advertising accepted: No

EDITORIAL DESCRIPTION

Scope: Publishes monograph studies about American, English, and European literatures. Emphasis is on Italian literature.
Reviews books: No
Publishes notes: No
Languages accepted: Italian; English
Prints abstracts: No
Author-anonymous submission: No

SUBMISSION REQUIREMENTS

Author pays submission fee: No
Author pays page charges: No
Length of books: 150-200 pp.
Style: MLA
Number of copies required: 2
Copyright ownership: A. Longo Editore
Rejected manuscripts: Not returned
Time before publication decision: 6 mos.
Time between decision and publication: 8-10 mos.
Number of reviewers: 2
Books submitted per year: 40
Books published per year: 10-15

(2205)
*Portuguese Studies

H. M. Macedo, Editor
Portuguese Dept.
King's College
Strand
London WC2R 2LS, England

Telephone: (44) 71 8732507
Fax: (44) 71 8732787
First published: 1985
Sponsoring organization: Modern Humanities Research Assn.; Calouste Gulbenkian Foundation; Luso-American Foundation; Portuguese Government
ISSN: 0267-5315
MLA acronym: PStud

SUBSCRIPTION INFORMATION

Frequency of publication: Annual
Available in microform: No
Subscription price: £24.00/yr. Europe; $58.00/yr. US
Year to which price refers: 1992
Subscription address: Modern Humanities Research Assn., c/o Dept. of German, King's College, Strand, London WC2R 2LS, England

ADVERTISING INFORMATION

Advertising accepted: No

EDITORIAL DESCRIPTION

Scope: Publishes articles on the literature, culture, and history of Portugal, Brazil, and the Portuguese-speaking countries of Africa.
Reviews books: Yes
Publishes notes: No
Languages accepted: English
Prints abstracts: No
Author-anonymous submission: No

SUBMISSION REQUIREMENTS

Author pays submission fee: No
Author pays page charges: No
Length of articles: 7,500 words
Length of book reviews: 350-1,000 words
Style: Modern Humanities Research Assn.
Number of copies required: 2
Copyright ownership: Modern Humanities Research Assn.
Rejected manuscripts: Returned by surface mail
Number of reviewers: 2
Articles published per year: 14
Book reviews published per year: 10

(2206)
*Post Script: Essays in Film and the Humanities

Gerald Duchovnay & J. P. Telotte, Editors
Dept. of Literature & Languages
East Texas State Univ.
Commerce, TX 75429

Telephone: 903 886-5260
Fax: 903 886-5918
First published: 1981
Sponsoring organization: Post Script, Inc.
ISSN: 0277-9897
MLA acronym: PostS

SUBSCRIPTION INFORMATION

Frequency of publication: 3 times/yr.
Circulation: 350-500
Available in microform: No
Subscription price: $20.00/yr. institutions US; $25.00/yr. institutions elsewhere; $12.00/yr. individuals US; $17.00/yr. individuals elsewhere
Year to which price refers: 1991-92

ADVERTISING INFORMATION

Advertising accepted: Yes
Advertising rates: $100.00/half page; $200.00/full page

EDITORIAL DESCRIPTION

Scope: Welcomes manuscripts on film as language and literature (narrative, character, imagery); ensemble acting; the actor as auteur; film music; film as visual art (painting and cinematic style, set design, costuming); film and photography; film history; aesthetics and ontology; the response of film and the humanities to technology; interdisciplinary studies in theme and genre; film and American studies; interviews. Includes bibliography of film studies for the year.
Reviews books: Yes
Publishes notes: Yes
Languages accepted: English
Prints abstracts: No
Author-anonymous submission: Yes

SUBMISSION REQUIREMENTS

Restrictions on contributors: None
Author pays submission fee: No
Author pays page charges: No
Length of articles: 2-20 pp.
Length of book reviews: 500-1,000 words
Length of notes: 1,000 words maximum
Style: MLA
Number of copies required: 3
Special requirements: Black and white photographs or photocopies may accompany article.
Copyright ownership: Journal
Rejected manuscripts: Returned; enclose SASE.
Time before publication decision: 4-6 mos.
Time between decision and publication: 4-18 mos.
Number of reviewers: 2-4
Articles submitted per year: 65-90
Articles published per year: 14-16
Book reviews submitted per year: 20-30
Book reviews published per year: 5-10
Notes submitted per year: 1-3
Notes published per year: 1-3

(2207)
Postilla Bohemica/Postylla Bohemica: Vierteljahresschrift der Konstanzer Hus-Gesellschaft e.V.

Frank Boldt, Editor
Verlag K-Presse
Vagtstr. 1
28 Bremen 1, Germany

First published: 1972
Sponsoring organization: Konstanzer Hus-Gesellschaft
MLA acronym: PostB

SUBSCRIPTION INFORMATION

Frequency of publication: 4 times/yr.
Circulation: 300

EDITORIAL DESCRIPTION

Scope: Specializes in articles on Czech linguistics, Czech history (literary and general), and the arts. Most of the articles are written by Czech scholars.
Reviews books: Yes
Languages accepted: German
Prints abstracts: No

(2208)
*Postmodern Culture: An Electronic Journal of Interdisciplinary Criticism

Eyal Amiran & John Unsworth, Editors
Box 8105
North Carolina State Univ.
Raleigh, NC 27695-8105

Telephone: 919 515-2687
Fax: 919 515-3628
E-mail: Pmc@ncsuvm.bitnet; pmc@ncsuvm.cc.ncsu.ecu
First published: 1990
Sponsoring organization: North Carolina State Univ.
ISSN: 1053-1920
MLA acronym: PMC

SUBSCRIPTION INFORMATION

Frequency of publication: 3 times/yr. (Jan., May, Sept.)
Circulation: 100 (diskette & fiche); 1,650 (e-mail)
Available in microform: Yes
Subscription price: Diskette or fiche version: $30.00/yr. institutions; $15.00/yr. individuals. Electronic mail version: free
Year to which price refers: 1992

ADVERTISING INFORMATION

Advertising accepted: Yes, on an exchange basis

EDITORIAL DESCRIPTION

Scope: An electronic journal of interdisciplinary studies. Focuses on postmodern literature, theory, and culture. Includes different kinds of writing from traditional analytical essays and reviews to video scripts and other new literary forms.
Reviews books: Yes
Publishes notes: No
Languages accepted: English
Prints abstracts: Yes
Author-anonymous submission: Yes

SUBMISSION REQUIREMENTS

Restrictions on contributors: None
Author pays submission fee: No
Author pays page charges: No
Length of articles: 3,000-8,000 words
Length of book reviews: 1,000-3,000 words
Style: MLA
Number of copies required: 1
Special requirements: Submission can be made by electronic mail, on diskette, or in hard copy; diskette submissions should be in WordPerfect or ASCII format, if possible.
Copyright ownership: Author
Rejected manuscripts: Returned at author's request
Time before publication decision: 6-8 weeks
Time between decision and publication: 4 mos. maximum
Number of reviewers: 5
Articles submitted per year: 100-150
Articles published per year: 15-20
Book reviews submitted per year: 25-30
Book reviews published per year: 12-15

(2209)
*Postmodern Studies

Theo D'haen & Hans Bertens, Editors
Dept. of English
Leiden Univ.
P.O.B. 9515
2300 RA Leiden, Netherlands

Additional editorial address: Hans Bertens, Dept. of English, Utrecht Univ., Trans 10, 3512 JK Utrecht, Netherlands
First published: 1988

ISSN: 0923-0483
MLA acronym: PmdnS

SUBSCRIPTION INFORMATION

Frequency of publication: Annual
Circulation: 450-700
Available in microform: No
Subscription address: Editions Rodopi, Keizersgracht 302-304, 1016 EX Amsterdam, Netherlands
Additional subscription address: Editions Rodopi, 233 Peachtree St., N.E., Suite 404, Atlanta, GA 30303-1504
Subscription telephone: (31) 20 6227507; 404 523-1964; 800 225-3998
Subscription fax: (31) 20 6380948; 404 522-7116

ADVERTISING INFORMATION

Advertising accepted: Yes, on an exchange basis

EDITORIAL DESCRIPTION

Scope: Publishes collections of articles on the phenomenon of postmodernism in literature. Includes theory, criticism, and cultural studies.
Reviews books: No
Publishes notes: No
Languages accepted: English
Prints abstracts: No
Author-anonymous submission: No

SUBMISSION REQUIREMENTS

Restrictions on contributors: None
Author pays submission fee: No
Author pays page charges: No
Length of books: 200-300 pp.
Style: MLA
Number of copies required: 2
Copyright ownership: Rodopi
Rejected manuscripts: Returned
Time before publication decision: 3 mos.
Time between decision and publication: 1 yr.
Number of reviewers: 2
Articles published per year: 10-15
Books published per year: 1

(2210)
*Powys Notes

Richard Maxwell, Editor
Dept. of English
Valparaiso Univ.
Valparaiso, IN 46383

Telephone: 219 464-5069
First published: 1985
Sponsoring organization: Powys Soc. of North America
ISSN: 1058-7691
MLA acronym: PowN

SUBSCRIPTION INFORMATION

Frequency of publication: 2 times/yr. (Spring, Fall)
Circulation: 125
Available in microform: No
Subscription price: $15.00/yr. institutions US; C$19.00/yr. institutions Canada; $12.00/yr. individuals US; C$15.00/yr. individuals Canada; £8.00/yr. United Kingdom
Year to which price refers: 1992
Subscription address: Constance Harsh, Dept. of English, 13 Oak Dr., Colgate Univ., Hamilton, NY 13346-1398
Additional subscription address: In Canada: Ben Jones, Dept. of English, Carleton Univ., Ottawa, ON K1S 5B6, Canada
Subscription telephone: 315 824-7294
Subscription fax: 315 824-7176

ADVERTISING INFORMATION

Advertising accepted: Yes

EDITORIAL DESCRIPTION

Scope: Presents scholarship, reviews, and bibliography of Powysian interest.
Reviews books: Yes
Publishes notes: Yes
Languages accepted: English
Prints abstracts: No
Author-anonymous submission: No

SUBMISSION REQUIREMENTS

Author pays submission fee: No
Author pays page charges: No
Length of articles: 4,000-10,000 words
Length of book reviews: 1,000-1,500 words
Length of notes: 2,000 words
Number of copies required: 2
Rejected manuscripts: Returned
Time before publication decision: 1 mo.
Time between decision and publication: 6-12 mos.
Number of reviewers: 2
Articles submitted per year: 8-10
Articles published per year: 4-5
Book reviews published per year: 2-10
Notes submitted per year: 20
Notes published per year: 15

(2211)
*The Powys Review

Belinda Humfrey & Simon Barker, Editors
Dept. of English
Saint David's Univ. College
Lampeter
Dyfed SA48 7ED, Wales

Telephone: (44) 570 422351 ext. 349
Fax: (44) 570 423423
First published: 1977
ISSN: 0309-1619
MLA acronym: PRev

SUBSCRIPTION INFORMATION

Frequency of publication: 2 times/yr.
Circulation: 1,000
Available in microform: No
Subscription price: £8.00/yr.
Year to which price refers: 1992
Subscription address: Gomer Press, Llandysul, Dyfed, Wales

ADVERTISING INFORMATION

Advertising accepted: Yes
Advertising rates: £50.00/half page; £100.00/full page

EDITORIAL DESCRIPTION

Scope: Publishes articles on the Powys family and their writing as well as on related literature, especially from 1890 to the present.
Reviews books: Yes
Publishes notes: Yes
Languages accepted: English
Prints abstracts: No
Author-anonymous submission: No

SUBMISSION REQUIREMENTS

Restrictions on contributors: None
Author pays submission fee: No
Author pays page charges: No
Length of articles: 4,000-6,000 words
Length of book reviews: 1,000 words
Length of notes: 750 words
Style: MLA; Oxford
Number of copies required: 2 for contributors from Great Britain; 1 otherwise
Copyright ownership: Editor
Rejected manuscripts: Returned; enclose return postage.

Time before publication decision: 1 mo. maximum
Time between decision and publication: 6-12 mos.
Number of reviewers: 2-3
Articles submitted per year: 24
Articles published per year: 14
Book reviews submitted per year: 19
Book reviews published per year: 18
Notes submitted per year: 15
Notes published per year: 6

(2212)
*Prace Językoznawcze

Kazimierz Polański, Editor
Ossolineum Publishing House of the Polish Academy of Sciences
Rynek 9
50-106 Wrocław, Poland

Telephone: (48) 71 38625
First published: 1954
Sponsoring organization: Polska Akademia Nauk, Komitet Językoznawstwa
ISSN: 0079-3485
MLA acronym: PANPJ

SUBSCRIPTION INFORMATION

Frequency of publication: Irregular
Circulation: 700-800
Available in microform: No
Subscription address: Foreign Trade Enterprise-Ars Polona, Krakowskie Przedmieście 7, 00-068 Warsaw, Poland
Additional subscription address: Dział Sprzedaży i Eksportu, Ossolineum, Rynek 9, 50-106 Wrocław, Poland
Subscription telephone: (48) 22 261201
Subscription fax: (48) 22 268673

ADVERTISING INFORMATION

Advertising accepted: No

EDITORIAL DESCRIPTION

Scope: Publishes monographs on problems of Polish language.
Reviews books: No
Publishes notes: No
Languages accepted: Polish; English; French; German; Slavic languages
Prints abstracts: Yes
Author-anonymous submission: No

SUBMISSION REQUIREMENTS

Restrictions on contributors: None
Author pays submission fee: No
Author pays page charges: No
Length of books: No restrictions
Style: None
Number of copies required: 2
Copyright ownership: Ossolineum
Rejected manuscripts: Returned
Time before publication decision: 3 mos.
Time between decision and publication: 1 yr.
Number of reviewers: 1
Books submitted per year: 2-4
Books published per year: 2-3

(2213)
Prace Komisji Językoznawstwa

Franciszek Sławski, Editor
Ossolineum Publishing House of the Polish Academy of Sciences
Rynek 9
50-106 Wrocław, Poland

First published: 1962
Sponsoring organization: Polska Akademia Nauk, Oddział w Krakowie
ISSN: 0079-3310

MLA acronym: PKJ

SUBSCRIPTION INFORMATION

Frequency of publication: Irregular
Circulation: 500-800
Available in microform: No
Subscription address: Foreign Trade Enterprise "Ars Polona", Krakowskie Przedmieście 7, 00-068 Warsaw, Poland

EDITORIAL DESCRIPTION

Scope: Publishes articles on all fields of linguistics.
Reviews books: No
Publishes notes: Yes
Languages accepted: Polish; English; German; French
Prints abstracts: Yes

SUBMISSION REQUIREMENTS

Author pays submission fee: No
Author pays page charges: No
Number of copies required: 2
Copyright ownership: Ossolineum

(2214)
Prace Komisji Słowianoznawstwa

Maria Bobrownicka, Wiesław Boryś, Ryszard Łużny, Zdzisław Niedziela, Franciszek Sławoski, & Stanisław Urbanczyk, Editors
Ossolineum Publishing House of the Polish Academy of Sciences
Rynek 9
50-106 Wrocław, Poland

First published: 1962
Sponsoring organization: Polska Akademia Nauk, Oddział w Krakowie
ISSN: 0079-3434
MLA acronym: PANPKS

SUBSCRIPTION INFORMATION

Frequency of publication: Irregular
Circulation: 800-1,500
Available in microform: No
Subscription address: Foreign Trade Enterprise "Ars Polona", Krakowskie Przedmieście 7, 00-068 Warsaw, Poland

ADVERTISING INFORMATION

Advertising accepted: No

EDITORIAL DESCRIPTION

Scope: Publishes monographs on Slavic literatures and linguistics.
Reviews books: No
Publishes notes: Yes
Languages accepted: Polish
Prints abstracts: Yes

SUBMISSION REQUIREMENTS

Restrictions on contributors: Contributors must be members of Polska Akademia Nauk.
Author pays submission fee: No
Author pays page charges: No
Number of copies required: 2
Copyright ownership: Ossolineum
Number of reviewers: 2
Books published per year: 1-2

(2215)
*Pragmatics: Quarterly Publication of the International Pragmatics Association

Marcyliena Morgan, Gunter Senft, & Masayoshi Shibatani, Editors
c/o IPrA Secretariat
P.O. Box 33
2018 Antwerp 11, Belgium

Additional editorial address: M. Morgan, Dept. of Anthropology, Univ. of California, Los Angeles, CA 90024; G. Senft, Max-Planck Research Group for Cognitive Anthropology, P.O. Box 310, 6500 AH Nijmegen, Netherlands; M. Shibatani, Kobe Univ., Faculty of Letters, Kobe 657, Japan
Telephone: (32) 3 2305574
Fax: (32) 3 2305574
E-mail: Ipra@ccu.uia.ac.be; morgan@anthro.sscnet.ucla.edu; cogant@mpi.nl; d54565@jpnkudpc.bitnet
First published: 1991
Sponsoring organization: International Pragmatics Assn. (IPrA)
ISSN: 1018-2101
MLA acronym: Pragmatics

SUBSCRIPTION INFORMATION

Frequency of publication: 4 times/yr. (Mar., June, Sept., Dec.)
Circulation: 800
Subscription price: $110.00 (3,900 BF)/yr. institutions; $55.00 (2,000 BF)/yr. individuals
Year to which price refers: 1993

ADVERTISING INFORMATION

Advertising accepted: Yes

EDITORIAL DESCRIPTION

Scope: Publishes articles, research reports, discussions, and news on the field of pragmatics in the widest sense as a functional (i.e., cognitive, social, and cultural) perspective on language and communication.
Publishes notes: Yes
Languages accepted: English

SUBMISSION REQUIREMENTS

Author pays submission fee: No
Author pays page charges: No
Number of copies required: 2
Special requirements: Final version of accepted articles should be camera-ready or accompanied by an IBM-compatible diskette in WordPerfect or ASCII format.
Copyright ownership: Author
Number of reviewers: 2

(2216)
*Pragmatics & Beyond: New Series

Herman Parret, Jacob L. Mey, & Jef Verschueren, Editors
Linguistics (GER)
Univ. of Antwerp (UIA)
Universiteitsplein 1
2610 Wilrijk, Belgium

Telephone: (32) 3 8202773
Fax: (32) 3 8202244
E-mail: Ipra@ccu.uia.ac.be
First published: 1980
ISSN: 0922-842X
MLA acronym: P&B

SUBSCRIPTION INFORMATION

Available in microform: No
Subscription address: John Benjamins North America, Inc., 821 Bethlehem Pike, Philadelphia, PA 19118
Additional subscription address: John Benjamins B.V., P.O. Box 75577, Amsteldijk 44, 1070 AN Amsterdam, Netherlands
Subscription telephone: 215 836-1200; (31) 20 6738156
Subscription fax: 215 836-1204; (31) 20 6739773

ADVERTISING INFORMATION

Advertising accepted: No

EDITORIAL DESCRIPTION

Scope: Publishes monographs on pragmatics, discourse analysis, text linguistics, semiotics, sociolinguistics, psycholinguistics, anthropological linguistics, communication theories, and related topics.
Reviews books: No
Publishes notes: No
Languages accepted: English; French
Prints abstracts: No

SUBMISSION REQUIREMENTS

Author pays submission fee: No
Author pays page charges: No
Length of books: 200-350 double-spaced typescript pp.
Style: Series; available upon request.
Number of copies required: 2
Copyright ownership: Series
Rejected manuscripts: Returned
Time before publication decision: 3 mos.
Time between decision and publication: 6-12 mos.
Number of reviewers: 2-3
Books submitted per year: 15
Books published per year: 5

(2217)
*Prague Bulletin of Mathematical Linguistics

Eva Hajičová, Editor
Malostranské n.25
11800 Prague 1, Czech Republic

Telephone: (42) 2 532132
Fax: (42) 2 532742
E-mail: HAJICOVA@CSPGUK11.BITNET
First published: 1964
Sponsoring organization: Univ. Karlova
ISSN: 0032-6585
MLA acronym: PBML

SUBSCRIPTION INFORMATION

Frequency of publication: 2 times/yr.
Circulation: 800
Available in microform: No

ADVERTISING INFORMATION

Advertising accepted: Yes
Advertising rates: $100.00/full page

EDITORIAL DESCRIPTION

Scope: Publishes articles on theoretical and computational linguistics.
Reviews books: Yes
Publishes notes: Yes
Languages accepted: English; French; German; Russian
Prints abstracts: No
Author-anonymous submission: No

SUBMISSION REQUIREMENTS

Restrictions on contributors: None
Author pays submission fee: No
Author pays page charges: No
Length of articles: 20-25 pp.
Length of book reviews: 1,000 words
Length of notes: 500 words
Style: None
Number of copies required: 2
Copyright ownership: Univ. Karlova
Rejected manuscripts: Returned
Time before publication decision: 3 mos.
Time between decision and publication: 6 mos.
Number of reviewers: 2
Articles submitted per year: 12-20
Articles published per year: 6-10
Book reviews submitted per year: 16
Book reviews published per year: 10-12
Notes submitted per year: 2-4
Notes published per year: 2-4

(2218)
Prapor: Literaturno-Khudozhniĭ ta Hromads'ko-Politychnyĭ Zhurnal

I. S. Maslov, Editor
Writers' Union of Ukraine
Vulyts'a Ordzhonikidze 2
Kiev, MSP, 252601, Ukraine

Additional editorial address: Vydavnytstvo Prapor, Vulyts'a Vlasa Chubar'a 11, Kharkov 310002, Ukraine; Redaktsiĭa Prapor, Vulyts'a Chernyshevs'koho 59, Kharkov, 310078 Ukraine
First published: 1956
Sponsoring organization: Spilka Pys'mennykiŭ Ukrainy
ISSN: 0130-1608
MLA acronym: Prapor

SUBSCRIPTION INFORMATION

Frequency of publication: 12 times/yr.
Circulation: 15,000
Available in microform: No
Subscription address: Victor Kamkin, Inc., 4956 Boiling Brook Pkwy., Rockville, MD 20852
Additional subscription address: "Soĭuzdruk" agency of the Ukraine, Druzhkivs'ka vulyts'a 10, Kiev, 252189, Ukraine

ADVERTISING INFORMATION

Advertising accepted: No

EDITORIAL DESCRIPTION

Scope: Publishes articles on Ukrainian literature and publicist writings.
Reviews books: Yes
Publishes notes: Yes
Languages accepted: Ukrainian
Prints abstracts: No
Author-anonymous submission: No

SUBMISSION REQUIREMENTS

Restrictions on contributors: None
Author pays page charges: No
Length of articles: 20,000 characters maximum
Length of book reviews: 20,000 characters maximum
Length of notes: 10,000 characters maximum
Style: None
Number of copies required: 2
Special requirements: Submit original typescript.
Copyright ownership: Author
Rejected manuscripts: Returned (if more than 20 pp.)
Time before publication decision: 1-3 mos.
Time between decision and publication: 3-12 mos.
Number of reviewers: 3
Articles submitted per year: 800
Articles published per year: 260
Book reviews submitted per year: 90
Book reviews published per year: 50
Notes submitted per year: 80
Notes published per year: 40

(2219)
Praxis: A Journal of Culture and Criticism

Ronald Reimers, Editor
Dickson Art Center
Univ. of California, Los Angeles
Los Angeles, CA 90024

First published: 1975
ISSN: 0743-880X
MLA acronym: Praxis

SUBSCRIPTION INFORMATION

Frequency of publication: 2 times/yr.

EDITORIAL DESCRIPTION

Reviews books: No
Languages accepted: English
Prints abstracts: No

SUBMISSION REQUIREMENTS

Rejected manuscripts: Returned; enclose SASE.

(2220)
*(Pré)publications

Svend Bach, Maj-Britt Munk Nielsen, Meretha Neubert, Richard Raskin, & Ole Wehner Rasmussen, Editors
Romansk Inst. Sekretariat
Aarhus Univ.
Niels Juelsgade 84
8200 Aarhus N, Denmark

Telephone: (45) 86 136711
Fax: (45) 86 104680
First published: 1973
Sponsoring organization: Romansk Inst.
ISSN: 0900-9507
MLA acronym: Prépub

SUBSCRIPTION INFORMATION

Frequency of publication: 7-8 times/yr.
Circulation: 300
Available in microform: No
Subscription price: 35 Dkr/yr.
Year to which price refers: 1992

ADVERTISING INFORMATION

Advertising accepted: No

EDITORIAL DESCRIPTION

Scope: Publishes literary and linguistic articles by students and professors at the Institut d'Etudes Romanes.
Reviews books: No
Publishes notes: No
Languages accepted: Danish; English; French; Italian; Spanish
Prints abstracts: Yes
Author-anonymous submission: No

SUBMISSION REQUIREMENTS

Restrictions on contributors: Contributors must be members of the Inst. d'Etudes Romanes.
Author pays submission fee: No
Author pays page charges: No
Number of copies required: 1
Special requirements: Submit camera-ready copy and abstract.
Copyright ownership: Author
Rejected manuscripts: Returned
Time before publication decision: 2 mos.
Time between decision and publication: 1 mo.
Number of reviewers: 3
Articles submitted per year: 30
Articles published per year: 24

(2221)
*Présence Africaine: Revue Culturelle du Monde Noir/Cultural Review of the Negro World

C. Mame Yande Diop, Editor
25 bis, rue des Ecoles
75005 Paris, France

Telephone: (33) 1 43541374
Fax: (33) 1 43259667
First published: 1947
ISSN: 0032-7638
MLA acronym: PA

SUBSCRIPTION INFORMATION

Frequency of publication: 4 times/yr.
Circulation: 2,500
Available in microform: No

ADVERTISING INFORMATION

Advertising accepted: No

EDITORIAL DESCRIPTION

Scope: Focuses on general fiction, belles lettres, poetry, history, philosophy, religion, and politics pertaining to Africa.
Reviews books: Yes
Publishes notes: Yes
Languages accepted: English; French
Prints abstracts: No
Author-anonymous submission: Yes

SUBMISSION REQUIREMENTS

Restrictions on contributors: None
Author pays submission fee: No
Author pays page charges: No
Length of articles: 5,000 words
Length of book reviews: 1,000 words maximum
Length of notes: 1,000 words maximum
Style: Journal
Number of copies required: 2
Special requirements: Submit double-spaced typescript with wide margins.
Copyright ownership: Assigned by author to journal
Rejected manuscripts: Not returned
Time before publication decision: 6 mos.
Time between decision and publication: 6 mos.
Number of reviewers: 2-3
Articles submitted per year: 60
Articles published per year: 30
Book reviews submitted per year: 60
Book reviews published per year: 30
Notes submitted per year: 25
Notes published per year: 10

(2222)
*Présence Francophone: Revue Internationale de Langue et de Littérature

Jacques Michon, Editor
Univ. de Sherbrooke
Sherbrooke, Québec J1K 2R1, Canada

Telephone: 819 821-7266
Fax: 819 821-7238
First published: 1970
Sponsoring organization: Univ. de Sherbrooke, Dépt. des Lettres & Communications
ISSN: 0048-5195
MLA acronym: PFr

SUBSCRIPTION INFORMATION

Frequency of publication: 2 times/yr. (Spring, Fall)
Circulation: 500
Available in microform: No
Subscription price: $25.00/yr. institutions; $20.00/yr. individuals; $10.00/single issue
Year to which price refers: 1992

ADVERTISING INFORMATION

Advertising accepted: Yes

EDITORIAL DESCRIPTION

Scope: Focuses on the study of authors and literary works of the Francophone world, and the French language outside France.
Reviews books: Yes
Publishes notes: Yes
Languages accepted: French
Prints abstracts: Yes
Author-anonymous submission: No

SUBMISSION REQUIREMENTS

Restrictions on contributors: None
Author pays submission fee: No
Author pays page charges: No
Length of articles: 5,000 words
Length of book reviews: 1,000 words
Length of notes: 400 words
Style: Guide du rédacteur de l'administration fédérale
Number of copies required: 1
Special requirements: Submit original typescript.
Copyright ownership: Author & journal
Rejected manuscripts: Not returned
Time before publication decision: 3 mos.
Time between decision and publication: 18 mos.
Number of reviewers: 3
Articles submitted per year: 40
Articles published per year: 20
Book reviews submitted per year: 25
Book reviews published per year: 20
Notes submitted per year: 5
Notes published per year: 5

(2223)
Pre/Text: A Journal of Rhetorical Theory

Victor J. Vitanza, Editor
Dept. of English
Box 19035
Univ. of Texas at Arlington
Arlington, TX 76019-0035

Telephone: 817 273-2494; 817 273-2692
First published: 1980
Sponsoring organization: Univ. of Texas, Arlington
ISSN: 0731-0714
MLA acronym: Pre/Text

SUBSCRIPTION INFORMATION

Frequency of publication: 4 times/yr.
Circulation: 500
Available in microform: No

ADVERTISING INFORMATION

Advertising accepted: Yes

EDITORIAL DESCRIPTION

Scope: Publishes exploratory articles and working papers on the interdisciplinary nature of rhetorical theory and rhetorical metatheory.
Reviews books: Yes
Publishes notes: Yes
Languages accepted: English
Prints abstracts: No
Author-anonymous submission: Yes

SUBMISSION REQUIREMENTS

Restrictions on contributors: Review articles are solicited.
Author pays submission fee: No
Author pays page charges: No
Length of articles: 20-30 pp.; longer articles are accepted
Length of book reviews: 20-30 pp.
Length of notes: 4-5 pp.
Style: MLA
Number of copies required: 3
Copyright ownership: Journal

Rejected manuscripts: Returned; enclose SASE.
Time before publication decision: 3-4 mos.
Time between decision and publication: 6-9 mos.
Number of reviewers: 3
Articles submitted per year: 50
Articles published per year: 12-15
Book reviews published per year: 4
Notes published per year: 12-15

(2224)
*Pretexts: Studies in Writing and Culture

John Higgins & David Schalkwyk, Editors
English Dept.
Univ. of Cape Town
Private Bag
Rondebosch
Cape Town 7700, South Africa

First published: 1989
ISSN: 1015-549X
MLA acronym: Pretexts

SUBSCRIPTION INFORMATION

Frequency of publication: 2 times/yr.
Circulation: 140
Available in microform: No
Subscription price: $20.00/yr.
Year to which price refers: 1992

ADVERTISING INFORMATION

Advertising accepted: Yes
Advertising rates: 150 R ($50.00, £30.00)/full page

EDITORIAL DESCRIPTION

Scope: Publishes literary and cultural criticism. Concerned with a broad spectrum of representations in literary and non-literary writing.
Reviews books: Yes
Publishes notes: Yes
Languages accepted: English
Prints abstracts: No
Author-anonymous submission: Yes

SUBMISSION REQUIREMENTS

Author pays submission fee: No
Author pays page charges: No
Length of articles: 5,000-8,000 words
Length of book reviews: 1,500-2,000 words
Length of notes: 500 words
Style: MLA; Harvard
Number of copies required: 1
Copyright ownership: Author
Rejected manuscripts: Returned
Time before publication decision: 2 mos.
Time between decision and publication: 4 mos. maximum
Number of reviewers: 2-3
Articles submitted per year: 24
Articles published per year: 12
Book reviews submitted per year: 4
Book reviews published per year: 2

(2225)
Prilozi Proučavanju Jezika

Aleksandar Mladenović, Editor
Inst. za Južnoslovenske Jezike
Filozofski Fakultet u Novom Sadu
Stevana Musića b.b.
21000 Novi Sad, Yugoslavia

First published: 1965
Sponsoring organization: Inst. za Južnoslovenske Jezike
ISSN: 0555-1137
MLA acronym: PPJ

SUBSCRIPTION INFORMATION

Frequency of publication: Annual
Circulation: 1,000
Available in microform: No
Subscription address: Izdavačko Preduzeće Matice Srpske, TRG Svetozara Markovića 2, 21000 Novi Sad, Yugoslavia

ADVERTISING INFORMATION

Advertising accepted: No

EDITORIAL DESCRIPTION

Scope: Publishes articles on Serbo-Croatian language and linguistics including onomastics, lexicology, dialectology, lexicography, history, and Old Church Slavic.
Reviews books: No
Publishes notes: No
Languages accepted: Serbo-Croatian
Prints abstracts: Yes

SUBMISSION REQUIREMENTS

Restrictions on contributors: Contributors must be affiliated with a university in Yugoslavia.
Author pays submission fee: No
Author pays page charges: No
Length of articles: 20 pp.
Style: None
Number of copies required: 1
Copyright ownership: Inst. za Južnoslovenske Jezike
Rejected manuscripts: Not returned
Time before publication decision: 6 mos.
Time between decision and publication: 1 yr.
Number of reviewers: 2
Articles submitted per year: 10-15
Articles published per year: 10-15

(2226)
*Prilozi za Književnost, Jezik, Istoriju i Folklor

Miroslav Pantić, Editor
Filološki Fakultet
Studentski trg. 3/I
Pošt. fax. 556
Belgrade 11000, Yugoslavia

Telephone: (38) 11 638622/136
Fax: (38) 11 630039
First published: 1921
ISSN: 0350-6673
MLA acronym: Prilozi

SUBSCRIPTION INFORMATION

Frequency of publication: Annual
Available in microform: No
Subscription price: $10.00/yr.
Year to which price refers: 1992
Subscription address: Filološki Fakultet, Fond za Publikacije (za Priloge), Studentski trg. 3/I, Belgrade 11000, Yugoslavia

ADVERTISING INFORMATION

Advertising accepted: No

EDITORIAL DESCRIPTION

Scope: Publishes articles on literature, language, history, and folklore.
Reviews books: Yes
Publishes notes: Yes
Languages accepted: Serbo-Croatian; French; German; Russian; Italian; English
Prints abstracts: No
Author-anonymous submission: No

SUBMISSION REQUIREMENTS

Author pays submission fee: No
Author pays page charges: No
Style: Scientific
Number of copies required: 1
Number of reviewers: 2
Articles submitted per year: 20-30
Articles published per year: 15
Book reviews submitted per year: 20-30
Book reviews published per year: 5-10
Notes submitted per year: 20
Notes published per year: 5-10

(2227)
*Primerjalna Književnost

Darko Dolinar, Editor
Slovensko Društvo za Primerjalno Književnost
Aškerčeva 12
61000 Ljubljana, Slovenia

Additional editorial address: Inst. za Slov. Literaturo in Lit. vede ZRC SAZU, Novi trg 5, 61000 Ljubljana, Slovenia
Telephone: (38) 61 156068
Fax: (38) 61 155253
First published: 1978
Sponsoring organization: Slovensko Društvo za Primerjalno Književnost
ISSN: 0351-1189
MLA acronym: PKn

SUBSCRIPTION INFORMATION

Frequency of publication: 2 times/yr.
Circulation: 350-400
Available in microform: No

ADVERTISING INFORMATION

Advertising accepted: Yes

EDITORIAL DESCRIPTION

Scope: Publishes articles on comparative literature, with an emphasis on Slovene literature, as well as theoretical, historical, and methodological aspects of literary criticism.
Reviews books: Yes
Publishes notes: Yes
Languages accepted: Slovenian; Serbo-Croatian; English; German
Prints abstracts: Yes
Author-anonymous submission: No

SUBMISSION REQUIREMENTS

Restrictions on contributors: None
Author pays submission fee: No
Author pays page charges: No
Length of articles: 5,000-7,000 words
Length of book reviews: 1,500-2,500 words
Length of notes: 500-1,000 words
Style: Poetics, Poetics Today (see PoT 2, iii for particulars)
Number of copies required: 2
Special requirements: Submit a 150-200 word abstract.
Copyright ownership: Author
Rejected manuscripts: Returned
Time before publication decision: 3-6 mos.
Time between decision and publication: 2-3 mos.
Number of reviewers: 3-4
Articles submitted per year: 8-12
Articles published per year: 7-10
Book reviews submitted per year: 15
Book reviews published per year: 12
Notes submitted per year: 5-7
Notes published per year: 3-5

(2228)
*Princeton University Library Chronicle

Patricia H. Marks, Editor
Princeton Univ. Library
One Washington Rd.
Princeton, NJ 08544

Telephone: 609 258-3155
First published: 1939
Sponsoring organization: Friends of the Princeton Univ. Library
ISSN: 0032-8456
MLA acronym: PULC

SUBSCRIPTION INFORMATION

Frequency of publication: 3 times/yr. (Fall, Winter, Spring)
Circulation: 1,800
Available in microform: Yes
Subscription price: $25.00/yr. institutions; $50.00/yr. individuals (includes membership)
Year to which price refers: 1991-92

ADVERTISING INFORMATION

Advertising accepted: No

EDITORIAL DESCRIPTION

Scope: Publishes articles based on research conducted in the Library's Department of Rare Books and Special Collections and other Princeton Collections. Articles in the humanities, social and natural sciences, and about books and book collecting are welcome, as are bibliographic essays. We seek articles of scholarly importance and general interest written for the educated nonspecialist.
Reviews books: No
Publishes notes: Yes
Languages accepted: English
Prints abstracts: No
Author-anonymous submission: No

SUBMISSION REQUIREMENTS

Restrictions on contributors: None
Author pays submission fee: No
Author pays page charges: No
Length of articles: 20-25 typescript pp.
Length of notes: 5 typescript pp.
Style: Chicago
Number of copies required: 2
Special requirements: Submit 2 paper copies or 1 copy with diskette using WordPerfect.
Copyright ownership: Princeton Univ. Library
Rejected manuscripts: Returned; enclose return postage.
Time before publication decision: 3-4 mos.
Time between decision and publication: 6-12 mos.
Number of reviewers: 9
Articles submitted per year: 25
Articles published per year: 12-15
Notes submitted per year: 10
Notes published per year: 5

(2229)
*Printing History

David Pankow, Editor
Melbert B. Cary, Jr. Collection
Rochester Inst. of Technology
One Lomb Memorial Dr.
Rochester, NY 14623

Telephone: 716 475-2408
Fax: 716 475-6900
First published: 1979
Sponsoring organization: American Printing History Assn.
ISSN: 0192-9205
MLA acronym: PHist

SUBSCRIPTION INFORMATION

Frequency of publication: 2 times/yr. (June, Dec.)
Circulation: 1,200
Available in microform: No
Subscription price: $35.00/yr. institutions; $30.00/yr. individuals
Year to which price refers: 1992
Subscription address: American Printing History Assn., P.O. Box 4922, Grand Central Station, New York, NY 10163-4922

ADVERTISING INFORMATION

Advertising accepted: Yes

EDITORIAL DESCRIPTION

Scope: A scholarly journal concerned with cultural and historical aspects of printing history, typography, and book arts.
Reviews books: Yes
Publishes notes: Yes
Languages accepted: English
Prints abstracts: No
Author-anonymous submission: Yes

SUBMISSION REQUIREMENTS

Author pays submission fee: No
Author pays page charges: No
Length of articles: 2,500-3,750 words
Length of book reviews: 1,000-1,500 words
Length of notes: 100 words
Style: Chicago
Number of copies required: 2
Special requirements: Submit double-spaced manuscript.
Copyright ownership: Journal
Rejected manuscripts: Returned
Time before publication decision: 4-6 weeks
Number of reviewers: 2
Articles submitted per year: 15-20
Articles published per year: 6-10
Book reviews submitted per year: 15-20
Book reviews published per year: 12-15

(2230)
Prismal/Cabral: Revista de Literatura Hispánica/Caderno Afro-Brasileiro Asiático Lusitano

Aleida Rodriguez, Editor
Dept. of Spanish & Portuguese
Univ. of Maryland
College Park, MD 20742

First published: 1977
Sponsoring organization: Univ. of Maryland, Dept. of Spanish
ISSN: 0738-8667
MLA acronym: Prismal/Cabral

SUBSCRIPTION INFORMATION

Frequency of publication: 2 times/yr.
Circulation: 225
Available in microform: No

ADVERTISING INFORMATION

Advertising accepted: Yes

EDITORIAL DESCRIPTION

Scope: Publishes critical essays on Spanish-American and Luso-Brazilian literature, as well as poetry, fiction, interviews, and drama.
Reviews books: Yes
Languages accepted: English; Portuguese; Spanish
Prints abstracts: No

SUBMISSION REQUIREMENTS

Restrictions on contributors: None
Author pays submission fee: No
Author pays page charges: No
Length of articles: 10-15 pp.
Length of book reviews: 2-4 pp.
Style: MLA
Number of copies required: 1
Copyright ownership: Journal
Rejected manuscripts: Returned at author's request
Time before publication decision: 6 mos.
Time between decision and publication: 6-12 mos.
Number of reviewers: 6
Articles submitted per year: 40
Articles published per year: 25-30
Book reviews submitted per year: 10
Book reviews published per year: 4

(2231)
*Pro Lingua

Otto Winkelmann, Editor
Gottfried Egert Verlag
Rainweg 4
6916 Wilhelmsfeld, Germany

Telephone: (49) 6220 1792
Fax: (49) 6220 6701
First published: 1988
MLA acronym: ProL

SUBSCRIPTION INFORMATION

Available in microform: No

ADVERTISING INFORMATION

Advertising accepted: No

EDITORIAL DESCRIPTION

Scope: Publishes monographs on linguistics.
Reviews books: No
Publishes notes: No
Languages accepted: German; English; all romance languages
Prints abstracts: No
Author-anonymous submission: No

SUBMISSION REQUIREMENTS

Author pays submission fee: No
Author pays page charges: No
Number of copies required: 2
Copyright ownership: Gottfried Egert Verlag
Rejected manuscripts: Returned
Time before publication decision: 6 mos.
Number of reviewers: 2
Books submitted per year: 15
Books published per year: 4

(2232)
*Problemata Semiotica

Kurt Reichenberger & Roswitha Reichenberger, Editors
Edition Reichenberger
Pfannkuchstr. 4
3500 Kassel, Germany

Telephone: (49) 561 775204
First published: 1984
MLA acronym: PSem

SUBSCRIPTION INFORMATION

Frequency of publication: Irregular
Available in microform: No

ADVERTISING INFORMATION

Advertising accepted: No

EDITORIAL DESCRIPTION

Scope: Series publishes monographs on subjects in the humanities, arts, and social sciences within the context of semiotics.
Reviews books: No
Publishes notes: No
Languages accepted: English; Spanish; German; French; Italian
Prints abstracts: No
Author-anonymous submission: No

SUBMISSION REQUIREMENTS

Restrictions on contributors: None
Author pays submission fee: No
Author pays page charges: No
Length of books: 100-200 pp. (350 words/page)
Style: Series
Number of copies required: 1
Special requirements: Submission of typescript and Macintosh-compatible diskette using Microsoft Word is preferred. Authors should attempt to secure subsidy from their universities for printing costs.
Copyright ownership: Edition Reichenberger
Rejected manuscripts: Returned
Time before publication decision: 2 mos.
Time between decision and publication: 8-12 mos.
Number of reviewers: 2-3
Books submitted per year: 2
Books published per year: 1

(2233)
Probleme de Lingvistică Generală

Al. Graur, L. Wald, & I. Coteanu, Editors
c/o Editura Academiei Române
Calea Victoriei 125
79717 Bucharest, Romania

First published: 1959
Sponsoring organization: Academia Română
ISSN: 0552-1645
MLA acronym: PLG

SUBSCRIPTION INFORMATION

Frequency of publication: Irregular

EDITORIAL DESCRIPTION

Scope: Focuses on general linguistics.
Reviews books: No
Languages accepted: Romanian; French; English
Prints abstracts: Yes

SUBMISSION REQUIREMENTS

Restrictions on contributors: None
Length of books: 20 double-spaced typescript pp. maximum
Style: Journal
Number of copies required: 2
Special requirements: Submit original typescript and 1 copy; include an abstract (100 words maximum).
Copyright ownership: Assigned by author to journal
Rejected manuscripts: Not returned
Number of reviewers: 3
Books published per year: 11

(2234)
Probleme der Dichtung

Hans Joachim Mähl
Inst. für Literaturwissenschaft
Univ. Kiel, Olshausenstr. 40-60
Fakultätenblock II, Haus 50c
2300 Kiel 1, Germany

First published: 1951
ISSN: 0555-2257

MLA acronym: PdD

SUBSCRIPTION INFORMATION

Frequency of publication: Irregular
Circulation: 800-1,500
Available in microform: No
Subscription address: Carl Winter Universitätsverlag GmbH, Lutherstr. 59, Postfach 106140, 6900 Heidelberg, Germany

ADVERTISING INFORMATION

Advertising accepted: No

EDITORIAL DESCRIPTION

Scope: Publishes monographs on German literature.
Reviews books: No
Languages accepted: German
Prints abstracts: No

SUBMISSION REQUIREMENTS

Restrictions on contributors: None
Length of books: No restrictions
Style: MLA
Number of copies required: 2
Copyright ownership: Carl Winter Universitätsverlag GmbH
Rejected manuscripts: Returned
Time before publication decision: 6 mos.
Time between decision and publication: 1 yr.
Number of reviewers: 3

(2235)
*Problemi: Periodico Quadrimestrale di Cultura

Giuseppe Petronio, Editor
Via Tripoli, 2
00199 Rome, Italy

Telephone: (39) 91 588850
Fax: (39) 91 6111848
First published: 1967
ISSN: 0032-9339
MLA acronym: Problemi

SUBSCRIPTION INFORMATION

Frequency of publication: 3 times/yr.
Circulation: 1,500
Available in microform: No
Subscription price: 84,000 Lit/yr.
Year to which price refers: 1992
Subscription address: G. B. Palumbo Editore, Via Ricasoli, 59, 90139 Palermo, Italy

ADVERTISING INFORMATION

Advertising accepted: Yes
Advertising rates: 1,000,000 Lit/full page

EDITORIAL DESCRIPTION

Scope: Publishes articles on modern languages and literatures.
Reviews books: No
Publishes notes: No
Languages accepted: Italian
Prints abstracts: No
Author-anonymous submission: No

SUBMISSION REQUIREMENTS

Restrictions on contributors: None
Author pays submission fee: No
Author pays page charges: No
Length of articles: 8,000 words
Number of copies required: 1
Copyright ownership: G. B. Palumbo Editore
Rejected manuscripts: Returned
Time before publication decision: 6 mos.
Time between decision and publication: 8 mos.
Articles submitted per year: 30
Articles published per year: 18

(2236)
Problemi di Ulisse

Maria Luisa Astaldi, Editor
Via Po, 11
00198 Rome, Italy

First published: 1947
ISSN: 0048-5411
MLA acronym: PU

SUBSCRIPTION INFORMATION

Frequency of publication: 4 times/yr.
Available in microform: No
Subscription address: Licosa SpA, Via Duca Di Calabria 1/1, 50125 Florence, Italy

ADVERTISING INFORMATION

Advertising accepted: No

EDITORIAL DESCRIPTION

Scope: Publishes articles on culture and literature.
Reviews books: No
Languages accepted: Italian
Prints abstracts: No

SUBMISSION REQUIREMENTS

Length of articles: 8 pp.
Time before publication decision: 4 mos.
Number of reviewers: 3
Articles published per year: 30

(2237)
*Probus: International Journal of Latin and Romance Linguistics

W. Leo Wetzels, Editor
Dept. of French
Univ. of Nijmegen
6525 GG Nijmegen, Netherlands

Additional editorial address: In the Americas and Canada: Rafael A. Núñez Cedeño, Dept. of Spanish, Italian & Portuguese, Univ. of Illinois, Chicago, IL 60680; Eduardo Raposo, Dept. of Spanish & Portuguese, Univ. of California, Santa Barbara, CA 93106
Telephone: (31) 80 612203
E-mail: U262003@HNYKUN11.bitnet
First published: 1989
ISSN: 0921-4771
MLA acronym: Probus

SUBSCRIPTION INFORMATION

Frequency of publication: 3 times/yr.
Circulation: 120
Available in microform: No
Subscription price: $100.00/yr. institutions; $44.00/yr. individuals
Year to which price refers: 1991
Subscription address: Walter de Gruyter & Co., Postfach 110240, 1000 Berlin 11, Germany
Additional subscription address: In N. America: Walter de Gruyter Inc., 200 Saw Mill River Rd., Hawthorne, NY 10532

ADVERTISING INFORMATION

Advertising accepted: Yes

EDITORIAL DESCRIPTION

Scope: Publishes articles on historical and synchronic research in the field of Latin and Romance linguistics. Special emphasis is on phonology, morphology, syntax, semantics, lexicon, and sociolinguistics. Encourages problem-oriented contributions that combine solid empirical foundations of philological and linguistic work with insights provided by modern theoretical approaches.
Reviews books: Yes

Publishes notes: Yes
Languages accepted: Primarily English; French; Italian; Spanish; Portuguese
Prints abstracts: No
Author-anonymous submission: Yes

SUBMISSION REQUIREMENTS

Author pays submission fee: No
Author pays page charges: No
Length of articles: No restrictions
Length of book reviews: No restrictions
Length of notes: No restrictions
Style: MLA
Number of copies required: 4
Special requirements: Submit 4 copies of double-spaced typescript and 1 diskette, preferably written in WordPerfect on an MS-DOS or compatible system. See inside back cover for complete details.
Copyright ownership: Walter de Gruyter & Co.
Rejected manuscripts: Not returned
Time before publication decision: 3-4 mos.
Time between decision and publication: 6-9 mos.
Number of reviewers: 2-3
Articles submitted per year: 30-40
Articles published per year: 15-20
Book reviews submitted per year: 10
Book reviews published per year: 3-5
Notes submitted per year: 5
Notes published per year: 1-3

(2238)
*Proceedings & Transactions Royal Society of Canada

Royal Soc. of Canada
P.O. Box 9734
Ottawa, Ontario K1G 5J4, Canada

Telephone: 613 991-6990
Fax: 613 991-6996
First published: 1882
ISSN: 0316-4616
MLA acronym: PTRSC

SUBSCRIPTION INFORMATION

Frequency of publication: Annual
Circulation: 1,200
Available in microform: Yes, through University Microfiche

ADVERTISING INFORMATION

Advertising accepted: No

EDITORIAL DESCRIPTION

Scope: Publishes selected papers given at the annual meeting of the Royal Society of Canada. Papers are of an interdisciplinary nature in the areas of the humanities and sciences.
Reviews books: No
Languages accepted: English; French
Prints abstracts: No

SUBMISSION REQUIREMENTS

Restrictions on contributors: Contributors must have presented the paper at the annual meeting.
Author pays submission fee: No
Author pays page charges: No
Length of articles: No restrictions
Copyright ownership: Royal Soc. of Canada
Rejected manuscripts: Returned
Time before publication decision: 8 mos.
Articles published per year: 30

(2239)
*Proceedings of the American Antiquarian Society: A Journal of American History and Culture Through 1876

John B. Hench, Editor
American Antiquarian Soc.
185 Salisbury St.
Worcester, MA 01609-1634

Telephone: 508 752-5813
First published: 1813
Sponsoring organization: American Antiquarian Soc.
ISSN: 0044-751X
MLA acronym: PAAS

SUBSCRIPTION INFORMATION

Frequency of publication: 2 times/yr. (Oct., Apr.)
Circulation: 900
Available in microform: Yes
Subscription price: $45.00/yr. US; $53.00/yr. elsewhere
Year to which price refers: 1992

ADVERTISING INFORMATION

Advertising accepted: No

EDITORIAL DESCRIPTION

Scope: Emphasizes publication of bibliographies, primary sources, and other basic tools for scholarship as well as other monographic literature within the general field of American history and culture through 1876.
Reviews books: No
Publishes notes: Yes
Languages accepted: English
Prints abstracts: No
Author-anonymous submission: No

SUBMISSION REQUIREMENTS

Restrictions on contributors: None
Author pays submission fee: No
Author pays page charges: No
Length of articles: No restrictions
Length of notes: No restrictions
Style: Chicago
Number of copies required: 2
Special requirements: Submit original typescript.
Copyright ownership: Assigned by author to journal
Rejected manuscripts: Returned
Time before publication decision: 1-5 mos.
Time between decision and publication: 6-12 mos.
Number of reviewers: 2-4
Articles submitted per year: 25
Articles published per year: 8
Notes submitted per year: 3-4
Notes published per year: 3-4

(2240)
*Proceedings of the American Philosophical Society Held at Philadelphia for Promoting Useful Knowledge

Herman H. Goldstine & Carole N. LeFaivre, Editors
American Philosophical Soc.
104 S. Fifth St.
Philadelphia, PA 19106

Telephone: 215 440-3427
Fax: 215 440-3450
First published: 1838
ISSN: 0003-049X
MLA acronym: PAPS

SUBSCRIPTION INFORMATION

Frequency of publication: 4 times/yr.
Circulation: 1,200
Available in microform: Yes
Subscription address: American Philosophical Soc., P.O. Box 40098, Philadelphia, PA 19106

ADVERTISING INFORMATION

Advertising accepted: No

EDITORIAL DESCRIPTION

Scope: Contains papers which have been read before the American Philosophical Society in addition to other papers which have been accepted for publication.
Reviews books: No
Languages accepted: English
Prints abstracts: No

SUBMISSION REQUIREMENTS

Restrictions on contributors: Publishes papers read at American Philosophical Soc. meetings or resulting from primary research.
Author pays submission fee: No
Author pays page charges: No
Length of articles: 10,000 words
Style: Chicago
Number of copies required: 2
Copyright ownership: American Philosophical Soc.
Rejected manuscripts: Returned
Time before publication decision: 6-12 mos.
Time between decision and publication: 1 yr.
Number of reviewers: 1
Articles submitted per year: 75
Articles published per year: 40

(2241)
*Proceedings of the Annual Meeting of the Western Society for French History

Norman Ravitch, Editor
Dept. of History
Univ. of California
Riverside, CA 92521-0204

Telephone: 714 787-5401
Fax: 714 787-5299
First published: 1974
Sponsoring organization: Western Soc. for French History
ISSN: 0099-0329
MLA acronym: PAMWS

SUBSCRIPTION INFORMATION

Frequency of publication: Annual
Circulation: 200
Available in microform: Yes, after original run of volumes is exhausted.
Subscription address: Western Soc. for French History, at the above address

ADVERTISING INFORMATION

Advertising accepted: Yes

EDITORIAL DESCRIPTION

Scope: Publishes papers presented at the annual meeting of the Western Society for French History.
Reviews books: No
Publishes notes: No
Languages accepted: English; French
Prints abstracts: No
Author-anonymous submission: Yes

SUBMISSION REQUIREMENTS

Restrictions on contributors: Contributors must have presented paper or commentary at annual meeting.

Author pays submission fee: No
Author pays page charges: No
Length of articles: 4,500 words including notes
Style: Chicago
Number of copies required: 1
Special requirements: Submit abstract and copyright permission form.
Copyright ownership: Journal
Rejected manuscripts: Not returned
Time before publication decision: 4-5 mos.
Time between decision and publication: 5 mos.
Number of reviewers: 2-3
Articles submitted per year: 60-70
Articles published per year: 30-40

(2242)
*Proceedings of the British Academy

J. M. H. Rivington, Publications Officer
British Academy
20-21 Cornwall Terrace
London NW1 4QP, England

Telephone: (44) 71 4875966
Fax: (44) 71 2243807
First published: 1902
Sponsoring organization: British Academy
ISSN: 0068-1202
MLA acronym: PBA

SUBSCRIPTION INFORMATION

Frequency of publication: Irregular (approx. 3 times/yr.)
Available in microform: No
Subscription address: Oxford Univ. Press, 200 Madison Ave., New York, NY 10016

ADVERTISING INFORMATION

Advertising accepted: No

EDITORIAL DESCRIPTION

Scope: Publishes texts of lectures and symposia on all aspects of the humanities and social sciences.
Reviews books: No
Publishes notes: No
Languages accepted: English
Prints abstracts: No
Author-anonymous submission: No

SUBMISSION REQUIREMENTS

Restrictions on contributors: Contributions are solicited.
Author pays submission fee: No
Author pays page charges: No
Copyright ownership: British Academy
Articles published per year: 30

(2243)
*Proceedings of the Leeds Philosophical and Literary Society, Literary & Historical Section

Ian Moxon, Editor
School of History
Univ. of Leeds
Leeds LS2 9JT
West Yorkshire, England

Telephone: (44) 532 333544
Fax: (44) 532 342759
First published: 1925
Sponsoring organization: Leeds Philosophical & Literary Soc.
ISSN: 0024-0281
MLA acronym: PLPLS-LHS

SUBSCRIPTION INFORMATION

Frequency of publication: Irregular
Circulation: 500
Available in microform: No
Subscription address: Leeds Philosophical & Literary Soc., City Museum, Calverley St., Leeds LS1 3AA, England

ADVERTISING INFORMATION

Advertising accepted: No

EDITORIAL DESCRIPTION

Scope: Publishes monographs on the humanities.
Reviews books: No
Publishes notes: No
Languages accepted: English; German; French; Italian
Prints abstracts: No
Author-anonymous submission: No

SUBMISSION REQUIREMENTS

Restrictions on contributors: None
Author pays submission fee: No
Author pays page charges: No
Length of articles: 5,000-50,000 words
Style: None
Number of copies required: 1
Copyright ownership: Assigned by author to publisher
Rejected manuscripts: Returned
Time before publication decision: 3 mos.
Time between decision and publication: 6-24 mos.
Number of reviewers: 2
Articles submitted per year: 6-10
Articles published per year: 2-3

(2244)
*Proceedings of the Massachusetts Historical Society

Conrad E. Wright, Editor
Massachusetts Historical Soc.
1154 Boylston St.
Boston, MA 02215

Telephone: 617 536-1608
First published: 1859
Sponsoring organization: Massachusetts Historical Soc.
ISSN: 0076-4981
MLA acronym: PMHS

SUBSCRIPTION INFORMATION

Frequency of publication: Annual
Circulation: 750
Available in microform: Yes, volume 1-70, through Univ. Microfilms International
Subscription price: $30.00/yr.
Year to which price refers: 1992
Subscription address: Northeastern Univ. Press, Box 6525, Ithaca, NY 14851
Subscription telephone: 617 437-5480

ADVERTISING INFORMATION

Advertising accepted: No

EDITORIAL DESCRIPTION

Scope: Publishes monographic and documentary articles relating to American history, particularly the history of Massachusetts and New England.
Reviews books: No
Publishes notes: Yes
Languages accepted: English
Prints abstracts: No
Author-anonymous submission: Yes

SUBMISSION REQUIREMENTS

Restrictions on contributors: None
Author pays submission fee: No
Author pays page charges: No
Length of articles: No restrictions
Length of notes: 1,000-12,500 words
Style: Chicago
Number of copies required: 2
Special requirements: Submit original typescript.
Copyright ownership: Massachusetts Historical Soc.
Rejected manuscripts: Returned
Time before publication decision: 3 mos.
Time between decision and publication: 15-18 mos.
Number of reviewers: 2-3
Articles submitted per year: 10-15
Articles published per year: 4-6
Notes submitted per year: 3-5
Notes published per year: 0-3

(2245)
Proceedings of the PMR Conference: Annual Publication of the International Patristic, Mediaeval and Renaissance Conference

Phillip Pulsiano, Editor
Augustinian Historical Inst.
Augustinian Rm., Old Falvey
Villanova Univ.
Villanova, PA 19085

First published: 1976
Sponsoring organization: Villanova Univ., Augustinian Historical Inst.
ISSN: 0272-8710
MLA acronym: PPMRC

SUBSCRIPTION INFORMATION

Frequency of publication: Annual
Circulation: 300
Available in microform: No

ADVERTISING INFORMATION

Advertising accepted: No

EDITORIAL DESCRIPTION

Scope: Publishes articles on Patristic, Medieval, and Renaissance culture.
Reviews books: No
Publishes notes: No
Languages accepted: English
Prints abstracts: No
Author-anonymous submission: No

SUBMISSION REQUIREMENTS

Restrictions on contributors: Contributors must have read paper at conference.
Author pays submission fee: No
Author pays page charges: No
Length of articles: 6,000-8,000 words
Style: Journal
Number of copies required: 2
Special requirements: Submit double-spaced typescript with footnotes on a separate page; include an abstract. Style sheet available from Augustinian Historical Inst.
Copyright ownership: Journal
Rejected manuscripts: Returned; enclose return postage.
Time before publication decision: 6 mos.
Time between decision and publication: 1 yr.
Number of reviewers: 2
Articles submitted per year: 60
Articles published per year: 14

(2246)
*Profession

Phyllis Franklin & Carol Zuses, Editors
Modern Language Assn.
10 Astor Place
New York, NY 10003

Telephone: 212 614-6302
Fax: 212 477-9863

E-mail: MLAOD@CUVMB.BITNET
First published: 1977
Sponsoring organization: Modern Language Assn. of America
MLA acronym: Profession

SUBSCRIPTION INFORMATION

Frequency of publication: Annual
Circulation: 32,000
Available in microform: No
Subscription price: $7.50/single issue
Year to which price refers: 1991

ADVERTISING INFORMATION

Advertising accepted: No

EDITORIAL DESCRIPTION

Scope: Publishes articles on current intellectual, curricular, and professional trends and issues affecting the study and teaching of the modern languages and their literatures.
Reviews books: No
Publishes notes: Yes
Languages accepted: English
Prints abstracts: No
Author-anonymous submission: No

SUBMISSION REQUIREMENTS

Author pays submission fee: No
Author pays page charges: No
Length of articles: 1,800-5,000 words
Length of notes: 800 words
Style: MLA
Number of copies required: 1
Copyright ownership: Modern Language Assn. of America
Rejected manuscripts: Returned
Time before publication decision: 3-4 mos.
Time between decision and publication: 5 mos.
Number of reviewers: 3
Articles submitted per year: 24-36
Articles published per year: 10-12
Notes submitted per year: 3-5
Notes published per year: 2-3

(2247)
Proměny

Zdenka Brodská, Managing Editor
33731 Kirby Ave.
Farmington Hills, MI 48335

Additional editorial address: Karel Hruby, Editor, Thiersteinerrain 90, 4059 Basel, Switzerland
First published: 1964
Sponsoring organization: Czechoslovak Soc. of Arts & Sciences in America, Inc.
ISSN: 0033-1058
MLA acronym: Proměny

SUBSCRIPTION INFORMATION

Frequency of publication: 4 times/yr. (Jan., Apr., July, Oct.)
Circulation: 1,000
Subscription address: R. Bunža, 190-17A 69th Ave., Flushing, NY 11365

EDITORIAL DESCRIPTION

Scope: Publishes articles on new events in arts and sciences.
Reviews books: Yes
Languages accepted: Czech; French; Slovak; English
Prints abstracts: No

SUBMISSION REQUIREMENTS

Restrictions on contributors: None
Length of articles: 2,500-5,000 words
Number of copies required: 2
Special requirements: Submit original typescript.

Copyright ownership: Assigned by author to journal
Rejected manuscripts: Returned
Time before publication decision: 3 mos.
Time between decision and publication: 6 mos.
Number of reviewers: 2
Articles published per year: 80

(2248)
Prooftexts: A Journal of Jewish Literary History

Alan Mintz & David G. Roskies, Editors
838 West End Ave., 6-C
New York, NY 10025

Additional editorial address: D. G. Roskies, Jewish Theological Seminary, 3080 Broadway, New York, NY 10027
First published: 1981
ISSN: 0272-9601
MLA acronym: Prooftexts

SUBSCRIPTION INFORMATION

Frequency of publication: 3 times/yr. (Jan., May, Sept.)
Circulation: 900
Subscription price: $47.00/yr. institutions US; $20.00/yr. individuals US; add $4.40/yr. postage Canada & Mexico, $5.00/yr. elsewhere
Year to which price refers: 1993
Subscription address: Johns Hopkins Univ. Press, Journals Publishing Division, 2715 North Charles St., Baltimore, MD 21218-4319

ADVERTISING INFORMATION

Advertising accepted: Yes

EDITORIAL DESCRIPTION

Scope: Encompasses literary approaches to classical Jewish sources, the study of modern Hebrew and Jewish literature, American and European literature, and Jewish writing in other languages. Concerned with the significance of both literary traditions and contemporary issues of textuality.
Reviews books: Yes
Publishes notes: Yes
Languages accepted: English; Hebrew
Prints abstracts: No
Author-anonymous submission: Yes

SUBMISSION REQUIREMENTS

Restrictions on contributors: Book reviews are generally solicited.
Author pays submission fee: No
Author pays page charges: No
Length of articles: No restrictions
Length of book reviews: No restrictions
Length of notes: No restrictions
Style: Chicago
Number of copies required: 4
Special requirements: Hebrew should be transliterated and conform to journal's transliteration.
Copyright ownership: Johns Hopkins Univ. Press
Rejected manuscripts: Not returned
Time before publication decision: 1 yr.
Time between decision and publication: 3-6 mos.
Number of reviewers: 4
Articles submitted per year: 40-50
Articles published per year: 15-20
Book reviews submitted per year: 20
Book reviews published per year: 10
Notes submitted per year: 13-20
Notes published per year: 4-6

(2249)
*Prose Studies: History, Theory, Criticism

Ronald J. Corthell, Editor
Dept. of English
Kent State Univ.
Kent, OH 44242

Additional editorial address: Thomas N. Corns, British Editor, Univ. College of North Wales, Bangor LL57 2DG, England; Jonathon Loesberg, Reviews Editor, Dept. of Literature, American Univ., Washington, DC 20016-8047
Telephone: 216 672-3211
Fax: 216 672-3152
First published: 1977
ISSN: 0144-0357
MLA acronym: PSt

SUBSCRIPTION INFORMATION

Frequency of publication: 3 times/yr. (May, Sept., Dec.)
Available in microform: No
Subscription price: $80.00 (£52.00)/yr. institutions; $35.00 (£24.00)/yr. individuals
Year to which price refers: 1992
Subscription address: Frank Cass & Co. Ltd., Gainsborough House, 11 Gainsborough Rd., London E11 1RS, England
Subscription telephone: (44) 81 5304226
Subscription fax: (44) 81 5307795

ADVERTISING INFORMATION

Advertising accepted: Yes

EDITORIAL DESCRIPTION

Scope: Publishes articles on nonfictional prose of all periods.
Reviews books: Yes
Publishes notes: Yes
Languages accepted: English
Prints abstracts: No
Author-anonymous submission: No

SUBMISSION REQUIREMENTS

Restrictions on contributors: None
Author pays submission fee: No
Author pays page charges: No
Length of articles: 3,000-15,000 words
Length of book reviews: 1,000-1,500 words
Length of notes: 1,500-3,000 words
Style: Chicago
Number of copies required: 2
Copyright ownership: Frank Cass & Co., Ltd.
Rejected manuscripts: Returned; enclose return postage.
Time before publication decision: 2 mos.
Time between decision and publication: 1 yr.
Number of reviewers: 2
Articles submitted per year: 200
Articles published per year: 18
Book reviews published per year: 30

(2250)
Prospects: An Annual Journal of American Cultural Studies

Jack Salzman, Editor
Center for American Studies
Columbia Univ.
603 Lewisohn Hall
New York, NY 10027

First published: 1975
ISSN: 0361-2333
MLA acronym: Prospects

SUBSCRIPTION INFORMATION

Frequency of publication: Annual
Circulation: 2,500
Available in microform: No

Subscription price: $73.00/yr. institutions; $41.00/yr. individuals
Year to which price refers: 1993
Subscription address: Periodicals Division, Cambridge Univ. Press, 40 W. 20th St., New York, NY 10011-4211
Additional subscription address: Outside the US & Canada: Cambridge Univ. Press, Edinburgh Bldg., Shaftesbury Rd., Cambridge CB2 2RU, England

ADVERTISING INFORMATION

Advertising accepted: No

EDITORIAL DESCRIPTION

Scope: A multidisciplinary journal that is neither partisan nor restrictive; presents works of criticism and scholarship that elucidate the essential nature of the American character, and that explore all aspects of American civilization. Is eclectic in its approach: its format is free, open, flexible, and articles vary considerably in length and subject matter.
Reviews books: Yes
Publishes notes: No
Languages accepted: English
Prints abstracts: No

SUBMISSION REQUIREMENTS

Restrictions on contributors: None
Author pays submission fee: No
Author pays page charges: No
Length of articles: No restrictions
Style: MLA
Number of copies required: 2
Copyright ownership: Cambridge Univ. Press
Rejected manuscripts: Returned
Time before publication decision: 2 mos.
Time between decision and publication: 9 mos.
Number of reviewers: 1
Articles published per year: 25

(2251)
*Proteus: A Journal of Ideas

Angelo Costanzo, Editor
Office of Publications & Public Information
302 Old Main
Shippensburg Univ.
Shippensburg, PA 17257

Telephone: 717 532-1206
Fax: 717 532-1253
First published: 1983
Sponsoring organization: Shippensburg Univ.
ISSN: 0889-6348
MLA acronym: Proteus

SUBSCRIPTION INFORMATION

Frequency of publication: 2 times/yr. (Mar., Oct.)
Available in microform: Yes
Subscription price: $10.00/yr.
Year to which price refers: 1992

ADVERTISING INFORMATION

Advertising accepted: Yes, on an exchange basis

EDITORIAL DESCRIPTION

Scope: Provides an interdisciplinary approach to ideas and literature, with each issue devoted to a single theme.
Reviews books: No
Publishes notes: No
Languages accepted: English
Prints abstracts: No
Author-anonymous submission: Yes

SUBMISSION REQUIREMENTS

Restrictions on contributors: None
Author pays submission fee: No

Author pays page charges: No
Length of articles: 3,000-5,000 words
Style: MLA; American Psychological Assn.; Chicago
Number of copies required: 4
Copyright ownership: Journal & Shippensburg Univ.
Rejected manuscripts: Returned; enclose SASE.
Time before publication decision: 4-5 mos.
Time between decision and publication: 2 mos.
Number of reviewers: 5
Articles submitted per year: 50-60
Articles published per year: 15-30

(2252)
Proust Research Association Newsletter

J. Theodore Johnson, Jr., Editor
Dept. of French & Italian
Univ. of Kansas
2056 Wescoe Hall
Lawrence, KS 66045-2120

First published: 1969
Sponsoring organization: Proust Assn.
ISSN: 0048-5659
MLA acronym: PRAN

SUBSCRIPTION INFORMATION

Frequency of publication: Irregular
Circulation: 350
Available in microform: No

ADVERTISING INFORMATION

Advertising accepted: No

EDITORIAL DESCRIPTION

Scope: Publishes brief articles and notes of a heuristic nature dealing with Proust manuscripts, doctoral dissertations, lectures, and works in progress.
Reviews books: Yes
Publishes notes: Yes
Languages accepted: English; French
Prints abstracts: No
Author-anonymous submission: No

SUBMISSION REQUIREMENTS

Restrictions on contributors: Contributors must be Proust scholars.
Author pays submission fee: No
Author pays page charges: No
Length of articles: 6-7 pp. maximum
Length of book reviews: 3 pp.
Length of notes: 6-7 pp.
Style: MLA
Number of copies required: 1
Copyright ownership: Author
Rejected manuscripts: Returned
Time before publication decision: 6 weeks
Time between decision and publication: 1 yr. maximum
Number of reviewers: 1-2
Articles submitted per year: 1-2
Articles published per year: 1-2
Book reviews submitted per year: 1-2
Book reviews published per year: 1-2
Notes submitted per year: 5-7
Notes published per year: 5-7

(2253)
*Proverbium: Yearbook of International Proverb Scholarship

Wolfgang Mieder, Editor
Dept. of Russian & German
Waterman Bldg.
Univ. of Vermont
Burlington, VT 05405

First published: 1984

Sponsoring organization: Univ. of Vermont
ISSN: 0743-782X
MLA acronym: ProverbiumY

SUBSCRIPTION INFORMATION

Frequency of publication: Annual
Circulation: 270
Available in microform: No
Subscription price: $25.00 yr. institutions; $20.00/yr. individuals
Year to which price refers: 1992
Subscription address: Richard Sweterlitsch, Managing Editor, Dept. of English, Old Mill, Univ. of Vermont, Burlington, VT 05405-0114

ADVERTISING INFORMATION

Advertising accepted: Yes

EDITORIAL DESCRIPTION

Scope: Publishes essays dealing with all facets of the proverb. It is international in scope, and features in addition to scholarly articles, book reviews, an annual bibliography, and brief notes.
Reviews books: Yes
Publishes notes: Yes
Languages accepted: English; German; French; Russian; Spanish
Prints abstracts: No
Author-anonymous submission: No

SUBMISSION REQUIREMENTS

Restrictions on contributors: None
Author pays submission fee: No
Author pays page charges: No
Length of book reviews: 7 pp. maximum
Length of notes: No restrictions
Style: MLA preferred
Number of copies required: 1
Special requirements: Submit double-spaced typescript and diskette using ASCII format.
Copyright ownership: Univ. of Vermont
Rejected manuscripts: Returned with comments
Time before publication decision: 12-18 mos.
Time between decision and publication: 1 yr.
Number of reviewers: 1-2
Articles submitted per year: 25
Articles published per year: 15-17
Book reviews submitted per year: 10-15
Book reviews published per year: 10-15
Notes submitted per year: 4-5
Notes published per year: 4-5

(2254)
Przegląd Humanistyczny

J. Z. Jakubowski, Editor
Panstwowe Wydawnictwo Naukowe
Miadowa 10
Warsaw, Poland

First published: 1957
ISSN: 0033-2194
MLA acronym: PHum

SUBSCRIPTION INFORMATION

Frequency of publication: 12 times/yr.
Subscription address: Ars Polona-Ruch, Krakowskie Przedmieście 7, P.O. Box 1001, 00-068 Warsaw, Poland

EDITORIAL DESCRIPTION

Reviews books: Yes
Languages accepted: Polish
Prints abstracts: No

(2255)
*PSA: The Official Publication of the Pirandello Society of America

Anne Paolucci, Editor
Dept. of English
St. John's Univ.
Jamaica, NY 11439

Telephone: 718 767-8380
Fax: 718 767-8380
First published: 1985
Sponsoring organization: Pirandello Soc. of America
MLA acronym: PSAm

SUBSCRIPTION INFORMATION

Frequency of publication: Annual
Circulation: 125
Available in microform: No
Subscription price: $30.00/yr. institutions; $15.00/yr. individuals
Year to which price refers: 1992

ADVERTISING INFORMATION

Advertising accepted: Yes

EDITORIAL DESCRIPTION

Scope: Publishes articles on fiction and drama studies; production news of Pirandello plays; and comparative assessments of 20th-century drama and fiction.
Reviews books: Yes
Publishes notes: Yes
Languages accepted: English
Prints abstracts: Occasionally
Author-anonymous submission: Yes

SUBMISSION REQUIREMENTS

Author pays submission fee: No
Author pays page charges: Yes, if extensive
Length of articles: 5-7 pp.
Length of book reviews: 300-500 pp.
Length of notes: 200-300 words
Style: MLA
Number of copies required: 2
Copyright ownership: Pirandello Soc. of America
Rejected manuscripts: Returned; enclose SASE.
Time before publication decision: 6 mos.
Time between decision and publication: 6-12 mos.
Number of reviewers: 3
Articles submitted per year: 12-20
Articles published per year: 4-5

(2256)
*Psychiatry: Interpersonal and Biological Processes

David Reiss, Editor
Dept. of Psychiatry & Behavioral Science
George Washington Univ. Medical School
2300 Eye St. NW, Room 613
Washington, DC 20037

First published: 1938
Sponsoring organization: Washington School of Psychiatry
ISSN: 0033-2747
MLA acronym: Psychiatry

SUBSCRIPTION INFORMATION

Frequency of publication: 4 times/yr. (Feb., May, Aug., Nov.)
Circulation: 2,000
Available in microform: Yes
Subscription address: Journals Dept., Guilford Press, 200 Park Ave. S., New York, NY 10003

ADVERTISING INFORMATION

Advertising accepted: Yes

EDITORIAL DESCRIPTION

Scope: Interdisciplinary journal focusing on joint concerns of psychiatry and such fields as psychology, sociology, anthropology, linguistics, philosophy, and biology. Includes clinical, research, and theoretical material.
Reviews books: Yes
Languages accepted: English
Prints abstracts: No
Author-anonymous submission: Yes

SUBMISSION REQUIREMENTS

Author pays submission fee: No
Author pays page charges: No
Length of articles: 10,000 words maximum
Length of book reviews: 750-1,500 words
Style: Journal
Number of copies required: 3
Special requirements: Indicate scope in first paragraph. Include a biographical footnote. Use tables, charts, and other illustrative material only for presentations not made clear in textual form. No multiple submissions.
Copyright ownership: Washington School of Psychiatry
Rejected manuscripts: Returned; enclose SASE.
Time before publication decision: 2-4 mos.
Time between decision and publication: 8-10 mos.
Number of reviewers: 2-3
Articles submitted per year: 120
Articles published per year: 32
Book reviews published per year: 8-10

(2257)
*Psychological Bulletin

Robert Sternberg, Editor
Dept. of Psychology
Yale Univ.
Yale Station, Box 11A
New Haven, CT 06520

Telephone: 203 432-4632
Fax: 203 432-7172
E-mail: STEROBJ@YALEVM
First published: 1904
Sponsoring organization: American Psychological Assn.
ISSN: 0033-2909
MLA acronym: PsyB

SUBSCRIPTION INFORMATION

Frequency of publication: 6 times/yr.
Circulation: 10,500
Available in microform: Yes
Subscription address: Subscription Section, American Psychological Assn., 1400 N. Uhle St., Arlington, VA 22201

ADVERTISING INFORMATION

Advertising accepted: No

EDITORIAL DESCRIPTION

Scope: Publishes evaluative integrative reviews and interpretations of substantive and methodological issues in scientific psychology. Reports original research only for illustrative purposes.
Reviews books: No
Publishes notes: Yes
Languages accepted: English
Prints abstracts: Yes
Author-anonymous submission: Yes, at author's request

SUBMISSION REQUIREMENTS

Restrictions on contributors: None
Author pays submission fee: No
Author pays page charges: No
Length of articles: No restrictions
Style: American Psychological Assn.
Number of copies required: 5
Special requirements: Include a 75-100 word abstract.
Copyright ownership: American Psychological Assn.
Rejected manuscripts: Not returned
Time before publication decision: 3 mos.
Time between decision and publication: 6-10 mos.
Number of reviewers: 2-4
Articles submitted per year: 325
Articles published per year: 70
Notes submitted per year: 30
Notes published per year: 10

(2258)
*Psychological Review

Walter Kintsch, Editor
Dept. of Psychology
Univ. of Colorado
Campus Box 345
Boulder, CO 80309

Additional editorial address: Susan Knapp, Executive Editor, 1400 N. Uhle St., Arlington, VA 22201
First published: 1894
Sponsoring organization: American Psychological Assn.
ISSN: 0033-295X
MLA acronym: PsychologR

SUBSCRIPTION INFORMATION

Frequency of publication: 4 times/yr.
Circulation: 6,500
Available in microform: Yes
Subscription address: American Psychological Assn., 1400 N. Uhle St., Arlington, VA 22201

ADVERTISING INFORMATION

Advertising accepted: Yes

EDITORIAL DESCRIPTION

Scope: Publishes original theoretical articles.
Reviews books: No
Publishes notes: Yes
Languages accepted: English
Prints abstracts: Yes
Author-anonymous submission: Yes, at author's request.

SUBMISSION REQUIREMENTS

Restrictions on contributors: None
Author pays submission fee: No
Author pays page charges: No
Length of articles: 10,000-20,000 words
Length of notes: 500-5,000 words
Style: American Psychological Assn.
Number of copies required: 4
Copyright ownership: American Psychological Assn.
Rejected manuscripts: Not returned
Time before publication decision: 5-40 weeks
Time between decision and publication: 4-6 mos.
Number of reviewers: 3
Articles submitted per year: 200
Articles published per year: 20
Notes submitted per year: 30
Notes published per year: 11

(2259)
*Public Culture: Bulletin of the Society for Transnational Cultural Studies

Carol A. Breckenridge, Editor
1010 East 59th St.
Univ. of Chicago
Chicago, IL 60637

Telephone: 312 702-0814; 312 702-5660
Fax: 312 702-9861
E-mail: Cbre@midway.uchicago.edu
First published: 1988
Sponsoring organization: Soc. for Transnational Cultural Studies
ISSN: 0899-2363
MLA acronym: PubCult

SUBSCRIPTION INFORMATION

Frequency of publication: 3 times/yr.
Circulation: 850
Available in microform: No
Subscription price: $20.00/yr.
Year to which price refers: 1993
Subscription address: P.O. Box 37005, Chicago, IL 66537
Subscription telephone: 312 753-3347
Subscription fax: 312 753-0811

ADVERTISING INFORMATION

Advertising accepted: Yes

EDITORIAL DESCRIPTION

Scope: Reports and reflects current research on the cultural flows that draw cities, societies, and states into larger transnational relationships, and on such cosmopolitan forms as cinema, sports, television and video, tourism, advertising, architecture, and museums.
Reviews books: Yes, review essays
Publishes notes: Yes
Languages accepted: English
Prints abstracts: No
Author-anonymous submission: Yes

SUBMISSION REQUIREMENTS

Author pays submission fee: No
Author pays page charges: No
Length of articles: 30 pp. maximum
Number of copies required: 2
Copyright ownership: Soc. for Transnational Cultural Studies
Rejected manuscripts: Returned; enclose SASE.
Time before publication decision: 2 mos.
Time between decision and publication: 4-8 mos.
Number of reviewers: 2
Articles submitted per year: 100
Articles published per year: 16

(2260)
*Publication of the American Dialect Society

Dennis E. Baron, Editor
Dept. of English
Univ. of Illinois
608 S. Wright St.
Urbana, IL 61801

Telephone: 217 333-2392
Fax: 217 333-4321
First published: 1944
Sponsoring organization: American Dialect Soc.
ISSN: 0002-8207
MLA acronym: PADS

SUBSCRIPTION INFORMATION

Frequency of publication: Irregular
Circulation: 1,000
Available in microform: No
Subscription address: Univ. of Alabama Press, Box 2877, University, AL 35486

ADVERTISING INFORMATION

Advertising accepted: No

EDITORIAL DESCRIPTION

Scope: Publishes monographs on the English language in North America and the languages that influence it or are influenced by it. Series publishes studies in regional dialects, social dialects, occupational vocabulary, place names, usage, non-English dialects, new words, proverbial sayings, and the literary use of dialect. Does not publish articles on general grammar without dialect emphasis or articles on literary figures not known as dialect writers.
Reviews books: No
Publishes notes: No
Languages accepted: English
Prints abstracts: No
Author-anonymous submission: No

SUBMISSION REQUIREMENTS

Restrictions on contributors: Contributors must be members of the American Dialect Soc.
Author pays submission fee: No
Author pays page charges: No
Length of books: 25,000-40,000 words
Style: MLA
Number of copies required: 2
Special requirements: Include a 200-word abstract.
Copyright ownership: American Dialect Soc.
Rejected manuscripts: Returned at author's request
Time before publication decision: 6 mos.
Time between decision and publication: 1 yr.
Number of reviewers: 3
Books submitted per year: 10
Books published per year: 1-2

(2261)
*Publications of the American Folklore Society

Patrick B. Mullen, Editor
Dept. of English
Ohio State Univ.
164 West 17th Ave.
Columbus, OH 43210-1370

Telephone: 614 292-6065
Fax: 614 292-7816
First published: 1894
Sponsoring organization: American Folklore Soc.
MLA acronym: PAFS

SUBSCRIPTION INFORMATION

Frequency of publication: Irregular
Available in microform: No

ADVERTISING INFORMATION

Advertising accepted: No

EDITORIAL DESCRIPTION

Scope: Publishes American and international folklore scholarship. Includes monographs, collections, manuals, indexes, and reference works.
Reviews books: No
Publishes notes: No
Languages accepted: English
Prints abstracts: No
Author-anonymous submission: No

SUBMISSION REQUIREMENTS

Restrictions on contributors: None
Author pays submission fee: No
Author pays page charges: No
Length of books: 50,000-75,000 words
Style: Chicago
Number of copies required: 2
Special requirements: Submit proposal before manuscript. Submit original typescript and 1 copy.
Copyright ownership: Author
Rejected manuscripts: Returned
Time before publication decision: 4-5 mos.
Time between decision and publication: 10-12 mos.
Number of reviewers: 3
Books submitted per year: 5-12
Books published per year: 2-4

(2262)
*Publications of the Arkansas Philological Association

Robert Lowrey, Editor
P.O. Box 4933
Univ. of Central Arkansas
Conway, AR 72032

Telephone: 501 450-5118
E-mail: REL@VM1.UCA.EDU
First published: 1974
Sponsoring organization: Univ. of Central Arkansas; Arkansas Philological Assn.
ISSN: 0160-3124
MLA acronym: PAPA

SUBSCRIPTION INFORMATION

Frequency of publication: 2 times/yr.
Circulation: 200
Available in microform: Yes
Subscription price: $25.00/yr. institutions; $20.00/yr. individuals
Year to which price refers: 1992

ADVERTISING INFORMATION

Advertising accepted: Yes
Advertising rates: $100.00/quarter page; $150.00/half page; $200.00/full page

EDITORIAL DESCRIPTION

Scope: Publishes papers presented at the annual Arkansas Philological Association meeting. Focuses on modern language and literature.
Reviews books: Yes
Publishes notes: No
Languages accepted: English; French; Spanish; German
Prints abstracts: No
Author-anonymous submission: Yes

SUBMISSION REQUIREMENTS

Restrictions on contributors: Contributors must be members of the Arkansas Philological Assn. and papers must be read at the annual meeting. Book reviews are solicited.
Author pays submission fee: No
Author pays page charges: No
Length of articles: 3,000-4,000 words
Length of book reviews: 500-1,000 words
Style: MLA
Number of copies required: 1
Special requirements: Submission on MS-DOS (Word Star) diskette is preferred.
Copyright ownership: Univ. of Central Arkansas Press
Rejected manuscripts: Returned; enclose return postage.
Time before publication decision: 5 mos.
Time between decision and publication: 1-6 mos.
Number of reviewers: 3
Articles submitted per year: 50-60
Articles published per year: 10-14
Book reviews submitted per year: 10
Book reviews published per year: 4-6

(2263)
*Publications of the English Goethe Society

J. D. Adler, Frank M. Fowler, & Ann C. Weaver, Editors
Dept. of German
Queen Mary & Westfield College
Mile End Rd.
London E1, England

First published: 1886
Sponsoring organization: English Goethe Soc.
ISSN: 0959-3683
MLA acronym: PEGS

SUBSCRIPTION INFORMATION

Frequency of publication: Annual
Available in microform: No
Subscription address: Dept. of German, University College, London WC1, England

ADVERTISING INFORMATION

Advertising accepted: No

EDITORIAL DESCRIPTION

Scope: Publishes articles on Goethe and German literature from 1700 to the present.
Reviews books: No
Publishes notes: No
Languages accepted: English; German
Prints abstracts: No
Author-anonymous submission: No

SUBMISSION REQUIREMENTS

Restrictions on contributors: Contributors must have read papers at the English Goethe Soc.
Author pays submission fee: No
Author pays page charges: No
Style: Modern Humanities Research Assn.
Number of copies required: 1
Copyright ownership: English Goethe Soc.
Rejected manuscripts: Returned; enclose return postage.
Time before publication decision: 2 mos.
Time between decision and publication: 18 mos.
Articles published per year: 5

(2264)
Publications of the Mississippi Philological Association

Wilton Beauchamp & Evans Harrington, Editors
Dept. of English
Jackson State Univ.
Jackson, MI 39217

First published: 1982
Sponsoring organization: Mississippi Philological Assn.
ISSN: 0740-9478
MLA acronym: POMPA

SUBSCRIPTION INFORMATION

Frequency of publication: Annual
Circulation: 500

ADVERTISING INFORMATION

Advertising accepted: Yes

EDITORIAL DESCRIPTION

Scope: Publishes articles on literature, linguistics, philology, semantics, and pedagogy relating to these fields.
Reviews books: No
Publishes notes: No
Languages accepted: English
Prints abstracts: No

SUBMISSION REQUIREMENTS

Restrictions on contributors: Manuscripts are not solicited. All manuscripts must be read at the annual meeting of the Mississippi Philological Assn.
Author pays submission fee: No
Author pays page charges: No
Length of articles: 8-10 pp.
Style: MLA
Number of copies required: 1
Copyright ownership: Journal
Rejected manuscripts: Returned; enclose SASE.
Time before publication decision: 6 mos.
Time between decision and publication: 6 mos.
Number of reviewers: 4
Articles submitted per year: 30
Articles published per year: 6-8

(2265)
*Publications of the Missouri Philological Association

James Obertino, Editor
Dept. of English
Central Missouri State Univ.
Warrensburg, MO 64093-5046

Telephone: 816 543-4568
First published: 1976
Sponsoring organization: Missouri Philological Assn.
ISSN: 0194-035X
MLA acronym: PMPA

SUBSCRIPTION INFORMATION

Frequency of publication: Annual
Circulation: 275
Available in microform: No
Subscription price: $10.00/yr.
Year to which price refers: 1992

ADVERTISING INFORMATION

Advertising accepted: No

EDITORIAL DESCRIPTION

Scope: Publishes articles in all areas of language and literature study.
Reviews books: No
Publishes notes: Yes
Languages accepted: English; French; German; Spanish
Prints abstracts: No

SUBMISSION REQUIREMENTS

Restrictions on contributors: Submission must have been read at annual Association meeting. Notes are considered when submitted, but are not published in every issue.
Author pays submission fee: No
Author pays page charges: No
Length of articles: 2,000-3,500 words
Length of notes: 1,000 words maximum
Style: MLA
Number of copies required: 2
Special requirements: Submit original typescript.
Copyright ownership: Journal
Rejected manuscripts: Returned at author's request; enclose SASE.
Time before publication decision: 3 mos.
Time between decision and publication: 4-6 mos.
Number of reviewers: 2-4
Articles submitted per year: 25-30
Articles published per year: 8-10

(2266)
*Publications of the Philological Society

Max W. Wheeler, Editor
School of European Studies
Univ. of Sussex
Falmer, Brighton BN1 9QN, England

Telephone: (44) 273 606755 ext. 2080
Fax: (44) 273 678466
First published: 1913
Sponsoring organization: Philological Soc.
ISSN: 0079-1636
MLA acronym: PPS

SUBSCRIPTION INFORMATION

Frequency of publication: Irregular
Circulation: 800
Available in microform: No
Subscription price: £10.00/yr. (includes membership)
Year to which price refers: 1992
Subscription address: Basil Blackwell, 108 Cowley Rd., Oxford OX4 1JF, England
Subscription telephone: (44) 865 791100
Subscription fax: (44) 865 791347

ADVERTISING INFORMATION

Advertising accepted: No

EDITORIAL DESCRIPTION

Scope: Publishes monographs or volumes of collected studies on philology and linguistics.
Reviews books: No
Publishes notes: No
Languages accepted: English
Prints abstracts: No
Author-anonymous submission: No

SUBMISSION REQUIREMENTS

Restrictions on contributors: None
Author pays submission fee: No
Author pays page charges: No
Number of copies required: 1
Special requirements: Submit double-spaced typescript with ample margins; notes should be separate.
Copyright ownership: Philological Soc.
Rejected manuscripts: Returned
Number of reviewers: 3

(2267)
*Publications of the Texas Folklore Society

Francis Edward Abernethy, Editor
Texas Folklore Soc.
Univ. Station
Nacogdoches, TX 75962

Telephone: 409 568-4407
Fax: 409 568-1117
First published: 1916
Sponsoring organization: Texas Folklore Soc.
ISSN: 0082-3023
MLA acronym: PTFS

SUBSCRIPTION INFORMATION

Frequency of publication: Annual
Circulation: 2,500
Available in microform: No
Subscription price: $15.00/yr.
Year to which price refers: 1992

ADVERTISING INFORMATION

Advertising accepted: No

EDITORIAL DESCRIPTION

Scope: Contains many papers read at Society's meetings and other articles both volunteered and solicited. Most contributions are the product of original collection in the various branches of folklore.
Reviews books: Yes
Publishes notes: No
Languages accepted: English
Prints abstracts: No
Author-anonymous submission: No

SUBMISSION REQUIREMENTS

Restrictions on contributors: None
Author pays submission fee: No
Author pays page charges: No
Style: MLA; Chicago
Number of copies required: 1
Copyright ownership: Texas Folklore Soc.
Rejected manuscripts: Returned; enclose return postage.
Time before publication decision: 6 mos.
Time between decision and publication: 1 yr.
Number of reviewers: 5
Books submitted per year: 1
Books published per year: 1

(2268)
*Publications Romanes et Françaises

Alexandre Micha, Editor
Librairie Droz
11, rue Massot
1211 Geneva 12, Switzerland

Telephone: (41) 22 466666
Fax: (41) 22 472391
First published: 1933
Sponsoring organization: Librairie Droz
ISSN: 0079-7812
MLA acronym: PRF

SUBSCRIPTION INFORMATION

Frequency of publication: Irregular
Circulation: 1,000
Available in microform: No

ADVERTISING INFORMATION

Advertising accepted: No

EDITORIAL DESCRIPTION

Scope: Publishes monographs on French literature.
Reviews books: No
Publishes notes: No
Languages accepted: French
Prints abstracts: No
Author-anonymous submission: No

SUBMISSION REQUIREMENTS

Restrictions on contributors: None
Author pays submission fee: No
Author pays page charges: No
Length of books: No restrictions
Style: None
Number of copies required: 1
Rejected manuscripts: Returned
Time before publication decision: 3 mos.
Time between decision and publication: 6 mos.

(2269)
*Publishing History: The Social, Economic and Literary History of Book, Newspaper and Magazine Publishing

Michael L. Turner & Simon Eliot, Editors
Chadwyck-Healey Ltd.
Cambridge Place
Cambridge CB2 1NR, England

Telephone: (44) 223 311479
Fax: (44) 223 66440
First published: 1977
ISSN: 0309-2445
MLA acronym: PubHist

SUBSCRIPTION INFORMATION

Frequency of publication: 2 times/yr. (Apr., Oct.)
Circulation: 500
Available in microform: Yes
Subscription price: £60.00 ($100.00)/yr. institutions; £28.00 ($48.00)/yr. individuals
Year to which price refers: 1992
Additional subscription address: In the USA: Chadwyck-Healey Inc., 1101 King St., Alexandria, VA 22314

ADVERTISING INFORMATION

Advertising accepted: Yes
Advertising rates: £60.00/half page; £95.00/full page

EDITORIAL DESCRIPTION

Scope: Publishes articles on all aspects of the history of publishing.
Reviews books: Yes
Publishes notes: Yes
Languages accepted: English
Prints abstracts: No
Author-anonymous submission: No

SUBMISSION REQUIREMENTS

Restrictions on contributors: None
Author pays submission fee: No
Author pays page charges: No
Length of articles: 9,000 words
Length of book reviews: 1,000 words
Length of notes: 1,000 words
Style: Request from Chadwyck-Healey
Special requirements: Submit original typescript.
Copyright ownership: Chadwyck-Healey Ltd.
Rejected manuscripts: Returned
Time before publication decision: 3 mos.
Time between decision and publication: 6-12 mos.
Number of reviewers: 1
Articles submitted per year: 12
Articles published per year: 8
Book reviews published per year: 2
Notes published per year: 1-2

(2270)
*Publishing Research Quarterly

Beth Luey, Editor
Dept. of History
Arizona State Univ.
Tempe, AZ 85287-2501

Telephone: 602 965-3226
Fax: 602 965-0310
First published: 1985
Historical variations in title: Formerly *Book Research Quarterly*
Sponsoring organization: Arizona State Univ.
ISSN: 1053-8801
MLA acronym: PRQ

SUBSCRIPTION INFORMATION

Frequency of publication: 4 times/yr. (Spring, Summer, Fall, Winter)
Circulation: 1,000
Available in microform: Yes
Subscription price: $72.00/yr. institutions; $36.00/yr. individuals
Year to which price refers: 1992
Subscription address: Dept. 4010, Transaction Periodicals Consortium, Rutgers Univ., New Brunswick, NJ 08903
Additional subscription address: In Europe & Israel: Swets Publishing Service, Heereweg 347, 2161 CA Lisse, Netherlands
Subscription telephone: 908 932-2280
Subscription fax: 908 932-3138

ADVERTISING INFORMATION

Advertising accepted: Yes
Advertising rates: $190.00/half page; $250.00/full page

EDITORIAL DESCRIPTION

Scope: Publishes research, information, and essays on publishing, including works on print media as well as on electronic media. Includes articles on the social, political, economic, and technological conditions that help shape this process throughout the world. It has special importance to publishers, authors, librarians, book manufacturers, and information specialists who, in the nature of their work life, must understand the current state of publishing.
Reviews books: Yes
Publishes notes: No
Languages accepted: English
Prints abstracts: Yes
Author-anonymous submission: Yes

SUBMISSION REQUIREMENTS

Restrictions on contributors: Book reviews and some articles are solicited.
Author pays submission fee: No
Author pays page charges: No
Length of articles: 50,000 words maximum
Length of book reviews: 500-1,500 words
Style: Chicago
Number of copies required: 2
Special requirements: Submit a brief abstract and biographical note. Provide camera-ready copy of tables and illustrations.
Copyright ownership: Publisher
Rejected manuscripts: Returned
Time before publication decision: 2-3 mos.
Time between decision and publication: 3-6 mos.
Number of reviewers: 1-3
Articles submitted per year: 60
Articles published per year: 40
Book reviews published per year: 30

(2271)
*Pynchon Notes

John M. Krafft, Khachig Tölölyan, & Bernard Duyfhuizen, Editors
Miami Univ.-Hamilton
1601 Peck Blvd.
Hamilton, OH 45011

Telephone: 513 863-8833
Fax: 513 863-1655
E-mail: JMKRAFFT@MIAVXZ.HAM.-MUOHIO.EDU
First published: 1979
Sponsoring organization: Univ. of Wisconsin-Eau Claire, English Dept.; Miami Univ.-Hamilton, English Dept.
ISSN: 0278-1891
MLA acronym: PNotes

SUBSCRIPTION INFORMATION

Frequency of publication: 2 times/yr. (Spring, Fall)

Circulation: 300
Available in microform: No
Subscription price: $9.00/yr. institutions US & Canada; $12.00/yr. institutions elsewhere
Year to which price refers: 1992
Subscription address: Bernard Duyfhuizen, English Dept., Univ. of Wisconsin-Eau Claire, Eau Claire, WI 54702-4004
Subscription telephone: 715 836-2639
Subscription fax: 715 836-2380

ADVERTISING INFORMATION

Advertising accepted: Yes, on an exchange basis

EDITORIAL DESCRIPTION

Scope: Focuses primarily on the works of Thomas Pynchon, considered both in themselves and in the broader contexts of contemporary American, modern, and comparative literature. Includes current bibliography.
Reviews books: Yes
Publishes notes: Yes
Languages accepted: English
Prints abstracts: No
Author-anonymous submission: No

SUBMISSION REQUIREMENTS

Restrictions on contributors: None
Author pays submission fee: No
Author pays page charges: No
Length of articles: No restrictions
Length of book reviews: No restrictions
Length of notes: No restrictions
Style: MLA
Number of copies required: 1
Special requirements: Submit original typescript or diskette.
Copyright ownership: Editors
Rejected manuscripts: Returned; enclose SASE.
Time before publication decision: 4-12 weeks
Time between decision and publication: 3-9 mos.
Number of reviewers: 3
Articles submitted per year: 30
Articles published per year: 6-12
Book reviews submitted per year: 4-8
Book reviews published per year: 4-8
Notes submitted per year: 12
Notes published per year: 6

(2272)
*Al- Qanṭara: Revista de Estudios Arabes

Manuela Marín, Editor
Instituto de Filología
Duque de Medinaceli, 6
28014 Madrid, Spain

Telephone: (34) 1 5856010
Fax: (34) 1 5856197
First published: 1933
Sponsoring organization: Consejo Superior de Investigaciones Científicas (C.S.I.C.)
ISSN: 0211-3589
MLA acronym: Qanṭara

SUBSCRIPTION INFORMATION

Frequency of publication: 2 times/yr.
Circulation: 1,000
Available in microform: No
Subscription price: 4,950 Pta/yr.
Year to which price refers: 1992

ADVERTISING INFORMATION

Advertising accepted: No

EDITORIAL DESCRIPTION

Scope: Publishes articles on Islamic and Arab culture, with major focus on the Islamic West.
Reviews books: Yes
Publishes notes: Yes

Languages accepted: Spanish; English; French
Prints abstracts: Yes

SUBMISSION REQUIREMENTS

Restrictions on contributors: None
Author pays submission fee: No
Author pays page charges: No
Length of articles: 40 pp. maximum
Length of book reviews: 4 pp.
Length of notes: 8 pp.
Number of copies required: 2
Special requirements: Submit original typescript and an abstract in English.
Copyright ownership: Assigned by author to journal
Rejected manuscripts: Returned
Time before publication decision: 2 mos.
Time between decision and publication: 9 mos.
Number of reviewers: 2
Articles submitted per year: 20-30
Articles published per year: 20
Book reviews published per year: 20
Notes published per year: 10

(2273)
*Quaderni del Dipartimento di Lingue e Letterature Straniere Moderne, Universita di Genova

Giorgio De Piaggi, Editor
Dpto. di Lingue & Litterature Straniere Moderne
Piazza S. Sabina 2
16124 Genoa, Italy

Telephone: (39) 10 2099551
Fax: (39) 10 281878
First published: 1987
Sponsoring organization: Univ. di Genova, Dpto. di Lingue & Letterature Straniere Moderne
MLA acronym: QDLLSM

SUBSCRIPTION INFORMATION

Frequency of publication: Annual
Circulation: 500
Available in microform: No
Subscription address: Schena Editore, Viale Stazione 177, 72015 Fasano, Brindisi, Italy

ADVERTISING INFORMATION

Advertising accepted: No

EDITORIAL DESCRIPTION

Scope: Publishes articles on linguistic and literary studies.
Reviews books: No
Publishes notes: No
Languages accepted: English; Italian; French; Russian; Polish; German; Spanish
Prints abstracts: No

SUBMISSION REQUIREMENTS

Restrictions on contributors: Articles are usually solicited but exceptions are made.
Author pays submission fee: No
Author pays page charges: No
Length of books: 7,000 words
Style: MLA
Number of copies required: 1
Copyright ownership: Schena Editore
Time before publication decision: 3 mos.
Time between decision and publication: 1 yr.
Number of reviewers: 5
Articles submitted per year: 14-20
Articles published per year: 12-14

(2274)
*Quaderni di Filologia Germanica della Facoltà di Lettere e Filosofia dell'Università di Bologna

Vita Fortunati, Editor
A. Longo Editore
P.O. Box 431
48100 Ravenna, Italy

Telephone: (39) 544 217026
Fax: (39) 544 217026
First published: 1980
Sponsoring organization: Univ. degli Studi di Bologna
ISSN: 0024-8215
MLA acronym: QFG

SUBSCRIPTION INFORMATION

Frequency of publication: Irregular
Circulation: 1,000
Available in microform: No
Subscription price: 30,000 Lit/yr.
Year to which price refers: 1988

ADVERTISING INFORMATION

Advertising accepted: No

EDITORIAL DESCRIPTION

Scope: Publishes literary criticism with an emphasis on English, German, American, and Finnish literature.
Reviews books: No
Publishes notes: Yes
Languages accepted: Italian; English; German
Prints abstracts: No

SUBMISSION REQUIREMENTS

Author pays submission fee: No
Author pays page charges: No
Length of articles: 5,000-7,500 words
Length of notes: 3,500 words
Style: MLA
Number of copies required: 2
Special requirements: Submit original typescript.
Copyright ownership: Journal
Rejected manuscripts: Not returned
Time before publication decision: 4 mos.
Time between decision and publication: 9 mos.
Number of reviewers: 2
Articles submitted per year: 25
Articles published per year: 15
Notes submitted per year: 20
Notes published per year: 10

(2275)
*I Quaderni di Gaia: Rivista Semestrale di Letteratura Comparata e di Cultura Transdisciplinare

Armando Gnisci, Editor
Cattedra di Letterature Comparate
Fac. di Lettere, Dipt. di Italianistica
Univ. di Roma "La Sapienza"
Piazzale A. Moro, 5
00185 Rome, Italy

Telephone: (39) 6 5806274
Fax: (39) 6 491609
First published: 1990
MLA acronym: IQdG

SUBSCRIPTION INFORMATION

Frequency of publication: 2 times/yr. (Apr., Oct.)
Circulation: 60
Available in microform: No
Subscription price: 40,000 Lit/yr. institutions Italy; 55,000 Lit/yr. institutions elsewhere; 28,000 Lit/yr. individuals Italy; 36,000 Lit/yr. individuals elsewhere

Year to which price refers: 1991
Subscription address: Carucci Editore, Viale Trastevere 60, 00153 Rome, Italy

ADVERTISING INFORMATION

Advertising accepted: Yes
Advertising rates: 2,000,000 Lit/full page

EDITORIAL DESCRIPTION

Scope: Publishes articles on comparative literature studies.
Reviews books: Yes
Publishes notes: Yes
Languages accepted: Italian; English; French; German; Spanish
Prints abstracts: No
Author-anonymous submission: No

SUBMISSION REQUIREMENTS

Author pays submission fee: No
Author pays page charges: No
Length of articles: 5,300 words
Length of book reviews: 360 words
Length of notes: 3,500-4,000 words
Number of copies required: 1
Special requirements: Submit typescript and diskette using MS-DOS.
Copyright ownership: Carucci Editore
Rejected manuscripts: Not returned
Time before publication decision: 3-6 mos.
Time between decision and publication: 1-2 yrs.
Number of reviewers: 2-3
Articles submitted per year: 30
Articles published per year: 8
Book reviews submitted per year: 60
Book reviews published per year: 25
Notes submitted per year: 5
Notes published per year: 5

(2276)
Quaderni di Lingue e Letterature

Univ. degli Studi di Verona
Facoltà di Lingue & Letterature Straniere
37129 Verona, Italy

Sponsoring organization: Univ. degli Studi di Verona, Fac. di Lingue & Letterature Straniere
MLA acronym: QLL

EDITORIAL DESCRIPTION

Scope: Publishes articles on literature and linguistics.
Languages accepted: Italian; English; French; German; Spanish

(2277)
*Quaderni di Semantica: Rivista Internazionale di Semantica Teorica e Applicata/An International Journal of Theoretical and Applied Semantics

Mario Alinei, Editor
Quintole per le Rose 131
50029 Tavarnuzze (Florence), Italy

Telephone: (39) 55 2034283
Fax: (39) 55 2034283
First published: 1980
ISSN: 0393-1226
MLA acronym: QSem

SUBSCRIPTION INFORMATION

Frequency of publication: 2 times/yr.
Available in microform: No
Subscription price: 60,000 Lit/yr.
Year to which price refers: 1992
Subscription address: Soc. Editrice il Mulino, Strada Maggiore 37, 40125 Bologna, Italy

ADVERTISING INFORMATION

Advertising accepted: Yes

EDITORIAL DESCRIPTION

Scope: Publishes articles on theoretical and applied semantics.
Reviews books: Yes
Publishes notes: Yes
Languages accepted: English; French; Italian; Spanish; German
Prints abstracts: No
Author-anonymous submission: No

SUBMISSION REQUIREMENTS

Author pays submission fee: No
Author pays page charges: No
Number of copies required: 2
Special requirements: Submit double-spaced typescript. Use IPA for phonetic transcriptions.
Copyright ownership: Author & journal
Rejected manuscripts: Returned
Time before publication decision: 4 mos.
Time between decision and publication: 1 yr.
Number of reviewers: 2
Articles submitted per year: 100
Articles published per year: 30
Book reviews submitted per year: 30
Book reviews published per year: 10

(2278)
*Quaderni d'Italianistica: Official Journal of the Canadian Society for Italian Studies

Antonio Franceschetti, Editor
Dept. of Italian Studies
Univ. of Toronto
Toronto M5S 1A1, Canada

Telephone: 416 978-5569
Fax: 416 978-5593
First published: 1980
Sponsoring organization: Canadian Soc. for Italian Studies
ISSN: 0226-8043
MLA acronym: QI

SUBSCRIPTION INFORMATION

Frequency of publication: 2 times/yr. (Spring, Fall)
Circulation: 450
Available in microform: No
Subscription price: C$24.00/yr. institutions; C$20.00/yr. individuals
Year to which price refers: 1991

ADVERTISING INFORMATION

Advertising accepted: Yes

EDITORIAL DESCRIPTION

Scope: Publishes articles that promote an international dialogue between Canadian and non-Canadian scholars on all aspects of Italian culture.
Reviews books: Yes
Publishes notes: Yes
Languages accepted: English; French; Italian
Prints abstracts: No
Author-anonymous submission: No

SUBMISSION REQUIREMENTS

Restrictions on contributors: None
Author pays submission fee: No
Author pays page charges: No
Length of articles: 5,000 words including notes
Length of book reviews: 500-750 words
Length of notes: 2,000 words
Style: MLA
Number of copies required: 2
Special requirements: Submit original typescript. Submission on diskette is welcome.
Copyright ownership: Author
Rejected manuscripts: Returned at author's request
Time before publication decision: 4-6 mos.
Time between decision and publication: 8 mos.
Number of reviewers: 4
Articles submitted per year: 20-25
Articles published per year: 8-10
Book reviews submitted per year: 20-25
Book reviews published per year: 15-20
Notes submitted per year: 10-15
Notes published per year: 10-12

(2279)
*Quaderni Ibero-Americani: Attualità Culturale della Penisola Iberica e America Latina

Giuseppe Bellini, Editor
Via Montebello, 21
10124 Torino, Italy

Telephone: (39) 11 832743
Fax: (39) 11 832584
First published: 1946
Sponsoring organization: Assoc. Studi Iberici
ISSN: 0033-4960
MLA acronym: QIA

SUBSCRIPTION INFORMATION

Frequency of publication: 2 times/yr.
Circulation: 1,200
Available in microform: No
Subscription price: $35.00/yr.
Year to which price refers: 1992

ADVERTISING INFORMATION

Advertising accepted: Yes

EDITORIAL DESCRIPTION

Scope: Publishes articles on Spanish and Latin American literature and culture.
Reviews books: Yes
Publishes notes: Yes
Languages accepted: English; French; Italian; Spanish; Portuguese
Prints abstracts: Yes
Author-anonymous submission: No

SUBMISSION REQUIREMENTS

Author pays submission fee: No
Author pays page charges: No
Length of articles: 5-20 pp.
Length of book reviews: 5 pp.
Length of notes: 5 pp.
Style: None
Number of copies required: 2
Copyright ownership: Author
Rejected manuscripts: Not returned
Time before publication decision: 6 mos.
Time between decision and publication: 6 mos.
Number of reviewers: 2
Articles submitted per year: 20-30
Articles published per year: 5-10
Book reviews submitted per year: 100
Book reviews published per year: 40
Notes submitted per year: 10-15
Notes published per year: 5

(2280)
*Quaderni Veneti

Giorgio Padoan, Editor
A. Longo Editore
Via P. Costa, 33
C.P. 431
48100 Ravenna, Italy

Telephone: (39) 544 217026
Fax: (39) 544 217026

First published: 1985
Sponsoring organization: Centro Interuniversitario di Studi Veneti
ISSN: 0394-2694
MLA acronym: QVen

SUBSCRIPTION INFORMATION

Frequency of publication: 2 times/yr.
Circulation: 2,000
Available in microform: No
Subscription price: 54,000 Lit/yr. Italy; 72,000 Lit/yr. elsewhere
Year to which price refers: 1993

ADVERTISING INFORMATION

Advertising accepted: No

EDITORIAL DESCRIPTION

Scope: Publishes literary criticism with an emphasis on Veneto literature, poetry, dialect, and language.
Reviews books: Yes
Publishes notes: Yes
Languages accepted: Italian
Prints abstracts: No
Author-anonymous submission: No

SUBMISSION REQUIREMENTS

Restrictions on contributors: None
Author pays submission fee: No
Author pays page charges: No
Length of articles: 5,000-7,500 words
Length of book reviews: 2,500 words
Length of notes: 2,000-2,500 words
Style: MLA
Number of copies required: 2
Special requirements: Submit original typescript and IBM or Macintosh diskette.
Copyright ownership: A. Longo Editore
Rejected manuscripts: Not returned
Time before publication decision: 4 mos.
Time between decision and publication: 1 yr.
Number of reviewers: 2
Articles submitted per year: 100-150
Articles published per year: 20-25
Book reviews submitted per year: 100-150
Book reviews published per year: 15
Notes submitted per year: 120-130
Notes published per year: 20

(2281)
*Quadrant

A. Roig, Editor
Univ. Paul Valéry
Route de Mende, B.P. 5043
34032 Montpellier-Cedex, France

Telephone: (33) 67522141
Fax: (33) 67142052
First published: 1984
ISSN: 0769-0126
MLA acronym: Qu

SUBSCRIPTION INFORMATION

Frequency of publication: Annual
Available in microform: No
Subscription price: 60 F/yr.
Year to which price refers: 1992

ADVERTISING INFORMATION

Advertising accepted: Yes, on an exchange basis

EDITORIAL DESCRIPTION

Scope: Publishes articles on Portuguese and Brazilian language and literature.
Reviews books: No
Publishes notes: No
Languages accepted: French; Spanish; Portuguese
Prints abstracts: No
Author-anonymous submission: No

SUBMISSION REQUIREMENTS

Author pays submission fee: No
Author pays page charges: No
Length of articles: 3,000-10,000 words
Number of copies required: 2
Rejected manuscripts: Returned
Time before publication decision: 8-10 mos.
Time between decision and publication: 3 mos.
Number of reviewers: 4
Articles submitted per year: 12-15
Articles published per year: 7-8

(2282)
*Quadrant

Robert Manne, Les Murray, & Robin Marsden, Editors
P.O. Box 1495
Collingwood
Victoria 3066, Australia

Telephone: (61) 3 4176855
Fax: (61) 3 4162980
First published: 1956
Sponsoring organization: Australian Assn. for Cultural Freedom
ISSN: 0033-5002
MLA acronym: Quadrant

SUBSCRIPTION INFORMATION

Frequency of publication: 10 times/yr.
Circulation: 6,500
Available in microform: Yes
Subscription price: A$45.00/yr.
Year to which price refers: 1992

ADVERTISING INFORMATION

Advertising accepted: Yes
Advertising rates: $100.00/quarter page; $200.00/half page; $400.00/full page; $500.00/insert

EDITORIAL DESCRIPTION

Scope: Publishes informed criticism of world affairs, literary criticism, creative writing, and cultural reflections on art, music and film.
Reviews books: Yes
Publishes notes: No
Languages accepted: English
Prints abstracts: No

SUBMISSION REQUIREMENTS

Restrictions on contributors: None
Author pays submission fee: No
Author pays page charges: No
Length of articles: 2,000-4,000 words
Length of book reviews: 1,000-2,000 words
Style: MLA
Number of copies required: 2
Special requirements: Submit double-spaced typescript on size A4 (8 1/4 in. x 11 3/4 in.) paper printed on one side only. Include author's address.
Copyright ownership: Author; journal has first publication rights.
Rejected manuscripts: Returned; enclose SASE.
Time before publication decision: 3 mos.
Time between decision and publication: 1-4 mos.
Number of reviewers: 1-3
Articles submitted per year: 1,200
Articles published per year: 200
Book reviews submitted per year: 60
Book reviews published per year: 50

(2283)
*Quantitative Linguistics

Burghard Rieger & Reinard Köhler, Editors
Univ. of Trier
Dept. of Computational Linguistics
FB II: LDV/CL
Postfach 3825
5500 Trier, Germany

Telephone: (49) 651 2012270
Fax: (49) 651 2013946
E-mail: Quantling@utrurt.uucp.de
First published: 1978
ISSN: 0932-7991
MLA acronym: QLing

SUBSCRIPTION INFORMATION

Frequency of publication: Irregular
Circulation: 1,000
Available in microform: No

ADVERTISING INFORMATION

Advertising accepted: Yes, on an exchange basis

EDITORIAL DESCRIPTION

Scope: Publishes articles and monographs on quantitative, mathematical modelling of language phenomena, including structures, functions, and processes.
Reviews books: Yes
Publishes notes: Yes
Languages accepted: English; French; German
Prints abstracts: Yes
Author-anonymous submission: No

SUBMISSION REQUIREMENTS

Restrictions on contributors: None
Author pays submission fee: No
Author pays page charges: No
Length of books: No restrictions
Length of book reviews: No restrictions
Style: American Psychological Assn.
Number of copies required: 3
Special requirements: Submit on diskette and include an English abstract.
Copyright ownership: Author
Rejected manuscripts: Returned
Time before publication decision: 3 mos.
Time between decision and publication: 6 mos.
Number of reviewers: 3
Articles submitted per year: 30
Articles published per year: 20
Books published per year: 3-4
Book reviews submitted per year: 8
Book reviews published per year: 10

(2284)
*The Quarterly Journal of Speech

Robert L. Ivie, Editor
Dept. of Speech Communication
Texas A&M Univ.
College Station, TX 77843-4234

Telephone: 409 845-3338
Fax: 409 845-6594
E-mail: E340ri@tamvm1.bitnet
First published: 1915
Sponsoring organization: Speech Communication Assn.
ISSN: 0033-5630
MLA acronym: QJS

SUBSCRIPTION INFORMATION

Frequency of publication: 4 times/yr. (Feb., May, Aug., Nov.)
Circulation: 6,750
Available in microform: No
Subscription address: James L. Gaudino, Executive Secretary, Speech Communication Assn., 5105 Backlick Rd., Annandale, VA 22003

Subscription telephone: 703 750-0533

ADVERTISING INFORMATION

Advertising accepted: Yes

EDITORIAL DESCRIPTION

Scope: Publishes essays on theoretical, historical, critical, and empirical aspects of human communication.
Reviews books: Yes
Publishes notes: Yes
Languages accepted: English
Prints abstracts: Yes
Author-anonymous submission: Yes

SUBMISSION REQUIREMENTS

Restrictions on contributors: None
Author pays submission fee: No
Author pays page charges: No
Length of articles: 9,000 words maximum
Length of book reviews: 1,200 words maximum
Style: MLA; American Psychological Assn.
Number of copies required: 4
Copyright ownership: Speech Communication Assn.
Rejected manuscripts: Not returned; reviews are sent to author.
Time before publication decision: 2-3 mos.
Time between decision and publication: 6-8 mos.
Number of reviewers: 2
Articles submitted per year: 250
Articles published per year: 30-35
Book reviews published per year: 60-80

(2285)
*Quarterly Review of Film and Video

Michael Renov, Editor
Univ. of Southern California
School of Cinema-Television
University Park
Los Angeles, CA 90089-2211

Telephone: 213 740-3334
Fax: 213 740-7682
First published: 1976
ISSN: 0146-0013
MLA acronym: QRFV

SUBSCRIPTION INFORMATION

Frequency of publication: 4 times/yr.
Circulation: 1,000
Subscription price: $24.00/yr. members; $48.00/yr. nonmembers
Year to which price refers: 1992
Subscription address: Harwood Academic Publishers, P.O. Box 786, Cooper Station, New York, NY 10276
Subscription telephone: 212 206-8900
Subscription fax: 212 645-2459

ADVERTISING INFORMATION

Advertising accepted: Yes

EDITORIAL DESCRIPTION

Scope: Publishes articles and review essays exploring historical, theoretical, and critical issues relevant to film and television/video studies. Topics covered include Hollywood film, network television, technology, pedagogy, popular culture, and issues of class, feminism and sexual politics.
Reviews books: Yes
Publishes notes: Yes
Languages accepted: English
Prints abstracts: No
Author-anonymous submission: No

SUBMISSION REQUIREMENTS

Restrictions on contributors: Most reviews are commissioned.

Author pays submission fee: No
Author pays page charges: No
Length of articles: 30 pp. maximum
Length of book reviews: 1,500-2,500 words
Length of notes: 100 words
Style: Chicago
Number of copies required: 3
Special requirements: Submit double-spaced typescript with 3 cm margins. Contributions must not have been published previously or be under consideration elsewhere. For further information see *Notes for Contributors* in journal.
Copyright ownership: Publisher
Time before publication decision: 1-3 mos.
Number of reviewers: 8

(2286)
*Queen's Quarterly

Boris Castel, Editor
Queen's Univ.
Kingston, Ontario K7L 3N6, Canada

Telephone: 613 545-2667
Fax: 613 545-6822
First published: 1893
Sponsoring organization: Queen's Univ.
ISSN: 0033-6041
MLA acronym: QQ

SUBSCRIPTION INFORMATION

Frequency of publication: 4 times/yr. (Spring, Summer, Autumn, Winter)
Circulation: 3,400
Available in microform: Yes
Subscription price: $22.00/yr.
Year to which price refers: 1992

ADVERTISING INFORMATION

Advertising accepted: Yes

EDITORIAL DESCRIPTION

Scope: Publishes articles on politics, history, literature, culture, science, and foreign affairs. The authors of these articles are specialists but articles are written for the general reader. Publishes some poetry and fiction as well as review articles, an extensive new books section, and reviews of gallery exhibition, musical, and dramatic performances.
Reviews books: Yes
Publishes notes: No
Languages accepted: English
Prints abstracts: No
Author-anonymous submission: No

SUBMISSION REQUIREMENTS

Restrictions on contributors: Book reviews are commissioned.
Author pays submission fee: No
Author pays page charges: No
Length of articles: 3,000-8,000 words
Style: MLA
Number of copies required: 1
Special requirements: Submit original double-spaced typescript.
Copyright ownership: Author
Rejected manuscripts: Returned; enclose SASE.
Time before publication decision: 2-3 mos.
Time between decision and publication: 1 yr.
Number of reviewers: 2
Articles submitted per year: 160
Articles published per year: 42
Book reviews published per year: 125

(2287)
Queensland Studies in German Language and Literature

Manfred Jurgensen, Editor
Univ. of Queensland
Dept. of German
Brisbane 4067, Queensland, Australia

First published: 1970
Sponsoring organization: Univ. of Queensland, Brisbane
ISSN: 0818-3279
MLA acronym: QSGLL

SUBSCRIPTION INFORMATION

Frequency of publication: Once every 2 yrs.
Circulation: 5,000
Available in microform: No
Subscription address: Francke Verlag, Postfach, 3001 Berne, Switzerland

ADVERTISING INFORMATION

Advertising accepted: Yes

EDITORIAL DESCRIPTION

Scope: Publishes articles on modern German literature in the form of critical anthologies. Volumes deal with one author only and are published in book-form.
Reviews books: No
Publishes notes: No
Languages accepted: German
Prints abstracts: No
Author-anonymous submission: Yes

SUBMISSION REQUIREMENTS

Restrictions on contributors: Prospective contributors are invited to write to the Editor to ascertain the subject of forthcoming publications.
Author pays submission fee: No
Author pays page charges: No
Length of articles: 5,000 words
Length of books: 45,000-50,000 words
Style: MLA
Number of copies required: 1
Special requirements: Submit original typescript.
Copyright ownership: Journal
Rejected manuscripts: Returned
Time before publication decision: 1 mo.
Time between decision and publication: 1 yr.
Number of reviewers: 3 plus Editorial Board

(2288)
*Quellen und Forschungen zur Sprach- und Kulturgeschichte der Germanischen Völker

Stefan Sonderegger, Editor
Deutsches Seminar
Rämistr. 74
8001 Zurich, Switzerland

First published: 1874
ISSN: 0481-3596
MLA acronym: QFSK

SUBSCRIPTION INFORMATION

Frequency of publication: Irregular
Circulation: 800-1,000
Available in microform: No
Subscription address: Walter de Gruyter & Co., Genthinerstr. 13, 1000 Berlin 30, Germany
Subscription telephone: (49) 30 260050
Subscription fax: (49) 30 26005251

ADVERTISING INFORMATION

Advertising accepted: No

EDITORIAL DESCRIPTION

Scope: Publishes monographs on German and Germanic philology and literature, as well as text editions.
Reviews books: No
Publishes notes: No
Languages accepted: German
Prints abstracts: No
Author-anonymous submission: No

SUBMISSION REQUIREMENTS

Restrictions on contributors: Contributors must have Ph.D. Submission of material written in English requires advance authorization.
Author pays submission fee: No
Author pays page charges: Yes
Length of books: 200-400 pp.
Style: Request from Walter de Gruyter & Co.
Number of copies required: 1
Copyright ownership: Walter de Gruyter & Co.
Rejected manuscripts: Returned; enclose return postage.
Time before publication decision: 2-6 mos.
Time between decision and publication: 6-12 mos.
Number of reviewers: 2 minimum
Books submitted per year: 4
Books published per year: 2-3

(2289)
***Qui Parle: A Journal of Literary and Critical Studies**

Michel Chaouli, David Levin, Elizabeth Maddock, Patrick Riley, Anne Cheng, & Natalie Melas, Editors
Doreen B. Townsend Center for the Humanities
460 Stephens Hall
Univ. of California
Berkeley, CA 94720

Telephone: 510 643-9670
First published: 1985
Sponsoring organization: Dept. of French, Dept. of English, Dept. of Comparative Literature, Doreen B. Townsend Center for the Humanities, & Graduate Division of the Univ. of California, Berkeley
ISSN: 1041-8385
MLA acronym: QPar

SUBSCRIPTION INFORMATION

Frequency of publication: 2 times/yr. (Sept., Feb.)
Circulation: 600
Available in microform: No
Subscription price: $20.00/yr., $40.00/2 yrs. institutions US; $10.00/yr., $17.00/2 yrs. individuals US; add $2.00/yr. postage Canada & Mexico; add $6.00/yr. postage elsewhere
Year to which price refers: 1992

ADVERTISING INFORMATION

Advertising accepted: Yes

EDITORIAL DESCRIPTION

Scope: Publishes articles and reviews dealing with literary theory, cultural studies, visual arts, history, philosophy, and popular culture.
Reviews books: Yes
Publishes notes: No
Languages accepted: English; French (seldomly)
Prints abstracts: No
Author-anonymous submission: Yes

SUBMISSION REQUIREMENTS

Restrictions on contributors: None
Author pays submission fee: No
Author pays page charges: No
Length of articles: 5,000 words
Length of book reviews: 1,000 words
Style: MLA
Number of copies required: 2
Copyright ownership: Author
Rejected manuscripts: Returned; enclose SASE.
Time before publication decision: 2-10 weeks
Time between decision and publication: 3-6 mos.
Number of reviewers: 6-9
Articles submitted per year: 75
Articles published per year: 20
Book reviews submitted per year: 15
Book reviews published per year: 8

(2290)
Quimera: Revista de Literatura

Miguel Riera, Editor
c/o Montesinos Editor SA
Maignón 26 3°
08024 Barcelona, Spain

Telephone: (34) 3 2106906
Fax: (34) 3 2106906
First published: 1980
ISSN: 0211-3325
MLA acronym: Quimera

SUBSCRIPTION INFORMATION

Frequency of publication: 11 times/yr.
Circulation: 25,000
Available in microform: No
Subscription price: 5,000 Pta/yr. Spain; 5,500 Pta/yr. Europe; $60.00/yr. US
Year to which price refers: 1992

ADVERTISING INFORMATION

Advertising accepted: Yes

EDITORIAL DESCRIPTION

Scope: Publishes articles on world literature.
Reviews books: Yes
Languages accepted: Spanish
Prints abstracts: No
Author-anonymous submission: Yes

SUBMISSION REQUIREMENTS

Restrictions on contributors: None
Author pays submission fee: No
Author pays page charges: No
Length of articles: 10 pp.
Length of book reviews: 5,000 characters
Number of copies required: 1
Copyright ownership: Journal
Rejected manuscripts: Not returned
Time before publication decision: 2 mos.
Time between decision and publication: 2 mos.
Number of reviewers: 1
Articles submitted per year: 1,000
Articles published per year: 200
Book reviews submitted per year: 500
Book reviews published per year: 200

(2291)
***La Quinzaine Littéraire**

Maurice Nadeau, Editor
43, rue du Temple
75004 Paris, France

Telephone: (33) 1 48874858
Fax: (33) 1 48871301
First published: 1966
ISSN: 0048-6493
MLA acronym: QL

SUBSCRIPTION INFORMATION

Frequency of publication: 23 times/yr.
Circulation: 30,000
Available in microform: Yes
Subscription price: 520 F/yr.
Year to which price refers: 1992

ADVERTISING INFORMATION

Advertising accepted: Yes

EDITORIAL DESCRIPTION

Scope: Publishes essays and book reviews about books published in French or translated into French.
Reviews books: Yes
Publishes notes: Yes
Languages accepted: French
Prints abstracts: Yes

SUBMISSION REQUIREMENTS

Restrictions on contributors: None
Author pays submission fee: No
Author pays page charges: No
Length of articles: 6,000 characters
Length of book reviews: 1,200-1,500 words
Number of copies required: 1
Copyright ownership: Author & journal
Rejected manuscripts: Returned at author's request
Time before publication decision: 15 days
Time between decision and publication: 15-60 days
Articles submitted per year: 1,000-1,200
Articles published per year: 600-800
Book reviews submitted per year: 800-1,000
Book reviews published per year: 600-800
Notes submitted per year: 500
Notes published per year: 150-200

(2292)
***Quondam et Futurus: A Journal of Arthurian Interpretations**

Henry Hall Peyton III, Editor
English Dept.
Memphis State Univ.
Memphis, TN 38152

Additional editorial address: Mildred Leake Day, 2212 Pinehurst Dr., Gardendale, AL 35071
Telephone: 901 678-4591
First published: 1991
ISSN: 8755-3627
MLA acronym: Q&F

SUBSCRIPTION INFORMATION

Frequency of publication: 4 times/yr.
Circulation: 400
Available in microform: No
Subscription price: $20.00/yr. US; $25.00/yr. Canada; $30.00/yr. elsewhere
Year to which price refers: 1992

ADVERTISING INFORMATION

Advertising accepted: Yes
Advertising rates: $75.00/quarter page, 4 issues; $150.00/half page, 4 issues; $300.00/full page, 4 issues

EDITORIAL DESCRIPTION

Scope: Publishes articles on Arthurian studies.
Reviews books: Yes
Publishes notes: Yes
Languages accepted: English
Prints abstracts: No
Author-anonymous submission: No

SUBMISSION REQUIREMENTS

Author pays submission fee: No
Author pays page charges: No
Length of articles: 10,000 words
Length of book reviews: 2,500 words
Length of notes: 2,000 words
Style: MLA
Number of copies required: 2
Copyright ownership: Journal & author
Rejected manuscripts: Returned
Time before publication decision: 2 mos.

Time between decision and publication: 4 mos.
Number of reviewers: 2
Articles submitted per year: 55
Articles published per year: 30
Book reviews submitted per year: 30
Book reviews published per year: 20

(2293)
*The Rackham Journal of the Arts and Humanities

Thomas Mussio, Editor
411 Mason Hall
Univ. of Michigan
Ann Arbor, MI 48109

First published: 1971
Sponsoring organization: Univ. of Michigan, Graduate School
ISSN: 0731-4817
MLA acronym: RaJAH

SUBSCRIPTION INFORMATION

Frequency of publication: Annual
Circulation: 300
Available in microform: No

ADVERTISING INFORMATION

Advertising accepted: Yes

EDITORIAL DESCRIPTION

Scope: Publishes articles on interdisciplinary and comparative literature studies. Invites essays on the language, literature, and art of all cultures, translations, original poetry, dramas, and short stories.
Reviews books: No
Publishes notes: No
Languages accepted: English; French; German; Spanish; Italian
Prints abstracts: No
Author-anonymous submission: No

SUBMISSION REQUIREMENTS

Restrictions on contributors: Contributors are primarily graduate students at the Univ. of Michigan.
Author pays submission fee: No
Author pays page charges: No
Length of articles: 10-25 pp.
Style: MLA
Number of copies required: 2
Copyright ownership: Journal
Rejected manuscripts: Returned; enclose SASE.
Time before publication decision: 4-6 mos.
Time between decision and publication: 3-4 mos.
Number of reviewers: 6-7
Articles submitted per year: 35-40
Articles published per year: 4-5

(2294)
Rad Jugoslavenske Akademije Znanosti i Umjetnosti

Jugoslavenske Akademija Znanosti i Umjetnosti
Zrinski trg 11
41000 Zagreb, Croatia

First published: 1867
ISSN: 0375-1015
MLA acronym: Rad

SUBSCRIPTION INFORMATION

Frequency of publication: Irregular

EDITORIAL DESCRIPTION

Scope: Publishes scientific works of the Yugoslav Academy members as well as those of other scientists.
Reviews books: No
Prints abstracts: Yes

SUBMISSION REQUIREMENTS

Restrictions on contributors: None
Length of articles: No restrictions
Style: None
Number of copies required: 1

(2295)
*Radovi Zavoda za Slavensku Filologiju

Zavod za Slavensku Filologiju, Filozofski Fak.
Univ. of Zagreb
Dure Salaja 3
41000 Zagreb, Croatia

Telephone: (38) 41 620111
Fax: (38) 41 513834
First published: 1956
Sponsoring organization: Ministarstvo Znanosti, Tehnologije & Informatike, Republike Hrvatske, Zagreb
ISSN: 0514-5090
MLA acronym: RZSF

SUBSCRIPTION INFORMATION

Frequency of publication: Annual
Available in microform: No
Subscription telephone: (38) 41 620035

ADVERTISING INFORMATION

Advertising accepted: No

EDITORIAL DESCRIPTION

Scope: Publishes articles on Slavic studies.
Reviews books: Yes
Languages accepted: Slavic languages
Prints abstracts: Yes
Author-anonymous submission: No

SUBMISSION REQUIREMENTS

Author pays submission fee: No
Author pays page charges: No
Length of articles: No restrictions
Length of book reviews: No restrictions
Style: MLA
Number of copies required: 1
Copyright ownership: Author
Rejected manuscripts: Returned
Time before publication decision: 6 mos.
Time between decision and publication: 6 mos.
Number of reviewers: 3

(2296)
Raduga

Viktor Kondratenko, Editor
Izdatel'stvo Radianskii Pismennik
Bul'var Lesi Ukrainki, 20
Kiev, Ukraine

First published: 1950
ISSN: 0033-8591
MLA acronym: Raduga

SUBSCRIPTION INFORMATION

Frequency of publication: 12 times/yr.
Circulation: 15,131
Subscription address: Soiuz Pisatelei Ukraïny, ul. Pushkinskaia 32, Kiev, Ukraine

EDITORIAL DESCRIPTION

Scope: Publishes articles on Ukrainian language and literature.
Reviews books: Yes
Languages accepted: Russian

(2297)
*Raft: A Journal of Armenian Poetry and Criticism

Vahé Oshagan & John A. C. Greppin, Editors
Program in Linguistics
Cleveland State Univ.
Cleveland, OH 44115

Additional editorial address: Vahé Oshagan, 11/635 Pacific Highway, Killara, NSW 2071, Australia
Telephone: 216 687-3967; (61) 2 4988342
Fax: 216 687-9366
E-mail: R0946@CSUOHIO
First published: 1987
ISSN: 0891-0545
MLA acronym: Raft

SUBSCRIPTION INFORMATION

Frequency of publication: Annual
Circulation: 210
Available in microform: No
Subscription price: $30.00/2 yrs. institutions; $17.50/2 yrs. individuals
Year to which price refers: 1992

ADVERTISING INFORMATION

Advertising accepted: Yes

EDITORIAL DESCRIPTION

Scope: Publishes Armenian poetry and criticism.
Reviews books: Yes
Publishes notes: Yes
Languages accepted: English
Prints abstracts: No
Author-anonymous submission: Yes, frequently

SUBMISSION REQUIREMENTS

Restrictions on contributors: Book reviews are solicited.
Author pays submission fee: No
Author pays page charges: No
Length of articles: 10-15 pp.
Length of book reviews: 3-5 pp.
Length of notes: 1,000 words maximum
Style: Chicago
Number of copies required: 1
Copyright ownership: Journal
Rejected manuscripts: Returned
Time before publication decision: 2-4
Time between decision and publication: 1 yr.
Number of reviewers: 2
Articles submitted per year: 10-12
Articles published per year: 4-5
Book reviews submitted per year: 3-4
Book reviews published per year: 3-4

(2298)
*Il Ragguaglio Librario: Rassegna Mensile Bibliografica Culturale

Giulio Madurini, Editor
Via G. Terruggia, 14
20162 Milan, Italy

Telephone: (39) 2 6473600
Fax: (39) 2 6610305
First published: 1933
ISSN: 0033-8648
MLA acronym: RagL

SUBSCRIPTION INFORMATION

Frequency of publication: 10 times/yr.
Available in microform: No
Subscription price: 50,000 Lit/yr. Italy; 60,000 Lit/yr. elsewhere
Year to which price refers: 1993

ADVERTISING INFORMATION

Advertising accepted: Yes

EDITORIAL DESCRIPTION

Scope: Publishes cultural bibliographies.
Reviews books: Yes
Publishes notes: No
Languages accepted: Italian; Spanish
Prints abstracts: No
Author-anonymous submission: No

SUBMISSION REQUIREMENTS

Restrictions on contributors: Unsolicited manuscripts are not accepted.
Author pays submission fee: No
Author pays page charges: No

(2299)
Raiṇa Gadagrāmata

Saulcerite Viese, Editor
Padomju bulvāris 24
Riga, Latvia

First published: 1975
Sponsoring organization: "Liesma" Publishing House
MLA acronym: RGad

SUBSCRIPTION INFORMATION

Frequency of publication: Annual
Subscription address: Victor Kamkin, Inc., 4956 Boiling Brook Pkwy., Rockville, MD 20852

EDITORIAL DESCRIPTION

Scope: Publishes articles on the literary heritage of Janis Rainis and Aspazija.
Reviews books: No
Languages accepted: Latvian
Prints abstracts: No

(2300)
Rajasthan University Studies in English

Jasbir Jain & A. Janakiram, Editors
Dept. of English
Rajasthan Univ.
Jaipur 302004, India

First published: 1963
Sponsoring organization: Univ. of Rajasthan
ISSN: 0448-1690
MLA acronym: RUSEng

SUBSCRIPTION INFORMATION

Frequency of publication: Annual
Circulation: 500
Available in microform: No

ADVERTISING INFORMATION

Advertising accepted: No

EDITORIAL DESCRIPTION

Scope: Publishes scholarly articles on literature and allied fields, especially on English, American, comparative, and Commonwealth literatures.
Reviews books: Yes
Publishes notes: Yes
Languages accepted: English
Prints abstracts: No
Author-anonymous submission: No

SUBMISSION REQUIREMENTS

Restrictions on contributors: None
Author pays submission fee: No
Author pays page charges: No
Length of articles: 5,000 words maximum
Length of book reviews: 250 words
Length of notes: 1,000 words
Style: MLA
Number of copies required: 1
Special requirements: Include a 200-word abstract.
Copyright ownership: Author
Rejected manuscripts: Not returned
Time before publication decision: 2 mos.
Time between decision and publication: 8 mos.
Number of reviewers: 2
Articles submitted per year: 30
Articles published per year: 12
Book reviews submitted per year: 8
Book reviews published per year: 4
Notes submitted per year: 4
Notes published per year: 2

(2301)
*Rapport d'Activités de l'Institut de Phonétique

M. Max Wajskop, Editor
Inst. de Phonetique
Univ. Libre de Bruxelles, C.P. 110
Ave. Franklin D. Roosevelt, 50
1050 Brussels, Belgium

Telephone: (32) 2 6422010
Fax: (32) 2 6422007
First published: 1967
Sponsoring organization: Univ. Libre de Bruxelles; Dept. of National Education
ISSN: 0777-3692
MLA acronym: RAIP

SUBSCRIPTION INFORMATION

Frequency of publication: Annual
Circulation: 350
Available in microform: No
Subscription price: Free
Year to which price refers: 1992

ADVERTISING INFORMATION

Advertising accepted: No

EDITORIAL DESCRIPTION

Scope: Publishes preliminary reports of research done by collaborators at the Institut de Phonetique. Includes articles on linguistics, language teaching, second language acquisition, phonetics, and speech perception.
Reviews books: No
Publishes notes: No
Languages accepted: Dutch; English; French
Prints abstracts: Yes
Author-anonymous submission: No

SUBMISSION REQUIREMENTS

Restrictions on contributors: Contributors must be members of the Univ. Libre de Bruxelles and/or formally linked to their research activities.
Author pays submission fee: No
Author pays page charges: No
Length of articles: No restrictions
Number of copies required: 2
Special requirements: Submit abstract in French and English.
Copyright ownership: Journal
Rejected manuscripts: Returned
Time before publication decision: 2 mos.
Number of reviewers: 2
Articles submitted per year: 10
Articles published per year: 7

(2302)
*Rare Books & Manuscripts Librarianship

Alice Schreyer, Editor
Special Collections
Univ. of Chicago Library
1100 E. 57th St.
Chicago, IL 60637

Additional editorial address: James N. Green, Book Review Editor, Library Company of Philadelphia, 1314 Locust St., Philadelphia, PA 19107-5698
Telephone: 312 702-8705
Fax: 312 702-0853
E-mail: Ads8@midway.uchicago.edu
First published: 1986
Sponsoring organization: Assn. of College & Research Libraries, American Library Assn.
ISSN: 0884-450X
MLA acronym: RBML

SUBSCRIPTION INFORMATION

Frequency of publication: 2 times/yr.
Circulation: 500
Available in microform: No
Subscription price: $30.00/yr. institutions; $25.00/yr. individuals
Year to which price refers: 1991
Subscription address: American Library Assn., 50 E. Huron St., Chicago, IL 60611

ADVERTISING INFORMATION

Advertising accepted: Yes

EDITORIAL DESCRIPTION

Scope: Publishes articles and reviews relating to the theory and practice of rare books and manuscripts librarianship. Includes works on acquisition and collection development, conservation, cataloguing, and computer applications in addition to other topics in librarianship.
Reviews books: Yes
Publishes notes: Yes
Languages accepted: English
Prints abstracts: No
Author-anonymous submission: Yes

SUBMISSION REQUIREMENTS

Restrictions on contributors: None
Author pays submission fee: No
Author pays page charges: No
Length of articles: 3,000-5,000 words
Length of book reviews: 500-1,000 words
Length of notes: 1,000 words
Style: Chicago
Number of copies required: 3
Special requirements: Submit original, camera-ready art for illustrations, figures, and graphs.
Copyright ownership: American Library Assn.
Rejected manuscripts: Returned
Time before publication decision: 6-8 weeks
Time between decision and publication: 6-9 mos.
Number of reviewers: 2
Articles submitted per year: 15-25
Articles published per year: 8-10
Book reviews published per year: 10-12
Notes published per year: 2-3

(2303)
*Raritan: A Quarterly Review

Richard Poirier, Editor
31 Milne St.
New Brunswick, NJ 08903

Telephone: 908 932-7887
Fax: 908 932-7855
First published: 1981
Sponsoring organization: Rutgers Univ.
ISSN: 0275-1607

MLA acronym: Raritan

SUBSCRIPTION INFORMATION

Frequency of publication: 4 times/yr.
Circulation: 3,500
Available in microform: Yes
Subscription price: $20.00/yr. institutions; $16.00/yr. individuals
Year to which price refers: 1991-92

ADVERTISING INFORMATION

Advertising accepted: Yes
Advertising rates: $275.00/full page; $325.00/cover

EDITORIAL DESCRIPTION

Scope: Publishes critical and theoretical essays and review articles on works, authors, and intellectual movements. Also publishes fiction and poetry.
Reviews books: Yes
Publishes notes: No
Languages accepted: English
Prints abstracts: No
Author-anonymous submission: No

SUBMISSION REQUIREMENTS

Restrictions on contributors: None
Author pays submission fee: No
Author pays page charges: No
Length of articles: 25 pp.
Length of book reviews: 20 pp.
Style: Chicago
Number of copies required: 1
Copyright ownership: Journal or author by request
Rejected manuscripts: Returned; enclose SASE.
Time before publication decision: 6 weeks
Time between decision and publication: 9 mos.
Number of reviewers: 4
Articles submitted per year: 200
Articles published per year: 25-30
Book reviews submitted per year: 25
Book reviews published per year: 15

(2304)
Rassegna della Letteratura Italiana

Walter Binni, Editor
Dpto. di Italianistica
Fac. di Lettere
Univ. di Roma
Rome, Italy

First published: 1893
ISSN: 0033-9423
MLA acronym: RLI

SUBSCRIPTION INFORMATION

Frequency of publication: 3 times/yr.
Circulation: 2,000
Available in microform: No
Subscription address: Casa Editrice G. C. Sansoni, Editore Nuova S.p.A., Via Benedetto Varchi 47, 50132 Florence, Italy

ADVERTISING INFORMATION

Advertising accepted: Yes

EDITORIAL DESCRIPTION

Scope: Publishes studies of Italian literature from a historical-critical point of view.
Reviews books: Yes
Publishes notes: Yes
Languages accepted: Italian
Prints abstracts: Yes

SUBMISSION REQUIREMENTS

Restrictions on contributors: None
Author pays submission fee: No
Length of articles: No restrictions

Style: None
Number of copies required: 1
Copyright ownership: Editor
Time before publication decision: 2 mos.
Time between decision and publication: 3 mos.
Number of reviewers: 1
Articles published per year: 20
Book reviews published per year: 350
Notes published per year: 12

(2305)
*Rassegna Iberistica

Franco Meregalli & Giuseppe Bellini, Editors
Dipt. di Iberistica
Fac. di Lingue e Letterature Straniere
Univ. degli Studi
S. Marco 3417, 30124 Venice, Italy

Telephone: (39) 41 5298458
Fax: (39) 41 5298427
First published: 1978
Sponsoring organization: Consiglio Nazionale delle Ricerche
ISSN: 0392-4777
MLA acronym: RIber

SUBSCRIPTION INFORMATION

Frequency of publication: 3 times/yr.
Available in microform: No
Subscription address: Bulzoni Editore, Via dei Liburni 14, 00185 Rome, Italy

ADVERTISING INFORMATION

Advertising accepted: Yes, on an exchange basis

EDITORIAL DESCRIPTION

Scope: Publishes articles and reviews on Iberian studies.
Reviews books: Yes
Publishes notes: No
Languages accepted: Italian; Portuguese; Spanish; Catalan
Prints abstracts: No
Author-anonymous submission: No

SUBMISSION REQUIREMENTS

Restrictions on contributors: Unsolicited manuscripts are not accepted.
Author pays submission fee: No
Author pays page charges: No
Length of articles: 6,000-8,000 words maximum
Length of book reviews: 2,400 words maximum
Style: MLA
Number of copies required: 1
Copyright ownership: Reverts to author after 1 yr.
Rejected manuscripts: Not returned
Time before publication decision: 6 mos.
Time between decision and publication: 3-4 mos.
Number of reviewers: 2
Articles published per year: 6
Book reviews published per year: 90

(2306)
*Rassegna Italiana di Linguistica Applicata

Renzo Titone, Editor
Via Madesimo 22
00135 Rome, Italy

Telephone: (39) 6 3016669
Fax: (39) 6 4462062
First published: 1968
Sponsoring organization: Centro Italiano di Linguistica Applicata
ISSN: 0033-9725
MLA acronym: RILA

SUBSCRIPTION INFORMATION

Frequency of publication: 3 times/yr.
Circulation: 2,000
Available in microform: No
Subscription price: 48,000 Lit/yr. Italy; 70,000 Lit/yr. elsewhere
Year to which price refers: 1991
Subscription address: Bulzoni Editore, Via dei Liburni, 14, 00185 Rome, Italy
Subscription fax: (39) 6 4450355

ADVERTISING INFORMATION

Advertising accepted: Yes

EDITORIAL DESCRIPTION

Scope: Publishes articles on applied linguistics.
Reviews books: Yes
Publishes notes: Yes
Languages accepted: English; French; Italian; Spanish; German
Prints abstracts: Yes
Author-anonymous submission: No

SUBMISSION REQUIREMENTS

Author pays submission fee: No
Author pays page charges: No
Length of articles: 5,000-10,000 words
Length of book reviews: 500 words
Length of notes: 300 words
Style: None
Number of copies required: 1
Copyright ownership: Bulzoni Editore
Rejected manuscripts: Not returned
Time before publication decision: 3 mos.
Time between decision and publication: 4 mos.
Number of reviewers: 4
Articles submitted per year: 80-90
Articles published per year: 50-60
Book reviews submitted per year: 100
Book reviews published per year: 60-70
Notes submitted per year: 20
Notes published per year: 15

(2307)
*Rassegna Storica del Risorgimento

Emilia Morelli, Editor
Ist. per la Storia del Risorgimento Italiano
Vittoriano Piazza Venezia
00186 Rome, Italy

Telephone: (39) 6 6793526; (39) 6 6793598
First published: 1914
Sponsoring organization: Ist. per la Storia del Risorgimento
ISSN: 0033-9873
MLA acronym: RSR

SUBSCRIPTION INFORMATION

Frequency of publication: 4 times/yr.
Circulation: 3,700
Available in microform: No
Subscription price: 50,000 Lit/yr. Italy; 60,000 Lit/yr. elsewhere
Year to which price refers: 1992

ADVERTISING INFORMATION

Advertising accepted: No

EDITORIAL DESCRIPTION

Scope: Publishes articles on 18th- and 19th-century Italian history.
Reviews books: Yes
Publishes notes: Yes
Languages accepted: Italian; French; English; Spanish
Prints abstracts: No
Author-anonymous submission: No

SUBMISSION REQUIREMENTS

Restrictions on contributors: None

Author pays submission fee: No
Author pays page charges: No
Length of articles: 20-30 pp.
Length of book reviews: 2 pp.
Style: None
Number of copies required: 1
Copyright ownership: Journal
Rejected manuscripts: Not returned
Time before publication decision: 1 mo.
Time between decision and publication: 6-8 mos.
Number of reviewers: 5
Articles submitted per year: 30-40
Articles published per year: 20-25
Book reviews submitted per year: 100-120
Book reviews published per year: 70-80
Notes submitted per year: 10
Notes published per year: 8

(2308)
Razgledi: Spisanie za Literatura Umetnost i Kultura

Danilo Kocevski, Editor
ul. "Ruzveltova" br. 8
Poštanski fah 345
91000 Skopje, Macedonia (Yugoslavia)

First published: 1959
ISSN: 0034-0227
MLA acronym: Razgledi

SUBSCRIPTION INFORMATION

Frequency of publication: 10 times/yr.
Circulation: 1,000

EDITORIAL DESCRIPTION

Scope: Publishes poems, stories, essays, criticism, literary history, and reviews (mostly of Yugoslav books).
Reviews books: Yes
Languages accepted: Macedonian
Prints abstracts: No

(2309)
*Razón y Fe: Revista Hispanoamericana de Cultura

Juan García-Pérez, Editor
Pablo Aranda, 3
28006 Madrid, Spain

Telephone: (34) 1 5624930
Fax: (34) 1 5634073
First published: 1901
Sponsoring organization: Casa de Escritores S.I.
ISSN: 0034-0235
MLA acronym: RyF

SUBSCRIPTION INFORMATION

Frequency of publication: 10 times/yr.
Circulation: 3,500
Available in microform: No
Subscription price: $58.00/yr.
Year to which price refers: 1992

ADVERTISING INFORMATION

Advertising accepted: Yes

EDITORIAL DESCRIPTION

Scope: Publishes articles on any aspect of culture related to actual problems treated from a Christian perspective.
Reviews books: Yes
Publishes notes: Yes
Languages accepted: Spanish
Prints abstracts: Yes
Author-anonymous submission: No

SUBMISSION REQUIREMENTS

Author pays submission fee: No
Author pays page charges: No
Length of articles: 10-15 pp.
Length of book reviews: 400 words
Length of notes: 3,000-3,500 words
Number of copies required: 1
Special requirements: Submit original typescript.
Copyright ownership: Journal
Rejected manuscripts: Returned
Time before publication decision: 2 weeks
Time between decision and publication: 2 mos.
Number of reviewers: 2-3
Articles submitted per year: 50-60
Articles published per year: 40-45
Book reviews published per year: 250-300
Notes published per year: 60-70

(2310)
*Razprave Razreda za Filološke in Literarne vede Slovenske Akademije Znanosti in Umetnosti

Slovenska Akademija Znanosti in Umetnosti
Novi trg 3
61000 Ljubljana, Slovenia

Telephone: (38) 61 156068
Fax: (38) 61 155232
First published: 1950
Sponsoring organization: Slovenska Akademija Znanosti in Umetnosti
ISSN: 0560-2920
MLA acronym: Raz SAZU

SUBSCRIPTION INFORMATION

Frequency of publication: Irregular
Circulation: 800
Available in microform: No
Subscription address: Cankarjeva Zalozba, Trg osvoboditve 7, 61000 Ljubljana, Slovenia
Subscription telephone: (38) 61 310791
Subscription fax: (38) 61 318782

ADVERTISING INFORMATION

Advertising accepted: No

EDITORIAL DESCRIPTION

Scope: Publishes articles on linguistics and literatures.
Reviews books: No
Publishes notes: No
Languages accepted: Slovenian
Prints abstracts: Yes

SUBMISSION REQUIREMENTS

Restrictions on contributors: None
Author pays submission fee: No
Author pays page charges: No
Length of articles: No restrictions
Style: None
Number of copies required: 1
Rejected manuscripts: Returned

(2311)
*RE Arts & Letters: A Liberal Arts Forum

Lee Schultz, Editor
School of Liberal Arts
Stephen F. Austin State Univ.
P.O. Box 13007, SFA Station
Nacogdoches, TX 75962

Telephone: 409 568-2101
First published: 1968
Sponsoring organization: Stephen F. Austin State Univ., School of Liberal Arts
ISSN: 0034-0286
MLA acronym: REAL

SUBSCRIPTION INFORMATION

Frequency of publication: 2 times/yr. (Fall, Spring)
Circulation: 400
Available in microform: No
Subscription price: $12.00/yr. institutions; $10.00/yr. individuals
Year to which price refers: 1993

ADVERTISING INFORMATION

Advertising accepted: No

EDITORIAL DESCRIPTION

Scope: Essays are invited from the liberal arts disciplines, anthropology, geography, history, languages, literature, philosophy, political science, psychology, religion, and sociology. Original poetry and short works of drama and fiction are also invited. Articles are reviewed based on the intrinsic merit of the scholarship and creative work and the appeal to a sophisticated international readership. No regional or other restrictions as to origins or content are imposed.
Reviews books: Yes
Publishes notes: Yes
Languages accepted: English; Spanish
Prints abstracts: No
Author-anonymous submission: Yes

SUBMISSION REQUIREMENTS

Restrictions on contributors: None
Author pays submission fee: No
Author pays page charges: No
Length of articles: 7,000 words maximum
Length of book reviews: 1,000-3,000 words
Length of notes: 500-1,000 words
Style: MLA
Number of copies required: 2
Special requirements: Query editor prior to submitting book reviews.
Copyright ownership: School of Liberal Arts, Stephen F. Austin Univ.; reverts to author after publication.
Rejected manuscripts: Returned; enclose return postage.
Time before publication decision: 1 mo.
Time between decision and publication: 6-12 mos.
Number of reviewers: 3
Articles submitted per year: 110
Articles published per year: 4-8
Book reviews published per year: 2-6
Notes submitted per year: 15-20
Notes published per year: 4

(2312)
*Reader: Essays in Reader-Oriented Theory, Criticism, and Pedagogy

Elizabeth A. Flynn & John Clifford, Editors
Dept. of Humanities
Michigan Technological Univ.
Houghton, MI 49931

Additional editorial address: Send submissions to: John Clifford, Dept. of English, Univ. of North Carolina, Wilmington, NC 28403
Telephone: 906 487-2447
First published: 1976
Sponsoring organization: Michigan Technological Univ.
ISSN: 0742-9681
MLA acronym: Reader

SUBSCRIPTION INFORMATION

Frequency of publication: 2 times/yr. (Fall, Spring)
Available in microform: No
Subscription price: $10.00/yr. institutions US; $12.00/yr. institutions elsewhere; $8.00/yr. individuals US; $10.00/yr. individuals elsewhere
Year to which price refers: 1992

ADVERTISING INFORMATION

Advertising accepted: Yes
Advertising rates: $100.00/full page

EDITORIAL DESCRIPTION

Scope: Publishes articles on reader-response theory, criticism, and pedagogy.
Reviews books: Yes
Publishes notes: Yes
Languages accepted: English
Prints abstracts: No
Author-anonymous submission: Yes

SUBMISSION REQUIREMENTS

Author pays submission fee: No
Author pays page charges: No
Length of articles: 20 double-spaced typescript pp. maximum
Length of book reviews: 500 words
Length of notes: 100 words
Style: MLA
Number of copies required: 3
Special requirements: Submit original typescript and 2 copies, as well as an IBM- or Macintosh-compatible diskette if possible.
Rejected manuscripts: Returned; enclose SASE.
Time before publication decision: 1-6 mos.
Time between decision and publication: 3-12 mos.
Number of reviewers: 2-3
Articles submitted per year: 20-30
Articles published per year: 8-10

(2313)
*Reading and Writing: An Interdisciplinary Journal

R. Malatesha Joshi, Editor
Reading Center
104 Gundersen Hall
College of Education
Oklahoma State Univ.
Stillwater, OK 74078-0146

Telephone: 405 744-8043
Fax: 405 744-7713
First published: 1989
ISSN: 0922-4777
MLA acronym: R&W

SUBSCRIPTION INFORMATION

Frequency of publication: 4 times/yr.
Available in microform: Yes
Subscription price: 282 f ($143.00)/yr. institutions; 141 f ($72.00)/yr. individuals
Year to which price refers: 1992
Subscription address: Kluwer Academic Publishers, P.O. Box 17, 3300 AA Dordrecht, Netherlands
Additional subscription address: Kluwer Academic Publishers, P.O. Box 358 Accord Station, Hingham, MA 02018-0358
Subscription telephone: (31) 78 334911
Subscription fax: (31) 78 334254

ADVERTISING INFORMATION

Advertising accepted: Yes

EDITORIAL DESCRIPTION

Scope: Publishes scientific articles pertaining to the processes, acquisition, and the loss of reading and writing skills. Some topics covered include: models of reading and writing; diagnosis and remediation of reading, writing, and spelling at all ages; orthography and its relation to reading and writing; computer literacy; cross-cultural studies; and developmental and acquired disorders of reading and writing.
Reviews books: Yes
Publishes notes: Yes
Languages accepted: English
Prints abstracts: Yes
Author-anonymous submission: Yes

SUBMISSION REQUIREMENTS

Author pays submission fee: No
Author pays page charges: No
Style: American Psychological Assn.
Special requirements: Submit original typescript and 2 copies.
Copyright ownership: Kluwer Academic Publishers
Time between decision and publication: 6 mos.
Number of reviewers: 2
Articles submitted per year: 80
Articles published per year: 24
Book reviews submitted per year: 5
Book reviews published per year: 2
Notes submitted per year: 15
Notes published per year: 2

(2314)
*Reading Medieval Studies

P. S. Noble, A. K. Bate, & A. Curry, Editors
Graduate Center for Medieval Studies
Univ. of Reading
Berkshire, RG6 2AH, Reading, England

Telephone: (44) 734 318124
First published: 1975
Sponsoring organization: Univ. of Reading, Graduate Center for Medieval Studies
ISSN: 0950-3129
MLA acronym: RMSt

SUBSCRIPTION INFORMATION

Frequency of publication: Annual (Oct.-Nov.)
Circulation: 120
Available in microform: No
Subscription price: £9.00/yr.
Year to which price refers: 1992

ADVERTISING INFORMATION

Advertising accepted: No

EDITORIAL DESCRIPTION

Scope: Publishes articles on medieval studies, especially history, literature, philosophy, and art.
Reviews books: Yes
Publishes notes: Yes
Languages accepted: English
Prints abstracts: No
Author-anonymous submission: No

SUBMISSION REQUIREMENTS

Restrictions on contributors: None
Author pays submission fee: No
Author pays page charges: No
Length of articles: No restrictions
Length of book reviews: 500 words
Length of notes: No restrictions
Style: MLA
Number of copies required: 1
Copyright ownership: Univ. of Reading, Graduate Center for Medieval Studies
Rejected manuscripts: Returned
Time before publication decision: 3 mos.
Time between decision and publication: 1 yr.
Number of reviewers: 2
Articles submitted per year: 5
Articles published per year: 4-7
Book reviews published per year: 2-3
Notes published per year: 1

(2315)
*Reading Psychology: An International Quarterly

William H. Rupley, Editor
Dept. Edc 1
College of Education
Texas A&M Univ.
College Station, TX 77843

Telephone: 409 845-7093
Fax: 409 845-9663
First published: 1979
Sponsoring organization: Texas A&M Univ.
ISSN: 0270-2711
MLA acronym: RPsych

SUBSCRIPTION INFORMATION

Frequency of publication: 4 times/yr.
Circulation: 1,200
Available in microform: Yes
Subscription address: Hemisphere Publishing Corp., 79 Madison Ave., Suite 1110, New York, NY 10016-7892

ADVERTISING INFORMATION

Advertising accepted: Yes

EDITORIAL DESCRIPTION

Scope: Publishes papers in the field of reading and related psychological disciplines. The focus is on psychology of reading, the reader, and reading instruction.
Reviews books: Yes
Publishes notes: Yes
Languages accepted: English
Prints abstracts: Yes
Author-anonymous submission: Yes

SUBMISSION REQUIREMENTS

Restrictions on contributors: Reviews are solicited.
Author pays submission fee: No
Author pays page charges: No
Length of articles: 10-20 pp.
Length of book reviews: 1,000 words maximum
Length of notes: 100 words maximum
Style: American Psychological Assn.
Number of copies required: 3
Special requirements: Include abstract.
Copyright ownership: Hemisphere Publishing Corp.
Rejected manuscripts: Returned; enclose SASE.
Time before publication decision: 3 mos.
Time between decision and publication: 6 mos.
Number of reviewers: 3
Articles submitted per year: 175
Articles published per year: 16-20
Book reviews submitted per year: 35
Book reviews published per year: 12-15
Notes submitted per year: 10
Notes published per year: 10

(2316)
*Reading Research Quarterly

Michael L. Kamil, Robert J. Tierney, & Judith Green, Editors
257 Arps Hall
Ohio State Univ.
1945 N. High St.
Colombus, OH 43210

Telephone: 614 292-1257
Fax: 614 292-7695
E-mail: READING@OHSTMVSA.BITNET
First published: 1965
Sponsoring organization: International Reading Assn.
ISSN: 0034-0553
MLA acronym: RRQ

SUBSCRIPTION INFORMATION

Frequency of publication: 4 times/yr. (Winter, Spring, Summer, Fall)
Circulation: 10,000
Available in microform: No
Subscription address: International Reading Assn., 800 Barksdale Rd., P.O. Box 8139, Newark, DE 19714-8139

ADVERTISING INFORMATION

Advertising accepted: No

EDITORIAL DESCRIPTION

Scope: Provides a forum for reading research and theories of the reading process.
Reviews books: No
Publishes notes: No
Languages accepted: All languages
Prints abstracts: Yes
Author-anonymous submission: Yes

SUBMISSION REQUIREMENTS

Restrictions on contributors: None
Author pays submission fee: No
Author pays page charges: No
Length of articles: No restrictions
Style: American Psychological Assn., 3rd ed.
Number of copies required: 7 for US; 1 elsewhere
Special requirements: An abstract must be included.
Copyright ownership: International Reading Assn.
Rejected manuscripts: Not returned.
Time before publication decision: 3-4 mos.
Time between decision and publication: 6 mos.
Number of reviewers: 3 minimum
Articles submitted per year: 150
Articles published per year: 24

(2317)
*REAL: The Yearbook of Research in English and American Literature

Herbert Grabes, Hans-Jürgen Diller, & Hartwig Isernhagen, Editors
Inst. für Anglistik & Amerikanistik der Univ. Giessen
Otto-Behaghel-Str. 10
6300 Giessen, Germany

Telephone: (49) 641 7025562
Fax: (49) 641 7025998
First published: 1982
Sponsoring organization: Franz Vogt Stiftung
ISSN: 0723-0338
MLA acronym: REALB

SUBSCRIPTION INFORMATION

Frequency of publication: Annual
Circulation: 265
Available in microform: No
Subscription address: Gunter Narr Verlag, Dischingerweg 5, 7400 Tübingen 5-Hirschau, Germany

ADVERTISING INFORMATION

Advertising accepted: Yes

EDITORIAL DESCRIPTION

Scope: Publishes research studies in English and American literature, other literatures written in English, philology (poetics, rhetoric, textual criticism), and the history of ideas.
Reviews books: No
Publishes notes: No
Languages accepted: English
Prints abstracts: No
Author-anonymous submission: No

SUBMISSION REQUIREMENTS

Restrictions on contributors: None
Author pays submission fee: No
Author pays page charges: No
Length of articles: 50 double-spaced typescript pp. maximum
Style: MLA
Number of copies required: 2
Special requirements: Include notes at end.
Copyright ownership: Reverts to author after 1 yr.
Rejected manuscripts: Returned
Time before publication decision: 3 mos. maximum
Time between decision and publication: 6-8 mos.
Number of reviewers: 3-5
Articles submitted per year: 50
Articles published per year: 9-10

(2318)
*Reappraisals: Canadian Writers

Lorraine McMullen, Editor
Dept. of English
Univ. of Ottawa
Ottawa, Ontario K1N 6N5, Canada

Telephone: 613 564-3411
Fax: 613 564-9175
First published: 1974
Sponsoring organization: Dept. of English, Univ. of Ottawa
MLA acronym: ReapprC

SUBSCRIPTION INFORMATION

Frequency of publication: Annual
Available in microform: No
Subscription address: Univ. of Ottawa Press, 603 Cumberland, Ottawa, Ontario K1N 6N5, Canada
Subscription telephone: 613 564-2270
Subscription fax: 613 564-9284

ADVERTISING INFORMATION

Advertising accepted: No

EDITORIAL DESCRIPTION

Scope: Publishes collections of articles on Canadian literature and writers.
Reviews books: No
Publishes notes: No
Languages accepted: English
Prints abstracts: No
Author-anonymous submission: No

SUBMISSION REQUIREMENTS

Restrictions on contributors: Contributors must have presented paper at the symposia on Canadian writers of the Department of English, University of Ottawa.
Author pays submission fee: No
Author pays page charges: No
Length of articles: 3,500-8,000 words
Length of books: 200-220 pp.
Style: MLA
Number of copies required: 1
Copyright ownership: Author
Rejected manuscripts: Returned
Time before publication decision: 8-12 mos.
Time between decision and publication: 8-10 mos.
Number of reviewers: 4
Articles published per year: 12-15
Books submitted per year: 1
Books published per year: 1

(2319)
Recherches Anglaises et Nord-Américaines

A. Bleikasten, Editor
Univ. des Sciences Humaines de Strasbourg
22, rue Descartes
67084 Strasbourg, France

Telephone: (33) 88417317
Fax: (33) 88417354
First published: 1987
Sponsoring organization: Univ. des Sciences Humaines de Strasbourg
ISSN: 0557-6989
MLA acronym: RANNAM

SUBSCRIPTION INFORMATION

Frequency of publication: Annual
Circulation: 1,000
Available in microform: No

ADVERTISING INFORMATION

Advertising accepted: Yes

EDITORIAL DESCRIPTION

Scope: Publishes articles on the literature and culture of Britain, the United States, and other English-speaking countries.
Reviews books: No
Publishes notes: No
Languages accepted: English; French
Prints abstracts: No

SUBMISSION REQUIREMENTS

Author pays submission fee: No
Author pays page charges: No
Length of articles: 15 pp.
Style: MLA for English articles
Number of copies required: 2
Copyright ownership: Assigned by author to journal
Rejected manuscripts: Not returned
Time before publication decision: 2 mos.
Time between decision and publication: 15 mos.
Number of reviewers: 2
Articles submitted per year: 30
Articles published per year: 15

(2320)
*Recherches Augustiniennes

Etudes Augustiniennes
3, rue de l'Abbaye
75006 Paris, France

First published: 1958
ISSN: 0484-0887
MLA acronym: RechA

SUBSCRIPTION INFORMATION

Frequency of publication: Irregular
Available in microform: No
Subscription address: Ed. Brepols, 23 Rue des Grands Augustins, 75006 Paris, France
Additional subscription address: Outside France: Baron Frans, Fourstr. 8, 2300 Turnhout, Belgium

ADVERTISING INFORMATION

Advertising accepted: No

EDITORIAL DESCRIPTION

Scope: Publishes studies on classical and medieval texts.
Reviews books: No
Publishes notes: No
Languages accepted: English; French; German; Spanish; Italian
Prints abstracts: No

SUBMISSION REQUIREMENTS

Author pays submission fee: No
Author pays page charges: No
Number of copies required: 1
Time before publication decision: 2 mos.
Time between decision and publication: 6-12 mos.
Number of reviewers: 4-5
Articles published per year: 5-10

(2321)
Recherches de Science Religieuse

Joseph Moingt, Editor
15, rue Monsieur
75007 Paris, France

First published: 1910
ISSN: 0034-1258
MLA acronym: RechSR

SUBSCRIPTION INFORMATION

Frequency of publication: 4 times/yr. (Mar., June, Sept., Dec.)
Circulation: 1,700
Available in microform: No

ADVERTISING INFORMATION

Advertising accepted: No

EDITORIAL DESCRIPTION

Scope: Publishes articles on theology, exegesis, history of Christianity, philosophy, and all religious sciences.
Reviews books: Yes
Languages accepted: French
Prints abstracts: Yes

SUBMISSION REQUIREMENTS

Restrictions on contributors: None
Author pays submission fee: No
Author pays page charges: No
Length of articles: 50,000-100,000 characters
Style: Journal
Number of copies required: 1
Special requirements: Submit original typescript.
Copyright ownership: Journal
Rejected manuscripts: Not returned
Time before publication decision: 3 mos.
Time between decision and publication: 2 yrs.
Number of reviewers: 3
Articles published per year: 25
Book reviews published per year: 200

(2322)
*Recherches de Théologie Ancienne et Médiévale

D. E. Manning, Editor
Abbaye du Mont Cesar
202 Mechelse Str.
3000 Louvain, Belgium

Telephone: (32) 16 224174
Fax: (32) 16 292788
First published: 1929
ISSN: 0034-1266
MLA acronym: RTAM

SUBSCRIPTION INFORMATION

Frequency of publication: Annual
Available in microform: No
Subscription price: 950 BF ($32.00)/yr.
Year to which price refers: 1991

ADVERTISING INFORMATION

Advertising accepted: Yes

EDITORIAL DESCRIPTION

Scope: Journal publishes on the study of publications about ancient and medieval theology.
Reviews books: Yes
Publishes notes: Yes
Languages accepted: English; French; German; Italian; Spanish
Prints abstracts: Yes
Author-anonymous submission: Yes

SUBMISSION REQUIREMENTS

Author pays submission fee: No
Author pays page charges: No, unless authors want manuscripts published before assigned date.
Length of articles: No restrictions
Length of book reviews: No restrictions
Length of notes: No restrictions
Style: Scientific
Number of copies required: 1
Special requirements: Submit typescript and diskette. Authors will be asked to correct their proofs.
Copyright ownership: Journal
Rejected manuscripts: Returned at author's request
Time before publication decision: 1-2 yrs.
Time between decision and publication: 2-3 weeks
Number of reviewers: 3
Articles submitted per year: 20-25
Articles published per year: 10
Book reviews submitted per year: 30-40
Book reviews published per year: 15
Notes submitted per year: 10-15
Notes published per year: 5

(2323)
*Recherches Germaniques

Gonthier-Louis Fink, Editor
Univ. des Sciences Humaines
22, rue Descartes
67084 Strasbourg Cedex, France

Telephone: (33) 88417300 ext. 7317
First published: 1971
Sponsoring organization: Univ. des Sciences Humaines de Strasbourg
ISSN: 0399-1989
MLA acronym: RGer

SUBSCRIPTION INFORMATION

Frequency of publication: Annual
Circulation: 800
Available in microform: No

ADVERTISING INFORMATION

Advertising accepted: Yes

EDITORIAL DESCRIPTION

Scope: The journal is a scientific review of German civilization and literature. Includes articles, unpublished manuscripts, inquests, and bibliographies.
Reviews books: No
Publishes notes: Yes
Languages accepted: French; German
Prints abstracts: Yes
Author-anonymous submission: No

SUBMISSION REQUIREMENTS

Restrictions on contributors: None
Author pays submission fee: No
Author pays page charges: No
Length of articles: 20 pp.
Length of notes: 10 pp.
Number of copies required: 2
Special requirements: Supply one abstract in French and one in German; each should be 150-200 words.
Copyright ownership: Journal for 2 yrs. and then reverts to author
Rejected manuscripts: Not returned
Time before publication decision: 6 mos.
Time between decision and publication: 6-13 mos.
Number of reviewers: 2-3
Articles submitted per year: 12-15
Articles published per year: 10

(2324)
*Recherches Linguistiques de Vincennes

Nicolas Ruwet, Editor
Univ. de Paris VIII
2, rue de la Liberté
93526 Saint-Denis Cedex 02, France

Telephone: (33) 1 49406788
Fax: (33) 1 48210446
First published: 1972
ISSN: 0986-6124
MLA acronym: RLdV

SUBSCRIPTION INFORMATION

Frequency of publication: Annual
Circulation: 400
Available in microform: No
Subscription price: $30.00/2 issues
Year to which price refers: 1991-92

ADVERTISING INFORMATION

Advertising accepted: Yes
Advertising rates: 800 F/full page

EDITORIAL DESCRIPTION

Scope: Publishes articles on grammatical topics of theoretical interest. Focuses on generative grammar.
Reviews books: No
Publishes notes: No
Languages accepted: French; English
Prints abstracts: Yes
Author-anonymous submission: Yes, for nonthematic papers

SUBMISSION REQUIREMENTS

Restrictions on contributors: Articles for thematic issues are solicited.
Author pays submission fee: No
Author pays page charges: No
Length of articles: 30,000-40,000 characters
Number of copies required: 3
Copyright ownership: Editor & Presses Universitaires de Vincennes
Rejected manuscripts: Returned
Time before publication decision: 6-12 mos.
Time between decision and publication: 6-24 mos.
Number of reviewers: 2
Articles published per year: 5-8

(2325)
Recherches Sémiotiques/Semiotic Inquiry

Pierre Ouellet, Jean Fisette, & Barbara Havercroft, Editors
Dépt. d'Etudes Littéraires
Univ. du Québec à Montréal
C.P. 8888, succ. A
Montreal, Quebec H3C 3P8, Canada

First published: 1981
Sponsoring organization: Assn. Canadienne de Sémiotique/Canadian Semiotic Assn.
ISSN: 0229-8651
MLA acronym: RSSI

SUBSCRIPTION INFORMATION

Frequency of publication: 2 times/yr. (July, Dec.)

Circulation: 600
Available in microform: Yes
Subscription address: Christian Vandendorpe, Secretary (ACS/CSA), Dépt. des Lettres Françaises, Univ. of Ottawa, Ottawa, Ontario KlN 6N5, Canada

ADVERTISING INFORMATION

Advertising accepted: No

EDITORIAL DESCRIPTION

Scope: Takes the field of semiotics in the broadest sense, to include both the theoretical and empirical study of signs, sign systems and processes, signalling and communicative behavior, and their foundations: biological, socio-anthropological, linguistic, philosophical, etc. in all the domains of culture
Reviews books: Yes
Publishes notes: Yes
Languages accepted: French; English
Prints abstracts: Yes
Author-anonymous submission: No

SUBMISSION REQUIREMENTS

Restrictions on contributors: None
Author pays submission fee: No
Author pays page charges: No
Length of articles: 10,000-12,500 words
Length of book reviews: 1,000-1,500 words
Length of notes: No restrictions
Style: Journal
Number of copies required: 4
Special requirements: Submit original double-spaced typescript on standard quality paper. A short abstract (approx. 300-600 words) in the language of the article should accompany manuscript. All graphic material must be submitted camera-ready.
Copyright ownership: Canadian Semiotic Assn.
Time before publication decision: 6-8 wks.
Time between decision and publication: 6 mos.
Number of reviewers: 3
Articles submitted per year: 50
Articles published per year: 9-12
Book reviews submitted per year: 10-12
Book reviews published per year: 10
Notes submitted per year: 5
Notes published per year: 2-3

(2326)
*Recherches sur Diderot et sur l'Encyclopédie

Anne-Marie Chouillet, Editor
7, route de la Reine
92100 Boulogne, France

Telephone: (33) 1 46058175
First published: 1986
Sponsoring organization: Soc. Diderot
ISSN: 0769-0888
MLA acronym: RDidE

SUBSCRIPTION INFORMATION

Frequency of publication: 2 times/yr.
Circulation: 500
Available in microform: No
Subscription price: $50.00/yr. institutions; $40.00/yr. individuals; $20.00/single issue
Year to which price refers: 1992
Subscription address: Klincksieck, 11 rue de Lille, 75007 Paris, France
Subscription fax: (33) 1 42964063

ADVERTISING INFORMATION

Advertising accepted: Yes
Advertising rates: 1,000 F/full page

EDITORIAL DESCRIPTION

Scope: Publishes articles on Denis Diderot, l'Encyclopédie, and his other works, including literature, philosophy, and history.

Reviews books: Yes
Publishes notes: Yes
Languages accepted: French
Prints abstracts: Yes, in English
Author-anonymous submission: No

SUBMISSION REQUIREMENTS

Restrictions on contributors: None
Author pays submission fee: No
Author pays page charges: No
Length of articles: 8-45 pp.
Length of book reviews: 4 pp. maximum
Length of notes: 2 pp. maximum
Number of copies required: 2
Special requirements: Submit an abstract in English or French.
Copyright ownership: Soc. Diderot
Rejected manuscripts: Not returned
Time before publication decision: 6 mos.
Time between decision and publication: 3-24 mos.
Number of reviewers: 3
Articles submitted per year: 25
Articles published per year: 20
Book reviews submitted per year: 12
Book reviews published per year: 12

(2327)
*Recherches sur le Français Parlé

Publications de l'Univ. de Provence, Aix-Marseille 1
29, av. R.-Schuman
13621 Aix-en-Provence Cedex 1, France

Telephone: (33) 42200916
First published: 1977
Sponsoring organization: Groupe Aixois de Recherches en Syntaxe (GARS); Univ. de Provence-Aix
MLA acronym: RFP

SUBSCRIPTION INFORMATION

Frequency of publication: Annual
Circulation: 500
Available in microform: No

ADVERTISING INFORMATION

Advertising accepted: No

EDITORIAL DESCRIPTION

Scope: Publishes articles on French linguistics, in particular on aspects of spoken French.
Languages accepted: French
Author-anonymous submission: No

SUBMISSION REQUIREMENTS

Author pays submission fee: No
Author pays page charges: No
Number of copies required: 1
Copyright ownership: Publications de Univ. de Provence
Rejected manuscripts: Returned

(2328)
Recherches sur l'Imaginaire

Univ. d'Angers
Centre de Recherches en Littérature & Linguistique
2 rue Lakanal
49045 Angers Cedex, France

MLA acronym: RsLI

SUBSCRIPTION INFORMATION

Frequency of publication: Annual
Available in microform: No

ADVERTISING INFORMATION

Advertising accepted: No

EDITORIAL DESCRIPTION

Scope: Publishes research on literary anthropology in French and foreign literatures of the 19th and 20th centuries.
Reviews books: No
Publishes notes: Yes
Languages accepted: French
Prints abstracts: No

SUBMISSION REQUIREMENTS

Length of books: 15-20 pp.
Number of copies required: 1
Rejected manuscripts: Returned
Time before publication decision: 3-6 mos.
Number of reviewers: 11
Books published per year: 20

(2329)
*Records of Early English Drama Newsletter

Jo Anna Dutka, Editor
English Dept.
Erindale College
Univ. of Toronto
Mississauga, Ontario L5L 1C6, Canada

Telephone: 416 828-3737
Fax: 416 828-5202
First published: 1976
Sponsoring organization: Univ. of Toronto, Erindale College
ISSN: 0700-9283
MLA acronym: REEDN

SUBSCRIPTION INFORMATION

Frequency of publication: 2 times/yr.
Circulation: 650
Available in microform: No
Subscription price: C$7.50/yr.
Year to which price refers: 1992
Subscription address: 150 Charles St. West, Toronto M5S 1K9, Canada
Subscription telephone: 416 585-4504

ADVERTISING INFORMATION

Advertising accepted: No

EDITORIAL DESCRIPTION

Scope: Publishes articles and notes dealing with external evidence of early drama.
Reviews books: No
Publishes notes: Yes
Languages accepted: English
Prints abstracts: No
Author-anonymous submission: No

SUBMISSION REQUIREMENTS

Restrictions on contributors: None
Author pays submission fee: No
Author pays page charges: No
Length of articles: No restrictions
Length of notes: No restrictions
Style: Journal
Number of copies required: 1
Copyright ownership: Assigned by author to journal
Rejected manuscripts: Returned
Time before publication decision: 1 mo.
Time between decision and publication: 6 mos.
Number of reviewers: 2
Articles submitted per year: 5-8
Articles published per year: 4-6
Notes submitted per year: 3-5
Notes published per year: 1-2

(2330)
*Recovering Literature: A Journal of Contextualist Criticism

Gerald J. Butler, Editor
P.O. Box 805
Alpine, CA 91903

Telephone: 619 659-0291
First published: 1972
ISSN: 0300-6425
MLA acronym: RecL

SUBSCRIPTION INFORMATION

Frequency of publication: 3 times/yr.
Circulation: 250
Available in microform: No
Subscription price: $6.00/yr.
Year to which price refers: 1992

ADVERTISING INFORMATION

Advertising accepted: Yes

EDITORIAL DESCRIPTION

Scope: Publishes literary criticism from a contextualist point of view. Text is viewed as undermining myth, habitualized perceptions, and cultural attitudes.
Reviews books: Yes
Publishes notes: Yes
Languages accepted: English; French; German; Spanish
Prints abstracts: No
Author-anonymous submission: No

SUBMISSION REQUIREMENTS

Restrictions on contributors: None
Author pays submission fee: No
Author pays page charges: No
Length of articles: No restrictions
Length of book reviews: No restrictions
Length of notes: No restrictions
Style: None
Number of copies required: 1
Copyright ownership: Journal
Rejected manuscripts: Returned
Time before publication decision: 1 mo.
Time between decision and publication: 3 mos.
Number of reviewers: 3
Articles submitted per year: 25
Articles published per year: 10
Book reviews submitted per year: 1-3
Book reviews published per year: 1-3
Notes submitted per year: 2-3
Notes published per year: 2-3

(2331)
Regensburger Beiträge zur Deutschen Sprach- und Literaturwissenschaft. Reihe B: Untersuchungen

Bernhard Gajek, Editor
Inst. für Germanistik
Univ. Regensburg
Postfach 397
8400 Regensburg 1, Germany

First published: 1975
Sponsoring organization: Univ. Regensburg
ISSN: 0170-8872
MLA acronym: RBSL

SUBSCRIPTION INFORMATION

Frequency of publication: Irregular
Circulation: 400
Available in microform: No
Subscription address: Verlag Peter Lang AG, Postfach 277, 3000 Bern 15, Switzerland

ADVERTISING INFORMATION

Advertising accepted: No

EDITORIAL DESCRIPTION

Scope: Publishes monographs on German language and literature.
Reviews books: No
Publishes notes: No
Languages accepted: German
Prints abstracts: No
Author-anonymous submission: No

SUBMISSION REQUIREMENTS

Restrictions on contributors: None
Author pays submission fee: No
Author pays page charges: Yes
Length of books: No restrictions
Style: Scientific
Number of copies required: 2
Special requirements: Submit original typescript.
Copyright ownership: Verlag Peter Lang
Rejected manuscripts: Returned
Time before publication decision: 1-3 mos.
Time between decision and publication: 3-6 mos.
Number of reviewers: 2-3
Books submitted per year: 4-6
Books published per year: 3-4

(2332)
*Regional Language Studies—Newfoundland

Graham Shorrocks, Editor
Dept. of English Language & Literature
Memorial Univ. of Newfoundland
St. John's, Newfoundland A1B 3X9, Canada

Telephone: 709 737-8983
Fax: 709 737-4000
E-mail: Gshorroc@kean.ucs.mun.ca
First published: 1968
Sponsoring organization: Dept. of English Language & Literature, Memorial Univ. of Newfoundland
ISSN: 0079-9335
MLA acronym: RLS

SUBSCRIPTION INFORMATION

Frequency of publication: Irregular
Circulation: 400
Available in microform: No

ADVERTISING INFORMATION

Advertising accepted: Yes

EDITORIAL DESCRIPTION

Scope: Promotes the study of varieties of English spoken in Newfoundland and Labrador. Aims to spread information about other languages spoken in the province, and about the linguistic research being conducted in the region. Publishes articles on synchronic and diachronic linguistics including phonology, morphology, syntax, and lexis, as well as regional and social dialects, specialized vocabularies (occupational dialects), and onomastics. Also concerned with the folklore, folk-life and material culture of the speech communities of the province. Contributions of a more general character may be included occasionally.
Reviews books: Yes
Publishes notes: Yes
Languages accepted: English; French; German
Prints abstracts: Yes
Author-anonymous submission: Usually

SUBMISSION REQUIREMENTS

Author pays submission fee: No
Author pays page charges: No
Length of articles: No restrictions
Length of book reviews: No restrictions
Length of notes: No restrictions
Style: MLA preferred
Number of copies required: 1
Copyright ownership: Author & Dept. of English Language & Literature, Memorial Univ. of Newfoundland
Rejected manuscripts: Returned
Time before publication decision: 3 weeks
Number of reviewers: 2-4

(2333)
*Reihe der Villa Vigoni: Deutsch-Italienische Studien

Max Niemeyer Verlag
Postfach 2140
7400 Tübingen, Germany

Telephone: (49) 7071 81104
Fax: (49) 7071 87419
First published: 1989
Sponsoring organization: Verein Villa Vigoni e.-V.
ISSN: 0936-8965
MLA acronym: RdVV

SUBSCRIPTION INFORMATION

Frequency of publication: Irregular
Available in microform: No

ADVERTISING INFORMATION

Advertising accepted: No

EDITORIAL DESCRIPTION

Scope: Publishes studies on the history of German-Italian relations in the fields of literature, culture, history, and education.
Reviews books: No
Publishes notes: No
Languages accepted: German
Prints abstracts: No
Author-anonymous submission: No

SUBMISSION REQUIREMENTS

Copyright ownership: Max Niemeyer Verlag
Time before publication decision: 6 mos.
Time between decision and publication: 1 yr.
Books published per year: 2-3

(2334)
*Reihe Germanistische Linguistik

Helmut Henne, Horst Sitta, & Herbert Ernst Wiegand, Editors
Max Niemeyer Verlag
Postfach 2140
7400 Tübingen, Germany

Telephone: (49) 7071 81104
Fax: (49) 7071 87419
First published: 1975
ISSN: 0344-6778
MLA acronym: RGL

SUBSCRIPTION INFORMATION

Frequency of publication: Irregular
Available in microform: No

ADVERTISING INFORMATION

Advertising accepted: No

EDITORIAL DESCRIPTION

Scope: Publishes studies in German language.
Reviews books: No
Publishes notes: No
Languages accepted: German
Prints abstracts: No
Author-anonymous submission: Yes

SUBMISSION REQUIREMENTS

Restrictions on contributors: None

Author pays submission fee: No
Author pays page charges: No
Length of books: No restrictions
Style: MLA; Series
Number of copies required: 2
Copyright ownership: Max Niemeyer Verlag
Rejected manuscripts: Returned
Time before publication decision: 3-6 mos.
Time between decision and publication: 6 mos.
Number of reviewers: 2-3
Books submitted per year: 8-12
Books published per year: 4-8

(2335)
Reihe Siegen: Beiträge zur Literatur-, Sprach- und Medienwissenschaft

Wolfgang Drost, Helmut Kreuzer, Wolfgang Raible, Karl Riha, & Christian W. Thomsen, Editors
Carl Winter Universitätverlag GmbH
Postfach 106140
6900 Heidelberg 1, Germany

Additional editorial address: C/o Fachbereich 3, Univ.-GH Adolf-Reichweinstr., 5900 Siegen, Germany
First published: 1977
Sponsoring organization: Ministerium für Wissenschaft & Forschung des Landes Nordrhein-Westfalen
MLA acronym: RSieg

SUBSCRIPTION INFORMATION

Frequency of publication: Irregular
Circulation: 700

ADVERTISING INFORMATION

Advertising accepted: No

EDITORIAL DESCRIPTION

Scope: Devoted to an extended concept of literature. Is also open to cultural history, language, and media studies. Publishes monographs on German, English-American, and Romance languages studies.
Reviews books: No
Publishes notes: No
Languages accepted: German; English; French
Prints abstracts: No
Author-anonymous submission: No

SUBMISSION REQUIREMENTS

Restrictions on contributors: None
Author pays submission fee: No
Author pays page charges: No
Length of books: 250 pp.
Style: MLA
Number of copies required: 2
Copyright ownership: Author
Rejected manuscripts: Returned
Time before publication decision: 15 mos. maximum
Time between decision and publication: 1 yr.
Number of reviewers: 2-3
Books submitted per year: 10-20
Books published per year: 4-7

(2336)
*Reinardus: Yearbook of the International Reynard Society/Annuaire de la Société Internationale Renardienne

Brian J. Levy & Paul Wackers, Editors
French Dept.
Univ. of Hull
Cottingham Rd.
Hull HU6 7RX, England

Additional editorial address: Paul Wackers, Inst. Nederlands, Katholieke Univ., P.B. 9103, 6500 HD Nijmegen, Netherlands
Telephone: (44) 482 465367
Fax: (44) 482 465991
E-mail: BJL18@UK.AC.HULL
First published: 1988
Sponsoring organization: International Reynard Soc.
ISSN: 0925-4757
MLA acronym: Reinardus

SUBSCRIPTION INFORMATION

Frequency of publication: Annual (May-June)
Available in microform: No
Subscription price: 100 f ($52.00)/yr.
Year to which price refers: 1992
Subscription address: Erwin Verzandvoort, Dommelborch 70, 5247 SG Rosmalen, Netherlands
Additional subscription address: Institutions contact: John Benjamins Publishing Company, P.O. Box 75577, Amsteldijk 44, 1070 AN Amsterdam, Netherlands; 821 Bethlehem Pike, Philadelphia, PA 19118

ADVERTISING INFORMATION

Advertising accepted: No

EDITORIAL DESCRIPTION

Scope: Publishes comparative research in the fields of medieval comic, and satirical, didactic and allegorical literature. Emphasizes beast epic, fable, and *fabliau*.
Reviews books: Yes
Publishes notes: No
Languages accepted: French; English; German; Italian
Prints abstracts: No
Author-anonymous submission: No

SUBMISSION REQUIREMENTS

Restrictions on contributors: None
Author pays submission fee: No
Author pays page charges: No
Length of articles: 5,000 words
Length of book reviews: 1,000 words
Style: Journal
Number of copies required: 2
Copyright ownership: John Benjamins Publishing Co.
Rejected manuscripts: Returned
Time before publication decision: 2-3 mos.
Time between decision and publication: 3-18 mos.
Number of reviewers: 2
Articles submitted per year: 20-25
Articles published per year: 15-18
Book reviews submitted per year: 1-2
Book reviews published per year: 1-2

(2337)
*RELC Journal: A Journal of Language Teaching and Research in Southeast Asia

Makhan L. Tickoo, Editor
Southeast Asian Ministers of Education Organization
Regional Language Centre
30 Orange Grove Rd.
Singapore 1025, Republic of Singapore

Telephone: (65) 7379044 ext. 605
Fax: (65) 7342753
E-mail: RELC@NUSVM.BITNET
First published: 1970
Sponsoring organization: Southeast Asian Ministers of Education Organization, Regional Language Centre
ISSN: 0033-6882
MLA acronym: RELC

SUBSCRIPTION INFORMATION

Frequency of publication: 2 times/yr. (June, Dec.)
Circulation: 1,500
Available in microform: Yes
Subscription price: $18.00/yr.
Year to which price refers: 1992
Subscription address: John Chow, at the above address

ADVERTISING INFORMATION

Advertising accepted: Yes

EDITORIAL DESCRIPTION

Scope: Presents information and ideas on theories, research, methods, and materials related to language learning in general and English in particular. Main articles, short notes, and book reviews are of general interest and of particular relevance to language teaching programs in Southeast Asia.
Reviews books: Yes
Publishes notes: Yes
Languages accepted: English
Prints abstracts: Yes
Author-anonymous submission: No

SUBMISSION REQUIREMENTS

Restrictions on contributors: None
Author pays submission fee: No
Author pays page charges: No
Length of articles: 1,000-5,000 words
Length of book reviews: 1,000-1,500 words
Length of notes: 500 words
Style: Linguistic Soc. of America
Number of copies required: 3
Special requirements: Submit original typscript and 2 copies. Include an abstract (200 words maximum).
Copyright ownership: Regional Language Centre
Rejected manuscripts: Not returned
Time before publication decision: 4-6 mos.
Time between decision and publication: 4 mos.
Number of reviewers: 5-6
Articles submitted per year: 70-90
Articles published per year: 20
Book reviews submitted per year: 10
Book reviews published per year: 4-7
Notes submitted per year: 8
Notes published per year: 3-5

(2338)
*Religion and Literature

Thomas Werge & James P. Dougherty, Editors
Dept. of English
Univ. of Notre Dame
Notre Dame, IN 46556

Telephone: 219 239-5725
Fax: 219 239-8609

First published: 1960
Sponsoring organization: Univ. of Notre Dame, Dept. of English
ISSN: 0029-4500
MLA acronym: R&L

SUBSCRIPTION INFORMATION

Frequency of publication: 3 times/yr. (Mar., July, Nov.)
Circulation: 500
Available in microform: Yes
Subscription price: $25.00/yr. institutions US; $20.00/yr. individuals US; $29.00/yr. elsewhere
Year to which price refers: 1992

ADVERTISING INFORMATION

Advertising accepted: Yes

EDITORIAL DESCRIPTION

Scope: Publishes critical and scholarly articles concerning the relations between religion in any form and literature in any genre.
Reviews books: Yes
Publishes notes: No
Languages accepted: English
Prints abstracts: No
Author-anonymous submission: No

SUBMISSION REQUIREMENTS

Restrictions on contributors: Book reviews are commissioned.
Author pays submission fee: No
Author pays page charges: No
Length of articles: 5,000 words
Length of book reviews: 1,500-2,500 words
Style: MLA; Chicago
Number of copies required: 3
Copyright ownership: Dept. of English, Univ. of Notre Dame
Rejected manuscripts: Returned; enclose return postage.
Time before publication decision: 3-5 mos.
Time between decision and publication: 1 yr.
Number of reviewers: 5
Articles submitted per year: 90
Articles published per year: 12
Book reviews published per year: 12

(2339)
*Renaissance & Modern Studies

M. I. Millington & C. M. Heywood, Editors
Dept. of Hispanic Studies
Univ. of Nottingham
Nottingham NG7 2RD, England

Telephone: (44) 602 484848 ext. 2528
Fax: (44) 602 420825
First published: 1957
Sponsoring organization: Univ. of Nottingham
ISSN: 0486-3720
MLA acronym: RMS

SUBSCRIPTION INFORMATION

Frequency of publication: Annual
Circulation: 500
Available in microform: Yes, in US
Subscription price: £7.50/yr.
Year to which price refers: 1992
Subscription address: Marlies Chrzanowski, Dept. of Hispanic Studies, Univ. of Nottingham, Nottingham NG7 2RD, England

ADVERTISING INFORMATION

Advertising accepted: No

EDITORIAL DESCRIPTION

Scope: Publishes articles of original research on topics drawn from all the humanities and ranging chronologically from 1500 to the present. Each issue is devoted to a single pre-advertised theme or area.
Reviews books: No
Publishes notes: No
Languages accepted: English
Prints abstracts: No
Author-anonymous submission: No

SUBMISSION REQUIREMENTS

Restrictions on contributors: Unsolicited articles are not accepted.
Author pays submission fee: No
Author pays page charges: No
Length of articles: 8,000 words; longer articles occasionally accepted
Style: Modern Humanities Research Assn.
Number of copies required: 2
Special requirements: Submit original typescript and diskette.
Copyright ownership: Author
Rejected manuscripts: Returned
Time before publication decision: 1 mo.
Time between decision and publication: 6 mos.
Number of reviewers: 2
Articles submitted per year: 9
Articles published per year: 9

(2340)
*Renaissance and Reformation/ Renaissance et Réforme

François Paré, Editor
Dept. of French Studies
Univ. of Guelph
Guelph, Ontario N1G 2W1, Canada

Telephone: 519 824-4120 ext. 3884
First published: 1963
Sponsoring organization: Canadian Soc. for Renaissance Studies/Soc. Canadienne d'Etudes de la Renaissance; North Central Conference, Renaissance Soc. of America; Pacific Northwest Renaissance Conference; Toronto Renaissance & Reformation Colloquium; Victoria Univ. Centre for Reformation & Renaissance Studies
ISSN: 0034-429X
MLA acronym: Ren&R

SUBSCRIPTION INFORMATION

Frequency of publication: 4 times/yr. (Feb., May, Aug., Nov.)
Circulation: 700
Available in microform: No
Subscription price: C$33.00/yr. institutions; C$20.00/yr. individuals
Year to which price refers: 1991-92
Subscription address: K. Eisenbichler, Business Manager, Victoria College, Univ. of Toronto, Toronto, Ontario M5S 1K7, Canada

ADVERTISING INFORMATION

Advertising accepted: No

EDITORIAL DESCRIPTION

Scope: Publishes articles on all aspects of the Renaissance and the Reformation.
Reviews books: Yes
Publishes notes: No
Languages accepted: English; French
Prints abstracts: No
Author-anonymous submission: Yes

SUBMISSION REQUIREMENTS

Restrictions on contributors: None
Author pays submission fee: No
Author pays page charges: No
Length of articles: 50 pp. maximum
Length of book reviews: 700 words

Style: MLA; French
Number of copies required: 2
Copyright ownership: Journal
Rejected manuscripts: Returned; enclose return postage.
Time before publication decision: 4 mos.
Time between decision and publication: 1 yr.
Number of reviewers: 2 minimum
Articles submitted per year: 75
Articles published per year: 12-15
Book reviews submitted per year: 30
Book reviews published per year: 30

(2341)
*The Renaissance Bulletin

Gorō Suzuki, Editor
c/o Renaissance Inst.
Sophia Univ.
7-1 Kioi-cho, Chiyoda-ku
Tokyo 102, Japan

Telephone: (81) 3 32383909
First published: 1974
Sponsoring organization: Renaissance Inst.
ISSN: 0388-0796
MLA acronym: RenB

SUBSCRIPTION INFORMATION

Frequency of publication: Annual
Circulation: 500
Available in microform: No

ADVERTISING INFORMATION

Advertising accepted: No

EDITORIAL DESCRIPTION

Scope: Publishes articles and studies from Japan on the English Renaissance, mainly in the field of literature.
Reviews books: Yes
Publishes notes: No
Languages accepted: English
Prints abstracts: No
Author-anonymous submission: No

SUBMISSION REQUIREMENTS

Restrictions on contributors: Contributors must be members of The Renaissance Inst.
Author pays submission fee: No
Author pays page charges: No
Length of articles: 1,500-3,000 words
Length of book reviews: 1,000-2,000 words
Style: MLA
Number of copies required: 1
Copyright ownership: Renaissance Inst.
Rejected manuscripts: Returned; enclose return postage.
Time before publication decision: 3 mos.
Time between decision and publication: 1 yr.
Number of reviewers: 3-4
Articles submitted per year: 1-5
Articles published per year: 1-3
Book reviews submitted per year: 1-5
Book reviews published per year: 1-5

(2342)
*Renaissance Drama

Mary Beth Rose, Editor
Newberry Library
60 West Walton St.
Chicago, IL 60610

Telephone: 312 943-9090
First published: 1956
Sponsoring organization: Newberry Library Center for Renaissance Studies; Northwestern Univ.
ISSN: 0486-3739
MLA acronym: RenD

SUBSCRIPTION INFORMATION

Frequency of publication: Annual (Spring)
Circulation: 500
Available in microform: No
Subscription address: Northwestern Univ. Press, 625 Colfax, Evanston, IL 60201
Subscription telephone: 708 491-5313

ADVERTISING INFORMATION

Advertising accepted: No

EDITORIAL DESCRIPTION

Scope: Journal is devoted to the understanding of drama of all nations in the 15th, 16th, and 17th centuries as a central feature of Renaissance culture. Essays are encouraged that explore the relationship of Renaissance dramatic traditions to their precursors and successors; have an interdisciplinary orientation; explore the relationship of drama to society and history; examine the impact of new forms of interpretation on Renaissance drama; and raise fresh questions about the texts and performances of Renaissance plays.
Reviews books: No
Publishes notes: Yes
Languages accepted: English
Prints abstracts: No
Author-anonymous submission: No

SUBMISSION REQUIREMENTS

Restrictions on contributors: None
Author pays submission fee: No
Author pays page charges: No
Length of articles: No restrictions
Style: MLA
Number of copies required: 1
Copyright ownership: Northwestern Univ. Press
Rejected manuscripts: Returned
Time before publication decision: 3-5 mos.
Time between decision and publication: 6-12 mos.
Number of reviewers: 2-3
Articles submitted per year: 85
Articles published per year: 9-10

(2343)
*Renaissance Monographs

Peter Milward, Editor
Renaissance Inst.
Sophia Univ.
7-1 Kioi-cho, Chiyoda-ku
Tokyo 102, Japan

Telephone: (81) 3 32383909
First published: 1974
Sponsoring organization: Renaissance Inst.
MLA acronym: RenM

SUBSCRIPTION INFORMATION

Frequency of publication: Annual
Circulation: 500
Available in microform: No

ADVERTISING INFORMATION

Advertising accepted: No

EDITORIAL DESCRIPTION

Scope: Publishes monographs on the writings and life of England and Europe in the Middle Ages and Renaissance.
Reviews books: No
Publishes notes: No
Languages accepted: English
Prints abstracts: No
Author-anonymous submission: No

SUBMISSION REQUIREMENTS

Restrictions on contributors: Contributors must be members of the Renaissance Inst. and must be Japanese and living in Japan.
Author pays submission fee: No
Author pays page charges: No
Length of books: 52,500 words
Style: MLA
Number of copies required: 2
Special requirements: Include an abstract.
Copyright ownership: Journal
Rejected manuscripts: Returned; enclose returned postage.
Time before publication decision: 6 mos.
Time between decision and publication: 2-4 mos.
Number of reviewers: 2-3
Books submitted per year: 1
Books published per year: 1

(2344)
*Renaissance Papers

George Walton Williams & Barbara J. Baines, Editors
Box 8105
Dept. of English
North Carolina State Univ.
Raleigh, NC 27695-8105

Telephone: 919 515-3870; 919 684-5827
Fax: 919 684-4871
First published: 1956
Sponsoring organization: Southeastern Renaissance Conference
ISSN: 0584-4207
MLA acronym: RenP

SUBSCRIPTION INFORMATION

Frequency of publication: Annual
Circulation: 600
Available in microform: No
Subscription price: $20.00/yr. institutions; $12.50/yr. individuals
Year to which price refers: 1991

ADVERTISING INFORMATION

Advertising accepted: No

EDITORIAL DESCRIPTION

Scope: Publishes papers selected from those presented at the Annual Meetings of the Southeastern Renaissance Conference.
Reviews books: No
Publishes notes: No
Languages accepted: English
Prints abstracts: No

SUBMISSION REQUIREMENTS

Restrictions on contributors: Contributors must be members of Southeastern Renaissance Conference.
Author pays submission fee: No
Author pays page charges: No
Length of articles: 10 pp.
Style: Chicago
Number of copies required: 1
Copyright ownership: Author & journal
Rejected manuscripts: Not returned
Time before publication decision: 2 mos.
Time between decision and publication: 6-8 mos.
Number of reviewers: 3
Articles submitted per year: 30
Articles published per year: 7-8

(2345)
*Renaissance Quarterly

Bridget Gellert Lyons & Rona Goffen, Editors
Renaissance Soc. of America, Inc.
1161 Amsterdam Ave.
New York, NY 10027

Telephone: 212 854-2318
Fax: 212 749-3163
First published: 1948
Sponsoring organization: Renaissance Soc. of America
ISSN: 0034-4338
MLA acronym: RenQ

SUBSCRIPTION INFORMATION

Frequency of publication: 4 times/yr. (Spring, Summer, Fall, Winter)
Circulation: 3,500
Available in microform: Yes
Subscription price: $55.00/yr. institutions; $50.00/yr. individuals; $25.00/yr. students
Year to which price refers: 1992

ADVERTISING INFORMATION

Advertising accepted: Yes
Advertising rates: $200.00/half page; $250.00/full page; $300.00/back cover

EDITORIAL DESCRIPTION

Scope: Publishes articles, book reviews, news and notes, and a bibliography on subjects involving all aspects (literary, historical, artistic) of the Renaissance.
Reviews books: Yes
Publishes notes: No
Languages accepted: English
Prints abstracts: No
Author-anonymous submission: Yes

SUBMISSION REQUIREMENTS

Restrictions on contributors: Book reviews are solicited.
Author pays submission fee: No
Author pays page charges: No
Length of articles: 2,000-12,500 words
Length of book reviews: 500-800 words
Style: Chicago
Number of copies required: 2
Special requirements: Submit double-spaced typescript. Author's name and affiliation should be on cover sheet or separate sheet only.
Copyright ownership: Journal
Rejected manuscripts: Returned; enclose SASE.
Time before publication decision: 2-6 mos.
Time between decision and publication: 12-18 mos.
Number of reviewers: 2-3
Articles submitted per year: 75
Articles published per year: 12-16
Book reviews published per year: 120-130

(2346)
*Renaissance Studies: Journal of the Society for Renaissance Studies

Gordon Campbell, Editor
English Dept.
Leicester Univ.
Leicester LE1 7RH, England

Telephone: (44) 533 522633
Fax: (44) 533 522065
E-mail: LEB@LEICESTER.AC.UK
First published: 1987
Sponsoring organization: Soc. for Renaissance Studies
ISSN: 0269-1213
MLA acronym: RenSt

SUBSCRIPTION INFORMATION

Frequency of publication: 4 times/yr.
Circulation: 550
Available in microform: Yes
Subscription price: £51.00/yr. United Kingdom & Europe; $100.00/yr. elsewhere
Year to which price refers: 1992
Subscription address: Journals Subscriptions, Oxford Univ. Press, Pinkhill House, Southfield Rd., Eynsham, Oxford OX8 1JJ, England
Subscription telephone: (44) 865 882283
Subscription fax: (44) 865 882890

ADVERTISING INFORMATION

Advertising accepted: Yes

EDITORIAL DESCRIPTION

Scope: Publishes articles on all aspects of Renaissance culture and history. Includes studies on the history, art, architecture, religion, literature and language of any European country or any country influenced by Europe during the Renaissance period.
Reviews books: Yes
Publishes notes: Yes
Languages accepted: English
Prints abstracts: No
Author-anonymous submission: Yes

SUBMISSION REQUIREMENTS

Restrictions on contributors: Book reviews are commissioned.
Author pays submission fee: No
Author pays page charges: No
Length of articles: 8,000 words
Length of book reviews: 2,500 words
Style: Journal
Number of copies required: 3
Special requirements: Machine-readable text preferred.
Copyright ownership: Soc. for Renaissance Studies & Oxford Univ. Press
Rejected manuscripts: Not returned
Time before publication decision: 1-2 mos.
Time between decision and publication: 2-3 yrs.
Number of reviewers: 2-3
Articles submitted per year: 50-60
Articles published per year: 10-15
Book reviews submitted per year: 20-25
Book reviews published per year: 20-25
Notes submitted per year: 6-8
Notes published per year: 2-3

(2347)
*Renascence: Essays on Value in Literature

Joseph Schwartz, Editor
Brooks Hall 200B
Marquette Univ.
Milwaukee, WI 53233

Telephone: 414 288-1417
First published: 1948
Sponsoring organization: Marquette Univ.
ISSN: 0034-4346
MLA acronym: Renascence

SUBSCRIPTION INFORMATION

Frequency of publication: 4 times/yr.
Circulation: 650
Available in microform: Yes
Subscription price: $20.00/yr. US; $23.00/yr. elsewhere; $6.00/single issue
Year to which price refers: 1991-92
Subscription address: Marquette Univ. Press, Holthusen Hall 409, Marquette Univ., Milwaukee, WI 53233
Subscription telephone: 414 288-7444

ADVERTISING INFORMATION

Advertising accepted: Yes, on an exchange basis

EDITORIAL DESCRIPTION

Scope: Elucidates the Christian perspective on literature and the meaning of values in literature, and explores the relation between criticism and values. Essays on Western literature from any period are welcome.
Reviews books: No
Publishes notes: No
Languages accepted: English
Prints abstracts: No
Author-anonymous submission: No

SUBMISSION REQUIREMENTS

Restrictions on contributors: None
Author pays submission fee: No
Author pays page charges: No
Length of articles: 3,000-7,500 words
Style: MLA
Number of copies required: 2
Special requirements: Submit original typescript; use minumum number of footnotes.
Copyright ownership: Journal
Rejected manuscripts: Returned; enclose SASE.
Time before publication decision: 3-6 mos.
Time between decision and publication: 18-24 mos.
Number of reviewers: 2
Articles submitted per year: 125
Articles published per year: 18-23

(2348)
Rendiconti dell'Istituto Lombardo Accademia di Scienze e Lettere

Alfonso Giordano, Editor
Ist. Lombardo
Accademia di Scienze e Lettere
Via Borgonuovo, 25
20121 Milan, Italy

First published: 1864
Sponsoring organization: Ist. Lombardo
ISSN: 0021-2504
MLA acronym: RIL

SUBSCRIPTION INFORMATION

Frequency of publication: Annual
Circulation: 500
Available in microform: No

ADVERTISING INFORMATION

Advertising accepted: No

EDITORIAL DESCRIPTION

Reviews books: No
Languages accepted: English; French; German; Italian; Latin
Prints abstracts: No

SUBMISSION REQUIREMENTS

Restrictions on contributors: Submissions must be presented by a member of the Ist. Lombardo.
Author pays submission fee: No
Author pays page charges: Yes, for science papers exceeding 8 pp. and for literature papers exceeding 12 pp.
Length of articles: 8-12 typescript pp.
Style: None
Number of copies required: 1
Copyright ownership: Ist. Lombardo
Time between decision and publication: 1 yr.
Number of reviewers: 2

(2349)
*Renditions: A Chinese-English Translation Magazine

Eva Hung, Editor
Research Centre for Translation
Chinese Univ. of Hong Kong
Shatin, N. T., Hong Kong

Telephone: (852) 6097399
Fax: (852) 6035149
First published: 1973
Sponsoring organization: Wing Lung Bank Fund for Promotion of Chinese Culture
ISSN: 0377-3515
MLA acronym: Renditions

SUBSCRIPTION INFORMATION

Frequency of publication: 2 times/yr. (Spring, Fall)
Circulation: 1,000-1,500
Available in microform: No
Subscription price: $20.00/yr.
Year to which price refers: 1992

ADVERTISING INFORMATION

Advertising accepted: Yes
Advertising rates: $110.00/half page; $200.00/full page

EDITORIAL DESCRIPTION

Scope: English-language magazine devoted primarily to translations of Chinese writings past and present in the field of literature and the humanities. Also publishes pertinent articles written originally in English.
Reviews books: Yes
Languages accepted: English
Prints abstracts: No
Author-anonymous submission: No

SUBMISSION REQUIREMENTS

Restrictions on contributors: None
Author pays submission fee: No
Author pays page charges: No
Length of articles: 5,000 words; longer articles and translations may be considered
Style: Journal
Number of copies required: 1
Special requirements: Original Chinese text should accompany translations.
Copyright ownership: Assigned by author to journal
Rejected manuscripts: Returned at author's request
Time before publication decision: 4 mos.
Time between decision and publication: 6-12 mos.
Number of reviewers: 3
Articles submitted per year: 80-100
Articles published per year: 20-25

(2350)
*Representations

Svetlana Alpers & Stephen Greenblatt, Editors
322 Wheeler Hall
Univ. of California
Berkeley, CA 94720

Telephone: 510 642-4671
First published: 1983
Sponsoring organization: Univ. of California
ISSN: 0734-6018
MLA acronym: Representations

SUBSCRIPTION INFORMATION

Frequency of publication: 4 times/yr. (Feb., May, Aug., Nov.)
Circulation: 1,800
Available in microform: Yes
Subscription price: $52.00/yr. institutions; $26.00/yr. individuals; $18.00/yr. students

Year to which price refers: 1991
Subscription address: Univ. of California Press, 2120 Berkeley Way, Berkeley, CA 94720
Subscription telephone: 510 642-4191
Subscription fax: 510 643-7127

ADVERTISING INFORMATION

Advertising accepted: Yes

EDITORIAL DESCRIPTION

Scope: The journal publishes in the humanities and interpretative social sciences focusing on recent developments in literary criticism, iconography, historiography, and social theory.
Reviews books: No
Publishes notes: No
Languages accepted: English
Prints abstracts: No
Author-anonymous submission: No

SUBMISSION REQUIREMENTS

Restrictions on contributors: None
Author pays submission fee: No
Author pays page charges: No
Length of articles: 6,000-20,000 words
Style: Chicago
Number of copies required: 2
Special requirements: Manuscripts must be double-spaced typescript with footnotes typed separately.
Copyright ownership: Publisher
Rejected manuscripts: Returned; enclose SASE.
Time before publication decision: 6-12 weeks
Time between decision and publication: 3-15 mos.
Number of reviewers: 15
Articles submitted per year: 300
Articles published per year: 24-30

(2351)
*República de las Letras

Andrés Sorel, Editor
Sagasta 28
5a Planta
28004 Madrid, Spain

Telephone: (34) 1 4467047
Fax: (34) 1 4462961
First published: 1978
Sponsoring organization: Asoc. Colegial de Escritores de España
MLA acronym: RLetras

SUBSCRIPTION INFORMATION

Frequency of publication: 4 times/yr.
Circulation: 2,000
Available in microform: No

ADVERTISING INFORMATION

Advertising accepted: Yes

EDITORIAL DESCRIPTION

Scope: Publishes articles on literature with an emphasis on Spanish and Latin American authors. It also includes articles on the theater. Monographic issues are also published and these concern publishing, criticism, the teaching of literature, etc. In addition, one issue per year concerns the literature of one foreign country.
Reviews books: Yes
Publishes notes: No
Languages accepted: Spanish

SUBMISSION REQUIREMENTS

Restrictions on contributors: None
Author pays submission fee: No
Author pays page charges: No
Length of articles: No restrictions
Length of book reviews: No restrictions
Number of copies required: 1

Copyright ownership: Author & Asoc. Colegial de Escritores de España
Rejected manuscripts: Returned
Time before publication decision: 6 mos.
Time between decision and publication: 6 mos.
Number of reviewers: 6
Articles submitted per year: 200
Articles published per year: 100

(2352)
*Res Publica Litterarum: Studies in the Classical Tradition

Piergiorgio Parroni, Editor
Via dell'Abbazia 40
61032 Fano, PS, Italy

Telephone: (39) 721 802750
First published: 1978
Sponsoring organization: Ist. Internazionale Studi Piceni, Centro Nazionale delle Ricerche
ISSN: 0275-4304
MLA acronym: RPLit

SUBSCRIPTION INFORMATION

Frequency of publication: Annual
Circulation: 130
Available in microform: No

ADVERTISING INFORMATION

Advertising accepted: No

EDITORIAL DESCRIPTION

Scope: Publishes articles from different humanistic disciplines that touch upon Classical, Medieval, and Renaissance topics.
Reviews books: Yes
Publishes notes: Yes
Languages accepted: English; French; German; Italian; Spanish; Latin; Greek
Prints abstracts: No
Author-anonymous submission: No

SUBMISSION REQUIREMENTS

Restrictions on contributors: None
Author pays submission fee: No
Author pays page charges: No
Length of articles: 20 pp.
Length of book reviews: 2 pp.
Style: Chicago
Number of copies required: 2
Special requirements: Include a cover letter.
Rejected manuscripts: Returned
Time before publication decision: 6 mo.
Time between decision and publication: 1-2 yrs.
Number of reviewers: 3
Articles submitted per year: 50
Articles published per year: 25-30
Book reviews submitted per year: 12-15
Book reviews published per year: 5-10

(2353)
*Research in African Literatures

Abiola Irele, Editor
Ohio State Univ.
P.O. Box 3509
Columbus, OH 43210-0709

First published: 1970
Sponsoring organization: MLA, Division on African Literatures; African Literature Assn.
ISSN: 0034-5210
MLA acronym: RAL

SUBSCRIPTION INFORMATION

Frequency of publication: 4 times/yr. (Feb., May, Aug., Nov.)
Circulation: 1,200
Available in microform: Yes

Subscription price: $40.00 (£20.00)/yr. institutions Africa; $55.00 (£27.50)/yr. institutions elsewhere; $30.00 (£15.00)/yr. individuals
Year to which price refers: 1992
Subscription address: Indiana Univ. Press, Journals Division, 601 N. Morton St., Bloomington, IN 47404
Subscription telephone: 812 855-3830
Subscription fax: 812 855-7931

ADVERTISING INFORMATION

Advertising accepted: Yes

EDITORIAL DESCRIPTION

Scope: Publishes articles on all aspects of the oral and written literatures of Africa. Also includes bibliographies, position papers, research reports, and book reviews.
Reviews books: Yes
Publishes notes: Yes
Languages accepted: English; French; German; Spanish; Portuguese
Prints abstracts: No
Author-anonymous submission: Yes

SUBMISSION REQUIREMENTS

Restrictions on contributors: None
Author pays submission fee: No
Author pays page charges: No
Length of articles: No restrictions
Length of book reviews: 1,500 words
Length of notes: No restrictions
Style: MLA
Number of copies required: 1
Special requirements: Footnotes should appear at the end. Articles not in French or English are accepted for translation into English.
Copyright ownership: Indiana Univ. Press
Rejected manuscripts: Returned
Time before publication decision: 3 mos.
Time between decision and publication: 9 mos.
Number of reviewers: 2-3
Articles submitted per year: 200-350
Articles published per year: 30-40
Book reviews submitted per year: 80
Book reviews published per year: 80
Notes submitted per year: 10-20
Notes published per year: 5-7

(2354)
*Research in Text Theory/ Untersuchungen zur Texttheorie

János S. Petöfi, Editor
Walter de Gruyter, Inc.
200 Saw Mill River Rd.
Hawthorne, NY 10532

First published: 1977
ISSN: 0179-4167
MLA acronym: RTT

SUBSCRIPTION INFORMATION

Frequency of publication: Irregular

ADVERTISING INFORMATION

Advertising accepted: Yes

EDITORIAL DESCRIPTION

Scope: Provides a general overview of the present state of text linguistics, various aspects of text processing, and basic questions of text theory.
Reviews books: No
Publishes notes: No
Languages accepted: German; English

(2355)
*Research in Yoruba Language and Literature

Lawrence Olufemi Adéwolé, Editor
Dept. of African Languages & Literatures
Obáfemi Awólowo Univ.
Ilé-Ifẹ, Nigeria

Telephone: (234) 36 230290-0 ext. 2706 or 2716
First published: 1991
Sponsoring organization: Yoruba Language & Literature Club, Obáfemi Awólowo Univ.
ISSN: 1115-4322
MLA acronym: RYLL

SUBSCRIPTION INFORMATION

Frequency of publication: 2-4 times/yr.
Available in microform: No
Subscription price: $30.00/issue institutions; $20.00/issue individuals
Year to which price refers: 1993
Subscription address: Technicians of the Sacred, 1317 North San Fernando Blvd., Suite 310, Burbank, CA 91504

ADVERTISING INFORMATION

Advertising accepted: Yes
Advertising rates: $25.00/quarter page; $45.00/half page; $80.00/full page

EDITORIAL DESCRIPTION

Scope: Publishes articles on Yoruba language and literature.
Reviews books: Yes
Publishes notes: Yes
Languages accepted: English
Prints abstracts: Yes
Author-anonymous submission: Yes

SUBMISSION REQUIREMENTS

Restrictions on contributors: None
Author pays submission fee: No
Author pays page charges: No
Length of articles: 3,000 words
Length of book reviews: 1,000 words
Length of notes: 1,500 words
Style: MLA
Number of copies required: 3
Copyright ownership: Journal
Rejected manuscripts: Returned; enclose SAE.
Number of reviewers: 2
Articles submitted per year: 50
Articles published per year: 14-28
Book reviews submitted per year: 30
Book reviews published per year: 10-15
Notes submitted per year: 20
Notes published per year: 5-10

(2356)
*Research Opportunities in Renaissance Drama

David M. Bergeron, Editor
English Dept.
Univ. of Kansas
Lawrence, KS 66045

Telephone: 913 864-3773; 913 864-4520
First published: 1956
ISSN: 0098-647X
MLA acronym: RORD

SUBSCRIPTION INFORMATION

Frequency of publication: Annual
Circulation: 400
Available in microform: No
Subscription price: $6.00/yr., $10.00/2 yrs.
Year to which price refers: 1992
Subscription address: Hall Center for the Humanities, Watkins Home, Univ. of Kansas, Lawrence, KS 66045
Subscription telephone: 913 864-4798

ADVERTISING INFORMATION

Advertising accepted: Yes

EDITORIAL DESCRIPTION

Scope: Reports on the MLA Sessions on Renaissance and Medieval Drama; includes bibliographies and research articles.
Reviews books: Yes
Publishes notes: Yes
Languages accepted: English
Prints abstracts: No
Author-anonymous submission: No

SUBMISSION REQUIREMENTS

Restrictions on contributors: None
Author pays submission fee: No
Author pays page charges: No
Length of articles: 30-40 pp. maximum
Length of book reviews: 2,500 words
Style: MLA
Number of copies required: 1
Copyright ownership: Editor
Rejected manuscripts: Returned
Time before publication decision: 2 mos.
Time between decision and publication: 8-12 mos.
Number of reviewers: 2-3
Articles submitted per year: 30
Articles published per year: 12
Book reviews published per year: 1

(2357)
*Resources for American Literary Study

Jackson R. Bryer & Carla Mulford, Editors
Journals Dept.
Pennsylvania State Univ. Press
820 N. University Dr.
University Park, PA 16802-1003

Telephone: 814 865-1327
Fax: 814 863-1408
First published: 1971
Sponsoring organization: Univ. of Maryland; Pennsylvania State Univ.
ISSN: 0048-7384
MLA acronym: RALS

SUBSCRIPTION INFORMATION

Frequency of publication: 2 times/yr. (Spring, Fall)
Circulation: 500
Available in microform: Yes
Subscription price: $20.00/yr. institutions US; $23.00/yr. institutions elsewhere; $17.50/yr. individuals US; $20.00/yr. individuals elsewhere
Year to which price refers: 1991-92
Subscription address: Suite C, Barbara Bldg.
Subscription telephone: 814 326-9180

ADVERTISING INFORMATION

Advertising accepted: Yes
Advertising rates: $100.00/half page; $200.00/full page

EDITORIAL DESCRIPTION

Scope: Publishes: (1) annotated and evaluative checklists of critical and biographical scholarship on the significant works of major authors, or the total work of minor authors; (2) evaluative bibliographical essays on major authors, works, genres, trends, and periods; (3) informative accounts or catalogues of significant collections of research materials of literary and cultural interest available in archives and libraries, with special attention to recent acquisitions; and (4) edited correspondence, personal papers, unpublished materials, and other documents and essays of interest to literary scholars and cultural historians.
Reviews books: Yes
Publishes notes: Yes
Languages accepted: English
Prints abstracts: No
Author-anonymous submission: No

SUBMISSION REQUIREMENTS

Restrictions on contributors: None
Author pays submission fee: No
Author pays page charges: No
Style: MLA
Number of copies required: 1
Special requirements: Type double-spaced throughout.
Copyright ownership: Pennsylvania State Univ. Press
Rejected manuscripts: Returned
Time before publication decision: 6 mos.
Time between decision and publication: 1 yr.
Number of reviewers: 2
Articles submitted per year: 25
Articles published per year: 12
Book reviews submitted per year: 25
Book reviews published per year: 25

(2358)
Restant: Tijdschrift voor Recente Semiotische Teorievorming en de Analyse van Teksten/Review for Semiotic Theories and the Analysis of Texts

Luk De Vos, André Lefèvre, Tony Meesdom, Kris Humbeeck, Rudi Horemans, Jeroen Olyslaeghers, & Stef Heyvaert, Editors
Generaal Eisenhowerlei 30
2140 Antwerp, Belgium

First published: 1970
Sponsoring organization: Univ. te Antwerpen
ISSN: 0771-095X
MLA acronym: Restant

SUBSCRIPTION INFORMATION

Frequency of publication: 4 times/yr.
Circulation: 500-1,000
Available in microform: No

ADVERTISING INFORMATION

Advertising accepted: Yes

EDITORIAL DESCRIPTION

Scope: Publishes articles on semiotics and Dutch and comparative literature, international film theory, communication, musical and cognitive theories, and the theory, philosophy, and sociology of literature.
Reviews books: Yes
Publishes notes: Yes
Languages accepted: English; French; German; Dutch; Afrikaans; Italian; Spanish
Prints abstracts: No
Author-anonymous submission: No

SUBMISSION REQUIREMENTS

Restrictions on contributors: None
Author pays submission fee: No
Author pays page charges: No
Length of articles: 15-35 pp.
Length of book reviews: 1,500 words minimum
Length of notes: 1,200 words minimum
Style: MLA
Number of copies required: 3
Special requirements: Submit a 5-8 line vita and an abstract if article is in Italian or Spanish.
Copyright ownership: Journal & author
Rejected manuscripts: Returned; enclose return postage.
Time before publication decision: 2-6 mos.
Time between decision and publication: 6 mos.
Number of reviewers: 5
Articles submitted per year: 350
Articles published per year: 40-75
Book reviews submitted per year: 200

Book reviews published per year: 20
Notes submitted per year: 50
Notes published per year: 5

(2359)
*Restoration: Studies in English Literary Culture, 1660-1700

J. M. Armistead, Editor
College of Letters & Sciences
James Madison Univ.
Harrisonburg, VA 22807

Telephone: 703 568-6261
Fax: 703 568-3561
First published: 1977
Sponsoring organization: James Madison Univ., College of Letters & Sciences
ISSN: 0162-9905
MLA acronym: Restoration

SUBSCRIPTION INFORMATION

Frequency of publication: 2 times/yr.
Circulation: 500
Available in microform: No
Subscription price: $8.00/yr. US; $12.00 ($18.00 airmail)/yr. elsewhere
Year to which price refers: 1992

ADVERTISING INFORMATION

Advertising accepted: Yes
Advertising rates: $150.00/full page; $200.00/ inside back cover

EDITORIAL DESCRIPTION

Scope: Journal publishes full-length articles and special essays on Restoration literary works and their contexts. Also includes an annotated bibliography, updated twice a year, and announcements.
Reviews books: Yes
Publishes notes: Yes
Languages accepted: English
Prints abstracts: No
Author-anonymous submission: Yes, at author's request.

SUBMISSION REQUIREMENTS

Restrictions on contributors: Book reviews are commissioned.
Author pays submission fee: No
Author pays page charges: No
Length of articles: 3,000-7,000 words
Length of notes: 500-3,000 words
Style: MLA
Number of copies required: 2
Copyright ownership: James Madison Univ.
Rejected manuscripts: Returned
Time before publication decision: 1-2 mos.
Time between decision and publication: 12-18 mos.
Number of reviewers: 2
Articles submitted per year: 25
Articles published per year: 10
Book reviews published per year: 2

(2360)
*Restoration and 18th Century Theatre Research

Douglas H. White, Editor
Loyola Univ. of Chicago
6525 No. Sheridan Road
Chicago, IL 60626

Telephone: 312 508-2682
First published: 1962
Sponsoring organization: Loyola Univ. of Chicago
ISSN: 0034-5822
MLA acronym: RECTR

SUBSCRIPTION INFORMATION

Frequency of publication: 2 times/yr.
Circulation: 650
Available in microform: No
Subscription price: $8.00/yr.
Year to which price refers: 1992

ADVERTISING INFORMATION

Advertising accepted: Yes

EDITORIAL DESCRIPTION

Scope: Publishes articles on Restoration and 18th-century British theater, including theater history. Also publishes articles on drama, opera, and American theater of the period.
Reviews books: Yes
Publishes notes: Yes
Languages accepted: English
Prints abstracts: No
Author-anonymous submission: Yes

SUBMISSION REQUIREMENTS

Restrictions on contributors: None
Author pays submission fee: No
Author pays page charges: No
Length of articles: 5,000 words maximum
Length of book reviews: 900-1,200 words
Length of notes: 600 words
Style: MLA
Number of copies required: 1
Copyright ownership: Assigned to journal
Rejected manuscripts: Returned
Time before publication decision: 4-6 mos.
Time between decision and publication: 6 mos.
Number of reviewers: 2
Articles submitted per year: 40
Articles published per year: 10-15
Books submitted per year: 6-8
Books published per year: 6-8

(2361)
*Review

James O. Hoge & James L. W. West III, Editors
Dept. of English
110B Williams Hall
Virginia Polytechnic Inst. & State Univ.
Blacksburg, VA 24061

Additional editorial address: James L. W. West III, Dept. of English, Pennsylvania State Univ., University Park, PA 16802
First published: 1979
ISSN: 0190-3233
MLA acronym: Rev

SUBSCRIPTION INFORMATION

Frequency of publication: Annual
Circulation: 750
Available in microform: No
Subscription address: Univ. Press of Virginia, P.O. Box 3608, University Station, Charlottesville, VA 22903

ADVERTISING INFORMATION

Advertising accepted: No

EDITORIAL DESCRIPTION

Scope: Publishes lengthy reviews of scholarly work in all periods and genres of English and American literature.
Reviews books: Yes
Publishes notes: No
Languages accepted: English
Prints abstracts: No

SUBMISSION REQUIREMENTS

Restrictions on contributors: Unsolicited manuscripts are not accepted.
Author pays submission fee: No
Author pays page charges: No
Length of articles: 2,000 words minimum
Style: Journal
Number of copies required: 2
Special requirements: Submit double-spaced typescript.
Copyright ownership: Univ. Press of Virginia
Rejected manuscripts: Returned
Time before publication decision: 6 weeks
Time between decision and publication: 9 mos.
Number of reviewers: 3
Articles submitted per year: 22
Articles published per year: 22

(2362)
*Review: Latin American Literature and Arts

Alfred J. Mac Adam, Editor
Americas Soc.
680 Park Ave.
New York, NY 10021

Telephone: 212 249-8950
Fax: 212 517-6247
First published: 1968
Sponsoring organization: Americas Soc., Inc.
ISSN: 0890-5762
MLA acronym: Review

SUBSCRIPTION INFORMATION

Frequency of publication: 2 times/yr.
Circulation: 4,000
Available in microform: Yes
Subscription price: $22.00/yr. institutions US; $14.00/yr. individuals US; $26.00/yr. elsewhere
Year to which price refers: 1992

ADVERTISING INFORMATION

Advertising accepted: Yes
Advertising rates: $400.00/half page; $800.00/ full page

EDITORIAL DESCRIPTION

Scope: Publishes critical studies on Latin American and Caribbean literature and arts. Includes translations.
Reviews books: Yes
Publishes notes: No
Languages accepted: English
Prints abstracts: No
Author-anonymous submission: No

SUBMISSION REQUIREMENTS

Author pays submission fee: No
Author pays page charges: No
Length of articles: 2,500-4,000 words
Length of book reviews: 600-1,500 words
Style: MLA
Number of copies required: 1
Special requirements: All translations must be accompanied by the original Spanish or Portuguese.
Copyright ownership: Journal
Rejected manuscripts: Returned; enclose SASE.
Time before publication decision: 2 mos.
Time between decision and publication: 1 yr.
Number of reviewers: 5
Articles published per year: 20-30
Book reviews published per year: 35-40

(2363)
*The Review of Contemporary Fiction

John O'Brien & Steven Moore, Editors
Fairchild Hall
Illinois State Univ.
Normal, IL 61761

First published: 1981
ISSN: 0276-0045
MLA acronym: RCF

SUBSCRIPTION INFORMATION

Frequency of publication: 3 times/yr. (Spring, Summer, Fall)
Circulation: 3,175
Available in microform: Yes
Subscription price: $24.00/yr. institutions; $17.00/yr. individuals
Year to which price refers: 1992

ADVERTISING INFORMATION

Advertising accepted: Yes
Advertising rates: $150.00/full page

EDITORIAL DESCRIPTION

Scope: Publishes articles on contemporary fiction. Each issue is devoted to criticism of one or two contemporary novelists.
Reviews books: Yes
Publishes notes: No
Languages accepted: English
Prints abstracts: No
Author-anonymous submission: No

SUBMISSION REQUIREMENTS

Author pays submission fee: No
Author pays page charges: No
Length of articles: 1,000-3,000 words
Length of book reviews: 300 words
Style: Chicago
Number of copies required: 2
Copyright ownership: Journal; reverts to author
Rejected manuscripts: Returned; enclose SASE.
Time before publication decision: 1 mo.
Time between decision and publication: 1 yr.
Number of reviewers: 1-3
Articles submitted per year: 350
Articles published per year: 75
Book reviews submitted per year: 125
Book reviews published per year: 90

(2364)
*Review of English Studies: A Quarterly Journal of English Literature and the English Language

R. E. Alton, Editor
Academic Publishing Division
Oxford Univ. Press
Walton St.
Oxford OX2 6DP, England

First published: 1925
ISSN: 0034-6551
MLA acronym: RES

SUBSCRIPTION INFORMATION

Frequency of publication: 4 times/yr. (Feb., May, Aug., Nov.)
Circulation: 2,600
Available in microform: Yes
Subscription price: £56.00/yr. United Kingdom; $106.00/yr. US
Year to which price refers: 1992
Subscription address: Journals Subscriptions Dept., Oxford Univ. Press, Pinkhill House, Southfield Rd., Eynsham, Oxford OX8 1JJ, England
Subscription telephone: (44) 865 882283
Subscription fax: (44) 865 882890

ADVERTISING INFORMATION

Advertising accepted: Yes

EDITORIAL DESCRIPTION

Scope: Publishes scholarly articles on English literature and language.
Reviews books: Yes
Publishes notes: Yes
Languages accepted: English
Prints abstracts: No
Author-anonymous submission: No

SUBMISSION REQUIREMENTS

Restrictions on contributors: Reviews are commissioned.
Author pays submission fee: No
Author pays page charges: No
Length of articles: 4,000-8,000 words
Length of book reviews: 700 words
Length of notes: 2,000-3,000 words
Style: Oxford Univ. Press
Number of copies required: 1
Copyright ownership: Oxford Univ. Press
Rejected manuscripts: Returned; enclose return postage.
Time before publication decision: 6 mos.
Time between decision and publication: 18 mos.
Number of reviewers: 1-2
Articles submitted per year: 150
Articles published per year: 12
Book reviews published per year: 200
Notes published per year: 8-10

(2365)
*Review of National Literatures

Anne Paolucci, Editor
Council on National Literatures
P.O. Box 81
Whitestone, NY 11357

Telephone: 718 767-5364
Fax: 718 767-8380
First published: 1970
Sponsoring organization: Council on National Literatures
ISSN: 0034-6640
MLA acronym: RNL

SUBSCRIPTION INFORMATION

Frequency of publication: Annual
Circulation: 1,000
Available in microform: No
Subscription price: $35.00/yr. US; $45.00/yr. elsewhere
Year to which price refers: 1992

ADVERTISING INFORMATION

Advertising accepted: Yes
Advertising rates: $200.00/full page; $400.00/ inside back cover

EDITORIAL DESCRIPTION

Scope: Each issue focuses on a national culture or a representative theme, author, literary movement, or critical tendency, in an effort to provide substantial and concentrated critical materials for comparative studies of Western and non-Western literatures.
Reviews books: Yes
Publishes notes: Yes
Languages accepted: English
Prints abstracts: No
Author-anonymous submission: No

SUBMISSION REQUIREMENTS

Restrictions on contributors: Unsolicited manuscripts are not accepted.
Author pays submission fee: No
Author pays page charges: No
Length of articles: 25-30 pp.
Length of book reviews: No restrictions
Style: Journal
Number of copies required: 2
Special requirements: Submit 2 copies of typescript or on IBM-compatible diskette using WordPerfect.
Copyright ownership: Council on National Literatures
Rejected manuscripts: Returned
Number of reviewers: 4
Articles published per year: 7-10

(2366)
*De Revisor

Maria van Daalen, Christien Kok, Dirk Ayelt Kooiman, & Jan Kuijper, Editors
De Revisor B.V.
Singel 262
1016 AC Amsterdam, Netherlands

Telephone: (31) 20 5511262
Fax: (31) 20 6203509
First published: 1974
ISSN: 0302-8852
MLA acronym: Revisor

SUBSCRIPTION INFORMATION

Frequency of publication: 6 times/yr.
Circulation: 1,200
Available in microform: No
Subscription price: 82.50 f/yr. Netherlands; 100 f/yr. elsewhere

ADVERTISING INFORMATION

Advertising accepted: Yes
Advertising rates: 195 f/quarter page; 360 f/ half page; 660 f/full page

EDITORIAL DESCRIPTION

Scope: Publishes prose, poetry, and articles on literature.
Reviews books: No
Publishes notes: No
Languages accepted: Dutch
Prints abstracts: No
Author-anonymous submission: No

SUBMISSION REQUIREMENTS

Author pays submission fee: No
Author pays page charges: No
Length of articles: 6,000-10,000 words
Number of copies required: 5
Special requirements: Manuscript must be typescript. Articles in English, French, Italian, Spanish, Norwegian, Swedish, and Russian are accepted for translation into Dutch.
Copyright ownership: Author
Rejected manuscripts: Returned; enclose return postage.
Time before publication decision: 1-2 mos.
Time between decision and publication: 2-6 mos.
Number of reviewers: 6
Articles submitted per year: 1,000
Articles published per year: 25

(2367)
*Revista Alicantina de Estudios Ingleses

Pedro Jesús Marcos-Pérez, Enrique Alcaraz-Varó, José Antonio Alvarez-Amorós, & M. Carmen Africa Vidal, Editors
c/o Secretaría
Dept. de Filología Inglesa
Univ. de Alicante
03071 Alicante, Spain

Telephone: (34) 6 5903440
Fax: (34) 6 5903464
First published: 1988
Sponsoring organization: Dept. de Filología Inglesa, Univ. de Alicante
ISSN: 0214-4808
MLA acronym: RAEI

SUBSCRIPTION INFORMATION

Frequency of publication: Annual (Nov.)
Circulation: 100
Available in microform: No
Subscription price: 4,500 Pta/4 issues institutions; 5,500 Pta/4 issues individuals
Year to which price refers: 1992

ADVERTISING INFORMATION

Advertising accepted: Yes

EDITORIAL DESCRIPTION

Scope: Publishes articles on the language, literature, linguistics, literary theory, criticism, history, and culture of English-speaking countries.
Reviews books: Yes
Publishes notes: No
Languages accepted: English; Occasionnally Spanish
Prints abstracts: Yes
Author-anonymous submission: Yes

SUBMISSION REQUIREMENTS

Restrictions on contributors: None
Author pays submission fee: No
Author pays page charges: No
Length of articles: 9,000 words
Length of book reviews: 1,000 words
Style: MLA
Number of copies required: 2
Special requirements: Include a 100-word maximum abstract. Submission on MS-DOS diskette using WordPerfect is required.
Copyright ownership: Dept. de Filología Inglesa, Univ. de Alicante
Rejected manuscripts: Returned at author's request
Time before publication decision: 2-3 mos.
Time between decision and publication: 1 yr.
Number of reviewers: 1
Articles submitted per year: 15-20
Articles published per year: 12-15
Book reviews submitted per year: 10-15
Book reviews published per year: 8-10

(2368)
*Revista Argentina de Lingüística

Victor M. Castel & César E. Quiroga S., Editors
Casilla de Correo 45
5511 Gral. Gutiérrez
Mendoza, Argentina

Telephone: (54) 61 978716
Fax: (54) 61 380370
First published: 1985
Sponsoring organization: Conicet
ISSN: 0326-6400
MLA acronym: RAdL

SUBSCRIPTION INFORMATION

Frequency of publication: 2 times/yr. (Mar., Sept.)
Circulation: 200
Available in microform: No
Subscription price: $45.00/yr.
Year to which price refers: 1992

ADVERTISING INFORMATION

Advertising accepted: Yes

EDITORIAL DESCRIPTION

Scope: Publishes studies on a wide range of linguistic topics.
Reviews books: Yes
Publishes notes: Yes
Languages accepted: Spanish
Prints abstracts: Yes
Author-anonymous submission: Yes

SUBMISSION REQUIREMENTS

Author pays submission fee: No
Author pays page charges: No
Style: Journal
Number of copies required: 3
Special requirements: Submit a 200-word abstract in English and Spanish.
Copyright ownership: Journal
Time before publication decision: 6 mos.

Time between decision and publication: 6 mos.
Number of reviewers: 2

(2369)
Revista Brasileira de Língua e Literatura

Leodegario A. de Azevedo Filho & Mario Camarinha da Silva, Editors
Soc. Brasileira de Língua e Literatura
Av. Epitácio Pessoa, 2094
Apt. 102
Rio de Janeiro 22471, Brazil

First published: 1979
ISSN: 0101-8248
MLA acronym: RBLL

SUBSCRIPTION INFORMATION

Frequency of publication: Irregular
Available in microform: No
Subscription address: Livraria Padrão, Rua Miguel Conto 40, Rio de Janeiro, Brazil

ADVERTISING INFORMATION

Advertising accepted: Yes

EDITORIAL DESCRIPTION

Scope: Publishes articles, reviews, notes, short poems, and stories.
Reviews books: Yes
Publishes notes: Yes
Languages accepted: Portuguese
Prints abstracts: Yes
Author-anonymous submission: No

SUBMISSION REQUIREMENTS

Restrictions on contributors: None
Author pays submission fee: No
Author pays page charges: No
Length of articles: 10,000 words maximum
Length of book reviews: 3,000 words maximum
Length of notes: 300 words maximum
Style: Journal
Number of copies required: 1
Copyright ownership: Author
Time between decision and publication: 1 mo.
Number of reviewers: 2
Articles published per year: 8
Book reviews published per year: 8
Notes published per year: 8

(2370)
Revista Brasileira de Lingüística

Cidmar Teodoro Pais, Editor
Ed. Leo Degario A. de Azeveho Filho
Soc. Brasileira de Lingua e Literatura
av. Epitacio Pessoa, 2094
22471 Rio de Janeiro, Brazil

First published: 1974
Sponsoring organization: Soc. Brasileira para Professores de Lingüística
ISSN: 0102-6798
MLA acronym: RBL

SUBSCRIPTION INFORMATION

Frequency of publication: 2 times/yr.

EDITORIAL DESCRIPTION

Scope: Publishes scholary articles on general linguistics and semiotics.
Languages accepted: Portuguese
Prints abstracts: Yes

(2371)
*Revista Canadiense de Estudios Hispánicos

Nigel Dennis, Editor
Dept. of Modern Languages & Literatures
Univ. of Ottawa
Ottawa, Ontario K1N 6N5, Canada

Additional editorial address: Victor Ouimette, Review Editor, Dept. of Hispanic Studies, McGill Univ., 1001 Sherbrooke St. W, Montreal, PQ, H3A 1G5, Canada
Telephone: 613 564-7419
Fax: 613 564-7527
First published: 1976
Sponsoring organization: Asoc. Canadiense de Hispanistas; Carleton Univ.
ISSN: 0384-8167
MLA acronym: RCEH

SUBSCRIPTION INFORMATION

Frequency of publication: 3 times/yr. (Fall, Winter, Spring)
Circulation: 1,000
Available in microform: No
Subscription price: C$30.00/yr. institutions; C$20.00/yr. individuals
Year to which price refers: 1992
Subscription address: C. A. Marsden, Spanish Dept., Carleton Univ., Ottawa K1S 5B6, Canada

ADVERTISING INFORMATION

Advertising accepted: No

EDITORIAL DESCRIPTION

Scope: Publishes articles on literature, philosophy, and history of the Hispanic world and its worldwide relations.
Reviews books: Yes
Publishes notes: Yes
Languages accepted: English; French; Spanish; Catalan; Portuguese; Galician
Prints abstracts: Yes
Author-anonymous submission: No

SUBMISSION REQUIREMENTS

Restrictions on contributors: Contributors must be subscribers. Unsolicited book reviews are not accepted.
Author pays submission fee: No
Author pays page charges: No
Length of articles: 20 double-spaced pp. maximum
Length of book reviews: 500-1,000 words
Length of notes: 2,000 words
Style: MLA
Number of copies required: 2
Special requirements: Include a summary in Castellano.
Copyright ownership: Journal
Rejected manuscripts: Returned
Time before publication decision: 3 mos.
Time between decision and publication: 18-24 mos.
Number of reviewers: 2-3
Articles submitted per year: 100-125
Articles published per year: 18-20
Book reviews published per year: 25
Notes submitted per year: 20-30
Notes published per year: 9

(2372)
*Revista Canaria de Estudios Ingleses

Dept. de Inglés
Fac. de Filogía
Univ. de La Laguna
Tenerife, Spain

First published: 1980
Sponsoring organization: Univ. de La Laguna, Secretariado de Publicaciones

ISSN: 0211-5913
MLA acronym: RCEI

SUBSCRIPTION INFORMATION

Frequency of publication: 2 times/yr. (Apr., Nov.)
Circulation: 500
Available in microform: No
Subscription price: $60.00/yr. institutions; $45.00/yr. individuals
Year to which price refers: 1992
Subscription address: Secretariado de Pubs., Univ. de La Laguna, San Augustín 30, 38201 La Laguna, Tenerife, Spain

ADVERTISING INFORMATION

Advertising accepted: Yes

EDITORIAL DESCRIPTION

Scope: Publishes articles on the English language (both historical and modern) and the literature of English-speaking countries.
Reviews books: Yes
Publishes notes: Yes
Languages accepted: English; Spanish
Prints abstracts: Yes
Author-anonymous submission: Yes

SUBMISSION REQUIREMENTS

Restrictions on contributors: None
Author pays submission fee: No
Author pays page charges: No
Length of articles: 4,000-10,000 words
Length of book reviews: 1,500-5,000 words
Length of notes: 1,000-4,000 words
Style: MLA
Number of copies required: 2
Copyright ownership: Journal
Rejected manuscripts: Returned; enclose return postage.
Time before publication decision: 6-8 weeks
Time between decision and publication: 4-8 mos.
Number of reviewers: 3
Articles submitted per year: 15
Articles published per year: 11
Book reviews submitted per year: 12
Book reviews published per year: 10
Notes submitted per year: 12
Notes published per year: 10

(2373)
*Revista Chilena de Literatura

Hugo Montes Brunet, Editor
Fac. de Filosofía & Humanidades
Dept. de Literatura, Univ. de Chile
Ignacio Carrera Pinto 1025-Ñuñoa
Casilla 10136 Correo Central
Santiago, Chile

Telephone: (56) 2 2725978
Fax: (56) 2 2716823
First published: 1970
Sponsoring organization: Univ. de Chile, Dept. de Literatura
ISSN: 0048-7651
MLA acronym: RChL

SUBSCRIPTION INFORMATION

Frequency of publication: 2 times/yr.
Available in microform: No
Subscription price: $30.00/yr.
Year to which price refers: 1992

ADVERTISING INFORMATION

Advertising accepted: No

EDITORIAL DESCRIPTION

Scope: Publishes articles on literary theory and criticism.
Reviews books: Yes
Publishes notes: Yes
Languages accepted: Spanish
Prints abstracts: No
Author-anonymous submission: No

SUBMISSION REQUIREMENTS

Restrictions on contributors: None
Author pays submission fee: No
Author pays page charges: No
Length of articles: No restrictions
Length of book reviews: No restrictions
Length of notes: No restrictions
Style: None
Number of copies required: 2
Special requirements: Submit original typescript.
Copyright ownership: Journal
Rejected manuscripts: Not returned
Time before publication decision: 3 mos.
Time between decision and publication: 3 mos.
Number of reviewers: 5
Articles submitted per year: 30
Articles published per year: 10-20
Book reviews submitted per year: 10
Book reviews published per year: 6-8
Notes submitted per year: 20
Notes published per year: 6

(2374)
*Revista de Crítica Literaria Latinoamericana

Antonio Cornejo Polar, Editor
Ave. Benavides 3074
La Castellana
Lima 18, Peru

Additional editorial address: 1309 Cathedral of Learning-Hispanic, Univ. of Pittsburgh, Pittsburgh, PA 15260
Telephone: (51) 54 486353; 412 624-5225
Fax: 412 624-8505
First published: 1975
Sponsoring organization: Univ. of Pittsburgh
ISSN: 0252-8843
MLA acronym: RCLL

SUBSCRIPTION INFORMATION

Frequency of publication: 2 times/yr. (July, Dec.)
Circulation: 1,500
Available in microform: No
Subscription price: $35.00/yr.
Year to which price refers: 1993

ADVERTISING INFORMATION

Advertising accepted: Yes
Advertising rates: $60.00/half page; $100.00/full page

EDITORIAL DESCRIPTION

Scope: Publishes critical articles on Latin American literature with a focus on the study of the relationship between literature and society.
Reviews books: Yes
Publishes notes: Yes
Languages accepted: Spanish; Portuguese
Prints abstracts: No
Author-anonymous submission: No

SUBMISSION REQUIREMENTS

Restrictions on contributors: None
Author pays submission fee: No
Author pays page charges: No
Length of articles: 30 pp. (25 lines/p.)
Length of book reviews: 6 pp. (25 lines/p.)
Length of notes: 12 pp. (25 lines/p.)
Style: MLA
Number of copies required: 1
Copyright ownership: Author
Rejected manuscripts: Not returned
Time before publication decision: 6-12 mos.
Time between decision and publication: 6-24 mos.
Number of reviewers: 3
Articles submitted per year: 160-180
Articles published per year: 25-30
Book reviews submitted per year: 50-60
Book reviews published per year: 20-25
Notes submitted per year: 50-60
Notes published per year: 8-10

(2375)
*Revista de Dialectología y Tradiciones Populares

Julio Caro Baroja, Editor
Inst. de Filología
Consejo Superior de Investigaciones Científicas
Duque de Medinaceli, 6
28014 Madrid, Spain

Telephone: (34) 1 5856156
Fax: (34) 1 5856197
First published: 1944
Sponsoring organization: Inst. de Filología, Consejo Superior de Investigaciones Científicas
ISSN: 0034-7981
MLA acronym: RDTP

SUBSCRIPTION INFORMATION

Frequency of publication: Annual
Circulation: 600
Available in microform: No
Subscription price: 3,300 Pta/yr.
Year to which price refers: 1992
Subscription address: Oficina de Pubs., C.S.I.C., Vitruvio, 8, 28006 Madrid, Spain
Subscription telephone: (34) 1 5855674

ADVERTISING INFORMATION

Advertising accepted: No

EDITORIAL DESCRIPTION

Scope: Publishes articles on ethnology, folklore, folk art, oral tradition, speech, and dialect of Spain. Includes bibliographies.
Reviews books: Yes
Publishes notes: Yes
Languages accepted: Spanish
Prints abstracts: Yes
Author-anonymous submission: No

SUBMISSION REQUIREMENTS

Restrictions on contributors: None
Author pays submission fee: No
Author pays page charges: No
Length of articles: 10,000 words
Length of book reviews: 600-1,000 words
Length of notes: 3,000 words
Style: Revista de Filología Española
Number of copies required: 2
Copyright ownership: Journal
Rejected manuscripts: Returned
Time before publication decision: 3 mos.
Time between decision and publication: 1 yr.
Number of reviewers: 3
Articles submitted per year: 20-30
Articles published per year: 15
Book reviews submitted per year: 30
Book reviews published per year: 15
Notes submitted per year: 10
Notes published per year: 5

(2376)
*Revista de Estudios Extremeños

Manuel Pecellín Lancharro, Director
Dept. de Publicaciones
Diputación Provincial de Badajoz
Felipe Checa 1
06071 Badajoz, Spain

Telephone: (34) 24 222518

First published: 1927
Sponsoring organization: Diputación Provincial
ISSN: 0210-2854
MLA acronym: REE

SUBSCRIPTION INFORMATION

Frequency of publication: 3 times/yr.
Available in microform: No
Subscription price: 1,000 Pta ($12.00)/yr.
Year to which price refers: 1992
Subscription address: Vasco Núñez, 54, P.O. Box 581, 06001 Badajoz, Spain

ADVERTISING INFORMATION

Advertising accepted: No

EDITORIAL DESCRIPTION

Scope: Fosters knowledge concerning the Spanish region of Extremadura.
Reviews books: Yes
Publishes notes: Yes
Languages accepted: Spanish; Portuguese; English
Prints abstracts: No
Author-anonymous submission: No

SUBMISSION REQUIREMENTS

Restrictions on contributors: None
Author pays submission fee: No
Author pays page charges: No
Length of articles: No restrictions
Length of book reviews: No restrictions
Length of notes: No restrictions
Style: None
Number of copies required: 1
Special requirements: Submit original typescript.
Copyright ownership: Journal
Rejected manuscripts: Returned
Time before publication decision: 4 mos.
Time between decision and publication: 1 mo.
Number of reviewers: 2
Articles submitted per year: 40
Articles published per year: 30
Book reviews submitted per year: 30
Book reviews published per year: 25
Notes submitted per year: 30
Notes published per year: 25

(2377)
*Revista de Estudios Hispánicos

Mercedes López-Baralt, Editor
Seminario de Estudios Hispánicos
"Federico de Onís"
Fac. de Humanidades
Univ. de Puerto Rico
Río Piedras, PR 00931

Telephone: 809 764-0000 ext. 2247, 3672, 3673, 3674
Fax: 809 763-5899
First published: 1971
Sponsoring organization: Seminario de Estudios Hispánicos "Federico de Onís"; Univ. of Puerto Rico, Fac. de Humanidades
ISSN: 0378-7974
MLA acronym: REH-PR

SUBSCRIPTION INFORMATION

Frequency of publication: Annual
Circulation: 1,000
Available in microform: No
Subscription price: $18.50/yr. institutions; $9.00/yr. individuals; $6.00/yr. students
Year to which price refers: 1992
Subscription address: Editorial de la Univ. de Puerto Rico, P.O. Box 23322, University Station, Río Piedras, PR 00931-3322

ADVERTISING INFORMATION

Advertising accepted: Yes

EDITORIAL DESCRIPTION

Scope: Publishes documents and unpublished research works, bibliographies, and criticism on Hispanic literature, linguistics, cultural history, and folklore.
Reviews books: Yes
Publishes notes: Yes
Languages accepted: Spanish; English; French
Prints abstracts: No
Author-anonymous submission: No

SUBMISSION REQUIREMENTS

Restrictions on contributors: None
Author pays submission fee: No
Author pays page charges: No
Length of articles: 9,000 words
Length of book reviews: 1,800 words
Style: MLA with modifications
Number of copies required: 1
Special requirements: Submit original typescript.
Copyright ownership: Journal
Rejected manuscripts: Returned
Time before publication decision: 1 mo.
Time between decision and publication: 6 mos.
Number of reviewers: 4
Articles submitted per year: 12-14
Articles published per year: 8-10
Book reviews submitted per year: 10
Book reviews published per year: 5
Notes submitted per year: 8

(2378)
*Revista de Estudios Hispánicos

Randolph D. Pope, Editor
Washington Univ.
One Brookings Dr.
St. Louis, MO 63130-4899

Telephone: 314 935-5175
Fax: 314 726-3494
First published: 1967
Sponsoring organization: Washington Univ.
ISSN: 0034-818X
MLA acronym: REH

SUBSCRIPTION INFORMATION

Frequency of publication: 3 times/yr. (Winter, Spring, Fall)
Circulation: 546
Available in microform: Yes, through Univ. Microfilms International
Subscription price: $33.00/yr. institutions; $21.00/yr. individuals; $15.00/yr. students
Year to which price refers: 1993
Subscription address: Michael Mudrovic, Managing Editor, at the above address

ADVERTISING INFORMATION

Advertising accepted: No

EDITORIAL DESCRIPTION

Scope: Publishes articles on Spanish and Spanish American language and literature.
Reviews books: Yes
Publishes notes: No
Languages accepted: English; Spanish
Prints abstracts: No
Author-anonymous submission: No

SUBMISSION REQUIREMENTS

Restrictions on contributors: Unsolicited book reviews are not accepted.
Author pays submission fee: No
Author pays page charges: No
Length of articles: 15-30 pp.
Length of book reviews: 500 words
Style: MLA
Number of copies required: 2
Special requirements: Submit original typescript or laser print and 1 copy.
Copyright ownership: Journal
Rejected manuscripts: Returned; enclose SASE.
Time before publication decision: 4 mos.
Time between decision and publication: 1 yr.
Number of reviewers: 3
Articles submitted per year: 150
Articles published per year: 20
Book reviews published per year: 40

(2379)
Revista de Etnografie şi Folclor

Alex Dobre, Editor
Editura Academiei Rômane
Calea Victoriei 125
79717 Bucharest, Romania

First published: 1956
Sponsoring organization: Academia Româná
ISSN: 0034-8198
MLA acronym: REF

SUBSCRIPTION INFORMATION

Subscription address: Rompresfilatelia, Calea Grivitei 64-66, P.O. Box 12-201, 78104 Bucharest, Romania

EDITORIAL DESCRIPTION

Scope: Publishes studies and materials on culture from the standpoint of ethnography and Romanian folklore, literature, music, and dance.
Reviews books: Yes
Languages accepted: Romanian
Prints abstracts: Yes

(2380)
Revista de Filologia de la Universidad de La Laguna

Fac. de Filologia
Univ. de La Laguna
Tenerife, Spain

ISSN: 0212-4130
MLA acronym: RFULL

SUBSCRIPTION INFORMATION

Frequency of publication: 2 times/yr.

EDITORIAL DESCRIPTION

Scope: Publishes articles on scholarship in classical and modern languages and literatures.
Reviews books: Yes
Languages accepted: Spanish
Prints abstracts: No

(2381)
Revista de Filología Española

Editorial Gómez, S.L., Editor
Plaza del Castillo 28
Apt. 86
Pamplona, Spain

First published: 1914
Sponsoring organization: Inst. Miguel de Cervantes
ISSN: 0556-5871
MLA acronym: RFE

SUBSCRIPTION INFORMATION

Frequency of publication: Annual

EDITORIAL DESCRIPTION

Scope: Each issue is devoted to one work with one author.

Languages accepted: Spanish
Prints abstracts: No

(2382)
*Revista de Filología y Lingüística de la Universidad de Costa Rica

Enrique Margery Peña, Director
Editorial de la Univ. de Costa Rica
A.P. 75
2060 Ciudad Universitaria Rodrigo Facio
San José, Costa Rica

Telephone: (506) 253133; (506) 247977; (506) 247071
Fax: (506) 249267
Sponsoring organization: Univ. de Costa Rica
ISSN: 0377-628X
MLA acronym: RFLUCR

SUBSCRIPTION INFORMATION

Frequency of publication: 2 times/yr.
Circulation: 300
Available in microform: No
Subscription price: 500 C/yr. Costa Rica; $20.00/yr. elsewhere
Year to which price refers: 1992

ADVERTISING INFORMATION

Advertising accepted: No

EDITORIAL DESCRIPTION

Scope: Publishes articles on Hispanic and other literatures, linguistics, and philology.
Reviews books: No
Publishes notes: Yes
Languages accepted: Spanish; English; French
Prints abstracts: Yes

SUBMISSION REQUIREMENTS

Author pays submission fee: No
Author pays page charges: No
Length of articles: 40 pp. maximum
Number of copies required: 3
Copyright ownership: Author
Time before publication decision: 1 yr.
Time between decision and publication: 1 yr.
Articles submitted per year: 30
Articles published per year: 24

(2383)
Revista de História

Euripedes Simoes de Paula, Editor
Dept. de História da USP
C.P. 8105
Cidade Universitária
São Paulo, Brazil

First published: 1950
Sponsoring organization: Univ. do São Paolo, Dept. de História
ISSN: 0034-8309
MLA acronym: RdH

SUBSCRIPTION INFORMATION

Frequency of publication: 4 times/yr.
Circulation: 3,000

ADVERTISING INFORMATION

Advertising accepted: No

EDITORIAL DESCRIPTION

Scope: Publishes articles on history and humanistic sciences.
Reviews books: Yes
Publishes notes: Yes
Languages accepted: Portuguese
Prints abstracts: No

Author-anonymous submission: No

SUBMISSION REQUIREMENTS

Restrictions on contributors: None
Author pays submission fee: No
Author pays page charges: No
Length of articles: No restrictions
Length of book reviews: 6-8 pp.
Style: None
Number of copies required: 1
Copyright ownership: Journal
Rejected manuscripts: Returned
Time before publication decision: 3 mos.
Number of reviewers: 1
Articles submitted per year: 45
Articles published per year: 30
Book reviews submitted per year: 50
Book reviews published per year: 45

(2384)
Revista de Istorie şi Teorie Literară

Zoe Dumitrescu Buşulenga, Editor
Editura Academiei Rômane
Calea Victoriei 125
71021 Bucharest, Romania

First published: 1952
Sponsoring organization: Academia de Ştiinţe Sociale şi Politice, Inst. de Istorie şi Teorie Literară George Călinescu
ISSN: 0034-8392
MLA acronym: RITL

SUBSCRIPTION INFORMATION

Frequency of publication: 4 times/yr.
Circulation: 1,500
Subscription address: ILEXIM, Export-Import Presa, Str. 13 Decembrie Nr. 3, Box 136-137, 70116 Bucharest, Romania

EDITORIAL DESCRIPTION

Scope: Contributes to the scientific appreciation of the national literary patrimony, to the development of studies and research in history and theory of literature, in world and comparative literature, aesthetics, and folklore. Publishes studies, articles, debates, commentaries on scientific life giving information about the results attained in these domains in Romania and abroad, at encouraging the exchange of ideas, initiatives, work hypotheses, points of view, new methods of exploration, and interpretation of the literary phenomenon. Addresses literary scholars and historians, comparatists, aestheticians, folklorists, critics, writers, research-workers, journalists, professors, and students.
Reviews books: Yes
Languages accepted: English; French; German; Romanian; Russian; Spanish; Italian
Prints abstracts: No

SUBMISSION REQUIREMENTS

Restrictions on contributors: None
Length of articles: 10-20 pp.
Number of copies required: 2
Special requirements: Submit original typescript.
Rejected manuscripts: Not returned
Time before publication decision: 1-2 mos.
Time between decision and publication: 18 mos.
Number of reviewers: 3 plus Editorial Board
Articles published per year: 50-60

(2385)
*Revista de Letras

Coordenadoria Geral de Bibliotecas da UNESP
Seção de Intercâmbio
Av. Vicente Ferreira, 1278
C.P. 603
17.500 Marília, São Paulo, Brazil

First published: 1959
Sponsoring organization: Univ. Estadual Paulista
ISSN: 0101-3505
MLA acronym: RDLet

SUBSCRIPTION INFORMATION

Frequency of publication: Annual
Available in microform: No
Subscription price: $30.00/yr.
Year to which price refers: 1991
Subscription address: FUNDUNESP-Fundação para o Desenvolvimento da UNESP, Diretoria de Publicações, Av. Rio Branco, 1210, Campos Elíseos, 01206 São Paulo SP, Brazil

ADVERTISING INFORMATION

Advertising accepted: No

EDITORIAL DESCRIPTION

Scope: Publishes original articles on literature written by UNESP professors and others.
Reviews books: Yes
Publishes notes: No
Languages accepted: Portuguese
Prints abstracts: Yes
Author-anonymous submission: Yes

SUBMISSION REQUIREMENTS

Author pays submission fee: No
Author pays page charges: No
Length of articles: 10-20 pp.
Length of book reviews: 5 pp.
Number of copies required: 3
Special requirements: Reference material (such as bibliographic citations, abstracts, key words) must be in English.
Copyright ownership: Journal
Rejected manuscripts: Returned
Time before publication decision: 8 mos.
Time between decision and publication: 3 mos.
Number of reviewers: 4
Articles submitted per year: 15-18
Articles published per year: 10-12
Book reviews submitted per year: 2-3
Book reviews published per year: 2-3

(2386)
*Revista de Literatura

Miguel A. Garrido-Gallardo & Juan M. Díez-Taboada, Editors
Inst. de Filología
c/o Consejo Superior de Investigaciones Científicas
Duque de Medinaceli, 6
28014 Madrid, Spain

Telephone: (34) 1 5856154
Fax: (34) 1 5856197
First published: 1952
Sponsoring organization: Consejo Superior de Investigaciones Científicas (C.S.I.C.)
ISSN: 0034-849X
MLA acronym: RL

SUBSCRIPTION INFORMATION

Frequency of publication: 2 times/yr.
Available in microform: No
Subscription address: Oficina de Publicaciones, Vitruvio, 8, 28006 Madrid, Spain
Subscription telephone: (34) 1 2629633

ADVERTISING INFORMATION

Advertising accepted: Yes

EDITORIAL DESCRIPTION

Scope: Publishes articles on contemporary theory and criticism of literature as well as on Spanish literature.
Reviews books: Yes
Publishes notes: Yes
Languages accepted: Spanish
Prints abstracts: Yes
Author-anonymous submission: Yes

SUBMISSION REQUIREMENTS

Author pays submission fee: No
Author pays page charges: No
Length of articles: No restrictions
Length of book reviews: No restrictions
Length of notes: No restrictions
Style: Journal
Number of copies required: 2
Copyright ownership: Consejo Superior de Investigaciones Científicas, Inst. de Filología
Rejected manuscripts: Returned
Time before publication decision: 6 mos.
Time between decision and publication: 6 mos.
Number of reviewers: 2
Articles submitted per year: 20-25
Articles published per year: 12-16
Book reviews submitted per year: 26-28
Book reviews published per year: 22-24
Notes submitted per year: 15
Notes published per year: 6-10

(2387)
*Revista de Occidente

Fundación José Ortega y Gasset
Fortuny, 53
28010 Madrid, Spain

Telephone: (34) 1 4104412
Fax: (34) 1 3084007
First published: 1923
Sponsoring organization: Fundación Ortega y Gasset
ISSN: 0034-8635
MLA acronym: RO

SUBSCRIPTION INFORMATION

Frequency of publication: 11 times/yr.
Circulation: 12,000
Available in microform: No
Subscription price: 7,600 Pta/yr. Spain; 9,700 Pta ($102.00)/yr. elsewhere
Year to which price refers: 1992
Snbscription telephone: (34) 1 4472700

ADVERTISING INFORMATION

Advertising accepted: Yes

EDITORIAL DESCRIPTION

Scope: Publishes articles related to the humanities and social sciences.
Reviews books: Yes
Languages accepted: Spanish
Prints abstracts: No
Author-anonymous submission: No

SUBMISSION REQUIREMENTS

Author pays submission fee: No
Author pays page charges: No
Length of articles: 3,500-4,500 words
Length of book reviews: 1,000-2,000 words
Number of copies required: 1
Copyright ownership: Author
Time between decision and publication: 2-6 mos.
Number of reviewers: 2-3
Articles submitted per year: 500
Articles published per year: 100-120
Book reviews published per year: 20-30

(2388)
*Revista de Teatro

Aldo Calvet, Editor
Av. Almte. Barroso, 97
3⁰ andar
Rio de Janeiro - RJ, Brazil

Additional editorial address: Rua da Quintanda, 194, 10⁰ andar, Rio de Janeiro, Brazil
Telephone: (55) 21 2539634; (55) 21 2407231
Fax: (55) 21 2407431
First published: 1955
Sponsoring organization: Soc. Brasileira de Autores Teatrais
ISSN: 0102-7336
MLA acronym: RdT

SUBSCRIPTION INFORMATION

Frequency of publication: 4 times/yr. (Mar., July, Sept., Dec.)
Available in microform: No
Subscription price: $30.00/yr.
Year to which price refers: 1992

ADVERTISING INFORMATION

Advertising accepted: Yes

EDITORIAL DESCRIPTION

Scope: Publishes works by Brazilian authors, notes on theater in Brazil, both on the professional and the amateur groups, anniversaries of famous world playrights, activities in the theater all over the world, Brazilian actors and actresses from the past and the present, etc.
Reviews books: No
Publishes notes: Yes
Languages accepted: Portuguese
Prints abstracts: No
Author-anonymous submission: No

SUBMISSION REQUIREMENTS

Author pays submission fee: No
Author pays page charges: No
Length of articles: 300 words
Length of notes: 50 words
Style: None
Number of copies required: 2
Copyright ownership: Journal
Rejected manuscripts: Not returned
Time before publication decision: 2 mos.
Time between decision and publication: 6 weeks
Number of reviewers: 2
Articles submitted per year: 12
Articles published per year: 6

(2389)
*La Revista del Centro de Estudios Avanzados de Puerto Rico y el Caribe

Ricardo E. Alegría, Director
Aptdo. S-4467
San Juan, PR 00904-4467

Telephone: 809 723-4481
Fax: 809 723-4481
First published: 1985
Sponsoring organization: Centro de Estudios Avanzados de Puerto Rico & el Caribe
MLA acronym: RCEPRC

SUBSCRIPTION INFORMATION

Frequency of publication: 2 times/yr.
Circulation: 100
Available in microform: No
Subscription price: $12.00/yr.
Year to which price refers: 1992

ADVERTISING INFORMATION

Advertising accepted: No

EDITORIAL DESCRIPTION

Scope: Publishes articles on Puerto Rican and Caribbean literature, history, and culture.
Reviews books: Yes
Publishes notes: No
Languages accepted: Spanish
Prints abstracts: No
Author-anonymous submission: No

SUBMISSION REQUIREMENTS

Author pays submission fee: No
Author pays page charges: No
Length of articles: 12-15 pp.
Length of book reviews: 1 p.
Number of copies required: 1
Copyright ownership: Author
Rejected manuscripts: Returned
Time before publication decision: 6 mos.
Time between decision and publication: 6 mos.
Number of reviewers: 2
Articles submitted per year: 40-45
Articles published per year: 20
Book reviews published per year: 8

(2390)
*Revista Española de Lingüística

Francisco R. Adrados, Editor
Soc. Española de Lingüística
Duque de Medinaceli, 6
Madrid-14, Spain

First published: 1971
Sponsoring organization: Soc. Española de Lingüística
ISSN: 0210-1874
MLA acronym: REspL

SUBSCRIPTION INFORMATION

Frequency of publication: 2 times/yr.
Circulation: 1,000
Available in microform: No
Subscription address: Editorial Gredos, Sanchez Pacheco, 81, Madrid-14, Spain

ADVERTISING INFORMATION

Advertising accepted: No

EDITORIAL DESCRIPTION

Scope: Concerned with synchronic and diachronic themes of general linguistics and with general interest studies on specific languages.
Reviews books: Yes
Publishes notes: Yes
Languages accepted: English; French; German; Spanish
Prints abstracts: Yes

SUBMISSION REQUIREMENTS

Restrictions on contributors: None
Length of articles: 15-25 pp.
Length of book reviews: 2-4 pp.
Number of copies required: 2
Copyright ownership: Editorial Gredos
Time before publication decision: 1 yr.
Time between decision and publication: 1 yr.
Articles published per year: 20
Book reviews published per year: 20

(2391)
*Revista Hispánica Moderna

Jaime Alazraki & Gonzalo Sobejano, Editors
Hispanic Inst.
Columbia Univ.
612 W. 116th St.
New York, NY 10027

Telephone: 212 854-8292
Fax: 212 854-4187

First published: 1934
Sponsoring organization: Columbia Univ., Hispanic Inst. of the US
ISSN: 0034-9593
MLA acronym: RHM

SUBSCRIPTION INFORMATION

Frequency of publication: 2 times/yr.
Circulation: 1,500
Available in microform: No
Subscription price: $30.00/yr. institutions; $20.00/yr. individuals; add $5.00/yr. postage outside US
Year to which price refers: 1992

ADVERTISING INFORMATION

Advertising accepted: No

EDITORIAL DESCRIPTION

Scope: Publishes articles on 19th- and 20th-century Spanish and Latin American literature.
Reviews books: Yes
Publishes notes: Yes
Languages accepted: English; Portuguese; Spanish
Prints abstracts: No
Author-anonymous submission: No

SUBMISSION REQUIREMENTS

Restrictions on contributors: Book reviews are solicited.
Author pays submission fee: No
Author pays page charges: No
Length of articles: 12-35 typescript pp.
Length of book reviews: 5 pp.
Length of notes: 10 pp.
Style: MLA
Number of copies required: 2
Special requirements: Submit original typescript.
Copyright ownership: Assigned by author to journal
Rejected manuscripts: Returned; enclose return postage.
Time before publication decision: 6-12 mos.
Time between decision and publication: 1-2 yrs.
Number of reviewers: 4
Articles submitted per year: 25-30
Articles published per year: 15-25
Book reviews published per year: 15-22
Notes submitted per year: 4-10
Notes published per year: 6

(2392)
*Revista Iberoamericana

Keith McDuffie, Editor
1312 C. L.
Univ. of Pittsburgh
Pittsburgh, PA 15260

Telephone: 412 624-3359; 412 624-5225
Fax: 412 624-8505
First published: 1938
Sponsoring organization: Inst. Internacional de Literatura Iberoamericana; Univ. of Pittsburgh
ISSN: 0034-9631
MLA acronym: RI

SUBSCRIPTION INFORMATION

Frequency of publication: 4 times/yr.
Circulation: 2,000
Available in microform: Yes, through Univ. Microfilms International
Subscription price: $60.00/yr. institutions; $40.00/yr. individuals; $25.00/yr. students; $25.00/yr. Latin America
Subscription address: Erika Braga, at the above address
Subscription telephone: 412 624-5246

ADVERTISING INFORMATION

Advertising accepted: No

EDITORIAL DESCRIPTION

Scope: Advances the study of Iberoamerican literature and promotes cultural relations among the peoples of the Americas.
Reviews books: Yes
Publishes notes: Yes
Languages accepted: Spanish; Portuguese
Prints abstracts: No
Author-anonymous submission: No

SUBMISSION REQUIREMENTS

Restrictions on contributors: Contributors must be members of the Inst. Internacional de Literatura.
Author pays submission fee: No
Author pays page charges: No
Length of articles: 20-30 pp.
Length of book reviews: 3-8 pp.
Length of notes: 10-19 pp.
Style: MLA
Number of copies required: 2
Special requirements: Submit original typescript and diskette using Microsoft Word or WordPerfect.
Copyright ownership: Inst. of Iberoamerican Literature
Rejected manuscripts: Returned; enclose SASE.
Time before publication decision: 3-24 mos.
Time between decision and publication: 6-12 mos.
Number of reviewers: 3
Articles submitted per year: 300
Articles published per year: 140-200
Book reviews submitted per year: 200
Book reviews published per year: 50-80
Notes submitted per year: 250
Notes published per year: 30-50

(2393)
*Revista Interamericana de Bibliografía/Inter-American Review of Bibliography

Celso Rodríguez, Editor
Dept. of Cultural Affairs
General Secretariat of the OAS
Washington, DC 20006

Telephone: 202 458-3242
Fax: 202 458-6115
First published: 1951
Sponsoring organization: Organization of American States, Dept. of Cultural Affairs
ISSN: 0250-6262
MLA acronym: RIB

SUBSCRIPTION INFORMATION

Frequency of publication: 4 times/yr. (Mar., June, Sept., Dec.)
Circulation: 900
Available in microform: Yes
Subscription price: $15.00/yr. Western hemisphere, except US & Canada; $20.00/yr. elsewhere
Year to which price refers: 1992
Subscription address: Sales & Promotion Unit, at the above address

ADVERTISING INFORMATION

Advertising accepted: No

EDITORIAL DESCRIPTION

Scope: Devoted to the study of the humanities and the social sciences in Latin America and the Caribbean. Publishes a listing of recent articles, dissertations, U.S. Congressional publications, and research in progress related to Latin America and the Caribbean.
Reviews books: Yes
Publishes notes: No
Languages accepted: English; Spanish; French; Portuguese
Prints abstracts: No
Author-anonymous submission: No

SUBMISSION REQUIREMENTS

Restrictions on contributors: Articles with bibliographical content are preferred. Book reviews are solicited.
Author pays submission fee: No
Author pays page charges: No
Length of articles: 20-30 double-spaced pp. including notes
Length of book reviews: 400 words
Style: MLA
Number of copies required: 3
Special requirements: Submit original typescript.
Copyright ownership: Author
Rejected manuscripts: Not returned
Time before publication decision: 4-5 weeks
Time between decision and publication: 12-18 mos.
Number of reviewers: 3
Articles submitted per year: 30
Articles published per year: 20
Book reviews published per year: 60-70

(2394)
*Revista Letras

Marta Morais da Costa, Editor
Setor de Ciências Humanas, Letras e Artes—Univ. Federal do Paraná
Rua General Carneiro, 460—11° andar
80060-150 Curitiba, Paraná, Brazil

Telephone: (55) 41 2633038 ext. 215
Fax: (55) 41 2642243
First published: 1953
ISSN: 0100-0888
MLA acronym: RLet

SUBSCRIPTION INFORMATION

Frequency of publication: Annual
Circulation: 700
Available in microform: No

ADVERTISING INFORMATION

Advertising accepted: No

EDITORIAL DESCRIPTION

Scope: Publishes articles on linguistics and literature of the Americas and Europe.
Reviews books: Yes
Publishes notes: No
Languages accepted: English; French; German; Italian; Portuguese; Spanish
Prints abstracts: Yes

SUBMISSION REQUIREMENTS

Restrictions on contributors: None
Author pays submission fee: No
Author pays page charges: No
Length of articles: 15 pp.
Length of book reviews: 1-3 pp.
Style: Associacão Brasileira de Normas Técnicas
Number of copies required: 3
Special requirements: Submit unpublished work with a 250-word abstract in Portuguese, and English, German, French, Spanish, or Italian.
Copyright ownership: Journal
Rejected manuscripts: Not returned
Time before publication decision: 2 mos.
Time between decision and publication: 6 mos.
Number of reviewers: 3
Articles submitted per year: 40
Articles published per year: 12
Book reviews published per year: 2-3

(2395)
Revista Portuguesa de Filologia

Manuel de Paiva Boléo, Editor
Inst. de Lingua & Literatura Portuguesas
Fac. de Letras
Univ. de Coimbra
3049 Coimbra Codex, Portugal

First published: 1947
ISSN: 0035-0400
MLA acronym: RPF

SUBSCRIPTION INFORMATION

Frequency of publication: Annual
Circulation: 850
Subscription address: Casa do Castelo, Rua da Sofia, 47, Coimbra, Portugal

EDITORIAL DESCRIPTION

Scope: Publishes articles on the Portuguese language (European, African, Brazilian) and its influence in territories in Asia; also includes articles on other Romance languages, especially when they present a methodological or comparative interest, as well as articles on general linguistics.
Reviews books: Yes
Languages accepted: English; French; Italian; Portuguese; Spanish
Prints abstracts: No

SUBMISSION REQUIREMENTS

Restrictions on contributors: None
Length of articles: No restrictions
Style: Journal
Number of copies required: 1
Special requirements: Submit original typescript.
Copyright ownership: Assigned by author to journal
Rejected manuscripts: Returned
Number of reviewers: 1

(2396)
*Revista Portuguesa de Filosofia

Lúcio Craveiro da Silva, Editor
Univ. Católica Portuguesa
Fac. de Filosofia
Praça de Faculdade, 1
4719 Braga Codex, Portugal

Telephone: (351) 53 616200
Fax: (351) 53 615631
First published: 1945
ISSN: 0035-0400
MLA acronym: RPFilos

SUBSCRIPTION INFORMATION

Frequency of publication: 4 times/yr.
Circulation: 1,500
Available in microform: No
Subscription price: $55.00/yr.
Year to which price refers: 1992

EDITORIAL DESCRIPTION

Scope: Publishes articles on philosophy.
Reviews books: Yes
Publishes notes: Yes
Languages accepted: Portuguese; Spanish; French; English; Italian; German
Prints abstracts: Yes

SUBMISSION REQUIREMENTS

Author pays submission fee: No
Author pays page charges: No
Length of articles: 20 pp.
Number of copies required: 1
Articles published per year: 16

(2397)
*Revista Signos: Estudios de Lengua y Literatura

Eduardo Godoy, Editor
Inst. de Literatura & Ciencias del Lenguaje
Univ. Católica de Valparaiso
Casilla 4059
Valparaiso, Chile

Telephone: (56) 32 251024
Fax: (56) 32 212746
First published: 1967
Sponsoring organization: Univ. Católica de Valparaiso, Inst. de Lenguas & Literatura
ISSN: 0035-0451
MLA acronym: RSV

SUBSCRIPTION INFORMATION

Frequency of publication: 2 times/yr.
Circulation: 1,000
Subscription price: $20.00/yr.
Year to which price refers: 1992
Subscription address: Ediciones Universitarias de Valparaiso, Yungay 2872, Of. 2, Casilla 1415, Valparaiso, Chile

ADVERTISING INFORMATION

Advertising accepted: No

EDITORIAL DESCRIPTION

Scope: Publishes articles on literature and linguistics.
Reviews books: Yes
Languages accepted: Spanish
Prints abstracts: Yes
Author-anonymous submission: No

SUBMISSION REQUIREMENTS

Author pays submission fee: No
Author pays page charges: No
Length of articles: 15 pp.
Length of book reviews: 2 pp.
Style: MLA
Number of copies required: 3
Rejected manuscripts: Not returned
Time before publication decision: 2 mos.
Time between decision and publication: 2 mos.
Number of reviewers: 3
Articles submitted per year: 30
Articles published per year: 20
Book reviews submitted per year: 10
Book reviews published per year: 8

(2398)
*Revista/Review Interamericana

Juan R. González Mendoza, Editor
Inter American Univ. of Puerto Rico
San Germán Campus
Call Box 5100
San Germán, PR 00683

Telephone: 809 264-1912 ext. 373
Fax: 809 892-6350
First published: 1971
Sponsoring organization: Inter American Univ. of Puerto Rico, San Germán campus
ISSN: 0360-7917
MLA acronym: RevI

SUBSCRIPTION INFORMATION

Frequency of publication: 2 times/yr.
Circulation: 500
Available in microform: Yes; back, out-of-print issues
Subscription price: $18.00/yr.
Year to which price refers: 1990

ADVERTISING INFORMATION

Advertising accepted: Yes

EDITORIAL DESCRIPTION

Scope: Addresses itself to the educated layman (and concerned specialist) with an interest in books, art, science, general cultural, literary, philosophical, social, economic, historical, and political subjects with emphasis on Puerto Rican, Caribbean, Latin American, and New World themes.
Reviews books: Yes
Publishes notes: Yes
Languages accepted: English preferred; Spanish preferred; Portuguese; French
Prints abstracts: No
Author-anonymous submission: Yes

SUBMISSION REQUIREMENTS

Author pays submission fee: No
Author pays page charges: No
Length of articles: 10,000 words maximum
Length of book reviews: 750-1,000 words
Length of notes: 750-1,000 words
Style: Chicago preferred; Real Academia; MLA acceptable
Number of copies required: 3
Special requirements: Submit original typescript and 2 copies. Identification must not appear on two of the copies. Query editor prior to submission.
Copyright ownership: Journal
Rejected manuscripts: Returned
Time before publication decision: 3 mos.
Time between decision and publication: 6-9 mos.
Number of reviewers: 2
Articles submitted per year: 75
Articles published per year: 40 (includes articles, poetry, short stories, and book reviews)

(2399)
*Revue André Malraux Review

Robert S. Thornberry, Editor
Dept. of Romance Languages
Univ. of Alberta
Edmonton, Alberta T6G 2E6, Canada

Telephone: 403 439-9393
Fax: 403 474-8149
First published: 1969
Sponsoring organization: Dept. of Romance Languages, Univ. of Alberta
ISSN: 0839-458X
MLA acronym: RAMR

SUBSCRIPTION INFORMATION

Frequency of publication: 2 times/yr. (Spring, Fall)
Circulation: 250
Available in microform: No
Subscription price: C$30.00/yr. institutions Canada; $30.00/yr. institutions US; $35.00/yr. institutions elsewhere; C$24.00/yr. individuals Canada; $25.00/yr. individuals US; $25.00/yr. individuals elsewhere
Year to which price refers: 1992
Subscription address: Susan McLean McGrath, Circulation Manager, Dept. of Foreign Languages, Literatures & Cultures, Central Michigan Univ., Mount Pleasant, MI 48859

ADVERTISING INFORMATION

Advertising accepted: No

EDITORIAL DESCRIPTION

Scope: An international journal devoted to all aspects of the life, works, and influence of André Malraux. Solicits manuscripts, both substantial essays and notes, from any critical, historical, or scholarly approach. Publishes comparative studies, research-oriented scholarship, biographical and bibliographical articles. Material on subjects broadly related to Malraux is also welcome. Occasional special issues are devoted to particular areas of Malraux's work.
Reviews books: Yes
Publishes notes: Yes
Languages accepted: English; French; Notes are also accepted in German, Italian, and Spanish
Prints abstracts: No
Author-anonymous submission: Yes

SUBMISSION REQUIREMENTS

Restrictions on contributors: None
Author pays submission fee: No
Author pays page charges: No
Length of articles: 15-25 typescript pp.
Length of book reviews: 2-6 typescript pp.
Length of notes: 1,000 words
Style: Chicago
Number of copies required: 4
Special requirements: Submit double-spaced typescript with one inch margins on all sides. Include footnotes at end and an 150-250 word abstract. Accepted contributions must be submitted on diskette.
Copyright ownership: Editor
Rejected manuscripts: Returned
Time before publication decision: 6-9 mos.
Time between decision and publication: 9-12 mos.
Number of reviewers: 3-5
Articles submitted per year: 20
Articles published per year: 8-10
Book reviews submitted per year: 12-15
Book reviews published per year: 12-15
Notes submitted per year: 2-5
Notes published per year: 2

(2400)
*Revue Bazmavep: Hayagitakan-Banasirakan-Grakan Handēs/Revue d'Etudes Arméniennes

Sahak Jemjemian, Editor
Academia Armena Sancti Lazari
San Lazzaro degli Armeni
30126 Venice-Lido, Italy

Telephone: (39) 41 5260104
Fax: (39) 41 5268690
First published: 1843
Sponsoring organization: Academia Armena Sancti Lazari
ISSN: 0080-2549
MLA acronym: Bazmavep

SUBSCRIPTION INFORMATION

Frequency of publication: 4 times/yr.
Circulation: 750
Available in microform: No
Subscription price: 60,000 Lit/yr.
Year to which price refers: 1992

ADVERTISING INFORMATION

Advertising accepted: No

EDITORIAL DESCRIPTION

Scope: Publishes articles on Armenian studies.
Reviews books: Yes
Publishes notes: No
Languages accepted: Armenian; French; English; Italian; German
Prints abstracts: Yes
Author-anonymous submission: No

SUBMISSION REQUIREMENTS

Restrictions on contributors: None
Author pays submission fee: No
Author pays page charges: No
Length of articles: 1-60 pp.
Length of book reviews: 350 words maximum
Style: None
Number of copies required: 1
Copyright ownership: Academia Armena Sancti Lazari
Rejected manuscripts: Not returned
Time before publication decision: 3-10 mos.
Time between decision and publication: 3-5 mos.
Number of reviewers: 4
Articles submitted per year: 15-20
Articles published per year: 15-20
Book reviews submitted per year: 3-5
Book reviews published per year: 3-6

(2401)
Revue Belge de Philologie et d'Histoire/Belgisch Tijdschrift voor Filologie en Geschiedenis

Jean-Marie Duvosquel, Jean Stengers, Roger Lambrechts, & Jean-Pierre van Noffen, Editors
4, boulevard de l'Empereur
1000 Brussels, Belgium

First published: 1922
Sponsoring organization: Soc. pour le Progrès des Etudes Philologiques & Historiques
ISSN: 0035-0818
MLA acronym: RBPH

SUBSCRIPTION INFORMATION

Frequency of publication: 4 times/yr.
Circulation: 1,200
Available in microform: No
Subscription address: Jean-Jacques Heirwegh, 210, chaussée de Malines, 1970 Wezembeek, Belgium

ADVERTISING INFORMATION

Advertising accepted: Yes

EDITORIAL DESCRIPTION

Scope: Publishes articles on history, classical and modern philology, and literary criticism.
Reviews books: Yes
Publishes notes: Yes
Languages accepted: French; English; Dutch; German; Italian; Latin; Portuguese; Spanish
Prints abstracts: No

SUBMISSION REQUIREMENTS

Restrictions on contributors: None
Author pays submission fee: No
Author pays page charges: No
Length of articles: 15-30 pp.
Length of book reviews: 1 p.
Number of copies required: 2
Special requirements: Articles on modern literature should be written in the language of the texts discussed.
Copyright ownership: Journal
Rejected manuscripts: Returned; enclose return postage.
Time before publication decision: 4-6 weeks
Time between decision and publication: 2 yrs.
Number of reviewers: 2
Articles published per year: 24
Book reviews published per year: 350-400

(2402)
*Revue Bénédictine

Dom Daniel Misonne, Editor
Abbaye de Maredsous
5198 Denée, Belgium

Telephone: (32) 82 699155
Fax: (32) 82 699625
First published: 1884
Sponsoring organization: Abbaye de Maredsous
ISSN: 0035-0893
MLA acronym: RB

SUBSCRIPTION INFORMATION

Frequency of publication: 2-4 times/yr.
Circulation: 1,000
Available in microform: No
Subscription price: 2,500 BF/yr.
Year to which price refers: 1992

ADVERTISING INFORMATION

Advertising accepted: No

EDITORIAL DESCRIPTION

Scope: Publishes articles on the criticism and history of religious literature. Publishes previously unpublished works, original studies, book reviews, and two critical indexes with separate pagination, the *Bulletin d'Histoire Bénédictine* and the *Bulletin d'Ancienne Littérature Chrétienne Latine*.
Reviews books: Yes
Publishes notes: No
Languages accepted: English; French; German; Italian
Prints abstracts: No
Author-anonymous submission: No

SUBMISSION REQUIREMENTS

Restrictions on contributors: Unsolicited book reviews are not accepted.
Author pays submission fee: No
Author pays page charges: No
Length of articles: No restrictions
Length of book reviews: No restrictions
Number of copies required: 1
Special requirements: Submit double-spaced typescript.
Copyright ownership: Author & journal
Rejected manuscripts: Returned
Time before publication decision: 1 mo.
Time between decision and publication: 1 yr.
Number of reviewers: 3
Articles submitted per year: 50
Articles published per year: 20
Book reviews submitted per year: 150
Book reviews published per year: 60

(2403)
*Revue Celfan/Celfan Review

Eric Sellin, Editor
Dept. of French & Italian
Tulane Univ.
New Orleans, LA 70118

Telephone: 504 865-5116
First published: 1981
Sponsoring organization: Center for the Study of the Francophone Literature of North Africa
ISSN: 0890-6998
MLA acronym: CelfanR

SUBSCRIPTION INFORMATION

Frequency of publication: 2 times/yr.
Circulation: 150
Available in microform: No

ADVERTISING INFORMATION

Advertising accepted: Yes, on an exchange basis

EDITORIAL DESCRIPTION

Scope: Publishes articles devoted to Francophone Maghrebine authors, to French authors of North Africa, and to the role of North Africa in the work of French authors.
Reviews books: Yes
Publishes notes: Yes
Languages accepted: English; French
Prints abstracts: No
Author-anonymous submission: No

SUBMISSION REQUIREMENTS

Restrictions on contributors: None
Author pays submission fee: No
Author pays page charges: No
Length of articles: 1,000 words maximum
Length of book reviews: 250 words maximum
Length of notes: 1,000 words maximum
Style: MLA; Chicago
Number of copies required: 1
Special requirements: Submit double-spaced typescript.
Copyright ownership: Reverts to author after publication but journal retains the right to re-use or reprint.
Rejected manuscripts: Returned
Time before publication decision: 2 mos.
Time between decision and publication: 6 mos.
Number of reviewers: 1-2
Articles published per year: 30-35
Book reviews published per year: 10-15

(2404)
Revue de l'Académie Arabe de Damas

Shakir Al-Faham, Editor
Arab Language Academy
P.B. 327
Damascus, Syria

Telephone: (963) 11 713145
ISSN: 0002-4031
MLA acronym: RAAD

SUBSCRIPTION INFORMATION

Frequency of publication: 4 times/yr.
Available in microform: No

ADVERTISING INFORMATION

Advertising accepted: No

EDITORIAL DESCRIPTION

Scope: Publishes linguistic and historical articles, as well as scientific terms in Arabic.
Reviews books: Yes
Publishes notes: Yes
Languages accepted: Arabic

SUBMISSION REQUIREMENTS

Author pays page charges: No
Length of articles: No restrictions
Length of book reviews: Depends on book length
Number of copies required: 1
Copyright ownership: Author
Articles submitted per year: 60
Articles published per year: 25
Book reviews submitted per year: 15
Book reviews published per year: 8

(2405)
Revue de l'ACLA/Journal of the CAAL

CAAL Secretariat
Univ. McGill
Fac. des Sciences de l'Education
3700, rue McTavish
Montreal, Quebec H3A 1Y2, Canada

Telephone: 514 398-6982
Fax: 514 398-4679
First published: 1979
Historical variations in title: Formerly *Bulletin de l'ACLA/Bulletin of the CAAL*
Sponsoring organization: Assn. Canadienne de Linguistique Appliquée/Canadian Assn. of Applied Linguistics
ISSN: 0709-9207
MLA acronym: RACLA

SUBSCRIPTION INFORMATION

Frequency of publication: 2 times/yr. (Spring, Autumn)
Circulation: 700
Available in microform: No
Subscription price: C$40.00/yr. Canada; C$45.00/yr. elsewhere
Year to which price refers: 1991

ADVERTISING INFORMATION

Advertising accepted: Yes

EDITORIAL DESCRIPTION

Reviews books: Yes
Publishes notes: No
Languages accepted: English; French
Prints abstracts: Yes
Author-anonymous submission: No

SUBMISSION REQUIREMENTS

Restrictions on contributors: None
Author pays submission fee: No
Author pays page charges: No
Length of articles: 20 pp.
Length of book reviews: 3 pp.
Style: Journal; MLA
Number of copies required: 1
Copyright ownership: Journal
Rejected manuscripts: Returned
Time before publication decision: 6 mos.
Time between decision and publication: 3-4 mos.
Number of reviewers: 5
Articles submitted per year: 30-40
Articles published per year: 15-20
Book reviews submitted per year: 30-50
Book reviews published per year: 30-50

(2406)
*Revue de Linguistique Romane

M. Georges Straka, Editor
8 Quai Rouget de l'Isle
67000 Strasbourg, France

Telephone: (33) 88350084
First published: 1925
Sponsoring organization: Soc. de Linguistique Romane
ISSN: 0035-1458
MLA acronym: RLiR

SUBSCRIPTION INFORMATION

Frequency of publication: 2 times/yr.
Available in microform: No
Subscription price: 440 F/yr. nonmembers; 240 F/yr. members
Subscription address: Gérard Gorcy, Trésor de la Langue Française, 44, ave. de la Libération, C.O. 3310, 54014 Nancy Cédex, France
Subscription telephone: (33) 83962176

ADVERTISING INFORMATION

Advertising accepted: No

EDITORIAL DESCRIPTION

Scope: Publishes articles on synchronic and diachronic Romance linguistics with heavy emphasis on dialect studies.
Reviews books: Yes
Publishes notes: Yes
Languages accepted: French; Spanish; Italian; Romanian; Portuguese; Catalan
Prints abstracts: No

SUBMISSION REQUIREMENTS

Restrictions on contributors: Contributors must be members of the Soc. de Linguistique Romane.
Author pays submission fee: No
Author pays page charges: No
Length of articles: 4-50 pp.
Length of book reviews: 1-4 pp.
Length of notes: 1-4 pp.
Number of copies required: 1
Special requirements: Submit original typescript.
Copyright ownership: Journal
Rejected manuscripts: Returned
Time before publication decision: 3 mos. maximum
Time between decision and publication: 6-18 mos.
Number of reviewers: 2 plus Editorial Board
Articles submitted per year: 50
Articles published per year: 10-20
Book reviews submitted per year: 150
Book reviews published per year: 120
Notes submitted per year: 5
Notes published per year: 3

(2407)
*Revue de Littérature Comparée

Muriel Détrie, Editor
Univ. de Tours
3, rue des Tanneurs
37000 Tours, France

First published: 1921
Sponsoring organization: Centre National de la Recherche Scientifique
ISSN: 0035-1466
MLA acronym: RLC

SUBSCRIPTION INFORMATION

Frequency of publication: 4 times/yr.
Circulation: 2,000
Available in microform: Yes
Subscription address: Soc. Nouvelle Didier Erudition, 6, rue de la Sorbonne, 75005 Paris, France

ADVERTISING INFORMATION

Advertising accepted: Yes

EDITORIAL DESCRIPTION

Scope: Publishes comparative studies of modern literatures, especially European. Includes articles on literary theory.
Reviews books: Yes
Publishes notes: Yes
Languages accepted: English; French
Prints abstracts: Yes
Author-anonymous submission: Yes

SUBMISSION REQUIREMENTS

Restrictions on contributors: None
Author pays submission fee: No
Author pays page charges: No
Length of articles: 20-25 pp.
Length of book reviews: 2 pp.
Length of notes: 5 pp.
Style: MLA

Number of copies required: 1
Special requirements: Submit original typescript.
Copyright ownership: Didier Erudition
Rejected manuscripts: Not returned
Time before publication decision: 6-9 mos.
Time between decision and publication: 6-12 mos.
Number of reviewers: 1-2
Articles submitted per year: 60
Articles published per year: 25
Book reviews submitted per year: 80
Book reviews published per year: 50
Notes submitted per year: 20
Notes published per year: 12

(2408)
*Revue de Métaphysique et de Morale

Paul Ricoeur, François Azouvi, M. B. de Launay, & Christian Berner, Editors
7, rue Laromiguière
75005 Paris, France

Telephone: (33) 1 46342160
Fax: (33) 1 45872999
First published: 1893
Sponsoring organization: Soc. Française de Philosophie
ISSN: 0035-1571
MLA acronym: RMM

SUBSCRIPTION INFORMATION

Frequency of publication: 4 times/yr.
Circulation: 1,700
Available in microform: No
Subscription address: Armand Colin, B.P. 22, 41353 Vineuil, France
Subscription telephone: (33) 1 46341219

ADVERTISING INFORMATION

Advertising accepted: Yes

EDITORIAL DESCRIPTION

Scope: Publishes articles on fundamental philosophy, history of philosophy, and ethics.
Reviews books: Yes
Publishes notes: Yes
Languages accepted: French; English; German
Prints abstracts: Yes
Author-anonymous submission: No

SUBMISSION REQUIREMENTS

Restrictions on contributors: None
Author pays submission fee: No
Author pays page charges: No
Length of articles: 25 pp.
Length of book reviews: 400 words
Length of notes: 100 words
Style: None
Number of copies required: 2
Special requirements: Submit original typescript.
Copyright ownership: Librairie Armand Colin
Rejected manuscripts: Not returned
Time before publication decision: 3 mos.
Time between decision and publication: 9 mos.
Number of reviewers: 3
Articles submitted per year: 90
Articles published per year: 26
Book reviews submitted per year: 100
Book reviews published per year: 80
Notes submitted per year: 40
Notes published per year: 20

(2409)
Revue de Philologie de Littérature et d'Histoire Anciennes

R. Weil & P. Flobert, Editors
Klincksieck Editions
11, rue de Lille
75007 Paris, France

First published: 1845
ISSN: 0035-1652
MLA acronym: RPLHA

SUBSCRIPTION INFORMATION

Frequency of publication: 2 times/yr.
Circulation: 1,000
Available in microform: No
Subscription address: S.P.P.I.F., B.P. 22, 41350 Vineuil, France

ADVERTISING INFORMATION

Advertising accepted: No

EDITORIAL DESCRIPTION

Scope: Publishes articles on languages, literatures, and history of classical antiquity.
Reviews books: Yes
Publishes notes: Yes
Languages accepted: French; English (occasionally)
Prints abstracts: Yes

SUBMISSION REQUIREMENTS

Restrictions on contributors: None
Author pays submission fee: No
Author pays page charges: No
Length of articles: 4,500 words maximum
Length of book reviews: 300-400 words
Length of notes: 1,000 words
Style: None
Number of copies required: 1
Special requirements: Submit original typescript.
Copyright ownership: Assigned by author to journal
Rejected manuscripts: Returned
Time before publication decision: 18 mos.
Time between decision and publication: 8 mos.
Number of reviewers: 2
Articles published per year: 20
Book reviews submitted per year: 120-150
Book reviews published per year: 120-150
Notes submitted per year: 8-10
Notes published per year: 11

(2410)
*Revue de Phonétique Appliquée

Raymond Renard, Editor
Dépt. de Phonétique & Psychoacoustique
Univ. de l'Etat à Mons
Place du Parc, 20
7000 Mons, Belgium

Telephone: (32) 65 373054
First published: 1965
Sponsoring organization: Ministère de l'Education de la Communauté Française de Belgique
ISSN: 0770-545X
MLA acronym: RevPL

SUBSCRIPTION INFORMATION

Frequency of publication: 4 times/yr.
Circulation: 1,000
Available in microform: Yes
Subscription address: Editions Didier Erudition, 6, rue de la Sorbonne, 75005 Paris, France

ADVERTISING INFORMATION

Advertising accepted: No

EDITORIAL DESCRIPTION

Scope: Publishes articles on the study of language as an oral phenomenon.
Reviews books: Yes
Publishes notes: Yes
Languages accepted: English; French; German
Prints abstracts: Yes
Author-anonymous submission: No

SUBMISSION REQUIREMENTS

Restrictions on contributors: None
Author pays submission fee: No
Author pays page charges: No
Length of articles: No restrictions
Length of book reviews: No restrictions
Length of notes: No restrictions
Style: None
Number of copies required: 3
Special requirements: Include a short title, the author's name, and institutional affiliation on a separate page. Include a 100-word summary in English, French, and German on a separate page.
Copyright ownership: Journal
Rejected manuscripts: Returned
Time before publication decision: 3 mos.
Time between decision and publication: 3 mos.
Number of reviewers: 3-5
Articles submitted per year: 25
Articles published per year: 15-20
Book reviews submitted per year: 5
Book reviews published per year: 5
Notes submitted per year: 5
Notes published per year: 5

(2411)
Revue des Etudes Anciennes

Pierre Debord, Editor
Univ. de Bordeaux III
Domaine Universitaire
33405 Talence Cedex, France

First published: 1899
Sponsoring organization: Univ. de Bordeaux III
ISSN: 0035-2004
MLA acronym: REAnc

SUBSCRIPTION INFORMATION

Frequency of publication: 2 times/yr.
Circulation: 1,000

EDITORIAL DESCRIPTION

Scope: Publishes articles on classical studies.
Reviews books: Yes
Prints abstracts: Yes

SUBMISSION REQUIREMENTS

Restrictions on contributors: None
Length of articles: No restrictions
Number of copies required: 1
Special requirements: Submit typescript.
Copyright ownership: Journal
Rejected manuscripts: Returned
Time before publication decision: 3 mos.
Time between decision and publication: 18 mos.
Number of reviewers: 2-3
Articles published per year: 15

(2412)
*Revue des Etudes Arméniennes

N. A. Garsoïan & Jean-Pierre Mahé, Editors
52 Boulevard Saint-Michel
75006 Paris, France

Telephone: (33) 1 43260662
First published: 1920
Sponsoring organization: Assn. de la Revue des Etudes Armeniennes
ISSN: 0080-2549

MLA acronym: REArmNS

SUBSCRIPTION INFORMATION

Frequency of publication: Annual
Circulation: 800
Available in microform: No
Subscription price: 350 F/yr.
Year to which price refers: 1992

ADVERTISING INFORMATION

Advertising accepted: Yes

EDITORIAL DESCRIPTION

Scope: Publishes articles on Armenian language, literature, art, and history.
Reviews books: Yes
Publishes notes: Yes
Languages accepted: English; French; German
Prints abstracts: Yes
Author-anonymous submission: No

SUBMISSION REQUIREMENTS

Restrictions on contributors: None
Author pays submission fee: No
Author pays page charges: No
Style: Journal; see volume 19-20
Number of copies required: 1
Special requirements: Use *Système Hübschmann-Meillet-Benveniste* for transliterations. Titles in Russian or Armenian should be transliterated and then translated into the language of the article.
Copyright ownership: Journal
Rejected manuscripts: Returned
Time before publication decision: 3 mos.
Time between decision and publication: 1 yr.
Number of reviewers: 2
Articles submitted per year: 25
Articles published per year: 20-25
Book reviews published per year: 10-20
Notes submitted per year: 4-5
Notes published per year: 4-5

(2413)
*Revue des Etudes Augustiniennes

Etudes Augustiniennes
3, rue de l'Abbaye
75006 Paris, France

First published: 1955
ISSN: 0035-2021
MLA acronym: REA

SUBSCRIPTION INFORMATION

Frequency of publication: 2 times/yr.
Available in microform: No
Subscription price: 350 F (2,000 BF)/yr.
Year to which price refers: 1992
Subscription address: Ed. Brepols, 23, rue des Grands Augustins, 75006 Paris, France

ADVERTISING INFORMATION

Advertising accepted: No

EDITORIAL DESCRIPTION

Scope: Publishes articles on patristic studies.
Reviews books: Yes
Publishes notes: Yes
Languages accepted: French; English; German; Spanish; Italian
Prints abstracts: Yes

SUBMISSION REQUIREMENTS

Author pays submission fee: No
Author pays page charges: No
Number of copies required: 1
Special requirements: Submission on diskette using Microsoft Word is preferred.
Rejected manuscripts: Returned
Time before publication decision: 1 mo.

Time between decision and publication: 2-6 mos.
Number of reviewers: 4-5
Articles submitted per year: 40
Articles published per year: 20
Book reviews published per year: 100
Notes submitted per year: 2-3

(2414)
*Revue des Etudes Grecques

Assn. des Etudes Grecques
16, rue de la Sorbonne
75005 Paris, France

First published: 1869
Sponsoring organization: Assn. des Etudes Grecques
ISSN: 0035-2039
MLA acronym: REG

SUBSCRIPTION INFORMATION

Frequency of publication: 2 times/yr.
Circulation: 1,500
Available in microform: No
Subscription price: 630 F/yr.
Year to which price refers: 1992
Subscription address: Soc. d'Edition "Les Belles Lettres", 95, boulevard Raspail, 75006 Paris, France

ADVERTISING INFORMATION

Advertising accepted: Yes

EDITORIAL DESCRIPTION

Scope: Publishes articles on language, literature, philosophy, and history of ancient and modern Greece.
Reviews books: Yes
Publishes notes: Yes
Languages accepted: French
Prints abstracts: Yes
Author-anonymous submission: No

SUBMISSION REQUIREMENTS

Restrictions on contributors: None
Author pays submission fee: No
Author pays page charges: No
Length of articles: No restrictions
Style: None
Number of copies required: 1
Special requirements: Submit typescript.
Copyright ownership: Assigned by author to journal
Rejected manuscripts: Returned
Time before publication decision: 6 mos.
Time between decision and publication: 1 yr.
Number of reviewers: 4
Articles submitted per year: 30-40
Articles published per year: 20-30
Book reviews submitted per year: 130
Book reviews published per year: 100
Notes published per year: 10-20

(2415)
*Revue des Etudes Islamiques

D. Sourdel, J. Sourdel-Thomine, & L. Kalus, Editors
c/o Secrétariat
7, rue Abel
75012 Paris, France

First published: 1927
ISSN: 0336-156X
MLA acronym: REIsl

SUBSCRIPTION INFORMATION

Frequency of publication: 2 times/yr.
Circulation: 500
Available in microform: No

Subscription address: Librairie Orientaliste Paul Geuthner S.A., 12, rue Vavin, 75006 Paris, France

ADVERTISING INFORMATION

Advertising accepted: Yes

EDITORIAL DESCRIPTION

Scope: Publishes articles on Islamic civilization and culture.
Reviews books: Yes
Publishes notes: Yes
Languages accepted: French; English
Prints abstracts: No

SUBMISSION REQUIREMENTS

Restrictions on contributors: None
Author pays submission fee: No
Author pays page charges: No
Length of articles: No restrictions
Length of book reviews: No restrictions
Length of notes: No restrictions
Style: Journal
Number of copies required: 1
Special requirements: Submit original typescript.
Copyright ownership: Assigned by author to journal
Rejected manuscripts: Returned
Time before publication decision: 3 mos.
Time between decision and publication: 1 yr.
Number of reviewers: 3
Articles published per year: 10-15

(2416)
*Revue des Etudes Italiennes

Christian Bec & Michel David, Editors
Grand Palais
Perron Alexandre III
Cours la Reine
75008 Paris, France

First published: 1936
Sponsoring organization: Soc. d'Etudes Italiennes
ISSN: 0035-2047
MLA acronym: REI

SUBSCRIPTION INFORMATION

Frequency of publication: 4 times/yr.
Circulation: 650
Available in microform: No
Subscription price: 200 F/yr. France; 210 F/yr. elsewhere
Year to which price refers: 1992

ADVERTISING INFORMATION

Advertising accepted: No

EDITORIAL DESCRIPTION

Scope: Publishes articles on Italian language and literature.
Reviews books: Yes
Publishes notes: Yes
Languages accepted: French; Italian
Prints abstracts: No

SUBMISSION REQUIREMENTS

Author pays submission fee: No
Author pays page charges: No
Length of articles: 40 pp. maximum
Number of copies required: 1
Rejected manuscripts: Returned
Time before publication decision: 1 yr.
Time between decision and publication: 6 mos.
Number of reviewers: 5
Articles published per year: 10

(2417)
*Revue des Etudes Latines

Marcel Durry, Pierre Grimal, & Alain Michel, Editors
Inst. d'Etudes Latines
Univ. de Paris IV-La Sorbonne
1, rue Victor-Cousin
75230 Paris, France

First published: 1923
Sponsoring organization: Soc. des Etudes Latines
ISSN: 0373-5737
MLA acronym: RELat

SUBSCRIPTION INFORMATION

Frequency of publication: Annual
Circulation: 2,000
Available in microform: No
Subscription price: 300 F/yr.
Year to which price refers: 1992
Subscription address: Soc. d'Edition "Les Belles Lettres", 95, boulevard Raspail, 75006 Paris, France

ADVERTISING INFORMATION

Advertising accepted: Yes

EDITORIAL DESCRIPTION

Scope: Publishes communications and discussions on any subject which touches on the science and teaching of Latin.
Reviews books: Yes
Publishes notes: Yes
Languages accepted: French; Latin
Prints abstracts: Yes
Author-anonymous submission: No

SUBMISSION REQUIREMENTS

Author pays submission fee: No
Author pays page charges: No
Length of articles: 15 pp.
Time before publication decision: 6 mos.
Time between decision and publication: 6 mos.

(2418)
*Revue des Langues Romanes

Gérard Gouiran, Editor
Centre d'Etudes Occitanes
Univ. Paul Valéry
B.P. 5043
34032 Montpellier Cedex, France

First published: 1870
Sponsoring organization: Univ. Paul-Valéry Montpellier III, Centre d'Etudes Occitanes; Centre National de la Recherche Scientifique
ISSN: 0223-3711
MLA acronym: RLR

SUBSCRIPTION INFORMATION

Frequency of publication: 2 times/yr.
Circulation: 600
Available in microform: No
Subscription price: 190 F/yr.
Year to which price refers: 1992

ADVERTISING INFORMATION

Advertising accepted: No

EDITORIAL DESCRIPTION

Scope: Covers Romance literatures and linguistics. Concentrates chiefly on Old French and Occitan material.
Reviews books: Yes
Publishes notes: Yes
Languages accepted: French; Spanish; Italian; Portuguese; Romanian; Occitan; Catalan
Prints abstracts: No

Author-anonymous submission: No

SUBMISSION REQUIREMENTS

Author pays submission fee: No
Author pays page charges: No
Length of articles: 15 pp.
Length of book reviews: 3 pp. maximum
Length of notes: 3 pp. maximum
Number of copies required: 1
Special requirements: Submit typescript.
Time before publication decision: 3 mos.
Time between decision and publication: 3 yrs. maximum
Number of reviewers: 6
Articles submitted per year: 15-25
Articles published per year: 8-15
Book reviews published per year: 50

(2419)
*La Revue des Lettres Modernes: Histoire des Idées et des Littératures

Michel J. Minard, Editor
Editions Lettres Modernes
73, rue du Cardinal-Lemoine
75005 Paris, France

Telephone: (33) 1 43544609
First published: 1954
ISSN: 0035-2136
MLA acronym: RLM

SUBSCRIPTION INFORMATION

Frequency of publication: Irregular
Available in microform: No
Subscription price: 940 F/yr.
Year to which price refers: 1992

ADVERTISING INFORMATION

Advertising accepted: No

EDITORIAL DESCRIPTION

Scope: Publishes articles on modern literature. Each issue is dedicated to a single author.
Reviews books: Yes
Publishes notes: No
Languages accepted: French
Prints abstracts: No

SUBMISSION REQUIREMENTS

Author pays submission fee: No
Author pays page charges: No
Length of articles: 20,000 characters
Style: Journal
Number of copies required: 1
Rejected manuscripts: Returned; enclose return postage or international reply coupons.
Time before publication decision: 1 mo.
Time between decision and publication: 4 mos.
Number of reviewers: 2

(2420)
Revue des Sciences Humaines

Philippe Bonnefis & Jean Decottingmies, Editors
Presses Universitaires de Lille
B.P. 149
59653 Villeneuve d'Ascq Cedex, France

First published: 1933
Sponsoring organization: Univ. de Lille III
ISSN: 0035-2195
MLA acronym: RSH

SUBSCRIPTION INFORMATION

Frequency of publication: 4 times/yr. (Mar., June, Sept., Dec.)
Circulation: 1,400

EDITORIAL DESCRIPTION

Scope: Publishes series of essays organized around a given theme or topic concerning chiefly French literature.
Reviews books: No
Languages accepted: French
Prints abstracts: No

SUBMISSION REQUIREMENTS

Restrictions on contributors: None
Length of articles: 20,000 words
Number of copies required: 1
Copyright ownership: Journal
Rejected manuscripts: Not returned
Time before publication decision: 2 mos.
Time between decision and publication: 6 mos.
Number of reviewers: 2
Articles published per year: 40-50

(2421)
*Revue d'Esthétique

Olivier Revault d'Allonnes & Mikel Dufrenne, Editors
162, rue Saint-Charles
75740 Paris Cedex 15, France

Fax: (33) 1 46347452
First published: 1948
Sponsoring organization: Soc. Française d'Esthétique
ISSN: 0035-2292
MLA acronym: RE

SUBSCRIPTION INFORMATION

Frequency of publication: 2 times/yr.
Available in microform: No
Subscription price: 500 F/yr. plus postage
Year to which price refers: 1992
Subscription address: Jean-Michel Place, 12 rue Pierre & Marie Curie, 75005 Paris, France
Subscription telephone: (33) 1 46330511

ADVERTISING INFORMATION

Advertising accepted: Yes

EDITORIAL DESCRIPTION

Scope: Publishes articles on aesthetics and the philosophy of art.
Reviews books: Yes
Publishes notes: No
Languages accepted: French
Prints abstracts: No

SUBMISSION REQUIREMENTS

Restrictions on contributors: None
Author pays submission fee: Yes
Author pays page charges: No
Length of articles: 10-15 pp.
Length of book reviews: 400 words
Number of copies required: 1
Copyright ownership: Journal & author
Rejected manuscripts: Returned; enclose SAE.
Time before publication decision: 6 mos.
Time between decision and publication: 1 yr.
Number of reviewers: 11
Articles submitted per year: 50
Articles published per year: 30
Book reviews submitted per year: 20
Book reviews published per year: 8

(2422)
*Revue d'Histoire du Théâtre

Soc. d'Histoire du Théâtre
98, boulevard Kellermann
75013 Paris, France

Telephone: (33) 1 45884655
First published: 1948

Sponsoring organization: Soc. d'Histoire du Théâtre
ISSN: 0035-2373
MLA acronym: RHT

SUBSCRIPTION INFORMATION

Frequency of publication: 4 times/yr. (Mar., June, Sept., Dec.)
Circulation: 1,000
Available in microform: No
Subscription price: 340 F/yr.
Year to which price refers: 1993

ADVERTISING INFORMATION

Advertising accepted: No

EDITORIAL DESCRIPTION

Scope: Publishes articles on the theater both past and present.
Reviews books: Yes
Publishes notes: No
Languages accepted: French
Prints abstracts: No

SUBMISSION REQUIREMENTS

Author pays submission fee: No
Author pays page charges: No
Length of articles: 16 pp.
Length of book reviews: 1 p.
Number of copies required: 1
Special requirements: Submit typescript.
Copyright ownership: Editor
Rejected manuscripts: Not returned
Time before publication decision: 1-3 mos.
Time between decision and publication: 1 yr. minimum
Number of reviewers: 6
Articles submitted per year: 40
Articles published per year: 30
Book reviews submitted per year: 10
Book reviews published per year: 1-8

(2423)
*Revue d'Histoire Ecclésiastique

Claude Soetens, Editor
Bibliothèque
Univ. Catholique de Louvain
Collège Erasme
1348 Louvain-la-Neuve, Belgium

First published: 1900
Sponsoring organization: Univ. de Louvain
ISSN: 0035-2381
MLA acronym: RHE

SUBSCRIPTION INFORMATION

Frequency of publication: 4 times/yr.
Circulation: 1,900
Available in microform: No
Subscription price: 3,500 BF/yr.
Year to which price refers: 1993

ADVERTISING INFORMATION

Advertising accepted: Yes
Advertising rates: 10,500 BF/full page

EDITORIAL DESCRIPTION

Scope: Publishes articles on the history of the church, such as institutions, culture, and theology. Includes book reviews and systematic bibliography.
Reviews books: Yes
Publishes notes: Yes
Languages accepted: French; English
Prints abstracts: No

SUBMISSION REQUIREMENTS

Restrictions on contributors: None
Author pays submission fee: No
Author pays page charges: No

Length of articles: 15-50 pp.
Length of book reviews: 50-2,000 words
Length of notes: 10-100 words
Number of copies required: 1-2
Copyright ownership: Journal
Rejected manuscripts: Returned; enclose return postage.
Time before publication decision: 3 mos.
Time between decision and publication: 6-18 mos.
Number of reviewers: 1-2
Articles submitted per year: 25-30
Articles published per year: 12-15
Book reviews submitted per year: 600-700
Book reviews published per year: 450-600
Notes submitted per year: 30-50
Notes published per year: 24-40

(2424)
*Revue d'Histoire Littéraire de la France

Sylvain Menant, Editor
11, rue Monticelli
75014 Paris, France

Additional editorial address: Send books for review to: 112 rue Monge, B.P. 173, 75005 Paris, France
First published: 1894
Sponsoring organization: Soc. d'Histoire Littéraire de la France
ISSN: 0035-2411
MLA acronym: RHL

SUBSCRIPTION INFORMATION

Frequency of publication: 6 times/yr.
Circulation: 2,500
Available in microform: No
Subscription price: 365 F/yr. France; $86.00/yr. elsewhere
Year to which price refers: 1992
Subscription address: Librairie Armand Colin, B.P. 22, 41353 Vineuil, France

ADVERTISING INFORMATION

Advertising accepted: Yes

EDITORIAL DESCRIPTION

Scope: Publishes articles on French literature of the 16th to 20th centuries.
Reviews books: Yes
Publishes notes: Yes
Languages accepted: French
Prints abstracts: Yes
Author-anonymous submission: No

SUBMISSION REQUIREMENTS

Author pays submission fee: No
Author pays page charges: No
Number of copies required: 2
Copyright ownership: Librairie Armand Colin
Rejected manuscripts: Not returned
Time before publication decision: 6 mos.
Time between decision and publication: 1 yr.
Number of reviewers: 2
Articles published per year: 40
Book reviews published per year: 230
Notes published per year: 15

(2425)
*Revue Française d'Etudes Américaines

Sophie Body-Gendrot & Michel Granger, Editors
EHESS
Centre d'Etudes Nord-Américaines
12, rue Corvisart
75013 Paris, France

Additional editorial address: S. Body-Gendrot, 105 rue Didot, 75014 Paris, France
Telephone: (33) 1 43956347

Fax: (33) 1 45449311
First published: 1976
Sponsoring organization: Assn. Française d'Etudes Américaines (AFEA)
ISSN: 0397-7870
MLA acronym: RFEA

SUBSCRIPTION INFORMATION

Frequency of publication: 4 times/yr.
Circulation: 800
Available in microform: No
Subscription price: 290 F/yr. France; 350 F/yr. elsewhere
Year to which price refers: 1992
Subscription address: Presses Universitaires de Nancy, 25 rue Baron-Louis, B.P. 454, 54001 Nancy Cedex, France

ADVERTISING INFORMATION

Advertising accepted: Yes
Advertising rates: 900 F/half page; 2,000 F/full page

EDITORIAL DESCRIPTION

Scope: Publishes articles on American literature, civilization, history, art, religion, and media.
Reviews books: Yes
Publishes notes: No
Languages accepted: English; French
Prints abstracts: Yes
Author-anonymous submission: No

SUBMISSION REQUIREMENTS

Restrictions on contributors: Essays in the May issue are papers read at previous AFEA conventions. Book reviews are solicited. Every issue deals with a particular theme established at least one year in advance of deadline, except July issue which is open.
Author pays submission fee: No
Author pays page charges: No
Length of articles: 27,000 characters
Length of book reviews: 1/2 p.
Style: MLA
Number of copies required: 3
Special requirements: Include a 1,000-character abstract in both English and French.
Copyright ownership: Journal for 1 yr.
Rejected manuscripts: Returned; enclose SASE.
Time before publication decision: 3 mos.
Time between decision and publication: 4-12 mos.
Number of reviewers: 3
Articles submitted per year: 60
Articles published per year: 30-40
Book reviews published per year: 90-100

(2426)
*Revue Francophone de Louisiane

A. David Barry, Editor
P.O. Box 43331
Univ. of Southwestern Louisiana
Lafayette, LA 70504-3331

Telephone: 318 231-6811
Fax: 318 231-6195
First published: 1986
Sponsoring organization: Univ. of Southwestern Louisiana; Conseil International d'Etudes Francophones
ISSN: 0890-9555
MLA acronym: RFdL

SUBSCRIPTION INFORMATION

Frequency of publication: 2 times/yr. (Spring, Winter)
Circulation: 400
Available in microform: No
Subscription price: $15.00/yr. institutions; $12.00/yr. individuals
Year to which price refers: 1992

ADVERTISING INFORMATION

Advertising accepted: Yes

EDITORIAL DESCRIPTION

Scope: Publishes articles on the literature, culture, history, and language of the Francophone world.
Reviews books: Yes
Publishes notes: No
Languages accepted: French; English
Prints abstracts: No
Author-anonymous submission: Yes

SUBMISSION REQUIREMENTS

Restrictions on contributors: None
Author pays submission fee: No
Author pays page charges: No
Length of articles: No restrictions
Length of book reviews: 250-400 words
Style: MLA
Number of copies required: 2
Copyright ownership: Univ. of Southwestern Louisiana
Rejected manuscripts: Not returned
Time before publication decision: 3-6 mos.
Time between decision and publication: 3-6 mos.
Number of reviewers: 3
Articles submitted per year: 40-60
Articles published per year: 20-30
Book reviews submitted per year: 70
Book reviews published per year: 45-50

(2427)
*Revue Frontenac Review

Catherine McGann & Stéphanie Nutting, Editors
Dept. of French Studies
Queen's Univ.
Kingston, Ontario K7L 3N6, Canada

Telephone: 613 545-2090
Fax: 613 545-6300
E-mail: LESSARDG@QUCDN.QueensU.Ca
First published: 1983
Sponsoring organization: Queen's Univ., Dept. of French; Queen's Univ., Graduate Students' Soc.
ISSN: 0715-9994
MLA acronym: FrontenacR

SUBSCRIPTION INFORMATION

Frequency of publication: Annual (Autumn)
Circulation: 200
Available in microform: No
Subscription price: C$10.00/yr. individuals; C$5.00/yr. students
Year to which price refers: 1991

ADVERTISING INFORMATION

Advertising accepted: Yes
Advertising rates: C$40.00/quarter page

EDITORIAL DESCRIPTION

Scope: Journal is a forum for graduate students in the humanities. It concentrates on literary/critical articles and also includes art history, architecture, and philosophy. Each issue is thematic.
Reviews books: No
Publishes notes: No
Languages accepted: French; English
Prints abstracts: No
Author-anonymous submission: Yes

SUBMISSION REQUIREMENTS

Restrictions on contributors: Only graduate students may submit articles.
Author pays submission fee: No
Author pays page charges: No
Length of articles: 4,000-10,000 words
Style: MLA

Number of copies required: 1
Copyright ownership: Author
Rejected manuscripts: Not returned
Time before publication decision: 3-5 mos.
Time between decision and publication: 3-5 mos.
Number of reviewers: 5
Articles submitted per year: 15-20
Articles published per year: 5-7

(2428)
*Revue Générale

Georges Sion, Jean Claude Ricquier, & France Bastia, Editors
Chaussée de Louvain, 41
1320 Hamme-Mille, Belgium

Telephone: (32) 10 866629
Fax: (32) 10 866691
First published: 1865
ISSN: 0770-8602
MLA acronym: RG

SUBSCRIPTION INFORMATION

Frequency of publication: 10 times/yr.
Circulation: 1,000
Available in microform: No
Subscription price: 1,900 BF/yr. Belgium; 2,300 BF/yr. elsewhere
Year to which price refers: 1992
Subscription address: Chaussée de la Croix 47, 1340 Ottignies-Louvain-la-Neuve, Belgium
Subscription telephone: (32) 10 415024
Subscription fax: (32) 10 412578

ADVERTISING INFORMATION

Advertising accepted: Yes

EDITORIAL DESCRIPTION

Scope: Publishes articles on modern humanities.
Reviews books: Yes
Publishes notes: Yes
Languages accepted: French
Prints abstracts: No
Author-anonymous submission: No

SUBMISSION REQUIREMENTS

Restrictions on contributors: None
Author pays submission fee: No
Author pays page charges: No
Length of articles: 10 pp.
Length of book reviews: 1 p.
Number of copies required: 1
Special requirements: Submit original typescript.
Copyright ownership: Journal & author
Rejected manuscripts: Returned at author's request
Time before publication decision: 1 mo.
Time between decision and publication: 1-12 mos.
Number of reviewers: 2
Articles submitted per year: 80-100
Articles published per year: 50-60
Book reviews submitted per year: 100
Book reviews published per year: 70

(2429)
*Revue Internationale de Philosophie

Michel Meyer, Editor
Univ. de Bruxelles
C.P. 188
Av. F. D. Roosevelt, 50
1050 Brussels, Belgium

First published: 1938
ISSN: 0048-8143
MLA acronym: RIPh

SUBSCRIPTION INFORMATION

Frequency of publication: 4 times/yr.
Subscription address: Imprimerie UNIVERSA, rue Hoender 24, 9200 Wetteren, Belgium

ADVERTISING INFORMATION

Advertising accepted: Yes

EDITORIAL DESCRIPTION

Scope: Publishes articles on philosophy.
Reviews books: Yes
Publishes notes: No
Languages accepted: German; English; French; Italian
Prints abstracts: No

SUBMISSION REQUIREMENTS

Restrictions on contributors: Uninvited contributions are not accepted.
Length of articles: 20 pp.
Length of book reviews: No restrictions
Number of copies required: 2
Copyright ownership: Journal
Time between decision and publication: 2 yrs. maximum

(2430)
*Revue Québécoise de Linguistique

Jacques Labelle, Editor
Dept. de Linguistique
Univ. du Québec à Montréal
C.P. 8888, Succursale "A"
Montreal H3C 3P8, Canada

Telephone: 514 987-4227
Fax: 514 987-4652
E-mail: RQLing@UQAM.Bitnet.CA
First published: 1971
Sponsoring organization: Fond pour la Formation de Chercheurs & l'Aide à la Recherche; Univ. du Québec à Montréal; CRSHC
ISSN: 0710-0167
MLA acronym: RQdL

SUBSCRIPTION INFORMATION

Frequency of publication: 2 times/yr.
Circulation: 350
Available in microform: No
Subscription price: C$29.00/yr.
Year to which price refers: 1991-92
Subscription address: Service des Pubs., Univ. du Québec à Montréal, C.P. 8888, Succursale "A", Montreal H3C 3P8, Canada
Subscription telephone: 514 987-7747

ADVERTISING INFORMATION

Advertising accepted: Yes

EDITORIAL DESCRIPTION

Scope: Publishes articles on linguistics.
Reviews books: Yes
Publishes notes: Yes
Languages accepted: English; French
Prints abstracts: Yes
Author-anonymous submission: No

SUBMISSION REQUIREMENTS

Restrictions on contributors: None
Author pays submission fee: No
Author pays page charges: No
Length of articles: 20-25 pp.
Length of book reviews: 4-6 pp.
Length of notes: 4-6 pp.
Style: Linguistic Soc. of America
Number of copies required: 1
Special requirements: Submission on diskette is preferred. If not possible, submit double-spaced typescript on one side of page.
Copyright ownership: Journal

Rejected manuscripts: Retained for at least 1 yr.
Time before publication decision: 6 mos.
Time between decision and publication: 6 mos.
Number of reviewers: 3-5
Articles submitted per year: 25-35
Articles published per year: 15-20
Book reviews submitted per year: 7-8
Book reviews published per year: 5-6
Notes submitted per year: 5-6
Notes published per year: 3-4

(2431)
*Revue Québécoise de Linguistique Théorique et Appliquée

Henri Wittmann, Editor
C.P. 95
Trois-Rivières G9A 5E3, Canada

Telephone: 819 378-8157
First published: 1974
Sponsoring organization: Assn. Québécoise de Linguistique
ISSN: 0835-3581
MLA acronym: RAQL

SUBSCRIPTION INFORMATION

Frequency of publication: 4 times/yr.
Circulation: 600
Available in microform: No

ADVERTISING INFORMATION

Advertising accepted: Yes

EDITORIAL DESCRIPTION

Scope: Publishes articles on linguistics.
Reviews books: Yes
Publishes notes: Yes
Languages accepted: French
Prints abstracts: Yes
Author-anonymous submission: Yes

SUBMISSION REQUIREMENTS

Restrictions on contributors: Restricted to AQL members and invited papers.
Author pays submission fee: No
Author pays page charges: No
Length of articles: No restrictions
Length of book reviews: No restrictions
Length of notes: No restrictions
Style: Journal; Linguistic Soc. of America
Number of copies required: 4
Special requirements: Include original typescript or diskette plus 3 printed copies.
Copyright ownership: Assn. Québécoise de Linguistique
Rejected manuscripts: Returned
Time before publication decision: 4 mos.
Time between decision and publication: 8 mos. maximum
Number of reviewers: 3
Articles submitted per year: 22
Articles published per year: 17
Book reviews submitted per year: 10
Book reviews published per year: 5
Notes submitted per year: 2
Notes published per year: 2

(2432)
*Revue Romane

John Pederson, Hans Peter Lund, Michael Herslund, Hanne Korzen, Ginette Kryssing-Berg, Berta Pallares, Ghani Merad, Lene Waage Petersen, & Nils Soelberg, Editors
Inst. d'Etudes Romanes
Københavns Univ.
Njalsgade 80
2300 Copenhagen S, Denmark

Fax: (45) 32 965014

First published: 1966
Sponsoring organization: Statens Humanistiske Forskningsråd
ISSN: 0035-3906
MLA acronym: RevR

SUBSCRIPTION INFORMATION

Frequency of publication: 2 times/yr. (June, Dec.)
Circulation: 400
Available in microform: No
Subscription address: Munksgaard International Publishers Ltd., Nørre Søgade 35, P.O. Box 2148, 1016 Copenhagen, Denmark

ADVERTISING INFORMATION

Advertising accepted: No

EDITORIAL DESCRIPTION

Scope: Publishes studies on Romance languages and literatures and book reviews of linguistic and literary works.
Reviews books: Yes
Publishes notes: Yes
Languages accepted: French; Spanish; Portuguese; Romanian; Italian
Prints abstracts: Yes
Author-anonymous submission: No

SUBMISSION REQUIREMENTS

Restrictions on contributors: None
Author pays submission fee: No
Author pays page charges: No
Length of articles: 15-25 pp.
Length of book reviews: 8,000-10,000 print units maximum
Length of notes: 15,000-25,000 print units
Style: Journal
Number of copies required: 1
Special requirements: Submit original typescript or good copy, and an 150-word abstract.
Copyright ownership: Journal
Rejected manuscripts: Not returned
Time before publication decision: 3 mos.
Time between decision and publication: 1-2 yrs.
Number of reviewers: 2
Articles submitted per year: 25-30
Articles published per year: 10-12
Book reviews submitted per year: 25-30
Book reviews published per year: 17-25
Notes submitted per year: 2-6
Notes published per year: 1-4

(2433)
Revue Roumaine de Linguistique

Editura Academiei Române
Calea Victoriei 125
79717 Bucharest, Romania

First published: 1956
Historical variations in title: Incorporates *Cahiers de Linguistique Théorique et Appliquée*
Sponsoring organization: Academia Română
ISSN: 0035-3957
MLA acronym: RRL

SUBSCRIPTION INFORMATION

Frequency of publication: 6 times/yr. (plus 2 issues combined with *Cahiers de Linguistique Théorique et Appliquée*)
Available in microform: No
Subscription address: ILEXIM, Departmentul Export-Import Presă, str. Decembrie nr. 3, P.O. Box 136-137, Bucharest, Romania

EDITORIAL DESCRIPTION

Scope: Publishes articles on general linguistics.
Reviews books: Yes
Languages accepted: English; French; German; Italian; Russian; Spanish; Portuguese
Prints abstracts: No

SUBMISSION REQUIREMENTS

Author pays submission fee: No
Author pays page charges: No
Number of copies required: 2
Time before publication decision: 6 mos.
Articles published per year: 50

(2434)
*Revue Thomiste: Revue Doctrinale de Théologie et de Philosophie

S.-Th. Bonino, Editor
Ecole de Théologie
1, avenue Lacordaire
31078 Toulouse Cedex, France

Telephone: (33) 61528470
Fax: (33) 61524724
First published: 1893
Sponsoring organization: Ordre des Prêcheurs, Province Dominicaine de Toulouse
ISSN: 0035-4295
MLA acronym: RThom

SUBSCRIPTION INFORMATION

Frequency of publication: 4 times/yr. (Mar., June, Sept., Dec.)
Circulation: 850
Available in microform: No
Subscription price: 380 F/yr. France; 450 F/yr. Europe; 480 F/yr. elsewhere
Year to which price refers: 1992

ADVERTISING INFORMATION

Advertising accepted: Yes

EDITORIAL DESCRIPTION

Scope: A doctrinal, theological, and philosophical review placed under the patronage of St. Thomas Aquinas, which seeks to safeguard the century-old riches of learning, and to extend its research to more up-to-date problems. Publishes essentially articles on theology, philosophy, and history of doctrines, and also a large number of chronicles and reviews of books.
Reviews books: Yes
Publishes notes: Yes
Languages accepted: French
Prints abstracts: No
Author-anonymous submission: No

SUBMISSION REQUIREMENTS

Restrictions on contributors: None
Author pays submission fee: No
Author pays page charges: No
Length of articles: 50,000-100,000 characters
Length of book reviews: 5,000-8,000 characters
Length of notes: 40,000 characters
Style: Journal
Number of copies required: 1
Special requirements: Submit original typescript with notes in separate section.
Copyright ownership: Journal
Rejected manuscripts: Returned
Time before publication decision: 2 mos.
Time between decision and publication: 3-18 mos.
Number of reviewers: 2
Articles submitted per year: 12
Articles published per year: 9-10
Book reviews submitted per year: 350-400
Book reviews published per year: 250-300
Notes submitted per year: 15
Notes published per year: 9-10

(2435)
Revue Tunisienne de Sciences Sociales

Centre d'Etudes & de Recherches Economiques & Sociales
Univ. de Tunis
23, rue d'Espagne
Tunis, Tunisia

First published: 1964
Sponsoring organization: Univ. de Tunis, Centre d'Etudes & de Recherches Economiques & Sociales
ISSN: 0035-4333
MLA acronym: RTSS

SUBSCRIPTION INFORMATION

Frequency of publication: 4 times/yr.

EDITORIAL DESCRIPTION

Reviews books: Yes
Languages accepted: French; Arabic
Prints abstracts: No

(2436)
*Rheinische Vierteljahrsblätter

H. L. Cox, W. Besch, W. Janssen, & M. Nikolay-Panter, Editors
Inst. für Geschichtliche Landeskunde
Am Hofgarten 22
5300 Bonn, Germany

Telephone: (49) 228 737502
Fax: (49) 228 737562
First published: 1931
Sponsoring organization: Inst. für Geschichtliche Landeskunde der Rheinland; Univ. Bonn; Landschaftsverband Rheinland, Cologne
ISSN: 0035-4473
MLA acronym: RhV

SUBSCRIPTION INFORMATION

Frequency of publication: Annual
Circulation: 2,000
Available in microform: No
Subscription price: 40 DM/yr.
Year to which price refers: 1992

ADVERTISING INFORMATION

Advertising accepted: No

EDITORIAL DESCRIPTION

Scope: Publishes articles on the regional history of the Rhineland, dialectology and historical linguistics, and European and regional ethnology.
Reviews books: Yes
Publishes notes: Yes
Languages accepted: German; French; English
Prints abstracts: No

SUBMISSION REQUIREMENTS

Restrictions on contributors: None
Author pays submission fee: No
Author pays page charges: No
Length of articles: 50 pp.
Length of book reviews: 3-5 pp.
Length of notes: 10 pp.
Number of copies required: 1
Special requirements: Submit original typescript.
Copyright ownership: Assigned by author to journal
Rejected manuscripts: Returned
Time before publication decision: 2 mos.
Time between decision and publication: 10 mos.
Number of reviewers: 3
Articles submitted per year: 20
Articles published per year: 10
Book reviews published per year: 70-80

Notes submitted per year: 8
Notes published per year: 2

(2437)
*Rheinisches Jahrbuch für Volkskunde

H. L. Cox, Editor
Am Hofgarten 22
5300 Bonn 1, Germany

Telephone: (49) 228 737618
Fax: (49) 228 737562
First published: 1950
Sponsoring organization: Landschaftsverband Rheinland
ISSN: 0080-2697
MLA acronym: RJV

SUBSCRIPTION INFORMATION

Frequency of publication: Annual
Circulation: 700-1,000
Available in microform: No
Subscription address: Dümmler Verlag, Kaiserstr. 31/37, 5300 Bonn 1, Germany
Subscription telephone: (49) 228 223031
Subscription fax: (49) 228 213040

ADVERTISING INFORMATION

Advertising accepted: No

EDITORIAL DESCRIPTION

Scope: Publishes articles on cultural anthropology of Europe and the Rheinland.
Reviews books: No
Publishes notes: No
Languages accepted: German; English; French; Dutch
Prints abstracts: No
Author-anonymous submission: No

SUBMISSION REQUIREMENTS

Restrictions on contributors: None
Author pays submission fee: No
Author pays page charges: No
Length of articles: 20-30 pp.
Style: MLA
Number of copies required: 1
Copyright ownership: Author
Rejected manuscripts: Returned
Time before publication decision: 3 mos.
Time between decision and publication: 6-12 mos.
Number of reviewers: 2
Articles submitted per year: 15-20
Articles published per year: 12-15

(2438)
*Rheinisches Museum für Philologie

Carl Werner Müller, Editor
Inst. für Klassische Philologie
Univ. des Saarlandes
6600 Saarbrücken, Germany

First published: 1827
ISSN: 0035-449X
MLA acronym: RMP

SUBSCRIPTION INFORMATION

Frequency of publication: 4 times/yr.
Circulation: 600
Available in microform: No
Subscription address: J. D. Sauerländer's Verlag, Finkenhofstr. 21, 6000 Frankfurt, Germany

ADVERTISING INFORMATION

Advertising accepted: No

EDITORIAL DESCRIPTION

Scope: Publishes articles on Greek and Latin culture, with an emphasis on literature.
Reviews books: No
Publishes notes: Yes
Languages accepted: English; German; Italian; French; Latin
Prints abstracts: No

SUBMISSION REQUIREMENTS

Restrictions on contributors: None
Author pays submission fee: No
Author pays page charges: No
Length of articles: 30 pp. maximum
Length of notes: 200 words maximum
Style: None
Number of copies required: 1
Special requirements: Submit typescript.
Copyright ownership: Editor for 2 yrs.
Rejected manuscripts: Returned, except overseas
Time before publication decision: 1 mo.
Time between decision and publication: 2-3 yrs.
Articles published per year: 35
Notes published per year: 10

(2439)
*Rhetoric Review

Theresa Enos, Editor
Dept. of English
Univ. of Arizona
Tucson, AZ 85721

Telephone: 602 621-3371
Fax: 602 621-8885
E-mail: RHETREV@ARIZVMS.BITNET; rhetrev@ccit.arizona.edu
First published: 1982
Sponsoring organization: Rhetoric Review Assn. of America
ISSN: 0735-0198
MLA acronym: RhetRev

SUBSCRIPTION INFORMATION

Frequency of publication: 2 times/yr.
Circulation: 1,500
Available in microform: No
Subscription price: $15.00/yr. institutions US; $17.00/yr. institutions elsewhere; $12.00/yr. individuals US; $14.00/yr. individuals elsewhere
Year to which price refers: 1992

ADVERTISING INFORMATION

Advertising accepted: Yes
Advertising rates: $200.00/full page

EDITORIAL DESCRIPTION

Scope: Publishes articles on the history and theory of rhetoric. Includes studies on postmodern rhetoric and literary theory.
Reviews books: Yes
Publishes notes: No
Languages accepted: English
Prints abstracts: No
Author-anonymous submission: Yes

SUBMISSION REQUIREMENTS

Restrictions on contributors: Book reviews are assigned.
Author pays submission fee: No
Author pays page charges: No
Length of articles: 6,000 words
Length of book reviews: 1,500 words
Style: MLA
Number of copies required: 3
Special requirements: Author's identification should appear on title page only.
Copyright ownership: Journal
Rejected manuscripts: Returned; enclose return postage.
Time before publication decision: 2 mos.

Time between decision and publication: 6-12 mos.
Number of reviewers: 3
Articles submitted per year: 150-200
Articles published per year: 20
Book reviews published per year: 8-10

(2440)
*Rhetoric Society Quarterly

Philip Keith & Eugene Garver, Editors
Dept. of English
St. Cloud State Univ.
720 Fourth St. South
St. Cloud, MN 56301-4498

Telephone: 612 255-3189
E-mail: RHETSOC@MSUS1.MSUS.EDU
First published: 1968
Sponsoring organization: Rhetoric Soc. of America
ISSN: 0277-3945
MLA acronym: RSQ

SUBSCRIPTION INFORMATION

Frequency of publication: 4 times/yr.
Circulation: 900
Available in microform: No
Subscription price: $20.00/yr. US (includes membership); $25.00/yr. elsewhere (includes membership); $5.00/yr. students
Year to which price refers: 1992
Subscription address: Dept. of Philosophy, St. Cloud State Univ., 720 Fourth St. South, St. Cloud, MN 56301-4498

ADVERTISING INFORMATION

Advertising accepted: Yes, on an exchange basis

EDITORIAL DESCRIPTION

Scope: Publishes manuscripts on rhetorical theory, rhetorical criticism, history of rhetoric, rhetorical pedagogy, rhetorical research, bibliographies, notes and information on rhetorical programs and conferences, reports on new developments in rhetoric, and reviews.
Reviews books: Yes
Publishes notes: Yes
Languages accepted: English
Prints abstracts: No
Author-anonymous submission: No

SUBMISSION REQUIREMENTS

Restrictions on contributors: None
Author pays submission fee: No
Author pays page charges: No
Length of articles: No restrictions
Length of book reviews: No restrictions
Length of notes: No restrictions
Style: MLA
Number of copies required: 2
Special requirements: Submit 2 copies of double-spaced manuscript which may be on computer paper.
Copyright ownership: Journal
Rejected manuscripts: Not returned
Time before publication decision: 6 mos.
Time between decision and publication: 6-9 mos.
Number of reviewers: 2
Articles submitted per year: 100
Articles published per year: 20-25
Book reviews submitted per year: 25-30
Book reviews published per year: 20-25
Notes submitted per year: 50
Notes published per year: 40

(2441)
Rhetorica: A Journal of the History of Rhetoric

James J. Murphy, Editor
Dept. of Rhetoric
Univ. of California
Davis, CA 95616

First published: 1983
Sponsoring organization: International Soc. for the History of Rhetoric
ISSN: 0734-8584
MLA acronym: Rhetorica

SUBSCRIPTION INFORMATION

Frequency of publication: 4 times/yr. (Feb., May, Aug., Nov.)
Circulation: 600
Available in microform: Yes
Subscription address: Univ. of California Press, 2120 Berkeley Way, Berkeley, CA 94720

ADVERTISING INFORMATION

Advertising accepted: Yes

EDITORIAL DESCRIPTION

Scope: Publishes articles on the theory and practice of rhetoric in all periods and languages.
Reviews books: Yes
Publishes notes: No
Languages accepted: English; French; German; Italian
Prints abstracts: No
Author-anonymous submission: Yes

SUBMISSION REQUIREMENTS

Restrictions on contributors: None
Author pays submission fee: No
Author pays page charges: No
Length of articles: No restrictions
Style: MLA
Number of copies required: 2
Special requirements: Submit author's name, address, and manuscript title on a separate page. Manuscript must be double-spaced typescript, including all quotations and footnotes.
Copyright ownership: Journal
Rejected manuscripts: Returned; enclose SASE.
Time before publication decision: 2 mos.
Time between decision and publication: 6 mos.
Number of reviewers: 2
Articles submitted per year: 30
Articles published per year: 16
Book reviews submitted per year: 10
Book reviews published per year: 8

(2442)
Ricerche Slavistiche

L. Constantini, S. Graciotti, & G. Brogi-Bercoff, Editors
Ist. di Filologia Slava
Fac. di Lettere
Via C. Fea 2
00161 Rome, Italy

Additional editorial address: G. Brogi-Bercoff, Via Sette Chiese 13, 00145 Rome, Italy
First published: 1952
Sponsoring organization: Univ. di Roma
ISSN: 0391-4127
MLA acronym: RSl

SUBSCRIPTION INFORMATION

Frequency of publication: Annual
Circulation: 250
Available in microform: No
Subscription address: IRSA Verlag GmbH, Rüdengasse 6, 1030 Vienna, Austria

ADVERTISING INFORMATION

Advertising accepted: Yes

EDITORIAL DESCRIPTION

Scope: Publishes articles on Slavic literatures and philology.
Reviews books: Yes
Publishes notes: Yes
Languages accepted: Italian; English; German; French; Russian; Polish; Czech; Serbo-Croatian; Bulgarian; Ukrainian
Prints abstracts: No
Author-anonymous submission: Yes

SUBMISSION REQUIREMENTS

Author pays submission fee: No
Author pays page charges: No
Length of articles: 50,000-60,000 words
Length of book reviews: 6,000-7,000 words
Length of notes: 8,000-9,000 words
Number of copies required: 2
Special requirements: Manuscripts submitted in Slavic languages are considered. Include a 1,000-word abstract.
Copyright ownership: Journal
Rejected manuscripts: Not returned
Time before publication decision: 4 mos.
Time between decision and publication: 1 yr.
Number of reviewers: 6
Articles submitted per year: 12-15
Articles published per year: 7-10
Book reviews published per year: 25-30

(2443)
*RILCE: Revista de Filología Hispánica

Jesús Cañedo, Director
Campus Universitario
Univ. de Navarra
31080 Pamplona, Spain

Telephone: (34) 48 252700 ext. 2498
Fax: (34) 48 173650
First published: 1985
Sponsoring organization: Univ. de Navarra
ISSN: 0213-2370
MLA acronym: RILCE

SUBSCRIPTION INFORMATION

Frequency of publication: 2 times/yr. (May, Nov.)
Circulation: 200
Available in microform: No
Subscription price: 2,400 Pta/yr. Spain; $30.00/yr. elsewhere
Year to which price refers: 1992
Subscription address: Biblioteca de Humanidades, Univ. de Navarra, 31080 Pamplona, Spain

ADVERTISING INFORMATION

Advertising accepted: No

EDITORIAL DESCRIPTION

Scope: Publishes articles on the language and literatures of Spain and Spanish America.
Reviews books: Yes
Publishes notes: Yes
Languages accepted: Spanish
Prints abstracts: Yes
Author-anonymous submission: Yes

SUBMISSION REQUIREMENTS

Restrictions on contributors: None
Author pays submission fee: No
Author pays page charges: No
Length of articles: 15 pp.
Length of book reviews: 5 pp.
Length of notes: 7 pp.
Number of copies required: 2

Special requirements: Include a 10-line abstract in Spanish and English.
Rejected manuscripts: Returned
Time before publication decision: 2-3 weeks
Time between decision and publication: 10 mos.
Number of reviewers: 2
Articles submitted per year: 25
Articles published per year: 12
Book reviews submitted per year: 30
Book reviews published per year: 15
Notes submitted per year: 3
Notes published per year: 2

(2444)
*RIMA: Review of Indonesian and Malaysian Affairs

Anthony Day, Editor
Dept. of Indonesian & Malayan Studies
Univ. of Sydney
Sydney, NSW 2006, Australia

Telephone: (61) 2 6923121
Fax: (61) 2 6923173
First published: 1967
Sponsoring organization: Univ. of Sydney; Royal Inst. for Anthropology & Linguistics, Leiden
ISSN: 0034-6594
MLA acronym: RevIMA

SUBSCRIPTION INFORMATION

Frequency of publication: 2 times/yr.
Circulation: 350
Available in microform: No
Subscription price: A$25.00/yr. Australia & New Zealand; A$33.00/yr. elsewhere
Year to which price refers: 1993

ADVERTISING INFORMATION

Advertising accepted: Yes

EDITORIAL DESCRIPTION

Scope: Publishes articles on political, economic, sociological, cultural, linguistic, and literary aspects of the Indonesian and Malayan area.
Reviews books: Yes
Publishes notes: No
Languages accepted: English; Bahasa Malay dialect
Prints abstracts: No
Author-anonymous submission: No

SUBMISSION REQUIREMENTS

Restrictions on contributors: None
Author pays submission fee: No
Author pays page charges: No
Length of articles: No restrictions
Length of book reviews: 900 words
Style: Chicago
Number of copies required: 1
Copyright ownership: Author
Rejected manuscripts: Returned
Time before publication decision: 4 mos.
Time between decision and publication: 3-4 mos.
Number of reviewers: 2
Articles submitted per year: 20
Articles published per year: 10-15
Book reviews submitted per year: 20
Book reviews published per year: 10-15

(2445)
*Rinascimento: Rivista dell'Istituto Nazionale di Studi sul Rinascimento

Gian Carlo Garfagnini, Editor
Ist. Nazionale di Studi sul Rinascimento
Palazzo Strozzi
50123 Florence, Italy

First published: 1950

Sponsoring organization: Ist. Nazionale di Studi sul Rinascimento
ISSN: 0080-3073
MLA acronym: Rinascimento

SUBSCRIPTION INFORMATION

Frequency of publication: Annual
Circulation: 800
Available in microform: No
Subscription price: 86,000 Lit/yr. Italy; 100,000 Lit/yr. elsewhere
Year to which price refers: 1991
Subscription address: Leo S. Olschki, Viuzzo del Pozzetto, C.P. 66, 50126 Florence, Italy

ADVERTISING INFORMATION

Advertising accepted: No

EDITORIAL DESCRIPTION

Scope: Publishes articles on aspects of Renaissance culture and civilization.
Reviews books: No
Publishes notes: Yes
Languages accepted: English; French; German; Italian; Spanish; Latin
Prints abstracts: No
Author-anonymous submission: No

SUBMISSION REQUIREMENTS

Restrictions on contributors: None
Author pays submission fee: No
Author pays page charges: No
Length of articles: 25-40 pp.
Length of notes: 10-15 pp.
Style: None
Number of copies required: 1
Special requirements: Include original typescript.
Copyright ownership: Journal
Rejected manuscripts: Not returned
Time before publication decision: 1 mo.
Time between decision and publication: 1 yr.
Number of reviewers: 2
Articles submitted per year: 10-14
Articles published per year: 6-12
Notes submitted per year: 6-8
Notes published per year: 1-4

(2446)
*Río de la Plata: Culturas

Paul Verdevoye, Director
CELCIRP
Inst. des Hautes Etudes d'Amérique Latine
28, rue Saint-Guillaume
75007 Paris, France

Additional editorial address: Claude Cymerman, 35 boulevard Sérurier, 75019 Paris, France
Telephone: (33) 1 42497357
First published: 1985
Sponsoring organization: Centro de Estudios de Literaturas & Civilizaciones del Río de la Plata (CELCIRP); Unión Latina; Assn. des Littératures Latino-Américaines & des Caraïbes & Africaines du XXème Siècle
ISSN: 0982-0582
MLA acronym: RíoPla

SUBSCRIPTION INFORMATION

Frequency of publication: 2 times/yr.
Circulation: 200
Available in microform: No
Subscription price: $30.00/yr. N. America, Europe, Africa, & Asia; $24.00/yr. Latin America
Year to which price refers: 1992
Subscription address: Nilda Díaz, 24 ave. du Général-Pierre-Billotte, 94000 Créteil, France
Additional subscription address: Assia Gómez, 150 rue du Maine, 75014 Paris, France
Subscription telephone: (33) 1 47898082 (Nora Parola-Leconte, Deputy Editor)

ADVERTISING INFORMATION

Advertising accepted: Yes

EDITORIAL DESCRIPTION

Scope: Publishes articles on the culture and civilization of Argentina, Paraguay, and Uruguay, through the humanities and social sciences. Includes studies on literature, language, linguistics, sociology, psychology, history, and political science.
Reviews books: Yes
Publishes notes: Yes
Languages accepted: Spanish; French; all Romance languages
Prints abstracts: No
Author-anonymous submission: No

SUBMISSION REQUIREMENTS

Restrictions on contributors: None
Author pays submission fee: No
Author pays page charges: No
Length of articles: 15 pp. maximum
Length of book reviews: 2 pp. maximum
Length of notes: 1 p. maximum
Number of copies required: 2
Special requirements: Each issue is thematic. Only articles corresponding to the topic are accepted.
Rejected manuscripts: Returned; enclose self-addressed envelope.
Time before publication decision: 6 mos.
Time between decision and publication: 6 mos.
Number of reviewers: 3
Articles submitted per year: 60
Articles published per year: 24-32
Book reviews submitted per year: 20
Book reviews published per year: 20
Notes submitted per year: 5
Notes published per year: 5

(2447)
Riscontri: Rivista Trimestrale di Cultura e di Attualità

Mario Gabriele Giordano, Editor
Via Vasto n. 29
83100 Avellino, Italy

First published: 1979
ISSN: 0392-5080
MLA acronym: Riscontri

SUBSCRIPTION INFORMATION

Frequency of publication: 4 times/yr.
Circulation: 100
Available in microform: No

ADVERTISING INFORMATION

Advertising accepted: Yes

EDITORIAL DESCRIPTION

Scope: Provides a cultural forum for the arts and for literature.
Reviews books: Yes
Publishes notes: Yes
Languages accepted: All languages
Prints abstracts: No
Author-anonymous submission: No

SUBMISSION REQUIREMENTS

Author pays submission fee: No
Author pays page charges: No
Length of articles: 20 pp.
Length of book reviews: 2 pp.
Style: Standard Italian
Number of copies required: 2
Special requirements: Consult inside cover of journal.
Copyright ownership: Sabatia Editrice
Rejected manuscripts: Returned; enclose return postage.
Time before publication decision: 6 mos.

Time between decision and publication: 6 mos.
Number of reviewers: 10
Articles submitted per year: 80
Articles published per year: 50
Book reviews submitted per year: 30
Book reviews published per year: 20
Notes submitted per year: 15
Notes published per year: 8

(2448)
*Riverside Quarterly

Leland Sapiro, Sheryl Smith, Redd Boggs, & Mary Emerson, Editors
Box 958
Big Sandy, TX 75755

Additional editorial address: Send fiction to: Redd Boggs, Box 1111, Berkeley, CA 94701. Send poetry to: Sheryl Smith, 515 Saratoga no. 2, Santa Clara, CA 95050
First published: 1964
ISSN: 0889-2326
MLA acronym: RQ

SUBSCRIPTION INFORMATION

Frequency of publication: Irregular
Circulation: 1,100
Available in microform: Yes
Subscription price: $8.00/4 issues
Year to which price refers: 1992

ADVERTISING INFORMATION

Advertising accepted: Yes, on an exchange or donation basis

EDITORIAL DESCRIPTION

Scope: Prints criticism and reviews of science fiction and fantasy. Emphasis is on current material rather than Victorian fantasy or science fiction of the Gilded Age.
Reviews books: Yes
Publishes notes: Yes
Languages accepted: English
Prints abstracts: No
Author-anonymous submission: No

SUBMISSION REQUIREMENTS

Restrictions on contributors: None
Author pays submission fee: No
Author pays page charges: No
Length of articles: No restrictions
Length of book reviews: No restrictions
Length of notes: No restrictions
Style: None
Number of copies required: 1
Special requirements: If author is affiliated with a college or university then page costs ($25.00/pg.) are charged to that institution.
Copyright ownership: Reverts to author upon publication
Rejected manuscripts: Returned; enclose return postage.
Time before publication decision: 10 days
Time between decision and publication: 9-12 mos.
Number of reviewers: 1

(2449)
*La Rivista Dalmatica

Nicolo' Luxardo de Franchi, Oddone Talpo, & Guido Cace, Editors
Archivio Dalmato della società "Dante Alighieri"
Piazza di Firenze, 27
00186 Rome, Italy

Telephone: (39) 6 6873686
First published: 1899
Sponsoring organization: Assn. Nazionale Dalmata di Roma
ISSN: 0393-4624

MLA acronym: RD

SUBSCRIPTION INFORMATION

Frequency of publication: 4 times/yr.
Circulation: 700
Available in microform: No
Subscription price: 30,000 Lit/yr. Italy; 35,000 Lit/yr. elsewhere
Year to which price refers: 1992

ADVERTISING INFORMATION

Advertising accepted: Yes

EDITORIAL DESCRIPTION

Scope: Publishes articles on history, folklore, literature, arts, and Italian traditions of Dalmatia.
Reviews books: Yes
Publishes notes: Yes
Languages accepted: Italian; Venetian dialects of Dalmatia
Prints abstracts: No
Author-anonymous submission: No

SUBMISSION REQUIREMENTS

Restrictions on contributors: None
Author pays submission fee: No
Author pays page charges: Sometimes, for large numeric tables, drawings, and photographs
Length of articles: 2,500-10,000 words
Length of book reviews: 500-1,500 words
Length of notes: 250-1,000 words
Style: Journal
Number of copies required: 1
Special requirements: Submit original, double-spaced typescript. Articles submitted in languages other than Italian or Venetian dialects of Dalmatia will be translated if accepted for publication.
Copyright ownership: Journal
Rejected manuscripts: Returned at author's request
Time before publication decision: 4-6 weeks
Time between decision and publication: 3-9 mos.
Number of reviewers: 2
Articles submitted per year: 30-35
Articles published per year: 25-30
Book reviews submitted per year: 15-20
Book reviews published per year: 15-20
Notes submitted per year: 15-25
Notes published per year: 10-15

(2450)
*Rivista degli Studi Orientali

Paolo Daffina & Biancamaria Sconcia Amoretti, Editors
Dpto. di Studi Orientali
Città Univ.
Rome, Italy

Telephone: (39) 6 4451209
Fax: (39) 6 4451209
First published: 1907
Sponsoring organization: Univ. di Roma, Dipartimento di Studi Orientali
ISSN: 0392-4869
MLA acronym: RdSO

SUBSCRIPTION INFORMATION

Frequency of publication: 2 times/yr.
Circulation: 500
Available in microform: No
Subscription price: 80,000 Lit/yr.
Year to which price refers: 1992
Subscription address: Bardi Editore, Salita dei Crescenzi 16, 00186 Rome, Italy

EDITORIAL DESCRIPTION

Scope: Publishes articles on Oriental studies.
Reviews books: Yes
Publishes notes: Yes

Languages accepted: English; French; German; Italian; Spanish
Prints abstracts: Occasionally
Author-anonymous submission: No

SUBMISSION REQUIREMENTS

Author pays submission fee: No
Author pays page charges: No
Length of articles: No restrictions
Length of book reviews: No restrictions
Length of notes: No restrictions
Number of copies required: 1
Copyright ownership: Univ. of Rome
Rejected manuscripts: Returned
Time before publication decision: 3 mos.
Time between decision and publication: 1 yr.
Articles submitted per year: 20
Articles published per year: 15
Book reviews submitted per year: 50
Book reviews published per year: 40
Notes submitted per year: 10
Notes published per year: 5

(2451)
Rivista di Cultura Classica e Medievale

Ettore Paratore, Editor
P.O. Box 7216
00100 Rome, Italy

First published: 1959
ISSN: 0035-6085
MLA acronym: RCCM

SUBSCRIPTION INFORMATION

Frequency of publication: 3 times/yr.
Circulation: 2,000
Available in microform: No

ADVERTISING INFORMATION

Advertising accepted: No

EDITORIAL DESCRIPTION

Scope: Publishes studies on classical and medieval culture.
Reviews books: Yes
Publishes notes: No
Languages accepted: English; French; German; Italian; Latin
Prints abstracts: No

SUBMISSION REQUIREMENTS

Restrictions on contributors: None
Author pays submission fee: No
Author pays page charges: No
Length of articles: No restrictions
Number of copies required: 1
Copyright ownership: Ettore Paratore
Rejected manuscripts: Not returned
Time before publication decision: 11 mos.

(2452)
*Rivista di Estetica

Gianni Vattimo, Editor
Rosenberg & Sellier
Via Andrea Doria, 14
10123 Turin, Italy

Telephone: (39) 11 8127820
Fax: (39) 11 8127744
First published: 1956
ISSN: 0035-6212
MLA acronym: RdE

SUBSCRIPTION INFORMATION

Frequency of publication: 3 times/yr.
Circulation: 1,500
Available in microform: No

ADVERTISING INFORMATION

Advertising accepted: Yes

EDITORIAL DESCRIPTION

Scope: Publishes articles on Italian philosophical culture and the development of aesthetics. Topics include philosophic theory of the arts, sociology, and psychology of the arts, poetics, methodology of the arts and literary criticism, hermeneutics, typology of culture and the art, and anthropology.
Reviews books: Yes
Publishes notes: Yes
Languages accepted: Italian; French; English; Spanish
Prints abstracts: No
Author-anonymous submission: No

SUBMISSION REQUIREMENTS

Restrictions on contributors: None
Author pays submission fee: No
Author pays page charges: No
Length of articles: 7,000-8,000 words
Length of book reviews: 1,000-2,000 words
Length of notes: 20-50 words
Style: Journal
Number of copies required: 2
Copyright ownership: Author
Rejected manuscripts: Returned
Time before publication decision: 2 mos.
Time between decision and publication: 1 yr.
Number of reviewers: 2
Articles submitted per year: 40
Articles published per year: 20
Book reviews submitted per year: 40
Book reviews published per year: 20
Notes submitted per year: 40
Notes published per year: 20

(2453)
*Rivista di Filosofia Neo-Scolastica

Adriano Bausola, Editor
Vita e Pensiero
Largo A. Gemelli, 1
20123 Milan, Italy

Telephone: (39) 2 8856252
Fax: (39) 2 8856260
First published: 1909
Sponsoring organization: Univ. Cattolica del Sacro Cuore
ISSN: 0035-6247
MLA acronym: RFNS

SUBSCRIPTION INFORMATION

Frequency of publication: 4 times/yr.
Circulation: 1,200
Available in microform: No
Subscription price: 118,000 Lit/yr.
Year to which price refers: 1992
Subscription address: For exchanges write to: Biblioteca/Scambi Periodici, Univ. Cattolica del Sacro Cuore, at the above address

ADVERTISING INFORMATION

Advertising accepted: Yes

EDITORIAL DESCRIPTION

Scope: Publishes neo-scholastic research which, in accordance with the Christian faith, contributes to a fuller understanding of contemporary philosophy.
Reviews books: Yes
Publishes notes: Yes
Languages accepted: French; Italian
Prints abstracts: No
Author-anonymous submission: No

SUBMISSION REQUIREMENTS

Restrictions on contributors: None
Author pays submission fee: No

Author pays page charges: No
Length of articles: 20-30 typescript pp.
Length of book reviews: 5-6 pp.
Length of notes: 5-10 pp.
Style: None
Number of copies required: 1
Special requirements: Submit original typescript.
Copyright ownership: Assigned by author to journal
Rejected manuscripts: Returned
Time before publication decision: 3-4 mos.
Time between decision and publication: 1 yr.
Number of reviewers: 2-3
Articles published per year: 35
Book reviews published per year: 50

(2454)
*Rivista di Letterature Moderne e Comparate

Giuliano Pellegrini, Arnaldo Pizzorusso, Claudia Corti, Elena Del Panta, Brunella Eruli, Antonio R. Parra, & Ivanna Rosi, Editors
Via della Cernaia 55
50129 Florence, Italy

First published: 1946
ISSN: 0391-2108
MLA acronym: RLMC

SUBSCRIPTION INFORMATION

Frequency of publication: 4 times/yr.
Circulation: 900
Available in microform: No
Subscription price: 55,000 Lit/yr. Italy; 85,000 Lit/yr. elsewhere
Year to which price refers: 1991
Subscription address: Pacini Editore, Via Gheradesca, 56014 Ospedaletto, Pisa, Italy

ADVERTISING INFORMATION

Advertising accepted: Yes

EDITORIAL DESCRIPTION

Scope: Publishes articles on modern and comparative literature including critical essays, text analyses, and essays on the history of ideas.
Reviews books: Yes
Publishes notes: No
Languages accepted: English; French; Italian
Prints abstracts: No
Author-anonymous submission: No

SUBMISSION REQUIREMENTS

Author pays submission fee: No
Author pays page charges: No
Length of articles: 15-25 pp.
Length of book reviews: 3-5 pp.
Number of copies required: 2
Copyright ownership: Pacini Editore
Rejected manuscripts: Not returned
Time before publication decision: 1 mo.
Time between decision and publication: 3-12 mos.
Number of reviewers: 2
Articles submitted per year: 50-60
Articles published per year: 16-20
Book reviews submitted per year: 30
Book reviews published per year: 20-25

(2455)
*Rivista di Linguistica

Pier Marco Bertinetto, Editor
Scuola Normale Superiore
P. dei Cavalieri 7
56100 Pisa, Italy

Telephone: (39) 50 597111
Fax: (39) 50 563513

E-mail: BERTINET@IPISNSIB
First published: 1989
MLA acronym: RdLing

SUBSCRIPTION INFORMATION

Frequency of publication: 2 times/yr.
Available in microform: No
Subscription address: Rosenberg & Sellier, Via Andrea Doria 14, 10123 Torino, Italy
Subscription telephone: (39) 11 8127820
Subscription fax: (39) 11 8127744

ADVERTISING INFORMATION

Advertising accepted: Yes

EDITORIAL DESCRIPTION

Scope: Publishes articles on linguistics.
Reviews books: Yes, review-essays
Publishes notes: Yes
Languages accepted: English; Italian; French; German; Esperanto
Prints abstracts: Yes
Author-anonymous submission: Yes

SUBMISSION REQUIREMENTS

Author pays submission fee: No
Author pays page charges: No
Style: Journal
Number of copies required: 3
Copyright ownership: Rosenberg & Sellier
Rejected manuscripts: Not returned
Time before publication decision: 4 mos.
Time between decision and publication: 6-12 mos.
Number of reviewers: 2
Articles submitted per year: 40
Articles published per year: 15

(2456)
*Rivista di Storia e Letteratura Religiosa

Franco Bolgiani, Carlo Ossola, Giorgio Cracco, & Mario Rosa, Editors
Biblioteca Erik Peterson
Fac. di Lettere
Univ. di Torino
Via S. Ottavio, 20
10124 Turin, Italy

Telephone: (39) 11 830556
First published: 1965
ISSN: 0035-6573
MLA acronym: RSLR

SUBSCRIPTION INFORMATION

Frequency of publication: 3 times/yr.
Circulation: 800
Available in microform: No
Subscription price: 65,000 Lit/yr. Italy; 85,000 Lit/yr. elsewhere
Year to which price refers: 1991
Subscription address: Casa Editrice Leo S. Olschki, C.P. 66, 50100 Florence, Italy
Subscription telephone: (39) 55 6530684
Subscription fax: (39) 55 6530214

ADVERTISING INFORMATION

Advertising accepted: Yes

EDITORIAL DESCRIPTION

Scope: Publishes studies and research in the fields of religious history and literature (especially Judeo-Christian), as well as comparative studies between Judeo-Christian and non-Christian religions (particularly those religions which, from a historical or phenomenological point of view, are close to Christianity).
Reviews books: Yes
Publishes notes: Yes

Languages accepted: English; French; Italian; German; Spanish
Prints abstracts: No
Author-anonymous submission: No

SUBMISSION REQUIREMENTS

Restrictions on contributors: None
Author pays submission fee: No
Author pays page charges: No
Length of articles: 8,000-12,000 words
Length of book reviews: 2,000-2,500 words
Length of notes: 800-1,000 words
Number of copies required: 1
Copyright ownership: Casa Editrice Leo S. Olschki
Rejected manuscripts: Not returned
Time before publication decision: 1 mo.
Time between decision and publication: 3-12 mos.
Number of reviewers: 3
Articles submitted per year: 15
Articles published per year: 6-8
Book reviews published per year: 30-40
Notes published per year: 75-100

(2457)
*Rivista di Studi Bizantini e Neoellenici

Enrica Follieri, Editor
Dpto. Filologia Greca e Latina
Univ. di Roma
Piazzale Aldo Moro, 5
00185 Rome, Italy

Telephone: (39) 6 49913586
First published: 1925
Sponsoring organization: Univ. di Roma
ISSN: 0557-1367
MLA acronym: RSBN

SUBSCRIPTION INFORMATION

Frequency of publication: 1-2 times/yr.
Circulation: 500
Available in microform: No
Subscription address: Libreria Tombolini, Via IV Novembre 146, Rome, Italy
Subscription telephone: (39) 6 6785925

ADVERTISING INFORMATION

Advertising accepted: No

EDITORIAL DESCRIPTION

Scope: Publishes articles on Byzantine and Neo-Hellenic literature.
Reviews books: Yes
Languages accepted: English; Greek; Italian; French; German
Prints abstracts: No

SUBMISSION REQUIREMENTS

Restrictions on contributors: None
Author pays submission fee: No
Author pays page charges: No
Length of articles: 20-30 pp.
Style: Journal
Number of copies required: 1
Special requirements: Submit original typescript.
Copyright ownership: Univ. di Roma, Dpto. Filologia Greca & Latina
Rejected manuscripts: Returned
Time before publication decision: 1 week
Time between decision and publication: 2 yrs.
Number of reviewers: 2
Articles submitted per year: 15-20
Articles published per year: 10-15
Book reviews published per year: 1

(2458)
*Rivista di Studi Italiani

Anthony Verna, Editor
Dept. of Italian Studies
Univ. of Toronto
Toronto, Ontario M5S 1A1, Canada

Telephone: 416 236-1519; 416 978-3325
Fax: 416 598-2471
First published: 1983
ISSN: 0821-3216
MLA acronym: RSItal

SUBSCRIPTION INFORMATION

Frequency of publication: 2 times/yr.
Circulation: 500
Available in microform: No
Subscription price: $30.00/yr. institutions; $25.00/yr. individuals
Year to which price refers: 1992

ADVERTISING INFORMATION

Advertising accepted: Yes
Advertising rates: C$100.00/full page

EDITORIAL DESCRIPTION

Scope: Publishes articles on Italian literature, linguistics, culture, and comparative literature.
Reviews books: Yes
Publishes notes: Yes
Languages accepted: Italian; French; English
Prints abstracts: No
Author-anonymous submission: Yes

SUBMISSION REQUIREMENTS

Restrictions on contributors: All contributions are solicited.
Author pays submission fee: No
Author pays page charges: No
Length of articles: 20 pp.
Length of book reviews: 600 words
Length of notes: 300 words
Style: MLA
Number of copies required: 2
Copyright ownership: Journal
Rejected manuscripts: Returned
Time before publication decision: 1 mo.
Time between decision and publication: 6-12 mos.
Number of reviewers: 3
Articles published per year: 20
Book reviews published per year: 20
Notes published per year: 3-6

(2459)
*Rivista Italiana di Dialettologia: Lingue Dialetti Società

Fabio Foresti, Editor
Ist. di Glottologia
Via Zamboni 16
40126 Bologna, Italy

Telephone: (39) 51 230414; (39) 51 235298
First published: 1977
Historical variations in title: Formerly *Rivista Italiana di Dialettologia: Scuola Società Territorio*
Sponsoring organization: Consiglio Nazionale delle Ricerche; Ministero Beni Culturali & Ambientali
MLA acronym: RID

SUBSCRIPTION INFORMATION

Frequency of publication: Annual
Circulation: 600
Available in microform: No
Subscription price: 38,000 Lit/yr. Italy; 66,000 Lit/yr. elsewhere
Year to which price refers: 1991
Subscription address: Cooperativa Libraria Universitaria Ed. Bologna, Via Marsala 24, 40126 Bologna, Italy
Subscription telephone: (39) 51 220736; (39) 51 224780
Subscription fax: (39) 51 237758

ADVERTISING INFORMATION

Advertising accepted: Yes

EDITORIAL DESCRIPTION

Scope: Publishes articles on general dialectology, Italian dialectology and linguistics, sociolinguistics, and linguistic training.
Reviews books: Yes
Publishes notes: Yes
Languages accepted: Italian; English; French
Prints abstracts: Yes
Author-anonymous submission: No

SUBMISSION REQUIREMENTS

Restrictions on contributors: Unsolicited manuscripts are not accepted.
Author pays submission fee: No
Author pays page charges: No
Length of articles: 40 double-spaced typescript pp. (32 lines or 2,000 words) maximum
Length of book reviews: 1 p.
Length of notes: 40 double-spaced typescript pp. (32 lines or 2,000 words) maximum
Style: Journal; style sheet in *RID* 8(1984):343-347
Number of copies required: 2
Special requirements: Submit original typescript plus 2 copies. Include a 20-line abstract in Italian and a 20-line author's bio-bibliography.
Copyright ownership: Cooperativa Libraria Universitaria Ed. Bologna
Rejected manuscripts: Not returned
Time before publication decision: 3 mos.
Time between decision and publication: 6 mos.
Number of reviewers: 2
Articles submitted per year: 20
Articles published per year: 10
Book reviews submitted per year: 100
Book reviews published per year: 300
Notes published per year: 6

(2460)
*Rivista Storica Italiana

Franco Venturi, Editor
Via Po, 17
10124 Turin, Italy

First published: 1884
ISSN: 0035-7073
MLA acronym: RSI

SUBSCRIPTION INFORMATION

Frequency of publication: 3 times/yr. (Apr., Aug., Dec.)
Circulation: 2,000
Available in microform: No
Subscription price: 120,000 Lit/yr. Italy; 210,000 Lit/yr. elsewhere
Year to which price refers: 1992
Subscription address: Edizioni Scientifiche Italiane, Via Chiatamone, 7, 80121 Naples, Italy

ADVERTISING INFORMATION

Advertising accepted: No

EDITORIAL DESCRIPTION

Scope: Publishes articles on history from the ancient to the contemporary world.
Reviews books: Yes
Publishes notes: No
Languages accepted: Italian
Prints abstracts: No
Author-anonymous submission: No

SUBMISSION REQUIREMENTS

Restrictions on contributors: None
Author pays submission fee: No
Author pays page charges: No
Length of articles: No restrictions
Length of book reviews: No restrictions
Style: Journal
Number of copies required: 1
Special requirements: Submit original typescript.
Copyright ownership: Assigned by author to journal
Rejected manuscripts: Returned
Time before publication decision: 3 mos.
Time between decision and publication: 1 yr.
Number of reviewers: Editors
Articles published per year: 30
Book reviews submitted per year: 250
Book reviews published per year: 50

(2461)
*RLA: Revista de Lingüística Teórica y Aplicada

Adalberto Salas & Max S. Echeverría, Editors
Casilla 82-C, Correo 3
Univ. de Concepción
Concepción, Chile

Telephone: (56) 41 234985 ext. 2143, 2313, 2530
Fax: (56) 41 240280
First published: 1963
Sponsoring organization: Univ. de Concepción, Chile
ISSN: 0033-698X
MLA acronym: RLTA

SUBSCRIPTION INFORMATION

Frequency of publication: Annual
Circulation: 400
Available in microform: No
Subscription price: $7.00/yr. plus postage
Year to which price refers: 1991
Subscription address: Graciela Alvarez C., Casilla 82-C, Correo 3, Concepción, Chile

ADVERTISING INFORMATION

Advertising accepted: Yes

EDITORIAL DESCRIPTION

Scope: Publishes articles on theoretical and applied linguistics.
Reviews books: Yes
Publishes notes: Yes
Languages accepted: Spanish; French; English
Prints abstracts: Yes
Author-anonymous submission: Yes

SUBMISSION REQUIREMENTS

Restrictions on contributors: Articles submitted must be previously unpublished.
Author pays submission fee: No
Author pays page charges: No
Length of articles: 3,200 words
Length of book reviews: 600 words
Length of notes: 400 words
Style: MLA
Number of copies required: 2
Special requirements: Submit a 200-word abstract in English.
Copyright ownership: Journal
Rejected manuscripts: Not returned
Time before publication decision: 6 mos.
Time between decision and publication: 6 mos.
Number of reviewers: 2
Articles submitted per year: 15
Articles published per year: 9
Book reviews submitted per year: 5
Book reviews published per year: 4
Notes submitted per year: 2
Notes published per year: 2

(2462)
*RLA: Romance Languages Annual

Jeanette Beer, Charles Ganelin, & Anthony J. Tamburri, Editors
Purdue Univ.
1359 Stanley Coulter Hall
West Lafayette, IN 47907-1359

Telephone: 317 494-7691
E-mail: Rla@purccvm (Bitnet); rla@vm.cc.-purcc.edu (Internet)
First published: 1990
Sponsoring organization: Purdue Research Foundation; Dept. of Foreign Languages & Literatures, Purdue Univ.
ISSN: 1050-0774
MLA acronym: RLAn

SUBSCRIPTION INFORMATION

Frequency of publication: Annual (Spring)
Circulation: 150
Available in microform: No
Subscription price: $30.00/yr. institutions US & Canada; $25.00/yr. individuals US & Canada; $35.00/yr. elsewhere
Year to which price refers: 1991

ADVERTISING INFORMATION

Advertising accepted: No

EDITORIAL DESCRIPTION

Scope: Publishes articles on Romance languages, literature, and film.
Reviews books: No
Publishes notes: No
Languages accepted: English; Spanish; French; Italian; Portuguese; Catalan
Prints abstracts: No
Author-anonymous submission: Yes

SUBMISSION REQUIREMENTS

Restrictions on contributors: Contributors must participate in Purdue Univ. Conference on Romance Languages.
Author pays submission fee: No
Author pays page charges: Yes, if article exceeds 7 printed pp.
Cost of page charges: $7.50/page exceeding 7 printed pp.
Length of articles: 5,000 words
Style: MLA
Number of copies required: 2
Copyright ownership: Purdue Research Foundation
Rejected manuscripts: Returned
Time before publication decision: 2 mos.
Time between decision and publication: 10 mos.
Number of reviewers: 2
Articles submitted per year: 200
Articles published per year: 100

(2463)
*Robert Frost Review

Earl J. Wilcox, Editor
Dept. of English
Winthrop Univ.
Rock Hill, SC 29733

Telephone: 803 323-4633
Fax: 803 323-2347
First published: 1991
Sponsoring organization: Robert Frost Soc.
ISSN: 1062-6999
MLA acronym: RFR

SUBSCRIPTION INFORMATION

Frequency of publication: Annual (Fall)
Circulation: 150
Available in microform: No
Subscription price: $15.00/yr.
Year to which price refers: 1992

ADVERTISING INFORMATION

Advertising accepted: No

EDITORIAL DESCRIPTION

Scope: Publishes articles on Robert Frost's life and poetry.
Reviews books: Yes
Publishes notes: Yes
Languages accepted: English
Prints abstracts: No
Author-anonymous submission: No

SUBMISSION REQUIREMENTS

Author pays submission fee: No
Author pays page charges: No
Length of articles: 2,000 words
Length of book reviews: 500 words
Length of notes: No restrictions
Style: MLA
Number of copies required: 1
Copyright ownership: Author
Rejected manuscripts: Returned; enclose SASE
Time before publication decision: 6 mos.
Time between decision and publication: 1 yr. maximum
Number of reviewers: 1-2
Articles submitted per year: 20-40
Articles published per year: 8-10
Book reviews submitted per year: 4
Book reviews published per year: 4
Notes submitted per year: 5-10
Notes published per year: 3-5

(2464)
*Robinson Jeffers Newsletter

Robert J. Brophy, Editor
Dept. of English
California State Univ. at Long Beach
1250 Bellflower Blvd.
Long Beach, CA 90840

Telephone: 213 985-4235
Fax: 310 985-2369
First published: 1962
Sponsoring organization: Occidental College; California State Univ., Long Beach
ISSN: 0300-7936
MLA acronym: RJN

SUBSCRIPTION INFORMATION

Frequency of publication: 4 times/yr.
Circulation: 300
Available in microform: Yes, for some back issues
Subscription price: $10.00/yr.
Year to which price refers: 1992

ADVERTISING INFORMATION

Advertising accepted: No

EDITORIAL DESCRIPTION

Scope: Publishes news notes, abstracts, reviews, bibliographic studies, manuscript resources, short articles, memoirs, letters by or about Robinson Jeffers and some photo-reproductions.
Reviews books: Yes
Publishes notes: Yes
Languages accepted: English
Prints abstracts: No
Author-anonymous submission: No

SUBMISSION REQUIREMENTS

Restrictions on contributors: None
Author pays submission fee: No
Author pays page charges: No
Length of articles: 400-1,000 words
Length of book reviews: 200-400 words
Length of notes: 400-800 words
Style: MLA
Number of copies required: 1

Special requirements: Keep footnotes to a minimum.
Copyright ownership: CSULB Univ. Press
Rejected manuscripts: Returned
Time before publication decision: 1 mo.
Time between decision and publication: 3-6 mos.
Number of reviewers: 1-2
Articles submitted per year: 16
Articles published per year: 8
Book reviews submitted per year: 5
Book reviews published per year: 4
Notes submitted per year: 12
Notes published per year: 10

(2465)
*Rocky Mountain Review of Language and Literature

Carol A. Martin, Editor
Dept. of English
Boise State Univ.
Boise, ID 83725

Telephone: 208 385-1199
First published: 1946
Sponsoring organization: Rocky Mountain Modern Language Assn.
ISSN: 0035-7626
MLA acronym: RMR

SUBSCRIPTION INFORMATION

Frequency of publication: 4 times/yr. (Feb., May, Aug., Nov.)
Circulation: 1,200
Available in microform: No
Subscription address: Charles Davis, 1910 University Dr., Boise, ID 83725

ADVERTISING INFORMATION

Advertising accepted: Yes

EDITORIAL DESCRIPTION

Scope: Publishes articles on language and literature and the related arts, directed toward an audience of scholars, writers, and teachers in the fields of English and foreign languages.
Reviews books: Yes
Publishes notes: No
Languages accepted: English; French; German; Italian; Portuguese; Spanish
Prints abstracts: No
Author-anonymous submission: Yes

SUBMISSION REQUIREMENTS

Restrictions on contributors: Contributors must be members of the Rocky Mountain Modern Language Assn.
Author pays submission fee: No
Author pays page charges: No
Length of articles: 4,500-7,500 words
Length of book reviews: 300-600 words
Style: MLA
Number of copies required: 2
Special requirements: Submit original manuscript; do not include author's name on manuscript.
Copyright ownership: Journal
Rejected manuscripts: Returned with anonymous referee comments; enclose SASE.
Time before publication decision: 3-4 mos.
Time between decision and publication: 6-12 mos.
Number of reviewers: 3
Articles submitted per year: 50
Articles published per year: 10-12
Book reviews submitted per year: 100
Book reviews published per year: 60-75

(2466)
*Rocznik Komisji Historycznoliterackiej

Stanisław Burkot, Editor
Ossolineum Publishing House of the Polish Academy of Sciences
Rynek 9
50-106 Wrocław, Poland

Telephone: (48) 71 369-61
Fax: (48) 71 488103
First published: 1963
Sponsoring organization: Polska Academia Nauk, Oddział w Krakowie, Komisja Historycznoliteracka
ISSN: 0079-337X
MLA acronym: RKH

SUBSCRIPTION INFORMATION

Frequency of publication: Annual
Circulation: 500-600
Available in microform: No
Subscription address: Foreign Trade Enterprise "Ars Polona", Krakowskie Przedmieście 7, 00-068 Warsaw, Poland

ADVERTISING INFORMATION

Advertising accepted: No

EDITORIAL DESCRIPTION

Scope: Publishes articles on Polish literature.
Reviews books: No
Publishes notes: No
Languages accepted: Polish
Prints abstracts: Yes
Author-anonymous submission: No

SUBMISSION REQUIREMENTS

Restrictions on contributors: None
Author pays submission fee: No
Author pays page charges: No
Length of articles: 40,000 words
Number of copies required: 2
Special requirements: Submit a 300-word abstract.
Copyright ownership: Ossolineum
Rejected manuscripts: Returned
Time before publication decision: 1 yr. minimum
Time between decision and publication: 12-15 mos.
Number of reviewers: 2
Articles submitted per year: 14
Articles published per year: 10-12

(2467)
*Rocznik Orientalistyczny

Edward Tryjarski, Editor
Inst. Orientalistyczny
Uniw. Warszawski
Krakowskie Przedmieście 26/28
00-927 Warsaw 64, Poland

First published: 1914
Sponsoring organization: Polska Akademia Nauk, Komitet Nauk Orientalistycznych
ISSN: 0080-3545
MLA acronym: RocO

SUBSCRIPTION INFORMATION

Frequency of publication: 2 times/yr.
Circulation: 500
Available in microform: No
Subscription address: Panstwowe Wydawnictwo Naukowe, ul. Miodowa 10, Warsaw, Poland

ADVERTISING INFORMATION

Advertising accepted: No

EDITORIAL DESCRIPTION

Scope: Publishes Oriental studies.
Reviews books: Yes
Publishes notes: No
Languages accepted: English; French; German; Russian
Prints abstracts: No

SUBMISSION REQUIREMENTS

Restrictions on contributors: None
Author pays submission fee: No
Author pays page charges: No
Length of articles: 20-30 typescript pp.
Length of book reviews: 5-10 typescript pp.
Style: None
Number of copies required: 1
Copyright ownership: Author
Rejected manuscripts: Returned
Time before publication decision: 2 mos.
Time between decision and publication: 2 yrs.
Number of reviewers: 2
Articles submitted per year: 25
Articles published per year: 15-20
Book reviews submitted per year: 10-15
Book reviews published per year: 10

(2468)
*Rocznik Slawistyczny/Revue Slavistique

Franciszek Sławski, Editor
ul. J. Piłsudskiego 6, II p.
31-109 Cracow, Poland

Additional editorial address: Ossolineum, Rynek 9, 50-106 Wrocław, Poland
First published: 1908
Sponsoring organization: Polska Akademia Nauk, Komitet Językoznawstwa; Polska Akademia Nauk, Komitet Słowianoznowstwa
ISSN: 0080-3588
MLA acronym: RoSlaw

SUBSCRIPTION INFORMATION

Frequency of publication: 2 times/yr.
Circulation: 400
Available in microform: No
Subscription address: Foreign Trade Enterprise "Ars Polona", Krakowskie Przedmieście 7, 00-068 Warsaw, Poland

ADVERTISING INFORMATION

Advertising accepted: No

EDITORIAL DESCRIPTION

Scope: Publishes articles, reviews, and bibliographies on Slavic linguistics.
Reviews books: Yes
Publishes notes: No
Languages accepted: Polish; French; German; English; Italian; Spanish; Bulgarian; Macedonian; Serbo-Croatian; Slovenian; Czech; Slovak; Sorbian; Russian; Belorussian; Ukrainian
Prints abstracts: Yes

SUBMISSION REQUIREMENTS

Restrictions on contributors: None
Author pays submission fee: No
Author pays page charges: No
Length of articles: 15 typescript pp.
Length of book reviews: 7 pp.
Style: None
Number of copies required: 2
Special requirements: Articles in Slavic languages are summarized in English, French, or German.
Copyright ownership: Ossolineum
Rejected manuscripts: Returned
Time before publication decision: 2-6 mos.
Time between decision and publication: 12-16 mos.
Number of reviewers: 1 plus Editorial Board
Articles submitted per year: 5-15

Articles published per year: 5-12
Book reviews submitted per year: 5-15
Book reviews published per year: 5-12

(2469)
Roczniki Humanistyczne: Annales de Lettres et Sciences Humaines/Annals of Arts

Towarzystwo Naukowe
Katolickiego Uniw. Lubelskiego
Al. Racławickie 14
20-027 Lublin, Poland

First published: 1949
Sponsoring organization: Towarzystwo Naukowe Katolickiego Uniw. Lubelskiego
ISSN: 0035-7707
MLA acronym: RoHum

SUBSCRIPTION INFORMATION

Frequency of publication: Annual
Available in microform: No

ADVERTISING INFORMATION

Advertising accepted: No

EDITORIAL DESCRIPTION

Scope: Publishes articles on languages, history, history of art, critical literature, and neophilology.
Reviews books: No
Languages accepted: Polish; English; French; German
Prints abstracts: Yes

SUBMISSION REQUIREMENTS

Restrictions on contributors: None
Author pays submission fee: No
Author pays page charges: No
Length of articles: No restrictions
Style: None
Number of copies required: 3
Copyright ownership: Author
Rejected manuscripts: Returned at author's request
Time before publication decision: 3 mos.
Time between decision and publication: 15-18 mos.
Number of reviewers: 2
Articles submitted per year: 10
Articles published per year: 5

(2470)
*Rodopi Perspectives on Modern Literature

David Bevan, Editor
Dept. of Romance Languages
Univ. of Auckland
Private Bag
Auckland, New Zealand

First published: 1988
ISSN: 0923-0416
MLA acronym: RPML

SUBSCRIPTION INFORMATION

Frequency of publication: Irregular
Available in microform: No
Subscription address: Editions Rodopi, 233 Peachtree St. NE, Suite 404, Atlanta, GA 30303-1504
Additional subscription address: Outside N. America: Editions Rodopi, Keizersgracht 302-304, 1016 EX Amsterdam, Netherlands

ADVERTISING INFORMATION

Advertising accepted: Yes

EDITORIAL DESCRIPTION

Scope: Publishes collections of articles on modern literature.
Reviews books: No
Publishes notes: No
Languages accepted: English
Prints abstracts: No
Author-anonymous submission: No

SUBMISSION REQUIREMENTS

Restrictions on contributors: Contributions are by invitation.
Author pays submission fee: No
Author pays page charges: No
Length of articles: 10-20 pp.
Style: MLA
Copyright ownership: Rodopi
Articles submitted per year: 10-20
Articles published per year: 10-20

(2471)
*Rolig-Papir

Karen Risager & Hartmut Haberland, Editors
ROLIG
Univ. of Roskilde
Dept. of Language and Culture
P.O. Box 260
4000 Roskilde, Denmark

Telephone: (45) 46 757711 ext. 2375
Fax: (45) 46 754410
E-mail: Tarzan@jane.ruc.dk
First published: 1974
Sponsoring organization: Univ. of Roskilde
ISSN: 0106-0821
MLA acronym: ROLIG

SUBSCRIPTION INFORMATION

Frequency of publication: Irregular
Circulation: 300
Subscription price: Free
Year to which price refers: 1992

ADVERTISING INFORMATION

Advertising accepted: No

EDITORIAL DESCRIPTION

Scope: The series publishes working papers written by members and guests of ROLIG, the linguistic circle of the University of Roskilde.
Reviews books: Occasionally
Publishes notes: Yes
Languages accepted: Danish; German; English; Norwegian; Swedish; French
Prints abstracts: No
Author-anonymous submission: No

SUBMISSION REQUIREMENTS

Restrictions on contributors: Contributors must be associated with the Roskilde Linguistic Circle.
Author pays submission fee: No
Author pays page charges: No
Length of articles: 20-50 pp.
Length of books: No restrictions
Length of notes: No restrictions
Number of copies required: 1
Copyright ownership: Author
Rejected manuscripts: Returned; enclose return postage.
Time before publication decision: 3-5 weeks
Time between decision and publication: 1-2 mos.
Number of reviewers: 2
Books submitted per year: 5-10
Books published per year: 2-6
Notes submitted per year: 0-2
Notes published per year: 0-2

(2472)
*Roman 20-50: Revue d'Etude du Roman du XXe Siècle

Monique Gosselin, Michel Raimond, André Karatson, Jacqueline Levi-Valensi, Bernard Alluin, Jacques Deguy, Paul Renard, & Christian Morzewski, Editors
Société Roman 20-50
56, rue Brûle-Maison
59000 Lille, France

Telephone: (33) 20542025
First published: 1986
Sponsoring organization: Univ. de Lille III; Centre National des Lettres
ISSN: 0295-5024
MLA acronym: RVC

SUBSCRIPTION INFORMATION

Frequency of publication: 2 times/yr.
Circulation: 400
Available in microform: No
Subscription price: 80 F/yr.
Year to which price refers: 1992

ADVERTISING INFORMATION

Advertising accepted: No

EDITORIAL DESCRIPTION

Scope: Publishes research on French novels, as well as novels from other countries, published between 1920 and 1950 and pedagogical application of the results of it. Also publishes reappraisals of forgotten masterpieces.
Reviews books: Yes
Publishes notes: Yes
Languages accepted: French
Prints abstracts: No
Author-anonymous submission: No

SUBMISSION REQUIREMENTS

Restrictions on contributors: Book reviews are solicited.
Author pays submission fee: No
Author pays page charges: No
Length of articles: 10 pp.
Length of book reviews: 1,200-1,500 words
Length of notes: 60 words
Style: MLA
Number of copies required: 2
Copyright ownership: Soc. Roman 20-50
Rejected manuscripts: Returned; enclose return postage.
Time before publication decision: 1 yr.
Time between decision and publication: 2 yrs.
Number of reviewers: 2
Articles submitted per year: 50
Articles published per year: 30
Book reviews submitted per year: 80
Book reviews published per year: 20
Notes submitted per year: 100
Notes published per year: 30

(2473)
*Romance Languages and Linguistics Series

Patrice La Liberté, Editor
Georgetown Univ. Press
Intercultural Center, Rm. 111
Georgetown Univ.
Washington, DC 20057-1079

Telephone: 202 687-6251
Fax: 202 687-6341
First published: 1966
MLA acronym: RL&LS

SUBSCRIPTION INFORMATION

Frequency of publication: Irregular
Available in microform: No

Subscription address: Order Dept., at the above address
Subscription telephone: 202 687-6063

ADVERTISING INFORMATION

Advertising accepted: No

EDITORIAL DESCRIPTION

Scope: Publishes studies in Romance languages and linguistics, with an emphasis on Spanish and Brazilian Portuguese.
Reviews books: No
Publishes notes: No
Languages accepted: Spanish; Portuguese; French; English; Latin
Prints abstracts: No
Author-anonymous submission: No

SUBMISSION REQUIREMENTS

Author pays submission fee: No
Author pays page charges: No
Style: Chicago
Number of copies required: 1
Special requirements: Contributors are urged to send cover letter and sample chapter, rather than an entire manuscript.
Copyright ownership: Georgetown Univ. Press
Rejected manuscripts: Returned; enclose return postage.
Number of reviewers: 2 minimum
Books published per year: 5-10

(2474)
*Romance Linguistics & Literature Review

Henry Biggs & Ivana Lyon, Editors
Romance Linguistics & Literature Program
359 Royce Hall, UCLA
405 Hilgard Ave.
Los Angeles, CA 90024-1532

First published: 1988
Sponsoring organization: Romance Linguistics & Literature Program, Univ. of California, Los Angeles; Graduate Students Assn., Univ. of California, Los Angeles
MLA acronym: RL&LR

SUBSCRIPTION INFORMATION

Frequency of publication: Annual (Fall)
Available in microform: No
Subscription price: $10.00/yr. institutions; $8.00/yr. individuals; $6.00/yr. students
Year to which price refers: 1991

ADVERTISING INFORMATION

Advertising accepted: Yes

EDITORIAL DESCRIPTION

Scope: Publishes articles on Romance linguistics and literatures; includes research dealing with one or more languages or literatures.
Publishes notes: Yes
Languages accepted: English; Catalan; French; Italian; Portuguese; Romanian
Prints abstracts: No
Author-anonymous submission: Yes

SUBMISSION REQUIREMENTS

Restrictions on contributors: Slight preference is given to students at UCLA.
Author pays submission fee: No
Author pays page charges: No
Length of articles: 4,500-9,000 words
Length of notes: 1,500-3,000 words
Style: MLA
Number of copies required: 3
Special requirements: Accepted manuscripts must be submitted on diskette using Microsoft Word.

Copyright ownership: Regents of the Univ. of California
Rejected manuscripts: Not returned
Time before publication decision: 4 mos.
Time between decision and publication: 4 mos.
Number of reviewers: 3-6
Articles submitted per year: 35-40
Articles published per year: 4-6
Notes submitted per year: 1-3
Notes published per year: 1-3

(2475)
Romance Linguistics [Croon Helm Romance Linguistics]

Martin Harris & Nigel Vincent, Editors
Routledge
11 New Fetter Lane
London EC4P 4EE, England

First published: 1990
MLA acronym: RomLi

SUBSCRIPTION INFORMATION

Available in microform: No
Subscription address: ITPS, North Way, Andover, Hampshire SP10 5BE, England

ADVERTISING INFORMATION

Advertising accepted: No

EDITORIAL DESCRIPTION

Scope: Publishes monographs and collections of articles on Romance philology and general linguistics. Recognizes and promotes the mutual interaction of these two subjects, and encompasses works in phonetics, phonology, morphology, syntax and lexis of Romance languages, as well as the history of Romance linguistics and linguistic thought in the Romance cultural area.
Reviews books: No
Publishes notes: No
Languages accepted: English
Prints abstracts: No

SUBMISSION REQUIREMENTS

Copyright ownership: Author
Rejected manuscripts: Returned
Number of reviewers: 2 maximum

(2476)
*Romance Monographs

Santo Arico, Melvin Arrington, Jack Brown, & Donald Dyer, Editors
Dept. of Modern Languages
Univ. of Mississippi
University, MS 38677-9800

Telephone: 601 232-7298
Fax: 601 232-5918
First published: 1972
Sponsoring organization: Dept. of Modern Languages, Univ. of Mississippi
MLA acronym: RMon

SUBSCRIPTION INFORMATION

Frequency of publication: Irregular
Available in microform: No

ADVERTISING INFORMATION

Advertising accepted: No

EDITORIAL DESCRIPTION

Scope: Publishes monographs on the literature and linguistics of Romance languages.
Reviews books: No
Publishes notes: No

Languages accepted: English; All Romance languages
Prints abstracts: No
Author-anonymous submission: No

SUBMISSION REQUIREMENTS

Author pays submission fee: No
Author pays page charges: Yes
Number of copies required: 1
Copyright ownership: Series
Rejected manuscripts: Returned
Number of reviewers: 2

(2477)
*Romance Notes

Edward Davidson Montgomery, Editor
Dept. of Romance Languages
Dey Hall CB 3170
Univ. of North Carolina
Chapel Hill, NC 27599-3170

Telephone: 919 962-1025
E-mail: HAL333@UNC.BITNET
First published: 1959
Sponsoring organization: Univ. of North Carolina, Chapel Hill
ISSN: 0035-7995
MLA acronym: RomN

SUBSCRIPTION INFORMATION

Frequency of publication: 3 times/yr. (Fall, Winter, Spring)
Circulation: 650
Available in microform: Yes
Subscription price: $18.00/yr. institutions; $15.00/yr. individuals; $8.00/yr. students
Year to which price refers: 1991

ADVERTISING INFORMATION

Advertising accepted: No

EDITORIAL DESCRIPTION

Scope: Publishes articles on all aspects of the Romance languages and literatures.
Reviews books: No
Publishes notes: Yes
Languages accepted: English; French; Italian; Spanish; Portuguese; Catalan
Prints abstracts: No
Author-anonymous submission: Yes

SUBMISSION REQUIREMENTS

Restrictions on contributors: None
Author pays submission fee: No
Author pays page charges: No
Length of articles: 10 pp. including footnotes
Style: MLA
Number of copies required: 2
Special requirements: Submit original manuscript and a 3-line abstract. Place author's name on separate sheet only.
Copyright ownership: Univ. of North Carolina
Rejected manuscripts: Returned; enclose return postage.
Time before publication decision: 3 mos.
Time between decision and publication: 1 yr.
Number of reviewers: 2 plus Editorial Board
Notes submitted per year: 200
Notes published per year: 40

(2478)
*Romance Philology

Jerry R. Craddock, Charles B. Faulhaber, Suzanne Fleischman, & Edward F. Tuttle, Editors
Dept. of French
4125 Dwinelle Hall
Univ. of California
Berkeley, CA 94720

Telephone: 510 642-6352
Fax: 510 642-6957
E-mail: Jerryc@garnet.berkeley.edu
First published: 1947
ISSN: 0035-8002
MLA acronym: RPh

SUBSCRIPTION INFORMATION

Frequency of publication: 4 times/yr. (Aug., Nov., Feb., May)
Circulation: 1,200
Available in microform: Yes
Subscription price: $54.00/yr. institutions; $27.00/yr. individuals; $15.00/yr. students
Year to which price refers: 1991-92
Subscription address: Periodicals Dept., Univ. of California Press, 2120 Berkeley Way, Berkeley, CA 94720
Subscription telephone: 510 642-4191
Subscription fax: 510 643-7127

ADVERTISING INFORMATION

Advertising accepted: Yes
Advertising rates: $130.00/half page; $225.00/full page

EDITORIAL DESCRIPTION

Scope: Publishes articles on historical and synchronic Romance linguistics and on medieval literature in the Romance languages.
Reviews books: Yes
Publishes notes: Yes
Languages accepted: English; French; Spanish; Italian; German
Prints abstracts: No
Author-anonymous submission: No

SUBMISSION REQUIREMENTS

Restrictions on contributors: Contributors must be subscribers, reside outside North America, or be unaffiliated with field. Reviews are commissioned.
Author pays submission fee: No
Author pays page charges: No
Length of articles: 10,000 words
Length of book reviews: 2,500 words
Length of notes: 5,000 words
Style: Chicago with modifications
Number of copies required: 3
Special requirements: All submissions must use the author-date system of documentation, keyed to a reference list.
Copyright ownership: Regents of Univ. of California
Rejected manuscripts: Returned; enclose SASE.
Time before publication decision: 4 mos.
Time between decision and publication: 2-4 yrs.
Number of reviewers: 2
Articles submitted per year: 25
Articles published per year: 10
Book reviews submitted per year: 75
Book reviews published per year: 75
Notes submitted per year: 10
Notes published per year: 3-5

(2479)
*Romance Quarterly

Brian J. Dendle, Editor
1115 Patterson Office Tower
Univ. of Kentucky
Lexington, KY 40506-0027

First published: 1954
Sponsoring organization: Univ. of Kentucky
ISSN: 0883-1157
MLA acronym: KRQ

SUBSCRIPTION INFORMATION

Frequency of publication: 4 times/yr. (Feb., May, Aug., Nov.)
Circulation: 550
Available in microform: Yes
Subscription address: Heldref Publications, 1319 Eighteenth St. NW, Washington, DC 20036-1802

ADVERTISING INFORMATION

Advertising accepted: Yes

EDITORIAL DESCRIPTION

Scope: Considers historical or interpretive articles in all areas of Romance scholarship—literary, cultural, etc.
Reviews books: Yes
Publishes notes: Yes
Languages accepted: English; Catalan; French; Italian; Portuguese; Spanish
Prints abstracts: No
Author-anonymous submission: No

SUBMISSION REQUIREMENTS

Restrictions on contributors: None
Author pays submission fee: No
Author pays page charges: No
Length of articles: 8-25 double-spaced pp. including endnotes
Length of book reviews: 500-600 words
Length of notes: 500-2,000 words
Style: MLA 1977 ed.
Number of copies required: 2
Special requirements: Submit original typescript plus 1 copy.
Copyright ownership: Heldref Publications
Rejected manuscripts: Returned; enclose loose return postage.
Time before publication decision: 6 weeks
Time between decision and publication: 18 mos.
Number of reviewers: 2
Articles submitted per year: 160
Articles published per year: 34-40
Book reviews submitted per year: 60
Book reviews published per year: 40-50
Notes submitted per year: 4
Notes published per year: 4

(2480)
*Romance Studies

Valerie Minogue & Brian Nelson, Editors
Dept. of French
School of European Languages
Univ. of Wales
Singleton Park
Swansea SA2 8PP, Wales

Additional editorial address: In Australia & New Zealand contact: Brian Nelson, Dept. of Romance Languages, Monash Univ., Clayton, Melbourne, Victoria 3168, Australia
Telephone: (44) 792 295754
Fax: (44) 792 295710
First published: 1982
ISSN: 0263-9904
MLA acronym: RSt

SUBSCRIPTION INFORMATION

Frequency of publication: 2 times/yr.
Circulation: 200
Available in microform: No
Subscription price: £15.00/yr. institutions United Kingdom & Europe; £20.00/yr. institutions elsewhere; £10.00/yr. individuals United Kingdom & Europe; £15.00/yr. individuals elsewhere
Year to which price refers: 1992
Subscription address: George Evans, at the above address
Subscription telephone: (44) 792 205678 ext. 4549

ADVERTISING INFORMATION

Advertising accepted: Yes
Advertising rates: £25.00/full page; also available on an exchange basis

EDITORIAL DESCRIPTION

Reviews books: No
Publishes notes: No
Languages accepted: English
Prints abstracts: No
Author-anonymous submission: Yes

SUBMISSION REQUIREMENTS

Restrictions on contributors: Since the journal collaborates in organizing colloquia, some articles are colloquium papers which were accepted for presentation.
Author pays submission fee: No
Author pays page charges: No
Length of articles: 6,000 words maximum
Style: MLA; Modern Humanities Research Assn.
Number of copies required: 2
Copyright ownership: Journal
Rejected manuscripts: Returned
Time before publication decision: 6-8 weeks
Time between decision and publication: 6-12 mos.
Number of reviewers: 2-3
Articles submitted per year: 30-30
Articles published per year: 15

(2481)
*Romania: Revue Consacrée à l'Etude des Langues et des Litératures Romanes

Jacques Monfrin, Editor
Soc. des Amis de la Romania
19, rue de la Sorbonne
75005 Paris, France

First published: 1872
Sponsoring organization: Soc. des Amis de la Romania; Centre National de la Recherche Scientifique
ISSN: 0035-8029
MLA acronym: Romania

SUBSCRIPTION INFORMATION

Frequency of publication: 4 times/yr.
Available in microform: No

ADVERTISING INFORMATION

Advertising accepted: No

EDITORIAL DESCRIPTION

Scope: Publishes articles on Romance language and literature of the medieval period.
Reviews books: Yes
Publishes notes: Yes
Languages accepted: English; French; Italian; Spanish; German
Prints abstracts: No

SUBMISSION REQUIREMENTS

Author pays submission fee: No
Author pays page charges: No
Length of articles: 2-40 pp.
Number of copies required: 2
Special requirements: Submit original typescript plus 1 copy.
Rejected manuscripts: Returned at author's request; enclose return postage.
Time before publication decision: 6 mos.
Time between decision and publication: 1 yr.
Number of reviewers: 3
Articles submitted per year: 50

(2482)
România Literară: Săptăminal de Literatură și Artă Editat de Uniunea Scriitorilor din Republica Socialistă România

George Ivașcu, Editor
Piața Scînteii 1
Bucharest, Romania

First published: 1968
Sponsoring organization: Uniunea Scriitorilor din România
ISSN: 0048-8550
MLA acronym: RoLit

SUBSCRIPTION INFORMATION

Frequency of publication: 52 times/yr.
Circulation: 25,000
Available in microform: No
Subscription address: ILEXIM, Calea Grivitei, 64-66, Box 12-201, 10876 Bucharest, Romania

ADVERTISING INFORMATION

Advertising accepted: Yes

EDITORIAL DESCRIPTION

Scope: Publishes news items pertaining to Romanian and international literary activities; critical articles, largely about Romanian literature, but also about non-Romanian; scholarly articles on both Romanian and non-Romanian writers; original poetry and prose.
Reviews books: Yes
Publishes notes: Yes
Languages accepted: Romanian
Prints abstracts: No
Author-anonymous submission: No

SUBMISSION REQUIREMENTS

Restrictions on contributors: None
Author pays submission fee: No
Author pays page charges: No
Length of articles: 300-2,500 words
Length of book reviews: 600-1,200 words
Length of notes: 100-300 words
Style: Modern Lit. Rom. (MLR)
Number of copies required: 2
Copyright ownership: Journal
Time before publication decision: 1-4 weeks
Time between decision and publication: 1-4 weeks
Number of reviewers: 3
Articles submitted per year: 2,500
Articles published per year: 2,000
Book reviews submitted per year: 520
Book reviews published per year: 450
Notes submitted per year: 1,600
Notes published per year: 1,200

(2483)
*Romanian Review

Nicolae Șarambei & Valentin Mihaescu, Editors
Piața Presei Libere 1
71341 Bucharest, Romania

Telephone: (40) 0 173836
First published: 1946
Sponsoring organization: Redacția Publicațiilor Pentru Străinătate "România"
ISSN: French: 0251-3528; English: 1220-1871; German: 1220-3327; Russian: 1220-5060
MLA acronym: RoR

SUBSCRIPTION INFORMATION

Frequency of publication: 12 times/yr.
Circulation: 7,500
Available in microform: No
Subscription price: $18.00/yr.
Year to which price refers: 1992

ADVERTISING INFORMATION

Advertising accepted: Yes
Advertising rates: $250.00/half page; $450.00/full page

EDITORIAL DESCRIPTION

Scope: Publishes literary criticism, poetry, excerpts from plays, novels, short stories, history, articles on science, the arts, sociology, and aesthetics.
Reviews books: Yes
Publishes notes: Yes
Languages accepted: English; French; German; Russian
Prints abstracts: No
Author-anonymous submission: No

SUBMISSION REQUIREMENTS

Restrictions on contributors: None
Author pays submission fee: No
Author pays page charges: No
Length of articles: 2,000-2,500 words
Length of book reviews: 1,200 words
Length of notes: 600 words
Style: MLA
Number of copies required: 2
Copyright ownership: Author
Rejected manuscripts: Not returned
Time before publication decision: 1 mo.
Time between decision and publication: 3 mos.
Number of reviewers: 3
Articles submitted per year: 80
Articles published per year: 40
Book reviews submitted per year: 30
Book reviews published per year: 20
Notes submitted per year: 60
Notes published per year: 60

(2484)
Romanic Review

Michael Riffaterre, Editor
Dept. of French & Romance Philology
Columbia Univ.
New York, NY 10027

First published: 1909
Sponsoring organization: Columbia Univ., Dept. of French & Romance Philology
ISSN: 0035-8118
MLA acronym: RR

SUBSCRIPTION INFORMATION

Frequency of publication: 4 times/yr. (Jan., Mar., May, Nov.)
Circulation: 1,500
Available in microform: No
Subscription price: $45.00/yr. institutions US & Canada; $50.00/yr. institutions elsewhere; $30.00/yr. individuals US & Canada; $35.00/yr. individuals elsewhere; $25.00/yr. students US & Canada; $30.00/yr. students elsewhere
Year to which price refers: 1992

ADVERTISING INFORMATION

Advertising accepted: Yes

EDITORIAL DESCRIPTION

Scope: Publishes work in all areas of Romanic literature. Especially interested in material deriving from the new critical methods (structuralist, post-structuralist, neo-Marxist, sociological, semiological).
Reviews books: Yes
Languages accepted: English; French
Prints abstracts: No

SUBMISSION REQUIREMENTS

Restrictions on contributors: None
Author pays submission fee: No
Length of articles: No restrictions
Length of book reviews: No restrictions
Style: MLA
Number of copies required: 1
Special requirements: Footnotes are not accepted; use double-spaced endnotes.
Copyright ownership: Columbia Univ.
Rejected manuscripts: Returned; enclose return postage.
Number of reviewers: 2
Articles published per year: 35
Book reviews published per year: 50

(2485)
*Romanica Gandensia

Philippe Verelst, Editor
Rijksuniv. te Gent
Faculteit der Letteren en Wijsbegeerte
Blandijnberg, 2
9000 Ghent, Belgium

First published: 1953
ISSN: 0080-3855
MLA acronym: RomG

SUBSCRIPTION INFORMATION

Frequency of publication: Irregular
Circulation: 600-800
Available in microform: No

ADVERTISING INFORMATION

Advertising accepted: No

EDITORIAL DESCRIPTION

Scope: Publishes studies in Romance philology.
Reviews books: No
Publishes notes: No
Languages accepted: French; Italian; Spanish
Prints abstracts: No
Author-anonymous submission: No

SUBMISSION REQUIREMENTS

Restrictions on contributors: Articles are either commissioned or contributed by Ghent students.
Author pays submission fee: No
Author pays page charges: No
Copyright ownership: Rijksuniversteit te Gent
Books published per year: 0-1

(2486)
*Romanica Gothoburgensia

Lars Lindvall, Editor
Acta Universitatis Gothoburgensis
Box 5096
402 22 Göteborg, Sweden

First published: 1955
ISSN: 0072-503X
MLA acronym: RomGoth

SUBSCRIPTION INFORMATION

Frequency of publication: Irregular
Available in microform: No

ADVERTISING INFORMATION

Advertising accepted: No

EDITORIAL DESCRIPTION

Scope: Publishes monographs on Romance languages and literatures.
Reviews books: No
Publishes notes: No

Articles published per year: 15-25
Book reviews published per year: 10-20
Notes published per year: 40-60

Languages accepted: French; Spanish
Prints abstracts: Sometimes
Author-anonymous submission: No

SUBMISSION REQUIREMENTS

Copyright ownership: Editor & author

(2487)
*Romanische Forschungen

Wido Hempel, Editor
Romanisches Seminar
Univ. Tübingen
Wilhelmstr. 50
7400 Tübingen, Germany

First published: 1883
ISSN: 0035-8126
MLA acronym: RF

SUBSCRIPTION INFORMATION

Frequency of publication: 4 times/yr.
Circulation: 500
Available in microform: No
Subscription address: Verlag Vittorio Klostermann, Postfach 90 06 01, 6000 Frankfurt 90, Germany

ADVERTISING INFORMATION

Advertising accepted: Yes

EDITORIAL DESCRIPTION

Scope: Publishes studies in Romance languages and literatures, e.g., French, Italian, Portuguese, Spanish, and Spanish American.
Reviews books: Yes
Publishes notes: Yes
Languages accepted: English; French; German; Italian; Spanish; Portuguese
Prints abstracts: No

SUBMISSION REQUIREMENTS

Author pays submission fee: No
Author pays page charges: No
Length of articles: 20-30 pp.
Length of notes: 8-16 pp.
Number of copies required: 1
Copyright ownership: Verlag Vittorio Klostermann
Rejected manuscripts: Returned; enclose return postage.
Time before publication decision: 6 mos.
Time between decision and publication: 1 yr.
Articles published per year: 12
Book reviews published per year: 90
Notes published per year: 8

(2488)
*Romanistische Arbeitshefte

Gustav Ineichen & Bernd Kielhöfer, Editors
Max Niemeyer Verlag
Postfach 2140
7400 Tübingen, Germany

First published: 1973
ISSN: 0344-676X
MLA acronym: RA

SUBSCRIPTION INFORMATION

Frequency of publication: Irregular
Available in microform: No

ADVERTISING INFORMATION

Advertising accepted: No

EDITORIAL DESCRIPTION

Scope: Publishes monographs on Romance linguistics, especially French.
Reviews books: No
Publishes notes: No
Languages accepted: German
Prints abstracts: No
Author-anonymous submission: Yes

SUBMISSION REQUIREMENTS

Restrictions on contributors: None
Author pays submission fee: No
Author pays page charges: No
Length of books: 110 pp.
Style: MLA
Number of copies required: 1
Special requirements: Submit typescript.
Copyright ownership: Max Niemeyer Verlag
Rejected manuscripts: Returned
Time before publication decision: 3 mos.
Time between decision and publication: 6 mos.
Number of reviewers: 2
Books submitted per year: 1-2
Books published per year: 1

(2489)
*Romanistisches Jahrbuch

Hans Flasche, B. König, Margot Kruse, W. Pabst, C. Schmitt, & W.-D. Stempel, Editors
Romanisches Seminar
Univ. Hamburg
Von-Melle-Park 6
2000 Hamburg 13, Germany

Telephone: (49) 40 41232731
First published: 1947
ISSN: 0080-3898
MLA acronym: RJ

SUBSCRIPTION INFORMATION

Frequency of publication: Annual (Autumn)
Circulation: 500
Available in microform: No
Subscription price: 238 DM/yr.
Year to which price refers: 1992
Subscription address: Walter de Gruyter & Co., Genthiner Str. 13, 1000 Berlin 30, Germany
Subscription telephone: (49) 30 260050
Subscription fax: (49) 30 26005251

ADVERTISING INFORMATION

Advertising accepted: Yes

EDITORIAL DESCRIPTION

Scope: Publishes articles on Romance literatures and linguistics.
Reviews books: Yes
Publishes notes: No
Languages accepted: German; French; Spanish; Italian; Portuguese; English
Prints abstracts: No
Author-anonymous submission: No

SUBMISSION REQUIREMENTS

Author pays submission fee: No
Author pays page charges: No
Length of articles: 10,000 words maximum
Length of book reviews: 1,000-1,500 words
Style: MLA with modifications
Number of copies required: 2
Special requirements: Specifications available from journal.
Copyright ownership: Walter de Gruyter & Co.
Rejected manuscripts: Returned
Time before publication decision: 3 mos.
Time between decision and publication: 9 mos.
Number of reviewers: 2
Articles submitted per year: 16-20
Articles published per year: 14
Book reviews submitted per year: 50-60
Book reviews published per year: 50

(2490)
Romanoslavica

Asoc. Slaviștilor din R. S. România
Str. Pitar Moș 7-13
Sectorul 1
70151 Bucharest, Romania

First published: 1958
Sponsoring organization: Asoc. Slaviștilor din Republica Socialistă România
ISSN: 0557-272X
MLA acronym: RomSl

SUBSCRIPTION INFORMATION

Frequency of publication: Irregular
Available in microform: No

ADVERTISING INFORMATION

Advertising accepted: No

EDITORIAL DESCRIPTION

Scope: Focuses on the linguistic, literary, and historical relationships between Romanians and Slavs.
Reviews books: Yes
Publishes notes: Yes
Languages accepted: Romanian; French
Prints abstracts: Yes

SUBMISSION REQUIREMENTS

Author pays submission fee: No
Author pays page charges: No
Length of articles: 4,000-7,000 words
Length of book reviews: 500-1,000 words
Length of notes: 200-300 words
Number of copies required: 2
Rejected manuscripts: Not returned
Time before publication decision: 3 mos.
Time between decision and publication: 1-2 yrs.
Number of reviewers: 2
Articles submitted per year: 50
Articles published per year: 25
Book reviews published per year: 20
Notes published per year: 20

(2491)
*Romantisme: Revue du Dix-Neuvième Siècle

Claude Duchet & Max Milner, Editors
Editions CDU & SEDES Réunis
88, boulevard Saint-Germain
75005 Paris, France

Additional editorial address: C. Duchet, 29 rue Boussingault, 75013 Paris, France
Telephone: (33) 1 43252323
Fax: (33) 1 46335715
First published: 1971
Sponsoring organization: Soc. des Etudes Romantiques & Dix-neuvièmistes; Centre National des Lettres; Centre National de la Recherche Scientifique
ISSN: 0048-8593
MLA acronym: Romantisme

SUBSCRIPTION INFORMATION

Frequency of publication: 4 times/yr.
Available in microform: No
Subscription price: 270 F/yr. France; 360 F/yr. elsewhere
Year to which price refers: 1992

ADVERTISING INFORMATION

Advertising accepted: No

EDITORIAL DESCRIPTION

Scope: Publishes articles on literature, sciences, history, and arts in the 19th century.
Reviews books: Yes

Publishes notes: Yes
Languages accepted: French
Prints abstracts: Yes
Author-anonymous submission: No

SUBMISSION REQUIREMENTS

Author pays submission fee: No
Author pays page charges: No
Length of articles: 8,000-10,000 words
Length of book reviews: 400-600 words
Length of notes: 800-1,000 words
Number of copies required: 2
Special requirements: Submit original typescript and 1 copy.
Copyright ownership: Author
Rejected manuscripts: Not returned
Time before publication decision: 3-4 mos.
Time between decision and publication: 6-12 mos.
Number of reviewers: 3
Articles published per year: 28-30
Book reviews submitted per year: 100
Book reviews published per year: 50-60
Notes submitted per year: 5-6
Notes published per year: 2

(2492)
*The Romantist

John Charles Moran, Steve Eng, & Jesse F. Knight, Editors
F. Marion Crawford Memorial Soc.
Saracinesca House
3610 Meadowbrook Ave.
Nashville, TN 37205

Telephone: 615 292-9695
First published: 1977
Sponsoring organization: F. Marion Crawford Memorial Soc.
ISSN: 0161-682X
MLA acronym: Romantist

SUBSCRIPTION INFORMATION

Frequency of publication: Annual
Circulation: 300
Available in microform: No

ADVERTISING INFORMATION

Advertising accepted: Yes

EDITORIAL DESCRIPTION

Scope: Publishes articles on the modern manifestations of the aesthetic and imaginative aspects of the Romantic tradition in literature and the arts, with a special section on Francis Marion Crawford, beginning with the late 19th century; emphasis on fantastic and imaginative literature.
Reviews books: Yes
Publishes notes: Yes
Languages accepted: English
Prints abstracts: No

SUBMISSION REQUIREMENTS

Restrictions on contributors: None
Author pays submission fee: No
Author pays page charges: No
Length of articles: No restrictions
Length of book reviews: No restrictions
Length of notes: No restrictions
Style: MLA preferred
Number of copies required: 1
Special requirements: Query editors before submitting article or book review. Approximately half of the articles and book reviews are commissioned.
Copyright ownership: F. Marion Memorial Soc.
Rejected manuscripts: Returned; enclose return postage.
Time before publication decision: 3 mos. maximum
Time between decision and publication: 1 yr.
Number of reviewers: 3

Articles submitted per year: 15-20
Articles published per year: 10-15
Book reviews submitted per year: 5-10
Book reviews published per year: 5-10
Notes submitted per year: 3-5
Notes published per year: 2-3

(2493)
*Römische Historische Mitteilungen

Otto Kresten & Adam Wandruszka, Editors
Österreichische Akademie der Wissenschaften
Historisches Inst. beim Österreichischen Kulturinstitut in Rome
113, Viale Bruno Buozzi
00197 Rome, Italy

Telephone: (39) 406 3224793
Fax: (39) 406 3224296
First published: 1958
Sponsoring organization: Österreichische Akademie der Wissenschaften
ISSN: 0080-3790
MLA acronym: RHistM

SUBSCRIPTION INFORMATION

Frequency of publication: Annual
Circulation: 500
Available in microform: No
Subscription address: Verlag der Österreichischen Akademie der Wissenschaften, c/o Ignaz-Seipel-Platz 2, Platz 2, 1010 Vienna, Austria

ADVERTISING INFORMATION

Advertising accepted: Yes, for publications from the Austrian Academy of Sciences

EDITORIAL DESCRIPTION

Scope: Publishes the research work of the Historisches Institut beim Österreichischen Kultur-Institut in Rome.
Reviews books: No
Publishes notes: Yes
Languages accepted: German; Italian; English; Spanish; French; Latin
Prints abstracts: No
Author-anonymous submission: No

SUBMISSION REQUIREMENTS

Restrictions on contributors: None
Author pays submission fee: No
Author pays page charges: No
Length of articles: No restrictions
Length of notes: No restrictions
Style: None
Number of copies required: 1
Special requirements: None
Copyright ownership: Österreichische Akademie der Wissenschaften
Rejected manuscripts: Returned
Time before publication decision: Immediate
Time between decision and publication: 6-12 mos.
Number of reviewers: 1-2
Articles submitted per year: 25
Articles published per year: 20
Notes submitted per year: 2
Notes published per year: 1

(2494)
*Römische Quartalschrift für Christliche Altertumskunde und Kirchengeschichte

Erwin Gatz, Hermann Hoberg, & Bernhard Kötting, Editors
I-120
Vatican City
Collegio Teutonico
Rome, Italy

Telephone: (39) 6 6983923

First published: 1887
ISSN: 0035-7812
MLA acronym: RQCAK

SUBSCRIPTION INFORMATION

Frequency of publication: 2 times/yr.
Circulation: 350
Available in microform: No
Subscription price: 198 DM/yr.
Year to which price refers: 1991
Subscription address: Verlag Herder KG, Hermann-Herder-Str. 4, Postfach, 7800 Freiburg/Br., Germany

ADVERTISING INFORMATION

Advertising accepted: Yes, on pages 3 and 4 of jacket

EDITORIAL DESCRIPTION

Scope: Publishes articles on church history.
Reviews books: Yes
Publishes notes: No
Languages accepted: English; German; Italian; French
Prints abstracts: No
Author-anonymous submission: No

SUBMISSION REQUIREMENTS

Restrictions on contributors: None
Author pays submission fee: No
Author pays page charges: No
Length of articles: 15 pp.
Length of book reviews: 1 1/2 pp.
Number of copies required: 2
Copyright ownership: Journal
Rejected manuscripts: Returned
Time before publication decision: 1 yr.
Time between decision and publication: 1 yr.
Number of reviewers: 1
Articles submitted per year: 20-25
Articles published per year: 6-10
Book reviews submitted per year: 35
Book reviews published per year: 8

(2495)
*Rongorongo Studies: A Forum for Polynesian Philology

Steven Roger Fischer, Editor
Droste-Hülshoff-Weg 1
7758 Meersburg, Germany

First published: 1991
ISSN: 0938-0795
MLA acronym: RSFPP

SUBSCRIPTION INFORMATION

Frequency of publication: 2 times/yr.
Circulation: 115
Available in microform: No
Subscription price: 20 DM/yr.
Year to which price refers: 1992

ADVERTISING INFORMATION

Advertising accepted: Yes
Advertising rates: 100 DM/full page

EDITORIAL DESCRIPTION

Scope: Publishes articles on Polynesian philology and linguistics. Includes studies on Polynesian chants, songs, tales, legends, myths, genealogies, etc., and offers interpretations and reviews of the latest creative literature written in contemporary Polynesian languages.
Reviews books: Yes
Publishes notes: Yes
Languages accepted: English; French; German; Spanish
Prints abstracts: Yes
Author-anonymous submission: No

SUBMISSION REQUIREMENTS

Restrictions on contributors: Book reviews are solicited.
Author pays submission fee: No
Author pays page charges: No
Length of articles: 12 pp. maximum
Length of book reviews: 2 typescript pp. maximum
Length of notes: 4 pp. maximum
Number of copies required: 1
Special requirements: Consult with editor for submission instruction. Submit original typescript and camera-ready illustrations. Articles not in English must include an English abstract.
Copyright ownership: Journal
Rejected manuscripts: Returned
Time before publication decision: 1-2 mos.
Time between decision and publication: 3-6 mos.
Number of reviewers: 12
Articles submitted per year: 12
Articles published per year: 8
Notes submitted per year: 8
Notes published per year: 4

(2496)
*Room of One's Own: A Feminist Journal of Literature and Criticism

Growing Room Collective
P.O. Box 46160
Station G
Vancouver, BC V6R 4G5, Canada

First published: 1975
Sponsoring organization: Growing Room Collective
ISSN: 0316-1609
MLA acronym: ROO

SUBSCRIPTION INFORMATION

Frequency of publication: 4 times/yr.
Circulation: 1,000
Available in microform: Yes
Subscription price: C$15.00/yr., C$25.00/2 yrs. Canada; C$20.00/yr. elsewhere
Year to which price refers: 1991

ADVERTISING INFORMATION

Advertising accepted: Yes

EDITORIAL DESCRIPTION

Scope: Publishes original poetry and prose by women as well as criticism and reviews of work by women or of feminist concern. The emphasis is on literature rather than on ideology.
Reviews books: Yes
Publishes notes: Yes
Languages accepted: English
Prints abstracts: No
Author-anonymous submission: No

SUBMISSION REQUIREMENTS

Restrictions on contributors: None
Author pays submission fee: No
Author pays page charges: No
Length of articles: 4,000 words
Length of book reviews: 1,500 words
Number of copies required: 1
Copyright ownership: Author
Rejected manuscripts: Returned; enclose SASE or international reply coupons.
Time before publication decision: 6 mos.
Time between decision and publication: 6-12 mos.
Number of reviewers: 6-8
Articles published per year: 16
Book reviews published per year: 12

(2497)
*Rowohlts Monographien

Wolfgang Müller, Editor
Rowohlt Verlag GmbH
Hamburger Str. 17
2057 Reinbek, Germany

Telephone: (49) 40 72720
Fax: (49) 40 7272319
First published: 1958
ISSN: 0485-5256
MLA acronym: RM

SUBSCRIPTION INFORMATION

Frequency of publication: 12 times/yr.
Available in microform: No

ADVERTISING INFORMATION

Advertising accepted: Yes

EDITORIAL DESCRIPTION

Scope: Publishes illustrated monographs on outstanding personalities in the arts and sciences, including film, history, politics, philosophy, education, and religion.
Reviews books: No
Publishes notes: No
Languages accepted: German
Prints abstracts: No

SUBMISSION REQUIREMENTS

Author pays submission fee: No
Author pays page charges: No
Length of books: 136,000 characters
Number of copies required: 1
Copyright ownership: Rowohlt Verlag
Rejected manuscripts: Returned
Time before publication decision: 6 weeks
Time between decision and publication: 6-18 mos.
Books published per year: 12

(2498)
*Rozprawy Komisji Językowej

Karol Dejna, Editor
Łódzkie Towarzystwo Naukowe
Piotrkowska 179
90-447 Łódź, Poland

Additional editorial address: Ossolineum Publishing House of the Polish Academy of Sciences, Rynek 9, 50-106 Wrocław, Poland
First published: 1954
Sponsoring organization: Łódzkie Towarzystwo Naukowe
ISSN: 0076-0390
MLA acronym: RKJ

SUBSCRIPTION INFORMATION

Frequency of publication: Annual
Circulation: 400-500
Available in microform: No
Subscription address: Foreign Trade Enterprise "Ars Polona", Krakowskie Przedmieście 7, 00-068 Warsaw, Poland

ADVERTISING INFORMATION

Advertising accepted: No

EDITORIAL DESCRIPTION

Scope: Publishes articles on general, Polish, and slavic linguistics.
Reviews books: Occasionally
Publishes notes: No
Languages accepted: Polish; all major languages
Prints abstracts: Yes
Author-anonymous submission: No

SUBMISSION REQUIREMENTS

Restrictions on contributors: None
Author pays submission fee: No
Author pays page charges: No
Length of articles: 60 pp.
Length of book reviews: 5 pp.
Style: None
Number of copies required: 3
Copyright ownership: Ossolineum
Rejected manuscripts: Returned
Time before publication decision: 2 yrs.
Time between decision and publication: 1 yr.
Number of reviewers: 1
Articles submitted per year: 20
Articles published per year: 10-15

(2499)
RSA Journal: Rivista di Studi Nord-Americani

Mario Materassi, Editor
Biblioteca Americana
Fac. di Magistero
Via San Gallo 10
50123 Florence, Italy

Fax: (39) 55 2757948
First published: 1990
Sponsoring organization: Assoc. Italiana di Studi Nord-Americani
MLA acronym: RSA

SUBSCRIPTION INFORMATION

Frequency of publication: Annual
Circulation: 500
Available in microform: No
Subscription price: 25,000 Lit/yr. Italy; 30,000 Lit/yr. elsewhere
Year to which price refers: 1991

ADVERTISING INFORMATION

Advertising accepted: Yes

EDITORIAL DESCRIPTION

Scope: Publishes articles on American studies including American literature, history, and culture.
Reviews books: No
Publishes notes: No
Languages accepted: English; Italian
Prints abstracts: Yes
Author-anonymous submission: No

SUBMISSION REQUIREMENTS

Author pays submission fee: No
Author pays page charges: No
Length of articles: 5,000-7,000 words
Style: MLA
Number of copies required: 5
Special requirements: Submission on IBM-compatible diskette is preferred.
Copyright ownership: Author
Rejected manuscripts: Not returned
Time before publication decision: 6 mos.
Time between decision and publication: 3 mos.
Number of reviewers: 7
Articles submitted per year: 20
Articles published per year: 7-8

(2500)
*Ruch Literacki

Franciszek Ziejka, Editor
ul. Sławkowska 17
31-016 Cracow, Poland

Additional editorial address: Ossolineum, Rynek 9, 50-106 Wrocław, Poland
Telephone: (48) 12 110190
First published: 1926

Sponsoring organization: Polska Akademia Nauk
ISSN: 0035-9602
MLA acronym: RuchL

SUBSCRIPTION INFORMATION

Frequency of publication: 6 times/yr.
Circulation: 1,700
Available in microform: No
Subscription price: 144,000 Zł/yr.
Year to which price refers: 1992
Subscription address: Foreign Trade Enterprise "Ars Polona", Krakowskie Przedmieście 7, 00-068 Warsaw, Poland

ADVERTISING INFORMATION

Advertising accepted: No

EDITORIAL DESCRIPTION

Scope: Publishes articles on Polish literary history and literary theory.
Reviews books: Yes
Publishes notes: Yes
Languages accepted: Polish
Prints abstracts: Yes
Author-anonymous submission: No

SUBMISSION REQUIREMENTS

Restrictions on contributors: None
Author pays submission fee: No
Author pays page charges: No
Length of articles: 20 pp.
Length of book reviews: 4 pp.
Length of notes: 1 p.
Style: MLA
Number of copies required: 2
Copyright ownership: Ossolineum
Rejected manuscripts: Not returned
Time before publication decision: 3 mos.
Time between decision and publication: 1 yr.
Number of reviewers: 2
Articles submitted per year: 80
Articles published per year: 30
Book reviews submitted per year: 150
Book reviews published per year: 100
Notes submitted per year: 30
Notes published per year: 10

(2501)
*Ruperto Carola: Heidelberger Universitätshefte

Jürgen Miethke, Editor
Historisches Seminar der Universität
Univ. Heidelberg
Postfach 105760
6900 Heidelberg, Germany

Telephone: (49) 6221 542441
Fax: (49) 6221 542618
First published: 1948
Sponsoring organization: Freundeskreises der Univ. Heidelberg
ISSN: 0035-998X
MLA acronym: RC

SUBSCRIPTION INFORMATION

Frequency of publication: 2 times/yr. (June, Dec.)
Circulation: 1,200
Available in microform: No
Subscription address: Heidelberger Verlagsanstalt,, Hauptstr. 23, 6900 Heidelberg, Germany

ADVERTISING INFORMATION

Advertising accepted: Yes

EDITORIAL DESCRIPTION

Scope: Publishes articles on the humanities, sciences, and history of Heidelberg, and in particular, on Heidelberg University.
Reviews books: Yes
Publishes notes: Yes
Languages accepted: German
Prints abstracts: No
Author-anonymous submission: No

SUBMISSION REQUIREMENTS

Restrictions on contributors: Book reviews are solicited.
Author pays submission fee: No
Author pays page charges: No
Length of articles: 40,000 characters
Length of book reviews: 5,000-10,000 characters
Length of notes: 5,000 characters
Style: None
Number of copies required: 1-2
Copyright ownership: Author
Rejected manuscripts: Returned; enclose return postage
Time before publication decision: 6 mos. maximum
Time between decision and publication: 6 mos.
Number of reviewers: 2
Articles submitted per year: 30
Articles published per year: 20
Book reviews published per year: 10
Notes submitted per year: 30
Notes published per year: 30

(2502)
*The Ruskin Gazette

O. E. Madden, Editor
351, Woodstock Rd.
Oxford OX2 7NX, England

Additional editorial address: Oxford Union Soc., Frewin Court, Oxford OX1 3JB, England
Telephone: (44) 865 310987
First published: 1987
Sponsoring organization: Ruskin Soc. of London
MLA acronym: RuskGaz

SUBSCRIPTION INFORMATION

Frequency of publication: Annual
Circulation: 100
Available in microform: No
Subscription price: £8.00/yr.
Year to which price refers: 1991

ADVERTISING INFORMATION

Advertising accepted: No

EDITORIAL DESCRIPTION

Scope: Publishes articles on John Ruskin and his circle.
Reviews books: Yes
Publishes notes: Yes
Languages accepted: English
Prints abstracts: Yes
Author-anonymous submission: Yes

SUBMISSION REQUIREMENTS

Author pays submission fee: No
Author pays page charges: No
Length of articles: 500 words
Length of book reviews: 60-100 words
Length of notes: 300 words
Copyright ownership: Ruskin Soc. of London
Time before publication decision: 4 mos.
Time between decision and publication: 3 mos.
Articles submitted per year: 5-6
Articles published per year: 5-6
Book reviews published per year: 1
Notes published per year: 100

(2503)
*Ruskin Newsletter

James S. Dearden, Editor
Ruskin Galleries
Bembridge School
Isle of Wight, England

Telephone: (44) 983 872101
First published: 1969
Sponsoring organization: Ruskin Assn.
ISSN: 0953-1130
MLA acronym: RuskN

SUBSCRIPTION INFORMATION

Frequency of publication: Irregular
Circulation: 100
Available in microform: No
Subscription price: $10.00/yr. US; £4.00/yr. elsewhere
Year to which price refers: 1992
Subscription address: US subscribers contact: G. A. Cate, Dept. of English, Univ. of Maryland, College Park, MD 20742

ADVERTISING INFORMATION

Advertising accepted: No

EDITORIAL DESCRIPTION

Scope: Publishes work on John Ruskin and his immediate circle. Includes items of interest to Ruskin scholars concerning news and events in their fields, as well as short articles.
Reviews books: Yes
Publishes notes: Yes
Languages accepted: English
Prints abstracts: No

SUBMISSION REQUIREMENTS

Restrictions on contributors: Unsolicited manuscripts are not accepted.
Author pays submission fee: No
Author pays page charges: No

(2504)
*Russian, Croatian and Serbian, Czech and Slovak, Polish Literature

J. van der Eng, N. Å. Nilsson, S. Lasić, M. Grygar, T. Winner, & R. Fieguth, Editors
Slavic Seminar
Univ. of Amsterdam
Spuistr. 210
1012 VT Amsterdam, Netherlands

Additional editorial address: N. Å. Nilsson, Tegnerlunden 12, 113 59 Stockholm, Sweden
Telephone: (31) 20 5253081
Fax: (31) 20 5253052
First published: 1971
ISSN: 0304-3479
MLA acronym: RCSCSPL

SUBSCRIPTION INFORMATION

Frequency of publication: 8 times/yr. (in 2 volumes)
Available in microform: Yes
Subscription price: 730 f/yr.
Year to which price refers: 1992
Subscription address: Elsevier Science Publishers B.V., Journals Dept., P.O. Box 211, 1000 AE Amsterdam, Netherlands

ADVERTISING INFORMATION

Advertising accepted: No

EDITORIAL DESCRIPTION

Scope: Publishes several issues devoted to special topics of Russian literature with contributions on related topics in Croatian, Serbian, Czech, Slovak, and Polish literatures. All methods and viewpoints will be welcomed, provided they contribute something new, original, or challenging to our understanding of Russian and other Slavic literatures.
Reviews books: Yes
Publishes notes: Yes
Languages accepted: English; Russian; German (occasionally); French (occasionally)
Prints abstracts: No
Author-anonymous submission: No

SUBMISSION REQUIREMENTS

Restrictions on contributors: None
Author pays submission fee: No
Author pays page charges: No
Length of articles: No restrictions
Length of book reviews: No restrictions
Length of notes: No restrictions
Style: None
Number of copies required: 1
Special requirements: Submit first page as title page only, stating title, author's name, full address, and an abbreviated title not exceeding 40 characters including spaces. Print this short title at the top of each page.
Copyright ownership: Assigned by author to publisher
Rejected manuscripts: Returned
Time before publication decision: 2-4 weeks
Number of reviewers: 2-4
Articles published per year: 40-45
Book reviews published per year: 1-4
Notes published per year: 0-1

(2505)
***Russian Language Journal**

Munir Sendich, Editor
A-601 Wells Hall
Michigan State Univ.
East Lansing, MI 48824

Telephone: 517 337-0162
First published: 1947
Sponsoring organization: Michigan State Univ.; American Council of Teachers of Russian; Purdue Univ.; Ohio State Univ.; Univ. of Oklahoma
ISSN: 0036-0252
MLA acronym: RLJ

SUBSCRIPTION INFORMATION

Frequency of publication: 3 times/yr. (Winter, Spring, Fall)
Circulation: 650
Available in microform: Yes
Subscription price: $25.00/yr.
Year to which price refers: 1991

ADVERTISING INFORMATION

Advertising accepted: Yes

EDITORIAL DESCRIPTION

Scope: Publishes scholarly articles on Russian language and literature and methods of their teaching in the US and Canada; notes on teaching hints that reflect one's own experience in the instruction of Russian language/literature and are helpful to the profession; occasional scholarly contributions on comparative research in Russian and other Slavic languages/literatures; unpublished documents, evaluations of the newest teaching materials in Russian, and book reviews of Russian publications useful to the profession; indexes to Russian literary journals.
Reviews books: Yes
Publishes notes: Yes
Languages accepted: English; Russian
Prints abstracts: Yes
Author-anonymous submission: No

SUBMISSION REQUIREMENTS

Restrictions on contributors: None
Author pays submission fee: No
Author pays page charges: No
Length of articles: 7,000 words; longer contributions accepted
Length of book reviews: 1,500 words maximum
Length of notes: 2,500 words
Style: Shaw; MLA; Turabian
Number of copies required: 2
Special requirements: Consult Editor regarding editorial policy.
Copyright ownership: Editor
Rejected manuscripts: Returned; enclose return postage.
Time before publication decision: 4 mos.
Time between decision and publication: 4-12 mos.
Number of reviewers: 5
Articles submitted per year: 75
Articles published per year: 49
Book reviews submitted per year: 68
Book reviews published per year: 60
Notes submitted per year: 25
Notes published per year: 15

(2506)
***Russian Linguistics: International Journal for the Study of the Russian Language**

L. Ďurovič, A. G. F. van Holk, & W. Lehfeldt, Editors
Kluwer Academic Publishers
P.O. Box 17
3300 AA Dordrecht, Netherlands

Additional editorial address: L. Ďurovič, Slaviska Inst., Lunds Univ., Finngt 12, 223 62 Lund, Sweden
Telephone: (46) 46 108822 (L. Ďurovič)
Fax: (46) 46 108825
First published: 1974
Sponsoring organization: Nederlandse Organisatie voor Zuiver-Wetenschappelijk Onderzoek; Swedish Council for Research in the Humanities & Social Sciences
ISSN: 0304-3487
MLA acronym: RusLing

SUBSCRIPTION INFORMATION

Frequency of publication: 3 times/yr.
Circulation: 400
Available in microform: Yes, through Univ. Microfilms International
Subscription price: 308 f ($175.00)/yr.
Year to which price refers: 1991
Subscription address: Kluwer Academic Publishers, P.O. Box 322, 3300 AH Dordrecht, Netherlands
Additional subscription address: Kluwer Academic Publishers, P.O. Box 358, Accord Station, Hingham, MA 02018-0358

ADVERTISING INFORMATION

Advertising accepted: Yes
Advertising rates: Request from Kluwer Academic Publishers.

EDITORIAL DESCRIPTION

Scope: Publishes scholarly articles on Russian linguistics and Russian and East Slavic languages.
Reviews books: Yes
Publishes notes: Yes
Languages accepted: English; Russian; German (occasionally); French (occasionally)
Prints abstracts: No
Author-anonymous submission: Yes

SUBMISSION REQUIREMENTS

Author pays submission fee: No
Author pays page charges: No
Length of articles: 6,000 words
Length of book reviews: 1,800 words
Length of notes: 600 words maximum
Style: Reidel style guide
Number of copies required: 2
Special requirements: Contact editors before submitting. Place notes at end, before references.
Copyright ownership: Kluwer Academic Publishers
Rejected manuscripts: Returned
Time before publication decision: 4-6 mos.
Time between decision and publication: 5-9 mos. minimum
Number of reviewers: 2
Articles submitted per year: 30-40
Articles published per year: 15-20
Book reviews submitted per year: 30-40
Book reviews published per year: 25-35
Notes submitted per year: 2-6
Notes published per year: 2-3

(2507)
The Russian Review: An American Quarterly Devoted to Russia Past and Present

Allan Wildman, Editor
Ohio State Univ.
Dulles Hall
230 W. 17th Ave.
Columbus, OH 43210

Telephone: 614 292-9252
Fax: 614 292-2282
First published: 1941
Sponsoring organization: Ohio State Univ.
ISSN: 0036-0341
MLA acronym: RusR

SUBSCRIPTION INFORMATION

Frequency of publication: 4 times/yr. (Jan., Apr., July, Oct.)
Circulation: 1,600
Available in microform: Yes
Subscription price: $46.00/yr. institutions; $28.00/yr. individuals; $20.00/yr. students
Year to which price refers: 1993
Subscription address: Ohio State Univ. Press, 1070 Carmack Rd., Columbus, OH 43210-1002

ADVERTISING INFORMATION

Advertising accepted: Yes

EDITORIAL DESCRIPTION

Scope: Publishes scholarly articles on various aspects of Russian culture, life, history, and political science.
Reviews books: Yes
Publishes notes: Yes
Languages accepted: English; Russian (for textual matter)
Prints abstracts: No
Author-anonymous submission: Yes

SUBMISSION REQUIREMENTS

Restrictions on contributors: Unsolicited book reviews are not accepted.
Author pays submission fee: No
Author pays page charges: No
Length of articles: 10,000 words maximum (excluding notes)
Length of book reviews: 500-800 words
Style: Chicago
Number of copies required: 3
Special requirements: Submit original typescript.
Copyright ownership: Assigned by author to Ohio State Univ. Press
Rejected manuscripts: Returned; enclose SASE.

Time before publication decision: 6-8 weeks
Time between decision and publication: 1 yr.
Number of reviewers: 2
Articles submitted per year: 150
Articles published per year: 20
Book reviews published per year: 120
Notes submitted per year: 4
Notes published per year: 2

(2508)
*Russian Studies in Literature: A Journal of Translations

Deming Brown, Editor
M. E. Sharpe, Inc.
80 Business Park Dr.
Armonk, NY 10504

Telephone: 914 273-1800
Fax: 914 273-2106
First published: 1962
Historical variations in title: Formerly *Soviet Studies in Literature*
ISSN: 1061-1975
MLA acronym: RSiL

SUBSCRIPTION INFORMATION

Frequency of publication: 4 times/yr.
Circulation: 250
Available in microform: No
Subscription price: $286.00/yr. US; $308.00/yr. elsewhere
Year to which price refers: 1992

ADVERTISING INFORMATION

Advertising accepted: Yes

EDITORIAL DESCRIPTION

Scope: Publishes English translations of articles published in Russian-language periodicals on literary criticism, aesthetics, and current literary controversy.
Reviews books: No
Publishes notes: Yes
Languages accepted: English
Prints abstracts: No
Author-anonymous submission: No

SUBMISSION REQUIREMENTS

Restrictions on contributors: Publishes only translations of material by Russian-language authors.
Author pays submission fee: No
Author pays page charges: No
Length of articles: No restrictions
Style: Chicago
Copyright ownership: M. E. Sharpe, Inc.
Number of reviewers: 2
Articles submitted per year: 500
Articles published per year: 25

(2509)
Russkaia Literatura: Istoriko-Literaturnyĭ Zhurnal

N. N. Skatov, Editor
nab. Makarova, d.4
199034 St. Petersburg, Russia

First published: 1958
Sponsoring organization: Inst. Russkoĭ Literatury Akademiia Nauk S.S.S.R. (Pushkinskiĭ Dom)
ISSN: 0131-6095
MLA acronym: RLit

SUBSCRIPTION INFORMATION

Frequency of publication: 4 times/yr.

EDITORIAL DESCRIPTION

Scope: Publishes articles on Russian literature.
Reviews books: Yes
Languages accepted: Russian
Prints abstracts: No

(2510)
*Russkaia Rech': Nauchno-Populiarnyĭ Zhurnal

V. P. Vomperski, Editor
ul. Volkhonka 18/2
121019 Moscow G-19, Russia

Telephone: (7) 95 2026525
First published: 1967
Sponsoring organization: Akademiia Nauk S.S.S.R.
ISSN: 0131-6117
MLA acronym: RusRe

SUBSCRIPTION INFORMATION

Frequency of publication: 6 times/yr.
Circulation: 23,000
Available in microform: No
Subscription address: Mezhdunarodnaia Kniga, Smolenskaia Sennaia 32/34, Moscow G-200, Russia

ADVERTISING INFORMATION

Advertising accepted: Yes

EDITORIAL DESCRIPTION

Scope: Publishes articles on the Russian languages and literature.
Reviews books: Yes
Publishes notes: Yes
Languages accepted: Russian
Prints abstracts: No
Author-anonymous submission: No

SUBMISSION REQUIREMENTS

Author pays submission fee: Yes
Author pays page charges: Yes
Length of articles: 15,000-20,000 printed signs
Length of book reviews: 6,400 printed signs
Length of notes: 1,000 printed signs
Style: Popular; scientific
Number of copies required: 2
Copyright ownership: Journal
Rejected manuscripts: Returned
Time before publication decision: 1-2 mos.
Time between decision and publication: 4-5 mos.
Number of reviewers: 2
Articles submitted per year: 250-300
Articles published per year: 180
Book reviews submitted per year: 15
Book reviews published per year: 12-15
Notes submitted per year: 80
Notes published per year: 50-60

(2511)
Russkiĭ Fol'klor: Materialy i Issledovaniia

Inst. Russkoĭ Literatury (Pushkinskiĭ Dom) AN SSSR
nab. Makarova, 4
St. Petersburg V-164, Russia

First published: 1956
MLA acronym: RusF

SUBSCRIPTION INFORMATION

Frequency of publication: Annual

EDITORIAL DESCRIPTION

Scope: Publishes articles on Russian folklore.

(2512)
Russkiĭ Iazyk v Shkole: Metodicheskiĭ Zhurnal

N. M. Shanskiĭ, Editor
Ministerstvo Prosveshcheniia RSFSR
3-i proezd Mar'inoĭ Roshchi 41
Moscow, Russia

First published: 1936
ISSN: 0036-0376
MLA acronym: RJŠ

SUBSCRIPTION INFORMATION

Frequency of publication: 6 times/yr.
Circulation: 191,300

EDITORIAL DESCRIPTION

Scope: Publishes articles on Russian language study.
Reviews books: Yes

(2513)
Russkiĭ Iazyk za Rubezhom

A. V. Abramovich, Editor
Inst. Russkogo yazika im Pushkina
ul. Volgina 6
Moscow 117485, Russia

First published: 1967
ISSN: 0036-0384
MLA acronym: RJR

SUBSCRIPTION INFORMATION

Frequency of publication: 6 times/yr.

EDITORIAL DESCRIPTION

Scope: Publishes articles on the Russian language.
Reviews books: No
Languages accepted: Russian
Prints abstracts: No

(2514)
*Sacred Heart University Review

Sidney Gottlieb, Editor
Sacred Heart Univ.
Dept. of English
5151 Park Ave.
Fairfield, CT 06432-1023

Telephone: 203 371-7810
First published: 1980
Sponsoring organization: Sacred Heart Univ.
ISSN: 0276-7643
MLA acronym: SHUR

SUBSCRIPTION INFORMATION

Frequency of publication: 2 times/yr. (Fall, Spring)
Available in microform: No
Subscription price: $10.00/yr.
Year to which price refers: 1992

ADVERTISING INFORMATION

Advertising accepted: Yes

EDITORIAL DESCRIPTION

Scope: Publishes essays on topics of general interest ranging from humanities to the sciences.

Reviews books: Yes
Publishes notes: No
Languages accepted: English
Prints abstracts: No
Author-anonymous submission: No

SUBMISSION REQUIREMENTS

Restrictions on contributors: Publishes primarily contributions from visiting as well as resident scholars at Sacred Heart Univ. Book reviews are commissioned.
Author pays submission fee: No
Author pays page charges: No
Length of articles: 2,000-4,000 words
Length of book reviews: 1,500 words
Style: Chicago
Number of copies required: 2
Special requirements: Final version of accepted articles should be submitted on an IBM-compatible diskette.
Copyright ownership: Journal & author
Rejected manuscripts: Returned; enclose return postage
Time before publication decision: 3-4 mos.
Time between decision and publication: 6 mos.
Number of reviewers: 2
Articles submitted per year: 20
Articles published per year: 8
Book reviews published per year: 4

(2515)
*Sacris Erudiri: Jaarboek voor Godsdienstwetenschappen

St. Pietersabdij van Steenbrugge
Baron Ruzettelaan 435
8310 Brugge 4, Belgium

Telephone: (32) 50 359112
Fax: (32) 50 371457
First published: 1948
ISSN: 0771-7776
MLA acronym: SacE

SUBSCRIPTION INFORMATION

Frequency of publication: Annual
Circulation: 425
Available in microform: No
Subscription price: 2,400 BF/yr.
Year to which price refers: 1991
Subscription address: Martinus Nÿhoff International, P.O. Box, 2501 AX The Hague, Netherlands
Additional subscription address: Brepols Publishers, Baron Frans du Fourstraat 8, 2300 Turnhout, Belgium

ADVERTISING INFORMATION

Advertising accepted: No

EDITORIAL DESCRIPTION

Scope: Publishes articles on patristics, history of liturgy, and early and medieval church history.
Reviews books: No
Publishes notes: Yes
Languages accepted: English; French; German; Italian; Spanish; Dutch
Prints abstracts: No
Author-anonymous submission: No

SUBMISSION REQUIREMENTS

Author pays submission fee: No
Author pays page charges: No
Length of articles: No restrictions
Length of notes: No restrictions
Number of copies required: 2
Special requirements: Quotations in Latin are permitted. Submit original typescript and 1 copy.
Copyright ownership: Author
Rejected manuscripts: Returned
Time before publication decision: 6 weeks
Time between decision and publication: 1 yr.

Number of reviewers: 2
Articles submitted per year: 15
Articles published per year: 10-12

(2516)
*Saga-Book

A. Faulkes, R. McTurk, & D. Slay, Editors
Viking Soc. for Northern Research
Univ. College London
Gower St.
London WC1E 6BT, England

First published: 1892
Sponsoring organization: Viking Soc. for Northern Research
ISSN: 0305-9219
MLA acronym: Saga-Book

SUBSCRIPTION INFORMATION

Frequency of publication: 2 times/yr.
Available in microform: No

EDITORIAL DESCRIPTION

Scope: Publishes articles on Old Norse and Icelandic literature, philology, and linguistics; studies of the Viking Age including Orkney, Shetland, and Scotland; and Scandinavian history.
Reviews books: Yes
Publishes notes: Yes
Languages accepted: English
Prints abstracts: No
Author-anonymous submission: No

SUBMISSION REQUIREMENTS

Author pays submission fee: No
Author pays page charges: No
Length of articles: No restrictions
Length of book reviews: No restrictions
Length of notes: No restrictions
Style: Journal
Number of copies required: 1
Copyright ownership: Viking Soc. for Northern Research
Rejected manuscripts: Returned with comments
Time before publication decision: 1-6 mos.
Time between decision and publication: 6-24 mos.
Number of reviewers: 3
Articles submitted per year: 6-10
Articles published per year: 3-4
Book reviews published per year: 12
Notes submitted per year: 2
Notes published per year: 1-2

(2517)
Saga och Sed, Kungl. Gustav Adolfs Akademiens Årsbok

Lennart Elmevik, Editor
Kungl. Gustav Adolfs Akademien
Klostergatan 2
753 21 Uppsala, Sweden

First published: 1934
Sponsoring organization: Humanistisk-Samhällsvetenskapliga Forskningsrådet; Kungliga Gustav Adolfs Akademien
ISSN: 0586-5360
MLA acronym: SagaS

SUBSCRIPTION INFORMATION

Frequency of publication: Annual
Available in microform: No
Subscription price: 195 NKr ($33.00)/yr.
Year to which price refers: 1992
Subscription address: Scandinavian Univ. Press, P.O. Box 2959 Tøyen, 0608 Oslo, Norway
Additional subscription address: Scandinavian Univ. Press, 200 Meacham Ave., Elmont, NY 11003

ADVERTISING INFORMATION

Advertising accepted: Yes

EDITORIAL DESCRIPTION

Scope: Publishes articles on folklore and folk beliefs.
Reviews books: No
Publishes notes: No
Languages accepted: Swedish; Danish; Norwegian; English; German; French
Prints abstracts: No

SUBMISSION REQUIREMENTS

Author pays submission fee: No
Author pays page charges: No
Number of copies required: 1
Copyright ownership: Journal
Rejected manuscripts: Returned
Time before publication decision: 1 mo.
Time between decision and publication: 6-12 mos.

(2518)
*SAGE: A Scholarly Journal on Black Women

Patricia Bell-Scott, Beverly Guy-Sheftall, Jacqueline Jones Royster, Janet Sims-Wood, Miriam DeCosta-Willis, & Lucille Fultz, Editors
P.O. Box 42741
Atlanta, GA 30311

Telephone: 404 223-7528
Fax: 404 753-8383
E-mail: PBSCOTT@UGA
First published: 1984
Sponsoring organization: Spelman College; Univ. of Georgia
ISSN: 0741-8639
MLA acronym: SAGE

SUBSCRIPTION INFORMATION

Frequency of publication: 2 times/yr. (Spring, Fall)
Circulation: 1,000
Available in microform: No
Subscription price: $25.00/yr. institutions; $15.00/yr. individuals
Year to which price refers: 1992

ADVERTISING INFORMATION

Advertising accepted: Yes

EDITORIAL DESCRIPTION

Scope: Publishes articles, critical essays, in-depth interviews, reviews of books, films, and exhibits, research reports, resource listings, documents, and announcements focusing on the lives and cultures of black women wherever they reside.
Reviews books: Yes
Publishes notes: Yes
Languages accepted: English
Prints abstracts: No
Author-anonymous submission: Yes

SUBMISSION REQUIREMENTS

Restrictions on contributors: Contributors are encouraged to query editor prior to submission since each issue has a thematic focus.
Author pays submission fee: No
Author pays page charges: No
Length of articles: 15 double-spaced pp.
Length of book reviews: 4 double-spaced pp.
Length of notes: No restrictions
Style: Chicago
Number of copies required: 3

Special requirements: Submit double-spaced typescript with one-inch margins at the top, bottom, and sides. Manuscripts must have a title page, which should include the author's name, address, phone number, and a one to three-sentence bio-sketch.
Copyright ownership: Journal & author
Rejected manuscripts: Returned at author's request; enclose return postage.
Time before publication decision: 3-6 mos.
Time between decision and publication: 6-12 mos.
Number of reviewers: 4-6
Articles submitted per year: 40
Articles published per year: 20
Book reviews submitted per year: 20
Book reviews published per year: 12-15
Notes submitted per year: 5
Notes published per year: 3

(2519)
*Sagetrieb: A Journal Devoted to Poets in the Imagist/Objectivist Tradition

Burton Hatlen, Editor
302 Nelville Hall
Univ. of Maine at Orono
Orono, ME 04469

First published: 1982
Sponsoring organization: National Poetry Foundation; Univ. of Maine, Orono
ISSN: 0735-4665
MLA acronym: SagetriebIO

SUBSCRIPTION INFORMATION

Frequency of publication: 3 times/yr.
Circulation: 1,000
Available in microform: No
Subscription price: $18.00/yr.
Year to which price refers: 1991-92
Subscription address: National Poetry Foundation, at the above address

ADVERTISING INFORMATION

Advertising accepted: Yes

EDITORIAL DESCRIPTION

Scope: Publishes critical, biographical, and exegetical work on 20th-century poets in the "open form" tradition, especially H.D., William Carlos Williams, Mina Loy, Marianne Moore, Louis Zukofsky, Basil Bunting, George Oppen, Charles Reznikoff, Lorine Niedecker, Charles Olson; and Black Mountain, San Francisco, and New York school of poets; and contemporary poets whose work has been influenced by these experimental currents.
Reviews books: Yes
Publishes notes: Yes
Languages accepted: English
Prints abstracts: No
Author-anonymous submission: Yes

SUBMISSION REQUIREMENTS

Restrictions on contributors: None
Author pays submission fee: No
Author pays page charges: No
Length of articles: No restrictions
Length of book reviews: No restrictions
Style: MLA
Number of copies required: 2
Special requirements: Submission on IBM-compatible diskette using Microsoft Word is preferred.
Copyright ownership: National Poetry Foundation
Rejected manuscripts: Returned; enclose SASE.
Time before publication decision: 1-3 mos.
Time between decision and publication: 1 yr. maximum
Number of reviewers: 2-3
Articles submitted per year: 50-60
Articles published per year: 20-30
Book reviews submitted per year: 10-20
Book reviews published per year: 5-10
Notes submitted per year: 10-20
Notes published per year: 10-20

(2520)
Saint Louis University Research Journal of the Graduate School of Arts and Sciences

Felino L. Lorente, Editor
Graduate School of Arts & Sciences
Saint Louis Univ.
P.O. Box 71
Baguio City 0216, Philippines

First published: 1970
Sponsoring organization: St. Louis Univ., Philippines, Graduate School of Arts & Sciences
ISSN: 0036-3014
MLA acronym: SLRJ

SUBSCRIPTION INFORMATION

Frequency of publication: 2 times/yr. (June, Dec.)
Circulation: 1,000
Available in microform: No
Subscription address: Business Dept., at the above address

ADVERTISING INFORMATION

Advertising accepted: No

EDITORIAL DESCRIPTION

Scope: Interdisciplinary journal of business administration, economics, education, management engineering, philosophy, and teaching. Publishes research materials prepared by students and faculty members of the different colleges of the University (Commerce, Education, Engineering and Architecture, Human Sciences, Natural Sciences, Medicine, Graduate School, and Law), and of the different research institutes of the University.
Reviews books: Yes
Publishes notes: Yes
Languages accepted: English
Prints abstracts: No
Author-anonymous submission: No

SUBMISSION REQUIREMENTS

Restrictions on contributors: Can publish at least one outside contribution per issue.
Author pays submission fee: No
Author pays page charges: No
Length of articles: 20 pp. minimum
Length of book reviews: 300-500 words
Length of notes: 1,000-1,500 words
Style: Campbell
Number of copies required: 2
Special requirements: Include a curriculum vitae on a separate sheet.
Copyright ownership: St. Louis Univ.
Rejected manuscripts: Returned
Time before publication decision: 3 mos.
Time between decision and publication: 2 mos.
Number of reviewers: 10
Articles submitted per year: 60
Articles published per year: 25
Book reviews submitted per year: 25
Book reviews published per year: 12
Notes submitted per year: 10
Notes published per year: 2

(2521)
*Salmagundi

Robert Boyers & Peggy Boyers, Editors
Skidmore College
Saratoga Springs, NY 12866

Telephone: 518 584-5000 ext. 2302
Fax: 518 584-3023
First published: 1965
Sponsoring organization: Skidmore College
ISSN: 0036-3529
MLA acronym: Salmagundi

SUBSCRIPTION INFORMATION

Frequency of publication: 4 times/yr.
Circulation: 5,000
Available in microform: No
Subscription price: $37.00/2 yrs. institutions; $25.00/2 yrs. individuals
Year to which price refers: 1992

ADVERTISING INFORMATION

Advertising accepted: Yes
Advertising rates: $250.00/full page

EDITORIAL DESCRIPTION

Scope: Publishes articles on the humanities and the social sciences. Also publishes original poetry and fiction, interviews, and symposia.
Reviews books: Yes
Publishes notes: Yes
Languages accepted: English
Prints abstracts: No
Author-anonymous submission: No

SUBMISSION REQUIREMENTS

Restrictions on contributors: None
Author pays submission fee: No
Author pays page charges: No
Length of articles: 2,500-10,000 words
Length of book reviews: 2,500-6,500 words
Length of notes: 200-2,000 words
Style: None
Number of copies required: 1
Copyright ownership: Journal
Rejected manuscripts: Returned; enclose return postage.
Time before publication decision: 1-4 mos.
Time between decision and publication: 8-12 mos.
Number of reviewers: 2-3
Articles submitted per year: 700
Articles published per year: 40-50
Book reviews submitted per year: 350
Book reviews published per year: 20
Notes submitted per year: 300
Notes published per year: 6-15

(2522)
*Salzburg English & American Studies

James Hogg, Editor
Univ. Salzburg
Inst. für Anglistik & Amerikanistik
Akademiestr. 24
5020 Salzburg, Austria

Telephone: (43) 6217 7084
First published: 1971
Historical variations in title: Formerly *Salzburger Studien zur Anglistik und Amerikanistik*
Sponsoring organization: Univ. Salzburg, Inst. für Anglistik & Amerikanistik
ISSN: 0080-5718
MLA acronym: SEAS

SUBSCRIPTION INFORMATION

Frequency of publication: Irregular
Circulation: 200
Available in microform: No

ADVERTISING INFORMATION

Advertising accepted: No

EDITORIAL DESCRIPTION

Scope: Publishes monographs on English and American studies.
Reviews books: No
Publishes notes: No

Languages accepted: English; German
Prints abstracts: No
Author-anonymous submission: No

SUBMISSION REQUIREMENTS

Restrictions on contributors: Authors must have some connection with Salzburg Univ.
Author pays submission fee: No
Author pays page charges: No
Length of books: No restrictions
Style: None
Number of copies required: 1
Copyright ownership: Author
Rejected manuscripts: Returned; enclose return postage.
Time before publication decision: 2 mos.
Time between decision and publication: 1 yr.
Number of reviewers: 2
Books submitted per year: 3-4
Books published per year: 2-3

(2523)
*Salzburg Studies in English: Jacobean Drama Studies

James Hogg, Editor
Inst. für Anglistik & Amerikanistik
Univ. Salzburg
Akademiestr. 24
5020 Salzburg, Austria

First published: 1972
Sponsoring organization: Univ. Salzburg, Inst. für Anglistik & Amerikanistik
MLA acronym: JDS

SUBSCRIPTION INFORMATION

Frequency of publication: Irregular (4 times/yr.)
Circulation: 200-300
Available in microform: No

ADVERTISING INFORMATION

Advertising accepted: No

EDITORIAL DESCRIPTION

Scope: Publishes recent research on the Jacobean playwrights and critical editions of plays not usually considered for commercial publication. Allows specialized studies on specific aspects of Jacobean Drama.
Reviews books: No
Publishes notes: Yes
Languages accepted: English; French; German
Prints abstracts: No
Author-anonymous submission: No

SUBMISSION REQUIREMENTS

Restrictions on contributors: None
Author pays submission fee: No
Author pays page charges: No
Length of books: No restrictions
Style: None
Number of copies required: 1
Copyright ownership: Author
Rejected manuscripts: Returned; enclose return postage.
Time before publication decision: 1-2 mos.
Time between decision and publication: 6 mos.
Number of reviewers: 1-2
Articles submitted per year: 10
Articles published per year: 5
Books submitted per year: 15
Books published per year: 4

(2524)
*Salzburg Studies in English Literature: Elizabethan & Renaissance Studies

James Hogg, Editor
Inst. für Anglistik & Amerikanistik
Akademiestr. 22-24
5020 Salzburg, Austria

Telephone: (43) 6217 7084
First published: 1972
Sponsoring organization: Univ. Salzburg, Inst. für Anglistik & Amerikanistik
MLA acronym: ElizS

SUBSCRIPTION INFORMATION

Frequency of publication: Irregular
Circulation: 250
Available in microform: No
Subscription price: 40 DM/volume
Year to which price refers: 1992

ADVERTISING INFORMATION

Advertising accepted: No

EDITORIAL DESCRIPTION

Scope: Publishes studies of Elizabethan authors; editions of rare texts.
Reviews books: No
Publishes notes: Yes
Languages accepted: English; French; German
Prints abstracts: No
Author-anonymous submission: No

SUBMISSION REQUIREMENTS

Restrictions on contributors: None
Author pays submission fee: No
Author pays page charges: No
Length of books: No restrictions
Length of notes: No restrictions
Style: None
Number of copies required: 1
Copyright ownership: Author
Rejected manuscripts: Returned; enclose return postage.
Time before publication decision: 1-2 mos.
Time between decision and publication: 6 mos.
Number of reviewers: 1-2
Books submitted per year: 25
Books published per year: 10

(2525)
*Salzburg Studies in English Literature: Poetic Drama & Poetic Theory

James Hogg, Editor
Univ. Salzburg
Inst. für Anglistik & Amerikanistik
Akademiestr. 24
5020 Salzburg, Austria

Telephone: (43) 6217 7084
First published: 1972
Sponsoring organization: Univ. Salzburg, Inst. für Anglistik & Amerikanistik
MLA acronym: PD

SUBSCRIPTION INFORMATION

Frequency of publication: Irregular
Circulation: 200
Available in microform: No
Subscription price: 40 DM/yr.
Year to which price refers: 1992

ADVERTISING INFORMATION

Advertising accepted: No

EDITORIAL DESCRIPTION

Scope: Publishes studies of poetic technique, theory, and dramatists and editions of rare texts.
Reviews books: No
Publishes notes: Yes
Languages accepted: English; French; German
Prints abstracts: No
Author-anonymous submission: No

SUBMISSION REQUIREMENTS

Restrictions on contributors: None
Author pays submission fee: No
Author pays page charges: No
Length of books: No restrictions
Length of notes: No restrictions
Number of copies required: 1
Copyright ownership: Author
Rejected manuscripts: Returned; enclose return postage.
Time before publication decision: 1-2 mos.
Time between decision and publication: 6 mos.
Number of reviewers: 1-2
Books submitted per year: 10-15
Books published per year: 8

(2526)
*Salzburg Studies in English Literature: Romantic Reassessment

James Hogg, Editor
Inst. für Anglistik & Amerikanistik
Univ. Salzburg
Akademiestr. 24
5020 Salzburg, Austria

Telephone: (43) 6217 7084
First published: 1972
Sponsoring organization: Univ. Salzburg, Inst. für Anglistik & Amerikanistik
MLA acronym: RcRt

SUBSCRIPTION INFORMATION

Frequency of publication: Irregular
Circulation: 250
Available in microform: No
Subscription price: 40 DM/volume
Year to which price refers: 1992

ADVERTISING INFORMATION

Advertising accepted: No

EDITORIAL DESCRIPTION

Scope: Publishes recent research on all topics connected with Romanticism, including the Victorians.
Reviews books: No
Publishes notes: Yes
Languages accepted: English; German; French
Prints abstracts: No
Author-anonymous submission: No

SUBMISSION REQUIREMENTS

Restrictions on contributors: None
Author pays submission fee: No
Author pays page charges: No
Length of articles: No restrictions
Length of books: No restrictions
Length of notes: No restrictions
Style: None
Number of copies required: 1
Copyright ownership: Author
Rejected manuscripts: Returned; enclose return postage.
Time before publication decision: 2 mos.
Time between decision and publication: 6 mos.
Number of reviewers: 1-2
Books submitted per year: 25-30
Books published per year: 12

(2527)
*Samlaren: Tidskrift för Svensk Litteraturvetenskaplig Forskning

Ulf Wittrock, Editor
Litteraturvetenskapliga Inst.
Uppsala Univ.
Slottet ing. AO
752 37 Uppsala, Sweden

Telephone: (46) 18 182943
First published: 1880
ISSN: 0348-6133
MLA acronym: Samlaren

SUBSCRIPTION INFORMATION

Frequency of publication: Annual
Circulation: 600
Available in microform: No
Subscription price: 150 Skr/yr.
Year to which price refers: 1991

ADVERTISING INFORMATION

Advertising accepted: No

EDITORIAL DESCRIPTION

Scope: Publishes studies on literature. Includes works on research and history of literature in Swedish and in other languages, from all time periods. Contains on annual bibliography of research of Swedish literature.
Reviews books: Yes
Publishes notes: Yes
Languages accepted: Swedish; English; German; French
Prints abstracts: No
Author-anonymous submission: No

SUBMISSION REQUIREMENTS

Author pays submission fee: No
Author pays page charges: No
Number of copies required: 2
Copyright ownership: Author
Rejected manuscripts: Not returned
Time before publication decision: 3 weeks
Time between decision and publication: 3-12 mos.
Articles published per year: 4-5
Book reviews published per year: 20
Notes published per year: 2-5

(2528)
*Sammlung Kurzer Grammatiken Germanischer Dialekte

Helmut Gneuss, Siegfried Grosse, & Klaus Matzel, Editors
Max Niemeyer Verlag
Postfach 2140
7400 Tübingen, Germany

Telephone: (49) 7071 81104
Fax: (49) 7071 87419
First published: 1886
ISSN: 0344-6646
MLA acronym: SkGgD

SUBSCRIPTION INFORMATION

Frequency of publication: Irregular
Available in microform: No

ADVERTISING INFORMATION

Advertising accepted: No

EDITORIAL DESCRIPTION

Scope: Publishes monographs and handbooks German dialects such as Old High German, Old English, etc.
Reviews books: No
Publishes notes: No
Languages accepted: German
Prints abstracts: No
Author-anonymous submission: Yes

SUBMISSION REQUIREMENTS

Restrictions on contributors: None
Author pays submission fee: No
Author pays page charges: No
Length of books: No restrictions
Style: None
Number of copies required: 1
Copyright ownership: Max Niemeyer Verlag
Rejected manuscripts: Returned
Time before publication decision: 6 mos.
Time between decision and publication: 1 yr.
Number of reviewers: 2-3
Books published per year: 1-3

(2529)
*Sammlung Metzler

J. B. Metzlersche Verlagsbuchhandlung
Kernerstr. 43
Postfach 103241
7000 Stuttgart 1, Germany

Fax: (49) 711 2290290
First published: 1961
ISSN: 0558-3667
MLA acronym: SM

SUBSCRIPTION INFORMATION

Frequency of publication: Irregular
Circulation: 5,000
Available in microform: No

ADVERTISING INFORMATION

Advertising accepted: No

EDITORIAL DESCRIPTION

Scope: Publishes monographs on literature and the arts, the teaching of literary methods, linguistics, history of literature and intellectual history, poetry, mutual relations between German and non-German literatures, and documents.
Reviews books: No
Publishes notes: No
Languages accepted: German
Prints abstracts: No
Author-anonymous submission: No

SUBMISSION REQUIREMENTS

Restrictions on contributors: None
Author pays submission fee: No
Author pays page charges: No
Length of books: 120-150 pp.
Style: Series
Number of copies required: 1
Copyright ownership: J. B. Metzlersche Verlagsbuchhandlung
Rejected manuscripts: Returned
Time before publication decision: 2 mos.
Time between decision and publication: 8 mos.
Number of reviewers: 2
Books submitted per year: 20-30
Books published per year: 5-10

(2530)
*Samtiden: Tidsskrift for Politikk, Litteratur og Samfunnsspørsmål

Thomas Hylland Eriksen, Editor
H. Aschehoug & Co.
Sehesteds gt. 3
0164 Oslo, Norway

Telephone: (47) 2 400406
Fax: (47) 2 206395
First published: 1890
Sponsoring organization: Norwegian Ministry of Culture
ISSN: 0036-3928
MLA acronym: Samtiden

SUBSCRIPTION INFORMATION

Frequency of publication: 6 times/yr.
Circulation: 5,500
Available in microform: No
Subscription price: 320 NKr/yr. institutions; 280 NKr/yr. individuals
Year to which price refers: 1992
Subscription address: Forlagsentralens Tidsskriftavdeling, P.B. 150, Furuset, 1001 Oslo, Norway
Additional subscription address: Postboks 363 Sentrum, 0102 Oslo, Norway
Subscription telephone: (47) 2 326050

ADVERTISING INFORMATION

Advertising accepted: Yes
Advertising rates: 3,000 NKr/full page

EDITORIAL DESCRIPTION

Scope: Publishes articles on literature, politics, and social issues.
Reviews books: Yes
Languages accepted: Norwegian; Swedish; Danish
Prints abstracts: No

SUBMISSION REQUIREMENTS

Restrictions on contributors: None
Author pays submission fee: No
Author pays page charges: No
Length of articles: 10 pp.
Length of book reviews: 3 pp.
Number of copies required: 1
Special requirements: Submit typescript on size A4 (8 1/4 in. x 11 3/4 in.) paper.
Copyright ownership: Journal & author
Rejected manuscripts: Returned
Time before publication decision: 1-3 mos.
Time between decision and publication: 6 mos.
Number of reviewers: 2
Articles published per year: 100
Book reviews published per year: 6

(2531)
*San José Studies

Fauneil J. Rinn, Editor
English Dept.
San Jose State Univ.
San Jose, CA 95192

Telephone: 408 924-4476
First published: 1975
Sponsoring organization: San Jose State Univ. Foundation
ISSN: 0097-8051
MLA acronym: SJS

SUBSCRIPTION INFORMATION

Frequency of publication: 3 times/yr. (Winter, Spring, Fall)
Circulation: 400
Available in microform: No
Subscription price: $18.00/yr. institutions; $12.00/yr. individuals
Year to which price refers: 1992
Subscription address: Allisón Diaz, Business Manager, School of Social Sciences, San Jose State Univ., San Jose, CA 95192

ADVERTISING INFORMATION

Advertising accepted: No

EDITORIAL DESCRIPTION

Scope: Publishes articles and literature appealing to the educated public. Critical, creative, and informative writing in the broad areas of the arts, humanities, sciences, and social sciences are considered.

Reviews books: No
Publishes notes: No
Languages accepted: English
Prints abstracts: No
Author-anonymous submission: Yes

SUBMISSION REQUIREMENTS

Restrictions on contributors: Previously published articles and multiple submissions are not acceptable.
Author pays submission fee: No
Author pays page charges: No
Length of articles: 5,000 words maximum
Style: MLA preferred
Number of copies required: 2
Special requirements: Author's name and address should appear only on cover sheet of original; identifying word from title should be on subsequent pages adjacent to page number.
Copyright ownership: First serial rights to San Jose State Univ. Foundation
Rejected manuscripts: Returned; enclose SASE or return postage.
Time before publication decision: 2 mos.
Time between decision and publication: 6-12 mos.
Number of reviewers: 2-3
Articles submitted per year: 250
Articles published per year: 30-35

(2532)
*Sananjalka: Suomen Kielen Seuran Vuosikirja

Aimo Hakanen, Editor
Henrikinkatu 3
20500 Turku, Finland

Telephone: (358) 21 6335280
First published: 1959
Sponsoring organization: Finnish Language Soc.; Academia Scientiarum Fennica
ISSN: 0558-4639
MLA acronym: Sananjalka

SUBSCRIPTION INFORMATION

Frequency of publication: Annual
Circulation: 700
Available in microform: No
Subscription price: 160 Fmk/yr. cloth; 100 Fmk/yr. paper
Year to which price refers: 1992
Subscription address: Akateeminen Kirjakauppa, Keskuskatu 1, 00100 Helsinki, Finland

ADVERTISING INFORMATION

Advertising accepted: Yes

EDITORIAL DESCRIPTION

Scope: Publishes articles on Finnish and related languages, Finnish ethnology, Finnish literature, Finnish folklore, and Finnish comparative religion.
Reviews books: Yes
Publishes notes: Yes
Languages accepted: Finnish
Prints abstracts: Yes
Author-anonymous submission: No

SUBMISSION REQUIREMENTS

Restrictions on contributors: None
Author pays submission fee: No
Author pays page charges: No
Length of articles: 5-20 pp.
Length of book reviews: 1-5 pp.
Length of notes: 1-3 pp.
Style: None
Number of copies required: 1
Special requirements: Include an abstract 10% of the length of the article.
Copyright ownership: Author
Rejected manuscripts: Returned
Time before publication decision: 2 mos.
Time between decision and publication: 8 mos.

Number of reviewers: 2
Articles submitted per year: 10-15
Articles published per year: 8-10
Book reviews submitted per year: 8-15
Book reviews published per year: 7-10
Notes submitted per year: 4-8
Notes published per year: 3-6

(2533)
Sapienza: Rivista di Filosofia e di Teologia

Michele Miele, Editor
Vicoletto S. Pietro a Maiella, 4
80134 Naples, Italy

Telephone: (39) 81 459003
First published: 1948
Sponsoring organization: Dominican Order
ISSN: 0036-4711
MLA acronym: Sapienza

SUBSCRIPTION INFORMATION

Frequency of publication: 4 times/yr.
Available in microform: No
Subscription price: 30,000 Lit ($30.50)/yr.
Year to which price refers: 1992
Subscription address: Editrice Domenicana Italiana, via Luigi Palmieri 19, 80133 Naples, Italy

ADVERTISING INFORMATION

Advertising accepted: Yes

EDITORIAL DESCRIPTION

Scope: Focuses on the scientific investigation of theological and philosophical problems in light of Catholic and Thomist ideas.
Reviews books: Yes
Publishes notes: Yes
Languages accepted: Italian; English; French
Prints abstracts: No

SUBMISSION REQUIREMENTS

Restrictions on contributors: None
Length of articles: No restrictions
Length of book reviews: 2-3 pp.
Length of notes: 3-4 pp.
Style: None
Number of copies required: 1
Special requirements: Submit original typescript.
Copyright ownership: Journal
Rejected manuscripts: Returned at author's request; enclose return postage.
Time before publication decision: 8 mos.
Time between decision and publication: 1 yr.
Articles submitted per year: 30
Articles published per year: 15-20
Book reviews submitted per year: 50-60
Book reviews published per year: 40-50
Notes submitted per year: 15-20
Notes published per year: 12-15

(2534)
*Saul Bellow Journal

Liela Goldman, Editor
6533 Post Oak Dr.
West Bloomfield, MI 48322

Telephone: 313 851-4441
Fax: 313 557-6636
First published: 1981
ISSN: 0735-1550
MLA acronym: SBN

SUBSCRIPTION INFORMATION

Frequency of publication: 2 times/yr. (Spring-Summer, Fall-Winter)
Available in microform: No

Subscription price: $28.00/yr. institutions; $16.00/yr. individuals US; $28.00/yr. individuals elsewhere
Year to which price refers: 1993

ADVERTISING INFORMATION

Advertising accepted: No

EDITORIAL DESCRIPTION

Scope: Publishes critical writing on Bellow's work.
Reviews books: Yes
Publishes notes: Yes
Languages accepted: English
Prints abstracts: No

SUBMISSION REQUIREMENTS

Author pays submission fee: No
Author pays page charges: No
Length of articles: 2,500-5,000 words
Length of book reviews: 500-1,000 words
Style: MLA
Number of copies required: 2
Special requirements: Submission on diskette accompanied by 2 copies of the typescript is preferred.
Copyright ownership: Editor
Rejected manuscripts: Returned; enclose return postage.
Time before publication decision: 2 mos.
Time between decision and publication: 6 mos.
Number of reviewers: 2
Articles published per year: 15
Book reviews submitted per year: 4
Book reviews published per year: 4

(2535)
Savacou: A Journal of the Caribbean Artists Movement

Edward Brathwaite, Editor
Dept. of History
U.W.I., Mona
Kingston 7
Jamaica, West Indies

First published: 1970
Sponsoring organization: Caribbean Artists' Movement
ISSN: 0036-5068
MLA acronym: Savacou

SUBSCRIPTION INFORMATION

Frequency of publication: Irregular
Circulation: 2,000
Subscription address: P.O. Box 170, Mona, Kingston 7, Jamaica, West Indies

EDITORIAL DESCRIPTION

Scope: Aims to present the work of creative writers (established, unknown, in exile, or at home), to examine and assess the significance of artistic expression through slavery to the present, with a view to recognizing continuities and submerged or "lost" traditions, and to help increase recognition of the whole Caribbean area as a meaningful historical and cultural entity. Issues concentrate on conceptual ideas, exploring the relationship between the arts, thought, and society. Each issue is concerned with a specific topic, the contributions being drawn from various disciplines.
Reviews books: Yes
Languages accepted: English
Prints abstracts: No

SUBMISSION REQUIREMENTS

Restrictions on contributors: None
Number of copies required: 1
Copyright ownership: Author
Rejected manuscripts: Returned at author's request

Number of reviewers: 2-3
Articles published per year: 10-12

(2536)
Savremenik: Mesečni Književni Časopis

Pavle Zorić, Editor
Knijezevne Novine
Francuska 7
11000 Belgrade, Yugoslavia

First published: 1955
Sponsoring organization: Serbian Assn. for Culture
ISSN: 0036-519X
MLA acronym: Savremenik

SUBSCRIPTION INFORMATION

Frequency of publication: 12 times/yr.
Circulation: 1,000

EDITORIAL DESCRIPTION

Scope: Publishes articles on modern literature.
Reviews books: Yes
Languages accepted: Serbo-Croatian
Prints abstracts: No

(2537)
Sborník Prací Filosofické Fakulty Brněnské University: Řada Jazykovědná—A

Sborník Prací a Spisy
Filosofické Fakulty Masarykovy Univ.
Arna Nováka 1
660 88 Brno, Czech Republic

MLA acronym: SPFFBUA

SUBSCRIPTION INFORMATION

Frequency of publication: Annual
Subscription address: Knižní Velkoobchod, Opatovická 18, 113 81 Prague 1-Nové Město, Czech Republic

EDITORIAL DESCRIPTION

Scope: Publishes articles on linguistics.
Languages accepted: Czech; Russian; Polish; English

(2538)
*Sborník Prací Filosofické Fakulty Brněnské University: Řada Literárněvědná—D

Milan Kopecký, Editor
Sborník Prací a Spisy
Filosofické Fakulty Masarykovy Univ.
A. Nováka 1
660 88 Brno, Czech Republic

Telephone: (42) 5 750050
Fax: (42) 5 753050
First published: 1955
ISSN: 0231-7818
MLA acronym: SPFFBUD

SUBSCRIPTION INFORMATION

Frequency of publication: Annual
Circulation: 500
Available in microform: No
Subscription price: 45 Kčs/yr.
Year to which price refers: 1991

ADVERTISING INFORMATION

Advertising accepted: No

EDITORIAL DESCRIPTION

Scope: Publishes articles on literary theory and on the history of Czech, Soviet, Russian, prerevolutionary, and other slavonic literatures.
Reviews books: Yes
Publishes notes: No
Languages accepted: Czech; Russian; Polish
Prints abstracts: Yes
Author-anonymous submission: No

SUBMISSION REQUIREMENTS

Author pays submission fee: No
Author pays page charges: No
Copyright ownership: Masarykovy Univ., Filosofické Fak.
Rejected manuscripts: Returned
Time before publication decision: 3 mos.
Time between decision and publication: 1 yr.
Number of reviewers: 1-2

(2539)
*Scandinavian Review

Lena Biörck Kaplan, Publisher
American-Scandinavian Foundation
725 Park Ave.
New York, NY 10021

Telephone: 212 879-9779
Fax: 212 249-3444
First published: 1913
Sponsoring organization: American-Scandinavian Foundation
ISSN: 0098-857X
MLA acronym: ScanR

SUBSCRIPTION INFORMATION

Frequency of publication: 3 times/yr. (Apr., Sept., Dec.)
Circulation: 3,500
Available in microform: Yes

ADVERTISING INFORMATION

Advertising accepted: Yes
Advertising rates: $400.00/full page

EDITORIAL DESCRIPTION

Scope: Publishes articles on culture, society, literature, politics, and economics of all Nordic countries.
Reviews books: Yes
Publishes notes: No
Languages accepted: English
Prints abstracts: No

SUBMISSION REQUIREMENTS

Restrictions on contributors: None
Author pays submission fee: No
Author pays page charges: No
Length of articles: 1,500 words
Length of book reviews: 200-300 words
Style: Chicago
Number of copies required: 1
Copyright ownership: Assigned by author to journal
Rejected manuscripts: Returned; enclose SASE.
Time before publication decision: 3 mos.
Time between decision and publication: 9 mos.
Number of reviewers: 3
Articles submitted per year: 150
Articles published per year: 40

(2540)
*Scandinavian Studies

Steven P. Sondrup & Peter Vinten-Johansen, Editors
3003 JKHB
Brigham Young Univ.
Provo, UT 84602

Additional editorial address: For history & social science: Peter Vinten-Johansen, Dept. of History, Michigan State Univ., East Lansing, MI 48824
Telephone: 801 378-2579; 801 378-5598
Fax: 801 378-4649
E-mail: Bitnet: SONDRUP@BYUVM
First published: 1911
Sponsoring organization: Soc. for the Advancement of Scandinavian Study
ISSN: 0036-5637
MLA acronym: SS

SUBSCRIPTION INFORMATION

Frequency of publication: 4 times/yr. (Winter, Spring, Summer, Fall)
Circulation: 1,000
Available in microform: Yes
Subscription price: $40.00/yr. institutions N. America; $45.00/yr. institutions elsewhere; $35.00/yr. members N. America; $38.00/yr. members elsewhere
Year to which price refers: 1993
Subscription address: George Tate, at the above address

ADVERTISING INFORMATION

Advertising accepted: Yes
Advertising rates: $150.00/full page

EDITORIAL DESCRIPTION

Scope: Publishes articles on Scandinavian literature, linguistics, and area studies.
Reviews books: Yes
Publishes notes: Yes
Languages accepted: English
Prints abstracts: No
Author-anonymous submission: No

SUBMISSION REQUIREMENTS

Restrictions on contributors: Considers only papers based on material examined in the original language. Unsolicited reviews are returned.
Author pays submission fee: No
Author pays page charges: No
Length of articles: 3,000-10,000 words
Length of book reviews: 750-1,250 words
Length of notes: 100-200 words
Style: MLA
Number of copies required: 2
Special requirements: Quotations from Danish, Norwegian, Old Norse, Swedish, Finnish, and Modern Icelandic should include a translation.
Copyright ownership: Soc. for the Advancement of Scandinavian Study
Rejected manuscripts: Returned
Time before publication decision: 3 mos.
Time between decision and publication: 8-12 mos.
Number of reviewers: 2
Articles submitted per year: 50-70
Articles published per year: 20-25
Book reviews submitted per year: 90-100
Book reviews published per year: 90-100
Notes submitted per year: 15
Notes published per year: 15

(2541)
*Scandinavica: An International Journal of Scandinavian Studies

Janet Garton, Editor
School of Modern Languages & European History
Univ. of East Anglia
Norwich NR4 7TJ, England

Telephone: (44) 603 56161 ext. 2142
Fax: (44) 603 58553
First published: 1962
ISSN: 0036-5653
MLA acronym: Scan

SUBSCRIPTION INFORMATION

Frequency of publication: 2 times/yr. (May, Nov.)
Circulation: 400
Available in microform: No
Subscription price: $45.00/yr.
Year to which price refers: 1993
Subscription address: Subscriptions Office (EUR), at the above address

ADVERTISING INFORMATION

Advertising accepted: Yes

EDITORIAL DESCRIPTION

Scope: Publishes articles on Scandinavian literature, especially modern.
Reviews books: Yes
Publishes notes: Yes
Languages accepted: English; French; German
Prints abstracts: No
Author-anonymous submission: No

SUBMISSION REQUIREMENTS

Restrictions on contributors: Reviews are commissioned.
Author pays submission fee: No
Author pays page charges: No
Length of articles: 2,500–12,500 words
Length of book reviews: 300–2,500 words
Length of notes: 1,500–3,000 words
Style: Modern Humanities Research Assn.
Number of copies required: 2
Special requirements: Number footnotes consecutively.
Copyright ownership: Assigned by author to Editor
Rejected manuscripts: Returned at author's request
Time before publication decision: 2–3 mos.
Time between decision and publication: 12–18 mos.
Number of reviewers: 2–4
Articles submitted per year: 20–30
Articles published per year: 8–12
Book reviews published per year: 20–30
Notes submitted per year: 3–6
Notes published per year: 2–3

(2542)
*Scando-Slavica

Erik Egeberg, Editor
ISL/Univ.
9000 Tromsø, Norway

Additional editorial address: Asst. Editor, Uppsala Univ., Slaviska Inst., Box 513, 751 20 Uppsala, Sweden
First published: 1954
Sponsoring organization: Assn. of Scandinavian Slavists & Baltologists
ISSN: 0080-6765
MLA acronym: SSl

SUBSCRIPTION INFORMATION

Frequency of publication: Annual
Circulation: 650
Available in microform: No
Subscription address: Munksgaard, International Publishers, Ltd., 35 Nørre Søgade, Postbox 2148, 1016 Copenhagen K, Denmark

ADVERTISING INFORMATION

Advertising accepted: Yes

EDITORIAL DESCRIPTION

Scope: Publication for Slavic and Baltic philology, literature, history, and archaeology. Presents an annual bibliography of books and articles by Scandinavian Slavists and Baltologists. Abstracts books.
Reviews books: No
Publishes notes: No
Languages accepted: English; French; German; Russian
Prints abstracts: No
Author-anonymous submission: No

SUBMISSION REQUIREMENTS

Restrictions on contributors: None
Author pays submission fee: No
Author pays page charges: No
Length of articles: 16 printed pp. maximum
Style: Journal
Number of copies required: 2
Special requirements: See journal for "Instructions to Contributors." Submissions must be received by 1 Mar. to be considered for that year; all entries received after 1 Mar. will be held for following year.
Copyright ownership: Assn. of Scandinavian Slavists & Baltologists
Rejected manuscripts: Returned
Time before publication decision: 2–14 mos.
Time between decision and publication: 6–8 mos.
Number of reviewers: 2–3
Articles submitted per year: 25
Articles published per year: 12

(2543)
*Scena: Časopis za Pozorišnu Umetnost

Radomir Putnik, Editor
Sterijino pozorje
Zmaj-Jovina 22/1
21000 Novi Sad, Yugoslavia

Telephone: (38) 21 612485
Fax: (38) 21 615976
First published: 1965
Sponsoring organization: Sterijino pozorje
ISSN: Serbo-Croatian issue: 0036-5734; English issue: 0351-3963
MLA acronym: Scena

SUBSCRIPTION INFORMATION

Frequency of publication: 6 times/yr.; one issue annually in English
Circulation: 1,000
Available in microform: No
Subscription price: 15 DM/yr.
Year to which price refers: 1992

ADVERTISING INFORMATION

Advertising accepted: No

EDITORIAL DESCRIPTION

Scope: Publishes articles, surveys, reviews, book reviews, notes, and original plays from the contemporary Yugoslav writers (predominantly Serbian, Croatian, Slovenian, Macedonian).
Reviews books: Yes
Publishes notes: Yes
Languages accepted: Serbo-Croatian; English
Prints abstracts: No
Author-anonymous submission: No

SUBMISSION REQUIREMENTS

Restrictions on contributors: None
Author pays submission fee: No
Author pays page charges: No
Length of articles: No restrictions
Length of book reviews: 8–10 typescript pp. maximum
Length of notes: 8–10 typescript pp. maximum
Number of copies required: 1
Copyright ownership: Author
Rejected manuscripts: Not returned
Time before publication decision: 2–3 mos.
Time between decision and publication: 1–3 mos.
Number of reviewers: 3
Articles submitted per year: 150–200
Articles published per year: 120–150
Book reviews submitted per year: 50
Book reviews published per year: 30

(2544)
*Schatzkammer der Deutschen Sprache, Dichtung und Geschichte

Pamela Saur, Robert H. Buchheit, & Horst Ludwig, Editors
Lamar Univ.
P.O. Box 10023
Beaumont, TX 77710

Telephone: 605 677-5583
First published: 1975
ISSN: 0740-1965
MLA acronym: Schatzkammer

SUBSCRIPTION INFORMATION

Frequency of publication: 2 times/yr. (Fall, Spring)
Circulation: 700
Available in microform: No
Subscription price: $10.00/yr., $25.00/3 yrs.
Year to which price refers: 1991–92
Subscription address: USD Press, Univ. of South Dakota, Vermillion, SD 57069-2390

ADVERTISING INFORMATION

Advertising accepted: Yes

EDITORIAL DESCRIPTION

Scope: Publishes articles on German linguistics, pedagogy, German American history, creative writing, and German culture.
Reviews books: Yes
Publishes notes: No
Languages accepted: German; English
Prints abstracts: No
Author-anonymous submission: Yes

SUBMISSION REQUIREMENTS

Author pays submission fee: Yes, for accepted articles
Cost of submission fee: $10.00 handling fee after acceptance
Author pays page charges: No
Length of articles: 15 typescript pp.
Length of book reviews: 500 words
Style: MLA
Number of copies required: 3
Special requirements: Submit original manuscript.
Copyright ownership: Univ. of South Dakota Press
Rejected manuscripts: Returned
Time before publication decision: 6 weeks
Time between decision and publication: 3–12 mos.
Number of reviewers: 3
Articles submitted per year: 15
Articles published per year: 7
Book reviews submitted per year: 15–20
Book reviews published per year: 15–20

(2545)
*Schlesien: Arts, Science, Folklore

Eberhard Günter Schulz, Editor
Postfach 110425
8700 Würzburg 11, Germany

Additional editorial address: E. G. Schulz, Fr.-
 Ebert-Str. 79, 3550 Marburg, Germany
Telephone: (49) 6421 42514
First published: 1956
Sponsoring organization: Verein der Freunde &
 Förderer der Sfiftung Kulturwerk Schlesien
ISSN: 0036-6153
MLA acronym: Schlesien

SUBSCRIPTION INFORMATION

Frequency of publication: 4 times/yr.
Available in microform: No
Subscription price: 38 DM/yr.
Year to which price refers: 1992
Subscription address: Bergstadtverlag W. G.
 Korn, Karlstr. 10, Postfach 546, 7480 Sig-
 maringen, Germany
Subscription telephone: (49) 7571 728125

ADVERTISING INFORMATION

Advertising accepted: No

EDITORIAL DESCRIPTION

Scope: Publishes articles on the arts and folk-
 lore of Silesia.
Reviews books: Yes
Publishes notes: Yes
Languages accepted: German
Prints abstracts: No
Author-anonymous submission: No

SUBMISSION REQUIREMENTS

Author pays page charges: No
Length of articles: 10 pp. maximum
Number of copies required: 1
Special requirements: Submit original type-
 script.
Copyright ownership: Editor
Time before publication decision: 2 mos.
Time between decision and publication: 6-12
 mos.
Articles submitted per year: 50
Articles published per year: 30
Book reviews submitted per year: 30
Book reviews published per year: 25
Notes published per year: 5

(2546)
*Scholarly Publishing: A Journal for Authors and Publishers

Mark Carroll & Ian Montagnes, Editors
Univ. of Toronto Press
10 St. Mary St., Suite 700
Toronto M4Y 2W8, Canada

First published: 1969
ISSN: 0036-634X
MLA acronym: SchP

SUBSCRIPTION INFORMATION

Frequency of publication: 4 times/yr.
Circulation: 2,000
Available in microform: Yes
Subscription price: $50.00/yr. institutions;
 $25.00/yr. individuals
Year to which price refers: 1992
Subscription address: Journals Dept., Univ. of
 Toronto Press, 5201 Dufferin St., Downsview,
 Ontario, M3H 5T8, Canada

ADVERTISING INFORMATION

Advertising accepted: Yes

EDITORIAL DESCRIPTION

Scope: Devoted to improving the writing and
 publishing of serious nonfiction by university
 and commercial presses, at all stages from au-
 thor to reader.
Reviews books: Yes
Publishes notes: No
Languages accepted: English
Prints abstracts: No
Author-anonymous submission: No

SUBMISSION REQUIREMENTS

Restrictions on contributors: None
Author pays submission fee: No
Author pays page charges: No
Length of articles: 2,500-5,000 words
Length of book reviews: 250-450 words
Style: Chicago preferred; Oxford spelling
Number of copies required: 1
Copyright ownership: Univ. of Toronto Press
Rejected manuscripts: Returned
Time before publication decision: 1 mo.
Time between decision and publication: 4-6
 mos.
Number of reviewers: 1-2
Articles submitted per year: 75
Articles published per year: 50
Book reviews submitted per year: 12
Book reviews published per year: 10

(2547)
*Scholars' Facsimiles & Reprints

Norman Mangouni, Editor
P.O. Box 344
Delmar, NY 12054-0344

Telephone: 518 439-5978
First published: 1936
ISSN: 0161-7729
MLA acronym: SF&R

SUBSCRIPTION INFORMATION

Frequency of publication: Irregular
Available in microform: Yes

ADVERTISING INFORMATION

Advertising accepted: No

EDITORIAL DESCRIPTION

Scope: Reprints rare books of seminal impor-
 tance in English and American literature,
 rhetoric, history, philosophy, psychology, and
 religion.
Reviews books: No
Publishes notes: No
Languages accepted: English
Prints abstracts: No

SUBMISSION REQUIREMENTS

Author pays submission fee: No
Author pays page charges: No
Length of books: 2,000-3,000 words
Style: Chicago
Number of copies required: 2
Copyright ownership: Publisher
Rejected manuscripts: Returned at author's re-
 quest
Time before publication decision: 1 mo.
Time between decision and publication: 4 mos.
Number of reviewers: 1
Books published per year: 30

(2548)
*Schriften der Gesellschaft für Theatergeschichte

Gesellschaft für Theatergeschichte
Mecklenburgische Str. 56
1000 Berlin 33, Germany

Telephone: (49) 30 82400123
Fax: (49) 30 82400111
First published: 1902
ISSN: 0176-8891
MLA acronym: SGT

SUBSCRIPTION INFORMATION

Frequency of publication: Irregular
Circulation: 350
Available in microform: No
Subscription price: 50 DM/volume
Year to which price refers: 1992

ADVERTISING INFORMATION

Advertising accepted: No

EDITORIAL DESCRIPTION

Scope: Series is devoted to the history of the
 theater.
Reviews books: No
Publishes notes: No
Languages accepted: German
Prints abstracts: No
Author-anonymous submission: No

SUBMISSION REQUIREMENTS

Restrictions on contributors: None
Author pays submission fee: No
Author pays page charges: No
Length of books: No restrictions
Style: MLA preferred
Number of copies required: 1
Special requirements: Notes and bibliography
 should come at the end of the text.
Copyright ownership: Gesellschaft für Theater-
 geschichte
Rejected manuscripts: Returned
Time before publication decision: 4-6 mos.
Number of reviewers: 2-3

(2549)
*Schriften der Theodor-Storm-Gesellschaft

Karl Ernst Laage & Gerd Eversberg, Editors
Theodor-Storm-Gesellschaft
Wasserreihe 31
im Storm-Haus
2250 Husum, Germany

First published: 1952
Sponsoring organization: Theodor-Storm-
 Gesellschaft
ISSN: 0082-3880
MLA acronym: SSG

SUBSCRIPTION INFORMATION

Frequency of publication: Annual
Circulation: 1,800
Available in microform: No

ADVERTISING INFORMATION

Advertising accepted: No

EDITORIAL DESCRIPTION

Scope: Publishes articles about Theodor Storm,
 and reviews about poetical realism.
Reviews books: Yes
Publishes notes: Yes
Languages accepted: German
Prints abstracts: No
Author-anonymous submission: No

SUBMISSION REQUIREMENTS

Restrictions on contributors: None
Author pays submission fee: Yes
Author pays page charges: No
Length of articles: 10-15 pp.
Length of notes: 2-3 pp.
Style: None
Number of copies required: 1
Special requirements: Submit typescript.
Copyright ownership: Journal
Rejected manuscripts: Returned
Time before publication decision: 15 mos.
Time between decision and publication: 8-10 mos.
Number of reviewers: 3
Articles submitted per year: 10
Articles published per year: 5
Book reviews published per year: 10
Notes submitted per year: 5
Notes published per year: 2-3

(2550)
*Schweizer Anglistische Arbeiten

Robert Fricker, Ernst Leisi, & Henri Petter, Editors
Francke Verlag
Dischingerweg 5
7400 Tübingen 5-Hirschau, Germany

Telephone: (49) 7071 78091
Fax: (49) 7071 75288
First published: 1936
ISSN: 0080-7214
MLA acronym: SAA

SUBSCRIPTION INFORMATION

Frequency of publication: Irregular
Available in microform: No

ADVERTISING INFORMATION

Advertising accepted: No

EDITORIAL DESCRIPTION

Scope: Publishes monographs on English language and literature.
Reviews books: No
Languages accepted: English; German
Prints abstracts: No

SUBMISSION REQUIREMENTS

Style: MLA
Number of copies required: 2
Copyright ownership: Francke Verlag
Rejected manuscripts: Returned
Time before publication decision: 2-3 mos.
Time between decision and publication: 6 mos.
Books submitted per year: 3-5
Books published per year: 2-4

(2551)
*Schweizer Volkskunde: Korrespondenzblatt der Schweizerischen Gesellschaft für Volkskunde

Schweizerische Gesellschaft für Volkskunde
Augustinergasse 19
4051 Basel, Switzerland

Telephone: (41) 61 2619900
First published: 1911
Sponsoring organization: Schweizerische Gesellschaft für Volkskunde
ISSN: 0048-9522
MLA acronym: SV

SUBSCRIPTION INFORMATION

Frequency of publication: 6 times/yr.
Circulation: 1,600
Available in microform: No
Subscription price: 45 SwF/yr.
Year to which price refers: 1992

ADVERTISING INFORMATION

Advertising accepted: Yes

EDITORIAL DESCRIPTION

Scope: Publishes articles on Swiss folklife and folk culture.
Reviews books: Yes
Publishes notes: Yes
Languages accepted: German
Prints abstracts: No
Author-anonymous submission: No

SUBMISSION REQUIREMENTS

Author pays submission fee: No
Author pays page charges: No
Length of articles: 5,000 words
Length of book reviews: 400 words
Length of notes: 1,000 words
Number of copies required: 2
Copyright ownership: Editor
Time before publication decision: 2 weeks
Time between decision and publication: 2-6 mos.
Number of reviewers: 1
Articles published per year: 10
Book reviews published per year: 15
Notes published per year: 10

(2552)
*Schweizerisches Archiv für Volkskunde

Ueli Gyr, Editor
Schweizerisches Archiv für Volkskunde Redaktion
Volkskundliches Seminar der Univ. Zurich
Zeltweg 67
8032 Zurich, Switzerland

First published: 1897
Sponsoring organization: Schweizerische Gesellschaft für Volkskunde
ISSN: 0036-794X
MLA acronym: SAV

SUBSCRIPTION INFORMATION

Frequency of publication: 2 times/yr.
Circulation: 1,100
Available in microform: No
Subscription address: G. Krebs Verlagsbuchhandlung AG, St. Alban-Vorstadt 56, 4006 Basel, Switzerland

ADVERTISING INFORMATION

Advertising accepted: No

EDITORIAL DESCRIPTION

Scope: Publishes articles on European folklore and ethnology.
Reviews books: Yes
Publishes notes: No
Languages accepted: French; German; Italian
Prints abstracts: No

SUBMISSION REQUIREMENTS

Restrictions on contributors: None
Author pays submission fee: No
Author pays page charges: No
Length of articles: 12-18 pp.
Length of book reviews: 1-2 1/2 p.
Style: None
Number of copies required: 1
Special requirements: Submit original typescript.
Copyright ownership: Schweizerische Gesellschaft für Volkskunde
Rejected manuscripts: Returned

Time before publication decision: 6 mos.
Time between decision and publication: 12-18 mos.
Number of reviewers: 3-4
Articles submitted per year: 12-15
Articles published per year: 12
Book reviews submitted per year: 80
Book reviews published per year: 60

(2553)
*Science et Esprit

Gilles Langevin, Editor
Bibliothèque de Theologie
5605, rue Decelles
Montreal, Quebec H3T 1W4, Canada

Telephone: 514 737-1465
Fax: 514 745-4299
First published: 1948
Sponsoring organization: Facultés Jesuites de Montréal
ISSN: 0316-5345
MLA acronym: ScEc

SUBSCRIPTION INFORMATION

Frequency of publication: 3 times/yr.
Circulation: 375
Available in microform: No
Subscription price: C$20.00/yr.
Year to which price refers: 1992
Subscription address: Editions Bellarmin, 165 rue Des lauriers, St.-Laurent, Quebec H4N 2S4, Canada

ADVERTISING INFORMATION

Advertising accepted: No

EDITORIAL DESCRIPTION

Scope: Publishes scientific studies in philosophy and theology.
Reviews books: Yes
Publishes notes: Yes
Languages accepted: English; French
Prints abstracts: Yes

SUBMISSION REQUIREMENTS

Restrictions on contributors: None
Author pays submission fee: No
Author pays page charges: No
Length of articles: 20-25 pp.
Length of book reviews: 300-400 words
Style: None
Number of copies required: 1
Copyright ownership: Assigned by author to journal
Rejected manuscripts: Returned
Time before publication decision: 2 mos.
Time between decision and publication: 2-6 mos.
Number of reviewers: 3
Articles submitted per year: 30
Articles published per year: 16-20
Book reviews submitted per year: 50
Book reviews published per year: 40-50
Notes submitted per year: 5
Notes published per year: 3

(2554)
*Science Fiction: A Review of Speculative Literature

Van Ikin, Editor
Dept. of English
Univ. of Western Australia
Nedlands, Western Australia, 6009, Australia

Telephone: (61) 9 3802280
Fax: (61) 9 3801030
First published: 1977
ISSN: 0314-6677
MLA acronym: SFic

SUBSCRIPTION INFORMATION

Frequency of publication: 3 times/yr.
Circulation: 1,500
Available in microform: No
Subscription price: A$24.00 (A$36.00 airmail)/yr.
Year to which price refers: 1992

ADVERTISING INFORMATION

Advertising accepted: Yes
Advertising rates: A$80.00/half page; A$150.00/full page

EDITORIAL DESCRIPTION

Scope: Publishes articles, interviews, and reviews related to science fiction.
Reviews books: Yes
Publishes notes: Yes
Languages accepted: English
Prints abstracts: No
Author-anonymous submission: No

SUBMISSION REQUIREMENTS

Restrictions on contributors: None
Author pays submission fee: No
Author pays page charges: No
Length of articles: 2,000-3,000 words
Length of book reviews: 500-1,500 words
Length of notes: 500-1,000 words
Style: MLA
Number of copies required: 2
Copyright ownership: Author
Rejected manuscripts: Returned; enclose return postage.
Time before publication decision: 3 mos.
Time between decision and publication: 6-12 mos.
Number of reviewers: 3
Articles submitted per year: 30
Articles published per year: 5-8
Book reviews submitted per year: 60
Book reviews published per year: 20
Notes submitted per year: 10
Notes published per year: 3

(2555)
*Science-Fiction Studies

R. D. Mullen, Arthur B. Evans, Istvan Csicsery-Ronay, Jr., & Veronica Hollinger, Editors
East College
DePauw Univ.
Greencastle, IN 46135

Telephone: 317 658-4758
Fax: 317 658-4177
E-mail: AEVANS@DEPAUW.BITNET
First published: 1973
Sponsoring organization: DePauw Univ.
ISSN: 0091-7729
MLA acronym: SFS

SUBSCRIPTION INFORMATION

Frequency of publication: 3 times/yr. (Mar., July, Nov.)
Circulation: 1,000
Available in microform: No
Subscription price: $22.00/yr. institutions US; C$25.00/yr. institutions Canada; $26.00 (£14.50)/yr. institutions elsewhere; $15.00/yr. individuals US; C$17.00/yr. individuals Canada; $18.00 (£11.00)/yr. individuals elsewhere
Year to which price refers: 1993

ADVERTISING INFORMATION

Advertising accepted: Yes
Advertising rates: $50.00/half page; $100.00/full page

EDITORIAL DESCRIPTION

Scope: Publishes articles on science fiction, including utopian fiction, but not, except for purposes of comparison and contrast, supernatural or mythological fantasy.
Reviews books: Yes
Publishes notes: Yes
Languages accepted: English
Prints abstracts: Yes
Author-anonymous submission: No

SUBMISSION REQUIREMENTS

Restrictions on contributors: Unsolicited book reviews are not accepted.
Author pays submission fee: No
Author pays page charges: No
Length of articles: 5,000-9,000 words maximum
Length of book reviews: 1,000 words
Length of notes: 100-1,500 words
Style: MLA; journal
Number of copies required: 2
Special requirements: Submit double-spaced typescript and, if possible, an IBM-compatible diskette in WordPerfect. Articles in French, German, Italian, Spanish, and Slavic languages are translated before publication.
Copyright ownership: Assigned by author to journal for specific uses only
Rejected manuscripts: Returned
Time before publication decision: 2-4 mos.
Time between decision and publication: 3-9 mos.
Number of reviewers: 1-2 plus editor
Articles submitted per year: 100
Articles published per year: 24
Book reviews published per year: 40
Notes submitted per year: 20
Notes published per year: 15

(2556)
*Scottish Gaelic Studies

Donald MacAulay & Colm Ó Baoill, Editors
Celtic Dept.
Univ. of Aberdeen
Old Aberdeen AB9 2UB, Scotland

Telephone: (44) 224 272547
Fax: (44) 224 487048
First published: 1926
ISSN: 0080-8024
MLA acronym: SGS

SUBSCRIPTION INFORMATION

Frequency of publication: Irregular
Circulation: 400
Available in microform: No
Subscription price: £10.00/yr.
Year to which price refers: 1990

ADVERTISING INFORMATION

Advertising accepted: Yes

EDITORIAL DESCRIPTION

Scope: Publishes articles on Scottish Gaelic language and literature, as well as on history and cultural studies.
Reviews books: Yes
Publishes notes: Yes
Languages accepted: English; Scottish Gaelic
Prints abstracts: No
Author-anonymous submission: No

SUBMISSION REQUIREMENTS

Restrictions on contributors: None
Author pays submission fee: No
Author pays page charges: No
Length of articles: No restrictions
Length of notes: No restrictions
Style: MLA
Number of copies required: 1
Special requirements: Submit only original, unpublished manuscripts.

Copyright ownership: Author
Rejected manuscripts: Returned
Time before publication decision: 1 mo.
Number of reviewers: 2

(2557)
*Scottish Language

J. Derrick McClure, Editor
Dept. of English, Taylor Bldg.
King's College
Old Aberdeen AB9 2UB, Scotland

Telephone: (44) 224 272625
Fax: (44) 224 272624
First published: 1982
Sponsoring organization: Assn. for Scottish Literary Studies
ISSN: 0264-0198
MLA acronym: ScotL

SUBSCRIPTION INFORMATION

Frequency of publication: Annual (Winter)
Circulation: 800
Available in microform: No
Subscription address: Assn. for Scottish Literary Studies, Dept. of English, Univ. of Aberdeen, Aberdeen AB9 2UB, Scotland

ADVERTISING INFORMATION

Advertising accepted: No

EDITORIAL DESCRIPTION

Scope: Publishes on the languages of Scotland: Gaelic, Lowland Scots, and Scottish English. Also publishes articles on linguistic, historical, social, and literary aspects of the languages, including Scottish lexicography and dialectology.
Reviews books: Yes
Publishes notes: Yes
Languages accepted: English
Prints abstracts: No
Author-anonymous submission: No

SUBMISSION REQUIREMENTS

Restrictions on contributors: None
Author pays submission fee: No
Author pays page charges: No
Length of articles: 4,000-8,000 words
Length of book reviews: 1,000-2,000 words
Length of notes: 1,000-2,000 words
Style: Modern Humanities Research Assn.
Number of copies required: 1
Copyright ownership: Author
Rejected manuscripts: Returned
Time before publication decision: 1 mo.
Time between decision and publication: 1 yr.
Number of reviewers: 2
Articles submitted per year: 8
Articles published per year: 4-7
Book reviews submitted per year: 2-3
Book reviews published per year: 1-3
Notes submitted per year: 1
Notes published per year: 1

(2558)
*Scottish Literary Journal

J. H. Alexander, Editor
Dept. of English
Univ. of Aberdeen
Aberdeen AB9 2UB, Scotland

Telephone: (44) 224 272626
Fax: (44) 224 272664
First published: 1974
Historical variations in title: Formerly *Scottish Literary Journal: A Review of Studies in Scottish Language and Literature*
Sponsoring organization: Assn. for Scottish Literary Studies

ISSN: 0305-0785
MLA acronym: ScLJ

SUBSCRIPTION INFORMATION

Frequency of publication: 2 times/yr. (May, Nov.); Supplements 2 times/yr.
Circulation: 800
Available in microform: No
Subscription price: £40.00/yr. institutions; £24.00/yr. individuals
Year to which price refers: 1991
Subscription address: David Hewitt, Treasurer, ASLS, at the above address
Subscription telephone: (44) 224 272634

ADVERTISING INFORMATION

Advertising accepted: Yes

EDITORIAL DESCRIPTION

Scope: Publishes articles on Scottish literature in Scots, English, and Gaelic from the beginnings to the present, including Scottish folklore. Also publishes cultural studies relevant to Scottish literature.
Reviews books: Yes
Publishes notes: Yes
Languages accepted: English
Prints abstracts: No
Author-anonymous submission: No

SUBMISSION REQUIREMENTS

Restrictions on contributors: None
Author pays submission fee: No
Author pays page charges: No
Length of articles: 5,000 words
Length of book reviews: 1,500 words
Length of notes: 1,500 words
Style: Modern Humanities Research Assn.
Number of copies required: 2
Copyright ownership: Author & Assn. for Scottish Literary Studies
Rejected manuscripts: Returned
Time before publication decision: 3 mos.
Time between decision and publication: 6-12 mos.
Number of reviewers: 2
Articles submitted per year: 20
Articles published per year: 10
Book reviews submitted per year: 50
Book reviews published per year: 50
Notes submitted per year: 4
Notes published per year: 3

(2559)
*Scottish Slavonic Review: An International Journal Promoting East-West Contacts

Peter Henry, Editor
53 Southpark Ave.
Univ. of Glasgow
Glasgow G12 8QQ, Scotland

Additional editorial address: Jekaterina Young, Review Editor, Dept. of Russian Studies, Univ. of Manchester, Manchester M13 9PL, England
Telephone: (44) 41 3398855 ext. 5599
Fax: (44) 41 3304808
First published: 1983
ISSN: 0265-3273
MLA acronym: SSR

SUBSCRIPTION INFORMATION

Frequency of publication: 2 times/yr. (Spring, Autumn)
Circulation: 300
Available in microform: No
Subscription price: $38.00/yr. institutions; $25.00/yr. individuals
Year to which price refers: 1992

ADVERTISING INFORMATION

Advertising accepted: Yes; contact J. Young

EDITORIAL DESCRIPTION

Scope: Publishes scholarly articles in the fields of Slavonic and East European studies, East-West cultural relations, translations of poetry and short prose fiction, documents heretofore unpublished, book reviews, reports, resumes, and illustrations.
Reviews books: Yes
Publishes notes: Yes
Languages accepted: English; Russian; Czech; German; Polish; Hungarian
Prints abstracts: No
Author-anonymous submission: Yes

SUBMISSION REQUIREMENTS

Restrictions on contributors: Notes are commissioned.
Author pays submission fee: No
Author pays page charges: No
Length of articles: 6,000-8,000 words
Length of book reviews: 400-600 words
Length of notes: 400 words
Style: Journal
Number of copies required: 2
Special requirements: Submit double-spaced typescript on size A4 (8 1/4 in. x 11 3/4 in.) paper.
Copyright ownership: Author
Rejected manuscripts: Returned
Time before publication decision: 6-8 weeks
Time between decision and publication: 6 mos.
Number of reviewers: 2
Articles submitted per year: 30
Articles published per year: 15-20
Book reviews submitted per year: 50-60
Book reviews published per year: 50-60
Notes submitted per year: 20-30
Notes published per year: 15-25

(2560)
Scottish Studies

D. J. Hamilton, Editor
School of Scottish Studies
Univ. of Edinburgh
27 George Square
Edinburgh EH8 9LD, Scotland

First published: 1957
Sponsoring organization: Univ. of Edinburgh, School of Scottish Studies
ISSN: 0036-9411
MLA acronym: ScS

SUBSCRIPTION INFORMATION

Frequency of publication: Annual
Circulation: 750
Available in microform: No

ADVERTISING INFORMATION

Advertising accepted: No

EDITORIAL DESCRIPTION

Scope: Publishes research on Scottish traditional life and cultural history. Contributions are made by both the staff of the School of Scottish Studies and by any other scholars in the field and take the form of full-scale articles, shorter notes, and book reviews. Notes include first-hand reports of field work and research and transcriptions from the School's manuscripts and tape-recorded archives. Occasionally includes bibliographies.
Reviews books: Yes
Publishes notes: Yes
Languages accepted: English; Scottish Gaelic
Prints abstracts: No
Author-anonymous submission: No

SUBMISSION REQUIREMENTS

Restrictions on contributors: None
Author pays submission fee: No
Author pays page charges: No
Length of articles: 4,000-8,000 words
Length of book reviews: 450-1,200 words
Length of notes: 2,000 words
Style: Journal
Number of copies required: 1
Special requirements: Submit original typescript.
Copyright ownership: Author & School of Scottish Studies
Rejected manuscripts: Returned
Time before publication decision: 3-6 mos.
Time between decision and publication: 1 yr.
Number of reviewers: 2 plus editorial staff
Articles submitted per year: 10-15
Articles published per year: 3-4
Book reviews submitted per year: 3-4
Book reviews published per year: 2-3
Notes submitted per year: 5-6
Notes published per year: 2-4

(2561)
Scottish Text Society

R. J. Lyall, Editor
Dept. of Scottish Literature
Univ. of Glasgow
Glasgow, Scotland

First published: 1884
MLA acronym: STS

SUBSCRIPTION INFORMATION

Frequency of publication: Annual
Circulation: 500
Available in microform: No
Subscription address: Dept. of English Studies, Univ. of Stirling, Stirling FK9 4LA, Scotland

ADVERTISING INFORMATION

Advertising accepted: No

EDITORIAL DESCRIPTION

Scope: Publishes monographs on Scottish language and literature especially of the medieval and Renaissance periods.
Reviews books: Yes
Languages accepted: Scottish Gaelic; English
Prints abstracts: No

SUBMISSION REQUIREMENTS

Restrictions on contributors: None
Author pays submission fee: No
Author pays page charges: No
Length of books: No restrictions
Number of copies required: 1
Copyright ownership: Journal
Rejected manuscripts: Returned
Time before publication decision: 1 yr. maximum
Time between decision and publication: 2-3 yrs.
Number of reviewers: 2
Books published per year: 1

(2562)
*Screen

John Caughie, Simon Frith, Sandra Kemp, Norman King, & Annette Kuhn, Editors
John Logie Baird Centre
Univ. of Glasgow
Glasgow G12 8QQ, Scotland

Telephone: (44) 41 3305035
Fax: (44) 41 3304808
First published: 1960
Sponsoring organization: John Logie Baird Centre

ISSN: 0036-9543
MLA acronym: Screen

SUBSCRIPTION INFORMATION

Frequency of publication: 4 times/yr. (Winter, Spring, Summer, Autumn)
Available in microform: Yes
Subscription price: £38.00/yr. institutions United Kingdom & Europe; $80.00/yr. institutions elsewhere; £21.00/yr. individuals United Kingdom & Europe: $45.00/yr. individuals elsewhere
Year to which price refers: 1991
Subscription address: Journals Subscription Dept., Oxford Univ. Press, Pinkhill House, Southfield Rd., Eynsham, Oxford OX8 1JJ, England
Subscription telephone: (44) 865 882283
Subscription fax: (44) 865 882890

ADVERTISING INFORMATION

Advertising accepted: Yes
Advertising rates: $80.00/quarter page; $145.00/half page; $270.00/full page; $865.00/ four color full page

EDITORIAL DESCRIPTION

Scope: Publishes articles on film and television studies. Is committed to the development of critical, theoretical and historical work in its field of interest.
Reviews books: Yes
Publishes notes: Yes
Languages accepted: English
Prints abstracts: No
Author-anonymous submission: No

SUBMISSION REQUIREMENTS

Restrictions on contributors: None
Author pays submission fee: No
Author pays page charges: No
Length of articles: 5,000 words
Length of book reviews: 2,500 words
Number of copies required: 2
Copyright ownership: John Logie Baird Centre
Number of reviewers: 2 minimum

(2563)
*The Scriblerian and the Kit Cats: A Newsjournal Devoted to Pope, Swift, and Their Circle

Peter A. Tasch, Arthur J. Weitzman, & Roy S. Wolper, Editors
Dept. of English
Temple Univ.
Philadelphia, PA 19122

Telephone: 215 787-4717
Fax: 215 787-9620
First published: 1968
Sponsoring organization: Temple Univ.; Northeastern Univ.; Univ. of Florida; Univ. of Tennessee
ISSN: 0036-9640
MLA acronym: Scriblerian

SUBSCRIPTION INFORMATION

Frequency of publication: 2 times/yr. (Fall, Spring)
Circulation: 1,200
Available in microform: No
Subscription price: $12.00/yr. institutions; $10.00/yr. individuals
Year to which price refers: 1991-92

ADVERTISING INFORMATION

Advertising accepted: Yes

EDITORIAL DESCRIPTION

Scope: Publishes reviews, notes, queries, illustrations, and ephemera on the Scriblerians and Kit-Cats and their acquaintances.
Reviews books: Yes
Publishes notes: Yes
Languages accepted: English
Prints abstracts: No
Author-anonymous submission: No

SUBMISSION REQUIREMENTS

Restrictions on contributors: None
Author pays submission fee: No
Author pays page charges: No
Length of book reviews: 250-1,200 words
Length of notes: 1,000-1,500 words
Style: MLA
Number of copies required: 1
Special requirements: Submit original manuscript.
Copyright ownership: Journal
Rejected manuscripts: Returned
Time before publication decision: 6 mos.
Time between decision and publication: 6 mos.
Number of reviewers: 3
Book reviews published per year: 50
Notes submitted per year: 20
Notes published per year: 8

(2564)
Scripsi

Peter Craven, Michael Heyward, & Andrew Rutherford, Editors
Ormond College
Univ. of Melbourne
Parkville 3052, Australia

First published: 1981
Sponsoring organization: Literature Board of the Australia Council, Victorian Ministry of the Arts, & Ormond College
ISSN: 9725-0096
MLA acronym: Scripsi

SUBSCRIPTION INFORMATION

Frequency of publication: 4 times/yr.
Circulation: 2,000
Available in microform: No

ADVERTISING INFORMATION

Advertising accepted: Yes

EDITORIAL DESCRIPTION

Scope: Scripsi is an international literary journal publishing poetry, prose, fiction, essays, reviews and interviews.
Reviews books: Yes
Publishes notes: No
Languages accepted: English
Prints abstracts: No

SUBMISSION REQUIREMENTS

Restrictions on contributors: None
Author pays submission fee: No
Author pays page charges: No
Length of articles: 2,000-5,000 words; 15,000 words maximum
Length of book reviews: 2,000 words
Number of copies required: 1
Copyright ownership: Author & journal
Time before publication decision: 2 mos.
Time between decision and publication: 3-9 mos.
Number of reviewers: 2
Articles submitted per year: 500
Articles published per year: 20
Book reviews submitted per year: 50
Book reviews published per year: 20

(2565)
*Scripta Humanistica

Bruno M. Damiani, Editor
1383 Kersey Lane
Potomac, MD 20854

Telephone: 301 294-7949
Fax: 301 424-9584
First published: 1974
MLA acronym: SHum

SUBSCRIPTION INFORMATION

Available in microform: No

ADVERTISING INFORMATION

Advertising accepted: No

EDITORIAL DESCRIPTION

Scope: Publishes monographs in the area of humanistic studies, including literature, linguistics, philosophy, history, and art, as well as creative writing in prose fiction and poetry.
Reviews books: No
Publishes notes: No
Languages accepted: All modern and classical languages
Prints abstracts: No
Author-anonymous submission: No

SUBMISSION REQUIREMENTS

Author pays submission fee: No
Author pays page charges: No
Length of books: 150-200 pp.
Style: MLA
Copyright ownership: Author
Rejected manuscripts: Returned
Time before publication decision: 3 mos.
Time between decision and publication: 3 mos.
Number of reviewers: 3
Books submitted per year: 100
Books published per year: 10-15

(2566)
*Scripta Islandica: Isländska Sällskapets Årsbok

Claes Åneman, Editor
Isländska Sällskapet
Institutionen för Nordiska Språk
Box 513
751 20 Uppsala, Sweden

Telephone: (46) 18 181273
Fax: (46) 18 181272
First published: 1950
Sponsoring organization: Isländska Sällskapet, Uppsala; Humanistisk-Samhällsvetenskapliga Forskningsrådet
ISSN: 0582-3234
MLA acronym: ScI

SUBSCRIPTION INFORMATION

Frequency of publication: Annual
Circulation: 800
Available in microform: No
Subscription price: 135 NKr ($22.00)/yr.
Year to which price refers: 1992
Subscription address: Scandinavian Univ. Press, P.O. Box 2959 Tøyen, 0608 Oslo, Norway
Additional subscription address: Scandinavian Univ. Press, 200 Meacham Ave., Elmont, NY 11003

ADVERTISING INFORMATION

Advertising accepted: Yes

EDITORIAL DESCRIPTION

Scope: Publishes papers contributing to the knowledge of the Icelandic and Faroese language, literature, and culture.

Reviews books: Yes
Publishes notes: No
Languages accepted: English; Swedish; German; French; Danish; Norwegian
Prints abstracts: No

SUBMISSION REQUIREMENTS

Restrictions on contributors: None
Author pays submission fee: No
Author pays page charges: No
Number of copies required: 1
Special requirements: Submit typescript.
Copyright ownership: Journal
Rejected manuscripts: Returned
Time before publication decision: 1 mo.
Time between decision and publication: 6 mos.
Number of reviewers: 1
Articles published per year: 3-6

(2567)
***Scriptorium: Revue Internationale des Etudes Relatives aux Manuscrits/ International Review of Manuscript Studies**

M. Garand & Pascale Bourgain, Editors
40, avenue d'Iéna
75116 Paris, France

Telephone: (33) 1 47238939
First published: 1946
ISSN: 0036-9772
MLA acronym: Scriptorium

SUBSCRIPTION INFORMATION

Frequency of publication: 2 times/yr.
Circulation: 1,200
Available in microform: No
Subscription price: 3,800 BF/yr.
Year to which price refers: 1991
Subscription address: Centre d'Etudes des Manuscrits, 4 Boulevard de l'Empereur, 1000 Brussels, Belgium

ADVERTISING INFORMATION

Advertising accepted: No

EDITORIAL DESCRIPTION

Scope: Publishes manuscript studies.
Reviews books: Yes
Publishes notes: Yes
Languages accepted: English; French; German; Italian; Spanish
Prints abstracts: No

SUBMISSION REQUIREMENTS

Author pays submission fee: No
Author pays page charges: No
Number of copies required: 2
Special requirements: Submit original typescript and 1 copy.
Copyright ownership: Centre d'Etudes des Manuscrits
Rejected manuscripts: Returned
Time before publication decision: 2 mos.
Time between decision and publication: 1 yr.
Number of reviewers: 6
Articles submitted per year: 30
Articles published per year: 15
Book reviews submitted per year: 1,100
Book reviews published per year: 900
Notes submitted per year: 20
Notes published per year: 10

(2568)
Seara Nova

Ulpiano Nascimento, Editor
Cooperativa Cultura Editora
Apdo. 2774
1119 Lisbon Codex, Portugal

First published: 1921
ISSN: 0037-0177
MLA acronym: SeN

SUBSCRIPTION INFORMATION

Frequency of publication: 6 times/yr.

EDITORIAL DESCRIPTION

Scope: Publishes articles on cultural subjects.
Reviews books: Yes
Languages accepted: Portuguese
Prints abstracts: No

(2569)
***The SECOL Review: Southeastern Conference on Linguistics**

Greta D. Little & Michael Montgomery, Editors
c/o Linguistics Program
Univ. of South Carolina-Columbia
Columbia, SC 29208

Telephone: 803 777-2171
Fax: 803 777-2300
First published: 1976
Sponsoring organization: Southeastern Conference on Linguistics; Univ. of South Carolina
ISSN: 0730-6245
MLA acronym: SECOLB

SUBSCRIPTION INFORMATION

Frequency of publication: 2 times/yr.
Circulation: 350
Available in microform: No
Subscription price: $20.00/yr. institutions; $12.00/yr. individuals; $8.00/yr. students
Year to which price refers: 1991

ADVERTISING INFORMATION

Advertising accepted: Yes

EDITORIAL DESCRIPTION

Scope: Publishes articles on all aspects of linguistics including literature.
Reviews books: Yes
Publishes notes: Yes
Languages accepted: English
Prints abstracts: No
Author-anonymous submission: No

SUBMISSION REQUIREMENTS

Restrictions on contributors: Contributors should be members of the Southeastern Conference on Linguistics.
Author pays submission fee: No
Author pays page charges: No
Length of articles: No restrictions
Length of book reviews: No restrictions
Length of notes: 100 words maximum
Style: MLA
Number of copies required: 3
Copyright ownership: Journal
Rejected manuscripts: Returned at author's request
Time before publication decision: 4 mos.
Time between decision and publication: 15 mos.
Number of reviewers: 3
Articles submitted per year: 80
Articles published per year: 12-15
Book reviews published per year: 10-15
Notes published per year: 15

(2570)
***SECOLAS Annals: Journal of the Southeastern Council on Latin American Studies**

T. Ray Shurbutt, Editor
L. B. 8054
Georgia Southern Univ.
Statesboro, GA 30460

Telephone: 912 681-5862
First published: 1970
Sponsoring organization: Southeastern Council on Latin American Studies; Georgia Southern Univ.
ISSN: 0081-2951
MLA acronym: SECOLASA

SUBSCRIPTION INFORMATION

Frequency of publication: Annual
Circulation: 450
Available in microform: Yes, vols. I-XIV
Subscription price: $4.00/yr.
Year to which price refers: 1992

ADVERTISING INFORMATION

Advertising accepted: No

EDITORIAL DESCRIPTION

Scope: Prints selected papers read at the Southeastern Council on Latin American Studies annual meeting.
Reviews books: No
Publishes notes: No
Languages accepted: English; Spanish
Prints abstracts: No
Author-anonymous submission: No

SUBMISSION REQUIREMENTS

Restrictions on contributors: Paper must have been read at annual Southeastern Council on Latin American Studies meeting.
Author pays submission fee: No
Author pays page charges: No
Length of articles: 30 double-spaced typescript pp. maximum
Style: Turabian
Number of copies required: 3
Copyright ownership: Author
Rejected manuscripts: Not returned
Time before publication decision: 4 mos.
Time between decision and publication: 4 mos.
Number of reviewers: 3
Articles submitted per year: 20-35
Articles published per year: 7-10

(2571)
Secolul 20

Dan Hăulică, Editor
Uniunea Scriitorilor din Republica Socialistă România
Calea Victoriei, 133
Sector 1, Bucharest, Romania

First published: 1961
Sponsoring organization: Uniunea Scriitorilor din România
ISSN: 0037-0517
MLA acronym: SXX

SUBSCRIPTION INFORMATION

Frequency of publication: 12 times/yr.
Circulation: 10,000
Available in microform: No
Subscription address: Calea Victoriei 115, Bucharest, Romania

ADVERTISING INFORMATION

Advertising accepted: Yes

EDITORIAL DESCRIPTION

Scope: Focuses on translation into Romanian of 20th-century non-Romanian and Romanian literature; critical articles on Romanian and non-Romanian writers of this century; news items about contemporary literature; arts and culture in general.
Reviews books: Yes
Publishes notes: Yes
Languages accepted: Romanian; English; French; Spanish; Italian
Prints abstracts: No

SUBMISSION REQUIREMENTS

Restrictions on contributors: None
Author pays submission fee: No
Author pays page charges: No
Length of articles: 3,000 words
Length of book reviews: 600 words
Length of notes: 300 words
Style: Encounter; World Literature Today; The Literary Review
Number of copies required: 3
Copyright ownership: Author
Rejected manuscripts: Returned
Time before publication decision: 6 mos.
Time between decision and publication: 1 yr.
Number of reviewers: 2
Articles submitted per year: 150
Articles published per year: 120
Book reviews published per year: 12
Notes published per year: 30

(2572)
*Second Language Research

J. N. Pankhurst & M. A. Sharwood Smith, Editors
Dept. of English
Univ. of Utrecht
Trans 10
3512 JK Utrecht, Netherlands

Telephone: (31) 30 392193
Fax: (31) 30 333380
E-mail: Smith@let.ruu.nl.earn
First published: 1985
ISSN: 0267-6583
MLA acronym: SLRe

SUBSCRIPTION INFORMATION

Frequency of publication: 3 times/yr. (Feb., June, Oct.)
Circulation: 450
Available in microform: No
Subscription price: £41.00/yr. United Kingdom; $76.00/yr. US & Canada; £44.00/yr. elsewhere
Year to which price refers: 1991
Subscription address: Subscriptions Dept., Edward Arnold Journals, Mill Rd., Dunton Green, Sevenoaks, Kent TN13 2YA, England
Additional subscription address: In N. America: Cambridge Univ. Press, 40 West 20th St., New York, NY 10011-4211
Subscription telephone: (44) 732 450111
Subscription fax: (44) 732 461321

ADVERTISING INFORMATION

Advertising accepted: Yes

EDITORIAL DESCRIPTION

Scope: Publishes theoretical and experimental papers in second language acquisition and second language performance as well as providing a forum for investigators in the field of nonnative language learning. Seeks to promote interdisciplinary research which links acquisition studies to neighboring theoretical and experimental disciplines, e.g., psycholinguistics, neurolinguistics and sociolinguistics.
Reviews books: Yes
Publishes notes: Yes
Languages accepted: English
Prints abstracts: Yes

Author-anonymous submission: No

SUBMISSION REQUIREMENTS

Author pays submission fee: No
Author pays page charges: No
Length of articles: 3,000-5,000 words
Length of book reviews: 1,000-3,000 words
Length of notes: 1,000-3,000 words
Style: Harvard
Number of copies required: 3
Copyright ownership: Edward Arnold (Publisher)
Rejected manuscripts: Returned at author's request
Time before publication decision: 6 mos.
Time between decision and publication: 6 mos.
Number of reviewers: 2
Articles submitted per year: 40
Articles published per year: 15
Book reviews submitted per year: 6
Book reviews published per year: 9
Notes submitted per year: 2
Notes published per year: 1

(2573)
*Sefarad: Revista de Estudios Hebraicos, Sefardies y de Oriente Proximo

Victoria Spottorno, Editor
Inst. de Filología
c/o Consejo Superior de Investigaciones Científicas
Duque de Medinaceli, 6
28014 Madrid, Spain

Telephone: (34) 1 5856000
Fax: (34) 1 5856197
First published: 1941
Sponsoring organization: Inst. de Filología, Consejo Superior de Investigaciones Científicas
ISSN: 0037-0894
MLA acronym: Sefarad

SUBSCRIPTION INFORMATION

Frequency of publication: 2 times/yr.
Circulation: 600
Available in microform: No
Subscription price: 6,000 Pta/yr. outside Spain
Year to which price refers: 1992
Subscription address: Dept. de Publicaciones del C.S.I.C., Vitruvio 8, 28006 Madrid, Spain
Subscription telephone: (34) 1 2629633
Subscription fax: (34) 1 2629634

ADVERTISING INFORMATION

Advertising accepted: No

EDITORIAL DESCRIPTION

Scope: Publishes articles on Hebraic, Near Eastern, and Sephardic studies.
Reviews books: Yes
Publishes notes: Yes
Languages accepted: English; French; German; Italian; Spanish
Prints abstracts: Yes

SUBMISSION REQUIREMENTS

Restrictions on contributors: None
Author pays submission fee: No
Author pays page charges: No
Length of articles: 25 pp.
Length of book reviews: No restrictions
Length of notes: No restrictions
Style: None
Number of copies required: 2
Special requirements: Submit original typescript and 1 copy. Notes and quotations in Hebrew, Greek, and other ancient languages are accepted in their original graphics. Transcriptions must follow *Sefarad* rules.
Copyright ownership: Journal
Rejected manuscripts: Returned

Time before publication decision: 1 mo.
Time between decision and publication: 1 yr.
Number of reviewers: 9
Articles submitted per year: 25
Articles published per year: 20
Book reviews published per year: 40

(2574)
*Seges: Etudes et Textes de Philologie et Littérature. Université de Fribourg Suisse/Studien und Texte zur Philologie und Literatur. Universität Freiburg Schweiz/Studi e Testi di Filologia e Letteratura. Università di Friburgo Svizzera

Rolf Fieguth & Edgar Marsch, Editors
Faculté des Lettres
Univ. de Fribourg
1700 Fribourg, Switzerland

Telephone: (41) 37 219546
Fax: (41) 37 219703
First published: 1963
Sponsoring organization: Conseil de l'Univ. de Fribourg
ISSN: 0582-3951
MLA acronym: Seges

SUBSCRIPTION INFORMATION

Frequency of publication: Irregular
Circulation: 600-2,500
Available in microform: No
Subscription address: Editions Universitaires, Pérolles, 1700 Fribourg, Switzerland

ADVERTISING INFORMATION

Advertising accepted: No

EDITORIAL DESCRIPTION

Scope: Publishes monographs on philological and literary texts and studies.
Reviews books: Yes
Publishes notes: No
Languages accepted: English; French; German; Italian
Prints abstracts: No
Author-anonymous submission: No

SUBMISSION REQUIREMENTS

Author pays submission fee: No
Author pays page charges: No
Length of books: No restrictions
Style: None
Number of copies required: 1
Copyright ownership: Author
Rejected manuscripts: Returned
Time before publication decision: 5 mos.
Time between decision and publication: 4-12 mos.
Number of reviewers: 2-4
Books published per year: 2-4

(2575)
*SEL: Studies in English Literature, 1500-1900

Robert L. Patten, Logan Browning, & Sally Hubbard, Editors
Rice Univ.
P.O. Box 1892
Houston, TX 77251-1892

Telephone: 713 527-8101 ext. 2649
Fax: 713 285-5207
First published: 1961
Sponsoring organization: Rice Univ.
ISSN: 0039-3657
MLA acronym: SEL

SUBSCRIPTION INFORMATION

Frequency of publication: 4 times/yr.
Circulation: 1,900
Available in microform: Yes
Subscription price: $30.00/yr. institutions US; $35.00/yr. institutions elsewhere; $25.00/yr. individuals; $8.00/single issue
Year to which price refers: 1992

ADVERTISING INFORMATION

Advertising accepted: Yes
Advertising rates: $150.00/half page; $250.00/full page; $300.00/back cover

EDITORIAL DESCRIPTION

Scope: Publishes articles on English literature, with each issue focusing on a specific period: Winter: English Renaissance; Spring: Elizabethan and Jacobean Drama; Summer: Restoration and Eighteenth Century; Autumn: Nineteenth Century.
Reviews books: Yes
Publishes notes: No
Languages accepted: English
Prints abstracts: No
Author-anonymous submission: Yes, at author's request.

SUBMISSION REQUIREMENTS

Restrictions on contributors: Unsolicited book reviews are not accepted.
Author pays submission fee: No
Author pays page charges: No
Length of articles: 20-25 pp.
Length of book reviews: 12,000 words
Style: Chicago
Number of copies required: 1
Special requirements: Submit original typescript or photocopy. No multiple submissions.
Copyright ownership: Assigned by author to Rice Univ.
Rejected manuscripts: Returned; enclose return postage.
Time before publication decision: 3 mos.
Time between decision and publication: 6-24 mos.
Number of reviewers: 2-3
Articles submitted per year: 160
Articles published per year: 36
Book reviews published per year: 4

(2576)
*Selecta: Journal of the Pacific Northwest Council on Foreign Languages

Craig W. Nickisch, Editor
Dept. of Foreign Languages
Campus Box 8067
Idaho State Univ.
Pocatello, ID 83209

First published: 1980
Sponsoring organization: Pacific Northwest Council on Foreign Languages (PNCFL)
ISSN: 0277-0598
MLA acronym: Selecta

SUBSCRIPTION INFORMATION

Frequency of publication: Annual
Circulation: 750
Available in microform: No
Subscription price: $12.00/yr.
Year to which price refers: 1992
Subscription address: Dept. of Foreign Languages & Literatures, Oregon State Univ., Kidder Hall 210, Corvallis, OR 97331-4603
Subscription telephone: 503 737-2146
Subscription fax: 503 737-2434

ADVERTISING INFORMATION

Advertising accepted: Yes
Advertising rates: $35.00/half page; $50.00/full page

EDITORIAL DESCRIPTION

Scope: Publishes articles on international literature, pedagogy, linguistics, and culture.
Reviews books: No
Publishes notes: No
Languages accepted: French; German; Spanish; Portuguese; Italian; English; Chinese transliterated; Japanese transliterated; Russian transliterated
Prints abstracts: No
Author-anonymous submission: Yes

SUBMISSION REQUIREMENTS

Restrictions on contributors: Contributors must be members of PNCFL and have delivered paper at annual meeting.
Author pays submission fee: No
Author pays page charges: No
Length of articles: 3,000 words
Style: MLA
Number of copies required: 2
Special requirements: Submit original manuscript and diskette.
Copyright ownership: PNCFL
Rejected manuscripts: Returned; enclose return postage.
Time before publication decision: 4-6 mos.
Time between decision and publication: 6 mos.
Number of reviewers: 3
Articles submitted per year: 60
Articles published per year: 25

(2577)
*Selected Bibliographies in Language and Literature

Joseph Gibaldi, Editor
Modern Language Assn. of America
10 Astor Place
New York, NY 10003-6981

Telephone: 212 614-6312
Fax: 212 477-9863
First published: 1980
Sponsoring organization: Modern Language Assn. of America
MLA acronym: SBLL

SUBSCRIPTION INFORMATION

Frequency of publication: Irregular
Available in microform: No

ADVERTISING INFORMATION

Advertising accepted: No

EDITORIAL DESCRIPTION

Scope: Publishes guides to reference and resource materials in languages and literatures.
Reviews books: No
Publishes notes: No
Languages accepted: English
Prints abstracts: No
Author-anonymous submission: No

SUBMISSION REQUIREMENTS

Restrictions on contributors: None
Author pays submission fee: No
Author pays page charges: No
Style: MLA
Number of copies required: 1
Copyright ownership: MLA
Rejected manuscripts: Returned
Time before publication decision: 3 mos.
Time between decision and publication: 1 yr.
Number of reviewers: 13

(2578)
Selected Reports in Ethnomusicology

Eran Fraenkel, Manager Editor
Ethnomusicology Publications
Dept. of Ethnomusicology & Systematic Musicology
Univ. of California, Los Angeles
405 Hilgard Ave.
Los Angeles, CA 90024-1657

First published: 1966
Sponsoring organization: Univ. of California, Los Angeles, Dept. of Ethnomusicology
ISSN: 0361-6622
MLA acronym: SRIELA

SUBSCRIPTION INFORMATION

Frequency of publication: Annual
Circulation: 1,000
Available in microform: No

ADVERTISING INFORMATION

Advertising accepted: No

EDITORIAL DESCRIPTION

Scope: Publishes articles on ethnomusicological theory, methods, world areas, comparative analysis in music, and anthropology of music.
Reviews books: No
Publishes notes: No
Languages accepted: English; French
Prints abstracts: No
Author-anonymous submission: Yes

SUBMISSION REQUIREMENTS

Restrictions on contributors: Articles are solicited.
Author pays submission fee: No
Author pays page charges: No
Style: Chicago
Number of copies required: 1
Special requirements: Submit original typescript and IBM or Macintosh format diskette.
Copyright ownership: Regents of Univ. of California
Rejected manuscripts: Returned
Time between decision and publication: 9-12 mos.
Number of reviewers: 2-3
Articles published per year: 7-10

(2579)
*Seminar: A Journal of Germanic Studies

Rodney Symington, Editor
Dept. of Germanic Studies
Univ. of Victoria
P.O. Box 3045
Victoria, BC V8W 3P4, Canada

Telephone: 604 721-7323
Fax: 604 721-8873
E-mail: SYMINGTO@UVVM.CA (Bitnet)
First published: 1965
Sponsoring organization: Canadian Assn. of Univ. Teachers of German
ISSN: 0037-1939
MLA acronym: Seminar

SUBSCRIPTION INFORMATION

Frequency of publication: 4 times/yr. (Feb., May, Sept., Nov.)
Circulation: 850-1,100
Available in microform: Yes
Subscription price: C$35.00/yr.
Year to which price refers: 1992
Subscription address: Periodicals Dept., Univ. of Toronto Press, Toronto, Ontario, M5S 1A6, Canada
Subscription fax: 416 667-7832

ADVERTISING INFORMATION

Advertising accepted: Yes

EDITORIAL DESCRIPTION

Scope: Publishes articles on Germanic studies.
Reviews books: Yes
Publishes notes: No
Languages accepted: English; French; German
Prints abstracts: No
Author-anonymous submission: Yes

SUBMISSION REQUIREMENTS

Restrictions on contributors: Book reviews are solicited.
Author pays submission fee: No
Author pays page charges: No
Length of articles: No restrictions
Length of book reviews: No restrictions
Style: MLA
Number of copies required: 2
Copyright ownership: Canadian Assn. of Univ. Teachers of German
Rejected manuscripts: Returned
Time before publication decision: 2-4 mos.
Time between decision and publication: 1 yr.
Number of reviewers: 3
Articles submitted per year: 50
Articles published per year: 20
Book reviews published per year: 40-50

(2580)
*Semiosis: Internationale Zeitschrift für Semiotik und Ästhetik

Elisabeth Walther, Udo Bayer, & Juliane Hansen, Editors
Am Gänsborg 16/1
7269 Deckenpfronn, Germany

Additional editorial address: Elisabeth Walther, Alte Weinsteige 98, 7000 Stuttgart 70, Germany
Telephone: (49) 7056 2324; (49) 711 764668
First published: 1976
Sponsoring organization: Vereinigung für Wissenschaftliche Semiotik; Forschungsgruppe für Semiotik & Wissensdraftsheorie der Univ. Stuttgart; Inst. de Recherche en Sciences de la Communication & de l'Education, Faculté Pluridisciplinaire des Sciences Humaines & Sociales, Perpignan
ISSN: 0170-219X
MLA acronym: Semiosis

SUBSCRIPTION INFORMATION

Frequency of publication: 4 times/yr.
Circulation: 30
Available in microform: No
Subscription price: 43 DM/yr.; 34.40 DM/yr. students
Year to which price refers: 1991
Subscription address: Agis-Verlag GmbH, Postfach 2220, 7570 Baden-Baden, Germany
Subscription telephone: (49) 7221 64024
Subscription fax: (49) 7221 66810

ADVERTISING INFORMATION

Advertising accepted: Yes

EDITORIAL DESCRIPTION

Scope: Publishes articles on general semiotics, Peirce studies, logical and philosophical semiotics, and informational and semiotical aesthetics.
Reviews books: Yes
Publishes notes: Yes
Languages accepted: English; French; German; Italian; Spanish
Prints abstracts: Yes
Author-anonymous submission: No

SUBMISSION REQUIREMENTS

Restrictions on contributors: None
Author pays submission fee: No
Author pays page charges: No
Length of articles: 15 pp.
Length of book reviews: 1-3 pp.
Length of notes: 200-300 words
Style: None
Number of copies required: 1
Special requirements: Include a summary.
Copyright ownership: Author
Rejected manuscripts: Returned
Time before publication decision: 3-6 mos.
Time between decision and publication: 3-6 mos.
Number of reviewers: 2-4
Articles submitted per year: 40-50
Articles published per year: 30-40
Book reviews submitted per year: 10-14
Book reviews published per year: 10
Notes submitted per year: 10-20
Notes published per year: 10

(2581)
Semiosis: Seminario de Semiótica, Teoría, Análsis

Renato Prada Oropeza, Editor
Centro de Investigaciones Linguístico-Literarias
Apartado Postal 369
91000 Xalapa, Veracruz, Mexico

First published: 1978
Sponsoring organization: Univ. Veracruzana
ISSN: 0187-9316
MLA acronym: SCSSL

SUBSCRIPTION INFORMATION

Frequency of publication: 2 times/yr.
Available in microform: No

ADVERTISING INFORMATION

Advertising accepted: Yes, on an exchange basis

EDITORIAL DESCRIPTION

Scope: Focuses on semiotic theories and analyses.
Reviews books: Yes
Publishes notes: Yes
Languages accepted: Spanish
Prints abstracts: No

SUBMISSION REQUIREMENTS

Restrictions on contributors: None
Author pays submission fee: No
Author pays page charges: No
Length of articles: 15-50 pp.
Length of book reviews: 10 pp.
Length of notes: 10 pp. maximum
Style: MLA
Number of copies required: 2
Special requirements: English, French, and Italian submissions are translated into Spanish. Submit original typescript. Each page should contain 28 lines of 10 words each.
Copyright ownership: Univ. Veracruzana
Rejected manuscripts: Not returned
Time before publication decision: 1 mo.
Time between decision and publication: 6 mos.
Number of reviewers: 2
Articles submitted per year: 15
Articles published per year: 12
Book reviews submitted per year: 2-4
Book reviews published per year: 2-4
Notes submitted per year: 12
Notes published per year: 10

(2582)
Semiotext(e)

Sylvère Lotringer & Jim Fleming, Editors
P.O. Box 568
Brooklyn, NY 11211-0568

Telephone: 718 387-6471
Fax: 718 387-6471
First published: 1974
Sponsoring organization: National Endowment for the Arts; New York State Council on the Arts; Coordinating Council of Literary Magazines
ISSN: 0093-9579
MLA acronym: Semiotext(e)

SUBSCRIPTION INFORMATION

Frequency of publication: 3 times/yr. (irregular)
Circulation: 5,000
Available in microform: No

ADVERTISING INFORMATION

Advertising accepted: No

EDITORIAL DESCRIPTION

Scope: Focus is on analyzing the power mechanisms which produce and maintain the present divisions of knowledge (psychoanalysis, linguistics, literature, philosophy, semiotics).
Reviews books: No
Publishes notes: No
Languages accepted: English
Prints abstracts: No
Author-anonymous submission: No

SUBMISSION REQUIREMENTS

Restrictions on contributors: None
Author pays submission fee: No
Author pays page charges: No
Length of articles: No restrictions
Style: MLA
Number of copies required: 2
Copyright ownership: Assigned to journal
Rejected manuscripts: Not returned
Time before publication decision: 3 mos.
Time between decision and publication: 12-18 mos.
Number of reviewers: Editors
Articles submitted per year: 20
Articles published per year: 50

(2583)
*Semiotic Crossroads

Paul Perron, Editor
Dept. of French
Univ. of Toronto
7 King's College Circle
Toronto, Ontario M5S 1A1, Canada

First published: 1988
ISSN: 0922-5072
MLA acronym: SemCross

SUBSCRIPTION INFORMATION

Frequency of publication: Irregular
Subscription address: John Benjamins B.V., Amsteldijk 44, P.O. Box 75577, 1070 AN Amsterdam, Netherlands
Additional subscription address: John Benjamins North America, Inc., 821 Bethlehem Pike, Philadelphia, PA 19118
Subscription fax: (31) 20 6739773; 215 836-1204

ADVERTISING INFORMATION

Advertising accepted: No

EDITORIAL DESCRIPTION

Scope: Publishes monographs on current tendencies in semiotic research.
Reviews books: No
Publishes notes: No
Languages accepted: English
Prints abstracts: No
Author-anonymous submission: No

SUBMISSION REQUIREMENTS

Author pays submission fee: No
Author pays page charges: No
Number of copies required: 2
Copyright ownership: John Benjamins B.V.
Rejected manuscripts: Returned
Time before publication decision: 6 mos.
Time between decision and publication: 1 yr.
Number of reviewers: 2
Books submitted per year: 6
Books published per year: 2-3

(2584)
*Semiotica: Journal of the International Association for Semiotic Studies/Revue de l'Association Internationale de Sémiotique

Thomas A. Sebeok, Editor
Research Center for Language & Semiotic Studies
Indiana Univ.
P.O. Box 10
Bloomington, IN 47402

Telephone: 812 855-1567
Fax: 812 855-1273
E-mail: SEBEOK@IUBACS (Bitnet);
 SEBEOK@UCS.INDIANA.EDU (Internet)
First published: 1969
Sponsoring organization: International Assn. for Semiotic Studies
ISSN: 0037-1998
MLA acronym: Semiotica

SUBSCRIPTION INFORMATION

Frequency of publication: 10 times/yr. (5 vols.-/yr., 2 double issues/vol.)
Available in microform: No
Subscription price: $473.55/yr. institutions; $181.20/yr. IASS members
Year to which price refers: 1991
Subscription address: Walter de Gruyter, Inc., 200 Saw Mill River Rd., Hawthorne, NY 10532
Subscription telephone: 914 747-0110
Subscription fax: 914 747-1326

ADVERTISING INFORMATION

Advertising accepted: Yes

EDITORIAL DESCRIPTION

Scope: The editor invites contributions from all who are interested in developing semiotic concepts within the lines of their own field of inquiry.
Reviews books: Yes
Publishes notes: No
Languages accepted: English; French
Prints abstracts: No
Author-anonymous submission: No

SUBMISSION REQUIREMENTS

Restrictions on contributors: None
Author pays submission fee: No
Author pays page charges: No
Length of articles: No restrictions
Length of book reviews: No restrictions
Style: Journal
Number of copies required: 2
Special requirements: Submit original typescript.

Copyright ownership: Mouton de Gruyter Publishers
Rejected manuscripts: Returned at author's request
Time before publication decision: 3 mos.
Time between decision and publication: 2 yrs.
Number of reviewers: 3
Articles submitted per year: 120
Articles published per year: 55
Book reviews submitted per year: 40
Book reviews published per year: 30

(2585)
Senara: Revista de Filoloxía

Manuel Cahada Gómez, Matilde Mansilla García, & José Ramón Losada Durán, Editors
Colegio Univ. de Vigo
Aptdo. 874
Vigo, Spain

First published: 1979
Sponsoring organization: Colegio Univ. de Vigo
ISSN: 0211-464X
MLA acronym: Senara

SUBSCRIPTION INFORMATION

Frequency of publication: Annual
Available in microform: No

ADVERTISING INFORMATION

Advertising accepted: No

EDITORIAL DESCRIPTION

Scope: Publishes articles on linguistics, literature, and literary theory with an emphasis on Spanish studies.
Reviews books: Yes
Publishes notes: Yes
Languages accepted: French; Galician; German; Basque; Italian; Portuguese; Catalan; English; Spanish
Prints abstracts: Yes

SUBMISSION REQUIREMENTS

Author pays submission fee: No
Author pays page charges: No
Length of articles: 25,000 words maximum
Length of book reviews: 1,000-2,000 words
Length of notes: 500-1,000 words
Style: MLA
Number of copies required: 2
Special requirements: Submit double-spaced typescript.
Time before publication decision: 3-12 mos.
Time between decision and publication: 1 mo.
Number of reviewers: 4
Articles submitted per year: 30
Articles published per year: 6
Book reviews submitted per year: 6

(2586)
*Serie de Vocabularios y Diccionarios Indigenas "Mariano Silva y Aceves"

Doris Bartholomew & Louise Schoenhals, Editors
Summer Inst. of Linguistics
P.O. Box 8987 CRB
Tucson, AZ 85738-0987

Additional editorial address: Inst. Linguistico de Verano, Hidalgo 78, Colonia Nino Jesus, Tlalpan, D.F. 14080, Mexico
Telephone: 602 825-6000
Fax: 602 825-6116
First published: 1959
Sponsoring organization: Summer Inst. of Linguistics
ISSN: 0559-5401
MLA acronym: SVDI

SUBSCRIPTION INFORMATION

Frequency of publication: Irregular
Circulation: 1,000
Available in microform: Yes

ADVERTISING INFORMATION

Advertising accepted: No

EDITORIAL DESCRIPTION

Scope: Publishes dictionaries of Mexican Indian languages.
Reviews books: No
Publishes notes: No
Languages accepted: Spanish
Prints abstracts: No
Author-anonymous submission: No

SUBMISSION REQUIREMENTS

Restrictions on contributors: Contributors must be members of the Summer Inst. of Linguistics.
Author pays submission fee: No
Author pays page charges: No
Length of books: 5,000 entries on Idiom side
Style: Own style for bilingual dictionary entries; outline for grammar sections
Number of copies required: 1
Special requirements: Manuscripts in individual indigenous languages are accepted.
Copyright ownership: Summer Inst. of Linguistics
Rejected manuscripts: Returned
Time before publication decision: 2-3 mos.
Time between decision and publication: 1-2 yrs.
Number of reviewers: 3
Books submitted per year: 2-3
Books published per year: 0-4

(2587)
*Serie Linguistica

Tribal Affairs Dept.
Summer Inst. of Linguistics
Dept. of Pesquisas Lingüísticas
SAIN, Lote D, Bloco 3
70770 Brasilia, D.F., Brazil

First published: 1973
Sponsoring organization: Summer Inst. of Linguistics, Brazil
ISSN: 0102-6526
MLA acronym: SerL

SUBSCRIPTION INFORMATION

Frequency of publication: Irregular
Circulation: 300
Available in microform: No

ADVERTISING INFORMATION

Advertising accepted: No

EDITORIAL DESCRIPTION

Scope: Publishes data-oriented linguistic papers on Brazilian indigenous languages.
Reviews books: No
Publishes notes: No
Languages accepted: Portuguese; English
Prints abstracts: Yes

SUBMISSION REQUIREMENTS

Restrictions on contributors: Contributors must be members or trainees of the Summer Inst. of Linguistics or have participated in one of its field seminars.
Author pays submission fee: No
Author pays page charges: No
Style: MLA
Number of copies required: 1
Special requirements: Submit original typescript.
Copyright ownership: Author

Rejected manuscripts: Returned to Brazilian authors only
Time before publication decision: 3 mos.
Time between decision and publication: 4 yrs.
Number of reviewers: 2

(2588)
*Serie Lingüística Peruana

Mary Ruth Wise, Editor
Inst. Lingüístico de Verano
Casilla 2492
Lima 100, Peru

Telephone: (51) 14 287993
Fax: (51) 14 629629
First published: 1963
Sponsoring organization: Summer Inst. of Linguistics
ISSN: 0885-8691
MLA acronym: SLP

SUBSCRIPTION INFORMATION

Frequency of publication: Irregular
Circulation: 300
Available in microform: Yes
Subscription address: E. Iturriaga y Cia., Jiron Ica 441-OF.202-203, Casilla 4640, Lima, Peru

ADVERTISING INFORMATION

Advertising accepted: No

EDITORIAL DESCRIPTION

Scope: Publishes descriptive and theoretical works on indigenous Peruvian languages, as well as bilingual dictionaries.
Reviews books: No
Publishes notes: Yes
Languages accepted: Spanish
Prints abstracts: No
Author-anonymous submission: No

SUBMISSION REQUIREMENTS

Restrictions on contributors: Contributors must be members or associates of the Summer Inst. of Linguistics.
Author pays submission fee: No
Author pays page charges: No
Length of books: 25,000-75,000 words
Length of notes: 2,000 words minimum
Style: MLA with modifications
Number of copies required: 1
Copyright ownership: Summer Inst. of Linguistics
Rejected manuscripts: Returned
Time before publication decision: 6-24 mos.
Time between decision and publication: 1-36 mos.
Number of reviewers: 2
Books submitted per year: 2-3
Books published per year: 1-3

(2589)
Serpe: Rivista Letteraria

Fausto Federici, Editor
Assn. dei Medici Scrittori Italiani
Via Concordia, 20
00183 Rome, Italy

First published: 1952
Sponsoring organization: Assn. dei Medici Scrittori Italiani
ISSN: 0037-2498
MLA acronym: Serpe

SUBSCRIPTION INFORMATION

Frequency of publication: 4 times/yr.
Circulation: 12,000
Available in microform: No

ADVERTISING INFORMATION

Advertising accepted: Yes

EDITORIAL DESCRIPTION

Scope: Publishes articles on modern literature.
Reviews books: Yes
Languages accepted: Italian; French
Prints abstracts: No

SUBMISSION REQUIREMENTS

Restrictions on contributors: None
Author pays submission fee: No
Author pays page charges: No
Length of articles: No restrictions
Style: None
Number of copies required: 1
Copyright ownership: Assigned by author to journal
Rejected manuscripts: Not returned
Time between decision and publication: 3 mos.
Number of reviewers: 2
Articles published per year: 50

(2590)
*The Seventeenth Century

Richard Maber, Editor
Centre for 17th Century Studies
Univ. Library
Palace Green
Durham, DH1 3RN, England

Telephone: (44) 91 3742721
Fax: (44) 91 3743740
First published: 1986
Sponsoring organization: Durham Centre for 17th Century Studies
ISSN: 0268-117X
MLA acronym: SCen

SUBSCRIPTION INFORMATION

Frequency of publication: 2 times/yr. (Spring, Autumn)
Circulation: 350
Available in microform: No
Subscription price: £18.00/yr. institutions; £12.00/yr. individuals
Year to which price refers: 1992

ADVERTISING INFORMATION

Advertising accepted: Yes
Advertising rates: £25.00/half page; £40.00/full page; £30.00/insert

EDITORIAL DESCRIPTION

Scope: Publishes articles on all aspects of the 17th century. Emphasizes articles of an interdisciplinary nature, as well as articles embodying original research.
Reviews books: No
Publishes notes: No
Languages accepted: English
Prints abstracts: No
Author-anonymous submission: No

SUBMISSION REQUIREMENTS

Restrictions on contributors: None
Author pays submission fee: No
Author pays page charges: No
Length of articles: 10,000 words maximum
Style: Modern Humanities Research Assn.
Number of copies required: 2
Copyright ownership: Journal
Rejected manuscripts: Returned
Time before publication decision: 3-4 mos.
Time between decision and publication: 6-12 mos
Number of reviewers: 2-3
Articles submitted per year: 40
Articles published per year: 10-12

(2591)
*Seventeenth-Century French Studies

C. N. Smith, Editor
School of Modern Languages & European Studies
Univ. of East Anglia
Norwich NR4 7TJ, England

Telephone: (44) 603 56161 ext. 2139
Fax: (44) 603 58553
First published: 1979
Sponsoring organization: Soc. for Seventeenth-Century French Studies
ISSN: 0265-1068
MLA acronym: SCFS

SUBSCRIPTION INFORMATION

Frequency of publication: Annual
Circulation: 300
Available in microform: No
Subscription price: £8.00/yr. institutions; £6.00/yr. individuals
Year to which price refers: 1992

ADVERTISING INFORMATION

Advertising accepted: Yes

EDITORIAL DESCRIPTION

Scope: Publishes articles on all aspects of French life, literature, art, culture, history, music and science in the 17th century.
Reviews books: Yes
Publishes notes: Yes
Languages accepted: English; French
Prints abstracts: No
Author-anonymous submission: No

SUBMISSION REQUIREMENTS

Restrictions on contributors: Book reviews are solicited.
Author pays submission fee: No
Author pays page charges: No
Length of articles: 6,000 words maximum
Length of book reviews: 2,500-6,000 words
Length of notes: No restrictions
Style: Modern Humanities Research Assn.
Number of copies required: 2
Special requirements: Notes should appear in single numerical sequence at end of manuscript.
Copyright ownership: Soc. for Seventeenth-Century French Studies
Rejected manuscripts: Returned
Time before publication decision: 1 yr.
Time between decision and publication: 3 mos.
Number of reviewers: 2
Articles submitted per year: 25
Articles published per year: 15
Book reviews published per year: 3
Notes submitted per year: 2
Notes published per year: 2

(2592)
*Seventeenth-Century News

Harrison T. Meserole & J. Max Patrick, Editors
English Dept.
Blocker Bldg.
Texas A&M Univ.
College Station, TX 77843-4227

Telephone: 409 845-3400
First published: 1941
Sponsoring organization: Milton Soc. of America; MLA, Milton Section of the Division on Seventeenth-Century English Studies
ISSN: 0037-3028
MLA acronym: SCN

SUBSCRIPTION INFORMATION

Frequency of publication: 4 times/yr. (Spring, Summer, Fall, Winter)
Circulation: 1,500

Available in microform: Yes
Subscription price: $9.00/yr. US; $13.00/yr. elsewhere
Year to which price refers: 1991

ADVERTISING INFORMATION

Advertising accepted: Yes
Advertising rates: $80.00/quarter page; $150.00/half page; $250.00/full page

EDITORIAL DESCRIPTION

Scope: Covers all aspects of 17th-century culture, English, American, and European, with emphasis on literature and history. It enables specialists and nonspecialists to keep abreast of new books and articles about Donne, Milton, and Dryden; Bacon, Browne, and Burton; the dramatists (except Shakespeare); the most recent work on the Metaphysicals and the Cavaliers; Meditative Poetry and Mannerism; the Baroque and Scientific Movements; and all other aspects, major and minor, of 17th-century life and thought. Published with *SCN* is *Neo-Latin News*, which covers all scholarship on literature and ideas in Latin from 1500 to the present.
Reviews books: Yes
Publishes notes: Yes
Languages accepted: English
Prints abstracts: Yes
Author-anonymous submission: No

SUBMISSION REQUIREMENTS

Restrictions on contributors: Reviews are commissioned.
Author pays submission fee: No
Author pays page charges: No
Length of articles: 3,500-4,000 words
Length of book reviews: 750-1,000 words
Length of notes: 1,000 words
Style: MLA
Number of copies required: 2
Special requirements: Submit original double-spaced typescript on 8 1/2 in. x 11 in. white paper.
Copyright ownership: Author
Rejected manuscripts: Returned; enclose return postage.
Time before publication decision: 8-10 weeks
Time between decision and publication: 12-18 mos.
Number of reviewers: 2-3
Articles submitted per year: 30-40
Articles published per year: 4-5
Book reviews published per year: 60-70
Notes submitted per year: 40-50
Notes published per year: 4-5

(2593)
Sewanee Review

George Core, Editor
Univ. of the South
Sewanee, TN 37375

First published: 1892
Sponsoring organization: Univ. of the South
ISSN: 0037-3052
MLA acronym: SR

SUBSCRIPTION INFORMATION

Frequency of publication: 4 times/yr. (Jan., Apr., July, Oct.)
Circulation: 3,500
Available in microform: Yes

ADVERTISING INFORMATION

Advertising accepted: Yes

EDITORIAL DESCRIPTION

Scope: A literary quarterly devoted to criticism, fiction, and poetry.
Reviews books: Yes
Publishes notes: No
Languages accepted: English
Prints abstracts: No
Author-anonymous submission: No

SUBMISSION REQUIREMENTS

Restrictions on contributors: Book reviews are solicited.
Author pays submission fee: No
Author pays page charges: No
Length of articles: 5,000-7,500 words
Length of book reviews: 900 words for short reviews; 1,500-4,000 words for review articles
Style: Chicago
Number of copies required: 1
Special requirements: Submit original typescript.
Copyright ownership: Partial rights may be assigned by author to journal for creative work. Publisher holds copyright for all commissioned work.
Rejected manuscripts: Returned; enclose return postage and envelope. Acknowledged if author sends stamped postcard.
Time before publication decision: 3-4 weeks
Time between decision and publication: 6-9 mos.
Number of reviewers: 1-2
Articles published per year: 130
Book reviews published per year: 56

(2594)
*Shakespeare and Renaissance Association of West Virginia—Selected Papers

Edmund M. Taft, Editor
Dept. of English
Marshall Univ.
Huntington, WV 25755-2646

Telephone: 304 696-3155
First published: 1976
Historical variations in title: Also known as *Selected Papers from the West Virginia Shakespeare and Renaissance Association*
Sponsoring organization: West Virginia Shakespeare & Renaissance Assn.
ISSN: 0885-9574
MLA acronym: SPWVSRA

SUBSCRIPTION INFORMATION

Frequency of publication: Annual
Circulation: 200
Available in microform: No
Subscription price: $5.00/yr.
Year to which price refers: 1992

ADVERTISING INFORMATION

Advertising accepted: No

EDITORIAL DESCRIPTION

Scope: Publishes articles from the annual conference concerning Shakespeare and Renaissance literature and pedagogy.
Reviews books: Yes
Publishes notes: No
Languages accepted: English
Prints abstracts: No
Author-anonymous submission: No

SUBMISSION REQUIREMENTS

Restrictions on contributors: Contributors must deliver paper at annual meeting.
Author pays submission fee: No
Author pays page charges: No
Length of articles: 2,500-5,000 words
Length of book reviews: 1,000-2,000 words
Style: MLA
Number of copies required: 1
Copyright ownership: West Virginia Shakespeare & Renaissance Assn.
Rejected manuscripts: Returned

Time before publication decision: 2 mos.
Time between decision and publication: 6 mos.
Number of reviewers: 2
Articles submitted per year: 24-30
Articles published per year: 6-10
Book reviews submitted per year: 1-3
Book reviews published per year: 1-3

(2595)
*Shakespeare Bulletin: A Journal of Performance Criticism and Scholarship

James P. Lusardi & June Schlueter, Editors
English Dept.
Lafayette College
Easton, PA 18042

Telephone: 215 250-5245; 215 250-5248
Fax: 215 250-9850
First published: 1982
Sponsoring organization: Lafayette College
ISSN: 0748-2558
MLA acronym: ShakB

SUBSCRIPTION INFORMATION

Frequency of publication: 4 times/yr.
Circulation: 500
Available in microform: No
Subscription price: $15.00/yr.
Year to which price refers: 1993

ADVERTISING INFORMATION

Advertising accepted: Yes
Advertising rates: $25.00/quarter page; $40.00/half page; $75.00/full page

EDITORIAL DESCRIPTION

Scope: Provides ongoing commentary on matters pertaining to Shakespeare and Renaissance drama through feature articles and theatre and book reviews.
Reviews books: Yes
Publishes notes: Yes
Languages accepted: English
Prints abstracts: No
Author-anonymous submission: No

SUBMISSION REQUIREMENTS

Restrictions on contributors: Theater and book reviews are commissioned.
Author pays submission fee: No
Author pays page charges: No
Length of articles: 20 pp. maximum
Length of book reviews: 750 words; Theater reviews: 1,000 words
Length of notes: 300 words
Style: MLA
Number of copies required: 1
Special requirements: Submit original single-spaced typescript or computer diskette using WordPerfect or Nota Bene.
Copyright ownership: Journal
Rejected manuscripts: Returned
Time before publication decision: 1-4 mos.
Time between decision and publication: 1-3 mos.
Number of reviewers: 2
Articles submitted per year: 50
Articles published per year: 20
Book reviews published per year: 30
Notes submitted per year: 10
Notes published per year: 5

(2596)
*Shakespeare in Southern Africa: Journal of the Shakespeare Society of Southern Africa

Laurence Wright, Hilary Semple, & Temple Hauptfleisch, Editors
Shakespeare Soc. of Southern Africa
Inst. for the Study of English in Africa
Rhodes Univ.
6140 Grahamstown, South Africa

First published: 1987
Sponsoring organization: Shakespeare Soc. of Southern Africa
ISSN: 1011-582X
MLA acronym: ShSA

SUBSCRIPTION INFORMATION

Frequency of publication: Annual (May)
Circulation: 350
Available in microform: No
Subscription price: 20 R ($20.00)/yr.
Year to which price refers: 1992

ADVERTISING INFORMATION

Advertising accepted: No

EDITORIAL DESCRIPTION

Scope: Publishes articles, commentary, and reviews on all aspects of Shakespearean studies and performance, with a particular emphasis on the response to Shakespeare in southern Africa.
Reviews books: Yes
Publishes notes: Yes
Languages accepted: English
Prints abstracts: No
Author-anonymous submission: Yes, at author's request

SUBMISSION REQUIREMENTS

Restrictions on contributors: None
Author pays submission fee: No
Author pays page charges: No
Length of articles: 10,000 words
Length of book reviews: 5,000 words
Length of notes: 1,000 words maximum
Style: MLA; Journal
Number of copies required: 2
Special requirements: Submit double-spaced typescript on size A4 (8 1/4 in. x 11 3/4 in.) paper. Submit also current professional designation (as appropriate) and details of recent publications.
Copyright ownership: Shakespeare Soc. of Southern Africa
Rejected manuscripts: Returned
Time before publication decision: 2 mos.
Time between decision and publication: 1-11 mos.
Number of reviewers: 4
Articles submitted per year: 10
Articles published per year: 5
Book reviews submitted per year: 5
Book reviews published per year: 5

(2597)
*Shakespeare-Jahrbuch

Günther Klotz, Editor
Berolinastr. 9
1020 Berlin, Germany

Telephone: (37) 2 4397274
Fax: (37) 2 4397274
First published: 1865
Sponsoring organization: Deutsche Shakespeare-Gesellschaft
ISSN: 0080-9128
MLA acronym: ShJE

SUBSCRIPTION INFORMATION

Frequency of publication: Annual (Apr.)
Available in microform: No
Subscription price: 32 DM/yr.
Year to which price refers: 1992
Subscription address: Deutsche Shakespeare-Gesellschaft, Markt 13, 5300 Weimar, Germany

ADVERTISING INFORMATION

Advertising accepted: No

EDITORIAL DESCRIPTION

Scope: Publishes Shakespeare studies.
Reviews books: Yes
Publishes notes: No
Languages accepted: German; English
Prints abstracts: No
Author-anonymous submission: No

SUBMISSION REQUIREMENTS

Restrictions on contributors: None
Author pays submission fee: No
Author pays page charges: No
Length of articles: 400-750 typescript lines
Length of book reviews: 90 typescript lines
Style: Journal
Number of copies required: 2
Copyright ownership: Author
Rejected manuscripts: Returned; enclose return postage.
Time before publication decision: 3 mos.
Time between decision and publication: 15 mos. maximum
Number of reviewers: 2-5
Articles submitted per year: 20-40
Articles published per year: 12-16
Book reviews published per year: 10-40

(2598)
*The Shakespeare Newsletter

John W. Mahon & Thomas A. Pendleton, Editors
English Dept.
Iona College
New Rochelle, NY 10801

Telephone: 914 633-2061
Fax: 914 633-2608
First published: 1951
ISSN: 0037-3214
MLA acronym: ShN

SUBSCRIPTION INFORMATION

Frequency of publication: 4 times/yr.
Circulation: 1,850
Available in microform: No
Subscription price: $12.00/yr. US; $14.00/yr. elsewhere
Year to which price refers: 1992

ADVERTISING INFORMATION

Advertising accepted: Yes
Advertising rates: $230.00/half page; $420.00/full page

EDITORIAL DESCRIPTION

Scope: Survey of scholarly and popular Shakespeareana. Includes digests of articles, lectures, dissertations, book news, brief original articles, and Shakespearean Festival programs.
Reviews books: Yes
Publishes notes: Yes
Languages accepted: English
Prints abstracts: Yes
Author-anonymous submission: No

SUBMISSION REQUIREMENTS

Restrictions on contributors: Articles are usually solicited but are also accepted if written for the journal. Reviews are solicited.
Author pays submission fee: No
Author pays page charges: No
Length of articles: 1,500 words maximum
Length of book reviews: 250 words
Length of notes: 250-1,500 words
Style: MLA; Chicago
Number of copies required: 1
Special requirements: Submit typescript. Factual articles are preferred. Purely critical articles may be accepted. Footnotes should be included in text. Inquiry to editor is recommended.
Copyright ownership: Author
Rejected manuscripts: Returned; enclose SASE.
Number of reviewers: 2
Articles submitted per year: 6-12
Articles published per year: 6-12
Book reviews published per year: 30-50
Notes published per year: 25

(2599)
*Shakespeare Quarterly

Barbara A. Mowat, Editor
Folger Shakespeare Library
201 E. Capitol St. SE
Washington, DC 20003-1094

Telephone: 202 544-4600 ext. 249
Fax: 202 544-4623
First published: 1950
Sponsoring organization: Folger Shakespeare Library
ISSN: 0037-3222
MLA acronym: SQ

SUBSCRIPTION INFORMATION

Frequency of publication: 4 times/yr. (Spring, Summer, Fall, Winter) plus Bibliography (Winter supplement)
Circulation: 3,500
Available in microform: Yes
Subscription price: $55.00/yr. institutions US; $60.00/yr. institutions elsewhere; $30.00-$40.00/yr. individuals US; $25.00-$50.00/yr. individuals elsewhere
Year to which price refers: 1992
Subscription telephone: 202 544-4600 ext. 251
Subscription fax: 202 544-4623

ADVERTISING INFORMATION

Advertising accepted: Yes
Advertising rates: $150.00/half page; $225.00/full page

EDITORIAL DESCRIPTION

Scope: Publishes critical articles and notes on Shakespeare, his works, and his age; book and theater reviews about current Shakespearean scholarship and drama; and the annual World Shakespeare Bibliography.
Reviews books: Yes
Publishes notes: Yes
Languages accepted: English
Prints abstracts: No
Author-anonymous submission: No

SUBMISSION REQUIREMENTS

Restrictions on contributors: None
Author pays submission fee: No
Author pays page charges: No
Length of articles: 20 typescript pp.
Length of book reviews: 1,000 words
Length of notes: 500-1,500 words
Style: MLA; Chicago, 12th ed.
Number of copies required: 1
Special requirements: Submit original typescript.
Copyright ownership: Folger Shakespeare Library

Rejected manuscripts: Returned; enclose return postage & SAE.
Time before publication decision: 3 mos.
Time between decision and publication: 1-2 yrs.
Number of reviewers: 2-5
Articles submitted per year: 200
Articles published per year: 20
Book reviews submitted per year: 45
Book reviews published per year: 45
Notes submitted per year: 40
Notes published per year: 5

(2600)
*Shakespeare Studies

Yasunari Takahashi, Editor
Shakespeare Soc. of Japan
501 Kenkyusha Bldg.
9, 2-chome, Kanda Surugadai
Chiyoda-Ku, Tokyo 101, Japan

Telephone: (81) 3 32921050
First published: 1962
Sponsoring organization: Shakespeare Soc. of Japan
ISSN: 0582-9402
MLA acronym: ShStud

SUBSCRIPTION INFORMATION

Frequency of publication: Annual
Circulation: 800
Available in microform: No
Subscription price: 6,000 yen/yr. Japan; $5.00/yr. elsewhere
Year to which price refers: 1992

ADVERTISING INFORMATION

Advertising accepted: No

EDITORIAL DESCRIPTION

Scope: Publishes scholarly articles on Shakespeare and Elizabethan drama.
Reviews books: No
Publishes notes: No
Languages accepted: English
Prints abstracts: No
Author-anonymous submission: No

SUBMISSION REQUIREMENTS

Restrictions on contributors: Contributors must be members of the Shakespeare Soc. of Japan.
Author pays submission fee: No
Author pays page charges: No
Length of articles: 5,000-8,000 words
Style: MLA
Number of copies required: 2
Copyright ownership: Journal
Rejected manuscripts: Returned
Time before publication decision: 1 mo.
Time between decision and publication: 3 mos.
Number of reviewers: 4
Articles submitted per year: 10
Articles published per year: 3

(2601)
*Shakespeare Studies

J. Leeds Barroll & Barry Gaines, Editors
Dept. of English
Univ. of New Mexico
Albuquerque, NM 87131

Telephone: 505 277-4436
Fax: 505 277-5573
First published: 1965
ISSN: 0582-9399
MLA acronym: ShakS

SUBSCRIPTION INFORMATION

Frequency of publication: Annual
Circulation: 2,000

Available in microform: No

ADVERTISING INFORMATION

Advertising accepted: No

EDITORIAL DESCRIPTION

Scope: Publishes Shakespeare research and criticism.
Reviews books: Yes
Publishes notes: No
Languages accepted: English
Prints abstracts: No
Author-anonymous submission: No

SUBMISSION REQUIREMENTS

Restrictions on contributors: None
Author pays submission fee: No
Author pays page charges: No
Length of articles: No restrictions
Length of book reviews: No restrictions
Style: MLA
Number of copies required: 1
Copyright ownership: Assigned by author to journal
Rejected manuscripts: Returned
Time before publication decision: 6 mos.
Time between decision and publication: 1 yr.
Number of reviewers: 2-3
Articles submitted per year: 150
Articles published per year: 15
Book reviews published per year: 20

(2602)
*Shakespeare Survey: An Annual Survey of Shakespeare Studies and Production

Stanley Wells, Editor
Shakespeare Inst.
Church St.
Stratford-upon-Avon
Warwickshire CV37 6HP, England

First published: 1948
ISSN: 0080-9152
MLA acronym: ShS

SUBSCRIPTION INFORMATION

Frequency of publication: Annual
Circulation: 4,000
Available in microform: No
Subscription address: Cambridge Univ. Press, Edinburgh Bldg., Shaftsbury Rd., Cambridge CB2 2RU, England

ADVERTISING INFORMATION

Advertising accepted: No

EDITORIAL DESCRIPTION

Scope: Publishes scholarly and critical articles on all aspects of Shakespeare's work with an emphasis on literary criticism and scholarship. Also includes review articles on the previous year's publications in the field and a review of selected productions including the Royal Shakespeare Company's previous Stratford season.
Reviews books: Yes
Publishes notes: No
Languages accepted: English
Prints abstracts: No
Author-anonymous submission: No

SUBMISSION REQUIREMENTS

Restrictions on contributors: Book reviews are commissioned.
Author pays submission fee: No
Author pays page charges: No
Length of articles: 5,000 words maximum
Style: Journal; request style sheet from Editor.
Number of copies required: 1

Copyright ownership: Cambridge Univ. Press
Rejected manuscripts: Returned; enclose international reply coupons.
Time before publication decision: 3 mos.
Time between decision and publication: 1-2 yrs.
Number of reviewers: 3
Articles submitted per year: 90-120
Articles published per year: 16
Book reviews published per year: 3 review articles

(2603)
*Shakespeare Yearbook

Linda Kay Hoff, Joan Hartwig, Nicholas Radel, Peter Milward, & Buford Jones, Editors
Edwin Mellen Press
P.O. Box 450
Lewiston, NY 14092

First published: 1990
ISSN: 1045-9456
MLA acronym: ShY

SUBSCRIPTION INFORMATION

Frequency of publication: Annual (Spring)
Circulation: 300
Available in microform: No
Subscription telephone: 716 754-2788

ADVERTISING INFORMATION

Advertising accepted: Yes

EDITORIAL DESCRIPTION

Scope: Focuses on cultural continuity from the late medieval to the Elizabethan period. Publishes articles which deal with all influences on the Shakespearean corpus and culture.
Reviews books: Yes
Publishes notes: Yes
Languages accepted: English; German; French
Prints abstracts: No
Author-anonymous submission: No

SUBMISSION REQUIREMENTS

Restrictions on contributors: None
Author pays submission fee: No
Author pays page charges: No
Length of articles: 2,500-8,000 words
Length of book reviews: 750-1,000 words
Length of notes: 300 words
Style: MLA; Chicago
Number of copies required: 2
Special requirements: Submit double-spaced typescript.
Copyright ownership: Edwin Mellen Press
Rejected manuscripts: Returned
Time before publication decision: 3-6 mos.
Time between decision and publication: 6-18 mos.
Number of reviewers: 2
Articles submitted per year: 15
Articles published per year: 10-12

(2604)
*The Shandean: An Annual Devoted to Laurence Sterne and His Works

Peter de Voogd, W. G. Day, & Kenneth Monkman, Editors
P.O. Box 71851
1008 EB Amsterdam, Netherlands

Telephone: (31) 30 333380
First published: 1989
Sponsoring organization: Laurence Sterne Trust
ISSN: 0956-3083
MLA acronym: Shandean

SUBSCRIPTION INFORMATION

Frequency of publication: Annual

Circulation: 500
Available in microform: No
Subscription price: £20.00/yr. institutions; £14.00/yr. individuals
Year to which price refers: 1992

ADVERTISING INFORMATION

Advertising accepted: Yes
Advertising rates: £90.00/half page; £170.00/full page

EDITORIAL DESCRIPTION

Scope: Publishes critical and historical articles on all aspects of the life and work of Laurence Sterne. Much of the contents are based on unpublished material at Shandy Hall.
Reviews books: Yes
Publishes notes: Yes
Languages accepted: English
Prints abstracts: No
Author-anonymous submission: No

SUBMISSION REQUIREMENTS

Restrictions on contributors: None
Author pays submission fee: No
Author pays page charges: No
Style: MLA
Number of copies required: 1
Special requirements: Submission on diskette in WordPerfect is preferred.
Copyright ownership: Author
Rejected manuscripts: Returned
Time before publication decision: 1 mo.
Time between decision and publication: 6 mos. maximum
Number of reviewers: 3
Articles published per year: 7
Book reviews published per year: 3
Notes published per year: 5

(2605)
*The Shavian: The Journal of the Shaw Society

T. F. Evans, Editor
5 Parkhouse Dr.
Stone
Staffordshire ST15 8QR, England

Telephone: (44) 785 813671
First published: 1946
Sponsoring organization: Bernard Shaw Soc.
ISSN: 0037-3346
MLA acronym: Shavian

SUBSCRIPTION INFORMATION

Frequency of publication: Annual
Circulation: 500
Available in microform: Yes

ADVERTISING INFORMATION

Advertising accepted: Yes

EDITORIAL DESCRIPTION

Scope: Publishes articles on the life, works, and times of Bernard Shaw and his contemporaries.
Reviews books: Yes
Publishes notes: Yes
Languages accepted: English
Prints abstracts: No

SUBMISSION REQUIREMENTS

Restrictions on contributors: Members of Bernard Shaw Soc. have priority.
Author pays submission fee: No
Author pays page charges: No
Length of articles: 1,000 words maximum
Length of book reviews: 500 words maximum
Length of notes: 250 words maximum
Style: MLA; Chicago

Number of copies required: 2
Special requirements: Will accept submissions in languages other than English if accompanied by English translation. Submit camera-ready copy, A5 format.
Copyright ownership: Reverts to author
Rejected manuscripts: 1 copy returned; enclose return postage.
Time before publication decision: 3 mos.
Number of reviewers: 1-3
Articles submitted per year: 6
Articles published per year: 3
Book reviews published per year: 10
Notes published per year: 10

(2606)
*Shaw: The Annual of Bernard Shaw Studies

Fred D. Crawford, Editor
1034 Hickory St.
Lansing, MI 48912-1711

Telephone: 517 487-2887
First published: 1951
Sponsoring organization: Pennsylvania State Univ.
ISSN: 0037-3354
MLA acronym: ShawR

SUBSCRIPTION INFORMATION

Frequency of publication: Annual (May-June)
Circulation: 1,600
Available in microform: No
Subscription address: Pennsylvania State Univ. Press, Suite C, Barbara Bldg., 820 N. University Dr., University Park, PA 16802
Subscription telephone: 814 865-1327; 800 326-9180

ADVERTISING INFORMATION

Advertising accepted: No

EDITORIAL DESCRIPTION

Scope: Publishes articles on Bernard Shaw and his milieu.
Reviews books: Yes
Publishes notes: Yes
Languages accepted: English
Prints abstracts: No
Author-anonymous submission: Yes

SUBMISSION REQUIREMENTS

Restrictions on contributors: Book reviews are assigned.
Author pays submission fee: No
Author pays page charges: No
Length of articles: 5,000 words maximum
Length of book reviews: 1,500 words
Length of notes: No restrictions
Style: MLA
Number of copies required: 3
Copyright ownership: Assigned by author to journal; author retains reprint rights.
Rejected manuscripts: Returned; enclose return postage.
Time before publication decision: 2 mos.
Time between decision and publication: 12-18 mos.
Number of reviewers: 3
Articles submitted per year: 40
Articles published per year: 12-15
Book reviews published per year: 3-4
Notes submitted per year: 2-3
Notes published per year: 2-3

(2607)
*Shenandoah: The Washington & Lee University Review

Dabney Stuart, Editor
P.O. Box 722
Lexington, VA 24450

Telephone: 703 463-8765
Fax: 703 463-8945
First published: 1950
Historical variations in title: Formerly *Shenendoah*
Sponsoring organization: Washington & Lee Univ.
ISSN: 0037-3583
MLA acronym: Shenandoah

SUBSCRIPTION INFORMATION

Frequency of publication: 4 times/yr.
Circulation: 1,000
Available in microform: Yes
Subscription price: $11.00/yr., $18.00/2 yrs. US; $14.00/yr., $24.00/2 yrs. elsewhere
Year to which price refers: 1991

ADVERTISING INFORMATION

Advertising accepted: Yes
Advertising rates: $100.00/half page; $200.00/full page

EDITORIAL DESCRIPTION

Scope: Publishes fiction, poetry, interviews, essays, and reviews.
Reviews books: Yes
Publishes notes: No
Languages accepted: English
Prints abstracts: No
Author-anonymous submission: No

SUBMISSION REQUIREMENTS

Restrictions on contributors: Most articles and all reviews are solicited.
Author pays submission fee: No
Author pays page charges: No
Length of articles: No restrictions
Length of book reviews: No restrictions
Style: None
Number of copies required: 1
Special requirements: Multiple submissions are not favored.
Copyright ownership: Journal; reverts to author after publication
Rejected manuscripts: Returned; enclose return postage and SAE.
Time before publication decision: 3-6 weeks
Time between decision and publication: 6-8 mos.
Number of reviewers: 1
Book reviews published per year: 4

(2608)
*Shiron

Zenzo Suzuki, Editor
Dept. of English Literature
Faculty of Arts & Letters
Tohoku Univ.
Kawauchi, Sendai 980, Japan

Telephone: (81) 22 2221800
Fax: (81) 22 2215207
First published: 1933
Sponsoring organization: Shiron Club
ISSN: 0387-7590
MLA acronym: Shiron

SUBSCRIPTION INFORMATION

Frequency of publication: Annual (July)
Circulation: 180
Available in microform: No
Subscription price: 8,000 yen/yr.
Year to which price refers: 1992

ADVERTISING INFORMATION

Advertising accepted: No

EDITORIAL DESCRIPTION

Scope: Journal publishes critical, scholarly, and interpretative articles about English and American literature.
Reviews books: No
Publishes notes: No
Languages accepted: Japanese; English
Prints abstracts: Yes
Author-anonymous submission: No

SUBMISSION REQUIREMENTS

Restrictions on contributors: Contributors must be members of Shiron Club.
Author pays submission fee: No
Author pays page charges: No
Length of articles: 5,000 words
Style: MLA
Number of copies required: 1
Copyright ownership: Author
Rejected manuscripts: Returned
Time before publication decision: 6 mos.
Time between decision and publication: 4 mos.
Number of reviewers: 7
Articles submitted per year: 10
Articles published per year: 4

(2609)
*Shoin Literary Review

Shoin Women's Univ.
Dept. of English
2-1, 1-chome
Shinoharaobanoyama-cho
Nada-ku, Kobe-657, Japan

Telephone: (81) 78 8826125
Fax: (81) 78 8226125
First published: 1968
Sponsoring organization: Soc. of English Literature, Shoin Women's Univ.
ISSN: 0288-6154
MLA acronym: ShLR

SUBSCRIPTION INFORMATION

Frequency of publication: Annual
Available in microform: No

ADVERTISING INFORMATION

Advertising accepted: No

EDITORIAL DESCRIPTION

Scope: Publishes articles on English literature and language.
Reviews books: No
Publishes notes: No
Languages accepted: English; Japanese
Prints abstracts: No
Author-anonymous submission: No

SUBMISSION REQUIREMENTS

Restrictions on contributors: Contributors must be staff members of Shoin Women's Univ.
Author pays submission fee: No
Author pays page charges: No

(2610)
Siculorum Gymnasium

Fac. di Lettere
Univ. degli Studi di Catania
Catania, Italy

First published: 1948
ISSN: 0037-458X
MLA acronym: SGym

SUBSCRIPTION INFORMATION

Frequency of publication: 2 times/yr.

EDITORIAL DESCRIPTION

Reviews books: No
Languages accepted: Italian
Prints abstracts: No

(2611)
*Sidney Newsletter & Journal

Gerald Rubio, Editor
Dept. of English
Univ. of Guelph
Guelph, Ontario N1G 2W1, Canada

Telephone: 519 821-0604
Fax: 519 836-2449
First published: 1980
Historical variations in title: Formerly *Sidney Newsletter*
ISSN: 1192-1757
MLA acronym: SNew

SUBSCRIPTION INFORMATION

Frequency of publication: 2 times/yr. (Spring, Fall)
Circulation: 300
Available in microform: No

ADVERTISING INFORMATION

Advertising accepted: No

EDITORIAL DESCRIPTION

Scope: Publishes articles on Sir Philip Sidney, his circle and milieu.
Reviews books: Yes
Publishes notes: Yes
Languages accepted: English
Author-anonymous submission: Yes

SUBMISSION REQUIREMENTS

Restrictions on contributors: None
Author pays submission fee: No
Author pays page charges: No
Length of articles: 2,000-25,000 words
Length of book reviews: 1,000-5,000 words
Length of notes: 2,000 words maximum
Style: MLA
Number of copies required: 1
Copyright ownership: Author
Rejected manuscripts: Returned at author's request
Time before publication decision: 3-6 mos.
Time between decision and publication: 3 mos.
Number of reviewers: 3
Articles submitted per year: 10
Articles published per year: 6
Book reviews submitted per year: 15
Book reviews published per year: 14
Notes submitted per year: 2
Notes published per year: 2

(2612)
*Sight and Sound

Philip Dodd, Editor
British Film Inst.
21 Stephen St.
London W1P 1PL, England

Telephone: (44) 71 2551444
Fax: (44) 71 4362327
First published: 1932
Sponsoring organization: British Film Inst.
ISSN: 0037-4806
MLA acronym: Sight&S

SUBSCRIPTION INFORMATION

Frequency of publication: 12 times/yr.
Circulation: 25,000
Available in microform: Yes
Subscription price: £25.00/yr. United Kingdom; £32.00/yr. Europe; £30.00 (£52.00 airmail)/yr. elsewhere
Year to which price refers: 1992
Subscription address: Subscription Dept., Tower House, Sovereign Park, Market Harborough, Leicestershire LE16 9EF, England
Subscription telephone: (44) 858 468888
Subscription fax: (44) 858 434958

ADVERTISING INFORMATION

Advertising accepted: Yes
Advertising rates: £800.00/full page, black & white; £1,200.00/full page, color

EDITORIAL DESCRIPTION

Scope: Publishes articles on film. Also includes an extensive film review section.
Reviews books: Yes
Publishes notes: Occasionally
Languages accepted: English
Prints abstracts: No
Author-anonymous submission: No

SUBMISSION REQUIREMENTS

Restrictions on contributors: Reviews are usually commissioned.
Author pays submission fee: No
Author pays page charges: No
Length of articles: 1,000-7,000 words
Length of book reviews: 600-2,000 words
Style: Modern Humanities Research Assn.
Number of copies required: 2
Copyright ownership: Author
Rejected manuscripts: Returned
Time before publication decision: 1 mo.
Time between decision and publication: 1-3 mos.
Number of reviewers: 1-2
Articles submitted per year: 700
Articles published per year: 80
Notes submitted per year: 200
Notes published per year: 20

(2613)
*Siglo XX/20th Century

Luis T. González-del-Valle, David Herzberger, & Djelal Kadir, Editors
Dept. of Spanish & Portuguese
Univ. of Colorado
McKenna Languages Building
Campus Box 278
Boulder, CO 80309-0278

Telephone: 303 492-7308
Fax: 303 492-3699
First published: 1983
Sponsoring organization: Twentieth Century Spanish Assn. of America
ISSN: 0740-946X
MLA acronym: Siglo

SUBSCRIPTION INFORMATION

Frequency of publication: 2 times/yr.
Circulation: 700
Available in microform: Yes
Subscription price: $25.00/yr.
Year to which price refers: 1992

ADVERTISING INFORMATION

Advertising accepted: No

EDITORIAL DESCRIPTION

Scope: Aims to contribute to the advancement of Spanish and Spanish American research in the fields of literary theory and criticism by fostering dialogue on 20th century Spanish and Spanish American literatures. It is concerned with the many issues affecting critical discourse.
Reviews books: Yes
Publishes notes: Yes
Languages accepted: English; Spanish
Prints abstracts: No
Author-anonymous submission: No

SUBMISSION REQUIREMENTS

Restrictions on contributors: None
Author pays submission fee: No
Author pays page charges: No
Length of articles: 10-25 pp.
Length of book reviews: 2-6 pp.
Length of notes: 5-9 pp.
Style: MLA
Number of copies required: 3
Copyright ownership: Soc. of Spanish & Spanish-American Studies
Rejected manuscripts: Returned with comments
Time before publication decision: 3 mos.
Time between decision and publication: 1 yr.
Number of reviewers: 5
Articles submitted per year: 80
Articles published per year: 12
Book reviews submitted per year: 18
Book reviews published per year: 12
Notes submitted per year: 6
Notes published per year: 1

(2614)
*Sigma: Linguistique Anglaise-Linguistique Générale

Publications de l'Univ. de Provence—Aix-Marseille I
29 Ave. R. Schumann
13621 Aix-en-Provence Cedex 1, France

Telephone: (33) 42200916
First published: 1976
Historical variations in title: Formerly *Sigma: Revue de Centre d'Etudes Linguistiques d'Aix*
Sponsoring organization: Univ. de Provence-Aix, Centre d'Etudes Linguistiques d'Aix (CELA) & Centre d'Etude des Sciences du Langage
ISSN: 0223-0100
MLA acronym: Sig

SUBSCRIPTION INFORMATION

Frequency of publication: Annual
Circulation: 350
Available in microform: No
Subscription price: 140 F/yr.
Year to which price refers: 1992
Subscription address: Service des Publications-Univ. de Provence, 29, Ave. R. Schuman, 13621 Aix-en-Provence Cedex 1, France
Subscription telephone: (33) 42599930 ext. 348

ADVERTISING INFORMATION

Advertising accepted: No

EDITORIAL DESCRIPTION

Scope: Publishes articles on English, French and general theoretical linguistics.
Reviews books: Yes
Publishes notes: Yes
Languages accepted: French; English
Prints abstracts: Yes
Author-anonymous submission: No

SUBMISSION REQUIREMENTS

Restrictions on contributors: None
Author pays submission fee: No
Author pays page charges: No

Length of articles: 16,000 words maximum
Length of book reviews: 3,000 words
Length of notes: No restrictions
Style: MLA
Number of copies required: 1
Special requirements: Submit manuscript before 15 Sept.
Copyright ownership: Publications de l'Univ. de Provence
Rejected manuscripts: Returned
Time before publication decision: 4-6 weeks
Time between decision and publication: 4 mos.
Number of reviewers: 2
Articles submitted per year: 10-12
Articles published per year: 7-9
Book reviews submitted per year: 3-6
Book reviews published per year: 2

(2615)
*Sign Language Studies

William C. Stokoe, Editor
Linstok Press Inc.
9306 Mintwood St.
Silver Spring, MD 20901

Telephone: 301 585-1939
E-mail: WCSTOKOE@GALLUA
First published: 1972
ISSN: 0302-1475
MLA acronym: SLS

SUBSCRIPTION INFORMATION

Frequency of publication: 4 times/yr. (Mar., June, Sept., Dec.)
Circulation: 500
Available in microform: No
Subscription price: $50.00/yr. institutions US; $55.00/yr. institutions elsewhere; $40.00/yr. individuals US; $46.00/yr. individuals elsewhere
Year to which price refers: 1993
Subscription address: Linstok Press Inc., 4020 Blackburn Lane, Burtonsville, MD 20866
Subscription telephone: 301 426-0268; 800 475-4756
Subscription fax: 301 421-0270

ADVERTISING INFORMATION

Advertising accepted: Yes
Advertising rates: $100.00/half page; $175.00/full page; $250.00/inside cover

EDITORIAL DESCRIPTION

Scope: Welcomes studies not only of gestural systems but also of nonvocal communication generally, facial expression, gesticulation, kinesics, language origins, communication networks, primate communication, proxemics, and semiotic systems.
Reviews books: Yes
Publishes notes: No
Languages accepted: English; French; German
Prints abstracts: Yes

SUBMISSION REQUIREMENTS

Restrictions on contributors: Contributors must be subscribers or members of subscribing institutions.
Author pays submission fee: No
Author pays page charges: No
Length of articles: No restrictions
Length of book reviews: No restrictions
Style: Journal
Number of copies required: 3
Special requirements: Submit abstract and biographical notes.
Copyright ownership: Assigned by author to journal
Rejected manuscripts: Returned; enclose return postage.
Time before publication decision: 2 mos.
Time between decision and publication: 2-4 mos.
Number of reviewers: 2-3

Articles submitted per year: 30-40
Articles published per year: 15-20
Book reviews submitted per year: 4
Book reviews published per year: 3-4

(2616)
*Signs: Journal of Women in Culture and Society

Ruth-Ellen Joeres & Barbara Laslett, Editors
Center for Advanced Feminist Studies
495 Ford Hall
Univ. of Minnesota
224 Church St. SE
Minneapolis, MN 55455

Telephone: 612 626-1695
Fax: 612 626-1697
First published: 1975
Sponsoring organization: Univ. of Chicago
ISSN: 0097-9740
MLA acronym: Signs

SUBSCRIPTION INFORMATION

Frequency of publication: 4 times/yr. (Autumn, Winter, Spring, Summer)
Circulation: 7,500
Available in microform: Yes
Subscription price: $74.00/yr. institutions; $32.50/yr. individuals; $23.00/yr. students
Year to which price refers: 1993
Subscription address: Univ. of Chicago Press, Journals Division, P.O. Box 37005, Chicago, IL 60637
Subscription telephone: 312 753-3347

ADVERTISING INFORMATION

Advertising accepted: Yes
Advertising rates: Request from Univ. of Chicago Press

EDITORIAL DESCRIPTION

Scope: International, multidisciplinary forum for current research and discussion about women. Includes research and theory-based articles, reports, review essays, book reviews, and commentary.
Reviews books: Yes
Publishes notes: Yes
Languages accepted: English
Prints abstracts: No
Author-anonymous submission: Yes

SUBMISSION REQUIREMENTS

Restrictions on contributors: Book reviews are solicited.
Author pays submission fee: No
Author pays page charges: No
Length of articles: 20-35 pp. with notes
Length of book reviews: 2-8 pp.
Length of notes: 100-150 words
Style: Chicago
Number of copies required: 3
Special requirements: Submit original manuscript. Omit name and identifying footnotes (name should appear on a separate title page). Avoid unnecessarily gendered language.
Copyright ownership: Assigned by author to journal
Rejected manuscripts: Returned; enclose SASE.
Time before publication decision: 2-6 mos.
Time between decision and publication: 9-15 mos.
Number of reviewers: 3
Articles submitted per year: 400
Articles published per year: 30
Book reviews published per year: 28

(2617)
*Sìlarus: Rassegna Bimestrale di Cultura

Italo Rocco, Editor
Via B. Buozzi, 47
C.P. 317
84091 Battipaglia (Salerno), Italy

First published: 1965
ISSN: 0037-5179
MLA acronym: Silarus

SUBSCRIPTION INFORMATION

Frequency of publication: 6 times/yr.
Circulation: 3,000
Available in microform: No

ADVERTISING INFORMATION

Advertising accepted: Yes

EDITORIAL DESCRIPTION

Scope: Publishes articles on the diffusion of culture in all its social aspects.
Reviews books: Yes
Publishes notes: Yes
Languages accepted: Italian; French; Latin; English
Prints abstracts: Yes

SUBMISSION REQUIREMENTS

Author pays submission fee: No
Author pays page charges: No
Number of copies required: 2
Copyright ownership: Editor
Rejected manuscripts: Not returned
Time before publication decision: 3 mos.
Time between decision and publication: 2 mos.
Number of reviewers: 20
Articles submitted per year: 50
Articles published per year: 50
Book reviews submitted per year: 50
Book reviews published per year: 50
Notes submitted per year: 60
Notes published per year: 60

(2618)
Silliman Journal

Joy Perez, Editor
Silliman Univ.
Dumaguete City 6501, Philippines

First published: 1954
Sponsoring organization: Silliman Univ.
ISSN: 0037-5284
MLA acronym: SJ

SUBSCRIPTION INFORMATION

Frequency of publication: 4 times/yr.
Circulation: 100
Available in microform: Yes

ADVERTISING INFORMATION

Advertising accepted: No

EDITORIAL DESCRIPTION

Scope: Publishes articles on the humanities and the sciences, with particular relevance to the Philippines, Asia, or the Pacific and special emphasis on cross-cultural studies.
Reviews books: Yes
Publishes notes: Yes
Languages accepted: English
Prints abstracts: Yes
Author-anonymous submission: No

SUBMISSION REQUIREMENTS

Restrictions on contributors: None
Author pays submission fee: No
Author pays page charges: No
Length of articles: No restrictions
Length of book reviews: 500-1,000 words
Length of notes: 1,000-2,000 words
Style: MLA
Number of copies required: 2
Special requirements: Submit original typescript.
Copyright ownership: Silliman Univ.
Rejected manuscripts: Returned; enclose return postage.
Time before publication decision: 1 mo.
Time between decision and publication: 6 mos.
Number of reviewers: 3
Articles submitted per year: 40
Articles published per year: 22
Book reviews published per year: 24
Notes published per year: 10

(2619)
*Simone de Beauvoir Studies

Yolanda Astarita Patterson, Editor
440 La Mesa Dr.
Menlo Park, CA 94028

Telephone: 415 854-4183
First published: 1983
Sponsoring organization: Simone de Beauvoir Soc.
MLA acronym: SdBS

SUBSCRIPTION INFORMATION

Frequency of publication: Annual
Circulation: 130
Available in microform: No
Subscription price: $20.00/yr.
Year to which price refers: 1992
Additional subscription address: Liliane Lazar, 37 Hill Lane, Rosalyn Heights, NY 11577

ADVERTISING INFORMATION

Advertising accepted: Yes
Advertising rates: $60.00/half page; $100.00/full page

EDITORIAL DESCRIPTION

Scope: Publishes articles, monographs, poetry, and reviews relating to Simone de Beauvoir.
Reviews books: Yes
Publishes notes: No
Languages accepted: English; French
Author-anonymous submission: No

SUBMISSION REQUIREMENTS

Restrictions on contributors: None
Author pays submission fee: No
Author pays page charges: No
Length of articles: 3,000-5,000 words
Length of book reviews: 1,000 words
Number of copies required: 3
Copyright ownership: Author
Rejected manuscripts: Returned
Time before publication decision: 4-5 mos.
Time between decision and publication: 4-5 mos.
Number of reviewers: 3
Articles submitted per year: 20
Articles published per year: 5-12

(2620)
*Sing Out!: The Folk Song Magazine

Mark Moss, Editor
Box 5253
Bethlehem, PA 18015-5253

Telephone: 215 865-5366
Fax: 215 865-5129
First published: 1950
ISSN: 0037-5624
MLA acronym: Sing Out

SUBSCRIPTION INFORMATION

Frequency of publication: 4 times/yr.
Circulation: 10,000
Available in microform: Yes
Subscription price: $25.00/yr. institutions; $18.00/yr. individuals
Year to which price refers: 1992

ADVERTISING INFORMATION

Advertising accepted: Yes

EDITORIAL DESCRIPTION

Scope: Publishes traditional and contemporary songs, articles, interviews, teach-ins, reviews, commentary on folk music and musicians from around the world, and coverage of folk music events. Also contains special columns on storytelling and children's music.
Reviews books: Yes
Languages accepted: English
Prints abstracts: No
Author-anonymous submission: No

SUBMISSION REQUIREMENTS

Restrictions on contributors: None
Author pays submission fee: No
Author pays page charges: No
Length of articles: 1,500 words
Length of book reviews: 250 words
Number of copies required: 1
Copyright ownership: Publisher
Rejected manuscripts: Returned; enclose return postage.
Time before publication decision: 6-12 mos.
Time between decision and publication: 3 mos.
Number of reviewers: 2
Articles published per year: 14
Book reviews published per year: 25-30

(2621)
The Single Hound: The Poetry and Image of Emily Dickinson

Andrew Leibs, Editor
Box 598
Newmarket, NH 03857

First published: 1989
ISSN: 1044-8934
MLA acronym: SHnd

SUBSCRIPTION INFORMATION

Frequency of publication: 2 times/yr. (May, Dec.)
Circulation: 100

ADVERTISING INFORMATION

Advertising accepted: No

EDITORIAL DESCRIPTION

Scope: Focuses on the discussion of the poetry and image of Emily Dickinson.
Reviews books: Yes
Publishes notes: Yes
Languages accepted: English
Prints abstracts: No
Author-anonymous submission: Yes

SUBMISSION REQUIREMENTS

Author pays submission fee: No
Author pays page charges: No
Length of articles: 2,500-3,000 words
Length of book reviews: 500-1,000 words
Length of notes: 300-600 words
Special requirements: Submit double-spaced typescript. Poem discussions should focus on lesser-known poems.
Copyright ownership: Journal
Time before publication decision: 2-4 weeks

(2622)
*Sinn und Form: Beiträge zur Literatur

Sebastian Kleinschmidt, Editor
Akademie der Künste zu Berlin
Robert-Koch-Platz 7
1040 Berlin, Germany

Telephone: (37) 2 2363398
Fax: (37) 2 2824675
First published: 1949
Sponsoring organization: Akademie der Künste zu Berlin
ISSN: 0037-5756
MLA acronym: SuF

SUBSCRIPTION INFORMATION

Frequency of publication: 6 times/yr.
Circulation: 3,500
Available in microform: No
Subscription price: 64.20 DM/yr.
Year to which price refers: 1992
Subscription address: VVA Bertelsmann Distribution GmbH/Zeitschriftenservice, PF 7777, Au der Autobahn, 4830 Gütersloh, Germany
Additional subscription address: Rütten & Loening Berlin GmbH, Französische Str. 32, 1086 Berlin, Germany
Subscription telephone: (49) 524 44115; (37) 2 2235223
Subscription fax: (37) 2 2298637

ADVERTISING INFORMATION

Advertising accepted: Yes

EDITORIAL DESCRIPTION

Scope: Publishes articles on all aspects of literature.
Reviews books: Yes
Publishes notes: No
Languages accepted: German
Prints abstracts: No
Author-anonymous submission: No

SUBMISSION REQUIREMENTS

Restrictions on contributors: None
Author pays submission fee: No
Author pays page charges: No
Length of articles: No restrictions
Length of book reviews: No restrictions
Style: None
Number of copies required: 2
Copyright ownership: Reverts from journal to author after 1 yr.
Rejected manuscripts: Returned; enclose return postage
Time before publication decision: 2-8 weeks
Number of reviewers: 3
Articles submitted per year: 232
Articles published per year: 120
Book reviews submitted per year: 10
Book reviews published per year: 10
Time between decision and publication: 2-4 mos.
Number of reviewers: 3
Articles submitted per year: 2-5
Articles published per year: 4
Book reviews published per year: 1-2
Notes submitted per year: 2-3
Notes published per year: 2-3

(2623)
*Siouan and Caddoan Linguistics

Allan R. Taylor & David S. Rood, Editors
Dept. of Linguistics
Campus Box 295
Univ. of Colorado
Boulder, CO 80309-0295

Telephone: 303 492-7082
First published: 1979
ISSN: 0748-724X
MLA acronym: SCLing

SUBSCRIPTION INFORMATION

Frequency of publication: Irregular
Circulation: 320
Available in microform: No
Subscription price: Free
Year to which price refers: 1992

ADVERTISING INFORMATION

Advertising accepted: No

EDITORIAL DESCRIPTION

Scope: Publishes on current events and ongoing research on Siouan and Caddoan languages and linguistics.
Reviews books: Yes
Publishes notes: Yes
Languages accepted: English
Prints abstracts: No
Author-anonymous submission: No

SUBMISSION REQUIREMENTS

Restrictions on contributors: None
Author pays submission fee: No
Author pays page charges: No
Length of articles: 2,500 words
Length of book reviews: 500 words
Length of notes: 500 words
Style: None
Number of copies required: 1
Special requirements: Submit camera-ready copy for articles and reviews.
Copyright ownership: Author
Rejected manuscripts: Returned
Time before publication decision: 2-4 weeks
Number of reviewers: 1-2
Articles submitted per year: 2-3
Articles published per year: 2-3
Book reviews submitted per year: 1-4
Book reviews published per year: 1-4
Notes submitted per year: 10-20
Notes published per year: 10-20

(2624)
Sipario: Il Mensile Italiano dello Spettacolo

Giacomo De Santis, Editor
Siparo Editrice, S. R. L.
Via Gaffurio 2
20124 Milan, Italy

First published: 1946
MLA acronym: Sipario

SUBSCRIPTION INFORMATION

Frequency of publication: 12 times/yr.
Circulation: 25,000

EDITORIAL DESCRIPTION

Scope: Review for theater, cinema, opera, TV, and ballet. Publishes original scripts, critical essays, inquiries, interviews, correspondence, and theater, film, and music reviews.
Reviews books: Yes
Languages accepted: Italian
Prints abstracts: No

SUBMISSION REQUIREMENTS

Restrictions on contributors: None
Length of articles: 2 pp.
Style: None
Number of copies required: 1
Time before publication decision: 2 weeks
Time between decision and publication: 1 mo.
Number of reviewers: 5
Articles published per year: 600

(2625)
Sirp ja Vasar

Leonhard Laks, Editor
Postkast 388
Pikk t. 40
200001 Tallinn, Estonia

First published: 1940
Sponsoring organization: Estonian Ministry of Culture; Creative Unions of Estonia
MLA acronym: SjV

SUBSCRIPTION INFORMATION

Frequency of publication: 52 times/yr.
Circulation: 59,500
Available in microform: No
Subscription address: Ajakirjanduslevi, Suur-Karja 20, Tallinn, Estonia

ADVERTISING INFORMATION

Advertising accepted: No

EDITORIAL DESCRIPTION

Scope: Covers Estonian cultural subjects, including literature, fine arts, music, architecture, theater, film, social problems, and general cultural and philosophical essays.
Reviews books: Yes
Publishes notes: Yes
Languages accepted: Estonian
Prints abstracts: No

SUBMISSION REQUIREMENTS

Restrictions on contributors: None
Author pays submission fee: No
Author pays page charges: No
Length of articles: 9 typescript pp. maximum
Length of book reviews: 4-5 typescript pp.
Length of notes: 2-3 typescript pp.
Number of copies required: 1
Special requirements: Submit original typescript. Submissions in languages other than Estonian are accepted, but articles must be published in Estonian translation.
Rejected manuscripts: Returned
Time before publication decision: 1 week
Time between decision and publication: 1 mo.
Number of reviewers: 3
Articles submitted per year: 1,000
Articles published per year: 500
Book reviews published per year: 50
Notes published per year: 100

(2626)
*Sitzungsberichte der Österreichischen Akademie der Wissenschaften in Wien, Philosophisch-Historische Klasse

Verlag der Österreichischen Akademie der Wissenschaften
Dr.-Ignaz-Seipel-Platz 2
1010 Vienna, Austria

Telephone: (43) 222 515810
Fax: (43) 222 5139541
First published: 1848
Sponsoring organization: Bundesministerium für Wissenschaft & Forschung, Vienna; Fonds der Wissenschaftlichen Forschung

MLA acronym: SÖAW

SUBSCRIPTION INFORMATION

Frequency of publication: Irregular
Circulation: 500-1,000
Available in microform: No

ADVERTISING INFORMATION

Advertising accepted: No

EDITORIAL DESCRIPTION

Scope: Publishes monographs on history, philosophy, music, numismatics, and folklore.
Reviews books: No
Publishes notes: No
Languages accepted: German; English; French
Prints abstracts: No

SUBMISSION REQUIREMENTS

Restrictions on contributors: Contributors must be members of Akademie der Wissenschaften in Vienna or have presented the manuscript at special meetings of the Academy.
Author pays submission fee: No
Author pays page charges: No
Length of books: No restrictions
Number of copies required: 1
Copyright ownership: Österreichische Akademie der Wissenschaften
Books published per year: 20

(2627)
*Sitzungsberichte der Sächsischen Akademie der Wissenschaften zu Leipzig: Philologisch-Historische Klasse

Sächsische Akademie der Wissenschaften zu Leipzig
Goethestr. 3-5
7010 Leipzig, Germany

First published: 1846
Sponsoring organization: Ministry of Science & Art, Germany
MLA acronym: SSAWL

SUBSCRIPTION INFORMATION

Frequency of publication: Irregular
Circulation: 800
Available in microform: No

ADVERTISING INFORMATION

Advertising accepted: Yes

EDITORIAL DESCRIPTION

Scope: Publishes lectures given at the plenary meeting of the Saxon Academy on the topics of natural, philological, and historical sciences.
Reviews books: No
Publishes notes: No
Languages accepted: German
Prints abstracts: No
Author-anonymous submission: No

SUBMISSION REQUIREMENTS

Restrictions on contributors: Contributors must be members of the Sächsische Akademie.
Author pays submission fee: No
Author pays page charges: No
Number of copies required: 3
Special requirements: Submit original typescript and 2 copies.
Copyright ownership: Sächsische Akademie der Wissenschaften zu Leipzig
Number of reviewers: 2

(2628)
*The Sixteenth Century Journal

Robert M. Kingdon, Robert A. Kolb, & Robert V. Schnucker, Editors
LB 115
Northeast Missouri State Univ.
Kirksville, MO 63501

Telephone: 816 785-4665
Fax: 816 785-4181
E-mail: SS18@NEMOMUS
First published: 1969
Sponsoring organization: Sixteenth Century Studies Conference
ISSN: 0361-0160
MLA acronym: SCJ

SUBSCRIPTION INFORMATION

Frequency of publication: 4 times/yr. (Apr., July, Oct., Jan.)
Circulation: 2,300
Available in microform: Yes
Subscription price: $40.00/yr institutions US; $45.00/yr. institutions elsewhere; $35.00/yr. individuals US; $40.00/yr. individuals elsewhere
Year to which price refers: 1992

ADVERTISING INFORMATION

Advertising accepted: Yes
Advertising rates: $100.00/full page

EDITORIAL DESCRIPTION

Scope: Publishes articles in most areas of scholarly activity, including literature, theology, demography, history, music history, and art history, covering the period 1450-1648.
Reviews books: Yes
Publishes notes: Yes
Languages accepted: English
Prints abstracts: Yes
Author-anonymous submission: Yes

SUBMISSION REQUIREMENTS

Restrictions on contributors: None
Author pays submission fee: No
Author pays page charges: Yes, if changes are made on galleys. Authors must also pay for charts at the rate determined by the typographer.
Length of articles: 20 double-spaced typescript pp. maximum
Length of book reviews: 500-550 words
Length of notes: 1,000-15,000 words
Style: Chicago
Number of copies required: 2
Special requirements: Submit original typescript plus 1 copy or ASCII diskette.
Copyright ownership: Journal
Rejected manuscripts: Returned with comments
Time before publication decision: 3-4 mos.
Time between decision and publication: 6-12 mos.
Number of reviewers: 4-5
Articles submitted per year: 150
Articles published per year: 35-40
Book reviews submitted per year: 200
Book reviews published per year: 200
Notes submitted per year: 6
Notes published per year: 1

(2629)
*Skandinavistik: Zeitschrift für Sprache, Literatur und Kultur der Nordischen Länder

Bernhard Glienke, Wilhelm Friese, Ulrich Groenke, Dietrich Hofmann, Gert Kreutzer, Klaus von See, Kurt Braunmüller, & Edith Marold, Editors
Nordisches Inst.
Univ. Kiel
Olshausenstr. 40
2300 Kiel, Germany

Telephone: (49) 431 8802323
First published: 1970
Sponsoring organization: Deutsche Forschungsgemeinschaft
ISSN: 0432-8427
MLA acronym: Skandinavistik

SUBSCRIPTION INFORMATION

Frequency of publication: 2 times/yr. (June, Dec.)
Circulation: 300
Available in microform: No
Subscription price: 68 DM/yr.
Year to which price refers: 1992
Subscription address: Verlag J. J. Augustin, Am Fleth 36/37, Postfach 6, 2208 Glückstadt, Germany

ADVERTISING INFORMATION

Advertising accepted: No

EDITORIAL DESCRIPTION

Scope: Publishes articles on literature, language, linguistics, and culture of Sweden, Denmark, Norway, and Iceland. Includes articles on Old Icelandic literature and language and literary relations between Germany and the Scandinavian countries.
Reviews books: Yes
Publishes notes: Yes
Languages accepted: German; English
Prints abstracts: No
Author-anonymous submission: No

SUBMISSION REQUIREMENTS

Restrictions on contributors: None
Author pays submission fee: No
Author pays page charges: No
Length of articles: 8-16 pp.
Length of book reviews: 2-3 pp.
Length of notes: 2-3 pp.
Number of copies required: 1
Copyright ownership: Author
Rejected manuscripts: Returned
Time before publication decision: 6 mos.
Time between decision and publication: 6 mos.
Number of reviewers: 6
Articles submitted per year: 20
Articles published per year: 6-8
Book reviews submitted per year: 20-25
Book reviews published per year: 16-22
Notes submitted per year: 6-8
Notes published per year: 4-6

(2630)
*Skírnir: Tímarit Hins Íslenska Bókmenntafélags

Vilhjálmur Árnason & Ástráður Eysteinsson, Editors
Hið Íslenska Bókmenntafélag
P.O. Box 8935
128 Reykjavik, Iceland

Additional editorial address: Tómasarhagi 53, 107 Reykjavik, Iceland
First published: 1827
ISSN: 0256-8446
MLA acronym: Skírnir

SUBSCRIPTION INFORMATION

Frequency of publication: 2 times/yr.
Circulation: 1,500
Available in microform: No

ADVERTISING INFORMATION

Advertising accepted: Yes

EDITORIAL DESCRIPTION

Scope: Publishes articles on Icelandic literature, culture, philosophy, biography, and historical geography.
Reviews books: Yes
Publishes notes: Yes
Languages accepted: Icelandic
Prints abstracts: No
Author-anonymous submission: No

SUBMISSION REQUIREMENTS

Restrictions on contributors: None
Author pays submission fee: No
Author pays page charges: No
Length of articles: 15-40 pp.
Length of book reviews: 6-10 pp.
Length of notes: 8-12 pp.
Style: None
Number of copies required: 1
Special requirements: Articles accepted in English, German, or Scandinavian languages are translated into Icelandic.
Copyright ownership: Journal
Rejected manuscripts: Returned
Time before publication decision: 1-3 mos.
Time between decision and publication: 1-6 mos.
Number of reviewers: 3
Articles submitted per year: 25
Articles published per year: 14
Book reviews submitted per year: 20
Book reviews published per year: 10-15
Notes submitted per year: 4-5
Notes published per year: 3-4

(2631)
*Skrifter Utgivna av Institutionen för Nordiska Språk vid Uppsala Universitet

Thorsten Andersson, Lennart Elmevik, Bengt Nordberg, & Mats Thelander, Editors
Uppsala Univ.
Inst. för Nordiska Språk
Box 513
751 20 Uppsala, Sweden

Telephone: (46) 18 181271
Fax: (46) 18 181272
First published: 1953
ISSN: 0083-4661
MLA acronym: SINSU

SUBSCRIPTION INFORMATION

Frequency of publication: Irregular
Subscription price: 120 Skr/yr.
Year to which price refers: 1992

ADVERTISING INFORMATION

Advertising accepted: No

EDITORIAL DESCRIPTION

Scope: Publishes studies on Scandinavian languages.
Reviews books: No
Publishes notes: No
Prints abstracts: Yes

(2632)
*Skrifter Utgivna av Litteraturvetenskapliga Institutionen vid Uppsala Universitet

Bengt Landgren, Editor
Litteraturvetenskapliga Inst.
Uppsala Univ.
Slottet ing. AO
752 37 Uppsala, Sweden

Telephone: (46) 18 182955
Fax: (46) 18 182950
First published: 1972
MLA acronym: SULI

SUBSCRIPTION INFORMATION

Frequency of publication: Irregular
Available in microform: No

ADVERTISING INFORMATION

Advertising accepted: No

EDITORIAL DESCRIPTION

Scope: Publishes monographs on Swedish literature.
Reviews books: No
Languages accepted: English; French; German
Prints abstracts: Yes

SUBMISSION REQUIREMENTS

Author pays submission fee: No
Author pays page charges: No
Length of books: 54,000 words
Style: MLA
Copyright ownership: Author
Rejected manuscripts: Returned
Books submitted per year: 2-4
Books published per year: 2-4

(2633)
*Skrifter Utgivna av Svenska Litteratursällskapet. Studier i Nordisk Filologi

Lars Huldén, Editor
Svenska Litteratursällskapet i Finland Förlag
Mariegatan 8
00170 Helsinki 17, Finland

Fax: (358) 0 632820
First published: 1910
ISSN: 0356-0376
MLA acronym: SSLSN

SUBSCRIPTION INFORMATION

Frequency of publication: Annual
Available in microform: No

ADVERTISING INFORMATION

Advertising accepted: No

EDITORIAL DESCRIPTION

Scope: Publishes articles on Nordic philology.
Reviews books: No
Publishes notes: Yes
Languages accepted: Swedish; Danish; Norwegian
Prints abstracts: No

SUBMISSION REQUIREMENTS

Author pays submission fee: No
Author pays page charges: No

(2634)
*Skrifter Utgivna av Svenska Litteratursällskapet i Finland

Helena Solstrand-Pipping, Lars Huldén, & Magnus Pettersson, Editors
Svenska Litteratursällskapets i Finland Förlag
Mariegaten 8
00170 Helsinki 17, Finland

Fax: (358) 0 632820
First published: 1886
Sponsoring organization: Svenska Litteratursällskapet i Finland
ISSN: 0039-6842
MLA acronym: SLF

SUBSCRIPTION INFORMATION

Frequency of publication: Irregular
Available in microform: No

ADVERTISING INFORMATION

Advertising accepted: No

EDITORIAL DESCRIPTION

Scope: Publishes articles on Swedish literature in Finland, as well as on history and sociology.
Reviews books: No
Publishes notes: Yes
Languages accepted: Swedish
Prints abstracts: Yes

SUBMISSION REQUIREMENTS

Number of copies required: 2
Copyright ownership: Author & series
Time between decision and publication: 6 mos.
Number of reviewers: 2
Books published per year: 6-8

(2635)
*Skrifter Utgivna av Svenska Språknämnden

Margareta Westman, Editor
Svenska Språknämnden
Lundagatan 42, uppg. 5
117 27 Stockholm, Sweden

Telephone: (46) 8 6680153
Fax: (46) 8 7206805
First published: 1946
ISSN: 0346-7724
MLA acronym: SNSS

SUBSCRIPTION INFORMATION

Frequency of publication: Irregular
Available in microform: No

ADVERTISING INFORMATION

Advertising accepted: No

EDITORIAL DESCRIPTION

Scope: Publishes monographs on language planning and cultivation, and modern Swedish usage.
Reviews books: No
Publishes notes: No
Languages accepted: Swedish; Norwegian; Danish
Prints abstracts: No
Author-anonymous submission: Yes

SUBMISSION REQUIREMENTS

Restrictions on contributors: None
Author pays submission fee: No
Author pays page charges: No
Length of books: No restrictions
Style: None

Number of copies required: 1
Copyright ownership: Author & series
Rejected manuscripts: Returned
Time before publication decision: 1-2 mos.
Time between decision and publication: 4-8 mos.
Number of reviewers: 2-5
Books submitted per year: 1-5
Books published per year: 1-3

(2636)
Skrifter Utgivna av Vetenskaps-Societeten i Lund

Vetenskaps-Societeten i Lund
Lund, Sweden

First published: 1921
ISSN: 0347-1772
MLA acronym: SUVSL

SUBSCRIPTION INFORMATION

Frequency of publication: Irregular
Circulation: 600
Available in microform: No

ADVERTISING INFORMATION

Advertising accepted: No

EDITORIAL DESCRIPTION

Scope: Publishes monographs on literature.
Reviews books: No
Prints abstracts: No

SUBMISSION REQUIREMENTS

Restrictions on contributors: None
Author pays submission fee: No
Number of copies required: 1
Copyright ownership: Vetenskaps-Societeten i Lund
Rejected manuscripts: Returned
Time before publication decision: 2 mos.
Number of reviewers: 1

(2637)
*Skrifter Utgivna genom Dialekt- och Folkminnesarkivet i Uppsala

Maj Reinhammar, Editor
Dialekt- & Folkminnesarkivet
Box 1743
751 47 Uppsala, Sweden

Telephone: (46) 18 156360
Fax: (46) 18 151342
First published: 1940
Sponsoring organization: Dialekt- & Folkminnesarkivet i Uppsala
ISSN: Ser. A, 0348-4475; Ser. B, 0348-4483; Ser. C, 0280-2651; Ser. D, 0348-0954
MLA acronym: SUDFU

SUBSCRIPTION INFORMATION

Frequency of publication: Irregular
Circulation: 1,000
Available in microform: No

ADVERTISING INFORMATION

Advertising accepted: No

EDITORIAL DESCRIPTION

Scope: Publishes theses, monographs, editions, and dictionaries on Swedish dialects (in Sweden, Finland, Ukraine, the US, etc.); Nordic, Lappish, and Finnish dialects within Sweden; Swedish, Nordic, Lappish, and Finnish ethnology and folklore. Four subseries comprise this series. Their focuses are: Series A, dialects; Series B, folklore and everyday life; Series C, Lappish languages and Lappish culture; Series D, dialect dictionaries from Dalarna, Gotland and other regions.
Reviews books: No
Publishes notes: No
Languages accepted: Swedish; Norwegian; Danish; English; German; French
Prints abstracts: No
Author-anonymous submission: No

SUBMISSION REQUIREMENTS

Restrictions on contributors: None
Author pays submission fee: No
Author pays page charges: No
Number of copies required: 1
Copyright ownership: Author & Dialekt- och Folkminnesarkivet i Uppsala
Rejected manuscripts: Returned
Time before publication decision: 2 mos.
Time between decision and publication: 12-18 mos.
Books published per year: 1-2

(2638)
Slavia: Časopis pro Slovanskou Filologii

Slavomir Wollman, Editor
Academia
Vodickova 40
122 29 Prague 1, Czech Republic

First published: 1922
ISSN: 0037-6736
MLA acronym: Slavia

SUBSCRIPTION INFORMATION

Frequency of publication: 4 times/yr.
Subscription address: Kubon & Sagner, Postfach 340108, 8000 Munich 34, Germany

EDITORIAL DESCRIPTION

Scope: Publishes articles on Slavic philology, linguistics, and literature.
Reviews books: Yes
Languages accepted: English; French; German
Prints abstracts: Yes

SUBMISSION REQUIREMENTS

Special requirements: Considers manuscripts in Slavic languages.

(2639)
*Slavia Orientalis

Lucjan Suchanek, Editor
Uniw. Jagielloński
Inst. Filologii Wschodniosłowianskiej
ul. Krupnicza 35
31-111 Cracow, Poland

Telephone: (48) 12 214876
First published: 1952
Sponsoring organization: Polska Akademia Nauk, Komitet Słowianoznawstwa
ISSN: 0037-6744
MLA acronym: SlOr

SUBSCRIPTION INFORMATION

Frequency of publication: 4 times/yr.
Circulation: 1,000
Available in microform: No
Subscription address: Jan Okuniewski, Wydawnictwo "Energeia", ul. Wiktorska 91 B/1, 02-582 Warsaw, Poland

ADVERTISING INFORMATION

Advertising accepted: No

EDITORIAL DESCRIPTION

Scope: Publishes articles on East Slavic languages and literatures.
Reviews books: Yes
Publishes notes: Yes
Languages accepted: Polish; Russian; English; Ukrainian; Belorussian
Prints abstracts: No
Author-anonymous submission: No

SUBMISSION REQUIREMENTS

Restrictions on contributors: None
Author pays submission fee: No
Author pays page charges: No
Length of articles: 20 pp.
Length of book reviews: 3-5 pp.
Length of notes: 1-2 pp.
Number of copies required: 2
Special requirements: Submit original typescript.
Copyright ownership: Author
Rejected manuscripts: Returned at author's request
Time before publication decision: 3 mos.
Time between decision and publication: 6 mos.
Number of reviewers: 2
Articles submitted per year: 45
Articles published per year: 32
Book reviews submitted per year: 40
Book reviews published per year: 30
Notes published per year: 40

(2640)
*Slavic and East European Arts

E. J. Czerwinski & Nicholas Rzhevsky, Editors
Dept. of Germanic & Slavic
State Univ. of New York at Stony Brook
Stony Brook, NY 11794-3367

Telephone: 516 632-7360
First published: 1982
Sponsoring organization: Slavic Cultural Center, Inc.; State Univ. of New York at Stony Brook
ISSN: 0737-7002
MLA acronym: SEEA

SUBSCRIPTION INFORMATION

Frequency of publication: 2 times/yr. (Spring, Winter)
Available in microform: No

ADVERTISING INFORMATION

Advertising accepted: Yes
Advertising rates: $50.00/full page

EDITORIAL DESCRIPTION

Scope: Journal is devoted to the arts of the Slavic and East European countries.
Reviews books: No
Publishes notes: Yes
Languages accepted: English
Prints abstracts: No
Author-anonymous submission: No

SUBMISSION REQUIREMENTS

Restrictions on contributors: None
Author pays submission fee: No
Author pays page charges: No
Length of articles: 3,000-55,000 words
Length of notes: 3,000 words
Style: MLA
Number of copies required: 2

Copyright ownership: Slavic Cultural Center, Inc.
Rejected manuscripts: Returned; enclose SASE.
Time before publication decision: 2 mos.
Number of reviewers: 2
Articles submitted per year: 40
Articles published per year: 20
Notes submitted per year: 5
Notes published per year: 3

(2641)
*Slavic and East European Journal

Gary R. Jahn, Editor
Dept. of Slavic & Central Asian Languages & Literatures
Univ. of Minnesota
Minneapolis, MN 55455

First published: 1957
Sponsoring organization: American Assn. of Teachers of Slavic & East European Languages
ISSN: 0037-6752
MLA acronym: SEEJ

SUBSCRIPTION INFORMATION

Frequency of publication: 4 times/yr. (Mar., June, Sept., Dec.)
Circulation: 2,000
Available in microform: Yes
Subscription address: George Gutsche, Executive Secretary-Treasurer, Dept. of Russian & Slavic Languages, Univ. of Arizona, Tucson, AZ 85721

ADVERTISING INFORMATION

Advertising accepted: Yes

EDITORIAL DESCRIPTION

Scope: Publishes articles on Slavic and East European languages, literatures, and pedagogy. Articles should be analytical or synthesizing studies which contain their own documentation and demonstrate a command of the basic materials in the original languages. Offers new contributions to scholarly knowledge, rather than to critical opinion. Does not publish translations, texts, documents, lists, glossaries, or other raw materials, although all of these may be incorporated briefly into articles and notes as documentation; nor is it an outlet for article-length reviews of new literary works, although scholarly surveys of contemporary writers will be considered. Pedagogical articles should attempt to advance language teaching on the basis of sound experimentation and research. Surveys of recent scholarship on particular authors, subjects, or fields, and compilations useful to the profession are published.
Reviews books: Yes
Publishes notes: Yes
Languages accepted: English
Prints abstracts: No
Author-anonymous submission: Yes

SUBMISSION REQUIREMENTS

Restrictions on contributors: Contributors must be members of American Assn. of Teachers of Slavic & East European Languages.
Author pays submission fee: No
Author pays page charges: No
Length of articles: 7,000 words maximum
Length of book reviews: 750-1,000 words
Length of notes: 2,500-3,500 words maximum
Style: MLA; Chicago
Number of copies required: 4
Special requirements: Cyrillic used for indented quotations (5 or more lines of verse or text). At least 3 copies of submission must contain no identification of the author.
Copyright ownership: American Assn. of Teachers of Slavic & East European Languages

Rejected manuscripts: One copy returned at author's request; enclose return postage.
Time before publication decision: 4 mos.
Time between decision and publication: 1 yr.
Number of reviewers: 2-3
Articles submitted per year: 75
Articles published per year: 25-30
Book reviews submitted per year: 100
Book reviews published per year: 90-120
Notes submitted per year: 10
Notes published per year: 4-5

(2642)
*Slavic Review: American Quarterly of Russian, Eurasian and East European Studies

Elliott Mossman, Editor
636 Williams Hall
Univ. of Pennsylvania
Philadelphia, PA 19104-6305

Telephone: 215 898-8096
Fax: 215 898-2998
First published: 1941
Historical variations in title: Formerly *Slavic Review: American Quarterly of Soviet and East European Studies*
Sponsoring organization: American Assn. for the Advancement of Slavic Studies, Inc.
ISSN: 0037-6779
MLA acronym: SlavR

SUBSCRIPTION INFORMATION

Frequency of publication: 4 times/yr. (Spring, Summer, Fall, Winter)
Circulation: 4,000
Available in microform: Yes, for early years, not current
Subscription address: Executive Director, American Assn. for the Advancement of Slavic Studies, Jordan Quad/Acacia, 125 Panama St., Stanford Univ., Stanford, CA, 94305-4130
Subscription telephone: 415 723-9668
Subscription fax: 415 725-7737

ADVERTISING INFORMATION

Advertising accepted: Yes

EDITORIAL DESCRIPTION

Scope: Aim is to publish the highest quality research in social science and the humanities on subjects dealing with Russia, Eurasia, and Eastern Europe. Articles should contain a conceptual point that is fresh, instructive, and accessible to a broad, educated public.
Reviews books: Yes
Publishes notes: Yes
Languages accepted: English
Prints abstracts: No
Author-anonymous submission: Yes

SUBMISSION REQUIREMENTS

Restrictions on contributors: Contributors should be members of the American Assn. for the Advancement of Slavic Studies, Inc.
Author pays submission fee: No
Author pays page charges: No
Length of articles: 25 pp.
Length of book reviews: 500-700 words
Length of notes: 12 pp.
Style: Chicago
Number of copies required: 4
Special requirements: Use Library of Congress transliteration.
Copyright ownership: American Assn. for the Advancement of Slavic Studies, Inc.
Rejected manuscripts: Additional copies returned; enclose return postage.
Time before publication decision: 3 mos.
Time between decision and publication: 3-8 mos.
Number of reviewers: 1-3
Articles submitted per year: 200
Articles published per year: 25

Book reviews submitted per year: 300
Book reviews published per year: 300
Notes submitted per year: 36
Notes published per year: 8

(2643)
*Slavica Helvetica

Peter Brang, Editor
Verlag Peter Lang AG
Jupiterstr. 15
3000 Bern 15, Switzerland

First published: 1969
ISSN: 0171-7316
MLA acronym: SlavH

SUBSCRIPTION INFORMATION

Frequency of publication: Irregular
Available in microform: No

ADVERTISING INFORMATION

Advertising accepted: No

EDITORIAL DESCRIPTION

Scope: Publishes monographs on Slavic literary history and linguistics.
Reviews books: No
Publishes notes: No
Languages accepted: French; German; Czech; English; Russian
Prints abstracts: No

SUBMISSION REQUIREMENTS

Author pays submission fee: No
Length of books: 150-400 pp.
Number of copies required: 1
Copyright ownership: Verlag Peter Lang
Rejected manuscripts: Returned
Time before publication decision: 1 mo.
Time between decision and publication: 3-6 mos.
Number of reviewers: 1
Books submitted per year: 1-4
Books published per year: 1-3

(2644)
*Slavica Othiniensia

Bent Jensen & Jaroslav Vincenc Pavlík, Editors
Odense Univ. Centr for Slaviske Studier
Campusvej 55
5230 Odense M, Denmark

First published: 1978
Sponsoring organization: Odense Univ.
ISSN: 0106-1313
MLA acronym: SlavO

SUBSCRIPTION INFORMATION

Frequency of publication: Annual
Available in microform: No

ADVERTISING INFORMATION

Advertising accepted: No

EDITORIAL DESCRIPTION

Scope: Publishes articles on Slavic studies.
Reviews books: Yes
Publishes notes: Yes
Languages accepted: Danish; Swedish; Norwegian; English; German; French; Russian
Prints abstracts: Yes

SUBMISSION REQUIREMENTS

Restrictions on contributors: Contributors must be affiliated with Odense Universitet.
Author pays submission fee: No

Author pays page charges: No
Length of articles: No restrictions
Length of book reviews: No restrictions
Length of notes: No restrictions
Style: Scando-Slavica
Number of copies required: 3
Special requirements: Submit original typescript plus 2 copies.
Copyright ownership: Author
Rejected manuscripts: Returned
Time before publication decision: 1 mo.
Time between decision and publication: 2 mos.
Number of reviewers: 1
Articles submitted per year: 5-12
Articles published per year: 4-9
Book reviews submitted per year: 1-6
Book reviews published per year: 1-3
Notes submitted per year: 2
Notes published per year: 1

(2645)
Slavistički Studii: Spisanie za Rusistika, Polonistika i Bohemistika

Boris Markov, Editor
Katedra za Slavistika
Filološki Fakultet
Univerzitet "Kiril i Metodij"
Skopje, Macedonia (Yugoslavia)

First published: 1976
Sponsoring organization: Republiča Zajednica za Naučni Dejnosti
MLA acronym: SlavS

SUBSCRIPTION INFORMATION

Frequency of publication: Annual
Circulation: 100
Available in microform: No

ADVERTISING INFORMATION

Advertising accepted: No

EDITORIAL DESCRIPTION

Scope: Publishes articles on language and literature.
Reviews books: Yes
Publishes notes: Yes
Languages accepted: Macedonian; Polish; Russian
Prints abstracts: Yes

SUBMISSION REQUIREMENTS

Restrictions on contributors: None
Author pays submission fee: No
Author pays page charges: No
Length of articles: 2,000 words
Length of book reviews: 300 words
Number of copies required: 2
Special requirements: Articles must be previously unpublished.
Copyright ownership: Katedra za Slavistika

(2646)
*Slavistična Revija

Franc Zadravec, Jože Toporišič, & Boris Paternu, Editors
Aškerčeva 12
61000 Ljubljana, Slovenia

Telephone: (38) 61 150001 ext. 237
Fax: (38) 61 159337
E-mail: Miran.hladnik@uni-lj.ac.mail.yu
First published: 1948
Sponsoring organization: Slavistično Društvo Slovenije
ISSN: 0350-6894
MLA acronym: SlR

SUBSCRIPTION INFORMATION

Frequency of publication: 4 times/yr.
Circulation: 1,100
Available in microform: No
Subscription price: $32.00/yr.
Year to which price refers: 1992

ADVERTISING INFORMATION

Advertising accepted: No

EDITORIAL DESCRIPTION

Scope: Publishes articles on linguistics and literary sciences concerning Slovene and Slavic languages and literatures.
Reviews books: Yes
Publishes notes: Yes
Languages accepted: Slovenian; German; Serbo-Croatian; French; Italian; English; Polish; Macedonian; Russian; Czech
Prints abstracts: Yes
Author-anonymous submission: No

SUBMISSION REQUIREMENTS

Restrictions on contributors: None
Author pays submission fee: No
Author pays page charges: No
Length of articles: 25 pp. suggested
Length of book reviews: 600-1,200 words
Length of notes: 600-1,200 words
Number of copies required: 2
Special requirements: Submit a 100-word abstract and a 30-word synopsis. If possible, submit on diskette in ASCII format.
Copyright ownership: Journal
Rejected manuscripts: Not returned
Time before publication decision: 2-12 weeks
Time between decision and publication: 1-6 mos.
Number of reviewers: 1-4
Articles submitted per year: 30
Articles published per year: 25
Book reviews submitted per year: 12
Book reviews published per year: 10
Notes submitted per year: 10
Notes published per year: 10

(2647)
*The Slavonic and East European Review

R. P. Bartlett, M. A. Branch, N. Cornwall, A. G. Cross, V. M. DuFeu, J. Graffy, L. A. J. Hughes, D. Kirby, M. Light, A. B. McMillin, W. F. Ryan, J. E. O. Screen, & D. Short, Editors
School of Slavonic & East European Studies
Univ. of London
Senate House, Malet St.
London WC1E 7HU, England

Telephone: (44) 71 6374934 ext. 4034
Fax: (44) 71 4368916
First published: 1922
Sponsoring organization: Univ. of London, School of Slavonic & East European Studies; Modern Humanities Research Assn.
ISSN: 0037-6795
MLA acronym: SEER

SUBSCRIPTION INFORMATION

Frequency of publication: 4 times/yr. (Jan., Apr., July, Oct.)
Circulation: 1,300
Available in microform: No
Subscription price: £71.00/yr.
Year to which price refers: 1992
Subscription address: Honorary Treasurer, Modern Humanities Research Assn., King's College, Strand, London WC2R 2LS, England

ADVERTISING INFORMATION

Advertising accepted: No

EDITORIAL DESCRIPTION

Scope: Publishes articles and documents on the linguistics, literature, history, and culture of Slavonic peoples, Eastern Europe, non-European peoples of the former Soviet Union and book reviews in the same fields.
Reviews books: Yes
Publishes notes: Yes
Languages accepted: English
Prints abstracts: No
Author-anonymous submission: Yes

SUBMISSION REQUIREMENTS

Restrictions on contributors: None
Author pays submission fee: No
Author pays page charges: No
Length of articles: 8,000 words maximum
Length of book reviews: 700 words
Length of notes: 100-300 words
Style: Modern Humanities Research Assn. with modifications
Number of copies required: 2
Special requirements: Submit double-spaced typescript using size A4 (8 1/4 in. x 11 3/4 in.) paper.
Copyright ownership: School of Slavonic & East European Studies, Univ. of London
Rejected manuscripts: Returned at author's request
Time before publication decision: 4-6 mos.
Time between decision and publication: 12-18 mos.
Number of reviewers: 2-4
Articles submitted per year: 60
Articles published per year: 25-30
Book reviews submitted per year: 400
Book reviews published per year: 300
Notes submitted per year: 30
Notes published per year: 30

(2648)
*Slovakia

M. Mark Stolarik, Editor
22 Bren-Maur Rd.
Nepean, Ontario K2J 327, Canada

Additional editorial address: Chair in Slovak History, Dept. of History, Univ. of Ottawa, Ottawa, Ontario K1N 6N5, Canada
Telephone: 613 825-6015
First published: 1950
Sponsoring organization: Slovak League of America
ISSN: 0583-5623
MLA acronym: Slovakia

SUBSCRIPTION INFORMATION

Frequency of publication: Annual
Circulation: 1,200
Available in microform: No
Subscription price: $6.00/yr.
Year to which price refers: 1992
Subscription address: Slovak League of America, John A. Holy, Secretary-Treasurer, 870 Rifle Camp Rd., West Paterson, NJ 07424

ADVERTISING INFORMATION

Advertising accepted: No

EDITORIAL DESCRIPTION

Scope: The publication is devoted to the history, literature, and culture of the Slovaks.
Reviews books: Yes
Publishes notes: Yes
Languages accepted: English
Prints abstracts: No
Author-anonymous submission: Yes

SUBMISSION REQUIREMENTS

Restrictions on contributors: None
Author pays submission fee: No
Author pays page charges: No

SUBMISSION REQUIREMENTS

Restrictions on contributors: None
Author pays submission fee: No
Author pays page charges: No
Length of articles: 15 pp.
Length of book reviews: 10 pp.
Style: Standard Czech
Number of copies required: 3
Special requirements: Submit original typescript and 2 copies.
Copyright ownership: Academic Publishing House of the Czechoslovak Academy of Sciences
Rejected manuscripts: Returned
Time before publication decision: 2 mos.
Time between decision and publication: 4 mos.
Number of reviewers: 2
Articles submitted per year: 20
Articles published per year: 15
Book reviews submitted per year: 25
Book reviews published per year: 20

(2657)
*Slovo na Storozhi

J. B. Rudnyckyi, Editor
Ukrainian Language Assn.
911 Carling Ave.
Ottawa, Ontario, Canada

Telephone: 613 484-3096
First published: 1964
Sponsoring organization: Ukrainian Language Assn.
ISSN: 0583-6263
MLA acronym: SNS

SUBSCRIPTION INFORMATION

Frequency of publication: Annual
Circulation: 750
Available in microform: No

ADVERTISING INFORMATION

Advertising accepted: Yes

EDITORIAL DESCRIPTION

Scope: Publishes articles on language retention and development, bilingualism vs. multilingualism, linguicide, and language and culture.
Reviews books: Yes
Publishes notes: Yes
Languages accepted: Ukrainian; English
Prints abstracts: Yes
Author-anonymous submission: No

SUBMISSION REQUIREMENTS

Restrictions on contributors: None
Author pays submission fee: No
Author pays page charges: No
Length of articles: 2-3 pp.
Length of book reviews: 1 1/2-2 pp.
Length of notes: 1/2 page
Style: MLA
Number of copies required: 2
Copyright ownership: Ukrainian Language Assn.
Rejected manuscripts: Returned
Time before publication decision: 1 yr.
Time between decision and publication: 6 mos.
Number of reviewers: 3
Articles submitted per year: 20
Articles published per year: 10
Book reviews submitted per year: 5
Book reviews published per year: 5
Notes submitted per year: 5
Notes published per year: 5

(2658)
Social Psychology Quarterly

Karen S. Cook, Editor
American Sociological Assn.
1722 N St., NW
Washington, DC 20036

First published: 1937
Sponsoring organization: American Sociological Assn.
ISSN: 0190-2725
MLA acronym: SPsy

SUBSCRIPTION INFORMATION

Frequency of publication: 4 times/yr. (Mar., June, Sept., Dec.)
Circulation: 3,650
Available in microform: No

ADVERTISING INFORMATION

Advertising accepted: Yes

EDITORIAL DESCRIPTION

Scope: Publishes articles concerning the processes and products of social interaction. This includes the study of the primary relations of individuals to one another or to groups, collectivities, or institutions, and also the study of intra-individual processes insofar as they substantially influence, or are influenced by, social forces.
Reviews books: No
Publishes notes: Yes
Languages accepted: English
Prints abstracts: Yes
Author-anonymous submission: No

SUBMISSION REQUIREMENTS

Restrictions on contributors: None
Author pays submission fee: Yes
Author pays page charges: Yes, if author has available funds.
Length of articles: 6,000 words
Length of notes: 2,000 words
Style: Journal
Number of copies required: 4
Copyright ownership: Assigned by author to American Sociological Assn.
Rejected manuscripts: Not returned
Time before publication decision: 3 mos.
Time between decision and publication: 3-5 mos.
Number of reviewers: 2-4
Articles submitted per year: 200
Articles published per year: 40
Notes submitted per year: 30
Notes published per year: 6

(2659)
Social Science Information/
Information sur les Sciences Sociales

Elina Almasy & Anne Rocha-Perazzo, Editors
Maison des Sciences de l'Homme
Bureaux 425-426
54, boulevard Raspail
75270 Paris Cédex 06, France

Telephone: (33) 1 49542026
Fax: (33) 1 45488353
First published: 1952
Sponsoring organization: Maison des Sciences de l'Homme; Ecole des Hautes Etudes en Sciences Sociales
ISSN: 0539-0184
MLA acronym: SSI

SUBSCRIPTION INFORMATION

Frequency of publication: 4 times/yr.
Circulation: 970
Available in microform: No

Subscription address: Sage Publications Ltd., 6 Bonhill St., London EC2A 4PU, England
Subscription telephone: (44) 71 3740645
Subscription fax: (44) 71 3748741

ADVERTISING INFORMATION

Advertising accepted: Yes

EDITORIAL DESCRIPTION

Reviews books: No
Publishes notes: No
Languages accepted: English; French
Prints abstracts: No
Author-anonymous submission: Yes

SUBMISSION REQUIREMENTS

Restrictions on contributors: None
Author pays submission fee: No
Author pays page charges: No
Length of articles: 30 pp.
Style: None
Number of copies required: 3
Copyright ownership: Publisher
Rejected manuscripts: Returned
Time before publication decision: 6 mos.
Time between decision and publication: 6 mos.
Number of reviewers: 2
Articles submitted per year: 100
Articles published per year: 40

(2660)
*Social Text

Bruce Robbins & Andrew Ross, Editors
Center for Critical Analysis of Contemporary Culture
Rutgers Univ.
8 Bishop Pl.
New Brunswick, NJ 08903

Additional editorial address: C/o Mariani, 141 Perry St., New York, NY 10014
Telephone: 908 932-1503; 212 627-8846
Fax: 908 932-8683
First published: 1978
Sponsoring organization: Rutgers Univ.
ISSN: 0164-2472
MLA acronym: SText

SUBSCRIPTION INFORMATION

Frequency of publication: 4 times/yr.
Circulation: 2,000
Available in microform: No
Subscription price: $60.00/yr. institutions; $24.00/yr. individuals; $16.00/yr. students; add $6.00/yr. postage outside US
Year to which price refers: 1992

ADVERTISING INFORMATION

Advertising accepted: Yes, on an exchange basis

EDITORIAL DESCRIPTION

Scope: Publishes studies on social issues. Includes interdisciplinary articles on literature, culture, politics, education, and language.
Reviews books: Yes
Publishes notes: No
Languages accepted: English
Prints abstracts: No
Author-anonymous submission: No

SUBMISSION REQUIREMENTS

Restrictions on contributors: None
Author pays submission fee: No
Author pays page charges: No
Length of articles: 7,500 words
Length of book reviews: 2,000 words
Style: Chicago
Number of copies required: 2
Copyright ownership: Duke Univ. Press
Rejected manuscripts: Not returned

Time before publication decision: 3 mos.
Time between decision and publication: 3 mos.
Number of reviewers: 6 minimum
Articles submitted per year: 200
Articles published per year: 40
Book reviews submitted per year: 15
Book reviews published per year: 4

(2661)
Société des Anciens Textes Français

40, Avenue d'Iéna
75116 Paris, France

First published: 1875
Sponsoring organization: Soc. des Anciens Textes
MLA acronym: SATF

SUBSCRIPTION INFORMATION

Frequency of publication: Irregular
Available in microform: No
Subscription address: Editions A. & J. Picard & Cie, 82, rue Bonaparte, 75006 Paris, France

ADVERTISING INFORMATION

Advertising accepted: No

EDITORIAL DESCRIPTION

Scope: Publishes Old French texts in the original language.
Reviews books: No
Publishes notes: No
Languages accepted: French
Prints abstracts: No
Author-anonymous submission: No

SUBMISSION REQUIREMENTS

Restrictions on contributors: None
Length of books: No restrictions
Style: Series
Copyright ownership: Soc. des Anciens Textes

(2662)
*Société des Textes Français Modernes

Editions Klincksieck
11, rue de Lille
75007 Paris, France

Telephone: (33) 1 42603825
Fax: (33) 1 42964063
First published: 1905
Sponsoring organization: Centre National des Lettres; Centre National de la Recherche Scientifique
ISSN: 0768-0821
MLA acronym: STFM

SUBSCRIPTION INFORMATION

Frequency of publication: 2 times/yr.
Available in microform: No
Subscription price: 210 F/yr.
Year to which price refers: 1992
Subscription address: Univ. de Paris IV, 1, rue V. Cousin, 75005 Paris, France

ADVERTISING INFORMATION

Advertising accepted: No

EDITORIAL DESCRIPTION

Scope: Publishes French texts of the 16th, 17th, and 18th centuries.
Reviews books: No
Publishes notes: No
Languages accepted: French
Prints abstracts: No
Author-anonymous submission: No

SUBMISSION REQUIREMENTS

Restrictions on contributors: None
Author pays submission fee: No
Author pays page charges: No
Length of books: 250-300 pp.
Style: RHLF
Number of copies required: 2
Copyright ownership: Series
Rejected manuscripts: Returned
Time before publication decision: 3-9 mos.
Number of reviewers: 2-4
Books submitted per year: 2-5
Books published per year: 2

(2663)
*Society for the Study of Midwestern Literature Newsletter

David D. Anderson, Editor
Ernst Bessey Hall
Michigan State Univ.
East Lansing, MI 48824-1033

Telephone: 517 353-4370; 517 355-2400
First published: 1971
Sponsoring organization: Soc. for the Study of Midwestern Literature
ISSN: 0085-6304
MLA acronym: SSMLN

SUBSCRIPTION INFORMATION

Frequency of publication: 3 times/yr. (Spring, Summer, Fall)
Circulation: 500
Available in microform: No

ADVERTISING INFORMATION

Advertising accepted: No

EDITORIAL DESCRIPTION

Reviews books: Yes
Publishes notes: Yes
Languages accepted: English
Prints abstracts: No

SUBMISSION REQUIREMENTS

Restrictions on contributors: Contributors must be members of the Soc. for the Study of Midwestern Literature.
Author pays submission fee: No
Author pays page charges: No
Length of articles: 1,000-5,000 words
Length of book reviews: 1,000 words
Length of notes: 500-1,000 words
Style: MLA
Number of copies required: 1
Copyright ownership: Reverts to author upon request
Time before publication decision: 3 mos.
Time between decision and publication: 3-6 mos.
Articles submitted per year: 50
Articles published per year: 12-15
Book reviews submitted per year: 15
Book reviews published per year: 9
Notes submitted per year: 10
Notes published per year: 5

(2664)
*Sociocriticism

Edmond Cros, Editor
Inst. International de Sociocritique
Univ. Paul Valéry
B.P. 5043
34032 Montpellier, France

Telephone: (33) 67142172
First published: 1985
MLA acronym: Sociocriticism

SUBSCRIPTION INFORMATION

Frequency of publication: 2 times/yr.
Available in microform: No
Subscription price: $50.00/yr. institutions
Year to which price refers: 1992
Subscription address: C.E.R.S., Univ. Paul Valéry, B.P. 5043, 34032 Montpellier Cedex, France

ADVERTISING INFORMATION

Advertising accepted: Yes

EDITORIAL DESCRIPTION

Scope: Publishes articles on sociological criticism with each issue organized around a specific theme.
Reviews books: No
Publishes notes: No
Languages accepted: French; Spanish; English
Prints abstracts: Yes
Author-anonymous submission: Yes

SUBMISSION REQUIREMENTS

Restrictions on contributors: None
Author pays submission fee: No
Author pays page charges: No
Length of articles: 8,000 words
Style: MLA
Number of copies required: 2
Special requirements: Include 100-word abstract.
Copyright ownership: Journal
Rejected manuscripts: Not returned
Articles published per year: 25

(2665)
Sociolinguistics

Tony Hak, Editor
Medical Sociology
P.O. Box 1738
3000 DR Rotterdam, Netherlands

First published: 1970
Sponsoring organization: International Sociological Assn., Research Committee on Sociolinguistics
ISSN: 0049-1217
MLA acronym: Socioling

SUBSCRIPTION INFORMATION

Frequency of publication: 2 times/yr.
Circulation: 300
Available in microform: No
Subscription address: Foris Publications, P.O. Box 509, 3300 AM Dordrecht, Netherlands

ADVERTISING INFORMATION

Advertising accepted: Yes

EDITORIAL DESCRIPTION

Scope: Stresses professional activities of the membership and readership, particularly on new developments in research and teaching in sociolinguistics. Hopes to draw attention to that most critical topic, the study of language involvements in society.
Reviews books: Yes
Publishes notes: Yes
Languages accepted: English; French; Spanish
Prints abstracts: Yes

SUBMISSION REQUIREMENTS

Restrictions on contributors: None
Author pays submission fee: No
Author pays page charges: No
Length of articles: 6-10 pp.
Length of book reviews: 1 p.
Length of notes: No restrictions
Style: American Sociolinguistics Assn.
Number of copies required: 1

Special requirements: Submit on diskette if possible, and supply a 150-word abstract, and a 150-word biographical note.
Copyright ownership: Foris Publications
Time before publication decision: 1 mo.
Time between decision and publication: 6 mos. maximum
Number of reviewers: 2
Articles submitted per year: 10-12
Articles published per year: 8-12

(2666) Sodobnost

Ciril Zlobec, Editor
Uredništvo Sodobnosti
Mestni trg 26
61000 Ljubljana, Slovenia

ISSN: 0038-0482
MLA acronym: Sodobnost

SUBSCRIPTION INFORMATION

Frequency of publication: 12 times/yr.
Subscription address: Državna Založba Slovenije, Knjižni Oddelek, Stritarjeva 3/11, Box 50-1, Ljubljana, Slovenia

EDITORIAL DESCRIPTION

Scope: Publishes articles on Slovenian literature and culture.
Languages accepted: Slovenian
Prints abstracts: No

(2667) *Sophia

Naoji Kimura, Board Chairman
Sophia Univ.
Kioicho 7-1
Chiyoda-ku
Tokyo 102, Japan

Telephone: (81) 3 32383541
Fax: (81) 3 32383541
First published: 1952
Sponsoring organization: Sophia Univ.
ISSN: 0489-6432
MLA acronym: SophiaT

SUBSCRIPTION INFORMATION

Frequency of publication: 4 times/yr.
Available in microform: No

ADVERTISING INFORMATION

Advertising accepted: No

EDITORIAL DESCRIPTION

Scope: Publishes articles on interdisciplinary studies on cultural exchange.
Reviews books: Yes
Publishes notes: Yes
Languages accepted: Japanese
Prints abstracts: No
Author-anonymous submission: No

SUBMISSION REQUIREMENTS

Restrictions on contributors: Contributors must be affiliated with Sophia Univ.
Author pays submission fee: No
Author pays page charges: No
Length of articles: No restrictions
Length of book reviews: 4,000 words
Length of notes: No restrictions
Style: None
Number of copies required: 1
Special requirements: Submit original typescript.
Copyright ownership: Author
Rejected manuscripts: Returned

Time before publication decision: 1 mo.
Time between decision and publication: 2 mos.
Number of reviewers: 2-3
Articles submitted per year: 100
Articles published per year: 80
Book reviews submitted per year: 30
Book reviews published per year: 20
Notes submitted per year: 30
Notes published per year: 20

(2668) *Sophia English Studies

Tetsuo Anzai, Editor
English Literary Soc. of Sophia Univ.
7-1 Kioicho, Chiyoda Ku,
Tokyo, Japan

First published: 1976
Sponsoring organization: Sophia Univ., English Literary Soc.
ISSN: 0388-6417
MLA acronym: SES

SUBSCRIPTION INFORMATION

Frequency of publication: Annual
Circulation: 700
Available in microform: No
Subscription price: 4,000 yen/yr.
Year to which price refers: 1991

ADVERTISING INFORMATION

Advertising accepted: No

EDITORIAL DESCRIPTION

Scope: Publishes articles on English literature and language.
Reviews books: No
Publishes notes: No
Languages accepted: English; Japanese
Prints abstracts: No
Author-anonymous submission: No

SUBMISSION REQUIREMENTS

Restrictions on contributors: Contributors must be members of the the English Literary Soc. of Sophia Univ.
Author pays submission fee: Yes
Author pays page charges: Yes
Length of articles: 2,500-12,500 words or 12,000 Japanese characters
Style: MLA
Number of copies required: 3
Copyright ownership: Assigned by author to journal
Rejected manuscripts: Returned
Time before publication decision: 1 mo.
Time between decision and publication: 2 mos.
Number of reviewers: 4
Articles submitted per year: 10
Articles published per year: 6

(2669) *Soundings: An Interdisciplinary Journal

Ralph V. Norman, Editor
306 Aconda Court
Univ. of Tennessee
Knoxville, TN 37996-0530

Telephone: 615 974-8252
First published: 1968
Sponsoring organization: Soc. for Values in Higher Education; Univ. of Tennessee
ISSN: 0038-1861
MLA acronym: Soundings

SUBSCRIPTION INFORMATION

Frequency of publication: 4 times/yr. (Mar., June, Sept., Dec.)

Circulation: 1,725
Available in microform: Yes
Subscription price: $27.00/yr. institutions US; $30.00/yr. institutions elsewhere; $18.00/yr. individuals US; $21.00/yr. individuals elsewhere
Year to which price refers: 1992

ADVERTISING INFORMATION

Advertising accepted: Yes
Advertising rates: $45.00/quarter page; $75.00/half page; $120.00/full page

EDITORIAL DESCRIPTION

Scope: Publishes interdisciplinary articles with emphasis on the humanities and the social sciences.
Reviews books: Yes
Publishes notes: Yes
Languages accepted: English
Prints abstracts: No
Author-anonymous submission: Yes

SUBMISSION REQUIREMENTS

Restrictions on contributors: None
Author pays submission fee: No
Author pays page charges: No
Length of articles: 8,000 words maximum
Length of book reviews: 5,000 words
Style: MLA
Number of copies required: 3
Special requirements: Submit original typescript plus 2 copies.
Copyright ownership: Soc. for Values in Higher Education & Univ. of Tennessee
Rejected manuscripts: Returned; enclose SASE.
Time before publication decision: 4-6 mos.
Time between decision and publication: 6-24 mos.
Number of reviewers: 3-4
Articles submitted per year: 150
Articles published per year: 24-30
Book reviews submitted per year: 5
Book reviews published per year: 2-4
Notes submitted per year: 4-8
Notes published per year: 2-3

(2670) *Soundings: Collections of the University Library, University of California, Santa Barbara

Donald E. Fitch, Editor
Librarian's Office
Univ. Library
Univ. of California
Santa Barbara, CA 93106

Telephone: 805 893-2649
First published: 1969
Sponsoring organization: Univ. of California, Santa Barbara, Library
ISSN: 0038-1853
MLA acronym: SCUL

SUBSCRIPTION INFORMATION

Frequency of publication: Annual
Circulation: 850
Available in microform: No
Subscription price: $4.00/yr.
Year to which price refers: 1992
Subscription address: Librarian's office, at the above address

ADVERTISING INFORMATION

Advertising accepted: No

EDITORIAL DESCRIPTION

Scope: Welcomes manuscripts descriptive of, or in some way related to, the collections of the Library. Occasionally publishes lectures delivered on the Santa Barbara campus.

Reviews books: No
Publishes notes: Yes
Languages accepted: English
Prints abstracts: No
Author-anonymous submission: No

SUBMISSION REQUIREMENTS

Restrictions on contributors: None
Author pays submission fee: No
Author pays page charges: No
Style: MLA
Number of copies required: 1
Copyright ownership: Univ. of California, Santa Barbara, Library
Rejected manuscripts: Returned
Time before publication decision: 1 mo.
Time between decision and publication: 2-10 mos.
Number of reviewers: 3
Articles published per year: 4-5
Notes published per year: 1-2

(2671)
*Sources Chrétiennes

Dominique Bertrand, Editor
29, rue du Plat
69002 Lyon, France

Telephone: (33) 78372708
Fax: (33) 72325019
First published: 1942
Sponsoring organization: Assn. des Amis de Sources Chrétiennes
ISSN: 0750-1978
MLA acronym: SCh

SUBSCRIPTION INFORMATION

Frequency of publication: Irregular
Circulation: 2,500
Available in microform: No
Subscription address: Les Editions du Cerf, 29, boulevard de Latour-Maubourg, 75340 Paris Cedex 07, France
Subscription telephone: (33) 1 44181212

ADVERTISING INFORMATION

Advertising accepted: Yes

EDITORIAL DESCRIPTION

Scope: Publishes editions of texts of eastern and western Christian literatures of the first fourteen centuries. Includes introductions, translations, annotations, and indexes.
Reviews books: Yes
Publishes notes: No
Languages accepted: French; Latin; Greek
Prints abstracts: No
Author-anonymous submission: No

SUBMISSION REQUIREMENTS

Restrictions on contributors: None
Author pays submission fee: No
Author pays page charges: No
Length of books: 80,000-160,000 words
Number of copies required: 2
Special requirements: Request from subscription address.
Copyright ownership: Editions du Cerf
Rejected manuscripts: Returned
Time before publication decision: 6 mos.
Time between decision and publication: 10-18 mos.
Number of reviewers: 2
Books submitted per year: 8-12
Books published per year: 8-10

(2672)
*South African Journal of African Languages/Suid-Afrikaanse Tydskrif vir Afrikatale

L. J. Louwrens & Louise Serfontein, Editors
Dept. of African Languages
Univ. of South Africa
P.O. Box 392
Pretoria 0001, South Africa

Telephone: (27) 12 4298271
Fax: (27) 12 4293355
First published: 1981
Sponsoring organization: Dept. of National Education
ISSN: 0257-2117
MLA acronym: SAJAL

SUBSCRIPTION INFORMATION

Frequency of publication: 4 times/yr.
Circulation: 1,500
Available in microform: No
Subscription price: 48 R/yr.
Year to which price refers: 1991
Subscription address: Bureau for Scientific Publications, P.O. Box 1758, Pretoria 0001, South Africa
Subscription telephone: (27) 12 3226422
Subscription fax: (27) 12 3226422

ADVERTISING INFORMATION

Advertising accepted: No

EDITORIAL DESCRIPTION

Scope: Publishes articles on the languages of Africa that are of a linguistic or literary nature.
Reviews books: Yes, in a supplement
Publishes notes: Yes
Languages accepted: Afrikaans; English; all African languages
Prints abstracts: Yes
Author-anonymous submission: Yes

SUBMISSION REQUIREMENTS

Author pays submission fee: No
Author pays page charges: No
Length of articles: 1,000-10,000 words
Length of book reviews: 900 words
Length of notes: 500 words
Number of copies required: 3
Special requirements: Submit original typescript and 2 copies. See "Instructions to Authors" in journal.
Copyright ownership: African Language Assn. of Southern Africa
Rejected manuscripts: Returned
Time before publication decision: 2 mos.
Time between decision and publication: 4-6 mos.
Number of reviewers: 2
Articles submitted per year: 40-50
Articles published per year: 24

(2673)
*South African Theatre Journal

Temple Hauptfleisch & Ian Steadman, Editors
School of Dramatic Art
Univ. of the Witwatersrand
P.O. Wits
2050, South Africa

Additional editorial address: Review editor: Drama Dept., Univ. of Stellenbosch, Stellenbosch, 7600, South Africa
Telephone: (27) 2231 773091
Fax: (27) 2231 774336
First published: 1987
Sponsoring organization: Dramatic, Artistic & Literary Rights Organization, Johannesburg; Univ. of Witwatersrand; Univ. of Stellenbosch; Oude Meester Foundation
MLA acronym: SATJ

SUBSCRIPTION INFORMATION

Frequency of publication: 2 times/yr. (May, Sept.)
Circulation: 300
Available in microform: No
Subscription price: 35 R/yr. institutions Africa; $30.00/yr. institutions elsewhere; 20 R/yr. individuals Africa; $20.00/yr. individuals elsewhere
Year to which price refers: 1992
Subscription address: P.O. Box 6054, Uniedal 7612, South Africa
Additional subscription address: Drama Dept., Univ. of Stellenbosch, Stellenbosch, 7600, South Africa

ADVERTISING INFORMATION

Advertising accepted: Yes
Advertising rates: 250 R/half page, 2 issues; 500 R/full page, 2 issues

EDITORIAL DESCRIPTION

Scope: Aims at providing a forum for the academic discussion of performance studies and the performing arts, especially as they manifest themselves in Southern Africa. Publishes articles on the history, theory, and practice of the performing arts, as well as on the methodology of theater research. It also contains theater reports, book reviews, commentary, and general announcements.
Reviews books: Yes
Publishes notes: Yes
Languages accepted: All languages
Prints abstracts: Yes
Author-anonymous submission: Yes

SUBMISSION REQUIREMENTS

Restrictions on contributors: None
Author pays submission fee: No
Author pays page charges: Yes
Cost of page charges: 25 R/page
Length of articles: 3,000-5,000 words
Length of book reviews: 800 words
Length of notes: 200 words
Style: MLA
Number of copies required: 3
Copyright ownership: Author
Rejected manuscripts: Returned; enclose SASE.
Time before publication decision: 2 mos.
Time between decision and publication: 6-12 mos.
Number of reviewers: 2
Articles submitted per year: 15-20
Articles published per year: 8-10
Book reviews submitted per year: 20
Book reviews published per year: 16
Notes submitted per year: 10
Notes published per year: 10

(2674)
*South Asian Review

Satya S. Pachori, Editor
Dept. of Language & Literature
Univ. of North Florida
4567 St. Johns Bluff Rd., S.
Jacksonville, FL 32216

Telephone: 904 646-2580
Fax: 904 646-2703
First published: 1977
Sponsoring organization: South Asian Literary Assn.
ISSN: 0275-9527
MLA acronym: SARev

SUBSCRIPTION INFORMATION

Frequency of publication: Annual
Circulation: 100
Available in microform: No

ADVERTISING INFORMATION

Advertising accepted: No

EDITORIAL DESCRIPTION

Scope: Publishes articles on South Asian languages, literatures, culture, philosophy, and religion and their impact on language and literature, and comparative literary studies of East and West.
Reviews books: Yes
Publishes notes: Yes
Languages accepted: English
Prints abstracts: No
Author-anonymous submission: No

SUBMISSION REQUIREMENTS

Restrictions on contributors: Contributors must be members of South Asian Literary Assn.
Author pays submission fee: Yes
Author pays page charges: No
Length of articles: 10-15 double-spaced typescript pp.
Length of book reviews: 500-1,000 words
Length of notes: 500-1,000 words
Style: MLA
Number of copies required: 2
Special requirements: Send a 250-word abstract before submitting manuscript.
Copyright ownership: South Asian Literary Assn.
Rejected manuscripts: Returned
Time before publication decision: 2-3 mos.
Time between decision and publication: 3-6 mos.
Number of reviewers: 2-3
Articles submitted per year: 20-25
Articles published per year: 9-12
Book reviews submitted per year: 2-4
Book reviews published per year: 2-3
Notes submitted per year: 2-4
Notes published per year: 2-3

(2675)
South Atlantic Quarterly

Frank Lentricchia, Editor
304-H Allen Bldg.
Duke Univ.
Durham, NC 27706

First published: 1902
Sponsoring organization: Duke Univ.
ISSN: 0038-2876
MLA acronym: SAQ

SUBSCRIPTION INFORMATION

Frequency of publication: 4 times/yr. (Winter, Spring, Summer, Fall)
Circulation: 1,700
Available in microform: Yes
Subscription price: $40.00/yr. institutions; $20.00/yr. individuals
Year to which price refers: 1991
Subscription address: Duke Univ. Press, Box 6697 College Station, Durham, NC 27708

ADVERTISING INFORMATION

Advertising accepted: Yes

EDITORIAL DESCRIPTION

Scope: Publishes articles in general humanities, social sciences, and events of current interest.
Reviews books: Yes
Publishes notes: No
Languages accepted: English
Prints abstracts: No
Author-anonymous submission: No

SUBMISSION REQUIREMENTS

Restrictions on contributors: Book reviews are solicited.
Author pays submission fee: No

Author pays page charges: No
Length of articles: 10,000 words
Length of book reviews: 5,000 words
Style: Chicago
Number of copies required: 2
Special requirements: Submit original typescript and 1 copy.
Copyright ownership: Assigned by author to Duke Univ. Press
Rejected manuscripts: Returned; enclose return postage.
Time before publication decision: 4-6 weeks
Time between decision and publication: 12-18 mos.
Number of reviewers: 2-3
Articles submitted per year: 200
Articles published per year: 32
Book reviews published per year: 3-4

(2676)
*South Atlantic Review

Robert F. Bell, Editor
South Atlantic MLA
Box 6109
104 Manly Hall
Univ. of Alabama
Tuscaloosa, AL 35486-6109

Telephone: 205 348-9067
Fax: 205 348-9642
First published: 1935
Sponsoring organization: South Atlantic Modern Language Assn.
ISSN: 0277-335X
MLA acronym: SoAR

SUBSCRIPTION INFORMATION

Frequency of publication: 4 times/yr. (Jan., May, Sept., Nov.)
Circulation: 4,500
Available in microform: Yes
Subscription price: $25.00/yr. institutions; $15.00/yr. individuals; $8.00/yr. students; add $10.00/yr. postage outside US
Year to which price refers: 1992

ADVERTISING INFORMATION

Advertising accepted: Yes

EDITORIAL DESCRIPTION

Scope: Publishes critical and scholarly essays in English and the modern languages on those languages and literatures that are in the province of the South Atlantic Modern Language Assn.
Reviews books: Yes
Publishes notes: No
Languages accepted: English
Prints abstracts: No
Author-anonymous submission: Yes

SUBMISSION REQUIREMENTS

Restrictions on contributors: Contributors must be members of the South Atlantic Modern Language Assn.
Author pays submission fee: No
Author pays page charges: No
Length of articles: 15-25 typescript pp.
Length of book reviews: 1,000 words
Style: MLA
Number of copies required: 2
Special requirements: Submit original typescript and photocopy.
Copyright ownership: Assigned by author to journal
Rejected manuscripts: Returned; enclose return postage.
Time before publication decision: 1-3 mos.
Time between decision and publication: 4-8 mos.
Number of reviewers: 3
Articles submitted per year: 100
Articles published per year: 20-25

Book reviews submitted per year: 120-150
Book reviews published per year: 120-150

(2677)
*South Carolina Review

Richard J. Calhoun, Editor
Dept. of English
Clemson Univ.
Clemson, SC 29634-1503

Telephone: 803 656-3229
First published: 1968
Sponsoring organization: Clemson Univ., College of Liberal Arts
ISSN: 0038-3163
MLA acronym: SCR

SUBSCRIPTION INFORMATION

Frequency of publication: 2 times/yr. (Sept., Mar.)
Circulation: 600
Available in microform: No
Subscription price: $7.00/yr. individuals US
Year to which price refers: 1992

ADVERTISING INFORMATION

Advertising accepted: Yes
Advertising rates: $75.00/half page; $125.00/full page

EDITORIAL DESCRIPTION

Scope: Solicits manuscripts of all kinds: essays, scholarly articles, criticism, poetry, and stories. Interests are not limited to any particular region.
Reviews books: Yes
Publishes notes: No
Languages accepted: English
Prints abstracts: No
Author-anonymous submission: No

SUBMISSION REQUIREMENTS

Restrictions on contributors: Book reviews are commissioned.
Author pays submission fee: No
Author pays page charges: No
Length of articles: 3,000-5,000 words
Length of book reviews: 900 words
Style: MLA
Number of copies required: 1
Special requirements: Submission on IBM ASCII diskette is requested for accepted manuscripts.
Copyright ownership: Assigned by author to journal
Rejected manuscripts: Returned; enclose return postage.
Time before publication decision: 6-9 mos.
Time between decision and publication: 2-3 yrs.
Number of reviewers: 5
Articles submitted per year: 50
Articles published per year: 10

(2678)
*South Central Review: The Journal of the South Central Modern Language Association

Richard Golsan, Editor
Dept. of English
Texas A&M Univ.
College Station, TX 77843-4227

First published: 1984
Sponsoring organization: South Central Modern Language Assn.
ISSN: 0743-6831
MLA acronym: SCRev

Frequency of publication: 4 times/yr. (Spring, Summer, Fall, Winter)
Circulation: 1,800
Available in microform: No
Subscription address: Executive Director, SCMLA, at the above address

ADVERTISING INFORMATION

Advertising accepted: Yes

EDITORIAL DESCRIPTION

Scope: Publishes research and scholarship in modern languages and literatures, critical essays, and book reviews.
Reviews books: Yes
Publishes notes: No
Languages accepted: English
Prints abstracts: No
Author-anonymous submission: Yes

SUBMISSION REQUIREMENTS

Restrictions on contributors: Contributors should be members of the South Central Modern Language Assn. Reviews are commissioned.
Author pays submission fee: No
Author pays page charges: No
Length of articles: 3,000-7,500 words
Length of book reviews: 750-1,000 words
Style: MLA (1985)
Number of copies required: 2
Special requirements: Submit original typescript and 1 author-anonymous copy.
Copyright ownership: South Central Modern Language Assn.
Rejected manuscripts: Returned; enclose SASE.
Time before publication decision: 2-4 mos.
Time between decision and publication: 6-12 mos.
Number of reviewers: 2-4
Articles submitted per year: 100-125
Articles published per year: 18-20
Book reviews submitted per year: 65-70
Book reviews published per year: 55-60

(2679)
*South Dakota Review

John R. Milton, Editor
P.O. Box 111
Univ. Exchange
Vermillion, SD 57069

Telephone: 605 677-5229
First published: 1963
Sponsoring organization: Univ. of South Dakota, College of Arts & Sciences
ISSN: 0038-3368
MLA acronym: SDR

SUBSCRIPTION INFORMATION

Frequency of publication: 4 times/yr.
Circulation: 500
Available in microform: Yes
Subscription price: $15.00/yr., $25.00/2 yrs. US & Canada; add $1.00/yr. postage elsewhere
Year to which price refers: 1992

ADVERTISING INFORMATION

Advertising accepted: No

EDITORIAL DESCRIPTION

Scope: Publishes fiction, poetry, essays. Flexible, but preference is given to writers in, or materials about, the western half of the US.
Reviews books: No
Publishes notes: No
Languages accepted: English
Prints abstracts: No
Author-anonymous submission: No

SUBMISSION REQUIREMENTS

Restrictions on contributors: None
Author pays submission fee: No
Author pays page charges: No
Length of articles: 5,000 words
Number of copies required: 1
Copyright ownership: Univ. of South Dakota
Rejected manuscripts: Returned
Time before publication decision: 2-4 weeks; longer in summer
Time between decision and publication: 3-6 mos.
Number of reviewers: 1-2
Articles submitted per year: 50
Articles published per year: 4-20

(2680)
*Southeast Asian Review of English

Margaret Yong, Editor
Dept. of English
Univ. of Malaya
59100 Kuala Lumpur, Malaysia

First published: 1980
Sponsoring organization: Assn. for Commonwealth Literature & Language Studies in Malaysia
ISSN: 0127-046X
MLA acronym: SARE

SUBSCRIPTION INFORMATION

Frequency of publication: 2 times/yr. (June, Dec.)
Circulation: 100-200
Available in microform: No
Subscription price: $15.00/yr. institutions; $10.00/yr. individuals
Year to which price refers: 1992
Subscription address: Serials Division, Univ. of Malaya Cooperative Bookstore, Univ. of Malaya, 59100 Kuala Lumpur, Malaysia

ADVERTISING INFORMATION

Advertising accepted: Yes, on an exchange basis

EDITORIAL DESCRIPTION

Scope: Publishes articles related to new literatures in English; teaching of English as a second language; and British and American literature.
Reviews books: Yes
Publishes notes: Yes
Languages accepted: English
Prints abstracts: No
Author-anonymous submission: Yes

SUBMISSION REQUIREMENTS

Restrictions on contributors: None
Author pays submission fee: No
Author pays page charges: No
Length of articles: No restrictions
Length of book reviews: No restrictions
Length of notes: No restrictions
Style: MLA
Number of copies required: 1
Special requirements: Submit double-spaced typescript. Poems in Southeast Asian languages are accepted for publication if accompanied by English translation.
Copyright ownership: Assn. for Commonwealth Language & Literature Studies in Malaysia
Rejected manuscripts: Returned; enclose return postage.
Time before publication decision: 3-6 mos.
Time between decision and publication: 6-12 mos.
Number of reviewers: 2-4
Articles submitted per year: 20-30
Articles published per year: 20
Book reviews published per year: 15-30
Notes submitted per year: 10-20
Notes published per year: 10-20

(2681)
*Southerly: A Review of Australian Literature

Elizabeth Webby, Editor
Dept. of English
Univ. of Sydney
Sydney, NSW 2006, Australia

Telephone: (61) 2 6922226
Fax: (61) 2 6922434
First published: 1939
Sponsoring organization: English Assn., Sydney
ISSN: 0038-3732
MLA acronym: Southerly

SUBSCRIPTION INFORMATION

Frequency of publication: 4 times/yr.
Circulation: 1,200
Available in microform: Yes, through Univ. Microfilms International
Subscription price: A$35.00/yr. Australia; A$45.00/yr. elsewhere
Year to which price refers: 1992
Subscription address: P.O. Box 187, Rozelle NSW, 2039, Australia
Subscription telephone: (61) 2 8182591
Subscription fax: (61) 2 8185332

ADVERTISING INFORMATION

Advertising accepted: Yes

EDITORIAL DESCRIPTION

Scope: Publishes creative and critical writing in the field of Australian literature.
Reviews books: Yes
Publishes notes: Yes
Languages accepted: English
Prints abstracts: No
Author-anonymous submission: No

SUBMISSION REQUIREMENTS

Restrictions on contributors: Contributors of original fiction and poetry must be Australian.
Author pays submission fee: No
Author pays page charges: No
Length of articles: 5,000 words
Length of book reviews: 1,000 words
Length of notes: 1,000 words
Style: MLA
Number of copies required: 1
Copyright ownership: Author
Rejected manuscripts: Returned; enclose return postage.
Time before publication decision: 6 weeks
Time between decision and publication: 1 yr.
Number of reviewers: 1-2
Articles submitted per year: 20-30
Articles published per year: 12-16
Book reviews submitted per year: 12
Book reviews published per year: 12

(2682)
*Southern Folklore

Erika Brady, Editor
Western Kentucky Univ.
Bowling Green, KY 42101

Additional editorial address: Send books for review to: Eric Montenyohl, Dept. of English, Univ. of Southwestern Louisiana, Lafayette, LA 70504-4691
First published: 1932
Sponsoring organization: Western Kentucky Univ.
ISSN: 0889-594X
MLA acronym: SFolk

SUBSCRIPTION INFORMATION

Frequency of publication: 3 times/yr.
Circulation: 1,200
Available in microform: Yes

Subscription price: $20.00/yr.
Year to which price refers: 1992
Subscription address: Univ. Press of Kentucky, 663 South Limestone St., Lexington, KY 40506-0336
Subscription telephone: 606 257-8439

ADVERTISING INFORMATION

Advertising accepted: Yes

EDITORIAL DESCRIPTION

Scope: Publishes articles on analytical, descriptive, comparative, and historical study of folklore and folklife, and recent developments in the discipline including the public sector and cultural conservation.
Reviews books: Yes
Publishes notes: No
Languages accepted: English
Prints abstracts: No
Author-anonymous submission: Yes

SUBMISSION REQUIREMENTS

Restrictions on contributors: None
Author pays submission fee: No
Author pays page charges: No
Length of articles: 4,000-5,000 words
Length of book reviews: 750 words
Style: Chicago
Number of copies required: 2
Special requirements: Submit original typescript and 1 copy. If possible, submit on diskette using WordPerfect. Use the author-date documentation system.
Copyright ownership: Journal & Univ. Press of Kentucky
Rejected manuscripts: Returned
Time before publication decision: 3 mos.
Time between decision and publication: 5 mos.
Number of reviewers: 2
Articles submitted per year: 60
Articles published per year: 15
Book reviews submitted per year: 20
Book reviews published per year: 15

(2683)
*Southern Humanities Review

Dan R. Latimer & R. T. Smith, Editors
9088 Haley Center
Auburn Univ.
Auburn, AL 36849

Telephone: 205 844-9088
First published: 1967
Sponsoring organization: Auburn Univ.
ISSN: 0038-4186
MLA acronym: SHR

SUBSCRIPTION INFORMATION

Frequency of publication: 4 times/yr. (Mar., June, Sept., Dec.)
Circulation: 700
Available in microform: Yes
Subscription price: $15.00/yr., $27.00/2 yrs. US; $20.00/yr., $36.00/2 yrs. elsewhere
Year to which price refers: 1992

ADVERTISING INFORMATION

Advertising accepted: Yes
Advertising rates: $100.00/inside back cover

EDITORIAL DESCRIPTION

Scope: Publishes fiction, poetry, and critical essays on the arts, literature, philosophy, religion, and history.
Reviews books: Yes
Publishes notes: No
Languages accepted: English
Prints abstracts: No
Author-anonymous submission: No

SUBMISSION REQUIREMENTS

Restrictions on contributors: Multiple submissions are not accepted. Manuscripts lacking return postage are not considered.
Author pays submission fee: No
Author pays page charges: No
Length of articles: 3,500-5,000 words
Length of book reviews: 750-1,000 words
Style: MLA
Number of copies required: 1
Copyright ownership: Journal
Rejected manuscripts: Returned; enclose return postage.
Time before publication decision: 1-3 mos. minimum
Time between decision and publication: 6-18 mos.
Number of reviewers: 4
Articles submitted per year: 75
Articles published per year: 8-10
Book reviews submitted per year: 75-80
Book reviews published per year: 50-65

(2684)
*Southern Literary Journal

Kimball King & Fred Hobson, Editors
Dept. of English
Greenlaw Hall
Univ. of North Carolina
Chapel Hill, NC 27599-3520

Telephone: 919 962-5481
First published: 1968
Sponsoring organization: Univ. of North Carolina, Chapel Hill, Dept. of English
ISSN: 0038-4291
MLA acronym: SLJ

SUBSCRIPTION INFORMATION

Frequency of publication: 2 times/yr. (Spring, Fall)
Circulation: 750
Available in microform: Yes
Subscription price: $15.00/yr. institutions; $12.00/yr. individuals
Year to which price refers: 1992-93
Subscription address: Univ. of North Carolina Press, Journals Dept., Chapel Hill, NC 27599-6215
Subscription telephone: 919 966-3561

ADVERTISING INFORMATION

Advertising accepted: Yes
Advertising rates: Request from Univ. of North Carolina Press

EDITORIAL DESCRIPTION

Scope: Focuses on the literary and intellectual life of the American South from colonial times to the present day. Includes articles on literary criticism, historical studies, and thematic and interpretative analysis. Each issue contains one or more review essays in which recent books are discussed in terms of the larger issues they raise.
Reviews books: Yes
Publishes notes: No
Languages accepted: English
Prints abstracts: No

SUBMISSION REQUIREMENTS

Restrictions on contributors: None
Author pays submission fee: No
Author pays page charges: No
Length of articles: 3,500 words
Length of book reviews: No restrictions
Style: MLA
Number of copies required: 1
Copyright ownership: Assigned by author to journal
Rejected manuscripts: Returned; enclose return postage.
Time before publication decision: 3-6 mos.
Time between decision and publication: 6-12 mos.
Number of reviewers: 2-3
Articles submitted per year: 100
Articles published per year: 18
Book reviews published per year: 10

(2685)
*The Southern Quarterly: A Journal of the Arts in the South

Stephan Flinn Young, Editor
P.O. Box 5078
Southern Station
Hattiesburg, MS 39406-5078

Telephone: 601 266-4370
First published: 1962
Sponsoring organization: Univ. of Southern Mississippi
ISSN: 0038-4496
MLA acronym: SoQ

SUBSCRIPTION INFORMATION

Frequency of publication: 4 times/yr. (Fall, Winter, Spring, Summer)
Circulation: 850
Available in microform: Yes
Subscription price: $20.00/yr. institutions; $9.00/yr., $16.00/2 yrs. individuals
Year to which price refers: 1992

ADVERTISING INFORMATION

Advertising accepted: Yes
Advertising rates: $75.00/half page; $100.00/full page; also available on an exchange basis

EDITORIAL DESCRIPTION

Scope: Publishes research and criticism on the arts in the South, past and present. Invites articles, essays, and reviews on both contemporary and earlier literature, music, visual arts, architecture, popular and folk arts, theater, and dance.
Reviews books: Yes
Publishes notes: No
Languages accepted: English
Prints abstracts: No
Author-anonymous submission: No

SUBMISSION REQUIREMENTS

Restrictions on contributors: None
Author pays submission fee: No
Author pays page charges: No
Length of articles: 15-20 manuscript pp.
Length of book reviews: 750 words
Style: MLA
Number of copies required: 1
Special requirements: Submit original typescript. Submit diskette upon acceptance.
Copyright ownership: Journal
Rejected manuscripts: Returned; enclose return postage.
Time before publication decision: 3-6 mos.
Time between decision and publication: 12-15 mos.
Number of reviewers: 2-3
Articles submitted per year: 150
Articles published per year: 40
Book reviews published per year: 15-20

(2686)
*The Southern Review

James Olney & Dave Smith, Editors
43 Allen Hall
Louisiana State Univ.
Baton Rouge, LA 70803

Telephone: 504 388-5108
Fax: 504 388-5098
First published: 1965

Sponsoring organization: Louisiana State Univ.
ISSN: 0038-4534
MLA acronym: SoR

SUBSCRIPTION INFORMATION

Frequency of publication: 4 times/yr. (Jan., Apr., July, Oct.)
Circulation: 3,100
Available in microform: Yes
Subscription price: $30.00/yr. institutions; $15.00/yr. individuals; $5.00/single issue
Year to which price refers: 1992

ADVERTISING INFORMATION

Advertising accepted: Yes
Advertising rates: $60.00/quarter page; $90.00/half page; $150.00/full page

EDITORIAL DESCRIPTION

Scope: Publishes poetry, fiction, literary criticism, and book reviews with an emphasis on contemporary literature in the United States and abroad, and with special interest in Southern culture and history.
Reviews books: Yes
Publishes notes: No
Languages accepted: English
Prints abstracts: No
Author-anonymous submission: No

SUBMISSION REQUIREMENTS

Restrictions on contributors: Reviews are solicited.
Author pays submission fee: No
Author pays page charges: No
Length of articles: 4,000-10,000 words
Length of book reviews: 1,000-4,500 words
Style: Chicago
Number of copies required: 1
Special requirements: No footnotes preferred
Copyright ownership: Author
Rejected manuscripts: Returned; enclose return postage.
Time before publication decision: 3 mos.
Time between decision and publication: 1 yr.
Number of reviewers: 1-2
Articles submitted per year: 1,000
Articles published per year: 25-30
Book reviews published per year: 10

(2687)
*Southern Review: Literary and Interdisciplinary Essays

Cathy Greenfield & Barbara Milech, Editors
Dept. of English
Univ. of Adelaide
Adelaide
South Australia, 5001, Australia

First published: 1963
Sponsoring organization: Univ. of Adelaide, English Dept.; Curtin Univ., School of Communication & Cultural Studies
ISSN: 0038-4526
MLA acronym: SoRA

SUBSCRIPTION INFORMATION

Frequency of publication: 3 times/yr. (Mar., July, Nov.)
Circulation: 500
Available in microform: No
Subscription price: A$49.00/yr. institutions; A$25.00/yr. individuals; A$15.00/yr. students & unemployed
Year to which price refers: 1992

ADVERTISING INFORMATION

Advertising accepted: Yes, on an exchange basis

EDITORIAL DESCRIPTION

Scope: Publishes critical articles, reviews, and review articles on literature, literary theory, and cultural studies, as well as poems and short stories. Invites essays that are interdisciplinary, relating literary criticism to other areas of study, and that move beyond the traditional formations of English literature to focus on literatures in English (African, Australian, Canadian, Caribbean, etc.). Welcomes particularly new and radical kinds of critical discourse. Southern Review hopes to present a wide range of critical opinions over a broad field of subject matter, at a level accessible to the general academic reader.
Reviews books: Yes
Publishes notes: No
Languages accepted: English
Prints abstracts: No
Author-anonymous submission: No

SUBMISSION REQUIREMENTS

Restrictions on contributors: Unsolicited reviews are not accepted.
Author pays submission fee: No
Author pays page charges: No
Length of articles: 5,000-6,000 words
Length of book reviews: 2,500-3,000 words
Style: MLA
Number of copies required: 1
Special requirements: If accepted, authors are asked to resubmit their articles on IBM- or Macintosh-compatible diskettes, preferably using Microsoft Word, Wordstar, or a plain ASCII file.
Copyright ownership: Author
Rejected manuscripts: Returned; enclose SASE.
Time before publication decision: 3 mos.
Time between decision and publication: 1 yr.
Number of reviewers: 9
Articles submitted per year: 150
Articles published per year: 15
Book reviews submitted per year: 20
Book reviews published per year: 12

(2688)
*Southern Studies: An Interdisciplinary Journal of the South

Maxine Taylor, Editor
Dept. of Social Sciences
Northwestern State Univ.
Natchitoches, LA 71497

Telephone: 318 357-5507
First published: 1961
Sponsoring organization: Northwestern State Univ., Natchitoches
ISSN: 0024-693X
MLA acronym: SoSt

SUBSCRIPTION INFORMATION

Frequency of publication: 4 times/yr.
Circulation: 4,000
Available in microform: Yes
Subscription price: $10.00/yr. US; $25.00/yr. elsewhere
Year to which price refers: 1992

ADVERTISING INFORMATION

Advertising accepted: Yes

EDITORIAL DESCRIPTION

Scope: Publishes studies in various fields which contribute to a greater knowledge and understanding of the South and its regional setting. Especially interested in Southern history and literature.
Reviews books: Yes
Publishes notes: No
Languages accepted: English
Prints abstracts: No
Author-anonymous submission: Yes

SUBMISSION REQUIREMENTS

Restrictions on contributors: Contributors must meet scholarly standards and editorial guidelines.
Author pays submission fee: No
Author pays page charges: No
Length of articles: 25 pp.
Style: MLA; Chicago
Number of copies required: 2
Special requirements: Submit original double-spaced typescript and 1 copy.
Copyright ownership: Journal
Rejected manuscripts: Returned
Time before publication decision: 4 mos.
Time between decision and publication: 9-12 mos.
Number of reviewers: 3
Articles submitted per year: 80-90
Articles published per year: 20-30

(2689)
Southwest Journal of Linguistics

Heather K. Hardy, Editor
Dept. of English, Box 13827
Univ. of North Texas
Denton, TX 76203

Telephone: 817 565-2147
First published: 1975
Sponsoring organization: Linguistic Assn. of the Southwest
ISSN: 0737-4143
MLA acronym: SJL

SUBSCRIPTION INFORMATION

Frequency of publication: 2 times/yr.
Circulation: 300
Available in microform: No
Subscription address: Donald E. Hardy, Executive Director, LASSO, Dept. of English, Denton, TX 76203-3827

ADVERTISING INFORMATION

Advertising accepted: Yes

EDITORIAL DESCRIPTION

Scope: Publishes articles on all aspects of linguistics.
Reviews books: Yes
Publishes notes: No
Languages accepted: English
Prints abstracts: No
Author-anonymous submission: No

SUBMISSION REQUIREMENTS

Restrictions on contributors: None
Author pays submission fee: No
Author pays page charges: No
Length of articles: 15-40 pp.
Length of book reviews: 1,000-5,000 words
Style: Linguistic Soc. of America
Number of copies required: 3
Special requirements: Submit final draft on diskette.
Copyright ownership: Journal
Rejected manuscripts: Returned at author's request
Time before publication decision: 2-5 mos.
Time between decision and publication: 9-12 mos.
Number of reviewers: 2-3
Articles submitted per year: 30-50
Articles published per year: 15-20
Book reviews submitted per year: 4
Book reviews published per year: 4

(2690)
*Southwest Review

Willard Spiegelman & Elizabeth Mills, Editors
307 Fondren Library West, Box 4374
Southern Methodist Univ.
Dallas, TX 75275

Telephone: 214 373-7440
First published: 1915
Sponsoring organization: Southern Methodist Univ.
ISSN: 0038-4712
MLA acronym: SWR

SUBSCRIPTION INFORMATION

Frequency of publication: 4 times/yr.
Circulation: 1,500
Available in microform: Yes

ADVERTISING INFORMATION

Advertising accepted: Yes
Advertising rates: $250.00/full page

EDITORIAL DESCRIPTION

Scope: Embraces almost every area of adult interest: contemporary affairs, history, folklore, fiction, poetry, literary criticism, interviews, art, music, and the theater.
Reviews books: No
Publishes notes: No
Languages accepted: English
Prints abstracts: No
Author-anonymous submission: No

SUBMISSION REQUIREMENTS

Author pays submission fee: No
Author pays page charges: No
Length of articles: 3,000-7,500 words
Style: Chicago
Number of copies required: 1
Special requirements: Submit original typescript or good quality copy; letter-quality printout preferred over dot matrix.
Copyright ownership: Author
Rejected manuscripts: Returned; enclose SASE.
Time before publication decision: 3 mos.
Time between decision and publication: 3-12 mos.
Number of reviewers: 2
Articles submitted per year: 150
Articles published per year: 20

(2691)
Sovetish Heymland/Sovetskaia Rodina: Ezhemesiachnyĭ Literaturno-Khudozhestvennyĭ Zhurnal

A. Vergelis, Editor
Tsentr
ul. Kirova, 17
101000 Moscow, Russia

First published: 1961
Sponsoring organization: Soiuz Pisateleĭ S.S.S.R.
ISSN: 0134-4315
MLA acronym: SovH

SUBSCRIPTION INFORMATION

Frequency of publication: 12 times/yr.
Circulation: 5,000
Available in microform: Yes
Subscription address: Mezhdunarodnaya Kniga, Dimitrova str., 39, 113095 Moscow, Russia

ADVERTISING INFORMATION

Advertising accepted: No

EDITORIAL DESCRIPTION

Scope: Publishes articles on Yiddish language and literature.
Reviews books: Yes
Publishes notes: Yes
Languages accepted: Yiddish
Prints abstracts: No
Author-anonymous submission: No

SUBMISSION REQUIREMENTS

Author pays submission fee: Yes
Author pays page charges: Yes
Length of articles: No restrictions
Length of book reviews: No restrictions
Length of notes: No restrictions
Number of copies required: 1
Copyright ownership: Author
Rejected manuscripts: Not returned
Time before publication decision: 1-2 mos
Time between decision and publication: 6 mos.
Number of reviewers: 1-2

(2692)
Soviet Literature

Alexander Prokhanov & Natalia Perova, Editors
1/7 Kutuzovsky Prospekt
121248 Moscow, Russia

First published: 1946
Sponsoring organization: Soiuz Pisateleĭ S.S.S.R.
ISSN: 0202-1870
MLA acronym: SovL

SUBSCRIPTION INFORMATION

Frequency of publication: 12 times/yr.
Circulation: 20,000
Available in microform: No
Subscription address: Sovinperiodika, Dimitrova str., 39, 113095 Moscow, Russia

ADVERTISING INFORMATION

Advertising accepted: No

EDITORIAL DESCRIPTION

Scope: Publishes fiction, poetry, and nonfiction which originally appeared in various languages of the peoples of the USSR, as well as commissioned material. Has regular sections devoted to literary criticism and the arts; gives information on new books by Soviet writers. Aims to introduce foreign readers to the present-day literary scene in the Soviet Union and to reflect the Soviet public's interest in foreign culture.
Reviews books: Yes
Publishes notes: Yes
Languages accepted: English; German; Spanish; French; Polish; Japanese; Hungarian; Czech; Slovak; Russian
Prints abstracts: Yes
Author-anonymous submission: No

SUBMISSION REQUIREMENTS

Restrictions on contributors: None
Author pays submission fee: No
Author pays page charges: No
Length of articles: No restrictions
Length of book reviews: No restrictions
Length of notes: No restrictions
Style: None
Number of copies required: 1
Special requirements: Submit original typescript.
Copyright ownership: Journal
Rejected manuscripts: Not returned
Time before publication decision: 1 mo.
Time between decision and publication: 4-6 mos.
Number of reviewers: 5

(2693)
*SPAN: Journal of the South Pacific Association for Commonwealth Literature and Language Studies

Kateryna Longley, Editor
Centre for Research in Culture & Communication
School of Humanities
Murdoch Univ.
Murdoch, Western Australia 6150, Australia

Telephone: (61) 9 3602313
Fax: (61) 9 3106285
First published: 1975
Sponsoring organization: South Pacific Assn. for Commonwealth Literature & Language Studies
ISSN: 0313-1459
MLA acronym: SPAN

SUBSCRIPTION INFORMATION

Frequency of publication: 2 times/yr.
Circulation: 300
Available in microform: No
Subscription price: A$30.00/yr. institutions; A$20.00/yr. individuals; A$10.00/yr. students
Year to which price refers: 1992

ADVERTISING INFORMATION

Advertising accepted: No

EDITORIAL DESCRIPTION

Scope: Publishes articles and reviews on literature and scholarship in the South Pacific, including Australia and New Zealand. Also publishes some stories and sets of poems.
Reviews books: Yes
Publishes notes: Yes
Languages accepted: English
Prints abstracts: No
Author-anonymous submission: No

SUBMISSION REQUIREMENTS

Restrictions on contributors: Reviews are commissioned.
Author pays submission fee: No
Author pays page charges: No
Length of articles: 3,000 words maximum
Length of book reviews: 500 words maximum
Length of notes: 1,000 words maximum
Style: MLA
Number of copies required: 1
Special requirements: Submission on Macintosh diskette is preferred.
Copyright ownership: Author
Rejected manuscripts: Returned by surface mail
Time before publication decision: 2 mos.
Time between decision and publication: 6 mos. maximum
Number of reviewers: 2-6
Articles submitted per year: 15
Articles published per year: 10
Book reviews submitted per year: 10-12
Book reviews published per year: 10
Notes submitted per year: 2
Notes published per year: 2

(2694)
*Speculum: A Journal of Medieval Studies

Luke Wenger, Editor
Medieval Academy of America
1430 Massachusetts Ave.
Cambridge, MA 02138

Telephone: 617 491-1622
First published: 1926
Sponsoring organization: Medieval Academy of America
ISSN: 0038-7134
MLA acronym: Speculum

SUBSCRIPTION INFORMATION

Frequency of publication: 4 times/yr. (Jan., Apr., July, Oct.)
Circulation: 6,000
Available in microform: Yes

ADVERTISING INFORMATION

Advertising accepted: Yes
Advertising rates: $200.00/half page; $325.00/full page

EDITORIAL DESCRIPTION

Scope: Concerned with medieval architecture, fine arts, geography, history, law, literature, music, numismatics, philosophy, science, social and economic institutions, and all other aspects of the civilization of the Middle Ages.
Reviews books: Yes
Publishes notes: Yes
Languages accepted: English
Prints abstracts: No
Author-anonymous submission: No

SUBMISSION REQUIREMENTS

Restrictions on contributors: Unsolicited reviews are not accepted.
Author pays submission fee: No
Author pays page charges: No
Length of articles: 15,000 words maximum
Length of book reviews: 1,200 words maximum; exceptions allowed
Length of notes: 2,500 words maximum
Style: Journal
Number of copies required: 1; 2 preferred
Copyright ownership: Publisher
Rejected manuscripts: Returned
Time before publication decision: 4-6 mos.
Time between decision and publication: 1 yr.
Number of reviewers: 4-6
Articles submitted per year: 100
Articles published per year: 20-25
Book reviews published per year: 350
Notes published per year: 2-5

(2695)
*Speculum Artium

Aldo Scaglione, Editor
Dept. of French & Italian
New York Univ.
19 University Pl., 6th Floor
New York, NY 10003

First published: 1977
MLA acronym: SArt

SUBSCRIPTION INFORMATION

Frequency of publication: Irregular
Circulation: 600
Available in microform: No
Subscription address: Angelo Longo Editore, C.P. 431, 48100 Ravenna, Italy

ADVERTISING INFORMATION

Advertising accepted: No

EDITORIAL DESCRIPTION

Scope: Publishes monograph studies concerning the relationships among the various arts, between art and ideas, art and science, the arts and social history, and between the literary or figurative arts and the techniques underlying them.
Reviews books: No
Publishes notes: No
Languages accepted: English; French; Italian; Spanish
Prints abstracts: Yes
Author-anonymous submission: No

SUBMISSION REQUIREMENTS

Restrictions on contributors: None
Author pays submission fee: No
Author pays page charges: Yes
Length of books: 150-200 pp.
Style: MLA
Number of copies required: 2
Copyright ownership: Angelo Longo Editore
Rejected manuscripts: Returned
Time before publication decision: 2 mos.
Time between decision and publication: 1-2 yrs.
Number of reviewers: 2
Books submitted per year: 5
Books published per year: 3

(2696)
*Spektator: Tijdschrift voor Neerlandistiek

J. van Marle & M. Mathijsen, Editors
Inst. voor Neerlandistiek, UvA
Spuistraat 134
1012 VB Amsterdam, Netherlands

Telephone: (31) 20 5254723
Fax: (31) 20 5254429
First published: 1971
ISSN: 0165-084X
MLA acronym: Spektator

SUBSCRIPTION INFORMATION

Frequency of publication: 4 times/yr.
Circulation: 500
Available in microform: No
Subscription address: Van Gorcum Publishers, P.O. Box 43, 9400 AA Assen, Netherlands
Subscription telephone: (31) 5920 46846
Subscription fax: (31) 5920 72064

ADVERTISING INFORMATION

Advertising accepted: Yes

EDITORIAL DESCRIPTION

Scope: Publishes articles and squibs on Dutch language and literature, and on general subjects concerning language and literature. Articles on linguistics often (but not necessarily) have a generative background.
Reviews books: Yes
Publishes notes: Yes
Languages accepted: Dutch; English
Prints abstracts: No
Author-anonymous submission: No

SUBMISSION REQUIREMENTS

Restrictions on contributors: None
Author pays submission fee: No
Author pays page charges: No
Length of articles: 5-12 pp.
Length of book reviews: 1,000 words
Style: Linguistic Soc. of America
Number of copies required: 3
Special requirements: Include a 150-word summary.
Copyright ownership: Van Gorcum Publishers
Rejected manuscripts: Returned at author's request
Time before publication decision: 2 mos.
Time between decision and publication: 6 mos.
Number of reviewers: 3-5
Articles submitted per year: 60
Articles published per year: 35
Book reviews submitted per year: 60
Book reviews published per year: 60

(2697)
*Spenser Studies: A Renaissance Poetry Annual

Thomas P. Roche, Jr. & Patrick Cullen, Editors
Dept. of English
Princeton Univ.
Princeton, NJ 08540

Additional editorial address: Patrick Cullen, 300 W. 108th St., Apt. 8D, New York, NY 10025
First published: 1980
ISSN: 0195-9468
MLA acronym: SSt

SUBSCRIPTION INFORMATION

Frequency of publication: Annual
Available in microform: No
Subscription address: AMS Press, 56 E. 13th St., New York, NY 10003

ADVERTISING INFORMATION

Advertising accepted: No

EDITORIAL DESCRIPTION

Scope: Publishes articles on all 16th-century English poets with emphasis on Spenser and Sidney. Also publishes articles on the literary/historical/intellectual context and influence of 16th-century English poetry, as well as occasional articles of general interest on Renaissance subjects.
Reviews books: Yes
Publishes notes: Yes
Languages accepted: English
Prints abstracts: Yes
Author-anonymous submission: No

SUBMISSION REQUIREMENTS

Restrictions on contributors: None
Author pays submission fee: No
Author pays page charges: No
Length of articles: 3,000-10,000 words
Length of notes: 3,000 words
Style: Journal
Number of copies required: 2
Special requirements: Send one copy to each editorial address. Include a 100-175 word abstract.
Copyright ownership: AMS Press
Rejected manuscripts: Returned; enclose SASE or international reply coupons.
Time before publication decision: 3 mos.
Time between decision and publication: 8-12 mos.
Number of reviewers: 1-3
Articles submitted per year: 35-50
Articles published per year: 10-14
Notes submitted per year: 10-15
Notes published per year: 5-7

(2698)
Spicilegio Moderno: Letteratura, Lingua, Idee

Ist. di Lingue e Letterature Straniere
Fac. di Magistero dell'Univ. di Bologna
Palazzo Hercolani
Strada Maggiore, 45,
Bologna, Italy

Sponsoring organization: Univ. di Bologna
ISSN: 0391-4216
MLA acronym: SpM

SUBSCRIPTION INFORMATION

Frequency of publication: 2 times/yr.
Circulation: 1,200
Subscription address: Editrice Libreria Goliardica, Via Oberdan 2-4, 56100 Pisa, Italy

EDITORIAL DESCRIPTION

Scope: Publishes articles on literary criticism and linguistics research.
Reviews books: Yes
Prints abstracts: Yes

SUBMISSION REQUIREMENTS

Restrictions on contributors: Contributors must be associated with Univ. di Bologna or article must be solicited by the Institute.
Length of articles: 25 pp.
Style: Journal
Number of copies required: 1
Special requirements: Submit original typescript.
Copyright ownership: Assigned by author to journal.
Time before publication decision: 6 mos.
Time between decision and publication: 3 mos.
Number of reviewers: 4
Articles published per year: 20

(2699)
*Spiegel der Letteren: Tijdschrift voor Nederlandse Literatuurgeschiedenis en voor Literatuurwetenschap

K. Porteman, Editor
Predikherenberg 59
3010 Louvain, Belgium

Telephone: (32) 16 284855
Fax: (32) 16 285068; (32) 16 285025
First published: 1956
Sponsoring organization: Univ. Stichting van België; Ministerie Nederlandse Cultuur
ISSN: 0038-7479
MLA acronym: SpL

SUBSCRIPTION INFORMATION

Frequency of publication: 4 times/yr.
Circulation: 1,000
Available in microform: No
Subscription price: 1,280 BF/yr.
Year to which price refers: 1992
Subscription address: Uitgeverij Peeters, Bondgenotenlaan 153, 3000 Louvain, Belgium
Subscription telephone: (32) 16 488102

ADVERTISING INFORMATION

Advertising accepted: No

EDITORIAL DESCRIPTION

Scope: Publishes articles on Dutch literature and on the theory of literature.
Reviews books: Yes
Publishes notes: Yes
Languages accepted: Dutch; English; German; French
Prints abstracts: No
Author-anonymous submission: No

SUBMISSION REQUIREMENTS

Restrictions on contributors: None
Author pays submission fee: No
Author pays page charges: No
Length of articles: 7,000 words
Length of book reviews: No restrictions
Length of notes: No restrictions
Number of copies required: 2
Special requirements: Submit original typescript.
Copyright ownership: Assigned by author to journal
Rejected manuscripts: Returned
Time before publication decision: 1 yr.
Time between decision and publication: 3-6 mos.
Number of reviewers: 2
Articles submitted per year: 25
Articles published per year: 12
Book reviews submitted per year: 60

Book reviews published per year: 40
Notes submitted per year: 12
Notes published per year: 8

(2700)
*SPIL: (Stellenbosch Papers in Linguistics)

Rudolf P. Botha, Melinda Sinclair, Walter Winckler, & Cecile le Roux, Editors
Dept. of General Linguistics
Univ. of Stellenbosch
Stellenbosch 7600, South Africa

Telephone: (27) 2231 772010
Fax: (27) 2231 774336
First published: 1978
Sponsoring organization: Univ. of Stellenbosch
MLA acronym: SPIL

SUBSCRIPTION INFORMATION

Frequency of publication: 1-2 times/yr.
Circulation: 240
Available in microform: No

ADVERTISING INFORMATION

Advertising accepted: No

EDITORIAL DESCRIPTION

Scope: Publishes papers on theoretical linguistics.
Reviews books: No
Publishes notes: No
Languages accepted: English
Prints abstracts: No
Author-anonymous submission: No

SUBMISSION REQUIREMENTS

Author pays submission fee: No
Author pays page charges: No
Length of books: No restrictions
Style: Adapted from *Linguistic Inquiry/Language*
Copyright ownership: Author
Rejected manuscripts: Returned
Time before publication decision: 1-6 mos.
Time between decision and publication: 1-2 mos.
Number of reviewers: 2
Articles submitted per year: 3-8
Articles published per year: 3-8

(2701)
*Spirit: A Magazine of Poetry

David Rogers, Editor
English Dept.
Seton Hall Univ.
South Orange, NJ 07079

Telephone: 201 761-9000 ext. 5101
Fax: 201 761-9596
First published: 1934
Sponsoring organization: Seton Hall Univ.
ISSN: 0038-7584
MLA acronym: Spirit

SUBSCRIPTION INFORMATION

Frequency of publication: 2 times/yr. (Spring-Summer, Fall-Winter)
Circulation: 675
Available in microform: Yes
Subscription price: $4.00/yr.
Year to which price refers: 1992

ADVERTISING INFORMATION

Advertising accepted: Yes

EDITORIAL DESCRIPTION

Scope: Publishes contemporary poetry and articles about poetry and poetics.
Reviews books: Yes
Publishes notes: No
Languages accepted: English
Prints abstracts: No

SUBMISSION REQUIREMENTS

Restrictions on contributors: None
Author pays submission fee: No
Author pays page charges: No
Length of articles: 10-15 pp.
Length of book reviews: 500-750 words
Style: MLA
Number of copies required: 1
Copyright ownership: Seton Hall Univ.
Rejected manuscripts: Returned
Time before publication decision: 2-4 weeks
Time between decision and publication: 2-4 mos.
Number of reviewers: 3
Articles published per year: 2-3
Book reviews submitted per year: 10
Book reviews published per year: 4-6

(2702)
*Der Sprachdienst

Hans Bickes, Editor
c/o Helmut Walther
Gesellschaft für Deutsche Sprache
Taunusstr. 11, Postfach 2669
6200 Wiesbaden 1, Germany

Telephone: (49) 611 520031
Fax: (49) 611 51313
First published: 1957
Sponsoring organization: Gesellschaft für Deutsche Sprache
ISSN: 0038-8459
MLA acronym: Sprachdienst

SUBSCRIPTION INFORMATION

Frequency of publication: 6 times/yr.
Circulation: 3,000
Available in microform: No
Subscription price: 66.60 DM/yr.
Year to which price refers: 1992

ADVERTISING INFORMATION

Advertising accepted: Yes

EDITORIAL DESCRIPTION

Scope: Publishes articles on the cultivation of and research on the modern German language. Deals mainly with linguistics, as opposed to literature (i.e., dialectology and etymology rather than grammar and syntax).
Reviews books: Yes
Publishes notes: Yes
Languages accepted: German
Prints abstracts: No
Author-anonymous submission: No

SUBMISSION REQUIREMENTS

Restrictions on contributors: None
Author pays submission fee: No
Author pays page charges: No
Length of articles: 5 pp.
Length of book reviews: 2 pp.
Length of notes: 1 p.
Style: None
Number of copies required: 1
Special requirements: Submit original typescript.
Copyright ownership: Gesellschaft für Deutsche Sprache
Rejected manuscripts: Returned
Time before publication decision: 2 mos.
Time between decision and publication: 5 mos.
Number of reviewers: 2
Articles submitted per year: 50

Articles published per year: 35
Book reviews submitted per year: 20
Book reviews published per year: 12
Notes submitted per year: 20
Notes published per year: 15

(2703)
*Die Sprache: Zeitschrift für Sprachwissenschaft

Jochem Schindler & Martin Peters, Editors
Inst. für Sprachwissenschaft
Univ. Wien
Luegerring 1
1010 Vienna, Austria

Telephone: (43) 1 401032318
First published: 1949
Sponsoring organization: Bundesministerium für Wissenschaft & Forschung, Vienna
ISSN: 0376-401X
MLA acronym: Sprache

SUBSCRIPTION INFORMATION

Frequency of publication: 2 times/yr.
Circulation: 650
Available in microform: No

ADVERTISING INFORMATION

Advertising accepted: Yes
Advertising rates: 580 DM/full page

EDITORIAL DESCRIPTION

Scope: Focuses on the investigation of Indo-European languages and linguistics as well as historical linguistics.
Reviews books: Yes
Publishes notes: Yes
Languages accepted: English; French; German; Italian
Prints abstracts: No
Author-anonymous submission: No

SUBMISSION REQUIREMENTS

Restrictions on contributors: None
Author pays submission fee: No
Author pays page charges: No
Length of articles: 30 typescript pp. maximum
Length of book reviews: 300 words
Length of notes: 4,000 words
Style: None
Number of copies required: 1
Special requirements: Submit typescript.
Copyright ownership: Verlag Harrassowitz
Rejected manuscripts: Returned
Time before publication decision: 3 mos. maximum
Time between decision and publication: 1-2 yrs.
Number of reviewers: 1-3
Articles submitted per year: 25
Articles published per year: 10-20
Book reviews submitted per year: 80
Book reviews published per year: 80
Notes submitted per year: 10
Notes published per year: 4

(2704)
*Sprache im Technischen Zeitalter

Walter Höllerer, Norbert Miller, & Joachim Sartorius, Editors
Literarisches Colloquium Berlin
Am Sandwerder 5
1000 Berlin, Germany

Telephone: (49) 30 8169960
Fax: (49) 30 81699619
First published: 1961
ISSN: 0038-8475
MLA acronym: SiTZ

SUBSCRIPTION INFORMATION

Frequency of publication: 4 times/yr. (Mar., June, Sept., Dec.)
Circulation: 1,500
Available in microform: No
Subscription price: 48 DM/yr.
Year to which price refers: 1992

ADVERTISING INFORMATION

Advertising accepted: Yes
Advertising rates: 600 DM/full page

EDITORIAL DESCRIPTION

Scope: Publishes articles on contemporary literature from around the world.
Reviews books: No
Publishes notes: No
Languages accepted: German
Prints abstracts: No
Author-anonymous submission: No

SUBMISSION REQUIREMENTS

Author pays submission fee: No
Author pays page charges: No
Copyright ownership: Publisher; reverts to author after 1 yr.
Time before publication decision: 6 mos.
Time between decision and publication: 2 mos.
Number of reviewers: 5
Articles submitted per year: 150
Articles published per year: 20

(2705)
Sprache und Datenverarbeitung: International Journal for Language Data Processing

Winfried Lenders, Harald H. Zimmermann, & Tom C. Gerhardt, Editors
c/o T. Gerhardt
IAI
Martin-Luther-Str. 14
6600 Saarbrücken, Germany

Telephone: (49) 228 735645
Fax: (49) 228 735639
First published: 1977
ISSN: 0343-5202
MLA acronym: SDv

SUBSCRIPTION INFORMATION

Frequency of publication: 2 times/yr.
Available in microform: No
Subscription address: Jan Brustkern, Inst. für Angewandte Kommunikations- & Sprachforschung, Poppelsdorfer Allee 47, 5300 Bonn 1, Germany

ADVERTISING INFORMATION

Advertising accepted: Yes

EDITORIAL DESCRIPTION

Scope: Publishes articles on linguistic data processing, computational linguistics, linguistic information science, research on language structures and communication processes related to speech, and computerized text analysis.
Reviews books: Yes
Publishes notes: No
Languages accepted: German; English; French
Prints abstracts: Yes

SUBMISSION REQUIREMENTS

Restrictions on contributors: None
Author pays submission fee: No
Author pays page charges: No
Length of articles: No restrictions
Length of book reviews: No restrictions
Style: Journal
Number of copies required: 2
Copyright ownership: Journal
Rejected manuscripts: Returned at author's request; enclose return postage.
Time before publication decision: 2 mos.
Time between decision and publication: 4-6 mos.
Number of reviewers: 2
Articles submitted per year: 20-25
Articles published per year: 20
Book reviews submitted per year: 8-10
Book reviews published per year: 5-10

(2706)
Sprache und Dichtung

M. Bindshedler, W. Kohlschmidt, & P. Zinsli, Editors
Univ. Bern
Deutsches Seminar
Schüzenmattstr. 14
3012 Bern, Switzerland

First published: 1956
ISSN: 0081-3826
MLA acronym: SuD

SUBSCRIPTION INFORMATION

Frequency of publication: Irregular
Available in microform: No
Subscription address: Verlag Paul Haupt, Falkenplatz 14, 3001 Bern, Switzerland

ADVERTISING INFORMATION

Advertising accepted: No

EDITORIAL DESCRIPTION

Scope: Publishes research in German language, literature, and folklore.
Reviews books: No
Publishes notes: No
Languages accepted: German
Prints abstracts: No

SUBMISSION REQUIREMENTS

Length of books: No restrictions
Number of copies required: 1
Copyright ownership: Verlag Paul Haupt
Rejected manuscripts: Returned

(2707)
Sprache und Geschichte in Afrika

Bernd Heine, Wilhelm J. G. Möhlig, Franz Rottland, Rainer Vossen, & Jürgen Christoph Winter, Editors
Inst. für Afrikanistik
Univ. zu Köln
5000 Cologne 41, Germany

Additional editorial address: Lehrstuhl für Afrikanistik II, Univ. Bayreuth, 8580 Bayreuth, Germany
ISSN: 0170-5946
MLA acronym: SUGIA

SUBSCRIPTION INFORMATION

Subscription address: Helmut Buske Verlag, Richardstr. 47, Postfach 760244, 2000 Hamburg 76, Germany

ADVERTISING INFORMATION

Advertising accepted: No

EDITORIAL DESCRIPTION

Scope: Publishes collections of articles on African languages and history.
Reviews books: No
Languages accepted: German; English; French
Prints abstracts: Yes

(2708)
***Sprache und Information: Beiträge zur Philologischen und Linguistischen Datenverarbeitung, Informatik, und Informationswissenschaft**

István Bátori, Walther von Hahn, Rainer Kuhlen, Winfried Lenders, Wolfgang Putschke, Hans Jochen Schneider, & Harald Zimmermann, Editors
Max Niemeyer Verlag
Postfach 2140
7400 Tübingen, Germany

Additional editorial address: IKP, Univ. Bonn, Poppelsdorfer Allee 47, 5300 Bonn, Germany
Fax: (49) 228 735638
E-mail: UPK000@DBNRHRZ1
First published: 1982
ISSN: 0722-298X
MLA acronym: S&I

SUBSCRIPTION INFORMATION

Frequency of publication: Irregular
Available in microform: No

ADVERTISING INFORMATION

Advertising accepted: No

EDITORIAL DESCRIPTION

Scope: Publishes monographs on linguistic data, information processing, and information science.
Reviews books: No
Publishes notes: No
Languages accepted: German; English
Prints abstracts: No
Author-anonymous submission: No

SUBMISSION REQUIREMENTS

Restrictions on contributors: None
Author pays submission fee: No
Author pays page charges: No
Length of books: 100-300 pp.
Style: MLA
Number of copies required: 2
Special requirements: Submit typescript.
Copyright ownership: Max Niemeyer Verlag
Rejected manuscripts: Returned
Time before publication decision: 6 mos.
Time between decision and publication: 3 mos.
Number of reviewers: 2-3 minimum
Books submitted per year: 2-4
Books published per year: 1-3

(2709)
Sprache & Kognition: Zeitschrift für Sprach- und Kognitionspsychologie und ihre Grenzgebiete

Dietrich Dörner, Johannes Engelkamp, & Hannelore Grimm, Editors
Univ. Bamberg
Lehrstuhl Psychologie II
Markusplatz 3
8600 Bamberg, Germany

First published: 1982
Sponsoring organization: Deutsche Forschungsgemeinschaft
ISSN: 0253-4533
MLA acronym: S&K

SUBSCRIPTION INFORMATION

Frequency of publication: 4 times/yr.
Circulation: 300
Available in microform: No
Subscription price: 235 SwF (144 DM)/yr. institutions; 86 SwF (99 DM)/yr. individuals; 63 SwF (72 DM)/yr. students
Year to which price refers: 1992

Subscription address: Verlag Hans Huber, Länggass-Str. 76, 3000 Bern 9, Switzerland

ADVERTISING INFORMATION

Advertising accepted: Yes

EDITORIAL DESCRIPTION

Scope: Publishes articles on cognitive and language processing and its interaction.
Reviews books: Yes
Publishes notes: No
Languages accepted: German
Prints abstracts: Yes
Author-anonymous submission: No

SUBMISSION REQUIREMENTS

Author pays submission fee: No
Author pays page charges: No
Length of articles: 8,000 words
Length of book reviews: 1,800 words
Style: American Psychological Assn.
Number of copies required: 6
Copyright ownership: Huber Verlag, Bern
Time before publication decision: 1 yr.
Time between decision and publication: 9 mos.
Number of reviewers: 2-3
Articles submitted per year: 35-40
Articles published per year: 16-20
Book reviews submitted per year: 4-6
Book reviews published per year: 4-5

(2710)
***Sprache und Literatur: Regensburger Arbeiten zur Anglistik und Amerikanistik**

Karl Heinz Göller, Hans Bungert, & Otto Hietsch, Editors
Univ. Regensburg
Inst. für Anglistik
Universitätsstr. 31
8400 Regensburg, Germany

Telephone: (49) 941 9433468
Fax: (49) 941 9432305
First published: 1970
ISSN: 0172-1178
MLA acronym: SLRAAA

SUBSCRIPTION INFORMATION

Frequency of publication: Irregular
Circulation: 300-350
Available in microform: No
Subscription address: Verlag Peter Lang AG, Jupiterstr. 15, 3015 Bern, Switzerland

ADVERTISING INFORMATION

Advertising accepted: No

EDITORIAL DESCRIPTION

Scope: Publishes studies of English and American language and literature.
Reviews books: No
Publishes notes: No
Languages accepted: English; German
Prints abstracts: Yes
Author-anonymous submission: No

SUBMISSION REQUIREMENTS

Restrictions on contributors: None
Author pays submission fee: No
Author pays page charges: No
Length of books: 400 pp. maximum
Style: MLA
Number of copies required: 1
Special requirements: Submit offset manuscripts.
Copyright ownership: Verlag Peter Lang
Rejected manuscripts: Returned
Time before publication decision: 2 mos.

Time between decision and publication: 9-12 mos.
Number of reviewers: 3
Books submitted per year: 2
Books published per year: 2

(2711)
***Sprachkunst: Beiträge zur Literaturwissenschaft**

Herbert Foltinek & Walter Weiss, Editors
Kommission für Literaturwissenschaft
c/o Hermann Blume
Postgasse 7/2
1010 Vienna, Austria

Telephone: (43) 1 51581481
Fax: (43) 1 5139541
First published: 1970
Sponsoring organization: Bundesministerium für Wissenschaft & Forschung, Vienna
ISSN: 0038-8483
MLA acronym: Sprachkunst

SUBSCRIPTION INFORMATION

Frequency of publication: 2 times/yr.
Circulation: 500
Available in microform: No
Subscription price: 490 S (70 DM)/yr.
Year to which price refers: 1992
Subscription address: Verlag der Österreichischen Akademie der Wissenschaften, Dr. Ignaz-Seipel-Platz 2, 1010 Vienna, Austria
Subscription telephone: (43) 1 51581403

ADVERTISING INFORMATION

Advertising accepted: Yes, on an exchange basis

EDITORIAL DESCRIPTION

Scope: A journal for literary studies. Publishes articles on poetry, literary history, and poetics. Includes critical discussions and scholarly reviews; in addition, abstracts of literary dissertations and *habilitationsschriften* at Austrian universities are listed annually. Endeavors to mediate between different schools of research and European literature.
Reviews books: Yes
Publishes notes: Yes
Languages accepted: German; English; French; Russian
Prints abstracts: No
Author-anonymous submission: No

SUBMISSION REQUIREMENTS

Restrictions on contributors: None
Author pays submission fee: No
Author pays page charges: No
Length of articles: No restrictions
Length of book reviews: No restrictions
Length of notes: No restrictions
Style: MLA
Number of copies required: 1
Copyright ownership: Assigned by author to journal
Rejected manuscripts: Returned
Time before publication decision: 3 mos.
Time between decision and publication: 15 mos.
Number of reviewers: 3
Articles submitted per year: 50
Articles published per year: 20
Book reviews submitted per year: 6
Book reviews published per year: 15
Notes submitted per year: 3
Notes published per year: 2

(2712)
*Sprachpflege und Sprachkultur: Zeitschrift für Gutes Deutsch

Herbert Görner, Editor
VEB Bibliographisches Inst. Leipzig
Grimmaische Str. 28
Postfach 130
7010 Leipzig, Germany

First published: 1952
ISSN: 0863-209X
MLA acronym: Spr&Spr

SUBSCRIPTION INFORMATION

Frequency of publication: 4 times/yr.
Circulation: 12,000
Available in microform: No
Subscription address: Adler's Foreign Books, Inc., 162 Fifth Ave., New York, NY 10010

ADVERTISING INFORMATION

Advertising accepted: No

EDITORIAL DESCRIPTION

Scope: Focuses on lexicology, orthography, stylistics, grammatics, and any question regarding the German language.
Reviews books: Yes
Publishes notes: Yes
Languages accepted: German
Prints abstracts: No

SUBMISSION REQUIREMENTS

Author pays submission fee: No
Author pays page charges: No
Length of articles: 2,000-5,000 words
Length of book reviews: 300-500 words
Length of notes: 300-600 words
Number of copies required: 2
Special requirements: Submit original typescript.
Copyright ownership: Author
Rejected manuscripts: Returned
Time before publication decision: 2 mos.
Time between decision and publication: 6 mos.
Number of reviewers: 2
Articles submitted per year: 60-80
Articles published per year: 40-50
Book reviews submitted per year: 20-30
Book reviews published per year: 20-25
Notes submitted per year: 15-20
Notes published per year: 15-20

(2713)
*Sprachspiegel: Schweizerische Zeitschrift für die deutsche Muttersprache

Werner Frick, Kurt Meyer, & Alfons Müller, Editors
Alpenstr. 7
6004 Lucerne, Switzerland

Telephone: (41) 41 511910
First published: 1945
Sponsoring organization: Deutschschweizerischer Sprachverein (DSSV)
ISSN: 0038-8513
MLA acronym: Spsp

SUBSCRIPTION INFORMATION

Frequency of publication: 6 times/yr.
Circulation: 1,400
Available in microform: No
Subscription price: 55 SwF/yr.
Year to which price refers: 1992

ADVERTISING INFORMATION

Advertising accepted: Yes

Advertising rates: 100 SwF/quarter page; 190 SwF/half page; 270 SwF/three-quarter page; 350 SwF/full page

EDITORIAL DESCRIPTION

Scope: The German-Swiss Linguistic Society is a league of language friends who cultivate the German language as their mother tongue and deepen the comprehension of it.
Reviews books: Yes
Publishes notes: Yes
Languages accepted: German
Prints abstracts: No
Author-anonymous submission: No

SUBMISSION REQUIREMENTS

Restrictions on contributors: None
Author pays submission fee: No
Author pays page charges: No
Length of articles: 3,000 words or 7 pp. maximum
Length of book reviews: 300 words or 1/2 p.
Length of notes: 1/4 p.
Style: None
Number of copies required: 1
Copyright ownership: Author
Rejected manuscripts: Returned
Time before publication decision: 2 mos.
Time between decision and publication: 1 yr.
Number of reviewers: 2
Articles submitted per year: 24
Articles published per year: 20
Book reviews submitted per year: 25
Book reviews published per year: 20
Notes submitted per year: 120
Notes published per year: 100

(2714)
Sprachstrukturen, Reihe A: Historische Sprachstrukturen

Herbert L. Kufner, Hugo Steger, & Otmar Werner, Editors
Cornell Univ.
College of Arts & Sciences
Dept. of Modern Languages & Linguistics
Morrill Hall
Ithaca, NY 14850

Additional editorial address: C/o Hugo Steger, Univ. Freiburg, Deutsches Seminar, Abt. f. Sprache & Altere Literatur, Lehrstuhl für Germanische Philologie, Werthmanplatz 3, 7800 Freiberg i.Br., Germany
First published: 1972
ISSN: 0344-6670
MLA acronym: SprachstrukA

SUBSCRIPTION INFORMATION

Frequency of publication: Irregular
Available in microform: No
Subscription address: Max Niemeyer Verlag, Postfach 2140, 7400 Tübingen, Germany

ADVERTISING INFORMATION

Advertising accepted: No

EDITORIAL DESCRIPTION

Scope: Focuses on grammatical descriptions of the older Germanic languages and their developments, as well as historical grammar in terms of modern linguistics.
Reviews books: No
Publishes notes: No
Languages accepted: German; English
Prints abstracts: No
Author-anonymous submission: No

SUBMISSION REQUIREMENTS

Restrictions on contributors: Authors are usually invited to contribute.
Author pays submission fee: No
Author pays page charges: No

Length of books: 100-140 pp.
Style: Request from Max Niemeyer Verlag
Copyright ownership: Max Niemeyer Verlag
Time before publication decision: 6 mos.
Time between decision and publication: 6 mos.
Books published per year: 1

(2715)
*Sprachwissenschaft

Rolf Bergmann & Theo Vennemann, Editors
Univ. Bamberg
Hornthalstr. 2
8600 Bamberg, Germany

Telephone: (49) 951 863634
Fax: (49) 951 863301
First published: 1976
Sponsoring organization: Deutsche Forschungsgemeinschaft
ISSN: 0344-8169
MLA acronym: Sprachwiss

SUBSCRIPTION INFORMATION

Frequency of publication: 4 times/yr.
Circulation: 500
Available in microform: No
Subscription price: 135 DM/yr.
Year to which price refers: 1991
Subscription address: Carl Winter Universitätsverlag, Lutherstr. 59, 6900 Heidelberg, Germany

ADVERTISING INFORMATION

Advertising accepted: No

EDITORIAL DESCRIPTION

Scope: Publishes articles of general and theoretical interest using examples from Germanic languages. Includes theoretical and descriptive articles on Germanic languages.
Reviews books: No
Publishes notes: No
Languages accepted: German; English; French
Prints abstracts: No
Author-anonymous submission: No

SUBMISSION REQUIREMENTS

Restrictions on contributors: None
Author pays submission fee: No
Author pays page charges: No
Length of articles: No restrictions
Style: Journal
Number of copies required: 1
Special requirements: Submit original typescript. Request style sheet from editor.
Copyright ownership: Author
Rejected manuscripts: Returned
Time before publication decision: 1-3 mos.
Time between decision and publication: 3-6 mos.
Number of reviewers: 2-3
Articles submitted per year: 30-40
Articles published per year: 20-30

(2716)
*Språkvård: Tidskrift Utgiven av Svenska Språknämnden

Margareta Westman, Editor
Svenska Språknämnden
Lundagatan 42, uppg. 5
117 27 Stockholm, Sweden

Telephone: (46) 8 6680153
Fax: (46) 8 7206805
First published: 1965
Sponsoring organization: Svenska Språknämnden
ISSN: 0038-8440
MLA acronym: Språkvård

SUBSCRIPTION INFORMATION

Frequency of publication: 4 times/yr.
Circulation: 4,000
Available in microform: No
Subscription price: 75 Skr/yr.
Year to which price refers: 1992

ADVERTISING INFORMATION

Advertising accepted: No

EDITORIAL DESCRIPTION

Scope: Concerns linguistics (communications, slang, grammar), language planning and cultivation, and modern Swedish usage.
Reviews books: Yes
Publishes notes: Yes
Languages accepted: Swedish; Danish; Norwegian
Prints abstracts: No
Author-anonymous submission: Yes

SUBMISSION REQUIREMENTS

Restrictions on contributors: None
Author pays submission fee: No
Author pays page charges: No
Length of articles: 15 typescript pp. maximum
Length of book reviews: 500-600 words
Length of notes: 200-400 words
Style: None
Number of copies required: 1
Copyright ownership: Author and/or journal
Rejected manuscripts: Returned
Time before publication decision: 1 mo.
Time between decision and publication: 2-4 mos.
Number of reviewers: 1-2
Articles submitted per year: 25-30
Articles published per year: 15-20
Book reviews submitted per year: 5-15
Book reviews published per year: 5-10

(2717)
*Spring: The Journal of the E. E. Cummings Society

Norman Friedman & David V. Forrest, Editors
33-54 164th St.
Flushing, NY 11358-1442

Telephone: 718 353-3631
First published: 1980
Sponsoring organization: E. E. Cummings Soc.
MLA acronym: SpringE

SUBSCRIPTION INFORMATION

Frequency of publication: Annual
Available in microform: No
Subscription price: $20.00/yr. institutions; $15.00/yr. individuals; $10.00/yr. students
Year to which price refers: 1992

EDITORIAL DESCRIPTION

Scope: Publishes articles on he life, works, and times of E. E. Cummings.
Reviews books: Yes
Publishes notes: Yes
Languages accepted: English
Prints abstracts: No
Author-anonymous submission: No

SUBMISSION REQUIREMENTS

Restrictions on contributors: None
Author pays submission fee: No
Author pays page charges: No
Length of articles: No restrictions
Length of book reviews: No restrictions
Length of notes: No restrictions
Style: MLA
Number of copies required: 1
Rejected manuscripts: Returned; enclose SASE.
Time before publication decision: 2 mos.
Number of reviewers: 2 minimum

(2718)
Sprog og Kultur

Aarhus Univ.
Inst. for Iysk Sprog- & Kulturforskning
Aarhus, Denmark

First published: 1932
ISSN: 0038-8645
MLA acronym: SoK

SUBSCRIPTION INFORMATION

Frequency of publication: Irregular
Subscription address: Scandinavian Univ. Press, P.O. Box 2929 Tøyen, 0608 Oslo, Norway
Additional subscription address: Scandinavian Univ. Press, 200 Meacham Ave., Elmont, NY 11003

(2719)
*Spunti e Ricerche: Rivista d'Italianistica

S. Kolsky & Walter Musolino, Editors
Italian Section, Dept. of French & Italian
Univ. of Melbourne
Parkville 3052, Australia

Telephone: (61) 3 4791120; (61) 3 4792355
Fax: (61) 3 4791700
First published: 1985
Sponsoring organization: Italian section of Dept. of French & Italian, Univ. of Melbourne
ISSN: 0816-5432
MLA acronym: SpRi

SUBSCRIPTION INFORMATION

Frequency of publication: Annual
Circulation: 100
Available in microform: No
Subscription price: A$15.00/yr. Australia; A$20.00 (A$25.00 airmail)/yr. elsewhere
Year to which price refers: 1990
Subscription address: W. Mussolino, Dept. of Italian Studies, La Trobe Univ., Bundoora, Victoria 3083, Australia

ADVERTISING INFORMATION

Advertising accepted: Yes

EDITORIAL DESCRIPTION

Scope: Concerned with Italian literature, politics, linguistics, economics, history, society, cinema, and art. Also studies and encourages the cultural work produced by Italians, or about Italians, in Australia.
Reviews books: Yes
Publishes notes: Yes
Languages accepted: Italian; English
Author-anonymous submission: No

SUBMISSION REQUIREMENTS

Restrictions on contributors: None
Author pays submission fee: No
Author pays page charges: No
Length of articles: No restrictions
Length of book reviews: 2-3 pp.
Length of notes: No restrictions
Style: MLA
Number of copies required: 2
Special requirements: Submit double-spaced typescript on size A4 (8 1/4 in. x 11 3/4 in.) paper. Notes should appear at the end of the article together with the contributor's name and city of residence or university affiliation.
Rejected manuscripts: Not returned
Time before publication decision: 3-6 mos.
Time between decision and publication: 1-9 mos.
Number of reviewers: 8
Articles submitted per year: 12
Articles published per year: 6-8

Book reviews submitted per year: 5-6
Book reviews published per year: 5-6

(2720)
*Stanford French and Italian Studies

Jean-Marie Apostolidès & Marc Bertrand, Editors
Dept. of French & Italian
Stanford Univ.
Stanford, CA 94305

First published: 1975
Sponsoring organization: Stanford Univ., Dept. of French & Italian
ISSN: 0886-0750
MLA acronym: SFIS

SUBSCRIPTION INFORMATION

Frequency of publication: Irregular
Available in microform: No
Subscription address: Anma Libri, P.O. Box 876, Saratoga, CA 95071

ADVERTISING INFORMATION

Advertising accepted: No

EDITORIAL DESCRIPTION

Scope: Collection of scholarly publications devoted to the study of French and Italian literature and language, culture and civilization. Publishes occasionally on related Romance topics.
Reviews books: No
Publishes notes: No
Languages accepted: English; French; Italian
Prints abstracts: No

SUBMISSION REQUIREMENTS

Restrictions on contributors: None
Author pays submission fee: No
Author pays page charges: Yes
Length of books: No restrictions
Style: MLA
Number of copies required: 2
Special requirements: Submit double-spaced manuscript. Original typescript required if manuscript is accepted.
Copyright ownership: Anma Libri
Rejected manuscripts: Returned
Time before publication decision: 4-6 mos.
Time between decision and publication: 15 mos.
Number of reviewers: 3

(2721)
Stanford French Review

Jean-Marie Apostolidès & Jean-Pierre Dupuy, Editors
Dept. of French & Italian
Stanford Univ.
Stanford, CA 94305-2010

First published: 1977
Sponsoring organization: Stanford Univ., Dept. of French & Italian
ISSN: 0163-657X
MLA acronym: SFR

SUBSCRIPTION INFORMATION

Frequency of publication: 3 times/yr.
Circulation: 600
Available in microform: No
Subscription address: Anma Libri, P.O. Box 876, Saratoga, CA 95071

ADVERTISING INFORMATION

Advertising accepted: Yes

EDITORIAL DESCRIPTION

Scope: Publishes articles dealing with French literature in its diverse culture.
Reviews books: Yes
Publishes notes: Yes
Languages accepted: English; French
Prints abstracts: No

SUBMISSION REQUIREMENTS

Restrictions on contributors: None
Author pays submission fee: No
Author pays page charges: No
Length of articles: 20 double-spaced pp.
Length of book reviews: 3 double-spaced typescript pp.
Length of notes: No restrictions
Style: MLA
Number of copies required: 2
Copyright ownership: Anma Libri
Rejected manuscripts: Destroyed unless accompanied by SASE.
Time before publication decision: 2-3 mos.
Time between decision and publication: 1 yr. minimum
Number of reviewers: 3-4
Articles submitted per year: 200
Articles published per year: 30
Book reviews published per year: 10

(2722)
*Stanford German Studies

Dept. of German Studies
Stanford Univ.
Stanford, CA 94305

First published: 1973
Sponsoring organization: Stanford Univ., Dept. of German Studies
ISSN: 0171-7219
MLA acronym: SGerS

SUBSCRIPTION INFORMATION

Frequency of publication: Irregular
Circulation: 500
Available in microform: No
Subscription address: Verlag Peter Lang & Cie. A.G., Jupiterstr. 15, 3015 Bern, Switzerland

ADVERTISING INFORMATION

Advertising accepted: No

EDITORIAL DESCRIPTION

Scope: Publishes monographs in German studies.
Reviews books: No
Publishes notes: No
Languages accepted: English; German
Prints abstracts: No
Author-anonymous submission: No

SUBMISSION REQUIREMENTS

Restrictions on contributors: None
Author pays submission fee: No
Author pays page charges: Yes
Length of books: 200-300 pp.
Style: MLA
Number of copies required: 2
Copyright ownership: Assigned by author to Verlag Peter Lang
Rejected manuscripts: Returned
Time before publication decision: 6 mos.
Time between decision and publication: 6-9 mos.
Number of reviewers: 2-4
Books submitted per year: 3-4
Books published per year: 2-3

(2723)
*Stanford Humanities Review

Maria Koundoura & Anahid Kassabian, Editors
Stanford Humanities Center
Mariposa House
Stanford, CA 94305-8630

Telephone: 415 725-6747
Fax: 415 723-1895
First published: 1989
ISSN: 1048-3721
MLA acronym: StHR

SUBSCRIPTION INFORMATION

Frequency of publication: 2 times/yr.
Circulation: 200
Subscription price: $40.00/yr. institutions; $20.00/yr. individuals
Year to which price refers: 1993

ADVERTISING INFORMATION

Advertising accepted: No

EDITORIAL DESCRIPTION

Scope: An interdisciplinary journal dedicated to publishing criticism, scholarship, fiction, poetry, and art.
Reviews books: Yes
Publishes notes: No
Languages accepted: English
Prints abstracts: No
Author-anonymous submission: No

SUBMISSION REQUIREMENTS

Author pays submission fee: No
Author pays page charges: No
Length of articles: 5,000-10,000 words
Length of book reviews: 1,000-2,000 words
Style: MLA
Number of copies required: 1
Special requirements: Submit typescript and Macintosh diskette.
Time before publication decision: 6 mos.
Time between decision and publication: 1 yr. maximum

(2724)
Stanford Italian Review

Jean-Marie Apostolidès & John Freccero, Editors
Dept. of French & Italian
Stanford Univ.
Stanford, CA 94305

First published: 1979
Sponsoring organization: Stanford Univ., Dept. of French & Italian
ISSN: 0730-6857
MLA acronym: StIR

SUBSCRIPTION INFORMATION

Frequency of publication: 2 times/yr.
Available in microform: No
Subscription price: $64.50/yr. institutions; $30.00/yr. individuals
Year to which price refers: 1992
Subscription address: Anma Libri, P.O. Box 876, Saratoga, CA 95071

ADVERTISING INFORMATION

Advertising accepted: Yes

EDITORIAL DESCRIPTION

Scope: Publishes critical essays in Italian studies.
Reviews books: No
Publishes notes: Yes
Languages accepted: Italian; English; French; German
Prints abstracts: No

SUBMISSION REQUIREMENTS

Author pays submission fee: No
Author pays page charges: No
Length of articles: 5,000 words
Length of notes: No restrictions
Style: MLA (1985)
Number of copies required: 2
Special requirements: Manuscripts must be double-spaced, including excerpts and footnotes.
Copyright ownership: Anma Libri
Rejected manuscripts: Destroyed unless accompanied by SASE.
Time before publication decision: 3 mos.
Time between decision and publication: 1 yr.
Number of reviewers: 2
Articles published per year: 18

(2725)
*Stanford Literature Review

Jean-Marie Apostolidès & Hans Ulrich Gumbrecht, Editors
Dept. of French & Italian & Comparative Literature
Stanford Univ.
Stanford, CA 94305

Telephone: 415 723-1251
First published: 1984
Sponsoring organization: Stanford Univ., Dept. of French & Italian
ISSN: 0886-666X
MLA acronym: SLRev

SUBSCRIPTION INFORMATION

Frequency of publication: 2 times/yr. (Spring, Fall)
Available in microform: No
Subscription address: Anma Libri, P.O. Box 876, Saratoga, CA 95071

ADVERTISING INFORMATION

Advertising accepted: Yes

EDITORIAL DESCRIPTION

Scope: An interdisciplinary journal intended not to represent a single theoretical, philosophical, or political position but rather to establish a high level of intellectual tension through plurality. Focuses on the contemporary multicultural transformations in the institutional and semantic aspects of the concept of literature.
Reviews books: No
Publishes notes: Yes
Languages accepted: English
Prints abstracts: No

SUBMISSION REQUIREMENTS

Author pays submission fee: No
Author pays page charges: No
Length of articles: 20 double-spaced typescript pp.
Length of notes: No restrictions
Style: MLA (1985)
Number of copies required: 2
Copyright ownership: Anma Libri
Rejected manuscripts: Destroyed unless accompanied by SASE.
Time before publication decision: 3 mos.
Time between decision and publication: 1 yr.
Number of reviewers: 2
Articles published per year: 10

(2726)
*Stanford Slavic Studies

Lazar Fleishman, Editor
Dept. of Slavic Languages & Literatures
Stanford Univ.
Stanford, CA 94305

Telephone: 415 723-4438
First published: 1987
ISSN: 0883-5365
MLA acronym: StSS

SUBSCRIPTION INFORMATION

Frequency of publication: Annual
Circulation: 700
Available in microform: No

ADVERTISING INFORMATION

Advertising accepted: No

EDITORIAL DESCRIPTION

Scope: Publishes articles on Russian literature, Slavic linguistics, literary theory, cultural studies, and archival research.
Reviews books: No
Publishes notes: Yes
Languages accepted: English; Russian; French; German
Prints abstracts: No

SUBMISSION REQUIREMENTS

Restrictions on contributors: None
Author pays submission fee: No
Author pays page charges: No
Style: None
Number of copies required: 2
Copyright ownership: Author
Rejected manuscripts: Returned; enclose SASE.
Time before publication decision: 1-2 yrs.
Time between decision and publication: 6-12 mos.
Number of reviewers: 2-3
Articles submitted per year: 20
Articles published per year: 10-15
Notes published per year: 2-3

(2727)
Stasinos: The Bulletin of the Greek Philologists

George Con. Ioannides, Managing Editor
Stasinos Greek Philologists Assn. of Cyprus
c/o Pedagogical Academy
P.O. Box 4813
Nicosia, Cyprus

First published: 1963
Sponsoring organization: Syndesmos Hellenon Philologon Kyprou "Stasinos"
ISSN: 0585-0959
MLA acronym: Stasinos

SUBSCRIPTION INFORMATION

Frequency of publication: Once every 2 yrs.
Circulation: 1,100

EDITORIAL DESCRIPTION

Scope: Publishes articles on classical, medieval, and modern literature (Greek and foreign), philosophy, archaeology, and education.
Reviews books: No
Languages accepted: English; French; Greek; German
Prints abstracts: Yes

SUBMISSION REQUIREMENTS

Restrictions on contributors: Contributors must be members of Syndesmos Hellenon Philologon Kyprou "Stasinos" or be well known authors in the field.

Length of articles: 5-15 pp.
Style: MLA
Number of copies required: 1
Special requirements: Submit original typescript.
Copyright ownership: Assigned by author to journal
Rejected manuscripts: Returned
Time before publication decision: 1 mo.
Time between decision and publication: 6 mos.
Number of reviewers: 4
Articles published per year: 20-36

(2728)
*Steaua

Aurel Răbu, Editor
Piata Libertatii nr. 1
3400 Cluj-Napoca, Romania

Telephone: (40) 95 112852
First published: 1949
Sponsoring organization: Uniunea Scriitorilor din România
ISSN: 0039-0852
MLA acronym: Steaua

SUBSCRIPTION INFORMATION

Frequency of publication: 12 times/yr.
Circulation: 2,000
Available in microform: No
Subscription price: $50.00/yr.
Year to which price refers: 1992
Subscription address: ILEXIM Departamentul Export-Import, Calea Griviței nr. 64-66, P.O. Box 136-137, Bucharest, Romania

ADVERTISING INFORMATION

Advertising accepted: Yes

EDITORIAL DESCRIPTION

Scope: Focuses on literature, art, and culture, with news items, critical articles, verse, fiction, and art reproductions. Primarily oriented toward Transylvanian art and literature.
Reviews books: Yes
Publishes notes: Yes
Languages accepted: Romanian
Prints abstracts: No
Author-anonymous submission: No

SUBMISSION REQUIREMENTS

Restrictions on contributors: None
Author pays submission fee: No
Author pays page charges: No
Length of articles: No restrictions
Number of copies required: 1
Special requirements: Submit typescript.
Copyright ownership: Author
Rejected manuscripts: Not returned
Time before publication decision: 2 mos.
Time between decision and publication: 1 mo.
Number of reviewers: 3
Articles published per year: 900-1,000

(2729)
*Steinbeck Monograph Series

Tetsumaro Hayashi, Editor
Steinbeck Research Inst.
English Dept.
Ball State Univ.
Muncie, IN 47306

Telephone: 317 285-5688
First published: 1971
Sponsoring organization: Steinbeck Research Inst.
MLA acronym: StMS

SUBSCRIPTION INFORMATION

Frequency of publication: Irregular
Circulation: 660
Available in microform: No
Subscription price: $15.00/volume US; $20.00/volume elsewhere
Year to which price refers: 1991
Subscription address: Steinbeck Soc., at the above address

ADVERTISING INFORMATION

Advertising accepted: Yes
Advertising rates: Request from editor.

EDITORIAL DESCRIPTION

Scope: Publishes articles and monographs on John Steinbeck's works.
Reviews books: No
Publishes notes: No
Languages accepted: English
Prints abstracts: No
Author-anonymous submission: No

SUBMISSION REQUIREMENTS

Restrictions on contributors: Submission is by invitation only.
Author pays submission fee: No
Author pays page charges: No
Length of articles: 12-15 pp.
Length of books: 50-100 pp.
Style: Chicago
Number of copies required: 2
Copyright ownership: Editor
Rejected manuscripts: Returned
Time before publication decision: 3 mos.
Time between decision and publication: 2 yrs.
Number of reviewers: 3

(2730)
*Steinbeck Quarterly

Tetsumaro Hayashi, Editor
Steinbeck Soc.
English Dept.
Ball State Univ.
Muncie, IN 47306

Telephone: 317 285-5688
First published: 1968
Sponsoring organization: Ball State Univ.; International Steinbeck Soc.
ISSN: 0039-100X
MLA acronym: StQ

SUBSCRIPTION INFORMATION

Frequency of publication: 2 combined issues/yr.
Circulation: 660
Available in microform: Yes
Subscription price: $25.00/yr. US; $30.00/yr. elsewhere
Year to which price refers: 1992

ADVERTISING INFORMATION

Advertising accepted: Yes

EDITORIAL DESCRIPTION

Scope: Publishes critical and biographical essays on John Steinbeck.
Reviews books: Yes
Publishes notes: Yes
Languages accepted: English
Prints abstracts: No
Author-anonymous submission: No

SUBMISSION REQUIREMENTS

Restrictions on contributors: Contributors must be members in good standing of the International Steinbeck Soc. Book reviews are solicited.
Author pays submission fee: No
Author pays page charges: No

Length of articles: 10-15 double-spaced pp.
Length of book reviews: 2-4 double-spaced pp.
Length of notes: 2-3 pp.
Style: Chicago
Number of copies required: 2
Special requirements: Submit original typescript; include a letter.
Copyright ownership: Editor
Rejected manuscripts: Returned; enclose SASE.
Time before publication decision: 2-3 mos.
Time between decision and publication: 1-2 yrs.
Number of reviewers: 3
Articles submitted per year: 70-80
Articles published per year: 6-10
Book reviews published per year: 10
Notes submitted per year: 30
Notes published per year: 5

(2731)
Stendhal Club: Revue Internationale d'Etudes Stendhaliennes. Nouvelle Série. Revue Trimestrielle

V. Del Litto, Editor
4, rue Lesdiguières
38000 Grenoble, France

First published: 1958
Sponsoring organization: Centre National des Lettres
ISSN: 0039-1158
MLA acronym: SC

SUBSCRIPTION INFORMATION

Frequency of publication: 4 times/yr. (Jan., Apr., July, Oct.)
Circulation: 1,000
Available in microform: No

ADVERTISING INFORMATION

Advertising accepted: Yes

EDITORIAL DESCRIPTION

Scope: Publishes articles on Stendhal.
Reviews books: Yes
Publishes notes: Yes
Languages accepted: French
Prints abstracts: No

SUBMISSION REQUIREMENTS

Restrictions on contributors: None
Author pays submission fee: Yes
Author pays page charges: No
Length of articles: 5,000 words
Length of book reviews: 2,000 words
Length of notes: 2,000 words
Style: Journal
Number of copies required: 2
Special requirements: Submit original typescript.
Copyright ownership: Journal
Rejected manuscripts: Not returned
Time before publication decision: 15 days
Time between decision and publication: 1 yr.
Number of reviewers: 2
Articles submitted per year: 50-60
Articles published per year: 20-30
Book reviews submitted per year: 30-40
Book reviews published per year: 15-30
Notes submitted per year: 20-25
Notes published per year: 15-20

(2732)
*Stimmen der Zeit

Wolfgang Seibel, S.J., Editor
Zuccalistr. 16
8000 Munich 19, Germany

Telephone: (49) 89 17900913
Fax: (49) 89 17900910
First published: 1865
ISSN: 0039-1492
MLA acronym: SZ

SUBSCRIPTION INFORMATION

Frequency of publication: 12 times/yr.
Circulation: 9,000
Available in microform: No
Subscription price: 130.80 DM/yr.
Year to which price refers: 1992
Subscription address: Herder KG, Hermann-Herder-Str. 4, 7800 Freiburg im Breisgau, Germany
Subscription telephone: (49) 761 2717333
Subscription fax: (44) 761 2717520

ADVERTISING INFORMATION

Advertising accepted: Yes

EDITORIAL DESCRIPTION

Reviews books: Yes
Publishes notes: Yes
Languages accepted: German
Prints abstracts: No

SUBMISSION REQUIREMENTS

Author pays submission fee: No
Author pays page charges: No
Length of articles: 2,500 words maximum
Number of copies required: 1
Copyright ownership: Assigned by author to journal for 1 yr.
Rejected manuscripts: Returned; enclose return postage
Time before publication decision: 2 weeks
Time between decision and publication: 4 mos.
Articles published per year: 80
Book reviews published per year: 150

(2733)
*Stockholm Studies in Baltic Languages

Inst. för Slaviska & Baltiska Språk
Stockholms Univ.
106 91 Stockholm, Sweden

Telephone: (46) 8 164385
Fax: (46) 8 159522
First published: 1983
Sponsoring organization: Stockholms Univ.
ISSN: 0281-5478
MLA acronym: SSBL

SUBSCRIPTION INFORMATION

Frequency of publication: Irregular
Available in microform: No
Subscription address: Almquist & Wiksell International, P.O. Box 4627, 116 91 Stockholm, Sweden

ADVERTISING INFORMATION

Advertising accepted: No

EDITORIAL DESCRIPTION

Scope: Publishes dissertations and monographs on Baltic languages, linguistics, literature, and folklore.
Reviews books: No
Publishes notes: No
Languages accepted: French; German; English; Latvian; Lithuanian; Swedish
Prints abstracts: Yes

SUBMISSION REQUIREMENTS

Restrictions on contributors: Contributors must be affiliated with Stockholms Univ.
Author pays submission fee: No
Length of books: 100-200 pp.
Copyright ownership: Author
Time before publication decision: 3 weeks
Time between decision and publication: 3 mos.
Number of reviewers: 3

(2734)
Stockholm Studies in English

Lennart A. Björk & Magnus Ljung, Editors
Engelska Inst.
Universitetet
106 91 Stockholm, Sweden

First published: 1937
Sponsoring organization: Univ. Stockholm
ISSN: 0346-6272
MLA acronym: SSEL

SUBSCRIPTION INFORMATION

Frequency of publication: Irregular
Circulation: 600-1,000
Available in microform: No
Subscription address: Almqvist & Wiksell International, P.O. Box 4627, 116 91 Stockholm, Sweden

ADVERTISING INFORMATION

Advertising accepted: No

EDITORIAL DESCRIPTION

Scope: Publishes books on English language and literature.
Reviews books: No
Languages accepted: English
Prints abstracts: No

SUBMISSION REQUIREMENTS

Restrictions on contributors: Contributors must be present or former teachers and students at the Univ. of Stockholm.
Author pays submission fee: No
Author pays page charges: No
Length of books: No restrictions
Style: None
Number of copies required: 1
Special requirements: Submit original typescript.
Copyright ownership: Assigned by author to series
Rejected manuscripts: Returned
Time between decision and publication: 3-6 mos.
Number of reviewers: 1
Books submitted per year: 2-3
Books published per year: 1-2

(2735)
*Stockholm Studies in Russian Literature

Peter Alberg Jensen, Editor
Univ. of Stockholm
106 91 Stockholm, Sweden

First published: 1974
Sponsoring organization: Univ. Stockholm
ISSN: 0346-8496
MLA acronym: SSRL

SUBSCRIPTION INFORMATION

Frequency of publication: Irregular
Circulation: Varies
Available in microform: No
Subscription address: Almqvist & Wiksell International, P.O. Box 4627, 116 91 Stockholm, Sweden

ADVERTISING INFORMATION

Advertising accepted: No

EDITORIAL DESCRIPTION

Scope: Publishes monographs and collections of articles on Russian literature.
Reviews books: No
Publishes notes: No
Languages accepted: English; Russian
Prints abstracts: No
Author-anonymous submission: No

SUBMISSION REQUIREMENTS

Restrictions on contributors: Contributors must be associated with Univ. of Stockholm.
Author pays submission fee: No
Author pays page charges: No
Copyright ownership: Author
Number of reviewers: 2

(2736)
*Stockholmer Germanistische Forschungen

Birgit Stolt, Editor
Germanistisches Inst. der Univ. Stockholm
106 91 Stockholm, Sweden

First published: 1956
Sponsoring organization: Univ. Stockholm
ISSN: 0491-0893
MLA acronym: SGF

SUBSCRIPTION INFORMATION

Frequency of publication: Irregular
Available in microform: No
Subscription address: Almqvist & Wiksell International, P.O. Box 4627, 116 91 Stockholm, Sweden

ADVERTISING INFORMATION

Advertising accepted: No

EDITORIAL DESCRIPTION

Scope: Publishes articles on philology, linguistics, and German literature.
Reviews books: No
Publishes notes: Yes
Languages accepted: English; German
Prints abstracts: Yes
Author-anonymous submission: No

SUBMISSION REQUIREMENTS

Author pays submission fee: No
Length of notes: No restrictions
Style: None
Number of copies required: 1
Copyright ownership: Author
Rejected manuscripts: Returned
Books submitted per year: 0-2
Books published per year: 0-2

(2737)
*Strindbergiana

Hans-Göran Ekman & Margareta Brundin, Editors
Strindbergsmuseet
Drottninggt. 85
111 60 Stockholm, Sweden

First published: 1985
Sponsoring organization: Strindbergssällskapet
ISSN: 0282-8006
MLA acronym: Strindbergiana

SUBSCRIPTION INFORMATION

Frequency of publication: Irregular (once a year)
Available in microform: No
Subscription price: 175 Skr/yr.
Year to which price refers: 1992

ADVERTISING INFORMATION

Advertising accepted: No

EDITORIAL DESCRIPTION

Scope: Publishes articles on August Strindberg.
Reviews books: No
Publishes notes: Yes
Languages accepted: Swedish; German
Prints abstracts: No
Author-anonymous submission: No

SUBMISSION REQUIREMENTS

Restrictions on contributors: None
Author pays submission fee: No
Author pays page charges: No
Length of articles: 10-30 pp.
Style: Oxford
Number of copies required: 1
Copyright ownership: Assigned by author to journal
Rejected manuscripts: Returned at author's request
Time before publication decision: 3-6 mos.
Time between decision and publication: 1 yr.
Number of reviewers: 2
Articles submitted per year: 5-10
Articles published per year: 10-15

(2738)
Strumenti Critici: Rivista Quadrimestrale di Cultura e Critica Letteraria

D'Arco Silvio Avalle, Maria Corti, Dante Isella, & Cesare Segre, Editors
Soc. Editrice il Mulino
Strada Maggiore, 37
40125 Bologna, Italy

First published: 1966
ISSN: 0039-2618
MLA acronym: SCr

SUBSCRIPTION INFORMATION

Frequency of publication: 3 times/yr.
Available in microform: No

ADVERTISING INFORMATION

Advertising accepted: No

EDITORIAL DESCRIPTION

Scope: Publishes studies in culture and literary criticism in general, including semiotics.
Reviews books: Yes
Publishes notes: Yes
Languages accepted: Italian; English; French
Prints abstracts: Yes

SUBMISSION REQUIREMENTS

Restrictions on contributors: Contributions are by invitation only.
Author pays submission fee: No
Author pays page charges: No
Length of articles: No restrictions
Length of book reviews: No restrictions
Length of notes: No restrictions
Number of copies required: 1
Copyright ownership: Editors
Rejected manuscripts: Returned
Time before publication decision: 1-24 weeks
Time between decision and publication: 5 mos.
Number of reviewers: 4
Articles submitted per year: 30
Articles published per year: 20
Book reviews submitted per year: 8
Book reviews published per year: 7
Notes submitted per year: 5
Notes published per year: 3

(2739)
Studi Danteschi

Francesco Mazzoni, Editor
Soc. Dantesca Italiana
Via Arte della Lana, 1
50123 Florence, Italy

First published: 1920
Sponsoring organization: Soc. Dantesca Italiana
ISSN: 0391-7835
MLA acronym: SD

SUBSCRIPTION INFORMATION

Frequency of publication: Annual
Circulation: 800
Available in microform: No
Subscription address: Ll. Co. SA. Libreria, Commissioneria Sansoni, Via Lamarmora, 45, 50121 Florence, Italy

ADVERTISING INFORMATION

Advertising accepted: No

EDITORIAL DESCRIPTION

Scope: Publishes articles on Dante's life, works, and culture.
Reviews books: Yes
Publishes notes: Yes
Languages accepted: Italian; English; French; German; Spanish; Portuguese
Prints abstracts: Yes
Author-anonymous submission: No

SUBMISSION REQUIREMENTS

Restrictions on contributors: None
Author pays submission fee: No
Author pays page charges: No
Length of articles: No restrictions
Length of book reviews: 500 words
Length of notes: 2,000 words
Number of copies required: 2
Special requirements: Submit original typescript plus 1 copy.
Copyright ownership: Author
Rejected manuscripts: Not returned
Time before publication decision: 2 yrs.
Time between decision and publication: 2 yrs.
Number of reviewers: 2 plus Editorial Board
Articles submitted per year: 10-15
Articles published per year: 6-8
Book reviews submitted per year: 50-60
Book reviews published per year: 30-40
Notes submitted per year: 5-6
Notes published per year: 2-3

(2740)
Studi dell'Istituto Linguistico

Mario Curreli, Editor
Ist. Linguistico
Fac. di Economia e Commercio
Via Curtatone, 1
50123 Florence, Italy

MLA acronym: StIL

(2741)
Studi di Filologia Italiana: Bollettino Annuale dell'Accademia della Crusca

Domenico De Robertis, Editor
Accademia della Crusca
Villa Medicea di Castello
Via di Castello, 46
50141 Florence, Italy

First published: 1927
Sponsoring organization: Accademia della Crusca
ISSN: 0392-5110
MLA acronym: SFI

SUBSCRIPTION INFORMATION

Frequency of publication: Annual
Circulation: 700
Available in microform: No
Subscription address: LICOSA S.p.A., Via Duca di Calabria, 1/1, 50125 Florence, Italy

ADVERTISING INFORMATION

Advertising accepted: No

EDITORIAL DESCRIPTION

Scope: Publishes textual criticism, historical studies of Italian language and dialects, and articles on the editing of documents in Italian.
Reviews books: No
Publishes notes: No
Languages accepted: Italian; English; French; Spanish; German
Prints abstracts: No
Author-anonymous submission: No

SUBMISSION REQUIREMENTS

Restrictions on contributors: None
Author pays submission fee: No
Author pays page charges: No
Length of articles: No restrictions
Style: Journal
Special requirements: Submit original typescript.
Copyright ownership: Author
Rejected manuscripts: Returned
Number of reviewers: 1

(2742)
*Studi di Grammatica Italiana

Giovanni Nencioni, Editor
Accademia della Crusca
Villa Medicea di Castello
Via di Castello 46
50141 Florence, Italy

First published: 1971
Sponsoring organization: Accademia della Crusca
MLA acronym: StGrI

SUBSCRIPTION INFORMATION

Frequency of publication: Irregular (approx. Annual)
Circulation: 700
Available in microform: No
Subscription address: LICOSA S.p.a, Via Duca di Calabria 1/1, 50125 Florence, Italy

ADVERTISING INFORMATION

Advertising accepted: No

EDITORIAL DESCRIPTION

Scope: Publishes studies of Italian language.
Reviews books: No
Languages accepted: Italian
Prints abstracts: No

SUBMISSION REQUIREMENTS

Restrictions on contributors: None
Author pays submission fee: No
Author pays page charges: No
Length of articles: No restrictions
Number of copies required: 1
Copyright ownership: Author
Rejected manuscripts: Returned
Time before publication decision: 2 mos.
Time between decision and publication: 1 yr.
Number of reviewers: 6
Articles submitted per year: 20
Articles published per year: 15-18

(2743)
*Studi di Letteratura Francese

Enea Balmas, Editor
Via Festa del Perdono, 7
20122 Milan, Italy

First published: 1967
Sponsoring organization: Consiglio Nazionale delle Ricerche
ISSN: 0585-4768
MLA acronym: StLF

SUBSCRIPTION INFORMATION

Frequency of publication: 1-2 times/yr.
Available in microform: No
Subscription address: Casa Editrice Leo S. Olschki, C.P. 66, 50100 Florence, Italy

ADVERTISING INFORMATION

Advertising accepted: No

EDITORIAL DESCRIPTION

Scope: Publishes articles on French literature.
Reviews books: Yes
Publishes notes: No
Languages accepted: Italian; French; English
Prints abstracts: No
Author-anonymous submission: Yes

SUBMISSION REQUIREMENTS

Restrictions on contributors: To be considered for publication, articles must conform to the theme of a particular volume.
Author pays submission fee: No
Author pays page charges: No
Length of articles: 5,000 words
Length of book reviews: 1,000 words
Style: Olschki
Number of copies required: 1
Copyright ownership: Author
Rejected manuscripts: Returned
Time before publication decision: 2 weeks
Number of reviewers: 1-2
Articles submitted per year: 10
Articles published per year: 10
Book reviews submitted per year: 30
Book reviews published per year: 20

(2744)
*Studi di Letteratura Ispano-Americana

Giuseppe Bellini, Editor
Cattedra di Letteratura Ispano-Americana
Ist. di Ling. & Lett. Iberiche & Ibero-americane, Fac. di Lett. & Filos.
Univ. degli Studi di Milano
via Festa del Perdono, 7
20122 Milan, Italy

First published: 1967
Sponsoring organization: Consiglio Nazionale delle Ricerche
ISSN: 0585-4776
MLA acronym: SLIA

SUBSCRIPTION INFORMATION

Frequency of publication: Annual
Available in microform: No
Subscription price: 30,000 Lit/yr.
Year to which price refers: 1992
Subscription address: Cisalpino-Goliardica, Via Rezia 4, 20135 Milan, Italy

ADVERTISING INFORMATION

Advertising accepted: No

EDITORIAL DESCRIPTION

Scope: Publishes articles on Spanish and Latin American literature and culture.
Reviews books: No
Publishes notes: No
Languages accepted: Italian; Spanish; Portuguese; French
Prints abstracts: Yes

SUBMISSION REQUIREMENTS

Author pays submission fee: No
Author pays page charges: No
Length of articles: 4,000 words
Style: MLA
Number of copies required: 2
Copyright ownership: Editor
Rejected manuscripts: Not returned
Time before publication decision: 6 mos.
Time between decision and publication: 2 mos.
Number of reviewers: 3
Articles submitted per year: 30
Articles published per year: 10-15

(2745)
*Studi d'Italianistica nell'Africa Australe/Italian Studies in Southern Africa

Piero d'Onofrio, Anna Meda, & Rita Wilson, Editors
c/o A. Meda
Dept. of Romance Languages
Univ. of South Africa
P.O. Box 392
Pretoria 0001, South Africa

Additional editorial address: R. Wilson, Dept. of Italian, Univ. of the Witwatersrand, P.O. Wits 2050, Johannesburg, South Africa
Telephone: (27) 12 4296249
Fax: (27) 12 4293414
First published: 1988
Sponsoring organization: Assn. Professori d'Italiano/Assn. of Professional Italianists; Univ. of South Africa
ISSN: 1012-2338
MLA acronym: SIAA

SUBSCRIPTION INFORMATION

Frequency of publication: 2 times/yr.
Circulation: 300
Available in microform: No
Subscription price: 60 R/yr. members S. Africa; $40.00/yr. institutions; $30.00/yr. individuals; $18.00/single issue
Year to which price refers: 1992
Subscription address: A. Poeti, Dept. of Italian, Univ. of Witwatersrand, P.O. Wits 2050, Johannesburg, South Africa

ADVERTISING INFORMATION

Advertising accepted: Yes

EDITORIAL DESCRIPTION

Scope: Publishes articles which foster multi- and interdisciplinary study and communication on Italian language and literature. Provides an insight into Italian culture, especially as it manifests itself in Southern Africa.
Reviews books: Yes
Publishes notes: Yes
Languages accepted: Italian; English
Prints abstracts: Yes
Author-anonymous submission: Yes

SUBMISSION REQUIREMENTS

Restrictions on contributors: None
Author pays submission fee: No
Author pays page charges: Yes (South Africa only)
Cost of page charges: 70 R
Length of articles: 15 pp.
Length of book reviews: 750-900 words
Length of notes: 150 words
Style: MLA
Number of copies required: 3

Special requirements: Submit original typescript and 2 copies. Include a 100-word abstract and a 50-word note on contributor. Name and affiliation of author should be on a separate sheet.
Copyright ownership: Assn. of Professional Italianists
Rejected manuscripts: Not returned
Time before publication decision: 4 mos.
Time between decision and publication: 18 mos. maximum
Number of reviewers: 3
Articles submitted per year: 15
Articles published per year: 10
Book reviews submitted per year: 40
Book reviews published per year: 30
Notes submitted per year: 5
Notes published per year: 3

(2746)
Studi e Problemi di Critica Testuale

R. Raffaele Spongano, Editor
Via Castiglione, 8
40124 Bologna, Italy

First published: 1970
ISSN: 0049-2361
MLA acronym: SPCT

SUBSCRIPTION INFORMATION

Frequency of publication: 2 times/yr.
Circulation: 600

EDITORIAL DESCRIPTION

Scope: Interested in Italian philology. Each volume is composed normally of six sections, assigned as follows: the first to articles, discussions, or essays methodological in character; the second to texts, edited or unedited, and to all that concerns their critical reconstruction, their edition, and their exegesis; the third to reviews of important works; the fourth to documentary notes of what is not reviewed (above); the fifth to notes from other Italian and foreign periodicals; and the sixth to indexes for consultation, bibliographies, and unedited or rare curiosities.
Languages accepted: Italian
Prints abstracts: No

SUBMISSION REQUIREMENTS

Rejected manuscripts: Not returned

(2747)
*Studi e Saggi Linguistici

Tristano Bolelli, Editor
Lungarno Mediceo 40
56127 Pisa, Italy

Telephone: (39) 50 542485
First published: 1961
ISSN: 0085-6827
MLA acronym: SeSL

SUBSCRIPTION INFORMATION

Frequency of publication: Annual
Circulation: 450
Available in microform: No
Subscription price: 70,000 Lit/yr. Italy; 140,000 Lit/yr. elsewhere
Year to which price refers: 1992
Subscription address: Giardini Editori, Via S. Bibbiana 28, 56100 Pisa, Italy
Subscription telephone: (39) 50 855390

ADVERTISING INFORMATION

Advertising accepted: No

EDITORIAL DESCRIPTION

Scope: Publishes articles on linguistics.
Reviews books: Yes
Publishes notes: Yes
Languages accepted: Italian; French; English; German
Prints abstracts: Yes
Author-anonymous submission: No

SUBMISSION REQUIREMENTS

Restrictions on contributors: None
Author pays submission fee: No
Author pays page charges: No
Length of articles: No restrictions
Length of book reviews: No restrictions
Length of notes: No restrictions
Style: None
Number of copies required: 1
Copyright ownership: Editor
Rejected manuscripts: Not returned
Time before publication decision: 4 mos.
Time between decision and publication: 6 mos.
Articles submitted per year: 18-30
Articles published per year: 8-10
Book reviews submitted per year: 6
Book reviews published per year: 0-6
Notes submitted per year: 6
Notes published per year: 2-6

(2748)
*Studi Francescani: Trimestrale di Vita Culturale e Religiosa a Cura dei Frati Minori d'Italia

Marino Damiata, Editor
A. Giacomini, 3
50132 Florence, Italy

First published: 1903
Sponsoring organization: Provincia Toscana di S. Francesco Stimmatizzato dei Frati Minori
ISSN: 0392-727X
MLA acronym: SFran

SUBSCRIPTION INFORMATION

Frequency of publication: 2 double issues/yr.
Circulation: 800
Available in microform: No

ADVERTISING INFORMATION

Advertising accepted: No

EDITORIAL DESCRIPTION

Scope: Publishes articles on Franciscan history, theology, philosophy, and spirituality.
Reviews books: Yes
Publishes notes: No
Languages accepted: Italian; French
Prints abstracts: No
Author-anonymous submission: No

SUBMISSION REQUIREMENTS

Author pays submission fee: No
Author pays page charges: No
Length of articles: 10-30 pp.
Length of book reviews: 1-3 pp.
Number of copies required: 1
Copyright ownership: Journal
Rejected manuscripts: Returned
Time before publication decision: 1 mo.
Time between decision and publication: 6 mos. minimum
Articles submitted per year: 15
Articles published per year: 10
Book reviews submitted per year: 50
Book reviews published per year: 50

(2749)
*Studi Francesi

Sergio Cigada, Giuseppe Di Stefano, Emanuele Kanceff, Gianni Mombello, Mario Richter, Cecilia Rizza, Corrado Rosso, & Lionello Sozzi, Editors
C. Vittorio Emanuele II 68
10121 Turin, Italy

Telephone: (39) 11 8127820
Fax: (39) 11 8127744
First published: 1957
Sponsoring organization: Consiglio Nazionale delle Ricerche & Ministero Pubblica Istruzione & Ist. Bancario S. Paolo di Torino
ISSN: 0039-2944
MLA acronym: SFr

SUBSCRIPTION INFORMATION

Frequency of publication: 3 times/yr.
Circulation: 1,000
Available in microform: No
Subscription address: Rosenberg & Sellier, Via Andrea Doria 14, 10123 Turin, Italy

ADVERTISING INFORMATION

Advertising accepted: Yes

EDITORIAL DESCRIPTION

Scope: Publishes historical and critical studies, texts and unedited documents that contribute to a deeper knowledge of French literature and civilization. Each issue includes a bibliographical review of the research dedicated to the representatives of French literary culture and discusses contemporary criticism in relation to reading works significant to French cultural history of all periods.
Reviews books: Yes
Publishes notes: Yes
Languages accepted: English; French; Italian
Prints abstracts: No
Author-anonymous submission: No

SUBMISSION REQUIREMENTS

Author pays submission fee: No
Author pays page charges: No
Length of articles: 5,000-7,000 words
Length of book reviews: 1,000-1,500 words
Length of notes: 1,500-2,500 words
Style: Journal
Number of copies required: 1
Copyright ownership: Rosenberg & Sellier
Rejected manuscripts: Not returned
Time before publication decision: 1 yr.
Time between decision and publication: 1-2 yr.
Number of reviewers: 2-3
Articles submitted per year: 40-50
Articles published per year: 12-30
Book reviews submitted per year: 20-30
Book reviews published per year: 15-20

(2750)
*Studi Germanici

Paolo Chiarini, Editor
Villa Sciarra-Wurts
Via Calandrelli, 25
00153 Rome, Italy

Telephone: (39) 6 5812465
Fax: (39) 6 5835929
First published: 1935
Sponsoring organization: Ist. Italiano di Studi Germanici
ISSN: 0039-2952
MLA acronym: StG

SUBSCRIPTION INFORMATION

Frequency of publication: 3 times/yr. (Feb., June, Oct.)
Circulation: 1,000

Available in microform: No
Subscription price: 50,000 Lit/yr. plus postage
Year to which price refers: 1992
Subscription address: Libreria Herder, Pzza di Montecitorio, 120-00186 Rome, Italy
Subscription fax: (39) 6 6784751

ADVERTISING INFORMATION

Advertising accepted: Yes

EDITORIAL DESCRIPTION

Scope: Publishes articles on German and Scandinavian literatures, philology, and languages.
Reviews books: Yes
Publishes notes: No
Languages accepted: German; Italian; English; French
Prints abstracts: No
Author-anonymous submission: No

SUBMISSION REQUIREMENTS

Restrictions on contributors: None
Author pays submission fee: No
Author pays page charges: No
Length of articles: 20-25 pp.
Length of book reviews: 3-10 pp.
Style: None
Number of copies required: 2
Copyright ownership: Ist. Italiano di Studi Germanici
Rejected manuscripts: Returned
Time before publication decision: 4-8 mos.
Time between decision and publication: 4-8 mos.
Number of reviewers: 2
Articles submitted per year: 30
Articles published per year: 24
Book reviews submitted per year: 30
Book reviews published per year: 25-30

(2751)
Studi Goldoniani

Nicola Mangini, Editor
Casa di Goldoni
Ist. di Studi Teatrali
S. Tomà 2794
30125 Venice, Italy

First published: 1968
Sponsoring organization: Comune di Venezia
MLA acronym: SGoldoniani

SUBSCRIPTION INFORMATION

Frequency of publication: Irregular
Available in microform: No

ADVERTISING INFORMATION

Advertising accepted: No

EDITORIAL DESCRIPTION

Scope: Publishes studies on Carlo Goldoni.
Reviews books: No
Publishes notes: No
Languages accepted: Italian
Prints abstracts: No

SUBMISSION REQUIREMENTS

Restrictions on contributors: None
Author pays submission fee: No
Author pays page charges: No
Length of articles: 30-40 pp.
Number of copies required: 1
Special requirements: None
Copyright ownership: Casa di Goldoni
Time before publication decision: 6 mos.
Time between decision and publication: 1 yr.
Number of reviewers: 2
Articles submitted per year: 10-15
Articles published per year: 10-12

(2752)
Studi Ispanici

Giardini Editori e Stampatori
Via Santa Bibbiana, 28
56100 Pisa, Italy

First published: 1976
Sponsoring organization: Consiglio Nazionale delle Ricerche
ISSN: 0585-492X
MLA acronym: SIs

SUBSCRIPTION INFORMATION

Frequency of publication: Annual
Available in microform: No

ADVERTISING INFORMATION

Advertising accepted: No

EDITORIAL DESCRIPTION

Scope: Publishes articles on Spanish literature and language.
Reviews books: Yes
Publishes notes: No
Languages accepted: Italian; Spanish
Prints abstracts: No

SUBMISSION REQUIREMENTS

Restrictions on contributors: None
Author pays submission fee: No
Author pays page charges: No
Length of articles: 20 pp.
Length of book reviews: 5 pp.
Style: MLA
Number of copies required: 1
Copyright ownership: Editor
Time before publication decision: 3 weeks
Time between decision and publication: 10 mos.
Number of reviewers: 5
Articles submitted per year: 19-20
Articles published per year: 8-10
Book reviews submitted per year: 6-8
Book reviews published per year: 2-3

(2753)
Studi Italiani di Linguistica Teorica ed Applicata

Enrico Arcaini, Editor
Liviana Editrice
Via Luigi Dottesio n.1
35138 Padua, Italy

First published: 1972
Sponsoring organization: Univ. di Bologna, Centro Interfacoltà di Linguistica Teorica e Applicata
ISSN: 0490-6809
MLA acronym: SILTA

SUBSCRIPTION INFORMATION

Frequency of publication: 3 times/yr.
Circulation: 2,000
Available in microform: No

ADVERTISING INFORMATION

Advertising accepted: Yes

EDITORIAL DESCRIPTION

Scope: Publishes technical studies, synthesis of research, theories, methods, discussions, notices, and a survey of publications of a broadly informative nature. Occasional special issues are devoted to problems of current interest.
Reviews books: Yes
Publishes notes: Yes
Languages accepted: English; French; Italian; German; Spanish
Prints abstracts: Yes
Author-anonymous submission: No

SUBMISSION REQUIREMENTS

Restrictions on contributors: None
Author pays submission fee: No
Author pays page charges: No
Length of articles: 4,000-10,000 characters
Length of book reviews: 2,000 characters
Length of notes: 2,500 characters
Style: Use the International Phonetic Assn.'s system of transcription.
Number of copies required: 2
Special requirements: Include a summary of 10 lines or less.
Copyright ownership: Assigned by author to journal
Rejected manuscripts: Returned; enclose return postage.
Time before publication decision: 2 mos.
Time between decision and publication: 1 yr.
Number of reviewers: 4
Articles submitted per year: 30
Articles published per year: 24
Book reviews submitted per year: 30
Book reviews published per year: 12-20
Notes submitted per year: 15
Notes published per year: 6-10

(2754)
*Studi Medievali

Claudio Leonardi, Editor
Via Lorenzo il Magnifico, 53
50129 Florence, Italy

Telephone: (39) 55 499131
First published: 1904
Sponsoring organization: Centro Italiano di Studi sull'Alto Medioevo
ISSN: 0039-0437
MLA acronym: SMed

SUBSCRIPTION INFORMATION

Frequency of publication: 2 times/yr. (June, Dec.)
Circulation: 1,400
Available in microform: No
Subscription address: Centro Italiano di Studi sull'Alto Medioevo, Palazzo Ancaiani, piazza Liberta 6, 06049 Spoleto (Perugia), Italy
Subscription telephone: (39) 743 220418; (39) 743 220485
Subscription fax: (39) 743 39107

ADVERTISING INFORMATION

Advertising accepted: No

EDITORIAL DESCRIPTION

Scope: Publishes articles on medieval civilization as well as editions of texts.
Reviews books: Yes
Publishes notes: Yes
Languages accepted: English; French; Italian; German; Spanish
Prints abstracts: No
Author-anonymous submission: No

SUBMISSION REQUIREMENTS

Restrictions on contributors: None
Author pays submission fee: No
Author pays page charges: No
Length of articles: No restrictions
Length of book reviews: No restrictions
Length of notes: No restrictions
Style: Journal
Number of copies required: 1
Copyright ownership: Journal
Time before publication decision: 6-12 mos.
Time between decision and publication: 12-18 mos.
Number of reviewers: 2
Articles submitted per year: 8
Articles published per year: 25
Book reviews submitted per year: 100
Book reviews published per year: 60
Notes published per year: 15

(2755)
*Studi Mediolatini e Volgari

Valeria Bertolucci Pizzorusso, Editor
Piazza S. Martino 3
56100 Pisa, Italy

Telephone: (39) 50 42409
Fax: (39) 50 983906
First published: 1953
ISSN: 0585-4962
MLA acronym: SMV

SUBSCRIPTION INFORMATION

Frequency of publication: Annual
Circulation: 500
Available in microform: No
Subscription price: 75,000 Lit/yr.
Year to which price refers: 1989
Subscription address: Pacini Editore, Via A. Gherardesca, 56014 Ospedaletto, Pisa, Italy
Subscription telephone: (39) 50 982439

ADVERTISING INFORMATION

Advertising accepted: No

EDITORIAL DESCRIPTION

Scope: Publishes philological, linguistic, literary, and Romance research.
Reviews books: Yes
Publishes notes: Yes
Languages accepted: English; German; French; Spanish; Italian; Romanian; Portuguese
Prints abstracts: No
Author-anonymous submission: No

SUBMISSION REQUIREMENTS

Restrictions on contributors: None
Author pays page charges: No
Length of articles: 20-30 pp.
Length of notes: 3-5 pp.
Style: None
Number of copies required: 2
Copyright ownership: Pacini Editori
Rejected manuscripts: Not returned
Time before publication decision: 1 yr.
Time between decision and publication: 6 mos.
Number of reviewers: 2
Articles submitted per year: 10
Articles published per year: 6
Book reviews submitted per year: 6
Book reviews published per year: 4
Notes submitted per year: 4
Notes published per year: 3

(2756)
Studi Micenei ed Egeo-Anatolici

Ernesto De Miro, Editor
Ist. per gli Studi Micenei ed Egeo-Anatolici
Consiglio Nazionale delle Ricerche
Via Giano Della Bella 18
00162 Rome, Italy

Sponsoring organization: Ist. per gli Studi Micenei ed Egeo-Anatolici
MLA acronym: SMEA

SUBSCRIPTION INFORMATION

Subscription address: Edizioni dell'Ateneo, Via Ruggero Bonghi, 11/b, 00184 Rome, Italy

EDITORIAL DESCRIPTION

Prints abstracts: No

SUBMISSION REQUIREMENTS

Copyright ownership: Ist. per gli Studi Micenei ed Egeo-Anatolici

(2757)
Studi Novecenteschi: Revista Semestrale di Storia della Letteratura Italiana Contemporanea

Cesare De Michelis, Editor
Ist. di Filologia e Letteratura Italiana
Univ. di Padova
Via Beato Pellegrino, 1
Padua, Italy

First published: 1972
ISSN: 0303-4615
MLA acronym: SNov

SUBSCRIPTION INFORMATION

Frequency of publication: 2 times/yr.
Available in microform: No
Subscription address: Giardini Editore, Via delle Sorgenti 23, 56010 Agnano Pisano, Italy

ADVERTISING INFORMATION

Advertising accepted: No

EDITORIAL DESCRIPTION

Scope: Publishes critical articles on contemporary Italian literature and history.
Reviews books: Yes
Publishes notes: Yes
Languages accepted: Italian
Prints abstracts: No

SUBMISSION REQUIREMENTS

Restrictions on contributors: None
Author pays submission fee: No
Author pays page charges: No
Length of articles: No restrictions
Length of book reviews: No restrictions
Length of notes: No restrictions
Style: None
Number of copies required: 1
Copyright ownership: Journal
Time before publication decision: 2 mos.
Time between decision and publication: 6 mos.
Number of reviewers: 3
Articles submitted per year: 18
Articles published per year: 6
Book reviews submitted per year: 30
Book reviews published per year: 15
Notes submitted per year: 8
Notes published per year: 4

(2758)
*Studi Romani: Rivista Trimestrale dell'Istituto Nazionale di Studi Romani

Ist. Nazionale di Studi Romani
Piazza dei Cavalieri di Malta, 2
00153 Rome, Italy

Telephone: (39) 6 5743442; (39) 6 5743445
First published: 1953
Sponsoring organization: Ist. Nazionale di Studi Romani
ISSN: 0039-2995
MLA acronym: SRo

SUBSCRIPTION INFORMATION

Frequency of publication: 2 times/yr.
Available in microform: No
Subscription price: 45,000 Lit/yr. Italy; 70,000 Lit/yr. elsewhere
Year to which price refers: 1992

ADVERTISING INFORMATION

Advertising accepted: No

EDITORIAL DESCRIPTION

Scope: Publishes articles on all aspects of Rome. Includes studies on Italian literature as well as studies on non-Italian writers in Rome.
Reviews books: Yes
Publishes notes: Yes
Languages accepted: Italian
Prints abstracts: No
Author-anonymous submission: No

SUBMISSION REQUIREMENTS

Restrictions on contributors: None
Author pays submission fee: No
Author pays page charges: No
Length of articles: 18 pp.
Length of book reviews: 12 pp.
Length of notes: 7 pp.
Style: None
Number of copies required: 1
Special requirements: Submit typescript.
Copyright ownership: Journal
Rejected manuscripts: Not returned
Time before publication decision: 2 mos.
Time between decision and publication: 1 yr.
Number of reviewers: 2
Articles submitted per year: 45
Articles published per year: 40
Book reviews submitted per year: 140
Book reviews published per year: 100
Notes submitted per year: 75
Notes published per year: 70

(2759)
*Studi Secenteschi

Martino Capucci, Editor
Editrice Leo S. Olschki
C.P. 66
50100 Florence, Italy

Telephone: (39) 55 6530684
Fax: (39) 55 6530214
First published: 1960
ISSN: 0081-6248
MLA acronym: SSe

SUBSCRIPTION INFORMATION

Frequency of publication: Annual
Circulation: 1,000
Available in microform: No
Subscription price: 76,000 Lit/yr.
Year to which price refers: 1991

ADVERTISING INFORMATION

Advertising accepted: No

EDITORIAL DESCRIPTION

Scope: Publishes studies on the 17th century.
Reviews books: No
Publishes notes: No
Languages accepted: English; French; Italian
Prints abstracts: No
Author-anonymous submission: No

SUBMISSION REQUIREMENTS

Author pays submission fee: No
Author pays page charges: No
Style: Olschki
Copyright ownership: Editrice Leo S. Olschki
Rejected manuscripts: Returned
Number of reviewers: 1

(2760)
*Studi sul Boccaccio

Vittore Branca, Giorgio Padoan, & Carlo Delcorno, Editors
S. Marco 2885
Venice, Italy

Additional editorial address: G. Padoan, S. Croce 1666a, Venice, Italy
First published: 1963
Sponsoring organization: Ente Nazionale Giovanni Boccaccio
ISSN: 0585-4997
MLA acronym: SBoc

SUBSCRIPTION INFORMATION

Frequency of publication: Generally annual
Circulation: 1,000
Available in microform: No
Subscription address: LICOSA S.p.A., Via Lamormora, 45, 50121 Florence, Italy

ADVERTISING INFORMATION

Advertising accepted: No

EDITORIAL DESCRIPTION

Scope: Publishes studies of Boccaccio in all aspects: biographical, historical, literary, and social.
Reviews books: Yes
Publishes notes: Yes
Languages accepted: English; Italian; French; German; Spanish
Prints abstracts: No
Author-anonymous submission: No

SUBMISSION REQUIREMENTS

Restrictions on contributors: Contributions are by invitation only.
Author pays submission fee: No
Author pays page charges: No
Length of articles: No restrictions
Length of book reviews: 5 pp.
Length of notes: 10 pp.
Style: None
Number of copies required: 2
Special requirements: Submit original typescript.
Copyright ownership: Editor
Rejected manuscripts: Returned
Time before publication decision: 2-3 mos.
Time between decision and publication: 6-12 mos.
Number of reviewers: 2
Articles submitted per year: 30-35
Articles published per year: 10-20
Book reviews submitted per year: 20-25
Book reviews published per year: 10
Notes submitted per year: 40
Notes published per year: 20-25

(2761)
*Studi Tassiani

Biblioteca Civica Angelo Mai
Piazza Vecchia, 15
24100 Bergamo, Italy

Telephone: (39) 35 399430; (39) 35 399431
Fax: (39) 35 240655
First published: 1951
Sponsoring organization: Centro di Studi Tassiani
ISSN: 0081-6256
MLA acronym: ST

SUBSCRIPTION INFORMATION

Frequency of publication: Annual
Circulation: 300
Available in microform: No
Subscription price: 60,000 Lit/yr.
Year to which price refers: 1992

ADVERTISING INFORMATION

Advertising accepted: No

EDITORIAL DESCRIPTION

Scope: Publishes essays on Torquato Tasso.
Reviews books: Yes
Publishes notes: No
Languages accepted: Italian
Prints abstracts: Yes
Author-anonymous submission: Yes

SUBMISSION REQUIREMENTS

Restrictions on contributors: None
Author pays submission fee: No
Author pays page charges: Yes
Length of articles: 10 pp.
Length of book reviews: 5 pp.
Number of copies required: 1
Copyright ownership: Author
Rejected manuscripts: Not returned
Time before publication decision: 2 mos.
Time between decision and publication: 2 mos.
Number of reviewers: 3
Articles submitted per year: 4
Articles published per year: 4
Book reviews submitted per year: 5
Book reviews published per year: 3

(2762)
*Studi Trentini di Scienze Storiche

Soc. Studi Trentini di Scienze Storiche
Via Petrarca, 36
C.P. n. 80
38100 Trento, Italy

Telephone: (39) 461 983388
First published: 1920
Sponsoring organization: Soc. di Studi Trentini di Scienze Storiche
MLA acronym: STr

SUBSCRIPTION INFORMATION

Frequency of publication: 4 times/yr.
Circulation: 1,300, 1st section; 2,300, 2nd section
Available in microform: No
Subscription price: 36,000 Lit/yr. 1st section; 100,000 Lit/yr. 2nd section
Year to which price refers: 1992

ADVERTISING INFORMATION

Advertising accepted: Yes

EDITORIAL DESCRIPTION

Scope: Publishes articles on the history, historical figures, culture, and linguistics of Trentino and on historians of Trentino.
Reviews books: Yes
Publishes notes: Yes
Languages accepted: Italian; German; Latin; English; French
Prints abstracts: Yes
Author-anonymous submission: No

SUBMISSION REQUIREMENTS

Restrictions on contributors: None
Author pays submission fee: No
Author pays page charges: No
Length of articles: No restrictions
Length of book reviews: No restrictions
Style: Scientific
Number of copies required: 1
Special requirements: Submit original typescript.
Copyright ownership: Journal; author occasionally by agreememt
Rejected manuscripts: Not returned
Time before publication decision: 1 mo.
Time between decision and publication: 6 mos.
Number of reviewers: 9
Articles submitted per year: 20-30
Articles published per year: 15-20
Book reviews submitted per year: 30
Book reviews published per year: 30
Notes submitted per year: 30
Notes published per year: 30

(2763)
*Studi Urbinati, Serie B3: Linguistica, Letteratura, Arte

Univ. degli Studi
Via Saffi 2
61029 Urbino, Italy

First published: 1950
Sponsoring organization: Univ. di Urbino
MLA acronym: SULLA

SUBSCRIPTION INFORMATION

Subscription address: Edizioni Quattro Venti, C.P. n. 156, 61029 Urbino, Italy

ADVERTISING INFORMATION

Advertising accepted: No

EDITORIAL DESCRIPTION

Scope: Publishes articles on linguistics, literature, and art.
Reviews books: No
Publishes notes: No
Languages accepted: Italian
Prints abstracts: No

SUBMISSION REQUIREMENTS

Author pays submission fee: No
Author pays page charges: No
Special requirements: Consult Editorial Board prior to submission.
Copyright ownership: Univ. degli Studi

(2764)
*Studia Albanica

Académie des Sciences d'Albanie
Section des Sciences Sociales
Rruga "Myslym Shyri" 7
Tirana, Albania

First published: 1964
ISSN: 0585-5047
MLA acronym: SAlb

SUBSCRIPTION INFORMATION

Frequency of publication: 2 times/yr.
Available in microform: No
Subscription price: $6.00/yr.
Year to which price refers: 1992
Subscription address: Shtypshkronja "Mihal Duri", Tirana, Albania

ADVERTISING INFORMATION

Advertising accepted: Yes

EDITORIAL DESCRIPTION

Reviews books: Yes
Publishes notes: Yes
Languages accepted: French; English; German; Italian
Prints abstracts: No
Author-anonymous submission: No

SUBMISSION REQUIREMENTS

Author pays submission fee: Yes
Author pays page charges: No
Length of notes: 4,000-5,000 words
Number of copies required: 2
Time before publication decision: 6 weeks
Time between decision and publication: 6 mos.

Number of reviewers: 3
Articles submitted per year: 60
Articles published per year: 35
Book reviews submitted per year: 30
Book reviews published per year: 20
Notes submitted per year: 30
Notes published per year: 20

(2765)
*Studia Anglica Posnaniensia: An International Review of English Studies

Jacek Fisiak, Editor
Inst. of English
Adam Mickiewicz Univ.
Marchlewskiego 124/126
61-874 Poznań, Poland

First published: 1968
Sponsoring organization: Adam Mickiewicz Univ.
ISSN: 0081-6272
MLA acronym: SAP

SUBSCRIPTION INFORMATION

Frequency of publication: Annual
Circulation: 1,500
Available in microform: No

ADVERTISING INFORMATION

Advertising accepted: Yes

EDITORIAL DESCRIPTION

Scope: An international review of English studies. Carries original articles on English linguistics and American and English literature as well as book reviews. Gives preference to linguistic contributions which occupy three quarters of its contents.
Reviews books: Yes
Publishes notes: Yes
Languages accepted: English
Prints abstracts: No
Author-anonymous submission: No

SUBMISSION REQUIREMENTS

Restrictions on contributors: None
Author pays submission fee: No
Author pays page charges: No
Length of articles: No restrictions
Length of book reviews: No restrictions
Length of notes: No restrictions
Style: Linguistic Soc. of America
Number of copies required: 3
Special requirements: Submit original typescript.
Copyright ownership: Assigned by author to journal
Rejected manuscripts: Returned
Time before publication decision: 2 mos.
Time between decision and publication: 6-18 mos.
Number of reviewers: 3
Articles submitted per year: 40-45
Articles published per year: 25
Book reviews submitted per year: 5-10
Book reviews published per year: 3-5
Notes submitted per year: 1-2
Notes published per year: 1-2

(2766)
*Studia Anthroponymica Scandinavica: Tidskrift för Nordisk Personnamnsforskning

Thorsten Andersson & Lena Peterson, Editors
Seminariet för Nordisk Ortnamnsforskning
S:t Johannesgatan 11
753 12 Uppsala, Sweden

Telephone: (46) 18 181289
Fax: (46) 18 181279
First published: 1983
Sponsoring organization: Nordiska Publiceringsnämnden för Humanistiska Tidskrifter
ISSN: 0280-8633
MLA acronym: StAS

SUBSCRIPTION INFORMATION

Frequency of publication: Annual (Autumn)
Circulation: 200
Available in microform: No
Subscription price: 190 Skr/yr. Sweden; 160 Skr/yr. other Scandinavian countries; 175 Skr/yr. elsewhere
Year to which price refers: 1992
Subscription address: Swedish Science Press, Box 118, 75104 Uppsala, Sweden
Subscription telephone: (46) 18 365566

ADVERTISING INFORMATION

Advertising accepted: No

EDITORIAL DESCRIPTION

Scope: Publishes studies dealing with the etymology, phonology, morphology, semantics, history, sociology, and stylistics of names, with an emphasis on personal names in all Nordic countries and the fate of Nordic names outside the Nordic region, both in the past and in modern times.
Reviews books: Yes
Publishes notes: No
Languages accepted: German; English; Danish; Swedish; Icelandic; Norwegian; Faroese
Prints abstracts: Yes
Author-anonymous submission: No

SUBMISSION REQUIREMENTS

Author pays submission fee: No
Author pays page charges: No
Length of articles: 1,000-15,000 words
Length of book reviews: 500-1,000 words
Style: Harvard, with modifications
Number of copies required: 1
Special requirements: Submit a short abstract for articles not in English or German.
Copyright ownership: Author
Rejected manuscripts: Returned
Time before publication decision: 1 mo.
Time between decision and publication: 8-20 mos.
Number of reviewers: 2
Articles submitted per year: 8-10
Articles published per year: 6-8
Book reviews submitted per year: 5-15
Book reviews published per year: 5-15

(2767)
*Studia Celtica

J. E. Caerwyn Williams, Editor
School of Advanced Welsh & Celtic Studies
Univ. College of Wales
Aberystwyth, Cards, Wales

First published: 1966
Sponsoring organization: Univ. of Wales, Board of Celtic Studies
ISSN: 0081-6353
MLA acronym: StC

SUBSCRIPTION INFORMATION

Frequency of publication: Once every 2 yrs.
Circulation: 500
Available in microform: No
Subscription address: Univ. of Wales Press, Univ. Registry, Cathays Pk., Cardiff, Wales

ADVERTISING INFORMATION

Advertising accepted: No

EDITORIAL DESCRIPTION

Scope: Devoted mainly to philological and linguistic studies of the Celtic languages. Also welcomes contributions on Celtic archaeology and early Celtic history. The journal helps to keep specialists in the different Celtic languages in touch with each other's work and with the work done in Celtic by Indo-Europeanists.
Reviews books: Yes
Publishes notes: Yes
Languages accepted: English; French; German; Welsh; Irish Gaelic; Breton; Scottish Gaelic
Prints abstracts: No
Author-anonymous submission: No

SUBMISSION REQUIREMENTS

Restrictions on contributors: None
Author pays submission fee: No
Author pays page charges: No
Length of articles: No restrictions
Length of book reviews: 600-1,000 words
Length of notes: No restrictions
Style: MLA
Number of copies required: 1
Special requirements: Submit typescript.
Copyright ownership: Author
Rejected manuscripts: Returned
Time before publication decision: 12-18 mos.
Time between decision and publication: 12-18 mos.
Number of reviewers: 1-2
Articles submitted per year: 20-30 every 2 yrs.
Articles published per year: 10-15 every 2 yrs.
Book reviews submitted per year: 10-15 every 2 yrs.
Book reviews published per year: 10-15 every 2 yrs.
Notes submitted per year: 5-10 every 2 yrs.
Notes published per year: 4-8 every 2 yrs.

(2768)
*Studia Fennica Ethnologica

Henni Ilomäki, Matti Räsänen, Anna-Leena Sükala, & Pentti Leino, Editors
Suomalaisen Kirjallisuuden Seura
Hallituskatu 1
00170 Helsinki 1, Finland

Telephone: (358) 0 13123210
Fax: (358) 0 13123220
First published: 1933
Historical variations in title: Supersedes *Studia Fennica*
Sponsoring organization: Suomalaisen Kirjallisuuden Seura
ISSN: 0085-6835
MLA acronym: SFenE

SUBSCRIPTION INFORMATION

Circulation: 1,000-1,500
Available in microform: No
Subscription telephone: (358) 0 131215

ADVERTISING INFORMATION

Advertising accepted: No

EDITORIAL DESCRIPTION

Scope: Publishes articles and monographs on ethnology.
Reviews books: No

Publishes notes: No
Languages accepted: English; French; German
Prints abstracts: No
Author-anonymous submission: No

SUBMISSION REQUIREMENTS

Restrictions on contributors: Unsolited manuscripts are not accepted.
Author pays submission fee: No
Author pays page charges: No
Number of copies required: 1
Copyright ownership: Author & Suomalaisen Kirjallisuuden Seura
Rejected manuscripts: Returned
Number of reviewers: 1-2

(2769)
*Studia Fennica Folkloristica

Henni Ilomäki, Matti Räsänen, Anna-Leena Sükala, & Pentti Leino, Editors
Suomalaisen Kirjallisuuden Seura
Hallituskatu 1
00170 Helsinki, Finland

Telephone: (358) 0 13123210
Fax: (358) 0 13123220
First published: 1933
Historical variations in title: Supersedes Studia Fennica
Sponsoring organization: Suomalaisen Kirjallisuuden Seura
ISSN: 1235-1946
MLA acronym: SFenF

SUBSCRIPTION INFORMATION

Circulation: 1,000-1,500
Available in microform: No
Subscription telephone: (358) 0 131215

ADVERTISING INFORMATION

Advertising accepted: No

EDITORIAL DESCRIPTION

Scope: Publishes articles and monographs on folklore.
Reviews books: No
Publishes notes: No
Languages accepted: English; French; German
Prints abstracts: No
Author-anonymous submission: No

SUBMISSION REQUIREMENTS

Restrictions on contributors: Unsolicited manuscripts are not accepted.
Author pays submission fee: No
Author pays page charges: No
Number of copies required: 1
Copyright ownership: Author & Suomalaisen Kirjallisuuden Seura
Rejected manuscripts: Returned
Number of reviewers: 1-2

(2770)
*Studia Fennica Linguistica

Henni Ilomäki, Matti Räsänen, Anna-Leena Sükala, & Pentti Leino, Editors
Suomalaisen Kirjallisuuden Seura
Hallituskatu 1
00170 Helsinki, Finland

Telephone: (358) 0 13123210
Fax: (358) 0 13123220
First published: 1933
Historical variations in title: Supersedes Studia Fennica
Sponsoring organization: Suomalaisen Kirjallisuuden Seura
ISSN: 0085-6835
MLA acronym: SFenL

SUBSCRIPTION INFORMATION

Circulation: 1,000-1,500
Available in microform: No
Subscription telephone: (358) 0 131215

ADVERTISING INFORMATION

Advertising accepted: No

EDITORIAL DESCRIPTION

Scope: Publishes articles and monographs on Finnish linguistics.
Reviews books: No
Publishes notes: No
Languages accepted: English; French; German
Prints abstracts: No
Author-anonymous submission: No

SUBMISSION REQUIREMENTS

Restrictions on contributors: Unsolicited manuscripts are not accepted.
Author pays submission fee: No
Author pays page charges: No
Number of copies required: 1
Copyright ownership: Author & Suomalaisen Kirjallisuuden Seura
Rejected manuscripts: Returned
Number of reviewers: 1-2

(2771)
Studia Germanica Gandensia

Seminaire voor Duitse Taalkunde
Blandijnberg 2
9000 Ghent, Belgium

First published: 1959
Sponsoring organization: Fac. van Letteren en Wijsbegeerte, Rijksuniv. te Gent
ISSN: 0081-6442
MLA acronym: SGG

SUBSCRIPTION INFORMATION

Frequency of publication: 3-4 times/yr.
Circulation: 150
Available in microform: No

ADVERTISING INFORMATION

Advertising accepted: No

EDITORIAL DESCRIPTION

Scope: Publishes studies of Germanic languages and literatures.
Reviews books: No
Publishes notes: No
Languages accepted: Dutch; English; German; Danish; Norwegian; Swedish
Prints abstracts: No

SUBMISSION REQUIREMENTS

Restrictions on contributors: None
Author pays submission fee: No
Author pays page charges: No
Length of articles: 20-50 pp.
Style: None
Number of copies required: 1
Copyright ownership: Assigned by author to journal
Rejected manuscripts: Returned
Time before publication decision: 5 mos.
Time between decision and publication: 5 mos.
Number of reviewers: 1
Articles published per year: 10-12

(2772)
Studia Ghisleriana

Collegio Ghislieri
Pavia, Italy

First published: 1948
Sponsoring organization: Collegio Ghislieri
MLA acronym: SGh

SUBSCRIPTION INFORMATION

Frequency of publication: Irregular
Available in microform: No

ADVERTISING INFORMATION

Advertising accepted: No

EDITORIAL DESCRIPTION

Reviews books: No
Languages accepted: All languages
Prints abstracts: No

SUBMISSION REQUIREMENTS

Restrictions on contributors: Contributors must be members of the Collegio Ghislieri; occasional exceptions are made.
Author pays submission fee: No
Author pays page charges: No
Special requirements: Considers manuscripts in all languages.
Copyright ownership: Author

(2773)
*Studia Grammatica

Manfred Bierwisch, Editor
Max Planck-Arbeitsgruppe "Strukturelle Grammatik"
Preuzlaner Promenade 149-152
1100 Berlin, Germany

Telephone: (49) 30 4797171
Fax: (49) 30 4797174
First published: 1962
ISSN: 0081-6469
MLA acronym: Stgr

SUBSCRIPTION INFORMATION

Frequency of publication: Irregular
Available in microform: No
Subscription address: Akademie-Verlag, Leipziger Str. 3-4, 1086 Berlin, Germany
Subscription telephone: (49) 30 2236390

ADVERTISING INFORMATION

Advertising accepted: No

EDITORIAL DESCRIPTION

Scope: Series considers grammatical and semantic research, as well as text analysis. In addition to studies of the theory of grammar of various languages, studies which deal with the problems of computational linguistics are also included.
Reviews books: No
Publishes notes: No
Languages accepted: German; English
Prints abstracts: Yes
Author-anonymous submission: No

SUBMISSION REQUIREMENTS

Restrictions on contributors: None
Author pays submission fee: No
Author pays page charges: No
Length of books: No restrictions
Style: None
Number of copies required: 2
Special requirements: Submit an abstract in English.
Copyright ownership: Akademie-Verlag

Rejected manuscripts: Returned
Time before publication decision: 3 mos.
Time between decision and publication: 8 mos.
Number of reviewers: 2
Books submitted per year: 1-2
Books published per year: 1-2

(2774)
*Studia Hibernica

Liam Mac Mathúna & Pauric Travers, Editors
St. Patrick's College
Dublin 9, Ireland

Telephone: (353) 1 376191
Fax: (353) 1 376197
First published: 1961
Sponsoring organization: St. Patrick's College
ISSN: 0081-6477
MLA acronym: SH

SUBSCRIPTION INFORMATION

Frequency of publication: Annual
Circulation: 1,000
Available in microform: No
Subscription price: IR£10.00/yr.
Year to which price refers: 1992

ADVERTISING INFORMATION

Advertising accepted: No

EDITORIAL DESCRIPTION

Scope: Devoted to the study of Irish language, literature, history, archaeology, folklore, place names, and related subjects. Aims at presenting the research of scholars in various fields of Irish studies. Endeavours to provide in each issue a proportion of articles, such as surveys of periods in history or literature, which will be of general interest. A long review section is a special feature of the journal and all new publications within its scope are there reviewed.
Reviews books: Yes
Publishes notes: No
Languages accepted: English; Irish Gaelic
Prints abstracts: No

SUBMISSION REQUIREMENTS

Author pays submission fee: No
Author pays page charges: No
Length of articles: 4,000-10,000 words
Length of book reviews: 500-1,500 words
Number of copies required: 1
Copyright ownership: Reverts to author after 1 yr.
Rejected manuscripts: Returned
Time before publication decision: 3 mos.
Time between decision and publication: 6-12 mos.
Number of reviewers: 3-4
Articles submitted per year: 10-15
Articles published per year: 6-8
Book reviews published per year: 10-20

(2775)
Studia Imagologica: Comparative Literature and European Diversity/Littérature Comparée et Diversité Européenne/Vergleichende Literaturwissenschaft und Europäische Diversität

Hugo Dyserinck & Joep Leerssen, Editors
Editions Rodopi B.V.
Keizersgracht 302-304
1016 EX Amsterdam, Netherlands

Telephone: (31) 20 6227507
Fax: (31) 20 6380948
First published: 1992
MLA acronym: StudIm

SUBSCRIPTION INFORMATION

Additional subscription address: Editions Rodopi, 233 Peachtree St. N.E., Suite 404, Atlanta, GA 30303-1504
Subscription telephone: 404 523-1964; 800 225-3998
Subscription fax: 404 522-7116

ADVERTISING INFORMATION

Advertising accepted: No

EDITORIAL DESCRIPTION

Scope: Publishes monographs on comparative and European literature.
Reviews books: No
Languages accepted: English; French; German

(2776)
*Studia Iranica

Assn. pour l'Avancement des Etudes Iraniennes
13, rue de Santeuil
75231 Paris Cedex 05, France

Telephone: (33) 1 45874069
First published: 1972
Sponsoring organization: Assn. pour l'Avancement des Etudes Iraniennes
ISSN: 0772-7852
MLA acronym: StudiaI

SUBSCRIPTION INFORMATION

Frequency of publication: 2 times/yr.; plus supplement *Abstracta Iranica*
Circulation: 600
Available in microform: Yes
Subscription price: 1,800 BF/yr.
Year to which price refers: 1991
Subscription address: E. Peeters, Imprimerie Orientaliste, B.P. 41, 3000 Louvain, Belgium
Additional subscription address: Philippe Gignoux, 5 allée du Mâconnais, Férolles-Attilly, 77150 Lesigny, France
Subscription telephone: (32) 16488102

EDITORIAL DESCRIPTION

Scope: Publishes studies on Iran.
Reviews books: Yes
Publishes notes: Yes
Languages accepted: French; English; German
Prints abstracts: Yes
Author-anonymous submission: No

SUBMISSION REQUIREMENTS

Restrictions on contributors: None
Author pays submission fee: No
Author pays page charges: No
Length of articles: No restrictions
Length of book reviews: 1-5 pp.
Length of notes: 1-10 pp.
Style: Journal
Number of copies required: 2
Copyright ownership: Assigned by author to Assn. pour l'Avancement des Etudes Iraniennes
Rejected manuscripts: Returned
Time before publication decision: 3-6 mos.
Time between decision and publication: 6 mos.
Number of reviewers: 2
Articles submitted per year: 15
Articles published per year: 12
Book reviews submitted per year: 6
Book reviews published per year: 5
Notes submitted per year: 3
Notes published per year: 2

(2777)
*Studia Islamica

A. L. Udovitch & A. M. Turki, Editors
Near Eastern Studies
Princeton Univ.
Princeton, NJ 08540

Additional editorial address: A. M. Turki, 1 bis, rue Gager-Gabillot, 75015 Paris, France
First published: 1953
Sponsoring organization: Princeton Univ.; Centre Nationale de Recherche Scientifique
ISSN: 0585-5292
MLA acronym: StIsl

SUBSCRIPTION INFORMATION

Frequency of publication: 2 times/yr.
Circulation: 1,000
Available in microform: No
Subscription address: G.-P. Maisonneuve & Larose, 11, rue Victor-Cousin, 75005 Paris, France

ADVERTISING INFORMATION

Advertising accepted: Yes

EDITORIAL DESCRIPTION

Scope: Publishes papers written by specialists on subjects from all sections of the field of Islamic studies. Emphasizes the general aspects of the subjects treated in these studies. Pays special attention to discussions of method, to comprehensive views, and to new conclusions.
Reviews books: Yes
Publishes notes: Yes
Languages accepted: English; French
Prints abstracts: No

SUBMISSION REQUIREMENTS

Restrictions on contributors: None
Author pays submission fee: No
Length of articles: 25-40 typescript pp.
Length of book reviews: 1,000 words
Number of copies required: 1
Copyright ownership: Author
Rejected manuscripts: Returned
Time before publication decision: 2 mos.
Time between decision and publication: 12-18 mos.
Number of reviewers: 2-4
Articles published per year: 14-16

(2778)
*Studia Islandica: Íslenzk Fræði

Sveinn Skorri Höskuldsson, Editor
Inst. of Literary Research
Univ. of Iceland
101 Reykjavik, Iceland

First published: 1937
Sponsoring organization: Inst. of Literary Studies, Univ. of Iceland
MLA acronym: StudIsl

SUBSCRIPTION INFORMATION

Frequency of publication: Annual
Circulation: 600

ADVERTISING INFORMATION

Advertising accepted: No

EDITORIAL DESCRIPTION

Scope: Publishes monographs on Icelandic studies.
Reviews books: No
Languages accepted: English; Icelandic
Prints abstracts: Yes

SUBMISSION REQUIREMENTS

Author pays submission fee: Yes
Author pays page charges: No
Number of copies required: 2
Copyright ownership: Inst. of Litrerary Studies
Rejected manuscripts: Returned
Number of reviewers: 3
Articles submitted per year: 6-7
Articles published per year: 1-3
Books published per year: 1

(2779)
*Studia Linguistica

Christer Platzack & Jan-Olof Svantesson, Editors
c/o Merle Horne, Ed. Secretary
Dept. of Linguistics
Lund Univ.
Helgonabacken 12
223 62 Lund, Sweden

Telephone: (46) 46 108440
Fax: (46) 46 104210
E-mail: Merle.Horne@lings.lu.se
First published: 1947
Sponsoring organization: Swedish Council for Research in the Humanities & Social Sciences
ISSN: 0038-3193
MLA acronym: SL

SUBSCRIPTION INFORMATION

Frequency of publication: 2 times/yr.
Circulation: 500
Available in microform: No
Subscription price: 275 NKr ($46.00)/yr.
Year to which price refers: 1992
Subscription address: Scandinavian Univ. Press, Subscription Dept., P.O. Box 2959 Tøyen, 0608 Oslo 6, Norway
Additional subscription address: Scandinavian Univ. Press, 200 Meacham Ave., Elmont, NY 11003
Subscription telephone: (47) 2 677600

ADVERTISING INFORMATION

Advertising accepted: Yes

EDITORIAL DESCRIPTION

Scope: Serves as a forum for Scandinavian linguists, but is open to scholars from all other countries.
Reviews books: Yes
Publishes notes: Yes
Languages accepted: English; French; German
Prints abstracts: Yes
Author-anonymous submission: No

SUBMISSION REQUIREMENTS

Restrictions on contributors: None
Author pays submission fee: No
Author pays page charges: No
Length of articles: 10-25 pp.
Length of book reviews: 1-4 pp.
Length of notes: 2-4 pp.
Style: Linguistic Soc. of America
Number of copies required: 3
Copyright ownership: Journal
Rejected manuscripts: Not returned
Time before publication decision: 2 mos.
Time between decision and publication: 6-12 mos.
Number of reviewers: 2
Articles submitted per year: 30
Articles published per year: 8
Book reviews submitted per year: 15
Book reviews published per year: 10
Notes submitted per year: 5
Notes published per year: 1-2

(2780)
*Studia Litteraria

István Bitskey & Attila Tamás, Editors
Magyar Irodalomtörténeti Intézet
4010 Debrecen, Hungary

First published: 1963
Sponsoring organization: Kossuth Lajos Tudományegyetem
ISSN: 0562-2867
MLA acronym: SLD

SUBSCRIPTION INFORMATION

Frequency of publication: Annual
Circulation: 300
Available in microform: No
Subscription address: Kossuth Lajos Tudományegyetem, 4010 Debrecen, Pf. 52, Hungary

ADVERTISING INFORMATION

Advertising accepted: No

EDITORIAL DESCRIPTION

Scope: Publishes papers on the history of Hungarian literature.
Reviews books: No
Publishes notes: No
Languages accepted: Hungarian; French; German; English
Prints abstracts: Yes

SUBMISSION REQUIREMENTS

Restrictions on contributors: Contributors are usually members of the Dept. of Hungarian Literature, Kossuth Lajos Univ.
Author pays submission fee: No
Author pays page charges: No
Length of articles: 2,000-5,000 words
Style: None
Number of copies required: 2
Special requirements: Submit original typescript.
Copyright ownership: Author
Rejected manuscripts: Returned
Time before publication decision: 2 mos.
Time between decision and publication: 1 yr.
Number of reviewers: 3
Articles submitted per year: 10
Articles published per year: 1-10

(2781)
*Studia Logica: An International Journal for Symbolic Logic

Ryszard Wójcicki, Editor
Skr. 61
U.P.T. Warsaw 37, Poland

Telephone: (48) 22 267181
E-mail: Logifis@pleavn.bitnet
First published: 1953
ISSN: 0039-3215
MLA acronym: SLog

SUBSCRIPTION INFORMATION

Frequency of publication: 4 times/yr.
Circulation: 480
Available in microform: No
Subscription price: $153.00/yr.
Year to which price refers: 1992
Subscription address: Kluwer Academic Publishers, P.O. Box 322, 3300 AH Dordecht, Netherlands
Additional subscription address: Kluwer Academic Publishers, Order Dept., P.O. Box 358, Accord Station, Hingham, MA 02018-0358

ADVERTISING INFORMATION

Advertising accepted: Yes, on an exchange basis

EDITORIAL DESCRIPTION

Scope: Publishes articles on all technical issues of contemporary logic, philosophical issues in linguistics, and logical systems including their semantics, methodology, and applications.
Reviews books: Yes
Publishes notes: Yes
Languages accepted: English
Prints abstracts: Yes
Author-anonymous submission: No

SUBMISSION REQUIREMENTS

Restrictions on contributors: None
Author pays submission fee: No
Author pays page charges: No
Length of articles: 10,000 words
Length of book reviews: 500 words
Length of notes: 500 words
Style: Journal
Number of copies required: 3
Copyright ownership: Kluwer Academic Publishers
Rejected manuscripts: Returned
Time before publication decision: 2-5 mos.
Time between decision and publication: 3-6 mos.
Number of reviewers: 2
Articles submitted per year: 60
Articles published per year: 40
Book reviews submitted per year: 20
Book reviews published per year: 20

(2782)
*Studia Mediewistyczne

Mieczysław Markowski, Editor
Dział Wydawnictw
Inst. Filozofii & Socjologii
Polskiej Akademii Nauk
ul. Nowy Świat 72
00-330 Warsaw, Poland

Telephone: (48) 22 336377 ext. 383, 384, 385
First published: 1958
Sponsoring organization: Polska Akademia Nauk, Inst. Filozofii & Socjologii
ISSN: 0039-3231
MLA acronym: StMed

SUBSCRIPTION INFORMATION

Frequency of publication: Annual
Available in microform: No
Additional subscription address: Wydawnictwo Ossolineum, Dział Handlowy, Rynek 9, 50-106 Warsaw, Poland
Subscription telephone: (48) 22 265231 ext. 97

ADVERTISING INFORMATION

Advertising accepted: No

EDITORIAL DESCRIPTION

Scope: Publishes articles and dissertations on medieval philosophy and intellectual life of the Middle Ages as well as editions of medieval texts (in Latin).
Reviews books: Yes
Publishes notes: Yes
Languages accepted: French; German; Polish; English; Latin; Italian
Prints abstracts: Yes
Author-anonymous submission: No

SUBMISSION REQUIREMENTS

Restrictions on contributors: None
Author pays submission fee: No
Author pays page charges: No
Length of articles: 500-300,000 words
Length of book reviews: 300-10,000 words
Length of notes: 300-10,000 words
Style: Journal
Number of copies required: 2-3
Special requirements: Submit original typescript and diskette.

Copyright ownership: Assigned by author to journal
Rejected manuscripts: Not returned
Time before publication decision: 6 mos.
Time between decision and publication: 15 mos.
Number of reviewers: 2
Articles submitted per year: 15
Articles published per year: 1-15
Book reviews submitted per year: 10
Book reviews published per year: 7
Notes submitted per year: 5
Notes published per year: 4

(2783)
Studia Monastica

Josep Massot Muntaner, Editor
L'Abadia de Montserrat
Barcelona, Spain

First published: 1959
Sponsoring organization: Abadia de Montserrat
ISSN: 0039-3258
MLA acronym: StM

SUBSCRIPTION INFORMATION

Frequency of publication: 2 times/yr.
Circulation: 800
Available in microform: No
Subscription address: Publicacions de l'Abadia de Montserrat, Ausias March 92-98, Barcelona-13, Spain

ADVERTISING INFORMATION

Advertising accepted: No

EDITORIAL DESCRIPTION

Scope: Publishes articles on monastic history.
Reviews books: Yes
Publishes notes: Yes
Languages accepted: Catalan; English; French; German; Italian; Latin; Portuguese; Spanish
Prints abstracts: No
Author-anonymous submission: No

SUBMISSION REQUIREMENTS

Restrictions on contributors: None
Author pays submission fee: No
Author pays page charges: No
Number of copies required: 1
Special requirements: Submit original typescript.
Copyright ownership: Author
Rejected manuscripts: Returned
Time before publication decision: 1 week
Time between decision and publication: 8-12 mos.
Number of reviewers: 1-2

(2784)
*Studia Musicologica Academiae Scientiarum Hungaricae

József Ujfalussy, Editor
Táncsics u. 7
1014 Budapest, Hungary

Telephone: (36) 1 1759011
Fax: (36) 1 1759282
First published: 1961
Sponsoring organization: Magyar Tudományos Akadémia
ISSN: 0039-3266
MLA acronym: SMus

SUBSCRIPTION INFORMATION

Frequency of publication: Annual
Available in microform: No
Subscription address: Akadémiai Kiadó, P.O. Box 245, 1519 Budapest, Hungary
Subscription telephone: (36) 1 1665545

ADVERTISING INFORMATION

Advertising accepted: Yes

EDITORIAL DESCRIPTION

Scope: Publishes papers on musicology.
Reviews books: Yes
Publishes notes: Yes
Languages accepted: English; French; German; Italian; Russian
Prints abstracts: No

SUBMISSION REQUIREMENTS

Author pays submission fee: No
Author pays page charges: No
Number of copies required: 2
Rejected manuscripts: Returned
Time before publication decision: 1-12 mos.
Time between decision and publication: 6 mos.
Number of reviewers: 8
Articles published per year: 20-30
Book reviews published per year: 5-10

(2785)
*Studia Mystica

Robert Boenig, Editor
Dept. of English
Texas A&M Univ.
College Station, TX 77843-4227

Telephone: 409 845-8318
Fax: 409 845-5164
E-mail: REB5335@VENUS.TAMU.EDU
First published: 1978
Sponsoring organization: Texas A&M Univ.; Skidmore College
ISSN: 0161-7222
MLA acronym: SMy

SUBSCRIPTION INFORMATION

Frequency of publication: 3 times/yr.
Circulation: 300
Available in microform: No
Subscription price: $14.00/yr.
Year to which price refers: 1992
Subscription address: Dept. of Humanities, California State Univ., Sacramento, CA 95819

ADVERTISING INFORMATION

Advertising accepted: No

EDITORIAL DESCRIPTION

Scope: Publishes articles on the interrelationship of mystical experience and aesthetic experience in literature, visual arts, music, philosophy, and religion.
Reviews books: Yes
Publishes notes: Yes
Languages accepted: English
Prints abstracts: No
Author-anonymous submission: No

SUBMISSION REQUIREMENTS

Restrictions on contributors: None
Author pays submission fee: No
Author pays page charges: No
Length of articles: 15-30 typescript pp.
Length of book reviews: 750-1,200 words
Length of notes: 1,500-2,000 words
Style: Chicago
Number of copies required: 2
Special requirements: Accepted articles must be submitted on diskette.
Copyright ownership: Journal, reverts to author
Rejected manuscripts: Returned; enclose return postage or international reply coupons.
Time before publication decision: 2-3 mos.
Time between decision and publication: 6-12 mos.
Number of reviewers: 2-3
Articles submitted per year: 40
Articles published per year: 15

Book reviews submitted per year: 16
Book reviews published per year: 16
Notes submitted per year: 6
Notes published per year: 2

(2786)
*Studia Neophilologica: A Journal of Germanic and Romance Languages and Literature

Lars Hermodsson, Editor
Uppsala Univ.
Tyska Inst.
Kyrkogårdsgatan 10
P.O. Box 513
751 20 Uppsala, Sweden

Telephone: (46) 18 181349
First published: 1928
Sponsoring organization: Humanistisk-Samhällsvetenskapliga Forskningsrådet
ISSN: 0039-3274
MLA acronym: SN

SUBSCRIPTION INFORMATION

Frequency of publication: 2 times/yr. (May, Dec.)
Circulation: 400
Available in microform: Yes
Subscription price: 410 Skr (450 NKr, $75.00)/yr.
Year to which price refers: 1992
Subscription address: Scandinavian Univ. Press, Stockholm Office, P.O. Box 3255, 103 65 Stockholm, Sweden
Additional subscription address: Scandinavian Univ. Press, 200 Meacham Ave., Elmont, NY 11003; Scandinavian Univ. Press, P.O. Box 2959 Tøyen, 0608 Oslo, Norway
Subscription telephone: (46) 8 6137050
Subscription fax: (46) 8 209982

ADVERTISING INFORMATION

Advertising accepted: Yes

EDITORIAL DESCRIPTION

Scope: Publishes articles on English, German, and Romance languages and literature and reviews of books in these fields.
Reviews books: Yes
Publishes notes: Yes
Languages accepted: English; French; German; Italian; Spanish
Prints abstracts: No
Author-anonymous submission: No

SUBMISSION REQUIREMENTS

Restrictions on contributors: None
Author pays submission fee: No
Author pays page charges: No
Length of articles: 30 pp. maximum
Length of book reviews: 6 pp. maximum
Style: Journal
Number of copies required: 1
Copyright ownership: Author
Rejected manuscripts: Returned; enclose return postage
Time before publication decision: 1-2 mos.
Time between decision and publication: 1-2 yrs.
Number of reviewers: 1-2
Articles submitted per year: 70-80
Articles published per year: 15-18
Book reviews published per year: 15-30
Notes published per year: 1-2

(2787)
*Studia Phonetica

Pierre R. Léon, Editor
Canadian Scholars' Press, Inc.
c/o Jack Wayne
211 Grenadier St.
Toronto, Ontario M6R 1R9, Canada

Additional editorial address: Experimental Phonetics Lab, New College, 300 Huron St., Toronto, Ontario M5S 2X6, Canada
First published: 1969
Sponsoring organization: Canadian Federation for the Humanities
ISSN: 0829-2167
MLA acronym: SPh

SUBSCRIPTION INFORMATION

Frequency of publication: Irregular
Circulation: 800
Available in microform: No

ADVERTISING INFORMATION

Advertising accepted: No

EDITORIAL DESCRIPTION

Scope: Publishes monographs on the phonetic and phonemic study of languages.
Reviews books: No
Publishes notes: No
Languages accepted: French; English
Prints abstracts: No
Author-anonymous submission: Yes

SUBMISSION REQUIREMENTS

Restrictions on contributors: None
Author pays submission fee: No
Author pays page charges: No
Length of books: No restrictions
Style: Chicago
Number of copies required: 2
Copyright ownership: Canadian Scholars' Press Inc.
Rejected manuscripts: Not returned
Time before publication decision: 2 mos.
Number of reviewers: 4

(2788)
Studia Slavica Academiae Scientiarum Hungaricae

Ferenc Papp, Editor
Akadémiai Kiadó
P.O. Box 24
1363 Budapest, Hungary

First published: 1955
Sponsoring organization: Magyar Tudományos Akadémia
ISSN: 0039-3363
MLA acronym: SSASH

SUBSCRIPTION INFORMATION

Frequency of publication: 4 times/yr.
Circulation: 450
Available in microform: No
Subscription address: Kultura, Postfach 149, 1389 Budapest, Hungary

ADVERTISING INFORMATION

Advertising accepted: Yes

EDITORIAL DESCRIPTION

Scope: Publishes papers in the field of linguistic, philological, and folkloristic research in Slavic studies.
Reviews books: Yes
Languages accepted: English; French; German; Russian; all Slavonic languages

SUBMISSION REQUIREMENTS

Restrictions on contributors: None
Author pays submission fee: No
Author pays page charges: No
Length of articles: 7,500 words
Length of book reviews: 1,500-2,000 words
Length of notes: 750-1,000 words
Style: Journal
Number of copies required: 2
Copyright ownership: Author
Rejected manuscripts: Not returned
Time before publication decision: 3 mos.
Time between decision and publication: 18 mos.
Number of reviewers: 2
Articles submitted per year: 35
Articles published per year: 30
Book reviews submitted per year: 25-30
Book reviews published per year: 20-30
Notes submitted per year: 4-5
Notes published per year: 4-5

(2789)
*Studia Slavica Finlandensia

Valdemar Melanko, Editor
Venäjän ja Itä-Euroopan Inst.
Armfeltintie 10
00150 Helsinki 15, Finland

Telephone: (358) 0 651166
Fax: (358) 0 628618
First published: 1984
Sponsoring organization: Inst. for Russian & East-European Studies
ISSN: 0781-3333
MLA acronym: SSFin

SUBSCRIPTION INFORMATION

Frequency of publication: Annual
Circulation: 800
Available in microform: No
Subscription price: 70 Fmk/yr.
Year to which price refers: 1991

ADVERTISING INFORMATION

Advertising accepted: Yes

EDITORIAL DESCRIPTION

Scope: Publishes articles by Finnish Slavicists including works about poetry, drama, Slavic linguistics, Russian language, and Finnish-Russian/Soviet relations.
Reviews books: Yes
Publishes notes: Yes
Languages accepted: Russian; English; German
Prints abstracts: No
Author-anonymous submission: No

SUBMISSION REQUIREMENTS

Restrictions on contributors: None
Author pays submission fee: No
Author pays page charges: No
Length of articles: 15-20 pp.
Length of book reviews: 1-2 pp.
Length of notes: No restrictions
Style: Journal; available upon request
Number of copies required: 2
Copyright ownership: Author
Rejected manuscripts: Returned
Time before publication decision: 2-3 mos.
Time between decision and publication: 6-10 mos.
Number of reviewers: 2
Articles submitted per year: 16-20
Articles published per year: 15
Book reviews submitted per year: 2-3
Book reviews published per year: 1-2
Notes submitted per year: 2-3
Notes published per year: 1-2

(2790)
Studia Staropolskie

Czesław Hernas, Editor
Zakład Narodowy im. Ossolinskich
Rynek 9
50-106 Wrocław, Poland

First published: 1953
Sponsoring organization: Polska Akademia Nauk, Inst. Badań Literackich
ISSN: 0081-6949
MLA acronym: StuSta

SUBSCRIPTION INFORMATION

Frequency of publication: Irregular
Circulation: 1,500
Available in microform: No
Subscription address: Foreign Trade Enterprise "Ars Polona", Krakowskie Przedmieście 7, 00 068 Warsaw, Poland

ADVERTISING INFORMATION

Advertising accepted: No

EDITORIAL DESCRIPTION

Scope: Publishes books focusing on the problems of Old Polish literature and culture.
Reviews books: No
Publishes notes: Yes
Languages accepted: Polish
Prints abstracts: Yes

SUBMISSION REQUIREMENTS

Restrictions on contributors: Contributors must be members of the Polish Academy of Sciences.
Author pays submission fee: No
Author pays page charges: No
Number of copies required: 2
Copyright ownership: Ossolineum
Rejected manuscripts: Returned
Time before publication decision: 2 mos.
Number of reviewers: 2
Books published per year: 0-3

(2791)
*Studiekamraten

Thomas Nydahl, Editor
Sätaröds Station
290 10 Tollarp, Sweden

Telephone: (46) 44 320165
First published: 1919
Historical variations in title: Formerly *Studiekamraten: Tidskrift för det Fria Bildningsarbetet*
Sponsoring organization: Statens Kulturråd
ISSN: 0039-3452
MLA acronym: Studiekamraten

SUBSCRIPTION INFORMATION

Frequency of publication: 5 times/yr.
Circulation: 1,000
Subscription price: 260 Skr/yr.
Year to which price refers: 1992
Subscription address: Postgiro 483 73 73-2, Studiekamraten, 290 10 Tollarp, Sweden

EDITORIAL DESCRIPTION

Scope: Publishes articles on Swedish and international literature, culture, and art.
Reviews books: Yes
Languages accepted: Swedish; Danish; Norwegian
Prints abstracts: No

SUBMISSION REQUIREMENTS

Restrictions on contributors: None
Author pays submission fee: No

Author pays page charges: No
Length of articles: 2-10 typescript pp.
Copyright ownership: Author
Rejected manuscripts: Returned at author's request
Number of reviewers: 1

(2792)
*Studien und Texte zur Sozialgeschichte der Literatur

Wolfgang Frühwald, Georg Jäger, Dieter Langewiesche, Alberto Martino, & Rainer Wohlfeil, Editors
Max Niemeyer Verlag
Postfach 2140
7400 Tübingen, Germany

Telephone: (49) 7071 81104
Fax: (49) 7071 87419
First published: 1981
ISSN: 0174-4410
MLA acronym: STSL

SUBSCRIPTION INFORMATION

Frequency of publication: Irregular
Circulation: 500
Available in microform: No

ADVERTISING INFORMATION

Advertising accepted: No

EDITORIAL DESCRIPTION

Scope: Publishes studies on the social history of literature from the beginnings to the 20th century.
Reviews books: No
Publishes notes: No
Languages accepted: German; English
Prints abstracts: No
Author-anonymous submission: Yes

SUBMISSION REQUIREMENTS

Restrictions on contributors: None
Author pays submission fee: No
Author pays page charges: No
Length of books: No restrictions
Style: MLA
Number of copies required: 2
Copyright ownership: Max Niemeyer Verlag
Rejected manuscripts: Returned
Time before publication decision: 6 mos.
Time between decision and publication: 1 yr.
Number of reviewers: 2
Books submitted per year: 5-6
Books published per year: 3-4

(2793)
*Studien zu den Boğazköy-Texten

Akademie der Wissenschaften & der Literatur
Geschwister-Stoll Str. 2
6500 Mainz 1, Germany

Fax: (49) 6131 57740
First published: 1965
Sponsoring organization: Kommission für den Alten Orient der Akademie der Wissenschaften & der Literatur
ISSN: 0585-5853
MLA acronym: StBoT

SUBSCRIPTION INFORMATION

Frequency of publication: Irregular
Circulation: 400
Available in microform: No

ADVERTISING INFORMATION

Advertising accepted: No

EDITORIAL DESCRIPTION

Scope: Publishes studies of the Bogazköy texts.
Reviews books: No
Publishes notes: No
Languages accepted: German; English
Prints abstracts: No
Author-anonymous submission: No

SUBMISSION REQUIREMENTS

Restrictions on contributors: None
Author pays submission fee: No
Author pays page charges: No
Length of books: No restrictions
Style: None
Number of copies required: 1
Copyright ownership: Akademie der Wissenschaften & der Literatur, Mainz
Rejected manuscripts: Returned
Time before publication decision: 3-5 mos.
Time between decision and publication: 1-2 yrs.
Number of reviewers: 2
Books submitted per year: 1-2
Books published per year: 1 book every 2-4 yrs.

(2794)
*Studien zum Kleinen Deutschen Sprachatlas

Wolfgang Putschke & Werner H. Veith, Editors
Max Niemeyer Verlag
Postfach 2140
7400 Tübingen, Germany

Telephone: (49) 7071 81104
Fax: (49) 7071 87419
First published: 1982
MLA acronym: SKDS

SUBSCRIPTION INFORMATION

Frequency of publication: Irregular
Available in microform: No

ADVERTISING INFORMATION

Advertising accepted: No

EDITORIAL DESCRIPTION

Scope: Publishes monographs and collections on German areal linguistics.
Reviews books: No
Publishes notes: No
Languages accepted: German
Author-anonymous submission: No

SUBMISSION REQUIREMENTS

Style: Series
Copyright ownership: Max Niemeyer Verlag

(2795)
*Studien zur Deutschen Literatur

Wilfried Barner, Richard Brinkmann, & Conrad Wiedemann, Editors
Max Niemeyer Verlag
Postfach 2140
7400 Tübingen, Germany

Telephone: (49) 7071 81104
Fax: (49) 7071 87419
First published: 1965
ISSN: 0081-7236
MLA acronym: SzDL

SUBSCRIPTION INFORMATION

Frequency of publication: Irregular
Available in microform: No

ADVERTISING INFORMATION

Advertising accepted: No

EDITORIAL DESCRIPTION

Scope: Publishes studies in modern German literature.
Reviews books: No
Publishes notes: No
Languages accepted: German; English
Prints abstracts: No
Author-anonymous submission: Yes

SUBMISSION REQUIREMENTS

Restrictions on contributors: None
Author pays submission fee: No
Author pays page charges: No
Length of books: No restrictions
Style: Journal
Number of copies required: 2
Copyright ownership: Max Niemeyer Verlag
Rejected manuscripts: Returned
Time before publication decision: 6 mos.
Time between decision and publication: 1 yr.
Number of reviewers: 1
Books submitted per year: 8-10
Books published per year: 3-6

(2796)
*Studien zur Deutschen Literatur des 19. und 20. Jahrhunderts

Dieter Kafitz, Franz Norbert Mennemeier, & Erwin Rotermund, Editors
Verlag Peter Lang
Jupiterstr. 15
3015 Bern, Switzerland

Telephone: (41) 31 321122
Fax: (41) 31 321131
First published: 1986
ISSN: 0930-2166
MLA acronym: SDLNZJ

EDITORIAL DESCRIPTION

Scope: Publishes monographs and collections of articles on studies on German literature from the 19th and 20th centuries.
Reviews books: No
Publishes notes: No
Languages accepted: German; English; French
Prints abstracts: No
Author-anonymous submission: No

SUBMISSION REQUIREMENTS

Author pays page charges: Yes
Number of copies required: 1
Special requirements: Submit original typescript.
Copyright ownership: Verlag Peter Lang
Time before publication decision: 1-2 mos.
Time between decision and publication: 6 mos.
Number of reviewers: 2
Books published per year: 3-4

(2797)
*Studien zur Englischen Philologie

Lothar Fietz, Gerhard Müller-Schwefe, Friedrich Schubel, & Jörg Fichte, Editors
Max Niemeyer Verlag
Postfach 2140
7400 Tübingen, Germany

Telephone: (49) 7071 81104
Fax: (49) 7071 87419
First published: 1963
ISSN: 0081-7244
MLA acronym: SzEP

SUBSCRIPTION INFORMATION

Frequency of publication: Irregular
Available in microform: No

ADVERTISING INFORMATION

Advertising accepted: No

EDITORIAL DESCRIPTION

Scope: Publishes studies in English language and literature.
Reviews books: No
Publishes notes: No
Languages accepted: English; German
Prints abstracts: Yes
Author-anonymous submission: Yes

SUBMISSION REQUIREMENTS

Restrictions on contributors: None
Author pays submission fee: No
Author pays page charges: No
Length of books: No restrictions
Style: MLA
Number of copies required: 2
Copyright ownership: Max Niemeyer Verlag
Rejected manuscripts: Returned
Time before publication decision: 3-6 mos.
Time between decision and publication: 1 yr.
Number of reviewers: 2-3
Books submitted per year: 3-4
Books published per year: 1-2

(2798)
*Studien zur Germanistik, Anglistik und Komparatistik

Armin Arnold & Alois Haas, Editors
HWV
Bifang 10
4600 Olten, Switzerland

First published: 1969
ISSN: 0340-594X
MLA acronym: SGAK

SUBSCRIPTION INFORMATION

Frequency of publication: Irregular
Circulation: 200
Available in microform: No
Subscription address: Verlag Bouvier & Co., Fürstenstr. 3, 5300 Bonn 1, Germany

ADVERTISING INFORMATION

Advertising accepted: No

EDITORIAL DESCRIPTION

Scope: Publishes monographs on German, English, and comparative studies.
Reviews books: No
Publishes notes: No
Languages accepted: German; English; French
Prints abstracts: No
Author-anonymous submission: No

SUBMISSION REQUIREMENTS

Restrictions on contributors: None
Author pays submission fee: No
Author pays page charges: No, if reproduced from manuscript.
Length of books: No restrictions
Style: MLA
Number of copies required: 1
Copyright ownership: Verlag Bouvier
Rejected manuscripts: Returned
Time before publication decision: 1-3 mos.
Time between decision and publication: 6-36 mos.
Number of reviewers: 1-2
Books submitted per year: 1-2
Books published per year: 0-1

(2799)
Studien zur Indologie und Iranistik

Georg Buddruss, Oskar von Hinüber, Gert Klingenschmitt, Albrecht Wezler, & Michael Witzel, Editors
Bernhard-Ihnen-Str. 18
2057 Reinbek, Germany

First published: 1975
ISSN: 0341-4191
MLA acronym: StII

SUBSCRIPTION INFORMATION

Frequency of publication: Annual
Circulation: 200-250
Available in microform: No
Subscription address: Dr. Inge Wezler Verlag, at the above address

ADVERTISING INFORMATION

Advertising accepted: Yes

EDITORIAL DESCRIPTION

Scope: Publishes articles on Old and New Indian and Iranian philology.
Reviews books: No
Languages accepted: English; French; German
Prints abstracts: Yes

SUBMISSION REQUIREMENTS

Restrictions on contributors: None
Author pays submission fee: No
Author pays page charges: No
Length of articles: 20-25 typescript pp.
Style: None
Number of copies required: 1
Special requirements: Contributions not written in English should be accompanied by an English summary of approximately 1,000 words.
Copyright ownership: Journal
Rejected manuscripts: Returned
Time before publication decision: 1 mo.
Time between decision and publication: 6-12 mos.
Number of reviewers: 1-2
Articles submitted per year: 10-15
Articles published per year: 6-10

(2800)
*Studien zur Literatur der Moderne

Helmut Koopmann, Editor
Univ. Augsburg
Universitätstr. 10
8900 Augsburg 1, Germany

First published: 1976
ISSN: 0340-9023
MLA acronym: StLM

SUBSCRIPTION INFORMATION

Frequency of publication: Irregular
Available in microform: No
Subscription address: Bouvier, Am Hof 32, Postfach 346, 5300 Bonn 1, Germany

ADVERTISING INFORMATION

Advertising accepted: No

EDITORIAL DESCRIPTION

Scope: Encompasses authors and topics dealing with the turn of the century and early 20th-century materials.
Reviews books: No
Publishes notes: No
Languages accepted: German; English
Prints abstracts: No
Author-anonymous submission: No

SUBMISSION REQUIREMENTS

Author pays submission fee: No
Author pays page charges: No
Length of books: No restrictions
Number of copies required: 1
Copyright ownership: Editor
Rejected manuscripts: Returned
Time before publication decision: 2-3 mos.
Time between decision and publication: 3 mos.
Number of reviewers: 1
Books published per year: 1

(2801)
*Studien zur Theoretischen Linguistik

Theo Vennemann, Editor
Wilhelm Fink Verlag GmbH & Co KG
Ohmstr. 5
8000 Munich 40, Germany

First published: 1983
Sponsoring organization: Univ. München
ISSN: 0178-126X
MLA acronym: STLing

SUBSCRIPTION INFORMATION

Frequency of publication: Irregular
Available in microform: No

ADVERTISING INFORMATION

Advertising accepted: No

EDITORIAL DESCRIPTION

Scope: Publishes monograph studies on linguistics.
Reviews books: No
Publishes notes: No
Languages accepted: German; English
Prints abstracts: No
Author-anonymous submission: No

SUBMISSION REQUIREMENTS

Restrictions on contributors: Contributors must be associated with Univ. München; all contributions are invited.
Author pays submission fee: No
Length of books: No restrictions
Style: None
Number of copies required: 1
Special requirements: Send inquiry before sending manuscripts.
Copyright ownership: Wilhelm Fink Verlag
Rejected manuscripts: Returned
Time between decision and publication: 1 yr.

(2802)
*Studier fra Sprog- og Oldtidsforskning

Minna Skafte Jensen, Editor
Inst. for Græsk og Latin
KBH.s. Univ. Nialsgade 80
2300 Copenhagen S, Denmark

First published: 1891
Sponsoring organization: Danish Philological-Historical Soc.
MLA acronym: SSO

SUBSCRIPTION INFORMATION

Frequency of publication: Annual
Available in microform: No

ADVERTISING INFORMATION

Advertising accepted: No

EDITORIAL DESCRIPTION

Scope: Publishes monographs on philology, history, and literature.
Reviews books: No
Languages accepted: Danish
Prints abstracts: No

SUBMISSION REQUIREMENTS

Author pays page charges: No
Length of books: 100 pp.
Number of copies required: 1
Copyright ownership: Publisher
Rejected manuscripts: Returned
Time before publication decision: 6 mos.
Time between decision and publication: 6 mos.
Number of reviewers: 2
Books published per year: 2

(2803)
*Studier i Modern Språkvetenskap

Kerstin Jonasson, Johan Falk, Gunnel Melchers, & Barbro Nilsson, Editors
Nyfilologiska Sällskapet i Stockholm
Univ. of Stockholm
106 91 Stockholm, Sweden

Telephone: (46) 8 163497
Fax: (46) 8 153910
E-mail: Paulus—D@ROM—SU.SU
First published: 1898
Sponsoring organization: Univ. of Stockholm
ISSN: 0585-3583
MLA acronym: SMS

SUBSCRIPTION INFORMATION

Frequency of publication: Irregular
Circulation: 600
Available in microform: No

ADVERTISING INFORMATION

Advertising accepted: No

EDITORIAL DESCRIPTION

Scope: Concerns literary, philological, and linguistic subjects in English, French, Spanish, German, Swedish, and occasionally other languages.
Reviews books: No
Languages accepted: English; French; German; Spanish; Italian
Prints abstracts: No

SUBMISSION REQUIREMENTS

Restrictions on contributors: None
Author pays submission fee: No
Author pays page charges: No
Length of articles: 20 pp. maximum
Style: None
Number of copies required: 2
Copyright ownership: Author
Rejected manuscripts: Returned
Time before publication decision: 1 mo.
Time between decision and publication: 1-2 yrs.
Number of reviewers: 2
Articles published per year: 8-10

(2804)
*Studies: An Irish Quarterly Review

Noel Barber, S.J.
35 Lower Leeson St.
Dublin 2, Ireland

Telephone: (353) 1 766785
Fax: (353) 1 762984
First published: 1912
Sponsoring organization: Jesuit Order
ISSN: 0039-3495
MLA acronym: Studies

SUBSCRIPTION INFORMATION

Frequency of publication: 4 times/yr.
Circulation: 1,500
Available in microform: Yes
Subscription price: $35.00/yr. institutions; $30.00/yr. individuals
Year to which price refers: 1993

ADVERTISING INFORMATION

Advertising accepted: Yes
Advertising rates: IR£140.00/full page

EDITORIAL DESCRIPTION

Scope: Publishes articles on Irish letters, politics, social justice, and theological questions.
Reviews books: Yes
Publishes notes: No
Languages accepted: English
Prints abstracts: No
Author-anonymous submission: No

SUBMISSION REQUIREMENTS

Restrictions on contributors: None
Author pays submission fee: No
Author pays page charges: Yes
Length of articles: 3,500-4,000 words
Length of book reviews: 600 words
Style: Oxford Univ. Press: *Collins' Authors and Printers Dictionary*
Number of copies required: 2
Special requirements: Submit original typescript.
Copyright ownership: Journal
Rejected manuscripts: Not returned
Time before publication decision: 6 mos.
Time between decision and publication: 3 yrs. maximum
Number of reviewers: 2
Articles submitted per year: 100
Articles published per year: 26-28
Book reviews submitted per year: 200
Book reviews published per year: 69

(2805)
*Studies in African Linguistics

Russell G. Schuh, Editor
Dept. of Linguistics
Univ. of California
Los Angeles, CA 90024

Telephone: 310 825-0634
First published: 1970
Sponsoring organization: African Studies Center, Univ. of California, Los Angeles
ISSN: 0039-3533
MLA acronym: SAL

SUBSCRIPTION INFORMATION

Frequency of publication: 3 times/yr.
Circulation: 400
Available in microform: No

ADVERTISING INFORMATION

Advertising accepted: Yes, on an exchange basis

EDITORIAL DESCRIPTION

Scope: Publishes descriptive linguistic articles on African languages or theoretical linguistic articles which rely entirely or principally on African-language data.
Reviews books: No
Publishes notes: Yes
Languages accepted: English; French
Prints abstracts: Yes
Author-anonymous submission: No

SUBMISSION REQUIREMENTS

Restrictions on contributors: None
Author pays submission fee: No

Author pays page charges: No
Length of articles: 35 double-spaced typescript pp. maximum
Length of notes: 1,000 words maximum
Style: Journal
Number of copies required: 2
Special requirements: Include abstract of 120 words maximum.
Copyright ownership: Univ. of California
Rejected manuscripts: Returned; enclose SASE.
Time before publication decision: 3-5 mos.
Time between decision and publication: 6-12 mos.
Number of reviewers: 2
Articles submitted per year: 20
Articles published per year: 15
Notes submitted per year: 2-5
Notes published per year: 2-3

(2806)
*Studies in African Literature

Heinemann Educational Books
361 Hanover St.
Portsmouth, NH 03801-3959

Telephone: 603 431-7894
Fax: 603 431-7840
First published: 1969
MLA acronym: SAfrL

SUBSCRIPTION INFORMATION

Frequency of publication: Irregular
Available in microform: No

ADVERTISING INFORMATION

Advertising accepted: No

EDITORIAL DESCRIPTION

Scope: Provides serious critical studies of writing from Africa.
Reviews books: No
Languages accepted: English
Prints abstracts: No

SUBMISSION REQUIREMENTS

Restrictions on contributors: None
Author pays submission fee: No
Author pays page charges: No
Length of books: No restrictions
Style: Chicago
Number of copies required: 2
Copyright ownership: Author
Rejected manuscripts: Returned

(2807)
*Studies in American Drama, 1945-Present

Philip C. Kolin & Colby H. Kullman, Editors
Dept. of English
Univ. of Southern Mississippi
Hattiesburg, MS 39406-8395

Additional editorial address: Colby H. Kullmann, Dept. of English, Univ. of Mississippi, University, MS 38677
First published: 1986
ISSN: 0886-7907
MLA acronym: SAD

SUBSCRIPTION INFORMATION

Frequency of publication: 2 times/yr.
Circulation: 600
Available in microform: Yes, through Univ. Microfilms International
Subscription price: $32.00/yr. institutions; $16.00/yr. individuals; $8.00/single issue
Year to which price refers: 1992

Subscription address: Journals Dept., Ohio State Univ. Press, 1070 Carmack Rd., Columbus, OH 43210-1002
Subscription telephone: 614 292-1407
Subscription fax: 614 292-2065

ADVERTISING INFORMATION

Advertising accepted: Yes
Advertising rates: $125.00/half page; $200.00/full page

EDITORIAL DESCRIPTION

Scope: Publishes articles on theater history, dramatic influence, performance, biography, and interpretation. Journal is especially interested in studies of Tennessee Williams, Edward Albee, David Mamet, Sam Shepard, David Rabe, Adrienne Kennedy, Megan Terry, August Wilson, and Lanford Wilson. Also publishes theater reviews and interviews with American dramatists.
Reviews books: No
Publishes notes: No
Languages accepted: English
Prints abstracts: No
Author-anonymous submission: Yes

SUBMISSION REQUIREMENTS

Restrictions on contributors: None
Author pays submission fee: No
Author pays page charges: No
Length of articles: 2,000-5,000 words maximum
Style: MLA
Number of copies required: 2
Special requirements: Written permission of playwright must be obtained to publish interviews.
Copyright ownership: Ohio State Univ. Press
Rejected manuscripts: Returned; enclose SASE.
Time before publication decision: 6-12 mos.
Time between decision and publication: 6-18 mos.
Number of reviewers: 2-3
Articles submitted per year: 100
Articles published per year: 10-12

(2808)
*Studies in American Fiction

James Nagel, Editor
Dept. of English
Northeastern Univ.
Boston, MA 02115

Telephone: 617 437-3687
First published: 1973
Sponsoring organization: Dept. of English, Northeastern Univ.
ISSN: 0091-8083
MLA acronym: SAF

SUBSCRIPTION INFORMATION

Frequency of publication: 2 times/yr. (Spring, Fall)
Circulation: 1,300
Available in microform: No
Subscription price: $12.00/yr. institutions; $7.00/yr. individuals
Year to which price refers: 1992

ADVERTISING INFORMATION

Advertising accepted: Yes
Advertising rates: $75.00/half page; $100.00/full page; $150.00/back cover

EDITORIAL DESCRIPTION

Scope: Publishes articles, notes, and reviews relating to authors, works, movements, and influences in American fiction from its beginnings to the present.
Reviews books: Yes
Publishes notes: Yes
Languages accepted: English

Prints abstracts: No
Author-anonymous submission: Yes, at author's request.

SUBMISSION REQUIREMENTS

Restrictions on contributors: Reviews are solicited.
Author pays submission fee: No
Author pays page charges: No
Length of articles: 2,500-6,500 words
Length of book reviews: 750 words
Length of notes: 2,500 words
Style: MLA
Number of copies required: 1
Special requirements: Submit original typescript.
Copyright ownership: Journal
Rejected manuscripts: Returned
Time before publication decision: 3 mos.
Time between decision and publication: 1 yr.
Number of reviewers: 3
Articles submitted per year: 500
Articles published per year: 20
Book reviews published per year: 15-20
Notes submitted per year: 150
Notes published per year: 8

(2809)
Studies in American Humor

John O. Rosenbalm, Editor
Dept. of English
Southwest Texas State Univ.
San Marcos, TX 78666

First published: 1974
ISSN: 0045-280X
MLA acronym: StAH

SUBSCRIPTION INFORMATION

Frequency of publication: 3 times/yr. (Spring, Fall, Winter)
Circulation: 350

ADVERTISING INFORMATION

Advertising accepted: Yes

EDITORIAL DESCRIPTION

Scope: Publishes articles on American humor.
Reviews books: Yes
Publishes notes: Yes
Languages accepted: English
Prints abstracts: No

SUBMISSION REQUIREMENTS

Restrictions on contributors: None
Author pays submission fee: No
Author pays page charges: No
Length of articles: 3,000-5,000 words
Length of book reviews: 750-1,000 words
Length of notes: 100-300 words
Style: MLA & Webster's New International Dictionary
Number of copies required: 2
Special requirements: Include a short biographical sketch.
Copyright ownership: Southwest Texas State Univ.
Rejected manuscripts: Returned; enclose return postage.
Time before publication decision: 2 mos.
Time between decision and publication: 6 mos.
Number of reviewers: 3
Articles submitted per year: 75
Articles published per year: 20
Book reviews submitted per year: 12-15
Book reviews published per year: 9

(2810)
*Studies in American Indian Literatures: The Journal of the Association for the Study of American Indian Literatures

Helen Jaskoski & Robert M. Nelson, Editors
Dept. of English
California State Univ. Fullerton
Fullerton, CA 92634

Telephone: 714 449-7039
Fax: 714 773-3990
First published: 1977
Sponsoring organization: Assn. for the Study of American Indian Literatures
ISSN: 0730-3238
MLA acronym: SAIL

SUBSCRIPTION INFORMATION

Frequency of publication: 4 times/yr. (Spring, Summer, Fall, Winter)
Circulation: 250
Available in microform: No
Subscription price: $35.00/yr. institutions; $25.00/yr. individuals
Year to which price refers: 1992
Subscription address: Box 112, Univ. of Richmond, Richmond, VA 23173
Subscription telephone: 804 289-8311
Subscription fax: 804 289-8313

ADVERTISING INFORMATION

Advertising accepted: Yes
Advertising rates: $100.00/full page

EDITORIAL DESCRIPTION

Scope: Publishes review essays, reviews, bibliographies, and scholarly articles on both contemporary American Indian literature and traditional literature, including some transcriptions of native language oral texts.
Reviews books: Yes
Publishes notes: Yes
Languages accepted: English
Prints abstracts: No
Author-anonymous submission: Yes

SUBMISSION REQUIREMENTS

Restrictions on contributors: None
Author pays submission fee: No
Author pays page charges: No
Length of articles: 1,200-7,000 words
Length of book reviews: 500-1,500 words
Length of notes: 500 words
Style: MLA
Number of copies required: 3
Copyright ownership: Author
Rejected manuscripts: Returned; enclose SASE.
Time before publication decision: 1-3 mos.
Time between decision and publication: 1 yr.
Number of reviewers: 2-4
Articles submitted per year: 25-30
Articles published per year: 12-15
Book reviews submitted per year: 30
Book reviews published per year: 30
Notes submitted per year: 20
Notes published per year: 10

(2811)
*Studies in American Jewish Literature

Daniel Walden, Editor
Dept. of English
117 Burrowes Bldg.
Pennsylvania State Univ.
University Park, PA 16802

Additional editorial address: Bonnie Lyons, Book Review Editor, Dept. of English, Univ. of Texas, San Antonio, TX 78285
Telephone: 814 863-3753

Fax: 814 863-7285
First published: 1975
Sponsoring organization: Studies in American Jewish Literature, Inc.; Univ. of Delaware
ISSN: 0271-9274
MLA acronym: SAJL

SUBSCRIPTION INFORMATION

Frequency of publication: Annual
Circulation: 400
Available in microform: Yes
Subscription price: $18.00/yr.
Year to which price refers: 1992
Subscription address: Univ. of Delaware Press, Newark, DE 19716

ADVERTISING INFORMATION

Advertising accepted: Yes
Advertising rates: Request from Univ. of Delaware Press

EDITORIAL DESCRIPTION

Scope: Devoted to examining Jewish life and experience in the American culture, particularly as revealed in the literature. Focuses on works by America Jewish authors. Also includes works by non-Jewish authors writing on the American Jewish experience.
Reviews books: Yes
Publishes notes: No
Languages accepted: English
Prints abstracts: No
Author-anonymous submission: No

SUBMISSION REQUIREMENTS

Restrictions on contributors: Articles and book reviews are generally commissioned, but all contributions are considered.
Author pays submission fee: No
Author pays page charges: No
Length of articles: 5,000 words
Length of book reviews: 500-750 words
Style: MLA
Number of copies required: 2
Copyright ownership: Journal & Univ. of Delaware Press
Rejected manuscripts: Returned
Time before publication decision: 3-6 mos.
Time between decision and publication: 6-12 mos.
Number of reviewers: 2-3
Articles submitted per year: 50
Articles published per year: 15-20
Book reviews submitted per year: 20-30
Book reviews published per year: 7-15

(2812)
*Studies in Austrian Literature, Culture, and Thought

Donald G. Daviau, Jorun B. Johns, & Richard H. Lawson, Editors
Ariadne Press
270 Goins Court
Riverside, CA 92507

Telephone: 714 684-9202
Fax: 714 684-9202
First published: 1989
MLA acronym: SALCT

ADVERTISING INFORMATION

Advertising accepted: No

EDITORIAL DESCRIPTION

Scope: Publishes monographs and collections of articles on Austrian literature, culture, and thought, as well as translations of Austrian authors.
Reviews books: No
Publishes notes: No
Languages accepted: English; German
Prints abstracts: No

Author-anonymous submission: Yes

SUBMISSION REQUIREMENTS

Author pays submission fee: No
Author pays page charges: No
Length of books: No restrictions
Style: MLA
Number of copies required: 2
Copyright ownership: Ariadne Press
Rejected manuscripts: Returned
Time before publication decision: 3 mos.
Time between decision and publication: 6-9 mos.
Number of reviewers: 3
Books submitted per year: 20
Books published per year: 10

(2813)
*Studies in Bibliography: Papers of the Bibliographical Society of the University of Virginia

David Vander Meulen, Editor
English Dept.
Wilson Hall
Univ. of Virginia
Charlottesville, VA 22903

First published: 1948
Sponsoring organization: Univ. of Virginia, Bibliographical Soc.
ISSN: 0081-7600
MLA acronym: SB

SUBSCRIPTION INFORMATION

Frequency of publication: Annual
Circulation: 1,100
Available in microform: No
Subscription price: $30.00/yr.; $15.00/yr. students
Year to which price refers: 1992
Subscription address: Penelope F. Weiss, Executive Secretary, Bibliographical Soc., Univ. of Virginia Library, Charlottesville, VA 22903

ADVERTISING INFORMATION

Advertising accepted: No

EDITORIAL DESCRIPTION

Scope: Publishes articles and notes on analytical bibliography, textual criticism, manuscript study, the history of printing and publishing, as well as related matters of method and evidence.
Reviews books: No
Publishes notes: No
Languages accepted: English
Prints abstracts: No
Author-anonymous submission: No

SUBMISSION REQUIREMENTS

Restrictions on contributors: None
Author pays submission fee: No
Author pays page charges: No
Length of articles: 500-15,000 words
Style: MLA
Number of copies required: 1
Copyright ownership: Univ. of Virginia
Rejected manuscripts: Returned; enclose return postage.
Time before publication decision: 1 mo.
Time between decision and publication: 1 yr.
Number of reviewers: 1-3
Articles submitted per year: 30-40
Articles published per year: 20

(2814)
*Studies in Browning and His Circle: A Journal of Criticism, History, and Bibliography

Rita S. Humphrey, Editor
P.O. Box 97152
Baylor Univ.
Waco, TX 76798

Telephone: 817 755-3566
First published: 1973
Sponsoring organization: Baylor Univ., Armstrong Browning Library
ISSN: 0095-4489
MLA acronym: SBHC

SUBSCRIPTION INFORMATION

Frequency of publication: Annual
Circulation: 350
Available in microform: No

ADVERTISING INFORMATION

Advertising accepted: No

EDITORIAL DESCRIPTION

Scope: Publishes scholarship related to the life and/or works of Robert and Elizabeth Barrett Browning.
Reviews books: Yes
Publishes notes: Yes
Languages accepted: English
Prints abstracts: No
Author-anonymous submission: No

SUBMISSION REQUIREMENTS

Restrictions on contributors: None
Author pays submission fee: No
Author pays page charges: No
Length of articles: 2,500-5,000 words
Length of book reviews: 600-800 words
Length of notes: 800-1,000 words
Style: MLA
Number of copies required: 2
Copyright ownership: Author
Rejected manuscripts: Returned; enclose return postage.
Time before publication decision: 3 mos.
Time between decision and publication: 3 mos.
Number of reviewers: 2
Articles submitted per year: 20
Articles published per year: 12
Book reviews submitted per year: 4
Book reviews published per year: 4
Notes submitted per year: 10
Notes published per year: 10

(2815)
*Studies in Canadian Literature/ Etudes en Littérature Canadienne

Kathleen Scherf, Editor
Dept. of English
Univ. of New Brunswick
P.O. Box 4400
Fredericton, New Brunswick E3B 5A3, Canada

Telephone: 506 453-4676; 506 453-4598
Fax: 506 453-5069
First published: 1976
Sponsoring organization: Univ. of New Brunswick
ISSN: 0380-6995
MLA acronym: SCL

SUBSCRIPTION INFORMATION

Frequency of publication: 2 times/yr.
Circulation: 450
Available in microform: Yes
Subscription price: C$20.00/yr. plus postage institutions; C$14.00/yr. plus postage individuals
Year to which price refers: 1992

Subscription telephone: 506 453-4598

ADVERTISING INFORMATION

Advertising accepted: Yes
Advertising rates: C$25.00/quarter page; C$40.00/half page; C$80.00/full page

EDITORIAL DESCRIPTION

Scope: Publishes scholarly and critical articles on all aspects of Canadian literature of all periods.
Reviews books: No
Publishes notes: Yes
Languages accepted: English; French
Prints abstracts: No
Author-anonymous submission: Yes

SUBMISSION REQUIREMENTS

Restrictions on contributors: None
Author pays submission fee: No
Author pays page charges: No
Length of articles: 2,500 words minimum
Style: MLA
Number of copies required: 2
Special requirements: Submit original typescript.
Copyright ownership: Author
Rejected manuscripts: Returned; enclose SASE.
Time before publication decision: 3-6 mos.
Time between decision and publication: 6 mos.
Number of reviewers: 4
Articles submitted per year: 75-100
Articles published per year: 30
Notes submitted per year: 2-4

(2816)
*Studies in Comparative Literature

Wendell M. Aycock, Editor
Dept. of English
Texas Tech Univ.
Lubbock, TX 79409-3091

Telephone: 806 742-2501
Fax: 806 742-0989
First published: 1968
ISSN: 0899-2193
MLA acronym: SCLit

SUBSCRIPTION INFORMATION

Frequency of publication: Annual
Available in microform: No
Subscription address: Texas Tech Univ. Press, Sales Office, Texas Tech Univ., Lubbock, TX 79409-1037

ADVERTISING INFORMATION

Advertising accepted: No

EDITORIAL DESCRIPTION

Scope: Publishes books on subjects in comparative literature.
Reviews books: No
Publishes notes: No
Languages accepted: English
Prints abstracts: No
Author-anonymous submission: No

SUBMISSION REQUIREMENTS

Author pays submission fee: No
Author pays page charges: No
Style: Chicago
Special requirements: Submit typescript and IBM-compatible diskette.
Copyright ownership: Texas Tech Univ. Press
Time before publication decision: 3-6 mos.
Time between decision and publication: 1 yr.
Number of reviewers: 2
Books published per year: 1

(2817)
*Studies in Contemporary Satire: A Creative and Critical Journal

C. Darrel Sheraw & Carole Pasquarette, Editors
Dept. of English
Clarion Univ. of Pennsylvania
Clarion, PA 16214

Telephone: 814 226-2531; 814 226-2482
First published: 1974
Sponsoring organization: English Dept., Clarion Univ.
ISSN: 0163-4143
MLA acronym: StCS

SUBSCRIPTION INFORMATION

Frequency of publication: Annual
Circulation: 450
Available in microform: No
Subscription price: $3.00/yr.
Year to which price refers: 1992

ADVERTISING INFORMATION

Advertising accepted: No
Advertising rates: $25.00/half page; $50.00/full page

EDITORIAL DESCRIPTION

Scope: Publishes critical articles on contemporary satiric fiction, poetry, drama, cinema, and graphic art; includes original satiric prose and verse written in French, German, Italian, Spanish, and Japanese.
Reviews books: Yes
Publishes notes: No
Languages accepted: English
Prints abstracts: No
Author-anonymous submission: Yes

SUBMISSION REQUIREMENTS

Restrictions on contributors: None
Author pays submission fee: No
Author pays page charges: No
Length of articles: 3,000 words
Length of book reviews: 1,000 words maximum
Style: MLA
Number of copies required: 2
Special requirements: Include a short (5-7 lines) biographical piece including publications for "Notes on Contributors Section".
Copyright ownership: Author
Rejected manuscripts: Returned
Time before publication decision: 3 mos.
Time between decision and publication: 1 yr.
Number of reviewers: 2-3
Articles submitted per year: 20
Articles published per year: 5
Book reviews submitted per year: 4-6
Book reviews published per year: 2-4

(2818)
*Studies in Descriptive Linguistics

Dietrich Nehls, Editor
Julius Groos Verlag
Postfach 102423
6900 Heidelberg 1, Germany

Telephone: (49) 6221 303621
Fax: (49) 6221 301993
First published: 1978
ISSN: 0171-6794
MLA acronym: SDL

SUBSCRIPTION INFORMATION

Frequency of publication: Irregular
Circulation: 1,000
Available in microform: No

ADVERTISING INFORMATION

Advertising accepted: No

EDITORIAL DESCRIPTION

Scope: The series contains anthologies of articles and also monographs dealing primarily with the description of English, German, French, Russian and Spanish languages. The descriptions concern more particularly the grammar, semantico-syntactical, and pragmatic levels of the languages.
Reviews books: No
Publishes notes: Yes
Languages accepted: English; Russian; French; German; Spanish
Prints abstracts: Yes
Author-anonymous submission: No

SUBMISSION REQUIREMENTS

Restrictions on contributors: Only solicited manuscripts are considered.
Author pays submission fee: No
Author pays page charges: No
Length of books: 20-30 pp.
Style: MLA
Number of copies required: 2
Copyright ownership: Julius Groos Verlag
Rejected manuscripts: Returned
Time before publication decision: 2 mos.
Time between decision and publication: 1 yr.
Number of reviewers: 2-5

(2819)
*Studies in Eighteenth-Century Culture

Carla H. Hay, Editor
Dept. of History
Marquette Univ.
Milwaukee, WI 53233

Telephone: 517 337-2929
Fax: 517 332-2150
First published: 1971
Sponsoring organization: American Soc. for Eighteenth-Century Studies
ISSN: 0360-2370
MLA acronym: SECC

SUBSCRIPTION INFORMATION

Frequency of publication: Annual
Circulation: 1,000
Available in microform: No
Subscription address: Colleagues Press, Inc., P.O. Box 4007, East Lansing, MI 48826
Additional subscription address: Outside N. America: Boydell & Brewer Ltd., P.O. Box 9, Woodbridge, Suffolk IP12 3DF, England

ADVERTISING INFORMATION

Advertising accepted: No

EDITORIAL DESCRIPTION

Scope: Publishes articles on 18th-century culture, especially literature, history, daily life, and arts.
Reviews books: No
Publishes notes: No
Languages accepted: English
Prints abstracts: No
Author-anonymous submission: No

SUBMISSION REQUIREMENTS

Restrictions on contributors: Papers must have been delivered at a regional or national meeting of the American Soc. for 18th-Century Studies.
Author pays submission fee: No
Author pays page charges: No
Length of articles: 5,000 words
Style: Chicago
Number of copies required: 4
Copyright ownership: American Soc. for Eighteenth-Century Studies
Rejected manuscripts: Returned; enclose SAE and loose postage.

(2820)
Studies in English and American

Tibor Frank, Editor
Pesti Barnabás Utca 1
1052 Budapest, V., Hungary

Sponsoring organization: L. Eötvös Univ.
ISSN: 0134-1790
MLA acronym: SEA

SUBSCRIPTION INFORMATION

Frequency of publication: Irregular
Available in microform: No

ADVERTISING INFORMATION

Advertising accepted: No

EDITORIAL DESCRIPTION

Scope: Publishes Hungarian studies in English and American language and literature.
Reviews books: No
Publishes notes: No
Languages accepted: English
Prints abstracts: No

SUBMISSION REQUIREMENTS

Restrictions on contributors: None, but Hungarian scholars are given preference.
Author pays submission fee: No
Author pays page charges: No
Length of articles: 20-40 pp.
Style: MLA
Number of copies required: 2
Copyright ownership: Author
Rejected manuscripts: Returned at author's request
Time before publication decision: 2 mos.
Time between decision and publication: 1 yr.
Number of reviewers: 1-2
Articles submitted per year: 25
Articles published per year: 15

(2821)
*Studies in English and American Literature, Linguistics, and Culture

Benjamin Franklin V, Editor
Camden House, Inc.
Drawer 2025
Columbia, SC 29202

First published: 1984
MLA acronym: SEALLC

SUBSCRIPTION INFORMATION

Frequency of publication: Irregular
Available in microform: No
Subscription address: P.O. Box 4836, Hampden Station, Baltimore, MD 21211

ADVERTISING INFORMATION

Advertising accepted: No

EDITORIAL DESCRIPTION

Scope: Publishes monograph studies on English literature, American literature, literary criticism, and linguistics.
Reviews books: No
Publishes notes: No
Languages accepted: English
Prints abstracts: No

Time before publication decision: 4 mos.
Time between decision and publication: 15-18 mos.
Number of reviewers: 2
Articles submitted per year: 100
Articles published per year: 15

Author-anonymous submission: Yes

SUBMISSION REQUIREMENTS

Restrictions on contributors: None
Author pays submission fee: No
Author pays page charges: No
Length of books: No restrictions
Style: Chicago
Number of copies required: 1
Copyright ownership: Camden House, Inc.
Rejected manuscripts: Returned
Time before publication decision: 1 mo.
Time between decision and publication: 5-7 mos.
Number of reviewers: 2
Books published per year: 3

(2822)
*Studies in English and Comparative Literature

Michael Kenneally & Wolfgang Zach, Editors
Marianopolis College
3880 Côte des Neiges Rd.
Montreal, Quebec H3H 1W1, Canada

Additional editorial address: In Europe: Wolfgang Zach, Inst. für Anglistik, Univ. Graz, Heinrichstr. 26/IV, 8010 Graz, Austria
Telephone: 514 489-7122; 514 931-8792
Fax: 514 931-8790
First published: 1987
MLA acronym: SECL

SUBSCRIPTION INFORMATION

Circulation: 400-800
Available in microform: No
Subscription address: Gunter Narr Verlag, Postfach 2567, 7400 Tübingen, Germany

ADVERTISING INFORMATION

Advertising accepted: No

EDITORIAL DESCRIPTION

Scope: Publishes monographs on selected aspects of English and world literature, with an emphasis on comparative literature.
Reviews books: No
Publishes notes: No
Languages accepted: English; German
Prints abstracts: No
Author-anonymous submission: No

SUBMISSION REQUIREMENTS

Restrictions on contributors: None
Author pays submission fee: No
Length of books: No restrictions
Style: MLA
Number of copies required: 2
Copyright ownership: Gunter Narr Verlag
Rejected manuscripts: Not returned
Time before publication decision: 2-3 mos.
Time between decision and publication: 9 mos.
Number of reviewers: 3
Books submitted per year: 6-8
Books published per year: 1

(2823)
*Studies in English Language and Literature

Hershel C. Johnson, Editor
Seinan Gakuin Univ.
6-2-92 Nishijin
Sawaraku, Fukuoka 814, Japan

Telephone: (81) 92 8411311 ext. 2527
Fax: (81) 92 8232506
First published: 1960
Sponsoring organization: Seinan Gakuin Univ.;

SUBSCRIPTION INFORMATION

Frequency of publication: 3 times/yr. (Mar., July, Oct.)
Circulation: 350-400
Available in microform: No

ADVERTISING INFORMATION

Advertising accepted: No

EDITORIAL DESCRIPTION

Scope: Publishes articles on studies of the English language and English language literature, including linguistics, English as a second language, communication, and business English.
Reviews books: No
Publishes notes: No
Languages accepted: English; Japanese
Prints abstracts: No
Author-anonymous submission: No

SUBMISSION REQUIREMENTS

Restrictions on contributors: Contributors must contribute to the teaching of English language and literature at Seinan Gakuin Univ.
Author pays submission fee: No
Author pays page charges: No
Length of articles: 2,500-8,000 words
Style: MLA, if in English
Number of copies required: 3
Copyright ownership: Seinan Gakuin Univ.
Rejected manuscripts: Returned
Time before publication decision: 6-9 mos.
Time between decision and publication: 1 yr.
Number of reviewers: 3
Articles submitted per year: 40
Articles published per year: 10-12

(2824)
*Studies in English Language and Literature

Osamu Ōsaka, Editor
Kyushu Univ. 01
Inst. of Languages & Cultures
English Language & Literature Soc.
2-1 Ropponmatsu 4-chome
Chuō-ku, Fukuoka-Shi 810, Japan

First published: 1951
Sponsoring organization: English Language & Literature Soc.
ISSN: 0422-7891
MLA acronym: SELL

SUBSCRIPTION INFORMATION

Frequency of publication: Annual
Available in microform: No

ADVERTISING INFORMATION

Advertising accepted: No

EDITORIAL DESCRIPTION

Scope: Publishes articles on English language and literature.
Reviews books: No
Publishes notes: No
Languages accepted: English; Japanese
Prints abstracts: Yes

SUBMISSION REQUIREMENTS

Restrictions on contributors: Contributors must be members of the English Language & Literature Soc.
Author pays submission fee: No
Author pays page charges: No
Length of articles: 30-50 double-spaced pp. for English; 30-50 (400-letter spaced writing paper) pp. for Japanese
Style: MLA
Number of copies required: 1

(2825)
*Studies in English Literature

Hiroyuki Ide, Editor
English Literary Soc. of Japan
501 Kenkyusha Building
9, Surugadai 2-Chome Kanda
Chiyoda-Ku, Tokyo 101, Japan

First published: 1919
Sponsoring organization: English Literary Soc. of Japan
ISSN: 0039-3649 (English & Japanese issues); 0387-3439 (English issues)
MLA acronym: SELit

SUBSCRIPTION INFORMATION

Frequency of publication: 3 times/yr.
Circulation: 4,000
Available in microform: No

ADVERTISING INFORMATION

Advertising accepted: No

EDITORIAL DESCRIPTION

Scope: Publishes studies in English and American literature, philology, and linguistics.
Reviews books: Yes
Publishes notes: No
Languages accepted: English; Japanese
Prints abstracts: Yes
Author-anonymous submission: No

SUBMISSION REQUIREMENTS

Restrictions on contributors: Contributors must be members of the English Literary Soc. of Japan.
Author pays submission fee: No
Author pays page charges: No
Length of articles: 20-25 double-spaced typescript pp.
Length of book reviews: 10-15 double-spaced typescript pp.
Style: MLA
Number of copies required: 3
Special requirements: Enclose brief CV.
Copyright ownership: Author
Rejected manuscripts: Returned at author's request
Time before publication decision: 3 mos.
Time between decision and publication: 6 mos.
Number of reviewers: 3
Articles submitted per year: 50-60
Articles published per year: 15-20
Book reviews submitted per year: 50-60
Book reviews published per year: 45-50

(2826)
*Studies in German Literature, Linguistics, and Culture

James Hardin & Gunther Holst, Editors
Camden House, Inc.
Drawer 2025
Columbia, SC 29202

Telephone: 803 765-2384
Fax: 803 736-9455
First published: 1980
MLA acronym: SGLLC

Copyright ownership: Author & English Language and Literature Soc.
Rejected manuscripts: Not returned
Time before publication decision: Immediate
Time between decision and publication: 5 mos.
Number of reviewers: 1-2
Articles submitted per year: 5-7
Articles published per year: 5-7

SUBSCRIPTION INFORMATION

Frequency of publication: Irregular
Available in microform: No
Subscription address: Camden House, Inc., P.O. Box 4836 Hampden Station, Baltimore, MD 21211

ADVERTISING INFORMATION

Advertising accepted: No

EDITORIAL DESCRIPTION

Scope: Publishes monograph studies including works on German and Austrian literature, poetry, linguistics, and culture.
Reviews books: No
Publishes notes: No
Languages accepted: English; German
Prints abstracts: No
Author-anonymous submission: No

SUBMISSION REQUIREMENTS

Author pays submission fee: No
Style: Chicago
Number of copies required: 1
Copyright ownership: Camden House, Inc.
Rejected manuscripts: Returned
Time before publication decision: 6-8 mos.
Time between decision and publication: 5-7 mos.
Number of reviewers: 2
Books submitted per year: 40-50
Books published per year: 15-25

(2827)
*Studies in Hogg and his World

Gillian H. Hughes, Editor
c/o Dept. of English Studies
Univ. of Stirling
Stirling FK9 4LA, Scotland

Additional editorial address: 37 Dalston Dr., Didsbury, Manchester M20 0LQ, England
First published: 1990
Sponsoring organization: James Hogg Soc.
ISSN: 0960-6025
MLA acronym: SHW

SUBSCRIPTION INFORMATION

Frequency of publication: Annual
Circulation: 60
Available in microform: No
Subscription price: £12.50/yr.; £6.50/yr. students & retired members
Year to which price refers: 1992
Subscription address: Robin MacLachlan, Treasurer, 8 Tybenham Rd., London SW19 3LA, England

ADVERTISING INFORMATION

Advertising accepted: Yes

EDITORIAL DESCRIPTION

Scope: Publishes articles on James Hogg, his work, and his society.
Reviews books: Yes
Publishes notes: Yes
Languages accepted: English; Scottish Gaelic
Prints abstracts: No
Author-anonymous submission: No

SUBMISSION REQUIREMENTS

Restrictions on contributors: None
Author pays submission fee: No
Author pays page charges: No
Length of articles: 5,000 words
Length of book reviews: 500-800 words
Length of notes: 1,000-2,000 words
Style: Modern Humanities Research Assn.
Number of copies required: 2

Copyright ownership: James Hogg Soc. & author
Rejected manuscripts: Returned; enclose SAE.
Number of reviewers: 1
Articles submitted per year: 10-15
Articles published per year: 10-15
Book reviews submitted per year: 5
Book reviews published per year: 5
Notes submitted per year: 3-4
Notes published per year: 3-4

(2828)
Studies in Iconography

Anthony Lacy Gully, Editor
School of Art
Arizona State Univ.
Tempe, AZ 85287

Additional editorial address: Gail Sigal, Assoc. Editor, Literature, Dept. of English, Wakeforest Univ., Winston-Salem, NC 27109
Telephone: 602 965-6439
Fax: 602 965-8338
First published: 1975
Sponsoring organization: Arizona State Univ.
ISSN: 0148-1029
MLA acronym: SIcon

SUBSCRIPTION INFORMATION

Frequency of publication: Annual
Circulation: 310
Available in microform: No

ADVERTISING INFORMATION

Advertising accepted: No

EDITORIAL DESCRIPTION

Scope: Publishes articles on iconographical problems in art and literature from any historical period, as well as on music criticism, philosophy, and cultural history.
Reviews books: Yes
Publishes notes: Yes
Languages accepted: English
Prints abstracts: No
Author-anonymous submission: Yes

SUBMISSION REQUIREMENTS

Restrictions on contributors: None
Author pays submission fee: No
Author pays page charges: No
Length of articles: 20 pp.
Length of book reviews: 1,000 words
Length of notes: 500 words
Style: MLA; Art Bulletin
Number of copies required: 2
Special requirements: Submit black and white photos (5x7 in. or 8x10 in.) for all illustrations. Type articles and notes double-spaced.
Copyright ownership: Journal
Rejected manuscripts: Returned; enclose return postage.
Time before publication decision: 3 mos.
Time between decision and publication: 6-9 mos.
Number of reviewers: 2-3
Articles submitted per year: 30-40
Articles published per year: 10-12
Book reviews submitted per year: 4-8
Book reviews published per year: 4
Notes submitted per year: 10
Notes published per year: 3

(2829)
Studies in Interactional Sociolinguistics

John J. Gumperz & Marion V. Smith, Editors
Cambridge Univ. Press
Edinburgh Bldg.
Shaftesbury Rd.
Cambridge CB2 2RU, England

Additional editorial address: Cambridge Univ. Press, 40 W. 20th St., New York, NY 10011
First published: 1982
MLA acronym: StIS

SUBSCRIPTION INFORMATION

Frequency of publication: Irregular
Available in microform: No
Subscription address: Cambridge Univ. Press, 110 Midland Ave., Port Chester, NY 10573

ADVERTISING INFORMATION

Advertising accepted: No

EDITORIAL DESCRIPTION

Scope: Publishes monographs and collections on sociolinguistics.
Reviews books: No
Publishes notes: No
Languages accepted: English
Prints abstracts: No

SUBMISSION REQUIREMENTS

Length of books: 250-350 pp.
Copyright ownership: Cambridge Univ. Press
Rejected manuscripts: Returned
Time before publication decision: 2-3 mos.
Time between decision and publication: 1 yr.
Number of reviewers: 2-3

(2830)
*Studies in Language: International Journal Sponsored by the Foundation "Foundations of Language"

Bernard Comrie, Michael Noonan, & Werner Abraham, Editors
Dept. of Linguistics
GFS-301
Univ. of Southern California
Los Angeles, CA 90089-1693

Additional editorial address: Submit reviews to Werner Abraham, Germanistisch Inst., R.U. Groningen, Oude Kijk in 't Intstr. 26, 9712 EK Groningen, Netherlands
First published: 1977
Sponsoring organization: Foundations of Language
ISSN: 0378-4177
MLA acronym: SLang

SUBSCRIPTION INFORMATION

Frequency of publication: 2 times/yr.
Circulation: 600
Available in microform: No
Subscription price: 352 f ($213.00)/yr.
Year to which price refers: 1993
Subscription address: John Benjamins B.V., Amsteldijk 44, P.O. Box 75577, 1070 AN Amsterdam, Netherlands
Additional subscription address: John Benjamins North America, Inc., 821 Bethlehem Pike, Philadelphia, PA 19118
Subscription telephone: (31) 20 6738156; 215 836-1200
Subscription fax: (31) 20 6739773; 215 836-1204

ADVERTISING INFORMATION

Advertising accepted: Yes

Advertising rates: 400 f ($220.00)/full page

EDITORIAL DESCRIPTION

Scope: Invites general or technical contributions, original or expository, in fields of research dealing specifically with: (1) traditional areas of linguistics, descriptive as well as formal and typological, i.e., phonology, morphology, syntax, semantics, and pragmatics; (2) linguistic theories derived from various methods of language analysis; (3) contributions to the study of the foundations of language made within such fields as sociology, anthropology, psychology, language acquisition, mathematics, communication theory, artificial intelligence, theory of argumentation, law, ethics, traditional areas of the philosophy of language (analytical philosophy, phenomenology, hermeneutics); (4) logical systems with strong compatability with natural languages; and (5) methodology of linguistics, etc.
Reviews books: Yes
Publishes notes: Yes
Languages accepted: English; French; German
Prints abstracts: Yes

SUBMISSION REQUIREMENTS

Restrictions on contributors: None
Author pays submission fee: No
Author pays page charges: No
Length of articles: 5,000-7,000 words
Length of book reviews: 2,000-2,500 words
Length of notes: 500-750 words
Style: Journal
Number of copies required: 2
Special requirements: No carbon copies; good photostats allowed.
Copyright ownership: John Benjamins B.V.
Rejected manuscripts: Not returned
Time before publication decision: 2-3 mos.
Time between decision and publication: 8-15 mos.
Number of reviewers: 1-2
Articles submitted per year: 20-40
Articles published per year: 10-12
Book reviews published per year: 20
Notes published per year: 2-6

(2831)
*Studies in Language Companion Series

Werner Abraham & Michael Noonan, Editors
Germanistisch Inst.
R.U. Groningen
Oude Kijk in 't Jatstr. 26
9712 EK Groningen, Netherlands

First published: 1978
Sponsoring organization: Foundations of Language
ISSN: 0165-7763
MLA acronym: SLCS

SUBSCRIPTION INFORMATION

Frequency of publication: Irregular
Available in microform: No
Subscription address: John Benjamins Publishing Co., P.O. Box 75577, Amsteldijk 44, 1070 AN Amsterdam, Netherlands
Additional subscription address: John Benjamins North America, Inc., 821 Bethlehem Pike, Philadelphia, PA 19118
Subscription telephone: (31) 20 6738156; 215 836-1200
Subscription fax: (31) 20 6739773; 215 836-1204

ADVERTISING INFORMATION

Advertising accepted: No

EDITORIAL DESCRIPTION

Scope: Publishes monographs on contemporary linguistics and philosophy.
Reviews books: No
Publishes notes: No
Languages accepted: English
Prints abstracts: No
Author-anonymous submission: Yes

SUBMISSION REQUIREMENTS

Author pays submission fee: No
Author pays page charges: No
Length of books: 250-350 pp.
Style: Series; request from editor.
Copyright ownership: John Benjamins Publishing Co.
Books submitted per year: 5
Books published per year: 2

(2832)
*Studies in Language Learning: An Interdisciplinary Review of Language Acquisition, Language Pedagogy, Stylistics and Language Planning

C. C. Cheng, Editor
Language Learning Laboratory
G70 Foreign Language Bldg.
707 S. Mathews St.
Univ. of Illinois
Urbana, IL 61801

Telephone: 217 333-9776
Fax: 217 244-0190
E-mail: CCCHENG@UIUCVMO.BITNET
First published: 1975
Sponsoring organization: Univ. of Illinois, Language Learning Laboratory
ISSN: 0736-9867
MLA acronym: SLL

SUBSCRIPTION INFORMATION

Frequency of publication: Irregular
Available in microform: No

ADVERTISING INFORMATION

Advertising accepted: No

EDITORIAL DESCRIPTION

Scope: Primarily concerned with applied linguistics, and specifically with language acquisition, language pedagogy, stylistics, and language planning. Gives preference to contributions of a theoretical and/or methodological interest. Aims at developing interdisciplinary cooperation between faculty and students working in language-related fields in humanities, social sciences, education, and other disciplines. Includes prepublication versions of contributions from faculty and students of the University of Illinois. Invited contributions from non-University of Illinois faculty and students are also included. Encourages detailed papers which present the state of the art of various sub-fields of applied linguistics and focus on current insights and controversies in the language-related fields. Shorter notes and comments published in the Notes and Comments section. One issue each year devoted to a special topic.
Reviews books: Yes
Publishes notes: Yes
Languages accepted: English
Prints abstracts: Yes
Author-anonymous submission: No

SUBMISSION REQUIREMENTS

Restrictions on contributors: Most articles are invited.
Author pays submission fee: No
Author pays page charges: No
Length of articles: 4,000-10,000 words
Length of book reviews: 750-1,000 words
Length of notes: 300-750 words
Style: Linguistic Soc. of America

(2833)
*Studies in Latin American Popular Culture

Harold E. Hinds, Jr. & Charles M. Tatum, Editors
Division of Social Sciences
Univ. of Minnesota, Morris
Morris, MN 56267

First published: 1982
Sponsoring organization: Univ. of Arizona; Univ. of Minnesota, Morris
ISSN: 0730-9139
MLA acronym: SLAPC

SUBSCRIPTION INFORMATION

Frequency of publication: Annual
Circulation: 400-450
Available in microform: No
Subscription address: Charles M. Tatum, Dept. of Spanish & Portuguese, Univ. of Arizona, Tucson, AZ 85721

ADVERTISING INFORMATION

Advertising accepted: Yes

EDITORIAL DESCRIPTION

Scope: Publishes scholarly articles, interviews, and review essays on all aspects of the theory and practice of popular culture in Latin America. Popular culture includes any aspect of culture which is accepted by significant numbers of people.
Reviews books: Yes
Publishes notes: No
Languages accepted: English
Prints abstracts: No
Author-anonymous submission: No

SUBMISSION REQUIREMENTS

Restrictions on contributors: None
Author pays submission fee: No
Author pays page charges: No
Length of articles: 20 pp. including notes, illustrations, graphs, etc.
Length of book reviews: 10 pp. including notes, illustrations, graphs, etc.
Style: Turabian
Number of copies required: 3
Special requirements: Submit original manuscript plus 2 photocopies. Include all footnotes at end of article. Translate all foreign titles, words, and quotes in text of article (but not in footnotes) and place them in brackets after the original. If a title, word, or quote is repeated, translate it only the first time it appears.
Copyright ownership: Journal
Rejected manuscripts: Returned; enclose SAE and loose postage.
Time before publication decision: 1-2 mos.
Time between decision and publication: 1-2 yrs.
Number of reviewers: 2 minimum
Articles published per year: 15-20
Book reviews published per year: 8-12

Number of copies required: 2 copies of reviews; 1 copy of short Notices or Publications Received
Copyright ownership: Univ. of Illinois
Rejected manuscripts: Returned
Time before publication decision: 2 mos.
Time between decision and publication: 6 mos.
Number of reviewers: 2

(2834)
*Studies in Medieval Culture

Thomas H. Seiler, Editor
Medieval Inst. Publications
Western Michigan Univ.
Kalamazoo, MI 49008-3851

Telephone: 616 387-4254
Fax: 616 387-4150
First published: 1971
Sponsoring organization: Western Michigan Univ., Medieval Inst.
ISSN: 0085-6878
MLA acronym: SMC

SUBSCRIPTION INFORMATION

Frequency of publication: Irregular (2-3 times/yr.)
Circulation: 200
Available in microform: No
Subscription telephone: 616 387-4155

ADVERTISING INFORMATION

Advertising accepted: No

EDITORIAL DESCRIPTION

Scope: Each volume focuses either on a single topic or on interdisciplinary approaches to a specific medieval subject.
Reviews books: No
Languages accepted: English
Prints abstracts: No
Author-anonymous submission: No

SUBMISSION REQUIREMENTS

Restrictions on contributors: Publications include papers presented at the International Congress on Medieval Studies.
Author pays submission fee: No
Author pays page charges: No
Style: Chicago
Number of copies required: 1
Copyright ownership: Board of the Medieval Inst.
Rejected manuscripts: Returned
Time before publication decision: 3-6 mos.
Time between decision and publication: 1-2 yrs.
Number of reviewers: 2
Books submitted per year: 3-4
Books published per year: 2-3

(2835)
Studies in Medieval English Language and Literature

Kinshiro Oshitari, Editor
c/o Tadahiro Ikegami
English Dept.
Seijo Univ.
6-1-20 Seijo, Setagaya-ku,
Tokyo 157, Japan

First published: 1986
Sponsoring organization: Japan Soc. for Medieval English Studies
ISSN: 0913-1507
MLA acronym: SMELL

SUBSCRIPTION INFORMATION

Frequency of publication: Annual
Circulation: 400
Available in microform: No

ADVERTISING INFORMATION

Advertising accepted: No

EDITORIAL DESCRIPTION

Scope: Publishes articles on medieval English language and literature and reports on the annual congress and branch meetings of the Japan Society for Medieval English Studies.
Reviews books: No
Publishes notes: No
Languages accepted: English; Japanese
Prints abstracts: No

SUBMISSION REQUIREMENTS

Restrictions on contributors: Contributors must be members or be asked by the editor.
Author pays submission fee: No
Author pays page charges: No
Length of articles: 6,000-10,000 words
Style: MLA
Number of copies required: 3
Copyright ownership: Japan Soc. for Medieval English Studies
Rejected manuscripts: Not returned
Time before publication decision: 6 mos.
Time between decision and publication: 6 mos.
Number of reviewers: 11
Articles submitted per year: 10-20
Articles published per year: 5-10

(2836)
*Studies in Medievalism

Leslie J. Workman, Editor
Dept. of English
Hope College
Holland, MI 49423

Telephone: 616 394-7626
Fax: 616 394-7922
First published: 1979
Sponsoring organization: Soc. for the Study of Medievalism
ISSN: 0738-7164
MLA acronym: SiM

SUBSCRIPTION INFORMATION

Frequency of publication: Annual (Spring)
Circulation: 200
Available in microform: No
Subscription address: Boydell & Brewer Inc., P.O. Box 41026, Rochester, NY 14604
Additional subscription address: Boydell & Brewer Ltd., P.O. Box 9, Woodbridge, Suffolk IP12 3DF, England
Subscription telephone: 716 275-0419
Subscription fax: 716 271-8778

ADVERTISING INFORMATION

Advertising accepted: No

EDITORIAL DESCRIPTION

Scope: An interdisciplinary forum for scholars in all fields, including the visual and other arts, concerned with any aspect of the post-medieval idea and the study of the Middle Ages, and the influence, both scholarly and popular, of this study on Western society after 1500.
Reviews books: Yes
Publishes notes: Yes
Languages accepted: English; German; French; Italian
Prints abstracts: No
Author-anonymous submission: Yes

SUBMISSION REQUIREMENTS

Author pays submission fee: No
Author pays page charges: No
Length of articles: 2,000-7,500 words
Length of book reviews: 1,000 words
Length of notes: 1,000 words
Style: MLA
Number of copies required: 2
Special requirements: Submit original typescript, 1 copy, and an abstract.

(2837)
*Studies in Modern German Literature

Peter D. G. Brown, Editor
Dept. of Foreign Languages
State Univ. of New York
New Paltz, NY 12561

Telephone: 914 257-3480
First published: 1987
ISSN: 0888-3904
MLA acronym: SMGL

SUBSCRIPTION INFORMATION

Available in microform: No
Subscription address: Peter Lang Publishing, Inc., 62 West 45th St., New York, NY 10036-4202
Subscription telephone: 212 302-6740

ADVERTISING INFORMATION

Advertising accepted: No

EDITORIAL DESCRIPTION

Scope: Publishes monographs on German literature since the 18th century.
Reviews books: No
Publishes notes: No
Languages accepted: English; German
Prints abstracts: No
Author-anonymous submission: No

SUBMISSION REQUIREMENTS

Restrictions on contributors: No
Author pays submission fee: No
Author pays page charges: No
Length of books: 200-425 pp.
Style: MLA
Number of copies required: 1
Copyright ownership: Peter Lang Publishing Co.
Rejected manuscripts: Returned
Time before publication decision: 2 mos.
Time between decision and publication: 9 mos.
Number of reviewers: 2
Books submitted per year: 20
Books published per year: 10

(2838)
*Studies in Philippine Linguistics

Fe T. Otanes & Hazel Wrigglesworth, Editors
Summer Inst. of Linguistics
Box 2270 C.P.O.
1099 Manila, Philippines

First published: 1977
Sponsoring organization: Linguistic Soc. of the Philippines & Summer Inst. of Linguistics
ISSN: 0116-0516
MLA acronym: SIPL

SUBSCRIPTION INFORMATION

Frequency of publication: 2 times/yr.
Circulation: 65
Available in microform: No
Subscription price: $12.00/yr.
Year to which price refers: 1992

ADVERTISING INFORMATION

Advertising accepted: No

EDITORIAL DESCRIPTION

Scope: Publishes papers of an empirical or theoretical nature which contribute to the study of language and communicative behavior in the Philippines.
Reviews books: No
Publishes notes: No
Languages accepted: English
Prints abstracts: No
Author-anonymous submission: No

SUBMISSION REQUIREMENTS

Restrictions on contributors: None
Author pays submission fee: No
Author pays page charges: No
Length of articles: 100 double-spaced typescript pp. maximum
Style: Linguistic Soc. of America
Number of copies required: 1
Copyright ownership: Author
Rejected manuscripts: Returned
Time before publication decision: 2 mos.
Time between decision and publication: 9 mos.
Number of reviewers: 2
Articles published per year: 25

(2839)
*Studies in Philology

Jerry Leath Mills, Editor
Dept. of English
Univ. of North Carolina at Chapel Hill
Greenlaw Hall, CB 3520
Chapel Hill, NC 27599-3520

Telephone: 919 962-5481
Fax: 919 962-3520
First published: 1906
Sponsoring organization: Univ. of North Carolina, Chapel Hill, Depts. of Languages & Literatures
ISSN: 0039-3738
MLA acronym: SP

SUBSCRIPTION INFORMATION

Frequency of publication: 4 times/yr. (Jan., Apr., July, Nov.)
Circulation: 1,900
Available in microform: No
Subscription price: $24.00/yr. institutions; $18.00/yr. individuals; add $6.00/yr. postage outside US
Year to which price refers: 1993
Subscription address: Univ. of North Carolina Press, P.O. Box 2288, Chapel Hill, NC 27514
Subscription telephone: 919 966-3561

ADVERTISING INFORMATION

Advertising accepted: Yes

EDITORIAL DESCRIPTION

Scope: Publishes studies of medieval and modern English literature, with emphasis on the Middle Ages and the Renaissance.
Reviews books: No
Publishes notes: No
Languages accepted: English
Prints abstracts: No
Author-anonymous submission: No

SUBMISSION REQUIREMENTS

Restrictions on contributors: None
Author pays submission fee: No
Author pays page charges: No
Length of articles: 20-40 typescript pp.
Style: Chicago
Number of copies required: 1
Copyright ownership: Assigned by author to Univ. of North Carolina Press
Rejected manuscripts: Returned
Time before publication decision: 3-6 mos.
Time between decision and publication: 18-24 mos.
Number of reviewers: 1-3
Articles submitted per year: 100-150
Articles published per year: 19-24

(2840)
*Studies in Popular Culture

Dennis R. Hall, Editor
Dept. of English
Univ. of Louisville
Louisville, KY 40292

Telephone: 502 588-6896
Fax: 502 588-5055
E-mail: DRHALL01@ULKYVM (Bitnet)
First published: 1977
Sponsoring organization: Popular Culture Assn. of the South
ISSN: 0888-5753
MLA acronym: SiPC

SUBSCRIPTION INFORMATION

Frequency of publication: 2 times/yr. (Oct., Apr.)
Circulation: 300
Available in microform: No
Subscription price: $15.00/yr. US; $20.00/yr. elsewhere
Year to which price refers: 1991-92
Subscription address: Diane Calhoun-French, Executive Secretary, Popular Culture Assn. of the South, c/o Office of the Academic Dean, Jefferson Community College-Southwest, Louisville, KY 40272
Subscription telephone: 502 935-9840 ext. 204

ADVERTISING INFORMATION

Advertising accepted: Yes
Advertising rates: $50.00/full page

EDITORIAL DESCRIPTION

Scope: Publishes articles on popular culture. Focus is on the popular artifact rather than the received classics. Seeks to examine popular culture phenomena in their social contexts and to explore multidisciplinary approaches.
Reviews books: Yes
Publishes notes: No
Languages accepted: English
Prints abstracts: No
Author-anonymous submission: No

SUBMISSION REQUIREMENTS

Restrictions on contributors: Contributors are asked to join PCAS, but are not required to do so. Book notices are written by a member of the editorial board.
Author pays submission fee: No
Author pays page charges: No
Length of articles: 10-20 pp.
Length of book reviews: 1 p. maximum
Style: MLA suggested
Number of copies required: 2
Special requirements: Submit 2 double-spaced typescripts. Manuscript should be available on diskette, using WordPerfect if possible.
Copyright ownership: Author
Rejected manuscripts: Returned; enclose SASE.
Time before publication decision: 3-6 mos.
Time between decision and publication: 6-12 mos.
Number of reviewers: 2 minimum
Articles submitted per year: 100-150
Articles published per year: 28-30

Copyright ownership: Journal
Rejected manuscripts: Returned; enclose SASE.
Time before publication decision: 3 mos.
Number of reviewers: 1-3
Articles submitted per year: 30
Articles published per year: 15

(2841)
*Studies in Puritan American Spirituality

Michael Schuldiner, Editor
305 Constitution Hall
Box 900119
Univ. of Alaska, Fairbanks
Fairbanks, AK 99775-1040

Telephone: 907 474-6374
Fax: 907 474-5817
E-mail: FFMJS@ALASKA
First published: 1990
ISSN: 1048-8553
MLA acronym: SPAS

SUBSCRIPTION INFORMATION

Frequency of publication: Annual
Available in microform: No
Subscription price: $30.00/yr. institutions (hard cover); $20.00/yr. individuals (paper)
Year to which price refers: 1992
Subscription address: Edward Mellen Press, Order Dept., P.O. Box 450, Lewiston, NY 14092
Subscription telephone: 716 754-2788
Subscription fax: 716 754-4056

ADVERTISING INFORMATION

Advertising accepted: No

EDITORIAL DESCRIPTION

Scope: Focuses on the history and theology of Puritan America; the form that spirituality was given by the writers, artists, artisans, and composers of the Puritan American period; and the influence of Puritan America on later generations.
Reviews books: Yes
Publishes notes: Yes
Languages accepted: English
Prints abstracts: No
Author-anonymous submission: No

SUBMISSION REQUIREMENTS

Author pays submission fee: No
Author pays page charges: No
Length of articles: 5,000-15,000 words
Length of book reviews: 3,500 words minimum
Number of copies required: 2
Copyright ownership: Edwin Mellen Press
Rejected manuscripts: Returned
Time before publication decision: 6-8 weeks
Number of reviewers: 2-3
Articles submitted per year: 35-45
Articles published per year: 7-13

(2842)
Studies in Religion/Sciences Religieuses: Revue Canadienne/A Canadian Journal

Roland Chagnon, Editor
Dept. des Sciences Religieuses
Univ. du Québec à Montréal
C.P. 8888, Succ. A
Montreal, Quebec H3C 3P8, Canada

First published: 1971
Sponsoring organization: Canadian Corporation for Studies in Religion
ISSN: 0008-4298
MLA acronym: SRC

SUBSCRIPTION INFORMATION

Frequency of publication: 4 times/yr.
Circulation: 1,305
Available in microform: No
Subscription address: Wilfrid Laurier Univ. Press, Wilfrid Laurier Univ., Waterloo, Ontario N2L 3C5, Canada

ADVERTISING INFORMATION

Advertising accepted: Yes

EDITORIAL DESCRIPTION

Scope: Publishes academic studies of religion.
Reviews books: Yes
Publishes notes: Yes
Languages accepted: English; French
Prints abstracts: No
Author-anonymous submission: No

SUBMISSION REQUIREMENTS

Restrictions on contributors: Book reviews are commissioned.
Author pays submission fee: No
Author pays page charges: No
Length of articles: 5,000 words maximum
Length of book reviews: 500-700 words
Length of notes: 150 words
Style: Journal
Number of copies required: 3
Special requirements: Include brief biographical statement and abstract.
Copyright ownership: Canadian Corporation for Studies in Religion
Rejected manuscripts: Returned; enclose SASE.
Time before publication decision: 2 mos.
Time between decision and publication: 16 mos.
Number of reviewers: 2
Articles submitted per year: 50
Articles published per year: 30
Book reviews published per year: 45
Notes published per year: 40

(2843)
*Studies in Romance Languages

John E. Keller, Editor
Dept. of Spanish & Italian
Univ. of Kentucky
Patterson Tower
Lexington, KY 40506-0027

Telephone: 606 257-8438
Fax: 606 257-2984
First published: 1970
ISSN: 0085-6894
MLA acronym: SRL

SUBSCRIPTION INFORMATION

Frequency of publication: Irregular
Available in microform: No
Subscription address: Univ. Press of Kentucky, Lexington, KY 40508-4008
Subscription telephone: 606 257-8439
Subscription fax: 606 257-2984

ADVERTISING INFORMATION

Advertising accepted: No

EDITORIAL DESCRIPTION

Scope: Publishes scholarly studies in a wide variety of areas, including folklore, associated with the Romance languages and literatures.
Reviews books: No
Publishes notes: No
Languages accepted: English
Prints abstracts: No
Author-anonymous submission: No

SUBMISSION REQUIREMENTS

Restrictions on contributors: None
Author pays submission fee: No
Author pays page charges: No
Length of books: 120-250 double-spaced typescript pp.
Style: MLA; Chicago
Number of copies required: 2
Special requirements: Quotations may be in original language.
Copyright ownership: Univ. Press of Kentucky
Rejected manuscripts: Returned

Time before publication decision: 3 mos.
Time between decision and publication: 1 yr.
Number of reviewers: 2
Books submitted per year: 10
Books published per year: 1-2

(2844)
*Studies in Romanticism

David Wagenknecht, Editor
236 Bay State Rd.
Boston, MA 02215

Telephone: 617 353-2505
First published: 1961
Sponsoring organization: Boston Univ., Graduate School
ISSN: 0039-3762
MLA acronym: SIR

SUBSCRIPTION INFORMATION

Frequency of publication: 4 times/yr. (Spring, Summer, Fall, Winter)
Circulation: 1,900
Available in microform: Yes
Subscription price: $55.00/yr. institutions; $20.00/yr. individuals
Year to which price refers: 1993
Subscription address: Subscription Dept., Boston Univ. Scholarly Publications, 985 Commonwealth Ave., Boston, MA 02215
Subscription telephone: 617 353-4106

ADVERTISING INFORMATION

Advertising accepted: Yes
Advertising rates: $120.00/half page; $200.00/full page

EDITORIAL DESCRIPTION

Scope: Publishes articles on studies in Romanticism. Some issues are devoted to a specific announced topic.
Reviews books: Yes
Publishes notes: No
Languages accepted: English
Prints abstracts: No
Author-anonymous submission: No

SUBMISSION REQUIREMENTS

Restrictions on contributors: None
Author pays submission fee: No
Author pays page charges: No
Length of articles: 4,000-10,000 words
Length of book reviews: 1,500 words
Style: MLA
Number of copies required: 2
Special requirements: Submit original typescript and an abstract. Quotations in all modern European languages are permitted if English translations are provided. Request translation policy from Editor.
Copyright ownership: Trustees of Boston Univ.
Rejected manuscripts: Returned
Time before publication decision: 2-4 mos.
Time between decision and publication: 1-2 yrs.
Number of reviewers: 1-4
Articles submitted per year: 100
Articles published per year: 20-24
Book reviews submitted per year: 35
Book reviews published per year: 20-25

(2845)
*Studies in Scottish Literature

G. Ross Roy, Editor
Dept. of English
Univ. of South Carolina
Columbia, SC 29208

Telephone: 803 777-2239; 803 777-4203
First published: 1963

Sponsoring organization: Dept. of English, Univ. of South Carolina
ISSN: 0039-3770
MLA acronym: SSL

SUBSCRIPTION INFORMATION

Frequency of publication: Annual
Circulation: 400
Available in microform: No
Subscription price: $16.00/yr. US; $18.50/yr. elsewhere
Year to which price refers: 1991
Subscription telephone: 803 787-6601

ADVERTISING INFORMATION

Advertising accepted: No

EDITORIAL DESCRIPTION

Scope: Devoted to all aspects of Scottish literature. Articles and notes welcome.
Reviews books: Yes
Publishes notes: Yes
Languages accepted: English
Prints abstracts: No
Author-anonymous submission: Yes

SUBMISSION REQUIREMENTS

Restrictions on contributors: Reviews are commissioned.
Author pays submission fee: No
Author pays page charges: No
Length of articles: 2,500-15,000 words
Length of book reviews: 500-2,000 words
Length of notes: 200-2,000 words
Style: MLA with modifications; publisher not noted in footnotes
Number of copies required: 2
Copyright ownership: Editor
Rejected manuscripts: Returned; enclose return postage.
Time before publication decision: 6 mos.
Time between decision and publication: 1 yr.
Number of reviewers: 2
Articles submitted per year: 50
Articles published per year: 16
Book reviews submitted per year: 15
Book reviews published per year: 15
Notes submitted per year: 10
Notes published per year: 5

(2846)
*Studies in Second Language Acquisition

Albert Valdman, Editor
Ballantine Hall 602
Indiana Univ.
Bloomington, IN 47405

Telephone: 812 855-0097
Fax: 812 855-5678
E-mail: Ssla@iubacs.bitnet; ssla@ucs.indiana.edu
First published: 1978
ISSN: 0272-2631
MLA acronym: SSLA

SUBSCRIPTION INFORMATION

Frequency of publication: 4 times/yr. (Mar., June, Sept., Dec.)
Circulation: 1,200
Available in microform: Yes
Subscription price: $79.00/yr. institutions; $41.00/yr. individuals
Year to which price refers: 1992
Subscription address: Cambridge Univ. Press, 40 W. 20th St., New York, NY 10011-4211
Additional subscription address: Cambridge Univ. Press, Edinburgh Bldg., Shaftesbury Rd., Cambridge CB2 2RU, England

ADVERTISING INFORMATION

Advertising accepted: No

EDITORIAL DESCRIPTION

Scope: Publishes articles on theory and research in second language acquisition and foreign language learning.
Reviews books: Yes
Publishes notes: No
Languages accepted: English
Prints abstracts: Yes
Author-anonymous submission: Yes

SUBMISSION REQUIREMENTS

Restrictions on contributors: None
Author pays submission fee: No
Author pays page charges: No
Length of articles: 7,500 words
Length of book reviews: 750 words
Style: American Psychological Assn.
Number of copies required: 4
Copyright ownership: Cambridge Univ. Press
Rejected manuscripts: Not returned
Time before publication decision: 5 mos.
Time between decision and publication: 6-8 mos.
Number of reviewers: 3-4
Articles submitted per year: 60-70
Articles published per year: 18-20
Book reviews submitted per year: 40-50
Book reviews published per year: 40-50

(2847)
*Studies in Short Fiction

Michael J. O'Shea, Editor
Newberry College
Newberry, SC 29108

Telephone: 803 321-5195
Fax: 803 321-5232
First published: 1963
Sponsoring organization: Newberry College
ISSN: 0039-3789
MLA acronym: SSF

SUBSCRIPTION INFORMATION

Frequency of publication: 4 times/yr. (Jan., Apr., July, Oct.)
Circulation: 1,700
Available in microform: Yes
Subscription price: $21.00/yr. institutions; $18.00/yr. individuals
Year to which price refers: 1991

ADVERTISING INFORMATION

Advertising accepted: No

EDITORIAL DESCRIPTION

Scope: Publishes serious commentary on short fiction.
Reviews books: Yes
Publishes notes: Yes
Languages accepted: English
Prints abstracts: No
Author-anonymous submission: No

SUBMISSION REQUIREMENTS

Restrictions on contributors: Book reviews are solicited.
Author pays submission fee: No
Author pays page charges: No
Length of articles: 3,750 words maximum
Length of book reviews: 1-1 1/2 printed pp.
Length of notes: 1,250 words
Style: MLA (1985)
Number of copies required: 2
Copyright ownership: Newberry College
Rejected manuscripts: Returned; enclose return postage & SAE.
Time before publication decision: 4-6 mos.
Time between decision and publication: 12-14 mos.
Number of reviewers: 3
Articles submitted per year: 175
Articles published per year: 40

Book reviews published per year: 45
Notes submitted per year: 25
Notes published per year: 8

(2848)
*Studies in Slavic and General Linguistics

A. A. Barentsen, B. M. Groen, & R. Sprenger, Editors
Vakgroep voor Slavische Taal- en Letterkunde
Postbus 9515
2300 RA Leiden, Netherlands

Telephone: (31) 71 272078
First published: 1980
ISSN: 0169-0124
MLA acronym: SSGL

SUBSCRIPTION INFORMATION

Frequency of publication: Annual
Circulation: 400
Available in microform: No
Subscription address: Editions Rodopi B.V., Keizersgracht 302-304, 1016 EX Amsterdam, Netherlands
Additional subscription address: In N. America: Editions Rodopi, 233 Peachtree St. N.E., Ste. 404, Atlanta, GA 30303-1504
Subscription telephone: (31) 20 6227507; 404 523-1964
Subscription fax: (31) 20 6380948; 404 522-7116

ADVERTISING INFORMATION

Advertising accepted: No

EDITORIAL DESCRIPTION

Scope: Series devoted mainly to descriptive linguistics. Emphasis is on Slavic linguistics, but discussions of non-Slavic languages and theoretical issues are included.
Reviews books: No
Publishes notes: No
Languages accepted: Czech; English; French; German; Polish; Russian; Serbo-Croatian; Bulgarian
Prints abstracts: No
Author-anonymous submission: No

SUBMISSION REQUIREMENTS

Restrictions on contributors: None
Author pays submission fee: No
Author pays page charges: Yes, for monographs
Cost of page charges: $12.00/page
Length of books: No restrictions
Style: Series
Number of copies required: 1
Copyright ownership: Author
Rejected manuscripts: Returned
Time before publication decision: 3 mos.
Time between decision and publication: 3 mos.
Number of reviewers: 3
Books published per year: 10-15 articles or one monograph

(2849)
*Studies in Slavic Literature and Poetics

J. J. van Baak, R. G. Grübel, A. G. F. van Holk, & W. G. Weststeÿn, Editors
Editions Rodopi B.V.
Keizersgracht 302-304
1016 EX Amsterdam, Netherlands

Additional editorial address: Slavic Inst., Groningen Univ., Oude Kijk in 't Jatstraat 26, 9712 EK Groningen, Netherlands
Telephone: (31) 20 6227507
Fax: (31) 20 6380948

First published: 1981
ISSN: 0169-0175
MLA acronym: SSLP

SUBSCRIPTION INFORMATION

Frequency of publication: Irregular
Circulation: 400-900
Available in microform: No
Additional subscription address: Editions Rodopi, 233 Peachtree St. N.E., Suite 404, Atlanta, GA 30303-1504
Subscription telephone: 404 523-1964; 800 225-3998
Subscription fax: 404 522-7116

ADVERTISING INFORMATION

Advertising accepted: Yes, on an exchange basis

EDITORIAL DESCRIPTION

Scope: Publishes monographs and collections of papers in the field of descriptive and theoretical Slavic poetics.
Reviews books: No
Publishes notes: No
Languages accepted: English; German; Russian
Prints abstracts: No
Author-anonymous submission: No

SUBMISSION REQUIREMENTS

Restrictions on contributors: None
Author pays submission fee: No
Author pays page charges: No
Length of books: 200 pp.
Style: MLA
Number of copies required: 4
Special requirements: Submit camera-ready copy and include a 200 word abstract.
Copyright ownership: Editions Rodopi B.V.
Rejected manuscripts: Returned; enclose SASE.
Time before publication decision: 3 mos.
Time between decision and publication: 6 mos.
Number of reviewers: 4
Articles submitted per year: 20
Articles published per year: 20
Books submitted per year: 5
Books published per year: 3

(2850)
Studies in Speech Pathology and Clinical Linguistics

Raymond D. Kent & Martin J. Ball, Editors
Dept. of Communicative Disorders
Univ. of Wisconsin
1975 Willow Dr.
Madison, WI 53706

Additional editorial address: M. Ball, Dept. of Communication, Univ. of Ulster at Jordanstown, Shore Rd., Newtownabbey BT37 0QB, United Kingdom
First published: 1991
ISSN: 0927-1813
MLA acronym: SSPCL

SUBSCRIPTION INFORMATION

Subscription address: John Benjamins Publishing Co., 821 Bethlehem Pike, Philadelphia, PA 19118
Additional subscription address: John Benjamins Publishing Co., Amsteldijk 44, P.O. Box 75577, 1070 AN Amsterdam, Netherlands

EDITORIAL DESCRIPTION

Scope: Publishes monographs and collections of articles on aspects of disordered communication, and the relation between language theory and language pathology.
Languages accepted: English

SUBMISSION REQUIREMENTS

Copyright ownership: John Benjamins B.V.

(2851)
*Studies in the Age of Chaucer: The Yearbook of the New Chaucer Society

Lisa J. Kiser, Editor
Dept. of English
Ohio State Univ.
164 W. 17th Ave.
Columbus, OH 43210-1370

Telephone: 614 292-6065
Fax: 614 292-7816
First published: 1979
Sponsoring organization: New Chaucer Soc.
ISSN: 0190-2407
MLA acronym: SAC

SUBSCRIPTION INFORMATION

Frequency of publication: Annual (Sept.)
Circulation: 900
Available in microform: No
Subscription price: $30.00/yr.; $15.00/yr. students
Year to which price refers: 1992
Subscription address: Christian Zacher, New Chaucer Soc., Dept. of English, Ohio State Univ., Columbus, OH 43210

ADVERTISING INFORMATION

Advertising accepted: No

EDITORIAL DESCRIPTION

Scope: Publishes articles on the art of Chaucer and his contemporaries, their literary relationships and reputations, and the artistic, economic, intellectual, religious, scientific, social, and historical backgrounds to their work. Includes an annotated bibliography and reviews of Chaucer-related publications.
Reviews books: Yes
Publishes notes: No
Languages accepted: English; French; German; Italian
Prints abstracts: No
Author-anonymous submission: Yes

SUBMISSION REQUIREMENTS

Restrictions on contributors: Unsolicited reviews are not accepted.
Author pays submission fee: No
Author pays page charges: No
Length of articles: 10,000-15,000 words
Length of book reviews: 1,000 words
Style: Chicago
Number of copies required: 2
Copyright ownership: New Chaucer Soc.
Rejected manuscripts: Returned; enclose return postage.
Time before publication decision: 4 mos.
Time between decision and publication: 9-12 mos.
Number of reviewers: 2-3
Articles submitted per year: 50
Articles published per year: 5-7
Book reviews published per year: 35-40

(2852)
*Studies in the American Renaissance

Joel Myerson, Editor
Dept. of English
Univ. of South Carolina
Columbia, SC 29208

Telephone: 803 777-2165
E-mail: N270031@UNIVSCVM
First published: 1977
Sponsoring organization: Univ. Press of Virginia
ISSN: 0149-015X
MLA acronym: SAR

SUBSCRIPTION INFORMATION

Frequency of publication: Annual
Circulation: 750
Available in microform: No
Subscription price: $40.00/yr.
Year to which price refers: 1991
Subscription address: Univ. Press of Virginia, Box 3608, University Station, Charlottesville, VA 22903

ADVERTISING INFORMATION

Advertising accepted: No

EDITORIAL DESCRIPTION

Scope: Examines the lives and works of mid-19th-century American authors and the circumstances in which they wrote, published, and were received. Includes biographical, historical, and bibliographical articles on the literature, history, philosophy, art, religion, and general culture of America, 1830-1860.
Reviews books: Yes
Publishes notes: Yes
Languages accepted: English
Prints abstracts: No
Author-anonymous submission: No

SUBMISSION REQUIREMENTS

Restrictions on contributors: None
Author pays submission fee: No
Author pays page charges: No
Length of articles: No restrictions
Length of book reviews: 1,000 words
Length of notes: 2,000 words
Style: Journal
Number of copies required: 2
Copyright ownership: Author
Rejected manuscripts: Returned; enclose return postage.
Time before publication decision: 3 mos.
Time between decision and publication: 12-18 mos.
Number of reviewers: 2
Articles submitted per year: 30-50
Articles published per year: 10-15
Notes submitted per year: 5
Notes published per year: 1-2

(2853)
*Studies in the Humanities

Patrick D. Murphy, Gail Ivy Berlin, & Geraldine Korb Zalazar, Editors
110 Leonard Hall
Indiana Univ. of Pennsylvania
Indiana, PA 15705-1094

Telephone: 412 357-2261
First published: 1969
Sponsoring organization: Indiana Univ. of Pennsylvania
ISSN: 0039-3800
MLA acronym: StHum

SUBSCRIPTION INFORMATION

Frequency of publication: 2 times/yr. (June, Dec.)
Circulation: 300
Available in microform: No
Subscription price: $12.00/yr. institutions; $6.00/yr. individuals
Year to which price refers: 1991

ADVERTISING INFORMATION

Advertising accepted: Yes, on an exchange basis

EDITORIAL DESCRIPTION

Scope: Publishes studies in literature, film, drama, theory and cultural studies. The journal encourages works which are multidisciplinary and cross-cultural.
Reviews books: Yes
Publishes notes: No
Languages accepted: English
Prints abstracts: No
Author-anonymous submission: Yes

SUBMISSION REQUIREMENTS

Restrictions on contributors: Most book reviews are solicited but proposals for multi-author reviews are welcome.
Author pays submission fee: No
Author pays page charges: No
Length of articles: 4,000 words
Length of book reviews: 300-500 words
Style: MLA
Number of copies required: 3
Copyright ownership: Indiana Univ. of Pennsylvania
Rejected manuscripts: Returned; enclose SASE.
Time before publication decision: 3 mos.
Time between decision and publication: 1 yr.
Number of reviewers: 2-3
Articles submitted per year: 60
Articles published per year: 10-15
Book reviews published per year: 10-12

(2854)
*Studies in the Humanities:
Literature-Politics-Society

Guy R. Mermier, Editor
Univ. of Michigan
Dept. of Romance Languages & Literatures
Ann Arbor, MI 48109-1275

Additional editorial address: Peter Lang Publishing, Inc., 62 West 45th St., 4th Floor, New York, NY 10036
Telephone: 212 302-6740
Fax: 212 302-7574
First published: 1984
ISSN: 0742-6712
MLA acronym: StH-LPS

SUBSCRIPTION INFORMATION

Frequency of publication: Irregular
Available in microform: No
Subscription telephone: 212 764-1471

EDITORIAL DESCRIPTION

Scope: Publishes monographs on studies in the humanities, with an emphasis on literature, politics, and society.
Reviews books: No
Publishes notes: No
Languages accepted: English; French; Italian; Spanish; German
Prints abstracts: No
Author-anonymous submission: No

SUBMISSION REQUIREMENTS

Author pays submission fee: No
Length of books: 200 pp.
Style: MLA
Number of copies required: 1
Copyright ownership: Peter Lang Publishing, Inc.
Rejected manuscripts: Returned
Time before publication decision: 3-6 mos.
Time between decision and publication: 9 mos.
Number of reviewers: 1-4
Books submitted per year: 6
Books published per year: 2

(2855)
*Studies in the Linguistic Sciences

Hans Henrich Hock, Editor
Dept. of Linguistics
Univ. of Illinois at Urbana-Champaign
707 S. Mathews St.
Urbana, IL 61801

Telephone: 217 333-3563
Fax: 217 244-0190
E-mail: Hhhock@ux1.cso.uiuc.edu
First published: 1971
Sponsoring organization: Dept. of Linguistics & School of Humanities, Univ. of Illinois
ISSN: 0049-2388
MLA acronym: SLSc

SUBSCRIPTION INFORMATION

Frequency of publication: 2 times/yr.
Circulation: 300
Available in microform: Yes

ADVERTISING INFORMATION

Advertising accepted: No

EDITORIAL DESCRIPTION

Scope: Publishes articles on general and specialized linguistics.
Reviews books: Yes
Publishes notes: No
Languages accepted: English
Prints abstracts: Yes
Author-anonymous submission: No

SUBMISSION REQUIREMENTS

Restrictions on contributors: Contributors must be members of the Univ. of Illinois Dept. of Linguistics or especially invited.
Author pays submission fee: No
Author pays page charges: No
Length of articles: 20 single-spaced typescript pp.
Style: Journal; Language
Number of copies required: 3
Special requirements: Include a half-page abstract.
Copyright ownership: Author
Rejected manuscripts: Returned
Time before publication decision: 2 mos.
Time between decision and publication: 3 mos.
Number of reviewers: 2 minimum
Articles submitted per year: 40
Articles published per year: 22

(2856)
*Studies in the Literary Imagination

R. Barton Palmer & Matthew C. Roudané, Editors
Dept. of English
Georgia State Univ.
Atlanta, GA 30303

Telephone: 404 651-2900
First published: 1968
Sponsoring organization: Georgia State Univ.
ISSN: 0039-3819
MLA acronym: SLitI

SUBSCRIPTION INFORMATION

Frequency of publication: 2 times/yr.
Circulation: 3,500
Available in microform: Yes

ADVERTISING INFORMATION

Advertising accepted: No

EDITORIAL DESCRIPTION

Scope: Each issue is devoted to a special topic in English and American literature.
Reviews books: No
Publishes notes: No
Languages accepted: English
Prints abstracts: No
Author-anonymous submission: No

SUBMISSION REQUIREMENTS

Restrictions on contributors: Unsolicited manuscripts are not accepted.
Author pays submission fee: No
Author pays page charges: No
Length of articles: 15-20 pp.
Style: MLA
Number of copies required: 1
Copyright ownership: Georgia State Univ., Dept. of English
Rejected manuscripts: Returned
Time before publication decision: 2 mos.
Time between decision and publication: 1 yr.
Number of reviewers: 2
Articles published per year: 20

(2857)
*Studies in the Novel

Gerald A. Kirk, Editor
Univ. of North Texas
P.O. Box 13706
N.T. Station
Denton, TX 76203

Telephone: 817 565-2025
First published: 1969
Sponsoring organization: Univ. of North Texas
ISSN: 0039-3827
MLA acronym: SNNTS

SUBSCRIPTION INFORMATION

Frequency of publication: 4 times/yr.
Circulation: 1,500
Available in microform: Yes
Subscription price: $25.00/yr. institutions US; $15.00/yr. individuals US; $35.00/yr. elsewhere
Year to which price refers: 1992
Subscription telephone: 817 565-2025

ADVERTISING INFORMATION

Advertising accepted: No

EDITORIAL DESCRIPTION

Scope: Publishes studies of novels, novelists, and literary theory. Material on minor or fairly recent novels is not generally included.
Reviews books: Yes
Publishes notes: No
Languages accepted: English
Prints abstracts: No
Author-anonymous submission: No

SUBMISSION REQUIREMENTS

Restrictions on contributors: Book reviews are commissioned.
Author pays submission fee: No
Author pays page charges: No
Length of articles: 25 typescript pp. maximum
Length of book reviews: 600-1,000 words
Style: Chicago
Number of copies required: 2
Special requirements: Submit on 5.25 in. diskette using WordPerfect, or a clean copy suitable for scanning.
Copyright ownership: Assigned by author to journal
Rejected manuscripts: Returned; enclose return postage.
Time before publication decision: 3 mos.
Time between decision and publication: 12-18 mos.
Number of reviewers: 2-3
Articles submitted per year: 350-400
Articles published per year: 20-25
Book reviews published per year: 40-45

(2858)
*Studies in the Sciences of Language Series

D. L. Goyvaerts, Editor
Hoge Weg 15
2130 Brasschaat, Belgium

First published: 1975
MLA acronym: SSLS

SUBSCRIPTION INFORMATION

Frequency of publication: Irregular
Subscription address: John Benjamins Publishing Co., P.O. Box 75577, Amsteldijk 44, 1070 AN Amsterdam, Netherlands
Additional subscription address: John Benjamins North America, Inc., 821 Bethlehem Pike, Philadelphia, PA 19118

EDITORIAL DESCRIPTION

Scope: Publishes monograph studies in linguistics.
Languages accepted: English
Prints abstracts: No
Author-anonymous submission: Yes

SUBMISSION REQUIREMENTS

Length of books: 300 pp.
Style: MLA
Number of copies required: 2
Copyright ownership: John Benjamins B.V.
Rejected manuscripts: Returned
Time before publication decision: 6 mos.
Time between decision and publication: 6 mos.
Number of reviewers: 1-2
Books submitted per year: 2-3
Books published per year: 1

(2859)
*Studies in Twentieth Century Literature

Michael Ossar & Marshall Olds, Editors
Dept. of Modern Languages
Kansas State Univ. Eisenhower Hall 104
Manhattan, KS 66506-1003

Additional editorial address: Dept. of Modern Languages, Oldfather Hall, Univ. of Nebraska, Lincoln, NE 68588-0318
Telephone: 913 532-6760; 402 472-3770
Fax: 913 532-7004
E-mail: MLO@KSUVM; MOLDS@UNLINFO.UNL.EDU
First published: 1976
Sponsoring organization: Univ. of Nebraska, Lincoln; Kansas State Univ.
ISSN: 0145-7888
MLA acronym: StTCL

SUBSCRIPTION INFORMATION

Frequency of publication: 2 times/yr. (Jan., July)
Circulation: 550
Available in microform: No
Subscription price: $20.00/yr., $35.00/2 yrs. institutions; $15.00/yr., $28.00/2 yrs. individuals
Year to which price refers: 1992

ADVERTISING INFORMATION

Advertising accepted: Yes, on a paid basis and also on an exchange basis.
Advertising rates: $50.00/half page; $100.00/full page

EDITORIAL DESCRIPTION

Scope: Devoted to literary theory and practical criticism, with exclusive emphasis upon 20th-century literature written in French, German, Russian, and Spanish (including Latin America). Essays should focus on poetry, prose, drama, or literary theory. Submissions on English or American literature are not considered.
Reviews books: Yes
Publishes notes: No
Languages accepted: English
Prints abstracts: Yes
Author-anonymous submission: Yes

SUBMISSION REQUIREMENTS

Restrictions on contributors: None
Author pays submission fee: No
Author pays page charges: No
Length of articles: 10-25 typescript pp.
Length of book reviews: 500-1,000 words
Style: MLA
Number of copies required: 4
Special requirements: Submit original typescript and 3 copies; include a 200-word abstract.
Copyright ownership: Journal
Rejected manuscripts: Returned at author's request; enclose SAE and loose return postage.
Time before publication decision: 3-4 mos.
Time between decision and publication: 1 yr.
Number of reviewers: 3
Articles submitted per year: 31
Articles published per year: 8-9
Book reviews submitted per year: 8-10
Book reviews published per year: 8-10

(2860)
*Studies in Weird Fiction

S. T. Joshi, Editor
607 First St. #3L
Hoboken, NJ 07030

First published: 1986
ISSN: 1050-1045
MLA acronym: StWF

SUBSCRIPTION INFORMATION

Frequency of publication: 2 times/yr.
Circulation: 500
Available in microform: No
Subscription price: $4.50/issue
Year to which price refers: 1991
Subscription address: Necronomicon Press, 101 Lockwood St., West Warwick, RI 02893

ADVERTISING INFORMATION

Advertising accepted: No

EDITORIAL DESCRIPTION

Scope: Designed to promote the criticism of fantasy, horror, and supernatural fiction subsequent to Poe.
Reviews books: Yes
Publishes notes: Yes
Languages accepted: English
Prints abstracts: No
Author-anonymous submission: No

SUBMISSION REQUIREMENTS

Restrictions on contributors: Book reviews are solicited.
Author pays submission fee: No
Author pays page charges: No
Length of articles: 1,000-10,000 words
Length of book reviews: 500-1,500 words
Length of notes: 250-500 words
Style: Chicago
Number of copies required: 1
Copyright ownership: Journal; copyright reverts to author after 1 yr.
Rejected manuscripts: Returned; enclose SASE.
Time before publication decision: 1 mo.
Time between decision and publication: 3-15 mos.
Number of reviewers: 1
Articles submitted per year: 20
Articles published per year: 6-10
Book reviews submitted per year: 6-8
Book reviews published per year: 6-8
Notes submitted per year: 8
Notes published per year: 2-4

(2861)
*Studies on Lucette Desvignes and the Twentieth Century

Patrick Brady, Editor
Dept. of Romance Languages
Univ. of Tennessee
Knoxville, TN 37919

Additional editorial address: New Paradigm Press, 5413 Neilwoods Dr., Knoxville, TN 37919
Telephone: 615 588-8878
First published: 1991
Sponsoring organization: Soc. des Amis de Lucette Desvignes
MLA acronym: StLD

SUBSCRIPTION INFORMATION

Frequency of publication: Annual
Subscription price: $10.00 (60 F)/yr. (includes membership)
Year to which price refers: 1991
Additional subscription address: 9 rue Paul Lippe, 21000 Dijon, France

ADVERTISING INFORMATION

Advertising accepted: Yes

EDITORIAL DESCRIPTION

Scope: Dedicated to the novelist Lucette Desvignes and to the latest and best twentieth-century novelists, but also publishes articles on all significant authors of this period writing in French or in English. Includes both contemporary and traditional modes of criticism.
Reviews books: Yes
Publishes notes: Yes
Languages accepted: French; English
Author-anonymous submission: No

SUBMISSION REQUIREMENTS

Author pays submission fee: No
Copyright ownership: New Paradigm Press
Rejected manuscripts: Returned; enclose return postage

(2862)
*Studies on Voltaire and the Eighteenth Century

H. T. Mason, Editor
Dept. of French
Univ. of Bristol
17-19 Woodland Rd.
Bristol BS8 1TE, England

Telephone: (44) 272 303416
Fax: (44) 272 303416
First published: 1955
Sponsoring organization: Voltaire Foundation
ISSN: 0435-2866
MLA acronym: SVEC

SUBSCRIPTION INFORMATION

Frequency of publication: 10-12 times/yr.
Circulation: 430
Available in microform: No
Subscription address: Voltaire Foundation, Taylor Inst., St. Giles, Oxford OX1 3NA, England

Subscription telephone: (44) 865 270251
Subscription fax: (44) 865 270740

ADVERTISING INFORMATION

Advertising accepted: No

EDITORIAL DESCRIPTION

Scope: Publishes articles on 18th-century studies in the humanities and social sciences in Europe and North America.
Reviews books: No
Publishes notes: No
Languages accepted: English; French
Prints abstracts: No
Author-anonymous submission: Yes

SUBMISSION REQUIREMENTS

Restrictions on contributors: None
Author pays submission fee: No
Author pays page charges: No
Length of articles: No restrictions
Style: Series
Number of copies required: 1
Special requirements: Submit original typescript.
Copyright ownership: Publisher
Rejected manuscripts: Returned; enclose return postage.
Time before publication decision: 1-4 mos.
Time between decision and publication: 1-2 yrs.
Number of reviewers: 1-3
Articles submitted per year: 80-100
Articles published per year: 40-50

(2863)
**Studii şi Cercetări Lingvistice*

I. Coteanu, Editor
Spiru Haret 12
79638 Bucharest, Romania

Telephone: (40) 0 157430 ext. 265
First published: 1950
Sponsoring organization: Academia Română
ISSN: 0039-405X
MLA acronym: StCL

SUBSCRIPTION INFORMATION

Frequency of publication: 6 times/yr.
Available in microform: No
Subscription price: 600 L/yr. institutions; 360 L/yr. individuals
Year to which price refers: 1992
Subscription address: Orion S.R.L., Splaiul Independentei 202 A, Sector 6, P.O. Box 74-19, Bucharest, Romania
Subscription fax: (40) 0 424169

ADVERTISING INFORMATION

Advertising accepted: Yes

EDITORIAL DESCRIPTION

Scope: Publishes research on the structure and history of the Romanian language, studies in general linguistics, and contributions to the fields of Romance, Slavonic, and Germanic linguistics and philology. Also publishes book reviews, information on works and publications in the above mentioned fields, and news regarding meetings of linguists both in Romania and abroad.
Reviews books: Yes
Publishes notes: Yes
Languages accepted: Romanian; English; French; German; Russian; Spanish; Italian
Prints abstracts: Yes
Author-anonymous submission: No

SUBMISSION REQUIREMENTS

Restrictions on contributors: None
Author pays submission fee: No
Author pays page charges: No

Length of articles: 20 double-spaced typescript pp. maximum
Length of book reviews: 3,500 words
Length of notes: 1,000-1,500 words
Style: Journal
Number of copies required: 2
Special requirements: Submit original typescript and a 100-word abstract.
Copyright ownership: Assigned by author to journal
Rejected manuscripts: Not returned
Time before publication decision: 2-3 mos.
Time between decision and publication: 2-3 mos.
Number of reviewers: 3
Articles submitted per year: 70
Articles published per year: 55
Book reviews submitted per year: 20
Book reviews published per year: 18
Notes submitted per year: 30
Notes published per year: 30

(2864)
Studime Filologjike

Academies des Sciences de la RPSA
Inst. i Gjuhësise dhe i Letersise
Rruga Naim Frashëri 7
Tirana, Albania

First published: 1964
ISSN: 0563-5780
MLA acronym: SFil

(2865)
*Studium

Edizioni Studium
via Cassiodoro, 14
00193 Rome, Italy

Telephone: (39) 6865846; (39) 6 6875456
First published: 1904
ISSN: 0039-4130
MLA acronym: Studium

SUBSCRIPTION INFORMATION

Frequency of publication: 6 times/yr.
Circulation: 3,000
Available in microform: No
Subscription address: C.P. 30100, 00100 Rome 47, Italy

ADVERTISING INFORMATION

Advertising accepted: Yes

EDITORIAL DESCRIPTION

Scope: Publishes articles on cultural events, philosophy, sociology, natural and applied sciences, politics, history, and religious sciences, as well as letters and bibliographic notes.
Reviews books: Yes
Publishes notes: Yes
Languages accepted: Italian
Prints abstracts: No

SUBMISSION REQUIREMENTS

Restrictions on contributors: None
Author pays submission fee: No
Author pays page charges: No
Length of articles: 10,000-40,000 words
Number of copies required: 1
Special requirements: Submit original typescript.
Rejected manuscripts: Not returned
Time before publication decision: 2 mos.
Time between decision and publication: 2 mos.
Number of reviewers: 3
Articles submitted per year: 160
Articles published per year: 100-120
Book reviews submitted per year: 150
Book reviews published per year: 130

(2866)
*Stuttgarter Arbeiten zur Germanistik

Ulrich Müller, Franz Hundsnurscher, & Cornelius Sommer, Editors
Akademischer Verlag Stuttgart
Hans-Dieter Heinz
Steiermärker Str. 132
7000 Stuttgart 30, Germany

Telephone: (49) 711 812413
Fax: (49) 711 816769 (c/o Sprint)
First published: 1975
ISSN: 0179-2482
MLA acronym: SAG

SUBSCRIPTION INFORMATION

Frequency of publication: Irregular
Circulation: 300-1,000
Available in microform: No

ADVERTISING INFORMATION

Advertising accepted: No

EDITORIAL DESCRIPTION

Scope: Publishes monographs in the field of modern German literature.
Reviews books: No
Languages accepted: German; English; French; Italian
Prints abstracts: No

SUBMISSION REQUIREMENTS

Restrictions on contributors: None
Author pays submission fee: No
Author pays page charges: No
Length of books: 80-500 pp.
Style: None
Number of copies required: 1
Special requirements: Submit camera-ready copy.
Copyright ownership: Author
Rejected manuscripts: Returned
Time before publication decision: 2-4 mos.
Time between decision and publication: 2-3 mos.
Number of reviewers: 1-2
Books submitted per year: 30
Books published per year: 15

(2867)
Stvaranje: Časopis za Književnost i Kulturu

Bulevar Revolucije, br. 11
Poštanski fah 73
81000 Titograd, Montenegro (Yugoslavia)

First published: 1946
ISSN: 0039-422X
MLA acronym: Stvaranje

SUBSCRIPTION INFORMATION

Frequency of publication: 12 times/yr.
Circulation: 2,100
Available in microform: No

ADVERTISING INFORMATION

Advertising accepted: No

EDITORIAL DESCRIPTION

Scope: Publishes poems, stories, novels in serial form, essays, criticism, literary history, and reviews (mostly of Yugoslav books).
Reviews books: Yes
Publishes notes: Yes
Languages accepted: Serbo-Croatian
Prints abstracts: No

SUBMISSION REQUIREMENTS

Author pays submission fee: No
Length of articles: No restrictions
Length of book reviews: No restrictions
Length of notes: No restrictions
Style: None
Number of copies required: 2
Copyright ownership: Author
Rejected manuscripts: Not returned
Time between decision and publication: 1 mo.
Number of reviewers: 2
Articles submitted per year: 280
Articles published per year: 110
Book reviews submitted per year: 120
Book reviews published per year: 40
Notes submitted per year: 30
Notes published per year: 17

(2868)
*Style

Harold F. Mosher, Jr., Editor
Dept. of English
Northern Illinois Univ.
DeKalb, IL 60115-2854

Telephone: 815 753-0611; 815 753-6653
Fax: 815 753-1824
First published: 1967
Sponsoring organization: Dept. of English, Northern Illinois Univ.
ISSN: 0039-4238
MLA acronym: Style

SUBSCRIPTION INFORMATION

Frequency of publication: 4 times/yr.
Circulation: 600
Available in microform: Yes
Subscription price: $36.00/yr. institutions; $24.00/yr. individuals; $15.00/yr. students; add $4.00/yr. postage outside US
Year to which price refers: 1992

ADVERTISING INFORMATION

Advertising accepted: Yes
Advertising rates: $60.00/half page; $100.00/full page

EDITORIAL DESCRIPTION

Scope: Journal has the following aims: (1) To publish theory, methodology, and analyses of style, particularly those that deal with literature in the English language and that provide systematic methods of description and evaluation of style. (2) To review all books that contribute significantly to an understanding of style, stylistics, and related literary problems. Reviewers should describe the contents of the book, compare it to similar books to establish its relative importance, and explain the contribution of the author's methodology to the study of style. (3) To present earlier and recent critical and theoretical work through bibliographical essays, check lists, and annotated bibliographies on topics of current interest and debate, English translations of contributions in foreign languages, and collected essays by eminent scholars.
Reviews books: Yes
Publishes notes: No
Languages accepted: English
Prints abstracts: Yes
Author-anonymous submission: No

SUBMISSION REQUIREMENTS

Restrictions on contributors: None
Author pays submission fee: No
Author pays page charges: No
Length of articles: 20-30 typescript pp. (4,000-6,000 words)
Length of book reviews: 1,500 words
Style: MLA
Number of copies required: 2

Special requirements: Submit a 150-word abstract; will accept floppy disc with hard copy. Will consider submissions in French, German, Spanish, Italian, Russian, and Czech for publication in English.
Copyright ownership: Editor
Rejected manuscripts: Returned; enclose SASE.
Time before publication decision: 3-4 mos.
Time between decision and publication: 6-12 mos.
Number of reviewers: 2-4
Articles submitted per year: 150
Articles published per year: 20-30
Book reviews submitted per year: 20-30
Book reviews published per year: 20-30

(2869)
*SubStance: A Review of Theory and Literary Criticism

Sydney Lévy & Michel Pierssens, Editors
Dept. of French & Italian
Univ. of California, Santa Barbara
Santa Barbara, CA 93106

Telephone: 805 893-8037
Fax: 805 893-8016
E-mail: FI00SUB@UCSBUXA.bitnet
First published: 1971
Sponsoring organization: Sub-stance, Inc.; Univ. of California, Santa Barbara, Dept. of French & Italian
ISSN: 0049-2426
MLA acronym: SubStance

SUBSCRIPTION INFORMATION

Frequency of publication: 3 times/yr.
Circulation: 600
Available in microform: Yes
Subscription price: $68.00/yr. institutions; $21.00/yr. individuals $14.00/yr. students
Year to which price refers: 1991
Subscription address: Journals Division, Univ. of Wisconsin Press, 114 No. Murray St., Madison, WI 53715
Subscription telephone: 608 262-4952

ADVERTISING INFORMATION

Advertising accepted: Yes
Advertising rates: $110.00/half page; $200.00/full page

EDITORIAL DESCRIPTION

Scope: Dedicated to the discussion and dissemination of contemporary experiments in literature, philosophy, the arts, and sciences. Proposes the reexamination of classical literary texts in the light of developments in contemporary disciplines. Welcomes the participation of all those (students and teachers) interested in making known their present research and results. Periodically publishes a special issue or section devoted to a single author, critic, or problem.
Reviews books: Yes
Publishes notes: No
Languages accepted: English
Prints abstracts: No
Author-anonymous submission: No

SUBMISSION REQUIREMENTS

Restrictions on contributors: None
Author pays submission fee: No
Author pays page charges: No
Length of articles: 15-25 pp.
Length of book reviews: 3-6 pp.
Style: MLA
Number of copies required: 2
Copyright ownership: Board of Regents, Univ. of Wisconsin
Rejected manuscripts: Returned; enclose return postage.
Time before publication decision: 2-4 mos.
Time between decision and publication: 6-12 mos.

Number of reviewers: 2
Articles submitted per year: 60-80
Articles published per year: 20
Book reviews submitted per year: 15-25
Book reviews published per year: 30

(2870)
*Sudetenland

Franz Peter Künzel, Editor
Egenhoferstr. 24
8039 Puchheim b. München, Germany

Telephone: (49) 89 803257
First published: 1958
Sponsoring organization: Gesellschaft zur Förderung ostmitteleuropäischer Literatur
ISSN: 0585-8682
MLA acronym: Sudetenland

SUBSCRIPTION INFORMATION

Frequency of publication: 4 times/yr.
Circulation: 2,800
Available in microform: No
Subscription price: 35 DM/yr.
Year to which price refers: 1993
Subscription address: Verlagshaus Sudetenland, Paul-Heyse-Str. 6/III, 8000 Munich 2, Germany

ADVERTISING INFORMATION

Advertising accepted: No

EDITORIAL DESCRIPTION

Scope: Publishes articles on Sudeten-German culture.
Reviews books: Yes
Publishes notes: Yes
Languages accepted: German
Prints abstracts: Yes
Author-anonymous submission: No

SUBMISSION REQUIREMENTS

Restrictions on contributors: None
Author pays submission fee: No
Author pays page charges: No
Length of articles: No restrictions
Length of book reviews: No restrictions
Length of notes: No restrictions
Style: None
Number of copies required: 1
Copyright ownership: Author
Rejected manuscripts: Returned
Time before publication decision: 3-12 mos.
Time between decision and publication: 3-12 mos.
Number of reviewers: 1
Articles submitted per year: 200
Articles published per year: 120-160
Book reviews submitted per year: 30
Book reviews published per year: 20
Notes submitted per year: 100
Notes published per year: 70

(2871)
*Südost-Forschungen

Edgar Hösch & Karl Nehring, Editors
Südost-Inst.
Güllstr. 7
8000 Munich 2, Germany

Telephone: (49) 89 7461330
Fax: (49) 89 74613333
First published: 1936
Sponsoring organization: Südost-Inst.
ISSN: 0081-9077
MLA acronym: SOF

SUBSCRIPTION INFORMATION

Frequency of publication: Annual

Circulation: 600
Available in microform: No
Subscription price: 136 DM/yr.
Year to which price refers: 1991
Subscription address: Oldenbourg Verlag, Rosenheimer Str. 145, 8000 München 80, Germany
Subscription telephone: (49) 8105 211144
Subscription fax: (49) 8105 5520

ADVERTISING INFORMATION

Advertising accepted: No

EDITORIAL DESCRIPTION

Scope: Publishes articles on the history, culture, and languages of Southeast Europe.
Reviews books: Yes
Publishes notes: No
Languages accepted: German; English; French; Italian
Prints abstracts: No
Author-anonymous submission: Yes

SUBMISSION REQUIREMENTS

Restrictions on contributors: None
Author pays submission fee: No
Author pays page charges: No
Length of articles: 20-30 pp.
Length of book reviews: 30-60 lines
Style: None
Number of copies required: 2
Copyright ownership: Journal
Rejected manuscripts: Returned
Number of reviewers: 3
Articles submitted per year: 30
Articles published per year: 10-15
Book reviews published per year: 150

(2872)
*Südostdeutsches Archiv

Friedrich Gottas, Gerhard Seewann, & Harald Zimmerman, Editors
Südostdeutsche Historische Kommission
Mohlstr. 18
74000 Tübingen 1, Germany

Telephone: (49) 7071 2002544
First published: 1985
Sponsoring organization: Südostdeutsche Historische Kommission
ISSN: 0081-9085
MLA acronym: SüdoA

SUBSCRIPTION INFORMATION

Frequency of publication: 1 double issue every 2 yrs.
Available in microform: No
Subscription address: R. Oldenbourg Verlag GmbH, Rosenheimer Str. 145, 8000 Munich 80, Germany

ADVERTISING INFORMATION

Advertising accepted: No

EDITORIAL DESCRIPTION

Scope: Publishes articles on German history, literature, and ethnography in the Southeastern European region.
Reviews books: Yes
Publishes notes: Yes
Languages accepted: German; English
Prints abstracts: No
Author-anonymous submission: No

SUBMISSION REQUIREMENTS

Restrictions on contributors: None
Author pays submission fee: No
Author pays page charges: No
Length of articles: 30 pp.
Length of book reviews: 1-5 pp.
Length of notes: 1 p.

Number of copies required: 1
Special requirements: Submit original typescript.
Copyright ownership: Journal
Rejected manuscripts: Returned
Time before publication decision: 6 mos.
Time between decision and publication: 6 mos.
Number of reviewers: 3
Articles submitted per year: 12
Articles published per year: 10
Book reviews submitted per year: 30-50
Book reviews published per year: 30

(2873)
*Sumlen: Årsbok för Vis- och Folkmusikforskning

Bengt R. Jonsson, Editor
c/o Svenskt Visarkiv
Hagagatan 23 B II
113 47 Stockholm, Sweden

Telephone: (46) 8 340935
Fax: (46) 8 314756
First published: 1976
Sponsoring organization: Samfundet för Visforskning, Stockholm
ISSN: 0346-8119
MLA acronym: Sumlen

SUBSCRIPTION INFORMATION

Frequency of publication: Annual
Circulation: 700
Available in microform: No

ADVERTISING INFORMATION

Advertising accepted: No

EDITORIAL DESCRIPTION

Scope: Publishes articles on folk songs and folk music.
Reviews books: Yes
Publishes notes: Yes
Languages accepted: Swedish; Danish; Norwegian; English; German
Prints abstracts: Yes

SUBMISSION REQUIREMENTS

Restrictions on contributors: None
Author pays submission fee: No
Author pays page charges: No
Length of articles: 10-35 pp.
Number of copies required: 2
Copyright ownership: Journal & author
Rejected manuscripts: Returned
Time before publication decision: 1 mo.
Number of reviewers: 3
Articles published per year: 6-8
Book reviews submitted per year: 15-20
Book reviews published per year: 15-20

(2874)
*Summer Institute of Linguistics and the University of Texas at Arlington Publications in Linguistics

William R. Merrifield & Donald A. Burquest, Editors
Academic Publications
Summer Inst. of Linguistics
7500 W. Camp Wisdom Rd.
Dallas, TX 75236

Telephone: 214 709-2403
Fax: 214 709-2404
First published: 1958
Sponsoring organization: Summer Inst. of Linguistics & the Univ. of Texas at Arlington
ISSN: 1040-0850
MLA acronym: SILUTAPL

SUBSCRIPTION INFORMATION

Frequency of publication: 5-7 times/yr.
Available in microform: Yes
Subscription address: International Academic Bookstore, Summer Inst. of Linguistics, 7500 W. Camp Wisdom Rd., Dallas, TX 75236
Subscription fax: 214 709-2433

ADVERTISING INFORMATION

Advertising accepted: No

EDITORIAL DESCRIPTION

Scope: Publishes monographs on linguistic theory and language data.
Reviews books: No
Publishes notes: No
Languages accepted: English
Prints abstracts: No
Author-anonymous submission: No

SUBMISSION REQUIREMENTS

Restrictions on contributors: Contributors are primarily Summer Inst. of Linguistics-Univ. of Texas at Arlington members; some exceptions are made.
Author pays submission fee: No
Author pays page charges: No
Length of books: 120-300 pp.
Style: Chicago
Number of copies required: 1
Special requirements: Submit typescript and electronic copy.
Copyright ownership: Summer Inst. of Linguistics, Inc.
Rejected manuscripts: Not returned
Time before publication decision: 2 mos.
Time between decision and publication: 9 mos.
Number of reviewers: 1-3
Books submitted per year: 10-12
Books published per year: 5-7

(2875)
SUNY Series in Cultural Perspectives

Antonio T. de Nicolás, Editor
SUNY Press
State Univ. Plaza
Albany, NY 12246

MLA acronym: SSCP

ADVERTISING INFORMATION

Advertising accepted: No

EDITORIAL DESCRIPTION

Reviews books: No
Languages accepted: English

(2876)
*Suomalais-Ugrilaisen Seuran Toimituksia/Mémoires de la Société Finno-Ougrienne

Juha Janhunen, Editor
Suomalais-Ugrilainen Seura
PL 320
00171 Helsinki, Finland

Telephone: (358) 0 662149
First published: 1890
Sponsoring organization: Soc. Finno-Ougrienne
ISSN: 0355-0230
MLA acronym: MSFO

SUBSCRIPTION INFORMATION

Frequency of publication: Irregular
Circulation: 600-800
Available in microform: No

ADVERTISING INFORMATION

Advertising accepted: No

EDITORIAL DESCRIPTION

Scope: Publishes monographs on Uralic and Altaic linguistics and ethnography.
Reviews books: No
Publishes notes: No
Languages accepted: Finnish; German; English; French; Russian
Prints abstracts: Occasionally

SUBMISSION REQUIREMENTS

Author pays submission fee: No
Author pays page charges: No
Length of books: 200-300 pp.
Style: Scientific
Number of copies required: 1
Special requirements: Submit camera-ready manuscript or diskette.
Copyright ownership: Soc. Finno-Ougrienne
Rejected manuscripts: Returned
Time before publication decision: 2 mos.
Time between decision and publication: 3-12 mos.
Number of reviewers: 2-3
Books published per year: 3-6

(2877)
*Suomalaisen Kirjallisuuden Seuran Toimituksia

Suomalaisen Kirjallisuuden Seura
PL 259
00171 Helsinki 17, Finland

Telephone: (358) 0 131231
Fax: (358) 0 13123220
First published: 1834
Sponsoring organization: Suomalaisen Kirjallisuuden Seura
ISSN: 0355-1768
MLA acronym: SKS

SUBSCRIPTION INFORMATION

Frequency of publication: Irregular
Circulation: 1,000-5,000
Available in microform: No

ADVERTISING INFORMATION

Advertising accepted: No

EDITORIAL DESCRIPTION

Scope: Publishes monographs on Finnish research in language, literature, folklore, and cultural history.
Reviews books: No
Languages accepted: Finnish; Swedish; English; German
Author-anonymous submission: No

SUBMISSION REQUIREMENTS

Restrictions on contributors: None
Author pays submission fee: No
Author pays page charges: No
Number of copies required: 1
Copyright ownership: Author & Suomalaisen Kirjalliuuden Seura
Rejected manuscripts: Returned
Number of reviewers: 2-3
Books submitted per year: 60
Books published per year: 20

(2878)
Suomen Antropologi/Antropologi i Finland

Matti Sarmela, Editor
Helsingen Yliopisto. Kultuuriantropologia
Fabianinkatu 33
00170 Helsinki, Finland

First published: 1976
Sponsoring organization: Suomen Antropologinen Seura
ISSN: 0355-3930
MLA acronym: SAnt

SUBSCRIPTION INFORMATION

Frequency of publication: 4 times/yr. (Feb. May, Sept., Nov.-Dec.)
Circulation: 800
Available in microform: No
Subscription price: 160 Fmk/yr.
Year to which price refers: 1991
Subscription address: Tuija Saarinen, Siltavoudintie 17 A 6, 00640 Helsinki, Finland

ADVERTISING INFORMATION

Advertising accepted: Yes, on an exchange basis

EDITORIAL DESCRIPTION

Scope: Publishes articles on cultural anthropology (including folk life and folkloristics) and physical anthropology.
Reviews books: Yes
Publishes notes: Yes
Languages accepted: Finnish; Swedish; English
Prints abstracts: Yes

SUBMISSION REQUIREMENTS

Author pays submission fee: No
Author pays page charges: No
Style: Journal
Number of copies required: 2
Special requirements: Include a short summary in English and biographical information about the author.
Copyright ownership: Author
Rejected manuscripts: Returned at author's request
Time before publication decision: 1-4 mos.
Time between decision and publication: 2 mos.
Number of reviewers: 2
Articles submitted per year: 16-20
Articles published per year: 12-16
Book reviews submitted per year: 10-15
Book reviews published per year: 10-15
Notes submitted per year: 2-3
Notes published per year: 2-3

(2879)
*Suplementos Anthropos: Materiales de Trabajo Intelectual

Ramón Gabarrós Cardona, Editor
Aptdo. 387
08190 Sant Cugat del Vallés, Spain

Telephone: (34) 3 5894884
Fax: (34) 3 6741713
First published: 1987
ISSN: 1130-2089
MLA acronym: SupA

SUBSCRIPTION INFORMATION

Frequency of publication: 6 times/yr.
Circulation: 2,000
Available in microform: No
Subscription price: 9,975 Pta/yr.
Year to which price refers: 1992
Additional subscription address: In US: Literal Books, P.O. Box 713, Adelphi, MD 20783
Subscription telephone: US: 800 366-8680; elsewhere: (34) 3 5894884

ADVERTISING INFORMATION

Advertising accepted: Yes
Advertising rates: 180,000 Pta/inside back cover

EDITORIAL DESCRIPTION

Scope: A supplement to *AnthroposS* and *DocumentosA*, it publishes monographic issues related to subjects included in those journals. Each issue is thematic and covers subjects including Spanish and Latin American literature, culture, and thought.
Reviews books: No
Publishes notes: No
Languages accepted: Spanish
Prints abstracts: No

SUBMISSION REQUIREMENTS

Restrictions on contributors: Contributions are solicited.
Author pays submission fee: No
Author pays page charges: No

(2880)
*Sŭpostavitelno Ezikoznanie/ Sopostavitel'noe Jazykoznanie/ Contrastive Linguistics

Zivko Bojadziev, Editor
Sofiĭski Universitet "Kliment Ohridski"
Kabinet 159a
15, Car Osvoboditel Blvd.
1040 Sofia, Bulgaria

Additional editorial address: P.O. Box 31, 1504 Sofia, Bulgaria
Telephone: (359) 2 443049
First published: 1976
Sponsoring organization: Sofia Univ.
ISSN: 0204-8701
MLA acronym: SEzik

SUBSCRIPTION INFORMATION

Frequency of publication: 6 times/yr.
Circulation: 700
Available in microform: No
Subscription price: $24.00/yr.
Year to which price refers: 1992
Subscription address: HEMUS Foreign Trade Organization, 7, Levski St., 1000 Sofia, Bulgaria

ADVERTISING INFORMATION

Advertising accepted: Yes

EDITORIAL DESCRIPTION

Scope: Focuses on the contrastive study of Bulgarian with other languages on various linguistic levels; general linguistics; the theory and practice of translation; and history of linguistics.
Reviews books: Yes
Publishes notes: Yes
Languages accepted: Bulgarian; Russian; English; German; French
Prints abstracts: Yes
Author-anonymous submission: No

SUBMISSION REQUIREMENTS

Restrictions on contributors: None
Author pays submission fee: No
Author pays page charges: No
Length of articles: 15 pp.
Length of book reviews: 6 pp.
Length of notes: 4 pp.
Style: Mouton
Number of copies required: 2

Special requirements: Include abstract (600 characters). Submit double-spaced typescript with 30 lines per page and 60 characters per line and one copy. Leave wide margin on left and cite references according to Mouton's style.
Copyright ownership: Sofia Univ. Publishing House
Rejected manuscripts: Returned at author's request
Time before publication decision: 1 mo.
Time between decision and publication: 12-18 mos.
Number of reviewers: 2-9
Articles submitted per year: 50
Articles published per year: 40
Book reviews submitted per year: 120-130
Book reviews published per year: 100-130
Notes submitted per year: 40
Notes published per year: 40

(2881)
*Surfaces [Electronic publication]

Jean-Claude Guédon & Bill Readings, Editors
Dépt. de Littérature Comparée
Univ. de Montréal
C.P. 6128, succ. A
Montreal, Quebec H3C 3J7, Canada

Telephone: 514 343-7793
Fax: 514 343-2211
E-mail: SURFACES@ERE.UMONTREAL.CA
First published: 1991
Sponsoring organization: Univ. de Montréal, Dépt. de Littérature Comparée
ISSN: 1188-2492
MLA acronym: Surfaces

SUBSCRIPTION INFORMATION

Frequency of publication: Paper: annual. On-line: continuous
Available in microform: No
Subscription price: Electronic mail version: free. Diskette version: $5.00/yr. Paper version: $0.20/page
Year to which price refers: 1991
Subscription telephone: 514 343-5863
Subscription fax: 514 343-5864

ADVERTISING INFORMATION

Advertising accepted: Yes, on an exchange basis

EDITORIAL DESCRIPTION

Scope: An electronic journal of interdisciplinary studies. Includes articles on literature, popular culture, music, film, etc.
Reviews books: Yes
Publishes notes: Yes
Languages accepted: English; French; German; Spanish
Prints abstracts: Yes
Author-anonymous submission: Yes

SUBMISSION REQUIREMENTS

Author pays submission fee: No
Author pays page charges: No
Length of articles: 8,000 words
Length of book reviews: 2,000 words
Length of notes: 2,000 words
Style: MLA
Number of copies required: 2
Special requirements: Submissions may be made by electronic mail, on diskette, or in hard copy. Include a 3-4 line abstract.
Copyright ownership: Author
Rejected manuscripts: Returned
Time before publication decision: 2 mos.
Time between decision and publication: 1 week
Number of reviewers: 2
Articles submitted per year: 30-40
Articles published per year: 20
Book reviews submitted per year: 20
Book reviews published per year: 20
Notes submitted per year: 10
Notes published per year: 10

(2882)
*Susquehanna University Studies

Ronald L. Dotterer, Editor
Susquehanna Univ.
Selinsgrove, PA 17870

Telephone: 717 372-4199
Fax: 717 372-4310
First published: 1936
Sponsoring organization: Susquehanna Univ. Press
ISSN: 0361-8250
MLA acronym: SUS

SUBSCRIPTION INFORMATION

Frequency of publication: Annual
Circulation: 1,000
Available in microform: No
Subscription address: Associated University Presses, 440 Forsgate Dr., Cranbury, NJ 08512

ADVERTISING INFORMATION

Advertising accepted: No

EDITORIAL DESCRIPTION

Scope: Publishes articles on interdisciplinary research with an emphasis on the humanities and the sciences. Collections are on a specific topic.
Reviews books: No
Publishes notes: No
Languages accepted: English; French; German
Prints abstracts: No
Author-anonymous submission: No

SUBMISSION REQUIREMENTS

Restrictions on contributors: None; guest editors are welcome.
Author pays submission fee: No
Author pays page charges: No
Length of articles: 8,000 words maximum
Style: Chicago
Number of copies required: 1
Copyright ownership: Journal
Rejected manuscripts: Returned
Time before publication decision: 3 mos.
Time between decision and publication: 18 mos.
Number of reviewers: 6
Articles submitted per year: 75
Articles published per year: 10-12

(2883)
*Suvremena Lingvistika

Zrinka Babić, Stjepan Damjanović, Snježana Kordić, Ivo Pranjković, Josip Silić, Vesna Muhvić-Dimanovski, & Milena Žic Fuchs, Editors
Salajeva 3
41000 Zagreb, Croatia

Telephone: (38) 41 620060
Fax: (38) 41 513834
First published: 1962
Sponsoring organization: Hrvatsko Filološko Društvo
ISSN: 0586-0290
MLA acronym: SuvL

SUBSCRIPTION INFORMATION

Frequency of publication: 2 times/yr.
Circulation: 1,000
Available in microform: No
Subscription price: $10.00/yr. institutions; $5.00/yr. individuals; $3.00/single issue
Year to which price refers: 1992
Subscription telephone: (38) 41 620068

ADVERTISING INFORMATION

Advertising accepted: Yes
Advertising rates: $40.00/full page

EDITORIAL DESCRIPTION

Scope: Publishes articles on contemporary trends in linguistics.
Reviews books: Yes
Publishes notes: Yes
Languages accepted: Croatian; English; French; German; Italian; Russian
Prints abstracts: Yes
Author-anonymous submission: Yes

SUBMISSION REQUIREMENTS

Restrictions on contributors: None
Author pays submission fee: No
Author pays page charges: No
Length of articles: 9,000 words
Length of books: 3,000 words
Length of book reviews: 900 words
Number of copies required: 3
Special requirements: Submit original typescript and 2 copies.
Copyright ownership: Author
Rejected manuscripts: Not returned
Time before publication decision: 1-3 mos.
Time between decision and publication: 5 mos.
Number of reviewers: 3
Articles submitted per year: 30
Articles published per year: 20
Book reviews submitted per year: 15
Book reviews published per year: 10
Notes submitted per year: 7
Notes published per year: 7

(2884)
Svantevit: Dansk Tidsskrift for Slavistik

Jens Nørgaard-Sørensen, Hans Kristian Mikkelsen, Kjeld Bjørnager, Kirsten Roos, Erik Kulavig, & Bronisław Swiderski, Editors
Slavisk Inst.
Ny Munkegade 116
8000 Aarhus C, Denmark

First published: 1975
Sponsoring organization: Dansk Slavistforbund
ISSN: 0106-5378
MLA acronym: Svantevit

SUBSCRIPTION INFORMATION

Frequency of publication: 2 times/yr.
Circulation: 250
Available in microform: No

ADVERTISING INFORMATION

Advertising accepted: No

EDITORIAL DESCRIPTION

Scope: Publishes articles on the languages, literatures, and history of the Slavic countries.
Reviews books: Yes
Publishes notes: No
Languages accepted: Danish; Norwegian; Swedish; English; French; German; Russian
Prints abstracts: No
Author-anonymous submission: No

SUBMISSION REQUIREMENTS

Restrictions on contributors: None
Author pays submission fee: No
Author pays page charges: No
Length of articles: 16 pp. maximum
Length of book reviews: 1,000-1,500 words
Style: Journal
Number of copies required: 1

Copyright ownership: Author & journal
Rejected manuscripts: Returned
Time before publication decision: 3 mos.
Time between decision and publication: 3-6 mos.
Number of reviewers: 2
Articles submitted per year: 30-35
Articles published per year: 15-20
Book reviews published per year: 20-25

(2885)
*Svenska Akademiens Handlingar

Svenska Akademien
P.O. Box 2118
103 13 Stockholm, Sweden

Telephone: (46) 8 249208
Fax: (46) 8 244225
First published: 1786
Sponsoring organization: Svenska Akademien
ISSN: 0349-4543
MLA acronym: SAH

SUBSCRIPTION INFORMATION

Frequency of publication: Annual
Available in microform: No
Subscription address: Norstedts Förlag, P.O. Box 2052, 103 12 Stockholm, Sweden
Subscription telephone: (46) 8 7893000
Subscription fax: (46) 8 214006

ADVERTISING INFORMATION

Advertising accepted: No

EDITORIAL DESCRIPTION

Scope: Publishes reports on the annual Grand Ceremony of the Academy and on awarded prizes, as well as memoirs written by members of the Academy.
Reviews books: No
Publishes notes: No
Languages accepted: Swedish
Prints abstracts: No
Author-anonymous submission: No

SUBMISSION REQUIREMENTS

Restrictions on contributors: Contributors must be members of the Swedish Academy, or have been commissioned by the Academy to contribute.
Author pays submission fee: No
Author pays page charges: No
Copyright ownership: Author & Svenska Akademien
Rejected manuscripts: Returned
Time between decision and publication: 1 yr.

(2886)
*Svenska Landsmål och Svenskt Folkliv

Maj Reinhammar, Editor
Dialekt- & Folkminnesarkivet i Uppsala
Box 1743
751 47 Uppsala, Sweden

Telephone: (46) 18 156360
Fax: (46) 18 151342
First published: 1878
Sponsoring organization: Dialekt- & Folkminnesarkivet i Uppsala
ISSN: 0347-1837
MLA acronym: SLSF

SUBSCRIPTION INFORMATION

Frequency of publication: Annual (plus one irregular issue of B-series)
Circulation: 650
Available in microform: No
Subscription price: 120 Skr/yr.

Year to which price refers: 1991

ADVERTISING INFORMATION

Advertising accepted: No

EDITORIAL DESCRIPTION

Scope: Publishes articles on Swedish dialects (in Sweden, Estonia, the Ukraine, Finland, Argentina, Canada and the US); Nordic, Lappish, and Finnish dialects; Swedish, Nordic, Lappish, and Finnish ethnology and folklore.
Reviews books: Yes
Publishes notes: Yes
Languages accepted: Swedish; Norwegian; Danish; English; French; German
Prints abstracts: Yes
Author-anonymous submission: No

SUBMISSION REQUIREMENTS

Restrictions on contributors: None
Author pays submission fee: No
Author pays page charges: No
Length of articles: No restrictions
Length of book reviews: No restrictions
Length of notes: No restrictions
Style: None
Number of copies required: 1
Special requirements: Submit a 200-word abstract.
Copyright ownership: Author & Dialekt- och Folkminnesarkivet i Uppsala
Rejected manuscripts: Returned
Time before publication decision: 2 mos.
Time between decision and publication: 8-12 mos.
Number of reviewers: 2
Articles published per year: 6-10
Book reviews published per year: 6-15
Notes published per year: 1-6

(2887)
Svensklärarföreningens Årsskrift

Åke Högström, Editor
Mossuägen 54
141 44 Huddinge, Sweden

First published: 1917
MLA acronym: SlfÅ

SUBSCRIPTION INFORMATION

Frequency of publication: Annual
Circulation: 3,500
Available in microform: No

ADVERTISING INFORMATION

Advertising accepted: No

EDITORIAL DESCRIPTION

Scope: Focuses on the education of teachers of the Swedish language.
Reviews books: No
Languages accepted: Swedish
Prints abstracts: No

SUBMISSION REQUIREMENTS

Restrictions on contributors: None
Author pays submission fee: Yes
Author pays page charges: No
Length of articles: 10,000 words
Number of copies required: 1
Copyright ownership: Journal
Rejected manuscripts: Returned
Time before publication decision: 6 mos.
Time between decision and publication: 6 mos.
Articles submitted per year: 20
Articles published per year: 6

(2888)
*Svoboda: Ukrainian Daily

Zenon Snylyk, Editor
Ukrainian National Assn., Inc.
30 Montgomery St.
Jersey City, NJ 07302

Telephone: 201 434-0237
Fax: 201 451-5486
First published: 1893
Sponsoring organization: Ukrainian National Assn.
ISSN: 0274-6964
MLA acronym: Svoboda

SUBSCRIPTION INFORMATION

Frequency of publication: Daily
Circulation: 13,500
Subscription price: $40.00/yr.
Year to which price refers: 1992

ADVERTISING INFORMATION

Advertising accepted: Yes

EDITORIAL DESCRIPTION

Scope: Focuses on Ukrainian current events.
Reviews books: Yes
Languages accepted: Ukrainian; English
Prints abstracts: No
Author-anonymous submission: No

SUBMISSION REQUIREMENTS

Restrictions on contributors: None
Author pays submission fee: No
Author pays page charges: No
Length of articles: 1,000 words
Length of book reviews: 500 words
Number of copies required: 1
Rejected manuscripts: Returned at author's request
Time before publication decision: 10 days
Time between decision and publication: 10 days
Number of reviewers: 2
Articles submitted per year: 1,500
Articles published per year: 1,200
Book reviews submitted per year: 100
Book reviews published per year: 100

(2889)
Swedish-American Historical Quarterly

H. Arnold Barton, Editor
Dept. of History
Southern Illinois Univ.
Carbondale, IL 62901

First published: 1950
Sponsoring organization: Swedish-American Historical Soc.
ISSN: 0039-7326
MLA acronym: SAHQ

SUBSCRIPTION INFORMATION

Frequency of publication: 4 times/yr. (Jan., Apr., July, Oct.)
Circulation: 1,500
Available in microform: Yes
Subscription address: Swedish-American Historical Soc., 5125 N. Spaulding Ave., Chicago, IL 60625

ADVERTISING INFORMATION

Advertising accepted: Yes

EDITORIAL DESCRIPTION

Scope: Publishes articles on the history of Swedish emigration and of Swedes in North America.
Reviews books: Yes

Publishes notes: Yes
Languages accepted: English
Prints abstracts: No
Author-anonymous submission: No

SUBMISSION REQUIREMENTS

Restrictions on contributors: None
Author pays submission fee: No
Author pays page charges: No
Length of articles: 3,000-8,500 words
Length of book reviews: 400-800 words
Length of notes: 100 words
Style: MLA; Chicago
Number of copies required: 1
Special requirements: Submit original typescript.
Copyright ownership: Assigned by author to journal
Rejected manuscripts: Returned
Time before publication decision: 2 mos.
Time between decision and publication: 1-2 yrs.
Articles submitted per year: 25-30
Articles published per year: 15-20
Book reviews submitted per year: 15-20
Book reviews published per year: 15-20
Notes submitted per year: 8-10
Notes published per year: 70-80

(2890)
*Swedish Book Review

Laurie Thompson, Editor
St. David's University College
Lampeter
Dyfed SA48 7ED, Wales

Telephone: (44) 570 422351
Fax: (44) 570 423782
First published: 1983
Sponsoring organization: Swedish Council for Cultural Affairs; Swedish Inst.; Swedish Information Service (NY); Swedish-English Literary Translators' Assn. (SELTA)
ISSN: 0265-8119
MLA acronym: SBR

SUBSCRIPTION INFORMATION

Frequency of publication: 2 times/yr. (Spring, Fall) plus supplement with Fall issue
Circulation: 750
Available in microform: No
Subscription price: £10.00/yr.
Year to which price refers: 1992
Additional subscription address: Valerie Gustaveson, 260 East San Jose Ave., Claremont, CA 91711; Linda Schenck, Mossgatan 5, 41321 Göteborg, Sweden

ADVERTISING INFORMATION

Advertising accepted: Yes

EDITORIAL DESCRIPTION

Scope: Publishes English translations of Swedish literature, presentations of Swedish authors and works, and reviews and bibliographies, as well as information on forthcoming Swedish books.
Reviews books: Yes
Publishes notes: No
Languages accepted: English
Prints abstracts: No
Author-anonymous submission: No

SUBMISSION REQUIREMENTS

Restrictions on contributors: None, but contributors usually reside outside Sweden. Some articles are commissioned.
Author pays submission fee: No
Author pays page charges: No
Style: Journal
Number of copies required: 1
Special requirements: Submission on Macintosh diskette is preferred.
Copyright ownership: Journal & author

Rejected manuscripts: Returned
Time before publication decision: 1-3 mos.
Number of reviewers: 1-2
Articles submitted per year: 15-20
Articles published per year: 8-12
Book reviews submitted per year: 20-50
Book reviews published per year: 15-20

(2891)
*Swift Studies: The Annual of the Ehrenpreis Center

Hermann J. Real & Heinz J. Vienken, Editors
Englisches Seminar
Westfälische Wilhelms-Univ. Münster
Johannisstr. 12-20
4400 Münster, Germany

Telephone: (49) 251 834548
First published: 1986
Sponsoring organization: Friends of the Ehrenpreis Center
MLA acronym: SStud

SUBSCRIPTION INFORMATION

Frequency of publication: Annual
Available in microform: No
Subscription price: 60 DM/yr.
Year to which price refers: 1991

ADVERTISING INFORMATION

Advertising accepted: No

EDITORIAL DESCRIPTION

Scope: Publishes articles relating to the works of Jonathan Swift.
Reviews books: No
Publishes notes: Yes
Languages accepted: English
Prints abstracts: No
Author-anonymous submission: Yes

SUBMISSION REQUIREMENTS

Restrictions on contributors: None
Author pays submission fee: No
Author pays page charges: No
Length of articles: 3,000-6,000 words
Length of notes: 800-1,500 words
Style: MLA
Number of copies required: 3
Copyright ownership: Editor
Rejected manuscripts: Returned; enclose SASE.
Time before publication decision: 2 mos.
Time between decision and publication: 10-18 mos.
Number of reviewers: 3
Articles submitted per year: 10-15
Articles published per year: 6-8
Notes submitted per year: 10-12
Notes published per year: 3-4

(2892)
*Swiss Papers in English Language and Literature

Max Nänny, Editor
Englisches Seminar
Univ. Zürich
Plattenstr. 47
8032 Zürich, Switzerland

Telephone: (47) 1 2573551
Fax: (41) 1 2621204
First published: 1984
Sponsoring organization: Swiss Assn. of Univ. Teachers of English; Schweizerische Akademie der Geisteswissenschaften (Swiss Academy of Humanities)
ISSN: 7196-8700
MLA acronym: SPELL

SUBSCRIPTION INFORMATION

Frequency of publication: Once every 2 yrs.
Circulation: 500
Available in microform: No
Subscription price: 46 DM/volume
Year to which price refers: 1991
Subscription address: Gunter Narr Verlag, P.O. Box 2567, 7400 Tübingen, Germany
Subscription telephone: (49) 7071 78091
Subscription fax: (49) 7071 75288

ADVERTISING INFORMATION

Advertising accepted: Yes
Advertising rates: 500 DM/full page

EDITORIAL DESCRIPTION

Scope: Publishes selected papers from biennial symposium on specific aspects of English and American language and literature.
Reviews books: No
Publishes notes: No
Languages accepted: English
Prints abstracts: No
Author-anonymous submission: No

SUBMISSION REQUIREMENTS

Restrictions on contributors: Contributors must be members of the Swiss Assn. of Univ. Teachers of English or be invited speakers at biennial symposia.
Author pays submission fee: No
Author pays page charges: No
Length of articles: 6,000 words
Style: MLA
Number of copies required: 2-3
Copyright ownership: Gunter Narr Verlag
Rejected manuscripts: Returned
Time before publication decision: 3-6 mos.
Time between decision and publication: 3-12 mos.
Number of reviewers: 3
Articles submitted per year: 12-15
Articles published per year: 10-12

(2893)
*Sydney Studies in English

G. A. Wilkes & A. P. Riemer, Editors
Dept. of English
Univ. of Sydney
Sydney, NSW 2006, Australia

First published: 1975
Sponsoring organization: Univ. of Sydney, Dept. of English; English Assn., Sydney
MLA acronym: SSEng

SUBSCRIPTION INFORMATION

Frequency of publication: Annual
Available in microform: No
Subscription price: A$8.50/yr.
Year to which price refers: 1992

ADVERTISING INFORMATION

Advertising accepted: No

EDITORIAL DESCRIPTION

Scope: Publishes criticism and scholarship in English literature and drama.
Reviews books: Yes
Publishes notes: Yes
Languages accepted: English
Prints abstracts: No
Author-anonymous submission: No

SUBMISSION REQUIREMENTS

Restrictions on contributors: None
Author pays submission fee: No
Author pays page charges: No
Length of articles: 5,000 words
Style: MLA

Number of copies required: 1
Copyright ownership: Author
Rejected manuscripts: Returned; enclose SASE.
Time before publication decision: 2 mos.
Articles published per year: 8-9

(2894)
*Sydsvenska Ortnamnssällskapets Årsskrift/The Annual Journal of the South Swedish Place-Name Society

Göran Hallberg, Editor
Helgonabacken 14
223 62 Lund, Sweden

Telephone: (46) 46 107469
Fax: (46) 46 152381
First published: 1925
Sponsoring organization: Swedish Council for Research in the Humanities & Social Sciences (HSFR)
ISSN: 0302-8348
MLA acronym: SOÅ

SUBSCRIPTION INFORMATION

Frequency of publication: Annual
Circulation: 600
Available in microform: No
Subscription price: 40 Skr/yr.
Year to which price refers: 1991

ADVERTISING INFORMATION

Advertising accepted: No

EDITORIAL DESCRIPTION

Scope: Publishes papers and research reports concerning South Swedish dialects and onomastics.
Reviews books: Yes
Publishes notes: Yes
Languages accepted: Danish; English; German; Norwegian; Swedish
Prints abstracts: Yes
Author-anonymous submission: No

SUBMISSION REQUIREMENTS

Restrictions on contributors: None
Author pays submission fee: No
Author pays page charges: No
Number of copies required: 1
Special requirements: Submit original typescript.
Copyright ownership: Journal
Rejected manuscripts: Returned
Time before publication decision: 2-3 weeks
Time between decision and publication: 1 yr. maximum
Number of reviewers: 3
Articles submitted per year: 5
Articles published per year: 5
Book reviews submitted per year: 1-5
Book reviews published per year: 1-5
Notes submitted per year: 1-5
Notes published per year: 1-5

(2895)
*Symbolae Osloenses

Egil Kraggerud, Editor
Classical Dept.
Univ. i Oslo
Postboks 1007
Blindern
0315 Oslo, Norway

Telephone: (47) 2 677600
Fax: (47) 2 677575
First published: 1922
Sponsoring organization: Norges Almenvitenskapelige Forskningsråd (Norwegian Research Council for Science & Humanities)
ISSN: 0039-7679
MLA acronym: SO

SUBSCRIPTION INFORMATION

Frequency of publication: Annual
Available in microform: No
Subscription address: Scandinavian Univ. Press, P.O. Box 2959 Tøyen, 0608 Oslo, Norway
Additional subscription address: Oxford Univ. Press, Distribution Services, Saxon Way West, Corby, Northants, NN18 9ES, England

ADVERTISING INFORMATION

Advertising accepted: No

EDITORIAL DESCRIPTION

Scope: Publishes articles on classical studies including philology, history, and art.
Reviews books: No
Publishes notes: No
Languages accepted: English; French; German; Latin; Italian
Prints abstracts: Yes
Author-anonymous submission: No

SUBMISSION REQUIREMENTS

Restrictions on contributors: Half of the volume presents Norwegian contributions or contributions on Norwegian material.
Author pays submission fee: No
Author pays page charges: No
Length of articles: 40 pp. maximum
Number of copies required: 2
Special requirements: Submit original typescript.
Copyright ownership: Universitetsforlaget
Rejected manuscripts: Returned
Time before publication decision: 6 mos. maximum
Number of reviewers: 2
Articles submitted per year: 20
Articles published per year: 10-12

(2896)
*Symposium: A Quarterly Journal in Modern Foreign Literatures

Paul J. Archambault, Editor
210 H. B. Crouse Hall
Syracuse Univ.
Syracuse, NY 13244-1160

Telephone: 315 443-5487
First published: 1946
Sponsoring organization: Syracuse Univ., Faculty of Foreign Languages & Literatures
ISSN: 0039-7709
MLA acronym: Symposium

SUBSCRIPTION INFORMATION

Frequency of publication: 4 times/yr.
Circulation: 1,000
Available in microform: Yes
Subscription price: $52.00/yr. institutions US; $30.00/yr. individuals US; $60.00/yr. elsewhere
Year to which price refers: 1992
Subscription address: Heldref Publications, 1319 Eighteenth St., NW, Washington, DC 20016-1802
Subscription telephone: 202 296-6267

ADVERTISING INFORMATION

Advertising accepted: Yes

EDITORIAL DESCRIPTION

Scope: Welcomes contributions pertinent to modern foreign literatures. Material dealing exclusively with British or American literature is not acceptable.
Reviews books: Yes
Publishes notes: No
Languages accepted: English; French; Spanish; Italian; German
Prints abstracts: No
Author-anonymous submission: No

SUBMISSION REQUIREMENTS

Restrictions on contributors: Reviews are solicited.
Author pays submission fee: No
Author pays page charges: No
Length of articles: 20-35 pp.
Length of book reviews: 500-700 words
Style: MLA
Number of copies required: 1
Special requirements: Articles written in languages other than English must be accompanied by a short paragraph describing their contents.
Copyright ownership: Heldref Publications
Rejected manuscripts: Returned; enclose SASE.
Time before publication decision: 4-6 weeks
Time between decision and publication: 6-12 mos.
Articles submitted per year: 100
Articles published per year: 20
Book reviews published per year: 10-20

(2897)
*Syn og Segn: Norsk Tidsskrift

Borghild Gramstad, Editor
Postboks 4672 Sofienberg
0506 Oslo, Norway

Telephone: (47) 2 687600
Fax: (47) 2 687502
First published: 1894
Sponsoring organization: Norske Samlaget
ISSN: 0039-7717
MLA acronym: SoS

SUBSCRIPTION INFORMATION

Frequency of publication: 4 times/yr.
Circulation: 4,000
Available in microform: No
Subscription price: 245 NKr/yr. institutions; 190 NKr/yr. individuals
Year to which price refers: 1992
Subscription address: Forlagsentralen, Tidsskriftavdelinga, Boks 150 Furuset, 1001 Oslo, Norway
Subscription telephone: (47) 2 326050

ADVERTISING INFORMATION

Advertising accepted: Yes

EDITORIAL DESCRIPTION

Scope: Publishes articles on politics and society, history, literature, and visual culture.
Reviews books: Yes
Publishes notes: Yes
Languages accepted: Norwegian
Prints abstracts: No

SUBMISSION REQUIREMENTS

Restrictions on contributors: None
Author pays submission fee: No
Author pays page charges: No
Length of articles: 3,000-9,000 words
Length of book reviews: 1,000-4,000 words
Length of notes: 20 words
Number of copies required: 1
Special requirements: Submit original typescript.
Copyright ownership: Author
Rejected manuscripts: Returned
Time before publication decision: 1 mo.
Time between decision and publication: 2-6 mos.
Number of reviewers: 1
Articles submitted per year: 150
Articles published per year: 60
Book reviews submitted per year: 5-10
Book reviews published per year: 5-8

Notes submitted per year: 1-5
Notes published per year: 4

(2898)
Syntax and Semantics

Stephen R. Anderson, Editor
Cognitive Science Center
Johns Hopkins Univ.
Baltimore, MD 21218

First published: 1973
ISSN: 0092-4563
MLA acronym: S&S

SUBSCRIPTION INFORMATION

Frequency of publication: Irregular
Available in microform: No
Subscription address: Academic Press, 111 Fifth Ave., New York, NY 10003

ADVERTISING INFORMATION

Advertising accepted: No

EDITORIAL DESCRIPTION

Scope: Publishes collections and monographs on syntactic and semantic theory.
Reviews books: No
Publishes notes: No
Languages accepted: English
Prints abstracts: No
Author-anonymous submission: No

SUBMISSION REQUIREMENTS

Author pays submission fee: No
Author pays page charges: No
Style: None
Number of copies required: 2
Special requirements: Separate articles are not accepted. Only entire books are considered for publication.
Copyright ownership: Academic Press
Rejected manuscripts: Returned at author's request
Time before publication decision: 3 mos.
Time between decision and publication: 9 mos.
Number of reviewers: 1-4

(2899)
*Synthese: An International Journal for Epistemology, Methodology and Philosophy of Science

Jaakko Hintikka, James H. Fetzer, Risto Hilpinen, Barry Richards, Paul Humphreys, & Michael Vasko, Editors
Dept. of Philosophy
Boston Univ.
Boston, MA 02215

Additional editorial address: Send articles to: Michael Vasko, Managing Editor, Dept. of Philosophy, Boston Univ., Boston, MA 02215. Send books for review to: Paul Humphreys, Book Review Editor, Dept. of Philosophy, Univ. of Virginia, Charlottesville, VA 22903
Telephone: 617 353-6807
Fax: 617 353-6805
First published: 1936
ISSN: 0039-7857
MLA acronym: Synthese

SUBSCRIPTION INFORMATION

Frequency of publication: 4 volumes/yr. of 3 issues each
Available in microform: No
Subscription price: 264 f ($150.00)/volume; 1,056 f ($600.00)/yr.
Year to which price refers: 1991

Subscription address: Kluwer Academic Publishers Group, P.O. Box 332, 3300 AH Dordrecht, Netherlands
Additional subscription address: In US: Kluwer Academic Publishers Group, P.O. Box 358, Accord Station, Hingham, MA 02018-0358

ADVERTISING INFORMATION

Advertising accepted: Yes

EDITORIAL DESCRIPTION

Scope: Publishes articles in the following fields: theory of knowledge, the general methodological problems of science, such as the problems of scientific discovery and scientific inference, of induction and probability, of causation and the role of mathematics, statistics and logic in science; the methodological and foundational problems of the different departmental sciences, in so far as they have philosophical interest; those aspects of symbolic logic and of the foundations of mathematics which are relevant to the philosophy and methodology of science; and those facets of the history and sociology of science which are important for contemporary topical pursuits. Special attention is paid to the role of mathematical, logical, and linguistic methods in the general methodology of science and in the foundations of different sciences, be they physical, biological, behavioral, or social.
Reviews books: Yes
Publishes notes: Yes
Languages accepted: English
Prints abstracts: Yes
Author-anonymous submission: Yes

SUBMISSION REQUIREMENTS

Restrictions on contributors: None
Author pays submission fee: No
Author pays page charges: No
Length of articles: 8,000 words
Length of book reviews: 3,000 words
Style: Journal
Number of copies required: 2
Special requirements: Consult journal regarding submission policy.
Copyright ownership: Kluwer Academic Publishers
Rejected manuscripts: Returned at author's request
Time before publication decision: 4 mos.
Number of reviewers: 2
Articles submitted per year: 450
Articles published per year: 80
Book reviews submitted per year: 30
Book reviews published per year: 20

(2900)
*Synthesis: Bulletin du Comité National Roumain de Littérature Comparée et de l'Institut d'Histoire et de Théorie Littéraire "G. Călinescu" de l'Académie Roumaine

Zoe Dumitrescu-Buşulenga & Mircea Anghelescu, Editors
1, bd. Schitu Măgureanu
70626 Bucharest, Romania

Additional editorial address: Editura Academiei Române, Calea Victoriei 125, Bucharest, Romania
Telephone: (40) 0 147898
First published: 1974
Sponsoring organization: Académie Roumaine; Comité National Roumain de Littérature Comparée; Inst. d'Histoire & de Théorie Littéraire "G. Călinescu" de l'Académie Roumaine
ISSN: 0256-7245
MLA acronym: Synthesis

SUBSCRIPTION INFORMATION

Frequency of publication: Annual
Circulation: 1,000
Available in microform: No
Subscription price: $83.00/yr.
Year to which price refers: 1992
Subscription address: Orion srl, Splaiul Independenţei 202A, Bucharest 6, Romania

ADVERTISING INFORMATION

Advertising accepted: No

EDITORIAL DESCRIPTION

Scope: Publishes scholarly papers and critical essays on the following topics: comparative literature, literary theory, and criticism which relate to Romanian or comparative literature.
Reviews books: Yes
Publishes notes: Yes
Languages accepted: English; French; German; Russian; Spanish; Italian
Prints abstracts: No
Author-anonymous submission: No

SUBMISSION REQUIREMENTS

Restrictions on contributors: None
Author pays submission fee: No
Author pays page charges: No
Length of articles: 10 pp. maximum
Length of book reviews: 500 words
Length of notes: 700-800 words
Style: Editura Academiei
Number of copies required: 2
Copyright ownership: Editura Academiei
Rejected manuscripts: Not returned
Time before publication decision: 3 mos.
Time between decision and publication: 1 yr.
Number of reviewers: 2
Articles submitted per year: 25-30
Articles published per year: 10-12
Book reviews submitted per year: 30-40
Book reviews published per year: 15-20
Notes submitted per year: 4-5
Notes published per year: 1-2

(2901)
*Syracuse University Library Associates Courier

Gwen G. Robinson, Editor
c/o Syracuse Univ. Library Associates
600 Bird Library
Syracuse Univ.
Syracuse, NY 13244-2010

Telephone: 315 443-2697
Fax: 315 443-9510
First published: 1958
Sponsoring organization: Syracuse Univ. Library Associates
ISSN: 0011-0418
MLA acronym: Courier

SUBSCRIPTION INFORMATION

Frequency of publication: 2 times/yr. (Spring, Fall)
Circulation: 600
Available in microform: No

ADVERTISING INFORMATION

Advertising accepted: No

EDITORIAL DESCRIPTION

Scope: Contains articles pertaining to the collections of the Syracuse University Library, along with news of recent acquisitions, library exhibits, lectures, and the affairs and interests of the Syracuse University Library Associates.
Reviews books: Yes
Publishes notes: Yes
Languages accepted: English
Prints abstracts: No

Author-anonymous submission: No

SUBMISSION REQUIREMENTS

Restrictions on contributors: None
Author pays submission fee: No
Author pays page charges: No
Length of articles: 2,000-8,000 words
Style: Chicago
Number of copies required: 1
Special requirements: Submit double-spaced typescript including notes and extracts.
Copyright ownership: Assigned by author to journal
Rejected manuscripts: Returned
Time before publication decision: 2 mos.
Time between decision and publication: 9 mos.
Number of reviewers: 3
Articles submitted per year: 20-30
Articles published per year: 10-20
Notes submitted per year: 6-8
Notes published per year: 3-4

(2902)
Syria: Revue d'Art Orientale et d'Archéologie

E. Will & J. Caquot, Editors
Librairie Orientaliste Paul Geuthner
12, rue Vavin
75006 Paris, France

First published: 1920
Sponsoring organization: Inst. Français d'Archéologie de Beyrouth
ISSN: 0039-7946
MLA acronym: Syria

SUBSCRIPTION INFORMATION

Frequency of publication: 2 double issues/yr.

EDITORIAL DESCRIPTION

Reviews books: Yes
Languages accepted: French
Prints abstracts: No

(2903)
***Szinház: Theatre, Theoretical and Critical Journal of Theatrical Arts**

Tamás Koltai, Editor
Báthori utca 10
1054 Budapest, Hungary

Telephone: (36) 1 1316308
First published: 1968
ISSN: 0039-8136
MLA acronym: Szinház

SUBSCRIPTION INFORMATION

Frequency of publication: 12 times/yr.
Circulation: 2,000
Available in microform: No
Additional subscription address: Posta Központi Hirlap Iroda, V. József nádor tér 1., 1900 Budapest, Hungary

ADVERTISING INFORMATION

Advertising accepted: Yes

EDITORIAL DESCRIPTION

Scope: Focuses on the critical examination of Hungarian and foreign performances and studies in theatrical trends.
Reviews books: Yes
Publishes notes: No
Languages accepted: Hungarian; English; German; French
Prints abstracts: Yes
Author-anonymous submission: No

SUBMISSION REQUIREMENTS

Restrictions on contributors: None
Author pays submission fee: No
Author pays page charges: No
Length of articles: 10 pp.
Length of book reviews: 5 pp.
Number of copies required: 2
Special requirements: Submit original typescript plus 1 copy.
Copyright ownership: Author
Rejected manuscripts: Not returned
Time before publication decision: 1 mo.
Time between decision and publication: 2 mos.
Number of reviewers: 3
Articles submitted per year: 350-400
Articles published per year: 160-180
Book reviews submitted per year: 40-50
Book reviews published per year: 10-20

(2904)
T. A. Informations: Revue Internationale du Traitement Automatique du Langage

André Deweze, Editor
Saint-Vincent-de-Mercuze
38660 Letouvet, France

First published: 1960
Sponsoring organization: Assn. pour l'Etude & le Developpement de la Traduction Automatique & de la Linguistique Appliquée; Centre Nationale de la Recherche Scientifique
ISSN: 0039-8217
MLA acronym: TAI

SUBSCRIPTION INFORMATION

Frequency of publication: 2 times/yr.
Circulation: 600
Subscription address: Librairie C. Klincksieck, 11, rue de Lille, 75007 Paris, France

EDITORIAL DESCRIPTION

Scope: Publishes articles on computational linguistics.
Reviews books: Yes
Languages accepted: English; French
Prints abstracts: Yes

SUBMISSION REQUIREMENTS

Length of articles: 10-30 pp.
Number of copies required: 2
Time before publication decision: 2 mos.
Time between decision and publication: 4 mos.
Number of reviewers: 3
Articles published per year: 6-8

(2905)
***T. E. Notes: A T. E. Lawrence Newsletter**

Denis W. McDonnell, Janet A. Riesman, & Mary E. McDonnell, Editors
653 Park St.
Honesdale, PA 18431

Telephone: 717 253-6706
Fax: 717 253-6786
First published: 1990
ISSN: 1054-514X
MLA acronym: TENotes

SUBSCRIPTION INFORMATION

Frequency of publication: 10 times/yr.
Circulation: 100
Available in microform: No
Subscription price: $25.00/yr. US; $30.00/yr. elsewhere
Year to which price refers: 1992

ADVERTISING INFORMATION

Advertising accepted: No

EDITORIAL DESCRIPTION

Scope: Publishes short articles and notes on T. E. Lawrence.
Reviews books: Yes
Publishes notes: Yes
Languages accepted: English
Prints abstracts: Yes

SUBMISSION REQUIREMENTS

Author pays submission fee: No
Author pays page charges: No
Length of articles: 500 words
Length of book reviews: 500 words
Length of notes: 500 words
Number of copies required: 3
Special requirements: Submit original typescript and 2 copies.
Copyright ownership: Author
Time before publication decision: 1 mo.
Time between decision and publication: 2 mos.
Number of reviewers: 2

(2906)
***Taal en Tongval**

G. de Schutter & J. B. Berns, Editors
Blandijnberg 2
9000 Ghent, Belgium

Additional editorial address: J. B. Berns, P.-J. Meertens Inst., Keizersgracht 569-571, Amsterdam DR 1002, Netherlands
Telephone: (32) 91 644075
Fax: (32) 91 644195
First published: 1949
Sponsoring organization: Seminarie voor Vlaamse Dialectologie (Ghent); Zuidnederlandse Dialectcentrale (Leuven); P.-J. Meertens-Inst.
ISSN: 0039-8691
MLA acronym: TeT

SUBSCRIPTION INFORMATION

Frequency of publication: 2 times/yr.
Circulation: 390
Available in microform: No
Subscription price: 650 BF/yr.
Year to which price refers: 1992

ADVERTISING INFORMATION

Advertising accepted: Yes

EDITORIAL DESCRIPTION

Scope: Publishes articles on Dutch dialectology and sociolinguistics.
Reviews books: Yes
Publishes notes: Yes
Languages accepted: Dutch
Prints abstracts: No
Author-anonymous submission: Yes

SUBMISSION REQUIREMENTS

Restrictions on contributors: None
Author pays submission fee: No
Author pays page charges: No
Length of articles: 30 pp. maximum
Length of book reviews: 2 pp.
Length of notes: 100 words
Number of copies required: 1
Copyright ownership: Author
Rejected manuscripts: Returned
Time before publication decision: 3 mos.
Time between decision and publication: 6 mos.
Number of reviewers: 3
Articles submitted per year: 15
Articles published per year: 12
Book reviews submitted per year: 12
Book reviews published per year: 10

Notes submitted per year: 5
Notes published per year: 4

(2907)
*Talisman: A Journal of Contemporary Poetry and Poetics

Edward Foster, Editor
Box 1117
Hoboken, NJ 07030

Telephone: 201 798-9093
First published: 1988
ISSN: 0898-8684
MLA acronym: Talisman

SUBSCRIPTION INFORMATION

Frequency of publication: 2 times/yr.
Circulation: 400
Available in microform: No
Subscription price: $13.00/yr. institutions; $9.00/yr. individuals
Year to which price refers: 1992

ADVERTISING INFORMATION

Advertising accepted: Yes
Advertising rates: $100.00/full page

EDITORIAL DESCRIPTION

Scope: Publishes contemporary poetry, interviews with poets, and criticism of poetry.
Reviews books: Yes
Publishes notes: No
Languages accepted: English
Prints abstracts: No
Author-anonymous submission: No

SUBMISSION REQUIREMENTS

Restrictions on contributors: None
Author pays submission fee: No
Author pays page charges: No
Length of articles: 1,000-2,000 words
Length of book reviews: 500 words
Style: Chicago preferred
Number of copies required: 1
Copyright ownership: Author
Rejected manuscripts: Returned
Time before publication decision: 1 mo.
Time between decision and publication: 1-5 mos.
Number of reviewers: 1-3
Articles submitted per year: 40
Articles published per year: 15
Book reviews submitted per year: 25
Book reviews published per year: 5

(2908)
*Taller de Letras

Ileana Cabrera Ponce, Editor
Avda. Jaime Guzmán E. 3300
Casilla 316-22
Santiago, Chile

Telephone: (56) 2 2744041 ext. 2153
Fax: (56) 2 2232577
First published: 1971
Historical variations in title: Formerly Taller de Letras: Revista del Instituto de Letras de la Ponfífica Universidad Católica de Chile
Sponsoring organization: Pontificia Univ. Católica de Chile
ISSN: 0716-0798
MLA acronym: TdL

SUBSCRIPTION INFORMATION

Frequency of publication: Annual (Nov.)
Circulation: 100
Available in microform: No
Subscription price: Ch$2,000/yr. Chile; $20.00/yr. elsewhere
Year to which price refers: 1992
Additional subscription address: Inst. de Letras, Pontificia Univ. Católica de Chile, Casilla 316, Correo 22 Santiago, Chile

ADVERTISING INFORMATION

Advertising accepted: Yes
Advertising rates: Ch$50,000/half page; Ch$100,000 ($300.00)/full page

EDITORIAL DESCRIPTION

Scope: Publishes articles on literature, linguistics, applied linguistics, and translation.
Reviews books: Yes
Publishes notes: Yes
Languages accepted: Spanish primarily; English; French; German
Prints abstracts: Yes

SUBMISSION REQUIREMENTS

Author pays submission fee: No
Author pays page charges: No
Length of articles: 4,500 words
Length of book reviews: 450 words
Length of notes: 1,000 words
Style: MLA
Number of copies required: 3
Special requirements: Request guidelines from editor.
Copyright ownership: Pontificia Univ. Católica de Chile
Rejected manuscripts: Not returned
Time before publication decision: 2 mos.
Time between decision and publication: 4 mos.
Number of reviewers: 2
Articles submitted per year: 20
Articles published per year: 12
Book reviews submitted per year: 5
Book reviews published per year: 3
Notes submitted per year: 5
Notes published per year: 3

(2909)
*Tamarack: Journal of the Edna St. Vincent Millay Society

Elizabeth Barnett & John J. Patton, Editors
Edna St. Vincent Millay Soc.
Steepletop
Austerlitz, NY 12017

First published: 1981
Sponsoring organization: Edna St. Vincent Millay Soc.
MLA acronym: Tamarack

SUBSCRIPTION INFORMATION

Frequency of publication: Irregular
Circulation: 400
Available in microform: No
Subscription address: 8A Chauncy St., 5, Cambridge, MA 02138

ADVERTISING INFORMATION

Advertising accepted: No

EDITORIAL DESCRIPTION

Scope: Concentrates on Edna St. Vincent Millay and her work. Includes articles and reviews of her contemporaries as well as the work of present day poets.
Reviews books: Yes
Languages accepted: English
Prints abstracts: Yes

SUBMISSION REQUIREMENTS

Restrictions on contributors: None
Author pays submission fee: No
Author pays page charges: No
Length of articles: 5-10 double-spaced typescript pp.
Length of book reviews: 700-1,000 words
Style: Chicago
Number of copies required: 2
Special requirements: Cite source of quoted material; manuscript must be double-spaced.
Copyright ownership: Journal
Rejected manuscripts: Returned
Time before publication decision: 3 mos.
Time between decision and publication: 5-6 mos.
Number of reviewers: 3
Articles submitted per year: 15-20
Articles published per year: 9-10
Book reviews submitted per year: 2-3
Book reviews published per year: 1

(2910)
*Tamkang Review: A Quarterly of Comparative Studies between Chinese and Foreign Literatures

Chang-fang Chen, Editor
Graduate School of Western Languages & Literature
LA 507, Tamkang Univ.
Tamsui, Taipei, Taiwan 25137, Republic of China

Fax: (886) 2 6211254
First published: 1970
Sponsoring organization: Tamkang Univ., Graduate School of Western Languages & Literatures
ISSN: 0049-2949
MLA acronym: TkR

SUBSCRIPTION INFORMATION

Frequency of publication: 4 times/yr.
Circulation: 1,000
Available in microform: No
Subscription price: $40.00/yr. institutions; $20.00/yr. individuals
Year to which price refers: 1991

ADVERTISING INFORMATION

Advertising accepted: Yes

EDITORIAL DESCRIPTION

Scope: Publishes comparative studies of Chinese and foreign literatures, including the classical and modern literatures of East Asia and the West. Also publishes studies of Chinese literature from a point of view or methodology which places a subject within the context of world literature.
Reviews books: Yes
Publishes notes: Yes
Languages accepted: English
Prints abstracts: Yes
Author-anonymous submission: Yes

SUBMISSION REQUIREMENTS

Restrictions on contributors: None
Author pays submission fee: No
Author pays page charges: No
Length of articles: 4,000-12,000 words
Length of book reviews: 500-2,000 words
Length of notes: 500 words
Style: MLA
Number of copies required: 2
Special requirements: All references to Chinese and Japanese must be accompanied by originals.
Copyright ownership: Journal
Rejected manuscripts: Returned at author's request
Time before publication decision: 6 mos.
Time between decision and publication: 6 mos.
Number of reviewers: 2-4
Articles submitted per year: 60
Articles published per year: 20-30
Book reviews submitted per year: 15-20
Book reviews published per year: 6-8

(2911)
*Tangence

Elisabeth Haghebaert, Secrétaire de Rédaction
300, allée des Ursulines
Rimouski, PQ G5L 3A1, Canada

Telephone: 418 724-1573
Fax: 418 724-1525
First published: 1981
Sponsoring organization: Ministère des Affaires Culturelles du Québec; Conseil des Arts du Canada; Univ. du Québec à Rimouski
ISSN: 1189-4563
MLA acronym: Tangence

SUBSCRIPTION INFORMATION

Frequency of publication: 4 times/yr.
Available in microform: No
Subscription price: C$30.00/yr. institutions Canada; C$25.00/yr. individuals Canada; C$22.00/yr. students & writers Canada; C$32.00/yr. elsewhere
Year to which price refers: 1992

ADVERTISING INFORMATION

Advertising accepted: Yes

EDITORIAL DESCRIPTION

Scope: Publishes articles on Québécois literature as well as literature from other parts of the world.
Reviews books: Yes
Publishes notes: Yes
Languages accepted: French
Prints abstracts: No
Author-anonymous submission: No

SUBMISSION REQUIREMENTS

Restrictions on contributors: Contributions are solicited.
Author pays submission fee: No
Author pays page charges: No
Length of articles: 35,000-40,000 characters
Length of book reviews: 10,000 characters
Length of notes: 5,000 characters
Style: Times
Number of copies required: 1
Copyright ownership: Author
Time between decision and publication: 3 mos.
Articles published per year: 32
Book reviews published per year: 12
Notes published per year: 12

(2912)
*Tarbiz: A Quarterly for Jewish Studies

Warren Z. Harvey, Y. Kaplan, & I. Ta-Shma, Editors
Inst. of Jewish Studies
Hebrew Univ.
91905 Jerusalem, Israel

First published: 1930
Sponsoring organization: Hebrew Univ.
ISSN: 0334-3650
MLA acronym: Tarbiz

SUBSCRIPTION INFORMATION

Frequency of publication: 4 times/yr. (Oct., Mar., June, Sept.)
Circulation: 1,500
Available in microform: No
Subscription address: Magnes Press, Hebrew Univ., 91076 Jerusalem, Israel
Subscription telephone: (972) 2 660341
Subscription fax: (972) 2 666804

ADVERTISING INFORMATION

Advertising accepted: No

EDITORIAL DESCRIPTION

Scope: Publishes articles on Judaica.
Reviews books: Yes
Publishes notes: Yes
Languages accepted: Hebrew
Prints abstracts: Yes
Author-anonymous submission: No

SUBMISSION REQUIREMENTS

Author pays submission fee: No
Author pays page charges: No
Number of copies required: 2 paper copies and 1 diskette
Special requirements: Manuscript should be submitted on IBM-compatible diskette.
Copyright ownership: Magnes Press
Rejected manuscripts: Not returned
Time before publication decision: 3 mos.
Time between decision and publication: 12-18 mos.
Articles submitted per year: 75
Articles published per year: 25
Book reviews submitted per year: 15
Book reviews published per year: 6
Notes submitted per year: 30
Notes published per year: 20

(2913)
*Target: International Journal of Translation Studies

Gideon Toury & José Lambert, Editors
M. Bernstein Chair of Translation Theory
Tel Aviv Univ.
P.O. Box 39085
Tel Aviv 69 978, Israel

Additional editorial address: J. Lambert, Dept. of Literary Theory - KU Leuven, Blijde Inkomststraat 21, 3000 Leuven, Belgium
Telephone: (972) 3 6422141
Fax: (972) 3 6408980
E-mail: TOURY@TAUNIVM
First published: 1989
ISSN: 0924-1881
MLA acronym: Target

SUBSCRIPTION INFORMATION

Frequency of publication: 2 times/yr.
Available in microform: No
Subscription price: 136 f ($82.00)/yr. institutions
Year to which price refers: 1991
Subscription address: John Benjamins Publishing Co., P.O. Box 75577, Amsteldijk 44, 1070 AN Amsterdam, Netherlands
Additional subscription address: John Benjamins North America, Inc., 821 Bethlehem Pike, Philadelphia, PA 19118
Subscription telephone: (31) 20 6738156; 215 836-1200
Subscription fax: (32) 20 6739773; 215 836-1204

ADVERTISING INFORMATION

Advertising accepted: No

EDITORIAL DESCRIPTION

Scope: Focuses on the interrelationships between the position of translating and translation in culture, the norms governing them, and the modes of performing translation processes under various circumstances.
Reviews books: Yes
Publishes notes: No
Languages accepted: English; French; German
Prints abstracts: Yes
Author-anonymous submission: No

SUBMISSION REQUIREMENTS

Restrictions on contributors: Most book reviews are solicited.
Author pays submission fee: No
Author pays page charges: No
Length of articles: 4,000-8,000 words
Length of book reviews: 800-1,500 words
Style: Journal
Number of copies required: 3
Special requirements: Manuscripts must be previously unpublished and not be under consideration elsewhere. Submit double-spaced typescript with wide margins. Notes, references, figures, and tables should be presented on separate sheets. Style sheet available from editors. Submission on IBM-compatible diskette is encouraged.
Copyright ownership: John Benjamins Publishing Co.
Time before publication decision: 2-3 mos.
Time between decision and publication: 6-12 mos.
Number of reviewers: 2 minimum
Articles submitted per year: 30-40
Articles published per year: 10-12
Book reviews submitted per year: 15-20
Book reviews published per year: 12-15

(2914)
*TDR: The Drama Review: A Journal of Performance Studies

Richard Schechner, Editor
Tisch School of the Arts
New York Univ.
721 Broadway, Rm. 626
New York, NY 10003

Telephone: 212 998-1626
Fax: 212 995-4060
First published: 1955
Sponsoring organization: New York Univ., Tisch School of the Arts
ISSN: 0012-5962
MLA acronym: TDRev

SUBSCRIPTION INFORMATION

Frequency of publication: 4 times/yr.
Circulation: 5,000
Available in microform: Yes
Subscription price: $70.00/yr. institutions US; $90.00/yr. institutions Canada; $84.00/yr. institutions elsewhere; $30.00/yr. individuals US; $47.00/yr. individuals Canada; $44.00/yr. individuals elsewhere; $20.00/yr. students US; $37.00/yr. students Canada; $34.00/yr. students elsewhere
Year to which price refers: 1992
Subscription address: MIT Press Journals, 55 Hayward St., Cambridge, MA 02142-1399
Subscription telephone: 617 253-2864
Subscription fax: 617 258-6779

ADVERTISING INFORMATION

Advertising accepted: Yes

EDITORIAL DESCRIPTION

Scope: Publishes articles on all types of performance by scholars and practitioners worldwide. Covers theater, dance, performance art, folk and ritual performance, performance in everyday life, performance in sports, etc.
Reviews books: Yes
Publishes notes: Yes
Languages accepted: English
Prints abstracts: No
Author-anonymous submission: No

SUBMISSION REQUIREMENTS

Restrictions on contributors: None
Author pays submission fee: No
Author pays page charges: No
Length of articles: 25-30 typescript pp.
Length of book reviews: 5-10 pp.
Style: Chicago
Number of copies required: 1

Special requirements: Submit double-spaced typescript, and diskette using WordPerfect, if possible. Include author's address and social security number.
Copyright ownership: Journal
Rejected manuscripts: Returned; enclose SASE.
Time before publication decision: 1-2 mos.
Time between decision and publication: 3-6 mos.
Number of reviewers: 2-3
Articles submitted per year: 80
Articles published per year: 40
Book reviews submitted per year: 20
Book reviews published per year: 8

(2915)
*Te Reo: Journal of the Linguistic Society of New Zealand

Ray Harlow, Editor
Linguistic Soc. of New Zealand
Univ. of Waikato
Linguistics
Private Bag
Hamilton, New Zealand

E-mail: RAYHARLOW@WAIKATO.AC.NZ
First published: 1958
Sponsoring organization: Linguistic Soc. of New Zealand, Inc.
ISSN: 0494-8440
MLA acronym: Te Reo

SUBSCRIPTION INFORMATION

Frequency of publication: Annual
Circulation: 300
Available in microform: No
Subscription price: NZ$15.00/yr. New Zealand (includes membership); NZ$18.00/yr. elsewhere (includes membership)
Year to which price refers: 1991
Subscription address: Linguistic Soc. of New Zealand, Univ. of New Zealand, Romance Languages, Private Bag, New Zealand

ADVERTISING INFORMATION

Advertising accepted: Yes, on an exchange basis

EDITORIAL DESCRIPTION

Scope: Publishes articles on oceanic linguistics, general linguistics and studies of specific languages, such as Creoles and Pigdins. Occasionally publishes review articles.
Reviews books: Yes
Publishes notes: Yes
Languages accepted: English; French
Prints abstracts: No
Author-anonymous submission: No

SUBMISSION REQUIREMENTS

Restrictions on contributors: Preference given to articles submitted by members.
Author pays submission fee: No
Author pays page charges: No
Length of articles: 50 printed pp. maximum; longer articles are considered
Length of book reviews: 2,000 words
Length of notes: 2-3 pp.
Style: Journal; Linguistic Soc. of America
Number of copies required: 1
Special requirements: Submit double-spaced typescript with wide margins; use one side of paper only. Also submit 100-word abstract. If possible, supply submission in machine-readable form.
Copyright ownership: Linguistic Soc. of New Zealand, Inc.
Rejected manuscripts: Returned with comments
Time before publication decision: 2 mos.
Time between decision and publication: 8 mos.
Number of reviewers: 2
Articles submitted per year: 1-10
Articles published per year: 4-6
Book reviews submitted per year: 1-2

Book reviews published per year: 0-2
Notes submitted per year: 0-2
Notes published per year: 0-1

(2916)
Teanga: Bliainiris na Teangeolaíochta Feidhmí in Éirinn/The Yearbook of Applied Linguistics

Dónall P. Ó Baoill, Editor
I.T.É.
31 Fitzwilliam Place
Dublin 2, Ireland

First published: 1979
Historical variations in title: Formerly *Teanga: Iris Chumann na Teangeolaíochta Feidhmí/Journal of the Irish Association for Applied Linguistics*
Sponsoring organization: Irish Assn. for Applied Linguistics
ISSN: 0332-205X
MLA acronym: Teanga

SUBSCRIPTION INFORMATION

Frequency of publication: Annual (Summer)
Circulation: 150-200
Available in microform: No

ADVERTISING INFORMATION

Advertising accepted: No

EDITORIAL DESCRIPTION

Scope: Publishes articles on research and development in all areas of applied linguistics and the teaching of modern languages.
Reviews books: Yes
Publishes notes: No
Languages accepted: Irish Gaelic; English
Prints abstracts: No
Author-anonymous submission: No

SUBMISSION REQUIREMENTS

Restrictions on contributors: None
Author pays submission fee: No
Author pays page charges: No
Length of articles: 3,500-4,500 words
Length of book reviews: 700-1,000 words
Style: Journal
Number of copies required: 1
Special requirements: Submit camera-ready copy.
Copyright ownership: Irish Assn. for Applied Linguistics
Rejected manuscripts: Returned
Time before publication decision: 3-6 mos.
Time between decision and publication: 3-6 mos.
Number of reviewers: 3
Articles submitted per year: 5-10
Articles published per year: 5-9
Book reviews submitted per year: 3-5
Book reviews published per year: 3-5

(2917)
*Teangeolas

Íosold Ó Deirg, Editor
Linguistics Inst. of Ireland
31 Fitzwilliam Pl.
Dublin 2, Ireland

Telephone: (353) 1 765489
Fax: (353) 1 610004
First published: 1975
Sponsoring organization: Linguistics Inst. of Ireland
ISSN: 0332-0294
MLA acronym: Teangeolas

SUBSCRIPTION INFORMATION

Frequency of publication: 2 times/yr.
Available in microform: No

ADVERTISING INFORMATION

Advertising accepted: No

EDITORIAL DESCRIPTION

Scope: Publishes articles on linguistics, language learning, and teaching in Ireland.
Reviews books: Yes
Publishes notes: Yes
Languages accepted: English; Irish Gaelic; French
Prints abstracts: No
Author-anonymous submission: No

SUBMISSION REQUIREMENTS

Author pays submission fee: No
Author pays page charges: No
Length of articles: 5,000 words
Length of book reviews: 3,000 words
Length of notes: 3,000 words
Number of copies required: 2
Copyright ownership: Journal
Rejected manuscripts: Returned
Time before publication decision: 1-2 mo.
Time between decision and publication: 1-2 mos.
Number of reviewers: 2
Articles published per year: 8
Book reviews submitted per year: 3-5
Book reviews published per year: 3-5
Notes submitted per year: 1-2
Notes published per year: 1-2

(2918)
*Teatro del Siglo de Oro: Ediciones Críticas

Kurt Reichenberger & Roswitha Reichenberger, Editors
Edition Reichenberger
Pfannkuchstr. 4
3500 Kassel, Germany

Telephone: (49) 561 775204
First published: 1982
MLA acronym: TSO

SUBSCRIPTION INFORMATION

Frequency of publication: 1-2 times/yr.
Circulation: 2,000
Available in microform: No

ADVERTISING INFORMATION

Advertising accepted: No

EDITORIAL DESCRIPTION

Scope: Series publishes critical editions of Spanish *comedias* or *auto sacramentales*.
Reviews books: No
Publishes notes: No
Languages accepted: English; Spanish; French
Prints abstracts: No
Author-anonymous submission: No

SUBMISSION REQUIREMENTS

Restrictions on contributors: None
Author pays submission fee: No
Author pays page charges: No
Length of books: 100,000 words
Style: Series; MLA
Number of copies required: 1
Special requirements: Submission of typescript and Macintosh-compatible diskette using Microsoft Word is preferred. Authors should attempt to secure subsidy from their universities for printing costs.
Copyright ownership: Edition Reichenberger

Rejected manuscripts: Returned
Time before publication decision: 2 mos.
Time between decision and publication: 10-12 mos.
Number of reviewers: 2
Books submitted per year: 4-5
Books published per year: 3-4

(2919)
*Teatro del Siglo de Oro: Estudios de Literatura

Kurt Reichenberger & Roswitha Reichenberger, Editors
Edition Reichenberger
Pfannkuchstr. 4
3500 Kassel, Germany

Telephone: (49) 561 775204
First published: 1984
MLA acronym: TSOL

SUBSCRIPTION INFORMATION

Frequency of publication: Irregular
Circulation: 200
Available in microform: No

ADVERTISING INFORMATION

Advertising accepted: No

EDITORIAL DESCRIPTION

Scope: Publishes monographs on Spanish theater of the 16th-18th centuries.
Reviews books: No
Publishes notes: No
Languages accepted: Spanish; English
Prints abstracts: No
Author-anonymous submission: No

SUBMISSION REQUIREMENTS

Restrictions on contributors: None
Author pays submission fee: No
Author pays page charges: No
Length of books: 100,000 words
Style: Series; MLA
Number of copies required: 1
Special requirements: Submit typescript and Macintosh-compatible diskette using Microsoft Word. Authors should attempt to secure subsidy from their universities for printing costs.
Copyright ownership: Editor
Rejected manuscripts: Returned
Time before publication decision: 1-2 mos.
Time between decision and publication: 8-12 mos.
Number of reviewers: 2
Books submitted per year: 4-5
Books published per year: 3-4

(2920)
*Technische Universität Berlin Arbeitspapiere zur Linguistik/ Working Papers in Linguistics

Manfred Kohrt & Klaus Robering, Editors
Technische Univ. Berlin
Inst. für Linguistik
Ernst Reuter Platz 7 (TEL 6)
1000 Berlin 10, Germany

First published: 1978
Sponsoring organization: Technische Univ. Berlin, Inst. für Linguistik
ISSN: 0343-8694
MLA acronym: TUBWPL

SUBSCRIPTION INFORMATION

Frequency of publication: Irregular (2 times/yr.)
Circulation: Varies
Available in microform: No

Subscription address: Universitätsbibliothek der Technischen Univ. Berlin, Abt. Publikationen, Str. des 17 Juni 135, 1000 Berlin 12, Germany

ADVERTISING INFORMATION

Advertising accepted: No

EDITORIAL DESCRIPTION

Scope: Series publishes reports on work in progress by members of the Institut für Linguistik at the Technische Universität, Berlin.
Reviews books: No
Publishes notes: No
Languages accepted: English; French; German
Prints abstracts: No

SUBMISSION REQUIREMENTS

Restrictions on contributors: Contributors must be members of Technische Univ. Berlin, Inst. für Linguistik; unsolicited manuscripts are not accepted.
Author pays submission fee: No
Author pays page charges: No
Style: None
Number of copies required: 1
Special requirements: Pages must be numbered on verso.
Copyright ownership: Technische Univ. Berlin
Time before publication decision: 2 mos.
Time between decision and publication: 6 mos.

(2921)
Teksty Drugie: Teoria Literatury—Krytyka—Interpretacja

Ryszard Nycz, Editor
Pałac Staszica, pokój 128
Nowy Świat 72
00-330 Warsaw, Poland

Telephone: (48) 22 265231 ext. 101
First published: 1990
Sponsoring organization: Inst. Badań Literackich, Polska Akademia Nauk
ISSN: 0867-0633
MLA acronym: TekstyD

SUBSCRIPTION INFORMATION

Frequency of publication: 6 times/yr.
Available in microform: No
Subscription price: $36.00/yr.
Year to which price refers: 1991

ADVERTISING INFORMATION

Advertising accepted: Yes, on an exchange basis

EDITORIAL DESCRIPTION

Scope: Publishes articles on literary criticism, theory and interpretation.
Reviews books: Yes
Publishes notes: No
Languages accepted: Polish
Prints abstracts: No
Author-anonymous submission: No

SUBMISSION REQUIREMENTS

Restrictions on contributors: None
Author pays submission fee: Yes
Length of articles: 10-15 pp.
Length of book reviews: 5 pp.
Style: MLA
Number of copies required: 1
Copyright ownership: Journal or Author
Rejected manuscripts: Returned at author's request
Time before publication decision: 2 mos.
Time between decision and publication: 2 mos.
Number of reviewers: 3-5
Articles submitted per year: 200

Articles published per year: 60
Book reviews submitted per year: 100
Book reviews published per year: 30

(2922)
Temenos: Studies in Comparative Religion Presented by Scholars in Denmark, Finland, Norway and Sweden

Lauri Honko, Editor
Inst. of Folklore & Comparative Religion
Univ. of Turku
Henrikinkatu 3
20500 Turku 50, Finland

First published: 1965
Sponsoring organization: Finnish Soc. for the Study of Comparative Religion
ISSN: 0497-1817
MLA acronym: Temenos

SUBSCRIPTION INFORMATION

Frequency of publication: Annual
Circulation: 500
Available in microform: No
Subscription address: Academic Bookstore, Keskuskatu 1, 00100 Helsinki 10, Finland

ADVERTISING INFORMATION

Advertising accepted: No

EDITORIAL DESCRIPTION

Scope: Publishes articles on comparative religion and related disciplines.
Reviews books: Yes
Publishes notes: Yes
Languages accepted: English; French; German
Prints abstracts: No

SUBMISSION REQUIREMENTS

Restrictions on contributors: Only one contribution from outside Nordic countries is accepted each year.
Author pays submission fee: No
Author pays page charges: No
Length of articles: 3,600-9,000 words
Length of book reviews: 500-1,500 words
Style: None
Number of copies required: 1
Special requirements: Submit original typescript. Notes should be typed with full references; do not submit separate bibliography.
Copyright ownership: Finnish Soc. for the Study of Comparative Religion
Rejected manuscripts: Returned
Time before publication decision: 2-5 mos.
Time between decision and publication: 1 yr.
Number of reviewers: 2
Articles submitted per year: 15-20
Articles published per year: 8-12
Book reviews submitted per year: 10-30
Book reviews published per year: 10-30

(2923)
Temps Modernes

26, rue de Conde
75006 Paris, France

First published: 1945
Sponsoring organization: Presses d'Aujourd'hui
ISSN: 0040-3075
MLA acronym: TM

SUBSCRIPTION INFORMATION

Frequency of publication: 12 times/yr.
Circulation: 11,000

EDITORIAL DESCRIPTION

Reviews books: No
Languages accepted: French
Prints abstracts: No

SUBMISSION REQUIREMENTS

Restrictions on contributors: None
Length of articles: 15-40 pp.
Style: MLA
Number of copies required: 1
Copyright ownership: Assigned by author to journal
Rejected manuscripts: Returned
Time before publication decision: 3 mos.
Time between decision and publication: 1-6 mos.
Number of reviewers: 3
Articles published per year: 100-150

(2924)
*Tennessee Folklore Society Bulletin

Charles K. Wolfe & Guy Anderson, Editors
Tennessee Folklore Soc.
Middle Tennessee State Univ.
Box 201
Murfreesboro, TN 37132

Telephone: 615 898-2576
First published: 1935
Sponsoring organization: Tennessee Folklore Soc.
ISSN: 0040-3253
MLA acronym: TFSB

SUBSCRIPTION INFORMATION

Frequency of publication: 3 times/yr. (Mar., June, Sept.)
Circulation: 400
Available in microform: Yes
Subscription price: $12.00/yr. institutions; $10.00/yr. individuals
Year to which price refers: 1992
Subscription address: Guy Anderson, Dept. of English, Middle Tennessee State Univ., Murfreesboro, TN 37132

ADVERTISING INFORMATION

Advertising accepted: No

EDITORIAL DESCRIPTION

Scope: Documents folk life, folk arts, and folk culture, as well as aspects of literature and language that relate to folk culture, of the mid-South and of Tennessee. This goal encompasses articles on literature and folklore, interpretative and theoretical essays about the nature of folk arts and folk culture, and the presentation of transcriptions, ballads, and other source material. Special interest is given to articles on applied folklore, accounts of research or presentation projects in the field, and accounts of services to the field.
Reviews books: Yes
Publishes notes: Yes
Languages accepted: English
Prints abstracts: Yes
Author-anonymous submission: No

SUBMISSION REQUIREMENTS

Restrictions on contributors: None
Author pays submission fee: No
Author pays page charges: No
Length of articles: 750-3,500 words
Length of book reviews: 250-1,500 words
Length of notes: 250-750 words
Style: MLA
Number of copies required: 1
Special requirements: None
Copyright ownership: Tennessee Folklore Soc.
Rejected manuscripts: Returned
Time before publication decision: 2 mos.
Time between decision and publication: 2 mos.

Number of reviewers: 2
Articles submitted per year: 30-40
Articles published per year: 20
Book reviews submitted per year: 12-15
Book reviews published per year: 12
Notes submitted per year: 10-12
Notes published per year: 8-9

(2925)
*Tennessee Philological Bulletin: Proceedings of the Annual Meeting of the Tennessee Philological Association

Sally B. Young, Editor
Dept. of English
Univ. of Tennessee at Chattanooga
Chattanooga, TN 37403

Telephone: 615 755-4621
First published: 1964
Sponsoring organization: Tennessee Philological Assn.
ISSN: 0735-0783
MLA acronym: TPB

SUBSCRIPTION INFORMATION

Frequency of publication: Annual
Circulation: 200
Available in microform: No
Subscription price: $7.00/yr.
Year to which price refers: 1992

ADVERTISING INFORMATION

Advertising accepted: No

EDITORIAL DESCRIPTION

Scope: Publishes articles on modern and classical languages and literatures. Publishes proceedings of annual meeting of the Tennessee Philological Assn.
Reviews books: No
Publishes notes: No
Languages accepted: English
Prints abstracts: Yes
Author-anonymous submission: Yes

SUBMISSION REQUIREMENTS

Restrictions on contributors: Contributors must be members of the Tennessee Philological Assn. Cost of reading paper at annual meeting is $25.00.
Author pays submission fee: No
Author pays page charges: No
Length of articles: 2,500 words
Style: MLA
Number of copies required: 3
Special requirements: Submit original typescript and 2 copies along with a 300-word abstract.
Copyright ownership: Journal
Rejected manuscripts: Returned; enclose return postage.
Time before publication decision: 3 mos.
Time between decision and publication: 6 mos.
Number of reviewers: 4
Articles submitted per year: 13-15
Articles published per year: 4-7

(2926)
*Tennessee Studies in Literature

Dept. of English
Univ. of Tennessee
Knoxville, TN 37996

Telephone: 615 974-5401
First published: 1956
Sponsoring organization: Dept. of English, Univ. of Tennessee, Knoxville
ISSN: 0497-2384
MLA acronym: TStL

SUBSCRIPTION INFORMATION

Frequency of publication: Annual
Circulation: 600
Available in microform: No
Subscription address: Univ. of Tennessee Press, 293 Communications Bldg., University Station, Knoxville, TN 37996

ADVERTISING INFORMATION

Advertising accepted: No

EDITORIAL DESCRIPTION

Scope: Publishes collections on literature. Each volume focuses on a particular literary topic.
Reviews books: No
Publishes notes: No
Languages accepted: English
Prints abstracts: No
Author-anonymous submission: No

SUBMISSION REQUIREMENTS

Restrictions on contributors: Articles are generally commissioned.
Author pays submission fee: No
Author pays page charges: No
Length of articles: 5,000 words maximum
Style: MLA
Number of copies required: 1
Copyright ownership: Univ. of Tennessee Press
Rejected manuscripts: Returned; enclose return postage.
Number of reviewers: 2-3

(2927)
*The Tennyson Research Bulletin

Marion Shaw, Editor
Dept. of English
The University
Hull HU6 7RX, England

First published: 1967
Sponsoring organization: Tennyson Soc.
ISSN: 0082-2841
MLA acronym: TRB

SUBSCRIPTION INFORMATION

Frequency of publication: Annual (Nov.)
Circulation: 500
Available in microform: No
Subscription price: £12.00/yr. institutions; £6.00/yr. individuals
Year to which price refers: 1992
Subscription address: Honorary Secretary, Tennyson Soc., Central Library, Free School Lane, Lincoln LN2 1EZ, England

ADVERTISING INFORMATION

Advertising accepted: Yes

EDITORIAL DESCRIPTION

Scope: Publishes new material on Tennyson, his life, his work, and his contemporaries.
Reviews books: Yes
Publishes notes: Yes
Languages accepted: English
Prints abstracts: No
Author-anonymous submission: No

SUBMISSION REQUIREMENTS

Restrictions on contributors: Reviews are commissioned.
Author pays submission fee: No
Author pays page charges: No
Length of articles: 5,000 words maximum
Length of book reviews: 2,000 words maximum
Length of notes: 750 words maximum
Style: Chicago
Number of copies required: 2
Copyright ownership: Author
Rejected manuscripts: Returned

Time before publication decision: 3 mos.
Time between decision and publication: 1 yr.
Number of reviewers: 3 maximum
Articles submitted per year: 20-25
Articles published per year: 5-6
Book reviews published per year: 2-5
Notes submitted per year: 5-10
Notes published per year: 1-5

(2928)
*Tennyson Society Monographs

Marion Shaw, Editor
Tennyson Soc.
Central Library
Free School Lane
Lincoln LN2 1E2, England

Telephone: (44) 522 552866
Fax: (44) 522 552858
Sponsoring organization: Tennyson Soc.
ISSN: 0082-285X
MLA acronym: TSMon

SUBSCRIPTION INFORMATION

Frequency of publication: Irregular
Available in microform: No
Subscription price: £12.00/yr. institutions; £6.00/yr. individuals
Year to which price refers: 1992
Subscription address: Honarary Secretary, at the above address

ADVERTISING INFORMATION

Advertising accepted: No

EDITORIAL DESCRIPTION

Scope: Publishes new material on Tennyson, his life, work, and contemporaries.
Reviews books: No
Publishes notes: No
Languages accepted: English
Prints abstracts: No
Author-anonymous submission: Yes

SUBMISSION REQUIREMENTS

Author pays submission fee: No
Author pays page charges: No
Length of articles: 7,000 words maximum
Style: Chicago
Number of copies required: 2
Copyright ownership: Author
Rejected manuscripts: Returned
Time before publication decision: 6 mos.
Time between decision and publication: 1-2 yrs.
Number of reviewers: 2-3

(2929)
*TENSO: Bulletin of the Societe Guilhem IX

Wendy Pfeffer, Editor
Classical & Modern Languages
Univ. of Louisville
Louisville, KY 40292

Telephone: 502 588-0493
Fax: 502 588-8885
First published: 1986
Sponsoring organization: Soc. Guilhem IX
ISSN: 0890-3352
MLA acronym: TENSO

SUBSCRIPTION INFORMATION

Frequency of publication: 2 times/yr. (Fall, Spring)
Available in microform: No
Subscription price: $15.00/yr. institutions; $10.00/yr. individuals; $5.00/yr. students; add $2.00/yr. postage outside US

Subscription address: E. W. Poe, Dept. of French & Italian, Tulane Univ., New Orleans, LA 70118

ADVERTISING INFORMATION

Advertising accepted: No

EDITORIAL DESCRIPTION

Scope: Publishes articles on any aspect of Occitan (Provençal, Langue d'Oc) studies, including literature, language, and linguistics of the medieval and modern periods.
Reviews books: Yes
Publishes notes: Yes
Languages accepted: English; French; Occitan; Catalan; Spanish; Italian; German
Author-anonymous submission: Yes

SUBMISSION REQUIREMENTS

Restrictions on contributors: None
Author pays submission fee: No
Author pays page charges: No
Length of articles: 5,000 words maximum
Length of book reviews: 1,000 words
Style: MLA
Number of copies required: 2
Special requirements: Submit double-spaced typescript, including notes and quotations. Please allow ample margins (1 in. at top and right, 1.5 in. at left and bottom)
Rejected manuscripts: Returned at author's request; enclose SASE.
Time before publication decision: 9 mos.
Time between decision and publication: 9 mos.
Number of reviewers: 2
Articles published per year: 6
Book reviews published per year: 8

(2930)
*Teología Espiritual

Esteban Pérez Delgado, Director
Fac. de Teología San Vicente Ferrer
Sección Dominicos
Pouet de Sant Vicent, 1
46003 Valencia, Spain

Additional editorial address: Apdo. 136, 46900 Torrente, Spain
First published: 1957
Sponsoring organization: Fac. de Teología de Valencia, Sección Dominicos
ISSN: 0495-1549
MLA acronym: TE

SUBSCRIPTION INFORMATION

Frequency of publication: 3 times/yr.
Circulation: 8,500
Available in microform: No

ADVERTISING INFORMATION

Advertising accepted: Yes

EDITORIAL DESCRIPTION

Scope: Focuses on the study and promulgation of authentic Christian spirituality.
Reviews books: Yes
Publishes notes: Yes
Languages accepted: Spanish
Prints abstracts: Yes

SUBMISSION REQUIREMENTS

Author pays submission fee: No
Author pays page charges: No
Length of articles: 25-30 printed pp.
Length of book reviews: 1/2 p.
Length of notes: Varies
Style: Scientific-theological
Number of copies required: 1
Special requirements: Submit typescript.
Copyright ownership: Journal
Rejected manuscripts: Returned

Time before publication decision: 2 weeks
Number of reviewers: 3
Articles submitted per year: 30
Articles published per year: 30
Book reviews submitted per year: 60-70
Book reviews published per year: 60-70
Notes submitted per year: 6
Notes published per year: 6

(2931)
*Teoría Literária: Texto y Teoría

Iris M. Zavala, Editor
Editions Rodopi B.V.
Keizersgracht 302-304
1016 EX Amsterdam, Netherlands

First published: 1987
ISSN: 0921-2523
MLA acronym: TLit

SUBSCRIPTION INFORMATION

Frequency of publication: Irregular
Circulation: 600
Available in microform: No
Additional subscription address: In N. America: Editions Rodopi, 233 Peachtree St. N.E., Suite 404, Atlanta, GA 30303-1504
Subscription telephone: (31) 20 6227507; 404 523-1964; 800 225-3998
Subscription fax: (31) 20 6380948; 404 522-7116

ADVERTISING INFORMATION

Advertising accepted: No

EDITORIAL DESCRIPTION

Scope: Publishes monographs of critical studies which raise fundamental questions about the status of the literary text and different types of discourse.
Reviews books: No
Publishes notes: No
Languages accepted: Spanish
Prints abstracts: No
Author-anonymous submission: No

SUBMISSION REQUIREMENTS

Author pays submission fee: No
Author pays page charges: No
Length of books: 250-300 pp.
Style: MLA; Chicago
Special requirements: Submit typescript and diskette.
Copyright ownership: Editions Rodopi B.V.
Time before publication decision: 10-12 mos.
Time between decision and publication: 10-12 mos.
Number of reviewers: 2
Books submitted per year: 4-5
Books published per year: 2-3

(2932)
*TESOL Quarterly

Sandra Silberstein, Editor
English, GN-30
Univ. of Washington
Seattle, WA 98195

Additional editorial address: Heidi Riggenbach, Reviews Editor, at the above address
Telephone: 206 543-7993
Fax: 206 543-5331
First published: 1966
Sponsoring organization: Teachers of English to Speakers of Other Languages (TESOL)
ISSN: 0039-8322
MLA acronym: TESOLQ

SUBSCRIPTION INFORMATION

Frequency of publication: 4 times/yr. (Spring, Summer, Autumn, Winter)
Circulation: 22,000
Available in microform: Yes
Subscription address: TESOL, 1600 Cameron St., Suite 300, Alexandria, VA 22314

ADVERTISING INFORMATION

Advertising accepted: Yes

EDITORIAL DESCRIPTION

Scope: Encourages submission of previously unpublished articles on topics of significance to teachers of English as a second or foreign language or of standard English as a second dialect. Manuscripts are invited in the following areas: (1)psychology and sociology of language learning and teaching; (2)curriculum design and development; (3)testing and evaluation; (4)professional preparation; (5)language planning; and (6)professional standards.
Reviews books: Yes
Publishes notes: Yes
Languages accepted: English
Prints abstracts: Yes
Author-anonymous submission: Yes

SUBMISSION REQUIREMENTS

Restrictions on contributors: None
Author pays submission fee: No
Author pays page charges: No
Length of articles: 20 pp. maximum
Length of book reviews: 1,250 words
Length of notes: 350-500 words
Style: American Psychological Assn.
Number of copies required: 3
Special requirements: Include an abstract (200 words maximum).
Copyright ownership: Journal
Rejected manuscripts: Filed in TESOL archives
Time before publication decision: 4 mos.
Time between decision and publication: 9 mos.
Number of reviewers: 3
Articles submitted per year: 225-250
Articles published per year: 24
Book reviews submitted per year: 25
Book reviews published per year: 9
Notes submitted per year: 80
Notes published per year: 40

(2933)
*Tessera

Barbara Godard, Managing Editor
350 Stong
York Univ.
4700 Keele St.
North York, ON M35 1P3, Canada

Telephone: 416 736-5166; 416 929-5919
Fax: 416 736-5735
First published: 1984
Sponsoring organization: Ontario Arts Council; Canada Council; York Univ.
ISSN: 0840-4631
MLA acronym: Tessera

SUBSCRIPTION INFORMATION

Frequency of publication: 2 times/yr.
Circulation: 400
Available in microform: No
Subscription price: C$20.00/yr. institutions; C$18.00/yr. individuals; add C$4.00/yr. postage outside Canada
Year to which price refers: 1992

ADVERTISING INFORMATION

Advertising accepted: No

EDITORIAL DESCRIPTION

Scope: Publishes articles on feminist literary theory with a focus on Canadian/Quebec women writers and experimental writing.
Reviews books: No
Publishes notes: No
Languages accepted: English; French
Prints abstracts: Yes
Author-anonymous submission: No

SUBMISSION REQUIREMENTS

Restrictions on contributors: Contributors must be women. Preference is given to Canadian writers.
Author pays submission fee: No
Author pays page charges: No
Style: MLA preferred
Number of copies required: 1
Copyright ownership: Author
Rejected manuscripts: Returned
Time before publication decision: 3 mos.
Time between decision and publication: 4 mos.
Number of reviewers: 5
Articles submitted per year: 50
Articles published per year: 20

(2934)
*Testi e Discorsi: Strumenti Linguistici e Letterari

Guy Aston, William Dodd, Roberta Mullini, Paola Pugliatti, & Romana Zacchi, Editors
Cooperativa Libraria Universitaria Editrice Bologna
via Marsala, 24
40126 Bologna, Italy

Telephone: (39) 51 220736
Fax: (39) 51 237758
First published: 1983
MLA acronym: T&D

SUBSCRIPTION INFORMATION

Frequency of publication: Irregular
Available in microform: No

ADVERTISING INFORMATION

Advertising accepted: No

EDITORIAL DESCRIPTION

Scope: Publishes monograph studies of literature and linguistics with an emphasis on literary theory, English literature, and applied and contrastive linguistics.
Reviews books: No
Publishes notes: No
Languages accepted: Italian; English
Prints abstracts: No
Author-anonymous submission: No

SUBMISSION REQUIREMENTS

Author pays submission fee: No
Number of copies required: 2
Special requirements: Submit camera-ready copy or diskette.
Copyright ownership: Publisher
Rejected manuscripts: Returned
Number of reviewers: 2

(2935)
*Texas Pan American Series

Univ. of Texas Press
P.O. Box 7819
Austin, TX 78713-7819

First published: 1962
MLA acronym: TPAS

SUBSCRIPTION INFORMATION

Frequency of publication: Irregular
Available in microform: Yes, through Univ. Microfilms International

ADVERTISING INFORMATION

Advertising accepted: No

EDITORIAL DESCRIPTION

Scope: Publishes monograph series on Latin American literature and English translations of Latin American literature.
Languages accepted: English
Prints abstracts: No
Author-anonymous submission: No

SUBMISSION REQUIREMENTS

Author pays submission fee: No
Author pays page charges: No
Length of books: No restrictions
Style: Chicago suggested
Number of copies required: 1
Special requirements: Submit original typescript.
Copyright ownership: Univ. of Texas Press
Rejected manuscripts: Returned
Time before publication decision: 3-6 mos.
Time between decision and publication: 18 mos.
Number of reviewers: 2

(2936)
*The Texas Review

Paul Ruffin & Donald Coers, Editors
Dept. of English
Sam Houston State Univ.
Huntsville, TX 77341

First published: 1979
Sponsoring organization: Dept. of English, Sam Houston State Univ.
ISSN: 0885-2685
MLA acronym: TexasR

SUBSCRIPTION INFORMATION

Frequency of publication: 2 times/yr.
Circulation: 500
Available in microform: No
Subscription price: $10.00/yr.
Year to which price refers: 1992

ADVERTISING INFORMATION

Advertising accepted: Yes

EDITORIAL DESCRIPTION

Scope: Publishes poetry, fiction, criticism, reviews, and interviews.
Reviews books: Yes
Publishes notes: Yes
Languages accepted: English
Prints abstracts: No
Author-anonymous submission: No

SUBMISSION REQUIREMENTS

Restrictions on contributors: None
Author pays submission fee: No
Author pays page charges: No
Length of articles: 10,000 words
Length of book reviews: 500-1,000 words
Length of notes: 1,500 words
Style: MLA
Number of copies required: 1
Copyright ownership: Journal
Rejected manuscripts: Returned
Time before publication decision: 3 mos.
Time between decision and publication: 6-12 mos.
Number of reviewers: 5
Articles submitted per year: 100
Articles published per year: 6
Book reviews submitted per year: 50
Book reviews published per year: 20

(2937)
*Texas Studies in Literature and Language

Anthony Hilfer, Editor
Dept. of English
Parlin Hall
Univ. of Texas
Austin, TX 78712-1164

Telephone: 512 471-8354
First published: 1911
Sponsoring organization: Dept. of English, Univ. of Texas
ISSN: 0040-4691
MLA acronym: TSLL

SUBSCRIPTION INFORMATION

Frequency of publication: 4 times/yr. (Spring, Summer, Fall, Winter)
Circulation: 1,000
Available in microform: Yes
Subscription price: $37.00/yr. institutions; $23.00/yr. individuals
Year to which price refers: 1991
Subscription address: P.O. Box 7819, Austin, TX 78713
Subscription telephone: 512 471-4278

ADVERTISING INFORMATION

Advertising accepted: Yes

EDITORIAL DESCRIPTION

Scope: Invites contributions of significance in all areas of literature and in American studies. Publishes review essays.
Reviews books: Yes
Publishes notes: No
Languages accepted: English
Prints abstracts: No
Author-anonymous submission: Yes, at author's request

SUBMISSION REQUIREMENTS

Restrictions on contributors: None
Author pays submission fee: No
Author pays page charges: No
Length of articles: 10,000-50,000 words
Length of book reviews: 17 pp.
Style: Chicago
Number of copies required: 1
Special requirements: If photocopy is submitted, author must state whether other journals are considering the essay.
Copyright ownership: Univ. of Texas Press
Rejected manuscripts: Returned; enclose SASE.
Time before publication decision: 2-4 mos.
Time between decision and publication: 6-12 mos.
Number of reviewers: 3-5
Articles submitted per year: 500
Articles published per year: 32
Book reviews published per year: 2-4 review essays

(2938)
*Text: Transactions of the Society for Textual Scholarship

D. C. Greetham, W. Speed Hill, & Peter L. Shillingsburg, Editors
Ph.D. Program in English
Graduate Center
City Univ. of New York
33 West 42 St.
New York, NY 10036

Telephone: 212 642-2227; 212 873-2442
First published: 1984
Sponsoring organization: Soc. for Textual Scholarship
ISSN: 0736-3974
MLA acronym: Text

SUBSCRIPTION INFORMATION

Frequency of publication: Annual
Circulation: 500
Available in microform: No
Subscription price: $45.00/yr. institutions & nonmembers; $22.50/yr. members
Year to which price refers: 1991
Subscription address: Institutions & nonmembers contact: AMS Press, Inc., 56 E. 13th St., New York, NY 10003
Additional subscription address: Members should contact Soc. for Textual Scholarship at the editional address

ADVERTISING INFORMATION

Advertising accepted: No

EDITORIAL DESCRIPTION

Scope: Publishes articles on textual theories and problems in all disciplines. Provides a forum for the interdisciplinary exchange of textual theory and practice in any field involving the enumeration, accessioning, description, analysis, transmission, editing, and annotating of texts. Articles emphasizing a strong theoretical component with an application to several disciplines are particularly encouraged, but empirical studies of specific textual projects or problems are also published.
Reviews books: Yes
Publishes notes: Yes
Languages accepted: English
Prints abstracts: No
Author-anonymous submission: No

SUBMISSION REQUIREMENTS

Restrictions on contributors: None
Author pays submission fee: No
Author pays page charges: No
Length of articles: No restrictions
Length of book reviews: No restrictions
Length of notes: No restrictions
Style: MLA; Chicago; individual discipline style
Number of copies required: 3
Copyright ownership: AMS Press
Rejected manuscripts: Returned
Time before publication decision: 1-2 mos.
Time between decision and publication: 12-18 mos.
Number of reviewers: 2-3
Articles submitted per year: 40-50
Articles published per year: 25-30
Book reviews published per year: 5-10

(2939)
Text & Context: A Journal of Interdisciplinary Studies

Alun Munslow, David Cairns, & Shaun Richards, Editors
Dept. of Humanities
Staffordshire Polytechnic
Beaconside, Stafford ST18 0AD, England

First published: 1986
Sponsoring organization: Staffordshire Polytechnic
ISSN: 0950-5865
MLA acronym: T&C

SUBSCRIPTION INFORMATION

Frequency of publication: Annual
Circulation: 150-200
Available in microform: No
Subscription price: £4.00/yr.
Year to which price refers: 1991

ADVERTISING INFORMATION

Advertising accepted: Yes
Advertising rates: £50.00/half page; £100.00/full page

EDITORIAL DESCRIPTION

Scope: Publishes articles which explore literature and history as cultural practices.
Reviews books: Yes
Publishes notes: Yes
Languages accepted: English
Prints abstracts: No
Author-anonymous submission: Yes

SUBMISSION REQUIREMENTS

Restrictions on contributors: None
Author pays submission fee: No
Author pays page charges: No
Length of articles: 5,000 words
Length of book reviews: 500 words
Style: MLA
Number of copies required: 2
Copyright ownership: Staffordshire Polytechnic
Rejected manuscripts: Returned
Time before publication decision: 3 mos.
Time between decision and publication: 1 yr. maximum
Number of reviewers: 3
Articles submitted per year: 20
Articles published per year: 4-5
Book reviews submitted per year: 30
Book reviews published per year: 12-15

(2940)
*Text and Performance Quarterly

Kristin M. Langellier, Editor
Univ. of Maine
315 Stevens Hall
Orono, ME 04469

Telephone: 207 581-1942
First published: 1989
Sponsoring organization: Speech Communication Assn.
ISSN: 1046-2937
MLA acronym: TPQ

SUBSCRIPTION INFORMATION

Frequency of publication: 4 times/yr. (Jan., Apr., July, Oct.)
Circulation: 2,300
Available in microform: Yes
Subscription price: $90.00/yr. institutions US; $96.00/yr. institutions elsewhere; $75.00/yr. individuals; $25.00/yr. students
Year to which price refers: 1992
Subscription address: Speech Communication Assn., 5105 Backlick Rd., Bldg. E, Annandale, VA 22003
Subscription telephone: 703 750-0533
Subscription fax: 703 941-9471

ADVERTISING INFORMATION

Advertising accepted: Yes

EDITORIAL DESCRIPTION

Scope: Publishes communicative perspectives on texts and performances, including written and oral traditions. Analyzes the nexus of texts, performers, and audiences in social, cultural, and historical contexts. Includes theory, criticism, and empirical analyses.
Reviews books: Yes
Publishes notes: No
Languages accepted: English
Prints abstracts: Yes
Author-anonymous submission: Yes

SUBMISSION REQUIREMENTS

Restrictions on contributors: Book reviews are assigned.
Author pays submission fee: No
Author pays page charges: No
Length of articles: 8,000-12,000 words
Length of book reviews: No restrictions
Style: MLA, 3rd edition
Number of copies required: 4

Special requirements: Submit a 150-word abstract and the history of the manuscript.
Copyright ownership: Speech Communication Assn.
Rejected manuscripts: Not returned
Time before publication decision: 6-8 weeks
Time between decision and publication: 6 mos.
Number of reviewers: 3
Articles submitted per year: 70
Articles published per year: 16-20
Book reviews published per year: 40

(2941)
*Text & Presentation: The Journal of the Comparative Drama Conference

Karelisa V. Hartigan, Editor
Dept. of Classics/3-C Dauer
Univ. of Florida
Gainesville, FL 32611-2005

Telephone: 904 377-2178
Fax: 904 392-3584
E-mail: KVHRTGN@UFPINE
First published: 1982
Historical variations in title: Formerly *Comparative Drama Conference Papers*
Sponsoring organization: Dept. of Classics, Univ. of Florida
ISSN: 1054-724X
MLA acronym: T&P

SUBSCRIPTION INFORMATION

Frequency of publication: Annual
Circulation: 100
Available in microform: No
Subscription price: $20.00/yr.
Year to which price refers: 1992
Subscription address: Maupin House, P.O. Box 90148, Gainesville, FL 32607-0148
Subscription telephone: 904 373-5588

ADVERTISING INFORMATION

Advertising accepted: No

EDITORIAL DESCRIPTION

Scope: Publishes papers on drama and theater history presented at annual conference.
Reviews books: No
Publishes notes: No
Languages accepted: English
Prints abstracts: No
Author-anonymous submission: No

SUBMISSION REQUIREMENTS

Restrictions on contributors: Restricted to papers presented at annual conference. Purchase of 2 copies of book by author is considered payment of submission fee.
Author pays submission fee: No
Author pays page charges: No
Length of articles: 10 pp.
Style: MLA
Number of copies required: 2
Special requirements: Foreign language quotations must be translated in the notes. Submit camera-ready copy.
Copyright ownership: Comparative Drama Conference
Rejected manuscripts: Returned at author's request
Time before publication decision: 3 mos.
Time between decision and publication: 9 mos.
Number of reviewers: 2-3
Articles submitted per year: 30-35
Articles published per year: 15

(2942)
Text & Kontext

Klaus Bohnen & Sven-Aage Jørgensen, Editors
Njalsgade 80, 18-2-74
2300 Copenhagen S, Denmark

First published: 1973
Sponsoring organization: Nordiska Publiceringsnämnden för Humanistiska Tidskrifter; Københavns Univ.
ISSN: 0105-7014
MLA acronym: T&K

SUBSCRIPTION INFORMATION

Frequency of publication: 2 times/yr.
Available in microform: No
Subscription address: Wilhelm Fink Verlag, Ohmstr. 5, 8000 Munich 40, Germany

ADVERTISING INFORMATION

Advertising accepted: Yes

EDITORIAL DESCRIPTION

Scope: Publishes articles on German literary studies.
Reviews books: Yes
Publishes notes: Yes
Languages accepted: German
Prints abstracts: Yes

SUBMISSION REQUIREMENTS

Author pays submission fee: No
Author pays page charges: No
Length of articles: 15-20 pp.
Length of book reviews: 5-8 pp.
Length of notes: 1-2 pp.
Number of copies required: 1
Copyright ownership: Publisher & author
Rejected manuscripts: Returned
Time before publication decision: 6-12 mos.
Time between decision and publication: 3-6 mos.
Number of reviewers: 2
Articles published per year: 16-20
Book reviews published per year: 5-10

(2943)
*Text + Kritik: Zeitschrift für Literatur

Heinz Ludwig Arnold, Editor
Postfach 1264
3400 Göttingen, Germany

Telephone: (49) 551 53156
Fax: (49) 551 53156
First published: 1963
ISSN: 0040-5329
MLA acronym: TuK

SUBSCRIPTION INFORMATION

Frequency of publication: 4 times/yr.
Circulation: 5,000
Subscription address: Edition Text + Kritik GmbH, Postfach 800529, 8000 Munich 80, Germany
Subscription telephone: (49) 89 432929
Subscription fax: (49) 89 433997

ADVERTISING INFORMATION

Advertising accepted: Yes

EDITORIAL DESCRIPTION

Scope: Publishes literary monographs dedicated to an author of New German literature. Includes previously unpublished texts, interpretations, critical analysis, and extensive, mostly annotated, bibliographies.
Reviews books: No
Publishes notes: No
Languages accepted: German

Prints abstracts: No
Author-anonymous submission: No

SUBMISSION REQUIREMENTS

Restrictions on contributors: None
Author pays submission fee: No
Author pays page charges: No
Length of articles: 8-12 pp.
Style: High German
Number of copies required: 1
Copyright ownership: Journal & author
Rejected manuscripts: Returned
Time before publication decision: 3 mos.
Number of reviewers: 3
Articles submitted per year: 20-25
Articles published per year: 20-25

(2944)
Texte: Revue de Critique et de Théorie Littéraire

Brian T. Fitch & Andrew Oliver, Editors
Trinity College
Univ. of Toronto
Toronto M5S 1H8, Canada

Telephone: 416 978-2652
Fax: 416 978-4949
E-mail: ANDREWO@EPAS.UTORONTO.CA
First published: 1982
ISSN: 0715-8920
MLA acronym: Texte

SUBSCRIPTION INFORMATION

Frequency of publication: Annual
Circulation: 650
Available in microform: No
Subscription price: $33.00/yr. institutions; $17.00/yr. individuals
Year to which price refers: 1991
Subscription address: Journals Dept., Univ. of Toronto Press, 5201 Dufferic St., Downsview, Ontario M3H 5T8, Canada
Subscription telephone: 416 667-7838
Subscription fax: 416 667-7832

ADVERTISING INFORMATION

Advertising accepted: No

EDITORIAL DESCRIPTION

Scope: Publishes articles on literary theory and criticism. Focuses on French literature but includes studies on literature from other regions.
Reviews books: No
Publishes notes: Yes
Languages accepted: French; English
Prints abstracts: Yes, for articles in English
Author-anonymous submission: Yes

SUBMISSION REQUIREMENTS

Restrictions on contributors: None
Author pays submission fee: No
Author pays page charges: No
Length of articles: No restrictions
Length of notes: No restrictions
Style: Journal
Number of copies required: 2
Special requirements: Submission on diskette or through electronic mail is welcome.
Copyright ownership: Author
Rejected manuscripts: Returned; enclose return postage.
Time before publication decision: 2 mos.
Time between decision and publication: 6 mos.
Number of reviewers: 2
Articles submitted per year: 60
Articles published per year: 15

(2945)
*Texte der Hethiter

A. Kammenhuber, Editor
Schneckenburgerstr. 11
Munich 80, Germany

Telephone: (49) 89 4703749
First published: 1971
ISSN: 0173-4865
MLA acronym: THeth

SUBSCRIPTION INFORMATION

Frequency of publication: Irregular
Circulation: 600-1,500
Available in microform: No
Subscription address: Carl Winter Universitätsverlag, Lutherstr. 59, 6900 Heidelberg, Germany
Subscription telephone: (49) 6221 41490

ADVERTISING INFORMATION

Advertising accepted: Yes

EDITORIAL DESCRIPTION

Scope: Publishes studies on the Hittites in Anatolia, including their culture, history language, texts, and relations to their neighbors
Reviews books: Yes
Languages accepted: English; German; French; Italian
Prints abstracts: No
Author-anonymous submission: No

SUBMISSION REQUIREMENTS

Restrictions on contributors: None
Author pays submission fee: No
Author pays page charges: No
Length of books: No restrictions
Length of book reviews: No restrictions
Length of notes: None
Style: MLA
Number of copies required: 1
Copyright ownership: Carl Winter Universitätsverlag
Rejected manuscripts: Returned
Time before publication decision: 2 weeks
Time between decision and publication: 3 mos.
Number of reviewers: 1
Books submitted per year: 1
Books published per year: 1
Book reviews submitted per year: 6
Book reviews published per year: 6

(2946)
Texte des Späten Mittelalters und der Frühen Neuzeit

Karl Stackmann & Stanley N. Werbow, Editors
Erich Schmidt Verlag
Genthiner Str. 30G
1000 Berlin 30, Germany

First published: 1956
ISSN: 0563-3079
MLA acronym: TSM

SUBSCRIPTION INFORMATION

Frequency of publication: Irregular
Available in microform: No
Subscription address: Erich Schmidt Verlag, Viktoriastr., 44a, 4800 Bielefeld 1, Berlin, Germany

ADVERTISING INFORMATION

Advertising accepted: No

EDITORIAL DESCRIPTION

Scope: Publishes texts of 14th-16th century manuscripts and printings made available for research and study. These critical editions often include introductions, commentaries, and glosses.
Reviews books: No
Languages accepted: German
Prints abstracts: No

(2947)
Texte zur Forschung

Wissenschaftliche Buchgesellschaft
Hindenburgstr. 40
Postfach 11-11-29
6100 Darmstadt 11, Germany

First published: 1970
ISSN: 0174-0474
MLA acronym: TzF

SUBSCRIPTION INFORMATION

Frequency of publication: Irregular
Available in microform: No

ADVERTISING INFORMATION

Advertising accepted: No

EDITORIAL DESCRIPTION

Scope: Publishes monograph studies about German literature.
Reviews books: No
Publishes notes: No
Languages accepted: German
Prints abstracts: No

SUBMISSION REQUIREMENTS

Author pays submission fee: No
Author pays page charges: No
Length of books: 160-240 pp.
Number of copies required: 2
Copyright ownership: Wissenschaftliche Buchgesellschaft & author
Rejected manuscripts: Returned
Time between decision and publication: 2-3 yrs.
Number of reviewers: 2

(2948)
*Textes Littéraires Français

Librairie Droz S.A.
11, rue Massot
1211 Geneva 12, Switzerland

Telephone: (41) 22 3466666
Fax: (41) 22 3472391
First published: 1945
Sponsoring organization: Librairie Droz S.A.
ISSN: 0257-4063
MLA acronym: TLF

SUBSCRIPTION INFORMATION

Frequency of publication: Irregular
Circulation: 500
Available in microform: No

ADVERTISING INFORMATION

Advertising accepted: No

EDITORIAL DESCRIPTION

Scope: Publishes French literary texts.
Reviews books: No
Publishes notes: No
Languages accepted: French
Prints abstracts: No
Author-anonymous submission: No

SUBMISSION REQUIREMENTS

Restrictions on contributors: None
Author pays submission fee: No
Author pays page charges: No
Number of copies required: 1
Copyright ownership: Librairie Droz S.A.
Rejected manuscripts: Returned
Time before publication decision: 4 mos.
Time between decision and publication: 8 mos.
Books submitted per year: 15
Books published per year: 10

(2949)
*Texto Crítico

Sixto Rodríguez Hernández, Editor
Centro de Investigaciones Lingüístico-Literarias
Inst. de Investigaciones Humanísticas
Univ. Veracruzana
Apartado Postal 369
91000 Xalapa, Veracruz, Mexico

First published: 1975
Sponsoring organization: Univ. Veracruzana, Centro de Investigaciones Linguistico-Literarias
ISSN: 0185-0830
MLA acronym: TCrit

SUBSCRIPTION INFORMATION

Frequency of publication: 2 times/yr.
Circulation: 1,000
Available in microform: No
Subscription price: $25.00/yr. plus postage
Year to which price refers: 1992

ADVERTISING INFORMATION

Advertising accepted: Yes

EDITORIAL DESCRIPTION

Scope: Publishes articles on Latin American literature, critical literary analysis, and linguistic research.
Reviews books: Yes
Publishes notes: Yes
Languages accepted: Spanish
Prints abstracts: No

SUBMISSION REQUIREMENTS

Restrictions on contributors: None
Author pays submission fee: No
Author pays page charges: No
Length of articles: 15-25 pp.
Length of book reviews: 3-6 pp.
Length of notes: 6-12 pp.
Style: MLA
Number of copies required: 2
Special requirements: Submit original typescript.
Copyright ownership: Assigned by author to journal
Rejected manuscripts: Returned
Time before publication decision: 1-2 mos.
Time between decision and publication: 8 mos.
Number of reviewers: 2
Articles submitted per year: 250
Articles published per year: 40
Book reviews submitted per year: 40
Book reviews published per year: 30

(2950)
*Textual Practice

Terence Hawkes, Editor
Dept. of English
Univ. of Wales, College of Cardiff
P.O. Box 94
Cardiff CF1 3XE, Wales

Additional editorial address: Jean Howard,
  Dept. of English & Comparative Literature,
  Columbia Univ., New York, NY 10027
Telephone: (44) 222 874245; 212 854-3215
Fax: (44) 222 874242; 212 854-5788
First published: 1987
ISSN: 0950-236X
MLA acronym: TexP

SUBSCRIPTION INFORMATION

Frequency of publication: 3 times/yr. (Spring, Autumn, Winter)
Circulation: 450
Available in microform: No
Subscription price: $78.00/yr. institutions; $54.00/yr. individuals
Year to which price refers: 1991
Subscription address: Subscriptions Dept., Associated Book Publishers, North Way, Andover,, Hants, SP10 5BE England
Additional subscription address: US subscriptions: Assoc. Book Publishers' Acct. No. 051-70 700-4, Barclays Bank Ltd., 300 Park Ave., New York, N.Y. 10022

ADVERTISING INFORMATION

Advertising accepted: Yes

EDITORIAL DESCRIPTION

Scope: Publishes interdisciplinary articles in the humanities.
Reviews books: Yes
Publishes notes: No
Languages accepted: English
Prints abstracts: No
Author-anonymous submission: No

SUBMISSION REQUIREMENTS

Restrictions on contributors: None
Author pays submission fee: No
Author pays page charges: No
Length of articles: 6,000 words
Length of book reviews: 1,500 words
Style: MLA
Number of copies required: 2
Special requirements: Submit double-spaced typescript, on one side of the paper, preferably on A4 (8 1/4 in. x 11 3/4 in.) size, with a 4cm margin on the left.
Copyright ownership: Routledge
Rejected manuscripts: Returned; enclose SASE.
Time before publication decision: 9 mos.
Time between decision and publication: 1 yr.
Number of reviewers: 1
Articles submitted per year: 50-60
Articles published per year: 16-20
Book reviews submitted per year: 30-40
Book reviews published per year: 25

(2951)
*Textus: Annual of the Hebrew University Bible Project

E. Tov, S. Talmon, & G. Marquis, Editors
c/o Magnes Press
P.O. Box 7695
91076 Jerusalem, Israel

Additional editorial address: Bible Project, Inst. of Jewish Studies, Hebrew Univ., 91905 Jerusalem, Israel
Telephone: (972) 2 660341; (972) 2 754656
Fax: (972) 2 633170
First published: 1960

Sponsoring organization: Hebrew Univ. Bible Project
ISSN: 0082-3797
MLA acronym: Textus

SUBSCRIPTION INFORMATION

Frequency of publication: Annual
Circulation: 1,000
Available in microform: No

ADVERTISING INFORMATION

Advertising accepted: No

EDITORIAL DESCRIPTION

Scope: Publishes studies on the textual criticism of the Bible.
Reviews books: No
Publishes notes: Yes
Languages accepted: English; Hebrew; French
Prints abstracts: Yes
Author-anonymous submission: No

SUBMISSION REQUIREMENTS

Restrictions on contributors: None
Author pays submission fee: No
Author pays page charges: No
Length of articles: No restrictions
Length of notes: No restrictions
Number of copies required: 1
Special requirements: Submit manuscript on IBM- or Macintosh-compatible diskette.
Copyright ownership: Author
Rejected manuscripts: Returned
Time before publication decision: 1 mo.
Time between decision and publication: 1-10 mos.
Number of reviewers: 1
Articles submitted per year: 10-15
Articles published per year: 10-12
Notes submitted per year: 4-6
Notes published per year: 4-6

(2952)
*Thalia: Studies in Literary Humor

Jacqueline Tavernier-Courbin, Editor
Dept. of English
Univ. of Ottawa
175 Waller
Ottawa, Ontario K1N 6N5, Canada

Telephone: 613 230-9505
Fax: 613 564-9175
First published: 1978
Sponsoring organization: Thalia: Assn. for the Study of Literary Humor
ISSN: 0706-5604
MLA acronym: Thalia

SUBSCRIPTION INFORMATION

Frequency of publication: 2 times/yr.
Circulation: 500
Available in microform: No
Subscription price: C$18.00/yr.
Year to which price refers: 1992

ADVERTISING INFORMATION

Advertising accepted: Yes
Advertising rates: C$100.00/half page; C$150.00/full page

EDITORIAL DESCRIPTION

Scope: Publishes articles on literary humor, popular culture, and visual arts, as well as occasional literary parodies.
Reviews books: Yes
Publishes notes: No
Languages accepted: English; French
Prints abstracts: No
Author-anonymous submission: Yes

SUBMISSION REQUIREMENTS

Restrictions on contributors: Reviews are usually solicited. Contributors must become subscribers.
Author pays submission fee: No
Author pays page charges: No
Length of articles: 20 pp.
Length of book reviews: 5 pp.
Style: MLA (1977)
Number of copies required: 3
Special requirements: Articles accepted for publication must be submitted on diskette.
Copyright ownership: Journal
Rejected manuscripts: Returned; enclose return postage.
Time before publication decision: 3-6 mos.
Time between decision and publication: 6-12 mos.
Number of reviewers: 2-3
Articles submitted per year: 100
Articles published per year: 18-22
Book reviews published per year: 10

(2953)
Theater

Joel Schechter, Editor
222 York St.
New Haven, CT 06520

First published: 1968
Sponsoring organization: Yale School of Drama & Yale Repertory Theater
ISSN: 0161-0775
MLA acronym: Theater

SUBSCRIPTION INFORMATION

Frequency of publication: 3 times/yr.
Circulation: 2,000
Available in microform: Yes
Subscription price: $24.00/yr. institutions; $20.00/yr. individuals
Year to which price refers: 1992

ADVERTISING INFORMATION

Advertising accepted: Yes

EDITORIAL DESCRIPTION

Scope: Publishes writing on diverse theater events throughout America and abroad, particularly on groups, playwrights, and plays. Welcomes essays, interviews, and retrospectives that locate theatrical events in a greater cultural, social, or aesthetic context, and not simply documentations that are time-bound to particular productions. Also publishes new plays by Dario Fo, Athol Fugard, Theodora Skipitares, and others.
Reviews books: Yes
Publishes notes: No
Languages accepted: English
Prints abstracts: No
Author-anonymous submission: No

SUBMISSION REQUIREMENTS

Restrictions on contributors: Most articles and plays are solicited.
Author pays submission fee: No
Author pays page charges: No
Length of book reviews: 1,000-2,000 words
Style: None
Number of copies required: 2
Copyright ownership: Varies
Rejected manuscripts: Returned; enclose return postage.
Time before publication decision: 3 mos.
Time between decision and publication: 6-12 mos.
Number of reviewers: 2-3
Articles published per year: 40
Book reviews submitted per year: 5-10
Book reviews published per year: 5

(2954)
*TheaterZeitSchrift: Beiträge zu Theater, Medien, Kulturpolitik

G. H. Susen, E. Wack, P. Roessler, & P. Oltmanns, Editors
Wochenschau Verlag
Adolf-Damaschke-Str. 103
6231 Schwalbach/Taunus, Germany

Additional editorial address: Hauptstr. 56, 1000 Berlin 62, Germany
Telephone: (49) 30 7849230
First published: 1982
ISSN: 0723-1172
MLA acronym: TZS

SUBSCRIPTION INFORMATION

Frequency of publication: 4 times/yr.
Circulation: 1,750
Available in microform: No
Subscription price: 43 DM/yr. plus postage
Year to which price refers: 1991
Subscription telephone: (49) 6196 84010

ADVERTISING INFORMATION

Advertising accepted: Yes
Advertising rates: 130 DM/quarter page; 165 DM/third page; 270 DM/half page; 490 DM/full page; 540 DM/inside cover

EDITORIAL DESCRIPTION

Scope: Publishes articles on theoretical issues concerning film, television, and theater, focusing on a particular theme in each issue. Includes information on media and cultural politics.
Reviews books: Yes
Publishes notes: Yes
Languages accepted: German; English
Prints abstracts: No
Author-anonymous submission: No

SUBMISSION REQUIREMENTS

Author pays submission fee: No
Author pays page charges: No
Length of articles: 5,000 words
Length of book reviews: 1,500 words
Number of copies required: 1
Copyright ownership: Wochenschau Verlag
Time before publication decision: 1 mo.
Time between decision and publication: 6 weeks
Number of reviewers: 2
Articles submitted per year: 20
Articles published per year: 40
Book reviews submitted per year: 5
Book reviews published per year: 20

(2955)
*Theatre Annual

Wallace Sterling, Editor
School of Theatre Arts
Univ. of Akron
Akron, OH 44325-1005

Telephone: 216 972-6081
Fax: 216 972-5101
First published: 1942
Sponsoring organization: Univ. of Akron
ISSN: 0082-3821
MLA acronym: TA

SUBSCRIPTION INFORMATION

Frequency of publication: Annual
Circulation: 400
Available in microform: No
Subscription price: $8.00/yr.
Year to which price refers: 1992

ADVERTISING INFORMATION

Advertising accepted: No

EDITORIAL DESCRIPTION

Scope: Publishes articles on theater history and criticism.
Reviews books: No
Publishes notes: No
Languages accepted: English
Prints abstracts: No
Author-anonymous submission: Yes

SUBMISSION REQUIREMENTS

Restrictions on contributors: None
Author pays submission fee: No
Author pays page charges: No
Length of articles: 1,500-7,500 words
Style: MLA; Chicago
Number of copies required: 3
Copyright ownership: Assigned by author to journal
Rejected manuscripts: Returned
Time before publication decision: 6 mos.
Time between decision and publication: 3-12 mos.
Number of reviewers: 3
Articles submitted per year: 25
Articles published per year: 4-8

(2956)
*Theatre History in Canada/Histoire du Théâtre au Canada

Leonard E. Doucette & Richard Plant, Editors
Graduate Centre for Study of Drama
Univ. of Toronto
214 College St.
Toronto, Ontario M5T 2Z9, Canada

Telephone: 416 978-7980
Fax: 416 971-1378
First published: 1980
Sponsoring organization: Assn. for Canadian Theatre Research
ISSN: 0226-5761
MLA acronym: THIC

SUBSCRIPTION INFORMATION

Frequency of publication: 2 times/yr. (Spring, Fall)
Circulation: 350
Available in microform: No
Subscription price: C$22.00/yr. institutions; C$15.00/yr. individuals; C$12.00/yr. students
Year to which price refers: 1992

ADVERTISING INFORMATION

Advertising accepted: No

EDITORIAL DESCRIPTION

Scope: Publishes articles on theater research in Canada, including the history of drama, troupes, performers, stage design, directors, and drama theory and criticism.
Reviews books: Yes
Publishes notes: No
Languages accepted: French; English
Prints abstracts: Yes
Author-anonymous submission: Yes

SUBMISSION REQUIREMENTS

Restrictions on contributors: None
Author pays submission fee: No
Author pays page charges: No
Length of articles: 4,000 words
Length of book reviews: 500-1,000 words
Style: MLA with modifications
Number of copies required: 1-2
Special requirements: Submit typescript and diskette or 2 copies of typescript.
Copyright ownership: Univ. of Toronto Graduate Centre for Study of Drama & Queen's Univ. in Kingston
Rejected manuscripts: Returned; enclose postage or international reply coupons.
Time before publication decision: 1 yr.
Time between decision and publication: 3-6 mos.
Number of reviewers: 4
Articles submitted per year: 20-25
Articles published per year: 12
Book reviews published per year: 10

(2957)
Theatre History Studies

Ron Engle, Editor
Theatre Arts Dept.
Box 8182
Univ. of North Dakota
Grand Forks, ND 58202

Additional editorial address: After 1993 contact new Editor: Robert A. Schanke, Director of Theatre, Central College, Pella, IA 50219
First published: 1981
Sponsoring organization: Mid-America Theatre Conference, Inc.; Univ. of North Dakota; Univ. of Nebraska-Lincoln; Kansas State Univ.; Univ. of Missouri
ISSN: 0733-2033
MLA acronym: THStud

SUBSCRIPTION INFORMATION

Frequency of publication: Annual
Circulation: 1,000
Available in microform: No
Subscription price: $13.00/yr. institutions US; $14.50/yr. institutions elsewhere; $8.00/yr. individuals US; $9.50/yr. individuals elsewhere
Year to which price refers: 1992

ADVERTISING INFORMATION

Advertising accepted: Yes

EDITORIAL DESCRIPTION

Scope: Journal is devoted to research and excellence in all areas of theater history for diverse national and international fields of interest.
Reviews books: Yes
Publishes notes: Yes
Languages accepted: English
Prints abstracts: No
Author-anonymous submission: No

SUBMISSION REQUIREMENTS

Restrictions on contributors: Book reviews are commissioned by editor.
Author pays submission fee: No
Author pays page charges: No
Length of articles: No restrictions
Length of book reviews: 900 words
Length of notes: 1,200 words
Style: Chicago
Number of copies required: 2
Copyright ownership: Univ. of North Dakota
Rejected manuscripts: Returned; enclose return postage.
Time before publication decision: 2-6 mos.
Time between decision and publication: 6-12 mos.
Number of reviewers: 2
Articles submitted per year: 50-70
Articles published per year: 9-12
Book reviews published per year: 9-12
Notes submitted per year: 5-10
Notes published per year: 1-2

(2958)
Theatre Journal

W. B. Worthen & Janelle Reinelt, Editors
Northwestern Univ.
Evanston, IL 60208

Additional editorial address: J. Reinelt, Dept. of Drama, California State Univ., Sacramento, CA 95819

First published: 1949
Sponsoring organization: Assn. for Theatre in Higher Education
ISSN: 0013-1989
MLA acronym: TJ

SUBSCRIPTION INFORMATION

Frequency of publication: 4 times/yr. (Mar., May, Oct., Dec.)
Circulation: 6,000
Available in microform: No
Subscription price: $49.50/yr. institutions US; $21.00/yr. individuals US; add $3.20/yr. postage Canada & Mexico, $11.10/yr. elsewhere
Year to which price refers: 1993
Subscription address: Johns Hopkins Univ. Press, Journals Publishing Division, 2715 North Charles St., Baltimore, MD 21218-4319
Subscription telephone: 800 537-5487
Subscription fax: 410 516-6998

ADVERTISING INFORMATION

Advertising accepted: Yes

EDITORIAL DESCRIPTION

Scope: Focuses on theory, criticism, and history in the theater arts.
Reviews books: Yes
Publishes notes: No
Languages accepted: English
Prints abstracts: No

SUBMISSION REQUIREMENTS

Restrictions on contributors: None
Author pays submission fee: No
Author pays page charges: No
Length of articles: 3,500-13,500 words
Length of book reviews: 750 words
Style: Chicago
Number of copies required: 3
Special requirements: Submit original typescript plus 2 copies.
Copyright ownership: Johns Hopkins Univ. Press
Rejected manuscripts: Returned; enclose return postage.
Time before publication decision: 2 mos.
Time between decision and publication: 6-8 mos.
Number of reviewers: 3-4
Articles submitted per year: 400
Articles published per year: 30
Book reviews published per year: 50

(2959)
*Theatre Notebook: A Journal of the History and Technique of the British Theatre

Russell Jackson, Katharine Worth, & Michael Booth, Editors
Shakespeare Inst.
Univ. of Birmingham
Masoncroft
Church St.
Stratford-upon-Avon, Warwickshire CV37 6HP, England

Additional editorial address: Editorial Manager, 105 High St., Maldon, Essex CM9 7EP, England
First published: 1945
Sponsoring organization: Soc. for Theatre Research
ISSN: 0040-5523
MLA acronym: TN

SUBSCRIPTION INFORMATION

Frequency of publication: 3 times/yr.
Circulation: 1,450
Available in microform: No
Subscription price: £12.00/yr. United Kingdom; £13.00 ($26.00)/yr. elsewhere
Year to which price refers: 1991
Subscription address: Soc. for Theatre Research, c/o Theatre Museum, 1c Tavistock St., London WC2E 7PA, England

ADVERTISING INFORMATION

Advertising accepted: Yes
Advertising rates: £40.00/half page; £60.00/full page

EDITORIAL DESCRIPTION

Scope: Journal's purpose is to record and encourage interest in British theater history.
Reviews books: Yes
Publishes notes: Yes
Languages accepted: English
Prints abstracts: No
Author-anonymous submission: No

SUBMISSION REQUIREMENTS

Restrictions on contributors: None
Author pays submission fee: No
Author pays page charges: No
Length of articles: 5,000 words maximum
Length of book reviews: 750 words maximum
Length of notes: 200 words maximum
Style: None
Number of copies required: 1
Copyright ownership: Author
Rejected manuscripts: Returned; enclose return postage.
Time before publication decision: 2 mos.
Time between decision and publication: 1 yr.
Number of reviewers: 3
Articles published per year: 12-14
Book reviews published per year: 15-20
Notes published per year: 20

(2960)
*Theatre Research International

Claude Schumacher, Editor
Dept. of Theater Studies
Univ. of Glasgow
Glasgow G12 8QF, Scotland

Telephone: (44) 41 3305162
Fax: (44) 41 3304808
First published: 1976
Sponsoring organization: International Federation for Theatre Research
ISSN: 0307-8833
MLA acronym: ThR

SUBSCRIPTION INFORMATION

Frequency of publication: 3 times/yr. (Feb., June, Nov.)
Circulation: 1,000
Available in microform: No
Subscription price: £44.00 ($84.00)/yr.
Year to which price refers: 1991
Subscription address: Journals Subscription Dept., Oxford Univ. Press, Pinkhill House, Southfield Rd., Eynsham, Oxford OX8 1JJ, England
Subscription telephone: (44) 865 882283
Subscription fax: (44) 865 882890

ADVERTISING INFORMATION

Advertising accepted: Yes

EDITORIAL DESCRIPTION

Scope: Publishes historical, critical, and theoretical study and documentation of drama, conceived of as the art of the theater.
Reviews books: Yes
Publishes notes: Yes
Languages accepted: English
Prints abstracts: Yes
Author-anonymous submission: No

SUBMISSION REQUIREMENTS

Restrictions on contributors: None
Author pays submission fee: No
Author pays page charges: No
Length of articles: 4,000 words maximum
Length of book reviews: 450-600 words
Style: Hart's Rules
Number of copies required: 3
Special requirements: Submit original manuscript; include a 200-word abstract.
Copyright ownership: Oxford Univ. Press for 1 yr.; then reverts to author provided acknowledgement is made to original publication.
Rejected manuscripts: Returned; enclose return postage.
Time before publication decision: 4 mos.
Time between decision and publication: 1 yr.
Number of reviewers: 2-3
Articles submitted per year: 40-50
Articles published per year: 12-18
Book reviews published per year: 50-70

(2961)
*Theatre Studies

Alan Woods & Brian Rose, Editors
Theatre Research Inst.
1430 Lincoln Tower, 1800 Cannon Dr.
Ohio State Univ.
Columbus, OH 43210-1230

Telephone: 614 292-6614
First published: 1955
Sponsoring organization: Lawrence & Lee Theatre Research Inst.
ISSN: 0362-0964
MLA acronym: TheatreS

SUBSCRIPTION INFORMATION

Frequency of publication: Annual
Circulation: 800
Available in microform: Yes
Subscription price: $10.00/yr. institutions; $8.00/yr. individuals
Year to which price refers: 1992

ADVERTISING INFORMATION

Advertising accepted: Yes
Advertising rates: $50.00/half page; $100.00/full page

EDITORIAL DESCRIPTION

Scope: Publishes articles in the areas of theater history, literature, criticism, and theory by graduate students of theater and drama. Also includes book review by graduate students.
Reviews books: Yes
Publishes notes: No
Languages accepted: English
Prints abstracts: No
Author-anonymous submission: Yes

SUBMISSION REQUIREMENTS

Restrictions on contributors: Contributors must be graduate students in drama or theater. Book reviews are solicited.
Author pays submission fee: No
Author pays page charges: No
Length of articles: 1,500-4,000 words
Length of book reviews: 600 words
Style: Chicago
Number of copies required: 3
Special requirements: Author's name should appear only on separate cover.
Copyright ownership: Journal
Rejected manuscripts: Returned; enclose return postage.
Time before publication decision: 4 mos.
Time between decision and publication: 10 mos.
Number of reviewers: 3
Articles submitted per year: 30
Articles published per year: 3-5
Book reviews published per year: 30

(2962)
Theatre Survey: The Journal of the American Society for Theatre Research

Judith Milhous, Editor
Ph.D. Program in Theatre
CUNY Graduate Center
33 West 42nd St.
New York, NY 10036

Additional editorial address: Patti P. Gillespie, Book Review Editor, Theatre Dept., Univ. of Maryland, College Park, MD 20742
Telephone: 212 642-2231
First published: 1960
Sponsoring organization: Indiana Univ.; American Soc. for Theatre Research
ISSN: 0040-5574
MLA acronym: ThS

SUBSCRIPTION INFORMATION

Frequency of publication: 2 times/yr. (May, Nov.)
Circulation: 1,200
Available in microform: No
Subscription price: $40.00/yr.
Year to which price refers: 1991
Additional subscription address: Individuals should contact: Cary Mazer, American Soc. for Theatre Research, Dept. of English, Univ. of Pennsylvania, Philadelphia, PA 19104
Subscription telephone: 212 642-2231 (institutions); 215 898-7382 (individuals)

ADVERTISING INFORMATION

Advertising accepted: Yes
Advertising rates: $150.00/full page

EDITORIAL DESCRIPTION

Scope: Publishes scholarly articles on theater history.
Reviews books: Yes
Publishes notes: Yes
Languages accepted: English
Prints abstracts: No
Author-anonymous submission: No

SUBMISSION REQUIREMENTS

Restrictions on contributors: Reviews are published by invitation only.
Author pays submission fee: No
Author pays page charges: No
Length of articles: 1,500-10,000 words
Length of book reviews: 1,000-2,000 words
Length of notes: 500-1,500 words
Style: MLA; Chicago
Number of copies required: 3
Copyright ownership: American Soc. for Theatre Research & author
Rejected manuscripts: Returned; enclose return postage
Time before publication decision: 4 mos.
Time between decision and publication: 1 yr.
Number of reviewers: 2-4
Articles submitted per year: 40
Articles published per year: 12
Book reviews published per year: 15-25
Notes submitted per year: 8-10
Notes published per year: 3-5

(2963)
*Theatron: Studien zur Geschichte und Theorie der Dramatischen Künste

Hans-Peter Bayerdörfer, Dieter Borchmeyer, & Andreas Höfele, Editors
Inst. für Theaterwissenschaft
Univ. München
Ludwigstr. 25
8000 Munich 22, Germany

First published: 1988
ISSN: 0934-6252
MLA acronym: Theatron

SUBSCRIPTION INFORMATION

Frequency of publication: Irregular
Available in microform: No
Subscription address: Max Niemeyer Verlag, Postfach 2140, 7400 Tübingen, Germany

ADVERTISING INFORMATION

Advertising accepted: No

EDITORIAL DESCRIPTION

Scope: Publishes monographs on drama and the theater. Topics covered include opera, dance, dramatic theory, and related subjects.
Reviews books: No
Publishes notes: No
Languages accepted: German; English; French
Prints abstracts: No
Author-anonymous submission: No

SUBMISSION REQUIREMENTS

Author pays submission fee: No
Author pays page charges: No
Style: None
Number of copies required: 1
Copyright ownership: Max Niemeyer Verlag
Rejected manuscripts: Returned
Time before publication decision: 3 mos.
Time between decision and publication: 10 mos.
Books submitted per year: 2-3
Books published per year: 2-3

(2964)
*Themes in Drama

James Redmond, Editor
Dept. of Drama
Westfield College
Univ. of London
Mile End Rd.
Hampstead, London E1 4NS, England

Telephone: (44) 71 7753204
Fax: (44) 71 9755500
First published: 1983
ISSN: 0263-676X
MLA acronym: ThD

SUBSCRIPTION INFORMATION

Frequency of publication: Annual (Mar.)
Available in microform: No
Subscription address: Cambridge Univ. Press, 40 W. 20th St., New York, NY 10011
Additional subscription address: Outside N. America: Cambridge Univ. Press, Edinburgh Bldg., Shaftesbury Rd., Cambridge CB2 2RU, England

ADVERTISING INFORMATION

Advertising accepted: No

EDITORIAL DESCRIPTION

Scope: Publishes reviews and articles on the theatrical activity of a wide range of cultures and periods. Each volume indicates connections between the various national traditions of theater by bringing together studies of a theme of central and continuing importance.
Reviews books: Yes
Publishes notes: No
Languages accepted: English
Prints abstracts: No
Author-anonymous submission: No

SUBMISSION REQUIREMENTS

Restrictions on contributors: Reviews are commissioned.
Author pays submission fee: No
Cost of page charges: No
Style: Cambridge Univ. Press
Number of copies required: 1
Copyright ownership: Cambridge Univ. Press
Time before publication decision: 3 mos.
Time between decision and publication: 6 mos.
Articles submitted per year: 60
Articles published per year: 20
Books published per year: 1

NOTE: Ceased publication in or before 1994

(2965)
*Theoria: A Journal of Studies in the Arts, Humanities and Social Sciences

D. Greaves, F. Hugo, R. de Kadt, & H. van Vuuren, Editors
Univ. of Natal Press
P.O. Box 375
3200 Pietermaritzburg
Natal, South Africa

Telephone: (27) 331 955226
Fax: (27) 331 955599
First published: 1947
Sponsoring organization: Univ. of Natal
ISSN: 0040-5817
MLA acronym: Theoria

SUBSCRIPTION INFORMATION

Frequency of publication: 2 times/yr. (May, Oct.)
Circulation: 320
Available in microform: Yes
Subscription price: $30.00/yr. institutions; $20.00/yr. individuals
Year to which price refers: 1992
Subscription address: Secretary, at the above address

ADVERTISING INFORMATION

Advertising accepted: No

EDITORIAL DESCRIPTION

Scope: Publishes critical studies in the arts, humanities, and social sciences. Correspondence is encouraged and letters are published.
Reviews books: Yes
Publishes notes: Yes
Languages accepted: English; Afrikaans
Prints abstracts: No
Author-anonymous submission: Yes

SUBMISSION REQUIREMENTS

Restrictions on contributors: None
Author pays submission fee: No
Author pays page charges: No
Length of articles: 5,000-10,000 words
Length of notes: Letters, 500-1,000 words
Style: MLA with modifications
Number of copies required: 2
Special requirements: Submit 2 copies of typescript plus diskette. Include an abstract (200 words maximum).
Copyright ownership: Assigned by author to journal
Rejected manuscripts: Not returned
Time before publication decision: 2-6 mos.
Time between decision and publication: 6-18 mos.
Number of reviewers: 2
Articles submitted per year: 40-50
Articles published per year: 18-20
Book reviews submitted per year: 4-8
Book reviews published per year: 2-4
Notes published per year: 2-5 letters

(2966)
*Theory and History of Literature

Wlad Godzich & Jochem Schulte-Sasse, Editors
Univ. of Minnesota Press
2037 University Ave. SE
Minneapolis, MN 55414

First published: 1981
MLA acronym: THL

SUBSCRIPTION INFORMATION

Available in microform: No

EDITORIAL DESCRIPTION

Scope: Publishes monographs on the development and understanding of literature through theory and history.
Reviews books: No
Publishes notes: No
Languages accepted: English
Prints abstracts: No
Author-anonymous submission: No

SUBMISSION REQUIREMENTS

Length of books: No restrictions
Style: Chicago
Number of copies required: 1
Copyright ownership: Author
Rejected manuscripts: Returned
Time before publication decision: 4 mos.
Time between decision and publication: 1 yr.
Number of reviewers: 3
Books published per year: 4

(2967)
*Thēsaurismata

N. M. Panayotakis, Editor
Ist. Ellenico di Studi Bizantini & Postbizantini
Castello 3412
30122 Venice, Italy

Telephone: (39) 41 5226581
Fax: (39) 41 5238248
First published: 1962
Sponsoring organization: Ist. Ellenico di Studi Bizantini & Postbizantini
ISSN: 0082-4097
MLA acronym: Thēsaurismata

SUBSCRIPTION INFORMATION

Frequency of publication: Annual
Circulation: 1,000
Available in microform: No

ADVERTISING INFORMATION

Advertising accepted: No

EDITORIAL DESCRIPTION

Scope: Publishes studies on the history and civilization of Byzantine and post-Byzantine Greece and of Hellenism, based on documents located in Italy, by researchers and collaborators of the Institute.
Reviews books: No
Publishes notes: Yes
Languages accepted: English; French; German; Greek; Italian
Prints abstracts: Yes
Author-anonymous submission: No

SUBMISSION REQUIREMENTS

Restrictions on contributors: None
Author pays submission fee: No
Author pays page charges: No
Length of articles: 32-48 pp.
Length of notes: 2-8 pp.
Style: MLA
Number of copies required: 2
Special requirements: Submit original typescript.
Copyright ownership: Editor
Rejected manuscripts: Returned
Time before publication decision: 1 mo.
Time between decision and publication: 6-12 mos.
Number of reviewers: 1
Articles submitted per year: 10-20
Articles published per year: 10-15
Notes submitted per year: 3-5
Notes published per year: 2-3

(2968)
Thesaurus: Boletín del Instituto Caro y Cuervo

Jose Manuel Rivas Sacconi & Ismael Enrique Delgado Téllez, Editors
Inst. Caro y Cuervo
Apartado Aéreo 51502
Bogota, Colombia

First published: 1945
Sponsoring organization: Inst. Caro y Cuervo
ISSN: 0040-604X
MLA acronym: Thesaurus

SUBSCRIPTION INFORMATION

Frequency of publication: 3 times/yr.
Circulation: 2,500
Available in microform: Yes, through Univ. Microfilm International

ADVERTISING INFORMATION

Advertising accepted: No

EDITORIAL DESCRIPTION

Scope: Publishes articles on linguistics, philology, and literary criticism. Primary focus is on the Spanish language and Spanish and Latin American literatures.
Reviews books: Yes
Publishes notes: Yes
Languages accepted: Spanish
Prints abstracts: No
Author-anonymous submission: No

SUBMISSION REQUIREMENTS

Restrictions on contributors: Articles are solicited.
Author pays submission fee: No
Author pays page charges: No
Length of articles: 7,000-22,000 words
Length of book reviews: 1,000-2,000 words
Length of notes: 2,000-3,000 words
Style: Inst. Caro y Cuervo
Number of copies required: 1
Special requirements: Submitted articles must be previously unpublished.
Copyright ownership: Journal
Rejected manuscripts: Returned at author's request
Time before publication decision: 1-6 mos.
Time between decision and publication: 1 yr.
Number of reviewers: 2
Articles submitted per year: 60
Articles published per year: 25
Book reviews submitted per year: 50
Book reviews published per year: 30
Notes submitted per year: 30
Notes published per year: 15

(2969)
Third Rail: A Review of International Arts & Literature

Uri Hertz, Editor
P.O. Box 46127
Los Angeles, CA 90046

First published: 1975
ISSN: 0741-5968
MLA acronym: ThirdR

SUBSCRIPTION INFORMATION

Frequency of publication: Annual
Circulation: 5,000
Available in microform: No

ADVERTISING INFORMATION

Advertising accepted: Yes

EDITORIAL DESCRIPTION

Scope: A review of international arts and literature, publishing original poetry and prose, translations of literary work from foreign languages, interviews, criticism, theater, film and book reviews. *Third Rail*'s aim is to provide readers with access to developing currents in literature and the arts to offer perspectives on the streams of tradition flowing into them.
Reviews books: Yes
Publishes notes: Yes
Languages accepted: English
Prints abstracts: Yes
Author-anonymous submission: No

SUBMISSION REQUIREMENTS

Author pays submission fee: No
Author pays page charges: No
Length of articles: 500-2,500 words
Length of book reviews: 200-1,500 words
Number of copies required: 1
Special requirements: Manuscripts should be typed, double-spaced. Translations from foreign languages should be accompanied by original text.
Copyright ownership: Journal; reverts to authors upon publication.
Rejected manuscripts: Returned; enclose SASE.
Time before publication decision: 3-6 mos.
Time between decision and publication: 3-6 mos.
Number of reviewers: 2
Articles submitted per year: 160
Articles published per year: 20
Book reviews submitted per year: 30
Book reviews published per year: 15

(2970)
*The Thomas Hardy Journal

Norman Page, Editor
Dept. of English
Univ. of Nottingham
Nottingham NG7 2RD, England

First published: 1985
Sponsoring organization: Thomas Hardy Soc.
ISSN: 0268-5418
MLA acronym: THJ

SUBSCRIPTION INFORMATION

Frequency of publication: 3 times/yr. (Feb., May, Oct.)
Circulation: 1,500
Available in microform: No
Subscription price: £20.00/yr.
Year to which price refers: 1992
Subscription address: Copper Trees, Salston Ride, Ottery St. Mary, Devon, EX11 1RH, England
Subscription telephone: (44) 404 813032

ADVERTISING INFORMATION

Advertising accepted: Yes
Advertising rates: £35.00/half page; £70.00/full page

EDITORIAL DESCRIPTION

Scope: Publishes articles, reviews, and letters related to the work and life of Thomas Hardy.
Reviews books: Yes

Publishes notes: Yes
Languages accepted: English
Prints abstracts: Yes
Author-anonymous submission: No

SUBMISSION REQUIREMENTS

Restrictions on contributors: None
Author pays submission fee: No
Author pays page charges: No
Length of articles: 4,000 words maximum
Length of book reviews: 800 words
Length of notes: 200 words
Style: MLA
Number of copies required: 1
Copyright ownership: Author
Rejected manuscripts: Returned; enclose SASE.
Time before publication decision: 3 mos.
Time between decision and publication: 3-6 mos.
Number of reviewers: 1-3
Articles submitted per year: 30
Articles published per year: 15-20
Book reviews submitted per year: 15
Book reviews published per year: 15
Notes submitted per year: 10
Notes published per year: 5

(2971)
The Thomas Hardy Yearbook

G. Stevens Cox, Editor
Toucan Press
Saravia
Rue des Monts
St. Sampson, Guernesy, Channel Islands

First published: 1970
ISSN: 0082-416X
MLA acronym: THY

SUBSCRIPTION INFORMATION

Frequency of publication: Annual
Circulation: 2,000-3,000
Available in microform: No

ADVERTISING INFORMATION

Advertising accepted: Yes

EDITORIAL DESCRIPTION

Scope: Publishes essays and articles about the life, times, and works of Thomas Hardy including his environment, both physical and cultural, and on Dorset writers, especially those of the 19th century.
Reviews books: Yes
Languages accepted: English; French

SUBMISSION REQUIREMENTS

Restrictions on contributors: None
Author pays submission fee: No
Author pays page charges: No
Length of articles: 500-8,000 words
Length of book reviews: 500-3,000 words
Style: MLA preferred
Number of copies required: 1
Special requirements: Submit typescript.
Copyright ownership: Toucan Press & author
Rejected manuscripts: Returned
Time before publication decision: 1 week
Time between decision and publication: 1-2 yrs.
Number of reviewers: 1-2
Articles published per year: 10-20

(2972)
*Thomas Mann Jahrbuch

Eckhard Heftrich & Hans Wysling, Editors
Germanistisches Inst. der Univ. Münster
Domplatz 20-22
4400 Münster, Germany

Additional editorial address: H. Wysling, Eidgenössische Hochschule Zurich, Thomas-Mann-Archiv, Schönberggasse 15, 8001 Zurich, Switzerland
Telephone: (49) 251 834603
First published: 1988
ISSN: 0935-6983
MLA acronym: TMJ

SUBSCRIPTION INFORMATION

Frequency of publication: Annual
Circulation: 600
Available in microform: No
Subscription price: 60 DM/yr. (includes membership)
Year to which price refers: 1991
Subscription address: Deutsche Thomas-Mann-Gesellschaft e.V., Geschäftsstelle, Buchhandlung Gustav Weiland Nachf., Königstr. 67a, 2400 Lübeck, Germany
Additional subscription address: Verlag Vittorio Klostermann GmbH, Postfach 90 06 01, 6000 Frankfurt 90, Germany

ADVERTISING INFORMATION

Advertising accepted: No

EDITORIAL DESCRIPTION

Scope: Publishes articles on the works and life of Thomas Mann. Focuses on research and the publication of as yet unpublished relevant historical material.
Reviews books: Yes
Publishes notes: Yes
Languages accepted: German
Prints abstracts: Yes
Author-anonymous submission: No

SUBMISSION REQUIREMENTS

Author pays submission fee: No
Author pays page charges: No
Length of articles: No restrictions
Length of book reviews: No restrictions
Length of notes: No restrictions
Style: Journal
Number of copies required: 2
Copyright ownership: Vittorio Klostermann GmbH
Rejected manuscripts: Not returned
Time before publication decision: 6 mos. maximum
Number of reviewers: 2
Articles submitted per year: 10-15
Articles published per year: 10-15
Book reviews submitted per year: 5
Book reviews published per year: 5
Notes submitted per year: 20
Notes published per year: 10

(2973)
*Thomas-Mann-Studien

Hans Wysling, Editor
Thomas Mann Archiv
Eidgenössischen Technischen Hochschule
Schönberggasse 15
8001 Zurich, Switzerland

Telephone: (41) 1 2564045
First published: 1967
Sponsoring organization: Eidgenössische Technische Hochschule
ISSN: 0563-4822
MLA acronym: ThMS

SUBSCRIPTION INFORMATION

Frequency of publication: Irregular (every 4-5 yrs.)
Circulation: 2,000
Available in microform: No
Subscription address: Vittorio Klostermann Verlag, Frauenlobstr. 22, 6000 Frankfurt 90, Germany

ADVERTISING INFORMATION

Advertising accepted: No

EDITORIAL DESCRIPTION

Scope: Publishes monograph on Thomas Mann.
Reviews books: No
Publishes notes: No
Languages accepted: German; English; French
Prints abstracts: No
Author-anonymous submission: No

SUBMISSION REQUIREMENTS

Restrictions on contributors: None
Author pays submission fee: No
Author pays page charges: No
Length of books: No restrictions
Style: MLA
Number of copies required: 2
Copyright ownership: Vittorio Klostermann Verlag
Rejected manuscripts: Returned
Time before publication decision: 6 mos.
Time between decision and publication: 9 mos.
Number of reviewers: 2-4

(2974)
*The Thomas Wolfe Review

John S. Phillipson, Aldo P. Magi, & Deborah A. Borland, Editors
Dept. of English
Buchtel College of Arts & Sciences
Univ. of Akron
Akron, OH 44325-1906

Telephone: 216 972-7470
First published: 1977
Sponsoring organization: Thomas Wolfe Soc.
ISSN: 0276-5683
MLA acronym: TWN

SUBSCRIPTION INFORMATION

Frequency of publication: 2 times/yr.
Circulation: 700
Available in microform: No
Subscription price: $10.00/yr.
Year to which price refers: 1992

ADVERTISING INFORMATION

Advertising accepted: No

EDITORIAL DESCRIPTION

Scope: Interested in all aspects of Wolfe: reminiscences (particularly those casting new light on him), criticism, bibliography, queries, forthcoming publications about him, and news of interest to those interested in Wolfe.
Reviews books: No
Publishes notes: Yes
Languages accepted: English
Prints abstracts: No
Author-anonymous submission: Yes

SUBMISSION REQUIREMENTS

Restrictions on contributors: None
Author pays submission fee: No
Author pays page charges: No
Length of articles: 1,000-2,000 words
Length of notes: 500-1,000 words
Style: Chicago
Number of copies required: 1

(2975)
*Thoreau Society Bulletin

Bradley P. Dean, Editor
Thoreau Soc., Inc.
Route 2 Box 36
Ayden, NC 28513

Telephone: 919 355-0620
Fax: 919 355-5280
E-mail: 72560,2472 (Compuserve); !TRANS-PAC (AT&T Mail/EasyPlex)
First published: 1941
Sponsoring organization: Thoreau Soc., Inc.
ISSN: 0040-6406
MLA acronym: TSB

SUBSCRIPTION INFORMATION

Frequency of publication: 4 times/yr.
Circulation: 1,600
Available in microform: Yes
Subscription price: $20.00/yr.; $10.00/yr. students
Year to which price refers: 1992
Subscription address: 156 Belknap St., Concord, MA 01742
Subscription telephone: 508 369-5912

ADVERTISING INFORMATION

Advertising accepted: No

EDITORIAL DESCRIPTION

Scope: Publishes articles on Henry David Thoreau.
Reviews books: Yes
Publishes notes: Yes
Languages accepted: English
Prints abstracts: No
Author-anonymous submission: Yes

SUBMISSION REQUIREMENTS

Restrictions on contributors: None
Author pays submission fee: No
Author pays page charges: No
Length of articles: 200-1,000 words
Length of book reviews: 500 words
Length of notes: 200-500 words
Style: MLA
Number of copies required: 1
Copyright ownership: Author may request.
Rejected manuscripts: Returned at author's request; enclose return postage.
Time before publication decision: 3 weeks
Time between decision and publication: 6-9 mos.
Number of reviewers: 1-3
Articles submitted per year: 25
Articles published per year: 10-15
Book reviews submitted per year: 10-20
Book reviews published per year: 10-20
Notes submitted per year: 20
Notes published per year: 10-15

Special requirements: Submit double-spaced typescript.
Copyright ownership: Univ. of Akron
Rejected manuscripts: Returned; enclose SASE.
Time before publication decision: 1 mo.
Time between decision and publication: 2 yrs.
Number of reviewers: 2
Articles submitted per year: 12-15
Articles published per year: 10-12

(2976)
*Thought: A Review of Culture and Idea

G. Richard Dimler, S.J., Editor
Fordham Univ. Press
Univ. Box L
Bronx, NY 10458

First published: 1926
Sponsoring organization: Fordham Univ.
ISSN: 0040-6457
MLA acronym: Thought

SUBSCRIPTION INFORMATION

Frequency of publication: 4 times/yr. (Mar., June, Sept., Dec.)
Circulation: 1,200
Available in microform: Yes
Subscription price: $30.00/yr. institutions; $20.00/yr. individuals
Year to which price refers: 1992
Subscription address: Attn.: Journal Dept., at the above address

ADVERTISING INFORMATION

Advertising accepted: Yes
Advertising rates: $150.00/half page; $250.00/full page

EDITORIAL DESCRIPTION

Scope: Publishes articles of general interest in the humanities and social sciences.
Reviews books: Yes
Publishes notes: Yes
Languages accepted: English
Prints abstracts: No
Author-anonymous submission: Yes

SUBMISSION REQUIREMENTS

Author pays submission fee: No
Author pays page charges: No
Length of articles: 20 double-spaced typescript pp.
Length of book reviews: 10 double-spaced typescript pp.
Length of notes: No restrictions
Style: MLA
Number of copies required: 2
Special requirements: Type footnotes double-spaced at end, and parenthetical within the text when possible.
Copyright ownership: Fordham Univ.
Rejected manuscripts: Returned; enclose return postage.
Time before publication decision: 3 mos.
Time between decision and publication: 9-10 mos.
Number of reviewers: 3-4
Articles submitted per year: 150
Articles published per year: 20
Book reviews submitted per year: 1-2
Book reviews published per year: 1-2

(2977)
*Thought Currents in English Literature

English Literary Soc. of Aoyama Gakuin Univ.
4-25 Shibuya 4 chome
Shibuya-ku
Tokyo, Japan

First published: 1927
Sponsoring organization: Aoyama Gakuin Univ., English Literary Soc.
MLA acronym: TCEL

SUBSCRIPTION INFORMATION

Frequency of publication: Annual
Available in microform: No

ADVERTISING INFORMATION

Advertising accepted: No

EDITORIAL DESCRIPTION

Scope: Publishes articles on English language and literature.
Reviews books: Yes
Publishes notes: Yes
Languages accepted: English; Japanese
Prints abstracts: No

SUBMISSION REQUIREMENTS

Restrictions on contributors: Contributors must be members of the English Literary Soc.
Author pays submission fee: No
Author pays page charges: No
Length of articles: 5,000 words
Length of book reviews: 750-1,000 words
Length of notes: 750-1,000 words
Style: MLA
Number of copies required: 1
Copyright ownership: Author
Rejected manuscripts: Returned
Time before publication decision: 3 mos.
Time between decision and publication: 5-6 mos.
Number of reviewers: 2
Articles submitted per year: 15-20
Articles published per year: 5-7
Book reviews submitted per year: 10
Book reviews published per year: 2
Notes submitted per year: 5-10
Notes published per year: 1-2

(2978)
*Tidskrift för Litteraturvetenskap

Clas Wahlin, Editor
Litteraturvetenskapliga Inst.
Stockholms Univ.
106 91 Stockholm, Sweden

Telephone: (46) 8 163510
Fax: (46) 8 155874
First published: 1971
Sponsoring organization: Föreningen för Utgivandet av Tidskrift för Litteraturvetenskap
MLA acronym: TfL

SUBSCRIPTION INFORMATION

Frequency of publication: 4 times/yr.
Circulation: 500
Available in microform: No
Subscription price: 180 Skr/yr.
Year to which price refers: 1993

ADVERTISING INFORMATION

Advertising accepted: No

EDITORIAL DESCRIPTION

Scope: Publishes articles on comparative literature. Emphasis is on Swedish literature.
Reviews books: Yes
Publishes notes: Yes
Languages accepted: Swedish; Danish; Norwegian

SUBMISSION REQUIREMENTS

Author pays submission fee: No
Author pays page charges: No
Number of copies required: 3
Time before publication decision: 1 mo.
Time between decision and publication: 3 mos.
Number of reviewers: 3
Articles submitted per year: 100
Articles published per year: 16-25
Book reviews submitted per year: 20
Book reviews published per year: 20
Notes submitted per year: 25
Notes published per year: 8

(2979)
*Tijdschrift voor Nederlandse Taal- en Letterkunde

G. R. W. Dibbets & J. L. A. Heestermans, Editors
G. C. Zieleman
Rondedans 160
2907 AH Capelle A.D. Ijssel, Netherlands

First published: 1881
ISSN: 0040-7550
MLA acronym: TNTL

SUBSCRIPTION INFORMATION

Frequency of publication: 4 times/yr.
Circulation: 380
Available in microform: No
Subscription price: 148 f/yr. institutions; 98 f/yr. individuals
Year to which price refers: 1992
Subscription address: E. J. Brill, Plantijnstr. 2, 2321 JC Leiden, Netherlands
Subscription telephone: (31) 71 312624

ADVERTISING INFORMATION

Advertising accepted: No

EDITORIAL DESCRIPTION

Scope: Publishes articles on Dutch linguistics and literature.
Reviews books: Yes
Publishes notes: No
Languages accepted: Dutch; English; German; French
Prints abstracts: No
Author-anonymous submission: No

SUBMISSION REQUIREMENTS

Restrictions on contributors: None
Author pays submission fee: No
Author pays page charges: No
Length of articles: 24 pp. maximum
Length of book reviews: 6 pp.
Style: None
Number of copies required: 2
Copyright ownership: Author & E. J. Brill
Rejected manuscripts: Returned
Time before publication decision: 2 mos. maximum
Time between decision and publication: 8 mos.
Number of reviewers: 2
Articles submitted per year: 20-25
Articles published per year: 13-20
Book reviews submitted per year: 0-4
Book reviews published per year: 20

(2980)
*Tijdschrift voor Skandinavistiek

G. Laureys, G. van der Toorn-Piebenga, & H. van der Liet, Editors
Skandinavisch Inst.
Rijksuniv. Groningen
Postbus 716
9700 AS Groningen, Netherlands

Telephone: (31) 50 635850
Fax: (31) 50 635821
E-mail: Vderliet@let.rug.nl
First published: 1980
ISSN: 0168-2148
MLA acronym: TS

SUBSCRIPTION INFORMATION

Frequency of publication: 2 times/yr.
Circulation: 250
Available in microform: No
Subscription price: 30 f/yr.
Year to which price refers: 1992
Subscription address: Skandinavisch Inst., Rijksuniv. Groningen, Oude Kijk in't Jatstr. 26, Postbus 716, 9700 AS Groningen, Netherlands

ADVERTISING INFORMATION

Advertising accepted: No

EDITORIAL DESCRIPTION

Scope: Publishes articles on Scandinavian studies, especially language and literature.
Reviews books: Yes
Publishes notes: Yes
Languages accepted: Dutch; Danish; Norwegian; Swedish
Prints abstracts: Yes

SUBMISSION REQUIREMENTS

Restrictions on contributors: None
Author pays submission fee: No
Author pays page charges: No
Length of articles: 20 typescript pp.
Length of book reviews: 4-5 pp.
Length of notes: 200-600 words
Number of copies required: 3
Copyright ownership: Journal
Rejected manuscripts: Returned
Time before publication decision: 3 mos.
Time between decision and publication: 4 mos.
Number of reviewers: 4
Articles submitted per year: 15-20
Articles published per year: 8-10
Book reviews published per year: 8

(2981)
Tinta

Gary Vessells & Sonia Zuniga-Lomeli, Editors
Spanish & Portuguese Dept.
Univ. of California at Santa Barbara
Santa Barbara, CA 93106

First published: 1981
Sponsoring organization: Univ. of California at Santa Barbara, Spanish & Portuguese Dept.
ISSN: 0739-7003
MLA acronym: Tinta

SUBSCRIPTION INFORMATION

Frequency of publication: Annual (June)
Circulation: 125
Available in microform: No

ADVERTISING INFORMATION

Advertising accepted: Yes

EDITORIAL DESCRIPTION

Scope: Journal aims to provide a forum for outstanding scholarly and creative expression written in Hispanic and Luso-Brazilian literature.
Reviews books: Yes
Publishes notes: Yes
Languages accepted: Spanish; Portuguese; English
Prints abstracts: No
Author-anonymous submission: No

SUBMISSION REQUIREMENTS

Author pays submission fee: No
Author pays page charges: No
Length of articles: 15-20 pp.
Length of book reviews: 3 pp.
Length of notes: 1 1/2 pp.
Style: MLA
Number of copies required: 3
Special requirements: Include a short autobiography and enclose SASE.
Copyright ownership: Journal
Rejected manuscripts: One copy retained, two returned
Time before publication decision: 5 mos.
Time between decision and publication: 1 mo.
Number of reviewers: 7
Articles submitted per year: 30
Articles published per year: 10-15

Book reviews submitted per year: 6
Book reviews published per year: 3-8

(2982)
*Tirade

R. Anker & T. Lieske, Editors
Uitgeversmaatschappij G. A. van Oorschot B.V.
Herengracht 613
1017 CE Amsterdam, Netherlands

Telephone: (31) 20 6231484
Fax: (31) 20 6254083
First published: 1957
ISSN: 0563-5691
MLA acronym: Tirade

SUBSCRIPTION INFORMATION

Frequency of publication: 6 times/yr.
Circulation: 1,250
Available in microform: No
Subscription price: 80 f/yr. Netherlands; 92.50 f/yr. elsewhere
Year to which price refers: 1992

ADVERTISING INFORMATION

Advertising accepted: Yes

EDITORIAL DESCRIPTION

Scope: Publishes prose, poetry, and articles on literature and literary history.
Reviews books: No
Publishes notes: Yes
Languages accepted: Dutch
Prints abstracts: No

SUBMISSION REQUIREMENTS

Restrictions on contributors: None
Author pays submission fee: Yes
Author pays page charges: No
Length of articles: 3,000-5,000 words
Style: None
Number of copies required: 1
Special requirements: Submit typescript.
Copyright ownership: Author
Rejected manuscripts: Returned
Time before publication decision: 2 mos.
Time between decision and publication: 3 mos.
Number of reviewers: 2
Articles published per year: 40

(2983)
*Tlalocan: Revista de Fuentes para el Conocimiento de las Culturas Indigenas de México

Karen Dakin, Editor
Inst. de Investigaciones Filológica
Seminario de Lenguas Indígenas
Circuito Mario de la Cueva-Univ. Nacional Autónoma de México
Ciudad Universitaria
04510 Mexico City, D.F., Mexico

Telephone: (52) 5 6227489
Fax: (52) 5 6657874
E-mail: DAKIN@UNAMVM1
First published: 1942
Sponsoring organization: Univ. Nacional Autónoma de México
ISSN: 0185-0989
MLA acronym: Tlalocan

SUBSCRIPTION INFORMATION

Frequency of publication: Irregular
Circulation: 2,000
Available in microform: No
Subscription price: $16.00/yr.
Year to which price refers: 1989

ADVERTISING INFORMATION

Advertising accepted: Yes, on an exchange basis

EDITORIAL DESCRIPTION

Scope: Publishes linguistic, ethnological, and historical sources related to the Indian cultures of Mexico and Central America.
Reviews books: Yes
Publishes notes: Yes
Languages accepted: English; French; Spanish; German
Prints abstracts: Yes
Author-anonymous submission: No

SUBMISSION REQUIREMENTS

Restrictions on contributors: None
Author pays submission fee: No
Author pays page charges: No
Length of articles: 11,000 words
Length of book reviews: 750-1,000 words
Length of notes: 150-300 words
Style: American Anthropologist
Number of copies required: 2
Special requirements: Articles in Spanish must have English abstracts, and vice versa. Journal will provide them, if necessary. Considers manuscripts in Indian languages of Mexico & Central America.
Copyright ownership: Author
Rejected manuscripts: Returned
Time before publication decision: 3 mos.
Time between decision and publication: 1 yr.
Number of reviewers: 2
Articles submitted per year: 35
Articles published per year: 25
Book reviews submitted per year: 2
Book reviews published per year: 1
Notes submitted per year: 15
Notes published per year: 10

(2984)
*Tōhōgaku: Eastern Studies

Jikidō Takasaki, Editor
Tōhō Gakkai/Inst. of Eastern Culture
4-1, Nishi-Kanda 2-chōme
Chiyoda-ku,
Tokyo, 101, Japan

Telephone: (81) 3 32627221
Fax: (81) 3 32637227
First published: 1951
Sponsoring organization: Tōhō Gakkai
ISSN: 0495-7199
MLA acronym: Tōhōgaku

SUBSCRIPTION INFORMATION

Frequency of publication: 2 times/yr.
Available in microform: No
Subscription price: 1,900 yen/yr. plus postage
Year to which price refers: 1992

ADVERTISING INFORMATION

Advertising accepted: No

EDITORIAL DESCRIPTION

Scope: Publishes articles on Eastern studies.
Reviews books: Yes
Publishes notes: No
Languages accepted: Japanese
Prints abstracts: Yes, in English
Author-anonymous submission: No

SUBMISSION REQUIREMENTS

Restrictions on contributors: Contributors must be members of Tōhō Gakkai.
Author pays submission fee: No
Author pays page charges: No
Length of articles: 16,000 words
Length of book reviews: 4,800 words
Number of copies required: 1

Copyright ownership: Tōhō Gakkai
Time before publication decision: 2 mos.
Time between decision and publication: 6 mos.
Number of reviewers: 13
Articles submitted per year: 30
Articles published per year: 20

(2985)
Tohoku Gakuin University Review: Essays and Studies in English Language and Literature [Tohoku Gakuin Daigaku Ronshu, Eigo-Eibungaku]

Yukio Igarashi, Editor
Tohoku Gakuin Univ.
3-1. Tsuchitoi 1 Chome
Sendai 980, Japan

First published: 1953
Sponsoring organization: Tohoku Gakuin Univ., Literary, Economic, & Juristic Assn.
ISSN: 0385-406X
MLA acronym: ESELL

SUBSCRIPTION INFORMATION

Frequency of publication: 2 times/yr.
Circulation: 1,500
Available in microform: No

ADVERTISING INFORMATION

Advertising accepted: No

EDITORIAL DESCRIPTION

Scope: Publishes articles on English language and literature. Includes treatment of authors, works, genre, methodology, criticism, and translation.
Reviews books: Yes
Publishes notes: Yes
Languages accepted: Japanese; English
Prints abstracts: No

SUBMISSION REQUIREMENTS

Restrictions on contributors: Most contributors are members of the Literary, Economic, & Juristic Assn. of Tohoku Gakuin Univ.
Author pays submission fee: No
Author pays page charges: No
Length of articles: 3,000 words
Length of notes: 1,000 words
Style: MLA
Copyright ownership: Author
Rejected manuscripts: Returned
Time before publication decision: 2-3 mos.
Time between decision and publication: 2 mos.
Number of reviewers: 1
Articles submitted per year: 4-5
Articles published per year: 4-5
Book reviews submitted per year: 1
Book reviews published per year: 1
Notes submitted per year: 1
Notes published per year: 1

(2986)
*Tolstoy Studies Journal

Amy Mandelker, Editor
Graduate Program in Comparative Literature
Graduate Center, City Univ. of New York
33 W. 42nd St.
New York, NY 10036-8099

Additional editorial address: Send bibliographical entries to Harold K. Schefski, Dept. of German, Russian & Classics, California State Univ., Long Beach, 1250 Bellflower Blvd., Long Beach, CA 90840
Telephone: 212 861-9527
First published: 1988

Sponsoring organization: City Univ. of New York-Graduate Center; City Univ. of New York-Graduate Center, Dept. of Comparative Literature
ISSN: 1044-1573
MLA acronym: TSJ

SUBSCRIPTION INFORMATION

Frequency of publication: Annual
Available in microform: No
Subscription price: $20.00/yr. faculty & institutions; $10.00/yr. emeriti, students, & independent scholars
Year to which price refers: 1992
Subscription address: Kathleen Parthé, 104 Jefferson Rd., Princeton, NJ 08540-3303

ADVERTISING INFORMATION

Advertising accepted: Yes

EDITORIAL DESCRIPTION

Scope: Publishes articles on the life and works of Lev Tolstoĭ as well as other topics relevant to Tolstoĭ scholarship.
Reviews books: Yes
Publishes notes: Yes
Languages accepted: English
Prints abstracts: Yes
Author-anonymous submission: Yes

SUBMISSION REQUIREMENTS

Restrictions on contributors: Most reviews are solicited.
Author pays submission fee: No
Author pays page charges: No
Length of articles: No restrictions
Length of book reviews: No restrictions
Length of notes: No restrictions
Style: MLA
Number of copies required: 2
Special requirements: Use Library of Congress system of transliteration for Russian and other Slavic languages. Russian surnames which have commonly been transliterated differently in English should be given their standardized form. Submission on diskette is encouraged; state type of program, operating system, and title of file.
Copyright ownership: Journal
Rejected manuscripts: Returned
Time before publication decision: 6 mos.
Time between decision and publication: 6 mos.
Number of reviewers: 2
Articles submitted per year: 12-15
Articles published per year: 5
Book reviews submitted per year: 4
Book reviews published per year: 3-4
Notes submitted per year: 3-4
Notes published per year: 3-4

(2987)
*Tools & Tillage: A Journal on the History of the Implements of Cultivation and Other Agricultural Processes

Grith Lerche, Axel Steensberg, & Alexander Fenton, Editors
International Secretariat for Research on the History of Agricultural Implements
National Museum, Brede
2800 Lyngby, Denmark

First published: 1968
Sponsoring organization: National Museum of Denmark; Danish Research Council for the Humanities
ISSN: 0563-8887
MLA acronym: T&T

SUBSCRIPTION INFORMATION

Frequency of publication: Annual
Circulation: 1,000

Available in microform: No

ADVERTISING INFORMATION

Advertising accepted: No

EDITORIAL DESCRIPTION

Scope: Concerned with cultivating equipment, field systems, and agricultural processes, methods of cultivation and cropping. Includes linguistic as well as functional aspects. Publishes primary research; coverage is from the beginning of cultivation to the industrial era in every part of the world.
Reviews books: Yes
Publishes notes: Yes
Languages accepted: English; German
Prints abstracts: Yes
Author-anonymous submission: No

SUBMISSION REQUIREMENTS

Restrictions on contributors: Contributions must be based on primary research.
Author pays submission fee: No
Author pays page charges: No
Length of articles: 16 printed pp. including notes, illustrations, and abstract
Length of book reviews: 300-400 words
Length of notes: 2-4 pp.
Style: Journal
Number of copies required: 3
Special requirements: Submit original typescript, illustrations, and a 200-word abstract.
Copyright ownership: Journal & author
Rejected manuscripts: Returned
Time before publication decision: 2-3 mos.
Time between decision and publication: 8-10 mos.
Number of reviewers: 3
Articles published per year: 4-5
Book reviews published per year: 1-3
Notes published per year: 1-2

(2988)
Topic: A Journal of the Liberal Arts

John Mark Scott, Jr., Editor
Washington & Jefferson College
Washington, PA 15301

First published: 1961
ISSN: 0049-4127
MLA acronym: Topic

SUBSCRIPTION INFORMATION

Frequency of publication: Annual
Circulation: 1,000

ADVERTISING INFORMATION

Advertising accepted: No

EDITORIAL DESCRIPTION

Scope: Each issue has a separate subtitle and covers a single topic, area of interest, or theme. Each issue includes articles from several disciplines written in such a way that colleagues in other disciplines will be interested in reading them. Invites contributions in all areas of the humanities and also in the sciences where they relate to the humanities. Out of these contributions subsequent *Topics* will evolve. Welcomes suggestions of *Topics* to which issues may be devoted.
Reviews books: No
Languages accepted: English; Spanish; French; German
Prints abstracts: No

SUBMISSION REQUIREMENTS

Author pays submission fee: No
Length of articles: 2,500-3,000 words
Style: MLA
Number of copies required: 1

Rejected manuscripts: Returned; enclose return postage.
Time before publication decision: 9 mos.
Time between decision and publication: 2-3 mos.
Number of reviewers: 3-5
Articles published per year: 4-8

(2989)
Topics in Sociolinguistics

Nessa Wolfson & Marinel Gerritsen, Editors
Graduate School of Education
Univ. of Pennsylvania
Philadelphia, PA 19104

Additional editorial address: P. J. Meertens Inst., Keizersgracht, 569-571, 1017 DR Amsterdam, Netherlands
First published: 1982
MLA acronym: TiS

SUBSCRIPTION INFORMATION

Frequency of publication: Irregular
Available in microform: No
Subscription address: Foris Publications, P.O. Box 509, 3300 AM Dordrecht, Netherlands

ADVERTISING INFORMATION

Advertising accepted: No

EDITORIAL DESCRIPTION

Scope: Publishes works which take as their unifying theme the interplay between linguistic, social, and cultural factors in human communication.
Reviews books: No
Publishes notes: No
Languages accepted: English
Prints abstracts: Yes

SUBMISSION REQUIREMENTS

Restrictions on contributors: Contributors must be sociolinguists.
Author pays submission fee: No
Author pays page charges: No
Style: Language
Number of copies required: 1
Copyright ownership: Author
Rejected manuscripts: Returned
Time before publication decision: 3-4 mos.
Time between decision and publication: 6-9 mos.
Number of reviewers: 3-4
Books submitted per year: 15-20
Book reviews published per year: 3

(2990)
*La Torre: Revista de la Universidad de Puerto Rico

Arturo Echavarría, Editor
Apdo. 23322, U.P.R.
San Juan, PR 00931-3322

Telephone: 809 758-0148
Fax: 809 753-9116
First published: 1953
Sponsoring organization: Univ. of Puerto Rico
ISSN: 0040-9588
MLA acronym: Torre

SUBSCRIPTION INFORMATION

Frequency of publication: 4 times/yr.
Circulation: 500
Available in microform: No
Subscription price: $28.00/yr. institutions; $16.00/yr. individuals
Year to which price refers: 1992

ADVERTISING INFORMATION

Advertising accepted: Yes, on an exchange basis

EDITORIAL DESCRIPTION

Scope: Publishes articles on Spanish, Spanish American, and Caribbean literature and linguistics.
Reviews books: Yes
Publishes notes: Yes
Languages accepted: Spanish
Prints abstracts: No
Author-anonymous submission: No

SUBMISSION REQUIREMENTS

Author pays submission fee: No
Author pays page charges: No
Length of articles: 6,900 words
Length of book reviews: 1,100 words
Length of notes: 1,640 words
Style: MLA
Number of copies required: 1
Special requirements: Submit original typescript.
Copyright ownership: Univ. of Puerto Rico
Rejected manuscripts: Returned
Time before publication decision: 4 mos.
Time between decision and publication: 18 mos.
Number of reviewers: 2
Articles published per year: 30
Book reviews published per year: 16

(2991)
*T'oung Pao: Revue Internationale de Sinologie

Jacques Gernet & E. Zürcher, Editors
Collège de France
11, place Marcelin-Berthelot
75231 Paris Cedex 05, France

Additional editorial address: Sinologische Inst., Arsenalstraat 1, 2311 VV Leiden, Netherlands
First published: 1890
ISSN: 0082-5433
MLA acronym: TPA

SUBSCRIPTION INFORMATION

Frequency of publication: 5 times/yr.
Circulation: 600
Available in microform: No
Subscription price: 135 f ($67.50)/yr.
Year to which price refers: 1991
Subscription address: E. J. Brill, P.O. Box 9000, 2300 PA Leiden, Netherlands
Additional subscription address: E. J. Brill, 24 Hudson St., Kinderhook, NY 12106

ADVERTISING INFORMATION

Advertising accepted: No

EDITORIAL DESCRIPTION

Scope: Publishes articles dealing with China before 1900.
Reviews books: Yes
Languages accepted: English; French; German
Prints abstracts: Yes

SUBMISSION REQUIREMENTS

Restrictions on contributors: None
Author pays submission fee: No
Author pays page charges: No
Length of articles: No restrictions
Length of book reviews: No restrictions
Style: None
Number of copies required: 2
Copyright ownership: E. J. Brill
Rejected manuscripts: Not returned
Time before publication decision: 2 mos.
Time between decision and publication: 1-2 yrs.
Number of reviewers: 3-4

(2992)
Trabalhos em Linguistica Aplicada

UNICAMP-Inst. de Estudos da Linguagem
Setor de Publicações
C.P. 6045
13081 Campinas-SP, Brazil

First published: 1983
Sponsoring organization: Dept. de Lingüística Aplicada do Inst. de Estudos da Linguagem, Univ. Estadual de Campinas
ISSN: 0103-1813
MLA acronym: TLA

SUBSCRIPTION INFORMATION

Frequency of publication: 2 times/yr.
Circulation: 800

EDITORIAL DESCRIPTION

Scope: Publishes articles on applied linguistics of first, second, and foreign language learning, as well as on translation.
Reviews books: Yes
Publishes notes: No
Languages accepted: Portuguese; English; French; Spanish
Prints abstracts: No
Author-anonymous submission: No

(2993)
*Tradisjon: Tidsskrift for Folkeminnevitskap

Reimund Kvideland, Editor
Nordic Inst. of Folklore
P.O. Box 107
20501 Turku, Finland

Telephone: (358) 21 326202
Fax: (358) 21 311523
First published: 1971
Sponsoring organization: Norges Almenvitenskapelige Forskningsråd
ISSN: 0332-5997
MLA acronym: Tradisjon

SUBSCRIPTION INFORMATION

Frequency of publication: Annual
Circulation: 1,000
Available in microform: No
Subscription price: 225 NKr ($42.00)/yr.
Year to which price refers: 1992
Subscription address: Scandinavian Univ. Press, P.O. Box 2959 Tøyen, 0608 Oslo, Norway
Additional subscription address: Scandinavian Univ. Press, 200 Meacham Ave., Elmont, NY 11003

ADVERTISING INFORMATION

Advertising accepted: Yes

EDITORIAL DESCRIPTION

Scope: Publishes articles on folklore with primary emphasis on the Nordic countries.
Reviews books: Yes
Publishes notes: Yes
Languages accepted: Danish; Norwegian; Swedish
Prints abstracts: Yes

SUBMISSION REQUIREMENTS

Restrictions on contributors: None
Author pays submission fee: No
Author pays page charges: No

Articles submitted per year: 15
Articles published per year: 8
Book reviews submitted per year: 50
Book reviews published per year: 20

Length of articles: 20 pp. maximum
Length of book reviews: 1/2-1 p.
Length of notes: 60-120 words
Number of copies required: 1
Special requirements: Include a summary in English.
Copyright ownership: Journal
Rejected manuscripts: Returned
Time before publication decision: 6 mos.
Time between decision and publication: 6 mos.
Number of reviewers: 2-5
Articles published per year: 8
Book reviews published per year: 26
Notes published per year: 8

(2994)
*Traditio: Studies in Ancient and Medieval History, Thought, and Religion

R. E. Kaske, Elizabeth A. R. Brown, Charles Lohr, Brian E. Daley, S.J. & James J. O'Donnell, Editors
Fordham Univ. Press
Univ. Box L
Bronx, NY 10458-5172

First published: 1943
Sponsoring organization: Fordham Univ. Press
ISSN: 0362-1529
MLA acronym: Traditio

SUBSCRIPTION INFORMATION

Frequency of publication: Annual
Circulation: 700
Available in microform: Yes, through Univ. Microfilms International

ADVERTISING INFORMATION

Advertising accepted: No

EDITORIAL DESCRIPTION

Scope: Publishes critical editions of texts and magisterial studies, in all fields of ancient and Medieval studies.
Reviews books: No
Publishes notes: Yes
Languages accepted: English; French; German; Greek; Italian; Latin; Spanish
Prints abstracts: No
Author-anonymous submission: No

SUBMISSION REQUIREMENTS

Restrictions on contributors: Submit manuscripts after the beginning of January in each year and before 1 July.
Author pays submission fee: No
Author pays page charges: No
Length of articles: No restrictions
Length of notes: No restrictions
Style: Journal
Number of copies required: 1
Special requirements: Articles should not be under consideration by another journal.
Copyright ownership: Author
Rejected manuscripts: Returned
Time before publication decision: 3-6 mos.
Time between decision and publication: 10-11 mos.
Number of reviewers: 2-5
Articles submitted per year: 75
Articles published per year: 12-15
Notes submitted per year: 20
Notes published per year: 4-6

(2995)
*Tradition: A Journal of Orthodox Jewish Thought

Emanuel Feldman, Editor
Rabbinical Council of America
275 Seventh Ave.
New York, NY 10001

First published: 1958
Sponsoring organization: Rabbinical Council of America
ISSN: 0041-0608
MLA acronym: Tradition

SUBSCRIPTION INFORMATION

Frequency of publication: 4 times/yr.
Circulation: 3,000
Subscription price: $31.00/yr. institutions; $20.00/yr. individuals
Year to which price refers: 1992

ADVERTISING INFORMATION

Advertising accepted: No

EDITORIAL DESCRIPTION

Scope: Publishes articles on Jewish thought.
Reviews books: Yes
Publishes notes: Yes
Languages accepted: English
Prints abstracts: No
Author-anonymous submission: Yes

SUBMISSION REQUIREMENTS

Restrictions on contributors: None
Author pays submission fee: No
Author pays page charges: No
Length of articles: 12-20 double-spaced typescript pp.
Style: MLA; *Encyclopedia Judaica*
Number of copies required: 3
Special requirements: Consult with editor before submission
Copyright ownership: Rabbinical Council of America
Rejected manuscripts: Not returned
Time before publication decision: 3 mos.
Time between decision and publication: 6-12 mos.
Number of reviewers: 5
Articles published per year: 24-30

(2996)
Traditional Music

Alan Ward, Editor
90 St. Julian's Farm Rd.
London SE27 ORS, England

First published: 1975
ISSN: 0306-7440
MLA acronym: TrM

SUBSCRIPTION INFORMATION

Frequency of publication: 3 times/yr.

EDITORIAL DESCRIPTION

Scope: Publishes articles on traditional music in the British Isles. Reviews records.
Reviews books: Yes
Languages accepted: English
Prints abstracts: No

SUBMISSION REQUIREMENTS

Restrictions on contributors: None
Length of articles: No restrictions
Style: None
Copyright ownership: Journal

(2997)
*Traditiones: Zbornik Inštituta za Slovensko Narodopisje

Mojca Ravnik, Editor
Znanstvenoraziskovalni Center
Slovenske Akademije Znanosti in Umetnosti
Novi trg 5
61000 Ljubljana, Slovenia

Telephone: (38) 61 156068
Fax: (38) 61 155232
E-mail: SAZU.SYSTEM; SAZU.INFOSAZU
First published: 1972
Sponsoring organization: Slovenska Akademija Znanosti in Umetnosti
ISSN: 0352-0447
MLA acronym: TZI

SUBSCRIPTION INFORMATION

Frequency of publication: Annual
Circulation: 600
Available in microform: No
Subscription telephone: (38) 61 123144

ADVERTISING INFORMATION

Advertising accepted: No

EDITORIAL DESCRIPTION

Scope: Publishes articles on folklore, ethnology, and anthropology, concerned with Slovenian territory.
Reviews books: Yes
Publishes notes: Yes
Languages accepted: Slovenian; German; French; Italian; English; all Slavic languages
Prints abstracts: Yes
Author-anonymous submission: No

SUBMISSION REQUIREMENTS

Restrictions on contributors: None
Author pays submission fee: No
Author pays page charges: No
Length of articles: 6,000-8,000 words
Length of book reviews: 1,500-2,500 words
Length of notes: 500-1,000 words
Style: SAZU
Number of copies required: 1
Copyright ownership: Author
Rejected manuscripts: Returned
Time before publication decision: 1-2 mos.
Time between decision and publication: 6-10 mos.
Number of reviewers: 3
Articles submitted per year: 10-12
Articles published per year: 9-12
Book reviews submitted per year: 20-25
Book reviews published per year: 20-25
Notes submitted per year: 10-15
Notes published per year: 10-15

(2998)
*The Transactions of the Asiatic Society of Japan

Roger Finch, Editor
Asiatic Soc. of Japan
Central P.O. Box 592
Tokyo, Japan

First published: 1872
Sponsoring organization: Asiatic Soc. of Japan
ISSN: 0287-6051
MLA acronym: TASJ

SUBSCRIPTION INFORMATION

Frequency of publication: Annual
Circulation: 500
Available in microform: No
Subscription price: 5,000 yen/yr. (includes membership)
Year to which price refers: 1992
Subscription telephone: (81) 3 35861548
Subscription fax: (81) 3 35870030

ADVERTISING INFORMATION

Advertising accepted: Yes, on an exchange basis

EDITORIAL DESCRIPTION

Scope: Publishes papers on Japanese and East Asian studies.
Reviews books: No
Publishes notes: Yes
Languages accepted: English
Prints abstracts: No
Author-anonymous submission: No

SUBMISSION REQUIREMENTS

Restrictions on contributors: Primarily publishes papers presented monthly, by invited speakers, to the Asiatic Soc. of Japan.
Author pays submission fee: No
Author pays page charges: No
Length of articles: 8,000 words
Number of copies required: 1
Copyright ownership: Asiatic Soc. of Japan
Rejected manuscripts: Returned
Time before publication decision: 2 mos.
Time between decision and publication: 6-12 mos.
Number of reviewers: 2-3
Articles submitted per year: 10-12
Articles published per year: 5-6

(2999)
*Transactions of the Cambridge Bibliographical Society

E. S. Leedham-Green, Editor
Cambridge Univ. Library
West Rd.
Cambridge CB3 9DR, England

Telephone: (44) 223 333148
Fax: (44) 223 333160
E-mail: ELIT@PHX.CAM.AC.UK; ELIT@UK.AC.CAM.PHX
First published: 1949
Sponsoring organization: Cambridge Bibliographical Soc.
ISSN: 0068-6611
MLA acronym: TCBS

SUBSCRIPTION INFORMATION

Frequency of publication: Annual
Circulation: 500
Available in microform: No
Subscription price: £8.00 ($18.00)/yr.
Year to which price refers: 1992
Subscription telephone: (44) 223 333122

ADVERTISING INFORMATION

Advertising accepted: Yes
Advertising rates: £100.00 ($200.00)/full page

EDITORIAL DESCRIPTION

Scope: Publishes contributions of general bibliographical interest, especially concerning Cambridge. Includes articles on manuscripts or printed books in Cambridge libraries, and books printed at Cambridge or written by Cambridge authors.
Reviews books: No
Publishes notes: Yes
Languages accepted: English
Prints abstracts: No
Author-anonymous submission: No

SUBMISSION REQUIREMENTS

Restrictions on contributors: None
Author pays submission fee: No
Author pays page charges: No
Length of articles: 10,000 words maximum
Style: MLA
Number of copies required: 1
Special requirements: Submit typescript or diskette.
Copyright ownership: Cambridge Bibliographical Soc.
Rejected manuscripts: Returned
Time before publication decision: 1 mo.
Time between decision and publication: 15 mos.
Number of reviewers: 2
Articles published per year: 8
Notes published per year: 2

(3000)
*Transactions of the Gaelic Society of Inverness

Hugh Barron, Honorary Secretary
Gaelic Soc. of Inverness
The Granary, Ness Side
Dores Rd.
Iverness, Scotland

First published: 1872
Sponsoring organization: Gaelic Soc. of Inverness
ISSN: 0958-5451
MLA acronym: TGSI

SUBSCRIPTION INFORMATION

Frequency of publication: Once every 2 yrs.
Circulation: 500
Available in microform: No

ADVERTISING INFORMATION

Advertising accepted: No

EDITORIAL DESCRIPTION

Scope: Publishes articles concerning the Gaelic language and Highland matters.
Reviews books: Yes
Publishes notes: No
Languages accepted: English; Scottish Gaelic
Prints abstracts: Yes
Author-anonymous submission: No

SUBMISSION REQUIREMENTS

Restrictions on contributors: Contributors must be members of the Gaelic Soc. of Inverness or have read a paper at a meeting of the Society.
Author pays submission fee: No
Author pays page charges: No
Length of articles: No restrictions
Style: None
Number of copies required: 1
Copyright ownership: Assigned by author to journal
Rejected manuscripts: Returned
Articles submitted per year: 5-8

(3001)
*Transactions of the Honourable Society of Cymmrodorion

R. Geraint Gruffydd & Llinos Beverley Smith, Editors
Centre for Advanced Welsh & Celtic Studies
Old College
Aberystwyth
Dyfed SY23 2AX, Wales

Telephone: (44) 970 622090
First published: 1892
Sponsoring organization: Honourable Soc. of Cymmrodorion
ISSN: 0959-3632
MLA acronym: THSC

SUBSCRIPTION INFORMATION

Frequency of publication: Annual
Circulation: 1,800

Available in microform: No
Subscription address: Honourable Soc. of Cymmrodorian, 30 Eastcastle St., London W1 7PD, England

ADVERTISING INFORMATION

Advertising accepted: No

EDITORIAL DESCRIPTION

Scope: Publishes lectures and papers delivered before the Society as well as other articles of interest to the society's membership.
Reviews books: No
Publishes notes: No
Languages accepted: English; Welsh
Prints abstracts: No
Author-anonymous submission: No

SUBMISSION REQUIREMENTS

Restrictions on contributors: Priority is given to lectures and papers delivered before, and at the invitation of, the Soc. of Cymmrodorion.
Author pays submission fee: No
Author pays page charges: No
Length of articles: 5,000 words
Style: Hart's Rules
Number of copies required: 1
Copyright ownership: Author
Rejected manuscripts: Returned
Time before publication decision: 3 mos.
Time between decision and publication: 2 yrs.
Number of reviewers: 2
Articles submitted per year: 15
Articles published per year: 9

(3002)
*Transactions of the International Conference of Orientalists in Japan

Jikidō Takasaki, Editor
Tōhō Gakkai/Inst. of Eastern Culture
4-1, Nishi-Kanda 2-chōme
Chiyoda-ku
Tokyo 101, Japan

Telephone: (81) 3 32627221
Fax: (81) 3 32627227
First published: 1956
Sponsoring organization: Tōhō Gakkai
ISSN: 0538-6012
MLA acronym: TICOJ

SUBSCRIPTION INFORMATION

Frequency of publication: Annual
Available in microform: No
Subscription price: 2,300 yen/yr. plus postage
Year to which price refers: 1992

ADVERTISING INFORMATION

Advertising accepted: No

EDITORIAL DESCRIPTION

Scope: Publishes papers on Oriental studies read before the International Conference of Orientalists.
Reviews books: No
Publishes notes: No
Languages accepted: English
Prints abstracts: Yes
Author-anonymous submission: No

SUBMISSION REQUIREMENTS

Restrictions on contributors: Contributors must be participants in the International Conference of Orientalists.
Author pays submission fee: No
Author pays page charges: No
Length of articles: 5,000 words
Style: Chicago
Copyright ownership: Tōhō Gakkai

Articles submitted per year: 60
Articles published per year: 5-6

(3003)
*Transactions of the Philological Society

Max W. Wheeler, Editor
School of European Studies
Univ. of Sussex
Falmer, Brighton BN1 9QN, England

Telephone: (44) 273 606755 ext. 2080
Fax: (44) 273 678466
First published: 1842
Sponsoring organization: Philological Soc.
ISSN: 0079-1636
MLA acronym: TPS

SUBSCRIPTION INFORMATION

Frequency of publication: 2 times/yr.
Circulation: 800
Available in microform: Yes; back issues to 1981 only
Subscription price: $133.50/yr. institutions; $81.00/yr. individuals; £10.00/yr. members
Year to which price refers: 1992
Subscription address: Basil Blackwell Ltd., c/o Marston Book Services, Journal Subscriptions Dept., P.O. Box 87, Oxford OX2 ODT, England
Subscription telephone: (44) 865 791155
Subscription fax: (44) 865 791927

ADVERTISING INFORMATION

Advertising accepted: Yes

EDITORIAL DESCRIPTION

Scope: Focuses on the study of the structure and history of languages.
Reviews books: No
Publishes notes: No
Languages accepted: English
Prints abstracts: No

SUBMISSION REQUIREMENTS

Restrictions on contributors: None
Author pays submission fee: No
Author pays page charges: No
Number of copies required: 3
Special requirements: Consult with editor for manuscript requirements.
Copyright ownership: Philological Soc.
Rejected manuscripts: Returned at author's request
Time before publication decision: 3 mos. maximum
Time between decision and publication: 1 yr. maximum
Number of reviewers: 2-3
Articles published per year: 8-10

(3004)
Transactions of the Samuel Johnson Society of the Northwest

K. J. Ericksen & R. H. Carnie, Editors
Samuel Johnson Soc.
English Dept.
Univ. of Calgary
2500 University Drive N. W.
Calgary, Alberta T2N 1N4, Canada

Sponsoring organization: Samuel Johnson Soc. of the Northwest
ISSN: 0828-6515
MLA acronym: TSJSNW

SUBSCRIPTION INFORMATION

Frequency of publication: Irregular
Circulation: 300

Available in microform: No

ADVERTISING INFORMATION

Advertising accepted: No

EDITORIAL DESCRIPTION

Scope: Publishes papers on Samuel Johnson and 18th-century literature read at the society's meetings.
Reviews books: No
Publishes notes: No
Languages accepted: English
Prints abstracts: No
Author-anonymous submission: Yes

SUBMISSION REQUIREMENTS

Restrictions on contributors: Contributors must be members of the Samuel Johnson Soc. of the Northwest, and have read paper at annual meeting.
Author pays submission fee: No
Author pays page charges: No
Length of articles: 5,000 words
Style: MLA
Number of copies required: 1
Special requirements: Submit camera-ready copy for all illustrations.
Copyright ownership: Journal
Rejected manuscripts: Returned; enclose return postage.
Time before publication decision: 3-4 mos.
Time between decision and publication: 8-12 mos.
Number of reviewers: 4
Articles submitted per year: 30-40
Articles published per year: 12

(3005)
*Transactions of the Wisconsin Academy of Sciences, Arts, and Letters

Carl Haywood, Editor
Univ. of Wisconsin-Oshkosh
College of Letters & Science
Oshkosh, WI 54901

Telephone: 414 424-1186
Fax: 414 424-7317
First published: 1870
Sponsoring organization: Wisconsin Academy of Sciences, Arts & Letters
ISSN: 0084-0505
MLA acronym: TWA

SUBSCRIPTION INFORMATION

Frequency of publication: Annual
Circulation: 1,550
Available in microform: No
Subscription price: $5.00/yr.
Year to which price refers: 1992
Subscription address: Wisconsin Academy of Sciences Arts, & Letters, 1922 University Ave., Madison, WI 53705-4099

ADVERTISING INFORMATION

Advertising accepted: No

EDITORIAL DESCRIPTION

Scope: Publishes articles on literature, the arts, and science, either with a Wisconsin focus or by Wisconsin authors.
Reviews books: No
Publishes notes: No
Languages accepted: English
Prints abstracts: Yes, for science papers.
Author-anonymous submission: No

SUBMISSION REQUIREMENTS

Restrictions on contributors: Preference is given to contributions from or about Wisconsin.

Author pays submission fee: No
Author pays page charges: No
Length of articles: No restrictions
Style: Varies with subject area; Chicago primarily
Number of copies required: 2
Special requirements: Submit double-spaced typescript.
Copyright ownership: Wisconsin Academy of Sciences, Arts & Letters
Rejected manuscripts: Returned
Time before publication decision: 3 mos.
Time between decision and publication: 6 mos.
Number of reviewers: 2
Articles submitted per year: 40-50
Articles published per year: 10-15

(3006)
Transactions of the Yorkshire Dialect Society

Arnold Kellett, Editor
22 Aspin Oval
Knaresborough
North Yorkshire HG5 8EL, England

First published: 1897
Sponsoring organization: Yorkshire Dialect Soc.
ISSN: 0954-6316
MLA acronym: TYDS

SUBSCRIPTION INFORMATION

Frequency of publication: Annual
Circulation: 750
Available in microform: No
Subscription price: £5.00/yr.
Year to which price refers: 1992
Subscription address: Cedric Sellers, Hon. Treasurer, 7 Brook Park, Briggswath, Sleights, Whitby YO21 1RT, United Kingdom

ADVERTISING INFORMATION

Advertising accepted: No

EDITORIAL DESCRIPTION

Scope: Publishes articles on the Yorkshire and other dialects.
Reviews books: Yes
Publishes notes: Yes
Languages accepted: English
Prints abstracts: No
Author-anonymous submission: No

SUBMISSION REQUIREMENTS

Restrictions on contributors: None
Author pays submission fee: No
Author pays page charges: No
Length of articles: 2,000-5,000 words
Length of book reviews: 300 words
Length of notes: 500 words
Style: MLA
Number of copies required: 1
Special requirements: Submit typescript.
Copyright ownership: Author & Yorkshire Dialect Soc.
Rejected manuscripts: Returned
Time before publication decision: 2 mos.
Time between decision and publication: 1 yr.
Number of reviewers: 1
Articles submitted per year: 5
Articles published per year: 3
Book reviews submitted per year: 5
Book reviews published per year: 3
Notes submitted per year: 2
Notes published per year: 1

(3007)
*Translation

Frank MacShane, Lori Carlson, & Timothy Sultan, Editors
412 Dodge
Columbia Univ.
New York, NY 10027

Telephone: 212 854-2305
Fax: 212 749-0397
First published: 1972
Sponsoring organization: Translation Center
ISSN: 0093-9307
MLA acronym: Translation

SUBSCRIPTION INFORMATION

Frequency of publication: 2 times/yr. (June, Dec.)
Circulation: 1,000
Available in microform: No
Subscription price: $18.00/yr. US; $20.00/yr. elsewhere
Year to which price refers: 1992

ADVERTISING INFORMATION

Advertising accepted: Yes
Advertising rates: $150.00/half page; $300.00/full page

EDITORIAL DESCRIPTION

Scope: Publishes new translations of important contemporary world literature.
Reviews books: No
Publishes notes: No
Languages accepted: English
Prints abstracts: No

SUBMISSION REQUIREMENTS

Restrictions on contributors: None
Author pays submission fee: No
Author pays page charges: No
Length of articles: 30 typescript pp. maximum
Style: Chicago
Number of copies required: 1
Special requirements: Contributor must have permission to publish translation. Include 10-line author biography, 10-line translator biography, and original foreign language text. Query editor before submitting.
Copyright ownership: Journal; reverts to author upon publication
Rejected manuscripts: Returned; enclose SASE.
Time before publication decision: 2-6 mos.
Time between decision and publication: 3 mos.
Number of reviewers: 3-5
Articles submitted per year: 200-300
Articles published per year: 70

(3008)
*Translation Perspectives

Marilyn Gaddis Rose, Managing Editor
CRIT/TRIP
State Univ. of New York
P.O. Box 6000
Binghamton, NY 13902-6000

Telephone: 607 777-6726
Fax: 607 777-4000
E-mail: BKUMIEGA@BINGVAXA
First published: 1982
Sponsoring organization: Center for Research in Translation, State Univ. of New York at Binghamton
ISSN: 0890-4758
MLA acronym: TrP

SUBSCRIPTION INFORMATION

Frequency of publication: Irregular
Circulation: 200
Available in microform: No
Subscription price: $20.00/issue
Year to which price refers: 1991

ADVERTISING INFORMATION

Advertising accepted: No

EDITORIAL DESCRIPTION

Scope: Publishes articles on all aspects of language and criticism as they intersect with translation.
Reviews books: No
Publishes notes: No
Languages accepted: English
Prints abstracts: No
Author-anonymous submission: No

SUBMISSION REQUIREMENTS

Restrictions on contributors: Some issues are thematic and solicited.
Author pays submission fee: No
Author pays page charges: No
Length of articles: 2,500-3,000 words
Style: MLA
Number of copies required: 1
Special requirements: Submit typescript and electronic copy.
Copyright ownership: SUNY, Binghamton
Rejected manuscripts: Returned
Time before publication decision: 2 mos.
Time between decision and publication: 10 mos.
Number of reviewers: 2
Articles submitted per year: 20
Articles published per year: 15

(3009)
*Translation Review

Rainer Schulte, Dennis Kratz, & Sheryl St. Germain, Editors
Box 830688
Univ. of Texas at Dallas
Richardson, TX 75083-0688

Telephone: 214 690-2093
Fax: 214 690-2989
First published: 1978
Sponsoring organization: American Literary Translators Assn.
ISSN: 0737-4836
MLA acronym: TRev

SUBSCRIPTION INFORMATION

Frequency of publication: 3 times/yr.
Circulation: 1,000
Available in microform: Yes, through Univ. Microfilms International
Subscription price: $25.00/yr. institutions; $30.00/yr. individuals; $20.00/yr. students
Year to which price refers: 1992

ADVERTISING INFORMATION

Advertising accepted: Yes
Advertising rates: $75.00/quarter page; $125.00/half page; $200.00/full page

EDITORIAL DESCRIPTION

Scope: Publishes reviews of all matters pertaining to literary translation and articles relating to the art and craft of translation.
Reviews books: Yes
Publishes notes: No
Languages accepted: English
Prints abstracts: No
Author-anonymous submission: No

SUBMISSION REQUIREMENTS

Restrictions on contributors: None
Author pays submission fee: No
Author pays page charges: No
Length of articles: No restrictions
Length of book reviews: 1,000 words
Length of notes: 100 words
Style: None

Number of copies required: 1
Copyright ownership: Journal
Rejected manuscripts: Returned
Time before publication decision: 4 mos.
Time between decision and publication: 4-6 mos.
Number of reviewers: 3
Articles submitted per year: 60
Articles published per year: 20
Book reviews submitted per year: 50
Book reviews published per year: 25

(3010)
*Travaux de Linguistique: Revue Internationale de Linguistique Française

Rika van Deyck, Editor
Dienst voor Franse Linguïstiek
Blandijnberg 2
9000 Ghent, Belgium

Telephone: (32) 91 644047
Fax: (32) 91 644195
First published: 1969
Historical variations in title: Formerly *Travaux de Linguistique: Publications du Service de Linguistique Française de l'Université de l'Etat à Gand*
ISSN: 0082-6049
MLA acronym: TL

SUBSCRIPTION INFORMATION

Frequency of publication: 2 times/yr.
Circulation: 500
Available in microform: No
Subscription price: 1,950 BF/yr.
Year to which price refers: 1992
Subscription address: Editions Duculot S.A., Ave. de Lauzelle, 65, 1348 Louvain-la-Neuve, Belgium
Subscription telephone: (32) 10 471911
Subscription fax: (32) 10 471925

ADVERTISING INFORMATION

Advertising accepted: No

EDITORIAL DESCRIPTION

Scope: Publishes studies on French linguistics and general linguistics.
Reviews books: Yes
Publishes notes: No
Languages accepted: French
Prints abstracts: No
Author-anonymous submission: No

SUBMISSION REQUIREMENTS

Restrictions on contributors: None
Author pays submission fee: No
Author pays page charges: No
Length of articles: 25 pp.
Length of book reviews: 5 pp.
Style: Journal
Number of copies required: 3
Special requirements: Submit original typescript and diskette.
Copyright ownership: Assigned by author to journal
Rejected manuscripts: Not returned
Time before publication decision: 3 mos.
Time between decision and publication: 1 yr. maximum
Number of reviewers: 3
Articles submitted per year: 25
Articles published per year: 20
Book reviews submitted per year: 5
Book reviews published per year: 1-2

(3011)
*Travaux de Linguistique et de Philologie

Georges Kleiber & Gilles Roques, Editors
Univ. des Sciences Humaines de Strasbourg
22, rue Descartes
67084 Strasbourg Cedex, France

Telephone: (33) 88417426
First published: 1963
Sponsoring organization: Centre National de la Recherche Scientifique
ISSN: 0082-6057
MLA acronym: TraLiPhi

SUBSCRIPTION INFORMATION

Frequency of publication: Annual
Available in microform: No
Subscription address: Librairie Klincksieck, 11, rue de Lille, 75007 Paris, France

ADVERTISING INFORMATION

Advertising accepted: No

EDITORIAL DESCRIPTION

Scope: Publishes original works on linguistics, philology, and stylistics, treating French and other Romance languages.
Reviews books: No
Publishes notes: Yes
Languages accepted: French
Prints abstracts: No

SUBMISSION REQUIREMENTS

Author pays submission fee: No
Author pays page charges: No
Number of copies required: 2
Copyright ownership: Librairie Klincksieck
Rejected manuscripts: Returned
Time before publication decision: 6 mos.
Time between decision and publication: 1 yr.
Number of reviewers: 1-3
Articles submitted per year: 15-20
Articles published per year: 8

(3012)
*Travaux de Linguistique Quantitative

Charles Muller, Editor
Slatkine Reprints
5 rue de Chaudronniers, P.O. Box 765
1211 Geneva 3, Switzerland

Telephone: (41) 22 7762551
Fax: (41) 22 7763527
First published: 1978
MLA acronym: TLQ

SUBSCRIPTION INFORMATION

Frequency of publication: Irregular
Available in microform: No

ADVERTISING INFORMATION

Advertising accepted: No

EDITORIAL DESCRIPTION

Scope: Publishes studies on quantitative linguistics.
Publishes notes: No
Languages accepted: French
Prints abstracts: No

(3013)
*Travaux de Littérature

Madeleine Bertaud, Director
ADIREL
17, rue du Pavillon
92100 Boulogne, France

First published: 1988
Sponsoring organization: Assn. pour la Diffusion de la Recherche Littéraire (ADIREL)
MLA acronym: TraLit

SUBSCRIPTION INFORMATION

Frequency of publication: Annual
Circulation: 900
Available in microform: No
Subscription price: 300 F/yr. institutions; 280 F/yr. members France; 310 F/yr. elsewhere
Year to which price refers: 1992
Additional subscription address: Institutions contact: Klincksieck, 11 rue de Lille, 75007 Paris, France

ADVERTISING INFORMATION

Advertising accepted: No

EDITORIAL DESCRIPTION

Scope: Publishes research on French literature from the Middle Ages to the present.
Reviews books: No
Publishes notes: No
Languages accepted: French
Prints abstracts: No
Author-anonymous submission: Yes

SUBMISSION REQUIREMENTS

Restrictions on contributors: None
Author pays submission fee: No
Author pays page charges: No
Length of articles: 6,000 words
Number of copies required: 2
Special requirements: Submit original typescript and 1 copy.
Copyright ownership: ADIREL
Rejected manuscripts: Not returned
Time before publication decision: 3 mos.
Time between decision and publication: 18 mos.
Number of reviewers: 8
Articles submitted per year: 60
Articles published per year: 20-30

(3014)
*Travaux d'Humanisme et Renaissance

Librairie Droz
11 rue Marrot
1211 Geneva 3, Switzerland

Telephone: (41) 22 3466666
Fax: (41) 22 3472391
First published: 1953
ISSN: 0082-6081
MLA acronym: THR

SUBSCRIPTION INFORMATION

Frequency of publication: Irregular
Circulation: 1,000
Available in microform: No

ADVERTISING INFORMATION

Advertising accepted: No

EDITORIAL DESCRIPTION

Scope: Publishes monographs on Renaissance literature and history.
Reviews books: No
Publishes notes: No
Languages accepted: French; English; Italian; German
Prints abstracts: No

Author-anonymous submission: No

SUBMISSION REQUIREMENTS

Restrictions on contributors: None
Author pays submission fee: No
Author pays page charges: No
Style: None
Number of copies required: 1
Copyright ownership: Librarie Droz S.A.
Rejected manuscripts: Returned
Time before publication decision: 3 mos.
Time between decision and publication: 8 mos.
Number of reviewers: 3
Books submitted per year: 40
Books published per year: 6

(3015)
*Travaux du CIEREC (Centre Interdisciplinaire d'Etudes et de Recherches sur l'Expression Contemporaine)

Louis Roux, Editor
CIEREC
Maison Rhône Alpes des Sciences de L'Homme
35, rue du Onze Novembre
42023 Saint-Etienne Cedex, France

Telephone: (33) 77421600
Fax: (33) 77421684
First published: 1971
Sponsoring organization: Centre Interdisciplinaire d'Etudes & de Recherches sur L'Expression Contemporaine
MLA acronym: TrCIEREC

SUBSCRIPTION INFORMATION

Frequency of publication: 4 times/yr.
Circulation: 500-1,000
Available in microform: No

ADVERTISING INFORMATION

Advertising accepted: No

EDITORIAL DESCRIPTION

Scope: Publishes monographs on linguistics, semiology, and epistemology, as well as literature and contemporary civilizations, and the history and criticism of modern contemporary art.
Reviews books: No
Publishes notes: No
Languages accepted: French; English; German; Italian; Spanish
Prints abstracts: Yes

SUBMISSION REQUIREMENTS

Author pays submission fee: No
Author pays page charges: No
Copyright ownership: CIEREC
Rejected manuscripts: Returned
Time before publication decision: 3 mos.
Time between decision and publication: 1 yr.
Number of reviewers: 2
Books submitted per year: 8
Books published per year: 4

(3016)
*Travessia

Zahidé L. Muzart, Editor
Curso de Pós-Graduação em Literatura Brasileira
Univ. Federal de Santa Catarina
88049 Florianópolis, S.C., Brazil

Telephone: (55) 482 319582
First published: 1980
Sponsoring organization: Editora da Univ. Federal de Santa Catarina
ISSN: 0101-9570
MLA acronym: Travessia

SUBSCRIPTION INFORMATION

Frequency of publication: 2 times/yr.
Circulation: 500-700
Available in microform: No
Subscription price: 11,000 Cz/2 yrs.
Year to which price refers: 1992
Subscription address: Editora de UFSC, C.P. 476, 88049 Florianópolis, S.C., Brazil

ADVERTISING INFORMATION

Advertising accepted: No

EDITORIAL DESCRIPTION

Scope: Publishes papers on Brazilian literature. Each issue is generally devoted to a special topic and includes the following features: critical articles on the subject, an updated bibliography, and reviews of recent publications.
Reviews books: Yes
Languages accepted: Portuguese; Spanish; English; French; Italian
Prints abstracts: No
Author-anonymous submission: No

SUBMISSION REQUIREMENTS

Author pays submission fee: No
Author pays page charges: No
Length of articles: 10 pp.
Length of book reviews: 2 pp.
Style: Ass. Bras.de Normas Técnicas for Portuguese
Number of copies required: 1
Copyright ownership: Author
Rejected manuscripts: Not returned
Time before publication decision: 2 mos.
Time between decision and publication: 6 mos.
Number of reviewers: 3
Articles submitted per year: 35-40
Articles published per year: 30
Book reviews submitted per year: 4-6
Book reviews published per year: 2-3

(3017)
*Trends in Linguistics: Documentation

Werner Winter & Richard Rhodes, Editors
Von Liliencronstr. 2
2308 Preetz, Germany

MLA acronym: TiLDoc

SUBSCRIPTION INFORMATION

Frequency of publication: Irregular
Available in microform: No
Subscription address: Mouton de Gruyter, Genthiner Str. 13, 1000 Berlin 30, Germany
Additional subscription address: Walter de Gruyter, Inc., 200 Saw Mill River Rd., Hawthorne, NY 10532
Subscription telephone: (49) 30 260050; 914 747-0110
Subscription fax: (49) 30 26005251; 914 747-1326

ADVERTISING INFORMATION

Advertising accepted: No

EDITORIAL DESCRIPTION

Scope: Publishes dictionaries and studies on linguistics.
Reviews books: No
Publishes notes: No
Languages accepted: English
Prints abstracts: No
Author-anonymous submission: No

SUBMISSION REQUIREMENTS

Author pays submission fee: No
Author pays page charges: No
Length of books: 400 pp.
Style: Mouton
Number of copies required: 1
Copyright ownership: Mouton de Gruyter
Rejected manuscripts: Returned
Time before publication decision: 4 mos.
Time between decision and publication: 1 yr.
Number of reviewers: 2-3

(3018)
*Trends in Linguistics: State-of-the-Art Reports

Werner Winter, Editor
Von Liliencronstr. 2
2308 Preetz, Germany

MLA acronym: TiLSAR

SUBSCRIPTION INFORMATION

Frequency of publication: Irregular
Available in microform: No
Subscription address: Mouton de Gruyter, Genthiner Str. 13, 1000 Berlin 30, Germany
Additional subscription address: Walter de Gruyter, Inc., 200 Saw Mill River Rd., Hawthorne, NY 10532
Subscription telephone: (49) 30 260050; 914 747-0110
Subscription fax: (49) 30 26005251; 914 747-1326

ADVERTISING INFORMATION

Advertising accepted: No

EDITORIAL DESCRIPTION

Scope: Publishes studies on linguistics.
Reviews books: No
Publishes notes: No
Languages accepted: English
Prints abstracts: No
Author-anonymous submission: No

SUBMISSION REQUIREMENTS

Author pays submission fee: No
Author pays page charges: No
Length of books: 400 pp.
Style: Mouton
Number of copies required: 1
Copyright ownership: Mouton de Gruyter
Rejected manuscripts: Returned
Time before publication decision: 4 mos.
Time between decision and publication: 1 yr.
Number of reviewers: 2-3

(3019)
*Trends in Linguistics: Studies and Monographs

Werner Winter, Editor
Von Liliencronstr. 2
2308 Preetz, Germany

First published: 1976
MLA acronym: TiLSaM

SUBSCRIPTION INFORMATION

Frequency of publication: Irregular
Available in microform: No
Subscription address: Mouton de Gruyter, Genthiner Str. 13, 1000 Berlin, Germany
Additional subscription address: Walter de Gruyter, Inc., 200 Saw Mill River Rd., Hawthorne, NY 10532
Subscription telephone: (49) 30 260050; 914 747-0110
Subscription fax: (49) 30 26005251; 914 747-1326

ADVERTISING INFORMATION

Advertising accepted: No

EDITORIAL DESCRIPTION

Scope: Publishes monographs and collections of articles on linguistics.
Reviews books: No
Publishes notes: No
Languages accepted: English
Prints abstracts: No
Author-anonymous submission: No

SUBMISSION REQUIREMENTS

Author pays submission fee: No
Author pays page charges: No
Length of books: 400 pp.
Style: Mouton
Number of copies required: 1
Copyright ownership: Mouton de Gruyter
Rejected manuscripts: Returned
Time before publication decision: 4 mos.
Time between decision and publication: 1 yr.
Number of reviewers: 2-3

(3020)
*Trierer Studien zur Literatur

Jörg Hasler, Karl Hölz, & Lothar Pikulik, Editors
Universität Trier
Fachbereich II
Postfach 3825
5500 Trier, Germany

Telephone: (49) 651 2012307
Fax: (49) 651 2014299
First published: 1979
ISSN: 0721-4294
MLA acronym: TSLit

SUBSCRIPTION INFORMATION

Frequency of publication: Irregular
Circulation: 120
Available in microform: No
Subscription address: Verlag Peter Lang GmbH, Eschborner Landstr. 42-50, 6000 Frankfurt a.M. 90, Germany

ADVERTISING INFORMATION

Advertising accepted: No

EDITORIAL DESCRIPTION

Scope: Publishes scholarly and critical monographs on German, English, American, and French literature.
Reviews books: No
Publishes notes: No
Languages accepted: German; English; French
Prints abstracts: No
Author-anonymous submission: No

SUBMISSION REQUIREMENTS

Restrictions on contributors: Contributors must be faculty members or doctoral candidates at the Univ. of Trier.
Author pays submission fee: No
Author pays page charges: Yes
Length of books: No restrictions
Number of copies required: 3
Copyright ownership: Verlag Peter Lang GmbH
Rejected manuscripts: Returned
Time before publication decision: 1 mo.
Time between decision and publication: 6 mos.
Number of reviewers: 3
Books submitted per year: 2-3
Books published per year: 2-3

(3021)
*Trimestre

Luciano Russi, Editor
Fac. di Scienze Politiche
Università
64100 Teramo, Italy

Telephone: (39) 861 266536
Fax: (39) 861 266537
First published: 1967
Sponsoring organization: Univ. G. D'Annunzio
ISSN: 0564-2523
MLA acronym: Trimestre

SUBSCRIPTION INFORMATION

Frequency of publication: 4 times/yr.
Circulation: 1,500
Available in microform: No
Subscription price: 60,000 Lit/yr. Italy; 90,000 Lit/yr. elsewhere
Year to which price refers: 1992
Subscription address: Trimestre, Via Bolzano, Sambuceto, 66100 Chieti, Italy
Subscription telephone: (39) 85 4461000

ADVERTISING INFORMATION

Advertising accepted: Yes

EDITORIAL DESCRIPTION

Scope: Publishes historical, philosophical, and social studies and research. Focus is mainly on Italian studies but not exclusively.
Reviews books: Yes
Publishes notes: Yes
Languages accepted: Italian; French; English; Spanish; German
Prints abstracts: No
Author-anonymous submission: No

SUBMISSION REQUIREMENTS

Restrictions on contributors: Collaboration is by invitation only.
Author pays submission fee: No
Author pays page charges: No
Length of articles: 20 pp.
Length of book reviews: 1/2 p.
Length of notes: 1/2 p.
Style: None
Number of copies required: 2
Special requirements: Submit original manuscript.
Copyright ownership: Author
Rejected manuscripts: Returned
Time before publication decision: 2 weeks
Time between decision and publication: 1 mo.
Number of reviewers: 2
Articles submitted per year: 60
Articles published per year: 15
Book reviews submitted per year: 40
Book reviews published per year: 12
Notes submitted per year: 30
Notes published per year: 10

(3022)
*TriQuarterly

Reginald Gibbons, Editor
2020 Ridge Ave.
Northwestern Univ.
Evanston, IL 60208

Telephone: 708 491-7614
First published: 1958
Sponsoring organization: Northwestern Univ.
ISSN: 0041-3097
MLA acronym: TriQ

SUBSCRIPTION INFORMATION

Frequency of publication: 3 times/yr. (Fall, Winter, Spring)
Circulation: 5,000
Available in microform: Yes
Subscription price: $18.00/yr.
Year to which price refers: 1992

ADVERTISING INFORMATION

Advertising accepted: Yes

EDITORIAL DESCRIPTION

Scope: Publishes American and international fiction and poetry; topical issues dealing with literature and culture of certain areas, such as contemporary Polish, Spanish and South African literature; special issues, such as little magazine history, essays on John Cage, Nabokov; and special features.
Reviews books: Yes
Publishes notes: No
Languages accepted: English
Prints abstracts: No
Author-anonymous submission: No

SUBMISSION REQUIREMENTS

Restrictions on contributors: Reviews are solicited.
Author pays submission fee: No
Author pays page charges: No
Length of articles: No restrictions
Length of book reviews: No restrictions
Style: Chicago
Number of copies required: 1
Special requirements: No simultaneous submissions.
Copyright ownership: Journal; reverts to author upon publication
Rejected manuscripts: Returned; enclose SASE.
Time before publication decision: 2 mos.
Time between decision and publication: 1 yr.
Number of reviewers: 2
Articles submitted per year: 7,000
Articles published per year: 100-105 stories, poems, and essays
Book reviews published per year: 0-6

(3023)
Tristania: A Journal Devoted to Tristan Studies

Lewis A. M. Sumberg, Editor
P.O. Box 11091
Chattanooga, TN 37401

First published: 1975
Sponsoring organization: Tristan Soc.
ISSN: 0360-3385
MLA acronym: Tristania

SUBSCRIPTION INFORMATION

Frequency of publication: 2 times/yr. (Autumn, Spring)
Available in microform: No

ADVERTISING INFORMATION

Advertising accepted: Yes, on an exchange basis

EDITORIAL DESCRIPTION

Scope: Devoted to the study of all aspects of the Tristan legend and materials. Traditional, nontraditonal, comparatist, and interdisciplinary approaches are welcome, as well as essays and notes on origins, the story itself, and influences at all periods of time.
Reviews books: Yes
Publishes notes: No
Languages accepted: English; French; German
Prints abstracts: No
Author-anonymous submission: Yes

(3024)
*Triveni: Journal of Indian Renaissance

Bhavaraju Narasimha Rao & C. V. N. Dhan, Editors
Triveni Publishers
Machilipatnam-521001, India

Telephone: 31546
First published: 1928
Sponsoring organization: Ravi Academic Soc. (Regd)
ISSN: 0041-3135
MLA acronym: Triveni

SUBSCRIPTION INFORMATION

Frequency of publication: 4 times/yr. (Apr., July, Oct., Jan.)
Circulation: 2,000
Available in microform: No
Subscription price: 70 Re ($26.00)/yr.
Year to which price refers: 1992
Subscription address: Ravi Academic Soc. (Regd), Brodiepet, Guntur-522002, India

ADVERTISING INFORMATION

Advertising accepted: Yes

EDITORIAL DESCRIPTION

Scope: Devoted to art, literature, and history.
Reviews books: Yes
Publishes notes: No
Languages accepted: English
Prints abstracts: No

SUBMISSION REQUIREMENTS

Author pays submission fee: No
Author pays page charges: No
Length of articles: 2,000-3,000 words
Length of book reviews: 250-500 words
Number of copies required: 1
Copyright ownership: Author
Rejected manuscripts: Returned; enclose SASE.
Time before publication decision: 2 mos.
Time between decision and publication: 2 mos.
Number of reviewers: 2
Articles submitted per year: 120
Articles published per year: 80
Book reviews submitted per year: 130
Book reviews published per year: 90

Restrictions on contributors: Article must not have been previously published. Reviews are solicited. Authors writing in French or German must be native speakers.
Author pays submission fee: No
Author pays page charges: No
Length of articles: 20 pp. maximum including notes
Length of book reviews: 1,000 words
Style: MLA
Number of copies required: 1
Special requirements: Type triple-spaced on 8 1/2 x 11 in. paper; include a 1-page abstract.
Copyright ownership: Journal
Rejected manuscripts: Returned
Time before publication decision: 2-3 mos.
Time between decision and publication: 6-12 mos.
Number of reviewers: 3
Articles submitted per year: 30
Articles published per year: 10-12
Book reviews submitted per year: 8-10
Book reviews published per year: 8-10

(3025)
*Trivium

C. C. Eldridge, Editor
St. David's Univ. College
Lampeter
Dyfed SA48 7ED, Wales

Telephone: (44) 570 422351
Fax: (44) 570 623423
First published: 1966
Sponsoring organization: St. David's Univ. College
MLA acronym: Trivium

SUBSCRIPTION INFORMATION

Frequency of publication: Annual
Circulation: 300
Available in microform: No
Subscription price: £7.00/yr.
Year to which price refers: 1992

ADVERTISING INFORMATION

Advertising accepted: No

EDITORIAL DESCRIPTION

Scope: Devoted to the arts and associated subjects, including cinema.
Reviews books: Yes
Publishes notes: Yes
Languages accepted: English; Welsh
Prints abstracts: No
Author-anonymous submission: No

SUBMISSION REQUIREMENTS

Restrictions on contributors: Book reviews are commissioned.
Author pays submission fee: No
Author pays page charges: No
Length of articles: 5,000 words
Style: Modern Humanities Research Assn.
Number of copies required: 1
Special requirements: Submit original typescript.
Copyright ownership: Journal
Rejected manuscripts: Returned
Time before publication decision: 6 weeks
Time between decision and publication: 1 yr.
Number of reviewers: 3
Articles published per year: 8

(3026)
Trondheim Workingpapers

F. J. J. Peters, Editor
English Dept.
Univ. of Trondheim
Trondheim, Norway

First published: 1982
Sponsoring organization: Dept. of English, Univ. i Trondheim
MLA acronym: TWP

SUBSCRIPTION INFORMATION

Frequency of publication: 2-3 times/yr.
Available in microform: No

ADVERTISING INFORMATION

Advertising accepted: No

EDITORIAL DESCRIPTION

Scope: Devotes each issue to a special theme dealing with language, literature, and civilization/culture in English language communities.
Reviews books: No
Publishes notes: No
Languages accepted: English; Norwegian

SUBMISSION REQUIREMENTS

Restrictions on contributors: Half the contributors in each issue must be present or former members of the Trondheim Univ. English Dept.
Author pays submission fee: No
Author pays page charges: No
Style: MLA; Chicago; style sheets of such European journals as *Lingua*
Number of copies required: 2
Copyright ownership: Author
Rejected manuscripts: Returned
Time before publication decision: 2 mos.
Time between decision and publication: 3 mos.
Number of reviewers: 3
Articles submitted per year: 8
Articles published per year: 4

(3027)
*Tropelías: Revista de Teoría de la Literatura y Literatura Comparada

Túa Blesa, Editor
Dept. de Lingüística General & Hispánia
Fac. de Filosofía & Letras
Univ. de Zaragoza
50009 Zaragoza, Spain

Telephone: (34) 976 551647 ext. 2116
Fax: (34) 976 567834
First published: 1990
Sponsoring organization: Univ. de Zaragoza; Banco Zaragozano; Gobierno de Aragón
ISSN: 1132-2373
MLA acronym: Tropelías

SUBSCRIPTION INFORMATION

Frequency of publication: Annual
Available in microform: No
Subscription price: 2,500 Pta/yr. institutions Spain; $30.00/yr. institutions elsewhere; 2,000 Pta/yr. individuals Spain; $25.00/yr. individuals elsewhere
Year to which price refers: 1992

ADVERTISING INFORMATION

Advertising accepted: Yes
Advertising rates: 20,000 Pta/full page

EDITORIAL DESCRIPTION

Scope: Publishes articles on literary theory and comparative literature. Emphasis is on Spanish literature.
Reviews books: No
Publishes notes: Yes
Languages accepted: Spanish; Catalan; Galician; English; French; German; Italian
Prints abstracts: No
Author-anonymous submission: Yes

SUBMISSION REQUIREMENTS

Author pays submission fee: No
Author pays page charges: No
Length of articles: 10-30 pp.
Length of notes: 1-10 pp.
Style: MLA; Chicago
Number of copies required: 1
Special requirements: Submit original typescript and 3.5 in. Macintosh-compatible diskette.
Copyright ownership: Author
Rejected manuscripts: Returned
Time before publication decision: 1 mo.
Time between decision and publication: 3-12 mos.
Number of reviewers: 2
Articles submitted per year: 25-30
Articles published per year: 13-15

(3028)
*Tropismes

Jean-Jacques Lecercle & André Topia, Editors
Centre de Recherches Anglo-Américaines
Univ. de Paris X-Nanterre
200, Avenue de la République
92001 Nanterre Cedex, France

First published: 1984
Sponsoring organization: Centre de Recherches Anglo-Américaines, Univ. de Paris X-Nanterre
ISSN: 0761-2591
MLA acronym: Tropismes

SUBSCRIPTION INFORMATION

Frequency of publication: Annual
Circulation: 200
Available in microform: No
Subscription price: 140 F/yr.
Year to which price refers: 1991
Subscription address: Editions de l'Espace Européen, 89 rue Sartoris, 92250 La Garenne-Colombes, France
Subscription telephone: (33) 1 47829732

ADVERTISING INFORMATION

Advertising accepted: No

EDITORIAL DESCRIPTION

Scope: Publishes articles on English and American literature. Each volume focuses on a specific literary topic.
Reviews books: No
Publishes notes: No
Languages accepted: French; English
Author-anonymous submission: No

SUBMISSION REQUIREMENTS

Author pays submission fee: No
Author pays page charges: No
Length of articles: 8,500 words
Style: MLA
Number of copies required: 2
Copyright ownership: Author
Rejected manuscripts: Not returned
Time before publication decision: 6 mos.
Time between decision and publication: 6 mos.
Number of reviewers: 2
Articles submitted per year: 10-12
Articles published per year: 6-8

(3029)
*Tropos

Karen Schoeman & Agnès Peysson Zeiss, Editors
Dept. of Romance & Classical Languages & Literatures
Old Horticulture Bldg.
Michigan State Univ.
East Lansing, MI 48824-1112

First published: 1971
MLA acronym: Tropos

SUBSCRIPTION INFORMATION

Frequency of publication: Annual
Circulation: 175
Available in microform: No
Subscription price: $7.50/yr.
Year to which price refers: 1992

ADVERTISING INFORMATION

Advertising accepted: No

EDITORIAL DESCRIPTION

Scope: Publishes articles relevant to the study of all aspects of Romance and Classical languages, literatures, and civilizations. Also publishes some creative works.
Reviews books: No
Publishes notes: No
Languages accepted: Spanish; French; English; Italian
Prints abstracts: No
Author-anonymous submission: Yes

SUBMISSION REQUIREMENTS

Restrictions on contributors: Contributors must be graduate students.
Author pays submission fee: No
Author pays page charges: No
Length of articles: 3,500-5,000 words
Style: MLA
Number of copies required: 2
Special requirements: Author's name should not appear on manuscript; attach a cover letter on manuscript.
Copyright ownership: Journal
Rejected manuscripts: Returned; enclose return postage.
Time before publication decision: 3-4 mos.
Time between decision and publication: 4 mos.
Number of reviewers: 3
Articles submitted per year: 20-25
Articles published per year: 4-8

(3030)
*Tsing Hua Journal of Chinese Studies

Kuo Po-wen, Editor
College of Humanities & Social Sciences
National Tsing Hua Univ.
Hsinchu, Taiwan 300, Republic of China

Telephone: (886) 35 715131 ext. 4545
Fax: (886) 35 722436
First published: 1956
Sponsoring organization: Tsing Hua Univ.
ISSN: 0577-9170
MLA acronym: THJCS

SUBSCRIPTION INFORMATION

Frequency of publication: 4 times/yr. (Mar., Sept.)
Circulation: 500
Available in microform: No
Subscription price: $40.00/yr.
Year to which price refers: 1992
Subscription address: Tsing Hua Journal of Chinese Studies, National Tsing Hua Univ., Hsinchu, Taiwan 300, Republic of China

ADVERTISING INFORMATION

Advertising accepted: No

EDITORIAL DESCRIPTION

Scope: Publishes scholarly articles and reviews in the fields of Chinese humanities and social sciences.
Reviews books: Yes
Publishes notes: No
Languages accepted: Chinese languages; English
Prints abstracts: Yes
Author-anonymous submission: No

SUBMISSION REQUIREMENTS

Restrictions on contributors: None
Author pays submission fee: No
Author pays page charges: No
Length of articles: 2,500-30,000 words
Length of book reviews: 3,000 words; review articles may be longer.
Style: MLA
Number of copies required: 1
Special requirements: Submit original typescript. Include original texts if article contains translations.
Copyright ownership: Journal
Rejected manuscripts: Returned
Time before publication decision: 3 mos.
Time between decision and publication: 6 mos.
Number of reviewers: 2-3
Articles submitted per year: 30-40
Articles published per year: 20
Book reviews submitted per year: 10-20
Book reviews published per year: 5-10

(3031)
*TTR: Traduction, Terminologie, Rédaction: Etudes Sur le Texte et Ses Transformations

Jean-Marc Gouanvic, Editor
Secrétariat
Bureau HB-400, Dépt. d'Etudes Françaises
Univ. Concordia
7141, rue Sherbrooke Ouest
Montreal, PQ H4B 1R6, Canada

Telephone: 514 848-7512
Fax: 514 848-3492
First published: 1988
Sponsoring organization: Assn. Canadienne de Traductologie/Canadian Assn. for Translation Studies
ISSN: 0835-8443
MLA acronym: TTR

SUBSCRIPTION INFORMATION

Frequency of publication: 2 times/yr. (June, Dec.)
Circulation: 300
Available in microform: No
Subscription price: $37.00/yr. institutions; $26.00/yr. individuals
Year to which price refers: 1992

ADVERTISING INFORMATION

Advertising accepted: Yes
Advertising rates: C$150.00/full page

EDITORIAL DESCRIPTION

Scope: A scientific and professional journal that publishes articles on translation studies, terminology, and writing. It is mainly oriented towards theoretical and cultural issues including translation and social discourse. Issues are thematic.
Reviews books: Yes
Publishes notes: Yes
Languages accepted: French; English
Prints abstracts: No
Author-anonymous submission: No

SUBMISSION REQUIREMENTS

Restrictions on contributors: None
Author pays submission fee: No
Author pays page charges: No
Length of articles: 20,000-50,000 characters
Length of book reviews: 5,000 characters
Length of notes: 2,000 characters
Style: Journal
Number of copies required: 3
Special requirements: Accepted articles must be submitted on diskette in ASCII format.
Copyright ownership: Journal & author
Rejected manuscripts: Not returned
Time before publication decision: 6 mos.
Time between decision and publication: 6-12 mos.
Number of reviewers: 6
Articles submitted per year: 40
Articles published per year: 25
Book reviews submitted per year: 10
Book reviews published per year: 10
Notes submitted per year: 5
Notes published per year: 2

(3032)
TTT: Interdisciplinair Tijdschrift voor Taal- & Tekstwetenschap

René Appel, Renate Bartsch, Machtelt Bolkestein, & Paul ten Have, Editors
Klassiek Seminarium
Oude Turfmarkt 129
1012 GC Amsterdam, Netherlands

Telephone: (31) 20 5252523
First published: 1981
ISSN: 0167-4773
MLA acronym: TTT

SUBSCRIPTION INFORMATION

Frequency of publication: 3 times/yr.
Circulation: 180
Available in microform: No
Subscription price: 121 f/yr. institutions; 80 f/yr. individuals
Year to which price refers: 1991
Subscription address: ICG Publications BV, Postbus 509, 3300 AM Dordrecht, Netherlands
Subscription telephone: (31) 78 510454
Subscription fax: (31) 78 510972

ADVERTISING INFORMATION

Advertising accepted: Yes

EDITORIAL DESCRIPTION

Scope: Publishes articles on languages and linguistics.
Reviews books: Yes
Publishes notes: Yes
Languages accepted: Dutch
Prints abstracts: Yes, in English

SUBMISSION REQUIREMENTS

Length of articles: 10,000 words maximum
Number of copies required: 6

(3033)
*Tübinger Studien zur Deutschen Literatur

Gotthart Wunberg, Editor
Deutsches Seminar der Universität
Wilhelmstr. 50
7400 Tübingen 1, Germany

Telephone: (49) 69 7807050
Fax: (49) 69 785893
First published: 1976
ISSN: 0171-7235
MLA acronym: TSDL

SUBSCRIPTION INFORMATION

Frequency of publication: Irregular
Available in microform: No
Subscription address: Peter Lang Verlag, Eschborner Landstr. 42-50, 6000 Frankfurt a.M. 90, Germany

ADVERTISING INFORMATION

Advertising accepted: No

EDITORIAL DESCRIPTION

Scope: Publishes monographs concerning German authors and topics in the 18th, 19th, and 20th centuries.
Reviews books: No
Publishes notes: No
Languages accepted: German; English; French
Prints abstracts: No
Author-anonymous submission: No

SUBMISSION REQUIREMENTS

Author pays page charges: Yes
Number of copies required: 2
Copyright ownership: Author or editor
Time before publication decision: 6 mos.
Time between decision and publication: 4 mos.
Books published per year: 1-2

(3034)
Tulimuld: Eesti Kirjanduse ja Kultuuri Ajakiri

Bernard Kangro, Editor
Skördevägen 1
222 38 Lund, Sweden

First published: 1950
ISSN: 0041-4034
MLA acronym: Tulimuld

SUBSCRIPTION INFORMATION

Frequency of publication: 4 times/yr.
Circulation: 1,000
Available in microform: No

ADVERTISING INFORMATION

Advertising accepted: No

EDITORIAL DESCRIPTION

Scope: Covers Estonian literary and cultural events in exile. Publishes short stories, poems, essays, and literary criticism.
Reviews books: Yes
Languages accepted: Estonian
Prints abstracts: No

SUBMISSION REQUIREMENTS

Author pays submission fee: No
Author pays page charges: No
Number of copies required: 1
Copyright ownership: Editor
Rejected manuscripts: Returned
Time before publication decision: 3 mos.
Time between decision and publication: 3 mos.
Number of reviewers: 1
Articles published per year: 50
Book reviews published per year: 12

(3035)
*Tulsa Studies in Women's Literature

Holly A. Laird, Editor
Univ. of Tulsa
600 S. College Ave.
Tulsa, OK 74104

Telephone: 918 631-2503
Fax: 918 631-2033
First published: 1982
Sponsoring organization: Univ. of Tulsa
ISSN: 0732-7730
MLA acronym: TSWL

SUBSCRIPTION INFORMATION

Frequency of publication: 2 times/yr.
Circulation: 500
Available in microform: No
Subscription price: $14.00/yr., $27.00/2 yrs., $40.00/3 yrs. institutions US; $16.00/yr., $31.00/2 yrs., $46.00/3 yrs. institutions elsewhere; $12.00/yr., $23.00/2 yrs., $34.00/3 yrs. individuals US; $15.00/yr., $29.00/2 yrs., $43.00/3 yrs. individuals elsewhere
Year to which price refers: 1992

ADVERTISING INFORMATION

Advertising accepted: Yes
Advertising rates: $75.00/half page; $150.00/full page; also on an exchange basis

EDITORIAL DESCRIPTION

Scope: Publishes articles, notes, archival research, and reviews dealing with the life and work of women writers of every period and in all languages.
Reviews books: Yes
Publishes notes: Yes
Languages accepted: English
Prints abstracts: No
Author-anonymous submission: Yes

SUBMISSION REQUIREMENTS

Restrictions on contributors: Book reviews are solicited.
Author pays submission fee: No
Author pays page charges: No
Length of articles: 20 pp.
Length of book reviews: 500 words
Length of notes: 300-500 words
Style: MLA (1977)
Number of copies required: 3
Special requirements: Submit original plus 2 copies.
Copyright ownership: Journal
Rejected manuscripts: Returned; enclose SASE.
Time before publication decision: 4-6 mos.
Time between decision and publication: 4 mos.
Number of reviewers: 3
Articles submitted per year: 300-400
Articles published per year: 10-12
Book reviews published per year: 15-20
Notes submitted per year: 5
Notes published per year: 5

(3036)
*Twayne's Critical History of Poetry Series

Melissa Solomon, Alan Shucard, & David O'Connell, Editors
Twayne Publishers
Macmillan Publishing co.
866 Third Ave.
New York, NY 10022

First published: 1988
MLA acronym: TCHPS

SUBSCRIPTION INFORMATION

Frequency of publication: Irregular
Available in microform: No

ADVERTISING INFORMATION

Advertising accepted: No

EDITORIAL DESCRIPTION

Scope: Publishes monographs on literary histories that focus on development of poetic genre in a particular time and place.
Reviews books: No
Publishes notes: No
Languages accepted: English
Prints abstracts: No
Author-anonymous submission: No

SUBMISSION REQUIREMENTS

Restrictions on contributors: Contributors must have Ph.D. in literature and demonstrate expertise in subject area.
Author pays submission fee: No
Author pays page charges: No
Length of books: 60,000-70,000 words
Style: Series
Number of copies required: 1
Special requirements: Submit typescript and diskette.
Copyright ownership: G. K. Hall & Co.
Rejected manuscripts: Returned; enclose SASE.
Time before publication decision: 3-6 mos.
Number of reviewers: 1
Books published per year: 1-2

(3037)
*Twayne's Critical History of the Novel

Melissa Solomon & Herbert Sussman, Editors
Twayne Publishers
Macmillan Publishing Co.
866 Third Ave.
New York, NY 10022

First published: 1988
MLA acronym: TCHN

SUBSCRIPTION INFORMATION

Frequency of publication: Irregular
Available in microform: No

ADVERTISING INFORMATION

Advertising accepted: No

EDITORIAL DESCRIPTION

Scope: Publishes monographs which provide a critical history of the novel as a genre, examining its development in various countries and traditions throughout the world.
Reviews books: No
Publishes notes: No
Languages accepted: English
Prints abstracts: No
Author-anonymous submission: No

SUBMISSION REQUIREMENTS

Author pays submission fee: No
Length of books: 200-250 pp.
Style: Chicago
Number of copies required: 1
Copyright ownership: G. K. Hall & Co.
Rejected manuscripts: Returned
Time before publication decision: 3 mos.
Time between decision and publication: 15-18 mos.
Number of reviewers: 2
Books submitted per year: 2
Books published per year: 1-2

(3038)
*Twayne's English Authors Series

Mark Zadrozny, Editor
Twayne Publishers
Macmillan Publishing Co.
866 Third Ave.
New York, NY 10022

Telephone: 212 702-2000
Fax: 212 605-9350
First published: 1964
ISSN: 0564-559X
MLA acronym: TEAS

SUBSCRIPTION INFORMATION

Frequency of publication: 10 times/yr.
Circulation: 1,500-2,000
Available in microform: No

ADVERTISING INFORMATION

Advertising accepted: No

EDITORIAL DESCRIPTION

Scope: Publishes critical studies of English authors.
Reviews books: No
Publishes notes: No
Languages accepted: English
Prints abstracts: No
Author-anonymous submission: No

SUBMISSION REQUIREMENTS

Restrictions on contributors: Contributors must hold Ph.D. in English literature and demonstrate expertise on proposed subject.
Author pays submission fee: No
Author pays page charges: No
Length of books: 175 pp.
Style: Chicago; series
Number of copies required: 1
Special requirements: Consult with editor prior to submission.
Copyright ownership: Twayne Publishers
Rejected manuscripts: Returned
Time before publication decision: 4 mos.
Time between decision and publication: 12-18 mos.
Number of reviewers: 2
Books published per year: 10

(3039)
*Twayne's Filmmakers Series

Mark Zadrozny & Frank Beaver, Editors
Twayne Publishers
Macmillan Publishing Co.
866 Third Ave.
New York, NY 10022

Additional editorial address: Frank Beaver, Dept. of Communication, Univ. of Michigan, 2020 Frieze Bldg., Ann Arbor, MI 48109
Telephone: 212 702-6881
Fax: 212 605-9350
First published: 1992
MLA acronym: TFS

SUBSCRIPTION INFORMATION

Frequency of publication: Irregular
Available in microform: No
Additional subscription address: Order Dept., 100 Front St., Box 500, Riverside, NJ 08075-7500
Subscription telephone: 800 257-5755
Subscription fax: 800 562-1272

ADVERTISING INFORMATION

Advertising accepted: No

EDITORIAL DESCRIPTION

Scope: Publishes monographs on the full panorama of motion picture history and art. Examines film movements and genres; analyzes cinema from a national perspective; and studies the work of individual directors.
Reviews books: No
Publishes notes: No
Languages accepted: English
Prints abstracts: No

SUBMISSION REQUIREMENTS

Length of books: 250 pp.
Number of copies required: 1
Books submitted per year: 5-6
Books published per year: 3-4

(3040)
*Twayne's Masterwork Studies

Mark Zadrozny, Editor
Twayne Publishers
Macmillan Publishing Co.
866 Third Ave.
New York, NY 10022

Telephone: 212 702-2000
Fax: 212 605-9350
First published: 1986
MLA acronym: TMS

SUBSCRIPTION INFORMATION

Frequency of publication: 15 times/yr.

ADVERTISING INFORMATION

Advertising accepted: No

EDITORIAL DESCRIPTION

Scope: Publishes monographs on explorations of major works of literature. Each work offers a chronology of the author's life, historical context of the work, critical reception, index, and a listing of primary and secondary sources.
Reviews books: No
Publishes notes: No
Languages accepted: English
Author-anonymous submission: No

SUBMISSION REQUIREMENTS

Restrictions on contributors: Unsolicited manuscripts are discouraged.
Length of books: 100-125 pp.
Style: Chicago; series
Number of copies required: 1
Copyright ownership: Twayne Publishers
Rejected manuscripts: Returned
Time before publication decision: 6 mos.
Time between decision and publication: 18 mos.
Number of reviewers: 2
Books submitted per year: 15
Books published per year: 15

(3041)
*Twayne's New Critical Introductions to Shakespeare

Twayne Publishers
Macmillan Publishing Co.
866 Third Ave.
New York, NY 10022

Telephone: 212 702-4399
Fax: 212 605-9350
First published: 1987
MLA acronym: TNCIS

SUBSCRIPTION INFORMATION

Frequency of publication: Irregular
Available in microform: No

ADVERTISING INFORMATION

Advertising accepted: No

EDITORIAL DESCRIPTION

Scope: Publishes critical studies of Shakespeare's plays, including stage histories and critical reception from Shakespeare's time to the present.
Reviews books: No
Publishes notes: No
Languages accepted: English
Prints abstracts: No
Author-anonymous submission: No

SUBMISSION REQUIREMENTS

Author pays submission fee: No
Length of books: 100-125 pp.
Style: Chicago
Copyright ownership: Twayne Publishers
Books submitted per year: 3-4
Books published per year: 2-3

(3042)
*Twayne's Studies in Short Fiction

Melissa Solomon & Gordon Weaver, Editors
Twayne Publishers
Macmillan Publishing Co.
866 Third Ave.
New York, NY 10022

First published: 1988
MLA acronym: TSSF

SUBSCRIPTION INFORMATION

Frequency of publication: 6 times/yr.
Available in microform: No

ADVERTISING INFORMATION

Advertising accepted: No

EDITORIAL DESCRIPTION

Scope: Aims to introduce readers to major short story writers. Each book contains three parts: a critical analysis of the author's short fiction, the writer at work, and excerpts from previously published criticism and reviews.
Reviews books: No
Publishes notes: No
Languages accepted: English
Prints abstracts: No
Author-anonymous submission: No

SUBMISSION REQUIREMENTS

Restrictions on contributors: Contributors must have Ph.D. in literature and demonstrate expertise in proposed subject.
Author pays submission fee: No
Author pays page charges: No
Length of books: 60,000-70,000 words
Style: Chicago
Number of copies required: 1
Special requirements: Consult with editor prior to submission.
Copyright ownership: G. K. Hall & Co.
Rejected manuscripts: Returned; enclose SASE.
Time before publication decision: 3-6 mos.
Number of reviewers: 2
Books published per year: 6

(3043)
*Twayne's United States Authors Series

Jacob Conrad, Editor
Twayne Publishers
Macmillan Publishing Co.
866 Third Ave.
New York, NY 10022

First published: 1961
ISSN: 0496-6015
MLA acronym: TUSAS

SUBSCRIPTION INFORMATION

Frequency of publication: 20 times/yr.
Available in microform: No

ADVERTISING INFORMATION

Advertising accepted: No

EDITORIAL DESCRIPTION

Scope: Publishes critical studies of American authors.
Reviews books: No
Publishes notes: No
Languages accepted: English
Prints abstracts: No
Author-anonymous submission: No

SUBMISSION REQUIREMENTS

Restrictions on contributors: Contributors must have Ph.D. in American literature and demonstrate expertise on the proposed subject.
Author pays submission fee: No
Author pays page charges: No
Length of books: 60,000 words
Style: Series; Chicago
Number of copies required: 1
Special requirements: Consult with editor prior to submission.
Copyright ownership: Twayne Publishers
Rejected manuscripts: Returned; enclose SASE.
Time before publication decision: 3-6 mos.
Number of reviewers: 2
Books published per year: 20

(3044)
*Twayne's Women and Literature Series

Melissa Solomon & Kinley E. Roby, Editors
Twayne Publishers
Macmillan Publishing Co.
866 Third Ave.
New York, NY 10022

Telephone: 212 702-9003
Fax: 212 605-9350
First published: 1992
MLA acronym: TWLS

SUBSCRIPTION INFORMATION

Frequency of publication: Irregular
Circulation: 350
Available in microform: No

ADVERTISING INFORMATION

Advertising accepted: No

EDITORIAL DESCRIPTION

Scope: Provides a critical history of British and American women writers from the Anglo-Saxon age to the modern era and presents women as the subject as well as the creators of literature. Each volume examines the cultural influences at work shaping women's roles during a particular period and the consequences for them as women and writers.
Reviews books: No
Languages accepted: English
Prints abstracts: No
Author-anonymous submission: No

SUBMISSION REQUIREMENTS

Author pays submission fee: No
Author pays page charges: No
Length of books: 60,000 words
Style: MLA
Number of copies required: 2
Copyright ownership: Twayne Publishers
Rejected manuscripts: Returned
Time before publication decision: 3 mos.
Time between decision and publication: 16 mos.
Number of reviewers: 2
Books submitted per year: 1-2
Books published per year: 1-2

(3045)
*Twayne's World Authors Series

Carol Chin, Senior Editor
Twayne Publishers
Macmillan Publishing Co.
866 Third Ave.
New York, NY 10022

Telephone: 212 702-7997
Fax: 212 605-9350
First published: 1966
ISSN: 0564-5603
MLA acronym: TWAS

SUBSCRIPTION INFORMATION

Frequency of publication: Irregular
Available in microform: No
Subscription address: Macmillan Distribution Center, Attn.: Order Dept., 100 Front St., Box 500, Riverside, NJ 08075-7500
Subscription telephone: 800 257-5755

ADVERTISING INFORMATION

Advertising accepted: No

EDITORIAL DESCRIPTION

Scope: Publishes literary/critical studies of the works of authors in Europe, Latin America, Asia, and Africa.
Reviews books: No
Publishes notes: No
Languages accepted: English
Prints abstracts: No
Author-anonymous submission: No

SUBMISSION REQUIREMENTS

Restrictions on contributors: Contributors must have Ph.D. in language or literature of author proposed.
Author pays submission fee: No
Author pays page charges: No
Length of books: 60,000-80,000 words
Style: Series; Chicago
Number of copies required: 1
Special requirements: Consult with editor prior to submission.
Copyright ownership: Author or Twayne Publishers
Rejected manuscripts: Returned; enclose SASE.
Time before publication decision: 3-6 mos.
Time between decision and publication: 12-18 mos.
Number of reviewers: 2
Books published per year: 8-10

(3046)
*Twentieth Century Literature: A Scholarly and Critical Journal

William McBrien, Editor
English Dept.
Hofstra Univ.
Hempstead, NY 11550

Telephone: 516 463-5460
Fax: 516 564-4296
First published: 1955
Sponsoring organization: Hofstra Univ.
ISSN: 0041-462X
MLA acronym: TCL

SUBSCRIPTION INFORMATION

Frequency of publication: 4 times/yr.
Circulation: 3,000
Available in microform: Yes
Subscription price: $30.00/yr. institutions US; $34.00/yr. institutions elsewhere; $25.00/yr. individuals US; $30.00/yr. individuals elsewhere
Year to which price refers: 1992
Subscription address: 49 Sheridan Ave., Albany, NY 12210-1413
Subscription telephone: 518 436-9686
Subscription fax: 516 436-7433

ADVERTISING INFORMATION

Advertising accepted: No

EDITORIAL DESCRIPTION

Scope: Considers manuscripts on all aspects of modern and contemporary literature, including articles in English on writers in other languages.

Reviews books: No
Publishes notes: No
Languages accepted: English
Prints abstracts: No
Author-anonymous submission: Yes

SUBMISSION REQUIREMENTS

Restrictions on contributors: None
Author pays submission fee: No
Author pays page charges: No
Length of articles: 15-20 typescript pp.
Style: MLA (1985)
Number of copies required: 3
Special requirements: Submit original typescript.
Copyright ownership: Assigned by author to journal
Rejected manuscripts: Returned; enclose return postage.
Time before publication decision: 2-3 mos.
Time between decision and publication: 9-15 mos.
Number of reviewers: 2
Articles submitted per year: 500
Articles published per year: 28

(3047)
Twórczość

Jerzy Lisowski, Editor
ul. Wiejska 16
00-490 Warsaw, Poland

First published: 1945
ISSN: 0041-4727
MLA acronym: Tw

SUBSCRIPTION INFORMATION

Frequency of publication: 12 times/yr.
Circulation: 10,000
Available in microform: No
Subscription address: Foreign Trade Enterprise Ars Polona-Ruch, Krakowskie Przedmieście 7, Warsaw, Poland

ADVERTISING INFORMATION

Advertising accepted: No

EDITORIAL DESCRIPTION

Scope: Publishes poetry, fiction, and essays.
Reviews books: Yes
Publishes notes: Yes
Languages accepted: Polish
Prints abstracts: No

SUBMISSION REQUIREMENTS

Restrictions on contributors: None
Author pays submission fee: No
Author pays page charges: No
Length of articles: 5,000-15,000 words
Length of book reviews: 1,000 words
Length of notes: 500-800 words
Number of copies required: 1
Copyright ownership: Author
Rejected manuscripts: Returned
Time before publication decision: 1 mo.
Time between decision and publication: 4 mos.
Number of reviewers: 3-5
Articles submitted per year: 1,800
Articles published per year: 300
Book reviews submitted per year: 100
Book reviews published per year: 90
Notes submitted per year: 200
Notes published per year: 60

(3048)
*Tydskrif vir Geesteswetenskappe

Edith Raidt, Managing Editor
Die Suid-Afrikaanse Akademie vir Wetenskap en Kuns
Akademiegebou, Hamiltonstr.
Posbus 538
Pretoria 0001, South Africa

Telephone: (27) 12 285082
Fax: (27) 12 285091
First published: 1961
Sponsoring organization: Suid-Afrikaanse Akademie vir Wetenskap en Kuns
ISSN: 0041-4751
MLA acronym: TvG

SUBSCRIPTION INFORMATION

Frequency of publication: 4 times/yr. (Mar., June, Sept., Dec.)
Circulation: 1,000
Available in microform: No
Subscription price: 44 R/yr.
Year to which price refers: 1992

ADVERTISING INFORMATION

Advertising accepted: No

EDITORIAL DESCRIPTION

Scope: Publishes original research articles on Afrikaans language and literature, theology, art, culture, social sciences, economics, and pedagogy, as well as book reviews.
Reviews books: Yes
Publishes notes: Yes
Languages accepted: Afrikaans; Dutch
Prints abstracts: Yes
Author-anonymous submission: No

SUBMISSION REQUIREMENTS

Restrictions on contributors: None
Author pays submission fee: No
Author pays page charges: Yes
Cost of page charges: 100 R/page
Length of articles: 6,000 words
Length of book reviews: 250-500 words
Length of notes: 500 words
Number of copies required: 3
Special requirements: Include a 100-250 word abstract in English, Dutch, French, or German.
Copyright ownership: Suid-Afrikaanse Akademie
Rejected manuscripts: Returned
Time before publication decision: 3 mos.
Time between decision and publication: 9-12 mos.
Number of reviewers: 2
Articles submitted per year: 35
Articles published per year: 25
Book reviews submitted per year: 40
Book reviews published per year: 40
Notes submitted per year: 2
Notes published per year: 2

(3049)
*Tydskrif vir Letterkunde

H. J. Pieterse, Editor
Posbus 1758
Pretoria 0001, South Africa

Additional editorial address: Dept. of Afrikaans, Unisa, Posbus 392, Pretoria 0001, South Africa
Telephone: (27) 12 3226404
Fax: (27) 12 3207803
First published: 1951
Sponsoring organization: Afrikaanse Skrywerskring, Die Afrikaanse Persfonds
ISSN: 0041-476X
MLA acronym: TvL

SUBSCRIPTION INFORMATION

Frequency of publication: 4 times/yr.
Circulation: 2,000
Available in microform: No
Subscription price: 15 R/yr.
Year to which price refers: 1992

ADVERTISING INFORMATION

Advertising accepted: No

EDITORIAL DESCRIPTION

Scope: Publishes creative and critical Afrikaans literature, reviews, and literary news.
Reviews books: Yes
Publishes notes: Yes
Languages accepted: Afrikaans; Dutch; English
Prints abstracts: No
Author-anonymous submission: No

SUBMISSION REQUIREMENTS

Restrictions on contributors: None
Author pays submission fee: No
Author pays page charges: No
Length of articles: 4,000-5,000
Length of book reviews: 1,600 words
Length of notes: 250-500 words
Style: MLA
Number of copies required: 1
Special requirements: Submit original typescript.
Copyright ownership: Author
Rejected manuscripts: Returned; enclose SASE.
Time before publication decision: 2-12 weeks
Time between decision and publication: 1-6 mos.
Number of reviewers: 2
Articles submitted per year: 40
Articles published per year: 25
Book reviews submitted per year: 50
Book reviews published per year: 40
Notes submitted per year: 3
Notes published per year: 3

(3050)
Typological Studies in Language

T. Givón, Editor
John Benjamins North America Inc.
821 Bethlehem Pike
Philadelphia, PA 19118

First published: 1982
ISSN: 0167-7373
MLA acronym: TSLang

SUBSCRIPTION INFORMATION

Frequency of publication: 2-4 times/yr.
Additional subscription address: John Benjamins B.V., Amsteldijk 44, P.O. Box 75577, 1070 AN Amsterdam, Netherlands

EDITORIAL DESCRIPTION

Scope: Functionally and typologically oriented, the series aims to investigate universals of human language via as broadly defined a data base as possible, leaning toward crosslinguistic, diachronic, developmental and live-discourse data.
Reviews books: No
Languages accepted: English
Prints abstracts: No

SUBMISSION REQUIREMENTS

Restrictions on contributors: None
Style: Language

(3051)
*UCLA Occasional Papers in Linguistics

Dept. of Linguistics
Univ. of California, Los Angeles
Los Angeles, CA 90024-1543

First published: 1975
Sponsoring organization: Dept. of Linguistics, Univ. of California, Los Angeles
MLA acronym: UCLAOPL

SUBSCRIPTION INFORMATION

Frequency of publication: Irregular
Available in microform: No

ADVERTISING INFORMATION

Advertising accepted: No

EDITORIAL DESCRIPTION

Scope: Presents research by the faculty and students of the University of California in Los Angeles on selected descriptive and theoretical topics in linguistics.
Reviews books: No
Publishes notes: No
Languages accepted: English; French
Prints abstracts: No

SUBMISSION REQUIREMENTS

Restrictions on contributors: Contributors must be faculty or students of Univ. of California, Los Angeles
Copyright ownership: Univ. of California Regents

(3052)
*UCLA Working Papers in Phonetics

Ian Maddieson, Editor
Phonetics Laboratory
Dept. of Linguistics
Univ. of California
Los Angeles, CA 90024-1543

Telephone: 310 825-0634
First published: 1964
Sponsoring organization: Dept. of Linguistics, Univ. of California, Los Angeles
ISSN: 0575-4836
MLA acronym: WPP

SUBSCRIPTION INFORMATION

Frequency of publication: Irregular; usually 2-3 times/yr.
Circulation: 200
Available in microform: Yes, through Univ. Microfilms International
Subscription price: $10.00/issue
Year to which price refers: 1993

ADVERTISING INFORMATION

Advertising accepted: No

EDITORIAL DESCRIPTION

Scope: Publishes studies in phonetics by faculty, researchers, and students associated with the UCLA Phonetics Laboratory. Contributions are considered work in progress.
Reviews books: No
Publishes notes: No
Languages accepted: English
Prints abstracts: No

SUBMISSION REQUIREMENTS

Restrictions on contributors: Contributors must be members of UCLA Phonetics Laboratory.

(3053)
*Ufahamu: Journal of the African Activist Association

Angaluki Muaka, Editor
African Activist Assn.
African Studies Center
Univ. of California
Los Angeles, CA 90024

Telephone: 310 825-3686
First published: 1970
Sponsoring organization: Univ. of California, Los Angeles, African Studies Center
ISSN: 0041-5715
MLA acronym: Ufahamu

SUBSCRIPTION INFORMATION

Frequency of publication: 3 times/yr.
Circulation: 300
Available in microform: No
Subscription price: $20.00/yr. institutions US; $29.50/yr. institutions elsewhere; $14.00/yr. individuals US; $23.50/yr. individuals elsewhere
Year to which price refers: 1992

ADVERTISING INFORMATION

Advertising accepted: Yes

EDITORIAL DESCRIPTION

Scope: Accepts contributions from anyone interested in Africa and related subject areas. Contributions range from progressive scholarly articles and book reviews to freelance writing and poetry.
Reviews books: Yes
Publishes notes: No
Languages accepted: English; French
Prints abstracts: No
Author-anonymous submission: No

SUBMISSION REQUIREMENTS

Restrictions on contributors: None
Author pays submission fee: No
Author pays page charges: No
Length of articles: 15-25 pp.
Length of book reviews: 500-1,500 words
Style: Chicago
Number of copies required: 1
Copyright ownership: Univ. of California Regents
Rejected manuscripts: Not returned
Time before publication decision: 3-6 mos.
Time between decision and publication: 3-6 mos.
Number of reviewers: 2-4
Articles published per year: 25
Book reviews published per year: 10

(3054)
*Ukrainian Quarterly: Journal of East European and Asian Affairs

Petro Matiaszek, Editor
203 Second Ave.
New York, NY 10003

Telephone: 212 228-6840
Fax: 212 254-4721
First published: 1944
Sponsoring organization: Ukrainian Congress Committee of America
ISSN: 0041-6010
MLA acronym: UQ

SUBSCRIPTION INFORMATION

Frequency of publication: 4 times/yr. (Spring, Summer, Fall, Winter)
Circulation: 5,000
Available in microform: No
Subscription price: $25.00/yr.
Year to which price refers: 1992

ADVERTISING INFORMATION

Advertising accepted: Yes

EDITORIAL DESCRIPTION

Scope: Publishes articles on East Europe, Asia, and Ukraine.
Reviews books: Yes
Publishes notes: No
Languages accepted: English
Prints abstracts: No
Author-anonymous submission: Yes

SUBMISSION REQUIREMENTS

Restrictions on contributors: None
Author pays submission fee: No
Length of articles: 6,500 words
Length of book reviews: 500-1,000 words
Style: MLA
Number of copies required: 2
Special requirements: Submit original typescript plus 1 copy.
Copyright ownership: Journal & author
Rejected manuscripts: Returned; enclose SASE.
Time before publication decision: 3 mos.
Time between decision and publication: 1 mo.
Number of reviewers: 3-4
Articles submitted per year: 60
Articles published per year: 25
Book reviews submitted per year: 50
Book reviews published per year: 20

(3055)
*The Ukrainian Review: A Quarterly Journal Devoted to the Study of Ukraine

Slava Stetsko, Nicholas L. Chirovsky, Lev Shankovsky, Oleh S. Romanyshyn, Volodymyr Zarycky, Sephen Oleskiw, Roman Zwarycz, & Borys Potapenko, Editors
Ukrainian Publishers, Ltd.
200 Liverpool Rd.
London N1 1LF, England

Additional editorial address: Zeppelinstr. 67, 8000 Munich 8, Germany
Telephone: (44) 71 6076266
Fax: (44) 71 6076737
E-mail: 100016,27 (Compuserve)
First published: 1954
Sponsoring organization: Assn. of Ukrainians in Great Britain, Ltd.; Organization for Defense of Four Freedoms for Ukraine, Inc.; Ukrainica Research Inst., Canada
ISSN: 0041-6029
MLA acronym: UkrR

SUBSCRIPTION INFORMATION

Frequency of publication: 4 times/yr.
Circulation: 1,500
Available in microform: No
Subscription price: $40.00/yr.
Year to which price refers: 1991
Subscription address: c/o Assn. of Ukrainians in Great Britain, Ltd., 49 Linden Gardens, London W2 4HG, England

ADVERTISING INFORMATION

Advertising accepted: Yes

EDITORIAL DESCRIPTION

Scope: Publishes studies of the present situation in Ukraine as well as its history, culture, literature, and political aspirations. Also studies Russian imperial designs toward its neighbors and the world.
Reviews books: Yes
Publishes notes: Yes
Languages accepted: English
Prints abstracts: No
Author-anonymous submission: No

SUBMISSION REQUIREMENTS

Restrictions on contributors: None
Author pays submission fee: No
Author pays page charges: No
Length of articles: 20 pp. maximum
Style: None
Number of copies required: 1
Special requirements: Submit typescript.
Copyright ownership: Author
Rejected manuscripts: Returned at author's request
Time before publication decision: 1 mo.
Time between decision and publication: 3 mos.
Number of reviewers: 3
Articles published per year: 20

(3056)
Ukraïns'ke Literaturoznavstvo: Mizhvidomchyĭ Respublikans'kyĭ Zbirnyk

L'vov Univ.
Universitetskaya Ul., 1
290000 L'vov, Ukraine

First published: 1966
Sponsoring organization: L'vov Univ.
ISSN: 0503-1230
MLA acronym: ULz

SUBSCRIPTION INFORMATION

Frequency of publication: 2 times/yr.
Circulation: 1,000
Available in microform: No

ADVERTISING INFORMATION

Advertising accepted: No

EDITORIAL DESCRIPTION

Scope: Publishes articles on Ukrainian literary history and theory.
Reviews books: No
Publishes notes: No
Languages accepted: Ukrainian
Author-anonymous submission: No

SUBMISSION REQUIREMENTS

Restrictions on contributors: None
Author pays submission fee: Yes
Author pays page charges: No
Style: Scientific
Number of copies required: 2
Special requirements: Submit original typescript and 1 copy.
Copyright ownership: Author
Rejected manuscripts: Returned
Time before publication decision: 4-6 mos.
Time between decision and publication: 6-8 mos.
Number of reviewers: 2
Articles submitted per year: 60
Articles published per year: 40

(3057)
*Ukraïns'ke Movoznavstvo: Mizhvidomchyĭ Naukovyĭ Zbirnyk

O. Bjilodid, Editor
Kiev State Univ. Press
10, Kreshchatik
Kiev-I, 252001, Ukraine

Telephone: (7) 44 2281093
First published: 1973
Sponsoring organization: Kiev State Univ.
ISSN: 0320-3077
MLA acronym: UkrMov

SUBSCRIPTION INFORMATION

Frequency of publication: Annual
Circulation: 700
Available in microform: No

ADVERTISING INFORMATION

Advertising accepted: No

EDITORIAL DESCRIPTION

Scope: Publishes articles on Ukrainian language.
Reviews books: No
Publishes notes: No
Languages accepted: Ukrainian
Prints abstracts: No

SUBMISSION REQUIREMENTS

Restrictions on contributors: None
Author pays submission fee: No
Length of articles: 12 pp.
Number of copies required: 2
Rejected manuscripts: Not returned
Time before publication decision: 3 mos.
Number of reviewers: 2
Articles published per year: 50-60

(3058)
*Ukraïns'kyĭ Istoryk

Lubomyr R. Wynar, Editor
P.O. Box 312
Kent, OH 44240

Additional editorial address: 3804 Oxford Ave., Montreal, PQ, H4A 2Y2, Canada
First published: 1963
Sponsoring organization: Ukrainian Historical Assn., Inc.
ISSN: 0041-6061
MLA acronym: UkrI

SUBSCRIPTION INFORMATION

Frequency of publication: 4 times/yr.
Circulation: 650-700
Available in microform: No
Subscription price: $40.00/yr. institutions; $35.00/yr. individuals
Year to which price refers: 1993
Subscription address: Ukrainian Historian, 165-16 Clinton Terrace, Jamaica, NY 11432
Additional subscription address: P.O. Box 95, Etobicoke, ON M9C 4U2, Canada

ADVERTISING INFORMATION

Advertising accepted: Yes

EDITORIAL DESCRIPTION

Scope: Publishes articles on Ukrainian and East European history and culture.
Reviews books: Yes
Publishes notes: Yes
Languages accepted: Ukrainian; English; German
Prints abstracts: Yes
Author-anonymous submission: No

SUBMISSION REQUIREMENTS

Restrictions on contributors: Preference given to contributors who are members of the Ukrainian Historical Assn., the American Historical Assn., and the American Assn. for the Advancement of Slavic Studies.
Author pays submission fee: No
Author pays page charges: No
Length of articles: 20-25 typescript pp.
Length of book reviews: 500-800 words
Length of notes: 100-200 words
Style: Chicago
Number of copies required: 3
Special requirements: Submit double-spaced original typescript; include 100-150 word abstract.
Copyright ownership: Ukrainian Historical Assn.
Rejected manuscripts: Returned; enclose SASE.
Time before publication decision: 2-6 mos.
Time between decision and publication: 4-8 mos.
Number of reviewers: 2-3
Articles submitted per year: 40-50
Articles published per year: 15-20
Book reviews submitted per year: 100
Book reviews published per year: 20-30
Notes submitted per year: 50-70
Notes published per year: 15-20

(3059)
*Ulster Folklife

Jonathan Bell, Editor
Ulster Folk & Transport Museum
Cultra
Holywood
County Down BT18 OEU, Northern Ireland

First published: 1955
Sponsoring organization: Ulster Folk & Transport Museum
ISSN: 0082-7347
MLA acronym: UF

SUBSCRIPTION INFORMATION

Frequency of publication: Annual
Circulation: 750
Available in microform: No
Subscription price: IR£7.00/yr.
Year to which price refers: 1992

ADVERTISING INFORMATION

Advertising accepted: No

EDITORIAL DESCRIPTION

Scope: Publishes articles and notes within subject area of folk cultural studies, European regional ethnology and folklore, dialectology and relevant peripheral studies in economic and social history, human geography, onomastics, and social anthropology. Articles are usually confined geographically to Ulster, and also more generally to Ireland. Occasionally comparative studies reach more widely into north-west Britain and Atlantic Europe.
Reviews books: Yes
Publishes notes: Yes
Languages accepted: English; Irish Gaelic
Prints abstracts: No
Author-anonymous submission: No

SUBMISSION REQUIREMENTS

Restrictions on contributors: None
Author pays submission fee: No
Author pays page charges: No
Length of articles: 5,000-15,000 words
Length of book reviews: No restrictions
Length of notes: 700-2,000 words
Style: Journal
Number of copies required: 1
Copyright ownership: Publisher & author
Rejected manuscripts: Returned
Time before publication decision: 6 weeks

Time between decision and publication: 6 mos.
Number of reviewers: 1
Articles submitted per year: 5-10
Articles published per year: 6-9
Book reviews submitted per year: 8-15
Book reviews published per year: 12-15
Notes submitted per year: 1-3
Notes published per year: 1-2

(3060)
ULULA: Graduate Studies in Romance Languages

Teresa M. Vilarós-Soler, Alberto Moreiras, Michael Lastinger, & Valérie Lastinger, Editors
Dept. of Romance Languages
Univ. of Georgia
Athens, GA 30602

First published: 1984
Sponsoring organization: Dept. of Romance Languages, Univ. of Georgia
ISSN: 0747-8011
MLA acronym: ULULA

SUBSCRIPTION INFORMATION

Frequency of publication: Annual
Available in microform: No

ADVERTISING INFORMATION

Advertising accepted: No

EDITORIAL DESCRIPTION

Scope: Journal publishes literary criticism about the Romance literatures.
Reviews books: Yes
Publishes notes: No
Languages accepted: English; Spanish; French; Italian; Portuguese; Catalan; Galician
Prints abstracts: No

SUBMISSION REQUIREMENTS

Restrictions on contributors: Contributors must be either graduate students or guest contributors.
Author pays submission fee: No
Author pays page charges: No
Length of articles: 4,000 words
Length of book reviews: 750 words
Style: MLA
Number of copies required: 2
Special requirements: None
Copyright ownership: Author
Rejected manuscripts: Returned; enclose SASE.
Time before publication decision: 1 yr. maximum
Time between decision and publication: 1 yr. maximum
Number of reviewers: 4
Articles submitted per year: 40
Articles published per year: 10
Book reviews submitted per year: 15
Book reviews published per year: 10

(3061)
Umma: A Magazine of Original Writing

Clement Ndulute, Editor
P.O. Box 35041
Dar es Salaam, Tanzania

First published: 1966
Sponsoring organization: Univ. of Dar es Salaam
ISSN: 0856-0854
MLA acronym: Umma

SUBSCRIPTION INFORMATION

Frequency of publication: Annual
Circulation: 2,000
Available in microform: No

ADVERTISING INFORMATION

Advertising accepted: No

EDITORIAL DESCRIPTION

Scope: Publishes work by aspiring writers and critics.
Reviews books: Yes
Publishes notes: Yes
Languages accepted: English; Swahili
Prints abstracts: No
Author-anonymous submission: No

SUBMISSION REQUIREMENTS

Restrictions on contributors: None
Author pays submission fee: No
Author pays page charges: No
Length of articles: 20 double-spaced quarto pp.
Length of book reviews: 3,500 words
Length of notes: No restrictions
Style: MLA preferred
Number of copies required: 1
Copyright ownership: Journal or author
Rejected manuscripts: Returned at author's request
Time before publication decision: 3 mos.
Time between decision and publication: 3 mos.
Number of reviewers: 2
Articles submitted per year: 20
Articles published per year: 10
Book reviews submitted per year: 10
Book reviews published per year: 5
Notes submitted per year: 5
Notes published per year: 4

(3062)
*Uncoverings: Research Papers of the American Quilt Study Group

Laurel Horton, Editor
American Quilt Study Group
660 Mission St., Ste. 400
San Francisco, CA 94105-4007

Telephone: 415 495-0163
Fax: 415 495-3516
First published: 1981
Sponsoring organization: American Quilt Study Group
ISSN: 0227-0628
MLA acronym: Uncoverings

SUBSCRIPTION INFORMATION

Frequency of publication: Annual (Oct.)
Subscription price: $20.00/yr.
Year to which price refers: 1991

EDITORIAL DESCRIPTION

Scope: Publishes articles on the social, technological and cultural history of quiltmaking, quilts, and related textiles.
Reviews books: No
Publishes notes: No
Languages accepted: English
Prints abstracts: Yes
Author-anonymous submission: Yes

SUBMISSION REQUIREMENTS

Restrictions on contributors: None
Author pays submission fee: No
Author pays page charges: No
Length of articles: 4,400-8,900 words
Style: Chicago
Number of copies required: 1
Special requirements: Submit abstract for consideration. Accepted papers, based on abstracts, will be presented at annual seminar, and then edited for publication the following year.
Copyright ownership: American Quilt Study Group; reverts to author upon publication.
Rejected manuscripts: Returned with comments
Time before publication decision: 1 mo.
Time between decision and publication: 18 mos.
Number of reviewers: 5
Articles submitted per year: 20-25
Articles published per year: 9

(3063)
*Understanding Contemporary American Literature

Matthew J. Bruccoli, Editor
Univ. of South Carolina Press
1716 College St.
Columbia, SC 29208

Telephone: 803 777-5243
Fax: 803 777-0160
First published: 1985
MLA acronym: UCAL

SUBSCRIPTION INFORMATION

Frequency of publication: Irregular

ADVERTISING INFORMATION

Advertising accepted: No

EDITORIAL DESCRIPTION

Scope: This is a series of guides or companions that introduce contemporary American writers by identifying and explicating their materials, themes, use of language, points of view, structures, symbolism, and responses to experience. The criticism and analysis are aimed at a level of general accessibility.
Reviews books: No
Publishes notes: No
Languages accepted: English
Prints abstracts: No
Author-anonymous submission: No

SUBMISSION REQUIREMENTS

Author pays submission fee: No
Author pays page charges: No
Length of books: 200 pp.
Style: Chicago
Number of copies required: 2
Copyright ownership: Univ. of South Carolina Press
Rejected manuscripts: Returned, with an explanation of rejection
Time before publication decision: 1 mo.
Time between decision and publication: 10-12 mos.
Number of reviewers: 1
Books submitted per year: 10
Books published per year: 2-5

(3064)
*Understanding Contemporary British Literature

Matthew J. Bruccoli, Editor
Univ. of South Carolina Press
1716 College St.
Columbia, SC 29208

Telephone: 803 777-5243
Fax: 803 777-0160
MLA acronym: UCBL

SUBSCRIPTION INFORMATION

Frequency of publication: Irregular

ADVERTISING INFORMATION

Advertising accepted: No

EDITORIAL DESCRIPTION

Scope: Introduces contemporary British writers by identifying and explaining their works, themes, language, points of view, structures, symbolism, and responses to experience. The series focuses on being accessible to a general audience.
Reviews books: No
Publishes notes: No
Languages accepted: English
Prints abstracts: No
Author-anonymous submission: No

SUBMISSION REQUIREMENTS

Author pays submission fee: No
Author pays page charges: No
Length of books: 200 pp.
Style: Chicago
Number of copies required: 2
Copyright ownership: Univ. of South Carolina
Rejected manuscripts: Returned with an explanation of rejection
Time before publication decision: 1 mo.
Time between decision and publication: 10-12 mos.
Number of reviewers: 1
Books submitted per year: 5
Books published per year: 1-3

(3065)
*Understanding Modern European and Latin American Literature

James Hardin, Editor
Univ. of South Carolina
Dept. of German & Slavic
Columbia, SC 29208

First published: 1988
MLA acronym: UMELAL

SUBSCRIPTION INFORMATION

Frequency of publication: Irregular
Available in microform: No
Subscription price: All contributions are commissioned.

ADVERTISING INFORMATION

Advertising accepted: No

EDITORIAL DESCRIPTION

Scope: Introduces modern European and Latin American writers by identifying and explaining their works, themes, language, points of view, structures, symbolism, and responses to experience. The series focuses on being accessible to a general audience.
Reviews books: No
Publishes notes: No
Languages accepted: English
Prints abstracts: No

SUBMISSION REQUIREMENTS

Author pays submission fee: No
Length of books: 180 pp.
Style: Chicago
Copyright ownership: Univ. of South Carolina
Number of reviewers: 2

(3066)
Unilit

Pothukuchi Sambasiva Rao, Editor
6-3-195 New Bhoiguda
Secunderabad-3, A.P., India

First published: 1960
Sponsoring organization: Viswa Sahithi
ISSN: 0041-6762
MLA acronym: Unilit

SUBSCRIPTION INFORMATION

Frequency of publication: 12 times/yr.
Circulation: 2,000

ADVERTISING INFORMATION

Advertising accepted: Yes

EDITORIAL DESCRIPTION

Reviews books: Yes
Publishes notes: Yes
Languages accepted: English
Prints abstracts: No

SUBMISSION REQUIREMENTS

Restrictions on contributors: None
Author pays submission fee: No
Author pays page charges: Yes
Length of articles: 3,000 words
Length of book reviews: 500 words
Length of notes: 500 words
Style: None
Number of copies required: 1
Special requirements: Include photographs if possible.
Rejected manuscripts: Returned; enclose return postage.
Time before publication decision: 1 mo.
Time between decision and publication: 1 mo.
Number of reviewers: 3
Articles submitted per year: 100
Articles published per year: 20
Book reviews submitted per year: 30
Book reviews published per year: 25
Notes submitted per year: 30
Notes published per year: 20

(3067)
*Unisa English Studies: Journal of the Department of English

S. G. Kossick, Editor
Dept. of English
Univ. of South Africa
P.O. Box 392
0001 Pretoria, South Africa

Telephone: (27) 12 4296714
Fax: (27) 12 4293221
First published: 1963
Sponsoring organization: Univ. of South Africa
ISSN: 0041-5359
MLA acronym: UES

SUBSCRIPTION INFORMATION

Frequency of publication: 2 times/yr. (Apr./May, Sept.)
Circulation: 4,500
Available in microform: No
Subscription price: 11 R/yr.
Year to which price refers: 1992
Subscription address: Dept. of Publishing Services, Unisa Box 392, Pretoria, South Africa
Subscription telephone: (27) 12 4293023

ADVERTISING INFORMATION

Advertising accepted: Yes
Advertising rates: 50 R/half page; 100 R/full page

EDITORIAL DESCRIPTION

Scope: Publishes articles on English-language literature.
Reviews books: Yes
Publishes notes: Yes
Languages accepted: English
Prints abstracts: No
Author-anonymous submission: No

SUBMISSION REQUIREMENTS

Restrictions on contributors: None
Author pays submission fee: No
Author pays page charges: No
Length of articles: 3,000-5,000 words
Length of book reviews: 1,000 words
Length of notes: 300 words
Style: MLA
Number of copies required: 1
Special requirements: Submit double-spaced typescript.
Copyright ownership: Univ. of South Africa
Rejected manuscripts: Returned
Time before publication decision: 2-4 weeks
Time between decision and publication: 6 mos.
Number of reviewers: 2-3
Articles submitted per year: 20
Articles published per year: 5-10
Book reviews submitted per year: 100
Book reviews published per year: 65-100
Notes submitted per year: 45-50
Notes published per year: 45-50

(3068)
Unitas: A Quarterly for the Arts and Sciences

Lamberto Pasión, O.P., Editor
Room 220, Main Bldg.
Univ. of Santo Tomas
España, Manila 2806, Philippines

First published: 1922
ISSN: 0041-7149
MLA acronym: Unitas

SUBSCRIPTION INFORMATION

Frequency of publication: 4 times/yr. (Mar., June, Sept., Dec.)
Circulation: 2,000

ADVERTISING INFORMATION

Advertising accepted: Yes

EDITORIAL DESCRIPTION

Scope: Publishes articles that appeal several notches above the level of the popular and the common, yet responsive enough to relate themselves to the changes and innovations around us.
Reviews books: Yes
Publishes notes: Yes
Languages accepted: English
Prints abstracts: No

SUBMISSION REQUIREMENTS

Restrictions on contributors: None
Author pays submission fee: No
Author pays page charges: No
Length of articles: 4,000 words minimum
Length of book reviews: 800 words minimum
Length of notes: 2,000 words minimum
Number of copies required: 1
Special requirements: Manuscripts should be typed double-spaced on one side of paper only.
Copyright ownership: Univ. of Santo Tomas
Rejected manuscripts: Returned; enclose SASE.
Time before publication decision: 4 mos.
Time between decision and publication: 3 1/2 mos.
Number of reviewers: 4
Articles submitted per year: 64
Articles published per year: 24
Book reviews submitted per year: 16
Book reviews published per year: 16

(3069)
Universidad de La Habana

Bernardo Callejas, Editor
Dirección de Extensión Universitaria
Edificio "Julio Antonio Mella"
Calle L 353, casi esquina a 21
2do. piso, El Vedado
Havana, Cuba

First published: 1934
ISSN: 0041-8420
MLA acronym: UdLH

SUBSCRIPTION INFORMATION

Frequency of publication: 2 times/yr.
Subscription address: Imprenta Universitaria "André Voisin", Univ. de La Habana, Havana, Cuba

EDITORIAL DESCRIPTION

Reviews books: Yes
Languages accepted: Spanish
Prints abstracts: No

(3070)
*Università degli Studi di Torino. Dipartimento di Scienze e del Linguaggio e Letterature Moderne e Comparate

Editrice Tirrenia Stampatori
Via Ferrari 5
10124 Turin, Italy

Telephone: (39) 11 877010
First published: 1987
Sponsoring organization: Univ. degli Studi di Torino, Dipto. di Scienze del Linguaggio & Letterature Moderne & Comparate
MLA acronym: USTSLL

SUBSCRIPTION INFORMATION

Frequency of publication: Annual
Available in microform: No

ADVERTISING INFORMATION

Advertising accepted: No

EDITORIAL DESCRIPTION

Scope: Publishes monographs on studies in language and modern comparative literature.
Reviews books: No
Publishes notes: No
Languages accepted: Italian; German; French
Prints abstracts: No
Author-anonymous submission: No

SUBMISSION REQUIREMENTS

Author pays submission fee: No
Author pays page charges: No

(3071)
Universitas: Zeitschrift für Wissenschaft, Kunst und Literatur

H. W. Bähr, Editor
Landhansstr. 18
7400 Tübingen, Germany

First published: 1946
ISSN: 0041-9079
MLA acronym: Univ

SUBSCRIPTION INFORMATION

Frequency of publication: 12 times/yr.
Circulation: 7,200
Subscription address: Wissenschaftliche Verlagsgesellschaft GmbH, Postfach 40, 7000 Stuttgart 1, Germany

EDITORIAL DESCRIPTION

Reviews books: Yes
Languages accepted: German; English; Spanish
Prints abstracts: No

SUBMISSION REQUIREMENTS

Restrictions on contributors: None
Number of copies required: 1
Copyright ownership: Author or publisher
Articles published per year: 120-140

(3072)
University of California Publications, Folklore and Mythology Studies

Eugene Anderson, Daniel Crowley, Patrick Ford, & Daniel Melia, Editors
Univ. of California Press
2120 Berkeley Way
Berkeley, CA 94720

First published: 1953
ISSN: 0068-6360
MLA acronym: UCPFS

SUBSCRIPTION INFORMATION

Frequency of publication: Irregular
Available in microform: No

ADVERTISING INFORMATION

Advertising accepted: No

EDITORIAL DESCRIPTION

Scope: Publishes monographs on folklore and mythology.
Reviews books: No
Publishes notes: No
Languages accepted: English
Prints abstracts: No
Author-anonymous submission: Yes

SUBMISSION REQUIREMENTS

Restrictions on contributors: Contributors must be affiliated with Univ. of California.
Author pays submission fee: No
Author pays page charges: No
Length of books: 50,000-300,000 words
Style: Chicago
Number of copies required: 2
Special requirements: If manuscript is accepted, author must supply camera-ready copy.
Copyright ownership: Regents, Univ. of California
Rejected manuscripts: Returned
Time before publication decision: 6 mos.
Time between decision and publication: 1 yr.
Number of reviewers: 2
Books submitted per year: 2
Books published per year: 1

(3073)
*University of California Publications in Linguistics

Margaret Langdon, Paul Schachter, Sandra Thompson, Johanna Nichols, & William Shipley, Editors
Univ. of California Press
2120 Berkeley Way
Berkeley, CA 94720

First published: 1943
ISSN: 0068-6484
MLA acronym: UCPL

SUBSCRIPTION INFORMATION

Frequency of publication: Irregular
Available in microform: No

ADVERTISING INFORMATION

Advertising accepted: No

EDITORIAL DESCRIPTION

Scope: Publishes monographs on linguistics.
Reviews books: No
Publishes notes: No
Prints abstracts: No
Author-anonymous submission: Yes

SUBMISSION REQUIREMENTS

Restrictions on contributors: Contributors must be affiliated with Univ. of California.
Author pays submission fee: No
Author pays page charges: No
Length of books: 50,000-300,000 words
Style: Linguistic Soc. of America
Number of copies required: 2
Special requirements: If manuscript is accepted, author must supply camera-ready copy.
Copyright ownership: Regents, Univ. of California
Rejected manuscripts: Returned
Time before publication decision: 6 mos.
Time between decision and publication: 1 yr.
Number of reviewers: 2
Books submitted per year: 5
Books published per year: 3

(3074)
*University of California Publications in Modern Philology

Samuel G. Armistead, Jean-Pierre Barricelli, Harold E. Toliver, & Andrew Wright, Editors
Univ. of California Press
2120 Berkeley Way
Berkeley, CA 94720

First published: 1909
ISSN: 0068-6492
MLA acronym: UCPMP

SUBSCRIPTION INFORMATION

Frequency of publication: Irregular
Available in microform: No

ADVERTISING INFORMATION

Advertising accepted: No

EDITORIAL DESCRIPTION

Scope: Welcomes manuscripts that deal with both Western and non-Western languages and literatures, including stylistics, criticism, literary theory, and interdisciplinary studies relating literature to other intellectual and aesthetic endeavors.
Reviews books: No
Publishes notes: No
Languages accepted: Spanish; French
Prints abstracts: No
Author-anonymous submission: Yes

SUBMISSION REQUIREMENTS

Restrictions on contributors: Contributors must be affiliated with Univ. of California.
Author pays submission fee: No
Author pays page charges: No
Length of books: 50,000-300,000 words
Style: Chicago
Number of copies required: 2
Special requirements: If manuscript is accepted, author must supply camera-ready copy.
Copyright ownership: Regents, Univ. of California
Rejected manuscripts: Returned

Time before publication decision: 6 mos.
Time between decision and publication: 1 yr.
Number of reviewers: 2
Books submitted per year: 4
Books published per year: 2

(3075)
*University of Dayton Review

Robert C. Conard, Editor
Dept. of Languages
Univ. of Dayton
Dayton, OH 45409

Telephone: 513 229-2425
Fax: 513 339-3433
First published: 1964
Sponsoring organization: Univ. of Dayton
ISSN: 0041-9525
MLA acronym: UDR

SUBSCRIPTION INFORMATION

Frequency of publication: Irregular; usually 3 times/yr.
Available in microform: No

ADVERTISING INFORMATION

Advertising accepted: No

EDITORIAL DESCRIPTION

Scope: Publishes work of humanistic and Christian concern. Welcomes articles relating to special disciplines in the humanities and those reflecting interdisciplinary scholarship.
Reviews books: No
Publishes notes: No
Languages accepted: English; German; French; Spanish
Prints abstracts: No
Author-anonymous submission: Yes, at author's request.

SUBMISSION REQUIREMENTS

Restrictions on contributors: None
Author pays submission fee: No
Author pays page charges: No
Length of articles: 6,000 words
Style: MLA; Chicago; standard style for the discipline
Number of copies required: 2
Special requirements: Submit original typescript.
Copyright ownership: Author
Rejected manuscripts: Returned
Time before publication decision: 3 mos.
Time between decision and publication: 1 yr.
Number of reviewers: 1-2
Articles published per year: 30

(3076)
*University of Florida Monographs, Humanities Series

Raymond Gay-Crosier, Editor
Dept. of Romance Languages & Literatures
Univ. of Florida
Gainesville, FL 32611

First published: 1952
ISSN: 0071-6189
MLA acronym: UFMH

SUBSCRIPTION INFORMATION

Frequency of publication: Irregular
Available in microform: No
Subscription address: Univ. Press of Florida, 15 N.W. 15th St., Gainesville, FL 32603

ADVERTISING INFORMATION

Advertising accepted: No

EDITORIAL DESCRIPTION

Scope: Publishes monographs on all aspects of the humanities.
Reviews books: No
Publishes notes: No
Languages accepted: English
Prints abstracts: No
Author-anonymous submission: No

SUBMISSION REQUIREMENTS

Restrictions on contributors: None
Author pays submission fee: No
Author pays page charges: No
Length of books: 100,000 words
Style: MLA; Chicago
Number of copies required: 1
Special requirements: Submission on Macintosh or IBM diskette, in addition to typescript, is preferred.
Copyright ownership: Board of Regents, State of Florida
Rejected manuscripts: Returned
Time before publication decision: 3-6 mos.
Time between decision and publication: 9-24 mos.
Number of reviewers: 2 minimum
Books submitted per year: 30
Books published per year: 2-4

(3077)
*University of Hartford Studies in Literature: A Journal of Interdisciplinary Criticism

Michael Walsh, Editor
Dept. of English
Univ. of Hartford
West Hartford, CT 06117

Telephone: 203 243-4574
First published: 1969
Sponsoring organization: Univ. of Hartford
ISSN: 0196-2280
MLA acronym: HSL

SUBSCRIPTION INFORMATION

Frequency of publication: 3 times/yr.
Circulation: 320
Available in microform: Yes
Subscription price: $9.00/yr. institutions US; $7.50/yr. individuals US; $12.00/yr. elsewhere
Year to which price refers: 1990

ADVERTISING INFORMATION

Advertising accepted: Yes
Advertising rates: $75.00/half page; $100.00/full page

EDITORIAL DESCRIPTION

Scope: An interdisciplinary journal publishing literary criticism and studies of literature as defined by another discipline. Includes cinema studies and studies on the place of language in culture.
Reviews books: Yes
Languages accepted: English
Prints abstracts: No
Author-anonymous submission: Yes, at author's request.

SUBMISSION REQUIREMENTS

Restrictions on contributors: None
Author pays submission fee: No
Author pays page charges: No
Length of articles: 3,750-7,500 words
Length of book reviews: 500-1,500 words
Style: MLA
Number of copies required: 3
Special requirements: Quotations are printed in original language with English translation. Submit author's name on separate page, not on the manuscript itself.
Copyright ownership: Univ. of Hartford
Rejected manuscripts: Returned; enclose return postage.
Time before publication decision: 3 mos.
Time between decision and publication: 6-12 mos.
Number of reviewers: 2 minimum
Articles submitted per year: 60-75
Articles published per year: 12-14
Book reviews submitted per year: 15-18
Book reviews published per year: 15

(3078)
*University of Kansas Humanistic Studies

David M. Bergeron, Editor
Hall Center for the Humanities
Watkins Home
Univ. of Kansas
Lawrence, KS 66045

Telephone: 913 864-4798
First published: 1912
Sponsoring organization: Univ. of Kansas, Hall Center for the Humanities
ISSN: 0085-2473
MLA acronym: UKPHS

SUBSCRIPTION INFORMATION

Frequency of publication: Irregular
Circulation: 700-1,200
Available in microform: No

ADVERTISING INFORMATION

Advertising accepted: No

EDITORIAL DESCRIPTION

Scope: Publishes monographs on humanistic subjects, such as literature, arts, language studies, philosophy, and history.
Reviews books: No
Languages accepted: English; French; Spanish
Prints abstracts: No

SUBMISSION REQUIREMENTS

Restrictions on contributors: None
Author pays submission fee: No
Author pays page charges: No
Length of books: 60,000 words
Style: MLA
Number of copies required: 1
Special requirements: Submit an abstract and table of contents.
Rejected manuscripts: Returned
Time before publication decision: 5 mos.
Time between decision and publication: 10 mos.
Number of reviewers: 3-4

(3079)
*University of Leeds Review

F. Felsenstein & Gwyneth Pitt, Editors
Publications Office
Univ. of Leeds
Leeds LS2 9JT, England

First published: 1948
Sponsoring organization: Univ. of Leeds
ISSN: 0041-9737
MLA acronym: ULR

SUBSCRIPTION INFORMATION

Frequency of publication: Annual
Circulation: 1,000
Available in microform: No
Subscription price: £8.35/yr. institutions; £5.10/yr. individuals
Year to which price refers: 1991-92

ADVERTISING INFORMATION

Advertising accepted: Yes

EDITORIAL DESCRIPTION

Scope: Publishes public and inaugural lectures given throughout the year as well as articles of general interest.
Reviews books: No
Publishes notes: No
Languages accepted: English
Prints abstracts: No
Author-anonymous submission: Yes

SUBMISSION REQUIREMENTS

Restrictions on contributors: All articles are commissioned.
Author pays submission fee: No
Author pays page charges: No
Length of articles: 6,000 words
Style: University
Number of copies required: 1
Copyright ownership: Assigned by author to journal
Rejected manuscripts: Returned
Time before publication decision: 2 mos.
Time between decision and publication: 15 mos.
Number of reviewers: 1
Articles published per year: 12-18

(3080)
*University of Mississippi Studies in English

Benjamin Franklin Fisher IV, Editor
P.O. Box 941
Oxford, MS 38655

First published: 1980
Sponsoring organization: Univ. of Mississippi
ISSN: 0278-310X
MLA acronym: UMSE

SUBSCRIPTION INFORMATION

Frequency of publication: Annual
Circulation: 450
Available in microform: Yes, through Univ. Microfilms International
Subscription address: Business Manager, Dept. of English, Univ. of Mississippi, University, MS 38677

ADVERTISING INFORMATION

Advertising accepted: No

EDITORIAL DESCRIPTION

Scope: Publishes articles on British and American literature.
Reviews books: Yes, as essay-reviews
Publishes notes: Yes
Languages accepted: English
Prints abstracts: No
Author-anonymous submission: No

SUBMISSION REQUIREMENTS

Restrictions on contributors: Reviews are solicited.
Author pays submission fee: No
Author pays page charges: No
Length of articles: 2,500 words minimum
Length of notes: 250-2,000 words
Style: Journal
Number of copies required: 2
Special requirements: Include notes at end of manuscript.
Copyright ownership: Journal
Rejected manuscripts: Returned; enclose return postage.
Time before publication decision: 1-3 mos.
Time between decision and publication: 12-18 mos.
Number of reviewers: 2-3

Articles submitted per year: 120
Articles published per year: 15-20
Book reviews published per year: 1-2 essay-reviews
Notes submitted per year: 12
Notes published per year: 3-5

(3081)
*University of North Carolina Studies in Comparative Literature

Diane R. Leonard, Editor
Curriculum of Comparative Literature
Univ. of North Carolina
341 Dey Hall 014A
Chapel Hill, NC 27514

First published: 1950
ISSN: 0081-7775
MLA acronym: UNCSCL

SUBSCRIPTION INFORMATION

Frequency of publication: Irregular
Circulation: 1,000
Available in microform: No
Subscription address: Univ. of North Carolina Press, Chapel Hill, NC 27514

ADVERTISING INFORMATION

Advertising accepted: No

EDITORIAL DESCRIPTION

Scope: Publishes monographs in comparative literature, criticism, and literary theory.
Reviews books: No
Publishes notes: No
Languages accepted: English
Prints abstracts: No

SUBMISSION REQUIREMENTS

Restrictions on contributors: None
Author pays submission fee: No
Author pays page charges: Yes
Style: Chicago
Number of copies required: 2
Copyright ownership: Univ. of North Carolina Press
Rejected manuscripts: Returned
Time before publication decision: 3-6 mos.
Time between decision and publication: 1 yr. maximum
Number of reviewers: 2

(3082)
*University of North Carolina Studies in the Germanic Languages and Literatures

Paul T. Roberge, Editor
Dept. of Germanic Languages
Univ. of North Carolina
CB 3160 Dey Hall
Chapel Hill, NC 27599-3160

Telephone: 919 966-1642
Fax: 919 962-5604 (c/o Univ. Fax Service)
E-mail: Prt@ecsvax.uncecs.edu
First published: 1949
Sponsoring organization: Dept. of Germanic Languages, Univ. of North Carolina, Chapel Hill
ISSN: 0081-8593
MLA acronym: UNCSGLL

SUBSCRIPTION INFORMATION

Frequency of publication: Irregular
Available in microform: No
Subscription address: Univ. of North Carolina Press, P.O. Box 2288, Chapel Hill, NC 27515-2288

Additional subscription address: In United Kingdom, Europe, Middle East, & Africa contact: Trevor Brown & Anna Simpson-Müllner, Univ. Book Marketing, 1st floor, Dilke House, Malet St., London WC1E 7JA, England
Subscription telephone: 919 966-3561; 800 848-6224
Subscription fax: 919 966-3829

ADVERTISING INFORMATION

Advertising accepted: No

EDITORIAL DESCRIPTION

Scope: Publishes book length manuscripts in the field of Germanic languages, including literature, linguistics, philology, and culture. Monographs are preferred but collections of essays will be considered.
Reviews books: No
Publishes notes: No
Languages accepted: English; German
Prints abstracts: No
Author-anonymous submission: No

SUBMISSION REQUIREMENTS

Restrictions on contributors: None
Author pays submission fee: No
Author pays page charges: Yes
Length of books: 125-400 pp.
Style: Chicago
Number of copies required: 2
Special requirements: Consult with editor for publication policy prior to submission.
Copyright ownership: Univ. of North Carolina Press
Rejected manuscripts: Returned
Time before publication decision: 3-6 mos.
Time between decision and publication: 10-12 mos.
Number of reviewers: 2
Books submitted per year: 8-10
Books published per year: 1-4

(3083)
*University of Pennsylvania Studies on South Asia

Rosane Rocher, Editor
Dept. of South Asia Regional Studies
820 Williams Hall/CU
Univ. of Pennsylvania
Philadelphia, PA 19104

First published: 1984
Sponsoring organization: Dept. of South Asia Regional Studies, Univ. of Pennsylvania
ISSN: 0169-0361
MLA acronym: UPSSA

SUBSCRIPTION INFORMATION

Frequency of publication: Irregular
Available in microform: No

ADVERTISING INFORMATION

Advertising accepted: No

EDITORIAL DESCRIPTION

Scope: Publishes monographs about South Asian culture and society.
Reviews books: No
Publishes notes: No
Languages accepted: English
Prints abstracts: No

SUBMISSION REQUIREMENTS

Author pays submission fee: No
Author pays page charges: No
Number of copies required: 1
Copyright ownership: South Asia Regional Studies, Univ. of Pennsylvania
Rejected manuscripts: Returned

Time before publication decision: 3 mos.
Time between decision and publication: 1 yr.
Number of reviewers: 3
Books submitted per year: 5
Books published per year: 1

(3084)
*The University of Saga Studies in English

Masahiko Agari & Masao Koike, Editors
Dept. of English
College of Liberal Arts
Univ. of Saga
1 Honjo
Saga 840, Japan

First published: 1967
Sponsoring organization: Dept. of English, College of Liberal Arts, Univ. of Saga
MLA acronym: USSE

SUBSCRIPTION INFORMATION

Frequency of publication: Annual
Available in microform: No

ADVERTISING INFORMATION

Advertising accepted: No

EDITORIAL DESCRIPTION

Scope: Publishes critical studies dealing with all aspects of English language and literature.
Reviews books: No
Publishes notes: Yes
Languages accepted: English; Japanese
Prints abstracts: No
Author-anonymous submission: No

SUBMISSION REQUIREMENTS

Restrictions on contributors: Contributors must be members of the Dept. of English of the Univ. of Saga.
Author pays submission fee: No
Author pays page charges: No
Style: MLA
Number of copies required: 1
Copyright ownership: English Dept., Univ. of Saga
Time before publication decision: 1 mo.
Articles submitted per year: 2-9
Articles published per year: 2-9

(3085)
*University of Toronto Italian Studies

Massimo Ciavolella, Editorial Committee Chair
Dept. of Italian Studies
Univ. of Toronto
Toronto, Ontario M5S 1A1, Canada

Telephone: 416 978-6062
Fax: 416 978-5593
First published: 1987
Sponsoring organization: Dept. of Italian Studies, Univ. of Toronto
MLA acronym: UTIS

SUBSCRIPTION INFORMATION

Frequency of publication: Annual
Circulation: 300
Available in microform: No

ADVERTISING INFORMATION

Advertising accepted: No

EDITORIAL DESCRIPTION

Scope: Publishes collections of articles on Italian studies.
Reviews books: No
Publishes notes: No
Languages accepted: English
Prints abstracts: No
Author-anonymous submission: No

SUBMISSION REQUIREMENTS

Restrictions on contributors: Contributions are by invitation only.
Author pays submission fee: No
Author pays page charges: No
Length of articles: 5,000 words
Length of books: 250 pp.
Style: MLA
Number of copies required: 2
Copyright ownership: Dovehouse Editions Inc.

(3086)
*University of Toronto Quarterly: A Canadian Journal of the Humanities

A. Bewell, Editor
Univ. of Toronto Press
Editorial Dept.
10 St. Mary St., Suite 700
Toronto, Ontario M4Y 2W8, Canada

First published: 1931
Sponsoring organization: Univ. of Toronto Press
ISSN: 0042-0247
MLA acronym: UTQ

SUBSCRIPTION INFORMATION

Frequency of publication: 4 times/yr.
Circulation: 1,200
Available in microform: Yes
Subscription price: C$45.00/yr. institutions; C$24.00/yr. individuals; C$16.50/yr. students; add C$5.00/yr. outside Canada
Year to which price refers: 1992
Subscription address: Univ. of Toronto Press, 5201 Dufferin St., Downsview, Ontario M3H 5T8, Canada

ADVERTISING INFORMATION

Advertising accepted: Yes

EDITORIAL DESCRIPTION

Scope: Publishes articles of criticism and scholarly analysis in all areas of the humanities. Favors articles that cross either periods or disciplines. Does not normally print thematically oriented criticism or the results of highly specialized research. Expects high quality criticism or intellectual argument.
Reviews books: Yes
Publishes notes: No
Languages accepted: English; French
Prints abstracts: No
Author-anonymous submission: No

SUBMISSION REQUIREMENTS

Restrictions on contributors: Book reviews are commissioned.
Author pays submission fee: No
Author pays page charges: No
Length of articles: 4,000-8,000 words
Length of book reviews: No restrictions
Style: Journal
Number of copies required: 1
Special requirements: Editors prefer a photocopy which does not have to be returned; computer printouts should have nonjustified right margins.
Copyright ownership: Univ. of Toronto Press
Rejected manuscripts: Returned at author's request; enclose return postage or international postal coupons.
Time before publication decision: 1-3 mos.
Time between decision and publication: 1 yr.
Number of reviewers: 1-3
Articles submitted per year: 140
Articles published per year: 14-18
Book reviews published per year: 120

(3087)
*University of Toronto Romance Series

Ronald Schoeffel, Editor
Univ. of Toronto Press
10 St. Mary St., Suite 700
Toronto, Ontario M4Y 2W8, Canada

Telephone: 416 978-4738
First published: 1942
ISSN: 0082-5336
MLA acronym: UTFS

SUBSCRIPTION INFORMATION

Frequency of publication: Irregular
Available in microform: No

ADVERTISING INFORMATION

Advertising accepted: No

EDITORIAL DESCRIPTION

Scope: Publishes monographs on Romance studies.
Reviews books: No
Publishes notes: No
Languages accepted: English
Prints abstracts: No
Author-anonymous submission: No

SUBMISSION REQUIREMENTS

Number of copies required: 2
Copyright ownership: Univ. of Toronto Press
Rejected manuscripts: Returned

(3088)
*Uniwersytet im. Adama Mickiewicza w Poznaniu: Seria Filologia Angielska

Jacek Fisiak, Editor
c/o Ewa Bosacka, Director
Wydawnictwo Naukowe UAM
ul. Nowowiejskiego 55
61-734 Poznań, Poland

Telephone: (48) 61 527701; (48) 61 527380
First published: 1966
MLA acronym: UAM

SUBSCRIPTION INFORMATION

Frequency of publication: Irregular
Available in microform: No
Subscription address: Ars Polona Ruch, Centrala Handlu Zagranicznego, ul. Krakowskie Przedmieście, 7, 00-068 Warsaw, Poland

ADVERTISING INFORMATION

Advertising accepted: No

EDITORIAL DESCRIPTION

Scope: Publishes monograph studies on English philology.
Reviews books: No
Publishes notes: No
Languages accepted: English
Prints abstracts: No
Author-anonymous submission: No

SUBMISSION REQUIREMENTS

Restrictions on contributors: Most contributions are dissertations.
Author pays submission fee: No
Author pays page charges: No
Length of books: 200 pp.
Style: MLA
Number of copies required: 3-4
Special requirements: Submit original typescript and 2-3 copies.

(3089)
*Die Unterrichtspraxis

George F. Peters, Editor
Dept. of Linguistics & Languages
A615 Wells Hall
Michigan State Univ.
East Lansing, MI 48824-1027

Telephone: 517 353-0740
Fax: 517 336-2736
E-mail: 22024.GFP@MSU
First published: 1968
Sponsoring organization: American Assn. of Teachers of German
ISSN: 0042-062X
MLA acronym: UP

SUBSCRIPTION INFORMATION

Frequency of publication: 2 times/yr.
Circulation: 7,800
Available in microform: No
Subscription address: American Assn. of Teachers of German, National Office no. 104, 112 Haddontowne Ct., Cherry Hill, NJ 08034
Subscription telephone: 609 795-5553
Subscription fax: 609 795-9398

ADVERTISING INFORMATION

Advertising accepted: Yes

EDITORIAL DESCRIPTION

Scope: Devoted to improving and increasing German instruction in the United States. Primarily pedagogical in nature, it considers for publication timely and significant articles, reports, news, discussions, reference material, and book reviews of interest to teachers of German language, literature, and culture at all instructional levels.
Reviews books: Yes
Publishes notes: No
Languages accepted: English; German
Prints abstracts: Yes
Author-anonymous submission: Yes

SUBMISSION REQUIREMENTS

Restrictions on contributors: None
Author pays submission fee: No
Author pays page charges: No
Length of articles: 15 pp.
Length of book reviews: No restrictions
Style: MLA
Number of copies required: 3
Special requirements: Author's name should not appear on manuscript. Include a short biographical statement in English and a 100-word abstract.
Copyright ownership: American Assn. of Teachers of German
Rejected manuscripts: Returned; enclose SAE and sufficient loose postage.
Time before publication decision: 3 mos.
Time between decision and publication: 1 yr.
Number of reviewers: 3
Articles submitted per year: 51
Articles published per year: 22
Book reviews submitted per year: 23
Book reviews published per year: 23

Copyright ownership: Publisher
Rejected manuscripts: Returned
Time before publication decision: 3 mo.
Time between decision and publication: 1 yr. maximum
Number of reviewers: 1-2

(3090)
*Untersuchungen zur Deutschen Literaturgeschichte

Max Niemeyer Verlag
Postfach 2140
7400 Tübingen, Germany

Telephone: (49) 7071 81104
Fax: (49) 7071 87419
First published: 1962
ISSN: 0083-4564
MLA acronym: UDL

SUBSCRIPTION INFORMATION

Frequency of publication: Irregular
Available in microform: No

ADVERTISING INFORMATION

Advertising accepted: No

EDITORIAL DESCRIPTION

Scope: Publishes monographs on German literary history.
Reviews books: No
Publishes notes: No
Languages accepted: German; English
Prints abstracts: No
Author-anonymous submission: Yes

SUBMISSION REQUIREMENTS

Restrictions on contributors: None
Author pays submission fee: No
Author pays page charges: No
Length of books: No restrictions
Style: MLA
Number of copies required: 1
Copyright ownership: Max Niemeyer Verlag
Rejected manuscripts: Returned
Time before publication decision: 3-6 mos.
Time between decision and publication: 9 mos.
Number of reviewers: 2-3
Books submitted per year: 4-5
Books published per year: 2-3

(3091)
Uomini e Libri: Periodico Bimestrale di Critica ed Informazione Letteraria

Mario Miccinesi, Editor
Viale Emilio Caldara, 8
20122 Milan, Italy

First published: 1965
ISSN: 0042-0654
MLA acronym: UeL

SUBSCRIPTION INFORMATION

Frequency of publication: 5 times/yr.
Circulation: 7,000
Available in microform: No

ADVERTISING INFORMATION

Advertising accepted: Yes

EDITORIAL DESCRIPTION

Scope: Publishes literary information and both Italian and foreign literary criticism.
Reviews books: Yes
Publishes notes: Yes
Languages accepted: Italian
Prints abstracts: No

SUBMISSION REQUIREMENTS

Restrictions on contributors: Collaboration is by invitation.
Author pays submission fee: No
Author pays page charges: No
Length of articles: No restrictions

Length of book reviews: No restrictions
Length of notes: No restrictions
Rejected manuscripts: Not returned
Articles submitted per year: 500
Articles published per year: 250
Book reviews published per year: 170
Notes published per year: 500

(3092)
The Upstart Crow

James R. Andreas, Editor
Drury College
900 North Benton Ave.
Springfield, MO 65802

First published: 1978
Sponsoring organization: Drury College
ISSN: 0886-2168
MLA acronym: UCrow

SUBSCRIPTION INFORMATION

Frequency of publication: Annual
Circulation: 500
Available in microform: No

ADVERTISING INFORMATION

Advertising accepted: No

EDITORIAL DESCRIPTION

Scope: Publishes critical essays on Shakespeare's plays and poems. Encourages any original idea or new approach which would stimulate thinking or rethinking.
Reviews books: Yes
Publishes notes: Yes
Languages accepted: English
Prints abstracts: No
Author-anonymous submission: No

SUBMISSION REQUIREMENTS

Restrictions on contributors: None
Author pays submission fee: No
Author pays page charges: No
Length of articles: 6,000-8,000 words
Length of book reviews: 2,000 words
Length of notes: 1,500 words
Style: MLA
Number of copies required: 2
Special requirements: Quotations should be single spaced in typescript. Submit original typescript. If possible, submit copy on IBM diskette in text-file format with left margins set at zero.
Copyright ownership: Drury College
Rejected manuscripts: Returned; enclose return postage.
Time before publication decision: 6 mos.
Time between decision and publication: 1 yr.
Number of reviewers: 2
Articles submitted per year: 50
Articles published per year: 10
Book reviews submitted per year: 5
Book reviews published per year: 1
Notes submitted per year: 10
Notes published per year: 2

(3093)
*Ural-Altaische Jahrbücher/Ural-Altaic Yearbook: Internationale Zeitschrift für Nord-Eurasien

Gyula Décsy & A. J. A. Bodrogligeti, Editors
Goodbody Hall 141
Indiana Univ.
Bloomington, IN 47405

Telephone: 812 332-8918
First published: 1921
Sponsoring organization: Eurasian Linguistic Assn.
ISSN: 0042-0786

MLA acronym: UAJ

SUBSCRIPTION INFORMATION

Frequency of publication: Annual
Circulation: 600
Available in microform: No
Subscription price: $74.00/yr.
Subscription address: Eurolingua, P.O. Box 101, Bloomington, IN 47402

ADVERTISING INFORMATION

Advertising accepted: Yes

EDITORIAL DESCRIPTION

Scope: Publishes generic and/or specific comparisons of, as well as individual treatments of, about 60 East-Eurasian languages, mainly from linguistic standpoints.
Reviews books: Yes
Publishes notes: Yes
Languages accepted: English; German
Prints abstracts: No
Author-anonymous submission: No

SUBMISSION REQUIREMENTS

Restrictions on contributors: None
Author pays submission fee: No
Author pays page charges: No
Length of articles: 30 pp.
Length of book reviews: 4 pp.
Length of notes: 1/2 p.
Style: MLA
Number of copies required: 1
Special requirements: Submission on diskette using Macintosh Microsoft Word or IBM WordPerfect is preferred; otherwise, submit original typescript.
Copyright ownership: Assigned by author to editor
Rejected manuscripts: Returned
Time before publication decision: 2 mos.
Time between decision and publication: 1 yr.
Number of reviewers: 2
Articles submitted per year: 15-20
Articles published per year: 5-10
Book reviews submitted per year: 50-60
Book reviews published per year: 40-50
Notes submitted per year: 30-40
Notes published per year: 30-40

(3094)
Urbe: Rivista Romana di Storia, Arte, Lettere, Costumanze

Manlio Barberito, Editor
Fratelli Palombi Editori
Via dei Gracchi, 181-185
00192 Rome, Italy

First published: 1936
ISSN: 0042-1030
MLA acronym: Urbe

SUBSCRIPTION INFORMATION

Frequency of publication: 6 times/yr.
Circulation: 1,000
Available in microform: No

ADVERTISING INFORMATION

Advertising accepted: Yes

EDITORIAL DESCRIPTION

Reviews books: Yes
Languages accepted: Italian
Prints abstracts: No

SUBMISSION REQUIREMENTS

Restrictions on contributors: None
Length of articles: 10 pp.
Style: None

Number of copies required: 1
Time before publication decision: 2 mos.
Time between decision and publication: 2 mos.
Articles published per year: 18

(3095)
*Us Wurk: Tydskrift foar Frisistyk

O. Vries, P. Breuker, E. J. Brouwer, & G. J. de Haan, Editors
Fries Inst. Rijksuniv. te Groningen
Oude Kijk in 't Jatstraat 26
9712 EK Groningen, Netherlands

Telephone: (31) 50 635947
First published: 1952
Sponsoring organization: Stifting Freonen Frysk Ynst. RUG
ISSN: 0042-1235
MLA acronym: UW

SUBSCRIPTION INFORMATION

Frequency of publication: 4 times/yr.
Circulation: 300
Available in microform: No
Subscription price: 25 f/yr.
Year to which price refers: 1992
Subscription telephone: (31) 50 635944

ADVERTISING INFORMATION

Advertising accepted: No

EDITORIAL DESCRIPTION

Scope: Publishes studies on Frisian language and literature.
Reviews books: No
Publishes notes: Yes
Languages accepted: Dutch; Frisian; English; German; French
Prints abstracts: Yes
Author-anonymous submission: No

SUBMISSION REQUIREMENTS

Restrictions on contributors: None
Author pays submission fee: No
Author pays page charges: No
Length of articles: 32 pp. maximum
Length of notes: No restrictions
Style: None
Number of copies required: 1
Special requirements: Submit typescript or diskette.
Copyright ownership: Author
Rejected manuscripts: Returned
Time before publication decision: 6 weeks
Time between decision and publication: 6-12 mos.
Number of reviewers: 4

(3096)
*Utah Studies in Literature and Linguistics

Wolff A. von Schmidt, Gerhard P. Knapp, & Luis Lorenzo-Rivero, Editors
Dept. of Languages & Literature
Univ. of Utah
Salt Lake City, UT 84112

Telephone: 801 581-7561
Fax: 801 581-7581
First published: 1974
Sponsoring organization: Univ. of Utah
ISSN: 0171-726X
MLA acronym: USLL

SUBSCRIPTION INFORMATION

Frequency of publication: Irregular
Circulation: 300-700
Available in microform: No

Subscription address: Verlag Peter Lang & Cie., AG., Jupiterstr. 15, 3000 Bern, Switzerland

ADVERTISING INFORMATION

Advertising accepted: No

EDITORIAL DESCRIPTION

Scope: Publishes monographs on comparative literature and on French, German, and Spanish literature.
Reviews books: Yes
Publishes notes: No
Languages accepted: English; French; German; Spanish
Prints abstracts: No
Author-anonymous submission: Yes

SUBMISSION REQUIREMENTS

Restrictions on contributors: None
Author pays submission fee: No
Length of books: No restrictions
Style: None
Number of copies required: 1
Copyright ownership: Verlag Peter Lang & Cie., AG
Rejected manuscripts: Returned
Time before publication decision: 1 mo.
Time between decision and publication: 9 mos.
Number of reviewers: 3
Books submitted per year: 5-8
Books published per year: 2-3

(3097)
*Utrechtse Publikaties voor Algemene Literatuurwetenschap/Utrecht Publications in General and Comparative Literature

Douwe W. Fokkema, Joost Kloek, Sophie Levie, Willie van Peer, & Bernhard F. Scholz, Editors
Inst. Algemene Literatuurwetenschap
Muntstr. 4
3512 EV Utrecht, Netherlands

First published: 1962
Sponsoring organization: Rijksuniv. te Utrecht, Inst. voor Vergelijkend Literatuur-Onderzoek
ISSN: 0167-8175
MLA acronym: UPAL

SUBSCRIPTION INFORMATION

Frequency of publication: Irregular
Available in microform: No
Subscription address: John Benjamins B.V., P.O. Box 75577, Amsteldijk 44, 1070 AN Amsterdam, Netherlands
Additional subscription address: John Benjamins North America, Inc., 821 Bethlehem Pike, Philadelphia, PA 19118
Subscription telephone: (31) 20 6738156; 215 836-1200
Subscription fax: (31) 20 6739773; 215 836-1204

ADVERTISING INFORMATION

Advertising accepted: No

EDITORIAL DESCRIPTION

Scope: Publishes articles on literary theory, general and comparative literature, and comparative literature from the Middle Ages to the present.
Reviews books: No
Publishes notes: No
Languages accepted: English
Prints abstracts: No
Author-anonymous submission: No

SUBMISSION REQUIREMENTS

Restrictions on contributors: None
Author pays submission fee: No

(3098)
*Vagant

Johann Grip, Alf van der Hagen, Pål Norheim, John Tore Aartveit, Cecilie Schram Hoel, Tone Hödnebö, Henning Hagerup, Torunn Borge, & Hege Imerslund, Editors
Postboks 894, Sentrum
0104 Oslo, Norway

Telephone: (47) 2 428626
First published: 1988
Sponsoring organization: Norwegian Cultur Fond
ISSN: 0802-0736
MLA acronym: Vagant

SUBSCRIPTION INFORMATION

Frequency of publication: 4 times/yr. (Jan., Apr., Aug., Nov.)
Circulation: 4,000

ADVERTISING INFORMATION

Advertising accepted: Yes

EDITORIAL DESCRIPTION

Scope: Publishes articles on literature, film, and rock music. Includes essays, interviews, poetry, and fiction.
Reviews books: Yes
Publishes notes: Yes
Languages accepted: Norwegian; Danish; Swedish
Prints abstracts: No

SUBMISSION REQUIREMENTS

Restrictions on contributors: None
Author pays submission fee: No
Author pays page charges: No
Style: New Century Schoolbook
Copyright ownership: Journal
Time between decision and publication: 1-6 mos.
Number of reviewers: 6
Articles published per year: 50-60
Book reviews submitted per year: 20
Book reviews published per year: 15
Notes submitted per year: 25
Notes published per year: 20

(3099)
Vagartha: Critical Quarterly of Indian Literature

Meenakshi Mukherjee, Editor
N-3 Panchsheel Park
New Delhi 110017, India

First published: 1972
Sponsoring organization: Joshi Foundation
MLA acronym: Vagartha

SUBSCRIPTION INFORMATION

Frequency of publication: 4 times/yr.
Circulation: 500

Author pays page charges: No
Length of books: 300-350 pp.
Style: Series; request from editor.
Number of copies required: 2
Copyright ownership: John Benjamins
Rejected manuscripts: Returned
Time before publication decision: 6 mos.
Time between decision and publication: 1 yr.
Number of reviewers: 1-2
Books submitted per year: 4-6
Books published per year: 2-3

EDITORIAL DESCRIPTION

Scope: Publishes articles on contemporary Indian literature.
Reviews books: Yes
Languages accepted: English
Prints abstracts: No

SUBMISSION REQUIREMENTS

Restrictions on contributors: None
Length of articles: 3,000-6,000 words
Number of copies required: 1
Special requirements: Submit original typescript.
Rejected manuscripts: Returned; enclose return postage.
Time before publication decision: 6 mos.
Time between decision and publication: 6-12 mos.
Number of reviewers: 4
Articles published per year: 20-25

(3100)
Varavīksne

Ligita Bībere, Editor
Šarlotes 5-8
1001 Riga, Latvia

First published: 1967
ISSN: 0506-4120
MLA acronym: Varaviksne

SUBSCRIPTION INFORMATION

Frequency of publication: Annual

EDITORIAL DESCRIPTION

Scope: Publishes articles on Latvian literature.

(3101)
Variétés

Giorgio Cerruti, Edda Melon, Sergio Zoppi
Tirrenia Stampatori
via Gaudenzio Ferrari, 5
10124 Torino, Italy

Telephone: (39) 11 877010
MLA acronym: Variétés

SUBSCRIPTION INFORMATION

Frequency of publication: Irregular

EDITORIAL DESCRIPTION

Scope: Publishes articles on French literature. Each issue is thematic.
Languages accepted: French

(3102)
Varieties of English Around the World

Manfred Görlach, Editor
Univ. zu Köln
Englisches Seminar
Albertus-Magnus-Platz
5000 Cologne 41, Germany

First published: 1979
ISSN: 0172-7362
MLA acronym: VEAW

SUBSCRIPTION INFORMATION

Circulation: 300-800
Available in microform: No
Subscription address: John Benjamins N.A. Inc., 821 Bethlehem Pike, Philadelphia, PA 19118
Additional subscription address: John Benjamins B.V., P.O. Box 75577, Amsteldijk 44, 1070 AN Amsterdam, Netherlands

ADVERTISING INFORMATION

Advertising accepted: No

EDITORIAL DESCRIPTION

Scope: Aims to serve both scholarship and teaching by providing up-to-date treatments of the forms and functions of English, region by region, including English-based pidgins and creoles.
Reviews books: No
Publishes notes: No
Languages accepted: English
Prints abstracts: No
Author-anonymous submission: No

SUBMISSION REQUIREMENTS

Restrictions on contributors: None
Author pays submission fee: No
Author pays page charges: No
Length of books: 120-200 pp.
Style: MLA
Number of copies required: 2
Special requirements: Submit camera-ready copy.
Copyright ownership: John Benjamins N.A.
Time before publication decision: 4-6 mos.
Time between decision and publication: 3 mos.
Number of reviewers: 1-2
Books published per year: 2-4

(3103)
*Il Veltro: Rivista della Civiltà Italiana

Vincenzo Cappelletti, Editor
Via S. Nicola de' Cesarini, 3
00186 Rome, Italy

Telephone: (39) 6 6592275
Fax: (39) 6 68300103
First published: 1957
Sponsoring organization: Presenza Italiana
ISSN: 0042-3254
MLA acronym: Veltro

SUBSCRIPTION INFORMATION

Frequency of publication: 6 times/yr.
Circulation: 6,000
Available in microform: No
Subscription price: 100,000 Lit/yr. Italy
Year to which price refers: 1992

ADVERTISING INFORMATION

Advertising accepted: Yes

EDITORIAL DESCRIPTION

Scope: Welcomes original research in the areas of past and current Italian social traditions, Italian ideal, creative, and humanitarian affirmations, values and problems that have guided Italy's historical course, and relations between Italy and other countries, cultures, and societies.
Reviews books: Yes
Publishes notes: Yes
Languages accepted: Italian
Prints abstracts: Yes
Author-anonymous submission: No

SUBMISSION REQUIREMENTS

Restrictions on contributors: None
Author pays submission fee: No
Author pays page charges: No
Length of articles: 10-20 pp.
Length of book reviews: 2-3 pp.
Length of notes: 1 p.
Style: MLA

Number of copies required: 2
Special requirements: Submit original typescript and 1 photocopy.
Copyright ownership: Assigned by author to journal
Rejected manuscripts: Returned
Time before publication decision: 2 mos.
Time between decision and publication: 4-6 mos.
Number of reviewers: 2
Articles submitted per year: 60
Articles published per year: 40
Book reviews submitted per year: 200
Book reviews published per year: 120-190
Notes submitted per year: 100
Notes published per year: 50

(3104)
*The Velvet Light Trap

Dept. of Communication Arts
Univ. of Wisconsin
Vilas Hall, 6th floor
821 University Ave.
Madison, WI 53706

Additional editorial address: Dept. of Radio-Television-Film, Univ. of Texas, CMA 6.118, Austin, TX 78712
Telephone: 608 262-2543 (Madison, WI); 512 471-4071 (Austin, TX)
First published: 1971
ISSN: 0149-1830
MLA acronym: VLT

SUBSCRIPTION INFORMATION

Frequency of publication: 2 times/yr. (Mar., Sept.)
Circulation: 600
Available in microform: Yes
Subscription address: Univ. of Texas Press, P.O. Box 7819, Austin, TX 78713
Subscription telephone: 512 471-4531

ADVERTISING INFORMATION

Advertising accepted: Yes

EDITORIAL DESCRIPTION

Scope: Publishes articles on the history of film and television.
Reviews books: Yes
Publishes notes: No
Languages accepted: English
Prints abstracts: No
Author-anonymous submission: No

SUBMISSION REQUIREMENTS

Restrictions on contributors: Book reviews are solicited.
Author pays submission fee: No
Author pays page charges: No
Length of articles: 35 pp.
Style: MLA
Number of copies required: 3
Special requirements: Submit double-spaced typescript with copies of illustrations. Quotations not in English should be accompanied by translation.
Copyright ownership: Univ. of Texas Press
Rejected manuscripts: Not returned
Time before publication decision: 3 mos.
Time between decision and publication: 6-12 mos.
Number of reviewers: 2
Articles submitted per year: 40-50
Articles published per year: 10-12
Book reviews published per year: 0-5

(3105)
Ventanal: Revista de Creación y Critica

Assn. Culturelle & Latino-Américaine
Univ. de Perpignan
Chemin de la Passió Vella
66025 Perpignan, France

First published: 1981
Sponsoring organization: Univ. de Perpignan
ISSN: 0292-9236
MLA acronym: Ventanal

SUBSCRIPTION INFORMATION

Frequency of publication: 2 times/yr.
Circulation: 300
Available in microform: No

ADVERTISING INFORMATION

Advertising accepted: No

EDITORIAL DESCRIPTION

Scope: Publishes articles on Spanish and Latin American literature.
Reviews books: Yes
Publishes notes: No
Languages accepted: Spanish; French; Catalan
Prints abstracts: No
Author-anonymous submission: No

SUBMISSION REQUIREMENTS

Restrictions on contributors: None
Author pays submission fee: No
Author pays page charges: No
Length of articles: 15 pp.
Length of book reviews: 1-2 pp.
Style: Journal
Number of copies required: 1
Rejected manuscripts: Returned
Time before publication decision: 2-3 mos.
Time between decision and publication: 5-6 mos.
Number of reviewers: 3
Articles submitted per year: 20
Articles published per year: 7-9
Book reviews submitted per year: 30
Book reviews published per year: 20

(3106)
*Verba: Anuario Galego de Filoloxía

Ramón Lorenzo, Editor
c/o Alexandre Veiga
Fac. de Filoloxía
Univ. de Santiago de Compostela
15771 Santiago de Compostela, Spain

Telephone: (34) 81 575340
Fax: (34) 81 574646
First published: 1974
Sponsoring organization: Univ. de Santiago de Compostela
ISSN: 0210-377X
MLA acronym: Verba

SUBSCRIPTION INFORMATION

Frequency of publication: Annual
Available in microform: No
Subscription price: 4,800 Pta/yr.
Year to which price refers: 1991
Subscription address: Servicio de Publicacións & Intercambio Científico, Univ. de Santiago de Compostela, Campus Universitario, 15771 Santiago de Compostela, Spain
Subscription telephone: (34) 81 563100 (request Servicio de Publicaciónes)
Subscription fax: (34) 81 593963

ADVERTISING INFORMATION

Advertising accepted: No

EDITORIAL DESCRIPTION

Scope: Publishes articles on linguistics and Galician and Romance philology.
Reviews books: Yes
Publishes notes: Yes
Languages accepted: Galician; Spanish; Portuguese; Catalan; French; Italian; English; German
Prints abstracts: No
Author-anonymous submission: No

SUBMISSION REQUIREMENTS

Restrictions on contributors: None
Author pays submission fee: No
Author pays page charges: No
Length of articles: 20,000 words maximum
Length of book reviews: 1,500 words maximum
Length of notes: 5,000 words maximum
Style: None
Number of copies required: 1
Rejected manuscripts: Returned
Time before publication decision: 3 mos. maximum
Time between decision and publication: 1 yr. maximum
Number of reviewers: 3
Articles submitted per year: 15
Articles published per year: 12
Book reviews submitted per year: 12
Book reviews published per year: 10
Notes submitted per year: 8
Notes published per year: 6

(3107)
*Verbatim: The Language Quarterly

Laurence Urdang, Editor
4 Laurel Heights
Old Lyme, CT 06371

Additional editorial address: P.O. Box 199, Aylesbury, Bucks HP20 2HY, England
Telephone: 203 434-2104; (44) 296 395880
First published: 1974
ISSN: 0162-0932
MLA acronym: Verbatim

SUBSCRIPTION INFORMATION

Frequency of publication: 4 times/yr. (Summer, Autumn, Winter, Spring)
Circulation: 10,000
Available in microform: No
Subscription price: $16.50/yr. US; £11.50/yr. United Kingdom
Year to which price refers: 1992-93
Subscription address: P.O. Box 78008, Indianapolis, IN 46278-0008
Additional subscription address: P.O. Box 199, Aylesbury, Bucks HP20 2HY, England
Subscription telephone: 800 999-2266

ADVERTISING INFORMATION

Advertising accepted: Yes
Advertising rates: $125.00/quarter page; $210.00/half page; $400.00/full page

EDITORIAL DESCRIPTION

Scope: Publishes articles on all aspects of language.
Reviews books: Yes
Publishes notes: Yes
Languages accepted: English
Prints abstracts: No
Author-anonymous submission: No

SUBMISSION REQUIREMENTS

Restrictions on contributors: Book reviews are assigned.
Author pays submission fee: No
Author pays page charges: No
Length of articles: 1,500 words maximum
Length of book reviews: 1,000 words
Length of notes: 100 words

Style: Chicago
Number of copies required: 1
Special requirements: Submit double-spaced typescript or printout.
Copyright ownership: Publisher
Rejected manuscripts: Returned; enclose SASE.
Time before publication decision: 6 weeks
Time between decision and publication: 3 mos.
Number of reviewers: 1
Articles submitted per year: 100
Articles published per year: 15
Book reviews submitted per year: 12-15
Book reviews published per year: 12-15
Notes submitted per year: 100
Notes published per year: 16-20

(3108)
*Verdad y Vida: Revista de las Ciencias del Espiritu

Franciscanos Españoles
Joaquin Costa, 36
28002 Madrid, Spain

Telephone: (34) 1 5619900; (34) 1 5619908
First published: 1943
Sponsoring organization: Franciscan Order, Spain
ISSN: 0042-3718
MLA acronym: VyV

SUBSCRIPTION INFORMATION

Frequency of publication: 4 times/yr.
Circulation: 500
Available in microform: No
Subscription price: $50.00/yr.
Year to which price refers: 1992

ADVERTISING INFORMATION

Advertising accepted: No

EDITORIAL DESCRIPTION

Scope: Focuses on the Franciscan interpretation of man and the modern world.
Reviews books: Yes
Publishes notes: Yes
Languages accepted: Spanish; Portuguese
Prints abstracts: No

SUBMISSION REQUIREMENTS

Restrictions on contributors: None
Author pays submission fee: Yes
Length of articles: 17 pp.
Number of copies required: 1
Rejected manuscripts: Returned
Time before publication decision: 6 mos.
Number of reviewers: 2
Articles published per year: 25
Book reviews published per year: 150
Notes published per year: 4

(3109)
*Veröffentlichungen der Abteilung für Slavische Sprachen und Literaturen des Osteuropa-Instituts (Slavisches Seminar) an der Freien Universität Berlin

Fred Otten, Klaus-Dieter Seemann, & Jurij Striedter, Editors
Osteuropa Inst.
Freie Univ. Berlin
Garystr. 55
1000 Berlin 33 (Dahlem), Germany

Fax: (49) 30 8383788
First published: 1953
Sponsoring organization: Freien Univ., Osteuropa-Inst.
ISSN: 0067-592X
MLA acronym: VOEI

SUBSCRIPTION INFORMATION

Frequency of publication: Irregular
Circulation: 500
Available in microform: No
Subscription address: Verlag Otto Harrassowitz, Postfach 2929, Taunusstr. 14, 6200 Wiesbaden 1, Germany

ADVERTISING INFORMATION

Advertising accepted: No

EDITORIAL DESCRIPTION

Scope: Publishes monographs on Slavic philology. Covers languages and literature.
Reviews books: No
Publishes notes: No
Languages accepted: German; English
Prints abstracts: No

SUBMISSION REQUIREMENTS

Restrictions on contributors: Manuscripts are solicited from authors connected with the institute.
Author pays submission fee: No
Author pays page charges: No
Length of books: No restrictions
Number of copies required: 1
Special requirements: Submit original typescript or copy from a laser printer, and if possible, a 3.5 in. diskette using Microsoft Word.
Copyright ownership: Freie Univ., Osteuropa-Inst.
Rejected manuscripts: Returned
Time before publication decision: 2 mos.
Time between decision and publication: 10 mos.
Number of reviewers: 2-3
Books submitted per year: 4
Books published per year: 2

(3110)
*Veröffentlichungen der Deutschen Akademie für Sprache und Dichtung

Deutsche Akademie für Sprache & Dichtung
Alexandraweg 23
6100 Darmstadt, Germany

Telephone: (49) 6151 44823
Fax: (49) 6151 46268
First published: 1954
Sponsoring organization: Deutsche Akademie für Sprache & Dichtung
MLA acronym: VDASD

SUBSCRIPTION INFORMATION

Frequency of publication: Irregular
Available in microform: No
Subscription address: Luchterhand Literaturverlag, Mühlenkamp 6C, 2000 Hamburg 6O, Germany
Subscription telephone: (49) 40 2795404
Subscription fax: (49) 40 2704966

ADVERTISING INFORMATION

Advertising accepted: No

EDITORIAL DESCRIPTION

Scope: Publishes monographs on German literature since 1900; original literature (especially from exiled authors from 1933-1945); letters.
Reviews books: No
Publishes notes: No
Languages accepted: German
Prints abstracts: No

SUBMISSION REQUIREMENTS

Restrictions on contributors: None
Author pays submission fee: No
Author pays page charges: No
Length of books: No restrictions
Number of copies required: 1
Copyright ownership: Author
Rejected manuscripts: Returned
Books published per year: 1-3

(3111)
Veröffentlichungen des Grabmann Instituts zur Erforschung der Mittelalterlichen Theologie und Philosophie

Werner Dettloff, Richard Heinzmann, & Michael Schmaus, Editors
Grabmann-Inst.
Geschwister-Scholl-Platz 1
8000 Munich 22, Germany

First published: 1967
Sponsoring organization: Univ. München
ISSN: 0580-2091
MLA acronym: VGIEMTP

SUBSCRIPTION INFORMATION

Frequency of publication: Irregular
Available in microform: No
Subscription address: Verlag Ferdinand Schöningh, Jühenplatz 1-3, 4790 Paderborn, Germany

ADVERTISING INFORMATION

Advertising accepted: No

EDITORIAL DESCRIPTION

Scope: Publishes texts and studies on Medieval theology and philosophy.
Reviews books: No
Publishes notes: No
Languages accepted: German
Prints abstracts: No

SUBMISSION REQUIREMENTS

Restrictions on contributors: None
Author pays submission fee: No
Author pays page charges: No
Length of books: No restrictions
Style: None
Number of copies required: 1
Copyright ownership: Author
Rejected manuscripts: Not returned
Time between decision and publication: 6-8 mos.
Number of reviewers: 3
Books published per year: 1-2

(3112)
*Il Verri: Rivista di Letteratura

Luciano Anceschi, Editor
Via Finelli, 3
40126 Bologna, Italy

Telephone: (39) 59 374094
First published: 1956
ISSN: 0506-7715
MLA acronym: Verri

SUBSCRIPTION INFORMATION

Frequency of publication: 4 times/yr.
Circulation: 3,500
Available in microform: No
Subscription address: Mucchi Editore, Via Emilia Est 1529, 41100 Modena, Italy

ADVERTISING INFORMATION

Advertising accepted: No

EDITORIAL DESCRIPTION

Scope: Aims at uniting the interest and discipline of the scientific method with an attentive participation in advanced literature, from the point of view of new phenomenological criticism. Special issues are devoted to particular themes, such as phenomenology, new music, Nietzsche, and structuralism.
Reviews books: Yes
Publishes notes: Yes
Languages accepted: Italian; French
Prints abstracts: Yes

SUBMISSION REQUIREMENTS

Restrictions on contributors: None
Author pays submission fee: No
Author pays page charges: No
Length of articles: 2,500-20,000 words
Style: None
Number of copies required: 2
Special requirements: Submit original typescript.
Copyright ownership: Assigned by author to journal
Rejected manuscripts: Not returned
Time before publication decision: 2 mos.
Time between decision and publication: 2 mos.
Number of reviewers: 2
Articles submitted per year: 100
Articles published per year: 40-50
Book reviews submitted per year: 100-120
Book reviews published per year: 50-60
Notes submitted per year: 80-100
Notes published per year: 30-40

(3113)
*Versants: Revue Suisse des Littératures Romanes/Rivista Svizzera di Letterature Romanze/ Schweizerische Zeitschrift für Romanische Literaturen

Antonio Stäuble, Editor
65 bis, Chemin du Devin
1012 Lausanne, Switzerland

Telephone: (41) 21 6520082
First published: 1981
Sponsoring organization: Collegium Romanicum; Académie Suisse des Sciences Humaines
MLA acronym: Versants

SUBSCRIPTION INFORMATION

Frequency of publication: 2 times/yr. (Apr., Nov.)
Available in microform: No
Subscription price: 42 SwF/yr.
Year to which price refers: 1992
Subscription address: Editions de la Baconnière SA, 19 ave. du Collège, C.P. 185, 2017 Boudry, Switzerland
Subscription telephone: (41) 38 421004

ADVERTISING INFORMATION

Advertising accepted: No

EDITORIAL DESCRIPTION

Scope: Publishes articles on Romance literatures.
Reviews books: No
Publishes notes: No
Languages accepted: French; Italian; Spanish; occasionnally German; occasionnally Catalan
Prints abstracts: No
Author-anonymous submission: No

SUBMISSION REQUIREMENTS

Author pays submission fee: No
Author pays page charges: No
Length of articles: 20 pp.
Number of copies required: 2
Special requirements: Submit original typescript and 1 copy.
Copyright ownership: Editions de la Baconnière
Rejected manuscripts: Returned
Time before publication decision: 1-6 mos.
Time between decision and publication: 6 mos.
Number of reviewers: 1-2
Articles published per year: 12-18

(3114)
*Verslagen en Mededelingen van de Koninklijke Academie voor Nederlandse Taal- en Letterkunde

Koninklijke Academie voor Nederlandse Taal- en Letterkunde
Koningstr. 18
9000 Ghent, Belgium

Telephone: (32) 91 252774
Fax: (32) 91 232718
First published: 1887
Sponsoring organization: Koninklijke Academie voor Nederlandse Taal- en Letterkunde, Ghent
ISSN: 0770-786X
MLA acronym: VMKAN

SUBSCRIPTION INFORMATION

Frequency of publication: 3 times/yr.
Available in microform: No
Subscription price: 1,000 BF/yr.
Year to which price refers: 1991

ADVERTISING INFORMATION

Advertising accepted: No

EDITORIAL DESCRIPTION

Scope: Publishes articles on Dutch language and literature, by members of the academy and other scholars.
Reviews books: No
Publishes notes: No
Languages accepted: Dutch; occasionnally German; occasionnally English; occasionnally French
Prints abstracts: No
Author-anonymous submission: No

SUBMISSION REQUIREMENTS

Author pays submission fee: No
Author pays page charges: No
Number of copies required: 1
Rejected manuscripts: Not returned
Time before publication decision: 3 mos.
Time between decision and publication: 3-4 mos.
Number of reviewers: 2
Articles published per year: 12-13

(3115)
*Versus: Quaderni di Studi Semiotici

Umberto Eco, Editor
Ist. di Discipline della Communicazione e dello Spettacolo
Univ. di Bologna
Via Toffano 2
40125 Bologna, Italy

Telephone: (39) 51 348797
Fax: (39) 51 300006
First published: 1971
MLA acronym: Versus

SUBSCRIPTION INFORMATION

Frequency of publication: 3 times/yr.
Available in microform: No
Subscription price: 24,000 Lit/yr. Italy; 48,000 Lit/yr. elsewhere
Year to which price refers: 1992
Subscription address: Via Mecenate 91, Versus-Bompiani, 20138 Milan, Italy
Subscription telephone: (39) 2 50951

ADVERTISING INFORMATION

Advertising accepted: Yes, on an exchange basis

EDITORIAL DESCRIPTION

Scope: Publishes articles on research in the fields of semiotics, linguistics, philosophy of language, and their history.
Reviews books: Yes
Publishes notes: Yes
Languages accepted: English; French; Italian
Prints abstracts: No
Author-anonymous submission: No

SUBMISSION REQUIREMENTS

Author pays submission fee: No
Author pays page charges: No
Length of articles: 10,000-15,000 words
Length of book reviews: 400-500 words
Length of notes: 400-500 words
Number of copies required: 1
Copyright ownership: Bompiani
Rejected manuscripts: Not returned
Time between decision and publication: 6 mos.
Number of reviewers: 3
Articles submitted per year: 30
Articles published per year: 20
Book reviews submitted per year: 30
Book reviews published per year: 30

(3116)
Vértice: Revista de Cultura e Arte

Francisco Melo, Manager
Editorial Caminho, S.A.
Rua de S. Bernardo, 14
1200 Lisbon, Portugal

Telephone: (351) 1 3952193/7
First published: 1942
ISSN: 0042-4447
MLA acronym: Vértice

SUBSCRIPTION INFORMATION

Frequency of publication: 6 times/yr.
Circulation: 4,800

ADVERTISING INFORMATION

Advertising accepted: Yes

EDITORIAL DESCRIPTION

Scope: Publishes articles on culture and art.
Reviews books: Yes
Languages accepted: Portuguese
Prints abstracts: No

SUBMISSION REQUIREMENTS

Restrictions on contributors: None
Author pays submission fee: No
Author pays page charges: No
Length of articles: 10 pp. (30 lines/p.)
Number of copies required: 2
Rejected manuscripts: Not returned
Time before publication decision: 1 mo.
Time between decision and publication: 2 mos.
Number of reviewers: 4

(3117)
Vestnik Leningradskogo Universiteta. Seriia 2, Istoriia, Iazykoznanie, Literaturovedenie

S. P. Merkur'ev, Editor
Universitetskaia Nab., 7/9
199034 St. Petersburg, Russia

First published: 1956
ISSN: 0024-0842
MLA acronym: VLU

SUBSCRIPTION INFORMATION

Subscription address: Mezhdunarodnaia Kniga, Moscow G-200, Russia

EDITORIAL DESCRIPTION

Scope: Publishes articles in the fields of history, language, and literature with an emphasis on theoretical, experimental, and applied studies. Included are articles on the history of Russian, Soviet, Arabic and other literatures, theoretical topics in literature studies, and linguistics.

SUBMISSION REQUIREMENTS

Style: MLA
Special requirements: Submit typescript. Include English abstract.
Copyright ownership: Author
Rejected manuscripts: Not returned
Number of reviewers: 2

(3118)
Vestnik Moskovskogo Universiteta. Seriia 9, Filologiia

I. F. Volkov, Editor
ul. Gertsena, 5/7
103009 Moscow, Russia

First published: 1946
ISSN: 0130-0075
MLA acronym: VMU

SUBSCRIPTION INFORMATION

Frequency of publication: 6 times/yr.
Circulation: 2,000
Available in microform: No

ADVERTISING INFORMATION

Advertising accepted: No

EDITORIAL DESCRIPTION

Scope: Pubishes articles on linguistics and literature.
Reviews books: Yes
Publishes notes: Yes
Languages accepted: Russian
Prints abstracts: No
Author-anonymous submission: No

SUBMISSION REQUIREMENTS

Author pays submission fee: No
Author pays page charges: No
Length of articles: 3,500-4,000 words
Length of book reviews: 1,500 words
Length of notes: 1,000-1,500 words
Number of copies required: 1
Copyright ownership: Journal
Rejected manuscripts: Not returned
Time before publication decision: 1 yr.
Time between decision and publication: 6 mos.
Number of reviewers: 2
Articles submitted per year: 105-132
Articles published per year: 70-88
Book reviews submitted per year: 27-30
Book reviews published per year: 18-20

Notes submitted per year: 27-30
Notes published per year: 18-20

(3119)
Vestsi Akadėmii Navuk Belarusi

M. V. Biryla, Editor
Leninski pr. 66
Pakoï 404
220072 Minsk, Belarus

First published: 1956
Historical variations in title: Formerly *Vestsi Akadėmii Navuk BSSR*
ISSN: 0321-1649
MLA acronym: VANBel

SUBSCRIPTION INFORMATION

Frequency of publication: 6 times/yr.

EDITORIAL DESCRIPTION

Scope: Publishes articles on the humanities with an emphasis on Belarus.
Reviews books: Yes
Languages accepted: Belorussian
Prints abstracts: Yes

(3120)
Vetenskaps-Societeten i Lund Årsbok

Vetenskaps-Soc.
Lund, Sweden

First published: 1920
ISSN: 0349-053X
MLA acronym: VSLÅ

SUBSCRIPTION INFORMATION

Frequency of publication: Annual
Circulation: 650
Available in microform: No

ADVERTISING INFORMATION

Advertising accepted: No

EDITORIAL DESCRIPTION

Scope: Publishes studies on literature.
Reviews books: No
Prints abstracts: No

SUBMISSION REQUIREMENTS

Restrictions on contributors: None
Author pays submission fee: No
Length of articles: No restrictions
Number of copies required: 1
Copyright ownership: Vetenskaps-Soc.
Rejected manuscripts: Returned
Time before publication decision: 2 weeks
Time between decision and publication: 6 mos.
Number of reviewers: 1-3

(3121)
*Vetera Christianorum

Antonio Quacquarelli, Editor
Ist. di Studi Classici & Cristiani
Univ. degli Studi di Bari
Strada San Giacomo, 7
70122 Bari, Italy

Telephone: (39) 80 317909
Fax: (39) 80 317918
First published: 1964
Sponsoring organization: Univ. degli Studi di Bari
ISSN: 0506-8126
MLA acronym: VChrist

SUBSCRIPTION INFORMATION

Frequency of publication: 2 times/yr.
Circulation: 1,500
Available in microform: No
Subscription price: 40,000 Lit/yr. Italy; 60,000 Lit/yr. elsewhere
Year to which price refers: 1992

ADVERTISING INFORMATION

Advertising accepted: No

EDITORIAL DESCRIPTION

Scope: Aims to contribute to the studies on the origins of Christian literature beginning with work by Francesco Di Capua. Publishes articles that trace the spiritual word, in its various phases and development, in the ancient Christian world. Intends primarily to examine ancient versions of the Holy Scripture, the biblical exegesis of the Fathers and liturgical expression, and the formative values of communication at every level. Also collects archaeological documentation in an effort to enlarge different aspects of Christian antiquity in Puglia.
Reviews books: Yes
Publishes notes: Yes
Languages accepted: German; Italian; French; Spanish; English
Prints abstracts: No
Author-anonymous submission: No

SUBMISSION REQUIREMENTS

Restrictions on contributors: None
Author pays submission fee: No
Author pays page charges: No
Length of articles: No restrictions
Length of book reviews: No restrictions
Length of notes: No restrictions
Style: None
Number of copies required: 1
Special requirements: Submit original typescript.
Copyright ownership: Ist. di Studi Classici & Cristiani
Rejected manuscripts: Returned
Time before publication decision: 1 mo.
Time between decision and publication: 6-12 mos.
Number of reviewers: 6
Articles submitted per year: 30-35
Articles published per year: 20-25
Book reviews submitted per year: 80
Book reviews published per year: 40
Notes submitted per year: 10
Notes published per year: 5

(3122)
*VIA: Voices in Italian Americana

Anthony J. Tamburri, Paolo A. Giordano, & Fred L. Gardaphè, Editors
Dept. of Foreign Languages & Literatures
Stanley Coulter Hall
Purdue Univ.
West Lafayette, IN 47907

Additional editorial address: Paolo A. Giordano, Dept. of Modern Languages, Loyola Univ. Chicago, 6525 North Sheridan Rd., Chicago, IL 60626; Fred L. Gardaphè, English Dept., Columbia College, Chicago, IL 60605
Telephone: 317 494-7691
Fax: 317 494-3660
E-mail: XVXA@PURCCVM
First published: 1990
Sponsoring organization: Dept. of Foreign Languages & Literatures, Purdue Univ.; Loyola Univ. of Chicago; Columbia College
ISSN: 1048-292X
MLA acronym: VIA

SUBSCRIPTION INFORMATION

Frequency of publication: 2 times/yr. (Spring, Fall)
Circulation: 150
Available in microform: No
Subscription price: $22.50/yr. institutions US; $15.00/yr. individuals US; $25.00/yr. elsewhere
Year to which price refers: 1991

ADVERTISING INFORMATION

Advertising accepted: Yes
Advertising rates: $75.00/half page; $100.00/ full page

EDITORIAL DESCRIPTION

Scope: Publishes essays, interviews, notes, and book reviews about Italian Americans in North America, as well as fiction and poetry by Italian Americans in North America.
Reviews books: Yes
Publishes notes: Yes
Languages accepted: English; Italian
Prints abstracts: No
Author-anonymous submission: Yes

SUBMISSION REQUIREMENTS

Restrictions on contributors: None
Author pays submission fee: No
Author pays page charges: No
Length of articles: 20 pp.
Length of book reviews: 500-1,000 words
Length of notes: 2,000 words
Style: MLA (1985)
Number of copies required: 3
Special requirements: Submission on Macintosh or IBM diskettes is preferred.
Copyright ownership: Bordighera, Inc.
Rejected manuscripts: Returned; enclose SASE.
Time before publication decision: 4 mos.
Time between decision and publication: 1 yr.
Number of reviewers: 3-5
Articles submitted per year: 20
Articles published per year: 6
Book reviews submitted per year: 20
Book reviews published per year: 15

(3123)
Viața Românească

Ioanichie Olteanu, Editor
Uniunea Sciitorilor din Republica Socialista România
Calea Victoriei 115
Bucharest 70179, Romania

First published: 1906
Sponsoring organization: Uniunea Scriitorilor din România
ISSN: 0042-5052
MLA acronym: ViR

SUBSCRIPTION INFORMATION

Frequency of publication: 12 times/yr.
Circulation: 2,000
Available in microform: No
Additional subscription address: ILEXIM, Export-Import Press, Str. 13 Decembrie Nr. 3, Box 136-137, 70116 Bucharest, Romania

ADVERTISING INFORMATION

Advertising accepted: Yes

EDITORIAL DESCRIPTION

Scope: Publishes literary articles and essays on Romanian and foreign literature, fiction, poetry, and philosophy.
Reviews books: Yes
Publishes notes: Yes
Languages accepted: Romanian
Prints abstracts: No

SUBMISSION REQUIREMENTS

Restrictions on contributors: None
Author pays submission fee: No
Author pays page charges: No
Length of articles: 2,750 words
Length of book reviews: 1,600 words
Length of notes: 800 words
Number of copies required: 1
Copyright ownership: Writer's Union of Romania
Rejected manuscripts: Not returned
Time before publication decision: 2 mos.
Time between decision and publication: 6 mos.
Articles submitted per year: 240
Articles published per year: 80
Book reviews submitted per year: 170
Book reviews published per year: 130
Notes submitted per year: 50
Notes published per year: 30

(3124)
*Viator: Medieval and Renaissance Studies

Robert L. Benson, A. R. Braunmuller, Robert I. Burns, S.J., Katherine C. King, & Joseph F. Nagy, Editors
Center for Medieval & Renaissance Studies
Univ. of California
Los Angeles, CA 90024-1485

Telephone: 310 825-5622
Fax: 310 825-0655
First published: 1970
Sponsoring organization: Univ. of California, Los Angeles, Center for Medieval & Renaissance Studies
ISSN: 0083-5897
MLA acronym: Viator

SUBSCRIPTION INFORMATION

Frequency of publication: Annual
Circulation: 450
Available in microform: No
Subscription price: $49.00/yr.
Year to which price refers: 1991-92
Subscription address: Univ. of California Press, Journals Division, 2120 Berkeley Way, Berkeley, CA 94720
Subscription telephone: 510 642-4191
Subscription fax: 510 643-7127

ADVERTISING INFORMATION

Advertising accepted: No

EDITORIAL DESCRIPTION

Scope: Publishes articles on the Middle Ages and Renaissance (roughly AD 350-1650), with emphasis on intercultural and interdisciplinary studies.
Reviews books: No
Publishes notes: No
Languages accepted: English; French; German; Italian; Spanish
Prints abstracts: No
Author-anonymous submission: No

SUBMISSION REQUIREMENTS

Restrictions on contributors: None
Author pays submission fee: No
Author pays page charges: No
Length of articles: 25-100 double-spaced typescript pp.
Style: Chicago; journal
Number of copies required: 1
Special requirements: Dot-matrix printouts are not accepted.
Copyright ownership: Regents of the Univ. of California
Rejected manuscripts: Returned
Time before publication decision: 4 mos.
Time between decision and publication: 18 mos.
Number of reviewers: 3 minimum

Articles submitted per year: 60
Articles published per year: 16-20

(3125)
*Victorian Fiction Research Guides

P. D. Edwards, Editor
Dept. of English
Univ. of Queensland
Queensland 4072, Australia

First published: 1979
Sponsoring organization: Univ. of Queensland
ISSN: 0158-3921
MLA acronym: VFR

SUBSCRIPTION INFORMATION

Frequency of publication: Irregular
Circulation: 200
Available in microform: No

ADVERTISING INFORMATION

Advertising accepted: No

EDITORIAL DESCRIPTION

Scope: Publishes bibliographies and indexes on minor or lesser known writers active during the period from about 1860 to 1910.
Reviews books: No
Publishes notes: No
Languages accepted: English
Prints abstracts: No

SUBMISSION REQUIREMENTS

Author pays submission fee: No
Author pays page charges: No
Length of books: No restrictions
Style: Chicago with modifications
Number of copies required: 1
Special requirements: Submit camera-ready typescript.
Copyright ownership: Author
Rejected manuscripts: Returned
Time before publication decision: 1 mo.
Time between decision and publication: 6 mos.
Number of reviewers: 2
Books published per year: 2

(3126)
*Victorian Literature and Culture

Adrienne Auslander Munich & John Maynard, Editors
Dept. of English
State Univ. of New York at Stony Brook
Stony Brook, NY 11794

Additional editorial address: Dept. of English, New York Univ., 19 University Pl., New York, NY 10003
Telephone: 516 632-9176; 212 998-8835
Fax: 516 632-6252; 212 995-4019
First published: 1973
Historical variations in title: Formerly *Browning Institute Studies*
Sponsoring organization: Browning Inst.
ISSN: 0092-4725
MLA acronym: VLC

SUBSCRIPTION INFORMATION

Frequency of publication: Annual
Circulation: 1,000
Available in microform: No
Subscription price: $47.50/yr. institutions; $27.50/yr. individuals US; $29.50/yr. individuals elsewhere
Year to which price refers: 1991
Subscription address: AMS Press, 56 E. 13th St., New York, NY 10003
Subscription telephone: 212 777-4700
Subscription fax: 212 995-5413

ADVERTISING INFORMATION

Advertising accepted: Yes

EDITORIAL DESCRIPTION

Scope: Focuses on Victorian literature and cultural history. Includes studies on relations among the arts and studies of the intersections of cultural or social issues with the arts.
Reviews books: Yes
Publishes notes: No
Languages accepted: English
Prints abstracts: No
Author-anonymous submission: Yes

SUBMISSION REQUIREMENTS

Restrictions on contributors: Book reviews are solicited.
Author pays submission fee: No
Author pays page charges: No
Length of articles: 8,000-20,000 words
Length of book reviews: 3,000 words
Style: MLA
Number of copies required: 2
Rejected manuscripts: Returned; enclose return postage
Time before publication decision: 2 mos.
Time between decision and publication: 1 yr.
Number of reviewers: 3
Articles submitted per year: 50-60
Articles published per year: 12-16

(3127)
Victorian Newsletter

Ward Hellstrom & Louise R. Hellstrom, Editors
FAC 200
Western Kentucky Univ.
Bowling Green, KY 42101

First published: 1952
Sponsoring organization: Western Kentucky Univ.
ISSN: 0042-5192
MLA acronym: VN

SUBSCRIPTION INFORMATION

Frequency of publication: 2 times/yr.
Circulation: 1,000
Available in microform: Yes
Subscription price: $5.00/yr. US; $6.00/yr. elsewhere
Year to which price refers: 1992

ADVERTISING INFORMATION

Advertising accepted: No

EDITORIAL DESCRIPTION

Scope: Publishes articles and notes on Victorian literature.
Reviews books: Yes
Publishes notes: Yes
Languages accepted: English
Prints abstracts: No
Author-anonymous submission: No

SUBMISSION REQUIREMENTS

Restrictions on contributors: None
Author pays submission fee: No
Author pays page charges: No
Length of articles: 7,500 words
Style: MLA
Number of copies required: 1
Copyright ownership: Journal
Rejected manuscripts: Returned; enclose SASE.
Time before publication decision: 3 mos. maximum
Time between decision and publication: 1 yr. minimum
Number of reviewers: 1
Articles submitted per year: 67
Articles published per year: 15

(3128)
*Victorian Periodicals Review

Barbara Quinn Schmidt, Editor
English Dept.
Southern Illinois Univ.
Edwardsville, IL 62026-1436

Telephone: 618 692-2326
Fax: 618 692-3509
First published: 1968
Sponsoring organization: Research Soc. for Victorian Periodicals
ISSN: 0709-4698
MLA acronym: VPR

SUBSCRIPTION INFORMATION

Frequency of publication: 4 times/yr.
Circulation: 650
Available in microform: Yes

ADVERTISING INFORMATION

Advertising accepted: Yes

EDITORIAL DESCRIPTION

Scope: Publishes articles or notes with a historical, critical, or bibliographical emphasis dealing with the editorial and publishing history of Victorian periodicals (newspapers, magazines, or reviews) or with the importance of periodicals for an understanding of the history and culture of Victorian and Edwardian Britain. The central focus is on Great Britain and Ireland during the Victorian and Edwardian eras, but is also interested in work dealing with the press in other parts of the Empire and in material relating to the earlier decades of the 19th century. Welcomes brief informal reports on work in progress.
Reviews books: Yes
Publishes notes: Yes
Languages accepted: English
Prints abstracts: No
Author-anonymous submission: Yes

SUBMISSION REQUIREMENTS

Restrictions on contributors: None
Author pays submission fee: No
Author pays page charges: No
Length of articles: No restrictions
Length of book reviews: 900-1,600 words
Style: MLA preferred
Number of copies required: 2
Special requirements: Submit typescript and diskette using Word4 for Macintosh.
Copyright ownership: Journal
Rejected manuscripts: Returned; enclose return postage or international reply coupons.
Time before publication decision: 6-12 mos.
Time between decision and publication: 1-2 yrs.
Number of reviewers: 2-3
Articles submitted per year: 30-50
Articles published per year: 12-20
Book reviews submitted per year: 30-45
Book reviews published per year: 20-35
Notes submitted per year: 5-15
Notes published per year: 5-15

(3129)
*Victorian Poetry

Hayden Ward, Editor
Dept. of English
West Virginia Univ.
Morgantown, WV 26506

Telephone: 304 293-3107
Fax: 304 293-6858
First published: 1963
Sponsoring organization: West Virginia Univ.
ISSN: 0042-5206
MLA acronym: VP

SUBSCRIPTION INFORMATION

Frequency of publication: 4 times/yr. (Spring, Summer, Autumn, Winter)
Circulation: 1,200
Available in microform: Yes
Subscription price: $25.00/yr. institutions; $15.00/yr. individuals; add $3.00/yr. postage outside US & Canada
Year to which price refers: 1991
Subscription address: Victorian Poetry-Subscriptions, Office of Publications, West Virginia Univ., Morgantown, WV 26506
Subscription telephone: 304 293-6368

ADVERTISING INFORMATION

Advertising accepted: Yes
Advertising rates: $75.00/half page; $150.00/full page

EDITORIAL DESCRIPTION

Scope: Publishes articles mainly on British and other English-language literatures from 1830 to 1914, sometimes in relation to texts from other periods and cultures. Treats primarily poetry and occasionally prose in aesthetic, historical, philosophical, and theoretical contexts.
Reviews books: Yes
Publishes notes: Yes
Languages accepted: English
Prints abstracts: No
Author-anonymous submission: Yes

SUBMISSION REQUIREMENTS

Restrictions on contributors: Reviews are solicited.
Author pays submission fee: No
Author pays page charges: No
Length of articles: 10-25 pp.
Length of book reviews: 1,500 words
Length of notes: 1,500-2,500 words
Style: Chicago
Number of copies required: 2
Special requirements: IBM formatted diskettes in ASCII or simple text file should be available, if possible.
Copyright ownership: West Virginia Univ.
Rejected manuscripts: Returned; enclose return postage.
Time before publication decision: 3 mos.
Time between decision and publication: 1 yr. maximum
Number of reviewers: 2
Articles submitted per year: 100
Articles published per year: 30-35
Book reviews published per year: 4-6
Notes submitted per year: 10-12
Notes published per year: 6-8

(3130)
*Victorian Review: The Journal of the Victorian Studies Association of Western Canada

Glennis Stephenson, Editor
Dept. of English
Univ. of Alberta
Edmonton, AB T6G 2E5, Canada

Telephone: 403 492-7821
Fax: 403 492-8142
First published: 1972
Sponsoring organization: Victorian Studies Assn. of Western Canada
ISSN: 0848-1512
MLA acronym: VRev

SUBSCRIPTION INFORMATION

Frequency of publication: 2 times/yr.
Circulation: 200
Available in microform: No
Subscription price: C$25.00/yr. institutions N. America; C$30.00/yr. institutions elsewhere; C$20.00/yr. individuals N. America; C$25.00/yr. individuals elsewhere

Year to which price refers: 1992

ADVERTISING INFORMATION

Advertising accepted: No

EDITORIAL DESCRIPTION

Scope: Publishes articles on all aspects of 19th-century studies.
Reviews books: Yes
Publishes notes: Yes
Languages accepted: English
Prints abstracts: No
Author-anonymous submission: Yes

SUBMISSION REQUIREMENTS

Author pays submission fee: No
Author pays page charges: No
Length of articles: 2,500-6,500 words
Style: MLA
Number of copies required: 2
Special requirements: Submit 2 copies of manuscript or 1 copy and 3.5 or 5.25 in. diskette in WordPerfect 4.2, 5.0, or 5.1, Multimate, Advantage I or II, Wordstar, or ASCII.
Copyright ownership: Victorian Studies Assn. of Western Canada
Rejected manuscripts: Returned; enclose return postage or international reply coupons.
Time before publication decision: 3 mos.
Time between decision and publication: 6-12 mos.
Number of reviewers: 3
Articles submitted per year: 50
Articles published per year: 8-10
Book reviews published per year: 20-25

(3131)
*Victorian Studies: A Journal of the Humanities, Arts and Sciences

Donald Gray, Editor
Ballantine Hall 338
Indiana Univ.
Bloomington, IN 47405

Telephone: 812 855-9533
First published: 1957
Sponsoring organization: Indiana Univ.
ISSN: 0042-5222
MLA acronym: VS

SUBSCRIPTION INFORMATION

Frequency of publication: 4 times/yr. (Fall, Winter, Spring, Summer)
Circulation: 3,000
Available in microform: Yes
Subscription price: $40.00/yr. institutions; $25.00/yr. individuals; add $12.50/yr. ($24.00 airmail) postage outside US
Year to which price refers: 1993
Subscription address: Indiana Univ. Press, 601 North Morton St., Bloomington, IN 47404-3797
Subscription telephone: 812 855-9449
Subscription fax: 812 855-7931

ADVERTISING INFORMATION

Advertising accepted: Yes
Advertising rates: $110.00/half page; $200.00/full page

EDITORIAL DESCRIPTION

Scope: Publishes articles on the humanities, arts, and sciences of Victorian Britain.
Reviews books: Yes
Publishes notes: No
Languages accepted: English
Prints abstracts: No
Author-anonymous submission: Yes

SUBMISSION REQUIREMENTS

Restrictions on contributors: Book reviews are commissioned.
Author pays submission fee: No
Author pays page charges: No
Length of articles: 6,000-8,000 words
Length of book reviews: 1,000 words
Style: MLA
Number of copies required: 2
Special requirements: Articles must be written with an interdisciplinary focus.
Copyright ownership: Indiana Univ. Trustees
Rejected manuscripts: Returned; enclose return postage or international reply coupons.
Time before publication decision: 4 mos.
Time between decision and publication: 6-12 mos.
Number of reviewers: 3
Articles submitted per year: 200
Articles published per year: 16
Book reviews published per year: 75

(3132)
*Vigiliae Christianae: A Review of Early Christian Life and Language

J. den Boeft, R. van den Broek, A. F. J. Klijn, G. Quispel, & J. C. M. van Winden, Editors
Van Effendreef 15
2353 BM Leiderdorp, Netherlands

Additional editorial address: Send manuscripts to above address; send books for review to: J. C. M. van Winden, Haarlemmerstr. 106, 2312 GD Leiden, Netherlands
Telephone: (31) 71 893908
First published: 1947
ISSN: 0042-6032
MLA acronym: VigC

SUBSCRIPTION INFORMATION

Frequency of publication: 4 times/yr.
Circulation: 800
Available in microform: Yes
Subscription price: 170 f /yr.
Year to which price refers: 1992
Subscription address: E. J. Brill, P.O. Box 9000, 2300 PA Leiden, Netherlands
Subscription telephone: (31) 71 312624
Subscription fax: (31) 71 317532

ADVERTISING INFORMATION

Advertising accepted: Yes

EDITORIAL DESCRIPTION

Scope: Contains articles and short notices of a historical and cultural, linguistic, or philological nature on Early Christian literature in the widest sense of the word, as well as on Christian epigraphy and archaeology. Church and dogmatic history will only be dealt with if they bear directly on social history; Byzantine and Mediaeval literature only insofar as it exhibits continuity with the Early Christian period. The journal will also contain reviews of important studies, published elsewhere. Covers period from post-New Testament to Gregory the Great.
Reviews books: Yes
Publishes notes: Yes
Languages accepted: English; French; German
Prints abstracts: No
Author-anonymous submission: No

SUBMISSION REQUIREMENTS

Restrictions on contributors: Book reviews are solicited. Articles larger than 25 pp. may be accommodated in a supplement series.
Author pays submission fee: No
Author pays page charges: No
Length of articles: 10-25 pp.
Length of book reviews: 500-1,500 words
Length of notes: 1,000-1,500 words
Style: None
Number of copies required: 2
Copyright ownership: E. J. Brill Publishing Co.
Rejected manuscripts: Returned at author's request
Time before publication decision: 2-3 mos.
Time between decision and publication: 12-18 mos.
Number of reviewers: 2-3
Articles submitted per year: 40-50
Articles published per year: 25-30
Book reviews submitted per year: 40-50
Book reviews published per year: 30-40

(3133)
*VIJ: Victorians Institute Journal

Donald L. Lawler, Editor
Dept. of English
East Carolina Univ.
Greenville, NC 27834

Additional editorial address: Assoc. ed. for texts: John Pfordresher, Dept. of English, Georgetown Univ., Washington, DC 20057; Assoc. ed. for Graphics: Joseph Kestner, Dept. of English, Univ. of Tulsa, Tulsa, OK; Assoc. ed. for Reviews: McKay Sundwall, Dept. of English, East Carolina Univ., Greenville, NC 27834
Telephone: 919 757-6660
Fax: 919 757-4889
First published: 1972
Sponsoring organization: Victorians Inst.; East Carolina Univ.
ISSN: 0886-3865
MLA acronym: VIJ

SUBSCRIPTION INFORMATION

Frequency of publication: Annual
Circulation: 1,000
Available in microform: No

ADVERTISING INFORMATION

Advertising accepted: No

EDITORIAL DESCRIPTION

Scope: Publishes work on Victorian literature, art, history, culture, and ideas.
Reviews books: Yes
Publishes notes: Yes
Languages accepted: English
Prints abstracts: Yes
Author-anonymous submission: No

SUBMISSION REQUIREMENTS

Restrictions on contributors: None
Author pays submission fee: No
Author pays page charges: No
Length of articles: 10-30 pp.
Length of book reviews: 1,500-3,000 words
Length of notes: 1,500-2,000 words
Style: MLA
Number of copies required: 2
Special requirements: Submit electronic copy/diskette for Macintosh or DOS, with file name enclosed.
Copyright ownership: East Carolina Univ. Publications
Rejected manuscripts: Returned; enclose return postage.
Time before publication decision: 3 mos.
Time between decision and publication: 1 yr.
Number of reviewers: 2-3
Articles submitted per year: 80
Articles published per year: 12
Book reviews submitted per year: 5-10
Book reviews published per year: 4-6
Notes submitted per year: 2-5
Notes published per year: 0-1

(3134)
*Vinduet

Halfdan W. Freihow, Editor
Gyldendal Norsk Forlag
Sehestedsgt. 4
0164 Oslo 1, Norway

Additional editorial address: P.O. Box 6860, St. Olavs plass, 0130 Oslo 1, Norway
Telephone: (47) 2 200710
First published: 1947
ISSN: 0042-6288
MLA acronym: Vinduet

SUBSCRIPTION INFORMATION

Frequency of publication: 4 times/yr.
Circulation: 4,000
Available in microform: No
Subscription address: Forlagsentralens Tidsskriftavdeling, Postboks 150 Furuset, 1001 Oslo 10, Norway

ADVERTISING INFORMATION

Advertising accepted: Yes

EDITORIAL DESCRIPTION

Scope: Publishes articles on Norwegian, Scandinavian and other literatures.
Reviews books: Yes
Publishes notes: No
Languages accepted: Norwegian; Swedish; Danish
Prints abstracts: No
Author-anonymous submission: No

SUBMISSION REQUIREMENTS

Restrictions on contributors: None
Author pays submission fee: No
Author pays page charges: No
Length of articles: No restrictions
Length of book reviews: No restrictions
Style: None
Number of copies required: 1
Copyright ownership: Gyldendal Norsk Forlag
Rejected manuscripts: Returned
Time before publication decision: 6-8 weeks
Time between decision and publication: 6-8 weeks
Articles submitted per year: 400
Articles published per year: 80
Book reviews submitted per year: 50
Book reviews published per year: 12

(3135)
*Vinyar Tengwar

Carl F. Hostetter, Editor
2509 Ambling Circle
Crofton, MD 21114

Telephone: 410 721-5690
First published: 1988
Sponsoring organization: Elvish Linguistic Fellowship; Mythopoeic Soc.
ISSN: 1054-7606
MLA acronym: VT

SUBSCRIPTION INFORMATION

Frequency of publication: 6 times/yr.
Circulation: 100
Available in microform: No
Subscription price: $12.00/yr. US; $15.00/yr. Canada; $15.00 ($18.00 airmail)/yr. elsewhere
Year to which price refers: 1992

ADVERTISING INFORMATION

Advertising accepted: No

EDITORIAL DESCRIPTION

Scope: Publishes articles on all aspects of the primary- and secondary- world of linguistic scholarship of J. R. R. Tolkien.
Reviews books: Yes
Publishes notes: Yes
Languages accepted: English
Prints abstracts: No
Author-anonymous submission: No

SUBMISSION REQUIREMENTS

Author pays submission fee: No
Author pays page charges: No
Length of book reviews: 1,000 words
Length of notes: 500 words
Style: MLA
Number of copies required: 1
Special requirements: Submission on 3.5-inch diskette is preferred.
Copyright ownership: Author
Rejected manuscripts: Returned; enclose SASE.
Time before publication decision: 1 mo.
Time between decision and publication: 1 mo.
Number of reviewers: 4
Articles submitted per year: 40
Articles published per year: 30
Book reviews submitted per year: 10
Book reviews published per year: 8
Notes submitted per year: 10
Notes published per year: 8

(3136)
*Virginia Cavalcade

Edward D. C. Campbell, Jr., Editor
Virginia State Library & Archives
11th Street at Capitol Square
Richmond, VA 23219-3491

Telephone: 804 786-2311
First published: 1951
Sponsoring organization: Virginia State Library & Archives
ISSN: 0042-6474
MLA acronym: VC

SUBSCRIPTION INFORMATION

Frequency of publication: 4 times/yr. (Jan., Apr., July, Oct.)
Circulation: 11,000
Available in microform: Yes
Subscription price: $6.00/yr., $10.00/2 yrs.
Year to which price refers: 1992
Additional subscription address: Claire T. Ward, Circulation Clerk, at the above address
Subscription telephone: 804 786-2329

ADVERTISING INFORMATION

Advertising accepted: No

EDITORIAL DESCRIPTION

Scope: Publishes articles on Virginia history and culture.
Reviews books: No
Publishes notes: No
Languages accepted: English
Prints abstracts: No
Author-anonymous submission: No

SUBMISSION REQUIREMENTS

Restrictions on contributors: None
Author pays submission fee: No
Author pays page charges: No
Length of articles: 3,500-4,000 words
Style: Chicago
Number of copies required: 1
Special requirements: Publication policies are fully explained in "Invitation to Authors," which is available upon request. Submit ribbon copy of manuscript.
Copyright ownership: Assigned by author to publisher
Rejected manuscripts: Returned

Time before publication decision: 2-3 mos.
Time between decision and publication: 9 mos.
Number of reviewers: 4
Articles submitted per year: 65
Articles published per year: 16

(3137)
*Virginia Quarterly Review: A National Journal of Literature and Discussion

Staige D. Blackford, Editor
1 West Range
Charlottesville, VA 22903

Telephone: 804 924-3124
First published: 1925
Sponsoring organization: Univ. of Virginia
ISSN: 0042-675X
MLA acronym: VQR

SUBSCRIPTION INFORMATION

Frequency of publication: 4 times/yr. (Jan., Apr., July, Oct.)
Circulation: 4,000
Available in microform: Yes
Subscription price: $15.00/yr.
Year to which price refers: 1992
Subscription address: Business Manager, at the above address

ADVERTISING INFORMATION

Advertising accepted: Yes

EDITORIAL DESCRIPTION

Scope: Publishes articles and discussions on contemporary literature.
Reviews books: Yes
Publishes notes: No
Languages accepted: English
Prints abstracts: No
Author-anonymous submission: Yes

SUBMISSION REQUIREMENTS

Restrictions on contributors: None
Author pays submission fee: No
Author pays page charges: No
Length of articles: 3,000-4,000 words
Length of book reviews: 1,000-3,000 words for essay reviews
Style: Chicago
Number of copies required: 1
Copyright ownership: Journal
Rejected manuscripts: Returned; enclose SASE.
Time before publication decision: 6 weeks
Time between decision and publication: 15-18 mos.
Number of reviewers: 3
Articles submitted per year: 183
Articles published per year: 20
Book reviews submitted per year: 40
Book reviews published per year: 30 essay reviews

(3138)
*Virginia Woolf Miscellany

Lucio Ruotolo, J. J. Wilson, Peter Stansky, & Mark Hussey, Editors
Dept. of English
Stanford Univ.
Stanford, CA 94305-2087

Additional editorial address: Patricia Laurence, Book Review Editor, City College of New York, New York, NY 10031
Telephone: 415 723-2635; 415 725-0712
First published: 1973
ISSN: 0736-251X
MLA acronym: VWM

SUBSCRIPTION INFORMATION

Frequency of publication: 2 times/yr.
Circulation: 1,100
Available in microform: No
Subscription address: c/o Dept. of English, Sonoma State Univ., Rohnert Park, CA 94928

ADVERTISING INFORMATION

Advertising accepted: No

EDITORIAL DESCRIPTION

Scope: Publishes scholarly information on Virginia Woolf studies.
Reviews books: Yes
Publishes notes: Yes
Languages accepted: English
Prints abstracts: No
Author-anonymous submission: No

SUBMISSION REQUIREMENTS

Author pays submission fee: No
Author pays page charges: No
Length of articles: 1,000 words maximum
Length of book reviews: 800 words
Length of notes: 400 words
Style: MLA
Number of copies required: 1
Copyright ownership: Author
Rejected manuscripts: Returned; enclose return postage.
Time before publication decision: 2 mos.
Time between decision and publication: 6 mos.
Number of reviewers: 2
Articles submitted per year: 30
Articles published per year: 10
Book reviews submitted per year: 15
Book reviews published per year: 5
Notes submitted per year: 20
Notes published per year: 5

(3139)
*Virittäjä: Journal de Kotikielen Seura

Matti Larjavaara, Editor
Fabianinkatu 33
00170 Helsinki 17, Finland

First published: 1897
Sponsoring organization: Kotikielen Seura (Mother Tongue Soc.)
ISSN: 0042-6806
MLA acronym: Vir

SUBSCRIPTION INFORMATION

Frequency of publication: 4 times/yr.
Circulation: 1,000
Available in microform: No

ADVERTISING INFORMATION

Advertising accepted: Yes

EDITORIAL DESCRIPTION

Scope: Publishes articles on Finnish and Finnic linguistics, teaching of mother language, and language planning.
Reviews books: Yes
Publishes notes: Yes
Languages accepted: Finnish
Prints abstracts: Yes

SUBMISSION REQUIREMENTS

Restrictions on contributors: None
Author pays submission fee: No
Author pays page charges: No
Length of articles: 8-25 pp.
Length of book reviews: 2-15 pp.
Length of notes: 1-5 pp.
Number of copies required: 2-3

Special requirements: Submit original, double-spaced typescript on size A4 (8 1/4 in. x 11 3/4 in.) paper.
Copyright ownership: Author
Rejected manuscripts: Not returned
Time before publication decision: 3 mos.
Time between decision and publication: 6-15 mos.
Number of reviewers: 1-3
Articles published per year: 16-20
Book reviews published per year: 20-30
Notes published per year: 8-10

(3140)
*Vishveshvaranand Indological Journal

Jai Narain Sharma, Chairman
Vishveshvaranand Vishva Bandhu Inst. of Sanskrit & Indological Studies
Panjab Univ.
P.O. Sadhu Ashram
Hoshiarpur 146021, India

First published: 1963
Sponsoring organization: Panjab Univ., Vishveshvaranand Vishva Bandhu Inst. of Sanskrit & Indological Studies
ISSN: 0507-1410
MLA acronym: VIndJ

SUBSCRIPTION INFORMATION

Frequency of publication: 2 times/yr. (June, Dec.)
Circulation: 250
Available in microform: No

ADVERTISING INFORMATION

Advertising accepted: No

EDITORIAL DESCRIPTION

Scope: Publishes research papers on all subjects of Indology: language and literature, religion, philosophy, sociology, history, and arts and sciences. Also includes sections on critical editions of old Sanskrit texts, monographs, reviews, etc.
Reviews books: Yes
Publishes notes: Yes
Languages accepted: English; Sanskrit
Prints abstracts: No
Author-anonymous submission: No

SUBMISSION REQUIREMENTS

Restrictions on contributors: None
Author pays submission fee: No
Author pays page charges: No
Length of articles: 12 pp.
Length of book reviews: 500 words
Length of notes: 250 words
Style: MLA
Number of copies required: 1
Special requirements: Submit typescript.
Copyright ownership: Panjab Univ., Vishveshvaranand Vishva Bandhu Inst. of Sanskrit & Indological Studies
Rejected manuscripts: Returned at author's request
Time before publication decision: 6 mos.
Time between decision and publication: 6 mos.
Number of reviewers: 6
Articles submitted per year: 50
Articles published per year: 30
Book reviews submitted per year: 70
Book reviews published per year: 50
Notes submitted per year: 75
Notes published per year: 50

(3141)
*Visible Language: The Quarterly Concerned with All That Is Involved in Our Being Literate

Sharon Helmer Poggenpohl, Editor
6 Hidden Bridge
Pittsford, NY 14534

Telephone: 716 381-1552
E-mail: SHP0159@RITVAX
First published: 1967
ISSN: 0022-2224
MLA acronym: VLang

SUBSCRIPTION INFORMATION

Frequency of publication: 4 times/yr.
Circulation: 1,300
Available in microform: Yes
Subscription price: $55.00/yr. institutions US; $62.00/yr. institutions elsewhere; $30.00/yr. individuals US; $37.00/yr. individuals elsewhere
Year to which price refers: 1993
Subscription address: Rhode Island School of Design, Graphic Design Dept., 2 College St., Providence, RI 02903
Subscription telephone: 401 454-6171

ADVERTISING INFORMATION

Advertising accepted: Yes

EDITORIAL DESCRIPTION

Scope: Publishes research and ideas that help define the unique role and properties of written language.
Reviews books: Yes
Publishes notes: Yes
Languages accepted: English
Prints abstracts: Yes
Author-anonymous submission: Yes

SUBMISSION REQUIREMENTS

Restrictions on contributors: None
Author pays submission fee: No
Author pays page charges: No
Length of articles: No restrictions
Length of book reviews: No restrictions
Length of notes: No restrictions
Style: Chicago
Number of copies required: 3
Special requirements: Stress graphic material to accompany text.
Copyright ownership: Journal or author
Rejected manuscripts: Returned; enclose return postage
Time before publication decision: 3 mos.
Time between decision and publication: 6 mos.
Number of reviewers: 3-5
Articles submitted per year: 45
Articles published per year: 18-20
Book reviews submitted per year: 10-12
Book reviews published per year: 6
Notes submitted per year: 10
Notes published per year: 5

(3142)
Vitchyzna: Literaturno-Khudozhniï ta Hromads'ko-Politychnyï Misiachnyk

Liubomyr Dmyterko, Editor
Izdatel'stvo Radyanskiï Pismennik
Bul'var Lesi Ukrainki, 20
Kiev, Ukraine

First published: 1930
ISSN: 0042-7470
MLA acronym: Vitchyzna

SUBSCRIPTION INFORMATION

Frequency of publication: 12 times/yr.
Circulation: 16,240

Additional subscription address: Victor Kamkin Inc., 4956 Boiling Brook Pkwy., Rockville, MD 20852

EDITORIAL DESCRIPTION

Reviews books: Yes

(3143)
*Vivarium: An International Journal for the Philosophy and Intellectual Life of the Middle Ages and Renaissance

C. H. Kneepkens, Secretary of the Editorial Board
Katholieke Univ.
Erasmusplein 1 - 9.18
P.O. Box 9103
6500 HD Nijmegen, Netherlands

First published: 1963
Sponsoring organization: Nederlandse Organisatie voor Zuiver-Wetenschappelijk Onderzoek
ISSN: 0042-7543
MLA acronym: Vivarium

SUBSCRIPTION INFORMATION

Frequency of publication: 2 times/yr. (Feb., Sept.)
Circulation: 600
Available in microform: No
Subscription address: E. J. Brill, P.O. Box 9000, 2300 PA Leiden, Netherlands

ADVERTISING INFORMATION

Advertising accepted: Yes

EDITORIAL DESCRIPTION

Scope: Publishes articles on the relation of philosophy to the whole of Medieval and Renaissance thought and learning as well as on the liberal arts in the Middle Ages and the Renaissance.
Reviews books: Yes
Publishes notes: Yes
Languages accepted: English; French; German
Prints abstracts: No

SUBMISSION REQUIREMENTS

Restrictions on contributors: None
Author pays submission fee: No
Author pays page charges: No
Length of articles: 1,750-12,000 words
Style: Journal; style sheet available on request
Number of copies required: 1
Special requirements: Submit original double-spaced typescript; footnotes should be numbered continuously throughout each article.
Copyright ownership: Assigned by author to journal
Rejected manuscripts: Returned
Time before publication decision: 5-6 mos.
Time between decision and publication: 1-2 yrs.
Number of reviewers: 3-5
Articles published per year: 8-10
Book reviews published per year: 2-3
Notes published per year: 2-3

(3144)
*De Vlaamse Gids

Uitg J. Hoste, Editor
Leopoldstr. 10
2000 Antwerp, Belgium

Telephone: (32) 3 4494937
First published: 1905
ISSN: 0042-7675
MLA acronym: VlG

SUBSCRIPTION INFORMATION

Frequency of publication: 6 times/yr.
Circulation: 9,000
Available in microform: No
Subscription price: 600 BF/yr. Belgium; 900 BF/yr. elsewhere
Year to which price refers: 1992

ADVERTISING INFORMATION

Advertising accepted: Yes

EDITORIAL DESCRIPTION

Scope: Publishes work on Netherlandic literature and poetry.
Reviews books: Yes
Publishes notes: Yes
Languages accepted: Dutch
Prints abstracts: No

SUBMISSION REQUIREMENTS

Author pays submission fee: Yes
Author pays page charges: No
Length of articles: 1,500 words
Length of book reviews: No restrictions
Number of copies required: 1
Copyright ownership: Author
Rejected manuscripts: Returned
Time before publication decision: 1-2 mos.
Time between decision and publication: 1-2 mos.
Number of reviewers: 1 plus Publishing Council
Articles published per year: 60

(3145)
*Voix et Images: Littérature Québécoise

Jacques Pelletier, Editor
Dept. d'Etudes Littéraires
Univ. du Québec, C.P. 8888, succ. A
Montréal, Québec H3C 3P8, Canada

Telephone: 514 987-6664
Fax: 514 987-8218
First published: 1975
Sponsoring organization: Univ. du Québec, Montréal, Dept. d'Etudes Littéraires
ISSN: 0318-9201
MLA acronym: V&I

SUBSCRIPTION INFORMATION

Frequency of publication: 3 times/yr. (Autumn, Winter, Spring)
Circulation: 1,000
Available in microform: No
Subscription price: C$23.00/yr. Canada; C$26.00/yr. elsewhere; C$18.00/yr. students
Year to which price refers: 1992
Subscription address: Service des Publications, Univ. de Québec à Montréal, C.P. 8888, "A", Montreal, Quebec H3C 3P8, Canada
Subscription telephone: 514 987-7747

ADVERTISING INFORMATION

Advertising accepted: Yes, on an exchange basis
Advertising rates: C$200.00/half page; C$275.00/full page

EDITORIAL DESCRIPTION

Scope: Publishes studies dealing exclusively with national literature. Welcomes analyses, using either traditional or modern methods, articles of recent productions, and interviews of writers of Quebec, and bibliographical notes regarding their literary place.
Reviews books: Yes
Publishes notes: No
Languages accepted: French
Prints abstracts: Yes
Author-anonymous submission: No

SUBMISSION REQUIREMENTS

Restrictions on contributors: None
Author pays submission fee: No
Author pays page charges: No
Length of articles: 7,500 words maximum
Length of book reviews: 700 words
Style: MLA
Number of copies required: 4
Copyright ownership: Journal
Rejected manuscripts: Not returned
Time before publication decision: 3 mos.
Time between decision and publication: 3-12 mos.
Number of reviewers: 3
Articles submitted per year: 75
Articles published per year: 30
Book reviews submitted per year: 30
Book reviews published per year: 25

(3146)
*Volkskunde: Driemaandelijks Tijdschrift voor de Studie van het Volksleven

J. Theuwissen & S. Top, Editors
Mercatorstraat 122
2018 Antwerp, Belgium

First published: 1888
ISSN: 0042-8523
MLA acronym: Volkskunde

SUBSCRIPTION INFORMATION

Frequency of publication: 4 times/yr.
Available in microform: No
Subscription price: 600 BF/yr.
Year to which price refers: 1992
Subscription address: Centrum voor Studie en Documentatie v.z.w., Jan de Voslei 37/6, 2020 Antwerp, Belgium

ADVERTISING INFORMATION

Advertising accepted: Yes

EDITORIAL DESCRIPTION

Scope: Publishes articles on Flemish folklore and ethnology.
Reviews books: Yes
Publishes notes: Yes
Languages accepted: Dutch
Prints abstracts: No

SUBMISSION REQUIREMENTS

Restrictions on contributors: None
Author pays submission fee: No
Author pays page charges: No
Length of articles: No restrictions
Length of book reviews: 300 words
Length of notes: 300 words
Number of copies required: 2
Copyright ownership: Author
Rejected manuscripts: Returned
Time before publication decision: 3 mos.
Time between decision and publication: 2 mos.
Number of reviewers: 2
Articles submitted per year: 18-20
Articles published per year: 10-12
Book reviews submitted per year: 40
Book reviews published per year: 40
Notes submitted per year: 10-15
Notes published per year: 10-12

(3147)
Voprosy Iazykoznaniia

T. V. Gamkrelidze, Editor
ul. Volkhonika 18/2
121019 Moscow G-19, Russia

First published: 1952

Sponsoring organization: Akademiia Nauk S.S.S.R., Dept. of Language & Literature, Moscow
ISSN: 0373-658X
MLA acronym: VJa

SUBSCRIPTION INFORMATION

Frequency of publication: 6 times/yr.
Circulation: 7,040
Available in microform: No
Subscription address: "Mezhdunarodnaja Kniga", Smolenskaja pl. 32/34, 121200 Moscow G-200, Russia

ADVERTISING INFORMATION

Advertising accepted: Yes

EDITORIAL DESCRIPTION

Scope: Publishes articles on general linguistics.
Reviews books: Yes
Publishes notes: No
Languages accepted: Russian
Prints abstracts: No

SUBMISSION REQUIREMENTS

Author pays submission fee: No
Author pays page charges: No
Length of articles: 24 pp.
Length of book reviews: 8-10 pp.
Number of copies required: 2
Time before publication decision: 1 yr.
Time between decision and publication: 6 mos.

(3148)
Voprosy Literatury

L. I. Lazarev, Editor
Bol'shoĭ Gnezdnikovskiĭ per, d.10
103009 Moscow K-9, Russia

First published: 1957
Sponsoring organization: Soiuz Pisateleĭ S.S.S.R.; Inst. Mirovoĭ Literatury im. A. M. Gor'kogo Akademiia Nauk S.S.S.R.
ISSN: 0042-8795
MLA acronym: VLit

SUBSCRIPTION INFORMATION

Frequency of publication: 12 times/yr.
Circulation: 25,000
Available in microform: No
Subscription address: Victor Kamkin, 4956 Boiling Brook Pkwy., Rockville, MD 20852

ADVERTISING INFORMATION

Advertising accepted: Yes

EDITORIAL DESCRIPTION

Scope: Publishes articles on the problems of theory and history of Russian and foreign literatures.
Reviews books: Yes
Publishes notes: Yes
Languages accepted: Russian
Prints abstracts: No
Author-anonymous submission: No

SUBMISSION REQUIREMENTS

Restrictions on contributors: None
Author pays submission fee: No
Author pays page charges: No
Length of articles: 24-50 typescript pp.
Length of book reviews: 8-10 pp.
Length of notes: 3 pp.
Style: MLA; Critical Inquiry
Number of copies required: 3
Special requirements: Submit original typescript.
Copyright ownership: Journal
Rejected manuscripts: Returned
Time before publication decision: 6 weeks

Time between decision and publication: 2 mos.
Number of reviewers: 3
Articles submitted per year: 420
Articles published per year: 110-120
Book reviews submitted per year: 360
Book reviews published per year: 100-110
Notes submitted per year: 600
Notes published per year: 48-50

(3149)
Voprosy Russkoĭ Literatury: Respublikanskiĭ Mezhvedomstvennyĭ Nauchnyĭ Sbornik

V. A. Merentsov, Editor
Kafedra Russkoĭ Literatury
Gosuniversitet
Ul. Kotsiubinskogo, 2
274012 Chernovtsy, Ukraine

ISSN: 0507-3871
MLA acronym: VRL

SUBSCRIPTION INFORMATION

Additional subscription address: Victor Kamkin Inc., 4956 Boiling Brook Pkwy., Rockville, MD 20852

(3150)
*Vox Romanica: Annales Helvetici Explorandis Linguis Romanicis Destinati

Ricarda Liver & Peter Wunderli, Editors
Romanisches Seminar der Univ.
Neuengasse 30
3011 Bern, Switzerland

Additional editorial address: Universitätsstr. 1, 4000 Dusseldorf 1, Germany
First published: 1936
Sponsoring organization: Collegium Romanicum
ISSN: 0042-899X
MLA acronym: VR

SUBSCRIPTION INFORMATION

Frequency of publication: Annual
Circulation: 550
Available in microform: No
Subscription address: A. Francke Verlag, Postfach 2560, 7400 Tübingen, Germany

ADVERTISING INFORMATION

Advertising accepted: No

EDITORIAL DESCRIPTION

Scope: Publishes articles on diachronic and synchronic Romance linguistics, general diachronic theory, some synchronic theory, and medieval Romance literatures.
Reviews books: Yes
Publishes notes: Yes
Languages accepted: English; French; German; Italian; Spanish
Prints abstracts: No
Author-anonymous submission: No

SUBMISSION REQUIREMENTS

Restrictions on contributors: None
Author pays submission fee: No
Author pays page charges: No
Length of articles: 4,000-12,500 words
Length of book reviews: 1,000-2,000 words
Length of notes: 500-800 words
Style: None
Number of copies required: 1
Special requirements: Submit original typescript.
Copyright ownership: Author

Rejected manuscripts: Returned
Time before publication decision: 3 mos.
Time between decision and publication: 1-2 yrs.
Number of reviewers: 2
Articles submitted per year: 15-20
Articles published per year: 10
Book reviews submitted per year: 20-25
Book reviews published per year: 20-25
Notes submitted per year: 50-60
Notes published per year: 50-60

(3151)
*Vsesvit: Zhurnal Inozemnoï Literatury. Literaturno-Mystets'kyĭ ta Hromads'ko-Politychnyĭ Misiachnyk. Orhan Spilky Pys'mennykiv Ukraïny, Ukraïns'koho Tovarystva Druzhby i Kul'turnykh Zv'iazkiv z Zarubizhnymy Kraïnamy, Ukraïns'koï Rady Myru

Oleg Mykytenko, Editor
34/1, M. Hrushevsky str.
252021 Kiev, Ukraine

Telephone: (7) 44 2931318; (7) 44 2930613
Fax: (7) 44 2931318
First published: 1925
ISSN: 0320-8370
MLA acronym: Vsesvit

SUBSCRIPTION INFORMATION

Frequency of publication: 12 times/yr.
Circulation: 42,000
Available in microform: No
Subscription price: $80.00/yr.
Year to which price refers: 1993
Additional subscription address: In the US & Canada: UPU, P.O. Box 009, Green Village, NJ 07935
Subscription fax: 201 701-0451

ADVERTISING INFORMATION

Advertising accepted: Yes
Advertising rates: $1,000.00/full page; $2,000.00/cover

EDITORIAL DESCRIPTION

Scope: Publishes translations of non-Ukraine literature, art, and critical articles on literature, art, and drama. Also includes articles on international affairs, and Ukrainian relations with the world.
Reviews books: Yes
Publishes notes: Yes
Languages accepted: Ukrainian
Prints abstracts: No
Author-anonymous submission: No

SUBMISSION REQUIREMENTS

Author pays submission fee: Yes
Author pays page charges: No
Length of articles: 2,500 words maximum
Length of book reviews: 125 words maximum
Length of notes: 80 words maximum
Number of copies required: 2
Copyright ownership: Author
Rejected manuscripts: Not returned
Time before publication decision: 1 mo.
Time between decision and publication: 3 mos.
Number of reviewers: 1-2
Articles submitted per year: 200-300
Articles published per year: 80-100
Book reviews submitted per year: 40
Book reviews published per year: 10-15
Notes submitted per year: 400
Notes published per year: 200

(3152)
*Vuelta

Octavio Paz, Enrique Kranze, & Aurelio Asiain, Editors
Presidente Carranza 210
Coyoacán
04000 Mexico City, D.F., Mexico

Telephone: (52) 5 5548980; (52) 5 5548811; (52) 5 5545686
Fax: (52) 5 6580074
First published: 1976
ISSN: 0185-1586
MLA acronym: Vuelta

SUBSCRIPTION INFORMATION

Frequency of publication: 12 times/yr.
Circulation: 20,000
Available in microform: No
Subscription price: Mex$120,000.00/yr. Mexico; $75.00/yr. N. America & Central America; $90.00/yr. Europe & S. America; $100.00/yr. Asia, Africa, & Oceania
Year to which price refers: 1993
Additional subscription address: Ebsco Subscription Services, P.O. Box 1943, Birmingham, AL 35201

ADVERTISING INFORMATION

Advertising accepted: Yes
Advertising rates: $940.00/quarter page; $1,505.00/half page; $2,225.00/full page; $3,887.00/full page, color

EDITORIAL DESCRIPTION

Scope: Publishes articles on international literature and politics.
Reviews books: Yes
Publishes notes: Yes
Languages accepted: Spanish
Author-anonymous submission: No

SUBMISSION REQUIREMENTS

Restrictions on contributors: None
Author pays submission fee: No
Author pays page charges: No
Length of articles: 15-20 pp.
Length of book reviews: 4-6 pp.
Length of notes: 6-8 pp.
Style: MLA
Number of copies required: 1
Copyright ownership: Author & journal
Rejected manuscripts: Not returned
Time before publication decision: 6 mos.
Time between decision and publication: 4-6 mos.
Number of reviewers: 3
Articles submitted per year: 700
Articles published per year: 105
Book reviews submitted per year: 200
Book reviews published per year: 60
Notes submitted per year: 180-200
Notes published per year: 36

(3153)
*[vwa]

Pascal Antonietti, Philippe Marthaler, & Marcelino Palomo, Editors
C.P. 172
2301 La Chaux-de-Fonds, Switzerland

Telephone: (41) 39 282418; (41) 39 282682
First published: 1983
ISSN: 0259-6512
MLA acronym: vwa

SUBSCRIPTION INFORMATION

Frequency of publication: 2 times/yr.
Available in microform: No
Subscription price: 62 SwF/3 issues
Year to which price refers: 1992

ADVERTISING INFORMATION

Advertising accepted: No

EDITORIAL DESCRIPTION

Scope: Publishes articles on literary theory and on literature with an emphasis on Swiss-French and French-language literature. Also publishes poetry, short stories, and illustrations.
Reviews books: No
Publishes notes: No
Languages accepted: French
Prints abstracts: Yes
Author-anonymous submission: No

SUBMISSION REQUIREMENTS

Author pays submission fee: No
Author pays page charges: No
Length of articles: 10 pp.
Number of copies required: 1
Special requirements: Submit typescript.
Copyright ownership: Journal
Rejected manuscripts: Not returned
Time before publication decision: 4 mos.
Time between decision and publication: 6 mos.
Number of reviewers: 3
Articles submitted per year: 50
Articles published per year: 20-25

(3154)
*Vyzvol'nyĭ Shliakh/Liberation Path

I. Dmytriw, Editor
Ukrainian Publishers Ltd.
200 Liverpool Rd.
London N1 1LF, England

Telephone: (44) 71 6076266
Fax: (44) 71 6076737
First published: 1954
ISSN: 0042-9422
MLA acronym: VyzSh

SUBSCRIPTION INFORMATION

Frequency of publication: 12 times/yr.
Circulation: 4,000
Available in microform: No
Subscription price: £30.00/yr. United Kingdom; $65.00/yr. US; $75.00/yr. Canada; 120 DM/yr. Germany; 350 F/yr. France
Year to which price refers: 1992

ADVERTISING INFORMATION

Advertising accepted: No

EDITORIAL DESCRIPTION

Scope: Publishes articles on Ukrainian politics, history, sociology, literature, poetry, and developments in Ukraine.
Reviews books: Yes
Publishes notes: Yes
Languages accepted: Ukrainian
Prints abstracts: No
Author-anonymous submission: No

SUBMISSION REQUIREMENTS

Restrictions on contributors: None
Author pays submission fee: No
Author pays page charges: No
Length of articles: No restrictions
Length of book reviews: 500-650 words
Length of notes: 500 words maximum
Style: None
Number of copies required: 1
Special requirements: Submit double-spaced typescript.
Copyright ownership: Author & Ukrainian Publishers, Ltd.
Rejected manuscripts: Returned at author's request
Time before publication decision: 1-2 mos.
Time between decision and publication: 1 mo.
Number of reviewers: 2-3
Articles submitted per year: 200-240
Articles published per year: 150-160
Book reviews submitted per year: 30-40
Book reviews published per year: 25-30
Notes submitted per year: 12-20
Notes published per year: 12-20

(3155)
*Waiguoyu

Dai Weidong, Editor
Shanghai International Studies Univ.
550 Da Lian Rd. W.
Shanghai 200083, People's Republic of China

Telephone: (86) 21 5420358; (86) 21 5420900-581
Fax: (86) 21 5420225
First published: 1979
Historical variations in title: Foreign Languages
Sponsoring organization: Shanghai International Studies Univ.
ISSN: 1004-5139
MLA acronym: Waiguoyu

SUBSCRIPTION INFORMATION

Frequency of publication: 6 times/yr.
Circulation: 10,000
Available in microform: No
Subscription address: Guoji Shudian, P.O. Box 2820, Beijing, People's Republic of China

ADVERTISING INFORMATION

Advertising accepted: Yes, on an exchange basis

EDITORIAL DESCRIPTION

Scope: Focuses on English, American (US), French, German, Russian, and Japanese languages and literatures, linguistics, translation, and pedagogy.
Reviews books: Yes
Publishes notes: Yes
Languages accepted: English; Chinese languages; Russian; German; French; Japanese; Spanish
Prints abstracts: Yes
Author-anonymous submission: Yes

SUBMISSION REQUIREMENTS

Restrictions on contributors: None
Author pays submission fee: No
Author pays page charges: No
Length of articles: 10,000 words
Length of book reviews: 1,500-2,000 words
Length of notes: 2,000-4,000 words
Style: MLA
Number of copies required: 1
Copyright ownership: Journal
Rejected manuscripts: Returned
Time before publication decision: 3 mos.
Time between decision and publication: 2 mos.
Number of reviewers: 3
Articles submitted per year: 500
Articles published per year: 100
Book reviews submitted per year: 30
Book reviews published per year: 10-15
Notes submitted per year: 12
Notes published per year: 6

(3156)
*The Wallace Stevens Journal: A Publication of the Wallace Stevens Society

John N. Serio, Editor
Liberal Studies
Clarkson Univ.
Potsdam, NY 13699-5750

Telephone: 315 268-3987

Fax: 315 268-3983
E-mail: Serio@crnft.camp.clarkson.edu
First published: 1977
Sponsoring organization: Wallace Stevens Soc.
ISSN: 0148-7132
MLA acronym: WSJour

SUBSCRIPTION INFORMATION

Frequency of publication: 2 times/yr.
Circulation: 500
Available in microform: No
Subscription price: $25.00/yr. institutions; $20.00/yr. individuals; add $5.00/yr. postage outside US
Year to which price refers: 1992

ADVERTISING INFORMATION

Advertising accepted: Yes
Advertising rates: $100.00/half page; $150.00/full page

EDITORIAL DESCRIPTION

Scope: Publishes articles, reviews, bibliographies, news and comments, and poems about Wallace Stevens.
Reviews books: Yes
Publishes notes: Yes
Languages accepted: English
Prints abstracts: No
Author-anonymous submission: No

SUBMISSION REQUIREMENTS

Restrictions on contributors: None
Author pays submission fee: No
Author pays page charges: No
Length of articles: 2,500-8,000 words
Length of book reviews: 1,200 words
Length of notes: 100-200 words
Style: MLA
Number of copies required: 2
Special requirements: Word-processed papers preferred.
Copyright ownership: Author
Rejected manuscripts: Not returned
Time before publication decision: 2-3 mos.
Time between decision and publication: 6-12 mos.
Number of reviewers: 3-4
Articles submitted per year: 40-50
Articles published per year: 12-15
Book reviews submitted per year: 10-15
Book reviews published per year: 10-15
Notes submitted per year: 2
Notes published per year: 2

(3157)
*Walt Whitman Quarterly Review

Edwin Folsom, Editor
308 English-Philosophy Bldg.
Univ. of Iowa
Iowa City, IA 52242

Telephone: 319 335-0454
Fax: 319 335-2535
First published: 1983
Sponsoring organization: Univ. of Iowa
ISSN: 0737-0679
MLA acronym: WWQR

SUBSCRIPTION INFORMATION

Frequency of publication: 4 times/yr. (Summer, Fall, Winter, Spring)
Circulation: 600
Available in microform: Yes
Subscription price: $15.00/yr. institutions; $12.00/yr. individuals; add $3.00/yr. postage outside US
Year to which price refers: 1992

ADVERTISING INFORMATION

Advertising accepted: Yes

EDITORIAL DESCRIPTION

Scope: Publishes scholarly discussions of Walt Whitman, his writing, influence, and relationship to his times, as well as reviews of Whitman books and bibliographies.
Reviews books: Yes
Publishes notes: Yes
Languages accepted: English
Prints abstracts: No
Author-anonymous submission: No

SUBMISSION REQUIREMENTS

Restrictions on contributors: None
Author pays submission fee: No
Author pays page charges: No
Length of articles: 5,000 words
Length of book reviews: 2,500 words
Length of notes: 2,000 words
Style: MLA
Number of copies required: 2
Special requirements: See "Guidelines for Contributors," printed in each issue.
Copyright ownership: Journal
Rejected manuscripts: Returned; enclose return postage.
Time before publication decision: 2 mos.
Time between decision and publication: 3-12 mos.
Number of reviewers: 2-3
Articles submitted per year: 50
Articles published per year: 15
Book reviews submitted per year: 15
Book reviews published per year: 12
Notes submitted per year: 20
Notes published per year: 10

(3158)
*War, Literature, and the Arts

Donald Anderson, Editor
Dept. of English
U.S. Air Force Academy, CO 80840-5701

Telephone: 719 472-3930
Fax: 719 472-3135
First published: 1989
Sponsoring organization: United States Air Force Academy
ISSN: 1046-6967
MLA acronym: WL&A

SUBSCRIPTION INFORMATION

Frequency of publication: 2 times/yr. (Spring, Fall)
Circulation: 200
Available in microform: No
Subscription price: $20.00/yr. institutions; $10.00/yr. individuals; add $5.00/yr. postage outside US
Year to which price refers: 1992

ADVERTISING INFORMATION

Advertising accepted: Yes
Advertising rates: $100.00/full page

EDITORIAL DESCRIPTION

Scope: Contributes to understanding war and art, by means of critical inquiry into artistic depictions of war from any culture or period. Although critical articles are the main focus, personal memoir, poetry, short fiction, and visual art are also considered.
Reviews books: Yes
Publishes notes: Yes
Languages accepted: English
Prints abstracts: No
Author-anonymous submission: Yes

SUBMISSION REQUIREMENTS

Restrictions on contributors: None
Author pays submission fee: No
Author pays page charges: No
Length of articles: 3,500-7,500 words
Length of book reviews: 1,250-2,500 words
Length of notes: 1,250-2,500 words
Style: MLA
Number of copies required: 2
Copyright ownership: Author
Rejected manuscripts: Returned; enclose SASE.
Time before publication decision: 3-6 mos.
Time between decision and publication: 6-12 mos.
Number of reviewers: 2-3
Articles published per year: 8
Book reviews published per year: 6-8
Notes submitted per year: 4-6

(3159)
*Wascana Review

Joan Givner & Karen Smythe, Editors
English Dept.
Univ. of Regina
Regina, Saskatchewan S4S 0A2, Canada

Telephone: 306 585-4311
First published: 1966
Sponsoring organization: Univ. of Regina
ISSN: 0043-0412
MLA acronym: WascanaR

SUBSCRIPTION INFORMATION

Frequency of publication: 2 times/yr.
Circulation: 500
Available in microform: No
Subscription price: C$7.00/yr. Canada; C$8.00/yr. elsewhere
Year to which price refers: 1992

ADVERTISING INFORMATION

Advertising accepted: No

EDITORIAL DESCRIPTION

Scope: Publishes English, Canadian, and American literary criticism, fiction, and poetry.
Reviews books: Yes
Publishes notes: No
Languages accepted: English
Prints abstracts: No
Author-anonymous submission: No

SUBMISSION REQUIREMENTS

Restrictions on contributors: Book reviews are assigned.
Author pays submission fee: No
Author pays page charges: No
Length of articles: 5,000-6,000 words
Length of book reviews: 3,000-4,000 words
Style: MLA
Number of copies required: 1
Copyright ownership: Journal
Rejected manuscripts: Returned; enclose return postage.
Time before publication decision: 6 weeks
Time between decision and publication: 6 mos.
Number of reviewers: 3
Articles submitted per year: 100
Articles published per year: 6-8
Book reviews published per year: 12

(3160)
*Weber Studies: An Interdisciplinary Humanities Journal

Neila C. Seshachari, Editor
Weber State Univ.
Ogden, UT 84408-1214

Telephone: 801 626-6473
First published: 1984
Sponsoring organization: Weber State Univ., College of Arts & Humanities
ISSN: 0891-8899
MLA acronym: WStu

SUBSCRIPTION INFORMATION

Frequency of publication: 3 times/yr. (Winter, Spring, Fall)
Circulation: 1,000
Available in microform: No
Subscription price: $20.00/yr. institutions; $10.00/yr. individuals
Year to which price refers: 1992

ADVERTISING INFORMATION

Advertising accepted: Yes, on an exchange basis

EDITORIAL DESCRIPTION

Scope: Publishes articles on interdisciplinary studies in the humanities, as well as poetry and fiction.
Reviews books: Yes
Publishes notes: No
Languages accepted: English
Prints abstracts: No
Author-anonymous submission: No

SUBMISSION REQUIREMENTS

Restrictions on contributors: Book reviews are solicited.
Author pays submission fee: No
Author pays page charges: No
Length of articles: 2,500-5,000 words
Length of book reviews: 1,500 words
Style: MLA
Number of copies required: 3
Special requirements: Submit double-spaced typescript.
Copyright ownership: Author
Rejected manuscripts: Returned; enclose SASE.
Time before publication decision: 3 mos.
Time between decision and publication: 6-12 mos.
Number of reviewers: 2
Articles submitted per year: 100-150
Articles published per year: 8-10
Book reviews published per year: 5-6

(3161)
Wege der Forschung

Wissenschaftliche Buchgesellschaft
Hindenburgstr. 40
Postfach 11-11-29
6100 Darmstadt 11, Germany

First published: 1956
ISSN: 0509-9609
MLA acronym: WdF

SUBSCRIPTION INFORMATION

Frequency of publication: Irregular
Available in microform: No

ADVERTISING INFORMATION

Advertising accepted: No

EDITORIAL DESCRIPTION

Scope: Publishes articles and monograph studies on literature and literary theory.
Reviews books: No
Publishes notes: No
Languages accepted: German; English
Prints abstracts: No

SUBMISSION REQUIREMENTS

Author pays submission fee: No
Author pays page charges: No
Length of books: 350 pp.
Number of copies required: 2
Copyright ownership: Wissenschaftliche Buchgesellschaft & editor
Rejected manuscripts: Returned
Time between decision and publication: 2-3 yrs.
Number of reviewers: 2

(3162)
*Weimarer Beiträge: Zeitschrift für Literaturwissenschaft, Ästhetik und Kulturwissenschaften

Peter Engelmann, Editor
Passagen Verlag
Walfischgasse 15/14
1010 Vienna, Austria

Additional editorial address: Karla Kliche, Aufbau-Verlag, Französische Str. 32, 1086 Berlin, Germany
Telephone: (43) 222 5137761
Fax: (43) 222 5126327
First published: 1955
Historical variations in title: Formerly Weimarer Beiträge: Zeitschrift für Literaturwissenschaft, Ästhetik und Kulturtheorie
Sponsoring organization: Kulturinitiative; Gesellschaft für Demokratische Kultur e.V., Berlin; Bundesministerium für Wissenschaft & Forschung, Vienna; Bundesministerium für Unterricht & Kunst, Vienna
ISSN: 0043-2199
MLA acronym: WB

SUBSCRIPTION INFORMATION

Frequency of publication: 4 times/yr.
Circulation: 1,000
Available in microform: No
Subscription price: 144 DM/yr.
Year to which price refers: 1992
Subscription address: Minerva Verlagsauslieferung, Sachsenplatz 4-6, Postfach 88, 1201 Vienna, Austria
Subscription telephone: (43) 222 3302433/248 ext. 250
Subscription fax: (43) 222 3302439/62

ADVERTISING INFORMATION

Advertising accepted: Yes

EDITORIAL DESCRIPTION

Scope: Publishes articles, interviews, reports, and reviews of literature, aesthetics, the theory of culture, and methodical problems. Subjects include the cultural heritage, world literature, and development of art and culture.
Reviews books: Yes
Publishes notes: No
Languages accepted: German
Prints abstracts: No
Author-anonymous submission: No

SUBMISSION REQUIREMENTS

Restrictions on contributors: None
Author pays submission fee: No
Author pays page charges: No
Length of articles: 18-20 pp.
Length of book reviews: 4 pp.
Style: None
Number of copies required: 2
Special requirements: Submit on 3.5 in. DOS diskette using WordPerfect.
Copyright ownership: Author
Rejected manuscripts: Returned; enclose return postage
Time before publication decision: 3 mos.
Time between decision and publication: 6 mos.
Number of reviewers: 2
Articles submitted per year: 120
Articles published per year: 30
Book reviews submitted per year: 20
Book reviews published per year: 18

(3163)
*The Wellsian: The Journal of the H. G. Wells Society

Michael Draper, Editor
c/o English Dept.
Luton Sixth Form College
Bradgers Hill Rd.
Bedfordshire
Luton LU2 7EW, England

Telephone: (44) 582 412005
First published: 1976
Sponsoring organization: H. G. Wells Soc.
ISSN: 0263-1776
MLA acronym: Wellsian

SUBSCRIPTION INFORMATION

Frequency of publication: Annual
Circulation: 200
Available in microform: No
Subscription price: £12.00/yr. institutions; £6.50/yr. individuals United Kingdom; £8.00/yr. individuals elsewhere
Year to which price refers: 1992
Subscription address: Sylvia Hardy, English Dept., Nene College, Moulton Park, Northampton NN2 7AL, England
Subscription telephone: (44) 604 715000
Subscription fax: (44) 604 720636

ADVERTISING INFORMATION

Advertising accepted: No
Advertising rates: £25.00/half page

EDITORIAL DESCRIPTION

Scope: Publishes articles on the writings, thought, and life of H. G. Wells.
Reviews books: Yes
Publishes notes: Yes
Languages accepted: English
Prints abstracts: No
Author-anonymous submission: No

SUBMISSION REQUIREMENTS

Restrictions on contributors: None
Author pays submission fee: No
Author pays page charges: No
Length of articles: 2,000-9,000 words
Length of book reviews: 1,000 words
Length of notes: 1,000 words
Style: MLA
Number of copies required: 1
Copyright ownership: Author
Rejected manuscripts: Returned
Time before publication decision: 1 mo.
Number of reviewers: 1
Articles submitted per year: 10
Articles published per year: 6-8
Book reviews submitted per year: 2
Book reviews published per year: 2
Notes submitted per year: 2
Notes published per year: 2

(3164)
Die Welt der Slaven: Halbjahresschrift für Slavistik

Heinrich Kunstmann, Editor
Inst. für Slavische Philologie
Geschwister-Scholl-Platz 1
8000 Munich 22, Germany

First published: 1955
ISSN: 0043-2520
MLA acronym: WSl

SUBSCRIPTION INFORMATION

Frequency of publication: 2 times/yr.
Circulation: 350
Available in microform: No
Subscription address: Otto Sagner Verlag, Postfach 340108, 8000 Munich 34, Germany

ADVERTISING INFORMATION

Advertising accepted: Yes

EDITORIAL DESCRIPTION

Scope: Publishes articles on Slavic philology (language and literature), folklore, and history.
Reviews books: Yes
Languages accepted: English; French; German; Russian
Prints abstracts: No

SUBMISSION REQUIREMENTS

Restrictions on contributors: None
Author pays submission fee: No
Author pays page charges: No
Length of articles: 10-20 pp.
Number of copies required: 1
Special requirements: Submit original typescript.
Copyright ownership: Editor
Rejected manuscripts: Returned
Time before publication decision: 2 mos.
Time between decision and publication: 1 yr.
Number of reviewers: 2-3
Articles submitted per year: 25-35
Articles published per year: 20
Book reviews published per year: 10

(3165)
*Die Welt des Islams: Internationale Zeitschrift für die Geschichte des Islams in der Neuzeit

S. Wild & W. Ende, Editors
Oriental Seminar
Regina Pacis-Weg 7
5300 Bonn 1, Germany

First published: 1913
Sponsoring organization: Deutsche Forschungsgemeinschaft
ISSN: 0043-2359
MLA acronym: WI

SUBSCRIPTION INFORMATION

Frequency of publication: 2 double-issues/yr.
Circulation: 500
Available in microform: No
Subscription price: 102 f ($51.00)/yr.
Year to which price refers: 1991
Subscription address: E. J. Brill N.V., P.O. Box 9000, 2300 PA Leiden, Netherlands
Additional subscription address: In US & Canada: E. J. Brill, 24 Hudson St., Kinderhook, NY 12106

ADVERTISING INFORMATION

Advertising accepted: Yes

EDITORIAL DESCRIPTION

Scope: Publishes articles on the history and culture of Islam, the Islamic countries, and Islamic contributions from the end of the 18th century to the present, with special attention given to literature.
Reviews books: Yes
Publishes notes: Yes
Languages accepted: English; French; German
Prints abstracts: No
Author-anonymous submission: No

SUBMISSION REQUIREMENTS

Restrictions on contributors: None
Author pays submission fee: No
Author pays page charges: No
Length of articles: 10-30 typescript pp.
Length of book reviews: 500 words
Number of copies required: 1
Copyright ownership: E. J. Brill
Rejected manuscripts: Returned
Time before publication decision: 1-2 mos.

Time between decision and publication: 2 yrs.
Number of reviewers: 3
Articles submitted per year: 15
Articles published per year: 6-10
Book reviews submitted per year: 50
Book reviews published per year: 20

(3166)
*Die Welt des Orients: Wissenschaftliche Beiträge zur Kunde des Morgenlandes

Wolfgang Röllig, Wolfram von Soden, & Heinz Halm, Editors
Corrensstr. 12
7400 Tübingen, Germany

Telephone: (49) 7071 292193
Fax: (49) 7071 296758
First published: 1947
Sponsoring organization: Deutsche Forschungsgemeinschaft
ISSN: 0340-6229
MLA acronym: WO

SUBSCRIPTION INFORMATION

Frequency of publication: Annual
Circulation: 500
Available in microform: No
Subscription address: Vandenhoeck & Ruprecht, Theaterstr. 13, 3400 Göttingen, Germany

ADVERTISING INFORMATION

Advertising accepted: No

EDITORIAL DESCRIPTION

Scope: Publishes articles on the history, culture, and languages of the modern and ancient Near East.
Reviews books: Yes
Publishes notes: No
Languages accepted: English; German; French; Italian
Prints abstracts: No
Author-anonymous submission: No

SUBMISSION REQUIREMENTS

Restrictions on contributors: None
Author pays submission fee: No
Author pays page charges: No
Length of articles: No restrictions
Length of book reviews: No restrictions
Style: None
Number of copies required: 1
Special requirements: Submit original typescript.
Copyright ownership: Journal
Rejected manuscripts: Returned
Time before publication decision: 2 mos.
Time between decision and publication: 1 yr.
Number of reviewers: 2
Articles submitted per year: 12
Articles published per year: 8-10
Book reviews submitted per year: 20
Book reviews published per year: 20

(3167)
*West Georgia College Review

Martha A. Saunders, Editor
English Dept.
West Georgia College
Carrollton, GA 30118

Telephone: 706 836-6512
Fax: 706 836-6717
First published: 1968
Sponsoring organization: West Georgia College
ISSN: 0043-3136
MLA acronym: WGCR

SUBSCRIPTION INFORMATION

Frequency of publication: Annual
Circulation: 500
Available in microform: No

ADVERTISING INFORMATION

Advertising accepted: No

EDITORIAL DESCRIPTION

Scope: Accepts original scholarly work with an interdisciplinary interest in humanities, social sciences, sciences, education, and business.
Reviews books: No
Publishes notes: No
Languages accepted: English
Prints abstracts: No
Author-anonymous submission: Yes

SUBMISSION REQUIREMENTS

Restrictions on contributors: Contributors are usually members of the West Georgia College faculty, but others will be considered.
Author pays submission fee: No
Author pays page charges: No
Length of articles: 5,000 words
Style: MLA
Number of copies required: 3
Special requirements: Submit double-spaced typescript with cited sources at the end of the article.
Copyright ownership: West Georgia College
Rejected manuscripts: Returned
Time before publication decision: 6 weeks
Time between decision and publication: 6 mos.
Number of reviewers: 3
Articles submitted per year: 10-12
Articles published per year: 3-5

(3168)
*West Virginia University Philological Papers

Armand E. Singer, Editor
Dept. of Foreign Languages
West Virginia Univ.
Morgantown, WV 26506

Telephone: 304 293-5121
Fax: 304 293-7655
First published: 1936
Sponsoring organization: Dept. of Foreign Languages, West Virginia Univ.
ISSN: 0363-3470
MLA acronym: WVUPP

SUBSCRIPTION INFORMATION

Frequency of publication: Annual
Circulation: 300
Available in microform: No
Subscription price: $10.00/yr.
Year to which price refers: 1992

ADVERTISING INFORMATION

Advertising accepted: Yes

EDITORIAL DESCRIPTION

Scope: Publishes literary studies.
Reviews books: No
Publishes notes: No
Languages accepted: English
Prints abstracts: No
Author-anonymous submission: No

SUBMISSION REQUIREMENTS

Restrictions on contributors: Contributions are currently limited to papers selected from those read at the West Virginia University annual Colloquium on Modern Literature and Film.
Author pays submission fee: No
Author pays page charges: No

(3169)
*Westerly: A Quarterly Review

Bruce Bennett, Peter Cowan, & Dennis Haskell, Editors
Center for Studies in Australian Literature
Dept. of English
Univ. of Western Australia
Nedlands 6009, Australia

Telephone: (61) 9 3802101
Fax: (61) 9 3801030
First published: 1956
Sponsoring organization: Univ. of Western Australia; Australia Council; Western Australian Dept. for Arts
ISSN: 0043-342X
MLA acronym: Westerly

SUBSCRIPTION INFORMATION

Frequency of publication: 4 times/yr.
Circulation: 1,000
Available in microform: No

ADVERTISING INFORMATION

Advertising accepted: Yes

EDITORIAL DESCRIPTION

Scope: Publishes creative and critical writing on the literature and culture of Australia and its neighboring regions.
Reviews books: Yes
Publishes notes: No
Languages accepted: English
Prints abstracts: No
Author-anonymous submission: No

SUBMISSION REQUIREMENTS

Restrictions on contributors: None
Author pays submission fee: No
Author pays page charges: No
Length of articles: 3,000 words
Length of book reviews: 800-1,000 words
Style: MLA
Number of copies required: 1
Special requirements: Submit original typescript; enclose return postage.
Copyright ownership: Author
Rejected manuscripts: Returned
Time before publication decision: 3 mos.
Time between decision and publication: 6 mos.
Number of reviewers: 3
Articles submitted per year: 100
Articles published per year: 16
Book reviews submitted per year: 80
Book reviews published per year: 16-20

Length of articles: 10-20 typescript pp.
Style: MLA with modifications
Number of copies required: 2
Special requirements: Original typescript and xerox duplicate preferred; no multiple works. Style sheet available from editor. Final version of accepted work must be submitted on diskette.
Copyright ownership: Assigned by author to journal
Rejected manuscripts: Returned; enclose loose return postage.
Time before publication decision: 5 mos.
Time between decision and publication: 18 mos.
Number of reviewers: 4 maximum
Articles submitted per year: 50-75
Articles published per year: 15

(3170)
*Western American Literature

Thomas J. Lyon, Editor
Dept. of English
Utah State Univ.
Logan, UT 84322-3200

Telephone: 801 750-1603
First published: 1966
Sponsoring organization: Western Literature Assn.; Utah State Univ.
ISSN: 0043-3462
MLA acronym: WAL

SUBSCRIPTION INFORMATION

Frequency of publication: 4 times/yr. (May, Aug., Nov., Feb.)
Circulation: 900
Available in microform: Yes
Subscription price: $30.00/yr. institutions; $15.00/yr. individuals
Year to which price refers: 1992

ADVERTISING INFORMATION

Advertising accepted: Yes
Advertising rates: $75.00/full page

EDITORIAL DESCRIPTION

Scope: Publishes manuscripts on any aspect of the literature of the American West. Also publishes reviews and review essays dealing with current literature of the American West.
Reviews books: Yes
Publishes notes: Yes
Languages accepted: English
Prints abstracts: No
Author-anonymous submission: No

SUBMISSION REQUIREMENTS

Restrictions on contributors: None
Author pays submission fee: No
Author pays page charges: No
Length of book reviews: 300 words
Style: MLA
Number of copies required: 2
Copyright ownership: Journal
Rejected manuscripts: Returned; enclose return postage.
Time before publication decision: 2 mos.
Time between decision and publication: 6-12 mos.
Number of reviewers: 1-3
Articles submitted per year: 100-150
Articles published per year: 16-20
Book reviews submitted per year: 200
Book reviews published per year: 150-200
Notes submitted per year: 6-8
Notes published per year: 4-20

(3171)
Western Folklore

Pack Carnes, Editor
Lake Forest College
Lake Forest, IL 60045

First published: 1942
Sponsoring organization: California Folklore Soc.
ISSN: 0043-373X
MLA acronym: WF

SUBSCRIPTION INFORMATION

Frequency of publication: 4 times/yr. (Jan., Apr., July, Oct.)
Circulation: 1,200
Available in microform: Yes
Subscription price: $30.00/yr. institutions (includes membership); $25.00/yr. individuals (includes membership); $15.00/yr. students & emeriti (includes membership)
Year to which price refers: 1992

Subscription address: Theodore C. Humphrey, 421 Baughman Ave., Claremont, CA 91711

ADVERTISING INFORMATION

Advertising accepted: Yes

EDITORIAL DESCRIPTION

Scope: Publishes articles on American and world folklore. Includes book, record, and film reviews.
Reviews books: Yes
Publishes notes: Yes
Languages accepted: English
Prints abstracts: No
Author-anonymous submission: Yes

SUBMISSION REQUIREMENTS

Restrictions on contributors: Contributions accepted from all sources, not solely from professional folklorists.
Author pays submission fee: No
Author pays page charges: No
Length of articles: 20-40 pp.
Length of book reviews: 300-500 words
Length of notes: 500-3,000 words
Style: Chicago
Number of copies required: 2
Special requirements: Submit double-spaced typescript.
Copyright ownership: California Folklore Soc.
Rejected manuscripts: Returned; enclose return postage.
Time before publication decision: 6 mos.
Time between decision and publication: 6 mos.
Number of reviewers: 2
Articles submitted per year: 75
Articles published per year: 15
Book reviews published per year: 30
Notes submitted per year: 25
Notes published per year: 10

(3172)
Western Humanities Review

Barry Weller, Richard Howard, David Kranes, Charles Berger, & Kristoffer Jacobson, Editors
Dept. of English
Univ. of Utah
Salt Lake City, UT 84112

Telephone: 801 581-6070
First published: 1947
Sponsoring organization: Dept. of English, Univ. of Utah
ISSN: 0043-3845
MLA acronym: WHR

SUBSCRIPTION INFORMATION

Frequency of publication: 4 times/yr. (Winter, Spring, Summer, Fall)
Circulation: 1,100
Available in microform: Yes
Subscription price: $24.00/yr. institutions; $18.00/yr. individuals
Year to which price refers: 1992

ADVERTISING INFORMATION

Advertising accepted: No

EDITORIAL DESCRIPTION

Scope: Publishes articles on any aspect of the humanities, including fiction and poetry of merit.
Reviews books: No
Publishes notes: Yes
Languages accepted: English
Prints abstracts: No
Author-anonymous submission: No

SUBMISSION REQUIREMENTS

Author pays submission fee: No
Author pays page charges: No

Length of articles: 2,000 words
Length of notes: 800 words
Style: MLA for nonfiction submissions
Number of copies required: 1
Copyright ownership: Journal
Rejected manuscripts: Returned; enclose SASE.
Time before publication decision: 1-3 mos.
Time between decision and publication: 3-6 mos.
Number of reviewers: 2-4
Articles submitted per year: 350
Articles published per year: 10
Notes submitted per year: 200
Notes published per year: 5

(3173)
*Western Writers Series

Wayne Chatterton & James H. Maguire, Editors
Dept. of English
Boise State Univ.
Boise, ID 83725

Telephone: 208 385-1182
First published: 1972
Sponsoring organization: Boise State Univ.
ISSN: 0886-7348
MLA acronym: WWS

SUBSCRIPTION INFORMATION

Frequency of publication: 5 times/yr.
Circulation: 750
Available in microform: No
Subscription price: $3.95/volume
Year to which price refers: 1992
Subscription address: Business Manager, BSU Western Writers Series, Dept. of English, Boise State Univ., Boise, ID 83725
Subscription telephone: 208 385-3584

ADVERTISING INFORMATION

Advertising accepted: No

EDITORIAL DESCRIPTION

Scope: Publishes brief introductions to the lives and works of Western American writers.
Reviews books: No
Publishes notes: No
Languages accepted: English
Prints abstracts: No
Author-anonymous submission: No

SUBMISSION REQUIREMENTS

Restrictions on contributors: No assignments are given to graduate students.
Author pays submission fee: No
Author pays page charges: No
Length of books: 15,000 words
Style: MLA; series
Number of copies required: 2
Special requirements: Request copy of series guidelines from editor prior to submission.
Copyright ownership: Series
Rejected manuscripts: Returned
Time before publication decision: 2 mos.
Time between decision and publication: 5 yrs.
Number of reviewers: 2
Books submitted per year: 20
Books published per year: 5

(3174)
Wetenschappelijke Tijdingen op het Gebied van de Geschiedenis van de Vlaamse Beweging

G. De Smet, Editor
Congreslaan 40
9000 Ghent, Belgium

First published: 1935
Sponsoring organization: Vereniging voor Wetenschap

ISSN: 0774-532X
MLA acronym: WT

SUBSCRIPTION INFORMATION

Frequency of publication: 4 times/yr.
Circulation: 600
Available in microform: No

ADVERTISING INFORMATION

Advertising accepted: Yes

EDITORIAL DESCRIPTION

Scope: Focuses on the scientific study of the history of the Flemish movement.
Reviews books: Yes
Publishes notes: No
Languages accepted: Dutch
Prints abstracts: No

SUBMISSION REQUIREMENTS

Restrictions on contributors: None
Author pays submission fee: No
Author pays page charges: No
Length of articles: 20-25 pp.
Style: None
Number of copies required: 1
Copyright ownership: Assigned by author & journal
Rejected manuscripts: Returned
Time before publication decision: 3-6 mos.
Time between decision and publication: 1-2 mos.
Number of reviewers: 2
Articles submitted per year: 20-30
Articles published per year: 20-25
Book reviews published per year: 10-15

(3175)
*The Wicazo SA Review: A Journal of Indian Studies

Elizabeth Cook-Lynn, Beatrice Medicine, William Willard, & Roger Buffalohead, Editors
Route 8 Box 510
Dakota Meadows
Rapid City, SD 57702

Telephone: 605 341-3228
First published: 1985
ISSN: 0749-6427
MLA acronym: WSaR

SUBSCRIPTION INFORMATION

Frequency of publication: 2 times/yr. (Spring, Fall)
Circulation: 500
Available in microform: No
Subscription price: $20.00/yr.
Year to which price refers: 1992

ADVERTISING INFORMATION

Advertising accepted: Yes
Advertising rates: $60.00/quarter page; $100.00/half page; $175.00/full page; $200.00/inside back cover; $200.00/half back cover

EDITORIAL DESCRIPTION

Scope: Journal is devoted to the development of Native American studies as an academic discipline.
Reviews books: Yes
Publishes notes: Yes
Languages accepted: English; Spanish; translations in Native American languages
Prints abstracts: Yes

SUBMISSION REQUIREMENTS

Restrictions on contributors: None
Author pays submission fee: No
Author pays page charges: No

Length of articles: 6,000-8,000 words
Style: MLA
Number of copies required: 2
Copyright ownership: Author
Rejected manuscripts: Returned; enclose SASE.
Time before publication decision: 10 weeks maximum
Time between decision and publication: 3 mos.
Number of reviewers: 2
Articles published per year: 6-8
Book reviews published per year: 8-10

(3176)
*Wide Angle: A Film Quarterly of Theory, Criticism, and Practice

Ruth Bradley, Editor
School of Film
378 Lindley Hall
Ohio Univ.
Athens, OH 45701

First published: 1978
Sponsoring organization: Ohio Univ.; Athens Center for Film & Video
ISSN: 0160-6840
MLA acronym: WAn

SUBSCRIPTION INFORMATION

Frequency of publication: 4 times/yr. (Jan., Apr., July, Oct.)
Circulation: 2,000
Available in microform: Yes
Subscription price: $52.00/yr. institutions US; $21.00/yr. individuals US; add $4.20/yr. postage Canada & Mexico, $11.00/yr. elsewhere
Year to which price refers: 1993
Subscription address: Johns Hopkins Univ. Press, Journals Publishing Division, 2715 North Charles St., Baltimore, MD 21218-4319
Subscription telephone: 410 516-6944; 800 537-5487
Subscription fax: 410 516-6998

ADVERTISING INFORMATION

Advertising accepted: Yes
Advertising rates: $125.00/half page; $200.00/full page

EDITORIAL DESCRIPTION

Scope: Publishes articles on classical and avant-garde films, film theory and interpretations; critical analyses; and coverage of national cinema from the United States, Europe, Japan, Australia, Latin America, and the Third World.
Reviews books: Yes
Languages accepted: English
Prints abstracts: No
Author-anonymous submission: No

SUBMISSION REQUIREMENTS

Restrictions on contributors: None
Author pays submission fee: No
Author pays page charges: No
Length of articles: 4,000 words
Length of book reviews: 2,000 words
Style: MLA
Number of copies required: 3
Special requirements: Submit an abstract of a maximum of 250 words, and a brief biographical sketch of the author.
Copyright ownership: Journal
Rejected manuscripts: Not returned
Time before publication decision: 4 mos.
Time between decision and publication: 1 yr.
Number of reviewers: 3
Articles published per year: 23
Book reviews published per year: 11

(3177)
*Wiener Arbeiten zur Deutschen Literatur

Hedwig Heger, Wendelin Schmidt-Dengler, & Werner Welzig, Editors
c/o Wilhelm Braumüller
Universitäts-Verlagsbuchhandlung GmbH
Servitengasse 5
1092 Vienna, Austria

Telephone: (43) 222 3191159; (43) 222 3191482
Fax: (43) 222 3102805
First published: 1970
Sponsoring organization: Univ. Wien, Inst. für Germanistik
ISSN: 0083-9906
MLA acronym: WADL

SUBSCRIPTION INFORMATION

Frequency of publication: Irregular
Circulation: 600
Available in microform: No

ADVERTISING INFORMATION

Advertising accepted: No

EDITORIAL DESCRIPTION

Scope: Publishes studies on German literature.
Reviews books: No
Publishes notes: No
Languages accepted: German
Prints abstracts: No

SUBMISSION REQUIREMENTS

Author pays submission fee: No
Author pays page charges: No
Length of books: No restrictions
Style: None
Number of copies required: 1
Special requirements: Submit typescript.
Copyright ownership: Wilhelm Braumüller
Rejected manuscripts: Returned
Time before publication decision: 4 mos.
Time between decision and publication: 1 yr.
Number of reviewers: 4

(3178)
*Wiener Beiträge zur Englischen Philologie

Siegfried Korninger, G. Bauer, H. Foltinek, H. Kühnelt, Franz Karl Stanzel, & E. Stürzl, Editors
c/o Wilhelm Braumüller
Universitäts-Verlagsbuchhandlung GmbH
Servitengasse 5
1092 Vienna, Austria

Telephone: (43) 222 3191159; (43) 22 3191482
Fax: (43) 222 3102805
First published: 1953
ISSN: 0083-9914
MLA acronym: WBEP

SUBSCRIPTION INFORMATION

Frequency of publication: Irregular
Circulation: 600
Available in microform: No

ADVERTISING INFORMATION

Advertising accepted: No

EDITORIAL DESCRIPTION

Scope: Publishes studies on English philology.
Reviews books: No
Publishes notes: No
Languages accepted: English; German
Prints abstracts: No

SUBMISSION REQUIREMENTS

Author pays submission fee: No
Author pays page charges: No
Copyright ownership: Wilhelm Braumüller

(3179)
Wiener Linguistische Gazette

John Rennison, Editor
Inst. für Sprachwissenschaft
Liechtensteinstr. 46a
1090 Vienna, Austria

First published: 1972
Sponsoring organization: Univ. Wien, Inst. für Sprachwissenschaft
MLA acronym: WLG

SUBSCRIPTION INFORMATION

Frequency of publication: 2-3 times/yr.
Circulation: 150
Available in microform: No

ADVERTISING INFORMATION

Advertising accepted: Yes

EDITORIAL DESCRIPTION

Scope: Publishes articles on general linguistics, theoretical and applied linguistics, sociolinguistics, psycholinguistics, and text linguistics.
Reviews books: No
Languages accepted: English; German
Prints abstracts: Yes

SUBMISSION REQUIREMENTS

Restrictions on contributors: Contributors must be associated with the Univ. of Vienna.
Author pays submission fee: No
Author pays page charges: No
Length of articles: 1,200-9,000 words
Style: MLA preferred
Number of copies required: 1
Special requirements: Submit camera-ready copy.
Copyright ownership: Author
Rejected manuscripts: Returned
Time before publication decision: 1 mo.
Time between decision and publication: 8 mos. maximum
Number of reviewers: 3-6
Articles submitted per year: 25
Articles published per year: 14

(3180)
*Wiener Slavistisches Jahrbuch

G. Hüttl-Folter, R. Katičić, F. V. Mareš, G. Wytrzenst, & Josef Vintr, Editors
c/o J. Vintr
Inst. für Slawistik
Univ. Wien
Liebiggasse 5
1010 Vienna, Austria

Telephone: (43) 222 51581402
Fax: (43) 222 5139541
First published: 1950
Sponsoring organization: Bundesministerium für Wissenschaft & Forschung, Vienna
ISSN: 0084-0041
MLA acronym: WSJ

SUBSCRIPTION INFORMATION

Frequency of publication: Annual
Circulation: 500
Available in microform: No
Subscription address: Verlag der Österreichischen, Akademie der Wissenschaften, Dr. Ignaz Seipel-Platz 2, 1010 Vienna, Austria

ADVERTISING INFORMATION

Advertising accepted: Yes

EDITORIAL DESCRIPTION

Scope: Publishes articles and reviews of Slavic studies.
Reviews books: Yes
Publishes notes: Yes
Languages accepted: English; French; German; Russian; Slavic languages
Prints abstracts: No
Author-anonymous submission: No

SUBMISSION REQUIREMENTS

Restrictions on contributors: None
Author pays submission fee: No
Author pays page charges: No
Length of articles: 15 pp.
Length of book reviews: 4 pp.
Length of notes: 2 pp.
Style: Journal
Number of copies required: 2
Special requirements: Submit original typescript.
Copyright ownership: Verlag der Österreichischen Akademie der Wissenschaften
Rejected manuscripts: Returned
Time before publication decision: 3 mos.
Time between decision and publication: 1-2 yrs.
Number of reviewers: 2
Articles submitted per year: 10-12
Articles published per year: 7-10
Book reviews submitted per year: 20
Book reviews published per year: 10-15
Notes submitted per year: 20
Notes published per year: 5-10

(3181)
*Wiener Slawistischer Almanach

Aage Hansen-Löve & Tilmann Reuther, Editors
Inst. für Slawistik der Univ. Wien
Liebiggasse 5
1010 Vienna, Austria

Additional editorial address: Inst. fü Slavische Philologie, Univ. München, Geschwister-Scholl-Platz 1, 8000 Munich 22, Germany
First published: 1978
ISSN: 0258-6819
MLA acronym: WSlA

SUBSCRIPTION INFORMATION

Frequency of publication: 2 times/yr.
Circulation: 180
Available in microform: No
Subscription price: 84 DM/yr.
Year to which price refers: 1991
Subscription address: Buchvertrieb A. Neimanis, Hans-Sachs-Str. 10, 8000 Munich 5, Germany
Subscription telephone: (49) 89 263076

ADVERTISING INFORMATION

Advertising accepted: No

EDITORIAL DESCRIPTION

Scope: Publishes articles on Slavic studies in linguistics and literature.
Reviews books: Yes
Publishes notes: No
Languages accepted: English; French; German; Italian; Russian; Czech; Polish; Serbo-Croatian; Slovenian
Prints abstracts: No
Author-anonymous submission: No

SUBMISSION REQUIREMENTS

Restrictions on contributors: None
Author pays submission fee: No
Author pays page charges: No
Length of articles: 30 pp.

Length of book reviews: 3 pp.
Style: MLA
Number of copies required: 1
Special requirements: Submit original typescript.
Copyright ownership: Journal
Rejected manuscripts: Returned
Time before publication decision: 3 mos.
Time between decision and publication: 1 yr.
Number of reviewers: 1-2
Articles submitted per year: 50
Articles published per year: 30
Book reviews submitted per year: 10
Book reviews published per year: 8

(3182)
*Wiener Zeitschrift für die Kunde Südasiens und Archiv für Indische Philosophie

G. Oberhammer, Editor
Inst. für Indologie der Univ. Wien
Universitätsstr. 7
1010 Vienna, Austria

Telephone: (43) 1 401032569
Fax: (43) 1 4020533
First published: 1957
Sponsoring organization: Bundesministerium für Wissenschaft & Forschung, Vienna
ISSN: 0084-0084
MLA acronym: WZKS

SUBSCRIPTION INFORMATION

Frequency of publication: Annual
Circulation: 420
Available in microform: No
Subscription price: 490 S/yr.
Year to which price refers: 1991
Subscription address: Österreichische Akademie der Wissenschaften, Dr. Ignaz-Seipel-Platz, 1010 Vienna, Austria
Subscription telephone: (43) 1 51581401
Subscription fax: (43) 1 5139541

ADVERTISING INFORMATION

Advertising accepted: No

EDITORIAL DESCRIPTION

Scope: Focuses on the propagation of philological studies in Vedic, Sanskrit, and Prakrit literatures with special regard to the history of Indian religions and philosophies.
Reviews books: Yes
Publishes notes: No
Languages accepted: English; French; German; Italian
Prints abstracts: No
Author-anonymous submission: No

SUBMISSION REQUIREMENTS

Restrictions on contributors: None
Author pays submission fee: No
Author pays page charges: No
Length of articles: 5-40 pp.
Length of book reviews: 1-3 pp.
Style: Journal
Number of copies required: 1
Special requirements: Include a short summary in English if the paper is written in a language other than English.
Copyright ownership: Österreichische Akademie der Wissenschaften
Rejected manuscripts: Returned
Time before publication decision: 1-2 weeks
Time between decision and publication: 1-2 yrs.
Number of reviewers: 1-2
Articles submitted per year: 15-18
Articles published per year: 8-12
Book reviews submitted per year: 15-25
Book reviews published per year: 15-20

(3183)
*Wild About Wilde Newsletter

Carmel McCaffrey, Editor
2542 Vance Dr.
Mount Airy, MD 21771

Telephone: 410 875-0699
First published: 1986
MLA acronym: WAWN

SUBSCRIPTION INFORMATION

Frequency of publication: 2 times/yr.
Circulation: 400
Available in microform: No
Subscription price: $6.00/yr.
Year to which price refers: 1992

ADVERTISING INFORMATION

Advertising accepted: No

EDITORIAL DESCRIPTION

Scope: Publishes short articles, book reviews, and news that deal with all aspects of Oscar Wilde's work. Also includes extracts from Oscar Wilde's works and letters.
Reviews books: Yes
Publishes notes: Yes
Languages accepted: English
Prints abstracts: No

SUBMISSION REQUIREMENTS

Author pays submission fee: No
Author pays page charges: No
Length of articles: 800 words
Length of book reviews: 500 words
Length of notes: 100 words
Number of copies required: 1
Copyright ownership: Editor
Rejected manuscripts: Returned at author's request
Time before publication decision: 1 mo.
Time between decision and publication: 6 mos. maximum
Number of reviewers: 1
Articles submitted per year: 10
Articles published per year: 7
Book reviews published per year: 2
Notes published per year: 2

(3184)
Wilkie Collins Society Journal

Kirk H. Beetz, Editor
1307 F St.
Davis, CA 95616-1101

First published: 1981
Sponsoring organization: Wilkie Collins Soc.
ISSN: 0897-2982
MLA acronym: WCSJ

SUBSCRIPTION INFORMATION

Frequency of publication: Annual (Sept.)
Available in microform: No

ADVERTISING INFORMATION

Advertising accepted: No

EDITORIAL DESCRIPTION

Scope: Journal publishes articles on Wilkie Collins and such related topics as mystery fiction, Gothic horror fiction, and the works of Dickens and Reade.
Reviews books: Yes
Publishes notes: Yes
Languages accepted: English
Prints abstracts: No
Author-anonymous submission: No

SUBMISSION REQUIREMENTS

Restrictions on contributors: None
Author pays submission fee: No
Author pays page charges: No
Length of articles: 10,000 words maximum
Length of book reviews: 500-2,000 words
Length of notes: 50-5,000 words
Style: MLA
Number of copies required: 1-2
Special requirements: Dot matrix printouts are not accepted.
Copyright ownership: Reverts to author
Rejected manuscripts: Returned; enclose SASE.
Time before publication decision: 1-3 mos.
Time between decision and publication: 4-16 mos.
Number of reviewers: 2
Articles submitted per year: 10
Articles published per year: 3
Book reviews submitted per year: 10
Book reviews published per year: 1
Notes submitted per year: 10
Notes published per year: 5

(3185)
*Willa Cather Pioneer Memorial Newsletter

John J. Murphy, Editor
326 North Webster
Red Cloud, NE 68970

Telephone: 402 746-2653
Fax: 402 746-2685
First published: 1957
Sponsoring organization: Willa Cather Pioneer Memorial & Educational Foundation
ISSN: 0197-663X
MLA acronym: WCPMN

SUBSCRIPTION INFORMATION

Frequency of publication: 4 times/yr.
Circulation: 1,700
Available in microform: No
Subscription price: $15.00/yr.
Year to which price refers: 1992

ADVERTISING INFORMATION

Advertising accepted: No

EDITORIAL DESCRIPTION

Scope: Promotes and assists in the development and preservation of the art, literature, and historical collection relating to the life, time, and work of Willa Cather.
Reviews books: Yes
Publishes notes: Yes
Languages accepted: English
Prints abstracts: No
Author-anonymous submission: Yes

SUBMISSION REQUIREMENTS

Restrictions on contributors: Notes are usually written by editor.
Author pays submission fee: No
Author pays page charges: No
Length of articles: 1,000 words
Length of book reviews: 50 words
Length of notes: 50 words
Style: MLA
Number of copies required: 1
Copyright ownership: Willa Cather Pioneer Memorial & Educational Foundation
Rejected manuscripts: Returned; enclose return postage.
Time before publication decision: 6 mos.
Time between decision and publication: 2 mos.
Number of reviewers: 3
Articles submitted per year: 25
Articles published per year: 20
Book reviews submitted per year: 5
Book reviews published per year: 5

(3186)
*The William and Mary Quarterly: A Magazine of Early American History and Culture

Michael McGiffert, John E. Selby, & Ann Gross, Editors
P.O. Box 220
Williamsburg, VA 23187

Telephone: 804 221-1125
Fax: 804 221-1287
First published: 1892
Sponsoring organization: Inst. of Early American History & Culture, Williamsburg, VA
ISSN: 0043-5597
MLA acronym: WMQ

SUBSCRIPTION INFORMATION

Frequency of publication: 4 times/yr. (Jan., Apr., July, Oct.)
Circulation: 3,700
Available in microform: Yes
Subscription price: $30.00/yr. institutions; $25.00/yr. individuals; $12.50/yr. students; add $4.00/yr. postage outside US
Year to which price refers: 1992
Subscription telephone: 804 221-1124

ADVERTISING INFORMATION

Advertising accepted: Yes
Advertising rates: $85.00/half page; $150.00/full page

EDITORIAL DESCRIPTION

Scope: Publishes scholarly articles and book reviews relating to the history and culture of colonial America and the early republic and related history of the British Isles, the European continent, Africa, and other areas of the New World to approximately 1815.
Reviews books: Yes
Publishes notes: Yes
Languages accepted: English
Prints abstracts: No
Author-anonymous submission: Yes

SUBMISSION REQUIREMENTS

Restrictions on contributors: None
Author pays submission fee: No
Author pays page charges: No
Length of articles: 40 typescript pp. including footnotes
Length of book reviews: 900 words
Style: Chicago with modifications
Number of copies required: 3
Copyright ownership: Author
Rejected manuscripts: Returned
Time before publication decision: 3 mos. maximum
Time between decision and publication: 12-18 mos.
Number of reviewers: 2-3
Articles submitted per year: 120
Articles published per year: 20
Book reviews submitted per year: 60
Book reviews published per year: 60
Notes published per year: 8-10

(3187)
*William Carlos Williams Review

Brian Bremen, Editor
Dept. of English
Univ. of Texas
Austin, TX 78712

Telephone: 512 471-7842
First published: 1975
Sponsoring organization: Univ. of Texas
ISSN: 0196-6258
MLA acronym: WCWR

SUBSCRIPTION INFORMATION

Frequency of publication: 2 times/yr. (Spring, Fall)
Circulation: 350
Available in microform: No
Subscription price: $10.00/yr. institutions; $8.00/yr. individuals
Year to which price refers: 1993

ADVERTISING INFORMATION

Advertising accepted: Yes
Advertising rates: $100.00/half page; $200.00/full page

EDITORIAL DESCRIPTION

Scope: Publishes articles, notes, and reviews relating to William Carlos Williams.
Reviews books: Yes
Publishes notes: Yes
Languages accepted: English
Prints abstracts: No
Author-anonymous submission: No

SUBMISSION REQUIREMENTS

Restrictions on contributors: None
Author pays submission fee: No
Author pays page charges: No
Length of articles: 10,000 words maximum; occasional exceptions are made
Length of book reviews: 1,500-2,000 words; occasional exceptions are made
Length of notes: 500-1,000 words
Style: MLA
Number of copies required: 1
Copyright ownership: Journal or author
Rejected manuscripts: Returned; enclose return postage.
Time before publication decision: 3-5 mos.
Time between decision and publication: 1-6 mos.
Number of reviewers: 2-4
Articles submitted per year: 15-20
Articles published per year: 6-10
Book reviews submitted per year: 6-10
Book reviews published per year: 6
Notes submitted per year: 6-10
Notes published per year: 6

(3188)
*The Winesburg Eagle: The Official Publication of the Sherwood Anderson Society

Charles E. Modlin & Hilbert H. Campbell, Editors
Dept. of English
Virginia Polytechnic Inst. & State Univ.
Blacksburg, VA 24061-0112

First published: 1975
Sponsoring organization: Sherwood Anderson Soc.
ISSN: 0147-3166
MLA acronym: WE

SUBSCRIPTION INFORMATION

Frequency of publication: 2 times/yr. (Jan., July)
Circulation: 200-300
Available in microform: No
Subscription price: $8.00/yr.
Year to which price refers: 1992

ADVERTISING INFORMATION

Advertising accepted: Yes

EDITORIAL DESCRIPTION

Scope: Publishes scholarship on Sherwood Anderson.
Reviews books: Yes
Publishes notes: Yes
Languages accepted: English
Prints abstracts: No
Author-anonymous submission: No

SUBMISSION REQUIREMENTS

Restrictions on contributors: None
Author pays submission fee: No
Author pays page charges: No
Length of articles: 4,000 words maximum
Length of book reviews: 750 words
Length of notes: 500 words
Style: MLA
Number of copies required: 1
Copyright ownership: Sherwood Anderson Soc.
Rejected manuscripts: Returned; enclose return postage.
Time before publication decision: 3 weeks
Time between decision and publication: 6 mos.
Number of reviewers: 1-3
Articles submitted per year: 12
Articles published per year: 8
Book reviews submitted per year: 2
Book reviews published per year: 2
Notes submitted per year: 4
Notes published per year: 1-2

(3189)
*Winterthur Portfolio: A Journal of American Material Culture

Catherine E. Hutchins, Susan Randolph, Onie Rollins, Teresa Gawinski, & Shirley Wajda, Editors
Winterthur Museum
Winterthur, DE 19735

Telephone: 302 888-4613
Fax: 302 888-4880
First published: 1979
Sponsoring organization: Henry Francis du Pont Winterthur Museum
ISSN: 0084-0416
MLA acronym: WPo

SUBSCRIPTION INFORMATION

Frequency of publication: 3 times/yr. (Spring, Summer-Autumn, Winter)
Circulation: 2,000
Available in microform: Yes
Subscription price: $30.00/yr. individuals; $24.00/yr. students
Year to which price refers: 1992
Subscription address: Univ. of Chicago Press, Journals Division, P.O. Box 37005, Chicago, IL 60637
Subscription fax: 312 702-0694

ADVERTISING INFORMATION

Advertising accepted: Yes

EDITORIAL DESCRIPTION

Scope: Publishes articles on the arts in America in such fields as architectural history, art history, folklore, and decorative arts. Analytical articles are preferred, as are articles that integrate artifacts into their cultural framework.
Reviews books: Yes
Publishes notes: Yes
Languages accepted: English
Prints abstracts: No
Author-anonymous submission: Yes

SUBMISSION REQUIREMENTS

Restrictions on contributors: None
Author pays submission fee: No
Author pays page charges: No
Length of articles: 5,000-15,000 words
Length of book reviews: 1,500-4,000 words
Length of notes: 4,000-5,000 words
Style: Chicago
Number of copies required: 1
Special requirements: Submit double-spaced manuscript. If pictures are to be used, submit 8 x 10 inch glossy black & white photographs.
Copyright ownership: Winterthur Museum

Rejected manuscripts: Returned
Time before publication decision: 4 mos.
Time between decision and publication: 8-12 mos.
Number of reviewers: 3
Articles submitted per year: 75
Articles published per year: 12
Book reviews submitted per year: 35-40
Book reviews published per year: 35-40
Notes submitted per year: 1-2

(3190)
*Wirkendes Wort: Deutsche Sprache und Literatur in Forschung und Lehre

Heinz Rölleke & Theodor Lewandowski, Editors
Bouvier Verlag
Am Hof 28
5300 Bonn 1, Germany

Additional editorial address: Lothar Bluhm, Bergische Univ., FB 4, Gauss Str. 20, 5600 Wuppertal 1, Germany
First published: 1950
ISSN: 0723-6778
MLA acronym: WWort

SUBSCRIPTION INFORMATION

Frequency of publication: 3 times/yr.
Circulation: 3,000
Available in microform: No

ADVERTISING INFORMATION

Advertising accepted: Yes

EDITORIAL DESCRIPTION

Scope: Publishes articles on German language and literature.
Reviews books: Yes
Publishes notes: No
Languages accepted: German
Prints abstracts: No

SUBMISSION REQUIREMENTS

Restrictions on contributors: None
Author pays submission fee: No
Author pays page charges: No
Length of articles: 8,000-10,000 words
Length of book reviews: 7,500 words
Style: Vierteljahresschrift
Number of copies required: 2
Copyright ownership: Author; reverts to journal after 1 yr.
Rejected manuscripts: Returned
Time before publication decision: 1-2 mos.
Time between decision and publication: 4-6 mos.
Number of reviewers: 2
Articles submitted per year: 80
Articles published per year: 30-35
Book reviews published per year: 15-20

(3191)
Wissenschaftliche Zeitschrift der Friedrich-Schiller-Universität Jena. Gesellschaftswissenschaftliche Reihe

Verlagsabteilung der Friedrich-Schiller-Univ.
Ernst-Thälmann-Ring 24a
6900 Jena, Germany

First published: 1951
Sponsoring organization: Friedrich-Schiller-Univ., Jena
ISSN: 0138-1652
MLA acronym: WZUJ

(3192)
Wissenschaftliche Zeitschrift der Humboldt-Universität zu Berlin. Gesellschaftswissenschaftliche Reihe

Günter Hellriegel, Editor
Mittelstr. 7-8
1086 Berlin, Germany

First published: 1951
Sponsoring organization: Humboldt-Univ., Berlin
ISSN: 0522-9855
MLA acronym: WZUB

SUBSCRIPTION INFORMATION

Frequency of publication: 6 times/yr.
Available in microform: No
Subscription address: Deutscher Buch Export-Import, Leninstr. 16, 7010 Leipzig, Germany

ADVERTISING INFORMATION

Advertising accepted: No

EDITORIAL DESCRIPTION

Scope: Publishes articles on social studies and philology.
Reviews books: No
Languages accepted: German; Russian; English; French
Prints abstracts: Yes

SUBMISSION REQUIREMENTS

Restrictions on contributors: Contributors must be affiliated with Berlin Univ.
Author pays submission fee: No
Author pays page charges: No
Length of articles: 25 pp.
Style: None
Number of copies required: 2
Special requirements: Submit original typescript and a short abstract in German, English, French, & Russian; use size A4 (8 1/4 in. x 11 3/4 in.) paper.
Copyright ownership: Author
Rejected manuscripts: Returned
Time before publication decision: 3 mos.
Time between decision and publication: 1 yr.
Number of reviewers: 3
Articles submitted per year: 120
Articles published per year: 90

(3193)
Wissenschaftliche Zeitschrift der Martin-Luther Universität Halle-Wittenberg. Gesellschafts- und Sprachwissenschaftliche Reihe

Günter Scholz, Editor
August-Bebel-Str. 13
4010 Halle (Saale), Germany

First published: 1951
Sponsoring organization: Martin Luther Univ.
ISSN: 0438-4385
MLA acronym: WZUH

SUBSCRIPTION INFORMATION

Frequency of publication: 6 times/yr.
Available in microform: No
Subscription address: Buchexport, Leninstr. 16, 7010 Leipzig, Germany

ADVERTISING INFORMATION

Advertising accepted: No

EDITORIAL DESCRIPTION

Reviews books: Yes
Publishes notes: Yes

Languages accepted: German; English; Russian; French
Prints abstracts: No
Author-anonymous submission: No

SUBMISSION REQUIREMENTS

Restrictions on contributors: None
Author pays submission fee: No
Author pays page charges: No
Length of articles: 10-15 pp.
Length of book reviews: 1-2 pp.
Length of notes: 1-2 pp.
Style: Journal
Number of copies required: 1
Special requirements: Submit original typescript.
Copyright ownership: Author
Rejected manuscripts: Not returned
Time before publication decision: 1 mo.
Time between decision and publication: 5-8 mos.
Articles submitted per year: 130
Articles published per year: 120
Book reviews submitted per year: 70
Book reviews published per year: 70
Notes submitted per year: 5-10
Notes published per year: 5-10

(3194)
Wissenschaftliche Zeitschrift der Wilhelm-Pieck-Universität Rostock. Gesellschaftswissenschaftliche Reihe

Wolfgang Brauer, Editor
Wilhelm-Pieck-Univ. Rostock
Abteilung Wissenschaftspublizistik
Vogelsang 13/14
2500 Rostock, Germany

First published: 1951
Sponsoring organization: Wilhelm-Pieck-Univ. Rostock
ISSN: 0323-4630
MLA acronym: WZUR

SUBSCRIPTION INFORMATION

Frequency of publication: 10 times/yr.
Circulation: 1,250
Available in microform: No
Subscription address: Buchexport, Leninstr. 16, 7010 Leipzig, Germany

ADVERTISING INFORMATION

Advertising accepted: No

EDITORIAL DESCRIPTION

Scope: Publishes scientific papers in all fields represented at Wilhelm-Pieck-University as well as lessons and lectures given by guests.
Reviews books: No
Publishes notes: No
Languages accepted: German; Russian; English; French; Spanish
Prints abstracts: Yes
Author-anonymous submission: No

SUBMISSION REQUIREMENTS

Restrictions on contributors: Authors must be associated with the Univ. of Rostock.
Author pays submission fee: No
Author pays page charges: No
Length of articles: No restrictions
Number of copies required: 1
Copyright ownership: Wilhelm-Pieck-Univ. Rostock
Time before publication decision: 2 mos.
Time between decision and publication: 10 mos.
Number of reviewers: 2-3
Articles submitted per year: 200-250
Articles published per year: 200

(3195)
*Wolfenbütteler Barock-Nachrichten

Jill Bepler & Barbara Strutz, Editors
Herzog August Bibliothek
Postfach 1364
3340 Wolfenbüttel, Germany

First published: 1974
Sponsoring organization: Herzog August Bibliothek; Wolfenbütteler Arbeitskreis für Barockforschung
ISSN: 0340-6318
MLA acronym: WBN

SUBSCRIPTION INFORMATION

Frequency of publication: 2 times/yr.
Circulation: 800
Available in microform: No
Subscription price: 58 DM/yr.
Year to which price refers: 1992
Subscription address: Otto Harrassowitz, Postfach 2929, 6200 Wiesbaden, Germany

ADVERTISING INFORMATION

Advertising accepted: Yes

EDITORIAL DESCRIPTION

Scope: Publishes short articles and notes concerning German authors of the Baroque period and bibliographies of material concerning the German Baroque period.
Reviews books: Yes
Publishes notes: Yes
Languages accepted: German; English
Prints abstracts: No
Author-anonymous submission: No

SUBMISSION REQUIREMENTS

Restrictions on contributors: None
Author pays submission fee: No
Author pays page charges: No
Number of copies required: 1
Copyright ownership: Otto Harrassowitz
Time before publication decision: 1 week
Time between decision and publication: 3-6 mos.
Articles published per year: 10
Book reviews published per year: 6
Notes published per year: 25

(3196)
*Wolfenbütteler Beiträge: Aus den Schätzen der Herzog August Bibliothek

Paul Raabe, Editor
Herzog August Bibliothek
Postfach 1364
3340 Wolfenbüttel, Germany

Telephone: (49) 5331 808209
Fax: (49) 5331 808266; (49) 5331 808173
E-mail: S2170101@DBSTU1
First published: 1972
Sponsoring organization: Herzog August Bibliothek
ISSN: 0300-2012
MLA acronym: WolfenbüttelerB

SUBSCRIPTION INFORMATION

Frequency of publication: Annual
Circulation: 1,000
Available in microform: No
Subscription address: Verlag Vittorio Klostermann, Frauenlobstr. 22, Postfach 900601, 6000 Frankfurt am Main 90, Germany

ADVERTISING INFORMATION

Advertising accepted: No

EDITORIAL DESCRIPTION

Scope: Publishes articles on the holdings of Herzog August Bibliothek.
Reviews books: No
Publishes notes: No
Languages accepted: German; English; French
Prints abstracts: No
Author-anonymous submission: No

SUBMISSION REQUIREMENTS

Author pays submission fee: No
Author pays page charges: No
Length of articles: No restrictions
Style: Journal
Number of copies required: 1
Copyright ownership: Verlag Vittorio Klostermann
Rejected manuscripts: Returned
Time before publication decision: 1 mo.
Time between decision and publication: 6-12 mos.
Number of reviewers: 3
Articles published per year: 10

(3197)
Wolfenbütteler Studien zur Aufklärung

Claus Ritterhoff, Editor
Lessing-Akademie
Rosenwall 16
3340 Wolfenbüttel, Germany

Additional editorial address: Max Niemeyer Verlag, Postfach 2140, 7400 Tübingen, Germany
First published: 1974
Sponsoring organization: Lessing-Akademie
ISSN: 0342-5940
MLA acronym: WSA

SUBSCRIPTION INFORMATION

Frequency of publication: 2 times/yr.
Circulation: 1,000

ADVERTISING INFORMATION

Advertising accepted: No

EDITORIAL DESCRIPTION

Scope: Publishes research concerning Lessing; the Enlightenment, largely in German culture, literature, and social history, but not exclusively German; and the culture and social history of the Jews in Germany, especially in the 18th and early 19th centuries.
Reviews books: No
Publishes notes: No
Languages accepted: German; English; French
Prints abstracts: No

SUBMISSION REQUIREMENTS

Restrictions on contributors: None
Author pays submission fee: No
Author pays page charges: No
Length of articles: 20-40 pp.
Copyright ownership: Max Niemeyer Verlag
Time before publication decision: 3 mos.
Time between decision and publication: 8-10 mos.
Number of reviewers: 2-3
Articles published per year: 20
Books published per year: 2

(3198)
*Women and Language

Anita Taylor, Editor
Communication Dept.
George Mason Univ.
Fairfax, VA 22030

Telephone: 703 993-1099
Fax: 703 993-1096
E-mail: ATAYLOR@GMUVAX
First published: 1976
Sponsoring organization: Organization for the Study of Communication, Language & Gender
ISSN: 8755-4550
MLA acronym: W&Lang

SUBSCRIPTION INFORMATION

Frequency of publication: 2 times/yr.
Circulation: 400
Available in microform: No
Subscription price: $15.00/yr. institutions US; $20.00/yr. institutions elsewhere; $10.00/yr. members US; $13.00/yr. members Canada; $18.00/yr. members elsewhere; $15.00/yr. nonmembers US; $18.00/yr. nonmembers Canada; $23.00/yr. nonmembers elsewhere
Year to which price refers: 1993

ADVERTISING INFORMATION

Advertising accepted: No

EDITORIAL DESCRIPTION

Scope: Reports books, journals, articles, research in progress; publishes short articles; identifies courses, conferences, and other events relevant to the study of language and gender; and communicates observations and information from magazines, newspapers, scholarly publications, and correspondents from all over the world. Includes scholarship from anthropology, communication, journalism, linguistics, library science, literary studies, etc.
Reviews books: Yes
Publishes notes: Yes
Languages accepted: English
Prints abstracts: No
Author-anonymous submission: No

SUBMISSION REQUIREMENTS

Restrictions on contributors: Most reviews are solicited.
Author pays submission fee: No
Author pays page charges: No
Length of articles: 2,000-3,000 words
Length of book reviews: 750 words
Length of notes: 500 words
Style: MLA; American Psychological Assn.
Number of copies required: 3
Special requirements: Submit original typescript and 2 copies.
Copyright ownership: Journal
Rejected manuscripts: Not returned
Time before publication decision: 2-3 mos.
Time between decision and publication: 6-9 mos.
Number of reviewers: 2
Articles submitted per year: 25-30
Articles published per year: 10-12
Book reviews submitted per year: 10-12
Book reviews published per year: 15-20
Notes published per year: 20-30

(3199)
Women & Literature

Holmes & Meier Publishers
30 Irving Place
New York, NY 10003

Telephone: 212 254-4100
Fax: 212 254-4104
First published: 1981

MLA acronym: W&L

SUBSCRIPTION INFORMATION

Frequency of publication: Irregular
Available in microform: No

ADVERTISING INFORMATION

Advertising accepted: No

EDITORIAL DESCRIPTION

Scope: Focuses on women writers and the treatment of women in literature.
Reviews books: No
Languages accepted: English
Prints abstracts: No

SUBMISSION REQUIREMENTS

Restrictions on contributors: None
Author pays submission fee: No
Style: MLA
Number of copies required: 2
Copyright ownership: Holmes & Meier Publishers
Rejected manuscripts: Returned; enclose return postage.
Number of reviewers: 3

(3200)
*Women & Performance: A Journal of Feminist Theory

Jill Dolan, Editor
NYU/Tisch School of the Arts
Performance Studies Dept.
721 Broadway, 6th Fl.
New York, NY 10003

First published: 1983
Sponsoring organization: Women & Performance Project, Inc.
ISSN: 0740-770X
MLA acronym: W&P

SUBSCRIPTION INFORMATION

Frequency of publication: Irregular
Circulation: 1,000
Available in microform: No

ADVERTISING INFORMATION

Advertising accepted: Yes

EDITORIAL DESCRIPTION

Scope: Publishes articles on feminist issues in dance, theater, film, music, video, and ritual. It includes articles on feminist performance, and reviews of both feminist and mainstream performance. Also publishes scripts of performance and film.
Reviews books: Yes
Languages accepted: English
Prints abstracts: No
Author-anonymous submission: Yes

SUBMISSION REQUIREMENTS

Author pays submission fee: No
Author pays page charges: No
Length of articles: 15-20 double-spaced pp.
Style: MLA; Chicago
Number of copies required: 2
Copyright ownership: Author
Rejected manuscripts: Returned; enclose SASE.
Time before publication decision: 1-2 mos.
Time between decision and publication: 1-2 mos.
Number of reviewers: 7
Articles submitted per year: 20

(3201)
*Women in German Yearbook: Feminist Studies in German Literature and Culture

Jeanette Clausen & Sara Friedrichmeyer, Editors
Dept. of Modern Foreign Languages
Indiana Univ. - Purdue Univ.
Fort Wayne, IN 46805-1499

Additional editorial address: Sara Friedrichmeyer, Foreign Languages, Univ. of Cincinnati-RWC, Cincinnati, OH 45236
Telephone: 219 481-6836 (J. Clausen); 513 745-5679 (S. Friedrichmeyer)
Fax: 219 481-6985 (J. Clausen); 513 745-5767 (S. Friedrichmeyer)
First published: 1985
Historical variations in title: Formerly *Women in German Yearbook: Feminist Studies and German Culture*
Sponsoring organization: Coalition of Women in German
ISSN: 1058-7446
MLA acronym: WGY

SUBSCRIPTION INFORMATION

Frequency of publication: Annual
Circulation: 550
Available in microform: No
Subscription address: Univ. of Nebraska Press, 328 Nebraska Hall, 901 North 17th St., Lincoln, NE 68588-0520
Subscription telephone: 402 472-3581
Subscription fax: 402 472-6214

ADVERTISING INFORMATION

Advertising accepted: No

EDITORIAL DESCRIPTION

Scope: Publishes articles on feminist scholarship related to any aspect of German literary, cultural, and language studies.
Reviews books: Yes
Publishes notes: No
Languages accepted: English; German
Prints abstracts: Yes
Author-anonymous submission: Yes

SUBMISSION REQUIREMENTS

Restrictions on contributors: Contributors are asked to join the Coalition of Women in German. Unsolicited reviews are not accepted.
Author pays submission fee: No
Author pays page charges: No
Length of articles: 7,500 words
Style: MLA
Number of copies required: 2
Special requirements: Submit original typescript and 1 copy. Typescript must be prepared for anonymous review.
Copyright ownership: Univ. of Nebraska Press
Rejected manuscripts: Returned
Time before publication decision: 3-6 mos.
Time between decision and publication: 6-12 mos.
Number of reviewers: 2 minimum
Articles submitted per year: 30
Articles published per year: 8-12
Book reviews published per year: 1-2

(3202)
Women's Studies: An Interdisciplinary Journal

Wendy Martin, Editor
Dept. of English
Claremont Graduate School
Claremont, CA 91711-6163

Telephone: 909 621-8555 ext. 2974
First published: 1972
Sponsoring organization: National Women's Studies Assn.
ISSN: 0049-7878
MLA acronym: WS

SUBSCRIPTION INFORMATION

Frequency of publication: 3 times/yr.
Circulation: 800
Available in microform: No
Subscription address: Gordon & Breach Science Publishers Ltd., Box 786, Cooper Station, New York, NY 10276
Subscription telephone: 212 206-8900
Subscription fax: 212 645-2459

ADVERTISING INFORMATION

Advertising accepted: Yes

EDITORIAL DESCRIPTION

Scope: A forum for the presentation of scholarship and criticism about women in the fields of literature, history, art, sociology, law, political science, economics, anthropology, and the sciences. Also publishes poetry, short fiction, film and book reviews.
Reviews books: Yes
Publishes notes: No
Languages accepted: English
Prints abstracts: Yes
Author-anonymous submission: Yes

SUBMISSION REQUIREMENTS

Restrictions on contributors: None
Author pays submission fee: No
Author pays page charges: No
Length of articles: 15-20 pp.
Length of book reviews: 500-1,000 words
Style: MLA
Number of copies required: 2
Special requirements: Submit double-spaced typescript; include a 100-150 word abstract.
Copyright ownership: Gordon & Breach Science Publishers, Ltd.
Rejected manuscripts: Returned; enclose SASE.
Time before publication decision: 3 mos.
Time between decision and publication: 1 yr.
Number of reviewers: 1-3
Articles submitted per year: 200-300
Articles published per year: 60
Book reviews submitted per year: 100
Book reviews published per year: 9-12

(3203)
*WORD: Journal of the International Linguistic Association

Ruth Brend, John R. Costello, Eugénio Chang-Rodríguez, & Sheila M. Embleton, Editors
3363 Burbank Dr.
Ann Arbor, MI 48105

Telephone: 313 665-2787
E-mail: USERSX6J@UMICHUM (Bitnet); RUTH.BREND@UM.CC.UMICH.EDU (Internet)
First published: 1945
Sponsoring organization: International Linguistic Assn.
ISSN: 0043-7956
MLA acronym: Word

SUBSCRIPTION INFORMATION

Frequency of publication: 3 times/yr. (Apr., Aug., Dec.)
Circulation: 1,500
Available in microform: Yes
Subscription price: $35.00/yr.
Year to which price refers: 1992
Subscription address: T. S. Beardsley, Jr., Hispanic Soc. of America, 613 W. 155th St., New York, NY 10032

ADVERTISING INFORMATION

Advertising accepted: No

EDITORIAL DESCRIPTION

Scope: Publishes contributions on the structure, function, or historical development of natural languages, or theoretical questions relating to these.
Reviews books: Yes
Publishes notes: Yes
Languages accepted: English
Prints abstracts: Yes
Author-anonymous submission: No

SUBMISSION REQUIREMENTS

Restrictions on contributors: None
Author pays submission fee: No
Author pays page charges: No
Length of articles: No restrictions
Length of book reviews: No restrictions
Length of notes: No restrictions
Style: Journal; available in vol. 35(1) or from Managing Editor.
Number of copies required: 4
Copyright ownership: International Linguistic Assn.
Rejected manuscripts: Returned; enclose return postage.
Time before publication decision: 4 mos.
Time between decision and publication: 6-9 mos.
Number of reviewers: 4
Articles submitted per year: 30-40
Articles published per year: 15-20
Book reviews submitted per year: 20-30
Book reviews published per year: 20-30
Notes submitted per year: 2-4
Notes published per year: 3

(3204)
*Word & Image: A Journal of Verbal/Visual Enquiry

John Dixon Hunt, Editor
3 Pembroke Studios
Pembroke Gardens
London W8 6HX, England

Additional editorial address: For reviews: Eric Homberger, Univ. of East Anglia, School of English & American Studies, Norwich NR4 7TJ, England
First published: 1985
ISSN: 0266-6286
MLA acronym: W&I

SUBSCRIPTION INFORMATION

Frequency of publication: 4 times/yr. (Jan.-Mar., Apr.-June, July-Sept., Oct.-Dec.)
Available in microform: No
Subscription price: $194.00/yr. institutions; $90.00/yr. individuals
Year to which price refers: 1991
Subscription address: Taylor & Francis Ltd., Rankine Rd., Basingstoke, Hampshire RG24 0PR, England
Subscription telephone: (44) 256 840366

ADVERTISING INFORMATION

Advertising accepted: Yes

EDITORIAL DESCRIPTION

Scope: Explores all aspects of the interrelation of verbal/visual languages.
Reviews books: Yes
Publishes notes: Yes
Languages accepted: English; French
Prints abstracts: Yes, for French articles
Author-anonymous submission: No

SUBMISSION REQUIREMENTS

Restrictions on contributors: Unsolicited book reviews are not accepted.
Author pays submission fee: No
Author pays page charges: No
Length of articles: 4,000-12,000 words
Length of book reviews: 500-2,000 words
Length of notes: 500-2,000 words
Style: MLA
Number of copies required: 2
Special requirements: Submit original typescript and 1 copy.
Copyright ownership: Taylor & Francis Ltd.
Rejected manuscripts: Returned
Time before publication decision: 3 mos.
Time between decision and publication: 1 yr.
Number of reviewers: 2-3
Articles submitted per year: 200
Articles published per year: 20-25
Book reviews published per year: 12-20
Notes submitted per year: 10
Notes published per year: 2

(3205)
*Word Ways: The Journal of Recreational Linguistics

A. Ross Eckler, Editor
Spring Valley Rd.
Morristown, NJ 07960

Telephone: 201 538-4584
First published: 1968
ISSN: 0043-7980
MLA acronym: WWays

SUBSCRIPTION INFORMATION

Frequency of publication: 4 times/yr. (Feb., May, Aug., Nov.)
Circulation: 450-600
Available in microform: Yes
Subscription price: $17.00/yr.
Year to which price refers: 1992
Subscription address: Faith W. Eckler, at the above address

ADVERTISING INFORMATION

Advertising accepted: Yes
Advertising rates: $65.00/full page

EDITORIAL DESCRIPTION

Scope: Focuses on language play, including research articles, puzzles, and constrained writing.
Reviews books: Yes
Publishes notes: Yes
Languages accepted: English
Prints abstracts: No
Author-anonymous submission: No

SUBMISSION REQUIREMENTS

Restrictions on contributors: Do not submit previously published material.
Author pays submission fee: No
Author pays page charges: No
Length of articles: 500-5,000 words
Length of book reviews: 250 words
Length of notes: 250 words
Style: None
Number of copies required: 1
Copyright ownership: Publisher
Rejected manuscripts: Returned; enclose return postage.
Time before publication decision: 1 mo.
Time between decision and publication: 4 mos.
Number of reviewers: 1
Articles submitted per year: 85
Articles published per year: 75
Book reviews submitted per year: 10
Book reviews published per year: 6-10
Notes submitted per year: 10
Notes published per year: 6-10

(3206)
*The Wordsworth Circle

Marilyn Gaull, Editor
Dept. of English
Temple Univ.
Philadelphia, PA 19122

Telephone: 215 787-7344
First published: 1970
Sponsoring organization: Wordsworth-Coleridge Assn.
ISSN: 0043-8006
MLA acronym: WC

SUBSCRIPTION INFORMATION

Frequency of publication: 4 times/yr.
Circulation: 1,000
Available in microform: Yes
Subscription price: $15.00/yr., $25.00/2 yrs.
Year to which price refers: 1992
Subscription telephone: 215 787-4716 ext. 215

ADVERTISING INFORMATION

Advertising accepted: Yes
Advertising rates: $125.00/full page

EDITORIAL DESCRIPTION

Scope: The journal was founded to improve communication among colleagues interested in the first generation English Romantic writers: Wordsworth, Coleridge, Hazlitt, De Quincey, Lamb, Southey, Landor, Jane Austen, Sir Walter Scott, the minor poets, and popular writers and their times. The editor invites contributions from subscribers in the form of essays, notes, queries, conference proceedings, library collections, special events, advance notices of works to be published, and suggestions for projects. The third number (Summer) is devoted to reviews of all works published on English, American, or Continental Romanticism during the previous year.
Reviews books: Yes
Publishes notes: Yes
Languages accepted: English
Prints abstracts: No
Author-anonymous submission: Yes

SUBMISSION REQUIREMENTS

Restrictions on contributors: Contributors must be subscribers.
Author pays submission fee: No
Author pays page charges: No
Length of articles: 5,000-10,000 words
Length of book reviews: 2,500 words
Length of notes: 1,500 words
Style: Journal; MLA
Number of copies required: 2
Copyright ownership: Author
Rejected manuscripts: Returned
Time before publication decision: 3 mos.
Time between decision and publication: 3 mos.
Number of reviewers: 2
Articles submitted per year: 100
Articles published per year: 40
Book reviews submitted per year: 30
Book reviews published per year: 30
Notes submitted per year: 5-10
Notes published per year: 5-10

(3207)
*Work Papers of the Summer Institute of Linguistics, University of North Dakota Session

Robert A. Dooley & J. Albert Bickford, Editors
Summer Inst. of Linguistics, North Dakota Session
P.O. Box 8217, University Station
Grand Forks, ND 58202

Additional editorial address: 7500 W. Camp Wisdom Rd., Dallas, TX 75236

Telephone: 214 283-5778; 214 709-2401
Fax: 214 709-2433
E-mail: 66276510 (Easylink)
First published: 1957
Sponsoring organization: Summer Inst. of Linguistics
MLA acronym: WPSILUNDS

SUBSCRIPTION INFORMATION

Frequency of publication: Annual (July)
Circulation: 100
Available in microform: No
Subscription price: $6.25/yr.
Year to which price refers: 1991
Subscription address: International Academic Bookstore, 7500 W. Camp Wisdom Rd., Dallas, TX 75236
Subscription telephone: 214 709-2404

ADVERTISING INFORMATION

Advertising accepted: No

EDITORIAL DESCRIPTION

Scope: Publishes provisional results of ongoing research by members of the faculty, and some advanced students, of the Summer Institute of Linguistics, University of North Dakota session.
Reviews books: No
Publishes notes: No
Languages accepted: English
Prints abstracts: No
Author-anonymous submission: No

SUBMISSION REQUIREMENTS

Restrictions on contributors: Contributors must be associated with the Summer Inst. of Linguistics at the Univ. of North Dakota. Guest lecturers are included.
Author pays submission fee: No
Author pays page charges: No
Length of articles: 6,000 words
Style: Journal
Number of copies required: 1
Rejected manuscripts: Returned
Time before publication decision: 1 mo.
Time between decision and publication: 3 mos.
Number of reviewers: 2
Articles submitted per year: 6-7
Articles published per year: 5-6

(3208)
*Working Papers

Dept. of Linguistics
Lund Univ.
Helgonabacken 12
223 62 Lund, Sweden

First published: 1969
Sponsoring organization: Dept. of Linguistics, Lund Univ.
ISSN: 0280-526X
MLA acronym: WPLU

SUBSCRIPTION INFORMATION

Frequency of publication: Irregular
Circulation: 300
Available in microform: No

ADVERTISING INFORMATION

Advertising accepted: No

EDITORIAL DESCRIPTION

Scope: Publishes articles on general linguistics and phonetics.
Reviews books: No
Publishes notes: No
Languages accepted: English; French; German; Swedish
Prints abstracts: No

SUBMISSION REQUIREMENTS

Restrictions on contributors: Contributors must be members of the Lund Univ. Dept. of Linguistics.
Author pays submission fee: No
Author pays page charges: No
Length of articles: 10,000 words
Number of copies required: 1
Special requirements: Use A4 page format.
Copyright ownership: Author
Articles submitted per year: 10-15
Articles published per year: 10-15

(3209)
*Working Papers in Linguistics

Dept. of Linguistics
222 Oxley Hall
1712 Neil Ave.
Ohio State Univ.
Columbus, OH 43210-1298

Telephone: 614 292-4052
First published: 1967
Sponsoring organization: Dept. of Linguistics, Ohio State Univ.
ISSN: 0473-9604
MLA acronym: WPL

SUBSCRIPTION INFORMATION

Frequency of publication: Irregular
Circulation: 500
Available in microform: No
Subscription price: $10.00/issue
Year to which price refers: 1992

ADVERTISING INFORMATION

Advertising accepted: No

EDITORIAL DESCRIPTION

Scope: Reports on current research by linguists associated with the Ohio State University.
Reviews books: Yes
Languages accepted: English
Prints abstracts: No

SUBMISSION REQUIREMENTS

Restrictions on contributors: Contributions are solicited by a separate editor for each volume.
Author pays submission fee: No
Author pays page charges: No
Length of articles: No restrictions
Style: None
Copyright ownership: Ohio State Univ., Dept. of Linguistics

(3210)
*Works and Days: Essays in the Socio-Historical Dimensions of Literature and the Arts

David B. Downing, Editor
Dept. of English
110 Leonard Hall
Indiana Univ. of Pennsylvania
Indiana, PA 15705

Fax: 412 357-6213
E-mail: Downing@IUP
First published: 1979
Sponsoring organization: Indiana Univ. of Pennsylvania
ISSN: 0886-2060
MLA acronym: W&D

SUBSCRIPTION INFORMATION

Frequency of publication: 2 times/yr. (Spring, Autumn)
Circulation: 300
Available in microform: No
Subscription price: $20.00/yr. institutions; $10.00/yr. individuals
Year to which price refers: 1992

ADVERTISING INFORMATION

Advertising accepted: Yes

EDITORIAL DESCRIPTION

Scope: Publishes articles which explore the relations between the arts and their sociohistorical and sociocultural contexts.
Reviews books: Yes
Publishes notes: No
Languages accepted: English
Prints abstracts: No
Author-anonymous submission: No

SUBMISSION REQUIREMENTS

Restrictions on contributors: None
Author pays submission fee: No
Author pays page charges: No
Length of articles: No restrictions
Style: MLA
Number of copies required: 2
Special requirements: Submit double-spaced typescript.
Copyright ownership: Editor
Rejected manuscripts: Returned; enclose SASE.
Time before publication decision: 3 mos.
Time between decision and publication: 3 mos.
Number of reviewers: 3
Articles submitted per year: 30-40
Articles published per year: 10-12
Book reviews submitted per year: 6-8
Book reviews published per year: 2-4

(3211)
*World Englishes: Journal of English as an International and Intranational Language

Braj B. Kachru & Larry E. Smith, Editors
Dept. of Linguistics
Univ. of Illinois
4088 Foreign Languages Bldg.
707 South Mathews Ave.
Urbana, IL 61801

Additional editorial address: Larry E. Smith, Inst. of Culture & Communication, East-West Center, 1777 East-West Rd., Honolulu, HI 96849. Send books for review to: Peter H. Lowenberg, Dept. of Linguistics, Georgetown Univ., Washington, DC 20057.
Telephone: 217 333-3563
Fax: 217 244-3050
First published: 1982
ISSN: 0883-2919
MLA acronym: WEng

SUBSCRIPTION INFORMATION

Frequency of publication: 3 times/yr.
Available in microform: Yes
Subscription price: $200.00/yr. institutions; $40.00/yr. individuals; $35.00/yr. members
Year to which price refers: 1992
Subscription address: Pergamon Press, Inc., 660 White Plains Rd., Tarrytown, NY 10591-5153
Additional subscription address: Pergamon Press Ltd., Headington Hill Hall, Oxford OX3 0BW, England
Subscription telephone: 914 524-9200; (44) 865 794141
Subscription fax: 914 333-2444; (44) 865 743911

ADVERTISING INFORMATION

Advertising accepted: Yes

EDITORIAL DESCRIPTION

Scope: Devoted to the study of the forms and functions of varieties of English, both native and non-native, in diverse cultural and sociolinguistic contexts. Publishes articles, notes, book reviews, conference reports, research-in-progress, theses and dissertations. Includes contributions on any aspect of English studies in the broadest sense, including language, literature, and methods of teaching English as a primary or additional language, but emphasis is on data-based research with a theoretical orientation. Also considers articles of interest to researchers and teachers of English in areas such as language acquisition, bilingualism, dialectology, lexicography, sociolinguistics, stylistics, and English-based pidgin and creole languages.
Reviews books: Yes
Publishes notes: Yes
Languages accepted: English
Prints abstracts: Yes
Author-anonymous submission: Yes

SUBMISSION REQUIREMENTS

Restrictions on contributors: Most reviews and notes are by invitation.
Author pays submission fee: No
Author pays page charges: No
Length of articles: 25-30 pp.
Length of book reviews: 2,000 words
Length of notes: 1,000 words
Style: Linguistic Soc. of America with modifications
Number of copies required: 3
Special requirements: Include an abstract of 150-200 words.
Copyright ownership: Publisher
Rejected manuscripts: Returned at author's request; enclose return postage
Time before publication decision: 4-6 mos.
Time between decision and publication: 6-9 mos.
Number of reviewers: 2-3
Book reviews published per year: 20-25
Notes published per year: 10-15

(3212)
*World Literature Today: A Literary Quarterly of the University of Oklahoma

Djelal Kadir, Editor
110 Monnet Hall
630 Parrington Oval
Univ. of Oklahoma
Norman, OK 73019-0375

Telephone: 405 325-4531
Fax: 405 325-7495
First published: 1927
Sponsoring organization: Univ. of Oklahoma
ISSN: 0196-3570
MLA acronym: WLT

SUBSCRIPTION INFORMATION

Frequency of publication: 4 times/yr. (Feb., May, Aug., Nov.)
Circulation: 2,000
Available in microform: Yes
Subscription price: $36.00/yr., $56.00/2 yrs. institutions US; $24.00/yr., $40.00/2 yrs. individuals US; add $6.00/yr. postage Canada; $8.00/yr. postage elsewhere
Year to which price refers: 1992

ADVERTISING INFORMATION

Advertising accepted: Yes

EDITORIAL DESCRIPTION

Scope: Publishes short articles on contemporary writers and literary cultural movements in all countries plus reviews of contemporary *belles lettres.*

Reviews books: Yes
Publishes notes: Yes
Languages accepted: English
Prints abstracts: No
Author-anonymous submission: No

SUBMISSION REQUIREMENTS

Restrictions on contributors: None
Author pays submission fee: No
Author pays page charges: No
Length of articles: 3,000-5,000 words
Length of book reviews: 500 words
Length of notes: 200 words
Style: Chicago
Number of copies required: 1
Copyright ownership: Oklahoma Univ. Press
Rejected manuscripts: Returned; enclose return postage.
Time before publication decision: 1 mo.
Time between decision and publication: 6-12 mos.
Number of reviewers: 3
Articles submitted per year: 100
Articles published per year: 40
Book reviews submitted per year: 1,300
Book reviews published per year: 1,200
Notes submitted per year: 250
Notes published per year: 200

(3213)
*World Literature Written in English

Diana Brydon, Editor
Dept. of English
Univ. of Guelph
Guelph, Ontario N1G 2W1, Canada

Telephone: 519 824-4120 ext. 3252; 519 856-1042
Fax: 519 837-1315
First published: 1962
Sponsoring organization: Univ. of Guelph
ISSN: 0093-1705
MLA acronym: WLWE

SUBSCRIPTION INFORMATION

Frequency of publication: 2 times/yr. (Spring, Fall)
Circulation: 445
Subscription price: C$30.00/yr. institutions; C$20.00/yr. individuals; add C$5.00/yr. outside N. America
Year to which price refers: 1992
Subscription address: Journals Dept., Univ. of Toronto Press, 5201 Dufferin St., Downsview, ON M3H 5T8, Canada
Subscription telephone: 416 978-2317; 416 978-2261
Subscription fax: 416 978-2554

ADVERTISING INFORMATION

Advertising accepted: Yes

EDITORIAL DESCRIPTION

Scope: Focuses on English language literature other than British and American. Publishes articles, interviews, bibliographies, reviews, and notes.
Reviews books: Yes
Publishes notes: Yes
Languages accepted: English
Prints abstracts: No
Author-anonymous submission: Yes

SUBMISSION REQUIREMENTS

Restrictions on contributors: No creative writing is published.
Author pays submission fee: No
Author pays page charges: No
Length of articles: 5,000 words maximum
Length of book reviews: 800 words
Length of notes: 250 words maximum
Style: MLA
Number of copies required: 2

Copyright ownership: Assigned by author to journal
Rejected manuscripts: Returned; enclose return postage.
Time before publication decision: 3 mos.
Time between decision and publication: 2 yr. maximum
Number of reviewers: 2-4
Articles submitted per year: 150
Articles published per year: 24
Book reviews submitted per year: 30
Book reviews published per year: 20
Notes submitted per year: 5
Notes published per year: 2

(3214)
*Xavier Review

Thomas Bonner, Jr. & Robert E. Skinner, Editors
Xavier Univ.
Box 110C
English Dept.
New Orleans, LA 70125

Telephone: 504 483-6484; 504 483-7304
Fax: 504 488-3320
First published: 1980
Sponsoring organization: Dept. of English, Xavier Univ.
ISSN: 0887-6881
MLA acronym: XUS

SUBSCRIPTION INFORMATION

Frequency of publication: 2 times/yr.
Circulation: 300
Available in microform: No
Subscription price: $15.00/yr. institutions; $10.00/yr. individuals
Year to which price refers: 1992

ADVERTISING INFORMATION

Advertising accepted: No

EDITORIAL DESCRIPTION

Scope: Publishes poetry, fiction, nonfiction, and reviews of contemporary literature with an emphasis on the South, black writers, Latin American subjects, religion, and literature.
Reviews books: Yes
Publishes notes: Yes
Languages accepted: English
Prints abstracts: No
Author-anonymous submission: No

SUBMISSION REQUIREMENTS

Restrictions on contributors: Book reviews are assigned.
Author pays submission fee: No
Author pays page charges: No
Length of articles: 10-20 pp.
Length of book reviews: 2-3 pp.
Length of notes: 3-5 pp.
Style: MLA
Number of copies required: 1
Copyright ownership: Journal; assigned on request
Rejected manuscripts: Returned; enclose SASE.
Time before publication decision: 3 mos.
Time between decision and publication: 6-12 mos.
Number of reviewers: 3
Articles submitted per year: 80-100
Articles published per year: 5
Book reviews published per year: 4
Notes submitted per year: 30-35
Notes published per year: 1-3

(3215)
*Y Traethodydd

J. E. Caerwyn Williams, Editor
Coleg Prifysgol Cymru
Aberystwyth, Dyfed, Wales

First published: 1845
Sponsoring organization: Presbyterian Church of Wales; Welsh Arts Council
MLA acronym: Y Traethodydd

SUBSCRIPTION INFORMATION

Frequency of publication: 4 times/yr.
Circulation: 700
Available in microform: No
Subscription address: Llyfrfa'r M. C./Gwasg Pantycelyn, Heol Dewi, Caernarfon, Gwynead, Wales

ADVERTISING INFORMATION

Advertising accepted: No

EDITORIAL DESCRIPTION

Scope: Publishes articles on theology, philosophy, and literature.
Reviews books: Yes
Publishes notes: Yes
Languages accepted: Welsh
Prints abstracts: No
Author-anonymous submission: Yes

SUBMISSION REQUIREMENTS

Restrictions on contributors: None
Author pays submission fee: No
Author pays page charges: No
Length of articles: 3,500 words
Length of book reviews: 300-500 words
Length of notes: 250-500 words
Style: MLA
Number of copies required: 1
Special requirements: Submit typescript.
Copyright ownership: Author
Rejected manuscripts: Returned; enclose return postage.
Time before publication decision: 1 yr.
Time between decision and publication: 1 yr.
Number of reviewers: 1
Articles submitted per year: 30-40
Articles published per year: 20
Book reviews submitted per year: 20-30
Book reviews published per year: 12-24
Notes submitted per year: 8-10
Notes published per year: 4-8

(3216)
*Yale French Studies

Liliane Greene, Editor
P.O. Box 2504A
Yale Station
Yale Univ.
New Haven, CT 06520

First published: 1948
Sponsoring organization: Dept. of French, Yale Univ.
ISSN: 0044-0078
MLA acronym: YFS

SUBSCRIPTION INFORMATION

Frequency of publication: 2 times/yr.
Circulation: 2,500
Available in microform: Yes
Subscription address: Customer Services, Yale Univ. Press, 92A Yale Station, New Haven, CT 06520

ADVERTISING INFORMATION

Advertising accepted: Yes

EDITORIAL DESCRIPTION

Scope: Publishes articles on French literature, culture, and related topics.
Reviews books: No
Publishes notes: No
Languages accepted: English
Prints abstracts: No

SUBMISSION REQUIREMENTS

Restrictions on contributors: Articles are solicited.
Author pays submission fee: No
Author pays page charges: No
Length of articles: 15-20 typescript pp.
Style: Chicago
Number of copies required: 1
Special requirements: Submit double-spaced typescript including footnotes, quotations, and notes.
Copyright ownership: Journal
Rejected manuscripts: Returned

(3217)
*The Yale Journal of Criticism: Interpretation in the Humanities

Ann Fabian, Esther Da Costa Meyer, Ian Duncan, Kevin Dunn, & Wayne Koestenbaum, Editors
Whitney Humanities Center
Box 2968, Yale Station
New Haven, CT 06520

Telephone: 203 432-0663
Fax: 203 432-1087
First published: 1987
Sponsoring organization: Whitney Humanities Center
ISSN: 0893-5378
MLA acronym: YJC

SUBSCRIPTION INFORMATION

Frequency of publication: 2 times/yr. (Apr., Oct.)
Available in microform: Yes
Subscription price: $75.00/yr. institutions N. America; £75.00/yr. institutions elsewhere; $27.50/yr. individuals N. America, £30.00/yr. individuals elsewhere
Year to which price refers: 1991-92
Subscription address: Blackwell Publishers, Subscriber Services Coordinator, 238 Main St., Suite 501, Cambridge, MA 02142
Additional subscription address: Blackwell Publishers, Journals Marketing Manager, 108 Cowley Rd., Oxford OX4 1JF, England
Subscription telephone: 617 225-0430
Subscription fax: 800 835-6770

ADVERTISING INFORMATION

Advertising accepted: Yes

EDITORIAL DESCRIPTION

Scope: Welcomes submissions of an interpretive or theoretical nature in all fields of the humanities. Interdisciplinary articles are especially encouraged.
Reviews books: No
Publishes notes: No
Languages accepted: English
Prints abstracts: No
Author-anonymous submission: No

SUBMISSION REQUIREMENTS

Restrictions on contributors: None
Author pays submission fee: No
Author pays page charges: No
Length of articles: 12,000 words maximum
Style: Chicago
Number of copies required: 2
Special requirements: Submit double-spaced typescript with endnotes, and, if electronic, produced on a letter-quality printer.
Copyright ownership: Yale Univ.
Rejected manuscripts: Returned; enclose SASE.
Time before publication decision: 1-2 mos.
Time between decision and publication: 6-12 mos.
Number of reviewers: 2
Articles submitted per year: 90
Articles published per year: 20

(3218)
*Yale Journal of Law & the Humanities

Greg Miller & Mark Ouweleen, Editors
401A Yale Station
New Haven, CT 06520

Additional editorial address: 127 Wall St., New Haven, CT 06511
Telephone: 203 432-4037
Fax: 203 432-2592
First published: 1988
ISSN: 1041-6374
MLA acronym: YJLH

SUBSCRIPTION INFORMATION

Frequency of publication: 2 times/yr. (Summer, Winter)
Circulation: 600
Available in microform: No
Subscription price: $30.00/yr. institutions US; $35.00/yr. institutions elsewhere; $15.00/yr. individuals US; $20.00/yr. individuals elsewhere
Year to which price refers: 1992

ADVERTISING INFORMATION

Advertising accepted: Yes
Advertising rates: $200.00/full page

EDITORIAL DESCRIPTION

Scope: Publishes articles linking law and legal issues with liberal arts topics.
Reviews books: Yes
Languages accepted: English
Prints abstracts: No
Author-anonymous submission: Yes

SUBMISSION REQUIREMENTS

Author pays submission fee: No
Author pays page charges: No
Style: Chicago; Blue Book
Number of copies required: 2
Copyright ownership: Journal; occasionally author
Rejected manuscripts: Not returned
Time before publication decision: 1 mo.
Time between decision and publication: 3-6 mos.
Number of reviewers: 20
Articles submitted per year: 250
Articles published per year: 12-14
Book reviews submitted per year: 30
Book reviews published per year: 4-8

(3219)
*The Yale Review

J. D. McClatchy, Ellen James, & Wendy Wipprecht, Editors
1902A Yale Station
New Haven, CT 06520

Telephone: 203 432-0499
Fax: 203 432-0510
First published: 1911
Sponsoring organization: Yale Univ.
ISSN: 0044-0124
MLA acronym: YR

SUBSCRIPTION INFORMATION

Frequency of publication: 4 times/yr. (Jan., Apr., July, Oct.)
Circulation: 6,000
Available in microform: Yes
Subscription price: $40.00/yr. institutions US; $45.00/yr. institutions elsewhere; $20.00/yr. individuals US; $30.00/yr. individuals elsewhere
Year to which price refers: 1992
Subscription address: Subscription Services, Blackwell Publishers, 238 Main St., Suite 501, Cambridge, MA 02142
Additional subscription address: Blackwell Publishers, 108 Cowley Rd., Oxford OX4 1JF, England
Subscription telephone: 800 835-6770

ADVERTISING INFORMATION

Advertising accepted: Yes

EDITORIAL DESCRIPTION

Scope: Publishes articles on domestic affairs, literary criticism, aspects of culture, fiction, poetry, and reviews of scholarly books, poetry, and fiction.
Reviews books: Yes
Publishes notes: No
Languages accepted: English
Prints abstracts: No
Author-anonymous submission: No

SUBMISSION REQUIREMENTS

Restrictions on contributors: None
Author pays submission fee: No
Author pays page charges: No
Length of articles: 4,000-5,000 words
Length of book reviews: 1,500-2,000 words
Style: Journal
Number of copies required: 1
Copyright ownership: Yale Univ.
Rejected manuscripts: Returned; enclose return postage.
Time before publication decision: 2 mos.
Time between decision and publication: 18 mos.
Number of reviewers: 3
Articles submitted per year: 750
Articles published per year: 20
Book reviews submitted per year: 75
Book reviews published per year: 25-30

(3220)
*Yale University Library Gazette

Stephen Parks, Editor
Yale Univ. Library
1603A Yale Station
New Haven, CT 06520

Telephone: 203 432-2967
Fax: 203 432-4047
First published: 1926
Sponsoring organization: Yale Univ. Library
ISSN: 0044-0175
MLA acronym: YULG

SUBSCRIPTION INFORMATION

Frequency of publication: 2 times/yr. (Apr., Oct.)
Circulation: 1,200
Available in microform: No
Subscription price: $20.00/yr.
Year to which price refers: 1992

ADVERTISING INFORMATION

Advertising accepted: No

EDITORIAL DESCRIPTION

Scope: Publishes articles based on collections in the various divisions of the Yale Library, along with news of recent acquisitions and, occasionally, catalogues of current exhibitions.
Reviews books: No
Publishes notes: Yes
Languages accepted: English
Prints abstracts: No
Author-anonymous submission: No

SUBMISSION REQUIREMENTS

Author pays submission fee: No
Author pays page charges: No
Style: Chicago
Number of copies required: 1
Rejected manuscripts: Returned
Time before publication decision: 1 mo.

(3221)
*Yearbook for Traditional Music

Dieter Christensen, Editor
International Council for Traditional Music
Dept. of Music
Columbia Univ.
New York, NY 10027

Telephone: 212 678-0332
First published: 1969
Sponsoring organization: UNESCO
ISSN: 0740-1558
MLA acronym: YTM

SUBSCRIPTION INFORMATION

Frequency of publication: Annual
Circulation: 1,300
Available in microform: No
Subscription price: $35.00/yr.
Year to which price refers: 1992

ADVERTISING INFORMATION

Advertising accepted: No

EDITORIAL DESCRIPTION

Scope: Publishes articles on ethnomusicology.
Reviews books: Yes
Publishes notes: No
Languages accepted: English; French; German
Prints abstracts: Yes
Author-anonymous submission: No

SUBMISSION REQUIREMENTS

Restrictions on contributors: None
Author pays submission fee: No
Author pays page charges: No
Length of articles: No restrictions
Length of book reviews: No restrictions
Style: MLA
Number of copies required: 2
Special requirements: Include a 50-100 word abstract. Foreign members may submit manuscripts in idiomatic English, along with a copy of the manuscript in their original language or, preferably, in French, German, or Spanish, and brief biographical data on the author.
Copyright ownership: Author
Rejected manuscripts: Returned at author's request
Time before publication decision: 2 mos.
Time between decision and publication: 10 mos.
Number of reviewers: 2
Articles submitted per year: 20-25
Articles published per year: 10-15
Book reviews published per year: 6-10

(3222)
*Yearbook of Comparative and General Literature

Gilbert D. Chaitin, Editor
Ballantine Hall 402
Indiana Univ.
Bloomington, IN 47405

Telephone: 812 855-2140
First published: 1952
Sponsoring organization: Indiana Univ., Comparative Literature Program; American Comparative Literature Assn.; National Council of Teachers of English
ISSN: 0084-3695
MLA acronym: YCGL

SUBSCRIPTION INFORMATION

Frequency of publication: Annual
Circulation: 980
Available in microform: Yes
Subscription price: $25.00/yr. institutions; $17.50/yr. individuals
Year to which price refers: 1992

ADVERTISING INFORMATION

Advertising accepted: Yes

EDITORIAL DESCRIPTION

Scope: Publishes methodologically oriented research in comparative literature: articles dealing with theory and practice in the study of genres and modes, themes and motifs, periods and movements, as well as of other intercultural and interdisciplinary phenomena; also, articles on the theory and history of comparative literature and the teaching of the subject on all levels and in all parts of the world. Emphases: Asian-Western literary relations, the comparative study of arts, film studies with a focus on literature, the theory and practice of translation. Special features: comprehensive reviews of research, comparative reviews of translation into English of important texts, annual bibliography of the relations of literature and other arts.
Reviews books: Yes
Publishes notes: No
Languages accepted: English; French; German; Spanish
Prints abstracts: No
Author-anonymous submission: Yes

SUBMISSION REQUIREMENTS

Restrictions on contributors: Book reviews are commissioned.
Author pays submission fee: No
Author pays page charges: No
Length of articles: 5,000-7,500 words
Length of book reviews: 800-1,200 words
Style: MLA
Number of copies required: 2
Special requirements: Submission of typescript and diskette is preferred.
Copyright ownership: Assigned by author to journal
Rejected manuscripts: Returned at author's request; enclose SASE.
Time before publication decision: 6-8 weeks
Time between decision and publication: 12-18 mos.
Number of reviewers: 5
Articles submitted per year: 12-15
Articles published per year: 5-6
Book reviews published per year: 20

(3223)
Yearbook of Comparative Criticism

Joseph P. Strelka, Editor
Dept. of Germanic Languages
State Univ. of New York
Albany, NY 12222

First published: 1968
ISSN: 0084-3709
MLA acronym: YCC

SUBSCRIPTION INFORMATION

Frequency of publication: 1-2 times/yr.
Subscription address: Pennsylvania State Univ. Press, 215 Wagner Bldg., University Park, PA 16802

EDITORIAL DESCRIPTION

Scope: Publishes articles on international literary theory and methods of literary scholarship.
Reviews books: No
Languages accepted: English
Prints abstracts: No

SUBMISSION REQUIREMENTS

Restrictions on contributors: Unsolicited manuscripts are not accepted.
Length of articles: 25-30 double-spaced typescript pp.
Style: Chicago
Number of copies required: 1
Copyright ownership: Journal
Rejected manuscripts: Returned
Number of reviewers: 1-2

(3224)
*Yearbook of English Studies

A. J. Gurr, Editor
English Dept.
Univ. of Reading
Box 218
Reading RG6 2AA, England

Telephone: (44) 734 318367
Fax: (44) 734 314404
First published: 1971
Sponsoring organization: Modern Humanities Research Assn.
ISSN: 0306-2473
MLA acronym: YES

SUBSCRIPTION INFORMATION

Frequency of publication: Annual
Circulation: 1,000
Available in microform: No
Subscription price: $26.00/yr.
Year to which price refers: 1992
Subscription address: R. A. Wisbey, Honorary Treasurer, Modern Humanities Research Assn., King's College, Strand, London WC2R 2LS, England

ADVERTISING INFORMATION

Advertising accepted: No

EDITORIAL DESCRIPTION

Scope: Publishes on language and literature of the English-speaking world. Now restructured, the journal is a supplement to *MLR* and likewise publishes articles on a particular theme. Each issue contains a section of Special Number essays, a smaller section of other articles submitted to *MLR* and *YES*, and a section of reviews.
Reviews books: Yes
Publishes notes: No
Languages accepted: English
Prints abstracts: No
Author-anonymous submission: No

SUBMISSION REQUIREMENTS

Restrictions on contributors: None
Author pays submission fee: No
Author pays page charges: No
Length of articles: 8,000 words
Length of book reviews: 800 words
Style: Modern Humanities Research Assn.
Number of copies required: 1
Special requirements: Submit original typescript.
Copyright ownership: Modern Humanities Research Assn.
Rejected manuscripts: Returned
Time before publication decision: 6 weeks
Time between decision and publication: 18 mos.
Number of reviewers: 2
Articles submitted per year: 35
Articles published per year: 16

Book reviews submitted per year: 80
Book reviews published per year: 80

(3225)
*Yearbook of Italian Studies

Antonio D'Andrea, Dante Della Terza, F. Fido, & Pamela D. Stewart, Editors
Dept. of Italian
McGill Univ.
1001 Sherbrooke St. W.
Montreal, Quebec H3A 1G5, Canada

Fax: (39) 55 598895 (Casalini Libri)
First published: 1971
ISSN: 0826-9661
MLA acronym: YIS

SUBSCRIPTION INFORMATION

Frequency of publication: Annual
Circulation: 1,500
Available in microform: Yes
Subscription address: Casalini Libri, Via Benedetto da Maiano 3, 50014 Fiesole (Florence), Italy

ADVERTISING INFORMATION

Advertising accepted: No

EDITORIAL DESCRIPTION

Scope: Intended to establish a closer cultural bond between Italy and North America by providing a meeting ground for scholars in Canada and the US actively involved in Italian studies and those Italian scholars who, having spent some time in the universities of the North American continent, are aware of the intellectual interests of their colleagues on the other side of the ocean. Does not deal exclusively with literary history and criticism, but is open to all aspects of Italian culture and its impact abroad.
Reviews books: Yes
Publishes notes: Yes
Languages accepted: English; French; Italian
Prints abstracts: No

SUBMISSION REQUIREMENTS

Restrictions on contributors: Contribution is by invitation only.
Author pays submission fee: No
Author pays page charges: No
Length of articles: 25 pp.
Style: MLA
Number of copies required: 1
Copyright ownership: Casalini Libri
Rejected manuscripts: Returned
Time before publication decision: 1 yr.
Time between decision and publication: 8 mos.
Number of reviewers: 2
Articles published per year: 10
Book reviews published per year: 2-3
Notes published per year: 2-3

(3226)
*The Yearbook of Langland Studies

John A. Alford & M. Teresa Tavormina, Editors
Dept. of English
Morrill Hall
Michigan State Univ.
East Lansing, MI 48824

Telephone: 517 355-7570
Fax: 517 332-2150
First published: 1987
Sponsoring organization: College of Arts & Letters, Michigan State Univ.
ISSN: 0890-2917
MLA acronym: YLS

SUBSCRIPTION INFORMATION

Frequency of publication: Annual
Circulation: 500
Available in microform: No
Subscription price: $28.00/yr. institutions; $18.00/yr. individuals
Year to which price refers: 1992
Subscription address: Colleagues Press, P.O. Box 4007, East Lansing, MI 48826
Additional subscription address: Outside US & Canada: Boydell & Brewer Ltd., P.O. Box 9, Woodbridge, Suffolk IP12 3DF, England

ADVERTISING INFORMATION

Advertising accepted: No

EDITORIAL DESCRIPTION

Scope: Publishes articles and bibliographies on *Piers Plowman* and related poems of the alliterative tradition.
Reviews books: Yes
Publishes notes: Yes
Languages accepted: English
Prints abstracts: No
Author-anonymous submission: No

SUBMISSION REQUIREMENTS

Restrictions on contributors: Book reviews are commissioned.
Author pays submission fee: No
Author pays page charges: No
Length of articles: No restrictions
Length of book reviews: No restrictions
Length of notes: No restrictions
Style: MLA with modifications
Number of copies required: 2
Copyright ownership: Author
Rejected manuscripts: Returned; enclose return postage.
Time before publication decision: 6 mos.
Time between decision and publication: 6 mos.
Number of reviewers: 2-3
Articles submitted per year: 20
Articles published per year: 6-8
Book reviews published per year: 6-10
Notes submitted per year: 8
Notes published per year: 3-4

(3227)
Yearbook of Romanian Studies: A Publication of the Romanian Studies Association of America

Paul G. Teodorescu, Editor
7 John Circle, #4
Salinas, CA 93905

First published: 1976
Sponsoring organization: Romanian Studies Assn. of America
ISSN: 0149-7219
MLA acronym: YRS

SUBSCRIPTION INFORMATION

Frequency of publication: Annual (Dec.)
Circulation: 125-200
Available in microform: No
Subscription price: $5.00/yr.
Year to which price refers: 1991
Subscription address: Raymonde A. Bulger, Graceland College, Lamoni, IA 50140

ADVERTISING INFORMATION

Advertising accepted: No

EDITORIAL DESCRIPTION

Scope: Publishes research in Romanian language, literature, philology, arts, folklore, and linguistics.
Reviews books: Yes
Publishes notes: Yes

Languages accepted: English; French; Italian; Spanish; Romanian
Prints abstracts: No
Author-anonymous submission: No

SUBMISSION REQUIREMENTS

Author pays submission fee: Yes
Author pays page charges: No
Length of articles: 3,500 words
Length of book reviews: 1,000 words
Length of notes: No restrictions
Style: MLA
Number of copies required: 1
Special requirements: Submit original typescript.
Copyright ownership: Romanian Studies Assn. of America
Rejected manuscripts: Returned; enclose return postage.
Time before publication decision: 3 mos.
Time between decision and publication: 1 yr.
Number of reviewers: 2
Articles submitted per year: 4
Articles published per year: 3-4
Book reviews submitted per year: 2
Book reviews published per year: 2

(3228)
*The Yearbook of the Society for Pirandello Studies

Elizabeth Schächter, Editor
Keynes College
Univ. of Kent
Canterbury, Kent CT2 7NP, England

Telephone: (44) 227 764000
Fax: (44) 227 475472
First published: 1981
Historical variations in title: Formerly *Yearbook of the British Pirandello Society*
Sponsoring organization: Soc. for Pirandello Studies
ISSN: 0260-9215
MLA acronym: YSPS

SUBSCRIPTION INFORMATION

Frequency of publication: Annual
Available in microform: No
Subscription price: £9.00/yr.
Year to which price refers: 1991

ADVERTISING INFORMATION

Advertising accepted: Yes

EDITORIAL DESCRIPTION

Scope: Publishes articles on Luigi Pirandello.
Reviews books: Yes
Publishes notes: Yes
Languages accepted: English; Italian
Prints abstracts: Yes
Author-anonymous submission: No

SUBMISSION REQUIREMENTS

Restrictions on contributors: Reviews are commissioned.
Author pays submission fee: No
Author pays page charges: No
Length of articles: 6,000 words maximum
Length of book reviews: 2,000 words maximum
Length of notes: 2,000 words
Style: MLA
Number of copies required: 2
Special requirements: Manuscripts in Italian should by accompanied by a 200-word abstract in English.
Copyright ownership: Author
Rejected manuscripts: Returned; enclose SASE
Time before publication decision: 3 mos.
Time between decision and publication: 3 mos.
Number of reviewers: 5
Articles submitted per year: 12
Articles published per year: 6
Book reviews published per year: 5

Notes submitted per year: 1
Notes published per year: 1

(3229)
*Year's Work in English Studies

Gordon Campbell, Editor
English Assn.
The Vicarage
Priory Gardens
London W4 1TT, England

Telephone: (44) 81 9954236
Fax: (44) 81 9954236
First published: 1919
Sponsoring organization: English Assn., London
ISSN: 0084-4144
MLA acronym: YWES

SUBSCRIPTION INFORMATION

Frequency of publication: Annual
Circulation: 3,000
Available in microform: No

ADVERTISING INFORMATION

Advertising accepted: No

EDITORIAL DESCRIPTION

Scope: Annual bibliographical survey of scholarly books and articles on English language and literature. Also includes two chapters on American literature, one on new literatures in English, and one on literary theory.
Reviews books: Yes
Publishes notes: No
Languages accepted: English
Prints abstracts: No

SUBMISSION REQUIREMENTS

Restrictions on contributors: All contributions are by staff of the English Assn.
Author pays submission fee: No
Author pays page charges: No
Style: Journal
Number of copies required: 3
Copyright ownership: English Assn.
Articles published per year: 19
Book reviews submitted per year: 1,300
Book reviews published per year: 1,300

(3230)
*The Year's Work in Modern Language Studies

David A. Wells, Glanville Price, John Lindon, Peter Mayo, & Stephen Parkinson, Editors
Birkbeck College
Malet St.
London WC1E 7HX, England

Telephone: (44) 7 6316103
First published: 1929
Sponsoring organization: Modern Humanities Research Assn.
ISSN: 0084-4152
MLA acronym: YWMLS

SUBSCRIPTION INFORMATION

Frequency of publication: Annual
Circulation: 1,400
Available in microform: No
Subscription address: Honorary Treasurer, Modern Humanities Research Assn., King's College, Strand, London WC2R 2LS, England

ADVERTISING INFORMATION

Advertising accepted: No

EDITORIAL DESCRIPTION

Scope: Bibliographical survey including short reviews of works published on Romance, Celtic, Germanic, and Slavonic languages and literatures.
Reviews books: Yes
Publishes notes: No
Languages accepted: English
Prints abstracts: No

SUBMISSION REQUIREMENTS

Restrictions on contributors: Submission is by invitation.
Author pays submission fee: No
Author pays page charges: No
Length of articles: No restrictions
Style: Modern Humanities Research Assn.
Number of copies required: 2
Copyright ownership: Modern Humanities Research Assn.
Rejected manuscripts: Returned
Time before publication decision: 1-2 weeks
Time between decision and publication: 1 yr.
Number of reviewers: 1
Articles submitted per year: 75-85
Articles published per year: 75-85
Book reviews submitted per year: Several thousand
Book reviews published per year: Several thousand

(3231)
*Yeats: An Annual of Critical and Textual Studies

Richard J. Finneran & Mary FitzGerald, Editors
Dept. of English
Univ. of Tennessee
Knoxville, TN 37996

Additional editorial address: Dept. of English, Univ. of New Orleans, New Orleans, LA 70148
Telephone: 615 974-6973
First published: 1983
ISSN: 0742-6224
MLA acronym: Yeats

SUBSCRIPTION INFORMATION

Frequency of publication: Annual (Nov.-Dec.)
Circulation: 500
Available in microform: No
Subscription price: $39.95/yr.
Year to which price refers: 1991
Subscription address: Univ. of Michigan Press, 839 Greene St., P.O. Box 1104, Ann Arbor, MI 48106-1104

ADVERTISING INFORMATION

Advertising accepted: No

EDITORIAL DESCRIPTION

Scope: Publishes Yeats scholarship in the form of articles, notes, editions, reviews, and an annual bibliography of criticism.
Reviews books: Yes
Publishes notes: Yes
Languages accepted: English
Prints abstracts: No
Author-anonymous submission: No

SUBMISSION REQUIREMENTS

Restrictions on contributors: Unsolicited reviews are not accepted.
Author pays submission fee: No
Author pays page charges: No
Length of articles: No restrictions
Length of book reviews: No restrictions
Length of notes: No restrictions
Style: MLA; journal
Number of copies required: 1
Copyright ownership: Univ. of Michigan Press

Rejected manuscripts: Returned
Time before publication decision: 3-6 mos.
Time between decision and publication: 14 mos.
Number of reviewers: 1-2
Articles submitted per year: 30
Articles published per year: 10
Book reviews published per year: 10
Notes submitted per year: 4
Notes published per year: 2

(3232)
*Yeats Annual

Warwick Gould, Editor
Dept. of English
Royal Holloway & Bedford New College, Univ. of London
Egham Hill
Egham, Surrey TW20 0EX, England

Telephone: (44) 784 443216
Fax: (44) 784 437520
First published: 1982
ISSN: 0278-7687
MLA acronym: YeA

SUBSCRIPTION INFORMATION

Frequency of publication: Annual
Available in microform: No
Subscription price: £50.00/yr.
Year to which price refers: 1992
Subscription address: Macmillan Press, Houndmills, Basingstoke, Hampshire RG21 2XS, England
Subscription telephone: (44) 256 29242

ADVERTISING INFORMATION

Advertising accepted: No

EDITORIAL DESCRIPTION

Scope: Publishes scholarly editions of works by Yeats, articles on Yeats, books reviews, and notes about works in progress. Includes a bibliography of recent work and of recently discovered items.
Reviews books: Yes
Publishes notes: Yes
Languages accepted: English; French
Prints abstracts: No
Author-anonymous submission: Yes

SUBMISSION REQUIREMENTS

Restrictions on contributors: Most book reviews are solicited.
Author pays submission fee: No
Author pays page charges: No
Length of articles: 20,000 words maximum
Length of book reviews: 3,000 words maximum
Length of notes: 10,000 words maximum
Style: Journal
Number of copies required: 3
Copyright ownership: Editor
Rejected manuscripts: Returned; enclose return postage.
Time before publication decision: 3 mos. maximum
Time between decision and publication: 12-15 mos.
Number of reviewers: 3-5
Articles submitted per year: 30-40
Articles published per year: 7-8
Book reviews published per year: 18-20
Notes submitted per year: 12-15
Notes published per year: 4-5

(3233)
*Yeats Eliot Review: A Journal of Criticism and Scholarship

Russell Elliott Murphy, Editor
English Dept.
Univ. of Arkansas at Little Rock
Little Rock, AR 72204

Telephone: 501 569-8324
Fax: 501 569-8323
First published: 1974
Sponsoring organization: Univ. of Arkansas at Little Rock
ISSN: 0704-5700
MLA acronym: YER

SUBSCRIPTION INFORMATION

Frequency of publication: 4 times/yr.
Circulation: 300
Available in microform: No
Subscription price: $12.00/yr. institutions US; $14.00/yr. institutions elsewhere; $10.00/yr. individuals US; $12.00/yr. individuals elsewhere
Year to which price refers: 1992

ADVERTISING INFORMATION

Advertising accepted: Yes

EDITORIAL DESCRIPTION

Scope: Research-based papers and notes on all aspects of Yeats and Eliot studies are invited. Also includes bibliographical update, book reviews, and review articles.
Reviews books: Yes
Publishes notes: Yes
Languages accepted: English
Prints abstracts: No
Author-anonymous submission: No

SUBMISSION REQUIREMENTS

Restrictions on contributors: None
Author pays submission fee: No
Author pays page charges: No
Length of articles: No restrictions
Length of book reviews: 1,000 words
Length of notes: No restrictions
Style: MLA
Number of copies required: 3
Copyright ownership: Author
Rejected manuscripts: Returned; enclose return postage.
Time before publication decision: 4-6 mos.
Time between decision and publication: 18 mos.
Number of reviewers: 3
Articles submitted per year: 50
Articles published per year: 15
Book reviews submitted per year: 25
Book reviews published per year: 8
Notes submitted per year: 5-10
Notes published per year: 4

(3234)
*Yed'a-'Am/Yeda-Am: Bamah le-Folklor Yehudi/Journal of the Israel Folklore Society

Itzchak Ganuz, Editor
10 Vitkin St.
P.O. Box 314
Tel-Aviv, Israel

Telephone: (972) 3 5463650
First published: 1948
Sponsoring organization: Israel Folklore Soc.
ISSN: 0334-4053
MLA acronym: YA

SUBSCRIPTION INFORMATION

Frequency of publication: Annual
Available in microform: No

ADVERTISING INFORMATION

Advertising accepted: No

EDITORIAL DESCRIPTION

Scope: Publishes articles on Israeli and Jewish folklore.
Reviews books: Yes
Publishes notes: Yes
Languages accepted: Hebrew
Prints abstracts: No
Author-anonymous submission: No

SUBMISSION REQUIREMENTS

Restrictions on contributors: None
Author pays submission fee: No
Author pays page charges: No
Number of copies required: 3
Rejected manuscripts: Not returned
Time before publication decision: 6 mos.
Time between decision and publication: 3 mos.
Articles submitted per year: 30
Articles published per year: 30
Book reviews submitted per year: 15
Book reviews published per year: 15
Notes submitted per year: 5
Notes published per year: 5

(3235)
Yerushalaymer Almanakh

Yoysef Kerler, Meir Charatz, & Efraim Shedletsky, Editors
12/6 Shderot Eshkol
Jerusalem, Israel

First published: 1973
Sponsoring organization: Yiddish Writers Group, Jerusalem
ISSN: 0334-9594
MLA acronym: YAlm

SUBSCRIPTION INFORMATION

Frequency of publication: Annual
Available in microform: No

ADVERTISING INFORMATION

Advertising accepted: No

EDITORIAL DESCRIPTION

Scope: Publishes fiction, poetry, reviews, review articles, and scholarly articles by Yiddish writers (mostly immigrants from the Soviet Union or Poland) residing in Israel.
Reviews books: Yes
Languages accepted: Yiddish
Prints abstracts: No

SUBMISSION REQUIREMENTS

Author pays submission fee: No
Author pays page charges: No
Articles published per year: 25-50
Book reviews published per year: 5-10

(3236)
*Yiddish

Joseph C. Landis, Editor
NSF 350
Queens College, City Univ. of New York
Flushing, NY 11367

First published: 1973
Sponsoring organization: American Assn. of Professors of Yiddish
ISSN: 0364-4308
MLA acronym: Yiddish

(3237)
Yiddishe Kultur

Itshe Goldberg, Editor
Yiddisher Kultur Farband, Inc.
1133 Broadway, Rm. 1019
New York, NY 10010

Telephone: 212 691-0708
First published: 1938
ISSN: 0044-0426
MLA acronym: YK

SUBSCRIPTION INFORMATION

Frequency of publication: 6 times/yr.
Circulation: 3,000
Available in microform: No
Subscription price: $15.00/yr.
Year to which price refers: 1992

ADVERTISING INFORMATION

Advertising accepted: No

EDITORIAL DESCRIPTION

Reviews books: Yes
Languages accepted: Yiddish

SUBSCRIPTION INFORMATION

Frequency of publication: 4 times/yr.
Circulation: 550
Available in microform: No
Subscription price: $15.00/yr.
Year to which price refers: 1992

ADVERTISING INFORMATION

Advertising accepted: No

EDITORIAL DESCRIPTION

Scope: Publishes articles on Yiddish literature and language, and on cultural context of Yiddish literature as well as translations of articles and literature from Yiddish into English. Every 4th issue is devoted to Jewish writing in any language and is titled *Modern Jewish Studies Annual.*
Reviews books: Yes
Publishes notes: Yes
Languages accepted: English; Yiddish
Prints abstracts: No
Author-anonymous submission: No

SUBMISSION REQUIREMENTS

Restrictions on contributors: None
Author pays submission fee: No
Author pays page charges: No
Length of articles: No restrictions
Length of book reviews: No restrictions
Length of notes: No restrictions
Style: MLA
Number of copies required: 1
Copyright ownership: Author
Rejected manuscripts: Returned
Time before publication decision: 1 yr.
Time between decision and publication: 18 mos.
Number of reviewers: 2
Articles submitted per year: 75
Articles published per year: 50
Book reviews submitted per year: 16
Book reviews published per year: 16

(3238)
*YOD: Revue des Etudes Hébraïques et Juives Modernes et Contemporaines

Mireille Hadas-Lebel, Editor
INALCO
2, rue de Lille
75343 Paris Cedex 07, France

Additional editorial address: Centre de Documentation & de Recherche, 104 quai de Clichy, 92110 Clichy, France
Telephone: (33) 1 49707040
Fax: (33) 1 49264299
First published: 1975
Sponsoring organization: Inst. National des Langues & Civilisations Orientales (INALCO)
ISSN: 0338-9316
MLA acronym: YOD

SUBSCRIPTION INFORMATION

Frequency of publication: 2 times/yr.
Circulation: 300
Available in microform: No
Subscription price: 95 F ($20.00)/yr.
Year to which price refers: 1991
Subscription telephone: (33) 1 49264209

ADVERTISING INFORMATION

Advertising accepted: No

EDITORIAL DESCRIPTION

Scope: Publishes articles on Hebrew language, contemporary Hebrew literature, and the history and sociology of Jewish communities.
Reviews books: Yes
Publishes notes: Yes
Languages accepted: French; English
Prints abstracts: No

SUBMISSION REQUIREMENTS

Author pays submission fee: No
Author pays page charges: No
Length of articles: 15 pp.
Length of book reviews: 1 p.
Copyright ownership: INALCO
Rejected manuscripts: Returned
Time before publication decision: 3 mos.
Time between decision and publication: 6 mos.
Number of reviewers: 2
Articles submitted per year: 25
Articles published per year: 20

(3239)
*Z: Filmtidsskrift

Jon Iversen, Editor
Teatergt. 3
0180 Oslo 1, Norway

Telephone: (47) 2 114217
Fax: (47) 2 207981
First published: 1983
Sponsoring organization: Norwegian Federation of Film Societies; Norwegian Cultural Foundation
ISSN: 0800-1464
MLA acronym: Z

SUBSCRIPTION INFORMATION

Frequency of publication: 4 times/yr.
Circulation: 1,750
Available in microform: No
Subscription price: 150 NKr/yr. Scandinavia; 180 NKr/yr. elsewhere
Year to which price refers: 1992

ADVERTISING INFORMATION

Advertising accepted: Yes
Advertising rates: 950 NKr/quarter page; 1,800 NKr/half page; 3,500 NKr/full page

EDITORIAL DESCRIPTION

Scope: Publishes articles on film theory, criticism, and history.
Reviews books: Yes
Publishes notes: Yes
Languages accepted: Norwegian
Prints abstracts: No
Author-anonymous submission: No

SUBMISSION REQUIREMENTS

Author pays submission fee: No
Author pays page charges: No
Number of copies required: 1
Copyright ownership: Author
Rejected manuscripts: Returned at author's request
Time before publication decision: 3 mos. maximum
Time between decision and publication: 3 mos.
Number of reviewers: 2-6
Articles submitted per year: 40
Articles published per year: 40
Book reviews submitted per year: 4
Book reviews published per year: 4
Notes submitted per year: 15
Notes published per year: 15

(3240)
Z Dziejów Form Artystycznych W Literaturze Polskiej

Janusz Sławinski, Editor
Inst. Badań Literackich
Polska Akademia Nauk
Rynek 9
50-106 Wrocław, Poland

First published: 1963
Sponsoring organization: Polska Akademie Nauk, Inst. Badań Literackich
ISSN: 0084-4411
MLA acronym: ZDFALP

SUBSCRIPTION INFORMATION

Frequency of publication: Irregular
Circulation: 1,500
Available in microform: No
Subscription address: Ars Polona-Ruch, Krakowskie Przedmieście 7, 00-068 Warsaw, Poland

ADVERTISING INFORMATION

Advertising accepted: No

EDITORIAL DESCRIPTION

Scope: Publishes monographs on Polish literature, artistic language, and theoretical poetics.
Reviews books: No
Languages accepted: Polish
Prints abstracts: No

SUBMISSION REQUIREMENTS

Restrictions on contributors: Contributors must be members of Inst. Badań Literackich.
Length of books: 100-200 pp.
Number of copies required: 2
Copyright ownership: Ars Polona-Ruch
Time before publication decision: 2 mos.
Number of reviewers: 2
Books published per year: 1-2

(3241)
*Zadarska Revija: Časopis za Kulturu i Društvena Pitanja

Dinko Foretić, Ante Franić, & Julije Derossi, Editors
Zagregačka ulica 1
Zadar, Croatia

Telephone: (38) 57 24070
First published: 1951
Sponsoring organization: Community Organization for Culture
ISSN: 0044-1589
MLA acronym: ZR

SUBSCRIPTION INFORMATION

Frequency of publication: 6 times/yr.
Circulation: 1,000
Available in microform: Yes
Subscription price: $50.00/yr.
Year to which price refers: 1992

ADVERTISING INFORMATION

Advertising accepted: Yes
Advertising rates: $100.00/full page

EDITORIAL DESCRIPTION

Scope: Publishes articles on history and literature.
Reviews books: Yes
Publishes notes: Yes
Languages accepted: Croatian
Prints abstracts: Yes

SUBMISSION REQUIREMENTS

Author pays submission fee: Yes
Author pays page charges: Yes
Length of articles: 10-30 pp.
Number of copies required: 1
Copyright ownership: Author
Rejected manuscripts: Not returned
Time before publication decision: 1-5 mos.
Time between decision and publication: 2 mos.
Number of reviewers: 4
Articles submitted per year: 200
Articles published per year: 80
Book reviews submitted per year: 40
Book reviews published per year: 20
Notes submitted per year: 100
Notes published per year: 100

(3242)
*Zagadnienia Rodzajów Literackich: Woprosy Literaturnych Żanrov/Les Problèmes des Genres Littéraires

Jan Trzynadlowski, Witold Ostrowski, & Grzegorz Gazda, Editors
Ul. Piotrkowska 179
90-447 Łódź, Poland

Additional editorial address: Ossolineum, Rynek 9, 50-106 Wrocław, Poland
First published: 1958
Sponsoring organization: Łódzkie Towarzystwo Naukowe
ISSN: 0084-4446
MLA acronym: ZRL

SUBSCRIPTION INFORMATION

Frequency of publication: 2 times/yr.
Circulation: 1,000
Available in microform: No
Subscription address: Ars Polona-Ruch, Krakowskie Przedmieście 7, 00-068 Warsaw, Poland

ADVERTISING INFORMATION

Advertising accepted: No

EDITORIAL DESCRIPTION

Scope: Publishes studies of literary genres and poetics.
Reviews books: Yes
Publishes notes: Yes
Languages accepted: English; French; Polish; Russian; German
Prints abstracts: Yes
Author-anonymous submission: No

SUBMISSION REQUIREMENTS

Restrictions on contributors: None
Author pays submission fee: No
Author pays page charges: No
Length of articles: 25-30 typescript pp.
Length of book reviews: 1-7 typescript pp.
Length of notes: 1-5 typescript pp.
Style: MLA
Number of copies required: 2
Special requirements: Submit original typescript.
Copyright ownership: Zakład Narodowy im Ossolińskich
Rejected manuscripts: Returned
Time before publication decision: 2 mos.
Time between decision and publication: 18 mos.
Number of reviewers: 3
Articles submitted per year: 25
Articles published per year: 12
Book reviews submitted per year: 14
Book reviews published per year: 12
Notes submitted per year: 4
Notes published per year: 3

(3243)
*Zaïre-Afrique

Kikassa Mwanalessa & René Beeckmans, Editors
Av. Père Boka n °9 (Vis-à-vis du Building des Aff. Etrangères)
B.P. 3375 Kinshasa/Gombe, Zaïre

First published: 1961
Sponsoring organization: Centre d'Etudes pour l'Action Sociale
ISSN: 0049-8513
MLA acronym: Z-A

SUBSCRIPTION INFORMATION

Frequency of publication: 10 times/yr.
Circulation: 5,000
Available in microform: No

ADVERTISING INFORMATION

Advertising accepted: Yes

EDITORIAL DESCRIPTION

Scope: Publishes articles on economic and sociocultural matters in order to promote the development of Zaïre and the African continent.
Reviews books: Yes
Publishes notes: No
Languages accepted: French
Prints abstracts: No

SUBMISSION REQUIREMENTS

Restrictions on contributors: None
Author pays submission fee: No
Author pays page charges: No
Length of articles: 15-20 double-spaced typescript pp.
Length of book reviews: 350 words
Style: MLA
Number of copies required: 2
Special requirements: Submit original typescript.
Copyright ownership: Journal
Rejected manuscripts: Returned at author's request
Time before publication decision: 2 mos.
Time between decision and publication: 1-3 mos.
Number of reviewers: 3
Articles submitted per year: 350
Articles published per year: 50-70
Book reviews submitted per year: 50
Book reviews published per year: 10-15

(3244)
*Zambezia: The Journal of the University of Zimbabwe

E. A. Ngara, Editor
c/o Publications Officer
Univ. of Zimbabwe
P.O. Box MP 203
Mount Pleasant, Harare, Zimbabwe

Telephone: (263) 4 303211 ext. 1236
Fax: (263) 4 732828
E-mail: STRINGER@zimbix.uz.zw (Internet)
First published: 1969
Sponsoring organization: Univ. of Zimbabwe
ISSN: 0379-0622
MLA acronym: Zambezia

SUBSCRIPTION INFORMATION

Frequency of publication: 2 times/yr.
Circulation: 300
Available in microform: No
Subscription price: $24.00/yr.
Year to which price refers: 1991

ADVERTISING INFORMATION

Advertising accepted: Yes

EDITORIAL DESCRIPTION

Scope: A multidisciplinary journal focusing on Zimbabwe and South Central Africa. Most articles submitted and accepted are in the disciplines of the social sciences, humanities, and arts, although articles from other disciplines are welcomed.
Reviews books: Yes
Publishes notes: Yes
Languages accepted: English
Prints abstracts: No
Author-anonymous submission: Yes

SUBMISSION REQUIREMENTS

Restrictions on contributors: None
Author pays submission fee: No
Author pays page charges: No
Length of articles: 6,000 words maximum
Length of book reviews: No restrictions
Length of notes: No restrictions
Style: Oxford Univ. Press
Number of copies required: 3
Copyright ownership: Univ. of Zimbabwe
Rejected manuscripts: Returned
Time before publication decision: 2 mos.
Time between decision and publication: 8 mos.
Number of reviewers: 3
Articles submitted per year: 16
Articles published per year: 10
Book reviews submitted per year: 16
Book reviews published per year: 16

(3245)
*Zapiski Russkoi Akademicheskoi Gruppy v S.Sh.A./Transactions of the Association of Russian-American Scholars in the U.S.A.

Nadja Jernakoff, Alexis Klimoff, & Eugene Magerovsky, Editors
85-20 114th St.
Richmond Hill, NY 11418

Additional editorial address: 11 Hawthorne Court, Loudonville, NY 12211
Telephone: 718 846-6410
First published: 1967

Sponsoring organization: Assn. of Russian-American Scholars in the U.S.A., Inc.
ISSN: 0066-9717
MLA acronym: TZ

SUBSCRIPTION INFORMATION

Frequency of publication: Annual (Dec.)
Circulation: 400
Available in microform: No
Subscription price: $25.00/yr. individuals
Year to which price refers: 1992

ADVERTISING INFORMATION

Advertising accepted: No

EDITORIAL DESCRIPTION

Scope: Publishes articles by members of the Association of Russian-American Scholars in the U.S.A. on a variety of subjects including Russian literature, history, art, sciences, and culture.
Reviews books: Yes
Publishes notes: Yes
Languages accepted: Russian; English; French; German
Prints abstracts: No
Author-anonymous submission: No

SUBMISSION REQUIREMENTS

Restrictions on contributors: None
Author pays submission fee: No
Author pays page charges: No
Length of articles: 15-25 double spaced pp.
Length of book reviews: 2-4 double-spaced pp.
Length of notes: 5-10 double spaced pp.
Style: MLA
Number of copies required: 4
Special requirements: Include complete bibliography and footnotes. Submit original typescript plus 3 copies.
Copyright ownership: Assn. of Russian-American Scholars in the U.S.A., Inc.
Rejected manuscripts: Returned
Time before publication decision: 6 mos
Time between decision and publication: 9-12 mos.
Number of reviewers: 3-4
Articles submitted per year: 15-25
Articles published per year: 15
Book reviews submitted per year: 5-6
Book reviews published per year: 5-6
Notes submitted per year: 3-4
Notes published per year: 3-4

(3246)
*Zapisy

Vitaŭt Kipel & Thomas E. Bird, Editors
230 Springfield Ave.
Rutherford, NJ 07070

Telephone: 201 933-6807
Fax: 201 438-4565
First published: 1952
Sponsoring organization: Belorussian Inst. of Arts & Sciences
ISSN: 0513-837X
MLA acronym: Zapisy

SUBSCRIPTION INFORMATION

Frequency of publication: Annual
Circulation: 500
Available in microform: No

ADVERTISING INFORMATION

Advertising accepted: No

EDITORIAL DESCRIPTION

Scope: Publishes articles on Belorussian history, literature, and art.
Reviews books: Yes
Publishes notes: Yes
Languages accepted: Belorussian; English
Prints abstracts: Yes

SUBMISSION REQUIREMENTS

Restrictions on contributors: None
Author pays submission fee: No
Author pays page charges: No
Length of articles: No restrictions
Length of book reviews: 500-700 words
Length of notes: 1,000 words
Style: None
Number of copies required: 1
Special requirements: Include English or Belorussian resume.
Copyright ownership: Varies
Rejected manuscripts: Returned
Time before publication decision: 1-2 yrs.
Time between decision and publication: 1 yr.
Number of reviewers: 3
Articles submitted per year: 1
Articles published per year: 1
Book reviews submitted per year: 5
Book reviews published per year: 10

(3247)
Zbirnyk Prats' Naukovoĭ Shevchenkivs'koĭ Konferentsiĭ

V. Borodin, Editor
Academy of Sciences
Naukova Dumka
ul. Repina, 3
252601 Kiev-601, GSP, Ukraine

First published: 1954
Sponsoring organization: T. H. Shevchenko Inst. of Literature
MLA acronym: ZbirP

SUBSCRIPTION INFORMATION

Frequency of publication: Annual
Circulation: 600
Available in microform: No

ADVERTISING INFORMATION

Advertising accepted: No

EDITORIAL DESCRIPTION

Scope: Publishes papers on the life, works, study, and reception of Taras Hryhorovych Shevchenko.
Reviews books: No
Publishes notes: No
Languages accepted: Ukrainian
Prints abstracts: No
Author-anonymous submission: No

SUBMISSION REQUIREMENTS

Restrictions on contributors: Only papers read at the annual Shevchenko conference are considered.
Author pays submission fee: No
Author pays page charges: No
Length of articles: 4,000 words
Style: Scientific
Number of copies required: 2
Copyright ownership: Naukova Dumka
Time before publication decision: 3 mos.
Time between decision and publication: 1 yr.
Number of reviewers: 2
Articles submitted per year: 30
Articles published per year: 30

(3248)
*Zeitschrift der Deutschen Morgenländischen Gesellschaft

Tilman Nagel, Editor
Seminar für Arabistik
Prinzenstr. 21
3400 Göttingen, Germany

First published: 1846
Sponsoring organization: Deutsche Morgenländische Gesellschaft
ISSN: 0341-0137
MLA acronym: ZDMG

SUBSCRIPTION INFORMATION

Frequency of publication: 2 times/yr.
Circulation: 900
Available in microform: No
Subscription address: Franz Steiner Verlag GmbH, Birkenwaldstr. 44, 7000 Stuttgart 1, Germany

ADVERTISING INFORMATION

Advertising accepted: Yes

EDITORIAL DESCRIPTION

Scope: Publishes articles on all aspects of Oriental studies including Ancient Orient, Semitic languages, and Egyptian, African, Islamic, Turkish, Iranian, Judaic, Chinese, Japanese and Korean studies.
Reviews books: Yes
Publishes notes: Yes
Languages accepted: German; English; French
Prints abstracts: No
Author-anonymous submission: No

SUBMISSION REQUIREMENTS

Restrictions on contributors: None
Author pays submission fee: No
Author pays page charges: No
Length of articles: 40 pp. maximum
Style: Journal
Number of copies required: 1
Special requirements: Submit typescript.
Copyright ownership: Journal
Rejected manuscripts: Returned
Time before publication decision: 1 mo.
Time between decision and publication: 2-3 yrs.
Number of reviewers: 1-2
Articles submitted per year: 25-30
Articles published per year: 20
Book reviews published per year: 150-200
Notes published per year: 5-10

(3249)
*Zeitschrift für Althebraistik

Hans-Peter Müller, Johannes Hendrik Hospers, Ernst Jenni, Benjamin Kedar-Kopfstein, H. Lichtenberger, Edward Lipiński, Stanislav Segert, & Wolfram von Soden, Editors
Alttestamentliches Seminar
Westfälischen Wilhelms-Univ.
Universitätsstr. 13-17
4400 Münster, Germany

Telephone: (49) 251 719701
Fax: (49) 251 832090
E-mail: Aat03@dmswwula
First published: 1988
ISSN: 0932-4461
MLA acronym: ZAH

SUBSCRIPTION INFORMATION

Frequency of publication: 2 times/yr.
Available in microform: Yes
Subscription price: 149 DM/yr.
Year to which price refers: 1991
Subscription address: W. Kohlhammer Verlag GmbH, Hessbrühlstr. 69, Postfach 80 04 30, 7000 Stuttgart 80, Germany

Subscription telephone: (49) 711 78630
Subscription fax: (49) 711 7863263

ADVERTISING INFORMATION

Advertising accepted: Yes

EDITORIAL DESCRIPTION

Scope: Treats philological and linguistic topics in the language of the Old Testament, epigraphy of Ancient Israel, and the Hebrew of Qumrān and of the Samaritans.
Reviews books: No
Publishes notes: Yes
Languages accepted: German; English; French
Prints abstracts: Yes
Author-anonymous submission: No

SUBMISSION REQUIREMENTS

Author pays submission fee: No
Author pays page charges: No
Length of articles: No restrictions
Length of notes: No restrictions
Style: None
Number of copies required: 2
Special requirements: Submission of typescript and diskette is preferred.
Copyright ownership: W. Kohlhammer Verlag GmbH
Time before publication decision: 1 yr.
Time between decision and publication: 10 mos.
Number of reviewers: 2-3
Articles submitted per year: 20
Articles published per year: 10-12
Notes submitted per year: 10
Notes published per year: 5-7

(3250)
*Zeitschrift für Anglistik und Amerikanistik

Helmut Findeisen, Editor
Mockauer Str. 118, 15/9
7025 Leipzig, Germany

Telephone: 2412785
First published: 1953
ISSN: 0044-2305
MLA acronym: ZAA

SUBSCRIPTION INFORMATION

Frequency of publication: 4 times/yr.
Circulation: 1,500
Available in microform: No
Subscription price: 72 DM/yr.
Year to which price refers: 1992
Subscription address: Langenscheidt KG, Crellestr. 28-30, 1000 Berlin 62, Germany
Additional subscription address: Langenscheidt KG, Neusser Str. 3, 8000 Munich 40, Germany
Subscription telephone: (49) 30 7800020
Subscription fax: (49) 89 36096258

ADVERTISING INFORMATION

Advertising accepted: Yes

EDITORIAL DESCRIPTION

Scope: Publishes articles on English and American language and literature.
Reviews books: Yes
Publishes notes: Yes
Languages accepted: English; German
Prints abstracts: No
Author-anonymous submission: No

SUBMISSION REQUIREMENTS

Restrictions on contributors: None
Author pays submission fee: No
Author pays page charges: No
Length of articles: 6,000-8,000 words
Length of book reviews: 1,200 words

Length of notes: 1,000-2,000 words
Style: MLA
Number of copies required: 2
Special requirements: Submit original typescript.
Copyright ownership: Assigned by author to publisher for 1 yr.
Rejected manuscripts: Returned; enclose return postage.
Time before publication decision: 2 mos.
Time between decision and publication: 10-15 mos.
Number of reviewers: 2-3
Articles submitted per year: 40-50
Articles published per year: 25
Book reviews submitted per year: 100
Book reviews published per year: 75
Notes submitted per year: 6
Notes published per year: 4

(3251)
Zeitschrift für Arabische Linguistik

Hartmut Bobzin & Otto Jastrow, Editors
Bismarckstr. 1
8520 Erlangen, Germany

First published: 1978
ISSN: 0170-026X
MLA acronym: ZAL

SUBSCRIPTION INFORMATION

Frequency of publication: 2 times/yr.
Circulation: 200
Available in microform: No
Subscription address: Verlag Otto Harrassowitz, Postfach 2929, 6200 Wiesbaden, Germany

ADVERTISING INFORMATION

Advertising accepted: Yes

EDITORIAL DESCRIPTION

Scope: Publishes articles on Arabic linguistics.
Reviews books: Yes
Publishes notes: Yes
Languages accepted: English; French; German; Italian; Spanish; Arabic
Prints abstracts: No
Author-anonymous submission: No

SUBMISSION REQUIREMENTS

Author pays submission fee: No
Author pays page charges: No
Length of articles: 20 pp.
Length of book reviews: No restrictions
Length of notes: No restrictions
Style: Journal
Number of copies required: 1
Copyright ownership: Verlag Otto Harrassowitz
Rejected manuscripts: Returned
Time before publication decision: 1 mo.
Time between decision and publication: 1-2 yrs.
Number of reviewers: 2
Articles submitted per year: 10-15
Articles published per year: 6-8
Book reviews submitted per year: 15
Book reviews published per year: 15
Notes submitted per year: 5
Notes published per year: 5

(3252)
*Zeitschrift für Assyriologie und Vorderasiatische Archäologie

D. O. Edzard, U. Seidl, H. Otten, & Wolfram von Soden, Editors
Inst. für Assyriologie & Hethitologie
Geschwister-Scholl-Platz
8000 Munich 22, Germany

Telephone: (49) 89 21803553
First published: 1886

Sponsoring organization: Deutsche Forschungsgemeinschaft
ISSN: 0084-5299
MLA acronym: ZAVA

SUBSCRIPTION INFORMATION

Frequency of publication: 2 times/yr.
Available in microform: No
Subscription address: Verlag Walter de Gruyter & Co., Genthiner Str. 13, Postfach 110240, 1000 Berlin 30, Germany

ADVERTISING INFORMATION

Advertising accepted: No

EDITORIAL DESCRIPTION

Scope: Publishes ancient Near Eastern studies.
Reviews books: Yes
Publishes notes: No
Languages accepted: English; German; French
Prints abstracts: Yes
Author-anonymous submission: No

SUBMISSION REQUIREMENTS

Author pays submission fee: No
Author pays page charges: No
Number of copies required: 1
Copyright ownership: Verlag Walter de Gruyter
Rejected manuscripts: Returned
Time before publication decision: 6-12 mos.

(3253)
*Zeitschrift für Balkanologie

Gabriella Schubert, Norbert Reiter, & Klaus-Detlev Grothusen, Editors
Inst. für Balkanologie
Garystr. 55
1000 Berlin 33, Germany

Telephone: (49) 30 8382039
Fax: (49) 30 8383788
First published: 1962
Sponsoring organization: Deutsche Forschungsgemeinschaft, Bonn-Bad Godesberg
ISSN: 0044-2356
MLA acronym: ZB

SUBSCRIPTION INFORMATION

Frequency of publication: 2 times/yr.
Circulation: 300
Available in microform: No
Subscription price: 92 DM/yr.; 46 DM/single issue
Year to which price refers: 1991
Subscription address: Verlag Otto Harrassowitz, Taunusstr. 6, Postfach 2929, 6200 Wiesbaden 1, Germany
Subscription telephone: (49) 611 530553
Subscription fax: (49) 611 530570

ADVERTISING INFORMATION

Advertising accepted: No

EDITORIAL DESCRIPTION

Scope: Publishes articles on the linguistics of Balkan languages including Albanian, Bulgarian, Modern Greek, Rumanian, Osmanic Turkish, Serbo-Croatian, and Hungarian. Questions of ethnology, folklore, and literature referring to Southeast Europe will also be discussed.
Reviews books: Yes
Publishes notes: No
Languages accepted: English; French; German; Italian; Russian
Prints abstracts: No
Author-anonymous submission: No

SUBMISSION REQUIREMENTS

Restrictions on contributors: None

Author pays submission fee: No
Author pays page charges: No
Length of articles: 30-40 pp.
Length of book reviews: 5 pp.
Style: Journal
Number of copies required: 1
Copyright ownership: Verlag Otto Harrassowitz
Rejected manuscripts: Returned
Time before publication decision: 2 mos.
Time between decision and publication: 1 yr.
Number of reviewers: 2
Articles submitted per year: 20
Articles published per year: 20
Book reviews submitted per year: 6
Book reviews published per year: 4-6

(3254)
*Zeitschrift für Celtische Philologie

Karl Horst Schmidt, Editor
Sprachwissenschaftliches Inst. der Univ. Bonn
An der Schlosskirche 2
5300 Bonn 1, Germany

First published: 1897
Sponsoring organization: Deutsche Forschungsgemeinschaft
ISSN: 0084-5302
MLA acronym: ZCP

SUBSCRIPTION INFORMATION

Frequency of publication: Irregular
Circulation: 200
Available in microform: No
Subscription address: Max Niemeyer Verlag, Postfach 2140, 7400 Tübingen, Germany

ADVERTISING INFORMATION

Advertising accepted: Yes

EDITORIAL DESCRIPTION

Scope: Publishes work on Celtic philology and linguistics.
Reviews books: Yes
Publishes notes: Yes
Languages accepted: English; German; French
Prints abstracts: No
Author-anonymous submission: No

SUBMISSION REQUIREMENTS

Restrictions on contributors: None
Author pays submission fee: No
Author pays page charges: No
Length of articles: No restrictions
Length of book reviews: No restrictions
Length of notes: No restrictions
Style: None
Number of copies required: 1
Special requirements: None
Copyright ownership: Max Niemeyer Verlag
Rejected manuscripts: Returned
Number of reviewers: 2-3

(3255)
*Zeitschrift für Deutsche Philologie

Werner Besch & Hartmut Steinecke, Editors
Hobsweg 64
5300 Bonn 1, Germany

Additional editorial address: Hartmut Steinecke, Sammtholzweg 13, 4790 Paderborn-Wever, Germany
Telephone: (49) 228 251119; (49) 5251 91152
First published: 1869
ISSN: 0044-2496
MLA acronym: ZDP

SUBSCRIPTION INFORMATION

Frequency of publication: 4 times/yr.
Circulation: 1,350
Available in microform: No
Subscription price: 208 DM/yr.
Year to which price refers: 1991
Subscription address: Erich Schmidt Verlag, Genthiner Str. 30G, 1000 Berlin 30, Germany

ADVERTISING INFORMATION

Advertising accepted: Yes

EDITORIAL DESCRIPTION

Scope: Publishes articles on German language, literature, and folklore.
Reviews books: Yes
Publishes notes: Yes
Languages accepted: German
Prints abstracts: Yes, in English
Author-anonymous submission: No

SUBMISSION REQUIREMENTS

Restrictions on contributors: None
Author pays submission fee: No
Author pays page charges: No
Length of articles: 15 pp.
Length of book reviews: 2-3 pp.
Length of notes: 4-6 pp.
Style: Journal
Number of copies required: 1
Copyright ownership: Journal & author
Rejected manuscripts: Returned
Time before publication decision: 1-3 mos.
Time between decision and publication: 12 mos.
Number of reviewers: 2
Articles submitted per year: 30-40
Articles published per year: 24
Book reviews submitted per year: 50-60
Book reviews published per year: 50
Notes submitted per year: 5-10
Notes published per year: 4-8

(3256)
*Zeitschrift für Deutsches Altertum und Deutsche Literatur

Franz Josef Worstbrock, Editor
Inst. für Deutsche Philologie
Schellingstr. 3
8000 Munich 40, Germany

Telephone: (49) 89 21802403
First published: 1841
Sponsoring organization: Deutsche Forschungsgemeinschaft, Bonn-Bad Godesberg
ISSN: 0044-2518
MLA acronym: ZDA

SUBSCRIPTION INFORMATION

Frequency of publication: 4 times/yr.
Circulation: 800
Available in microform: No
Subscription price: 180 DM/yr.
Year to which price refers: 1992
Subscription address: Franz Steiner Verlag Wiesbaden GmbH, Birkenwaldstr. 44, Postfach 101526, 7000 Stuttgart 10, Germany
Subscription telephone: (49) 711 25682229

ADVERTISING INFORMATION

Advertising accepted: Yes

EDITORIAL DESCRIPTION

Scope: Publishes articles on medieval German language and literature and German language history.
Reviews books: Yes
Publishes notes: No
Languages accepted: German; English
Prints abstracts: No
Author-anonymous submission: No

SUBMISSION REQUIREMENTS

Restrictions on contributors: None
Author pays submission fee: No
Author pays page charges: No
Length of articles: No restrictions
Length of book reviews: No restrictions
Style: Request from Franz Steiner Verlag
Number of copies required: 1
Special requirements: Consult with editor for submission instructions; submit original typescript.
Copyright ownership: Journal; reverts to author after 1 yr.
Rejected manuscripts: Returned
Time before publication decision: 1-2 mos.
Time between decision and publication: 9-12 mos.
Number of reviewers: 1
Articles submitted per year: 25-35
Articles published per year: 17-22
Book reviews submitted per year: 30-35
Book reviews published per year: 27-35

(3257)
*Zeitschrift für Dialektologie und Linguistik

Joachim Göschel, Rudolf Freudenberg, & Dieter Stellmacher, Editors
Wilhelm-Röpke-Str. 6, Block A
3550 Marburg/Lahn, Germany

Telephone: (49) 6421 284693; (49) 6421 284696
First published: 1924
Sponsoring organization: Deutsche Forschungsgemeinschaft, Bonn a.Rh.
ISSN: 0044-1449
MLA acronym: ZDL

SUBSCRIPTION INFORMATION

Frequency of publication: 3 times/yr.
Circulation: 600
Available in microform: No
Subscription price: 120 DM/yr.; 44 DM/single issue
Year to which price refers: 1992
Subscription address: Franz Steiner Verlag Wiesbaden GmbH, Birkenwaldstr. 44, Postfach 10 15 26, 7000 Stuttgart 10, Germany
Subscription telephone: (49) 711 2582218

ADVERTISING INFORMATION

Advertising accepted: Yes

EDITORIAL DESCRIPTION

Scope: Publishes articles, notes, reviews, and bibliographies on dialectology and general linguistics.
Reviews books: Yes
Publishes notes: Yes
Languages accepted: English; German
Prints abstracts: Yes
Author-anonymous submission: Yes

SUBMISSION REQUIREMENTS

Restrictions on contributors: None
Author pays submission fee: No
Author pays page charges: No
Length of articles: 10-25 pp.
Length of book reviews: 1-5 pp.
Length of notes: 1-2 pp.
Style: Journal
Number of copies required: 2
Special requirements: Write to editor for journal's style sheet prior to submission; include abstract; submit original typescript and 1 copy.
Copyright ownership: Franz Steiner Verlag
Rejected manuscripts: Returned
Time before publication decision: 2 mos.
Time between decision and publication: 16 mos.
Number of reviewers: 2-3
Articles submitted per year: 25-30
Articles published per year: 15-22
Book reviews submitted per year: 90
Book reviews published per year: 80

Notes submitted per year: 30
Notes published per year: 20

(3258)
*Zeitschrift für Französische Sprache und Literatur

Klaus W. Hempfer & Peter Blumenthal, Editors
Inst. für Romanische Philologie
Habelschwerdter Allee 45
1000 Berlin 33, Germany

Additional editorial address: P. Blumenthal, Univ. Stuttgart, Inst. für Linguistik, Romanistik, Keplerstr. 17, 7000 Stuttgart, Germany
Telephone: (49) 30 8382043
Fax: (49) 30 8386749
First published: 1879
Sponsoring organization: Deutsche Forschungsgemeinschaft
ISSN: 0044-2747
MLA acronym: ZFSL

SUBSCRIPTION INFORMATION

Frequency of publication: 3 times/yr.
Circulation: 500
Available in microform: No
Subscription price: 128 DM/yr.
Year to which price refers: 1992
Subscription address: Franz Steiner Verlag Wiesbaden GmbH, Birkenwaldstr. 44, Postfach 10 15 26, 7000 Stuttgart 1, Germany
Subscription telephone: (49) 711 25820
Subscription fax: (49) 711 2582290

ADVERTISING INFORMATION

Advertising accepted: Yes

EDITORIAL DESCRIPTION

Scope: Publishes articles on French and Provençal languages and literatures.
Reviews books: Yes
Publishes notes: Yes
Languages accepted: English; French; German; Spanish; Italian
Prints abstracts: Yes
Author-anonymous submission: No

SUBMISSION REQUIREMENTS

Restrictions on contributors: Book reviews are solicited.
Author pays submission fee: No
Author pays page charges: No
Length of articles: 2,000-12,000 words
Length of book reviews: 500-4,000 words
Length of notes: 1,000-3,000 words
Style: MLA
Number of copies required: 1
Special requirements: Submit original typescript.
Copyright ownership: Assigned by author to journal; reverts to author after 1 yr.
Rejected manuscripts: Returned; enclose return postage.
Time before publication decision: 2-3 mos.
Time between decision and publication: 1-2 yrs.
Number of reviewers: 2-3
Articles submitted per year: 30-50
Articles published per year: 12-16
Book reviews published per year: 40-45
Notes submitted per year: 20-30
Notes published per year: 2-4

(3259)
*Zeitschrift für Germanistik

Klaus-Dieter Hährel, Editor
Humboldt-Univ.
Postfach 1297
1086 Berlin, Germany

Telephone: (37) 2 9765539

First published: 1980
ISSN: 0323-7982
MLA acronym: ZG

SUBSCRIPTION INFORMATION

Frequency of publication: 3 times/yr.
Available in microform: No
Subscription address: Peter Lang GmbH, Europäischen Verlag der Wissenschaften, Jupiterstr. 15, 3000 Bern 15, Switzerland

ADVERTISING INFORMATION

Advertising accepted: Yes

EDITORIAL DESCRIPTION

Scope: Publishes articles on German philology and on the history of German literature in East Germany, West Germany, Austria, and Switzerland.
Reviews books: Yes
Publishes notes: Yes
Languages accepted: German
Prints abstracts: No
Author-anonymous submission: No

SUBMISSION REQUIREMENTS

Author pays submission fee: No
Length of articles: 600 words
Length of book reviews: 180 words
Length of notes: 100 words
Style: MLA; Berlin
Number of copies required: 2
Copyright ownership: Peter Lang GmbH
Time before publication decision: 2 yrs.
Time between decision and publication: 4 mos.
Articles submitted per year: 200
Articles published per year: 150
Book reviews submitted per year: 150
Book reviews published per year: 90
Notes submitted per year: 15
Notes published per year: 15

(3260)
Zeitschrift für Germanistische Linguistik

Els Oksaar, Helmut Henne, Peter von Polenz, & Herbert Ernst Wiegand, Editors
Inst. für Allgemeine Sprachwissenschaft & Indogermanistik
Univ. Hamburg
von-Melle-Park 6
2000 Hamburg 13, Germany

Additional editorial address: P. von Polenz, Fachbereich Sprach- & Literaturwissenschaft, Univ. Trier, Postfach 3825, 5500 Trier, Germany
First published: 1973
ISSN: 0301-3294
MLA acronym: ZGL

SUBSCRIPTION INFORMATION

Frequency of publication: 3 times/yr.
Circulation: 800
Available in microform: Yes
Subscription address: Walter de Gruyter & Co., Genthiner Str. 13, 1000 Berlin 30, Germany

ADVERTISING INFORMATION

Advertising accepted: Yes

EDITORIAL DESCRIPTION

Scope: Contains essays and criticism on topics of scientific research in the German language and its history, with focus in grammar, lexical semantics, pragmatics, stylistics, text linguistics, sociolinguistics, and linguistic criticism. Also includes reports about meetings and congresses, discussion and controversy about current subjects, abstracts of contributions to journals, and an annual survey of new books.
Reviews books: No
Publishes notes: Yes
Languages accepted: German
Prints abstracts: Yes
Author-anonymous submission: No

SUBMISSION REQUIREMENTS

Author pays submission fee: No
Author pays page charges: No
Style: MLA with modifications
Number of copies required: 1
Special requirements: Use as few footnotes as possible and provide a list of quoted literature.
Copyright ownership: Walter de Gruyter & Co.
Rejected manuscripts: Returned
Time before publication decision: 2-5 mos.
Time between decision and publication: 3-7 mos.
Number of reviewers: 4
Articles submitted per year: 20-30
Articles published per year: 13-17
Notes submitted per year: 15-20
Notes published per year: 10-15

(3261)
*Zeitschrift für Katalanistik: Revista d'Estudis Catalans

Christine Bierbach, Brigitte Schlieben-Lange, Axel Schönberger, & Tilbert Dídac Stegmann, Editors
c/o Katalanisches Kulturbüro
Jordanstr. 10
6000 Frankfurt am Main 90, Germany

Telephone: (49) 69 7073744
Fax: (49) 69 7073745
First published: 1988
Sponsoring organization: Deutsch-Katalanische Gesellschaft; Johann Wolfgang Goethe-Univ.; Centre UNESCO de Catalunya; Höchst Ibèrica; Dept. de Cultura, Generalität de Catalunya
ISSN: 0932-2221
MLA acronym: ZfK

SUBSCRIPTION INFORMATION

Frequency of publication: Annual
Circulation: 2,000
Available in microform: No
Subscription price: 35 DM/yr.
Year to which price refers: 1992

ADVERTISING INFORMATION

Advertising accepted: Yes
Advertising rates: 500 DM/full page

EDITORIAL DESCRIPTION

Scope: Publishes articles on Catalan studies, including Catalan literature and linguistics.
Reviews books: Yes
Publishes notes: Yes
Languages accepted: German; Catalan
Prints abstracts: Yes
Author-anonymous submission: No

SUBMISSION REQUIREMENTS

Author pays submission fee: No
Author pays page charges: No
Length of articles: 12-15 pp.
Length of book reviews: 3 pp. maximum
Length of notes: 3 pp. maximum
Style: Duden

Number of copies required: 1
Copyright ownership: Deutsch-Katalanische Gesellschaft e.V.
Rejected manuscripts: Not returned
Time before publication decision: 2 mos.
Time between decision and publication: 2-6 mos.
Number of reviewers: 4
Articles submitted per year: 15-25
Articles published per year: 10-20
Book reviews submitted per year: 5-10
Book reviews published per year: 5-10
Notes submitted per year: 0-5
Notes published per year: 0-5

(3262)
*Zeitschrift für Ostforschung: Länder und Völker im Östlichen Mitteleuropa

Friedrich Benninghoven, Stefan Hartmann, Winfried Irgang, Ludwig Petry, Gert von Pistohlkors, Friedrich Prinz, Roderich Schmidt, Hugo Weczerka, & Hellmuth Weiss, Editors
Gisonenweg 7
3550 Marburg a.d. Lahn 1, Germany

Telephone: (49) 6421 1840
Fax: (49) 6421 184139
First published: 1952
Sponsoring organization: Johann-Gottfried-Herder-Forschungsrat e.V.
ISSN: 0044-3239
MLA acronym: ZOF

SUBSCRIPTION INFORMATION

Frequency of publication: 4 times/yr.
Circulation: 750
Available in microform: No
Subscription price: 98 DM/yr.
Year to which price refers: 1991
Subscription address: Verlag J. G. Herder-Inst., at the above address

ADVERTISING INFORMATION

Advertising accepted: No

EDITORIAL DESCRIPTION

Scope: Publishes the most recent research results from Middle East Europe in the areas of history, cultural history, art history, geography, folklore, economics, and trade, in the form of essays, research reports, announcements, literary reports, book reviews, and selected bibliographies.
Reviews books: Yes
Publishes notes: No
Languages accepted: German; English
Prints abstracts: Yes
Author-anonymous submission: No

SUBMISSION REQUIREMENTS

Restrictions on contributors: None
Author pays submission fee: Yes
Author pays page charges: No
Length of articles: 40 pp. maximum
Length of book reviews: 1/2-1 p.
Style: None
Number of copies required: 1
Special requirements: Submit original typescript.
Copyright ownership: Journal; reverts to author after 1 yr.
Rejected manuscripts: Returned
Number of reviewers: 2
Articles published per year: 10-19

(3263)
*Zeitschrift für Romanische Philologie

Max Pfister, Editor
Steinbergstr. 20
6550 Hamburg, Germany

First published: 1877
ISSN: 0049-8661
MLA acronym: ZRP

SUBSCRIPTION INFORMATION

Frequency of publication: 3 times/yr.
Circulation: 610
Available in microform: No
Subscription address: Max Niemeyer Verlag, Postfach 2140, 7400 Tübingen, Germany

ADVERTISING INFORMATION

Advertising accepted: Yes

EDITORIAL DESCRIPTION

Scope: Covers the literary historical area of Romance literature to the Renaissance and Romance philology. Also includes articles on related general linguistics when space is available.
Reviews books: Yes
Publishes notes: Yes
Languages accepted: French; German; Portuguese; Spanish; Italian; Romanian; English occasionally
Prints abstracts: No
Author-anonymous submission: No

SUBMISSION REQUIREMENTS

Restrictions on contributors: None
Author pays submission fee: No
Author pays page charges: No
Length of articles: 9,000 words
Length of book reviews: 1,500 words
Length of notes: 300 words
Style: Journal
Number of copies required: 1
Special requirements: Submit original typescript.
Copyright ownership: Max Niemeyer Verlag
Rejected manuscripts: Returned; enclose return postage.
Time before publication decision: 3-90 days
Time between decision and publication: 1-3 yrs.
Number of reviewers: 1-3
Articles submitted per year: 40
Articles published per year: 20
Book reviews submitted per year: 160
Book reviews published per year: 140
Notes submitted per year: 100
Notes published per year: 90

(3264)
*Zeitschrift für Slavische Philologie

Peter Brang & Helmut Keipert, Editors
Carl Winter Universitätsverlag
Lutherstr. 59
6900 Heidelberg, Germany

Additional editorial address: Send articles on Slavic literatures to: Peter Brang, Bundtstr. 20, 8127 Forch/ZH, Switzerland. Send articles on Slavic linguistics to: Helmut Keipert, Slavistisches Seminar, Lennéstr. 1, 5300 Bonn, Germany
Telephone: (41) 1 9800950 (P. Brang); (49) 228 737272 (H. Keipert)
First published: 1924
Sponsoring organization: Deutsche Forschungsgemeinschaft, Bad Godesberg
ISSN: 0044-3492
MLA acronym: ZSP

SUBSCRIPTION INFORMATION

Frequency of publication: 2 times/yr.

Available in microform: No
Subscription price: 200 DM/yr.
Year to which price refers: 1992
Subscription telephone: (49) 6221 41490 (Carl Winter Universitätsverlag)

ADVERTISING INFORMATION

Advertising accepted: Yes

EDITORIAL DESCRIPTION

Scope: Publishes articles on Slavic languages and literatures.
Reviews books: Yes
Languages accepted: German; Russian; English
Prints abstracts: No

SUBMISSION REQUIREMENTS

Restrictions on contributors: None
Author pays submission fee: No
Author pays page charges: No
Length of articles: No restrictions
Length of book reviews: No restrictions
Style: None
Number of copies required: 1
Special requirements: Submit original typescript, and, if possible, Macintosh diskette.
Copyright ownership: Assigned by author to journal
Rejected manuscripts: Returned
Time before publication decision: 3 mos.
Time between decision and publication: 12-18 mos.
Number of reviewers: 2
Articles published per year: 20-25
Book reviews published per year: 15-20

(3265)
*Zeitschrift für Slawistik

Klaus Dieter Seemann, Witold Kośny, Karl Gutschmidt, & Ulf Lehmann, Editors
Freie Univ. Berlin
Osteuropa-Inst., Abteilung Slavistik
Garystr. 55
1000 Berlin 33, Germany

Telephone: (49) 30 8382028
Fax: (49) 30 8383788
First published: 1956
ISSN: 0044-3506
MLA acronym: ZS

SUBSCRIPTION INFORMATION

Frequency of publication: 4 times/yr.
Circulation: 1,000
Available in microform: No
Subscription price: 160 DM/yr. Germany; 171 DM/yr. elsewhere
Year to which price refers: 1992
Subscription address: Akademie Verlag, Leipziger Str. 3-4, 1086 Berlin, Germany
Additional subscription address: Buchexport, Volkseigener Aussenhandelsbetrieb, Postfach 160, 7010 Leipzig, Germany

ADVERTISING INFORMATION

Advertising accepted: Yes

EDITORIAL DESCRIPTION

Scope: Publishes articles on Slavic languages and literatures.
Reviews books: Yes
Publishes notes: Yes
Languages accepted: German; English
Prints abstracts: No
Author-anonymous submission: No

SUBMISSION REQUIREMENTS

Restrictions on contributors: None
Author pays submission fee: No
Author pays page charges: No
Length of articles: 20 pp.

Length of book reviews: 5 pp.
Length of notes: No restrictions
Style: Journal
Number of copies required: 2
Special requirements: Manuscripts must be double-spaced.
Copyright ownership: Akademie Verlag
Rejected manuscripts: Returned
Time before publication decision: 3 mos.
Time between decision and publication: 1 yr.
Number of reviewers: 1-2
Articles submitted per year: 60
Articles published per year: 50
Book reviews submitted per year: 50
Book reviews published per year: 40
Notes submitted per year: 10
Notes published per year: 10

(3266)
*Zeitschrift für Volkskunde: Halbjahreschrift der Deutschen Ges. f. Volkskunde

Gottfried Korff, Martin Scharfe, Klaus Roth, & Siegried Becker, Editors
Schloss (Ludwig-Uhland-Inst.)
7400 Tübingen, Germany

Additional editorial address: Martin Scharfe, Inst. für Europäische Ethnologie & Kulturforschung, Bahnhofstr. 3, 3550 Marburg, Germany
Telephone: (49) 7071 294886
Fax: (49) 7071 295330
First published: 1891
Sponsoring organization: Deutsche Gesellschaft für Volkskunde
ISSN: 0044-3700
MLA acronym: ZV

SUBSCRIPTION INFORMATION

Frequency of publication: 2 times/yr.
Circulation: 1,300
Available in microform: No
Subscription price: 96 DM/yr.
Year to which price refers: 1992
Subscription address: Verlag Otto Schwartz & Co., Annastr. 7, 3400 Göttingen, Germany

ADVERTISING INFORMATION

Advertising accepted: Yes
Advertising rates: 190 DM/quarter page; 360 DM/half page; 700 DM/full page

EDITORIAL DESCRIPTION

Scope: Publishes articles on all fields of German folklore and European ethnology.
Reviews books: Yes
Publishes notes: Yes
Languages accepted: German
Prints abstracts: Yes, in English

SUBMISSION REQUIREMENTS

Restrictions on contributors: None
Author pays submission fee: No
Author pays page charges: No
Length of articles: 20 pp.
Length of book reviews: 2 pp.
Number of copies required: 1
Copyright ownership: Author
Rejected manuscripts: Returned
Time before publication decision: 2 mos.
Time between decision and publication: 8 mos.
Number of reviewers: 1-3
Articles submitted per year: 15-20
Articles published per year: 10
Book reviews submitted per year: 50-80
Book reviews published per year: 40-50
Notes submitted per year: 8
Notes published per year: 5-8

(3267)
*Zeszyty Literackie

Barbara Toruńczyk, Editor
B.P. 234
75464 Paris Cedex 10, France

Additional editorial address: 13 rue Jarry, 75010 Paris, France; Agora, ul. Nowy Świat 27, 00-029 Warsaw, Poland
Telephone: (33) 1 42463253
Fax: (33) 1 42461371
First published: 1983
Sponsoring organization: Agora
ISSN: 0751-0357
MLA acronym: ZL

SUBSCRIPTION INFORMATION

Frequency of publication: 4 times/yr.
Circulation: 8,000
Available in microform: No
Subscription price: $52.00 (260 F)/yr. institutions; $40.00 (200 F)/yr. individuals
Year to which price refers: 1991
Subscription address: Librairie Libella, 12, rue Saint Louis-en-l'Ile, 75004 Paris, France
Additional subscription address: Agora, ul. Nowy Świat 27, 00-029 Warsaw, Poland
Subscription telephone: (33) 1 43265109
Subscription fax: (33) 1 43251421

ADVERTISING INFORMATION

Advertising accepted: Yes

EDITORIAL DESCRIPTION

Scope: Publishes articles on Polish and other East European literatures. Also includes creative works by Polish writers.
Reviews books: Yes
Publishes notes: Yes
Languages accepted: Polish
Prints abstracts: Yes
Author-anonymous submission: No

SUBMISSION REQUIREMENTS

Restrictions on contributors: None
Author pays submission fee: No
Author pays page charges: No
Length of articles: 9 pp.
Length of book reviews: 7 pp.
Length of notes: 4 pp.
Style: MLA
Number of copies required: 3
Copyright ownership: Author & journal
Rejected manuscripts: Not returned
Time before publication decision: 6 weeks
Time between decision and publication: 6 weeks
Number of reviewers: 2
Articles submitted per year: 500
Articles published per year: 100
Book reviews submitted per year: 50
Book reviews published per year: 25
Notes submitted per year: 110
Notes published per year: 25

(3268)
*Zeta: Rivista Internazionale di Poesia

Carlo Marcello Conti, Editor
Via Michelini 1
33100 Udine, Italy

Additional editorial address: Zeta Factory, Via Marano, 33037 Pasian di Prato, Udine, Italy
Telephone: (39) 432 699390
Fax: (39) 432 699390
First published: 1978
ISSN: 0393-2362
MLA acronym: Zeta

SUBSCRIPTION INFORMATION

Frequency of publication: 2 times/yr.
Circulation: 2,000
Available in microform: Yes
Subscription price: 50,000 Lit/yr.
Year to which price refers: 1992
Subscription address: Franca Campanotto, at the above address

ADVERTISING INFORMATION

Advertising accepted: Yes

EDITORIAL DESCRIPTION

Scope: Publishes poetry and articles on Italian and international poetry.
Reviews books: Yes
Publishes notes: Yes
Languages accepted: English; Italian; French; Spanish; German
Prints abstracts: Yes

SUBMISSION REQUIREMENTS

Author pays submission fee: No
Author pays page charges: No
Length of articles: 2,000 words
Length of book reviews: 500 words
Length of notes: 150 words
Number of copies required: 2
Special requirements: Submit typescript.
Rejected manuscripts: Not returned
Time before publication decision: 6 mos.
Time between decision and publication: 6 mos.
Number of reviewers: 15
Articles submitted per year: 60
Articles published per year: 20
Book reviews submitted per year: 150
Book reviews published per year: 20
Notes submitted per year: 200
Notes published per year: 20

(3269)
*Zielsprache Deutsch: Zeitschrift für Unterrichtsmethodik und Angewandte Sprachwissenschaft

Elmar Winters-Ohle, Editor
Arneckestr. 5
4600 Dortmund 1, Germany

Telephone: (49) 231 102690
Fax: (49) 231 101509
First published: 1970
ISSN: 0341-5864
MLA acronym: ZD

SUBSCRIPTION INFORMATION

Frequency of publication: 4 times/yr. (Mar., June, Sept., Dec.)
Circulation: 3,000
Available in microform: No
Subscription price: 28 DM/yr. plus postage
Year to which price refers: 1992
Subscription address: Max Hueber Verlag, Max Hueber Str. 4, 8045 Ismaning bei München, Germany
Subscription telephone: (49) 89 9602-0
Subscription fax: (49) 89 9602-358

ADVERTISING INFORMATION

Advertising accepted: Yes

EDITORIAL DESCRIPTION

Scope: Publishes work on methods of teaching German and applied linguistics.
Reviews books: Yes
Publishes notes: Yes
Languages accepted: German
Prints abstracts: Yes
Author-anonymous submission: No

SUBMISSION REQUIREMENTS

Restrictions on contributors: None
Author pays submission fee: No
Author pays page charges: No

Length of articles: 12 pp.
Length of book reviews: 2 pp.
Length of notes: 80-100 words
Style: MLA
Number of copies required: 2
Copyright ownership: Author & Max Hueber Verlag
Rejected manuscripts: Returned
Time before publication decision: 6-8 weeks
Time between decision and publication: 6 mos. maximum
Number of reviewers: 1
Articles submitted per year: 35-45
Articles published per year: 20-25
Book reviews submitted per year: 20-30
Book reviews published per year: 10-20

(3270)
*Živa Antika

Petar Hr. Ilievski, Editor
Seminar za Klasična Filologija
Filosofski Fakultet
Skopje, Macedonia (Yugoslavia)

Telephone: (38) 91 222311
First published: 1951
Sponsoring organization: Macedonian Assn. for Classical Studies
ISSN: 0514-7727
MLA acronym: ŽA

SUBSCRIPTION INFORMATION

Frequency of publication: 2 times/yr.
Available in microform: Yes

ADVERTISING INFORMATION

Advertising accepted: No

EDITORIAL DESCRIPTION

Scope: Publishes articles on classical philology, archaeology, and ancient history.
Reviews books: Yes
Publishes notes: Yes
Languages accepted: English; French; Latin; Slovenian; Macedonian; German; Italian; Russian; Serbo-Croatian
Prints abstracts: Yes

SUBMISSION REQUIREMENTS

Restrictions on contributors: None
Author pays submission fee: No
Author pays page charges: No
Length of articles: 30 pp.
Length of book reviews: 15 pp.
Length of notes: 1 p.
Number of copies required: 1
Special requirements: Submit original typescript.
Copyright ownership: Journal & author
Time before publication decision: 1 yr.
Time between decision and publication: 6-12 mos.
Number of reviewers: 2
Articles submitted per year: 50
Articles published per year: 40-50
Book reviews published per year: 20-30
Notes published per year: 10

(3271)
Život: Časopis za Književnost i Kulturu

Ranko Sladojević, Editor
P. Preradovića 3, Fach 129
71000 Sarajevo, Bosnia and Herzegovina

First published: 1952
Sponsoring organization: Republican Union of Culture
ISSN: 0514-776X
MLA acronym: Život

SUBSCRIPTION INFORMATION

Frequency of publication: 12 times/yr.
Circulation: 1,300
Available in microform: No
Subscription address: Sour "Svjetlost", at the above address

ADVERTISING INFORMATION

Advertising accepted: No

EDITORIAL DESCRIPTION

Scope: Publishes poetry, prose, and criticism in and of Yugoslavian and world literature, concentrating on Bosnia and Herzegovina.
Reviews books: Yes
Publishes notes: Yes
Languages accepted: Serbo-Croatian
Prints abstracts: Yes
Author-anonymous submission: No

SUBMISSION REQUIREMENTS

Restrictions on contributors: None
Author pays submission fee: Yes
Author pays page charges: No
Length of articles: No restrictions
Length of book reviews: No restrictions
Length of notes: No restrictions
Style: None
Number of copies required: 1
Copyright ownership: Author
Rejected manuscripts: Not returned
Time before publication decision: 1 mo.
Time between decision and publication: 1-4 mos.
Number of reviewers: 3
Articles submitted per year: 800-1,000
Articles published per year: 200-220
Book reviews submitted per year: 150-180
Book reviews published per year: 80-100
Notes submitted per year: 30-50
Notes published per year: 20-30

(3272)
Znak: Miesięcznik

Stefan Wilkanowicz, Editor
Spoleczny Inst. Wydawniczy "Znak"
ul. Kosciuszki 37
30-106 Cracow, Poland

ISSN: 0044-488X
MLA acronym: Znak

SUBSCRIPTION INFORMATION

Frequency of publication: 12 times/yr.

EDITORIAL DESCRIPTION

Reviews books: No
Languages accepted: Polish

(3273)
*Znamenje

Ivan Arzenšek, Editor
Petrovče 199
63301 Petrovče, Slovenia

Telephone: (38) 63 776209
First published: 1971
Sponsoring organization: Kulturna Skupnost Slovenije
MLA acronym: Znamenje

SUBSCRIPTION INFORMATION

Frequency of publication: 3 times/yr.
Available in microform: No
Subscription address: Založba Znamenje, d.o.o. Petrovče, Petrovče 199, 63301 Petrovče, Slovenia

ADVERTISING INFORMATION

Advertising accepted: No

EDITORIAL DESCRIPTION

Scope: Publishes articles on theology, philosophy, and culture.
Reviews books: Yes
Publishes notes: Yes
Languages accepted: Slovenian
Prints abstracts: No
Author-anonymous submission: No

SUBMISSION REQUIREMENTS

Restrictions on contributors: None
Author pays submission fee: Yes
Author pays page charges: No
Length of articles: No restrictions
Length of book reviews: No restrictions
Length of notes: No restrictions
Number of copies required: 1
Copyright ownership: Author
Rejected manuscripts: Returned
Time before publication decision: 3 weeks
Time between decision and publication: 4 mos.
Number of reviewers: 3
Articles submitted per year: 1,000
Articles published per year: 80
Book reviews submitted per year: 40
Book reviews published per year: 30
Notes submitted per year: 70
Notes published per year: 60

(3274)
Znamia: Literaturno-Khudozhestvennyĭ i Obshchestvenno-Politicheskiĭ Zhurnal

G. Ia. Baklanov, Editor
Ul. Nikol'skaia, 8/1
103863 GSP Moscow, Russia

Sponsoring organization: Soiuz Pisateleĭ S.S.S.R.
ISSN: 0130-1616
MLA acronym: Znamia

SUBSCRIPTION INFORMATION

Frequency of publication: 12 times/yr.

EDITORIAL DESCRIPTION

Scope: Publishes primarily original short stories and poetry by Russian writers. Also includes articles on Russian literature.
Reviews books: Yes
Languages accepted: Russian
Prints abstracts: Yes

(3275)
The Zora Neale Hurston Forum

Ruthe T. Sheffey, Editor
P.O. Box 550
Morgan State Univ.
Baltimore, MD 21239

First published: 1986
Sponsoring organization: Zora Neale Hurston Soc.
MLA acronym: ZNHF

SUBSCRIPTION INFORMATION

Frequency of publication: 2 times/yr. (Spring, Fall)
Circulation: 200
Available in microform: No

ADVERTISING INFORMATION

Advertising accepted: Yes

EDITORIAL DESCRIPTION

Scope: Publishes essays and creative writing which promote the appreciation of the life, works, and legacy of Zora Neale Hurston, and of the creative African American circles in which she moved in the first half of the 20th century.
Reviews books: Yes
Publishes notes: Yes
Languages accepted: English
Prints abstracts: No
Author-anonymous submission: No

SUBMISSION REQUIREMENTS

Restrictions on contributors: Contributors must be members of Zora Neale Hurston Soc.
Author pays submission fee: No
Author pays page charges: No
Length of articles: 6-8 pp.
Style: MLA
Number of copies required: 3
Special requirements: Submit original typescript and 2 copies
Copyright ownership: Author
Rejected manuscripts: Returned; enclose SASE.
Time before publication decision: 1 mo.
Time between decision and publication: 6 mos.
Number of reviewers: 3
Articles published per year: 12
Book reviews published per year: 4
Notes published per year: 4

(3276)
Zvezda

G. F. Nikolaev, Editor
Mokhovaia 20
191028 St. Petersburg, Russia

First published: 1924
Sponsoring organization: Hudozhestvennaya Literatura Publishing House
ISSN: 0321-1878
MLA acronym: Zvezda

SUBSCRIPTION INFORMATION

Frequency of publication: 12 times/yr.
Circulation: 210,000
Available in microform: No

ADVERTISING INFORMATION

Advertising accepted: No

EDITORIAL DESCRIPTION

Scope: Publishes novels, poetry, and articles on modern literature, economics, and sociology.
Reviews books: Yes
Publishes notes: Yes
Languages accepted: Russian
Prints abstracts: No
Author-anonymous submission: No

SUBMISSION REQUIREMENTS

Restrictions on contributors: None
Author pays submission fee: No
Author pays page charges: No
Length of articles: 800-1,000 words
Length of book reviews: 1,000-3,000 words
Style: None
Number of copies required: 2
Special requirements: Submit original typescript.
Copyright ownership: Author
Rejected manuscripts: Returned
Time before publication decision: 2-3 mos.
Time between decision and publication: 10 mos. maximum

Number of reviewers: 2-3
Articles submitted per year: 900 minimum
Articles published per year: 90-100
Book reviews submitted per year: 400-500
Book reviews published per year: 40-50
Notes submitted per year: 200-250
Notes published per year: 20-25

(3277)
Życie Literackie

Wydawnictwo Wspolczesne RSW Prasa
ul. Wiejska 12
00-420 Warsaw, Poland

First published: 1951
Sponsoring organization: Zwiazek Literatów Polskich
ISSN: 0591-2369
MLA acronym: ŻLit

SUBSCRIPTION INFORMATION

Frequency of publication: 52 times/yr.
Additional subscription address: Ars Polona-Ruch, Krakowskie Przedmieście 7, 00-068 Warsaw, Poland

EDITORIAL DESCRIPTION

Author-anonymous submission: No

INDEX TO SUBJECTS

Acoustic phonetics   2173
Acoustical research   1446
Adventure novel   790
Aegean epigraphy   1491
Aegean philology   1843
Aegean studies   2756
Aesthetics   359, 412, 645, 681, 792, 914, 1206, 1353, 1378, 2191, 2384, 2421, 2452, 2483, 2853, 3162
  Biblical literature and   1648
  Chinese   1373
  Hispanic   786
  Indian   1402
  literary   495, 2166
  Pre-Raphaelite Brotherhood   1438
  Russian   2508
  semiotics and   754, 2580
Afghanistan studies   1267
Africa
  books and audio-visual materials   659
  culture in Portuguese-speaking countries   2205
  English language in   862
  history of Portuguese-speaking countries   2205
  Italian culture in   2745
  literature of Portuguese-speaking countries   2205
  Portuguese language in   2395
  publishing and book trade in   48
African   see also Central African; North African; Southern African; West African
African American folklore   1137
African American literature   46, 365, 1137, 1552, 1675, 1779, 3275
African American music   1723
African American studies   109, 506
African anthropology   52, 476, 1257, 1884, 2102
African arts   47, 61, 506, 1257
  Zimbabwe   3244
African culture   42, 47, 51, 56, 239, 262, 506, 714, 926, 1052
  language and   49
  sociology of   658
  Sub-Saharan   45
African education   1884
African ethnology   476, 1052
African fiction   2221
African folk culture   2102
  Botswana   401
African folklore   525, 1137
  Zimbabwe   3244
African history   43, 52, 56, 239, 476, 1052, 1257, 1884, 2102, 2221
  Botswana   401
African languages   42, 49, 52, 59-60, 262, 525, 952, 956, 1052, 1354, 1680, 2672, 2805
  history and   2707
  West Africa   1484
African linguistics   57, 434, 476, 956, 1052, 1257, 1346, 1354, 1661, 1884, 2805
  Botswana   401
African literature   43, 50, 52, 54, 56, 59, 124, 185, 262, 365, 506, 525, 714, 862, 926, 952, 1137, 1257, 1375, 1401, 1536, 1675, 1680, 1777, 1779-1780, 1884, 2022, 2058, 2221, 2353, 2672, 2806, 3045, 3049, 3053, 3243
  English language   409
  French language   2426
  Indian Ocean   2022
  Portuguese language   1738
  sociology of   658
African music   1257, 1780
African philosophy   1884, 2221
African poetics   658
African poetry   2221
African religions   2221
African society   42
African studies   43-44, 52-53, 55, 58-59, 184, 264, 453, 476, 525, 917, 952, 1030, 1257, 1594, 1777, 1780, 3053, 3243, 3248
  bibliographies   42, 48, 56, 734
  Botswana   401
  contemporary   1420
  methodology   658

African studies (*cont.*)
  Sierra Leone   58
  Yoruba   2355
Afrikaans language   1514, 1680
Afrikaans language literature   1514, 1680, 3048-3049
Afro-   see also Black
Afro-Asiatic languages   2902
Afro-Asiatic linguistics   63, 352, 1355
Afro-Hispanic culture   62
Afro-Hispanic literature   62, 1734
Albanian folklore   730
Albanian linguistics   3253
Albanian literature   1938, 2764
Albanian studies   730, 1613, 2764
Albee, Edward   2807
Alchemy   555
Alcohol, literature and   793
Aleut   see Eskimo-Aleut
Alfonso el Sabio   448
Alger, Horatio, Jr.   1981
Algerian literature   2403
Algonquian culture   2119
Algonquian linguistics   2119
Allegory   2336
Alto Adige, Italy   243
Altaic ethnography   26, 2876
Altaic languages   26, 1241, 3093
Altaic linguistics   2876, 3093
Altaic studies   1241
Alto Adige, Italy   243
American anthropology   113
  Native American   97
  Southwestern   2105
American art   109, 113, 1497
  1830-1860   2852
  18th century   839
  Kansas and Great Plains   1175
  Southern   2685
  Southwestern   2105
American civilization   229, 2250, 2425
American cultural history   2357
American culture   85, 101, 109, 113, 130-131, 174-176, 254, 262, 280, 939, 1016, 1071, 1217, 1356, 1753, 2239, 2250, 2319, 2686
  colonial   3186
  18th century   285
  facsimile reprints   285
  mid-Atlantic   2142
  Midwestern   1497, 1835, 2063
  early national   3186
  19th century   116, 2852
  Old Northwest Territory   2063
  17th century   285, 2592
  Southern   1848, 2684-2686
  Southwestern   1480
  Virginia   3136
American dance, Southern   2685
American drama   96, 1092
  20th century   964
American-European studies   1753
American fiction   2808
  contemporary   3022
  novel   105
American film   2250, 3104
American folk art   3062
  Southern   2685
  Southwestern   2105
American folk culture   995, 1016
  New Jersey   1963
  North Carolina   2004
  Northwestern   2011
  Pennsylvania   2141
  Southern   2682
American folk song   2010
American folklore   109, 223, 684, 995, 1016, 1849, 2261, 3171
  Central region   1829
  Georgia   1042
  Great Plains   1135
  Kansas and Great Plains   1175
  Midwestern   1834
  Mississippi   1847
  New England   2010
  New Jersey   1963
  North Carolina   1042, 2004
  Northwestern   2011
  Southern   1847, 2682
  Southwestern   1480

American folklore (*cont.*)
  Tennessee   2924
American-German linguistics   1753
American-German literary relations   1753
American history   85, 130-131, 280, 1219, 1358, 1450, 2239, 2244, 2499
  Civil War   1226
  colonial   3186
  1830-1860   2852
  18th century   839
  Great Plains   1135
  Illinois   1226
  Kansas and Great Plains   1175
  literature and   1226, 1850
  Maine   622
  mid-Atlantic   2142
  Midwestern   1497, 2107
  early national   3186
  New England   1956
  North Carolina   2005
  Northwestern Ohio   2012
  17th century   2592
  Southern   2688
  Southwestern   1480, 2105
  Virginia   3136
American humor   2809
American language   see English language, in North America; Native American languages
American linguistics   1221, 1263, 2394, 2825
American literary history   101
  19th century   906
American literary theory and criticism   848, 1205
American literature   7, 20, 28, 65, 85, 95, 101, 103-105, 109, 113-115, 127, 130-131, 173-178, 187, 208, 229, 253-254, 262, 280, 316, 406, 409, 415, 419, 454, 465, 467, 504, 511, 534, 556, 574, 591, 629, 660, 663, 682, 694, 848, 864, 873-875, 912, 925, 939, 978, 983, 1035, 1071, 1091-1092, 1109, 1153, 1164, 1217, 1219, 1225, 1358, 1389-1390, 1450, 1458, 1477, 1497, 1506, 1546, 1593, 1610, 1612, 1673, 1684, 1699, 1713, 1753, 1775-1776, 1830, 1855, 1872, 1874-1875, 1946, 2015, 2076, 2123, 2135, 2145, 2170, 2204, 2239, 2242, 2249-2250, 2274, 2300, 2317, 2319, 2361, 2363, 2367, 2394, 2425, 2499, 2608, 2680, 2710, 2732, 2765, 2821, 2823-2825, 2856, 2892, 2936, 3020, 3028, 3043, 3067, 3075, 3122, 3159, 3224, 3250
  Appalachian   223, 1451, 2033
  bibliographies   102, 906, 2357, 3229
  18th century   285, 823, 839
  ethnic   101, 1806
  facsimile reprints   285
  Great Plains   1135, 1175
  Hispanic   129, 360
  history and   1226
  Hungarian studies   2820
  Jewish   2811
  Kansas   1175
  Louisiana   1731
  Maine   622
  mid-Atlantic   2142
  midwestern   1226, 1831, 1835, 2663
  Mississippi   2019
  modern   1144
  Mormon   410
  narrative   1424
  New England   906, 1956
  19th century   116, 622, 782, 823, 906, 1051, 1174, 1772, 1807, 1928, 1989-1991, 2187, 2621, 2852, 2975, 3157
  North Carolina   2005
  Northwestern Ohio   2012
  Puritan   2841
  rare book reprints   2547
  realism (1870-1910)   102
  Richmond, Virginia   850
  Romantic   3206
  17th century   285, 823, 2592
  Southern   1848, 2684-2685, 2688, 2924
  Southwestern   1480, 1968
  study resources   2357
  teaching   627
  Transcendentalist   906

American literature (*cont.*)
   20th century 153, 320, 366, 554, 813, 832, 850, 963, 982, 990-991, 1006, 1144, 1173, 1205, 1334, 1494, 1552, 1678, 1730, 1732, 1813, 1815, 1889, 1917, 1981, 2072, 2101, 2138, 2271, 2463-2464, 2534, 2717, 2729-2730, 2807, 2909, 2974, 3063, 3185, 3187-3188, 3275
   Virginia 850
   Western 2679, 3170, 3173
   women and 3044
American music 109, 113
   African American 1723
   bluegrass 371
   18th century 839
   Kansas and Great Plains 1175
   Southern 2685
American philosophy 2852
American poetry 107, 1334, 1612
   Kansas and Great Plains 1175
   19th century 854
   20th century 1144, 2463, 2519, 2909, 3156
American popular culture 109, 1356
   18th century 839
   Northwestern 2011
American religions 109
   1830-1860 2852
American Renaissance (1830-1860) 2852
American studies 113-115, 130, 178, 229, 465, 511, 534, 799, 809, 939, 1024, 1358, 1450, 1546, 1855, 2425, 2499, 2522, 2937, 3062, 3080
   Asian 92
   French-speaking peoples 2426
   Iowa 2107
   Midwestern 1497, 2063, 2107
   Pacific 92
   Puritan 2841
   Southern 1848
American theater 2953
   bibliographies 2807
   Southern 2685
   20th century 2807
Americas *see* Central American; Latin American; Native American; North American; South American
Amsterdam 144
Analytic philosophy 2830
Anatolian studies 2756
Ancient *see* Classical, *and early and ancient as subheadings under main topic, e.g.,* History, ancient; Literature, ancient; Greek language, ancient
Ancient inscriptions *see* Epigraphy
Andean linguistics 1623
Andean literature 1623
Anderson, Sherwood 3188
Anglo-American studies 467, 925
   17th-18th century 431
Anglo-Irish literature 1290, 2020
Anglo-Italian studies 1359
Anglo-Norman texts 179
Anglo-Saxon studies 180, 512, 2062, 2150
Animal communication 936
Anthropological linguistics 210, 1263, 1763, 2216, 2461
Anthropology 93, 209, 212, 358, 733, 792, 935, 1199, 1210, 1440, 1481, 1763, 1900, 2043, 2126, 2311, 2520, 2578
   see also Cultural anthropology; Ethnography; Ethnology; Social anthropology, *and entries for anthropology in specific countries or regions, e.g.,* Indian anthropology; African anthropology
   archaeology and 3189
   Balto-Slavic 14
   communication and 1439
   Indo-European 953
   language and 2830
   language teaching and 2932
   Latin American 1411
   linguistics and 474
   literary theory and 2191
   literature and 2328
   Native American 97
   New Zealand Maori and other Pacific peoples 1471

Anthropology (*cont.*)
   religion and 1805
   typology 2452
Antiquaries 2016
   American 2239
   Irish 1474
Antiquity 11
   classical 853, 880, 1133, 1907, 2171, 2409
Aphasia 619, 1949
Appalachian studies 223, 1042, 1451, 2033
Applied linguistics 68, 206, 224, 309, 333, 425-426, 493, 507, 676, 837, 948, 1038-1039, 1048, 1055, 1104, 1119, 1134, 1235, 1259, 1264, 1272, 1296, 1313, 1414, 1437, 1454, 1560, 1569, 1579, 1596-1597, 1599, 1647, 1666, 1871, 1900, 1947, 1950, 2041, 2301, 2306, 2337, 2405, 2461, 2753, 2832, 2846, 2908, 2913, 2916, 2992, 3179, 3269
   abstracts 1574
   Hebrew 1162
   Slavic 333
Aquinas, Thomas, Saint 2533
Arab-Muslim civilization 1222
Arabic dialectology 3251
Arabic language 1349, 2080, 2272
   teaching 72
Arabic linguistics 72, 1630, 3251
   history of 3251
Arabic literature 72, 81, 228, 1267, 1361, 2080
   modern 3165
Arabic studies 228, 1011, 1267
Aramaic linguistics 1601
Architecture 144, 602, 657, 1506, 1778, 2427, 3189
   contemporary 37
   Estonian 2625
   medieval 2694
   theaters 2961
Archives
   American literary and cultural collections 2357
   performing arts 2149
   psychology 108
Argentinian literature 1603
Argumentation
   rhetoric and 2168
   theory of 2830
Armenian art 2412
Armenian history 2412
Armenian language 820, 2400, 2412
Armenian linguistics 203
Armenian literature 820, 1710, 2297, 2400, 2412
Armenian philology 1151
Armenian poetry 2297
Armenian studies 2137, 2400, 2412
Art 4, 69, 189, 273, 289, 511, 548, 575, 604, 666, 690, 736, 741, 775, 787, 893, 1203, 1282, 1394, 1506, 1691, 1712, 1743, 1778, 1840, 1927, 1935, 1954, 2083, 2242, 2293, 2421, 2690, 2695, 2728, 2763, 2791, 3048, 3071, 3094, 3116, 3142, 3245
   see also Arts; Fine arts, *and entries for art in specific countries or regions, e.g.,* American art
   Celtic 509, 943
   classical 2895
   1890s 1457
   18th century 841
   folk 1920
   Humanist 356
   Italian American 1303
   literature and 622, 3162
   medieval 824, 1418, 1472, 1790, 1799, 2314
   modern 307
   mystical 2785
   religion and 1447
   Renaissance 356, 824, 1418, 1472, 1799, 2345-2346
   Romantic 290, 2492
   typology 2452
   women in 3202
Art criticism 1314, 1353, 2182, 2282, 3015
Art history 792, 852, 947, 1091, 1348, 1463, 1481, 1525, 1793, 2350, 2427, 2469, 2628, 2828, 3124

Art history (*cont.*)
   East European 3262
   English 1219
   medieval 1418, 1790
   Middle Eastern 195
   modern 3015
   Netherlands 819
   Renaissance 980, 1418
Art theory 706
   Chinese 1373
Arthurian legend 260
Arthurian literature 260
Arthurian studies 260, 424, 2292
Artificial intelligence 621, 1441
   language and 2830
Arts 80, 86, 110, 144, 231, 275, 281, 400, 450, 555, 596, 602, 657, 670, 679, 684, 772, 818, 858, 881, 909, 1194, 1275, 1409, 1440, 1499, 1547, 1694, 1728, 1775, 1823, 1877, 1942, 2003, 2029, 2135, 2143, 2219, 2452, 2483, 2531, 2545, 2683, 2969, 3005, 3025, 3068
   see also Art; Fine arts, *and entries for arts in specific countries or regions, e.g.,* Czech arts
   Baroque 317
   Blacks and 506
   comparative studies 3222
   contemporary 37, 1820, 2247, 2869
   decorative 3189
   figurative 2128
   literature and 647, 708, 2529
   19th century 2491
   philosophy, theory of 2452
   religious aspects 94
   reviews 1727
   17th century 2590
   style 1564
   20th century 407
   war and 3158
   women in the 518
Asia, Portuguese language in 2395
Asia Minor
   civilization 168
   languages 168
Asian *see also* Central Asian; East Asian; Eastern, *and entries for specific nationalities, e.g.,* Chinese; Japanese, *etc.*
Asian American studies 92
Asian art 265, 1448, 2169
Asian civilizations 2169
Asian culture 12, 21, 168, 239, 1201, 1810, 1970
Asian dance 266
Asian folk culture 265
Asian folklore 265
Asian history 22, 239, 1810
Asian languages 22, 168, 193, 453, 1386, 1448, 2467
Asian linguistics 1201
Asian literatures 21, 193, 403, 686, 1448, 2467, 3045
   philosophy and 2169
Asian music 265-266
Asian philology 21
Asian philosophy 2169
Asian religions 22, 265, 1447
Asian society 239, 2169
Asian studies 195, 263-264, 268, 453, 917, 979, 1011, 1154, 1347, 1362, 1473, 1881, 2079, 2081-2082, 2169, 2450, 2618, 2984, 2998, 3054, 3248
   18th century 841
   Ural-Altaic 1241
Asian theater 266-267
Aspazija *see* Pliekšāne, Elza
Assyriology 1382, 3252
Asturian studies 385
Atlante Linguistico Italiano 389
Atlases
   German linguistics 2794
   Italian linguistics 389
   Mediterranean linguistics 390
Audio-visual media 1950
Augustine, Saint 286-287
Augustinian Order 605
Austen, Jane 2152, 3206

Australian *see also* Commonwealth
Australian anthropology 2047
Australian culture 297, 301, 714, 1217, 1784, 3169
Australian drama 294
Australian dramatists 302
Australian folklore 298
Australian history 1784
Australian languages 300, 2048
Australian linguistics 300, 2114
Australian literature 217, 295, 297, 301, 714, 1217, 1363, 1375, 1784, 1967, 2681, 3169
Australian poetry 1784
Australian society 301
Australian studies 295
Australian theater 302
Austria
  German literature in 3259
  in history and literature 2088
Austrian culture 2087, 2812
  19th-20th century 1865
Austrian folklore 2090
Austrian history 1029, 2088, 2812
Austrian literary history 36
Austrian literature 1328, 1683, 1686, 2087-2088, 2812, 2826
  19th-20th century 1865
Austrian philology 36
Austrian philosophy 2812
Austrian studies 951, 2812
  Eastern 2089
Austroasiatic folklore 1879
Austroasiatic studies 1879
Austronesian linguistics 751, 1560, 2048, 2154
Autobiography
  of science fiction writers 1040
  as subject 2
Autograph manuscripts 1627
Automatic text processing 2705
Avant-garde studies 307, 741
Azerbaijani language 1926
Azerbaijani literature 1926
Aztecs 919
Bacon, Sir Francis 2592
Balkan *see also entries for specific nationalities, e.g.,* Bulgarian; Romanian, *etc.*
Balkan culture 312
Balkan folklore 940
Balkan history 312, 464
Balkan languages 313, 464, 940, 3253
Balkan linguistics 313, 3253
Balkan literatures 464, 940
Balkan studies 311-312, 1122
Ballad 1333
Ballet 2624
Baltic *see also* Estonian; Latvian; Lithuanian
Baltic arts 1587, 1720
Baltic folklore 1587, 2733
Baltic history 2542
Baltic languages 14, 315, 1785, 2733
Baltic linguistics 1587, 1633, 1785, 2733
Baltic literatures 14, 1587, 1785, 2542, 2733
  East Baltic 1337
Baltic philology 2542
Baltic religions 13
Baltic studies 1364, 1720
  East Baltic 1337
Balto-Slavic ethnography 14
Balto-Slavic relations 14
Balzac, Honoré de 201
Bantu linguistics 57
Baroque literature 317
  French 671
  German 750, 3195
  Neo-Latin 1211
  Spanish 449
Baroque period 2592
  arts 317
  culture 3195
Basque culture 1479
Basque language 1479, 1515
Basque literature 1479, 1515
Basque studies 1479
Baudelaire, Charles 423, 941
Baum, L. Frank 320

Beast fable 341, 2336
Beat Generation 1889
Beauvoir, Simone de 2619
Beckett, Samuel 323, 1365
Behavioral research 324, 936, 1351, 1426
Belgian French dialectology 773
Belgian literature, French language 2426
Belgian studies, French-speaking peoples 2426
Bellman, Carl Michael 337
Bellow, Saul 2534
Belorussian art 3246
Belorussian-Baltic relations 14
Belorussian bibliography 3246
Belorussian history 3246
Belorussian language 333-334, 3119
Belorussian literature 3119, 3246
Belorussian studies 3119
Benedictine Order 94, 2402
Bergman, Hjalmar Fredrik Elgerius 1195
Beyle, Marie Henri *see* Stendhal
Bible 344, 1161, 2951
  see also Old Testament; New Testament
  ancient versions 3121
  translations 2021
Biblical language 1648
  Old Testament 3249
Biblical literature 1447
  oral literature and 1648
  poetics and 1648
  semiotics and 1648
  textual criticism 2951
Biblical studies 344, 1011
  Old Testament studies 1425
Bibliographies 95, 1258, 2298, 2577
  African American literature 46
  African literature 2353
  African studies 42, 48, 56, 659, 734, 1884
  American history and culture 2239
  American literary realism (1870-1910) 102
  American literature 104, 178, 2357, 3229
  American literature, 19th century 906
  American Renaissance (1830-1860) 2852
  American theater 2807
  Anglo-Saxon studies 180
  Arthurian studies 424
  Australian literature 301
  Aztecs 919
  Baltic literature 2542
  Belorussian 3246
  biographical scholarship 361, 553
  Black literature 2044
  Bodleian Library 374
  British literature 178
  Brown University Library collections 396
  Cabell, James Branch 1494
  Canadian literature 915, 1366
  Casanova de Seingalt, Giacomo 1260
  Chaucer, Geoffrey 2851
  Chinese literature 1165
  Cistercian Order 602
  classical studies 1121
  Colombian 378
  Commonwealth literatures 178, 1375
  courtly literature 857
  detective fiction 257
  dialectology 3257
  East Baltic studies 1337
  East European 3262
  Edwardian fiction 3125
  1890s 1457
  English literature 3229
  English literature, except British and American 3213
  English literature and culture, 1880-1920 869
  English-Polish contrastive linguistics 2112
  English Renaissance literature 866
  Finnish literature 1510
  French language 1898
  French linguistics 1577
  French literary culture 2749
  French literature 1060, 1898, 2054
  French-speaking peoples, literature 2022
  genres 2357
  German Baroque period 3195
  German civilization 2323

Bibliographies (*cont.*)
  German literature 2323
  Hawthorne, Nathaniel 1928
  Hispanic philology 2036
  Hispanic studies 2377
  Hofmannsthal, Hugo von 1196
  humanities 444, 1077
  Irish studies 1406
  Italian American studies 1303
  Italian philology 2746
  Italian studies 527
  Japanese literature 1165
  Joyce, James 1335
  Kafka, Franz 1465
  Korean literature 1165
  Latin American Indians 1581
  Latin American literature 571
  Lawrence, D. H. 739
  Léger, Alexis Saint-Léger 496
  Lessing, Doris 810
  linguistics 148, 493, 3257
  linguistics, history of 1189
  literary history 240
  literary periods 2357
  Lowry, Malcolm 1758
  Malraux, André 2399
  medieval drama 2356
  Morris Library collections 1223
  Native American studies 1980
  Neo-Latin studies 1211
  Norwegian literature 2002
  Old English studies 2061
  onomastics 2065
  Pérez Galdós, Benito 165
  performing arts 2149
  philology 2803
  Pynchon, Thomas 2271
  Québécois writers 3145
  recorded sound 271
  Renaissance drama 2356
  Renaissance studies 2345
  rhetoric 2440
  Romance linguistics, comparative 653
  Romance literature 1615
  Russian and Soviet literature 1712
  Scottish studies 354, 2560
  Serbo-Croatian translations 1893
  Shakespeare, William 2599
  Slavic linguistics 2468
  Slavic literature 2542
  Slavic studies 2097
  social sciences 444
  Southeast Asian studies 1885
  Southern American art 2685
  Spanish drama, Baroque and Renaissance 449
  Stevens, Wallace 3156
  stylistics 2868
  of translations 1165
  Victorian fiction 3125
  Victorian periodicals 3128
  Welty, Eudora 963
  Whitman, Walt 3157
  Wolfe, Thomas 2974
  world literature 1712
  Yugoslavian linguistics 1489
  Zola, Emile 494
Bibliography, as subject 8, 167, 208, 375, 394, 450, 1522, 1628, 1677, 1999, 2100, 2120-2121, 2813, 2938, 2999
  African 48
  documentation and 1383
  Estonian 2098
  history 346
Bibliophilism 1627, 2158
Bilingual education 224, 360
Bilingual lexicography 783
Bilingualism 360, 619, 1423, 1565, 1901, 2846
  English-Spanish 360
  multilingualism vs. 2657
Bio-bibliography, 20th century 553
Biography 2497
  see also Autobiography
  American writers 1699, 3063
  British writers 1700, 3064
  1890s 1457
  European writers 3065
  hagiography 2930

Bibliography (*cont.*)
   Latin American writers 3065
   medieval 1075
   Rutgers University Library materials 1475
   Samar-Leyte 1624
   Steinbeck, John 2730
   as subject 2, 361, 2151
   Western American writers 3173
   writers 784, 1701
Black American *see* African American
Black culture
   in Spanish-speaking countries 62
   of the United States, Caribbean, Canada,
     and South America 506
Black literature 1552, 1675
   English language 2044
   in Spanish-speaking countries 62
   of the United States, Caribbean, Canada,
     and South America 506
   women writers 3275
Black Mountain poets 2519
Black poetry 46, 2044
Black studies 979, 1675, 2176
Black women 2518
Blake, William 367
Blasphemy 1759
Bloch, Ernst 370
Bluegrass music 371
Blues 372, 1723
Boccaccio, Giovanni 2760
Bodleian Library 374
Boece, Hector 546
Bogazköy texts 2793
Bohemian studies 2645
Bolivian studies 386
Book binding 236, 1627
   history of 1628
Book collecting 95, 375, 394, 396, 1626,
   2158, 2302
   history of 236, 1628
Book preservation 1626, 2302
Book printing 1142
Book production in 1890 1457
Book publishing 2269-2270
   in Africa 48
Book reviews 395, 1198, 1616, 1726-1727,
   1975, 2291
   African studies 659
   Irish literature 1406
   Italian books and periodicals 1304
   medieval literature 879
   poetry 2133
   Swedish books 2890
   Yugoslavian books 2308, 2867
Book trade 95, 236, 1627, 2302, 2826
   African 48
Books 236, 2270, 2302
   see also Rare books; Texts
   Cambridge University libraries 2999
   Finnish 398
   history of 346, 350, 1522, 1631, 1748, 1999,
     2120, 2938
Bosco, Henri 489
Bosnian and Herzegovinian literature 399,
   3271
Botswana studies 401
Brasillach, Robert 475
Brazil, Portuguese language in 2395
Brazilian *see also* Luso-Brazilian
Brazilian culture 2205
Brazilian history 2205
Brazilian indigenous languages 462, 2587
Brazilian literature 405, 463, 1181, 1738,
   1817, 2204-2205, 2281, 3016
   women writers 1605
Brecht, Bertolt 407, 645, 1108
Breton language 1202, 1515
Breton literature 1202, 1515
Bridges, Robert 1200
British *see also* Commonwealth; English;
   Irish; Scottish; Welsh
British art, 18th century 839
British culture 175, 178, 2319
   18th century 285
   facsimile reprints 285
   17th century 285
British ethnology 1013

British folk culture 1013
   comparative studies related to Ireland 3059
British folklore 1729
British history
   American colonial period to 1815 3186
   18th century 839
British Library 414
British literature 65, 175, 912, 1092, 1700,
   2145, 2319
   18th century 285, 839
   facsimile reprints 285
   interdisciplinary studies 178
   modern 3064, 3232
   19th century 1990-1991
   17th century 285
   women and 3044
British music
   18th century 839
   traditional 2996
British periodicals, Victorian 3128
British popular culture, 18th century 839
British studies 2242
British theater
   history and technique 2959
   Restoration 2360
Brontë, Anne 416
Brontë, Charlotte 416
Brontë, Emily 416
Brontë, Patrick Branwell 416
Browne, Thomas 2592
Browning, Elizabeth Barrett 418, 2814
Browning, Robert 418, 2814
Buddhism 1242
   Chinese 1373
Buddhist studies 268
Budé, Guillaume 436
Bulgarian language 422, 2880
Bulgarian lexicology 422
Bulgarian linguistics 3253
Bulgarian literature 311, 422, 1709
Bunting, Basil 2519
Bunyan, John 456
Burton, Robert 2592
Byron, George Gordon Byron, Baron 457,
   1501
Byzantine art 460, 882, 1324, 2967
Byzantine culture 1324, 2084
Byzantine history 460, 882, 1008, 1324, 2967
Byzantine literature 340, 460, 882, 1324,
   2967, 3132
Byzantine philology 460
Byzantine studies 340, 458-460, 1399, 2137,
   2457
   early period 218
   Slavic and 459
Cabell, James Branch 1494
Caddoan languages 2623
Čakavian dialect 500
Camões, Luis Vaz de 377
Canada
   ethnic groups 521
   teaching German in 1880
   teaching Russian in 2505
Canadian *see also* Commonwealth; French
   Canadian
Canadian-American cultural relations 534
Canadian culture 297, 714, 1217
   Québécois 3145
Canadian dialects 2332
Canadian drama 2956
Canadian folk culture 524
   Western 2011
Canadian folk music 522-523
Canadian folklore 524, 729
   Atlantic provinces 2010
   Labrador 2332
   Newfoundland 2332
   Western 2011
Canadian German studies 1093
Canadian linguistics
   Labrador 2332
   Newfoundland 2332
Canadian literature 187, 297, 531, 534, 714,
   875, 915, 1217, 1366, 1375, 1684, 2318,
   2496, 2815, 2911, 2933, 3159
   comparative studies 535
   German language 1093
   Québécois 950, 957, 1614, 1625, 2933, 3145

Canadian literature (*cont.*)
   women writers 2933
Canadian music 523
Canadian onomastics 2332
Canadian poetry 533, 1367
Canadian popular culture 524
   Western 2011
Canadian studies 1368, 2121, 2241
   Ukrainian culture 1033
Canadian theater 538, 2956
Canon law 171, 219
   medieval 1789
Carian language 1491
Caribbean anthropology 1369
Caribbean arts 1369, 2362, 2535
Caribbean culture 262, 2389, 2398
Caribbean folk culture 1369
Caribbean folklore 1137
Caribbean geography 1369
Caribbean history 1369, 2535
Caribbean languages 262, 1369
Caribbean linguistics 1369
Caribbean literature 262, 1137, 1369, 1375,
   1485, 1675, 1777, 2022, 2362, 2389, 2398,
   2535, 2990
   in English 714
   in French 2426
Caribbean music 1369
Caribbean philosophy 1369
Caribbean religions 1369
Caribbean society 2535
Caribbean studies 1369, 1434, 1777, 2389,
   2393, 2398
   French-speaking peoples 2426
Carlyle, Jane 544
Carlyle, Thomas 544-545
Carroll, Lewis *see* Dodgson, Charles
   Lutwidge
Carthusian Order 155
Casanova de Seingalt, Giacomo 1260
Castilian literature 976
Catalan language 1184, 3261
Catalan linguistics 1734
Catalan literature 1046, 1734, 2462, 3060,
   3113, 3261
Cather, Willa 554, 3185
Catholicism 1212
   Thomist ideas 802, 2533
Caucasian studies 2137
Cavalier poets 2592
Celestina 557
Celtic *see also* Breton; Gaelic; Irish; Scottish;
   Welsh
Celtic art 509, 943
Celtic epigraphy 943
Celtic folklore 322, 509
Celtic history 509, 2767
Celtic languages 447, 509, 943, 1202, 1370,
   2767, 3230
Celtic linguistics 420, 509, 943, 1370, 2767,
   3254
Celtic literatures 447, 509, 892, 943, 1202,
   1588, 3001, 3230
Celtic paleography 509
Celtic philology 420, 943, 2767, 3254
Celtic place names 509
Celtic religions 943
Celtic studies 447, 509, 558, 943, 2055, 2242,
   2767, 3001
Cemeteries 1773
Censorship 1233
Central African studies 3244
Central American Indian cultures 2983
Central American linguistics 1263
Central American literatures 1496, 1695
Central Asian studies 561
Central European studies 536, 3262
Cervantes Saavedra, Miguel de 160, 566,
   2138
Chaucer, Geoffrey 486, 572, 2851
Chesterton, Gilbert Keith 573, 1252
Chicano *see* Mexican American
Child development 576
   language and 1245
   language and communication 225
Child language 577, 1371
Children's folklore 578

Children's literature 579-581, 790, 1668
  education and 581
  teaching 580
Children's music 2620
Chilean literature 18, 162, 164, 380, 1689, 1695
Chinese art 451
Chinese Buddhism 1373
Chinese culture 263, 583-584, 1416
Chinese languages 451, 473, 1372, 1416
  teaching 1454
Chinese linguistics 1068, 1372, 1374, 1386, 1454
Chinese literature 205, 263, 445, 451, 584-585, 592-593, 1068, 1154, 1165, 1374, 1454, 1866, 2349, 2991
  comparative studies 582, 2910
Chinese philosophy 1373
Chinese religions 1373
Chinese studies 268, 583, 846, 1362, 2349, 2991, 3030
Chinese theater 1374
Chivalry 616
Christian churches
  language and 1648
  Mormon 410
Christian culture 2309
Christian epigraphy 3132
Christian literature 2402, 2413, 2671, 3121, 3132
Christian-Muslim relations 1911
Christian social history 3132
Christian studies 2494
Christian theology 818
Christian thought 588
Christianity 2084, 2456, 2930, 3075
  history 1447, 2321
  Judeo-Christian tradition 603
  literature and 588-589, 2347
  modern culture and 712
  monasticism 2783
  neoscholasticism 2453
Church history 154, 158, 219, 2423, 2494, 2515, 3132
  Low Countries 2070
Church Slavonic language 2655
Cinema see Film
Cistercian Order 156, 602
Civilization
  see also entries for civilization in specific countries or regions, e.g., English civilization
  Arab-Muslim 228, 1222
  comparative studies 648
  history of 1481
  medieval 468, 1788, 2694, 2754
  Renaissance 2445
  Ural-Altaic 1241
Clare, John 1344
Classical see also Greek; Latin; Roman
Classical antiquity 853, 880, 1133, 1907, 2171, 2409
  manuscript research 1764
  reception in Middle Ages 1121
Classical art 2895
Classical culture 2451
Classical history 610, 2409, 2895
  manuscript research 1764
Classical languages 189, 3029
Classical literature 189, 608, 610, 638, 944, 1167, 1586, 2409, 2727, 2925, 3029
  contemporary criticism 2869
Classical philology 41, 218, 610, 853, 891, 1114, 1150, 1177, 1256, 1860, 2100, 2161, 2401, 2895, 3270
Classical philosophy 610, 2166
Classical studies 41, 944, 1143, 1170, 1586, 1669, 2352, 2411, 3029
Classical texts 944, 2320
Classification, in libraries 1383
Claudel, Paul-Louis-Charles-Marie 612
Clemens, Samuel 1772
Cocteau, Jean 491
Cognition 619, 1281, 1351, 1430, 1812, 2146, 2313, 2358, 2709
  language and 618, 1557
Cognitive linguistics 618

Cognitive psychology 617, 620-621, 1396, 1645, 1949
Cognitive science 617-618, 621, 1441, 1557
Coins see Numismatics
Coleridge, Samuel Taylor 570, 3206
Collection study, Russian archival materials 2726
Collins, William Wilkie 3184
Colombian culture 378
Colombian literature 378, 380
Colonialism 714, 800
  in the Americas 1971
  in Australia 301
Comedy 1214, 2336, 2952
Commonwealth see also Australian; British; English, etc.
Commonwealth literatures 173, 295, 406, 419, 639-642, 663, 873-874, 1375, 1673, 1676, 1684, 1967, 2300, 2680, 2693, 3213, 3250
  interdisciplinary studies 178
Commonwealth novel 640
Commonwealth studies 178, 295, 467, 809
Communication 644, 936, 1249, 1281, 1376-1377, 1410, 1439, 1554, 1882, 1900, 2270, 2284, 2358, 2410, 2823, 3198
  brain and language studies 404
  cultural 2192
  discourse studies 797
  interpersonal and small-group 643
  language teaching and 2932
  literary theory and 2191
  networks 2615
  nonverbal 643, 1268, 1428, 1554, 2615
  pathology 225, 968, 1012
  in the Philippines 2838
  primate 2615
  semiotics 754, 985
  in Sweden 2716
  teaching and 643
  therapy 968
Communication processes, related to speech 2705
Communication theory 1376-1377, 2216
  Biblical literature and 1648
  language and 2830
Communism 2091
  education and 805
Comparative linguistics 145, 242, 334, 771, 1010, 1081, 1386, 1680, 1803, 1936, 2112, 2798
  English and Japanese 865
  Romance 653
Comparative literary history 1, 3222
Comparative literature 19, 81, 120, 163, 170, 232, 405, 467, 495, 535, 593, 629, 631, 647, 649, 651, 683, 795, 798, 811, 905, 1073, 1099, 1101, 1156, 1164, 1275, 1277, 1310, 1319, 1378, 1476, 1485, 1566, 1595, 1671, 1676, 1680, 1722, 1803, 1859, 1872, 1874, 1939-1940, 1953, 2076, 2099, 2103, 2227, 2271, 2275, 2292-2293, 2300, 2358, 2365, 2384, 2407, 2454, 2458, 2529, 2650, 2687, 2775, 2798, 2816, 2822, 2881, 2900, 2910, 2913, 2978, 3027, 3031, 3070, 3081, 3096-3097, 3148, 3162, 3217, 3222-3223
  Chinese and Western 582
  East and West 2674
  European with North and South American 652
  Germanic, Romance, and English 1100
  19th century 1987
Comparative philology 1190, 1640
Comparative philosophy 2169
Comparative religion 212, 1282, 1763, 2038, 2111, 2456, 2922
  Finnish 2532
Comparative studies 1378
Composition 1352
  teaching 626-627
Computational linguistics 621, 646, 655, 1572, 2217, 2705, 2773, 2904
  Hebrew 1162
Computer see also Automatic; Machine
Computer-assisted analysis, linguistics 654
Computer-assisted instruction 656

Computer-assisted language learning 1672
Computer research
  humanities 656
  Japanese linguistics 1504
  linguistics 1558
  literature 1672
Computer science 646, 2781
Computers 1181
Conan Doyle, Sir Arthur 310
Concordances, for literary and linguistic research 654
Confucianism 1373, 1373
Conrad, Joseph 664-665, 887
Contemporary see contemporary, modern, and 20th century as subheadings under main topic, e.g., History, contemporary; Art, modern; American literature, 20th century
Contextualist criticism 2330
Continental see European
Contrastive linguistics 672, 920-921, 1259, 1490, 2112, 2880
Cork County, Ireland 1455
Costa Rican literature 1496, 2382
Country music, North American 1379
Courtly literature, bibliographies 857
Courtly love, Arthurian studies 424
Crawford, Francis Marion 2492
Creole languages 688, 1434, 1560, 2116, 2915
  Western hemisphere 112, 1263
Creole literature 945
Creole studies 688, 945
Critical debate 663
Critical theory 402, 518, 728, 972, 1352, 1703, 1842, 1859, 1892
  contemporary literature 856
  literature and arts 708
Criticism 700, 1203
  see also Art criticism; Literary theory and criticism; Textual criticism
  avant-garde 715
  contemporary 772
  cultural 703, 1208, 1815, 1842
  feminist 2518, 3201
  see also Feminist literary theory and criticism
  historical 335
  rhetorical 2440
Croatian see also Serbo-Croatian
Croatian dialects, Čakavian 500
Croatian language 1340, 1380
  Čakavian dialect 500
Croatian literature 311, 1380, 1521, 1877, 2295, 2504
Croatian studies 1380
Cross-cultural communication 1900, 2667
Cross-cultural studies 828, 1490, 2618
  French and English 1048
Cuban American literature 360
Cultural anthropology 14-15, 209, 211, 928, 934, 1735
  European 2437
  Finnish 2878
  Rhein region 2437
  Western Pacific 2047
Cultural criticism 703, 707, 856, 972, 1208, 1815, 2059, 2881, 3077
Cultural geography 1381, 3189
Cultural history 237, 511, 2828
  see also Culture, and entries for cultural history in specific countries or regions, e.g., French cultural history; European cultural history
Cultural issues, related to teaching of language and literature 1469
Cultural performance 2940
Cultural relations 1, 2789
  American-European 1753
  Balto-Slavic 14
  Canadian-American 534
  Canadian ethnic groups 521
  East-West 2559
  Franco-British 1048
  Franco-Portuguese 258
  German-Scandinavian 292
Cultural studies 81, 629, 1855, 1962, 2687, 3031

Cultural theory and criticism 800, 1842
Culture 86, 198, 211, 230, 249, 304, 402, 541,
    559, 605, 637, 666, 693, 700, 704-705,
    726, 728, 745, 776, 855, 886, 904, 938,
    1004, 1017, 1146, 1301, 1357, 1378, 1481,
    1495, 1537, 1539, 1547, 1559, 1667,
    1697-1698, 1781, 1877, 1892, 1942-1943,
    1955, 2092, 2123, 2219, 2224, 2236, 2259,
    2282, 2286, 2289, 2303, 2568, 2617, 2660,
    2718, 2728, 2738, 2791, 2939, 2950, 3022,
    3048, 3094, 3116, 3210, 3219, 3273
  see also Civilization; Cultural history; Folk
    culture; Popular culture; Society;
    Sociocultural studies, and entries for
    culture of specific countries or regions,
    e.g., Brazilian culture; Middle Eastern
    culture
  ancient 11, 2438
  Arab influence on Western 228
  Catholic 1212
  Christian 2309, 3132
  classical 1121, 2451
  communist countries 2091
  cross-cultural studies 2618
  18th century 2819
  English-speaking countries 2319, 3026
  15th century 997
  folklore and 1692
  French-speaking peoples 933
  Greek-speaking peoples 1421
  Hispanic 1000
  Hispanic American 484
  history and 3162
  language and 2657
  Latin American Indians 1581
  literature and 1512, 2059
  medieval 1418, 1799, 2245, 2451, 2834
  modern 712
  New World 2398
  19th century 1987
  Portuguese-speaking countries 284, 2205
  Renaissance 1418, 1799, 2245, 2346, 2445
  rhetoric and 2168
  Sephardic 923
  17th century 2592
  theory of 3162
  typology 2452
  Western hemisphere 128, 829
  women in 2616
  Yiddish 3237
Cummings, E. E. 2717
Cuneiform 1382
Customs 1921, 3094
  Eastern 1473
Cyprian culture 2160
Cyprian epigraphy 1491
Cyprian ethnology 883
Cyprian folklore 883, 1544, 2160
Cyprian history 883, 1544
Cyprian language 2160
Cyprian linguistics 883
Cyprian literature 2160
Czech see also Slovak
Czech arts 2207
Czech culture, Sudetenland 2870
Czech ethnography 568
Czech folklore 568
Czech history 2207
Czech language, medieval 1669
Czech linguistics 1924, 2207
Czech literary history 2207
Czech literature 567-568, 713, 2504, 2538
  medieval 1669
  Sudetenland 2870
Dada 741
Dalmatian arts 2449
Dalmatian folklore 2449
Dalmatian language 2449
Dalmatian literature 1877, 2449
Dalmatian studies 2449
Dance 684, 924, 2149, 2578, 2963
  American 2685
  Asian 266
  ballet 2624
  feminist studies 3200
  Indian 1018
  Southern United States 2685

Danish cultural history 1996
Danish ethnology 1015
Danish folk culture 747, 1015
Danish folklore 748, 1996
Danish language 748, 2629
  dialects 747
  German language and 1528
Danish linguistics 747, 2629
Danish literature 745, 748, 831, 1192, 1996,
    2629
  19th century 1140
Dante 84, 749, 767, 1590, 1617, 2739
De Quincey, Thomas 570, 3206
Decorative arts 3189
Defoe, Daniel 2563
Demographics 2628
Descriptive linguistics 429, 837, 1038, 1045,
    1081, 2113, 2715, 2818, 2830, 2874
Desvignes, Lucette 2861
Detective fiction 257, 614, 2187, 3184
Developmental psychology 769
Devotional literature 1913
Dewey, John 2138
Diachronic linguistics 147, 149, 282, 429,
    1081, 1190, 1550, 1763, 2277, 2390, 2406,
    2703, 2707, 3150, 3260
  functional theory and 1660
  German 1936, 2714
  Hungarian 1749
  Iberian 1400
  Indo-European 1243
  language change 771, 2714
  North-Western European 2034
  Romance 2237, 2478
Dialectology 355, 379, 389, 1117, 1750, 1787,
    1821, 1983, 2212, 2332, 2375, 2436, 2459,
    2886, 3257
  Afro-Asiatic 63
  Arabic 3251
  Dutch 2906
  English 112
  French 773
  German 760, 1101, 2172, 2702, 2794
  Irish 3059
  Italian 1300, 2459
  Mexican American 308
  Romanian 1635
  Serbo-Croatian 2225
Dialects 1729, 3006
  American English 112
  Arabic 3251
  Asturian Spanish 385
  Belgian French 773
  Čakavian 500
  Danish 747
  English 112, 3102
  Finnish 2637, 2886
  French 773
  Galician Portuguese 1184
  German 760, 1101, 1224, 2794
  Germanic 1824, 2528
  Hungarian 1749, 1751
  Italian 1639, 2449, 2741
  Labrador 2332
  Lancashire 1466
  Lappish 2637, 2886
  in literature 2260
  Lorrain French 773
  Lowland Scots 2557
  Newfoundland 2332
  North American 1982, 2260
  Picard French 773
  Romance languages 2406
  Swedish 2637, 2886, 2894
  Wallon French 773
  Yorkshire 3006
Diary, as subject 2, 153
Dickens, Charles 779-781
Dickey, James L. 1334
Dickinson, Emily 782, 854, 2621
Dictionaries 1266, 1622, 3017
  Mexican Indian languages 2586
  Peruvian languages 2588
Dictionary of the Real Academia Española
    380
Didactics 986
Diderot, Denis 785, 2326

Dime novel 790
Discographies 271
  English Renaissance 486
Discourse 797, 1410
  social 3031
  theory of 795, 2191
Discourse analysis 224, 379, 483, 707, 795,
    972, 1259, 1599, 1900, 2216
Dissertations 1870
  abstracts 801
  humanities 181
  Romance 1148
Dixon, Richard W. 1200
Dodgson, Charles Lutwidge 1318
Dominican literature 723
Dominican Order 595
Donne, John 1345, 2592
Doolittle, Hilda 1144, 2519
Dostoevskiĭ, Fëdor Mikhaĭlovich 811
Drama 267, 269, 407, 681, 894, 914, 1384,
    1954, 1972, 2123, 2148, 2673, 2853, 2914,
    2934, 2940, 2953, 2955, 2960, 2963-2964,
    3151, 3210
  see also Performing arts; Theater, and
    entries for drama in specific countries,
    e.g., Australian drama
  Australasian 294
  by Black dramatists 2044
  comparative 650, 2941
  Elizabethan 486, 2575, 2600
  15th century 2342
  folk 1014, 1921
  history of 2962
  Italian American 1303
  medieval 650, 824-826, 1592, 1795-1796,
    2356
  modern 774, 1867
  Mormon 410
  19th century 1867
  Renaissance 824, 2342, 2356, 2594-2595,
    2599
  reviews 1616
  Romantic 3206
  satiric 2817
  17th century 2342, 2592
  16th century 2342
  Slovak 2652
  theory 1384
  20th century 37, 1867, 2255, 2859
  verse 2525
Dramatists 2953
  women 2807
Dravidian linguistics 1265
Dravidian studies 1242
Dreiser, Theodore 813
Dreyfus affair 494
Dryden, John 2563, 2592
Duras, Marguerite 1385
Dutch see also Netherlandic
Dutch dialectology 2906
Dutch language 819, 1331-1332, 1824, 1986,
    2696, 2906
Dutch onomastics 1916
East Asian culture 1152, 1154
East Asian history 1152
East Asian languages 473, 1386
East Asian literatures 1152
East Asian studies 268, 1152, 1154, 2467,
    3002
East European art 2640
East European cultural history 3262
East European culture 2091, 2559, 2647
East European ethnic minorities 1930
East European folklore 3262
East European history 2647, 3058, 3262
East European languages 2641
East European linguistics 713, 2647
East European literatures 19, 713, 752, 1875,
    2640-2641, 2647, 3267
East European studies 536, 713, 1159, 1216,
    1720, 2089, 2091, 2091, 2642, 3054, 3262
East German literature 1079
East German place names 339
East German studies 1079
East Slavic languages 2506, 2639
East Slavic literatures 2639
East-West cultural relations 2559

East-West literary relations 647, 652, 1705, 3222
East-West relations 763
Eastern *see also* Asian; Far Eastern; Middle Eastern; Near Eastern
Eastern art 1448, 1473
Eastern culture 12, 21
Eastern history 22, 202, 1473
Eastern languages 22, 1448, 2080
Eastern literatures 403, 1448, 1473, 2080
Eastern philology 202
Eastern religions 22
Eastern studies 453, 917, 1011, 1347, 1473, 1853, 2450, 2984, 3248
Eastern writing systems 2902
Editing 661, 833, 2120
Education 858, 863, 1194, 1343, 1571, 1579, 1656, 2246, 2520, 2727
  see also Pedagogy; Teaching
  Africa 1884
  bilingual 360
  children's literature and 581
  Eastern Europe 2091
  humanities 1213
  Hungary 80
  India 501, 1018
  institutions 1343
  Korea 1529
  language development *see* Language teaching
  literature and 581, 1414
  medieval 1902
  policy 1343, 1945
  psycholinguistics and 543, 1439
  psychology 797
  Socialist 805
  society and 1945
  Southeast Asia 1885
  theory 627
  Zimbabwe 3244
Edwardian literature 499, 3125
Edwardian society 499
Egyptian language 590
Egyptology 40, 590, 1425
Eichendorff, Joseph Karl Benedict, Freiherr von 290-291
Eighteenth century studies 138, 337, 411, 803, 841-842, 1260, 1761, 1973, 2819, 2862
For other 18th century references, see subheadings under primary topics of interest, e.g. Art, 18th century
  Anglo-American 431
  British, American, and European 839
Electronic publishing 2270
Eliot, George 1085-1086
Eliot, T. S. 3233
Elizabethan drama 486, 2575, 2600
Elizabethan literature 486, 2524, 2575, 2603
Elizabethan theater 849
Emblems 139, 852
  Biblical literature and 1648
Emerson, Ralph Waldo 906
Encyclopédie 785, 2326
English *see also* Anglo-; British; Commonwealth
English art
  15th-17th century 623
  history 1219
  19th century 1438
  Pre-Raphaelite Brotherhood 1438
  Victorian 3133
English civilization 229, 540
  Edwardian 499
  Victorian 499
English composition, teaching 626-627
English culture 85, 174-176, 280, 939, 942, 1217
  19th century 869
  17th century 2592
  20th century 869
  Victorian 3126
English dialects 112, 3102
  Lancashire 1466
  North America 1982, 2260
  Scots English 2557
  Yorkshire 3006

English drama 2893
  Elizabethan 486, 2575, 2600
  15th century 623
  Jacobean 2523, 2575
  medieval 1792, 2329
  Renaissance 1792, 2329
  Restoration 486
  17th century 623, 2523
  16th century 623, 2523
English folk dance 861
English folk song 861
English folklore 684, 861
English history 85, 280, 2016
  medieval to 20th century 1219
  17th century 2592
  Victorian 3133
English language 28, 112, 121, 166, 172-176, 229, 409, 415, 419, 465, 508, 737, 843, 864, 868, 873, 876-877, 907, 925, 939, 1035, 1179, 1229, 1389-1392, 1458-1459, 1591-1592, 1680, 1736, 1824, 1948, 2016, 2051, 2106, 2364, 2367, 2372, 2550, 2668, 2680, 2710, 2734, 2786, 2797, 2821, 2823-2824, 2892, 2977, 2985, 3026, 3084, 3107, 3211, 3224, 3250
  in Africa 862
  in Australia 300
  for business 2823
  history 112, 406
  Hungarian studies 2820
  interdisciplinary studies 178
  Middle 873, 1229, 2835
  in New Zealand 2915
  in North America 112, 130-131, 174, 591, 864, 925, 939, 1035, 1175, 1753, 1982, 2260, 2820, 2892, 3250
  Old 873, 1229, 2061-2062
  Polish language and 2112
  in Scotland 2557
  for special purposes 409
  teaching 229, 562, 574, 606, 627, 716, 863, 871, 1279, 2337, 2932
English lexicography 2016
English linguistics 112, 406, 409, 1387, 1391, 1459, 1662, 2367, 2614, 2765, 2803, 2825, 3211
  contrastive analysis 2112
  diachronic and synchronic 865
English literary theory and criticism 848
English literature 7, 28, 65, 85, 95, 121, 157, 166, 173-177, 208, 229, 253, 280, 316, 406, 409, 415, 419, 454, 465, 467, 503-504, 510, 540, 556, 574, 622, 629, 660, 663, 682, 695, 737, 843, 848, 860, 864, 867-868, 870, 873-875, 903, 907, 910, 912, 925, 939, 942, 971, 978, 983, 1048, 1100, 1153, 1164, 1179, 1217, 1219, 1225, 1359, 1387, 1389-1390, 1392, 1409, 1458-1459, 1477, 1506, 1506, 1612, 1667, 1673, 1684, 1746, 1776, 1824, 1855, 1872, 1874-1875, 1946, 1948, 1974, 2016, 2051, 2093, 2099, 2106, 2123, 2170, 2204, 2249, 2274, 2300, 2317, 2319, 2361, 2363-2364, 2367, 2372, 2550, 2608-2609, 2668, 2680, 2687, 2710, 2734, 2765, 2786, 2797, 2803, 2821-2825, 2856, 2892-2893, 2934, 2936, 2977, 2985, 3020, 3027-3028, 3038, 3067, 3075, 3084, 3159, 3184, 3211, 3224, 3250
  bibliographies 3229
  except British and American 714, 3213
  Commonwealth 253, 642
  Dorset writers 2971
  Edwardian 499, 3125
  18th century 64, 367, 431, 840, 2563, 2575, 2604, 3004
  Elizabethan 486, 2524, 2575, 2603
  Hungarian studies 2820
  interdisciplinary studies 178
  Latin language 815, 1837-1838, 2592
  Mannerism 2592
  Middle English period 572, 873, 1229, 1591-1592, 1832, 2150, 2343, 2834-2835, 2839, 2851
  modern 3064
  modern, to 1900 2839
  narrative 1424

English literature (*cont.*)
  new literatures in English 642, 714, 1375, 1541, 1967, 2680, 2693
  19th century 310, 416, 418, 457, 544-545, 570, 779-781, 869, 887, 1078, 1085-1086, 1116, 1200, 1318, 1344, 1438, 1482, 1501-1502, 1509, 1989, 2152, 2502-2503, 2526, 2575, 2814, 2927-2928, 2970-2971, 3184, 3206
  Old English period 873, 1229, 1591-1592, 2061-2062
  postcolonial 253
  Pre-Raphaelite Brotherhood 1438
  rare book reprints 2547
  Reformation 1132
  Renaissance 486, 866, 872, 1132, 2341, 2343, 2575, 2839
  Restoration 2359, 2575
  Romantic 570, 2575, 3206
  17th century 431, 456, 815, 1087, 1345, 1837-1838, 2359, 2563, 2575, 2592, 2594
  16th century 82-83, 486, 761, 815, 1149, 1345, 1890, 2242, 2575, 2594-2602, 2611, 3041
  Stuart 866
  teaching 627, 716, 2061
  Tudor 866
  20th century 573, 664, 717, 738-739, 810, 859, 869, 887, 955, 973, 1009, 1207, 1232, 1252, 1338, 1758, 1760, 1816, 1915, 2138-2139, 2177, 2210-2211, 2905, 3135, 3138, 3163, 3233
  Victorian 416, 418, 499, 780-781, 2009, 2575, 3125-3127, 3129-3130, 3133, 3184
English manuscripts 870
English music
  15th-17th century 623
  Renaissance 486
English onomastics 1994
English philology 157, 1389, 1500, 1832, 2372, 2797, 2803, 2825, 3088, 3178
English poetry 1229, 1459, 1612
  15th century 623
  Middle English period 1229, 3226
  Old English period 1229
  17th century 623, 2592
  16th century 623, 2697
  Victorian 3129
English-Spanish bilingualism 360
English-speaking countries 172, 2319
  literature 3026
English studies 38, 83, 177, 229, 465, 809, 939, 942, 1128, 1167, 1359, 1736, 1855, 2242, 2522, 2765, 2797-2798, 3080, 3224, 3229
  Middle English period 2343
  professional topics 38
  Renaissance 486, 2524
English texts
  Middle English language 1832
  early period 827
English theater
  Elizabethan 849
  19th century 1992
  Restoration 2360
  Shakespearean 2602
English translations
  of ancient Sanskrit and Oriental texts 403
  of Brazilian literature 405
  from Chinese 2349
  of Croatian short stories and poetry 1380
  of Hebrew literature 1869
  of Iranian literature 1284
  of Latin American literature 1582
  related to Norwegian Americans 2015
  from Russian publications 2508
  of Scandinavian literature 2539
  of South Asian literature 1443
  from Tamil 1445
  of Ukrainian literature 1483
  of world literature 3007
  from Yiddish 3236
Enlightenment 803, 1602, 1739, 2029, 3197
  French 671, 2029
  German 750, 3197
  Hispanic 786
  Hungarian 19
  Italian 2029

Epic literature, Romance 2064
Epigraphy 2902
 Aegean 1491
 Celtic 943
 early Christian 3132
 Cyprian 1491
 Greek 1860
 Northwest-Semitic 3249
Epistemology 1206, 2899, 3015
 Indian 1402
Erasmus, Desiderius 1890
Eskimo-Aleut linguistics 1263
Esperanto 808, 846, 900-902, 1570, 1690
Esthetics see Aesthetics
Estonian art 1728, 1762, 2625
Estonian culture 13, 1762, 2625, 3034
Estonian film 2625
Estonian folklore 1762, 2098
Estonian history 13
Estonian language 13, 851, 1364, 1503
Estonian literature 13, 1364, 1503, 1728, 1762, 2098, 2625, 3034
Estonian music 2625
Estonian studies 1728, 1762
Estonian theater 2625
Ethics 1158, 2164, 2309, 2408
 Indian 1402
 language and 2830
 psychology and 617
 religion and 1447
Ethnic literature, American 101, 1806
Ethnic slurs 1759
Ethnic studies 979, 2578
 Canadian 521
 East European 1930
Ethnography 14-15, 210, 928, 935, 1545, 1735, 1920, 2379
 Altaic 26, 2876
 Balto-Slavic 14
 Czech 568
 European 929, 2552
 Hungarian 26
 Latvian 250
 Slovak 568
 Uralic 26, 2876
Ethnolinguistics 210, 355, 1117, 1599, 2277, 2461
 Native American 132
Ethnology 212, 792, 934, 937, 1018, 1498, 1735, 2043, 2436, 2768
 see also Folk culture and entries for ethnology in specific countries or regions, e.g., Danish ethnology
 Finno-Ugric 1003, 1493
 French-speaking peoples 933
 Mexican and Central American Indian peoples 2983
 New Zealand Maori and other Pacific peoples 1471
Ethnomethodology 795, 797, 1210
Ethnomusicology 523, 935, 1333, 1583, 2578, 2733, 2784, 2873, 3221
 see also Folk music
 African 51
Ethology, comparative 936
Etymology
 German 1912, 2702
 Germanic 1804
 Hungarian 1749
 Italian 1639
 Romanian 1635
 Swedish 1804
Euboean studies 233
European see also East European; Indo-European; Southeast European; West European, etc., and entries for specific nationalities, e.g., French; German, etc.
European cultural anthropology 2437
European cultural history 1393
 Northern 1996
European culture 262, 1886
 17th century 2592
 Southeast 2871
European ethnography 929, 2552
European ethnology 929, 3266
European folk culture 929, 3059
European folklore 2090, 2552

European history 245, 2460
 American colonial period to 1815 3186
 medieval 2150
 17th century 2592
European languages 331, 953, 997, 1515, 1886
 Ibero-Romance 1221
 modern 262, 1035, 1256, 2917
European linguistics 1010, 1886, 2394
European literary history 19, 1393
 Northern 1996
European literature 3, 162, 245, 262, 903, 953, 965, 971, 1031, 1035, 1515, 1686, 1713, 1875, 1886, 2076, 2135, 2145, 2394, 2711, 2775, 2936, 3045
 Baroque arts and 317
 comparative studies 19, 2407
 18th century 839
 15th century 997
 history and 2493
 Humanist 19
 Hungarian literature and 19
 Ibero-Romance 1221
 medieval 19, 766, 2150, 2343
 modern 912, 1256, 3065
 19th century 1990-1991
 North America and 652
 Renaissance 2343
 Romantic 970, 3206
 17th century 2592
 South America and 652
European philosophy, medieval 330
European studies 1, 763, 966, 971, 1193
 18th century 839, 841
 medieval 2150, 2343
 Northern 1996
European theater 3228
European theology, medieval 330
Evans, Marian see Eliot, George
Exoticism 547
Experimental linguistics 493, 1433
Experimental phonetics 1654, 2173
Experimental psychology 452, 1812
Extremadura region, Spain 2376
Fable, beast 341, 2336
Facsimile reprints, rare 17th- and 18th-century British and American works 285
Fantasy fiction 981, 987, 1915, 2139, 2448, 2492, 2555, 2860
Far Eastern music 266
Far Eastern studies 2078
Faroese studies 1065, 2566
Faulkner, William 990-991
Feminist literary theory and criticism 1842, 2496, 2518, 2933, 3201
Feminist studies 153, 198, 402, 518, 728, 993-994, 1066, 1859, 2933, 3200-3201
Festivals 995
Fiction
 see also Novel; Science fiction; Short fiction; Short story, etc., and entries for fiction in specific countries, e.g., Canadian fiction
 detective 257, 614, 2187, 3184
 18th century 840
 in English translation 2184
 history and theory 2030
 Italian American 1303
 mystery 257, 3184
 19th century 840
 satiric 2817
 17th century 840
 20th century 711, 1261, 1868
Film 510, 598-600, 681, 700, 713, 741, 772, 828, 856, 957, 983, 998-999, 1007, 1206, 1378, 1394, 1436, 1506, 1690, 1712, 1718, 1725, 1859, 1952, 2149, 2206, 2259, 2285, 2462, 2562, 2612, 2853, 2940, 2954, 2969, 3039, 3077, 3098, 3176, 3210
 American 3104
 Estonian 2625
 feminist studies 3200
 French 594, 1057, 1061
 gender and sexuality in 1080
 history 594, 828, 2206, 3104, 3239
 interviews 1706
 Italian 1305, 1308, 2719
 Italian American 1303

Film (cont.)
 literature and 1706, 3222
 philosophy and 2166
 reviews 1091, 1616, 1706, 2206, 2282, 2612, 2624
 satire in 2817
 Slovak 2652
 teaching 1706
 theory and criticism 518, 706, 972, 1206, 1969, 2358, 3176, 3239
 war and 3158
 women and 3202
Fine arts 1378, 2111
 see also Art; Arts
 American 2105
 Croatian 1380
 Estonian 2625
 Indian 1234
 Italian 1305
 medieval 2694
Finnic languages 3139
Finnish anthropology 2878
Finnish culture 1493, 1540
Finnish dialects 2637
 Sweden 2886
Finnish ethnology 930, 2532, 2768, 2877
Finnish folklore 2532, 2769, 2877-2878
Finnish-German studies 1329
Finnish language 2532
 language planning 3139
Finnish linguistics 1998, 2770, 3139
Finnish literature 398, 831, 1192, 1329, 1510, 1540, 2274, 2532, 2877
 Swedish language 398
Finno-Ugric ethnology 1003, 1493
Finno-Ugric folklore 1003, 1493
Finno-Ugric languages 33, 949, 1003, 1503, 2041, 3139
Finno-Ugric linguistics 851, 949, 1003, 1652
Finno-Ugric studies 1493
Flemish folk culture 3146
Flemish folklore 1317
Flemish history 3174
Flemish language 2906
Flemish onomastics 1916
Folk see also Popular
Folk arts 1773, 1920, 2199, 3062, 3189
 Euboean 233
 Polish 2199, 2199
 Spanish 2375
 United States 2105, 2685
Folk beliefs 1019, 1350, 1921, 2517
 Southeast Asia 358
 speech and 2253
 women and 207
 Zimbabwe 3244
Folk craft 2987
Folk culture 728, 995, 1015-1016, 1020-1021, 1357, 1778, 1908, 2551, 3062, 3146
 see also Ethnology
 African 401, 2102
 Asian 265
 British 1013, 3059
 children's 578
 Danish 747, 1015
 European 929, 3059
 Finnish 2878
 Flemish 3146
 Irish 1013, 3059
 Jewish 1339
 Labrador 2332
 Newfoundland 2332
 North Carolina 2004
 Pennsylvania 2141
 Slovak 2654
 Swiss 1022
Folk dance 1014, 1333, 1921
 English 861
Folk drama 1014, 1921
Folk histories 1042, 2073
Folk literature 984, 1921
Folk music 935, 1014, 1333, 1921, 2620, 2784, 2873, 2924, 3221
 see also Ethnomusicology
 African American 1723
 blues 1723
 Canadian 522-523

Folk rituals 733
  Southeast Asia 358
Folk song 1014, 1333, 2620, 2873
  Atlantic provinces 2010
  Canadian 523
  English 861
  Indian 1018
  Latin American Indian 1581
  New England 2010
Folklife see Folk culture
Folklore 15, 75, 220, 222, 261, 298, 341, 668, 729, 851, 881, 928, 984, 995, 1016-1017, 1019-1021, 1262, 1357, 1397, 1450, 1503, 1506, 1692, 1729, 1735, 1834, 1847, 1921-1922, 2074-2075, 2090, 2126, 2226, 2253, 2261, 2267, 2277, 2336, 2379, 2384, 2517, 2545, 2578, 2626, 2690, 2769, 2993, 3072, 3171, 3189
  see also entries for folklore in specific countries or regions, e.g., Estonian folklore; Latin American folklore
  African American 1137
  ancient Greek 1688
  Appalachian region 1451
  Asian 265
  Austroasiatic 1879
  Biblical literature and 1648
  Celtic 509
  children's 578
  Creole 688
  European 2552
  Finno-Ugric 1003, 1493
  Flemish 1317
  Germanic 1097
  Gypsy 1461
  Hispanic 2377
  history 1021
  Jewish 3234
  Labrador 2332
  Latin 1688
  literature and 1894
  Newfoundland 2332
  performance 2940
  Romance 2479, 2843
  theory 1834
Fontane, Theodor 1023
Foreign language teaching see Language teaching
Foreign languages, professional topics 39
Foreign literatures, professional topics 39
Formalist literary theory and criticism 913
France see also French
France, foreign language teaching in 1579
Franciscan Order 1054, 2748, 3108
  history 247, 1047
  literature 1047
  philosophy 1047
Franco-Portuguese cultural relations 258
Franconia, Germany 1330
Francophone see French-speaking peoples
French art 1057, 1063
  17th century 482
French Canadian see also Québécois
French Canadian language see French language, in Canada
French Canadian literature 539, 950, 957, 1614, 1625, 2054, 2426, 2815, 2911, 3145
  politics and 34
  women writers 2933
French Canadian studies, Quebec 2241, 3145
French civilization 299, 1055, 1061-1062, 1595, 2720, 2749
  in the Americas 34
French colonial history 2241
French cultural history 2749
French culture 513, 547, 1050, 1057, 1595, 1978, 2241, 2720, 3216
  French literature and 2721
French dialects 773, 1046
French drama 1057
French film 594, 1057, 1061
French history 1062-1063, 2023, 2241, 2591
  Dreyfus affair 494
  17th century 482
  southern 188, 1046
French language 78, 433, 773, 946, 992, 1044, 1057, 1061-1063, 1247, 1398, 1632, 1978, 2023, 2222, 2426, 2487, 2720, 3258

French language (cont.)
  bibliographies 1898
  in Canada 34, 539
  15th century 1898
  14th century 1898
  spoken 2327
  teaching 532, 562, 606, 1043-1044, 1055, 1061
  20th century 483
French linguistics 78, 1045, 1049, 1061, 1250, 1398, 1577, 1632, 1662, 1664-1665, 2327, 2418, 2488, 2614, 2803, 3010
  20th century 483
French literary history 2424
French literature 119, 157, 183, 188, 299, 433, 436, 467, 469, 513, 547, 624, 697, 743, 753, 817, 905, 911, 946, 950, 957-958, 962, 967, 971, 992, 1043-1044, 1046, 1048-1050, 1055, 1057-1063, 1248, 1250, 1287, 1595, 1608, 1612, 1632, 1717-1719, 1839, 1859, 1978, 2023, 2028-2029, 2054, 2123, 2134, 2204, 2222, 2241, 2268, 2363, 2420, 2426, 2462, 2487, 2529, 2591, 2720, 2743, 2749, 2803, 2944, 2948, 3013, 3020, 3027, 3060, 3075, 3096, 3101, 3113, 3153, 3216, 3258
  bibliographies 1898
  culture 2721
  18th century 671, 785, 840, 2326, 2662, 2862
  Enlightenment 671, 2029
  15th century 671, 1898
  14th century 1898
  medieval 611, 836, 2064, 2418, 2834
  early modern 671
  Naturalist movement 494
  19th century 201, 423, 432, 441, 443, 488, 494, 498, 941, 1088, 1988, 2252, 2731
  North Africa 2403
  Old French 2418
  philosophy and 428
  Reformation 1132
  Renaissance 1132
  17th century 345, 482, 671, 804, 2122, 2662
  16th century 430, 435, 671, 960, 1887, 2662
  20th century 134, 323, 438-439, 475, 489, 491-492, 496-497, 612, 1027, 1365, 1385, 2328, 2399, 2472, 2619, 2859, 2861
French music 2591
  17th century 482
French novel, 20th century 2472
French onomastics 2026
French philology 157, 1500, 2803
French philosophy 428, 1063, 2023
  17th century 482
French poetry 513, 624, 1612
  19th century 2127
  Parnassian 440
  Symbolist 440
French popular culture 1057
French-speaking peoples 3013
  culture 2426
  ethnology 933
  literature 753, 958, 1595, 2022, 2054, 2222, 2426
French studies 469, 513, 1057, 1062-1063, 2134, 2241
  17th century 482
  southern 188
  in Southern Africa 1064
  Western France 183
French texts 2662
  ancient 2661
Frisian language 1299, 2906, 3095
Frisian literature 3095
Frisian studies 1299, 1997
Frost, Robert 2463
Functional linguistics 1069
Gaelic studies 1588
  see also Celtic; Irish; Scottish
  Irish 2774
  Scottish 2556, 3000
Galician culture 1136
Galician literature 448, 1136, 3060
Galician philology 3106
Galician poetry 448
Galician Portuguese dialect 1136, 3106
Galician studies 720

Game theory, Biblical literature and 1648
García Lorca, Federico 383
Gascon literature 1046
Gaskell, Elisabeth C. 1078
Gautier, Théophile 432
Gender 1080, 2138, 3198
Genealogy 144, 616
  Germanic 1097
Generación del 1927 383
Generative grammar 1645, 2324
Generative poetics 1648
Genres 912, 1083, 1966, 2076, 2193, 2227, 3222, 3242
  bibliographies 2357
  teaching 627
Geolinguistics 1084, 2277
George, Stefan 553
Georgia folklore 1042
German-American literary relations 1753
German American studies 1099, 2544
German art 1327
  Schleswig-Holstein and Northern 1996
German Canadian studies 1093
German culture 136, 514, 645, 763, 1094, 1959, 2323, 2544, 2826, 3082
  Enlightenment 3197
  history 328, 1996
  Sudetenland 2870
German dialectology 2702
German dialects 760, 1101, 2794
  southwest 1224
German etymology 1912, 2702
German folklore 328, 1101, 2706, 3255, 3266
  Alemannic-Suebian region 77
  Schleswig-Holstein and Northern 1996
German history 763, 1096
  of Jews 3197
  Southeastern Europe 2872
German-Hungarian literary relations 1936
German-Italian studies 2333
German Jews, history 3197
German language 29, 296, 319, 537, 630, 762, 952, 1095, 1101, 1103, 1127, 1141, 1176, 1224, 1256, 1320, 1331-1332, 1389, 1513, 1824, 1880, 1948, 2106, 2172, 2331, 2436, 2706, 2712, 2750, 2786, 2826, 2947, 3082, 3190, 3255, 3260
  Alemannic-Suebian region 77
  Danish language and 1528
  feminist approach 3201
  history of 329, 339, 1101, 3256
  Low 1515, 1531, 1983-1984
  medieval 3256
  modern 151, 329, 1977, 2702
  New High 2702
  Switzerland 2713
  teaching 532, 562, 606, 757, 768, 1880, 3089, 3269
  technical 1912
  United States 3089
German lexicology 2712
German linguistics 551, 757, 1103-1104, 1138, 1513, 1618, 2172, 2334, 2544, 2702, 2794, 2803, 3161, 3179, 3260
  diachronic 1936
German literary history 325, 1682, 3259
  Schleswig-Holstein and Northern 1996
German literature 16, 29, 118, 136, 152, 235, 237, 293, 296, 319, 325, 327, 332, 391, 514, 537, 587, 630, 698, 763, 791, 817, 833, 952, 965, 971, 1079, 1094-1102, 1104-1105, 1127, 1141, 1176, 1228, 1256, 1320, 1327, 1329, 1331-1332, 1389, 1531, 1683-1686, 1718, 1791, 1824, 1859, 1863, 1872, 1880, 1903, 1936, 1943-1944, 1948, 1959-1960, 1983-1984, 2106, 2189, 2234, 2274, 2288, 2323, 2331, 2333, 2363, 2501, 2529, 2544, 2579, 2622, 2627, 2706, 2722, 2736, 2750, 2786, 2803, 2826, 2942, 2947, 3020, 3075, 3082, 3090, 3096, 3162, 3177, 3190, 3230, 3255, 3259
  Baroque 750, 3195
  Canada and 1093
  18th century 151, 750, 1123-1124, 1322, 1326-1328, 1602, 1682, 1767, 2263, 3033, 3197
  Enlightenment 750, 3197
  feminist approach 3201

German literature (*cont.*)
  to 1500   90
  15th century   750
  14th century   750
  humanist   750
  Latin language   1856
  Low German   1515
  Mannerism   750
  medieval   329, 347, 750, 764, 1028, 1856, 1905, 3256
  modern   151, 1977, 2287, 2795, 2800, 2837, 2866
  Neo-Latin   750
  19th century   36, 151, 290-291, 613, 1023, 1160, 1168, 1197, 1321, 1323, 1325, 1515, 1682, 1767, 1854, 1985, 2263, 2549, 2796, 3033
  Old German   1126
  Reformation   750, 1132
  Renaissance   1132
  Rhein region   2436
  Rococo   750
  17th century   750, 1682
  Silesia   2545
  16th century   750, 1740, 1770, 1890
  social history   1274
  Southeastern Europe   2872
  Sudetenland   2870
  teaching   768
  20th century   151, 368-370, 407-408, 553, 645, 1108, 1196, 1465, 1515, 1682, 1767, 1910, 2153, 2263, 2796, 2859, 2943, 2972-2973, 3033, 3110
  women and   3201
German manuscripts   1902
German-Netherlandic literary relations   553
German onomastics   339, 758, 1101
German orthography   2712
German pedagogy   2544
German philology   327, 896, 1139, 1141, 1331, 1389, 1500, 1912, 2288, 2750, 2803, 2947, 3161, 3255, 3259
German philosophy   514
  Enlightenment   1602
  20th century   408
German poetry   514, 2189, 2826
  Low German   1515
German popular culture   3266
German-Scandinavian cultural relations   292
German-Scandinavian literary relations   2629
German semantics   1912
German-Slavic studies   758
German studies   29, 118, 514, 763, 951-952, 1079, 1096, 1104, 1167, 1959, 1961, 2094, 2333, 2722
  Alemannic-Suebian region   77
  Franconian region   1330
  Heidelberg   1167, 2501
  northern   1996
  Rhein region   2436-2437
  Schleswig-Holstein   1996
German stylistics   2712
German texts   1902, 1941
  medieval   1905
German theater   1101
Germanic dialects   1824, 2528
Germanic etymology   1804
Germanic folklore   1097
Germanic genealogy   1097
Germanic languages   98, 118, 152, 1097, 1389, 1808, 1960, 2714-2715, 2771, 3082, 3230
  Old   150, 1126
Germanic linguistics   98, 757, 1492, 1528, 1662, 2062, 2528, 2715, 2863, 3082
  comparative   2034
  Old Germanic   1126
Germanic literature   98, 152, 1097, 1100, 1389, 2288, 2771, 3082, 3230
  Old Germanic   1126
Germanic numismatics   1097
Germanic onomastics   1097, 2085
Germanic philology   1099, 1389, 1618, 2034, 2288, 2863, 3082
Germanic studies   542, 951, 1053, 1097, 1737, 1824, 1903, 2579, 2798
  comparative   1106
Gesture   1268, 1759, 2615

Gezelle, Guido Pierre Théodore Joseph   1110
Gide, André   438
Giraudoux, Jean   492
Gissing, George   1116
Glasgow, Ellen   850
Glossaries   1589
Goethe, Johann Wolfgang von   1123-1124, 1326-1328, 2263
Goldoni, Carlo   2751
Gothic literature   2187
Graffiti   1759
Grammar   1572, 1821, 1851-1852, 2324
  Bulgarian   422
  French   1045
  German   2712
  Labrador   2332
  Native American   1263
  Newfoundland   2332
  Romanian   1635
  Swedish   2716
  universal   1431
Graphic arts   1627
  satire in   2817
Graves, Robert   1009
Gravestones   1773
Great Plains studies   1135, 1175
Greek   *see also* Byzantine; Classical
Greek art   461
  Byzantine and post-Byzantine   2967
Greek culture   1462
  ancient   436
  modern   1171
Greek epigraphy   1860
Greek folklore   1755
  ancient   1688
  Cyprus   1544
  modern   884, 1172
Greek historiography   609
Greek history   218, 461, 1172, 1421, 1462, 1861
  ancient   609, 1133, 2414
  Byzantine and post-Byzantine   2967
  Ionian Islands   1508
Greek language   944, 1801
  ancient   41, 218, 277, 427, 590, 609-610, 853, 891, 1118, 1121, 1143, 1171, 1177, 1399, 1491, 1669, 1752, 1843, 1860, 1907, 2171, 2409, 2414, 2438, 2895, 3270
  Macedonian Greek dialect   1755
  modern   1171, 1421, 2414
  Mycenaean Greek dialect   1843
Greek linguistics   461, 1172, 1755, 3253
  Cyprus   1544
Greek literature   157, 311, 461, 1172, 1462, 1755, 2438, 2727
  ancient   218, 436, 609, 1121, 1171, 1399, 1688, 1752, 2414, 2727
  Byzantine and post-Byzantine   2967
  medieval   2727
  modern   1171, 1421, 2185, 2414, 2457, 2727
Greek philology   157, 218, 891
  ancient   891, 1133
Greek philosophy, ancient   1399
Greek religion, ancient   1399
Greek studies   1421, 1462
  ancient   218, 1121, 1399, 2895, 2967
  Euboean   233
  Ionian Islands   1508
  Macedonia   1755
  Mycenaean   1860, 2756
Gregory, Lady Isabella Augusta   622
Grillparzer, Franz   1321
Groth, Klaus Johann   1515
Grundtvig, Nikolai Frederik Severin   1140
Gutenberg, Johann   1142
Gypsy studies   1461
Hagiography   154, 2930
Haiku   1145
Hamlet   1149
Hardy, Thomas   622, 2138, 2970-2971
Hawthorne, Nathaniel   1928
Hazlitt, William   570, 3206
Hearing disorders   822
Hearing research   822, 1444
Hebbel, Friedrich   1160
Hebrew language   1161, 1163, 1349, 1600-1601, 2951, 3238

Hebrew language (*cont.*)
  Qumrân   3249
  Samaritans   3249
Hebrew linguistics   1162-1163, 1601
Hebrew literature   359, 1161, 1163, 1869, 1899, 2248, 3234
  English translations   1869
Hebrew philology   1845
Hegel, Georg Wilhelm Friedrich   613
Heidelberg, Germany   2501
Heine, Heinrich   1168
Hemingway, Ernest   1173
Hemito-Semitic linguistics   1355
Heraldry   616
Herbert, George   1087
Hermeneutics   1966, 2452
  language and   2830
Hermeticism   555
Hispanic   *see also* Ibero-; Latin American; Luso-Brazilian; Spanish; Spanish American
Hispanic aesthetics   786
Hispanic American culture   484
Hispanic American literature   251, 484, 898, 922, 2036
Hispanic cultural history   2377
Hispanic culture   216, 800, 1181, 1183, 1186, 1405
Hispanic Enlightenment   786
Hispanic folklore   2377
Hispanic history   2371
Hispanic languages   216, 251, 1000, 2378
  teaching   1181
Hispanic linguistics   691, 1181, 1183, 1623, 1695, 1734, 2036-2037, 2377, 2990
  United States   381
Hispanic literature   74, 216, 251, 349, 691, 786, 800, 1000, 1181, 1183, 1186, 1188, 1405, 1623, 1721, 1883, 2037, 2351, 2371, 2377, 2935, 3060
  through 1700   1400
  in the United States   129, 360
Hispanic pedagogy   1181
Hispanic philology   1400, 2036
Hispanic philosophy   878, 1183, 2371
Hispanic society   1405
Hispanic studies   442, 446, 798, 979, 1181, 1734, 2981
  in the United States   381
Hispanic theater   1107
Historical anthropology, Indo-European   1404
Historical criticism   335
Historical linguistics   *see* Diachronic linguistics; Philology
Historiography   1463
  18th century   387
  Greek   609
  literature and   613
History   3, 69, 184, 189, 222, 283, 289, 350, 354, 392, 467, 511, 625, 633, 638, 666, 670, 681, 690, 700, 736, 744, 758, 881, 1017, 1091, 1146, 1150, 1167, 1348, 1408-1409, 1447, 1481, 1506, 1525, 1545, 1547, 1685, 1809, 1864, 1927, 2038, 2092, 2111, 2163-2164, 2168, 2226, 2240, 2243, 2286, 2311, 2321, 2350, 2383, 2401-2402, 2408, 2440, 2469, 2483, 2545, 2626-2628, 2634, 2683, 2690, 2783, 2802, 2813, 2865, 2897, 2965, 2969, 3021-3022, 3058, 3094, 3117, 3124, 3132, 3189, 3210, 3241
  see also Classical history *and entries for the history of specific countries or regions, e.g.,* English history; African history
  African languages   2707
  ancient   2994, 3270
  Celtic   509, 2767, 3001
  church   154, 158, 2494
  contemporary   1820
  culture and   2939, 3162
  of doctrines   2434
  18th century   138, 839, 841, 2307
  European literature and   2493
  15th century   997
  Flemish   3174
  folklore and   1021
  Franco-British relations   1048
  German American   2544
  Germanic   1097

History (cont.)
  Hispanic 2371
  Humanist 356
  of ideas 555, 652, 737, 906, 1463, 2317
  intellectual 165, 2529
  interdisciplinary studies 1463, 1698
  Islamic 1295, 3165
  language and 2707
  literary theory and 2191
  literature and 613, 622, 1414, 1683, 1698, 2493
  medieval 1418, 1798
  Mexican and Central American Indian cultures 2983
  New World 2398
  19th century 141, 2307, 2491
  oral 1042, 2073
  philosophy of 613
  Portuguese-speaking countries 284
  pre-Hellenic and pre-Roman 218
  rare book reprints 2547
  Reformation 238
  Renaissance 142, 356, 980, 1418, 1472, 1799, 2345-2346, 3014
  Roman 218, 1133, 1586
  17th century 143, 2590, 2592
  Slavic-Romanian relations 2490
  social 1463, 1481, 2144, 3021
  Tamil 1445
  of theater 1516, 2422, 2548, 2955, 2957, 2959, 2961-2962
  women's 1066, 3202
Hittite studies 2793, 2945
Hoffmann, E. T. A. 1854
Hofmannsthal, Hugo von 1196
Hogg, James 2827
Hölderlin, Friedrich 1197
Holmes, Sherlock 310
Homosexuality, in literature 1036
Hopkins, Gerard Manley 1200
Horror fiction 2860
Housman, Alfred Edward 1207
Housman, Clemence 1207
Housman, Laurence 1207
Hughes, Langston 1552
Human behavior 1426
Human development 1209
Humanism 356, 792, 1132, 1155, 1211, 2254, 2345, 2383, 3075, 3078
  Czech 1669
  Italian 1302
Humanist literature 356
  European 19
  German 750
  Hungarian 19
Humanist philology 1114
Humanities 27, 66, 182, 185, 198, 321, 417, 502, 607, 666, 706, 710, 728, 765, 818, 874, 885, 895, 1034, 1077, 1146, 1253, 1401, 1467, 1506, 1533, 1547, 1594, 1629, 1698, 1783, 1828, 1926, 2007, 2050, 2084, 2104, 2228, 2242, 2289, 2339, 2387, 2428, 2501, 2514, 2521, 2531, 2618, 2659, 2664, 2675, 2683, 2723, 2853-2854, 2937, 2976, 2988, 3025, 3076, 3079, 3086, 3119, 3172, 3194, 3217
  bibliographies 444
  biographical scholarship 361
  Caribbean 2393
  Chinese 2349, 3030
  comparative civilization studies 648
  comparative studies 2115
  computer research 656
  dissertation abstracts 801
  dissertations 181
  East European ethnic minorities 1930
  higher education 1213
  interdisciplinary studies 421, 1825, 2293, 2669, 3075, 3160
  Italian American studies 1303
  Latin America 2393
  law and 3218
  Persian 1754
  professional topics 2246
  religion and 94
  Southern United States 1848
  Soviet nationalities 1930
  Ukrainian studies 1483

Humor 1214
  American 2809
  literary 2952
Hungarian arts 80
Hungarian dialects 1749, 1751
Hungarian ethnography 15, 26, 2040
Hungarian etymology 1749
Hungarian folklore 15
Hungarian-German literary relations 1936
Hungarian language 26, 949, 1749, 1751
Hungarian linguistics 1749, 2040, 3253
Hungarian literary history 2780
Hungarian literature 19, 24, 80, 713, 1215-1216, 1292-1294, 1532, 1751, 2040
  modern 1687
Hungarian phonetics 1749
Hungarian studies 1216, 1218
Hungarian theater 2903
Hunt, Leigh 1501
Hurston, Zora Neale 3275
Hymns 1220
Iberian culture 515
Iberian history 442
Iberian languages 442, 689, 1400
Iberian literature 442, 515, 689
  medieval 448
  through 1700 1400
Iberian poetry 515
Iberian studies 689, 2305
Ibero-American languages 689
Ibero-American literature 689, 2392
Ibero-American studies 164, 689
Ibero-Romance languages 1221
Ibero-Romance literatures 1221
Ibsen, Henrik 667
Icelandic see also Old Norse
Icelandic culture 2566, 2630
Icelandic language 1074, 2516, 2566, 2629
Icelandic linguistics 2629
Icelandic literature 353, 834, 1074, 2516, 2566, 2629-2630
Icelandic philology 353
Icelandic studies 1074, 2778
Iconography 139, 825-826
  Near Eastern 1349
Iconology 1348
Ideas
  see also Philosophy; Thought
  18th century 839
  history of 652, 906, 1463, 2144, 2144, 2317
Ideology 693
  communism 2091
Illinois history 1226
Illuminated manuscripts 1764
Illustration 1627, 2139
Illyrian culture 1122
Imagery 139
Impressionism 1457
Indexes
  documentation and 1383
  Edwardian fiction 3125
  of humanities and social science journals 1077
  for literary and linguistic research 654
  to performing arts 2149
  to religious literature 2402
  Victorian fiction 3125
Indian refers to the state of India, its people, history, language, and culture. For entries for indigenous peoples of North and South American continents see Native American
Indian aesthetics 1402
Indian anthropology 1018
Indian art 1234, 3140
  Renaissance 3024
Indian culture 343, 501, 1234, 1970
Indian dance 1018
Indian ethics 1402
Indian folklore 1018
Indian history 1460, 3140
  Renaissance 3024
Indian languages 1237, 1402, 3140
Indian linguistics 1236-1237, 1265, 1566
Indian literature 403, 1018, 1234, 1238-1240, 1242, 1375, 1403, 3140
  English language 687, 714

Indian literature (cont.)
  regional 641
  Renaissance 3024
  20th century 3099
Indian music 1018
Indian performing arts 1234
Indian philology 2799
Indian philosophy 403, 1402, 1460, 3140, 3182
Indian religions 403, 1402, 1460, 3140, 3182
Indian Renaissance 3024
Indian society 501
Indian song 1018
Indian studies 199, 343, 403, 1011, 1242, 1452, 1460, 1470, 3083, 3140, 3182
  Tamil 1445
Indic languages 403, 1242, 1470
Indic linguistics 3182
Indo-English literature 316, 1392
Indo-European anthropology 953
Indo-European cultural history 1404
Indo-European languages 313, 953, 1801, 2703, 2902
  Phrygian 1491
Indo-European linguistics 242, 313, 953, 1243, 1404, 2703
Indo-European onomastics 313
Indo-European philology 1404
Indo-European studies 953, 1404, 1763
Indo-Iranian studies 1242
Indological studies 268
Indonesian anthropology 358, 1244
Indonesian culture 2444
Indonesian folklore 1244
Indonesian history 358, 1244
Indonesian linguistics 358, 1244, 2048, 2444
Indonesian literature 1244
Indonesian studies 1244, 2444
  Irian Jaya 1285
  Lesser Sunda Islands 2155
Information sciences 1631, 2705
  information processing 2708
  information theory, Biblical literature and 1648
Inge, William Motter 2807
Inklings 1252
Inscriptions see Epigraphy
Institutions
  academic 1343
  educational 1343
  medieval 1418, 2694
  religious 1805
  Renaissance 1418
Intellectual history 165, 2529
Intellectual life, medieval 2782
Intensional logic 1657
Interdisciplinary studies 555, 560, 742, 826, 1214, 1378, 1554, 1892, 1987, 2007, 2059, 2190, 2208, 2238, 2289, 2350, 2520, 2660, 2667, 2723, 2725, 2881-2882, 2939, 3167, 3217, 3222
  African 55
  American culture 109
  American literature 178
  Americas 1971
  Australian 297
  biographical scholarship 361
  books 395
  British literature 178
  Canadian 297
  Central European 536
  Commonwealth literature 178
  communication and language 1554
  comparative literature 535
  drama 650
  East European 536
  18th century 842
  English language 178
  ethnology 933
  historical 1463
  humanities 421, 1825, 2115, 2293, 2669, 3075
  Hungarian 1218
  Indo-European 1404
  Japanese 1407
  language 1270, 1554, 1654, 2183, 2293
  language acquisition 2832
  late medieval and Renaissance 1418
  linguistics 754, 1654

Interdisciplinary studies (*cont.*)
 literature   879, 1129, 2183, 2293, 2687, 3077
 literature and history   613, 1698
 medieval   10, 1790, 3124
 Renaissance   3124
 Romanticism   2844
 Russian   536
 Southern United States   2688
 Soviet Union   536
 Ukrainian   536
 women   1066, 3202
Interlanguage communication   1900
Interpersonal communication   643
Interpreting   1589, 1900
 translation and   1818
Interviews
 American dramatists   2807
 Australian writers   301
 Black culture   46
 Black literature   2044
 Canadian writers   1366, 3145
 children's literature   1668
 contemporary poets   2907
 contemporary writers   669, 1747, 1850
 East German writers   1079
 English literature, except British and American   3213
 film   1706
 folk song   2620
 performing arts   2624
 Québécois writers   3145
 science fiction   2554
 Spanish theater   916
 theater productions   2953
Ionian Islands studies   1508
Iowa history   2107
Iqbal, Muhammed   1282
Iranian   *see also* Persian
Iranian art   1283
Iranian culture   1283-1284
Iranian history   1267, 1283
Iranian languages   1242, 2776
Iranian literature   1267, 1283, 2776
 translations   1284
Iranian philology   2799
Iranian society   1284
Iranian studies   988, 1011, 1242, 1267, 1283-1284, 2776
Iranian theology   1267
Irian Jaya anthropology   1285
Irian Jaya linguistics   1285
Irish antiquaries   1474
Irish culture   635, 845, 1290
Irish dialectology   3059
Irish ethnology   3059
Irish folk culture   1013
Irish folklore   322, 2774, 3059
Irish Gaelic language   558, 844, 892, 2150, 2774, 2917, 3059
Irish history   558, 954, 1288, 1290, 1455, 1474, 2774, 3059
 medieval   2150
Irish law, medieval   2150
Irish linguistics   2917
Irish literature   28, 695, 864, 875, 954, 1406, 1455, 1684, 1781, 2020, 2774, 2804
 18th century   2563, 2891
 Irish Gaelic   558, 635, 844, 892, 1588
 medieval   2150
 modern   622, 1291
 19th century   3183
 20th century   323, 622, 969, 1335, 1365, 1487, 2605-2606, 3231-3233
Irish material culture   1455
Irish onomastics   1994, 3059
Irish place names   2774
Irish studies   526, 845, 892, 954, 1290, 2774
 medieval   2150
Islamic   *see also* Muslim
Islamic culture   1295, 2272, 2415
Islamic studies   228, 268, 1282, 1295, 1349, 1425, 1442, 1911, 2415, 2777, 3165
Israeli anthropology   1267
Israeli art   252
Israeli culture   252
Israeli folklore   1267, 3234
Israeli literature   252, 1163, 1267, 1869, 2248

Israeli philosophy   1267
Israeli studies   1267
Israeli theater   269
Israeli writers   1163
Italian American literature   1303, 1937, 3122
Italian American studies   1303, 1937, 3122
Italian art   91, 2719
 Veneto region   244
Italian books, reviews   1304
Italian civilization   2720
Italian culture   194, 519, 549, 788, 1037, 1071, 1305, 1308, 1311, 1607, 1937, 2278, 2447, 2720, 2724, 2745, 3103, 3225
 Renaissance   563
 Trentino   2762
 Venetian   274
Italian dialects   1300, 1639, 2459
 Dalmatian   2449
 historical studies   2741
 Venetian   2280
Italian etymology   1639
Italian film   549, 1305, 1308, 2719
Italian fine arts   1305
Italian-German studies   2333
Italian history   91, 197, 245, 1305, 1308, 2719, 2724, 2757, 3021
 Alto Adige region   243
 18th-19th centuries   2307
 Risorgimento   2307
 social and cultural   3103
 Trentino   2762
 Veneto region   244
Italian humanism   1302
Italian language   91, 197, 1037, 1305, 1308, 1311-1312, 1639, 1801, 2280, 2416, 2458-2459, 2487, 2720, 2742, 2745
 Dalmatia   2449
 history of   1639, 2741
 teaching   532, 1310, 1639
 Venetian Italian dialect   2280
Italian linguistics   242, 389, 807, 1311, 1639, 2278, 2459, 2488, 2719
 Alto Adige region   243
 Mediterranean region   390
 Trentino   2762
 Veneto region   244
Italian literature   8, 91, 192, 194, 197, 245, 311, 335, 519, 527, 549, 690, 692, 726, 807, 903, 1037, 1071, 1073, 1115, 1129, 1277, 1305-1306, 1308-1312, 1359, 1580, 1611-1612, 1718, 1839, 1859, 1937, 2029, 2123, 2204, 2278, 2280, 2304, 2333, 2352, 2416, 2445, 2447, 2458, 2462, 2487, 2610, 2617, 2695, 2719-2720, 2724, 2745, 2758, 3060, 3085, 3091, 3113, 3225
 Dalmatia   2449
 18th century   1260, 2751
 Latin language   84, 802, 1590, 1617, 2434, 2739
 medieval   84, 247, 749, 802, 1302, 1590, 1617, 2434, 2739, 2760
 19th century   170, 388
 Reformation   1132
 Renaissance   563, 1132, 1302
 16th century   2761
 20th century   170, 1609, 2255, 2757, 3228
 Veneto region   244
Italian music   1305
Italian onomastics   1639
Italian philology   673, 1639, 2280, 2746
Italian philosophy   788, 1113, 2452, 3021
Italian poetry   91, 549, 1612, 3268
Italian society   2719
Italian studies   91, 527, 1306-1308, 1359, 2278, 2333, 2416, 2458, 3021, 3085, 3225
 Bergamo   338
 Rome   2758
 in South Africa   2745
 Veneto region   244, 2280
Italian texts   2746
Italian theater   3228
Jacobean drama   2523, 2575
Jainism   1402
James, Henry, Jr.   622, 1174
Japanese art   451, 1336, 1888
Japanese culture   1336, 1407
Japanese folklore   1888

Japanese history   1888
Japanese language   451, 1453
 mathematical research   1504
Japanese linguistics   865, 1082, 1386, 1453, 1504
Japanese literature   205, 445, 451, 1154, 1165, 1409, 1453, 1888
Japanese religions   1888
Japanese studies   268, 1336, 1362, 1407, 2998
Jean Paul   1322
Jeffers, Robinson   2464
Jewish   *see also* Hebrew; Israeli; Yiddish
Jewish American literature   2811
Jewish culture   1339
 in America   2811
 in Germany   3197
Jewish ethnology   1339
Jewish folk culture   1339
Jewish folklore   1339, 3234
Jewish history, German   3197
Jewish literature   362, 1993, 2248, 3236, 3238
Jewish Orthodox thought   2995
Jewish studies   362, 637, 1339, 1349, 1442, 1845, 1993, 2248, 2573, 2912
 Sephardic   923
Johnson, Samuel   64, 3004
Journal indexes, humanities and social sciences   1077
Journalism   1377, 1486
 history of   1748
Joyce, James   622, 969, 1335, 1487
Judaic studies   3238
Judaism   1212, 1447, 1488
 modern culture and   712
Judeo-Christian studies   603, 2456
Kafka, Franz   1465
Kansas studies   1175
Keats, John   1501-1502
Kerouac, Jack   1889
Kinesics   2615
Kipling, Rudyard   1509
Kit-Cat Club   2563
Korean art   451
Korean culture   1529
Korean history   1529
Korean language   451, 1572
Korean linguistics   1386
Korean literature   451, 1165, 1529
Korean studies   1362, 1529
Kurdish language   1926
Kurdish literature   1926
Labrador dialects   2332
Labrador linguistics   2332
Labrador onomastics   2332
Ladin language   243
Ladino language   923
Lamb, Charles   570, 3206
Lancashire dialect   1466
Landor, Walter Savage   3206
Langland, William   3226
Language, languages   184, 192, 471-472, 502, 562, 619, 628, 759, 1089-1090, 1194, 1228, 1237, 1263, 1273, 1286, 1315, 1409-1410, 1412, 1476, 1527, 1551, 1559, 1570-1571, 1598, 1641, 1656, 1713, 1809, 1822, 1840, 1919, 1931, 2000, 2040, 2045, 2111, 2159, 2167, 2203, 2226, 2246, 2311, 2335, 2421, 2465, 2469, 2696, 2703, 2709, 2718, 2766, 2882, 2913, 2917, 3032, 3048, 3051, 3070, 3210
 see also Linguistic; Linguistics; Philology, *and entries for specific languages, e.g.,* Swedish language
 abusive and offensive   1759
 ancient   11
 of Bible and theology   1648
 brain and   404
 of children   1371
 classical   189, 3029
 cognition   618, 1557
 comprehension, production, acquisition   1024, 1419
 Creole   688
 culture and   2657
 East European   2641
 ethics and   2830
 European   331, 953, 997, 1515, 1886

Language, languages (*cont.*)
 figurative 1819
 functional theory of 1660
 gender and 3198
 hearing and 822
 hermeneutics and 2830
 Hispanic 216, 251, 1000, 1181, 2378
 history and 2707
 history of 1469, 1763, 3003
 interdisciplinary studies 1270, 1554, 1654, 2183, 2293, 2832
 Latin American 442, 446, 2446
 law 2830
 literature and 663, 2397
 logical structure 1431
 mathematical models 2283
 mathematical research 1504
 medieval 234
 Mediterranean 1801
 modern 41, 189, 193, 234, 551, 678, 1408, 1619, 1808, 1873-1874, 1876, 1940, 2096, 2183, 2235, 2676, 3230
 Near Eastern, ancient 344
 perception and 620, 1657, 2146
 philosophy of 275, 428, 778, 797, 1069, 1189, 1402, 1638, 1657, 1782, 2162, 2164, 2166, 2830, 3115
 politics 1084
 religion and 171
 Renaissance 2346
 sexuality in 796
 sign languages 1268, 2615
 society and 210, 1270, 1550, 1567-1568, 1657, 2665
 special purposes 409, 676, 757, 986
 style and 1638
 theory of 706, 921
 written 3141
Language acquisition 543, 1005, 1024, 1272, 1419, 1555-1556, 1563, 1569, 1654, 1657, 1782, 2337, 2397, 2405, 2830, 2832, 2917
Language attrition 1556
Language development 225, 576, 769, 1371, 1439, 1556, 2461
Language disorders 225, 577, 1556, 1949
 brain and 404
Language learning 224, 948, 1005, 1084, 1412, 1423, 1556, 1656, 1901, 2832, 2992
 computer-assisted 543
 psychology and sociology of 1555, 2932
 in Thailand 2136
Language maintenance 2657
Language obsolescence 2657
Language origins 2615
Language planning 1570, 1900, 2832
 see also Language teaching
 English as foreign language 2932
 Finnish 3139
 Swedish 2635, 2716
Language play 3205
Language poets 2519
Language processing 620, 655, 2846
Language remediation 577
Language structure 1561, 2705, 3003
Language teaching 39, 224, 426, 532, 543, 757, 948, 1024, 1039, 1084, 1225, 1259, 1388, 1423, 1469, 1490, 1821, 1871, 1876, 1900, 1947, 1950, 2046, 2301, 2405, 2410, 2465, 2832, 2917, 3211
 see also Language planning
 abstracts 1574
 Afrikaans 1514
 applied linguistics in 507, 1272
 Arabic 72
 Chinese 1454
 East European languages 2641
 English 229, 562, 574, 606, 627, 716, 863, 871, 1279, 2337, 2932
 first language 2461
 in France 1579
 French 532, 562, 606, 1043-1044, 1055, 1061
 German 532, 562, 606, 757, 768, 1880, 3089, 3269
 Hispanic 1181
 Hungarian 1751
 Italian 532, 1310, 1639

Language teaching (*cont.*)
 Japanese 1453
 Latin 606
 linguistics and 1255, 2932
 Luso-Brazilian 1181
 Old English 2061
 in Poland 1119
 Portuguese 1181
 Romanian 1635
 Russian 562, 2505
 second languages 1569
 Slavic 2641
 in Southeast Asia 2337
 Spanish 532, 606, 1181
 Swedish 2887
 in Thailand 2136
Language testing 224, 975, 1575
Languages for special purposes 676, 757, 986
 English 409
Languedocian Occitan dialect 1046
Lappish dialects 2637, 2886
Lappish linguistics 1998
Lappish literature 398
Latin American *see also* Hispanic; Luso-Brazilian; South American; Spanish American
Latin American arts 550, 1582, 2362
Latin American culture 213, 239, 446, 515, 718, 806, 1183, 1186, 1411, 2279, 2398, 2446, 2879
Latin American drama 1584
Latin American Enlightenment 786
Latin American fiction, in English translation 1582
Latin American folklore 1411, 1769
Latin American history 239, 442, 1411, 1734
Latin American Indian studies 1581
Latin American languages 442, 446, 2446
Latin American literary theory and criticism 615
Latin American literature 18, 74, 76, 126, 128, 163, 213, 349, 442, 446, 515, 550, 571, 586, 615, 718-719, 723, 732, 740, 798, 806, 976, 1026, 1183, 1186, 1278, 1411, 1496, 1582, 1610, 1653, 1689, 1721, 1734, 1769, 1875, 1993, 2036, 2086, 2204, 2279, 2305, 2351, 2362, 2374, 2382, 2398, 2446, 2744, 2879, 2935, 2949, 3045, 3105
 modern 1286, 3065
 19th-20th century 2391
Latin American music 1583
Latin American philosophy 76
Latin American poetry 76, 515, 2188
 in English translation 1582
Latin American popular culture 1411, 2833
Latin American society 239
Latin American studies 35, 76, 128, 550, 1721, 1971, 2393, 2398, 2446, 2570
Latin American theater 76, 1107, 1584
Latin *see also* Classical; Neo-Latin; Roman
Latin language 41, 218, 277, 590, 609-610, 853, 880, 891-892, 944, 1118, 1121, 1143, 1585-1586, 1669, 1752, 1860, 1907, 2171, 2409, 2417, 2438, 2895
 medieval 1857
 teaching 606
Latin language literature 154, 157, 218, 602, 609, 1121, 1132, 1211, 1585-1586, 1688, 1752, 1890, 2417, 2438, 2755
 Christian 2402
 1500 to present 2592
 manuscript research 1764
 medieval 84, 247-248, 329, 802, 1590, 1617, 1669, 1857, 1905, 2434, 2739
 17th century 815, 1837-1838, 2592
 vernacular 1789
Latin linguistics 2755
Latin philology 157, 218, 891, 1133, 2755
 medieval 1302
Latin studies 2417
Latin texts 1902, 1905
 medieval 2782
Latvian art 1587
Latvian culture 13, 70
Latvian ethnography 250
Latvian folklore 1587
Latvian history 13, 70, 1337

Latvian language 13, 1364
Latvian linguistics 1587
Latvian literature 13, 752, 1337, 1337, 1364, 1535, 1587, 3100
 20th century 2299
Latvian philology 70
Latvian philosophy 70
Latvian-Slavic relations 14
Latvian studies 70, 246
Law
 humanities and 3218
 Irish, medieval 2150
 language and 2830
 literature and 541, 3218
 manuscript research 1764
 medieval 2694
 religion and 1805
 women in 3202
Lawrence, D. H. 738-739, 955, 2138
Lawrence, T. E. 2905
Learning disabilities, language and 1412
Legend
 see also Myth
 Atlantic provinces 2010
 modern 668
 New England 2010
Léger, Alexis Saint-Léger 496
Lesbian studies 1066
Lessing, Doris 810
Lessing, Gotthold Ephraim 1602, 3197
Letters, as subject 2
Lewes, George Henry 1085
Lewis, C. S. 717, 1252, 1915
Lewis, Wyndham 859
Lexicography 224, 248, 470, 746, 975, 1266, 1620-1621, 1900, 3107
 bilingual 783
 Danish 747
 English 2016
 Italian 1639
 monolingual 783
 translation and 1818
Lexicology 470, 1117, 1266, 1621-1622, 1821, 3205
 see also entries for lexicology in specific countries, e.g., German lexicology
 Hebrew 1162
 offensive words 1759
 Serbo-Croatian 2225
Leyte language 1624
Leyte literature 1624
Leyte studies 1624
Libraries 625, 1626-1627, 1999, 2302
 Abidjan University 186
 American studies 2357
 Biblioteca Civica "A. Mai" di Bergamo 338
 Bodleian Library 374
 British Library 414
 Brown University 396
 Cambridge University 2999
 Columbia University 633
 Harvard University 1155
 Herzog August Bibliothek 3196
 history of 236, 374, 1522, 1628
 John Rylands University, Manchester 450
 Kippenberg collection, Düsseldorf 1326
 Miller Library (Maine) 622
 Morris Library, Southern Illinois University, Carbondale 1223
 National Library of Wales 1929
 Princeton University Library 2228
 Rutgers University 1475
 Syracuse University 2901
 University of California, Santa Barbara 2670
 University of Iowa 397
 University of Miami 548
 University of Southern California 677
 University of Texas, Austin 1629
 Yale University 3220
Library science 8, 350, 605, 858, 1383, 1408, 1522, 1626, 1631, 1999, 2158, 2302
 catalogues 1077
Liceo Classico G. Garibaldi di Palermo 189
Limousin literature 1046
Linguistic analysis 795, 1642
 English-Polish contrastive analysis 2112

Linguistic atlases 389-390
  German languages 2794
Linguistic data processing 1672, 2705
Linguistic literary theory and criticism 327
Linguistic relations, American-European 1753
Linguistic theology 1648
Linguistic theory 112, 778, 865, 936, 1000, 1024, 1069, 1572, 1578, 1642, 1681, 1782, 1855, 2036, 2125, 2162, 2283, 2614
Linguistics 17, 79, 89, 123, 145, 149, 159, 184, 200, 205, 212, 220, 222, 226, 249, 283, 288, 300, 336, 348, 355, 359, 364, 376, 379, 425, 445, 462-463, 471-472, 474, 481, 487, 507-508, 516, 532, 551, 562, 565, 569, 619, 634, 660, 672, 678, 722-723, 731, 735, 757, 762, 792, 837, 877, 896, 920, 922, 961, 975, 986, 1010, 1024, 1034, 1038-1039, 1045, 1068, 1081-1082, 1089-1091, 1101, 1117, 1134, 1147, 1150, 1210, 1225, 1229, 1231, 1247, 1249, 1251, 1263, 1266, 1272, 1296, 1401, 1413, 1437, 1441, 1444, 1461, 1489, 1503, 1523, 1527, 1543, 1549-1551, 1553, 1560, 1562, 1566, 1571, 1573, 1576, 1578-1579, 1597-1599, 1623, 1634-1636, 1638, 1640-1641, 1643, 1646, 1651, 1653-1654, 1656-1657, 1659, 1662-1665, 1729, 1811, 1821-1822, 1828, 1862, 1891, 1896, 1931, 1998, 2000, 2008, 2014, 2018, 2041, 2045-2046, 2099, 2174, 2198, 2213, 2231, 2233, 2264, 2266, 2273, 2276, 2301, 2310, 2324, 2334, 2368, 2370, 2382, 2395, 2404, 2430-2431, 2433, 2455, 2461, 2471, 2475, 2498, 2520, 2529, 2537, 2565, 2569, 2576, 2585, 2623, 2656, 2678, 2689, 2695-2696, 2698, 2700, 2708, 2736, 2747, 2755, 2763, 2765, 2779, 2801, 2823, 2830, 2848, 2855, 2858, 2863, 2874, 2880, 2883, 2898, 2908, 2917, 2920, 2934, 2949, 2965, 2968, 2987, 3003, 3010, 3015, 3017-3019, 3032, 3050-3052, 3073, 3102, 3106-3107, 3115, 3118, 3147, 3155, 3194, 3203, 3207-3209, 3257
  see also Ethnolinguistics; Psycholinguistics; Sociolinguistics, etc., and entries for linguistics in specific countries or regions, e.g., Chinese linguistics; European linguistics
  abstracts 1655
  Afro-Asiatic 63, 352, 1355
  ancient Eastern 590
  anthropological 210, 1263, 1763, 2216, 2461
  applied see Applied linguistics
  bibliographies 148
  brain and 404
  cognitive studies 618, 1557
  comparative see Comparative linguistics
  composition and 626, 1352
  computer-assisted analysis 654
  computers and 1558, 1672
  contrastive 2112, 2880
  descriptive see Descriptive linguistics
  diachronic see Diachronic linguistics
  18th century 841
  experimental 493, 1433, 1654, 2173
  Finno-Ugric 851, 949, 1003, 1652
  functional 1069, 1660
  geolinguistics 1084, 2277
  Hemito-Semitic 1355
  historical see Diachronic linguistics
  history of 145-146, 149, 379, 1189, 2880
  Indo-European 242, 313, 953, 1243, 1404, 2703
  interdisciplinary studies 754, 1654
  Irian Jaya 1285
  language teaching and 1255, 2932
  Lappish 1998
  literary theory and 2191
  literature and 714, 1298, 1561, 1966, 3240
  logic and 1431
  mathematical see Mathematical linguistics
  medieval 1940
  methodology 1342, 1998
  Mexican American 308
  Mexican and Central American Indian 2983
  modern 2831, 1940

Linguistics (cont.)
  Mon-Khmer 1879
  New Zealand Maori and other Pacific peoples 1471
  philosophy and 1657
  psychiatry and 2256
  rhetoric and 1352
  science and 2899
  sign languages and 1268
  textual 2125, 2216
  theoretical see Theoretical linguistics
  theory of 1573, 1654, 2899
  Tolkien, J. R. R. 3135
Literacy 543, 1352, 1656, 2270, 2313
Literary criticism see Literary theory and criticism
Literary genres see names of specific genres, e.g., Poetry
Literary history 19, 240, 375, 495, 535, 651-652, 708, 792, 848, 852, 972, 1100, 1169, 1293, 1463, 1469, 1481, 1517, 1606, 1733, 1872, 1962, 1966, 2030, 2076, 2123, 2191, 2227, 2308, 2384, 2529, 2650, 2828, 2867, 2966, 2982
  see also entries for literary history of specific countries or regions, e.g., Czech literary history; European literary history
  Jewish 2248
  modern 332
  Neo-Latin 1211
Literary periods 912, 1939, 1966, 2076, 2193
  bibliographies 2357
  teaching 627
Literary relations
  American-European 1753
  East-West 647, 652, 1705, 3222
  European with North and South America 652
  German and non-German 2529
  German-Dutch 553
  German-Hungarian 1936
  German-Scandinavian 2629
  Romanian-Slavic 2490
Literary research 1677
  computer-assisted analysis 654
  methods 535
Literary semantics 1414
Literary style 1561, 1564, 1638, 1966
  Bulgarian writers 422
Literary theory and criticism 18, 101, 125, 163, 198, 205, 254, 270, 288, 402, 463, 466, 535, 562, 627, 629, 631-632, 649, 651, 700, 704, 706-707, 723, 728, 755, 765, 772, 778, 795, 879, 898, 912-913, 920, 950, 957, 961-962, 972, 983, 985, 1000, 1070, 1100, 1164, 1169, 1213, 1277, 1308, 1378, 1415, 1476, 1503, 1518, 1526-1527, 1561-1562, 1623, 1648, 1670-1671, 1678, 1687, 1715, 1717, 1776, 1827-1828, 1863, 1891, 1910, 1952-1953, 1962, 1966, 2030, 2036, 2040, 2054, 2059, 2076, 2095, 2108, 2129, 2134, 2166, 2191-2193, 2227, 2289, 2303, 2312, 2350, 2358, 2365, 2367, 2373, 2384, 2386, 2407, 2439, 2452, 2484, 2538, 2555, 2585, 2613, 2650, 2699, 2704, 2725-2726, 2857, 2868, 2881, 2921, 2931, 2934, 2938, 2944, 2950, 2966, 3027, 3067, 3077, 3148, 3153, 3161, 3210
  see also Poetics and entries for literary theory and criticism in specific countries, e.g., American literary theory and criticism
  American literature, 19th century 906
  comparative literature 535, 2900, 3081, 3223
  contextualist 2330
  culture and 1967
  depth psychology and 1703
  feminist 1842, 2518, 3201
  French 905
  generic 1083
  history of 2191
  Italian literature 1129
  linguistics and 2191
  medieval 1940
  methodology 1469
  modern 1940
  narrative 2191

Literary theory and criticism (cont.)
  phenomenological 3112
  psychology and 2191
  Romanian literature 2900
  sociology and 2191
  teaching 627
  theory of 2166
  20th century 2859, 2869
  values and 2347
Literature 4, 9, 65, 69, 110, 120, 135, 159, 184, 186, 190-192, 200, 214-215, 220, 222, 231, 249, 273, 275, 281, 288-289, 305, 335, 348, 351, 359, 393, 400, 445, 450, 455, 510, 548, 562, 575, 596, 625, 628, 632-633, 638, 657, 666, 670, 674, 679, 681, 690, 696, 703-705, 707-708, 722, 728, 736, 744-745, 759, 772, 775-776, 784, 787, 795-796, 818, 855, 858, 886, 890, 893-895, 898, 904, 908-909, 914, 922, 947, 957, 967, 977, 993, 1007, 1025, 1032, 1034, 1089, 1091, 1111, 1130-1131, 1146-1147, 1150, 1164, 1178, 1194, 1198, 1203, 1208, 1228, 1246, 1280, 1297, 1314-1315, 1348, 1383, 1394, 1401, 1440, 1476, 1495-1496, 1499, 1505-1508, 1518, 1520, 1525, 1533, 1543, 1545, 1547, 1559, 1571, 1598, 1603, 1625, 1634, 1653, 1670, 1674, 1690-1691, 1694, 1701, 1705, 1707, 1716, 1725-1728, 1733, 1743, 1747, 1775, 1781, 1786, 1791, 1809, 1811, 1814, 1823, 1830, 1840, 1842, 1863, 1873, 1877, 1892, 1895, 1906, 1914, 1927, 1933, 1935, 1942, 1944, 1954, 1957, 1964-1966, 1969, 1975, 2003, 2007, 2027-2028, 2037, 2039, 2045, 2083, 2092, 2099, 2111, 2128-2129, 2131-2132, 2138, 2140, 2159, 2178-2180, 2182, 2184, 2190, 2200-2201, 2206, 2224, 2226, 2236, 2243, 2246, 2251, 2264, 2273, 2276, 2282, 2286, 2289-2290, 2300, 2303, 2308, 2310-2311, 2335, 2348, 2366, 2369, 2373, 2382, 2385-2387, 2401, 2421, 2427, 2447, 2465, 2469, 2482-2483, 2520, 2527, 2530-2531, 2564-2565, 2574, 2585, 2593, 2607, 2622, 2626-2628, 2636, 2653, 2677-2678, 2683, 2686, 2690, 2695-2696, 2698, 2724, 2725, 2728, 2738, 2763, 2789, 2791-2792, 2802, 2853, 2865, 2867, 2882, 2897, 2908, 2911, 2926, 2934, 2937, 2944, 2965-2966, 2969, 2982, 3005, 3022, 3034, 3040, 3047-3048, 3061, 3071, 3079, 3086, 3091, 3094, 3097-3098, 3117-3118, 3120, 3137, 3142, 3151-3152, 3155, 3161, 3214-3215, 3219, 3241, 3271, 3277
  see also Comparative literature; World literature, etc. and entries for specific literary genres, e.g., Poetry; literary periods, e.g., Renaissance literature; and national or regional literatures, e.g., French literature; British literature
  alcohol and 793
  allegorical 2336
  American history and 1850
  ancient 11
  anthropology and 2328
  arts and 622, 647, 2529, 3162, 3204
  Austria in 2088
  bibliographies 1258
  biomedical ethics and 1702
  children's 579-580, 790, 1668
  Christianity and 588-589, 2347
  colonial 714
  comic 2336
  computer-assisted research 1672
  conservative political theory and 1864
  culture and 1512, 1955, 2059, 2939
  devotional 1913
  East Baltic 1337
  East European 713, 752, 1875, 2641, 2647
  1890s 1457
  18th century 138, 411, 839, 841, 1761, 2819
  English language 7, 28, 172, 406, 642, 714, 737, 860, 925, 1375, 1541, 1967, 2317, 2319, 2680, 2680, 2693, 2823, 3026, 3211
  film and 1706
  folklore and 1692, 1894
  Franciscan Order 1047
  French language 753, 1049, 2222

Literature (*cont.*)
  gender and sexuality in 1080, 2138
  Gothic 2187
  history and 613, 622, 1414, 1683, 1698
  history of *see* Literary history
  homosexuality and 1036
  human body in 2138
  humanist 19, 356, 750
  interdisciplinary studies 879, 1129, 2183, 2293, 2687, 2723, 3077
  language and 663, 2397
  Lappish 398
  law and 541, 3218
  linguistics and 714, 1298, 1561-1562, 3240
  medicine and 1702
  medieval 41, 140, 234, 241, 270, 478, 765, 816, 879, 1008, 1075, 1418, 1472, 1789-1790, 1793-1794, 1797-1799, 1802, 1857, 1875, 1897, 1940, 2314, 2336, 2694, 2727, 2929, 3132
  modern 41, 71, 137, 189, 193, 234, 307, 342, 608, 710, 756, 765, 881, 1001, 1365, 1422, 1519, 1875, 1940, 2183, 2235, 2262, 2271, 2419, 2454, 2470, 2536, 2589, 2676, 2727, 2896, 2925, 3015, 3046, 3168
  music and 1909
  mystical 1913, 2785
  myth and 1915
  Native American 97, 2810
  neurophysiology and 1414
  new literatures in English 642, 1541, 1967, 2680, 2693
  1950s 1889
  19th century 141, 1457, 1987, 2491, 2800
  performance 2940
  philosophy and 428, 530, 2165-2167, 2358, 2408, 2453, 2687
  politics and 1463, 1864, 2144, 2854
  Portuguese-speaking countries 2205
  postcolonial 714, 1967, 2693
  postmodern 307
  postmodernism in 2209
  pseudoscience in 555
  psychiatry and 1702, 2256
  psychology and 99, 530, 622
  Reformation 238
  religion and 171, 207, 437, 588, 588-589, 604, 1212, 1447, 1696, 2338, 2347, 2402, 2423, 2453, 2456, 2687
  science and 2687
  semantics and 1414
  semiotics and 754, 800, 2582
  17th century 143, 2590
  society and 903, 2687, 2854
  sociology and 1227, 2358
  speech and 1681
  teaching 629, 1388, 1469, 1876, 1950
  theology and 1704
  theory of *see* Literary theory and criticism
  Third World 629, 642, 2680
  20th century 137, 153, 255, 366, 402, 573, 669, 687, 702, 856, 981, 1109, 1820, 1889, 1899, 1934, 2013, 2017, 2056, 2181, 2255, 2571, 2686, 2800, 2861, 2869, 3046, 3212
  values in 2347
  war and 3158
  women in 279, 701, 3044, 3199, 3202
  women writers 3044
  women's 1066, 1593, 1779
Lithuanian arts 1720
Lithuanian culture 13, 67, 1539
Lithuanian folklore 1688
Lithuanian history 13
Lithuanian language 13, 1112, 1364, 1539
Lithuanian linguistics 1492, 1633
Lithuanian literature 13, 67, 1364, 1539, 1688, 1691, 1820
Lithuanian poetry 1820
Lithuanian-Slavic relations 14
Lithuanian studies 1720
Liturgy 1440
  Cistercian Order 156, 602
  history 2515
Logic 1431, 1822, 2164, 2781
  Chinese 1373
  Indian 1402
  intensional 1657
  language and 1431

Logic (*cont.*)
  literary theory and 2191
  manuscript studies 1764
  modal 1657
  natural language and 1657, 2830
  philosophy and semantics 1431
  rhetoric and 2168
  science and 2899
  semiotics and 2580
Lorraine French dialectology 773
Lost Generation 1205, 1730
Louisiana literature 1731
Lovecraft, Howard Phillips 1732
Lowry, Malcolm 1758
Loy, Mina 2519
Low German language *see* German language, Low
Low German literature *see* German literature, Low German
Luso-Brazilian culture 484, 1181
Luso-Brazilian languages, teaching 1181
Luso-Brazilian linguistics 1181
Luso-Brazilian literature 484, 740, 1181, 1188, 1734, 1817, 2230, 2462
Luso-Brazilian studies 1181, 1738
Luther, Martin 1739-1740, 1890
Lyrics 259
MacDonald, George 1252, 2009
Macedonian culture 1744
Macedonian Greek dialect 1755
Macedonian history 1744
Macedonian language 1708, 1756
Macedonian literature 311, 1708, 1744
Machine translation 1745, 2708
Maghrebi literature 2022, 2403
Maine studies 622
Malayan culture 2444
Malayan linguistics 2048, 2444
Malayan studies 2444
Malayo-Polynesian linguistics 2048
Malaysian studies 1468
Malraux, André 2399
Mamet, David 2807
Mann, Thomas 369, 2972-2973
Mannerism
  English literature 2592
  German literature 750
Manuscripts 247, 374, 625, 870, 1764-1765, 2120, 2302, 2567, 2782, 2813
  in Cambridge University libraries 2999
  14th-16th century 2946
  German 1902
  illumination 1764
  Latin 1857, 1902
  medieval 1789, 1797, 1902
Maori studies 1471
Marxist theory and criticism 1842
  Romance literature 2484
Mass media 693, 972, 1376, 1486, 1634, 1791, 2335, 2792
Material culture 1381, 1773, 1778, 2987, 3062, 3189
  Canadian 524
  Ireland 1455
  Labrador 2332
  Latin America 128
  Newfoundland 2332
  Sub-Saharan Africa 45
Mathematical linguistics 306, 646, 1504, 1564, 1666, 2217, 2283, 3012
Mathematics
  language and 2830
  literary theory and 2191
  literature and 1414
Maumee River Valley 2012
May, Karl 1323
Mayan culture 564, 918
Mayan languages 918, 1417
Mayan linguistics 1417
Mazzini, Giuseppe 388
Media 796, 2259
Medicine, literature and 1702
Medieval *see also* Middle Ages, and medieval as subheading under main topic of interest, e.g., Literature, medieval
Medieval studies 41, 87, 140, 241, 248, 468, 478, 636, 766, 857, 974, 997, 1047, 1067, 1092, 1121, 1418, 1472, 1789, 1793-1794, 1797-1799, 1846, 1897, 2024, 2084, 2130, 2202, 2314, 2352, 2413, 2694, 2994, 3124

Medieval texts 816, 1075, 1794, 1797-1798, 1902, 2202, 2320, 2754
Medievalism 2836
Meditative poetry 2592
Melville, Herman 1807
Memoir, war and 3158
Memory 452, 620, 1419, 1812
Mencken, H. L. 1813
Merton, Thomas 1815
Metaphor 210, 1819
Metaphysical poetry 1087, 2592
Metaphysics 2164
  Chinese 1373
Metrics 838
  Italian 1639
  literary theory and 2191
Mexican American folklore 308
Mexican American literature 129, 308, 360, 1605, 1693, 1817
Mexican American theater 1107
Mexican Indian cultures 2983
Mexican Indian languages, dictionaries 2586
Mexican literature 897, 1693, 3152
  20th century 3022
Mexican studies 1480
Middle Ages 2836
  history 1008, 1418, 1472, 1790, 1793, 1902, 2314, 2694, 2994
  languages 41, 1802, 1940
Middle Eastern *see also* Eastern; Near Eastern
Middle Eastern anthropology 1267
Middle Eastern culture 195
  ancient 1853
Middle Eastern folklore 1267
Middle Eastern history 195, 1267
Middle Eastern linguistics 195
Middle Eastern literature 195
Middle Eastern music 266
Middle Eastern philology 1267
Middle Eastern philosophy 195, 1267
Middle Eastern religions 195, 1267
Middle Eastern studies 6, 81, 264, 1267, 1442
Middle English language *see* English language, Middle
Middle English literature *see* English literature, Middle English period
Midwestern United States 2107
  culture 1497, 1835, 2063
  folklore 1834
  literature 1226, 1831, 1835, 2663
  Old Northwest Territory 2063
Millay, Edna St. Vincent 2909
Milton, John 815, 1837-1838, 2592
Mindanao, Philippines 2155
Minorities 109, 2176
  see also entries under ethnic studies and specific ethnic groups, e.g., Mexican American
Minority discourse 728
Minority literature 1779
Mississippi folklore 1847
Mississippi literature 2019
Modal logic 1657
Modern *see contemporary, modern, and 20th century as subheadings under main topic, e.g.,* History, contemporary; Art, modern; American literature, 20th century
Modernism 1338, 1422
Mon-Khmer studies 1879
Monastic life *see* Religious orders
Monasticism, history of 2783
Mongol languages 1881
Mongolian culture 479
Mongolian linguistics 479
Mongolian literature 1881
Mongolian studies 1241, 1881
Montaigne, Michel Eyquem de 430, 1887
Moore, Marianne Craig 2519
Moral philosophy, Chinese 1373
More, Sir Thomas 1890
Mormons 410
Moroccan literature 2403
Morphology 79, 1622, 1645, 1654, 1782, 1851-1852, 1931, 2237, 2830
  Balkan languages 313
  functional theory and 1660
  Indo-European languages 313

Morphology (cont.)
  Labrador 2332
  Newfoundland 2332
Morphophonology, Hebrew 1162
Morris, William 1482
Moslem see Muslim
Motor skills 2147
Multicultural studies 683
Multiculturalism 714, 1423, 1565, 1901
Multilingualism 1423, 1900-1901
  bilingualism and 2657
Munda language 1242
Munster province, Ireland 1455
Museum studies 1908
  German 328
  Schiller-Nationalmuseum 1767
Music 4, 222, 259, 271, 307, 681, 700, 706,
  935, 1014, 1091, 1506, 1583, 1718, 1725,
  1909, 1954, 2149, 2578, 2626, 2690, 2828,
  2873, 3221
  see also Folk music, and entries for music in
    specific countries or regions, e.g.,
    American music; Latin American music
  African American 1723
  bluegrass 371
  blues 372
  children's 2620
  contemporary 37
  country 371, 1379
  criticism 2282
  drama and 825
  18th century 839, 841
  Far Eastern 266
  feminist studies 3200
  in film 2206
  folklore and 1921
  history of 1909
  hymns 1220
  literature and 1909
  medieval 824, 1418, 1799, 2694
  politics and 1233
  Renaissance 824, 980, 1418, 1799
  reviews 1616, 2624
  rock 3098
  Romantic 2492
  theory 2358
Musical instruments
  bluegrass 371
  folk music 1333
Musicians, bluegrass 371
Musicology 935, 1583, 2578, 2784
  see also Ethnomusicology
Musil, Robert 1910
Muslim see also Islamic
Muslim-Christian relations 1911
Muslim civilization 1222
  Spain 2272
Muzeul Literaturii Române 1766
Mycenaean Greek dialect 1843
Mycenaean studies 1860, 2756
Mystery fiction 257, 3184
Mysticism 1913, 2785
Myth 1440, 1763, 1914-1915, 2126, 3072
  see also Legend
  criticism and 627
  Indo-European 1404
  Latin American Indian 1581
Mythology, Roman 1688
Nabokov, Vladimir 1917
Nahuatl culture 919
Nahuatl language 919
Names 1918, 2067-2068, 2924
  Netherlandic 1916
  Scandinavian 2766
Narrative 668, 1424
Native American see also entries under
  specific groups of Native Americans
Native American culture 2983
Native American languages 1069, 1263, 2623
  Mayan 918, 1417
  Mexican Indian 1069, 2586
  Peruvian 2588
Native American linguistics 132
Native American literature 97, 2810
Native American studies 97, 979, 1971, 3175
  bibliographies 1980
  Southwest United States 2983

Natural language 1441, 1657
  mathematical research 1504
  processing 655
Naturalism 494, 1457
Nautical languages 390
Near Eastern see also Eastern; Middle
  Eastern
Near Eastern culture 344, 3166
  ancient 1349, 1829, 1853
Near Eastern history 195, 3166
  ancient 1349, 1425
  medieval 1425
Near Eastern iconography 1349
Near Eastern languages 195, 3166
  ancient 344
  Northwest Semitic, ancient 1429
Near Eastern music 266
Near Eastern studies 2573, 3165, 3252
  ancient 1425
  18th century 841
  medieval 1425
Neo-Latin literature 1211, 2592
  German 750
Neo-Latin studies 727, 896, 1211
Neoclassicism 1170
Neologisms
  Italian 1639
  North America 2260
Neoscholastic philosophy 2453
Nerval, Gérard de 488
Netherlandic see also Dutch
Netherlandic culture 2069
Netherlandic-German literary relations 553
Netherlandic history 819
  Amsterdam 144
Netherlandic linguistics 2696, 2979, 3114
Netherlandic literature 144, 529, 787, 819,
  1331-1332, 1743, 1824, 1986, 2069, 2358,
  2696, 2699, 2979, 3114, 3144, 3174
  19th century 1110
  16th century 1890
Netherlandic poetry 3144
Netherlandic sociolinguistics 2906
Netherlandic studies 951, 2070
Neurolinguistics 481, 619, 822, 1134, 1412,
  1426, 1654, 1782, 1949
  history of 1189
Neurophysiology
  brain and language studies 404
  literature and 1414
Neuropsychology 1949
  brain and language studies 619
New England folklore 2010
New England history 1956
New England literature 1956
  Transcendentalism 906
New Guinea anthropology 2047
New Guinea linguistics 751, 1560
New High German language see German
  language, New High
New Jersey folklore 1983
New literatures in English 642, 714, 1375,
  1541, 1967, 2680, 2693
New Testament 344
New words see Neologisms
New World studies 2398
New Zealand drama 294
New Zealand linguistics 2915
New Zealand literature 295, 714, 1375, 1548
New Zealand studies 295
  Maori studies 1471
Newfoundland dialects 2332
Newfoundland linguistics 2332
Newfoundland onomastics 2332
Newspapers see Periodicals
Niedecker, Lorine 2519
Nietzsche, Friedrich Wilhelm 1985
Nigeria, teaching French in 1043
Nigerian culture, traditional 51
Nigerian languages 1346
Nikolaus von Cües 1856
Nin, Anaïs 153
Nineteenth century studies 141, 970, 1987,
  3130
For other 19th century references, see
  subheadings under primary topics of
  interest, e.g., Art, 19th century

Nonfiction
  19th-century prose 1990
  publishing 2546
Nonverbal communication 643, 1268, 1428,
  2615
Nordic see Old Norse; Scandinavian
Norris, Frank 1051
North African anthropology 1267
North African literature 2403
North American dialects 1982, 2260
North American-European literary relations
  652
North American linguistics 1263
North American music 1379
North American place names 2260
North American studies 1971
North Carolina folklore 1042, 2004
North Carolina history 2005
Northern European folklore 1996
Northern European studies 1996
Northwest Semitic languages 1429
Northwest Territory (United States) 2063
Norwegian-American studies 2015
Norwegian language 2001, 2629
Norwegian linguistics 1742, 2001, 2629
Norwegian literature 831, 2002, 2015, 2629,
  3134
  19th century 667
Norwegian place names 1742
Norwegian puppet theater 169
Norwegian studies 1742
Novel 2030, 2123, 2857, 3037, 3184
  American 105
  Commonwealth 640
  dime 790
  18th century 840
  1920-1950 2472
  Spanish 165
  20th century 541, 2472
Numismatics 2626
  Celtic 943
  Germanic 1097
  medieval 2694
Objectivists 2519
Occitan see also Provençal
Occitan language 188, 272, 1046, 1515
Occitan linguistics 1072, 2418, 2929
Occitan literature 188, 272, 1046, 1072, 1515,
  2418, 2929, 3258
Occitan studies 2929
Occultism, in literature 555
Oceanic see also Pacific
Oceanic anthropology 358
Oceanic history 358
Oceanic linguistics 358, 2048-2049, 2915
Oceanic literature 714
O'Connor, Flannery 1006
Ohio, history of northwestern region 2012
Old Church Slavonic language 2225, 2655
Old English language see English language,
  Old
Old English literature see English literature,
  Old English period
Old German literature see German literature,
  Old German
Old Norse civilization 1788
Old Norse language 1101, 1591, 2516, 2629
Old Norse literature 256, 329, 353, 831, 834,
  1101, 1591-1592, 1742, 2516, 2629
Old Norse philology 353
Old Testament 344, 1163, 1425, 3249
Olson, Charles 2519
O'Neill, Eugene 964
Onomastics 331, 1750, 1787, 1918-1919,
  1994, 2026, 2066-2068, 2766
  see also Names; Personal names; Place
    names, and entries for onomastics in
    specific countries, e.g., German
    onomastics
  Balkan 313
  bibliographies 2065
  German-Slavic 758
  Germanic 1097, 2085
  Indo-European 313
  Labrador 2332
  Netherlands 1916
  Newfoundland 2332

Onomastics (cont.)
  Romance languages 2026
Opera 259, 1909, 2624, 2963
Oppen, George 2519
Oral history 2073-2074
  Atlantic provinces 2010
  Georgia 1042
  New England 2010
  North Carolina 1042
Oral literature 75, 1019, 1921, 2075, 2810
  African 2353
  Biblical literature and 1648
  Latin American Indian 1581
Oral tradition 75, 2075
  African 1257
  Asian 265
  Canadian 524
  Spanish 2375
Oratory see Rhetoric
Oriental see Asian; Eastern, and entries for specific nationalities, e.g., Chinese; Japanese; etc.
Orthography
  German 2712
  Romanian 1635
Oz, Land of 320
Pacific see also Oceanic
Pacific American studies 92
Pacific anthropology 2047
Pacific linguistics 2114, 2118
Pacific studies 1471, 2693
Pakistani literature 1375
  20th century 1282
Pakistani studies 1267
Paleography 450, 1425, 1628, 2938
  Celtic 509
  Irish 892
  Southeast Asia 1879
Palestine, ancient and medieval studies 1425
Pantomime 924
Papuan languages 751, 1560, 2048
Papyrology 40, 590
Parnassian poetry 440
Parœmia 2253
Patmore, Coventry 1200
Patristic studies 286, 2245, 2320, 2515
Peake, Mervyn 1816, 2139
Pedagogy 39, 425-426, 627, 660, 1343, 1863, 2087, 2576, 2916, 3048, 3155
  see also Education; Language teaching; Teaching
  college composition and communication 626
  German 2544
  Hispanic 1181
  Luso-Brazilian 1181
  rhetorical 2440
Péguy, Charles 134
Pennsylvania folk culture 2141
Pepper, Stephen Coburn 2138
Perception 1281, 2147
  language and 620, 1657, 2146
Pérez Galdós, Benito 165
Performance studies 1384, 1440, 2914
Performing arts 924, 1384, 1774, 2111, 2148, 2595, 2673, 2914, 2940, 2960
  see also Dance; Music; Opera; Theater
  bibliographies 2149
  indexes 2149
  Indian 1234
  reviews 2624
Periodicals
  magazines 106, 2269, 3022
  publishing 1427, 2269-2270
  Victorian 3128
Persian see also Iranian
Persian language 1926, 2776
Persian literature 1754, 1926, 3165
Persian studies 553, 1754, 2776
Personal names 1918, 2067-2068
  see also Onomastics
  Dutch and Flemish 1916
  Scandinavian 2766
Peruvian languages, indigenous 2588
Peruvian literature 1623
Phenomenology 1210, 3112
  language and 2830

Philippine anthropology 2155-2156
Philippine art 2157
Philippine culture 2155
Philippine drama 2157
Philippine folklore 2155
Philippine history 2155, 2157
Philippine linguistics 2154-2155, 2838
Philippine literature 789, 2157
Philippine philosophy 2157
Philippine sociology 2156
Philippine studies 789, 1624, 2155-2157, 2618
Philology 3, 41, 69, 135, 145, 191, 221-222, 283, 376, 441, 551, 638, 722, 893, 1147, 1348, 1505, 1525, 1545, 1808, 1811, 1904, 2099, 2262, 2264-2266, 2317, 2382, 2469, 2574, 2626-2627, 2736, 2802-2803, 2839, 2863-2864, 2925, 2968, 3003, 3118, 3191-3193
  see also entries for philology in specific countries or regions, e.g., French philology
  Aegean 1843
  Celtic 420, 943, 2767, 3254
  early Christian literature 3132
  classical 218, 610, 853, 891, 1114, 1150, 1177, 1256, 1860, 2100, 2161, 2401, 2895, 3270
  comparative 1190, 1640
  Hispanic 1400, 2036
  Humanist 1114
  Indo-European 1404
  medieval 1114, 1897
  modern 2100, 2401, 3074
  Old Norse 353
  Old Testament 3249
  Romance 196, 1734, 2475, 2478, 2485, 2803, 3263, 2755, 3011, 3106
Philosophical logic 1431
Philosophy 3, 9, 76, 81, 171, 184, 189-192, 219, 230-231, 304, 417, 604-605, 690, 700, 744, 778, 792, 847, 904, 947, 959, 1041, 1056, 1091, 1167, 1210, 1212, 1246, 1276, 1282, 1378, 1409, 1432, 1481, 1506, 1525, 1533, 1694, 1841, 1864, 1927, 2025, 2095, 2111, 2143, 2162-2164, 2167, 2186, 2242, 2256, 2311, 2396, 2427, 2429, 2520, 2529, 2583, 2683, 2727, 2865, 2937, 2965, 3021, 3215, 3273
  see also Ideas; Thought and entries for philosophy in specific countries or regions, e.g., Chinese philosophy; Latin American philosophy
  analytic 2830
  of art 412, 1353
  Catholic 802, 2533
  comparative 2169
  contemporary 2869
  East-West comparative studies 2169
  18th century 387, 841, 1973
  film and 2166
  Franciscan Order 1047
  Hispanic 2371
  of history 613
  history of 235, 1431, 1463, 2408
  Judaic 1488
  of language see Philosophy of language
  literary theory and 2191
  of literature 2358
  literature and 428, 530, 2165-2167, 2408, 2453, 2687
  logic and 1431
  manuscript research 1764
  medieval 241, 330, 478, 1047, 1418, 1789-1790, 2314, 2694, 2782, 3111, 3143, 1799
  myth and 1915
  neoscholastic 2453
  Portuguese-speaking countries 284
  rare book reprints 2547
  of religion 1158, 1447
  religion and 94, 1805, 2321
  Renaissance 980, 1418, 1799, 2345, 3143
  rhetoric and 2168
  of science 1209, 2899
  science and 2553
  semiotics and 2580, 2582
  17th century 2590
  theater and 2166

Philosophy (cont.)
  theology and 2434
  Thomist 802, 2533
  20th century 402, 1820, 2831
Philosophy of language 275, 428, 778, 797, 1069, 1189, 1402, 1638, 1657, 1782, 2162, 2164, 2166, 2830, 3115
Phonetics 79, 184, 204, 562, 1413, 1433, 1446, 1464, 1645, 2041, 2071, 2174, 2301, 2410, 2787, 3052, 3208
  Danish 747
  experimental 1654, 2173
  Hebrew 1162
  Hungarian 1749
Phonology 1433, 1464, 1642, 1645, 1654, 1664, 1782, 1821, 1851-1852, 1931, 2174-2175, 2237, 2805, 2830
  Balkan 313
  Bulgarian 422
  functional theory and 1660
  Hebrew 1162
  Indo-European languages 313
  Labrador 2332
  Newfoundland 2332
Phraseology 3205
Phrygian language 1491
Picard French dialectology 773
Pidgin languages 688, 1434, 1560, 2116, 2915
  Western hemisphere 1263
Pierce, Charles Sanders 2580
Pinter, Harold 2177
Pirandello, Luigi 2255, 3228
Pirckheimer, Willibald 1770
Place names 1918, 2067-2068
  see also Onomastics; Toponymy
  Celtic 509
  Dutch 1916
  East German 339
  Flemish 1916
  Irish 2774
  North American 2260
  Norwegian 1742
  Scandinavian 1919
Pliekšane, Elza 2299
Pliekšans, Janis 2299
Poe, Edgar Allan 2187
Poetics 81, 107, 838, 913, 1164, 1562, 1648, 2191-2192, 2452, 2525, 2701, 2907, 3242
  African 658
  Biblical literature and 1648
  Slavic 1269, 2849
  20th century 996, 2056
Poetry 445, 681, 685, 690, 702, 723, 755, 821, 838, 894, 977, 1532, 1741, 1954, 2123, 2133, 2186, 2188, 2242, 2529, 2621, 2695, 2701, 2907, 3268
  see also entries for poetry in specific countries or regions, e.g., Australian poetry
  Cavalier 2592
  Croatian, in English translation 1380
  English language 2184
  in English translation 1380, 2184
  Haiku 1145
  history of 3036
  meditative 2592
  metaphysical 1087, 2592
  Mormon 410
  narrative technique 1424
  19th century 440
  Parnassian 440
  psychoanalysis of 2003
  Renaissance 2697
  satiric 2817
  17th century 1087, 2592
  Symbolist 440
  20th century 996, 1833, 2056, 2194, 2859
Polish anthropology 2199
Polish art 2196-2197
Polish-Baltic relations 14
Polish culture 2097, 2196-2197, 2199, 2790
Polish drama 774, 2110
Polish folk art 2199
Polish folklore 1692, 2199
Polish history 1679, 1979, 2097, 2196-2197
Polish language 1342, 1979, 2097, 2790
  English language and 2112

Polish linguistics 364, 2198, 2212, 2498
    contrastive analysis 2112
Polish literary theory and criticism 363
Polish literature 351, 363, 713, 1537, 1679,
    1715, 1836, 1979, 2097, 2108, 2197, 2466,
    2500, 2504, 2790, 2921, 3240, 3267
    20th century 3022
Polish studies 2196, 2645
    Silesia 2545
Polish theater 2110
Political ideas, history of 1463, 2144
Political prose 2144
Politics
    French-Canadian literature and 34
    literature and 1233, 1463, 2138, 2144
    manuscript research 1764
Polynesian linguistics 2048, 2495
Polynesian philology 2495
Polynesian studies 1471
Popular see also Folk
Popular culture 402, 518, 600, 700, 728, 790,
    828, 1376-1377, 1435-1436, 1450, 1952,
    2289, 2375, 2840, 2881, 3062
    American 109, 1356, 2011
    Canadian 524, 2011
    18th century 839
    folklore and 1692
    French 1057
    German 3266
    Latin American 1411, 2833
    Swiss 1022
Popular literature 984
Popular music 935
Portuguese see also Luso-Brazilian
Portuguese American drama 1584
Portuguese American theater 1584
Portuguese civilization 446
Portuguese culture 258, 926, 2205
Portuguese Enlightenment 786
Portuguese history 442, 1811, 2205
Portuguese language 284, 442, 446, 462, 632,
    1184, 1738, 2281, 2395, 2473, 2487
    Galician Portuguese dialect 1136, 1184,
        3106
    teaching 1181
Portuguese linguistics 376, 463, 1734, 1817,
    2473
Portuguese literature 258, 284, 442, 446, 632,
    798, 926, 1181, 1580, 1738, 1817,
    2204-2205, 2281, 2305, 2487, 2568, 2981,
    3060, 3116
    modern 1286
    16th century 377
Portuguese philology 2395
Portuguese-speaking countries 284, 1697
Postcolonial literature 1375
Postcolonialism 714, 800
Postmodern literature 755
Postmodernism 307, 402, 2208-2209
Poststructuralist theory and criticism 913
    Romance literature 2484
Pound, Ezra 982, 2101
Powys, John Cowper 2210-2211
Powys, Llewelyn 2210-2211
Powys, Theodore Francis 2210-2211
Pragmatics 23, 379, 920, 1431, 1437, 1654,
    2215-2216, 2830, 3260
    in Biblical and theological language 1648
    literature and 2191
    philosophy and 1657, 2124
Pre-Raphaelite Brotherhood 1438
Print collecting 2158
Printing 236, 396, 2999
    history of 346, 354, 1142, 1628, 1748,
        2120-2121, 2229, 2813
Pronunciation
    Labrador 2332
    Newfoundland 2332
Prose 977, 2249
    see also Fiction
    American 1990
    British 1990
    diary 153
    English 623, 872
    European 1990
    15th-17th century 623
    19th century 1990

Prose (cont.)
    political 2144
    Renaissance 872
    satiric 2817
    20th century 2859
Prosody 838
Protestantism 1212
Proust, Marcel 441, 443, 2252
Provençal see also Occitan
Provençal language 2929, 3258
Proverbs 2253, 2260
Proxemics 2615
Prussian language 14
Prussian-Slavic relations 14
Psychiatry 1426
    brain and language studies 404
    linguistics and 2256
    literature and 1702, 2256
Psychoacoustics 1446
Psychoanalysis 466
    film and 518
    linguistics and 474
    literature and 99, 794, 1703, 2095, 3077
    poetry and 2003
    semiotics and 2582
Psycholinguistics 99, 146, 210, 225, 379, 481,
    530, 576-577, 618, 620, 769, 797, 822,
    921, 1005, 1012, 1117, 1134, 1259,
    1272-1273, 1351, 1395-1396, 1419, 1426,
    1430, 1441, 1444, 1446, 1549-1550, 1555,
    1557, 1563, 1575, 1599, 1654, 1812, 1819,
    1949-1950, 2041, 2146-2147, 2216, 2258,
    2306, 2313, 2316, 2337, 2461, 3179
    applied 2306
    education and 1439
    history and 1189
Psychology 108, 413, 425, 792, 1091, 1210,
    1394, 1396, 1426, 2256-2258
    abnormal 1351
    brain and language studies 404
    cognitive 617, 620
    depth psychology 1703
    developmental 769, 1209
    educational 797
    experimental 452, 1812
    history and 622
    language and 2830
    language learning 1555, 2932
    literary theory and 2191
    literature and 99, 622, 1414, 1703
    memory and cognition 1812
    phonetics and 2410
    rare book reprints 2547
    of reading 2315
    of rhetoric 2168
    social 1430, 2658
Psychopathology 1351
    psycholinguistic issues 1439
Public address see Rhetoric
Publishing 236, 375, 1233, 1627, 2270, 2999
    see also Book publishing
    editing 661, 833, 2120
    electronic 2270
    history of 167, 1628, 1631, 2120-2121,
        2138, 2269, 2813, 2938
    magazines 106, 2269
    newspapers 1427, 2269
    periodicals 1427, 2270
    scholarly 835, 2546
Puerto Rican culture 2398
Puerto Rican literature 129, 360, 732, 2389,
    2398
Puerto Rican studies 732, 2389, 2398
Puppet theater 169
Puritan American literature 2841
Puritanism 2841
Pynchon, Thomas 2271
Québécois see also French Canadian
Québécois culture 3145
Québécois literature 950, 957, 1614, 2426,
    2815, 2911, 2933, 3145
    women writers 2933
Québécois studies 957, 2241, 3145
Quilts 3062
Raabe, Wilhelm 1325
Rabe, David 2807

Rabelais, François 435, 960
Race relations, in the Americas 1971
Radio, Slovak 2652
Rainis, Janis see Pliekšāns, Jānis
Rare books 95, 625, 2302
    reprints 2547
Rare texts
    Elizabethan 2524
    verse drama 2525
Reader-response theory 2312
Reading 1281, 1563, 1656, 2270, 2312-2313,
    2315-2316
Realism
    American literature 102
    19th century 1325, 1457
    Spanish novel 165
Reference materials
    see also Bibliographies; Indexes
    humanities and social sciences 1077
    linguistics 1266
Reformation literature
    English 1132
    European 19
    French 1132
    German 750, 1132
    Hungarian 19
    Italian 1132
Reformation studies 238, 1132, 2340
Reich, Wilhelm 2138
Religion 604, 670, 938, 1378, 1440, 1447, 1815,
    1914, 2126, 2311, 2456, 2628, 2683, 2842
    see also entries for specific religions and
        denominations and entries for religions in
        specific countries or regions, e.g., Indian
        religions
    ancient 11, 1019, 2994
    art and 1447
    Celtic 943
    comparative 212, 1282, 1763, 2038, 2111,
        2456, 2922
    18th century 841
    ethics and 1447
    Finnish 2532
    history of 792, 1158, 1463, 1481, 1764,
        1805, 2038, 2456
    Humanist period 356
    literature and 171, 207, 437, 588-589, 604,
        1212, 1447, 1696, 2338, 2347, 2423, 2453,
        2687
    medieval 2994
    modern culture and 712
    philosophy of 1158, 1447
    politics and 1233
    rare book reprints 2547
    Renaissance 356
    Roman 1860
    social sciences and 1350, 1447
    women and 207
Religious literature 437, 1805, 1832, 2402,
    2456
Religious orders
    Augustinian 605
    Benedictine 94
    Carthusian 155
    Cistercian 156, 602
    Dominican 595
    Franciscan 247, 1054, 3108
Religious studies 94, 171, 595, 1047, 1805,
    2321, 2865, 3108
Religious thought, Jewish 2995
Renaissance art 356, 824, 1418, 1472,
    2345-2346
Renaissance civilization 2445
Renaissance culture 563, 1418, 1799, 2245,
    2346, 2445
Renaissance drama 824, 2342, 2356,
    2594-2595, 2599
    English 1792, 2329
Renaissance history 142, 356, 980, 1418,
    1472, 1799, 2345-2346, 3014
Renaissance literature 41, 142, 270, 356, 980,
    1170, 1418, 1472, 1793-1794, 1799,
    2345-2346, 2594, 3014
    English 486, 866, 872, 1132, 2341, 2575,
        2839, 2343
    European 2343
    French 671, 1132, 2029

Renaissance literature (cont.)
  German 750
  Italian 563, 1132, 1302, 2029
  Neo-Latin 1211
  translations 87
Renaissance music 824, 980, 1418, 2345
Renaissance philosophy 980, 1418, 1799, 2345, 3143
Renaissance poetry 2697
Renaissance religion 356
Renaissance studies 41, 87, 91, 142, 356, 636, 974, 980, 1132, 1418, 1472, 1793-1794, 2029, 2130, 2340, 2342, 2344-2345, 2352, 2594, 3124
  English 486, 2343, 2524
  European 2343
  humanities 2339
Renaissance texts 1794
  translations 87
Renaissance theology 1418
Reprints see Facsimile reprints
Restoration drama 486
Restoration literature 2359, 2575
Restoration theater 2360
Reznikoff, Charles 2519
Rhein region 2436
  cultural anthropology 2437
Rhetoric 569, 660, 1146, 1352, 1973, 2284, 2439-2441, 3210
  Biblical literature and 1648
  composition and 556, 626
  history of 2440
  Italian 1639
  philosophy and 2168
  rare book reprints 2547
  teaching 627
  theory of 2223
Rhetorical analysis 1564
Rhetorical theory 2440
Rhys, Jean 1338
Richmond, Virginia, literature 850
Rilke, Rainer Maria 368
Rimbaud, Arthur 2127
Rituals 1019, 1440
  feminist studies 3200
Rococo literature, German 750
Rojas, Fernando de 557
Roman see also Classical; Latin
Roman empire 1008
Roman historiography 609
Romance languages 30, 196, 326, 376, 597, 961-962, 1000, 1157, 1166, 1256, 1808, 1826, 1948, 2006, 2395, 2432, 2473-2475, 2477, 2481, 2486, 2720, 2755, 2786, 2843, 3029, 3113, 3230
  see also entries for specific languages, e.g., French language
  Ibero-Romance 1221
  medieval 1800
  onomastics 2026
Romance linguistics 5, 326, 551, 962, 1166, 1492, 2220, 2418, 2432, 2462, 2473-2476, 2479, 2488-2489, 2863, 3011
  see also entries for specific languages and regions, e.g., Italian linguistics
  comparative studies 242, 653
  synchronic and diachronic 2237, 2406, 2478, 3150
Romance literatures 5, 30, 480, 597, 961-962, 1100, 1157, 1166, 1256, 1580, 1615, 1826, 1872, 1948, 2006, 2220, 2418, 2432, 2462, 2474, 2476-2477, 2479-2480, 2484, 2486, 2489, 2720, 2786, 2843, 3029, 3087, 3230
  medieval 1800, 2064, 2478, 2481, 3150
Romance philology 196, 1734, 2475, 2478, 2485, 2755, 2803, 2863, 3011, 3106, 3263
Romance studies 25, 1524, 1768, 2477, 2479, 2487, 2720, 3029, 3087
  dissertations 1148
  medieval 1800, 2481
Romances, Arthurian 424
Romanian arts 3227
Romanian culture 1844
Romanian etymology 1635
Romanian folklore 1844, 2728, 3227
Romanian history 1844

Romanian language 220, 1449, 1635, 1844, 2863, 3227
Romanian linguistics 565, 1449, 1635, 3227, 3253
Romanian literature 220, 311, 675, 713, 1449, 1580, 1635, 1733, 1766, 1844, 2083, 2384, 2482-2483, 2728, 2900, 3123, 3227
  comparative studies 495
  20th century 2571
Romanian onomastics 1635
Romanian orthography 1635
Romanian philology 1635, 3227
Romanian-Slavic studies 2490
Romanian studies 1844, 3227
  Timiş region 2083
Romantic literature 290-291, 2492
  American 3206
  American Transcendentalism 906
  English 570, 2575, 3206
  European 970, 3206
Romantic music 2492
Romanticism 290-291, 970, 2187, 2491, 2526, 2844
  British 367
Rome, Italy 2758
Royal Shakespeare Company 2602
Ruskin, John 2502-2503
Russian see also Soviet
Russian art 202
Russian-Baltic relations 14
Russian culture 2097, 2507, 2647, 2726, 3245
Russian drama 517
Russian folklore 1688, 2511
Russian history 485, 1289, 1979, 2097, 2507, 2647, 3245
Russian language 122, 303, 357, 1289, 1315, 1896, 1979, 2097, 2506, 2510, 2512-2513, 2789, 3117
  Slavic comparative studies 2505
  teaching 562, 2505
Russian linguistics 1492, 2506, 2789
Russian literary theory and criticism 2508
Russian literature 122, 303, 357, 485, 517, 817, 913, 1289, 1315, 1688, 1711-1712, 1878, 1925, 1951, 1979, 2031-2032, 2060, 2091, 2097, 2504, 2507, 2509-2510, 2538, 2647, 2726, 2735, 3117, 3148, 3245, 3274
  English translations 2508
  19th century 811, 2986
  Slavic comparative studies 2505
  teaching 2505
  20th century 1917, 2859
  Yiddish language 2691
Russian philology 1002
Russian poetry 357, 517
Russian studies 536, 1289, 2642, 2645, 2647
Saga 668
Saint see entries under given names
Saivism 1402
Samar language 1624
Samar literature 1624
Samar studies 1624
Samizdat literature 1233
Samoyedic languages 1652, 2041
Sand, George 1088
Sanskrit language 1242, 1470
Sanskrit literature 403
Sanskrit studies 199, 1460, 3182
Sanskrit texts 403, 3140
Satire 1214, 2336, 2817
Saussure, Ferdinand de 487
Scandinavian see also Old Norse, and entries for specific nationalities, e.g., Danish, Swedish, etc.
Scandinavian civilization, medieval 1788
Scandinavian culture 931, 1534, 1540, 2077, 2539, 2629
Scandinavian ethnology 931, 1995, 2637, 2886
Scandinavian folklore 261, 1995, 2637, 2886, 2993
Scandinavian-German cultural relations 292
Scandinavian-German literary relations 2629
Scandinavian history 1191-1192, 1995, 2516
Scandinavian languages 256, 1331-1332, 1389, 1824, 1998, 2001, 2106, 2540, 2629, 2631, 2750, 2980

Scandinavian linguistics 256, 1998, 2540
Scandinavian literatures 256, 831, 1331-1332, 1389, 1534, 1540, 1824, 2002, 2077, 2106, 2527, 2540-2541, 2629, 2980, 3134
  in English translation 2539
Scandinavian onomastics 1919
Scandinavian philology 256, 1389, 2633, 2750
Scandinavian puppet theater 169
Scandinavian studies 951, 1995, 2539-2540, 2980
  Vikings 2516
Schiller-Nationalmuseum 1767
Schleswig-Holstein studies 1996
Science 775, 1194, 3005
  18th century 841
  epistemology of 2899
  history of 1463, 1481, 1822, 2240, 2899
  humanistic 2383
  interdisciplinary studies 421
  of language 1573, 1654
  linguistics and 2899
  literature and 2687
  logic and 1431
  medieval 2694
  19th century 2491
  philosophy of 1822, 2899
  religion and 94, 595
  17th century 2592
  women in 3202
Science fiction 981, 987, 1040, 1976, 2123, 2139, 2448, 2554-2555, 2860
  Soviet 2692
Scots English dialect 2557
Scott, Sir Walter 3206
Scottish culture 2556, 2560
Scottish folklore 2558
Scottish Gaelic language 1515, 2556-2557, 3000
  Renaissance 2561
Scottish history 2556
Scottish languages, Lowland dialects 2557
Scottish literature 1515, 2845, 3000
  bibliography 354
  English language 2558
  Latin language 546
  19th century 1252, 2009, 2827, 3206
  Renaissance 2561
  Scots English dialect 2558
  Scottish Gaelic language 2556, 2558
  16th century 546
Scottish onomastics 1994
Scottish studies 2556, 2560
Scottish texts 2561
Screenwriters 1706
Scriblerus Club 2563
Scripts, original 2624
Scriptural studies 1158, 3121
Second language learning 921, 1490, 2572, 2846
Semantic analysis 1666
Semantics 79, 470, 927, 975, 1134, 1439, 1441, 1622, 1642, 1645, 1654, 1664, 1782, 1821, 1931, 2162, 2164, 2167, 2237, 2264, 2277, 2773, 2781, 2830, 2898, 3260
  see also Semiotics
  Biblical and theological language 1648
  comparative 210
  French 78
  functional theory and 1660
  German 1912
  Hebrew 1162
  Italian 1639
  literary 1414
  literary theory and 2191
  philosophy and 1657, 2124
Semiotic theory and criticism, Romance literature 2484
Semiotics 23, 100, 226, 275, 463, 569, 754, 795, 897, 920, 972, 985, 1041, 1206, 1268, 1523, 1882, 1891, 2025, 2216, 2232, 2325, 2358, 2370, 2580-2584, 2615, 3015, 3115
  see also Semantics
  aesthetics and 754, 2580
  African literatures 658
  Biblical literature and 1648
  communication and 754
  French 1250
  literature and 754, 800, 985

Semiotics (*cont.*)
  logic and 2580
  philosophy and 2580
Semitic languages 1349, 1442, 1601, 1801
  ancient Northwest 1429
Semitic literatures 31
Semitic philology 2100
Semitic studies 1442
Sensory processes 2146
Sephardic literature 923
Sephardic studies 111, 923, 2573
Serbian literature 1517, 1521, 1979, 2504
Serbo-Croatian *see also* Croatian; Serbian
Serbo-Croatian dialectology 2225
Serbo-Croatian language 1489, 1521, 1923, 2225
  history 2225
  translations 1893
Serbo-Croatian lexicology 2225
Serbo-Croatian linguistics 3253
Serbo-Croatian onomastics 2225
Seventeenth century studies 143, 431, 804, 2590, 2592, 2759
  For other 17th century references, see subheadings under primary topics of interest, e.g. History, 17th century
Sexuality 1036, 1080, 2138
  language and 796
Shakespeare, William 82-83, 486, 761, 2242, 2594-2603, 3041, 3092
  Hamlet 1149
Shaw, George Bernard 1232, 2605-2606
Shelley, Percy Bysshe 1501-1502
Shepard, Sam 2807
Shevchenko, Taras Hryhorovych 3247
Short fiction 1477, 2123, 2847
  see also Fiction; Short story
  Black writers 2044
  related to Kansas and Great Plains 1175
  Mormon 410
  women writers 3202
Short story 1477, 2847, 3042
Siberian culture 479
Siberian languages 479
Sidney, Sir Philip 2611, 2697
Sidney Circle 2611
Sign languages 1268, 2615
Silesian studies 2545
Sino-Tibetan languages 1372
Sinology *see* Chinese
Siouan languages 2623
Slang, Swedish 2716
Slavic arts 2640
Slavic-Baltic relations 14
Slavic culture 2097, 2109
Slavic ethnology 932
Slavic folklore 3164
Slavic history 32, 202, 303, 1159, 1979, 2097, 2542, 2647, 2788, 2884, 3058, 3164
Slavic languages 14, 32, 122, 303, 333, 551, 1289, 1489, 1718, 1785, 1979, 2097, 2295, 2506, 2559, 2639, 2641, 2646, 2726, 2884, 3109, 3164, 3230, 3264-3265
  Church Slavonic 2655
  comparative studies 2505
  Old Church Slavonic 2655
  Siberia 479
Slavic linguistics 1159, 1269, 1643, 1785, 2212, 2468, 2498, 2638, 2643, 2647, 2726, 2788-2789, 2848, 2863, 3181
Slavic literatures 14, 32, 122, 303, 1289, 1341, 1785, 1827, 1979, 2097, 2109, 2295, 2504, 2538, 2542, 2559, 2638-2641, 2643-2644, 2646-2647, 2788, 2849, 2884, 3109, 3164, 3181, 3230, 3264-3265
  comparative studies 2505
  modern 3276
Slavic onomastics 758
Slavic philology 202, 2117, 2542, 2638, 2863, 3109, 3164, 3264
Slavic poetics 1269, 2849
Slavic-Prussian relations 14
Slavic-Romanian studies 2490
Slavic studies 505, 520, 1159, 1827, 1932, 2214, 2295, 2442, 2559, 2642, 2644, 2646, 3180, 3265
  Byzantine 459
  comparative 1106

Slovak *see also* Czech
Slovak culture 1538, 2648
Slovak drama 2652
Slovak ethnography 568
Slovak ethnology 2654
Slovak film 2652
Slovak folk culture 2654
Slovak folklore 568, 2654
Slovak history 2648
Slovak language 2651
Slovak linguistics 2651
Slovak literature 568, 2504, 2648, 2650, 2653
Slovak radio 2652
Slovak social anthropology 568
Slovak television 2652
Slovak theater 2652
Slovenian anthropology 2997
Slovenian culture 1714, 2666
Slovenian ethnography 2649
Slovenian ethnology 2997
Slovenian folklore 2997
Slovenian history 1530, 2649
Slovenian language 1341, 1858, 2646, 2649
Slovenian literary history 1530
Slovenian literature 1341, 1530, 1671, 1714, 1858, 2227, 2646, 2649, 2666
  translations 1714
Slovenian studies 2646, 2649
Social anthropology 14-15, 209, 211, 928, 934, 1735
  Czech 568
  Irish 3059
  Slovak 568
  Western Pacific 2047
Social criticism 795, 2664
Social development 1970
Social dialects, North American 2260
Social history 1463, 1481, 2144, 3021, 3021
  German literature 1274
  Irish 3059
  Jews in Germany 3197
  17th century 2590
Social institutions, medieval 2694
Social movements, history of 1463
Social psychology 1410, 1430, 2658
Social relations, language and 1568
Social sciences 502, 1146, 1426
  Caribbean 2393
  history of 1463
  language acquisition and 2832
  Latin America 2393
  religion and 1350, 1447
Social studies 2660, 3191-3193
  comparative civilization studies 648
  East European ethnic minorities 1930
  18th century 841
  non-Russian Soviet nationalities 1930
Society 211, 745, 938, 1495, 2897
  see also Civilization; Culture *and entries for society in specific countries, e.g., German society*
  Communist countries 2091
  Greek-speaking peoples 1421
  language and 210, 1270, 1550, 1567-1568, 1657, 2665
  literature and 903, 2687, 2854
  politics and 2854
  women in 2616
Sociocultural studies 2792
  African 3243
  Australian 301
Sociolinguistics 112, 210, 355, 379, 688, 797, 877, 920-921, 1081, 1084, 1117, 1134, 1273, 1416, 1437, 1550, 1563, 1572, 1599, 1656, 1690, 1750, 1782, 1787, 1819, 1900, 2041, 2216, 2237, 2665, 2829, 2989, 3102, 3179
  Danish 747
  French 483
  German 2172
  Italian 2459
  Netherlandic 2906
Sociological theory and criticism, Romance literature 2484
Sociology 69, 184, 1210, 2965
  American 131
  of language 877, 1270

Sociology (*cont.*)
  language and 2830
  of language learning 1555, 2932
  linguistics and 474
  literary theory and 2191
  of literature 1227, 2358
  of rhetoric 2168
Songs 259
  see also Folk song
Sound recordings, collections 271
South African drama 2673
South African literature 862, 2224, 3022, 3067
South African studies 2965
  Shakespeare 2596
South African theater 2673
South American *see also* Latin American; Native American; Spanish American
South American-European literary relations 652
South American Indian languages
  Brazil 462, 2587
  Peru 2588
South American linguistics 1263
South American literature 897, 1180, 1695
South Asian civilization 403
South Asian culture 2674
South Asian languages 2674
South Asian literature 403, 1443, 2674, 3182
South Asian philosophy 403
South Asian religions 403
South Asian studies 268, 1362, 2674, 3083
Southeast Asian anthropology 358, 1885
Southeast Asian history 358, 1885
Southeast Asian languages 1658, 1879
Southeast Asian linguistics 358, 1885, 2118
Southeast Asian literature 1885
Southeast Asian studies 1362, 1879, 1885
Southeast European ethnology 3253
Southeast European folklore 3253
Southeast European history 2871
Southeast European literature 3253
Southeast European studies 311, 2089, 2871
  Middle Eastern influences 1267
Southern African studies 3244
  French studies 1064
Southern United States
  arts 2685
  culture 2684-2686
  history 2688
  literature 1848, 2684-2685, 2688
Southey, Robert 3206
Southwestern United States 1450, 1480, 2105
Soviet *see also entries for nationalities that comprised the Soviet Union, e.g.,* Latvian; Russian; Ukrainian; *etc.*
Soviet arts 2692
Soviet culture 814, 2091
Soviet literature 814, 1712, 2538, 2692
Soviet science fiction 2692
Soviet studies 536, 1720, 1930, 2089, 2091
Spain
  ancient, languages of 853
  Franciscan Order in 3108
  Middle Eastern influences on 1267
  Muslim culture 2272
Spanish *see also* Hispanic; Iberian; Ibero-; Latin American; South American
Spanish American art 725
Spanish American culture 662, 1000, 1182
Spanish American drama 1584
Spanish American linguistics 164, 381, 777, 2394, 2443
Spanish American literature 382, 601, 662, 699, 725, 777, 922, 1180-1182, 1185, 1187-1188, 1278, 1817, 2230, 2378, 2380, 2394, 2443, 2487, 2968, 2990
  modern 1286
  20th century 2613, 2859
  women writers 1605
Spanish American studies 164
Spanish American theater 1584
Spanish art 725
Spanish culture 213, 662, 719, 806, 1182-1183, 2279, 2879
  Pyrenees 1186
Spanish dialects, Asturian 385

Spanish drama
  Renaissance and Baroque 449
  20th century 916
Spanish-English bilingualism 360
Spanish Enlightenment 786
Spanish ethnology 2375
Spanish folk art 2375
Spanish folklore 1769
Spanish history 442, 719, 1734
  Muslim 2272
  19th century 165
Spanish language 162, 379-380, 384, 442, 446, 709, 899, 920, 922, 1184-1186, 1604, 1653, 1769, 2375, 2378, 2443, 2446, 2473, 2487, 2585, 2752, 3106
  Asturian Spanish dialect 385
  medieval 680
  Old 853
  teaching 532, 606, 1181
Spanish linguistics 164, 384, 691, 777, 798, 888, 897, 922, 1183, 1649, 1817, 2086, 2368, 2382, 2443, 2461, 2473, 2488, 2803
Spanish literature 18, 73-74, 119, 157, 161-164, 213, 221, 349, 380, 382, 384-385, 442, 446, 552, 601, 662, 691, 699, 709, 719, 723, 725, 740, 777, 798, 806, 817, 888, 899, 922, 1136, 1181-1183, 1185, 1187-1188, 1227, 1230, 1278, 1580, 1604, 1606, 1695, 1769, 1817, 1839, 1859, 1883, 2036, 2086, 2123, 2204, 2279, 2305, 2351, 2363, 2376, 2378, 2380, 2382, 2386-2387, 2443, 2462, 2487, 2585, 2744, 2752, 2803, 2879, 2918, 2968, 2981, 2990, 3027, 3060, 3075, 3096, 3105, 3113
  Castilian 976
  18th century 2057, 2919
  Galician 448
    medieval 448, 557, 680, 2064
    modern 1286
  Muslim 2272
  19th century 165, 2057, 2391
  Pyrenees 1186
  Realism 165
  17th century 160, 566, 830, 2138, 2919
  16th century 830, 2919
  20th century 383, 2057, 2391, 2613, 2859, 3022
  women writers 1605
Spanish novel, 19th century 165
Spanish philology 157, 2381, 2443, 2803
  Arabic 2272
Spanish poetry 73, 2188
Spanish studies 446
  Asturias 385
  Extremadura 2376
Spanish theater 724, 1107, 2918-2919
  20th century 916
Speech 471-472, 822, 1281, 1439, 1444, 1446, 1657, 2284, 2410, 2705
  church and 1648
  communication 643
  literature and 1681
  social aspects 1568
Speech and language pathology 225, 576-577, 643, 1012, 1412, 1426, 1949, 2850
  brain and language studies 404
  ear and hearing studies 822
Speech perception 1563, 2173, 2301
Speech processing, acoustic 2173
Speech production 1563, 2173
Speech synthesis 2173
Speech therapy 1012
Spenser, Edmund 815, 2697
Spirituality 219, 787
  Carthusian 155
  Christian 2930
  Cistercian 156
  history of 602
  Low Countries 2070
  myth and 1915
Staël-Holstein, Anne-Louise-Germaine, baronne de 498
Stage design 924
Steinbeck, John 2729-2730
Stendhal 2731
Stereotypes 1
Sterne, Laurence 2563, 2604

Stevens, Wallace 3156
Stifter, Adalbert 36
Stories see Fiction; Short fiction; Short story
Storm, Theodor 2549
Storytelling 2620
Strindberg, August 2737
Structuralist literary theory and criticism 913
  Biblical literature and 1648
  Romance literature 2484
Style 1564, 1638, 1821, 2042
  see also Literary style
Stylistic analysis 1562
Stylistics 224, 379, 569, 1259, 2191, 2832, 2868, 3011, 3155
  French 1045
  German 2712
  Hebrew 1162
  Italian 1639
  postcolonial literatures in English 714
  Romanian 1635
Sudetenland culture 2870
Summer Institute of Linguistics 2021
Supernatural 2492
Surrealism 741
Suspense fiction see Mystery fiction
Svenska Akademien 2885
Swahili language 1511
Swahili literature 1511
Swedish art 2791
Swedish cultural history 989
Swedish culture 1540, 2791
Swedish dialects 2637, 2886
  southern 2894
Swedish etymology 1804
Swedish history, in North America 2889
Swedish language 2042, 2629, 2635, 2716
  dialects 2637, 2886
  teaching 2887
Swedish linguistics 2629, 2716, 2803
Swedish literature 831, 1192, 1540, 2527, 2629, 2632, 2791, 2803, 2890, 2978
  18th century 337
  in Finland 398, 2634
  19th century 2737
  20th century 1195
Swedish onomastics, southern 2894
Swedish philology 2803
Swift, Jonathan 2563, 2891
Swiss folk culture 1022, 2551
Swiss folklore 1022
Swiss literature
  French 3153
  German 2826
Swiss popular culture 1022
Swiss studies 951
Switzerland
  German language in 2713
  German literature in 2826, 3259
Symbolic activity 1819
Symbolic logic, science of 2899
Symbolism 490
  1890s 1457
Symbolist poetry 440
Synchronic linguistics 2390, 2406, 3150
  functional theory and 1660
  Romance 2237, 2478
Syntactic analysis 1666
Syntax 79, 1642, 1645, 1654, 1664, 1782, 1851-1852, 1931, 2237, 2773, 2830, 2898
  Biblical and theological language 1648
  Creole and Pidgin 688
  functional theory and 1660
  Hebrew 1162
  literature and 2191
  philosophy and 1657
  theory of 2805
Taboo words and expressions 1759
Tagalog language 2154
Tale
  Atlantic provinces 2010
  New England 2010
Tamil culture 1445
Tamil folklore 1445
Tamil linguistics 1445
Tamil literature 1445
Tamil studies 1445
Tantrism 1402

Taoism 1373
Tasso, Torquato 2761
Teaching 2246, 2520
  see also Education; Language teaching; Pedagogy
  American literature 627
  Arabic literature 72
  children's literature 580
  composition 626
  English literature 627, 716
  film 1706
  Japanese literature 1453
  linguistics 1024
  literature 1388, 1469, 1876, 1950, 2529
  reading 2315
  Russian literature 2505
  speech communication 643
Technical language 986
  German 1912
Technical writing 3031
Television 518, 600, 1436, 1952, 2149, 2285, 2562, 2612, 2624, 2954, 3104
  Slovak 2652
Tennessee folklore 2924
Tennyson, Alfred Tennyson, Baron 2927-2928
Tense logic 1657
Terminology 1266, 1589, 3031
  translation and 1818
Text linguistics 920, 1562, 1599, 1782, 2125, 2216, 2354, 3179
Text processing 2354
  automatic 2705
  Japanese 1504
Text theory 2354, 2938
Texts 1870
  see also Books; Manuscripts
  ancient 2994
  Anglo-Norman 179
  Bogazköy 2793
  Christian 2671
  classical 2320
  Elizabethan 2524
  English, early 827
  folklore 1692
  French 2661-2662
  German 1902, 1905, 1941
  Hittite 2793, 2945
  humanities 1077
  Italian 2746
  Latin 1902, 1905, 2782
  medieval 1076, 1902, 1905, 2202, 2320, 2754, 2782, 2994, 3111
  Middle English language 1832
  philosophy, medieval 3111
  Romance 1157, 2006
  Sanskrit 403, 3140
  theology, medieval 3111
  verse drama 2525
Textual criticism 167, 1681, 2103, 2813, 2938, 2950
  Bible 2951
  French 78, 1250
  Spanish literary texts 1230
  Tamil 1445
Textual editing 2120, 2938, 3031
Thai folklore 1478
Thai literature 1478
Thai studies 1478
Thailand, language teaching in 2136
Theater 69, 267, 269, 557, 645, 914, 924, 957, 1108, 1440, 1690, 1712, 1725, 1774, 1958, 1972, 2148-2149, 2388, 2422, 2624, 2673, 2690, 2695, 2903, 2918, 2934, 2940, 2954, 2960, 2964, 2969
  see also Drama; Performing arts, and entries for theater in specific countries or regions, e.g., Italian theater; Latin American theater
  of the absurd 2255
  architecture 2961
  culture and 2807
  1890s 1457
  18th century 2360
  Elizabethan 849
  feminist studies 3200
  Hispanic 1107

Theater (*cont.*)
   history of 1516, 2422, 2548, 2941, 2955, 2957-2959, 2961-2963
   19th century 1457, 1992
   philosophy and 2166
   productions 2953
   Slovak 2652
   stage design 924
   staging 2961
   theater criticism 2955, 2957-2958
   theory 1107, 2958, 2961, 2963
   20th century 774
Theme 1863
Theology 94, 171, 219, 417, 450, 595, 605, 1056, 1158, 1771, 1805, 2321, 2628, 3048, 3215, 3273
   ancient 2322
   Catholic 1212, 2533
   Christian 818, 2930
   classical antiquity to Renaissance, manuscript research 1764
   Franciscan Order 1047
   German Enlightenment 1602
   history 2423
   linguistic 1648
   literature and 1704
   medieval 330, 1047, 1418, 1789, 2322, 3111
   Middle Eastern 1267
   Mormon 410
   Portuguese-speaking countries 284
   Renaissance 1418
   science and 2553
   Thomist 802, 2434, 2533
Theoretical linguistics 147, 493, 502, 516, 528, 676, 837, 1038, 1386, 1414, 1564, 1572, 1596, 1643-1645, 1647, 1851-1852, 1936, 1998, 2113, 2124, 2212, 2217, 2581, 2614, 2700, 2715, 2753, 2773, 2830, 2874, 3179
Theory of linguistics *see* Linguistics, theory of
Third World literatures 629, 642, 647, 2680
Third World studies 402
Thomas Aquinas, Saint 802, 2434
Thomism 802, 2434, 2533
Thoreau, Henry David 2975
Thought
   see also Ideas; Philosophy
   Arabic 228
   Caribbean 2535
   Christian 588
   German 514
   Hispanic 878, 1183
   Islamic 228
   Jewish 2995
   Mormon 410
   19th-20th century 1833
Tibetan studies 1241-1242
Tibeto-Burman languages 1658
Timișoara, Romania 2083
Tolkien, J. R. R. 1252, 1760, 1915, 3135
Tolstoĭ, Lev Nikolaevich 2986
Toponymy 2067
   see also Onomastics; Place names
Transcendentalism 906, 2852
Translation 117, 224, 227, 309, 428, 465, 631, 672, 746, 889, 1048, 1165, 1259, 1271, 1549, 1589, 1641, 1818, 1893, 1953, 2880, 2908, 2913, 2992, 3008-3009, 3155
   documentation and 1383
   machine 1745, 2708
   Summer Institute of Linguistics 2021
   theory 2021, 2227, 2913, 3008, 3031, 3222
Translations 65, 107, 649, 791, 996, 1244, 1957, 1964, 2103, 2145, 2180
   Celestina 557
   into Chinese 1025
   of Chinese literature 1165
   into French, of literary criticism 240
   of Hebrew literature 1869
   into Italian 1639
   of Japanese literature 1165
   of Korean literature 1165
   of linguistic texts 493
   of Macedonian poetry and prose 1744
   of medieval literature 87, 1075
   into modern Greek 2185

Translations (*cont.*)
   of Neo-Latin texts 1211
   of poetry 1830, 2367
   of poetry into Spanish 2188
   into Polish 774
   of Renaissance literature 87
   into Romanian 2571
   Serbo-Croatian 1893
   of Slovenian creative writing 1714
   from Swedish into English 2890
   into Ukrainian 3151
Transylvanian art 2728
Transylvanian literature 2728
Trentino, Italy 2762
Tristan legend 3023
Tungusic languages 1241
Turkish linguistics 3253
Turkish literature 3165
Turkish studies 1011, 1241, 1267
Turkmen culture 1316
Turkmen language 1316
Turkmen literature 1316
Twain, Mark *see* Clemens, Samuel
Typography 2229
Typology 1069, 1821
Ukrainian culture 1033, 3055
   in the United States 1033
Ukrainian folk art 1920
Ukrainian folk culture 1033
Ukrainian folklore 2035
Ukrainian history 1033, 1159, 3055, 3058
   in the United States 1033
Ukrainian language 1159, 1538, 1896, 2035, 2296, 3057
Ukrainian literary theory and criticism 3056
Ukrainian literature 88, 1033, 1159, 2035, 2218, 2296, 3055-3056, 3151, 3154
   19th century 3247
   Ukrainian language and 1896
   Yiddish language 2691
Ukrainian poetry 2195
Ukrainian studies 133, 536, 1159, 1483, 2888, 3054, 3058, 3154
United States
   cultural relations with Canada 534
   English-Spanish bilingualism 360
   German language teaching 1880, 3089
   Hispanic linguistics 381
   Kansas and Great Plains region 1175
   religion in 109
   Ukrainian culture 1033
Universal grammar 1431
Universidad Católica de Puerto Rico 1204
University presses 2546
Uralic ethnography 26, 2876
Uralic languages 26, 33, 1241, 3093
Uralic linguistics 33, 2876, 3093
Uralic studies 1241, 2041
Utopian fiction 2555
Valéry, Paul Ambroise 439, 1027
Values
   Christian 2309
   in literature 2347
Venetian culture 274
Venetian studies 2280
Veneto, Italy 244
Verse drama 2525
Versification 838
Vico, Giambattista 387, 1973
Victorian art 781, 3126, 3133
Victorian culture 781, 3126
Victorian history 3133
Victorian literature 416, 418, 499, 780-781, 2009, 2575, 3125-3126, 3126-3127, 3129-3130, 3133, 3184
Victorian periodicals 3128
Victorian poetry 3129
Victorian society 499
Victorian studies 3127-3128, 3131
   Romanticism 2526
Vikings 2516
Virgin Mary 1771
Virginia history 3136
Virginia literature, Richmond 850
Visayas, Philippines 2155
Visual arts 700, 1164, 1964
   literature and 3204

Vocabulary
   Labrador 2332
   Newfoundland 2332
   Romanian 1635
Voltaire 2862
Vormärz 1168
Wales *see* Welsh
Wallon French dialectology 773
Wallon onomastics 773
War 3158
Waugh, Evelyn 973
Weil, Simone 497
Weiss, Peter 2153
Wells, H. G. 3163
Welsh, Jane Baillie *see* Carlyle, Jane
Welsh history 447
Welsh language 447, 1515
Welsh literature 447, 1515, 1724
   English language 1974
Welsh onomastics 1994
Welty, Eudora 963
West African languages 1484
West African studies 2053
West Asian literature 403
West Asian studies 1470
West-East literary relations 647, 652
West European folklore 1688
West European literature 20, 1518, 1688, 1764
Western culture 829
Western hemisphere
   English language in 112
   linguistics 1263
Western literature 593, 829, 1068
   values in 2347
Western United States
   fiction and poetry related to 2679
   literature 3170, 3173
Wharton, Edith 832
Whitman, Walt 3157
Wilde, Oscar 3183
Williams, Charles 1252, 1915
Williams, Tennessee 2807
Williams, William Carlos 2519, 3187
Wolfe, Thomas 2974
Women
   see also Feminist
   literature and 3044, 3199, 3202
   19th century 1987
   religion and 207
Women writers 153, 554, 1066, 1144, 1385, 1593, 3035, 3044, 3199, 3202
   black women 2518, 3275
   dramatists 2807
   German 3201
   Spanish language literature 1605
Women's literature 1066, 1593, 1779, 2933
Women's speech 3198
Women's studies 109, 207-208, 279, 701, 707, 994, 1066, 1338, 1955, 2496, 2499, 2616, 3062
   black women 2518
The Wonderful Wizard of Oz 320
Woolf, Virginia 2138, 3138
Word games 3205
Wordsworth, William 570, 3206
World literature 1169, 1510, 1709, 1712, 1939, 2384, 2576
   comparative studies 495, 683
   English language 7, 2822, 3213
   in English translation 3007
   Hungarian literature and 19
   20th century 1678
Writers
   see also Women writers
   Anglo-Irish 2020
   Bosnian and Herzegovinian 399
   physicians 1702
Writing 626, 1656, 2313
   technical 3031
Writing systems 218, 283, 344, 450, 590, 1425, 2938, 3270
   Celtic 509
   Eastern 2902
   Irish 892
   Mediterranean 1843
Yeats, William Butler 622, 3231-3233

Yiddish culture   1125, 3237
Yiddish language   2691, 3236
Yiddish literature   1125, 2248, 2691, 3235-3236
Yorkshire English dialect   3006
Yoruba language   2355
Yoruba literature   2355

Yugoslavian   *see also* Croatian; Macedonian; Serbian; Serbo-Croatian; Slovenian, *etc.*
Yugoslavian history   1979
Yugoslavian languages   1979
Yugoslavian literature   1517, 1877, 3271
  Bosnia and Herzegovina   399, 3271
  Croatia   1521
Yugoslavian theater   2543

Zaïre studies   3243
Zimbabwe folklore   3244
Zimbabwe linguistics   3244
Zimbabwe literature   3244
Zimbabwe studies   3244
Zola, Emile   494
Zukofsky, Louis   2519

INDEX TO SPONSORING ORGANIZATIONS

Aarhus Univ., Dept. of English 809
Abadia de Montserrat 2783
Abbaye de Maredsous 2402
Academia Armena Sancti Lazari 2400
Academia das Ciências de Lisboa 1811
Academia de Științe Sociale și Politice, Inst. de Istorie și Teorie Literară George Călinescu 2384
Academia Norteamericana de la Lengua Española 381
Academia Română 220, 1635, 2040, 2233, 2379, 2433, 2863, 2900
   Inst. d'Histoire & de Théorie Littéraire "G. Călinescu" 2900
Academia Scientiarum Fennica 182, 930, 1019, 2532
Académie des Sciences de la RPS d'Albanie, Inst. de Culture Populaire 730
Académie Royale de Langue & de Littérature Françaises 433, 1768
Academy of the Hebrew Language 1601
   Scientific Secretariat 1600
Accademia della Crusca 2741-2742
Acoustical Soc. of America 1446
Adam Mickiewicz Univ. 1186, 2112, 2765
   Dept. of Glottodidactics 1119
Adolf Noreen-sällskapet för Nysvensk Språk & Stilforskning 2042
African Activist Assn. 3053
African-American Inst. 44
African Literature Assn. 2353
African Studies Assn. 53
Afrika Brug 59
Afrikaanse Skrywerskring 3049
Agence de Coopération Culturelle & Technique 945
Agora 3267
Ahmadu Bello Univ., English Literary Assn. 1536
Akadēmia Athēnōn 884
Akademie der Künste zu Berlin 2622
Akademie der Wissenschaften & der Literatur, Kommission für den Alten Orient 2793
Akademie der Wissenschaften Berlin
   Zentralinst. für Alte Geschichte & Archäologie 2161
   Zentralinst. für Sprachwissenschaft 339
Akademie der Wissenschaften Berlin/Brandenburg 764
Akademie der Wissenschaften in Göttingen 3
Akademiia Nauk Armianskoĭ 2137
Akademiia Nauk Belorusskoĭ 333
Akademiia Nauk S.S.S.R. 2510
   Dept. of Language & Literature 3147
   Inst. Mirovoĭ Literatury im. A. M. Gor'kogo 1526, 3148
   Inst. Russkoĭ Literatury 2509
Akademiia Nauk Ukraïny
   Inst. Movoznavstva 1896
   Inst. Mystetstva-Znavstva, Folkloru ta Etnografii 1920
   Inst. Ukraïns'koĭ Movy 1538
Akademija Nauka i Umjetnosti Bosne i Hercegovine Sarajevo 1122
Al. I Cuza Univ. 159
Albertus-Magnus-Kolleg 13
Alemannisches Inst. 77
Aligarh Muslim Univ. 83
Allegheny College 998
American Academy of Arts & Sciences 742
American Academy of Religion 1447
American Anthropological Assn. 93
American Antiquarian Soc. 2239
American Assn. for Applied Linguistics 224
American Assn. for Chinese Studies 1374
American Assn. for Italian Studies 1305
American Assn. for the Advancement of Slavic Studies 2642
American Assn. of Australian Literary Studies 217
American Assn. of Professors of Yiddish 3236
American Assn. of Teachers of Arabic 72
American Assn. of Teachers of French 1061
American Assn. of Teachers of German 1095, 3089
American Assn. of Teachers of Italian 1310

American Assn. of Teachers of Slavic & East European Languages 2641
American Assn. of Teachers of Spanish & Portuguese 1181
American Auditory Soc. 822
American Cassinese Federation of Benedictines, Abbeys & Priories 94
American Comparative Literature Assn. 651, 3222
American Council of Learned Societies 1463
American Council of Teachers of Russian 2505
American Culture Assn. 1356
American Dialect Soc. 112, 1982, 2260
American Drama Inst. 96
American Folklore Soc. 1357, 2261
   Children's Folklore Section 578
   Folklore & History Section 1021
   Jewish Folklore & Ethnology Section 1339
American Italian Historical Assn. 1303
American Jewish Committee 637
American Jewish Congress 1488
American Library Assn., Assn. of College & Research Libraries 2302
American Literary Translators Assn. 3009
American Name Soc. 1918
American Oriental Soc. 1448
American Printing History Assn. 2229
American Psychological Assn. 108, 769, 1351, 1395-1396, 1430, 2257-2258
American Quilt Study Group 3062
American Romanian Academy of Arts & Sciences 1449
American-Scandinavian Foundation 2539
American Schools of Oriental Research 344, 1382
American Soc. for Aesthetics 1353
American Soc. for Eighteenth-Century Studies 842, 2819
American Soc. for Reformation Research 238
American Soc. for Theatre Research 2962
American Soc. of Geolinguistics 1084
American Sociological Assn. 2658
American Speech-Language-Hearing Assn. 1444
American Studies Assn. 109
American Studies Assn. of Texas 1450
American Translators Assn. 117
American Univ. in Cairo, Dept. of English & Comparative Literature 81
Americas Soc. 2362
Amherst College 1775
Amici Thomae Mori 1890
Amis de la Tradition Celtique 2055
Amitié Charles Péguy 134
Amitié Henri Bosco 489
Anaïs Nin Foundation 153
Anglo-Norman Text Soc. 179
Anthropos-Inst. 212
Antioch College 215
Anton-und-Katharina-Kippenberg-Stiftung 1326
Aoynama Gakuin Univ., English Literary Soc. 2977
Appalachian State Univ. 2004
   Center for Appalachian Studies 223
Appalachian Studies Assn. 1451
Arbeo-Gesellschaft 1902
Archives & Musée de la Littérature 685
Arizona State Univ. 2164, 2270, 2828
   Hispanic Research Center 360
Arkansas Philological Assn. 2262
Arthur Christensens Folkemindefond 1015
Arts Council of Great Britain 65, 1726, 2184
A.S.B.L. Soc. des Etudes Classiques 944
Asiatic Soc. of Bombay 1452
Asiatic Soc. of Japan 2998
Asoc. Canadiense de Hispanistas 2371
Asoc. Colegial de Escritores de España 2351
Asoc. de Licenciados & Doctores en los Estados Unidos 719
Asoc. de Literatura Femenina Hispanica 1605
Asoc. Española de Estudios Anglo-Norteamericanos 280
Asoc. Internacional de Escritores Judíos en Lengua Hispaña y Portuguesa 1993

Asoc. Slaviștilor din Republica Socialistă România 2490
Assessorato Regionale Beni Culturali 189
Assn. Canadienne de Linguistique Appliquée 2405
Assn. Canadienne de Littérature Comparée 535
Assn. Canadienne de Sémiotique 2325
Assn. Canadienne de Traductologie 3031
Assn. Canadienne d'Ethnologie & de Folklore 524
Assn. de la Revue des Etudes Armeniennes 2412
Assn. dei Medici Scrittori Italiani 2589
Assn. des Amis de Rabelais & de la Devinière 435
Assn. des Amis de Robert Brasillach 475
Assn. des Amis de *Sources Chrétiennes* 2671
Assn. des Ecrivains Slovènes 1714
Assn. des Etudes Grecques 2414
Assn. des Littératures Latino-Américaines & des Caraïbes & Africaines du XXème Siècle 2446
Assn. des Professeurs de Langues Vivantes de l'Enseignement Public 1579
Assn. des Traducteurs Littéraires de Slovénie 1714
Assn. des Univs. Partiellement ou Entièrement de Langue Française 945
Assn. d'Humanisme & Renaissance 356
Assn. for Asian Performance 267
Assn. for Canadian Studies in Australia & New Zealand 297
Assn. for Canadian Theatre Research 2956
Assn. for Commonwealth Literature & Language Studies in Malaysia 2680
Assn. for Computational Linguistics 655
Assn. for Computers & the Humanities 656
Assn. for Computing Machinery 646
Assn. for Education in Journalism & Mass Communication 1486
Assn. for French Language Studies 1398
Assn. for French Studies in Southern Africa 1064
Assn. for Gravestone Studies 1773
Assn. for Literary & Linguistic Computing 1672
Assn. for Recorded Sound Collections 271
Assn. for Scottish Literary Studies 2557-2558
Assn. for Symbolic Logic 1431
Assn. for the Advancement of Baltic Studies 1364
Assn. for the Advancement of Psychoanalysis 99
Assn. for the Study of American Indian Literatures 2810
Assn. for the Study of Dada & Surrealism 741
Assn. for the Study of the Nationalities (U.S.S.R. & East Europe) 1930
Assn. for Theatre in Higher Education 2958
Assn. Française d'Etudes Américaines 2425
Assn. Guillaume Budé 436
Assn. Internationale de Linguistique Appliquée 68
Assn. Internationale des Etudes Françaises 469
Assn. Italiana di Anglistica 166
Assn. Lyonnaise pour le Développement des Relations Universitaires Internationales 440
Assn. Nazionale Dalmata di Roma 2449
Assn. of Canadian Univ. Teachers of English 875
Assn. of Depts. of English 38
Assn. of Depts. of Foreign Languages 39
Assn. of Northwest Semitic Languages 1429
Assn. of Professional Italianists 2745
Assn. of Russian-American Scholars in the U.S.A. 3245
Assn. of Scandinavian Slavists & Baltologists 2542
Assn. of Teachers of Advanced Composition 1352
Assn. of Teachers of Japanese 1453
Assn. of Ukrainians in Great Britain 3055

Assn. pour la Diffusion de la Recherche Littéraire 3013
Assn. pour la Promotion de l'Etude des Langues Modernes 889
Assn. pour l'Avancement des Etudes Iraniennes 2776
Assn. pour le Développement des Etudes Contrastives 672
Assn. pour le Développement des Etudes Finno-Ougriennes 949
Assn. pour l'Étude de la Pensée de Simone Weil 497
Assn. pour l'Étude & le Développement de la Traduction Automatique & de la Linguistique Appliquée 2904
Assn. Professori d'Italiano 2745
Assn. Québécoise de Linguistique 2431
Assn. Suisse de Littérature Générale & Comparée 631
Assn. Suisse des Sciences Humaines 631
Assoc. Brasileira de Professores Universitários de Inglés 925
Assoc. Italiana di Studi Nord-Americani 2499
Assoc. Studi Iberici 2279
Ateneo Veneto 274
Athens Center for Film & Video 3176
Atlanta Univ. 2176
Atlantic Provinces Linguistic Assn. 2113
Attila József Univ. 24-25
   Dept. of Philosophy 26
Auburn Univ. 2683
Augustan Reprint Soc. 285
Augustinian Fathers of the Real Monasterio de San Lorenzo de El Escorial 605
Augustinian Order 286
Australasian Univs. Language & Literature Assn. 288
Australia & New Zealand Slavists' Assn. 303
Australia Council of the Arts 3169
   Literature Board 301, 2564
Australian & New Zealand Assn. for Medieval & Renaissance Studies 2130
Australian Assn. for Cultural Freedom 2282
Australian Folklore Assn. 298
Australian Linguistic Soc. 300
Australian National Univ.
   Research School of Pacific Studies, Dept. of Linguistics 2114, 2116, 2118
   Research School of Social Sciences 703
Austrian Inst. of Culture 2087
Austrian Ministry of Education 1328
Austrian Ministry of Science 986, 1134
Autobiography Soc. 2
Baker Street Irregulars 310
Ball State Univ. 2730
Banasthali-Vidyapith 316
Banco de la República 378
Banco Zaragozano 3027
Bar-Ilan Univ. 359, 1162
Bayerische Akademie der Wissenschaften 321, 1905
Bayerisches Staatsministerium für Wissenschaft & Kunst 1855
Baylor Univ., Armstrong Browning Library 2814
Beijing Foreign Studies Univ. 1024-1025
Belgian Government 1313
Belgischen Germanisten- & Deutschlehrerverband 1104
Bellmanssällskapet 337
Belmont Univ. 1477
Belorussian Inst. of Arts & Sciences 3246
Berea College, Black Cultural Center 1137
Bernard Shaw Soc. 1232, 2605
Bhandarkar Oriental Research Inst. 199
Bharatiya Vidya Bhavan 343
Bibliographical Soc., London 1628
Bibliographical Soc. of America 2120
Bibliographical Soc. of Canada 2121
Bibliographical Soc. of Northern Illinois 167
Biblioteca Balmes 158
Biblioteca Luis Angel Arango 378
Bluefield State College, Center for International Understanding 640
Board of Celtic Studies 1724
Bodleian Library 374

Boise State Univ. 3173
Börsenverein des Deutschen Buchhandels 236
Boston Critic 400
Boston Univ. 2135
   African Studies Center 1346
   Graduate School 2844
Botswana Soc. 401
Bowdoin College 1928
Bowling Green State Univ.
   Dept. of English 1830
   Popular Culture Center 1436
Brazilian Soc. of Professors of Linguistics 23
Brecht Soc. of America 1108
Brigham Young Univ. 410
   Center for the Study of Christian Values in Literature 1696
British Academy 2242
British Assn. for American Studies 1358
British Assn. for Applied Linguistics 224
British Comparative Literature Assn. 649, 1953
British Council 166
   English Language Services Dept. 1574
British Film Inst. 2612
British Inst. in Paris 1048
British Inst. of Persian Studies 1283
British Library 414, 870
British Psychological Soc. 413
British Soc. for Eighteenth-Century Studies 411
British Soc. of Aesthetics 412
Brontë Soc. 416
Brown Univ. 405, 1874, 2030
   Afro-American Studies Program 1552
   Friends of the Library 396
Browning Inst. 3126
Browning Soc. 418
Bucknell Univ. 421
Bŭlgarska Akademija na Naukite 313
   Inst. za Bŭlgarska Literatura 1709
   Inst. za Bŭlgarski Ezik pri Bŭlgarskata 422
Bundesministerium für Unterricht & Kunst 1686, 3162
Bundesministerium für Wissenschaft & Forschung, Vienna 229, 1133, 1774, 2626, 2703, 2711, 3162, 3180, 3182
Bymålslaget 1742
Byron Soc., UK 457
Cabildo Insular de Gran Canaria 165
California Folklore Soc. 3171
California State Univ., Fresno, Dept. of Linguistics 1658
California State Univ., Long Beach 2464
California State Univ., Sacramento, Dept. of Foreign Languages 976
Calouste Gulbenkian Foundation 2205
Cambridge Bibliographical Soc. 2999
Cambridge Philological Soc. 610
Cambridge Univ. 516
Canada Council 214, 2933
Canadian Assn. for American Studies 534
Canadian Assn. for Irish Studies 526
Canadian Assn. for the Advancement of Netherlandic Studies 529
Canadian Assn. for Translation Studies 3031
Canadian Assn. of African Studies 525
Canadian Assn. of Applied Linguistics 2405
Canadian Assn. of Slavists 536
Canadian Assn. of Univ. Teachers of German 537, 2579
Canadian Comparative Literature Assn. 535
Canadian Corporation for Studies in Religion 2842
Canadian Council 1625
Canadian Ethnic Studies Assn. 521
Canadian Federation for the Humanities 2787
Canadian Linguistic Assn. 528
Canadian Philosophical Assn. 778
Canadian Semiotic Assn. 2325
Canadian Soc. for Eighteenth-Century Studies 1761
Canadian Soc. for Italian Studies 2278
Canadian Soc. for Musical Traditions 522-523
Canadian Soc. for Renaissance Studies 2340
Canadian Soc. for the Study of Names 2067
Capuchin Italian Inst. 1301

Cardozo School of Law 541
Caribbean Artists' Movement 2535
Carleton Univ. 542-543, 1008, 2371
Carlyle Soc. 545
Casa di Dante 84
Catholic Univ. of America, Dept. of Anthropology 211
Center for Great Plains Studies 1135
Center for Research & Documentation on World Language Problems 1570
Center for the Study of the Francophone Literature of North Africa 2403
Central Inst. of English & Foreign Languages 562, 1388
Central Missouri State Univ., Dept. of English 2180
Centre de Recherches Littéraires & Historiques 467
Centre de Recherches sur l'Amérique Anglophone 187
Centre d'Ethnologie Française 933
Centre d'Etudes & Recherches Semiotiques 615
Centre d'Etudes & Recherches Sociocritiques 1227
Centre d'Etudes Freudiennes du Montpellier 794
Centre d'Etudes Gidiennes 438
Centre d'Etudes pour l'Action Sociale 3243
Centre Inter-Disciplinaire de Recherches Afro-Indian-Océaniques 467
Centre Interdisciplinaire d'Etudes & de Recherches sur l'Expression Contemporaine 3015
Centre International de Synthèse du Baroque 317
Centre National de la Recherche Scientifique 132, 228, 241, 429, 441, 468, 473, 479, 484, 486, 563, 623, 803, 933, 939, 943, 954, 983, 1347, 1661, 1897, 2407, 2418, 2481, 2491, 2662, 2777, 2904, 3011
   Inst. National de la Langue Française 470
   Laboratoire d'Automatique Documentaire & Linguistique 1664-1665
Centre National des Lettres 438, 466, 484, 498, 681, 939, 1798, 2054, 2186, 2472, 2491, 2662, 2731
Centro de Estudios Avanzados de Puerto Rico & el Caribe 2389
Centro de Estudios de Economía & Sociedad 798
Centro de Estudios de Literaturas & Civilizaciones del Río de la Plata 2446
Centro de Estudios Latinoamericanos "Rómulo Gallegos" 35
Centro di Cultura dell'Alto Adige 690
Centro di Studi Tassiani 2761
Centro Interuniversitario di Studi Veneti 2280
Centro Italiano di Linguistica Applicata 2306
Centro Italiano di Studi sull'Alto Medioevo 2754
Centro Nazionale delle Ricerche, Ist. Internazionale Studi Piceni 2352
Cercle Ferdinand de Saussure 487
Cervantes Soc. of America 566
Československá Akademie Věd 459, 551, 1924, 2656
   Inst. for Greek, Roman & Latin Studies 1669
   Oriental Inst. 239
   Ústav pro Českou a Světovou Literaturu 567
   Ústav pro Etnografii & Folkloristiku 568
   Ústav pro Jazyk Český 2068
Charles Lamb Soc. 570
Chiang Ching-kuo Foundation 451
Chiba English Literary Soc. 574
Children's Literature Assn. 579-580
China Academy, Inst. for Advanced Chinese Studies 583
Chinese Comparative Literature Assn., American Chapter 582
Chinese Language Teachers' Assn. 1454
Chu-Shikoku American Literature Soc. 591
Chūgoku Bungakukai 592
Chulalongkorn Univ. 2136

Círculo de Cultura Panamericano 601
Cistercian Order 602
Citadel 1991
City Univ. of New York
    Graduate Center 780, 2986
    Graduate Center, Dept. of Comparative
        Literature 2986
    Graduate Center, Peyre Inst. 741
    Graduate Center, Ph.D. Program in
        Linguistics 731
    John Jay College 1439
    Queens College 544, 780, 788, 1564
    Victorian Committee 544
Claflin College 607
Clarion Univ., Dept. of English 2817
Classical Assn. of Canada 2171
Classical Assn. of the Middle West & South 609
Clemson Univ. 1928
    College of Liberal Arts 2677
Coalition of Women in German 3201
Cognitive Science Soc. 621
Colby College 622
Colegio de México 917, 2036
Colegio Univ. de la Rioja 722
Colegio Univ. de Vigo 2585
College English Assn. 556
College Language Assn. 628
College of Idaho, Regional Studies Center 2011
College of Speech & Language Therapists, London 968
Collegio Ghislieri 2772
Collegio San Bonaventura, Historical Commission 247
Collegium Romanicum 3113, 3150
Colonial Soc. of Massachusetts 1956
Columbia College 3122
Columbia Univ.
    Center for American Culture Studies 799
    Dept. of English & Comparative Literature 879
    Dept. of French & Romance Philology 2484
    Dept. of Germanic Languages 1098
    Dept. of Linguistics 634
    Friends of Columbia Libraries 633
    Hispanic Inst. of the U.S. 2391
    Inst. on East Central Europe 2649
Comediantes 449
Comenius Univ. 932
Comhar Teoranta 635
Comité Doyeu Jean Lépine 489
Comité National Roumain de Littérature Comparée 2900
Comitetul de Cultură și Educație Socialisiță Timiș 2083
Commission d'Initiative & de Développement Culturels de la Ville de Montréal 1614
Commission Interuniversitaire Suisse de Linguistique Appliquée 426
Communauté Française de Belgique 1615
Community Organization for Culture 3241
Compagnia di Gesù 1616
Compañía Nacional de Teatro Clásico 724
Comune di Bergamo 338
Comune di Venezia 2751
Conference of College Teachers of English of Texas 660
Conference on Christianity & Literature 589
Conseil de Recherches en Sciences Humaines du Canada 478, 957
Conseil des Arts de la Communauté Urbaine de Montréal 1614, 1625
Conseil des Arts du Canada 1614, 2911
Conseil Général de la Réunion 467
Conseil International d'Etudes Francophones 2426
Consejo Nacional de Investigaciones Científicas & Técnicas, Argentina 1230
Consejo Superior de Investigaciones Científicas 230, 923, 2272, 2386
    Inst. de Filología 160, 853, 2375, 2573
Conselho Nacional de Pesquisa 985
Consiglio Nazionale delle Ricerche 348, 389, 1638, 2305, 2459, 2743-2744, 2749, 2752
    Centro di Studi Vichiani 387

Conventual Order, Provincia Toscana Frati Minori Conventuali 604
Convergence 712
Coordinating Council of Literary Magazines 2140, 2582
Copenhagen Business School, Faculty of Languages 676
Cork Historical & Archaeological Soc. 1455
Cornell Univ. 1959
    Dept. of Modern Languages & Linguistics 678
    Dept. of Romance Studies 772
    Sage School of Philosophy 2163
    Southeast Asia Program 1244
Council for Name Studies in Great Britain & Ireland 1994
Council of Editors of Learned Journals 835
Council on National Literatures 683, 2365
Country Dance & Song Soc. of America 684
Country Music Foundation 1379
Courtauld Inst. 1481
Creative Unions of Estonia 2625
Critical Arts Projects 693
Critical Quarterly Soc. 705
Croatian Academy of America 1380
Curia Generalis Ordinis Cisterciensis 156
Curtin Univ. of Technology, School of Communication & Cultural Studies 2687
Cusanus Assn. Union for Cusanus Research 1856
Cyprus Research Centre 883
Cyril W. Nave Foundation 1738
Czechoslovak Soc. of Arts & Sciences in America 2247
D. H. Lawrence Soc. 738
Daito Bunka Univ. 445
Dalhousie Univ. 743-744
    Dept. of French 78, 1250
Dallas Inst. of Humanities & Culture 1144
Danish Oriental Soc. 22
Danish Philological-Historical Soc. 2802
Danish Research Council for the Humanities 17, 1788, 2987
Dansk Slavistforbund 2884
Dante Soc. of America 749
DeKalb College 1334
Delta State Univ. 1847
DePauw Univ. 2555
Deputazione di Storia Patria, Toscana 245
Deutsch-Italienische Vereinigung 1311
Deutsch-Katalanische Gesellschaft 3261
Deutsche Akademie für Sprache & Dichtung 759, 3110
Deutsche Bibliothek, Helsinki 1329
Deutsche Dante-Gesellschaft 767
Deutsche Forschungsgemeinschaft 60, 758, 766, 1102, 1118, 1190, 1221, 1295, 1491, 1857, 2078, 2190, 2629, 2709, 2715, 3165-3166, 3252-3254, 3256-3258
Deutsche Forschungsgemeinschaft, Bad Godesberg 3264
Deutsche Forschungsgemeinschaft, Bonn 234
Deutsche Gesellschaft für Amerikastudien 130-131
Deutsche Gesellschaft für Osteuropakunde 2091
Deutsche Gesellschaft für Volkskunde 3266
Deutsche Morgenländische Gesellschaft 3248
Deutsche Orient-Gesellschaft 1853
Deutsche Schillergesellschaft 1320
Deutsche Shakespeare-Gesellschaft 2597
Deutsche Shakespeare-Gesellschaft West 761
Deutscher Altphilologenverband 1143
Deutscher Sprachatlas 760
Deutsches Volksliedarchiv 1333
Deutschschweizerischer Sprachverein 2713
Dialekt- & Folkminnesarkivet 2637, 2886
Dickens Fellowship 781
Dickens Soc. 779
Dictionary Soc. of North America 783, 1266, 1620-1621
Diputació de Barcelona 924
Disputación Provincial 2376
Divine Word Univ. 1624
Dominican Order 2533
Domus Mazziniana 388
Doris Lessing Soc. 810

Dramatic, Artistic & Literary Rights Organization 2673
Dravidian Linguistics Assn. 1265
Drury College 3092
Društvo za Srpskohrvatski Jezik i Književnost NR Srbije 1521
Dublin Inst. for Advanced Studies, School of Celtic Studies 558
Duke Univ. 1418, 2675
Duquesne Univ.
    Dept. of English 815
    Dept. of Modern Languages 691
Duras Soc. 1385
Durham Center for 17th Century Studies 2590
E. E. Cummings Soc. 2717
East Carolina Univ. 3133
    Dept. of English 1842
East Tennessee State Univ., Center for Appalachian Studies & Services 2033
East-West Sign Language Assn. 1573
Eastern Michigan Univ. 1424
Ecole des Hautes Etudes en Sciences Sociales 476, 485, 1199, 2659
Ecole Française d'Athenes 427
Ecole Normale Supérieure, Paris 441
Ecole Normale Supérieure de Fontenay-St.-Cloud 425, 483
Edith Wharton Soc. 832
Edna St. Vincent Millay Soc. 2909
Eesti Kirjanike Liidu 1503, 1728
Eesti Teaduste Akadeemia 1503, 1652, 2098
    Mother Tongue Soc. 851
Eichendorff-Gesellschaft 290
Eidgenössische Technische Hochschule 2973
Eighteen Nineties Soc. 1457
Ellen Glasgow Soc. 850
Elvish Linguistic Fellowship 3135
Emerson College 2181
Emily Dickinson International Soc. 854
Emporia State Univ. 1175
    Office of Graduate Studies & Research 855
English Assn., London 860, 907, 3229
English Assn., Sydney 2681, 2893
English Folk Dance & Song Soc. 1014
English Goethe Soc. 2263
English Language & Literature Assn. 1667
English Language & Literature Assn. of Korea 1390
    Chungbuk Branch 1459
English Language & Literature Soc. 2824
English Linguistic Soc. of Japan 865
English Literary Soc. of Japan 2825
Enoch Pratt Free Library 1813
Ente Nazionale Giovanni Boccaccio 2760
Ernst H. Klett Stiftung Merkur 1814
Escòla Occitana 1072
Estonian Ministry of Culture 2625
Estudio Teológico de San Esteban 595
Eugene O'Neill Soc. 964
Eurasian Linguistic Assn. 3093
European Assn. for Lexicography 1266, 1620-1621
European Cultural Foundation 1, 1193
Evelyn Waugh Soc. 973
F. Marion Crawford Memorial Soc. 2492
Fachverband Moderne Fremdsprachen 1950
Facultad de Teología de Valencia, Sección Dominicos 2930
Facultés Catholiques de Lille 1805
Facultés Jesuites de Montréal 2553
Fairleigh Dickinson Univ. 1678
Fernando Rielo Foundation 890
Finnish Language Soc. 2532
Finnish Ministery of Education 1329
Finnish Oriental Soc. 22
Finnish Soc. for the Study of Comparative Religion 2922
Five Colleges, Inc. 1992
Florida State Univ.
    College of Arts & Sciences 1007
    Comparative Literature & Film Circle 1007
    Dept. of English 1365
Folger Shakespeare Library 2599
Folklore of Ireland Soc. 322
Folklore Soc., London 1017
Folklore Studies Assn. of Canada 524

Index to Sponsoring Organizations

Fond pour la Formation de Chercheurs & l'Aide à la Recherche 2430
Fondation Egyptologique Reine Elisabeth 590
Fondation Saint-John Perse 496
Fondation Universitaire de Belgique 1615
Fondazione G. Cini-CNRS It. 390
Fonds der Wissenschaftlichen Forschung 2626
Fonds F.C.A.R. pour l'Aide & le Soutien à la Recherche 957
Fonds National de la Recherche Scientifique 1768
Fonds zur Förderung der Wissenschaftlichen Forschung 1683
Fordham Univ. 2976, 2994
Foreign Languages Publication & Distribution Bureau 584
Föreningen för Utgivandet av Tidskrift för Litteraturvetenskap 2978
Föreningen Granskaren 1004
Forschungsinst. für Deutsche Sprache 760
Fort Hare Univ. 1030
Foundation Castrum Peregrini 553
Foundation for Cultural Review 1954
Foundation for Education, Science & Technology 716, 1514
Foundation for the Creative Arts 1680
Foundations of Language 2830-2831
Franciscan Inst. 1047
Franciscan Order 1054, 3108
  Provincia Toscana di S. Francesco Stimmatizzato dei Frati Minori 2748
Frank Norris Soc. 1051
Franz Vogt Stiftung 2317
Frederick May Foundation for Italian Studies 91
Freien Univ., Osteuropa-Inst. 3109
Frente de Afirmácion Hispanista 2003
Friedrich-Alexander-Univ. Erlangen-Nürnberg, Zentralinst. für Fränkische Landeskunde & Allgemeine Regionalforschung 1330
Friedrich-Schiller-Univ., Jena 3191
Friends of George Sand 1088
Friends of the Ehrenpreis Center 2891
Frobenius-Gesellschaft 2102
Fryske Akademy 1299
Fu Jen Univ., College of Foreign Languages 1068
Fundação Calouste Gulbenkian 258, 632
Fundación Amado Alonso 1000
Fundación Federico García Lorca 383
Fundación Ortega y Gasset 2387
Furman Univ. 1070
G. K. Chesterton Soc. 573
Gaelic Soc. of Inverness 3000
Gaskell Soc. 1078
General Federation of Labor of Israel 1125
Generalität de Catalunya, Dept. de Cultura 3261
George MacDonald Soc. 2009
George Washington Univ. 115
Georgetown Univ., School of Languages & Linguistics 1089-1090
Georgia College 1006
Georgia Southern Univ. 2570
Georgia State Univ. 1092, 2856
German Assn. of Univ. Professors of English 1855
German Ministry of Science & Art 2627
German Studies Assn. 1096
Germanistenverband im Südlichen Afrika 16
Gesamthochschule Kassel 1500
Gesellschaft für Demokratische Kultur 3162
Gesellschaft für Deutsche Sprache 1912, 2702
Gesellschaft für Kanada-Studien 539
Gesellschaft für Schleswig-Holsteinische Geschichte 1996
Gesellschaft zur Förderung Literarwissenschaftlicher Homostudien 1036
Gesellschaft zur Förderung ostmitteleuropäischer Literatur 2870
Gettysburg College 1109
Gissing Trust 1116
Global Black Expressive Culture Studies Assn. 1675
Gobierno de Aragón 3027

Goethe-Gesellschaft in Weimar 1123
Goethe Soc. of North America 1124
Golden Gate Baptist Theological Seminary 1163
Gomel'skiĭ Gosudarstvennyĭ Univ. 334
Görres Gesellschaft 2165
Görres-Gesellschaft zur Pflege der Wissenschaft 284, 330, 1713
Göteborgs Univ.
  Inst. de Lenguas Románicas 164
  Publications Committee 1
Governo do Estado de Minas Gerais 1840
Groupe Aixois de Recherches en Syntaxe 2327
Groupe d'Etudes Balzaciennes 201
Growing Room Collective 2496
Grundtvig-Center 1140
Gunvor & Josef Arnérs Stiftelse 891
Gutenberg-Gesellschaft 1142
Gypsy Lore Soc. 1461
H. G. Wells Soc. 3163
Hall Center for the Humanities 1384
Hampshire College 1775
Hannoverscher Künstlerverein 1203
Happy Hours Brotherhood 790
Hartford Seminary Foundation 1911
Harvard Univ.
  Council on East Asian Studies 1152
  Dept. of Comparative Literature 1156
  Dept. of English & American Literature & Language 1153
  Dept. of Romance Languages 1157
  Divinity School 1158
  Library 1155
  Ukrainian Research Inst. 1159
  Yenching Inst. 1154
Hebbel-Gesellschaft 1160
Hebrew Literary Foundation 362
Hebrew Univ. of Jerusalem 2912
  Bible Project 2951
  Inst. of Languages & Literatures 1164
Hebrew Writers Assn. of Israel 1899
Heinrich-Heine-Gesellschaft 1168
Heinrich-Heine-Inst. der Landeshauptstadt 1168
Helen Dwight Reid Educational Foundation 977
Helsingfors Universitetsbibliotek 398
Hemingway Soc. 1173
Henry Francis du Pont Winterthur Museum 3189
Henry James Soc. 1174
Heraldry Soc. 616
Herzog August Bibliothek 3195-3196
Hetaireia Byzantinōn Spoudōn 882
Hetaireia Historikōn Spoudōn epi tou Neō terou Hellēnismou 1861
Hiroshima Univ., English Literary Assn. 1179
Hispanic Soc. of America 1185
Historical Soc. of Mecklenburg, Upper Canada 1093
Historical Soc. of Pennsylvania 2142
Hitotsubashi Daigaku Koenkai 1194
Höchst Ibèrica 3261
Hofstra Univ. 3046
Hokkaido Univ. 205, 1201
  Inst. of Language & Culture Studies 1559
Hölderlin-Gesellschaft 1197
Hollins College 1198
Honourable Soc. of Cymmrodorion 3001
Hoosier Folklore Soc. 1834
Horatio Alger Soc. 1981
Housman Soc. 1207
Hrvatsko Filološko Društvo 1340, 2883
Hugo von Hofmannsthal-Gesellschaft 1196
Humanistisk-Samhällsvetenskapliga Forskningsrådet 27, 451, 891, 1074, 1919, 2082, 2517, 2566, 2786
Humanistiske Forskningsråd 1716
Humboldt-Univ., Berlin 3192
Hungarian Ministry of Foreign Affairs 1216
Hungarian PEN Club 1215
Hungarian Readers' Service Inc. 1218
Huntington Library, Art Collections, & Botanical Gardens 1219
Iași Soc. "Junimea" 675

Illinois Historic Preservation Agency 1226
Illinois State Historical Soc. 1226
Indian Assn. for Cultural Freedom 1970
Indian Council for Cultural Relations 1234
Indian Soc. for Commonwealth Studies 642
Indiana State Univ. 46, 1834
Indiana State Univ., Terre Haute, Dept. of English 813
Indiana Univ. 585, 2962, 3131
  Chicano-Riqueño Studies 586
  College of Arts & Sciences 599
  Comparative Literature Program 3222
  Dept. of Anthropology 210
  Dept. of Russian & East European Studies 2649
  Folklore Inst. 1397
  Research Inst. for Inner Asian Studies 1241
Indiana Univ. of Pennsylvania 2853, 3210
  Dept. of Spanish & Classical Languages 1183
  Graduate School 1183
Indiana Univ.-Purdue Univ. at Fort Wayne 613
Inklings-Gesellschaft 1252
Inst. Caro y Cuervo 2968
Inst. Catholique de Toulouse 437
Inst. d'Anglais Charles V 465
Inst. de Cine & RTV/Fundación Inst. Shakespeare 972
Inst. de Cooperación Iberoamericana 725, 899, 1649
Inst. de France, Académie des Inscriptions & Belles-Lettres 1348
Inst. de la Communication Parlée 471-472
Inst. de Langue & Littérature d'Oc 1046
Inst. de Linguistică și Istorie Literară din Cluj-Napoca 565
Inst. de Philologie & d'Histoire Orientales, Groupe d'Etudes Orientales & Slaves 202
Inst. de Recherche en Sciences de la Communication & de l'Education, Faculté Pluridisciplinaire des Sciences Humaines & Sociales, Perpignan 2580
Inst. des Belles Lettres Arabes 1222
Inst. for Balkan Studies 312
Inst. for Evolutionary Psychology 1394
Inst. for Perception Research/IPO 1281
Inst. for Russian & East-European Studies 2789
Inst. for the Medical Humanities 1702
Inst. for the Study of Man 1404, 1763
Inst. for Vico Studies 1973
Inst. Français d'Archéologie de Beyrouth 2902
Inst. für Deutsche Philologie, Munich 1274
Inst. für Deutsche Sprache 762
Inst. für Geschichtliche Landeskunde der Rheinland 2436
Inst. für Österreichkunde 2088
Inst. Historique & Archéologique Néerlandais à Istanbul 168
Inst. Internacional de Literatura Iberoamericana 2392
Inst. Libre Marie Haps 1549
Inst. Literario & Cultural Hispánico 74
Inst. Littéraire 1537
Inst. Meyer 1117
Inst. Miguel de Cervantes 2381
Inst. National des Langues & Civilisations Orientales 464, 3238
Inst. of Bolivian Studies 386
Inst. of Commonwealth & American Studies & English Language 1676
Inst. of Culture & Communication 828
Inst. of Early American History & Culture 3186
Inst. of Latin-American Studies 1583
Inst. of Linguists 1641
Inst. of Research in Foreign Literatures 1025
Inst. of Semitic Studies 1355
Inst. Sénégalo-Britannique 409
Inst. Supérieur de l'Etat de Traducteurs & d'Interprètes 889
Inst. voor Naamkunde 1916
Inst. Vox, Madrid 216
Inst. za Etnologiju i Folkloristiku 1921

Inst. za Srpskohrvatski Jezik 1489
Inter American Univ. of Puerto Rico, San Germán 2398
Intercollegiate Studies Inst. 1864
Interdisciplinary Nineteenth-Century Studies 1987
International African Inst. 42
International Arthur Schnitzler Research Assn. 1865
International Arthurian Soc. 424
International Assn. for Semiotic Studies 2584
International Assn. for the History of Religions 2038
International Assn. of Logopedics & Phoniatrics 1012
International Boethius Soc. 546
International Brecht Soc. 407, 645
International Byron Soc. 457
International Committee of Onomastic Sciences 2065
International Communication Assn. 1376
International Comparative Literature Assn. 1939
International Courtly Literature Soc. 857
International Dostoevsky Soc. 811
International Federation for Theatre Research 2960
International Fiction Assn. 1261
International Galdós Assn. 165
International Hopkins Assn. 1200
International Inst. of Tamil Studies 1445
International Linguistic Assn. 3203
International Maledicta Soc. 1759
International Phenomenological Soc. 2167
International Phonetic Assn. 1464
International Pragmatics Assn. 2215
International Reading Assn. 2316
International Reynard Soc. 2336
International Sign Linguistics Assn. 1268
International Slavic Center of the Republic of Serbia 1932
International Soc. for Chinese Philosophy 1373
International Soc. for Contemporary Legend 668
International Soc. for General Semantics 927
International Soc. for Humor Studies 1214
International Soc. for Infant Studies 1245
International Soc. for the Comparative Study of Civilizations 648
International Soc. for the History of Rhetoric 2441
International Soc. of Functional Linguistics 1660
International Sociological Assn., Research Committee on Sociolinguistics 2665
International Steinbeck Soc. 2730
International Union of Academies 248
International Wizard of Oz Club 320
Internationale Vereinigung für Germanische Sprach- & Literaturwissenschaft 1331-1332
Iowa Council of Teachers of English 1279
Iqbal Academy 1282
Irish American Cultural Inst. 845
Irish Assn. for Applied Linguistics 2916
Irish Historical Soc. 1288
Irish Slavists' Assn. 1289
Isländska Sällskapet, Uppsala 2566
Israel Folklore Soc. 3234
Israel Ministry of Foreign Affairs 252
Ist. Bancario S. Paolo di Torino 2749
Ist. Ellenico di Studi Bizantini & Postbizantini 2967
Ist. Enciclopedia Italiana 726
Ist. Italiano di Studi Germanici 2750
Ist. Italiano per gli Studi Filosofici 2029
Ist. Italo-Africano 43
Ist. Lombardo 1297-1298, 2348
Ist. Nazionale di Studi Romani 2758
Ist. Nazionale di Studi sul Rinascimento 2445
Ist. per gli Studi Micenei ed Egeo-Anatolici 2756
Ist. per la Storia del Risorgimento 2307
Ist. Universitario Orientale, Napoli 196
   Dipt. di Studi Asiatici 195

Dipt. di Studi e Ricerche su Africa e Paesi Arabi 195
Italian Cultural Centre 1312
Jadavpur Univ. 1319
James Branch Cabell Soc. 1494
James Hogg Soc. 2827
James Madison Univ., College of Letters & Sciences 2359
Jane Austen Soc. of North America 2152
Japan Ministry of Education 1810
Japan Soc. for Medieval English Studies 2835
Jawaharlal Nehru Univ. 1476
Jean-Paul Gesellschaft 1322
Jesuit Order 2804
Johann-Gottfried-Herder-Forschungsrat 3262
Johann Wolfgang Goethe-Univ. 3261
John Clare Soc. 1344
John Donne Soc. 1345
John Logic Baird Centre, Glasgow 2562
John Rylands Univ. Library of Manchester 450
Johns Hopkins Univ. 848, 1859
Joseph Conrad Soc. 664
Joshi Foundation 3099
Jugoslavenska Akademija Znanosti i Umjetnosti 1032
Julia Whitney Foundation 2032
Kafka Soc. of America 1465
Kansas State Univ. 2859, 2957
   Dept. of English 1497
Karl-May-Gesellschaft 1323
Karla Zarina Fonds 246
Katedra za Južnoslovenske Jezike 2225
Katholieke Univ. Nijmegen 1787
Katholieke Univ. te Leuven 1618
   Afdeling Toegepaste Linguïstiek 1313
   Dept. Orientalistiek 2081
   Fakulteit Letteren & Wijsbegeerte 1916
   Seminarium Philologiae Humanisticae 1211
Katolicki Uniw. Lubelskiego, Towarzystwo Naukowe 2469
Keats-Shelley Assn. of America 1501
Keats-Shelley Memorial Assn. 1502
Keiryō Kokugo Gakkai 1504
Kentucky Philological Assn. 1505
Kenyon College 1507
Kiev State Univ. 3057
King Alfred's College 1698
King Saud Univ. 1408
Kipling Soc. 1509
Klaus-Groth-Gesellschaft 1515
Književni Krug Split 1877
Københavns Univ. 204, 747, 1528, 2942
   Arnamagnæan Commission 353, 834
   Center for Oversættelsesvidenskab & Leksikografi 746
   Faculty of Humanities 172, 174
Kongelige Danske Videnskabernes Selskab 1525
Koninklijk Inst. voor Taal-, Land- en Volkenkunde 358
Koninklijke Academie voor Nederlandse Taal- en Letterkunde 3114
Koninklijke Nederlandse Akademie van Wetenschappen, Amsterdam 1786
Konstanzer Hus-Gesellschaft 2207
Kooperativo de Literatura Foiro 1690
Korea Univ., Dept. of English 2170
Korean National Commission for UNESCO 1529
Kossuth Lajos Tudományegyetem 1936, 2780
   Dept. of English 1217
Kotikielen Seura 3139
Kulturamt der Landeshauptstadt Hannover 1203
Kulturna Skupnost Slovenije 3273
Kungliga Gustav Adolfs Akademien 261, 931, 1919, 2517
Kwansei Gakuin Univ. 1542
Kyoristen Joshi Gakuen 1409
Kyushu American Literature Soc. 1546
L. Eötvös Univ. 2820
L. J. Skaggs & Mary C. Skaggs Foundation 2011
La Trobe Univ. 216
Lafayette College 612, 2595

Lamar Univ., College of Arts & Sciences 1547
Lancaster Univ. 1987
Landschaftsverband Westfalen-Lippe 1984
Langston Hughes Soc. 1552
Latinitas Foundation 1585
Latvian Academic Club 70
Latvian Academy of Sciences 250
Latvian Council of Science 1587
Laurence Sterne Trust 2604
Lawrence & Lee Theatre Research Inst. 2961
Leeds Philosophical & Literary Soc. 2243
Leningradskiĭ Univ. 1666
Lessing-Akademie 3197
Lessing Soc. 1602
Levy Humanities Series 978, 980
Lewis Carroll Soc. 1318
Library Assn., Univ., College, & Research Section, Scottish Group 354
Library of Congress, American Folklife Center 1016
Liceo Classico G. Garibaldi di Palermoturali 189
Lietuvių Kalbos Inst. 1633
Lietuvos Respublikos Kultūros ir Švietimo Ministerija 1112
Ligue d'Action Nationale 34
Lincolnshire & Humberside Arts Assn. 342
Linguistic Assn. of Canada & the United States 837, 1038
Linguistic Assn. of Nigeria 1346
Linguistic Assn. of the Southwest 2689
Linguistic Soc. of America 1553
Linguistic Soc. of Belgium 336
Linguistic Soc. of India 1237
Linguistic Soc. of Japan 1082
Linguistic Soc. of New Zealand 2915
Linguistic Soc. of Papua New Guinea 1560
Linguistic Soc. of the Philippines 2154, 2838
Linguistics Assn. of Great Britain 1413
Linguistics Inst. of Ireland 1565, 2917
Literary Criterion Centre 1673
Literary Research Assn. 1677
Lithuanian Franciscan Friars 67
Lituanus Foundation 1720
Ljubljana Univ., Faculty of Philosophy 20
Łódzkie Towarzystwo Naukowe 2498, 3242
Louisiana Endowment for the Humanities 1731
Louisiana State Univ. 1174, 1417, 2686
   Dept. of French & Italian 905
Loyola Univ., New Orleans 974, 1969
Loyola Univ. of Chicago 2360, 3122
Lund Univ. 1736
   Dept. of Linguistics 3208
Luso-American Foundation 2205
Luther-Gesellschaft 1739-1740
L'vov Univ. 1256, 3056
Lyrica Soc. 259
Macedonian Assn. for Classical Studies 3270
Magyar Irodalomtörténeti Társaság 1292
Magyar Irószövetség 1532
Magyar Tudományos Akadémia 11, 15, 19, 21, 928, 1001, 1293, 1687, 1748-1749, 1751, 2041, 2784, 2788
   Irodalomtudományi Intézet 1294
   Irodalomtudományi Intézetének Folyóirata 1169
   Nyelvtudomány Intézete 89
Maharaja Sayajirao Univ. of Baroda 1467, 1470
Mahidol Univ. 1879
Maine Folklife Center 2010
Maison des Sciences de l'Homme 1550, 2659
Makerere Univ. 1780
Manchester Univ. 702
Manila Univ., Ateneo 2157
Mankato State Univ. 1668
Manuscript Soc. 1765
Marquette Univ. 2347
Marshall Univ., West Virginia Assn. of College Teachers of English 454
Martin Luther Univ. 3193
Masarykovy Univ. 961
Massachusetts Historical Soc. 2244
Massachusetts Inst. of Technology 1851-1852

Massey Univ., Dept. of Modern Languages 1978
Maumee Valley Historical Soc. 2012
Maximilian-Gesellschaft 2158
McGill Univ.
  Dept. of Linguistics 1782
  Inter-University Center for Discourse Analysis & Text Sociocriticism 795
McMaster Univ. 840
McNeese State Univ. 1783
Mechitarist Congregation 1151
Medieval Academy of America 2694
Medieval Academy of Ireland 2150
Medieval & Renaissance Collegium 1793
Medieval Inst. 824-826, 997
Meerut Univ., Dept. of English 1803
Meijerbergs Inst. för Svensk Etymologisk Forskning 1804
Melville Soc. of America 1807
Memorial Univ. of Newfoundland, Dept. of English Language & Literature 2332
Mentunargrunnur Føroya Løgtings 1065
Mervyn Peake Soc. 1816
Mesa State College 1990
Miami Univ. 2063
Miami Univ., Hamilton, Dept. of English 2271
Michigan Academy of Science, Arts, & Letters 1823
Michigan State Univ. 2505
  Asian Studies Center 1443
  College of Arts & Letters 560, 3226
Michigan Technological Univ. 2312
Mid-America Folklore Soc. 1829
Mid-American Theatre Conference 2957
Middle-Atlantic Writers Assn. 1779
Middle East Studies Assn. of North America 1267
Middlebury College 1957
Midwest Modern Language Assn. 1469
Milton Soc. of America 1837, 2592
Mind Assn. 1841
Ministarstvo Znanosti, Tehnologije & Informatike, Republike Hrvatske, Zagreb 2295, 2655
Ministère de la Communauté Française de Belgique 773
Ministère de la Coopération & du Développement, France 2022
Ministère de l'Education de la Communauté Française de Belgique 2410
Ministère de l'Education Nationale, Belgium 1150, 1768
  Fondation Universitaire, Belgium 1586
Ministère des Affaires Culturelles du Québec 1614, 1625, 2911
Ministère des Affaires Etrangères, France 2022
Ministerie Nederlandse Cultuur 2699
Ministerie van de Vlaamse Gemeenschap 787, 1916
Ministerium für Wissenschaft & Forschung des Landes Nordrhein-Westfalen 2335
Ministero Beni Culturali & Ambientali 2459
Ministero dell'educazione Nationale, Italy 348
Ministero Pubblica Istruzione 2749
Ministerstvo Kultúry Slovenskej Republiky 2653
Ministerstvo Skolstva Slovenskej Socialistickej Republiky 606
Ministerstvo Skolstvi Ceske Socialisticke Republiky 606
Ministerstvo Vysšego Obrazovanija Litovskoj S.S.R. 315, 1688
Ministerul Culturii, Romania 350
Ministrstva za Kulturo Republike Slovenije 937
Ministry of Intergerman Relations 763
Minskiĭ Gosudarstvennyĭ Pedagogicheskiĭ Inst. Inostrannykh Iazykov 1821
Mississippi Folklore Soc. 1847
Mississippi Philological Assn. 2264
Mississippi State Univ., College of Arts & Sciences 1848
Missouri Folklore Soc. 1849
Missouri Philological Assn. 2265

Modern Critical Theory Group 2129
Modern Greek Studies Assn. 1421
Modern Humanities Research Assn. 1870, 1873, 2205, 2647, 3224, 3230
Modern Language Assn. of America 2183, 2246, 2577
  American Literature Section 103-104
  Discussion Group on Comparative Romance Linguistics 653
  Division on African Literatures 2353
  Division on American Literature to 1800 823
  Division on Chaucer 572
  Division on Children's Literature 579
  Division on Comparative Studies in Medieval Literature 1799
  Division on Old English Language & Literature 2061
  Division on Seventeenth-Century English Literature, Milton Section 2592
  Division on Spanish Medieval Language & Literature 680
Modern Language Soc. of Helsinki 1948
Modern Language Teachers' Assn. of Sweden 1876
Mombushō 2823
Monash Univ. 299
Mongolia Soc. 1881
Montana Committee for the Humanities 679
Montana State Univ., Research & Endowment Organization 679
Monumenta Germaniae Historica 766
Moody Street Irregulars 1889
Mount Holyoke College 1775
Mount Olive College 1895
Mount Saint Vincent Univ. 279
Münchener Sprachwissenschaftliche Studienkreis 1904
Musée de l'Homme 2043
Musée Royal de l'Afrique Centrale 45, 57
Museum für Hamburgische Geschichte 328
Museum of New Mexico Foundation 2105
Museums Assn. 1908
Muzeul Literaturii Române 1766
Mythopoeic Soc. 1915, 3135
Nanzan Anthropological Inst. 265
Nathaniel Hawthorne Soc. 1928
National Assn. for Ethnic Studies 979
National Assn. for Psychoanalytic Criticism 1703
National Assn. of Professors of Hebrew in American Insts. of Higher Learning 1163
National Council of Teachers of English 627, 863, 3222
  Conference on College Composition & Communication 626
National Endowment for the Arts 2140, 2145, 2582
National Endowment for the Humanities 679
National Federation of Modern Language Teachers Assns. 1871
National Library of Wales 1929
National Museum of Denmark 2987
National Park Service 995
National Poetry Foundation 982, 2101, 2519
National Taiwan Univ. 593
National Univ. of Ireland 844
National Women's Studies Assn. 3202
Naučnye Doklady Vysšej Školy 1002
Nederlandse Organisatie voor Zuiver-Wetenschappelijk Onderzoek 1034, 2506, 3143
Nederlandse Taalunie 819
Nevada Humanities Committee 1146
New Chaucer Soc. 2851
New England Theatre Conference 1958
New Jersey Folklore Soc. 1963
New Mexico Inst. of Mining & Technology 1968
New Orleans Poetry Forum 1964
New York Academy of Sciences 200
New York C. S. Lewis Soc. 717
New York State Council on the Arts 2145, 2582
New York State English Council 871

New York Univ. 2145
  School of Education, Inst. of Hebrew Culture & Education 362
  Tisch School of the Arts 2914
Newberry College 2847
Newberry Library 1980
  Center for Renaissance Studies 2342
Niedersächsisches Ministerium für Wissenschaft & Kunst, Hannover 1203
Nigerian Assn. of French Teachers 1043
Nordfriesischer Verein 1997
Nordic Assn. for American Studies 114
Nordic Humanities Research Councils 931, 1998
Nordisk Inst. for Hymnologi 1220
Nordiska Publiceringsnämnden för Humanistiska Tidskrifter 22, 929, 1264, 1995, 1999, 2766, 2942
Norges Almenvitenskapelige Forskningsråd 667, 831, 2001, 2895, 2993
Norske Samlaget 2897
North Carolina Arts Council 2140
North Carolina Folklore Soc. 2004
North Carolina State Univ. 2208
  Dept. of English 2044
Northeast Archives of Folklore & Oral History 2010
Northeast Missouri State Univ. 341, 2103
Northeast Modern Language Assn. 1874
  Italian Section 1937
Northeastern Univ. 1956, 2563
  Dept. of English 2808
Northern Illinois Univ. 428
  Dept. of English 1085, 2868
  Graduate School 1085
  Libraries 1085
Northwestern State Univ. 2688
Northwestern Univ. 2342, 3022
  Dept. of Linguistics 2014
Norwegian-American Historical Assn. 2015
Norwegian Cultur Fond 3098, 3239
Norwegian Federation of Film Socs. 3239
Norwegian Ministry of Culture 2530
Norwegian Oriental Soc. 22
Notre Dame Univ. 1987
Nottingham Univ. 2023-2024
Obáfẹmi Awólọwọ Univ. 2053
  Yoruba Language & Literature Club 2355
Oberlin College 996
Occidental College 2464
Odense Univ. 962, 2051, 2644
Ohio State Univ. 1454, 1698, 2505, 2507
  Dept. of English 1894
  Dept. of Linguistics 3209
  Division of Comparative Studies 2115
  Melton Center 1161
Ohio Univ. 2056, 3176
  Center for International Studies 1884-1885
  Dept. of English 1837
Okike Arts Centre 2058
Oklahoma State Univ., College of Arts & Sciences 596
Onarest-Inst. des Sciences Humaines 434
Ontario Arts Council 533, 2933
Opera di Dante 1617
Oral History Assn. 2074
Oral History Soc. 2073
Ordre des Prêcheurs, Province Dominicaine de Toulouse 2434
Organization for Defense of Four Freedoms for Ukraine 3055
Organization for the Study of Communication, Language & Gender 3198
Organization of American States 128
  Dept. of Cultural Affairs 2393
Ormond College 2564
Ortnamnssällskapet i Uppsala 2085
Österreichische Akademie der Wissenschaften 222, 2493
  Kommission für Byzantinistik 1324
Österreichisches Ost- & Südosteuropa-Inst. 2089
Otdelenie Literatury i Iazyka AN 1315
Oude Meester Foundation 2673
Overland Soc. 2092
P. J. Meertens-Inst. 1916, 2906
Pacific Northwest Council on Foreign Languages 2576

Pacific Northwest Renaissance Conference 2340
Panjab Univ., Chandigarh 2111
Panjab Univ., Hoshiarpur, Vishveshvaranand Vishva Bandhu Inst. of Sanskrit & Indological Studies 3140
Panstwowe Wydawnictwo Naukowe 1543
Parnassos Literary Soc. 2132
Pembroke State Univ. 2140
PEN
  All-India Centre 1240
  Centre Slovène 1714
Pennsylvania College English Assn. 1746
Pennsylvania Folklife Soc. 2141
Pennsylvania State Univ. 1343, 2357, 2606
  College of Liberal Arts 2168
Personhistoriska Samfundet 2151
Phi Beta Kappa 110
Philippine National Science Development Board 2154
Philippine Social Science Council 2154
Philippine Sociological Soc. 2156
Philological Assn. of the Pacific Coast 2099
Philological Soc. 2266, 3003
Phonetic Soc. of Japan 2071
Pioneer America Soc. 1778
Pirandello Soc. of America 2255
Pirckheimer Gesellschaft 1770
Pittsburg State Univ., Kansas 1833
Poetics & Linguistics Assn. 1562
Poetry in Review Foundation 2133
Poetry Soc. 2194
Polish Inst. of Arts & Sciences of America 2197
Polish Inst. of International Affairs 2196
Polish Linguistics Assn. 364
Polish Ministry of Culture 2052
Polska Akademia Nauk 880, 1640, 1679, 2500
  Inst. Badan Literackich 363, 2108, 2790, 2921, 3240
  Inst. Filozofii & Socjologii 2782
  Inst. Języka Polskiego 2198
  Inst. Słowianoznawstwa 14
  Inst. Sztuki 2199
  Komisja Historycznoliteracka, Oddział w Krakowie 2466
  Komisja Orientalistyczna 1011
  Komitet Językoznawstwa 2066, 2212, 2468
  Komitet Nauk Etnologicznych 1735
  Komitet Nauk Orientalistycznych 2467
  Komitet Słowianoznawstwa 2109, 2468, 2639
  Oddział w Katowicach 1651
  Oddział w Krakowie 2213-2214
  Wrocławskie Towarzystwo Naukowe 1715
Polskie Towarzystwo Ludoznawcze 1692, 1735
Polynesian Soc. 1471
Pontifical Inst. of Mediaeval Studies 1789, 2202
Pontificia Facoltà Teologica Marianum 1771
Pontificia Univ. Católica, Rio Grande do Sul 405
Pontificia Univ. Católica de Chile 2908
Pontificia Univ. Católica de São Paulo 985
Pontificia Univ. Católica del Perú, Dept. de Humanidades 1623
Popular Culture Assn. 1435
Popular Culture Assn. in the South 2840
Portuguese Government 2205
Post Script 2206
Potchefstroomse Univ. 1680
Powys Soc. of North America 2210
PRB Foundation of Pre-Raphaelite & Aesthetic Studies 2210
Presbyterian Church of Wales 3215
Princeton Univ. 2777
  Friends of the Library 2228
  Program in East Asian Studies 263
Pro Helvetia 559
Proust Assn. 2252
Providence Assn. for Ukrainian Catholics in America 133
Providence College 1278
Psychonomic Soc. 452, 1812, 2146
Purdue Research Foundation 2462

Purdue Univ. 2505
  Dept. of English 1868
  Dept. of Foreign Languages & Literatures 2462, 3122
Queen's Univ. 2286
  Dept. of French 2427
  Graduate Students' Soc. 2427
Raabe-Gesellschaft 1325
Rabbinical Council of America 2995
Rashtriya Sanskrit Samsthan 1460
Ravi Academic Soc. 3024
Real Inst. de Estudios Asturianos 385
Redacţia Publicaţiilor Pentru Străinătate "România" 2483
Regent's College, Centre for Information on Language Teaching & Research 1574
Renaissance Inst. 2341, 2343
Renaissance Soc. of America 2345
  North Central Conference 2340
Republica Zajedničga Naučni 2645
Republican Union of Culture 1314, 3271
Republiski Sekretariat nov Kulturo R Slovenije 1341
Research Club in Language Learning 1569
Research Soc. for American Periodicals 106
Research Soc. for Victorian Periodicals 3128
Réunion des Musées Nationaux 933
Rhetoric Soc. of America 2440
Rhode Island College 1703
Rhodes Univ., Inst. for the Study of English in Africa 862
Rice Univ. 2575
Rijksuniv. Centrum Antwerpen, Hoger Inst. voor Vertalers en Tolken 1647
Rijksuniv. te Gent 2079
  Faculteit van Letteren en Wijsbegeerte 2771
Rijksuniv. te Groningen 1138
  Stifting Freonen Frysk Ynst. 3095
Rijksuniv. te Leiden, Dept. of African Linguistics 1354
Rijksuniv. te Utrecht, Inst. voor Vergelijkend Literatuur-Onderzoek 3097
Rilke-Gesellschaft 368
Robert Frost Soc. 2463
Robert-Musil-Archiv 1910
Rocky Mountain Medieval & Renaissance Assn. 1472
Rocky Mountain Modern Language Assn. 2465
Romanian Studies Assn. of America 3227
Romansk Inst. 2220
Royal Asiatic Soc. 1473
  Malaysian Branch 1468
Royal Inst. for Anthropology & Linguistics, Leiden 2444
Royal Irish Academy 892
Royal Soc. of Antiquaries of Ireland 1474
Royal Soc. of Literature 908
Ruskin Assn. 2503
Ruskin Soc. of London 2502
Rutgers Univ. 1306, 1463, 2303, 2660
  Dept. of Italian 1071, 1937
  Friends of the Library 1475
Sächsische Akademie der Wissenschaften 758
Sacred Heart Univ. 2514
Sahitya Akademi 1239
St. Bonaventure Univ. 603
St. David's Univ. College 3025
St. Francis Xavier Univ. 214
St. Louis Univ., Missouri 1764
St. Louis Univ., Philippines, Graduate School of Arts & Sciences 2520
St. Patrick's College 2774
  Faculty of Celtic Studies 1588
Salisbury State Univ. 1706
Sällskapet Bokvännerna 375
Salmehistorisk Selskab 1220
Sam Houston State Univ., Dept. of English 2936
Samfundet för Visforskning, Stockholm 2873
Samfundet Sverige-Island 1074
Samoupravna Interesna Zajednica Srbije 1517
Samuel Johnson Soc. of the Northwest 3004
San Francisco State Univ. 1866
San Jose State Univ. Foundation 2531
Sana'a Univ. 1387
Scandinavian Councils of the Humanities 256

Schiller-Nationalmuseum 1767
Schleswig-Holstein Ministry of Education 1684
School of Oriental & African Studies 49
Schweizerische Akademie der Geisteswissenschaften 268, 2892, 3113
Schweizerische Asiengesellschaft 268
Schweizerische Bibliophilen-Gesellschaft 1627
Schweizerische Geisteswissenschaftliche Gesellschaft 1907
Schweizerische Gesellschaft für Volkskunde 1022, 2551-2552
Schweizerische Vereinigung für Altertumswissenschaft 1907
Science Fiction Foundation 1040
Scientific Assn., Republic of Serbia 1923
Scots Philosophical Club 2162
Scott Christian College, Post-Graduate Dept. of English 1392
Seinan Gakuin Univ. 2823
Seminarie voor Vlaamse Dialectologie, Ghent 2906
Seminario de Estudios Hispánicos "Federico de Onís" 2377
Semiotic Soc. of America 100
Seoul National Univ. 1572
Serbian Assn. for Culture 2536
Seton Hall Univ. 2701
Shakespeare Soc. of Japan 2600
Shakespeare Soc. of Southern Africa 2596
Shanghai International Studies Univ. 3155
Sherwood Anderson Soc. 3188
Shevchenko Inst. of Literature 3247
Shippensburg Univ. 2251
Shiron Club 2608
Shoin Women's Univ., Soc. of English Literature 2609
Siam Soc. 1478
Silliman Univ. 2618
Simone de Beauvoir Soc. 2619
Sixteenth Century Studies Conference 2628
Skidmore College 2521, 2785
Slavic Cultural Center 2640
Slavistično Društvo Slovenije 2646
Slovak League of America 2648
Slovenská Akadémia Vied
  Bratislava 2652
  Jazykovedný Ústav L Štúra 2651
  Národopisny Ústav 2654
Slovenska Akademija Znanosti in Umetnosti 1530, 2310, 2997
  Znanstvenoraziskovalni Center, Inšt. za Slovensko Literaturo in Literarne Vede 1671
Slovensko Društvo za Primerjalno Knjževnost 2227
Smith College 1775
Smithsonian Inst. 995
Soc. Américaine de Philosophie de Langue Française 428
Soc. Asiatique 1347
Soc. Brasileira de Autores Teatrais 2388
Soc. Brasiliera para Professores de Lingüística 2370
Soc. Canadienne des Etudes Classiques 2171
Soc. Canadienne d'Etude du Dix-Huitième Siècle 1761
Soc. Canadienne d'Etudes de la Renaissance 2340
Soc. Conradienne Française 887
Soc. Dantesca Italiana 2739
Soc. de Langue & de Littérature Wallonnes 773
Soc. de Letras Peninsulares 1606
Soc. de Linguistique Romane 2406
Soc. d'Edition les Belles Lettres 1248
Soc. des Amis de Jean Cocteau 491
Soc. des Amis de Jean Giraudoux 492
Soc. des Amis de la Romania 2481
Soc. des Amis de Lucette Desvignes 2861
Soc. des Amis de Marcel Proust & des Amis de Combray 443
Soc. des Anciens Textes 2661
Soc. des Bollandistes 154
Soc. des Etudes de Lettres 947
Soc. des Etudes Germaniques 951
Soc. des Etudes Latines 2417

Soc. des Etudes Romantiques & Dix-neuviémistes 2491
Soc. des Etudes Staëliennes 498
Soc. des Langues Néo-Latines 1580
Soc. des Professeurs Français & Francophones d'Amérique 1050
Soc. d'Etude du XVIIᵉ Siècle 804
Soc. d'Etudes Anglaises Contemporaines 942
Soc. d'Etudes Anglo-Américaines des XVIIᵉ & XVIIIᵉ Siècles 431
Soc. d'Etudes Italiennes 2416
Soc. d'Etudes Philosophiques 959
Soc. d'Histoire du Théâtre 2422
Soc. d'Histoire Littéraire de la France 2424
Soc. di Studi Trentini di Scienze Storiche 2762
Soc. Diderot 2326
Soc. Española de Didáctica de Lengua & Literatura 1598
Soc. Española de Lingüistica 2390
Soc. Filologica Friulana "G.I. Ascoli" di Udine 389
Soc. Finno-Ougrienne 2876
Soc. for Asian Music 266
Soc. for Cinema Studies 600
Soc. for Cultural Critique 728
Soc. for Ethnomusicology 935
Soc. for Folk Life Studies 1013
Soc. for French Studies 1062-1063
Soc. for Germanic Philology 98
Soc. for Iranian Studies 1284
Soc. for Italian Studies 1307
Soc. for Japanese Studies 1407
Soc. for Macedonian Studies 1172, 1755
Soc. for New Language Study 1229
Soc. for Phenomenology & the Human Sciences 1210
Soc. for Pirandello Studies 3228
Soc. for Renaissance Studies 2346
Soc. for Research in Child Development 576
Soc. for Seventeenth Century French Studies 2591
Soc. for Slovene Studies 2649
Soc. for Textual Scholarship 2938
Soc. for the Advancement of Scandinavian Study 2540
Soc. for the Promotion of Hellenic Studies 1399
Soc. for the Scientific Study of Religion 1350
Soc. for the Study of Contemporary Hispanic & Lusophone Revolutionary Literatures 1697
Soc. for the Study of Mediaeval Languages & Literature 1802
Soc. for the Study of Medievalism 2836
Soc. for the Study of Midwestern Literature 1831, 1835, 2663
Soc. for the Study of Myth & Tradition 2126
Soc. for the Study of the Multi-Ethnic Literature of the United States 1806
Soc. for Theatre Research 2959
Soc. for Transnational Cultural Studies 2259
Soc. for Values in Higher Education 2669
Soc. Française de Philosophie 2408
Soc. Française des Seiziémistes 2027
Soc. Française d'Esthétique 2421
Soc. Française d'Etude du 18ᵉ Siècle 803
Soc. Française d'Etudes des Pays du Commonwealth 639
Soc. Française d'Onomastique 2026
Soc. Gérard de Nerval 488
Soc. Guilhem IX 2929
Soc. Internationale des Amis de Montaigne 430
Soc. Italiana di Geografia 243
Soc. Japonaise de Langue & Littérature Françaises 946
Soc. Linguistica Europaea 1010
Soc. Littéraire des Amis d'Emile Zola 494
Soc. Menéndez Pelayo 382
Soc. Néophilologique de Helsinki 1808
Soc. of Basque Studies in America 1479
Soc. of Corfiote Studies 1508
Soc. of Cypriot Studies 1544
Soc. of English Folk Dance & Song 861
Soc. of Euboean Studies 233

Soc. of Spanish & Spanish-American Studies 161
Soc. of the Cantigueiros de Santa Maria 448
Soc. on Pidgins & Creoles in Melanesia 1560
Soc. per il Progresso delle Scienze 243
Soc. pour le Progrès des Etudes Philologiques & Historiques 2401
Soc. pour l'Information Grammaticale 1247
Soc. Rencesvals, American-Canadian Branch 2064
Soc. Scientiarum Fennicae 638
Soc. Suisse de Philosophie 1056
Soc. Suisse des Traditions Populaires 1022
Soc. Théophile Gautier 432
Social Sciences & Humanities Research Council of Canada 279, 533, 744, 1892
Sodalizio Glottologico Milanese 282
Sofia Univ. 2880
Soiuz Pisateleĭ Armenii 1710
Soiuz Pisateleĭ Belorussii 2200
Soiuz Pisateleĭ Latvii 752
Soiuz Pisateleĭ R.S.F.S.R. 1925, 2060
  Leningradskoe Otdelenie 1951
Soiuz Pisateleĭ S.S.S.R. 1711-1712, 2691-2692, 3148, 3274
Sojuz na Društvata za Makedonski Jazik i Literatura na SR Makedonski 1708
Sophia Univ. 1888, 2667
  English Literary Soc. 2668
  Faculty of Literature 868
South African Assn. of General Literary Studies 1415
South African Dept. of Education & Culture 1680
South African Dept. of National Education 2672
South Asian Literary Assn. 2674
South Atlantic Modern Language Assn. 2676
South Central Modern Language Assn. 2678
South Central Renaissance Conference 980
South Pacific Assn. for Commonwealth Literature & Language Studies 2693
Southeast American Soc. for French Seventeenth-Century Studies 482
Southeast Asian Ministers of Education Organization, Regional Language Centre 2337
Southeastern Conference on Linguistics 2569
Southeastern Council on Latin American Studies 2570
Southeastern Medieval Assn. 1797
Southeastern Nineteenth-Century Studies Assn. 1991
Southeastern Renaissance Conference 2344
Southern African Soc. for Semitics 1349
Southern Comparative Literature Assn. 647
Southern Conference on Afro-American Studies, Inc. 1137
Southern Humanities Council 1213
Southern Illinois Univ., Carbondale
  College of Liberal Arts 1434
  Dept. of Linguistics 1434, 2046
  Friends of Morris Library 1223
  Graduate School 1434
Southern Illinois Univ., Edwardsville 2123
Southern Methodist Univ. 2690
Southern Oregon State College 1698
Speech Communication Assn. 643-644, 2284, 2940
Spelman College 2518
Spilka Pys'mennykiŭ Ukrainy 2218
Sprachwissenschaftliches Inst. & Seminaren 1663
Srpska Akademija Nauka i Umetnosti, Balkanološki Inst. 311
Stadt Ludwigshafen 370
Staffordshire Polytechnic 2939
Stanford Univ. 1866
  Dept. of Comparative Literature 666
  Dept. of French & Italian 666, 2720-2721, 2724-2725
  Dept. of German Studies 2722
  Program of Interdisciplinary Research 666
Staroslavenski Zavod 2655
State Historical Soc. of Iowa 2107
State of North Carolina 2005
State Univ. of New York, Binghamton 117

Center for Medieval & Early Renaissance Studies 10, 974, 1790, 1794, 2061-2062
Center for Research in Translation 3008
Medieval & Renaissance Texts & Studies 974
State Univ. of New York, College at Fredonia 1988
State Univ. of New York, College at Potsdam 66
State Univ. of New York, Nassau Community College 1927
State Univ. of New York, Stony Brook 2640
Statens Humanistiske Forskningsråd 1512, 2432
Statens Kulturråd 2791
Stato del Cantone Ticino 559
Steinbeck Research Inst. 2729
Stephen F. Austin State Univ., School of Liberal Arts 2311
Sterijino Pozorje 2543
Stichting Ons Erfdeel 2069
Strindbergssällskapet 2737
Subgerencia Cultural 378
Südost-Inst. 2871
Südostdeutsche Historische Kommission 2872
Suffolk Univ. 964
Suid-Afrikaanse Akademie vir Wetenskap en Kuns 3048
Summer Inst. of Linguistics 751, 1879, 2021, 2154, 2586, 2588, 2838, 2874, 3207
  Linguistics Dept. 2018
Summer Inst. of Linguistics, Brazil 2587
Suomalais-ugrilainen Seura 1003
Suomalaisen Kirjallisuuden Seura 1493, 1510, 2768-2770, 2877
Suomalaisuuden Liitto 1495
Suomen Antropologinen Seura 2878
Suomen Muinaismuistoyhdistys 1498
Susquehanna Univ. 2882
Svenska Akademien 2885
Svenska Litteratursällskapet i Finland 1192, 2634
Svenska Österbottens Litteraturförening 1540
Svenska Språknämnden 2716
Swedish-American Historical Soc. 2889
Swedish Council for Cultural Affairs 2890
Swedish Council for Research in the Humanities & Social Sciences 2506, 2779, 2894
Swedish-English Literary Translators' Assn. 2890
Swedish Information Service 2890
Swedish Inst. 2890
Swedish Oriental Soc. 22
Swiss Assn. of Univ. Teachers of English 2892
Syndesmos Hellenon Philologon Kyprou "Stasinos" 2727
Syracuse Univ.
  Faculty of Foreign Languages & Literatures 2896
  Library Associates 2901
Tamkang Univ., Graduate School of Western Languages & Literatures 2910
Teachers of English to Speakers of Other Languages 2932
Technische Univ. Berlin, Inst. für Linguistik 2920
Tel Aviv Univ. 269
  Faculty of Humanities 1801
  Porter Inst. for Poetics & Semiotics 2192
Temple Univ. 1422, 2563
Tennessee Folklore Soc. 770, 2924
Tennessee Philological Assn. 2925
Tennyson Soc. 2927-2928
Texas A&M Univ. 2315, 2785
  Dept. of English 87
  Dept. of Modern Languages 87
Texas Folklore Soc. 2267
Texas Tech Univ. 839
Thalia, Assn. for the Study of Literary Humor 2952
Theatre Library Assn. 2149
Theodor-Storm-Gesellschaft 2549
Theosophical Soc., Adyar Library & Research Centre 403
Thomas Hardy Soc. 2970

Thomas Mann Gesellschaft 369
Thomas Merton Studies Center 1815
Thomas Wolfe Soc. 2974
Thoreau Soc. 2975
Tōhō Gakkai 12, 2984, 3002
Tohoku Gakuin Univ.
  English Inst. 1458
  Literary, Economic, & Juristic Assn. 2985
Tokyo Univ. of Foreign Studies 249
Tolkien Soc. 1760
Toronto Renaissance & Reformation
  Colloquium 2340
Toronto Semiotic Circle 1882
Towarzystwo Miłośników Języka Polskiego
  1342
Trägerverein Germanistik 1101
Translation Center 3007
Trent Univ. 1368
Trinity Univ. 1561
Tristan Soc. 3023
Tsing Hua Univ. 3030
Twentieth Century Spanish Assn. of America
  161, 2613
Udruženje Književnih Prevodilaca Srbije 1893
Ukrainian Congress Committee of America
  3054
Ukrainian Fraternal Assn. 1033
Ukrainian Historical Assn. 3058
Ukrainian Language Assn. 2657
Ukrainian Ministry of Higher Education
  1256
Ukrainian National Assn. 88, 2888
Ukrainica Research Inst. 3055
Ulster Folk & Transport Museum 3059
Ulster Soc. for Irish Historical Studies 1288
UNESCO 309, 1273, 3221
  Centre de Catalunya 3261
  International Council for Philosophy &
    Humanistic Studies 792
  Korean National Commission 1529
UNIMA 169
Union des Amis de la France Latine 1046
Union des Assns. des Folkorists de
  Yougoslavie 1922
Union des Ecrivains & des Artistes d'Albanie
  1613
Unión Latina 2446
United States Air Force Academy 3158
Uniunea Scriitorilor din România 675, 1733,
  2482, 2571, 2728, 3123
Univ. Austral de Chile 922
Univ. Autónoma 830
Univ. Autónoma de Puebla, Centro de
  Ciencias del Lenguaje 897
Univ. Blas Cañas 1695
Univ. Bonn 2436
  Historisches Seminar 392
Univ. Catholique de Louvain 1615
  Inst. de Linguistique 474
Univ. Católica de Puerto Rico 1204
Univ. Católica de Valparaiso, Inst. de Lenguas
  & Literatura 2397
Univ. Cattolica del Sacro Cuore 40, 2453
Univ. Cattolica Milano, Facoltà di Lettere 41
Univ. Central de Venezuela 898
Univ. Cheikh Anta Diop de Dakar 184
Univ. College 1291
Univ. d'Abidjan 186
Univ. d'Aix-Marseille 188
Univ. d'Angers 1477
Univ. d'Avignon 1914
Univ. de Alicante 163, 920
  Dept. de Filología Inglesa 2367
Univ. de Antioquia, Dept. de Lingüística &
  Literatura 1653
Univ. de Bordeaux 188, 442
Univ. de Bordeaux III 2411
Univ. de Buenos Aires
  Fac. de Filosofía & Letras 323
  Fac. de Filosofía & Letras, Inst. de Filología
    & Literaturas Hispánicas Dr. Amado
    Alonso 1000
Univ. de Caen 954
Univ. de Carabobo 2188
Univ. de Chile 162
  Centro de Estudios Bizantinos &
    Neohelénicos 461

Dept. de Linguistica 379, 1599
Dept. de Literatura 2373
Univ. de Concepción 18, 273, 2461
Univ. de Costa Rica 1496, 2382
Univ. de Deusto 1604
Univ. de Fribourg, Conseil de l'Univ. 2574
Univ. de Granada 1845
Univ. de Guadalajara 1069
Univ. de La Laguna, Secretariado de
  Publicaciones 2372
Univ. de La Réunion, Fac. des Lettres 85
Univ. de Lausanne
  Dépt. des Langues & des Sciences du
    Langage 481
  Faculté des Lettres 947
Univ. de Lille 954
Univ. de Lille III 983, 2420, 2472
Univ. de Limoges 188, 2025
  Fac. des Lettres & Sciences 887
Univ. de Lisboa 376
Univ. de Louvain 2423
Univ. de Malaga 157
Univ. de Mons (Ciéphum), Assn. sans But
  Lucratif Centre Interdisciplinaire d'Etudes
  Philosophiques 490
Univ. de Montréal 950
  Dépt. de Littérature Comparée 2881
  Inst. d'Etudes Médiévales 478
Univ. de Navarra 2443
Univ. de Nice 188
  Centre de Recherche sur les Ecritures de
    Langue Anglaise 737
Univ. de Paris III (Sorbonne Nouvelle) 563
Univ. de Paris VII (Vincennes) 465, 1661
  Dépt. de Linguistique 1664-1665
  Dept. de Littérature Française 1717
Univ. de Paris X (Nanterre) 479, 955
  Centre de Recherches Anglo-Américaines
    3028
  Centre de Recherches Ibériques &
    Ibéro-Américaines 689
  Centre de Recherches Italiennes 807
Univ. de Pau et des pays de l'Adour 188
Univ. de Perpignan 188, 1769
  Assn. Culturelle Ibérique &
    Latino-Américaine 3105
Univ. de Poitiers 442
  Fac. des Lettres & Langues 1632
Univ. de Provence-Aix 540, 2327, 2614
Univ. de Rennes 954
Univ. de Salamanca, Secretariado de
  Publicaciones 1843
Univ. de Santiago de Compostela 161, 3106
Univ. de Sherbrooke, Dépt. des Lettres &
  Communications 2222
Univ. de Toulouse 188, 442, 1718
Univ. de Toulouse-Le Mirail 484, 503
Univ. de Tunis, Centre d'Etudes & de
  Recherches Economiques & Sociales
  2435
Univ. de Valladolid, Dept. de Literatura
  Española 552
Univ. de Yaoundé, Faculté des Lettres &
  Sciences Humaines 185
Univ. de Zaragoza 3027
Univ. degli Studi di Bari 3121
Univ. degli Studi di Bologna 2274
Univ. degli Studi di Macerata 190
Univ. degli Studi di Perugia 191
Univ. degli Studi di Torino, Dipto. di Scienze
  del Linguaggio & Letterature Moderne &
  Comparate 3070
Univ. degli Studi di Udine e Trieste 1231
Univ. degli Studi di Venezia 193
Univ. degli Studi di Verona, Fac. di Lingue &
  Letterature Straniere 2276
Univ. del Norte, Asunción 798
Univ. del Pais Vasio-Euskal Herriko Univ.,
  Servicio Editorial 1843
Univ. del Valle 1596
Univ. des Sciences Humaines de Strasbourg
  2319, 2323
Univ. di Bari, Ist. Filosofia del Linguaggio
  275
Univ. di Bologna 1049, 2698
  Centro Interfacoltà di Linguistica Teorica e
    Applicata 2753

Univ. di Genova, Dpto. di Lingue &
  Letterature Straniere Moderne 2273
Univ. di Milano 9
Univ. di Roma 2442, 2457
  Dpto. di Studi Orientali 2450
  Ist. di Filologia Romanza 727
  La Sapienza 1610
Univ. di Torino 389
Univ. di Urbino 2763
Univ. do São Paolo, Dept. de História 2383
Univ. du Québec, Montréal 2430
  Dept. d'Etudes Littéraires 3145
Univ. du Québec, Rimouski 2911
Univ. Estadual de Campinas
  Inst. de Estudos da Linguagem, Dept. de
    Lingüística 462
  Inst. de Estudos da Linguagem, Dept. de
    Lingüística Aplicada 2992
  Inst. de Estudos da Linguagem, Núcleo de
    Estudos de Cultura de Expressão
    Portuguesa 926
Univ. Estadual Paulista 79, 2385
Univ. Faculteiten Sint-Ignatius te Antwerpen
  Centrum voor Gezelledstudie 1110
  Ruusbroecgenootschap Centrum voor
    Spiritualiteit 2070
Univ. Federal de Minas Gerais 463
  Centro de Estudos Mineiros 318
Univ. Federal de Santa Catarina 1225, 3016
Univ. G. D'Annunzio 3021
Univ. Hamburg 60
Univ. Heidelberg
  Freundeskreises 2501
  Gesellschaft der Freunde 1167
Univ. i Tromsø, Inst. for Språk & Litteratur
  2000
Univ. i Trondheim, Dept. of English 3026
Univ. Italiana per Stranieri 197
Univ.-Jubilæets Danske Samfund 748
Univ. Karlova 2217
  Filosofickǎ Fakulta 940
Univ. Köln 1524
  Thomas-Inst. 1846
Univ. Laval, Dept. de Langues & Linguistique
  1578
Univ. Libre de Bruxelles 2301
  Faculté de Philosophie & Lettres, Section de
    Slavistique 202
Univ. Metropolitana 732
Univ. Microfilms International 801
Univ. München 2801, 3111
Univ. Nacional Autónoma de México 718,
  1693, 2983
  Centro de Enseñanza de Lenguas Extrajeras
    921
  Centro de Estudios Mayas 564, 918
  Inst. de Investigaciones Historicas 919
Univ. Nacional de Educacion a Distancia, Fac.
  de Filología 888
Univ. Nacional de Trujillo 1597
Univ. of Adelaide, Dept. of English 2687
Univ. of Akron 990, 2955
Univ. of Alabama 366
Univ. of Alberta
  Canadian Inst. of Ukrainian Studies 1483
  Dept. of Romance Languages 2399
Univ. of Arizona 254, 2833
  Southwest Center 1480
Univ. of Arkansas, Little Rock 3233
Univ. of Auckland 216
Univ. of British Columbia 531
Univ. of Calgary 253
  Graduate Student Assn. 502
Univ. of California 505, 999, 1372, 1866,
  1989, 2350
Univ. of California, Berkeley
  Center for South & Southeast Asian
    Languages & Literature 1658
  Dept. of Comparative Literature 2289
  Dept. of English 2289
  Dept. of French 2289
  Dept. of Linguistics 1658
  Dept. of Spanish & Portuguese 1734
  Doreen B. Townsend Center for the
    Humanities 2289
  Graduate Division 2289
Univ. of California, Irvine 1107

Univ. of California, Los Angeles 47, 285
  African Studies Center 2805, 3053
  Asian American Studies Center 92
  Center for Medieval & Renaissance Studies 636, 3124
  Chicano Studies Research Center 308
  Dept. of Applied Linguistics 1296
  Dept. of Ethnomusicology 2578
  Dept. of Italian 549
  Dept. of Linguistics 3051-3052
  Dept. of Spanish & Portuguese 1817
  Graduate Students' Assn. 1296, 1817, 1960, 2134, 2474
  Latin American Center 1411
  Romance Linguistics & Literature Program 2474
Univ. of California, Riverside 73
Univ. of California, Santa Barbara 518
  Dept. of French & Italian 2869
  Dept. of Spanish & Portuguese 2981
  Library 2670
Univ. of Cambridge, Dept. of Anglo-Saxon, Norse & Celtic 509
Univ. of Cape Coast 262
Univ. of Cenderawasih 1285
Univ. of Central Arkansas 2262
  Dept. of English 879
Univ. of Chicago 575, 700, 2616
  Dept. of Near Eastern Languages & Civilizations 1425
  Division of Humanities 1875
Univ. of Cincinnati 1913
  College of Arts & Sciences 96
  Helen Weinberger Center for the Study of Drama & Playwriting 96
Univ. of Colorado 161, 864
Univ. of Colorado, Boulder 1080
Univ. of Connecticut 1670
Univ. of Dallas 612
Univ. of Dar es Salaam 3061
  Inst. of Kiswahili Research 1511
Univ. of Dayton 3075
Univ. of Debrecen 1750
Univ. of Delaware 2811
  Library Associates 625
Univ. of Denver, Dept. of English 756
Univ. of Durham 817
  Senate 818
Univ. of Edinburgh, School of Scottish Studies 2560
Univ. of Exeter 975
Univ. of Ferdowsi, Faculty of Letters & Humanities 1754
Univ. of Florida 974, 2563
  Dept. of Classics 2941
Univ. of Georgia 1091, 2518
  Dept. of Romance Languages 482, 3060
  Georgia Series on Hispanic Thought 878
Univ. of Ghana 1594
Univ. of Guelph 3213
  Dept. of Drama 914
Univ. of Hartford 3077
Univ. of Hawaii 1373, 2048-2049, 2169
  Center for Biographical Research 361
  College of Languages, Linguistics & Literature 98
Univ. of Hull 1886
  Dept. of German 1961
Univ. of Ibadan, Inst. of African Studies 1257
Univ. of Iceland, Inst. of Literary Studies 2778
Univ. of Illinois 1389
  Dept. of Linguistics 2855
  Language Learning Laboratory 2832
  School of Humanities 2855
Univ. of Iowa 2159, 3157
  Friends of the Libraries 397
  Iowa Center for Communication Study 1377
  School of Journalism & Mass Communication 1377
  School of Letters & Graduate College 1280
Univ. of Italy 348
Univ. of Jyväskylä, Dept. of English 1490
Univ. of Kansas 1384
  Center of Latin American Studies 1584

Hall Center for the Humanities 3078
  Mid-America American Studies Assn. 113
Univ. of Kent, Canterbury, School of European & Modern Language Studies 1414
Univ. of Kentucky 630, 2479
  Library Associates 1506
  Spanish & Italian Graduate Student Assn. 251
Univ. of Leeds 3079
  School of English 1591-1592
Univ. of Liverpool 446
Univ. of London
  School of Oriental & African Studies 453
  School of Slavonic & East European Studies 2647
Univ. of Louisville, Academic Publications 779
Univ. of Maine, Orono 2101, 2519
  Dept. of Anthropology 2010
Univ. of Malawi, Research & Publications Committee 1401
Univ. of Malta, Inst. of Anglo-Italian Studies 1359
Univ. of Manchester 1442
Univ. of Manitoba 1892
Univ. of Maryland 994, 2357
  Dept. of Spanish 2230
  European Division 1009
Univ. of Massachusetts 1775, 1992
  Dept. of English 866
  Graduate School 866
Univ. of Massachusetts, Amherst, Dept. of English 1776
Univ. of Melbourne 303, 1784
  Dept. of Classical & Near Eastern Studies 6
  Dept. of French & Italian, Italian section 2719
Univ. of Miami, Friends of the Library 548
Univ. of Michigan 1362, 1825, 1827
  Dept. of Romance Languages 800, 1826
  German Dept. 1824
  Graduate School 2293
  Program in American Culture 800
  Slavic Dept. 713, 1828, 2117
Univ. of Minnesota 1120, 1182
  College of Liberal Arts 1184
  Dept. of Spanish & Portuguese 972, 1184
Univ. of Minnesota, Morris 2833
Univ. of Mississippi 3080
  Dept. of Modern Languages 2476
Univ. of Missouri 2957
  Center for Studies in Oral Tradition 75, 2075
  Curators 1850
Univ. of Missouri, Columbia 62
Univ. of Missouri, Kansas City 1965
Univ. of Mysore 1676
Univ. of Natal 2965
Univ. of Nebraska, Kearney 2179
Univ. of Nebraska, Lincoln 554, 1405, 2859, 2957
  Dept. of Modern Languages 1605
Univ. of Nevada 1146
Univ. of New Brunswick 2815
Univ. of New England, Australia 297
Univ. of New Haven 909
Univ. of New Mexico 1360
  Dept. of English 102
Univ. of Nigeria, Nsukka, English Assn. 1906
Univ. of North Carolina, Chapel Hill 2477
  Dept. of English 823, 2684
  Dept. of Germanic Languages 3082
  Dept. of Romance Languages 1188, 2006
  Depts. of Languages & Literatures 2839
Univ. of North Dakota 2007, 2957
Univ. of North Texas 2857
Univ. of Northern Colorado, Dept. of Hispanic Studies 662
Univ. of Northern Iowa 971
Univ. of Notre Dame, Dept. of English 2338
Univ. of Nottingham 2339
Univ. of Oklahoma 97, 1083, 2059, 2505, 3212
Univ. of Oregon 2013

Univ. of Oslo, Inst. of Slavic & Baltic Studies 1785
Univ. of Ottawa
  Dept. of English 2318
  Dept. of Linguistics 493
Univ. of Pennsylvania 1185
  Dept. of South Asia Regional Studies 3083
Univ. of Pittsburgh 934, 1582, 2374, 2392
  Dept. of English 402
  Dept. of Hispanic Languages & Literatures 2086
  Dept. of Religious Studies 1440
Univ. of Playa Ancha 2037
Univ. of Puerto Rico 2990
  Fac. de Humanidades 2377
Univ. of Queensland 301, 2287, 3125
Univ. of Rajasthan 2300
Univ. of Reading
  Dept. of Italian Studies 1308
  Graduate Center for Medieval Studies 2314
Univ. of Regina 3159
Univ. of Rhode Island 1303
Univ. of Rochester
  Dept. of English 367
  Dept. of Foreign Languages, Literatures, & Linguistics 1844
Univ. of Roskilde 2471
Univ. of Saga, Dept. of English 3084
Univ. of St. Andrews 1035, 2162
Univ. of St. Thomas 1026
Univ. of San Carlos 2155
Univ. of Sheffield, Centre for English Cultural Tradition & Language 1729
Univ. of Sierra Leone 58
Univ. of South Africa 2745, 3067
Univ. of South Carolina 2569
  Dept. of English 2845
  Dept. of French & Classics 1060
Univ. of South Dakota, College of Arts & Sciences 2679
Univ. of South Florida, Tampa, College of Arts & Letters, Division of Language 1571
Univ. of Southern California
  Comparative Literature Program 1275
  Friends of the Univ. of Southern California Libraries 677
Univ. of Southern Mississippi 2685
  Dept. of English 2019
Univ. of Southwestern Louisiana 2426
Univ. of Stellenbosch 2673, 2700
Univ. of Sydney 2047, 2444
  Dept. of English 2893
Univ. of Tabriz 1926
Univ. of Tampa, Harold Pinter Soc. 2177
Univ. of Tennessee 2563, 2669
Univ. of Tennessee, Knoxville, Dept. of English 2926
Univ. of Texas 3187
  Dept. of English 2937
  General Libraries 1629
  Harry Ransom Humanities Research Center 1629
Univ. of Texas, Arlington 2223, 2874
Univ. of Texas, Austin
  Dept. of Oriental & African Languages & Literature 1705
  Dept. of Spanish & Portuguese 740
  Graduate School of Library & Information Science 1626
  Harry Ransom Humanities Research Center 1487
  Inter Nationes 791
Univ. of Texas, Pan American, Dept. of English 1722
Univ. of the Philippines
  College of Arts & Letters 789
  College of Science 789
  College of Social Sciences & Philosophy 789
Univ. of the South 2593
Univ. of the West Indies, Dept. of English 1485
Univ. of Thessaloniki, Faculty of Philosophy 885
Univ. of Toronto 3086
  Chair of Hungarian Studies 1218

Conference on Editorial Problems 661
Dept. of Italian Studies 3085
Erindale College 2329
Experimental Phonetics Lab 1249
Graduate Centre for Study of Drama 1867
Univ. of Tulsa 1335, 3035
Univ. of Utah 520, 3096
   Dept. of English 3172
Univ. of Vermont 2253
Univ. of Victoria 867
Univ. of Virginia 506, 1590, 1966, 3137
   Bibliographical Soc. 2813
   Center for Advanced Studies 671
   College of Arts & Sciences 671
   Dept. of French 671
Univ. of Wales
   Assn. for the Study of Welsh Writing in English 1974
   Board of Celtic Studies 447, 2767
Univ. of Warwick, Dept. of English 1086
Univ. of Washington 1872
Univ. of Waterloo 1106
Univ. of West Florida 1173
Univ. of Western Australia 3169
   Dept. of French Studies 911
Univ. of Western Ontario, Faculty of Arts 295
Univ. of Wisconsin 585, 669, 1362
   Dept. of German 1880
   Dept. of History 1738
   Dept. of Spanish & Portuguese 1738
   Ibero-American Center 1738
Univ. of Wisconsin, Eau Claire, Dept. of English 2271
Univ. of Wisconsin, Madison
   Dept. of French & Italian 1287
   Dept. of Hebrew & Semitic Studies 1163
Univ. of Wisconsin, Milwaukee, Center for Twentieth Century Studies 796
Univ. of Wisconsin, Superior 793
Univ. of Witwatersrand 52, 2673
Univ. of Zimbabwe 3244
Univ. Paul Valéry 188, 1286
   Centre d'Etudes & de Recherches Elisabéthaines 486
   Centre d'Etudes & de Recherches Victoriennes & Edouardiennes 499
   Centre d'Etudes Occitanes 2418
   Centre d'Etudes Valéryennes 439
   Conseil Scientifique 623
Univ. Regensburg 2331
Univ. S. Tommaso 171
Univ. Salzburg, Inst. für Anglistik & Amerikanistik 2522-2526
Univ. Siegen 1634
Univ. Stichting van België 1916, 2699
Univ. Stockholm 2733-2736, 2803
Univ. Stuttgart, Forschungsgruppe für Semiotik & Wissenschaftstheorie 2580
Univ. te Antwerpen 2358
Univ. v Ljubljani, Filozofska Fakulteta 1646
Univ. van Amsterdam 1405

Univ. Veracruzana 2104, 2581
   Centro de Investigaciones Lingüístico-Literarias 2949
Univ. Wien
   Inst. für Byzantinistik & Neogräzistik 1324
   Inst. für Germanistik 3177
   Inst. für Sprachwissenschaft 3179
   Inst. für Theaterwissenschaft 1774
Universala Esperanto-Asocio 808, 900-902
Universitätsbund Erlangen-Nürnberg 894
Uniw. Warszawski 55
Uppsala Univ. 28-33
Ursinus College 2141
Utah Academy of Sciences, Arts, & Letters 858
Utah State Univ. 3170
Vanderbilt Univ., W. T. Bandy Center for Baudelaire Studies 423
Verein der Freunde & Förderer der Sfiftung Kulturwerk Schlesien 2545
Verein für Niederdeutsche Sprachforschung 1531, 1983
Verein für Reformationsgeschichte 238
Verein für Volkskunde 2090
Verein Nordfriesisches Inst. 1997
Verein Villa Vigoni 2333
Vereinigung der Deutsch-Griechischen Gesellschaften 1171
Vereinigung der Französischlehrer 1055
Vereinigung für Wissenschaftliche Semiotik 2580
Vereniging van Leraren in Levende Talen 1619
Vereniging voor Wetenschap 3174
Victoria Univ., Center for Reformation & Renaissance Studies 2340
Victoria Univ. of Wellington 1979
Victorian Ministry of the Arts 2564
Victorian Studies Assn. of Western Canada 3130
Victorians Inst. 3133
Viking Soc. for Northern Research 2516
Villanova Univ., Augustinian Historical Inst. 2245
Vilnius Univ. 1492, 1522
Virginia Commonwealth Univ., Dept. of English 647
Virginia State Library & Archives 3136
Vishvanatha Kaviraja Inst. 1378
Viswa Sahithi 3066
Vlaamse Economische Hogeschool, Dept. of Translation 1259
Vladimir Nabokov Soc. 1917
Voltaire Foundation 2862
Wallace Stevens Soc. 3156
Warburg Inst. 1481
Washington & Lee Univ. 2607
Washington School of Psychiatry 2256
Washington State Univ., Dept. of English 555, 906, 2187
Washington Univ. 585, 2378
   Dept. of Germanic Languages & Literatures 1079

Weber State Univ., College of Arts & Humanities 3160
Welsh Arts Council 1974, 3215
Wenner-Gren Foundation for Anthropological Research 733
West African Linguistic Soc. 1484
West Bengal Inst. of Linguistics 1236
West Chester Univ. 629
West Georgia College 3167
West Virginia Shakespeare & Renaissance Assn. 2594
West Virginia Univ. 3129
   Dept. of Foreign Languages 3168
Western Australian Dept. for Arts 3169
Western Illinois Univ., College of Arts & Sciences 912
Western Kentucky Univ. 2682, 3127
Western Literature Assn. 3170
Western Michigan Univ., Medieval Inst. 2834
Western Soc. for French History 2241
Westfälische Wilhelms-Univ. 663
Whitman College 2166
Whitney Humanities Center 3217
Wilfrid Laurier Univ. 209
   Dept. of English 1758
   Dept. of Religion & Culture 1440
Wilhelm-Pieck-Univ. Rostock 3194
Wilkie Collins Soc. 3184
Willa Cather Pioneer Memorial & Educational Foundation 554, 3185
William Morris Soc. 1482
Wing Lung Bank Fund for Promotion of Chinese Culture 2349
Wisconsin Academy of Sciences, Arts & Letters 3005
Wolfenbütteler Arbeitskreis für Barockforschung 3195
Women & Performance Project 3200
Wordsworth-Coleridge Assn. 3206
World Federation of Free Latvians 246
Writers & Scholars International Ltd. 1233
Writers Union of Lithuania 1691
Wydawnictwa Szkolne & Pedagogiczne 351
Wyndham Lewis Soc. 859
Xavier Univ., Dept. of English 3214
Yale Repertory Theater 2953
Yale Univ. 3219
   Dept. of French 3216
   Library 3220
   School of Drama 2953
Yeshiva Univ. 111
   Cardozo School of Law 541
Yiddish Writers Group in Jerusalem 3235
Yonsei Univ., Liberal Arts College 1253
York Univ. 2933
Yorkshire Dialect Soc. 3006
Yr Academi Gymreig, English Language Section 1974
Zajednica za Kulturu SR Srbije 1518
Zora Neale Hurston Soc. 3275
Zuidnederlandse Dialectcentrale, Leuven 2906
Zwiazek Literatów Polskich 3277

INDEX TO EDITORIAL PERSONNEL

Aarts, Jan 1558
Aartveit, John Tore 3098
Abad, Ricardo G. 2156
Abádi-Nagy, Zoltán 1217
Abastillas, Vivencio 789
Abberton, Evelyn 968
Abbi, Anvita 1237
Abellán, Manuel L. 1405
Abernethy, Francis Edward 2267
Abiteboul, Maurice 1914
Abraham, Arthur 58
Abraham, Werner 1138, 1659, 2830-2831
Abramovich, A. V. 2513
Abramson, Arthur S. 1563
Achard, Pierre 1550
Ackmann, Martha 1593
Adam, Wolfgang 965
Adami, Giacomo 388
Adams, Gillian 580
Adams, Kathleen 1086
Adams, Timothy Dow 2
Adda, R. 425
Adediran, Biodun 2053
Adelberger, Jörg 1052
Adéwọlé, Lawrence Olufemi 2355
Adinarayana, L. 1674
Adler, J. D. 2263
Adrados, Francisco R. 853, 2390
Adwiraah, Eleonore 1052
Afshar, Iraj 988
Agari, Masahiko 3084
Agnihotri, Ramakant 1271
Agnoletti, Enzo Enriques 2201
Ahrens, Rüdiger 1855
Ainsley, Frank 1778
Aitchison, Jean 508
Akker, W. J. van den 1986
Alatis, James E. 1089-1090
Alaveras, Tilemachos 1933
Alazraki, Jaime 2391
Alba-Buffill, Elio 601
Albeck, Gustav 1140
Albright, Carol Bonomo 1303
Alcaraz-Varó, Enrique 2367
Alcira Arancibia, Juana 74
Alegría, Ricardo E. 2389
Alexander, Philip S. 1442
Alford, John A. 3226
Alhoniemi, Alho 1003
Alinei, Mario 2277
Allard, Guy H. 478
Allard, Jean-Paul 953
Allen, Cynthia 300
Allen, Gilbert 1070
Allen, James F. 655
Allén, Sture 1621
Allonnes, Olivier Revault d' 2421
Alluin, Bernard 2472
Almasy, Elina 2659
Almqvist, Bo 322
Alonso Turienzo, Teodoro 605
Alpago-Novello, Adriano 244
Alpers, Svetlana 2350
Altenhofer, Norbert 1053
Alton, R. E. 2364
Alvar, Manuel 899, 1649
Alvarez-Amorós, José Antonio 2367
Alvarez Turienzo, Saturnino 605
Amacker, René 487
Amalric, Jean-Claude 499
Aman, Reinhold A. 1759
Amanat, Abbas 1284
Amann, Klaus 1683
Ambrazas, V. 1633
Ambrière-Fargeaud, Madeleine 201
Ames, Roger T. 2169
Amigo Fernández de Arroyabe, María Luisa 1604
Amiran, Eyal 2208
Ammons, C. H. 2147
Ammons, R. B. 2147
Amo, Mercedes del 1258
Amoretti, Biancamaria Sconcia 2450
Amoretti H., María 1496
Amort, Čestmír 940
Amselle, Jean-Loup 476
Anan'ev, A. A. 2060

Anceschi, Luciano 3112
Andersen, Henning 17
Andersen, Stefan B. 2051
Anderson, Andrew A. 383
Anderson, David D. 1831, 1835, 2663
Anderson, Donald 3158
Anderson, Eugene 3072
Anderson, G. R. 1994
Anderson, Guy 2924
Anderson, Hilton 2019
Anderson, Hugh 298
Anderson, J. M. 1636
Anderson, Jon 706
Anderson, Stephen R. 2898
Anderson, Wilda 1859
Andersson, Sven-Gunnar 1127
Andersson, Thorsten 1919, 2631, 2766
Andreas, James R. 3092
Andrew, Joseph M. 913
Andrews, Alan 744
Andrews, Malcolm 781
Andrews, William 2
Andriekus, Leonardas, O.F.M. 67
Andriescu, Al. 159
Åneman, Claes 2566
Angelini, Ester Cason 244
Anghelescu, Mircea 2900
Anichenko, V. V. 334
Anker, R. 2982
Anozie, Sunday O. 658-659
Ansari, Asloob Ahmad 82
Antoni, Klaus 2078
Antonietti, Pascal 3153
Anzai, Tetsuo 2668
Apostolidès, Jean-Marie 2720-2721, 2724-2725
Appel, René 3032
Arai, Hiroshi 1194
Araya, Guillermo 349
Arcaini, Enrico 2753
Archambault, Paul J. 2896
Archibald, Douglas 622
Areška, V. 1688
Argenot, Marc 795
Århammar, Nils 1997
Arias de la Canal, Fredo 2003
Arico, Santo 2476
Arieşanu, Ion 2083
Arkoun, Mohammad 228
Armendarés, Vincent 1046
Armin, Arnold 2798
Armistead, J. M. 2359
Armistead, Samuel G. 3074
Armstrong, Alan 1698
Armstrong, Elizabeth Psakis 1913
Arnason, Vilhjálmur 2630
Arnaud, Pierre 431
Arnold, Armin 537
Arnold, Heinz Ludwig 2943
Arnow, Pat 1451, 2033
Arntzen, Helmut 1681
Arrington, Melvin 2476
Arsovska, Ljubitsa 1744
Arthur, David 861
Arzenšek, Ivan 3273
As, Saskia van 1034
Ashcroft, Bill 1967
Ashcroft, J. R. 1035
Asher, J. A. 296
Ashton-Jones, Evelyn 1352
Asiain, Aurelio 3152
Asker, Björn 2151
Assaf, Francis B. 482
Assmann, Michael 759
Astaldi, Maria Luisa 2236
Aste, Mario 1305
Astington, John H. 1867
Aston, Guy 2934
Åström, Anna-Maria 930
Attebery, Louie W. 2011
Aub-Buscher, Gertrud 1398
Aubenque, Pierre 959
Augst, Gerhard 768
Auld, Louis E. 259
Avalle, D'Arco Silvio 1800, 2738
Avellaneda, Andrés 993
Avendaño, Fausto 976

Aycock, Wendell M. 2816
Azevedo Filho, Leodegario A. de 2369
Azouvi, François 2408
Baacke, Dieter 1791
Baak, J. J. van 2849
Baba, Hirotoshi 1546
Babić, Stjepan 1340
Babić, Zrinka 2883
Bach, Svend 2220
Bachellery, Edward 943
Bachofen, Wolfgang 347
Bäckman, Sven 1736
Badawi, M. M. 1361
Bader, Françoise 429
Baena Z., Luis Angel 1596
Bahat, Shoshana 1600
Bähr, H. W. 3071
Bahri, Ravinder K. 687
Bahri, Ujjal Singh 687, 1235, 1271, 1566
Baines, Barbara J. 2344
Bains, Yashdip 96
Bair, Jeffrey H. 855
Bakalla, Muhammad Hasan 1630
Bakary, Touré 186
Baker, David 1507
Baker, Judith 1548
Baker, Linda 1557
Baker, Ronald L. 1021, 1834
Baker, William 1085
Bakker, N. 1110
Baklanov, G. Ia. 3274
Balaišius, Vytautas 1492
Baldi, Philip H. 1081
Baldwin, Spurgeon 680
Ball, Martin J. 2850
Balmas, Enea 2743
Balsamo, Luigi 346
Bamforth, S. J. 2023
Bammesberger, Alfred 1190
Bance, A. F. 1873
Bańczerowski, Jerzy 1640
Banerjee, Swapan 1236
Bankovskis, Pēteris 1694
Bantz, Charles R. 644
Barański, Zygmunt G. 1308
Barber, Noel, S.J. 2804
Barberito, Manlio 3094
Bardeleben, Renate von 1753
Barentsen, A. A. 2848
Barfoot, C. C. 682
Barham, Wayne 1830
Barker, Clive 1972
Barker, Nicolas 394
Barker, Simon 2211
Barna, Gábor 15
Barner, Wilfried 1320, 2795
Barnes, Daniel R. 1894
Barnes, Michael 2034
Barnes-Karol, Gwendolyn 1182
Barnett, Elizabeth 2909
Barnett, Teresa 2074
Barnwell, Katharine 2021
Baron, Dennis E. 2260
Baron, Michael 860
Baron, Virginia 2126
Barone, Francesco 1822
Barrax, Gerald 2044
Barreca, Regina 1670
Barrenechea, Ana Maria 1000
Barrett, Martyn 1005
Barricelli, Jean-Pierre 3074
Barroll, J. Leeds 1792, 2601
Barron, Hugh 3000
Barry, A. David 2426
Barry, Peter 860
Barry, William 2174
Barshay, Daniel 1746
Barsky, Robert 795
Bartana, Ortsion 1899
Bartholomew, Doris 2586
Bartlett, R. P. 2647
Barton, H. Arnold 2889
Bartsch, Renate 3032
Baruzzi, Arno 2165
Basile, Bruno 1638
Baskin, Andrew 1137
Bassalou, Lawrence W. 1396

Bastaire, Jean 134
Bastia, France 2428
Bataille, Gretchen M. 979
Batchelor, R. E. 2023
Bate, A. K. 2314
Bathrick, David 1959
Bátori, István 2708
Batts, Michael S. 537
Baudot, Georges 484
Bauer, G. 3178
Bauer, Matthias 663
Baum, Richard 5
Baumgarten, Rolf 892
Baumgartner, Hans-Michael 2165
Baumgartner, Joseph 2155
Baumgärtner, Klaus 1527
Baus, Wolf 1165
Bausola, Adriano 2453
Bayer, Udo 2580
Bayerdörfer, Hans-Peter 2963
Beal, Peter 870
Beam, Patricia 1387
Beardsley, T. S., Jr. 3203
Beatty, Bernard 457
Beauchamp, Wilton 2264
Beaver, Frank 3039
Bec, Christian 2416
Bec, Pierre 468
Bechert, Johannes 2124
Becker, Gerold 1945
Becker, Hellmut 1945
Becker, Siegried 3266
Becker-Cantarino, Barbara 587, 750
Beckett, J. R. 2047
Beckman, Mary E. 1433
Beeckmans, René 3243
Beegel, Susan F. 1173
Beekman, Klaus 307
Beer, Jeanette 2462
Beetz, Kirk H. 3184
Beffa, Marie-Lise 479
Béhague, Gerard 1583
Behler, Ernst 958, 1985
Behrendt, Poul 1534
Beitl, Klaus 2090
Bekker-Nielsen, Hans 1788
Béla, Márkus 80
Belamarić, Josip 1877
Belchior, Maria de Lourdes 258
Bell, Jonathan 3059
Bell, Robert F. 2676
Bell-Scott, Patricia 2518
Bellini, Giuseppe 2279, 2305, 2744
Ben-Shaul, Moshe 1899
Benac, Alojz 1122
Bender, Byron W. 2048-2049
Bender, Mark 686
Bendor-Samuel, John 1484
Benedyktowicz, Zbigniew 2199
Benkő, Loránd 1749
Bennani, Benjamin 341, 2103
Bennett, Betty T. 1501
Bennett, Bruce 3169
Benninghoven, Friedrich 3262
Bennington, Geoffrey 2095
Benseler, David P. 1871
Benson, Robert L. 3124
Benthem van den Bergh, G. van 1111
Bentley, D. M. R. 533
Bentley, G. E., Jr. 661
Bentringer, Rudolf 764
Benz, Ernst 13
Bepler, Jill 3195
Berchem, Theodor 1713
Berenger, Jean 187
Berg, Stephen 107
Berger, Charles 3172
Bergeron, David M. 2356, 3078
Bergh, Birger 891
Bergmann, Rolf 331, 2715
Bergner, Gwen 701
Berkhout, Carl T. 2061
Berkman, Anne E. 1874
Berlant, Lauren 700
Berlin, Gail Ivy 2853
Berlinger, Rudolph 847
Berner, Christian 2408

Bernik, France 1530
Berns, J. B. 2906
Berry, Eleanor 838
Bertaud, Madeleine 3013
Bertens, Hans 682, 2209
Berti, Giovanni 1302
Bertinetto, Pier Marco 2455
Bertini, Ferruccio 1752
Bertman, Martin A. 66
Bertozzi, Gabriele-Aldo 1608
Bertrand, Dominique 2671
Bertrand, Marc 2720
Berwick, Robert 1555
Besch, W. 2436
Besch, Werner 1139, 3255
Besien, Fred van 1259
Besserman, Lawrence 1164
Best, Alan D. 1961
Best, Anita 729
Bevan, David 2470
Bewell, A. 3086
Bex, Tony 1562
Beyer, Richard 1934
Bézzola, Guido 9
Bhatt, Parth 1249
Bhattacharya, Krishna 1236
Bibire, Ligita 3100
Bibire, Paul 816
Bichel, Ulf 1515
Bickes, Hans 2702
Bickford, J. Albert 3207
Bidler, Rose M. 1898
Bien, Peter 1421
Bierbach, Christine 3261
Bierbaumer, Peter 986
Bierwisch, Manfred 2773
Biggs, Henry 2474
Biggs, Robert D. 1425
Bigi, E. 1115
Bihler, Heinrich 1221
Bijlefeld, Willem A. 1911
Billick, David J. 801
Billy, Pierre-Henri 2026
Bindshedler, M. 2706
Bingen, Jean 590
Binni, Walter 2304
Bircher, Martin 587, 750
Bird, Thomas E. 3246
Birmingham, William 712
Birnbaum, Henrik 505
Birrell, T. A. 873
Biryla, M. V. 3119
Bishop, Michaël 624
Bisztray, George 1218
Bitskey, István 2780
Bjerre-Poulsen, Niels 114
Bjertrup, Susanne 1716
Bjilodid, O. 3057
Björk, Lennart A. 1128, 2734
Bjørnager, Kjeld 2884
Bjornson, Richard 2115
Black, L. G. 2016
Black, Robert A. 97
Blackford, Staige D. 3137
Blagojević, Slobodan 755
Blanken, Gerhard 1949
Blau, Joshua 1601
Blayac, Alain 942
Bledsoe, Wayne M. 648
Bleicken, Jochen 1177
Bleikasten, A. 2319
Blesa, Túa 3027
Blewett, David 840
Blicher, Henrik 1716
Blockley, Roger C. 1008
Blodgett, E. D. 535
Blom, J. M. 873
Bloom, Leonard 1479
Bloom, Steven F. 964
Bloome, David 1656
Bludau, Michael 1950
Blüher, Karl Alfred 1027
Blum, Claude 430
Blümel, Wolfgang 1491
Blumenthal, Peter 3258
Bly, Peter A. 165, 1721
Boafo, Y. S. 262

Boak, Denis 911
Bobrownicka, Maria 2214
Bobrowski, Ireneusz 2198
Bobzin, Hartmut 3251
Bocaz, Aura 1599
Bock, Hans-Manfred 1595
Bock, Philip K. 1360
Bodewitz, H. W. 1242
Bodrogligeti, A. J. A. 3093
Body-Gendrot, Sophie 2425
Boeft, J. den 3132
Boenig, Robert 2785
Boer, Peter de 1743
Boesch, Paula 734
Bogaards, Winnifred M. 973
Boggs, Redd 2448
Boheemen, Christine van 969
Bohm, A. 542
Böhm, Rudolf 1684
Bohn, Hilario I. 925
Bohnen, Klaus 2942
Bohrer, Karl Heinz 1814
Bois, Yve-Alain 2050
Bojadziev, Zivko 2880
Bojović, Zlata 1521
Boland, Bill 200
Boland, Roy C. 216
Bolaños, Patricia 251
Bold, Christine 534
Boldt, Frank 2207
Bolelli, Tristano 1300, 2747
Boléo, Manuel de Paiva 2395
Bolgiani, Franco 2456
Bolkestein, Machtelt 3032
Bömer, Franz 1143
Bonanno, David 107
Bonifassi, Georges 1046
Bonino, S.-Th. 2434
Bonnefis, Philippe 2420
Bonner, Thomas, Jr. 3214
Bonora, E. 1115
Booth, Michael 2959
Borchmeyer, Dieter 2963
Bordoni, Maria da Glória 405
Boretzky, Norbert 373
Borg, Alexander 1801
Borge, Torunn 3098
Borgonio, Guadalupe 919
Borland, Deborah A. 2974
Bormann, Thomas 808, 901-902
Born, Brad 2
Bornat, Joanna 2073
Bornéo Funck, Susana 1225
Börner, Holger 1943
Borodin, V. 3247
Borrel, Anne 443
Borrello, Alfred W. 973
Boryś, Wiesław 2214
Bos, F. C. 1786
Bosacka, Ewa 3088
Bosch, Peter 1441
Böschenstein, Bernhard 1197
Bose, Amalendu 501
Boshof, Egon 237
Bosworth, Edmund 1283
Botha, Rudolf P. 2700
Boulas, Marie Claire 1580
Bourgain, Pascale 2567
Bourjea, Serge 439
Bové, Paul A. 402
Bowden, Russell 1631
Bowen, Zack 695
Bowers, Bege K. 556
Bowie, Malcolm 513
Boyd, Ian 573
Boyd, Katrina 599
Boyers, Peggy 2521
Boyers, Robert 2521
Bracker, Jörgen 328
Bradac, James J. 1410
Bradley, Jerry 1968
Bradley, Ruth 3176
Brady, Erika 2682
Brady, Patrick 2861
Braga, Erika 2392
Brame, Michael K. 1642
Branca, Vittore 1611, 2760

Branch, M. A. 2647
Branciforti, Francesco 1800
Brang, Peter 2643, 3264
Bransford, Deborah 596
Brantschen, J.-B. 1056
Brathwaite, Edward 2535
Brauer, Wolfgang 3194
Braumüller, Wilhelm 3178
Braun, Hartmut 1333
Braunmuller, A. R. 3124
Braunmüller, Kurt 2629
Breatnach, Liam 892
Breatnach, Pádraig A. 844
Breckenridge, Carol A. 2259
Brednich, Rolf Wilhelm 984
Breitbart-Samsonowa, E. 1131
Brekle, Herbert E. 1662
Bremen, Brian 3187
Brend, Ruth 3203
Bresnan, J. 516
Breuker, P. 3095
Briesemeister, Dietrich 284, 1221
Brigden, Roy 1013
Bright, William 1568
Bringéus, Nils-Arvid 931
Brinkmann, Richard 765, 2795
Brockmann, Jane 936
Brodská, Zdenka 2247
Brody, Eugene B. 1426
Brody, Jill 1417
Broeck, Raymond van den 227
Broek, R. van den 3132
Brogi-Bercoff, G. 2442
Broich, Ulrich 2190
Bronkhorst, Johannes 268
Brooke, George J. 1442
Brooke-Little, John P. 616
Brooks, Randy 1145
Brooks, Shirley 1145
Brophy, Robert J. 2464
Brothers, Barbara 556
Brouwer, E. J. 3095
Brown, Deming 2508
Brown, Elizabeth A. R. 2994
Brown, Jack 2476
Brown, Joanne 1279
Brown, Peter D. G. 2837
Browne, Pat 614
Browne, Ray B. 1356, 1435
Browning, Logan 2575
Brownstein, Marilyn 674
Bruccoli, Matthew J. 784, 3063-3064
Bruce, Anselma 670
Bruckmüller, Ernst 2088
Brun, Bernard 441
Brundin, Margareta 2737
Brunet, Hugo Montes 2373
Brunner, Horst 234
Bruss, Paul 1424
Brustkern, Jan 2705
Bruyère, Claire 465
Bryant, John 1807
Brydon, Diana 3213
Bryer, Jackson R. 2357
Bubser, Reinhold 971
Buchheit, Robert H. 2544
Buchloh, Benjamin H. D. 2050
Buck, David 1362
Buddecke, Wolfram 1500
Buddruss, Georg 2799
Buffalohead, Roger 3175
Bulger, Raymonde A. 3227
Bull, Reimer 1515
Bulmanis, I. 1337
Bumke, Joachim 1028
Bungert, Hans 2710
Bunnens, G. 6
Bunža, R. 2247
Burchardt, Jørgen 1995
Burck, Erich 1121
Bürgel, J. Christoph 268
Burger, H. O. 1100
Burkot, Stanisław 2466
Burnett, Leon 1953
Burnier, Radha 403
Burns, Robert I., S.J. 3124
Burquest, Donald A. 2874

Burrell, Margaret 288
Burwick, Frederick 970
Burwick, Roswitha 1987
Busby, Keith 260, 992
Busch, Günther 1944
Buschmeier, M. 176
Busk-Jensen, Lise 1512
Buskirk, Martha 706
Bustos Trejo, Gerardo 918
Bușulenga, Zoe Dumitrescu 2384
Buthlay, Kenneth 2558
Butler, Christopher 2093
Butler, Clark 613
Butler, G. P. G. 1094
Butler, Gerald J. 2330
Butler, K. G. 1012
Butters, Ronald R. 112
Butts, William 1205
Butts, Yolanda 1205
Buurman, Margreet den 1034
Buzard, James 706
Byrman, Gunilla 1074
Cabrera Ponce, Ileana 2908
Cace, Guido 2449
Cacmica, P. 1361
Caesar, M. 1307
Caffi, Claudia 1437
Cagni, Luigi 195
Cahada Gómez, Manuel 2585
Cahn, Elizabeth 1066
Cairns, David 2939
Calabuig Adàn, Ignacio M. 1771
Calhoun, Richard J. 2677
Calhoun-French, Diane 2840
Callejas, Bernardo 3069
Calomino, Salvatore 1880
Calvet, Aldo 2388
Calvez, Jean-Yves 938
Camacho, Roberto Gomes 79
Campanotto, Franca 3268
Campbell, Edward D. C., Jr. 3136
Campbell, Gordon 2346, 3229
Campbell, Hilbert H. 3188
Campbell, Ian 544-545
Campbell, Josie P. 116
Campbell, Lorne 1481
Campos, Christophe 1048
Cañedo, Jesús 2443
Cano Pérez, M. J. 1845
Cap, Jean-Pierre 612
Cappelletti, Vincenzo 3103
Capucci, Martino 2759
Caputo-Mayr, Maria Luise 1465, 2087
Caquot, J. 2902
Carbonne, Philippe 1072
Carlson, Alvar W. 1381
Carlson, Greg 1657
Carlson, Lori 3007
Carlton, Charles M. 1844
Carmosino, Roger B. 1278
Carnero, Guillermo 163
Carnes, Pack 3171
Carney, Arlene E. 1444
Carnie, R. H. 3004
Caro Baroja, Julio 2375
Carothers, James B. 990
Carpenter, Cimberli 599
Carpenter, Kenneth E. 1155
Carpenter, Sarah 1795
Carr, Diana Guiragossian 785
Carranza, José 1183
Carravetta, Peter 788
Carreño, Antonio 1278
Carroll, Mark 2546
Carter, Timothy 1909
Carton, Philippe 498
Carvalho, Alfredo Leme Coelho de 925
Casado, Pablo Gil 2057
Casanova, Antoine 2143
Casanova, Eduardo 35
Casares, Carlos 1136
Caspar, Marie-Hélène 807
Castan, Félix 317
Castel, Boris 2286
Castel, Victor M. 2368
Castillo Peralta, Tito 273
Castro, I. 376

Castro García, Oscar 1653
Cate, G. A. 2503
Caudery, Tim 809
Caughie, John 2562
Cauty, André 132
Caws, Mary Ann 741
Cayton, Andrew R. L. 2063
Cazemajou, Jean 187
Celani, M. Antonieta A. 925
Černy, Lothar 663
Cerrato, Laura 323
Cerruti, Giorgio 3101
Červenka, Miroslav 567
Cervigni, Dino S. 194
Céspedes, Diógenes 723
Chagnon, Roland 2842
Chai, Kyu-Tae 1459
Chaitin, Gilbert D. 3222
Chambers, David 1481
Chametzky, Jules 1775
Champion, H. 611
Chaney, Edward 1359
Chang, Victor L. 1485
Chang-Rodríguez, Eugenio 381, 3203
Chaouli, Michel 2289
Chapman, Antony J. 413
Chapman, R. A. 2023
Charatz, Meir 3235
Charles, Michel 2193
Charnigo, Barbara A. 736
Charnigo, Richard 736
Charot, Georges 497
Charpentier, Françoise 430
Chatham, James R. 1181
Chatterton, Wayne 3173
Chaudron, Craig 224
Chaurand, J. 1045
Chaves McClendon, Carmen 878
Chen, Chang-fang 2910
Chen, Guohua 1024
Cheney, Patrick 652
Cheng, Anne 2289
Cheng, C. C. 2832
Cheng, Chung-ying 1373
Cherubim, Dieter 2106
Chesnutt, David R. 1765
Chevalier, Jean-Claude 1664-1665
Chew, Shirley 1375
Chiarini, Paolo 2750
Childers, Joseph 706
Chin, Carol 3045
Chirovsky, Nicholas L. 3055
Chisholm, William S. 783
Chock, Phyllis Pease 211
Choi, Young 1390
Cholakova, Kr. 422
Chorváthová, L'ubica 2654
Chouillet, Anne-Marie 2326
Chow, John 2337
Christensen, Dieter 3221
Christensen, Johs. H. 1534
Christodis, A.-Ph. 885
Chrysanthis, Kypros 2160, 2185
Chrzanowski, Marlies 2339
Chung, Chong Wha 2170
Ciavolella, Massimo 3085
Cifoletti, G. 1231
Cifuentes Honrubia, José Luis 920
Cigada, Sergio 2749
Cimmino, N. F. 775
Claassen, Walter T. 1429
Claessen, Henri J. M. 358
Clahsen, Harald 1556
Clamurro, William H. 566
Clancey, William J. 621
Clark, C. E. Frazer 784
Clark, Fred M. 1188
Clark, Paul 828
Clark, Sandy 981
Clarke, Bruce 839
Clas, André 1818
Classen, Carl Joachim 1121
Clausen, Jeanette 3201
Clausen, Peter Balslev 1220
Claut, Sergio 244
Clay, Jenny S. 609
Clayton, Dorothy J. 450

Clegg, Cyndia Susan 2099
Clere, Sarah V. 1895
Clifford, John 2312
Clift, G. W. 1497
Clifton, John M. 751, 1560
Clogan, Paul Maurice 1799
Clothey, Fred W. 1440
Cobban, James L. 1885
Cobo Borda, J. G. 829
Coca, Jordi 924
Cochran, William R. 310
Codell, Julie 1438
Coers, Donald 2936
Cohen, Joshua 400
Cohen, Ralph 1966
Cohen-Stratyner, Barbara Naomi 2149
Cohn, Alan M. 1223
Colaiacomo, Paola 504
Colclough, Margaret A. 1360
Coldewey, John C. 1872
Cole, Roger W. 1571
Coleman, Anne 1455
Collier, Gordon 714
Collins, Floyd 255
Collomb, Gérard 933
Coltheart, Max 619
Colvin, Daniel L. 912
Combrink, A. L. 1680
Combs, Charles E. 1958
Como, James 717
Comparato, V. I. 2144
Compernolle, René van 202
Comrie, B. 516
Conard, Robert C. 3075
Conrad, Jacob 3043
Conte, Paolo 244
Conti, Carlo Marcello 3268
Cook, Karen S. 2658
Cook, M. C. 1873
Cook, Robert Francis 2064
Cook-Lynn, Elizabeth 3175
Cookson, William 65
Cooper, Helen 1802
Cooper, Michael 1888
Cooper, N. L. 2162
Copjec, Joan 2050
Coppola, Carlo 1443
Corbin, Pierre 1621-1622
Cordié, Carlo 2100
Core, George 2593
Ćorić, Božo 1932
Cornejo Polar, Antonio 2374
Cornis-Pope, Marcel 647
Corns, Thomas N. 2249
Cornwall, N. 2647
Cornwell, Gareth 862
Cortelazzo, Manlio 390
Corthell, Ronald J. 2249
Corti, Claudia 2454
Corti, Maria 2738
Costa, Aida 1637
Costa, Marta Morais da 2394
Costa, Paola 792
Costantini, L. 2442
Costanzo, Angelo 2251
Coste, D. 948
Costello, John R. 3203
Coteanu, I. 2233, 2863
Courty, Michel 272
Coustillas, Pierre 1116
Couttenier, P. 1110
Cowan, Peter 3169
Cowan, William 528, 2119
Cowen, Roy C. 1824
Cowrie, Bernard 2830
Cox, Bonnie Jean 1506
Cox, C. Brian 702
Cox, G. Stevens 2971
Cox, H. L. 2436-2437
Cracco, Giorgio 2456
Craddock, Jerry R. 2478
Craig, Holly K. 1444
Cram, David 1370
Cramer, Kathryn 1976
Cramer, Thomas 1028
Craven, Peter 2564
Crawford, Donald W. 1353

Crawford, Fred D. 2606
Crevatin, F. 1231
Crisler, Jesse C. 1051
Cro, Stelio 527
Cros, Edmond 615, 1227, 2664
Cross, A. G. 1393, 2647
Cross, John 39
Crow, Jeffrey J. 2005
Crowdus, Gary 598
Crowley, Daniel 3072
Crozier, Alan 1074
Cruz, Jacqueline 1817
Crystal, David 577, 876, 1655
Csicsery-Ronay, Istvan, Jr. 2555
Cubberley, Paul 303
Čulić, Hrvoje 1877
Cullen, Patrick 2697
Cummins, Walter 1678
Cunneen, Joseph 712
Curley, Edwin M. 235
Curran, Stuart 1571
Curreli, Mario 2740
Currey, L. W. 1976
Curry, A. 2314
Curti, Aldo 289
Curti, Carmelo 2084
Curtis, Vesta 1283
Cutting, James E. 1395
Cuypers, J.-B. 45
Cymerman, Claude 2446
Czerwinski, E. J. 2640
Da Costa Meyer, Esther 3217
Daalen, Maria van 2366
D'Addario, Arnaldo 245
Daffina, Paolo 2450
Daggy, Robert E. 1815
Daghlian, Carlos 925
D'Agostino, Giovanni 549
Dai, Weidong 3155
Daigrepont, Lloyd M. 1547
Dakin, Karen 2983
Dale, Corinne 1477
Dale, Peter 65
Daley, Brian E. 2994
Dalfen, Joachim 1133
Dalidovich, Henrykh 1757
Dalla Valle, Tino 1612
Dallett, J. 542
Dalney, M. 2035
Daly, M. J. 453
Daly, Peter M. 136, 139, 852
Damiani, Bruno M. 2565
Damiata, Marino 2748
Damjanović, Stjepan 2883
Dammann, E. 60
Danaher, Kathleen 1406
Dandekar, R. N. 199
D'Andrea, Antonio 3225
Dandurand, Karen 1593
Danesi, Marcel 1882
Dangerfield, Elma 457
Daniel, Mary L. 1738
D'Anna, Gabriella 1609
Dantanus, Ulf 1876
Daphnes, K. 1508
Darras, Jacques 887
Dasgupta, Arun Kumar 1456
Dasgupta, Gautam 2148
Dasgupta, Kanad 1018
Dasgupta, Probal 1570
Dathorne, O. R. 1369
Datlof, Natalie 1088
Dato', Tan Sri 1468
Daum, Josef 1325
Dave, J. H. 343
Daviau, Donald G. 1865, 2812
David, Jack 915
David, Michel 2416
Davidsen-Nielsen, Niels 676
Davidson, Arnold I. 700
Davidson, Cathy 104
Davidson, Clifford 650, 824-826
Davies, Alan 1575
Davies, Martin 1628
Davies, Maurice 1908
Davies, Phillips G. 979
Davis, Charles 2465

Davis, Donald G., Jr. 1626
Davis, Geoffrey 714
Davis, Robert Con 2059
Davis, Robert Murray 973
Davis, Stephen F. 770
Davis, Steven 778
Davis, Thadious M. 1552
Day, Anthony 2444
Day, Mildred Leake 2292
Day, W. G. 2604
De Bot, Koes 224
De Camilli, Davide 1309
De Fina, Anna 921
De Michelis, Cesare 2757
De Miro, Ernesto 2756
De Nicolás, Antonio T. 2875
De Piaggi, Giorgio 2273
De Robertis, Domenico 2741
De Santis, Giacomo 2624
Dean, Bradley P. 2975
Dearden, James S. 2503
Debord, Pierre 2411
Debus, Friedrich 1103
Decaluwé, Jacques 1768
DeCosta-Willis, Miriam 2518
Decottingmies, Jean 2420
Decraene, Paulette 61
Décsy, Gyula 3093
DeFeu, V. M. 2647
Deguy, Jacques 2472
Deguy, Michel 2186
Dehn, Wilhelm 768
Deighton, Alan A. 1961
Deitz, Paula 1208
DeJean, Joan 1955
Dejna, Karol 2498
Del Panta, Elena 2454
Del Principe, David 1071
DeLancey, Mark W. 53
Delany, Samuel R. 1976
Delbecque, N. 1313
Delcorno, Carlo 2760
Delcourt, Christian 1768
Delcourt-Angélique, Janine 1768
Deleu, Jozef 2069
Delgado Téllez, Ismael Enrique 2968
Dell, Gary S. 1419
Della Terza, Dante 3225
Dell'Aquila, Michele 1309
Dendle, Brian J. 2479
Denez, Per 1202
Denison, Norman 1134
Denizot, Paul 431
Dennis, Harry J. 976
Dennis, Nigel 2371
Deretić, Jovan 1517
Derossi, Julije 3241
Derouau, W. 944
Deroux, C. 1586
Desai, R. W. 1149
Desgranges, M. 1248
Desné, Roland 803
Dessons, Gérard 1632
Détrie, Muriel 2407
Dettloff, Werner 3111
Dev, Amiya 1319
Devlamminck, Bernard 1549
Devoize, Jeanne 1477
Dewey, Barbara I. 397
Deweze, André 2904
Deyck, Rika van 3010
Deyermond, A. D. 699
Dezon-Jones, Elyane 443
D'haen, Theo 682
Dhan, C. V. N. 3024
Dhawan, R. K. 642
Di Cesare, Mario A. 1794
Di Crocco, James V. 1478
Di Gaeta, Daniela 549
Di Prisco, Rafael 898
Di Stefano, Giuseppe 1898, 2749
Diaz, Allisón 2531
Díaz, Gonzalo 605
Díaz, Nilda 2446
Díaz-Diocaretz, Myriam 704, 707
Dibbets, G. R. W. 2979
Dibon, Paul 2029

Didier, Béatrice 681
Diehl, Randy 2173
Díez Taboada, Juan M. 2386
Diffey, T. J. 412
Dihle, Albrecht 1167
Dillard, R. H. W. 579
Diller, Hans-Jürgen 176, 2317
Dimara, Daan 1285
Dimić, M. V. 535
Dimler, G. Richard, S.J. 2976
Dimmendaal, Gerrit J. 1354
Dinklage, Karl 1910
Diop, C. Mame Yande 2221
Dirkst, Walter 1943
Dissanayake, Wimal 828
Dittmar, Jürgen 1333
Diver, William 634
Dixon, Gordon 1672
Dmyterko, Liubomyr 3142
Dmytriw, I. 3154
Dobozy, Maria 857
Dobre, Alex 2379
Dobrovenskiĭ, R. 752
Dobson, Bob 1466
Dobson, Joanne 1593
Dobzynski, Charles 967
Dodd, Philip 2612
Dodd, Wayne 2056
Dodd, William 2934
DoDoo, J. N. 1594
Doerries, Reinhard R. 130
Dolan, Jill 3200
Dolby, Sandra K. 1397
Dolgin, Stacey L. 2057
Dolinar, Darko 1671, 2227
Dollerup, Cay 746
Dolnycky, Mstyslaw B. 133
Dominicy, Marc 336
Donald, J. Wallace 864
Donelson, Ken 863
Dongmo, Jean Louis 185
D'Onofrio, Piero 2745
Donohue, E. Dolores 934
Donohue, Joseph 1992
Donovan, Laurence 548
Dooley, Robert A. 3207
Doria, M. 1231
Dörner, Dietrich 2709
Doroszewski, Witold 2203
Dörries, Reinhard R. 131
Dossett, Anne Matson 452
Dotoli, Giovanni 348
Dotterer, Ronald L. 2882
Doucette, Leonard E. 2956
Doudna, Eileen 2152
Dougherty, James P. 2338
Downie, J. A. 2563
Downing, David B. 3210
Doxey, William S. 2017
Doyle, Paul A. 973, 1927
Draper, Ellen Dooling 2126
Draper, Michael 3163
Dravnieks, Aina 70
Dreisziger, Nandor F. 1218
Dressler, W. 516
Dressler, Wolfgang U. 1010
Dreyer, H. J. 1349
Drijkoningen, Fernand 307
Driskill, Clarence 395
Drost, Wolfgang 2335
Drugovats, Miodrag 1708
Drumond, Carlos 1637
Dryden, Edgar A. 254
DuBruck, Edelgard E. 997
Duby, G. 1897
Duchet, Claude 2491
Duchovnay, Gerald 2206
Dufour, A. 356
Dufour, Raymond 957
Dufournet, J. 1897
Dufrenne, Mikel 2421
Duhoux, Yves 474
Duke, Kathleen 1823
Dulai, Surjit S. 1443
Dumistrăcel, Stelian 220
Dumitrescu-Bușulenga, Zoe 2900
Duncan, Ian 3217

Dunmore, John 1978
Dunn, J. Michael 1431
Dunn, Kevin 3217
Dunsdorfs, Edgars 246
Dupas, Jean-Claude 983
Dupuy, Jean-Pierre 2721
DuQuesnay, Maurice W. 978
Durand, Jacques 1398
Durand, R. 983
Duridanov, Ivan V. 313
Durix, Jean-Pierre 639
Durkin, Kevin 1005
Ďurovič, L. 2506
Durry, Marcel 2417
Dutka, Jo Anna 2329
Dutton, Denis 2166
Duvosquel, Jean-Marie 2401
Duyfhuizen, Bernard 2271
Dworacki, Silvester 880
Dworkin, Kenya C. 1734
Dwyer, Sean 586
Dyer, Donald 2476
Dyhr, Mogens 1528
Dyke, Chuck 1987
Dyserinck, Hugo 1, 2775
Dziechcińska, Hanna 1679
Eapen, Rachel Lalitha 1388
Early, Robert 1830
Eaton, Trevor 1414
Eaves, Morris 367
Ebbinghaus, Ernst A. 1081
Echavarría, Arturo 2990
Echeverría, Max S. 2461
Eckhardt, Ernst Dietrich 1327
Eckler, A. Ross 3205
Eckler, Faith W. 3205
Eco, Umberto 3115
Edmondson, William 1268
Edwards, A. S. G. 1076
Edwards, John 1423
Edwards, P. D. 3125
Edwards, Robert R. 652
Edwards, Suzanne O. 1991
Edwards, Viviane 532
Edzard, D. O. 3252
Eekman, Thomas 505
Efron, Arthur 2138
Egeberg, Erik 2542
Egerod, Søren 17, 22
Egger, Carolus 1585
Ehling, Holger G. 1777
Eichler, Ernst 758
Eichner, Hans 537
Eid, Mushira 72
Eisenberg, Daniel 1400
Eklund, Sten 891
Ekman, Hans-Göran 2737
Elbert, E. Duane 1226
Eldridge, C. C. 3025
Eldridge, Patricia J. 1650
Eliot, Simon 2269
Elkhadem, Saad 305, 1261
Ellenberg, Karen T. 1506
Ellenbogen, Rudolph 633
Elliot, Emory 105
Ellison, John 1760
Ellwood, Robert S. 1275
Elman, Jeffrey 621
Elmevik, Lennart 2042, 2517, 2631
Embleton, Sheila M. 771, 3203
Emerson, Mary 2448
Ende, W. 3165
Enekwe, Ossie 2058
Eng, J. van der 2504
Eng, Steve 2492
Engelkamp, Johannes 2709
Engelmann, Peter 3162
England, Nora C. 1263
Engle, Ron 2957
Engler, Rudolf 487
English, Edward D. 1789
Enninger, Werner 373
Enoki, Kazuo 1810
Enos, Theresa 2439
Entract, Norman 1509
Eoyang, Eugene C. 585
Epstein, Barbara 1975

Epstein, Edmund L. 1564
Epstein, Joseph 110
Epstein, Steven A. 1472
Erbse, Hartmut 1118, 1177
Ericksen, K. J. 3004
Erickson, John D. 905
Eriksen, Charles W. 2146
Eriksen, Thomas Hylland 2530
Erikson, Olof 1876
Ermalenko, S. 1538
Ermatinger, Charles J. 1764
Ertis, E. 2098
Ertl, István 900
Eruli, Brunella 2454
Erzgräber, Willi 1946
Eschbach, Achim 1041, 1523
Eskola, Seikko 1495
Essen, Catharine von 337
Estermann, Monika 236
Euler, Arno 1311
Evans, A. B. 2555
Evans, D. Ellis 447
Evans, George 2480
Evans, T. F. 2605
Even-Zohar, Itamar 2192
Eversberg, Gerd 2549
Ewen, Colin J. 2175
Eyoh, Hansel 185
Eysteinsson, Ástráður 2630
Ezekiel, Nissim 1240
Fabian, Ann 3217
Fagundo, Ann Maria 73
Faham, Shakir Al- 2404
Falk, Johan 1876, 2803
Fallis, Richard 1290
Fant, Lars 1876
Fasold, Ralph 1567
Fasquelle, Jean Claude 1747
Faulhaber, Charles B. 2478
Faulkes, A. 2516
Faulkner, Peter 1482
Fauser, Peter 1945
Favreau, Robert 468
Fawaz, Leila 1267
Fecher, Charles A. 1813
Federici, Fausto 2589
Feintuch, Burt 1357
Feldman, Emanuel 2995
Feldstein, Richard 1703
Fellows, Otis 785
Felsenstein, F. 3079
Fenoulhet, J. 819
Fenton, Alexander 2987
Fenyő, István 1293
Ferdinand, Christine 1628
Ferguson, Charles 206
Fernández-Jiménez, Juan 719
Fernández-Montesinos, Manuel 383
Fernández Retamar, Roberto 550
Ferrari, Mirella 41
Ferrerio, Luisa Alpago-Novello 244
Ferrero, Mauro 549
Fetzer, James 2899
Feuillet, Jack 464
Fex, S. 1012
Fichte, Jörg 2797
Fidjestøl, Bjarne 1742
Fido, F. 3225
Fiedler, Leonhard M. 1196
Fieguth, R. 2504
Fieguth, Rolf 2574
Fields, Albert W. 978, 980
Fietz, Lothar 2797
Fife, James 1370
Filesi, Teobaldo 43
Filewod, Alan 538
Filinich Oregui, Maria Isabel 1891
Finan, Martha 1507
Finch, Roger 2998
Findeisen, Helmut 3250
Fink, Gonthier-Louis 2323
Finke, Wayne 1918
Finneran, Richard J. 3231
Firbas, Jan 415
Fischer, Steven Roger 2495
Fisette, Jean 2325
Fishburn, Katherine 810

Fisher, Benjamin Franklin, IV 3080
Fishman, Joshua A. 1270
Fisiak, Jacek 2112, 2765, 3088
Fisković, Igor 1877
Fitch, Brian T. 2944
Fitch, Donald E. 2670
FitzGerald, Mary 3231
Fitzpatrick, Frank 859
Flamini, Michael J. 118-127
Flannagan, Roy C. 1837
Flasche, Hans 284, 2489
Flashar, Hellmut 2190
Fleischer, Wolfgang 758
Fleischman, Suzanne 2478
Fleishman, Lazar 2726
Fleming, Anne 457
Fleming, Jim 2582
Fleming, Robert E. 102
Flemming, B. 168
Fletcher, Lea 993
Fletcher, Pauline 421
Flier, Michael S. 1159
Flobert, P. 2409
Flower, J. E. 1393
Flynn, Elizabeth A. 2312
Fogarty, Robert S. 215
Fogel, Daniel Mark 1174
Fokkema, Douwe W. 3097
Folena, Gianfranco 390, 1800
Foley, John Miles 75, 2075
Folkerts, Jean 1486
Follieri, Enrica 2457
Folsom, William 3157
Foltinek, H. 3178
Foltinek, Herbert 2711
Foltz, David A. 1183
Fontaine, Jean 1222
Fontanella, Luigi 1129
Fontanille, J. 2025
Forbes, Peter 2194
Ford, C. 819
Ford, Patrick 3072
Forero, Manuel-José 380
Foresti, Carlos 164
Foresti, Fabio 2459
Foretić, Dinko 3241
Forkner, Ben 1477
Forrest, David V. 2717
Forseth, Roger 793
Forsgren, Mats 30
Forster, Leonard W. 587, 750, 1094
Fortescue, Michael 17
Fortunati, Vita 2274
Fortune, Nigel 1909
Foster, Edward 2907
Foster, Hal 2050
Foster, Morris 97
Fotheringham, Richard 294
Fowke, Edith 523
Fowler, Frank M. 2263
Fowler, Raymond D. 108
Fowler, William M., Jr. 1956
Fox, Geoff 581
Fox, Jay 1696
Fox, Michael V. 1163
Fox, Thomas C. 1079
Fraenkel, Eran 2578
Fraiman, Susan 706
Francescato, G. 1231
Franceschetti, Antonio 2278
Francis, R. A. 2023
Franić, Ante 3241
Frank, Armin P. 2106
Frank, Robert W., Jr. 572
Frank, Tibor 2820
Franklin, A. J. 1392
Franklin, Benjamin, V 2821
Franklin, Phyllis 2246
Fraser, Howard M. 571
Freccero, John 2724
Freedle, Roy O. 797
Freeman, H. 992
Freeman, John 1994
Freihow, Halfdan W. 3134
Frenk, Margit 1693
Fretheim, Thorstein 1998
Freudenberg, Rudolf 3257

Frick, Werner 2713
Fricker, Robert 2550
Frideres, James 521
Friebert, Stuart 996
Friedman, Norman 2717
Friedrichmeyer, Sara 3201
Friese, Wilhelm 2629
Frigeri, Pier Riccardo 559
Frink, Orrin 2045
Frisch, Michael 2074
Frith, Simon 2562
Fritze, Ronald H. 1547
Froeschle, Hartmut 1093
Fromm, Hans 329, 1176, 1329
Frommann, Anne 1945
Fruchtman, Maya 1162
Frühwald, Wolfgang 290, 1274, 2792
Fuchs, Reimar W. 2158
Fuente, Ricardo de la 552
Fuhrmann, Horst 766
Fultz, Lucille 2518
Füssel, Stephan 1132
Gabarrós Cardona, Ramón 213, 2879
Gabba, Emilio 277
Gächter, Othmar 212
Gadler, Hanspeter 1134
Gadow, H. von 331
Gaier, Ulrich 1197
Gaines, Barry 2601
Gaines, Nora 1338
Gajek, Bernhard 2331
Galdon, Joseph A., S.J. 2157
Gale, Steven H. 2177
Galindo, Martívon 1734
Galisson, Robert 948
Gallarques, Dominique 475
Galliou, P. 943
Galloway, Margaret E. 1450
Gamkrelidze, T. V. 3147
Gandelman, Claude 275
Ganelin, Charles 2462
Ganesh, Kamala 1452
Ganuz, Itzchak 3234
Garand, M. 2567
Garcia, E. C. 1636
García de la Concha, Víctor 1258
García de la Fuente, Olegario 157
García Lorca, Isabel 383
García Lorenzo, Luciano 724
García-Pérez, Juan 2309
Gardaphè, Fred L. 3122
Garfagnini, Gian Carlo 2445
Garin, Eugenio 1113
Garrido-Gallardo, Miguel A. 2386
Garsoïan, N. A. 2412
Garton, Janet 2541
Garver, Eugene 2440
Garza, Mercedes de la 564
Garza Cuarón, Beatriz 2036
Gasque, Thomas J. 1918
Gassen, Heiner 594
Gassman Robert 268
Gast, Wolfgang 1791
Gatz, Erwin 2494
Gaudard, François-Charles 569
Gaudino, James L. 643, 2284
Gauger, Hans-Martin 1221
Gaugler, Nancy K. 2141
Gaull, Marilyn 3206
Gauss, Karl-Markus 1686
Gautreaux, Tim 1731
Gawinski, Teresa 3189
Gay-Crosier, Raymond 3076
Gazda, Grzegorz 3242
Geary, Patrick 974
Gebhardt, Richard C. 626
Geckeler, Horst 1221
Geen, Russell G. 1430
Geeraerts, Dirk 618
Geerts, G. 1618
Geh, Hans-Peter 1631
Geltman, Nancy Lenihan 977
Gelzer, Thomas 1907
Genot, Gérard 807
Geoffroy, Alain 85
Georgakas, Dan 598
Georghallides, G. S. 883

Georgiev, Marin 1707
Geraldi, João Wanderley 926
Gerhardt, L. 60
Gerhardt, Tom C. 2705
Gerke, Robert 454
German, Norman 1731
Gernet, Jacques 2991
Gerow, Edwin 1448
Gerritsen, Marinel 2989
Gerritsen, W. P. 1986
Gervais, D. C. 510
Gessel, Michael 320
Ghazoul, Ferial 81
Ghinassi, Ghino 1639
Giacomelli, Roberto 282
Giannantonio, Pompeo 692
Giarrizzo, Giuseppe 387
Gibaldi, Joseph 2577
Gibbons, Reginald 3022
Gidion, Jürgen 1945
Giedroyc, Jerzy 1537
Giesecke, Hermann 1945
Gignoux, Philippe 2776
Gilbar, Gad G. 264
Gilbert, Glenn G. 1434
Gildin, Hilail 1276
Giles, Richard F. 1200
Gill, H. S. 1476
Gill, Stephen 2093
Gillen, Francis X. 2177
Gillespie, G. 1094
Gillespie, Patti P. 2962
Gimaret, Daniel 1347
Giorcelli, Cristina 1610
Giordano, Alfonso 1297-1298, 2348
Giordano, Mario Gabriele 2447
Giordano, Paolo A. 3122
Giovannini, Adalberto 1907
Giraud, Yves 631
Girault, Claude 489
Girdenis, Aleksas 1492
Girdzijauskas, J. 1688
Givner, Joan 3159
Givón, T. 3050
Glenberg, Arthur M. 1396
Glienke, Bernhard 2629
Glinka, Luis 219
Gmoser, Gerda 1327
Gneuss, Helmut 173, 419, 2528
Gnisci, Armando 1073, 2275
Godard, Barbara 2933
Godden, Malcolm 180
Godoy, Eduardo 2397
Godzich, Wlad 1120, 2966
Goebel-Schilling, Gerhard 1311
Goetsch, Paul 1946
Goetz, Thomas H. 1988
Goffin, Rona 2345
Goheen, J. 542
Gojković, Drinka 1893
Goldberg, David 39
Goldberg, Florinda F. 1993
Goldberg, Itshe 3237
Goldberg, S. L. 703
Goldblatt, Howard 1866
Goldman, Liela 2534
Goldschmidt, M. R. 553
Goldstein, Laurence 1825
Goldstine, Herman H. 1809, 2240
Golisano, C. F. 283
Göller, Karl Heinz 2710
Golsan, Richard 2678
Gómez, Assia 2446
Gómez-Martínez, José Luis 878
Gómez-Soliño, José S. 280
Gontarski, S. E. 1365
Gonzalez, Andrew B. 2154
González-del-Valle, Luis T. 161, 2613
González Mendoza, Juan R. 2398
Goodacre, Selwyn H. 1318
Gooder, R. D. 510
GoodKnight, Glen H. 1915
Goodman, Howard L. 263
Goodridge, John 1344
Goossens, Jan 1984
Gorcy, Gérard 2406
Gordon, J. Janet 1882

Gordon, Sarah 1006
Göres, Jörn 1326
Görlach, Manfred 877, 1832, 3102
Görner, Herbert 2712
Gorsse, Odette 709
Göschel, Joachim 3257
Gosselin, Monique 2472
Gottas, Friedrich 2872
Gottesman, Ronald 1275
Gottlieb, Sidney 1087, 2514
Gouanvic, Jean-Marc 3031
Goudaillier, Jean-Pierre 1660
Gouiran, Gérard 2418
Gould, R. 542
Gould, Warwick 3232
Gowda, Anniah 1676
Gowen, William R. 1981
Goyvaerts, D. L. 2858
Grabbi, Hellar 1762
Gräbe, Ina 1415
Grabe, William 206
Grabes, Herbert 2317
Grabowicz, George G. 1159
Grace, George W. 2049
Graciotti, S. 2442
Graevenitz, Gerhart 765
Graffy, J. 2647
Graham, Ruth 198
Graham-Yooll, Andrew 1233
Gramstad, Borghild 2897
Grande, Félix 725
Granderoute, Robert 803
Granger, Michel 2425
Granoff, Phillis 1402
Grass, Günter 1943
Grassegger, Hans 1134
Graubard, Stephen R. 742
Graur, Al. 1635, 2233
Gray, Beryl 1086
Gray, Donald 3131
Gray, Douglas 2093
Gray, Floyd 1826
Grayson, C. 2096
Greaves, D. 2965
Green, James N. 2302
Green, Judith 2316
Green, Martin 1678
Green, William Scott 1447
Greenblatt, Stephen 1962, 2350
Greene, Liliane 3216
Greenfield, Cathy 2687
Greenland, Colin 1040
Greensmith, Bill 372
Greenspahn, Frederick E. 1163
Greenwald, Melissa J. 2142
Greer, Robert O., Jr. 1178
Greetham, D. C. 2938
Gregoire, Cl. 57
Gregorovich, Andrew 1033
Gregory, Eileen 1144
Gregory, Tullio 2029
Greppin, John A. C. 203, 2297
Gresenegger, Wolfgang 1774
Gresset, Michel 991
Grewendorf, Günther 1663
Grezsa, F. 24
Grieshofer, Franz 2090
Griffin, Daniel J. 1155
Griffiths, Jeremy 870
Grigsby, Lucy C. 2176
Grimal, Pierre 2417
Grimes, Ronald L. 1440
Grimm, Hannelore 2709
Grimm, Jürgen 5
Grimm, Reinhold 1095
Grimm, Reinhold R. 1839
Grindea, Miron 37
Grip, Johann 3098
Gritsopoulos, Tassos 1861
Groen, B. M. 2848
Groenke, Ulrich 2629
Gronbeck-Tedesco, John 1384
Gross, Ann 3186
Gross, Maurice 1664-1665
Grosse, Rudolf 758
Grosse, Siegfried 762, 2528
Grossi, V. 286

Grothusen, Klaus-Detlev 3253
Grover, Dorys C. 1494
Grübel, R. G. 2849
Gruber, Loren C. 1229
Grubmüller, Klaus 329, 1028
Grue, Lee Meitzen 1964
Gruenter, Rainer 325
Gruffydd, R. Geraint 3001
Grundmann, Roy 598
Grygar, M. 2504
Guarino, Guido 1306
Guback, Denise 648
Guédon, Jean-Claude 2881
Guenther, Mathias G. 209
Gueritz, M. E. 1283
Guesnier, Jean-François 231
Guesnier, Zoé 231
Guggisberg, Hans R. 238
Guildenhuys, F. 875
Guiliano, Edward 780
Guiora, A. Z. 1569
Guiraud, Pierre 1251
Gully, Anthony Lacy 2828
Gumperz, John J. 2829
Gunda, Béla 15
Günther, Joachim 1942
Gupta, Anil 1431
Gupta, G. S. Balarama 1403
Gupta, Rameshwar 316
Gura, Philip F. 823
Gurr, A. J. 1873, 3224
Gusmani, R. 1231
Gustaveson, Valerie 2890
Gustavsson, Sven R. 32
Gut, M. 1056
Gutiérrez, Franklin 76
Gutiérrez, Jesús 786
Gutiérrez Girardot, Rafael 1187
Gutknecht, Christoph 178, 1039
Gutsche, George 2641
Gutschmidt, K. 339
Gutschmidt, Karl 3265
Güttgemanns, Erhardt 1648
Guttilla, Giuseppe 189
Guy-Sheftall, Beverly 2518
Guyovarc'h, Christian J. 2055
Guyton, Juanita 1848
Gyr, Ueli 2552
Haan, G. J. de 3095
Haas, Alois 2798
Haas, Walter 2172
Haavaldsen, Ellen 1785
Haberland, Eike 2102
Haberland, Hartmut 1437, 2471
Habicht, Werner 761
Hackens, T. 218
Hacker, Marilyn 1507
Hacksley, M. M. 716
Hadas-Lebel, Mireille 3238
Haddad, Lahen 599
Haddad, Wadi' Z. 1911
Hadidi, J. 1754
Hadravivá-Dohnalová, Alena 1669
Haen, Theo D' 2209
Haensch, Günther 1589
Haes, F. de 685
Haeseryn, René 309
Hagen, A. 1787
Hagen, Alf van der 3098
Hagerup, Henning 3098
Haghebaert, Elisabeth 2911
Hahn, Walther von 2708
Hähnel, Klaus-Dieter 3259
Haider, Siegfried 1029
Hajdú, Péter 2041
Hajičová, Eva 2217
Hajko, Dalimir 2650
Hak, Tony 2665
Hakanen, Aimo 2532
Halder, Alois 2165
Hall, Dennis R. 2840
Hall, John F. 609
Hall, Judith A. 1428
Hallberg, Göran 2894
Halm, Heinz 3166
Halpert, Inge D. 1098

Halsey, Martha T. 916
Hamacher, Werner 1859
Hamaguchi, Osamu 591
Hamers, Marlene 2191
Hamilton, D. J. 2560
Hamilton, David 1280
Hamlin, Frank 2067
Hammond, Alexander 2187
Hammond, Brean 411
Hammond-Tooke, W. D. 52
Hamp, Eric P. 1263
Hampson, Robert 664
Handley, Graham 1086
Hanley, Keith 1987
Hanley, Susan 1407
Hansen, Juliane 2580
Hansen, Miriam 1959
Hansen, Niels Bugge 172
Hansen-Löve, Aage 3181
Hanson, Philip 530
Häntzschel, Günter 1160
Harbert, Wayne 678
Härd, John Evert 29
Harder, Peter 172
Hardin, James 1016, 2826, 3065
Hardy, Donald E. 2689
Hardy, Heather K. 2689
Hareide, Jorunn 831
Harkins, Conrad L., O.F.M. 1047
Härle, Gerhard 1036
Harlow, Benjamin C. 1783
Harlow, Ray 2915
Harms, Wolfgang 1903
Harnett, Gerald 1170
Harootunian, Harry 700
Harrington, Evans 2264
Harris, Edward P. 842
Harris, Martin 2475
Harris, Michael 1427
Harris, Roy 1554
Harsh, Constance 2210
Hart, Patrick 1815
Hart, Thomas R. 651
Hartigan, Karelisa V. 2941
Hartley, Robert A. 1501
Hartmann, Carl T. 1981
Hartmann, R. R. K. 975
Hartmann, Reinhard R. K. 1621
Hartmann, Stefan 3262
Hartwell, David G. 1976
Hartwig, Joan 2603
Harvey, Sally 216
Harvey, Warren Z. 2912
Hashim, S. R. 1467
Haskell, Dennis 3169
Haskell, Guy H. 1339
Hasker, William 588
Hasler, Jörg 3020
Hassán, Iacob M. 923
Hassler, Donald M. 981
Hatch, Martin 266
Hatlen, Burton 2519
Haubrichs, Wolfgang 1634
Haubst, Rudolf 1856
Haug, Walter 765, 1031
Hauge, Kjetil Rå 1785
Haule, James M. 1722
Häulică, Dan 2571
Hauptfleisch, Temple 2596, 2673
Hauser, Gerard A. 2168
Hausmann, Frank-Rutger 5
Hausmann, Franz Josef 1621
Have, Paul ten 3032
Havercroft, Barbara 2325
Haverkate, Henk 777
Hawkes, Terence 1952, 2950
Hay, Carla H. 2819
Hayashi, Tetsumaro 2729-2730
Hayes, John B. 352
Hays, William 1847
Haywood, Carl 3005
Hazael-Massieux, Marie-Christine 945
He, Jingzhi 584
Heale, Michael 1358
Healey, John F. 1442
Heath, Mary 1775
Hébert, François 1625

Heckel, Ilsa 921
Hed, Sven Åke 30
Heestermans, J. L. A. 2979
Heftrich, Eckhard 1713, 1985, 2972
Hegde, K. T. M. 1467
Hegel, Robert E. 585
Heger, Hedwig 3177
Heiduk, Franz 290-291
Heikkinen, Kaija 930
Heil, John 2162
Heilingsetzer, Georg 1029
Heine, Bernd 2707
Heinemann, Henri 438
Heintze, Beatrix 2102
Heinzmann, Richard 3111
Heirwegh, Jean-Jacques 2401
Heitmann, Friedrich 2549
Heitmann, Klaus 234
Helbig, Gerhard 757
Helbo, André 754
Helgesen, Anne 169
Hellriegel, Günter 3192
Hellstrom, Louise S. 3127
Hellstrom, Ward 3127
Helsinger, Elizabeth 700
Hemmer, Bjørn 667
Hempel, Wido 2487
Hempfer, Klaus W. 3258
Hench, John B. 2239
Henderson, Heather 779
Hendrickx, F. 2070
Henn, D. F. 1873
Henne, Helmut 2334, 3260
Henry, DeWitt 2181
Henry, Freeman G. 1060
Henry, Patrick 2166
Henry, Peter 2559
Hentig, Hartmut V. 1945
Hentzi, Gary 706
Herault, Georges 1661
Hergenhan, L. T. 301
Herget, Winfried 1753
Heringer, Hans Jürgen 1662
Herity, Michael 1474
Hermans, T. 819
Hermodsson, Lars 2786
Hernández, Mario 383
Hernández Viveros, Raúl 2104
Hernas, Czesław 1692, 2790
Herslund, Michael 2432
Hertz, Uri 2969
Herz, Julius M. 1465
Herzberger, David 2613
Hess-Lüttich, Ernest W. B. 1523
Hesse, Eva 2101
Hester, M. Thomas 1345
Hettrich, Heinrich 1904
Hetzler, Leo 573
Hetzron, Robert 1355
Hewitt, D. 2016
Hewitt, N. 2023
Heydebrand, Renate von 1903
Heyvaert, Stef 2358
Heyward, Mic 2564
Heywood, C. M. 2339
Hibbett, Howard S. 1154
Hickey, Joseph V. 1175
Hicks, Eric 947
Hietsch, Otto 2710
Higdon, David Leon 665
Higgins, I. R. W. 1035
Higgins, James 1721
Higgins, John 2224
Higgins, Orlie 1263
Higgins, Sue 1698
Hiiemäe, M. 2098
Hildebrandt, Reiner 760
Hildebrandt, W. 763
Hilfer, Anthony 2937
Hill, Cason L. 628
Hill, Joyce 816, 1592
Hill, Leslie 2129
Hill, Ordelle G. 1797
Hill, Ronald 1289
Hill, W. Speed 2938
Hillery, D. 817
Hillmann, Michael C. 1705

Hilpinen, Risto 2899
Hindley, Alan 1063
Hinds, Harold E., Jr. 2833
Hintikka, Jaakko 2899
Hinüber, Oskar von 2799
Hinz, Evelyn J. 1892
Hirsch, David H. 1874
Hirschheydt, Harro V. 314
Hiura, Barbara L. 979
Hjorth, Poul Lindegård 1525
Hladký, Josef 415
Hlavsa, Zdeněk 2656
Hoberg, Hermann 2494
Hoberg, Rudolf 1912
Hobson, Fred 2684
Hochstedler, Carol 1453
Hock, Hans Henrich 2855
Hoctor, Marion A. 556
Hodges, Carolyn R. 647
Hödl, Ludwig 330
Hödnebö, Tone 3098
Hoek Ostende, J. H. van den 144
Hoekstra, T. 1636
Hoel, Cecilie Schram 3098
Hof, Renate 130
Höfele, Andreas 2963
Hoff, Linda Kay 2603
Hoffer, Bates L. 1561
Hoffman, Lothar 986
Hoffmann, Gerhard 130-131
Hofmann, Dietrich 2629
Hogan, Joseph 2
Hogan, Rebecca 2
Hogan, Robert 1406
Hoge, James O. 2361
Hogg, James 155, 2522-2526
Högström, Åke 2887
Hohendahl, Peter U. 1959
Holbek, Bengt 1015
Holden, Alan W. 1207
Holk, A. G. F. van 2506, 2849
Höllerer, Walter 2704
Hollier, Denis 2050
Hollinger, Veronica 2555
Hollis, A. S. 610
Hollis, Burney J. 1779
Holmes, Glyn 656
Holmgaard, Jørgen 1512
Holst, Gunther 2826
Holthof, Jean-François 602
Holy, John A. 2648
Holyoak, Keith J. 621
Hölz, Karl 3020
Holzapfel, Otto 1333
Holzner, Johann 1254
Hong, Yunsook 1390
Honko, Lauri 1003, 1019, 2922
Hopper, John 135, 137-138, 140-143
Hörandner, Wolfram 1324
Horemans, Rudi 2358
Horne, Merle 2779
Horner, Bruce 1279
Horner, David 1048
Hornung, Alfred 130-131
Horton, Laurel 3062
Horton, Thomas B. 1672
Horvath, Barbara 300
Hösch, Edgar 2871
Hosey, Brenda 2115
Höskuldsson, Sveinn Skorri 2778
Hospers, Johannes Hendrik 3249
Hoste, Uitg J. 3144
Hostetter, Carl F. 3135
Houppermans, Sjef 992
Hövelmann, Hartmut 1739
Howard, Jean 2950
Howard, Patricia 1867
Howard, Rhoda 525
Howard, Richard 3172
Hruby, Karel 2247
Hruška, Blahoslav 239
Huang, C.-T. James 1386
Hubbard, Sally 2575
Huddleston, R. 516
Hudgens, Brenda 2180
Hudry, Françoise 241
Hughes, G. I. 874

Hughes, Gillian H. 2827
Hughes, L. A. J. 2647
Hugo, F. 2965
Huldén, Lars 2633-2634
Hulst, Harry van der 1645
Humbeeck, Kris 2358
Humfrey, Belinda 2211
Hummer, T. R. 1957
Humphrey, Rita S. 2814
Humphrey, Theodore C. 3171
Humphreys, Paul 2899
Hundsnurscher, Franz 1126, 2866
Hung, Eva 2349
Hunger, Herbert 1324
Hüning, Matthias 1034
Hunt, John Dixon 3204
Hunter, Bruce 530
Huntsman, J. 1471
Huré, Jacques 488
Hurka, Thomas 530
Hussey, Mark 3138
Hutchins, Catherine E. 3189
Hutner, Gordon 101
Huttenbach, Henry R. 1930
Hüttl-Folter, G. 3180
Huyssen, Andreas 1959
Hyams, P. J. E. 1940
Hyldgaard-Jensen, Karl 1528
Iartseva, V. N. 1315
Ickstadt, Heinz 130
Ide, Hiroyuki 2825
Idol, John L., Jr. 1928
Igarashi, Yukio 2985
Ignatieva, Natalia 921
Ihwe, Jens 2125
IJsewijn, Jozef 1211
Ikegami, Tadahiro 2835
Ikin, Van 2554
Ilievski, Petar Hr. 3270
Ilomäki, Henni 2768-2770
Ilson, Robert 1266
Imbach, R. 1056
Imerslund, Hege 3098
Ineichen, Gustav 2488
Ingen, Ferdinand van 587, 750
Ingram, Douglas H. 99
Innes, Christopher 1867
Intons-Peterson, Margaret Jean 1812
Ioannides, George Con. 2727
Irele, Abiola 2353
Irgang, Winfried 3262
Irimia, D. 159
Isebaert, L. 944
Isella, Dante 2738
Isern, Tom 855
Isernhagen, Hartwig 2317
Ishii, Hisao 1504
Itkonen, Erkki 1003
Iturrioz Leza, José Luis 1069
Ivanchev, Sv. 422
Ivanov, Anatoliĭ 1878
Ivanova, K. 422
Ivașcu, George 2482
Iversen, Jon 3239
Ives, Edward D. 2010
Ivić, Milka 1489
Ivie, Robert L. 2284
Iwara, A. U. 1043
Izu, Yamato 591
Jackowski, Aleksander 2199
Jackson, Dennis 739
Jackson, Russell 2959
Jacobi, Klaus 2165
Jacobs, M. 2096
Jacobsen, Elin Súsanna 1065
Jacobson, Kristoffer 3172
Jacobus, Lee A. 1670
Jacoebée, W. Pierre 753
Jacques, Georges 1615
Jäger, Dietrich 1684
Jäger, Georg 1274, 2792
Jaggar, Philip J. 49
Jahn, Gary R. 2641
Jahr, Ernst Håkon 1264, 2000-2001
Jain, Jasbir 2300
Jakubowski, J. Z. 2254
James, Edward 1040

James, Ellen 3219
Jammes, Robert 709
Janakiram, A. 2300
Janaszek-Ivaničkova, Halina 2109
Janhunen, Juha 2876
Janik, Allan 408
Jankhandi, Sudhakar Ratnakar 640
Janney, Richard W. 1437
Janota, Johannes 1100
Janssen, L. F. 1860
Janssen, W. 2436
Janssens, Marcel 787
Jara, René 972
Jareb, Jerome 1380
Jasiewicz, Zbigniew 1735
Jaskoski, Helen 2810
Jasper, David 1704
Jastrow, Otto 3251
Jauralde Pou, Pablo 830
Jay, Mary 48
Jeffery, Keith 1288
Jelsma, G. H. 1299
Jemjemian, Sahak 2400
Jenckes, Norma 96
Jenkins, Fred 1061
Jenkins, Paul 1775
Jenni, Ernst 3249
Jensen, Bent 2644
Jensen, Jens 1512
Jensen, John T. 493
Jensen, Minna Skafte 2802
Jensen, Peter Alberg 2735
Jeon, Hong-Shil 1459
Jeon, Jo-Yong 1459
Jeremić, Dragan M. 1519
Jerger, Susan 822
Jernakoff, Nadja 3245
Jersild, Devon 1957
Jessen, Karsten 292
Jessing, Benedict 373
Jinzaki, Katsuhiro 591
Joensen, Jóan Pauli 1065
Joeres, Ruth-Ellen 2616
Jog, K. P. 1452
Johns, Jorun B. 1865, 2812
Johnson, Anthony 166
Johnson, Christopher 2129
Johnson, Hershel C. 2823
Johnson, J. Theodore, Jr. 2252
Johnson, R. 2009
Johnstone, Henry W., Jr. 2168
Joly, André 1862
Jonasson, Kerstin 2803
Jones, Anne Hudson 1702
Jones, Ben 2210
Jones, Buford 2603
Jones, Catherine 2064
Jones, Eldred Durosimi 50
Jones, Emily 2093
Jones, Howard J. 1137
Jones, Malcolm 517
Jones, Marjorie 50
Jones, Michael 2024
Jong, J. W. de 1242
Jonsson, Bengt R. 2873
Jørgensen, Charlotte 1716
Jørgensen, Sven-Aage 2942
Joris, A. 1897
Joseph, Brian D. 771
Joshi, R. Malatesha 2313
Joshi, S. T. 1732, 2860
Joswick, Thomas P. 912
Jucquois, Guy 474
Juhasz, Suzanne 854
Julseth, David 740
Junghans, Helmar 1740
Jurgensen, Manfred 2287
Jurt, Joseph 1839
Kachanian-Toutenu, Mireille 488
Kachru, Braj B. 3211
Kadare, Ismail 1613
Kadir, Djelal 2613, 3212
Kadt, R. de 2965
Kafitz, Dieter 2796
Kahin, Audrey 1244
Kähler-Meyer, E. 60
Kaiser, Gerhard 1682

Kaiser, Gert 1028
Kaisse, Ellen M. 2175
Kalinka, L. 1587
Kalinke, Marianne 1389
Kallendorf, Craig 87
Kalmre, E. 2098
Kalus, L. 2415
Kamenetskaya, N. P. 1255
Kamil, Michael L. 2316
Kammenhuber, A. 2945
Kanceff, Emanuele 2749
Kandji, Mamadou 409
Kangro, Bernard 3034
Kapera, Zdzisław 1011
Kaphagawani, Didier N. 1401
Kaplan, Fred 780
Kaplan, Lena Biörck 2539
Kaplan, Morton 1703
Kaplan, Robert B. 206
Kaplan, Y. 2912
Kapp, Volker 1713
Karahasan, Dževad 1314
Karaliūnas, S. 1633
Karatson, André 2472
Kardong, Terrence 94
Károly, S. 26
Karpova, L. A. 1666
Kashkarov, Yuri 2032
Kaske, R. E. 2994
Käsmann, Hans 173, 419
Kassabian, Anahid 2723
Kassai, Georges 672
Kastovsky, Dieter 1010
Katičić, R. 3180
Katičić, Radoslav 1340
Katz-Roy, Ginette 955
Katzman, David 113
Kaunas, Domas 1522
Kavolis, Vytautas 648, 1820
Kawamura, Katsumi 946
Kaye, Alan 1355
Kaye, Frances W. 1135
Kaye, Jonathan 1645
Kaylor, Noel H., Jr. 546
Kazancigil, Ali 1273
Kedar-Kopfstein, Benjamin 3249
Keenum, Katherine 1152
Keipert, Helmut 3264
Keith, Philip 2440
Keller, Gary D. 360
Keller, Hagen 1067
Keller, Janet Dixon 93
Keller, John E. 448, 2843
Keller, Werner 1123
Kellermann, Kathy 1410
Kellett, Arnold 3006
Kelley, Charles Greg 1020
Kelley, Donald R. 1463
Kelly, Douglas 424
Kelly, Michael 1432
Kelly, Veronica 294
Kelly, W. A. 354
Kemp, Sandra 2562
Kempton, Adrian 1048
Kendall, Martha B. 210
Kenneally, Michael 2822
Kennedy, Anne 1548
Kennedy, Elspeth 1802
Kennedy, Judy 1438
Kenner, Hugh 2101
Kent, Raymond D. 2850
Kerdchouay, Euayporn 1478
Kerler, Yosyef 3235
Kern, Rudolf 1104
Kerr, David A. 1911
Keserü, B. 24
Kestner, Joseph 3133
Kettemann, Bernhard 229
Ketterman, Kathleen 1980
Kettle-Williams, J. L. 1641
Kettler, Robert R. 2063
Keyishian, Harry 1678
Keynes, Simon 180, 512
Keyser, Elizabeth 579
Keyser, Samuel Jay 735, 1644
Khattab, Ezzat A. 1408
Kibbey, Ann 1080

Kibler, Louis 1310
Kiefer, Ferenc 89
Kielhöfer, Bernd 2488
Killheffer, Robert K. J. 1976
Killy, Walther 2106
Kim, Seong-Jong 1459
Kim, Wook-Dong 1390
Kimber, Richard T. 1383
Kimble, David 1420
Kimura, Naoji 2667
Kinder, Rose Marie 2180
Kindstrand, J. F. 891
King, John N. 1698
King, Katherine C. 3124
King, Kimball 2684
King, Norman 498, 2562
King, R. S. 2023
King-Farlow, John 530
Kingdon, Robert M. 2628
Kingsbury, Paul 1379
Kingstone, Basil D. 529
Kinney, Arthur F. 866
Kinsella, Valerie 1574
Kintsch, Walter 2258
Kipel, Vitaŭt 3246
Kippenberg, Hans. G. 2038
Kirby, D. 2647
Kirk, Gerald A. 2857
Kirkpatrick, Gwen 1278
Kirsop, Wallace 299
Kiser, Lisa J. 2851
Kitroeff, Alexander 1462
Kjær, Iver 748
Kjonegaard, Vernon 1971
Klaus, Väino 1652
Klee, Carol A. 1184
Kleiber, Georges 3011
Klein, Holger 1953
Klein, Jeremy 927
Klein, Richard 772
Klein, Wolfgang 1634, 1654
Kleinewillinghöfer, Ulrich 1052
Kleinfeld, Gerald R. 1096
Kleinhenz, Christopher 749
Kleinschmidt, Sebastian 2622
Kliche, Karla 3162
Klijn, A. F. J. 3132
Klimas, Antanas 1720
Klimoff, Alexis 3245
Klingenschmitt, Gert 2799
Klinkowitz, Jerome 715
Kloek, Joost 3097
Klopfenstein, Eduard 268
Klöpsch, Volker 1165
Klotz, Günther 2597
Kluxen, Wolfgang 330
Knape, Joachim 1132
Knapp, Gerhard P. 3096
Knapp, Mona 810
Knapp, Peggy A. 270
Knapp, Susan 2258
Knappová, Miloslava 2068
Knecht, Peter 265
Kneepkens, C. H. 3143
Knight, D. M. 2023
Knight, Jesse F. 2492
Knoop, Ulrich 1103
Knowles, Owen 664
Kocevski, Danilo 2308
Koch, David V. 1223
Koch, Rainer 2153
Kochev, Iv. 422
Kočiš, František 2651
Kocourek, Rostislav 78, 1250
Koerner, E. F. Konrad 145-149, 771, 1189
Koestenbaum, Wayne 3217
Koester, Helmut 1158
Kohl, Stephan 176
Köhler, Erich 1100
Kohler, Klaus 2173
Köhler, Reinard 2283
Kohli, Devindra 1238
Kohli, Suresh 1238
Kohlschmidt, W. 2706
Kohrt, Manfred 2920
Kohsakra, Junichi 445
Kohut, Zenon 1483

Koike, Masao 3084
Kok, Christien 2366
Kókay, György 1748
Kokkinos, Demosthenes 881
Kokla, Paul 1652
Kolb, Robert A. 2628
Kolin, Philip C. 2807
Kolsky, S. 2719
Koltai, Tamás 2903
Kom, Ambroise 185
Komlovszki, Tibor 1294
Kondis, B. 312
Kondratenko, Viktor 2296
König, B. 2489
Konstantinov, Gueozgui 2178
Kooiman, Dirk Ayelt 2366
Kooper, Erik 682
Koopman, W. F. 1940
Koopmann, Helmut 290-291, 2800
Kopecký, Milan 2538
Köpeczi, Béla 1169
Köppe, Walter 16
Koppel, Gene 2152
Kopper, Edward A., Jr. 2020
Koppitz, H.-J. 1142
Kordić, Snježana 2883
Korff, Gottfried 3266
Kornelius, Joachim 176
Körner, Karl-Hermann 284
Korninger, Siegfried 3178
Korper, Phyllis 1077
Korshin, Paul J. 64
Korzen, Hanne 2432
Korzeniewski, Bohdan 2110
Kos, Janko 1530, 1671
Kośny, Witold 3265
Kosok, Heinz 973
Kossick, S. G. 3067
Kostink, O. H. 1920
Kotby, N. 1012
Kötting, Bernhard 2494
Kottje, Raymund 392
Koundoura, Maria 2723
Kovač, Zvonko 1877
Kovacs, L. 464
Kozicki, Henry 613
Kozodoy, Neal 637
Krafft, John M. 2271
Kraggerud, Egil 2895
Krailsheimer, A. J. 2096
Kramer, Dale 1389
Kramer, Dewey Weiss 1815
Kramer, Hilton 1954
Kramer, Victor A. 1092, 1815
Kranes, David 3172
Kranz, Gisbert 1252
Kranze, Enrique 3152
Krappmann, Lothar 1945
Krasić, Stjepan 171
Kratz, Bernd 630
Kraus, Jiří 1924
Krauss, Rosalind 2050
Krenn, Heliéna 1068
Kresten, Otto 2493
Kretschmer, Doris 1962
Kretzschmar, William A., Jr. 1391
Kreutzer, Gert 2629
Kreuzer, Helmut 1634, 2335
Krings, Hermann 2165
Krishnamurti, G. 1457
Krnjevic, Vuk 1520
Kroch, Anthony 1576
Krodel, Gottfried G. 238
Krollmann, Friedrich 1589
Kromann, Hans-Peder 1621
Kronholm, Tryggve 31
Krueger, John R. 1881
Krüger, Michael 71
Krummacher, Hans-Henrik 1941
Krummel, Richard F. 1097
Kruse, Horst 1684
Kruse, Joseph A. 1168
Kruse, Margot 1148, 2489
Kryssing-Berg, Ginette 2432
Kučera, Antonín 1620
Kucich, Greg 1987
Kudravets, A. P. 1935

Kuenzli, Rudolf E. 741, 1469
Kufner, Herbert L. 2714
Kuhlen, Rainer 2708
Kühlmann, Wilhelm 587, 750
Kuhn, Annette 2562
Kuhn, D. 1209
Kühnelt, H. 3178
Kuijper, Jan 2366
Kulavig, Erik 2884
Kulenović, Tvrtko 399
Kulik, Gary 109
Kulin, Katalin 19
Kullman, Colby H. 2807
Kumar, Suresh 1237
Kuna, K. M. 1393
Kuniaev, S. Iu. 1925
Kunstmann, Heinrich 3164
Künzel, Franz Peter 2870
Kuo, Po-wen 3030
Kuper, Adam J. 733
Kupersmith, William 2159
Kuris, Gary 1077
Kurk, Katherine C. 1505
Kuroda, S.-Y. 1386
Kurzová, Helena 1669
Kuschert, Rolf 1997
Kusko, K. Ja. 1256
Kuykendall, Peter V. 371
Kvideland, Reimund 2993
La Charité, Raymond C. 1058-1059
La Charité, Virginia A. 1058-1059
La Liberté, Patrice 2473
La Penna, Antonio 1752
Laaksonen, Pekka 1493
Labarbe, Jules 218
Labastida, Jaime 2182
Labelle, Jacques 2430
Labov, William 1567, 1576
Labriola, Albert C. 815, 1838
Labroisse, Gerd 151
Lachinger, Johann 36
Lachmann, Renate 2190
Lacoste, Claudine 432
LaCroix, Jean-Michel 187
Laddu, S. D. 199
Ladenburg, Paula 1077
Lagny, Michèle 1206
Lago Alba, Luis 595
Lahosa, Joan-Enric 924
Laine, Jarkko 2131
Laird, Holly A. 3035
Lajos, Kantor 1533
Laks, Leonhard 2625
Lakshimi, M. Vijaya 641
Lalanne, Jean-Louis 496
Lambert, José 2913
Lambert, P. Y. 943
Lambrechts, Roger 2401
Lamphere, Louise 1066
Lance, Donald M. 1849
Landgren, Bengt 2632
Landis, Joseph C. 3236
Lane, Harry 914
Lang, Lothar 1770
Langdon, Margaret 3073
Lange, Gerald 677
Langellier, Kristin M. 2940
Langemets, Andres 1728
Langendonck, W. van 1916, 2065
Langenfeld, Robert 869
Langevin, Gilles 2553
Langewiesche, Dieter 1274, 2792
Lankford, George 1829
Lapidge, Michael 180, 512
Larivaille, Paul 807
Larjavaara, Matti 3139
Laroque, François G. 623
Larsson, Lars-Gunnar 33
Lasić, S. 2504
Laslett, Barbara 2616
Lass, R. 516
Lasso de la Vega, Jośe S. 721
Last, Murray 42
Lastinger, Michael 3060
Lastinger, Valérie 3060
Lastra, Pedro 1278
Latimer, Dan R. 2683

Launay, N. B. de 2408
Laurence, Anne 456
Laurence, David 38
Laurence, Patricia 3138
Laureys, G. 2980
Laurie, Douglas 1232
Lavlinskiĭ, Leonard 1712
Law, Howard 2018
Lawal, Olu 1906
Lawler, Donald L. 3133
Lawson, E. Thomas 2038
Lawson, Richard H. 2812
Layiwola, Dele 51, 1257
Layman, Richard 784
Layoun, Mary 1421
Lazar, Liliane 2619
Lazar, Moshe 1275
Lazard, Gilbert 429
Lazarev, L. I. 3148
Le Roux, Cecile 2700
Leach, Joan 1078
Leaf, Hayim 362
LeBlanc, Edward T. 790
LeBlanc, Jacqueline 1776
Leblon, Bernard 1769
Lecercle, Jean-Jacques 3028
Lechanteur, Jean 773
Lecker, Robert 696, 915
Leclaire, J. 639
Leclere, Christian 1664-1665
Lederer, Herbert 2087
Lee, Chong-young 1253
Lee, Chungmin 1572
Lee, Jenny 1784
Lee, Peter 1723
Lee, Sang-Oak 1572
Lee, Sangsup 1390
Lee, Seung-Hwan 1529
Leeder, John 522
Leedham-Green, E. S. 2999
Leeman, Danielle 1577
Leenhardt, Jacques 1595
Leerssen, Joep 2775
LeFaivre, Carole N. 1809, 2240
Lefebvre, Anne 1660
Lefèvre, André 2358
Leger, Rudolf 1052
Leggott, Michelle 1548
Lehfeldt, W. 2506
Lehmann, Ulf 3265
Lehrer, Keith 2164
Lehtola, Erkka 398
Lehtonen, Jaakko 1490
Lehtonen, Soila 398
Leibowitz, Herbert 2133
Leibs, Andrew 2621
Leimberg, Inge 663
Leiner, Jacqueline 958
Leiner, Wolfgang 345, 958, 2054, 2122
Leino, Pentti 2768-2770
Leisi, Ernst 2550
Leistner-Opfermann, Detlef B. 895
Leiter, Samuel L. 267
Leitz, Robert C., III 1051
Lejeune, Claire 490
LeMaster, J. R. 1450
Lenders, Winfried 2705, 2708
Lenk, Patience-Anne 622
Lentricchia, Frank 2675
Léon, Pierre R. 2787
León de Vivero, Virginia 608
León-Portilla, Miguel 919
Leonard, Diane R. 3081
Leonardi, Claudio 2754
Leong, Russell C. 92
Lepschy, G. 1307
Lerche, Grith 2987
Leroy-Molinghen, Alice 460
Leščak, Milan 2654
Lessells, C. 936
Leuven-Zwart, Kitty van 227
Levi-Valensi, Jacqueline 2472
Levie, Sophie 3097
Levin, David 2289
Levin, Saul 1081
Levine, Paul 114
Levine, Robert M. 1738

Levitt, Jesse 1084
Levitt, John 1466
Levitt, Morton P. 1422
Levy, Brian J. 1886, 2336
Levy, Mark 1376
Lévy, Sydney 2869
Lewandowski, Theodor 3190
Lewis, C. W. 1724
Lewis, J. M. 1062
Lewis, Marvin A. 62
Lewis, Peter E. 818
Lewis, Robert W. 2007
Lewis, Theodore 1161
Lewis, Ward B. 407, 645
Leys, Odo 762
Li, De-en 1025
Liao, Hsien-hao Sebastian 593
Lichtenberger, H. 3249
Lichtlé, Michel 201
Liébaert, Jacques 1805
Lierheimer, Linda 701
Lieske, T. 2982
Liet, H. van der 2980
Light, M. 2647
Lightfoot, D. 516
Linck, Charles E., Jr. 973
Lindberg, Stanley W. 1091
Lindemann, Klaus 1863
Linden, Stanton J. 555
Lindon, John 3230
Lindvall, Lars 1876, 2486
Link, Franz 1713
Link, Victor 406
Linsky, Bernard 530
Lint, Th. van 820
Lipiński, Edward 3249
Lipkowitz, Ina 706
Lisowski, Jerzy 3047
Little, Greta D. 2569
Little, Roger 697
Litto, V. Del 2731
Livadaras, Nikolaos 2132
Livens, Robin G. 447
Liver, Ricarda 3150
Livorni, Ernesto 170
Ljung, Magnus 2734
Lo, Mou-pin 583
Locke, John 225
Lodge, R. Anthony 1398
Loebell, E. 1012
Loesberg, Jonathan 2249
Loffler-Laurian, Anne-Marie 672
Logan, Marie-Rose 198
Loganbill, Dean 1229
Lohf, Kenneth A. 633
Lohmeier, Dieter 1996
Lohr, Charles 2994
Lohr, Stephan 768
Lomke, Evander 1699-1701
Long, Michael H. 507
Longley, Kateryna 2693
Lönngren, Lennart 32
Lonsdale, Roger 2093
Looney, George 1830
Loos, Eugene 2018
Looy, H. van 218
López-Baralt, Mercedes 2377
López de Martínez, Adelaida 1605
Lorch, J. 1307
Lorente, Felino L. 2520
Lorenz, Kathryn M. 597
Lorenzo, Ramón 3106
Lorenzo-Rivero, Luis 3096
Lorian, Alexander 1164
Lory, B. 464
Losada Durán, José Ramón 2585
Lösche, Peter 130
Lotringer, Sylvère 2582
Lott, Eric 706
Loughrey, Bryan 705
Louwrens, L. J. 2672
Lovoll, Odd S. 2015
Lowenberg, Peter H. 3211
Lowrey, Robert 2262
Loyd, James O. 608
Loyola, Sister Mary 573
Luangco, Gregorio C. 1624

Lucano, Pino 86
Lucarini, Luciano 1608
Lucas, Alain 473
Luccichenti, Furio 1260
Lucente, Carla 1305
Luchsinger, R. 1012
Lucia, Cynthia 598
Lučin, Bratislav 1877
Luck, R. 368
Luczyk, Krzysztof 14
Ludwig, Horst 2544
Luey, Beth 2270
Lukács, László 928
Lukan, Walter 2089
Lukiv, Mykola 805
Lund, Hans Peter 2432
Lund, Vagner 1220
Lundeby, Einar 1742
Lundén, Rolf 28
Lundgreen-Nielsen, Flemming 748
Lupu, Ioana 350
Lusardi, James P. 2595
Lüv, E. 2098
Luxardo de Franchi, Nicolo' 2449
Luxemburg, Jan van 1034
Luxton, Richard N. 1581
Łużny, Ryszard 2214
Lyall, R. J. 2561
Lynn, David 1507
Lyon, Elisabeth 518
Lyon, George 522
Lyon, Ivana 2474
Lyon, Ted 571
Lyon, Thomas J. 3170
Lyons, Andrew P. 209
Lyons, Bonnie 2811
Lyons, Bridget Gellert 2345
Lyons, Harriet D. 209
Lyons, J. 516
Lyons, M. C. 1361
Lyster, Jens 1220
Maber, Richard 2590
Mac Adam, Alfred J. 2362
Mac Cana, Proinsias 892
Mac Mathúna, Liam 2774
Mac Síomóin, Tomás 635
MacAogáin, Eoghan 1565
Macary, Jean 1050
MacAulay, Donald 2556
MacCabe, Colin 702
MacCannell, Dean 100
MacCannell, Juliet 100
Maccubbin, Robert P. 841
Macedo, H. M. 2205
Macey, Samuel L. 867
Mackenzie, Ann Logan 446
Macksey, Richard 1859
MacLachlan, Robin 2827
MacRobert, C. M. 2097
MacShane, Frank 3007
Madden, O. E. 2502
Maddieson, Ian 1464, 3052
Maddock, Elizabeth 2289
Maddux, John S. 612
Madrigal, José A. 449
Madurini, Giulio 2298
Maes-Jelinek, Hena 714
Magerovsky, Eugene 3245
Maggioni, Giorgio 244
Magi, Aldo P. 2974
Magnusson, A. L. 849
Magnusson, Lars 1191
Maguin, Jean-Marie 486
Maguire, James H. 3173
Mahanti, J. C. 562
Mahé, Jean-Pierre 2412
Mähl, Hans-Joachim 1176, 2234
Mahon, John W. 2598
Mahoney, Dhira 857
Major, René 466
Majumdar, Neepa 599
Makkai, Adam 837, 1038
Makkai, Valerie Becker 837, 1038
Maksimchuk, B. V. 1256
Malaviya, Maya 1460
Maling, Joan 1931
Mallik, Bhakti P. 1236

Malmberg, Bertil 1272
Malone, Nancy M. 712
Maly, Ellen 792
Mandelker, Amy 2986
Manea, Ion 1449
Manfredi, Victor 1346
Mangini, Nicola 2751
Mangouni, Norman 2547
Mann, C. N. J. 2096
Mann, Michael 2180
Mannack, Eberhard 587, 750
Manne, Robert 2282
Manning, D. E. 2322
Mansilla García, Matilde 2585
Mäntäri, Pia 1948
Maransoko, H. J. M. 1511
Marc'hadour, Germain 1890
Marchand, F. 948
Marchetti, P. 944
Marcos, Juan Manuel 798
Marcos-Pérez, Pedro Jesús 2367
Marcuse, Michael J. 1677
Mareš, F. V. 3180
Margery Peña, Enrique 2382
Mariani, Umberto C. 1937
Mariconda, Steven J. 1732
Marín, Manuela 2272
Marino, James A. 978
Marken, Ron 526
Markey, Thomas L. 1650
Markley, Robert M. 839
Markov, Boris 2645
Markowski, Mieczysław 2782
Marks, Patricia H. 2228
Marle, J. van 2696
Marold, Edith 2629
Marotti, Arthur F. 708
Marquette, J. B. 188
Marquis, G. 2951
Marranca, Bonnie 2148
Marsch, Edgar 2574
Marsden, C. A. 2371
Marsden, Michael T. 1436
Marsden, Robin 2282
Marthaler, Philippe 3153
Marti, M. 1115
Martin, Ann 999
Martin, Biddy 1959
Martin, Carol A. 2465
Martin, Daniel R. 1887
Martin, Daniel W. 1446
Martín, Gregorio C. 691
Martin, Philip 1698
Martin, Wendy 3202
Martinelli, Perla Ari 1690
Martínez-San Miguel, Yolanda 1734
Martino, Alberto 587, 750, 1274, 2792
Maslov, I. S. 2218
Maslyko, E. A. 1821
Mason, H. A. 510
Mason, H. T. 2862
Massobrio, Lorenzo 389
Masson, Pierre 438
Massot Muntaner, Josep 2783
Mastellone, S. 2144
Mastrelli, Carlo Alberto 243
Matejka, Ladislav 1828, 2117
Materassi, Mario 2499
Matheeusen, Constant 1211
Mathews, Alice 660
Mathieu, Vittorio 726
Mathijsen, M. 2696
Matias, D. N. 453
Matiaszek, Petro 3054
Matisoff, James A. 1658
Matos, Francisco Gomes de 925
Matsumoto, Hiroshi 1179
Matter, Johan F. 68
Matthen, Mohan 530
Matthews, Adrian 1048
Matthews, John 1782
Matthews, John T. 990
Matthews, P. H. 516
Mattock, J. N. 1361
Matus Olivier, Alfredo 379
Matzel, Klaus 2528
Maude-Gembler, C. 1290

Maurer, Christopher 383
Mauss, Armand L. 1350
Maver, Marij 1858
Maxwell, Richard 2210
May, Jacques 268
May, Robert 1645
Mayer, Dieter 1682
Mayerthaler, Willi 2124
Maynard, John 3126
Mayo, Peter 3230
Mazejko, E. 536
Mazouer, Charles 469
Mazzarolli, Leopoldo 281
Mazzoni, Francesco 2739
Mbangwana, Paul 185
McArthur, Tom 876
McBrien, William 3046
McCaffrey, Carmel 3183
McCallom, Pamela 253
McClatchy, J. D. 3219
McClure, J. Derrick 2557
McCown, Robert A. 397
McDonald, W. U., Jr. 963
McDonald, William C. 997
McDonnell, Denis W. 2905
McDonnell, Mary E. 2905
McDuffie, Keith 2392
McGaha, Michael 566
McGann, Catherine 2427
McGee, C. E. 849
McGiffert, Michael 3186
McGowan, Thomas 2004
McGrath, Elizabeth 1481
McGrath, Susan McLean 2399
McGuinness, Arthur 842
McGuire, J. I. 1288
McHale, Brian 2192
McKaughan, Howard P. 2049
McKeever, Jerome M. 736
McKinley, James 1965
McKinnell, John 816
McLaughlin, M. 1307
McLean, Andrew 613
McLean, Hugh 505
McLean, Robert C. 906
McMillin, A. B. 2647
McMullen, Lorraine 2318
McNab, James P. 753
McNeil, W. K. 1829
McTigue, Bernard 95
McTigue, Bernard F. 444
McTurk, R. 2516
McWatt, Mark 1485
Meadows, Karen 2105
Meda, Anna 2745
Medicine, Beatrice 3175
Medin, Douglas L. 620
Medlar, Frank 1915
Medrano, Rebecca Read 128
Meerschen, Jean-Marie van der 889
Meesdom, Tony 2358
Mehl, Dieter 234
Mehler, Jacques 617
Meijer, W. 168
Meijs, Willem 1558
Meiners, R. K. 560
Melanko, Valdemar 2789
Melas, Natalie 2289
Melchers, Gunnel 2803
Melena, J. L. 1843
Melia, Daniel 3072
Melnichuk, O. S. 1896
Melo, Francisco 3116
Melon, Edda 3101
Meltzer, Françoise 700
Menant, Sylvain 2424
Ménard, Philippe 424
Menarini, Piero 383
Mennemeier, Franz Norbert 2796
Merad, Ghani 2432
Meredith, Michael 418
Meredith, Peter 1592, 1795-1796
Meregalli, Franco 2305
Merentsov, V. A. 3149
Mergen, Bernard 115
Meri, Mart 851
Merkt, Gérard 426

Merkur'ev, S. P. 3117
Merlan, F. C. 2047
Mermier, Guy R. 1793, 2854
Merrett, R. J. 1761
Merrifield, William R. 2874
Merrill, Paul W. 2134
Meserole, Harrison T. 2592
Metcalf, Allan 112, 1982
Methlagl, Walter 408
Mettomäki, Sirkka-Liisa 1493
Meulenaere, H. de 590
Mey, Jacob L. 1437, 2216
Meyer, Fred M. 320
Meyer, Kurt 2713
Meyer, L. de 2079
Meyer, Michel 2429
Meyer, Richard E. 1773
Meyer-Bahlburg, H. 60
Meÿer Drees, M. E. 1986
Meyers, Eric M. 344
Meyran, Daniel 1769
Miccinesi, Mario 3091
Micha, Alexandre 2268
Michael, Colette 428
Michaels, I. Lloyd 998
Michalowski, Piotr 1382
Michalson, Greg 1850
Michaud, Ginette 950
Michel, Alain 2417
Michel, M. 436
Michelsen, Peter 1167
Michelsen, William 1140
Michelson, Annette 2050
Michon, Jacques 2222
Middleton, Roger H. 1063, 2023
Mieder, Wolfgang 2253
Miele, Michele 2533
Miethke, Jürgen 2501
Mignolo, Walter D. 800
Mihaescu, Valentin 2483
Mihalić, Slavko 1032
Mikhailov, A. I. 306
Mikkelsen, Hans Kristian 2884
Mikola, T. 26
Milagros Pérez, María de los 1204
Milano, Benjamín 740
Milech, Barbara 2687
Milhous, Judith 2962
Miller, Greg 3218
Miller, John F. 609
Miller, Karl 1726
Miller, Norbert 2704
Miller, Norman 1430
Miller, Yvette Espinosa 1582
Millett, P. C. 610
Millington, M. I. 2339
Mills, David O. 1453
Mills, Elizabeth 2690
Mills, Jerry Leath 2839
Milner, Max 2491
Milton, John R. 2679
Milward, Peter 2343, 2603
Minard, Michel J. 240, 2419
Mineka, Susan 1351
Minelli, Stefano 1212
Minguet, Charles 689
Minogue, Valerie 2480
Mintz, Alan 2248
Mircheva, D. 422
Mirth, Karlo 1380
Misonne, Daniel, Dom 2402
Mistrík, Miloš 2652
Mitchell, Rosamond 224
Mitchell, W. J. T. 700
Mitsutomi, Shogo 1546
Mladenović, Alexandar 2225
Mobärg, Mats 1876
Mochet, Marie-Anne 483
Möcker, Hermann 2088
Modlin, Charles E. 3188
Mogridge, B. 542
Mohamed, Abdul Jan 728
Möhlig, Wilhelm J. G. 2707
Möhn, Dieter 986
Moingt, Joseph 2321
Molinié, G. 804
Mombello, Gianni 2749

Mommsen, Katharina 1099
Monday, William 7
Monfrin, Jacques 248, 2481
Mongin, Olivier 904
Monke, Arthur 1928
Monkman, Kenneth 2604
Montagnes, Ian 2546
Montandon, Alain 1595
Montenyohl, Eric 2682
Montevecchi, Orsolina 40
Montgomery, Edward Davidson 2477
Montgomery, Michael 2569
Moog-Grünewald, Maria 232
Moon, Michael 104
Moore, John Rees 1198
Moore, Peter 636
Moore, Steven 2363
Morahg, Gilead 1163
Morales Piñna, Eddie 2037
Moran, John Charles 2492
Morano, Rocco Mario 519
Morawietz, Kurt 1203
Mörch, Audun 1785
Moreau, Jean-Pierre 887
Moreiras, Alberto 3060
Morelli, Emilia 2307
Morey, Frederick L. 782
Morgan, D. O. 1473
Morgan, Frederick 1208
Morgan, Marcyliena 2215
Morgan, Speer 1850
Morin, Rosaire 34
Moriya, Mineo 843
Moron Arroyo, Ciriaco 786
Mortensen, Klaus P. 1534
Morzewski, Christian 2472
Moser, Hans 1254
Moser, Hugo 1139
Moser-Verrey, Monique 957
Moses, Claire G. 994
Mosher, Harold F., Jr. 2868
Mosier, John 1969
Moss, Anita 581
Moss, Mark 2620
Mossay, Justin 460
Mossman, Elliott 2642
Mott, Glenn 366
Motta, Paschoal 1840
Mount, Ferdinand 1727
Mourão-Ferreira, David 632
Moustgaard, Poul 1015
Mowat, Barbara A. 2599
Moxon, Ian 2243
Moye, Richard 706
Moyle, Richard M. 1471
Muaka, Angaluki 3053
Mudoola, Dan M. 1780
Mudrovic, Michael 2378
Mueller, Janel 1875
Mueller, Roswitha 796
Mufwene, Salikoko 1434
Mugurēvičs, E. 250
Muhvić-Dimanovski, Vesna 2883
Mukerji, Nirmal 2111
Mukherjee, Meenakshi 3099
Mulford, Carla 2142, 2357
Mullen, Edward J. 62
Mullen, Patrick B. 2261
Mullen, R. D. 2555
Mullen, Richard 670
Muller, A. 1012
Müller, Alfons 2713
Müller, Bodo 1166
Müller, Carl Werner 2438
Muller, Charles 3012
Müller, Hans-Peter 3249
Müller, Kurt 1713
Müller, Ulrich 1126, 2866
Müller, Wolfgang 2497
Müller-Lauter, Wolfgang 1985
Müller-Schwefe, Gerhard 2797
Müller-Seidel, Walter 1320
Mullini, Roberta 2934
Mulryan, John 603
Munawwar, Muhammed 1282
Münchberg, Harry 1679
Munich, Adrienne Auslander 3126

Muñoz G., Luis 18
Munslow, Alun 2939
Munteanu, Romul 495
Murphy, James J. 2441
Murphy, John J. 3185
Murphy, Patrick D. 2853
Murphy, Russell Elliott 3233
Murphy, Steve 2127
Murray, Christopher 1291
Murray, Les 2282
Musolino, Walter 2719
Müssenger, Helmut 1876
Mussio, Thomas 2293
Muysken, Pieter 688
Muzart, Zahidé L. 3016
Mwanalessa, Kikassa 3243
Myers, Lois 1450
Myerson, Joel 2852
Mykytenko, Oleg 3151
Myrsiades, Kostas 629, 1462
Nachbar, John G. 1436
Nachnibida, M. 2195
Nadeau, Maurice 2291
Nagel, James 694, 2808
Nagel, Tilman 3248
Nagucka, Ruta 364
Nagy, Joseph F. 3124
Nagy, Moses M. 612
Nagy, Péter 1292
Nalbandian, Al'bert 1710
Namjoshi, M. V. 1970
Nänny, Max 2892
Narasimhaiah, C. D. 1673
Narcy, Michel 497
Nascimento, Ulpiano 2568
Nash, Susan Smith 255
Navarat, Pavinee 2136
Navarro Carrosco, Ana Isabel 920
Naylor, Ronald P. 548
Nazor, Anica 2655
Ndulute, Clement 3061
Nedeljković, Dušan 1922
Neefs, Jacques 1717
Négrel, Dominique 485
Negri, Giuseppe 690
Nehls, Dietrich 1272, 2818
Nehring, Karl 2871
Nelde, Peter 1104
Nellemann, George 1015
Nelson, Brian 2480
Nelson, David 1723
Nelson, Lowry, Jr. 1075
Nelson, Robert M. 2810
Némedi, Lajos 1936
Nenci, Giuseppe 192
Nencioni, Giovanni 2742
Néraudau, M. 1248
Nercissian, M. G. 2137
Nerlich, Michael 1595
Neubert, Meretha 2220
Neuhäuser, Rudolf 811
Neuland, Eva 768
Neumann, Günter 1190
Neumann, Peter Horst 290-291
Neumarkt, Paul 1394
Neuschäfer, Hans-Jörg 1221
Nevala, Maria-Liisa 1329
Nevo, Ruth 1164
New, W. H. 531
Newall, Venetia 1262
Newey, Vincent 457
Newman, Paul-Bernard 198
Newton, A. P. 510
Ngara, E. A. 3244
Ngijol Ngijol, Pierre 185
Nicholls, David 575
Nichols, Johanna 3073
Nichols, Nina daVinci 198
Nickaŭ, Klaŭs 1118
Nickel, Catherine 1405
Nickel, Gerhard 1272
Nickisch, Craig W. 2576
Nickson, Richard 1232
Nicolaisen, Peter 1684
Niebaum, Hermann 1983
Niederehe, Hans-Josef 539, 1189
Niedziela, Zdzisław 2214

Nielsen, Hans F. 2034
Nielsen, Kai 530
Nielsen, Maj-Britt Munk 2220
Nienhauser, William H., Jr. 585
Niessen, Frits 2069
Nijland, C. 168
Nikolaev, G. F. 3276
Nikolay-Panter, M. 2436
Nikol'skiĭ, Boris N. 1951
Nilsen, Alleen 863
Nilson, Don L. F. 1214
Nilsson, Barbro 2803
Nilsson, N. Å. 2504
Nirenburg, Sergei 1745
Nisbet, H. B. 514
Nishimae, Takashi 591
Noble, P. S. 2314
Noël, Roger 1364
Noffen, Jean-Pierre van 2401
Nogueira Dobarro, Ángel 806
Nøjgaard, Morten 962, 2076
Nolla, Olga 732
Nollendorfs, Valters 1880
Noonan, Michael 2830-2831
Nordberg, Bengt 2631
Nordloh, David J. 103
Nørgaard-Sørensen, Jens 2884
Norheim, Pål 3098
Noriguchi, Shinichoro 1546
Norman, Ralph V. 2669
Nörrevang, Arne 1065
Norton, Barbara 257
Noth, Albrecht 1295
Novak, Maximilian 285
Novicki, Margaret A. 44
Nteta, Doreen A. N. 401
Núñez Cedeño, Rafael A. 2237
Nutting, Stéphanie 2427
Nutz, Maximilian 1682
Nwachukwu, P. Akụjụọobi 1346
Nyberg, Ben 1497
Nycz, Ryszard 2921
Nydahl, Thomas 2791
Nye, Russel B. 1356
Nyholm, Kurt 1329
Nynäs, Carina 1004
Ó Baoill, Colm 2556
Ó Baoill, Dónall P. 1370, 2916
Ó Corráin, Donnchadh 2150
Ó Deirg, Íosold 2917
Ó Fiannachta, Pádraig 1588
Ó Héalaí, Pádraig 322
Ó Murchadha, Diarmuid 1455
Ó Riagáin, Pádraig 1565
Oakleaf, David 253
Oates, Joyce Carol 2072
Öberg, Johan 2077
Oberhammer, G. 3182
Obertino, James 2265
O'Brien, John 2363
Obst, Ulrich 331
O'Connell, David 3036
O'Donnell, James J. 2994
O'Donnell, Patrick J. 1868
Oellers, Norbert 391
Offer, Yoseph 1600
Offord, M. H. 2023
Ogede, Oge 1536
Ohashi, Kenzaburo 991
Ohrt, Claus 1876
Oishi, Yūji 1336
O'Kane, John 856
O'Keeffe, Paul 859
Okruhlik, Kathleen 530
Okuma, Jacqueline 921
Olbert, Jürgen 1055
Olds, Marshall 2859
Oleskiw, Stephen 3055
Oliphant, Dave 1629
Olivares, Julián 129
Oliver, Andrew 2944
Oliver, Douglas 1048
Olney, James 2686
Olsen, Jørgen 1528
Olsen, Stephen 38
Olson, Gary 1352

Olteanu, Ioanichie 3123
Oltmanns, P. 2954
Olyslaeghers, Jeroen 2358
Omatsu, Glenn 92
O'Meara, Patrick 1289
Onatzky-Malin, Marie 202
Ondona, Pius 185
O'Neil, Charmian 483
Onishi, Masao 2071
Ono, Kazuto 1546
Ono, Kiyoyuki 574, 991
Opačić, Petar 1877
Opali, Fred 1780
Oppenheimer, E. 542
Orduna, Germán 1230
Orioles, V. 1231
Ormesson, Jean d' 792
Oroz Reta, José 287
Orski, Mieczysław 2052
Ortega, Julio 1278
Ōsaka, Osamu 2824
Osborn, Judi 2180
Osborne, John 342
Oshagan, Vahe 2297
O'Shea, Michael J. 2847
Oshitari, Kinshiro 2835
Ossar, Michael 2859
Ossola, Carlo 2456
Ostrowski, Witold 3242
Otanes, Fe T. 2838
Ōtsu, Yukio 1645
Ott, Ulrich 1320, 1767
Otten, Fred 3109
Otten, H. 3252
Otto, Erwin 176
Otto, Walter 1912
Ouellet, Pierre 2325
Ouimette, Victor 2371
Ouweleen, Mark 3218
Owen, D. D. R. 1035
Owens, W. R. 456
Oyer, H. 1012
Özdogan, M. 168
Ozolins, Sulamite 70
Pabst, W. 2489
Pachori, Satya S. 2674
Paczkowski, Renate 1996
Padel, O. J. 1994
Padluzhny, A. I. 333
Padoan, Giorgio 2280, 2760
Padron, Justo Jorge 890
Pae, Doo-Bon 1459
Page, Norman 2970
Pagès, Alain 494
Pahl, Kate 702
Paige, Lori 1776
Paine, J. H. E. 1477
Pair, Joyce M. 1334
Pais, Cidmar Teodoro 23, 2370
Paley, Morton D. 367
Pallares, Berta 2432
Palmer, Eustace J. T. 50
Palmer, N. F. 2094
Palmer, Nigel 1802
Palmer, R. Barton 2856
Palomo, Marcelino 3153
Pamp, Bengt 256
Panaccio, Claude 778
Panayotakis, N. M. 2967
Panichas, George A. 1864
Pankhurst, J. N. 2572
Pankow, David 2229
Panten, Albert A. 1997
Pantić, Miroslav 2226
Paolucci, Anne 683, 2255, 2365
Papadopoullos, Theodore 1544
Papamichael-Koutroubas, Anna 884
Papp, Ferenc 2788
Paquette, Jerre 7
Para, Jean-Baptiste 967
Paradis, Annie 484
Paratore, Ettore 2451
Paré, François 2340
Paredes, Raymund A. 308
Parikh, P. V. 1467
Park, Joo-Hyun 1459
Parker, Stephen Jan 1917

Parkinson, Stephen 3230
Parks, Stephen 3220
Paroissien, David 779
Parola-Leconte, Nora 2446
Parr, James A. 449
Parra, Antonio R. 2454
Parret, Herman 2216
Parrill, William 1731
Parroni, Piergiorgio 2352
Parsons, Terence 1431
Parthé, Kathleen 2986
Pasión, Lamberto, O.P. 3068
Pasquarette, Carole 2817
Pastor, Ricardo 386
Paternu, Boris 2646
Patrick, J. Max 2592
Pătruț, Ioan 565
Patten, Robert L. 2575
Patterson, Annabel 1418
Patterson, Yolanda Astarita 2619
Pattison, D. G. 1802
Patton, John J. 2909
Patty, James S. 423
Paul, Fritz 2106
Paul, Waltraud 473
Paula, Euripedes Simoes de 2383
Paulson, Ronald 848
Pavlík, Jaroslav Vincenc 2644
Paz, Consuelo 789
Paz, Octavio 3152
Pazukhin, Rostislav 1186
Pearce, Richard 2030
Pecellin Lancharro, Manuel 2376
Pécheur, Jacques 1044
Pedersen, Viggo Hjørnager 746
Pederson, John 2432
Peer, Willie van 3097
Peeters, Leopold 1064
Pehrson, G. 1195
Pelckmans, Paul 992
Pelegrin, J. Battesti 480
Pellegrini, Giuliano 2454
Pellegrini, Luigi 1607
Pelletier, Francis J. 1657
Pelletier, Jacques 3145
Penchoen, Tom 63
Pendleton, Thomas A. 2598
Peng, Fred C. C. 1573
Penley, Constance 518
Pennanen, Jukka 930
Perello, J. 1012
Perels, Christoph 1327
Perera, Katharine 1371
Pérez, Genaro J. 1883
Pérez, Janet 1883
Perez, Joy 2618
Pérez Delgado, Esteban 2930
Pérez Priego, Miguel Angel 888
Pérez Só, Reynaldo 2188
Perkins, Elizabeth 1667
Perks, Robert 2073
Perova, Natalia 2692
Perron, Paul 2583
Perrot, Jean 429, 949
Pertile, L. 1307
Peschel-Rentsch, Dietmar 895
Pešikan, Mitar 1923
Peterman, Michael A. 1368
Peters, F. J. J. 3026
Peters, George F. 3089
Peters, Martin 2703
Petersen, Peter 300
Petersmann, Gerhard 1133
Peterson, Lena 2766
Peterson, William S. 2120
Petöfi, János S. 2125, 2354
Petr, Jan 940
Petroni, Liano 1049
Petronio, Giuseppe 2235
Petry, Ludwig 3262
Petter, Henri 2550
Pettersson, Magnus 2634
Pettis, Joyce 2044
Peyton, Henry Hall, III 2292
Pfeffer, Wendy 2929
Pfeiffer, Waldemar 1119
Pfeil, Fred 1842

Pfister, Max 326, 3263
Pflug, Günther 1912
Pflumm, Walter 936
Pfordresher, John 3133
Philips, Margaret 702
Phillips, Evelyn 1185
Phillips, John 1213
Phillips, Robert L., Jr. 1848
Phillips, William 2135
Phillipson, John S. 2974
Picard, Olivier 427
Picchio, Luciana Stegagno 1610
Pich, Edgard 440
Pichl, Robert 1321
Pichois, Claude 423, 941
Pickering, O. S. 1832
Piel, Jean 710
Piepke, Joachim 212
Pieretti, Antonio 191
Pierssens, Michel 2869
Pieterse, Cosmo 1884
Pieterse, H. J. 3049
Pikulik, Lothar 3020
Pineda de Valderrama, Clemencia 1117
Pintér, Imre Kis 1532
Piö, Iørn 1015
Piromalli, Antonio 2204
Pisani, Vittore 282
Pisarkowa, Krystyna 364
Pistohlkors, Gert von 3262
Pitt, Gwyneth 3079
Pizzorusso, Arnaldo 2454
Pizzorusso, Valeria Bertolucci 2755
Plambeck, Vernon L. 2179
Plant, Richard 2956
Platzack, Christer 256, 2779
Pleavin, Noreen 860
Plouvier, Paule 794
Plummer, Joseph R. 1296
Podhoretz, Norman 637
Podolák, Ján 932
Poe, E. W. 2929
Poelstra, Wardy 1034
Poff, Deborah C. 279
Poggenpohl, Sharon Helmer 3141
Poirier, Richard 2303
Polan, Dana 600
Polański, Kazimierz 364, 1651, 2212
Polenz, Peter von 3260
Polk, Noel 991
Pollack, Lars-Ove 375
Pollet, G. 2081
Pollio, Howard R. 1819
Polomé, Edgar C. 1404, 1763
Pommier, Colette 1580
Pomogáts, Béla 1687
Ponzio, Augusto 275
Pope, Randolph D. 2378
Popp, Wolfgang 1036
Poppe, Erich 1370
Porcelli, Bruno 1309
Porteman, K. 2699
Porter, D. S. 374
Pörtl, Klaus 1221
Posadas, Roger 789
Posner, R. 516
Possin, H.-J. 406
Potapenko, Borys 3055
Pötscher, Walter 1133
Pouillon, Jean 1199
Poulsen, Jóan Hendrik W. 1065
Povejšil, Jaromír 551
Povey, John F. 47
Powell, David A. 1088
Pozzi, M. 1115
Prada Oropeza, Renato 2581
Pranjković, Ivo 2883
Preiss, Nathalie 201
Prelas, Mirko 1877
Premsrirat, Suwilai 1879
Preston, Edward 781
Preston, Peter 738
Pretzel, Ulrich 347
Preuss, Mary H. 1581
Price, Glanville 3230
Priestly, Tom M. S. 2649
Prins, M. J. 1030

Prinz, Friedrich 3262
Pritsak, Omeljan 1159
Prokhanov, Alexander 2692
Prophet, Carl W. 855
Przybylowicz, Donna 728
Psathas, George 1210
Puccini, Dario 1610
Pueyrredon, Victoria 1603
Pugh, Scott 1546
Pugliatti, Paola 2934
Pulbrook, Martin 1781
Pulsano, Phillip 2245
Punen, Christian 1579
Pupkis, Aldonas 1112
Pupo-Walker, Enrique 515
Putnik, Radomir 2543
Putschke, Wolfgang 1103, 2708, 2794
Putz, Otto 1165
Pütz, Peter 391
Putzer, Oskar 1254
Quack, Anton 212
Quacquarelli, Antonio 3121
Quak, Arend 150, 152
Quart, Leonard 598
Quartucci, Guillermo 917
Quella-Villéger, Alain 547
Quemada, Bernard 470
Queniart, J. 183
Quere, H. 983
Quimby, Ian M. G. 2142
Quindoza-Santiago, Lilia 789
Quinn, Brian 1546
Quinn, J. 2130
Quinn, Patrick 1009
Quintanilla, Miguel Angel 230
Quiroga S., César E. 2368
Quispel, G. 3132
Raabe, Paul 3196
Råberg, Per 27
Rabinbach, Anson G. 1959
Racault, Jean-Michel 467
Rachman, S. 324
Radel, Nicholas 2603
Radford, C. B. 1063
Raeper, William 2009
Raepsaet, G. 218
Ragen, Brian Abel 2123
Rahn, Jay 523
Raible, Wolfgang 2335
Raidt, Edith 3048
Raimond, Michel 2472
Raina, M. L. 1970
Rainey, Dora 255
Rainwater, Catherine 850
Raitt, A. W. 2096
Raja, K. Kunjunni 403
Rajchman, John 2050
Rajh, Bernard 776
Rajković, Zorica 1921
Rall, Dietrich 921
Ralph, Bo 1804
Ramge, H. 327
Ramos-Gascón, Antonio 1182
Ramraj, Victor 253
Rand, Nicholas T. 466
Randall, Stephen 534
Randolph, Susan 3189
Rankin, Thomas S. 1847
Rao, Bhavaraju Narasimha 3024
Rao, Pothukuchi Sambasiva 3066
Raposo, Eduardo 2237
Räsänen, Matti 930, 2768-2770
Raskin, Richard 2220
Raskin, Victor 1214
Rasmussen, Jens Elmegård 17
Rasmussen, Ole Wehner 2220
Rasporich, A. W. 521
Raszewski, Zbigniew 2110
Ratcliff, James L. 1343
Ratsimihah, Jean-Louis 1287
Rattunde, E. 1947
Răo, Aurel 2728
Rau, Johannes 1943
Rauer, Christian 1879
Raupach, Manfred 1500
Ravitch, Norman 2241
Ravnik, Mojca 2997

Raymond, James C. 627
Rayner, Keith 1396
Readings, Bill 2881
Real, Hermann J. 2891
Rector, Martin 2153
Réda, Jacques 2028
Redden, James E. 2046
Rédei, Károly 2041
Redmond, James 2964
Redon, Odile 1798
Redshaw, Thomas Dillon 845
Reed, Joel 839
Reed, T. J. 2094
Rees, Cees J. van 2191
Rees, Daniel, Dom 812
Rees, John 1497
Reeves, Robin 1974
Rege, M. P. 1970
Rehorick, Sally 532
Reichenberger, Kurt 2232, 2918-2919
Reichenberger, Roswitha 2232, 2918-2919
Reichmann, Oskar 1621
Reid, Barrett 2092
Reid, Robert 913
Reifegerste, Matthias 1101
Reigstad, Thomas J. 871
Reimers, Ronald 2219
Reinelt, Janelle 2958
Reinhammar, Maj 2637, 2886
Reis, Marga 329
Reiss, David 2256
Reiter, Norbert 3253
Reitterer, Hubert 1321
Renard, Paul 2472
Renard, Raymond 2410
Rendall, Steven 651
Rennison, John 3179
Renov, Michael 2285
Restrepo, Javier 798
Retsö, Jan 2080
Reuther, Tilman 3181
Revell, Donald 756
Revuelta Sañudo, Manuel 382
Rewa, Natalie 538
Rey, Alain 1251, 1620
Reyes, Portia 789
Reynolds, Fred 1352
Reynolds, Patricia 1760
Rhea, Barbara 1223
Rhoads, Linda Smith 1956
Rhodes, Jack 1991
Rhodes, Richard 618, 3017
Riasanovsky, Nicholas V. 505
Ricci, Julio 1026
Ricciardelli, M. 1037
Richards, Barry 2899
Richards, Jack C. 507
Richards, Pamela Spence 1475
Richards, Shaun 2939
Richardson, B. 1307
Richardson, L. Barbara 1084
Richardson, Margaret 397
Richardson, Mervyn E. J. 1442
Richardson, Roger 1698
Řichová, B. 239
Richter, Mario 2749
Ricks, Christopher 910
Ricoeur, Paul 2408
Ricouart, Janine 1385
Ricquier, Jean Claude 2428
Riddell, Barry 525
Ridderstad, Per S. 1999
Rieber, R. W. 1439
Rieger, Burghard 2283
Riemer, A. P. 2893
Riendeau, Roger 525
Riera, Miguel 1725, 2290
Rieser, Hannes 2125
Riesman, Janet A. 2905
Riewerts, Brar V. 1997
Riffaterre, Michael 2484
Rigbey, Ann 1034
Rigby, Brian 1057
Riggenbach, Heidi 2932
Riha, Karl 2335
Riley, Patrick 2289
Ringle, Martin 621

Rini, Joel 653
Rinn, Fauneil J. 2531
Risager, Karen 2471
Rischel, Andreas 1716
Rischel, Jørgen 17, 204
Rissanen, Matti 1948
Ritchie, J. M. 1094
Ritoók, Zsigmond 11
Ritterhoff, Claus 3197
Rivarola, José Luis 1623
Rivas Sacconi, José Manuel 2968
Rivington, J. M. H. 2242
Rix, Walter Torsten 1684
Rizza, Cecilia 2749
Roach, Peter 1464
Robbins, Bruce 2660
Roberge, Paul T. 3082
Robering, Klaus 2920
Roberts, Brynley F. 1929
Roberts, John 1560
Robine, C. 425
Robinson, Gwen G. 2901
Roby, Kinley E. 3044
Rocard, Marcienne 503
Rocco, Italo 2617
Rocha-Perazzo, Anne 2659
Roche, Thomas P., Jr. 2697
Rocher, Rosane 3083
Roddewig, Marcella 767
Rodini, Robert J. 1310
Rodriguez, Aleida 2230
Rodríguez, Celso 2393
Rodríguez, D. Plácido 557
Rodríguez Hernández, Sixto 2949
Rodríguez López-Vázquez, Alfredo 1598
Rodríquez, Alfonso 662
Roelandts, K. 1916
Roemer, Danielle 578
Roeper, Thomas 1555
Roessler, P. 2954
Rogers, David 2701
Rogers, Thomas F. 858
Rohrer, Christian 1662
Roig, A. 2281
Rolfe, Christopher 3163
Rölleke, Heinz 3190
Röllig, Wolfgang 3166
Rollins, Onie 3189
Roloff, Hans-Gert 587, 750, 1331
Romaine, S. 516
Romaine, Suzanne 1568
Romanyshyn, Oleh S. 3055
Rombach, Heinrich 2165
Romero, Elena 923
Romero, James 2105
Róna Tas, A. 26
Roncaglia, Aurelio 727
Ronen, Ruth 2192
Rood, David S. 2623
Roodenberg, J. J. 168
Rooney, Ellen 2030
Roos, J. de 168
Roos, Kirsten 2884
Ropars, Marie-Claire 1206
Roques, Gilles 3011
Ros, Martin 1743
Rosa, Mario 2456
Rose, Brian 2961
Rose, Marilyn Gaddis 117, 3008
Rose, Mary Beth 2342
Rosenbalm, John O. 2809
Rosenbaum, Karol 2650
Rosenberg, Jerome H. 2063
Rosenfeld, Lawrence B. 643
Rosengren, Inger 1737
Rosenthal-Kamarinea, Isidora 1171
Rosi, Ivanna 2454
Rosiello, Luigi 1638
Rosito, Massimiliano Giuseppe 604
Roskies, David G. 2248
Rosliakov, A. A. 1316
Rosner, Mary 779
Rosowski, Susan J. 554
Ross, Andrew 2660
Ross, Bruce Clunies 174
Ross, Robert 217
Rosslyn, F. M. 510

Rosso, Corrado 2749
Rotermund, Erwin 2796
Roth, Klaus 3266
Rothe-Rotowski, Monica 738
Rother, Rainer 2153
Rothfork, John 1968
Rottland, Franz 2707
Roudané, Matthew C. 2856
Roux, Louis 3015
Rovatti, Pier Aldo 304
Rovee-Collier, Carolyn K. 1245
Rowe, Mike 372
Rowehl, John 2163
Rowell, Charles H. 506
Rowsell, Lorna 502
Roxin, Claus 1323
Roy, G. Ross 2845
Royster, Jacqueline Jones 2518
Rozentāle, Magdalēne 70
Rozik, Eli 269
Rubavičius, Vytautas 1691
Rubin, David-Hillel 1841
Rubincam, C. I. R. 2171
Rubio, Gerald 2611
Rudat, Eva M. Kahiluoto 786
Ruddick, William 570
Rudenko-Desniak, Aleksandr 814
Rudman, Mark 2145
Rudnyckyj, J. B. 2657
Rudy, Jill Terry 1020
Ruffin, Paul 2936
Ruiz de Elvira, Antonio 721
Rumble, R. 1994
Rumpel, Heinrich 369
Rundgren, Sten 1074
Runte, Hans R. 743, 1250
Runtelata, Nicolae Dan 1733
Ruoff, Arno 1224
Ruotolo, Lucio 3138
Rupley, William H. 2315
Rupprecht, Bernhard 893
Rusch, Frederic E. 813
Russell, Daniel S. 139, 852
Russell, Ian 1014
Russell, R. 1873
Russi, Luciano 3021
Russo, Carlo Ferdinando 335
Russo, John Paul 1303
Russo, Sandy 702
Rutherford, Andrew 2564
Rutherford, Anna 1541
Rutherford, William 1556
Ruwet, Nicolas 2324
Ruxandra, Mihaila 1766
Ruÿgh, C. J. 1860
Ryan, J. S. 298
Ryan, Phyllis 921
Ryan, R. 1415
Ryan, Tomás L. 111
Ryan, W. F. 2647
Rydén, L. 891
Rydén, Mats 28
Rymut, Kazimierz 2066
Rzhevsky, Nicholas 2640
Saarinen, Tuija 2878
Sabatini, Francesco 1800
Saccone, Eduardo 1859
Sackett, Theodore A. 1181
Sacré, Dirk 1211
Sadgrove, Philip C. 1442
Sadji, Amadou Booker 952
Sáez Godoy, Leopoldo 1695
Safarewicz, Jan 14, 1342
Saha, Subhas Chandra 1363
Sahal, Pierre 540
Saine, Thomas P. 1124
Sainsbury, Mark 1841
St. Laurent, Marie-France 729
Sajavaara, Kari 1490
Sakamoto, Koretada 249
Salas, Adalberto 2461
Salgado, María A. 2006
Salinero Cascante, Maria Jesús 722
Salo, Sheila 1461
Salomon, Herman P. 111
Salzman, Jack 799, 2250
Sammallahti, Leena 930, 1498

Sampson, Dennis 526
Samsons, V. 1587
Sánchez, Alberto 160
Sánchez Gil, Francisco Victor 247
Sanders, Carol 1398
Sanderson, George 214
Sandford, J. 1094
Sandin, Maria 1540
Sandoval, Adriana 1693
Sandred, Karl Inge 2085
Sandstedt, Lynn A. 662
Sankaranarayanan, S. 403
Sankoff, David 1576
Sanna, Salvatore A. 1311
Šanski, N. M. 2512
Sansoni, G. C. 2128
Santaella, Lucia 985
Santana, Jorge A. 976
Santoro, Marco 903
Sapiro, Leland 2448
Şarambei, Nicolae 2483
Sárközi, Alice 21
Sarma, K. V. 403
Sarmar, E. R. Sreekrishna 403
Sarmela, Matti 2878
Sarrocco, Clara 717
Sartor, D. 442
Sartori, Franco 244
Sartorius, Joachim 2704
Satchidanandan, K. 1239
Sauer, Michael 768
Saunders, Martha A. 3167
Saur, Pamela 2544
Savukynas, Bronys 1539
Saxman, John H. 1444
Saxton, Ruth 810
Scaglione, Aldo 1277, 2695
Scalise, Sergio 1638
Scarborough, Connie L. 448
Scarpat, Giuseppe 2100
Schabram, Hans 2106
Schächter, Elizabeth 3228
Schachter, Paul 3073
Schade, Richard E. 1602
Schäfer, H.-P. 763
Schalhorn, B. 763
Schalkwyk, David 2224
Schaller, Hans Martin 766
Schamoni, Wolfgang 1165
Schanke, Robert A. 2957
Scharfe, Martin 3266
Scharnhorst, Gary 102
Schaub, Thomas 669
Schechner, Richard 2914
Schechter, Joel 2953
Scheel, Kurt 1814
Schefski, Harold K. 2986
Scheichl, Sigurd Paul 408, 1254
Schellbach-Kopra, Ingrid 1003, 1329
Scheller, Erich 1515
Schenkeveld-Van Der Dussen, M. A. 1986
Scherf, Kathleen 2815
Schetter, Willy 1177
Scheuer, Helmut 768
Schick, James B. M. 1833
Schindler, Jochem 2703
Schjørring, Jens Holger 1140
Schlacks, Charles, Jr. 520, 811
Schleifer, Ronald 1083, 2059
Schlieben-Lange, Brigitte 1634, 3261
Schlinpert, G. 339
Schlueter, June 2595
Schmaus, Michael 3111
Schmid, Wolfgang P. 1243
Schmidt, Barbara Quinn 3128
Schmidt, Ernst Günther 2161
Schmidt, H. 339
Schmidt, Karl Horst 420, 3254
Schmidt, Michael 2184
Schmidt, Peter 835
Schmidt, Roderich 3262
Schmidt, Torbjörn 1741
Schmidt-Bergmann, Hansgeorg 368
Schmidt-Dengler, Wendelin 3177
Schmidt-Radefeldt, Jürgen 1027
Schmitt, C. 2489
Schmitt, L. E. 327

Schmitt, Ludwig Erich 760, 1103
Schmitt, Matthias 1912
Schmitthenner, Walter 1121
Schneider, Hans Jochen 2708
Schneider, Roland 2078
Schnucker, R. V. 2628
Schoeffel, Ronald 3087
Schoeler, Gregor 268
Schoeman, Karen 3029
Schoenhals, Louise 2586
Scholz, Bernhard F. 3097
Scholz, Günter 3193
Schönberger, Axel 3261
Schöne, Albrecht 2106
Schoonover, David E. 397
Schottenius, Maria 393
Schousboe, Steen 174
Schrader, Hans-Jürgen 1325
Schrader, Wiebke 847
Schreiner, Peter 458
Schreyer, Alice 2302
Schröder, K. 1947
Schubel, Friedrich 2797
Schubert, Gabriella 3253
Schubert, Klaus 1570
Schuh, Russell G. 2805
Schuldiner, Michael 2841
Schüle, Bernard 1022
Schulte, Rainer 3009
Schulte-Sasse, Jochem 2966
Schulte-Wuelwer, Ulrich 1996
Schultz, Lee 2311
Schulz, Eberhard Günter 2545
Schulz, Gerhard 296
Schulz, Volker 1160
Schulze, Martin 1500
Schumacher, Claude 2960
Schupp, Volker 2190
Schutter, G. de 2906
Schütz, Albert J. 2049
Schützeichel, Rudolf 331
Schwartz, Joseph 2347
Schwarz, Ferdinand 1133
Schwitalla, Johannes 762
Sciascia, Leonardo 2039
Scivoletto, Nino 1114
Scott, Graham 300
Scott, Grant F. 970
Scott, John Mark, Jr. 2988
Screen, J. E. O. 2647
Searles, A. Langley 987
Seaward, Mark R. D. 416
Sebeok, Thomas A. 226, 2584
Sebestyén, Á. 1750
Sebold, Russell P. 1185
Secor, Marie J. 2168
See, Klaus von 1053, 2629
Seemann, Klaus-Dieter 3109, 3265
Seesholtz, Mel 1746
Seewann, Gerhard 2872
Šega, Drago 1671
Segal, Gail 2828
Segel, Elizabeth 581
Segert, Stanislav 3249
Segre, Cesare 1800, 2738
Seibel, Wolfgang, S.J. 2732
Seidl, Ivan 961
Seidl, U. 3252
Seigneuret, Jean-Charles 597
Seiler, Thomas H. 2834
Seitel, Peter 995
Selberg, Ole Michael 1785
Selby, John E. 3186
Sellers, Cedric 3006
Sellin, Eric 56, 2403
Semple, Hilary 2596
Sendich, Munir 2505
Senft, Gunter 2215
Senkman, Leonardo 1993
Senn, Fritz 969
Seppänen, Aimo 1128
Serbat, Guy 1247
Serfontein, Louise 2672
Sergeant, Jean-Claude 1048
Serio, John N. 835, 3156
Serper, Arieh 1164
Serralta, Frédéric 709

Serrano Osorio, Francisco 897
Sesé, Bernard 689
Seshachari, Neila C. 3160
Sevaldsen, Jørgen 172
Ševčenko, Ihor 1159
Severin, Dorothy Sherman 446
Sexson, Lynda 679
Sexson, Michael 679
Seymour, Richard K. 98
Sgall, Petr 1643
Shaer, Ben 1782
Shafer, Yvonne 964
Shaffer, Elinor 649
Shalsed, Gershon 1869
Shankovsky, Lev 3055
Shapiro, James S. 1792
Shapllo, Dalan 730, 1938
Sharma, Arvind 207
Sharma, Jai Narain 3140
Sharma, T. R. 1803
Sharp, Derrick 1901
Sharrad, Paul 1967
Sharwood Smith, M. A. 2572
Shaw, Marion 2927-2928
Shaw, R. 1207
Shedletsky, Efraim 3235
Sheffey, Ruthe T. 3275
Sheldon, Ted P. 271
Shelston, Alan 1078
Sheppard, Mubin 1468
Sheraw, C. Darrel 2817
Sherzer, Joel 1568
Shibatani, Masayoshi 1082, 2215
Shillingsburg, Peter L. 2938
Shipley, William 3073
Shoaf, Judith P. 974
Shoaf, R. A. 974
Shoben, Edward J. 1419
Shorrocks, Graham 2332
Short, D. 2647
Short, Mick 1562
Shucard, Alan 3036
Shurbutt, T. Ray 2570
Sicard, Claude 1718
Sicat, Rogelio 789
Siciliano, Enzo 2039
Siebenmann, Gustav 1221
Sieber, Harry 1859
Siehoff, John-Thomas 1960
Sieradzki, Jacek 774
Sierocka, Krystyna 363
Silagi, Gabriel 1902
Silberman, Marc 407
Silberstein, Sandra 2932
Silfer, Giorgio 1690
Silić, Josip 2883
Siller, Max 1254
Silva, António da 417
Silva, Lúcio Craveiro da 2396
Silva, Mario Camarinha da 2369
Silvers, Robert B. 1975
Silvestro, Elio 1304
Silzer, Peter J. 1285
Simms, Norman 1844
Simons, L. 1110
Simpson, Jacqueline 1017
Sims-Williams, Patrick 509
Sims-Wood, Janet 2518
Simson, George 361
Sinclair, Melinda 2700
Singer, Armand E. 3168
Singh, U. N. 1236
Singler, John V. 688
Sinisalo, Hannu 930
Sinor, Denis 1241
Sion, Georges 2428
Sirri, Raffaele 196
Sitaramayya, K. B. 1392
Sitta, Horst 2334
Šivic-Dular, Alenka 1341
Sivula, Anna 1948
Skaggs, David Curtis 2012
Škarić, Ivo 1340
Skatov, N. N. 2509
Skei, Hans H. 2002
Skerrett, Joseph T., Jr. 1806
Skinner, Robert E. 3214

Sklar, Robert 598
Skreija, Andris 1930
Skubic, Mitja 1646
Skurupijs, Eižens 70
Skydsgaard, Niels Jørgen 2076
Sladojević, Ranko 3271
Slagter, P. J. 1619
Slaughter, Jane 1066
Sławinski, Janusz 3240
Sławski, Franciszek 2213-2214, 2468
Slay, D. 2516
Sloane, David E. E. 106, 684, 909
Smart, Veronica 1994
Smerdel, Inja 937
Smet, G. de 3174
Smet, Rudolf de 1150
Smith, C. N. 2591
Smith, Dave 2686
Smith, David R. 1765
Smith, G. Rex 1442
Smith, G. S. 2097
Smith, J. Beverly 447
Smith, Joanna Handlin 1154
Smith, Larry E. 3211
Smith, Llinos Beverley 3001
Smith, Louisa 1668
Smith, Marion V. 2829
Smith, N. V. 516, 1636
Smith, Paul 668
Smith, Paul R. 607
Smith, R. T. 2683
Smith, Raymond J. 2072
Smith, Sheryl 2448
Smith, Thomas 2
Smith-Rosenberg, Carroll 1955
Smyth, Sarah 1289
Smythe, Karen 3159
Snow, Catherine 225
Snow, Joseph T. 557
Snyder, Joel 700
Snyder, Robert 589
Snylyk, Zenon 88, 2888
Snyman, Nico J. 1514
Sobejano, Gonzalo 2391
Soden, Wolfram von 3166, 3249, 3252
Soelberg, Nils 2432
Soetens, Claude 2423
Šojat, Antun 1340
Sokorski, Włodzimierz 1836
Solà, Francisco de P., S.J. 158
Sollers, Philippe 1246
Solomon, Melissa 3036-3037, 3042, 3044
Solstrand-Pipping, Helena 1192, 2634
Somenzi, Vittorio 1822
Somers, Harold 1745
Somerville, Susan C. 576
Sommer, Cornelius 1126, 2866
Sommerstein, Alan H. 1399
Sonderegger, Stefan 2288
Sondrup, Steven P. 2540
Sontrop, Th. A. 1743
Sorel, Andrés 2351
Sorelius, Gunnar 28
Sørensen, Bengt Algot 2076
Sorfleet, John Robert 1366
Sorlin, Pierre 1206
Sornig, Karl 1134
Sosa, Ernest 2167
Sosnowski, Saúl 1180
Soupel, Serge 939
Sourdel, D. 2415
Sourdel-Thomine, J. 2415
Sozzi, Lionello 2749
Spadaccini, Nicholas 972, 1182
Spahr, Blake Lee 587, 750
Specht, Rainer 235
Speed, D. 2130
Spellerberg, Gerhard 587, 750
Spencer, Paul 1494
Spiegelman, Willard 2690
Spies, Bernhard 1682
Spigel, Lynn 518
Spilka, Mark 2030
Spillenger, Paul 879
Spitella, Giorgio 197
Spongano, R. Raffaele 2746

Spoo, Robert 1335
Spottorno, Victoria 2573
Sprenger, R. 2848
Spriet, Pierre 187
Squires, J. E. R. 2162
Srebrnik, Patricia 253
Srinath, C. N. 1673
Srinivasan, A. 1234
Stachowski, Stanisław 1011
Stackmann, Karl 2106, 2946
Staines, David 1367
Staley, Thomas F. 1487
Stallybrass, Peter 1955
Stankiewicz, Edward 1269
Stankov, V. 422
Stanley, E. G. 2016
Stanley, John H. 396
Stanonik, Janez 20
Stanovnik, Majda 1671
Stansky, Peter 3138
Stanton, Domna C. 2183
Stanzel, Franz Karl 1100, 3178
Starewicz, Artur 2196
Stary, Giovanni 561
Stäuble, Antonio 3113
Stäuble, Michèle 631
Stauf, Renate 1100
Steadman, Ian 2673
Steakley, James 1880
Stechow, Arnim V. 1663
Steenberg, D. H. 1680
Steensberg, Axel 2987
Steeves, Edna L. 835, 1874
Steger, Hugo 2714
Stegmann, Tilbert Dídac 3261
Stegmann, Vera 645
Stein, Jean 1130
Stein, Rafaela 236
Steinecke, Hartmut 1139, 3255
Steininger, Alexander 2091
Steinthal, Hermann 1143
Stellmacher, Dieter 3257
Stempel, W.-D. 2489
Stengers, Jean 2401
Stephenson, Glennis 3130
Stephenson, Shelby 2140
Steponavičius, Albertas 1492
Steppat, Michael 663
Sterling, Wallace 2955
Stern, Carola 1943
Sternberg, Robert 2257
Stetsko, Slava 3055
Stevens, C. 1013
Steward, Dwight 1108
Stewart, Pamela D. 3225
Stickel, Gerhard 762
Stiehm, Lothar 2189
Stierle, Karlheinz 2190
Stine, Kate 257
Stitt, Peter 1109
Stjernfelt, Frederik 1716
Stoessel, Franz 1133
Stohlmann, Jürgen 1857
Stoklund, Bjarne 929
Stokoe, William C. 2615
Stolarik, M. Mark 2648
Stolt, Birgit 2736
Stolte, Heinz 1323
Stolz, Benjamin A. 1827, 2117
Stolz, Thomas 373
Stone, G. C. 2096-2097
Storm, Melvin 855
Straka, M. Georges 2406
Strang, Helen 711
Strasser, Erich 1791
Strasser, Gerhard 652
Štrasser, Ján 2653
Stratmann, Gerd 176
Straus, Barrie Ruth 974
Strelka, Joseph P. 1977, 3223
Striedter, Jurij 3109
Stroupe, John H. 650
Strunk, Klaus 1118, 1904
Strutz, Barbara 3195
Strutz, Josef 1910
Stuart, Dabney 2607
Stubington, Jill 298

Stuhlmann, Gunther 153
Stumpfeldt, Hans 2078
Sturm, Fred Gillette 1374
Stürzl, F. 3178
Sturzu, Corneliu 675
Stylianou, Petros S. 1545
Suarez, Juan 599
Subbarao, K. V. 1237
Subramoniam, V. I. 1265
Suchanek, Lucjan 2639
Suda, Minoru 1458
Sudavičiene, Lilija 1492
Sükala, Anna-Leena 2768-2770
Sukla, A. C. 1378
Sullivan, C. W., III 578
Sullivan, Lawrence E. 1411
Sultan, Timothy 3007
Sumberg, Lewis A. M. 3023
Sun, Jingyao 686
Sundquist, Eric 511
Sundwall, McKay 3133
Sung, Shee 583
Susen, G. H. 2954
Sussman, Henry 1120
Sussman, Herbert 3037
Sutherland, Guilland 1219
Sutton, Donald S. 1440
Sutzkever, Avrom 1125
Suvanto, Pekka 181-182
Suzuki, Gorō 2341
Suzuki, Zenzo 2608
Svantesson, Jan-Olof 2779
Svartvik, Jan 1736
Svobodová, Ivana 1924
Swagerty, William R. 1980
Swaim, Ginalie 2107
Swales, Martin 514, 698
Sweterlitsch, Richard 2253
Swiderski, Bronisław 2884
Symington, Rodney 2579
Szabics, Imre 1001
Szabó, Zoltán 2040
Szabolcsi, Miklós 1939
Szarmach, Paul E. 1790, 2061-2062
Szász, Imre 1215
Szekula, P. Augustin, C.M.V. 1151
Szporluk, Roman 1159
Szuberla, Guy 2063
Szulc, Aleksander 364
Szyrocki, Marian 587, 750
Ta-Shma, I. 2912
Tadić, Novica 1518
Taft, Edmund M. 2594
Taghavi, Nematollah 1926
Tagliacozzo, Giorgio 1973
Tai, James H-Y. 1454
Taillefer, M. 188
Takahashi, Yasunari 2600
Takasaki, Jikidō 12, 2984, 3002
Talamantez, Inés 1971
Talens, Jenaro 972, 1182
Talmon, S. 2951
Talmor, Ezra 1193
Talmor, Sascha 1193
Talpo, Oddone 2449
Talshir, David 1600
Tamani, Giuliano 193
Tamás, Attila 2780
Tamba, Irène 1247
Tamburri, Anthony J. 2462, 3122
Tamis, Ferdinando 244
Tamm, Aksel 1503
Tangco, Roberto 789
Tannen, Deborah 1568
Tanner, James T. F. 106
Tanner, John S. 1472
Tanter, Marcy 1776
Tariq, A. 83
Tasch, Peter A. 2563
Tasić, Nikola 311
Tassara Chávez, Gilda 2037
Tate, George 2540
Tatum, Charles M. 2833
Tausky, Thomas E. 295
Tavernier-Courbin, Jacqueline 2952
Tavormina, M. Teresa 3226
Taylor, Allan R. 2623

Taylor, Anita 3198
Taylor, Cheryl 1667
Taylor, Maxine 2688
Taylor, Talbot J. 1554
Teixeira, Manuel 377
Telotte, J. P. 2206
Tenney, Thomas A. 1772
Tennyson, G. B. 1989
Teodorescu, Paul G. 3227
Tering, H. 2098
Terrell, Carroll F. 982, 2101
Tesser, Abraham 1430
Tessitore, Fulvio 387
Tetel, Marcel 1418
Tharaud, Barry 1990
Thelander, Mats 2042, 2631
Théodoridès, Aristide 202
Thesleff, Holger 638
Theuwissen, J. 3146
Thieme, John 1375
Thiolier-Méjean, Suzanne 1046
Thomas, David 1879
Thomason, Sarah G. 1553
Thompson, Laurie 2890
Thompson, Paul 2073
Thompson, Sandra 3073
Thomsen, Christian W. 2335
Thomson, Al 2073
Thomson, Ron B. 1789
Thornberry, Robert S. 2399
Thorsen, Niels 114, 174
Tickoo, Makhan L. 2337
Tierney, Robert J. 2316
Tiessen, Paul 1758
Timko, Michael 544, 780
Titon, Jeff Todd 935
Titone, Renzo 2306
Titunik, Irwin R. 1828
Tobin, Ronald W. 1061
Todorovová, Jiřina 568
Toftdahl, Helmut 1140
Toliver, Harold E. 3074
Tölölyan, Khachig 2271
Tomadakis, N. B. 882
Toman, Jindrich 1827
Tomaselli, Keyan Gray 693
Tomita, Masaru 1745
Tomory, Eva 1218
Tonkin, Humphrey 1570
Tonnet, Henri 464
Toorn, M. C. van den 1986
Toorn-Piebenga, G. van der 2980
Top, S. 3146
Topia, André 3028
Toporišič, Jože 2646
Topping, Donald M. 2049
Toruńczyk, Barbara 3267
Tötösy de Zepetnek, S. 535
Toubert, P. 1897
Toubert, Pierre 1348
Tournoy, Gilbert 1211
Toury, Gideon 2913
Touzot, Jean 258
Tov, E. 2951
Towers, Tom H. 1356
Trabant, Jürgen 1523
Trahean, Joseph B., Jr. 2061
Traoré, Ousseynou B. 1675
Travers, Pauric 2774
Tripathi, Gaya C. 1460
Tromp, Bart 1743
Trouard, Dawn 990
Trudgill, Peter 1567
Trujillo, Colleen 1411
Truman, R. W. 2096
Trussler, Simon 1972
Tryjarski, Edward 2467
Trzynadlowski, Jan 1715, 3242
Tsau, Yifun 599
Tucker, G. Richard 206
Tukia, Marc 672
Tuller, Laurie 1645
Tumku, Shanta 1452
Turcotte, Gerry 297
Turgeon, Laurier 524
Turk, Horst 2106
Turki, A. M. 2777

Turner, Bez 372
Turner, Michael L. 2269
Tuttle, Edward F. 2478
Twycross, Meg 816, 1795-1796
Tye, Diane 524
Tyler, Lorraine K. 1557
Ucelay, Margarita 383
Udal'tsov, A. 1711
Udovitch, A. L. 2777
Uhlig, S. 60
Uitti, Karl D. 836
Ujfalussy, József 2784
Uledi-Kamanga, Brighton J. 1401
Undank, Jack 753
Unsworth, John 2208
Untermann, Jürgen 331
Unwin, Vicky 54
Upadhyaya, S. A. 343
Upshur, J. 1575
Upshur, J. A. 1569
Urban, William 1364
Urban, Ždeněk 940
Urbańczyk, Stanisław 2214
Urdang, Laurence 3107
Urs, S. N. Vikramraj 641
Ury, Marian 1453
Uther, Hans Jörg 984
Vago, Robert M. 731
Vajda, György Mihály 1939
Vajda, Miklós 1216
Valdman, Albert 2846
Valente, Luiz Fernando 405
Valentin, Jean-Marie 587, 750, 951
Valetas, Kostas 69
Välikangas, Olli 1948
Valjalo, David 1689
Vallbona, Rima de 1026
Vallone, Aldo 84
Van Emden, Wolfgang 697
Van Gelder, Gordon 1976
Van Hooft, Karen S. 360
Van Schooneveld, C. H. 1269
Van Wermeskerken, J. Herman 529
Vanagas, A. 1633
Vanasse, André 1614
Vancil, David 813
Vandendorpe, Christian 2325
Vander Meulen, David L. 2813
Vanderheyden, Ildefons 1054
Vannebo, Einar 2002
Vanovičová, Zora 2654
Varey, J. E. 699
Varnier, Marie-Hélène 477
Várvaro, Alberto 1800
Vaškelis, Aleksas 1820
Vasko, Michael 2899
Vásquez, Mary S. 1606
Vassallo, Peter 1359
Vater, Heinz 1513, 1662
Vattimo, Gianni 2452
Vaughan, W. E. 1288
Vaughn, Mary 507
Vavřínek, Vladimír 459
Veiga, Alexandre 3106
Veith, Werner H. 2794
Velmans, T. 464
Vennemann, Theo 1903, 2715, 2801
Venturi, Franco 2460
Verdevoye, Paul 2446
Verelst, Philippe 2485
Verene, Donald Phillip 1973
Vergauwen, G. 1056
Vergelis, A. 2691
Verhagen, Arie 1034
Verhesen, F. 685
Verkuyl, H. J. 1986
Vermeyden, Paula 150
Verna, Antony 2458
Verschueren, Jef 2216
Verzandvoort, Erwin 2336
Vessels, Gary 2981
Vet, Co 992
Vickery, Walter N. 1269
Vidal, Hernan 1697
Vidal, M. Carmen Africa 2367
Vidoeski, Božidar 1756
Vidović, Radovan 500

Vieira, Nelson H. 405, 1874
Vienken, Heinz J. 2891
Viese, Saulcerite 2299
Vigil-Piñón, Evangelina 129
Viikari, Auli 1510
Vilarós-Soler, Teresa M. 3060
Vilasco, Gilles 186
Villani, Sergio 1719
Villegas, Juan 1107
Vinall, Shirley W. 1308
Vincent, Nigel 516, 1413, 2475
Vincent, T. 365
Vinten-Johansen, Peter 2540
Vintr, Josef 3180
Viola, André 737
Virk, Jani 1714
Višinski, Boris 1744
Vitanza, Victor J. 2223
Vitse, Marc 709
Viudas Camarasa, Antonio 221
Vivier, Jack 435
Vizioli, Paolo 925, 1637
Vizzutti, Flavio 244
Vogel, Hans-Jochen 1943
Vogelsang, Arthur 107
Vogt, Ernst 1121
Vogt, Jochen 2153
Volkov, I. F. 3118
Voller, Jack G. 2123
Vomperski, V. P. 2510
Von Schmidt, Wolff A. 3096
Voogd, Peter de 2604
Vos, A. de 1110
Vos, Luk de 2358
Vos, Morris 912
Vossen, Rainer 2707
Vowell, Faye N. 855
Vries, O. 3095
Vuarchex, François 2022
Vuillet, Dominique 471-472
Vuuren, H. van 2965
Vyas, R. T. 1470
Waage Petersen, Lene 2432
Wachinger, Burghart 90, 329, 1031
Wack, E. 2954
Wackers, Paul 2336
Waddingtorpe, P. H. 1979
Wadhwani, Y. 1237
Wagener, Peter 2172
Wagenknecht, Christian J. 2106
Wagenknecht, David 2844
Wagner, Claudio 922
Wagner, Fritz 1857
Wahlin, Clas 2978
Wainwright, J. A. 744
Wajda, Shirley 3189
Wajskop, M. Max 2301
Wald, L. 2233
Walden, Daniel 2811
Waldman, Marilyn R. 2115
Wales, Katie 1562
Walker, Donald E. 655
Walker, R. M. 1873
Walker, Ron 1934
Walker, Steven 1696
Walker, Sue 1934
Wall, Stephen 910
Wall, William G. 779
Wallesch, Claus-W. 1949
Walsh, Joy 1889
Walsh, Michael 3077
Walters, William D., Jr. 1778
Walther, Elisabeth 2580
Walther, Hans 758
Walther, Helmut 2702
Wandruszka, Adam 2493
Wang, William S-Y. 1372
Wang, Zuoliang 1025
Wankenne, A., S.J. 944
Warburg, Gabriel R. 264
Ward, Alan 2996
Ward, Claire T. 3136
Ward, Dunstan 1048
Ward, Hayden 3129
Ward, Robert 845
Ware, Robert 530
Warner, Alfred 1912

Warwick, Ronald 1375
Wasserman, Julian N. 974
Watanabe, H. 1094
Watkins, Teresa 2073
Watson, Ruth 1548
Watts, Richard J. 1900
Watts, William 546
Watzlawick, Helmut 1260
Wawn, Andrew 1591
Waxman, Ruth B. 1488
Weaver, Ann C. 2263
Weaver, Gordon 596, 3042
Webb, G. H. 1509
Webb, Timothy 1502
Webby, Elizabeth 2681
Weber, Samuel 1120
Weczerka, Hugo 3262
Weigand, Karl-Heinz 370
Weijnen, A. 1787
Weil, R. 2409
Weill, Asher 252
Weisberg, Richard H. 541
Weiss, H. 359
Weiss, Hellmuth 3262
Weiss, Penelope F. 2813
Weiss, Walter 2711
Weissberger, Barbara 680
Weissenborn, Georg K. 1093
Weitenberg, J. J. S. 820
Weitzman, Arthur J. 2563
Weixlmann, Joe 46
Welch, John W. 410
Weller, Barry 3172
Weller, F.-R. 1947
Wells, David A. 3230
Wells, Stanley 2602
Welsh, James M. 1706
Welzig, Werner 3177
Wendehorst, Alfred 1330
Wenger, Luke 2694
Wenk, Klaus 2078
Wenke, John 1807
Wenzel, Heinz 1985
Wenzel, Horst 1028
Werbow, Stanley N. 2946
Werge, Thomas 2338
Werner, Otmar 1662, 2714
Wertheimer, Jürgen 232
Wertheimer, Molly 2168
Wesana-Chomi, E. 1511
West, Geoffrey 557
West, James L. W., III 2361
Westerman, William 1963
Westman, Margareta 2635, 2716
Weststeÿn, W. G. 2849
Wetzel, Hermann H. 1311
Wetzel, Patricia 1453
Wetzels, W. Leo 2237
Wexler, Kenneth 1555
Wexler, Paul 1801
Wezler, Albrecht 2799
Wheeler, Max W. 2266, 3003
Whitaker, Harry A. 404
White, Douglas H. 2360
White, Gertrude 573
White, J. J. 1094
Whiteman, Bruce 2121
Whiton, J. 1106
Wickler, Wolfgang 936
Widdowson, H. G. 206
Widdowson, J. D. A. 1729
Wieczerzak, Joseph W. 2197
Wiedemann, C. 327
Wiedemann, Conrad 1100, 2795
Wiederholt, J. Lee 1412
Wiegand, Herbert Ernst 1103, 1620, 2334, 3260
Wiehl, Reiner 1167
Wielandt, Ulf 1055
Wiese, Benno von 391
Wiesmüller, Wolfgang 408
Wiggen, Geirr 1264
Wigginton, Eliot 1042
Wilbert, Johannes 1411
Wilcox, Earl J. 2463
Wild, S. 3165
Wilder, Joseph Carleton 1480

Wildman, Allan 2507
Wilhelm, James J. 1075
Wilkanowicz, Stefan 3272
Wilkes, G. A. 2893
Wilkins, Frederick 964
Will, E. 2902
Willard, William 3175
Williams, Anne 530
Williams, David 697
Williams, Edith Whitehurst 1797
Williams, George Walton 2344
Williams, J. E. Caerwyn 2767, 3215
Williams, Jeffrey 1842
Williams, Mark 1548
Williams, William P. 167
Williamson, Elaine 1048
Williamson, J. W. 223
Willingham, David R. 1642
Willis, Sharon 518
Willson, A. Leslie 791
Wilmers, Mary-Kay 1726
Wilson, Ann 914
Wilson, Carol 1213
Wilson, J. J. 3138
Wilson, Rita 2745
Winckler, Walter 2700
Winden, J. C. M. van 3132
Windross, M. 1647
Winge, Vibeke 1531
Winid, Bogodar 55
Winkelmann, Friedhelm 340
Winkelmann, Kerstin 1052
Winkelmann, Otto 2231
Winner, T. 2504
Winnington, G. Peter 481, 2139
Winter, Carl 177, 332
Winter, Jürgen Christoph 2707
Winter, Werner 3017-3019
Winters-Ohle, Elmar 3269
Wintle, M. 819
Wipprecht, Wendy 3219
Wirgin, Jan 451
Wis, Marjatta 1948
Wisbey, R. A. 654, 1873, 3224
Wise, Derek 457
Wise, Mary Ruth 2588
Witchell, Elizabeth 1481
Witkowski, T. 339
Witte, John 2013
Wittmann, Henri 2431
Wittmann, Reinhard 236
Wittrock, Ulf 2527
Wittstock, Uwe 1944
Witzel, Michael 1242, 2799
Wlassics, Tibor 1590
Woesler, Winfried 833
Wohlfeil, Rainer 2792
Wójcicki, Ryszard 2781
Wójcik, Andreas 880
Wojcik-Andrews, Ian 1424
Wolf, Alois 1713
Wolf, Lothar 539
Wolf-Knuts, Ulrika 261
Wolfe, Charles K. 2924
Wölfel, Kurt 1322
Wolff, D. 1947
Wolff, Erwin 173, 419
Wolfson, Nessa 2989
Wolfzettel, Friedrich 1839
Wolgast, Eike 1167
Wollasch, Joachim 1067
Wollman, Slavomir 2638
Wollschläger, Hans 1323
Wolper, Roy S. 2563
Wolpers, Theodor 173, 419, 2106
Wolski, Werner 1620
Wood, David 1546
Wood, Deloris Gray 1730
Woodfield, Richard 412
Woodhouse, J. R. 1873
Woods, Alan 2961
Woodward, Kathleen 796
Woodyard, George W. 1584
Workman, Leslie J. 2836
Wormell, Irene 1631
Worstbrock, Franz Josef 3256
Worth, Dean S. 1269

Worth, Katharine 2959
Wortham, Thomas 1989
Worthen, W. B. 2958
Worthington, Pepper 1895
Wrigglesworth, Hazel 2838
Wright, Andrew 3074
Wright, C. J. 414
Wright, Conrad E. 2244
Wright, Laurence 2596
Wright, Michelle R. 666
Wright, Peter 1466
Wright, Roger 1721
Wright, Thomas C. 1146
Wrobel, Arthur 208
Wrobel, Henryk 2198
Wu, Beiling 582
Wu, Duncan 570
Wu, Xunnan 846
Wunberg, Gotthart 3033
Wunderli, Peter 3150
Wurtele, Douglas J. 875, 1008
Wuttke, Dieter 1132
Wyche, Kathleen B. 2005
Wynar, Lubomyr R. 3058
Wysling, Hans 2972-2973
Wytrzenst, G. 3180
Xu, Guozhang 1024
Yamamoto, Hiroshi 868
Yao, Xiaoping 1024
Yetman, Norman 113
Yip, Po-Ching 1416
Yong, Margaret 2680
Young, David 996
Young, Jekaterina 2559
Young, Katherine K. 207
Young, Lynne 543
Young, R. V. 1345
Young, Robert 2095
Young, Sally B. 2925
Young, Stephen Flinn 2685
Yperen, Maria J. L. van 358
Ystad, Vigdis 667
Yuniyev, V. I. 1255
Zacchi, Romana 2934
Zach, Wolfgang 2822
Zacher, Christian 2851
Zacks, Rose T. 1396
Zadravec, Franc 2646
Zadrozny, Mark 3038-3040
Zahn-Waxler, Carolyn 769
Zakar, P. Polycarpus 156
Zakonnikaŭ, Siarheĭ 2200
Zakrzewski, Bogdan 2108
Zalazar, Geraldine Korb 2853
Zālīte, Māra 1499
Zaluskowski, G. 763
Zalygin, S. P. 2031
Zandbergs, L. 1337
Zander, William 1678
Zanderigo Rosolo, Giandomenico 244
Zanenga, Bartolomeo 244
Zanker, Paul 1121
Zarev, Panteleĭ 1709
Zarycky, Volodymyr 3055
Zăstroiu, Remus 220
Zavala, Iris M. 707, 2931
Zea, Leopoldo 718
Zeifman, Hersh 1867
Zeiss, Agnès Peysson 3029
Zell, Hans M. 48
Zeman, Herbert 1328
Zennaro, Silvio 84
Zgusta, Ladislav 1620-1621
Žic-Fuchs, Milena 2883
Ziejka, Franciszek 2500
Zierer, Ernesto 1597
Zilberman, Regina 405
Zilversmit, Annette 832
Zimmer, Jürgen 1945
Zimmermann, Albert 1846
Zimmermann, Hans-Joachim 1167
Zimmermann, Harald 2705, 2708, 2872
Zimmermann, Lothar 1093
Zimmermann, Werner 1863
Zimmermann, Werner G. 1627
Zinsli, P. 2706
Zipes, Jack 1668, 1959

Zlobec, Ciril 2666
Zonneveld, W. 1986
Zoppi, Sergio 3101
Zorbas, Alejandro 461
Zorić, Pavle 2536

Zorzi, Marino 274
Zorzi, Renzo 657
Zuber-Skerritt, Ortrum 302
Zuniga-Lomeli, Sonia 2981

Zürcher, E. 2991
Zuses, Carol 2246
Zwarycz, Roman 3055
Zwernemann, J. 60

INDEX TO LANGUAGES PUBLISHED

Because of the many items involved, references to journals and series publishing in English, French, German, Italian, and Spanish are not included here. To include them would, in the view of the editors, make this index excessively large without increasing its usefulness. Users are urged to consult the main listing for additional information on languages published.

Afrikaans 52, 1030, 1349, 1415, 1514, 1680, 2358, 2672, 2965, 3048-3049
Albanian 1938
Arabic 72, 81, 228, 348, 1089, 1222, 1234, 1388, 1408, 1511, 1630, 2404, 2435, 3251
Armenian 1151, 2137, 2400
Bahasa Malay dialect 1285, 2444
Basque 1479, 2585
Belorussian 333-334, 1757, 1821, 2200, 2468, 2639, 3119, 3246
Bengali 1319
Breton 1202, 2767
Bulgarian 422, 1489, 1707, 1709, 2066, 2178, 2442, 2468, 2655, 2848, 2880
Catalan 158, 163, 446, 920, 924, 1046, 1072, 1184, 1186-1187, 1221, 1400, 1405, 1646, 1725, 1734, 1789, 1800, 1876, 2305, 2371, 2406, 2418, 2462, 2474, 2477, 2479, 2585, 2783, 2929, 3027, 3060, 3105-3106, 3261
Chinese languages 445, 473, 592-593, 686, 1024-1025, 1089, 1194, 1253, 1372, 1416, 1454, 1559, 3030, 3155
Croatian 1340, 2883, 3241
Czech 551, 567-568, 606, 1233, 1489, 1669, 1827-1828, 1924, 2066, 2068, 2117, 2247, 2442, 2468, 2537-2538, 2559, 2643, 2646, 2650, 2653-2656, 2692, 2848, 3181
Danish 150, 169, 174, 256, 337, 353, 375, 745-748, 831, 834, 1004, 1015, 1074, 1140, 1191-1192, 1220, 1389, 1512, 1525, 1534, 1540, 1716, 1742, 1804, 1876, 1919, 1934, 1995, 1999, 2002, 2042, 2051, 2085, 2220, 2471, 2517, 2530, 2566, 2633, 2635, 2637, 2644, 2716, 2766, 2771, 2791, 2802, 2873, 2884, 2886, 2894, 2978, 2980, 2993, 3098, 3134
Dutch 45, 57, 59, 144, 150, 218, 336, 355, 358, 474, 529, 590, 602, 787, 889, 1034, 1110-1111, 1150, 1259, 1299, 1313, 1317, 1331, 1349, 1514, 1531, 1549, 1618-1619, 1647, 1680, 1786-1787, 1916, 1983-1984, 1986, 2069-2070, 2079, 2301, 2358, 2366, 2401, 2437, 2515, 2696, 2699, 2771, 2906, 2979-2980, 2982, 3032, 3048-3049, 3095, 3114, 3144, 3146, 3174
Esperanto 846, 900, 902, 1570, 1690, 2455
Estonian 851, 1503, 1728, 1762, 2098, 2625, 3034
Faroese 1065, 1919, 2766
Filipino 1624, 2156
Finnish 33, 398, 1004, 1493, 1495, 1498, 1510, 2041, 2131, 2532, 2876-2878, 3139
French Creole 945
Frisian 1299, 1997, 3095
Galician 376, 1136, 1184, 2371, 2585, 3027, 3060, 3106
Greek 3, 69, 189, 233, 276, 348, 458, 460, 464, 881-886, 1172, 1324, 1462, 1508, 1544-1545, 1755, 1789, 1794, 1861, 1933, 2132, 2160, 2185, 2352, 2457, 2671, 2727, 2967, 2994
Gujarati 1467
Hebrew 359, 362, 1162-1163, 1600-1601, 1845, 1869, 1899, 2248, 2912, 2951, 3234
Hindi 316, 1460
Hindi-Urdu 1018, 1282, 1467, 2111

Hungarian 25-26, 80, 89, 928, 1001, 1169, 1216, 1218, 1292-1294, 1532-1533, 1687, 1748-1751, 2040-2041, 2559, 2692, 2780, 2903
Icelandic 150, 256, 353, 834, 1919, 2630, 2766, 2778
Irish Gaelic 322, 526, 558, 635, 844-845, 892, 1291, 1406, 1455, 1474, 1588, 1781, 2767, 2774, 2916-2917, 3059
Japanese 205, 249, 445, 455, 574, 591-592, 843, 868, 1082, 1089, 1145, 1179, 1201, 1336, 1409, 1458, 1504, 1559, 2608-2609, 2667-2668, 2692, 2823-2825, 2835, 2977, 2984-2985, 3084, 3155
Korean 1253, 1390, 1459, 1572, 2170
Latin 3, 11, 40, 155, 158, 171, 181, 189, 219, 241, 243, 247, 283, 638, 802, 880, 885, 1114, 1118, 1121, 1132-1133, 1177, 1211, 1324, 1585-1586, 1646, 1669, 1764, 1766, 1771, 1789, 1794, 1802, 1857, 1860, 1907, 2026, 2070, 2161, 2188, 2202, 2348, 2352, 2401, 2417, 2438, 2445, 2451, 2473, 2493, 2617, 2671, 2762, 2782-2783, 2895, 2994, 3270
Latvian 70, 246, 250, 315, 1337, 1499, 1535, 1587, 1633, 1694, 2299, 2733
Lithuanian 67, 315, 1112, 1492, 1522, 1539, 1633, 1688, 1691, 1820, 2733
Macedonian 1489, 1708, 2308, 2468, 2645-2646, 2655, 3270
Mongol languages 479, 1881
Native American languages 2105
Norwegian 150, 169, 256, 337, 353, 375, 748, 831, 834, 1004, 1074, 1140, 1191-1192, 1220, 1389, 1512, 1540, 1742, 1785, 1804, 1876, 1919, 1995, 1999-2002, 2042, 2085, 2471, 2517, 2530, 2566, 2633, 2635, 2637, 2644, 2716, 2766, 2771, 2791, 2873, 2884, 2886, 2894, 2897, 2978, 2980, 2993, 3026, 3098, 3134, 3239
Occitan 272, 1046, 1072, 2418, 2929
Panjabi 2111
Pennsylvania German dialect 2141
Persian 988, 1754, 1926
Philippine languages 2157
Polish 14, 32, 351, 363-364, 774, 880, 1342, 1489, 1522, 1537, 1543, 1692, 1715, 1735, 1827-1828, 1836, 2052, 2066, 2108-2110, 2117, 2198-2199, 2203, 2212-2214, 2254, 2273, 2442, 2466, 2468-2469, 2498, 2500, 2537-2538, 2559, 2639, 2645-2646, 2655, 2692, 2782, 2790, 2848, 2921, 3047, 3181, 3240, 3242, 3267, 3272
Portuguese 52, 79, 126, 132, 164, 184, 196, 212, 221, 258, 284, 348, 376-377, 405, 417, 446, 462, 480, 484, 571, 586, 602, 632, 689, 740, 786, 798, 878, 920, 925-926, 962, 972, 985, 1037, 1089, 1145, 1157, 1181, 1184-1188, 1221, 1225, 1286, 1400, 1411, 1570, 1583-1584, 1597-1598, 1605, 1610, 1646-1647, 1697, 1734, 1738, 1771, 1800, 1811, 1817, 1840, 1883, 1890, 1934, 1940, 1993, 2003, 2026, 2086, 2182, 2186, 2230, 2237, 2279, 2281, 2305, 2353, 2369-2371, 2374, 2376, 2383, 2385, 2388, 2391-2396, 2398, 2401, 2406, 2418, 2432-2433, 2462, 2465, 2473-2474, 2477, 2479, 2487, 2489, 2568, 2576, 2585, 2587, 2739, 2744, 2755, 2783, 2981, 2992, 3016, 3060, 3106, 3108, 3116, 3263

Romanian 159, 196, 220, 350, 565, 675, 1157, 1449, 1635, 1646, 1733, 1766, 1800, 1844, 2083, 2233, 2379, 2384, 2406, 2418, 2432, 2474, 2482, 2490, 2571, 2728, 2755, 2863, 3123, 3227, 3263
Russian 9, 11, 14-15, 19, 21, 26, 32-33, 159, 239, 252, 303, 309, 311, 313, 315, 331, 357, 364, 459, 495, 505, 520, 535, 561, 675, 752, 755, 805, 811, 817, 883, 949, 1002, 1081, 1089, 1119, 1131, 1151, 1194, 1233, 1255, 1315, 1388, 1489, 1492, 1522, 1526, 1539, 1587, 1597, 1619, 1633, 1640, 1642, 1646-1647, 1651-1652, 1666, 1669, 1688, 1709-1712, 1766, 1785, 1821, 1827-1828, 1874, 1878, 1896, 1925, 1930, 1935, 1939, 1951, 2031-2032, 2041, 2060, 2066, 2068, 2071, 2117, 2137, 2161, 2217, 2226, 2253, 2273, 2296, 2384, 2433, 2442, 2467-2468, 2483, 2504-2506, 2509-2510, 2513, 2537-2538, 2542, 2559, 2639, 2643-2646, 2655, 2692, 2711, 2726, 2735, 2784, 2788-2789, 2818, 2848-2849, 2863, 2876, 2880, 2883-2884, 2900, 3118, 3147-3148, 3155, 3164, 3180-3181, 3192-3194, 3242, 3245, 3253, 3264, 3270, 3274, 3276
Sanskrit 199, 343, 403, 1452, 1460, 2111, 3140
Scottish Gaelic 844, 2556, 2560-2561, 2767, 2827, 3000
Serbo-Croatian 311, 348, 500, 755, 1032, 1122, 1134, 1314, 1489, 1517-1521, 1646, 1827-1828, 1877, 1893, 1921-1923, 1932, 2066, 2117, 2225-2227, 2442, 2468, 2536, 2543, 2646, 2655, 2848, 2867, 3181, 3270-3271
Slovak 568, 606, 2066, 2247, 2468, 2650-2655, 2692
Slovenian 776, 937, 1341, 1489, 1530, 1646, 1671, 1858, 2227, 2310, 2468, 2646, 2655, 2666, 2997, 3181, 3270, 3273
Sorbian 2468
Swahili 1511, 3061
Swedish 20, 32-33, 150, 169, 256, 337, 353, 375, 393, 398, 748, 831, 834, 931, 989, 1004, 1074, 1140, 1191-1192, 1195, 1220, 1389, 1498, 1512, 1540, 1742, 1804, 1876, 1919, 1995, 1999, 2002, 2042, 2077, 2085, 2151, 2471, 2517, 2527, 2530, 2566, 2633-2635, 2637, 2644, 2716, 2733, 2737, 2766, 2771, 2791, 2873, 2877-2878, 2884-2887, 2894, 2978, 2980, 2993, 3098, 3134, 3208
Tagalog 789, 2154
Tamil 1445
Thai 1478
Tok Pisin English Pidgin 1560
Turkish 883, 1312
Ukrainian 88, 133, 805, 1256, 1483, 1538, 1896, 1920, 2035, 2066, 2195, 2218, 2442, 2468, 2639, 2655, 2657, 2888, 3056-3058, 3151, 3154, 3247
Waray 1624
Welsh 447, 1724, 1929, 2767, 3001, 3025, 3215
Yiddish 1125, 2691, 3235-3237

PERIODICALS WITH AUTHOR-ANONYMOUS SUBMISSION POLICY

Abr-Nahrain 6
Acta Germanica 16
ADFL Bulletin 39
Africa Report 44
African Notes 51
African Studies 52
African Studies Review 53
Afro-Hispanic Review 62
Agenda 65
Al-'Arabiyya 72
Alba de América 74
Alemannisches Jahrbuch 77
Alif 81
Allegorica 87
Általános Nyelvészeti Tanulmányok 89
Amerasia Journal 92
American Benedictine Review 94
American Drama 96
American Journal of Germanic Linguistics and Literatures 98
American Journal of Semiotics 100
American Literary History 101
American Literary Realism, 1870-1910 102
American Psychologist 108
American Quarterly 109
American Speech 112
American Studies 113
American Transcendental Quarterly 116
Amerikastudien/American Studies 130
Amsterdam Studies in the Theory and History of Linguistic Science IV 147
Amsterdamer Beiträge zur Älteren Germanistik 150
Amsterdamer Publikationen zur Sprache und Literatur 152
Anales Galdosianos 165
Anello Che Non Tiene 170
Anglica et Americana 174
Annales de Bretagne et des Pays de l'Ouest 183
Annali Università per Stranieri 197
Annals of Scholarship 198
Annual of Armenian Linguistics 203
Anthropologica 209
Anthropological Quarterly 211
Anthropos 212
Antípodas 216
Antipodes 217
Appalachian Journal 223
Approaches to Translation Studies 227
Arbor 230
Archiv für Geschichte der Philosophie 235
Ariel 251
Ariel: A Review of International English Literature 253
Arkansas Quarterly: A Journal of Criticism 255
Ars Lyrica: Journal of Lyrica, Society for Word-Music Relations 259
Arthurian Yearbook 260
Asian Music 266
Assays 270
Association for Recorded Sound Collections Journal 271
Atlantis 279
Australian-Canadian Studies 297
Aztlán 308
Behavior Research and Therapy 324
Beihefte zur Zeitschrift für Romanische Philologie 326
Bestia 341
Bibliothèque des Cahiers de l'Institut de Linguistique de Louvain 355
Bijdragen tot de Taal-, Land- en Volkenkunde 358
*Brain and Language 404
Brasil/Brazil 405
British Journal of Aesthetics 412
British Journal of Psychology 413
Bulletin de la Société Américaine de Philosophie de Langue Française 428
Cahiers de Linguistique—Asie Orientale 473
Cahiers du Dix-septième 482
Canadian-American Slavic Studies 520
Canadian Ethnic Studies/Etudes Ethniques au Canada 521
Canadian Folklore Canadien 524

Canadian Journal of Irish Studies 526
Canadian Journal of Italian Studies 527
Canadian Journal of Netherlandic Studies/Revue Canadienne d'Etudes Néerlandaises 529
Canadian Journal of Philosophy 530
Canadian Modern Language Review/La Revue Canadienne des Langues Vivantes 532
Canadian Review of American Studies 534
Canadian Slavonic Papers 536
Canadiana Romanica 539
CARA 540
Cardozo Studies in Law and Literature 541
Carleton Germanic Papers 542
Časopis pro Moderní Filologii 551
Cather Studies 554
Celestinesca 557
Cervantes 566
Champs du Signe 569
Chasqui 571
Child Development 576
Children's Folklore Review 578
Children's Literature Association Quarterly 580
Chinese Literature 585
Christianity and Literature 589
Cincinnati Romance Review 597
Cinema Journal 600
Classical and Modern Literature 608
Classical Journal 609
Clues 614
*Cognitive Neuropsychology 619
*Cognitive Psychology 620
Cognitive Science 621
College Composition and Communication 626
College English 627
College Literature 629
Comitatus 636
Communication Education 643
Communication Monographs 644
Comparatist 647
Comparative Civilizations Review 648
Conference of College Teachers of English Studies 660
Constructions 666
Contemporary Legend 668
*Contemporary Review 670
Continuum 671
Council on National Literatures/World Report 683
Country Dance and Song 684
Creole Language Library 688
Critical Arts 693
Critical Studies 704
Critical Theory 707
Criticón 709
Cuadernos de Poética 723
Cultural Critique 728
Current Bibliography on African Affairs 734
Dalhousie French Studies 743
Dalhousie Review 744
Daphnis 750
Degré Second 753
Degrés 754
Dialogue 778
Dickens Studies Annual 780
Diderot Studies 785
Dieciocho 786
Discours Social/Social Discourse 795
Discurso 798
Divus Thomas 802
Dix-Huitième Siècle 803
Dostoevsky Studies 811
Durham University Journal 818
Edad de Oro 830
Edward Sapir Monograph Series in Language, Culture, and Cognition 837
Eighteenth-Century Fiction 840
Eighteenth-Century Life 841
Eighteenth-Century Studies 842
El Popola Ĉinio 846
Elementa 847
Emblematica 852
Emporia State Research Studies 855

Encyclia 858
English in Africa 862
English Language Notes 864
English Linguistics 865
English Studies in Africa 874
English Studies in Canada 875
Epos 888
Esprit Créateur 905
Essays in Arts and Sciences 909
Essays in Theatre/Etudes Théâtrales 914
Essays on Canadian Writing 915
Estreno 916
Estudios de Lingüística 920
Estudios de Lingüística Aplicada 921
Ethnology 934
Ethnomusicology 935
Etudes Anglaises 939
Etudes Créoles 945
Etudes Littéraires 957
European Romantic Review 970
European Studies Journal 971
Evelyn Waugh Newsletter and Studies 973
Explorations in Ethnic Studies 979
Faulkner Journal 990
Feminaria 993
Feminist Studies 994
Field 996
Film Criticism 998
Filología 1000
Finnisch-Ugrische Forschungen 1003
First Language 1005
Flannery O'Connor Bulletin 1006
Florilegium 1008
Folk Life 1013
Folklore Forum 1020
Folklore Historian 1021
Folklore Suisse/Folclore Svizzero 1022
Foreign Literatures 1025
Forschungen zu Paul Valéry—Recherches Valéryennes 1027
Forum 1032
Forum der Letteren 1034
Forum Linguisticum 1038
Foundations of Semiotics 1041
Français au Nigéria 1043
French Cultural Studies 1057
French Forum 1058
French Literature Series 1060
French Review 1061
Fróðskaparrit 1065
Frontiers 1066
Garland Library of Medieval Literature 1075
Genders 1080
General Linguistics 1081
Gengo Kenkyū 1082
George Sand Studies 1088
German Life and Letters 1094
German Quarterly 1095
German Studies Review 1096
Germanic Review 1098
Gezelliana 1110
Great Plains Quarterly 1135
Hamlet Studies 1149
Harvard Library Bulletin 1155
Hebrew Annual Review 1161
Hebrew Studies 1163
Hemingway Review 1173
Henry James Review 1174
Heritage of the Great Plains 1175
Hispania 1181
Hispanic Linguistics 1184
Hispanica Posnaniensia 1186
History of European Ideas 1193
*Human Development 1209
Human Studies 1210
Huntington Library Quarterly 1219
Illinois Historical Journal 1226
Indian Journal of Applied Linguistics 1235
Information/Communication 1249
Institute of African Studies, Occasional Publications 1257
International Fiction Review 1261
International Journal of Lexicography 1266
International Journal of Middle East Studies 1267
Interpretation 1276

*only at author's request

Issues in Applied Linguistics 1296
Italian Americana 1303
Italian Studies 1307
Italica 1310
ITL 1313
Jezik 1340
Journal for Semitics/Tydskrif vir Semitistiek 1349
Journal for the Scientific Study of Religion 1350
*Journal of Abnormal Psychology 1351
Journal of Advanced Composition 1352
Journal of Aesthetics and Art Criticism 1353
Journal of American Culture 1356
Journal of Anthropological Research 1360
Journal of Asian Studies 1362
Journal of Beckett Studies 1365
Journal of Canadian Poetry 1367
Journal of Canadian Studies/Revue d'Etudes Canadiennes 1368
Journal of Caribbean Studies 1369
*Journal of Celtic Linguistics 1370
Journal of Child Language 1371
Journal of Communication 1376
Journal of Communication Inquiry 1377
Journal of Cultural Geography 1381
Journal of Dramatic Theory and Criticism 1384
Journal of Durassian Studies 1385
Journal of East Asian Linguistics 1386
Journal of European Studies 1393
*Journal of Experimental Psychology: Human Perception and Performance 1395
*Journal of Experimental Psychology: Learning, Memory, and Cognition 1396
Journal of Folklore Research 1397
Journal of French Language Studies 1398
*Journal of Hispanic Philology 1400
Journal of Indo-European Studies 1404
Journal of Japanese Studies 1407
Journal of King Saud University, Arts 1408
Journal of Language and Social Psychology 1410
Journal of Latin American Lore 1411
Journal of Literary Studies/Tydskrif Vir Literaturwetenskap 1415
*Journal of Memory and Language 1419
Journal of Modern Greek Studies 1421
Journal of Modern Literature 1422
Journal of Nervous and Mental Disease 1426
*Journal of Nonverbal Behavior 1428
Journal of Northwest Semitic Languages 1429
*Journal of Personality and Social Psychology 1430
Journal of Philosophical Logic 1431
Journal of Phonetics 1433
Journal of Pidgin and Creole Languages 1434
Journal of Pre-Raphaelite Studies 1438
Journal of Ritual Studies 1440
Journal of Semitic Studies 1442
*Journal of Speech and Hearing Research 1444
Journal of the Acoustical Society of America 1446
Journal of the American Oriental Society 1448
Journal of the American Studies Association of Texas 1450
Journal of the Gypsy Lore Society 1461
Journal of the Hellenic Diaspora 1462
Journal of the History of Ideas 1463
Journal of the Midwest Modern Language Association 1469
Journal of the Rocky Mountain Medieval and Renaissance Association 1472
Journal of the Southwest 1480
Journal of Ukrainian Studies 1483
Journal of West Indian Literature 1485
Journalism Quarterly 1486
*Keats-Shelley Journal 1501
Konzepte der Sprach- und Literaturwissenschaft 1527
Langage et Société 1550

Language 1553
*Language and Cognitive Processes 1557
Language and Linguistics in Melanesia 1560
Language and Literature 1562
Language Problems and Language Planning/Lingvaj Problemoj kaj Lingvo-Planado 1570
Language Sciences 1573
Language Testing 1575
Latin American Theatre Review 1584
Latvijas Zinātņu Akadēmijas Vēstis 1587
Lectura Dantis 1590
Legacy 1593
Lenguaje y Texto 1598
Lessing Yearbook/Jahrbuch 1602
Letras Peninsulares 1606
Lexicographica 1621
Libraries & Culture 1626
Linguistic and Literary Studies in Eastern Europe 1643
Linguistic Review 1645
Linguistics and Education 1656
Linguistique Africaine 1661
Linguistische Arbeiten 1662
Linguistische Berichte 1663
Lingvisticæ Investigationes 1664
Lingvisticæ Investigationes: Supplementa 1665
Literary Half-Yearly 1676
Literary Research 1677
Literator 1680
Literatura Mexicana 1693
Literature and Belief 1696
Literature and Contemporary Revolutionary Culture 1697
Literature and Medicine 1702
LittéRéalité 1719
Lletra de Canvi 1725
Lost Generation Journal 1730
Lucero 1734
Magazine 1746
Magyar Könyvszemle 1748
Man and Nature/L'Homme et La Nature 1761
Mankind Quarterly 1763
Maske und Kothurn 1774
Massachusetts Studies in English 1776
Material Culture 1778
Mawazo 1780
Mediaeval Studies 1789
Mediaevalia 1790
Medien in Forschung Unterricht 1791
Medieval and Renaissance Monograph Series 1793
Medieval Perspectives 1797
Medievalia et Humanistica 1799
MELUS 1806
Melville Society Extracts 1807
Memory & Cognition 1812
Mester 1817
Meta 1818
*Metaphor and Symbolic Activity 1819
Metmenys 1820
Michigan Academician 1823
Midwest Quarterly 1833
Midwestern Folklore 1834
Milton Quarterly 1837
*Mind 1841
Miscelanea de Estudios Arabes y Hebraicos 1845
Mississippi Folklore Register 1847
Modern Austrian Literature 1865
Modern Fiction Studies 1868
Modern Language Journal 1871
Modern Language Studies 1874
Modern Philology 1875
Monograph Series of the Toronto Semiotic Circle 1882
Monumenta Nipponica 1888
Moody Street Irregulars 1889
Mount Olive Review 1895
Mystics Quarterly 1913
Mythlore 1915
Naamkunde 1916
Names 1918
Nassau Review 1927
Nathaniel Hawthorne Review 1928

Nationalities Papers 1930
Natural Language & Linguistic Theory 1931
Neohelicon 1939
New England Theatre Journal 1958
New German Review 1960
New Scholar 1971
Nineteenth-Century French Studies 1988
Nineteenth-Century Prose 1990
Nineteenth-Century Studies 1991
North Carolina Historical Review 2005
Notes on Modern Irish Literature 2020
Nottingham French Studies 2023
*Novyĭ Zhurnal/The New Review 2032
NOWELE 2034
Oceania 2047
Oceanic Linguistics 2048
Odù 2053
Okike 2058
Old English Newsletter 2061
Old English Newsletter, Subsidia 2062
Old Northwest 2063
Onoma 2065
Onomastica Canadiana 2067
Oral History Review 2074
Oral Tradition 2075
Oxford English Monographs 2093
Palimpsest 2107
Papiere zur Linguistik 2124
Paragraph 2129
Parergon 2130
Paroles Gelées 2134
Pembroke Magazine 2140
Pennsylvania Magazine of History and Biography 2142
*Perceptual and Motor Skills 2147
*Philosophical Quarterly 2162
Philosophical Review 2163
Philosophy and Literature 2166
*Philosophy and Phenomenological Research 2167
Philosophy East and West 2169
Phoenix 2171
Phonology 2175
Phylon 2176
Plamŭk 2178
PMLA 2183
Poetics 2191
Polish Review 2197
Pontifical Institute of Mediaeval Studies, Studies and Texts 2202
Post Script 2206
Postmodern Culture 2208
Présence Africaine 2221
Pre/Text 2223
Pretexts 2224
Printing History 2229
Probus 2237
Proceedings of the Annual Meeting of the Western Society for French History 2241
Proceedings of the Massachusetts Historical Society 2244
Prooftexts 2248
Proteus 2251
PSA 2255
Psychiatry 2256
*Psychological Bulletin 2257
*Psychological Review 2258
Public Culture 2259
Publications of the Arkansas Philological Association 2262
Publishing Research Quarterly 2270
Quarterly Journal of Speech 2284
Queensland Studies in German Language and Literature 2287
Qui Parle 2289
Quimera 2290
Raft 2297
Rare Books & Manuscripts Librarianship 2302
RE Arts & Letters 2311
Reader 2312
Reading and Writing 2313
Reading Psychology 2315
Reading Research Quarterly 2316
Recherches de Théologie Ancienne et Médiévale 2322

*only at author's request

Recherches Linguistiques de Vincennes 2324
Reihe Germanistische Linguistik 2334
Renaissance and Reformation/Renaissance et Réforme 2340
Renaissance Quarterly 2345
Renaissance Studies 2346
Research in African Literatures 2353
Research in Yoruba Language and Literature 2355
*Restoration 2359
Restoration and 18th Century Theatre Research 2360
Revista Alicantina de Estudios Ingleses 2367
Revista Argentina de Lingüística 2368
Revista Canaria de Estudios Ingleses 2372
Revista de Letras 2385
Revista de Literatura 2386
Revista/Review Interamericana 2398
Revue André Malraux Review 2399
Revue de Littérature Comparée 2407
Revue Francophone de Louisiane 2426
Revue Frontenac Review 2427
Revue Québécoise de Linguistique Théorique et Appliquée 2431
Rhetoric Review 2439
Rhetorica 2441
Ricerche Slavistiche 2442
RILCE 2443
Rivista di Linguistica 2455
Rivista di Studi Italiani 2458
RLA: Revista de Lingüística Teórica y Aplicada 2461
RLA: Romance Languages Annual 2462
Rocky Mountain Review of Language and Literature 2465
Romance Linguistics & Literature Review 2474
Romance Notes 2477
Romance Studies 2480
Romanistische Arbeitshefte 2488
Ruskin Gazette 2502
Russian Linguistics 2506
Russian Review 2507
SAGE 2518
Sagetrieb 2519
Sammlung Kurzer Grammatiken Germanischer Dialekte 2528
San José Studies 2531
Schatzkammer der Deutschen Sprache, Dichtung und Geschichte 2544
Scottish Slavonic Review 2559
*SEL 2575
Selecta 2576
Selected Reports in Ethnomusicology 2578
Seminar 2579
*Shakespeare in Southern Africa 2596
Shaw 2606
Sidney Newsletter & Journal 2611
Signs 2616
Single Hound 2621
Sixteenth Century Journal 2628
Skrifter Utgivna av Svenska Språknämnden 2635
Slavic and East European Journal 2641
Slavic Review 2642
Slavonic and East European Review 2647
Slovakia 2648
Slovenské Divadlo 2652
Social Science Information/Information sur les Sciences Sociales 2659
Sociocriticism 2664
Soundings 2669
South African Journal of African Languages/Suid-Afrikaanse Tydskrif vir Afrikatale 2672
South African Theatre Journal 2673
South Atlantic Review 2676
South Central Review 2678
Southeast Asian Review of English 2680
Southern Folklore 2682
Southern Studies 2688
Språkvård 2716
Studi di Letteratura Francese 2743
Studi d'Italianistica nell'Africa Australe/Italian Studies in Southern Africa 2745
Studi Tassiani 2761
Studia Phonetica 2787
Studien und Texte zur Sozialgeschichte der Literatur 2792
Studien zur Deutschen Literatur 2795
Studien zur Englischen Philologie 2797
Studies in American Drama, 1945-Present 2807
*Studies in American Fiction 2808
Studies in American Indian Literatures 2810
Studies in Austrian Literature, Culture, and Thought 2812
Studies in Canadian Literature/Etudes en Littérature Canadienne 2815
Studies in Contemporary Satire 2817
Studies in English and American Literature, Linguistics, and Culture 2821
Studies in Iconography 2828
Studies in Language Companion Series 2831
Studies in Medievalism 2836
Studies in Scottish Literature 2845
Studies in Second Language Acquisition 2846
Studies in the Age of Chaucer 2851
Studies in the Humanities 2853
Studies in the Sciences of Language Series 2858
Studies in Twentieth Century Literature 2859
Studies on Voltaire and the Eighteenth Century 2862
Südost-Forschungen 2871
Surfaces [Electronic publication] 2881
Suvremena Lingvistika 2883
Swift Studies 2891
Synthese 2899
Taal en Tongval 2906
Tamkang Review 2910
Tennessee Philological Bulletin 2925
Tennyson Society Monographs 2928
TENSO 2929
TESOL Quarterly 2932
*Texas Studies in Literature and Language 2937
Text & Context 2939
Text and Performance Quarterly 2940
Texte 2944
Thalia 2952
Theatre Annual 2955
Theatre History in Canada/Histoire du Théâtre au Canada 2956
Theatre Studies 2961
Theoria 2965
Thomas Wolfe Review 2974
Thoreau Society Bulletin 2975
Thought 2976
Tolstoy Studies Journal 2986
Tradition 2995
Transactions of the Samuel Johnson Society of the Northwest 3004
Travaux de Littérature 3013
Tristania 3023
Tropelías 3027
Tropos 3029
Tulsa Studies in Women's Literature 3035
Twentieth Century Literature 3046
Ukrainian Quarterly 3054
Uncoverings 3062
University of California Publications, Folklore and Mythology Studies 3072
University of California Publications in Linguistics 3073
University of California Publications in Modern Philology 3074
*University of Dayton Review 3075
*University of Hartford Studies in Literature 3077
University of Leeds Review 3079
Unterrichtspraxis 3089
Untersuchungen zur Deutschen Literaturgeschichte 3090
Utah Studies in Literature and Linguistics 3096
VIA 3122
Victorian Literature and Culture 3126
Victorian Periodicals Review 3128
Victorian Poetry 3129
Victorian Review 3130
Victorian Studies 3131
Virginia Quarterly Review 3137
Visible Language 3141
Waiguoyu 3155
War, Literature, and the Arts 3158
West Georgia College Review 3167
Western Folklore 3171
Willa Cather Pioneer Memorial Newsletter 3185
William and Mary Quarterly 3186
Winterthur Portfolio 3189
Women & Performance 3200
Women in German Yearbook 3201
Women's Studies 3202
Wordsworth Circle 3206
World Englishes 3211
World Literature Written in English 3213
Y Traethodydd 3215
Yale Journal of Law & the Humanities 3218
Yearbook of Comparative and General Literature 3222
Yeats Annual 3232
Zambezia 3244
Zeitschrift für Dialektologie und Linguistik 3257

*only at author's request

DATE DUE

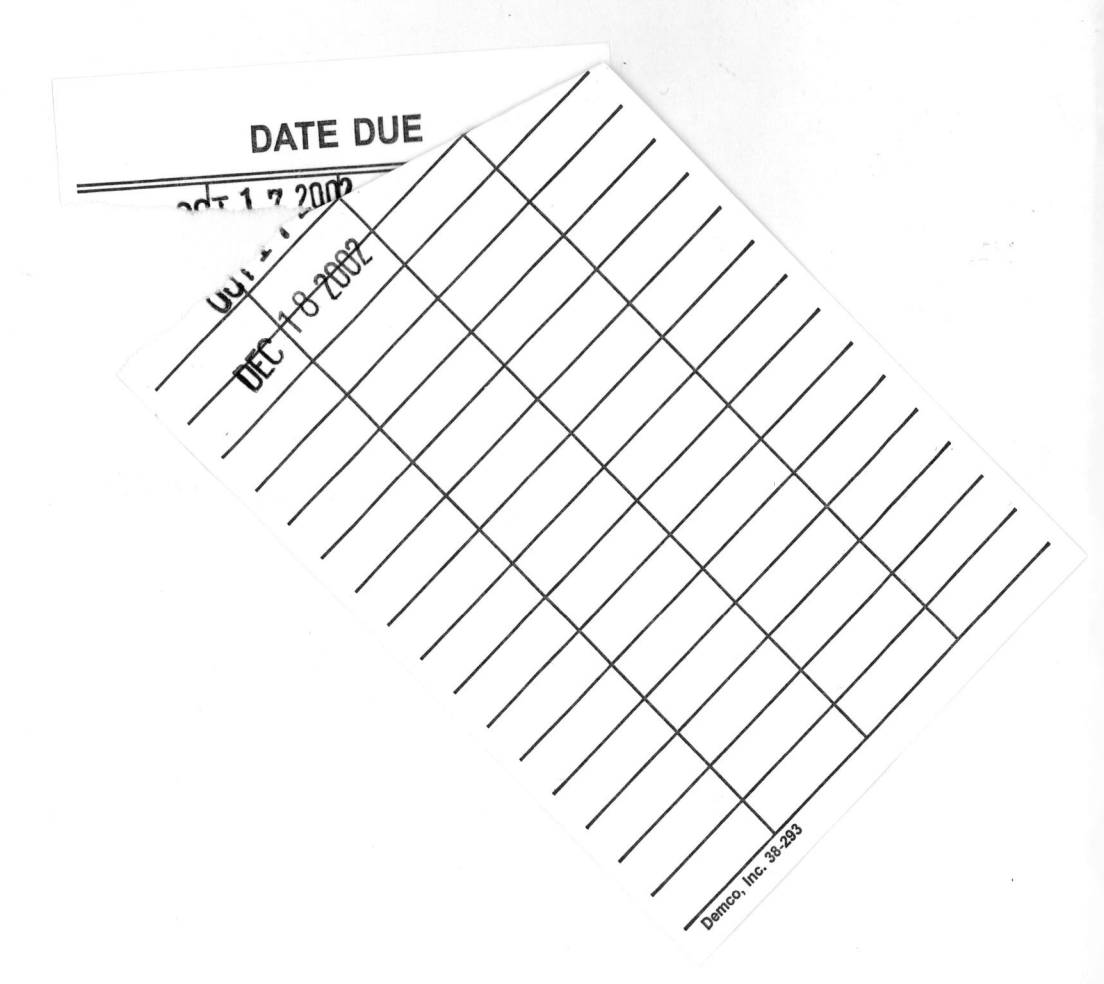

OCT 1 7 2002

DEC 1 8 2002

Demco, Inc. 38-293